International Dictionary of
OPERA

International Dictionary of

OPERA

EDITOR
C. STEVEN LARUE

PICTURE EDITOR
LEANDA SHRIMPTON

Volume 1: A-K

St J
St James Press

Detroit   London   Washington DC

STAFF

C. Steven LaRue, *Editor*
Leanda Shrimpton, *Picture Editor*
Emily J. McMurray, *Project Coordinator*
Paul E. Schellinger, *Associate Editor*
Robin Armstrong, David Ross Hurley, Robynn J. Stilwell, and Jeffrey Taylor, *Contributing Editors*

Cynthia Baldwin, *Art Director*
Mary Krzewinski, *Designer*
C. J. Jonik, *Keyliner*

Mary Beth Trimper, *Production Director*
Evi Seoud, *Assistant Production Manager*
Mary Kelley, *Production Assistant*

Cover photo: Luciano Pavarotti in *L'elisir d'amore*, 1990. Photo © Donald Cooper/Photostage, London.

Library of Congress Cataloging-in-Publication Data
International dictionary of opera / editor, C. Steven LaRue ; picture
editor, Leanda Shrimpton
    p.   cm.
Includes bibliographical references and indexes.
Contents: v. 1. A-K -- v. 2. L-Z/Indexes
ISBN 1-55862-081-8 (set : alk. paper) : $250.00. -- ISBN
1-55862-112-1 (v.1 : alk. paper). -- ISBN 1-55862-113-X (v.2. :
alk. paper)
    1. Opera--Dictionaries. I. LaRue, C. Steven.
ML102.O6I6 1993
782.1'03--dc20   92-44271
                                                        CIP
                                                        MN

British Library Cataloguing in Publication Data
    International Dictionary of Opera
    I. Larue, C. Steven II. Shrimpton, Leanda
    782.103
    ISBN 1-55862-081-8

∞™ The paper used in this publication meets the minimum requirements
of American National Standard for Information Sciences—Permanence
Paper for Printed Library Materials, ANSI Z39.48-1984.

Printed in the United States of America.
Published simultaneously in the United Kingdom.

CONTENTS

INTRODUCTION   *page* vii

ADVISERS   xi

LIST OF ENTRIES INCLUDED   xiii

ENTRIES

    Volume 1: A-K   1

    Volume 2: L-Z   719

TITLE INDEX   1487

NATIONALITY INDEX   1519

NOTES ON ADVISERS AND CONTRIBUTORS   1527

PICTURE ACKNOWLEDGMENTS   1541

INTRODUCTION

Scope

The *International Dictionary of Opera* provides students, teachers, researchers, and opera enthusiasts with a comprehensive source of biographical, bibliographical, and musicological information on people and works important to the history and development of opera. This two-volume set contains nearly 1100 entries on influential composers, librettists, performers, conductors, designers, directors, producers, and works representative of the genre from its beginnings to the present time.

Advisory Board

Entries were included in the *International Dictionary of Opera* based on the recommendations of advisers drawn from a number of fields associated with the study, performance, and recording of opera in both the United States and England. Advisers provided lists of suggested entries based on their individual expertise and their knowledge of the genre as a whole, from which the editor compiled the final selection of entries.

Entry Content

Each entry consists of a headnote containing biographical and bibliographical data followed by a signed critical essay. Headnotes were prepared by the editor and his staff from a number of different sources as well as from information supplied by individual contributors and advisers; thus the responsibility for the accuracy of the headnotes lies strictly with the editor and his staff, not with the contributors. Essays were provided by more than 200 music historians, theorists, teachers, critics, journalists, performers, recording executives, editors, publishers, and other individuals qualified to present interested readers with an informed critical opinion on the operatic work or person discussed. Viewpoints and interpretations found in the dictionary range from philosophical discussions of art and aesthetics to pragmatic considerations of performance and production.

Entries in the *International Dictionary of Opera* typically contain the following information:

- *BIOGRAPHICAL OUTLINE:* occupation; dates and places of birth and death; marriages and names of children; education and musical training, including institutions attended and names of teachers; career data, including musical posts held, milestones reached, and important performances, achievements, and awards; circle of important friends, associates, and students.

● *COMPOSITION AND PRODUCTION INFORMATION:* see the chart below for data unique to entry type:

Entry Type	Information Provided	Data Includes (where available)
Composer	List of Operas	Title (variant type; composer collaborators), librettist (source of libretto, including author and title of work), dates of composition, city, theater, and date of first performance, revisions under the composer's supervision, places and dates of performance.
Librettist	List of Librettos (selected)	Title, composer collaborator, date of first performance. (Note: further information can be found in the appropriate composer headnotes.)
Producer/ Director/ Designer	List of Productions (selected)	Title, city, theater, and date of performance.
Opera	Name of composer and librettist, and first performance information	List of roles and their general ranges. (Note: further information can be found in the appropriate composer headnote.)

● *SELECTED PRIMARY AND SECONDARY BIBLIOGRAPHIES:* title-by-title chronological lists of books and articles written and edited by the listee, including autobiographies and correspondence; and lists of books and articles written about the listee, including biographies, critical studies, chronologies, and dissertations. Readers seeking in-depth information about individual operas or librettists should also check appropriate composer bibliographies for additional sources to consult.

● *SIGNED CRITICAL ESSAY:* an evaluation or analysis of the contributions of the individual or importance of the work in question.

Illustrations

Individuals and operas in the *International Dictionary of Opera* come to life in 450 illustrations ranging from scenes from the contemporary opera stage to reproductions of period etchings, title pages of first-edition scores, portraits, and photographs.

Title and Nationality Indexes

Readers gain additional access to operas and individuals in the *International Dictionary of Opera* through the Title and Nationality indexes found in Volume 2. Titles in the "Operas" listing in each of the composer entries are indexed alphabetically, along with the composer's name and page number of the composer entry on which full composition information can be found. Operas for which full entries exist are further identified by boldface page numbers. In addition, users can explore national musical traditions by consulting the Nationality Index, in which individuals are arranged alphabetically by country of birth and/or citizenship and/or national affiliation.

Notes on Advisers and Contributors

Information about the areas of specialization of and additional music publications by the advisers and contributors to the *International Dictionary of Opera* can be found in the Notes on Advisers and Contributors section in Volume 2.

Acknowledgments

The editor wishes to recognize the pioneering efforts of Jim Vinson, founding editor of the *International Dictionary of Opera* and numerous other St James reference works, who died in 1991. Recognition is due as well to the late Greg Salmon, Russian music specialist and contributor of material for the essays on Glinka, Rimsky-Korsakov, Rubinstein, and Tchaikovsky. Special acknowledgment is also due to contributors Stephen Willier and Michael Sims, and advisers Bruce Burroughs, Andrew Farkas, and Thomas G. Kaufman for their editorial assistance in the late phases of this project; to the Gale Research Permissions Department for their help with photo sizing; and to Polly Vedder and Ken Shepherd for their technical assistance in the preparation of these volumes.

ADVISERS

Steven Barwick

Alan Blyth

Julian Budden

Bruce Burroughs

Norman Del Mar

Andrew Farkas

Paul Griffiths

Arthur Groos

Christopher Headington

John Higgins

Thomas G. Kaufman

Joseph Kerman

Herbert Lindenberger

George Martin

William R. Moran

Anthony Newcomb

Julian Rushton

John B. Steane

Denis Stevens

Michael Talbot

Alan Tyson

Arnold Whittall

LIST OF ENTRIES

COMPOSERS

Adam, Adolphe
Adams, John
Albert, Eugen d'
  See d'Albert, Eugen
Argento, Dominick
Arne, Thomas
Auber, Daniel-François-Esprit
Balfe, Michael
Barber, Samuel
Bartók, Béla
Beeson, Jack
Beethoven, Ludwig van
Bellini, Vincenzo
Benedict, Julius
Berg, Alban
Berio, Luciano
Berlioz, Hector
Bernstein, Leonard
Birtwistle, Harrison
Bizet, Georges
Blitzstein, Marc
Bloch, Ernest
Blomdahl, Karl-Birger
Blow, John
Boieldieu, Adrien
Boito, Arrigo
Borodin, Alexander
Boughton, Rutland
Britten, Benjamin
Bruneau, Alfred
Busoni, Ferruccio
Caccini, Giulio
Catalani, Alfredo
Cavalli, Francesco
Cesti, Antonio
Chabrier, Emmanuel
Charpentier, Gustave
Charpentier, Marc-Antoine
Chausson, Ernest
Cherubini, Luigi
Cilèa, Francesco
Cimarosa, Domenico
Copland, Aaron
Cornelius, Peter
Crosse, Gordon
d'Albert, Eugen
Dallapiccola, Luigi
Dargomïzhsky, Alexander

Davies, Peter Maxwell
Debussy, Claude
Delibes, Léo
Delius, Frederick
d'Indy, Vincent
Donizetti, Gaetano
Dukas, Paul
Dvořák, Antonín
Eaton, John
Egk, Werner
Einem, Gottfried von
Erkel, Ferenc
Falla, Manuel de
Fauré, Gabriel
Flotow, Friedrich von
Floyd, Carlisle
Foss, Lukas
Gagliano, Marco da
Galuppi, Baldassare
Gershwin, George
Ginastera, Alberto
Giordano, Umberto
Glass, Philip
Glinka, Mikhail
Gluck, Christoph Willibald von
Goehr, Alexander
Goldmark, Karl
Gomes, Antonio Carlos
Gounod, Charles François
Granados, Enrique
Graun, Carl
Grétry, André-Ernest-Modeste
Gruenberg, Louis
Halévy, Jacques
Handel, George Frideric
Hasse, Johann
Haydn, Franz Joseph
Henze, Hans Werner
Hérold, Ferdinand
Hindemith, Paul
Hoffmann, E. T. A.
Holst, Gustav
Honegger, Arthur
Humperdinck, Engelbert
Janáček, Leoš
Jommelli, Niccolò
Joplin, Scott
Kabalevsky, Dimitry

Kagel, Mauricio
Keiser, Reinhard
Knussen, Oliver
Kodály, Zoltán
Korngold, Erich Wolfgang
Krenek, Ernst
Kurka, Robert
Lalo, Edouard
Leoncavallo, Ruggero
Ligeti, György
Lortzing, Albert
Lully, Jean-Baptiste
Magnard, Albéric
Malipiero, Gian Francesco
Marschner, Heinrich
Martín y Soler, Vicente
Martinů, Bohuslav
Mascagni, Pietro
Massenet, Jules
Mattheson, Johann
Maw, Nicolas
Mayr, Simon
Méhul, Étienne-Nicolas
Menotti, Gian Carlo
Mercadante, Saverio
Messiaen, Olivier
Meyerbeer, Giacomo
Milhaud, Darius
Moniuszko, Stanislaw
Montemezzi, Italo
Monteverdi, Claudio
Moore, Douglas
Mozart, Wolfgang Amadeus
Musorgsky, Modest
Nicolai, Otto
Nielsen, Carl
Nono, Luigi
Offenbach, Jacques
Orff, Carl
Pacini, Giovanni
Paer, Ferdinando
Paisiello, Giovanni
Penderecki, Krzysztof
Pepusch, Johann Christoph
Pergolesi, Giovanni Battista
Peri, Jacopo
Pfitzner, Hans Erich
Piccinni, Niccolò
Pizzetti, Ildebrando
Ponchielli, Amilcare
Porpora, Nicola Antonio
Poulenc, Francis

Pousseur, Henri
Prokofiev, Sergei
Puccini, Giacomo
Purcell, Henry
Rameau, Jean-Philippe
Ravel, Maurice
Reimann, Aribert
Rimsky-Korsakov, Nicolai
Rossini, Gioachino
Rousseau, Jean-Jacques
Rubinstein, Anton
Sacchini, Antonio
Saint-Saëns, Camille
Salieri, Antonio
Sallinen, Aulis
Scarlatti, Alessandro
Schmidt, Franz
Schoenberg, Arnold
Schreker, Franz
Schubert, Franz
Schumann, Robert
Sessions, Roger
Shostakovich, Dmitri
Smetana, Bedřich
Smyth, Ethel
Spohr, Ludewig
Spontini, Gaspare
Stockhausen, Karlheinz
Strauss, Richard
Stravinsky, Igor
Szymanowski, Karol
Tchaikovsky, Piotr Ilyich
Telemann, Georg Philipp
Thomas, Ambroise
Thomson, Virgil
Tippett, Michael
Vaughan Williams, Ralph
Verdi, Giuseppe
Villa-Lobos, Heitor
Vivaldi, Antonio
Wagner, Richard
Wallace, Vincent
Walton, William
Ward, Robert
Weber, Carl Maria von
Weill, Kurt
Weinberger, Jaromir
Wolf, Hugo
Wolf-Ferrari, Ermanno
Zandonai, Riccardo
Zemlinsky, Alexander von
Zimmermann, Bernd Alois

CONDUCTORS

Abbado, Claudio
Beecham, Thomas
Blech, Leo
Bodanzky, Artur

Böhm, Karl
Boulez, Pierre
Bülow, Hans von
Busch, Fritz

Caldwell, Sarah
Campanini, Cleofonte
Chailly, Riccardo
Cluytens, André
Coates, Albert
Damrosch, Leopold
Davis, Colin
De Sabata, Victor
Faccio, Franco
Furtwängler, Wilhelm
Giulini, Carlo Maria
Goodall, Reginald
Karajan, Herbert von
Keilberth, Joseph
Kempe, Rudolf
Kleiber, Carlos
Kleiber, Erich
Klemperer, Otto
Knappertsbusch, Hans
Krauss, Clemens
Krips, Josef
Kubelík, Rafael
Leinsdorf, Erich
Leppard, Raymond
Levi, Hermann
Levine, James
Maazel, Lorin
Mackerras, Charles

Mahler, Gustav
Mariani, Angelo
Monteux, Pierre
Mottl, Felix
Muck, Karl
Mugnone, Leopoldo
Muti, Riccardo
Nikisch, Arthur
Prêtre, Georges
Pritchard, John
Reiner, Fritz
Richter, Hans
Rosbaud, Hans
Rudel, Julius
Sanzogno, Nino
Sawallisch, Wolfgang
Schalk, Franz
Schippers, Thomas
Schuch, Ernst von
Seidl, Anton
Serafin, Tullio
Sinopoli, Giuseppe
Solti, Georg
Szell, George
Toscanini, Arturo
Walter, Bruno
Weingartner, Felix
Wolff, Albert

LIBRETTISTS

Auden, W. H.
Aureli, Aurelio
Boito, Arrigo
Brecht, Bertolt
Busenello, Giovanni Francesco
Calzabigi, Ranieri de
Cammarano, Salvadore
Cicognini, Giacinto Andrea
Da Ponte, Lorenzo
Forzano, Giovacchino
Gallet, Louis
Gay, John
Ghislanzoni, Antonio
Giacosa, Giuseppe
Goldoni, Carlo
Gregor, Joseph
Halévy, Jacques

Haym, Nicola Francesco
Hofmannsthal, Hugo von
Illica, Luigi
Meilhac, Henri
Metastasio, Pietro
Piave, Francesco Maria
Quinault, Philippe
Rinuccini, Ottavio
Rolli, Paolo Antonio
Romani, Felice
Rospigliosi, Giulio
Schikaneder, Emanuel
Scribe, Eugène
Solera, Temistocle
Striggio, Alessandro
Zeno, Apostolo

PERFORMERS

Albanese, Licia
Albani, Emma
Alboni, Marietta
Alda, Frances
Allen, Thomas

Alva, Luigi
Amato, Pasquale
Anders, Peter
Anderson, June
Anderson, Marian

Araiza, Francesco
Arnoldson, Sigrid
Arroyo, Martina
Baccaloni, Salvatore
Bacquier, Gabriel
Bahr-Mildenburg, Anna
Bailey, Norman
Baker, Janet
Bampton, Rose
Barbieri, Fedora
Barrientos, Maria
Battistini, Mattia
Battle, Kathleen
Behrens, Hildegard
Bellincioni, Gemma
Bene, Adriana Gabrieli del
Benucci, Francesco
Berganza, Teresa
Berger, Erna
Berglund, Joel
Bergonzi, Carlo
Bernacchi, Antonio Maria
Berry, Walter
Björling, Jussi
Blachut, Beno
Bockelmann, Rudolf
Bohnen, Michael
Bonci, Alessandro
Boninsegna, Celestina
Bordoni, Faustina
Borgatti, Giuseppe
Borgioli, Dino
Bori, Lucrezia
Borkh, Inge
Brouwenstijn, Gré
Bruscantini, Sesto
Bumbry, Grace
Burian, Karel
Burrows, Stuart
Caballé, Montserrat
Caffarelli
Callas, Maria
Calvé, Emma
Campanini, Italo
Caniglia, Maria
Cappuccilli, Piero
Carreras, José
Caruso, Enrico
Cavalieri, Catarina
Cavalieri, Lina
Cebotari, Maria
Chaliapin, Feodor
Christoff, Boris
Cigna, Gina
Corelli, Franco
Corena, Fernando
Cossutta, Carlo
Cotrubas, Ileana
Crespin, Régine
Cuénod, Hugues
Curtin, Phyllis
Cuzzoni, Francesca
Dal Monte, Toti

Danco, Suzanne
Del Bene, Adriana Gabrieli
  See Bene, Adriana Gabrieli del
Della Casa, Lisa
Del Monaco, Mario
De Los Angeles, Victoria
De Luca, Giuseppe
De Lucia, Fernando
De Reszke, Edouard
De Reszke, Jean
Dermota, Anton
Dernesch, Helga
Destinn, Emmy
Di Stefano, Giuseppe
Domingo, Plácido
Duprez, Gilbert-Louis
Eames, Emma
Elias, Rosalind
Evans, Geraint
Ewing, Maria
Falcon, Marie Cornélie
Farinelli
Farrar, Geraldine
Farrell, Eileen
Fassbaender, Brigitte
Faure, Jean-Baptiste
Ferrier, Kathleen
Figner, Medea
  See Mei-Figner, Medea
Figner, Nikolay
Fischer-Dieskau, Dietrich
Flagstad, Kirsten
Fleta, Miguel
Fremstad, Olive
Freni, Mirella
Frick, Gottlob
Gadski, Johanna
Galli-Curci, Amelita
Galli-Marié, Celestine
Garcia, Manuel
Garden, Mary
Gedda, Nicolai
Ghijaurov, Nicolai
Giannini, Dusolina
Gigli, Beniamino
Glossop, Peter
Gluck, Alma
Gobbi, Tito
Gorr, Rita
Grisi, Giuditta
Grisi, Giulia
Grist, Reri
Gruberova, Edita
Guadagni, Gaetano
Gueden, Hilde
Hammond, Joan
Heldy, Fanny
Hempel, Frieda
Hidalgo, Elvira de
Hines, Jerome
Homer, Louise
Horne, Marilyn
Hotter, Hans

Ivogün, Maria
Jadlowker, Hermann
Janowitz, Gundula
Janssen, Herbert
Jeritza, Maria
Jerusalem, Siegfried
Johnson, Edward
Jones, Gwyneth
Journet, Marcel
Jurinac, Sena
Kelly, Michael
Kiepura, Jan
King, James
Kipnis, Alexander
Kollo, René
Konetzni, Anny
Konetzni, Hilde
Köth, Erika
Kraus, Alfredo
Kunz, Erich
Kurz, Selma
Lablache, Luigi
Lauri-Volpi, Giacomo
Lawrence, Marjorie
Lear, Evelyn
Lehmann, Lilli
Lehmann, Lotte
Leider, Frida
Lemnitz, Tiana
Lewis, Richard
Lind, Jenny
Lipp, Wilma
London, George
Lorengar, Pilar
Lorenz, Max
Los Angeles, Victoria de
  See de Los Angeles, Victoria
Lubin, Germaine
Ludwig, Christa
MacNeil, Cornell
Malibran, Maria
Marcoux, Vanni
Mario, Giovanni
Martón, Eva
Mathis, Edith
Matzenauer, Margaret
Maurel, Victor
McCormack, John
McIntyre, Donald
Mei-Figner, Medea
Melba, Nellie
Melchior, Lauritz
Merrill, Robert
Merriman, Nan
Milanov, Zinka
Mildenburg, Anna von
  See Bahr-Mildenburg, Anna
Milnes, Sherrill
Minton, Yvonne
Mödl, Martha
Moffo, Anna
Moll, Kurt
Moore, Grace

Morris, James
Muzio, Claudia
Neidlinger, Gustav
Nesterenko, Evgeny
Nilsson, Birgit
Nilsson, Christine
Nordica, Lillian
Norman, Jessye
Nourrit, Adolphe
Novotná, Jarmila
Olivero, Magda
Onegin, Sigrid
Pagliughi, Lina
Pasero, Tancredi
Pasta, Giuditta
Patti, Adelina
Patzak, Julius
Pavarotti, Luciano
Pears, Peter
Peerce, Jan
Pertile, Aureliano
Peters, Roberta
Pilarczyk, Helga
Pinza, Ezio
Pons, Lily
Ponselle, Rosa
Popp, Lucia
Prey, Hermann
Price, Leontyne
Price, Margaret
Raaff, Anton
Raisa, Rosa
Ramey, Samuel
Raskin, Judith
Resnik, Regina
Rethberg, Elisabeth
Ricciarelli, Katia
Rossi-Lemeni, Nicola
Roswaenge, Helge
Rothenberger, Anneliese
Rubini, Giovanni-Battista
Ruffo, Titta
Rysanek, Leonie
Sammarco, Mario
Sanderson, Sybil
Sass, Sylvia
Sayão, Bidú
Schipa, Tito
Schlusnus, Heinrich
Schorr, Friedrich
Schreier, Peter
Schröder-Devrient, Wilhemine
Schumann, Elisabeth
Schumann-Heink, Ernestine
Schwarzkopf, Elisabeth
Scotti, Antonio
Scotto, Renata
Seefried, Irmgard
Sembrich, Marcella
Senesino
Shirley, George
Shirley-Quirk, John
Siems, Margarethe

Siepi, Cesare
Silja, Anja
Sills, Beverly
Simionato, Giulietta
Simoneau, Léopold
Singher, Martial
Slezak, Leo
Smirnov, Dmitri
Söderström, Elisabeth
Sontag, Henriette
Soyer, Roger
Stabile, Mariano
Stade, Frederica Von
  See Von Stade, Frederica
Steber, Eleanor
Stevens, Risë
Stich-Randall, Teresa
Stignani, Ebe
Stolz, Teresa
Storace, Nancy
Storchio, Rosina
Stracciari, Riccardo
Stratas, Teresa
Streich, Rita
Strepponi, Giuseppina
Supervia, Conchita
Sutherland, Joan
Svanholm, Set
Tagliavini, Ferruccio
Tajo, Italo
Talvela, Martti
Tamagno, Francesco
Tamberlick, Enrico
Tauber, Richard

Tebaldi, Renata
Te Kanawa, Kiri
Tetrazzini, Luisa
Teyte, Maggie
Thill, Georges
Thorborg, Kerstin
Tibbett, Lawrence
Tietjens, Therese
Tourel, Jennie
Tozzi, Giorgio
Traubel, Helen
Treigle, Norman
Troyanos, Tatiana
Tucker, Richard
Turner, Eva
Valletti, Cesare
Vallin, Ninon
Van Dam, José
Varady, Julia
Verrett, Shirley
Viardot, Pauline
Vickers, Jon
Vinay, Ramón
Vishnevskaya, Galina
Von Stade, Frederica
Wächter, Eberhard
Warren, Leonard
Weber, Ludwig
Weikl, Bernd
Welitsch, Ljuba
Windgassen, Wolfgang
Wunderlich, Fritz
Zenatello, Giovanni

PRODUCERS, DIRECTORS, and DESIGNERS

Appia, Adolphe
Arundell, Dennis
Benois, Alexandre
Benois, Nicola
Berghaus, Ruth
Bergman, Ingmar
Brook, Peter
Chéreau, Patrice
Ciceri, Pierre-Luc-Charles
Copley, John
Corsaro, Frank
Cox, John
Craig, Edward Gordon
Dexter, John
Ebert, Carl
Everding, August
Felsenstein, Walter
Freeman, David
Friedrich, Götz
Gentele, Göran
Graf, Herbert
Graham, Colin
Guthrie, Tyrone

Hartmann, Rudolf
Hall, Peter
Herz, Joachim
Hockney, David
Koltai, Ralph
Kupfer, Harry
Meyerhold, Vsevolod
Miller, Jonathan
Moshinsky, Elijah
Nemirovich-Danchenko,
  Vladimir
Pizzi, Pier Luigi
Ponnelle, Jean-Pierre
Pountney, David
Prince, Harold
Reinhardt, Max
Rennert, Günther
Roller, Alfred
Sanquirico, Alessandro
Schenk, Otto
Schneider-Siemssen, Günther
Sellars, Peter
Sendak, Maurice

Serban, Andrei
Shaw, Glen Byam
Stanislavsky, Konstantin
Strehler, Giorgio
Svoboda, Josef
Urban, Joseph
Visconti, Luchino

Wagner, Wieland
Wagner, Wolfgang
Wallerstein, Lothar
Wallmann, Margherita
Wilson, Robert
Zeffirelli, Franco

OPERAS

Abaris, or The Boreads
  See *Abaris, ou Les Boréades*
Abaris, ou Les Boréades (*Abaris, or The Boreads*)
Abduction from the Seraglio, The
  See *Entführung aus dem Serail, Die*
Adriana Lecouvreur
Adriano in Siria (*Hadrian in Syria*)
Africaine, L' (*The African Maid*)
African Maid, The
  See *Africaine, L'*
Ägyptische Helena, Die (*Helen in Egypt*)
Aida
Akhnaten
  See *Triptych*
Albert Herring
Alceste [Gluck]
Alceste [Lully]
Alcina
All Women Do Thus
  See *Così fan tutte*
Amahl and the Night Visitors
Amelia al ballo (*Amelia Goes to the Ball*)
Amelia Goes to the Ball
  See *Amelia al ballo*
Amico Fritz, L' (*Friend Fritz*)
Amore dei tre re, L' (*The Love of Three Kings*)
Andrea Chénier
Aniara
Anima del Filosofo, L' (*The Soul of the Philosopher*)
Anna Bolena (*Anne Boleyn*)
Anne Boleyn
  See *Anna Bolena*
Antigonae
Antony and Cleopatra
Arabella
Arbore di Diana, L'
Arden Must Die
Ariadne and Bluebeard
  See *Ariane et Barbe-Bleue*
Ariadne auf Naxos (*Ariadne on Naxos*)
Ariadne on Naxos
  See *Ariadne auf Naxos*
Ariane et Barbe-Bleue

Arlecchino, oder, Die Fenster (*Harlequin, or, The Windows*)
Armide [Gluck]
Armide [Lully]
Artaxerxes
Aspern Papers, The
Attack on the Mill, The
  See *Attaque du moulin, L'*
Attaque du moulin, L' (*The Attack on the Mill*)
Attila
Atys
Ballad of Baby Doe, The
Ballo in maschera, Un (*A Masked Ball*)
Bánk Bán
Barber of Bagdad, The
  See *Barbier von Bagdad, Der*
Barber of Seville, The
  See *Barbiere di Siviglia, Il*
Barbier von Bagdad, Der (*The Barber of Bagdad*)
Barbiere di Siviglia, Il (*The Barber of Seville*) [Paisiello]
Barbiere di Siviglia, Il (*The Barber of Seville*) [Rossini]
Bartered Bride, The
Bassariden, Die (*The Bassarids*)
Bassarids, The
  See *Bassariden, Die*
Bastien and Bastienne
  See *Bastien und Bastienne*
Bastien und Bastienne (*Bastien and Bastienne*)
Battaglia di Legnano, La (*The Battle of Legnano*)
Battle of Legnano, The
  See *Battaglia di Legnano, La*
Bear, The
Beatrice and Benedict
  See *Béatrice et Bénédict*
Beatrice di Tenda (*Beatrice of Tenda*)
Béatrice et Bénédict
Beatrice of Tenda
  See *Beatrice di Tenda*
Beggar's Opera, The
Benvenuto Cellini
Bernauerin, Die (*The Wife of Bernauer*)

Betrothal in a Monastery
Bewitched Child, The
　　See *Enfant et les sortilèges, L'*
Billy Budd
Bohème, La [Leoncavallo]
Bohème, La [Puccini]
Bohemian Girl, The
Boris Godunov
Breasts of Tiresias, The
　　See *Mamelles de Tirésias, Les*
Brother Devil
　　See *Fra Diavolo*
Buona figliuola, La (The Good Daughter)
Burning Fiery Furnace
　　See *Church Parables*
Calisto, La
Capriccio
Capuleti ed i Montecchi, I (The Capulets
　　and the Montagues)
Capulets and the Montagues, The
　　See *Capuleti ed i Montecchi, I*
Cardillac
Carmen
Castor and Pollux
　　See *Castor et Pollux*
Castor et Pollux (Castor and Pollux)
Cavalleria rusticana (Rustic Chivalry)
Cendrillon (Cinderella)
Cenerentola, La (Cinderella)
Christophe Colomb (Christopher Columbus)
Christopher Columbus
　　See *Christophe Colomb*
Church Parables
Cid, Le
Cinderella
　　See *Cendrillon*
Cinderella
　　See *Cenerentola, La*
Clemenza di Tito, La (The Mercy of Titus)
Cleopatra
　　See *Unglückselige Cleopatra, Die*
Clowns, The
　　See *Pagliacci, I*
Coachman of Longjumeau, The
　　See *Postillon de Longjumeau, Le*
Colas Breugnon
Comedy on the Bridge
Comte Ory, Le (Count Ory)
Congenial Indies, The
　　See *Indes galantes, Les*
Consul, The
Contes d'Hoffmann, Les (The Tales of
　　Hoffmann)
Coronation of Poppea, The
　　See *Incoronazione di Poppea, L'*
Corregidor, Der (The Magistrate)
Cosa Rara, Una (A Rare Occurence)
Così fan tutte (All Women Do Thus)
Count Ory
　　See *Comte Ory, Le*
Country Philosopher, The
　　See *Filosofo di campagna, Il*

Cradle Will Rock, The
Crucible, The
Cry of Clytaemnestra, The
Cunning Little Vixen, The
Curlew River
　　See *Church Parables*
Dafne, La
Dalibor
Dame blanche, La (The White Lady)
Danton's Death
　　See *Dantons Tod*
Dantons Tod (Danton's Death)
Daphne
Dardanus
Daughter of the Regiment, The
　　See *Fille du régiment, La*
Dead City, The
　　See *Tote Stadt, Die*
Death in Venice
Demon, The
Deux Journées, Les (The Two Days)
Devil and Kate, The
Devils of Loudon, The
Devin du village, Le (The Village
　　Soothsayer)
Dialogues des Carmélites (Dialogues of the
　　Carmelites)
Dialogues of the Carmelites
　　See *Dialogues des Carmélites*
Dido and Aeneas
Disguised Gardener, The
　　See *Finta giardiniera, La*
Distant Sound, The
　　See *Ferne Klang, Der*
Doktor Faust
Don Carlos
Don Giovanni
Donna del lago, La (The Lady of the Lake)
Don Pasquale
Don Quichotte (Don Quixote)
Don Quixote
　　See *Don Quichotte*
Dreigroschenoper, Die (The Threepenny
　　Opera)
Due Foscari, I (The Two Foscari)
Duke Bluebeard's Castle
Edgar
Einstein on the Beach
　　See *Triptych*
Elegy for Young Lovers
Elektra
Elisir d'amore, L' (The Elixir of Love)
Elixir of Love, The
　　See *Elisir d'amore, L'*
Emperor Jones, The
Enfant et les sortilèges, L' (The Bewitched
　　Child)
Entführung aus dem Serail, Die (The
　　Abduction from the Seraglio)
Ernani
Erwartung (Expectation)
Esclarmonde

Eugene Onegin
Euridice, L' [Caccini]
Euridice, L' [Peri]
Euryanthe
Expectation
  See *Erwartung*
Fable of Orpheus, The
  See *Favola d'Orfeo, La*
Fair Maid of Perth, The
  See *Jolie fille de Perth, La*
Fairy Queen, The
Faithful Nymph, The
  See *Fida ninfa, La*
Falstaff
Fanciulla del West, La (*The Girl of the Golden West*)
Faust
Favola d'Orfeo, La (*The Fable of Orpheus*)
Favorite, La (*The Favorite*)
Fedeltà premiata, La (*Fidelity Rewarded*)
Fedora
Ferne Klang, Der (*The Distant Sound*)
Fervaal
Feuersnot (*Fire Famine; St. John's Eve*)
Fida ninfa, La (*The Faithful Nymph*)
Fidelio
Fidelity Rewarded
  See *Fedeltà premiata, La*
Fierabras
Fiery Angel, The
Fille du régiment, La (*The Daughter of the Regiment*)
Filosofo di campagna, Il (*The Country Philosopher*)
Finta giardiniera, La (*The Disguised Gardener*)
Fire Famine
  See *Feuersnot*
Fliegende Holländer, Der (*The Flying Dutchman*)
Florentine Tragedy, A
  See *Florentinische Tragödie, Eine*
Florentinische Tragödie, Eine (*A Florentine Tragedy*)
Flying Dutchman, The
  See *Fliegende Holländer, Der*
Force of Destiny, The
  See *Forza del Destino, La*
Foreign Lady, The
  See *Straniera, La*
Forza del Destino, La (*The Force of Destiny*)
Four Saints in Three Acts
Fra Diavolo (*Brother Devil*)
Francesca da Rimini
Frau ohne Schatten, Die (*The Woman without a Shadow*)
Free-Shooter, The
  See *Freischütz, Der*
Freischütz, Der (*The Free-Shooter*)
Friend Fritz
  See *Amico Fritz, L'*

From the House of the Dead
From Today till Tomorrow
  See *Von Heute auf Morgen*
Gambler, The
Genoveva
Gianni Schicchi
  See *Trittico*
Gioconda, La (*The Joyful Girl*)
Gioielli della Madonna, I (*The Jewels of the Madonna*)
Girl of the Golden West, The
  See *Fanciulla del West, La*
Girl of the West, The
  See *Fanciulla del West, La*
Giulio Cesare in Egitto (*Julius Caesar in Egypt*)
Gloriana
Glückliche Hand, Die (*The Lucky Hand*)
Golden Apple, The
  See *Pomo d'oro, Il*
Golden Cockerel, The
Good Daughter, The
  See *Buona Figliuola, La*
Good Soldier Schweik, The
Götterdämmerung (*Twilight of the Gods*)
  See *Ring des Nibelungen, Der*
Goyescas
Grand Macabre, Le
Greek Passion, The
Guillaume Tell (*William Tell*)
Gwendoline
Hadrian in Syria
  See *Adriano in Siria*
Halka
Hamlet
Hansel and Gretel
  See *Hänsel und Gretel*
Hänsel und Gretel
Hans Heiling
Harlequin, or The Windows
  See *Arlecchino, oder, Die Fenster*
Harmonie der Welt, Die (*The Harmony of the World*)
Harmony of the World, The
  See *Harmonie der Welt, Die*
Háry János
Helen in Egypt
  See *Ägyptische Helena, Die*
Hérodiade (*Herodias*)
Herodias
  See *Hérodiade*
Heure espagnole, L' (*The Spanish Hour*)
Hugh the Drover
Huguenots, Les
Human Voice, The
  See *Voix Humaine, La*
Ice Break, The
Idomeneo, King of Crete
  See *Idomeneo, Rè di Creta*
Idomeneo, Rè di Creta (*Idomeneo, King of Crete*)
Impresario, The
  See *Schauspieldirektor, Der*

Incoronazione di Poppea, L' (The
   Coronation of Poppea)
Indes galantes, Les (The Congenial Indies)
Intermezzo
Iolanta
Iphigenia in Aulis
  See *Iphigénie en Aulide*
Iphigenia in Tauris
  See *Iphigénie en Tauride*
Iphigénie en Aulide (*Iphigenia in Aulis*)
Iphigénie en Tauride (*Iphigenia in Tauris*)
Iris
Italiana in Algeri, L' (The Italian Girl in
   Algiers)
Italian Girl in Algiers, The
  See *Italiana in Algeri, L'*
Jenůfa
Jessonda
Jewels of the Madonna, The
  See *Gioielli della Madonna, I*
Jewess, The
  See *Juive, La*
Jolie fille de Perth, La (The Fair Maid of
   Perth)
Jongleur de Notre Dame, Le (The Juggler
of Our Lady)
Jonny spielt auf (Jonny Strikes up the
Band)
Jonny Strikes up the Band
  See *Jonny spielt auf*
Joseph
Joyful Girl, The
  See *Gioconda, La*
Juggler of Our Lady, The
  See *Jongleur de Notre Dame, La*
Juive, La (The Jewess)
Julietta
Julius Caesar in Egypt
  See *Giulio Cesare in Egitto*
Junge Lord, Der (The Young Lord)
Katia Kabanová
Khovanshchina (The Khovansky Plot)
Khovansky Plot, The
  See *Khovanshchina*
King Arthur
  See *Roi Arthus, Le*
King Arthur
King in Spite of Himself, The
  See *Roi Malgré Lui, Le*
King Listens, A
  See *Rè in Ascolto, Un*
King of Lahore, The
  See *Roi de Lahore, Le*
King of Ys, The
  See *Roi d'Ys, Le*
King Priam
King Roger
  See *Król Roger*
King's Children, The
  See *Königskinder, Die*
Kitezh
  See *Legend of the Invisible City of Kitezh*

Kluge, Die (The Wise Woman)
Knight of the Rose, The
  See *Rosenkavalier, Der*
Knot Garden, The
Koanga
Königin von Saba, Die (The Queen of
   Sheba)
Königskinder, Die (The King's Children)
Król Roger (King Roger)
Lady Macbeth of Mtsensk District, The
Lady of the Lake, The
  See *Donna del lago, La*
Lakmé
Lear
Legend of the Invisible City of Kitezh
Leonora
Libuše
Licht Cycle (Light Cycle)
  See *Licht: die sieben Tage der Woche*
Licht: die sieben Tage der Woche (Light:
   The Seven Days of the Week)
Life for the Tsar, A
Light Cycle
  See *Licht: die sieben Tage der Woche*
Light: The Seven Days of the Week
  See *Licht: die sieben Tage der Woche*
Lighthouse, The
Lily of Killarney
Lithuanians, The
  See *Lituani, I*
Lituani, I (The Lithuanians)
Lizzie Borden
Lohengrin
Lombardi alla Prima Crociata, I (The
   Lombards at the First Crusade)
Lombards at the First Crusade, The
  See *Lombardi alla Prima Crociata, I*
Louise
Love for Three Oranges, The
Love of Three Kings, The
  See *Amore dei tre re, L'*
Lowlands, The
  See *Tiefland*
Lucia di Lammermoor
Lucio Silla
Lucky Hand, The
  See *Die glückliche Hand*
Lucrezia Borgia
Luisa Miller
Lulu
Lustigen Weiber von Windsor (The Merry
   Wives of Windsor)
Macbeth [Bloch]
Macbeth [Verdi]
Madama Butterfly
Magic Flute, The
  See *Zauberflöte, Die*
Magistrate, The
  See *Corregidor, Der*
Mahagonny
Maid of Orleans, The
Maid Turned Mistress, The
  See *Serva Padrona, La*

Makropoulos Case, The
Mamelles de Tirésias, Les (The Breasts of
    Tiresias)
Manon
Manon Lescaut
Maria Stuarda (Mary Stuart)
Maritana
Marriage of Figaro, The
  See Nozze di Figaro, Le
Martha
Mary Stuart
  See Maria Stuarda
Mask of Orpheus, The
Maskarade (Masquerade)
Masked Ball, A
  See Ballo in maschera, Un
Masnadieri, I (The Robbers)
Masquerade
  See Maskarade
Master Peter's Puppet Show
  See Retablo de Maese Pedro, El
Mastersingers of Nuremburg, The
  See Meistersinger von Nürnberg, Die
Mathias the Painter
  See Mathis der Maler
Mathis der Maler (Mathias the Painter)
Matrimonio segreto, Il (The Secret
    Marriage)
Mavra
May Night
Mazeppa
Medea
  See Médée
Médée (Medea) [Charpentier]
Médée (Medea) [Cherubini]
Medium, The
Mefistofele
Meistersinger von Nürnberg, Die (The
    Mastersingers of Nuremburg)
Mercy of Titus, The
  See Clemenza di Tito, La
Merry Wives of Windsor, The
  See Lustigen Weiber von Windsor, Die
Midsummer Marriage, The
Midsummer Night's Dream, A
Mignon
Mireille
Mitridate Eupatore, Il
Mitridate, Rè di Ponto
Mond, Der (The Moon)
Mondo della luna, Il (The World of the
    Moon)
Montezuma [Graun]
Montezuma [Sessions]
Moon, The
  See Mond, Der
Mosè in Egitto (Moses in Egypt)
Moses and Aaron
  See Moses und Aron
Moses in Egypt
  See Mosè in Egitto
Moses und Aron (Moses and Aaron)

Mother of Us All, The
Muette de Portici, La (The Mute Girl of
    Portici)
Mute Girl of Portici, The
  See Muette de Portici, La
Nabucco
Nero
  See Nerone
Nerone (Nero)
Neues vom Tage (News of the Day)
News of the Day
  See Neues vom Tage
New Year
Nightengale, The
  See Rossignol, Le
Nina
Nixon in China
Norma
Nose, The (Nos)
Nozze di Figaro, Le (The Marriage of
    Figaro)
Oberon
Oedipe à Colone (Oedipus at Colonus)
Oedipus at Colonus
  See Oedipe à Colone
Oedipus Rex
Opera
Orfeo ed Euridice (Orpheus and Eurydice)
    [Gluck]
Orfeo ed Euridice [Haydn]
  See Anima del Filosofo, L
Orfeo ed Euridice [Monteverdi]
  See Favola d'Orfeo, La
Orlando [Handel]
Orlando [Vivaldi]
Ormindo, L'
Orpheus and Eurydice [Gluck]
  See Orfeo ed Euridice
Orpheus and Eurydice [Haydn]
  See Anima del Filosofo, L'
Orpheus and Eurydice [Monteverdi]
  See Favola d'Orfeo, La
Otello (Othello) [Rossini]
Otello (Othello) [Verdi]
Othello
  See Otello
Owen Wingrave
Pagliacci, I (The Clowns)
Palestrina
Parsifal
Paul Bunyan
Pauvre matelot, Le (The Poor Sailor)
Pearl Fishers, The
  See Pêcheurs de Perles, Les
Pêcheurs de perles, Les (The Pearl Fishers)
Peer Gynt
Pelleas and Melisande
  See Pelléas and Mélisande
Pelléas et Mélisande
Pénélope
Peter Grimes
Pilgrim's Progress, The

Pimpinone
Pirata, Il (The Pirate)
Pirate, The
  See Pirata, Il
Poacher, The
  See Wildschütz, Der
Pomo d'oro, Il (The Golden Apple)
Poor Sailor, The
  See Pauvre matelot, Le
Porgy and Bess
Postcard from Morocco
Postillon de Longjumeau, Le (The
    Coachman of Longjumeau)
Prigioniero, Il (The Prisoner)
Prince Igor
Prisoner, The
  See Prigioniero, Il
Prodigal Son
  See Church Parables
Prophet, The
  See Prophète, Le
Prophète, Le (The Prophet)
Punch and Judy
Purgatory
Puritani, I (The Puritans)
Puritans, The
  See Puritani, I
Queen of Spades, The
Queen of Sheba, The
  See Königin von Saba, Die
Quiet Place, A
  See Trouble in Tahiti [and] A Quiet Place
Radamisto
Rake's Progress, The
Rape of Lucretia, The
Rare Occurence, A
  See Cosa Rara, Una
Rè in Ascolto, Un (A King Listens)
Rè pastore, Il (The Shepherd King)
Red Line, The
Regina
Retablo de Maese Pedro, El (Master
    Peter's Puppet Show)
Return of Ulysses to the Homeland, The
  See Ritorno d'Ulisse in patria, Il
Rheingold, Das (The Rheingold)
  See Ring des Nibelungen, Der
Richard Coeur-de-Lion
Richard the Lionhearted
  See Richard Coeur-de-Lion
Riders to the Sea
Rienzi
Rigoletto
Rinaldo
Ring Cycle
  See Ring des Nibelung, Der
Ring des Nibelungen, Der (The Ring of the
    Nibelung)
Ring of the Nibelung, The
  See Ring des Nibelungen, Der
Rise and Fall of the City of Mahagonny
  See Mahagonny

Rising of the Moon, The
Ritorno d'Ulisse in Patria, Il (The Return
    of Ulysses to the Homeland)
Robbers, The
  See Masnadieri, I
Robert le Diable (Robert the Devil)
Robert the Devil
  See Robert le Diable
Roberto Devereux
Rodelinda
Roi Arthus, Le (King Arthur)
Roi de Lahore, Le (The King of Lahore)
Roi d'Ys, Le (The King of Ys)
Roi malgré lui, Le (The King in Spite of
    Himself)
Roland
Romeo and Juliet
  See Roméo et Juliette
Roméo et Juliette (Romeo and Juliet)
Rondine, La (The Swallow)
Rosenkavalier, Der (The Knight of the Rose)
Rossignol, Le (The Nightingale)
Rusalka
Ruslan and Lyudmila
Rustic Chivalry
  See Cavalleria rusticana
Sadko
Saffo
St Francis of Assisi
  See St François d'Assise
St François d'Assise (St Francis of Assisi)
St John's Eve
  See Feuersnot
Saint of Bleecker Street, The
Salome
Samson and Delilah
  See Samson et Dalila
Samson et Dalila (Samson and Delilah)
Satyagraha
  See Triptych
Saul and David
  See Saul og David
Saul og David (Saul and David)
Savitri
Schauspieldirektor, Der (The Impresario)
Schweigsame Frau, Die (The Silent Woman)
Secret Marriage, The
  See Matrimonio segreto, Il
Secret of Susanna, The
  See Segreto di Susanna, Il
Segreto di Susanna, Il (The Secret of
    Susanna)
Semiramide
Serse (Xerxes)
Serva Padrona, La (The Maid Turned
    Mistress)
Shepherd King, The
  See Rè pastore, Il
Short Life, The
  See Vida breve, La
Sicilian Vespers, The
  See Vêpres siciliennes, Les

Siège de Corinthe, Le (The Siege of
    Corinth)
Siege of Corinth, The
  See *Siège de Corinthe, Le*
Siegfried
  See *Ring des Nibelungen, Der*
Silent Woman, The
  See *Schweigsame Frau, Die*
Simon Boccanegra
Sleepwalker, The
  See *Sonnambula, La*
Snow Maiden, The
Soldaten, Die (The Soldiers)
Soldiers, The
  See *Soldaten, Die*
Sonnambula, La (The Sleepwalker)
Soul of the Philosopher, The
  See *L'anima del Filosofo*
Spanish Hour, The
  See *Heure espagnole, L'*
Staatstheater (State Theater)
State Theatre
  See *Staatstheatre*
Stiffelio
Stone Guest, The
Straniera, La (The Foreign Lady)
Strayed Woman, The
  See *Traviata, La*
Street Scene
Suor Angelica
  See *Trittico*
Susannah
Swallow, The
  See *Rondine, La*
Tabarro, Il
  See *Trittico*
Tales of Hoffmann, The
  See *Contes d'Hoffmann, Les*
Tamerlano
Tancredi
Tannhäuser
Tarare
Taverner
Tender Land
Thaïs
Thésée (Theseus)
Theseus
  See *Thésée*
Threepenny Opera, The
  See *Dreigroschenoper, Die*
Tiefland (The Lowlands)
Tosca
Tote Stadt, Die (The Dead City)
Traviata, La (The Strayed Woman)
Treemonisha
Triptych [Glass]
Triptych [Puccini]
  See *Trittico, Il*
Tristan and Isolde
  See *Tristan und Isolde*
Tristan und Isolde (Tristan and Isolde)
Trittico, Il (Triptych)

Troilus and Cressida
Trojans, The
  See *Troyens, Les*
Troubadour, The
  See *Trovatore, Il*
Trouble in Tahiti [and] A Quiet Place
Trovatore, Il (The Troubadour)
Troyens, Les (The Trojans)
Tsar and Carpenter
  See *Zar und Zimmermann*
Turandot [Busoni]
Turandot [Puccini]
Turco in Italia, Il (The Turk in Italy)
Turk in Italy, The
  See *Turco in Italia, Il*
Turn of the Screw
Twilight of the Gods
  See *Ring des Nibelungen, Der*
Two Days, The
  See *Deux Journées, Les*
Two Foscari, The
  See *Due Foscari, I*
Two Widows, The
Ulisse (Ulysses)
Ulysses
  See *Ulisse*
Undine [Hoffmann]
Undine [Lortzing]
Unglückselige Cleopatra, Die (The Unhappy
    Cleopatra)
Valkyrie, The
  See *Ring des Nibelungen, Der*
Vampire, The
  See *Vampyr, Der*
Vampyr, Der (The Vampire)
Vanessa
Venus and Adonis
Vêpres siciliennes, Les (The Sicilian
    Vespers)
Vestal Virgin, The
  See *Vestale, La*
Vestale, La (The Vestal Virgin)
Vida breve, La (The Short Life)
Village Romeo and Juliet, A
Village Soothsayer, The
  See *Devin du Village, Le*
Villi, Le (The Willis)
Voix Humaine, La (The Human Voice)
Von Heute auf Morgen (From Today till
    Tomorrow)
Walküre, Die (The Valkyrie)
  See *Ring des Nibelungen, Der*
Wally, La
War and Peace
Werther
White Lady, The
  See *Dame blanche, La*
Wife of Bernauer, The
  See *Bernauerin, Die*
Wildschütz, Der (The Poacher)
William Tell
  See *Guillaume Tell*

Willis, The
  See *Villi, Le*
Woman without a Shadow, The
  See *Frau ohne Schatten, Die*
World of the Moon, The
  See *Mondo della luna, Il*
Wozzeck
Wreckers, The
Xerxes
  See *Serse*

Yerma
Young Lord, The
  See *Junge Lord, Der*
Zampa
Zar und Zimmermann (Tsar and Carpenter)
Zauberflöte, Die (The Magic Flute)
Zazà
Zémire et Azor

International Dictionary of
OPERA

A

ABARIS, OR THE BOREADS
See ABARIS, OU LES BORÉADES

ABARIS, ou Les Boréades [Abaris, or The Boreads].

Composer: Jean-Philippe Rameau.

Librettist: L. de Cahusac.

First Performance: intended for fall 1763; first concert performance, London, 14 April 1975; first staged performance, Aix-en-Provence, July 1982.

Roles: Alphise; Sémire; Polymnie; A Nymph; Abaris; Calisis; Borée; Borilée; Adamas; Apollo; L'Amour; chorus.

Publications

articles–

Sadler, G. "Rameau's Last Opera: Abaris, ou Les Boréades." *Musical Times* 116 (1975): 327.
Donnington, Robert. "Rameau's *Les Boréades.*" *Early Music* 3 (1975).

unpublished–

Smith, Mary-Térey. "Jean-Philippe Rameau: Abaris ou les Boréades, a Critical Edition." Ph.D. dissertation, University of Rochester, 1971.

* * *

Abaris, ou Les Boréades, Rameau's last opera, was composed toward the end of his life. After a decade of ballet operas, pastorals, and similar works in a lighter vein, he returned to the form of his first successes, the *tragédie lyrique.* Three scores, the holograph and two copies with two sets of vocal/instrumental partbooks, contain the music. Rameau's original manuscript and a copy with parts are housed in the Bibliothèque Nationale, Paris. French musicologist Sylvie Bouissou recently discovered the third score and matching parts in the Nationale Archives—copied by Durand in 1763—which include a list of singers and instrumentalists participating in rehearsals in April 1763. Although the recently discovered music holds references to a fall 1763 premiere, *Les Boréades* was not performed in the eighteenth century. Musicological interest in Baroque music brought about the rediscovery of the opera: Paul Masson described it in his pioneering book on Rameau's operas in 1930. A true recognition, however, had to wait for Girdlestone's detailed study (1957) which emphasized the inventiveness of the score and quoted numerous musical examples.

Uncertainty surrounds the identity of the librettist. Decroix, a personal acquaintance of Rameau's, and a collector of his music, attributes the text to Cahusac, who collaborated with the composer frequently. If so, Rameau must have owned the story for several years since the poet had died in 1759.

Although the first performance of *Abaris ou Les Boréades*—a barely noticed broadcast by the O.R.T.F.—took place in 1963 in France, the real premiere was given at the Queen Elisabeth Hall, London, on 14 April 1975, in concert version with the Monteverdi Choir and Orchestra conducted by John Eliot Gardiner (who also prepared the edition). The cast included Jennifer Smith, Philip Landridge, Thomas Hemsley, Raimund Herincx, Anne-Marie Rodde, Jean-Claude Orliac, Dale Dusing, and Mary Beverly. It was the public's enthusiastic reaction to the concert presentation that led eventually to the first ever staged production at the Festival of Aix-en-Provence in July 1982. A recording, based on this production, followed in 1984. The first North American performance, shortened to suit local conditions, was given on 21 March 1982 at the Town Hall in New York City, also in concert form. Under Richard Kapp's direction, Ruth Welting, Abram Morales, David Arnold, and James Dietsch sang the leading parts with the Schola Cantorum Singers and the Philharmonia Virtuosi Orchestra. For this presentation the ensemble used a critical edition reconstructed and realized by Mary Térey-Smith.

Located in the ancient kingdom of Bactria, the story centers on the love between the young queen, Alphise, and Abaris, a noble foreigner of unknown origin who serves in Apollo's temple. According to tradition, Alphise must marry a descendent of Borée (Boreas), the god of the north wind. Pressed by the two "proper" suitors, Calisis and Borilée, to make a choice, the queen abdicates and publicly announces her love for Abaris. Borée manifests his displeasure with a violent storm; the winds envelop Alphise and carry her to the god's realm to be punished. With the assistence of Polimnie, Abaris finds the imprisoned queen and stuns Borée and the threatening suitors with Love's magic arrow. Apollo's appearance resolves the situation: Abaris is his son by a nymph (daughter of Borée), thus the obstacles for the marriage between Alphise and Abaris are removed. A general rejoicing ends the opera.

Stylistically, *Abaris, ou Les Boréades* is a highly complex work that displays a wide range of musical elements from the traditional to the boldly original. Rameau's concern to integrate music and drama is the main driving force in the piece starting with the overture, where the closing horn-calls are transformed into the fanfares of the hunting party in scene i. His preoccupation to combine the growing dramatic tension with musical continuity is especially evident in the last three acts and results in extended passages using thematic development in a symphonic context. An example of this is found in the last act, where a five-note descending scale pattern (first used in the accompaniment of *"Le sauvage avec nous"* in scene i) becomes the germ-motive of the entire torment section in scenes ii and iii, in which Borée and the suitors try to force Alphise into submission. In place of the continuous orchestral drive, Rameau builds up the excitement by unexpected changes and interruptions as he switches from solo air to fast-paced dance movement, and from recitatives to choir, all the time expanding Borée's menacing "Qu'elle gémisse" into a threatening choral ensemble. Mozart's late Italian opera finales come to mind as we admire the skilfull treatment of transitions and the elimination of set numbers to maintain dramatic continuity.

Inspired scoring is not limited to large scale dramatic scenes; imaginative melodic, harmonic, and formal writing can be found in vocal solos. At eighty, the composer seems to have pushed caution and practical considerations aside to make room for passionate outbursts (Alphise: "Songe affreux"—act III, scene i; Abaris: "Lieux désolés"—act IV, scene ii), ravishingly beautiful melodies (Alphise and Abaris: "Que ces moments sont doux"—act V, scene ii) and symbolic use of nature in comparison with deeply felt emotions (Nymph: "Un horizon serein"—act I, scene iv, and Abaris: "Que l'amour"—act V, scene v).

The instrumental pieces in *Les Boréades*—dances, *entrées* and *symphonies*—are as valuable as those in Rameau's earlier operas. It is true that the characteristic mosaic-style setting of *divertissements* (a series of short dances interspersed with solo and choral airs) is maintained here, as critics point out, at a time of symphonic development in Italy and Germany with emphasis on longer movements, but the multiplicity of contrasting themes, orchestral colors and rhythmic variety create a richly versatile musical tapestry which flows constantly. To enhance the meaning of titles, the composer often employs program music in orchestral numbers. In *Gavotte pour les Heures et les Zéphirs* (act IV, scene iv) he instructs the strings to imitate the striking of the clocks; against this ticking background the two *petit flutes* and bassoons represent the gently blowing winds. Country dances may have prompted the spirited nature of two fast-moving, virtuosic *Contredanses en Rondeau*.

Tenderly crafted expressive music announces the arrival of Polimnie and her *entourage* (act IV, scene iv). This *entrée* presents a rare occurance of contrapuntal texture in a lyrical context: the bassoon imitates the oboe/violin part against the slow moving counter themes of the violas and bass instruments. In an introductory *symphonie* the genre's dramatic aspect is tested with a graphic portrayal of the destructive subterranean winds (act V, scene i); fragmented scale runs and sudden break-offs bring forth a vivid, frightening image of gusting north winds ready to burst upon the earth and wreak havoc. Rameau's ingeniously scattered orchestration accentuates the thematic fragments and paints a brief yet amazingly realistic, modern sounding tone poem.

Is *Abaris ou Les Boréades* a significant work deserving a permanent place in the repertory of opera companies, or is it only an interesting but uneven composition of historical interest by an aging master? The opera's shortcomings are those of an anachronistic idiom: by 1764 the Lullian *tragédie lyrique* was *passé*. Rameau, aware of the changing public taste, filled the old form with vivid, exciting, at times ingenious music, and experimented with large-scale continuous writing to achieve unity. As the audience reaction to performances of *Les Boréades* shows, stylistically well-prepared performances under imaginative, knowledgeable leadership are appreciated by lovers of early opera regardless whether the music was

written by Rameau, Monteverdi, Purcell, Cavalli, Handel, Scarlatti, Keiser or other first-rate Baroque composers.
—Mary Térey-Smith

ABBADO, Claudio.

Conductor. Born 26 June 1933, in Milan. Studied music with his father, then at the Milan Conservatory, where he received a piano degree, 1955; studied conducting with Antonio Votto and piano with Friedrich Gulda, 1955; studied conducting with Hans Swarowsky at the Vienna Academy of Music, and with Carlo Zecchi and Alceo Galliera at the Accademia Chigiana in Siena, 1956-58; conducting debut in Trieste, 1958; Koussevitzky conducting prize, Berkshire Music Center, Tanglewood, 1963; American conducting debut with the New York Philharmonic, 7 April 1963; symphonic conductor at the Teatro alla Scala, Milan; conducted the Vienna Philharmonic, 1965; opera conductor at La Scala, 1968; principal guest conductor of the London Symphony, 1972; took the Vienna Philharmonic to Japan and China, 1972-73; Mozart Medal of the Mozart-Gemeinde of Vienna, 1973; conducted the La Scala company in the Soviet Union, 1974; conducted the Vienna Philharmonic and the La Scala company in the United States, 1976; founded the European Community Youth Orchestra, 1978; principal conductor of the Chamber Orchestra of Europe, 1981-; principal conductor of the London Symphony Orchestra, 1979; Golden Nicolai Medal of the Vienna Philharmonic, 1980; principal guest conductor of the Chicago Symphony, 1982-86; founded La Filarmonica della Scala in Milan, 1982; music director of the London Symphony Orchestra, 1983-88; Gran Croce, 1984; Mahler Medal of Vienna, 1985; principal conductor of the Vienna State Opera, 1986; founded the Mahler Orchestra, Vienna, 1986; member of the Légion d'honneur of France, 1986; artistic director of the Berlin Philharmonic, succeeding Herbert von Karajan, 1989.

Publications

By ABBADO: interviews–

Matheopoulos, Helena. *Maestro: Encounters with Conductors of Today.* London, 1982.
Chesterman, Robert, ed. *Conductors in Conversation.* London, 1990.

About ABBADO: articles–

Rhein, J. von. "Claudio Abbado." *Ovation* May (1984).

*　　*　　*

Perhaps more than any other late twentieth-century conductor, Claudio Abbado has demonstrated a complete mastery of both the standard symphonic literature and the operatic repertory. His commitment to opera has allowed him to create a vast repertoire, ranging from the works of Mozart to those of the late twentieth century. In doing so he has established himself as one of the foremost interpreters of opera of his generation.

Claudio Abbado

Abbado's opera debut came in 1958 at the Teatro Communale in Trieste, where he conducted Prokofiev's *Love for Three Oranges*. According to some critics his early conducting displayed elements of self-consciousness and showmanship that interfered with the overall interpretative effect. But even at this early point in his career, Abbado was commended for his close adherence to the composer's intentions and for an amazing ability to balance the orchestral and vocal resources. In 1963 he shared the Mitropoulos Prize for conducting with Zdenek Kosler and Pedro Calderon. Although predicted by some to be the least likely to fulfill the high expectations suggested by the prize, he now represents the only one to have unquestionably realized his potential.

From early in his career critics have almost unanimously commented on his individuality of approach and his ability to draw vivid musical detail from the orchestra. In this regard he has been compared favorably to his countrymen and predecessors Carlo Maria Giulini and Arturo Toscanini. Abbado generally acknowledges that Wilhelm Furtwängler has been one of the great influences on his career. He admired particularly Furtwängler's freedom of interpretation which, as Abbado explains, Furtwängler always justified. Similarly, Abbado always attempts to justify any apparent license he takes with a score. He also venerated Toscanini's extreme precision and control in handling the orchestra, and furthermore acknowledges the influence of Erich and Carlos Kleiber, Dmitri Mitropoulos, and Bruno Walter with helping him master the technical aspects of his craft.

In addition to the inevitable comparisons with Giulini and Toscanini, Abbado has also been equated with Herbert von Karajan, Karl Böhm, and fellow Italian Victor De Sabata. However much he has been compared with anyone in this illustrious group, his adoption of their techniques has not been superficial. Rather, while he may possess something of each of them, he nevertheless remains totally individual in his approach.

Certainly one of Abbado's most important contributions has proved his fruitful association with the prestigious opera at the Teatro alla Scala, Milan, from 1968 until his resignation as artistic director in 1980. Some of his La Scala collaborations with director Giorgio Strehler represent landmarks in late twentieth-century operatic production. When on tour with the La Scala company, he has similarly revealed new perspectives in the standard operatic repertoire. The 1976 La Scala production of *Simon Boccanegra* at Covent Garden, for example, was described by one enthusiastic critic as ". . . one of the few truly great operatic experiences of the post-war era."

Another of Abbado's most important contributions derives from his support of contemporary opera. He has always championed new and unusual works, such as operas by Luciano Berio, Pierre Boulez, Karlheinz Stockhausen, and Krzysztof Penderecki for performance at La Scala. In a July 1979 interview he stated specifically that "we will continue to introduce a new contemporary opera every season, as we have done works, for instance, of Nono and Penderecki. Next year there will be a premiere of an opera by Luciano Berio based on a story of Calvino."

Abbado has also enhanced the standard repertory by often choosing unconventional versions of operas. For his last production at La Scala, *Boris Godunov* (1979), Abbado utilized Musorgsky's original version of the score edited by Paul Lamm (1928) and David Lloyd-Jones (1975) in place of the more usual and colorful orchestration by Rimsky-Korsakov. Abbado viewed this not as a concession to current fashion for the "early version at any cost," but as a reflection of his sincere belief in its musical value.

Abbado clearly, and perhaps not unexpectedly, possesses a natural affinity for the interpretation of Verdi. British audiences at Covent Garden have been especially receptive to his Verdi productions. In 1975 his Verdi conducting was hailed as the finest since Giulini last appeared at Covent Garden. Similarly, the visit of Abbado and the La Scala company in September, 1976 to the Opera House of Washington's Kennedy Center proved an extraordinary revelation to American audiences.

Finally, Abbado has not confined himself to one orchestra and location, but has conducted liberally and conscientiously at opera houses all over the world. An excellent example was his critically acclaimed conducting of Alban Berg's *Wozzeck* in the late 1980s with the Vienna State Opera, from which an equally acclaimed live recording resulted. The interpretation stands as one of the finest recorded performances of this work to date and achieves high points both in the performing history of the work, and in Abbado's career as a conductor of twentieth-century opera.

—William Thornhill

THE ABDUCTION FROM THE SERAGLIO
See DIE ENTFÜHRUNG AUS DEM SERAIL

ADAM, Adolphe (-Charles).

Composer. Born 24 July 1803, in Paris. Died 3 May 1856, in Paris. Son of the composer and pianist Louis Adam. Studied piano with Henry Lemoine and composition with Boieldieu at the Paris Conservatory; began composing songs for vaudevilles in 1824; first dramatic work the one act operetta *Pierre et Catherine*, 1829; first success the comic opera *Le châlet*, 1834; as a result of a dispute with the director of the Opéra-Comique, Adam began a new opera theater in 1847 called the Opéra-National, for the purpose of performing works of young, aspiring composers, but it was forced to close at the outbreak of the revolution in February, 1848; contributed music criticism to the *Constitutionnel,* the *Assemblée National,* and the *Gazette Musical;* elected a member of the Institut in 1844; appointed professor of composition at the Paris Conservatory in 1849. Adam is best known for his ballets *Giselle* (Paris, Opéra, 28 June 1841), and *Le corsaire* (Paris, Opéra, 23 January 1856).

Operas

Pierre et Catherine, J.H. Vernoy de Saint-Georges, Paris, Opéra-Comique, 9 February 1829.

Henry V et ses compagnons (pasticcio), Paris, Nouveautés, 27 February 1830.

Danilowa, Jean Baptiste Vial and D. Duport, Paris, Opéra-Comique, 23 April 1830.

Rafaël (pasticcio), Paris, Nouveautés, 26 April 1830.

Trois jours en une heure (in collaboration with Romagnesi), Gabriel [J.J.G. de Lurier] and Masson, Paris, Opéra-Comique, 21 August 1830.

Joséphine, ou Le retour de Wagram, Gabriel and Delaboullaye, Paris, Opéra-Comique, 2 December 1830.

Le morceau d'ensemble, Carmouche and F. de Courcy, Paris, Opéra-Comique, 7 March 1831.

Le grand prix, ou Le voyage à frais communs, Gabriel and Masson, Paris, Opéra-Comique, 9 July 1831.

The Dark Diamond (historical melodrama), London, Covent Garden, 5 November 1832.

Le proscrit, ou Le tribunal invisible, Carmouche and Saintine, Paris, Opéra-Comique, 18 September 1833.

Une bonne fortune, Féréol and Edouard, Paris, Opéra-Comique, 23 January 1834.

Le châlet, Eugène Scribe and Anne Honoré Joseph Mélesville, Paris, Opéra-Comique, 25 September 1834.

La marquise, J.H. Vernoy de Saint-Georges and Adolphe de Leuven, Paris, Opéra-Comique, 28 February 1835.

Micheline, ou L'heure d'esprit, Saint-Hilaire, Masson, and Villeneuve, Paris, Opéra-Comique, 29 June 1835.

Le postillon de Longjumeau, Adolphe de Leuven and (Léon Lévy) Thérie Brunswick, Paris, Opéra-Comique, 13 October 1836.

Adolphe Adam

Le fidèle berger, Eugène Scribe and J.H. Vernoy de Saint-Georges, Paris, Opéra-Comique, 6 January 1838.

Le brasseur de Preston, Adolphe de Leuven and (Léon Lévy) Thérie Brunswick, Paris, Opéra-Comique, 31 October 1838.

Régine, ou Les deux nuits, Eugène Scribe, Paris, Opéra-Comique, 17 January 1839.

La reine d'un jour, Eugène Scribe and J.H. Vernoy de Saint-Georges, Paris, Opéra-Comique, 19 September 1839.

La rose de Péronne, Adolphe de Leuven and Adolphe Philippe d'Ennery, Paris, Opéra-Comique, 12 December 1840.

La main de fer, ou Le mariage secret, Eugène Scribe and Adolphe de Leuven, Paris, Opéra-Comique, 26 October 1841.

Le roi d'Yvetot, Adolphe de Leuven and Brunswick (after a poem by Béranger), Paris, Opéra-Comique, 13 October 1842.

Lambert Simnel [completion of a work by H. Monpou], Eugène Scribe and Anne Honoré Joseph Mélesville, Paris, Opéra-Comique, 14 September 1843.

Cagliostro, Eugène Scribe and J.H. Vernoy de Saint-Georges, Paris, Opéra-Comique, 10 February 1844.

Richard en Palestine, Paul Foucher, Paris, Opéra, 7 October 1844.

La bouquetière, H. Lucas, Paris, Opéra, 31 May 1847.

Les premiers pas (in collaboration with Auber, Carafa, and Halévy), Vaëz and Royer, Paris, Opéra-National, 15 November 1847.

Le toréador, ou L'accord parfait, Thomas Marie François Sauvage, Paris, Opéra-Comique, 18 May 1849.

Le fanal, J.H. Vernoy de Saint-Georges, Paris, Opéra, 24 December 1849.

Giralda, ou La nouvelle Psyché, Eugène Scribe, Paris, Opéra-Comique, 20 July 1850.

La poupée de Nuremberg, Adolphe de Leuven and Arthur de Beauplan, Paris, Opéra-National, 21 February 1852.

Le farfadet, François Antoine Eugène de Planard, Paris, Opéra-Comique, 19 March 1852.

Si j'étais roi, D'Ennery and Jules Brésil, Paris, Théâtre-Lyrique, 4 September 1852.

La faridondaine (drama with songs) (with A. De Groot), Dupeuty and Ernest Bourget, Porte Saint-Martin, 30 December 1852.

Le sourd, ou L'auberge plein, Adolphe de Leuven and Ferdinand Langlé (after P.J.B. Choudard Desforges), Paris, Opéra-Comique, 2 February 1853.

Le roi des halles, Adolphe de Leuven and Brunswick, Paris, Théâtre-Lyrique, 11 April 1853.

Le bijou perdu, Adolphe de Leuven and P.A.A. Pittaud De Forges, Paris, Théâtre-Lyrique, 6 October 1853.

Le muletier de Tolèdo, D'Ennery and Clairville, Paris, Théâtre-Lyrique, 16 December 1854.

A Clichy, D'Ennery and E. Grangé, Paris, Théâtre-Lyrique, 24 December 1854.

Le houzard de Berchini, Rosier, Paris, Opéra-Comique, 17 October 1855.

Falstaff, J.H. Vernoy de Saint-Georges and Adolphe de Leuven (after Shakespeare), Paris, Théâtre-Lyrique, 18 January 1856.

Mam'zelle Geneviève, Brunswick and Beauplan, Paris, Théâtre-Lyrique, 24 March 1856.

Les pantins de Violette, Léon Battu, Paris, Bouffes-Parisiens, 29 April 1856.

Other works: ballets, choral works, piano music, songs.

Publications

By ADAM: books–

E.H. Méhul. L.J.F. Hérold: Biographien. Kassel, 1855.
Souvenirs d'un musicien. Paris, 1857.
Derniers souvenirs d'un musicien. Paris, 1859.

articles–

"Lettres sur la musique française, 1836-1850." *La revue de Paris* August-September (1903).

About ADAM: books–

Neumann, William. *Adrien François Boieldieu: Adolph Adam: Biographien.* Kassel, 1855.
Halévy, F. *Notice sur la vie et ouvrages de M. Adolphe Adam.* Paris, 1859; reprinted as "Adolphe Adam" in Halévy, *Souvenirs et portraits,* Paris, 1861.
Mirecourt, E. de. *Adolphe Adam.* Paris, 1868.
Pougin, Arthur. *Adolphe Adam.* Paris, 1877.
Walsh, Thomas Joseph. *Second Empire opera; the Théâtre-Lyrique, Paris, 1851-1870.* London, 1981.
Studwell, William E. *Adolphe Adam and Léo Delibes: A Guide to Research.* New York, 1987.

articles–

Landormy, Paul, and Joseph Loisel, "Adam." In *Encyclopédie de la musique et dictionnaire du conservatoire.* Paris, 1913-31.
Cooper, Martin. "Before Broadway: Musical Comedy Has an Ancestor in Opéra Comique." *Opera News* 30/April 9 (1960): 9.
Hering, P. "Louis Joseph Ferdinand Herold (1791-1833), Adolphe Adam (1803-1856), Emile Waldteufel (1837-1915)." In *La musique en Alsace hier et aujourd'hui.* Paris, 1970.

* * *

A dominant figure from the 1830s through the 1850s, Adolphe Adam is known today only for his carol *Cantique de Noël,* several ballets and several operas. In a time span of thirty-two years, however, he produced 71 operatic works (mostly light), 15 ballets, and about 300 other compositions. His sole true masterpiece is the enduring ballet *Giselle,* one of the favorites of the choreographic repertory. Some other ballets, *La jolie fille de Gand, Le diable à quatre,* and *Le corsaire,* have also been performed in recent decades.

Perhaps most importantly, Adam was a pioneer of comic opera. Five such works by him are worth noting. *Le châlet* was Adam's most successful operatic work inside of France, but today it is rarely performed. *Giralda* appears to be all but forgotten as a viable production, but the lively, Spanish-flavor overture is occasionally played on classic music stations. The overture to *La poupée de Nuremberg,* with slight touches of brilliance, similarly appears from time to time on such stations. The quality of the overture, plus the work's at least borderline survival in the light operatic repertory, suggest a degree of underappreciation.

Si j'étais roi is Adam's second most popular opera. Its delightful, colorful, exotic, pseudo-oriental overture is a minor concert favorite. As a whole production exhibiting similar characteristics of charm, *Si j'étais roi* is no stranger to post-

World War II stages, particularly in Germany. It is a minor work, certainly, but not inconsequential.

Adam's best known opera is *Le postillon de Lonjumeau.* (Note that the "g" in the name of the town was dropped in the original title). Light hearted and even vulgar, the lively *Postillon* is the closest Adam got to an operatic masterwork. At times it is described as a masterpiece, but such a label would probably be stretching our artistic sensibilities. Yet it is a likeable and very good work, and it still retains a significant place in the world of light opera. Like *Si j'étais roi,* it remains a vital, living organism with a fair amount of appeal to contemporary audiences, most notably those in Germany.

The twentieth century view of Adam has been mixed, at times highly negative, but with recent commentary tending to be more positive. Although deserving of some of the criticism cast upon him, Adam merits a better fate than the general level of commentary on his contributions. Adam is decidedly not a great composer, but he should not be trivialized either. His ballets directly led to those of his protégé Delibes, thereby planting the seeds for Delibes's maturation into "the father of modern ballet music." He was in addition one of the key figures in the development of light opera, or in other words was a major link in the evolution of twentieth century musical comedy. Neither of these two historical functions should be overlooked, and neither should those several works which have survived about a century and a half in reasonably good health.

—William E. Studwell

ADAMS, John.

Composer. Born 15 February 1947, in Worchester, Massachusetts. Initially studied clarinet with his father, then with Felix Viscuglia; B.A. (magna cum lauda) 1969, and M.A. (in composition), 1971, Harvard University, where he studied with Leon Kirchner, David Del Tredici, Roger Sessions, and Earl Kim; an accomplished clarinettist, he played the solo part in Walter Piston's *Clarinet Concerto,* Carnegie Hall, 1969; head of composition department, San Francisco Conservatory, 1971-81; Guggenheim fellowship, 1982; new music adviser, San Francisco Symphony Orchestra, beginning in 1978, composer in residence, 1982–85; creative chair, St. Paul Chamber Orchestra, beginning in 1988.

Operas

Publisher: Associated.

Nixon in China. Alice Goodman, Houston, Houston Grand Opera, 22 October 1987.
The Death of Klinghoffer, Alice Goodman, Brussels, Théâtre Royal de la Monnaie, March 1991.

Other works: various works for both conventional and unconventional ensembles and mediums.

Publications

By ADAMS: interview–

"Nixon in China." [Conversation with Andrew Porter] *Tempo* December (1988).

Adams studied composition at Harvard University with Leon Kirchner, Roger Sessions, Earl Kim and Mario di Bonaventura. While at Harvard he distinguished himself as the first undergraduate permitted to submit a musical composition as his required senior thesis. He completed a BA in 1969 and an MA in 1971. During the summer of 1970 he served as composer-in-residence at the Marlboro Festival in Vermont. In 1972, he became director of the "New Music Ensemble" at the San Francisco Conservatory of Music, a post which he held until 1982.

Adams' association with the San Francisco Symphony Orchestra began in 1978, when he became the new music advisor for the orchestra under Edo de Waart. Under the auspices of that orchestra, he founded and directed the "New and Unusual Music Series," which served as a model for the nationwide "Meet the Composer" program. In 1982, under this residence program, Adams was appointed composer-in-residence with the San Francisco Symphony Orchestra and served until 1985.

Particularly important from this collaboration are his early works using voices, *Harmonium* and *Grand Pianola Music.* These pieces, although still influenced by minimalistic principles, show Adams as a composer with a commanding gift for sweeping lyrical melody, and the ability to combine modern and classical idioms with superior craftsmanship.

Harmonium (1981), commissioned by the San Francisco Symphony Orchestra, sets the poems of John Donne and Emily Dickinson. Of the young composer's first work for chorus, Alan Rich of *Newsweek* (March 18, 1985) said that the cantata was "among the major choral works of the era." Rich especially admired the "amazing range of sound" that Adams was able to elicit from the chorus. In *Grand Pianola Music* (1983) scored for wind, brass, two pianos, percussion ensemble, and three female vocalists, Adams abandoned pure minimalism for material that is reminiscent of early twentieth-century American popular music, particularly marches and player-piano music. Although *Grand Pianola Music* was not well received, the EMI/Angel recording went on to be a best seller.

Adams' opera *Nixon in China* (1985) represents a major contribution to late twentieth-century opera. Based on President Richard Nixon's historic seven day trip to the People's Republic of China in February of 1972, the opera was created in collaboration with American producer Peter Sellars and the poet/librettist Alice Goodman. The idea for the opera was offered by Sellars, a director whose imaginative and unusual settings of classical plays and operas have won critical respect. In 1984, the three collaborators gathered in Washington D.C. to study news reports and television footage of the historic visit. Adams told Stephanie Buchau in her *Opera News* interview (October 1987) that they had focused on Nixon's "more heroic aspects," finding Nixon an "interesting character" because of his vulnerability. Alice Goodman's beautifully written libretto succeeds in focusing on the heroic qualities of each character.

The opera is uniquely constructed in that its structural units decrease proportionally throughout the opera. There are three scenes in the first act, two scenes in the second act and one scene in the third act. The dramatic plot parallels the diminishing size of the acts in that it moves from a larger public sphere to a smaller personal one throughout the course of the opera.

Despite his foundations in minimalism, as a composer of opera, Adams uses melodic material in dramatic rather than repetitive ways. K. Robert Schwartz (*Fanfare,* June 1985) suggests that the dramatic requirements of Adams's music transcend the "deliberate austerity" inherent in minimalistic music. Adams has not abandoned the repetition and arpeggiation of minimalism; he simply relegates them to the orchestral accompaniment, and by doing so makes the vocal lines stand out in dramatic relief. This preservation of minimalistic elements in the orchestral scoring allows a freedom of vocal writing previously not seen in minimalistic opera.

Nixon in China was premiered on October 22, 1987, by the Houston Grand Opera. Two months later the production traveled to the "Next Wave Festival" at the Brooklyn Academy of Music and the Kennedy Center in Washington D.C. These performances took place amidst a storm of publicity and strongly divided critical controversy. The production was also mounted at the Netherlands Opera in Amsterdam (June 1988) and at the Edinburgh Festival (August 1988).

—Patricia Robertson

ADRIANA LECOUVREUR.

Composer: Francesco Cilèa.

Librettist: Arturo Colautti (after Scribe and Legouvé).

First Performance: Milan, Lirico, 6 November 1902.

Roles: Adriana Lecouvreur (soprano); Princess de Bouillon (mezzo-soprano); Maurice (tenor); Michonnet (baritone); Mlle Jouvenot (soprano); Mlle Dangeville (mezzo-soprano); Poisson (tenor); Quinault (bass); Abbé de Chazeuil (tenor); Prince de Bouillon (bass); Majordomo (speaking); chorus (SSATTBB).

Publications

articles–

Olivero, Magda. "Cilèa and *Adriana Lecouvreur.*" *Opera* August (1963).

*   *   *

Although it is not the most popular opera with critics or with audiences, *Adriana Lecouvreur* is very popular with singers, and has thus stayed in the repertoire for decades. The music is charming and pleasant, but the plot (involving death by

poisoned posies) is slightly week. The title role, based on an historical figure, provides great dramatic potential, beautiful melodies, and a relatively untaxing tessitura for the soprano. Several other meaty roles make this a singer's opera.

The plot, typical for its time, spins a complex web of tragedy and deceit. The opera opens as the troupe of the Comédie Française prepares for a performance of Racine's *Bajazet.* Michonnet, the stage manager, expresses his hidden love for the famous and fascinating leading lady, Adriana Lecouvreur. The Prince of Bouillon is also present to express his admiration for the actress Mlle Duclos. Both of these women are to appear in the evening's entertainment. Adriana enters, book in hand, rehearsing her part. Michonnet begins to confess his love for her, but is forestalled by her confession of her love for the young officer, Maurice de Saxe, not knowing that he is as renowned for his conquests in the boudoir as for those on the field. Maurice appears to wish her luck and promises to meet her after the show is over; she gives him a bouquet of violets as a token of her love. The Prince re-enters and intercepts a letter written to Maurice by Mlle Duclos; in his jealousy over his mistress, he does not realize that she was writing not for herself, but for his wife the Princess. The note proposes a rendezvous at the Prince's villa, La Grange; the Prince passes the letter along its original course, but determines to be there himself to surprise the lovers. After he receives the letter, Maurice makes his excuses to Adriana, for in order to keep his meeting with the Princess he must neglect the actress. After the play, the Prince invites the jilted Adriana to join him for supper at La Grange, and she accepts.

The second act opens at La Grange where the Princess waits for Maurice. He does not love her, but wants to make use of her—he is the rightful heir to the throne of Poland and needs money to secure it. When he arrives, she sees the bouquet of violets and falls into a jealous rage, so he gives the flowers to her. When she hears the approaching coach, she hides; as the Prince enters, he sees her fleeing, but still believes her to be his mistress rather than his wife, and wants to keep her trapped in hiding until the right moment. Adriana arrives and is surprised to find Maurice there. He tells her he was obliged to meet a lady for political reasons, a lady who is now in hiding, and asks Adriana to guard the hiding place so the woman might flee unharmed. Adriana does help the Princess flee, but in the process they both discover that they love the same man—although in the dark they do not know each other's identity. The Princess flees, and Maurice joins her, much to the sorrow of the actress. Adriana is overcome with grief as the others trot merrily down to supper.

The third act takes place at the salon of the Princess. Maurice is there, and Adriana, who has been asked to recite, is also present. The two women recognize each other as the unknown rivals for Maurice's affections. Adriana chooses the great speech from *Phèdre,* so she can use it to denounce her hostess. In her momentary triumph, she does not realize that the Princess will exact a slower, more permanent revenge.

The fourth act opens on a disconsolate Adriana; she feels neglected by Maurice, who is off fighting for his throne. It is her birthday, and she is visited by friends and fellow actors, and is receiving many gifts. One of the gifts is a casket which contains her bouquet of violets. Believing that this gift means he has forsaken her, she cries over them and kisses them, not realizing they have been poisoned and sent by her rival. Maurice arrives to explain his absence, and vows faithful love ever more. It is too late, however: the poison does its work, and she dies in his arms.

The real Adrienne Lecouvreur was a famous actress at the Comédie Française during the eighteenth century, who revolutionized French theater of the time by introducing natural declamation as the preferred mode of presentation. She was considered the greatest actress of her time and was a rival of the older, traditional actress, Mlle Duclos. In 1725, she met and became the devoted mistress to the pretender to the Polish throne, Hermann-Maurice, Compte de Saxe. The duchess de Bouillon also loved Maurice, but he rejected her romantic overtures, so she hatched a plot to poison her rival, Adrienne. The plot was unsuccessful, but when Adrienne died in 1730 from dysentery, rumors stemming from the unsuccessful poison plot grew wildly. A century later, Eugène Scribe and Ernest Legouvé shaped the myth into a highly successful drama; the greatest actresses of the time vied for the lead. In 1902, Francesco Cilèa premiered his opera of the same story.

Cilèa had a definite knack for melody, and the opera is filled with pretty tunes that do not tax the virtuosity of the singers. The parts lend themselves to great dramatic license, providing a perfect vehicle to demonstrate a singer's acting ability. As the play became the scene for great competition among actresses, the opera likewise engendered competition among divas, and a long chain of sopranos have passed the role on through the century, including Joan Hammond, Magda Olivero, and Renata Tebaldi. Surprisingly, few recordings have been made of this work. In one of the finest, Renata Scotto makes a great impression in the lead. Claims Raymond Monelle of *Opera* magazine: "Scotto's performance . . . is quite staggering, even for her. She is abundant, poised, infinitely moving, with gentle portamentos that grab at the heart, and her tone is uniformly warm and smooth. It is one of the greatest performances on record."

In the first few years after its composition, the opera made the rounds of the Italian opera houses, and appeared throughout the rest of the continent as well. Cilèa's most successful work, it demonstrates both his strengths and his weaknesses. The music, while charming and pretty, lacks substance, and the plot is weak. While it has never become a permanent part of the operatic canon, it does still receive performances, due primarily to the dramatic appeal of the roles.

—Robin Armstrong

ADRIANO IN SIRIA [Hadrian in Syria].

Composer: Giovanni Battista Pergolesi.

Librettist: Metastasio.

First Performance: Naples, San Bartolomeo, 25 October 1734.

*　　*　　*

Of all the major vocal compositions by Pergolesi, *Adriano in Siria* best reflects the composer's skill and attitudes towards the most prestigious musical genre of his day, *opera seria*. This was the first libretto by Metastasio that Pergolesi set (*L'olimpiade* is the other) and the only work written with a true castrato virtuoso in its cast: Caffarelli (Gaetano Majorano).

Adriano (Hadrian) has conquered the Parthian empire. Its vanquished king, Osroa, hides in disguise. Farnaspe, a Parthian prince (Caffarelli's role), asks Adriano to release Osroa's daughter Emirena from her captivity; she is Farnaspe's promised wife. Aquilio, a tribune and confidant to Adriano, succeeds in convincing Emirena to hide her affection for Farnaspe. She now fears (unjustly) that Adriano's resulting wrath would lead to Farnaspe's death. Aquilio hopes by this stratagem to encourage Adriano's ardent, concealed affection for Emirena and thus win Sabina (who has previously been promised in marriage to Adriano) for himself. Farnaspe is left despondent and confused by Emirena's ensuing cold reception. Adriano's own pleas to Emirena are thwarted by Sabina's sudden arrival from Rome. Osroa and other conspirators that night set the imperial palace aflame, but Farnaspe, fearing for Emirena's safety, rushes inside; he is captured as the supposed author of the arson.

In act II, Sabina arranges for Farnaspe and Emirena to escape, hoping to recapture Adriano's heart. As they flee together they meet Osroa with a bloody sword, who reports that he has just slain Adriano. Yet Adriano soon appears (an error in identity had led to the demise of Adriano's servant instead) and arrests them all. In the third act Aquilio tells Sabina that Adriano commands her to leave, while he informs Adriano that Sabina cannot be restrained from leaving. Adriano hopes to barter Osroa's safety for Emirena's hand, but Osroa betrays him and entreats his daughter to hate the emperor, and later, in private, encourages her to assassinate him. In the end Aquilio's plot is exposed, and Adriano, moved by Emirena's pleas and the noble virtue of Sabina, restores all to its natural order: to Osroa is returned the throne, Farnaspe is given Emirena's hand, Adriano resumes his loyalty to Sabina, and Aquilio is forgiven.

Pergolesi's libretto was substantially altered from Metastasio's original text. Of the original twenty-seven arias only ten were retained, while ten new arias and one new duet were inserted. Caffarelli, the single most important castrato singer of the second quarter of the eighteenth century, appeared in Naples for the first time in this 1734 operatic season. His three arias and duet are all new, and the plot was altered to close each act with Caffarelli on stage. His aria to end the first act, "Lieto così tal volta," with obbligato oboe, is one of Pergolesi's finest creations, displaying a lyric simplicity and elegant embroidery. Here the oboe and voice intertwine as equals, with the alternating coloratura climaxing in a double cadenza. Likewise, his aria to end the second act is exceptional; "Torbido in volto e nero" includes a double orchestra in fiery counterpoint. This aria was particularly popular, as its large manuscript transmission attests, and Pergolesi included it as a substitute, inserted aria in *L'olimpiade* for Rome the following year (altogether, five *Adriano* were reused or reworked for that production). Caffarelli aside, the other cast members were treated more or less equally. Emirena, Sabina, and Osroa each sing in four set pieces, and Adriano and Aquilio are given three each.

—Dale E. Monson

L'AFRICAINE [The African Maid].

Composer: Giacomo Meyerbeer.

Librettist: Eugène Scribe.

First Performance: Paris, Opéra, 28 April 1865 [posthumous; final revisions by Fétis].

Roles: Ines (soprano); Selika (soprano); Vasco da Gama (tenor); Nelusco (baritone); Don Pedro (bass); Don Diego (bass); Anna (mezzo-soprano); Don Alvar (tenor); Grand Inquisitor (bass); High Priest of Brahma (baritone); chorus (SSAATTBB).

Publications

article–

Servières, G. "Les transformations et tribulations de L'africaine." Rivista musicale italiana 34 (1927): 80.

unpublished–

Roberts, John H. "The Genesis of Meyerbeer's L'Africaine." Ph.D. dissertation, University of California, Berkeley, 1977.

* * *

But for a stroke of fate, L'Africaine might have been Meyerbeer's third opera composed for Paris, following Robert le diable and Les Huguenots and preceding Le prophète. Whenever possible, the composer wrote his music for specific voices, and in the person of Cornélie Falcon, who had triumphed as Valentine in Les Huguenots, he had found a remarkable soprano, possessor of a voice that must have somewhat resembled, in expressive range if not in timbre, those of Shirley Verrett or Régine Crespin in our time. It was a voice capable of both secure projection in the high mezzo register and solid extension into the lyrico-dramatic. With Falcon's voice in mind, Meyerbeer turned to a libretto by Eugène Scribe in which a humble Spanish sailor falls in love with an African princess.

But when Falcon, who in her brief six-year career gave her name to a specific type of voice, the "sopran falcon," lost her voice three years after the premiere of Les Huguenots, Meyerbeer laid the larger project aside, after having completed a piano score to the L'Africaine libretto in 1840 to satisfy his contract with the Opéra. According to the research of John H. Roberts, he turned to it again in 1849, following the success of Le prophète, and on the advice of a friend Meyerbeer asked Scribe to move the scene from Africa to India. Scribe finished the new libretto in 1853, having altered the story to conform more closely to his successful formula of building fictional stories around historical personages. The Spanish sailor became the Portuguese explorer, Vasco da Gama, sole survivor of an expedition seeking lands beyond Africa; the African princess, Selika, now inhabited a Hinduized Madagascar and was in love with Vasco, who had purchased her at a slave market. He, however, loves the noblewoman Ines. Imprisoned by the Inquisition, Vasco is freed when Ines agrees to marry his rival, Don Pedro, who then sets sail for the Indian Ocean, followed by Vasco. Thanks to Selika's jealous slave Nelusco, Don Pedro's ship is sunk. Vasco comes ashore to the beautiful new land, where he faces death until Selika swears he is her husband. But Ines, too, has survived, and Selika sends the lovers off. She commits suicide by inhaling the poisonous fumes of the hallucinatory flowers of the manchineel tree.

Meyerbeer died after having scored more than enough music for the evening's entertainment, leaving the musicologist Francois-Joseph Fétis to pare it to manageable proportions, consigning over an hour's worth to a companion volume of the performance score. For the most part, his excisions and inclusions reflect what Meyerbeer would probably have done in rehearsal. As Roberts notes (in an informative essay for San Francisco's 1988 program booklet) he changed both the text and orchestration of the most famous single piece of the score, Vasco's "O paradis," which should, at least for comparison, be recorded in its original scoring.

Despite its posthumous construction, L'Africaine has been rightly judged Meyerbeer's most mature score. It echoes and surpasses the best of his previous efforts in most respects. He had made the chorus a protagonist in Les Huguenots, contrasting Catholic and Protestant in the tavern scene of act III. In L'Africaine's first act, the liberal and conservative factions of the Grand Council debate the veracity of Vasco's story in a fiery exchange, punctuated by the sinister threats of the Grand Inquisitor's entourage. His tenors from Robert le diable onward had won applause with dramatic ariosos rather than full-fledged arias; "O paradis" successfully integrates the melodically-varied arioso with traditional aria structure, even adding a conventional but rousing cabaletta, "Conduisez-moi vers ce navire." Perhaps having learned something from Verdi's Rigoletto, Meyerbeer gives the baritone a remarkable two-part aria, and at the conclusion of the fifth act, when Selika inhales the hallucinogenic fumes of the deadly manchineel, he constructs a mini-symphony of vocal movements comparable to Fides' "O prêtres de Baal" in Le prophète or Dido's "Adieu, fiere cité" from Berlioz' Les Troyens, which itself owes much to Fides' scena.

Perhaps Fétis' only real error lies in his introduction of Nelusko, who has secretly loved Selika, in that finale. Both musically and dramatically his appearance is anticlimactic. Scribe has been unjustly blamed for other perceived flaws, predominantly the title, as the opera no longer has much to do with Africa; but Fétis argued that Paris had been waiting for a Meyerbeer opera called L'Africaine for a quarter-century, not for one titled Vasco da Gama. Scribe has also been criticized for Vasco's apparent fickleness, his falling into Selika's arms as soon as he thinks Ines is dead; but key lines explaining that he has drunk a love potion were truncated in the performance version. Even with its questionable revisions, L'Africaine, when played in French by a stellar cast, can overcome its dramatic deficiencies as effectively as does Verdi's Il trovatore to provide a moving evening of musical theater.

—William J. Collins

THE AFRICAN MAID
See L'AFRICAINE

A poster for the first performance of *L'Africaine,* **Paris, 1865**

DIE ÄGYPTISCHE HELENA [Helen in Egypt].

Composer: Richard Strauss.

Librettist: Hugo von Hofmannsthal.

First Performance: Dresden, Staatsoper, 6 June 1928; revised (act II), L. Wallerstein, Salzburg, Festspielhaus, 14 August 1933.

Roles: Helena (soprano); Menelaus (tenor); Aithra (soprano); Altair (baritone); Da-ud (tenor); Sea-Shell (contralto); Servants (soprano, mezzo-soprano); Hermione (soprano); Armed Youths (tenors); chorus (SATB).

Publications

book—

Lenz, Eva-Marie. *Hugo von Hofmannsthals mythologische Oper "Die ägyptische Helene".* Tübingen, 1972.

article—

Kohler, Stephan. "Machen wir mythologische Opern. . . . Zur Ägyptischen Helena von Hugo von Hofmannsthal und Richard Strauss." In *Richard Strauss-Blätter* new series 4 (1980): 43.

*   *   *

Richard Strauss's *Die ägyptische Helena* remains one of his least performed and certainly least understood operas, despite the revival of other formerly lesser-known stage works by the composer. Many commentators ascribe this to failings in Strauss's music, although contemporary reviews of both performances and recordings indicate that some have not bothered to consult a score. While the opera has its longueurs, especially in the second act, many of its problems lie in Hugo von Hofmannsthal's obtuse libretto. "Nur wer eine Melodie versteht, darf "Helenas" Richter sein" (Only he who understands a melody may be *Helena's* judge!), wrote Strauss to conductor Clemens Krauss. It is, as Strauss described it, an opera of beautiful melodies.

The first act takes place on an island off Egypt in the palace of Aithra, an enchantress and Poseidon's lover. Aithra learns that Menelaus is about to kill his wife Helen on a ship off her island, and she conjures up a storm to wreck them. Menelaus and Helena stagger into her palace. Helena tries to calm him, but he feels duty-bound to kill her. Aithra stays his hand by magic and calls upon her elves to fool the confused Menelaus into thinking that the Trojan War is raging outside. He rushes out. Aithra gives Helena a drink of lotus to calm her and has servants put her to bed. Menelaus reappears, thinking he has just killed Helena and her (already dead, of course) lover Paris. Aithra gives him a drink of the lotus and tells him that the Helena he brought back from Troy was a phantom, and that the real Helena has been here on the island with her all the while. Helena and Menelaus are reconciled, and Aithra makes preparations to whisk them away for a second honeymoon.

The second act opens in an oasis in the Atlas mountains. Helena sings the aria "Zweite Brautnacht" (Second Wedding Night). Menelaus awakes, with the effects of the lotus wearing off. He thinks he really did kill the real Helena the night before, and that this one is the phantom. As he is about to

run off into the desert, a band of Arabs ride in, led by their sheikh Altair and his son Da-ud. All of the men in the band are immediately infatuated with Helena. Altair invites Menelaus to a hunt with his son Da-ud. Aithra appears with an antidote for the lotus, a drink of remembrance. Helena declares that this is the only thing that can truly reconcile her and Menelaus. Altair woos Helena and threatens to take her by force. In the hunt Menelaus imagines Da-ud to be another Paris and kills him. This gives a shock to his memory; he begins to return to reality. Helena gives him the drink, and he recognizes her as the real Helena. But as he is about to kill her, he realizes that he has always loved her and she him, and drops his knife. Altair bursts in to claim Helena, but troops sent by Poseidon suddenly appear. Helena and Menelaus's daughter appears, and they mount magic horses to return to Sparta.

Hofmannsthal based his Helen plot on Euripides, Stesichoros, Claudel, Bachofen, and others. There had always been a problem in explaining how this unfaithful woman had been taken back by her seemingly forgiving husband. The explanation that the ancients came up with was that it was not really Helen who had fled to Troy, that Helen had been spirited off to Egypt by the gods and a phantom Helen sent in her place. When this phantom and Menelaus wandered off course to Egypt on their homeward trip, the phantom dissolved into a mist and the real Helen took its place.

Hofmannsthal's mistake was that he took this relatively simple story, which indeed may have made the Offenbach-like satire that Strauss had been begging for for so many years, and loaded psychological and war-related interpretations onto it: elves as a representation of unconscious processes; Menelaus suffering from World War I-like shell shock; reconciliation based on magic versus reconciliation based on recognition of eternal love. If act I had been the complete opera—although as Strauss noted early in his composition, the first scene between Menelaus and Helen immediately goes into dialectics beyond the limits of satire—Strauss might have had his little light opera. But Hofmannsthal needed a second act to resolve all of his ethical issues.

Helena is indeed an opera of beautiful melodies: Helena's "Bei jener Nacht" (Think of that Night), the orchestral interlude "Helenas Erwachen" (Helena's Awakening), and her "Zweiter Brautnacht" are just a few of the opera's treasures. The long, arching vocal lines in the arias are fiendishly difficult: the part of Helena was composed with Maria Jeritza in mind, so Strauss doubtless felt he could let himself go. There are also a number of lovely, soaring ensembles; the finales of both acts form ensemble complexes. In between the arias and ensembles Strauss employs an arioso that seems new, a development of the parlando style used in his preceding opera, *Intermezzo.*

Strauss composed this as a "number opera," with arias and ensembles more clearly delineated than in any opera since *Ariadne auf Naxos.* In the second act he tended toward a more through-composed style, but this was due to the more serious turn of the plot and Hofmannsthal's interlocking structure. Conductor Clemens Krauss convinced Strauss to revise this act for a 1933 production at Salzburg; they and producer Lothar Wallerstein simplified the dramatic structure. Some new music was composed, notably a prayer for Aithra, which develops into a trio for her, Helena, and Menelaus, but Strauss primarily reused or revised music from the first version.

Helena both sums up earlier stylistic trends in Strauss's operas and anticipates later ones. Some passages recall the polytonality of *Elektra,* while others utilize the neoclassic simplicity of *Ariadne.* The orchestration moves forward from

A program cover for *Die Ägyptische Helena,* **Dresden, 1928**

the mix of chamber passages and Wagnerian overscoring in *Die Frau ohne Schatten.* Strauss's new melodic style here, begun in *Intermezzo,* would find its way into *Die schweigsame Frau* and *Daphne,* and his turn toward Greek antiquity and melody would direct the most important of his last works—opera, song, and instrumental works.

—David Anderson

AIDA.

Composer: Giuseppe Verdi.

Librettist: Antonio Ghislanzoni (after a scenario by François Auguste Ferdinand Mariette as sketched in French by Camille du Locle).

First Performance: Cairo, New Opera House, 24 December 1871.

Roles: Aida (soprano); Amneris (mezzo-soprano); Radames (tenor); Amonasro (baritone); Ramfis (bass); Pharaoh (bass); Priestess (soprano or mezzo-soprano); Messenger (tenor); chorus (SSATTTTBBB).

Publications

books–

Geck, A. *Aida, die Oper: Schriftenreihe über musikalische Bühnenwerke.* Berlin, 1973.
Knaust, Rebecca. *The Complete Guide to "Aida".* New York, 1978.
Busch, Hans. *Verdi's Aida: the History of an Opera in Letters and Documents.* Minneapolis, 1978.
John, Nicholas, ed. *Giuseppe Verdi: Aida.* London, 1980.

articles–

Quaderni dell' Istituto di Studi Verdiani 4 (1971) [genesis of *Aida* issue].
Günther, Ursula. "Zur Entstehung von Verdis *Aida.*" *Studi musicali* 2 (1973).
Avant-scène opéra July-August (1976) [*Aida* issue].
Humbert, J. "A propos de l'égyptomanie dans l'oeuvre de Verdi: attribution à August Mariette d'un scénario anonyme de l'opéra *Aïda.*" *Revue de musicologie* 62 (1976): 229.
Alberti, L. "I progressi attuali [1872] del dramma musicale: note sulla disposizione scenica per l'opera *Aida.*" In *Il melodramma italiano dell' ottocento: studi e richerche per Massimo Mila,* 125. Turin, 1977.
Palden, Kurt. "Zur Geschichte der *Aida.*" *Österreichische Musikzeitung* 34 (1979): 334.

Aida, **act II, Paris, 1880**

Marchesi, Gustavo. "L'*Aida* come fiaba." In *Aida al Cairo,*
  91. Parma, 1982.
Della Seta, Fabrizio. " 'O cieli azzurri': Exoticism and Dramatic Discourse in *Aida.*" *Cambridge Opera Journal* 3
  (1991): 49.

*   *   *

Aida, the daughter of King Amonasro of Ethiopia, has been taken captive in an Egyptian war and made to serve as a slave in Memphis to the Pharaoh's daughter Amneris. She has kept her royal status secret, and fallen in love with the soldier Radames, who is ironically chosen to lead the Egyptian forces against her people. Amneris, also enamored of Radames, tricks Aida into revealing her concealed passion for him. Radames is victorious in war, and brings home as one of his captives Aida's father, who has kept his true identity secret. The Pharaoh announces that Radames will have as his victor's reward the hand of Amneris in marriage. Aida, in despair, meets Radames on the banks of the Nile and, induced by her father, convinces her lover that they must flee together. He unsuspectingly reveals the military secrets the concealed Amonasro has wanted to hear. Amneris has also overheard. She sends a guard after Amonasro, who is killed. Aida escapes. Radames, to save his honor, surrenders, and Amneris repents of her jealousy when Egypt's priests, led by the implacable Ramfis, condemn Radames to be buried alive. Sealed in his tomb, Radames finds that Aida has already found her way there to die with him. As Amneris prays in the temple above, Aida and Radames sing below that their souls are flying upwards to eternal day.

Archaeology was an exciting new science when *Aida* was written. Heinrich Schliemann unearthed Homer's Troy the very year of *Aida*'s premiere, and other excavations were revealing much of ancient Egypt itself. Verdi wanted archaeological correctness in his Egyptian opera. Specifically, he wanted on stage the long, straight, valveless instrument that was the only trumpet known to antiquity. He had six of them specially made in Milan to play his triumphal march, which called for just six brassy notes (the four a bugler plays in "Taps" plus two passing notes).

Verdi was careful to ensure that his archaeological correctness would sound, not embarrassingly primitive, but grandly barbaric: after three of his long trumpets have played the tune in the key of A flat, he has the other three, pitched a tone-and-a-half higher, repeat it from across the stage in the higher key of B natural; then he restores the march to its earlier key and, in a simple but very telling effect, has the two sets of trumpets play together, using as a descant the only note the second set has in common with the first. The effect was as grand as anything Meyerbeer had done for Paris. And without knowing it, Verdi was archaeologically right about the trumpets. When King Tut's tomb was opened in 1925, two trumpets were found within, one tuned in A flat, the other in B—incredibly, the very two keys Verdi had used.

Verdi had to be persuaded to write *Aida.* He had twenty-three operas behind him, regarded the old battles as won, and wanted to retire to his farm. But one of his Paris librettists, Camille du Locle, eventually interested him in a four-page synopsis for an opera for Cairo, to be set in ancient Egypt, written—so du Locle implied—by the Khedive of Egypt himself, the munificent Ismail Pasha, first of the three viceroys appointed by the Ottoman empire to rule Egypt during and after the construction of the Suez Canal.

Du Locle probably got the synopsis from Auguste Mariette, a cataloguist at the Louvre who had found archaeological fame in the Egyptian sands and was given the title of Bey and made Inspector General of Monuments by the Khedive. Mariette had the beginnings of *Aida*'s story in his own experience: he had actually uncovered a walled-up skeleton when excavating his Serapeum.

Du Locle visited Verdi on his Italian farm, and in less than a week the four-page scenario became, between the two of them, the four acts of *Aida,* in French prose. Verdi then had the French translated into Italian verse by the man who had already helped with the revision of *La forza del destino,* Antonio Ghislanzoni. We have thirty-four of the letters that passed between the composer and librettist, so we can still read how Verdi bullied Ghislanzoni till he got, instead of libretto language, the simple, heartfelt dialogue he wanted. Sometimes, tired of waiting, Verdi simply wrote his own Italian lines and set them to music. So in effect, Verdi is the librettist of *Aida.* He also suggested some of the best details in the staging, including the split levels in the last act.

The music of *Aida* is of a new richness and complexity, yet accessible even when heard for the first time. Act III, the Nile scene, contains solos and duets as impassioned and beautifully wrought as anything in opera. The scene is also a master textbook on how to write evocatively for woodwinds. Flute and oboe, clarinet and bassoon, wave and undulate in intricate patterns and conjure up the steamy, shimmering night, the ebb and swell of the river with all its creatures. But Verdi surpasses everything that has gone before in the duet "O terra, addio" in the last act. This grandest of operas ends, as it began, with music that is quiet, luminous, and delicately nuanced. The lovers voice their farewell to earth in a great, spreading arc of melody while the whole orchestra seems to quiver in one vast, cosmic tremolo. In no other music is there anything quite to equal this feeling of leaving earth for sky, of quietly walking through space.

Since the Cairo premiere, delayed for almost a year when the Franco-Prussian war broke out and Mariette and all the scenery were closed off in beleaguered Paris, *Aida* has become one of the most popular operas in the world. But a great operatic success does not always mean triumph and fulfillment for its creators. For the creators of *Aida,* it was almost as if they had inherited the curse laid on those who opened King Tut's tomb. The Khedive was dismissed by the Ottomans for administrative incompetence. Mariette lost his wife and five of his children to cholera and most of his records to the Nile when it flooded his house. Du Locle took over the management of the Opéra-Comique in Paris, saw it go bankrupt with the initial failure of Bizet's *Carmen,* and had a temporary but bitter falling out with Verdi over money. Ghislanzoni wrote over eighty other librettos, but never had a success remotely like *Aida.*

Finally, Verdi was angered that his new work, while widely admired, reminded some critics of Wagner. "If only I had never written *Aida!*" he said, ruefully. "To end up, after more than thirty-five years in the theater, an imitator!" We, with hindsight, have come to see *Aida* as not Wagnerian at all, but as crafted dramatically along the lines of French grand opera and musically the vindication and renewal of Italian vocal art in the face of the onslaughts of German symphonic drama. But Verdi was so saddened about being praised for the wrong reasons that he went into another period of virtual retirement. When he resurfaced sixteen years later, in his late seventies, after Wagner's death, it was to write the two greatest of all

Italian works for the musical stage, the ultimate reconciliation in opera of the vocal and the orchestral—*Otello* and *Falstaff.*

—M. Owen Lee

AKHNATEN
See TRIPTYCH

ALBANESE, Licia.

Soprano. Born 22 July 1913 in Bari, Italy. Married Italian-American businessman Joseph Gimma, 1945; studied with Emanuel De Rosa in Bari and with Giuseppina Baldassare-Tedeschi in Milan; professional debut in 1934 at the Teatro Lirico in Milan, replacing a soprano who had become ill during the first act in the part of Cio-Cio-San in *Madama Butterfly*; debut at Parma as Cio-Cio-San, 10 December 1935; Metropolitan Opera debut in the same role, 9 February 1940; received Order of Merit in Italy; received from Pope Pius XII award of the Lady Grand Cross of the Equestrian Order of the Holy Sepulchre; final Metropolitan Opera performance on 16 April 1966; a noted Puccini singer, her other roles include Marguerite in *Faust*, Violetta in *La Traviata*, and Desdemona in *Otello.*

Publications

About ALBANESE: books–

Celletti, R. *Le grandi voci*. Rome, 1964.
Ewen, D. *Musicians since 1900*. New York, 1978.

articles–

Green, L. "Licia Albanese and Verismo: 'I Always Tell the Truth'." *The Opera Quarterly* 7, no. 4 (1990-91): 53.

*   *   *

Licia Albanese had what she called "tricks for beauty": vocal and histrionic effects that were entirely legitimate, apposite, heartfelt, and uniquely hers, ways in which she shaped phrases ineffably and unforgettably, and movements (never, in her case, anything as obvious as the stock operatic "gesture") that both illuminated a character's deepest emotions and profoundly stirred those of her hearers.

Nowhere was Albanese's mastery of her art more palpable than during the moments that required her to "expire" on-stage, something she invariably accomplished with the most exquisite expressivity, whether called upon to demonstrate a gradual, quiet fading away (Mimì, *La bohème*), a final feverish outburst (Violetta, *La traviata*), an intense losing battle to cheat death (Manon Lescaut), or an act of unbearable poignancy such as the suicide of Butterfly.

The effect Albanese made as Cio-Cio-San in *Madama Butterfly* after she had sung the geisha's final words, made all the ceremonial preparations for her hara-kiri, committed the

act behind the shoji, and knocked the screen over to writhe and die before our eyes, remains one of the most indelible visual memories ever created by any opera singer. With her legs bound according to ritual, Butterfly's arms were still free to express both the pain of her mortal wound and the ascendancy of her spirit, which exults because she has redeemed her disgraced honor by making the ultimate sacrifices: giving up her son to his father and taking her own life. In a specially designed kimono with very large, beautifully colored sleeves, Albanese was in fact a butterfly, fluttering—but not melodramatically—until the moment there was no life remaining. She appeared to respond to the offstage voice of Pinkerton calling her name while at the same time making it clear that the temporal world was fast sliding away from her and that the voice might actually be one summoning her to the next plane—an altogether remarkable achievement.

Albanese was the fifth of seven children in a close-knit southern Italian family, all of whom had good voices. She was the one with ambition, instinct, and passion, and she began to study singing in her teens. She flourished under the tutelage of Giuseppina Baldassare-Tedeschi in Milan and at twenty-two won the first Italian government-sponsored vocal competition over three hundred other entrants. Her initial operatic appearance (Teatro Lirico, Milan, 1934, as an emergency substitute) and her "official" debut (Parma, 1935) were as Butterfly. She was soon championed by such artists as Gigli (who requested her for Mimì when he was about to record *La bohème*) and Muzio, whom she succeeded as Italy's principal interpreter of the title role of Refice's *Cecilia*. In the first five years of her career, Albanese sang at Teatro alla Scala, Covent Garden (debut 1937, Liù), and the Rome Opera, while working regularly in smaller houses in order to perfect her repertory. She went as far as to sing Elsa in *Lohengrin* at Modena but learned that Wagner, even in Italian, was not for her.

In 1939, when a number of distinguished Italian artists left New York for Italy to fulfill their engagements at the Teatro alla Scala, unaware that Mussolini would forbid them to leave the country again, Albanese went in the opposite direction. Seeking a career in America, she managed to get herself to Portugal and onto a boat for the United States, armed only with the enthusiasm of youth and her great talent.

Almost from the moment of her American debut at the Metropolitan (9 February 1940, again as Cio-Cio-San) a special rapport existed between her and the New York public. Despite the fact that this was the Metropolitan's 246th performance of *Madama Butterfly*, Albanese was only the third Italian soprano to perform the part with the company (and her two predecessors, Claudia Muzio and Augusta Oltrabella, had only sung it once each). Albanese struck an authentic chord not previously touched, and no singer ever became more beloved by the Italian-American opera audience. She endured until the closing of the old Metropolitan Opera House in 1966 in spite of the fact that her bright, penetrating, emotionally charged voice, with its strong top, was not really large enough to fill that huge theater as historically great voices have done. Albanese nonetheless made her points unequivocally, with the most detailed and nuanced artistry, and her most delicate moments registered clearly. Although remembered most vividly for her Puccini heroines and her Toscanini-endorsed Violetta, she also loved to sing Mozart, and brought a Mediterranean warmth and piquancy to his operas that was quite beyond the "Viennese School" singers.

Through the Puccini Foundation, begun with her late husband, Joseph Gimma, Albanese works tirelessly for the furtherance of those artistic values she considers indispensable to the survival of opera as an art form. In 1985 and 1987 she stepped out of retirement to enjoy a personal triumph in New York and Houston revivals of Sondheim's *Follies,* singing "One More Kiss" with prodigal tone and definitive understanding.

—Bruce Burroughs

ALBANI, Emma (born Marie Louise Cécile Lajeunesse).

Soprano. Born 1 November 1847 in Chambly, near Montreal. Died 3 April 1930. In 1878 married impresario Ernest Gye, who became lessee of Covent Garden after his father's death. Educated at Couvent du Sacré-Coeur at Montreal; soloist at St Joseph's Church in Albany, New York; in 1868 she began lessons with Duprez in Paris; in 1870 she studied in Milan with Francesco Lamperti, who dedicated his treatise on the trill to her; professional debut at Messina as Amina in Bellini's *La sonnambula* in 1870; debut at Covent Garden on 2 April 1872, where she continued to sing until 1896; debut at Metropolitan Opera as Gilda in 1891; farewell concert at Albert Hall, 1911; premieres include Elgar's *The Apostles* and *St Elizabeth*; Dame Commander of the Order of the British Empire June 1925.

Emma Albani as Elsa in *Lohengrin*

Publications

By ALBANI: books–

Forty Years of Song. London, 1911; reprinted New York, 1977.

About ALBANI: books–

Charbonneau, H. *L'Albani: Sa carrière artistique et triomphale.* Montreal, 1938.
MacDonald, Cheryl. *Emma Albani.* Toronto, 1984.

articles–

Ridley, N.A. "Emma Albani," *Record Collector* 11 (1959): 77.

*   *   *

The first Canadian performer to achieve an international reputation, Emma Albani became one of the most acclaimed divas of the late nineteenth century. In a career that spanned four decades, she sang more than forty operatic roles of remarkable stylistic diversity.

In her autobiography, *Forty Years of Song,* Albani attributed her celebrated facility for assimilating music to her early training with her father. Under his strict tutelage, she became a proficient composer, pianist, organist and harpist as well as singer. Her position as soprano soloist, organist and choir director at St. Joseph's church in Albany, NY (1865-1868) further contributed to her highly developed general musicianship. She traveled to Europe in 1868 where her teachers included Gilbert-Louis Duprez in Paris and Francesco Lamperti in Milan. The latter in particular was an important mentor, and she always subscribed to the "Lamperti method."

Her highly successful debut as Amina in Bellini's *La sonnambula* (Messina, 1870) marked the beginning of her public career. It was at this time that she assumed her stage name of Albani. In 1872, she repeated the role of Amina for her debut at Covent Garden in London. The critic for the *Musical Times* (May 1872) recognized the presence of "a genuine soprano voice, a facile and unexaggerated execution, and a remarkable power of *sostenuto* in the higher part of her register." These characteristics continued to earn critics' admiration; her natural and ingenuous stage manner also won the devotion of audiences, and even of royalty (she was a personal favorite of Queen Victoria). In 1878, she married Ernest Gye, who had just taken over from his father the position of manager of Covent Garden.

While continuing to sing at Covent Garden almost every season until 1896, Emma Albani also performed in many other countries, including France, Russia, Germany, the United States (where she sang several times at the Metropolitan Opera), and her native country, Canada. Her success as an opera diva was matched by her fame as a singer of oratorios and cantatas; for many years she sang to great acclaim at the English festivals. After retiring from the opera stage near the end of the century, she continued to tour and perform until 1911, when she gave her farewell recital at the Royal Albert Hall in London. Her final years, clouded by financial strain, were spent teaching and even singing in music halls. In recognition of her contribution to British music, she was made a Dame Commander of the British Empire in 1925.

Albani's vocal style changed significantly in the course of her career. Her earliest roles—such as Amina (*La sonnambula*), Lucia (*Lucia di Lammermoor*) and Elvira (*I puritani*)—required a light coloratura, but in the mid 1870s she expanded her repertoire to include the more dramatic vocal roles of Wagnerian opera. Always a believer in thorough preparation, she traveled to Germany to study the methods and practices of German opera with the conductor and coach, Franz Wüllner. She became especially celebrated for her interpretation of Wagner; one of her last great triumphs was a performance of *Tristan und Isolde* with Jean and Edouard de Reszke (1896).

The noted critic Herman Klein commented dispassionately and at some length on Albani's 1874 performance in *Lucia di Lammermoor,* observing that: "Her voice, a soprano of considerable range, with fine notes in the head register, was then clear and resonant if somewhat thin in timbre; perhaps more remarkable for its flexibility and a remarkable *sostenuto* (due to perfect breath-control) than for that peculiar sweetness and charm which haunts the ear. Neither then nor subsequently was there much power in the chest and lower medium notes."

The only known recordings of Albani's voice to survive are a handful of pieces recorded on wax cylinder in the first years of this century, some of which have been reissued. Keeping in mind that these date from the end of her career when she was in her late fifties, the recordings show a very clear voice, with great agility and a delicate *mezza voce.* They can only hint at the qualities that made her one of the most distinguished singers of her time.

—Joan Backus

ALBERT, EUGEN D'
See D'ALBERT, EUGEN

ALBERT HERRING.

Composer: Benjamin Britten.

Librettist: Eric Crozier (after Maupassant).

First Performance: Glyndebourne, 20 June 1947.

Roles: Lady Billows (soprano); Florence Pike (contralto); Miss Wordsworth (soprano); Mr Gedge (baritone); Mr Upfold (tenor); Superintendent Budd (bass); Sid (baritone); Albert Herring (tenor); Nancy (mezzo-soprano); Mrs. Herring (mezzo-soprano); Emmie (soprano); Cis (soprano); Harry (boy soprano).

Publications

articles–

Crozier, Eric. "Forward to *Albert Herring.*" 4 *Tempo* (1947).
_____. "Form in Opera: 'Albert Herring' Examined." *Tempo* new series/no. 5 (1947): 4.

Law, Jack. "Daring to Eat a Peach: Literary Allusion in *Albert Herring.*" *Opera Quarterly* (1987).
Mitchell, Donald. "The Serious Comedy of *Albert Herring.*" *About the House* spring (1989).

*   *   *

The life expectancy of comic operas is appallingly brief. Few outlive their composers. The effervescent tunes soon go flat (even if the singers stay on pitch), and the porous characters turn stale after an airing or two. To survive, comedy needs more than bubbles and yeast. If the characters are necessarily shallow, their postures and reactions must ring true. Some vicariously fulfill our egoistic wishes suppressed by mores and conventions. Don Giovanni, Figaro, Dr. Dulcamara, Falstaff, and Gianni Schicchi all live by their wits and do as they please, propriety be damned.

The hero of *Albert Herring* could hardly match wits with this rogues gallery. Feckless and obtuse, he nonetheless has his way in the end, subverting his mother's will and shocking the village dignitaries. Benjamin Britten and his librettist Eric Crozier caricature Albert's adversaries while satirizing puritanism, Victorian music and manners, operatic clichés, ceremonious busybodies, and anything decorously British. Irony is their ultimate weapon, and with it they impugn formality and expose hypocrisy. Britten especially delights in piercing the flatulent rhetoric of high-minded prigs with musical absurdities until their despotic pronouncements dwindle to flurries of self-righteous indignation. Unburdened and unimpressed, Albert walks away from them and the town of Loxford a free man.

In conceiving the libretto for *Albert Herring,* Crozier transplanted Maupassant's story "Le Rosier de Madame Husson" to Loxford (close to Britten's home in Aldeburgh), gave it a lighthearted ending, and Anglified everyone and everything. In act I, the imperious Lady Billows and a committee of distinguished citizens are attempting to select a virtuous girl as Loxford's Queen of the May. Several names are advanced, but none of the candidates meets Lady Billows' rigorous standards. Finally the Police Superintendent suggests a King of the May instead, and nominates Albert Herring, a young man with no vices, whose mother shelters and dominates him. Despite initial misgivings, Lady Billows enthusiastically endorses this modest proposal.

Scene ii shows us Albert tending his mother's grocery shop. The action contrasts him with the butcher's boy Sid, his girlfriend Nancy, and three rambunctious children who swipe fruit behind Albert's back. All accentuate the servile young man's stifled and joyless life. Abstemious, scrupulous, and lonely, Albert wonders why he alone has no fun. When the May Day delegation arrives to tell Albert how they plan to honor him, his mother is at first skeptical, but approves wholeheartedly after learning that the crown comes with twenty-five pounds from Lady Billows. Albert demurs, however, incurring his mother's wrath. Affronted by his protests and calling him ungrateful, "Mum" forcibly sends Albert to bed as the onlooking children taunt him in song.

As the Second Act curtain rises, the ceremonies are about to begin. In one of the opera's funniest bits, Miss Wordsworth, head teacher at the Church School, rehearses the children in a song of praise she has composed for King Albert. Sid furtively spikes Albert's glass of lemonade with rum. Finally King Albert himself arrives wearing a white suit and a crown of orange blossoms. To the copious speeches and presentations, he flatly responds, "Thank you very much." His loyal subjects acclaim him nonetheless, but Albert has a sudden attack of

Albert Herring, **Royal Opera, London, 1989 (Glyndebourne production)**

hiccups, prompting gratuitous remedies from all sides until Lady Billows bids the celebrants get on with the feast. Albert, meanwhile, upon witnessing an intimate scene between Sid and Nancy, decides to go in search of romance himself.

The next afternoon (act III), everyone is searching for Albert under the disgruntled Superintendent's direction. Already grieving for her son, "Mum" faints when Albert's crown is retrieved from a well. This unpropitious discovery inspires a threnodic ensemble climaxed by Albert's timely or untimely return. After a little grilling, he tells his astounded mourners that he has been out all night drinking, and has spent three pounds of the prize money. Scandalized, the upright citizens stalk out, and "Mum" retreats upstairs in near hysterics. Cheered on by Nancy, Sid, and the children, Albert sails the remains of his crown out over the heads of the audience.

Britten composed *Albert Herring* for the newly formed English Opera Group as a companion piece to *The Rape of Lucretia.* Like its predecessor, it is a chamber opera with an orchestra of single strings including harp, single woodwinds, one horn, and a versatile percussionist. There is no chorus. The conductor accompanies the recitatives on a piano. Although the more conventional scoring sometimes begs for a larger ensemble, it interchanges with more resourceful color schemes better suited to the small instrumental forces.

Like Schubert, Britten had a keen ear for adroitly applying inventive harmony. He also matched Debussy's skill in linking melodic fragments of disparate tonality. His style is at once practiced and original, protean but carefully pruned.

The reticular vocal ensembles demand absolute precision, though some are intentionally jumbled to produce the "cocktail party effect."

Albert Herring is unpretentious entertainment about pretentious people. Its bland, humorless protagonist escapes Loxford's hyperbolic populace, leaving the provincial luminaries to spout platitudes and venerate banalities. Britten, however, broadened the parody to include opera itself, a genre long encumbered by conventions and affectations. Like Albert, the composer went his own way, taking English opera with him. Pedantic thunder resounded from Loxford to Covent Garden, but he never looked back.

—James Allen Feldman

ALBONI, Marietta.

Contralto. Born 6 March 1823, in Città di Castello. Died 23 June 1894, in Ville d'Avray. Married: 1) Count Pepoli, 1853 (died, 1867); 2) Charles Ziéger, 1877. Studied with Mombelli in Bologna; in 1841 met Rossini, from whom she received lessons; debut in Pacini's *Saffo,* Bologna, 1842; Teatro alla Scala debut in Rossini's *Le siège de Corinthe,* 1842; sang in Russia (including St Petersburg, 1844-45), Prague, Berlin, and Hamburg; sang in Rome and at Covent Garden, 1847; Paris Opéra debut in *Semiramide,* 1847; sang premiere of

Marietta Alboni in *La Cenerentola,* **Her Majesty's Theatre, London, 1849**

Auber's *Zéline* (written for her), 1851; American tour 1852-53.

Publications

Pougin, Arthur. *Marietta Alboni.* Paris, 1912.
Pleasants, H. *The Great Singers.* London, 1967.

*   *   *

Alboni was only nineteen years old when she participated in performances of Rossini's *Stabat Mater* in Parma, Mantua and Verona with Donizetti conducting. The performances had been arranged at Rossini's behest because he had never heard the work complete. To an extent Rossini regarded Alboni as his protégée, and helped arrange her debut at Bologna's Teatro Communale in autumn 1842 and shortly thereafter, her first appearance at the Teatro alla Scala in his own "Siege of Corinth."

Alboni began at the top and remained one of the outstanding contralto voices for a quarter of a century. In two seasons at the Teatro alla Scala she undertook such roles as Maffeo Orsini in *Lucrezia Borgia,* Adalgisa in *Norma* and Arsace in *Semiramide.* Thereafter the bulk of her career was to be as an international artist; after appearing in Turin at the end of 1851 she seems not to have performed in opera in her home country again. Following appearances in St. Petersburg, Vienna and Prague, she gravitated to Paris and London. Her first season at Covent Garden coincided with its becoming a permanent opera house in 1847. As Arsace in *Semiramide* Alboni was the sensation of the first night, although the cast included such celebrated artists as Grisi and Tamburini. "A greater sensation probably was never before produced by any debutante," wrote Hogarth.

Alboni sang in ten of the seventeen operas presented in that first season at Covent Garden. It was a small company, and this accounted for one of her most remarkable achievements. When Verdi's *Ernani* was mounted, there was no baritone available; Alboni took on this major role, which later generations would associate with Battistini and de Luca.

During 1852 and 1853 Alboni sang in various centers in North America, including the role of Norma rather than Adalgisa. The great music critic Henry Chorley offers an interesting insight into the possible restlessness that led Alboni to sing roles that he felt were unsuited to her voice. Although Chorley was a great champion of Alboni's voice, which he described as "a rich, deep, real contralto of two octaves from G to G as sweet as honey . . . and with that tremulous quality which reminds fanciful speculators of the quiver in the air of the calm, blazing summer's noon," he also found that Alboni's singing lacked variety; she would settle on a phrase or ornament and therafter stick to it. Chorley felt that even "the most mellow of voices (with) the most exact musical execution" would pall without "other elements to charm." Chorley goes on to suggest that, sensing the weakness, Alboni sought to compensate by developing new repertory, including soprano roles such as Amina in *La Sonnambula* and Zerlina in *Don Giovanni* which ultimately damaged her contralto voice.

By way of contrast, Herman Klein, who heard Alboni in Rossini's Mass after she had left the operatic stage, felt that the damage was not permanent and that her voice remained as "fresh, rich and powerful as that of a woman half her age." It is interesting in light of this critical controversy that in her second London season Alboni took on the role of the page in *Les huguenots;* Meyerbeer had written the role for soprano, but the composer now transposed it for contralto, whose preserve it remained—without doubt a more appropriate "breeches" role for Alboni than her previous appearance as baritone in *Ernani!*

—Stanley Henig

ALCESTE.

Composer: Christoph Willibald von Gluck.

Librettist: Ranieri de Calzabigi (after Euripides).

First Performance: Vienna, Burgtheater, 26 December 1767; revised, François Louis-Grand Lebland du Roullet (translation and revision of Calzabigi), Paris, Académie Royale, 23 April 1776.

Roles: Alceste (soprano); Admetus (tenor); High Priest (bass-baritone); Apollo (baritone); Hercules (bass); Thanatos (bass); Evander (tenor); Herald (bass); Chorus Leaders (soprano, mezzo-soprano, tenor; bass); Eumelos, Aspasia (both mute); chorus (SSAATTBB).

Publications

articles–

Rousseau, J.-J. "Fragment d'observations sur l'*Alceste* italien de M. le Chevalier Gluck." In *Projet concernant de nouveaux signes pour la musique.* Geneva, 1781; reprinted in *Oeuvres complètes,* vol. 4, p. 463, Paris, 1857.
Sternfeld, F.W. "Expression and Revision in Gluck's *Orfeo* and *Alceste.*" In *Essays Presented to Egon Wellesz,* edited by Jack Westrup, 114. London, 1966.
Howard, Patricia. "Gluck's Two Alcestes." *Musical Times* 115 (1974): 642.
Candiana, Rosy. "L'*Alceste* da Vienna a Milano." *Giornale storico della letteratura italiana* 159 (1984): 227.

*   *   *

Alceste, dramma per musica in three acts by Christoph Willibald Gluck to a libretto by Ranieri de' Calzabigi based on the tragedy by Euripides, was premiered at the Vienna Burgtheater on 26 December 1767. A French version with text adapted and translated by Lebland du Roullet and with significant changes to the score, was first heard in Paris on 23 April 1776. This French version is the one that has most frequently been revived and the one that figures in the following plot synopsis. The action of the opera takes place some years after the Trojan War. The people of Thessaly invoke the gods to cure their dying king, Admetus. His wife, Alceste, touched by the concern for her husband, enters the crowd with her children and displays her grief by asking the gods for pity. Scene ii occurs inside the temple of Apollo, where the High Priest is seen invoking the god. The temple quakes and flames leap up from the altar as the terrifying voice of the oracle is heard. It declares that unless someone is sacrificed in his place, the king must die.· After a great deal of torment, Alceste offers her own life to save that of her husband. In act II there is general rejoicing at the king's recovery; the king believes he owes his life to a stranger. Noting his wife's troubled face, however, he questions her and eventually learns it is she who has made the sacrifice. Admetus determines to suffer the same fate as his wife. The people beg Alceste to save herself but she has decided to resign herself to the will of the gods. Act III, scene i takes place in front of the royal palace where Hercules learns of Alceste's fate and swears to rescue her. In scene ii Alceste has reached Hades but must wait until dark to enter. Admetus, determined not to be separated from Alceste, joins her. Thanatos appears with infernal spirits and declares that only one of the pair may enter Hades. As Alceste and Admetus express their desire to die for each other, Apollo declares that they are the perfect example of conjugal love and that they shall both live. The people rejoice.

Alceste was Gluck's second collaboration with the poet Calzabigi. In the famous dedication to the opera, a letter to Grand-Duke Leopold of Tuscany, Gluck stated his reform goals, which applied equally to his earlier Calzabigi setting, *Orfeo ed Euridice* of 1762. Gluck gave Calzabigi most of the credit for the formulation of these reforms, and indeed the wording of the *Alceste* dedication was undoubtedly by Calzabigi rather than Gluck. The stated intention was "to rid it [the music] altogether of those abuses that, introduced either by the inappropriate vanity of the singers or an exaggerated complaisance on the part of the composers, have long disgraced the Italian opera, and which have transformed the most stately and the most beautiful of all spectacles into the most foolish and boring one." The desire to make the drama believable meant that there must be a close union between the music and the libretto so that the music could, in the words of the dedication, "serve the poetry." This entailed the abolition of both superfluous embellishment and repetition, both prominent features of the da capo aria then in vogue. The da capo aria and secco recitative—at opposite ends of the musical spectrum in *opera seria*—were to be brought closer together by means of expressive declamation, with the accompaniment of either the harpsichord or the orchestra.

Although both *Orfeo ed Euridice* and *Alceste* are reform operas from the 1760s to texts by Calzabigi, the latter is a far darker story than the Orpheus legend, with no opportunity for the inclusion of a lighter pastoral element. The opening measures of Gluck's overture, which he called "Intrada," probably because it leads without break into the opening scene, provide the context for the entire opera: they consist of a massive D-minor arpeggio in the bass, a figure that recurs throughout the opera always in association with the supernatural. Alfred Einstein has labeled this the "first truly tragic introduction to an opera." Because of the prominence of the Underworld, three trombones are used. To a great extent Gluck carried out his reform theories in this work: the tone of tragedy and suffering is unbroken; there are no superfluous ballets, only ballets that form an organic part of the action; and there is no bravura vocal writing. The recitatives, however, seem to be a return to the old secco recitative, a decided regression in terms of *Orfeo*. The chorus has an important function; they and the character of Alceste share almost the entire dramatic and musical interest of the work.

Alceste was very successful in Vienna and to a great extent even in Italy. For Paris Gluck made a number of significant changes, more than in any other of his works, including some scene changes, a new finale, addition of choral parts, and the inclusion of a new character, Hercules. The opera touched off one of the constant French opera polemics, in this case one involving the relative merits of Gluck and Piccinni. The conflict came to a head in 1777 when both composers were given Quinault's libretto of *Roland* to set.

—Stephen Willier

ALCESTE, ou Le triomphe d'Alcide [Alcestis, or the Triumph of Alcides].

Composer: Jean-Baptiste Lully.

Librettist: Philippe Quinault.

First Performance: Paris, Opéra, 19 January 1674.

Roles: The Nymph of the Seine (soprano); La Gloire (soprano); The Nymph of the Tuileries (soprano); The Nymph of the Marne (soprano); Alcide (bass); Lychas (countertenor); Céphise (soprano); Straton (bass); Licomède (bass); Phérès (tenor); Admète (tenor); Cléante (bass); Alceste (soprano); Two Tritons (countertenor); Thétis (soprano); Eoleus (bass); Apollo (countertenor); A Woman in Mourning (soprano); A Man in Mourning (bass); Diana (soprano); Mercury (mute); Charon (bass); A Ghost (soprano); Pluto (bass); Proserpine (soprano); Ghost of Alceste (mute); Alecton (countertenor); chorus; mute figures in the Prologue.

Publications

book–

Winterfeld, C. von. *"Alceste" von Lully, Händel, und Gluck.* Berlin, 1851.

article–

Howard, Patricia. "Lully's Alceste." *Musical Times* 114 (1973): 21.

*   *   *

Alceste begins with an extended prologue in which the nymph of the Seine River and other pastoral divinities long for their unnamed "hero" (i.e., King Louis XIV) to return from battle. The central drama, set in ancient Thessaly, is very loosely based on Euripides' *Alcestis*. King Admète and Princess Alceste are about to be married. Under the guise of giving the couple a party, the jealous King Licomède of Scyros abducts Alceste. Admète, his friend Alcide (Hercules), and the Thessalian army defeat Licomède's forces and rescue Alceste, but Admète is mortally wounded. When the god Apollo offers immortal glory to anyone who dies in Admète's place, only Alceste will sacrifice herself. After Alceste's funeral, Alcide declares his own love for her and his intent to rescue her from Hades; Admète reluctantly agrees to relinquish Alceste to Alcide in the hope of seeing her alive again. Alcide succeeds in bringing Alceste back from the underworld. As Alceste and Admète sadly prepare to part, Alcide announces that,

having conquered an army and conquered death, he will now conquer his own desires and allow the lovers to remain together. A comic sub-plot runs parallel to the main plot: while Alceste is unwavering in her faithfulness to Admète, her young companion Céphise teases two suitors and celebrates fickleness.

Alceste was the second *tragédie en musique* by Lully and Quinault. The first, *Cadmus et Hermione,* had been so successful that the authors' enemies organized a cabal to discredit *Alceste.* They failed in the attempt, but their attack led Perrault (either Charles or Pierre) to write an important essay, *Critique de l'opéra, ou examen de la tragédie intitulée Alceste, ou le Triomphe d'Alcide* (1674). Perrault defended *Alceste,* ostensibly by comparing it with Euripides' tragedy but more importantly by clarifying ways that the conventions of opera differed from those of spoken tragedy or comedy.

Like most *tragédies en musique, Alceste* contains plenty of heroic action but no exploration of a tragic dilemma: Alceste sacrifices her life without apparent second thoughts; Admète and Alceste choose duty to Alcide over love for each other regretfully but without discussion; and even the hero Alcide chooses *gloire* over *amour* without evident internal struggle.

In place of human dilemma and discussion, the genre offers human and supernatural spectacle, and *Alceste* provides these brilliantly. There are the customary *dei ex machina,* which not only advance the plot but also bring about spectacular changes of scenery. For instance, it is thanks to the gods Diana and Mercury that Alcide is given passage from the worldly setting of Alceste's funeral to the entrance to the Underworld; the stage machinery at the Paris Opéra would have transformed the setting instantaneously during a very brief musical entr'acte. The wonderfully evocative ballet *divertissements* present a catalogue of stock topics, to which French librettists and composers would return many times: maritime celebration, tempest, battle scene, funeral, underworld scene, and pastoral celebration. The seaside wedding festival is clearly a "diversion" from the dramatic dialogue, but the return to high drama—Licomède's abduction of Alceste, followed by Admète's pursuit—is accomplished with additional ballet: a tempest stirred up by the North Winds, represented by four scurrying dancers, is subsequently calmed by the West Winds, four "flying" creatures. (The tempest scene was apparently inspired by a similar episode in Virgil's *Aeneid.*) In the battle between Admète's and Licomède's armies, punctuated by martial trumpets and timpani, half the dance troupe and stationary chorus represent the "besiegers" and the other half the "besieged." Alceste's funeral is a monumental scene, framed by a massive choral introduction and a concluding choral chaconne, including a pantomime ballet during which mourners tear their clothes and hair.

In comparison with Lully's mature operas of the 1680s, *Alceste* makes relatively sparing use of the full orchestra, and it virtually never exploits subtle conflict between poetic and musical meter; still, the composer's flexible mixture of gently expressive recitative with brief short-breathed airs and ensemble passages was well developed by the time he wrote *Alceste.* All scenes are successful, and some are gems—for instance, the moving farewell between Alceste and the dying Admète, in which intertwined solo fragments grow progressively shorter and gradually give way to a duet. An obvious feature that marks *Alceste* as an early work is the presence of comic scenes and a humorous sub-plot, in the manner of contemporaneous Italian opera. French attitudes toward seemliness and unity of action led Lully and Quinault to abandon these plot elements after 1675—an unfortunate development from our modern point of view, since Lully was a gifted musical comedian. One of the best loved passages in all of Lully's operas occurs as Alcide attempts to enter the underworld: a comical Charon sings cheerfully of the inevitability of death (over a bass line representing the flowing River Acheron), then, in the manner of an efficient Parisian shopkeeper, collects a fare from the shades before granting them passage to Hades.

Alceste was the first opera by Lully to be recorded in its entirety (in 1974); it has thus become one of his best known works.

—Lois Rosow

ALCINA.

Composer: George Frideric Handel.

Librettist: Unknown (after *L'isola di Alcina,* 1728, based on Ariosto, *Orlando furioso*).

First Performance: London, Covent Garden, 16 April 1735; revised 6 November 1736.

Roles: Alcina (soprano); Ruggiero (soprano); Morgana (soprano); Bradamante (contralto); Oronte (tenor); Melisso (bass); Oberto (soprano); chorus (SATB).

*　　*　　*

Alcina recounts the episode from Ariosto's *Orlando furioso* in which the knight Ruggiero is held prisoner on the sorceress Alcina's island of pleasure and forgets his obligations to love and duty in his bewitched passion for Alcina. In Ariosto's telling, Bradamante, the warrior maiden beloved by Ruggiero, seeks help from her mentor, the enchantress Melissa, who disguises herself as Ruggiero's teacher, the magician Atlante, and rescues the knight with the help of a magic ring.

Handel's libretto is directly based on an earlier, anonymous libretto performed in Rome, 1728, and Parma, 1729. In this version, Bradamante's tutor becomes the male sorcerer Melisso, and Bradamante accompanies him on his rescue mission disguised in male clothing as her brother Ricciardo. Thus the rescue by a sorcerer and the cross-dressing are both maintained. By adding Bradamante, however, the librettist allows for scenes of anger, despair, recrimination, and reconciliation between the lovers.

The source libretto further adds Oronte, a general in Alcina's forces, and Morgana, Alcina's sister, as a squabbling second pair of lovers. Morgana falls in love with Ricciardo (Bradamante in disguise), and Oronte, wanting to spread the jealousy he feels, convinces Ruggiero that it is Alcina who now loves Ricciardo. Their inclusion provides complication to the story not only as a foil to the other love interests, but also as a way of capitalizing on the male disguise of Bradamante.

A new episode in Handel's opera not included in the source libretto concerns Astolfo, a cousin of Bradamante's and a former victim of Alcina. In Handel's version, Astolfo has been transformed into a lion. He is rescued and reunited with his son, Oberto, when Ruggiero destroys Alcina's realm. This episode was added for the sheer spectacle it provided during a period in Handel's career when such scenes were eagerly anticipated by the audience. For example, in Handel's *Arianna (Ariadne)* of 1733, Teseo (Theseus) combats the Minotaur, and in *Atalanta* (1736) there is a wild boar chase and killing on stage. Oberto's confrontation with the lion whom he miraculously recognizes as his father arises from the same tradition.

The aspect of spectacle in *Alcina* is also evident in the impressive scenic transformations. Act I opens in "A desart [sic] Place terminated by high craggy Mountains, which, after A Noise of Thunder, and Lightning, . . . suddenly opens and breaks to Pieces, and vanishing, leaves to View the beautiful Palace of Alcina. . . ." In act II when "Melisso puts the Ring (formerly Angelica's) on Rogero's [Ruggiero's] Finger," the scene "immediately changes to a horrid desart Place." Similarly, in the last scene, Ruggiero breaks the spell, whereupon "the Scene wholly disappears, changing to the Sea, which is seen thro' a vast subterraneous Cavern, where many Stones are chang'd into Men. . . ."

Alcina and Handel's previous opera, *Ariodante* (1734), which is also based on Ariosto's *Orlando furioso,* are Handel's only operas for London conceived and written with a resident ballet troupe in mind. The French prima ballerina Marie Sallé had spent many seasons in London and was famous for her naturalistic approach to dance; her association with Handel was her first with Italian opera. In *Alcina,* the sorceress, tricked and deserted by Ruggiero, calls in vain on the spirits of the night for assistance. In frustration, she throws down her magical wand and leaves, after which the spirits and phantoms appear and dance.

In addition to the closing scene of act II for Alcina, including the accompanied recitative, "Ah! Ruggiero crudel" ("Ah! Cruel Ruggiero"), and the aria, "Ombre pallide" ("You pale shadows"), which led to the ballet, *Alcina* contains much remarkable music. In particular, Handel has eloquently depicted the sorceress who falls victim to her own emotions and the hero who is rescued from the sorceress's spell but leaves the enchanted isle with more than a touch of regret. In Alcina's aria "Ah! mio cor" ("Ah! my heart"), the sorceress (sung by Anna Strada) fully confesses the depth of her love for Ruggiero in short, broken phrases against a pulsating string accompaniment reminiscent of heartbeats and teardrops. In the second section Alcina briefly pulls herself together and remembers that as a sorceress she can punish the offender; the strings, now bowed, play repeated sixteenth notes that seem to resonate with her anger. But before she can act, her first emotion returns and overpowers her. Thus falling in the typical *da capo* form, in which an aria in two sections is completed by the return of the first, this aria nevertheless rises above the commonplace by using the form in a passionate, dramatic way.

Alcina also illustrates the importance of aria placement. In Ruggiero's "Verdi prati" ("Green meadows"), Handel summed up all of the knight's ambivalence about facing reality and responsibility. In the source libretto, this text occurred at the end of the first act and was sung by Bradamante, who looks forward to the destruction of Alcina's realm. In Handel's version, the text was moved to the second act and reassigned to Ruggiero. About to leave with Bradamante, he looks back on the "green meadows and charming woods whose charm and beauty will soon be lost." Handel's setting eschews the normative *da capo* form for rondo form (refrain form), where the phrase "Verdi prati" is heard three times, as if Ruggiero cannot easily let it go. The music is very simple, the strings and voice moving slowly together with no virtuosic display. The castrato Giovanni Carestini who first sang Ruggiero initially rejected this aria because of its simplicity. According to Charles Burney, Handel responded with an angry tongue-lashing, and Carestini sang the aria.

One audience member wrote of *Alcina* that the opera was "so fine I have not words to describe it. Strada has a whole scene of charming recitative—there are a thousand beauties. While Mr. Handel was playing his part, I could not help thinking him a necromancer in the midst of his own enchantments."

—Ellen T. Harris

ALDA (born Davis), Frances (Jeanne).

Soprano. Born 31 May 1879, in Christchurch, New Zealand. Died 18 September 1952, in Venice. Married Giulio Gatti-Casazza, manager of the Metropolitan Opera, in 1910 (divorced in 1928). Studied with Mathilde Marchesi in Paris; debut as Manon at Opéra-Comique in Paris, 1904; appearances at Brussels, 1905-08, Covent Garden, 1906, and Teatro alla Scala, 1908; debut as Gilda at the Metropolitan Opera, where she sang more than 250 performances until 1930; premiered Damrosch's *Cyrano* (1913) as Roxanne, Herbert's *Madeleine* (1914), and Hadley's *Cleopatra's Night* (1920); also appeared in Buenos Aires, Boston, and Chicago.

Frances Alda as Ophelia in Thomas's *Hamlet*

Publications

By ALDA: books–

Men, Women, and Tenors. Boston, 1937.

About ALDA: articles–

Favia-Artsay, A. "Frances Alda." *Record Collector* 6 (1951): 228.
Simpson, A. "This Country May Well be Proud of Her." *Music in New Zealand* 6 (1989): 36.
_____. "Frances Alda." In *Opera in New Zealand: Aspects of History and Performance.* Wellington, New Zealand, 1990.
Simpson, A. and P. Downes. In *Southern Voices: International Singers of New Zealand.* Auckland, 1992.

*   *   *

It was Alda's misfortune to sing at the Metropolitan Opera during what can be seen in hindsight as a golden age of sopranos. Lacking the charisma (and American birth) which made Geraldine Farrar a superstar, too outspoken and acerbic to win the hearts of colleagues and critics, and handicapped in her career by her ill-advised marriage to the Metropolitan's General Manager, Giulio Gatti-Casazza, Alda had to work harder than most to maintain her position. Her success was a tribute to her fighting qualities and to the genuineness of her talent.

That Alda deserves to rank amongst the leading lyric sopranos of her day is attested by some 130 gramophone recordings which she made for the Victor Company between 1909 and 1928. These show her clean attack and elegant line, and the sheer beauty of her voice. To quote J.B. Steane in *The Grand Tradition* (London, 1974), "she is probably the most consistently satisfying lyric soprano on pre-electrical records."

The most immediately notable aspect of Alda's recordings is her scrupulous attention to matters of rhythm, intonation and phrasing. She was undoubtedly better schooled in musicianship than many of her colleagues. Born into one of Australia's most notable operatic families, she was thoroughly grounded in piano and violin before she ever had a singing lesson. Her technical security and beautiful head tones were largely the product of her studies with Mathilde Marchesi prior to her European debut in 1904. Also characteristic of the Marchesi schooling is her forward voice production; she uses a tremendous amount of head resonance, and deliberately brightens her vowels to assist in this. At times the process adversely affects her diction, as in the charming recording of "A Perfect Day" from Victor Herbert's *Madeleine,* in which the word 'day' emerges as 'dee' throughout. On the other hand, few sopranos of any era can match the clean, clear figuration, free of intrusive aspirates, which she displays in negotiating the difficulties of "L'altra notte" from Boito's *Mefistofele.* Made in 1920, this was one of her own favorite recordings.

Another fine example of her art is "Ah, dunque" from Catalani's *Loreley,* where her technical security and excellent intonation in an aria beset with awkward intervallic leaps excites admiration. The recording is one of many which display her particularly close and precise trills. As a performance, "Ah, dunque" is amongst her most passionate. However, musical feeling rather than passion is the hall-mark of her interpretations. While her private life was colorful, on stage and on record she excelled in portraying lyrical, gentle, and often doomed heroines. Mimì in *La bohème* was her favourite. She sang the role at the Metropolitan more often than any other soprano, partnering all the leading tenors of her day—from Caruso to Gigli.

Desdemona in Verdi's *Otello,* Massenet's Manon and Puccini's *Manon Lescaut,* Marguerite in Gounod's *Faust,* Lady Harriet in *Martha,* and Nannetta in Verdi's *Falstaff* were other roles in which she made her mark. Her recordings of excerpts from Puccini's *Madama Butterfly* show that she was equally suited to that role, but opportunities to sing it were denied her once she moved to America. The lyricism of Micaela's aria (*Carmen*) and Lauretta's "O mio babbino caro" (*Gianni Schicchi*) fall naturally within her compass, and in recordings of both she displays a lovely warmth of tone allied to tasteful restraint. By applying the same care to popular music as she did to the finest operatic arias, she lent distinction to her many recordings of ballads and other lighter repertoire.

The modern listener needs to make few stylistic concessions in listening to an Alda recording. She generally concentrates on singing the notes the composer wrote, while emotional tricks, such as over-indulgence in portamento, are foreign to her style. Alda was an early advocate of radio broadcasting, which she described as "the greatest medium the world has ever seen for disseminating culture, particularly musical culture." She also felt that the movies were the only medium in which one would ever be able to see perfect operatic productions. In 1937 Alda completed her autobiography, *Men, Women and Tenors,* which is notable for its lively style and forthright views on contemporary singers and singing.

—Adrienne Simpson

ALL WOMEN DO THUS
See COSÌ FAN TUTTE

ALLEN, Thomas.

Baritone. Born 10 September 1944 in Seaham Harbour, County Durham, England. Married Margaret Holley, 1968 (one son). Studied at the Royal College of Music, London, 1964-8; professional debut at the Welsh National Opera as Figaro in *Il barbiere di Siviglia,* 1969; Covent Garden debut as Donald in *Billy Budd* in 1971 and joined company the following year; appeared at Glyndebourne as Papageno in *Die Zauberflöte* in 1973, returned as Figaro in 1974, Guglielmo in 1975 and Don Giovanni in 1977; created role of count in Musgrave's *The Voice of Ariadne* at 1974 Aldeburgh Festival; Metropolitan Opera debut as Papageno, 1981; appeared at Salzburg in *Il ritorno d'Ulisse,* 1985; in English National Opera's production of Busoni's *Doktor Faust,* London Coliseum, 1986.

*   *   *

Hailed by the *Guardian* as the best English baritone of his day, Thomas Allen reached fame in his mid-twenties with his

portrayal for the Welsh National Opera of Figaro in Rossini's *Il barbiere di Siviglia.* His musicianship, vocal elegance and flexibility were never in doubt, and after taking on this buffo role he also quickly proved his further range as a singing actor by playing such Mozart roles as the Count in *Le nozze di Figaro,* the officer-lover Guglielmo in *Così fan tutte* and the simple bird-catcher Papageno in *Die Zauberflöte.* His good looks and stage presence also made a considerable impression as Britten's handsome, doomed, young sailor in *Billy Budd* in a production by the same company that helped to make him the best interpreter of this demanding role for nearly two decades. In fact, Allen appeared as Budd in the late 1980s for English National Opera and BBC Television when he was already in his forties, admitting with some humor that soon he would have to give it up on account of his age alone.

At Covent Garden from 1971, Allen widened his experience by singing some supporting roles such as the politician Paolo Albiani in Verdi's *Simon Boccanegra* and the musician Schaunard in Puccini's *La bohème,* and he brought the same sense of good natured comedy to the role of Marcello, the hero Rodolfo's other artist friend in the same opera. He was a vivid soldier and would-be lover as Belcore in Donizetti's *L'elisir d'amore.* His experience as Mozart's Count Almaviva, a more complex character and a mature man, must have stood him in good stead when he took on the challenging Mozart role of Don Giovanni in 1977 for Glyndebourne. It was also in the 1970s and at another British venue, Benjamin Britten's Aldeburgh, that he proved again his ability to convince in new music when he created the role of the Count in Thea Musgrave's *The Voice of Ariadne.* He played the cynical but perhaps likable apothecary Ned Keene in the Philips recording of Britten's *Peter Grimes* that was made in the late 1970s; perhaps he thought himself (or was thought) unsuitable to take the older role of Captain Balstrode.

Thomas Allen possesses both vocal flexibility and an alert stage personality. Together these have given him a wide range, and made him good casting in operetta, for example Johann Strauss's *Die Fledermaus* at the New York Metropolitan Opera. As he approaches fifty, he seems to be concentrating on character roles such as Mozart's Count and Don Giovanni, and he has also sung the Count in Strauss's *Capriccio,* Faust in Busoni's *Doktor Faust* and the Forester in Janáček's *The Cunning Little Vixen.* This latter performance was recorded (EMI), and besides Mozart's Almaviva and Don Giovanni he has also recorded his portrayals of the somewhat unsympathetic Onegin in Tchaikovsky's *Eugene Onegin,* the heroine's brother Valentin in Gounod's *Faust,* the hero's friend Albert in Massenet's *Werther,* the unhappy, guilt-ridden Orestes in Gluck's *Iphigénie en Tauride* and Prince Hector in Tippett's *King Priam.*

Although it might be a disappointment to Thomas Allen that his baritone range largely prohibits him from playing strictly Romantic roles, he has nonetheless championed much of the Romantic repertory. He has appeared as Strauss's wealthy and idealistic "Croatian landowner" Mandryka in *Arabella,* and, being capable of a high baritone register, as Debussy's doomed young hero Pelléas in *Pelléas et Mélisande.* Allen has also played the Trojan Prince Aeneas in Purcell's *Dido and Aeneas,* but though this is nominally a romantic lead, the role is quite small and dramatically unsatisfying. Allen sang it opposite Jessye Norman in a recorded performance conducted for Philips by Raymond Leppard and brought to the vacillating Prince a touching quality of flawed nobility. He was no less dignified as yet another Prince, the romantic widower Andrei in Prokofiev's *War and Peace.* His vocal finesse has also allowed him to succeed as a lieder singer and in oratorio, and here too his recorded repertory is wide-ranging.

—Christopher Headington

ALVA, Luigi (born Luis Ernesto Alva Talledo).

Tenor. Born 10 April 1927, in Lima, Peru. Studied with Rosa Morales in Lima, with Emilio Ghirardini in Milan and with Ettore Campogalliani; opera debut in *I pagliacci* in Lima, 1950; European debut at Teatro Nuovo in Milan as Alfredo, 1954; sang Paolino in *Il matrimonio segreto* at the opening of Piccola Scala in Milan, 1955; debut at Teatro alla Scala as Almaviva, 1956; debut at Salzburg, 1957; debut at Covent Garden, 1960; debut as Fenton at the Metropolitan Opera, 1964, where he sang more than 80 performances in 8 roles until 1976; also sang in Chicago, Glyndebourne, Edinburgh, Vienna.

Publications

About ALVA: books–

Celletti, R. *Le grandi voci.* Rome, 1964.

*   *   *

Few singers have been able to match the cheerfulness, delicacy and gentle melancholy that Luigi Alva brought to his performances of leading tenor roles in late eighteenth- and early nineteenth-century comic opera. Alva was a lyric tenor of great musicality and sweetness of voice—characteristics he shared with his contemporary Peter Schreier. Although Alva did not have Schreier's vocal power and dramatic urgency, he often surpassed his German colleague in the warmth and charm of his interpretations and in the pure beauty of his voice. Like Schreier, Alva specialized in Mozart; but the Mozart operas represented an exception for both singers: Alva's repertory was mostly limited to the works of Italian composers while Schreier limited himself primarily to operas in German.

Early in his career Alva revealed his talents in a memorable portrayal of Paulino, the secret newly-wed in Cimarosa's *Il matrimonio segreto*. Near the end of his career he returned to the role with as much success as earlier. Although this reflects well on Alva's strength, it also suggests that he was not the type of singer-actor who could easily develop new repertory and new kinds of characters to portray as he got older. He sang young, rather innocent lovers throughout his career, never making a full transition to more mature tenor roles such as Mozart's Idomeneo.

Alva's interpretations of Rossini's young romantic leads won him great applause throughout his career. In a recording of *Il barbiere di Siviglia* under Abbado we can hear Alva's Almaviva. The voice is light and clear, sometimes (especially in dialogue and ensembles, when Alva is not trying to project his voice) with a distinctly (and perhaps to some listeners annoyingly) boyish quality. He rarely strains his voice: his high notes are strong without being forced. He spins out strands of coloratura with ease and grace, although his tendency to aspirate each syllable in runs might strike some listeners as mincing and effeminate. As Lindoro in *L'italiana in Algeri*, recorded under Silvio Varviso, Alva projects much

the same character as he does in *Il barbiere:* he is the same gentle, young lover. In the big aria "Languir per una bella" Alva's excellent breath control allows him to stretch out the opening slow melody to wonderful effect. He attacks the many high B-flats in the fast section with confidence and conquers them with rich, full-blooded tones. This is splendid, virile singing; this is Alva at his lyric best.

Although he is primarily remembered today as an interpreter of Mozart and Rossini, Alva's repertory was considerably more diverse than that. His performance of the role of Oronte in Handel's *Alcina* (as recorded under Bonynge) makes one wish that he had devoted more attention to Baroque opera. He is a spirited Handel singer, bringing to arias like "Semplicetto! a donna credi?" and "È un folle" a strong sense of character, vividly conveying each aria's meaning to the listener.

—John A. Rice

AMAHL AND THE NIGHT VISITORS.

Composer: Gian Carlo Menotti.

Librettist: Gian Carlo Menotti.

First Performance: National Broadcasting Company, 24 December 1951; stage premiere, Bloomington, Indiana, 21 February 1952.

Roles: Amahl (soprano); His Mother (mezzo-soprano); King Kaspar (tenor); King Melchior (baritone); King Balthazar (bass); Page (bass); chorus (SATB).

*   *   *

Menotti calls *Amahl and the Night Visitors* "an opera for children, because it tries to capture my own childhood." Having agreed to write the first opera ever commissioned for television, Menotti drew upon memories of happy childhood Christmases which were triggered by a chance encounter with Hieronymus Bosch's painting, *The Adoration of the Magi,* in New York's Metropolitan Museum of Art. The score and libretto arose instinctively and remained mostly free of alterations, as if the composer himself recognized that it could not be bettered. The original orchestral score bears not only Menotti's handwriting but also that of Samuel Barber, who had to assist in readying the work for rehearsals and the impending premiere.

A crippled boy who plays his shepherd's pipe and is possessed of a grand imagination, Amahl lives with his mother in a hut amid great poverty. The Three Kings, following the Star to find the Christ Child, knock at the door, seeking a brief rest on their way. When the Mother can finally be persuaded that Amahl is not spinning another foolish tale, she welcomes the Kings, and soon afterward the neighboring shepherds appear, singing and carrying baskets of fruit and vegetables, from which they present gifts to the visitors. Encouraged by the Mother to dance for the guests, the shepherds shyly begin a faltering folk dance that moves with increasing confidence from *lento, ma non troppo* to a whirling, excited *tarantella,* with music extracted from a string quartet Menotti wrote as a young student. When the neighbors leave, everyone is soon asleep, except for the Mother, who sings the only aria in the opera, a soliloquy reflecting on how she could help her son with just a piece of "all that gold." As she reaches for the gold, the aroused Page seizes the Mother, whereupon Amahl in great distress rises at once to her defense and tries to beat off the Page with his crutch. King Melchior tells the Mother she may keep the gold, for "the Child we seek doesn't need [it] . . . On love alone He will build His kingdom." The Mother sinks to her knees in tears, and wishes she could afford to send a gift of her own. Amahl breaks in and offers his hand-made crutch as a present to the Christ Child. Eagerly lifting the crutch, he steps toward the Kings, and in a dramatic hush, they all realize that he is walking without it for the first time. The Kings are awed by this "sign from the Holy Child," and when the procession departs, Amahl goes with them, to take his gift personally to the Child.

Amahl and The Night Visitors immediately became a classic among music for the Christmas season. Translated into more than twenty languages, it remains Menotti's most popular work, and the most frequently performed. The starkly simple stage requirements and modest instrumentation provide a wide choice of locale in which to perform it; Menotti chose to think of "a stage within a stage," and ignored the unique capabilities of television. With repeated melodic motives and the use of major triads at emotional climaxes, the unified elements of music and libretto produce in this work a strong emotional response that is by no means confined to children.

—Jean C. Sloop

AMATO, Pasquale.

Baritone. Born 1878 in Naples. Died 12 August 1942 in Jackson Heights, New York. Attended Conservatory of San Pietro a Majella, Naples; studied first with Beniamo Carelli and later Vincenzo Lombardi; professional debut as Germont in *La Traviata* at Teatro Bellini in Naples, 1900; Covent Garden debut as Amonasro, 1904; Toscanini secured him a position at Teatro alla Scala in 1907-8, where he was Golaud in first Teatro alla Scala performance of *Pélleas,* Kurwenal in *Tristan und Isolde;* began 12 seasons at the Metropolitan Opera after appearing as Germont on 20 November 1908; he created Rance in world premiere of Puccini's *Fanciulla del West,* 1910, Gaston in Damrosch's *Cyrano,* 1913, and Napoleone in Giordano's *Mme Sans-Gène,* 1913; departed from Metropolitan Opera in 1921; settled in New York as singing teacher.

Publications

About AMATO: articles–

Kenyon, P. and C. Williams: "Pasquale Amato." *Record Collector* 21 (1973): 3.

*   *   *

In the final analysis, Pasquale Amato's greatest professional achievement was his position as lead Italian baritone at the Metropolitan Opera, for twelve years, where he performed on the highest level. He was engaged by the Met frequently, singing on the average ten times a month. This is not so

remarkable given performance practices of the time. In Italian theaters, for example, a lead performer often sang up to five times a week, but this was usually the same role in a long "run" of an opera, in theaters with seating capacities of a thousand to fifteen hundred. The Metropolitan Opera seats 3600. No matter how conscientious and conservative the artist, he has to 'push' a bit more in the large auditoriums of North America. The constant grinding out of performances takes its toll on even the richest voices; very few have escaped without some erosion of their powers. This perhaps partially explains why certain treasured artists have been less successful in North American opera houses than in the smaller, more congenial theaters of Europe.

At the Metropolitan, Amato performed regularly with Caruso, Destinn, Farrar, and Toscanini. There is ultimately something thankless in such professional stability. Amato had to be content with endless Barnabas, Iagos, Tonios, Amonasaros, and Germonts. These regular roles were occasionally interspersed with such plums as Rance in *Fanciulla* and Napoleon in *Mme. Sans-Gène* (both world premières)—and Amato would have created Tabarro, had he not been absent for illness.

If sheer solidity is Amato's hallmark in an era blessed with so many first-rate baritones, this is hardly an insult. Not every gifted artist can reach all the peaks, and Amato touched many. Amato's recorded legacy stands up favorably with his illustrious contemporaries, even if only a few stand out as 'immortal' performances. The early (1907-10) Fonotipia recordings reveal a young bronze voice of ingratiating quality and range with only the heavy vibrato setting him apart from his peers. By the time he recorded for Victor, early in his association with the Metropolitan Opera, his voice was almost perfectly balanced from top to bottom, with merely a hint of vibrato. The *I due foscari* aria "O vecchio cor, che batti" stands out as gloriously controlled singing, while the 1911 *Forza* duet with Caruso forces the listener to consult the score to determine who is singing, so well matched and similar are their voices.

At the age of forty, Amato suffered a severe ailment that resulted in the loss of his right kidney. He never regained his full strength, and his career lost focus. By the time he recorded for Homocord in 1924, after his departure from the Metropolitan, his large voice and command of big gestures are still apparent but the voice lacks its previous lustre and one hears only the underlying roar.

During the 1920s and early 1930s Amato made extensive guest appearances in Europe and North America, but never again found a home theater. Many of these guest engagements were in theaters and venues that would have been unthinkable in his great years. As a teacher he found a permanant home at the University of Louisiana at Baton Rouge, where he died in 1942.

—Charles B. Mintzer

AMELIA AL BALLO [Amelia Goes to the Ball].

Composer: Gian Carlo Menotti.

Librettist: Gian Carlo Menotti.

First Performance: Philadelphia, 1 April 1937 (English version by George Mead).

Pasquale Amato as Jack Rance in *La fanciulla del West,* **Metropolitan Opera, New York, 1910**

Roles: Amelia (soprano); The Husband (baritone); The Lover (tenor); Amelia's Friend (mezzo-soprano or contralto); Chief of Police (bass); First and Second Maids (sopranos); chorus (SATB).

*   *   *

Written and inspired within the environs of Vienna, *Amelia al ballo,* the Opus 1 of Menotti's career as a composer, has justly been compared to *Le nozze di Figaro, Il barbiere di Siviglia,* and *Falstaff,* thanks to its madcap antics and action-filled score. Although the libretto was written in Menotti's native tongue, the first two performances were in an English translation by George Mead; it would be seventeen years before the original Italian was heard, at La Scala. Mary Curtis Bok's insistence on programming this student work in Philadelphia was vindicated by its adoption into the New York Metropolitan Opera repertory the following year. New York critics heralded the young man of twenty-six as a fresh addition to the Italian operatic tradition.

The score bears all the marks of Menotti's studies in traditional forms with Scalero. It portrays the frenzied antics of a young socialite preparing to leave for the first ball of the season, only to be confronted by her irate husband. He has just discovered a letter from Amelia's secret lover, who lives upstairs. In the ensuing quarrel, the husband agrees to go to the ball, but only after he has shot the lover. He leaves on this errand, and locks Amelia in the apartment. What follows is great fun: a two-storey balcony exchange as Amelia rushes to warn her beau; a wonderful face-off between husband and lover, while Amelia frets over getting to the ball; the heated argument in which Amelia shoots her husband, attracting much of the neighborhood when the policeman appears; Amelia's false version of the incident; the lover's arrest; and, as the still-breathing husband is borne off to the hospital, Amelia's triumphant departure for the ball on the arm of the policeman.

The superstructure of the opera is formed by seven set pieces: two duets; a *romanza* aria for each of the three principals; a trio; and an exuberant choral finale. Introduced by an overture in sonata-form, the entire opera is alive with contrapuntal activity: melodic arioso elements in the orchestra render the vocal line here and there to temporary status of an obligato. The traditional forms are woven into a smooth musical flow without orchestral introductions, but each of the first two arias comes to a full close, followed by a space that allows for applause. The frequent meter changes, to accommodate both speech rhythms and shifting emotions, will remain a characteristic of Menotti's entire *oeuvre,* and give a slight modern tinge to the fast-moving Mozartian patter of Italian.

—Jean C. Sloop

AMELIA GOES TO THE BALL
See AMELIA AL BALLO

L'AMICO FRITZ [Friend Fritz].

Composer: Pietro Mascagni

Librettist: P. Suardon [=N. Daspuro] (after Erckmann-Chatrian).

First Performance: Rome, Costanzi, 31 October 1891.

Roles: Fritz Kobus (tenor); Suzel (soprano); Beppe (mezzo-soprano); David (baritone); Hanezo (bass); Federico (tenor); Caterina (soprano).

*   *   *

Perhaps any opera Mascagni attempted after the extraordinary success of his first, prize-winning one-act *Cavalleria rusticana* would have seemed a disappointment, and therefore the relative neglect suffered by *L'Amico Fritz* is understandable in that context. Mascagni had wished to find a light and comic story in contrast to the dramatic *Cavalleria* to demonstrate his versatility, and *L'Amico Fritz* met his requirements, with its slight, charming plot and lightly sketched characters. But if the result lacks the dramatic punch of *Cavalleria* and also lacked that work's first-class libretto, *Fritz*'s lyrical and passionate sweetness make it work equally well on its own terms.

Fritz, a wealthy landowner, tells his matchmaking friend David that he will never marry. For Fritz's birthday celebration, Suzel, the daughter of his tenant farmer, brings a bouquet. A gypsy violin announces Beppe, who sings for Fritz. When Suzel hurries home, David notes how charmed Fritz was by her innocent loveliness. David declares he will find Suzel a husband. When Fritz crossly insists that she is too young, David wagers that Fritz will marry soon. Fritz bets a vineyard that he will not.

In act II, set at dawn, Suzel wakes to find the cherry tree in blossom. Fritz, who is visiting the farm, appears, and he catches the cherries that she throws down from the tree for him. But Fritz's friends descend on them: they've missed him in town. David, recognizing that Suzel is in love with Fritz, again broaches the idea of finding a husband for the girl, but Fritz becomes enraged. To himself, Fritz admits that he loves Suzel but, embarrassed by these new emotions, he rushes back to town, leaving Suzel bereft.

Songs of the peasants and of Beppe provoke Fritz's longing for Suzel. David announces that he has arranged a marriage for Suzel, which upsets Fritz even more. Suzel, in despair at having to marry someone she doesn't love, appeals to Fritz to stop the wedding. Fritz realizes she loves him, and admits his love for her. David's matchmaking has worked, and he gives Suzel the vineyard as a wedding present.

Mahler himself had noted Mascagni's musical progress since *Cavalleria.* His harmonies became more sophisticated, with a striking use of chromaticism and dissonance, and the orchestral colors in *Fritz* are well-suited to the story. There is a predominant use of strings and woodwind, with touches of brass that make telling comments. Only occasionally does Mascagni use the full orchestra, as in the intermezzo before act III, where its rich sound characterizes the unspoken passion of Fritz and Suzel.

The first, spritely pentatonic chords of the preludietto carry the promise of the opera's lighthearted story. A tender little theme, followed by a lovely yearning melody over throbbing accompaniment, give evidence of the love story to follow. A return to the opening chords and a whisper of the yearning melody precede the curtain's rising on a quiet 6/8 andante, as David and Fritz discuss the dowry for one of David's successful matchmaking attempts. Spritely woodwind chords announce the arrival of Fritz's friends for the birthday celebrations, and a teasing bassoon echoes the teasing of David by the young men, all of which contrasts with the sweet and simple greeting of Suzel's first entrance. Deftly and with instant effect, Mascagni paints the portrait of a loving and innocently gentle girl, as she offers her bouquet with "Son pochi fiori."

A simple melody at the beginning of act II evokes the quiet and peace of the country morning, which is then reinforced by Mascagni's use of a plaintive Alsatian folk song, "Es trag ein Mädelein," played first on the oboe, and then repeated in a more decorated version by an offstage chorus of peasants, trudging to the fields. Suzel's little song, "Bel cavalier," carries the same folk song feeling, with its simple words and repeated eight-bar phrase; but Mascagni embellishes it with a haunting oboe threnody between the verses, and the verses themselves are each written a tone higher than the last, suggesting Suzel's rising spirits.

With Fritz's entrance comes the famous Cherry Duet. Its opening andante sostenuto begins and ends with an easy 6/8 melody, almost like a popular canzona, with a freer lyrical middle section. This is followed by an andante amoroso sostenuto in the minor, Fritz expressing in a beautiful, melancholic phrase his amazement at the joys of spring, with Suzel joining in. This leads to a "Poco più," back in the major key of the opening andante. Its sweet lyrical phrases and constantly changing time signatures reinforce the sense of heady delight in the springtime around them. The mood is broken with a busy and happy little motive which announces the arrival of Fritz's friends, followed by Suzel's duet with David, its biblical theme of Rebecca at the well solemnly characterized by the changing tonalities of its cadential accompaniment.

Fritz's introspective and passionate "Quale strano" acknowledges both his love for Suzel and his determination not to give in to it; and then a repeat of the busy orchestral motives that brought the friends to the farm now takes them away, along with Fritz. As Suzel despairs, we hear the melancholy theme of the Cherry Duet's andante amoroso sostenuto, and at the act's end Suzel repeats the sad refrain of "Ein Mädelein": "The lover who goes away will never return."

A sorrowing theme in the bass opens the last act, highlighting Fritz's tormenting struggle between love and sworn bachelorhood. Beppe's little paean to love, accompanied by string pizzicato and touches of woodwind, heightens Fritz's sorrow, and in "O amore, o bella luce," with its great sweeping melody, Fritz bares the passion in his soul.

Suzel's poignant arietta "Non mi resta," with its tiptoeing chromatic opening phrase repeated throughout, leads to her passionate outcry, "Ah ditela per me quella parola," possibly the most beautiful melody in the opera, which blends into the final sweeping phrases of the lovers' declaration of their true feelings. All ends in a repeat of Fritz's "O amore," led by Fritz and joined by the six other principals.

Critics have complained about the imbalance between the simple plot and undeveloped characters of *L'Amico Fritz* and the weight of Mascagni's continuous and flowing melodic invention. This may be a major reason why the work has been relatively neglected outside Italy, although it is still popular at home. But it is that very outpouring of melody that makes it well worth reviving for the glorious voices of the contemporary opera stage.

—Louise Stein

L'AMORE DEI TRE RE [The Love of Three Kings].

Composer: Italo Montemezzi.

Librettist: Sem Benelli.

First Performance: Milan, Teatro alla Scala, 10 April 1913.

Roles: Archibaldo (bass); Avito (tenor); Fiora (soprano); Manfredo (baritone); Flaminio (tenor); Handmaiden (soprano); Young Girl (soprano); Old Woman (mezzo-soprano); chorus (SSAATTBB).

Publications

article–

Lualdi, A. "L'amore dei tre re di Montemezzi alla Scala." In *Serate musicali*, 237. Milan, 1928.

Italo Montemezzi's three-act *L'amore dei tre re,* to a libretto by Sem Benelli based closely on his verse tragedy, was premiered on 10 April 1913 under the baton of Tullio Serafin. On 2 January 1914 Toscanini presented it at the Metropolitan Opera in New York. In its medieval setting and subject matter the opera reflects the influence in Italy of Wagner's *Tristan und Isolde*. The action takes place at a remote Italian castle in the tenth century. In act I, Fiora, an Italian princess who had been betrothed to the Italian prince Avito, is forced instead to marry Manfredo, son of King Archibaldo, the Barbarian conqueror of Italy. Manfredo is away and Archibaldo begins to suspect Fiora of adultery. The old blind king is led around the castle by his guard Flaminio who, as an Italian, protects Fiora. Her trysts with Avito are heard by Archibaldo, whom Fiora cannot convince of her innocence. As the act ends everyone is anxiously awaiting Manfredo's return. In act II Manfredo, about to return to war, requests Fiora to wave to him from the castle battlements as he is leaving. As she is waving a long veil, Avito begins to embrace her and the two declare their passionate love for each other. Archibaldo approaches and Flaminio prevents Avito from killing him. Meanwhile Manfredo, noticing that Fiora's waving has stopped, has returned to the castle. Avito escapes. When Fiora and Archibaldo are alone, she taunts him and refuses to reveal her lover's identity until he loses control and strangles her. Manfredo forgives his wife. In act III Fiora is laid among flowers in the crypt and mourned by all. Avito kisses her but is seized by a chill, for Archibaldo has placed poison on her lips. Unwilling to live, Manfredo too kisses her and dies. The blind Archibaldo stumbles over a body that he assumes is Fiora's lover, but it is that of his own son.

The title, "The Love of Three Kings," may be explained in terms of Archibaldo's love for his son, Avito's love for Fiora, and Manfredo's unrequited passion for Fiora. Likewise, the three kings are all desirous of ruling Italy, represented symbolically by Fiora. According to Kobbé, "Tragic is the outcome of the conqueror's effort to win and rule over an unwilling people. Truly, he is blind." Avito becomes the symbol of the rightful native ruler prevented by the foreign invaders from possessing Fiora (Italy). Benelli's libretto consists of swift, concise action and sure characterization. In addition to Wagner's *Tristan* (and by implication the Romeo and Juliet story), *L'amore dei tre re* shares elements with Maeterlinck-Debussy's *Pelléas et Mélisande*. Montemezzi's

Rosa Ponselle as Fiora in *L'amore dei tre re*

work is in the tradition, along with *Pelléas* and other early twentieth-century operas such as Strauss' *Salome* and Berg's *Wozzeck*, of through-composed "sung play." A few parallels between *L'amore* and variously *Tristan/Roméo/Pelléas* include a beautiful young princess living in a castle with foreign kings, a passionate illicit love scene, the signal from the tower, a fatal draught and kiss, the heroine's true love being a man she has grown up with and with whom she has much in common, the scene in the crypt with the soliloquy at the bier, and the element of "love-death."

Benelli's libretto is generally considered superb, but the quality of Montemezzi's musical setting is more controversial. Many have held this relatively unfamiliar work, much more popular in America than in Italy, in high regard, and it has been a favorite vehicle of such singing actresses as Lucrezia Bori, Mary Garden, Claudio Muzio, Rosa Ponselle, and Dorothy Kirsten. The score contains few set-pieces, with the vocal writing perhaps developed from the continuous *declamato* of Verdi's *Otello*. The music is minutely expressive of the stage action but is rarely melodically expansive; the melodic lines are Italianate, but arias, and indeed even long vocal phrases, are few. The orchestration is vivid and intimately reflects actions, thoughts, people, and objects through recurring motifs. The score remains by far the best-known of Montemezzi's several operas. Not only have famous sopranos sung the part of Fiora, but the other principal roles have been portrayed by such illustrious singers as Pasquale Amato, Giovanni Martinelli, Edward Johnson, and Ezio Pinza. To the four principals Montemezzi provides music that clearly captures the character, thoughts, and passions of each; each has a major scene to himself. The two love duets between Fiora and Avito are extremely passionate, evoking not only passages from *Tristan* but also from act I of Verdi's *Otello*. The second-act duet from *L'amore* is interrupted, as in *Tristan*, in this case by the arrival of a servant bringing the white veil that Fiora is to wave to Manfredo.

In addition to Verdi, *verismo,* and Wagner, Richard Strauss (in the lush yet transparent orchestral textures) and Debussy (in a certain pervasive mystical quality) have influenced the score of *L'amore dei tre re*. This mixture of styles has been criticized by some. Patrick Smith wrote of *L'amore* that "It is weak-water stuff, expertly put together but sounding like this or that late nineteenth-century composer." Yet *L'amore dei tre re* is a work unlike any other Italian opera, similar perhaps only to the works of Montemezzi's contemporary, Zandonai, such as his *Francesca da Rimini* or *Giulietta e Romeo.*

—Stephen A. Willier

ANDERS, Peter.

Tenor. Born 1 July 1908, in Essen. Died 10 September 1954, in Hamburg. Studied with Grenzenbach and Lula Mysz-Gmeiner in Berlin; in chorus of Reinhardt's *La Belle Hélène* in 1931; engaged at Heidelberg, 1932; Darmstadt, 1933-34; Cologne, 1935-36; Hanover, 1937-8; Munich, 1938-40; Berlin, 1940-48; Hamburg, 1948-54; sang Tamino at Salzburg, 1943; Bacchus in *Ariadne auf Naxos* at Edinburgh Festival

in 1950; Walther in *Die Meistersinger* at Covent Garden in 1951.

*   *   *

The era of the 1930s and 40s may justly be regarded as a golden age of the German lyric tenor. The period also coincided with the development of the electrical recording process and produced an embarassment of riches that has served record collectors handsomely. Through the recording medium names like Richard Tauber, Julius Patzak, Helge Roswaenge, Josef Schmidt, Walther Ludwig, Herbert Ernst Groh and Marcel Wittrisch became famous throughout the world as exponents of opera, operetta and German Lied. The list would not be complete without the name of Peter Anders.

Anders made his operatic debut in 1932 in Heidelberg. In 1938 the noted conductor Clemens Krauss engaged him for the Munich Opera and subsequently Anders became a principal tenor at the Berlin Staatsoper during the war years. After the war, he sang principally at the Hamburg Opera. In 1950 he appeared at the Edinburgh Festival under Sir Thomas Beecham, who also conducted his Covent Garden appearance the following year as Walther von Stolzing in *Die Meistersinger.*

His earliest recordings date from 1933 for Telefunken, and he continued his association with that label through 1951. He then made a few recordings for Electrola, and his last recordings were issued by Deutsche Grammophon. He is also featured on a number of recordings from Berlin Radio published on Acanta and BASF. He recorded one role in a complete opera set, that of Lionel in *Martha*. At present two CDs are available, one on Electrola and one on Acanta.

His repertoire, typical of the German tenors of his generation, was wide ranging—German opera from Mozart to Wagner, Italian opera from Donizetti through Verdi to Mascagni and Puccini, operetta and German lied. Like his contemporaries he sang almost exclusively in German, the only exceptions being an "Una furtiva lagrima" and a "Funiculì-funiculà" in Italian. He was a serious and cultivated artist and recorded little from the popular song repertoire.

His early recordings reveal a lyric tenor voice with a distinctive bright, metallic timbre, combined with an excellent technique, faultless intonation and exemplary breath control. He was a dependable singer, always correct and eminently musical. His voice was not particularly flexible, although he manages the long run in "Il mio tesoro" (sung in German) on one breath. He did not have an extreme top range and therefore perhaps unwisely recorded the "Postillion lied" from *Le postillion de Longjumeau* without the climactic high D.

The Telefunken series of recordings are undoubtedly his best. The vocal quality is equalized throughout the range and is always used artistically. He disdained any use of *falsetto;* the vocal quality ranged from a pure head voice in soft passages through *mezza-voce*, to a ringing *forte* chest voice. A. G. Ross, writing in *Record News*, notes that Anders "took his Lehar, Millocker and Johann Strauss seriously and treated them with understanding and respect, giving a virile straightforward presentation of these melodies without Schmalz or egotistic virtuosity." The statement also applies to his operatic recordings, but paradoxically the virtues of his approach to music also reveal its weakness. The drawback is that his singing is mechanical, always musically correct, but lacking a distinctive personality.

Toward the end of his career he attempted the transformation from lyric to dramatic tenor. In his prime his voice was basically lyrico-spinto. Since his life was cut short by an unfortunate automobile accident, it is not possible to know whether or not he would have achieved success as a dramatic tenor. The evidence of his late recordings, however, suggests the possibility of decline. They reveal a loss of focus and evidence of strain in the high notes as well as a forced baritone-like quality in the middle register. The distinctive ease of production of his earlier records has vanished.

On the whole his Electrola recordings are probably his least successful, and unfortunately they have been the ones that have been released on CD. Close miking is a part of the problem, for it emphasizes the strained quality of his singing during this late period. The Deutsche Grammophon recordings are not entirely successful either, although the *Meistersinger* and *Undine* selections come off well.

His consumate musicality served him well in his recordings of Lieder. Like most of his contemporaries, his recordings from the Italian repertoire suffer from the use of the German text, and the exception, the 1944 "Una furtiva lagrima," is not successful. In fact, his 1942 version of the aria in German shows that he is more comfortable in his native language.

Critical evaluation of vocal quality is, of course, entirely subjective. The recordings of Peter Anders, particularly those by Telefunken, will always satisfy those who admire a clear, bright tenor voice used with taste and discernment. But that is also the drawback—they merely satisfy, they do not thrill. What Anders lacks is that spark of individualty and personality, that "egotistic virtuosity," that separates the great singer from the very good one.

—Bob Rose

ANDERSON, June.

Soprano. Born 1955, in Boston. Studied with Robert Leonard, New York. Debut as Queen of the Night with New York Center Opera, 1978; Rome debut as Rossini's Semiramide, 1982; appeared in Verdi's *Il corsaro,* San Diego, 1982; performed Rossini's *Armida* at Aix-en Provence and *Maometto II* in San Francisco, 1988; Metropolitan Opera debut as Gilda in *Rigoletto,* 1989; has sung at the Teatro alla Scala, Vienna, Rome, Paris, and Chicago.

* * *

Born in Boston, Massachusetts, June Anderson graduated from Yale University with a major in French Literature. She studied voice in New York City with Robert Leonard, and made her American debut in 1978 at the New York City Opera singing the Queen of the Night in Mozart's *Die Zauberflöte.* She made several other appearances with the New York City Opera, including Gilda in Verdi's *Rigoletto,* Rosina in Rossini's *Il barbiere di Siviglia,* Elvira in Bellini's *I puritani* and a concert version of Wagner's *Die Feen.* During the 1981-82 season she began to attract considerable critical attention. Theodore W. Libbey, Jr. of the *New York Times,* reviewing Anderson's *I puritani* at the New York City Opera, described her coloratura as "effortless" and with "touching vocal expressiveness." John Rockwell, also of the *New York Times,* reviewing Anderson's performance of Wagner's *Die Feen,* compared her coloratura and agility to that of "an early Anja Silja."

After a number of appearances in the United States, she moved to Italy, where she quickly achieved a series of successful performances which helped to launch her international career. In quick succession, she performed *Semiramide, Lucia di Lammermoor* and *Il barbiere di Siviglia* during the 1982-83 season at the Rome, Florence and Palermo Operas, respectively. Throughout this period she continued to perform in festivals in the United States and Canada.

Her Venice debut in April 1984, in Bellini's *La sonnambula* is particularly noteworthy in that the role of Amina had not been heard in the Teatro Malibran since Maria Malibran herself had sung it in 1835. In her *Opera News* (July 1984) review, Elizabeth Forbes described Anderson's voice as one which combined "flexibility, firmness of line and purity of tone in ideal proportions for this music." She also admired her characterization and "expressive strength."

By her own admission, Anderson has learned to say "no" to offers that do not fit the direction she has chosen for her career, even though this has meant turning down "performances in major places, major theaters with major conductors." This strategy has not seemed to hurt her prospects as she continues to strengthen her hold on the "bel canto" heroines. She recently performed a concert version of Rossini's *Semiramide* at Covent Garden with Marilyn Horne and Samuel Ramey.

Among her recordings are some unusual and less well-known works, such as Rossini's *Mosè in Egitto* and *Maometto Secondo* for Philips, Wagner's *Die Feen* for Orfeo and Bizet's *La jolie fille de Perth* with Alfredo Kraus for EMI/Angel. Her most recent disc, "Live from the Paris Opera" with Alfredo Kraus, contains a stunning version of "Bel raggio lusinghier" from Rossini's *Semiramide* which is, to date, the most representative recorded example of her ability and formidable talent.

—Patricia Robertson

ANDERSON, Marian.

Contralto. Born 17 February 1902, in Philadelphia. Studied with Giuseppe Boghetti in New York. First African-American soloist to appear in a major role at the Metropolitan Opera, as Ulrica in *Un ballo in maschera,* 1955; retired 1965; primarily known as a concert artist.

Publications

By ANDERSON: books–

My Lord, What a Morning: An Autobiography. New York, 1956.

About ANDERSON: books–

Vehanen, Kosti. *Marian Anderson: A Portrait.* New York, 1941.
Newman, Shirlee Petkin. *Marian Anderson: Lady from Philadelphia.* Philadelphia, c.1965.
Dobrin, Arnold. *Voices of Joy, Voices of Freedom.* New York, 1972.
Sims-Wood, Janet L. *Marian Anderson: An Annotated Bibliography and Discography.* Westport, 1981.

Marian Anderson as Ulrica in *Un ballo in maschera*, **Metropolitan Opera, New York, 1955**

Westlake, Neda M. *Marian Anderson: A Catalog of the Collection at the University of Pennsylvania Library*. Philadelphia, 1981.

Haskins, James. *One More River to Cross: The Stories of Twelve Black Americans*. New York, 1992.

articles–

Embree, Edwin Rogers. "Marian Anderson: Deep River of Song." In *Thirteen Against the Odds*. Port Washington, c.1944.

Schonberg, Harold. "The Other Voice of Marian Anderson." *The New York Times Magazine*, 10 August 1958.

Turner, P. "Afro-American Singers: An Index and Discography of Opera, Choral Music and Song." *Black Perspectives in Music* 9/1 (1981): 75.

"Reflected Glory." *Opera News* 48/October (1983): 64.

Lipman, Samuel. "Marian Anderson: The Diva from Philadelphia." *The New Criterion* 8/October (1989): 43.

Black, Allida M. "Championing a Champion: Eleanor Roosevelt and the Marian Anderson 'Freedom Concert'." *Presidential Studies Quarterly* 20/Fall (1990): 719.

"Another View (First Black to Sing a Major Role at the Met)." *Opera News* 55 (19 January 1991): 33.

* * *

When Marian Anderson returned to the United States for the 1935-36 concert season after her successful European tour, Olin Downes (*NYT*, 1/21/36) acclaimed her as "a born singer and a very sincere and thoughtful musician . . . She is a person of natural dignity and distinction . . . distinction, intelligence and taste are invariably reflected in her singing. The voice is a rare one, a deep contralto, rich in color and of a sensuous quality, save in the upper tones, which have a measure of nasality not displeasing . . . The middle register is best developed of all. The lowest octave has depth and beauty which haunt the ear and the memory." Downes lauded her artistic integrity: "[Miss Anderson] never distorts a rhythm or the contour of a phrase and is fortunately far from that type which stresses a high note or hangs on some advantageous effect in order to arouse the audience. It is not necessary for Miss Anderson so to attempt to arouse an audience, and she would not dream of doing so. She has palpably a real knowledge of her score in all its details, a fine control of breath, a knowledge of the laws of singing."

Noel Straus (*NYT*, 4/13/37) concurred with Downes, crediting Anderson with "the humbleness of spirit and unaffected simplicity which seem invariably to accompany greatness in any field of endeavor." At Carnegie Hall in 1937, he found that "the effect of her work was heightened by the sincerity and directness of her approach. . . . When the contralto employed mezzavoce in sustained passages . . . her singing was at its best. When used at its full power, the voice was less perfectly produced, often losing that perfection of sound which marked it in softer work. But as interpreter, Miss Anderson was ever impressive, whatever the mood and content of the selection."

Throughout her career, Anderson continued to impress critics by not allowing her extraordinary success to lead her into complacency. "The expressive capacities of her voice are constantly expanding," Downes wrote in 1939 (*NYT*, 1/7/39), "and she is becoming always more skilled in employing it for purposes of dramatic interpretation. . . . Miss Anderson can bridge registers and blend the tone of one into the other when that is her purpose. At the same time the dark color of

the low octave and the degree of reediness which occurs higher up represent only two of the natural tone colors which are at her disposal. Add to this her control and reserve of breath, and the quality, always vibrant and emotional of the voice itself. It has been developed . . . by the most serious and thoughtful work." Likewise Howard Taubman in 1942 (*NYT*, 1/6/42): "Marian Anderson's art grows deeper and richer with the years, even though the voice has not quite the magnificent lustre of half a dozen years ago . . . [She] sings with more restraint now, and with even greater variety of color effects. She can still let the voice out in stirring climaxes, but she saves these properly for big moments."

In addition to artistic and dramatic sincerity, the concert presentation of spirituals became an Anderson trademark. Again, Olin Downes commented that "Miss Anderson sings music by classic masters not as a lesson learned, or a duty carefully performed, but as an interpreter who has fully grasped and deeply felt the import of the song. When she interprets . . . Negro spirituals, she invests them with extraordinary distinction . . . One would not call this mere singing in the folk manner. The old folksongs were re-interpreted by an artist with special gifts that served to heighten and make the more complete expression of the things which had inspired the unknown composer of the melody."

Both Taubman and Downes expressed some disappointment, however, when Anderson ventured beyond Lieder and spirituals. "She is at her greatest in songs of profound compassion and soaring ecstasy; she can also manage a light, lyrical song with grace and sweetness;" but "when she tackles an operatic aria she leaves something to be desired," wrote Taubman. On the occasion of an appearance with the Philharmonic Orchestra in 1946, Downes (*NYT*, 4/5/46) conceded that "it may be that Miss Anderson is a singer primarily for the recital platform. Her rich voice fascinated the ear; her musicianship and her sincerity were unquestionable, but she sang apparently with constraint and inhibitory caution with the orchestra. No one would accuse her of musical misrepresentation, but the conviction as well as the mastery of nuance which is hers when she is accompanied by a piano was rather lost in the orchestral shuffle." Of course, because of limited operatic opportunities for African-American artists prior to her celebrated Metropolitan Opera debut in 1955, the solo recital platform was in fact her primary venue during the height of her concertizing years—it is not surprising that the more large-scale performances reflected a lack of experience.

Anderson's debut at the Met elicited a storm of praise, but also criticism at the tardiness of the event. "[The engagement] comes late—at least 15 years late. Miss Anderson's beautiful voice is not now in its prime" (Downes, *NYT* 10/17/54); "it would have been even happier as the tenth anniversary of an honor she richly merited long before, when she had vocal youth on her side as well as artistic experience" (Irving Kolodin, *Saturday Review*, 1/22/55); the performance "was long overdue, not only as far as the Metropolitan was concerned but also as far as Miss Anderson herself was concerned. And because of this I found the evening an occasion for sadness as well as rejoicing. Miss Anderson's voice—once so lovely, limpid, and unforgettably evocative—is far past its prime . . . She showed, understandably, considerable nervousness . . . and even when this initial nervousness had worn off, she failed to produce the brilliant result that the historic event seemed to demand. The audience gave her a thundering ovation, but I'm afraid that its applause was for the principle of the thing, and not for the specific artistic contribution she made. Her voice was unexpectedly small and tremulous in the vast spaces of the Metropolitan, and her stage personality . . . was timid and lacking in authority. The event should have occurred years before; coming at this time, it was hardly more than a gesture" (Winthrop Sargeant, *New Yorker,* 1/15/55).

Ronald Eyer (*Musical America,* 1/15/55), on the other hand, was thoroughly impressed by Anderson's Metropolitan Opera performance. "The contralto was a little unsettled at the beginning . . . but the powerful controls of a great and long-experienced artist took hold and she was singing with all her accustomed security, richness and warmth of tone and innate musicianship. Particularly notable was her contribution to the exacting quintet at the end of the act. Notable, too, was the deep penetration of the text, the meaning of the words given her to sing. For all the attention she gave to mood, inflection and tone coloration, she might have been singing the subtlest of lieder." Finally, Olin Downes again, who had followed Anderson's career for two decades: "there was no moment in which Miss Anderson's interpretation was commonplace or repetitive in effect. In Ulrica's one half-act, Miss Anderson stamped herself in the memory and the lasting esteem of those who listened."

Marian Anderson is also reknowned as an exemplary humanitarian as well as musician. When she was nominated to the United Nations delegation in 1958, Harold Schonberg wrote about "The Other Voice of Marian Anderson" (*NYT Mag,* 8/10/58) and how "she has always represented something that transcends singing and embraces humanity . . . Bolstered by faith, by a love for people and by a sincere desire to see and understand the other person's point of view . . . she manages to communicate that faith, love and sincerity as much through her meetings with people as through her singing."

—Kiko Nobusawa

ANDREA CHÉNIER.

Composer: Umberto Giordano.

Librettist: Luigi Illica.

First Performance: Milan, Teatro alla Scala, 28 March 1896.

Roles: Maddalena di Coigny (soprano); Chénier (tenor); Carlo Gérard (baritone); Contesse di Coigny (mezzo-soprano); Bersi (mezzo-soprano); Madelon (mezzo-soprano); Pietro Fleville (bass or baritone); Mathieu (baritone); Incredibile (tenor); Roucher (bass or baritone); Majordomo (bass); Fouquier-Tinville (bass or baritone); Schmidt (bass); Abbé (tenor); Dumas (bass); chorus (SSSSAATTBB).

Publications

articles–

Pinzauti, Leonardo. "Le ragioni di *Andrea Chénier.*" *Nuovo rivista musicale italiana* 15 (1981): 216.
Avant-scène opéra June (1989) [*Andrea Chénier* issue].

*   *   *

A report in *Opera* from a 1986 conference in Verona on Umberto Giordano and nineteenth-century *verismo* made the rather surprising point that ninety years after its Teatro alla Scala premiere, *Andrea Chénier* can still, in Italy at least, be the occasion of fiercely partisan controversy rather than the subject of cool critical appraisal. In most other operatic centers Giordano's best known work has, by and large, secured for itself a place in the ongoing repertory, while his other operas, except for an occasional performance of the later *Fedora,* have disappeared. Few critics regard *Andrea Chénier* as an unqualified masterpiece; indeed the then-editor of *Opera,* Harold Rosenthal, questioned the need for Covent Garden's 1983 revival on the grounds that the opera is "contrived." Nevertheless, despite gaps caused by the absence of suitable singers—the work requires three big Italianate voices—most houses now see it as worthy of periodic revival. And indeed, most audiences, untroubled by the critics' reservations, tend to respond enthusiastically to a good performance of the work.

Giordano had written three operas, *Marina, Mala vita,* and *Regina Diaz*—the latter two of which experienced some success—before being offered the libretto for *Andrea Chénier* which Luigi Illica had committed himself to write while still working on the libretto for what was to become Puccini's *La bohème.* Based very approximately on the life of the historical André Chénier, a poet who was first a supporter and then a victim of the French Revolution, the libretto is tautly effective in its condensation of the pertinent action into four acts. The first act, a kind of prelude to the other three, is set in the ballroom of the Comtesse de Coigny in 1789 on the eve of the Revolution. The three primary figures are clearly established: Carlo Gérard, a budding revolutionary but as yet still a servant, who secretly loves the daughter of the household, Maddalena di Coigny; she, in her turn, falls under the spell of one of the guests, the poet Andrea Chénier, when he responds to her challenge to improvise on the theme of *amor* by singing of his love for his country ("*Un dì, all'azzuro spazio*"). The unyielding insensitivity of the idle nobility toward the oppressed poor and the portents of the retribution about to come are vividly depicted. The remaining three acts, set in the Paris of the Reign of Terror five years later, depict Chénier's final days. In act II Chénier succeeds in meeting a mysterious woman who has been writing to him. It is Maddalena, hunted and threatened, sustained and protected only by Bersi, her faithful mulatto servant; she has continued to love Chénier since that first evening in her mother's home. The spy, Incredibile, reports their meeting to Gérard who is also searching for Maddalena; Gérard and Chénier fight, the former is wounded but recognizing Chénier whispers to him to escape because the Tribunal is seeking him. Act III takes place in the court of the Tribunal where Gérard, after initial hesitation, signs the warrant against Chénier, his rival. In a moment of self-disgust, he reflects on the degeneration of his Revolutionary ideals ("*Nemico della patria*"), but when Maddalena appears looking for Chénier who has now been arrested, he reveals his passion for her. She offers herself in exchange for Chénier's safety but, moved by her description of what she has undergone ("*La mamma morta*") and her love for the poet, he tries unsuccessfully to save Chénier from the Tribunal. Awaiting execution in act IV, Chénier sings an apostrophe to spring and new life ("*Come un bel dì di Maggio*"); he is joined by Maddalena, who has bribed a guard to let her change places with a condemned woman. Absorbed totally in each other, singing a magnificently climactic duet ("*Vicino a te*"), they move joyfully towards execution as the sun rises and a new day begins to dawn.

Andrea Chénier, though it is a thoroughly *verismo* work, has little of the earthiness of feeling or setting of the *verismo* prototype, *Cavalleria rusticana* (1890); its mixture of literary Romanticism and overtly passionate lyricism derives more

Engraving showing act III of *Andrea Chénier,* Teatro alla Scala, Milan, 1896

from the example set by *Manon Lescaut* (1893). The characters, the "literary" language, the epoch, the situations all belong to the high Romantic school and are based on the well-worn premise that "*Amor* is all." However, the premise, taken as seriously and absolutely as it is in *Tristan und Isolde,* lacks the philosophical and intellectual strength necessary to give it total conviction. The result is a persuasion, dramatic and musical, which never gets beyond the rhetorical; it convinces for the moment but fails to make any lasting effect. Giordano's chief instruments in effecting this persuasion are, first, a cunning sense of pace which structures each act and aria towards an effective climax: and second, a gift for creating passionately lyric outpourings which provide thrilling moments of emotional release for an audience. In *Andrea Chénier* at least, Giordano's gifts rarely fail.

—Peter Dyson

ANIARA.

Composer: Karl-Birger Blomdahl.

Librettist: Erik Lindegren (after Harry Martinson).

First Performance: Stockholm, 31 May 1959.

Roles: The Blind Poetess (soprano); Daisy Doody/La Garçonne (soprano); The Mimarobe (bass-baritone); Chefore (baritone); Three Technicians (two tenors, baritone); Sandon (tenor); chorus.

Publications

articles–

Hambraeus, Bengt. "Aniara." *Anno* (1959).
Schack, Erik. "Karl-Birger Blomdahls Aniara." *Dansk Musiktidskrift* (1959).
Törnblom, Folke. "Är Aniara en riktig Opera?" *Bonniers Litterära Magasin* (1959).
Wallner, Bo. "Vägen till Aniara." *Kungl Teaterns program book* (1959).
Balzer, Jürgen. "Karl-Birger Blomdahls Aniara." *Dansk Musiktidskrift* (1960).
Tegen, Martin. "Aniara." *Musik och Ljudteknik* 3 (1960).
Algulin, Ingemar. "Gestalterna i Aniara." *Nutida Musik* 4 (1983-84).
Lindegren, Erik. "Innehållet i Aniara samt Libretton." *Nutida Musik* 4 (1983-84).
Tobeck, Christina. "Aniara: ett skri av förtvivlan—en vadjan om besinning." *Nutida Musik* 4 (1983-84).

*   *   *

In *Aniara* Blomdahl, despite the experimental and controversial nature of his means of expression, was not concerned to play the innovator in trying to re-invent the form for his own ends (for example, the vocal music is far simpler and less experimental than in his oratorios), but the operatic conventions that he did use had new life breathed into them. Part of this was due to the storyline: if not now (after Tippett and Glass) the only opera to feature a spaceship, it is still the only one to be set entirely aboard one in outer space. A masterly compression of the 103 songs of Harry Martinson's apocalyptic poem of earthly holocaust and astronautical disaster, Erik Lindegren's libretto gave Blomdahl plenty of opportunities for musical and special effects. One such is the repeated spelling out of the name Aniara in Morse Code in the upper strings (with which the opera both opens and closes) to depict the vast emptiness of space. The then (in the 1950s) outlandish nature of the technology of computers and space travel and their implications (to which former concern he was to return in his unfinished last opera, *The Story Of The Great Computer*) allowed Blomdahl the chance to experiment with different musics in order to match his subject, while the scale of the operatic medium itself provided him with the chance to synthesize the disparate elements of his style that abstract musical forms, such as the symphony (his third and last, *Facets,* was written in 1950), seem increasingly to have been unable to do. Electronic music was familiar from a few experimental scores and American science-fiction films of the period (such as *Forbidden Planet*), but there was no research activity at the time in Sweden into what was considered a dead-end curiosity. With the assistance of two technicians at Swedish Radio, Blomdahl created the three electronic Mima-tapes, used to accompany the communications from the Mima (the super-advanced onboard computer, which is possessed of a "soul"). For the different elements among the voyagers he composed symphonic jazz (for the charismatic Daisy Doody and her acolytes), folk-like strains for the comedian Sandon that could almost have strayed from an Alfven score, and hollow, mechanical music for the chief technicians' jargon, which Sandon later tries, hysterically and unsuccessfully in the face of the holocaust, to parody. Blomdahl's use of contemporary popular idioms, jarringly out-of-date in the 1970s, seem in the 1990s much less self-conscious than those of, for example, Tippett in his later operas, and their development to depict the voyagers' increasingly desperate attempts to blot out their terrible predicament by descending into drug-taking, lesbianism, or cult-worship is masterly, and provides ample musical and dramatic justification for their use.

While undoubtedly a product of the 1950s, *Aniara* has proved more resilient than other contemporary "period pieces," due to the constant topicality of imminent Armageddon (whether from nuclear war or global pollution) and to the integrity and consistently high quality of the music. It should not be thought, however, that the opera works only, or better, as music than as theater, even though it is primarily familiar outside of Sweden through recordings. *Aniara* is not, and does not work as, an oratorio. The authors styled the work as a "revue about man in space and time" with good reason, and performances bereft of the visual staging constrict the overall view of the work. The first act charts the emotional progress of the voyagers on their way to Mars: initial relief at escaping from the catastrophe on Earth, through the traumas first of the accident which irreversibly throws the spaceship off course, and second the Mima's visualization of the full reality of the nuclear war that has destroyed the Earth (referred to as Doris, and the main city as Dorisburg, in the text) and set it ablaze.

In the second act, when hopelessness and death eventually overtake the voyagers, the music reflects both the increasing isolation of the survivors as they drift out of control, and the utter desolation of the void. Textures thin out, lines become more exposed, often scored for just a single voice or an unaccompanied instrument. Blomdahl was an acute enough composer to balance out his musical resources in the most satisfying way, and he took every opportunity to vary the topography of the scoring where the plot allowed (as in the libidinous dance for voice and orchestra in the Hall Of Mirrors scene, or the technician's "Mass Of Repentance," scored powerfully for male chorus, or the full orchestral bombast of the twentieth anniversary celebration), but the musical means are always at the service of the text first and foremost.

Aniara is not a comfortable or an easy opera. The apocalyptic setting, a vast sarcophagus fleeing a blasted planet, drifting beyond hope into the void, might be thought too appalling, the shock of the events portrayed too numbing, to contemplate. There is a detachment at times to the music (not to be confused with the resigned air of the Mimarobe) which undermines one's pity of the doomed voyagers as they descend into dictatorship, shamanism and mental anasthaesia of every sort, before finally dying of despair. Their tragedy may not have been of their making, yet they become somehow less sympathetic as events overtake them and injustices override their humanity. It is no accident that one of the most touching moments is the "suicide" of the Mima, who could no longer bear the burden of suffering inflicted on the passengers having been forced to reveal the truth of the holocaust. And yet it is a most immediate, catastrophic tragedy and is most affectingly realized. It is this duality of response that makes *Aniara* so compelling and so disturbing an experience.

—Guy Rickards

L'ANIMA DEL FILOSOFO OSSIA ORFEO ED EURIDICE [The Soul of the Philosopher, or Orpheus and Eurydice].

Composer: Franz Joseph Haydn.

Librettist: C.F. Badini.

First Performance: Florence, 1951 (composed 1791).

Roles: Orfeo (tenor); Euridice (soprano); Creonte (bass); Genius (soprano); Pluto (bass); chorus.

Publications

book–

Wirth, H. *Joseph Haydn: Orfeo ed Euridice: Analytical Notes.* Boston, 1951.

article–

Leopold, Silke. "Haydn und die Tradition der Orpheus-Opern." *Musica* 36 (1982): 131.

*   *   *

Haydn's setting of the Orpheus myth begins with Euridice fleeing the advances of Arideo. Warned by the chorus not to enter the dangerous forest, she is rescued by Orfeo, who tames the wild forest denizens with his lyric song, "Rendete a questo seno." The couple is married in the second act, but Euridice, again pursued by an agent of Arideo, steps on a serpent and dies after singing the exquisite aria, "Del mio core." Most of the third act is then spent in lamentation. The fourth act has Orfeo visiting the underworld and placating the Furies and Pluto. Euridice is returned to him. As the reunited couple prepare to leave, however, Euridice moves in front of her husband so he cannot avert his glance. Frustrated that his wife should have thus died a second time, Orfeo renounces heterosexual company and, following the Ovidian story, is killed by angry Bacchantes. He is poisoned, and just as the Bacchantes are about to tear his body to pieces, the River Lethe floods and drowns the orgiastic women. Orfeo's body is carried on the waters to its final resting place in Lesbos. Haydn's correspondence from the period makes mention of a fifth act, so there is some question about the organization of the opera as it has come to us.

Alternately (and even preferably) listed as *L'anima del filosofo,* Badini's setting of Ovid's Orpheus episodes differs fundamentally from those used by Haydn's immediate predecessors. Eschewing the happy ending usually inserted into the myth by the seventeenth century, Badini chose instead to follow more closely the Ovidian denouement, although in *Metamorphoses* XI Orpheus is in fact torn to pieces and only his head is thrown into the River Hebrus and carried to Lesbos.

Modern scholars concur in pointing out that *L'anima del filosofo* suffers from some basic dramatic deficiencies, particularly in its absence of incident in Orfeo's underworld journey and its failure of appropriately exploiting poetically or musically Euridice's second death. In addition, the title, *L'anima del filosofo,* suggests how much of the libretto's emphasis is spent on undramatic inactivity. In accounting for these "oversights," however, one wonders how much the specter of Gluck and Calzabigi made Haydn and Badini look to the spectacular Bacchic inundation to replace what had already been done so effectively before.

Haydn was clearly not in command of the project, however, for before he even left the Esterházy court to visit London in the early 1790s, he was apparently already commissioned by Sir John Gallini to compose an opera. Haydn's great and various talents did not include choosing his libretti well to begin with, but in this case Carlo Badini, one of the most respected librettists in London at the time, may bear more of the blame for the dramatic miscalculations listed above. Nonetheless, Haydn's correspondence from the period suggests that he was initially quite pleased to take on the project, if for no other reason than because it was his first opera commissioned since *Armida* (1783). It was also to be his last.

Much of the musical composition is of the highest quality. Worth mention are the opening chorus in which Euridice is warned about the dangers of the forest, Euridice's first death, the ensuing *bravura* aria by Orfeo, the Furies' chorus, and the music accompanying the final spectacle. Even H.C. Robbins Landon (*Haydn in England*), who describes *Orfeo* as "basically a magnificent failure," demonstrates considerable admiration for much of Haydn's composition and orchestration, especially his extraordinary use of the solo harp, trombone ("with chilling effect" in the Furies' chorus), cor anglais, and clarinet.

Because Gallini had difficulties with the theatrical arrangements, the work was never performed in London. In fact,

scholars have had to reconstruct the score from four incomplete sources. Although certain passages had been published and performed separately, the complete opera was not performed until 1951 (in Florence).

—Jon Solomon

ANNA BOLENA [Anne Boleyn].

Composer: Gaetano Donizetti.

Librettist: Felice Romani (after Pindemone and Pepoli).

First Performance: Milan, Carcano, 26 December 1830.

Roles: Enrico (bass); Anna (soprano); Giovanna (mezzo-soprano); Ricardo Percy (tenor); Lord Rochefort (bass); Smeton (contralto); Sir Harvey (tenor); chorus (SSATTB).

Publications

books–

Hauser, Richard. *Felice Romani—Gaetano Donizetti—"Anna Bolena." Zur Ästhetik politischer Oper in Italien zwischen 1826 und 1831.* Emmendingen, 1980.
Gossett, Philip. *Anna Bolena and the Artistic Maturity of Gaetano Donizetti.* Oxford, 1985.

*   *   *

In Felice Romani's libretto of *Anna Bolena,* Anna has been supplanted in the affections of Henry VIII (Enrico) by Jane Seymour (Giovanna), her lady-in-waiting. Enrico invites Riccardo Percy to return to court from exile in order to compromise his unwanted wife. Mark Smeaton (Smeton), a page who is in love with Anna, comes to her defense, with the result that all three—Anna, Percy, and Smeton, as well as her brother Lord Rochefort—are imprisoned. Despite Giovanna's impassioned attempts to save Anna, a corrupt council of ministers declares the queen guilty of adultery. In the Tower of London Anna recalls her childhood happiness and her adolescent love for Percy. Hearing the tumult of Enrico's marriage to Giovanna in the street outside, she recovers her senses and goes to the block with dignity amid the laments of her ladies.

Anna Bolena not only brought Donizetti his first taste of international fame, but also assembled all the necessary strands of his maturing talent: dramatic flexibility, an instinct for musical eloquence, and a seemingly limitless melodic flow. It marked that moment in the career of the composer when all the ingredients for triumph were at hand.

The year 1830 was a turning-point for Donizetti, but *Anna Bolena* was far from being his first successful opera. Many of the novelties ascribed to *Anna Bolena* had been tried out earlier, most notably in the opera *Imelda de' Lambertazzi* which immediately preceeded it. Donizetti made no sudden stylistic breakthrough; his ascent to mastery was unusually gradual and perfectly deliberate.

The genesis of *Anna Bolena* was long and painful. In collaborating with Felice Romani, Donizetti risked the ire of Bellini, whose star was at its zenith in the wake of several Bellini/

Anna Bolena, **with Joan Sutherland in the title role and Suzanne Mentzer as Jane Seymour, Royal Opera, London, 1988**

Romani scores which had brought the Italian peninsula to a pitch of excitement unknown since Rossini's departure. If Donizetti elected to write an ultra-dramatic opera, he was, in part, avoiding the latter's ultra-lyrical trademarks.

Anna Bolena is also the most important serious opera of Donizetti's early career. In it, he depicts real people instead of the operatic stereotypes familiar to audiences at that time, and for the first time he displays his taste for *"il vero,"* that elusive veracity which obsessed Giuseppe Verdi for the whole of his musical lifetime. It is this quality that raises the emotional temperature of many of Donizetti's subsequent scores, such as *Lucia di Lammermoor* (1835), *Roberto Devereux* (1837), *Le duc d'Albe* (unfinished 1839), and *Maria di Rohan* (1843), all of which transcend the cardboard characters and feeble texts of the day with music of exceptional flair and dramatic insight.

True to the Romantic age, both Romani and Donizetti were increasingly committed to exact portraiture instead of the vague generalizations of their predecessors. In arias like Anna's "Come innocente giovane," when she bursts into Smeton's sentimental ditty, the composer begins to probe a complex personality far more pointedly than ever before in a scene that perhaps is fiction but is dramatically credible. Many of the subsidiary roles, however, remain inert: Percy is a vignette (the usual yelping tenor of Italian opera), Smeton lacks real motivation, and Rochefort scarcely exists. Anna's act II confrontation with Giovanna, however, is magnificently conceived, displaying two fully-rounded portraits. Enrico, though deprived of a showpiece aria, is also brilliantly drawn as the perfect depiction of tyranny, quite repellently true to life.

Anna's final *scena* was recognized to be a major offering on first hearing. Giuditta Pasta, who created the role of Anna, transfixed audiences with this long series of *arie* and *ariosi* punctuated with orchestrally supported recitative. The three sections, the larghetto "Al dolce guidami," the lento "Cielo a'miei lunghi spasimi" (based, perhaps, on what Donizetti thought of as a Sicilian air), and the traumatic cabaletta "Coppia iniqua"—furious, and leaping to the extremes of register in painful anguish too poignant to be borne. This was music which reinvested Italian opera with meaning; *Anna Bolena* not only brought the composer to the attention of the world but reasserted the validity of *dramma per musica* once and for all.

—Alexander Weatherson

    ———

ANNE BOLEYN
See ANNA BOLENA

    ———

ANTIGONAE.

Composer: Carl Orff.

Librettist: after Sophocles (German translation by Friedrich Hölderlin).

First Performance: Salzburg, 9 August 1949.

Roles: Antigonae (soprano); Ismene (soprano); Creon (bass); Haemon (tenor); Tiresias (tenor); Messenger (bass); Eurydice (soprano or mezzo-soprano); Watchman (tenor); chorus (TB).

Publications

book–

Keller, W. *Carl Orffs Antigonae.* Mainz, 1950.

articles–

Thomas, Werner. "Carl Orffs *Antigonae.* Wieder-Gabe einer antiken Tragödie." In *Werk und Wiedergabe,* edited by Sigrid Wiesmann, 349. Bayreuth, 1980.
Orff, Carl. "*Antigonae.* Ein Trauerspiel des Sophokles von Friedrich Hölderlin." *Neue Festschrift für Musik* 143 (1982): 19.

* * *

The libretto of *Antigonae* is Hölderlin's translation of Sophocles' original tragedy of 442 B.C. The demise of Oedipus has left in chaos both the city of Thebes and his own family. His sons Eteocles and Polynices have just killed one another, but Creon, King of Thebes, has forbidden the burial of the traitor Polynices. Oedipus' daughters, Antigonae and Ismene, quarrel over the right course of action, but Antigonae claims a divine right that supersedes human edict and defiantly buries Polynices. This sets in motion a tragic chain reaction which results in the suicides of Antigonae, Haemon (her fiancé and son of Creon), and Eurydice (Creon's wife). Creon is left alone to bewail his own tragedy.

The innovative musical style which Carl Orff had developed throughout the war years lent itself quite naturally to this ancient Sophoclean drama. Sophocles' *Antigone* had been written at the height of Periclean Athens, while the Parthenon was under construction and before the devastating war against Sparta; Orff's *Antigonae* was written just after the demise of the Third Reich, and the events of the previous decade must have confirmed for the Munich-born composer that tragic consequences attend hubristic human confrontations with divine will. The ever-present element underlying the ancient Greek view of life, pervasive pessimism, which came naturally to Sophocles and allowed him to comprehend in his *Antigone* the hubris inherent in political empire before its collapse, had not entered the German spirit until the forced collapse of its new empire. This profound historical parallel found Orff at the peak of his creative powers.

With the success of *Carmina Burana* in 1937, Orff had created a musical style most appropriate for delivering text; he "disowned" all his previous works (although he would later revive his arrangements of Monteverdi operas). Concentrating on choral settings of ancient and medieval texts, Orff reinvigorated them by plying non-melodic phrases with extensive punctuation and emphasis from an enormous variety of percussion. There was no apparent attempt at recreating an historically accurate sound, only the expectation that the eternal spirituality of ancient and medieval texts could still be successfully restated in musical terms so modern that they echoed the primitive.

Antigonae represents Orff's most ambitious and successful attempt at extracting from a previously mute text a tragically profound musical experience, although one's experience of it can hardly be considered traditionally "operatic." The text is variously recited, chanted, and only rarely sung. Arias are replaced by lengthy set speeches, and polyphony is almost entirely absent. The accompaniment (which includes six pianos, four harps, nine string basses, and two xylophones) serves no melodic purpose, particularly since most of the text is chanted on recitation tones (sometimes with an obtrusive *initium*). Orff's purpose is to highlight the text, and since the original tragic text still presents its audience with such a discomforting portrayal of humans undergoing and accepting the inevitable results of the decision-making process, the effect is extremely powerful. The omnipresent quiet of the textual delivery is only irregularly interrupted by thunderous, extraordinarily repetitive and lengthy instrumental outbursts. Each outburst, however, punctuates the tragedies of Antigonae herself, Ismene, Haemon, Eurydice and, ultimately, Creon. When the normal quietude returns, we see that Orff has skillfully left each of these tragic figures in desperate isolation.

Because its style is so melodically minimal, *Antigonae's* few recognizable motifs create great impact when they occur. The descending, three-note chromaticism serves this purpose throughout the score, appearing first in Ismene's lament that she and her sister Antigonae are "left alone" (*allein geblieben*), and then frequently in Creon's final downfall. This chromaticism bears a remarkable resemblance to that appearing prominently and initially in the Euripidean *Orestes* fragment from the fifth-century B.C. If the similarity is not due to conscious historical revival by Orff, then it testifies to his ability to (re)create the simple, "primitive" sound he quite consciously sought in order to emphasize the isolation of Sophocles' characters.

Orff employed Hölderlin's much criticized German translation of the *Antigonae* for his text. Because Orff only rarely gave interviews about himself and his work, we will never know whether he intentionally chose this specific translation because the poet had produced it shortly before he went completely insane. Although Orff never scored Hölderlin's demise with a poignantly descending, three-note, primitive-sounding chromaticism, Hölderlin's ultimate isolation caused by his creative genius turned to lunacy puts into high relief Antigonae's political and familial isolation caused by her apparent lunacy vindicated finally as genius.

—Jon Solomon

ANTONY AND CLEOPATRA.

Composer: Samuel Barber.

Librettist: F. Zeffirelli (after Shakespeare).

First Performance: New York, Metropolitan Opera, 16 September 1966; revised, with libretto revisions by C. Menotti, 1975.

Roles: Cleopatra (soprano); Antony (bass); Caesar (tenor); Enobarbus (bass); Octavia (soprano); Charmian (mezzo-soprano); Iras (contralto); Dolabella (baritone); Mardian (tenor); Soothsayer (bass); Thidias (tenor or high baritone); Agrippa (bass); Lepidus (tenor); Maecenas (baritone); Eros (tenor); Candidus (baritone); Demetrius (tenor); Scarus (bass); Decretas (bass); A Rustic (baritone or bass); Messenger (tenor); Alexas (bass); Voice offstage (soprano); chorus (SSATB).

* * *

Samuel Barber's opera *Antony and Cleopatra* has achieved notoriety as one of the twentieth century's most heralded, lavish, and expensive operatic failures. Commissioned for the opening of New York City's new Metropolitan Opera House at Lincoln Center for the Performing Arts, the opera was conceived on a grand scale. Its creators undoubtedly aspired to present a work which captured the glamour and magnificence of the new house. They chose their subject well in the entanglement of the exotic, seductive Egyptian queen, Cleopatra, with the power and grandeur of ancient Rome embodied in Marc Antony. Yet *Antony and Cleopatra* fell victim to its own press—it could not hope to meet the inflated expectations of such a hyped audience—and a mismatch of creative talents.

It would not steal from Barber's achievements as a composer to partially attribute the opera's failed reception (and subsequent dearth of productions) to the composer's idiom. Barber, trained as a singer, developed a lyrical style that was well-suited to intimate vocal forms, less well-suited to extended symphonic structures. His language, which used tonal materials in a highly chromatic manner, seems to lack the potential for convincing large-scale dramatic structure that successful operatic writing requires. Dramatic momentum was achieved mostly through lengthy sequential developments, which, through their ubiquity, rapidly descends to mannerism and thus loses expressive power.

The best music of the opera is found when Barber evokes the contrasts between the principal locales of the drama. The opening scene, in which the chorus of Romans chides Antony for his decadence, is marked by skilled contrapuntal invention and harmonic clarity. With its hammered rhythms and furious quality, the scene establishes an energy which, sadly, is not maintained in subsequent scenes. In Cleopatra's first solo scene (act I, scene iii) the music evokes the allure of ancient Egypt through dazzlingly colorful orchestration and sinuous melody. Barber's evocation of the exotic stands in sharp contrast to the stolid, abrupt music of the Romans.

Overall, Barber's skillful orchestration and clear text-setting clarify the action of the libretto compellingly. Thus the weaknesses in the libretto are made more glaringly apparent. Barber's own compositional strengths underscore the opera's weaknesses.

Antony and Cleopatra was extensively revised after its premiere. The currently published score and the recording each reflect the revisions. Franco Zeffirelli, who wrote the first libretto and staged the first production, adapted Shakespeare's play for the operatic stage mostly by cutting characters, switching the sequence of the play's lines, and shrinking and rearranging scenes. This editing was necessary because the extreme length of Shakespeare's play rendered it far too cumbersome even for a full-length grand opera. Zeffirelli maintained Shakespeare's Elizabethan English, causing Barber some consternation; he was afraid that the language would compel him to write in a mannered style. In addition,

a huge chorus was added, compromising the intimacy of the web of relationships between the principle characters in the drama.

Menotti's revisions clarify the text considerably, lessen the amount of spectacle, and eliminate many tangential characters, streamlining the cast and clarifying relationships. The action was made more compact, relationships between principal characters strengthened, and crucial lines of the libretto underscored.

Perhaps the most damaging addition to Shakespeare's drama is the central love duet sung by Antony and Cleopatra, "Oh take, oh take those lips away." No such love scene appears in Shakespeare's play; Barber's setting of these words, to a languid and melodramatic tune, colors the scene with shallow emotion and seems more suited to operetta than opera. The first version of the opera lacked a love scene between Antony and Cleopatra, and this omission was felt by many critics to be seriously detrimental to the opera's success. In heeding the advice of his critics Barber weakened the expressive thrust of the work, lowering it to bathos.

Shakespeare's rich language suffers from the librettist's deletions. The characters often speak lines which are cryptic and rhythmically awkward: for example, note Caesar's statement in act I, scene ii, "You have broken/the article of your oath, which you shall never/Have tongue to charge me with." In the absence of a strong text, the composer is forced to rely on surface portrayals of turbulence. In this case, as mentioned above, tension is too often weakly suggested by the use of literal sequences of melodic/harmonic progressions that, being highly chromatic, possess a basic neutrality.

Other composers writing post-tonal opera in the twentieth century have relied on strong associative techniques to convey drama. One need only consider Berg's operas or Bernd Alois Zimmerman's *Die Soldaten* to see that opera can achieve high drama without tonality. Yet in these examples a strong libretto was given, and the composers were willing to utilize expressionistic effects in their orchestrations and vocal writing, stylistic elements that Barber, by nature a conservative, eschewed.

While Barber was a skilled musical craftsman, possessed of a facile and strong technique, long-range structural drama was not his strong suit. While many passages of *Antony and Cleopatra* are engaging, beautifully lyrical and moving in expression, overall the work is not particularly compelling. Perhaps if the libretto had been more engaging Barber's gifts would have served him better.

—Jonathan Elliott

APPIA, Adolphe.

Designer. Born 1 September 1862, in Geneva. Died 29 February 1928, in Nyon. Educated at the Leipzig Conservatory, 1882-84; in Dresden, 1884-89; worked on theories of staging Wagner, 1889-1904; opera set design debut with *Manfred,* Paris, 1903; began collaborating with Emile Jaques-Dalcroze in eurhythmic theory, 1906; helped found the Hellerau Institute, 1910; produced Gluck's *Orfeo,* Hellerau, 1913; designer at the Geneva Festival, 1914; staged *Tristan und Isolde,* Teatro alla Scala, Milan, 1923; staged *Das Rheingold,* 1924, and *Die Walküre,* 1925, in Basel. Many of Appia's design plans survive; Appia maintained a correspondence with Edward Gordon Craig.

Publications

By APPIA: books–

La mise en scene du Drame Wagnerien. Paris, 1885.
Die Musik und die Inszenierung. Monaco, 1899.

About APPIA: books–

Bonifas, Henry C. *Adolphe Appia.* Zurich, 1929.
Volbach, W. *Adolphe Appia: Prophet of the Modern Theatre.* Zurich, 1968.
Beacham, R. *Adolphe Appia: Theatre Artist.* Cambridge, 1987.
Beacham, R., ed. and W. Volbach, trans. *Adolphe Appia: Essays, Scenarios and Designs.* Ann Arbor, Michigan, 1989.

articles–

Copeau, Jacques. "L'art de l'oeuvre d'Adolphe Appia." *Comoedia* March (1928).
Simonson, Lee. "Appia's Contribution to the Modern Stage." *Theatre Arts Monthly* August (1932).
Beacham, R. "Adolphe Appia and Eurhythmics." *Maske und Kothurn* 29/nos. 1-4 (1983).
_____. "Adolphe Appia and the Wagnerian Opera." *Opera Quarterly* fall (1983).
_____. "Adolphe Appia, Emile Jaques-Dalcroze; and Hellerau. Part One: 'Music Made Visible'." *New Theatre Quarterly* 1/May (1985).
_____. "Adolphe Appia, Emile Jaques-Dalcroze, and Hellerau. Part Two: 'Poetry in Motion'." *New Theatre Quarterly* 1/August (1985).
_____. "Brothers in Suffering and Joy: the Appia-Craig correspondence." *New Theatre Quarterly* 4/August (1988).

*   *   *

In the last decade of the nineteenth century, Adolphe Appia, working virtually in isolation, laid out both the theoretical and practical foundations for a fundamental and permanent change in theatrical art. Through his extensive commentary, detailed scenarios, and unprecedented designs—all inspired by his analysis of Wagnerian opera—Appia first provided a complete and devastating critique of the disastrous state of contemporary practice, and then, with quite astonishing foresight, suggested the solutions which, in time and frequently at the hands of others, would re-establish it upon an entirely different basis.

In his revolutionary work, *Die Musik und die Inszenierung (Music and the Art of the Theater),* published in 1899, Appia suggested that, essentially, music was the measure of all things. The score itself should dictate not only the duration of the performance, but also all the movement and gestures of the actors, and by extension, the physical area itself, that is, the scenic space in which the performance took place. Appia built upon this radical concept what became known as the "New Art" of the theater. He called for three-dimensional scenery, for the use of creative, form-revealing light (developing the concept of the "lighting plot"), and for settings the overall conception of which would be expressive of the inner reality *as art* of works of musical drama. Through music all the arts of the theater could be integrated into an hierarchically ordered, balanced, conceptually coherent, and uniquely expressive new form of art.

Appia demanded that the actor be set free from the mockery of flat, painted settings, in order to practice a purified craft within a supportive and responsive setting. Light, symbolic coloring, and a dynamic sculptured space would be used to evoke for the first time mood, atmosphere and psychological nuance. All these expressive elements would be harmoniously correlated by the new theatrical artist, whom Appia termed the "Designer-Director," and whose work of art would be the operatic production itself. The audience, benefiting in turn from such reforms, would no longer be thought of as mere passive spectators, for Appia believed that experiments along the lines he suggested could more fully involve them in the theatrical act in order to experience and determine it more directly.

The second phase of Appia's creative career arose from his involvement with the system of eurhythmics devised by his fellow countryman, Emile Jaques-Dalcroze. The system was designed to enhance performers' perception of musical nuance and sensitivity to musical rhythm and tempo through the responsive movement of their own bodies in space. In 1906 Appia encountered it for the first time, and perceived at once that it provided the key to realizing his earlier theoretical principle that the performer must be motivated by music and through his movement determine the nature of the scenic environment. He began to prepare for Dalcroze's use a series of designs, termed "rhythmic spaces," which were to further revolutionize future scenic practice. These were essentially abstract arrangements of solid stairs, platforms, podia, and the like, whose rigidity, sharp lines and angles, and immobility, when confronted by the softness, subtlety, and movement of the body, would, by opposition, take on a kind of borrowed life. Settings were no longer to be thought of as illustrations of fictive environments, but as particular spaces in which a performance was to take place, and which themselves evoked the inner meaning of the opera.

Together with Dalcroze, Appia helped to plan and present a series of extraordinary demonstrations highlighting the potential of eurhythmics both for performance and design at Dalcroze's institute, established in 1911 at the garden city of Hellerau, near Dresden, in Germany. In 1912 and 1913, festivals were held, the center-piece of which was a production of Gluck's opera *Orfeo ed Euridice* performed by Dalcroze's eurhythmicists in Appia's unprecedented settings. The proscenium arch was abolished, and the lighting, operated from a central "organ," was carefully coordinated with the music and movement, as well as the emotional "flow" of the performance. Attended by the leading theatrical artists of the day, the festivals caused astonishment and admiration, and exercised profound influence upon later scenic practice, as well as directly and indirectly upon the development of modern dance.

In 1923 Appia was invited by Toscanini to present a new production of *Tristan und Isolde* at the Teatro alla Scala, Milan. Thus, at age 61, Appia had at last found the opportunity to stage Wagner according to the detailed theory and scenarios he had first drawn up in the 1890s. His ideas on the whole, however, did not win popular approval at La Scala, which was a bastion of conservative tradition. Objections were raised primarily against what was perceived as non-realistic and therefore illogical scenery. Paradoxically, it was precisely Appia's insistence that, scenically, the external world in *Tristan* must be deemphasized to encourage the audience's perception of the inner and spiritual essence of the opera that caused the greatest distress. Spectators were perplexed by the relative drabness of color, the absence of elaborately painted scenery, and the austere simplicity of the decor.

The following year Appia was asked to stage the entire *Ring* cycle at Basel, for which he prepared a scenario, together with an entirely new set of radical designs which were striking in their use of solid geometric forms to create abstract settings completely divorced from any lingering suggestion of realism that could still be found in his earlier versions. Unfortunately, the production of *Das Rheingold* and *Die Walküre* provoked such outrage and protest amongst a minority of reactionaries, determined at all costs to preserve the traditional Wagnerian settings, that the rest of the project had to be canceled.

It is perhaps a telling measure of Appia's innovative force and prophetic stature that at the end of his life, the ideas first formulated decades earlier were still thought too advanced. Full recognition came only in 1951 with the advent of the "New Bayreuth Style" under Wieland Wagner. Wagner whole-heartedly embraced Appia's ideas, which continue to provide the theoretical basis (though often unacknowledged) for much of the most successful operatic design and staging of the late twentieth-century.

—Richard C. Beacham

Viorica Ursuleac in the title role in *Arabella*

ARABELLA.

Composer: Richard Strauss.

Librettist: Hugo von Hofmannsthal.

First Performance: Dresden, Staatsoper, 1 July 1933.

Roles: Count Waldner (bass); Adelaide (mezzo-soprano); Arabella (soprano); Zdenka (soprano); Mandryka (baritone); Matteo (tenor); Count Elemer (tenor); Count Dominik (baritone); Count Lamoral (bass); Fiakermilli (soprano); Fortuneteller (soprano); several small roles from chorus; chorus (SATB).

Publications

books–

Schäfer, R.H. *Hugo von Hofmannsthals "Arabella"*. Bern, 1967.
Birkin, Kenneth W. *Richard Strauss: Arabella.* Cambridge, 1989.

articles–

Schuh, W. "Eine nicht komponierte Szene zur *Arabella.*" *Schweizerische Musikzeitung/Revue musicale suisse* 84 (1944): 231.
Tenschert, R. "*Arabella:* die letzte Gemeinschaft von Hugo von Hofmannsthal und Richard Strauss." *Österreichische Musikzeitschrift* 13 (1958).

*   *   *

Arabella was the last opera of the Strauss/Hofmannsthal collaboration. The idea for the opera arose in November 1927, after which events moved quickly. By December 1928 the complete text was in Strauss's hands and, during the spring of 1929, a painstaking revision of act I was satisfactorily

accomplished. Sadly, Hofmannsthal never knew how much this had delighted the composer: after his fatal heart attack of July the 15th, 1929, Strauss's congratulatory telegram was discovered, unopened. Hofmannsthal's revised first act is, indeed, a masterpiece of lyric theater offering the composer a musical challenge to which he rose magnificently. It is fashionable to criticize acts II and III, with whose text, in homage to the dead Hofmannsthal, Strauss refused to tamper. In fact, despite a somewhat looser dramatic organization, both acts work very well, giving Strauss openings for some of his most memorable music, including the Arabella/Mandryka meeting, and Arabella's farewell to her suitors in act II, and the marvellous "staircase" music of the final scene of act III.

The opera is set in 1860s Vienna. The Waldners aim to revive their fortunes by marrying off Arabella. Matteo, rejected by Arabella, is loved by her sister, Zdenka, (masquerading as a boy), who falsely encourages his suit with forged letters in her sister's hand. Of Arabella's current suitors, Elemer is the most eligible: time is short, and despite dreams of an attractive stranger she has encountered in the street, Arabella resigns herself to her fate. Now Waldner, to his delight, has an unexpected visitor, Mandryka, nephew of a rich former colleague, who seeks Arabella's hand. The two are introduced at the "Cabbies" ball; Arabella recognizes her stranger and begins to think dreams can come true. Mandryka socializes; she bids farewell to erstwhile suitors. Later, he overhears Zdenka offering Matteo the key to (supposedly) Arabella's room. Outraged, he creates an ugly scene before leaving in search of her. Fresh from his rendezvous (Zdenka has impersonated her sister in the darkness) Matteo is surprised to find Arabella in the hotel lobby. Mandryka enters, and upon seeing them together his suspicions are confirmed. He accuses; she protests. A duel is averted by a repentant (now female-clad) Zdenka, who confesses her guilt. Matteo is charmed. Ashamed, Mandryka intercedes on the lovers' behalf. All save Mandryka retire—Arabella, re-enacting an old Slav custom, descends from her room with a glass of water; he drinks exultantly before smashing the glass to seal their betrothal.

After a critically chequered career, *Arabella* is now firmly established in the repertoire. Nevertheless, accusations of triviality persist, and the work has too often, in some quarters, been dismissed as a pale reflection of *Der Rosenkavalier.* Critics seldom define their terms, but the substitution of "charm" for "triviality" (a commodity no opera was ever the worse for) gives perhaps a more faithful picture. Furthermore, it is a mistake to view this delightful opera as mere imitation; it constitutes the refinement of a process that, indeed, commenced with *Der Rosenkavalier,* but which led through the "parlando" experiment of the *Ariadne* "Vorspiel," via *Intermezzo* to reach ultimate fulfilment in *Capriccio* and the orchestral music of Strauss's last years. Leaner and conciser than *Der Rosenkavalier,* less innovative than *Intermezzo,* its generic importance lies in a successful attempt to capture the natural intimacy of Viennese spoken theater for the musical stage. The work springs naturally from the Viennese comedy tradition, already celebrated by Hofmannsthal's stage plays, *Der Schwierige* (*The Difficult Man,* 1921) and *Der Unbestechliche* (*The Incorruptible Man,* 1923). It provided the poet with an opportunity to exploit the musicality dormant in his prose writing, while the musician gloated with anticipatory relish over an essentially modern, absolutely realistic domestic character comedy, which would avoid previous mistakes and "longueurs."

There is, then, a new subtlety apparent in *Arabella.* Structurally better proportioned than *Der Rosenkavalier,* its slimmer format is also more easily damaged by those seemingly now statutory cuts which too often bedevil the final act. Handled with a delicacy born of the *Ariadne/Intermezzo* experience, the orchestra offers an imaginative solution to the problems of accompanimental balance, allowing much greater audibility to the text. This ideal balance between words and music was built into the Strauss/Hofmannsthal concept of music-theater: it was defined by the poet as "less of music, where the lead, the melody would be given more to the voice, where the orchestra would accompany . . . and be subordinate to the singers." It is this operetta-like, communicable human warmth, this lightness of touch and lyric subtlety, often sought but not always achieved in this longstanding partnership, which makes *Arabella* such a fine example of its genre.

Both *Der Rosenkavalier* and *Arabella* sprang from a pressing post-*Elektra* need to "detour around" the "Wagner mountain." One must, however, accept the work on its own merits—for its stage-worthiness, for its musical delights and Viennese authenticity, and for its charm of character and gently humorous situations. It demonstrates the refinement of an idiom, as well as being arguably among the most mature manifestations of a unique collaborative genius. Historically it is representative of a new species, the "conversation" opera, of which, as a supreme example, it occupies a significant place in the development of twentieth-century music theater.

—Kenneth W. Birkin

ARAIZA, Francesco.

Tenor. Born 4 October 1950, in Mexico City. Studied at the University of Mexico City, where he sang in University choir; concert debut in Mexico City in 1969 and subsequently sang in opera there; joined Karlsruhe Opera in 1974; lessons in Munich with Richard Holm and Erik Werba; appeared as Ferrando in *Così fan tutte* at Aix-en-Provence Festival, 1977; Metropolitan Opera debut as Belmonte in *Die Entführung aus dem Serail,* 1984; other roles include Tamino in *Zauberflöte* in 1980, Title role in *Faust* and Pong in *Turandot* in 1982, Ramiro in *Cenerentola* in 1986; appearances with opera houses in Zurich, Düsseldorf, Stuttgart, Munich, and the Salzburg Festival.

After declining for 150 years, vocal virtuosity is on the upswing. Twenty-five years ago few tenors sang roulades or high Cs. Today the number who do so is steadily burgeoning, though their singing sometimes lacks personality, passion and charm.

The differences between Nicola Monti on a Melodram recording of a Naples performance of *La cenerentola* in 1958 and Francisco Araiza on a CBS studio recording of the opera from 1980 are representative of the typical differences between tenors then and now. Monti is sunny and ingratiating, his mezza voce caressing. But he omits the trills, smudges the coloratura at conductor Mario Rossi's fast clip and sounds uncomfortable in the high register. The technical demands are beyond him and his range is simply too narrow: had the more difficult high passages not been cut, he probably would have been unable to sing the part.

Araiza sings it uncut, hitting all the notes except the trills, which he too avoids. He has marvelous agility and velocity, and the high Cs hold no terrors. But despite his proficiency, he is charmless and mechanical. There is little evidence that anyone in Rossini's day produced a tone as does Araiza, with the locus of resonation far forward in the face.

Compared to such turn-of-the-century interpreters of the part of Almaviva in *Il barbiere di Siviglia* as Fernando de Lucia and Alessandro Bonci, Araiza is less inspired in his treatment of rhythm. Their singing abounds in rubato; his is comparatively four square. De Lucia admittedly imposes his period's romanticism on the music, underscoring with accentuation and rubato its nascent romantic trends, overstepping stylistic boundaries expressively. He is heuristic. No less sensitive to the music, Bonci is less extreme in his liberties—as is his successor Dino Borgioli.

Araiza is probably the best recent Belmonte in *Die Entführung aus dem Serail.* At a 1984 performance at the Metropolitan Opera, he hit most of the notes dead on, with big, bright tones so well focused as to make intonation lapses more noticeable. In the notoriously florid "Ich baue ganz," he was accurate in the stepwise passages but less so in the arpeggiated ones. He interpolated a small cadenza before the repeat, followed by a little ornamentation—and a few extra breaths. He pronounced German well (unusual in an Hispanic singer) and acted energetically. But his singing was more impressive than beautiful, and he did not arouse interest. His dynamics were sometimes random, sometimes inert. He failed to emphasize melodic climaxes and to distinguish melody from ornamentation and sang with little tenderness. He hardly ever shaded his tone and managed to be vigorous yet dull.

To obtain precise articulation of florid passages Araiza aspirated. Many listeners—and some reviewers—find aspiration unendurable, yet musicologists and performers point to period writings suggesting that in the seventeenth and eighteenth centuries aspiration, or at least "detached" singing, was accepted practice. Admittedly the clarity of articulation achievable with aspiration can prove useful in certain contexts. In the quartet in Rossini's *La scala di seta,* for instance, the tenor sings triplets against the others' duplets, and aspiration helps him to clarify the rhythms. In *Die Entführung,* however, Araiza aspirated too heavily for my taste.

Singers sustain interest through temperament no less than through careful planning: Luciano Pavarotti does so through charisma; Tito Schipa, through charisma, charm and musical sensitivity; Giuseppe Di Stefano, through passion and feeling for words; Enrico Caruso, through warmth and emotion. Araiza isn't endowed with an extraordinary supply of these qualities. On a recording of lirico-spinto warhorses made in 1986, he relies instead on musical effects, such as contrasting soft singing with loud. His interpretations of the album's two Puccini pieces, "Che gelida manina" and "E lucevan le stelle," are satisfying, for in addition to alternating dynamics, he sings with tenderness and fervor. But in the aria from *Eugene Onegin,* one misses Dmitri Smirnoff's plaintive quality, his wistful yearning. In the *Arlesiana* aria, Araiza lacks both bitter melancholy for the opening and desperation and *slancio* (surge, "oomph") for the end—as well as punch and substance on the high As, where the voice is unassertive and veiled, particularly on dark vowels. Perhaps the recording's most underinterpreted selection is "Ah! fuyez, douce image," where Araiza sings as if he hadn't considered the importance of the notes in relation to each other or thought about which leads to which. In the middle voice he produces a strong round tone, but he doesn't imbue the high B-flats with longing, pleading and desperation, nor is he able, in the alternative, to trumpet them forth; however, on higher notes, such as the *Bohème* aria's C or the interpolated high D at the end of "Possente amor," the voice takes on brilliance. Stylistically he is an anomaly: a Latin singer with a German sound who achieves legato in the German manner since World War I—almost without portamento. The music on the record, mostly from the late nineteenth century, was first performed by singers who used portamento generously.

Araiza is never tasteless. At his worst he is earthbound, offering conscientious observance of markings in the score without going beyond them. At his best he is an excellent singer who just misses striking sparks.

Since 1983 he gradually has undertaken more dramatic repertory, although he has said that it may force him to abandon high parts. Having already performed Rodolfo, Faust and Lohengrin, he is scheduled for Chénier and wants to sing Alvaro, Don Carlo, Manrico (*Il trovatore*) and Max. He succeeded in florid repertory by virtue of technical prowess. In these parts, however, his relatively bland vocal personality probably will tell against him. Further, he may be producing a more heroic sound at the expense of vocal gleam. On a recent recording of *Maria Stuarda,* his tone is brassier but also thicker and coarser—the classic tradeoff.

Araiza has said that Neil Shicoff and Luis Lima are at the same point in their careers as he and are performing much of the same repertory. Of the three, Shicoff has the prettiest middle voice but is the least expressive and musically secure, Lima has the greatest emotional intensity and Araiza the most proficiency.

—Stefan Zucker

L'ARBORE DI DIANA.

Composer: Vicente Martín y Soler.

Librettist: Lorenzo Da Ponte.

First Performance: Vienna, Burgtheater, 1 October 1787.

Roles: Diana (soprano); Amor (soprano); Silvius (tenor); Endymion (tenor); chorus.

Publications

article–

Jesson R. "Martin y Soler's 'L'arbore di Diana'." *Musical Times* 113 (1972): 551.

* * *

The story of *L'arbore di Diana* is very loosely based on the Greek myth of Diana and Endymion. Diana and her three nymphs live in a beautiful garden at the center of which is a magic tree. The tree emits lovely music and light as long as the nymphs are true to their vows of chastity, but if a nymph should ever lapse, the tree will pelt her with disfiguring fruit. Amor seeks to overthrow Diana's tyranny. Disguising himself as a shepherdess, he invades Diana's garden with two young men, Silvius, a hunter, and Endymion, a shepherd, whom he encourages to seduce Diana and her nymphs. Diana's rage when she first encounters this attack on her chastity is as indignant as that of Fiordiligi and Dorabella when they first meet their "Albanian" suitors; but her nymphs soon succumb, and eventually so does Diana herself. The tree disappears, and a kingdom of love is established.

Da Ponte considered *L'arbore di Diana,* which he intended as an allegorical commentary on Joseph II's attempts to suppress many of the monasteries in his realm, to be his best libretto: "it was voluptuous without overstepping into the lascivious," and at the same time well suited to Martín y Soler's particular strengths: "those sweet melodies of his, which one feels deep in the spirit, but which few know how to imitate."

The music is indeed sweet. At the same time it is rich in its variety of orchestral textures and timbres, of rhythmic patterns, and of simple yet satisfying musical structures, always well suited to the dramatic situation and to the personalities of the characters. As in most of Da Ponte's Viennese operas, the librettist provided plenty of opportunity for ensembles, and Martín y Soler set them effectively. The intensely dramatic duet "Pian pianino," which begins in C major with Endymion asleep and Diana hesitantly drawing close to him, modulates suddenly from G major to E flat at the point where Endymion opens his eyes and sees Diana, and ends with a passionate passage in thirds and sixths, has been cited as a precurser of Mozart's seduction duet "Fra gli amplessi" in *Così fan tutte.*

Though it did not achieve the fame of *Una cosa rara,* Martín y Soler's previous opera, *L'arbore di Diana* was successfully performed in Vienna and elsewhere. It enjoyed widespread popularity in Germany as *Der Baum der Diana,* and when it was performed in London in 1797 "many of the airs were rapturously encored," according to one critic, who added that "more charming music we have seldom had the satisfaction of hearing."

—John A. Rice

ARDEN MUST DIE.

Composer: Alexander Goehr.

Librettist: E. Fried (after the sixteenth-century play *Arden of Faversham*).

First Performance: Hamburg, 5 March 1967.

Roles: Arden (bass); Franklin (bass); Alice (mezzo-soprano); Mosbie (tenor); Susan (soprano); Michael (tenor); Mrs Bradshaw (contralto); Greene (baritone); Reede (bass); Shakebag (tenor); Black Will (bass); Ferryman (bass); Shepherd (soprano); Mayor of Faversham (baritone); Apprentice (speaking part); chorus (SATB).

Publications

articles–

Drew, D. "Why Must Arden Die?" *The Listener* 78 (1967): 412, 445.
Northcott, Bayan. ". . . most wickedlye murdered. . . ." *Music and Musicians* 22 (1974): 26.

*   *   *

Arden Must Die takes as its source the anonymous sixteenth-century play *Arden of Faversham,* which in its turn derived from a true story related in Holinshed's Chronicles. Alexander Goehr and his librettist Erich Fried were both drawn to the subject matter of the play (which was suggested by the composer's wife), and saw in it issues of universal significance, most especially "the way we behave in the crises in which we are involved."

Alice, the wife of Arden, a wealthy and unscrupulous merchant responsible for the ruin of neighboring landowners Greene and Reede, wishes to have her husband murdered so that she can marry her lover Mosbie. In furtherance of her aims, she employs two notorious cut-throats, Black Will and Shakebag. After several unsuccessful attempts, first of all on the riverbank, where the fog thwarts their endeavours, and then in Arden's London lodgings, where his servant Michael, another conspirator, unintentionally draws the attention of Arden and his companion Franklin to the unbarred door, he is finally murdered in his own home surrounded by his family and neighbors.

The two paid assassins magnanimously offer their services as hangmen for the execution of the unrepentant Alice and Mosbie while Mrs Bradshaw, a hypocritical neighbor who has played an ambivalent role throughout, claiming abhorrence for the deed on one hand while acting as an intermediary between the conspirators on the other, finally turns king's evidence. The work ends with the ironic moral sung by a chorus of constables: "This is the remorse which makes upright men out of sinners,/ This is human kindness drawing its milk from strife./ This is the faithful dog that serves all who serve it dinners,/ This is the rule of law, restoring the past to life."

Goehr and Fried recognized the danger inherent in modern serious opera of involuntary self-parody, and suggested that the conscious exploitation of the tensions created by such self-satire could be dramatically potent. Thus we find the deeply serious issues of avarice, murder, personal morality, and hypocrisy presented in the context of black comedy with a libretto that draws on the techniques of Brechtian epic theater, eschewing psychologism, driven by narrative and rationality, and assuming a musico-dramatic shape that plays cat and mouse with operatic convention.

Fried's most original creation was the figure of Mrs Bradshaw. In a sense the central figure of the opera, she is the only one who undergoes any real development, all the others being somewhat one-dimensional figures whose actions and behavior seem mechanically contrived. Her manner at the outset, as she questions the motives of the conspirators, smacks of the detached interrogation of the newspaper journalist. Easily subdued by fear of reprisal, she lapses into pietism, directly addressing the audience with the words: "And if it's said that I to this deed assented,/ You know it is a lie: I always was against it!" By the beginning of act II she has turned collaborator, acting as a negotiator between Alice and the cut-throats. She is present at Arden's murder, slipping away before the recrimination begins and is eventually spared on account of her remorse.

It is easy to see why some members of the Hamburg audience took offense at the opera's premiere, with its implicit attack on the hypocrisy of those Germans who had survived the second world war by keeping their heads down, and had now been restored to bourgeois respectability. Fried's concluding comment in his note in the program book for the first performance read "Wer sich beleidigt fühlt, der ist gemeint" (Whoever feels himself insulted, he is intended).

Goehr's music underlines the dramatic tensions already alluded to, on one hand flirting with diatonicism and on the other employing the technique he describes as modal serialism. Although the heterogeneity of the material, which ranges from the quasi-Stravinskyan stratification of the opening and closing scenes, through the translucent impressionism of the riverbank scene, the pietistic chorale of Mrs Bradshaw, the paraphrase of an SA song, to the anachronistic modality of Gibbon's *Cries of London,* all suggest an eclecticism which could act against a cohesive musical edifice, the work does create a consistent and coherent artistic experience.

The edgy, restless, and brittle quality of the first scene, partly caused by the rapid interchange of short-breathed blocks of material that tend to preclude the evolution of forward momentum, gives way to a greater stability towards the opera's center with the more expansive music associated with the murder attempts, and the graphic illustration of the lovers' off-stage sexual athleticism depicted by the first of a pair of musical interludes. Indeed, the overall shape of the opera tends towards a kind of arch-shape and a very approximate mirror-symmetry which neatly parallels the fall and rise of Mrs Bradshaw as much as the rise and fall of Arden.

The set of pitches E-F-A-F♯ projected by the chorus of conspirators in the opening scene to the words "Arden must die," in quasi-lehrstück fashion, acts as a germinal motif for many of the work's melodic ideas. Throughout the opera Goehr creates areas of harmonic stability with clearly defined pitch centers, and the tonal node of E established in the opening scene gradually gives way to the unambiguous D major of Arden's act I entrance. His aria, which is underpinned by the articulation of a decorated arpeggio of D, presents a melodic shape derived from the germ motif, a shape which is taken over by Alice and dominates much of the rest of the first section of the act, as it is transformed into an ecstatic love duet, redolent of Janáček, which she sings with her lover, Mosbie. The pivotal center of the scene shifts towards F# in the impressionistic mists of the riverside murder attempt, before eventually settling, by way of Mrs Bradshaw's pietistic D major, onto F at the end of the act.

The second act, which opens with the hired assassins Shakebag and Black Will contemplating the "balmy evening light" over and around a pedal B, soon gives way to the modality of Gibbon's *Cries of London,* whose cadence point is D. The central section of the act is rather more acerbic and tonally ambiguous than the first, with less quasi-triadic relief as it moves towards the final and successful murder attempt, an event which is followed by an extraordinarily passionate, and pathologically sado-erotic, lyrical passage clearly focused on F and redolent of both Berg and Richard Strauss. The final scene reflects and transforms much of the material from the beginning of the first act with tonal centers shifting from C through to E before Goehr brings the work to a close with a harmonically ambiguous gesture.

—David Cooper

ARGENTO, Dominick.

Composer. Born 27 October 1927, in York, Pennsylvania. Studied with Nicolas Nabokov, Henry Cowell, and Hugo Weisgall at the Peabody Conservatory (B.A. 1951); studied with Dallapiccola at the Conservatorio Cherubini in Florence; studied with Bernard Rogers, Howard Hanson, and Alan Hovhaness at the Eastman School of Music, where he was awarded a Ph.D. in 1957; two Guggenheim fellowships, 1957, 1964; on the faculty of the University of Minnesota since 1958; in 1964, co-founder of the Center Opera Company, now the Minnesota Opera; Pulitzer Prize for his song cycle *From the Diary of Virginia Woolf,* 1975; elected a member of the American Academy and Institute of Arts and Letters; member of the American Academy of Arts and Sciences, 1980.

Operas

Publisher: Boosey and Hawkes.

Sicilian Lines, New York, 1 October 1954.
The Boor, J. Olon-Scrymgeour (after Chekhov), 1957, Rochester, 6 May 1957.
Colonel Jonathan the Saint, J. Olon-Scrymgeour, 1958-61, Denver, Denver Opera Company, 31 December 1961.
Christopher Sly, J. Manlove (after a scene from Shakespeare, *The Taming of the Shrew*), 1962-63, Minneapolis, University of Minnesota, 31 May 1963.
The Masque of Angels, J. Olon-Scrymgeour, 1963, Minneapolis, 9 January 1964.
The Shoemaker's Holiday, J. Olon-Scrymgeour (after the comedy by Thomas Dekker), 1967, Minneapolis, Center Opera Company, 1 June 1967.
Postcard from Morocco, J. Donahue, Minneapolis, Center Opera Company, 14 October 1971.
A Water Bird Talk, Argento (based on Chekhov, *On the Harmful Effects of Tobacco,* and J.J. Audubon, *The Birds of America*), 1974, Brooklyn, New York, 19 May 1977.
The Voyage of Edgar Allan Poe, Charles M. Nolte, 1975-76, Minneapolis, 24 April 1976.
Miss Havisham's Fire, J. Olon-Scrymgeour (after Dickens, *Great Expectations*), 1977-78, New York, New York City Opera, 22 March 1979.
Miss Havisham's Wedding Night, J. Olon-Scrymgeour (after Dickens, *Great Expectations*), 1980, Minneapolis, 1 May 1981.
Casanova's Homecoming, Argento, 1980-84, St Paul, 12 April 1985.
The Aspern Papers, Argento (after Henry James), Dallas, November, 1988.

Other works: orchestral works, ballets, choral works, songs.

Publications/Writings

By ARGENTO: articles–

"The Matter of Text." *National Association of Teachers of Singing* March/April (1988).

About ARGENTO: books–

Speer, D.J., ed. *Commemorating the World Premiere of "The Voyage of Edgar Allan Poe".* St. Paul, 1976.

articles–

Altman, Peter. "The Voyage of Dominick Argento." *Opera News* 40/no. 21 (1976).
Heinsheimer, Hans. "Great Expectations: for Argento's *Miss Havisham's Fire." Opera News* 43/no. 18 (1979).

unpublished–

Saya, Virginia Montgomery. "The Operas of Dominick Argento." Ph.D. dissertation, Cincinnati Conservatory of Music, 1989.

*   *   *

Dominick Argento was studying at Peabody Conservatory in the mid 1950s when he turned away from writing sonatas, quartets and symphonic pieces and began to focus his attention on writing for the voice with the composition of *Songs About Spring.* From that point forward his compositional output was dominated by works for the voice. His operatic emphasis was secured not only as a part of his normal studies, but through his private work with Hugo Weisgall, who was artistic director of the Hilltop Opera in Baltimore.

Over the years Argento has composed over one dozen operas, the first of which was a chamber opera, *The Boor,* completed in 1957. His first full-length opera was *Colonel Jonathan the Saint,* which was composed during his Guggenheim Fellowship between 1958-61. It was not premiered until 31 December 1961 by the Denver Opera Company. *Christopher Sly* is a comic opera based on the opening of Shakespeare's *The Taming of the Shrew.* It was first performed at the University of Minnesota in 1963 and was quite well received. The following year Argento became co-founder of the Center Opera in Minnesota, which was later renamed the Minnesota Opera. During the company's first season they premiered Argento's religious comedy, *The Masque of Angels,* for chorus and small orchestra, which was met with critical acclaim. This was followed three years later with the ballad opera, *The Shoemaker's Holiday,* adapted from the comedy of Thomas Dekker, and in 1971 by *Postcard from Morocco.*

Argento's *The Voyage of Edgar Allan Poe,* **Lyric Opera of Chicago, 1990**

Argento received national attention when he received the 1975 Pulitzer Prize in music for *From the Diary of Virginia Woolf,* which was introduced in Minneapolis on 9 January, 1975 by Dame Janet Baker. In commemoration of the American bicentennial Argento completed *The Voyage of Edgar Allan Poe,* based upon a libretto by Charles M. Nolte which describes the last crazed days of Poe's life. *A Water Bird Talk,* a one-act opera for baritone and twelve instrumentalists, was produced in Brooklyn, New York on 19 May 1977. The libretto is loosely based upon Chekhov's *On the Harmful Effects of Tobacco* and J. J. Audubon's *The Birds of America.* Within two years, his two-act opera with prologue and epilogue, *Miss Havisham's Fire* was premiered by the New York City Opera on 22 March 1979. It is based on Charles Dickens's *Great Expectations* with the libretto by John Olon-Scrymgeour.

Argento's compositional style has its roots in the voice. He has a deep respect for the human voice and does not view it as just another instrument. As he once explained, "It is a *part* of the performer rather than an adjunct to him." Thus, it is only natural that we find his writing focussed upon melodic line with a typically dramatic character that is unashamed of deep emotion. Argento views himself as a traditionalist "in the broadest sense . . . If you want a school, include me in the Mozart, Verdi, Mussorgsky school." His melodic and harmonic vocabulary is versatile, including such diverse elements as Gregorian chant, quotes from Wagner, folk music, jazz, and serialism.

Almost all of his operas deal with the underlying theme of self-discovery and self-knowledge. Over the years the plots of his operas have manifested these themes in a variety of ways. Argento describes them as follows: "*Christopher Sly* elaborates it farcically: a drunken ne'er-do-well is discovered unconscious, he is taken to a fine home, dressed as a Lord, supplied with a wife and servants. When he comes to, they convince him that his past life has all been a dream, that he is wealthy, respected, etc. For a long time he believes the prank to be reality, but eventually he learns who he really is, and in turn pulls a prank on the pranksters. The *Masque of Angels* puts the theme in a religious context; *Postcard From Morocco* treats it surrealistically; *The Voyage of Edgar Allan Poe* does it fantastically; *A Water Bird Talk* handles it tragicomically; and *Casanova's Homecoming* does it very deliberately."

—Roger E. Foltz

ARIADNE AND BLUEBEARD
See ARIANE ET BARBE-BLEUE

ARIADNE AUF NAXOS [Ariadne on Naxos].

Composer: Richard Strauss.

Librettist: Hugo von Hofmannsthal.

First Performance: Stuttgart, Court Theater, 25 October 1912; revised, Vienna, Court Opera, 4 October 1916.

Roles: Ariadne (soprano); Bacchus (tenor); Zerbinetta (soprano); Composer (soprano); Music Master (baritone); Dancing Master (tenor); Naiad (soprano); Dryad (contralto); Echo (soprano); Harlequin (baritone); Brighella (tenor); Scaramouche (tenor); Truffaldin (bass); Lackey (bass); Officer (tenor); Wigmaker (bass); Majordomo (speaking part).

Publications

books–

Daviau, D.G., and George J. Buelow. *The "Ariadne auf Naxos" of Hugo von Hofmannsthal and Richard Strauss.* Chapel Hill, 1975.

Forsyth, Karen. *Ariadne auf Naxos by Hugo von Hofmannsthal and Richard Strauss: its Genesis and Meaning.* Oxford, 1982.

articles–

Diebold, B. "Die ironische *Ariadne* und der *Bürger als Edelmann.*" *Deutsche Bühne* 1 (1918): 219.

Mühler, Robert. "Hugo von Hofmannsthals Oper *Ariadne auf Naxos.*" *Interpretation zur Österreichischen Literatur* 6 (1971).

Könneker, Barbara. "Die Funktion des Vorspiels in Hofmannsthals *Ariadne auf Naxos.*" *Germanisch-romanische Monatsschrift* 12 (1972).

Schuh, Willi. "Hofmannsthals Randnotizen für Richard Strauss im *Ariadne* Libretto." In *Für Rudolf Hirsch zum siebzigsten Geburtstag.* Frankfurt, 1975.

Brosche, Günther. "Der Schluss der Oper *Ariadne auf Naxos.* Neue Aspekte zur Entstehung des Werkes." *Österreichische Musikzeitschrift* 34 (1979): 329.

Erwin, C. "Richard Strauss's Presketch Planning for *Ariadne auf Naxos.*" *Musical Quarterly* 67 (1981): 348.

Avant-scène opéra July (1985) [*Ariadne à Naxos* issue].

* * *

The first version of *Ariadne auf Naxos* (1912) was intended as a short *divertissement,* to be appended to Max Reinhardt's production of Molière's *Le bourgeois gentilhomme.* Strauss and Hofmannsthal felt that the little opera would serve two functions at once: it would be an offer of thanks to Reinhardt, whose last-minute attention had saved the Dresden premiere

Ariadne auf Naxos, **with Edith Davis as the Prima Donna and Anne-Marie Sands as the Composer, Welsh National Opera, 1989**

of *Der Rosenkavalier* the year before, and it would allow Strauss and Hofmannsthal to work on a small piece as they developed ideas more suitable for a grand opera. This rather inauspicious beginning for *Ariadne,* the most elliptical of their operas, was ironic, for it would prove the most protracted and problematic fruit of the legendary collaboration. Indeed, the often stormy letters between Strauss and Hofmannsthal around the writing of *Ariadne* (a situation quite singular in their normally placid correspondence) attests to the significance of the work, and to its special place in their hearts.

The original *Ariadne auf Naxos* (connected to *Le bourgeois gentilhomme* by means of a prose scene written by Hofmannsthal) was generally met by critics and public with incomprehension. A rewrite was in order. The result was a full-length version of *Ariadne,* in which the prose scene was replaced by an extended musical prologue, which also shifted the action to eighteenth-century Vienna. The full-length *Ariadne auf Naxos* was first presented in 1916 to better response, but still there was a sense that the new opera was rather odd, something of a hybrid, most certainly a piece for highly specialized tastes. This reputation continues, and although *Ariadne* has found a place in the repertoire of international opera houses, it has never achieved the popular success of *Der Rosenkavalier* or even *Elektra.*

The lack of *Ariadne*'s general appeal is due in great part to its complex plot, which juxtaposes in a seemingly arbitrary way the political and social attitudes of characters who exist in several unrelated historical contexts (eighteenth-century Vienna, Greek antiquity, Renaissance Italy). Critical interpretation of the enigmatic libretto has fallen rather generally into two different, and perhaps opposing, readings. The more prevalent focuses on the idea of an "allomatic transformation," a notion put forward by Hofmannsthal himself in his celebrated "Ariadne letter" of 1911, and suggesting that Ariadne herself, through her suffering and loss, is genuinely purged and transformed, or reborn. This interpretation accounts for the presence of Zerbinetta chiefly as a dramaturgical device to provide contrast: her "false" understanding of transformation as an ever-present element of courtship and sex serves to underscore the "truth" of Ariadne's renewal. At the other extreme, formalist critics see *Ariadne*'s meaning in its multiple settings; in this view, the juxtaposition of historically and socially disparate elements represents a pluralistic world without a fixed reality.

There certainly is room for further interpretation. The turmoil and evolving social order of Strauss and Hofmannsthal's own *fin-de-siècle* Vienna have intriguing parallels with the eighteenth-century world of *Ariadne*'s prologue and its *nouveau-riche* nobleman who undertakes sponsorship of the little *opera seria.* The role of the chimerical Composer in the prologue offers marvelous insights into Strauss and Hofmannsthal's own attitudes to the process of artistic creation. And the very different perspectives on male/female relations offered by Ariadne and Zerbinetta make the work ripe for a feminist reading. Yet such notable critics as Herbert Lindenberger and Catherine Clement have largely ignored *Ariadne auf Naxos* in their recent books on opera; the work remains under-appreciated by the scholarly community as well as by the general public.

Such popular acclaim as *Ariadne* has received is due, no doubt, to its superb score. The multiple contexts of the story gave Strauss an opportunity to blend the lush romantic style of his "Vienna operas" (*Rosenkavalier, Arabella, Intermezzo*) with the more dissonant chromatic writing we find in his settings of mythological and ancient subjects (*Salome, Elektra, Die Frau ohne Schatten*). The resulting admixture—orchestrated with Strauss' typical mastery—is among the most

piquant and unusual sound-worlds in opera. Interestingly, the orchestra in *Ariadne*—the score calls for thirty-six players—is one of Strauss' smallest. This poses some difficulties to theaters presenting the opera, for the chamber-sized instrumental ensemble suggests one kind of opera house, while the nearly-Wagnerian vocal demands of the score seems to call for quite another.

Strauss' great gift for creating character through music is never better displayed than in *Ariadne auf Naxos.* The trouser role of the Composer, written in a conscious attempt to capitalize on the success of the similar character of Octavian in *Der Rosenkavalier,* is actually an improvement on its predecessor, and is crowned by a monologue on the nature of writing music ("Musik ist eine heilige Kunst"), which is one of the most beautiful and moving in the Strauss canon. The small ensembles for the comedians who support Zerbinetta and the three nymphs who comfort and serenade Ariadne are endlessly imaginative and elegant. And if, in this context, the tenor music for Bacchus is stiffer than one expects, that is entirely in keeping with the artificial and one-dimensional nature of the character.

The marvelous parts of the *prima donne* are two of Strauss' most superb musical portraits. Ariadne's monologues are sombre, elevated, fashioned in a neo-classical style reminiscent of Gluck's music for Alceste or Orphée, while at the same time the arching vocal line and autumnal glow of the orchestrations are unmistakably Strauss. By contrast, Zerbinetta's music makes use of the highly virtuosic coloratura conventions of *bel canto* Italian opera, culminating in an aria ("Grossmächtige Prinzessin"), nearly ten minutes in length, which is probably the most difficult and exacting music for soprano in our century. In one of the opera's cleverest devices, the monologues of the two women are juxtaposed so as to maximize a sense of rivalry and to galvanize the audience into factions. At the premiere of the revised *Ariadne auf Naxos* in 1916, the combination of the great Maria Jeritza as Ariadne and the equally-famous Selma Kurz as Zerbinetta created a furor; in recent years, the comparable star casting of Jessye Norman and Kathleen Battle in the roles has also stirred audience interest, and has ensured the opera a well-deserved place on the roster of the Metropolitan Opera, Covent Garden, and other major theaters.

—David Anthony Fox

ARIADNE ON NAXOS
See ARIADNE AUF NAXOS

ARIANE ET BARBE-BLEUE [Ariadne and Bluebeard].

Composer: Paul Dukas.

Librettist: Maurice Maeterlinck.

First Performance: Paris, Opéra-Comique, 10 May 1907.

Roles: Barbe-bleue (bass); Ariane (mezzo-soprano); Nurse (contralto); Selysette (mezzo-soprano); Ygraine (soprano);

Mélisande (soprano); Bellangere (soprano); Alladine (mime); Old Peasant (bass); Two Peasants (tenor and bass); chorus (TTBB).

*   *   *

The Bluebeard story has hovered around the edges of the operatic repertoire for centuries without ever quite becoming the basis for a standard work. Utilized by Grétry in the eighteenth century, deployed by the inimitable Offenbach for one of his finest spoofs in the nineteenth and the inspiration for Bartok's psychological case study in the 20th, the famous plot probably found its lushest musical evocation in Paul Dukas' only opera *Ariane et Barbe-bleue,* first performed in Paris in 1907.

The work is written to a text by Maurice Maeterlinck which takes a predictably symbol-fraught view of the characters and situation. Unlike his more famous play *Pelléas et Mélisande,* which Debussy set virtually intact, *Ariane* was conceived by the author as a libretto from the very start, specifically for an opera which could star his mistress, soprano Georgette Leblanc. The very plot reflects an incident in this lady's life, as she had spent a great deal of time and trouble trying to help a friend only to realize that said help was not wanted. Thus the subtitle of the libretto (but not the opera) is "The Useless Deliverance," and it is on this irony that Maeterlinck's treatment of the subject turns.

Act I finds us in Bluebeard's castle. An offstage chorus of rioting villagers is heard, giving us background information about the situation (i.e., that Bluebeard is a hated tyrant, that a new wife is arriving, etc.) which we need to know, but which is inevitably incomprehensible on stage: when it came to opera Maeterlinck was quite capable of astounding amateurism.

Ariane soon arrives with her old nurse. She is a creature of wisdom and light, and although she is carrying all the keys which Bluebeard has given her, she announces that the only one of any value is that to the final, forbidden door. However, the nurse convinces her to open the other ones, and out of each in turn spews a fantastic spate of precious stones, almost drowning the women in their splendor. Effusions of emeralds, rubies, etc., finally give way to Ariane's climactically lavish "Diamond Aria" at the end of the sequence, after which the action passes on to the opening of the forbidden door. In the second act Ariane and the Nurse enter the final portal and pass through to the dungeons of the castle where they encounter the living wraiths that are Bluebeard's other wives. They include Mélisande, to whom Maeterlinck has given an intriguing pre-history by recycling her into this story, to which Dukas responded with citations from Debussy's score. This second act, an overwhelming journey from darkness into light as Ariane contrives the release of the women, is probably Dukas' greatest achievement. With superb irony, act III shows Ariane trying to liberate the others. However, they are too used to a situation they somehow understand, and refuse to leave the castle with her. They choose to remain with Bluebeard, now emotionally broken by Ariane's bravery and clear-headedness. She grants them all a last farewell and leaves, her actions strongly underlining the opera's motto "The darkness has seen the light, and failed to understand it."

The work is an exciting piece of French mystical allure, full of haunting melodies and orchestral frissons, so it is no wonder that many musicians have championed it despite a rather static text. Famous portrayals of Ariane have included Leblanc, who in fact sang the premiere, and Geraldine Farrar

during the opera's brief sojourn at the Metropolitan under the baton of Toscanini, an ardent admirer of the piece.

After decades of neglect *Ariane et Barbe-bleue* is currently enjoying a well-deserved flurry of revivals, and while it will probably never be a repertoire staple, its musical beauties are many, and it is assuredly deserving of its recent acclaim.

—Dennis W. Wakeling

ARLECCHINO, oder, Die Fenster [Harlequin, or, The Windows].

Composer: Ferruccio Busoni.

Librettist: Ferruccio Busoni.

First Performance: Zurich, 11 May 1917.

Roles: Columbina (mezzo-soprano); Matteo (baritone); Abbate Conspicuo (baritone); Dottor Bombasto (bass); Leandro (tenor); Arlecchino (speaking); Annunziata (mute); two Soldiers (mute).

*   *   *

Busoni once wrote that *Arlecchino* was "an opera that turns itself against opera." Certainly its music frequently parodies popular operatic styles both general and specific; but the whole conception is a prime example of his conviction that the proper domain of opera is the artificial and fantastic. It was his interest in the revival of marionette theatre that led Busoni to base his libretto around the familiar characters of the seventeenth-century *Commedia dell'arte,* which seemed for him to possess many of the essential qualities of puppets, acting out predetermined roles in unreflective felicity.

The plot, set in a timeless Bergamo of the Italian imagination, involves Arlecchino's attempt to carry off Annuziata, wife of the ever-duped and Dante-loving tailor Matteo. Arlecchino convinces Matteo that the city is threatened by besieging barbarians, steals his coat to get hold of his house-key, and packs him off to war. He quarrels with his own wife Columbina; she turns for consolation to the knight Leandro, whom Arlecchino then wounds in a duel. Columbina, with the Abbot and Doctor, take Leandro off to the hospital in a providentially passing donkey-cart, while Arlecchino elopes with Annunziata, and Matteo, returning from his guard duty, sits down to read his Dante and await his absent wife.

The characters of *Arlecchino* are attitudes and actions, stock figures, not individuals (apart perhaps from the easygoing Abbate Conspicuo, who gives voice to some characteristically Busonian praise of wine, women, and the composer's native Tuscany). The knight Leandro, addle-brained *inammorato* of Arlecchino's wife Columbina, is in himself a whole tiring-room of old operatic attitudes, passing from a fiery Verdian revenge aria ('Vendetta, vendetta!') to bovine *Lohengrin*-ish adoration in the space of a few bars.

The exception is Arlecchino himself. In one sense he is no more "real" a character, but he is puppet-master—or rather superhuman *Übermarionette*—rather than puppet; he is protean in his adoption of roles and grasp of possibilities. He is a rogue, a trickster, a resourceful lover or rather unfaithful husband (of an unfaithful wife), a swordsman—in short, a

Arlecchino, **Landestheater, Darmstadt, 1925**

free spirit. Above all he is a conscious intellect, ironic and critical, throwing out quips of caustic philosophy. Whereas the other characters are defined by their voice-ranges and vocal themes, he never sings (except for a mocking tralala as he vanishes off-stage); his quickfire speech cuts through cliché conventions and runs rings round his opponents. And at the beginning and end of the opera he stands forth before the curtain to address the audience directly, breaking out of the dramatic frame, a genie out of the bottle.

Though Busoni is on the alert to undermine any hint of pathos or unnecessary sentiment, in its elegantly comic fashion *Arlecchino* is an anti-war opera, composed in neutral Switzerland during the ruinous years of the Great War. The illusory "Barbarians" provoke real fear; military music sometimes sounds harshly through the score; the characters are brought face to face with death (though Leandro miraculously revives) and they get short shrift from the good citizens of Bergamo whom they turn to for help. Serious issues are mocked, but they are also considered: Busoni wrote of the "constant play of colour between grim jest and playful seriousness" in the work; and elsewhere he remarked that "after that of *Die Zauberflöte* (which I value highly) it is the most moral libretto there is."

Mozart is the tutelary deity of Busoni's music for *Arlecchino* (Matteo even manages to put some of his favourite Dante—from the tale of Paolo and Francesca—to the "Champagne" Aria from *Don Giovanni*). But like the roguish hero himself he makes play with a kaleidoscopic range of possibilities, from operatic parody through folksong and troubadour song to the full resources of early twentieth-century harmony; this is embodied in Arlecchino's own trumpet theme, which encompasses all twelve notes of the chromatic scale arranged as triads of different keys—the musical secret of his protean adaptability. The tone is light, dry, quick-witted, tuneful, rhythmically vivacious, packing a scintillating variety of incident and musical reference into a scant hour of performance time. This is "Young Classicality" (*Junge Klassizíit*) indeed, and that principle finds its ideal statement in Arlecchino's triumphant peroration: "Now shines my star! The world stands open! The earth is young! Love is free!"

—Malcolm MacDonald

ARMIDE.

Composer: Christoph Willibald von Gluck.

Librettist: Philippe Quinault.

First Performance: Paris, Académie Royale, 23 September 1777.

Roles: Armide (soprano); Rénaud (tenor); Artemidor (tenor); Fury of Hate (contralto); Hidraot (baritone); Ubaldo (baritone); Danish Knight (tenor); Phenice (soprano); Sidonie (soprano); Aront (bass); Demon as Lucinda (soprano); Demon as Melissa (soprano); Naiad (soprano); chorus (SATB).

Publications

articles–

Reichardt, J.F. "Über Gluck und dessen Armide." *Berlinische musikalische Zeitung* 1 (1805): 109; 2 (1806): 57.
Favart, C.S. "Etwas über Glucks Iphigenia in Tauris und dessen Armide." *Mémoires et correspondance,* edited by A.P.C. Favart and H.F. Dumolard. Paris, 1808.

Eighteenth-century opera "reform" created a sensation in Viennese musical and intellectual circles when Gluck's *Orfeo ed Euridice* with Calzabigi's libretto premiered in 1762. Their *Alceste* was mounted five years later in 1767; the last of their three Italian "reform" operas, *Paride ed Elena,* saw the light of day in Vienna in 1770. The realization of elegant verbal and musical simplicity, which refocused prevalent conventions in the music theater, brought both librettist and composer great fame.

At the behest of Marie Antoinette, his former pupil, Gluck went to Paris to tackle French opera on its home grounds.

Iphigénie en Aulide, 1772, was followed two years later by *Orphée et Eurydice,* a revision of *Orfeo ed Euridice.* A French version of *Alceste* appeared in 1776. Critical response was fierce during these years, and only after the French *Alceste* did Gluck seem at ease in facing French traditions head-on when he composed *Armide,* produced in 1777 and based on a libretto Philippe Quinault had prepared for Jean Baptiste Lully almost a hundred years earlier. By utilizing this drama Gluck challenged the long-standing and apparently inviolable ideals of French practice, and in the process he revealed these values capable of renewal through "modern" compositional sensitivities.

The text for *Armide* is based on episodes from Tasso's epic *Gerusalemme liberata,* which explore Armide's infatuation with Rénaud. The libretto is a sensual one which proceeds by means of a series of confrontations, personal as between Armide and Rénaud, or allegorical as between Armide and the personification of Hate. Extravagant adventure scenes are revealed through stage craft and decoration only the French tradition could fully realize. Rénaud's ultimate rejection of Armide and her final destruction, together with her palace and all its glory, are among the great moments in French opera.

Critical response and resultant polemic resulted in one of those grand imbroglios common to French intellectual life. Gluck struck a nerve in French sensitivities, and whereas *Armide* was not one of his more popular works, it remained a critical touchstone for aesthetic and cultural concerns of French opera. The composer weathered the storm, and two

A set design for Gluck's *Armide* by Karl Friedrich Schinkel, Berlin, 1819

years later in 1779 his final major opera, *Iphigénie en Tauride,* marked the culmination of those arguments which had pitted supporters of Lully and Rameau as "true" French stylists against foreigners such as Gluck.

Whereas both the Italian and French versions of the Orpheus and Alcestis operas, together with Gluck's presentations of the two Iphigenia stories, have long held the admiration of critics, musicians, and stage directors alike, *Armide* remains a special case. It is an obvious *hommage à France,* well-shaped on its own terms. Recent stage productions reveal *Armide* to be a musical and stage entity worthy of modern consideration. With the right combination of musical and production resources the cynical statement that Gluck is either the dullest of great composers or the greatest of dull composers, perhaps both, becomes invalid.

—Aubrey S. Garlington

ARMIDE.

Composer: Jean-Baptiste Lully.

Librettist: Philippe Quinault (after Tasso, *La Gerusalemme liberata*).

First Performance: Paris, Opéra, 15 February 1686.

Roles: La Gloire (soprano); La Sagesse (soprano); Armide (soprano); Phénice (soprano); Sidonie (soprano); Hidraot (bass); Aronte (bass); Renaud (countertenor); Artémidore (tenor); La Haine (tenor); Ubalde (bass); A Danish Knight (countertenor); Demon as Melisse (soprano); Demon as Lucinde (soprano); A Nymph (soprano); A Shepherdess (soprano); A Lover (countertenor); chorus; ballet; mute figures in the Prologue.

Publications

article–

Torrefranca, F. "La prima opera francese in Italia?: L'Armida di Lulli, Roma 1690." In *Musikwissenschaftliche Beiträge: Festschrift für Johannes Wolf,* 191. Berlin, 1929.

*   *   *

Armide begins with an extended prologue in which allegorical representations of Wisdom and Glory dispute their relative power over an unnamed "hero" (King Louis XIV). The central drama, set in Damascus during the First Crusade, is based on a portion of Torquato Tasso's *Gerusalemme liberata.* The sorceress Armide, enemy of the Crusaders, has captured nearly an entire camp but is obsessed by Renaud, the one knight who has eluded her. With the help of demons in pleasant pastoral disguise, she traps Renaud, intending to kill him as he sleeps; however, as she stands over him, dagger in hand, she falls in love with him. She places Renaud under a magical spell so that he will return her love, and has the demons transport them both to an enchanted palace in a faraway place. Armide is ashamed and calls on Hatred to destroy her love; Hatred's followers attempt to obey (an action presented in pantomime ballet), but Armide cannot go

through with the operation. Having given in to love, she then concentrates on defeating Glory, her rival for Renaud's affections. She is unsuccessful: two knights find Renaud, break his enchantment, and lead him away to glorious knightly duty. Armide, in despair, orders the demons to destroy the magical palace and, with it, her fatal love. (The crumbling palace was one of Jean Bérain's most famous pieces of stage machinery.)

Eighteenth-century critics regarded *Armide* as Lully's and Quinault's masterpiece. Their last *tragédie en musique,* it represents their style at its most mature. Unlike most of Lully's operas, *Armide* concentrates on the sustained psychological development of a character—not Renaud, whose supposed heroic conflict between love and duty disappears the moment his enchantment is broken, but Armide, who repeatedly tries without success to choose vengeance over love and ultimately achieves neither. Lully's star soprano, Marie (or Marthe) le Rochois, was best remembered for this role; in 1743, Titon du Tillet wrote that her opening utterance in act I completely eclipsed the two confidants who had held the stage until then.

Thanks to the subtlety of expression in Lully's mature recitative and to his use of the orchestra, both in evocative entrance preludes and as accompaniment for solo voices, the music beautifully expresses Armide's state of mind. A parenthetical phrase in the sub-dominant key—the "flat side," representing weakness and shame, as Rameau would later point out—hints at Armide's ambivalence even in act I: "The conqueror of Renaud (if someone can be that) will be worthy of me." (Neither this suggestion that Renaud is invincible nor Armide's nightmare, in which she imagines herself conquered by Renaud, is in Tasso.) Armide's internal debate as she points her dagger at the sleeping Renaud became Lully's most famous recitative monologue; in the mid-eighteenth century it was held up as a masterpiece by Diderot and others, criticized at length by Rousseau, and defended in detailed analysis by Rameau. Armide's invocation of Hatred takes place over a savage repeated-note bass line; the invocation and ensuing dialogue are accompanied by the orchestra from start to finish. Moreover, Hatred and her followers are all represented by male performers; thus, when Armide finally begs them to stop their horrifying activities, her soprano voice stands out plaintively.

Act V begins with the only love scene in the opera, whose lush duets cannot mask Armide's concern about her rival, Glory; it ends with a lengthy orchestrally-accompanied recitative monologue, in which Armide's voice alternately breaks in sobs and soars in rage. This is the only Lullian opera to end intimately rather than with a *divertissement,* and the powerful effect of the ending on audiences was reported by Lecerf de la Viéville.

Finally, Quinault and Lully used Armide's sorcery as a tool for creating contrast: juxtaposed with the moments of horror and indecision are lovely pastoral scenes, none of them real; all are enchanted settings created at Armide's request, and in each case the shepherds and other characters are actually demons in disguise. Renaud's "air de sommeil" (slumber song), in which recorders and muted strings paint a flowing river and lush landscape, is justifiably famous. So is the lengthy passacaille in the final act, a hypnotic ballet intended to entertain Renaud in Armide's absence; recorders, strings, and voices weave a seemingly endless series of continuous variations over a ground bass—the well-known descending minor tetrachord, often a symbol of lament but here and elsewhere a symbol of happy love.

The only portion of *Armide* considered unsuccessful by early commentators, largely because it seemed merely an

Lully's *Armide*: drawing by Jean Bérain showing the destruction of the palace of Armide, for the title-page of the printed score, 1686

extended digression from the main action, was the fourth act. Here Renaud's colleagues attempt to find him but are hindered by Armide's traps. In eighteenth-century Parisian productions, the act was routinely "improved"; it is omitted altogether in the one recording of *Armide.*

—Lois Rosow

ARNE, Thomas Augustine.

Composer. Born 12 March 1710, in London. Died 5 March 1778, in London. Married: Celia Young, 15 March 1737. Educated at Eton; University of Oxford conferred upon him the title Doctor of Music, 6 July 1759. His sister Suzanna Maria was the famous tragic actress and singer Mrs. Cibber. First opera was his setting of Addison's *Rosamond,* 1733; the composition of many dramatic works followed, the best-known of which is his setting of Dalton's adaptation of Milton's *Comus,* 1738; Arne attempted to create an Italian style recitative using the English language with his *Artaxerxes,* a translation and setting of Metastasio's libretto of the same name, 1762. The well known song "Rule Britannia" comes from his opera *Alfred.*

Operas and Masques

Rosamond, Joseph Addison, London, Lincoln's Inn Fields Theatre, 7 March 1733.

The Opera of Operas, or Tom Thumb the Great, Eliza Haywood and William Hatchett (after Henry Fielding, *Tom Thumb*), London, Haymarket Theatre, 29 October 1733.

Dido and Aeneas, Barton Booth, London, Haymarket Theatre, 12 January 1734.

Comus, John Dalton (after Milton), London, Drury Lane Theatre, 4 March 1738.

A Hospital for Fools, James Miller, London, Drury Lane Theatre, 15 November 1739.

Alfred, James Thomson and David Mallet, London, Clivedon House, 1 August 1740.

The Judgment of Paris, William Congreve, London, Clivedon House, 1 August 1740.

The Blind Beggar of Bethnal Green, Robert Dodsley, London, Drury Lane Theatre, 3 April 1741.

The Rehearsal, G. Villiers, Drury Lane Theatre, 21 November 1741.

Miss Lucy in Town, Henry Fielding, London, Drury Lane Theatre, 6 May 1742.

The Temple of Dullness, (after the interludes in Lewis Theobald's *The Happy Captives*), London, Drury Lane Theatre, 17 January 1745.

The Picture or The Cuckold in Conceit, James Miller (after Molière), Drury Lane Theatre, 11 February 1745.

King Pepin's Campaign, William Shirley, London, Drury Lane Theatre, 15 April 1745.

Neptune and Amphitrite, London, Drury Lane Theatre, 31 January 1746.

Harlequin Incendiary, or Columbine Cameron, London, Drury Lane Theatre, 3 March 1746.

The Triumph of Peace, Robert Dodsley, London, Drury Lane Theatre, 21 February 1748.

The Muses' Looking Glass, T. Randolph, London, Covent Garden Theatre, 9 March 1749.

Henry and Emma, or The Nut-brown Maid. Matthew Prior, London, Covent Garden Theatre, 31 March 1749.

Don Saverio, Arne, London, Drury Lane Theatre, 15 February 1750.

Harlequin Sorcerer, (after Lewis Theobald), London, Covent Garden Theatre, 11 February 1752.

The Sheep-Shearing, or Florizel and Perdita, MacNamara Morgan (after Shakespeare's *The Winter's Tale*), London, Covent Garden Theatre, 25 March 1754.

Eliza, Richard Rolt, London, Haymarket Theatre, 29 May 1754.

Britannia, David Mallet, London, Drury Lane Theatre, 9 May 1755.

The Pincushion, John Gay, Dublin, Smock Alley Theatre, 20 March 1756.

Mercury Harlequin, Henry Woodward, London, Drury Lane Theatre, 27 December 1756.

The Sultan, or Solyman and Zayade, London, Covent Garden Theatre, 23 November 1758.

Thomas and Sally, or The Sailor's Return, Isaac Bickerstaffe, London, Covent Garden Theatre, 28 November 1760.

Artaxerxes, (Arne translation of Metastasio), London, Covent Garden Theatre, 2 February 1762.

Love in a Village, Isaac Bickerstaffe, London, Covent Garden Theatre, 8 December 1762.

The Guardian Outwitted, Arne, Covent Garden Theatre, 12 December 1764.

L'Olimpiade, Bottarelli (after Metastasio), London, King's Theatre, 27 April 1765.

The Fairy Prince, G. Colman (after B. Jonson, *Oberon*), London, Covent Garden Theatre, 12 November 1771.

Thomas Arne, etching after Bartolozzi

Squire Badger, Arne (after Fielding, *Don Quixote in England*), London, Little Hay Market Theatre, 16 March 1772.

The Cooper, Arne (after Audinot, *Quétant*), London, Little Hay Market Theatre, 10 June 1772.

Elfrida, Colman (after W. Mason), London, Covent Garden Theatre, 21 November 1772.

The Rose, Arne?, London, Drury Lane Theatre, 2 December 1772.

Henry and Emma (2nd version), H. Bates (after Prior), London, Covent Garden Theatre, 13 April 1774.

May-Day, or The Little Gipsy, David Garrick, London, Drury Lane Theatre, 28 October 1775.

Phoebe at Court, Arne (after R. Lloyd, *Capricious Lovers*), London, King's Theatre, 22 February 1776.

Caractacus, W. Mason, London, Covent Garden Theatre, 6 December 1776.

The Birth of Hercules, Shirley [not performed].

Other works: oratorios, odes, cantatas, songs, catches, canons, glees, instrumental music.

Publications/Writings

About ARNE: books–

Davies, T. *Memoirs of the Life of David Garrick.* London, 1780.

Genest, J. *Some Account of the English Stage.* London, 1832.

Hogarth, G. *Memoirs of the Musical Drama.* London, 1838.

Horner, B.H. *Life and Works of Dr Arne.* London, 1893.

Langley, Hubert. *Doctor Arne.* Cambridge, 1938.

Stockholm. *Garrick's Folly.* London, 1964.

Hartnoll, P. ed. *Shakespeare in Music.* London, 1964.

Parkinson, J.A. *An Index to the Vocal Works of Thomas Augustine Arne and Michael Arne.* Detroit, 1972.

Fiske, R. *English Theatre Music in the Eighteenth Century.* London, 1973.

Walsh, T.J. *Opera in Dublin 1705-1797.* Dublin, 1973.

articles–

Sonneck, O.G. "Caractacus not Arne's Caractacus." In *Miscellaneous Studies in the History of Music.* New York, 1921.

Roscoe, P.C. "Arne and 'The Guardian Outwitted'." *Music and Letters* 24 (1943): 237.

Herbage, Julian. "The Vocal Style of Thomas Augustine Arne," *Proceedings of the Royal Music Association* 78 (1951-1952): 83.

_____. "The Opera of Operas." *Monthly Musical Record* 89 (1959): 83.

_____. "T.A. Arne." *Musical Times* 101 (1960): 623.

_____. "Arne, His Character and His Environment." *Proceedings of the Royal Musical Association* 87 (1960-61).

Farncombe, C. "Arne and Artaxerxes." *Opera* 13 (1962): 159.

Herbage, Julian. "Artaxerxes." *Opera* 13 (1962): 333.

Lord, P. "The English-Italian Opera Companies 1732-3." *Music and Letters* 45 (1964): 239.

Scott, A. "Arne's 'Alfred'," *Music and Letters* 55 (1974): 385.

unpublished–

Farish, Stephen. "The Vauxhall Songs of Thomas Augustine Arne." Ph.D. dissertation, University of Illinois, Urbana, 1962.

Thomas Augustine Arne was a man of the theater, of the *English* musical theater. More so than any of his contemporaries, Arne conceived music in theatrical terms. Almost singlehandedly he preserved indigenous music drama in eighteenth–century England. Considering Handel's potent presence and the almost total domination of the London stage by Italian opera, this was a prodigious achievement.

Arne's first opera was Addison's *Rosamond* (1733), which included his sister, Susannah, in the title role (Charles Burney, *A General History of Music,* 1789). During that year he composed music "after the Italian Manner" for Fielding's *Tom Thumb.* Originally called *Tragedy of Tragedies,* Arne renamed it, *Opera of Operas* (Burney). The *Masque of Comus* (1738) begins his most productive stage. Arne's new score, linked with Dalton's libretto, converted Milton's masque into an operatic idiom acceptable to contemporary taste. Arne's setting of Congreve's masque, *The Judgement of Paris* (1740), revealed Arne's contrapuntal skill. George Hogarth considered its overture "by far the best of his instrumental compositions . . ." (*Memoirs of the Opera,* 1851). The vocal writing of both recitatives and airs skillfully combine florid Italian characteristics with accurate verbal prosody. The air "Gentle Swain! Hither Turn Thee" features a virtuoso cello obligato, written for Cervetto, who had recently introduced that instrument to England. The following trio employs transverse flutes in double obligato with voices, a concerted style then almost unknown on the stage. The *Masque of Alfred* (1740) along with other notable music, concludes with what is likely the best national song ever written, "Ode in Honour of Great Britain," better known as "Rule, Britannia!"

While there were numerous ballad operas during the 1740s, this period marked Arne's Shakespearean decade. Beginning in 1741 he contributed music to revivals: *As You Like It* (1740), *The Tempest* (1740, revived 1746), *Twelfth Night* (1741), *The Merchant of Venice* (1741-1742), *Cymbeline* (1746), *Much Ado About Nothing* (1746), *Love's Labours Lost* (1747), and *Romeo and Juliet* (1750).

In 1745, Arne was appointed composer to Vauxhall Gardens, retaining this position until shortly before his death. Success at Vauxhall expanded his fame, but presented an irresistible temptation to mass-produce. Nevertheless, many fine songs were heard at the gardens. Few memorable productions were staged during the 1750s. An opera, *Eliza* (1754), was called "a dull piece" by Hogarth (*Memoirs*).

Following Handel's death in 1758, Arne embarked on a new phase of theatrical productivity. His prior stormy association with David Garrick at Drury Lane was marked by ballad operas and farces of forgettable merit. Following a dispute with Garrick over the employment of his pupil, Charlotte Brent, he turned to Covent Garden, where his old friend, John Beard, was now involved in the theater's management. At Covent Garden, the short comic opera, *Thomas and Sally* (1760) on a libretto by Isaac Bickerstaffe, met immediate approval. A true opera, with dialogue in recitative, its scoring was innovative, including the introduction of clarinets into English opera. Inspired, perhaps, by the growing interest in *opera buffa,* Arne continued to compose comic operas and farces: *Love in a Village* (1762). *The Cooper* (1772), and *Achilles in Petticoats* (1773). His second, and only successful oratorio, *Judith,* was introduced early 1761 at Drury Lane, and, a year later, *Artaxerxes,* was staged at Covent Garden. Based on Metastasio's libretto, *Artaxerxes* was the first full-length English *opera seria.* It unleashed vehement criticism for its florid manner, and provoked debate about the very capacity of English recitative. In spite of critical disapproval, the opera enjoyed long-lasting acceptance.

Arne's sole Italian opera, *L'Olimpiade* (1765), was composed for the castrato, Giovanni Manzuoli. It did not meet with public approval, and the score was never printed. Charles Burney's condemnation was vicious: ". . . the doctor had kept bad company . . . too long to be able to comport himself properly at the Opera-house, . . . He had but little to say to good company" (Burney). Although Arne's reputation suffered greatly from Burney's adverse testimony, Burney, who began his career as the composer's apprentice, was not an objective observer. Arne gave young Burney abundant work, but little tutelage. Seizing an opportunity for quick profit, he abruptly sold his apprentice's contract. Burney's *General History of Music* acknowledges Arne as an important figure in eighteenth–century English music, yet slights the importance of Arne's achievements.

The eighteenth century was not a propitious time for an English dramatic composer. Arne's early development was overshadowed by popular *opera serie* by Bononcini, Porpora, and others. Subsequently, the comic operas of Pergolesi, Galuppi and Piccinni gained favor. Throughout this period, there was the overwhelming influence of Handel. One important question, however, is manifest: how would English musical theater have been different were it not for the legacy of Thomas Arne? He did not invent the ballad opera, but he did elevate its musical status. He did not reject Italian techniques; from beginning to end, he embraced them and made them his own. European musical sophistication elevated his musical style, infusing it with vocal virtuosity and innovations in orchestration.

Arne generated an English school of singing which supported and enhanced his contributions to the theatre. Thoroughly trained in ornamentation by Festing, a pupil of Geminiani, Arne demanded from his artists not only virtuosity, but dramatic integrity and careful, precise English declamation. Also trained by Geminiani was his wife, the former Cecilia Young, who figured prominently in Arne's early compositions. His first singing student was his sister, who, as Mrs Cibber, became the leading singing actress of her day. At her death in 1760, Garrick exclaimed, "Tragedy is dead!" The successful career of Beard, whose musicianship and acting competence far exceeded his vocal prowess, was largely because of the dramatic opportunities in Arne's theater music. Brent, known later as Mrs Pinto, acquitted herself with distinction among the most celebrated Italian virtuosi. A contemporary observer remarked, "Though she owed a great deal to nature, she owed a great deal to ARNE, without whose careful hand her singing might perhaps have been too luxuriant" (Charles Dibdin, *A Complete History of the Stage,* n.d.). The quintessence of his vocal style was not the actor who could sing, nor the singer who could act. It was the singing actor. This sense of theater enabled him to elevate serious English music theater of the eighteenth century above mere show, and to lift comedy over farce.

—Stephen Farish

ARNOLDSON, Sigrid.

Soprano. Born 20 March 1861, in Stockholm. Died 7 February 1943, in Stockholm. Married: impresario Alfred Fischof, 1888. Studied with Maurice Strakosch and Désirée Artôt; debut as Rosina in *Il barbiere di Siviglia,* Prague, 1885; London debut as Rosina at Drury Lane Theatre, 1887; Covent Garden debut as Zerlina in *Don Giovanni,* 1888; Metropolitan Opera debut, 1893; other roles included Cherubino, Carmen, Micaela, Nedda, Papagena; retired 1916; taught in Vienna and Berlin after retirement.

Swedish-born Sigrid Arnoldson possessed a voice that combined the agility of the leggera with the weight and power of the dramatic soprano. It spanned three octaves and allowed her to perform a range of roles that encompassed the lyric-coloratura repertoire as well as roles usually associated with mezzo-sopranos; this practice reflects a time in which vocal categories were less strictly observed than they are today.

Arnoldson made her debut as Rosina in Rossini's *Il barbiere di Siviglia* in Prague in 1885. The following year she sang as a guest artist in Moscow. First appearing at Monte Carlo in 1888, when she performed Delibes's Lakmé, she returned to sing Rosina and Thomas's Mignon (1891), Bizet's Carmen and Meyerbeer's Dinorah (1893), and Juliette in Gounod's *Roméo et Juliette* (1902). She first appeared in London in 1887, at the Drury Lane Theatre, as Rosina opposite another debutant, tenor Fernando de Lucia. She made her Covent Garden debut in 1888 as Zerlina in Mozart's *Don Giovanni,* and subsequently sang Papagena in Mozart's *Die Zauberflöte,* Rosina, and Cherubino in Mozart's *Le nozze di Figaro;* she also sang Oscar in Verdi's *Un ballo in maschera* when Nellie Melba declined to sing the role. Not an overwhelming success, perhaps because she was in Melba's shadow, she did not return to Covent Garden until 1892; in her seasons there she sang both Carmen and Micaela in *Carmen,* Nedda in Leoncavallo's *I pagliacci,* the Queen in Meyerbeer's *Les Huguenots,* Baucis in Gounod's *Philémon et Baucis,* Eudoxie in Halévy's *La juive,* Gemma in Cowen's *Signa,* and, in 1894, Sophie in Massenet's *Werther* (in the single performance of this opera at Covent Garden until 1979).

This relative paucity of roles may have been the result of the influential Melba's appropriation of the best parts. Arnoldson's London career ended abruptly, apparently as a result of a contretemps between her husband and Augustus Harris, the impresario of the Drury Lane Theatre, over an apparent slight (Harris did not introduce Arnoldson to Queen Victoria after a performance at Windsor Castle, and Arnoldson's husband's subsequent appeal to the Danish-born Princess of Wales was not met kindly by Harris). She also appeared in Paris (one season only), Nice, and Rome. She performed at the Metropolitan Opera in the 1893-94 season—her only season there—as Carmen, Micaela, Zerlina, the Queen in *Les Huguenots,* Cherubino, Nedda, Baucis, and Sophie in *Werther.* During the later years of her career she appeared in Hungary, Sweden, and Germany. She retired in 1916.

Arnoldson made approximately twenty-five records between 1906 and 1910, all in Berlin. They show a voice with an ability to move lightly throughout *fiorature,* with subtle rubato and a sense of style apparent even through the early recording. Her intonation was excellent, even on her highest notes, although there is some unsteadiness in the lowest range.

A slight darkness of tone, an artifact of her second identity as a mezzo-soprano, lends an unusual color to her singing of soprano arias. Contemporary reviews reveal that her phrasing was broad, and she employed appoggiaturas—unwritten ornaments characteristic of Mozart's time that have been eschewed by adherents to the more literal approach characteristic of our century. It was an expressive voice, capable of being both placid and playful, marked by an accurate technique and an abundance of tone color, with subtle shadings and a beautiful lyric sound.

—Michael Sims

ARROYO, Martina.

Soprano. Born 2 February 1937, in New York. Studied with Joseph Turnau at Hunter College, New York; co-winner with Grace Bumbry of the 1958 Metropolitan Opera Auditions; professional debut in Pizzetti's *Assassinio,* Carnegie Hall, 1958; Metropolitan Opera debut as Celestial Voice in *Don Carlos,* 1959; also sang in Vienna, Frankfurt, Berlin, and under contract in Zurich in 1963-68, returning to the Metropolitan Opera in 1965; at Covent Garden, 1968–80; other roles include Butterfly, Gioconda, Liu, Santuzza, and Elsa.

Publications

About ARROYO: books–

Steane, J.B. *The Grand Tradition.* London, 1974.

articles–

Story, R. "Positively Martina." *Opera News* (September 1991): 26.

* * *

Martina Arroyo was one of several outstanding black American singers to figure prominently on the roster of the Metropolitan Opera during the 1960s and 1970s. Leontyne Price was the pioneer and role model among the sopranos, and to a great extent Arroyo has lived up to the high standards established by Price in certain roles. Both excelled in the great Verdi operas calling for a lirico-spinto soprano voice, notably Aïda, Amelia in *Un ballo in maschera,* Leonora in *La forza del destino* and the *Messa da requiem;* and both were superb Mozarteans as Donna Anna and Donna Elvira in *Don Giovanni.*

Arroyo has recorded a number of the above roles. The consensus is that on her recordings as on the stage, Arroyo displays extremely beautiful vocalism with healthy, rounded tone, but that she is seldom dramatically involved. Ethan Mordden has described her Donna Anna under Colin Davis as "gutlessly beautiful" and her *Forza* Leonora as "temperate and smoothed-out in the modern manner." Yet her recorded *Forza* is dark, opulent, and soaring and she provides an effective *messa di voce* for the opening of "Pace, pace, mio Dio," capping the aria with a fine high B-flat. She has also recorded Donna Elvira with Karl Böhm; in this role, too, she does little characterization with the voice, but the singing is thrilling as

pure sound and the technical demands are executed in masterly fashion. On balance, the timbre of the voice is perhaps better suited to Donna Anna, although Arroyo, like many other big-voiced sopranos, finds "Non mì dir" a bit treacherous and sings "Or sai chi l'onore" without tension and urgency. Similarly, her recording of Valentine in *Les Huguenots* under Richard Bonynge finds her in sumptuous voice but dramatically unconvincing. In the recording of *I vespri siciliani* in which she filled in for Montserrat Caballé, the "Bolero" is performed in a perfunctory manner, carefully, as though it were a vocalise, lacking the requisite sparkle in the fioriture and missing tonal nuances when the music changes mode. As with *Forza,* her singing of Amelia in *Un ballo* with Muti is very strong, yet if one compares her delivery of the dramatic recitative in "Ecco l'orrido campo" with that of Callas, Arroyo seems tentative and rather lacklustre.

In short, Arroyo was a truly stunning vocalist, one of the great voices of our time, but her recordings do not present stage portraits. Much the same criticism has been leveled at her stage performances. Andrew Porter noted of her Amelia in the 1974 Chicago Lyric Opera production of *Simon Boccanegra* that she "merely produced imposing and beautiful sounds" and of her *Forza* Leonora at the Metropolitan in 1975 that she "made some sweet, full sounds, but her performance did not have much character." In that same year at the Metropolitan, her first Gioconda fulfilled similar expectations, but her fourth Gioconda was "passionate, both amply and powerfully sung," according to Porter, who also has a memory of an Arroyo-Shirley Verrett *Il trovatore* in which they sang and acted so well as to eliminate mid-scene applause. Reasons for Miss Arroyo's usual lack of dramatic verve might be her own temperament and the basically sweet, rounded tone of her voice, which lacks "bite" and incisiveness, especially in the low register.

Onstage Arroyo performed many more roles than she recorded. After winning the Metropolitan Auditions of the Air along with Grace Bumbry in 1958, her early career was spent in Germany and Austria, where she sang Aida, among other roles. In 1965 she returned to the Metropolitan, her principal operatic home, as Aida and appeared in 1966 in *Don Carlos.* Other performances include Selika in Meyerbeer's *L'Africaine,* Rezia in Weber's *Oberon,* Senta in *Der fliegende Holländer,* Elsa in *Lohengrin,* the lyrical Puccini roles, Rossini's *Stabat mater,* Beethoven's Ninth Symphony, and such twentieth-century masterpieces as Stockhausen's *Momente* and Schoenberg's *Gurrelieder.*

—Stephen Willier

ARTAXERXES.

Composer: Thomas Arne.

Librettist: Thomas Arne (translation of work by P. Metastasio).

First Performance: London, Covent Garden Theatre, 2 February 1762.

Roles: Artabanes (tenor); Arbaces (soprano); Artaxerxes (soprano); Rimines (tenor); Mandane (soprano); Semira (soprano); chorus.

Artaxerxes, Covent Garden, London, 1763 (the engraving shows a riot which occurred during a performance, caused by the decision to stop half-price admission for those entering the theater during the intermission)

Publications

articles–

Farncombe, C. "Arne and Artaxerxes." *Opera* 13 (1962): 159.
Herbage, Julian. "Artaxerxes." *Opera* 13 (1962): 333.

*   *   *

Artaxerxes was an anachronism, a Metastasian *opera seria* created during the twilight of the genre. The vocal gymnastics of the Italians still pleased the public, but voices were raised in opposition to the dominance of show over dramatic substance. In 1750, *opera buffa* had made its appearance in Pergolesi's *La serva padrona.* Serious Italian opera was challenged by the pasticcios of Galuppi and others. Patrons of English opera preferred ballad operas with spoken dialogue. Encouraged by the success of his comic opera, *Thomas and Sally* (1760), Thomas Augustine Arne departed from the ballad style that had established his reputation and ventured to write a serious English opera in the Italian style.

The story of *Artaxerxes* was well known; Attilio Ariosti had set Apostolo Zeno's version of the story in 1724. The drama, set in ancient Persia, emerges from the intrigues following the assassination of King Xerxes by Artabanes, Commander of the Royal Guards. Presuming Darius to be the assassin, Artaxerxes causes his brother's death and becomes heir to the throne. In Arne's version, the action centers on

Arbaces, son of Artabanes and friend of Artaxerxes. The principal female role is Arbaces' beloved Princess Mandane. Other characters include Artabanes' daughter, Semira, who is in love with Artaxerxes, and Rimines, Artabanes' lieutenant. The murderous conspiracy calculated by "Generalissimo" Artabanes to divert suspicion from himself imperils the life of his son, not once but twice. First he causes Arbaces to be found with the murder weapon. Near the end of the opera, when Artaxerxes invites the exonerated Arbaces to seal his loyalty by sharing the coronation goblet, Artabanes intervenes. Compelled to admit that he poisoned the draught in one final effort to usurp the throne, he confesses the murder of Xerxes. Parental affection ultimately conquers megalomania.

The successful premiere of *Artaxerxes* at Covent Garden did not assuage doubts about the efficacy of grand opera in English. Burney attributed the acceptance of *Artaxerxes* to its superior music and the impressiveness of the singing, but denigrated the recitative. Hogarth claimed that Arne's opera proved that English was not suitable for *secco* recitative. Even in Arne's accompanied recitatives, the musical merits of which Hogarth highly esteemed, the singers sounded as though they were singing English with an Italian accent. Although people flocked to hear the vocal pyrotechnics of Italian opera, it was evident the English public never fancied recitative. In *Artaxerxes,* Arne capitalized on the former, without overburdening his audience with the latter. Their appetite for vocal display was more than satisfied by the virtuoso airs specially written for the able castrati Tenducci (as Arbaces) and Peretti (as Artaxerxes). The role of Mandane, played by Arne's talented pupil, Charlotte Brent, became the acid test for English prima donnas. Even the composer's wife, much admired in her heyday, could not resist coming out of retirement to try her hand at Mandane during the 1768-69 season. In 1791, Drury Lane and Covent Garden mounted rival productions of *Artaxerxes*, pitting Covent Garden's exciting young soprano, Elizabeth Billington, against Drury Lane's experienced Mandane, the noted German soprano Gertrud Elizabeth Mara.

Arne's translation of Metastasio's libretto abbreviated many of the recitatives and focused on the emotional aspects of episodes within the narrative. This permitted the composer to concentrate on the airs while adhering to the conventions of *opera seria*, where dialogue advanced the story and the airs expressed the underlying passions. To enhance the opera's appeal, Arne departed from the old aria forms, introducing several airs resembling the songs written for the ballad operas and the public pleasure gardens. There was criticism for this infusion of popular elements into grand opera, but posterity has judged these songs favorably. Artaxerxes' touching "Water Parted from the Sea" retains its currency.

Whether *Artaxerxes* truly constitutes Arne's *magnum opus* can be debated, but the seriousness of his intent is incontrovertible. Added to the three virtuoso roles, the part of Artabanes became an acting *tour de force*. No mere poster board villain, the character of Artabanes is unusually complex. The portrayal of Artabanes was entrusted to John Beard, renowned for musicianship and intelligence as an actor. Beard appeared regularly in Arne's dramatic works from *Comus* (1738) to *Thomas and Sally*. Arne assigned the lesser roles of Semira and Rimines to Mrs Vernon (née Poitier) and George Mattocks, both with lengthy experience in his productions. Arne knew his actors and composed to utilize their strengths.

Artaxerxes combines all the powers of the composer's muse. Besides careful and perceptive casting, Arne refined and extended the recent orchestral innovations made in *Thomas and Sally*, including the use of the clarinet. *Artaxerxes* encompasses the lyricism of Arne's ballads and demonstrates an astute sense of theater. Above all it shows a unique ability to exploit the virtuosity of the singing voice honed over many years of working with and training some of the best English singers of his day.

—Stephen Farish

ARUNDELL, Dennis Drew.

Producer. Born 22 July 1898, in Finchley, England. Died 10 December 1988, in London. Educated at St John's College, Cambridge; Fellow at St John's College, 1923-29; professional debut as an actor in Nigel Playfair's revue *Riverside Nights*, 1926; operatic debut Cyril Rootham's *Two Sisters* (Cambridge, 1922); produced Handel's *Semele*, St John's College, 1926; taught at Royal College of Music and the Northern College of Music, Manchester; composed operas *Ghost of Abel* and *A Midsummer Night's Dream*, 1930; Chief Producer Sadler's Wells, 1946-63; translated numerous operas into English; staged world premieres of George Lloyd's *John Socman*, 1951, Frederick Delius's *Irmelin*, 1953, and Elizabeth Maconchy's *Sofa*, 1967; staged first British productions of Ermanno Wolf-Ferrari's *I quattro rusteghi*, Sadler's Wells,

1946, and Leoš Janáček's *Katya Kabanová*, Sadler's Wells, 1951; produced film version of *Les contes d'Hoffmann* conducted by Sir Thomas Beecham; awarded OBE in 1978.

Opera Productions (selected)

Semele, St John's College, Cambridge, 1926.
The Fairy Queen, Hyde Park, 1927.
Histoire du soldat, Cambridge, 1928.
Le roi David (King David), 1928.
Tosca, Oxford, 1949.
I quattro rusteghi, Sadler's Wells, 1946.
Faust, Sadler's Wells, 1947.
Peter Grimes, Helsinki, 1949.
John Socman, Manchester, 1951.
Katya Kabanová, Sadler's Wells, 1951.
The Bohemian Girl, Covent Garden, 1951.
Irmelin, Oxford, 1953.
The Pilgrim's Progress, Cambridge, 1954.
Der fliegende Holländer, Sadler's Wells, 1958.
Tosca, Sadler's Wells, 1960.
Sofa, Camden Fest, London, 1967.
Hänsel und Gretel, Melbourne, 1975-76.
Don Pasquale, Melbourne, 1975-76.

Opera Films

Les contes d'Hoffmann, with Sir Thomas Beecham.

Publications

By ARUNDELL: books–

Henry Purcell. London, 1927.
The Critic at the Opera. London, 1957.
The Story of Sadler's Wells, 1683-1964. London, 1965.
Introduction to Le nozze di Figaro *and* Cosi fan tutte. London, 1971.

articles–

"Purcell and Natural Speech." *Musical Times* 100 (1959): 323.
"*Tosca* Re-Studied." *Opera* 11 (1960): 262.
"The Producer." *Opera* 12 (1961): 631.
"New Light on *Dido and Aeneas*." *Opera* 13 (1962): 445.
"Opera in English or ... ?" *Music and Musicians* 11 (1962): 23.
"Readers' Letters: *Dido and Aeneas*." *Opera* 13 (1962): 765.
"Character and Reality." *Opera* 16 (1965): 17.
"Haydn Text." *Musical Times* 106 (1965): 680.
" 'Now Critics, Lie Snug!' " *Opera* 16 (1965): 717.
"Old Doctor Sam Johnson and All." *Opera* 19 (1968): 278.
"Readers' Letters: Opportunities for Young Singers." *Opera* 24 (1973): 850.
"The Translator at Work." *Opera* 25 (1974): 1061.
"Amy Shuard—A Personal Tribute." *Opera* 26 (1975): 542.
"A Producer's Reply." *Music and Musicians* 23 (1975): 18.
"Birthday Honours (OBE)." *Music and Musicians* 26 (1978): 6.
"Valetta Iacopi—An Appreciation." *Opera* 29 (1978): 139.
"Readers' Letters: The true *Dido*." *Opera* 32 (1981): 361.
" '*Dove sono*' Le nozze di Figaro?" *Opera* 35 (1984): 612.

About ARUNDELL: articles–

Blyth, Alan. "*Hugh the Drover;* Royal College of Music." *Opera* 23 (1972): 762.
Milnes, Rodney. "Obituary." *Opera* 40 (1989): 148.
"Obituary." *Musical Times* 130 (1989): 174.
"Obituary." *Notes* 46 (1990): 933.

*   *   *

Dennis Arundell, conductor, actor, composer, musicologist, stage historian, and translator, was also the author of a great deal of music criticism, especially on Wolfgang Amadeus Mozart and Henry Purcell. An influential force in the British theatrical world beginning in the mid-1920s, he produced the first staging of George Frideric Handel's *Semele* (1926) at St. John's College, Cambridge, England. He conducted and produced Purcell's *The Fairy Queen* in Hyde Park in 1927, a production also seen in Cambridge in 1931.

In 1928 Arundell produced a staged version of Igor Stravinsky's *Histoire du soldat* (*Soldier's Tale*), the British premiere. He produced the first British production of Arthur Honegger's *Le roi David* in 1929, for which he also provided the translation. For Sadler's Wells he produced Ermanno Wolf-Ferrari's *I quattro rusteghi* (*The Four Curmudgeons/The School for Fathers,* 1946), Charles Gounod's *Faust* (1947), the first British performance of Leos Janáček's *Katya Kabanová* (1951), Giacomo Puccini's *Tosca* (two productions, the latter in 1960), and Richard Wagner's *Der fliegende Holländer* (1958, a production that also ran at the London Coliseum in 1969). In 1949 he produced Benjamin Britten's *Peter Grimes* in Helsinki.

Arundell was invited to Covent Garden to produce Michael William Balfe's *The Bohemian Girl* in 1951, with performances conducted by Sir Thomas Beecham. This was his only Royal Opera production, apparently because at that time it was the policy that producers associated with Sadler's Wells would not be engaged for Covent Garden productions. He created the premiere of Frederick Delius's *Irmelin* (Oxford, 1953) and, in Cambridge, a production of Ralph Vaughan Williams's *The Pilgrim's Progress* (1954).

Arundell was put in charge of opera at the Royal College of Music in 1959, having become a member of the faculty in 1956, and he remained there until 1973. In 1974 he joined the Royal Northern College of Music in Manchester as opera coach. During the 1975-76 season in Melbourne, he produced Engelbert Humperdinck's *Hänsel und Gretel* and Gaetano Donizetti's *Don Pasquale.*

Arundell took a scholarly approach to opera production. He was one of the first musical scholars to analyze Mozart's tempos, and his conclusions are largely the ones followed today. His productions are remembered today for their stylistic integrity and their dramatic intensity. His philosophy was to maintain fidelity to the composer's intentions, without imposing his own interpretation on the opera. He held closely to the composer's stage directions and the letter of the score and stressed that it was vital for producers to have a thorough grounding in musical scholarship and a full knowledge of the social and historical context of the operas.

—Michael Sims

THE ASPERN PAPERS.

Composer: Dominick Argento.

Librettist: Dominick Argento (after Henry James).

First Performance: Dallas, November 1988.

*   *   *

Dominick Argento has composed several highly evocative operas, of which the latest (as of this writing) is *The Aspern Papers.* The plot is of course based on Henry James' short story of the same name, but Argento (who wrote his own libretto) has opened up the original considerably, showing us characters and scenes merely alluded to in James, their existence being only a distant memory of the protagonist Juliana Bordereau.

Simultaneous to this broadening of the tale's scope and compass, Argento has made its content more operatic; Aspern himself is no longer a Byronesque author but rather a leading composer of the bel canto era. Thus Juliana is not merely his paramour but also a famous diva of the time and creatrix of his leading roles. The treasured papers which she so zealously retains of the dead composer are now not merely a stray love letter or two, but the manuscript of Aspern's final and long-suppressed opera, *Medea.*

All these events, including Aspern's betrayal of Juliana with the young opera singer Sonia and their dealings with the impresario Barelli, are shown in scenes occurring in the summer of 1835. These episodes are interwoven with others from 1895 in which Juliana is an old lady living with her shy and unattractive spinster niece, Tina. This part of the story comes from James' original novella, whose prose Argento has closely followed. A young scholar of Aspern's life and works (known only as The Lodger) arrives at the ladies' villa and, hoping to use Tina as a means of getting his hands on the ancient Juliana's trove of manuscripts, woos the ungainly woman. When the old lady dies, Tina offers the young man the surviving papers on condition that he agree to marry her. Shocked, he refuses and bolts from the scene, but shortly returns. Tina tells him she has destroyed the papers, and in agony he leaves for a second and final time. Then, all alone, Tina withdraws the score of *Medea* from its hiding place and burns it, page by page, as we simultaneously see a vision of all the *Medea* characters (Juliana costumed as the title role, etc.) going up in flames.

The opera is a real *tour de force* for the two female leads, with Elisabeth Söderström as Juliana (both old and young: a particularly challenging part) and Frederica von Stade as Tina in the Dallas premiere of this work in November 1988. Argento's texture is through-composed, but the opera still separates into noticeable musical numbers. Especially memorable are the love duet of Juliana and Aspern in act II and the barcarole (supposedly written by Aspern) whose melody permeates the score at several crucial moments. Argento's subtle attention to the nuances of his text suggests the Debussy of *Pelléas et Mélisande,* but there is also an Italianate richness to his melody. While it is obviously too soon to comment on the opera's staying power, it certainly is as good as any other score to emerge in the last few years and a good deal better than most.

—Dennis Wakeling

THE ATTACK ON THE MILL
See L'ATTAQUE DU MOULIN

L'ATTAQUE DU MOULIN [The Attack on the Mill].

Composer: Alfred Bruneau.

Librettist: L. Gallet (after Zola).

First Performance: Paris, Opéra-Comique, 23 November 1893.

Roles: Dominique (tenor); Merlier (baritone); Enemy Captain (baritone); Guard (tenor): Public Crier (bass); Françoise (soprano); Marcelline (mezzo-soprano); Geneviève (soprano); French Captain (tenor or baritone); Young Man (baritone); Officer (baritone); chorus.

*   *   *

A review of Alfred Bruneau's artistic development would be quite helpful in understanding his most famous and successful opera, *L'attaque du moulin.* Bruneau was an advocate of the "naturalism" propounded by the great French novelist Émile Zola. Naturalism, supposedly based on scientific principles, was a reaction to the perceived unnatural and therefore unsatisfactory traits of modern industrial society and the overly restrictive parameters of Christian dogma and practice. The virtues of nature and the freedom of the individual were stressed.

This all sounds logical and idyllic, although in reality the results on stage were not nearly as easy to take. In an effort to simulate or imitate the overall style of Richard Wagner, including emphasis on substantial orchestration and a preference for individual vocal passages over combined voices, the much less talented Bruneau ended up with works which tended toward disharmony, disorder, and dissonance. Nevertheless, his promotion of realism on the musical stage was a major step in the development of modern French opera. But as a whole his innovative and iconoclastic ideas and methods, once regarded as the product of a master, are today looked upon with considerably less favor.

Yet Bruneau is not a complete dinosaur, and some of his operas, particularly *L'attaque du moulin,* are at least occasionally performed today. *L'attaque du moulin* came in Bruneau's middle period of development, and thereby apparently benefited from a more middle of the road artistic psychology. His earlier works, including one substantial success (*La rêve,* or *The Dream*), were harsher and more severe. Works after *L'attaque du moulin* were more moderate, but at the same time apparently lost some of the brash innovation of the earlier works.

Even though *L'attaque du moulin* was more mainstream than earlier Bruneau operas, it was hardly conventional. Bruneau described his theory of musical drama as follows: "It is music uniting itself intimately to the poetry . . . the orchestra comments upon the inward thoughts of the individual characters." This unorthodox philosophy, combined with only a moderate amount of skill (especially in melody), had controversial results. Bruneau's earliest works, and to a lesser extent *L'attaque du moulin,* could be characterized as an attack on

musical beauty and order. *L'attaque du moulin,* however, managed to be Bruneau's best compromise between convention and philosophical conviction.

The story of the opera was relatively conventional but, of artistic necessity, also tragic. The setting is France during the Franco-Prussian War of 1870-71. Françoise, the miller's daughter, is to be married to Dominique, a native of Flanders. Before the wedding takes place, war is declared with Germany. The Germans attack the mill and imprison Dominique in it. Françoise is able to get a knife to Dominique and distract the German sentry. Dominique kills the guard and escapes to the woods. Merlier, the miller, is summoned by the German commander and is given the option of revealing Dominique's hiding place or being shot. Merlier refuses to be an informant. Dominique returns with a contingent of French soldiers, who recapture the mill. Just as Dominique and the French troops enter, Merlier is executed before his daughter's eyes.

L'attaque du moulin was not initially well received, yet in time it gained significant public favor. In the first several decades of the twentieth century, it was fairly highly regarded, but by World War II its reputation noticeably declined. Today it is at best a modest member of the contemporary repertory.

—William E. Studwell

ATTILA.

Composer: Giuseppe Verdi.

Librettists: Temistocle Solera and Francesco Maria Piave (after Z. Werner).

First Performance: Venice, La Fenice, 17 March 1846.

Roles: Odabella (soprano); Foresto (tenor); Ezio (baritone); Attila (bass); Uldino (tenor); Pope Leo I (bass); chorus (SSAATTBB).

Publications

articles–

Noiray, M., and Roger Parker. "La composition d'*Attila*: étude de quelques variantes." *Revue de musicologie* 62 (1976): 104.
Mila, Massimo. "Lettura dell' *Attila* di Verdi." *Nuova rivista musicale italiana* 17 (1983): 247.

*   *   *

Verdi's version of the Attila story presents the King of the Huns fresh from his victory at Aquileia and poised to march on Rome. The plot is mainly concerned with his courageous albeit barbarian greatness pitted against three rather unsavory and scheming Italians, a surprising structural balance given the patriotic furor it incited on the peninsula.

The amazon-like Odabella, as close to being a Valkyrie as any character Verdi ever created, wins Attila's trust and favor through her courage and warlike prowess. The Roman general Ezio first tries to cut a deal with Attila to share the world between them, only to join the conspiracy against him

Ruggiero Raimondi with Josephine Barstow in *Attila*, Royal Opera, London, 1990

when rebuffed. The patriot Foresto, Odabella's lover, is first seen with refugees from Aquileia in the grand act of founding the city of Venice. His next entrance, however, places him in the thick of plot and counterplot, whence he never re-emerges.

In the opera's strongest sequence, Attila describes a dream in which he is turned back at the gates of Rome by a saintly vision. Soon thereafter the vision turns to reality when Pope Leo I bars his way in a scene reproducing the famous fresco by Raphael in the Vatican. The remainder of the opera is devoted to the schemes of the Italian trio until in the end Odabella stabs Attila in the heart, claiming that she thus has avenged her father.

This strange and brutal mishmash of an opera is the result of the work of two librettists. In 1845 Verdi, badly in need of a success after the dismal reception accorded *Alzira,* turned for a text to Temistocle Solera, who had proven a tried and true collaborator with *Nabucco* and *I Lombardi.* However, his version of the original play (a flamboyant and mystical farrago entitled *Attila, König der Hunnen* by Zacharias Werner) was not well received by Verdi, especially the final act. A break between the two men occurred, and the composer called his faithful Francesco Maria Piave onto the scene to patch up the ending. The result is a work of brusque noisiness in an epically broad manner with an utterly mismatched finale in which Verdi tries through intimacy to humanize his cardboard characters, to little avail. Yet it must be noted that *Attila* was in fact wildly popular in its day, representing a sort of culmination for Verdi of his "Risorgimento" style.

When Ezio offered Attila to "Take the universe, but leave Italy to me" ("Avrai tu l'universo, resti l'Italia a me") an audience battlecry was born. Likewise, the founding of Venice with its attendant sunrise effect was praised, especially by Venetian audiences at the premiere, this despite its oxymoronic chorus of hermits.

In our renewal of interest in the early Verdian canon, *Attila* has not fared so well as other works. While moments such as Attila's dream and the ensemble with Pope Leo, some of Odabella's solos, and the tenor/baritone duet still evoke enthusiasm, the abrupt and formulaic simplicity of much of the rest, plus the two-dimensional characterization of all save the title role, sits poorly on a public ready to savor, say, the woes of a Doge Foscari or even the cross-cultural clash of an Alzira. *Attila,* therefore, will probably remain on the fringes: often unsatisfactory yet worthy of a revival when a basso of great vocal and histrionic gifts is seized by an understandable yen to perform the title role.

—Dennis Wakeling

ATYS.

Composer: Jean-Baptiste Lully.

Librettist: Philippe Quinault.

First Performance: Saint-Germain, 10 January 1676.

Roles: Le Temps (bass); Flore (soprano); A Zephyr (countertenor); Melpomène (soprano); Atys (countertenor); Idas (bass); Sangaride (soprano); Doris (soprano); Cybèle (soprano); Mélisse (soprano); Célénus (bass); God of Slumber (countertenor); Morpheus (countertenor); Phantase (tenor); Phobétor (bass); chorus; ballet; mute figures in the Prologue.

Publications

articles–

Avant-scène opéra January (1987) [*Atys* issue].

*   *   *

In the prologue of *Atys* Lully pays hommage to Louis XIV: Time promises the king eternal fame, and Flora, goddess of spring, complains that she cannot properly honor the monarch because he routinely leaves for wars in March. Melpomène, Muse of Tragedy, seeks to relieve royal concerns for a while by relating the story of *Atys*.

The five acts unfold on the common theme of Lully's *tragédies lyriques,* the conflict of love and duty. Atys, favorite of Célénus (son of Neptune and King of the Phrygians), boasts that he is indifferent to love, but he secretly loves his king's betrothed, Sangaride, who returns Atys's affection. Cybèle, Queen of the Gods, arrives on the pretext of attending the nuptials. She secretly loves Atys and has come to declare her love for him, but is incapable of doing so openly. In the second act Cybèle chooses Atys over Célénus for the honor of High Sacrificer, granting Atys great honor and fame.

In the third act Atys questions the value of fame and fortune when he is wretched because of a hopeless love. He struggles with his conflict, and ultimately decides to surrender duty to love. Having done so, he falls into a deep sleep under a spell cast by Cybèle, who plans to apprise him of her love. Atys has good and bad dreams on the themes of love and duty, and awakens suddenly to be comforted by Cybèle. Sangaride interrupts them, confesses her feelings to Cybèle, and begs for help. After the couple has gone, Cybèle laments.

Atys, using his powers as Cybèle's High Priest, speaks to Sangaride's father and commands him to break off the wedding. Célénus and Cybèle, after discovering Atys's perfidy, conspire to inflict torment on the lovers. Atys, driven insane by an artifice of Cybèle, perceives Sangaride as a monster and kills her. When he comprehends his terrible act he tries to kill himself, but the goddess prevents him and turns him into a pine tree. Having done so, Cybèle again laments her loss in the company of woodland and water divinities, and her attendants.

Atys, the fourth of Lully's monumental collaborations with Quinault in the form of the *tragédie lyrique,* followed *Cadmus et Hermione, Alceste,* and *Thésée.* Thus, by the composition of *Atys,* the stage form that marked the beginning of French opera was emerging in its mature form. Quinault based his adaptation on Ovid, preserving the essential character of Ovid's tale, but altering the text considerably.

Set design by Carlo Vigaroni for act I of *Atys,* Paris Opéra, 1676

Several elements identify *Atys* as a milestone in Lully's works. One is the absence of comic elements: Lully must have responded to criticism leveled at the comic passages in the earlier *tragédies lyriques,* most notably *Alceste* and *Thésée,* for, as James R. Anthony has observed, the comic muse was subsequently banished from Lully operas. A second is the work's exceptional unity: contemporary accounts indicate that in *Atys* Lully worked assiduously to connect each detail to the whole, thus reaching a new level in subordinating every element to overall dramatic unity. In doing so, Lully abandoned the inclusion of opulent musical scoring except when it was fully justified by the dramatic action. Consequently, the exceptional passages of compelling beauty and power that he composed heightened the overall dramatic effect to an extreme degree. The third act of *Atys* offers an excellent example in the famous *sommeil.* This slumber scene, long recognized as among Lully's most masterful writings, depicts Atys asleep while dreams and visions appear to him to underscore his conflict. Another particularly effective passage, in act V, scene iii, presents the chorus observing and commenting on the murder of Sangaride, very much in the manner of the chorus in Greek tragedy.

Louis XIV displayed great affection for the opera, such that he had it repeated at Saint-Germain in 1678 and 1682, and it became known as "the king's opera." Madame de Sévigné held it with less esteem, finding the characters weak. Its reception in Paris was relatively indifferent.

—John Hajdu Heyer

Daniel Auber

AUBER, Daniel-François-Esprit

Composer. Born 29 January 1782, in Caen. Died 12 May 1871, in Paris. Student of Ladurner and Cherubini. In London in his teens, where his vocal compositions met with success; in Paris, 1803; first dramatic work the comic opera *L'erreur d'un moment,* 1805; first opera publicly performed *Le séjour militaire,* 1813; first successful opera *La bergère châtelaine,* 1820; the grand opera *La muette de Portici,* upon which much of his reputation is based, premiered in 1828; succeeded Gossec as a member of the Académie in 1829; appointed director of the Paris Conservatoire in 1842 by Louis Philippe; given the title of imperial *maître de chapelle* in 1852 by Napoleon III.

Operas

L'erreur d'un moment, Jacques Marie Boutet de Monvel, Paris, Salle Doyen, 1805.

Jean de Couvin, Népomucène Lemercier, Belgium, Château de Chimay, September 1812.

Le séjour militaire, Jean Nicolas Bouilly and Emanuel Mercier-Dupaty, Paris, Opéra-Comique, 27 February 1813.

Le testament et les billets-doux, François Antoine Eugène de Planard, Paris, Opéra-Comique, 18 September 1819.

La bergère châtelaine, François Antoine Eugène de Planard, Paris, Salle Feydeau, 27 January 1820.

Emma, ou La promesse imprudente, François Antoine Eugène de Planard, Paris, Opéra-Comique, 7 July 1821.

Leicester, ou Le château de Kenilworth, Eugène Scribe and Anne Honoré Joseph Mélesville (after Scott), Paris, Opéra-Comique, 25 January 1823.

La neige, ou Le nouvel éginard, Eugène Scribe and Casimir Delavigne, Paris, Opéra-Comique, 8 October 1823.

Vendôme en Espagne (with Hérold), Adolphe Joseph Simonis d'Empis and Edouard Mennechet, Paris, Opéra, 5 December 1823.

Les trois genres (with Boieldieu), Eugène Scribe, Emanuel Mercier-Dupaty, and Michel Pichat, Paris, Odéon, 27 April 1824.

Le concert à la cour, ou La débutante, Eugène Scribe and Anne Honoré Joseph Mélesville, Paris, Opéra-Comique, 3 June 1824.

Léocadie, Eugène Scribe and Anne Honoré Joseph Mélesville (after Cervantes, *La fuerça del sangre*), Paris, Opéra-Comique, 4 November 1824.

Le maçon, Eugène Scribe and Casimir Delavigne, Paris, Opéra-Comique, 3 May 1825.

Le timide, ou Le nouveau séducteur, Eugène Scribe and Xavier Boniface Saintine, Paris, Opéra-Comique, 30 May 1826.

Fiorella, Eugène Scribe, Paris, Opéra-Comique, 28 November 1826.

La muette de Portici (*Masaniello*), Eugène Scribe and Casimir Delavigne, Paris, Opéra, 29 February 1828.

La fiancée, Eugène Scribe, Paris, Opéra-Comique, 10 January 1829.

Fra Diavolo, ou L'hôtellerie de Terracine, Eugène Scribe, Paris, Opéra-Comique, 28 January 1830.

Le dieu et la bayadère ou La courtisane amoureuse (opera-ballet), Eugène Scribe, Paris, Opéra, 13 October 1830.

Le philtre, Eugène Scribe, Paris, Opéra, 20 June 1831.

La Marquise de Brinvilliers (with Batton, Berton, Blangini, Boieldieu, Carafa, Cherubini, Hérold, and Paer), Eugène Scribe, and François Henri Joseph Castil-Blaze, Paris, Opéra, 31 October 1831.

Le serment, ou Les faux-monnayeurs, Eugène Scribe, and Édouard Joseph Ennemond Mazères, Paris, Opéra, 1 October 1832.

Gustave III ou Le bal masqué, Eugène Scribe, Paris, Opéra, 27 February 1833.

Lestocq, ou L'intrigue et l'amour, Eugène Scribe, Paris, Opéra-Comique, 24 May 1834.

Le cheval de bronze (opéra féerique), Eugène Scribe, Paris, Opéra-Comique, 23 March 1835; revised as opéra-ballet, 21 September 1857.

Actéon, Eugène Scribe, Paris, Opéra-Comique, 23 January 1836.

Les chaperons blancs, Eugène Scribe, Paris, Opéra-Comique, 9 April 1836.

L'ambassadrice, Eugène Scribe, Paris, Opéra-Comique, 21 December 1836.

Le domino noir, Eugène Scribe, Paris, Opéra-Comique, 2 December 1837.

Le lac des fées, Eugène Scribe and Anne Honoré Joseph Mélesville, Paris, Opéra, 1 April 1839.

Zanetta, ou Jouer avec le feu, Eugène Scribe and Jules Henri Vernoy de Saint-Georges, Paris, Opéra-Comique, 18 May 1840.

Les diamants de la couronne, Eugène Scribe and Jules Henri Vernoy de Saint-Georges, Paris, Opéra-Comique, 6 March 1841.

Le Duc d'Olonne, Eugène Scribe and Xavier Boniface Saintine, Paris, Opéra-Comique, 4 February 1842.

La part du diable, Eugène Scribe, Paris, Opéra-Comique, 16 January 1843.

La sirène, Eugène Scribe, Paris, Opéra-Comique, 26 March 1844.

La barcarolle, ou L'amour et la musique, Eugène Scribe, Paris, Opéra-Comique, 22 April 1845.

Les premiers pas (with Adam, Carafa, and Halévy), Alphonse Royer and Gustave Vaëz, Paris, Opéra-National, 15 November 1847.

Haydée ou Le secret, Eugène Scribe (after a Russian story translated by Prosper Merimée, *Six et quatre*), Paris, Opéra-Comique, 28 December 1847.

L'enfant prodigue, Eugène Scribe, Paris, Opéra, 6 December 1850.

Zerline, ou La corbeille d'oranges, Eugène Scribe, Paris, Opéra, 16 May 1851.

Marco Spada (first version: opéra-comique), Eugène Scribe and Casimir Delavigne, Paris, Opéra-Comique, 21 December 1852.

Jenny Bell, Eugène Scribe, Paris, Opéra-Comique, 2 June 1855.

Manon Lescaut, Eugène Scribe (after Prévost), Paris, Opéra-Comique, 23 February 1856.

La circassienne, Eugène Scribe, Paris, Opéra-Comique, 2 February 1861.

La fiancée du Roi de Garbe, Eugène Scribe and Jules Henri Vernoy de Saint-Georges, Paris, Opéra-Comique, 11 January 1864.

Le premier jour de bonheur, Adolphe Philippe d'Ennery and Eugène Cormon, Paris, Opéra-Comique, 15 February 1868.

Rêve d'amour, Adolphe Philippe d'Ennery and Eugène Cormon, Paris, Opéra-Comique, 20 December 1869.

Other works: choral works, orchestral works, and chamber music.

Publications/Writings

By AUBER: books–

Règles de contrepoint. 1808.
Observations . . . sur la méthode de musique de M. le docteur Emile Chevé. Paris, 1860.
Recueil des leçons de solfège à changements de clef. Paris, 1886.

unpublished–

Quelques sujets de fugue.
Fugues et contrepoints, sujets de fugues pour les concours, datés de 1833 à 1870, esquisses et réalisations.
Leçons de solfège à changements de clef, 1842-69.
Leçons pour la lecture à première vue, 1844-70.

About AUBER: books–

Pougin, Arthur. *Auber.* Paris, 1873.
Wagner, Richard. "Reminiscences of Auber." In *Richard Wagner's Prose Works,* vol. 5, translated by W.A. Ellis, 35. London, 1892-99.
Kohut, A. *Auber.* Leipzig, 1895.
Hanslick, Eduard. *Die moderne Oper.* Berlin, 1900.
Berlioz, Hector. *Les musiciens et la musique.* Paris, 1903.
Malherbe, Charles. *Auber. Les musiciens celèbres.* Paris, 1911.
Pendle, Karin. *Eugène Scribe and French Opera of the Nineteenth Century.* Ann Arbor, 1979.
Dean, Winton. "French Opera." In *The New Oxford History of Music,* vol. 8. Oxford and London, 1982.
Fulcher, Jane F. *The Nation's Image: French Grand Opera as Politics and Politicized Art.* Cambridge, London, and New York, 1987.

articles–

Hanslick, Eduard. "Von Gounod, Thomas und Auber." *Musikalische Stationen* (1888): 115.
Prout, E. "Auber's *Le philtre* and Donizetti's *L'elisire d'amour.*" *Monthly Musical Record* (1900): 25; 49; 73.
Longyear, R. "La Muette de Portici." *Music Review* 19 (1958): 37.
———. "Le Livret bien fait." *Southern Quarterly* 1 (1963): 169.
Klein, John W. "Daniel François Auber." *Opera* (August 1971).
Pendle, Karin. "Scribe, Auber, and the Count of Monte Cristo." *Music Review* 34 (1973): 210.
Chabot, Carole. "Ballet in the operas of Eugène Scribe: an apology for the presence of dance in opera." *Studies in Music* 5 (1980): 7.
Finscher, Ludwig. "Aubers *La muette de Portici* und die Anfänge der Grand-opéra." In *Festschrift Heinz Becker zum 60. Geburtstag am 26, Juni 1982,* edited by Jürgen Schläder and Reinhold Quandt, 87. Laaber, 1982.

Wild, Nicole and Anne-Charlotte Rémond. *Auber et l'opéra romanique (catalogue d'exposition)*. Paris, 1982.

Stampp, Kenneth M., Jr. "Reviving Daniel Auber." *Opera Quarterly* 4 (1983): 82.

unpublished—

Longyear, R.M. "D.F.E. Auber: A Chapter in French Opéra Comique 1800-1870." Ph.D. dissertation, Cornell University, 1957.

From the 1820s until his death during the Paris Commune of 1871, Auber retained a pre-eminent position in the field of French *opéra comique*. In his hands this genre shed the frequently stiff, classicizing traits of the preceding generation (Dalayrac, Méhul, Cherubini, Le Sueur); at the same time it shed its more earnest dramatic ambitions of the Revolutionary period in favor of a witty, sophisticated entertainment suited to the tastes of Restoration society and the "bourgeois monarchy" of Louis-Philippe. The historical significance of his grand opera *La muette de Portici* (1828)—an important prototype in the development of that new genre—was realized through its influence on others rather than in the composer's own subsequent works.

Auber was born into relatively comfortable circumstances, and spent some time in London as a youth in preparation for a mercantile career. Only after the failure of his father's business (as a print dealer) in 1819 did Auber turn to music as a profession. Before this, however, he had already studied with Cherubini, composed several concertos and a mass, and had the opportunity of mounting informally two small-scale stage works under the aegis of an aristocratic family acquaintance, the Prince de Chimay. Auber achieved his first public success with the 3-act *opéra comique, La bergère châtelaine,* at the Salle Feydeau in 1820. Three years later he entered into what became a life-long association with the gifted and prolific man of the theatre, Eugène Scribe (*Leicester ou Le château de Kenilworth* after Scott and, more successful from the dramatic point of view, *La neige*). Both of these scores remain strongly in the thrall of Rossini, whose athletic vocal writing and other mannerisms were more easily imitated than was his genuine, but elusive, melodic charm. With *Le maçon* in 1825 the torch of French *opéra comique* was passed, so to speak, to Auber from Boieldieu, who celebrated his last and most enduring success in that year with *La dame blanche* (both had texts by Scribe). The plot of *Le maçon*—based on a supposedly factual account of a rich Turk living outside Paris who tries to foil his daughter's elopement by kidnapping a local mason and locksmith to seal up his *château*—exemplifies Scribe's ability to fashion clever, colorful librettos from the most varied sources. The posthumous fame of Auber's first and most significant grand opera, *La muette de Portici,* rests especially on the report that the patriotic fervor of the tenor-baritone duet in Act II ("Amour sacré de la patrie") set off the ultimately successful struggle for Belgian independence from Holland in 1830. *La muette* was the first of three operas of this period (with Rossini's *Guillaume Tell,* 1829, and Meyerbeer's *Robert le diable,* 1831), which together established a musical and dramaturgical model for the historical-spectacular 'grand opera' type that would remain influential through the 1880s. The novelty of a mute heroine (Fenella, played by a dancer to passages of orchestral pantomime) inspired Scribe and Auber to collaborate on the opera-

ballet *Le dieu et la bayadère,* principally conceived as a vehicle for the famed dancer Marie Taglioni. *Gustave III ou Le bal masqué* of 1833 was already Auber's last attempt at a full-scale grand opera (here designated an *opéra historique* by Scribe), except for the relatively unsuccessful biblical drama, *L'enfant prodigue,* of 1850. *Gustave III* has of course been eclipsed by the musically tauter, much more dynamic treatment of the material by Verdi as *Un ballo in maschera.*

After their comic masterpiece, *Fra Diavolo* (1830), the next two most enduring creations of the Scribe-Auber team in the genre of *opéra comique* were two equally lighthearted works in Iberian settings: *Le domino noir* (1837) and *Les diamants de la couronne* (1841). Auber's swan song was *Le premier jour de bonheur,* produced (without Scribe, who had since died) in 1868, at the age of 87. In the meantime he had continued to provide a steady stream of works for the Parisian musical stage, although his production tapered off somewhat (understandably) after 1850. Among the other later works deserving mention are *Haydée ou le secret* (1847, after a Russian story translated by Prosper Merimée) and an *opéra comique* version of Prévost's *Manon Lescaut* from 1856. The aria from the latter work known as "L'éclat de rire" remained a favorite coloratura vehicle into the early age of recording, while the closing scene (death of Manon) represents a "unique page in the works of Auber for its simple grandeur and deeply felt emotion," according to Charles Malherbe.

Auber's achievement in *La muette* may not consist so much in the creation of a "new form" of opera (which would in any case have owed as much to Scribe's contribution) as in the synthesis of elements from the *opéra comique* with others from Rossinian *opera seria*. To the extensive, vocally demanding solo and duo scene structures of the latter, he—and Scribe—added the colorful historical setting, characteristic chorus and dance numbers (Barcarolle, Tarantella, etc.), a more active musical and dramatic role for chorus, all within the context of a compelling dramatic plot. The preponderance of jaunty, dotted rhythms and the tendency to foursquare phrase structures in this score also betray its proximity to *opéra comique*. Wagner, who was well acquainted with the work from his youth, praised its "drastic concision and economy" of form and the vibrant, vital energy of the musical style, which seemed to make all previous efforts at "serious" opera obsolete at one stroke. Franz Liszt also wrote approvingly of the work, although he felt it to be less substantial than Rossini's *Guillaume Tell*; and, like Wagner, registered disapproval of the essential frivolity of Auber's musical nature as manifested in most of his other works.

It was, nonetheless, the charm, grace, and wit of his lighter works on which Auber's reputation ultimately rested. A number of critics noted his increasing dependency on the rhythms and phraseology of the popular dance (contredanse, quadrille, waltz) in his later works. Berlioz complained of this already in *Les diamants de la couronne* (1841). But on the foundation of such simplistic rhythmic structures Auber was able to float a supple, naturalistic musical dialogue that won the admiration of Eduard Hanslick, who pointed to the opening trio (ball scene) in *Le domino noir* as a "classic example" of Auber's virtuosity in passing freely between *cantabile* and declamatory styles to create a true "musical conversation" style.

—Thomas S. Grey

AUDEN, W(ystan) H(ugh).

Librettist/Poet. Born 21 February 1907, in York. Died 29 September 1973, in Vienna. Studied at Christ Church College, Oxford University; taught secondary school in Scotland, 1930; ambulence driver in the Spanish Civil War, 1937; became U.S. citizen, 1946; wrote numerous texts for Benjamin Britten, 1935-41; collaborated with Chester Kallman on the libretto for Stravinsky's *The Rake's Progress,* 1948 (first performed 1951); collaborated with Kallman on *Delia,* intended for Stravinsky but never set, 1953; also with Kallman, two librettos for Henze and an adaptation of *Love's Labour's Lost* for Nabokov, 1973. Auden's poetry has been set by Berio, Berkeley, M.D. Levy, Maw, and Walton.

Librettos

Paul Bunyan, B. Britten, 1941.
The Rake's Progress (with C. Kallman), I. Stravinsky, 1951.
Elegy for Young Lovers (with C. Kallman), H.W. Henze, 1961.
The Bassarids (with C. Kallman), H.W. Henze, 1966.
Moralities, H.W. Henze, 1969.
Love's Labour's Lost (with C. Kallman), N. Nabokov, 1973.

Publications/Writings

By AUDEN: books (on music)–

The Dyer's Hand [includes essays on music]. New York, 1962.
Forewords and Afterwords [includes essays on music]. New York, 1973.

articles (on music)–

"Operas in American Legend: Problems of Putting the Story of Paul Bunyan on the Stage." *New York Times* (1941).
Introduction to *An Elizabethan Song Book.* Garden City, New York, 1955.
"A Public Art." *Opera* 12 (1961): 12.
"The World of Opera." In *Secondary Worlds.* London, 1969.

About AUDEN: books–

Beach, J.W. *The Making of the Auden Canon.* Minneapolis, 1957.
Stravinsky, I., and R. Craft. *Memories and Commentaries.* New York, 1960.
Spears, M.K. *The Poetry of W.H. Auden: the Disenchanted Island.* New York, 1963.
Stravinsky, I., and R. Craft. *Dialogues and a Diary.* New York, 1963.
Henze, H.W. *Essays.* Mainz, 1964.
Blair, J.C. *The Poetic Art of W.H. Auden.* Princeton, 1965.
Stravinsky, I. and R. Craft. *Themes and Episodes.* New York, 1966.
White, E.W. *Stravinsky: the Composer and his Works.* London, [2nd ed.] 1966.
Stravinsky, I. and R. Craft. *Retrospectives and Conclusions.* New York, 1969.
White, E.W. *Benjamin Britten.* London, [2nd ed.] 1970.
Bloomfield, B.C., and E. Mendelson. *W.H. Auden: a Bibliography.* Charlottesville, [2nd ed.] 1972.
Mitchell, D. *Britten and Auden in the Thirties.* London, 1981.
Craft, R., ed. *Stravinsky: Selected Correspondence.* London, 1982.
Farnan, D.J. *Auden in Love.* New York, 1984.

articles–

Kerman, J. "Opera à la mode." *Hudson Review* 6 (1954): 560; revised in *Opera as Drama,* New York, 1956; 2nd ed., 1988.
Wright, B. "Britten and Documentary." *Musical Times* 104 (1963): 779.
Salus, P.H. "Auden and Opera." In *Quest* vol. 2, p. 7. New York, 1967.
Weisstein, Ulrich. "Reflections on a Golden Age: W.H. Auden's Theory of Opera." *Comparative Literature* 22 (1970): 108.
Spiegelman, W. "The Rake's Progress: an Operatic Version of Pastoral." *Southwest Review* 63 (1978): 28.
Alvey, R.G. "Toward an Appreciation of Auden's Use of Folksong." *Southern Folklore Quarterly* 43 (1979): 71.
Roth, M.A. "The Sound of a Poet Singing Loudly: a Look at *Elegy for Young Lovers.*" *Comparative Drama* 13 (1979): 99.
Spiegelman, W. "The Rake, the Don, the Flute: W.H. Auden as Librettist." *Parnassus* 10/no. 2 (1982): 171.
Zimmermann, M. "W.H. Audens Bekehrung zur Oper." *Musica* 38 (1984): 248.

unpublished–

Engelbert, Barbara. "Wystan Hugh Auden, 1907-1973. Seine opern-ästhetische Anschauung und seine Tätigkeit als Librettist." Ph.D. dissertation, University of Cologne, 1982.

* * *

One of the most distinguished English poets of the twentieth century, W.H. Auden came to libretto writing comparatively late in his career. Following his collaboration on several orchestral song cycles and film scores with Benjamin Britten, Auden's first operatic project was Britten's *Paul Bunyan* (1941). Clearly influenced by Brechtian epic drama, Auden's text attempts to fuse American folklore, Jungian psychology, and social commentary; the book also draws much attention to its own verbal cleverness. Considering the work a failure, Auden did not return to the form until 1947, when Igor Stravinsky invited him to provide words for an opera based on Hogarth's *The Rake's Progress.*

By 1947, Auden's appreciation of Mozartian and nineteenth-century Italian opera had been deepened by his close friendship with Chester Kallman, whom he had met in 1939. Auden enlisted Kallman as his collaborator, and the resulting opera employs the conventional forms (recitatives, arias, ensembles) of the old "number" opera. Compared to the words of *Paul Bunyan,* where self-consciously witty rhymes and paradoxes often seem to dominate—or at least vie for attention with—the music, the verse here is uncomplicated and direct, its elegant simplicity easily comprehended by listeners. At the same time, the delicately allusive quality of the libretto and the mythic dimensions of Auden and Kallman's moral fable offer audiences much intellectual substance as well.

The same combination of thought-provoking content and unaffected verbal polish marks Auden and Kallman's other collaborations, both as librettists and translators. In Hans Werner Henze's *Elegy for Young Lovers,* for example, the writers leave the closed forms of *The Rake's Progress* for more fluid psychological drama as they examine the figure of the artist-genius of the late nineteenth and early twentieth centuries. The final scene is of particular interest for the degree to which the librettists subordinate words to the demands of music. In that scene the action calls for the central character to produce a poetic masterpiece; rather than providing a text, however, Auden and Kallman ask for wordless vocalizing from those characters whose experience has produced that masterpiece. For Henze's *Bassarids,* based on Euripides' *Bacchae,* they emphasized the play's contemporary relevance by specifying that characters wear costumes from different historical periods (e.g., Dionysus as a Regency dandy, Tiresias as an Anglican archdeacon, the Bassarids as hippies) particularly associated with the beliefs of that character.

Auden and Kallman have written that a too-literal translation falsifies a work, and their application of this principle is particularly striking in their treatment of *The Magic Flute.* Rather than merely replacing German words with English equivalents, their version attempts to clarify both the motivations of the characters and the symbolic meaning of the action. These efforts extend to establishing new relationships among the characters and even to rearranging the sequence of the musical numbers of the second act.

An articulate and engaging critic, Auden has written frequently about opera, libretto-writing and translation. His most extended comments appear in *Secondary Worlds,* in which he makes clear the subordinate role of words to music, yet also suggests that the libretto is the last refuge of the poetic high style. There he also describes the composition of the libretti written for Stravinsky and Henze. Several shorter essays on opera are collected in *The Dyer's Hand.*

—Joe K. Law

AURELI, Aurelio.

Librettist. Born in the first half of the seventeenth century, in Murano. Died 1708, in Venice. Member of the Accademico degl' Imperfetti; in Vienna, 1659; in Venice, 1660-90; in the service of the Duke of Parma, 1688-94.

Librettos

L'Erginda, G. Sartorio, 1652.
L'Erismena, F. Cavalli, 1655.
Le fortune di Rodope e di Damira, P.A. Ziani, 1657.
Il Medoro, F. Luccio, 1658.
La costanza di Rosmonda, G.B. Rovettino, 1659.
La virtù guerriera, G. Tricarico, 1659.
L'Antigona delusa da Alceste, P.A. Ziani, 1660.
Gli amori infruttuosi di Pirro, A. Sartorio, 1661.
Gli scherzi di Fortuna, P.A. Ziani, 1662.
Le fatiche di Ercole per Deianira, P.A. Ziani, 1662.
Gli amori di Apollo e di Leucotoe, G.B. Rovettino, 1663.
La Rosilena, G.B. Rovettino, 1664.
Perseo, A. Mattioli, 1665.
Eliogabalo, G.A. Boretti, 1668; revised as *Il Vitio depresso e la Virtù coronata,* T. Orgiani, 1687; revised as *L'Eliogabalo rifformato col titolo del Vitio depresso.*
D'Artaxerse overo l'Ormonda costante, C. Grossi, 1669.
Claudio Cesare, G.A. Boretti, 1672.
L'Orfeo, A. Sartorio, 1673; as *Amor spesso inganna,* B. Sabadini, 1689; as *Orfeo a torto geloso overo Amore spesso inganna,* 1697.
Medea in Atene, A. Giannettini, 1675; as *Teseo in Atene,* 1677.

Helena rapita da Paride, G.D. Freschi, 1677; as *Le due rivali in amore,* T. Albinoni, 1728.
Alessandro Magno in Sidone, M.A. Ziani, 1679; as *La virtù sublimata dal grande, overo Il Macedone continente,* 1707.
L'Alcibiade, M.A. Ziani, 1680.
Pompeo Magno in Cilicia, G.D. Freschi, 1681.
Olimpia placata, G.D. Freschi, 1682; as *Olimpia vendicata,* B. Sabadini, 1688.
Massimo Puppiano G. Pallavincino, 1684.
Teseo tra le rivali, G.D. Freschi, 1685; as *Le due regine rivali,* 1708.
Ermione, A. Giannettini, 1686.
Hierone tiranno di Siracusa, B. Sabadini, 1688; as *Geronte tiranno di Siracusa,* G.F. Gasparini, 1700.
Pompeo continente B. Sabadini, 1690.
La gloria d'amore e Il favore degli dei, B. Sabadini, 1690.
Diomede punito da Alcide, B. Sabadini, 1690; T. Albinoni, 1701.
Circe abbandonata da Ulisse, B. Sabadini, 1692; G.F. Pollarolo, 1697.
Il Massimino, B. Sabadini, 1692.
Talestri innamorata d' Alessandro Magno, B. Sabadini, 1693.
Demetrio tiranno, B. Sabadini, 1694.
Il riso nato fra il pianto, B. Sabadini, 1694.
Isifile Amazzone di Lenno, P. Porfiri, 1697.
La ninfa bizzarra, M.A. Ziani, 1697; as *Gli amanti delusi,* G. Polani, 1706; as *Il cieco geloso,* 1708.
Rosane Imperatrice degli Assiri, 1699.
Prassitele in Gnido, A. Bonaventura Coletti, 1700; G. Polani, 1707.
La magia delusa, 1702.
Creso tolto a le Fiamme, G. Polani, 1705.
La pace fra Pompejani e Cesariani, 1708.
Irene regina di Sparta, 1708.
Amore e gelosia, G.M. Buini, 1729.

Publications

About AURELI: books—

Wolff, H.C. *Die Venetianische Oper in der Zweiten Hälfte des 17. Jahrhunderts.* Berlin, 1937.
Abert, A.A. *C. Monteverdi und das musikalische Drama.* Lippstadt, 1954.
Fabri, Paolo. *Il secolo cantate: per una sturia del libretto d'opera nel seicento.* Bologna, 1990.
Rosand, Ellen. *Opera in Seventeenth-Century Venice.* Berkeley, 1991.

articles—

Sandberger, A. "Zur Venetianischen Oper, II." *Jahrbuch der Musikbibliothek Peters* (1924): 53.
Rosand, Ellen. " 'L'ovidio transformato.' The Metamorphosis of a Musical Myth." *Israel Studies in Musicology* 2 (1980): 101.
————. "L'ovidio transformato." In Aurelio Aureli and Antonio Sartorio, *Orfeo,* ed. Ellen Rosand. *Drammaturgia musicale veneta* 6 (1983).

unpublished—

Glixon, Beth. "Recitative in Seventeenth Century Venetian Opera: Its Dramatic Function and Musical Language." Ph.D. dissertation, Rutgers University, 1985.
Saunders, Harris Sheridan, Jr. "The Repertoire of a Venetian Opera House (1678-1714): The Teatro Grimini di San

Giovanni Grisostomo." Ph.D. dissertation, Harvard University, 1985.

*　　*　　*

Aurelio Aureli was one of the most successful and prolific librettists during the second half of the seventeenth century. For over thirty years, he was associated almost exclusively with the Venetian opera theater, collaborating with nearly all of Venice's major opera composers including Francesco Cavalli, Pietro Antonio Ziani and his nephew Marco Antonio, Carlo Pallavicino and Antonio Sartorio. Thus, his works provide an unusually clear view of the development of the rich and complex web of literary, dramatic, and musical conventions of which opera is comprised.

Like his colleague Nicolò Minato, Aureli was a lawyer by profession. Yet unlike many of their predecessors, both Minato and Aureli were professional librettists—that is to say, their literary energies were devoted entirely to the writing of librettos. That professional librettists existed is an important indication as to the success and popularity of this young genre in Venice. The demand for opera in Venice was high, and the new generation of librettists such as Aureli, Minato, and Matteo Noris based their careers upon satisfying this demand. Nevertheless, this same popularity created a dilemma, for if Aureli and his contemporaries are to be believed, it was the constant demands for innovation—within the context of familiar norms and conventions—that placed the greatest strain upon these Venetian librettists. In the prefaces of his librettos, for example, Aureli repeatedly tried to justify his literary efforts, apologizing for their lack of adherence to classical tenets, and placing blame upon the increasingly jaded tastes of their audience. While we might wonder to what extent he "protests too much," his writings, as Ellen Rosand has suggested "articulate the aesthetic issues raised by opera as a genre."

Aureli's works are representative of the style of libretto favored in the Venetian theaters in the second half of the seventeenth century. Allowing his imagination free rein, Aureli would graft intrigues and complications onto the familiar characters, settings, and situations of legend and history. In many instances these stories were well-known to much of the audience. The suspense lay in the nature of the individual realization—the means by which the inevitable happy ending was achieved. This invariably involved a series of misunderstandings created by such devices as disguise and mistaken identity (causing gender and or social class confusion), by letters gone astray, or by mislabeled portraits. In his *argomenti,* Aureli would usually begin by separately recounting those aspects of the plot derived from classical sources, and then explain the complications and intrigues that were added for the sake of entertainment. In *L'Antigona delusa d'Alceste,* for example, Aureli describes the story of Alceste and Admeto as the "fantastic invention of the ancient poets": Alceste, who dies in order to restore her husband Admeto to health, is rescued from Hades by Hercules, at her husband's request. Aureli then describes the ways in which he has altered and added to the story for the sake of the entertainment. In this instance, Aureli focuses on the question of fidelity in both a spouse and a brother. Though mourning his self-sacrificing wife, Admeto is attracted to Antigona whom he loved "by fame" prior to his marriage to Alceste, and whom he had been prevented from marrying due to the dishonest plotting of his brother. The plot is propelled by such conventional devices as mistaken identity in which social classes are scrambled (Antigona disguises herself as a shepherdess), wrongly attributed portraits (which cause one to fall in or out of love with the wrong person) and a decidedly non-classical variety of stage settings (castles and forests, in addition to the classical Hades.) In the inevitable happy ending, all of the couples are properly realigned with one another without having committed any significant moral transgressions.

Aureli may well have been concerned about the difficulties of satisfying his audience's increasing demands for novelty; nevertheless, he did not allow his imagination to be stifled either by undue loyalty to his sources or by moral qualms. Indeed, in the 1670s and early 1680s, Aureli's librettos—and those written by many of his contemporaries—show a decided tendency towards the anti-heroic. As Ellen Rosand has shown, Aureli's *Orfeo ed Euridice* distorts the classical legend, reducing the mythically heroic Orfeo to a somewhat mundane jealous husband. Aureli's later Venetian works also show a distinct taste for the erotic. In *L'Antigona delusa d'Alceste* the question of adultery was raised but answered with a firm negative; yet *Alessandro Magno in Sidone,* written nearly twenty years later, begins with the act of adultery in progress. The young, ineffectual Eumene is discovered by his wife in bed with the "interesting, lascivious, beautiful, and intelligent Taide." While virtue is eventually rewarded and vice punished or forgiven, it is not without considerable attention focused on weak and ineffectual men, powerful and dangerous women, and the pleasure and consequences of illicit acts.

This tendency towards anti-heroism, the resulting mixture of comic and serious, and a greater emphasis on aria and singers—at the expense of what some critics called "decorum"—was undoubtedly part of what motivated the opera reformers at the end of the century. Indeed, with their implausible complications, untraditional portrayal of heroes and heroines, overly-clever servants, and not infrequent use of eroticism, Aureli's librettos likely epitomized the very features to which the reformers objected so virulently. Nevertheless, it is precisely these qualities that so engaged and influenced audiences in both Venice and elsewhere. As cultural historian Jose Maravall has written, it is "the external features of baroque art: the elaborate, the exaggerated, the spectacular, the irrational, and lack of restraint are all part of the means by which the audiences were enticed and ultimately controlled." With their emphasis on visual and aural spectacle, suspense, and exaggeration, preoccupation with disguise and gender confusion, the operas of Aureli and his contemporaries were well in keeping with the baroque aesthetic.

—Wendy Heller

B

BACCALONI, Salvatore.

Bass. Born 14 April 1900, in Rome. Died 31 December 1969, in New York. Attended Sistine Chapel Choir School, then studied with Giuseppe Kaschmann from 1921. Professional debut as Bartolo in *Il barbiere di Siviglia* in Rome, Adriano, 1922; sang at Teatro alla Scala, 1926-40, specializing in buffo roles; debut at Covent Garden as Timur in *Turandot*, 1928; United States debut in Chicago as Melitone in *La forza del destino*, 1930; debut at San Francisco as Leporello, 1938; debut at Metropolitan Opera as Bartolo, 1940, and he appeared in almost 300 performances there until 1962; roles include Don Pasquale, Dulcamara, Varlaam, Gianni Schicchi, Osmin, and Falstaff.

Publications

About BACCALONI: books–

Celletti, R. *Le grandi voci*. Rome, 1964.

*   *   *

Salvatore Baccaloni reigned from the 1920s to the 1950s as one of the twentieth century's leading comic basses. He made his debut in Rome in 1920, in the role of Bartolo in Rossini's *Il barbiere di Siviglia*, a role to which he often returned. During the 1920s he sang mostly in Italy, building a reputation that soon brought him requests to sing in many countries. The following decade was the most hectic of his long career. Baccaloni travelled widely, making many appearances at the Teatro Colón in Buenos Aires as well as in several theaters in North America and in Europe. He sang at Covent Garden from 1928; from 1936 to 1939 he sang at Glyndebourne. The last two decades of Baccaloni's career were a little more sedentary. From 1940 until the end of his singing career in the early 1960s he sang at the Metropolitan Opera in New York as a regular member of the company.

Baccaloni's repertory, like that of his successors, Italian comic basses Rolando Panerai and Sesto Bruscantini, was limited almost exclusively to opera in Italian. (All three of these singers were more limited in dramatic, linguistic, and musical range than the German bass Walter Berry; which is not to say that they did not rival or even excell Berry in some parts of their chosen repertory.) Baccaloni specialized in Mozart's buffo roles as well as in those of Rossini and Donizetti; perhaps his greatest role was that of the title role in Donizetti's *Don Pasquale*. Among his other roles were Geronimo in Cimarosa's *Il matrimonio segreto*, the title role in Puccini's *Gianni Schicchi*, and Uberto in Pergolesi's *La serva padrona*.

Conrad L. Osborne's discussion (in *High Fidelity*) of Baccaloni's portrayal of Leporello in the recording of Mozart's *Don Giovanni* made by Fritz Busch at Glyndebourne in 1936 points to the strengths and weaknesses of Baccaloni as a buffo artist: "He had a fluent, fruity light bass of true singing properties, and is up to a piece of serious work here, quite different from all those later Met evenings of slithering pitch and corn-pone antics (*polenta*, I guess it'd be, and lots of it) . . . . this ranks with the best of the Leporellos." The recording shows Baccaloni to have been a fine musician and singer who conveyed emotions vividly. He was capable of a wide range of vocal colors and used this variety with great dramatic effectiveness. Late in his career, in the 1950s, Baccaloni's vocal powers declined. Osborne's criticism refers to the comic exaggeration that Baccaloni increasingly depended on at the Metropolitan as his voice grew weaker. Yet even then his commanding stage presence did not desert him; a report in *Opera* about a performance of Mozart's *Entführung* at the Teatro alla Scala in 1952 (with Callas as Constanze) praised Baccaloni's Osmin. The fifty-two year old bass, "despite having very little voice left, showed that he is still a master of the stage."

—John A. Rice

———————

BACQUIER, Gabriel.

Baritone. Born 17 May 1924 in Béziers. Studied at Paris Conservatory, where he gained three *premiers prix*; debut in Landowski's *Le Fou* in Nice, 1950; with Théatre de la Monnaie in Brussels, 1953-56; Opéra-Comique in Paris, 1956-58; joined Paris Opéra as Germont, 1958; at Covent Garden as Almaviva, Riccardo in Bellini's *I puritani*, and Scarpia, 1964; United States debut in Chicago as high priest in *Samson et Dalila*, 1962; Metropolitan Opera debut in same role, 1964, and has sung over 115 performances since, including Scarpia, Don Pasquale, Iago, Lescaut, Leporello, Bartolo; created role of Abdul in *Last Savage*; was made a Chevalier of the Légion d'Honneur in 1975.

Publications

About BACQUIER: articles–

Segalini, S. "Gabriel Bacquier." *Opéra* (June 1982).
Erikson, F. "Gabriel Bacquier, Portrait," *Avant-scène opéra* December (1985).

*   *   *

During an era when the official critical lobby insisted that good French singing, and French singers typical of the best of the old school, were things of the past, Gabriel Bacquier was one of a not-inconsiderable group of French singers who gave the lie to this received opinion. Because French opera in general had gone out of fashion in the standard repertory, with even *Faust* by the 1960s becoming something of a rarity, the demand for French singers at an international level was thin. Like Crespin, Bacquier made his reputation, singing eventually all over the world, often in non-French roles: Don Giovanni, Leporello, Scarpia, Malatesta, Don Pasquale, Dulcamara and the Count in *Le nozze di Figaro.* Though eventually his interpretation of the four villains in *Les Contes d'Hoffmann,* his Golaud in *Pelléas et Mélisande* and Sancho in *Don Quichotte* became the cornerstones of his repertory, one cannot help feeling that in the atmosphere of a later era with a more adventurous spirit both in the programming of opera houses and the schedules of recording studios, his reputation, had he been able to concentrate more on the French repertoire, would have been even greater.

Bacquier's stage presence was not flamboyant; he was an actor of subtlety and restraint. His Scarpia was not a bully but a refined sadist, all the more troublesome for being so gentlemanly. In *Don Giovanni* his assurance had none of the later fashionable groping lechery, but was that of a seducer who had always had his way through a belief in his rights, rather than a love of the chase.

Bacquier's voice was smooth, not without a dryish quality which aided his diction; like Bernac and Souzay before him he excelled at fining down his tone when performing *mélodies*—one of his most languorous recorded performances is of Maurice Yvain's *Porquerolles.* He was a singing-actor in the best sense of that term, but he never sacrificed the beauty of tone or line to a point of drama, and he always maintained his fine diction. His devotion to the French and Italian repertory seems never to have swerved and he added no roles from German operas, and few modern works, although he created roles in Menotti's *The Last Savage,* Rivière's *Pour un Don Quichotte* (at the Piccola Scala, 1962) and in Daniel Lesur's *Andrea del Sarto* at Marseilles in 1969. "Rarely has a singer shown such complete mastery, both as vocalist and as an actor," wrote Tony Mayer in *Opera.* "As the action unfolds itself, so does Bacquier's involvement grow and the death scene was memorable."

In the early 1960s Bacquier sang with Joan Sutherland, as Germont in *La traviata;* he made his Covent Garden debut opposite Sutherland's Elvira in *I puritani* in 1964 and subsequently recorded *Don Giovanni, Les Huguenots, Lakmé* and *Les Contes d'Hoffmann* with Sutherland and Bonynge. Although all these dramatic and tragic roles were successes for Bacquier, it was perhaps as a comic performer that he excelled, in the operas by Donizetti mentioned and in Offenbach's *La Perichole* and *La vie parisienne* and in the role of Melitone in *La forza del destino,* which he recorded with Levine. His Iago, Falstaff, Leporello and Don Alfonso in *Così fan tutte* were all recorded under Solti and the Count in *Le nozze di Figaro* with Klemperer; even the comparatively small role of the Comte des Grieux in Massenet's *Manon* in the Rudel-Sills-Gedda recording is immediately impressive, his ironic conversation with Manon about the fleeting charm of young love drawing a full picture of the manipulative father. Unlike more flamboyant singers with a similar repertory, Bacquier did not achieve star status of the solo-record-album kind; instead he became the most reliable and elegant of all baritones of his time.

—Patrick O'Connor

BAHR-MILDENBURG, Anna.

Soprano. Born 29 November 1872, in Vienna. Died 27 January 1947, in Vienna. Married author Hermann Bahr, 1909.

Studied with Rosa Papier and with Ress. Debut as Brünnhilde in *Die Walküre* conducted by Mahler in Hamburg, 1895, and began a relation with Mahler; went with Mahler to Vienna, 1898-1916; Kundry at Bayreuth, 1897-1914; roles also include Donna Anna, Fidelio, Norma, and Strauss's Klytemnestra.

Publications

By BAHR-MILDENBURG: books–

With H. Bahr. *Bayreuth und das Wagner-Theater.* Leipzig, 1910; English translation, 1912.
Erinnerungen. Vienna, 1921.
Tristan und Isolde: Darstellung des Werkes aus dem Geiste der Dichtung und Musik. Leipzig, 1936.

About BAHR-MILDENBURG: books–

Stefan, P. *Anna Bahr-Mildenburg.* Vienna, 1922.

*   *   *

In operatic history the name of Anna Mildenburg is indissolubly linked with Gustav Mahler. Her vocal talent seems to have developed late and she was already nineteen when she commenced study with the influential Rosa Papier-Paumgartner. Four years later Mildenburg went with her teacher to audition for Pollini, the dictatorial director of the Hamburg Opera. The young artist sang arias from *Oberon, Don Giovanni,* and *Die Zauberflöte* and rounded off a bravura

Anna Bahr-Mildenburg as Kundry in *Parsifal*

performance with Ortrud's curse from *Lohengrin* and Brünn-hilde's cry. Pollini, a prodigious talent spotter, gave her an immediate engagement and she was asked to make her debut in that most demanding of roles, Brünnhilde in *Die Walküre.*

During rehearsals Mildenburg first met Mahler, who took over her training and the direction of her career. Her debut was a triumph, although, interestingly enough, one critic felt that her voice was overly lyrical! Nonetheless, it was as an outstanding dramatic soprano that Mildenburg's career was to develop; while still in her mid-twenties she sang in major Wagnerian roles as well as Rezia in *Oberon,* Donna Anna in *Don Giovanni,* Norma, and Leonore in *Fidelio.* Contemporary critics particularly praised her dramatic gifts and there is no doubt that Mahler was responsible for developing these.

The artistic partnership between Mildenburg and Mahler was matched by a passionate love affair during their Hamburg years, but this had certainly ended when Mildenburg sang in Vienna for the first time in 1898. Mahler was by then Director of the Vienna Hofoper, but this was not the reason for her engagement. Indeed, Mildenburg might not have accepted the contract had not Rosa Papier intervened to advise the erstwhile lovers as to the basis for renewing their professional collaboration. Mildenburg was a regular member of the Vienna Hofoper for nearly twenty years until 1917, making subsequent guest appearances there until 1921, but as a member of the peerless Mahler ensemble at the Opera. Indeed, by the time Mahler left the Opera in 1907 her voice was held by some to be in decline—possibly the result of early assumptions of the heaviest dramatic roles.

Curiously, Mildenburg sang only in *Lohengrin* and *Parsifal* at Bayreuth and not in the *Ring* (the role of Brünnhilde in the years of her prime was almost totally monopolized by the Swede, Ellen Gulbranson). She sang Isolde and Elisabeth in *Tannhäuser* at Covent Garden in 1906 and four years later she appeared in the first London performance of *Elektra.* On her London debut as Isolde the *Times* reviewer commented on her remarkably powerful voice and on its quality, but was critical of the singing in softer passages. This is an interesting contrast with the critique of her Hamburg debut and may indeed reinforce the notion that she was already past her best. That her histrionic abilities remained supreme is attested by the comment in the same newspaper on her Klytemnestra in *Elektra*—"so vivid a picture of decadence that while she was on the stage it was possible to forget all about the music".

The only known recording of Mildenburg was made in 1905. It is the recitative of Rezia's "Ocean" aria from *Oberon,* which she had sung at her audition in Hamburg. On this one record Mildenburg shows a powerful and penetrating voice with a superb attack. The singing is effortless and free, the overall impression that of a superb dramatic artist who never held herself back. Giving so freely of her talents probably ensured some vocal decline, but the sheer quality of voice explains the excitement of both Pollini and Mahler.

—Stanley Henig

BAILEY, Norman.

Baritone. Born 21 March 1933, in Birmingham, England. Married Doreen Simpson in 1957 (divorced 1983; two sons, one daughter); married the singer Kristine Ciesinski in 1985. Studied at Rhodes University in South Africa and at Vienna Music Academy with Adolf Vogel, Josef Witt, and Julius

Patzek; professional debut in Rossini's *La cambiale di matrimonio,* Vienna Chamber Opera, 1959; sang in Linz (1960-63), Wuppertal (1963-64), Dusseldorf (1964-67), and Sadler's Wells (1967-71), especially in Wagner roles; Teatro alla Scala debut as Dallapiccola's *Job,* 1967; debut in New York as Hans Sachs for New York City Opera (1975) and Metropolitan Opera (1976); made CBE in 1977.

Publications

About BAILEY: articles–

Forbes, E. "Norman Bailey." *Opera* (September 1973): 774.

*   *   *

During 1973 the English baritone Norman Bailey sang no fewer than eight different major roles from the Wagnerian repertory. This extraordinary achievement confirms his affinity with Wagner, but it would be misleading and grossly unfair to label him a specialist, since his career places him as a leading exponent of a wide range of roles and styles.

Norman Bailey was born in Birmingham, but studied at Rhodes University, South Africa after his family emigrated to that country. Having diverted his studies from theology to music, he spent a further two years at the Vienna Academy of Music, and this enabled him to launch his career in Austria. His professional debut was as Tobias Mill in the Vienna Chamber Opera's 1959 production of Rossini's *La cambiale di matrimonio,* and a year later he became a member of the company at the Landestheater, Linz. There he performed many contrasted roles ranging through the German and Italian repertories. Further experience in Germany, mainly at Wuppertal and with the Deutsche Oper am Rhein in Düsseldorf, preceded his membership of the Sadlers Wells (now English National) Opera in London, from 1967 until 1971.

When he took the part of Hans Sachs in the celebrated 1968 performances of *Die Meistersinger* under Reginald Goodall, he immediately impressed as a Wagnerian singer of major importance. Soon he was able to confirm the fact through his appearances at Covent Garden and Bayreuth, at Hamburg, Brussels and Munich.

When the English *Ring* was launched at the Coliseum in January 1970, Bailey's Wotan proved the ideal complement to Rita Hunter's Brünnhilde and Alberto Remedios's Siegfried. The magisterial command he brought to the role was impressive indeed, while at Bayreuth and other centers he extended his reputation in Wagner with successful portrayals of Günther and Amfortas.

Inevitably these years brought a concentration of roles, Bailey tending to reserve himself for the *Heldenbariton* rather than the higher Italianate style, of which also he had already shown himself an adept interpreter. But in 1972 he responded positively to a request from English National Opera to sing the Count di Luna in the new production of Verdi's *Il trovatore;* and, soon after, he took on the role of Ford in the same composer's *Falstaff* for BBC television. The result was that his career gained in flexibility, and his voice confirmed its ability to cope with a high *tessitura,* even if the singer admitted that he was under strain unless he felt in perfect health. Other notable successes, beyond Wagner, have included Jochanaan (*Salome*) and Pizarro (*Fidelio*), while some critics regard his performance as Kutuzov in the English National Opera's production of Prokofiev's *War and Peace* as the most spectacular of all his achievements. Certainly it was typical of the commanding stature and the depth of characterization with which Bailey brings roles to life. This rare ability, which he shares with but a handful of singers, was found to the full in this remarkable portrayal of Balstrode in Britten's *Peter Grimes* at Covent Garden, which was played alongside Jon Vickers's intense realization of the title role.

Only careful preparation and complete dedication can bring about the standards for which Norman Bailey is known. His vocal timbre, firm but not rich, does not always help to fill large halls, but in terms of clarity and musical intelligence few singers have been able to match him, while he has consistently displayed his mastery of dramatic understanding. Above all, his career reflects his commitment to the medium of opera itself, for he continues to explore new roles at the same time as confirming his stature in those with which he has become firmly identified.

—Terry Barfoot

BAKER, Janet (Abbott).

Mezzo-soprano. Born 21 August 1933, in Hatfield, Yorkshire. Married James Keith Shelley in 1957. Studied with Helene Isepp in 1953 and later with Meriel St Clair, and at Salzburg Mozarteum; won second prize in the Kathleen Ferrier Awards, 1956; opera debut as Roza in Smetana's *The Secret,* Oxford University Club, 1956; Eduige in Handel Opera Society's *Rodelinda* (1959), also Ariodante (1964) and Orlando (1966); debut with English opera group as Purcell's Dido at Aldeburgh, 1962; Covent Garden debut as Hermia in *Midsummer Night's Dream,* 1966; Scottish Opera debut as Dorabella, 1967; other roles include Pippo in *La gazza ladra,* Gluck's Orfeo (1958), Strauss's Octavian; Britten composed the part of Kate Julian in the 1971 television opera *Owen Wingrave* for her; Hamburg Shakespeare prize, 1971; honorary degrees from universities of London, Birmingham, and Oxford; made Commander of the Order of the British Empire in 1970 and Dame Commander in 1976.

Publications

By BAKER: books–

Full Circle: An Autobiographical Journal. London and New York, 1982.

About BAKER: books–

Blyth, A. *Janet Baker.* London and New York, 1973.
Steane, J.B. *The Grand Tradition.* London, 1974.
Ewen, D. *Musicians since 1900.* New York, 1978.

articles–

Wadsworth, S. "Sense and Sensibility." *Opera News* July (1977): 8.
Hirschman, P. "Janet Baker: The Operatic Roles." *Opera* February (1983): 146.

* * *

The career of the English mezzo-soprano Janet Baker has been equally remarkable in its three different aspects: the opera house, the Lieder recital and the concert hall. Her distinctive and beautiful voice has thus proved itself a flexible instrument, and her sure technique and warm personality have together made her the singer the British musical public has taken most closely to its heart since the days of Kathleen Ferrier.

In 1956 Janet Baker won second prize in the Kathleen Ferrier Competition; that same year she sang in the chorus at Glyndebourne and made her solo opera debut as Roza in Smetana's *The Secret* for the Oxford University Opera Club. Her operatic work rapidly developed, though at all times she has been careful in her selection of roles. She sang her first Orpheus (Gluck) in 1958, following it the next year with Eduige in the Handel Opera Society's production of *Rodelinda.* This association with pre-classical opera she maintained throughout her career, and her understanding of style and her commitment to the expressive nature of such works produced a series of memorable performances.

Though less frequently linked with Monteverdi, Baker has shown a clear sense of this style also: in Ottavio's solos in *L'incoronazione di Poppea,* such as the Act I lament and, in Act III, "Addio Roma," where the natural grandeur of her voice was enhanced by the most subtle colorings. Such things were even more true of her Purcell, Gluck and Handel performances. Her emotional commitment to Purcell's Dido, for instance, was matched by that to Gluck's Orpheus.

In 1962 Baker made her debut with the English Opera Group at Aldeburgh, where the following year she sang Polly in Benjamin Britten's realisation of *The Beggar's Opera.* She has written of the remarkable intensity created in the Aldeburgh environment, dominated by Britten and Peter Pears, and of the special influence it had on both her career and her musical personality: ". . . the debt I owe those two wonderful men is incalculable. Most performers who went through the experience of Aldeburgh must have known this feeling of being burned at the sacred fire. We survived the ordeal or we did not; but if we did, we were always changed, and I feel I was changed for the better. Ben and Peter gave us standards which turned us from national to international performers, and the alteration in status which British performers are now accorded, the respect we are unreservedly given all over the world, is due in large measure to them." (*Full Circle,* 1982, pp. 245-6)

Baker's special feeling for Britten's music was particularly evident in her performances in *The Rape of Lucretia;* and the composer recognised her achievement in creative terms, for in 1971 he wrote the part of Kate Julian for her in his television opera *Owen Wingrave.* Here her very positive sense of characterization was shown in a new way, for her Kate was a personality at once cold and unpleasant, whose outlook provided the necessary expression to emphasize Owen's situation as the outsider in an unsympathetic society.

Baker's 1967 Scottish Opera Dorabella (*Così fan tutte*) preceded her magnificent portrayal of Berlioz's Dido (*Les Troyens*) with the same company. This success she repeated at Covent Garden, and her feeling for the emotion and the fundamental nature of the tragic Queen enabled her to rise to one of the heights of her career. During these years her work expanded further: the double role of Diana-Jupiter in Cavalli's *La Calisto,* Penelope in Monteverdi's *Il ritorno d'Ulisse in patria,* Vitellia in Mozart's *La clemenza di Tito.*

Through the 1970s, Janet Baker maintained close links with three companies: Glyndebourne, Covent Garden and English National Opera. For the latter her Charlotte in Massenet's *Werther* was especially moving, and confirmed her strength in the French repertory; but her appearance as Donizetti's Mary Stuart perhaps reached even greater heights.

Janet Baker in the title role of Handel's *Julius Caesar,* English National Opera, London, 1979

Baker first sang Mary Stuart at the Coliseum in 1973, and nearly ten years later she did so again in a performance which has been preserved in a memorable recording. 1981-2 was in fact the season she chose to retire from the opera house, giving farewell performances also with Covent Garden, in Gluck's *Alceste,* and at Glyndebourne in Gluck's *Orfeo.* That season she chose to preserve her experiences in the form of a diary under the title *Full Circle,* a reference to the fact that her operatic career ended at Glyndebourne, the place where it had begun. In the text her thoughts return to the theme of the pressures opera places on the singer, to the demands of performing at the highest level; and certainly the expressive commitment for which she was noted must have been demanding in the extreme.

Janet Baker has in recent years, therefore, concentrated on the concert hall, but her work in the theatre has made its indelible mark on operatic life. Her achievements have been wide-ranging, through three hundred years of music, through many varying styles, through tragic and comic roles. In all these fields she was outstanding: Janet Baker must be ranked as one of the finest artists of recent times.

—Terry Barfoot

BALFE, Michael William.

Composer. Born 15 May 1808, in Dublin. Died 20 October 1870, in Rowney Abbey, Hertfordshire. Married: the Hungarian singer Lina Roser (1808-88); one daughter, Victoire, also a singer. Violinist in his youth; in London, 1823, and a member of the Drury Lane Theatre orchestra; in Rome, 1825, where he lived with his patron Count Mazzara and studied with Paer; in Milan, he studied counterpoint with Federici and singing with Filippo Galli; first dramatic work, the ballet *La Pérouse* (1826); met Rossini in Paris, sang Figaro in *Le Barbier de Séville* (1827); continued singing in Italy in Palermo and Milan, and sang with Malibran at La Scala; in London 1833; manager of the Lyceum Theatre, 1841-42; composed English operas 1835-41, as well as one Italian opera for the London stage (*Falstaff,* 19 July 1838); continued his career as both singer and opera composer in Paris, London, Berlin, St. Petersburg, and Trieste between 1841 and 1864. Balfe's English opera *The Bohemian Girl* (1843) was translated into German, Italian, and French, and continued throughout his life to be an international success.

Operas

Atala, after Chateaubriand, Paris, 1827 [lost].
I rivali di se stessi, A. Alcozor (after Le Brun), Palermo, 1829.
Un avvertimento ai gelosi, G. Foppa, Pavia, 1830.
Hamlet, after Shakespeare, 1832 [unfinished; lost].
Elfrida, intended for Paris, 1832 [unfinished; lost].
Enrico IV al passo della Marna, Milan, Teatro alla Scala, 19 February 1833.
The Siege of Rochelle, E. Fitzball (after Mme de Genlis), London, Drury Lane Theatre, 29 October 1835.
The Maid of Artois, A. Bunn, London, Drury Lane Theatre, 27 May 1836.
Catherine Grey, G. Linley, London, Drury Lane Theatre, 27 May 1837.
Joan of Arc, E. Fitzball, London, Drury Lane Theatre, 30 November 1837.

Diadeste, or The Veiled Lady, E. Fitzball, London, Drury Lane Theatre, 17 May 1838.
Falstaff (in Italian), S. Maggione, London, Her Majesty's Theatre, 19 July 1838.
Keolanthe, or The Unearthly Bride, E. Fitzball, London, Lyceum Theatre, 9 March 1841.
Le puits d'amour, Eugène Scribe and J.H. Vernoy de Saint-Georges, Paris, Opéra-Comique, 20 April 1843 (performed in English as *Geraldine, or The Lover's Well,* translated by G.A. à Beckett, London, Princess's Theatre, 14 August 1843).
The Bohemian Girl, A. Bunn (after J.H. Vernoy de Saint-Georges), London, Drury Lane Theatre, 27 November, 1843 (performed in Italian as *La zingara,* London, Her Majesty's Theatre, 6 February 1858).
Les quatre fils Aymon. Eugène Scribe and J.H. Vernoy de Saint-Georges, Paris, Opéra-Comique, 29 July 1844 (performed in English as *The Castle of Aymon, or The Four Brothers,* Leuwen and Brunswick, London, Princess's Theatre, 20 November 1844).
The Daughter of St. Mark, A. Bunn (after J.H. Vernoy de Saint-Georges), London, Drury Lane Theatre, 27 November 1844.
The Enchantress, A. Bunn (after J.H. Vernoy de Saint-Georges), London, Drury Lane Theatre, 14 May 1845.
L'étoile de Séville, H. Lucas (after Lope de Vega), Paris, Opéra, 17 December 1845.
The Bondman, A. Bunn (after Dumas), London, Drury Lane Theatre, 11 December 1846.
The Maid of Honour, E. Fitzball, London, Drury Lane Theatre, 20 December 1847.
[untitled work], after Hugo, *Le roi s'amuse,* 1848 [unfinished].
The Sicilian Bride, A. Bunn (after J.H. Vernoy de Saint-Georges), London, Drury Lane Theatre, 6 March 1852.
The Devil's In It, A. Bunn (after Eugène Scribe), London, Surrey Theatre, 26 July 1852.
Pittore e duca, F.M. Piave, Trieste, 21 November 1854 (performed in English as *Moro, or The Painter of Antwerp,* W.A. Barrett, London, Her Majesty's Theatre, 28 January 1882).
The Rose of Castille, A. Harris and E. Falconer (after D'Ennery and Claireville) London, Lyceum, 29 October 1857.
Satanella, or The Power of Love, A. Harris and E. Falconer (after Le Sage), London, Covent Garden Theatre, 20 December, 1858.
Bianca, or The Bravo's Bride, P. Simpson (after M.G. Lewis), London, Covent Garden Theatre, 6 December 1860.
The Puritan's Daughter, J.V. Bridgeman, London, Covent Garden, 30 November 1861.
Blanche de Nevers, J. Brougham (after Le Bossu), London, Covent Garden, 21 November 1862.
The Armourer of Nantes, J.V. Bridgeman, London, Covent Garden, 12 February 1863.
The Sleeping Queen, Mazeppa, H.B. Farnie, London, Gallery of Illustration, 31 August 1864.
The Knight of the Leopard, A. Matthison (after Scott, *The Talisman*), unfinished, arranged by Costa as *Il talismano,* G. Zaffira, London, Drury Lane Theatre, 11 June 1874.

Other works: Vocal works, including cantatas and songs, and chamber music.

Publications

By BALFE: books–

Indispensable Studies for a Bass Voice. London, 1851.
Indispensable Studies for a Soprano Voice. London, 1851.
A New Universal Method of Singing. London, 1857.

About BALFE: books–

Bunn, A. *The Stage.* London, 1840.
Kenney, C.L. *Memoir of Michael William Balfe.* London, 1875; 1978.
Barrett, W.A. *Balfe: his Life and Work.* London, 1882.
White, E.W. *The Rise of English Opera.* London, 1951.

articles–

Temperley, Nicholas. "The English Romantic Opera." *Victorian Studies* 9 (1966): 293.
Carr, B. "The First All-sung English 19th century Opera." *Musical Times* 115 (1974): 125.

* * *

England's relationship with opera, from its beginnings through the early twentieth century, involved both acceptance and envy of the continental product and fitful attempts at the development of an indigenous approach to the vocal art form. Dr Samuel Johnson had characterized Italian opera, as exemplified by Handel and Piccini, as "an exotick and irrational entertainment." The success of ballad operas, drawing for their music on popular tunes of the street, drove Handel into oratorio and English opera composition into a hybrid form which reflected middle-class rather the "elite" taste, more comparable, despite the sophisticated contributions of Thomas Arne and Stefano Storace, to the mid-twentieth century's Broadway and West End musicals than to the Italian, German, and French models at hand.

The success of Carl Maria von Weber's *Oberon,* to a preposterous English libretto, and the reform of the theatre patents by Parliament in 1843 combined to renew the demand for a musical drama which would reflect both the sophistication of continental opera and the ingenuous appeal of the ballad opera. Of those who advanced to the fore in this endeavor, none was as particularly gifted for the task as Balfe. Born in Ireland, he had trained as a violinist, playing in the Drury Lane Theatre orchestra before traveling to Italy to begin a short but successful career as principal baritone, singing the works of Mozart, Rossini, and Bellini, in the major Italian opera houses.

He volunteered to compose a short opera during an engagement in Naples when a chorus strike nullified the scheduled large-scale works. In his third opera, *Enrico Quarto,* he became the only well-known composer to create a major role in his own opera, a feat he repeated in England in *Geraldine, or the Lover's Well* (he later also sang in his own *The Siege of Rochelle* and *Catherine Grey,* but was not part of the original cast).

Others besides Balfe had musical credentials with which to challenge him for English opera supremacy, but they lacked his ability to merge the best in continental ensemble music with arias that echoed the native ballad opera tradition. Edward Loder proved too sophisticated, though his *The Night Dancers* (based on the plot of Adam's ballet, *Giselle*) and *Raymond and Agnes* are probably, as a whole, musically superior to any of Balfe's operas. But Loder also lacked the talent for prolific output which Balfe possessed to a Rossinian degree; John Barnett and George MacFarren, other talented contemporaries, also suffered this defect.

Balfe himself contributed the first major English opera without spoken dialogue, *Catherine Grey.* The success of *The Bohemian Girl* eight years later confirmed his place as the foremost composer of English opera, which, to his death, in spite of challenges by Julius Benedict and William Vincent Wallace, he retained.

Balfe's reputation today rests almost solely on *The Bohemian Girl,* the only one of his operas that continues, though with increasing infrequency, to be given on provincial stages. What popularity it has comes from the ballad arias, Arline's "I dreamt I dwelt in marble halls," Thaddeus' "When other lips," and Count Arnheim's "The heart bow'd down." Ballad arias celebrated in his own time, such as "With rapture dwelling" and "The light of other days," introduced by Maria Malibran in *The Maid of Artois,* and "When I beheld the anchor weigh'd" from *The Siege of Rochelle* have been totally forgotten, as have his most ambitious operas, *The Daughter of St. Mark, The Talisman,* and *Satanella.*

Balfe's choice of libretti, especially those by Alfred Bunn and Edward Fitzball, reflect a conscious choice to respond to the socio-economic preconceptions of his audience. At a time when Meyerbeer was setting his own highly successful Parisian operas to libretti reflecting sophisticated religious and political themes, Verdi was beginning to investigate the influence of such great themes on individuals caught in their forces, and even the musically conservative Lortzing was celebrating labor unrest in his *Regina,* Balfe was setting simplistic class-conscious fairy tales which the British public sought out as an antidote to reality.

It appears to have become difficult if not impossible for most contemporary listeners to judge the music of a simple melodist such as Balfe (or Auber, Marschner, the Ricci brothers, etc.) on its own merits, laying aside both the sophistication of hindsight and a sense of frustration that he did not use his considerable gifts in more challenging ways. If he did not, after all, establish an ongoing tradition of English opera (that would await the coming of Benjamin Britten a century later), his is the most representative response to one chapter in the quest for a national approach to an international art form, fascinating on a sociological level and naively charming musically.

—William J. Collins

THE BALLAD OF BABY DOE.

Composer: Douglas Moore.

Librettist: J. Latouche.

First Performance: Central City, Colorado, 7 July 1958.

Roles: Baby Doe (soprano); Augusta (mezzo-soprano); Horace Tabor (bass-baritone); William Jennings Bryan (bass); Mama McCourt (contralto); Sam (tenor); Bushy (tenor); Barney (bass); Jacob (bass); Sarah (soprano); Mary (soprano); Emily (contralto); Effie (contralto); McCourt Family (soprano, alto, tenor, bass); Four Washington Dandies (tenors, basses); many bit parts which may be doubled or tripled; chorus (SATB).

* * *

The story of *The Ballad of Baby Doe* has its roots in the American West of a century ago, and its chief characters are fashioned from actual historical figures. Horace Tabor, a rich owner of silver mines in Colorado, becomes infatuated with the much younger Elizabeth "Baby" Doe (Mrs. Harvey Doe). Horace's wife Augusta discovers her husband's secret liaison and threatens to drive her rival from town. She fails, and the affection between Horace and Baby Doe grows stronger. After both are divorced, their wedding is celebrated in Washington, D.C., with the President of the United States in attendance. Yet reputable folk continue to snub them, and Horace starts to encounter financial reverses. His career ends in ruins despite an attempt to recoup by supporting new political allies. After his death Baby Doe's unshakable devotion leads her to live out her lonely days near one of his abandoned mines.

The very title of *The Ballad of Baby Doe* hints at the simplicity and the reliance on convention that mark the work both in its tone and in the dramatic content. Horace, Augusta, and Baby Doe exemplify an archetypal love-triangle in the plainest way—a hero caught between women who represent respectively the power of love and the demands of social obligations. The characters themselves are almost reducible to humors. Horace is all ardor and ambition, Baby Doe radiant sweetness, and Augusta possessiveness and embitterment.

These characters, creatures more of feeling than of thought, exist at some remove from the political issues that are introduced midway in the opera, including the question of whether gold or silver should be the proper monetary standard for American currency. Crowd scenes set about dealing with this question through slogans rather than argument; the operatic equivalent of poster art conveys the politics of the day. Thus the level of stylization here matches the work's formulaic approach to characterization.

Douglas Moore's music skillfully delineates the nature of each character. The vocal parts for the two leading women especially stand in sharp relief. Baby Doe's placid charm displays itself in easy songfulness and flurries of coloratura writing, while Augusta's resentment finds expression in more jagged melodies and unexpected rhythms. In addition, Moore had the gift of creating a role that makes the singer appear to best advantage. For instance, Baby Doe has as her most prominent numbers three well-placed arias—a "willow song" in the second scene, a hymn of sorts "to the silver moon" during the first-act finale, and the opera's epilogue, a piece of almost Handelian serenity—and all three are guaranteed applause-getters. The epilogue is a homespun Liebestod, though musically it is akin to the close of Wagner's *Tristan und Isolde* mainly in its choice of key, B major. To set its opening words, "Always through the changing of sun and shadow, time and space," Moore has come upon a melody like the one Arthur Sullivan uses in setting other thoughts on the passing of the years, namely, "Silvered is the raven hair," from Gilbert and Sullivan's *Patience*.

During the nineteenth century, German composers were sometimes advised to strive for "ballad tone" in their works and, *mutatis mutandis,* this is what Moore achieves in *Baby Doe.* His score overflows with pieces in American popular, so-called vernacular, styles from a hundred-or-so years before. Marches and dances (in particular, several notable waltzes), sentimental airs suitable for the front parlor and rousing songs like some of Stephen Foster's comic efforts press in on one another throughout the opera. Even the more operatic numbers, however spiced with dissonance, always avoid the intense complexity of twentieth-century musical modernism; they have lucid tonal harmonies and concise formal shapes.

And when once-heard music reappears in later scenes, its recurrence resembles as much a Broadway musical's reprise of tunes as it does an insistent Wagnerian Leitmotiv.

In a masterful fashion Moore, together with John Latouche, simplified and mingled traditional ingredients in *The Ballad of Baby Doe.* It is a singers' opera that has memorable melodies, elements of spectacle, points of national and historical interest, including musical Americana, and time-honored characters and plot.

—Christopher Hatch

UN BALLO IN MASCHERA [A Masked Ball].

Composer: Giuseppe Verdi.

Librettist: Antonio Somma (after Eugène Scribe, *Gustave III*).

First Performance: Rome, Apollo, 17 February 1859.

Roles: Riccardo (tenor); Renato (baritone); Amelia (soprano); Oscar (soprano); Ulrica (contralto or mezzo-soprano); Samuel (bass); Tom (bass); Judge (tenor); Silvano (baritone or bass).

Publications

articles–

Bollettino dell' Istitute de Studi Verdiani [Parma] 1 (1960) [*Un ballo in maschera* issue].

Levarie, Siegmund. "Key Relationships in Verdi's *Un ballo in maschera.*" *Nineteenth-Century Music* 2 (1978): 143.

Avant-scène opéra March-April (1981) [*Un bal masqué* issue].

Levarie, Siegmund. "A Pitch Cell in Verdi's *Un ballo in maschera.*" *Journal of Musicological Research* 3 (1981): 399.

Parker, Roger, and Matthew Brown. "Motivic and Tonal Interaction in Verdi's *Un ballo in maschera.*" *Journal of the American Musicological Society* 36 (1983): 243.

Ross, Peter. "Amelias Auftrittsarie im *Maskenball.* Verdis Vertonung in dramaturgisch-textlichern Zusammenhang." *Archiv für Musikwissenschaft* 40/no. 2 (1983): 126.

* * *

Due to all sorts of difficulties with censors, Verdi and his librettist for *Un ballo in maschera* twice found it necessary to change the title as well as the names of characters and locales from Scribe's *Gustave III* in order to gain permission for performance. First they changed the title to *La vendetta in domino,* and the setting to seventeenth-century Stettin. Then, again at the censor's demand, the title became *Un ballo in maschera,* and the setting, seventeenth-century Boston. In the process, King Gustavus, the original victim of regicide, becomes Riccardo, variously Earl of Warwicke, or Governor of Boston. Anckarström, the original assassin, becomes Renato, and his wife, Countess Anckarström, becomes Amelia, or even sometimes Adelia. Oscar, a page, remains constant, as do other minor characters; but the two main conspirators appear as Tom and Sam, American negroes, consigned to the

Un ballo in maschera, **frontispiece of Ricordi piano-vocal score, c. 1860**

Boston scenario, which Verdi was forced to adopt for the first Roman production.

After a synoptic overture, which forecasts the dramatic development of the opera by presenting the main dramatic themes, Count Riccardo, who has fallen in love with the wife of his secretary, Renato, holds audience to receive proof of the loyalty and love of his subjects. Among those present, lurking in the background, are Samuel and Tom, negroes who conspire with other dissidents in a plan to murder Riccardo. Also present is Ulrica, a black fortune-teller, who is to be banished from the realm as a witch if Riccardo accepts the recommendation of his ministers. Listening to the light-hearted advice of his page, Oscar, he decides that he will first visit Ulrica in disguise, that very night, before making a final decision.

Dressed as a common fisherman, Riccardo briefly observes Ulrica's black magic before quickly hiding when Renato's wife, Amelia, arrives seeking a magical solution to her problem. As he listens, Riccardo learns that she has come to find a cure for the love she feels for him. For remedy, Ulrica directs her to go at midnight to pick a plant growing under a gibbet just outside town. Riccardo plans to meet her there, but first hears Ulrica's prophecy that he will be murdered by the next person whose hand he shakes. Renato arrives just then, and the two shake hands.

Amelia, heavily disguised, arrives at the gibbet just before midnight, and is startled by the sudden appearance of Riccardo, who soon persuades her to confess that she does love him indeed, which disclosure unleashes a glorious love duet.

Meanwhile the assassins have discovered Riccardo's whereabouts. But before they can actually accost him, Renato, unaware of the budding love affair and still loyal to Riccardo, arrives to warn him of the danger that threatens. He agrees to escort to safety the veiled figure who actually is his wife, while the count escapes to safety. Only later, when he and his disguised wife are accosted by Tom and Sam, does Renato discover her true identity.

Renato, increasingly furious, soon joins the conspiracy against Riccardo. At home the next day, Renato tells his wife she must die. Then, relenting a little, he forces her to draw lots to decide which of the conspirators will actually assassinate Riccardo. Renato wins. Despite a warning to stay away from the ball, Riccardo attends, is inadvertently identified by the page, Oscar, and fatally stabbed by Renato. He dies, forgiving all.

Un ballo in maschera shares several characteristics with four other operas Verdi wrote in the 1850s, *Luisa Miller, Rigoletto, Il trovatore,* and *La traviata.* In the first place, the libretto is dramatically convincing, and the story it tells is interesting and credible. This last named quality stems from the realism which *Un ballo in maschera* shares with the above named, except, possibly, for *Il trovatore.* Musically, it measures up to the new high standards Verdi had achieved in these operas, particularly with regard to melody, tonal adventurousness, and rhythmic vitality. In musical characterization Verdi introduced a new type in the role of Oscar, and in orchestration he found new finesse, variety, and power of expression, anticipating in these the great orchestral mastery of his late works. In short, *Un ballo in maschera,* with its successful premiere in Rome on 17 February 1859, marked a fitting close to a remarkable decade of creative growth for Verdi.

—Franklin Zimmerman

BAMPTON, Rose.

Soprano, mezzo-soprano. Born 28 November 1909, in Lakewood, Ohio, near Cleveland. Married: conductor Wilfrid Pelletier, 1937. Educated at the Curtis Institute; studied with Horatio Connell, Queena Mario, Martha Graham, Elena Gerhardt, and Lotte Lehmann; debut as Siebel in *Faust,* Chautauqua, 1929; minor roles with Philadelphia Opera, 1929-32; Metropolitan Opera debut as Laura, *La gioconda,* 1932; sixteen roles with the Metropolitan Opera, including Aida and Amneris in *Aida,* Donna Anna in *Don Giovanni,* the title role in *Alceste,* and a number of Wagnerian heroines; soprano debut as Leonora in *Il trovatore;* Covent Garden debut as Amneris in *Aida,* 1937; also sang with the New York City Opera; retired 1950. Taught at the Manhattan School, North Carolina School of the Arts, Drake University, the Juilliard School.

Publications:

About BAMPTON: articles–

"Reflected Glory." *Opera News* 48/October (1983): 64.
Freeman, John W. "The Subject is Rose." *Opera News* 53/March (1989): 8.

Rose Bampton's mother was born in America of German descent; her father came from Great Britain. Both were music-lovers, and the mother was an accomplished pianist, but their son, who studied the violin, decided not to pursue music professionally. Though born just outside Cleveland, which had a thriving musical life, Bampton did not study music until after the family had moved to Buffalo, New York. There her first voice teacher, a church organist named Seth Clark, recommended that the girl attend the Curtis Institute in Philadelphia, an all-scholarship institution, and she was accepted there, studying with Horatio Connell and later Queena Mario.

At first her voice was judged to be a coloratura soprano, and by studying the appropriate repertory she acquired technical agility, but she suffered uncertainty as to her rightful vocal range, and Curtis, thinking her too tall for the opera stage, gave her little preparation for opera. During student years she sang solo as a contralto in some concerts with the Philadelphia Orchestra under Stokowski; with him she recorded the "Wood Dove" in Schoenberg's *Gurre-Lieder* for RCA Victor. An appearance as Siebel in *Faust* at Chautauqua in 1929 actually preceded her Curtis studies, and while at Curtis she made a few appearances with the Philadelphia Opera in minor roles, 1929-32.

Invited to audition for the Metropolitan Opera as a result of the *Gurre-Lieder* recording, she sang mezzo-soprano repertory but was diagnosed as a soprano by the conducting staff,

including Wilfrid Pelletier, whom she later married (in 1937). His coaching proved invaluable to her career, as did work in stage deportment with the dancer Martha Graham and the Greek tragedienne Margaret Anglin. She was also coached in the Lieder repertory by Elena Gerhardt during a visit to England and later by Lotte Lehmann in California.

Starting at the Metropolitan as Laura in *La gioconda* on 28 November 1932, she eventually assumed sixteen roles with the company, appearing sixty-eight times at the Opera House and twenty-six times on tour before retiring with the advent of the Rudolf Bing administration in 1950. Her transition from mezzo to soprano was signaled by taking on Aida instead of Amneris, though as late as 1940 she sang both roles in the same season when Bruna Castagna, the scheduled Amneris, was taken ill. At Covent Garden she had sung Amneris to Eva Turner's Aida in 1937. Her other major roles at the Metropolitan included Leonora in *Il trovatore,* Donna Anna in *Don Giovanni,* Gluck's Alceste and four Wagner heroines—Sieglinde, Elisabeth, Elsa and Kundry. She was chosen by Arturo Toscanini for his 1944 National Broadcasting Company Symphony broadcasts of *Fidelio,* later released on records; her other recordings consist mainly of arias.

From these records it is possible to judge Bampton's scrupulous musicianship and thorough stylistic coaching, though not the sheer size of her voice, which amply filled the large Metropolitan. In matters of detail, such as vowel elision and arbitrary breath breaks, where Italian-trained singers are apt to fall back on "tradition" and expediency, Bampton was more likely to adhere to the composer's original. Yet her singing possessed ample feeling and temperament, together with an aptitude for classical restraint and nobility, notably in the *Alceste* arias. Hers was not the heart-on-sleeve artistry that appeals to the gallery, but it benefited from uncommon intelligence, solid musical discipline and adaptability to different musical styles.

Both in her extensive recital and radio work and in the theater, Bampton exemplified the sort of well-trained all-round singer for which America became increasingly known after World War II. Herself a teacher at the Manhattan School, North Carolina School of the Arts, Drake University and finally at the Juilliard School, she has passed on to younger singers her belief in a broad-based knowledge of music and practical experience before the public in a wide variety of repertory.

—John W. Freeman

BÁNK BÁN.

Composer: Ferenc Erkel.

Librettist: Béni Egressy (after József Katona).

First Performance: Pest, National Theater, 9 March 1861.

Roles: Endre II (baritone); Gertrude (mezzo-soprano); Otto (tenor); Count Bank (tenor); Melinda (soprano); Count Petur (baritone); Knight from Biberach (baritone); Tiborc (baritone); Master Solom (baritone); A Knight (tenor); chorus.

Publications

book–

Nagy, I.V., and P. Várnai. *Bánk bán az operaszinpadon.* Budapest, 1958.

articles–

Badacsonyi, George. "Bánk bán—Hungary's National Opera." *Opera* February (1968).

Bónis, F. "Erkel über seine Oper Bánk bán." *Studia musicologica Academiae scientiarum hungaricae* 11 (1969): 69.

* * *

Before considering Erkel's opera it may be as well to look at its source, the play *Bánk bán,* by József Katona. Katona (1791-1830) was born, and died, in the town of Kecskemét, the birthplace, incidentally, of Kodály. He was of the middle class and trained first as a lawyer before becoming an actor. Of several plays only *Bánk bán* (1814), a Shakespearian-type tragedy in five acts, has survived his death, and because of its sharp psychological insight as much as its tightly constructed plot it has achieved classic status. It was entered for a competition but failed on the grounds that it was too "daring" (i.e. subversive) and was not actually staged until 1833.

Like most Hungarians of his generation, Katona was an ardent nationalist, which in effect meant anti-Austrian. Hungarians considered themselves victims of Vienna-based Hapsburg domination, and *Bánk bán* was a barely disguised piece of nationalist propaganda. In common with most subversive writers, Katona chose a historical context in which to proclaim that which might not be openly stated. But the play transcends its propagandist element and becomes as well a searching study of the tragic history of its eponymous hero.

The action is set in historical times, during the reign of Endre II (1205-1235), a period of continuous warfare and great upheaval in Hungary. Count ("Bán"; titles and forenames in Hungarian follow the family name) Bánk is Regent during the absence of the king. He is, of course, a hero and an unswerving patriot, devoted husband and father, just master and fearless warrior. His path of duty is made thorny by the intrigues of Endre's foreign-born queen, Gertrude, and her relatives. One, her brother Otto, ravishes Bánk's wife Melinda, causing her to reject her husband in shame and eventually to drown herself and their child. The propagandist element is hammered home by a peasant, Tiborc, who pours out an impassioned catalogue of the miseries of a people crushed under a foreign yoke. Bánk, in an effort to win freedom for his countrymen, kills the queen but is himself destroyed by the condemnation of Endre, now returned, and by the sight of the drowned bodies of his wife and child.

It was no doubt the nationalist elements in the play that drew Erkel to it in the first place, and by 1851 or 1852 a three act libretto by Béni Egressy had been prepared. Having already scored a success with *Hunyadi László* in 1845 it was inevitable that he should try to capitalize on the country's nationalist aspirations. However, the time was inopportune. In 1848 Kossuth had led a short-lived rebellion against Austria which was bloodily suppressed, and *Bánk bán* had to be shelved until the political climate improved. In 1867 the "Ausgleich" (Settlement) between Austria and Hungary ceded to the latter a great deal of autonomy, resulting in the foundation of the Austro-Hungarian Empire over which Franz Josef ruled as emperor but separately as King of Hungary.

The opera was performed for the first time at the National Theater in Pest on 9 March 1861 under Erkel's direction and was an immediate (and lasting) success. During the 1930s the National Opera ordered Kálmán Nádasdy to revise Egressy's libretto on the grounds that it was inferior to both music and play. Nádasdy clarified Egressy's often tortuous syntax and,

in addition, hardened the sociological aspects of Tiborc's outburst. Revisions were also made to Erkel's score by the Opera's music director, Nándor Rékai, who reduced some of Erkel's taxing coloratura and revised the parts of Bánk and Tiborc for baritone and bass respectively. This version was staged in March 1940. In 1953 an alternative version was adopted, and Bánk and Tiborc became once again tenor and baritone and Melinda's coloratura was restored.

Part of the opera's success stemmed from Erkel's use of what was erroneously believed to be traditional Hungarian music. This had contributed to the success of *Hunyadi László* and had its origin in the *verbunkos* or dance music originally used as an adjunct to army recruitment. This, and its later manifestation the *csárdás* which appeared around 1830, was associated with gypsies who were for long thought to be the keepers of the true Hungarian folk tradition. This music, by turns lively and melancholic, rests on a few formulae. Alternately slow (*lassu*) and fast (*friss*) with a brisk, richly ornamented coda (*disz*), the melodies are usually broad, melismatic and punctuated by triplets and dotted rhythms. As a type the *verbunkos* is familiar through Brahms's Hungarian Dances, the Hungarian Rhapsodies of Liszt and the offerings of innumerable 'Gypsy' orchestras around the world. Curiously, Erkel did stumble on material closely related to the real thing (e.g., Introduction to act III), but this seems to have been an uncalculated choice.

These "Magyar" influences are immediately evident in the overture to *Bánk bán,* in which a melody used later by Bartók and Kodály also occurs. They surface throughout the opera in association with its expressly nationalistic sentiments (the Dances, Count Petur, Tiborc) and culminate in the Introduction to act III and Melinda's two arias "Ah, ember!" in act II, which features the cimbalom, and the "Nightingale" aria ("Tudsz-e mádárrol éneket?") in act III which deserves to be at least as well known as Rusalka's "Měsíčku na nebi hlubokém" (O Moon) in Dvořák's opera. Erkel's score also strongly reflects the influence of Romantic opera beyond Hungary, most notably that of Donizetti and Bellini, and, as Gertrude's second act aria "Reszkess. . . nagyur, reszkess!" (Tremble. . .great lord, tremble!) shows, he was capable of making powerful dramatic statements. As in Kodály's *Háry Janos* later, this "European" idiom is used largely to characterize the foreign (i.e., villainous) elements (Gertrude, Otto, etc.) and where it comes into conflict with the heroic (Otto-Melinda; Bánk-Gertrude) tends to be submerged by the *verbunkos* aspects of the music.

With *Bánk bán* Erkel seems to have realized he had exhausted this vein of nationalistic sentiment. Henceforth he turned to other sources of inspiration (ultimately, in *Istvan Király,* to Wagner), but, like his source Katona, he never again achieved so great or so deserved a success.

—Kenneth Dommett

BARBER, Samuel.

Composer. Born 9 March 1910, in West Chester, Pennsylvania. Died 23 January 1981, in New York. Nephew of contralto Louise Homer. Studied composition with Rosario Scalero, piano with Isabelle Vengerova, singing with Emilio de Gogorza, and conducting with Fritz Reiner at the Curtis Institute of Music, graduating 1932; taught at Curtis, 1939-1942, honorary doctorate awarded 1945; American Prix de

Rome, 1935; Pulitzer Scholarships, 1935, 1936; his *Symphony No. 1* became the first American work to be presented at the Salzburg Festival of Contemporary Music, 25 July 1937; served in the United States Army Air Force, 1942-45; Post Service Guggenheim Fellowships, 1945, 1947, 1949; Critics Award for his Cello Concerto, 1946; consultant at the American Academy in Rome in 1947 and 1948; Pulitzer Prize for *Vanessa*, 1958; honorary doctorate, Harvard University, 1959; Pulitzer Prize for his *Piano Concerto*, 1962. Barber's works have been performed by many major orchestras, including the Boston Symphony under Serge Koussevitzky and the Philadelphia Orchestra under Eugene Ormandy.

Operas

Publisher: G. Schirmer.

The Rose Tree, A.S. Brosius, 1920.
A Hand of Bridge, C. Menotti, 1953, Spoleto, 17 June 1959.
Vanessa, C. Menotti, 1956-57, New York, Metropolitan Opera, 15 January 1958.
Antony and Cleopatra, F. Zeffirelli (after Shakespeare), New York, Metropolitan Opera, 16 September 1966; revised, with libretto revisions by C. Menotti, 1975.

Other works: ballets, orchestral works, concertos, vocal works, chamber music, songs, solo piano works.

Publications

About BARBER: books–

Broder, Nathan. *Samuel Barber.* New York, 1954.
Hennessee, Don A. *Samuel Barber: A Bio-bibliography.* Westport, Connecticut, 1985.

*   *   *

Lyricism seems almost synonymous with the music of the American composer Samuel Barber. He is represented on the concert platform today more by his instrumental works than by his songs or operas, but one senses in all his pieces—even in the most abstract, and even in those few that hint at twelve-tone serial techniques—an expressive urge best satisfied through deeply meaningful melody. He was a "conservative" composer throughout his career. The several works that are deliberately angular and atonal—the 1939 Violin Concerto, the 1942 *Second Essay for Orchestra*, the 1949 Piano Sonata— stand out in marked contrast from the rest of his output; Barber flirted with musical modernism, and he did so successfully, but he never strayed far from the tonal harmonic language and basically diatonic melodic style to which he had early on pledged his allegiance.

His two best-known operas are the 1958 *Vanessa*, with a libretto by his long-time associate and companion Gian Carlo Menotti, and the 1966 *Antony and Cleopatra*, with a libretto by Franco Zeffirelli after the Shakespeare play; both were written for and produced by New York's Metropolitan Opera. *Vanessa*, a stormy drama about an older woman attempting to recapture her youth by means of a romantic involvement with a younger man, won the Pulitzer Prize for Music and it has enjoyed a fair number of subsequent productions; *Antony and Cleopatra*, commissioned for the opening of the Met's new opera house at Lincoln Center, was generally a failure as much with critics as with the public. Barber also wrote a one-act chamber opera titled *A Hand of Bridge*, for Menotti's

Festival of Two Worlds in Spoleto, Italy, in 1959; among the many works he produced as a child is a still unpublished opera—written at age ten—titled *The Rose Tree*.

As noted, Barber's instrumental music—in particular the 1933 *School for Scandal* overture, the *Adagio for Strings* extracted from his 1936 String Quartet, the 1962 *Piano Concerto*, the first two of the three *Essays for Orchestra* (from 1937 and 1942) and the 1955 *Summer Music* for wind quintet—is in general heard more frequently than his vocal pieces. Among the latter, the most enduringly popular seem to be the 1931 *Dover Beach*, for string quartet and mezzo-soprano or baritone, and the 1947 *Knoxville; Summer of 1915*, for soprano and orchestra, based on the prologue to James Agee's novel *A Death in the Family.*

—James Wierzbicki

———

THE BARBER OF BAGDAD
See DER BARBIER VON BAGDAD

———

THE BARBER OF SEVILLE
See IL BARBIERE DI SIVIGLIA

———

DER BARBIER VON BAGDAD [The Barber of Bagdad].

Composer: Peter Cornelius.

Librettist: Peter Cornelius.

First Performance: Weimar, 15 December 1858.

Roles: Abul Hassan (bass); Nureddin (tenor); Margiana (soprano); The Caliph (baritone); Baba Mustapha, The Cadi (tenor); Bostana (mezzo-soprano); Three Muezzins (bass, two tenors); chorus (SATB).

Publications

book–

Hasse, Max. *Peter Cornelius und sein "Barbier von Bagdad."* Leipzig, 1904.

articles–

Bartlett, K.W. "Peter Cornelius and *The Barber of Bagdad.*" *Opera* August (1956).
Wurmser, Leo. "Cornelius and his *Barber.*" *Opera* December (1965).

*   *   *

The fate of Peter Cornelius's *Der Barbier von Bagdad* was inextricably bound up with Franz Liszt's fate as *Kapellmeister* in Weimar. Still in his twenties, Cornelius had gone to Weimar to serve as Liszt's assistant in matters both musical and literary. Thus Cornelius became familiar with *Benvenuto Cellini,* Berlioz's first opera and the work that would influence him more than any other during the composition of *Der Barbier.* Although *Cellini* had been poorly received at its Paris premiere in 1838, Liszt, an ardent champion of musical modernism, conducted the German premiere of the opera in Weimar in 1852. Berlioz had specifically revised *Cellini* for Weimar, and the polylingual Cornelius was pressed into service to provide a German translation for the occasion. Later, on 15 December 1858, Liszt would lead the first performance of *Der Barbier von Bagdad.* The work was greeted with open derision at its premiere, but the hostility was directed as much at Liszt's modernist activities as at Cornelius's hapless *Barbier.* After this fiasco, which bankrupted Liszt's opera company and marked the end of his Weimar experience, the opera did not receive any further performances during Cornelius's lifetime. *Der Barbier* was only revived in various corrupt arrangements after the composer's death in 1874, and it was not until 1905 that a faithful edition by Max Hasse based on manuscript sources was finally published.

Der Barbier von Bagdad was a late pendant to the tradition of German comic operas on oriental tales that includes Mozart's *Die Entführung aus dem Serail* and Weber's *Abu Hassan.* Cornelius wrote to a friend that German opera, like the classical Greek theater, had found its great tragedians, but that it still lacked its Aristophanes, a role Cornelius himself hoped to fill with the composition of *Der Barbier von Bagdad.* Like Weber's opera, Cornelius's is based on a tale about that old windbag, Der Barber Abu (or, here, Abul) Hassan from the Arabian *Thousand and One Nights.* The first act reveals the lovesick Nureddin pining away for Margiana, beautiful daughter of the Cadi Mustapha. Expecting to be rewarded, Bostana, elderly maid servant to the cadi, volunteers to aid the young suitor in his quest. Having arranged for Nureddin to meet Margiana when the devout cadi leaves to pray at the mosque that very afternoon, Bostana urges Nureddin to summon a barber—the garrulous Abul Hassan—so that he will look his very best. The second act takes place in the cadi's home. From the wealthy Selim of Damascus, the cadi receives both a chest full of costly jewels and the announcement that Selim will arrive that day to seek Margiana's hand in marriage. The Cadi is elated at this news, but when he leaves for the mosque, Bostana smuggles in Nureddin. The tryst of Nureddin and Margiana is short-lived, however. Unbeknownst to Nureddin, the meddlesome Abul Hassan has followed him in hopes that he might be able to aid him in outwitting his old enemy, the cadi. Meanwhile, upon leaving for the mosque, the cadi has discovered that a clumsy slave has broken a valuable vase. The slave cries out when the enraged cadi applies a bastinado to his back. Overhearing these cries, Abul Hassan believes that the cadi is murdering Nureddin and creates a great commotion. Margiana conceals Nureddin in the chest in which Selim's gifts had been sent, Nureddin's servants attempt to remove the chest with Abul Hassan's help, the cadi believes that he is being robbed, pandemonium breaks out, and the Caliph of Bagdad arrives with troops to restore order. When the cadi informs the caliph that there has been an attempted robbery, Abul Hassan counters with the claim that the chest contains Nureddin's body, "shaved this morning, this afternoon a corpse." When the chest is opened, the bemused caliph grants his blessing to the young lovers, and the cadi is unable to oppose their betrothal.

Der Barbier von Bagdad is a remarkably self-assured compositional statement for a first opera by a composer who had previously written only songs. If it owes something to the German Romantic opera of Weber, Spohr, and Marschner, that influence is vague and generalized. The opera's harmonic language is more consistently chromatic, its orchestration more elaborate, and, in a word, its style more "modern" than those of any of these composers. The sophisticated command of orchestral sonority and of chromatic harmony that *Der Barbier* exhibits must certainly have owed a great deal to Cornelius's absorption of the music of Liszt and Wagner (the Wagner of *Lohengrin,* which was written in 1845), yet the music in the opera sounds remarkably remote from that of either of these Romantic revolutionaries. Mendelssohn's music for *A Midsummer Night's Dream* is suggested by some of the gossamer woodwind writing in the opera's overture and elsewhere, but, again, this is more a question of kinship than of influence. Even the opera's two most explicit models, Berlioz's *Benvenuto Cellini* and Rossini's *Il barbiere di Siviglia,* were conscious and therefore essentially superficial influences. The duet for Nureddin and Bostana in act I, "Wenn zum Gebet vom Minaret" (When he goes to pray at the Minaret), is unmistakably modeled on the fast second section of the duet for Teresa and Cellini in act I of *Benvenuto Cellini,* "Demain soir, Mardi Gras" (Tomorrow evening at Mardi Gras). The dramatic situation—in both operas a lovers' *rendezvous* is being planned—the quicksilver melody in six-eight time, the manner in which the second singer parrots each phrase of the first, all of these are directly cloned from Berlioz's duet. Nevertheless, Cornelius's duet amounts to an *hommage* written by a composer working within a different tonal tradition. The towering example of Rossini's *Il barbiere di Siviglia* is suggested by many of the comic situations to be found in *Der Barbier von Bagdad,* but again, it seems to be a case of Cornelius accepting the challenge to attempt Rossinian feats within his own German idiom.

Rarely in the history of opera can so original a voice have had so little effect. *Der Barbier von Bagdad* itself remains sealed off from the history of music by its initial failure. Cornelius once styled himself:

A pale and candid Lisztian
To his last breath and tone;
A Berlioz-Wagner-Weimar-Christian,
And yet Cornelius-like in mind and bone.

Yet he seems to have been content to remain in the shadow of the creativity of his heroes. After Liszt left Weimar, Cornelius spent most of his life as Wagner's amanuensis, never attempting to secure further performances of his comic masterwork, completing only one other opera. If posthumous revivals of *Der Barbier von Bagdad* occurred too late to have a direct influence on the subsequent history of opera, it remains an enchanting and original work in its own right. Although probably doomed to remain a "local classic," *Der Barbier* has found a secure place on operatic stages, however belatedly, if only in the German-speaking world.

—David Gable

IL BARBIERE DI SIVIGLIA, ovvero la precauzione inutile [The Barber of Seville].

Composer: Giovanni Paisiello.

Librettist: Giuseppe Petrosellini (after Beaumarchais).

First Performance: St Petersburg, Court, 26 September 1782.

Roles: Dr Bartolo (bass); Rosina (soprano); Count Almaviva (tenor); Figaro (baritone); Don Basilio (baritone); Giovinetto (tenor); Svegliato (bass); A Notary (bass); Chief of Police (tenor).

Publications

articles–

Loewenberg, Alfred. "Paisiello's and Rossini's 'Barbiere di Siviglia'." *Music and Letters* 20 (1939): 157.
Tartak, Marvin. "The Two *Barbieri.*" *Music and Letters* October (1969).
Scherliess, Volker. "*Il barbiere di Siviglia:* Paisiello und Rossini." *Analecta musicologica* 21 (1982): 100.
Lang, Paul Henry. "The Original *Barber:* Paisiello's Great Model for Mozart and Rossini." *Opus* 3/no. 1 (1986): 20.

*   *   *

Paisiello composed *Il barbiere di Siviglia* in 1782, while serving as *maestro di cappella* at the Russian court in St Petersburg. In his dedication of the opera to Catherine II he reveals how he came to choose the subject: "In the knowledge that (the play) *Le Barbier de Seville* amused your Imperial Majesty, I believed that it would not displease you in the form of an Italian opera. Accordingly, I have had it prepared as a libretto, endeavoring to render it as concisely as possible, while adding nothing to the original text, and preserving as many of the expressions of the play as the genius of Italian poetry will permit." As was customary and necessary, much of the play's dialogue was eliminated by Paisiello's librettist, Giuseppe Petrosellini (1727-99). With it, clearly by design, went much of the sparkling social criticism that distinguished Beaumarchais' *Le Barbier* (Paris, 1775). In addition, although Petrosellini adhered closely to the plot and the four-act structure of the play, he shifted its emphasis from Figaro to Dr Bartolo and he made all of the characters as conventional as they are in traditional Italian *opera buffa*. Despite its apparent complexity, the play rests upon a simple traditional plot, not unlike those of the *commedia dell' arte*. The playwright himself outlined it as follows: "An old man in love determines to marry his ward tomorrow; a young suitor cleverer than he defeats him by marrying the girl today right under the guardian's nose and in his house."

In keeping recitative to a minimum and the length of *Il barbiere* under two hours, Paisiello was simply responding to the express demands of Catherine II. His decision to balance the number of solo arias with an equal number of ensembles (four duets, two trios, one quintet, and one septet), on the other hand, followed the trend of the later eighteenth century towards increasing the importance of ensemble singing in comic opera. Three of the four scenes that comprise the two acts of the opera conclude with ensembles, and two of them open in that manner. The last scene closes with an ensemble-finale in seven sections that are unified by key and by the prevailing *buffo* style. Perhaps the opera's high point for

farce comes in the remarkable trio that begins act I, scene ii: Bartolo and his yawning and sneezing servants are each strikingly depicted musically in the course of an intricate musical structure freely adapted to the flow of the action. Also worthy of special mention is the quintet that closes act II, scene i, with its through-composed ritornello structure, unifying motives, and underlying sonata form, its apt changes of character and texture, and its characteristic orchestral use of a short repeated motive against which the voices sing in declamatory style.

Paisiello's solo arias reflect the freedom of *opera buffa,* whether in structure (as in the recitative passages that interrupt Figaro's entrance aria) or in rhythmic character (as in the many meter changes of Bartolo's grotesque Spanish seguidilla in act II). The composer even finds occasions to borrow aria-types from *opera seria,* the first of which (Rosina's "Giusto ciel") emulates the grand tragic manner, while the second (Rosina's "Gia riede primavera") displays the composer's bent for lachrymose sentimentality in its siciliana section.

It is perhaps in the solo arias of Paisiello's *Barber* that the clearest models may be found for the more famous settings of Beaumarchais' plays by Mozart and Rossini. In act I of *Il barbiere* by Paisiello, for example, Rosina is serenaded by Count Almaviva ("Saper bramate") in a manner very much like Cherubino's "Voi che sapete" in *Le nozze di Figaro.* In addition, the minuet sung by Mozart's Figaro in act I certainly reminds the listener of the minuet sung by Paisiello's Figaro as the second part of his catalog aria in act I of *Il barbiere.* That Mozart knew Paisiello's opera before setting Lorenzo Da Ponte's libretto based on Beaumarchais' sequel to *Le barbier* is quite certain, since Paisiello's *Il barbiere* was in the repertory of the Burgtheater in Vienna from 1783 through the first performance there of Mozart's *Le nozze di Figaro* in 1786. Rossini's *Barbiere* (Rome, 1816), which was actually based upon Paisiello's opera rather than upon the Beaumarchais play, reveals his debt to his Italian predecessor most strongly in Basilio's "La calunnia" and Dr Bartolo's "A un dottor della mia sorte," both of which draw freely upon the character, the *buffo* mannerisms, and even the keys of their respective models in the earlier opera.

Paisiello's *Il barbiere* would seem to represent the late eighteenth-century style of traditional Italian *opera buffa* at its best. Unfortunately for the composer's reputation, the genre was all too soon transfigured by the genius of Mozart and its *buffo* style rendered old-fashioned by Rossini. Nevertheless, despite a mannered indulgence in literal repetition (especially in the closing sections of ensembles) and eclectic reminiscences of styles as early as that of Pergolesi, Paisiello's setting of *Il barbiere* fully deserves occasional revival for its skillful characterization through music, its progressive use of the orchestra (as in the concertante solo woodwinds of Rosina's "Gia riede primavera"), and its highly developed ensemble and finale-writing.

—David Poultney

IL BARBIERE DI SIVIGLIA (Almaviva, ossia L'inutile precauzione) [The Barber of Seville].

Composer: Gioachino Rossini.

Librettist: C. Sterbini (after Beaumarchais and G. Petrosellini).

First Performance: Rome, Torre Argentina, 20 February 1816.

Roles: Rosina (soprano); Count Almaviva (tenor); Figaro (baritone); Dr Bartolo (bass); Basilio (bass); Berta (mezzo-soprano or soprano); Fiorello (baritone); Sergeant (tenor); Ambroggio (bass); Notary, Magistrate (mute); chorus (TTB).

Publications

books—

Gatti, G.M. *"Le 'Barbier de Séville' de Rossini."* Paris, 1925.
John, Nicholas, ed. *Il barbiere di Siviglia and Moïse et Pharaon.* London and New York, 1985.

articles—

Zedda, A. "Appunti per una lettura filologica del 'Barbieri'." *L'opera* 2 (1966): 13.
Tartak, M. "The Two 'Barbieri'." *Music and Letters* 1 (1969): 453.
Gallarati, P. "Dramma e ludus dall' *Italiana* al *Barbiere.*" In *Il melodramma italiano dell' ottocento: studi e ricerche per Massimo Mila.* Turin, 1977.
Avant-scène opéra November-December (1981) [*Le barbier de Séville* issue].

Scherliess, Volker. *"Il barbiere di Siviglia:* Paisiello und Rossini." *Analecta Musicologica* 21 (1982): 100.

*   *   *

No less an operatic authority than Giuseppe Verdi once said: "For abundance of real musical ideas, for comic verve, and for truthful declamation, *Il barbiere di Siviglia* is the finest *opera buffa* in existence." No one has ever seriously disputed Verdi's appraisal. Rossini himself realized the scope of his achievement, for in his later years he remarked: "I hope to be survived by, if nothing else, the third act of *Otello,* the second act of *William Tell,* and the whole of *The Barber of Seville.*" Rossini's *Otello,* alas, has been effaced by Verdi's; *Guillaume Tell* lives on principally as an overture; only *Il barbiere* has never worn out its welcome on the world's operatic stages.

Rossini composed it when he was twenty-four and already regarded as a budding genius, with *Tancredi* and *L'italiana in Algeri* already to his credit. The libretto (by Cesare Sterbini) was drawn from *Le barbier de Séville* of Beaumarchais, the French playwright whose *Le mariage de Figaro* had already provided Mozart with an excellent operatic subject.

Figaro, that most ebullient of barbers, also is the centerpiece of Rossini's comedy. The Count Almaviva, a Spanish grandee, has arrived in Seville disguised as a poor student named Lindoro, to serenade and otherwise lay siege to Ro-

Rossini's *Il barbiere di Siviglia,* **Royal Opera, London, 1990**

sina, the ward of the pompous Dr Bartolo, who plans to marry her himself. Almaviva, after his opening serenade, runs into his former attendant Figaro and enlists him in his campaign. On Figaro's advice, Almaviva makes two forays into Bartolo's house to woo Rosina, in act I pretending to be a drunken soldier and in act II a singing teacher replacing her regular instructor, the slippery Don Basilio. Rosina, who detests Dr Bartolo, encourages Almaviva. Despite all of Bartolo's machinations, Almaviva (who reveals his true identity at the last minute) manages to marry Rosina, while Figaro, his work done, happily extinguishes his lantern.

Out of deference to Giovanni Paisiello, then seventy-five years old, who had written a *Barbiere* also based on Beaumarchais some thirty-five years previously, Rossini decided to entitle his opera *Almaviva, ossia L'inutile precauzione* (*The Useless Precaution*). It was, as you might say, a useless precaution, for Paisiello's supporters effectively sabotaged the opening of Rossini's opera at the Torre Argentina Theater in Rome on 20 February 1816, turning it into a fiasco. By the third night, however, Rossini's opera was a roaring success, casting poor Paisiello's version quite into the shade, where it has remained ever since.

The American author James M. Cain, in his novel *Serenade,* has an operatic baritone describe Rossini's overtures this way: "Rossini loved the theater, and that's why he could write an overture. He takes you into the theater—hell, you can even feel them getting into their seats, and smell the theater smell, and see the lights go up on the curtain." In fact, Rossini liked some of his overtures so much that he recycled them from opera to opera. The sparkling and beautifully scored *Barbiere* overture, which seems so admirably suited to setting the mood for the buffoonery that follows, had already seen service in two earlier operas called *Aureliano in Palmira* and *Elisabetta, regina d'Inghilterra.*

From start to finish *Il barbiere* is so marvellously crafted, brilliantly inventive and uproariously funny that it becomes, as Verdi indicated, the ultimate *opera buffa.* Rossini once observed that he could set a laundry list to music, but far more important, he also knew how to create characters. Figaro, the mercurial barber himself, seems molded out of music. His rippling rhythms, agile phrases, infectious melodies, acrobatic leaps, even his repetitions and reiterations, all describe his character with a clarity that pages of descriptive text could scarcely match. He hardly needs words—indeed, at times in that most dazzling of all patter songs, the "Largo al factotum" in which he introduces himself, he actually gives language up in favor of a string of "la-la-la-la-las."

Similarly, Rosina's music admirably meets the requirements of both a kittenish young woman expressing the joys of first love and an operatic soprano seeking to make a brilliant impression. Rossini's first Rosina, Maria Giorgi-Righetti, was a contralto, so the role authentically belongs, if not to contraltos, at least to mezzo-sopranos. However, the role nowadays is perhaps most frequently sung by high sopranos, permitting some dazzling vocalizations in Rosina's introductory aria "Una voce poco fa." Rosina also has a chance to shine in the act-II "Lesson Scene," in which the supposed singing master, Almaviva in disguise, invites the girl to present a song of her choice. Rossini actually wrote an aria to be used at this point, but that hasn't prevented *prima donnas* from inserting selections of their own, ranging from the mad scene of *Lucia di Lammermoor* to "Home, Sweet Home."

Almaviva, with his impersonations of a drunken soldier and the unctuous music master, comes across more strongly than many a romantic lead, while Doctor Bartolo is a tonal image of inane pomposity, as in his aria "A un dottor della

mia sorte," and the artful intriguer Don Basilio discloses both his intentions and his character in his "Calumny" aria.

Yet for all its individual depictions, *Il barbiere* is essentially an ensemble opera, with its duets, trios, and larger groupings that manage to be farcical and touching at the same time. Also very much in evidence throughout are the "Rossini crescendo," in which the music increases dizzily in tempo and volume, and the "ensemble of perplexity," in which the various personages in overlapping combinations insist melodiously and repeatedly that the situation is most vexing and they really don't know what to do. Somehow, they always manage to do something, and it usually turns out for the best.

Il barbiere di Siviglia even drew praise from Beethoven, who counseled Rossini, however, not to try anything but *opera buffa.* "Wanting to succeed in another style would be to stretch your luck," he said, adding: "Above all, make a lot of *Barbers.*" One, as it turned out, was enough.

—Herbert Kupferberg

BARBIERI, Fedora.

Mezzo-soprano. Born 4 June 1920, in Trieste, Italy. Married impresario Barzoletti. Studied at Trieste with Luigi Toffolo and at school of Teatro Comunale, Florence with Giulia Tess; debut in Florence as Fidelma in *Matrimonio segreto* in 1940; created Dariola in Alfano's *Don Juan de Manara* in 1941 at Florence Festival; Teatro alla Scala debut as Meg Page in *Falstaff* in 1942, and sang regularly at the Teatro alla Scala from 1946; Metropolitan Opera debut in 1950 as Eboli in Verdi's *Don Carlos* on opening night of Sir Rudolf Bing's regime, and appeared there 1950-54, 1956-57, and 1967-68; sang at Covent Garden with Teatro alla Scala tour in 1950, and as guest, 1957-58 and 1964; created the Wife in Chailly's *L'idiota* at the Rome Opera.

Publications

About BARBIERI: books–

Natan, A. *Prima donna.* Basle, 1962.
Celletti, R. *Le grandi voci.* Rome, 1964.

* * *

One of the voice types that seem to be missing from stages today is the earthy, voluptuous mezzo/contralto: a voice born to sing Verdi's Azucena with as much naturalness as ease of power. Chloë Elmo had such a voice, and she was followed by Fedora Barbieri. Others sing these roles, but who really followed Elmo and Barbieri? Giulietta Simionato's sound was gorgeous but more refined in timbre.

The "meaty" vocal lines of such characters from Italian opera as Laura, La Principessa di Bouillon, Ulrica (*Un ballo in maschera*), and especially Dame Quickly were not Barbieri's only successes; her repertoire was large and extremely varied. She had a style and technique that encompassed Gluck, Handel, Cherubini, Rossini and Bellini, as well as Verdi. She was also a noted Carmen.

After her 1940 stage debut in Florence, her career enjoyed a steep upward rise, aided in part by her marriage to the director of Florence's Maggio Musicale. Successful debuts in many international houses came in rapid succession: she first sang in London with an Italian ensemble in 1950, and in the same year she debuted as Eboli (*Don Carlos*) in Rudolf Bing's original opening night at the Metropolitan, with Björling and Siepi. She subsequently sang eight roles at the Metropolitan; the final one, Quickly, in 1967 when she returned after several years' absence. Barbieri immediately became a favorite with audiences everywhere she appeared.

Barbieri's portrayal of Adalgisa (*Norma*) was often given with Maria Callas as Norma. She also sang that role with Zinka Milanov, with whom she also appeared in *Aïda*. Del Monaco was often her partner in *Carmen*.

Commercial recordings do not abound with Fedora Barbieri, and that is a definite loss. The best known are the two complete operas with RCA, *Trovatore* and *Aïda*, making up the dream operatic quartet of Milanov, Barbieri, Jussi Björling and Leonard Warren. In spite of magnificent singing and vocal style, the recorded performances are somewhat marred because the principals strive for perfection at the expense of visceral excitement. If a "pirate" copy of the Met's *Don Carlo* with Björling, Robert Merrill and Cesare Siepi can be found, certainly listen to that. "Pirate" copies of *Norma* with Callas and Barbieri are generally available. Late in her career, James Levine called on Barbieri to sing Berta in his recording of *Il barbiere* but intonation problems do not help the memory of her triumphs.

We still await the true successor to Fedora Barbieri.

—Bert Wechsler

BARRIENTOS, Maria.

Soprano. Born 10 March 1884 in Barcelona. Died 8 August 1946 in Ciboure, Basses-Pyrénées in France. Studied with Francesco Bonet; debut in *La sonnambula* at Teatro Lirico, Barcelona, 1898; sang at Covent Garden in *Il barbiere di Siviglia* in 1903; appeared at Teatro alla Scala in Meyerbeer's *Dinorah* and in *Il barbiere di Siviglia*, 1904-5; spent five seasons in Buenos Aires; Metropolitan Opera debut on 31 January 1916 in *Lucia di Lammermoor*, remained there until 1920, then returned to Europe.

Publications

About BARRIENTOS: books–

Colomer Pujol, J.M. *Maria Barrientos*. Barcelona.

*   *   *

The term *coloratura* refers to decoration of a vocal melody in the shape of runs, roulades, trills and florid passages. *Coloratura* can in fact be sung by any sort of voice but, over the years, it has come to be commonly applied to the light, high soprano voice as typified by Amelita Galli-Curci, Luisa Tetrazzini, Toti dal Monte, Lina Pagliughi, Beverly Sills and Kathleen Battle. The *coloratura soprano* might more accurately be described as a *soprano leggero* (literally, light soprano). To her fall such roles as Gilda (*Rigoletto*), Lucia (*Lucia di Lammermoor*), Elvira (*I puritani*) and Amina (*La sonnambula*). Maria Barrientos was a typical *soprano leggero*

who achieved considerable fame in the first two decades of this century.

Contemporary reports suggest that Barrientos' voice was not large (the *leggero* voice rarely is), but nonetheless exceptionally brilliant in the upper register, pure in tone, with accurate intonation and precise *coloratura*. A particular feature of her singing appears to have been a diamond-like staccato which, combined with her sure sense of pitch, no doubt contributed to her success in roles such as Lakmé (particularly in the famous "Bell Song") and Amina.

Her popularity was not universal, however. Although Barrientos sang with some success in Italy, she did not make much of an impression at the Teatro alla Scala or at Covent Garden. She never sang at all in several important European houses. Her appeal would mainly seem to have been centered on Spanish-speaking countries. She was adored in Spain and a great favorite in South America. She did appear with success at the Metropolitan Opera, however, for five seasons, at a time when there was a dearth of good light sopranos. Her only competition there was Frieda Hempel, but both were somewhat overshadowed by the arrival of Amelita Galli-Curci in 1921. Some idea of her reception at the Met can be gleaned from the critic of the *New York Times*, Richard Aldrich, writing of her debut as Lucia in 1915: "It is not too much to call Mme. Barrientos a singer of high accomplishment in the singing of such parts as Lucia in Donizetti's opera; it would be too much to call her a great one, but she is an artist whose addition to the company is likely to be interesting. It is a voice of light and fine-spun texture and great delicacy; it showed last evening little power. Its quality is agreeable, frequently very charming, though it is not always especially in its highest tones of the finest purity and smoothness. She sang the music of the "mad scene" with great fluency, and in a generally smoother style than she had shown earlier. She made no attempt to gain dramatically incisive power in this scene, but sought her effects in a subtler way by extreme delicacy and a fine chiseling of phrase, matching her pose and gesture. Her highest tones, sung pianissimo, had an exquisite quality. One of Mme. Barrientos' most noteworthy accomplishments is her ability to swell and diminish a tone with perfect evenness; the so-called *messa di voce*, which, used as she used it, is of striking effect. She lacks, unfortunately, the power of keeping quality and color of her voice intact on different vowel sounds. There is much to admire in her phrasing and in the dramatic suggestion and implication by methods of the less obvious sort that she put into much of her singing. And one element of her art that cannot be too highly esteemed is the almost invariable correctness of her intonation, even in the most elaborate passages."

Barrientos continued to appear with success in the twenties, but her operatic appearances began to become less frequent in favour of a new-found interest in the concert platform. In this repertoire, she was moderately successful, particularly in her association with Manuel de Falla, of whose songs she became a noted interpreter.

Barrientos had a fine and prolific recording career. She recorded first for Fonotipia between 1904 and 1906, and later for Columbia, between 1916 and 1920. The voice as recorded is merely attractive rather than especially beautiful, and we can hear largely the same qualities as are mentioned in reviews of her singing: accurate intonation, a brilliant staccato and remarkable agility. As is common in this kind of voice, the lower register sounds somewhat weak but is compensated for by a shining top. One odd mannerism, mentioned by Aldrich and evident on record, is her habit of opening vowel sounds in rapid passage work.

In the late twenties, Barrientos recorded for Columbia de Falla's *Canciones populares españolas* with the composer at the piano. These electrical recordings show a deepening of interpretative insight and a warmth of voice missing from her earlier recordings. Whether this warmer quality was owing to the greater fidelity of the electrical process or a greater maturity of voice is now hard to say. What is indisputable is the historical significance of these recordings for the student of de Falla's music.

In the final analysis, Barrientos was a good singer rather than a great one, but her association with de Falla assures her a place in the history of music in the twentieth century.

—Larry Lustig

THE BARTERED BRIDE [Prodaná nevěsta].

Composer: Bedřich Smetana.

Librettist: K. Sabina.

First Performance: Prague, Provisional Theater, 30 May 1866.

Roles: Mařenka (soprano); Jeník (tenor); Krusina (baritone); Ludmilla (soprano); Micha (bass); Hata (mezzo-soprano); Vašek (tenor); Kečal (bass); Circus Manager (tenor); Esmeralda (soprano); Circus Indian (tenor); chorus (SATB).

Publications

book–

Pražák, P. *Smetanova Prodaná nevěsta: vznik a osudy díla* [the origins of *The Bartered Bride*]. Prague, 1962.

articles–

Abraham, Gerald. "The Genesis of The Bartered Bride." *Music and Letters* 28 (1947): 36.
Pospíšil, V. "Talichova Prodaná nevěsta" [Talich's *Bartered Bride*]. *Hudebni revue* 10 (1957): 741.
Jiránek, Jaroslav. "Vstah hudby a slova ve Smetanově Prodané nevěstě" [word-music relations in *The Bartered Bride*]. *Hudebni veda* 8 (1971): 19; German summary, 123.
Jareš S. "Obrazová dokumentace nejstarších inscenací Prodané nevěsty" [Pictoral documentation of the first production of *The Bartered Bride*]. *Hudebni veda* 11 (1974): 195; German summary, 198.
Jiránek, Jaroslav. "K problému operníko libreta a jeho analýzy [analysis of *The Bartered Bride* libretto]. *Hudebni veda* 17 (1980): 221.

*　　*　　*

After a bustling overture, the action of *The Bartered Bride* opens on a spring holiday in a Bohemian village. At once we are introduced to the young lovers Mařenka and Jeník, who are shocked by the news that Mařenka's parents have promised her in marriage to the "only" son of their rich neighbor Micha, whom she has not even met. (There has been another son from a first marriage, but he has left home). Mařenka confesses her pledge to Jeník; after a vigorous exchange with the marriage broker Kečal and her parents, she remains defiant, and the act ends with a festive polka danced by the villagers.

Act II begins with a drinking song, with contributions in praise of money by Kečal and in praise of love by Jeník, while the villagers dance a vigorous *furiant*. Now at last we meet Vašek, Kečal's choice to be Mařenka's husband, a shy, simple, but good-natured lad with a stammer. He is terrified at the thought of marriage and by chance confesses this to Mařenka, who does not identify herself but seizes the opportunity to tell him that his prospective bride is flighty and that there is a prettier and nicer girl who loves him. In the meantime Kečal offers Jeník three hundred guilders if he will give up Mařenka, and surprisingly he agrees on the condition that she shall marry only Micha's elder son. When Kečal exits, Jeník tells us why: he is Micha's long-lost son, and now not only can he marry Mařenka, he can get her a dowry as well! Now the marriage contract between Mařenka and Vašek is read out publicly together with Jeník's renunciation of her, but when Kečal mentions the money the villagers, angry that Jeník should abandon Mařenka for gain, turn on him.

In the meantime, poor Vašek is searching anxiously for the nice girl who gave him good advice, in a comic aria marked *lamentoso*. He is cheered by the arrival of circus entertainers with a beautiful dancer called Esmeralda and a performing bear. But the man who should be in the bearskin is drunk, and Vašek, who agrees to take his place so as to dance with Esmeralda, starts practicing some steps, escaping from his parents who want him to meet the dreaded Mařenka. She in turn appears, furious at the news that Jeník has deserted her for money. When Vašek comes back to learn with delight who she really is, and all four parents urge her to marry him, she becomes even more confused, and after a touching ensemble she is left alone to bewail her situation. The appearance of Jeník provokes her to fury, and she cannot understand why he remains so cheerful. The dénouement comes when the official betrothal is to take place. Jeník, recognized by his father as his long-lost elder son, offers himself to Mařenka to the happiness of all present save Kečal.

For most operagoers, *The Bartered Bride* is the quintessential Czech national opera, although Smetana himself regarded his *Dalibor* and *Libuše* as more seriously nationalistic and was occasionally somewhat dismissive about this most popular of his works. He said that in writing it his model had been Mozart, and certainly the overture has the same vivacity, while the light-hearted intrigues of plot and counter-plot also owe something to Mozart (both *Le nozze di Figaro* and *The Bartered Bride* feature the rediscovery of a long-lost son), as well as perhaps such Italian composers as Rossini and Donizetti. As for Kečal, Smetana may have modeled him on the character Van Bett in Lortzing's *Zar und Zimmermann*.

It took some time before *The Bartered Bride* reached the form in which we know it today, for after the premiere Smetana made a number of major revisions that took him four years in all, not the least of which was the addition of the dances in each act—the polka that ends act I, the *furiant* in act II, and the circus clowns' *skočná* in act III. Another addition was the drinking song in praise of beer as "a gift from heaven" at the start of act II. Although the dances needed to be added for a planned Paris production—the French insisted on it—their incorporation is a gain in every way, while they and the drinking song also give the villagers more to do than simply observe and comment.

Good humor and *joie de vivre* abound in *The Bartered Bride*. But there is much more to the opera than this, with such touching moments as the quintet (later sextet) near the

A playbill for the premiere of *The Bartered Bride*, Prague, 1866

end, where it seems that Mařenka really must marry a man she does not love. The scheming broker Kečal provides comedy and has some effective scenes of frustration and anger too. But it is Vašek who provides the really inventive comic figure; here is a youth who is too sympathetic to be merely a figure of fun, and as sung by Peter Pears in 1943 in a Sadler's Wells production he provided the librettist Eric Crozier with a model for the Suffolk lad Albert Herring in Britten's comic opera of that name four years later.

—Christopher Headington

BARTÓK, Béla.

Composer. Born 25 March 1881, in Nagyszentmiklós, Hungary (now Sînnicolau Mare, Rumania). Died 26 September 1945, in New York City. Married: 1) the pianist Márta Ziegler (two sons); 2) Ditta Pásztory (died 21 November 1982). A child prodigy on the piano, he was initially taught by his parents, then by Ferenc Kersch, Ludwig Berger, and László Erkel; studied harmony with Anton Hyrtl; studied composition with János Koessler and piano with István Thomán at the Budapest Royal Academy of Music, 1899-1903; interested in folksongs as both an ethnomusicologist and a composer—commissioned by the Hungarian Academy of Sciences in 1904 to edit a folksong collection of 13,000 items; taught piano at the Budapest Royal Academy of Music from 1907-1934; moved to New York City in 1940; honorary doctorate, Columbia University, 1940; worked on a collection of Yugoslavian folksongs at Columbia University, 1941-1942. Bartók's only opera is *Duke Bluebeard's Castle* (1918).

Operas

Publishers: Boosey and Hawkes, Universal.

Duke Bluebeard's Castle (*A Kékszakállú herceg vara*), Béla Balázs, 1911 (revised 1912, 1918), Budapest, Budapest Opera, 24 May 1918.

Other works: ballets, orchestral works, chamber music, piano music, vocal works.

Publications

By BARTÓK: books–

Hungarian Folk Music. London, 1931. Originally published as *A magyar népdal.* Budapest, 1924.
Bartók, Béla, and Lord, Albert B. *Serbo-Croatian Folk Songs.* New York, 1951.
Carpitella, D., ed. *Béla Bartók: Scritti sulla musica popolare.* Turin, 1955.
Lord, Albert B., ed. *Serbo-Croatian Heroic Folk Songs.* Cambridge and Belgrade, 1954.

Béla Bartók, c. 1940

Suchoff, Benjamin, ed. *Rumanian Folk Music*. 2 vols. The Hague, 1967-75.
Suchoff, Benjamin, ed. *Turkish Folk Music from Asia Minor. Princeton, 1976.*
Yugoslav Folk Music. Albany, 1978.

Note: for a complete list of Bartók's writings, see Antokoletz, 1988.

Demény, János, ed. Letters. London, 1971.
Suchoff, Benjamin, ed. *Béla Bartók: Essays*. London, 1976.
Bartók, Béla Jr. *Családi levelei* [family letters]. Budapest, 1981.

About BARTÓK: books–

Stevens, Halsey. *The Life and Music of Béla Bartók*. New York, 1953; 1964.
Kroó, György. *Bartók színpadi müvei* [Bartok's stage works]. Budapest, 1962.
Lendvai, E. *Bartóks dramaturgiája*. Budapest, 1964.
Lendvai, E. *Béla Bartók: an Analysis of his Music*. London, 1971.
Leznais, Lajos. *Bartók*. London, 1973.
Kroó, György. *Bartók halauz*. Budapest, 1971; English translation as *A Guide to Bartók,* Budapest, 1974.
Crow, Todd, ed. *Bartók Studies*. Detroit, 1976.
Bonís, Ferenc. *Béla Bartók: his Life in Pictures and Documents*. Budapest, 1972; 1981.
Bartók, Béla Jr. *Apam életének krónikája* [Bartók's life]. Budapest, 1981.

Bartók, Béla Jr. *Béla Bartók mühelyében* [Bartók's workshop]. Budapest, 1982.
Lendvai, E. *The Workshop of Bartók and Kodaly*. Budapest, 1983.
Antokoletz, Elliot. *The Music of Béla Bartók: a study of Tonality and Progression in Twentieth-Century Music.* Berkeley, 1984.
———, ed. *Béla Bartók: a Guide to Research.* New York, 1988.
Griffiths, Paul. *Bartók*. London, 1984.
László, F., ed. *Bartók-dolgoyatok* [Bartók studies]. Bucharest, 1971.

articles–

Nüll, Edwin von der. "Stilelemente in Bartók's Opera." *Melos* May-June (1929).
Oláh, Gustáv. "Bartók and the Theatre." *Tempo* 13-14 (1949-1950).
Veress, Sándor. "Bluebeard's Castle." *Tempo* 13-4 (1949-1950).
Kroó, György. "Duke Bluebeard's Castle." *Studia Musicologica Academiae Scientiarum Hungaricae* 1 (1961): 251.
———. "Data on the Genesis of *Duke Bluebeard's Castle.*" *Studia Musicologica Academiae Scientiarum Hungaricae* 23 (1981).
Mauser, Siegfried. "Die musikdramatische Konzeption in *Herzog Blaubarts Burg.*" *Musik-Konzepte* 22 (1981): 169.

*   *   *

Bartók composed only one opera, *Duke Bluebeard's Castle,* based on the "mystery play" by the contemporary poet Béla Balász. It was also his first vocal work, and the text was offered to him at a highly appropriate time, both in his musical and in his personal development.

By 1911 Bartók had devoted several years to an intensive study of Hungarian folk music, and the fruits of this work had begun to emerge in his own music, in particular in the First String Quartet and the Violin Concerto no. 1. It gave him the courage to throw off the early influences on his style, especially that of Liszt, and he became fascinated by the music of Debussy, who also employed the lydian and whole-tone scales, which are frequently found in Hungarian folk-music.

Bartók had passed through a period of introspection in 1911. An intensely private and self-contained person, he had been obliged first by his unrequited love for the violinist Stefi Geyer, and then by marriage to his young pupil Márta Ziegler, to brood on the violation of individuality which is involved in any close relationship between man and woman. Balász's text is a direct symbolic dramatization of his idea.

The musical style of *Bluebeard* was partially influenced by Debussy's approach to the setting of Maeterlinck's *Pelléas and Mélisande*. Like Debussy, Bartók often uses his large orchestra to create coloristic tone-pictures of setting and landscape. He also displays an acute sensitivity to word-setting; the vocal line follows the intonations and cadences of the spoken Hungarian language, and totally avoids melismas.

Bartók's voice parts are far more passionate than those in *Pelléas,* and the declamation is often of Wagnerian power. The orchestra also plays a role in *Bluebeard* which is opposed to Debussy's aesthetics, despite his influence on its sound. Bartók employs impressionistic devices to evoke the contents of the first six rooms (and memorably adapts the sustained triads of *La cathédrale engloutie* to his own purposes in the climactic revelation at the fifth door), but the overall conception of his opera is post-Straussian. Bartók broke with Strauss in an adverse review of *Elektra* shortly before composing *Bluebeard,* but his one act opera is akin to Strauss' in its grandeur, power, and harmonic savagery. It is also composed on the same principle, as a symphonic poem with an ending which recapitulates the opening (to reflect the movement on stage from darkness to light and then back into utter darkness).

The use of tonal symbolism is also Straussian. Bartók's opera is dominated by a conflict between Judit's tonality of F natural and Bluebeard's F sharp; and this conflict is reinforced by the repeated use of a dissonant *leitmotif,* consisting simply of a repeated minor second, to portray the blood that Judit finds throughout the castle.

The violence and emphatic statement of many passages in the score of *Bluebeard* remove it decisively from Debussy's aesthetic. The debt to Strauss is also transcended by the features which gives Bartók's score its greatest individuality—the folk melancholy of the exquisite woodwind solos which establish the atmosphere in the opening sections of the work, and the predominantly linear, rather than vertical, harmonic procedures.

Bartók submitted *Duke Bluebeard's Castle* to a competition for a new opera; it was unsuccessful, and remained unperformed until 1918. His ballet *The Wooden Prince,* also to a text by Balász, was acclaimed on its first production in 1911, but rarely performed thereafter, and the pantomime *The Miraculous Mandarin*—one of Bartók's greatest scores, if also his most ferocious—was withdrawn after one performance in Cologne in 1926, and not heard in Hungary during the composer's lifetime.

These experiences partially explain why Bartók never wrote another opera, and his personal and financial situation was for many years so precarious that after *The Miraculous Mandarin* he wrote only one more work for orchestra (the *Cantata Profana*) without a commission.

Bartók's musical thinking also became more appropriate to concert than to stage music. During the 1920s and 1930s he was increasingly preoccupied with symmetrical construction, complex numerically based structures, counterpoint and fugue, approaches to composition which are not easily combined with a flexible response to text and stage action.

Hindemith and Berg, among others, have shown that these formal means can be employed successfully in opera. Bartók's reasons for not returning to this medium lie elsewhere. The difficulties he had encountered in achieving performance for his three stage works undoubtedly deterred him, but the fundamental reason is that in *Duke Bluebeard's Castle,* he had found a text which allowed him to express the one subject to which he wished to give lyric and dramatic expression.

—Michael Ewans

DIE BASSARIDEN [The Bassarids].

Composer: Hans Werner Henze.

Librettists: W.H. Auden and C. Kallman (after Euripides).

First Performance: Salzburg, 6 August 1966.

Roles: Dionysus (also Voice and Stranger; tenor); Pentheus (baritone); Cadmus (bass); Tiresias (also Calliope; tenor); Captain (also Adonis; baritone); Agave (also Venus; mezzo-soprano); Autonoe (also Proserpine; soprano); Beroe (mezzo-soprano); Slave (mute); Daughter (mute); chorus (SSAATTBB).

Publications

articles—

Österreichische Musikzeitung 21/no. 369 (1966) [*The Bassarids* issue].
Henderson, Robert. "Henze's Progress: From *Boulevard Solitude* to *The Bassarids.*" *Opera* October (1974).

* * *

When an offstage voice announces Dionysus' arrival in Boeotia (the territory of Thebes and Mt Cithaeron), most Thebans rush off to welcome him. King Pentheus remains sceptical and forbids the worship of Semele, paramour/wife of Zeus and mother of Dionysus, even though (or because) his own mother Agave and his aunt Autonoe are among the Bacchantes. Pentheus sends his Captain of the Guard to arrest all those worshiping on Mt Cithaeron, and he brings back Agave, Autonoe, the blind prophet Tiresias, and a stranger. When Pentheus orders that the prisoner be tortured, the sky darkens and the earth trembles. The stranger shows Pentheus a mirror in which he can observe the rituals on the mountain. Following an intermezzo—the opera is not divided into acts in the traditional manner—Pentheus dresses as a Bacchant and approaches Cithaeron. His mother, in an orgiastic trance, discovers him and leads a group of Bacchantes in tearing him to pieces. When they return to Thebes, however, she comes to realize the horror she has perpetrated. Dionysus orders her, her sisters, and their father, Cadmus (founder of Thebes), into exile.

Bassarids, elsewhere called "Bacchae" or "Bacchantes," are generally Thracian devotees of the god Dionysus (Bacchus). Although Aeschylus had written a tragedy called *The Bassarids,* the story of Henze's opera is an adaptation of Euripides' *Bacchae.* There had been few previous operatic settings of the Euripidean tragedy, the most interesting of which are Egon Wellesz' *Die Bakchantinnen* (1931) and G.F. Ghedini's *Le baccanti* (1948). W.H. Auden and Chester Kallman prepared this libretto for Henze, the same duo who had so ingeniously prepared *The Rake's Progress* for Stravinsky. Their adaptation of the tragedy conveys the horrifying, anti-civilizing forces of the original, which caused Nietzsche to contrast strongly the irrational elements in the worship of Dionysus with rational Apollonian worship. At the same time, Auden and Kallman extend the musical, poetic drama beyond the original text to the realms of commentary and variation, almost to the realm of parody.

Henze, who dislikes the term "eclectic" applied to his music, employs a wide range of musical styles throughout the opera, with modernized fugues, oratorio-style choral singing, and twelve-tone series. Shortly after composing *Die Bassariden,* Henze himself wrote (in *Tradition und Kulturerbe,* 1966) that he conceived of the opera as a nineteenth-century symphony of which the four parts consisted of sonata, scherzo (with Bacchic dances), adagio with fugue (interrupted by the intermezzo), and passacaglia. Above all his model was Mahler, whose music was beginning to experience a great renaissance in the 1960s. Henze found in Mahler's music the same basic struggle between man and nature characterized so markedly in Pentheus' human and rational struggle against Dionysiac natural forces. It provided the musical basis for Henze's psychological exploration of freedom, repression, and revolt.

—Jon Solomon

THE BASSARIDS
See DIE BASSARIDEN

BASTIEN AND BASTIENNE
See BASTIEN UND BASTIENNE

BASTIEN UND BASTIENNE.

Composer: Wolfgang Amadeus Mozart.

Librettist: Friedrich Wilhelm Weiskern and J.A. Schachtner (after J.-J. Rousseau, *Le devin du village,* and Favart, *Les amours de Bastien et Bastienne*).

First Performance: Dr F. Anton Mesmer's garden theater (?), September/October (?) 1768.

Roles: Bastien (tenor); Bastienne (soprano); Colas (bass).

Publications

articles–

Angermüller, Rudolf. "*Les époux esclaves ou Bastien et Bastienne à Alger.* Zur Stoffgeschichte der Entführung aus dem Serail." In *Mozart und seine Umwelt,* edited by the Internationale Stiftung Mozarteum Salzburg, 70. Kassel, 1979.
Tyler, Linda. "*Bastien und Bastienne:* The Libretto, Its Derivation, and Mozart's Text-Setting." *Journal of Musicology* 8 (1990): 197.

*   *   *

Mozart composed his first German opera, *Bastien und Bastienne,* in Vienna at the age of twelve. He and his family spent the entire year of 1768 in the capital hoping to further the young musician's career. One of Mozart's earliest biographers, Georg Nikolaus Nissen, wrote in 1828 that *Bastien und Bastienne* had been composed for a performance at the home of Franz Anton Mesmer, the famous physician, but unfortunately no documents survive to corroborate or refute Nissen's claim.

The plot of the one-act operetta involves only three characters. The shepherdess Bastienne is troubled because the shepherd Bastien has left her. The village soothsayer, Colas, advises Bastienne to feign indifference toward Bastien in order to inspire jealousy. The magician then warns Bastien of Bastienne's new disdain and recites a magic spell to make her appear. After she arrives the two lovers exchange accusations but soon reconcile and vow eternal fidelity.

The libretto of the operetta had gone through at least two major rewritings in France and Austria before Mozart set it to music. It was originally conceived as *Le devin du village* (1752) by Jean-Jacques Rousseau. After Rousseau's work proved a success in Paris, it was parodied in a comic version, entitled *Les amours de Bastien et Bastiene* (1753), written by Marie-Justine-Benoîte Favart and Harny de Guerville. The parody was picked up in Vienna in 1764, translated and adapted into a German comedy by Friedrich Wilhelm Weiskern, an actor and playwright at the Kärntnertor Theater. Mozart set this Viennese version to music in 1768, but a final overlay of textual revision was offered to Mozart after he returned home, by the Salzburg trumpeter Johann Andreas Schachtner. Mozart adopted some of Schachtner's suggestions into his setting, including recitatives to replace the spoken dialogue, but he did not complete his revision of the work. The complex derivation of the text from Paris to Vienna to Salzburg left it a distinctive interfusion of various operatic traditions.

Mozart allowed the diverse layers of his libretto to suggest the directions his musical setting would take. Reflecting the Viennese influence on the text, *Bastien und Bastienne* bears some resemblance to German folk comedy from the early eighteenth century, or genre which had consisted mostly of improvised comic plays dotted with relatively simple musical numbers. This influence is evident in Mozart's prominent use of syllabic declamation, in his occasional satire of *opera seria* rhetoric, and in his avoidance of traditional operatic formal schemes (such as da capo, ternary, binary, and rondeau). But Mozart drew on other traditions as well. Comic "patter" passages, frequent tempo changes within individual numbers, and flexible phrasing patterns testify to the young composer's growing mastery of contemporary *opera buffa* techniques. The French *opéra comique* tradition is evident, too, in the simple yet agile melodic style and the several instances of minor-key middle sections.

Mozart put these different conventions to use in his musical depiction of the opera's three characters. Bastienne's solos are, on the whole, more expansive than those of the two men. Four of her five arias encompass several sections in different tempi or meters, whereas the solos of Bastien and Colas are each set to a single time signature and tempo. Her relatively simple melodic style—attributable partly, no doubt, to the amateur status of the singers for whom Mozart composed the opera—resembles the French and north-German vocal styles more than the Italian tradition, but her arias nonetheless explore a greater emotional range than those of the other characters. The shepherd Bastien maintains a more pastoral character in his three solos. His consistently square-cut phrasing, triadic melodies, and simple repeated rhythmic patterns serve to set him apart from the other two. Colas avails himself more liberally of *buffo* rhetoric. For his charming "Diggi, daggi" aria, Mozart pursued a mock heroic style, beginning slowly, ominously, and in a minor key in the first section before turning to light, Italianate patter in the second.

Like other Austro-German composers working on German opera in the 1760s, Mozart experimented with the blending of many diverse operatic traditions in *Bastien und Bastienne.* His subsequent forays into the genre—*Zaide, Die Entführung aus dem Serail, Der Schauspieldirektor,* and *Die Zauber-flöte*—would testify to new developments in the German operatic tradition as a whole and to a growing maturity in Mozart's own operatic voice, a voice already distinctively resonant in *Bastien und Bastienne.*

—Linda Tyler

LA BATTAGLIA DI LEGNANO [The Battle of Legnano].

Composer: Giuseppe Verdi.

Librettist: Salvatore Cammarano (after J. Méry, *La bataille de Toulouse*).

First Performance: Rome, Torre Argentina, 27 January 1849.

Roles: Lida (soprano); Arrigo (tenor); Rolando (baritone); Marcovaldo (baritone); Federico Barbarossa (bass); First Consul (bass); Second Consul (bass); Podestà of Como (baritone); Imelda (mezzo-soprano); Herald (tenor); chorus (SSATTBB).

* * *

La battaglia di Legnano was Verdi's heartfelt response to the famed "Cinque Giornate," those heady five days of 1848 when a Milanese popular uprising managed, albeit briefly, to oust the hated Austrian overlords. Reflecting the seemingly imminent achievement of Italian independence, the opera is unabashedly patriotic and by rights should have been the *ne plus ultra* of all the composer's risorgimento works. That it turned out to be at once something less and something far more is one of the great ironies of Verdi's creative life.

Due to the political upheavals, Verdi was able to collaborate with veteran librettist Salvatore Cammarano without tying himself to the poet's home theater, the San Carlo in Naples (which, for several reasons, including an overstrict censorship, Verdi wished to avoid). Cammarano proposed to use a play by Frenchman Joseph Méry entitled *La bataille de Toulouse* but backdated its action while interweaving its domestic plot with events in the Italy of 1176 when forces of the Lombard League defeated a teutonic invasion of Friedrich Barbarossa at the Battle of Legnano.

The opening scene depicts forces gathering in Milan to withstand the anticipated German invasion. At their head is the fiery young Arrigo and his old friend Rolando. Everyone thought Arrigo to have been slain at the Battle of Susa, so there is great rejoicing followed by a stirring general oath to defend the fatherland. Meanwhile Rolando's wife, Lida, is in dire distress, as she and Arrigo had previously planned to be wed. On news of his death, and following the wishes of her own dying father, she agreed to marry Rolando. Now Arrigo has returned to the living and wildly berates her for failing to be eternally true to him. Rolando, unaware of all this, joins Arrigo at Como where in the presence of the vacillating civic establishment they defy the threats of Barbarossa. Preparing for the upcoming battle, Arrigo in a secret ceremony is initiated as leader of the "Cavalieri delle Morte" (Knights of Death) while Rolando takes heartfelt leave of his wife and young son. However, at this point Marcovaldo, a German prisoner of war who has himself been spurned by Lida and

noticed her attachment to Arrigo, treacherously informs Rolando of the situation. The enraged husband finds the two of them together in Arrigo's quarters high in a tower, whence Lida has gone to bid her former lover a chaste and final farewell. Assuming the worst, Rolando locks them in the room, as Arrigo's failure to appear at the morning's battle will brand him as cowardly, a fate worse than death to the young hero.

In despair, yet with an exultant cry of "Viva Italia!" Arrigo leaps from the tower window. In the original play the corresponding character was killed by this action, but here he miraculously survives to join his comrades and personally slay Barbarossa in the battle. All this is related to us in the final scene, after which Arrigo, mortally wounded, convinces Rolando of Lida's innocence and dies kissing the flag as a bereaved populace offers benediction.

La battaglia di Legnano is the first opera Verdi conceived *in toto* after his crucial exposure to Parisian musical sophistication and, perhaps even more significantly, after the composition of *Macbeth,* that epochal forward leap which embodies his initial response to the subtleties of Shakespearian dramaturgy. As a result the score is shot through with astounding musical refinements, which while enriching the ear also tend to sap the blatantly nationalistic moments of their primal vigor. Thus superb technical finesse abounds on virtually every page, and a prime example is the Lida/Arrigo duet from act I: the text offers the typical fustian of an irate tenor mindlessly ranting at a grieving soprano for her perfectly understandable decision to marry another, while Verdi's musical response is a finely constructed and thematically organic quasi-sonata movement. Other highlights include Lida's extraordinary solo in act III, not an aria but a series of brief arioso moments linked into a recitative of impressive flexibility. Although the opera has been dismissed as a "pièce d'occasion," a strong case could be made that of all the composer's works prior to *Luisa Miller* that have not found their way into at least the fringes of the repertoire, this opera is most worthy of such inclusion in future. Despite its strident libretto, it is a musical achievement of a very high order.

—Dennis Wakeling

BATTISTINI, Mattia.

Baritone. Born 27 February 1856, in Rome. Died 7 November 1928, in Colle Baccaro, near Rome. Studied briefly with Venceslao Persichini and Eugenio Terziana; traveled in Russia and to South America, but never visited United States; debut at the Torre Argentina, Rome in 1878; Covent Garden debut as Riccardo in Bellini's *I puritani,* 1883; Teatro alla Scala debut in 1888 as Nelusko in *L'africaine;* St Petersburg debut as Hamlet, 1893, thereafter visited Russia annually until 1914; roles include Rigoletto, Don Giovanni, Simon Boccanegra, Wolfram, Telramund; sang until 1926.

Publications

About BATTISTINI: books—

Fracassini, G. *Mattia Battistini: Profilo artistico illustrato.* Milan, 1914.
Palmegiani, F. *Mattia Battistini: il re dei baritone.* Milan, 1945; reprinted 1977.

Mattia Battistini in *Les Huguenots*

articles–

Shawe-Taylor, D. "Mattia Battistini" *Opera* (May 1957): 283.

*   *   *

Battistini was one of the first generation of great singers to leave behind a significant recorded legacy. His career, lasting fifty years—the length of his adult life—began and ended at the top. His debut was in late 1878 as King Alfonso in *La favorita* at the Torre Argentina in Rome. It was an enormous success and was followed within a few months by leading roles in *Il trovatore, La forza del destino* and *Rigoletto.* Although he was to sing in various Italian towns during the next decade culminating in his first Teatro alla Scala season in 1888, Battistini's international career was to begin almost immediately. During 1881 and 1882 he sang extensively in South America, returning there in 1889. In addition to appearances in both London and Paris he also sang frequently in Madrid and Lisbon.

In many ways the decisive step in Battistini's career was his journey to Russia in the winter of 1893 for his first performances in St. Petersburg and Moscow. In both he was to become an enormous favorite. For the next twenty years, until the First World War, the regular pattern of his year was to perform in St. Petersburg and Moscow during the winter months and in Warsaw en route in spring, autumn or both. He appeared in many other Russian cities as well as in Berlin, Vienna, Bucharest, but his performances in Italy were relatively few and far between.

Levik's memoirs include marvellous descriptions of Battistini's Russian appearances: "Battistini was particularly rich in overtones which continued to sound long after he had ceased to sing. You saw that the singer had closed his mouth, but certain sounds still held you in their power. The unusually attractive timbre of his voice caressed the listener, as though enveloping him in warmth." Levik also makes an important point which may help explain the length of Battistini's career: "If Battistini's greatest asset was his voice, then his second was his marvellous training. He attached great importance to work on his voice."

After his youthful journeys to South America Battistini never again crossed the Atlantic and thus never appeared in the USA. His first appearances at Covent Garden were in 1883, but neither then nor later in 1905 and 1906 did he make quite the same impact as he did further East. He was clearly effective in the first London performances of *Eugene Onegin,* but the opera itself had little success. P.G. Hurst claims that in *La traviata* he overshadowed Caruso and Melba, but this was probably not a widely held view. Much later in the 1920s he appeared in several concerts in London and the critics, marvelling at the longevity of his career, vied with each other in a battle of superlatives.

"My school is in my records." Clearly Battistini was very aware of the importance of his recorded legacy. His first records were made in Warsaw in 1902, but while historically fascinating, they do not demonstrate the best in the singer's art. His 1906 series, however, include some of the greatest records ever made.

Battistini recorded until the early 1920s and it becomes easy to appreciate the sobriquet 'King of baritones and baritone of kings'. The style seems aristocratic; vocal production seems easy; there is a finely flowing legato line; the overall effect is frequently of rare beauty. We have to remember that this style of singing has long since vanished for it reflects the age in which Battistini learned his trade. Expression is as important as legato and the singer is profligate with ornamentation which might not be acceptable today. Certainly it seems inappropriate in Mozart and verismo, but Battistini is simply superb in Bellini, Donizetti and early Verdi and, if acceptable in Italian, Massenet and Thomas. All his recordings from *La favorita* are fine. If the legato cannot quite match Renaud, Battistini has the edge in expression. His 1906 recording of 'Il mio Lionel' from *Martha* seems the acme of perfection, whilst there is regal splendor to the wonderful series from *Ernani.* In all his records Battistini seems to be tireless. A less well-trained artist could not have sustained such a career, with almost fifty years devoted to eighty different roles.

—Stanley Henig

BATTLE, Kathleen.

Soprano. Born 13 August 1948 in Portsmouth, Ohio. Studied with Franklin Bens at Cincinnati College-Conservatory (B.M. 1970; M.M. 1971); professional debut at Spoleto Festival in *Ein Deutsches Requiem,* 1972; sang Susanna with New York City Opera, 1976; debut at Metropolitan Opera as Shepherd in *Tannhäuser,* 1978, and has sung over 100 performances there, including Strauss's Zdenka, Rossini's Rosina, Despina, Zerlina, Blondchen, Susanna, Cleopatra in first Metropolitan Opera performance of Handel's *Giulio Cesare* in 1988, and Pamina in 1991; received Laurence Olivier

Award for the Best Performance in a New Opera Production for her Covent Garden debut as Zerbinetta in *Ariadne auf Naxos*; has also appeared with Opéra of Paris, Vienna State Opera, and Lyric Opera, Chicago; honorary doctoral degrees from the University of Cincinnati, Westminster Choir College in Princeton, New Jersey, Ohio University in Athens, Ohio, Xavier University in Cincinnati, and Amherst College.

* * *

Soprano Kathleen Battle has established herself as one of the leading *leggero* sopranos of the 1980s and 1990s. This term designates the vocal type situated between the agile coloratura and the slightly weightier lyric. Throughout her career Battle has remained within her voice category, although she has sung some lyric roles and, with her facility in fioritura, a few coloratura ones as well, choosing roles that require some agility and do not necessitate a particularly large instrument. She has avoided the tendency common in lyric sopranos to venture into the heavier, vocally dangerous spinto roles—roles that can take a physical and emotional toll on a singer.

Battle's repertoire includes Susanna in Mozart's *Le nozze di Figaro,* Blondchen in Mozart's *Die Entführung aus dem Serail,* Despina in Mozart's *Così fan tutte,* Pamina and Papagena in Mozart's *Die Zauberflöte,* Zerlina in Mozart's *Don Giovanni,* Norina in Donizetti's *Don Pasquale,* Adina in Donizetti's *L'elisir d'amore,* Sophie in Massenet's *Werther,* Sophie in Richard Strauss's *Der Rosenkavalier,* Zerbinetta in Richard Strauss's *Ariadne auf Naxos,* Zdenka in Richard Strauss's *Arabella,* the Shepherd in Wagner's *Tannhäuser,* Elvira in Rossini's *L'italiana in Algeri,* Rosina in Rossini's *Il barbiere di Siviglia,* Oscar in Verdi's *Un ballo in maschera,* and Cleopatra in Handel's *Giulio Cesare.*

Although Battle has sung extensively with the Metropolitan Opera (where she made her debut in 1978), she has also sung in the opera houses of Zurich, Chicago, San Francisco, Paris, London, and at the Salzburg Festival. She has also participated in concert performances of Handel's *Semele* and Verdi's *Falstaff* (as Nannetta) at Carnegie Hall.

Battle's voice is pure, light, and lyrical, and it is marked by an exceptional beauty of tone. The purity of her voice is not marked by a "whiteness," the characteristic vibratoless sound of some voices of its type. Although she does not have great power, she has the ability to float high pianissimo notes. Her high range is extended, encompassing the highest notes of Zerbinetta's aria, although it thins out somewhat at the very top. Her voice has been described as ravishing, radiant, and silvery, with effortless high notes of soaring purity; her voice is secure and well controlled. Within a relatively limited dramatic range, she is capable of expressive singing through nuances of tone color, and is able to convey coquetry and charm as well as deeper feelings. Her acting is aided by her clear diction and close attention to the words.

Critics have sometimes found her singing too beautiful for certain of her roles, and they note an excessive coyness in her manner, with the natural sweetness of her voice becoming cloying. Some critics have made reference to her tendency—to use their evocative term—to coo. They have noted that in some roles she emphasizes the soubrettishness of the character at the expense of the wisdom and wit that lie beneath the surface.

Battle has made recordings of some of her roles, including Elvira in Rossini's *L'italiana in Algeri* (under Scimone), Oscar (under Solti), Adina (under Levine), Zerbinetta (under Levine), Papagena (under Lombard), Despina (under Muti), Zerlina (under Karajan), Blondchen (under Solti), Susanna

(under Muti), and the Woodbird in Levine's complete recording of Wagner's *Der Ring des Nibelungen.*

—Michael Sims

———

THE BATTLE OF LEGNANO
See LA BATTAGLIA DI LEGNANO

———

THE BEAR.

Composer: William Walton.

Librettist: P. Dehn (after Chekhov).

First Performance: Aldeburgh, 1967.

Roles: Mme Popova (mezzo-soprano); Smirnov (baritone); Luka (bass); Cook (mute); Groom (mute).

* * *

The Bear was William Walton's second opera. The first, *Troilus and Cressida,* was composed in 1954 in the "grand" tradition of the nineteenth century. *The Bear,* which stands at the other end of the scale from this earlier work, is more closely related to a vaudeville than to grand opera. The libretto was skillfully adapted from Anton Chekhov's one-act play *The Bear* by Paul Dehn and the composer. The action takes place in the drawing room of a young widow, Madame Yeliena Ivanova Popova. The time is 1888. Madame clings to her widowhood, vowing to remain faithful to the memory of her late husband, who was anything but a paragon of virtue. Luka, her bailiff/manservant, announces the arrival of Gregory Stepanovitch Smirnov, a middle-aged landowner to whom Popova's late husband owed 1,300 rubles for oats for the family horse, Toby. Smirnov has come to collect. Popova assures him that her bailiff will pay at the end of the week, but Smirnov insists that he needs the money immediately. Popova exits. Smirnov carries on, moving from lamentation to shouting. Popova re-enters, bothered by the shouting. After an argument, Smirnov challenges her to a duel and she accepts. She gets her husband's pistols. While they brandish pistols and threaten one another, Luka alternately begs Smirnov to leave and prays to God for mercy. Just before shots are fired, Smirnov declares his love for the widow. They embrace.

The music, essentially diatonic, is composed in a style more akin to the music of Walton's *Façade* in its various versions. With such a light-hearted libretto, Walton is able to indulge himself, revealing the extent of his wit and tongue-in-cheek attitude towards his characters. He revels in parody. The music itself is a masterful interweaving of original composition, quotations, and allusions to other composers' works (not to mention a subtle snippet from Walton himself from time to time).

For instance, critics have often suggested that early in the work, while Madame Popova is contemplating a photograph of her late husband, the music is at times pure Tchaikovsky.

A more blatant allusion is apparent during the exchange between Popova and Smirnov, when she admonishes him about his lack of manners, declaring that he is coarse and ill-bred while she is a lady. Smirnov's response is in the style of a French singer; the music strongly suggests Fauré. Smirnov's use of French, of course, is pure conceit, given that the use of that language by nineteenth-century Russians signified refinement and breeding. Critics have also detected bits of Strauss, Offenbach, Verdi, and Britten, in addition to Walton's quotes from himself.

The Bear exhibits a strong rhythmic drive. The action is pushed along by the music, punctuated quite dramatically at appropriate times in the score. Although the instrumentation is light (including a single woodwind, one horn, one trumpet, one trombone, percussion, harp, piano and strings), the composer's skill is evident in the changes of texture that accompany changes of mood in the libretto.

The Bear has been described as "high-spirited" and "rollicking"; it is a farce from start to finish. It is also one of a small number of one-act operas that lend themselves to performance by amateurs as well as professionals. It is effective in its own right, not necessarily requiring all the trappings of elaborate sets and costumes.

—Carolyn J. Smith

BEATRICE AND BENEDICT
See BÉATRICE ET BÉNÉDICT

BEATRICE DI TENDA [Beatrice of Tenda].

Composer: Vincenzo Bellini.

Librettist: Felice Romani (after a novel by Carlo Tebaldi Fores and a ballet by Antonio Monticini).

First Performance: Venice, La Fenice, 16 March 1833.

Roles: Filippo (baritone); Beatrice (soprano); Agnese (soprano); Orombello (tenor); Anichino (tenor); Rizzardo del Maino (baritone or bass); chorus (SSATTBB).

Publications

articles–

Boromé, Joseph A. "Bellini and *Beatrice di Tenda*." *Music and Letters* October (1961): 319.
Lippmann, Friedrich. "Pagine sconosciute de *I Capuleti e i Montecchi* e *Beatrice di Tenda* di Vincenzo Bellini." *Rivista italiana di musicologia* 2 (1967): 140.
Gui, V. "*Beatrice di Tenda*." *Musica d'oggi* 2 (1969): 194.
Galatopoulos, Stelios. "The Romani-Bellini Partnership." *Opera* November (1972).

Brauner, Charles S. "Textual Problems in Bellini's *Norma* and *Beatrice di Tenda*." *Journal of the American Musicological Society* 29 (1976): 99.

*   *   *

The plot of *Beatrice di Tenda* is propelled by each of the principal characters loving someone who does not return his or her love. Filippo Visconti, a fifteenth-century Duke of Milan and husband of Beatrice di Tenda, through whom he rose to power, loves Agnese del Maino, Beatrice's lady-in-waiting. Agnese, while aware of Filippo's feelings, is in love with Orombello, Lord of Ventimiglia. Orombello, however, loves Beatrice. Beatrice, although she complains of Filippo's ingratitude, seems to love neither Filippo nor Orombello; she sings affectionately about her deceased husband. The plot moves through a series of accusations and betrayals. In act I, Orombello foolishly reveals to Agnese that he loves Beatrice. Filippo accusingly confronts Beatrice with a bundle of compromising secret papers, which Beatrice claims are petitions from her loyal subjects. Orombello begs Beatrice to run away with him and rally her supporters to overthrow Filippo, who has failed her both as a husband and as a ruler. Beatrice refuses and orders Orombello to leave, but at that moment they are surprised by Filippo and his retinue. Filippo has them both arrested.

The two main scenes of the second act are a trial scene and the final scene preceding Beatrice's execution. At the trial Beatrice does not defend herself against the accusations but rather questions the legality of being tried by her own vassals. Orombello who, offstage, had confessed under torture, retracts his confession before the judges. Both Agnese and Beatrice express sympathy for his sufferings. Filippo attempts to call off the trial, but now the judges declare that Beatrice must undergo torture. Agnese pleads with Filippo to pardon Beatrice and Orombello, but an attempted uprising by Beatrice's followers convinces Filippo that Beatrice is too great a threat to him. In the final scene Agnese begs Beatrice for forgiveness. Beatrice adds her forgiveness to Orombello's and bravely goes to her death.

Beatrice is the work of the mature Bellini, but it is not Bellini at his peak. The story suggests that the characters are driven by political desires as well as emotional ones. But rather than enhancing the drama, the overabundance of motives just diffuses the focus. Does Filippo believe Beatrice to be guilty of treason or adultery?—or both? or neither? With his motives unclear, both his decision to forgive Beatrice and to condemn her seem equally contrived. Beatrice's inner life is likewise opaque to the audience. What is the source of her abundant courage and fortitude? She has two full-scale arias—one in each act—but the musical effect of these numbers is routine, and when she has sung them our knowledge of her and sympathy for her do not increase much. It is possible that, in creating Beatrice, Bellini set out to generate a character who would outdo Norma in nobility and stature. Unfortunately, he formed a passionless character whom it is hard to care about.

Compared to several of his earlier operas, *Beatrice* has fewer of the long, long lines for which Bellini is so justly famous. A large number of melodies are constructed by accumulating repetitions of a single motive. There are also several open-ended melodies, which are responsible for much of the propulsive force of the opera, but also for a certain sense of incompletion and frustration. Probably the two most successful numbers in the opera are both ensembles of reconciliation—the quintet in act II beginning with Beatrice's text "Al tuo fallo" and the trio at the end of the second act, "Angiol di pace." Bellini borrowed the melody for "Angiol di pace" from one of his earlier operas, *Zaira.*

—Charlotte Greenspan

BÉATRICE ET BÉNÉDICT [Beatrice and Benedict].

Composer: Hector Berlioz.

Librettist: Hector Berlioz (after Shakespeare, *Much Ado about Nothing*).

First Performance: Baden-Baden, 9 August 1862.

Roles: Béatrice (mezzo-soprano); Hero (soprano); Bénédict (tenor); Ursula (contralto); Somarone (bass); Claudio (baritone); Don Pedro (bass); Leonato (mute); Messenger (speaking part); Scrivener (speaking part); Two Servants (speaking parts); chorus (SSATTBB).

Publications

articles–

Addison, A. "*Beatrice and Benedict:* The German Edition." *Berlioz Society Bulletin* 33 (1960): 1.

Rushton, Julian. "Berlioz's Swan-Song: Towards a Criticism of Beatrice et Benedict." *Proceedings of the Royal Musical Association* 109 (1982-83): 105.

* * *

Don Pedro returns from defeating the Moors to stay with the governor of Sicily, Leonato. Among his officers are Claudio, who is betrothed to the governor's daughter Hero, and Bénédict. After a celebratory chorus and Hero's meditation on her love, Hero's cousin Béatrice and Bénédict resume their long-standing war of words in a duet; but aside they admit their fascination with each other. Pedro and Claudio rail at Bénédict's intention to die a bachelor. They plot to have him fall in love with Béatrice; their success leads to his aria of gleeful acquiescence. The first act ends with a nocturnal duet for Hero and her maid Ursula. After a roistering drinking-song, a parallel plot causes Béatrice to fall in love with Bénédict. Following a great internal struggle, revealed in her magnificent aria and a trio with Hero and Ursula, she and Bénédict join Hero and Claudio in a double wedding.

An unkind summary of this slender plot would be *Much Ado about Nothing* without the much ado; the main thread of Shakespeare's drama, the conspiracy against Hero's virtue, is omitted. Instead of the comic police Berlioz invented the Kapellmeister Somarone, affectionately if rather heavily pilloried in his act I fugal epithalamium and act II drinking song. The dialogue is mostly taken from Shakespeare, but the opera suffers from the difficulty singers find in speaking verse, while singing actors certainly cannot manage such sophisticated music.

The tale of Béatrice and Bénédict contains just enough dramatic substance to keep the work afloat, but performance is justified mainly for the sake of the music. The brilliant overture is intricately built on several themes from the opera, yet it forms a secure sonata-form with introduction, enlivened with counterpoint of theme against theme and exuberant modulations. The arias for the title-roles and Hero, and several ensembles of biting wit (notably the act I duet and the men's trio) and delicate sentiment (the Nocturne and the women's trio in act II) form a substantial dramatic score. They are framed by good choruses: the celebration of victory; the pedantic epithalamium; the drinking-song "improvised" by Somarone; a distant chorus with guitar accompaniment which softens Béatrice's heart; and a sturdy processional march. There is also a delicious Siciliano which Berlioz based on a song of his youth.

The most enchanting number, although it stands outside the plot, is the Nocturne for Hero and Ursula, a piece of unsurpassed instrumental delicacy and melodic bloom. But the spirit of Berlioz's swan-song is best summed up in the final Scherzino-duettino (which provides the main theme of the overture). Amid the sparkle of the orchestra the lovers swear to become enemies tomorrow, but through their very levity the brittle textures and deceptive rhythms convey a sense of the gravity of existence which has only previously been hinted at in the melting Nocturne and Béatrice's fiery aria.

—Julian Rushton

BEATRICE OF TENDA
See BEATRICE DI TENDA

BEECHAM, (Sir) Thomas.

Conductor. Born 29 April 1879, in St Helens, near Liverpool. Died 8 March 1961, in London. Married: 1) Utica Celesia Wells, 1903 (divorced, 1942); 2) Betty Hambly, 1943 (died, 1957); 3) Shirley Hudson, 1959. Attended the Rossall School, Lancashire, 1892-97; studied at Wadham College, Oxford; founded the St Helen's Orchestra Society, 1899; conducted with the Hallé Orchestra in Manchester, 1899; conductor of K. Trueman's traveling opera company, 1902; conducted members of the Queen's Hall Orchestra, London, 1905; founded and led the New Symphony Orchestra, 1906-08; founded the Beecham Symphony Orchestra, 1909; worked at Covent Garden and His Majesty's Theatre, 1910-13; conducted opera at the Theatre Royal at Drury Lane; conductor of the Royal Philharmonic Concerts, 1916; knighted, 1916; declared bankruptcy, 1919; conducted the New York Philharmonic, 1928; founded the Delius Festival in London, 1929; founded the London Philharmonic Orchestra, 1932; tour of Berlin with the London Symphony, 1936; toured the United States and Australia, 1940; music director and conductor of the Seattle Symphony Orchestra, 1941-43; guest conductor at the Metropolitan Opera, New York, 1942-44; founded the Royal Philharmonic, 1946; conductor of Covent Garden, 1951; made a Companion of Honour by Queen Elizabeth II.

Publications

By BEECHAM: books–

A Mingled Chime: Leaves from an Autobiography. London, 1944.
Delius. London, 1959.

About BEECHAM: books–

Smyth, E. *Beecham and Pharaoh.* London, 1935.
Cardus, Neville. *Sir Thomas Beecham: a Memoir.* London, 1961.
Reid, C. *Thomas Beecham: an Independent Biography.* London, 1961.
Procter-Gregg, H., ed. *Sir Thomas Beecham, Conductor and Impresario: as Remembered by his Friends and Colleagues.* London, 1975.
Atkins, Harold, and Archie Newman, eds. *Beecham Stories: Anecdotes, Sayings, and Impressions of Sir Thomas Beecham.* London, 1978.
Jefferson, A. *Sir Thomas Beecham: a Centenary Tribute.* London, 1979.

articles–

Legge, Walter. "Sir Thomas." *Opera* May, June, July (1979).
Abromeit, Kathleen A. "Ethel Smyth, *The Wreckers,* and Sir Thomas Beecham." *Musical Quarterly* 73 (1989).

*   *   *

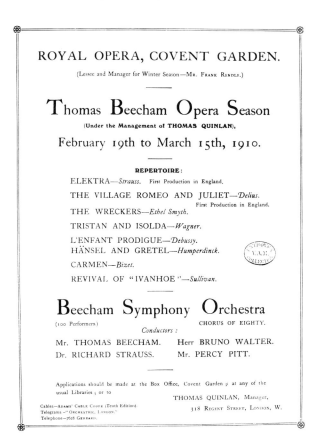

A poster for Thomas Beecham's 1910 opera season, Royal Opera, Covent Garden

During the course of his career, Thomas Beecham founded three major symphony orchestras, raised another to supremacy and saved two more from disaster during World War I. Beecham also established his own opera company and ran it, and he absorbed another into it to save the singers' careers. He introduced the early operas of Richard Strauss to England and presented first performances of two English composers' operas in London—Ethel Smyth and Frederick Delius. He conducted all these enterprises himself and seemed able to make the lightest and apparently the most trivial music sound elevated.

After a period of half-hearted education and whole-hearted opera-going abroad, Beecham became accompanist and assistant conductor to a small, South London opera company for a few weeks. In 1909 he undertook to conduct Ethel Smyth's *The Wreckers* in London, partly as a result of which his father, the millionaire Joseph Beecham, was reconciled with his self-willed son and at once the two of them laid plans to become an operatic force in Britain.

A spring season led by Beecham at Covent Garden and a winter season following it, in 1910, framed another during the summer at His Majesty's Theatre, which all caused some concern to the "reigning" management of Summer Season Grand Opera at Covent Garden. The Beechams allied themselves with Covent Garden during Oscar Hammerstein's ill-fated, ill-conceived occupation of Kingsway in 1911-12, but in 1913 and again in 1914 the Beechams presented the two most magnificent seasons of opera and ballet ever seen in London, at which Sergei Diaghilev's company was the star attraction. Thomas Beecham was the greatest impresario of his time, and probably of all time among Englishmen.

These substantial achievements, however, are only part of the man who devoted a good deal of energy to philandering, to witty and argumentative statements and speeches, to the gaining of profound knowledge on a diversity of subjects, and to his effort to make England the musical capital of Europe—if not of the world—with himself as leader.

As a practicing musician he was an indifferent pianist (he had altogether received little formal training), but he was a born conductor of such magnetism and inspiration that certain players believed themselves able to follow him if he were directing them from another room, out of sight. His conducting methods were not only very personal but completely unconventional. He admitted to not caring about "baton technique" as taught in the music schools that he despised, and gained his control of singers and orchestras and their effects in several ways. He personally and scrupulously marked all section leaders' parts for nuances of dynamics and phrasing, while his intuitive feeling for the music he was playing, coupled with a remarkable memory, personality and enthusiasm, caused all concerned to follow him willingly and precisely. His verbal direction was generally encouraging, and he liked to stress enjoyment above all else. Needless to say, he relied a lot upon his successive leaders, but even so, he sometimes lost his place in the score. His ability to digest complicated works (as demonstrated by his success in carrying out Diaghilev's demand that he conduct a performance of the ballet *Petrouchka* "in two days" time') was sometimes offset by accusations that he only bothered to read the top line in a score.

Joseph Beecham, knighted for his Drury Lane seasons and subsequently created a baronet, bought fourteen acres of London that included Covent Garden and Drury Lane Theatres as well as the fruit and vegetable market. Because of the war, plans were laid to ensure the safe amortization of payments at a meeting on a certain day in 1916, but on the early morning of that day, Sir Joseph Beecham was found dead.

His son, the new Sir Thomas Beecham Bart, was left with an enormous debt. The bankruptcy that resulted necessitated the immediate cancellation of all his plans, and forced his retirement from music.

Between the wars, Beecham made a come-back by conducting a spirited performance of *Die Meistersinger* with the British National Opera Company, overcoming, for one hot summer's evening only, what he considered a slap-dash attitude in the company. Between 1932 and 1939 he was established as conductor, musical director and impresario at Covent Garden, but his hopes of continuing there after the war in 1946 were never fulfilled. Artistic enterprises in Britain were increasingly becoming controlled by accountants, not by "eccentrics." This was one of the worst disappointments— among many—in Beecham's life, for he had striven since the first decade of the century to establish a truly national opera, and had gone a long way toward doing so.

Beechams operatic activities abroad were many and varied. He was the first non-German to conduct *Der Rosenkavalier* in Hamburg and from memory, and he was an associate conductor at the Metropolitan Opera in New York during part of World War II. His last operatic venture was at Bath in 1955, when he presented and conducted performances of *Zémire et Azor* by Grétry, although he was scheduled—at last—to direct Mozart's *Die Zauberflöte* at Glyndebourne, when he became too ill to do so.

The complete operas which Beecham recorded stand today as landmarks in this genre, and perhaps one way of getting to grips with the man Beecham is by listening to a record compiled from snatches at rehearsals with the Royal Philharmonic Orchestra. This includes a side devoted to *Die Entführung aus dem Serail*, when many facets of his musical knowledge and ability, his wit and gentle vulgarity, his appropriate attitudes towards people on differing occasions and his secure handling of singers and musicians alike are all combined in this audio portrait of one of the most remarkable Lancastrian-Englishmen there have ever been.

—Alan Jefferson

BEESON, Jack.

Composer. Born 15 July 1921, in Muncie, Indiana. Studied with Burrill Philips, Bernard Rogers, and Howard Hanson at the Eastman School of Music, New York (M.M. 1943); private study with Bartók while attending Columbia University as a graduate student; joined Columbia faculty in 1945; MacDowell Professor of Music, 1967-88; American Prix de Rome, 1948-50; Guggenheim fellowship, 1958-59; member, American Academy and Institute of Arts and Letters, 1976.

Operas

Publishers: Boosey and Hawkes, MCA, Mills, Presser.

Jonah, Beeson (after P. Goodman), 1950.
Hello Out There, Beeson (after Saroyan), 1954, New York, 27 May 1954.
The Sweet Bye and Bye, K. Elmslie, 1965, New York, 21 November 1957.
Lizzie Borden, K. Elmslie, 1960-65, New York, New York City Opera, 25 March 1965.

My Heart's in the Highlands, Beeson (after Saroyan), 1969, performance on National Educational Television, 17 March 1970.
Captain Jinks of the Horse Marines, S. Harnick (after C. Fitch), 1975, Kansas City, 20 September 1975.
Dr. Heidegger's Fountain of Youth, S. Harnick (after Hawthorne), 1978, New York, 17 November 1978.

Other works: orchestral works, vocal works, choral works, piano pieces.

Publications

By BEESON: articles–

"Grand and not so Grand." *Contemporary Composers on Contemporary Music,* edited by E. Schwartz and B. Childs, 316. New York, 1967.
"Magic, Music and Money." *The Columbia University Forum Anthology,* 22. New York, 1968.
"The Autobiography of Lizzie Borden." *Opera Quarterly* 4 (1986): 15.
"Composers and Librettists: Marriages of Convenience." *Opera Quarterly* 6 (1988-89): 1.

About BEESON: articles–

Eaton, Q. *"Hello Out There," "The Sweet Bye and Bye," "Lizzie Borden," "My Heart's in the Highlands."* In *Opera Production: A Handbook.* St Paul, 1961-74.

Jack Beeson has been associated with American opera as both a composer, champion, and conductor. He was involved in the premiere of the Virgil Thomson/Gertrude Stein collaboration, *The Mother of Us All,* in 1947, at the same time as he was writing his opera, *Jonah,* which he completed as a recipient of the Prix de Rome Fellowship and as a Fulbright Fellow in Rome. He would return to Rome as a Guggenheim Fellow in 1958-1959, to compose a number of orchestral and chamber works.

Beeson's operas draw on material from the American tradition. Perhaps his most renowned effort is *Lizzie Borden,* with a libretto by Kenward Elmslie, based on the true story of a daughter who brutally murdered her own parents. This opera, composed between 1960-1965, was premiered by the New York City Opera, and later broadcast on public television. He received a number of prestigious commissions for other operas, most notably from the National Endowment for the Arts for *Captain Jinks of the Horse Marines* (1975), with a libretto by Sheldon Harnick, from the National Educational Television Opera for *My Heart's in the Highlands* (1969), for which he wrote his own libretto, and from the National Arts Club for *Doctor Heidegger's Fountain of Youth* (1978), with a libretto by Sheldon Harnick.

In addition to the Prix de Rome and the Guggenheim Fellowship, Beeson has received the Marc Blitzstein Award for the Musical Theater, awarded by the American Academy and Institute of Arts and Letters, the National Arts Club Gold Medal for Music, and the Columbia University Great Teacher's Award.

Beeson's music is marked by simplicity and lyricism. He was greatly influenced by the American operatic composer Douglas Moore (*The Ballad of Baby Doe*), who promoted an American operatic style characterized by immediacy in both music and action. Never inclined to modernism, Beeson prefers harmony which is largely diatonic, often with vestiges of modality reminiscent of folk music. His accessible idiom stood at odds with much American music produced at universities and conservatories in the 1950s and 1960s. Nevertheless, he has remained true to his commitment to a populist idiom for American opera in the tradition of Moore and Carlisle Floyd, drawing upon native lore and history for his subject matter, and composing music with a rustic cast.

—Jonathan Elliott

BEETHOVEN, Ludwig van.

Composer. Born 15 or 16 December 1770, in Bonn. Died 26 March 1827 in Vienna. Basic music instruction with his father, then piano lessons with Tobias Friedrich Pfeiffer; keyboard and music theory instruction with Gilles van Eeden; violin and viola lessons with Franz Rovantini; enrolled at the University of Bonn, 1789, but never finished his formal training; composition study with Christian Gottlob Neefe; appointed deputy court organist by the elector Maximilian Franz, 1784; violinist in theater orchestras, 1788-92; studied with Haydn in Vienna, 1792; counterpoint lessons with Johann-Georg Albrechtsberger, 1794-95; lessons in vocal composition with Salieri, 1801-02; Prince Karl von Lichnowsky a benefactor, beginning 1800; first public appearance in Vienna, 29 March 1795, playing one of his piano concertos; performance of his works and competitions in Prague, Dresden, Leipzig, Berlin, and Vienna, 1796-1800; "Heiligenstadt Testament," 6 and 10 October 1802 [Beethoven's document concerning his growing deafness]; composition of *Symphony No. 3,* "Eroica," 1803-04; asked by Emanuel Schikaneder in 1803 to set his libretto, *Vestas Feuer (The Vestal Flame),* which he began but did not finish; began work on *Fidelio,* first performed 1805; numerous concerto, chamber, and solo piano works composed 1802-14; *Symphony No. 9,* 1824; last string quartets (op. 127, 130, 131, 132, 133, 135), 1824-26.

Operas

Editions:

L. van Beethovens Werke: Vollständige kritisch durchgesehene überall berechtigte Ausgabe, 24 vols. Leipzig, 1862-5; [supplement] vol. 25, Leipzig, 1888.
L. van Beethoven: Sämtliche Werke: Supplement zur Gesamtausgabe, Edited by W. Hess. Wiesbaden, 1959-71.
L. van Beethoven: Werke: Neue Ausgabe sämtlicher Werke, Edited by J. Schmidt-Görg et. al. Munich and Duisburg, 1961-.

Vestas Feuer, Emanuel Schikaneder, 1803 [fragment].
Fidelio, oder Die eheliche Liebe, J. Sonnleithner (after J.N. Bouilly, *Léonore ou L'amour coniugal),* 1804-05, Vienna, Theater an der Wien, 20 November 1805; revised 1805-06, Vienna, Theater an der Wien, 29 March 1806; revised 1814, Vienna, Kärntnertor, 23 May 1814.

Other works: symphonies, concertos, chamber music, piano solo music, choral works, songs, ballets, dances.

Publications

By BEETHOVEN: books–

Hamburger, M., ed. *Beethoven: Letters, Journals and Conversations.* London, 1951.
Anderson, Emily, ed. and trans. *The Letters of Beethoven.* London, 1961.
Köhler, K.-H., and G. Herre. *Ludwig van Beethovens Konversationshefte.* Leipzig, 1968.

Note: for a complete list of Beethoven's writings, see *The New Grove Dictionary of Music and Musicians,* 1980 ed.

About BEETHOVEN: books–

Kufferath, M. *Fidelio de L. van Beethoven.* Paris, 1913.
Hess, W. *Beethovens Oper Fidelio und ihre drei Fassungen.* Zurich, 1953.
————. *Beethovens Bühnenwerke.* Göttingen, 1962.
Solomon, Maynard B. *Beethoven.* New York, 1977.
Pahlen, Kurt. *Ludwig van Beethoven-"Fidelio" Ein Opernführer.* Munich, 1978.
Csampai, Attila, and Dietmar Holland, eds. *Ludwig van Beethoven. "Fidelio." Texte, Materialien, Kommentare.* Reinbek bei Hamburg, 1981.
Mayer, Hans. *Versuch über die Oper.* Frankfurt am Main, 1981.
John, Nicholas, ed. *Ludwig van Beethoven. "Fidelio." English National Opera Guides* 4. London, 1988.
May, Robin. *Beethoven.* London, 1990.

articles–

Schiederman, L. "Über Beethovens 'Lenore'." *Zeitschrift der Internationalen Musik-Gesellschaft* 8 (1906-07): 115.
Engländer, R. "Paers *Lenora* und Beethovens *Fidelio.*" *Neues Beethoven-Jahrbuch* 4 (1930): 118.
Anderson, Emily. "Beethoven's Operatic Plans." *Proceedings of the Royal Musical Association* 88 (1961-62): 61.
Dean, Winton. "Beethoven and Opera." In *The Beethoven Companion,* edited by Denis Arnold and Nigel Fortune, 374. London, 1971.
Ruhnke, Martin. "Die Librettisten des *Fidelio.*" In *Opernstudien: Anna Amalie Abert zum 65. Geburtstag.* 121. Tutzing, 1975.
Tyson, Alan. "The Problem of Beethoven's 'First' *Lenore* Overture." *Journal of the American Musicological Society* 28 (1975): 292.
————. "Das Leonoreskizzenbuch (Mendelssohn 15): Probleme der Rekonstruktion und der Chronologie." *Beethoven-Jahrbuch* (1977): 469.
Avant-Scene Opera May-June (1977) [*Fidelio* issue].
Tyson, Alan. "Yet Another 'Leonore' Overture?" *Music and Letters* 58 (1977): 192.
Pulkert, Oldrich. "Die Partitur der zweiten Fassung von Beethovens Oper *Lenore* im Musikarchiv des Nationaltheaters in Prag." In *Bericht über dem Internationalen Beethoven-Kongress 20,* edited by Harry Goldschmidt, Karl-Heinz Kohler, and Konrad Niemann, 247. Leipzig, 1978.
Carner, Mosco. "Fidelio." In *Major and minor* [a collection of essays by Carner]. London, 1980.
Schuler, Manfred. "Zwei unbekannte *Fidelio*-Partiturabschriften aus dem Jahre 1814." *Archiv für Musikwissenschaft* 39 (1982): 151.

Wagner, Manfred. "Rocco, Beethovens Zeichnung eines Funktionärs." *Österreichische Musikzeitschrift* 37 (1982): 369.

Gossett, Philip. "The arias of Marzelline: Beethoven as a composer of opera." *Beethoven-Jahrbuch* 10 (1983): 141.

Pulkert, Oldrich. "Historische Aspekte der Fidelio-Subjekts." In *Ars iocundissimo: Festschrift für Kurt Dorfmüller zum 60. Geburtstag,* edited by Horst Leuchtmann and Robert Münster, 257. Tutzing, 1984.

Robinson, Paul. "*Fidelio* and the French Revolution." *Cambrige Opera Journal* 3 (1991): 23.

*   *   *

In the face of Beethoven's extensive output in the other leading genres of his day—five piano concertos, nine symphonies, sixteen string quartets, thirty-two piano sonatas—his one completed opera *Fidelio* in many ways stands as an anomaly. Why only one, and one existing in three versions and with no less than four different overtures? Although many critics have suggested a lack of empathy for the art form, a more compelling answer is to be had in the composer's lifelong adherence to the tenets of the Enlightenment, a philosophy that, among other things, taught that humans can overcome the antagonisms that separate them one from another, that any problem can be overcome by sufficient and untrammeled use of reason, that nature provides an unerring source of joy and wisdom, and, as Immanuel Kant (a philosopher Beethoven greatly esteemed) proclaimed in 1784, that happiness can be granted to all who would "dare to be wise."

Beethoven's faith in the tenets of the Enlightenment is reflected on the one hand in his attraction to philosophically idealistic literary works in general and on the other hand in the texts he set to music. A telling, albeit extreme case in point is his thirty-year fascination with Friedrich Schiller's 1785 poem "An die Freude" ("To Joy"); first documented in 1793, when the Bonn jurist B. L. Fischenich wrote to the poet's wife reporting the twenty-three year-old composer's desire to set the poem to music as well as his dedication to the "great and the sublime," it was not until the choral finale of the Ninth Symphony in 1824 that the ambition bore fruit. In a sense, then, *Fidelio* is but one chapter within a much larger creative undertaking, one in which Beethoven's dedication to the poetically exalted impelled him to ever "strive," as he wrote to Christine Gerhardi in 1797, "toward the inaccessible goal which art and nature have set us."

A cursory survey of just a few of the many operatic librettos Beethoven rejected bears this out. Heinrich Collin's 1809 proposal for an opera on *Bradamante* was abandoned because the composer found it had "a soporific effect on feeling and reason." Emanuel Schikaneder's 1803 *Vestas Feuer* (The Vestal Flame) was discarded after Beethoven had completed the opening scene because he found the "language and verses" were of the sort "such as could only proceed out of the mouths of our Viennese apple-women." The plan for an opera on Goethe's *Faust,* first broached in 1808, was squelched when Beethoven met Goethe in 1812 and formed the opinion that the venerated poet enjoyed the trappings of the courtier "far more than is becoming to a poet." "Glitter," Beethoven grumbled to his publishers Breitkopf & Härtel, was more important to Goethe than being the "leading teacher of a nation." (For his part Goethe found the composer "an absolutely uncontrolled personality.") The same high-mindedness underlies his assessment of the subjects other composers deemed worthy of operatic treatment. Thus he found the story of Mozart's *The Marriage of Figaro* ridiculous and that of *Don Giovanni*

offensive. And although in 1822 he praised Rossini's comic opera *The Barber of Seville,* he advised him to stay away from serious opera as it was "ill suited to Italians. You do not possess sufficient musical knowledge to deal with real drama."

Needless to say, a taste for the idealistic does not a satisfactory opera make, particularly if the ethical values are pursued at the expense of character development or musical interest. In addition, there is always the risk the allied philosophy will gain the upper hand, or—far worse—ring insincere, which the American critic and composer Virgil Thomson obviously believed Beethoven succumbed to now and again when he berated him (in his once-famous essay "Mozart's Leftism") as "an old fraud who just talked about human rights and dignity but who was really an irascible, intolerant, and scheming careerist." Yet Chopin, surely the Romantic composer least influenced by Beethoven but one who knew well the full possibilities of musical expression, maintained that "Beethoven embraced the universe with the power of his spirit."

For all Thomson's vituperative spleen-venting, it is Chopin's pronouncement that rings with greater authority. The reason why—apparent especially in *Fidelio,* a work with a text that makes clear its meaning—is that Beethoven succeeds so well in musically realizing the philosophical implications of the libretto. Joseph Kerman has persuasively put forward the notion that starting with the "Eroica" Third Symphony (composed two years before the first version of *Fidelio*) "Beethoven's compositions become to a cardinal degree pointed individuals," individuals moreover that "one meets and reacts to . . . with the same sort of particularity, intimacy, and concern as one does to another human being." While the principal characters of *Fidelio* may occasionally strike us as of the cardboard variety, the concerns and emotions they voice nevertheless are expressed with universal persuasiveness, a manifestation of the composer's abiding interest in humanity as a whole. Indeed, one is moved to agree with Beethoven's own statement made in 1814 that the opera succeeds in speaking to and in turn engendering "kindred souls and sympathetic hearts for that which is great and beautiful."

Far from displaying a lack of empathy for opera, Beethoven, in aspiring to the "great and beautiful" in *Fidelio,* succeeded not only in that, but also in creating a work steeped in mastery of the medium. One need not doubt that the author of the glorious canon quartet "Mir ist so wunderbar," Leonore's "Abscheulicher! Wo eilst du hin?," the prisoner's chorus "O welche Lust!," the gradually-mounting intensity of Florestan's recitative and aria "Gott! welch ein Dunkel hier!," or the ecstatic duet "O namenlose Freude," sung by Leonore and Florestan in celebration of their long-awaited reunion, was anything less than an operatic composer of the first rank.

—James Parsons

THE BEGGAR'S OPERA.

Composer: Johann Christoph Pepusch (and others).

Librettist: John Gay.

First Performance: London, Lincoln's Inn Fields, 28 January 1728.

Roles: Mr Peachum (bass); Mrs Peachum (mezzo-soprano); Polly (mezzo-soprano); Captain Macheath (tenor); Filch (tenor or speaking); Lockit (baritone); Lucy (soprano); Mrs Trapes (contralto); Beggar (speaking); Player (speaking); several lesser roles for all voice ranges; chorus (SATB).

* * *

The Beggar's Opera is a "ballad opera," so called because the structure involves dialogue alternating with familiar tunes. The style grew out of a French vaudevillian practice of ridiculing grand opera; as French touring companies visited England, the genre gained instant popularity, and the practice was quickly adopted. For years England had subsisted on mostly Italianate opera that was considered effete by the general public. Singers were imported from many countries who might sing in their own language; also, most lead roles in Italian opera were given to castrato singers. The English considered the practice of castration barbaric and disliked the sound produced by castrati, and foreign opera came to be considered affected and unnatural.

A ballad opera by Scottish composer Allan Ramsay entitled *The Gentle Shepherd* had been published around 1725. This work, which contained verse in Scottish dialect and songs set to Scottish tunes, was not performed in England until the year following the success of *The Beggar's Opera*. The published score of *The Gentle Shepherd,* however, was well known among intellectual circles in London, and came to the notice of a group including Alexander Pope, Dean

Swift, and John Gay. Pope later wrote that Ramsay's pastoral was on Swift's mind when he suggested that their mutual friend Gay should write a set of Quaker Pastorales, or a pastoral set in Newgate (the notorious London prison which held suspects awaiting trial) among the whores and thieves. From this comment supposedly arose the idea for the opera, although Gay changed the form from a pastoral to a comedy.

The plot deals with the intrigues of several characters associated with Newgate prison: Mr Peachum (a receiver of stolen goods and an informer), his "wife" and their daughter Polly; Lockit (the keeper of Newgate); his daughter, Lucy; Captain Macheath (a highwayman); Filch (Peachum's young assistant); and assorted male and female criminals. In a prologue, a beggar explains to a player that the opera was written for a celebration of the marriage of two ballad singers, Moll Lay and James Chanter. The beggar then goes on to satirize and ridicule foreign opera.

In the first scene Peachum and Filch are discussing a jailed woman when Mrs Peachum enters and expresses her concern about Polly and Macheath. Filch reveals that Polly and Macheath have been secretly married. Polly enters and they chide her for this indiscretion. Finally, they decide that Macheath must hang in order to keep the reward in the family (as well as Macheath's knowledge of Peachum's operations). Polly protests, but to no avail; she is sent to hang him, but decides instead to warn him.

Macheath's gang have been drinking in their hideout, where Macheath tells them that he must go into hiding. They leave, and Macheath, proclaiming his love for women, sends

A ticket for a benefit performance of *The Beggar's Opera,* **London, c. 1728 (engraving after Hogarth)**

for some dancers. The women gradually seduce Macheath, removing his weapons playfully. When he is disarmed, Peachum enters and takes Macheath prisoner. Macheath is fettered in Newgate, where he must pay extortion money for a lighter set of irons. Lucy Lockit enters and berates him for his marriage. (Macheath is a rake who is chasing both Polly and Lucy.) He denies that he is already married and promises Lucy that he will marry her.

Meanwhile, Peachum and Lockit are quarreling about sharing the reward for Macheath. Lucy tries unsuccessfully to bargain for Macheath's release and returns to his cell with the bad news. Macheath suggests a bribe. Polly enters, insists that she is Macheath's legal spouse, and begins to fight with Lucy. Peachum drags Polly off, after which Macheath makes more promises to Lucy, who steals the key and sets him free.

There is a short scene in a gaming house, followed by a scene in which Lockit and Peachum learn of Macheath's escape. Lucy tries to poison Polly; meanwhile, Macheath is recaptured, but warns his gang against Peachum and Lockit. Polly and Lucy visit Macheath to say goodbye. He advises them to go to the West Indies to get married. The Jailer announces that Macheath has five more wives (each with a child) waiting to say goodbye; Macheath announces that he is quite ready to be hanged immediately.

Finally, the beggar and player re-enter. The player insists that the beggar can't hang Macheath; the beggar retorts that he can and will. The player insists that that would make the opera into a tragedy, and that it must end happily because it is a comedy; the beggar concurs, and Macheath is saved.

The Beggar's Opera is distinguished by several innovations. All of the characters in it were expected to both sing and act, unlike the performers of the masques of the time, and there was a total absence of recitative, unlike the practice in Italian operas. The music was almost entirely borrowed—twenty-eight of the tunes are Old English, fifteen Irish, five Scottish and three French songs with the remaining eighteen tunes by individual composers; three by Henry Purcell, two each by John Barrett, Henry Carey, Jeremiah Clarke and G.F. Handel, and one each by G.M. Bononcini, John Eccles, G. Frescobaldi, F. Geminiani, J.F. Pepusch, Lewis Ramondon, and John Wilford. (A list of the sources and attributions of the sixty-nine airs can be found in Edward J. Dent's edition of *The Beggar's Opera,* London, Oxford University Press, 1954.) *The Beggar's Opera* provoked much controversy on the grounds of immorality, and its immediate success was phenomenal—during the first season, ending in June 1728, it received sixty-two performances.

—Meredith Wynne

BEHRENS, Hildegard.

Soprano. Born 9 February 1937, in Oldenburg. Law degree from the University of Freiburg; studied voice with Ines Leuwen at Freiburg Music Academy; debut as Countess in *Le*

Hildegard Behrens as Brünnhilde in *Siegfried,* from Peter Hall's production of *Der Ring des Nibelungen,* Bayreuth, 1983

nozze di Figaro, Freiburg, 1971; sang at Deutsche Oper am Rhein in Düsseldorf, 1971; in Düsseldorf and Frankfurt she sang Fiordiligi in *Così fan tutte,* Agathe in Weber's *Der Freischütz,* Elsa, Musetta, Katya Kabanova, and Marie in Berg's *Wozzeck*; Salome at Salzburg, 1977; debut as Giorgetta in *Tabarro* at Covent Garden and Metropolitan Opera in 1976; sang Brünnhilde at Bayreuth, 1983.

German dramatic soprano Hildegard Behrens has had a successful career as a Wagnerian soprano. Many would argue, however, that her chief strengths lie elsewhere, that her voice is basically unsuited to the demands of the Wagnerian roles. Known as an intelligent and committed singer, Behrens has demonstrated that a lyric instrument can be employed in heavier repertoire, but at a cost. She has shown that dramatic involvement and dedication can carry a singer through even when the purely vocal requirements cannot fully be met.

Behrens's breakthrough came in 1977 with her performance of the title character in Richard Strauss's *Salome* in Salzburg under Herbert von Karajan. Since then she has performed Elettra in Mozart's *Idomeneo* (a role for which she is more suited dramatically than vocally), Elena in Janáček's *The Makropoulos Case,* Katya Kabanová, Isolde in Wagner's *Tristan und Isolde,* and the Empress in Richard Strauss's *Die Frau ohne Schatten,* as well as Richard Strauss's Ariadne. She first sang the three Brünnhildes in 1983 at Bayreuth under Georg Solti's baton.

Known as an intelligent singer (she studied law at the University of Freiburg), Behrens researches her characters before she performs them for the first time. Her performances are rarely less than interesting, and Behrens's intentions are generally clear even when they are not completely realized. She is best at portraying psychologically complex characters. An instinctive actor, she objects to directors who impose outlandish concepts on the operas. She sees opera as a medium for catharsis, the revelation of truth to the audience. Few would question Behrens's dedication; her performances possess a riveting intensity, combining vocal frailty and dramatic power. At its best, her singing has a majesty and stateliness.

Behrens's strength has always been in her gleaming, powerful top notes, notes that have remained stunningly effective even while the rest of her voice has shown signs of wear. Her assumption of roles that put excessive strain on her voice has undoubtedly contributed to the vocal problems critics have noticed in some of her performances. Defects that were incipient in her early years, and which were concealed by her many virtues, have, inevitably, become more prominent. Even early in her career, her voice had an unfocused, tremulous quality in its middle register, an unsteadiness that may have contributed to her ability to portray vulnerable characters but that can be disconcerting for the listener.

Although much of her career has been founded on the Wagnerian heroines—Sieglinde, Brünnhilde, Isolde—it is arguably in two Richard Strauss roles, Salome and Elektra, that she has created her greatest achievements. Her Elektra, especially as heard in concert performances with the Boston Symphony, is an astonishing welding of dramatic and vocal qualities, both in the bloodcurdling portrayal of Elektra's obsession and in the tenderness of the recognition scene, as well as in the heartbreaking moment when Elektra recalls the beauty she once possessed. This role, in which the title character holds the stage from her first appearance a few minutes after the rise of the curtain until the end, allowed her to demonstrate what she has described (in another context) as the necessity for both the passion and the steel of a role to be there from the beginning.

Behrens's Wagnerian characterizations have been well received, largely because of her combination of effective acting—she is able to convey searing passion as well as vulnerability—and the necessary strong high notes. She is relatively deficient in such aspects as stamina (the effort sometimes shows) and the sense of being in possession of unlimited resources; although she generally rises to the occasion, the listener may find it difficult to relax in the confident belief that Behrens will not run out of voice. She also lacks the ideal smoothness of the middle register and solidity of tone for Wagnerian roles.

Her recordings of complete operas, other than ones taken from staged performances, include the roles of Salome (under Karajan), Brünnhilde in James Levine's complete *Ring* cycle, Isolde (under Bernstein), Agathe in *Der Freischütz* (under Kubelik), Truth in Magnard's *Guercoeur* (under Plasson), and the Dyer's Wife in Richard Strauss's *Die Frau ohne Schatten* (under Solti).

—Michael Sims

BELLINCIONI, Gemma.

Soprano. Born 18 August 1864, in Monza, daughter of bass Cesare Bellincioni and contralto Carlotta Savoldini. Died 23

Gemma Bellincioni as Fedora

April 1950. Married tenor Roberto Stagno, whom she met in 1886; studied with her father and Stagno; debut in Pedrotti's *Tutti in Maschera,* 1880; further study under Luigia Ponti dell'Armi and Giovanni Corsi; sang in Spain and Portugal, 1882; sang in Rome 1885; appeared at Teatro alla Scala, 1886; she and Stagno created Turiddu and Santuzza in *Cavalleria rusticana* in Rome, 1890; created Giordano's Fedora; first Italian Salome under Strauss's baton, Turin, 1906; occasional appearances in Holland into the 1920s.

* * *

In the world premiere of *Cavalleria rusticana* in Rome in 1890, Gemma Bellincioni and her tenor partner, Roberto Stagno, created the parts of Santuzza and Turiddu. The public was transfixed by two singers of exceptional histrionic ability who were able to bring the drama set in the Sicilian village so vividly to life.

Bellincioni had already enjoyed an active career of some eleven years prior to this performance. Her characterizations were already unorthodox in that she was not content just to sing a role, but strove to create realism in her portrayals and thus was not always understood by the public. At the Teatro alla Scala, for example, her Violetta (*La traviata*) was coolly received by a public used to more conventional interpretations, though she had had great success in other theaters. She was obviously an artist still to find her métier.

After the first performance of *Cavalleria rusticana,* Bellincioni soon found herself in demand all over the world and before long became acknowledged as the supreme exponent of the art of verismo singing. She was idolized in Italy and won great acclaim in the great operatic centers of Europe, where her career was mainly centered. Many of her former colleagues adapted to the new style and she soon found herself singing with a rising, young generation of artists already versed in the requirements of the verismo school. Many were fine actors as well as singers: Enrico Caruso, Mario Sammarco, Eugenio Giraldoni, Edoardo Garbin and Giovanni Zenatello, among others.

Bellincioni's records are of exceptional interest to the collector. In their way they are as important to posterity as her contribution is to operatic history. She recorded just four titles for the Gramophone and Typewriter Company in 1903 and a further ten for Pathé in 1905. Of the four titles in 1903, two of the discs are of arias from roles she created, "Voi lo sapete" from *Cavalleria rusticana* and "O grandi occhi lucenti" from *Fedora.*

By the time she recorded, Bellincioni had been singing for about twenty-four years, including many verismo roles which may have taken their toll on her voice. It is quite possible, therefore, that by the time she came to record, the voice was no longer at its best; at the very least, it is unlikely to have been the same voice that created a sensation in 1890. In all her recordings her singing is characterized by a strong vibrato and extensive use of the chest register, both qualities she would almost certainly have employed to good effect on the stage. There is also a strong sense of drama, a wide range of vocal color and a keen pointing of the text. But also evident is a fine technique (she was, after all, initially trained in belcanto), obvious in the rapid coloratura (swift execution of florid scalework) of the aria from *La traviata* and the fine trills in the *Mefistofele* aria. Her recording of the aria from *Cavalleria rusticana* is of the utmost interest, and it is said that her interpretation of that aria was a model for many subsequent interpreters of the role of Santuzza.

Bellincioni was of supreme importance in operatic history and future generations can consider themselves fortunate that the gramophone arrived in time to capture her art for posterity.

—Larry Lustig

BELLINI, Vincenzo.

Composer. Born 3 November 1801, in Catania, Sicily. Died 23 September 1835, in Puteaux, near Paris. Studied with his father, Rosario Bellini, and grandfather Vincenzo Tobia Bellini, and at the Real Collegio di Musica di San Sebastiano (Naples) with Giovanni Furno, Giacomo Tritto, Carlo Conti, Girolamo Crescentini and Niccolò Zingarelli; *Il pirata* commissioned for Teatro alla Scala, Milan, 1827; various successes in Milan and Venice, 1827-31; unsuccessful production of *Beatrice di Tenda,* Venice, 1833; in London and then Paris, where, on the recommendation of Rossini, he was commissioned to write *I Puritani* produced at the Théâtre-Italien in 1835. His principal librettist was Felice Romani; he was closely associated with the tenor Rubini from 1827, and the soprano Giuditta Pasta from 1830.

Operas

Adelson e Salvini, Andrea Leone Tottola, Naples, Teatrino del Collegio San Sebastiano, January 1825.
Bianca e Gernando, Domenico Gilardoni, Naples, Teatro San Carlo, 30 May 1826.
Bianca e Fernando (second version of *Bianca e Gernando*), Felice Romani (after Gilardoni), Genoa, Teatro Carlo Felice, 7 April 1828.
Il pirata, Felice Romani (after M. Raimond, *Bertram ou Le pirate*), Milan, Teatro alla Scala, 27 October 1827.
La straniera, Felice Romani (after Victor–Charles Prévost, vicomte d'Arlincourt, *L'étrangère*), Milan, Teatro alla Scala, 14 February 1829.
Zaira, Felice Romani (after Voltaire), Parma, Teatro Ducale, 16 May 1829.
I Capuleti ed i Montecchi, Felice Romani (after Scevola, *Giulietta e Romeo* and Ducis, *Roméo et Juliette,* Venice, Teatro La Fenice, 11 March 1830.
Ernani, Felice Romani, late 1830 [unfinished].
La sonnambula, Felice Romani (after a ballet-pantomime by Eugène Scribe and Jean-Pierre Aumer), Milan, Teatro Carcano, 6 March 1831.
Norma, Felice Romani (after Louis Alexandre Soumet), Milan, Teatro alla Scala, 26 December 1831.
Beatrice di Tenda, Felice Romani (after a novel by Carlo Tebaldi Fores and a ballet by Antonio Monticini), Venice, Teatro La Fenice, 16 March 1833.
I Puritani, Carlo Pepoli (after Jacques-Arsène Ancelot and Joseph Xavier Boniface *Têtes rondes et cavaliers,* Paris, Théâtre-Italien, 24 January 1835.

Other works: early orchestral works, sacred and secular vocal works.

Publications

By BELLINI: books–

Pastura, F., ed. *Le lettere di Bellini*. Catania, 1935.
Cambi, L., ed. *Vincenzo Bellini: epistolario*. Milan, 1943.

About BELLINI: books–

Damerini, A. *Vincenzo Bellini, 'Norma': guida attraverso il dramma e la musica*. Milan, 1923.
Andolfi, O. *Norma di Vincenzo Bellini*. Rome, 1928.
_____. *La sonnambula di V. Bellini*. Rome, 1930.
Schlitzer, F. *"I Capuleti e i Montecchi" di Vincenzo Bellini: l'autografo della partitura*. Florence, 1956.
Pastura, Francesco. *Bellini secondo la storia*. Parma, 1959.
Rinaldi, M. *Felice Romani*. Rome, 1965.
Lippmann, Friedrich. *Vincenzo Bellini und die italienische Opera Seria seiner Zeit*. Cologne, 1969.
Orrey, Leslie. *Bellini*. London, 1969.
Weinstock, Herbert. *Vincenzo Bellini: his Life and his Operas*. New York, 1971; London, 1972.
Ricci, Franco Carlo. *Momenti drammatici nel treatro belliniano*. Rome, 1973.
Oehlmann, W. *Vincenzo Bellini*. Zurich, 1974.
Atti del convegno di studi sull' opera "Bianca e Fernando" di Vincenzo Bellini. Genoa, 1978.
Cataldo, G. *Il teatro di Bellini—Guida critica a tutte le opere*. Bologna, 1980.
Adamo, Maria Rosaria, and Friedrich Lippmann. *Vincenzo Bellini*. Turin, 1981.
Brunel, Pierre. *Vincenzo Bellini*. Paris, 1981.

Vincenzo Bellini, c. 1825, portrait by Carlo Arienti

Atti del simposio Belliniano celebrato in occasione del 150° anniversario della 1° esecuzione di "Norma." Catania, 1981.
Tintori, Giampiero. *Bellini*. Milan, 1983.
Metzger, Heinz-Klaus and Rainer Riehn, eds. *Vincenzo Bellini*. Munich, 1985.
Tintori, Giampiero. *I teatri di Vincenzo Bellini*. Palermo, 1986.
Maguire, Simon. *Vincenzo Bellini and the Aesthetics of Early Nineteenth-Century Italian Opera*. New York, 1989.

articles–

Wagner, Richard. "Bellini: ein Wort zu seiner Zeit." *Zuschauer* 7 (1837); reprint in *Bayreuther Blatter* (1885); English translation by W.A. Ellis in *Richard Wagner's Prose Works*. vol. 8, London, 1899; 1972.
Gray, Cecil. "Bellini." *Music and Letters* 7 (1926): 49.
Tonelli, L. "I libretti di Bellini." *Bollettino dei musicisti* 2 (1934): 75.
Einstein, Alfred. "Vincenzo Bellini." *Music and Letters* 16 (1935): 325.
Pannain G. "'Norma': Cento anni." In *Ottocento musicale italiano*, 49, Milan, 1936.
Porter, Andrew. "Bellini's Last Opera." *Opera* May (1960): 315.
_____. "An Introduction to *La sonnambula*." *Opera* October (1960): 665.
Boromé, Joseph A. "Bellini and *Beatrice di Tenda*." *Music and Letters* October (1961): 319.
Lippmann, Friedrich. "Pagine sconosciute de *I Capuletti e i Montecchi* e *Beatrice di Tenda* di Vincenzo Bellini." *Rivista Italiana di Musicologia* 2 (1967): 140.
Gui, V. "*Beatrice di Tenda*." *Musica d' oggi* 2 (1969): 194.
Lippman, Friedrich. "Su *La straniera* di Bellini." *Nuova rivista musicale italiana* 5 (1971): 565.
Galatopoulos, Stelios. "The Romani-Bellini Partnership." *Opera* November (1972).
Petrobelli, P. "Nota sulla poetica di Bellini: a proposito de *I puritani*." *Muzikoloski zbornik* 8 (1972): 70.
Monterosso, R. "Per un' edizione di *Norma*." In *Scritti in onore di Luigi Ronga*, 415, Milan and Naples, 1973.
Orrey, L. "The Literary Sources of Bellini's First Opera." *Music and Letters* 65 (1974): 24.
Brauner, Charles S. "Textual Problems in Bellini's *Norma* and *Beatrice di Tenda*." *Journal of the American Musicological Society* 29 (1976): 99.
Degrada, Francesco. "Prolegomeni a una lettera della *Sonnambula*." In *Il melodramma italiano dell' ottocento: studi e ricerche per Massimo Mila*. Turin, 1977.
Petrobelli, Pierluigi. "Bellini e Paisiello: altri documenti sulla nascita dei *Puritani*." In *Il melodramma italiano dell' ottocento: studi e ricerche per Massimo Mila*. Turin, 1977.
Avant-scène opéra September-October (1980) [*Norma* issue].
Gherardi, Luciano. "Una novella di Matteo Bandello 'riletta' da Felici Romani per Vincenzo Bellini." *Arte Musica Spettacolo* 4 (1981).
Collins, Michael. "The Literary Background to Bellini's *I Capuleti e i Montecchi*." *Journal of the American Musicological Society* 35 (1982): 532.
Avant-scène opéra March (1987) [*Les Puritains* issue].
Joly Jacques. "Felice Romani; ou, Le Classicisme romantique." *Avant-Scène Opéra* July (1989).
Avant-scène opéra July (1989) [*Les Capulets et Les Montaigus* issue].

Willier, Stephen A. "Madness, the Gothic, and Bellini's *Il pirata." Opera Quarterly* summer (1989).

*　　*　　*

Vincenzo Bellini may be considered the most efficient of the Italian operatic composers of the first half of the nineteenth century in that he made the greatest impact with the smallest product. Rossini composed about thirty-eight operas in about twenty years, Donizetti sixty-five operas in twenty-seven years and Verdi twenty-eight operas in fifty-four years. Bellini composed only ten operas in a ten year period, but on the basis of these works (or, in fact, a subset of these works), his importance in the history of opera and his value to lovers of opera is secure.

The principal events of Bellini's development as a composer were his acquisition of the eighteenth-century Neapolitan heritage, his mastery of the musical style of his day (shaped in part by Rossini's legacy and subject to currents of romantic thought), and finally his formulation of a unique personal style. His ten operas may be viewed in four stylistic categories.

Bellini's first two operas, *Adelson e Salvini* (1825) and *Bianca e Gernando* (1826) are well-crafted copies of already out-of-date stylistic models. *Adelson e Salvini,* Bellini's graduation piece, composed in his last year at the Naples Conservatory, is an *opera semiseria* having among the characters a noble lover, a comic servant who speaks Neapolitan dialect, and an impulsive artist. The libretto of *Bianca e Gernando,* with noble characteristics and a tyrant bloodlessly deposed at the conclusion, suggests a conservative *opera seria.* Musically, however, *Bianca* shows Bellini coming to terms with a more modern, Rossini-influenced musical style, particularly in the construction of multi-tempo arias.

Bellini's next two operas, *Il pirata* (1827) and *La straniera* (1829) are his most innovative, progressive works. They were composed for Milan, a city in which opera-goers were less steeped in and reverent towards eighteenth-century styles than in Naples. They were composed to librettos written by Felice Romani, Bellini's partner in the creation of all his mature operas except for *I Puritani.* These two operas show clear Romantic tendencies both in text and music. Both operas derive their stories from nineteenth-century depictions of medieval times. *Il pirata,* set in thirteenth-century Sicily, is based on a melodrama, *Bertram, ou le pirate,* by M. Raimond (possibly a pseudonym for Isadore Taylor) first performed in Paris in 1826. *La straniera,* set in thirteenth-century Brittany, is based on a novel by Victor-Charles Prévost, vicomte d'Arlincourt. In both operas the characters are propelled to their doom by overwhelming passions. Gualtiero in *Il pirata* and Arturo in *La straniera* both die at their own hands when they recognize they cannot be united with the women they love. For these works Bellini developed a melodic style, sometimes called *canto declamato* and sometimes *canto d'azione* which, standing somewhere between recitative-like and aria-like vocal writing, allowed a more flexible progression of the drama. Emotional texts were declaimed in a more direct, less embellished way. Formal shapes of the arias are more varied. In the case of Arturo in *La straniera,* the aria is abandoned entirely as a means of presenting the character.

Bellini's next two operas, *Zaira* (1829) and *I Capuleti ed i Montecchi* (1830) represent a kind of retrenchment from Romantic strivings with respect to texts, although Bellini continued to work with increasingly fluid and flexible melodic ideas between the borders of recitative and aria. *La sonnambula* (1831) and *Norma* (1831) attain a superb classical equipoise, a perfect balance between musical means and dramatic

ends. In Bellini's last two operas, *Beatrice di Tenda* (1833) and *I Puritani* (1835), this balance is once more disturbed. *Beatrice,* with a tenor who is dragged onstage after undergoing torture, would seem to adumbrate the *verismo* violence of *Tosca.* But one gets the impression that neither Romani's nor Bellini's heart was in this work. *I Puritani,* which, like *La sonnambula,* has a last-minute happy ending, moves on emotional ground more comfortable for Bellini. Unfortunately, Bellini was deprived of Romani's skills and support when he composed *I Puritani.* Thus, although *I Puritani* is among Bellini's richest and most advanced musical scores, the effect of the opera is weakened by an amateurish libretto by Carlo Pepoli.

One of Bellini's most significant distinguishing features, setting him apart from and in some ways above Rossini and Donizetti, was his sensitivity to the text he was setting. Bellini himself was the first to recognize and proclaim his dependence on good texts, specifically good texts written by his preferred poet, Felice Romani. In 1828, when Bellini's friend Francesco Florimo suggested that Bellini might set a libretto by Rossi, Bellini responded, "however much Rossi could make a good libretto for me, nevertheless he never, never, could be a poet like Romani, and especially for me, for I am so reliant on good words." In 1835, after a breach with Romani had led Bellini to set a libretto by another poet (*I Puritani* by Carlo Pepoli) Bellini again wrote to Florimo, "I shall try to make peace with Romani; I have great need of him if I want to compose for Italy again; after him nobody else can satisfy me." Richard Wagner who, of course, thought a good deal himself on the interrelations of words and music in musical drama, recognized Bellini's skillful handling of texts. He told Florimo, in 1880, "Bellini is one of my predilections: his music is all heart, closely, intimately linked to the words."

However, to say simply that Bellini was sensitive to his texts could be misleading. He cared about texts on the level of poetry and within the bounds of the single scene. All evidence indicates that Bellini viewed a libretto as a collection of parts—scenes or set numbers. He seems not to have thought of a libretto as a whole as having a structural integrity or dramatic consistency. After a story had been decided on, Bellini began composing when he had the texts for the first few scenes; he did not wait to see a completed libretto before he began composing. Similarly, work on an opera stopped when Bellini had composed three to four hours worth of music. *Norma* and *I Puritani* both shorten the endings of their source plays, at least in part because enough music had already been composed.

It is also a mistake to think that good texts were necessarily the inspiration of Bellini's fine melodies. Bellini routinely wrote wordless melodies—vocalises or *solfeggietti*—as a kind of compositional exercise. Many of his operas make use of melodies borrowed from earlier works. Thus, what Bellini sometimes needed from Romani was not a text to inspire him, but a text that would flawlessly fit a pre-existing melody.

No Bellini opera is performer-proof. Without a sympathetic and informed performance, his operas may fail to make a strong effect. Bellini himself seemed aware of and comfortable with his dependence on good singers for successful performances. When negotiating with representatives of various opera houses about the composition of a new work, Bellini's first concern was the singers who would give the premiere. (That Romani would provide the libretto for the new opera was not a negotiating point but a given.) When Bellini found satisfactory singers he was loyal to them. Bellini composed *La sonnambula, Norma,* and *Beatrice di Tenda* fully mindful of the talents of the prima donna Giuditta Pasta. The roles of Gernando in *Bianca e Gernando,* Gualtiero in *Il pirata,* Elvino in *La sonnambula,* and Arturo in *I Puritani* were composed for the unique vocal talents of Giovanni-Battista Rubini. Antonio Tamburini was Bellini's baritone in the revised *Bianca e Fernando, Il pirata, La straniera,* and *I Puritani;* Luigi Lablanche his bass in *Bianca e Gernando, Zaira,* and *I Puritani.* For his leading ladies, Bellini preferred singers with considerable dramatic gifts. He admired Pasta and also Maria Malibran, whom he heard perform *La sonnambula,* in English, in London. He considered Giulia Grisi, who created the role of Adalgisa in *Norma* and Elvira in *I Puritani* a rather cool singer.

Musicologists disagree as to where to place Bellini on the classic-romantic continuum. Simon Maguire emphasized Bellini's classical roots, Gary Tomlinson calls Bellini an "ambivalent Romantic," while Friedrich Lippman characterizes Bellini as "a composer who took a strong sensual delight in sound, and who in passages of ecstatic sonority proved himself a Romantic *par excellence.*" Certainly, particularly at the beginning of his career, Bellini was pleased to think of himself as an innovator and as a composer with a distinct personal style.

In 1834 Bellini wrote to Carlo Pepoli, "opera, through singing, must make one weep, shudder, die." This remark may be taken as the composer's credo. Curiously, if one reads through Bellini's letters for examples of the composer's own evaluation of his works, one can find him most often praising a cleverly conceived chorus or a good stroke of orchestration. After the premiere of an opera he often pointed to the good effect this or that number had when this or that singer performed it. The instances in which he praises one of his melodies, as such, are rare. Nevertheless, Bellini's contributions to the art of melody must be considered his most important artistic legacy. Tomlinson has commented, "no later Italian composer, and least of all Verdi, failed to be touched by the sweeping changes in melodic style that he more than any other single composer brought about. These changes included, in addition to his lyricism of heavenly lengths—his *"melodie lunghe lunghe lunghe"* in Verdi's famous phrase—the incisive *canto declamato* and enhanced recitative styles." Bellini fashioned a style of melodic utterance which, denuded of coloratura ornamentation, could have a direct emotional impact even in the space of a phrase or two.

An important innovation of Bellini's with regard to melodic structure was his placement of the climax close to the end of the piece. "Qui la voce" in *I puritani* is a particularly exquisite example of this type of construction. Interestingly, this change in the placement of the melodic climax parallels a change in dramaturgy in Italian Romantic opera; the climax of the drama is pushed as close to the final curtain as comprehensibility will allow. As the hero or heroine walks or plunges to his or her death, no time is allowed for a final peroration given by a secondary character or by the chorus. The audience is given just enough time to react emotionally, not to reflect. One may return to Bellini's statement that "opera, through singing, must make one weep, shudder, die," not consider, draw conclusions, intellectualize.

—Charlotte Greenspan

BENE, Adriana Gabrieli del (La Ferraresi).

Soprano. Born c. 1755, in Ferrara; died after 1799, in Venice. Married: Luigi del Bene, 1783. Studied at the Conservatorio dei Mendicanti in Venice, and with Antonio Sacchini; sang in London, 1785-86; sang at Teatro alla Scala, 1787; sang in Vienna, 1788-91; premiered Mozart's *Così fan tutte,* 1790; sang in Warsaw, 1792-93; sang in Italy, 1797-99.

Publications:

About BENE: books–

Burney, C. *The Present State of Music in France and Italy.* London, 1771.
Da Ponte, L. *Memorie.* New York, 1823-29.
Michtner, O. *Das alte Burgtheater als Opernbühne.* Vienna, 1970.
Hodges, Sheila. *Lorenzo Da Ponte.* London, 1985.

The first reference to Adriana Gabrieli del Bene occurs in Charles Burney's *The Present State of Music in France and Italy,* published in 1771. He heard her sing at the Conservatorio dei Mendicanti, one of four institutions in Venice where illegitimate girls were brought up and given an outstanding musical education by the finest masters in Italy—the composer Antònio Sacchini was among del Bene's teachers. "One of [the girls], la Ferrarese, sung very well," Burney wrote, "and had a very extraordinary compass of voice, as she was able to reach the highest E of our harpsichords, upon which she could dwell a considerable time in a fair, natural voice."

Only after her elopement in 1783, when she was nearly thirty, could she begin her operatic career. Two years later she was singing leading roles at the King's Theatre in London. Her reception was mixed. Many critics praised her brilliant execution, but Earl Mount Edgcumbe, an indefatigable opera goer, was not enthusiastic. "The late first woman Ferrarese del Bene, who had been . . . extolled to me," he recorded in his memoirs, "was but a very moderate performer. She was this year degraded to *prima buffa,* but even in that subordinate line was so ineffective, that Sestini was recalled to strengthen the company." However, her reputation was high enough for the Burgtheater in Vienna to engage her as their *prima donna.* The public was enthusiastic, although the Emperor Joseph II did not like her, describing her voice as weak and her person as ugly. But press and audiences alike were astounded by the extraordinary range of her voice, from an astonishing top note to a strikingly low one. The *Rapport von Wien* commented that not within living memory had such a voice been heard within the walls of Vienna.

Before long she became the mistress of Lorenzo Da Ponte, the librettist of the Burgtheater, who wrote, "Her voice was a delight, her technique new and marvellously affecting; her figure was not especially pleasing and she was not a particularly good actress, but with two ravishing eyes and a charming mouth, there were few operas in which she did not please immensely." But she had a violent and jealous disposition, and an arrogant attitude towards her public, and this, combined with Da Ponte's extreme partisanship, aroused the envy and dislike of the other singers and the hostility of the directors of the opera house.

However, in the early days all went well. She took the roles which had formerly been sung by Nancy Storace (q.v.), including the part of Susanna in a revival in 1789 of *Le nozze di Figaro.* Mozart composed two new arias for her on this occasion. Of one of them, "Un moto di gioia," he remarked that it should be a success if she was capable of singing it naïvely, which he very much doubted. The arias which he wrote for her in the role of Fiordiligi in *Così fan tutte* bear witness to the remarkable compass of her voice, especially the immensely taxing "Come scoglio."

After Vienna she no longer sang in leading opera houses. But during her brief career even her most severe critics acknowledged her profound knowledge of music—a legacy of her education at the Conservatorio dei Mendicanti—the unsurpassed range of her voice, and her versatility, for her roles included *prima donna* parts in both *opera seria* and *opera buffa.*

—Sheila Hodges

BENEDICT, (Sir) Julius.

Composer. Born 27 November 1804, in Stuttgart. Died 5 June 1885, in London. Studied with J. C. L. Abeille in Stuttgart and Hummel in Weimar; became a private pupil of Weber; conductor at the Kärntnertor Theater, Vienna, 1823, and at the Teatro San Carlo and the Teatro Fondo, Naples, 1825; in Paris, 1834; in London, 1835; music director of the Opera Buffa at the Lyceum Theatre, 1836; conducted opera at the Drury Lane Theatre, 1838-48; conducted the Monday Popular Concerts at Covent Garden; director of the Norwich Festivals, 1845-1878; accompanied Jenny Lind on her American tour, 1850-52; conducted the Liverpool Philharmonic Society, 1876-80. Benedict was knighted in 1871.

Operas

Giacinta ed Ernesto, L. Riciutti, Naples, Teatro Fondo, c. 1827.

I portoghesi in Goa, V. Torelli, Naples, Teatro San Carlo, 28 June 1830.

Un anno ed un giorno, D. Andreotti, Naples, Teatro Fondo, 19 October 1836.

The Gypsy's Warning, G. Linley and R.B. Peake, London, Drury Lane Theatre, 19 April 1838.

The Brides of Venice, A. Bunn, London, Drury Lane Theatre, 22 April 1844.

The Crusaders, A. Bunn, London, Drury Lane Theatre, 26 February 1846.

The Lake of Glenaston, 1862.

The Lily of Killarney, John Oxenford (after Dion Boucicault), London, Covent Garden Theatre, 8 February 1862.

The Bride of Song, H. B. Farnie, London, Covent Garden Theatre, 3 December 1864.

Other Works: cantatas, one symphony, instrumental works, two piano concertos, songs, piano pieces.

A scene from the first performance of Julius Benedict's *The Lily of Killarney,* **London, 1862**

Publications

By BENEDICT: books–

A Sketch of the Life and Works of the late F. Mendelssohn-Bartholdy. London, 1850.
Carl Maria von Weber. London, 1881; 2nd ed. 1913.

About BENEDICT: books–

Bunn, A. *The Stage.* London, 1840.
Legge, R.H. *Annals of the Norfolk Music Festival, 1834-93.* London, 1896.
Barnett, J.F. *Musical Reminiscences and Impressions.* London, 1906.
Bennett, J. *Forty Years of Music.* London, 1908.
De Filippis, F. *Cronache del Teatro di S. Carlo.* Naples, 1961.
Warrack, J. *Carl Maria von Weber.* London, 1968.

If Benedict's operas are somewhat eclectic in character, this is hardly surprising, since he was himself European in the widest sense of the word. The son of a Stuttgart banker, he studied with Weber, spent nine years in Italy, then moved to London for the rest of his life, where he was knighted in 1871. All of these varied influences left their mark on his musical compositions, though, as might be expected in his early years, the Germanic elements in his work sometimes proved too much for Italian audiences, while the Italian elements were not always to the taste of the nationalistic Germans.

Benedict's first three operas were all written and produced during his time in Naples, where he was conductor of the San Carlo and Fondo theatres. His *Giacinta ed Ernesto* was given in 1829, though it proved too "German" for Italian consumption. His *I portoghesi in Goa,* given in 1830, was successful in Naples but less so when performed in Stuttgart a few months later. His third opera, the one-act *Un anno ed un giorno* was given first in Naples in 1836 and then in London the next year, following his appointment as musical director of the Opera Buffa at the Lyceum Theatre.

During his time as musical director of Drury Lane (1838-48), he was not only responsible for two immensely successful productions of the period—Balfe's *The Bohemian Girl* and Wallace's *Maritana*—but he also composed three operas of his own: *The Gypsy's Warning* (1838), *The Brides of Venice* (1844) and *The Crusaders* (1846). None of them achieved any lasting success, the nature of his music being neither as positive as that of Weber nor as melodious as that of Rossini. In his late 50's, however, the melding of his various talents combined to produce a minor masterpiece in the form of *The Lily of Killarney* (words by Dion Boucicault and John Oxenford), which, given at Covent Garden in 1862, became so successful that it was performed not only in Europe but in Australia and the U.S.A. as well. The success of *The Lily of Killarney* was never repeated, however, and though his final opera, *The Bride of Song* (a one-act work with words by H.B. Farnie), was given at Covent Garden in 1864, it failed to capture the popular imagination as well; only the rather Weberish overture is still to be found in popular collections of nineteenth century music.

Taken as a whole, Benedict's operas are primarily of historical rather than musical interest, and though musically literate, their structure is usually more like that of operetta, with a series of short, small-scale numbers, than like that of true opera.

—Gerald Seaman

BENOIS, Alexandre [Aleksander Nikolayevich].

Designer. Born 4 May 1870, in St Petersburg. Died 9 February 1960, in Paris. His great-grandfather was director of Venice's Teatro La Fenice, and his grandfather designed the Bolshoi Theater, Moscow; primarily associated with Diaghilev's Ballet Russe; operatic debut: *La vendetta dell' Amore,* Court Theater of the Hermitage, 1900.

Opera Productions (selected)

Boris Godunov (second act only), Paris, 1908.
Le rossignol, Paris, 1914.
Le médicin malgré lui, Paris, 1924.
Philémon et Baucis, Paris, 1924.
L'impératrice aux rochers, Paris, 1927.
Le coq d'or, Paris, 1927.
Manon, Buenos Aires, 1931.
Le jongleur de Notre Dame, Milan, 1938.
La bohème, London, 1946.

Publications

About BENOIS: books–

Ernst, S. *Alexandre Benois.* Petrograd, 1921.
Gregor, J., and R. Fulop-Miller. *Das Russische Theater.* Vienna, 1928.
Cogniat, R. *Décor de Théatre.* Paris, 1930.
Leven, P. *The Birth of the Ballet Russe.* London, 1936.
Armani, F., and G. Bascape. *La Scala.* Milan, 1951.
Bestetti, C. *Cinquecenti anni di opera e balletto in Italia.* Rome, 1954.
Cinquante ans de spectacles en France [Librairie Théatrale]. Paris, 1955.
Thyssen-Bornemiza Collection: Set and Costume Designs [Sotheby's Catalogue]. London, 1987.
I Benois del Teatro alla Scala. Milan, 1988.

articles–

Jaremic, S. "Alexandre Benois." *Iskusstvo* [Kiev] (1911).

The name of Alexandre Benois is likely to be associated forever with the designs he did for Diaghilev's 1911 production of *Petroushka* in Paris and the fourteen other productions of this ballet he was to design, the last being in 1958. His other ballet designs included well-known versions of *Giselle* (Adam), *Les sylphides,* and *Swan Lake.* The operas on which Alexandre Benois worked were few in number but did include the premiere of *Le rossignol* (1914) and two Gounod operas: *Le médecin malgré lui* and *Philémon et Baucis* (1924), all of which were designed for Diaghilev. Benois wanted his son, Nicola, to work with him on the Gounod works, but Nicola's

Set design by Alexandre Benois for Rimsky-Korsakov's *The Golden Cockerel*, Paris, 1927

relations with Diaghilev were strained at the time, and he worked instead for the Teatro alla Scala.

The Benois family, of French origin, had had links with the theater for several generations; Alexandre's great-grandfather had been a director of the Teatro La Fenice. After growing up and studying in St Petersburg, where the family had settled, Benois became a member of the "Mir Isskoustva" group, named after the arts magazine which Diaghilev had founded. Benois became a painter and art historian, both of which accomplishments can be seen in his stage designs. His first operatic designs were for an unstaged production of *Orfeo ed Euridice* (Gluck) in 1895, and his first designs to reach the stage were for a Mariinsky *Götterdämmerung* in 1903. The first opera designs he did for Diaghilev were those for the second, "Polish," act of *Boris Godunov* with Chaliapin in the title role, part of Diaghilev 1908 Paris season.

Benois stayed in Russia until 1926, where he taught, painted, and designed for the stage, including a production of *The Queen of Spades* in 1921. In the West, he worked mainly for Ida Rubinstein, although he did design operas for Paris and Buenos Aires. After the break-up of the Rubinstein company, he continued to design ballets and occasional opera, mostly for La Scala, until his death in 1960.

—Oliver Smith

BENOIS, Nicola [Nicolai Aleksandrovich].

Designer. Born 2 May 1901, in St Petersburg. Died 30 March 1988, in Coidropo. Son of Alexandre Benois. Began work with his father in Paris; operatic debut with *Boris Godunov* and *Khovanshchina*, Paris, 1925; moved to Italy, where he became a scenic designer in Rome, 1927-32, and then chief scenic designer for the Teatro alla Scala, Milan, 1936-1970.

Opera productions (selected)

Boris Godunov, Paris, 1925.
Khovanschina, Paris, 1925.
Der Ring des Nibelungen, Rome, 1927-1931.
Tsar Saltan, Milan, 1929.
Ernani, Milan, 1936.
Mosè, Milan, 1936-37.
Aida, Verona, 1938.
Boris Godunov, Florence, 1940.
Lucrezia Borgia, Milan, 1951-52.
Anna Bolena, Milan.
L'assedio di Corinto, New York, 1975.

Publications

About BENOIS: books–

Cinquante ans de spectacles en France [Librairie Théatrale]. Paris, 1955.

Ardoin, J. *Callas: the Art, the Life.* London, 1974.
Due centi anni di Teatro alla Scala—la scenographia. Bergamo, 1977.
Visualità del Maggio. Florence, 1979.
Thyssen-Bornemiza Collection: Set and Costume Designs [Sotheby's Catalogue]. London, 1987.
I Benois del Teatro alla Scala. Milan, 1988.

*   *   *

Whereas his father, Alexandre, designed more ballets than operas, Nicola Benois is remembered mainly for the operas he designed at the Teatro alla Scala, Milan, especially the Visconti/Callas *Anna Bolena* (1957). His career in the theater was a long one, and it spanned a period which went from Constructivism to Pop Art—none of which was reflected in his work.

After working for an experimental group in Paris, Nicola Benois designed Toscanini's 1925 production of *Khovanshchina* at the Teatro alla Scala. His early work reflected the painterly style of his father, Alexandre, particularly his scenery for more "realistic" operas (both father and son often included figures in their sketches.) For costume design, both men drew their inspiration from paintings of the same time in which the opera is set (e.g. Dürer for *Faust,* Chardin for *Manon Lescaut,* etc.) but Nicola's sketches show more expression of character.

In 1937, after designing operas for various theaters, Nicola Benois was appointed director of productions at La Scala, a post he would occupy until 1970. He continued to study with Italian painters, and his style became much less realistic than that of his father. For Russian opera his designs showed the influence of the pre-revolutionary school; for German works there were hints of expressionism (Slevogt especially); while for Italian opera Benois seems to have based his designs on the styles which were current at the time of the creation of the opera in question. Benois's scenery and costumes for the 1962 revival of *Les Huguenots* were probably the last to convey the impression of the way opera had always been staged; his last opera designs for the Teatro alla Scala were for *Tosca* in 1974.

—Oliver Smith

BENUCCI, Francesco.

Bass. Born c. 1745, in Livorno; died 5 April 1824, in Florence. Appeared in Pistoia in 1769 and in Italy for next ten years; leading character buffo in Venice, 1778-9, and in Milan 1779-82; in Vienna 1783, 1784-1795 as a member of group of Italian singers that included Nancy Storace; created Figaro in *Le nozze di Figaro* in 1786, Leporello in *Don Giovanni* in 1788, Guglielmo in *Così fan tutte* in 1790, and Count Robinson in Cimarosa's *Il matrimonio segreto* in 1792; also appeared in operas by Sarti, Galuppi, Salieri, Paisiello, and Martín y Soler.

Publications

About BENUCCI: books–

Michtner, O. *Der alte Burgtheater als Opernbühne.* Vienna, 1970.

*   *   *

Francesco Benucci, a comic bass of exceptional ability as an actor as well as a singer, contributed much to Viennese musical life during the 1780s and early 1790s. He created roles in operas by all the leading composers of comic opera in Vienna, including Salieri, Martín y Soler and Mozart, who wrote for him the roles of Figaro and Guglielmo. After Martín's departure from Vienna and Mozart's death Benucci continued to sing in Vienna; in the 1790s he was especially successful in the role of Count Robinson in Cimarosa's *Il matrimonio segreto.*

Benucci's place of birth, Livorno, was until recently unknown: it is not mentioned in *The New Grove Dictionary.* But several libretti printed for operatic productions in which Benucci took part contain cast-lists that refer to Benucci as "di [or "da"] Livorno" (e.g. Cimarosa's *L'amore costante,* performed in Rome during Carnival, 1782). Benucci enjoyed a successful career in Italy before coming north to Vienna in 1783. He sang in many of the major operatic centers of Italy during the 1770s and early 1780s, including Venice, Rome and Florence. His repertory in Vienna included operas that he had successfully performed in Italy.

When Emperor Joseph II organized a troupe for the performance of opera buffa in 1783 Benucci became a mainstay of the company. Mozart was impressed with Benucci's singing, describing him in a letter to his father as "particularly good"; Benucci's talents may well have helped to attract Mozart's attention to opera buffa and to encourage him to write comic operas for Joseph's troupe.

A discussion of Benucci published in the *Berlinische musikalische Zeitung* in 1793 praised his "exceptionally round, beautiful, full bass voice" and his "unaffected, excellent acting." It goes on to remark that Benucci "has a rare habit that few Italian singers share: *he never exaggerates.*" Benucci won such popularity in Vienna that Emperor Joseph II, making plans to disband the Italian opera troupe in 1786, asked his brother Leopold, Grand Duke of Tuscany, to give him employment in Florence. Leopold responded positively, doubtless moved partly by Benucci's Tuscan birth. But the Viennese troupe survived and Benucci, after singing for a short time in London, returned to Vienna.

Not all of Benucci's best roles were newly composed. One of his roles in London was that of Tagliaferro, the German soldier in Piccinni's *La buona figliuola.* A London newspaper praised his performance as being better than any of the other interpreters of that role in earlier productions of Piccinni's opera in London.

We can get some idea of Benucci's abilities from the music that Mozart and other Viennese composers wrote for him. In arias such as "Se vuol ballare" and "Non più andrai" in Mozart's *Figaro* we can see that Benucci's voice was not particularly wide in range. His tessitura covered the octave from D in the bass clef to D above middle C. Benucci was certainly no *basso profondo,* like Ludwig Fischer, who created the role of Osmin in *Die Entführung aus dem Serail,* or Franz Gerl, the first Sarastro: Mozart rarely asked him to go below C in the bass clef. Benucci could evidently sing out occasional, isolated high notes with accuracy and power: Mozart had him do so in "Se vuol ballare", writing several isolated Fs above middle C.

—John A. Rice

BENVENUTO CELLINI.

Composer: Hector Berlioz.

Librettists: Léon de Wailly and Auguste Barbier (after Cellini's autobiography).

First Performance: Paris, Opéra, 10 September 1838.

Roles: Balducci (bass); Teresa (soprano); Benvenuto Cellini (tenor); Ascanio (mezzo-soprano); Fieramosca (baritone); Pompeo (baritone); Francesco (tenor); Bernardino (bass); Innkeeper (tenor); Officer (baritone); chorus (SATTBB).

Publications

books–

Piatier, F. *Benvenuto Cellini de Berlioz; ou, Le mythe de l'artiste.* Paris, 1979.

A caricature of the first production of Berlioz's *Benvenuto Cellini*, Paris, 1838

articles–

Von Bülow, Hans. "Hector Berlioz: Benvenuto Cellini." *Neue Zeitschrift für Musik* 47 (1852).

Prod'homme, P.-G. "Les deux Benvenuto Cellini de Berlioz." *Sammelbände der Internationalen Musik-Gesellschaft* 14 (1913): 449.

Hammond, A. "Benvenuto Cellini." *Opera* 8 (1957): 205.

Searle, Humphrey. "Berlioz and *Benvenuto*." *Opera* December (1966).

Macdonald, Hugh. "The Original Benvenuto Cellini." *Musical Times* 109 (1968): 142.

La May, T.K. "A New Look at the Weimar Versions of Berlioz' *Benvenuto Cellini*." *Musical Quarterly* 65 (1979): 559.

* * *

On the last Monday of Carnival, the Papal treasurer Balducci is grumbling at having to pay Cellini for work on an unfinished statue. Meanwhile Cellini serenades Balducci's daughter Teresa. Fieramosca, an inferior sculptor but the suitor preferred by Balducci, overhears Cellini make an assignation with Teresa; but he is caught hiding in her bedroom and ejected as a libertine. On Shrove Tuesday, Cellini and his men have nothing to drink until his apprentice Ascanio brings the Pope's money, reminding him that the statue is already overdue. They sing a hymn to their art, repeated at the end of the opera. During the Carnival Cellini has Harlequin pillory Balducci; then he tries to elope with Teresa. Fieramosca rashly intervenes but is humiliated by Ascanio while his friend Pompeo is killed by Cellini. The extinction of lights at midnight, marking the start of Lent, allows Cellini to escape.

On Ash Wednesday Cellini and Teresa are reunited in his workshop, but he is denounced by Fieramosca, Balducci, and finally the Pope (whom the censors insisted should be merely "the Cardinal"). But the Pope is more interested in the great statue of Perseus; and when Cellini threatens to destroy the mould he is granted the rest of the day to save his skin by finishing it. After difficulties with workmen and materials the statue is cast, Cellini's enemies fawn on him, and art and love are triumphantly vindicated.

Berlioz planned *Benvenuto Cellini* with spoken dialogue, and with a major climax to each act: the Carnival and the casting of Perseus. The Paris Opéra required recitatives, retained in the three-act Weimar version, for which he divided the first act and shortened the original second. In the latter the Weimar version alters the order of scenes, improbably allowing Cellini an hour rather than a day to finish Perseus; Berlioz also abbreviated the sextet with the Pope and the casting scene, which in the original version are magnificently developed, and cut the beautiful slow movement of the lovers' duet. Although it presents difficulties in the theater, the first version is musically preferable, and it is represented on the only recording. The Carnival makes, perhaps, too brilliant a first climax, anticipating *Die Meistersinger* in its handling of a stage filled with principals and a festive crowd which turns ugly. In both versions the final act contains excellent numbers (Ascanio's aria, a prayer heard against a passing procession of monks, Cellini's narration), but in neither is it as cogent as the earlier scenes. These unexpectedly reveal Berlioz as a master of comedy. The serenade interrupted by the furious grumbling of Balducci make a hilarious introduction, and the trio in which Fieramosca overhears the lovers perfectly blends enchanting music with farce. The overture and Fieramosca's aria, where he practices duelling in mixed metres, exemplify the explosive and capricious rhythmic inventions abounding in a score which is still, to some palates, over-rich for the opera house.

—Julian Rushton

BERG, Alban (Maria Johannes).

Composer. Born 9 February 1885, in Vienna. Died 24 December 1935, in Vienna. Married: Helene Nohowski, May 1911. Little musical training before meeting Schoenberg in October of 1904; in his youth, he was friends with Zweig, Kraus, Klimt, Loos, Altenberg, and Kokoschka; saw a performance of Büchner's *Woyzeck* in May of 1914, and immediately began sketches for a musical setting of the play; army service from 1914-1918; part of *Wozzeck* completed during a period of leave from the army in 1917; management of Schoenberg's Verein für Musikalische Privataufführungen in 1918; act I and first two scenes of *Wozzeck* completed in 1919, short score completed in autumn of 1921, orchestration completed in the spring of 1922, published by the composer in 1923; performance of *Drei Bruchstücke aus "Wozzeck"* in Frankfurt, June 1924; premiere at the Berlin Staatsoper, 14 December 1925; *Lyric Suite* published 1927; composition of *Lulu* from 1929-1935: short score completed spring 1934; *Symphonische Stücke aus der Oper "Lulu"* performed 30 November 1934; work on *Lulu* interrupted by composition of the Violin Concerto in 1935; *Lulu* suite performed in Vienna on 11

Alban Berg: portrait photograph with an autograph extract from *Wozzeck*

December 1935; orchestration of *Lulu* only through the beginning of act III; posthumous premiere in Zurich, 2 June 1937, but with only the parts of act III found in the *Lulu* suite. The materials for *Lulu*, act III, were withheld by Berg's widow until her death in 1976, and publication of the complete vocal score was in 1979, in an edition by the Viennese composer Friedrich Cerha, who completed the full score as well; first complete performance of *Lulu* 24 February 1979.

Operas

Publisher: Universal

Wozzeck, libretto arranged by the composer (after Georg Büchner), 1917-22, Berlin, Staatsoper, 14 December 1925.
Lulu, libretto arranged by the composer (after Frank Wedekind's *Erdgeist* and *Die Büchse der Pandora*), 1929-35, incomplete performance Zurich, 2 June 1937; first complete performance, Paris, Opéra, 24 February 1979.

Other works: songs, piano music, chamber music, orchestral works, a violin concerto.

Publications/Writings

By BERG: books—

Arnold Schoenberg, Gurrelieder: Führer. Vienna, 1913.
Arnold Schoenberg, Pelleas und Melisande, op. 5: thematische Analyse. Vienna, n.d.
Der Verein für musikalische Privataufführungen. Vienna, 1919; reprinted in Willi Reich, *Alban Berg*, Zurich, 1963; English translation by Cornelius Cardew in *The Life and Work of Alban Berg*, London, 1965; New York, 1982.
Berg, Helen, ed. *Alban Berg: Briefe an seine Frau.* Munich, 1965; English translation, London and New York, 1971.
Brand, Juliane, Christopher Haily, and Donald Harris, eds. *The Berg-Schoenberg Correspondence: Selected Letters.* London, 1987.

articles—

"Die musikalische Impotenz der 'neuen Ästhetik' Hans Pfitzners." *Musikblätter des Anbruch* 2 (1920); reprinted in Willi Reich, *Alban Berg*, Zurich, 1963; English translation by Cornelius Cardew in *The Life and Work of Alban Berg*, London, 1965; New York, 1982.
"Warum ist Schoenbergs Musik so schwer verständlich?" *Musikblätter des Anbruch* 6 (1924); reprinted in Willi Reich, *Alban Berg*, Zurich, 1963; English translation by Cornelius Cardew in *The Life and Work of Alban Berg*, London, 1965; New York, 1982.
"Offener Brief an Arnold Schoenberg." *Pult und Taktstock* February (1925); reprinted in Willi Reich, *Alban Berg*, Zurich, 1963; English translation by Cornelius Cardew in *The Life and Work of Alban Berg*, London, 1965; New York, 1982.
"A Word about 'Wozzeck'." *Modern Music* 5 (1927):22; reprinted in Willi Reich, *Alban Berg*, Zurich, 1963; English translation by Cornelius Cardew in *The Life and Work of Alban Berg*, London, 1965; New York, 1982.
Lecture on *Wozzeck*, 1929; printed in Hans Redlich, *Alban Berg: Versuch einer Würdigung*, Vienna, 1957; English translation in Redlich, *Alban Berg: the Man and his Music*, London, 1957.

"Die Stimme in der Oper." *Gesang: Jahrbuch 1929 der UE.* Vienna, 1929; reprinted in Willi Reich, *Alban Berg*, Zurich, 1963; English translation by Cornelius Cardew in *The Life and Work of Alban Berg*, London, 1965; New York, 1982.
"Was ist Atonal?" Radio interview, Vienna, 23 April 1930; English translation in Nicholas Slonimsky, *Music since 1900*, New York, 1938.

About BERG: books—

Musikblätter des Anbruch: Alban Bergs "Wozzeck" und die Musikkritik. Vienna, 1926.
Mahler, Fritz. *Zu Alban Berg's Oper "Wozzeck."* Vienna, 1957.
Redlich, Hans. *Alban Berg: Versuch einer Würdigung.* Vienna, 1957. Translated into English and abridged as *Alban Berg: the Man and his Music.* London, 1957.
Reich, Willi. *Alban Berg.* Zurich, 1963; English translation by Cornelius Cardew as *The Life and Work of Alban Berg*, London, 1965; New York, 1982.
Adorno, Theodor W. *Alban Berg.* Vienna, 1968.
Ploebsch, G. *Alban Bergs "Wozzeck".* Strasbourg, 1968.
Schweizer, K. *Die Sonatensatzform im Schaffen Alban Bergs.* Stuttgart, 1970.
Reiter, M. *Die Zwölftontechnik in Alban Bergs Oper Lulu.* Regensburg, 1973.
Carner, Mosco. *Alban Berg.* London, 1975; revised 2nd ed., 1983.
Hilmar, E. *Wozzeck von Alban Berg: Entstehung—erste Erfolge—Repressionen (1914-1935).* Vienna, 1975.
Berg, E. A., ed. *Alban Berg: Leben und Werk in Daten und Bildern.* Frankfurt, 1976.
Petazzi, P. *Alban Berg: La vita, l'opera, i testi musicali.* Milan, 1977.
Vogelsand, L. *Dokumentation zur Oper "Wozzeck" von Alban Berg: die Jahre des Durchbruchs 1925-32.* Laaber, 1977.
Barilier, E. *Alban Berg: Essai d'interprétation.* Lausanne, 1978.
Kolleritsch, O., ed. *50 Jahre Wozzeck von Alban Berg: Vorgeschichte und Auswirkungen in der Opernästhetik.* Gratz, 1978.
Cerha, F. *Arbeitsbericht zur Herstellung des 3. Akts der Oper Lulu von Alban Berg.* Vienna, 1979.
Lulu II. Musique et Musiciens [issued by the Opéra de Paris]. Paris, 1979.
Jarman, Douglas. *The Music of Alban Berg.* London, 1979; reprint Berkeley, 1985.
Monson, Karen. *Alban Berg: A Biography.* Boston, 1979; London, 1980.
Perle, George. *The Operas of Alban Berg, I: Wozzeck.* Berkeley, 1980.
Klein, R., ed. *Alban Berg Symposium: Vienna 1980.* Vienna, 1981.
Dahlhaus, Carl. *Vom Musikdrama zur Literaturoper.* Munich and Salzburg, 1983.
Neighbor, Oliver, Paul Griffiths, and George Perle. *Second Viennese School: Schoenberg, Webern, Berg.* New Grove Composer Biographies. London and New York, 1983.
Schmalfeldt, Janet. *Berg's "Wozzeck": Harmonic Language and Dramatic Design.* New Haven, 1983.
Perle, George. *The Operas of Alban Berg, II: Lulu.* Berkeley, 1985.
Jarman, Douglas. *Alban Berg: Wozzeck.* Cambridge, 1989.
———. *The Berg Companion.* London, 1989.

articles–

Viebig, E. "Alban Bergs 'Wozzeck': ein Beitrag zum Opern-problem." *Die Musik* 15 (1923): 506.

Berio, Luciano. "Invito a Wozzeck." *Il diapasion* 3 (1952): 14.

Blaukopf, K. *Autobiographische Elemente in Alban Bergs 'Wozzeck'.* Österreichische Musikzeitschrift 9 (1954): 155.

Offergeld, R. "Some Questions about *Lulu*'." *HiFi/Stereo Review* 13/4 (1964): 58.

Jarman, Douglas. "Dr. Schön's Five-Strophe Aria: Some Notes on Tonality and Pitch Association in Berg's *Lulu*." *Perspectives of New Music* 8 (1970): 23.

———. "Some Rhythmic and Metric Techniques in Alban Berg's *Lulu*." *Musical Quarterly* 56 (1970): 349.

Treitler, Leo. " 'Wozzeck' et l'Apocalypse." *Schweizerische Musikzeitung/Revue musicale suisse* 106 (1976): 249; English version in *Critical Inquiry* winter (1976).

Schmidt, Henry J. "Alban Berg's Wozzeck." In *Georg Büchner: The complete collected works,* translated and edited by Henry J. Schmidt, 388-92. New York, 1977.

Herschkowitz, F. "Some Thoughts on *Lulu*." *International Alban Berg Society Newsletter* 7 (1978): 11.

Jarman, Douglas. "*Lulu*: the Sketches." *International Alban Berg Society Newsletter* 6 (1978): 4.

Bachmann, Claus-Henning. "*Lulu* bisher: '. . . ein Anschlag auf den Dramatiker Berg.' Herstellung des dritten Aktes-Gespräch mit Friedrich Cerha." *Neue Zeitschrift für Musik* 140 (1979): 264.

Holloway, Robin. "The Complete *Lulu*." *Tempo* 129 (1979): 36.

Perle, George. "The Cerha edition" [of *Lulu,* act III]. *Perspectives of New Music* 17 (1979): 251.

———. "The complete *Lulu*." *Musical Times* 120 (1979): 115.

Stephan, Rudolph. "Zur Sprachmelodie in Alban Bergs *Lulu*-Musik." in *Dichtung und Musik,* edited by Günter Schnitzler, 246. Stuttgart, 1979.

Molkow, Wolfgang. "Klang und Einklang im Morgenrot. Zur Geschichte eines Natur-Topos." *Neue Zeitschrift für Musik* 141 (1980): 234.

Petersen, Peter. "Wozzecks persönliche Leitmotive." *Hamburger Jahrbuch für Musikwissenschaft* 4 (1980): 33.

Radice, Mark A. "The anatomy of a libretto: the music inherent in Büchner's *Wozzeck*." *Music Review* 41 (1980): 233.

Ringer, Alexander L. "Weill, Schönberg und die 'Zeitoper'." *Die Musikforschung* 33 (1980): 465.

Jarman, Douglas. "Countess Geschwitz's series: a controversy resolved?" *Proceedings of the Royal Musical Association* 107 (1981): 111.

Perle, George. "Das Film-Zwischenspiel in Bergs Oper *Lulu*." *Österreichische Musikzeitschrift* 36 (1981): 631.

———. "The tone-row as symbol in Berg's *Lulu*." In *Essays on the Music of J. S. Bach and other Diverse Subjects: A Tribute to Gerhard Herz.* edited by Robert L. Weaver 304. Louisville, Kentucky, 1981.

Avant-scène opéra 36 (1981) [*Wozzeck* issue].

Carner, Mosco. "Alban Berg's *Lulu*—A Reconsideration." *Musical Times* 124 (1983): 477.

Pople, Anthony. "Serial and Tonal Aspects of Pitch Structure in Act III of Berg's *Lulu*." *Soundings* 10 (1983): 36.

Carner, Mosco. "Berg e il riesame di *Lulu*." *Nuova Rivista Musicale Italiana* 18 (1984): 434.

Müller, Gerhard, "Georg Büchner als Musikdramatiker: Anmerkungen zu einer Aporie." *Theater der Zeit* 39 (1984): 10.

Rosenfeld, Gerhard, Siegfried Matthus, and Pavel Eckstein. "Der epochale *Wozzeck*: zum 100. Geburtstag von Alban Berg." *Oper Heute* 7 (1984): 110.

Ardoin, John. "Apropos *Wozzeck*." *Opera Quarterly* 3 (1985): 68.

Greene, Susan. "Wozzeck, and Marie: Outcast in Search of an Honest Morality." *Opera Quarterly* 3 (1985): 75.

Green, London. "Lulu Wakens." *Opera Quarterly* 3 (1985): 112.

Perle, George. "Some Thoughts on an Ideal Production of *Lulu*." *Journal of Musicology* 7 (1989).

* * *

Berg's natural feeling for the voice is heard in the many songs which were his first essays in composition. Written both before and during his period of study with Schoenberg, these show a secure command of late-Romantic Viennese musical language and a gift for lyrical word-setting through sensitivity of melodic contour and rhythmic characterisation. Understandably, one of his teacher's main aims was to encourage Berg towards a more instrumental style, less dominated by melody, more motivic in material and polyphonic in texture. Schoenberg also introduced his pupil to the expanded harmonic resources through which he himself was moving determinedly towards a psychological break with the conventions of tonality.

Though dominated throughout his life by the personality of Schoenberg, Berg remained true to his own instincts through the strength of his innate sensibility. Accepting Schoenberg's criticism of the brevity of the *Altenberg Lieder* and the *Four Pieces* for Clarinet and Piano, he composed the *Three Orchestral Pieces* in a style which, while reaping the benefits of Schoenbergian expressionism, owes a more direct debt to Mahler. Another irony of this work is that Schoenberg himself was unable to sustain music in larger forms at this time. Arguably, having found for himself a path through the impasse that Schoenberg had identified, Berg was from now on to prove the more artistically consistent and successful composer of the two.

Berg's major works number just twelve, composed over a span of nearly thirty years. His operas are thus better understood within the chronological progression of his output in all genres than by considering them together as a pair. At the same time, his tendency towards conservatism and his responsiveness to inspiration from sources beyond Schoenbergian modernism demand that his work be placed in a broader context. Thus while *Wozzeck* may be seen to follow the musical style of the *Three Orchestral Pieces* in all essentials, and was for many years thought of as the most successful "atonal" opera, its musical language in fact retains many links with the extended tonality developed by Strauss and others (including Schoenberg) during the first decade of the century and also restores to some extent the primacy of melody Berg had shown in his earliest compositions. In line with other developments in post-war music, the opera is notable for its use of conventional forms within the framework of a through-composed music-drama, and the revival of works by Zemlinsky and Schreker has confirmed *Wozzeck* as a work rooted in the time and place of its composition.

Moving towards serial technique in the mid 1920s under the inescapable influence of Schoenberg, Berg nonetheless maintained the prominence of tonalistic devices in his later works. Even more than *Wozzeck*'s blend of artificial formal construction with an eclectic mix of late-Romantic and post-Expressionist musical languages, these works constantly explore the historical tension between the conventions of tonal Romanticism and modernist musical constructivism, in contrast to Schoenberg's clear but uncertain commitment to the latter aesthetic.

Berg's last years were dominated by his work on *Lulu*. This task remained incomplete at his death, having been interrupted by the composition of the concert aria *Der Wein* and the *Violin Concerto,* both of which were undertaken for financial reasons. These three works are linked stylistically by an overt tonalism which makes their musical language more accessible than that of *Wozzeck*. At the same time, this is complemented by an ingenuity of construction which, particularly in *Lulu,* anticipates the 'tonal serialism' of the 1950s, while being all the more remarkable for its virtual inaudibility—an art which conceals art. The link between music and drama in *Lulu* is less onomatopoeic than in *Wozzeck,* however, and the subject matter less immediately appealing. The title role, for coloratura soprano, makes extraordinary vocal demands, and until the release in 1979 of Friedrich Cerha's realization of its third act the opera could only be performed as a fragment. All these factors prevented its proper appreciation for many years after Berg's death, during which period his reputation was carried largely by *Wozzeck* and the *Violin Concerto.*

The fuller acquaintance with *Lulu* which has become possible in recent years has been central to a revision of critical attitudes towards the composer. His earlier reputation for approachability through artistic compromise has now been replaced by a fascination with his ability to combine serialism with tonalistic elements, and an attractive sound-world with a forbidding array of hidden complexities in construction. Berg's second opera has found its place through the pluralistic climate of post-Modernist criticism. At the same time, there can be little doubt that the reputation of *Wozzeck* will in due course be restored to equal heights. For many musicians, these two operas stand alongside some by Strauss and Puccini, and perhaps a handful of other works, as the greatest of their century.

—Anthony Pople

BERGANZA, Teresa.

Mezzo-soprano. Born 16 March 1935. Married to the composer Felix Lavilla. Studied with Lola Rodriguez Aragon; won singing prize at Madrid in 1954; operatic debut as Dorabella in *Così fan tutte* at Aix-en-Provence Festival, 1957; debut at Piccola Scala as Isolier in *Comte Ory,* 1958; Glyndebourne debut as Cherubino in *Le nozze di Figaro,* 1958; U.S. debut at Dallas, 1958 appeared at Covent Garden as Rosina, 1960; Chicago as Cherubino, 1962; Metropolitan Opera debut as Cherubino, 1967.

Publications

About BERGANZA: books–

Steane, J.B. *The Grand Tradition.* London, 1974.
Segalini, S. *Teresa Berganza.* Paris, 1982.

articles–

Loveland, K. "Teresa Berganza." *Audio and Record Review* 3 (1964).
Harewood, M. "Teresa Berganza" *Opera* (March 1967).

* * *

Teresa Berganza specialized in Italian opera of the 17th, 18th and early 19th centuries. With few roles in the operas of Verdi and Puccini for her sweet, light mezzo-soprano voice and gentle stage personality she explored earlier repertory. She sang with great success some of the best roles in baroque opera, including works by Monteverdi, Purcell, and Handel. Although she is best known today for her performances in comic opera, especially those of Mozart and Rossini, Berganza's work in baroque opera showed that she was also capable of bringing tragic characters such as Ottavia (*L'incoronazione di Poppea*) and Dido (*Dido and Aeneas*) to life.

A recording of Handel's *Alcina* under Bonynge shows how fine Berganza was as a singer of baroque opera. Berganza's Ruggiero is strong and heroic. With perfectly executed coloratura she portrays him as a dashing, almost reckless figure (as, for example, in the brilliant aria "Bramo di triomfar"). Yet Ruggiero is also thoughtful and gentle; Berganza reveals this side of his character most beautifully in slow, lyrical arias like "Col celarvi", "Mio bel tesoro" and the famous "Verdi prati, selve amene".

One of Berganza's first professional roles was that of Dorabella (*Così fan tutte*), at Aix in 1957; she went on to sing several other Mozart roles. She won much applause for her portrayal of Cherubino at Glyndebourne in 1958; fourteen years later, she was still delighting audiences with the same role (Salzburg, 1972). Her performances of the role of Sesto in Mozart's *La clemenza di Tito* in two recordings (under Kertesz and Böhm) show that she was as effective in evoking the tragic and heroic aspects of Mozart as she was the comic.

It was especially as an interpreter of Rossini's comic heroines that Berganza revealed the full extent of her musical and dramatic talents. Her many performances of Rosina (*Il barbiere di Siviglia*) and Cinderella will long be remembered for their wit, charm and polished musicality. A recording of *Il barbiere* under Abbado shows Berganza to be a fine Rosina after singing the role for more than a decade. In her performance of "Una voce poco fa" one can hear the strength and flexibility of her voice; she attacks the sudden high notes (as she names Lindoro) with confidence and perfect accuracy without shouting or screeching; her voice blends beautifully with the orchestra. Her low notes are rich and strong. One could complain only that the performance is a little hurried, a little stiff. The pure beauty of Berganza's voice makes one wish that she took more time at fermatas; she seems to rush through coloratura where she might have slowed a little and let listeners savor her voice. Berganza's performance of Isabella (*L'italiana in Algeri*) as recorded under Silvio Varviso lacks some of the heroic and mock-heroic qualities that Marilyn Horne could bring to the role (especially in the aria "Pensa alla patria" and the recitative that precedes it). But the sweetness of her voice, the deftness of her coloratura, the beauty of her appearance and the liveliness of her acting all combine to make Berganza's Isabella one that can hardly be bettered.

—John A. Rice

BERGER, Erna.

Soprano. Born 19 October 1900, in Cossebaude, near Dresden. Died 14 June 1990, in Essen. Studied piano and singing with Hertha Boeckel and Melitza Hirzel in Dresden; debut at Dresden as first boy in *Die Zauberflöte,* 1925; in Berlin and Bayreuth, 1930-33, where she sang the Shepherd in *Tannhäuser;* appeared at Salzburg, 1932-54 as Blondchen and Zerlina; debut at Covent Garden as Marzelline in *Fidelio,* 1934; 1949-51 returned to London; also at Metropolitan Opera as Sophie, Queen of the Night, Gilda, and Rosina; in premieres of *Die ägyptische Helena,* 1924 and *Daphne,* 1938; continued to appear in opera in Germany and Austria until 1955; taught at Hamburg Musikhochschule after 1959.

Publications

By BERGER: books–

Berger, E. *Auf Flügeln des Gesangs: Erinnerungen einer Sängerin.* Zurich, 1988.

About BERGER: books–

Höcker, K. *Erna Berger, die singende Botschafterin.* Berlin, 1961.

*   *   *

Erna Berger, often called "the German Nightingale," was born in Cossebaude near Dresden on the 19th of October 1900. Her father, a railroad engineer interned in India from 1914 to 1918, returned to Dresden to find an eighteen year old daughter who liked to sing, but who worked as a stenotypist at a local bank. Soon after the family bought unimproved land in the interior of Paraguay and moved to South America. Erna Berger lived in a tent on the farm for a short while and then was sent to Montevideo, where she took a position of tutor in a private family and studied voice and piano. In 1924 she returned to Germany with her family by ship. On this sailing the Berger family had booked one of the least expensive cabins and Erna decided to give a ship's concert in order to earn some money to help with the passage. The concert was a big success. It was agreed by knowledgeable members of the audience that the young singer had a voice worthy of serious study. In Dresden Berger studied voice with Hertha Boeckel and Melitta Hirzel and in 1925 she auditioned for Fritz Busch, the general music director of the Dresden Opera. Instead of winning a scholarship for further study, Berger was immediately engaged for small roles and made her debut as the First Boy in Mozart's *Die Zauberflöte.* When a colleague who was to sing Olympia in Offenbach's *Les contes d'Hoffmann* suddenly became ill Berger was able to sing the role with no orchestra rehearsal. The audience gave her a huge ovation and one of the greatest coloratura soprano careers in German opera was begun. Erna Berger was a member of the Dresden Opera from 1926 to 1934. In 1927 she sang the title role in the premiere performance of Graener's *Hanneles Himmelfahrt,* the Dresden first performance of Krenek's *Jonny spielt auf,* in Wolf-Ferrari's *La dama boba* with the composer present, and on November 6, 1928 the first performance of Richard Strauss's *Die ägyptische Helena.* Other contemporary first performances included roles in Werner Egk's *Die Zaubergeige* and Stravinsky's *The Rake's Progress.*

In 1930 Toscanini asked her to sing the role of the Shepherd in Bayreuth's production of *Tannhäuser.* She was also the Forest Bird in the festival's *Siegfried.* Salzburg audiences heard her sing Blondchen in 1932 and Zerlina (*Don Giovanni*) and in several concert and recital performances during the 1953 and 1954 festivals. She made her Metropolitan Opera debut in 1949 as Sophie during the opening night's performance of *Rosenkavalier* and sang there through 1953. The New York *Post* critic wrote that Berger "achieved the best all-around portrayal of the evening. She has personality, combined with a voice which does her bidding in effective fashion. . . . Altogether she is a charming singing-actress and should be a major asset to the organization" (Nov. 21, 1949). Erna Berger was one of the first German singers to perform in London and New York with critical success and audience acceptance after the Second World War. She became a regular guest at Covent Garden singing the roles of Queen of the Night (*Die Zauberflöte*), Gilda (*Rigoletto*), and Sophie. She was also successful in guest performance at the Vienna Staatsoper. Erna Berger made extensive concert tours in North and South America between 1946 and 1953, spent several months in Australia in 1948, and in 1952 made a tour of Africa which continued on to Japan in 1953.

Erna Berger's major operatic home was, however, Berlin. Initially she sang as a guest under such conductors as Leo Blech (Frasquita in *Carmen* and Leila in Bizet's *Les pêcheurs de perles*) and Furtwängler (Ännchen). In 1929 she took part in the Berlin performances of Pfitzner's opera *The Christmas Elf* ("Christ-elflein") and in 1932 she sang the role of Oscar in the famous production of Verdi's *Un ballo in maschera* directed by Busch and staged by Carl Ebert. Beginning in 1934 and ending with her final performance during the 1953 season, she sang successively as a member of the Berlin Städtische Oper, the Berlin Staatsoper, and again after the war with the newly revived Städtische Oper. In 1946 she took part in the premiere of Rimsky-Korsakov's *Sadko.* Other important repertoire included the roles of Zerbinette, Gretel, Butterfly, Mimi, Zerline (which was filmed), Violetta, Rosina, Gilda, Queen of the Night, Constanze, Blondchen, and a series of unforgettable Sophies in the early 1950s partnered by Elisabeth Grümmer as Octavian.

But Erna Berger's career was not limited to the operatic stage. She was a Lieder singer of the first rank. Her intuitive musicality and a seemingly ageless soprano voice of seldom surpassed beauty and purity enabled her to have a hugely successful concert and recital career which thrilled audiences until her retirement from singing in 1964. Her repertoire extended from the works of Johann Christian Bach, Telemann, Pergolesi, Rameau, Caccini, Scarlatti, and Veracini to Stravinsky and Hindemith. She was a leading interpreter of Mozart concert arias, of the Lieder of Schubert, Brahms, Schumann, Pfitzner, and, not least, of the great treasure of Hugo Wolf's masterful songs.

Erna Berger was a tiny woman. She once described herself as much too small to have a stage career because "audiences would have to look for her with a magnifying glass." However, her absolutely exquisite voice, "coloratura like diamonds strung on a silver thread," her immaculate intonation and timbre of an ageless purity, and the modernity of her interpretations place Berger among the greatest German singers of her generation.

Erna Berger accepted a professorship at the Hochschule in Hamburg in 1959-60. Among her list of students in both Berlin and Hamburg was another famous coloratura, Rita Streich.

The West German government bestowed two levels of the German Service Cross on the singer in 1953 and 1976. She was an honorary member of the Berlin Academy of Arts (Akademie der Künste) and on her eightieth birthday she was made an honorary member of the Berlin Staatsoper as well. Erna Berger died on the 14th of June, 1990 in Essen. She was active in the musical life of Essen until the very end. A biography, *Erna Berger* by Karla Höcker, was published in Berlin in 1961.

—Suzanne Summerville

BERGHAUS, Ruth.

Producer and choreographer. Born 2 July 1927 in Dresden. Married: composer Paul Dessau (died 1979). Trained in dance and choreography at the Pauluccaschule, Dresden; began working professionally as choreographer in 1950; choreographer for the Theater der Freundschaft from 1951 to 1964; first professional operatic assignment was as choreographer for Joachim Herz's production of *Rigoletto* in Dresden, 1951; joined the Berliner Ensemble in 1964, and was the Ensemble's director 1971-77; in 1971 became a member of the Berlin City Parliament; producer, Deutsche Staatsoper, Berlin, 1977-79; planned complete performance of *Der Ring des Nibelungen* but project was cancelled after two widely-criticized performances of *Das Rheingold* (1979); during the 1980s collaborated with Michael Gielen on several productions for the Frankfurt Opera; successfully staged a complete production of Wagner's *Ring* in 1986-87; continued to stage operas throughout Europe in the 1980s and early 1990s. One of the most inventive and controversial directors of the post-World War II era, Berghaus was strongly influenced by Walter Felsenstein at the Komische Oper in Berlin, as well as Bertolt Brecht, and Götz Friedrich.

Opera Productions (selected)

Die Verurteilung des Lukullus (Dessau), Berlin, Deutsche Staatsoper, 1960.
Puntilla (Dessau), Berlin, Deutsche Staatsoper, 1966.
Elektra, Berlin, Deutsche Staatsoper, 1967.
Il barbiere di Siviglia, Munich, 1974.
Einstein (Dessau), Berlin, Deutsche Staatsoper, 1973.
Die Fledermaus, Munich, c. 1977.
La clemenza di Tito, Berlin, Deutsche Staatsoper, 1978.
Das Rheingold, Berlin, Deutsche Staatsoper, 1979.
Elektra, Mannheim, 1980.
Die Zauberflöte, Frankfurt, 1980.
Die Entführung aus dem Serail, Frankfurt, 1981.
Idomeneo, Berlin, Deutsche Staatsoper, 1981.
The Makropoulos Case (Janáček), Frankfurt, 1982.
Parsifal, Frankfurt, 1982.
Salome, Mannheim, 1982.
Aschenputtel (Rossini's *Cenerentola*), Berlin, Deutsche Staatsoper, 1983.
Les Troyens, Frankfurt, 1983.
Die Verurteilung des Lukullus, Berlin, Deutsche Staatsoper, 1983.
Don Giovanni, Cardiff, Welsh National Opera, 1984.
Wozzeck, Berlin, Deutsche Staatsoper, 1984.
Così fan tutte, Freiburg, 1985.
Wozzeck, Paris, Opéra, 1985.
Orpheus (Henze), Vienna, Staatsoper, 1986.
Der Ring des Nibelungen, Frankfurt, 1986-87.
Moses und Aron, Berlin, Deutsche Staatsoper, 1987.
Fierrabras (Schubert), Vienna, Theater an der Wien, 1988.

Lulu, Brussels, 1988.
Tristan und Isolde, Hamburg, 1988.
Così fan tutte, Berlin, Deutsche Staatsoper, 1989.
Lohengrin, Graz, Opernhaus, 1990.
Patmos (Schweinitz), Cassel, 1990.
Elektra, Zurich, 1991.
Pelléas et Mélisande, Berlin, Deutsche Staatsoper, 1991.

Publications

About BERGHAUS: books—

Jungheinrich, H.K., et al, eds. *Musiktheater.* Cassel, 1986.
Neef, S. *Das Theater der Ruth Berghaus.* Berlin, 1989.
Bertisch, K. *Ruth Berghaus.* Frankfurt-am-Main, c. 1990.

articles—

Bartels, Karsten. "Opernregie als szenischräumliche Umsetzung der Partitur: Zur Arbeit von Ruth Berghaus." In Ingrid Brunne and Harmut Grimm, eds., *Musikhören als Kommunikationsprozess.* Berlin, 1985.
Deisinger, H. "Figuren in ihren Widersprüchen zeigen: de Regisseurin Ruth Berghaus im Gespräch." *Neue Zeitschrift für Musik* no. 5 (May 1986): 27.
Kupfer, Hans, et al. "Noch nicht am Ende, aber . . ." *Bühne* (Summer 1991): 29.

One of the most talented, original and controversial opera producers of the second half of the twentieth century, Ruth Berghaus was born and educated in Dresden. After training in dance, choreography, and dance pedagogy at the Paulucca School, she began her professional career in 1950 as a choreographer. In the meantime, a visit while still a student to see Brecht's play *Mutter Courage,* presented by the Berlin Ensemble at the Theater on the Schiffbauerdamm in East Berlin, had radically influenced her political and theatrical outlook. In 1951, as her first operatic assignment, she provided the choreography for *Rigoletto,* produced in Dresden by Joachim Herz. A few years later she worked with Herz again on productions of Mascagni's *Cavalleria rusticana* and Leoncavallo's *Pagliacci* at Leipzig.

Berghaus was married to the composer Paul Dessau; her first opera productions were of his works. In 1960 she produced *Die Verurteilung des Lukullus,* first at the Berlin State Opera, and then in Mainz and Rostock. After directing the premiere of Dessau's *Puntila* in Berlin (1966), she staged her first production of another composer's opera, Strauss's *Elektra* (1967), which earned, as she herself admitted, "the first booing heard at the State Opera." It was not the last.

As Berghaus grew more experienced as an opera director, her productions became more controversial. Brechtian principles, which she had so successfully applied to the operas of Dessau (himself a Brecht collaborator), caused uproar in East Berlin as well as at the Bavarian State Opera, Munich, when applied to Rossini's *Il barbiere di Siviglia.*

Berghaus, named by Brecht's widow, Helene Weigel as her successor as Artistic Director of the Berlin Ensemble, took over the company on Weigel's death in 1971. During the seven years that she ran the ensemble, Berghaus did not stop working at the State Opera, where her productions included *Einstein* (probably the most successful of all her stagings of Dessau's operas), the Johann Strauss operetta *Die Fledermaus,* and, after resigning from the directorship of the Berlin

Ensemble, *La clemenza di Tito,* her first staging of an opera by Mozart. In 1979 Dessau died; his final opera, *Leonce und Lena,* was produced posthumously by his widow, who then started work on her largest operatic project so far, a complete production of Wagner's *Der Ring des Nibelungen.* However, her staging of *Das Rheingold* raised such a furor at the State Opera that after two performances the production was withdrawn and the other operas in the cycle were canceled.

Although she continued to direct in Berlin throughout the 1980s, Berghaus widened her horizons; she became a European celebrity, working in Mannheim, with the Welsh National Opera, at the Paris Opéra, at the Théâtre de la Monnaie (Brussels), at the Hamburg State Opera, and at Frankfurt-am-Main, where her eight-year collaboration with Michael Gielen, artistic and musical director of the Frankfurt Opera, resulted in the most exciting and stimulating work of her career. Having made her debut at Frankfurt in 1980 with a production of *Die Zauberflöte* that aroused tremendous fury in the audience, Berghaus staged *Die Entführung aus dem Serail* which, although it was booed on the opening night by a small section of the audience, quickly gained the interest of large numbers of intelligent opera goers. This remained the pattern for her next productions at Frankfurt, Janáček's *The Makropoulos Case* and Wagner's *Parsifal.* Mindful of the city's position as financial center of West Germany, the staging of *Parsifal* substituted the worship of money for conventional religious beliefs, turning the Knights of the Grail into black-suited business men clutching their briefcases.

With *Les Troyens* and *Der Ring des Nibelungen,* Berghaus and Gielen reached the apotheosis of their fruitful collaboration. Berlioz' two-part epic, with both halves given on the same evening, won unstinting praise from critics and public alike. *The Ring,* its four operas introduced over two years, achieved an even more spectacular success, especially when the whole cycle was performed in sequence and the power of its overall conception became clear. Because her own ideas were so strongly formulated and so firmly expressed, Berghaus was most successful when staging the operas of composers who themselves held strong ideas and expressed them forcefully.

Though her work in Frankfurt formed the peak of her career, Berghaus scored other triumphs during the 1980s. *Elektra* and *Salome,* operas particularly well suited to her approach, were greatly admired at Mannheim, while *Don Giovanni* for Welsh National Opera won cautious praise, though the production bewildered audiences unused to the wide cross-cultural sources of Berghaus's artistic references. Berg's *Wozzeck,* which she staged in Paris as well as in Berlin, and the same composer's *Lulu,* produced at Brussels, were notably successful, though *Tristan und Isolde* in Hamburg, the first production that she had done there, was received with furious cat-calls. Berghaus defended her staging (set in a space ship) by saying that her ideas were derived, as always, from the music alone.

This claim is evidently true. Ruth Berghaus, who started as a dancer and choreographer, who was married for a quarter of a century to a well-known composer, who directed one of the most famous theatrical companies in Europe for seven years, derived all her ideas from the scores of the operas that she directed. If, because of her immense knowledge and experience of theater in all its forms, those ideas were sometimes incomprehensible to the general public, that does not invalidate them. It does, however, help to explain why her staging of Schoenberg's *Moses und Aron,* an opera about which few people have pre-conceived opinions, given at Berlin in 1987, scored a great success, while *Così fan tutte,* a work about which everyone has their own ideas, and which she

produced there in 1989, was heartily booed, like the *Elektra* of twenty-two years earlier.

—Elizabeth Forbes

BERGLUND, Joel (Ingemar).

Bass-baritone. Born 4 June 1903, in Torsaker, Sweden. Studied at Stockholm Conservatory, 1922-28; debut at Stockholm Royal Opera as Monterone in *Rigoletto,* 1929, where he sang for thirty years and directed between 1949-52; appeared at Bayreuth in *Der fliegende Holländer,* 1942; Metropolitan Opera debut as Hans Sachs in 1946; has sung many Wagner roles as well as Gounod's Mephistopheles, Figaro, Simon Boccanegra and Jochanaan in *Salome,* among others.

With tenors Jussi Björling and Set Svanholm and mezzo Kirsten Thorborg, baritone Joel Berglund was one of Carl Johann (John) Forsell's best voice students. Berglund's career took place mostly in Sweden, where he was the director of the Royal Swedish Opera from 1949-1952, but he was also known and appreciated internationally. Berglund's professional debut, at the Stockholm Opera, was as Lothario in 1929. He sang in Zürich, Vienna, Buenos Aires and in Chicago, and toured North America in a quartet of opera singers. In 1942 he sang the Dutchman at Bayreuth.

Berglund's Metropolitan Opera debut, as Hans Sachs in *Die Meistersinger,* was in January of 1946 under George Szell. It received excellent reviews, which praised Berglund's extensive range and evenness of tone. That same season he sang the *Walküre* Wotan (with a cast of Traubel, Varnay, Thorborg, Melchior, and Kipnis), and then Kurwenal under Fritz Busch. The next season he added the Wanderer and Gurnemanz. On 4 February 1949, Berglund stood in for an ailing colleague as Jokanaan (*Salome*), thereby participating in the historic Metropolitan Opera debut of Ljuba Welitsch as Salome. His contribution to that evening was duly noted, and is still talked about.

As his repertoire also included such repertoire roles as Mozart's Figaro, Leporello (*Don Giovanni*), Boris (*Boris Godunov*), Simon Boccanegra, King Philip, the four villains in *Les contes d'Hoffmann,* and Mephistopheles, one can easily marvel at his stylistic versatility and a vocal range that encompassed Boccanegra to Gurnemanz.

It is a pity that Joel Berglund is not well represented on recordings. An RCA *Der fliegende Holländer* monologue on a 78 rpm disc is well-remembered, as are recordings of Wolfram's two monologues from *Tannhäuser.* A 1943 Telefunken Hans Sachs' "Wahnmonolog" is reproduced on Bluebell of Sweden's "Swedish Singers in New York" and Bluebell also published a live "Madamina, il catalogo" from a 1950 outdoor concert from Stockholm's Gröna Lund. Most interestingly, and most importantly, a performance of "Wotan's

Farewell" from 10 November 1952 appeared on Swedish Radio's short-lived label, SR records. Berglund sings magnificently and King Frederik IX of Denmark, who conducted the performance, commands the music as if he were Furtwängler.

—Bert Wechsler

BERGMAN, Ingmar.

Director. Born 14 July 1918, in Uppsala, Sweden. Married: Ingrid von Rosen, 1971; eight children by various marriages. Most famous contemporary Swedish film producer, known for extensive use of symbolism; enrolled at the University of Stockholm to study art history and literature, 1937; started his career in the Swedish theater, 1938; assistant at the Royal Opera House in Stockholm; worked in the script department at Svensk Filmindustri, 1940-44; from 1944 on divided his time between stage and film; began work as a theater director at the City Theatre, Hälsingborg, 1944-46; also theater director at Gothenburg, 1946-49, and at Malmo, 1952-59; first screen credits as scriptwriter and assistant director on Alf Sjöberg's *Frenzy* (*Hets*), 1944; first film as director *Crisis* (*Kris*), which he also wrote, 1945; international acclaim with *The Seventh Seal* (*Det Sjunde Inseglet*), 1956; head of the Royal Dramatic Theatre in Stockholm, 1963-66. Bergman's personal awards and honors include Swedish Film Society Honorary Diploma and Gold Plaque, FIB Mauritz Statue for Best Film Artist, Sorrento Festival's Sirena d'Oro, Honorary Doctorates and Professorship, French Legion of Honor Award, and others.

Opera Productions (selected)

The Rake's Progress, Stockholm Opera, 1961.
The Magic Flute (*Trollflöjten*), for television, 1975.

Publications

By BERGMAN: books–

Four Screenplays. Translated by Lars Malmström and David Kushner. New York, 1960.
The Seventh Seal: A Film. Translated by Lars Malmström and David Kushner. New York, 1960.
Scenes from a Marriage: Six Dialogues for Television. Translated by Alan Blair. New York, 1974.
Four Stories. Translated by Alan Blair. Garden City, New York, 1976.
Autumn Sonata: A Film. Translated by Alan Blair. New York, 1978.
From the Life of the Marionettes. Translated by Alan Blair. New York, 1980.
Fanny and Alexander. Translated by Alan Blair. New York, 1982.
A Project for the Theatre. Edited by Frederick J. Marker and Lise-Lone Marker. New York, 1983.
The Magic Lantern: An Autobiography. New York, 1988.

articles–

James, Caryn. "Film Makers' Youth: Outsiders Looking In. (Autobiographies by Directors Martin Scorsese, John Huston, and Ingmar Bergman)." *The New York Times* 139 (3 January 1990).

About BERGMAN: books–

Donner, Jörn. *The Personal Vision of Ingmar Bergman.* Translated by Holger Lundbergh. Bloomington, Indiana, 1964.
Steene, Birgitta. *Ingmar Bergman.* New York, 1968.
Gibson, Arthur. *The Silence of God; Creative Response to the Films of Ingmar Bergman.* New York, 1969.
Wood, Robin. *Ingmar Bergman.* New York, 1970.
Young, Vernon. *Cinema Borealis; Ingmar Bergman and the Swedish Ethos.* New York, 1971.
Simon, John Ivan. *Ingmar Bergman Directs.* New York, 1972.
Kawin, Bruce F. *Mindscreen: Bergman, Godard, and the First-Person Film.* Princeton, New Jersey, 1978.
Mosley, Philip. *Ingmar Bergman: The Cinema as Mistress.* Boston, 1981.
Cowie, Peter. *Ingmar Bergman: A Critical Biography.* New York, 1982.
Livingston, Paisley. *Ingmar Bergman and the Rituals of Art.* Ithaca, New York, 1982.
Gado, Frank. *The Passion of Ingmar Bergman.* Durham, North Carolina, 1986.
Steene, Birgitta. *Ingmar Bergman: A Guide to References and Resources.* Boston, 1987.

articles–

Wiskari, W. "Ingmar Bergman's Way with *The Rake.*" *New York Times* 110 (7 May 1961): 11.
Link, R. "Bergman's *Rake.*" *Musical America* 81 (June 1961): 30.
Diefenbronner, E. "Stockholm (*The Rake's Progress*)." *Musical Courier* 163 (1961).
Palatsky, E.H. "Stravinsky in Stockholm." *Opera News* 26 (30 September 1961): 28.
Burke, P.E. "Stockholm's New *Rake.*" *Music and Musicians* 10 (November 1961): 31.
Janzon, Bengt. "Bergman on Opera." *Opera* 13 (October 1962) 650-54 and *Opera News* 26 (5 May 1962): 12-14.
Hedlund, O. "The Genius As a Listener." *Philips Music Herald* (Summer 1963): 4-6.
Hedlund, O. "Ingmar Bergman, the Listener." *The Saturday Review* 47 (29 February 1964): 47-49.
Aghed, Jan. *Sydsvenska dagbladet snällposten* (31 December 1974): 10.
Lagercrantz, Olof. "Efter *Trollflöjten.*" *Dagens nyheter* (3 January 1975): 2.
Uppström, T. "*Trollflöjten* ett nederlag." *Aftonbladet* (6 January 1975): 2.
Zern, Leif. "Ingmar Bergman och finkulturen." *Dagens nyheter* (10 January 1975): 6.
Ahlgren, Stig. "Kontrollflöjten." *Vecko-Journalen* (15 January 1975): 28.
Fischbach, L. "Regissoerernas operor." *Musikrevy* 30, no. 1 (1975): 1-3.
Maegaard, K. "Bergmans *Tryllefloejte.*" *Dansk Musiktidsskrift* 50, no. 1 (1975): 40.
Dannenberg, P. "Ingmar Bergman inszeniert *Die Zauberfloete* (Fernsehen)." *Opern Welt; die deutsche Opernzeitschrift* no. 4 (April 1975): 42.
Lehmann-Braunsova, E. "Ingmar Bergman inscenoval *Kouzelnou Fletnu.*" *Hudebni Rozhledy; casopis Svazu ceskoslovenskych skladatelu* 28, no. 5 (1975): 221-22.

Evidon, R. "Bergman and *The Magic Flute.*" *The Musical Times* 117 (February 1976): 130-31.

Horowitz, J. *"The Magic Flute* opera verite (Bergman's Film)." *Music Journal* 34 (February 1976): 18.

Osborne, C.L. "The *Flute* on Film: It Works; Bergman's Camera Captures Mozart." *High Fidelity/Musical America* 26 (February 1976): MA16-18.

Lienert, K.R. "Zur Bergman-Verfilmung von W.A. Mozarts *Zauberflöte.*" *Schweizerische Musikzeitung* 116, no. 2 (1976): 102.

Flothuis, M. "Een gemiste kans." *Mens en Melodie* 31 (May 1976): 135-37.

Kirchberg, K. "Der Musik gehorsame Töchter—zu Ingmar Bergmans *Zauberflöten*-Film." *Musica; Zweimonatssch-rift für alle Gebiete des Musiklebens* 30, no. 6 (1976): 503-05.

Nattiez, J.J. "Ingmar Bergman ou l'autre survie de l'art lyrique." *Musique en Jeu* no. 24 (September 1976): 116-20.

Fabian, I. *"Die Zauberflöte* auf schwedisch—Die Originalein-spielung zu Ingmar Bergmans Fernsehfilm." *Opern Welt; die deutsche Opernzeitschrift* no. 10 (October 1976): 56-57.

Steene, Birgitta. *Positif* no. 177 (1976): 5-9.

Werba, E. "Zwei Mozart-Filme." *Oesterreichische Musik-zeitschrift* 32 (July-August 1977): 363.

Epertiere, R. "Mozart selon Bergman et Losey." *Harmonie* no. 152 (November 1979): 34-39.

Wangermee, R. "Quelques mystères de *La flute enchantée.*" *Revue Belge de Musicologie* 34-35 (1980-81): 153.

Schreiber, U. "Das Gold im Zahn, oder; Die andere Zugehörigkeit; zu den Mozart-Filmen von Ingmar Bergman und Joseph Losey." *Hifi-Stereophonie; Musik-Musikwiedergabe* 20 (March 1981): 240-42.

Lindblom, P. "Tredje Staandpunkten, Ingmar Bergman och jazz." *Nutida Musik* 25, no. 2 (1981-82): 38-39.

Kureishi, Hanif. *"The Magic Lantern* by Ingmar Bergman." *New Statesman & Society* 2 (7 July 1989): 37.

Clark, Sedgwick. *"Smiles of a Summer Night."* *Video Review* 12 (August 1991): 78.

Sheward, David. "Bergman on Stage." *Back Stage* 32 (28 June 1991): 36.

Redvall, Eva. "Bortz: Backanterna." *Opera News* 56 (11 April 1992): 52.

*   *   *

Internationally famous as a film and theater director, Ingmar Bergman won rave reviews for his debut at the Stockholm Royal Opera with his production of Stravinsky's *The Rake's Progress.* Despite offers from opera houses all over the world, he did not produce another opera until he directed Mozart's *Die Zauberflöte* for Swedish television. Both of these operas deal with themes that are prevalent in Bergman's work: the exploration of man's spiritual existence, the search for love, and questions of morality.

Bergman claimed that he was motivated to direct Stravinsky's *The Rake's Progress* when he saw a poor production of it. Although Bergman had not met the composer, he had read Stravinsky's ideas on interpretation and had seen him conduct. Bergman sensed what Stravinsky was saying with this opera and, with all of his theatrical skill and passion, set about to achieve it on the stage. As in his films, Bergman used the visual elements and symbolism of the characters to bypass reason and communicate directly to the heart of the viewer. Especially effective was the madhouse scene in which the madmen writhe in their private hells of dissonance and

shadows until the lighting changes, the motion stops, and the music resolves into Anne's beautiful farewell to Tom.

Ten years after the premiere of *The Rake's Progress* in Venice, which Stravinsky conducted, the composer attended Bergman's production. Despite cuts, deviations from stage directions, and translation into Swedish, Stravinsky was deeply moved and claimed that he had never seen a better production of *The Rake's Progress.*

When asked what other operas he would like to direct, Bergman named Mozart's *The Magic Flute.* As a child, he had been fascinated with this opera and had tried to stage it in his dollhouse theater. As a production assistant at the Swedish Opera House, Bergman had heard directors speak of the many problems of scenery and music. After having successfully directed the challenging *Rake's Progress,* he considered Mozart's *Magic Flute* to be the most fascinating and difficult opera ever written. An ideal vehicle for Bergman, it is an opera where the individual is simultaneously a symbol, a fairy story becomes an expression of humanistic ideals, and the stage becomes a glass through which we see ourselves.

Bergman's interpretation is shaped by his conviction that *The Magic Flute* fairy tale is nothing less than a mythic expression of truth. He saw the contradictions in the story as dreamlike patterns that speak directly to the subconscious. Bergman recreated the original production of 1791 with stage and props, even using lighting that simulated candlelight. To this authentic presentation, he added cut-ins to a modern audience, glimpses of the cast relaxing backstage, and placards with the texts of certain passages.

Bergman was profoundly moved by the scene in act II when Tamino cries out: "Oh, eternal night! When will you vanish? When shall I find light in the darkness?" and the chorus of priests answers from within the temple: "Soon, soon, or never more!" This moment in the opera seemed to be laden with spiritual meaning. He had tried to create this scene in an earlier film, *The Hour of the Wolf.*

The main contribution that Bergman made to opera is his method of interpretation. He felt handicapped by his inability to memorize a musical score and, to compensate, spent a great deal of time listening to and studying the music. The message that Bergman heard in the music was the foundation upon which he built the production. He then shaped the rhythmic sequences, harmonies, colors, relations, and forms of the visual and dramatic elements to clarify that message and make a powerful statement.

—Barbara A.K. Holm

BERGONZI, Carlo.

Tenor. Born 13 July 1924, in Polisene, near Parma. Studied with Edmondo Grandini in Brescia and under Ettore Campagalliani at Boito Conservatory in Parma, 1945-48; imprisoned for anti-Nazi activities during World War II; began career in baritone roles, singing Schaunard in Catania, 1947, and Rossini's Figaro in Lecce, 1948; tenor debut as Andrea Chénier in Bari, 1951; created role of Napoli's *Masaniello* for his Teatro alla Scala debut in 1953; sang Alvaro in *La forza del destino* for his London debut at Stoll Theatre in 1953, and for his Covent Garden debut in 1962; Metropolitan debut as Radames, 1956, and sang at the Metropolitan Opera until 1983 in 249 performances of 21 roles, including Alfredo, Manrico, Pollione, and Nemorino.

Publications

About BERGONZI: books–

Celletti, R. *Le grandi voci.* Rome 1964.
Matheopulos, Helena. *Bravo.* London, 1986.

articles–

Gualerzi, Giorgio. "Carlo Bergonzi." *Opera* (March 1978).

*   *   *

"A great Verdi stylist" is a description most often accorded to Carlo Bergonzi. In fact, Bergonzi has epitomized more of the essential qualities of an outstanding Verdi interpreter than most of the important tenors of the post-War period. In that respect he is the legitimate heir of a long line of Verdi stylists, and the logical successor to Pertile and Lauri-Volpi.

Though lacking the ringing top and heroic qualities of a Corelli or the dark, robust coloration of a Vinay, Bergonzi has managed, by sheer dint of hard study and a lifelong dedication to his art, to encompass the qualities necessary for the ideal Verdi interpreter. He is justly proud of his achievement of recording, after a nearly thirty year career, all the tenor arias of the Verdi repertoire in a 3-disc set for Philips: an outstanding achievement recognized as such by the awards of the Deutscher Schallplattenpreis, the Premio della critica discografica Italiana and the *Stereo Review* "Record of the Year."

How has Bergonzi achieved this reputation as a great Verdi stylist? In some respects his sympathy for Verdian style is to a large extent innate, as he was born and raised in the same area as Verdi himself. But added to this is a superlative vocal technique wedded to a beautiful voice used with sensitivity, superior musicality and intelligence. These qualities have enabled him to surmount many of the difficulties presented by Verdi's arias, many of which sound deceptively easy to sing. Much of Verdi's writing is around the *passaggio,* the notes E, F and G, where the male voice encounters a natural 'break' between the chest and the head registers. The tenor must learn to bridge these notes and "cover" (protect) the voice from this break if it is to last throughout a long career.

Bergonzi himself feels that an essential requirement of the Verdi specialist is to find the correct vocal color for each of his tenor roles. The color needed for the carefree, licentious Duke of Mantua is quite different from that appropriate for the heroic Radames. This is one reason why he has never attempted one of the most difficult of Verdi's tenor roles: Otello. He feels Otello demands a dark color that could never be his, either by nature or by study.

A somewhat stolid figure on stage, Bergonzi nevertheless succeeds in conveying the character he is portraying by vocal means, a factor which has no doubt been significant in his success in transferring his greatest Verdi roles to disc.

Yet, it is not just in Verdi's operas that Bergonzi has been acclaimed. He has sung many of Puccini's tenor roles: Cavaradossi (*Tosca*), Des Grieux (*Manon Lescaut*), Calaf (*Turandot*) and Rodolfo (*La Bohème*), has been acclaimed in the music of Giordano (*Andrea Chénier*), Boïto (*Mefistofele*), Catalani (*La Wally*), Massenet (*Werther*) and Ponchielli (*La Gioconda*) and is in much demand as a recitalist. Few tenors have demonstrated such versatility during the course of a career of more than forty years.

At the time of writing, Bergonzi is in his 66th year and is still singing beautifully. The highest notes of the tenor may now elude him, but the remainder of the voice is practically unimpaired by time. His singing is still beautiful, perfectly steady and commands the same remarkable breath control that has always enabled him to shape long, legato lines. He remains a testimony to the value of a sound technique and the wisdom of realising the capabilities of the voice and remaining within those limitations.

His association with Verdi remains, for in Verdi's birthplace, Busseto, he has formed a singing-school and shows a keen interest in passing on his experience and technique to young singers. He is also the driving force behind the "Concorso internazionale di voci verdiane," a competition dedicated to the furtherance of Verdian art. Perhaps from this enterprise a worthy successor to the master's crown will arise. Certainly Bergonzi's career is one of which any singer could be proud, and an inspiration to any young artist.

—Larry Lustig

BERIO, Luciano.

Composer. Born 24 October 1925, in Oneglia, Italy. Married: 1) singer Cathy Berberian, 1950 (divorced 1966; one daughter); 2) Susan Dyama, 1964 (divorced 1971; one son, one daughter); 3) Talia Pecker, 1977 (two sons). Studied composition with Ghedini and conducting with Giulini at the Milan Conservatory (composition degree, 1950); studied composition with Dallapiccola at Tanglewood; contacts with Darmstadt school, 1954; interest in electronic music and directorship of Studio di Fonologia Musicale, 1955-61, Milan; editor, *Incontri Musicali*; worked with Pierre Boulez at the Institut de Recherche et de Coordination Acoustique/Musique (IRCAM), Paris; on the faculty of the Juilliard School (1965-72), the Tanglewood Festival, and Harvard University since 1960; moved to the United States in 1963, returned to Italy in 1972; Artistic Director, Maggio Musicale, Florence, 1984; honorary member of the Royal Academy of Music, London, 1988; British Broadcasting Company Berio Festival at the Barbican, London, 1990.

Operas

Publishers: Belwin-Mills, Schott, Suvini Zerboni, Universal.

Opera, Berio, U. Eco, and F. Colombo, 1969-70, Santa Fe, New Mexico, 12 August 1970; revised, 1976.
La vera storia, Italo Calvino, 1977-81 Milan, Teatro alla Scala, 9 March 1982.
Un re in ascolto, Italo Calvino, Salzburg, 7 August 1984.

Other works: ballets, orchestral works, vocal music, chamber music, music for various solo instruments, music for tape.

Publications

By BERIO: books–

Kaltenecker, Martin, ed. and trans. *Entretiens avec Rossana Dalmonte.* Paris, 1983.

articles–

"Invito a Wozzeck." *Il diapasion* 3 (1952): 14.
"Poesia e musica: un'esperienza." *Incontri musicali* no. 3 (1959): 98.
"Verdi?" *Studi Verdiani* 1 (1982): 99.
"Eco in Ascolto." *Contemporary Music Review* 5 (1989).
Note: Berio's writings are extensive; for a more complete listing, see *The New Grove Dictionary of Music and Musicians,* 1980 edition.

About BERIO: books–

Azzaroni, Loris, et. al. *Il gesto della forma. Musica, poesia, teatro nell'opera di Luciano Berio.* Milano, 1981.
Mackay, Andy. *Electronic Music.* Oxford: 1981.
Dressen, Norbert. *Sprache und Musik bei Luciano Berio. Kölner Beiträge zur Musikforschung* 124. Regensburg, 1982.
Schrader, Barry. *Introduction to electro-acoustic music.* Englewood Cliffs, New Jersey, 1982.
Osmond-Smith, David. *Berio.* Oxford, 1991.

articles–

Konold, W. "Musik zwischen Sprache und Aktion: einige Aspekte zum Schaffen von Luciano Berio." *Musica* 25 (1971): 453.
Flynn, G. W. "Listening to Berio's Music." *Musical Quarterly* 61 (1975): 388.
Osmond-Smith, D. "Berio and the Art of Commentary." *Musical Times* 116 (1975): 871.
Stoianowa, Iwanka. "Über die Brechtschen Prinzipien der Operndramaturgie bei Luciano Berio: Musikalische Erzähltechnik und zeitgenössisches episches Theater." In *Gesellschaft für Musikforschung, Report, Bayreuth 1981,* edited by Christian-Hellmut Mahling and Sigrid Wiesmann, 520. Kassel, 1984.
Vogt, Matthias Theodor, "Listening as a Letter of Uriah: A Note on on Berio's *Un re in ascolto* (1984)." *Cambridge Opera Journal* 2 (1990): 173.

*　　*　　*

Luciano Berio was born into a family of musicians in Northern Italy. He is, with Luigi Nono, one of Italy's leading composers and intellectuals. Berio is first and foremost a musician, followed closely by the activities of pedagogue, lecturer, conductor and musical innovator.

Berio studied with Dallapiccola in the United States and Ghedini in Italy. He has been on the faculty of the Juilliard School of Music in New York, and taught at Harvard and Tanglewood as well. One of the earliest proponents and exponents of electronic music, he has worked alongside Pierre Boulez at IRCAM (Institut de Recherche et de Coordination Acoustique/Musique) at the Pompidou center in Paris, and ran a series of broadcast workshops on electronic music for RAI (Italian State Radio) in the late fifties and early sixties.

Berio's extraordinarily wide intellect has, over the years, brought him into contact, and in many cases close friendship with the leading Italian intellectual and literary figures of our day. His fascination with literature from Shakespeare to James Joyce has provided endless and fertile ground for seemingly limitless musical innovation, especially for the voice.

His marriage to the great American soprano Cathy Berberian produced a rare partnership in avant-garde music. Berberian had a voice of incredible range and flexibility which, combined with an exciting theatrical stage presence, was to lead to some of Berio's most original and memorable early work.

Partnerships have always played a major role in Berio's career. Most of these collaborations are with writers, but he has worked with other composers (Bruno Maderna and Mauricio Kapel for example) and choreographers. The music for Maurice Béjart's ballet *I Trionfi* was created in 1974 and was premiered in Florence. Much of his concert music has been used by choreographers in the modern dance idiom.

Luciano Berio's preoccupation with the voice verges on an obsessional interest. In his opera *Un re in ascolto* (A King Listens), the composer almost requires the audience to participate in the action by actually "listening" as well as "hearing" the work. Despite the fact that in the Italian language the word is the same for both concepts, it is Berio's particular interest in semantics and linguistics that helped create this intriguing opera.

Un re in ascolto was the second opera Berio composed in collaboration with the great Italian writer Italo Calvino (who died in 1985), the first being *La vera storia,* first staged at La Scala in 1982. It is typical of Berio that the first idea for *Un Re* came from an essay by the French intellectual Roland Barthes, was further influenced by W.H. Auden's writings on "The Tempest," and had program notes by Umberto Eco in the Royal Opera House program when the opera was produced there in 1989.

Luciano Berio loves the open-mindedness of the young, and has a strong following. In today's world he remains one of the most approachable (in human terms), challenging and prolific composers. With such a brilliant mind and eclectic approach to all cultural activity his many disciples, both professional and amateur can look forward with eager anticipation to further stimulus and possible provocation in the years to come.

—Sally Whyte

BERLIOZ, (Louis-) Hector.

Composer. Born 11 December 1803, in La Côte-St.-André. Died 8 March 1869, in Paris. Married: 1) Harriet Smithson, actress, 3 October 1833 (died 1854; one son), 2) Marie Recio, singer, 1854 (died 1862). Studied flute with Imbert and guitar with Dorant in Grenoble; self-taught in theory; medical student in Paris, 1821-24; studied composition with Jean François Le Sueur and counterpoint and fugue with Anton Reicha at the Paris Conservatoire, 1826-30; wrote for several Paris journals from 1823-63, including *Le Rénovateur, Gazette Musicale* (later merged with *Revue Musicale), Le Corsaire,* and *Journal des Débats,* among many others; sang in the chorus at the Théâtre des Nouveautés; awarded the Prix de Rome for his cantata *La mort de Sardanapale* in 1830; order of the Légion d'Honneur, 1839; Assistant Librarian 1839-50 and Librarian 1850 at the Paris Conservatoire; frequent concert engagements in Germany, Austria, and England, from 1842; visited Russia, 1847; in England, 1848; replaced Adolphe Adam at the Institute, 1856.

Hector Berlioz conducting a concert of the Société Philharmonique at the Jardin d'Hiver, Paris. Engraving by Gustav Doré from *Le Journal pour rire*, 22 June 1856

Operas

Editions:

H. Berlioz: Werke. Edited By C. Malherbe and F. Weingartner. Leipzig, 1900-10.
New Berlioz Edition. Edited by Hugh Macdonald et. al. Kassel, 1967-.

Estelle et Némorin, Gerono (after Florian), 1823 [not performed; score lost].
Les francs-juges, Humbert Ferrand, 1826 (revised 1829, and 1833 as *Le cri de guerre de Brisgaw,* T. Gounet) [not performed; only overture and five movements survive].
Benvenuto Cellini, Léon de Wailly and Auguste Barbier (after Cellini's autobiography), composed 1834-37, Paris, Opéra, 10 September 1838; revised 1852 for Weimar, 17 November 1852.
La nonne sanglante, Eugène Scribe, 1841-47 [unfinished].
Les troyens, Berlioz (after Virgil), 1856-58, Paris, Théâtre-Lyrique, 4 November 1863; revised 1859-60; divided into two parts, 1863.
Béatrice et Bénédict, Berlioz (after Shakespeare, *Much Ado about Nothing*), composed 1860-62, Baden-Baden (in German), 9 August 1862.

Other works: *La damnation de Faust* (légende dramatique) orchestral works including symphonies, choral works, works for solo voice and orchestra, songs.

Publications

By BERLIOZ: books–

Grand traité d'instrumentation et d'orchestration modernes. Paris, 1843; revised edition, 1855; translated as *Modern Instrumentation and Orchestration.* London, 1855.
Voyage musical en Allemagne et en Italie. Paris, 1844; 1970.
Les soirées de l'orchestre. Paris, 1852; translated by C. Roche, with an introduction by Ernest Newman, as *Evenings in the Orchestra,* New York, 1929; edited by Léon Guichard. Paris, 1968; translated by J. Barzun as *Evenings with the Orchestra,* New York, 1956; 2nd ed. 1973.
Les grotesques de la musique. Paris, 1859; edited by Léon Guichard, Paris, 1969.
A travers chants. Paris, 1862; edited Léon Guichard, Paris, 1971; translated by Edwin Evans as *Mozart, Weber, and Wagner; Gluck and his Operas;* and *Beethoven's Symphonies,* 3 vols., 1913-18.
Hallays, A, ed. *Les musiciens et la musique.* Paris, 1903.
Hector Berlioz: A Selection from his Letters. London, 1966.
Mémoires de Hector Berlioz. Paris, 1870; 2nd ed. in 2 vols, 1878; in English, London, 1884; new English translation by R. and E. Holmes, with annotations by Ernest Newman, New York, 1932; edited by P. Citron, Paris, 1969; translated into English and edited by David Cairns, London, 1969, New York, 1975, London, 1977.
Citron, Pierre, ed. *Correspondance générale.* 7 vols. Paris, 1972-.
Condé, Gérhard, ed. *Cauchemars et passions.* Paris, 1981.

About BERLIOZ: books–

Ernst, A. *L'oeuvre dramatique de H. Berlioz.* Paris, 1884.
Destranges, E. *Les Troyens de Berlioz: étude analytique.* Paris, 1897.

Tiersot, Julien. *La musique aux temps romantiques.* Paris, 1930; 1983.
Barzun, Jacques. *Berlioz and the Romantic Century.* 2 vols. Boston, 1950; London, 1951; revised and abridged as *Berlioz and his Century,* New York, 1956; 3rd ed., 1969; reprint Chicago, 1982.
Ganz, A.W. *Berlioz in London.* London, 1950.
Hopkinson, Cecil. *A Bibliography of the Musical and Literary Works of Hector Berlioz.* Edinburgh, 1951; revised by R. MacNutt, Tunbridge Wells, 1980.
Ballif, Claude. *Berlioz.* Paris, 1968; 1984.
Smith, Patrick J. *The Tenth Muse.* New York, 1970.
Dickinson, A.E.F. *The Music of Berlioz.* London, 1972.
Newman, Ernest. *Berlioz, Romantic and Classic.* Edited by Peter Heyworth. London, 1972.
Primmer, Brian. *The Berlioz Style.* London, 1973.
Dömling, W. *Berlioz.* Reinbeck, 1977.
Piatier, F. *Benvenuto Cellini de Berlioz; ou, Le Mythe de l'artiste.* Paris, 1979.
Walsh, Thomas Joseph. *Second Empire opera: the Théâtre Lyrique, Paris, 1851-1870. The history of opera.* London and New York, 1981.
Macdonald, Hugh. *Berlioz. Master Musicians.* London, 1982.
Clarson-Leach, Robert. *Berlioz: His Life and Times.* New York and Tunbridge Wells, Kent, 1983.
Rushton, Julian. *The Musical Language of Berlioz.* Cambridge, 1983.
Kemp, Ian, ed. *Hector Berlioz: Les Troyens.* Cambridge, 1988.
Murphy, Brian. *Hector Berlioz and the Development of French Music Criticism.* Ann Arbor, 1988.
Cairns, David. *Berlioz. Vol. 1: The Making of an Artist.* London, 1989.
Holoman, D. Kern. *Berlioz.* Cambridge, Massachusetts, and London, 1989.

articles–

Von Bülow, Hans. "Hector Berlioz: Benvenuto Cellini." *Neue Zeitschrift für Musik* 47 (1852).
Jullien, A. "Les Troyens." *Musica* 7 (1908): 43.
Prod'homme. "Les deux Benvenuto Cellini de Berlioz." *Sammelbände der Internationalen Musik-Gesellschaft* 14 (1913): 449.
Tiersot, J. "Hector Berlioz and Richard Wagner." *Musical Quarterly* 3 (1917): 453.
Servières, G. "Pièces inédits relatives aux Troyens." *La revue musicale* 5 (1924): 147.
Newman, E. "Les Troyens." In *Opera Nights,* 283. London, 1943.
Hammond, A. "Benvenuto Cellini." *Opera* 8 (1957): 205.
Klein, J.W. "*Les Troyens.*" *Monthly Musical Record* 87 (1957): 83.
Dickinson, A.E.F. "Berlioz and The Trojans." *Durham University Journal* 20 (1958): 24.
———. "Music for the Aeneid." In *Greece and Rome,* 2nd series 6 (1959): 129.
Addison, A. "*Beatrice and Benedict*: The German Edition." *Berlioz Society Bulletin* 33 (1960): 1.
Klein, J.W. "Berlioz as Musical Dramatist." *The Chesterian* 35 (1960): 35.
Wallis, C. "Berlioz and the Lyric Stage." *Musical Times* 101 (1960): 358.
Fraenkel, Gottfired. "Berlioz, the Princess, and *Les Troyens.*" *Music and Letters* 44 (1963): 249.
Rushton, Julian. "Berlioz's Roots in 18th-Century French Opera." *Berlioz Society Bulletin* no. 50 (1965): 3.

Cairns, David. "Berlioz's Epic Opera." *The Listener* 76 (1966): 364.

Searle, Humphrey. "Berlioz and *Benvenuto.*" *Opera* December (1966).

Macdonald, Hugh. "The Original Benvenuto Cellini." *Musical Times* 109 (1968): 142.

Cairns, David. "Berlioz and Virgil." *Proceedings of the Royal Musical Association* 45 (1968-69): 97; revised in *Responses,* London, 1973.

Kuhn, H. "Antike Massen: Zu einigen Motiven in *Les Troyens* von Hector Berlioz." In *Opernstudien: Anna Amalie Abert zum 65. Geburtstag,* 141. Tutzing, 1975.

Cairns, David. "Spontini's Influence on Berlioz." In *From Parnassus: Essays in Honor of Jacques Barzun.* New York, 1976.

La May, T.K. "A New Look at the Weimar Versions of Berlioz' *Benvenuto Cellini.*" *Musical Quarterly* 65 (1979): 559.

Langford, Jeffrey. "Berlioz, Cassandra, and the French operatic tradition." *Music and Letters* 62 (1981): 310.

Beye, Charles Rowan. "Sunt lacrimae serum." *Parnassus* 10 (1982): 75. [on the libretto of *Les troyens*]

Cockrell, Dale. "A study in French Romanticism: Berlioz and Shakespeare." *Journal of Musicological Research* 4 (1982): 85.

Rushton, Julian. "Berlioz's Swan-Song: Towards a Criticism of *Béatrice et Bénédict.*" *Proceedings of the Royal Music Association* 109 (1982-83): 105.

————. "The Overture to Les Troyens." *Music Analysis* 4 (1985): 119.

*　　*　　*

Berlioz's first eighteen years were passed remote from any major cultural center. His earliest experience of music was in small genres: chamber-music, to which he contributed nothing in his maturity; songs, including operatic arias arranged for the drawing-room; provincial examples of church and municipal music; folk-music. He fed his imagination on literature, thoughts of distant climes, and lives of great composers, but not until he came to Paris to study medicine did he experience theater, symphonic music, and opera.

Although nineteenth-century Paris was host to an unprecedented variety and richness of artistic achievement, opera remained the dominant art-form. Berlioz's contemporaries and friends included representatives of a great epoch in literature and spoken theater (Hugo, Nerval, Dumas, Balzac, Gautier, Vigny) and at least one great painter (Delacroix), as well as musicians who concentrated on the piano (Chopin, Thalberg, Liszt). But opera combined poetry, the music of voices and instruments, and the spectacle of elaborate scenery and dancing in the most fascinating of total experiences; and as in the age of Louis XIV it was both art and business, the cultural flagship of a rapidly developing nation. The Mecca of aspiring singers, dancers, and composers, Paris boasted three major opera companies: the Opéra itself, dominated by the grand operas of Rossini, Halévy, Meyerbeer, and later Verdi; the Opéra–Comique of Boieldieu, Hérold, Auber and Adam; and the Italian theatre which both imported and commissioned works by Rossini, Donizetti and Bellini.

Opera was at the center of Berlioz's livelihood, but he seldom took the parts he desired, of conductor and composer. He first attended the opera as an outspoken enthusiast, then as a newspaper critic and essayist whose judgment was respected and whose wit was feared. His comments, elegantly conveyed in *Les Soirées de l'orchestre* (in which orchestral musicians tell stories during dull or pretentious operas), are harsh, but history has tended to bear out his verdicts. He conducted a number of operas in London and Germany, and concert extracts from many more, but he was constantly passed over for posts in Paris for which, as a musician, he was the best qualified candidate.

His career as a composer was always primary for him, but his training and habits of thought were unconventional, and his greatest successes fell outside prevailing trends. No pianist, he was fascinated by the expressive instrumental music of Beethoven, and his earliest successes were in the unfashionable genres of concert overture and symphony. He gave concerts in France, Belgium, Germany, Russia, and England throughout his career, which were often highly successful, but they did little to further his operatic ambitions. The success of his innovative programmatic works, notably the *Symphonie fantastique* (1830) and *Harold en Italie* (1834), combined with a reputation for eccentricity and extravagance fed by such pieces as his huge (but state-commissioned) *Requiem* (1837), combined to make the Parisian establishment of Conservatoire and theater wary of him; nor did his reputation as a critic help acceptance of his own compositions.

For his time, Berlioz had unusual and decided tastes in opera. Despite his love of Weber and his sympathetic understanding of the best contemporary work, such as Meyerbeer and Verdi, he based his operatic aesthetic on Gluck and his successor Spontini. At the inception of his career he appeared as a flagrant romantic before Romanticism was widely acceptable; by the time the public and establishment had caught up with him, he had embraced a very personal form of neoclassicism. As a result none of his operas fitted with prevailing tastes, and none was remotely successful in his lifetime.

Berlioz's only completely romantic opera was his first, *Les francs-juges* (1826, revised 1829), to a libretto by his close friend Humbert Ferrand. This tale of sinister political violence in medieval Germany never reached the stage. He later destroyed much of the score, finding a place for its best ideas in other works; enough remains to show his ready assimilation of the French pre-Romantics, Méhul and his own teacher Le Sueur, as well as the recent and controversial works of Weber. The overture still holds its place in the concert-hall.

Frustrated in his attempts to obtain a theater commission, Berlioz could still develop his dramatic gifts in the annual competition cantatas for the Rome Prize, notably *Herminie* (1828) and *Cléopâtre* (1829), and in a group of *Eight Scenes,* using lyrics from Nerval's translation of Goethe's *Faust* (1829). He finally won the prize in 1830, subsequently destroying the winning cantata, *Sardanapale,* which he claimed to have written in a deliberately conventional style. After the required sojourn in Italy, where he denounced the quality of music and performance in opera as well as church music, he carved out a place for himself in Parisian concert life, promoting his own works at huge expense of money and effort.

He remained at heart a dramatic composer. In 1833 he married Harriet Smithson, whose assumption of the roles of Ophelia and Juliet had moved him, and all Paris, in 1827. His love and understanding of Shakespeare emerged in an entertaining fantasia on *The Tempest* (1830), the stirring *King Lear* overture (1831), and the huge 'dramatic symphony' *Romeo and Juliet* (1839). Meanwhile he had at last achieved a staged performance when *Benvenuto Cellini,* loosely based on the memoirs of the Florentine goldsmith and sculptor, was given at the Paris Opéra late in 1838. The libretto was a collaboration, Berlioz having a controlling hand; inexperience led to serious dramatic weaknesses in construction, notably a too-episodic final act following a brilliant climax in the previous finale, the Roman Carnival from which Berlioz later derived a popular concert overture. The semi-serious genre, mingling comedy with violence and the expression of artistic idealism, also created difficulties. But the reasons for its perhaps predictable failure are more mundane. The libretto was naturalistic in its language, evading the usual operatic euphemisms; the musicians, including the tenor Duprez and the conductor Habeneck, could not grasp Berlioz's electric rhythms and complex melodic phrasing. There were only four complete performances until *Benvenuto Cellini* was revived in London and Weimar in the 1850s, eventually with extensive revisions; the German performances obtained the success that the music deserved under the committed direction of Liszt.

In the 1840s Berlioz was persuaded to compose recitatives to Weber's *Der Freischütz* for the Opéra, and accepted a libretto from Scribe, *La nonne sanglante*. He never finished the music; the libretto was withdrawn and eventually set by Gounod. The main work of this period is the concert-length "dramatic legend" *La damnation de Faust* (1846), incorporating the earlier *Eight Scenes*. Despite being conceived for the concert-hall, much of this masterpiece is overtly operatic; partly because of this generic mix, *Faust* is the last of Berlioz's works which might be considered romantically extravagant. A project to adapt it for the London stage (1847) came to nothing, but the 20th century has seen several operatic productions. Its style of dramatic presentation is designed to appeal to the visual imagination rather than to complement a spectacle, and some scenes, notably those in hell and heaven, are near-impossible theatrically. It was while working on *Faust* that Berlioz became his own librettist; he never again relied on other poets, writing his own texts for the successful oratorio *L'enfance du Christ* (1850-54) and his last two operas.

Les Troyens (1855-9) was written without a commission, under the influence of a lifelong passion for Virgil's *Aeneid*, and upon persuasion from Liszt's mistress Carolyne Sayn-Wittgenstein. Nevertheless, always practical, Berlioz designed it for the resources of the Paris Opéra. Its huge scale, its ritual and processional scenes involving chorus and dancing (especially in the first and third acts), the spectacular effects required (the fall of Troy, the royal hunt and storm, the vision of imperial Rome), and the centering of a wide-ranging action upon noble, suffering women align it superficially with grand opera. But in essence it is deeply opposed to the prevailing bourgeois aesthetic; it is a work of idealism, tracing its stylistic ancestry to Gluck and Spontini rather than the fashionable Italians and Meyerbeer. It is no accident that in this period Berlioz produced his most-often performed stage work, an adaptation of Gluck's *Orpheus* for Pauline Viardot-Garcia which retained the revisions and enlargements made for Paris while restoring the key-scheme with the vocal tessitura of the original Vienna version.

Les Troyens is a classical epic, remote in spirit from the historical and religious subject-matter favoured by Grand Opera. Berlioz was under no illusions about the likely reaction of the public, but he had every right to expect immediate interest in his longest work; instead, unfounded rumors began to circulate about its absurd length and colossal instrumentation. In fact it is chastely scored, reserving large forces for ceremonial scenes, and is no longer than contemporary works of Meyerbeer and Wagner. The indifference of the authorities, including the Emperor Napoleon III, was unpardonable; soon after its completion the Opéra tried to repair its fortunes by calling in Wagner for *Tannhäuser*. Finally a magnificently unified conception was shattered by division into two operas, *La prise de Troie* (Acts I and II) and *Les Troyens à Carthage*

(Acts III to V). Only the latter was performed in Berlioz's lifetime (1863), savagely cut, at the inadequately equipped and funded Théâtre Lyrique, but with enough success to enable him to give up criticism; his last article is a warm appraisal of Bizet's *Les pêcheurs de perles*.

After finishing *Les Troyens* Berlioz contemplated a Cleopatra opera, and was asked for one on a Thirty Years' War subject. Successive bereavements and declining health make it doubtful that he would have had the strength for major projects; the gaps between his larger works had been growing since 1840, and his production of lesser pieces also declined. However, his friendly relationship with the impresario at Baden led him to agree to write his last and shortest opera, for which he returned to his beloved Shakespeare. "A caprice written with the point of a needle" was Berlioz's summary of *Béatrice et Bénédict*, as fresh and surprising an end to his career as is Verdi's *Falstaff*. But it is no surprise to find that he conceived an opera on *Much Ado about Nothing* in the productive 1830s, although there is no evidence of composition prior to 1860. Although it is ostensibly an opéra comique with spoken dialogue, *Béatrice et Bénédict* bears little resemblance to that genre as generally understood in Paris; it is designed as a sophisticated entertainment for a spa audience, and performing it in a large theatre is as damaging as putting on *Les Troyens* in a small one.

Throughout his career, Berlioz dreamed, conducted, and planned opera, but was continually frustrated in his efforts to create successful works for the stage. We cannot now regret the abortion of *La nonne sanglante* and the absence of other works on conventional librettos, but for Berlioz the refusal of the powers that were to recognize his operatic potential was a life-long tribulation. He understood the theatre thoroughly, and given intelligent singing and production his operas can all hold the stage; *Benvenuto Cellini* has unquenchable fire and spirit, *Béatrice et Bénédict* a uniquely intricate charm, and modern performances and recording have shown *Les Troyens* to be among the greatest works of the entire century.

—Julian Rushton

BERNACCHI, Antonio Maria.

Alto castrato. Born 23 June 1685, in Bologna. Died March 1756 in Bologna. Studied in Bologna with Pistocchi and G.A. Ricieri; soprano at San Petronio, Bologna; opera debut in Genoa, 1703; sang in Ruggeri's *Arato in Sparta*, Venice, 1712; Gasparini's *Il Bajazet*, 1719; premiere of Scarlatti's *Griselda*, 1721; in Munich from 1720; in Scarlatti's *Pirro e Demetrio* in London, 1717; sang Goffredo in Handel's *Rinaldo* and Dardano in Handel's *Amadigi*; in 1729 Handel engaged him as leading man for the Second Royal Academy, for which he sang the title roles in the premiere of *Lotario* (1729), in *Giulio Cesare*, and in *Tolomeo* in 1730, as well as Arsace in the premiere of *Partenope*; retired from stage in 1736 and established a singing school in Bologna; pupils include Guarducci and Raaff.

Publications

About BERNACCHI: books–

Heriot, Angus. *The Castrati in Opera.* London, 1956.
Pleasants, H. *The Great Singers.* New York, 1966; 1981.

articles–

Frati, L. "Antonio Bernacchi e la sua scuola di canto," *Rivista musicale italiana* 29 (1922): 473.

*   *   *

Bernacchi, an alto castrato, was one of the most famous and skilled singers of the early eighteenth century. As was typical for his time, he traveled widely. Following an early musical education and short service in San Petronio in Bologna, his operatic debut occurred in Genoa in 1703. He made several other early appearances at the courts of Mannheim, Vienna, and Munich (where he frequently sang in the 1720s), but his principal career was centered in Italy, where he appeared in Venice (for eight seasons before 1735), Bologna, Parma, Rome (in Alessandro Scarlatti's *Griselda* in 1721), Naples, Turin, and numerous other locations.

Bernacchi became well known to London audiences, appearing there first in two short seasons in 1716-17, singing in works by (among others) Handel and A. Scarlatti; for Handel he sang Goffredo in *Rinaldo* and Dardano in *Amadigi*. His third and most important London season, however, occurred over ten years later in 1729, after leaving an engagement in Naples over a falling out with another great singer, Giovanni Carestini. Now again in London, Bernacchi created the title role of Handel's *Lotario* and sang Arsace in the composer's *Partenope,* as well as appearing in several other revivals and *pasticci.* He returned to Italy in 1730, where he continued to sing until 1736 with much success.

Opinion of Bernacchi in London in the 1729-30 season seemed to vary, but often suffered in comparison with his immediate predecessor as first man for Handel, Senesino. Mrs. Pendarves in 1729 characterized Bernacchi as having "a vast compass, his voice mellow and clear, but not so sweet as Senesino, his manner better; his person not so good, for he is as big as a Spanish friar." Burney was more critical, finding him "past his meridian; his voice was never good, but now little was left, except a refined taste and an artificial manner of singing, which only professors and a few of the most intelligent part of the audience could feel or comprehend."

Bernacchi's principal glory rested on his powers of improvisation and embellishment, which he achieved in a style often said to have been instrumental in character and versatility; Pistocchi, Bernacchi's early teacher in Bologna, chided him: "I have taught you to sing, but you only want to play ['suonare,' to play an instrument]." Porpora also was highly critical of his "affected" manner. Zanetti caricatured Bernacchi standing near the Venice campanile with streams of acrobatic embellishment spewing through the air above.

Bernacchi's relationship to another influential singer, Farinelli (who probably studied with Bernacchi briefly in 1727), might have been influential on his own manner of singing. They appeared together in a revival of Orlandini's *Antigona* (under the title *La fedeltà coronata*) in Bologna in 1727, during which a lofty, ornate cadenza by Farinelli brought wild accolades from the audience. As Bernacchi then stepped forward, however, he embellished even more profusely and sang in such a refined, polished manner that the audience

was won over. Conjecture has it that each made a great impression on the other. Farinelli organized a memorial service for Bernacchi at his death.

One of Bernacchi's most important legacies was the students he tutored in Bologna after his retirement in the late 1730s. Among these were such tenors as Raaff and Carlani, the castrati Tedeschi (Amadori), Guarducci, and Gizziello, and the female alto Vittoria Tesi-Tramontini.

—Dale E. Monson

———

DIE BERNAUERIN [The Wife of Bernauer].

Composer: Carl Orff.

Librettist: Carl Orff.

First Performance: Stuttgart, 15 June 1947.

*   *   *

Frequently referred to as the "Bavarian *Antigone*", *Die Bernauerin* is an example, as Werner Thomas says, of "*Welttheater* transcending history." Orff's subtitle, "Ein Bayerische Stück," is not meant to indicate a dialect-centered vernacular play, but rather a theater drama in which the elements of sound and rhythm within the dialect have inspired musical counterparts and fused with them. *Die Bernauerin* marks the first of four such works in the transition from his "romantic" period to the late theatre settings of epic proportions on Greek themes.

The story, based on real figures in fifteenth-century Germany, relates the fate of Agnes, the daughter of a bath-house proprietor in Augsburg, who works as an attendant in her father's business. Young and attractive, she has caught the eye of Albrecht, a handsome young nobleman who, ignoring his father's plans for a dynastic union elsewhere, carries Agnes off to a castle in Straubing he had inherited and there secretly marries her. Not knowing the true details of their union, the townspeople are soon embroiled in vicious gossip. At the high point of their frenzy they declare that Agnes is a witch and should be dealt with as such. Word reaches Albrecht's father in Munich, and in the night, when Albrecht is away on business, armed guards break into the castle, take Agnes prisoner, and drag her to the river where she is thrown from the bridge and drowned. Albrecht returns later that night to be greeted by news of Agnes' demise, and in a fury he rouses his private guard to ride against his father and avenge his wife's death. The neighbors, meanwhile, have second thoughts about Agnes' guilt, and overnight she becomes a heroine in Bavarian folklore: to this day, a special mass is said annually for "die Bernauerin" in the little church in Straubing.

Orff's exhaustive source materials for this work included several versions of the tale which vary considerably. For musical theatre, Carl Orff chose certain dramatic additions of his own to enhance the effect: a mad monk foments the gossip; the local people are inclined to think that Agnes may be the cause of the Black Plague; and the Shakespearean-like witches relate the sordid details of the drowning as Agnes' hair is entangled by a long pole to push her head under the water. Orff's historical elements were given a fitting vehicle thanks to a 1940 edition of Johann Andreas Schmeller's early nineteenth-century Bavarian dictionary (four volumes). The composer immersed himself in the Bavarian dialect as one would experiment with musical rhythm and timbre, seeking to use the "music" of the language as an added dimension: a source of sound and rhythm that could be interwoven with tone and voice and instrumental elements. The result is a theatre piece that is not *"Mundart"*, but as Werner Thomas says, *"Welttheater* transcending history . . .".

The accessibility of this work for performance and its time-less subject matter merit closer consideration, particularly now that an English translation is available. The close unity of Bavarian dialect with the music demands a similarly ar-chaic text in a translated performance, akin to Shakespearean dialogue. There are elements of all the earlier works, together with new textual qualities, woven skillfully by means of a narrator, sections of spoken dialogue, and an extensive rhythm ensemble within the orchestra. The chorus is ex-tremely important to this theater piece, and the two main characters must be excellent actors.

—Jean C. Sloop

BERNSTEIN, Leonard.

Composer/Conductor. Born 25 August 1918, in Lawrence, Massachusetts. Died 14 October 1990, in New York. Mar-ried: Felicia Montealegre, actress, 9 September 1951 (died 1978). Studied piano with Helen Coates and Heinrich Gebh-ard; studied orchestration with E. B. Hill and counterpoint and fugue with Walter Piston at Harvard University, 1935-39; studied orchestration with Randall Thompson, piano with Isabella Vengerova, and conducting with Fritz Reiner at the Curtis Institute; studied conducting with Serge Koussevitzky at Tanglewood, summers of 1940 and 1941; Assistant Con-ductor, 1943, and Music Director, 1958-69, New York Phil-harmonic; guest conducting with Vienna Philharmonic and London Symphony Orchestra, among many others; awarded Order of Merit, Chile, 1964; Chevalier of the French Legion of Honor, 1968; Cavaliere, Italy, 1969; Austrian Honorary Distinction in Science and Art, 1976; Albert Einstein Com-memorative Award in the Arts; International Education Award; George Foster Peabody Award; honorary doctorate of letters, University of Warwick, England, 1974. Bernstein's stage works include the musicals *On the Town,* 1944, *Wonder-ful Town,* 1953, *Candide,* 1956, and *West Side Story,* 1957.

Operas

Publisher: G. Schirmer.

Trouble in Tahiti, Bernstein, Waltham, Massachusetts, Bran-deis University, 12 June 1952.
A Quiet Place, S. Wadsworth, Houston, Houston Grand Op-era, 17 June 1983 [revised 1984].

Other works: ballets, musicals, orchestral works, chamber music, film scores, songs.

Publications/Writings

By BERNSTEIN: books–

The Joy of Music. New York, 1959; 1963; London, 1974.
Leonard Bernstein's Young People's Concerts for Reading and Listening. New York, 1962; 1970.

The Infinite Variety of Music. New York and London, 1966.
The Unanswered Question. Cambridge, Massachusetts, 1976.
Findings. New York, 1982.

articles–

"Leonard Bernstein in Conversation with Robert Ches-terman." In *Conversations with Conductors,* edited by Rob-ert Chesterman, 53, 69. Totowa, New Jersey, and London, 1976.

About BERNSTEIN: books–

Briggs, John. *Leonard Bernstein: The Man, his Work, and his World.* Cleveland, 1961.
Holde, Artur. *Leonard Bernstein.* Berlin, 1961.
Ewen, David. *Leonard Bernstein.* London, 1967.
Gruen, John. *The Private World of Leonard Bernstein.* New York, 1968.
Ames, Evelyn. *A Wind from the West: Bernstein and the New York Philharmonic Abroad.* Boston, 1970.
Cone, M. *Leonard Bernstein.* New York, 1970.
Weber, J.W. *Leonard Bernstein.* Utica, 1975.
Matheopoulos, Helena. *Maestro....* London, 1982.
Robinson, Paul. *Leonard Bernstein.* New York and London, 1982.
Gradenwitz, Peter. *Leonard Bernstein.* Zurich, 1984; trans-lated as *Leonard Bernstein: The Infinite Variety of a Musi-cian.* Leamington Spa, 1987.
Freedland, Michael. *Leonard Bernstein.* London, 1987.
Peyser, Joan. *Leonard Bernstein.* New York and London, 1987.

articles–

Gradenwitz, P. "Leonard Bernstein." *Music Review* 10 (1949): 191.
Gow, D. "Leonard Bernstein, Musician of Many Talents." *Musical Times* 101 (1960): 427.
Gruen, John. "In Love with the Stage." *Opera News* 37 (1972): 16.
Wadsworth, S. "A Quiet Place: Librettist's Notes." Notes for *A Quiet Place,* Deutsche Grammophon 419 761-2 (1987).

unpublished–

Snyder, Linda Jane. "Leonard Bernstein's works for the musi-cal theatre: how the music functions dramatically." DMA dissertation, University of Illinois, Urbana-Champaign, 1982.

*　　*　　*

Leonard Bernstein devoted much of his career to various aspects of the opera and musical theater. He composed works for the Broadway stage that straddle the fine line between musical comedy, opera, and operetta; he composed works that adhere much more closely to the traditional European concept of opera; and he conducted major engagements at many of the world's most respected and renowned opera houses.

Whereas Bernstein's Broadway shows frequently contain operatic elements, such as the aria "Glitter and Be Gay" from *Candide* (1956), which requires a highly-developed and flexible operatic voice, in general they conform most closely to the forms and idioms established by his musical comedy predecessors Jerome Kern, Irving Berlin, Cole Porter, George Gershwin, and Richard Rodgers. His earliest collaborations for the Broadway stage, including the ballet *Fancy Free* (1944) and its musical comedy companion *On the Town* (1944), surely helped prepare him to some extent for the operatic stage. The popular song idiom, which inspired much of his first opera, clearly derives from his early Broadway and Tin Pan Alley song-writing experience.

Bernstein's two works that best represent traditional European opera are the one act *Trouble in Tahiti* (1952) and its sequel *A Quiet Place* (1983, which incorporates *Trouble in Tahiti* as two flashbacks). However, to call these two essentially autobiographical works traditional in any sense stretches considerably the accepted boundaries of opera. Elements of the popular theater and the conventional opera house merge and contrast throughout to create a hybrid form of musical theater. Bernstein has stated about *Trouble in Tahiti:* "It's a lightweight piece. The whole thing is popular-song inspired and the roots are in musical comedy, or, even better, the American musical theater." Certainly some of the roots may lie in musical comedy, but Bernstein's statement seems unusually reserved and restrained. Both the nature of the subject matter and its musical setting clearly reveal a genre that skirts the middle ground between traditional opera and musical comedy. And his allusion to "a lightweight piece" really misrepresents both *Trouble in Tahiti* and *A Quiet Place*. These two works attempt to convey substantially more serious subject matter than the typical Broadway musical; they are composed throughout, and they include musical techniques, forms, and idioms far removed from the Broadway theater. Even *Candide* represents an exception to his Broadway works because through various revisions and transformations it too now seems most at home in the opera house.

Although by no means best known as a conductor of opera, Bernstein enhanced his international reputation markedly through his association with individual operatic productions. In 1953 he became the first American to conduct at the Teatro alla Scala in Milan when he conducted Maria Callas in a production of Cherubini's *Médée*. He has also introduced some of the major operatic works of the twentieth century to the American public. For example, in the summer of 1946 he conducted the American premiere of Benjamin Britten's *Peter Grimes* at the Berkshire Music Center.

The predominant conflict in Bernstein's career as a theatrical composer has been whether to write popularly influenced music or music more closely allied with mainstream opera. In fact, this conflict between his obvious talent for the Broadway stage and his attraction to the European tradition represents the crucial dilemma of Bernstein's entire composing career. *A Quiet Place* would seem to be his partial response to those critics who have questioned his operatic credentials, since it attempts to reconcile the two seemingly incompatible idioms. While the sections based on *Trouble in Tahiti* (only a few passages of which were modified for the new work) utilize a language heavily influenced by popular musical techniques, the newly composed sections of *A Quiet Place* employ a musical language derived largely from the musical idioms of contemporary opera. The integration and juxtaposition of the contrasting styles creates a unique, if somewhat precariously balanced, theatrical composition.

Bernstein's most important theatrical contributions will almost certainly be remembered as those written specifically for the Broadway stage. Although both *Trouble in Tahiti* and *A Quiet Place* introduce some startlingly fresh elements to

American opera, such as the biting commentary on contemporary life and the attempt to blend popular and contemporary musical idioms, they are undoubtedly not as innovatory or influential as the Broadway shows, particularly *West Side Story* (1957). While Bernstein should not be regarded among the foremost American composers of opera, his two works should find and retain a secure place in the repertory of American opera.

—William Thornhill

BERRY, Walter.

Bass-baritone. Born 8 April 1929, in Vienna. Married Christa Ludwig in 1957 (divorced 1970). Studied with Hermann Gallos at the Vienna Academy. Joined Vienna State Opera in 1950. Metropolitan opera debut as Barak in Strauss's *Die Frau ohne Schatten,* 1966; from 1952 was a regular soloist at the Salzburg Festival, creating roles in Liebermann's *Penelope* (1954), Egk's *Die Irische Legende* (1955), and Einem's *Der Prozess* (1953).

Publications

About BERRY: books–

Lorenz, P. *Christa Ludwig, Walter Berry.* Vienna, 1968.

*   *   *

Walter Berry is one of the most accomplished bass-baritones of the second half of the twentieth century. With a beautiful, rich voice, accuracy of intonation, and unusual vividness of characterization, Berry has brought memorably to life roles as diverse as Leporello (Mozart's *Don Giovanni*), Pizarro (Beethoven's *Fidelio*), Kurwenal (Wagner's *Tristan*), Barak (Strauss's *Die Frau ohne Schatten*) and the title role in Berg's *Wozzeck.*

Berry's talents won praise from the beginning of his international career in the 1950s. In a recording of *Don Giovanni* made in the mid-1950s under Rudolf Moralt, Berry's Leporello stands out for its clear enunciation, its wit and sense of style. A later recording of the same opera, under Klemperer, shows Berry in even better form. Notice, in "Notte e giorno faticar," the extraordinary energy that Berry brings to the music, his alertness to the meaning of the words. Leporello's annoyance and impatience could hardly be expressed in a more lively, entertaining manner.

Another Mozart role in which Berry has been successful is Papageno (*Die Zauberflöte*). In the recording conducted by Sawallisch, Berry presents Papageno with plenty of high spirits and a wonderful variety of vocal color, while the clarity of Berry's enunciation breathes life into the music. Papageno's strophic songs benefit especially from Berry's musical and dramatic skills. In "Der Vogelfänger bin ich ja" Berry brings out individual words with subtle variations of vocal color; there is something new and interesting in each repetition of the melody. Yet the richness and sophistication of his performance does not keep Berry from remaining very much in character: his Papageno remains a simple, good-hearted man throughout.

Berry has won much praise for his many performances in the operas of Richard Strauss. His portrayal of Baron Ochs (*Der Rosenkavalier*) is celebrated. When he performed the role in Vienna in 1972 critics admired his diction, his *parlando,* and applauded him for never exaggerating; all of these features of his performance can be heard in a recording of an excerpt from act II, conducted by Heinrich Hollreiser (issued in 1967). Berry brings his accustomed energy and variety to his performance, expressing with subtle gradations of dynamics and tone color a wide spectrum of emotions. Berry's Ochs is a real person, not a caricature. The same recording shows that Berry could bring to life with equal vividness Strauss's Barak and Orest (in *Elektra*). Also recorded (under Leinsdorf) is Berry's fine portrayal of the Music Master in *Ariadne auf Naxos.*

Berry has devoted much more attention to twentieth-century opera (in addition to Strauss) than many opera singers. His gripping portrayals of Berg's Wozzeck have been acclaimed by critics and audiences alike. Among the many less familiar twentieth-century operas in which he has sung is Werner Egk's *Irische Legende.* Berry's fine performance was not enough in itself to save the opera from failure when it was performed in Salzburg in 1955, but there are other recent operas (Liebermann's *Penelope* and Einem's *Der Prozess,* for example) whose success owed much to Berry's talents.

—John A. Rice

BETROTHAL IN A MONASTERY [Obrucheniye v monastyre].

Composer: Sergei Prokofiev.

Librettists: Sergei Prokofiev and Myra Mendelson (after Sheridan, *The Duenna*).

First Performance: Leningrad, Kirov, 3 November 1946.

Roles: Don Jerome (tenor); Louisa (soprano); Ferdinand (baritone); Mendoza (bass); The Duenna, Margaret (contralto); Antonio (tenor); Clara (mezzo-soprano); Don Carlos (baritone); Father Augustine (baritone); Brother Elixir (tenor); Brother Chartreuse (baritone); Brother Benedictine (bass); Lopez (tenor); Rosina (mezzo-soprano); Lauretta (contralto); Two Servants (tenors); Three Fishwives (sopranos, mezzo-soprano); Three Maskers (tenor, baritones); Friend of Don Jerome (mute); Servant of Don Jerome (mute); chorus (SAATTBB).

*   *   *

The inspiration for Sergei Prokofiev's fifth full-length opera, *Obrucheniye v monastyre* (*Betrothal In a Monastery*), completed in 1940, came from Richard Brinsley Sheridan's 1775 comic opera, *The Duenna*. (Some sources also refer to Prokofiev's opera as *The Duenna—Duen'ia*—although the composer disliked this title, which sounds clumsy in Russian.) *Betrothal* was the first of three operatic collaborations between Prokofiev and the Soviet writer Myra Mendelson, who eventually became his second wife. Indeed, Mendelson later

claimed credit for persuading the composer to create a modern version of Sheridan's popular work, whose verses she had been translating into Russian. After hearing the plot of *The Duenna,* Prokofiev reportedly exclaimed, "But that's champagne—it could make an opera in the style of Mozart, Rossini!" And that's exactly what he produced, returning amidst the grim realities of Nazism and Stalin's Russia to his beloved eighteenth century, revisiting the self-conscious, ironic, theatrical world of his best-known opera, *Love for Three Oranges.*

By now an experienced librettist, Prokofiev wrote most of the book for *Betrothal*. Mendelson supplied editorial advice and some verse texts (both her own and translations from Sheridan) for arias and ensembles. In four acts and nine scenes further subdivided into forty-eight fast-moving episodes, a structure clearly exhibiting the dynamic influence of Prokofiev's recent work on film scores (including *Alexander Nevsky*), the adaptation diverges significantly in detail and emphasis from the original Sheridan. Only six of Sheridan's twenty-seven verses survive. Even more important, the style and level of language are more folksy and crude. Together with the often satirical spirit of the score, this verbal earthiness introduces a grotesque element absent in the original ballad opera.

Relying heavily on Mozartian devices such as exchanged and mistaken identities, local Spanish color, and the contrast between real and counterfeit love, the action of *Betrothal* takes place in a single day in Seville. Act I, in one scene, introduces the nobleman Don Jerome and his unsavory sidekick, the wily fish merchant Mendoza. They strike a business deal that includes Mendoza's marriage to Don Jerome's daughter Louisa. But Louisa is in love with the dashing young Antonio, who reciprocates her passion—as a memorable lyrical serenade and duet make clear. Meanwhile, Don Jerome's son Ferdinand loves Louisa's friend Clara, who has sought refuge in a convent to escape her evil parents. And the Duenna, Don Jerome's corrupt and bawdy housekeeper, wants to marry the rich Mendoza. These romantic complications play out against an enchanting choreographic background of masqueraders dancing and strolling through the city.

The intrigue thickens in the three scenes of act II. Louisa and the Duenna exchange identities. Louisa next assumes Clara's identity and appeals to Mendoza on Louisa's behalf. The Duenna persuades Mendoza to abduct her. In act III, Don Jerome unknowingly approves of his daughter's marriage to Antonio, clearing the way for Antonio to wed Louisa, Ferdinand to wed Clara, and the Duenna to wed Mendoza. The triple ceremony, heavy with humor, takes place in the first scene of act IV in a debauched monastery, whose monks spend most of their time drinking. True love and classical symmetry having triumphed over greed and chaos, all that's left for act IV, scene ii, is to return to Don Jerome's house, where in the course of yet another masquerade ball, the benevolent nobleman eventually accepts the inevitable in true classical fashion.

That the subject's mixture of satire, irony, and romance suited Prokofiev's temperament and mood seems clear from the speed with which he completed *Betrothal*. It took him only about two months from start to finish. While working, he decided to stress the romantic over the comic elements, although the blunders of Don Jerome and Mendoza clearly stimulated his mischievous imagination. Wisely, he controlled his natural tendency towards brittle cardboard caricature, so obvious in *Love for Three Oranges,* and chose to humanize the roles. Similarly, Prokofiev made use of numerous operatic conventions—arias clearly set off in the musical texture, ensembles, rhymed verses—which he had previously rejected as old-fashioned and static. *Betrothal* represents a return to classical traditions, and a conscious abandonment of the at times uncompromisingly radical views on opera that Prokofiev had espoused early in his career.

At the same time, many of the opera's notable features can be traced to the composer's experimentalism: distaste for dramatically stagnant scenes, a fondness for "physical" images (here, of drunkeness), close attention to the rhythm and intonation of language. Act III, scene vi, the "music-making" scene, is one of Prokofiev's liveliest and most imaginative pieces of stage business. Against the background of a constantly interrupted domestic trio (clarinet, trumpet, bass drum) played with humorous lack of polish by Don Jerome and two friends, Don Jerome reads two letters and unwittingly agrees to give his daughter in marriage to Antonio (thinking he is Mendoza). The interruptions in the music-making become comically repetitive, the humor heightened by the trumpeter's reluctance, and then the drummer's, to stop playing when Don Jerome does.

Although Prokofiev completed *Betrothal* very quickly, in the same sort of burst of inspiration that produced the "Classical" Symphony and *Peter and the Wolf,* he had to wait six years to see it produced on stage. Originally scheduled to open at Moscow's Stanislavsky Musical Theater in the summer of 1941, it was postponed after Hitler's invasion of Russia. Among the most accessible, skillfully crafted, entertaining, and emotionally rewarding of Prokofiev's seven operas, *Betrothal* deserves to be much better known in the Western repertoire.

—Harlow Robinson

THE BEWITCHED CHILD
See SEE L'ENFANT ET LES SORTILÈGES

BILLY BUDD.

Composer: Benjamin Britten.

Librettists: E.M. Forster and Eric Crozier (after Herman Melville).

First Performance: London, Covent Garden, 1 December 1951; revised 1960.

Roles: Edward Fairfax Vere (tenor); Billy Budd (baritone); John Claggart (bass); Mr Redburn (baritone); Mr Flint (bass-baritone); Lieutenant Ratcliff (bass); Red Whiskers (tenor); Donald (baritone); Dansker (bass); Novice (tenor); Squeak (tenor); Bosun (baritone); First Mate (baritone); Second Mate (baritone); Maintop (tenor); Novice's Friend (baritone); Arthur Jones (baritone); Four Midshipmen (boys' voices); Cabin Boy (speaking part); chorus (TTBB).

Publications

articles–

Mitchell, D. "More off than on 'Billy Budd'." *Music Survey* 4 (1951-52): 386.

Tempo no. 21 (1952) [*Billy Bud* issue].

Porter, Andrew. "Britten's *Billy Budd.*" *Music and Letters* 33 (1952): 11.

Stein, Erwin. "The Music of *Billy Budd.*" *Opera* 3 (1952): 206.

Mitchell, D. "A *Billy Budd* Notebook." *Opera News* 43/no. 19 (1979).

Brett, Philip, "Salvation at Sea: *Billy Budd.*" In *The Britten Companion,* edited by Christopher Palmer. London, 1984.

Hindley, Clifford. "Love and Salvation in Britten's *Billy Budd.*" *Music and Letters* (1989).

Whittall, Arnold. " 'Twisted relations': Method and Meaning in Britten's Billy Budd." *Cambridge Opera Journal* 2 (1990): 145.

*   *   *

Based upon Herman Melville's *Billy Budd, Sailor,* Benjamin Britten's opera is set on board ship during the French wars, shortly after the mutinies of 1797. Edward Fairfax Vere is Captain of HMS Indomitable, and John Claggart is its Master at Arms. Billy Budd, a young seaman, is impressed from a passing merchantman; he is a paradigm of beauty and goodness, his only flaw being his stammer. He excites the envy and hatred of the evil Claggart, who schemes to destroy him by falsely accusing him of mutiny. When, however, Vere arranges a confrontation between Billy and Claggart, Billy's stammer prevents him from answering the charges, and he strikes Claggart a fatal blow. The officers, bound by the Articles of War, find Billy guilty of murder, and sentence him to death. Vere accepts the verdict, and, behind closed doors, conveys this to Billy in a manner left to the audience's imagination. That night Billy, in chains, unflinchingly accepts his fate in a searching meditation; then, facing a dawn execution, is moved to cry before the assembled ship's company, "Starry Vere, God bless you!" He is hanged at the yardarm while the officers quell an incipient mutiny against the injustice. A Prologue and Epilogue show Vere in old age reflecting on his experiences. Now convinced that the execution had been a tragic mistake, he is assured that, blessed by Billy, he has found salvation and the love that passes understanding. Originally in four acts, the opera also provides graphic episodes depicting both the brutality and the comradeship of life on board, the excitement of impending battle and a ship's muster which elevates Vere as a patriotic commander. The latter scene was omitted when, for the revival of 1960, the opera was re-arranged in two acts.

The librettists, E.M. Forster and Eric Crozier, wrote in prose, though often a "heightened" prose, which Britten found well suited to musical setting. Musically the opera marks a development in Britten's style, embodying the complex inter-relationships of many short motifs in an overall structure which has been described as "symphonic." There is a developed symbolism in the use of tonal centers: for example, the ambiguity of the opening bars, rocking between B flat major and B minor, symbolic at once of the mist and of Vere's uncertainty, finds a final triumphant resolution in the blazing chord of B flat major in the Epilogue, as Vere affirms his assurance of salvation. The use of intervals, such as the fourth to mark Claggart's depravity, can be equally symbolic. All Britten's skill, both in characterizing individuals and in portraying different moods, from the intimate to the spectacularly grand, is evidenced, and so skilful is the writing even for a large orchestra, that the confinement of the vocal range to male voices only is hardly noticed. Particularly

Billy Budd, with Philip Langridge as Captain Vere (left) and Thomas Allen (right) as Billy, English National Opera, London, 1988

moving is the solemn succession of thirty-four variously orchestrated triads which marks the veiled interview between Billy and Vere.

The drama reflects a contest between fate and love. Forster saw in Melville's tale a prophetic utterance, "reaching back into the universal." It is pervaded by ineluctable fate—seen in the cruelly flogged novice, in Claggart's sense of predestination, in the "We've no choice" of the officers at the trial, in Billy's final reflection on the inevitability of Claggart's death and his own. The ship is an image of mankind "lost on the infinite sea." But strength to overcome this predicament is found through love, even though love perverted (in Claggart) can also destroy.

Though indirectly conveyed, the love which in their different ways Claggart and Vere feel for Billy is thus pivotal. For Claggart, that love is so deeply repressed and frustrated that it issues in a diabolical desire to destroy its object. But Vere is also drawn to the handsome sailor, and recent research has shown how in successive libretto drafts the relationship between Vere and Billy was developed far beyond Melville's portrayal of the Captain as an aloof disciplinarian. He is emotionally involved with the young man, while Billy responds with the ardor of personal devotion to Vere's goodness. The tragedy for Vere lies in the conflict between his love for Billy and his overriding sense that naval discipline requires the execution of the death sentence.

The love implicit in these relationships is symbolized in a recurring harmony of consecutive thirds and sixths. This harmony transforms the emotional atmosphere in the duet between Billy and Vere (act II, scene 2). It is also heard in the agitated quarter-deck interview between Claggart and Vere, with Claggart's innuendo that Vere is unduly moved by the young seaman's beauty. But at the climax it is the love between Billy and Vere (the "far-shining sail"—identified as love in a surviving note by Forster) which provides the strength to withstand fate. The point is made musically when Billy's melody for the far-shining sail is underpinned by the consecutive thirds/tenths of love: and when, at the hanging, the fearful orchestral fortissimo dissolves into tranquil high sixths, as forgiveness eclipses pain. In this context, reinforced by the recurring thirds in Vere's melodic line and Billy's arpeggio-like motif, the "Interview Chords," which reiterate the thirds of the common triad, are to be heard as the affirmation of a love which strengthens both Billy (in the darbies) and Vere (at the execution) in their resolve to hold to the path of duty. The Epilogue, in its combination of the Interview Chords with the tenths of the far-shining sail, confirms, however paradoxically, that this love has brought salvation.

Many other themes emerge from this inexhaustible score: the universal struggle of good and evil; the vulnerability of innocence; the power of forgiveness, with Billy seen as a Christ-figure; the misery, injustice and oppression, as well as the heroism and camaraderie, of life in Nelson's navy; the evil of war. Britten himself indicated that his interest was kindled by the conflict in Vere's mind. Perhaps only the obligatory reticence about homosexual desire inhibited a more overt statement of this theme in the opera as a conflict between love and duty.

—Clifford Hindley

BIRTWISTLE, (Sir) Harrison.

Composer. Born 15 July 1934, in Accrington, Lancashire. Married: Sheila Birtwistle (3 sons). Studied at Royal Manchester College of Music and the Royal Academy of Music. Director of Music, Cranborne Chase School, 1962-65; visiting professor at Princeton University, 1968-69, Swarthmore College, 1973, and the State University of New York at Buffalo, 1974-75; Music Director of the National Theatre, South Bank, London, 1975-83; instrumental music for productions at the National Theatre, including *Oresteia,* 1981. Knighted 1988.

Operas

Publisher: Universal

Punch and Judy, S. Pruslin, 1966-67, Aldeburgh Festival, Jubilee Hall, 8 June 1968; revised London, 3 March 1970.
Down by the Greenwood Side ("dramatic pastoral"), M. Nyman, Brighton, Pier Pavilion, 8 May 1969.
The Mask of Orpheus, P. Zinovieff, 1973-83, London, English National Opera, 21 May 1986.
Yan Tan Tethera ("mechanical pastoral"), Tony Harrison, 1983-86, London, Queen Elizabeth Hall, 7 August 1986.
Gawain, D. Harsent, 1989-91, London, Royal Opera House Covent Garden, 30 May 1991.

Other works: various vocal, instrumental, and combined pieces for a number of different ensembles.

Publications

About BIRTWISTLE: books–

Hall, Michael. *Harrison Birtwistle. The Contemporary Composers.* London, 1984.

articles–

Henderson, R. "Harrison Birtwistle." *Musical Times* 105 (1964): 188.
Crosse, G. "Birtwistle's *Punch and Judy.*" *Tempo* no. 85 (1968): 24.
Chanan, M. "Birtwistle's *Down by the Greenwood Side.*" *Tempo* no. 89 (1969): 19.
Bowen, M. "Harrison Birtwistle." In *British Music Now.* Elek, 1975.
Hall, M. "Birtwistle in Good Measure." *Contact* no. 26 (1983).
———. "The Sanctity of the Context." *Musical Times* January (1988).

*   *   *

Birtwistle belongs to that generation of British composers that came to maturity in the late 1950s, when the extremely radical ideas of the Darmstadt school of composers still retained their influence but were gradually losing ground to a less rigid, more spontaneous approach to composition. The New Music Manchester Group, which Birtwistle founded with Alexander Goehr and Peter Maxwell Davies in 1953 (when all three of them were students), was established to promote the cause of advanced music that had not completely abandoned tradition. Like his colleagues, Birtwistle was not prepared to be a "pointillist." He wanted to preserve a sense of line, a sense of observable continuity, even though he remained totally opposed to what he called the "goal orientation" of classical and romantic music. In contrast to the "pointillism" of the Darmstadt school, which produced virtually static music, he wanted to write music in which the line (to quote his favorite text—Paul Klee's *Pedagogical Sketchbook*) was "an active line on a walk, moving freely, without goal. A walk for a walk's sake."

Fundamental to this approach is the new sense of time flow which emerged in the fifties. Birtwistle's lines are essentially cyclic, and are not dissimilar to the isorhythmic tenors of a medieval motet in that rhythm and pitch cycles rotate independently of each other to form a larger cycle. It is this cyclic approach which determines not only the form of his music but also the plots he selects for his operas. *Punch and Judy* contains four cycles each involving a ritual murder and a quest for "pretty Poll." These revolve within a single cycle of the seasons. Being a comedy, it inevitably ends in a marriage, and in this sense it achieves a goal. But the marriage takes place in spring and therefore the start of a larger cycle is implied.

The Mask of Orpheus also takes place within a single cycle of the seasons, but here the outcome is tragic. Birtwistle selected the myth because it survives in dozens of different versions which he can go through almost simultaneously (Ovid's version revolving within Virgil's version, and so forth). The result fulfills Birtwistle's strange ambition to compose not only the most recent but also the original version of Orpheus, a version in which all that have gone before have their origin. But this is only a rather bizarre way of looking at events cyclically. He is merely going back to the beginning.

It could be said that Birtwistle was fated to write operas. In the fifties, composers of the Darmstadt school focused their attention on abstract processes, but, from the very first, Birtwistle involved himself with drama, even when writing purely instrumental pieces. At the very heart of his music is the notion of role playing; all who perform his music must act out a part. His very first piece was a work for wind quintet called *Refrains and Choruses.* To make a drama out of it, he needed a protagonist, someone who disrupts the cohesiveness of the group by his willful and capricious behaviour. To play this role, he selected the horn, the only brass instrument in the ensemble and therefore the odd-man-out. This relationship is clearly based on the very earliest form of Greek theater, and could be considered a metaphor for the relationship between chance and necessity, the need to balance life-enhancing capriciousness with the stability of necessity and predictability.

Birtwistle pursues this relationship in every aspect of his work, even down to the smallest details of building up chords. No figure has ever been more willful than Mr. Punch, but his caprice goes beyond the limits when he murders his alter ego, the showman Choregos (traditionally the man who subsidized the chorus in the Greek theater). His only salvation therefore is to defeat the hangman Jack Ketch (a metaphor for the devil lying within him). When he has done so his "pretty Poll" accepts him. Orpheus disrupts the established order because he disobeys or goes beyond the limitations imposed upon him not only by Pluto but, more significantly, by his father Apollo. He is guilty of hubris on a grand scale, and for this he must perish. But the balance between man and nature is only restored when the bee-keeper Aristaeus, who initiated the tragedy by attempting to rape Euridice, makes the necessary sacrifices, finds forgiveness and has his bees restored to him.

In 1975, on the evidence of *Punch and Judy* and the dramatic pastoral *Down by the Greenwood Side,* Birtwistle was appointed Musical Director of The National Theatre, a position he relinquished in the mid-eighties when he went to live in France to devote himself exclusively to composition. The experience has made him one of the most imaginative and skilled men of the theater, and this is clearly reflected not only in *The Mask of Orpheus* but also in *Yan Tan Tethera* and *Gawain,* his most recent opera. His object is to create "total theatre," and as a consequence he has become bitterly opposed to all forms of naturalism. In this he was probably influenced by the theatrical movements which were so prominent in the fifties and sixties when he was formulating his style: the Theater of the Absurd (the theater of Adamov, Beckett, Genet and Ionesco), which emphasizes a state of being rather than a state of becoming, and Antonin Artaud's Theater of Cruelty, "where theatre," said Artaud, "will recapture from cinema, music-hall, the circus and life itself those things that always belonged to it." The most famous example of the Theater of Cruelty was Peter Brook's production of Peter Weiss's *The Marat/Sade,* which took place in London just when Birtwistle was assembling his initial ideas for *Punch and Judy* in 1965. Occasionally Birtwistle takes his vision of total theater to almost unworkable extremes. In *The Mask of Orpheus* he includes a number of electronic inserts during which a troup of dancers must act out the stories Orpheus told to the animals, trees and rocks when sitting on his mountain top. But the action must take place in the accelerated pace used in the films of Mack Sennett, Max Linder, Buster Keaton and Charlie Chaplin. Although not impossible on the stage, the amount of rehearsal required for the ideal realisation of this style would be prohibitive in most present circumstances. Some of Birtwistle's operas may not come into their own until there emerges a generation of directors who can cope with such stylized procedures with ease.

—Michael Hall

BIZET, Georges (Alexandre-César-Léopold)

Composer. Born 25 October 1838, in Paris. Died 3 June 1875, in Bougival, near Paris. Married: Geneviève Halévy (daughter of the composer), 1869 (one son). Bizet's father was a voice teacher and composer, and his mother was a pianist; initially he studied with his parents, then fugue and composition with Zimmerman at the Paris Conservatory from the age of 9, where he also studied piano with Marmontel, organ with Benoist, and composition with Halévy; became a prodigious pianist, and was praised by Liszt. His cantatas *David* (1856) and *Clovis et Clotilde* (1857) won second and first prizes (Charles Colin was also awarded a first prize in 1857), respectively, in the competition for the Prix de Rome; in 1857, Bizet tied with Lecocq for first place in a competition sponsored by Jacques Offenbach for the composition of a one act stage work, *Le docteur miracle;* in Rome from January 1858-1860; *Les pêcheurs de perles* (Paris, 1863) praised by

Berlioz; the well known incidental music to Daudet's *L'Arlésienne* was composed in 1872; Bizet died during the initial run of *Carmen* (1875), which did not achieve critical success until after his death. Bizet was made Chevalier of the Légion d'Honneur in 1875.

Operas

La maison du docteur (opéra-comique), Henry Boisseaux, c. 1854-55.

Le docteur miracle (operetta), Léon Battu and Ludovic Halévy, 1856 or 1857, Paris, Théâtre des Bouffes-Parisiens, 9 April 1857.

Don Procopio (Italian opera buffa), Carlo Cambiaggio, 1858-59, posthumously produced in Monte Carlo, 10 March 1906.

L'amour peintre, Bizet (after Molière), 1860 [unfinished].

La prêtesse (operetta), Philippe Gille, c. 1861?.

La guzla de l'emir, Jules Barbier, Michel Carré, 1862.

Les pêcheurs de perles, Michel Carré and E. Cormon, 1863, Paris, Théâtre-Lyrique, 30 September 1863.

Ivan IV, F. H. LeRoy and François-Hippolyte Trianon, 1862-63?, revised 1864-65, posthumously produced in Württemberg, Möhringen Castle, 1946.

Malbrough s'en va-t-en guerre (with Legouix, Jonas, Delibes), Paul Siraudin and William Busnach, 1867, Théâtre de l'Athénée, 13 December 1867.

La jolie fille de Perth, Jules-Henry Vernoy de Saint-Georges and Jules Adenis (after Walter Scott), 1866, Paris, Théâtre-Lyrique, 26 December 1867.

La coupe du roi de Thulé, Louis Gallet and Édouard Blau, 1868-69.

Completed Halévy's biblical opera *Noë,* 1869.

Clarisse Harlowe (opéra-comique), Philippe Gille et Adolphe Jaime the younger (after Richardson), 1870-71 [unfinished].

Grisélidis (opéra-comique), Victorien Sardou, 1870-71 [unfinished].

Djamileh (opéra-comique), Louis Gallet, 1871, Paris, Opéra-Comique, 22 May 1872.

Sol-si-ré-pif-pan (operetta), William Busnach, 1872, Château d'Eau, 16 November 1872.

Don Rodrigue, Louis Gallet and Édouard Blau (after Guilhem da Castro, *La Jeunesse du Cid*), 1873 [unfinished].

Carmen, Henri Meilhac and Ludovic Halévy (after Mérimée), 1873-74, Paris, Opéra-Comique, 3 March 1875.

Other works: orchestral works, including two symphonies, choral works, piano music, songs.

Publications/Writings

By BIZET: books–

Ganderax, L., ed. *Lettres: Impressions de Rome, 1857-60; La Commune, 1871.* Paris, 1908.

Galabert, E., ed. *Lettres à un ami.* Paris, 1909.

Wright, Lesley A., ed. *Georges Bizet: Letters in the Nydahl Collection.* Stockholm, 1988.

About BIZET: books–

Pigot, C. *Georges Bizet et son oeuvre.* Paris, 1886; enlarged, 1911.

Gallet, L. *Notes d'un librettiste.* Paris, 1891.

Nietzsche, F. *Randglossen zu Bizets "Carmen."* Edited by H. Daffner. Regensburg, 1912.

Georges Bizet

Hühne, F. *Die Oper "Carmen" als ein Typus musikalischer Poetik*. Greifswald, 1915.

Imsan, D. *Carmen: Charakter-Entwicklung für die Bühne*. Darmstadt, 1917.

Gaudier, C. *Carmen de Bizet*. Paris, 1922.

Istel, E. *Bizet und Carmen*. Stuttgart, 1927.

Laparra, P. *Bizet et l'Espagne*. Paris, 1935.

Exposition Georges Bizet au Théâtre National de l'Opéra [catalogue]. Paris, 1938.

Cooper, Martin. *Carmen*. London, 1947.

Dean, Winton. *Georges Bizet: His Life and Work*. London, 1948; enlarged 1965; revised, 1975.

————. *Carmen*. London, 1949.

————. *Introduction to the Music of Bizet*. London, 1950.

Malherbe, Henry. *Carmen*. Paris, 1951.

Stefan-Gruenfeldt, P. *Georges Bizet*. Zurich, 1952.

Curtiss, Mina. *Bizet and His World*. New York, 1958.

Robert, F. *Georges Bizet*. Paris, 1965; 1981.

Pintorno, Giuseppe. *Georges Bizet, Museo Teatrale alla Scala—cataloghi*. Milan, 1975.

Knaust, Rebecca. *The Complete Guide to Carmen*. New York, 1978.

Cardoze, M. *Georges Bizet*. Paris, 1982.

Dahlhaus, Carl. *Musikalischer Realismus, Zur Musikgeschichte des 19. Jahrhunderts*. Munich, 1982; English translation by M. Whittall, Cambridge and London, 1985.

John, Nicholas, ed. *Georges Bizet: Carmen, English National Opera Guides* 13. London and New York, 1982.

Roy, Jean. *Bizet*. Paris, 1983.

Maingueneau, D. *Carmen: Les racines d'un mythe*. Paris, 1984.

Fornari, F. *Carmen adorate: psicoanalisi della donna demoniaca*. Milan, 1985.

McClary, S. *Feminine Endings: Music, Gender and Sexuality*. Minneapolis, 1991.

articles—

Charlot, A. and J. "A propos de la millième de Carmen." *L'art du théâtre* 5 (1905): 9.

Halévy, L. "La millième représentation de Carmen." *Le théâtre* January (1905).

Musica June (1912) [Bizet issue].

Tiersot, J. "Bizet and Spanish Music." *Musical Quarterly* 13 (1927): 566.

Revue de musicologie 20 (1938) [Bizet issue].

Dean, Winton. "An Unfinished Opera by Bizet." *Music and Letters* 28 (1947): 347.

Changeur, J.-P. Six articles on *Ivan IV. La vie bordelaise* 12 October-16 November (1951).

Dean, Winton. "Bizet's Ivan IV." In *Fanfare for Ernest Newman*, 58. London, 1955.

Dean, Winton. "The True Carmen?" *Musical Times* 106 (1965): 846.

Poupet, Michael. "Les infidélités posthumes de partitions lyriques de Georges Bizet: *Les Pêcheurs de perles*." *Revue de musicologie* 51 (1965): 170.

Westrup, Jack. "Bizet's *La Jolie Fille de Perth*." In *Essays Presented to Egon Wellesz*, 157. Oxford, 1966.

Dean, Winton. "The Corruption of *Carmen*: The Perils of Pseudo-Musicology." *Musical Newsletter* 3 (1973).

Wright, Lesley A. "A New Source for *Carmen*." *19th-Century Music* 2 (1978): 61.

Avant-scène opéra, March-April (1980) [*Carmen* issue].

Kestner, J. "Joyce, Wagner and Bizet: Exiles, Tannhäuser, and Carmen." *Modern British Literature* 5 (1980): 53.

Leukel, J. "Puccini et Bizet." *Revue musicale de Suisse Romanda* 35/May (1982): 61.

Maingueneau, Dominique. "Signification du décor: l'exemple de *Carmen*." *Romantisme* 38 (1982): 87.

Poupet, M. "Gounod et Bizet." *Avant-scène opéra* 41/May-June (1982): 106.

Wangermée, R. "L'Opéra sur la scène et à l'écran: À propos de Carmen." In *Approches de l'opéra*. edited by A. Helbo, 251. Paris, 1986.

Wright, Lesley A. "*Les Pêcheurs de perles*: Before the Premiere." *Studies in Music* 20 (1986): 27.

Clarkson, A. "Carmen: Bride of Dionysus." *Quadrant* 20/ no. 1 (1987): 51.

Edwards, G. "Carmen." In *Catholic Tastes and Times: Essays in Honour of Michael F. Williams*, edited by M. Rees, 127. Leeds, 1987.

Furman, N. "The Languages of Love in Carmen." In *Reading Opera*, edited by A. Groos and R. Parker, 168. Princeton, 1988.

Avant-scène opéra October (1989) [*Les pêcheurs de perles* issue].

Beardsley, T.S. "The Spanish Musical Sources of Bizet's *Carmen*." *Inter-American Music Review* 10/spring (1989): 143.

Siebenmann, G. "Carmen von Mérimée über Bizet zu Saura und Gades: Ein Spanienbild im Spiel der Medlen." In *Einheit und Vielfalt in der überoromania: Geschichte und Gegenwart*, edited by C. Strosetzki and M. Tietz, 169. Hamburg, 1989.

Baker, E. "The scene designs for the first performances of Bizet's *Carmen*." *Nineteenth-Century Music* 13 (1990): 230.

unpublished–

Wright, Lesley A. "Bizet before Carmen." Ph.D. dissertation, Princeton University, 1981.

Minor, M. "Hispanic Influences on the Works of French Composers of the Nineteenth and Twentieth Centuries." Ph.D. dissertation, University of Kansas, 1983.

Clay, S. "Henri Meilac-Ludovic Halévy; Des Bouffes-Parisiens à l'Opéra-Comique." Ph.D. dissertation, University of California, Davis, 1987.

*   *   *

Bizet is often credited with helping to introduce realism into opera with *Carmen,* now widely popular but largely rejected by the Parisian critics in 1875 both for its harsh libretto and the colorful score. Bizet influenced his contemporaries in less obvious ways, too, as they learned from his virtuoso orchestration techniques or from ideas they borrowed (Tchaikovsky clearly modeled the boys' march in *The Queen of Spades* [1890] on a similar piece in act I of *Carmen*). Bizet, however, did not leave direct descendants in opera, partially because he died so soon after achieving true artistic maturity. Furthermore, he did not establish new forms or revolutionize the concept of scene structure; instead, Bizet absorbed influences from Italian, German and French composers and, within the number opera tradition, combined these with his own innate gifts for melody and orchestration. At their best his scores combine a vital dramatic sense with colorful, tuneful, sometimes exotic-sounding music and create unforgettable passages that may range in their depictions from wittiness to tragic passion.

Though Bizet died at thirty-six, only three months after the controversial *Carmen* premiere, his operas span twenty years. In addition to his operatic projects and the incidental music for Daudet's tragedy *L'Arlésienne,* he also wrote songs, choral works, piano pieces, two symphonies and other orchestral pieces. Thus, Bizet's development as a composer can not be summarized in a single genre, and even for an assessment of his achievements in opera, it is necessary to study all the manuscripts, since a number of his works were abandoned or failed in the theater and were then either issued or re-issued in untrustworthy, posthumous editions.

While still a student at the Paris Conservatoire in the 1850s, Bizet turned to writing opera, but his individual musical personality took time to assert itself with consistency. These unpretentious early works show that he had successfully absorbed the lighter styles then current in France and Italy and had mastered a sparkling orchestration technique. Even his earliest opera, *La maison du docteur,* has some melodic charm, but it was never scored and was probably prepared for an informal performance with his Conservatoire friends. *Le docteur miracle,* with a standard comic plot featuring thwarted young love and disguise, won a competition and was staged at Offenbach's theater in 1857. Within the light comic style Bizet wrote fresh-sounding tunes for his solo numbers and several appealing ensembles; he responded to the most intriguing dramatic opportunity with a masterful and deliciously witty quartet, "Voici l'omelette." After winning the Prix de Rome later that year, he left for Italy and claimed to have changed his tastes in music. "I am more than ever convinced that Mozart and Rossini are the two greatest musicians. Though I still admire Beethoven and Meyerbeer with all my faculties, I feel that my nature is inclined more toward loving pure and accessible art than that of dramatic

passion," he wrote to his mother in October 1858. Not surprisingly, *Don Procopio* quite convincingly appropriates the manner of Rossini and Donizetti, and incorporates Italianate accompaniment figures and an attractive vocal style. The more even and accomplished score was praised by the Academy of Fine Arts: "This work is distinguished by an easy and brilliant touch, a youthful and bold style, valuable qualities for the genre of comedy toward which the composer has shown a marked propensity."

In the 1860s Bizet expanded his range and absorbed the more dramatic and grandiose styles. His operas of this period incorporate and juxtapose elements derived from Gounod, Félicien David, Meyerbeer, Weber and even Verdi; however, more and more passages also strike the ear as distinctive to Bizet's personal style. A music critic's remark on *Djamileh* in 1872 describes Bizet and his two staged operas of the 1860s, *Les pêcheurs de perles* and La jolie fille de Perth: "The composer who stumbles in taking a step forward is worth more attention than a composer who shows how easy it is to take a step backwards." This statement applies as well to the abandoned *Ivan IV,* where Bizet turned to Meyerbeer as a model for grand opera. Though the orchestration and massed effects are at times overblown and the pacing not always well controlled, the score teems with good ideas which Bizet quarried for years thereafter. *Les pêcheurs de perles* also attempts grandiose effects in some scenes, but here there are more lyrical moments, especially for the soloists, and effective use of musical exoticism.

Surprisingly large portions of *La jolie fille de Perth* sound like pre-echoes of the *opéra-comique* style that would flower in *Carmen.* Although the influence of Weber and Verdi's *Rigoletto* lingers in the background, there are passages of wit, tunefulness and masterfully delicate orchestral effects that could only have been written by Bizet. Despite important style consolidation, however, he also made concessions to fashion in an Italianate coloratura part, and could not consistently find inspiration in the weakest libretto he ever set.

Perhaps the greatest loss of the 1860s is *La coupe du roi de Thulé,* submitted to an Opéra competition in 1869; even the surviving fragments of this manuscript reveal much originality and dramatic power. More abandoned projects followed. Two *(Clarisse Harlow* and *Grisélidis)* were intended for the Opéra-Comique; another, the grand opera *Don Rodrigue,* for the Opéra. Even though sketches and drafts for these operas permit some understanding of Bizet's intentions, his theater works that have not gone through the rehearsal process are far from finished. During the *Carmen* rehearsals, for example, Bizet greatly improved the pacing of the work, rewrote three of the four finales, cut and reworked a great deal of music for the chorus, removed most of the *mélodrames,* and even wrote solo material as striking as the Habanera.

Both of Bizet's staged operas from the 1870s feature exotic subjects, masterful scoring, interesting harmonies, and unforgettable melodies. The libretto of *Djamileh* has quite lovely poetry but is dramatically weak, with little action and a hero whose appeal remains a mystery to all but Djamileh herself. Perhaps these weaknesses have kept the lovely, one-act score from the wide popularity that it richly deserves. *Carmen,* on the other hand, is supported by one of the half-dozen best libretti ever written. Bizet recognized the quality of his work and wrote to a friend: "They claim that I am obscure, complicated, tedious, more fettered by technical skill than lit by inspiration. Well, this time I have written a work that is all clarity and vivacity, full of color and melody."

Bizet correctly assessed his skills and should be regarded as one of the greatest melodists and orchestrators of France.

His themes may be traditional and four-square (as the main theme of the famous tenor/baritone duet "Au fond du temple saint" from *Les pêcheurs de perles*) or spun-out with phrases run together so seamlessly that they form an indivisible sentence (as in the "flower song" from *Carmen*) or sinuous and exotic. Even many of the youthful melodies have an ageless charm and freshness.

Generalizations about Bizet's melodic style are complicated by his practice of borrowing from his earlier works that had not been publicly performed. The graceful flute duet in the prelude of *La jolie fille de Perth* was written several years earlier for *Ivan IV*. Most of Don José's flower song was rescued from a baritone piece abandoned in the sketches for *Grisélidis.* Only occasionally does the melodic style betray a borrowing, as in the old-fashioned choral passage "Ah, Chante, chante encore" (close of act I, *Les pêcheurs de perles*), which was pulled from its context in *Don Procopio.*

Bizet's skill at orchestration is also evident throughout his career. Except in a few blatantly Meyerbeerian passages his scores sparkle with woodwind color and the occasional brass accent. Strings serve as the foundation of his orchestral sound. A favorite Bizet combination, flute and harp, opens one of the loveliest orchestral pieces in opera, the entr'acte before act III in *Carmen.* Later in the score, flutes and bassoons play a delicate counterpoint to Frasquita's and Mercédès' warning to Carmen that Don Jose is nearby the bullring. The examples of imaginative and striking scoring could go on and on.

Bizet's music is perhaps most characteristic when he is creating an exotic atmosphere. Although in *Carmen* he used several real Spanish tunes, he had basically one generic exotic mode; thus, he felt it appropriate to take a bolero from his ode symphony *Vasco da Gama* (1860) and place it in the mouth of the young Bulgarian called upon to entertain Ivan IV with a song from his homeland. The exotic vocabulary often includes chromatic harmonies and sinuous or chromatic melodies over the tonal security of a pedal note (as near the end of each strophe of Djamileh's "Ghazel"). The laughing figure that represents Carmen and is later transformed into the "fate" motif may be called exotic since it incorporates the distinctive sound of an augmented second. In Bizet's exotic mode accompaniment figures focus on a repeated rhythm (often involving drone fifths or syncopation); harmonies shift ambiguously between major and minor. Bizet's harmonic experiments are probably most noticeable within this style, but are not confined to these pieces. The opening of Carmen's séguedille dances along without solidly confirming the tonic for twenty-nine bars; but in the next act the feather-light quintet, squarely within the *opéra comique* tradition, slides effortlessly from a distant G major to the tonic D-flat major. Accented dissonances, on the other hand, like those in Djamileh's lamento probably gave fuel to Bizet's contemporary critics, who hurled the epithet "Wagnerian" at his scores.

In the combination of drama with music Bizet achieved a unique and highly successful balance, at first only in individual numbers, then in the entire second act of *La jolie fille de Perth,* then in much of *Djamileh* and virtually all of *Carmen.* Though Bizet received few libretti of high quality, he did work with his librettists to try to refine the dramatic impact of each scene. The quality of the text and the interest of the situation was strongly linked to the quality and interest of his musical response. Witty and ironic situations appealed to him, as evidenced by the imaginatively scored "marche et choeur des gamins" of *Carmen* where children parody the adults' ritual. In *La jolie fille de Perth* an elegant minuet backstage wryly comments on the insincerity of the Duke of Rothsay's practiced seduction technique as he attempts to seduce his old mistress disguised as another. Given the quality of his invention in humorous dramatic situations, we might wish that Bizet had had the opportunity to write a full-length comic opera in the 1870s.

At the other end of the spectrum, Bizet also found inspiration in intense or desperate situations and in the pure flame of tragic passion. The final tragic duet of *Carmen* combines drama and music so convincingly that at moments a listener can also forget that there are two arts combined, and the unbearable intensity removes any distance between audience and performers. Though it is one of the greatest of operatic duets, it cannot be successfully excerpted because it is so wedded to the dramatic situation. Bizet's success with dramatic situations is by no means confined to his last work. At her investiture Léila, the high priestess of *Les pêcheurs de perles* refuses in a line of flexible recitative worthy of Carmen ("Je reste ici quand j'y devais mourir") to back away from an equally impossible situation. On the other hand, religious ceremony may also stimulate a more conventional response. Here Bizet may depend on Meyerbeer, and such passages sound curiously dated next to the exotic portions of his scores. Tenderness and conventional love tend to inspire a derivative (Gounodesque) style. It is not by chance that the duet of Marie and the young Bulgarian (act I of *Ivan IV*) and of Catherine and Smith (act I of *La jolie fille*) sound much like the act I duet of Micaela and Don Jose.

The works of the 1850s reveal much skill and appealing charm but only glimpses of Bizet's individuality; in the 1860s they are more original but also more eclectic; and in the 1870s they are too few in number. But Bizet has left a body of work that maintains its vitality and appeal. It demonstrates, too, a surprisingly wide range—from wit to tragic passion, from delicacy to dramatic power—and at its best a balance of music and drama that few have equaled.

—Lesley A. Wright

BJÖRLING, Jussi.

Tenor. Born 5 February 1911, in Tuna, Sweden. Died 9 September 1960 in Stockholm. Married soprano Ann-Lisa Berg, 1935—and sometimes sang opposite her. Entered Stockholm Conservatory in 1928, studied with Joseph Hirlop and John Forsell; appeared as Lamplighter in *Manon Lescaut,* but official debut as Don Ottavio, both in Stockholm in 1930; sang regularly in Stockholm until 1939; Vienna debut as Manrico, 1936; Chicago debut in *Rigoletto,* 1937; Metropolitan Opera debut as Rodolfo, 1938, and appeared with Metropolitan Opera until 1959 as Manrico, Faust, Riccardo (in *Un ballo in maschera*), Don Carlos, and Romeo, among others; San Francisco debut as Rodolfo, 1940.

Publications

By BJÖRLING: books–

Med bagaget i strupen [autobiography]. Stockholm, 1945.

About BJÖRLING: books–

Björling, G. *Jussi: Boken om storebror.* Stockholm, 1945.
Hagman, B. *Jussi Björling: En minnesbok.* Stockholm, 1960.

Henrysson, H. and J.W. Porter. *A Jussi Björling Phonography.*
Stockholm, 1984.

articles—

Bruun, C.L. and K. Stubington. "Jussi Björling." *Record
News* 4: 117; 5: 176.
Thielen, H. "Jussi Björling: Schallplattenverzeichnis." *Fono
forum* 4 (1975): 358.
Blyth, A. "Jussi Björling." *Opera* September (1985).

Arguably the finest lyric tenor of the century, Jussi Björling
was one of a long line of eminent Swedish singers whose
musical achievements have contributed immeasurably to opera. Jenny Lind, Kirsten Flagstad, Lauritz Melchior, Christine Nilsson, Birgit Nilsson, Karin Branzell, Astrid Varnay,
Nicolai Gedda, John Forsell, and many others have all helped
to establish Sweden as a major source of vocal genius. Yet
few have come to define a benchmark of such supreme musical taste, secure vocal production, and disciplined performance as that set by Björling. His remarkable achievement was
the result of a fortuitous combination of the gift of a voice
with a timbre of rare beauty and the advantage of a long,
careful musical tutelage that provided a pedagogical foundation of uncommon soundness. Björling, though often compared inappropriately with Caruso, certainly should be considered the great singer's successor as the preeminent tenor
of his time. For it would be difficult to bring forth another
candidate who could clearly exceed Björling's artistic and
commercial success.

Björling was born into a musical family, the atmosphere of
which contributed substantially to his early growth. His father, David, had studied voice early in the century at the
Metropolitan Opera School, and later at the Vienna Conservatory. He relinquished a modest opera career in Sweden to
devote himself to the education of his sons, Olle, Jussi, Gösta,
and Karl (the youngest). With the older three, David formed
the Björling Male Quartet, which concertized until the latter's
death in 1926. The elder Björling evidently was a gifted and
patient pedagogue, for it is clear that much of the sound,
disciplined approach to fundamentals of vocal production
that characterized the mature Jussi Björling was owed in no
small way to his father's influence. Evidently his father would
not allow him to sing one note without his personal supervision.

Björling's musical development was assisted considerably
by his early association (1928) in Sweden with John Forsell,
director of the Royal Opera in Stockholm, and gifted teacher.
It would be difficult to overestimate the value of Forsell's
guidance. His was a disciplined school which stressed musical
expressivity; slow, careful development of technique; ease of
vocal production; and memorization of a wide variety of basic
repertoire.

Securely under Forsell's wing, Björling made his first operatic appearance in 1930 as the Lamplighter in *Manon,* but
almost immediately made a far greater impact in his debut
roles as Ottavio in *Don Giovanni* and as Arnold in Rossini's
Guillaume Tell. The latter role, with its demanding *tessitura*
and *coloratura,* evidently was a perfect vehicle for Björling's
secure high register and technical prowess and is revealing of
the nature of his early capabilities. During the next few years
at the Royal Opera in Stockholm, Björling sang over 50
roles—early evidence of his reliable memory, which perhaps

explains his well-known distaste for rehearsing. He took pride
in his absolute knowledge of his parts and his ability to sing
them at a moment's notice.

After the beginning of his international career in 1936,
his active repertoire decreased considerably. He ultimately
narrowed his efforts to a dozen familiar works, most of which
are available on recordings and establish his unerring mastery
of the Italian style. His gift for singing in the Italian language
(although he did not speak it) and his supreme execution of its
characteristic *cantabile* lines clearly sustained his judgment in
restricting his artistic purview.

Of his operatic roles, Björling expressed a preference for des
Grieux in *Manon,* and it must be said that his performances in
this role were particularly well done. Late in his career Björling declared an interest in singing more performances as
Radames (*Aïda*), as well as in the roles of Lohengrin and
Otello. To those dubious as to the suitability of these heavy
parts for his lyric voice, he characteristically dismissed the
challenge as of no consequence for him. Björling had an
implicit faith in the ability of a singer with a mastery of
technique to sing "anything." Nevertheless, it must be said
that on the whole he chose his operatic roles with discretion,
notwithstanding the frequent performances of *Il trovatore,*
which many consider to have been less than ideal for his
voice. Appropriately, the demands of a stage performance
of *Turandot* held no allure for Björling, though he often
performed "Nessun dorma" in recital. It is a commonplace
to speak critically of Björling's acting ability, and it must be
admitted that he often performed with an undeniable dramatic stiffness that belied his otherwise complete command
of the requisite skills of a world-class lyric tenor. Nevertheless, most agree that on the stage his consummate musicianship and expressive delivery usually more than atoned for
this deficiency.

To various degrees the voices of all great singers may be
characterized as distinctive. Of no one may this be said more
truly than of Björling. His timbre was unique and his voice
distinguished throughout its range for an uncommon evenness of production. Personally, he dismissed the concept of
vocal "registers," and maintained that the voice should never
have a break in the scale. He possessed an extraordinary
mezza voce, but derided the cultivation or use of *falsetto.*
Though some critics have pointed to a brightness of tone that
could become tiresome or even a bit harsh, Björling is known
for his pure vowels and a youthful quality that he preserved
throughout his career. He did acknowledge some change in
his sound as he aged, describing it as possibly a "lyric *spinto,*"
and, not surprisingly, the repertoire of his maturity eschewed
the Rossini *coloratura* of his youth. His was never an exceptionally powerful voice, and there were those who questioned
its carrying power in the larger houses. Nevertheless, whatever it lacked in this respect was strongly countered by its
fundamental focus and clarity. In comparison with his peers
he possessed superior control, maintaining pitch and tone
quality in the most demanding of melodic lines—regardless
of dynamic constraints. Like many, he occasionally pushed
pitch on the highest notes, but this was not a constant problem. In his remarks on singing he always stressed correct and
appropriate breathing—not only for support of the production, but for intelligent musical and poetic phrasing. He was
quick to condemn poor phrasing that garbled and distorted
the meaning of the words and his own style was exemplary
in avoiding that. He possessed an adroit command of shading
of tone and of the use of *legato* in spinning out a melodic line.
His mastery of the Italian style in vowels, diction, and tone
quality was accompanied by disciplined approach to rubato
and phrasing not often matched by other leading tenors.

Finally, he rarely indulged himself at the expense of the composer. He acknowledged that the conductor with whom he sang so frequently, Grevillius, helped inculcate this all-too-rare attitude.

Not yet fifty years of age when he died, Björling's career not only immeasurably enriched his times, but, thanks to an abundance of recordings, continues to generate admiration as each generation encounters his legacy. His artistic accomplishment stands as a model for those who value integrity, moderation, and discipline in interpretation; who respect deft surety in technical execution; and who prize uncommon beauty of tone. Although his remarkable gift was innate, Björling's devotion to its assiduous preparation and intelligent use serves as a peerless example.

—William E. Runyan

BLACHUT, Beno.

Tenor. Born 14 June 1913, in Vítkovice, Czechoslavakia (now Mahrische Ostrau-Wittkowitz). Died 10 January 1985. Studied at Prague Conservatory with Louis Kadeřábek, 1935-39; debut as Jeník in Smetana's *The Bartered Bride,* Olomouc, 1939; sang with Prague National Theatre from 1941, specializing in Czech repertory and heroic tenor roles; guest at Amsterdam and Vienna.

Publications

About BLACHUT: books–

Šíp, L. *Pěvci před mikrofonem* [singers]. Prague, 1960.
Brožovská, J. *Beno Blachut.* Prague, 1964.
Kopecký, E. and V. Pospíšil. *Slavní pěvci Národnicho divadla* [National theatre singers]. Prague, 1968.

articles–

Pospíšil, V. "Beno Blachut." *Hudebni rozhledy* 5/no. 1 (1952): 16.

*   *   *

Beno Blachut was born in Ostrava, Czechoslovakia in 1913, and after early studies in his home town, went to Prague to enroll in the Conservatory. After graduation he pursued a career in various provincial opera houses in Czechoslovakia. After five years of singing lyric tenor roles in the Brno Opera Company, he became a member, in 1941, of the Prague National Opera, and remained there until his retirement in 1980. For the majority of this time he was their first tenor in the dramatic repertoire, which means that his voice had developed considerably since the days of his early career. Information is difficult to locate about Eastern European opera companies and their singers, but certain facts are known, and other things may be conjectured. It is reasonably certain that Blachut specialized in major roles in the Czech repertoire, and that they took the majority of his time and energy. It is also a fact that the National Opera has always produced a certain number of operas every year which are part of the international repertoire. It is reasonable to assume that Blachut sang roles in such operas, and it is also a fact that he

appeared at the Vienna Staatsoper. Contemporary accounts of his Viennese performances in the role of Otello were extremely enthusiastic.

It is known that Blachut sang in various Russian companies with some frequency. Whatever the complete record of his guest appearances, it is certain that his time was spent mostly in Prague, and he was apparently one of the really prominent members of the company. A visit to the beautiful National Theater would reveal various portraits, photographs, and sculptures of honored Czech artists including portraits of Kavorovic, Talich, Chalabala, and the legendary Emmy Destinn. The only contemporary singer so honored is Beno Blachut, of whom there is a handsome bust in the corridor leading to the first balcony.

It is difficult, at best, to describe the quality of a singer's voice and musicianship. Still, perhaps a few things can be said that will be helpful. His was a big voice, or so it sounds on available recordings. The bright tenor sonority is conspicuous, with little hint of the baritone-like qualities found in other dramatic tenors such as Ramon Vinay or Lauritz Melchior. The general production is not unusually effortless in the Italian manner of a Gigli, but neither is it labored; Blachut maneuvers his voice exactly where and how he wishes and his range is evenly produced from bottom to top. His usable range is wide and, from recordings, seems to extend from "a" below middle "c" to the high "c" more than two octaves above it. Blachut's pitch is extremely good, and usually, he avoids the mannerism of approaching high notes with a portamento from below. Legato singing is exemplary, and his control and use of varied dynamics is much above average indeed.

This is merely a description of the fundamental level of his physical achievements, however; it is Blachut's qualities of musicianship, and his ability to dramatize words and operatic situations which puts him in a class with only a very few singers who used their art for the total integration of all possible musical-dramatic values. Blachut is one of those few artists whose intellect operates at an unusually high level. His achievements are the product of a kind of artistic discrimination that one associates most often with important conductors. Rhythms aren't just precise—they are part of the creation of a total character. The musical ability to shape phrases operates to wonderful effect, and, above all, the impression of a dedicated artist, totally free from what one might call the singer's ego, is deeply moving and very rare.

There are a few minor problems having nothing to do with Blachut's achievements. His work, of course, is available only through recordings, and fortunately, he recorded a great deal. But with the lone exception of a performance of the aria "Celeste Aïda" by Verdi, all of his other records are from the Czech repertoire. These works are marginal, at best, to the knowledge of most people in the West, but it must be said that this has the advantage to the opera buff of providing a new and exciting repertoire.

Blachut's roles were the dramatic ones in the operas of Smetana, Dvořák, Janáček, Suchon and some lesser lights. Unfortunately, some of his best performances, such as the performance of *Dalibor,* conducted by Krombhole, in which Blachut sings the title role, were recorded in the early 50s, and are no longer available except in secondhand stores. Throughout a period of about thirty years (1950-1980) Blachut recorded virtually every role for his voice-type in the Czech literature and these are definitely worth searching out.

In 1980 Blachut recorded one of the two main tenor roles in Dvořák's opera *The Jacobin.* At the age of 67, he provided a sensational demonstration of what a singer who knows his art can do even at a vocally advanced age. There is little indication of vocal deterioration despite well over forty years of constant activity.

In Blachut's recorded performance, Leoš Janáček's song cycle *The Diary of One Who Vanished* receives a terrifying interpretation, which virtually defines great singing.

Blachut recorded only for Supraphon of Prague, as far as is known. Supraphon's availability is variable, but the problems of ordering are not usually too serious.

—Harris Crohn

BLECH, Leo.

Conductor. Born 21 April 1871, in Aachen. Died 25 August 1958, in Berlin. Studied at the Hochschule für Musik in Berlin; conducted at the Municipal Theater in Aachen, 1893-99; summer study of composition with Humperdinck, 1893-96; opera conductor in Prague, 1899-1906; conductor at the Berlin Royal Opera, 1906, and Generalmusikdirektor, 1913; conductor of the Deutsche Opernhaus in Berlin, 1923; conductor at the Berlin Volksoper, 1924; conductor at the Vienna Volksoper, 1925; conductor at the Berlin Staatsoper, 1926-37; conductor at the Riga Oper, 1937-41; conducted in Stockholm, 1941-49; Generalmusikdirektor of the Städtische Oper in Berlin, 1949-53.

Publications

About BLECH: books–

Rychnowsky, E. *Leo Blech.* Prague, 1905.
Jacob, W. *Leo Blech: Ein Brevier anlässlich des 60. Geburtstages.* Hamburg, 1931.

*   *   *

Leo Blech reigned supreme in Berlin for many years prior to the Second World War and at one point was part of the quadrumvirate with Furtwängler, Kleiber and Klemperer, who held sway in the capital during the 1920s. Like so many of the conductors of the nineteenth century whose influence and legacy spilled over into the twentieth, Blech was also a composer, of operas as well as concert works. His operas, which owed much to Humperdinck, achieved a considerable popularity during his own lifetime (in particular *Versiegelt,* 1908) and helped his conducting career.

Blech's reputation in opera as a solid *routinier* in the best sense of the word was legendary; he was at his best with Wagner and Verdi. His Wagner was learned not only at Humperdinck's feet, but also in Prague, where he (like fellow apprentices Muck, Schalk and Bodanzky) worked for Angelo Neumann, promoter and director of the first touring opera company to stage Wagner's works in the 1880s. In the Italian repertoire Blech made a particular speciality of *Bohème, Butterfly* and *Aida,* but he was also a considerable exponent of the works of his contemporaries Richard Strauss and Ferruccio Busoni (*Doktor Faust*). His French repertory was dominated by a love for Bizet's *Carmen,* for which he became justly famed with more than six hundred performances during his career. Berlioz's *Les Troyens,* a more unusual work, was given a complete performance by Blech in May 1930 at the Berlin Festival, where he had earlier presented Prokofiev's *Love for Three Oranges.*

Blech was extremely fussy and a meticulous perfectionist who used to send notes to his singers correcting their errors (however trivial), not only between performances, but during the intervals between the acts. He memorized his vast repertoire, which contributed to his reputation for reliability in the opera pit. He also won considerable fame as a trainer of orchestras and as a conductor in the burgeoning field of recordings (his name is to be found on many HMV black-label recordings of the 78rpm era). His predominance in this area of music-making was largely due to his excellence as an accompanist. Furtwängler declared himself an admirer of Blech, whose art he described in a publication on Blech's sixtieth birthday as based on an amalgam of safety and clarity combined with elegance and flexibility. Another admirer was Erich Kleiber, with whom Blech worked for many years in the rarest harmony.

Though Blech was cast in the same rock-like mould as Hans Richter (solid and broad interpretations given with undisturbable assurance), he was also known to be quite swift in his performances of the Wagner canon. The stage-director's log books in Berlin recorded anything up to twenty minutes off a Wagner opera compared with performances conducted by the younger Kleiber. In his recordings (and one thinks in particular of his *Walküre* with Leider and Schorr) a thoughtful and sensitive reading can be perceived. Leo Blech's contribution during the so-called Golden Years of the Berlin Opera between the two world wars, was significant, even if it was overshadowed by a younger generation of conductors whose fame was to spread further.

—Christopher Fifield

BLITZSTEIN, Marc.

Composer. Born 2 March 1905, in Philadelphia. Died 22 January 1964, in Fort-de-France, Martinique. Married: Eva Goldbeck (died 1936). Studied composition with Rosario Scalero at the Curtis Institute; studied piano with Alexander Siloti in New York; studied with Nadia Boulanger in Paris, 1926-27 and with Schoenberg in Berlin, 1927; Guggenheim fellowship, 1940; stationed in England with United States Armed Forces during World War II. At the time of his death, Blitzstein was working on an opera on the subject of Sacco and Vanzetti, composed under the aegis of the Ford Foundation for performance at the Metropolitan Opera in New York.

Operas

Publisher: Chappell.

Triple Sec, R. Jeans, 1928, Philadelphia, 6 May 1929.
Parabola and Circula (opera-ballet), G. Whitsett, 1929.
The Condemned (choral opera), Blitzstein, 1932.
The Harpies, Blitzstein, 1931, New York, 25 May 1953.
The Cradle Will Rock, Blitzstein, 1936, New York, 16 June 1937.
No for an Answer, Blitzstein, 1937-40, New York, 5 January 1941.
Regina, Blitzstein (after Lillian Hellman, *The Little Foxes*), 1946-49, New York, 31 October 1949.
Reuben Reuben, Blitzstein, 1949-55.

Juno, J. Stein (after S. O'Casey, *Juno and the Paycock*), 1957-59.

Sacco and Vanzetti, Blitzstein, 1959-64 [unfinished].

The Magic Barrel, Blitzstein (after B. Malamud), 1963 [unfinished].

Idiots First, Blitzstein (after B. Malamud), 1963 [unfinished]; completed by L. Lehrman, Ithaca, New York, August 1974.

Other works: orchestral works, choral and vocal works, a piano concerto, a string quartet, and many piano pieces.

Publications/Writings

By BLITZSTEIN: books–

English Translation of Kurt Weill and Bertolt Brecht, *Die Dreigroschenoper,* as *The Threepenny Opera.* New York, 1954.

About BLITZSTEIN: books–

Copland, A. *The New Music.* New York, 1968.
Davis, C. *The Sun in Mid-Career.* New York, 1975.
Zuck, Barbara. *A History of Musical Americanisms. Studies in Musicology* 18. Ann Arbor, 1980.
Gordon, Eric. *Mark the Music.* New York, 1989.

articles–

Brant, H. "Marc Blitzstein." *Modern Music* 23 (1946): 170.
Hunter, J.O. "Marc Blitzstein's 'The Cradle Will Rock' as a Document of America, 1937." *American Quarterly* 16 (1964): 227.
Lederman, M. "Memories of Marc Blitzstein, Music's Angry Man." *Show* 4 (1964):18.
Peyser, J. "The Troubled Time of Marc Blitzstein." *Columbia University Forum* 9 (1966): 32.
Dietz, R.J. "Marc Blitzstein and the 'Agit-Prop' Theater of the 1930s." *Yearbook of the Inter-American Institute for Musical Research* 6 (1970): 51.
Gordon, Eric. "The Roots of 'Regina'." *Performing Arts* 3 (1980): 6.
———. "Of the People: Marc Blitzstein Remembered." *Opera News* 44 (1980): 26.
———. "The Musical Theater of Marc Blitzstein." *American Music* 3 (1985): 413.
Oja, C.J. "Marc Blitzstein's *The Cradle Will Rock* and Mass-Song Style of the 1930s." *Musical Quarterly* 73 (1989): 445.

unpublished–

Talley, P.M. "Social Criticism in the Original Theater Librettos of Marc Blitzstein." Ph.D. dissertation, University of Wisconson, 1965.
Dietz, R.J. "The Operatic Style of Marc Blitzstein." Ph.D. dissertation, University of Iowa, 1970.

*　　*　　*

One of the most important American composers from the late 1930s through the 1950s, Marc Blitzstein is now remembered for only a few works: *The Cradle Will Rock,* his opera with Orson Welles and the Federal Theatre Group that the government tried to ban in 1937; *Regina,* an opera based on

Lillian Hellman's *The Little Foxes,* which has been unlucky in revivals; and the *Airborne Symphony,* a cantata for male voices which has seen sporadic performances. But those more familiar with Blitzstein know a much richer body of work: the agitprop opera *No for an Answer,* his 1950s cold war Faust story *Reuben Reuben,* and his late musical version of Sean O'Casey's *Juno and the Paycock.*

Blitzstein was one of the few composers of his time who used his works to make social statements, considering this more important than plots that would guarantee box office success. His stage works of the thirties and early forties took up labor issues and were written so they could be performed by the very people he was writing about. Even when he turned to a more difficult, operatic style in *Regina* and his later works, Blitzstein took on unpopular subjects: racial issues, alienation, and the position of women in society. Blitzstein stayed with a tonal idiom throughout his career to keep his message accessible to audiences.

The 1941 opera/musical *No for an Answer* shows a move forward from some of the Weill-like numbers and the lack of variety in *The Cradle Will Rock* of four years before. Although still a stage work for and about the masses, Blitzstein used a variety of styles: the patter in the clever "Penny Candy"; full-blown lyricism in "Secret Singing"; a *Lehrstück* (teaching piece), "The Song of the Bat"; and a marvelous torch song, "Fraught." "Fraught," with its clever text and sophisticated nightclub idiom, is the best number in the show and one of the best Blitzstein ever wrote. Blitzstein attempted an interesting experiment in the love duet, "Francie," in which the male role Joe keeps repeating his love Francie's name. It is not entirely successful because the repeated vocal line requires a little more development to avoid monotony, but it shows the composer willing to depart from the standard Broadway conventions of his day. Blitzstein developed a better sense of line and phrasing in his later stage works, perhaps helped by his composition of the *Airborne Symphony,* a work for male chorus, in the 1940s.

Reuben Reuben, which closed in 1955 before it reached Broadway, is truly a through-composed opera, as opposed to Blitzstein's next work, *Juno. Juno* has discrete musical numbers separated by spoken dialogue and thus is akin to other Broadway musicals of its era. *Reuben* has musical numbers, listed as such in the program, but most of the dialogue between these numbers is underscored by music. Blitzstein uses unaccompanied dialogue only for important points in the story. To illustrate how Blitzstein creates a scene: in the first scene Reuben's exposition of his past is spoken over music. When he is unable to give directions because of his aphonia, the music stops. A song for Reuben, "Thank You," comes next, followed by circus-like music under a partly spoken, partly sung scene with some pickpockets. A lyrical duet for an argumentative couple expands into a trio with a girl asking directions and into a quartet with Reuben joining in ("Never Get Lost"). The music stops again when Reuben contemplates dying like his father. A jazzy interlude leads into the next scene in a bar.

This through-composed style in *Reuben* is an advance from that in *Regina.* Much of the dialogue in *Regina* had been set to music for the second production, and it occasionally sounds like interpolations. The music in *Reuben,* on the other hand, has a more developed flow and a better unity. This is an extravaganza of a score, with the boisterous scene at the street fair, the villain Bart's brooding music, another successful nightclub number, and the lovely duet "There Goes My Love." In this opera Blitzstein composes those developed, arching melodic lines that are missing in places in his early work. Although his book would need extensive reworking, this is a score that deserves to be resurrected.

One of the greatest hindrances to Blitzstein's career was his insistence on writing his own libretti. He claimed that he could not find any suitable collaborators, but working alone also allowed him to procrastinate, where a partner might have forced him to focus his work. Blitzstein achieved his best results when he used preexisting plays, in *Regina* and *Juno*. Reviewers commented on his problem with dramatic construction in *No for an Answer*, based on an original idea. Years later Blitzstein's muddled plot crippled the musically accomplished *Reuben Reuben*. His unfinished opera about Sacco and Vanzetti was held up by his insistence on working on his own and by other projects. This piece had the potential for being his greatest work, both as a social statement and as music drama. It is our loss that Blitzstein was killed before he could finish it.

—David E. Anderson

BLOCH, Ernest.

Composer. Born 24 July 1880, in Geneva, Switzerland. Died 15 July 1959, in Portland, Oregon. Studied solfeggio with Jaques-Dalcroze and violin with Louis Rey in Geneva, 1894-97; studied violin with Eugene Ysaÿe and composition with François Rasse in Brussels, 1897-1899; studied music theory with Iwan Knorr at the Conservatory in Frankfurt and took private lessons with Ludwig Thuille in Munich, 1900; met Debussy in Paris; first published work *Historiettes au crépuscule,* 1903; returned to Geneva in 1904, began working on *Macbeth;* conducted symphonic concerts in 1909-10 in Laussanne and Neuchâtel; conductor of the American tour accompanying the dancer Maud Allan, 1916; taught at the Mannes School of Music, New York, 1917; became an American citizen, 1924; director of the Institute of Music in Cleveland, 1920-1925; director of the San Francisco Conservatory, 1925-30; won first prize for his *America* in the 1927 competition for symphonic works sponsored by the magazine *Musical America;* in Switzerland, 1930-39; taught at the University of California at Berkeley, 1940-1952. Bloch's students included Roger Sessions, Ernst Bacon, George Antheil, Douglas Moore, Bernard Rogers, Randall Thompson, Quincy Porter, Halsey Stevens, Herbert Elwell, Isadore Freed, Frederick Jacobi, and Leon Kirchner.

Operas

Publishers: American Music, Boosey and Hawkes, Broude, Carisch, Eschig, C. Fischer, Leuckart, Mills, G. Schirmer, Summy-Birchard, Suvini Zerboni.

Macbeth, E. Fleg (after Shakespeare), 1904-9, Paris, Opéra-Comique, 30 November 1910.

Other works: orchestral works, choral and other vocal works, chamber music, piano pieces.

Publications

By BLOCH: books–

Tappy, José, ed. *Ernest Bloch—Romain Rolland: Lettres 1911-1933.* Lausanne, 1984.

articles–

"Man and Music." *Musical Quarterly* 19 (1933): 374.
article in Mack, Dietrich, ed. *Richard Wagner, Das Betroffensein der Nachwelt: Beiträge zur Wirkungsgeschichte.* Darmstadt, 1984.

About BLOCH: books–

Tibaldi-Chiesa, M. *Ernest Bloch.* Turin, 1933.
Bloch, Suzanne, with Irene Heskes. *Ernest Bloch: Creative Spirit.* New York, 1976.
Strassburg, Robert. *Ernest Bloch: Voice in the Wilderness.* Los Angeles, 1977.
Kushner, David Z. *Ernest Bloch: A Guide to Research.* New York, 1988.

articles–

Gatti, Guido. "Ernest Bloch." *Musical Quarterly* 7 (1921): 20.
Sessions, Roger. "Ernest Bloch." *Modern Music* 5 (1927-8): 3.
Hall, Raymond. "The *Macbeth* of Bloch." *Modern Music* 15 (1938): 209.
Griffel, M. "Bibliography of Writings on Ernest Bloch." *Current Musicology* 6 (1968): 142.
Kushner, David Z. "The Revivals of Bloch's *Macbeth.*" *Opera Journal* 4 (1971): 9.
———. "Ernest Bloch: A Retrospective on the Centenary of His Birth." *College Music Symposium* fall (1980): 77.
Brody, E. "Romain Rolland and Ernest Bloch." *Musical Quarterly* 68 (1982): 60.
Kushner, David Z. "The Jewish Works of Ernest Bloch." *Journal of Synagogue Music* June (1985): 28.
Weisser, Albert. "The 'Prologue' to *Jewish Music in Twentieth-Century America: Four Representative Figures.*" *Musica Judaica* 6 (1983-84): 60.
Sills, David L. "Ruminations on *Macbeth.*" *Ernest Bloch Society Bulletin* (1986-1987): 11.

* * *

Ernest Bloch, a nomadic cosmopolite, combined his own innate originality with influences derived from his native Switzerland, from his Jewish heritage, from his adopted country, the United States, and from the French and German traditions represented by his principal teachers.

A violinist, Bloch studied that instrument with Eugène Ysaÿe. His composition teachers included François Rasse, Iwan Knorr, and Ludwig Thuille. During the period 1909-10, he conducted orchestral concerts at Neuchâtel and Lausanne; from 1911-1915, he lectured on aesthetics at the Geneva Conservatoire. His spare time was spent on composition.

Bloch came to the United States in 1916 as conductor for Maud Allan's dance company. He taught in New York at the David Mannes School of Music, 1917-1920, while conducting concerts of his own works with major American orchestras (including the symphony orchestras of New York, Boston, and Philadelphia). His reputation as a "Jewish composer" stems from this period when he presented to the public such works as *Schelomo,* a Hebraic rhapsody for violoncello and orchestra. From 1920-1925, his stature now recognized, he served as the first director of the Cleveland Institute of Music, where his proposals to reform the traditional music curricula were met with opposition and resulted in his resignation. In

1924, he became a citizen of the United States, and, from 1925-1930, he assumed the position of director of the San Francisco Conservatory of Music. In 1927, he received first prize in *Musical America*'s prize competition for his epic rhapsody in three parts, *America*.

During the 1930s, Bloch lived mostly in Switzerland, but he made occasional trips to European capitals and to the United States to conduct his works. Because of the anti-Semitic tide engulfing the European continent and also because he wanted to retain his US citizenship, Bloch returned to America and, in 1941, settled in Agate Beach, Oregon. Shortly thereafter, he took a position as professor of music at the University of California at Berkeley, where he taught summer courses until his retirement in 1952. During these later years, he was recognized by such organizations as the American Academy of Arts and Sciences (first Gold Medal in Music, 1947), and the New York Music Critics' Circle (awarded for chamber music and orchestral music, 1952, for, respectively *String Quartet No. 3* and *Concerto Grosso no. 2*. In 1958, Bloch underwent cancer surgery which was not successful. An Ernest Bloch Society was founded in California in 1968, largely through the efforts of the three Bloch children, Ivan, Suzanne, and Lucienne. An earlier Bloch Society flourished in London during the late 1930s; Alex Cohen was its leading light.

Bloch's early compositions (e.g., *Symphonie orientale*) are derivative romantic effusions, but the *Symphony in C-Sharp Minor* and *Hiver-printemps,* although indicating the influences of the late 19th century German school and the early French impressionist school, are works of genuinely original content. With the lyric drama, *Macbeth,* produced in 1910 at the Opéra-Comique, Bloch emerged as a significant dramatic composer. Synthesizing elements drawn from such sources as the Wagnerian music drama, Debussy's *Pelléas et Mélisande,* and Mussorgsky's *Boris Godounov* with his own creative energy, Bloch reveals in *Macbeth* certain techniques which became characteristic of his compositional style: frequent changes of meter, tempo, and tonality, augmented intervals (mainly 2nds and 4ths), open 4ths and 5ths, cross relations, modal flavoring, use of the lower ranges of the various instruments, repeated-note patters, ostinatos, pedal points, leitmotifs, and cyclic formal procedures.

Bloch's search for a musical identity resulted in a series of epic works of heroic grandeur, based on or inspired by the Holy Scriptures, and known collectively as the "Jewish Cycle." In these works of deep emotive power, the orchestra is a veritable riot of kaleidoscopic color. The "oriental" or quasi-Hebraic character of, for example *Schelomo* or *Israel,* is heightened by the prominence of augmented intervals and the general overlay of exoticism. The Scotch-snap rhythm, with its many variants, is so pervasive that this writer refers to its usage here as the "Bloch rhythm."

During the 1920s, Bloch produced a number of important neo-classical works, such as the *Concerto grosso no. 1* for string orchestra with piano obbligato, which begins with a prelude and closes with a 5-part fugue, the two sonatas for violin and piano, and the first *Quintet* for piano and strings, with its use of quarter-tones in the first and last movements. But even in these works, Bloch continues to employ extra-musical references; for example, in the "Dirge" and "Pastoral" movements in the *Concerto grosso* and in the references to the Gregorian mass *Kyrie fons bonitatis* in the *Violin Sonata No. 2.* A return to large-scale compositions marks the music of the 1930s. The monumental *Arodath Hakodesh* and the *Violin Concerto,* with its American Indian motto, are representative. The unifying motto, as in the earlier *America,* became a major structural feature of the music of the final

years. The compositions from the Agate Beach period are, in essence, an amalgam of the composer's career as a creative artist. The works are generally less subjective than those of earlier years. Some may be categorized as neo-classical (e.g., *Concerto grosso no. 2* for string quartet and string orchestra), some as neo-romantic (e.g., *Concerto symphonique* for piano and orchestra). In other pieces, Bloch flirts with 12-tone technique, but not in a systematic or continuous fashion; the *Symphony in E-Flat Major* and the *Sinfonia breve* exemplify this category of composition. The later works are, in the main, bereft of the rhetorical features which characterize such earlier masterpieces as the "Jewish Cycle."

Bloch taught his many eminent students (including Sessions, Moore, Porter, Rogers, and Freed) to develop their own musical personalities according to their individual personal and artistic temperaments. He did not found any school nor was he a pioneer; rather, he developed a uniquely identifiable and original style from the ingredients he found already in use. Bloch, who viewed the creative act as a spiritual expression, produced a large number of works whose quality is high, most importantly in the chamber music and orchestral media. Bloch did not believe in fads or fetishes, he did not jump from "ism" to "ism" for the sake of novelty, and he always held firm to his own musical convictions. He was a singular figure in the history of 20th-century art music.

—David Z. Kushner

BLOMDAHL, Karl-Birger.

Composer. Born 19 October 1916, in Växjö, Sweden. Died 14 June 1968, in Kungsängen, near Stockholm. Studied composition with Hilding Rosenberg and conducting with Thor Mann in Stockholm; in France and Italy, 1946; studied at Tanglewood, 1954-55; taught composition at the Royal College of Music in Stockholm, 1960-64; music director of the Swedish Radio, 1964; his opera *Aniara* brought him international fame. Blomdahl was working on an opera entitled *Tale of the Great Computer* at the time of his death.

Operas

Publisher: Schott.

Aniara, Erik Lindegren (after a novel by Harry Martinson), 1957-58, Stockholm, 31 May 1959.
Herr von Hancken, Erik Lindegren (after a novel by Hjalmar Bergman), 1962-63, Stockholm, 2 September 1965.
Sagan om den stora datan [*Tale of the Great Computer*] after H. Alfvén [unfinished].

Other works: orchestral music, including three symphonies, chamber music, various works for voice, including an oratorio, ballets, works for tape.

Publications

By BLOMDAHL: articles–

"Hindemiths kompositionslära." *Musikvärlden* no. 5 (1945); no. 2 (1946).
"Ung svensk tonkunst." *Musikvärlden* no. 2 (1946).

with S.E. Bäck. "Tva tonkonstnärer." *Prisma* no. 1
  (1948): 94.
"Tolvtonsteknik." *Musikrevy* 5 (1950).
"Facetter." In *Modern nordisk musik,* edited by J. Bengtsson.
  Stockholm, 1957.
"Varför skiver jag opera?" *Kungl. Teaterns program book*
  (1959).
"Aniara." In *The Modern Composer and his World,* edited
  by R.M. Schafer. Toronto, 1961.
"In the Halls of Mirrors and Anabase." In *The Composer's
  Point of View,* edited by R.S. Hines. Norman, Oklahoma,
  1963.
"En snak om min musik." *Musikalske selvportraeter.* Copen-
  hagen, 1966.
"Musiken som vittnesmål om tidsmedvetenhet, engagemang,
  socialt patos." In *En Bok Till Hilding Rosenberg.* 1977.
"Rösternas dramatik." *Nutida Musik* 4 (1983-84).

About BLOMDAHL: articles–

Hambraeus, Bengt. "Aniara." *Anno* (1959).
Schack, Erik. "Karl-Birger Blomdahls Aniara." *Dansk Mu-
  siktidskrift* (1959).
Törnblom, Folke. "Är Aniara en riktig Opera?" *Bonniers
  Litterära Magasin* (1959).
Wallner, Bo. "Vägen till Aniara." *Kungl. Teaterns program
  book* (1959).
Balzer, Jürgen. "Karl-Birger Blomdahls Aniara." *Dansk
  Musiktidskrift* (1960).
Tegen, Martin. "Aniara." *Musik och Ljudteknik* 3 (1960).
Wallner, Bo. "Revue vom Menschen in Zeit und Raum."
  Melos (1960).
Tegen, Martin. "Även i Facetter." *STIM* (1970).
Wallner, Bo. "Även på svenska i Facetter." *STIM* (1970).
Inglefield, Ruth K. "Karl-Birger Blomdahl: A Portrait." *Mu-
  sical Quarterly* 58 (1972): 67.
Bucht, Gunnar. "Karl-Birger Blomdahl som musikdramati-
  ker." In *Jubelboken. Operan 200 år.* Stockholm, 1973.
Andersen, Sten. "Vi börjar långsamt." *Musikdramatik* no. 4
  (1982).
Algulin, Ingemar. "Gestalterna i Aniara." *Nutida Musik* 4
  (1983-84).
Lindegren, Erik. "Innehållet i Aniara samt Libretton." *Nut-
  ida Musik* 4 (1983-84).
Tobeck, Christina. "Aniara: ett skri av förtvivlan—en vadjan
  om besinning." *Nutida Musik* 4 (1983-84).

*   *   *

The career of Karl-Birger Blomdahl at first glance seems to
track the course of a tumbleweed, blown here and there by
every prevailing fashion from continental Europe, never settling for long on any one style, but never changing its essential
nature. While it is certainly true that he was ultrasensitive
and responsive to artistic trends occurring in Central Europe,
this really was no more than his highly active intellect being
as aware as possible of what his peers were creating around
him. There is a thread of consistency and continuity running
through all his music that belies the charge sometimes made
against him that he was uncritical in his responses to foreign
trends. His mature music is always readily identifiable as
Blomdahl (which cannot be said of many other composers,
such as Stravinsky in his late, serial mood,) even when it
betrays the influence of others. These influences were widely
drawn at all times of his career, reflecting varying passions
for the music of Hindemith, Bartok and Stravinksy early on,

through the Second Viennese School and serialism, to later
dabblings in electronic music. Had he lived on past 1968, his
response to "minimalism," then in its infancy but soon to
gain considerable ground in Scandinavia, would have made
fascinating listening. Whatever musical star he may have
followed from time to time, the music itself was always expertly crafted with many calculated and extraordinary effects
(for example the famous passage in the introduction to his
oratorio *I Speglarnas Sal [In The Hall Of Mirrors]* where the
strings play behind the bridge).
   Blomdahl struck up two notable artistic collaborations in
his music for the stage: first, with choreographer Birgit Akesson in several works including the two *Dance Suites,* the
ballets *Sisyphus, Minotauros* and *Spel for Atta (Game for
Eight),* as well as the dance episodes for the opera *Aniara;*
second, with the poet Erik Lindegren in the oratorios *I
Speglarnas Sal* and *Anabase* (for which Lindegren translated
St John Perse's text), libretti for the three operas, plus other
settings including the cantata *. . . resan i detta natt (A Journey
Through This Night).* These collaborations united in the three
ballets, which all had scenarios provided by Lindegren, as
well as the first opera, *Aniara* (1956-8), where Akesson provided the means of expression for a silent but important
character, the female pilot Isagel. Whatever the extra-musical
inspiration, however, Blomdahl's primary concern was musical integrity. He himself outlined his attitude in an article
published in 1959: "With text or without, it is *music* I am
composing. The text—whether lyric poetry or epic, drama,
comedy or parody—must arouse a musical response within
me, must 'sing' and imbue me with sounds and rhythms
which insist on being given form, concreteness."
   Always at the forefront of musical developments in Sweden
(so much so that in some quarters he was held to be subversive), he is best remembered as the composer of the first opera
to be set on board a spaceship, *Aniara.* This was first produced
in Sweden in 1959 and has been subsequently revived several
times (including one production for Swedish television), as
well as being produced in Germany and Belgium in the early
1960s. Since then it has retained its reputation as Blomdahl's
most singular work, for which he is best known, and has
become widely disseminated through two recordings (the second and better of which, conducted in 1983 by Stig West-
erberg, has made the essential transition onto compact disc).
Aniara's topicality, the unconventional aspects of the musical
idiom and subject matter all rendered its initial productions
highly publicized events, and its musical integrity has assured
the work a lasting, if undeservedly peripheral, place in the
opera house.
   If *Aniara* revealed a natural talent for the stage already
fully formed, the rest of Blomdahl's career sadly failed to
build on the experience. His second opera, *Herr von Hancken*
(1962-3, premiered in Stockholm, 1965), did not quite achieve
the artistic, still less the critical heights of *Aniara.* It is a
chamber comic opera, Lindegren's libretto being derived
from the novel by Hjalmar Bergman, and has never made the
leap into the general realm that *Aniara* has. *Herr von Hancken*
remains, outside if not inside Sweden, nothing more than a
reference in musical lexicons and would scarcely be even that
were it not for *Aniara's* fame.
   Blomdahl's third and last operatic venture, *Sagan om den
stora datan (The Story of the Great Computer),* has more
affinity with *Aniara,* at least in general subject matter (both
works feature computers), but was left unfinished at his early
death. This bleak and pessimistic work set during the future
was based on a book by the physicist Hannes Alfvén (under
the pen-name of Olof Johanesson), who in 1970 was awarded
the Nobel Prize for Physics. *Sagan om den stora datan,* which

was to extend much further the use of electronic music in a theatrical context, would certainly have broken new ground both for Blomdahl and for opera in general, and its incompleteness is as tragic as the story it would have endeavoured to tell.

—Guy Rickards

BLOW, John.

Composer. Born February (baptized 23 February) 1648 or 1649, in Newark-on-Trent, Nottinghamshire. Died 1 October 1708, in Westminster (London). Married: Elizabeth Braddock, 1674 (died 1683; five children). In the Chapel Royal choir under Henry Cooke, 1660-61; studied organ with Christopher Gibbons; appointed organist of Westminster Abbey, 3 December 1668, a post which he left to his student Henry Purcell in 1679; upon Purcell's death in 1695, Blow reassumed the position of organist of Westminster Abbey until his death; Gentleman of the Chapel Royal, 16 March 1673 or 1674; succeeded Humphrey as the Master of the Children of the Chapel Royal, 23 July 1674; Master of the Choristers, St. Paul's, 1687-1702 or 1703; appointed Composer of the Chapel Royal, 1699; honorary Lambeth degree of Doctor of Music, conferred 1677 by the Dean of Canterbury. Blow is buried in the north aisle of Westminster Abbey.

John Blow, engraving by Robert White from *Amphion Anglicus,* **London, 1700**

Operas/Masques

Masque for the Entertainment of the King: Venus and Adonis, c. 1682.

Other works: odes, anthems, songs, works for harpsichord.

Publications

About BLOW: books–

Dent, E.J. *Foundations of English Opera.* Cambridge, 1928; 1965.
Lewis, Anthony. Introduction to *J. Blow: Venus and Adonis.* Paris, 1939.
Price, Curtis A. *Henry Purcell and the London Stage.* [227, 245]. Cambridge, 1984.

articles–

Shaw, H. Watkins. "John Blow, Doctor of Music." *Musical Times* 78 (1937): 865, 946, 1025.
Clarke, H.L. "John Blow: a Tercentenary Survey." *Musical Quarterly* 35 (1949): 412.
Shaw, H. Watkins. "John Blow." *Musical Times* 99 (1958): 544.
Lewis, Anthony. "Purcell and Blow's 'Venus and Adonis'." *Music and Letters* 44 (1963): 266.
Shaw, H. Watkins. "The Autographs of John Blow." *Music Review* 25 (1964): 85.
McLean, H. "Blow and Purcell in Japan." *Musical Times* 104 (1963): 702; see also 878.
Luckett, Richard. "A New Source for 'Venus and Adonis.'" *Musical Times* 130 (1989): 76.

unpublished–

Wood, Bruce. "John Blow: Anthems with Orchestra." Ph.D. dissertation, Cambridge University, 1977.

John Blow's posthumous reputation has suffered well into this century as a result of the harsh evaluation of his music made by Charles Burney in *A General History of Music* (London, 1789). Burney described Blow's use of contrapuntal dissonance as "unwarrantable licentiousness," providing a series of examples to display his "crudities." But in fact Blow was only slightly extending the stylistic materials that had come into common use in seventeenth century England, and much of his music is not only competent but inspired, comparing quite favorably to that of his younger and ultimately more famous colleague, Henry Purcell.

Throughout his career Blow was a faithful servant in his duties as church and court composer as is verified by his extant works, which are dominated by anthems and court odes. Blow in fact came to prominence as a chorister in the Chapel Royal, composing several anthems by his mid-teenage years. While Henry Cooke probably provided Blow with his first formal lessons in composition, the young composer may have learned more from Christopher Gibbons and other older masters, who were the senior members of the restored Chapel Royal in the 1660s, and who were more experienced in the art of composition than Cooke.

While the works of Blow's youth are sometimes crafted in a rather stiff fashion, by about 1680 his style begins to show real maturity. In his anthems and odes from the 1680s and after, works which were often extended and multipartite, alternating soloist(s), chorus, and orchestra, Blow afforded himself the opportunity to work out his interests in the musical subtleties of the Italian, French, and of course English styles, some of these derived from dramatic genres. The 1680s also marked Blow's only direct work in an operatic medium, that coming in his miniature masterpiece *Venus and Adonis,* which was first given before Charles II around 1682. The composition of this remarkable little work was a singular occurrence in Blow's career, and its overall quality leads one to regret that Blow never again wrote for the stage.

Blow did, though, continue to exhibit a flair for the dramatic in his many secular songs, produced quite steadily in the 1680s and 1690s. Unlike Purcell's song output, however, which was produced mainly as a result of his close relationship with the London theater scene, Blow's songs were mostly written apart from any attendant dramatic work, appearing initially in a number of published collections which culminated in the vast anthology *Amphion Anglicus* of 1700, itself a companion to Purcell's *Orpheus Britannicus,* of 1695.

Some of Blow's last works display a move toward historicism: in a set of fourteen anthems produced in the first decade of the eighteenth century, Blow adapts the polyphonic language of Tudor and early Stuart England, enriching it with up-to-date harmonic underpinnings and forward-looking fugal writing. These works indicate a final shift in Blow's interests away from dramatic writing and further point to *Venus and Adonis* as a true anomaly within a career mostly devoted to music for church services and court ceremonies.

While partially indebted to the indigenous masque tradition, *Venus and Adonis,* together with its close relation, Purcell's *Dido and Aeneas,* seems to derive more closely from the *tragédies lyriques* of Lully, which were not unfamiliar in Restoration England. Both works prominently feature a French-style prologue, though only in Blow's case does the music for this integral part of the opera survive. The recent discovery of the printed libretto for *Venus and Adonis* (see Luckett) has helped to clarify what has previously only been a speculative dating. The surviving libretto is not from the first performance but from one shortly thereafter, and it bills the work not as a masque (as it is called in the surviving score) but as "an OPERA Perform'd before the KING [and] afterwards at Mr. JOSIAS PRIEST's Boarding School at Chelsey by Young Gentlewomen." Some handwritten notes further say that this performance took place on 17 April 1684 and, interestingly, that the part of Adonis was sung by Mr. Priest's daughter. Thus Blow's work is further linked to *Dido and Aeneas,* which received it premiere at Priest's School some five years later.

—Robert Shay

BOCKELMANN, Rudolf (August Louis Wilhelm).

Bass-baritone. Born 2 April 1892 near Luneberg, Germany. Died 9 October 1958. Studied with Scheidemantel and Oscar Lassner, in Leipzig, 1920-23; debut as the Herald in *Lohengrin* in Leipzig, 1923; in Hamburg 1926-1932, where he created the title role of Krenek's *Leben des Orest*; in Berlin, 1932-45; in Hamburg, 1946-51; at Bayreuth, 1928-42 as the Dutchman, Gunther, Kurwenal, Sachs, and Wotan; at Covent Garden in 1929-30 and 1934-38; in Chicago, 1930-32.

Publications

By BOCKELMANN: books–

Sämmelbände der Robert-Schumann-Gesellschaft II/1966 [Bockelmann's own notation on operatic techniques]. Leipzig, 1967.

About BOCKELMANN: books–

Wessling, B.W. *Verachtet mir die Meister nicht!* Celle, 1963.

A specialist in the roles of Wagner, German bass-baritone Rudolf Bockelmann made his first operatic appearance at Celle and his professional debut in Leipzig in 1923 as the Herald in *Lohengrin.* A prominent *Heldenbariton,* he sang in Hamburg between 1926 and 1932 and in Berlin from 1932 to 1945, singing such roles as Tchaikovsky's Eugene Onegin, Rossini's Guillaume Tell, Padre Guardiano in Verdi's *La forza del destino,* and Glinka's Ivan Susanin. He made his Covent Garden debut in 1929, and he sang there until 1938 in such roles as Telramund in *Lohengrin,* Hans Sachs in *Die Meistersinger,* Wotan in *Das Rheingold* and *Die Walküre,* and the Wanderer in *Siegfried.* He sang in numerous opera houses throughout Europe and the United States, including Bayreuth (from 1928), where he was the company's leading Wotan until the end of World War II; Chicago (1930-32); and Paris (where he appeared as Hans Sachs in 1934). He created the title role in Krenek's *Leben des Orest* in 1930, and appeared in the world premieres of Pfitzner's *Das Herz,* von Klenau's *Rembrandt von Rijn,* and Korngold's *Das Wunder der Heliane.* His repertoire also included Kurwenal in Wagner's *Tristan und Isolde,* which he sang under Toscanini's direction at Bayreuth in 1929. His Hans Sachs was considered one of the greatest of the century, at least if considered in vocal, rather than dramatic, terms.

Critics felt that Bockelmann possessed a beautiful voice with a sympathetic quality, a warmly lyrical, mellow sound, and a feeling for poetry, all conveyed artistically. His voice had substantial weight, despite its baritonal character and strong top, and he was able to sustain with ease the marathon-length Wagnerian roles. His demeanor was dignified and authoritarian. On the occasion of Bockelmann's appearance at Covent Garden in 1934, recording producer Walter Legge wrote that his Wotan "was a magnificent piece of work; his voice is like finely polished mahogany, dark, rich, and smooth, and with his enormous reserve of power and his admirably controlled breathing he was both in wrath and repose a superbly godlike being." He did not, however, create quite as well-rounded a Wotan, or as moral a Hans Sachs, as did Hans Hotter or Friedrich Schorr.

Bockelmann's ties to the Nazis kept him from maintaining his international career; the Nazis considered him one of their most honored singers, and they took pains to keep him in Germany to perform (his only excursions outside his fatherland were a few officially sanctioned trips to England to perform at Covent Garden under Furtwängler). After the Second World War, his international career was curtailed by the stigma of his collaboration with the Nazis; he continued to sing only in the German provinces and occasionally in Hamburg. As a result, Bockelmann is relatively little known today, in contrast to the many artists exiled during the Nazi period, who were able to maintain international performance and recording schedules.

Bockelmann made a number of recordings in Germany. These include excerpts from act III of *Siegfried,* as the Wanderer opposite Lauritz Melchior's Siegfried, which were committed to disc in 1929 and 1930. He also left souvenirs of his Dapertutto in Offenbach's *Les contes d'Hoffmann* ("Scintille, diamant"); his Hans Sachs ("Jerum! Jerum!" "Verachtet mir die Meister nicht," and the *Fliedermonolog*); and his Wotan ("Abendlich strahlt" and "Der Augen leuchtendes Paar"), all recorded in the early 1930s.

—Michael Sims

BODANZKY, Artur.

Conductor. Born 16 December 1877, in Vienna. Died 23 November 1939, in New York. Studied at the Vienna Conservatory and privately with Zemlinsky; violinist in the Vienna Court Opera Orchestra; conductor of the operetta season in Budweis, 1900; assistant to Mahler at the Vienna Court Opera, 1902; conducted in Berlin, 1905; conducted in Prague, 1906-09; music director at Mannheim, 1909; organized and led the memorial Mahler Festival in 1912; conducted *Parsifal* at Covent Garden, London, 1914; conducted the German repertoire at the Metropolitan Opera, New York, 1915-39; director of the Society of Friends of Music, New York, 1916-31; conductor of the New Symphony Orchestra, 1919-22.

*   *   *

During the 1915-1939 reign of Artur Bodanzky at the Metropolitan Opera, he presided over what was perhaps the most burnished Golden Age of Wagnerian performance in history. Under his baton, Leider, Flagstad, Lehmann, Rethberg, Thorborg, Melchior, Lorenz, and Schorr sang regularly. While rehearsal was not a normal practice at that time anywhere but at Bayreuth or Salzburg, Bodanzky set up a consistent performance framework into which singers of merit and stylistic knowledge could fit without too much inconvenience.

As evident in Metropolitan Opera performance air checks of the time, Bodanzky continued the tradition of conducting he learned from Zemlinsky and Mahler, and consequently attracted noble, magnificent playing from the orchestra. His Wagner performances were both idiomatic and glowing. He allowed his singers to shine, to enjoy the stardom they had earned, and accommodated their individual vagaries. Even without rehearsal, he welded ensemble singing, not only from the artists who sang the same operas together all year internationally, but from artists who did not enjoy the knowledge of everyday Wagner routine (as in an electrifying and suspenseful 1936 *Tannhäuser* song contest with Melchior and the normally non-Wagnerian Lawrence Tibbett as Wolfram).

Bodanzky is often excoriated for cutting, sometimes drastically, the works of Wagner, but this practice must be looked at from the perspective of the time and place in which he worked. First, almost everyone shortened Wagner then (and there is a small movement toward that end today). Also, at the Metropolitan, the works of Wagner were popular opera, as popular as *La bohème.* The reason for this may have been the great talent performing them, but attending Wagner then was not particularly an intellectual search for transcendental experience; it was entertainment and the enjoyment of great voices. Wagner was sung up to four times a week and nobody,

not even one possessed of Melchior's iron lungs, could survive singing uncut Wagner in a large house that often without grave vocal harm.

Bodanzky did not only conduct Wagner: he led the first Metropolitan performances of *Elektra* and Weinberger's *Schwanda,* and had a repertoire in that house that ranged from *Der Rosenkavalier* and *Salome* to Gluck's *Orfeo* and Mozart.

In later years, Bodanzky shared the Wagnerian repertoire with the young Erich Leinsdorf, even to conducting only the outer acts of *Parsifal* while Leinsdorf lead the "worldly" second act.

While his time and "style" may now be of the past, Bodanzky's importance and command would be remembered more clearly today if he had been recorded regularly on commercial discs or more universally distributed on "pirate" ones. As it is, the live performances of the same repertoire by Reiner, Busch and Beecham, not to mention those of Furtwängler, are the ones known best to the world.

—Bert Wechsler

LA BOHÈME.

Composer: Ruggero Leoncavallo.

Librettist: Ruggero Leoncavallo (after Henri Murger).

First Performance: Venice, Teatro La Fenice, 6 May 1897; revised as *Mimi Pinson,* Palermo, Massimo, 14 April 1913.

Roles: Marcello (tenor); Rodolfo (baritone); Schaunard (baritone); Barbemuche (bass); Visconte Paolo (baritone); Gustavro Colline (baritone); Gaudenzio (tenor); Durand (tenor); Musetta (mezzo-soprano); Mimi (soprano); Eufemia (mezzo-soprano); chorus.

Publications

articles–

Hanslick, E. "Die Bohème von Leoncavallo." In *Die moderne Oper,* vol 8. *Am Ende des Jahrhunderts (1895-1899): musikalische Kritiken und Schilderungen,* 123. Berlin, 1899.
Greenfield, E. "The Other Bohème." *Opera Annual* 5 (1958): 77.
Maehder, Jürgen. "Immagini di Parigi. La trasformazione del romanzo 'Scènes de la vie de Bohème' di Henry Murger nelle opere di Puccini e Leoncavallo." *Nuova rivista musicale italiana* 3 (1990): 403.

*   *   *

Sometime before 1893, Ruggero Leoncavallo completed a libretto based on scenes from Henri Murger's novel *Scènes de la Vie de Bohème,* and titled the opera *La Bohème.* He had shown Puccini the libretto the previous winter, and at that time offered it to him, but Puccini refused, saying that he was toying with the idea of writing an opera based on the life of the Buddha. Leoncavallo then decided to compose his own opera on the subject.

While Leoncavallo's version of *La Bohème* was more popular than Puccini's at its premier, Puccini's version has become, without question, the version that is more widely performed. It is interesting to note that Leoncavallo quoted popular tunes of the time, such as an air from Meyerbeer's *Les Hugenots.* Perhaps it was the use of popular tunes that caused Leoncavallo's successful premier, but as the tunes lost their popularity, so did his *La Bohème.*

Although both versions were founded on the same novel by Murger the two composers treat the story differently, except in the last act. The story is quite well known. The main characters are Marcello, a painter; Rodolfo, a poet; Musetta, Marcello's old lover; and Mimi, Rodolfo's lover. The relationships of both couples are quite stormy: Marcello recovers his old lover, Musetta, from a wealthy admirer, and Mimi accepts a rich admirer's offer to live with him. When Mimi tries to return to Rodolfo, he has nothing to do with her. Mimi becomes very sick and is prematurely discharged from the hospital because she cannot pay the bill. The height of the opera is Mimi's death. In Leoncavallo's version, Marcello and Musetta are the central figures, while Mimi and Rodolfo are presented as reflections of the principal pair. It is not until act IV that the relationship between Mimi and Rodolfo becomes of central interest.

Leoncavallo makes a strong effort to portray his characters working at their trades as real people. For example, in act II, Schaunard, a musician in the opera, performs one of his compositions at the piano. Similarly, Rodolfo recites one of his poems in the opening of act IV.

The strength of this opera is its libretto. Leoncavallo follows Murger's novel quite closely, which results in a tight plot with no unanswered questions. However, the drama in acts I and II has been criticized for being too slow. The music shows signs of "padding" throughout, with large sections of arpeggios, scales, and sequences. To convey a joyous atmosphere, Leoncavallo relies heavily on the device of making singers laugh in unison in staccato rhythms, which quickly loses its effectiveness. Despite a few clumsy spots, however, the music generally works well with the libretto.

—Kathleen A. Abromeit

LA BOHÈME.

Composer: Giacomo Puccini.

Librettists: Giuseppe Giacosa and Luigi Illica (after Mürger).

First Performance: Turin, Regio, 1 February 1896.

Roles: Rodolfo (tenor); Marcello (baritone); Schaunard (baritone); Colline (bass); Benoit (bass); Mimi (soprano); Musetta (soprano); Alcindoro (bass); Parpignol (tenor); Customs Guard (bass); chorus (SATB).

Publications

books–

Knaust, Rebecca. *The Complete Guide to "La bohème".* New York, 1978.
Csampai, Attila, and Dietmar Holland, ed. *La Bohème: Texte, Materialien, Kommentare.* Reinbek, 1981.
John, Nicholas, ed. *Giacomo Puccini: "La bohème."* London and New York, 1982.
Stewart, Robert S., ed. *Giacomo Puccini: La bohème.* London, 1983.
Groos, Arthur, and Roger Parker. *Giacomo Puccini: La bohème.* Cambridge, 1986.

articles–

Avant-scène opéra March-April (1979) [*La bohème* issue].
Lederer, Josef-Horst. "Mahler und die beiden Bohèmes." In *Festschrift Othmar Wessely zum 60. Geburtstag,* edited by Manfred Angerer et al., 399. Tutzing, 1982.

During the second half of the nineteenth century, a new movement appeared in the arts which was to have profound repercussions throughout Europe. The social upheaval resulting in the Revolution of 1848 in France brought about radically new approaches in artistic expression as well. Endowed with a new social awareness, many artists now saw it as their primary mission to depict the world "as it really was," with no idealizing tinsel attached. Painters such as Courbet and Millet produced "realistic" paintings, showing ordinary working people in lifelike settings. While the first dramas of Dumas *fils* can be seen as early examples of realism in the work of a French writer, it was Émile Zola during the last third of the century whose novels became the prime representatives of "realism" in French literature.

A more localized version of "realism" came about in Italy as well. Referred to as *verismo,* its foremost representative was the novelist Giovanni Verga, whose short stories and novels dealt primarily with rural characters, placed in realistic settings, who find themselves in extraordinary crises which result in violent outbursts of emotion. It was this display of crude passion which had a particular appeal to the realists in both France and Italy.

One of Verga's Sicilian short stories, included in his collection *Vita dei campi* (1880), was *Cavalleria rusticana.* It served as the model for the opera with the same name by Pietro Mascagni, a work, premiered in 1890, which is now considered the first Italian *verismo* opera. The great success of this work gave rise to a number of operas in the same mold by composers such as Spinelli, Giordano, Cilèa, and Leoncavallo, whose *I pagliacci* (1892) had won the Sonzogno opera competition, as Mascagni's *Cavalleria rusticana* had before.

Giacomo Puccini is often listed among these "veristic" composers as well, and specific reference is made to his *Tosca* and *Il tabarro,* mainly for the spine-chilling display of crass emotions and deadly violence in these operas. But the portrayal of common, real-life characters in a realistic setting was of concern to Puccini in other operas as well in which no connection can be seen with the more local tradition of literary *verismo.* This is true, more specifically, for *La fanciulla del West, Madama Butterfly,* and *La bohème.*

The model for Puccini's *La bohème* is the novel *Scènes de la vie de bohème* by the French writer Henry Mürger, originally published in various episodes in the magazine *Le Corsair* between 1845 and 1848. In 1849, a stage adaptation of the story by Théodore Barrière and Henry Mürger followed, which was a great success. In 1851, the novel was reissued in book form. It is not a structurally unified novel, but rather a collection of vignettes presenting the joys, woes, and aspirations of young people, mostly artists, and their struggles to survive. In portraying characters from the lower social strata,

La bohème, title-page of piano score, 1895, illustrated by Adolfo Hohenstein, who also designed the sets and costumes for the premiere in Turin

without any effort at concealing the less pleasant aspects of their existence, Mürger hit upon a raw nerve among his readers. Given the new vogue for "veristic" operas in the early 1880s, it is thus not surprising to find Puccini attracted to the "realistic" story of *La Bohème*. The libretto by Giuseppe Giacosa and Luigi Illica is based primarily on the novel, and not the stage play.

The opera, set in Paris around 1830, tells the story of four Bohemians, the poet Rodolfo, the painter Marcello, the philosopher Colline, and the musician Schaunard, who are chronically without money and live in the most wretched conditions in a shared attic apartment. In act I, Rodolfo meets his neighbor Mimi, who knocks on his door to ask for a light for her candle. She has an ominous cough and does not seem at all well. During their conversation, Rodolfo and Mimi fall in love. It is Christmas eve, and they decide to join the other Bohemians, who had gone out to celebrate at the Café Momus.

Act II takes place later the same day. Rodolfo and Mimi have joined the other Bohemians at the Café, and shortly thereafter Musetta, a vivacious woman and former love of Marcello's, appears in the company of a wealthy paramour, Alcindoro, for whom she shows no respect at all. As she still loves Marcello, she sends Alcindoro away on a pretext, and no sooner is he gone than she and Marcello immediately make up.

In act III, Rodolfo has left Mimi after a quarrel. Mimi tells Marcello of Rodolfo's jealousy, but when she overhears that Rodolfo is despairing over her failing health, she is deeply moved. Although Rodolfo and Mimi feel that their relationship is coming to an end, they decide to stay together until the spring.

In act IV, both Rodolfo and Marcello have ended their affairs with Mimi and Musetta. In the garret, the four Bohemians are having a Spartan meal consisting of a herring and some bread. Trying to cheer one another up, they engage in some exaggeratedly farcical activities, including a courtly dance and a mock duel. Unexpectedly, Musetta bursts in and announces the arrival of Mimi, whose health has further deteriorated. All past grudges are forgotten as everyone gathers around Mimi. While the others go off to fetch a doctor, some medicine, and a muff for Mimi's cold hands, Rodolfo and Mimi have a chance to express their feelings for each other. But Mimi is more ill than anyone had thought. When the others have returned to the room, she dies.

Comparison of the opera and Mürger's novel reveals, of course, both similarities and discrepancies. To analyze what the opera has retained, what is has discarded, and what it has transformed, provides important insight into the aesthetic choices made by Puccini and his librettists. The manner in which the opera deals with its "realistic" subject also provides a reference point vis-à-vis some of the "veristic" operas written at about the same time.

While Mürger's *Scènes de la vie de bohème* is one of the earliest examples of French "realist" literature, one would be hard-pressed to detect any explicit social criticism, and in this respect Mürger differs drastically from Zola or Verga. Mürger's Bohemians struggle not *against* the system, but rather for success *within* it; his characters do not seem to suffer from or resign themselves to the sociological and economic conditions; rather, they can almost be seen as taking a sort of sardonic, bitter-sweet pleasure in it. Mimi's death does not strike us so much as the shocking result of society's injustice, but rather as the product of her own carelessness. In their excessive lifestyles, the Bohemians are still very much "romantic"; new in Mürger is the insight that these romantics have to face up to a "real world."

Puccini's *Bohème* in its non-violent presentation of the story captures Mürger's brand of realism therefore very well; the opera is devoid of social criticism and commentary, yet full of attention to realistic detail. Great care was taken to create an ambience that seems as lifelike as possible, and the dialogue between the characters has none of the traditional poetic diction of Italian opera, but indulges instead in unabashed colloquial speech. Nevertheless, the differences between the novel and the opera reveal how far Puccini and his librettists were willing to take "realism" on the opera stage. Mimi, for instance, is by no means an altogether sympathetic character in Mürger's book; she shows, in fact, some rather unpleasant personality traits. In the opera, however, Mimi is a transformed, "purified" character, and this transformation brought her closer to operatic tradition as a heroine with whom the audience could identify. Realism notwithstanding, Puccini was not willing to risk an opera in which the tragic character would not be a sympathetic one whose fate would arouse pity. More than that: in the novel, Mimi dies abandoned in a charity hospital. Her body, after being subjected to experiments in an anatomy class, was buried in a pauper's grave. Clearly, this end was out of the question for Puccini and his librettists.

While the opera retains much of the essential character of the novel, a significant reversal of priorities has occurred: whereas love, or "amorous episodes," in Mürger's novel do not play the dominant role (the friendship of the Bohemians and their artistic aspirations are rather the main theme), Puccini's *Bohème* places love, more specifically the love between Mimi and Rodolfo, at the center of attention. Mürger and Barrière felt it necessary to do the same in their stage adaptation. Clearly, friendship or artistic ambition was not felt to be apt for dramatic development.

Structurally, *Scènes de la vie de bohème* can be seen to reflect "realism" in the seemingly random order of the episodes. Tragic, comic, and "sober" elements are freely juxtaposed—just as in real life. This structural principle had a formative influence on Puccini's *La bohème*. In the preface to the libretto, Giacosa and Illica pointed out, among other things, that they have strived to reproduce the spirit of the novel; to remain faithful to Mürger's characters; and to follow Mürger's method of presenting the story in distinct tableaux. Indeed, the four acts of the opera do represent four distinct tableaux, and they show only a vague dramatic connection with each other. With this, Giacosa and Illica had stepped onto new ground. In fact, it was this lack of dramatic unity which prompted considerable criticism at the premiere.

The free juxtaposition of tragic and comic, serious and not-so-serious episodes in the novel is masterfully reflected in the opera in those instances when such sentiments are fused together. This can be observed during Musetta's waltz, "*Quando me'n vo'* " (act II), where Puccini weaves the sentiments of Marcello, Alcindoro, Mimi, Rodolfo, Schaunard, and Colline into the musical structure. Similarly, the closing scene of act III shows Mimi and Rodolfo deciding to stay together until spring, and their emotional conversation is perpetually interrupted by the ranting argument between Musetta and Marcello. Arguably the most striking instance of this sort of juxtaposition occurs when, in act IV, Musetta bursts into the room and interrupts the silly behavior of the four Bohemians with the announcement of the arrival of the ailing Mimi.

How is "realism" reflected in Puccini's music? One would have to say, not very well, but this answer would be misleading. The very fact that in opera all the text is sung, with accompaniment by an orchestra, is in itself "unrealistic": in real life, people don't sing to each other, but talk. In this respect, all "veristic" operas are unrealistic. It is not coincidental, therefore, that in those moments when the "veristic" composers wanted to be as realistic as possible—namely at the point of heightened tension, when raw passion comes to the surface—the characters often stop singing and start screaming. This type of "lyricism," often referred to as *aria d'urlo,* became one of the trademarks of *verismo* operas. There is such a moment in *La bohème* as well, namely at the very conclusion of the opera, when the tragedy unfolds. In that moment of terrible recognition, all singing stops, and Rodolfo starts screaming as he finds out that Mimi has died.

Another way in which *verismo* composers attempted to infuse realism into their scores was by incorporating folkloristic songs, such as "ordinary" people might sing. Giordano did this in his *Mala vita,* which incorporates several popular Neapolitan tunes. Such real-life quotes are absent from Puccini's score, except for the military tattoo marching across the stage in act II (as Mosco Carner has pointed out, it is based on an authentic French march of the time of King Louis Philippe). But Puccini creates atmosphere by paying close attention to dramatic details. There is a good bit of descriptive music, illustrating, for instance, the flickering of the fire in the stove in act I, or the snowfall at the beginning of act III. His orchestration pays close attention to the dramatic situation as well. The more intimate the scene is, the more chamber-like is the orchestration. The full orchestra is dutifully employed for the portrayal of the crowd scenes in act II.

What impresses most about Puccini's score, however, is the virtually perfect pacing of the music. There is never a dull moment in the music, and Puccini abstains from musical verbosity. The result is a score consisting of musical units which say exactly as much as needed, and then move on to the next unit. Each act is relatively short as well: Puccini presents precisely what is needed, and not more. There is never a moment of boredom.

Whereas Puccini's first opera, *Le villi,* as well as his third, *Manon Lescaut,* revealed decided traces of Wagnerian influence, no Wagnerisms can be detected in *La bohème.* The tonal language is predominantly diatonic, and chromatic counterpoint is virtually non-existent. Even though Puccini does make use of extended harmonies, the tonal center is rarely in question. But above all, melody is the most important ingredient of the score, and in *La bohème* Puccini's genius for melodic invention has come to full fruition.

La bohème was arguably the work which established Puccini as the leading voice in Italian opera, indeed as one of the foremost opera composers anywhere around the turn of the century. Despite an initially cool reception, *La bohème* has always maintained itself in the repertoire, and may well have been performed more often than any other opera ever written. While the work reflects the general preoccupation with realistic subjects in opera at the time, it illustrates a marked detachment from some of the baser aspects of *verismo* opera.

—Jürgen Selk

THE BOHEMIAN GIRL.

Composer: Michael William Balfe.

Librettist: A. Bunn (after J.H. Vernoy de Saint-Georges).

First Performance: London, Drury Lane Theatre, 27 November 1843.

Roles: Arline (soprano); Thaddeus (tenor); Queen of the Gypsies (contralto); Devilshoof (bass); Count Arnheim (bass); Florestein (tenor); Captain of the Guard (bass); Officer (tenor); Buda (soprano).

The Bohemian Girl, Michael William Balfe's most enduring opera, has been described as a work of "charming sentimentality." Both words are apt. The music has undeniable charm, if little sophistication, a quality it does not, after all, seek. Alfred Bunn's libretto reflects the nineteenth-century middle-class preference for the highly sentimental, and in this Bunn succeeds where other of Balfe's librettists failed, striking the precise note that would inspire the composer to his best effort.

Bunn has rightly been accused of both banality and oversimplicity. His plot is a *mélange* of elements from familiar works. Thaddeus, a Polish soldier hiding from Austrian authorities disguised as a gypsy, saves the life of little Arline, the Count of Arnheim's daughter. When the gypsies are threatened with punishment for disloyalty to the Austrian flag, the gypsy Devilshoof kidnaps Arline. Twelve years pass, during which time Arline's memory of her former life seems to her only a dream, but her love for Thaddeus, and his for her, is real. Thaddeus, however, is also desired by the Queen of the Gypsies, who gives Arline an amulet she knows will be recognized as stolen, causing Arline's arrest. The plan works, but Arline is recognized by the count as his long-lost daughter. She is restored to her estates, but her love for a gypsy, Thaddeus, cannot be tolerated. He meets Arline secretly, but is betrayed by the queen. Thaddeus reveals to the count that he is no gypsy; he too has noble blood, which fact is enough for the count to accept him. Her plot foiled, the queen menaces Arline, but is shot dead by Devilshoof, leaving the lovers to rejoice.

Certainly Bunn's libretto appeals to the most obvious, uncomplicated emotions. But aside from the jarring transition at the close of act III—Devilshoof's shooting of the Queen leading directly into a chorus in praise of the young lovers (ameliorated in the 1978 Central City production by director Robert Darling's interpolation for the count: "Let not this awesome event mar our joy")—Bunn provided a clear story, one whose assumptions its public shared. Thaddeus is worthy of Arline not because he saved her life or has loved her regardless of her station, but because, as it turns out, he too is of her social class. When his right to Arline's hand is questioned by the count, he relies not on his goodness but on his blood to justify his suit. The gypsies are lighthearted but treacherous (as the audience knew all gypsies to be). Arline and the count are stereotypes, as is Florestein, the count's inept nephew. There are no surprises in this libretto, except to the characters on stage.

But a libretto cannot make an opera by itself, nor overly mar one written by a composer upon whom genius is smiling. Verdi converted the ridiculous book of *Il trovatore* into the quintessential Italian romantic opera, while far superior libretti (Boito's to Faccio's *Hamlet,* for example) lie forgotten, wedded to unmemorable music. Balfe poured into *The Bohemian Girl* some of his best ideas and created for it perhaps his three best arias. If the opera ever becomes as totally forgotten as those of his contemporary (some would suggest, superior), Edward Loder, the last notes of Balfe to be heard will surely be those of Arline's "I Dreamt I Dwelt in Marble Halls," whose haunting descending cadences possess a charm

The Bohemian Girl, title-page from a piano arrangement, 1843

that only the most determinedly intellectual listener can reject. The quintessential Italian tenor of the century, Beniamino Gigli, recognized the visceral appeal of Thaddeus' "When Other Lips" (for some reason better known by its closing words "Then You'll Remember Me"), while the absence of the Count's "The Heart Bow'd Down" from contemporary baritone recitals and recordings perhaps reflects more a fear of being thought old-fashioned than an adverse judgment on the aria's singability or capacity to please an audience. In the concerted passages, Balfe advances the action with an undeniable skill and innate conviction, though without building a musical structure anywhere as interesting as the ensembles in his own *Satanella* or in Loder's *The Night Dancers*.

Beyond the unsophisticated pleasure its music can give, *The Bohemian Girl* has the unsought burden of being the only example of English romantic opera one is likely to encounter in live performance (though even these are becoming rarer). As one of the best and most representative (the two are not always synonymous) works of its subgenre, it requires a production (such as those of Covent Garden in 1951 and Central City in 1978) which does not flinch in taking the opera seriously and reproducing it without deconstruction or irony. Given such a production, the opera has much to tell us about the taste of a vanished age. *The Bohemian Girl* has an uncomplicated honesty that transcends its banality, and tests our capacity to participate in a relentlessly unsophisticated pleasure, so very alien to our own age, in responding to it.

—William J. Collins

Karl Böhm

BÖHM, Karl.

Conductor. Born 28 August 1894, in Graz. Died 14 August 1981, in Salzburg. Studied piano and theory at the Graz Conservatory; studied music theory with Mandyczewski at the Vienna Conservatory; served in the Austrian Army during World War I; conductor of the Municipal Theater at Graz; received his Dr Jur., 1919; conducted at the Bavarian State Opera, Munich, 1921; Generalmusikdirektor, Darmstadt, 1927; conducted Berg's *Wozzeck*, 1931; Generalmusikdirektor of the Hamburg Opera, 1931-33; director of the Dresden State Opera, 1934-43, where he premiered Richard Strauss's operas *Die schweigsame Frau*, 1935, and *Daphne*, 1938; conductor at the Vienna State Opera during the war; cleared of charges of direct involvement with the Nazi party by the Allied postwar trials; organized and led a series of German operas at the Teatro Colón in Buenos Aires, Argentina, 1950; principal conductor of the Vienna State Opera, 1954-56; conducted the Chicago Symphony, 9 February 1956; Metropolitan Opera debut, 31 October 1957; United States tour with the Berlin Philharmonic, 1961; Japan tour with the Berlin Philharmonic, 1963-64; honorary title of Generalmusikdirektor of Austria, 1964; conducted a United States tour with the Deutsche Oper of Berlin, 1975; elected president of the London Symphony Orchestra, 1977; United States tour with the Vienna State Opera, 1979.

Publications

By BÖHM: books–

Dostal, Franz Eugen, ed. *Begegnung mit Richard Strauss.* Munich, 1964.
Ich erinnere mich ganz genau. Zurich, 1968; Munich, 1979.

interviews–

Matheopoulos, Helena. *Maestro: Encounters with Conductors of Today.* London, 1982.

About BÖHM: books–

Roemer, Margarete. *Karl Böhm.* Berlin, 1966.
Richter, Karl. *Karl Böhm: Selbstverständlich empfängt mich ihre Gnaden.* Augsburg, 1977.
Endler, Franz. *Karl Böhm: Ein Dirigentenleben.* Hamburg, 1981.
Hoyer, H. *Karl Böhm an der Wiener Staatsoper: Eine Dokumentation.* Vienna, 1981.

articles–

Schmiedel, Gottfried. "Karl Böhm and the Dresden Opera." *Opera* May (1960).
Wechsberg, Joseph. "Karl Böhm." *Opera* December (1977).

*   *   *

Karl Böhm's conducting career links him closely to Mozart, Wagner and Strauss. Throughout his tenure at the Dresden State Opera, the Vienna State Opera, the Metropolitan Opera and other houses, Böhm secured a reputation as a conductor in the service of music. This may seem like an obvious point, but it is not. Other more flamboyant conductors contemporary with Böhm were making the rounds of the opera circuit, such as Furtwängler, Toscanini, and Klemperer. Böhm was notable for the understatement of his conducting, and it is eventually what earned him fame. His dedication to the score was evident in the way he drew power from the orchestras he conducted; when he attracted attention, it was because of his unusual stance as a conductor lacking in ostentation.

Though Böhm favored understatement and privileged the music he performed over his status as a conductor, he was by no means a retiring pushover. Blunt in his demands for rehearsals, perfection, and commitment from his singers and players, Böhm often frightened and intimidated his performers. He had the advantage of not being especially vocal except in cases when he thought things were not going well; when he offered a suggestion, therefore, he received results. To those acquainted with his style of conducting, he seemed unassertive, and even to other musicians, he explained himself in only the most basic terms. Franz Endler's essay about Böhm from the Deutsche Grammophon recording of Strauss's *Die Frau ohne Schatten* suggests that Böhm "hardly lifted a finger to draw attention to his own role or its merits."

Böhm's dedication to music is all the more apparent when one realizes that the repertoire he favored is comprised mainly of German twentieth-century works (although he did not neglect nineteenth-century or earlier opera). He believed in the achievements of twentieth-century composers and relied on a high standard of performance as the way to convince listeners that they were indeed hearing masterpieces rather than curiosities. He developed lasting relationships with Richard Strauss and Alban Berg and put himself at the disposal of their music. He conducted Berg's *Wozzeck* in 1931, and continued to be a devoted promoter of that work. He also conducted the premieres of two Strauss operas, *Die schweigsame Frau* (1935) and *Daphne* (1938).

Böhm made his musical home across the globe. Of course, he had long tenures at certain houses like Dresden and Vienna, but he also conducted regularly at London, Salzburg, Bayreuth, Munich, Milan and New York. His character during performance showed vitality and freshness, although his gestures were functional rather than flamboyant. He possessed the magnetism which comes from surety and conviction of purpose. Pictures of him conducting reveal him also to be a performer, because his attention seems so concentrated on the performance.

—Timothy O. Gray

BOHNEN, Michael.

Bass-baritone. Born 2 May 1887, in Cologne. Died 26 April 1965 in Berlin. Married singer Mary Lewis (divorced). Studied with Fritz Steinbach and Schulz-Dornburg in Cologne, 1910; debut as Kaspar in *Der Freischütz* in Düsseldorf in 1910; sang in Wiesbaden, 1910-14; debut in Berlin as Gurnemanz in *Parsifal,* 1914; Covent Garden debut as King Heinrich in *Lohengrin,* 1914; debut at Bayreuth as Daland and Hunding, 1914; active in Berlin Hofoper (1913-21) and

in Vienna after World War 1; Metropolitan Opera debut as Tourist/Francesco in *Mona Lisa,* 1923, where he remained for ten seasons as King Mark, Hagen, Wotan, Kezal in *The Bartered Bride,* Mephistopheles, and Hans Sachs, among others; created leading role in the first American performance of Krenek's *Johnny spielt auf* in 1929; with Deutches Opernhaus, Berlin, 1933-45, serving as its administrator, 1945-47.

*   *   *

Michael Bohnen was called "the last of Opera's giants." Relatively unknown in America despite 177 performances at the Metropolitan Opera, he was a film star in Europe, a champion athlete, and a *Kammersänger* for Kaiser Wilhelm. His voice was universally praised, but his dramatic flourishes were considered by some to be overly eccentric. He was a character to be either loved or hated, but always noticed.

Bohnen debuted in *Der Freischütz* at Düsseldorf in 1910. Two years later, Cosima Wagner invited him to learn the Wagnerian tradition at Beyreuth. He did not limit himself to opera during these years. He boxed and wrestled professionally, won swimming championships and auto races, painted and sculpted. After World War I, he became interested in films and started his own production company. He starred in over thirty films, and audiences loved him. He sang at New York's Metropolitan Opera from 1923 until 1932 in both Wagnerian and other roles. He returned to Germany in 1933. During the war years, he had trouble under the Nazis and was not allowed to perform. After the war, he was appointed president of the Chamber of Arts, and brought all of his prodigious powers to bear in rebuilding Berlin's state opera. Because of his association with a dancer thought to be a Nazi sympathizer, he was shunned in musical circles after the war. Not allowed to work, he spent the last years of his life in poverty. His American reputation saved him at the end, however, for the Metropolitan Opera Company gave him a small honorary pension to ease his final months.

Bohnen sang 20 roles at the Metropolitan Opera. He debuted there in Max von Schilling's *Mona Lisa.* He performed in Weber's *Der Freischütz,* Smetana's *The Bartered Bride,* Gounod's *Faust,* Leoncavallo's *I pagliacci,* and a number of Wagner's operas. He created the title role in Krenek's *Jonny spielt auf* for the company. His rich voice entranced audiences. As his biographer Hans Borgelt wrote, "[His] voice was seductive, disquieting, appealing to the entire nervous system; it did not report a fact, it expressed editorial comment." He had an enormous range; when he was the director for the Berlin State Opera, he was supposedly able to demonstrate the low C for the basses and the high A for the tenor in the same scene.

While his voice was loved universally, Bohnen's dramatic intensity was less accepted. He was a gifted actor, but not terribly subtle or refined. David Prosser, writing for *Opera News,* called him "a contradictory amalgam of near-genius and semi-slapstick." In his recordings, he took musical liberties and shaded his vocal coloring for expressive purposes. In live performances he approached each part in a unique and individual way; his unpredictability caused great confusion among his colleagues. His Mephistopheles in *Faust* was covered in gray to represent the "earthbound" qualities, rather than the more traditional red of the devil. He created his own costumes and make-up with more thought to drama than consistency: in three successive performances of *Götterdämmerung* he had three different costumes—one with a shaved skull, the next with a flaming red wig and beard, the final with a long black beard and wig. He used his athletic prowess in performing, adding handsprings and cartwheels to his Tonio of *I pagliacci,* and a tap-danced finale to *Jonny spielt auf.*

At first the critics admired Bohnen's expressiveness. Henderson wrote of his performance in *Der Freischütz,* "[He was a] magnificent force [whose] dramatic power vitalizes the whole performance." Eccentricities began to wear thin, however, and Henderson wrote later that "The buffooneries of Mr. Bohnen are correct because they draw money." Other critics used words such as "bumptious," "erratic," and "inartistic." By the end of Bohnen's stay at the Metropolitan Opera Henderson had grown to despise him. In an article he titled "Male Singers Put in Their Places," he wrote "Michael Bohnen has a mercilessly hard metallic tone, a brutal attack and a generally barbaric style. He abuses the *portamento* much of the time and with very little temptation slides into a *parlando* that is almost plain speech. . . . His interpretations of famous operatic personages such as King Henry and Hagen are too frequently brilliant productions of Mr. Bohnen's own ideas of himself." Yet other critics loved him. Irving Kolodin wrote "He was one of the truly great operatic artists of the twenties. When you went to a Bohnen performance in which he was at his best you could not separate the vocal experience from the dramatic, for they were both completely interrelated."

While his imaginative flair may have annoyed his critics in New York, Bohnen was loved in Germany. As a film star, he was a great box office draw. Just before he retired, with his "larger-than-life" style, he single-handedly revitalized the Berlin State Opera after the decimation wrought by the Second World War. He created opera in a bombed building on a stage with no back wall. When the stage proved too narrow, he moved the cast into the audience. With his imagination he was able to create costumes and sets before textiles and paints were generally available in the city. He wrought similar miracles with his shell-shocked cast. As a vocal trainer he had phenomenal patience, working long hours with his singers to achieve dramatic and vocal accuracy. He coached the young Hans Beirer from a thin, operetta voice into the largest *heldontenor* in Europe. He labored unceasingly to retain Germany's operatic culture and dignity.

Modern audiences can get an unbiased sample of Bohnen's performing abilities from his recordings. They attest to his fine vocal technique and dramatic sensibilities. His voice was rich and smooth throughout his large range, and his registers were well blended. Yet he could tint his vocal color for dramatic purposes to produce any characterization from malevolent to humorous. Although he sometimes took expressive musical liberties, his pitch and rhythm were generally accurate even in the most difficult of passages. His colleagues might have quailed at his eccentricities, but today's listeners can revel in his consummate musicianship.

While recordings have assured Bohnen's immortality, even without them his character and imagination have reserved for him a place in the annals of opera. He was a figure some hated, some loved, but everyone remembered.

—Robin Armstrong

BOIELDIEU, (François) Adrien.

Composer. Born 16 December 1775, in Rouen. Died 8 October 1834, in Jarcy. Married: 1) the dancer Clotilde Mafleurai, 19 March 1802 (separated 1803); 2) the singer Philis Desoyres, 22 January 1827; had a son, Adrien-Louis-Victor Boieldieu (also a composer) by the singer Thérèse Regnault. Studied with Charles Broche at the church St André in Rouen, where he became assistant organist; as the guest of the composer Jadin and the Erards family (piano manufacturers) in Paris, he met many leading composers of the day, including Cherubini and Méhul; Parisian premiere with *La famille suisse,* 1797; professor of the pianoforte at the Paris Conservatory, 1798-1809; studied counterpoint with Cherubini in Paris, according to anecdotes; conductor of the Imperial Opera, St Petersburg, 1803; returned to Paris, 1811; professor of composition at the Conservatory, 1817-26; Chevalier of the Legion of Honor, 1821; retired 1833. Among Boieldieu's students were Fétis, Adam, and P.J.G. Zimmerman.

Operas

La fille coupable, Jacques François Adrien Boieldieu (composer's father), Rouen, Théâtre des Arts, 2 November 1793.

Rosalie et Myrza, Jacques François Adrien Boieldieu (composer's father), Rouen, Théâtre des Arts, 28 October 1795.

La famille suisse, Claude Godard d'Aucour de Saint-Just, Paris, Théâtre Feydeau, 11 February 1797.

L'heureuse nouvelle, Claude Godard d'Aucour de Saint-Just, and Charles de Longchamps, Paris, Théâtre Feydeau, 7 November 1797.

Le pari, ou Mombreuil et Merville, Charles de Longchamps, Paris, Salle Favart, 15 December 1797.

Zoraïme et Zulnar, Claude Godard d'Aucour de Saint-Just, Paris, Salle Favart, 10 May 1798.

La dot de Suzette, Jean Élie Bédéno Dejaure (after a novel by Joseph Fiévée), Paris, Salle Favart, 5 September 1798.

Les méprises espagnoles, Claude Godard d'Aucour de Saint-Just, Paris, Théâtre Feydeau, 18 April 1799.

Emma, ou La prisonnière (with Cherubini), Victor Joseph Étienne de Jouy, Claude Godard d'Aucour de Saint-Just, and Charles de Longchamps, Paris, Théâtre Montansier, 12 September 1799.

Béniowski, ou Les exilés du Kamchatka, Alexandre Duval (after a play by Kotzebue), Paris, Salle Favart, 8 June 1800; revised for the Opéra-Comique, 20 July 1824.

Le calife de Bagdad, Claude Godard D'Aucour de Saint-Just, Paris, Salle Favart, 16 September 1800.

Ma tante Aurore, ou Le roman impromptu, Charles de Longchamps, Paris, Opéra-Comique, 13 January 1803.

Le baiser et la quittance, ou Une aventure de garnison (with Méhul, R. Kreutzer, and Nicolò Isouard), Louis Picard, Michel Dieulafoy, and Charles de Longchamps, Paris, Opéra-Comique, 18 June 1803.

Aline, reine de Golconde, Jean Baptiste Charles Vial and Étienne Guillaume François de Favières, St Petersburg, Hermitage, 17 March 1804.

Abderkhan, Déligny, St Petersburg, Petershof Palace, 7 August 1804.

La jeune femme colère, Claparède (after a comedy by Étienne), St Petersburg, Hermitage, 30 April 1805.

Un tour de soubrette, St Petersburg, Hermitage, 28 April 1806.

Télémaque, P. Dercy, St Petersburg, Hermitage, 28 December 1806.

Amour et mystère, ou Lequel est mon cousin?, Joseph Marie Pain, St Petersburg, 1807.

La dame invisible, Alexis Daudet and Randon, St Petersburg, 1808.

Adrien Boieldieu, portrait by Louis Leopold Boilly (Musée des Beaux-Arts, Rouen)

Les voitures versées, Émanuel Mercier-Dupaty, St Petersburg, 26 April 1808.

Rien de trop, ou les deux paravents, Joseph Marie Pain, St Petersburg, Hermitage, 16 April 1808; revised for the Opéra-Comique, 29 April 1820.

Jean de Paris, Claude Godard D'Aucour de Saint-Just, Paris, Opéra-Comique, 4 April 1812.

Le nouveau seigneur de village, Augustin François Creuzé de Lesser and Étienne Guillame François de Favières, Paris, Opéra-Comique, 29 June 1813.

Bayard à Mézières (with Cherubini, Catel, and N. Isouard), André René Polydore Alissan de Chazet and Émanuel Mercier-Dupaty, Paris, Opéra-Comique, 12 February 1814.

Les béarnais, ou Henri IV en voyage (with R. Kreutzer), Charles Augustin Bassompierre Sewrin, Paris, Opéra-Comique, 21 May 1814.

Angéla, ou L'atelier de Jean Cousin (with S. Gail), C. Montcloux d'Épinay, Paris, Opéra-Comique, 13 June 1814.

La fête du village voisin, Charles Augustin Bassompierre Sewrin, Paris, Opéra-Comique, 5 March 1816.

Charles de France, ou Amour et Gloire (with Hérold), Marguerite Théaulon de Lambert, and François Victor Armand d'Artois de Bournonville, Paris, Opéra-Comique, 18 June 1816.

Le petit chaperon rouge, Marguerite Théaulon de Lambert, Paris, Opéra-Comique, 30 June 1818.

Blanche de Provence, ou La cour des fées (with Berton, Cherubini, R. Kreutzer, and Paër), Marguerite Théaulon de Lambert and Emmanuel Guillaume De Rancé, Paris, Académie Royale de Musique, 3 May 1821.

Pharamond (with Berton and R. Kreutzer), François Ancelot, Alexandre Pierre Guiraud, and Louis Alexandre Soumet, Paris, Académie Royale de Musique, 10 June 1825.

La dame blanche, Eugène Scribe (after Scott's *The Monastery* and *Guy Mannering*), Paris, Opéra-Comique, 10 December 1825.

Les deux nuits, Eugène Scribe (after Jean Nicolas Bouilly), Paris, Opéra-Comique, 20 May 1829.

Marguerite, Eugène Scribe [unfinished].

Les jeux floraux [unfinished].

La marquise de Brinvilliers (with Auber, Batton, Berton, Blangini, Carafa, Cherubini, Hérold, and Paër), Eugène Scribe and Castil-Blaze, Paris, Opéra-Comique, 31 October 1831.

Publications

About BOIELDIEU: books–

Cherubini, Luigi. *Discours prononcé aux funérailles de M. Boieldieu.* Paris, 1834.

Adam, Adolphe. *Souvenirs d'un musicien.* Paris, 1857.

Berlioz, Hector. *Mémoires de Hector Berlioz.* Paris, 1870; translated in English and edited by David Cairns, London, 1969; New York, 1975; London, 1977.

Adam, Adolphe. *Derniers souvenirs d'un musicien.* Paris, 1871.

Duval, E. *Boieldieu, notes et fragments inédits.* Paris, 1883.

Augé de Lassus, Lucien. *Boieldieu. Les musiciens célèbres.* Paris, 1908.

Mooser, R.A. *L'opéra-comique français en Russie au XVIIIe siècle.* Geneva, 1932.

Favre, Georges. *Boieldieu: sa vie, son oeuvre,* 2 vols. Paris, 1944-45.

Héquet, J. *Adrien Boieldieu: sa vie et ses oeuvres.* Paris, 1864.

Pougin, Arthur. *Boieldieu.* Paris, 1875.

Thannberg, H. de. *Le Centenaire de Boieldieu.* Paris, 1875.

Pendle, Karin. *Eugène Scribe and French Opera of the Nineteenth Century.* Ann Arbor, 1979.

articles–

Berlioz, Hector. "Boieldieu." *Le rénovateur* 14 October (1834).

Fétis, F.-J. "Boieldieu." *Revue musicale* 19 and 26 October (1834).

Robert, P.-L. "Lettres de Boieldieu (1830-1834)." *Bulletin français de la Société Internationale de Musique* 5 (1909): 899.

———. "Correspondance de Boieldieu." *Rivista musicale italiana* 19 (1912): 75; 22 (1915): 520.

———. "Lettres inédites d'Adrien Boieldieu." *La revue musicale* 7 (1926): 111.

Schaeffner, A. "À propos de *La dame blanche.*" *La Revue musicale* 7 (1926): 97.

Halévy, F. "Boieldieu." *Gazette musicale de Paris* 12, 19, and 26 October (1934).

Favre, Georges. "Quelques lettres inédites de Boieldieu." *La revue musicale* no. 185 (1938): 1.

———. "L'amitié de deux musiciens: Boieldieu et Cherubini." *La revue musicale* no. 201 (1946): 217.

Mirimonde, A.-P. de. "Musiciens isolés et portraits de l'école française du XVIIIe siècle dans les collections nationales." *Revue du Louvre* 17 (1967): 81.

Dean, Winton. "French Opera." In *The New Oxford History of Music.* vol. 8, 26-119. Oxford and London, 1982.

Études normandes 2 (1984) [special issue: *Boieldieu musicien normand*].

*   *   *

Following the "Revolutionary" generation including Dalayrac, Cherubini, Méhul, Kreutzer, Berton, et al., Boieldieu emerged as the most significant composer of *opéra comique* during the period of the Restoration, primarily the decade 1815-25. While the previous generation had fostered a new serious type of *opéra comique* involving suspenseful dramatic plots and high ethical principles, in keeping with the tenor of the times, Boieldieu tended to reintegrate lighter pastoral and comic elements of the original genre into the musically more developed form he inherited. With his most famous work, *La dame blanche* (1825), he introduced elements of popular romanticism, inspired above all by the works of Sir Walter Scott on which the opera is based.

Boieldieu's earliest training was with the cathedral organist of his native Rouen, Charles Broche. (An *opéra comique* by Ourry produced in the year of Boieldieu's death, *L'enfance de Boieldieu,* depicted the tribulations of the young composer under this supposedly harsh taskmaster.) The closure of the French churches in 1791 directed the young musician's attention to the theater, and he debuted at the Théâtre des Arts in Rouen with a two-act work, *La fille coupable* (to a text by his father) in 1793. Aside from a number of collections of popular romances for voice and piano and a few early instrumental works, the *opéra comique* remained his sole field of activity. (Two works performed at the Paris Opéra—*Blanche de Provence* and *Pharamond*—were collaborations with other composers.)

A year after marrying the dancer Clothilde Mafleurai he separated from her and, with eleven mostly successful operas for the Parisian stage to his name, Boieldieu left for an extended sojourn with the Russian court in St Petersburg. While he prospered well enough in Russia, there was little chance of his works reaching a wider audience during these years. Political tensions hastened his permanent return to France eight years later. Soon after this return Boieldieu scored a major success with *Jean de Paris* (4 April 1812), one of relatively few works that would remain in the repertory after his death. The principal operas created over the next decade, aside from collaborations, include *Le nouveau seigneur de village* (1813), *La fête du village voisin* (1816), and *Le petit chaperon rouge* (1818), an adaptation of the "Little Red Riding-Hood" story in which the heroine is pursued by an unscrupulous nobleman, in place of the wolf, and containing numerous magic elements akin to the contemporary Viennese popular theater. *La dame blanche* (1825), written with the soon-to-be famous Eugène Scribe, quickly proved to be far and away the most successful of Boieldieu's many operas. A more ambitious project, *Les deux nuits*, followed several years later but met with little popular acclaim. After this Boieldieu's health declined seriously and a third collaboration with Scribe (*Marguerite*, begun 1830) was never completed.

Much of Boieldieu's popularity in his own day can be attributed to the simple, undemanding character of his music. His style combines an unconstrained tunefulness with a facility for fluent vocal declamation in ensembles, where the melody may be carried by the orchestra or by one of the soloists (usually soprano). As with much earlier *opéra comique*, the success of many works depended heavily on the interest of the libretto as a play.

Beniowski ou les exilés de Kamchatka (1800, after Kotzebue) belongs to the "rescue opera" type, with an action-filled plot and romantically exotic settings (a Siberian cave, a snow-covered mountain range) similar to contemporary works by Le Sueur, Méhul, and Cherubini. More characteristic of Boieldieu is the element of light-hearted social satire found in *Ma tante Aurore* (1803), involving an old woman obsessed by the stuff of gothic romances, and *Les voitures versées* (1808), about an eccentric country gentleman who booby-traps the road by his estate in order to procure interesting visitors. It is indicative of the relative importance attached to the elements of play and music that Boieldieu's revisions of both these works, responding to their critical reception, involving a reworking of the dramatic layout, not of the music.

Boieldieu's style—unlike that of his successor Auber—is firmly rooted in the musical vocabulary of the later eighteenth century: his more extended ensembles (like those of Cherubini) too often tend toward a rather mechanical application of classical syntactic formulae, lacking a compelling sense of larger shape or direction. His harmonic palette is limited, and long stretches of music often fail to escape from the simplest tonic-dominant relationships, reinforced by flat, predictable "textbook" phrase structures (see for example the overtures to *Le calife de Bagdad* or *Jean de Paris*, or even that to *La dame blanche*).

Despite these limitations, Boieldieu's better works, such as *Le petit chaperon rouge* and *La dame blanche* recommend themselves by a naive, early Romantic charm. Their unpretentious musical idiom and the dialogue format make them best suited to small-scale or amateur productions; indeed, none of Boieldieu's works is appropriate to the large modern opera house. A lively, sympathetic and appropriately scaled approach, however, might reveal the appealing qualities that

made *La dame blanche* one of the most often performed operas of the entire nineteenth century.

—Thomas S. Grey

BOITO, Arrigo.

Composer/Librettist. Born 24 February 1842, in Padua. Died 10 June 1918, in Milan. Studied composition with Alberto Mazzucato and Ronchetti-Monteviti at the Milan Conservatory, 1853-61; in collaboration with Faccio, the composition of two cantatas (1860-61) won for them a two year travel grant from the Italian government, with which Boito travelled to Paris, Poland, Germany, Belgium, and England; wrote the text for Verdi's cantata *Inno delle Nazioni*, and later for Verdi's *Otello* and *Falstaff*; served in Garibaldi's army, 1866; first production of his *Mefistofele* at the Teatro alla Scala in 1868 was controversial and consequently unsuccessful, but his revisions of the original score led to later successful runs in Italy and elsewhere; appointed inspector general of Italian conservatories by the King of Italy, 1892; honorary doctorates from Cambridge and Oxford Universities; made a senator by the King of Italy, 1912. Boito also published verses under the pen name Tobia Gorrio, as well as translations of operas (Wagner's *Rienzi* and *Tristan und Isolde*), opera librettos for various composers (most notably Verdi), and novels.

Operas

Ero e Leander.
Nerone, 1862-1916; revised for performance by Toscanini, Milan, Teatro alla Scala, 1 May 1924.
Mefistofele, Boito, Milan, Teatro alla Scala, 5 March 1868.

Librettos

Amleto, F. Faccio, 1865.
Mefistofele, Boito, 1868.
Un tramonto, G. Coronaro, 1873.
La falce, A. Catalani, 1875.
La Gioconda, A. Ponchielli, 1876.
Ero e Leandro, G. Bottesini, 1879; L. Mancinelli, 1897.
Simon Boccanegra (after F. Piave), G. Verdi, 1881.
Otello, G. Verdi, 1887.
Falstaff, G. Verdi, 1893.
Semira (La regina di Babilù) [not performed].
Pier Luigi Farnese [not performed].
Iràm [not performed].
Nerone, Boito, 1924 [posthumous].
Basi e bote, R. Pick-Mangiagalli, 1927.

Other works: cantatas and songs.

Publications/Writings

By BOITO: books–

Rensis, Raffaello de, ed. *Lettere*. Rome, n.d.
Nardi, Pietro, ed. *Tutti gli scritti*. Milan, 1942 (includes all librettos and writings).
Opere. Milan, 1979 [with a bibliographic guide by Mario Lavagette]
Medici, Mario and Marcello Conato, eds. *Carteggio Verdi-Boito*. 2 vols. Parma, 1978.

articles–

"Cronaca musicale parigina." *La perseveranza* 2 March (1862).
"Cronache dei teatri." *Figaro* 7, 21 January; 4, 11, 18 February; 10, 17, 24 March (1864).
"Trattenimento musicale de Giovanni Noseda." *Figaro* 28 January (1864).
"Experimenti della Società del Quartetto." *Giornale della Società del Quartetto* 29 June (1864); 8 January, 6 April, 7, 4, May (1865).
"Il *Freischütz* davanti al pubblico della Scala." *Gazzetta musicale di Milano* 27 (1872).
" 'Nella selva' sinfonia di Giochino Raff." *Gazzetta musicale di Milano* 27 (1872).
"Mendelssohn in Italia." *Giornale della Società del Quartetto* 20 July - 31 December (1864).
"A Sua Eccelenza il Ministro della Istruzione Pubblica: lettera in quattro paragrafi." *Pungolo* 21 May (1868).
"La musica in piazza." *Gazzetta musicale di Milano* 25 (1870); 26 (1871).

About BOITO: books–

Risolo, M. *Il primo 'Mefistofele' di Arrigo Boito*. Naples, 1916.
Ricci, C. *Arrigo Boito* Milan, 1919; 2nd editon, 1924.
Bonaventura, Arnaldo. *Mefistofele: Guido attraverso il poema e la musica*. Milan, 1924.
Borriello, Antonio. *Il re orso di Ariggo Boito*. Rome, 1926.
Rensis, Rafaello de. *L'amleto di Arrigo Boito*. Ancona, 1927.
Vittadini, S. *Il primo libretto del "Mefistofele" di Arrigo Boito*. Milan, 1938.
Ballo, F. *Arrigo Boito*. Turin, 1939.
Pöschl, W. *Arrigo Boito: ein Vertreter der italianischen Spätromantik*. Berlin, 1939; 1967.
Nardi, Pietro. *Vita di Arrigo Boito*. Milan, 1942, 2nd edtion, 1944.
Rensis, R. de. *Arrigo Boito: anedotti e bizzarrie poetiche musicali*. Rome, 1942.
––––––. *Arrigo Boito: capitoli biografici*. Florence, 1942.
Nardi, Pietro. *Arrigo Boito, scritti e documenti*. Milan, 1948.
Borriello, Antonio. *Mito poesia e musica nel Mefistofele di Arrigo Boita*. Naples, 1950.
Mariani, G. *Arrigo Boito*. Parma, 1973.
Scarsi, G. *Rapporto poesia - musica in Arrigo Boito*. Rome, 1973.
Tedeschi, Rubens, *Addio, fiorito asil. Il melodramma italiano da Boito al Verismo*. Milan, 1978.

articles–

Filippi, F. "Il 'Mefistofele' di Arrigo Boito." *La perseveranza* 9, 16 March (1868).
Ricordi, G. "Analisi musicale del 'Mefistofele' di Boito." *Gazzetta musicale di Milano* 23 (1868): 81.

Giani, R. *Il "Nerone" di Arrigo Boito*. Milan. 1901; reprinted in *Rivista musicale italiana* 31 (1924): 235.
Huneker, J. "Verdi and Boito," and "Boito's Mefistofele." In *Overtones: a Book of Temperaments,* 236, 272. New York, 1904.
Forzano, G. "La preparazione sceneca del 'Nerone'." *Lettura* March (1924).
Gui, V. "Arrigo Boito e il 'Nerone'." *Rivista musicale italiana* 31 (1924): 2.
Pagliai, Morena. "I libretti di Arrigo Boito." In *La rassegna della letteratura italiana,* 1962.
Orselli, Cesare. "Arrigo Boito: Un riesame." *Chigiana* 25 (1968): 197.
Nicolaisen, Jay Reed. "The First *Mefistofele.* " *19th Century Music* 1 (1978): 221.
Grim, William E. "Faust Manqué: Boito's *Mefistofele.* " In *The Faust Legend in Jusic and Literature,* 29. New York, 1988.
Taddie, Daniel. "The Devil, You Say: Reflections on Verdi's and Boito's Iago." *Opera Quarterly* spring (1990).

unpublished–

Nicolaisen, Jay Reed. "Italian Opera in Transition 1871-1893." Ph.D. dissertation, University of California, Berkeley, 1978.

* * *

Arrigo Boito (1842-1918) was a significant opera composer, librettist, and man of letters. He is best known today as the composer of *Mefistofele* (1868; revised 1875 and 1881) and as librettist for Verdi's *Otello* (1887) and *Falstaff* (1893) and Ponchielli's *La Gioconda* (1876).

Although Boito was a composition graduate of the Milan Conservatory, he composed relatively few musical works, the bulk of his creative output being in the literary domain. Boito managed in his long lifetime to compose only two operas, *Mefistofele* and *Nerone* (first performed in 1924) of which only the former was completed.

Boito was associated in the 1860s and 1870s with the *Scapigliatura* (literally translated, the "disheveled ones"), a loosely-knit group of young Italian intellectuals and artists. The members of the *Scapigliatura* emphasized the darker side of human nature and exhibited a penchant for extreme pessimism, resembling in certain respects the earlier *Weltschmerz* movement in Germany and the naturalism evident in the contemporaneous works of the French. It was precisely this pessimistic streak that attracted Boito to the ambivalent character of Faust and the malevolent Nero.

Ironically, it is with the opera *Mefistofele* that Boito scored both his greatest disaster and triumph as a composer. The literary-minded Boito wanted to set both parts of Goethe's *Faust,* not just a truncated version of Part I as is the case with Gounod's *Faust.* The original version of *Mefistofele* was six hours in length and was very poorly received when it was premiered at the Teatro alla Scala on 5 March, 1868. Boito then began a lengthy process of revision in which half of the opera's original material was excised. *Mefistofele* was first performed in its revised version in 1875, was well received, and remains to this day as part of the standard opera repertoire.

Boito's experience with *Mefistofele,* while revealing his limitations as a composer, clearly demonstrated his formidable powers as a librettist. He was able to condense the many strands and subplots of Goethe's drama into a workable size for an opera, reducing the complexities of the original drama to an essential conflict between the real (as symbolized by Margherita) and the ideal (as represented by Helen of Troy). This ability to condense a complicated literary work to its essence also proved invaluable when Boito collaborated with Verdi on *Otello* and *Falstaff.* The latter opera, in fact, skillfully combines three Shakespeare plays, *Henry IV,* parts I and II, and *The Merry Wives of Windsor.* Another important factor in Boito's greatness as a librettist was his outstanding ability as a linguist. Being able to read Goethe and Shakespeare in their original languages gave Boito a distinct advantage over his colleagues since he was able to comprehend not only the author's precise poetic meanings but also the rhetoric and cadences of their languages. Finally, Boito's knowledge of musical composition gave him an intimate knowledge of the ways in which music and words are able to be combined successfully (or unsuccessfully as the case may be).

For all of his shortcomings as a composer, Boito did leave behind one masterpiece in *Mefistofele,* although it may be argued that this is the result of the opera's total effect being greater than the sum total of its musical, literary, and dramatic aspects. It is primarily as a librettist that Boito will be remembered and it is in this category that he ranks with such notable figures as Lorenzo da Ponte and Hugo von Hofmannsthal.

—William E. Grim

*   *   *

Arrigo Boito and Verdi at Sant' Agata

As critic, composer, and librettist, Arrigo Boito exerted a powerful influence over the direction of Italian opera in the second half of the nineteenth century. Although an overall assessment of all his work is difficult, there appears to be general agreement over Boito's achievements (or lack thereof) as a critic and a composer; as a librettist, Boito is generally praised, but the quality of his librettos for Verdi's final masterpieces, *Otello* and *Falstaff,* and their influence on Verdi's compositional thought, are still debated.

Boito's writings as a critic are notable principally for their erudition and wit and, especially early in his career, for their provocative attacks on the operatic establishment. As a member of the *scapigliatura,* Boito was one of the first to introduce and advocate Wagnerian ideals. The impact of his writings on nineteenth-century Italian opera composers, including Verdi, is documented by Walker and Budden.

Boito's talent for composition, however, is generally acknowledged to be lacking. Most critics today still agree with Verdi's judgement of 21 March 1877 that: "[Boito] has much talent, aspires to originality but succeeds only in being strange. He lacks spontaneity and he lacks invention." Andrew Porter found *Mefistofele* "untouched by poetry—except at one or two moments of lyric inspiration" (*The New Yorker,* April 17, 1978), and dismissed the music for *Nerone* outright: "The music was . . . dull. It is dull" (June 14, 1982). Yet William Ashbrook in his *New Grove* article has provided a mild defense, noting that despite profound flaws in the music "Boito's peculiar kind of eclecticism in *Nerone* has a morbid fascination. . . . Though *Nerone* has not held the stage, it remains a unique and awesome monument to the spirit of decadence in art."

The high quality of the librettos, though, makes the overall assessment of Boito's operas a more complex issue. Despite the harsh evaluation of the music for *Nerone,* Porter characterized the libretto as "enthralling, not dull at all: a mingling of mythical, classical, and Christian history, and of love pure with love polluted and perverse. The contrasts are violent" (*The New Yorker,* June 14, 1982). Most scholars find that the librettos to *Mefistofele* and *Nerone* represent radical departures from both the conventions of early nineteenth-century Italian opera (see Ashbrook 1988), and Boito's work for Ponchieli, Catalani, and Verdi. In particular, Patrick Smith (*The Tenth Muse*) notes a fundamentally "creative" (versus "adaptive": see below) aspect to these two librettos: "*Mefistofele* and *Nerone* inhabit another world entirely. The epic nature of their librettos is expressed not only in their scope but also in the[ir] grotesqueries. . . . In [these] operas the characters have shed the bonds of humanity and aspire to ideal characterizations" (p. 335). Ashbrook concurs but also notes that these highly innovative librettos remain perhaps idealized forms, impossible to set satisfactorily to music: "It is nonetheless dismaying to think that Boito ever seriously believed that his first sprawling text [to *Mefistofele*] could have served as the libretto to a viable opera." And Joseph Kerman (*Opera as Drama*) ties the value in the experiment of *Mefistofele* to Boito's progressive aesthetic stance: "[Boito] was well aware of the stress in later nineteenth-century opera. He had tried to meet it in *Mefistofele,* the most high-minded Italian opera since the days of Gluck; if he failed, he did so because of his insufficiencies as a composer, not because of any lack of boldness, skill, or understanding of the problem" (pp. 110–11).

More significant critical attention has been given to the librettos that Boito wrote on commission, specifically to those for Verdi's *Otello* and *Falstaff.* The discussion has tended either to praise as unique and innovative or attack as needlessly excessive the two unique features of Boito's work: 1) the design of the libretto—Boito's attempted fidelity to the original drama and his ability to establish a well-defined and workable operatic structure; and 2) the literary quality of the verse—specifically the metric flexibility and ingenuity of his verse and the often obscure and deliberately antique vocabulary. Scholars have also focused on broader issues such as the ability of the text to inspire the composer and the aesthetic ramifications in the choice of subject. Although critics have tended to agree on the general qualities of Boito's work, they have disagreed as to the import and relevance of the final product. The libretto for *Otello* has often come under scrutiny and criticism for oversimplification of Shakespeare's original characters. On the other hand, *Falstaff* is generally regarded as more appropriate for Boito's metric and poetic talents, thus resulting in a work "more truly Shakespearean than its Shakespearean sources" (G. Bradshaw, in *Giuseppe Verdi: Falstaff,* p. 152).

As stated above, Patrick Smith's survey presents the critical assessment in terms of adaption versus creation: Boito as a librettist followed the "adaptive ethos" integral to the Italian libretto, but "Boito as an artistic mind should have been [a creator]" (*The Tenth Muse,* p. 332). Therefore, according to Smith, any study of Boito must "concentrate on his [adaptive] strengths, yet do the man the credit of examining . . . just how much Boito the creator slipped through" (p. 333). Boito's adaptive abilities rest principally on "his secret of getting to the core of the story and the characters . . . [in] being able to express both in a dramatic and concise way," and in "demonstrat[ing] how a faithful adaption could be done" (p. 345, 342). The loss which occurs in the process is inevitable: "Verdi and Boito are hardly to blame [for the omissions in Otello]: the nineteenth century saw *Otello* as they adapted it" (p. 343). Smith also contends that the principal characteristics of Boito's verse—the tendency towards short lines, concentration on sibilants, sharp contrasts of vocal sounds and color, its pithy quality (the ability to sum up a scene in a single phrase), and its archaic language—were far from "mere intellectual gamesmanship. . . . What Boito was attempting to do in his works was not . . . to break open once and for all the closed-in work of the Italian libretto with its ingrained and ever-repeated formulas" (p. 338). Ultimately, "the music to which the text should be text can be inferred from the chameleon-like musicality of the words themselves" (p. 340).

Gabriele Baldini (*The Story of Giuseppe Verdi*) offers a markedly different assessment from Smith, finding that though "Boito was an artist and a man of letters . . . he never fully understood Verdi and so continually tried to bend him towards his own ideas (p. 71). For Baldini, it is Piave's librettos that are "best suited to Verdi's music." William Weaver (in "Verdi and His Librettists," *The Verdi Companion*) agrees that Boito's librettos have been overpraised: "Boito's verses are often unnecessarily elaborate, even murky; and some of his philosophical ideas—as in Iago's 'Credo,' which was totally of his own invention—are obvious and even banal." Graham Bradshaw and others find fault with the conventionalized dramaturgy of *Otello:* "[Boito and Verdi] ignored the complicating critical elements in Shakespeare's characterization. . . . larger issues are either contracted in Boito's libretto or appear, like Iago's over-explicit nihilism, in the simplified terms of Italian *melodramma*" (p. 155). Bradshaw also downplays Boito's contribution to *Falstaff:* "In preparing the libretto for *Falstaff,* Boito's decisive contribution was to present Verdi with six tautly related scenes. . . . The local literary miracles are a glorious bonus, to which Verdi was no less gloriously responsive; but in compressing and streamlining *The Merry Wives* [*of Windsor*], Boito was not so much pointing the way for Verdi as brilliantly clearing it" (p. 162).

Boito's defenders, such as Julian Budden (*The Operas of Verdi*) argue that the librettist's greatness resides in "his ability to aid and stimulate the thought of the composer" (p. 304); the choice of *Otello* is "precisely suited to Verdi's means. . . . Of all Shakespeare's dramas it is the best constructed and the most vividly theatrical (pp. 302-03). Hepokoski (*Giuseppe Verdi: Otello*) considers how the nineteenth-century view of Shakespeare affected Boito's decisions to simplify the principal characters in *Otello* and may have inspired Iago's "Credo." Hepokoski also focuses attention on the precise dramatic/musical implications behind the complexities of Boito's verse and how they were realized or ignored by Verdi. Hepokoski ventures that "we are much closer to understanding *Otello* when we realize that the poetry and the music present us with visions that differ in certain important respects; or, better, that the special quality of the opera is to be found in the interlocking of two powerful, gigantic casts of mind." Regarding *Falstaff,* Hepokoski (*Giuseppe Verdi: Falstaff*) points to the larger aesthetic issues as justification in considering certain aspects of Boito's libretto: "Surely one of the functions of th[e] playful manipulation of traditional Italian metres, as well as the references to such native writers as Boccaccio and Foscolo, was to insist on the essentially Italian character of Falstaff. For Boito, and probably for Verdi as well, the opera was at least partially an aesthetic statement, in many ways a counterthrust to . . . the immediate association of progress with German Wagnerianism and the recent vogue of *verismo* in Italy" (p. 33).

Despite the mixed critical assessment, Boito's powerful import on the great era of Italian opera is undeniable. Frank Walker closes his biography of Verdi (*The Man Verdi*) with Boito's death, declaring that Boito "had really fulfilled his destiny in causing the 'bronze colossus', as he called Verdi, to resound twice. He lives still, less as a composer than as a personality, an influence, a letter-writer, and as Verdi's incomparable librettist" (p.510).

—David Pacun

BONCI, Alessandro.

Tenor. Born 10 February 1870, in Cesena, near Rimini, Italy. Died 9 August 1940, in Viserba near Rimini. Studied with Carlo Pedrotti and Felice Coen in Pesaro, and with Enrico delle Sedie in Paris; debut as Fenton in *Falstaff* in Parma, 1896; sang at Teatro alla Scala in Bellini's *I puritani* and *La sonnambula,* 1897; Covent Garden debut as Rodolfo in *La Bohème,* 1900; first appeared in the United States in *I puritani* in 1906 at the opening of Hamilton's Manhattan Opera House, New York; debut as the Duke of Mantua at Metropolitan Opera, 1907, and remained there until 1910, where his roles included Rodolfo, Don Ottavio, and Wilhelm Meister in *Mignon;* also appeared in South America and Australia; in 1925 retired from the stage to teach in Milan.

*　　*　　*

The recorded legacy of Alessandro Bonci has a special importance in the history of operatic singing. Along with his close contemporary, Fernando de Lucia, Bonci was one of the last great exponents of the art of pure bel canto singing, although the pattern of their careers was quite different. De Lucia

Alessandro Bonci in *Un ballo in maschera*

became closely identified with contemporary composers, and ultimately the operas of Bellini and Donizetti played only a limited role in his career. Unlike his Neapolitan rival, Bonci made no serious attempt to sing other repertoire and was certainly never tempted by verismo. The result was a major and very long international career based on supreme, even unrivaled performances of a very small number of roles.

From the very outset of his career in 1896 Bonci was praised for the sheer beauty of his singing and his exquisite vocal control. Even though he was clearly indisposed at the time, Bonci's performance as Arturo in *I puritani* at his Teatro alla Scala debut early in 1897 led the critic of *Gazzetta Musicale di Milano* to refer to perfection in the art of singing. Bonci appeared subsequently at all the major Italian opera houses with his final performance at the Costanzi in Rome in 1923, although four years later he emerged from retirement to sing in Verdi's *Requiem* in his home town of Cesena.

Bonci's international career began in 1898 with a series of performances in Barcelona. After appearances in Lisbon, St. Petersburg and London, he crossed the Atlantic to join Hammerstein's Manhattan Company as principal tenor. The impressario's crying need throughout the years of his rivalry with the Metropolitan was for a tenor whose popularity could challenge Caruso's. Purely in regard to singing, Bonci might have solved the problem: Henry Krehbiel opined that in "nearly all things which enter into the art of vocalization he is incomparably finer than his rival. . . . . . his tones are impeccably pure, his command of breath perfect, his enunciation unrivalled". But no other tenor could compete with Caruso's overwhelming public support. Because Hammerstein's company included few tenors, Bonci was clearly overworked

during his first U.S. season, at the end of which he moved to the Metropolitan to join the same company as Caruso.

The high regard in which Bonci continued to be held by critics and musicians during his North American years is best revealed by a remarkable tribute by H. T. Parker: "a singer of delicate voice and perfectly mastered artistry. . . . . He is master of exquisitely sustained tone in flowing and songful passages. He can 'spin' his voice with a pliance that our generation has almost ceased to expect in singers of his sex. . . . a pure tenor voice that is an emotion in itself."

From 1909 Bonci's activities were to spread even further as he sang extensively throughout the Americas—in Mexico, Argentina, Uruguay and Brazil. But throughout all these activities his basic repertoire remained amazingly constant— Bellini's *I puritani* and *La sonnambula;* Donizetti's *Don Pasquale, L'elisir d'amore, La favorita* and *Lucia;* Rossini's *Il barbiere di Siviglia.* These seven operas by the three great masters of early nineteenth-century Italian opera were the core of his operatic career. Of Verdi there seems to have been little beyond *Rigoletto* and *Un ballo in maschera.* Bonci first appeared as Riccardo in the latter in Rome early in 1914 and it became a favored role. His final recorded excerpts are also from that opera. The only Puccini opera appears to have been *La Bohème,* while *Faust* embodied his main excursion into the French repertoire.

The bulk of Bonci's recorded output was for the Italian firm of Fonotipia, whose recordings of singers are among the best of the period. A recording of "A te o cara" from *I puritani* demonstrates all the virtues ascribed by H. T. Parker and suggest that Bonci must indeed have been the Arturo of the century. Equally outstanding is his performance of "Una furtiva lagrima" from *L'elisir d'amore.* On these Fonotipia discs Bonci offers some of the most naturally beautiful lyric singing ever recorded. If his later Columbia recordings lack the near vocal perfection of many of the Fonotipia recordings, some of the magic remained—even in the final concerted numbers, recorded electrically, from *Un ballo in maschera.*

A great singer, the shape and success of Bonci's career were inevitably determined by the times in which he lived and by the tastes of those times. Fifty years earlier he would have been the true successor to Rubini; fifty years later he would surely have partnered Callas and Sutherland in the great bel-canto revival.

—Stanley Henig

BONINSEGNA, Celestina.

Soprano. Born 26 February 1877, in Reggio Emilia. Died 14 February 1947, in Milan. Studied with Mattieli at Reggio Emilia; appeared as Norina in Reggio Emilia, 1892, then studied with Virginia Boccabadati in Pesaro, and made second debut in *Faust* in Bari, 1897; sang Rosaura in first performance in Rome of Mascagni's *Le maschere* (Costanzi), 1901; Covent Garden, 1904; Teatro alla Scala, 1904-5; Metropolitan Opera debut as Aida, 1906-7; Boston (1909-10), Barcelona (1912), St Petersburg (1913); retired from stage in 1923.

Publications

About BONINSEGNA: articles–

de Schauensee, M. "The Enigma of Boninsegna." *Opera News* 33 no. 16 (1965): 12.
Moran, W.R. "Celestina Boninsegna in the United States: Contemporary Critics Speak." *Record Collector* February (1960).

*   *   *

Celestina Boninsegna is an enigma among the singers of her age, a dramatic soprano of profound vocal endowment who knew only marginal success on the stage, but who managed to leave behind a large number of splendid recordings made for several companies between 1904 and about 1919—all of them documents befitting a major artist. Her career was something less than a pageant of great events. Throughout her prime she sang the most demanding roles alongside some of the most famous singers active at the time, and did so in some of the most prestigious houses in the world. But in all cases, though her repertory remained challenging and her

Celestina Boninsegna as Elena in *Mefistophele*

engagements reasonably constant, lasting tenure was denied her, and her stay in the important companies was short. She was acknowledged to be a fine singer, but her standing as a genuinely accomplished artist seems always to have been uncertain, and so she remained vulnerable to critical disparagement and public indifference throughout her career. There were always significant reservations, usually tendered in the form of deferential concessions to her rivals—and her career was certainly filled with rivals. She had the misfortune to arrive at the Teatro alla Scala during the heyday of Giannina Russ, whose repertory overlapped her own, and with whom she was often ruthlessly compared. At Covent Garden she had not only Russ to contend with, but also Destinn; and after only two performances of Aïda during her short stay at the Metropolitan Opera in 1906-1907 (with Russ again offering stiff competition from Hammerstein's Manhattan Opera House) she lost the role to Emma Eames, who was allowed to reclaim it for the balance of the season.

Boninsegna herself claimed that jealousy rather than simple professional rivalry smoldered at the foundation of the intrigues against her. Critic Max de Schauensee interviewed her in the summer of 1937, and suggested that the singer's reluctance to assert herself in these hostilities may well have accounted for her undistinguished career, aided by her obvious lack of driving ambition. Historian Leo Riemans, seeking some binding artistic explanation for Boninsegna's lackluster success, concluded that she was "essentially a 19th century artist lost in an unappreciative period . . . a singer first and foremost," doomed to fail in an age when verismo and its excesses prevailed and "good singing," as Riemans put it, "was not appreciated." In many respects this seems to accord with the contemporary view of Boninsegna as a somehow incomplete artist—a fine stylist with a strikingly beautiful voice who was never able to fully develop on the stage at a time when operatic histrionics were no longer a secondary concern. By some accounts her acting was squarely to blame, and was often criticized as primitive and subject to broad, overstated gestures and predictable stage business. Elsewhere, her physical appearance was seen as a major obstacle, and few critics were discrete enough to overlook it. She was a large woman, uncommonly tall, and dark complected, and this, coupled with her awkward bearing, was apparently unforgivable—especially in America, where the opera-going public had grown accustomed to her more glamourous colleagues.

Boninsegna generally confined herself to the earlier 19th-century repertory, though her voice would surely have been appropriate for the verismo roles of her generation. The closest she ever really came to a genuine patronage of the verismo repertory was Mascagni: Santuzza (*Cavalleria rusticana*) remained a fixture of her repertory. She created the role of Rosaura under the composer's direction in one of the six simultaneous premieres of his *Le maschera,* and later added *L'amico Fritz* and *Guglielmo Ratcliff.* Her entire repertory amounted to just over half a dozen Verdi heroines, the Marguerites of Gounod and Berlioz, Elena in Boïto's *Mefistofele,* Catalini's Wally, Elsa in *Lohengrin* (her only Wagnerian role), Valentine in Meyerbeer's *Les huguenots,* Ponchielli's Gioconda, and Donizetti's Maria di Rohan. Remarkably, Tosca was the only Puccini role she ever undertook on the stage. She was best suited to middle and late Verdi—specifically, the two Leonoras (*Il trovatore* and *La forza del destino*) and Aïda. In recordings from these works, she appears to have possessed in striking abundance the ideal attributes that once defined the "Verdi soprano"—the true spinto. Baritone Riccardo Stracciari described Boninsegna's voice as ". . . big and beautiful, all silver and velvet," and was moved to insist that she was the finest Aïda his memory could summon. The voice we hear is an unusually attractive one, dark and resonant, with a spectacular chest register and a clear, ringing top. Her passage between registers was cumbersome, however, and she often indulged in the kind of reckless leaps above and below the staff that left the breaks exposed. Her range, from A below middle C up two octaves, was not so exceptional in compass as it was in its expressive potential. The ease and precision with which she was able to negotiate the most difficult passage work, often lifting herself above the staff in the process without so much as a sign of forcing anywhere throughout the scale, was extraordinary by any standard, as was the smoothness of her tone, which lacked virtually any signs of the agitated tremolo so common among Italian dramatic sopranos of this and later periods.

Boninsegna's brief stay in America was symptomatic of her reception elsewhere. Contemporary assessments of her artistry are plentiful but wildly inconsistent. At the Met, her voice was dismissed as lacking sufficient weight and power to sustain the dramatic roles she began immediately to undertake (Aïda and Santuzza), and her careless management of vocal registers was considered annoying. Her phrasing, especially in Aïda, was similarly taken to task, one critic observing that she was constantly "chopping musical sentences into bits," a tendency that survives, regrettably, in many of her recordings. Kinder criticism insisted that her phrasing was merely conventional, lacking either musical or textual logic. Her seasons in Boston were a bit more encouraging but did not lead to her re-engagement. There, her voice was praised as powerful and resonant, even limpid, and her acting was often singled out as intelligent and intense—graceful enough, as one critic put it, "to distract from her physical proportions." Her Tosca was a highlight of the 1910 Boston season, and was compared favorably to Geraldine Farrar's.

It was as a recording artist that she enjoyed her greatest celebrity. In all she left just over 100 records, the first of them made in Milan for Gramophone & Typewriter Ltd. in 1904. She was recorded by Pathé in Paris and Milan between 1905 and about 1919, by Edison in London in 1911, and continued to record for the Gramophone Company through 1917. During her stay in the U.S., she made a number of discs for Columbia, and another set for them in Milan between 1910 and 1914. The repertory does little to supplement what she sang on the stage, and there is a good deal of repetition over many labels, but her greatest roles, Aïda and Verdi's two Leonoras, are well documented. The ensembles are among the most valuable of her recordings as they preserve some of the less well-traveled excerpts from these roles, but regrettably, she was given obscure partners such as Luigi Bolis, Emanuel Ischierdo, and Giovanni Vals more often than first-rate artists such as Fernando De Lucia and Francesco Cigada. Ironically, she has managed through her recordings to outmaneuver much of the competition, simply because her singing, the greatest of her assets, is allowed to stand alone, unburdened by contemporary judgements of her appearance: however "complete" the artistry of her rivals may have been in comparison to hers, their records clearly demonstrate that few had voices comparable to Boninsegna's.

—William Shaman

BORDONI, Faustina.

Mezzo-soprano. Born c. 1700, in Venice. Died 4 November 1781, in Venice. Married the composer Johann Adolf Hasse in 1730. Studied with M. Gasparini; debut in Pollarolo's *Ariodante*, Venice, 1716, and sang in Venice until 1725; Reggio, 1719; Modena, 1720; Bologna, 1721-2; Naples, 1721-3; Rome, 1722; German debut at Munich in P. Torri's *Griselda*, 1723; Parma, 1724-25; Vienna, 1725-6; London debut as Rossane in Handel's *Alessandro*, 1726; created several Handel roles, including Alcestis in *Admeto* (1727), Pulchiera in *Riccardo Primo* (1727), Elmira in *Siroe* (1728) and Elisa in *Tolomeo* (1728); Florence, 1728-9; Parma, 1729-30; Turin, 1729, 1731; Milan, 1730; Rome, 1731; Venice, 1729-32; in Dresden in 1731; Hasse's *Ciro riconosciuto* (1751) was her farewell to the stage; virtuosa da camera in Dresden until 1763; lived in Vienna, 1763-73, and then in Venice.

Publications

About BORDONI: books—

Tosi, P.F. *Opinioni de' cantore antichi e moderni*. Bologna, 1723; 1978; English translation 1742; 1969.

Niggle, Arnold. *Faustina Bordoni-Hasse: Eine Primadonna des achtzehnten Jahrhunderts*. Leipzig, 1880.

Hoegg, Margarete. *Die Gesangkunst der Faustina Hasse und der Sängerinnenwesen ihrer Zeit in Deutschland*. Königsbruck, 1931.

Mennicke, C. *Hasse und die Brüder Graun als Symphoniker*. Leipzig 1906.

Pleasants, H. *The Great Singers*. New York, 1966; 1981.

Faustina Bordoni, pastel portrait by Rosalba Carriera, c. 1720

articles–

Buelow, G.J. "A Lesson in Operatic Performance Practice by Madame Faustina Bordoni." In *Essays in Honor of Martin Bernstein.* New York, 1977.

unpublished–

LaRue, C.S. "The Composer's Choice: Aspects of Compositional Context and Creative Process in Selected Operas from Handel's Royal Academy Period." Ph.D. dissertation, University of Chicago, 1990.

Daughter of a patrician family in Venice, Bordoni received her early musical education there under Michelangelo Gasparini, who was primarily responsible for her vocal training, and Alessandro and Benedetto Marcello, to whom she undoubtedly owed some part of her musical expertise. From the time she made her début at sixteen in Pollarolo's *Ariodante,* she was an assured success and in Venice alone appeared in some thirty operas. Her later career took her all over Europe, and she made a lasting impression on London audiences as a protégée of Handel, her debut taking place in his *Alessandro* (5 May 1726).

She had a flexible and penetrating voice with a written compass of b'-flat to a", this last note being used sparingly. Later in life she would sing down to g or a', and though at no time could her voice be described as extensive, it was always completely at her service, especially in the clarity and speed of her ornamentation. Dr. Burney, who heard her in London, stressed her expertise in "a new kind of singing, by running divisions [rapid variations] with a neatness and velocity which astonished all who heard her. She had the art of sustaining a note longer . . . than any other singer, by taking her breath imperceptibly. Her beats and trills were strong and rapid; her intonation [was] perfect."

Her quick ability to memorize new roles made her an admirable operatic artist, and composers were only too anxious and willing to co-operate with her, despite a schedule of engagements almost as dense as that of many modern divas. The Jesuit musical historian Esteban Arteaga, a friend of Padre Martini, listed qualities corresponding almost exactly to those mentioned by Burney, adding that "a thousand other qualities contributed to inscribe her name among the first singers in Europe."

At the age of thirty she began what was virtually a new career, meeting in her home town a German phenomenon, Johann Adolph Hasse, only one year older than she was, and fully conversant with the Italian tongue through having studied with Alessandro Scarlatti. They married in 1730 and made an admirable pair. Hasse composed for Faustina a series of operas beginning with *Artaserse* (first version) and *Dalisa,* both performed in Venice. Moving to Dresden in 1731, Hasse held the post of court music director while she served as *virtuosa da camera* (chamber singer) until 1763, when both were dismissed by King Frederick as an economy measure.

They spent the rest of their lives in Vienna and Venice, and were visited in the former city by Burney who found "a short, brown, sensible, and lively old woman" with "good remains, for seventy-two, of that beauty for which she was so much celebrated in her youth, but none of her fine voice."

It was Quantz who praised not only her abilities as a virtuoso singer but her powers as an actress. "As she perfectly possessed that flexibility of muscles and features, which constitutes face-playing, she succeeded equally well in furious, amorous, and tender parts; in short, she was born for singing and for acting." Her portrait was twice painted by Rosalba Carriera, and later by Torelli; caricatures also exist by Zanetti, Ricci and Ghezzi.

—Denis Stevens

BORGATTI, Giuseppe

Tenor. Born 17 March 1871 in Cento. Died 18 October 1950 in Reno, Lago Maggiore. Married his teacher Elena Cuccoli; also studied with Alessandro Busi at Bologna and Carlo d'Ormeville in Milan; debut in *Faust,* Castelfranco Veneto, 1892, and then performed in *Fra Diavolo* and *Don Pasquale* there; title role in *Lohengrin,* Milan, 1894; spent 1894-95 in Madrid; in St Petersburg, 1895; created title role in Giordano's *Andrea Chénier,* Teatro alla Scala, 1896; best known as a singer of Wagner, but also appeared as Faust in Boito's *Mefistofele,* Alfredo in *La traviata,* and in Giordano's *Siberia,* among others; retired from the stage in 1914 because of glaucoma.

Publications

By BORGATTI: books–

La mia vita d'artista. Bologna, 1927.

About BORGATTI: books–

Gara, E. *Le grandi voci.* Rome, 1964.

articles–

Gara, E. "Il San Paolo dei wagneriani, Giuseppe Borgatti." In *La lettura,* Milan, 1938.

Giuseppe Borgatti was Italy's first Wagnerian tenor. When Arturo Toscanini introduced Wagner's *Siegfried* and *Tristan und Isolde* to the Teatro alla Scala audience, Borgatti was his tenor of choice, and he proved to combine the power of the German Heldentenor with the lyrical style of the Italian tradition.

Borgatti was born in Cento, Italy, in 1871, and reportedly was working as a mason when his operatic potential was discovered. His operatic debut came in 1892 as Faust in Gounod's opera in Castelfranco Veneto, where he also sang Ernesto in Donizetti's *Don Pasquale* and Auber's *Fra Diavolo.* His first Wagnerian role was Lohengrin, which he sang at the Teatro dal Verme in Milan in 1894. Performances of the tenor roles in Verdi's *Falstaff,* Donizetti's *Lucia di Lammermoor,* and Puccini's *Manon Lescaut* followed, and Borgatti also made his first trip to South America for performances in the major Italian theaters there.

Borgatti's Teatro alla Scala career lasted from 1896 until 1914. In 1896 he created the title role in Giordano's *Andrea Chénier* as a last-minute replacement for Alfonso Garulli, a performance that was favorably received by the composer.

That same year Toscanini conducted excerpts from *Götterdäm-merung* in a concert at La Scala with Borgatti in the role of Siegfried. Toscanini's 1899 performances of *Siegfried,* the first in Italy, featured Borgatti in the title role.

Borgatti had been scheduled to sing in the first Italian performance of *Tristan und Isolde* at the season opening of La Scala in December 1900, but his illness led to the replacement of *Tristan* with Puccini's *La bohème* (the performance in which Enrico Caruso made his La Scala debut). After his recovery, Borgatti sang his (and Italy's) first Tristan at the end of December opposite Amelia Pinto; at a later performance Wagner's son Siegfried praised the high quality of the performance. He sang the role again during the 1907 season. During the summer of 1901 Toscanini brought some of La Scala's greatest singers, among them Borgatti and Caruso, to Buenos Aires. Borgatti accompanied Toscanini to Argentina again in 1904. These performances were followed by more *Siegfrieds* in Bologna, again under Toscanini's baton. Back at La Scala, Borgatti appeared in the first Italian performances of *Das Rheingold* in 1903, in the role of Loge, again under Toscanini. In 1910 he again appeared as Siegfried, this time under Tullio Serafin. In 1913 Borgatti sang his first complete *Parsifal* at La Scala, an opera that was mounted despite Cosima Wagner's stricture against performances of the work outside Bayreuth; Borgatti had previously sung the role in a concert performance of act III in 1903. He repeated his Parsifal under Serafin in 1914.

Borgatti sang a relatively small number of roles outside the Wagner canon at La Scala. In 1900 he performed the title role in Galeotti's *Anton.* Later that year, for the Milanese premiere of Puccini's *Tosca,* which had been performed for the first time two months earlier in Rome, Toscanini again chose Borgatti to be his tenor. In 1901 he performed the role of Astarat in Goldmark's *Die Königen von Saba.* On the occasion of the death of Verdi in 1901, the Teatro alla Scala mounted a memorial program featuring excerpts from ten Verdi operas; the conductor was Toscanini, the tenors Caruso, Tamagno (who had created the role of Otello), and Borgatti. Nineteen hundred and six saw his first assumption of Herod in Richard Strauss's *Salome.*

Borgatti made a few recordings during the first decade of the twentieth century. These include Otello's "Niun mi tema," "Am stillen Herd" from Wagner's *Die Meistersinger,* "Winterstürme" from Wagner's *Die Walküre,* and "Atmest du nicht" from Wagner's *Lohengrin.* These recordings offer evidence that the demands that Wagner's orchestration makes on singers need not be incompatible with a relatively light voice or a lyrical approach. Paying attention to phrasing and employing the legato characteristic of the Italian style, Borgatti succeeded in singing Wagner with expression and a variety of color. Although his voice apparently was not large, he had the technique to produce his tone so as to be heard over the Wagnerian orchestra.

Deteriorating eyesight curtailed Borgatti's singing career; he had left the operatic stage by 1914, but continued singing in recital until 1928.

—Michael Sims

BORGIOLI, Dino.

Tenor. Born 15 February 1891, in Florence. Died 12 or 13 September 1960. Married singer Patricia Moore. Studied with Eugenio Giachetti, Florence; debut as Arturo in Bellini's *I puritani* in Milan, 1914; Teatro alla Scala debut as Ernesto in *Don Pasquale,* 1918; Covent Garden debut as Edgardo, 1925; San Francisco debut as Cavaradossi, 1933; Metropolitan Opera debut as Rodolfo, 1934; appeared at Glyndebourne as Ottavio, 1937.

* * *

By the time Dino Borgioli made his operatic debut in 1914 in Bellini's *I puritani,* the repertoire of the principal opera houses of the world had undergone a transformation. The dual influence of the concepts of Wagnerian music drama along with the dramatic style of the late Verdi had produced the Italian verismo school with its more powerful orchestration. Dramatic declamation combined with sheer power became the new standard of vocalization, and the tenor who popularized and significantly changed the taste and critical evaluation of vocal artistry was, of course, Enrico Caruso.

The older school of bel canto (beautiful singing, a style characterized by brilliant vocal display and purity of tone) of the early 19th century and the works of Rossini, Bellini and Donizetti, was no longer fashionable. Rossini had principally written for the *tenore leggiero,* a light tenor voice with emphasis on agility. The style of Bellini and Donizetti produced the *tenore di grazia,* emphasizing gracefulness. During the period between the two world wars (1917-1939) only two Italian artists who represented the style of *leggiero* and *di grazia* achieved international recognition; the more famous was Tito Schipa, the other was Dino Borgioli.

Dino Borgioli as Des Grieux in Massenet's *Manon*

Although Borgioli quickly established himself as an artist of the first rank, debuting at the Teatro alla Scala as Ernesto (*Don Pasquale*) in 1918, two roles in which he had established his reputation, in smaller houses, Fernando (*La favorita*) and Arturo (*I puritani*) were in operas that were no longer given during his career. Those works that endured, Rossini's *Il barbiere di Siviglia,* Bellini's *La sonnambula,* Donizetti's *L'elisir d'amore, Don Pasquale, Lucia di Lammermoor,* along with Verdi's lyrical tenor repertoire, *La traviata* and *Rigoletto,* provided the basic outlet for Borgioli's talent in operas of the older Italian school. Fortunately, the genre of lyric French opera represented by Massenet (*Manon*), Thomas (*Mignon*) and Bizet (*Les pêcheurs de perles*) was also congenial to his talent. Puccini's *La Bohème, Tosca,* and Mascagni's *L'amico Fritz* were the more modern operas in which he sang. The Mozart revival of the late 1920s added the role of Ottavio (*Don Giovanni*) to his repertoire.

Borgioli was not a prolific recorder. In 1923-24 he made 27 acoustical sides of operatic arias and duets, and in 1926-29 another thirty electrical sides, again of arias and duets, all principally from the repertoire listed above. Fortunately, he made two commercially issued recordings of complete operas, *Il barbiere di Siviglia* (1928) and *Rigoletto* (1930) both with Mercedes Capsir and Riccardo Stracciari. There is a published air check of a Salzburg *Don Giovanni* (1937) and a dim sounding air check of act I of *Tosca* with Claudia Muzio— the broadcast of the opening night of the San Francisco War Memorial Opera House on October 15, 1932.

In a review of the *Barbiere* recording, Irving Kolodin noted: "Capsir is a skillful singer, and Borgioli (on these discs at least) a great one." In correct Rossini style Borgioli sings the high lying *roulades* (runs) in head voice, cleanly articulating each note without ever resorting to aspirates. It is regrettable that he was restricted to the then customary simplified version of "Ecco ridente in cielo." However, in "Se il mio nome" he exhibits a fine trill and a marvelous *diminuendo* (the technique of beginning a note full voice and gradually diminishing the sound quality on the same note). In 1945, Philip L. Miller, in another review of this recording, hailed Borgioli (perhaps prematurely) "as a representative of a vanishing art."

Borgioli's lyrical Duke in the *Rigoletto* recording is characterized by a graceful "Questa o quella," marked by the appropriate chuckle and a marvelous *diminuendo.* In the love duet, at "Ah inseparabile" through the first part of "E il sol dell'anima," his dulcet use of *mezza voce* (half voice) avidly portrays the young seducer "whispering sweet nothings into Gilda's ears." In "La donna è mobile," his repeated *diminuendos* on "d'accento" are ravishing. The air check of *Don Giovanni,* although of variable pitch, clearly shows why he was regarded as an exemplary Don Ottavio.

Borgioli was a "long" tenor who had easy access to high notes. He is reputed to have been one of the few tenors to have sung the role of Arturo (*I puritani*) in the original key. His voice itself cannot be described as mellifluous. The chest register is bright sounding with a tinge of *squillo* (ringing, blasting quality). The head voice is always exquisitely floated. Thus critics have suggested that his *legato* (connected, smooth method of singing) is questionable, because the ringing bright quality of the chest voice contrasts with the soft quality of the head voice, so that the sound quality is not equalized throughout its range. However, his excellent technique enabled him to excel in the *diminuendo,* and to pass on one note from the bright chest register to the floating head voice smoothly, without any break.

After his retirement from the opera stage in 1939, Borgioli continued to concertize and broadcast over the BBC. Air checks of his concerts as late as 1950 show that he preserved his voice. His approach to music was intellectual; he disdained the popular Neapolitan song repertoire in favor of classical *arie antiche* and art songs of contemporary composers.

His eminence in his own day is confirmed by the list of star prima donnas with whom he sang: Toti Dal Monte, Claudia Muzio, Rosa Ponselle, Lucrezia Bori, Eva Turner and Conchita Supervia. He preserved the bel canto style of his predecessors, notably Fernando De Lucia and Alessandro Bonci, in an age when the style almost did become "a vanishing art," and thus helped pave the way for his successors in the current revival of bel canto.

—Bob Rose

BORI, Lucrezia [Lucrecia Borja y Gonzalez de Riancho].

Soprano. Born 4 December 1887, in Valencia. Died 14 May 1960, in New York. Studied at Valencia Conservatory and with Melchiorre Vidal in Milan; debut as Micaela in *Carmen* in Rome, 1908; at Teatro alla Scala in 1909; sang in Paris in 1910; New York Metropolitan Opera debut in *Manon Lescaut,* 1912; singer at Metropolitan Opera, 1912-36; on the board of directors of the Met, 1935-60.

Lucrezia Bori as Manon

Publications

About BORI: books–

Gatti-Casazza, G. *Memories of Opera.* New York, 1941.
Seltsam, W.H. *Metropolitan Opera Annals.* New York, 1947.
Lauri-Volpi, G. *Voci parallele.* Milan, 1955.
Marion, J.F. *Lucrezia Bori of the Metropolitan Opera.* New York, 1962.
Rasponi, L. *The Last Prima Donnas.* New York, 1982.

articles–

Richards, J.B. "Lucrezia Bori." *Record Collector* 9 (1954): 105.
Celletti, R. "Lucrezia Bori." *Musica e dischi* 107 (1955): 10.

*   *   *

The greatest triumph of Lucrezia Bori's career, notwithstanding the myriad times that the love of her exceptionally affectionate public flowed toward her across the footlights, actually took place offstage. This protracted victory over adversity began in 1915, when nodules developed on the twenty-eight-year-old soprano's vocal cords and the inescapable operation to remove them proved unsuccessful, or at least unskillful. A Milanese surgeon tried another procedure in 1916, and afterwards told Bori that a long silence was the only hope for restoration of the voice. Her lengthy ordeal and eventual return to singing with absolutely unimpaired resources constitutes one of the most famous chapters in operatic lore.

Lucrecia Borja y Gonzales de Riancho originated at Valencia, where her initial studies took place at the local conservatory. After further instruction in Italy, she made her operatic debut in Rome in 1908 as Micaela in *Carmen*. Here she adopted the Italian spelling of her first name and altered that of the last in order to minimize her connection with the sinister Borgias, from whom she was in fact one of the many Spanish descendants.

Bori did not have to struggle for recognition of her special, though fragile, gifts. She was at the Teatro alla Scala within a year of her debut (and sang Octavian in the Italian premiere of *Der Rosenkavalier* there in 1911), and on the Metropolitan Opera's first European visit in 1910 she was engaged to replace Lina Cavalieri as Manon Lescaut in five performances in Paris. This role served as well for her American debut with the company on opening night of the 1912 season.

The virtues that won for Bori the deep affection of the American audience were evident from the outset in what Henry Krehbiel, reviewing her first New York performance, called "the real fineness of her vocal art . . . an exquisite exhibition of legato singing . . . exquisite diction, impeccable intonation and moving pathos."

Bori's last appearance prior to her surgery was with the Metropolitan in Atlanta (Fiora in *L'amore dei tre re*, 30 April 1915). After the second operation, she had the devotion and the discipline to remain completely silent for an entire year and to speak in no more than a whisper for most of the next, so that healing might be without further intervention or incident. A deeply devout Roman Catholic—despite rumors of a romantic entanglement with tenor and later Metropolitan Opera general manager Edward Johnson, those closest to Bori believe her to have been celibate—her faith sustained her through the anguish and uncertainty of her period of enforced silence. Whatever brought on the problem (which developed shortly after she took on the title role of Mascagni's

Iris), when Bori was able to return to singing she consecrated her life completely to her art and to her public. She tested the waters first in the 600-seat theater at Monte Carlo in 1919 (as Zerlina in *Don Giovanni*) and returned to New York as Mimì (*La Bohème*) on 28 January 1921. Every performance thereafter was for her the repayment of a nonreimbursable debt to God and to those who gave her their devotion by coming to hear her sing. The love affair between Bori and the American public (her career after this was almost exclusively in the United States) continued unimpeded until her formal farewell to the stage on 29 March 1936. At that time, W. J. Henderson called her "America's opera sweetheart" and said that "there was every reason for thanksgiving that we had all been so fortunate as to live in Miss Bori's time." (She actually sang once more, a Mimì four days later with the Metropolitan in Baltimore.)

The soprano's recordings reveal a voice of warm and beautiful timbre, an unfailingly affecting delivery, some brilliance when necessary (though her preference was for repertory short on this requirement), a complete understanding of style, emotional power in tragedy, and a quite irresistible charm that suffuses every measure. In the theater she was recognized as a superb and nuanced actress-interpreter equally at home as Mélisande and Despina, Mimì and Mignon, no less persuasive in *Peter Ibbetson* than in *La vida breve*.

When the Great Depression hit, Bori was still a prominent artist in the company, but she spent all of her free time campaigning for funds to save the Metropolitan and "keep opera going." She became an indefatigable letter-writer and an ardent speech-maker who would appear at any meeting or before any group, and opera lovers heard her speaking voice for the first time in eloquent appeals over the radio. Even before retirement, she became the first singer *and* the first woman elected to the Metropolitan's board of directors. After she stopped singing, she fulfilled her vow to serve the company for the rest of her life by doing so up until the very day of her death from a brain hemorrhage. She remained on the board until that day, and was also honorary chairman of the Metropolitan Opera Guild (1936-60, with a term as active chairman 1943-48). Moreover, she was for many years president of the Bagby Music Lovers Foundation, which provided financial assistance to her less fortunate colleagues in retirement.

She remembered her own people as well, and worked tirelessly to raise relief funds following the devastating floods in Valencia in 1957. Three years later, thousands lined the streets there to pay homage and watch the soprano's funeral cortège, in a demonstration as great as that for any political figure. Franco bestowed upon her posthumously the Gran Cruz de la Beneficencia, the highest honor awarded in Spain for charitable work. "It is because of her that I have a roof over my head" said one mourner. Anyone working inside the old Metropolitan Opera House that day could legitimately have said the same thing.

—Bruce Burroughs

—————

BORIS GODUNOV.

Composer: Modest Musorgsky.

Librettist: Modest Musorgsky (after Pushkin and Karamzin).

First Performance: St Petersburg, Maryinsky Theater, 8 February 1874; revised posthumous production, Leningrad, 16 February 1928.

Roles: Boris Godunov (bass-baritone); Fyodor (mezzo-soprano); Xenia (soprano); Nurse (contralto or mezzo-soprano); Prince Shuisky (tenor); Brother Pimen (bass); Gregory Otrepiev, later The Pretender, Dimitri (tenor); Marina Mnishek (mezzo-soprano or soprano); Rangoni (baritone or bass); Varlaam (bass); Missail (tenor); Innkeeper (mezzo-soprano); Simpleton (tenor); Shchelkalov (baritone); Nikitich (bass); A Boyar (tenor); Lavitsky (bass); Cherniavsky (bass); Officer of Frontier Guard (bass); Mityukh (baritone); A Woman (soprano); chorus (SSAATTBB).

Publications

books–

Godet, Robert. *En marge de Boris Godounof.* 2 vols., Paris and London, 1926.
Belyayev, Victor. *"Boris Godounov" in its Genuine Version.* London, 1928.
———. et al. *Boris Godunov: stat'i i issledovaniya.* Moscow, 1930.
Nilsson, Kurt. *Die Rimskij-Korsakoffsche Bearbeitung des "Boris Godunoff" von Mussorgskij als Objekt der vergleichenden Musikwissenschaft.* Münster, 1937.

Lloyd-Jones, David. *Boris Godunov: Critical Commentary.* London, 1975.
Schandert, M. *Das Problem der originalen Instrumentation des "Boris Godunov" von M.P. Mussorgski.* Hamburg, 1979.
Le Roux, Maurice. *Moussorgski: Boris Godounov.* Paris, 1980.
Csampai, Attila, and Dietmar Holland, eds. *Mussorgsky, Modest. Boris Godunow. Texte—Materialien—Kommentare.* Reinbek, 1982.
John, Nicholas, ed. *Modest Petrovich Mussorgsky: "Boris Godunov".* Libretto translation by David Lloyd-Jones. *English National Opera Guide* 11. London and New York, 1982.
Emerson, Caryl. *"Boris Godunov": Transposition of a Russian Theme.* Bloomington, Indiana, 1986.

articles–

Abraham, Gerald. "Mussorgsky's 'Boris' and Pushkin's." *Music and Letters* 26 (1945): 31.
Nagy, Ferenc. "És a Borisz kié?" *Muzsika* 21 (1978): 29.
Oldani, Robert W. "Boris Godunov and the Censor." *19th Century Music* 2 (1978-79): 245.
Avant-scène opéra May-August (1980) [*Boris Godounov* issue].
Taruskin, Richard. "Musorgsky vs. Musorgsky: The Versions of *Boris Godunov*." *19th Century Music* 8 (1984): 91.

Boris Godunov, **with Paata Burchuladze in the title role, Royal Opera, 1991**

Oldani, Robert W. "Musorgsky's Boris on the Stage of the Maryinski Theater: A Chronicle of the First Production." *Opera Quarterly* summer (1986).

*   *   *

The intriguing sound of Musorgsky's *Boris Godunov* has captured the attention of audiences for well over one hundred years. Yet the opera in its initial form (1869) was considered inadequate by the Board of Directors of the Imperial Theater. The Committee's rejection of the 1869 version had to do primarily with the absence of a significant female role.

Soon after Musorgsky received word of the committee's criticism, he added the Polish act, which revolves around the Princess Marina. Though the act set in Poland appears only in the revision of 1872, there is evidence that Musorgsky had thought of it from the beginning. In addition to the Polish act, Musorgsky added the Revolution scene (act IV, scene i), also known as the "Scene Near Kromy." He deleted the St Basil scene and rewrote most of act II (Boris and his children).

After completing the revisions of 1872, Musorgsky won the approval of the Committee for a performance of *Boris,* which took place on 8 February 1874 at the Maryinsky Theater in St Petersburg, with Melnikov as Boris. According to David Lloyd-Jones, the definitive version of the opera was performed only twenty-six times between 1874 and 1882 in St Petersburg, the Revolution scene being omitted in the last fourteen of these; and then ten times in Moscow between 1888 and 1890.

In commemoration of Paul Lamm's 1928 edition of *Boris Godunov,* a performance of it was given on 16 February 1928 in Leningrad. One of the photographs of scenes from this production is entitled: "The Square by the Cathedral of St Basil at Moscow. The starving people implore the Czar to give them bread." The St Basil scene which Musorgsky excluded from the premiere performance of the opera in 1874 made its debut in the 1928 performance in Leningrad. Originally the St Basil scene came in the last act, just before the death of Boris. In the 1872 version, however, the St Basil scene was replaced by the Revolution scene, which Musorgsky placed after Boris' death. Except for the not very long lament of the Simpleton, almost the same in both versions, there is little in common between these scenes in dramatic or musical content. Still, they share some elements of style, modal textures being the more prevalent. Both close with the Simpleton singing, "Weep, weep, Russian folk, poor starving folk." In productions which include the St Basil scene (1869) as well as the Revolution scene (1872), the song of the Simpleton, which appears in both scenes, becomes a kind of ritornello mourning the vicissitudes of Mother Russia.

The St Basil scene is closer to Pushkin than the Revolution scene. In musical style, the Revolution scene is closer to the Polish act, both having been added for 1872. The death of Boris, composed in 1869, is in turn stylistically closer to the St Basil scene, also composed in 1869. Just before Boris dies, the static harmonies of the Coronation scene are heard; through rhythmic transformation they become his death knell, reminding us also of the chiming of the clock. The music introducing Boris' Coronation is unusual for the feeling of stasis created by two chords of like quality repeated over and over, imitating the sound of clanging bells.

The 1869 version, then, is the more individualistic and original in style. On the other hand, the 1872 version is dramatically more complete and musically more varied. The composer has expanded his scheme of events, adding the clock scene, the Innkeeper's song, the Polish act, and the

Revolution scene, all of which increase the scope and human interest of the work. Cosmopolitan musical style makes the revised score more varied, interesting, and accessible to a general audience.

—Maureen A. Carr

BORKH, Inge [real name Ingeborg Simon].

Soprano. Born 26 May 1917, in Mannheim. Married the singer Alexander Welitsch. Studied acting in Max Reinhardt seminary in Vienna and singing in Milan and at the Salzburg Mozarteum; debut in Lucerne, 1940 or 1941, and was engaged there 1941-44; first major success as Magda Sorel in *The Consul* in Basel, 1951; appeared in Munich, Vienna, Berlin, Stuttgart and London; U.S. debut in San Francisco as Elektra in 1953 and she returned to San Francisco as Verdi's Lady MacBeth in 1955; debut at Metropolitan Opera as Salome, 1958; Dyer's wife in first Covent Garden performance of *Die Frau ohne Schatten,* 1967.

Publications

About BORKH: books–

Celletti, R. *Le grandi voci.* Rome, 1964.

*   *   *

Inge Borkh as Elektra

Had Inge Borkh been singing at almost any other time in recent history, it seems certain that her fame would have been far greater. But it was perhaps her misfortune that she appeared on the scene during what may have been the last golden age for dramatic sopranos. Much of her Strauss and Wagner repertoire was shared with, among others, the internationally-celebrated Birgit Nilsson, whose clarion trumpet of a voice is certainly unique in our time, as well as with Astrid Varnay, whose vocal gifts were not the equal of Nilsson's, but whose intensely charismatic theatricality was much beloved by critics and audiences alike. And the years during which Borkh sang much of the Italian lyrico-spinto repertoire were also the years of Callas and Tebaldi, Milanov and Price. In this very distinguished company Borkh's own achievements tended to get lost, and she seemed a less immediately distinctive artist than these other singers.

Yet as we listen to the recordings which Borkh has left us, we realize that she possessed a rare excellence all her own. The breadth of her repertoire especially impresses; few singers have performed both German and Italian roles with equal security, and Borkh sounds absolutely idiomatic in both. She is one of a very small number of German sopranos who might actually be mistaken for an Italian when she performs Italian music; the language, although slightly accented, is stressed and the words pointed with the fluency and ease of a native speaker. Even more, Borkh's positive and natural way of sculpting the musical line is in the grand tradition of true bel canto singing. Recorded recitals preserve arias from *Un ballo in maschera, Andrea Chénier, Macbeth, Cavalleria rusticana* and more—a broad cross-section of the lyrico-spinto and dramatic repertoires. In all of these, Borkh's performances are warmly voiced and boldly projected. The tone itself is less immediately recognizable than some of the more famous voices of the time, but ironically Borkh's performance may in fact be better sung and as strongly characterized as several of the others. Her complete recording of *Turandot* is a good example of Borkh's artistry in Italian music. While Borkh lacks the gleaming top notes which are so exciting in Nilsson's performance of the role, she presents a more specific and in many ways more interesting interpretation of the troubled princess. And on the other hand, if Borkh's handling of text is almost inevitably less detailed than that of Maria Callas, her handling of the fearsome tessitura is far more secure.

As formidable as many of Borkh's performances in Italian music are, it is in the German repertoire that she especially excelled, and here her recordings need fear no comparisons. A radio transcription of her Sieglinde is predictably strongly sung and touchingly characterized, with Borkh skillfully projecting the fragility and nervousness of the young girl. She is even more impressive in an off-the-air performance of Salome from the Metropolitan Opera, excitingly conducted by Dimitri Mitropolous. Critics who saw Borkh perform this role in the theater invariably speak of her very fine acting, and this certainly comes through on purely aural terms. A comparison with the celebrated Salome of Ljuba Welitsch is revealing— where Welitsch is more overtly dramatic (sometimes rather too much so), her electrifying performance is achieved through some of the most idiosyncratic singing in memory; in truth, she often allows the musical line to all but vanish in search for "character." Borkh is equally vivid and her singing is far more consistent and true to Strauss' score. Her musical scrupulousness is, in fact, one of Borkh's great distinctions in this repertoire—like Callas, she never alters or abandons the musical line for dramatic effect and instead chooses to create character through the written notes.

Nowhere are these virtues more welcome than in the role of Elektra, and this portrayal was probably Borkh's crowning achievement. There exists a famous record of scenes conducted by Fritz Reiner, as well as a complete performance of the opera under Karl Böhm and several live recordings which are in wide circulation. In all of them Borkh distinguishes herself first by truly singing the difficult Strauss music, the tone always rich and firm, the awkward intervals meticulously observed. And once again always within the confines of her vocal achievement, Borkh is among the most intense and heart-wrenching of Elektras. Her performance is a splendid achievement, setting a standard for many years to come in this most difficult and exacting of operatic roles.

—David Anthony Fox

BORODIN, Alexander (Porfirevich).

Composer. Born 12 November 1833, in St. Petersburg. Died 27 February 1887, in St. Petersburg. Married: Catherine Sergeyevna Protopopova, a pianist, 1863. Attended the Academy of Medicine in St. Petersburg, 1850-56; learned to play the flute and the piano and composed some small piano pieces; graduated with honors from the Academy and joined the faculty, 1856; doctorate in chemistry, 1858; met Balakirev, 1862, and became involved in the Russian nationalist movement.

Operas

The Bogatïrs (Bogatïri), V.A. Krïlov, 1867, Moscow, Bol'shoy, 18 November 1867.
The Tsar's Bride (Tsarskaya nevesta), Borodin (after L.A. Mey), 1867-68 [lost].
Mlada (opera-ballet, with Rimsky-Korsakov, Cui, and Mussorgsky), Krïlov (after a scenario by S.A. Gedeonov), 1872 [not performed].
Prince Igor (Kniaz' Igor') (begun 1869, completed posthumously by Rimsky-Korsakov and Glazunov), Borodin (after a scenario by V.V. Stasov based on the medieval chronicle *Tale of Igor's Campaign*), St Petersburg, Mariinsky, 16 November 1890.

Other works: orchestral works, including symphonies, chamber music, piano works, and vocal pieces.

Publications

By BORODIN: books–

Pisma [letters]. Edited by S.A. Dianin, 3 vols. Moscow, 1928-50.

About BORODIN: books–

Dianin, S.A., editor. *Borodin: Zhizneopisaniye, materiali, dokumenti* [Biography, Materials, Documents]. Moscow, 1955; revised 2nd edition, 1969; English translation, 1963.
Bobeth, Marek. *Borodin und seine Opera "Fürst Igor": Geschichte - Analyse - Konsequenzen.* Munich, 1982.
Tigurovskii, N.A., and Yu I. Solov'ev. *Aleksandr Porfir'evich Borodin—A Chemist's Biography.* Translated by Charlene Steinburg and George B. Kauffmann. Berlin, 1988.

articles–

Abraham, Gerald. "Prince Igor." In *Studies in Russian Music,* 119. London, n.d.

Glazunov, A.K. "Zapiski o redaktsii Knzazya Igorya Borodina" [notes on the editing of *Prince Igor*]. *Russkaya muzikal'naya gazeta* 3 (1896): 155.

_____. "The History of 'Prince Igor'." In *On Russian Music,* 147. London. 1939.

Dmitriyev, A. "K istorii sozdaniya operï A.P. Borodina Knayaz' Igor" [history of the composition of *Prince Igor*]. *Sovetskaya muzyka* no. 11 (1950): 82.

Lloyd-Jones, D. "The Bogatyrs: Russia's First Operetta." *Monthly Musical Record* 89 (1959): 123.

Listova, N.A. "Iz istorii sozdaniya operï *Knyaz' Igor*' A.P. Borodina" [history of the composition of *Prince Igor*] *Soobshcheniya Instituta istorii iskusstv* 15 (1959): 36.

Kiselyov, V.A., et al., eds. "Noviye pis'ma Borodina" [new Borodin letters]. In *Muzikal' noye nasledstvo* 3, edited by M.P. Alexeyev and others, 208. Moscow, 1970.

Kiselyov, V.A. "Stsenicheskaya istoriya pervoy postanovki Knyazya Igorya." [history of the first performance of *Prince Igor*]. In *Muzikal' noye nasledstvo* 3, edited by M.P. Alexeyev and others, 284. Moscow, 1970.

Abraham, Gerald. "Arab Melodies in Rimsky-Korsakov and Borodin." *Music and Letters* 56 (1975): 313.

Seaman, Gerald. "The Rise of Slavonic Opera, I." *New Zealand Slavonic Journal* 2 (1978): 1.

Vyzgo-Ivanova, Irina and Ivanov-Ehvet, A. "Esce Raz ob istokah *Knjazja Igoria*" [More of the sources of *Prince Igor*] *Sovetskaya muzyka* 4 (1982): 89.

Lamm, Pavel. "K podlinnomu tekstu *Knjazja Igoria*." [toward an authentic text of *Prince Igor*]. *Sovetskaya muzyka* 12 (1983): 104.

Temirbekova, Alma. "Iz istorii russko - kazahskih muzykal' nyh svjazej" [historical connections between *Prince Igor* and Kayah music]. *Prostor* 1 (1983): 194.

Seaman, Gerald. "Borodin's Letters." *Musical Quarterly* 70 (1984): 476.

*   *   *

A single opera, *Kniaz' Igor' (Prince Igor),* a sprawling historical-folk epic set in twelfth-century Kievan Russia, represents Alexander Borodin in the Soviet and international repertoire. One of five members (with Rimsky-Korsakov, Mussorgsky, Cui, and Balakirev) of the *moguchaia kuchka* ("the mighty handful"), a group dedicated to developing a native Russian school of classical composition, Borodin received a rather desultory musical education, and divided his energies between music and his full-time profession of chemist. In a letter written while he was at work on *Igor,* Borodin admitted that "I'm always slightly ashamed to admit that I compose." For him, music was "a recreation, an idle pastime which provides diversion from my real work as professor and scientist."

As a result, his output was rather small, although it includes a number of successful art-songs (including a magnificent setting of Pushkin's poem "For the shores of thy far native land"); two very popular string quartets; and the evocative orchestral "musical picture" "V srednei Azii" ("In the Steppes of Central Asia," 1880), closely related in its "Oriental" musical style and subject matter to the "Polovtsian" acts (acts II and III) of *Igor.* Overworked and distracted by his many professional and family responsibilities, Borodin toiled on *Igor* sporadically for nearly eighteen years (from 1869), but still left it unfinished when he died in 1887.

Throughout his career, Borodin worked very closely with his colleagues in and around the *kuchka.* Indeed, his first completed work in opera (in 1872) was act IV of the communal fairy-tale opera-ballet *Mlada,* whose other acts were contributed by Rimsky-Korsakov, Cui and Mussorgsky. And it was critic Vladimir Stasov, a staunch supporter of the nationalist goals of the *kuchka,* who suggested to Borodin the idea of writing an opera on the subject of the failed campaign of Prince Igor Sviatoslavich (1151-1202) against the Polovtsy. Borodin continued to consult closely with his colleagues while working on *Igor,* often incorporating their suggestions and advice. Rimsky-Korsakov, who with Alexander Glazunov completed the opera after Borodin's death, played an important role throughout its composition.

Both musically and thematically, Borodin followed in the footsteps of the first internationally recognized Russian opera composer, Mikhail Glinka. *Igor,* in fact, combines the patriotic sweep of *A Life for the Tsar* with the exotic "Orientalism" of *Ruslan and Lyudmila.* Unlike the more radical Mussorgsky, who shunned conventional operatic forms in a search for greater verbal, dramatic and psychological truth, Borodin preferred "closed" melodic forms and an Italianate style. "The purely recitative style doesn't suit my nature or my character," he wrote. "I am drawn to song, to cantilena, and not to recitative. I am drawn to forms that are more closed, more rounded, broader. In opera and in stage design, there is no place for small forms, the unimportant or the trivial. Everything should be clear, vivid, and as 'performable' as possible for both voices and orchestra. The voices must come first, the orchestra second." Even when writing in a folksong idiom (he very rarely used actual folk tunes, instead composing his own on folk models), Borodin often employed a *bel canto* vocal style.

Somewhat overshadowed in Russia by the vogue for Tchaikovsky in the years before the 1917 Revolution, Borodin's operatic legacy gained in official popularity under the Soviet regime, and especially under Stalin's artistic "policy" of Socialist Realism. Because it was melodic, lyrical, emotionally straightforward, populist, optimistic, folksy within a conventional tonal framework, intellectually unchallenging, and patriotic, Borodin's music, and especially *Prince Igor,* found favor with the cultural bureaucrats, who encouraged Soviet composers to follow his model. Perhaps the best examples are Sergei Prokofiev's film scores to *Alexander Nevsky* and *Ivan the Terrible,* as well as his historical opera-epic *War and Peace.*

—Harlow Robinson

BOUGHTON, Rutland.

Composer. Born 23 January 1878, in Aylesbury. Died 25 January 1960, in London. Married: Christina Walshe (common-law). Studied at the Royal College of Music with Charles Stanford and Walford Davies; member of the orchestra of the Haymarket Theatre; taught at Midland Institute in Birmingham, 1905-11; heavily influenced by Wagner, and in collaboration with the poet Reginald Buckley wrote *The Music Drama of the Future,* 1911; organized stage festivals at Glastonbury to realize his artistic ideals.

Operas

Publishers: Curwen, Joseph Williams, Stainer and Bell, Novello.

Eolf, Boughton, 1901-3.
The Birth of Arthur, Reginald Buckley and Boughton, 1908-9, Glastonbury, 1909.
Uther and Igraine, Reginald Buckley, 1909.
The Immortal Hour, Boughton (after plays and poems by Fiona Macleod), 1912-13, Glastonbury, 26 August 1914.
Bethlehem, Boughton (after a 15th-century nativity play), 1915.
The Round Table, Reginald Buckley and Boughton, 1915-16, Glastonbury, August 1916.
The Moon Maiden, 1918.
Alkestis, Euripides, translated by Gilbert Murray, 1920-22, Glastonbury, 26 August 1922.
The Queen of Cornwall, Boughton (after the play by Thomas Hardy), 1923-24, Glastonbury, 26 August 1924.
The Ever-Young, Boughton, 1928-29, Bath, 1935.
The Lily Maid, Boughton, 1933-34, Stroud, 10 September 1934.
Galahad, Boughton, 1943-44.
Avalon, Boughton, 1944-45.

Other works: choral works, orchestral works, works for voice and orchestra, concertos, chamber music, songs.

Publications

By BOUGHTON: books–

Bach. London, 1907; 1930.
with Reginald Buckley. *The Music Drama of the Future.* London, 1911.
The Self-Advertisement of Rutland Boughton. London, 1911.
The Death and Resurrection of the Music Festival. London, 1913.
The Glastonbury Festival. London, 1917.
Parsifal. London, 1920.
The Glastonbury Festival Movement. London, 1922.
The Reality of Music. London, 1934.

articles–

"Festivalediction III." *Sackbut* 11 (1930): 35.
"The Immortal Hour." *Philharmonic Post* 4 (1949): 7.

About BOUGHTON: books–

Grew, S. *Our Favourite Musicians* [pp. 105-222]. London, 1924.
Holbrooke, J. *Contemporary British Composers* [p. 108 ff.]. London, 1925.
Brooke, D. *Composer's Gallery* [p. 29 ff.]. London, 1946.
White, E.W. *The Rise of English Opera* [pp. 148 ff, 195 ff.]. London, 1951.
Hurd, Michael. *Immortal Hour: the Life and Period of Rutland Boughton.* London, 1962.

articles–

Hurd, Michael. "The Glastonbury Festival." *Theatre Notebook* 17 (1963): 51.
––––––. "The Queen of Cornwall." *Musical Times* 104 (1963): 700.

––––––. "Rutland Boughton, 1878-1960." *Musical Times* 119 (1978): 31.

* * *

The position of Rutland Boughton in the history of British opera in the first half of the twentieth century was, and has remained, an unusual and controversial one. Although he composed a large quantity of music in other genres, particularly songs and choral works, such as *Midnight* (1909), his creative output is dominated by his twelve music-dramas. In these works (only four of which have been published; two in full score), and also in his polemical writings, Boughton conceived a distinctly English type of "choral-drama" within the post-Wagnerian aesthetic of the time. Boughton's earliest surviving attempt at operatic composition, *Eolf* (1901-3), written immediately following his studies at the Royal College of Music under Stanford and Davies, was the first of several works based on Arthurian legend in which he attempted to found a truly popular English art. Boughton's libretto, centered on a festival at which a prize-song by Eolf prompts King Arthur to release his slaves, reveals the influence of both Tolstoy and Wagner in the way that art serves the interests of the populace rather than an elite. The musical idiom of this and his two subsequent works based on medieval legend is strongly Wagnerian: *The Birth of Arthur* (1909), the first work in the Arthurian cycle, and *Uther and Igraine* (1909), the first of a projected series of works based on folk subjects dealing with the problems of contemporary Britain, to a libretto by an Arthurian poet, Reginald Buckley. Buckley and Boughton also produced a book, *Music Drama of the Future* (1911), in which they discussed their ideas as an extension of Wagnerian *Gesamtkunstwerk* philosophy and practice. For Boughton, associations of this type with other artists, notably the composer Granville Bantock, the socialist philosopher Edward Carpenter, the designer Christina Walshe and the critic George Bernard Shaw, proved fruitful throughout his working life.

Boughton dedicated a substantial part of his career to developing a concept of festival, inspired by the aesthetic philosophies of major thinkers of the recent past (Marx, Morris, Ruskin, Tolstoy, Wagner and Whitman). Following his 1911 visit to Bayreuth, Boughton promoted various schemes for realizing his dreams of establishing a temple theater and artistic community in England, pursuing these ideas further in *The Death and Resurrection of the Music Festival* (1913). However, plans for a large-scale festival at Glastonbury in the summer of 1913 were thwarted by controversy surrounding his personal life, which had already driven him from his teaching post at the Midland Institute of Music in Birmingham.

The first performance of parts of *The Birth of Arthur* did take place that summer in Bournemouth, a production notable for the 'dancing scenery' devised by Margaret Morris, and, with continued support from fellow artists, including Bantock, Elgar, Gordon Craig and George Moore, an inaugural Glastonbury Festival was established in the summer of 1914. Festivals took place there in the spring, summer and winter of every year, except for a short period when Boughton was on war service, providing (until July 1927) a unique collaborative atmosphere in which he thrived.

Facilities were far removed from the ideals of Bayreuth to which the project was sometimes compared by contemporaries. In spite of this, Glastonbury 1914 is memorable for the initial triumph of *The Immortal Hour,* Boughton's most famous and best-loved work, which blended a simple folk lyricism with the fairytale enchantment of the Celtic twilit underworld evoked in Fiona Macleod's poetry. First performed in the shadow of war, with only a grand piano for an orchestra and a cast made up of assorted friends and amateurs, the work might have seemed to have an uncertain future. However, this was far from being the case: it still holds the world record for the largest number of consecutive performances of any serious operatic composition. Stylistically, with *The Immortal Hour,* Boughton succeeded in breaking the rather heavy Wagnerian spell which had characterized earlier compositions.

Bethlehem, composed and performed in 1915 to a text by Boughton after a 15th century Coventry nativity play, continued in the simple folk vein which was coming to be recognized as an important feature of his style through the repeated success in London of *The Immortal Hour.* The dramatic tableaux are framed by traditional carols, subtly varied, which also act as a bridge between music and drama in the way that they both provide a commentary on the scenes (rather like the chorales in Bach's Passions), encouraging audience participation, and feature in the staged drama as well (the street scene of act 2). It was the scandal provoked by a production of *Bethlehem* at Christmas 1926, which Boughton, a committed communist, insisted on setting in a miner's cottage to express his solidarity with the General Strike, that led to the collapse of the Glastonbury dream, when fellow directors withdrew their support.

While they lasted, the Glastonbury festivals were a significant achievement both for Boughton and British opera. Over 350 staged performances took place there, including important revivals of neglected English works by Purcell, Blow and Locke, as well as some of Gluck's operas, and productions of six of Boughton's own works. Parts of the Arthurian cycle were performed: the first part, *The Birth of Arthur,* in its entirety in 1920, the second part, *The Round Table,* was premiered four years earlier. They were both eclipsed, however, by two other works of greater dramatic impact and musical innovation. The mythologically-inspired *Alkestis* (1922), which entered the repertory of the newly-formed British National Opera Company and was staged by them at Covent Garden in 1924, experimented with choral techniques inspired by conventions of Greek drama. The neo-classicist tendencies exhibited in its deliberately simple harmonic organization also won it many admirers, although more on tour in the provinces than in London. Both *Alkestis* and *The Queen of Cornwall* (1924), based on Hardy's play version of the Tristan legend, rely to an extent on the idiom of *The Immortal Hour,* although *The Queen of Cornwall* is more closely related in its use of folk song and occasionally passionate romantic lyricism. An off-stage chorus of spirits is used to enhance the overall orchestral effect.

When the Glastonbury period came to an end, Boughton moved to Kilcot, although he was often in London as conductor of the Labour Choral Union. He became involved in the key British music debates of the day concerning government subsidy for British opera and performing rights. By 1934, Boughton succeeded in organizing a new festival at Stroud and produced his latest music-drama, *The Lily Maid,* the central episode of the Arthurian cycle. Here the chorus is used to punctuate the action in prologues and epilogues to different sections. The following year he set up a festival at Bath to introduce *The Ever-Young* (1928), a richly expressive work with some musical and dramatic cross references to *The Immortal Hour.* Although the plot about a mortal woman married to an immortal God reverses the situation of the latter work, it was in no sense intended as a sequel.

Toward the end of his life, Boughton returned to work on his dream project, the completion of the Arthurian cycle, with two more works: *Galahad* (1944) and *Avalon* (1945). With little possibility of production, Boughton concentrated on the philosophical aspect, the collapse of Christian civilization, to the detriment of their theatrical appeal, making unrealistic dramatic demands and reverting to an unwieldy orchestral texture.

Boughton's life-long allegiance to a specifically English tradition of socialism was always at the forefront of his art. His methods of self-promotion and production were unique in British opera of the period. His ability to focus on the human situation and to express artistic cooperation through innovative use of chorus and dance, together with a blend of folk realism distinguished by sheer beauty of sound, brought his music-dramas to large numbers of people.

—Charlotte Purkis

BOULEZ, Pierre.

Conductor. Born 26 March 1925, in Montbrison. Studied composition with Olivier Messiaen at the Paris Conservatory (graduated 1945); lessons with René Leibowitz; theater conductor in Paris, 1948; tour of the United States with a French ballet troupe in 1952; organized the "Domaine Musical" concert series, Paris, 1954; gave courses at the Darmstadt festival, 1958; gave a lecture series at Harvard University, 1963; United States conducting debut, New York, 1964; conducted opera in Germany; conducted the *Ring* cycle at Bayreuth, 1976; guest conductor with the Cleveland Orchestra; music director of the New York Philharmonic, 1971-77; chief conductor of the London British Broadcasting Corporation Symphony Orchestra, 1971-75; founded the Institut de Recherche et Coordination Acoustique/Musique, 1974; Praemium Imperiale prize of Japan, 1989.

Publications

By BOULEZ: books–

with Chereau et al. *Histoire d'un "Ring": Bayreuth 1976-1980.* Paris, 1980.
Nattiez, J.-J., ed. *Points de repère.* Paris, 1981, 1985; English translation by M. Cooper as *Orientations: Collected Writings of Pierre Boulez,* London, 1986; 1990.

interviews–

Matheopoulos, Helena. *Maestro: Encounters with Conductors of Today.* London, 1982.

About BOULEZ: books–

Goléa, A. *Rencontres avec Pierre Boulez.* Paris, 1958.
Peyser, J. *Boulez, Composer, Conductor, Enigma.* New York, 1976.
Glock, W. ed. *Pierre Boulez: a Symposium.* London, 1986.

*   *   *

Pierre Boulez

Pierre Boulez has established a solid reputation as one of the most important avante-garde composers of the twentieth century. He is particularly noteworthy for his expansion of musical serialism to involve virtually all elements of music, thus advancing beyond systems devised by Schoenberg and his two pupils, Alban Berg and Anton Webern.

Boulez oeuvre to date numbers some forty compositions, among which there are at least a dozen works of major dimensions. As a brilliant student at the Paris Conservatory, and as a star pupil of Olivier Messiaen, Boulez soon attracted international notice for his ingenious and original adaptation of the principles of serialism to contemporary French style. He was particularly recognized for his unique penchant for sonorities and textures reflecting his interest in music of non-Western cultures, and for his experiments with electronic and indeterminate music.

The main connection that Boulez has had with the world of opera has been through his conducting. As chief conductor of the British Broadcasting Corporation Symphony and the New York Philharmonic, he of course had little direct contact with opera. But in the course of events, he has conducted an ever-increasing repertoire of dramatic works, many of which were fully staged. Perhaps his outstanding accomplishment in this area was his masterful 1976 presentation of Wagner's cycle, *Der Ring des Nibelungen,* the exquisitely detailed quality of which may have been obscured in the public mind by Patrice Cherou's revolutionary production. Cherou produced the work with scenes, costumes, lighting, and staging interpreted as if the action had taken place in late nineteenth-century Germany, as it existed after the Industrial Revolution had fairly well run its course. The subtle musical realizations of Boulez were so overshadowed by the enormous license of Cherou's direction as to escape both critical and public notice. Other important opera productions by Boulez include his presentations of Alban Berg's *Wozzeck* in 1963, and *Lulu* in 1979.

Careful listening shows that Boulez's attention to detail in a highly concentrated, yet multi-directional communication to his players has produced one of the clearest, firmest and most convincing arrays of Wagnerian drama ever called forth from a company. Although he has left both the New York Philharmonic and British Broadcasting Corporation Symphony orchestras to return to his native France, Boulez continues to be active as one of the most important conductors of the twentieth century.

—Franklin B. Zimmerman

THE BREASTS OF TIRESIAS
See LES MAMELLES DE TIRÉSIAS

BRECHT, Bertolt (Eugen Friedrich).

Librettist/Dramatist. Born 10 February 1898, in Augsburg. Died 14 August 1956, in Berlin. Recognition among literary circles for his play *Trommeln in die Nacht,* 1922; librettist for Kurt Weill's *Aufstieg und Fall der Stadt Mahagonny,* 1927-29, *Die Dreigroschenoper,* 1928, *Happy End,* 1929 *Der*

Jasager, 1930; opposed Weill's approach to opera in the article "Anmerkungen zur Oper 'Aufstieg und Fall der Stadt Mahagonny',", 1930; sixteen years of exile from Germany, 1933-49, during which many of his most important plays were written; return to East Berlin, 1949; establishment of the Berliner Ensemble, which achieved international recognition. Among the composers who set Brecht's texts are Hindemith, Eisler, Dessau, Einem, and Cerha.

Librettos

Mahagonny (Songspiel), K. Weill, 1927; revised as *Aufstieg und Fall der Stadt Mahagonny,* K. Weill, 1927-29.
Die Dreigroschenoper (with E. Hauptmann), K. Weill, 1928.
Happy End (with E. Hauptmann), K. Weill, 1929.
Der Jasager, K. Weill, 1930.
The Trial of Lucullus (after the radio play *Das Verhör des Lukullus,* translated by H.R. Hays), R. Sessions, 1947.
Puntila, after the play *Herr Puntila und sein Knecht Matti,* P. Dessau, 1957-59.
Der gute Mensch von Sezuan, S. Pironkov, 1965.
Baal, F. Cerha, 1976-78.

Publications/Writings

By BRECHT: books (on music)–

Unseld, S., ed. *Bertolt Brechts Dreigroschenbuch. Texte, Materialien, Dokumente.* Frankfurt, 1960.
Hauptmann, E., ed. *B. Brecht: Gesammelte Werke.* Frankfurt, 1967.
Hecht, W., ed. *Bertolt Brecht: Arbeitsjournal.* Frankfurt, 1973.

unpublished–

Note: many of the following essays are published in Italian translation in *Scritti teatrali,* 3 vols, Turin, 1975.

"Über die "Dreigroschenoper." 1929.
"Das moderne Theater ist das epische Theater. Anmerkungen über die Oper 'Aufstieg und Fall der Stadt Mahagonny." 1930.
"Literarisierung des Theaters. Anmerkungen zur 'Dreigroschenoper'." 1931.
"Anmerkungen zum 'Badener Lehrstück vom Einverständnis'." 1931.
"Anmerkungen zur 'Massnahme'." 1931.
"Aus der Musiklehre" [incomplete]. c. 1931.
"Die mittelbare Wirkung des epischen Theaters. Anmerkungen zur 'Mutter'." 1932.
"Über gestische Musik."1932.
"Über Bühnenmusik." n.d.
"Über die Verwendung von Musik für ein episches Theater." 1935.
"Vergnügungstheater oder Lehrtheater?" c. 1936.
"Über reimlose Lyrik mit unregelmässigen Rhythmen." 1939.
" 'Mutter Courage.' Anmerkungen zur Aufführung." 1949.
with P. Dessau. "Anmerkungen zur Oper 'Die Verurteilung des Lukullus' Diskussion über die Oper." 1951.
"Die Gesänge." 1951.

About BRECHT: books–

Hennenberg, F. *Dessau-Brecht: musikalische Arbeiten.* Berlin, 1963.

Bertolt Brecht, Berlin, 1927

Eisler, H. *Musik und Politik.* Leipzig, 1972.

Irmer, H.-J. *Brecht und das musikalische Theater.* Berlin, 1972.

McLean, S. *The Bänkelsang and the Works of Bertolt Brecht.* The Hague, 1972.

Thole, B. *Die Gesänge in den Stücken Bertolt Brechts: zur Geschichte und Ästhetik des Liedes im Drama.* Göppingen, 1973.

Hennenberg, F., and P. Pachnicke, eds. *Paul Dessau aus Gesprächen.* Leipzig, 1974.

Wagner, G. *Weill und Brecht: das musikalische Zeittheater.* Munich, 1977.

articles–

Heuss, A. "Bertolt Brechts Schulstück vom Jasager." *Zeitschrift für Musik* (1930).

Leibowitz, R. "Brecht et la musique de scène." *Théâtre populaire* no. 11 (1955).

Dessau, P. "Anmerkungen zur musikalischen Arbeiten mit Brecht." In Paul Dessau and Bertolt Brecht, *Lieder und Gesänge,* Berlin, 1957.

Drew, D. "Brecht versus Opera: some Comments." *The Score* (1958).

Hartung, G. "Zur epischen Oper Brechts und Weills." *Wissenschaftliche Zeitschrift der Martin-Luther-Universität* 8 (1959): 659.

Branscombe, P. "Brecht, Weill and 'Mahagonny'." *Musical Times* (1961).

Pestalozza, L. "Brecht e la musica." In P. Chiarini et al., *Nuovi studi su Bertolt Brecht.* Milan, 1961.

Weisstein, U. "Cocteau, Stravinsky, Brecht, and the Birth of Epic Opera." *Modern Drama* (1962).

Willet, J. "Brecht, the Music." In *Bertolt Brecht,* edited by P. Demetz. Englewood Cliffs, New Jersey, 1962.

Kuhnert, H. "Zur Rolle der Songs im Werk von Bertolt Brecht." *Deutsche Literatur* no. 3 (1963).

Dessau, P. "Wie es zum 'Lukullus' kam." In *Errinnerungen an Brecht.* Leipzig, 1964.

Reinhardt, M. "Brecht und das musikalische Theater." *Melos* (1967).

Pischner, H. "Brecht und die gesellschaftliche Funktion der Musik." *Musik und Gesellschaft* (1968).

Schebera, J. "Zur Funktion der Bühnenmusik in der sozialistischen Dramatik der DDR. Ergebnisse und Positionen sowie Überlegungen für die künftige Theaterarbeit." *Theater der Zeit* (1972).

Rognoni, L. "Funzione della musica nel teatro di Bertolt Brecht." *Fenomenologia della musica radicale.* Milan, [2nd ed.] 1974.

Volker, K. "Brecht und die Musik." *Musik und Bildung* (1976).

Kahnt, H. "Die Opernversuche Weills und Brechts mit *Mahagonny.*" In *Musiktheater heute,* edited by Helmut Kühn. Mainz, 1981.

Collisani, A. " 'Der Jasager': musica e distacco." *Rivista italiana di musicologia* (1982).

Borowick, S.H. "Weill's and Brecht's Theories on Music in Drama." *Journal of Musicological Research* (1982).

unpublished–

Tolksdorf, C. "J. Gays *Beggar's Opera* und Bertolt Brechts *Dreigroschenoper.*" Ph.D. dissertation, University of Bonn, 1951.
Borwick, S.H. "The Music for the Stage Collaborations of Weill and Brecht." Ph.D dissertation, University of North Carolina, 1972.
Wagner, G. "Weill und Brecht: das musikalische Zeittheater." Ph.D. dissertation, University of Monaco, 1977.
Lucchesi, J. *Zur Funktion und Geschichte der zeitgenössischen Schauspielmusik und zu einigen Aspekten der schauspielmusikalischen Praxis.* Ph.D. dissertation, Humboldt University, Berlin, 1977.
Nadar, T.R. "The Music of Kurt Weill, Hanns Eisler and Paul Dessau in the Dramatic Works of Bertolt Brecht." Ph.D. dissertation, University of Michigan, 1979.

*   *   *

Although a number of his plays have been set by composers in Germany and the United States as operas, Brecht wrote only two librettos that, in the accepted sense, can be termed operas: *Aufstieg und Fall der Stadt Mahagonny* and *Der Jasager.* Despite its title, and the occasional attempt by an opera company to include it in its repertory, *Die Dreigroschenoper* must always remain as Brecht described it to Giorgio Strehler in the 1950s, when he was involved with Strehler's first production of it: "the starting-point must always be a poor theatre trying to do its best."

Of Weill's operas, *Aufstieg und Fall der Stadt Mahagonny* remains the most epic in scale but also one of the most misunderstood. This is partly because it was preceded by the *Mahagonny Songspiel,* in which a fraction of the music was first heard, and after its initial performances, it was presented in Berlin and Vienna in a reduced, music-theater version (with Lotte Lenya as Jenny). People have thus assumed that it was in some way a follow-up to *Dreigroschenoper,* whereas it in fact preceded it as a project for Weill and Brecht. Brecht had little or no sympathy with the world of the conventional opera-house. His stage instructions and the slogans he wrote to be projected during performances amount to a scenario for the production which has seldom been followed.

The extent to which Brecht relied upon his "invisible" collaborator, Elisabeth Hauptmann, who not only provided the English-language songs in the opera *Mahagonny* but nearly all of *Happy End,* is a subject of enduring but frustrating interest to Brecht scholars. Beyond his librettos for Weill, Brecht's greatest influence on the world of opera is not as a dramatist but as a theorist. Ever since the end of the Second World War, there has been a long succession of opera stagings, the philosophy behind which is totally "Brechtian." The work of stage directors including Götz Friedrich, Ruth Berghaus, Harry Kupfer, and Joachim Herz, all of whom grew up in the shadow of Brecht, has had a worldwide impact (considered by some critics to be disastrous for the traditions of opera staging). Nevertheless, the formality of opera and its rituals and unrealistic conventions lend themselves perfectly to the Brechtian "alienation" technique. The way of singing, an entirely inappropriate one for opera, which has become known as the "Brechtian bark," is in fact a continuation of the popular beer-hall or street-corner style adopted by dozens of Berlin singers around the turn of the century prior to the advent of microphone-amplification. It has nothing to with Brecht himself, but it was a convenient vocal method to mouth the typical slogan-ballads which occur throughout his music-theater works (for instance the songs by Dessau for *Mutter Courage* or those by Eisler for *Die Rundköpfe und die Spitzköpfe*).

Brecht does not, in his published writings, seem to have had much comment to make on traditional opera: he would have been opposed to anything that he perceived as being "bourgeois." Nevertheless, his first wife, Marianne Zoff, was an opera-singer, and most his musical collaborators (Weill, Dessau, Eisler and Sessions) are composers who worked strictly within the conventional framework of concert and opera music. In his letters, Brecht seldom mentions singers or singing; it is said, however, that the famous "silent scream" at the end of *Mutter Courage* was partly inspired by a performance that Brecht saw of *Annie Get Your Gun* with Ethel Merman.

—Patrick O'Connor

BRITTEN, (Edward) Benjamin.

Composer. Born 22 November 1913, in Lowestoft, Suffolk. Died 4 December 1976, in Aldeburgh. Studied viola with Audrey Alston and composition with Frank Bridge; studied piano with Arthur Benjamin and Harold Samuel, and composition with John Ireland at the Royal College of Music, 1930; *Fantasy Quartet* performed at the International Society for Contemporary Music in Florence, 5 April 1934; film scores from 1935-1942; organized the English Opera Group, 1947, and the Aldeburgh Festival, 1948; Companion of Honour, 1952; Order of Merit, 1965; made a Lord by Queen Elizabeth II, 1976.

Operas

Publishers: Boosey and Hawkes, Faber.

Paul Bunyan, W.H. Auden, 1941, New York, Columbia University, Brander Matthews Hall, 5 May 1941.
Peter Grimes, M. Slater (after a poem by Crabbe), 1944-45, London, Sadler's Wells, 7 June 1945.
The Rape of Lucretia, Ronald Duncan (after A. Obey), 1946, Glyndebourne, 12 July 1946; revised, 1947.
Albert Herring, Eric Crozier (after Maupassant), 1947, Glyndebourne, 20 June 1947.
The Little Sweep, or Let's Make an Opera ("entertainment for young people"), Eric Crozier, 1949, Aldeburgh, Jubilee Hall, 14 June 1949.
Billy Budd (revised 1960), Forster and Crozier (after Herman Melville), 1951, London, Covent Garden, 1 December 1951.
Gloriana, W. Plomer, 1953, London, Covent Garden, 8 June 1953.
The Turn of the Screw, M. Piper (after Henry James), 1954, Venice, Teatro La Fenice, 14 September 1954.
Noye's Fludde (children's opera), Orford Church, 18 June 1958.
A Midsummer Night's Dream, Britten and Pears (after Shakespeare), 1960. Aldeburgh, Jubilee Hall, 11 June 1960.
Curlew River (church parable), W. Plomer, 1964, Orford Church, 12 June 1964.

Benjamin Britten with Peter Pears, Long Island, New York, 1939

The Burning Fiery Furnace (church parable), W. Plomer, 1966, Orford Church, 9 June 1966.

The Prodigal Son (church parable), W. Plomer, 1968, Orford Church, 10 June 1968.

Owen Wingrave, M. Piper (after Henry James), 1970, broadcast premiere: BBC, 16 May 1971; stage premiere: London, Covent Garden, 10 May 1973.

Death in Venice, M. Piper (after Thomas Mann), 1973, Snape Maltings, 16 June 1973.

Other works: orchestral works, choral works, chamber works, incidental music.

Publications/Writings

By BRITTEN: books–

On Receiving the First Aspen Award. London, 1964, 1978.

The Story of Music, With Imogen Holst. London, 1958; reprinted as *The Wonderful World of Music,* London, 1968.

Mitchell, Donald, and Philip Reed. *Letters from a Life.* Berkeley, 1991.

articles–

"An English Composer Sees America." *Tempo* 1 (1940).

"On Behalf of Gustav Mahler." *Tempo* 2 (1942).

"On Reading the Continuo in Purcell's Songs." In *Henry Purcell: 1659-1695*, edited by Imogen Holst. London. 1964, 1978.

"Frank Bridge (1879-1941)." *Faber Music News* fall (1966): 17.

About BRITTEN: books–

Crozier, Eric. *Peter Grimes*. London, 1945.

Keller, H. *The Rape of Lucretia; Albert Herring*. London, 1947.

Stuart, C. *Peter Grimes*. London, 1947.

Crozier, Eric, ed. *The Rape of Lucretia: A Symposium*. London, 1948.

White, Eric Walter. *Benjamin Britten: A Sketch of His Life and Works*. London, 1948; reprint Seattle, 1954; revised as *Britten: His Life and Operas*, edited by John Evans, Berkeley, 1983.

Abbiati, F. *Peter Grimes*. Milan, 1949.

Mitchell, Donald, and Hans Keller, eds. *Benjamin Britten: A Commentary on His Works from a Group of Specialists*. London, 1952; New York, 1953.

Lindler, H. *Benjamin Britten: das Opernwerk*. Bonn, 1955.

Gishford, Anthony, ed. *Tribute to Benjamin Britten on His Fiftieth Birthday*. London, 1963.

Holst, Imogen. *Britten*. London, 1966; 2nd ed., 1970; 3rd ed, 1980.

Hurd, Michael. *Benjamin Britten*. London. 1966.

Young, Percy M. *Benjamin Britten*. London, 1966.

Howard, Patricia. *The Operas of Benjamin Britten*. London, 1969.

Kendall, Alan. *Benjamin Britten*. London, 1973.

Schmidgall, Gary. *Literature as Opera*. New York. 1977.

Mitchell, Donald. *Benjamin Britten: Pictures from a Life*. New York and London, 1978.

Evans, Peter. *The Music of Benjamin Britten*. Minneapolis and London, 1979.

Herbert, David. *The Operas of Benjamin Britten*. London, 1979.

Blyth, Alan. *Remembering Britten*. London, 1981.

Duncan, Ronald. *Working with Britten*. Devon, 1981.

Kennedy, Michael. *Britten*. London, 1981.

Mitchell, Donald. *Britten and Auden in the Thirties: The Year 1936*. London, 1981.

Headington, Christopher. *Britten*. New York, 1982.

Whittall, Arnold. *The Music of Britten and Tippett*. Cambridge, 1982, 1990.

Brett, Philip. *Britten: Peter Grimes*. Cambridge Opera Guides. Cambridge, 1983.

John, Nicholas, ed. *Benjamin Britten: Peter Grimes and Gloriana*. Opera Guide 24. London and New York, 1983.

Palmer, Christopher, ed. *The Britten Companion*. New York, 1984.

Howard, Patricia. *Britten: The Turn of the Screw*. Cambridge Opera Guides. Cambridge, 1985.

Welford, Beth. *My Brother Benjamin*. Buckinghamshire, 1986.

Evans, John, Philip Reed, and Paul Wilson. *A Britten Source Book*. Aldeburgh, 1987.

Mitchell, Donald. *Britten: Death in Venice*. Cambridge Opera Guides. Cambridge, 1987.

articles–

Stein, Erwin. "Opera and *Peter Grimes*." *Tempo* 1st series/ no. 12 (1945): 2.

Crozier, Eric. "Forward to *Albert Herring*." *Tempo* (1947).

Stein, Erwin. "Form in Opera: 'Albert Herring' Examined." *Tempo* new series/no. 5 (1947): 4.

Music Survey 2 (1950) [Britten issue].

Stein, Erwin. "Benjamin Britten's Operas." *Opera* 1 (1950): 16.

Opera 2 (1951) [Britten issue].

Mitchell, D. "More off than on 'Billy Budd'." *Music Survey* 4 (1951-2): 386.

Tempo no. 21 (1952) [*Billy Budd* issue].

Porter, Andrew. "Britten's *Billy Budd*." *Music and Letters* 33 (1952): 111.

Stein, Erwin. "The Music of *Billy Bud*." *Opera* 3 (1952): 206.

"*Gloriana*: A Symposium." *Opera* August (1953).

Tempo no. 28 (1953) [*Gloriana* issue].

Klein, J. "Reflections on 'Gloriana'." *Tempo* no. 29 (1953): 16.

Porter, Andrew. "Britten's Gloriana'." *Music and Letters* 34 (1953): 277.

Roseberry, Eric. "*The Turn of the Screw* and its Musical Idiom." *Tempo* no. 34 (1955): 6.

Stein, Erwin. "Britten's New Opera for Children: *Noye's Fludde*." *Tempo* no. 48 (1958): 7.

Roseberry, Eric. "The Music of *Noye's Fludde*." *Tempo* no. 49 (1958): 2.

Evans, Peter. "Britten's *A Midsummer Night's Dream*." *Tempo* no. 53–54 (1960): 34.

Tempo no. 66–67 (1963) [Britten issue].

Evans, P. "Britten's Television Opera." *Musical Times* 112 (1971): 425.

Mitchell, D. "Britten's Church Parables." In *Aldeburgh Anthology*, edited by R. Blythe. Aldeburgh, 1972.

Evans, Peter, "Britten's *Death in Venice*." *Opera* 24 (1973): 490.

Opera 28 (1977).

Brett, Philip. "Britten and Grimes." *Musical Times* 118 (1977); 995.

Mitchell, D. "A *Billy Budd* Notebook." *Opera News* 43/no. 19 (1979).

Avant-Scène Opéra January/February (1981) [*Peter Grimes* issue].

Keller, Hans. "Zu Benjamin Brittens Opernschaffen." *Österreichische Musikzeitschrift* 36 (1981): 379.

Flynn, William T. "Britten the Progressive." *Music Review* 44 (1983): 44.

Mitchell, D. "Catching on to the Technique in Pagoda-Land." *Tempo* no. 146 (1983).

Reininghaus, Frieder. "Wie ein spannender Kriminalfilm. Benjamin Brittens *The Turn of the Screw*. *Neue Zeitschrift für Musik* 144 (1983): 28.

Bray, Trevor. "Frank Bridge and his quasi-adopted son." *Music Review* 45 (1984): 135.

Alexander, Peter F. "The Process of Composition of the Libretto of Britten's *Gloriana*." *Music and Letters* 67 (1986).

Opera Quarterly, 4 (1986).

Brett, Philip. "Grimes and Lucretia." In *Music and Theatre: Essays in Honour of Winton Dean*. Cambridge, 1987.

Corse, Sandra. "Owen Wingrave." In *Opera and the Uses of Language: Mozart, Verdi, and Britten*. New Jersey, 1987.

Law, Jack. "Daring to Eat a Peach: Literary Allusion in *Albert Herring*." *Opera Quarterly* (1987).

Mitchell, D. "The Origin, Evolution and Metamorphoses of Paul Bunyan, Auden's and Britten's 'American Opera'." In *W.H. Auden: Paul Bunyan*. London, 1988.

Hindley, Clifford. "Love and Salvation in Britten's *Billy Budd*." *Music and Letters* (1989).

Mitchell, Donald. "The Serious Comedy of *Albert Herring.*" *About the House* spring (1989).

Whittall, Arnold. " 'Twisted relations': Method and Meaning in Britten's *Billy Budd.*" *Cambridge Opera Journal* 2 (1990): 145.

unpublished–

Milliman, Joan Ann. "Benjamin Britten's Symbolic Treatment of Sleep, Dream, and Death as Manifest in his Opera *Death in Venice.*" Ph.D. dissertation, University of Southern California, 1977.

*　　*　　*

In the opening of *A Time There Was,* the filmed profile of Benjamin Britten's life directed by Tony Palmer, American composer/conductor Leonard Bernstein is quoted saying that Britten was "a man at odds with the world . . . ." At that time, shortly after Britten's death, it sounded strangely incompatible with the general impression of the composer's seemingly charmed life. Britten was, after all, the most prominent musician in England, and was hailed by many as the greatest English composer since Henry Purcell. Closer examination of his early life, however, reveals clues to the darker side to which Bernstein alludes, and Britten's life-long struggle is manifested in the themes and character of his vocal music, in particular the operas.

By the time Britten was in his mid-twenties, several personal and professional circumstances coalesced that are fundamental to a deeper understanding of his life and work. First, Britten, who exhibited a prodigious musical talent early on, felt unappreciated by the conservative English musical establishment of the 1920s and 1930s. Second, as a pacifist, Britten found himself aligned with the minority who opposed England's increased involvement in the approaching war. Third, Britten was a homosexual at a time and in a place that offered him little recourse but repression. Together, these circumstances resulted in overwhelming feelings of isolation, alienation, and oppression, feelings with which Britten struggled for the rest of his life, and about which, through his operas, he spoke eloquently.

It is not surprising, then, that Britten fled to America as World War II began, as did many European artists. He desired to live and work in an atmosphere free from social and political pressures, and one more conducive to creative expression. It was in the United States that his first operatic venture, *Paul Bunyan,* was written and produced (to decidedly less than enthusiastic reviews), along with other works, though it was not long before he realized that England, in particular that part of East Anglia close to his birthplace, was indeed the source of his creative roots and inspiration. Britten returned to England in 1942, along with a commission for an opera (which was to become *Peter Grimes*) from Serge Koussevitzky, and made Aldeburgh, on the North Sea coast, his home. He never ventured very far away, for any length of time, from then on.

Interestingly, his decision to return to England did not signal an end to his feelings of isolation. His continued hypersensitivity to criticism, and his (relative) physical isolation in Aldeburgh, surrounded by a protective shield of friends and close colleagues, at least suggest unresolved personal and creative issues. It is possible even to view the forming of the English Opera Group and the Aldeburgh Festival, both populated with close associates, as an attempt to ensure a certain artistic distance.

The themes of Britten's operas are quite personal, and in them one catches more than just a glimpse of their creator. Britten wrote about people and their relationships rather than about events, and this drew him to a wide variety of sources for libretti. Many, like Melville's *Billy Budd* or Henry James's *The Turn of The Screw,* were considered too problematic for operatic treatment, yet all contained the textual resources to meet Britten's thematic criteria. The result is a legacy of dramatic works, rich in formal variety, but unified in their examination of isolation, alienation and oppression.

Britten's musical style is eclectic. His vocabulary and techniques come from composers of all periods, though he assimilated them into an expression that is uniquely his own. He clearly favors those composers whose styles reflect the clarity of form and texture associated with "classicism" over the thicker texture and more harmonically dense "romanticism" of others. Purcell, Mozart, Schubert, Mahler and Shostakovich were particular favorites of Britten's and influential in forming his style. He was also thoroughly conversant with the techniques of the twelve-tone (dodecaphonic) school of composers, and utilized them when, as in *The Turn of the Screw* and *A Midsummer Night's Dream,* for example, they served his purpose. To this must be added the influence of music from the Far East, experienced most directly during Britten's tour of Japan and Bali in 1955-56, although Britten was first introduced to Balinese music in the late 1930s by fellow composer and authority on Balinese music, Colin McPhee. From Britten's exposure to Far Eastern music came an increased interest in the expressive potential of percussion instruments, and a more economical, linear texture in his subsequent works.

Among the compositional processes that Britten mastered, the principle of variation was central to his style, from the earliest compositions through nearly six decades of creativity. This ranged from large scale theme and variation structures, as in *A Boy Was Born, Variations on a Theme of Frank Bridge* and even the opera *The Turn of the Screw,* to the smallest, most elemental use of the process, such as basing a whole composition on a melody or motive that becomes the source for musical ideas and development. One observes this especially in Britten's later (post-1964) works, such as the church parables *(Curlew River, The Burning Fiery Furnace, The Prodigal Son), Owen Wingrave,* and *Death in Venice.*

The most characteristic use of the variation principle in Britten's music is through the passacaglia (variations above a repeated harmonic/melodic foundation). Virtually all of his operas contain at least one extended passacaglia, placed in significant dramatic situations. The most recognizable, perhaps, is the orchestral passacaglia in *Peter Grimes* (Interlude IV) which is based on the melody and harmonic implications of Grimes's climactic and prophetic cry, ". . . and God have mercy upon me!" in act II, scene 1. Equally important are those found in *Albert Herring* ("The Threnody" in act III), the "chase" scene in *Billy Budd* (act II, scene 1), the final scenes in *The Turn of the Screw* and *The Rape of Lucretia,* and act II, scene 9 ("The Pursuit") in *Death in Venice.*

In addition to his skills as a composer, Britten was an extraordinary pianist and gifted conductor. His musical collaborations with artists like Peter Pears, Dietrich Fischer-Dieskau, Mstislav Rostropovitch, and many others, are legendary, and his consummate musicianship is widely acknowledged. His popularity as a composer is in some measure reflected by the large number of his works that have remained in the repertoire. In terms of quality and quantity, the works of Benjamin Britten have dominated the post-World War II operatic stage, through the composer's keen sense of what works theatrically, his gift for melody and vocal writing in general, and his thorough craftsmanship.

In his acceptance speech upon being chosen the first recipient of the Aspen Award in the Humanities in 1964, Britten articulated those "human" characteristics which were so much a part of his conscious compositional process (his friend, the writer E.M. Forster, called it Britten's "Confession of Faith"): "I certainly write for human beings—directly and deliberately. I consider their voices, the range, the power, the subtlety, the colour potentialities of them. I consider the instruments they play—their most expressive and suitable individual sonorities . . . . I also take note of the *human* circumstances of music, of its environment and conventions; for instance I try to write dramatically effective music for the theatre—I certainly don't think opera is better for not being effective on the stage (some people think that effectiveness *must* be superficial)" (from *On Receiving the First Aspen Award,* London, 1978). By his personal testimony, Britten did not write for posterity, wisely pointing out that to try to do so would be impossible. Rather he wanted his music to be performed and enjoyed for the present, leaving others to worry about its place in music history. Assuming, though, that truly great music demands sufficient subjective (and emotional) response *and* objective (intellectual, analytical) appeal, Britten's operas of dramatic power, beauty, and technical skill argue impressively for inclusion in that category.

—Michael Sells

BROOK, Peter (Stephen Paul).

Director. Born 21 March 1925, in London. Married: actress Natasha Perry, 1951 (one daughter, one son). Educated Gresham School, Magdalen College, Oxford; director of productions, Royal Opera at Covent Garden, 1947-50; co-director of the Royal Shakespeare Company 1962-; staged world premiere of *The Olympians,* Covent Garden, 1949. Awards: New York Drama Critics Awards for Best Director—*Marat/Sade,* 1965-66; Commander of the British Empire (C.B.E.), 1965.

Opera Productions (selected)

Boris Godunov, London, Covent Garden, 1947.
La bohème, London, Covent Garden, 1948.
Le nozze di Figaro, London, Covent Garden, 1948.
The Olympians (Bliss), London, Covent Garden, 1949.
Dark of the Moon, London, Covent Garden, 1949.
Salome, London, Covent Garden, 1949.
Faust, New York, Metropolitan Opera, 1953.
Eugene Onegin, New York, Metropolitan Opera, 1957.
La tragédie de Carmen, Paris, 1981.

Publications

By BROOK: books–

The Empty Space, London, 1968.
The Shifting Point: Theatre, Film, Opera. London, 1988.
Peter Brook: A Theatrical Casebook. London, 1988.

articles–

Preface to Anouilh, Jean, *Ring Round the Moon.* London, 1951.
Preface to Anouilh, Jean, *Colombe, a Comedy.* London, 1952.
Introduction to Shakespeare, William, *As You Like It.* London, 1953.
"A Realistic Approach to *Eugene Onegin.*" *The New York Times* 107 (27 October 1957): 9, Section 2.
"Keep 'Em Still." *Musical American* 79/June (1959): 11.
Contributor to Melchinger, Siegfried, *Shakespeare auf dem modernen Welttheater.* Velber bei Hannover, 1964.
Preface to Warre, Michael, *Designing and Making Stage Scenery.* New York, 1966.
Introduction to Weiss, Peter, *The Persecution and Assassination of Jean-Paul Marat as Performed by the Inmates of the Asylum of Charenton Under the Direction of the Marquis de Sade.* New York, 1966.
Preface to Kott, Jan, *Shakespeare Our Contemporary.* London, 1967.
Preface to Grotowski, Jerzy, *Towards a Poor Theatre.* New York, 1968.
"The Influence of Gordon Craig in Theory and Practice." *Drama* 173 (1989): 40.
"Grotowski, Art as a Vehicle." *The Drama Review* 35/Spring (1991): 92.

interviews–

"The Art of Fine Tuning; Penetrating the Surface." *Parabola* 13/Summer (1988): 57.

About BROOK: books–

Trewin, J.C. *Peter Brook.* London, 1971.
Roose-Evans, James. *Experimental Theatre from Stanislavsky to Peter Brook.* London, 1984.
Jones, Edward Trostle. *Following Directions: A Study of Peter Brook.* c.1985.
Jones, David Richard. *Great Directors at Work.* Berkeley, 1986.
Cott, Jonathan. *Visions and Voices.* New York, 1987.
Leiter, Samuel L. *From Belasco to Brook: Representative Directors of the English-Speaking Stage.* New York, 1991.

articles–

Savage, R. "The Shakespeare-Purcell 'Fairy Queen'; A Defence and Recommendation." *Early Music* 1/4 (1973): 200.
Renk, H.E. "Die Krise des französischen Theaters." *Opernwelt* 23/8-9 (1982): 61.
Loney, Glenn. "The Carmen Connection." *Opera News* 48/September (1983): 11.
Auslander, Philip. "Holy Theatre and Catharsis." *Theatre Research International* 9/Spring (1984): 16.
Persche, G. "Die Femme fatale als Wende-Marke? Bemerkungen zur 'Carmen-Welle'." *Opernwelt* 25 (Yearbook 1984): 110.
Koltai, Tamas. "A reformizmus keves; beszelgetes Peter Brookkal." *Muzika* 27/December (1984): 11.
Acocella, Joan. "Theater: Apocalypse Then—And Now." *Art in America* 76/March (1988): 29.
Tonkin, Boyd. "The discovery of fire." *New Statesman* 115 (14 April 1988): 38.
———. "The Reluctant Hero Comes Home." *New Statesman* 115 (22 April 1988): 22.

"Getting Past Shakespeare: The Trials of a Theatre Director." *The Economist* 307 (23 April 1988): 99.

Meduri, Avanthi. "More Aftermath after Peter Brook." *The Drama Review* 32/Summer (1988): 14.

Baker, Rob. "Reaching for the Trapeze: An Interview with Peter Brook." *Parabola* 15/Spring (1990): 104.

Cohen, Paul B. "Peter Brook and the 'Two Worlds' of Theatre." *New Theatre Quarterly* 7 (May 1991): 147.

*　　*　　*

Producer Peter Brook was director of productions for the Royal Opera, Covent Garden, from 1947 to 1950. Aside from his non-operatic production credits on Broadway, in London's West End, at Stratford, England, and with the Royal Shakespeare Company, Brook has produced opera at the Metropolitan Opera (Gounod's *Faust* [1953] and Tchaikovsky's *Eugene Onegin* [1957]).

In 1981 Brook staged an adaptation of Bizet's *Carmen* as *La tragédie de Carmen* in Paris (a production that was later seen in New York) with four singers, two actors, fifteen instrumentalists, no chorus, a reordering and sometimes shortening of musical numbers, and a single, all-purpose set. The production was an attempt to reduce the opera to something closer to Merimée's novella, as, over the years, the opera has become inflated beyond Bizet's intentions through the use of sung recitatives replacing Bizet's spoken dialogue and through increasingly elaborate stage settings.

With a reputation as an iconoclast, Brook appeared to mark the beginning of a new era for the relatively stolid, conservative Royal Opera, a change welcomed by General Administrator David Webster. Later describing opera as "the Deadly Theater carried to absurdity," Brook arrived at the Royal Opera with substantial theatrical but little operatic experience. He anticipated the shift from the dominance of the singer or conductor to what is now referred to as the tyranny of the producer. His approach to operatic directing was fluid and dynamic, with a propensity for making frequent changes during the course of rehearsal and asking the singers—soloists and chorus—to move around the stage far more than was customary at the time.

Brook's first production at the Royal Opera was Musorgsky's *Boris Godunov,* the first at Covent Garden to use the composer's original version rather than Rimsky-Korsakov's reorchestration. This was a highly detailed, almost cinematic production with scenery that threatened to—and according to some critics did—overwhelm the performers. It proved to be a controversial staging, one praised for its excitement and psychological relevance as furiously as it was condemned for dwarfing the work. The production included sliding doors in the Kremlin, the use of recorded bells, and a procession of ghosts in the clock scene. According to Richard Temple Savage, the chorus was encouraged to behave like true revolutionaries, with the result that they left the singer playing Kruschev battered and bruised.

Puccini's *La bohème* followed, a production dominated by Ljuba Welitsch's Musetta rather than Brook's staging. Brook's next production, Mozart's *Le nozze di Figaro,* was hailed for its clarity and careful delineation of the class distinctions that are central to the plot. The 1949 season opened with Bliss's *The Olympians,* the first new English opera produced at Covent Garden after World War II. However, Brook's staging could not turn the work into a success, largely because the dearth of English opera singers at the time led to the casting of non-native speakers—not an ideal situation for a work intended to launch English opera at Covent Garden.

The production was criticized for being overloaded with detail and for the extent of movement of the singers. The efforts expended on the preparation of *The Olympians* had a detrimental effect on the remaining productions of the season.

For Brook's new *Salome,* starring Welitsch, the director chose Salvador Dali to design the sets. This production was looked to as the salvation of the season, and it provided Brook with the potential to create another spectacle, which the works since *Boris Godunov* had not. In the event, Musical Director Karl Rankl's edict against guest conductors led to a conflict with Brook, who wanted Strauss specialist Fritz Reiner to lead the performance. Rankl's reaction to the production may have been influenced by its explicit eroticism; what he revealed publicly was that he strongly disapproved of Dali's set, feeling that the singers would be inaudible because they would be placed too far back and because, as he complained in a telegram to Webster, there was no room on the stage for the Jews. The singers found the surreal costumes uncomfortable at best and, with their various sharp projections, even dangerous; the set, with numerous gaps in the flooring, had to be modified before the first performance to ensure the singers' safety. The production, described by *Opera* magazine as London's "first important postwar operatic scandal," was a popular but not a critical success. The critics felt that Brook, in this production as well as in the others, had tampered excessively with an established masterpiece. Brook, stating publicly that the opera world apparently was not ready for productions that challenged its intelligence, did not renew his contract for a third season.

Brook brought controversy to the Metropolitan Opera as well, with a production of *Faust,* first seen in 1953, that was updated to the nineteenth century—the composer's period—again anticipating a modern trend.

In 1981, thirty years after his departure from Covent Garden, a Brook production of Mozart's *Don Giovanni* was announced, but it did not take place.

—Michael Sims

BROTHER DEVIL
See FRA DIAVOLO

BROUWENSTIJN, Gré (born Gerarda Damphina).

Soprano. Born 26 August 1915 in Den Helder, Netherlands. Studied with Jaap Stroomenberg, Boris Pelsky and Ruth Horna in Amsterdam; debut as one of the three ladies in *Die Zauberflöte,* Amsterdam, 1940; joined the Netherlands opera, 1946; debut at Covent Garden as Aïda, 1951, and sang Verdi roles there until 1964, including Elisabeth in *Don Carlos,* 1958; sang Elisabeth, Gutrune, Sieglinde and Eva at Bayreuth, 1954-56; Chicago debut as Jenufa, 1959; debut at Glyndebourne as Leonore in *Fidelio,* 1959, and sang the same role in her farewell performance in Amsterdam, 1971.

Publications

By BROUWENSTIJN: books–

Gré Brouwenstijn met en zonder make-up. Bessum. 1971.

About BROUWENSTIJN: articles–

Rosenthal, H. "Gré Brouwenstijn." *Opera* (July 1959).

* * *

Critics invariably seem to refer to Dutch soprano Gré Brouwenstijn as a "great singing actress," an encomium which carries with it an implied apology: that personal charisma and stageworthiness compensated for a voice that was not in itself really first rate. While this does Brouwenstijn something of a disservice—she had quite a fine voice in addition to being a superb actress—it is true enough that her relatively small number of recordings do not alone entirely capture her greatness.

Audiences lucky enough to see Brouwenstijn in opera, for example, still speak of the overwhelming humanity of her Desdemona in Verdi's *Otello,* the passion of her Leonore in *Fidelio,* the radiance of her Elisabeth in *Tannhäuser,* and the nobility of her Elisabetta in *Don Carlo* as unique experiences, incomparable—in the truest sense of that overused word—with those of any other singer. Of these performances, the first two, like so many of Brouwenstijn's operatic roles, are preserved on disc only in scenes and arias excerpted out of context—a particularly inadequate document for this artist of the theatre. For the latter two roles we are luckier; radio transcription recordings of famous performances have been issued complete and are readily available.

It must be said at the outset that neither the excerpts nor the complete performances preserve Brouwenstijn's marvelous physical presence: her statuesque and mobile body and her remarkably expressive face, alive and responsive to every nuance of character. They do capture her vocal characterizations, and even through these limited means we are immediately struck by the power of her commitment, the depth and involvement of her acting. We also note that she does not always have the means at her disposal to neatly execute all of her extraordinary ideas: sometimes her breath control cannot quite support the arching line she clearly wants to make in an aria like Elisabetta's "Tu che le vanità," for instance; sometimes her intonation will go awry in the heat of passion. The voice itself is instantly recognizable, beautiful and warm, and of a thoroughly individual character—due in part to a somewhat tremulous quality that will not be to every listener's taste.

It is, however, this very tremulousness that in good part gives Brouwenstijn's performances the overwhelming intensity and sense of compassion that they all share. It was her great gift to invest even the grandest and most regal of heroines with a basic humanity which other singers—even other "great singing actresses"—have often found surprisingly elusive. Many other sopranos have, for example, performed Desdemona with success and have made something vivid and touching of the "Willow Song," but few, if any, have so poignantly revealed the humble young woman behind the regal persona.

Her performance as Sieglinde in Erich Leinsdorf's recording of *Die Walküre* is probably Brouwenstijn's best commercial record. She does not possess the sheer power and silvery top of several other notable interpreters, but her specificity and sense of wonderment are paralleled only by Lotte Lehmann. The extended narrative "Der Männer Sippe" in the first act, which in less skilled hands can seem like expository recitation, in Brouwenstijn's performance has a touch of revelation and luminescence that are quite unique. And though she may lack the natural vocal heft we have come to expect in the climactic passages of "Du bist der Lenz" and "O hehrstes Wunder," there is ample compensation in a sense of rapture that satisfies in a way purely vocal means never could.

Still, even this wonderful record is no more than a partial souvenir of Brouwenstijn. What a pity that her career predated the "age of videotape"! Had she appeared perhaps twenty years later, she might have preserved for later generations more complete documentation of her artistry. Instead, younger listeners must make use of what is left, the tantalizing but incomplete mementos of this most special and individual of artists.

—David Anthony Fox

BRUNEAU, (Louis-Charles-Bonaventure-) Alfred.

Composer. Born 3 March 1857, in Paris. Died 15 June 1934, in Paris. Student of Franchomme at the Paris Conservatory, 1873, and later studied harmony with Savard and composition with Massenet; Prix de Rome for his cantata *Sainte-Geneviève,* 1881; music critic for *Gil Blas,* 1892-95, *Le Figaro,* and *Le Matin;* Knight of the Légion d'Honneur, 1895; member of "Conseil Supérieur" at the Paris Conservatory, 1900; first conductor at the Opéra-Comique, 1903-4; Commandeur de St.-Charles, 1907; inspector of music instruction, 1909; tours of Russia, England, Spain, and the Netherlands conducting his own works; member of the Académie des Beaux Arts, 1925.

Operas

Kérim, Milliet and H. Lavedan, 1885-86, Château d'Eau, 9 June 1887.
Le rêve, Gallet (after Zola), 1890, Paris, Opéra-Comique, 18 June 1891.
L'attaque du moulin, Gallet (after Zola), 1892-93, Paris, Opéra-Comique, 23 November 1893.
Messidor, Zola, 1894-96, Paris, Opéra, 19 February 1897.
L'ouragan, Zola, 1897-1900, Paris, Opéra-Comique, 29 April 1901.
Lazare, Zola, 1902.
L'enfant roi, Zola, 1902, Paris, Opéra-Comique, 3 March 1905.
Nias Micoulin, Bruneau (after Zola, *La douleur de Toine*), 1906, Monte Carlo, 2 February 1907.
Les quatre journées, Bruneau (after Zola), 1908-16, Paris, Opéra-Comique, 25 December 1916.
Le jardin du paradis, R. de Flers and G.-A. de Caillavet (after H. C. Anderson), 1913-21, Paris, Opéra, 31 October 1923.
Le roi Candaule, M. Donnay, 1917-19, Paris, Opéra-Comique, 1 December 1920.
Angelo, tyran de Padoue, Méré (after Hugo), 1923-25, Paris, Opéra-Comique, 16 January 1928.
Virginie, H. Duvernois, 1928-30, Paris, Opéra, 7 January 1931.

Publications

By BRUNEAU: books–

Musiques d'hier et de demain. Paris, 1900.
La musique française. Paris, 1901.
Musiques de Russie et musiciens de France, Paris, 1903.
La vie et les oeuvres de Gabriel Fauré. Paris, 1925.
A l'ombre d'un grand coeur [on Zola]. Paris, 1932.
Massenet. Paris, 1935.

articles–

Articles in *Revue indépendente* (1889-90), *Revue illustrée* (1891), *Gil Blas* (1892-95), *Grande revue* (1902), as well as *Le Figaro* and *Le Matin.*

About BRUNEAU: books–

Hervey, A. *Alfred Bruneau.* London, 1907.
Séré, O. *Musiciens français d'aujourd'hui* [pp. 53 ff, 416 ff]. Paris, 1921.
Boschot, A. *La vie et les oeuvres de Alfred Bruneau.* Paris, 1937.
Cooper, M. *French Music from the Death of Berlioz to the Death of Fauré* [p. 102 ff]. London, 1951.
Guieu, Jean-Max. *Le théâtre lyrique d'Émile Zola.* Paris, 1983.

articles–

Wallon, S. "Chronologie des oeuvres d'Alfred Bruneau." *Revue de musicologie* 29 (1947): 25.
Longyear, R.M. "Political and Social Criticism in French Opera 1827-1920." In *Essays on the Music of J.S. Bach and Other Divers Subjects: A Tribute to Gerhard Herz,* edited by Robert L. Weaver, 245. Louisville, 1981.
Nicoladi, Fiamma. "Parigi e l'opera verista: dibattiti, riflessioni, polemiche." *Nuova rivista musicale italiana* 15 (1981): 577.

*   *   *

To many music lovers, Alfred Bruneau is an obscure relic of the past. During his rise to prominence, however, Bruneau was regarded as a successor to or at least a promising follower of Richard Wagner. He did utilize some of Wagner's concepts and techniques, notably the extensive employment of individual voice (as opposed to duets, trios, etc.) and the heavy use of orchestration, but he fell far short of his predecessor's genius, and conspicuously lacked the wonderful Wagnerian gift of melody.

Another outstanding artist who strongly influenced Bruneau was the great French writer Émile Zola. Six of Bruneau's seven most significant operas had librettos written by or based on Zola. Bruneau was an avid disciple of Zola's "naturalism" ("scientifically" based emphasis on nature and freedom), and of his political activities; when the novelist championed the cause of Dreyfus in the infamous Dreyfus affair, Bruneau followed in his path. Unfortunately, the political fallout from his controversial stand in the late 1890s negatively affected public acceptance of his works.

It was Bruneau's controversial musical style, however, that played the largest part in the public's hostile reaction to his works. His involvement with realistic and naturalistic themes, his frequent use of harsh dissonance, his general disregard for traditional harmony, and his overemphasis on the individual voice in his operas all combined to evoke displeasure among the generally conservative French critics.

Despite all of this, Bruneau had a major impact on his time due to his introduction of realism to the musical stage. Although his operas are neither widely nor frequently performed today, he did have an important role in the evolution of modern French opera. Seven of his operatic works are particularly significant. *Le rêve* (*The Dream*) was probably Bruneau's second most successful opera and the most stylistically severe of his better known works. *L'attaque du Moulin* (*The Attack on the Mill*), his most successful work, was not quite as intensely iconoclastic as its predecessor. *Messidor* (*Messidor,* or the tenth month of the French Republican calendar) and the spectacular *L'ouragan* (*The Hurricane*) moved somewhat away from the purer and stricter naturalism of the earlier works. *L'enfant roi* (*The Child King*) and *Le roi Candaule* (*King Candaule*), two of his later works, were lighter in mood, but another later work, *Les quatres journées* (*The Four Days*), is tragic with a definite touch of heroism.

Bruneau's innovations helped mold the future of his country's operatic productions, but his unconventional ideas also detracted from the quality of his works. What once seemed daring now seemed awkward and inartistic. What his idol Wagner could get away with the less well endowed Bruneau could not.

—William E. Studwell

BRUSCANTINI, Sesto.

Baritone. Born 10 December 1919, in Porto Civitanova, Italy. Married: the singer Sena Jurinac, 1953. Studied music with Luigi Ricci in Rome; Teatro alla Scala debut in the bass role of Don Geronimo in Cimarosa's *Il matrimonio segreto,* 1949; sang at Glyndebourne, 1951-56; appeared at the Salzburg Festival, 1952; U.S. debut with the Chicago Lyric Opera, 1961.

*   *   *

During a career spanning more than forty years, Sesto Bruscantini has won a name for himself as one of the leading bass-baritones in Italian opera of the eighteenth and nineteenth centuries. He has sung several serious, dramatic roles (Germont in Verdi's *La traviata,* for example), but his fame lies in his portrayal of comic characters. Judged solely as a musician, Bruscantini might receive low marks from many opera-goers; judged as a singer-actor, he is unsurpassed on the comic stage.

Bruscantini specializes in funny old men. He has done so since he was a young man, making his Teatro alla Scala debut in 1949 as Geronimo, the foolish father in Cimarosa's *Il matrimonio segreto.* Unlike the lyric tenor Luigi Alva, who specialized in the portrayal of very young men even as he himself grew older, Bruscantini has found himself growing increasingly suited to the roles he sings best.

Bruscantini has never been satisfied to stay, together with many other opera-singers, within the safe and easy confines of the standard repertory. He helped to revive many fine comic operas of the late eighteenth century, including works by Paisiello, Piccinni and Cimarosa. In a recording of one of these, Piccinni's *La buona figliola* (under Franco Caracciolo),

Bruscantini reveals many of his strengths. The voice is certainly not a beautiful one: a wide vibrato and vague sense of pitch is especially evident in his delivery of recitative. These features of his singing are so pervasive that they may eventually begin to annoy some listeners. But Bruscantini conveys the words, their sound and their meaning, so vividly that it is easy not to notice the vocal weaknesses. The character that he sings, Mengotto, is close to Mozart's Masetto in personality as well as name. Bruscantini's portrayal of the hapless peasant is funny and touching; after the opera is over we feel that we know and understand Mengotto.

Bruscantini has sung several Mozart roles, but not always with equal success. His portrayal of Leporello (Rome, 1954) was criticized as lacking sufficient vocal power. He has sung Don Alfonso throughout his career, from Glyndebourne in 1951 to Salzburg in 1985. It is a perfect role for him: one in which his skills as an actor and comedian are of great use, and the vocal demands relatively light. One critic at Salzburg described Bruscantini's performance as "more spoken than sung"; yet his portrayal of Don Alfonso was "of the highest class."

Late in his career critics tended to blame the purely musical shortcomings of Bruscantini's performances on old age. "He is now obliged to reduce the part to Sprechgesang," according to a critic of his performance of the title role of Donizetti's *Don Pasquale* at the Teatro alla Scala in 1985. The implication was that earlier in his career Bruscantini was more accurate in pitch, but similar complaints were aimed at him from near the beginning of his career. When he sang the same role at Salzburg in 1952, a critic complained that his Don Pasquale "sang too little and pattered too much."

Since the 1970s Bruscantini has combined directing with singing. A triple bill of Italian comic operas at the Wexford Festival (1977), under Bruscantini's direction and with him starring, was greeted with great laughter and applause. A double bill that he presented at the Dallas Opera in 1985 (Cimarosa's one-man show *Il maestro di cappella* and Rossini's *La cambiale di matrimonio*), was likewise much applauded. These performances have served as opportunities not only for audiences to enjoy Bruscantini's talents, but also for Bruscantini to pass his theatrical experience on to a younger generation.

—John A. Rice

BÜLOW, Hans (Guido) von.

Conductor. Born 8 January 1830, in Dresden. Died 12 February 1894, in Cairo. Married: 1) Cosima Liszt (daughter of Franz Liszt), 1857 (divorced, 1870); 2) Marie Schanzer, actress, 1882. Studied piano with Friedrich Wieck and theory with Max Eberwein, beginning 1839; took a music course with Moritz Hauptmann, and studied law at the University of Leipzig; studied piano with Plaidy; in Stuttgart, 1846-48; studied at the University of Berlin, 1849; met Wagner in Zurich; studied with Liszt in Weimar; tour as a pianist through Germany and Austria, 1853; head of the piano department at the Sterns Conservatory, Berlin, 1855-64; court pianist and conductor to Ludwig II of Munich, 1864; conducted the premiere of Wagner's *Tristan und Isolde* at the Court Opera in Munich, 10 June 1865; conducted the premiere of *Die Meistersinger von Nürnberg*, 21 June 1868; in Florence, 1872; tours of England and Russia as a pianist;

United States piano tour, 1875-76; Hofkapellmeister in Hanover, 1878-80; Hofkapellmeister in Meiningen, 1880-85; conductor of the Berlin Philharmonic, 1887-1893; in Cairo for treatment of a lung disorder.

Publications

By BÜLOW: books–

Bülow, Marie von, ed. *Briefe und Schriften Hans von Bülows.* 8 vols. Leipzig, 1895-1908.
Bache, C., trans. *The Early Correspondence of Hans von Bülow.* London, 1896.
with Richard Strauss. *Correspondence.* Edited by Willi Schuh and Franz Trenner, translated by A. Gishford. Westport, Connecticut, 1979.

About BÜLOW: books–

Zabel, E. *Hans von Bülow.* Hamburg, 1894.
Sternfeld, R. *Hans von Bülow.* Leipzig, 1894.
Pfeiffer, T. *Studien bei Hans von Bülow.* Berlin, 1894; 6th ed., 1909.
Vianna da Motta, J. *Nachtrag zu den Pfeifferschen "Studien bei Hans von Bülow".* Leipzig, 1895.
Heimann, H. *Hans von Bülow: Sein Leben und sein Wirken.* Berlin, 1909.
Bülow, Marie von. *Hans von Bülows Leben dargestellt aus seinen Briefen.* Leipzig, 1919.
Du Moulin-Eckart, R. *Hans von Bülow.* Berlin, 1921.
Bülow, Marie von. *Hans von Bülow in Leben und Wort.* Berlin, 1925.

Hans von Bülow

Schonberg, Harold C. *The Great Conductors.* New York, 1967.

articles–

Freitag, W. "An Annotated Biography of Hans von Bülow in the Harvard College Library." *Harvard Library Bulletin* July (1967).

* * *

Hans von Bülow, after hearing Wagner conduct in Dresden in 1849 and the premiere of *Lohengrin* under Liszt at Weimar in 1850, abandoned the law career chosen for him by his mother. He sought advice from Liszt and practical help from Wagner (then in Zurich), who arranged his first operatic conducting experience with Donizetti's *La fille du régiment.* Bülow's lack of tact soon led to his dismissal from Zurich, whereupon he moved to the small opera house in St Gallen as musical director and began with *Der Freischütz.* It was well received, not least because he conducted it without the score, a feature of his working methods which was to become renowned.

Bülow's conducting work was then interrupted by Liszt, who accepted him as a piano student. After teaching in Berlin and undertaking concert tours as a pianist, Bülow began a significant conducting phase in his career when he was appointed Hofkapellmeister in Munich, where he gave the premieres of *Tristan und Isolde* (1865) and *Die Meistersinger* (1868). In his meticulous preparation and rehearsal from memory of both operas (for five years he had been preparing a piano score of *Tristan*), Bülow virtually developed the procedure by which operas have since come to be staged in Germany and elsewhere. He began with individual coaching of his répétiteurs so that they in turn could prepare the singers to his satisfaction. He would then rehearse the singers both singly and in ensembles before they began production rehearsals with piano. This schedule of preparation was also used for the orchestra with first sectional and then full orchestral rehearsals before combining players and singers in *Sitzproben* and stage rehearsals (there were eleven pre-dress rehearsals for *Tristan* before the final dress rehearsal).

In 1869, Bülow resigned from Munich, unable to cope when his wife (Liszt's daughter Cosima) left him for Wagner, also foreseeing the scenic problems of staging the premiere of *Das Rheingold* demanded by King Ludwig against the composer's wishes. After more concert tours, he spent the years 1878-80 as Hofkapellmeister in Hanover, but resigned after a quarrel with the tenor Anton Schott (during *Lohengrin* he described the singer as a Knight of the Swine rather than of the Swan). Bülow moved on to Meiningen as Hofmusikdirektor, where he moulded the orchestra into one of Germany's finest, insisting that they play standing up and from memory. His last years were spent touring, teaching or guest-conducting at the Berlin or Hamburg opera houses.

Bülow was a musician of formidable ability, with absolute self-command and an acute intellectual power of interpretation whether of the established classics or of new works, though his repertoire was largely limited to German and Austrian music. He also possessed an irascible and quick-tempered nature; he was quarrelsome, nervous, passionate and given to extremes of mood. Weingartner thought he lacked the necessary instinct for working in opera and that by devoting his entire attention to the orchestra, he ignored his singers. Bülow's 1887 performance of *Carmen* in Hamburg horrified Weingartner with its musical aberrations and excessive rubato. However, Richard Strauss, a Bülow protégé, had the highest regard for his intellect, his analysis of phrasing and his grasp of the psychological content of the music of Beethoven and Wagner.

—Christopher Fifield

BUMBRY, Grace (Melzia Ann).

Mezzo-soprano and soprano. Born 4 January 1937, in St. Louis. Married the tenor Erwin Jaeckel in 1963. Studied at Boston University, Northwestern University and with Lotte Lehmann in Santa Barbara, 1955-58; winner (with Martina Arroyo) of the Metropolitan Opera auditions, 1958; operatic debut as Amneris in *Aida* at the Paris Opera, 1960; first black artist to appear at Bayreuth, 1961; debut at Covent Garden as Eboli, 1963; debut at Chicago as Ulrica, 1963; debut at Salzburg as Lady Macbeth, 1964; debut at Metropolitan Opera as Eboli, 1965, where she appeared in more than 170 performances; first soprano role was Santuzza in 1970.

Publications

About BUMBRY: articles–

Blyth, A. "Grace Bumbry." *Opera* June (1970): 506.

* * *

Grace Bumbry was one of several black female singers to arrive on the international operatic stage in the 1960s. Her emergence to this position progressed through a series of events that began in her childhood—singing both in her church and school choirs, beginning formal vocal study, entering local talent competitions, and appearing and winning first prize by singing the aria "O don fatale" from Verdi's *Don Carlos* on Arthur Godfrey's Talent Scouts in 1954 after her graduation from high school in St. Louis, Missouri. The singing of this aria allowed her to be heard by many Americans. The role of Princess Eboli in *Don Carlos* has continued to be one of her most successful endeavors on the operatic stage.

A scholarship enabled Bumbry to attend Boston University, but her true progress as a student of voice did not come about until she met and sang for Lotte Lehmann in a series of Master Classes in 1955, after transferring to Northwestern University near Chicago. It would appear that Lehmann was immensely impressed with Grace Bumbry because she was able to entice Bumbry to begin a very thorough and intensive three and a half years of study with her at the Music Academy of the West in Santa Barbara, California. She was, during her study, the recipient of a Marian Anderson Scholarship and a John Hay Whitney Award. During her final year of study with Lehmann, she was a joint winner (with Martina Arroyo) of the Metropolitan Opera Auditions of the Air. Even after this prestigious award, it was still not easy for her to launch a creditable career in the United States. Lehmann took her to England and Europe in 1959, where her most significant success took place at the Paris Opéra with her portrayal of Amneris in *Aida.* The acclaim she received in Paris helped her secure a three-year contract with Basel Opera in Switzerland. She began to add numerous roles to her repertory there.

Bumbry reached true international status in 1961 with her performance in Wagner's *Tannhäuser* for the Bayreuth Wagner Festival. She became the first black artist ever to sing in this great house. Her opportunity to portray the role of the traditionally blond-headed goddess was the result of a recommendation from the conductor Wolfgang Sawallisch to Wieland Wagner. In spite of protests from racist groups and neo-Nazi factions, Bumbry received thunderous applause. Critics were quick to make predictions about her future. For example, Ronald Eyer, writing in the New York Herald Tribune, prophesied that she would be the first great black Wagnerian. She did make a repeat appearance in Bayreuth later in the year in the same opera and for companies in Lyons and Chicago; but these prognostications did not completely materialize, in spite of her development into a singer of dramatic soprano roles. Her debuts at Covent Garden in 1963 and at the Metropolitan Opera in 1965 were both as Princess Eboli in *Don Carlos.* Reviewers were lavish in their praise of her commanding presence on stage (at 5'7″ with weight of 140 pounds, she is extremely striking in appearance), and critics lauded the excitement and dramatic qualities she brought to roles she interpreted for the stage.

Bumbry's singing also captured the hearts of spectators and reviewers, as is evidenced by statements such as those made by Alan Rich in the New York Herald Tribune of her debut at the Metropolitan Opera: "It is a big voice, but flexible and beautifully focused."

After 1970 when Bumbry began to perform soprano roles, conductors such as Karajan, Böhm, and Solti encouraged her upon hearing the way her top tones were developing. Her debut as Santuzza in Mascagni's *Cavalleria rusticana,* her first soprano role, came with the Vienna Staatsoper. She continued singing soprano repertoire as Salome in the same year (1970), and in 1971 she sang her first Tosca at the Metropolitan Opera. She performed the same role at Covent Garden in 1973. Reviewers and audiences have not been as consistent in their praise of her singing since her transition from a mezzo-soprano to a dramatic soprano. Notes in her upper range are not always as warm and resonant as those in her middle and lower tessituras. Other critics fault her languages and ability to execute phrases effectively. Despite such criticism, Bumbry, with her ability to exude magnetism from the stage, is still in 1992 singing in the major opera houses throughout the world. Because of her mastery of both mezzo-soprano and soprano roles, she has been successful as both Elisabetta and Eboli in *Don Carlos,* the roles of Venus and Elisabeth in *Tannhäuser,* and the Aïda and Amneris in *Aïda*—she sang both of these roles in a 1975 British Broadcasting Corporation telecast of *Aïda.* Her first major recording was with Joan Sutherland in Handel's *Messiah* in 1961. Opera discs that followed include *Aïda,* Bayreuth *Tannhäuser, Orfeo, Carmen,* and *Il trovatore,* to name a few.

—Rose Mary Owens

LA BUONA FIGLIUOLA, ossia La Cecchina [The Good Daughter, or Cecchina].

Composer: Niccolò Piccinni.

Librettist: C. Goldoni.

First Performance: Rome, Teatro delle Dame, 6 February 1760.

Publications

book–

Popovici, Josefine Dagmar. *La buona figliuola von Nicolo Piccinni.* Vienna, 1920.

article–

Torrefranca, T. "Strumentalità della commedia musicale: *Buona figliuola, Barbiere,* e *Falstaff.*" *Nuova rivista musicale italiana* 18 (1984): 1.

At the height of Carlo Goldoni's extraordinary career as a writer of spoken comedies and operatic *drammi giocosi* (mostly in collaboration with the composer Galuppi), he was invited to write for the court at Parma. Among the works filling that commission was the libretto for *La buona figliuola,* first set to music by Dunì in 1757. Three years later the young Piccinni tried his hand at the text, and the resulting spectacle was produced in Rome on 6 February 1760. It was the singularly most popular comic opera of the next twenty years, and swept over Europe in a barrage of performances; it was revived over thirty times in the next ten years alone. The tender, sentimental nature of this libretto (adapted from Richardson's *Pamela*) was well suited to Piccinni's facile, endearing melodies and lively finales.

The plot of *La buona figliuola* revolves around one of Goldoni's favorite themes: the follies of class distinction. Cecchina, the supposed orphan gardener at the palace of the marquis, secretly loves her master. The peasant Mengotto confesses his love for her, but Cecchina can offer only friendship. The marquis himself confesses his love, but she, too shy to respond (and too aware of her station), runs away. He tries to persuade another servant of the house, Sandrina, to intercede for him, to no avail. Armidoro learns of the marquis' affection for Cecchina and reconsiders his own marriage to the marquis' sister, since he could not possibly have a commoner for a sister-in-law! The marchioness conspires to save her betrothal by sending Cecchina away, but the marquis intervenes and commands Cecchina to stay. Caught in the middle of their argument, Cecchina runs off. In the country, she is discovered by Sandrina and Paoluccia, the marchioness's handmaid, and is roundly scolded (for stealing away the hearts of all the men). Mengotto again offers her his companionship, but Sandrina and Paoluccia tell him of Cecchina's affection for the marquis, so he abandons her. The marquis happens along, and the two female conspirators now say Cecchina is leaving with Mengotto, and the marquis rejects her as well. He later learns the truth and searches frantically for Cecchina outside the palace. Armidoro has kidnapped her, but she is rescued by Mengotto; the marquis finds her and whisks her away to the castle. Mengotto is talked out of suicide by a new figure, the drunken soldier Tagliaferro, who (in terrible Italian) entices Mengotto into becoming a soldier. Cecchina, pursued by the marquis, bluntly tells him that she is beneath his station. Tagliaferro appears and informs the marquis that Cecchina, who was found abandoned on the road as a baby twenty years earlier, is really the daughter of a German baron. The marquis is elated, as this will expedite his marriage. Cecchina continues to be the subject of accusations by Sandrina and Paoluccia, but the marquis believes none of it. In the end everything is worked out: Cecchina learns of her birthright and proclaims her love for the marquis; the wedding guests, at first surprised to see Cecchina when a marriage to a German baroness had been announced, are shown documents by Tagliaferro as proof of her heritage; Armidoro and the marchioness agree to marriage; and all sing in praise of Cupid's power.

Much of Piccinni's (perhaps overstressed) reputation for mastery of pathetic, emotive arias springs from this work; Cecchina is, after all, a quintessential mistreated and unfortunate character. Her aria near the end of the first act, "Una povera ragazza," explores her misfortune and is perhaps most representative of her station: no father or mother, mistreated, abused. It ends with her statement that Heaven will not abandon "innocence and honesty." The melancholy mood of Piccinni's musical setting carries over into the first closing ensemble finale, in which the ridiculing, frivolous accusations of Sandrina and Paoluccia, set in presto thirds, alternates with Cecchina's cries for mercy (in a slow minor key).

Among the more important musical contributions by Piccinni in this work are the ensembles. Piccinni was likely the first to bring the northern ensemble finale tradition, begun by Galuppi and Logroscino (which featured a flexible alternation of tempos, keys, moods, and motives, all dictated by shifts of the plot), south to Rome and Naples, as seen in this early work. The finales of *La buona figliuola* are particularly well planned, with juxtaposed pathetic and comic sections, recurring rondo-like motives, and an overall convincing harmonic design supported with a lucid orchestration. The second-act finale, for example, is highly sectional, with each nuance in the action supported by musical embroidery. Sandrina and Paolucia first accuse Cecchina of amorous advances to Tagliaferro in derisive thirds, after which she denies their words vigorously. The marquis believes her and answers in a minuet, lightly ornamented. A brisk presto closing section ensues, in which the two women sarcastically review the situation, Cecchina stands confused, and the men ridicule the women's attack.

—Dale E. Monson

Karel Burian as Herod in *Salome*, Dresden, 1905

Publications

By BURIAN: books–

Burian, K. *Z mých paměti* [memoirs]. Prague, 1913.

About BURIAN: books–

Burian, E.F. *Karel Burian.* Prague, 1948.

articles–

Dennis, J. et al. "Karel Burian." *Record Collector* 18 (1969): 149.

*   *   *

BURIAN, Karel (Carl Burrian).

Tenor. Born 12 January 1870, in Rousínov, near Rakovník, Bohemia. Died 25 September 1924, in Senomaty, Czechoslavakia. Studied with Wallerstein in Pivoda and von Kraus in Prague and Munich; debut as Jenik in *The Bartered Bride,* Brno, 1891; sang at several European houses, then at Dresden, 1902-10, specializing in Wagner; created Herod in *Salome,* 1905; at Covent Garden in Wagner roles, 1904-14; at Bayreuth, 1908; debut at Metropolitan Opera as Tannhäuser, 1906, and remained there for several seasons; joined Vienna State Opera.

Karel Burian's place in operatic history is assured by his creation of the role of Herod in *Salome,* but to be remembered for this alone would do an injustice to one of the greatest singers ever produced by Czechoslovakia. Though he achieved international fame, he remained faithful to his native country and became a noted interpreter of Czech opera and song.

Burian's voice was a large tenor of robust quality, Germanic rather than Italianate in tone and production and ideally suited to the *Heldentenor* repertoire. Indeed, it was as one of the finest interpreters of the role of Tristan that he appeared with great success on many of the world's most important stages. His fame in middle European countries was considerable, particularly as Tristan, Siegfried, Parsifal and

Dalibor. In the marvellous seasons at Dresden, at the time a major centre of operatic activity, notably for performances of Verdi and Wagner, he was greatly admired.

Burian's fame spread to the Met, to which he was invited, doubtless on the strength of his creation of Herod, for the planned premiere there of *Salome*. But the usefulness of a *Heldentenor* of his reputation could not be denied, especially at a time when there was still a strong German influence at that house, and regular performances of the *Ring* and other Wagnerian operas, but few tenors who specialized in Wagner. He appeared every season between 1906 and 1913, virtually monopolizing performances of the *Ring, Tristan und Isolde, Parsifal* and *Tannhäuser*. After one performance of *Tristan* with Burian and Fremstad in 1908, Gustav Mahler declared that he had never known a performance of *Tristan* to equal it. The New York critic, W.J. Henderson, wrote ". . . Mr Burian has been heard as Tristan (before) but has not sung the music with so much tenderness, with so much finish of phrase, tone and nuance. [He] rose far above his former level."

Burian recorded for the Gramophone and Typewriter Co. between 1905 and 1908, the Gramophone Co. in 1912, Pathé in 1907 and one solitary title for Parlophon in 1913. Though the records encompass a wide repertoire, representing German and Czech operas in which he excelled and more lyric roles such as Rodolfo (*La Bohème*), they are generally disappointing for they fail to capture the special qualities of Burian's voice. The acoustic techniques of the time often failed with the big, heroic voices. In order to avoid blasting and distortion it was usually necessary to place the singer away from the horn. If the loud singing was successfully captured, the delicacy and nuance could be lost. In addition, Burian's recordings are all sung in German or Czech, regardless of the provenance of the music. Burian himself, something of a poet, expressed disappointment with his recordings: "My voice was not of glassy stone, / Though that's what the gramophone captured. / Today and forever 'twill sound dull. / It's difficult to can one's soul."

What does emerge from the discs is nonetheless an obviously important voice, relatively without vibrato or rubato, but somewhat crudely projected. However, some of the many Czech songs are impressive for their more intimate quality, drawing from the singer a welcomed softening of the somewhat unrelenting tone and revealing an obvious love of the idiom.

It is unfortunate that Burian's voice was not well preserved for posterity. His fame must rest on the laurels of contemporary success and critical approbation.

—Larry Lustig

BURNING FIERY FURNACE
See CHURCH PARABLES

BURROWS, (James) Stuart.

Tenor. Born 7 February 1933, in Pontypridd. Attended Trinity College, Carmarthen, and taught school until 1963; operatic debut as Ismaele in Verdi's *Nabucco* for the Welsh National Opera, 1963; U.S. debut in San Francisco, 1967; debut at Metropolitan Opera as Don Ottavio in *Don Giovanni,* 1971, and appeared there as Tamino, 1972; has also appeared in Vienna and Salzburg.

*　　*　　*

Stuart Burrows has put his warm lyric tenor to good effect in a wide range of repertory. Comedy is not his strong point; he has ceded Rossini's comic tenor roles to others, such as Luigi Alva, who can perform them with a wit and charm that Burrows cannot match. But in more serious roles few if any lyric tenors can surpass him. Burrows is a brilliant interpreter of Mozart's tenor roles. He also sings many leading roles in nineteenth- and twentieth-century opera, and in several different languages, thus demonstrating a versatility rare among leading Mozart tenors.

Burrows' portrayals of Mozart heroes rival and sometimes excell those of Peter Schreier. As Tamino in *Die Zauberflöte*, Burrows has won praise for his sweet tone and convincing characterization, tender yet heroic. Tenderness and heroism can be sensed too in his performance of another great Mozart tenor role, the title role of *La clemenza di Tito*, which he performed at Covent Garden in the 1970s and recorded under Colin Davis. Burrows is one of the very few tenors who has been able to put this role across dramatically as well as technically. He is a strong Titus, firm and manly in his virtue. In "Del più sublime soglio" (Act I), his singing is warmly lyrical, beautifully evoking the nobility and humanity of Tito's character. He is capable of expressing anger; he does so vividly in the second-act accompanied recitative "Che orror! che tradimento!" His rendition of the triumphal aria "Se all'impero", later in Act II, with its fiendishly difficult coloratura, is a technical and dramatic tour-de-force.

Mozart wrote the role of Tito for Antonio Baglioni, for whom he had written the role of Ottavio four years earlier. It should come as no surprise that Burrows makes an admirable Ottavio, exhibiting in his performances of "Il mio tesoro" beautiful tone, exceptional breath control, and perfect command of coloratura. He portrays Ottavio as a young man who is dignified, yet capable of expressing warmth, affection and sympathy to his beloved. A critic praised his portrayal of Don Ottavio in Paris as "one of the best . . . in recent memory".

Burrows is equally effective in nineteenth-century opera, French, Russian and Italian. He has sung Des Grieux (Massenet's *Manon*) with great success; another of his best roles in French opera is the title role in Gounod's *Faust*. When he sang Faust at Covent Garden he won praise from one critic for his "limpid and liquid tones." He has won applause for his sweetly sung portrayals of Lensky (Tchaikovsky's *Eugene Onegin*); as recorded under Solti, Burrows' Lensky "can hardly be bettered", according to one critic. His performance of Pinkerton (Puccini's *Madama Butterfly*) in San Francisco (1971) was praised as "glorious" and "magnificently touching." Burrows' Verdi roles are relatively few; he won praise for his portrayal of Alfredo in *La traviata* (Boston 1972);

but in general his voice may be a little too light for Verdi's demands.

—John A. Rice

BUSCH, Fritz.

Conductor. Born 13 March 1890, in Siegen, Westphalia. Died 14 September 1951, in London. Studied with Steinbach, Boettcher, Uzielli, and Klauwell at the Cologne Conservatory; conductor at the Deutsche Theater in Riga, 1909-10; music director of the city of Aachen, 1912; music director of the Stuttgart Opera, 1918; Generalmusikdirektor of the Dresden State Opera, 1922, where he conducted the premiere of Richard Strauss's *Intermezzo* and *Die ägyptische Helena;* fired from his post at the Dresden State Opera by the Nazis, 1933; conducting engagements with the Danish Radio Symphony Orchestra and the Stockholm Philharmonic; music director of the Glyndebourne Festivals, 1934-39; conducting engagements in South America, 1940-45; conductor at the Metropolitan Opera in New York, 1945-49.

Publications

By BUSCH: books–

Aus dem Leben eines Musikers. Zurich, 1949; English translation as *Pages from a Musician's Life,* London, 1953.

About BUSCH: books–

Burbach, Wolfgang, ed. *In Memoriam Fritz Busch.* Dahlbruch, 1964; 1968.
Busch, G. *Fritz Busch, Dirigent.* Frankfurt, 1970.
Dopheide, B. *Fritz Busch.* Tutzing, 1970.

articles–

Schmiedel, Gottfried. "Fritz Busch and the Dresden Opera." *Opera* March (1960).

*   *   *

Conductor Fritz Busch was one of the major figures on the international music scene from the 1920s to his death in 1951. Busch's importance comes from his several fields of activity: his roles in the German Verdi revival in the 1920s and the English Mozart revival in the 1930s; his posts as music director in Stuttgart and Dresden where he championed new compositions by both established and young composers; and his work in Buenos Aires and with the Danish Radio Symphony Orchestra during his exile from Germany.

Busch conducted most of the major Verdi operas during his career, including those that were rarely performed in Germany until that time, such as *Macbeth.* Curiously enough he never conducted *La traviata,* which one suspects he found too sentimental. His first landmark production in the German Verdi revival was one of *Un ballo in maschera* in Berlin in 1932, produced by Carl Ebert. While in Dresden he staged Franz Werfel's adaptation of *La forza del destino* (Werfel also "rewrote" *Don Carlos* and *Simon Boccanegra*) and prepared

Macbeth, a work which became the first Verdi opera to be produced at Glyndebourne.

The Glyndebourne Festival in England is heavily indebted to Busch as its first music director for setting the standards of excellence that have distinguished it to this day. Busch and producer Ebert instilled an ensemble style and musical élan in the first Glyndebourne season of three Mozart operas that astonished British audiences accustomed to slapdash performances. Mozart became the kernel of the Glyndebourne season, with *Die Entführung aus dem Serail* (never in Busch's mind a "minor," light opera) an important part of it from the beginning and *Idomeneo* added shortly before Busch's death. Busch put Mozart stylists in an uproar, however, by insisting on playing the secco recitatives on the piano and not adding ornamentation. This became a Glyndebourne tradition.

Busch's Mozart recordings exhibit line, rhythmic precision, grace, élan—all those qualities for which Mozart at Glyndebourne is famous. His recitatives seem true conversation, with the words tripping off the singers' tongues. The arias exhibit a fine sense of line and sensitivity to the singers; ensembles often seem almost Rossinian, or perhaps one should say Donizettian, as *Don Pasquale* was a Busch calling card. One drawback may be the tempi, which overall are fairly quick. In the finale of *Così fan tutte,* for example, the singers smudge their runs keeping up with Busch. But these tempi may be due in part to recording requirements at the time. Busch's legendary aversion to ornamentation in Mozart has been (only slightly) overstated. Listening to his Glyndebourne recordings, one hears that the singers often add appoggiaturas at cadence points, although within recitatives and individual numbers ornamentation is indeed rare.

As music director in Stuttgart and Dresden, Busch championed new works by Pfitzner (*Palestrina* and lesser-known works like *Christelflein* and *Die Rose vom Liebesgarten*), Othmar Schoeck (the premiere of *Vom Fischer un syner Fru*), Busoni (the premiere of *Doktor Faust*), and his friends Reger (orchestral works) and Richard Strauss. Busch conducted the premieres of Strauss's *Intermezzo* and *Die ägyptische Helena,* and he was the codedicatee of *Arabella;* he conducted it for the first time in Buenos Aires. Busch also championed younger composers: he conducted the premieres of Hindemith's *Cardillac, Das Nusch-Nuschi,* and *Mörder, Hoffnung der Frauen,* as well as Kurt Weill's *Der Protagonist.*

During his self-exile from Germany in the 1930s and 1940s Busch developed the Danish Radio Symphony Orchestra into an outstanding ensemble; he also conducted extensively the Stockholm Philharmonic. The Teatro Colón in Buenos Aires became his base for opera. Busch also conducted various orchestral concerts there and in other South American cities, and during the Second World War he divided his activities between South and North America. After the war he worked primarily in the United States, conducting opera at the Metropolitan Opera (primarily Wagner, but also Mozart, Donizetti, Verdi, and Strauss) and symphonic concerts in New York, Cincinnati, Chicago, and elsewhere. Before his death Busch returned to Germany where he conducted a radio performance of *Un ballo in maschera.* His son Hans is a distinguished opera producer and teacher.

—David E. Anderson

BUSENELLO, Giovanni Francesco.

Librettist. Born 24 September 1598, in Venice. Died 27 October 1659, in Legnaro, near Padua. Probably studied at the University of Padua prior to 1620; Dean of the Scuola Grande della Misericordia della Val Verde, 1620; practicing lawer, 1623; Busenello was a member of the academies of Delfici, the Umoristi, the Imperfetti, and the Accademia degli Incogniti.

Librettos

Gli amori d'Apollo e di Dafne, Francesco Cavalli, 1640.
La Didone, Francesco Cavalli, 1641.
L'incoronazione di Poppea, Claudio Monteverdi, 1642; revised [by Busenello?], 1651.
La prosperità infelice di Giulio Cesare dittatore, Francesco Cavalli? [perhaps not set], 1646?.
La Statira, principessa di Persia, Venice, 1655.
La dicesa d'Enea all'inferno [not set].

Publications

By BUSENELLO: books–

Delle hore ociose [complete works]. Venice, 1656.

About BUSENELLO: books–

Ivanovich, C. *Minerva al tavolino.* Venice, 1681; 1688.
Mazzuchelli, G.M. *Gli scrittori d' Italia,* vol. 2. Brescia, 1763.
Livingston, A. *Una scappatella di Polo Vendramino e un sonetto di Gian Francesco Busenello.* Rome, 1911.
_____. *La vita veneziana nelle opere di Gian Francesco Busenello.* Venice, 1913.
Spini, G. *Ricerca dei libertini.* Rome, 1950.
_____., and Abert, A.A. *Claudio Monteverdi und das musikalische Drama.* Lippstadt, 1954.
Osthoff, W. *Das dramatische Spätwerk Claudio Monteverdis.* Tutzing, 1960.
Smith, P.J. *The Tenth Muse.* New York, 1970.

articles–

Osthoff, W. "Die venezianische und neapolitanische Fassung von Monteverdis *Incoronazione di Poppea.*" *Acta Musicologica* 26 (1954): 96.
_____. "Neue Beobachtungen zu Quellen und Geschichte von Monteverdis *Incoronazione di Poppea.*" *Die Musikforschung* 11 (1958): 135.
Degrada, F. "Gian Francesco Busenello e il libretto della *Incoronazione di Poppea.*" In *Congresso internazionale sul tema Claudio Monteverdi e il suo tempo: Venezia, Mantova e Cremona 1968,* 81.
Fischer, K. von. "Eine wenig beachtete Quelle zu Busenellos *L' incoronazione di Poppea.*" *Congresso internazionale sul tema Claudio Monteverdi e il suo tempo: Venezia, Mantova e Cremona 1968,* 75.
Chiarelli, A. "*L'incoronazione di Poppea* o *Il Nerone:* problemi di filologia." *Rivista italiana di musicologia* 9 (1974): 117.
Bianconi, L. and T. Walker. "Dalla *Finta pazzo* alla *Veremonda:* storie di Febiarmonici." *Rivista italiana di musicologia* 10 (1975): 379.

Brizi, B. "Teoria e prassi selodrammatica di G.F. Busenello e 'L'Incoronazione di Poppea'." In *Venezia e il melodramma nel Seicento,* edited by M.T. Muraro. Florence, 1976.

*   *   *

Born into a wealthy Venetian family, Giovanni Francesco Busenello studied law at Padua before establishing himself in Venice. Here he took advantage of the opening of the first "public" opera house in 1637 to provide texts for two operatic composers now catering to a popular audience rather than to a courtly patron: Busenello wrote the librettos for Claudio Monteverdi's *L'incoronazione di Poppea* (1643) and Francesco Cavalli's *Gli amori d'Apollo e di Dafne* (1640), *Didone* (1641), *La prosperità infelice di Giulio Cesare dittatore* (1646; possibly never composed) and *Statira, principessa di Persia* (1655 or 1656). Busenello was also a member of the libertine Accademia degli Incogniti in Venice: their sceptical stance towards moral and ethical issues may as well have influenced his work for the theatre, particularly in *L'incoronazione di Poppea,* where the exaltation of Nero's illicit love for his mistress, Poppea, has created significant problems for modern commentators on Monteverdi's last opera. But dubious morality is only to be expected in these new social contexts for opera. So, too, are the tentative experiments in various pastoral and historical genres seen in his librettos for Cavalli. All this typifies the uncertainty of opera in a changing world. Thus Busenello's significance lies chiefly in his attempt to accommodate traditional operatic styles to new social, political, and philosophical environments.

L'incoronazione di Poppea was only one of several librettos that Busenello included in the edition of his "complete works" of 1656, entitled *Delle hore ociose* ("Hours of Leisure": the title is significant). Nevertheless *Poppea* remains his most significant achievement. The choice of an historical subject rather than a pastoral-mythological one (the plot derives from Tacitus, Suetonius, and Seneca) reflects new operatic tendencies in turn influenced by the new audience for opera in Italy in the 1640s. To be sure, Busenello retains a supernatural framework typical of opera from its origins in the late sixteenth century: for example, the prologue establishes an intention to prove Cupid superior to Fortune and Virtue. But the bulk of the action concerns real-life (if unpleasant) characters in real-life emotional situations: the amoral Nero, the scheming Poppea, the rejected Octavia (Nero's wife) and the too-sententious Seneca. The shift in favor of dialogue rather than monologue allows a new naturalism in the presentation of the drama. Moreover, Busenello casts his verse in flexible metrical and structural formats that give full play to the stylistic tendencies of contemporary Venetian music, not least in its new use of triple- and duple-time aria styles to formalize and articulate specific moments of emotional significance. With Busenello, for better or for worse, opera sought to come of age.

—Tim Carter

BUSONI, Ferruccio (Dante Michelangelo Benvenuto).

Composer. Born 1 April 1866, in Empoli, near Florence. Died 27 July 1924, in Berlin. Married: Gerda Sjostrand (two sons). Child prodigy as a pianist; studied with Wilhelm Mayer in Graz, 1877; a member of the Academia Filarmonica in Bologna, 1881; studied Bach's music in Leipzig, 1886; professor of piano, Helsingfors Conservatory, where Sibelius was a student of his; first prize in the Rubinstein Competition for his *Konzertstück* for piano and orchestra, 1890; piano teacher at the Moscow Conservatory, 1890-91; professor at the New England Conservatory of Music, 1891-94; concert tour of Russia, 1912-13; director of the Liceo Musicale in Bologna, 1913; received the order of Chevalier de la Légion d'Honneur from the French government, 1913; in Zurich, 1914-1920, then Berlin until his death. Among Busoni's piano students were Brailovsky, Rudolf Ganz, Egon Petri, Mitropoulos, and Percy Grainger; among his composition students were Kurt Weill, Jarnach, and Wladimir Vogel. Busoni greatly influenced the works of Edgar Varèse.

Operas

Sigune, oder Das stille Dorf, F. Schanz (after a fairy tale), 1885-9 [never orchestrated].
Die Brautwahl, Busoni (after E.T.A. Hoffmann), 1906-11, Hamburg, 12 April 1912.
Arlecchino, oder, Die Fenster, Busoni, 1916-17, Zurich, 11 May 1917.
Turandot, Busoni (after Carlo Gozzi), 1916-17, Zurich, 11 May 1917.
Doktor Faust, Busoni (after the Faust legend and Marlowe), 1916-24 [unfinished; completed by Philipp Jarnach, first performed Dresden, 21 May 1925].

Ferruccio Busoni

Other works: orchestral works, vocal works, chamber music, piano music, songs.

Publications/Writings

By BUSONI: books–

Lehre von der Übertragung von Orgelwerken auf das Klavier, Bach-Busoni gesammelte Ausgabe 5. Leipzig, 1894.
Versuche einer organischen Klavier-Notenschrift. Leipzig, 1910; reprinted in *Bach-Busoni gesammelte Ausgabe* 7, Leipzig, 1920.
Entwurf einer neuen Aesthetic der Tonkunst. Trieste, 1907; English translation as *Sketch of a New Esthetic of Music,* by T. Baker, New York, 1911; reprinted in *Three Classics in the Aesthetics of Music,* New York, 1962.
Über die Möglichkeiten der Oper. Leipzig, 1926.
Schnapp, Friedrich, ed. *Briefe an seine Frau.* Zurich, 1935; English translation by Rosamond Ley, London, 1938; New York, 1975.
Selden-Goth, Gisella, ed. *Fünfundzwanzig Busoni-Briefe.* Vienna, Leipzig, and Zurich, 1937.
Refardt, Edgar, ed. *Briefe . . . an Hans Huber.* Zurich and Leipzig, 1939.
Gesammelte Aufsätze von der Einheit der Musik. Berlin, 1922; revised, edited by J. Henmann as *Wesen und Einheit der Musik.* Berlin, 1956; Italian translation as *Scritte e pensieri sulla musica,* edited by Luigi Dallapiccola and G.M. Gatti, Florence, 1941; English translation, London, 1957.
Beaumont, Antony, ed. *Selected Letters.* London, 1987.
Briner, A., ed. *Briefe Busonis an Edith Andreae.* Zurich, 1979.

librettos–

Der Arlecchineide Fortsetzung und Erde.
Die Götterbraut, written for L.T. Gruenberg.
Die mächtige Zauber, after Gobineau, 1905; published Trieste, 1907, 1910, 1974.
Das Wandbild, set by Schoek, 1920; published Leipzig, 1920.
Das Geheimnis, after Villiers de l'Isle-Adam, 1924; published in *Blätter der Staatsoper* November (1924).

About BUSONI: books–

Leichentritt, Hugo, *Ferruccio Busoni.* Leipzig, 1916.
Selden-Goth, Gisella. *Ferruccio Busoni.* Leipzig and Vienna, 1922.
Pfitzner, Hans. *Futuristengefahr: bei Gelegenheit von Busonis Ästhetik.* Augsburg, 1926.
Jemoli, Hans. *Ferruccio Busonis Zürcherjahre.* Zurich, 1929.
Nadel, S.F. *Ferruccio Busoni.* Leipzig, 1931.
Dent, Edward J. *Ferruccio Busoni: a Biography.* London, 1933; 1974.
Guerrini, Guido, and Paolo Fragapane. *Il "Doctor Faust" di Ferruccio Busoni.* Florence, 1942.
Selden-Goth, Gisella. *Ferruccio Busoni: la vita, la figura, l'opera.* Florence, 1944.
Debusmann, E. *Ferruccio Busoni.* Wiesbaden, 1949.
Busoni, Gerda. *Erinnerungen an Ferruccio Busoni.* Berlin, 1958.
Stuckenschmidt, H.H. *Ferruccio Busoni: Zeittafel eines Europäers.* Zurich, 1967; English translation, London, 1970.
Sablich, Sergio. *Busoni.* Turin, 1982.
Beaumont, Antony. *Busoni the Composer.* London, 1985.
Riethmüller, Albrecht. *Busonis Poetik.* Mainz, 1988.

articles–

Dent, Edward J. "Busoni's 'Doktor Faust'." *Music and Letters* 7 (1926): 196.

———. "Busoni and his Operas." *Opera* July (1954).

Stevenson, Ronald. "Busoni and Mozart." *The Score* September (1955).

Flinois, Pierre. "Ferruccio Busoni: une autre Turandot." *Avant-scène opéra* May–June (1981).

Henderson, Robert. "Busoni, Gozzi, Prokofiev, and The Oranges." *Opera* May (1982).

Jones, Patricia Collins. "Richard Strauss, Ferruccio Busoni and Arnold Schönberg: "Some Imperfect Wagnerites'." *Music Review* 43 (1982): 169.

Beaumont, Antony. "Busoni and the Theatre." *Opera* April (1986).

Baricelli, Jean Pierre. "Faust and the Music of Evil." *Journal of European Studies* (1983): 1.

Roberge, Marc-André. "Le retour au catalogue du *Doktor Faust* de Busoni." *Sonances* [Canada] 2 (1983): 24.

Busoni may still be better known as a transcriber of Bach (as in the "Bach-Busoni" Chaconne and many other keyboard recreations) than as a composer in his own right, but his music and thinking have been a seminal influence in the 20th century. A searching, speculative mind, a mystic and an ironic humorist, he was an inspired synthesizer of opposites, impaled from his earliest years upon the conflicting poles of Italian and German musical and linguistic culture. (His operas are all in German despite their imaginative infusions of Mediterranean warmth and clarity.)

Busoni's earliest influences were in fact the massive formal and contrapuntal logic of Bach (which his father, an itinerant clarinet virtuoso, forced him to study), and the *bel canto* melodic style of Italian opera (his father's repertoire consisted chiefly of operatic fantasies). These he soon combined with Brahmsian romanticism and the revolutionary harmonic thinking (and troubled spiritual atmosphere) of late Liszt: the results can be seen in the spacious virtuosity and startling stylistic juxtapositions of Busoni's huge *Piano Concerto* of 1904, with its final Lisztian "chorus mysticus."

From the *Piano Concerto* on, his idiom became increasingly exploratory. A profound and stimulating writer, in his *Aesthetic der Tonkunst (Sketch for a New Aesthetic of Music)* (1907), Busoni proposed the 12-note chromatic scale as the basic unit of tonality, with the abolition of "consonance" and "dissonance"; he also forecast microtonal systems and the invention of new instruments, including electronic ones. His own music passed through a period of eerily disembodied chromaticism that issued at length in a neo-Mozartian manner Busoni termed *junge Klassizität*—"renewed [literally, "youthful"] classicality"—which ultimately signified the rejection of all competing systems of composition, and the self-conscious (but masterly) employment of whichever artistic means were most appropriate to a given artistic situation.

Busoni had decided views on the role and proper subject of opera. In a 1913 essay, *The Future of Opera,* he stated most categorically that opera: ". . . should take possession of the supernatural or unnatural as its only proper sphere of representation and feeling and should create a pretence world in such a way that life is reflected in either a magic or a comic mirror, presenting consciously that which is not to be found in real life. The magic mirror is for grand opera, the comic for light opera. And dances and masks and apparitions should be interwoven, so that the onlooker never loses sight of the charms of pretence or gives himself up to it as an actual experience." Busoni's personal aesthetic was resolutely antipathetic to Wagner, and this dual stress on the importance of the fantastic and the magical, and on its ironic distancing, ultimately derived from his admiration for Mozart's *Don Giovanni* and *Die Zauberflöte.* In his own work, this aesthetic leads in apparently contradictory directions—on the one hand toward mythic, metaphysical fantasy with an almost religious dimension, and on the other toward an adumbration of Brechtian "alienation." The latter impulse is clearly developed in the stage works of Busoni's pupil Kurt Weill; the former finds perhaps its most resonant echo in the operas of a later admirer, Luigi Dallapiccola. But Busoni's own operas—above all *Doktor Faust*—matchlessly reconcile spiritual yearning and pungent irony, producing a uniquely potent and troubling atmosphere that makes the unseen almost palpable, and eludes easy popularity or facile classification.

Busoni wrote five operas, although the earliest, *Sigune, oder das stille Dorf (Sigune, or the Quiet Village),* composed 1885-89 on a fairy-tale subject, was never orchestrated. The others all belong to the exploratory and consolidatory periods of his last two creative decades. *Die Brautwahl (The Bridal Choice),* composed 1906-11 as Busoni's musical language was beginning to develop new attitudes toward melody and harmony, is by his own above-quoted criteria only a limited success. In this three-act "musical-fantastical comedy," closely based on a tale by E.T.A. Hoffmann (on whom Busoni was an acknowledged authority), comedy and magic are curiously intermingled as the petit-bourgeois society of 1820s Berlin is subverted by the action of magicians—and presented at a length that suggests grand rather than comic opera. Very rarely performed, *Die Brautwahl* contains much fascinating and attractive music, but displays problems of scale and stagecraft. It is both over-leisurely and almost too full of incident; it modulates alarmingly between farce, high seriousness and diablerie, and the libretto (in which Busoni was anxious to alter Hoffmann's dialogue as little as possible) remains undeniably wordy.

Far more successful (because it is concise, fast-moving and unified) is the one-act "theatrical capriccio" *Arlecchino (Harlequin,* 1916-17), a mercurial neo-Mozartian comedy, inspired by the artificiality of marionette-theater. The libretto—Busoni's own—involves the traditional characters of the *Commedia dell'arte* in a satirical anti-war fable, with the trickster Harlequin now in the magician's role, upsetting and energizing the complacent burghers of Bergamo. The 'Chinese fable' *Turandot,* in two short acts, was also composed in 1916-17—to be performed with *Arlecchino* as a double bill. A comparatively minor work, it is built up from extensive incidental music Busoni had written in 1905 and 1911 for Gozzi's play, which is here turned in the direction of studied artificiality, a "light and unreal tone" and fairy-tale exoticism (increased by the use of some actual oriental elements). It thus stands at the furthest possible remove from Puccini's opera on the same subject.

Busoni's choice of subjects and libretti reflect his fascination—and identification—with the powerfully symbolic figures of the magician, or the great artist: indeed, the magician is ultimately a symbol for the artist as seen at the most daring phase of creativity. At various times Busoni projected operas on the subject of the Wandering Jew, of Merlin (Karl Goldmark's opera *Merlin* was an early inspiration), and of Leonardo da Vinci (apparently foreshadowed in Leonhard, the good magician of *Die Brautwahl*). He published a libretto *Die mächtige Zauberer (The Mighty Magician)* for which he wrote no music, and also wrote, in 1918, the libretto of an *Arlecchino*

Part II, or the Geese of the Capitol, which remains unpublished. A bitter and fantastical satire on contemporary art and society, this libretto reputedly introduces a powerful figure who is at once Leonhard, Leonardo—and Faust. In fact, it is in Busoni's *Doktor Faust,* whose libretto was written between 1910 and 1914, that the summation of his life-work is to be found.

Busoni composed the music of *Doktor Faust,* his last opera, between 1916 and his death in 1924, at which point two portions of the work, including the final scene, remained unfinished (completions have been made by his pupil Philipp Jarnach and by Anthony Beaumont). Most of his other compositions during this period have been viewed as "studies" for *Faust,* and many were eventually woven into the opera's fabric in whole or in part. The view, sometimes expressed, that this renders *Faust* some kind of compilation or palimpsest, however, is utterly wrong. The result is Busoni's masterpiece and testament. Based not on Goethe but on the ancient puppet-plays, it is a profoundly, even achingly spiritual work, unsettlingly unattached to any conventional religious purpose save the protagonist's desperation to transcend his human condition. With seeming familiarity it expresses the extremes of mortal terror and spiritual radiance: a religious ardor directed, like that of the Renaissance alchemists, toward a new and magical world, symbolized by the naked youth born from the body of the dying Faust. Its message of psychic struggle, which still intermittently haunts the music of later generations, defines one of the most potent ambiences in 20th century opera.

—Malcolm MacDonald

C

CABALLÉ, Montserrat.

Soprano. Born 12 April 1933, in Barcelona. Studied at Barcelona Conservatorio del Liceo and with Eugenia Kemeny, Conchita Badia and Napoleone Annovazzi; awarded Liceo Gold medal in 1954; debut in *La serva padrona* at Reus, near Barcelona; appeared in Basel and Vienna in the late 1950s; debut at Teatro alla Scala as Flowermaiden in *Parsifal,* 1960; in Massenet's *Manon* in Mexico City, 1964; achieved international fame in concert performance of Lucrezia Borgia at Carnegie Hall, 1965; sang Marschallin in *Der Rosenkavalier* and Countess in *Le nozze di Figaro* at Glyndebourne, 1965; debut at Metropolitan Opera as Marguerite in *Faust,* 1965; debut in Chicago as Violetta, 1970; Covent Garden debut as Violetta, 1970; other roles include Luisa Miller, Desdemona, Ariadne and Tosca.

Publications

About CABALLÉ: books–

Steane, J.B. *The Grand Tradition.* London, 1974.
Farret, G. *Montserrat Caballé.* Paris, 1980.

articles–

Blyth, A. "Montserrat Caballé talks." *Grammaphone* (1973): 174.
Barker, F.G. "Montserrat Caballé" *Opera* April (1975): 342.

* * *

Montserrat Caballé is one of a handful of the greatest prima donnas of the twentieth century. Her limpid tone, seemingly inexhaustible breath capacity, ethereal, high, floated *pianissimi,* and sensitive musicality all combine to make her an exquisite vocalist, one with the ability to drive audiences into a frenzy. As a child she listened to recordings played by her father of Miguel Fleta, who was able to float high notes extremely softly, and she decided that a female could master that also. André Tubeuf has called Caballé's "a slow voice . . . spreading out like a becalmed sea," and Rupert Christiansen has characterized her as "fuller-voiced than Milanov, more individual than Tebaldi, more versatile than Leontyne Price," conceding that "even on an off-night [she] can produce *belles minutes* of a splendor that none of her contemporaries can match." Caballé's ability to spin out a pure legato line in an effortless manner comes from the many years (from age eight through age twenty) she studied at the Liceo Conservatory in her native Barcelona. She was taught breath control by Eugenia Kemeny, who trained her pupils as if they were long-distance runners—they had to learn how to spend the breath to have enough to finish the phrase, the aria, the opera with plenty to spare. At the Conservatory, Caballé learned her first operatic roles—Fiordiligi (*Così fan tutte*), Susanna in *Le nozze di Figaro*, Lucia, and the Queen of the Night (*Die Zauberflöte*)—from its music director, Napoleone

Annovazzi. After leaving her studies with the Gold Medal for Singing, Caballé unsuccessfully made the rounds of auditions in Italy. She began her career in Basel, where she stayed for three years, singing an astonishing number and variety of roles, among them Mimì (when another soprano fell ill), Nedda (*I pagliacci*), Marta in d'Albert's *Tiefland,* Pamina (*Die Zauberflöte*), Marina in *Boris Godunov,* Salome, all three heroines in Offenbach's *Les contes d'Hoffmann,* Leonora in *Il trovatore,* twenty-six Aïdas in the second season, and numerous Donna Elviras (*Don Giovanni*). From there she went to Bremen, where she added Violetta (*La traviata*), Ariadne, Tatiana, Armida, and Rosina (*Il barbiere di Siviglia*). Altogether Caballé sang forty-seven different roles in seven years in the late 1950s and early 1960s. She won a prize from the Vienna Staatsoper for her performance of Salome, her "very favorite" role and one that she has recorded stunningly for RCA Victor under Leinsdorf. Her Teatro alla Scala debut came in 1960 as the First Flower Maiden in Wagner's *Parsifal.* In 1962 she sang for the first time at the Teatro del Liceo in Barcelona, where she met her future husband, the tenor Bernabé Martí. He was Pinkerton to her Butterfly. A wealthy Barcelona family, the Bertrands, had helped the young Caballé, born during the Spanish Civil War, to finance her studies; for this Caballé promised them she would appear every season at the Barcelona theater. Recent undertakings there have included Sieglinde in *Die Walküre,* Respighi's *La fiamma,* Salome, and Isolde.

Caballé has a vast repertoire, ranging from Mozart and before through Bellini's *Norma,* the *non plus ultra* of soprano operatic endeavors, to Wagner and Strauss and beyond. As a young singer she preferred Strauss (there is an exquisite Strauss Lieder recital on RCA with Miguel Zanetti accompanying) and Mozart above all, never intending to tackle the bel canto operas of Rossini, Bellini, and Donizetti. Elisabeth Grümmer was Caballé's idol in Mozart singers. When the opportunity came for Caballé to make her New York debut at Carnegie Hall, substituting for the pregnant Marilyn Horne in Donizetti's *Lucrezia Borgia,* she decided to approach the music as if it were Mozart—whose music she considers a tonic for the voice—but with the proper early-nineteenth-century style. Her success was overwhelming and she has since revived such bel canto rarities as Bellini's *La straniera* and Donizetti's *Caterina Cornaro, Parisina d'Este,* and *Gemma di Vergy.* All of these are available on "live" recordings, the *Gemma di Vergy* from a Carnegie Hall performance in March of 1976 under Eve Queler that captures the soprano at her transcendant best. The final half hour is a model of magical, rapt bel canto singing of a very rare kind. Likewise, few have done more than Caballé to bring to life the early works of Verdi—*Il corsaro* and *I masnadieri* among them, both recorded on the Philips label.

Although Caballé has recorded extensively, rivaled among sopranos only by Joan Sutherland, and even though many of her performances are easily found on "pirates," there remain certain gaps that frustrate her many admirers. There should have been commercial recordings of three Verdi roles with which she had a great success—the Leonoras in *Il trovatore* and *La forza del destino* and Desdemona in *Otello*. Fortunately there are "live" recordings available of the two Leonoras. There is, however, much to be thankful for; in Verdi recordings alone, aside from the early operas mentioned, there is a fine *Traviata* (Caballé being one of the few sopranos after Callas who was a successful Violetta) under Prêtre, a *Don Carlos* under Muti that could hardly be bettered (included in the cast are Domingo and Verrett), a *Luisa Miller* with Pavarotti that outstrips all recorded competition, an *Aïda* under Muti with Domingo and Cossotto with an appropriately ethereal Tomb Scene, and a *Messa da requiem* under Barbirolli (with Cossotto, Vickers, and Raimondi) that is sheer perfection exactly where Verdi demands it—on the ultra-soft high B-flat in the "Libera me." Other recordings that stand out among the many that she has made are a *Così fan tutte* under Colin Davis, in which she and Janet Baker blend beautifully (this is the only commercial example of Caballé's Mozart, when there should have been a Countess and a Donna Elvira, the latter of which she sang over four hundred times); an early *Lucrezia Borgia* on RCA that displays her astonishing coloratura technique, the only hole in which is a weak trill (the live performance of her New York debut is also available); a definitive reading of Bellini's seminal *Il pirata;* and numerous recital discs, among them Puccini arias, French opera arias, duets with Martí, duets with Verrett, and Spanish song literature, which she studied with Conchita Badia.

In the last several years Caballé's career has been confined mainly to Europe. The Metropolitan Opera has not particularly served her well, giving her roles such as Tosca, when she would have been better as Semiramide or the Marschallin. Due to her sound early training Caballé has had a long career with no great deterioration in vocal quality. She attributes this in part to singing so much Mozart early in her career. Of her singing in Salieri's *Les Danaïdes* in Perugia in 1984 the correspondent for *Opera* wrote that "The most warmly applauded singer was Montserrat Caballe, an imposing yet very sweet Hypermestra, torn between love for her father and her lover, and distinguished for her sensitive *mezza-voce* singing and some powerful vocal outbursts." Numerous cancellations because of ill health have in the last decade marred an otherwise glorious career.

—Stephen Willier

CACCINI, Giulio.

Composer. Born c. 1550, Tivoli. Died (buried) 10 December 1618, in Florence. Studied singing and lute with Scipione delle Palla; singer in the Tuscan court, 1565; publication of his opera *Euridice*, 1601. Caccini was one of the founders of the Florentine Camerata, a group of artists and literati who met at the houses of Bardi and Corsi; Caccini was a pioneer of *musica in stile rappresentativo.*

Operas

L' Euridice, Ottavio Rinuccini, Florence, Palazzo Pitti, 6 October 1600.

Il rapimento di Cefalo (with S. Ventori del Nibbio, L. Bati, and P. Strozzi), G. Chiabrera, Florence, Gran sala delle commedie, Uffizi, 9 October 1600.

Other works: madrigals, monodies.

Publications

By CACCINI: books–

Preface to *Le nuove musiche*. Florence, 1602; Venice, 1607, 1615; English translations in *Source Readings in Music History,* edited by Oliver Strunk, 377, New York, 1950, and *Recent Researches in the Music of the Baroque Era* 9 (1970): 7.

About CACCINI: books–

Palisca, Claude V. *Girolamo Mei. Letters on Ancient and Modern Music to Vincenzo Galilei and Giovanni Bardi,* 2nd ed. 1977.
Hanning, Barbara R. *Of Poetry and Music's Power: Humanism and the Creation of Opera.* Ann Arbor, 1980.

articles–

Fortune, Nigel. "Italian Secular Monody from 1600 to 1635: an Introductory Survey." *Musical Quarterly* 39 (1953): 171.
Pirrotta, Nino. "Temperaments and Tendencies in the Florentine Camerata." *Musical Quarterly* 40 (1954): 169.
Bianconi, L. "Giulio Caccini e il manerismo musicale." *Chigiana* 25 (1968): 21.
Palisca, Claude V. "The First Performace of *Euridice.*" *Queens College Department of Music Twenty-fifth Anniversary Festschrift, 1937-1962.* New York, 1964.
Pirrotta, Nino, "Early Opera and Aria." In *New Looks at Italian Opera: Essays in Honor of Donald J. Grout,* edited by William Austin, 39. Ithaca, 1968; reprinted in Nino Pirrotta, *Music and Theater from Poliziano to Monteverdi,* Cambridge, 1982.
Brown, Howard M. "How Opera Began: an Introduction to Jacopo Peri's *Euridice* (1600)." *The Late Italian Renaissance,* edited by Eric Cochrane, 401. New York, 1970.
Hitchcock, H. Wiley, ed. Introduction to *G. Caccini: Le nuove musiche. Recent Researches in the Music of the Baroque Era* 9 (1970): 7.
Palisca, Claude V. "The Camerata Fiorentina: a Reappraisal." *Studi musicali* 1 (1972): 203.
Hitchcock, H. Wiley. "A New Biographical Source for Caccini." *Journal of the American Musicological Society* 26 (1973): 145.
Bacherini Bartoli, Maria Adelaide, "Giulio Caccini. Nuove fonti biografiche e lettere inedite." *Studies in Music* [Canada] 9 (1980): 59.
Brown, Howard M. "The Geography of Florentine Monody: Caccini at Home and Abroad." *Early Music* 9 (1981): 147-68.
Palisca, Claude V. "Peri and the Theory of Recitative." *Studies in Music* [Australia] 15 (1981): 51.
Hill, John Walter. "Realized Continuo Accompaniments from Florence c. 1600." *Early Music* 11 (1983): 194.
Willier, Stephen. "Rhythmic Variants in Early Manuscript Versions of Caccini's Monodies." *Journal of the American Musicological Society* 36 (1983): 481.

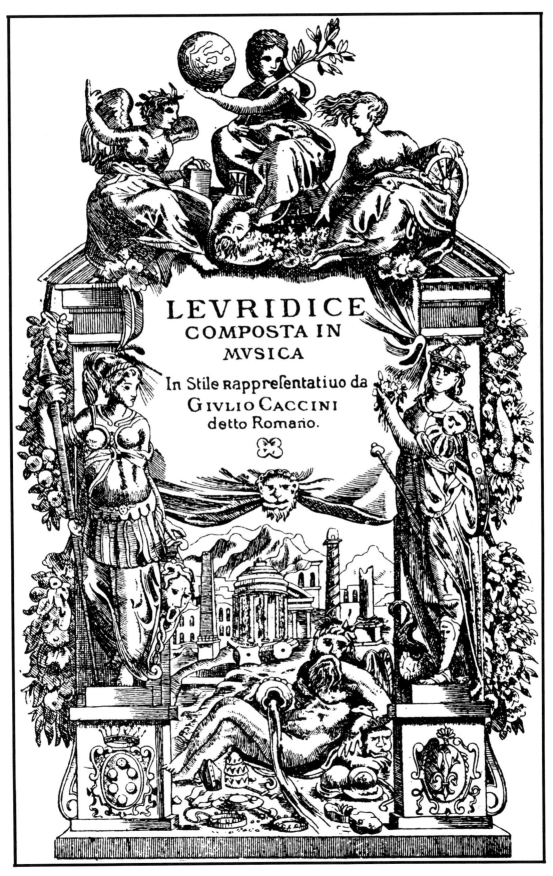

Caccini's *Euridice,* **title-page of first edition of score, Florence, 1600**

Sternfeld, Frederick W. "A Note on *stile recitativo.*" *Proceedings of the Royal Musical Association* 110 (1983-84): 41.

*   *   *

Caccini, as a participant in the discussions of Giovanni de' Bardi's Camerata in Florence in the late 1570s and early 1580s, and as a highly skilled and well-respected singer, was well equipped to become one of the main exponents of the newly-evolving monodic style. Shortly before 1580 Bardi published a *Discourse on Ancient Music and Good Singing,* which he addressed directly to Caccini. Bardi praises Caccini as musically unsurpassed in all of Italy and summarizes Camerata discussions on recapturing the powers of the music of the ancient Greeks. Caccini, for his part, mentions in his preface to the published score of *L'Euridice* (1600) the names of several of his pieces composed in monodic style and performed during the period of the meetings of the Camerata.

That Caccini took Bardi's advice as found in his *Discourse* is evident in the music of Caccini's complete, published setting of Ottavio Rinuccini's *L'Euridice* (1600), in his contribution to Peri's setting of the same libretto (1600), and in his collection of vocal chamber music, *Le nuove musiche* (1602). A case in point is the use of melodies composed of smaller, well-behaved intervals except when the text might reasonably indicate otherwise. Bardi's theory is, however, tempered in Caccini's works by Caccini's practice as a virtuoso singer. Bardi counsels that intelligibility of the words should govern the setting of texts to music, an area in which Caccini is careful, but Caccini does not neglect the interests of the virtuoso singer. To the speech-like quality incorporated in melody as recommended by Bardi, Caccini sometimes adds a *coloratura* flourish to enhance a cadence or to illustrate a particular word. Caccini's aim was not merely to delight or to impress but rather to move his listener to participate in the emotional state, the affect, suggested by the text.

Caccini's emphasis on the *basso continuo* texture throughout his works is noteworthy, and he gives a description of his use of the new texture in his preface to *L'Euridice.* The bass line is fixed, being fully notated, and the principal chord inversions and dissonances are indicated by Arabic numerals above the staff, but other particulars of realizing the harmony from the bass line are not indicated and are left to the taste of the performer. Caccini flaunts his willingness to override some conventional musical practices, such as the proscription against parallel octaves and parallel fifths, in order to make a particular effect.

The preface to *Le nuove musiche,* though not directly concerning opera, nevertheless gives valuable information about singing style and performance practice. Caccini discusses at length matters of ornamentation, tempo, and moving the passions of the listener, and he gives numerous musical examples to illustrate his points. The monodic compositions found in *Le nuove musiche* contain, unusually, written-out ornamentation which well repays study for its application to Caccini's theatrical style as found in *L'Euridice.*

Caccini is of prime importance both as a composer in the vanguard of early seventeenth century musical style (in his application of principles recommended by Bardi) and as a commentator on the methods of his own vocal performance (in serving the goal of moving the passions of the listener).

—Edward Rutschman

CAFFARELLI (Gaetano Majorano).

Mezzo-soprano castrato. Born 12 April 1710, in Bitonto, Italy. Died 31 January 1783, in Naples. Took his name from his teacher, Domenico Caffarelli; also studied voice in Naples with Nicola Porpora; debut in Sarro's *Valdemaro* in Rome, 1726; by 1734 he had appeared in Venice, Turin, Rome, and Bologna in operas by Lampugnani, Porpora and Hasse, among others; Naples debut in Leo's *Il castello d'Atlante* in 1734, after which he decided to settle in Naples, taking a post at the royal chapel; visited Rome in 1735; sang Lampugnani's *Ezio* at Milan, 1736; in London, 1737-38, where he created the title role in Handel's *Faramondo* and *Serse;* sang for wedding of Infante Philip in Madrid, 1739; in France 1753-54, singing in royal palaces near Paris; in Rome and Madrid, 1754; engaged for Lisbon court opera, 1755.

Publications

About CAFFARELLI: articles–

Prod'homme, J.G. "Un chanteur italien à Paris—le voyage de Caffarelli en 1753." *Bulletin française de la SIM* 6-7 (1911).
Faustini-Fasini, E. "Gli astri maggiori del bel canto napoletano Gaetano Majorano detto "Caffarelli." *Note d'archivio per la storia musicale* (1938): 121, 157, 258.

This mezzo–soprano castrato singer deserves to be remembered if only for the fact that he gave the premiere of one of Handel's best-known melodies, "Ombra mai fù" ("Never was there shade . . .") in the opera *Serse* (*Xerxes*), in London on 15 April 1738. Dr. Burney, who was present at the first performance, described "Ombra mai fù" as a "charming slow cavatina in a clear and majestic style, out of the reach of time and fashion." Known as "Handel's *Largo*" from the late 19th century onwards, this aria is often performed as an instrumental piece.

Caffarelli, one of the triumvirate (or, more properly, triumevirate) of castrati virtuosi who radiated outwards from Naples, differed from Farinelli and Gizziello in one major respect. They had on the whole become reconciled to their strange fate, accepting their change of nature with something approaching equanimity, whereas Caffarelli throughout his active career was quarrelsome, vain and insolent, to the extent that he was more than once under house-arrest for the insults and injuries he heaped upon those who in some way upset him.

Nevertheless, for those who were content to appreciate his art or to converse with him from the point of view of a non-rival, he could be a tolerable companion for a short time, and towards the end of his life he certainly had no cause for complaint since, like Farinelli and Gizziello, he had amassed a considerable fortune and was able to live in comfort and luxury. Aside from his singing, which had a powerful virtuoso character somewhat deficient in true expression, he occasionally composed and was known in London for his setting of a cantabile aria in the pastiche *Attalo,* written "in the fine style of grand pathetic," to quote Burney, and performed by Giusto Tenducci on 11 November 1758.

Caffarelli occasionally suffered from a kind of arrogant laziness, which once caused him to behave impertinently to Victor Amadeus, prince of Savoy. The prince, about to marry the Infanta of Spain in Turin, asked the King of Naples to send Caffarelli as a guest singer, who claimed on arrival to have lost a book of ready-made cadential ornaments on the road and was thus unable to appear. The prince entreated Caffarelli to do his best and thus overcome the prejudice of the Infanta, who had studied for a long time with Farinelli. Caffarelli pulled himself together and promised that the royal pair should hear two Farinellis that evening, and in the event he excelled himself and was restored to favor.

The singer's real name was Majorano, and he together with two brothers had the same patron from whom they took their name: Domenico Caffarelli, an accountant at the Papal Nuncio's office in Naples. His principal teacher was Nicolò Porpora, who after supervising his studies for several years claimed that he was the greatest singer in Italy, although personally not very likable.

Baron Grimm, who heard Caffarelli in Paris in 1754, said that he possessed an angelic voice noted for "remarkable facility and precision," and lending enchantment to the senses. Ten years later the actor-manager David Garrick attended a liturgical ceremony in Naples when a duke's daughter took the veil and Caffarelli sang, pleasing Garrick more than any other he had heard: "He touched me—and it was the first time I have been touched since I came into Italy." Dr. Burney, though admitting that Caffarelli was seldom at his best in London (possibly due to the climate), states that Handel had such respect for him that he gave him *ad libitum* passages—space to extemporize or ornament—and that the granting of such artistic freedom was a rare occurrence.

—Denis Stevens

CALDWELL, Sarah.

Conductor/Producer/Director/Designer. Born 6 March 1924, in Maryville, Missouri. Psychology student at the University of Arkansas; studied violin with Richard Burgin at the New England Conservatory; studied viola with Georges Fourel; assistant to Boris Goldovsky, head of the opera department at the New England Conservatory, 1947; head of the opera workshop, Boston University, 1952-60; founded the Opera Group of Boston, 1957 (name changed to the Opera Company of Boston, 1965); produced the United States premieres of Tippett's *The Ice Break* and Zimmermann's *Die Soldaten;* became the first woman to conduct the Metropolitan Opera, New York, 13 January 1976, and at the Ravinia Festival, Chicago, 3 August 1976.

*　　*　　*

Sarah Caldwell was educated at the University of Arkansas, Hendrix College, and at the New England Conservatory. Unlike most conductors, she studied violin and did not follow the typical keyboard-to-podium progression. While she had the opportunity to develop as a professional violinist with the Minneapolis Symphony and several other orchestras, she turned them down because of her passion for both the theater and music. Her opera conducting career began at Tanglewood in 1947 with the production of Vaughan William's *Riders to the Sea.* In 1952, she was named head of the Boston University opera workshop, and continued in this post until 1960. In 1957, she became founder and artistic director of the Opera Group of Boston, which was later to be renamed the Opera Company of Boston.

The company was originally housed in the Orpheum Theater, an old cinema and vaudeville house. By 1977, Caldwell became frustrated with the limitations of the Orpheum Theater. In a 4 October 1977 article in the Boston Globe, Caldwell announced that "planning for the future [of the opera company] hinges on the question of the opera house. . . . I feel we have fully exploited the production potential of the Orpheum Theater." After a great deal of determination and hard work, Caldwell and her troupe got a new opera house. In October of 1978, the Opera Company of Boston was moved to the Savoy Theater, which was built in the late 1920s for vaudeville. In August of the following year, the mortgage was finally paid off, and Caldwell had the pleasure of burning the mortgage papers. The ritual took place in a hibachi on the stage of the company's new home, during a rehearsal for *Madama Butterfly.*

In an effort to promote opera, an agreement between the Opera Company of Boston and the Philippines First Lady, Imelda R. Marcos, was signed in 1982. The program was established to create a counterpart operatic company in the Philippines. The agreement was established such that Caldwell and her staff would advise and assist the Cultural Center of the Philippines in creating an active operatic life in the Philippines. Many Bostonians did not condone this involvement, as they saw the action as direct support of a dictatorship.

Caldwell's contributions to the genre of opera have not gone unnoticed. On 13 January 1976, Sarah Caldwell triumphed as the first woman to conduct at the New York Metropolitan Opera. In this momentous performance, she conducted Verdi's *La traviata,* featuring soprano Beverly Sills. The performance received rave reviews and was aired on a national radio broadcast.

In addition to being the first woman to conduct at the Metropolitan Opera, Caldwell was also the first woman to conduct at the Ravinia Festival in Chicago. On 3 August 1976, Caldwell conducted the Chicago Symphony Orchestra in a special opera program featuring Beverly Sills.

Caldwell has conducted many American premieres, such as Prokofiev's *War and Peace,* Nono's *Intolleranza,* Schoenberg's *Moses und Aron,* Sessions *Montezuma,* and Tippett's *Ice Break. Montezuma's* only production, prior to Caldwell's U.S. premiere, was in Berlin in 1964. Due to Caldwell's commitment to promote opera, and her willingness to stage difficult and demanding scores, many works such as these are being given an opportunity for revival.

In addition to Caldwell's operatic work, she is also an orchestral conductor. She has appeared with the New York Philharmonic Orchestra, the Pittsburgh Symphony Orchestra, and the Boston Symphony Orchestra.

—Kathleen A. Abromeit

LA CALISTO.

Composer: Francesco Cavalli.

Librettist: Giovanni Faustini.

First Performance: Venice, Sant' Apollinare, November 1651.

Roles: Nature (contralto); Eternity (soprano); Destiny (soprano); Jove (bass); Mercury (tenor); Calisto (soprano); Endymion (contralto); Linfea (soprano); Satirino (soprano); Pan (contralto); Silvano (bass); Juno (soprano); Furies (2 sopranos); chorus.

Publications

articles–

Hicks, Anthony. "Cavalli and *La Calisto.*" *Musical Times* 111 (1970): 486.

* * *

At the opening of Cavalli's *La Calisto,* wars have destroyed much of the vegetation of the earth. Jove, concerned about the fate of the world, has descended from Olympus to restore man and nature. He is immediately diverted from his noble task by a glimpse of the nymph Calisto, with whom he becomes instantly enamoured. However, his plans for seduction are initially foiled because Calisto, as a follower of Diana, has taken a vow of chastity. Jove asserts himself as the bringer of miracles and causes a dried-up spring to renew itself before Calisto's astonished eyes. She refuses to be lured by the god's tricks and repulses him with sharp words. Mercury suggests that Jove can win Calisto's heart by taking the form of the goddess Diana. Thus, disguised as Diana, Jove succeeds in seducing Calisto. Later the unlucky nymph approaches her adored goddess and begs for more kisses. Diana, horrified and insulted, banishes the bewildered Calisto from her inner circle. The hypocritical goddess then returns—chastely, it would seem—to her dalliance with the shepherd Endymion.

Juno's arrival on the scene adds further complication. Having heard Echo's rumors of new conquests by Jove, she once again seeks her errant husband and wonders how he has this time changed his identity to achieve a favorable result to his pursuit. The first person she meets is none other than poor Calisto, the object of her husband's latest digression. Juno loses little time in taking her revenge at Jove's duplicity; she summons the Furies, who turn the nymph into a bear. However, Jove comes to Calisto's rescue, changes her back to a human, and at last wins her loving favor. He finds her a place among the stars of the heavens, where she discovers eternal life and "celestial harmony" as the constellation Ursa Minor.

La Calisto is the ninth of eleven early operas that Cavalli composed with one of his most successful and imaginative collaborators, the librettist Giovanni Faustini. Their subject, in this opera entirely derived from mythology, characterizes the gods in human terms of nobility mixed with frailty. Humans display weaknesses that make them the obvious victims of the gods. The naive and gentle Calisto has a counterpart in the shepherd Endymion. Both these gracious humans are in love with one goddess, Diana, who presumes a sanctimonious chasteness that will admit neither fluctuation nor treachery. All three are undone by the stronger characters of Jove and Juno. Ironically, this weakness and foolishness is mocked— as it so often is in Cavalli's operas—by two comic figures: an old and cantankerous nymph Linfea and a young satyr, known only as Satirino. Linfea is a familiar type in seventeenth-century opera: the old crone longing for lost opportunities to love. Satirino is the youthful spy, the manipulative partner in deceit, and the vicious commentator on the character of women, whom he admits he is too young to know much about. These two, with their witty and pointed remarks,

represent the chorus and explain in part the emotions of the elite.

—Martha Novak Clinkscale

CALLAS, Maria (born Kalogeropoulos, Cecilia Sophia Ann Marie).

Soprano. Born 3 December 1923, in New York. Died 16 September 1977 in Paris. Married Giovanni Battista Meneghini, 1949 (divorced 1959). Studied in Greece with Maria Trivella at National Conservatory, 1937-39; student debut as Santuzza in *Cavalleria rusticana,* Athens, 1939; sang Beatrice in *Boccaccio,* Tosca, Marta, Santuzza, and Fidelio in Greece; Italian debut as Gioconda in Verona Arena, 1947; Elvira in *Puritani* and other florid parts in Venice, 1949; Teatro alla Scala debut as Aida, 1950; joined La Scala in 1951; Covent Garden debut as Norma, 1952; Chicago debut in *Norma,* 1954; Metropolitan Opera debut, 1956; recital tour with di Stefano, 1973-74.

Publications

About CALLAS: books–

Jellinek, G. *Callas: Portrait of a Prima Donna.* New York, 1960; 1986.
Cederna, C. *Callas.* Milan, 1968.

Maria Callas in *La traviata*

Ardoin, J. and G. Fitzgerald. *Callas.* New York, 1974.

Wisneski, H. *Maria Callas: The Art Behind the Legend.* New York, 1975.

Galatopoulos, S. *Callas: Prima Donna Assoluta.* London, 1976.

Gastel Chiarelli, Christina. *Maria Callas: Vita, immagini, parole, musica.* Venice, 1981.

Ardoin, J. *The Callas Legacy: A Biography of a Career,* rev. ed. New York, 1982.

Meneghini, G.B. *My Wife, Maria Callas.* New York, 1982.

Stassinopoulos, A. *Maria Callas: The Woman Behind the Legend.* New York, 1982.

Rasponi, L. *The Last Prima Donnas.* New York, 1982.

Lowe, D.A., ed. *Callas: As They Saw Her.* New York, 1986.

Ardoin, J., ed. *Callas at Juilliard: The Master Classes.* New York, 1987; London, 1988.

Stancioff, N. *Maria Callas Remembered.* London, 1988.

articles–

Lord Harewood and H. Rosenthal. "Maria Callas." *Opera* November (1952).

Avant-scène opéra October (1982).

Fairman, R. "Callas—The Juilliard Master Classes." *Opera* September (1983).

Had Maria Callas been able to cope as effectively with persons and events as she did with the scores she absorbed and the roles she re-created, her life might not have ended prematurely in a tragedy of almost Greek proportion.

Maria Kalogeropoulos was born in New York in 1923, the second of two daughters of an emigré Greek family. She returned to Greece with her mother and sister in 1937, a spotty, short-sighted, over-weight adolescent with thick, ungainly legs, but she had an untrained voice of extraordinary potential and great determination to become a singer.

Elvira de Hidalgo, a once celebrated Spanish soprano who became a professor at the Athens Academy of Music, took Maria as her personal pupil free of charge. De Hidalgo perceived that the girl had three disconnected voices: a rich, veiled lower one; an insecure middle one; and an upper voice placed at the back of the throat and likely to go out of control when too much pressure was put upon it. All these voices needed to be brought together with no 'gaps' between them, and to be made to sound pleasant, if not beautiful, all the time. They never were.

De Hidalgo strongly advised her pupil to use the flexibility in her voice to its best advantage by concentrating on bel canto roles (for which de Hidalgo herself had been admired). This would be the best way of allowing the voice time to become strong enough in all its three registers to take on heavier roles later. So Maria, with great willingness and ability for intense concentration, quick study and endless patience, applied herself to the heroines of Bellini, Donizetti and Rossini.

Before she was eighteen years of age, Callas yielded to the first of many damaging temptations by accepting four roles with the Athens Opera during the German occupation of Greece: *Boccacio, Cavalleria rusticana,* Tosca, and Leonore in *Fidelio.* She was determined to sing any major role offered in spite of de Hidalgo's advice and warnings. Such stubbornness—and foolishness—was later seen as one of Callas's ineradicable characteristics.

In 1947 she made her first important debut at the Verona Arena as La Gioconda in Ponchielli's opera. There was still much wrong with the voice: noticeable breaks between the registers, a general unevenness of tone and some very crudely placed notes at the top. But her performance was ecstatically received and she was marked as a singer of high quality indeed.

Callas's conductor in Verona was Tullio Serafin, experienced director and voice-trainer who had founded the Verona Festival. He was greatly excited by Callas's voice and ability, and wanted her to profit from his instruction. He was to have both a good and a malign influence upon her career and began by encouraging her to sing the *Walküre* Brünnhilde and Kundry in *Parsifal,* side by side, as it were, with *I puritani, Il Turco in Italia, La traviata;* then Isolde, Norma and Turandot. In retrospect, it is difficult to understand what prompted Serafin to do such a thing, but he gave Callas the advantage of support and confidence which she so much lacked and seemed to find only from much older men. One of these, thirty years her senior, was an industrialist called Giovanni Battista Meneghini. He was old enough to be her father and rich enough to give her the security and pampering she sought. He attentively chaperoned her until they married and then gave up his business interests to become her sole agent and manager, although he was temperamentally unsuited to the task.

Callas went on singing, conquering audiences in Europe and America, blazing her own trail and becoming richer every time her husband maliciously doubled her fee. She began to live more than ever on her nerves instead of nursing her natural physical and vocal resources. When she was not singing in opera houses, she was making more recordings than any other singer of her time. She managed—some say "contrived"—to upset her family, her friends and colleagues, and as "The Tigress" she was grist to the newshounds whenever and wherever she caused a stir: public aggressiveness, cancelled performances, even poorer performances than her best (which would have gone unremarked in other singers) all made "La Callas" a merciless target for adverse publicity.

After ten years she had slimmed and was now very beautiful indeed. She had conquered the Teatro alla Scala, Milan, the Met, Covent Garden, Vienna and was tired of old Meneghini. The multi-millionaire Aristotle Onassis took her up, divorced his wife Tina, and gave Callas the entrée to the highest of High Society. She was fêted, adored, followed everywhere but sang less, because she had allowed her voice to get into a precarious state. All she wanted now was to settle down peacefully and have a child, but this was not what Onassis wanted. In 1968 he suddenly told her that he was "marrying Jackie Kennedy" (widow of the assassinated US President) "in two days' time." Her last hope of security and support instantly vanished and the physical and mental shock to Callas was deep-seated.

Most of the final artistic events in her career pale before the early achievements and are best overlooked, except for two. In 1971 and 1972 she gave exceptional and vivid master classes at the Juilliard School, New York. Fortunately they are preserved in book form and on tape/disc, and they indicate much of the deep natural perception she had acquired for a variety of operatic roles—and not only her own—as well as how to sing them. Callas was not an intellectual. Her innate understanding of her forty or so different operatic roles coupled with her extraordinary vocal quality, make those assumptions unique.

Maria Callas died suddenly in her Paris house in 1977. It was really a mercy for her. She was only fifty-four, but her voice was worn out and consequently there was nothing for her to live for. Those who heard her in her prime will not—cannot—forget the impression which she made; nor will memory of her perish because of the many records which she left as proof of her fine, flawed genius.

—Alan Jefferson

CALVÉ, Emma.

Soprano. Born 15 August 1858, Décazeville. Died 6 January 1942, Millau. Married tenor Galileo Gaspari. Studied with Jules Puget, 1879-82, Mathilde Marchesi in 1882, and Rosina Laborde in 1887; debut as Marguerite in Gounod's *Faust,* Brussels, 1881; performed at the Opéra-Comique, Paris, in 1880s; debut at Teatro alla Scala in Samara's *Flora Mirabilis,* 1887; created Suzel in Mascagni's *L'amico Fritz,* Rome, 1891; debut at Metropolitan Opera as Santuzza, 1893; performed 61 Carmens at Met as well as Boito's Marguerite and Elena, Ophélie in Thomas's *Hamlet* and the title role in *Messaline*; Massenet composed Anita in *Navarraise* (1894) and Fanny in *Sapho* (1897) for her; at Manhattan Opera, 1907-09; Boston, 1912; and Nice, 1914.

Publications

By CALVÉ: books–

My Life. New York, 1922, 1977.
Sous tous les ciels j'ai chanté: Souvenirs. Paris, 1940.

Emma Calvé as Carmen

About CALVÉ: books–

Gallus, A. *Emma Calvé.* New York, 1902.
Girard, G. *Emma Calvé: La Cantatrice sous tous les ciels.* Millau, 1983.

articles–

Shawe-Taylor, D. "Emma Calvé." *Opera* (April 1955).
Barves, H. and W. Moran. "Emma Calvé: a Discography." *Recorded Sound* 59 (1975): 450.

* * *

Admonishing young singers in a 1922 essay entitled "Practical Aspects on the Art of Studying Singing," soprano Emma Calvé outlined the binding principle that guided her own extraordinary career: "People do not go to the opera or the concert hall merely to hear solfeggios, trills and runs. They want to hear a human message from a human being who has experienced great things and trained the mind and soul in finer discipline than mere exercises. The singer must be a personality, must understand the bond of sympathy with mankind which, even more than a beautiful voice, commands the attention and interest of the audience." Emerging at a time when verismo was at the height of its international popularity, when the standard operatic repertory was in a state of transition and the demands made upon singers were being reassessed, Calvé was a uniquely resourceful performer, and summoned in great abundance the flexibility to adapt. She was among the most accomplished singers of her generation, perhaps its most inspired actress, and certainly one of its most celebrated personalities. She had little sympathy for the kind of theatrical posturing that prevailed in the opera house—the "false and conventional standards of lyric expression," as she described them, and looked instead to the dramatic stage for inspiration. The brilliant tragedian Eleanora Duse (1859-1924), in particular, had a profound effect on Calvé: "All my life," she wrote in her 1922 autobiography, "I have loved and admired her [Duse] deeply . . . Hers was the spark that set my fires alight. Her art, simple, human, passionately sincere, was a revelation to me." Just as Duse had triumphed as Santuzza in a dramatization of Verga's *Cavalleria rusticana,* Calvé's impersonation of the role in Mascagni's musical setting was equally successful, and brought her immediate recognition. Marveling not so much at the shrewdness of her stage business as at the integrity of its every detail, Herman Klein called her "the first *real* Santuzza" he had ever seen, bringing to the opera "the Sicilian atmosphere of Verga's story, just as Duse had brought it into the theater." Similarly, Bernard Shaw, an unabashed admirer of Calvé during her heyday at Covent Garden, described her Santuzza as "irresistibly moving and beautiful, and fully capable of sustaining the inevitable comparison with Duse's impersonation of the same part."

Until her first brief retirement from the operatic stage in 1904, she enjoyed great success in the standard repertory of Mozart, Bellini, and Donizetti, and was associated with the premieres of many important contemporary works—several of them written for her. But her fiery portrayals of Santuzza and Carmen made an even more lasting impression, and led to prestigious engagements at Covent Garden and the Metropolitan Opera. Carmen especially came to dominate her career and to compromise her early versatility, and to this day she remains inseparably linked to the role. London and New

York were both shocked and delighted by her brooding portrayal, leaving critics in the challenging position of remaining detached from the ensuing hysteria: in his review of her first Carmen at the Metropolitan Opera in December, 1893, W. J. Henderson wryly observed that "the audience was much moved by Mme. Calvé's Carmen, but what will be thought of it in the calmer light of the morning's remembrance, it is not easy to tell." Shaw wrote with some ambivalence of Calvé's Carmen and her brutalization of the character, making clear his displeasure in seeing the restraint and subtlety that so distinguished her Santuzza yielding to such extravagance. "Her death-scene," he concluded, "is horribly real. The young lady Carmen is never so effectively alive as when she falls, stage dead, beneath José's cruel knife. But to see Calvé's Carmen changing from a live creature . . . into a reeling, staggering, flopping, disorganized thing, and finally tumble down a mere heap of carrion, is to get much the same sensation as might be given by the reality of a brutal murder." Just as her compulsion to embody Santuzza had gone deeper than simply immersing herself into the coarse realism of the drama and the excesses of the score, the preparations for her first Carmen at the Opéra-Comique in 1891 led her to Granada to observe life among the gypsies. She later wrote that the "absorption of one's personality in a role requires adaptability, a chameleonlike change of one's whole aspect and being." Even her costumes—whether Italian peasant rags or Spanish gypsy garments—were entirely authentic in both spirit and detail.

Herman Klein described Calvé's voice best as having "the somber quality of a contralto miraculously impinged upon the acute timbre and high range of a soprano . . . the ideal voice," he added—perhaps in deference to the general nature of her repertory—"for the expression of mental anguish, suffering, pleading, and despair." Its compass was extraordinary. She had the naturally high range of a lyric-spinto, aided by an almost falsetto-like upper extension, but the more striking disposition of a true dramatic soprano, with a sumptuous middle register and dark, alluring chest tones.

Calvé's range allowed her to cultivate a diverse repertory that often included more than one prominent role in the same opera—she appeared variously as Salomé and Hérodias in Massenet's Hérodiade, and was a notable interpreter of both Margherita and Elena in Boïto's Mefistofele. The different registers of her voice were more dissimilar in texture than in temperament, but the warmth and resonance of the tone remained the same throughout her natural scale. Her passage between the extremes—often exhibited with virtuosic force in her recordings—was always calculated wisely for dramatic effect. An exquisitely controlled head voice, if indeed it was that (Calvé called it her "fourth voice"), produced with her mouth shut in coloratura fashion, allowed her virtually seamless access above the staff. She claimed to have learned its secret from Domenico Mustafà (1829-1912), last of the Sistine Chapel's virtuoso castrati, and though it was rather small and distant in context, she used it unhesitatingly even on the stage, as we can hear in one of the Faust fragments recorded live from the stage of the Metropolitan Opera in February, 1902. It is featured prominently and very effectively in many of her studio recordings as well.

Her records disappoint only insofar as they present a rather limited repertory further circumscribed by the repetition of some of the least substantial titles. They offer only a glimpse of the drama that contemporary critics insisted was as much a part of her singing as it was her acting. The voice itself recorded with great fidelity, leaving a splendid account of its size, its range, and its silvery tone. Apart from the five Mapleson cylinder fragments recorded at the Metropolitan Opera during the 1901-1902 season, and a few irretrievable Bettini cylinders from about 1900, there are just over fifty records made for four commercial companies between 1902 and about 1919. Of these, only fifteen titles are operatic. There is surprisingly little from Cavalleria rusticana and Carmen: in addition to three Mapleson ensembles, her Santuzza is represented by only four recordings of "Voi lo sapete;" from Carmen there are four recordings of the "Habanera," two each of the "Chanson Bohème" and "Seguidilla," a single "Card Scene" reduced to a solo, and a second-act duet recorded with tenor Charles Dalmores in March, 1908—her only commercially recorded duet. The Victor discs, made in 1907, 1908, and 1916 offer the finest account of her voice and her best operatic interpretations, and seem to represent the singer's most serious efforts to preserve something of herself for posterity. Her last recordings as a singer, made for the Pathé Company in Paris in about 1919 when she was past sixty, suggest that her voice and technique were largely unimpaired by age. Richard Aldrich, reviewing her Aeolian Hall recital of February, 1915, noted that the voice seemed "to have lost little in its high ranges, and even to have gained something in the rich lower tones of a purely contralto quality." It still showed "remarkable power, brilliancy and beauty of quality and the evidence of firm control and easy mastery of it." Deplorable as they are from a technical standpoint, the Pathés bear this out, especially the Carmen excerpts, the haunting "Pendant un an je fus ta femme" from Sapho (her only "creator" recording), and the lovely "L'Heure exquise" of Reynaldo Hahn, all of which are among her most effective and hauntingly memorable recordings. A poignant spoken excerpt from her autobiography, long thought to have been recorded on her deathbed, appeared shortly after Calvé's death, but was probably made in Millau, Aveyron in 1940, in the wake of the German offensive.

—William Shaman

CALZABIGI, Ranieri (Simone Francesco Maria) de.

Librettist/Poet. Born 23 December 1714, in Livorno. Died July 1795, in Naples. Member of the Accademia Etrusca of Cortona and the Arcadian Academy of Rome by 1740; in Naples, where he was under the patronage of the French ambassador to Naples, Marquis d'Hospital, 1741-50; published a critical edition of Metastasio's works, 1755; in Vienna, 1761, where he met the court theater intendent Count Durazzo, and began to collaborate with the court composer Christoph Willibald Gluck; in Pisa, 1775; back in Naples, 1780, where he published his Riposta (1790), in which he attacked Arteaga's criticisms of his reforms.

Librettos

L'impero dell'universo diviso con Giove (componimento drammatico), G. Manna, 1745.
La gara fra l'Amore e la Virtù (componimento drammatico), 1745.
Orfeo ed Euridice (azione teatrale per musica), C.W. Gluck, 1762.
Alceste, C.W. Gluck, 1767.
La critica teatrale o L'opera seria, F.L. Gassmann, 1769.

Paride ed Elena, C.W. Gluck, 1770.
Le donne letterate, A. Salieri and G.G. Boccherini, 1770.
L'amor innocente, A. Salieri and G.G. Boccherini, 1770.
Comala (componimento drammatico per musica), P. Morandi, 1780.
Ipermestra, written for Gluck, 1778; revised by Du Roullet and Tschudi as *Les Danaïdes,* set by A. Salieri, 1784.
Elfrida, G. Paisiello, 1792.
Elvira, G. Paisiello, 1794.
Amiti ed Ontario o I selvaggi [not performed].
Epitalamio.
Il sogno d'Olimpia (festa teatrale), G. de Majo, 1747 [lost?].
Semiramide, 1778 [lost].
La Lulliade o I buffi italiani scacciati da Parigi (poema eroicomico).

Publications/Writings

By CALZABIGI: books—

with G. Angiolini. *Dissertation sur les ballets pantomimes des anciens pour servir de programme . . . de Semiramis.* Vienna, 1765; 1956.
Poesie di Ranieri de' Calsabigi. Livorno, 1774.
Lettera di Ranieri de' Calsabigi al sig. Conte Vittorio Alfieri sulle quattro sue prime tragedie e risposta. n.p., 1784?
Lettera del C.D.C. ad un suo amico sopra i novi commenti alle poesie d'Orazio dell' Abate Galiani, pubblicati in Parigi nella Gazzetta letteraria degli anni 1764 e seguenti. Livorno, 1788.
Riposta che ritrovò casualmente nella gran città di Napoli il licenziato Don Santigliano di Gilblas y Guzman, y Tonnes, y Alfarace: discendente per linea paterna e materna da tutti quegli insigni personnaggi delle Spagne alla critica ragionatissima delle poesie drammatiche del C. de' Calsabigi fatta dal baccelliere D. Stefano Arteaga suo illustre compatriotto. Venice, 1790.
Poesie e prose diverse di Ranieri de' Calsabigi. Naples, 1793.

articles–

"Dissertazione su le poesie drammatiche del sig. Abate Pietro Metastasio." In *Poesie del Signor Abate Pietro Metastasio,* vol. 1, edited by Ranieri Calzabigi. Paris, 1755.
"Dissertazione sopra due marmi figurati dell'antica città di Ercolano." In *Saggi de dissertazioni accademiche . . . Accademia Etrusca . . . Cortona.* Rome, 1758.
with G. Angiolini. Preface to Gluck, C.W., *Don Juan.* Vienna, 1761.
"Riposta del consigliere di S.M. imperiale Ranieri de' Calsabigi alla lettera scrittagli dall'autore (Alessandro Pepoli) sopra le prime quattro tragedie del. sig. Conte Alfieri." In *Teatro del Conte Alessandro Pepoli.* Venice, 1787.
"Lettera del sig. Consigliere Calsabigi a S. Ecc. il sig. Conte Alessandro Pepoli." In *Giornale enciclopedico di Vicenza.* Vicenza, 1789.
"Lettera del sig. Consigliere imperiale Ranieri de'Calzabigi all'autore." In *Adelinda tragedia del Conte Alessandro Pepoli.* Parma, 1791.

About CALZABIGI: books–

Arteaga, S. *Le rivoluzioni del teatro musicale italiano.* Bologna, 1783-85; 2nd ed., 1785.
Ricci, C. *I teatri di Bologna nei secoli XVII e XVIII* [631 ff.]. Bologna, 1888; 1965.
Croce, B. *I teatri di Napoli.* Naples, 1891; 1968.

Lazzeri, G. *La vita e l'opera letteraria di Ranieri Calzabigi.* Città di Castello, 1907.
Giazotto, R. *Poesia melodrammatica e pensiero critico nel settecento.* Milan, 1952.
Gallarati, P. *Musica e maschera: Il libretto italiano del settecento.* Turin, 1984.
Marri, Federico, ed. *La figura e l'opera di Ranieri de' Calzabigi.* Florence, 1989.
Pozzoli, Barbara Eleonora. *Dell'alma amato oggetto: Gli affetti nell' "Orfeo ed Euridice" di Gluck a Calzabigi.* Milan, 1989.

articles–

Welti, H. "Gluck und Calsabigi." *Vierteljahrsschrift für Musikwissenschaft* 7 (1891): 26.
Einstein, A. "Calzabigis 'Erwiderung' von 1790." *Gluck-Jahrbuch* 2 (1915): 56; 3 (1917): 25.
———. "Ein unbekannter Operntext Calzabigis." *Gluck-Jahrbuch* 2 (1915): 103.
Prod'homme, J.G. "Deux collaborateurs italiens de Gluck." *Rivista musicale italiana* 23 (1916): 33.
Michel, H. "Ranieri Calzabigi als Dichter von Musikdramen und als Kritiker." *Gluck-Jahrbuch* 4 (1918) 99.
Haas, R. "Josse de Villeneuves Brief über den Mechanismus der italienischen Oper von 1756." *Zeitschrift für Musikwissenschaft* 7 (1924-25): 129.
Fubini, M., and E. Bonora. "L'opera per musica dopo Metastasio." In *P. Metastasio: Opere,* edited by M. Fubini. Milan, 1968.
Corona, R. del. "Calzabigi." *Rassegna musicale Curci* 22/no. 4 (1969): 17.
Hammelmann, H., and M. Rose. "New Light on Calzabigi and Gluck." *Musical Times* 110 (1969): 609.
Hortschansky, K. "Unbekannte Aufführungsberichte zu Glucks Opern der Jahre 1748 bis 1765." *Jahrbuch des Staatlichen Instituts für Musikforschung* (1969): 19.
Ballola, G.C. "L'ultimo Calzabigi, Paisiello e l'*Elfrida.*" *Chigiana* 9-10 (1972-73): 309.
Fubini, E. "Presupposti estetici e letterari della riforma di Gluck." *Chigiana* 9-10 (1972-73): 235.
Donà, M. "Dagli archivi milanesi: lettere di Ranieri di Calzabigi e di Antonia Bernasconi." *Analecta musicologica* no. 14 (1974): 268.
Gallerati, P. "L'estetica musicale di R. de' Calzabigi: 'La Lulliade'." *Nuova rivista musicale italiana* (1979).
———. "L'estetica musicale di R. de' Calzabigi: il caso Metastasio." *Nuova rivista musicale italiana* (1980).
Robinson, M.F. "The Ancient and the Modern: a Comparison of Metastasio and Calzabigi." *Studies in Music* [Canada] 7 (1982): 137.
Krieger, M. "Orpheus *Mit Glück:* the Deceiving Gratification of Presence." *Theatre Journal* 35 (1983): 295.
Candiani, R. "L'*Alceste* da Vienna a Milano." *Giornale storico della letteratura italiana* 161 (1984): 227.
———. "Gli anni napoletani di Ranieri de' Calzabigi nelle lettere inedite a Giovanni Fantoni." *Studi settecenteschi* 6 (1984): 169.

unpublished–

Candiani, R. "L'attività di Ranieri de' Calzabigi nel periodo napoletano (1780-1795)." Ph.D. dissertation, Università degli Studi, Milan, 1981-81.

*　　*　　*

Before he was a poet, Calzabigi was what is nowadays called a "wheeler-dealer," if not an outright scamp. He was good with money, able in business, "learned in history, wit, poet and great lover of women." This was in spite of an unfortunate skin condition that caused him to scratch constantly, a habit particularly disliked by the French. He fled from Naples in 1750 to escape a murder trial (he was accused of poisoning a relative); his departure from Paris for Vienna in 1760 may have been connected with the debacle of a fraudulent lottery which he and Casanova had organized. And when he finally left Vienna, an affair with an actress may have been to blame.

Calzabigi's reputation rests on two texts set by Gluck, *Orfeo* and *Alceste,* which were supposed to have brought about a "reform" of opera. Everything else—the third libretto for Gluck, *Paride ed Elena,* a group of satirical and contemporary comedies including *La finta giardiniera* for Mozart, and two mediocre historical dramas for Paisiello—is insignificant.

In the famous preface to *Alceste* (signed by Gluck but probably written by Calzabigi) a program is laid down for operatic reform. Long ritornelli before arias must be banished. There will be no elaborate coloratura that makes nonsense of the words. The wearisome repetitions of *da capo* form must be suppressed. The sharp division of recitative and aria should be overcome, the orchestra being introduced wherever the emotional temperature of the text demands it. All must aim at a "beautiful simplicity."

Orfeo and *Alceste* were novel in other ways as well. Both were based on mythology (*opera seria* most often had historical subjects) and both made extensive use of the chorus. But here we must be cautious; *Orfeo* was classified as an "azione teatrale," an established occasional genre in Vienna in which mythology and elaborate choral passages were standard. *Alceste* was later called a "tragedia in musica," a genre invented for the occasion.

The abuses which Calzabigi wished to purge from Italian opera were exactly those that a devotee of French opera would have condemned. While in Paris, Gluck had certainly heard the operas of Rameau and that composer's dramatic use of the chorus, his short arias, his passionate ariosi and recitatives are very like the French manner. He later wrote, "When I staged *Orfeo* and *Alceste,* I had already been accustomed to the French theater for twenty years, and I liked the true, the lifelike, the natural; passion, sentiment, terror and compassion. . . ." French music was popular in Vienna, as it was in Stuttgart, where Jommelli had embarked on a similar Frenchifying of Italian opera. In Parma, Tommaso Traetta was adapting Rameau's operas to Italian texts.

Calzabigi did not really create a new Italian manner; his language is conventional and Metastasian (he had, after all, published an edition of Metastasio's dramas in 1755), and his characters are still the tender, garrulous, delicate spirits of *opera seria.* Orfeo and Euridice are "two wilting lovers of the eighteenth century, masked *all'antica*" (Ghino Lazzeri). It is true that Calzabigi's scenario for *Alceste* is nearer to Euripides than to the old libretto of Quinault, written for Lully; the marriage of Alcestis and Admetus is already past, and at the outset the chorus laments the dying king. But Calzabigi delays the death of Alcestis until act III, devoting two acts to the deliberations and sorrow of the self-sacrificing heroine.

Further elements enhanced the novel effect *Orfeo* and *Alceste* had when they were first produced. Gaetano Guadagni, the first Orfeo, had been trained in London by David Garrick, and Gluck himself, during his time in London, had got to know Garrick's new style of acting. The passionate, naturalistic way in which the operas were presented must have seemed a revelation to the Viennese audiences. Furthermore, the dance sequences in *Orfeo* were devised by Gasparo Angiolini,

an exponent of the "danza parlante" that had been influenced by the creative Frenchman Noverre, himself an admirer of Garrick.

Neither *Orfeo* nor *Alceste* gained a foothold in Italy (*Alceste* flopped in Bologna in 1778), but both were adapted to French librettos and were successful in Paris, where Gluck's final works were written. When Calzabigi found that his career as a librettist declined after the collaboration with Gluck, he was more and more insistent that the "reform" was his idea. However, the great thing about these two works is not any 'reform' they brought about, but their sublime dramatic music.

—Raymond Monelle

CAMMARANO, Salvadore.

Librettist. Born 19 March 1801, in Naples. Died 17 July 1852, in Naples. Trained by his father to be a painter; his tragedy *Baldovino* presented at the Teatro dei Fiorentini, 1819; his first libretto written for Vignozzi, 1834; first libretto for Donizetti *Lucia di Lammermoor,* 1835; first libretto for Verdi *Alzira,* 1841.

Librettos (selected)

Lucia di Lammermoor, G. Donizetti, 1835.
Belisario, G. Donizetti, 1836.
L' assedio di Calais, G. Donizetti, 1836.
Pia de' Tolomei, G. Donizetti, 1837.
Roberto Devereux, G. Donizetti, 1837.
Maria di Rudenz, G. Donizetti, 1838.
Elena da Feltre, S. Mercadante, 1838.
Poliuto, G. Donizetti, 1838 [performed 1848].
La vestale, S. Mercadante, 1840.
Il proscritto, S. Mercadante, 1842.
Il reggente, S. Mercadante, 1843.
Maria di Rohan, G. Donizetti, 1843.
Il vascello de Gama, S. Mercadante, 1845.
Alzira, G. Verdi, 1845.
Orazi e Curiazi, S. Mercadante, 1846.
La battaglia di Legnano, G. Verdi, 1849.
Luisa Miller, G. Verdi, 1849.
with L.E. Bardare. *Il trovatore,* G. Verdi, 1853.
Saffo, G. Pacini, 1840.
La fidanzata corsa, G. Pacini, 1842.
Bondelmonte, G. Pacini, 1845.
Stella di Napoli, G. Pacini, 1845.
Merope, G. Pacini, 1847.
Virginia, S. Mercadante, early 1850s
Medea, S. Mercadante, 1851.
Malvina di Scozia, G. Pacini, 1851.
L'orfano di Brono, ossia Caterina de' Medici, S. Mercadante [not finished by composer].

Additional librettos for V. Battista, L. Cammarano, N. de Giosa, G. Lillo, A. Nini, A. Peri, G. Persiani, F. Ricci, L. Rossi, G. Staffa, and E. Vignozzi.

Publications

About CAMMARANO: books–

Di Giacomo, S. *Cronaca del Teatro S. Carlino.* Napoli, 1891.
Rolandi, U. *Libretti e librettisti verdiani.* Rome, 1941.
Della Corte, A. *Le sei più belle opere di G. Verdi.* Milano, 1946.
Viviani, V. *Libretti e librettisti in cento anni del teatro S. Carlo (1848-1948).* Napoli, 1948.
Zavadini, G. *Donizetti.* Bergamo, 1948.
Dapino, C., and F. Portinari, eds. *Il teatro italiano,* vol. 5. Turin, 1983.
Black, J. *The Italian Romantic Libretto: a Study of Salvatore Cammarano.* Edinburgh, 1985.

articles–

Di Giacomo, S. "Musicisti e librettisti: Salvatore Cammarano, il librettista del 'Trovatore' e G. Verdi." *Musica e musicisti* 59 (1904): 81.
Mantovani, T. "Librettisti verdiani: Salvatore Cammarano." *Musica d'oggi* 8 (1926): 18.
Black, J.N. "Cammarano's Libretti for Donizetti." *Studi Donizettiani* (1978).
————. "Salvatore Cammarano's Programme for *Il trovatore* and the Problems of the Finale." *Studi verdiani* 2 (1983): 78.
Avant-scène opéra 60 (1984) [Verdi, *Le trouvère* issue].

*   *   *

It is safe to say that Salvadore Cammarano was most influenced by Bellini's favorite poet, Felice Romani, and for Neapolitan productions he revised four of Romani's librettos (including *Medea* and *Anna Bolena*). To a great extent Cammarano's success as a librettist was a result of his extensive theatrical background. His grandfather, Vincenzo Cammarano, was the leading comic actor in Naples for the last three decades of the eighteenth century; an uncle, Filippo, was an actor, author, composer and librettist; his father, Giuseppe, was a painter, scene designer and actor; and other members of the family were opera singers, actors and composers. In addition, Naples itself was an important influence. In the nineteenth century it was the most populous city in Italy and had the richest theatrical life. Operas were performed more than 300 days of the year, and often performances of lyric stage works were held simultaneously in several different houses, sometimes of the same work.

Salvadore (he preferred that spelling) was first trained as a painter. He then wrote dramas before he became a librettist at the relatively late age of thirty-three. At that time, the poet functioned as both librettist and stage director, and from 1834 to his death Cammarano's official title at San Carlo, one of the leading opera houses in the world, was "Poeta concertatore."

Because of his broad background, Cammarano visualized well the production of an opera, and his stage directions are exceptionally full (often accompanied by diagrams and sketches). In the first stage of preparing the libretto, the prose outline (sometimes called a *programma*), Cammarano even describes at times the kind of music he felt would be appropriate. In *Il trovatore,* for example, Verdi followed almost all the poet's musical suggestions, and to good effect.

Cammarano was a slow, thoughtful worker who spent considerable time polishing his verses. In searching for subjects, he displayed familiarity with much contemporary European literature in addition to the usual classical history and mythology. Among his strengths was his ability to find especially felicitous, concise phrases both suitable to the dramatic situation and eminently singable that could be repeated at length by the composer (Verdi referred to such words as "le parole sceniche"). According to William Ashbrook, "in his overall competence at handling dramatic structure and in his mastery of effective verbal climaxes at the ends of stanzas . . . Cammarano displays a level of skill that few of his contemporaries could match." He also had a rare ability to negotiate well with the everpresent censors of his day.

Cammarano's weaknesses included a tendency toward formal conventionality and, frequently, a disregard for some of the most important elements of his literary source (see, for example, his libretto *Luisa Miller,* based on Schiller's *Kabale und Liebe*). His language was often highflown with a diction deliberately avoiding ordinary speech. This, it has been suggested, he felt to be appropriate for *melodramma,* the term used by Italians for the serious opera of his day. At times, obscurities disfigure his plots. These obscurities generally derived either from problems in the original source or the need to condense the literature to allow time for the music to expand in a natural and logical manner.

Cammarano's letters, not all published, reveal a man of much innate dignity and modesty with an eminently logical mind and a thorough grasp of the theater.

—Martin Chusid

———

CAMPANINI, Cleofonte.

Conductor. Born 1 September 1860, in Parma. Died 19 December 1919, in Chicago. Married: the soprano Eva Tetrazzini, 15 May 1887. Studied violin at the Parma Conservatory and at the Milan Conservatory; conducting debut with Bizet's *Carmen* in Parma, 1882; conducted the United States premiere of Verdi's *Otello* at the New York Academy of Music, 1888; conducted world premiers of *Adriana Lecouvreur,* 1902, *Siberia,* 1903, and *Madama Butterfly,* 1904; conductor for the new Manhattan Opera House in New York, 1906-09; principal conductor, 1910, and general director, 1913-19, of the Chicago Opera Company.

*   *   *

Campanini was an illustrious name on the musical scene on both sides of the Atlantic for well over fifty years. Italo Campanini started it all by becoming one of the foremost tenors of the last century, and his younger brother, Cleofonte, continued the tradition well into this century as a conductor.

Cleofonte Campanini came to America in 1883 as an assistant conductor for the new Metropolitan Opera Company, no doubt through the influence of Italo, who had the distinction of being in the opening night cast of *Faust.* During the following decade, Cleofonte rose to prominence in Italy conducting several world opera premiers. He met Oscar Hammerstein, the impresario of the Manhattan Opera Company, in 1906. He served as both music director and artistic director, and the combination of Hammerstein's money and his abilities made the newborn Manhattan Opera a formidable rival to the by then venerable Metropolitan Opera.

The second season of the Manhattan Opera, 1907-08, saw the arrival of Mary Garden. Upon Garden's arrival, a musical collaboration began between her and Campanini that was directly responsible for turning the operatic scene in New York completely around. Both artists championed the new, and Garden, who considered herself to be quintessentially Gallic, found in Campanini someone she could trust to recreate faithfully "her" French operas on American soil. The 1907-08 season saw the premieres of Massenet's *Thaïs,* Charpentier's *Louise* and Debussy's *Pelléas et Mélisande,* all Garden vehicles and all guaranteed to create controversy. Each was successful above the wildest imagining and gave way to speculation that the New York public had become tired of the old operas. Campanini was extolled by the press for his expert conducting of scores which had no tradition to draw upon. He handled them as easily as older music and found his way through them as though he had been conducting them all his life.

As rewarding as the partnership was between maestro and prima donna, however, it soon became evident that with *Pelléas et Mélisande,* Garden had replaced Campanini as artistic director. She attended all rehearsals, dictated casting, interjected her will on exact duplication of scenic designs of the Opéra-Comique originals, coached her colleagues, and did everything but conduct. Rumor had it that Campanini was one of her students and learned the score from her. He could not have had a better teacher, however, and he profited by Garden's advice when he received accolades for his accomplishments. Under his baton, the orchestra brought out all the myriad colors of Debussy's palette and created the mood of timelessness which is so essential to *Pelléas.*

In spite of suspicion in some quarters that Garden was his Svengali, Campanini's musical instincts were unfailing, and it was his suggestion to eliminate many of the minor characters in *Louise* that made the opera flow more smoothly. Relations grew cool between Campanini and Garden, and they drifted apart when he resigned in 1909. Rumor again had it that he did so when he found that he could not buck Garden's influence over Hammerstein. They were to join forces again in Chicago several years later, and all hard feelings vanished when they entered upon another fruitful period of operatic collaborations, but this time Campanini was in total command.

Campanini had no end of troubles with his *prima donne,* and his feud with his sister-in-law, Luisa Tetrazzini, is well known. Tetrazzini's time with him prior to and during the Manhattan years was quite cordial, although those who were thought to be in the know swore to a certain coolness between Luisa and her sister, Eva. Each denied even a hint of uncordiality, and Luisa made a point of declaring that she owed her phenomenal technique to listening both to the birds and to Eva. Campanini managed to remain on good terms with his sister-in-law until all communication suddenly ceased between them; no one really knows for sure what happened.

Campanini spent the last six years of his life as general director of the Chicago Opera. His impact on opera in Chicago is reflected in the description of his funeral by Ronald Davis: "Early in the morning of Friday, December 19, Chicago's beloved Campanini was dead." Davis continues, "The following Sunday the coffin bearing his body was brought to the Auditorium, where the company gave him a farewell as theatrical as his life had been. The casket was placed in the center of the stage, surrounded by masses of flowers and sets of the "Transformation Scene" from *Parsifal.* At either end of the coffin was a burning wax candle, while on a stand nearby was his baton and one of his scores. The company paid their respects in a musical service, the Chicago public paid theirs filing by the bier for three full hours, and then, as Mary Garden tells it, 'the curtain came down slowly, and that was the last we saw of Cleofonte Campanini'."

—John Pennino

CAMPANINI, Italo.

Tenor. Born 30 June 1845, in Parma. Died 22 November 1896, in Corcagno, near Parma. Studied with Griffini and Lamperti; appeared in *Lohengrin* at Bologna, 1871; London debut as Gennaro in *Lucrezia Borgia,* 1872; American debut in same role, at New York Academy of Music, 1873; appeared in *Faust* at the opening of the Metropolitan Opera, New York, 22 October 1883.

Elder brother of the acclaimed conductor Cleofonte Campanini (much later a pivotal figure in the performance of opera in Chicago), Italo studied in Parma and debuted in comprimario roles in 1863. He began his career as a first tenor in Odessa. After three years in Russia, he returned to Italy, where his creation of Lohengrin for that country (Bologna, 1871; conducted by Angelo Mariani), combined with his success during the 1871 Teatro alla Scala season in traditional Italian roles, assured his place among the leading singers of the decade. Perhaps his most significant contribution, aside from his Lohengrins throughout the peninsula, was his creation of Faust in the revision of Boito's *Mefistofele* (Bologna, 1875).

Rodolfo Celletti describes his voice, from contemporary accounts, as being "not of great volume, and in some ways uneven, but sweet, tractable, extended and quite brilliant in the high register, beautifully produced, and with an intuitive musical understanding." Throughout the 1870s he maintained a high standard and was in demand in Italy in a variety of roles from the extremely dramatic (Lohengrin, Eléazar in Halévy's *La Juive*) through traditional bel canto (Elvino in Bellini's *La sonnambula,* Gennaro in Donizetti's *Lucrezia Borgia*). He extended his career in these years to Spain, Austria, and again Russia.

He had also conquered New York and London in the 1870s, and, following a vocal crisis in early 1883, opened the Metropolitan Opera's first season on 22 October, 1883, as Faust in an Italian-language performance of Gounod's *Faust* with Christine Nilsson and Franco Novara (actually the Briton Frank Nash). The diminution of his powers was then noted by omission of extended discussion of his known virtues; later appearances (for example, Don Jose in Bizet's *Carmen*) emphasized his dramatic intensity and sought to minimize his increasing vocal limitations. Italian audiences were less sympathetic than New York critics, whistling his *Mefistofele* Faust off stage at Napoli's Teatro San Carlo in 1886.

Always sensitive to a formerly great singer's problems, London received his Almaviva (1892) and Faust (Gounod, 1894) with decorum, and applauded his creation of Berlioz' Faust (*La damnation de Faust*) at Albert Hall in 1894. Italo's vocal decline did not allow him to participate in his younger brother Cleofonte's successes in Turin, Milan, and other Italian cities beyond a triumphal season in Parma just before his vocal difficulties began. He retired before the advent of recordings; rumors that private cylinders made by millionaire Charles Schwab in the 1890s at one time existed are highly suspect, though Eva Tetrazzini has been quoted as saying that cylinders of his voice were made in Italy at the same time. They have never surfaced and are probably (if they ever existed) lost forever.

Italo Campanini is remembered for two significant contributions to vocal art: as Lohengrin, he popularized Wagner for an Italian audience that, guided first by Mariani and later by Toscanini, would come to embrace the ultramontane music of the German genius, and he provided for a generation of operagoers in Europe and the United States a reminder for those whose memory did not encompass the performances of Mario in the 1850s and 60s, that "the Italian tenor" need not be a mindless boor intent only on applause garnered by stentorian high notes at the expense of dramatic verity.

—William J. Collins

CANIGLIA, Maria.

Soprano. Born 5 May 1905, in Naples. Died 15 April 1979, in Rome. Married: Pino Donati, 1939. Studied at the Conservatory San Pietro a Maiella, in Naples; debut as Chrysothemis in *Elektra,* Turin, 1930; Teatro alla Scala debut as Maria in Pizzetti's *Lo straniero,* 1931; sang in Rome, 1930–51; created the roles of Manuela in Montemezzi's *La notte di Zoraïma,* Milan, 1931; Roxanne in Alfano's *Cyrano de Bergerac,* Rome, 1936; and the title role in Respighi's *Maria Egiziaca,* 1937; Covent Garden debut, 1937; Metropolitan Opera debut, 1938.

Publications:

About CANIGLIA: articles–

Lauri-Volpi, G. "Le grandi voci della lirica contemporanea: Maria Caniglia." *Musica e dischi* 8 (1969): 38.
Rasponi, Lanfranco. "Maria Caniglia, May 5, 1906—April 16, 1979. [*sic*]" *Opera News* 44/July (1979): 23.
Pedemonte, V. "Maria Caniglia, un ricordo." *Rassegna Musicale Curci* 33/2 (1980): 45.
Ludwig, H. "Der vergessene Generation? Die Trias Maria Caniglia, Benjamino Gigli, Gino Bechi und die italienische Sängergarde der dreissiger und vierziger Jahre." *Opernwelt* 23/8-9 (1982): 101.

* * *

To the 1940s generation of collectors, Maria Caniglia was the foremost spinto voice of complete recordings of Italian opera: Gigli's soprano in *Tosca, Andrea Chénier, Un ballo in maschera, Aida,* and the Verdi *Requiem,* and Leonora in the only *La forza del destino* then available. On the Italian stage she had her rivals—Iva Pacetti, Gina Cigna, Giuseppina Cobelli, and Lina Bruna Rasa among them, and in America there were Zinka Milanov and occasionally Stella Roman on the radio, but when you wanted to hear in modern sound some of the classic operatic confrontation scenes—the second act of *Tosca,* the third of *Andrea Chénier,* or the second of *La forza del destino,* say—you had to go to Caniglia. Her tone itself was a dramatic statement: an unforgettable mass of rubies and brass. She could attack the ear without offending it; the pain itself could be bewitching and the quality was uniquely weighty and lyrical at once.

Caniglia began her career at the height of the *verismo* approach and, like Magda Olivero, carried on with it to her retirement, in the early 1960s. By that time she had sung for twenty years at the Teatro alla Scala and an additional ten in Rome. Her idols had been Muzio and Cobelli and her self-chosen coaches were often such earlier singing actresses as Carmen Melis and Gilda dalla Rizza. Caniglia's records re-create that *verismo* world. Moments—indeed, entire passages—of crudeness have been noted, from her day through our own. She could obliterate a phrase on first attack, thrash a vocal line into submission, and play the lady baritone at the drop of a betrayal. Her Magnani manner might destroy a character: Caniglia's Aïda, for example, has a toughness at odds with everything we are told about that heroine. When she was tired her top voice could be metallic, colorless, and flat, and in the quest for drama she could forget whatever she knew about legato. Others sang more beautifully and some more movingly, but few had her theatrical sting, her sweeping sense of dramatic line, and, when she worked at it, her instinct for vibrant delicacy.

One sees her working at this last in *Andrea Chénier,* when at the start she really tries for an abstracted, youthful tone, in act II for fragility, and in "La mama morta," where Maddalena describes her degradation during the French Revolution, for sorrowful vulnerability. Her voice hasn't the poetry of Muzio's but the impulses are the same. Her greatest accomplishments, though, are as Tosca and Leonora, both possessed of an unique theatrical vibrance and dramatic range. In *Tosca* the voice is luscious. She manages some flirtatiousness at the start but really comes into her own in her first bitter confrontation with Scarpia. The second act is played with a brilliant impression of spontaneity. The rich, biting voice and her vibrant defenselessness are made for the music and the murder, and she handles the *parlando* closing with extraordinary believability. In act III, the narrative of Scarpia's death has a welcome lyricism, the love duet both languor and animal vigor, and the final scene a *verismo* conviction unsurpassed on records. The *Forza* Leonora is, all told, her masterpiece, and reveals her gifts more fully than any other recording. Here she appears both powerful and touchingly distraught. The few coarse moments are never cheap, and she is quite equal to the lyric grandeur of the role. In the long and difficult scene with Padre Guardiano, the voice is radiant with hope, and the prayer at the end (Caniglia worshiped this music) voiced with an earthy purity unique to this artist. "Pace, pace, mio Dio" shares this quality; no faceless beauty here. Caniglia at her best struck both the senses and the heart.

—London Green

CAPPUCCILLI, Piero.

Baritone. Born 9 November 1929 in Trieste, Italy. Married Graziella Bossi. Studied with Luciano Donnaggio in Trieste, 1970-75; debut as Tonio in *I pagliacci* at Teatro Nuovo in Milan, 1957; debut at Teatro alla Scala as Enrico in *Lucia di Lammermoor,* 1964; first Covent Garden appearance in *La traviata,* 1967, then sang *Otello* (1974) and *Un ballo in maschera* (1975) there; first Chicago appearance, 1969; sang the role of Don Carlos in 1975 Salzburg Festival under Herbert von Karajan.

Publications

About CAPPUCCILLI: books–

Matheopoulos, H. *Bravo.* London, 1986.

*   *   *

Piero Cappuccilli has been one of the leading baritones of the Italian repertoire of the past three decades, with a special affinity for the roles of Verdi. After studying with Luciano Donaggio in Trieste, he made his debut as Tonio in Leoncavallo's *Pagliacci* at the Teatro Nuovo, Milan, in 1957. The following year he sang in Verdi's *I vespri siciliani* in Palermo, where conductor Tullio Serafin was impressed by his performance and signed him to record the part of Enrico in Donizetti's *Lucia di Lammermoor,* the role of his Teatro alla Scala debut in 1964.

Cappuccilli has sung at the major opera houses of Italy, in roles including Nottingham in Donizetti's *Roberto Devereux*; Ernesto in Bellini's *Il pirata*; Don Carlo di Vargas in Verdi's *La forza del destino*; Simon Boccanegra; Iago in Verdi's *Otello*; Verdi's *Rigoletto*; and Rodrigo in Verdi's *Don Carlo.* Outside of Italy he has appeared as Filippo in Bellini's *Beatrice di Tenda* in Monte Carlo, 1986; Riccardo in Bellini's *I Puritani* in Chicago, 1969; Miller in *Luisa Miller* at the Edinburgh Festival, 1963; Rodrigo at the Salzburg Festival, 1975 (under Herbert von Karajan); and Di Luna in Verdi's *Il trovatore* in Paris, 1973.

Cappuccilli was hastily signed by the Metropolitan Opera as one of three baritones hired to take on roles that needed to be filled upon the death of Leonard Warren on the Metropolitan Opera House stage in March 1960. He sang a single performance, Germont *père* in Verdi's *La traviata* on 26 March 1960 and has not returned (he was announced for Verdi's *Rigoletto* in the 1984-85 season but canceled his appearances).

His Covent Garden debut was as the elder Germont in Verdi's *La traviata* in 1967; he later sang Iago in Verdi's *Otello* (1974) and Renato in Verdi's *Un ballo in maschera* (1975).

Cappuccilli may be described a an singer in the central tradition of Italian baritones, with a solid technique and a highly intelligent approach to the music. The possessor of a voice that some consider not intrinsically beautiful, he is capable of producing a warmth of sound when it is needed. Cappuccilli is most successful at portraying the fatherly Verdi figures, such as Rigoletto, Francesco Foscari and—especially—Simon Boccanegra, where his dignity, nobility, authority, and sturdiness of voice complement the maturity of the characters. He is also a fine Macbeth, vocally and dramatically refined, but with a trace of a snarl in the voice to add a touch of instability to the character. The color of his voice conveys the melancholy of many of Verdi's father-figures and lends an aura of pathos to his portrayals; it also contributes to his singing of villainous parts. The more romantic figures take less well to his vocal quality. As a vocal actor he has developed greater expressiveness in his singing. His earlier performances exhibited a tendency toward interpretive blandness and portrayals that were somewhat generalized. He can convey character without histrionic excess

through careful attention to the words. His sure breath control facilitates his legato phrasing and his mastery of the long line, an important asset in the arching contours of Verdi's writing. He is also capable of sustained high *pianissimi* (as, for example, on the word *"figlia"* at the end of the Boccanegra-Amelia duet in his second *Simon Boccanegra* recording). He is less adept at the roles of Bellini and other composers who demand skill in florid singing.

—Michael Sims

CAPRICCIO.

Composer: Richard Strauss.

Librettists: Clemens Krauss and Richard Strauss.

First Performance: Munich, Staatsoper, 28 October 1942.

Roles: The Countess (soprano); The Count (baritone); Flamand (tenor); Olivier (baritone); La Roche (bass); Clairon (contralto); Monsieur Taupe (tenor); Italian Singers (soprano, tenor); Majordomo (bass); Servants (four tenors, four basses).

Publications

books–

Kende, G.K. *Richard Strauss und Clemens Krauss: eine Künstlerfreundschaft und ihr Zusammenarbeit an "Capriccio".* Munich, 1960.
Wilhelm, Kurt. *Fürs Wort brauche ich Hilfe—Die Geburt der Oper "Capriccio" von Richard Strauss.* Munich, 1984.

article–

Tenschert, R. "The Sonnet in Richard Strauss's Opera *Capriccio." Tempo* 47 (1958).

*   *   *

It is hard to decide what is most remarkable about *Capriccio,* Richard Strauss' fifteenth and final opera: that it was premiered amid the air-raids on Munich during the height of World War II; that, especially given its unveiling during that period of unparalleled conflagration and clashing world-views, it takes as its anachronistic and seemingly irrelevant setting the aristocratic salon-life of the *ancien régime* in France, at which time social civility allowed people of a certain class the leisure to discuss abstract artistic theories; or that Strauss should still be able, in his late 70s, to write a work of such compositional savvy, intellectual rigor, unhackneyed wit, and glowing humanness.

Since Strauss no doubt intended *Capriccio* as his operatic testament, he used the opportunity to fill the work with a multitude of forms: arias, scenas, small ensembles, large ensembles, dances, fugues, orchestral interludes, self-contained chamber music. It's as if Strauss were re-inventing the "number opera" of his beloved Mozart by incorporating it into the continuous texture of his perhaps even more beloved Wagner

Kiri Te Kanawa in *Capriccio,* **Royal Opera, London, 1991**

to produce a one-act synthesis termed by its authors "a conversation-piece for music."

The subject matter of *Capriccio*—whether words or music are more important in opera—was suggested by Stefan Zweig, Strauss' librettist for *Die schweigsame Frau,* who happened across a copy of the libretto to *Primo la musica e poi le parole* that the Abbé Casti had written for Antonio Salieri (the opera of which was first performed on a double bill with Mozart's *Der Schauspieldirektor* in 1786). When Zweig, who was Jewish, necessarily fell from political acceptability with the newly installed Nazi Régime, Strauss turned first to Joseph Gregor (librettist for *Friedenstag, Daphne,* and *Die Liebe der Danae*), whose literary attempts on the project were unsatisfactory to Strauss, and then to the conductor Clemens Krauss, with whom he finally collaborated on the text.

Capriccio takes place about 1775 in the salon of a château near Paris, where a birthday celebration for the Countess Madeleine is being planned by the composer Flamand, the poet Olivier, the theater director La Roche, and the count, brother of the countess and himself an amateur actor. Flamand has written an instrumental sextet, Olivier a sonnet-play, and La Roche is conceiving a large-scale spectacle in two parts. Clairon, an actress, arrives from Paris to participate in the rehearsals, and La Roche brings along a dancer and two Italian singers.

Flamand and Olivier, in addition to vying with each other over the intrinsic merits of music and words, are each seeking the hand of the countess, a still-young widow. The artistic sparks begin to fly when Olivier recites a sonnet to Madeleine and the sonnet is impetuously set to music by Flamand. Madeleine realizes the new life that the sonnet now assumes, and though Flamand presses her to make a decision— music or words, Flamand or Olivier—Madeleine asks for a day to decide.

Meanwhile La Roche, the practical man of the theater, ridicules both Flamand and Olivier for their remote and high-minded notions, and demonstrates with his dancer and Italian singers what entertainment is meant to be: melodious and understandable, not abstruse and arcane. The center of the opera is devoted to La Roche's passionate espousal of the direct and unforced allure of his brand of theater. (There's more than a little autobiographical comment here by Strauss, who, over the preceding thirty years, had seen his own musical palette patronized and discredited by the more "advanced" twentieth-century composers.)

Arguments ensue among all those present, from which the count makes the suggestion that an opera be created based on the events of that very day. Now Olivier needs to know what ending to write: he or Flamand. Life has, in a modernistic twist, become art. Madeleine likewise puts Olivier off until the next day, and the opera ends, in an extended monologue, with her inability to choose.

Though a few sections of *Capriccio* bog down into flavorless recitative (the characters of the count, Clairon, and even Olivier are, musically, not very richly defined, perhaps because they represent words, not music), the rest of the opera comprises one glorious musical inspiration after another: the opening sextet; the sonnet and, especially, the trio that develops out of it; Flamand's love scene with Madeleine; the neo-Baroque dances; the Italian singers' duet (at once a scathing parody and an affectionate homage); the laughing and quarreling ensembles; and La Roche's monumental *cri du coeur.* And just when it appears that Strauss may have wound down comes the dessert: the marvelously funny servants' ensemble, the wry appearance (in mixed metres) of the prompter, the moonlit orchestral intermezzo, and the countess' neo-*Rosenkavalier* monologue of tender introspection.

There are hundreds of places in this wise and witty score where Strauss must have, at the 1942 premiere, chuckled to himself in barely containable glee. His famous statement that "Isn't this D-flat major the best possible conclusion to my life's work in the theatre?" seems utterly and self-knowingly genuine. He had ended his cycle of fifteen operas in the same luminescent tranquility of D-flat major as Wagner had ended his cycle of the four *Ring* operas. For Strauss, there could have been no greater fulfillment.

—Gerald Moshell

I CAPULETI ED I MONTECCHI [The Capulets and the Montagues].

Composer: Vincenzo Bellini.

Librettist: Felice Romani (after Scevola, *Giulietta e Romeo* and Ducis, *Romeo et Juliette*).

First Performance: Venice, La Fenice, 11 March 1830.

Roles: Capellio (bass); Giulietta (soprano); Romeo (mezzo-soprano); Tebaldo (tenor); Lorenzo (bass); chorus (SATB).

Publications

book–

Schlitzer, F. *"I Capuleti e i Montecchi" di Vincenzo Bellini: l'autografo della partitura.* Florence, 1956.

articles–

Lippmann, Friedrich. "Pagine sconosciute de *I Capuletti e i Montecchi* e *Beatrice di Tenda* di Vincenzo Bellini." *Rivista italiana di musicologia* 2 (1967): 140.
Galatopoulos, Stelios. "The Romani-Bellini Partnership." *Opera* November (1972).
Collins, Michael. "The Literary Background to Bellini's *I Capuleti e i Montecchi.*" *Journal of the American Musicological Society* 35 (1982): 532.
Brauner, Charles S. "Parody and Melodic Style in Bellini's *I Capuleti e i Montecchi.*" In *Studies in the History of Music,* vol. 2, 124. New York, 1988.
Avant-scène opéra March (1989) [*Les Capulets et Les Montaigues* issue].

*   *   *

The libretto of *I Capuleti ed i Montecchi* is Romani's revision of his *Giulietta e Romeo,* written for Nicola Vaccai in 1825. The immediate source for the story was not Shakespeare but a play *Giulietta e Romeo* by Luigi Scevola of 1818. The action in the libretto for Bellini is as follows. Giulietta and Romeo have already met and fallen in love before the opera begins. Act I: Romeo, disguised as a messenger, offers peace between the warring families, to be cemented by the marriage of Giulietta and Romeo. However, Giulietta is promised by her father Capellio, leader of the Capuleti, to his ally Tebaldo. Although Giulietta is distraught over her impending marriage to Tebaldo, she rejects Romeo's entreaties to run away

I Capuleti ed i Montecchi, Wilhelmine Schröder-Devrient as Romeo, Dresden, 1831

with him. The wedding festivities are interrupted by the sound of the Montecchi attacking. Romeo again tries to convince Giulietta to flee, is confronted by Capellio and Tebaldo, and is rescued by the Montecchi. Act II: Lorenzo, a physician, gives Giulietta the potion that will make her appear dead. Romeo and Tebaldo meet and are about to fight when they hear the funeral procession approaching. At the tomb, Romeo takes poison. Giulietta awakens, and the lovers bid each other farewell. As Romeo dies, Giulietta falls lifeless upon him. The Montecchi, Lorenzo, and Capellio enter and discover the tragedy.

Despite the inevitable unfavorable comparison between the libretto and Shakespeare's play (Berlioz is particularly scathing), Romani's drama is concise and well constructed. In part, the concision is the result of accident: Romani had to supply the libretto quickly because Bellini received the commission at the last minute after another composer had defaulted. Whatever the reason, the drama proceeds fairly logically, with the tragedy growing out of the irreconcilable conflicts of Romeo's ardor, Giulietta's vacillation between love and filial loyalty, and Capellio's stubbornness. (We are, however, left asking why Romeo is not recognized as the messenger of the opening scene and why Giulietta would refuse to run away with him but agree to take the potion.) There are no superfluous characters and subplots.

The haste required of Romani also affected Bellini, and just as the librettist reused old material, so did the composer. His previous opera, *Zaira,* had been a failure, and Bellini adapted many of its melodies for *I Capuleti.* However, in the

majority of cases the text in *I Capuleti* bears little resemblance to the text in *Zaira* that had served for the same melody; they differ in poetic form or dramatic context or both. The process of adaptation sometimes led to awkward results, as in Romeo's aria at Giulietta's tomb, "Deh! tu, bell'anima," in which the composer had to repeat the opening words of each line to make the text fit the music ("Deh! tu, deh! tu, bell'anima / A me, a me rivolgiti" ["Ah! you, ah! you, fair spirit / Turn to me, to me"], etc.). In addition to the self-borrowings, Bellini relied on the example of Vaccai in using a mezzo-soprano in the role of Romeo and in forming the two finales, numbers whose structures lie outside the usual conventions of bel-canto opera.

In modern times *I Capuleti ed i Montecchi* has not had the popularity of the two operas that followed it, *La sonnambula* and *Norma.* And indeed the score is uneven. After a slow start, the opera comes to life with Giulietta's entrance to a beautiful horn solo that will also accompany part of the ensuing recitative (several of the most striking melodies in the score are instrumental introductions; in addition to this horn solo, there is one for violoncello that opens act II and one for clarinet before the confrontation between Romeo and Tebaldo). This is followed by her elegiac *romanza* "Oh! quante volte, oh! quante" ("Oh! how many times"), whose melody, borrowed from his first opera, *Adelson e Salvini,* is testimony to the presence of Bellini's melodic gift even in his earliest works. Most of the remaining pieces in *I Capuleti,* while rarely reaching the heights of lyrical beauty attained in *Norma,* are attractive and dramatically apt. One might single out Giulietta's solo in the finale to act I, with its unsettling syncopated accompaniment, and the following duet with Romeo. Of the longer, more formal melodies, the slow section of the earlier Giulietta-Romeo duet in act I and both tempi of Giulietta's aria in act II are especially effective.

For most observers, the greatest scene of the opera is the finale, at the Capulets' tomb. It is unconventionally constructed of recitative, a one-tempo aria for Romeo, more recitative, a brief duet, and an even briefer conclusion after the lovers' deaths. The recitatives are particularly expressive; note the surge of melody when Romeo addresses Giulietta's corpse and the despairing fall of an octave when Romeo informs Giulietta that he will be staying in the tomb forever. Romeo's aria has a moving simplicity, despite the problems of text-setting mentioned above. And the duet, "Ah! crudel! che mai facesti?" ("Ah! cruel one! what did you do?")— whose structure Bellini derived from Vaccai but which he imbued with far greater musical power—is heart-rending with its brief spurts of lyricism defeated by the bleak changes from major to minor when Romeo starts to feel the effects of the poison and again as he enters his death throes. Unfortunately, because Vaccai's finale is somewhat more brilliant for Romeo, Maria Malibran in 1832 began the practice of using it in place of Bellini's, thereby depriving the audience of Bellini's finest dramatic achievement to date and perhaps contributing to the opera's descent into oblivion, from which it has only recently begun to emerge.

—Charles S. Brauner

CARDILLAC.

Composer: Paul Hindemith.

Librettist: Ferdinand Lion (after Hoffmann, *Das Fräulein von Scuderi*).

First Performance: Dresden, Staatsoper, 9 November 1926; revised by Hindemith (after Lion's libretto), first performed Zurich, Stadttheater, 20 June 1952.

Roles: Cardillac (baritone); His Daughter (soprano); Apprentice (tenor); First Singer at Opera (soprano); Officer (bass); Young Cavalier (tenor); Klymene (contralto); Phaeton (tenor); Apollo (bass); Rich Marquis (mute); tenors; chorus (SATB).

Publications

books–

Schilling, H.L. *Paul Hindemiths Cardillac.* Würzburg, 1962.

articles–

Lion, F. "Cardillac I und II." *Akzente* 4 (1957): 126.
Rexroth, Dieter. "Zum Stellenwert der Oper *Cardillac* im Schaffen Hindemiths." In *Erprobungen und Erfahrungen. Zu Paul Hindemiths Schaffen in den Zwanziger Jahren,* edited by Dieter Rexroth, 56. Mainz, 1978.

*　　*　　*

Paul Hindemith's first full-length opera, *Cardillac,* is also the first of a trilogy of works for the stage, which span three different periods of his dramatic writing. *Cardillac, Mathis der Maler,* and *Die Harmonie der Welt* all deal with the problem of the creative artist's relationship to his work and to society.

During the 1920s the alienation of the artist was a prevailing theme, and at this time Hindemith himself, pondering new directions for his dramatic writing, was experiencing a turbulent period in his development. Hence E.T.A. Hoffmann's novella of 1820, *Das Fräulein von Scuderi,* with its artist-in-society subject matter, proved to be a very attractive and challenging topic for the composer's first major confrontation with the problems of 20th-century opera.

At Hindemith's request, Ferdinand Lion, the Alsatian poet and essayist, produced a terse, theatrical libretto, freely based on Hoffmann's compelling portrait of the gifted, but psychotic goldsmith, René Cardillac, a highly renowned artist but isolated member of society in the Paris of Louis XIV. His obsessive self-identity with his creations and his pathological compulsion never to become separated from them, impel him to murder his clients in order to recover the precious objects they have purchased. Interwoven in this tale of terror is a love story of Cardillac's daughter and a young man, which interlocks with the dark side of the life of the father and heightens the pathos and tragedy as Cardillac is finally exposed and killed by the mob.

In his desire to maintain a creative distance from the explosive text, Hindemith avoided writing psychological music by supporting his architectonic concept with terse, dissonant, strict polyphony, thus controlling the psychological tensions of the work through the discipline of the orchestral music, and by placing the two stylistic elements—musical and literary—on different levels. In the rehearsals for the 1926 premiere under Fritz Busch, Hindemith insisted that the production not be static, but generate its own dramatic tensions with strong stage movement in contrast to the concertante orchestral music. As Felix Wolfes observed after the first performance, "The main attraction of this remarkable work consists in the curious union of dramatically forceful musical full-bloodedness with the strictest formal and stylistic asceticism, almost without parallel in opera." David Neumeyer, in his analysis of the 1926 *Cardillac* published in 1986, regards the work as "the most characteristic German opera in modern style of the mid and late twenties," because only *Cardillac* represents the "new objective" manner: i.e., through musical formal principles, subjective-psychological powers become objective-musical. Music and drama, in a juxtaposition of stylistic and expressive components, stand in a new relationship.

However, the "revolutionary élan" of the young Hindemith for "new objectivism" in opera as a counter force against the romanticism of Richard Strauss and Wagner, prevented him from recognizing the romanticism within his own nature, and ironically, against his intentions, the romantic element endemic to the subject matter returned strongly in the concept of the opera, resulting in a revision twenty-five years later.

Adaptations, revisions, new settings are not unusual in the history of opera. However, Hindemith's 1952 revision was so drastic that except for the title, some leading characters, and a few musical scenes, the new version had very little in common with the original. Moreover, the libretto was replaced by the composer's own text. In addition to adding new characters and scenes, Hindemith enlarged the work to four acts by creating a new act (act III, a "play within a play") which includes the performance of part of Lully's *Phaeton.* This insertion not only provides a virtuosic, declamatory scene,

Cardillac, **Landestheater, Darmstadt, 1927**

which brilliantly contrasts with the lugubrious environment of the impending crime, but this injection of baroque music into the drama with another level of activity increases the observational objectivity of the work.

As in most revisions, a certain amount of stylistic unity is sacrificed in Hindemith's effort to approach a new esthetic principle, and critical response varied. Some felt the emphasis placed on the expressionistic, abstract qualities of the score weakened the dramatic power of the work; others thought the philosophy and terror of the piece were not well combined. There were complaints that the vocal line was mostly declamatory, while the orchestral music carried the "tunes." Nevertheless, Hindemith ordered his publisher to permit only the revised score for performance, and not until the composer's death was the original version made available again. A champion of the original version in spite of the composer's wishes was the conductor Joseph Keilberth, who shortly before his death in 1968 initiated for Cologne Radio an authoritative recording, which Deutsche Grammaphon issued as the first commercial recording of the work in either version—an invaluable documentary event.

—Muriel Hebert Wolf

CARMEN.

Composer: Georges Bizet.

Librettists: Henri Meilhac and Ludovic Halévy (after Mérimée).

First Performance: Paris, Opéra-Comique, 3 March 1875.

Roles: Carmen (mezzo-soprano); Don José (tenor); Escamillo (baritone); Micaëla (soprano); Frasquita (soprano); Mercedes (mezzo-soprano); Le Remendado (tenor); Le Dancaire (tenor); Zuniga (bass); Morales (baritone); chorus (SATTBB), chorus (children).

Publications

books–

Nietzsche, F. *Randglossen zu Bizets "Carmen."* Edited by H. Daffner. Regensburg, 1912.
Hühne, F. *Die Oper "Carmen" als ein Typus musikalischer Poetik.* Greifswald, 1915.
Imsan, D. *Carmen: Charakter-Entwicklung für die Bühne.* Darmstadt, 1917.
Gaudier, C. *Carmen de Bizet.* Paris, 1922.
Istel, E. *Bizet und Carmen.* Stuttgart, 1927.
Laparra, P. *Bizet et l'Espagne.* Paris, 1935.

Célestine Galli-Marié, the first Carmen, 1875

Cooper, Martin. *Carmen*. London, 1947.

Dean, Winton. *Carmen*. London, 1949.

Malherbe, Henry. *Carmen*. Paris, 1951.

Knaust, Rebecca. *The Complete Guide to Carmen*. New York, 1978.

Dahlhaus, Carl. *Musikalischer Realismus, Zur Musikgeschichte des 19. Jahrhunderts*. Munich, 1982; English translation by M. Whittall, Cambridge and London, 1985.

John, Nicholas, ed. *Georges Bizet: Carmen. English National Opera Guides* 13. London and New York, 1982.

Roy, Jean. *Bizet*. Paris, 1983.

Maingueneau, D. *Carmen: Les racines d'un mythe*. Paris, 1984.

Fornari, F. *Carmen adorate: psicoanalisi della donna demoniaca*. Milan, 1985.

Clément, C. *L'opéra ou la défaite des femmes*. Paris, 1979; English translation, Minneapolis, 1988.

McClary, S. *Feminine Endings: Music, Gender and Sexuality*. Minneapolis, 1991.

articles–

Charlot, A. and J. "A propos de la millième de Carmen." *L'art du théâtre* 5 (1905): 9.

Halévy, L. "La millième représentation de Carmen." *Le théâtre* January (1905).

Tiersot, J. "Bizet and Spanish Music." *Musical Quarterly* 13 (1927): 566.

Revue de musicologie 20 (1938) [Bizet issue].

Dean, Winton. "The True Carmen?" *Musical Times* 106 (1965): 846.

Dean, Winton. "The Corruption of *Carmen*: The Perils of Pseudo-Musicology." *Musical Newsletter* 3 (1973).

Wright, Lesley A. "A New Source for *Carmen*." *Nineteenth-Century Music* 2 (1978): 61.

Avant-scène opéra, March-April (1980) [*Carmen* issue].

Kestner, J. "Joyce, Wagner and Bizet: Exiles, Tannhäuser, and Carmen." *Modern British Literature* 5 (1980): 53.

Maingueneau, D. "Signification du décor: l'exemple de *Carmen*." *Romantisme* 38 (1982): 87.

Wangermée, R. "L'Opéra sur la scène et à l'écran: À propos de Carmen." In *Approches de l'opéra*, edited by A. Helbo, 251. Paris, 1986.

Clarkson, A. "Carmen: Bride of Dionysus." *Quadrant* 20/no. 1 (1987): 51.

Edwards, G. "Carmen." In *Catholic Tastes and Times: Essays in Honour of Michael F. Williams*, edited by M. Rees, 127. Leeds, 1987.

Furman, N. "The Languages of Love in Carmen." In *Reading Opera*, edited by A. Groos and R. Parker, 168. Princeton, 1988.

Beardsley, T.S. "The Spanish Musical Sources of Bizet's *Carmen*." *Inter-American Music Review* 10/spring (1989): 143.

Siebenmann, G. "*Carmen* von Mérimée über Bizet zu Saura und Gades: Ein Spanienbild im Spiel der Medlen." In *Einheit und Vielfalt in der iberoromania: Geschichte und Gegenwart*, edited by C. Strosetzki and M. Tietz, 169, Hamburg, 1989.

Baker, E. "The scene designs for the first performances of Bizet's *Carmen*." *Nineteenth-Century Music* 13 (1990): 230.

*   *   *

Hostile reviews and talk of scandal greeted the 1875 premiere of *Carmen*, Georges Bizet's best known work, which was to become the world's most popular opera. For Bizet, *Carmen*'s debut was a bitter disappointment. He had worked for two years on the score, and he expected a hit: "People make me out to be obscure, complicated, tedious, more fettered by technical skill than lit by inspiration. Well, this time I have written a work that is all clarity and vivacity, full of colour and melody. It will be entertaining. . . ." While these qualities may account for *Carmen*'s subsequent success, it's less-than-enthusiastic initial reception could be attributed, in part at least, to the frustrated expectations of the middle-class families that regularly attended the performances of the Opéra-Comique. A passionate affair between a wanton Gypsy and a weak soldier set in the company of smoking working girls, lighthearted smugglers and ribald soldiers was hardly the kind of love story or social milieu that reflected the values of this bourgeois public. Moreover, the on-stage stabbing at the conclusion of the work broke the conventions of dramatic decorum, further offending the audience's sense of propriety. The original *Carmen* was composed of a Prélude followed by twenty-seven pieces that were separated by scenes in spoken dialogue, but it was an amended version produced in October 1875 at the Vienna Opera, after Bizet's death, that was to become the *Carmen* in the Grand Opera tradition now performed throughout the world. In its new format, the spoken dialogues were replaced by recitatives composed by Ernest Guiraud.

Stationed in Seville, far from his native Basque country, Corporal Don José arrests Carmen, the beguiling Gypsy, accused of attacking another woman during a fight in the tobacco factory. In exchange for a rendez-vous, José allows her to escape, and he is sent to prison. Upon his release, José arrives at the tavern of Lillas Pastia to meet Carmen. Their evening comes to an abrupt end when José hears the bugle sound the retreat and decides over Carmen's objections to go back to the barracks. As he is about to leave, Lieutenant Zuniga comes in with the express purpose of courting Carmen's favors; the two soldiers exchange words and draw their swords; they are separated by Carmen's Gypsy companions. His military career now jeopardized, José joins up with Carmen and her friends. When Micaëla, José's former sweetheart, fetches him at the request of his dying mother, Carmen, tired of their relationship and José's constant jealousy, begins a liaison with the toreador Escamillo. On the day of the corrida, outside the bullfighting arena, José urges Carmen to come back to him. In spite of his pleas and his threats, Carmen refuses to follow him, affirming that she would rather die than not be free to live and love as she pleases. As the shouts of the public in the background announce the victory of the toreador over the bull, José stabs her.

For the libretto, which is based on a short story by Prosper Mérimée published in 1845, Georges Bizet relied on two seasoned dramatists, Henri Meilhac and Ludovic Halévy, who had previously authored the libretti of Jacques Offenbach's very popular *opera bouffes*.

Bizet's *Carmen* changed the traditions of the French lyrical stage by blurring the distinctions between operatic genres. For example, Micaëla and Escamillo, whose roles were invented by Meilhac and Halévy, are stock characters in the Opéra Comique tradition—as are Carmen's companions—but the impossible love story between the Gypsy and the soldier is a tragedy that belongs to Grand Opera. In this story of romantic passion, the incompatible protagonists never sing of love in unison. Carmen's lower range mezzo and José's lyrical tenor are also mismatched, for the usual coupling of voices in nineteenth-century opera casts a soprano as the tenor's lover. In the aria "Ma mère, je la vois!" Micaëla's soprano blends with José's voice in a traditional duet which only calls attention to the unconventional nature of Carmen's and José's relationship. Bizet introduced another innovation when he insisted on a realistic staging that respected the opera's dramatic unity and that transformed the then motionless chorus into kinetic performers, and turned the lead singers into actors.

Tchaikovsky described *Carmen* as "a masterpiece in the fullest meaning of the word, that is to say, one of those rare works that translates the efforts of a whole musical period," and Nietzsche wrote to his friend, the composer Peter Gast, that Bizet's opus was "the best opera that existed . . . the opera of operas." Bizet's score offers a dazzling variety of moods and textures from the most delicate and hauntingly seductive to the tackiest of tunes, as in the case of the Toreador Song. For Richard Strauss, Bizet's composition stands as a masterpiece of orchestration. "If you want to learn how to orchestrate," he writes, "study the score of *Carmen.* What wonderful economy, and how every note and rest is in its proper place." *Carmen* has been hailed by pro- and anti-Wagnerians alike, and admired by a variety of composers, including Brahms, Gounod, Wolf, Debussy, Puccini, Stravinsky, Grieg, and Prokofiev.

Because the last act makes the bullfighting arena the referential backdrop of the story, the corrida has been the most commonly used critical topos for the interpretation of the opera. A fight to the death between man and beast, the corrida has been seen as a test of manly courage, and also as an event that averts the latent violence inherent in society through the ritual sacrifice of a scapegoat. But bull and matador can also be viewed as mirror images of each other, both torturer as well as victim, and the reversibility of their positions leaves open the possibility of divergent, even contradictory, interpretations. Thus, while critics in the past have judged Carmen's death to be a just retribution for causing a man's downfall, today a feminist critic, Catherine Clément, eulogizes Carmen as a heroine "who chooses to die before a man decides it for her." For Nietzsche, Bizet's work illustrated the war between the sexes, but a contemporary public might feel that it is Micaëla and Escamillo who better represent their sex—and there is no interaction between them—rather than the protagonists who seem equally distant from ideals of femininity and masculinity. A story about unrequited love, Bizet's *Carmen* demonstrates the tragedy of passion as a form of desire that negates the desire of the other.

From sexual politics to partisan causes, *Carmen* has often been used to represent political ideologies. In a 1984 production by Frank Corsaro at the New York City Opera, the opera is set during the Spanish Civil War with Carmen portrayed as a freedom fighter who falls in the struggle against fascism; yet, in a similar staging performed in Pforzheim during the Third Reich, Bizet's opera may have served rather to remind Nazi soldiers of the dangers awaiting those who fraternized with so-called "non-aryan" women. For Theodor Adorno, the greatness of Bizet's opera resides in its oppositional structure which continuously challenges the ascription of any fixed meaning, making it possible for the story of Carmen to become a myth. From the exotic temptress and the bewitching vamp to the incarnation of the modern free woman, the popularity of Bizet's *Carmen* launched a cultural industry which has already produced over thirty films, several ballets, and numerous plays bearing the unofficial trademark of her name.

—Nelly Furman

CARRERAS, José.

Tenor. Born 5 December 1946 in Barcelona. Studied with Jaime Puig at Barcelona Conservatory and with Juan Ruax; debut as Flavio in *Norma,* Barcelona, 1970; sang Gennaro in *Lucrezia Borgia,* 1970; London debut in concert version of *Maria Stuarda*; at New York City Opera, 1972-75; San Francisco debut, 1973, as Rodolfo in *La bohème*; Metropolitan Opera debut, 1975; Salzburg debut as Don Carlos, 1976; Chicago debut as Riccardo, 1976.

Publications

By CARRERAS: books–

Singing from the Soul. Seattle, 1991.

About CARRERAS: books–

Nadal, P. *Carreras—La pasion de Vivir.* Barcelona, 1988.

*   *   *

José Carreras has recently made a return to public performance after a bout with leukemia. He is evidently still a very affecting singer but the strain the illness has had on his vocal apparatus is apparent. Carreras in any case always tended to push his naturally lyric tenor voice to the limit, singing Andrea Chénier, Calaf, and even Radamès; the first role he sang gloriously as a young poet and artist, the others with only partial success. His dark, rich timbre, he claims, "can be dangerous because at times it makes me seem to have a bigger voice than I really do." Herbert von Karajan principally persuaded him to sing many of the heavier roles in his repertoire. Carreras is vocally, physically, and temperamentally a perfect Rodolfo in Puccini's *La bohème.* Yet even if there was some sense of vocal strain as he went from the essentially lyric roles in *La bohème, Luisa Miller, La traviata, Rigoletto,* and *Lucia di Lammermoor* to heavier ones in *Andrea Chénier, Don Carlos, Carmen, Il trovatore, La forza del destino,* and *Turandot,* there was a corresponding improvement in Carreras's acting ability and believability on stage. One role that Carreras always sang with particular success was Don José in *Carmen,* a part that he performed with Agnes Baltsa alone over one hundred times. Of Carreras's José, Alan Blyth wrote in *Gramophone:* "Carreras's Flower Song, ending with a marvelous *pianissimo* high B flat, is a thing of light and shade, finely shaped, not quite idiomatically French either in verbal or tonal accent, but very appealing." Of the above list the only role that has positively eluded him has been Radamès with Karajan, a role that Carreras immediately dropped.

The Barcelona native who, like Corelli and Domingo, is largely self-taught, was discovered at age 22 by Montserrat Caballé's brother Carlos. The soprano quickly recognized the young tenor's great talent, and Caballé and Carreras have subsequently appeared together numerous times both in live performance and on recordings. Carreras's official stage debut took place in 1970 in Barcelona as Flavio to Caballé's Norma. That same year he and Caballé appeared together at the Liceu in Donizetti's *Lucrezia Borgia.* In 1971 Carreras sang Rodolfo in Parma, where he won the International Verdi Competition in that year, and in 1972 he made his debut as Rodolfo at the New York City Opera. There he was given a three-year contract and learned eleven new roles in sixteen months. Debuts in important opera centers around the world followed. Carreras has been especially active in Salzburg,

Vienna, and at Covent Garden. His collaboration with Karajan began in 1976 with a Verdi *Messa da Requiem* at the Salzburg Easter Festival and a recording and stage performances of Verdi's *Don Carlos*.

Carreras not only pushed his voice but appeared on stage with great regularity. He has likewise had a prolific recording career, even as a "crossover" artist, having recorded not only Spanish and Italian folk and love songs but also *West Side Story* with Bernstein himself conducting (he was Bernstein's third choice and it was not a particularly happy collaboration) and *South Pacific,* both of these musicals with Kiri Te Kanawa. In the opera repertoire Carreras has been especially active recording the works of Verdi, not only the well-known masterpieces but also the less often performed earlier works such as *Un giorno di regno, Il corsaro, I due Foscari,* and *Stiffelio,* all for Philips. Carreras sings elegantly in *Il corsaro* with Caballé and Norman and is perhaps at his very best in *I due Foscari,* impassioned and gorgeous of tone in the prison scene. He has recorded a superb *Otello* of Rossini with von Stade under López Cobos on Philips. His Edgardo in *Lucia di Lammermoor* with Caballé is suitably ardent, reminiscent of the young Giuseppe Di Stefano. Carreras sings a high E at the conclusion of "Verrano a te." In *Il trovatore* under Colin Davis on Philips, Carreras follows Verdi's markings scrupulously, singing "Con espressione" in "Ah si, ben mio," and performing "Di quella pira" in the correct key of C major topped by a thrilling high note. His Don Carlos on EMI under Karajan is an ideal youth burning from unrequited love and political fervor; he is likewise ardent as Riccardo in *Un ballo in maschera* with Caballé under Davis, but here another similarity with Di Stefano is evident in that the voice shows signs of strain. Carreras's Cavaradossi in *Tosca,* likewise on Philips with Caballé and conducted by Davis, is sung heroically with a glorious thrust and a breathtakingly slow tempo for "E lucevan le stelle" that Carreras sustains beautifully, but the *Turandot* on which he sings Calaf (Caballé is Turandot) is marred by Alain Lombard's dull conducting. With Caballé there are also a number of live recordings, notable among them a 1974 *Maria Stuarda* from the Salle Pleyel and a 1977 *Roberto Devereux* from Aix-en-Provence. These give a good account of Carreras in his prime.

Blessed with a highly individual voice of a dark hue, superb physical looks, and intelligence, Carreras has had a thrilling international career, if not quite on the par with his contemporary tenor superstars Domingo and Pavarotti. Carreras appears in a number of videos of complete operas including a visually appealing Zeffirelli production of *La bohème* with Teresa Stratas as Mimi, a film about the Spanish tenor Julian Gayarre, the tenor "with the voice of an angel" who lived from 1844 to 1890, and in 1991 a compact disc of the songs of Andrew Lloyd Webber.

—Stephen A. Willier

CARUSO, Enrico.

Tenor. Born 25 February 1873, Naples. Died 2 August 1921 in Naples. Two sons by singer Ada Giachetti. One daughter by Dorothy Park Benjamin. Studied with Guglielmo Vergine, 1891-94, and Vincenzo Lombardi; debut in *L'Amico Francesco* in Naples, 1895; created Maurizio in *Adriana Lecouvreur,* Loris in *Fedora* and Dick Johnson in *La fanciulla del West*; sang at Teatro alla Scala, 1900-02; Covent Garden debut in *Rigoletto* with Nellie Melba, 1902; debut at Metropolitan Opera in *Rigoletto,* 1903, and sang there for eighteen seasons; operation for node on vocal cords in 1909.

Publications

By CARUSO: books–

The New Book of Caricatures. New York, 1965.

About CARUSO: books–

Key, P. and B. Zirato. *Enrico Caruso: A Biography.* 1922.
Caruso, D. *Enrico Caruso: His Life and Death.* New York 1945; London, 1946.
Ybarra, T.R. *Caruso: the Man of Naples and the Voice of Gold.* New York, 1953.
Robinson, F. *Caruso: His Life in Pictures.* New York, 1957.
Mouchon, J. *Enrico Caruso: sa vie et sa voix.* Longres, 1966; English translation, 1974.
Bolig, J.R. *The Recordings of Enrico Caruso: A Discography.* Delaware, 1973.
Greenfeld, H. *Caruso.* New York, 1983.
Paul, B. *A Cadenza for Caruso.* New York, 1984.
Rubboli, D. *Lo "scugnizzo" che conquisto il mondo: vita di Enrico Caruso.* Naples, 1987.
Scott, M. *The Great Caruso.* New York and London, 1988.

Enrico Caruso as the Duke in *Rigoletto*

Caruso, E., Jr., and A. Farkas. *Enrico Caruso: My Father and My Family.* Portland, 1990.

articles—

Favia-Artsay, A. "The Impossible Dream." *Hobbies* November (1972): 5.
Mayer-Reinach, U. "Die Gesangkunst Enrico Carusos und unsere Zeit." *Musica* 27 (1973): 563.
Villella, T. "Caruso: The Tenor of the Century." *Le Grand Baton* September (1975): 3.
Farkas, A. "Caruso and Budapest." *Record Collector* 28 (1984): 245.
———. "Enrico Caruso: Tenor, Baritone, Bass." *Opera Quarterly* 4/no. 4 (1986-87): 53.

*   *   *

Enrico Caruso had just turned twenty-two when he made his professional debut in Domenico Morelli's new opera, *L'amico Francesco,* on 15 March 1895. During the engagements that followed, mostly in the provincial Italian theaters, he built a repertory at an astonishing rate. The record shows that he learned 16 major roles in two years. With each successive and successful engagement Caruso's name gained currency. In 1897, he sang in the world premiere of *L'Arlesiana,* and upon the sudden death of Roberto Stagno for whom Giordano composed *Fedora,* Caruso was chosen to take his place at the world premiere on 17 November 1898. As he later said: "After that the contracts descended on me like a big rainstorm." It marked the beginning of his rise through the ranks of Italian tenors to preeminence.

After tours of Russia (1899 and 1900) and Buenos Aires (1899, 1900, 1901), his ascendancy began to accelerate. The series of important debuts that followed included Teatro alla Scala (1900), Teatro San Carlo of Naples (1901), Covent Garden (1902), Paris (1904), and Vienna (1906). In retrospect, Caruso's most important debut was with the Metropolitan Opera, as the Duke in *Rigoletto* on 23 November 1903. The Met became his artistic home for the rest of his career; he sang 628 performances in the house including galas, and 234 at the Brooklyn Academy of Music, in Philadelphia, and on tour. During his 18 seasons with the Met he was featured in 17 opening nights; he performed 39 of the 64 roles in his repertoire, among them Canio (*I pagliacci*), Radames (*Aïda*), Manrico (*Il trovatore*), Samson, Faust, Don José, Lionel, Cavaradossi, Rodolfo, the Duke of Mantua, and Riccardo. His only Wagnerian role was Lohengrin (three performances, Buenos Aires, 1901) and his only Mozart role Don Ottavio in *Don Giovanni* (Covent Garden). During his career he took part in ten world premieres, and he created Dick Johnson in *La Fanciulla del West.*

By his mid-thirties, Caruso became the most sought after and highest paid singer in the world. His fees at the Metropolitan eventually rose to $2,500 a performance, a fee limited, rather than set, by the tenor himself. His cachet elsewhere was much higher, $10,000 a performance in Cuba (1920) and $15,000 in Mexico City (1919). His last Victor contract (scheduled to run until 1934) guaranteed him an annual minimum of $100,000 in royalties, and his two silent movies (*My Cousin* and *A Splendid Romance,* 1918) allegedly brought him $100,000 each.

Caruso made his first recordings in 1902. The ten sides he recorded for the Gramophone and Typewriter Company in Milan on 19 April 1902 were so successful that Caruso has been generally credited with turning the gramophone, until then regarded as a toy, into a musical instrument. He signed an exclusive contract with the Victor Talking Machine Company in 1904, and all of his subsequent records were made either in New York City or in Camden, New Jersey. The majority of these acoustic recordings have never been out of the catalog, and despite the sonic deficiencies, his entire recorded legacy has been repeatedly reissued on long playing records and compact discs.

Although Guglielmo Vergine was Caruso's only singing teacher, conductor Vincenzo Lombardi helped him conquer his difficulties with his high notes, and he received help from his common-law wife, Ada Giachetti, herself an accomplished conservatory-trained singer and pianist. Thereafter, he firmed up his own technique by daily practice. His voice, initially light and lyrical, grew heavier and more dramatic with age. The baritone timbre and the solid lower range had been there from the beginning; in fact, in his youth he had some doubts whether he was a baritone or a tenor. His recordings show that he was able to sing a high D flat ("Cujus animam" from *Stabat Mater*) and color his voice to deliver a beautiful rendition of the bass aria "Vecchia zimarra" from *La bohème,* the latter commemorating the occasion when he sang the aria onstage for an indisposed Andrès de Segurola (23 December 1913). Remarkably, the two recordings were made only three years apart.

In stylistic terms, Caruso represented the bridge between the bel canto tenors of the late 19th century—Angelo Masini, Francesco Marconi, Fernando de Lucia, Alessandro Bonci—and the more robust verismo singers who followed him. Caruso did not abandon the merits of the old school but rather built on them, combining the old with the new style of singing. He would not distort the music, but allow the weight and meaning of the words to dominate the vocal line, thereby achieving a dramatic involvement and communicative effect greater and more immediate than any of his contemporaries. An example that bears out this assertion is his three *fortissimo* outbursts of "Sangue!" in the duet from *Otello* with Titta Ruffo. He is possibly the only singer on record who actually sings—not screams—these words.

Aurally, Caruso's voice had a sensuous appeal, "carnal," as described by Geraldine Farrar. His vocal production was flawless: a solid column of air supported an unwavering sound of exceptional beauty. The quality of the voice has been consistently described in many languages as "golden" and "velvet." It had a caressing warmth, a heroic ring, and sufficient flexibility to respond to the singer's demands. In his best years he could produce at will a *diminuendo,* piano, head tone, falsetto, or *voce mista* with the same ease as a forte or fortissimo. He took pride in his ability to color his voice according to the character of the music—light for Nemorino, heavy for Radames or Samson. Although his voice darkened and grew more robust, his increasingly "muscular" singing near the end appears to have been a matter of choice rather than limitations. His light and playful "'A vucchella" recorded in September 1919, shows the singer still in full control of his *mezza voce.*

He worked on his interpretations throughout his career. In some of his roles—Canio, the Duke of Mantua, Radames, Eléazar (*La Juive*)—he established standards that have not been equaled, much less surpassed. His style, modern if compared with that of any of his contemporaries, had a lasting influence on operatic singing in this century. His initially crude and elementary acting improved over the years, culminating in Eléazar in *La Juive,* his last role, which was uniformly regarded as a great histrionic as well as vocal achievement.

Caruso was a serious man in private, and a kind, gregarious, fun-loving person in company. His warm humanity endeared him to his public, his generosity was legendary. Always ready to extend a helping hand, he is said to have supported or helped over a hundred friends and relatives with monthly checks. The international publicity he generated was unsought and unpaid; it came of itself, the product of his accomplishments and celebrity and the love of his public.

Dying at the relatively young age of 48, Caruso's professional career spanned only 26 years. Although he performed in opera and concert in most countries of Europe, North and South America, a single televised concert of present-day superstars can reach more listeners than all the audiences who heard Caruso in his lifetime. He has been dead for seventy years, yet his name is synonymous with opera and great singing throughout the entire civilized world. Some authorities maintain that toward the end of his life, Caruso's voice showed signs of decline. Bearing in mind a chronic chest cold he could not shake in the fall of 1920, and conceding the effects of the inevitable aging process, it was still the Caruso voice. Mount Everest has eroded several feet over the enturies; it is still the tallest peak in the world.

—Andrew Farkas

CASTOR AND POLLUX
See CASTOR ET POLLUX

CASTOR ET POLLUX [Castor and Pollux].

Composer: Jean-Philippe Rameau.

Librettist: P.-J. Bernard.

First Performance: Paris, Opéra, 24 October 1737; revised, 8 June 1754.

Roles (Many may be doubled): Minerve (soprano); Vénus (soprano); L'Amour (tenor); Mars (bass); Telaira (soprano); Phoebe (soprano); Pollux (baritone or bass); Jupiter (bass); High Priest (tenor); Follower of Hebe (soprano); A Planet (soprano); Mercury (mute); Athlete I (tenor); Athlete II (bass); Happy Spirit (soprano); Castor (countertenor); chorus (SSATB).

Publications

article–

Libin, Laurence. "A Rediscovered Portrayal of Rameau and *Castor and Pollux*." *Early Music* 11 (1983): 510.

* * *

Castor et Pollux, Rameau's second *tragédie,* was hailed as his masterpiece during the eighteenth century, especially from 1754, when it was performed in its revised form. With *Hippolyte et Aricie* and *Les Boréades,* it occupies a place among Rameau's finest works in the tragic genre and holds particular appeal for the strength of human emotions portrayed in three characters: Castor, Pollux and Telaira. The story draws upon the themes of love, jealousy, and vengeance, but the strongest sentiment is the mutual devotion of the two brothers.

Castor, a mortal, is the half-brother of Pollux, a demigod and son of Jupiter. The original version opens with a magnificent tomb scene for Castor, who has died in battle. Pollux offers his affection to Telaira, daughter of Jupiter's grand priest, but she loves only Castor and wants Pollux to retrieve him from the underworld. Jupiter warns Pollux that to do so, he must take his brother's place. Aided by the demonguards of the underworld, Pollux successfully fends off the jealous Phoebe and her followers. Desolate, Phoebe reveals her love for Pollux before killing herself. Castor consents to return to Telaira only to say farewell so that Pollux can return to earth. Their fraternal love is rewarded by Jupiter's proclamation of immortality for the three, and the opera ends with a celestial celebration.

For the 1754 revival, the librettist Pierre-Joseph Bernard eliminated the allegorical prologue, and the opera begins before Castor's death, necessitating the addition of an entirely new first act. There were numerous other changes, such as the strengthening of Phoebe, now more strongly portrayed as a sorceress with magical powers. Capable of engaging Mercury's help at the entrance to the underworld, she is nevertheless unsuccessful. The new version provided more opportunity for spectacles and stage machinery so appreciated at the time, with descents of gods, a battle scene, and Castor's death on the field. The new fourth act was judged to be the finest at the revival, with its trio and chorus of demons, and the attempts of the *ombres heureuses* (happy shades of the Elysian Fields) to please Castor. Contrasts between scenes were also heightened in this version, such as the change from the flaming grotto and demons of the underworld to the peace of the Elysian Fields in act IV.

Rameau took advantage of changes in the libretto to recast airs and recitatives, insert new vocal and instrumental pieces, and integrate some of the spectacles and *divertissements* (interludes) more closely into the drama. In the first act, for example, the suite of airs and dances comprising the *divertissement* is no longer relegated to its traditional place at the end of the act, but incorporated within it, and the subsequent attack, ensuing battle, and Castor's death form a tragic end to the act. The chorus also became more integrated into the drama in the 1754 version. It witnesses and reacts immediately to the death of Castor with the outcry "O perte irréparable" ("Oh, irreparable loss," act I, scene v), a brilliant dramatic stroke. Other changes include more accompanied recitative, particularly at moments of solemnity or extreme emotion, such as Castor's vow to return to the underworld to redeem his brother (act IV, scene vii) and Jupiter's pronouncement of immortality for the brothers (act V, scene v), and two new florid *ariettes* (extended vocal solos) for Castor, "Quel bonheur règne dans mon âme" ("What happiness dwells in my soul," act I, scene iv) and "Tendre amour" ("Tender love," act V, scene iv) sung by the *haute-contre* (high tenor) Pierre Jélyotte, who created many of Rameau's leading roles.

The opera was performed at court in 1763 and was chosen to inaugurate the opera house at the Tuileries in 1764, the year of Rameau's death. It remained in the repertory until at least 1781 and achieved well over 200 performances during the eighteenth century.

—Mary Cyr

CATALANI, Alfredo.

Composer. Born 19 June 1854, in Lucca. Died 7 August 1893, in Milan. Studied with his father, and then studied counterpoint with Fortunato Magi at the Istituto Musicale Pacini in Lucca, 1872; studied composition with Bazin and piano with Marmontel in Paris, 1872; returned to Italy, 1873; studied composition with Bozzini at the Milan Conservatory, 1873; professor of composition at the Milan Conservatory, 1886, where he met Toscanini.

Operas

La falce, Arrigo Boito, Milan, Milan Conservatory, 19 July 1875.
Elda, Carlo D'Ormeville, Turin, Teatro Regio, 31 January 1880.
Dejanice, Angelo Zanardini, Milan, Teatro alla Scala, 17 March 1883.
Edmea, Antonio Ghislanzoni, Milan, Teatro alla Scala, 27 February 1886.
Loreley, Angelo Zanardini (after D'Ormeville), Turin, Teatro Regio, 16 February 1890.
La Wally, Luigi Illica (after the novel by Wilhelmine von Hillern), Milan, Teatro alla Scala, 20 January 1892.

Other works: orchestral works, choral works, songs, and piano pieces.

Publications

By CATALANI: books–

Gatti, Carlo, ed. *Lettere di Alfredo Catalani a Giuseppe Depanis.* Milan, 1946.

About CATALANI: books–

Depanis. *Alfredo Catalani: appunti e ricordi.* Turin, 1893.
C. P. "Un maestro di musica e due poeti da teatro: alcune lettere inedite di Alfredo Catalani." *Musica e musicisti* 58 (1903): 1041.
Adami, G. *G. Ricordi e i suoi musicisti.* Milan. 1933.
Pardini, D.L. *Alfredo Catalani.* Lucca, 1935.
Luzio, A. *Carteggi verdiani.* Rome, 1935-37.
Bonaccorsi, A. *Alfredo Catalani.* Turin, 1942.
Gatti, Carlo. *Catalani: la vita e le opere.* Milan, 1953.
Cortopani, R. *Il dramma di Alfredo Catalani.* Florence, 1954.
Pagani, Severino. *Alfredo Catalani: ombre e luci nella sua vite e nella sua arte.* Milan, 1957.
Bonaccorsi, A. *Maestri di Lucca.* Florence, 1967.
Sartori, Claudio. *L'avventura del violino. L'Italia musicale dell'Ottocento nella biografia e nei carteggi di Antonio Bazzini.* Turin, 1978.
Tedeschi, Rubens. *Addio, fiorito asil. Il melodramma italiano da Boito al Verismo.* Milan. 1978.
Nicolaisen, Jay. *Italian Opera in Transition 1871-93.* Ann Arbor, 1980.
Zurletti, Michelangelo. *Catalani.* Turin, 1982.

articles–

Barblan, G. "Presagio di gloria e ombre di mestizia ne *La falce* di Alfredo Catalani." *Musicisti toscani, Chigiana* 11 (1954): 65.
Klein, John W. "Alfredo Catalani." *Music and Letters* 35 (1954): 40.

_____. "Catalani and his Operas." *Monthly Musical Record* 88 (1958): 67, 101.
Walker, Frank. "Verdian Forgeries: Letters Hostile to Catalani." *Music Review* 19 (1958): 273; 20 (1959): 28.
Klein, John W. "Verdian Forgeries: a Summing-up." *Music Review* 20 (1959): 244.
_____. "Toscanini and Alfredo Catalani: A Unique Friendship." *Music and Letters* 48 (1967): 213.

* * *

As a composer of Italian opera, Alfredo Catalani was something of an anomaly. Representing an independent current in the history of nineteenth century Italian opera, Catalani's style had little in common with Giuseppe Verdi's or Giacomo Puccini's. Catalani's style remained surprisingly free of Verdi's direct influence. The Verdian aspects of Catalani's style largely derived from the operas of Amilcare Ponchielli, which were important models in the Milan of the 1870s and 80s, particularly during the period of Verdi's hiatus following the composition of *Aïda.* Even more striking was Catalani's resistance to the contemporary "naturalist" currents and French operatic dramaturgy that animated Puccini and other young Italian composers of Puccini's generation, this despite an enthusiasm for Émile Zola dating from Catalani's year as a student at the Conservatoire in Paris. In some respects, Catalani may be viewed as a spiritual heir of Vincenzo Bellini, and commentators have often remarked a Bellinian *morbidezza* (morbidity) in Catalani's work, although Bellini could hardly have exerted much of a direct influence, given Catalani's birthdate. Above all, it may have been Catalani's fascination with early German Romanticism and all things Northern, his allegiance to Arrigo Boïto (composer of *Mefistofele* and librettist for Verdi's *Otello* and *Falstaff*) and the *Scapigliatura* movement, that lent his operatic output its distinctive character.

Through Antonio Bazzini, his teacher at the conservatory in Milan, Catalani gained entrée to the salon of the countess Clara Maffei, where he was befriended by Boïto and the composer/conductor Franco Faccio, who would later lead the premiere of Verdi's *Otello.* Boïto and Faccio were active in the bohemian *Scapigliatura* (from the Italian for "dishevelled") movement, essentially a literary movement along the lines of the French "decadence" formed during the period of disillusionment among intellectuals following the unification of Italy. The *Scapigliatura* championed various ultramontane Romantic and avant-garde movements from Goethe and the Lake Poets to Wagnerism, but Boïto and Catalani were less than perfect Wagnerites. If his scores bespeak a real familiarity with Wagner's *Lohengrin,* Catalani resented the charges of "Wagnerism" and "*avvenirismo*" ("futurism") that were routinely laid at his doorstep, and, like Boïto, he was at least as enamored of Carl Maria von Weber as of the master of Bayreuth. Boïto prepared an Italian translation of Weber's *Der Freischütz* for its Teatro alla Scala premiere in 1872, while Weber's influence on Catalani's style of early German Romantic opera was palpable and abiding. This is directly reflected in Catalani's choices of subject matter for his first and last full-length operas, *Elda* and *La Wally;* the former is based on the legend of the Lorelei, the latter on a German novella set in the Tyrol.

Catalani's mature style is best reflected in the rustic drama of *Edmea,* despite a crippling libretto by Ghislanzoni, the librettist of Verdi's *Aïda;* in *Loreley,* an extensively revised version of *Elda;* and in *La Wally,* his last and best-known work. With *Dejanice,* Catalani tried his hand at Italian grand opera in the manner of Ponchielli. Ponchielli's *La Gioconda* (with a libretto by Boïto after Victor Hugo) was the more or less explicit model for *Dejanice*. Both operas freely avail themselves of the *convenienze* (conventions or conventional layout) of Verdian *melodramma* and Meyerbeerian French grand opera with their abundant opportunities for striking set pieces of various kinds. Like Wagner's, however, Catalani's was primarily an art of transition, and in the later operas, some of the most original music is to be found in the fluid developments linking the set pieces with their subtle and flexible use of *arioso* and *parlando*. Catalani's quasi-symphonic developments with their references to *ländler*, horn calls, and other effects of local color are so effective that the set pieces can seem like throw-backs to an earlier aesthetic, however successfully they may be elided in context. Consequently, the most successful set-pieces in Catalani's operas tend to be either atmospheric orchestral passages evoking natural or, in *Loreley*, supernatural phenomena, or genre scenes in which atmosphere and local color impinge on the dramatic transaction, as with the hushed and effective funeral procession in *Loreley* or the *Walzer del bacio* (Waltz of the kiss) in *La Wally*.

Catalani exploited his rich harmonic and orchestral palettes with real mastery. His mature works are orchestrated in a "symphonic" manner remote from that of earlier Italian opera. Catalani's instrumentation was beholden to the German symphonic tradition, to Beethoven and Weber—Beethoven's Seventh Symphony is evoked at one point in *La Wally*—and like them Catalani employed combinations of clean primary colors rather than Wagner's subtly shifting and imperceptibly blended timbres. Catalani exploited his harmonic language with great originality and with all of the flexibility that harmony had acquired in the later nineteenth century.

In Catalani's operas there is an odd amalgam of Italian conventions and German Romanticism, numbers opera and symphonic continuity, Italianate lyricism and motivic development that is not always perfectly reconciled. If he was no more fully successful in his particular quest for that late-nineteenth-century chimera, continuous opera, than many other composers of the period, on the basis of the finest pages in *Loreley* and *La Wally*, we can endorse Verdi's summation of Catalani as "brav'uomo ed eccelente musicista" ("a brave fellow and an excellent musician").

—David Gable

CAVALIERI, Catarina [born Franziska Cavalier].

Soprano. Born 19 February 1760, in Währing, near Vienna. Died 30 June 1801, in Vienna. Studied with Salieri; debut as Sandrina in Anfossi's *La finta giardiniera*, Vienna, 1775; created several roles for Salieri and Mozart, including those of Constanze in Mozart's *Die Entführung aus dem Serail*, 1782, and Mlle Silberklang in *Der Schauspieldirektor*, 1786.

*　　*　　*

Catarina Cavalieri was a soprano of remarkable qualities and accomplishments even when considered in light of the standards of eighteenth-century music theater. She was barely fourteen years old when she made a highly regarded opera debut at the Kärntnerthortheater in April, 1775. Two years later she was successful as an actress in a play by Lessing. Early on Cavalieri came under the "protection" of Antonio Salieri, and she was to remain his mistress for many years. Despite this connection and her change of name, she sang in only two of Salieri's Italian operas and found her greatest fame and critical acclaim as a leading soprano in German works at the newly established National Theater devoted to the *Singspiel*. Her lack of physical beauty—one contemporary went so far as to describe her as unusually ugly as well as one-eyed—was no impediment to her career. Joseph II claimed she was "very good" indeed, and Mozart had the highest regard for her musical abilities. In fact, Cavalieri's singing and acting capabilities were responsible in large part for the shape of Constanze's music in *Die Entführung aus dem Serail* (1782). At that time Mozart spoke admiringly of "Mlle. Cavalieri's flexible throat," and modern opera buffs may gain some idea of her expertise from "Martern aller Arten," that veritable "symphonia concertante" for soprano, chamber ensemble, and orchestra in act II of *Die Entführung*. Although active in a variety of musical styles and genres in such an international center as Vienna, there is no record that Cavalieri ever performed outside her native city.

Despite connections with Salieri she participated in more performances of Mozart compositions than any other singer in Vienna during the composer's lifetime, and the two seemed to have been good friends, a rare occurrence in the dog-eat-dog world of the music theater. Following *Die Entführung*, Cavalieri was scheduled to sing in *La sposa delusa* before Mozart abandoned that project. In 1786 she was the soprano soloist for the premiere of *Davidde Penitente*, and she was the original "Mlle Silberklang" in *Der Schauspieldirektor* in the same year. (It would seem unusually tongue-in-cheek for Mozart intentionally to compose Mlle Silberklang's aria as a model of Italian practice, both in terms of verse and musical structure, to be sung by a German soprano with an Italian *nom de plume* who performed in German in a *Singspiel*.)

Cavalieri also participated in the first performance of Mozart's version of Handel's *Acis and Galatea* in 1788 and appeared as Donna Elvira for the Viennese performance of *Don Giovanni* the same year. With her abilities in mind, Mozart composed "Mi tradì" for this occasion. In 1789 she sang Susanna for a revival of *Le nozze di Figaro*, and later, Mozart wrote his wife that Catarina and Salieri were very enthusiastic about *Die Zauberflöte*, which they attended with him shortly before his death.

Cavalieri had the good sense to retire from public performance in 1793 when she began to experience vocal difficulties; under comfortable circumstances she lived quietly in Vienna until her death some eight years later. Her career was short but successful, her life apparently a happy one. Her connections with Mozart assure her of more than an honorable position in the history of opera.

—Aubrey S. Garlington

CAVALIERI, Lina.

Soprano. Born 25 December 1874, in Viterbo. Died 7 February 1944, in Florence. Husbands included Prince Bariatinsky in 1890s, millionaire Winthrop Chandler in 1907, tenor Lucien Muratore (divorced 1927), and Giuseppe Campari. Studied with Maddelena Mariani-Masi after beginning career as a café singer; debut as Mimi in *La Bohème* at San Carlo in Naples, 1900; Metropolitan Opera debut as Fedora, 1906; appeared at Covent Garden, 1906; mostly engaged in Paris, Monte Carlo and St Petersburg.

Publications

By CAVALIERI: books–

La mia verità, ed P. d'Arvanni. Rome, 1936.

About CAVALIERI: books–

Tegani, U. *Cantani d'una volta.* Milan, 1945.
Rosenthal, H. *Two Centuries of Opera at Covent Garden.* London, 1958.

*   *   *

Lina Cavalieri is one of the very few twentieth-century artists whose claim to inclusion in this work is founded on other than vocal or artistic prowess. Although she may have had predecessors of her type in the nineteenth century, there is no mystery as to her notable successors in our century.

Blessed with an incredibly beautiful appearance she rose from the slums of Rome, where she performed in cafés and eventually on the "variety" stages, to London (The Empire)

Lina Cavalieri, 1903

and Paris (Folies-Bergère). In this evolution she was encouraged to study for the operatic stage with Maddelena Marianli-Masi in Milan.

Qualified successes at the San Carlos of both Lisbon and Naples and some of the lesser theaters of Italy aroused sufficient interest in her potential that she secured engagements in Poland and Russia. In the land of the czars she achieved a level of stardom enabling her to present her wide repertoire: from 1904 to 1913 she was featured in almost all the glamorous international Italian seasons in St. Petersburg. Her roles were invariably the Massanet Manon, Violetta in *La traviata,* and Mimì all usually sung with Anselmi, and after 1906 Thais with Battistini. In later seasons she added such personality roles as Carmen and Tosca.

A marriage to a Russian nobleman, Count Alexander Bariatinsky, was nullified by the Czar on grounds that the count had married beneath his station. Cavalieri received a generous financial settlement. Throughout her career she was famous for her jewels, many of which were gifts of the Czar himself and other royalty.

Billed as "The Most Beautiful Woman in the World," her appearances at the Metropolitan Opera, Covent Garden, and Oscar Hammerstein's Manhattan Opera aroused curiosity as the public quite naturally wondered whether someone so beautiful could really sing grand opera. Period critiques suggest that her well-used but small-scale vocal resources were reasonably appreciated in the context of her splendid "persona." There is no suggestion that her acting abilities were in any measure remarkable. Her handful of recordings made in 1910-1913 for Columbia reveal a beautiful lyric voice, albeit of low volume, reasonable technical skills, including a correct trill, a fairly easy top register when not pressed (at which point she loses pitch), and an academic vocal correctness.

Public relations professionals were kept busy as her photographs appeared regularly in newspapers and magazines as well as articles about her fabled beauty, jewels, clothes, and husbands. One can only conclude that she spent more time in the photographer's than in the vocal studio.

By the time she married the French tenor matinee idol Lucien Muratore her active singing days were over, although they did some joint concerts. Her silent movies (including *Manon* with Muratore) were modestly successful. Like so many celebrities of her day, she did a publicized stint as a field nurse during the Great War. Periodic attempts at an operatic comeback failed. Her talents ultimately led her to Paris where she was the successful operator of a beauty salon. Her life tragically ended in a 1944 Allied bombing raid of Florence. She was the inevitable subject of a cinema biography, "La donna pui bella del mondo," (1957), starring Gina Lollobrigida.

One concludes that Cavalieri is not an historically important singer but rather a fascinating footnote to her epoch—a gloriously beautiful celebrity who stalked the operatic world. It should be noted in fairness that although she was no operatic giant neither was she a joke, as was the beauteous and much publicized Ganna Walska. She has to be considered one of the most successful creations of Public Relations at a time when that industry was in its infancy. Though she loomed large in the print media of her day one questions whether her talents could be equally successfully packaged for the more demanding electronic media of our time.

—Charles B. Mintzer

CAVALLERIA RUSTICANA [Rustic Chivalry].

Composer: Pietro Mascagni.

Librettists: G. Targioni-Tozzetti and G. Menasci (after Verga).

First Performance: Rome, Costanzi, 17 May 1890.

Roles: Santuzza (soprano); Turiddu (tenor); Lola (mezzo-soprano); Alfio (baritone); Lucia (mezzo-soprano or contralto); chorus (SSATTB).

Publications

books–

Cellamare, D. *Mascagni e la Cavalleria visti da Cerignola.* Rome, 1941.
Ostali, P., and N. Ostali, eds. *"Cavalleria rusticana" 1890-1990: cento anni di un capolavoro.* Milan, 1990.

articles–

Sansone, Matteo. "Vergo and Mascagni: The Critics' Response to *Cavalleria rusticana.*" *Music and Letters* May (1990).

* * *

Gemma Bellincioni and Roberto Stagno in *Cavalleria rusticana*, c.1890

Cavalleria rusticana is universally regarded as the archetype of operatic *verismo*, a term which defined the literary source of the libretto and was also adopted for the musico-dramatic structures of the opera. Stripped of all its operatic embellishments, *Cavalleria*, set in a Sicilian village, is about a case of adultery, with the complication of a seduced girl who triggers off the revenge of the betrayed husband.

A critical assessment of the opera should first distinguish between the veristic literary source—Giovanni Verga's one-act play *Cavalleria rusticana* (1884)—and the libretto arranged by Targioni-Tozzetti and Menasci. Subtitled "Sicilian popular scenes," Verga's text marked a turning point in the theater of post-unity Italy for the originality of the subject and its innovative dramatic conception.

The play is organized as a series of duets encompassed by two choral scenes. The action takes place on Easter Sunday. Alfio is the Sicilian "man of honor," the stern believer in an unwritten code of conduct which empowers a wronged man to take justice into his own hands with no need of intermediaries. The silent presence of two *carabinieri* (policemen) in the first and last scenes acquires a special relevance in the context: Alfio's own justice is set against the law and order established in Sicily by the new Italian state. An old-time mafioso component surfaces in the characterization of Alfio and Turiddu. It is exemplified by the ritual and public challenge of the bite on the ear-lobe. Turiddu's death in the ensuing off-stage duel is accepted by the villagers as the right punishment for someone who infringed the common law that defends the family and condemns adultery as a threat to its integrity. The spine-chilling cry signaling the catastrophe: "Hanno ammazzato compare Turiddu!" ("Turiddu has been killed!"), phrased in the impersonal form, relates the final act of violence to a well-defined social context.

In the libretto, the skilfully coordinated movement of well individualized villagers is lost. Mascagni does manage to suggest a festive atmosphere in musical terms, opening with resounding church bells and adding, later on, organ music and Latin hymns, but these devices tend to remain exterior and decorative. They do not permeate the people on stage. In fact, Verga's villagers are gone. Their place has been taken by a chorus of blissful peasants who are made to sing an incongruous, anodyne work-song full of "birds," "myrtles," "oranges," and "humming spindles." From the crude dialect of the opening *Siciliana*—a sort of folkloric token of what is about to unravel on stage—we are taken back to the world of Arcadia.

Alfio is no longer the modest, hard-working carter of the play. His entry, modeled on Escamillo's first appearance in *Carmen*, shows us a vociferous local hero who braves icy winds, rain and snow, and boasts about his wife's faithfulness. On the other hand, Santuzza is very much the desperate and passionate peasant girl of the original story. Yet the last scene of the opera contains an incongruity that distances the opera, once more, from the *verismo* of the play: Santuzza reappears at the very end and throws herself into Lucia's arms. In the last scene of the play, instead, Verga leaves Turiddu's mother, Lola, and the minor characters on stage but keeps Santuzza well out of the way. She is left alone with her shame and sense of guilt. She is not only "dishonored" but *scellerata* (wicked), since, by exposing Lola's adultery, she has indirectly sentenced Turiddu to death. Her expiration begins with her seeing herself as an outcast in her own village. Her despair can hardly be shared with the mother of the man she has caused to be killed.

As remorse and isolation await Santuzza, institutional justice pursues Alfio, the murderer. At the end of the play, the two *carabinieri* dash off towards the place of the duel. In the opera the presence of policemen patrolling the village square would have spoilt the picturesqueness of the Sicilian setting and made it all too realistic, so there is no trace of that.

Having removed or distorted some essential, realistic features of the story, Mascagni and his librettists introduced their own pseudo-veristic ingredients: the serenade in Sicilian dialect inserted in the orchestral prelude, Lola's *stornello* (flower song, more Tuscan than Sicilian) and Turiddu's drinking song. These pieces of on-stage music, as well as the mellifluous intermezzo, spaced and enhanced the lyrical numbers of the opera such as Santuzza's romanza "Voi lo sapete, o mamma" ("You know that, mother") or Turiddu's farewell to his mother. The result was an intriguing melodrama where the thrill of novelty was balanced by the warm melodiousness of the Italian operatic tradition.

Mascagni's coarse-grained, impassioned music introduced a realistic, "earthy" dimension that was easily seen as a new style, indeed as the transposition of *verismo* from literature into opera. No less alluring was the veristic interpretation of Gemma Bellincioni and Roberto Stagno as Santuzza and Turiddu in the Roman premiere of *Cavalleria*. Their agitated confrontations, their dramatic gestures, such as Santuzza's curse "A te la mala Pasqua!" ("An evil Easter to you!"), helped establish a new vocal style and led to similar interpretations even in operas, such as *Carmen,* that belong to a different genre (i.e. *opéra-comique*). The casual encounter with literary *verismo* would be of little consequence in Mascagni's later production. *Cavalleria rusticana,* however, was to remain his greatest success, and the genre it inaugurated in 1890 would be primarily linked to this composer.

—Matteo Sansone

CAVALLI, Francesco (born Pietro Francesco Caletti).

Composer. Born 14 February 1602, in Crema. Died 14 January 1676, in Venice. Married: Maria Sozomeno, 1630 (died 1652). Studied with his father, Giovanni Battista Caletti, who was the maestro di cappella at Crema; taken to Venice for further musical study by the Venetian nobleman and mayor of Crema, Federico Cavalli, whose name Cavalli adopted; joined the choir of San Marco, under the direction of Claudio Monteverdi, 1616; second organist at San Marco, 1639; first opera *Le nozze di Teti e di Peleo,* 1639; *Il Xerse* (1654) performed for the marriage of Louis XIV, 1660; principal organist at San Marco, 1655, and maestro di cappella, 1668.

Operas

Le nozze di Teti e di Peleo, Orazio Persiani, Venice, San Cassiano, 20 January 1639.
Gli amori d'Apollo e di Dafne, Giovanni Francesco Busenello, Venice, San Cassiano, Carnival 1640.
La Didone, Giovanni Francesco Busenello, Venice, San Cassiano, Carnival 1641.
L'Amore innamorato, Giovanni Battista Fusconi (after G. F. Toredan and P. Michiel), Venice, San Moisè, 1 January 1642 [lost].
La virtù de' strali d'Amore, Giovanni Faustini, Venice, San Cassiano, Carnival 1642.
L'Egisto, Giovanni Faustini, Venice, San Cassiano, fall 1643.
L'Ormindo, Giovanni Faustini, Venice, San Cassiano, Carnival 1644.

La Doriclea, Giovanni Faustini, Venice, San Cassiano, Carnival 1645.
Il Titone, Giovanni Faustini, Venice, San Cassiano, Carnival 1645 [lost].
Il Giasone, Giacinto Andrea Cicognini, Venice, San Cassiano, 5 January 1649.
L'Euripo, Giovanni Faustini, San Moisè, 1649 [lost].
L'Orimonte, Nicolò Minato, Venice, San Cassiano, 20 February 1650.
L'Oristeo, Giovanni Faustini, Venice. Sant' Apollinare, Carnival 1651.
La Rosinda, Giovanni Faustini, Venice, Sant' Apollinare, 1651.
La Calisto, Giovanni Faustini, Venice, Sant' Apollinare, 28 November 1651.
L'Eritrea, Giovanni Faustini, Venice, Sant' Apollinare, 17 February 1652.
La Veremonda, l'Amazzone di Aragona, arranged by Luigi Zorzisto [G. Strozzi] (after G. A. Cicognini, *Celio*), Venice, SS. Giovanni e Paolo, 28 January 1653.
L'Orione, Francesco Melosio, Milan, Regio, June 1653.
Il Xerse, Nicolò Minato, Venice, SS. Giovanni e Paolo, 12 January 1654.
Il Ciro [music by Francesco Provenzale, originally performed in Naples; Cavalli composed changes for Venice], Giulio Cesare Sorrentino, Venice, SS. Giovanni e Paolo, 30 January 1654.
La Statira, principessa di Persia, Giovanni Francesco Busenello, Venice, SS. Giovanni e Paolo, 18 January 1655.
L' Erismena, Aurelio Aureli, Venice Sant' Apollinare, 30 December 1655.
L' Artemisia, Nicolò Minato, Venice, SS. Giovanni e Paolo, 10 January 1656 [lost].
L' Antioco, Nicolò Minato, Venice, San Cassiano, 25 January 1659 [lost].
L' Hipermestra, Giovanni Moniglia, 1654, Florence Teatro della Pergola, 18 June 1658.
Elena, Giovanni Faustini and Nicolò Minato, Venice, San Cassiano, c. 1659-60.
Ercole amante, Francesco Buti, Paris, Tuileries, 7 February 1662.
Scipione affricano, Nicolò Minato, Venice, SS. Giovanni e Paolo, 9 February 1664.
Mutio Scevola, Nicolò Minato, Venice, San Salvatore, 26 January 1665.
Pompeo magno, Nicolò Minato, Venice, San Salvatore, 20 February 1666.
Eliogabalo, anonymous libretto completed by Aurelio Aureli, composed for SS. Giovanni e Paolo, 1668; not performed.
Il Coriolano, Cristoforo Ivanovich, Piacenza, Ducale, 28 May 1669.
Massenzio, G. F. Busani, composed for San Salvatore, 1673; not performed [lost].

Other works: vocal and instrumental sacred music.

Publications/Writings

About CAVALLI: books–

Doglioni, N., et. al. *Le cose notabili et maravigliose della città di Venezia* [page 207]. Venice, 1671.
Ivanovich, C. *Minerva al tavolino.* Venice, 1681; 1688.
Bonlini, G.C. *Le glorie della poesia e della musica.* Venice, 1730.
Rolland, Romain. *Histoire de l'opéra en Europe avant Lully et Scarlatti.* Paris, 1895.

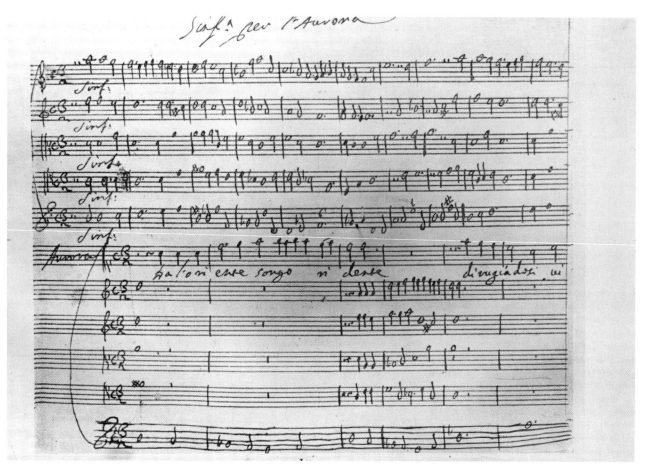

The prologue from Cavalli's autograph score of *L'Egisto*, 1642

Goldschmidt, H. *Studien zur Geschichte der italianischen Oper im 17. Jahrhundert.* Leipzig, 1901; 1967.

Prunières, Henry. *Cavalli et l'opéra italien au XVIIe siècle.* Paris, 1931.

Wolff, H.C. *Die venezianische Oper in der zweiten Hälfte des 17. Jahrhunderts.* Berlin, 1937; 1975.

Abert, A.A. *Claudio Monteverdi und das musikalische Drama.* Lippstadt, 1954.

Worsthorne, Simon. *Venetian Opera in the Seventeenth Century.* Oxford, 1954; 1968.

Glover, Jane. *Cavalli.* London, 1978.

Yans, G. *Un opéra de Francesco Cavalli pour la cour de Florence: L'Hipermestra.* Bologna, 1979.

Morelli, G. ed. *Scompiglio e lamento (simmetrie dell' incostanza e incostanza delle simmetrie): L'Egisto di Faustina e Cavalli.* Venice, 1982.

Rosand, Ellen. *Opera in Seventeenth Century Venice.* Berkeley, 1991.

articles–

Ambros, A.W. "Francesco Cavalli." *Neue Zeitschrift für Musik* 65 (1869): 313.

Kretzschmar, H. "Die Venetianische Oper und der Werke Cavallis und Cestis." *Vierteljahrsschrift für Musikwissenschaft* 8 (1892): 1.

Goldschmidt, H. *Cavalli als dramatischer Komponist. Monatshefte für Musikgeschichte* 25 (1893): 45, 53, 61.

Rolland, Romain. "L'opéra populaire à Venise: Francesco Cavalli." *Bulletin français de la Société Internationale de Musique* 2 (1906): 1, 60, 151.

Kretzschmar, H. "Beitrage zur Geschichte der Venetianischen Oper." *Jahrbuch der Musikbibliothek Peters* (1907): 71.

Wellesz, Egon. *Cavalli und der Stil der venetianischen Oper von 1640-1660. Studien zur Musikwissenschaft* 1 (1913): 1.

Prunières, Henry. "Notes sur une partition faussement attribuée à Cavalli." *Rivista musicale italiana* 27 (1920): 267.

Rolandi, U. "Le opere teatrali di Francesco Cavalli." *La scuola veneziana (secoli XVI-XVIII): note e documenti. Chigiana* 3 (1941): 15.

Powers, Harold S. "*Il Serse* trasformato." *Musical Quarterly* 47 (1961): 421; 48 (1962); 73.

Hjelmborg, Bjorn. "Aspects of the Aria in the Early Operas of Cavalli." In *Natalica Musicologica Knud Jeppeson,* 173. Copenhagen, 1962.

Osthoff, W. "Maske und Musik: die Gestaltwerdung der Opera in Venedig." *Castrum peregrini* 65 (1964): 10; Italian translation in *Nuova rivista musicale italiana* i (1967): 16.

Arnold, Denis. "Francesco Cavalli: Some Recently Discovered Documents." *Music and Letters* 46 (1965): 50.

Crain, G.F. "Francesco Cavalli and the Venetian Opera." *Opera* 18 (1967): 446.

Leppard, Raymond. "Cavalli's Operas." *Proceedings of the Royal Musical Association* 93 (1966-67): 67.

Pirrotta, Nino. "Early Opera and Aria." *New Looks at Italian Opera: Essays in Honor of Donald J. Grout,* edited by William Austin, 39. Ithaca, 1968.

Powers, Harold S. "*L'Erismena* travestita." In *Studies in Music History: Essays for Oliver Strunk,* edited by Harold S. Powers, 259. Princeton, 1968.

Swale, David. "Cavalli: The *Ersimena of 1665*." *Miscellanea Musicologia* 3 (1968): 146.

Hicks, Anthony. "Cavalli and *La Calisto*." *Musical Times* 111 (1970): 486.

Glover, Jane. "Cavalli and *Rosinda*." *Musical Times* 114 (1973): 133.

Bianconi, Lorenzo, and Thomas Walker. "Dalla 'Finta pazza' alla 'Veremonda': Storie di Febiarmonici." *Rivista italiana di Musicologia* 10 (1975): 379.

Rosand, Ellen. " 'Ormindo travestito' in *Erismena*." *Journal of the American Musicological Society* 28 (1975): 268.

Bianconi, Lorenzo. 'L'Ercole in Rialto.' In *Venezia e il melodramma nel seicento,* edited by Maria Teresa Muraro, 259. Florence, 1976.

Powers, Harold S. "*Il Mutio* tramutato." In *Venezia e il melodramma nel seicento,* edited by Maria Teresa Muraro. Florence. 1976.

Walker, Thomas. "Gli errori di 'Minerva al tavolini': osservazioni sulla cronologia delle prime opere veneziane." In *Venezia e il melodramma nel seicento,* edited by Maria Teresa Muraro, 7. Florence, 1976.

Glover, Jane. "Aria and Closed Form in the Operas of Francesco Cavalli." *The Consort* 32 (1976): 167.

Rosand, Ellen. "Aria as Drama in the Early Operas of Francesco Cavalli." In *Venezia e il melodramma nel seicento,* edited by Maria Teresa Muraro 75. Florence, 1976.

———. "Comic Contrast and Dramatic Continuity: Observations on the Form and Function of Aria in the Operas of Francesco Cavalli." *Music Review* 37 (1976): 92.

Murata, Margaret. "The Recitative Soliloquy." *Journal of the American Musicological Society* 32 (1979): 45.

Rosand, Ellen. "The Descending Tetrachord: An Emblem of Lament." *Musical Quarterly* 65 (1979): 346.

Rosand, Ellen. "Francesco Cavalli in Modern Edition." *Current Musicology* 27 (1979).

Glover, Jane. "Cavalli and *L'Egisto*." *Opera* January (1982).

unpublished–

Clinkscale, Martha Novak, "Pier Francesco Cavalli's *Xerse*." Ph.D. dissertation, University of Minnesota, 1970.

Rosand, Ellen. "Aria in the Early Operas of Francesco Cavalli." Ph.D. dissertation, New York University, 1971.

Rutschmann, Edward Raymond. "The Minato-Cavalli Operas. The Search for Structure in Libretto and Solo Scene." Ph.D. dissertation, University of Washington, 1979.

Jeffrey, Peter. "The Autograph Manuscripts of Francesco Cavalli." Ph.D. dissertation. Princeton University, 1980.

*   *   *

Unquestionably the most prolific Italian opera composer of the seventeenth century, Francesco Cavalli wrote more than thirty operas. Indeed, his contemporaries so admired this achievement that they attributed to him several operas by other composers. Together with his principal librettists, Giovanni Faustini, Giovanni Busenello, and Nicolò Minato, Cavalli vitalized the musical theater through a sympathetic regard for the dramatic sense of the word and by a flair for creating compelling scenic action.

In recent years Cavalli has been overshadowed as an opera composer by his older contemporary, the magnificent Claudio Monteverdi. However, it is Cavalli who can be credited with the formulation of the normal operatic divisions of scenes within acts, the interlocking of recitative with aria, the insertion of the plaintive lament, and the interjection of choral comment by large or small groups. Cavalli was also responsible for exporting this Venetian operatic style to other European cities after his works had achieved unparalleled success in public and private court theaters throughout the Italian peninsula.

During his lifetime Cavalli was respected not only as a composer of operas but of church music as well. Additionally, he was a performing artist throughout his musical career, having achieved success as a tenor singer and organist at the Church of San Marco in Venice. Eventually he earned the rank of maestro di cappella at San Marco and, as part of his duties in this capacity, furnished a considerable number of ceremonial works for liturgical use. Prominent and significant as Cavalli was as a church musician, however, his contribution to church music remained a local Venetian one.

Opera for the public arrived in Venice in 1637 with the opening of the Teatro San Cassiano. The proliferation of additional theaters throughout the city during the 1640s inaugurated a vivid and colorful world of singing actors, impresarios, and librettists. Cavalli succumbed to the enticements of this atmosphere and recognized its opportunities for the advancement of his own talent. With his 1639 debut opera, *Le nozze di Teti e di Peleo* (*The wedding of Thetis and Peleus*), at the Teatro San Cassiano, Cavalli was acclaimed by his Venetian contemporaries as a theatrical composer of exceptional imagination. Although most of his operas—and indeed all the earliest ones—were written on commission from one or another of the public Venetian opera houses, most of them received performances by traveling troupes or by resident court companies in other major Italian cities, such as Milan, Naples, Palermo, Rome, and Bologna.

The success of his earliest operas, especially *La Didone* (*Dido*), written to a libretto by Busenello, and *Egisto* (*Aegisthus*) and *Ormindo,* both written to libretti by Faustini, caused Cavalli to be praised throughout the Italian peninsula as a paragon among composers and a genius of the musical theater. International recognition followed when *Egisto* was repeated in Paris. *Giasone* (*Jason*), with its fiery libretto by G. A. Cicognini, was probably the most frequently performed opera during the seventeenth century. It became a brilliant symbol of a new demand for opera in Italy. *Xerxes* continued the exultant reception accorded the earlier works and was eventually chosen for performance at the Court of Louis XIV of France. While Cavalli was toasted in France and Austria, his success continued in Italy. One of Cavalli's latest and finest operas, *Scipione Affricano* (*Scipio Africanus*) and his ubiquitous *Giasone* were performed at the opening of the Teatro Tordinona in Rome at the behest of Queen Cristina of Sweden.

Cavalli's operas are meant to divert and entertain through music devised to complement word and story. Short vivacious arias and pungent, often colloquial, recitatives cleverly illuminate situations of comedy or mock heroism. Although the plots must certainly be fraught with political significance, the insinuations are lost to us through the passage of centuries. One general tendency can be appreciated for its immediacy: the presence of two sets of characters, one set historical, heroic or godlike, and the other group lower in social status and usually emanating from the servant class. The latter set of characters exhibits shrewdness, incisive wit, and admirable practicality, all of which engagingly illuminate and propel the action. These sprightly servants demand our sympathy through their shrewd dominance over their masters and their fates. Nobles and gods, on the other hand, act as genial commentators or revel in the agonies of love as they bemoan the paralysis brought on by their destinies.

Cavalli and his later librettists have occasionally been dismissed as superficial by a few recent critics for what they consider an unfortunate surrender to weak plots and the inferior poetic structures preferred by "public taste." One may agree that such a change in emphasis from the noble to the mundane does not represent a positive development; however, the action did become more lively, the scenic shifts more deft and ingenious, and the music more concise as it smartly underscored the characters' emotions. The result is immediate identification with plot and character on the part of Cavalli's audience—during both his time and ours. His works thus can be considered significant harbingers of the popularity accorded eighteenth-century opera buffa and dramma giocoso.

—Martha Novak Clinkscale

CEBOTARI, Maria.

Soprano. Born 10 February 1910, in Kishinev, Bessarabia. Died 9 June 1949, in Vienna. Studied at Kishinev Conservatory, 1924-29, and with Oskar Daniel at Hochschule für Musik in Berlin; debut as Mimi at Dresden Staatsoper, 1931, and sang there until 1936; created Aminta in *Die schweigsame Frau,* 1935; appeared at Covent Garden in 1936 and 1947; sang in Berlin, 1936-44, Vienna, 1946-49; created Lucille in *Dantons Tod,* 1947, Salzburg; created Iseut in Martin's *Vin herbé,* 1948; appeared in six films between 1933 and 1941.

Publications

About CEBOTARI: books–

Mingotti, A. *Maria Cebotari: Das Leben einer Sängerin.* Salzburg, 1950.

* * *

One of the world's most beautiful women, a glorious voice, a meteoric career, and dead at thirty-nine: this was the story of the soprano Maria Cebotari. Today one has only to watch the 1936 *Premiere der Butterfly,* one of her many films, to fall completely and utterly under her spell. Cebotari's recordings are equally exciting. Her *Ariadne* "Es gibt ein Reich" has been an unmatched classic since its first release on 78 rpm, and her final scene from *Salome* is the only real competition for Ljuba Welitsch's later ones, not to mention Cebotari's many Mozart recordings.

Cebotari's early life was almost that of a gypsy. After joining a troupe of itinerant Russian actors who visited her small Bessarabian town and whose leader she married (and later divorced for a film actor), she made her operatic debut in Paris. She then studied in Berlin, joining the Dresden Opera in 1931. Her Dresden appearances included the title role in the world premiere of Strauss' *Die Schweigsame Frau,* only one of the Strauss roles for which she was celebrated. Both before and after the War she appeared in London. Other guest appearances during her short eighteen-year career were in Berlin, Munich, Vienna, Salzburg, Zurich, Bucharest, Rome, and Milan. Invited to New York in 1940, Cebotari was among those great singers who could not accept American engagements because of the War and were unfortunately never heard on that continent.

A favorite singer of Richard Strauss', it is quite possible that she would also have been one of Mozart's, having excelled in a surprising number and variety of his roles. Verdi and Puccini were not forgotten; she sang Russian opera in Russian; was in the premiere of von Einem's *Dantons Tod;* and her humor was celebrated in *The Merry Wives of Windsor.* Maria Cebotari was also a unique star of operetta, singing just two months before her death in a performance of *The Beggar Student.* Beniamino Gigli, with whom she sang in Berlin as well as in a film, wrote later of the beauty of her voice.

Of her recordings, there is a wonderful complete *Rigoletto* and excerpts from *La traviata,* both with Roswaenger and Schlusnus. In the early 1970s, BASF released many radio tapes with Cebotari and her contemporaries, many of which have since been re-released by other labels. Her commercial recordings reappear with great regularity.

—Bert Wechsler

CENDRILLON [Cinderella].

Composer: Jules Massenet.

Librettist: Henri Cain (after Perrault).

First Performance: Paris, Opéra-Comique, 24 May 1899.

Roles: Cendrillon (soprano); Pandolphe (bass); Madame de la Haltière (contralto); Noémie (soprano); Dorothée (mezzo-soprano); Fairy Godmother (soprano); Prince (tenor); Major-domo of Entertainment (baritone); Dean of Faculty (tenor); King (baritone); Prime Minister (bass); Herald (speaking); chorus (SSATTBB).

* * *

After decades of neglect, Massenet's *Cendrillon* has enjoyed a revival since the late 1980s, to the pleasure of audiences and critics alike. *Opera* magazine called it "a lightweight piece, using the Cinderella story as a vehicle for gorgeous ceremonial, seductive melody and dazzling virtuosity, with snatches of neo-Baroque archaism and nursery rhyme to ensure a fairy-tale flavor." Critics agree that it makes a charming departure from "the usual depressing parade of Carmens and Cavallerias."

The libretto by Henri Cain remains true to the original tale by Charles Perrault with only slightly more emphasis on magic and fairies. The opera opens in the house of Madame de la Haltière—Cinderella's stepmother—as the Madame and her two daughters prepare for the Prince's ball. After the family leaves, Cendrillon, who is of course not included, sits by her hearth bemoaning her fate to the only live creatures around, the crickets, before falling asleep. She dreams of going to the ball; the fairies and sprites change her rags into a magnificent ball gown, give her jewels to wear and a carriage to ride in. She joyfully rushes away to the ball while the fairies warn her to return by midnight.

A poster for *Cendrillon,* **Paris, 1899**

The second act presents the Prince's ball. The Prince stands miserably alone; he has not chosen his bride as he was supposed to, and is quite annoyed by the attentions of Cendrillon's two step sisters. None of the fair maidens delight him until Cendrillon arrives and he falls instantly in love with her. He courts her all evening and she tells him she is his, but she behaves mysteriously. She won't tell him her name, and then races out at midnight. She loses a glass slipper in her haste; he picks it up and tries to follow her, but the fairies prevent him.

The third act begins in Madame de la Haltière's house. Cendrillon, who has already returned from the ball, sits weeping. Her stepmother and stepsisters return and tell her of the scandalous arrival of a stranger, and lead her to suspect that the Prince doubts her innocence. Upset, she decides to run away to the farm where she and her father were happy before he married his second wife. The scene changes to the forest of the fairies. Cendrillon asks the fairies for help and comfort. The Prince then finds Cendrillon and declares his love for her, offering her his heart as proof of his sincerity. The fairies send them both to sleep. She awakes months later—in act IV—and is told she is recovering from a long illness after being found unconscious in the woods. In response to her questions, her father tells her that during her fever she mumbled incoherent words about love and shoes. On the street below, a herald announces that the Prince is searching for the girl who lost her slipper, and Cendrillon begins to realize that all has not been a dream. She goes to the Palace. A crowd has gathered to watch the procession of young ladies. The Prince watches anxiously as girl after girl tries on the slipper unsuccessfully. At last the fairies lead Cendrillon to him; she carries the heart he gave her in the woods, whereupon the Prince recognizes her, and everyone rejoices.

Cendrillon was born in the Cavendish hotel where Massenet and his librettist, Henri Cain, were staying for the London premier of *Le Cid.* After hours of discussion, they settled on Perrault's story as the right vehicle for their next venture. Months later when he finished the music, Massenet then worked with the director of the Opéra-Comique in Paris, Albert Carré, to fashion the costumes, scenery, and staging. The result was a glittering production perfectly suited to this romantic tale of fairies. The contemporary French critic Willy was amazed at the spectacle: "The clever composer has spared nothing to make this operetta of apparitions successful—neither the iridescent polychrome of fairie's wings, nor humming choruses, nor castanets, nor the Mustel organ, nor the abundance of fourths and sixths, nor real turtledoves, nor the pizzicati of mandolas, nor *buffo* ensembles in the Italian manner, nor the archaic prettiness of imitation minuets . . ." The rich costumes, the splendid scenery, and the elaborate stage machinery required to transform the local setting into a world of magic, all guaranteed the opera's success with the French public.

In his music, Massenet always aimed to please his public; his compositions were rarely innovative. One critic in *Opera* magazine found it "distressing to read the score through and see how few original ideas he has. . . ." Critics claim that *Cendrillon* is musically flawed: the overture is "wooden," the chorus is "dull," and the work is "overburdened with repetitive musical schemes." Yet the music is also charmingly lyrical and expressive. To give his work a slightly old-fashioned flavor, Massenet used eighteenth-century musical styles. He matched the glittering fairy world on stage with gossamer-light textures from the orchestra. Cendrillon's magical fairy-godmother sings sparkling coloratura. The beauty of the melodies serve to hide any problems the work might have, and audiences have loved the work from the beginning.

The first production of *Cendrillon* ran for sixty performances at the Opéra-Comique in Paris; when it opened in Milan shortly afterwards, it did as well. The critic Willy witnessed opening night and said: "It would have been impossible to understand if, with so many aces in his hand, M Massenet had lost the game: he has won it triumphantly. To deny it would be dishonest." As new works replace old works, *Cendrillon* was dropped from the repertoire. In the 1980s during a general Massenet revival, opera companies discovered its charm and wondered why they had waited so long to perform it. In 1988, *Opera* magazine wrote: "Massenet's *Cendrillon* is a rarity in Britain. It is difficult to understand why this delicate, late romantic opera should apparently be so unattractive to those who plan the repertory of our opera companies, particularly at Christmas time." Audiences loved the contrast this light opera made to the traditional repertoire of tragic and *verismo* works.

—Robin Armstrong

LA CENERENTOLA, ossia La bontà in trionfo [Cinderella, or The Triumph of Goodness].

Composer: Gioachino Rossini.

Librettist: G. Ferretti (after Perrault, *Cendrillon;* C.-G. Etienne, and F. Fiorini).

First Performance: Rome, Valle, 25 January 1817.

Roles: Don Ramiro (tenor); Dandini (bass); Don Magnifico (bass); Clorinda (soprano); Tisbe (mezzo-soprano); Angelini, known as La Cenerentola or Cinderella (mezzo-soprano); Alidoro (bass); chorus.

Publications

book–

John, Nicholas, ed. *Gioachino Rossini: "La Cenerentola".* London and New York, 1980.

articles–

Zedda, A. "Problemi testuali della *Cenerentola.*" *Bollettino del Centro rossiniano di studi* no. 3 (1971).
Avant-scène opéra March (1986) [*La Cenerentola* issue].

From 1815 to 1823 Rossini was composer and musical and artistic director for the Royal Theater of San Carlo in Naples, engaged largely in composing serious operas. His contract permitted him to accept commissions from other theaters, and among those compositions are found *Il barbiere di Siviglia* (Rome, 20 February 1816) and *La Cenerentola.* The eleven months between them saw the premieres of two operas in Naples (*La gazzetta,* 26 September 1816, and *Otello,* 4 December 1816). With such a schedule it is no wonder that legends arose about the speed with which Rossini composed. In the case of *La Cenerentola,* legend and fact seem to be in agreement, for the theme was chosen on 23 December 1816, and the opera had its premiere a month later.

The original commission from the Teatro Valle had specified a different libretto, but the Roman censors caused so much difficulty that Rossini requested an entirely new subject. The shortness of time prevented Ferretti from writing an entirely new text; rather he adapted two previous libretti on the same topic. Most of the familiar fairy-tale elements (wicked stepmother, fairy godmother, pumpkin and mice transformed into coach and horses) are absent from those sources and thus from Ferretti's libretto. Even the glass slipper is missing, its place being taken by a pair of matching bracelets.

Need for haste also affected the music. Rossini re-used his overture to *La gazzetta* and, as frequently happened, assigned all the *secco* recitative and three numbers (a chorus and arias for Alidoro and Clorinda) to a Roman musician, Luca Agolini. In 1821 Rossini replaced the Alidoro aria with a new one of his own composing, "Là del ciel nell' arcano profondo" (There from heaven in profound mystery).

The opera presents the fairy-tale transformation of a scullery maid into a princess. Cinderella herself sets the sentimental theme in her opening song about a king who chose as his bride a kind-hearted girl rather than a beautiful one ("Una volta c'era un Re": Once there was a King). She demonstrates her own kindness by giving some food to a beggar, who is actually prince Ramiro's tutor Alidoro in disguise. Heralds announce the prince's imminent arrival: he will choose a wife from among the women he will invite to a ball. The beggar foretells that Cinderella will be happy by the next day. Clorinda and Tisbe, Cinderella's stepsisters, awaken their father, the impoverished Don Magnifico, who envisions himself as grandfather of kings.

Ramiro, having exchanged clothing with his valet Dandini in order to travel incognito, enters the house, and he and Cinderella immediately fall in love. When Alidoro, now functioning as royal tutor, asks Don Magnifico about his daughters, the father acknowledges only two, saying the third died; the tutor invites Cinderella to the ball.

At the ball Clorinda and Tisbe scornfully mistreat Ramiro, believing him to be the squire. A veiled lady, strangely resembling Cinderella, arrives, and Ramiro asks her to be his wife. She tells him he must seek for the mate of the bracelet she gives him; if he still loves her when he finds it, she will marry him. When Ramiro goes in search of the mysterious lady his carriage overturns in front of Magnifico's house—a happy accident arranged by Alidoro. Cinderella and Ramiro recognize each other. At the wedding banquet the father and stepsisters are forgiven so that all may live happily ever after.

Rossini uses a variety of musical styles to develop the sentimental love story and its various comic interludes. Cinderella's arias range from the folk-like opening song to the elaborate *rondò finale*, "Nacqui all'affano e al pianto" (I was born to grief and weeping). Equally ornate is Ramiro's second-act aria ("Sì, ritrovarla, io giuro": Yes, I will find her, I swear it), a piece that would not be out of place in an *opera seria*. For Don Magnifico, Rossini writes a standard comic patter song; however, Dandini, who spends much of the opera pretending to be the prince, has a grand mock-heroic cavatina, *buffo* declamation alternating with coloratura. In his duet with Dandini, Magnifico babbles in confusion; the following sextet, "Questo è un nodo avviluppato" (This is a tangled knot), is among the most wonderful of Rossini's ensembles.

—Patricia Brauner

CESTI, Antonio (Pietro).

Composer. Baptized 5 August 1623 in Arezzo. Died 14 October 1669, in Florence. Cesti became a Franciscan friar in Votterra, 1637; studied in Rome with Carissimi and Abbatini, 1640-45; first opera *Orontea* produced in Venice, 1649; maestro di cappella to Ferdinand II de' Medici; tenor in the papal choir, 1660; assistant kapellmeister to Emperor Leopold I at the Hapsburg court in Innsbruck, then in Vienna; *Il pomo d' oro*, 1668; returned to Florence.

Operas

Orontea, Giacinto Andrea Cicognini, Venice, SS. Apostoli, 20 January 1649.
Alessandro il vincitor di se stesso, Franco Sbarra, Venice, SS. Giovanni e Paolo, 1651.
Il Cesare amante, Dario Varotari, Venice, Grimano, fall 1651.
La Cleopatra, Dario Varotari (same as *Il Cesare amante*, with new prologue and ballets), Innsbruck, Sant' Arciduca Fernando Carlo di Austria, 1654.
L'Argia, Giovanni Filippo Apolloni, Innsbruck, 4 November 1655.
La Dori, ovvero La schiava fedele, Giovanni Filippo Apolloni, Innsbruck, 1657.
La magnanimità d'Alessandro, Franco Sbarra, Innsbruck, May 1662.
Il Tito, Niccolò Beregan, Venice, Grimano, 13 February 1666.
Nettuno e Flora festeggianti, Franco Sbarra, Vienna, Carnival 1667.
La Semirami, Giovani Andrea Moniglia, Vienna, 9 June 1667.
La Germania esultante, Franco Sbarra, Vienna, Favorita, 12 July 1667.
Il pomo d'oro, Franco Sbarra, Vienna, 13-14 July 1668.

Publications

About CESTI: books–

Wellesz, Egon. *Essays on Opera*. London, 1950.
Senn, W. *Musik und Theater am Hof zu Innsbruck*. Innsbruck, 1954.
Schlitzer, F. *Intorno alla "Dori" di Antonio Cesti*. Florence, 1957.
_____. *"L'Orontea" di Antonio Cesti: storia e bibliografia*. Florence, 1960.
Rosand, Ellen. *Opera in Seventeenth-Century Venice*. Berkeley, 1991.

articles–

Kretzschmar, H. "Die Venetianische Oper und der Werke Cavallis und Cestis." *Vierteljahrschrift für Musikwissenschaft* 8 (1892): 1.
Wellesz, Egon. "Zwei Studien zur Geschichte der Oper in XVII. Jahrhundert." *Sammelbände der Internationalen Musik-Gesellschaft* 15 (1913-14): 124.
Coradini, F. "P. Antonio Cesti, ... nuove notizie biografiche." *Rivista musicale italiana* (1923).
Sandberger, A. "Beziehungen der Königin Christine von Schweden, zur italienischen Oper und Musik, insbesondere zu ... Cesti. Mit einem Anhang über Cestis Innsbrucker Aufenthalt." *Bulletin de la Société Union Musicologique* 5 (1925): 121.

Cesti's *Il pomo d'oro*, set design for act II, scene 10, engraving by Matthaeus Küsel after Burnacini, 1668

Tessier, A. "L'Orontée de Lorenzani et l' Orontea du Padre Cesti." *La revue musicale* 9 (1928): 169.

Pirrotta, Nino. "Le prime opere di Antonio Cesti." In *L'orchestra*, edited by P. Castiglia. 153. Florence, 1954.

Osthoff, W. "Antonio Cestis 'Alessandro vincitor di se stesso'." *Studien zur Musikwissenschaft* 24 (1960): 13.

Shock, D.H. "Costuming for 'Il pomo d'oro'." *Gazette des beaux-arts* 69 (1967): 251.

Holmes, William C. "Comedy-Opera-Comic Opera." *Analecta Musicologica* 5 (1968): 92.

————. "Giacinto Andrea Cicognini's and Antonio Cesti's *Orontea* (1649)." In *New Looks at Italian Opera: Essays in Honor of Donald J. Grout,* edited by William Austin, 108. Ithaca, 1968.

Antonicek. "Antonio Cesti alla Corte di Vienna." *Nuova rivista musicale italiana* 4 (1970): 93.

Holmes, William C. "Cesti's 'L'Argia': an Entertainment for a Royal Convert." *Chigiana* 26-28 (1971): 35.

Seifert, H. "Die Festlichkeiten zur ersten Hochzeit Keiser Leopolds I." *Österreichische Musikzeitschrift* 29 (1974): 6.

Schmidt, Carl B. "Antonio Cesti's *La Dori:* a Study of Sources, Performance Traditions and Musical Style." *Rivista italiana di musicologia* 10 (1975): 455.

Hill, John Walter. "Le relazioni di Antonio Cesti con la corte e i teatri di Firenze." *Rivista italiana di musicologia* 11 (1976): 27.

Schmidt, Carl B. " 'La Dori' di Antonio Cesti: sussidi bibliografici." *Rivista italiana di musicologia* 11 (1976): 197.

Walker, Thomas. 'Gil errori di 'Minerva al tavolini': osservazioni sulla cronologia delle prime opere veneziane." In *Venezia e il melodramma nel seicento,* edited by Maria Teresa Muraro, 7. Florence, 1976.

Schmidt, Carl B. "Antonio Cesti's *Il pomo d' oro:* a Reexamination of a Famous Hapsburg Court Spectacle." *Journal of the American Musicological Society* 29 (1976): 381.

Schmidt, Carl B. "An Episode in the History of the Venetian Opera: the *Tito* Commission (1665-6)." *Journal of the American Musicological Society* 13 (1978): 442.

*   *   *

Antonio Cesti, one of the most important composers of mid-seventeenth century Italian opera, had a wide-ranging international career. Writing first for the public opera houses of Venice, he later composed operas for private consumption by the nobility, first in Innsbruck and then, toward the end of his career, at the Austrian imperial court in Vienna. Composer of more than a dozen operas, he helped to serve the operatic connection running from Venice to Vienna, and a comparison of his Venetian works and his Viennese works shows how he adapted to the resources available in each situation.

Cesti received his early training as a boy chorister in his native Arezzo, and he probably studied in Rome as well. He was a member of the Franciscan order for more than twenty years, until he was released in 1659. He also sang briefly as a member of the papal choir. His earliest documented essay in the genre of opera, *L'Orontea* (libretto by Giacinto Andrea Cicognini, produced in Venice in 1649), was wildly successful and continued to be revived throughout much of the rest of the century. After composing three operas for Venice, Cesti moved to Innsbruck to accept a position as composer in the service of Archduke Ferdinand Karl.

Cesti's Venetian operas are in the normal mid-century Venetian vein. They are three-act works featuring solo singing accompanied by basso continuo, with a three-part ensemble representing the thickest available texture. The division of the roles of recitative and aria is clear, often even clearer than in the works of the older composer Cavalli, who was active, mostly in Venice, during the entire span of Cesti's career. With the operas written for Innsbruck, the resources for performance were more extensive and are reflected in the greater use of the services of the machine builder and the ballet master. *La Dori* (libretto by Giovanni Filippo Apolloni, produced in 1657), composed for Innsbruck, was widely exported. At the Viennese court Cesti had the resources of an imperial court available, and they all converged in the festival opera *Il pomo d'oro* (libretto by Francesco Sbarra, produced in 1668). Here a large orchestra, a chorus used both for singing and as supernumeraries, extensive sets, and spectacular stage machinery all played a role in making a production which was long remembered. In Vienna Cesti followed the fashion of the court in setting mythological stories or allegorical libretti, the latter with the intention that the veiled allusions would be recognized by the members of the court audience.

Cesti is a master of declamation, and his recitative is well worth studying as a model of clear text setting. He is also important as a pioneer in the development of the singer's opera, in which there is a strong musical focus on the aria. Each successive aria provides part of a portrait of the character who sings it, and a cumulative picture emerges gradually as the character sings additional arias. This provides opportunities for the performer to sing more than one type of aria and allows ample scope for virtuoso treatment of the voice. Cesti is remembered as a composer successful in both the public opera house and the court opera house, as an important figure in the history of the clarification of the relationship between recitative and aria, and as a high-quality composer in his own right.

—Edward Rutschman

CHABRIER, (Alexis-) Emmanuel.

Composer. Born 18 January 1841, in Ambert, Puy-de-Dome. Died 13 September 1894, in Paris. Married: Marie Alice Dejean, 27 December 1873. Piano lessons beginning at the age of six; studied composition with the violinist Tarnowski at the Lycée Impérial at Clermont-Ferrand, 1851; began law study, 1858; studied piano with Edouard Wolff and counterpoint and fugue with Semet and Aristide Hignard; entered the Ministry of the Interior, 1861; with Duparc, visited Germany, where he heard a performance of Wagner's *Tristan und Isolde* in Munich, 1879; resigned from the ministry, 12 November 1880; visited Spain, 1882; chorus master for the Wagner concerts led by Lamoureux at Château d'Eau, 1884-85. His circle of friends included the painter Manet, the poet Verlaine, and the composers Duparc, d'Indy, Fauré, and Messager.

Operas

Fisch-Ton-Kan, Paul Verlaine, Paris, Salle de l'ancien Conservatoire, 1863-4.

Vaucochard et fils Ier, Paul Verlaine and L. Viotti, Paris, Salle de l'ancien Conservatoire, 1864.

Jean Hunyade, Henri Fouquier, 1867 [unfinished; parts used for *Gwendoline*].

L'étoile, Eugène Leterrier and Albert Vanloo, Paris, Bouffes-Parisiens, 28 November 1877.

Le Sabbat, A. Silvestre, 1877 [unfinished].

Une éducation manquée, Eugène Leterrier and Albert Vanloo, Paris, Cercle de la Presse, 1 May 1879.

Les muscadins, Clarétie, Silvestre, 1880 [unfinished].

Gwendoline, Catulle Mendès, 1885, Brussels, Théâtre de la Monnaie, 10 April 1886.

Le roi malgré lui, Emile de Najac, Paul Burani, and J. Richepin (after a comedy by A. and M. Ancelot), Paris, Opéra-Comique, 18 May 1887.

Briséis, ou Les amants de Corinthe [incomplete], Ephraim Mikhaël and Catulle Mendès (after Goethe *Die Braut von Corinth*) [composition begun 1888; first act completed 1891; produced posthumously in 1896].

Other Works: choral works, orchestral works, piano pieces, and songs.

Publications

By CHABRIER: books–

Legrand, A. and M. Chabrier, eds. *Lettres à Nanine.* 1909.

articles–

"Lettres inédites d'Emmanuel Chabrier." Edited by R. Brussel. *Bulletin français de la Société Internationale de Musique* 5 (1909): 1, 113.

"Lettres d'Emmanuel Chabrier." Edited by A. Chabrier. *Bulletin français de la Société Internationale de Musique* 7 (1911): 15.

About CHABRIER: books–

Destranges, E. *Un chef-d'oeuvre inachevé: 'Briséis'.* Paris, 1897.

Desaymard, Joseph. *Emmanuel Chabrier et 'Gwendoline',* Paris, 1904.

_____. *Un artiste auvergnat Emmanuel Chabrier.* Clermont-Ferrand. 1908.

Martineau, René. *Emmanuel Chabrier.* Paris, 1910.

Desaymard, J. et. al. *Emmanuel Chabrier: in Memoriam.* Paris, 1912.

Séré, Octave. *Musiciens français d'aujourd'hui.* Paris, 1912.

Servières, Georges. *Emmanuel Chabrier.* Paris, 1912.

Desaymard, Joseph. *Chabrier d'après ses lettres.* Paris. 1934.

Martin, A., ed. *Exposition Emmanuel Chabrier . . . catalogue.* Paris, 1941.

Tienot, Y. *Chabrier.* Paris and Brussels, 1964.

Poulenc, Francis. *Emmanuel Chabrier.* Paris, 1961; English translation. London 1981.

Myers, Rollo. *Emmanuel Chabrier and His Circle.* London. 1969.

Robert, Frédéric. *Emmanuel Chabrier: L'homme et son oeuvre.* Paris. 1969.

Delage, Roger. *Chabrier.* Paris. 1982.

articles–

Brussel, R. "Emmanuel Chabrier et le rire musical." *Revue d'art dramatique* 8 (1899); 55, 81.

Legrand, A. and M. Chabrier. "En hommage à Emmanuel Chabrier." *Bulletin français de la Société Internationale de Musique* 7 (1911): 1.

Blom, Eric, "The Tragedy of a Comic Opera." In *Stepchildren of Music,* 173. London, 1925.

Gorer, R. "Emmanuel Chabrier." *Music Review* 2 (1941): 132.

Delage, Roger. "Correspondance inédite entre Emmanuel Chabrier et Félix Mottl." *Revue de Musicologie* 49 (1963): 61.

———. "Ravel and Chabrier." *Musical Quarterly* 61 (1975): 4.

* * *

Chabrier is perhaps better known for a couple of short orchestral pieces, several piano works and a few songs than for any of the four works for the stage that he managed to complete. Indeed, the overture to *Gwendoline* and two orchestral excerpts from *Le roi malgré lui* remain far more familiar than the operas from which they are taken. At almost every stage in his relatively brief composing life Chabrier, in common with many of his French contemporaries, was continually preoccupied to a greater or lesser degree with the stage. Yet his resignation as a civil servant in 1880 resulted in a period of less than a dozen years or so as a full-time professional composer.

Chabrier's early enthusiasm for the other arts in addition to music—notably literature and painting—ensured that by the early 1860s his sights were already set upon the theater. At this time, his friendship with Paul Verlaine was turned to good account, as the poet supplied the librettos for Chabrier's first two operettas, *Fisch-Ton-Kan* and *Vaucochard et fils Ier.* Both works were destined to remain incomplete, although the torsos were staged in Paris in 1941. A more ambitious enterprise—*Jean Hunyade* to a libretto by Henri Fouquier—was also never finished, although the historical theme and "elevated" subject later paved the way for *Gwendoline,* in which a few fragments from *Jean Hunyade* were refurbished.

Chabrier's marriage, destined to be a happy one, took place in 1873, after which he embarked upon some orchestral and piano pieces. After an operatic lacuna of several years, the later 1870s saw the composer turning once again to the stage. Two works, *Le Sabbat* and *Les muscadins* remained unfinished. But *L'etoile* and *Une éducation manquée* remain among Chabrier's most enduring operettas. This is especially the case with *L'etoile.* Here, Chabrier's unerring sense for apt characterization, his superb theatrical timing, his wit and ebullience make for a thoroughly delightful stage work. Dance rhythms, piquant orchestration, a harmonic idiom both racy and subtle, memorable melodies—tender or impassioned, energetic or vital, as required—all these characteristics combine to produce a score of sparkling wit and undeniable skill.

The 1880s saw the composition and production of Chabrier's two masterpieces for the stage, *Gwendoline* and *Le roi malgré lui,* works which consolidated, indeed confirmed, Chabrier's reputation as a major French composer of opera. Having collaborated with the poet Catulle Mendès, who had supplied the libretto of *Gwendoline,* Chabrier again worked with the same writer in his last opera *Briséis, ou Les amants de Corinthe,* based on a story by Goethe. Like Fauré's *Pénélope,* the work was described as a "lyrical drama." Chabrier worked relentlessly on the opera for three years from 1888, but thereafter the syphilitic disease from which he had been suffering during the opera's composition took an increasing hold on him, with the result that by 1891 only one act had been completed. The rest of the opera was destined to remain unwritten. The surviving music is full of beauty and works surprisingly well as a concert performance, an expedient undertaken when it was given its première in Paris some two years after Chabrier's death.

In his excellent book on French music, first published in 1951, Martin Cooper somewhat underrated Chabrier as a composer of opera. But Cooper was the first to employ the phrase "café-concert atmosphere" as one of the many characteristics which made Chabrier's music so exciting and innovative when it was first heard. The catch phrase is useful, provided that due notice is taken of Chabrier's harmonic originality and professional skill. His fondness for sharply dissonant accented passing notes, and for equally dissonant pedal points that are foreign to the prevailing harmony, proclaim Chabrier as one of the most forward-looking French composers of his day. In the same way, a propensity for abrupt shifts to unexpected tonal regions foreshadowed many later developments of a similar kind. Debussy, Ravel and Stravinsky represent only three later composers who publicly acknowledged their debt to Chabrier.

During his lifetime Chabrier's operas were dogged by ill luck, theaters being closed by virtue of their owners' bankruptcy, because of fire, and for various other reasons, none of which can be related to Chabrier's music. Due to the enthusiastic support of the Viennese conductor Felix Mottl, the two best known of Chabrier's operas enjoyed some success in Germany, particularly in Karlsruhe, Leipzig and Munich. This success Chabrier lived to enjoy. However, 40 years after Cooper's book, Chabrier's stage works have yet to make an impact in the English-speaking world. It is fashionable to deride the clumsiness of the librettos. It would perhaps be fairer to admit that the eighth century English setting of *Gwendoline* and the historical/comic situation of sixteenth century Poland in *Le roi malgré lui* do not adapt well in translation either to English or to American taste. However, from a purely musical point of view, Chabrier's stage works are fully worthy both of their period and of their composer. They furnish further proof of that remarkable renaissance of French music which took place in the last quarter of the nineteenth century.

—J. Barrie Jones

CHAILLY, Riccardo.

Conductor. Born 20 February 1953, in Milan. Studied composition with his father, Luciano Chailly, and with Bruno Bettinelli at the Milan Conservatory; studied conducting with Piero Guarino in Perugia, Franco Caracciolo in Milan, and Franco Ferrara in Siena; assistant conductor of symphonic concerts at the Teatro alla Scala, Milan, 1972-74; conducted *Madama Butterfly* at the Chicago Lyric Opera, 1974; guest conductor at the San Francisco Opera, the Teatro alla Scala, Covent Garden, and the Vienna State Opera; Metropolitan Opera debut with Offenbach's *Les contes d'Hoffmann,* 1982; chief conductor of the Berlin Radio Symphony Orchestra,

1982-89; principal guest conductor of the London Philharmonic, 1982-85; artistic director of the Teatro Comunale in Bologna, 1986-89; chief conductor of the Concertgebouw Orchestra of Amsterdam (renamed the Royal Concertgebouw Orchestra), 1988.

* * *

There exists a tendency among some conductors to strive for an objective, scholarly approach to music, marked by performances that are high in surface excitement and technical expertise but are often unidiomatic, deficient in emotion, sentiment, and a sense of tradition. Riccardo Chailly's performances, at their best, have managed to exhibit the more positive aspects of this approach with relatively few of its deficiencies.

After studies with his father, the composer Luciano Chailly, Riccardo Chailly made his operatic debut at the Teatro Nuovo in Milan, leading Massenet's *Werther*. In 1974 he made his American conducting debut with Puccini's *Madama Butterfly* at the Chicago Lyric Opera, where he later led Verdi's *Rigoletto*, Leoncavallo's *Pagliacci*, and Puccini's *La bohème*. He conducted Gluck's *Iphigénie en Tauride* at the Teatro Massimo, Palermo, in 1975. In San Francisco in 1977 he led Jean-Pierre Ponnelle's production of Puccini's *Turandot*. He has conducted at the major opera houses of Europe, including *Les contes d'Hoffmann* in Munich, *La traviata* in Bologna, Rossini's *La Cenerentola* in Salzburg (a performance preserved on videotape), Wagner's *Die Walküre* in Bologna, and Prokofiev's *The Fiery Angel* in Amsterdam.

At the Teatro alla Scala in Milan, Chailly was assistant to Claudio Abbado for two years. During this period he conducted Verdi's *I due Foscari*, in 1979, and Stravinsky's *The Rake's Progress*, in 1980; in later seasons he led Musorgsky's *Sorochintsy Fair* and Giordano's *Andrea Chénier*.

In 1979 Chailly made his Stuttgart debut, conducting Verdi's *Rigoletto;* the critics hailed the production as a triumph, writing that he combined taut rhythm and strong accentuation with respect for Verdi's melodies. That year he also led performances of Stravinsky's *The Rake's Progress* with the London Sinfonietta at the Teatro Lirico, Milan. In 1981 he led Verdi's *Simon Boccanegra* at the Munich Festival.

Chailly's Metropolitan Opera debut—his only performances in that house—was with Offenbach's *Les contes d'Hoffmann* in 1982; one critic described his conducting as "lively and bumptious, all extroversion and zing." Other performances that year included Puccini's *Manon Lescaut* in Munich, Puccini's *La bohème* at Covent Garden, and Stravinsky's *The Rake's Progress* (in Ken Russell's production) at the Teatro della Pergola, as part of the Maggio Musicale. More Verdi followed in 1984, when he opened the Salzburg Festival with *Macbeth* and, later, that year, *Un ballo in maschera* in Geneva.

In 1986 Chailly became permanent conductor of the Teatro Comunale, Bologna. He began his tenure there with a performance of Verdi's *I vespri siciliani*, followed the next year by the same composer's *La traviata*, and, the year after, *Falstaff*, further reflecting his close association with the operas of Verdi, especially the middle- and late-period works. Although he has had success with Verdi's *Macbeth*, he admits to finding other early Verdi operas difficult to conduct, feeling they can easily sound banal and merely bombastic; he has, in fact, been criticized for rushing through these early scores. He appears more comfortable with the later, more sophisticated, more complexly orchestrated operas, bringing out the modernity of the works' symphonic style.

Chailly's career has encompassed operas ranging from the classical to the modern. He has developed a reputation as an intelligent—even intellectual—conductor, but not one who adheres to a strict literalism or purism in operatic performance; he combines study of the score with a consideration of tradition in terms of cuts and interpolations of high notes. His conducting has been described as alert and energetic, occasionally calling attention to itself, but rarely excessively so. This approach is effective in Verdi and other operas that thrive on the grand gesture, but is slightly less successful in conveying nuance and charm, or the lightness and humor of comic operas.

Chailly's experience in conducting the symphonic repertoire has prepared him well for handling the orchestral component of opera performances and in achieving a proper balance between the orchestra and the singers. He has been described as effective in highlighting details of the score, bringing out the color. His performances have been praised for being spirited and buoyant, brilliant yet sensitive, filled with temperament and rhythmic impetus; nevertheless, he is willing to linger over lyrical passages without interrupting the flow. He is said to have an ear for texture and an ability to differentiate between sentiment and sentimentality. He has been criticized for sometimes giving superficial readings and for a rather heavy-handed, slightly vulgar, approach, without any great emotional involvement and with a tendency to overplay climaxes.

Chailly is aware that the complexity of opera performances—the musical, dramatic, and technical aspects and the large number of participants—often requires compromises by the conductor; he sometimes must sacrifice control over some elements in the interest of the whole.

He has made several recordings of complete operas, including Massenet's *Werther* (1979); Giordano's *Andrea Chénier* (1984); Rossini's *Guglielmo Tell* (1980), *Il barbiere di Siviglia* (1982), and *Il Turco in Italia* (1981); and Puccini's *Manon Lescaut* (1988). He has also recorded the soundtrack for Claude d'Anna's film of Verdi's *Macbeth* (1987).

—Michael Sims

CHALIAPIN, Feodor Ivanovich.

Bass. Born 13 February 1873, near Kazan. Died 12 April 1938, in Paris. Studied in Tbilisi (1892-93) with D.A. Usatov; joined chorus of traveling opera at age fourteen; debut as Stolnik in *Halka*, Ufa, 1890; belonged to Imperial Opera at Mariinsky Theater, St Petersburg; first major successes with Mamontov's company in Moscow, 1896-99, where he sang Boris, Dosifey in *Khovanshchina*; Ivan the Terrible in *Maid of Pskov*, created Salieri in *Mozart and Salieri*; associated with Bolshoi, 1899-1914; at Teatro alla Scala in Boito's *Mefistofele*, 1901; created Massenet's Don Quichotte, 1910; debut at Metropolitan Opera as Mefistofele, 1907; director of Mariinsky Theater from 1918 to 1921; sang every season at the Metropolitan Opera 1921-29; appeared in films *Tsar Ivan the Terrible* (1915) and *Don Quixote* (1933).

Feodor Chaliapin as Boris Godunov

Publications

By CHALIAPIN: books–

Pages from my Life. London, 1927.
An Autobiography, as told to Maxim Gorky, edited by Nina Froud and James Hanley. London, 1968.

About CHALIAPIN: books–

Newmarch, R. *The Russian Opera.* London, 1914.
Semenoff, B . *Man and Mask: Forty Years in the Life of a Singer.* New York & London, 1932.
Grosheva, E.A., ed. *Fyodor Ivanovich Chaliapin.* Moscow, 1976-79.
Borovsky, V. *Chaliapin: A Critical Biography.* New York and London, 1988.

articles–

Semenoff, B. "Feodor Chaliapin." *Record Collector* 5/no. 6 (1950): 124.
Semenoff, B. "Chaliapin's Repertoire and Recordings." *Record Collector* 20/nos. 8-10 (1972): 173.
Borovsky, V. "The Art of Chaliapin." *Opera* January (1982).

*   *   *

Chaliapin was one of the greatest singers, not only of Russia but of all time. Possessing a deep lyrical bass voice of very wide range, he stressed vocal declamation, being much aware of the relationship between words and music. Contemporary accounts speak of the "exceptional softness and beauty of timbre," combining "sincerity with depth and power." He was able to convey extremes of emotion, being capable of warm tenderness to lofty tragedy and biting sarcasm. In preparing himself for a role, Chaliapin would go to immense trouble, not only reading historical literature about the character in question but visiting museums and art galleries. Thus, when undertaking the part of Ivan the Terrible in Rimsky-Korsakov's *The Maid of Pskov,* he studied the various portraits of the tsar by Shvarts (Schwarz), Repin, Vasnetsov and the sculptor Antokol'sky. Before applying his make-up, he would make sketches of the role in question, paying special attention to costume and other details. In fact, his ability to think himself psychologically into a particular part was such that it influenced the work of the great Russian producer, Konstantin Stanislavsky, who based his own theories of acting and performances on Chaliapin's stage roles. Nijinsky, too, is said to have watched Chaliapin's performances from the wings. Chaliapin himself was a true disciple of the Russian realist school, manifest in Russian literature by such writers as Gogol, Dostoevsky, and Gorky (with whom he had a close friendship), painters such as Repin, and, of course, with composers such as Borodin and Musorgsky; indeed, his performance of Tsar Boris in Musorgsky's *Boris Godunov,* still remains unsurpassed to this day. But Chaliapin was never content simply to rest on his laurels and repeat himself *ad nauseam.* Striving incessantly for self-improvement, he often sought to interpret standard roles in new ways. That this was the case is evidenced by the many surviving accounts in a multitude of foreign languages describing his performances as Don Basilio in Rossini's *Il barbiere di Siviglia,* Leporello in Mozart's *Don Giovanni,* Mephistopheles in both Gounod's *Faust* and Boito's *Mefistofele,* Oroveso in Bellini's *Norma* and a host of other characters, whilst his renderings of great Russian parts such as Galitsky, Igor and Konchak in Borodin's *Prince Igor,* Farlaf in Glinka's *Ruslan and Lyudmila,* Boris and Pimen in Musorgsky's *Boris Godunov* and Dosifey in the same composer's *Khovanshchina* have all served as paradigms for subsequent performers. Whether tsar or peasant, passionate lover or mad miller, all were infused with living power so that in Chaliapin's hands they were not motley stage figures but vital beings of flesh and blood. His interpretation of Salieri in Rimsky-Korsakov's much neglected *Mozart and Salieri* was said to be electrifying. No doubt Chaliapin was helped in all this by his own fine profile and excellent physique, which served him well up to his final years, as may be heard from recordings made as late as 1931; even though the voice is no longer in its prime, his magnetic personality and passionate intensity are still evident. Chaliapin was also an excellent chamber singer and had a repertoire of some 400 pieces. Critics praised in particular his performance of Schubert's "Der Doppelgänger," Schumann's "Die beiden Grenadiere," selected songs of Glinka, Dargomyzhsky, Rimsky-Korsakov and Rubinstein, his singing of Musorgsky's "Song of the Flea" becoming world famous. In all his work his excellent sense of phrasing, subtle nuances and awareness of the meaning of the text enabled him, as one writer has put it, "to imbue each musical phrase with imagery and profound psychological meaning." His performances of Russian folk-songs, especially "The Volga Boatmen" and "Dubinushka," which he sang on 26 November 1905 in the Bol'shoy Theater at the height of the revolutionary uprising, have never been forgotten. Finally it should be mentioned that he was both a stage director, giving Massenet's *Don Quixote* (1910), *Khovanshchina* (1911), and Verdi's *Don Carlos* (1917), and a screen actor appearing in the films *Tsar Ivan*

Vasil'evich Grozny (based on Rimsky-Korsakov's *The Maid of Pskov*) in 1915 and *Don Quixote,* with music by Ibert, in 1933. His surviving drawings, paintings, sketches and sculptures reveal still further facets of his remarkable personality as well as his autobiography, translated as *Man and Mask.*

—Gerald Seaman

CHARPENTIER, Gustave.

Composer. Born 25 June 1860, in Dieuze. Died 18 February 1956, in Paris. Studied violin with Massart, harmony with Pessard, and composition with Massenet at the Paris Conservatory, 1881-87; Grand Prix de Rome for his cantata *Didon,* 1887; formed the society "L'Oeuvre de Mimi Pinson," a service organization devoted to providing music and dance for the poor, 1900. Charpentier's fame is largely the result of his opera, *Louise,* which saw immediate success.

Operas

Louise ("roman musical"), Charpentier, 1889-96, Paris, Opéra-Comique, 2 February 1900.
Julien, ou La vie du poète, Charpentier, 1913, Paris, Opéra-Comique, 4 June 1913.
L'amour au faubourg, c. 1913 [unperformed].
Orphée, 1931 [unfinished].

Publications

About CHARPENTIER: books–

Paoli, D. de. *Luisa.* Milan, 1922.
Himonet, A. *Louise de G. Charpentier.* Châteaurox, 1922.
Delmas, Marc. *Gustave Charpentier et le lyrisme français,* Coulommiers, 1931.
Elkin, R. "Gustave Charpentier (1860)." In *The Music Masters* 3, edited by A. Bacharach. London, 1952; revised 1958.
Longyear, Rey M. "Political and Social Criticism in French Opera, 1827-1920." In *Essays on the Music of J.S. Bach and other Divers Subjects: A Tribute to Gerhard Herz,* edited by Robert L. Weaver, 245. Louisville, 1981.

articles–

Rolland, Romain. "Louise." *Rivista musicale italiana* 7 (1900): 361.
Laloy, L. "Le drame musical moderne: les véristes français; Gustave Charpentier." *Mercure musical* 1 (1905): 169.
Hoover, K. O'Donnell. "Gustave Charpentier." *Musical Quarterly* 25 (1939): 334.
Schmidt-Garre, H. "Oper im Jahre 1900: zwischen Naturalismus und Décadence." *Neue Zeitschrift für Musik* 124 (1963): 3.

*   *   *

When Charpentier died in 1956 at the age of ninety-five he was already a legend. Bearded, cloaked, and wearing an artist's hat flopping rakishly over his brow, Charpentier was the incarnation of old Montmartre where he had spent much of his adult life. As a young lad up from the provinces he studied at the Conservatoire under Massenet, a brilliant teacher, and became one of his star pupils. Inevitably he won the Prix de Rome and, under the terms of his scholarship, spent the regulation number of years in the Italian capital. These years were of vital importance to his career, for it was in Rome that he composed or drafted pretty well all the music for which he is famous today. This included the orchestral suite *Impressions d'Italie,* the "symphonie-drame" called *La vie du poète* which is a naturalistic counterpart of Berlioz's *Lélio,* and the first act of what later became *Louise.* Gounod was much impressed by *La vie du poète.* "Would you believe it," he wrote to a friend, "Charpentier composes in the key of C major, and you know, only God Almighty knows how to write in C!"

Charpentier was a romantic socialist who refused to write chamber music because he thought it an undemocratic medium. He founded a charitable organization intended to put good music within the reach of working girls. In 1897 he sponsored the election of a "Muse of Work," and the girl chosen and duly crowned in Montmartre was fêted with songs and dances grouped under the title of *Le couronnement de la muse,* a sort of pageant which provided much of the music in Act III of *Louise.* Like the composers of the French Revolution, Charpentier wrote works expressly designed for performance in the open air. This was, he believed, the best way of bringing music to the people, and he organized many street festivals to this end. The working classes gave him the larger part of his inspiration, and *Louise* is his sentimental tribute to them.

Charpentier's only other published opera is *Julien,* although for years he was rumoured to be working on other stage pieces. *Julien,* first given in 1913, failed to equal the glittering success of *Louise.* Based largely on *La vie du poète,* it is an uneven mixture of naturalistic elements and symbolism quite different from the realistic approach of *Louise,* and that, perhaps, is why it failed and was withdrawn from the Opéra-Comique after only twenty performances. Even so, it is blessed with an intermittent flow of luscious melody and ripe orchestration which provide moments of genuine pleasure.

To a certain extent Charpentier continues the style of his teacher Massenet with tunes that make a direct appeal to the heart. From Puccini he learned the technique of *verismo,* or realism. From Wagner he absorbed the art of writing for a large orchestra, of scoring with richness and variety and of repeating particular melodies identified with a given character. All these attributes are superbly displayed in *Louise,* the opera for which he will always be remembered. It has an honoured place in the history of French opera as a link in the chain that stretches from Massenet to the present day.

—James Harding

CHARPENTIER, Marc-Antoine.

Composer. Born c. 1634 in Paris. Died 24 February 1704, in Paris. Studied music with Carissimi in Italy; collaborated with Molière in the production of the comédie-ballets *Le mariage forcé* (1672) and *Le malade imaginaire* (1673) at the Théâtre-Français, and stayed with the company after Molière's death (1673) until 1685; appointed maître de chapelle to the Dauphin, c. 1679; granted a pension by Louis XIV,

1683; maître de musique and music teacher to Mlle. de Guise, c. 1670s-1688; intendant to the Duke of Orléans; maître de musique of the Jesuit Maison-professe, 1684; maître de musique of Sainte-Chapelle, 1698.

Operas/Pastorales

Operas–

Les amours d'Acis et de Galatée, Châlet M. de Rians, Paris, January 1678.
Endimion, Paris, 22 July 1681.
La descente d'Orphée aux enfers. c. 1685.
Les arts florissants. 1685-86.
Celse Martyr, Collège Louis–le–Grand, 1687 [lost].
David et Jonathan. Collège Louis–le–Grand, 1688.
Médée (tragédie lyrique), Thomas Corneille, Paris, 4 December 1693.
Philomèle (with the Duke of Chartres), Paris, Palais-Royal.

Pastorales–

Le sort d'Andromède, c. 1670.
Petite pastorale, c. 1675 [incomplete].
Le retour de printemps [lost].
Le jugement de Pan [lost].
La fête de Rueil, 1685.
Actéon, 1683-85; revised as *Actéon changé en biche,* 1683-85.
Les plaisirs de Versailles, c. 1680.
Sur la naissance de notre Seigneur Jésus Christ, 1683-85.
Pastorale sur la naissance de notre Seigneur Jésus Christ, 1683-85.
La couronne de fleurs, 1685.
Dialogue de Vénus et Médor.

Other works: sacred vocal works, songs, instrumental music.

Publications/Writings

By CHARPENTIER: unpublished–

Remarques sur les messes à 16 parties d'Italie. c. 1670.
Règles de composition par MᴿCharpentier. c. 1692.
Abrégé des règles de l'accompagnement de MᴿCharpentier. c. 1692.

About CHARPENTIER: books–

Tillet, E. Titon du. *Description de Parnasse français [p. 144 ff]. Paris, 1727.*
Brenet, Michel. *Les musiciens de la Sainte-Chapelle du Palais.* Paris. 1910.
Crussard, Claude. *Un musicien français oublié: Marc-Antoine Charpentier. 1634-1704.* Paris, 1945.
Lowe, Robert W. *Marc-Antoine Charpentier et l'opéra de collège.* Paris, 1966.
Anthony, James R. *French Baroque Music from Beaujoyeulx to Rameau.* London, 1973; revised 1978.
Cessac, Catherine. *Marc-Antoine Charpentier.* Paris, 1988.
Hitchcock, H. Wiley. *Marc-Antoine Charpentier.* Oxford, 1990.

articles–

Anon. articles in *Le mercure galant* (1699) and *Le nouveau mercure galant* (1678).

Brenet, Michel. "Marc-Antoine Charpentier." *Tribune de Saint-Gervais* March (1900).
Quittard, H. See articles in *Revue d'histoire et de critiques musicales* (1902, 1904, 1908), and his article in *Zeitschrift I.M.G.* (1905).
La Laurencie, L. de. "Un opéra inédit de M.-A. Charpentier: La descente d'Orphée aux enfers." *Revue de musicologie* 13 (1932): 184.
Oliver, A.R. "Molière's Contribution to the Lyric Stage." *Musical Quarterly* 33 (1947): 350.
Hitchcock, H. Wiley. "Marc-Antoine Charpentier and the Comédies-Français." *Journal of the American Musicological Society* 24 (1971): 225.
Duron, Jean. "L'année musicale 1688." *XVII siècle* 139 (1983): 224.
Avant-scène opéra 68 (1984) [*Médée* issue].

*   *   *

It is an odd twist of fate that French Baroque opera has been more or less defined by an Italian, Jean Baptiste Lully, while the Italian Baroque style was represented by a Frenchman, Marc-Antoine Charpentier. Charpentier was a respected composer in seventeenth-century France, but it was Lully who became the major court composer—a virtual musical monarch—in the court of King Louis XIV. He was *the* dominant French opera composer. Further, Lully obtained royal decrees in 1671, 1672, and again in 1685, giving him a musical monopoly which made it possible for him to completely dominate French theater and restrict any competition. Marc-Antoine Charpentier's operatic output was therefore somewhat limited; the majority of his compositions, including dramatic ones, are sacred works, for which he was highly esteemed.

A prolific composer of over 550 works, Marc-Antoine Charpentier was rediscovered only in the twentieth-century (musicologist H. Wiley Hitchcock is particularly known for his work on the composer). There is a remarkable lack of primary information about Charpentier. Much of the biographical material about him is based on secondary sources and comparative speculation. The date of his birth, for example, has been estimated to be as early as 1634 and as late as 1645 (1643 is now considered to be the probable year). We know nothing of his appearance or personality. Only the details of the latter part of his life can be determined with certainty.

As a young man, Charpentier spent several years studying in Italy, notably with Carissimi. His work as a composer for drama began in collaboration with the playwright Molière and his company, the Comédiens du Roi, in 1672 (*La Comtesse d'Escarbagnas, Le mariage forcé*). Though Molière died in 1673 after the fourth performance of *Le malade imaginaire,* Charpentier continued to compose for what in 1680 became the Comédie-Française until the mid 1680s. Thomas Corneille, brother of famous dramatist Pierre Corneille, and Donneau de Vise, editor of the *Mercure galant* newspaper, became Charpentier's two principal dramatic collaborators. A particularly notable production which required stage machines was Thomas Corneille's elaborate play, *Circé* (1675).

During the time he provided music for the Comédie-Française, Charpentier also worked for Marie de Lorraine, the Duchess de Guise. She employed a number of musicians in what became a remarkable musical establishment. For her, Charpentier composed at least eight secular dramatic works, including *La descente d'Orphée aux enfers.*

From 1679 or 1680 until about 1683, Charpentier served as musical director for the chapel of the Grand Dauphin. The

Dauphin was probably the source of a commission to write music for two stage works, *Les plaisirs de Versailles* and *La fête de Rueil*. In 1683 Charpentier was a candidate for a post of *sous-maître* of the royal chapel, but could not complete the competition due to illness.

From about 1684 to 1698, Charpentier was employed by the Jesuits at the Collège Louis-le-Grand and at the Église St. Louis (called "l'église de l'opéra" by his contemporary, Le Cerf de la Vieville). For the Jesuits and their colleges Charpentier wrote sacred French opera as well as Latin church music. The opera *David et Jonathan* (1688), perhaps the most important of these works, was his first dramatic work to be written without the limitations of Lully's monopoly.

The death of Lully in 1687 opened up the "official" Parisian musical scene to other composers. In 1693, Charpentier's most famous dramatic work, the opera *Médée* (libretto by Thomas Corneille), was commissioned and produced by the Académie Royale de Musique. In 1694, the publisher Ballard printed the score to *Médée,* the only major publication of Charpentier's music during his lifetime.

In the early 1690s, Charpentier was employed to teach music to Philippe, Duke of Chartres, a nephew of the King who in 1701 became the Duke of Orléans and from 1715-1723 was Regent of France. For him, Charpentier wrote treatises on composition and accompaniment. Teacher and student collaborated on an opera, *Philomèle* (now lost), which was performed three times in the royal palace.

Of Charpentier's over 200 motets, thirty-five are classified by H. Wiley Hitchcock as dramatic motets. Sometimes referred to as oratorios because of their specific characters and structure, these diverse works were designated by the composer's terms *motet, historia, canticum,* and *dialogus,* and were designed for use in church services. Topics include biblical stories (Abraham and Isaac, Joshua, Esther, the prodigal son, etc.), church history (such as the 1576 plague of Milan), and several Christmas works. From these compositions comes one of Charpentier's last works, *Judicium Salomonis* (*The Judgment of Solomon*), written in 1702 for the "Messe Rouge" "Red Mass," because of the red robes of the officials) at the opening of the French Parliament.

—Donald Oglesby

CHAUSSON, (Amédée-) Ernest.

Composer. Born 20 January 1855, in Paris. Died 10 June 1899, in Limay, near Mantes. Studied with Massenet at the Paris Conservatory, and then privately with César Franck; secretary of the Société Nationale de Musique.

Operas

Le roi Arthus. Chausson, 1886-95, Brussels, Théâtre de la Monnaie, 30 November 1903 [posthumous production].

Other works: orchestral works, vocal works, chamber works, piano music, songs.

Publications

About CHAUSSON: books–

Séré, O. *Musiciens français d'aujourd'hui.* Paris, 1911, 1921.
Oulmont, C. *Henri Duparc.* Paris, 1935; 1970 [analysis of *Arthus*].
Catalogue de l'Exposition Chausson. Paris, 1949.
Barricelli, J.-P. and L. Weinstein. *Ernest Chausson: the Composer's Life and Works.* Norman, 1955.
Davies, L. *César Franck and his Circle.* London, 1970.
Gallois, Jean. *Ernest Chausson: l'homme et l'oeuvre.* Paris, 1967.
Grover, Ralph Scott. *Ernest Chausson: The Man and his Music.* London, 1980.

articles–

D'Indy, Vincent. "Ernest Chausson." *Tribune de St. Gervais* September (1899).
Dukas, P. "Ernest Chausson." *Le Figaro* November (1903).
Hallays, A. "Le Roi Arthus." *Revue de Paris* 10 (1903): 846.
La revue musicale 1 (1925) [Chausson issue].
Oulmont, C. "Deux amis: Claude Debussy et Ernest Chausson: documents inédits." *Mercure de France* 1 December (1934).
Feschotte, J. "Chausson et la poésie." *Musica* 42 (1957): 2.
Hirsbrunner, Theo. "Enttauschte Hoffnung. Zu Leben und Werk von Ernest Chausson." *Neue Zürcher* 271 (1981): 67.
_____. "Debussy, Maeterlinck, Chausson: Literary and Musical Connections." *Miscellanea musicologica* 13 (1984): 57.

* * *

Chausson's slender musical output—partly explained, certainly, by a tragic and untimely death at the age of forty-four—cannot be adequately understood and evaluated unless and until some notice is taken of the circumstances into which this composer was born and nurtured. Thus, unlike Mozart and Schubert, for example, whose music bears little relationship to outer circumstances, Chausson's character and life were closely associated and intimately interconnected with everything he wrote, and his only opera, *Le roi Arthus* (*King Arthur*), is in no way an exception. In fact, these external factors played a more crucial role in *Arthus* than they did anywhere else (with the possible exception of parts of the Symphony).

Born into a well-to-do family whose wealth resulted from the position his father held as a public works contractor associated with Baron Haussmann in the construction of the Parisian boulevards, Chausson was not obliged to compose or, indeed, to work at all in order to support himself. During his childhood and early youth he was tutored privately by a young man, Brethous-Lafargue, who was well-educated conventionally and also conversant in the arts. Brethous-Lafargue took the youth to art museums, concerts, and salons such as that of Mme Saint-Cyr de Rayssac, where he met important painters of the day as well as persons prominent— or soon to become so—in the other arts. It was here that he became acquainted with the music of Beethoven, Schubert, Schumann, and Mendelssohn. He was attracted to literature (he wrote short stories, and sketches for a novel), and a fairly extensive portfolio shows conclusively that he was also talented in drawing.

Later, the elegant, cultured atmosphere of Mme de Rayssac's salon was transferred to Chausson's large mansion at 22 Boulevard de Courcelles where there was an impressive collection of paintings, a fine, well-stocked library, and a guest list that included many of the most prominent figures in the arts. Here, Chausson and his wife entertained Manet, Monet, Renoir and Degas, among other painters. Franck and his important followers, as well as Debussy were among the composers who visited the Chausson's residence, as were the performers Cortot and Ysaÿe, the writers Mallarmé, the young Gide, Colette, and Rodin, the sculptor.

Chausson's eventual decision to become a composer was dependent upon first satisfying his father's requirement that he train for the legal profession, a postponement that probably did little to boost his self-esteem or confidence. Chausson's private education meant that he grew up apart from other children, while in the salons he mingled with persons much older than himself, and in each instance his natural seriousness and tendency towards melancholy were reinforced. In a letter to Mme de Rayssac some years later he confessed that during his childhood and early youth he "was often sad without ever really knowing why." She became his confidante and adviser when, at the successful conclusion of his legal training (he qualified as a barrister in 1877), he enrolled in Massenet's orchestration course at the Paris Conservatory (1879). However, Franck's classes in composition, which he audited following the completion of his studies with Massenet, proved far more valuable, and were to bear fruit, although the Franckian influence which resulted was largely confined to Chausson's adoption of cyclical structure. His self-confidence was weakened in this period when he failed to obtain the Prix de Rome, for which he had been nominated.

The greatest test in Chausson's ever-continuing battle to prove his worth as a serious composer (he was keenly aware that his wealth could brand him a dilettante) came in 1880, when he first heard Wagner's *Tristan und Isolde* in Munich. Following his exposure to *Tristan*, Chausson planned and eventually completed *Le roi Arthus*, which occupied Chausson intermittently from 1886 to 1895. Some of the gaps can be attributed to a temporary loss of interest, probably occasioned by discouragement concerning Wagner's hold, while others indicate work on his Symphony in B flat. Passages from letters to friends reveal the intensity of the struggle he was undergoing: "the red specter of Wagner is always before me!"; "Well, Wagner is dead, but he wrote *Tristan*"; "O, if only I could de-wagnerize myself!" In the autumn of 1893 Chausson returned to *Arthus,* telling Debussy in a letter that he had resumed work on the third act "without too much trouble," and further informing him that he believed it was "becoming clear and de-wagnerized."

Had Chausson not been killed in a bicycle accident, he would probably have written other operas, for over the years he had developed a keen interest in composing for the theater. Indeed, he kept a small notebook in which are recorded the titles of projected works, *Arthus* included. But certainly any opera following *Arthus* would have shown quite different characteristics, for at the time of his death Chausson had exorcized the Wagnerian influence, moved away from the largely Germanic and heavy-handed idealism of the Franckists, and forged a link—albeit unconsciously—between them and the subtle, impressionistic language of Debussy. More significantly, perhaps, he had become aware of typically French characteristics, like formal balance and understatement. Yet the central feature of Chausson's music remains it elegiac quality—the product of his personality and background. What the fusion of some or all of these traits might have produced in future operas as well as works in other genres (which he was confidently planning) we shall, unfortunately, never know.

—Ralph S. Grover

CHÉREAU, Patrice.

Director. Born 2 November 1944, in Lézigné, Maine-et-Loire, France; educated at the Sorbonne in the early 1960s; began artistic apprenticeship by watching his father, a painter, and mother, a fabric designer; while at the Sorbonne, staged first production, Victor Hugo's *L'intervention,* at Louis-le-Grand; first came to the attention of the public in 1966, with a production of Eugène Labiche's nineteenth-century farce *L'affaire de la rue de Lourcine;* directed first opera, Rossini's *L'italiana in Algeri,* at the Spoleto Festival in 1969; became co-director of the Théâtre de la Cité (later the Théâtre National Populaire) in Villeurbanne, 1971; directed a controversial production of *Les Contes d'Hoffmann* at the Paris Opéra in 1974; chosen by conductor Pierre Boulez and Paris Opéra director Rolf Liebermann to stage Bayreuth's centennial production of *Der Ring des Nibelungen* in 1976; the production was repeated the following four seasons and videotaped in 1979 and 1980 for international release; staged the first complete three-act production of Berg's *Lulu* in 1979; became artistic director in chief of the Théâtre des Amandiers of Nanterre, 1982; after mounting a production of Mozart's *Lucia Silla* at the Teatro alla Scala in 1984, Chéreau began focusing mainly on directing films; he was contracted to direct three Mozart operas for the bicentennial of the composer's death in 1991, but withdrew in protest when conductor Daniel Barenboim was fired.

Opera Productions (selected)

L'italiana in Algeri, Spoleto Festival, 1969.
Les Contes d'Hoffmann, Paris, Opéra, 1974.
Der Ring des Nibelungen, Bayreuth, 1976.
Lulu, Paris, Opéra, 1979.
Lucia Silla, Teatro alla Scala, Paris and Brussels (joint production), 1984.

Publications

By CHÉREAU: books–

L'homme blessé: scénario et notes. Paris, c. 1983.

About CHÉREAU: books–

Bergfeld, Joachim. *Ich wollte Wagner vom Podest holen: Anmerkungen zur Bayreuther Ringinszenierung durch Patrice Chéreau im Jubiläumsjahr der Festspiele 1976.* Bayreuth, 1977.
Nattiez, Jean Jacques. *Tétralogies, Wagner, Boulez, Chéreau: essai sur l'infidélité.* Paris, c. 1983.
Treatt, Nicolas. *Treatt Chéreau.* Paris, c. 1984.
Nussac, Sylvie de. *Nanterre Amandiers: les années Chéreau, 1982-1990.* Paris, c. 1990.

Patrice Chéreau's production of *Das Rheingold*, Bayreuth, 1976

articles–

"Oper soll die Ausname bleiben" (interview). *Das Orchester* 26 (November 1978): 815.

Bonnenmeyer, W. "Es war eine positive Erfahrung" (interview). *Opernwelt* 21/10 (1980): 19.

"Patrice Chéreau vindt opera nu een onmogelijk genre" (interview). *Mens en Melodie* 38 (December 1983): 526.

Ewans, Michael Christopher. "Two Centenary Productions of *The Ring* at Bayreuth. I: The Bayreuth Centenary *Ring* by Patrice Chéreau and Pierre Boulez." *Miscellanea musicologica* 14 (July 1985): 167.

By the time he started producing opera, Patrice Chéreau was already something of an "enfant terrible" (he was only twenty-one when he began to make a name for himself in Paris) with a reputation for radical productions aimed at bringing a new, less conservative public into the theater. His work was marked by what he had seen at the Berliner Ensemble and the Picolla Scala (of whose director, Strehler, he was a great admirer).

In 1969, Chéreau agreed for the first time to produce an opera. This was Rossini's *L'italiana in Algeri* at the Spoleto Festival. He took with him, as designers, Richard Peduzzi (sets) and Jacques Schmidt (costumes), who would become his associates on all his opera productions. Convinced that he had nothing to say to the average opera audience of the

time, Chéreau set *L'italiana* in a semi-ruined Italianate theater, thus enabling the audience to reflect on the nature of opera as much as on the opera itself. The seriousness of Chéreau's approach was never in doubt. His ability to avoid pretention while striving for perfection after weeks of rehearsals reminded some critics of Walter Felsenstein.

Chéreau's work in the straight theater evolved towards the use of somber sets which seemed to act as much as the characters in them: lighting and costumes added to the eerie stage pictures. This was to become more apparent in the first opera Chéreau would produce for a major opera-house, Offenbach's *Les contes d'Hoffmann* (1974). This was one of the controversial stagings with which Rolf Liebermann was to revitalize the hidebound Paris Opéra. By going back to the spirit of Hoffmann's original tales and setting the opera in a haunted Baltic dockland, Chéreau turned the action into something far more sinister than what is suggested by the score. The production created a furor, which explains why he felt that audiences for opera still could not appreciate his work—a feeling that would be reinforced when Chéreau (with Boulez conducting) undertook the centenary *Ring* at Bayreuth in 1976.

The very temple of conservatism (which had at last digested the work of Wieland Wagner) was in an uproar after the premiere of the first Chéreau-produced *Ring* cycle. Making great use of nineteenth century industrialization and its imagery, together with scarcely-veiled attacks on capitalism, Chéreau was, in fact, only bringing into the Holy of Holies a number of trends that had already been adumbrated elsewhere in Europe. By creating visual effects that were striking, beautiful, and technically breath-taking, Chéreau delighted the younger (or more iconoclastic) element in the Bayreuth audience. By the time of the last performances in 1980, Chéreau's *Ring* was being cheered to the rafters. The whole production, with various modifications made by Chéreau over the years, was later filmed and shown world-wide on television. Audiences today would find it hard to see what all the fuss was about, since so much of Chéreau's thinking has been plundered by producers who came after him.

In 1979, the Paris Opéra was to put on what many considered to be Liebermann's finest achievement as an *intendant*— the completed three-act version of Berg's *Lulu*. Working again with Boulez, Chéreau was able to draw on his production of Wedekind's original play (Piccola Scala, 1972), e.g., staging the last scene in a public lavatory, and, by setting the opera in a corrupt pre-war Europe, to draw parallels between the fall of the opera's heroine and the rise of Fascism. This time, Chéreau met with no audience opposition, although only nine performances were ever given of what seemed to be a definitive production. Even so, Chéreau would not return to opera for another five years.

Mozart's *Lucio Silla* had rarely been staged when it was decided to mount the work as a joint venture in Milan, Paris and Brussels. By this time, the visual aspects of Chéreau's productions had become more austere. Peduzzi designed sets that were somewhat abstract, merely hinting at the Roman background, and Schmidt provided eighteenth century costumes. All this was in line with the direction that Chéreau's stagings were taking in the mid-eighties, and the evening was more a "succès d'estime" than an epoch-making operatic experience.

Since 1984, no new Chéreau opera productions have actually reached the stage. He has not neglected the straight theater but has devoted a lot of time to directing films. Various reports have suggested that Chéreau could be tempted back into the opera-house, but so far nothing has come to fruition.

—Oliver Smith

CHERUBINI, (Maria-) Luigi (-Carlo-Zenobio-Salvatore).

Composer. Born 8? September 1760, in Florence. Died 15 March 1842, in Paris. Married: Anne Cécile Tourette, 12 April 1794 (one son, two daughters). Studied music with his father, then with Bartolomeo Felici and his son Alessandro, Pietro Bizzarri, and Giuseppe Castrucci; sent to Bologna and Milan by Duke Leopold of Tuscany to study with Sarti, 1778-81; in London, 1784-86; composed sacred music and operas, 1778-88; settled in Paris, 1787; conductor and composer at the Théâtre de Monsieur (later the Théâtre de la rue Feydeau), 1789-1800; appointed inspector at the Paris Conservatory, 1 November 1794; inspector and professor at the Paris Conservatory, 1794-1822; in Vienna, 1805-06; in London, 1815; composed French operas, 1788-1814; surintendant of the royal chapel, 1814-30; member of the Institut de France, 1814; Chevalier of the Légion d'honneur, 1814; director of the Paris Conservatory, 1822-42; Commander of the Légion d'honneur, 1841. Cherubini's students include Auber and Halévy.

Luigi Cherubini, engraving after portrait by Ingres, 1842

Operas

Amore artigiano (intermezzo), Fiesole, San Domenico, 22 October 1773 [lost].

Il Giocatore (intermezzo), Florence, 1775.

Untitled intermezzo, Florence, Serviti, 16 February 1778.

Il Quinto Fabio, Apostolo Zeno, Alessandria, Paglia, fall 1779 [lost]: revised, Rome, Torre Argentina, January 1783.

Untitled opera, 1781 [unfinished].

Armida abbandonata, Jacopo Durandi, Florence, Teatro della Pergola, 25 January 1782.

Adriano in Siria, Metastasio, Livorno, Teatro degli Armeni, 16 April 1782.

Mesenzio, re d'Etruria, Ferdinando Casori, Florence, Teatro della Pergola, 6 September 1782.

Lo sposo di tre e marito di nessuna, Filippo Livigni, Venice, San Samuele, November 1783.

Olimpiade, Metastasio, 1783.

L'Alessandro nell'Indie, Metastasio, Mantua Nuovo Regio Ducale, April 1784.

L'Idalide, Ferdinando Moretti, Florence, Teatro della Pergola, 26 December 1784.

Demetrio (pasticcio) Mestastasio, London, King's Theatre, 1785 [four pieces by Cherubini].

La finta principessa, Filippo Livigni, London, King's Theatre, 2 April 1785.

Il Giulio Sabino, London, King's Theatre, 30 March 1786.

Ifigenia in Aulide, Ferdinando Moretti, Turin, Regio, 12 January 1788.

Démophon, Jean François Marmontel (after Metastasio, *Demofoonte*), Paris, Opéra, 5 December 1788.

Marguerite d'Anjou, 1790 [unfinished].

Lodoïska, Claude-François Fillette-Loraux (after Jean-Baptiste Louvet de Couvrai, *Les amours du chevalier de Faublas*), Paris, Théâtre Feydeau, 18 July 1791.

Koukourgi, Anne-Honore-Joseph Duveyrier [=Melesville], Paris, written for the Théâtre Feydeau, 1793 [not performed; part of the music used for *Ali Baba*].

Sélico, 1794 [fragments only].

Le congrès des rois (pasticcio), A.F. Eve Desmaillot, Paris, Favart, 26 February 1794 [lost].

Eliza, ou Le voyage aux glaciers du Mont St-Bernard, Jacques-Antoine Saint-Cyr, Paris, Théâtre Feydeau, 13 December 1794.

Médée, François Benoît Hoffman, Paris, Théâtre Feydeau, 13 March 1797.

L'hôtellerie portugaise, Étienne Saint-Aigan, Paris, Théâtre Feydeau, 25 July 1798.

La punition, Jean-Louis Brousse Desfaucherets, Paris, Théâtre Feydeau, 23 February 1799.

La prisonnière (with Boieldieu), Victor Joseph Étienne de Jouy, Charles de Longchamps, and Claude Godard d'Aucour de Saint-Just, Paris, Théâtre Montansier, 12 September 1799.

Les deux journées, Jean-Nicolas Bouilly, Paris, Théâtre Feydeau, 16 January 1800.

Epicure (with Méhul), Charles-Albert Demoustier, Paris, Théâtre Favart, 14 March 1800.

Untitled opéra-comique, 1802 [unfinished].

Anacréon, ou L'amour fugitif (opéra-ballet), R. Mendouze, Paris, Opéra, 4 October 1803.

Les arrêts, 1804 [unfinished].

Faniska, Josef von Sonnleithner (after René-Charles Guilbert de Pixérécourt, *Les mines de Pologne*), Vienna, Kärntner-tor Theater, 25 February 1806.

La petite guerre, 1807 [unfinished].

Pimmalione, Stefano Vestris (after Antonio Simone Sografi's Italian version of Rousseau's *Pigmalion*), Paris, Tuileries, 30 November 1809.

La crescendo, Charles Augustin de Bassompierre [=Sewrin], Paris, Opéra-comique, 1 September 1810.

Les abencérages, ou L'étendard de Grenade, Victor Joseph Étienne de Jouy (after Jean Pierre Claris de Florian, *Gozalve de Cordoue*), Paris, Opéra, 6 April 1813.

Bayard à Mézières (with Boieldieu, Catel, and Isouard), E. Dupaty and R.A. de Chazet, Paris, Opéra-comique, 12 February 1814 [lost].

Blanche de Provence, ou La cour des fées (with Berton, Boieldieu, Kreutzer, and Paër), M.E.G.M. Théaulon and de Rancé, Paris, Tuileries, 1 May 1821.

La marquise de Brinvilliers (with Auber, Batton, Berton, Blangini, Boieldieu, Carafa, Hérold, and Paër), Eugène Scribe and François Henri Joseph Blaze [=Castil-Blaze], Paris, Ventadour, 31 October 1831 [lost].

Ali Baba, ou Les quarante voleurs, Eugène Scribe and Anne-Honoré Joseph Duveyrier [=Melesville], Paris, Opéra, 22 July 1833 [part of music from *Koukourgi*].

Publications/Writings

By CHERUBINI: books–

with F.J. Gossec, A. Grétry, E.-N. Méhul, and J.F. Lesueur. *Eclaircissemens sur le Conservatoire de musique.* Paris, 1796.

with others. *Principes élémentaires de musique arrêtés par les membres du Conservatoire,. . . .* Paris, 1799-1802.

Rapport à son excellence le Ministre de l'interieur sur l'orgue expressif. Paris, 1812.

with R.J. Haüy, C. de Prony, et. al. *Académie des sciences: mémoire.* Paris, 1819.

Discours prononcé aux funerailles de M. Catel . . . par Cherubini. Paris, 1830.

Solfèges à changements de clefs. Paris, 1830.

Cours de contrepoint et de fugue. Paris, 1832; English translation by J.A. Hamilton, London, 1837; English translation by M.C. Clarke, London, 1854; German translation by F. Stoepel, Leipzig, 1836; German translation by G. Jensen, Cologne, 1896; German translation by R. Heuberger, Leipzig, 1911.

Académies royale de France: discours prononcé aux funérailles de M. Boieldieu, le lundi 16 octobre 1834. Paris, 1834.

with Halévy. *Cours de contrepoint et de fugue.* Paris, 1835; English translation, 1837.

Prefaces to C. Baudiot. *Traité de transposition musicale.* Paris, 1837.

Toulmon, A. Bottée de, ed. *Notice des manuscrits autographes de la musique composée par feu M.-L.-C.-Z.-S. Cherubini.* Paris, 1843, 1967.

Ed. *Marches d'harmonie.* Paris, 1847.

Pougin, A. ed. *Notice sur Méhul par Cherubini.* Paris, 1817; reprint in *Rivista musicale italiana* 16 (1909): 750.

articles–

"Review." *Le mercure de France* 26 May (1804).

About CHERUBINI: books–

Arnold, I.T.F.C. *Luigi Cherubini: Seine kurze Biographie und ästhetische Darstellung seiner Werke.* Erfurt, 1810.

Miel, E.F.M.A. *Notice sur la vie et les ouvrages de Cherubini.* Paris, 1842.

Place, C. *Essai sur la composition musicale: biographie et analyse phrénologique de Cherubini.* Paris, 1842.

Picchianti, L. *Notizie sulla vita e sulle opere di Luigi Cherubini.* Milan, 1843.

Raoul-Rochette, Désiré. *Notice historique sur la vie et les ouvrages de M. Cherubini.* Paris, 1844.

Gambini, C.A. *Hommage à Cherubini.* Paris, 1844.

Loménie, Louis de. *Cherubini.* Paris, 1847.

Neumann, W. *Luigi Cherubini: eine Biographie.* Cassel, 1854.

Adam, A. *Dernier souvenirs d'un musicien.* Paris, 1859.

Denne-Baron, R.D. *Mémoires historiques d'un musicien: Cherubini, sa vie, ses travaux, leur influence sur l'art.* Paris, 1862.

Torfs, T.E.X.N. *Cherubini.* Le Mans, 1867.

Gamucci, B. *Intorno alla vita ed alle opere di Luigi Cherubini.* Florence, 1869.

Bellasis, Edward. *Cherubini: Memorials Illustrative of his Life and Work.* London, 1874; German translation, Munich, 1876; 2nd ed., 1905; 3rd ed., 1912; 1971.

Lipsius, Ida M. *Musikalische Studienköpfe.* Leipzig, 1881-88.

Bennett, Joseph. *Luigi Cherubini.* London, 1884.

Crowest, Frederick J. *Cherubini.* London, 1890.

Wittmann, Maximilian E. *Cherubini.* Leipzig, 1895.

Carreras y Bulbena, José. *Luigi Cherubini: estudio musical.* Barcelona, 1896.

Nodnagel, Ernst O. *Der Wasserträger: Textlich und musikalisch Erläutert.* Leipzig, 1900.

Lega, Antonio. *Cherubini e l'opera "Medea": Cenno biografico con brani musicale.* Milan, 1909.

Hohenemser, Richard H. *Luigi Cherubini: Sein Leben und seine Werke.* Leipzig, 1913; 1969.

Quatrelles-L'Epine, M. *Cherubini (1760-1842): notes et documents inédits.* Lille, 1913.

Schemann, L. *Cherubini.* Stuttgart, 1925.

Espril, P. *Les voyages de Cherubini, ou L'enfance de Mozart.* Bayonne, 1946.

Confalonieri, Giulio. *Prigionia di un artista: il romanzo di Luigi Cherubini.* Milan, 1948; 2nd ed., 1978.

Schlitzer, F. *Richerche su Cherubini.* Sienna, 1954.

Damerini, Adelmo, ed. *Luigi Cherubini nel Il centenario della nascità.* Florence, 1962.

Reynolds, C.F. *Luigi Cherubini.* Ilfracombe, 1963.

Deane, Basil S. *Cherubini.* London, 1965.

Selden, Margery J.S. *The French Operas of Luigi Cherubini.* Ann Arbor, Michigan, 1972.

Della Croce, Vittorio. *Cherubini e i musicisti italiani del suo tempo.* Turin, 1983.

Buschmeier, G. *Die Entwicklung von Arie und Szene in der französichen Oper von Gluck bis Spontini.* Tutzing, 1991.

articles—

Blaze, François H.J. "Chérubini." *Revue de Paris* 52 (1833): 86, 165.

Cianchi, Emilio. "Cenno analitico sopra *Le Due Giornate,* opera teatrale di Luigi Cherubini." *Atti dell'Accademia del Regio Istituto musicale de Firenze* 1 (1863): 31.

Pougin, A. "Chérubini: sa vie, ses oeuvres, son rôle artistique." *Le ménestrel* 47-49 (1881-82).

Prout, Ebenezer. "Some Forgotten Operas. IV.-Cherubini's *Medea.*" *Monthly Musical Record* 35 (1905): 21, 41, 62.

Kretzschmar, Hermann. "Über die Bedeutung von Cherubinis Ouverturen uns Hauptopern für die Gegenwart." *Jahrbuch der Musikbibliothek Peters* 13 (1906): 75.

Hohenemser, Richard H. "Cherubinis *Wasserträger.*" *Die Musik* 13 (1913): 131.

Schemann, Ludwig. "Cherubinis dramatisches Erstlingsschaffen." *Die Musik* 17 (1925): 641.

Saponaro, Giacomo. "Luigi Cherubini (1760-1842): note biografiche." *Bolletino Bibliografico musicale* 5 (1930): 9.

Capri, A. "Luigi Cherubini nel centenario della morte (1812-1942)." *Musica* 1 (1942): 72.

Favre, G. "L'amitié de deux musiciens: Boïeldieu et Chérubini." *La revue musicale* no. 201 (1946): 217.

Sear, H.G. "Background for Cherubini." *Music and Letters* 24 (1953): 15.

Damerini, Adelmo. "Rivive *Medea* di Cherubini." *Rivista musicale italiana* 56 (1954): 61.

Cooper, Martin. "Cherubini's *Medea.*" *Opera* 10 (1959): 349.

Schröder, Cornelia. "Chronologisches Verzeichnis der Werke Luigi Cherubinis unter Kennzeichnung der in der Musikabteilung der Berliner Staatsbibliothek erhaltenen Handschriften." *Beiträge zur Musikwissenschaft* 3 (1961): 24.

Chusid, Martin. "Schubert's Overture for String Quartet and Cherubini's Overture to *Faniska.*" *Journal of the American Musicological Society* 15 (1962): 78.

Ghislanzoni, A. "Letteratura cherubiniana in ordine chronologico." *Collectinea historiae musicae* 3 (1963).

Selden, M.J.S. "Cherubini: the Italian 'Image'." *Journal of the American Musicological Society* 17 (1964): 378.

Dean, Winton. "Opera under the French Revolution." *Proceedings of the Royal Musical Association* 54 (1967-68): 77.

Ringer, Alexander. "Cherubini's *Médée* and the Spirit of French Revolutionary Opera." In *Essays in Musicology in Honor of Dragan Plamenac on his 70th Birthday,* 281. Pittsburgh, 1969; 1977.

Selden, M.J.S. "Cherubini and England." *Musical Quarterly* 60 (1974): 421.

Carli Ballola, Giovanni. "Da *Lodoiska* a *Les deux journées:* i canti di un viandante solitario." *Chigiani* 33 (1979): 103.

Tozzi, Lorenzo. "*La punition* ovvero di un ritrovato gioiello comico cherubiniano." *Chigiana* 33 (1979): 3.

Selden, M.J.S. "*Pymalion:* a Little-Known Opera by Cherubini." *Performing Arts* 11 (1981): 94.

Willis, Stephen. "Cherubini: from *Opera Seria* to *Opéra-comique.*" *Studies in Music* [Canada] 7 (1982): 155.

Deane, Basil S. "Cherubini and opéra-comique." *Opera* 40 (1989): 1305.

Murray, David. "*Médée.*" *Opera* 51 (1990): 103.

unpublished—

Haft, Virginia G. "Cherubini: a Critical Bibliography." Ph.D. dissertation, Columbia University, 1952.

Willis, Stephen. "Luigi Cherubini: a Study of his Life and Dramatic Music, 1795-1815." Ph.D. dissertation, Columbia University, 1975.

* * *

In an era when the freer, more liberalizing forms of *opera buffa* and *opéra comique* were coming to the fore, Cherubini seemed to be more interested in *opera seria* and *tragédie lyrique*. It is difficult to assess his contribution to *opera seria* because of the present inaccessibility of the original scores. (Although originally housed in the Deutsches Staatsbibliothek in Berlin, the manuscripts of Cherubini's early works were among those sent to Poland during World War II and are now kept in the Jagellonian Library, Cracow.) A brief look at what is available and a referral to contemporary criticism does indicate that Cherubini belonged to the "reform" school.

Cherubini's first interest in opera was probably due to his father, Bartolomeo. As he was *maestro al cembalo* at the Teatro della Pergola in Florence, his son must have been a frequent spectator there. Luigi's choice of Giuseppe Sarti (1729-1802), a reknowned composer of *opera seria*, as his teacher would indicate that, at the age of eighteen, he already had a preference for dramatic music. He frequently contributed arias to Sarti's operas as part of the learning process, so that, by the time of the appearance of his first *opera seria, Il Quinto Fabio*, in 1779, he was already showing a predilection for the new school of Italian dramatic music as espoused by Niccolo Jommelli (1714-74), Tommaso Michele Francesco Saverio Traette (1727-79), Antonio Maria Gaspero Gioacchino Sacchini (1730-86), as well as his teacher Sarti. In this first opera, Cherubini showed signs of uncommon use of orchestral color through imaginative instrumentation. The score of *Armida abbandonata* (1782) reveals the use of the orchestra to heighten dramatic moments, even to the detriment of the vocal line. In *Adriano in Siria* (1782), the instrumentation is somewhat unusual in its use of flutes, oboes, bassoons, French horns, trumpets, and kettle drums in addition to the strings.

By 1783, Cherubini was already finding the *opera seria* form restrictive in its limitations. In that year, he wrote his first *opera buffa, Lo sposo di tre e marito di nessuna*. He returned to *opera seria* with *L'Alessandro nell'Indie* (1784), where he first used the "recall-motive." There are several places in the text where the poet has characters refer to previous events or feelings, and Cherubini uses musical recall to emphasize these moments. Further, the instrumentation continues to be interesting: flutes, oboes, English horn, bassoons, trumpets, and four French horns. Cherubini also made use of the recapitulation aria, but not necessarily with a tonal progression of tonic-dominant-tonic.

By now, Cherubini was feeling stifled in his native Italy and decided to travel. He went first to London, where the *opera buffa La finta principessa* and the *opera seria Il Giulio Sabino* (1786) were presented. The latter was a fiasco. The critics blamed the disaster on the singers' inadequacy, but the fault was also Cherubini's, as he was still experimenting with *opera seria* form and was not yet sure of the direction he wished to take. During the summer of 1785, he visited Paris where he met his compatriot Jean-Baptiste Viotti (1755-1824). Except for a visit to London at the end of 1785 and one to Italy for the performance of his next operatic creation, he spent the rest of his life in France.

The culmination of Cherubini's *opera seria* output was *Ifigenia in Aulide* (1788). The single most important element which differentiated this work from previous ones was Cherubini's use of music to delineate character. Perhaps it was his thorough grounding in counterpoint which suggested to him this musical interpretation of character; perhaps it was a personal trait which allowed him to empathize more fully with a libretto that demanded development of the text through music. Whatever the reason, Cherubini's most successful operas were always those requiring the revelation of character traits through dramatic, out-of-the-ordinary situations. It must be assumed that *opera seria* was more suited to the demands of Cherubini's musical genius. It appears also that he preferred the Greek and Roman plots typical of *opera seria,* or perhaps historical subjects in general, to more mundane situations.

When Cherubini arrived in France, he was offered the music directorship of the Théâtre de "Monsieur," which opened its doors to the public in the Tuileries on 26 January 1789. He jumped at the chance, and for good reason. In 1786, he had accepted a commission to write an opera for the Académie royale de musique on a libretto by Jean François Marmontel (1723-99). Despite lack of experience in dealing with the difficult French metrical texts, he made his debut in Paris with *Démophon* on 5 December 1788. The results were mediocre. The critics complained that Cherubini did not yet possess the necessary technique to set a French text properly. His directorship would provide him with a job while he familiarized himself with the French language and acquired a name amongst French music lovers. His post obliged him to add arias and ensembles in a musical style currently in vogue to the mediocre and sometimes outdated Italian operas presented by the company.

In 1792, Cherubini signed a new contract with the Théâtre de la rue Feydeau (the reincarnation of the earlier Théâtre de "Monsieur") which paid him 6,000 livres a year for the continuation of his duties, plus 2,000 for the first two completely new operas written by him each year and another 4,000 for each additional opera. The result was a ten-year period of creativity which produced the following works: *Lodoïska* (1791), *Eliza ou Le voyage aux glaciers du Mont St-Bernard* (1794), *Médée* (1797), *L'hôtellerie portugaise* (1798), *La punition* (1799) and *Les deux journées* (1800). Work was also begun on *Koukourgi* (1793) but was never finished. The music was later reused and completed as *Ali-Baba ou les quarante voleurs.* In essence, the Théâtre de la rue Feydeau gave Cherubini financial stability and a stage which he used to experiment with the *opéra comique* form.

The first of this series of *opéras comiques, Lodoïska,* was also the first of a shorter series of "rescue" operas which included *Eliza,* and *Les deux journées.* Even *Médée* fits into this category, in which the action culminates with the rescue of one or more of the main protagonists from a sticky situation. Although the libretto of *Lodoïska* was not a masterpiece, the music was beautiful and effective and the stage devices were sensational. Its success was assured because of its flowing vocal lines, its unusually new and expanded orchestral elements, and its romantic plot which seized the imagination of revolutionary Paris by portraying the righteousness of heroism, liberty, and fraternity as opposed to the evilness of tyranny. With this opera, Cherubini embarked on a course of development of the *opéra comique* form which would lead to the eradication of almost all differences between it and *opera seria,* except for the spoken dialogue. The simple strophic ariettes become fully developed emotive arias, the ensemble becomes the norm rather than the exception, and the orchestration acquires symphonic proportions.

This trend continued with *Eliza,* which drew large audiences to view the onstage depiction of an avalanche. The musical numbers are no longer pauses in the plot allowing a character to sing quickly a couple of stanzas expressing his sentiments; they are scintillating with action and display a continuity which sometimes makes the spoken dialogue seem intrusive. This piece is considered by some to be the most consciously romantic of Cherubini's operas. *Médée* was the culmination of this style of Cherubini's dramatic development. In spite of the spoken dialogue, this is musically closer to a true *tragédie lyrique* than most of the works presented at the Académie.

With *Les deux journées,* Cherubini returned to a happier, if less interesting, compositional style, and he experienced a success which he never repeated in his lifetime. This was partly due to the libretto, judged by Beethoven and Goethe to be one of the finest of the period. Beethoven considered Cherubini the greatest living operatic composer based on his knowledge of this opera, and Mendelssohn remarked that the first three bars of the overture were worth more than all of the Berlin opera's repertory. Musically, it was successful because Cherubini conformed to the French concept of the *opéra comique*—short musical numbers with an emphasis on spoken dialogue and ensemble. Only two of the fifteen musical items are arias. Although this was Cherubini's most popular dramatic work, it contains none of the innovations characterizing his other efforts in this genre.

With his move to France, the logical continuation of Cherubini's developments of *opera seria* would be in the exploitation of *tragédie lyrique.* However, he was never able to break into the clique which ruled the tastes of the Académie royale (or impériale) de musique and his three works in the form—*Anacréon* (1803), *Les abencérages ou L'étendard de Grenade* (1813) and *Ali-Baba ou Les quarante voleurs* (1833)—were never successful. As well, Cherubini was unable to overcome two problems of the *tragédie lyrique* form—the use of recitative and the need for ballet, even if it did not fit into the plot. Consequently, all his most important contributions to nineteenth-century opera took place within the mold of *opéra comique.* In fact, almost half a century before Wagner, Cherubini evolved an operatic style which was criticized for being unsingable, unmelodic, for putting emphasis on the orchestra and making it play loudly, and for creating long musical numbers which slowed down the action even if they did underline the emotions and actions of the protagonists.

Although Cherubini stopped composing for the stage almost entirely after 1813, his dramatic sense was evident in other musical forms. His Symphonie (1815), composed for the Royal Philharmonic Society of London, has been described as a play without words. His numerous settings of the Mass continued the operatic tradition begun by Mozart. And his two *Messe des morts* established a new style for this form which culminated in Verdi's *Requiem*. The intrigues of the world of French opera defeated Cherubini but did not stifle the dramatic qualities of his creativity.

Many books and musical dictionaries have mistakenly hypothesized that Cherubini had no effect on future schools of composition. The names of his pupils, friends, and visitors read like a musical Who's Who of the nineteenth century: Bellini, Berlioz, Chopin, Donizetti, Fétis, Halévy, Hérold, Liszt, Mendelssohn, Meyerbeer, Rossini, Schumann, just to mention the most important and obvious. But his influence extended beyond the circle of his personal acquaintances. His developments in *opéra comique* were continued by Halévy (1799-1862) and Hérold (1791-1833) and culminated in Bizet's *Carmen;* in Germany, Carl Maria von Weber (1786-1826) examined every work of Cherubini that he could find, and the new style of *Singspiel* owed its origin in some part to the French master. In the *tragédie lyrique,* Spontini copied most of what his colleague had done, and thus, starting with Rossini and Meyerbeer, a direct link with Romantic Grand Opera, which pervaded the French stage during the mid-nineteenth century, was established. Later musicians who studied Cherubini included Brahms, Bruckner, Bülow and Wagner. German Music Drama, as epitomized by the works of Wagner, can also trace its existence directly to Cherubini.

There are good reasons why Cherubini's works disappeared from European stages after his death, despite their affinity with the romantic era: his *opéras comiques* were soon surpassed by those of his pupils and admirers, and his *tragédies lyriques* were too long and boring to excite much interest, especially after the subsequent reforms of Rossini and Meyerbeer. More importantly, he was unlucky in his librettists, and the music of the majority of his lyric works outdistances their texts. However, it is impossible to study operatic development in the nineteenth century without acknowledging Cherubini's place. A judicious editing of many of his stage compositions would render them agreeable to contemporary ears, thus assuring Cherubini's rightful survival as one of the principal architects of Romantic opera.

—Stephen C. Willis

CHRISTOFF, Boris.

Bass. Born 18 May 1914, in Plovdiv, Bulgaria. Received a law degree from the University of Sofia, then sang with Gussla Choir and Sofia Cathedral Choir where King Boris heard him and provided him with funds to study with Riccardo Stracciari in Rome; later studied with Muratti in Salzburg, 1945; opera debut as Colline in Reggio Calabria, 1946, then sang in Rome at the Teatro alla Scala as Pimen, 1947; U.S. debut in San Francisco as Boris, 1956; Chicago, 1957-63.

Publications

About CHRISTOFF: books–

Barker, F. *Voice of the Opera: Boris Christoff.* London, 1951.
Lauri-Volpi, G. *Voci parallele: Boris Christoff.* Milan, 1955.
Goury, J. *Boris Christoff.* Paris, 1970.

Boris Christoff as King Philip in *Don Carlos*

articles–

Bourgeois, J. "Boris Christoff." *Opera* November (1958).

* * *

In a career that spans from 1946 until well into the 1980s, Bulgarian bass Boris Christoff has sung with most of the major opera companies of the world, with the notable exception of the Metropolitan Opera. His earliest successes occurred in Italy; his debut was as Colline in Puccini's *La bohème* in Reggio Calabria, but his first major roles were as Pimen in Musorgsky's *Boris Godunov* in Rome in 1946 and at the Teatro alla Scala in 1947, and as King Marke at the Teatro la Fenice in Venice in late 1947. He was scheduled to sing King Philip II in Verdi's *Don Carlos* in the inaugural production of Rudolf Bing's regime at the Metropolitan Opera (1950). Christoff was prevented from entering the country, however, because he had a Bulgarian passport (which, under the terms of the McCarthy period's McCarran Act, was an insurmountable problem), and he has never appeared there.

Christoff did, however, sing King Philip at Covent Garden in 1958, and it proved to be one of his most memorable portrayals. His Covent Garden career had begun in 1949, and its problematic beginnings evaporated in the light of his subsequent triumphs there. His first performance, as Boris Godunov, was preceded by three conflicts that threatened its cancelation: Christoff insisted on singing the role in Russian (in the event, the rest of the cast sang in English, even though mixed-language performances were contrary to policy);

Christoff knew, and insisted on following, the Rimsky-Korsakov version of the score (he was allowed to employ this version while the rest of the cast followed the original Musorgsky); and he disagreed with director Peter Brook—not his only disagreement with a director—over several aspects of the staging, including a giant clock that he feared would dwarf his own efforts (general manager David Webster's intervention was needed to appease Christoff). Christoff's career came to a temporary halt in 1964 when it was discovered that he was suffering from a brain tumor, but Covent Garden was the first to rehire him, in 1965, for another Boris.

Musorgsky's tsar also served as the role of Christoff's San Francisco debut in 1956. He made frequent appearances in Chicago between 1957 and 1963, including performances of Verdi's *Don Carlos* in 1957 and Verdi's *Nabucco* in 1963. His New York debut came in a concert version of Rossini's *Mosè*.

Many considered Christoff to be Chaliapin's successor. Like that of his great Slavic predecessor, Christoff's singing was marked by an authority and an intensity, as well as substantial theatricality. It was a well-schooled, sonorous voice of substantial size, powerful and imposing, with a true legato, but it was not a richly honeyed, Italianate sound (the voice was a bit lacking in the warmth characteristic of that style). Despite this, he became a notable interpreter of Verdi's bass roles (he was more successful in this repertoire than Chaliapin had been), including, in addition to Zaccaria and King Philip, Ramfis in Verdi's *Aida*, Fiesco in *Simon Boccanegra*, and Procida in *Les vêpres siciliennes*. Other roles include Agamemnon in Gluck's *Ifigenia in Aulide*, Oroveso in Bellini's *Norma*, Count Rodolfo in Bellini's *La sonnambula*, Seneca in Monteverdi's *L'incoronazione di Poppea*, Méphistophélès in Gounod's *Faust*, Rocco in Beethoven's *Fidelio*, Gurnemanz in Wagner's *Parsifal*, Handel's Giulio Cesare, Massenet's Don Quichotte, and Boito's Mefistofele.

Voluminous but not especially large, Christoff's voice had the distinctive character frequently associated with Slavic singers. It possessed an inherent dignity and nobility that were significant assets in his portrayals of kings and tsars. To this was added an ability simultaneously to convey menace and evoke sympathy. Besides his apparent technical command and his exemplary breath control, Christoff had substantial stage presence, was capable of realistic acting, and demonstrated an admirable ability to project the text. Much of his acting was distinguished by its naturalness, its authority, and especially by its introspective quality. Only occasionally, as in his traversal of the role of Méphistophélès in *Faust*, was he guilty of exaggeration, even overacting.

Christoff's impersonation of King Philip II was perhaps his greatest role. It offered him the opportunity to demonstrate his ability to portray a multidimensional character, distinguishing between the public and private sides of the man. It also exhibited, in the great monologue "Ella giammai m'amo . . . Dormirò sol nel manto mio regal," his ability to produce a sustained pianissimo line, conveying the introspection and revealing the most personal thoughts of the character. It showed Christoff's ability to convey the sadness and resignation of the character as well as his essential nobility in a detailed, well-rounded portrait of the king.

In addition to numerous recordings of individual arias, Christoff participated in several recordings of complete operas. These include Fiesco (under Santini, 1957); Philip II (under Santini, 1954, 1961); Ramfis (under Perlea, 1955);

Méphistophélès (under Cluytens, 1954, 1958); Pimen, Varlaam, and Boris in the same recording (1952, under Dobrowen; 1962, under Cluytens); and Galitzky and Konchak in Borodin's *Prince Igor* (1967, under Semkow).

—Michael Sims

CHRISTOPHE COLOMB [Christopher Columbus].

Composer: Darius Milhaud.

Librettist: Paul Claudel.

First Performance: Berlin, State Opera, 5 May 1930.

Roles: Columbus (baritone); Isabella (soprano); Narrator (speaking); Accuser (speaking); Messenger (speaking); Steward (tenor); Master of Ceremonies (tenor); Cook (tenor); King of Spain (bass); several lesser roles, many from chorus.

Publications

article–

Knapp, Bettina. "Paul Claudel's *The Diary of Christopher Columbus*: a Demiurge Journeys Forth." *Theatrical Journal* 33 (1981): 145.

*   *   *

The encounter of the two remarkable creative personalities, Paul Claudel and Darius Milhaud, led to the creation of many works of art that were more than just a sum total of poetry and music. Claudel's mysticism and Catholic piety found their complement in Milhaud's humanism and Jewish sensibility. The result was a matching of superb poetic and musical technique with the most profound and multi-faceted emotional insight. Nowhere is the effect of this collaboration more evident than in *Christophe Colomb*, one of Milhaud's landmark compositions.

With five operas behind him, Milhaud had already begun to collaborate with Franz Werfel on *Maximilien* when Claudel approached him with the first part of his Columbus drama. Milhaud immediately concentrated all his artistic resources on the composition of the opera, which he completed within the year.

Claudel presents Columbus partly as an historic figure, partly as allegory, and partly as a religious symbol. The opera has no plot as such. Rather, Claudel probes and Milhaud illumines the journey of a soul inspired by God, encumbered with the pettiness of mankind, tortured by its own flaws, and finally proved worthy of redemption. A few historical episodes lend a framework to scenes in which imagery, symbolism, and dialectic embellish the underlying concept of the play.

The numerous scenes are grouped into two acts (whose order of performance is open to question). One act carries most of the dramatic action and includes a scene at the Inn at Valladolid just before Columbus' death; an encounter with a personified "posterity" that welcomes him to eternal glory and invites him to review the events of his life; a visit to the court of the King of Spain where he is met by Envy, Ignorance, Vanity, and Avarice; and scenes showing him recruiting the sailors, confronting their mutiny, and eventually reaching land. The other act is mostly allegorical. After the King and his advisors assess Columbus' accomplishments, Columbus is seen returning in chains from the West Indies, where he has been deposed as governor. He holds to the mast throughout the fury of a storm as he has held to his purpose against all odds. The next scenes show him beseiged by conscience and by the knowledge that his accomplishments were only partial. Finally, he lies dying at Valladolid. Everything worldly has been stripped from him.

Four scenes revolve around the mystical relationship between Columbus and Queen Isabella, who is shown as a child who places her ring on the foot of a dove and then sets it free. Then, in an intensely religious episode, Saint James, the patron saint of Spain, reminds her that the same ring is now on Columbus' finger and she must send him forth as she did the dove of her childhood. Finally, there are the scenes of her funeral and of her entry into Paradise where she prepares a place for Columbus. Claudel makes a great deal of the symbolism implied in Columbus' name. He is both Christ-bearer (Christopher) and recipient of God's grace (the colombe, or dove, being a symbol of the Holy Spirit).

Controversy surrounds the order in which the two acts should be presented. As originally conceived, the more dramatic of the two came first, followed by the allegorical one. Whereas intellectually this seems the best arrangement, on stage this sequence appeared anti-climactic. In the 1950s, author and composer agreed to reverse the order. A 1984 Marseilles Opera production, however, returned the opera to its original version, apparently with great success.

No matter which order is adopted, the fact remains that the disparity between the two parts and the great variety of subject matter within each act, as well as the wordiness of much of the libretto, presented very special challenges to the composer. Milhaud responded with a score that contrasts complexity and simplicity, massive orchestral sound and chamber orchestra sonority, soaring melody and spoken declamation. A narrator provides a continuing thread, as does the use of a chorus that sometimes comments on, sometimes takes part in the action and often serves as a tribunal. There is tremendous vigor to the music, from the use of percussion underlying the spoken passages, to the introduction of almost folk-like melodies and dance rhythms, the arching, ephemeral vocal lines, the powerful choral interjections, and the sheer brilliance of the composer's imagination in suiting musical material to emotional content. Visually, too, the opera is enormously attractive. Scenes change rapidly, and opportunities for lavish stage effects and costuming abound. The use of film projections adds to the mystical feeling of the work.

—Jane Hohfeld Galante

CHRISTOPHER COLUMBUS
See CHRISTOPHE COLOMB

CHURCH PARABLES.

Composer: Benjamin Britten.

Librettist: William Plomer.

Curlew River
First Performance, Orford Church, Suffolk, 12 June 1964.
The Burning Fiery Furnace
First Performance, Orford Church, Suffolk, 9 June 1966.
The Prodigal Son
First Performance, Orford Church, Suffolk, 10 June 1968.

Publications

article–

Mitchell, D. "Britten's Church Parables." In *Aldeburgh Anthology,* edited by R. Blythe. Aldeburgh, 1972.

*   *   *

Britten, working in collaboration with his librettist, William Plomer, did not conceive *Curlew River* as forming the first part of a trilogy. This should condition our expectations when we consider the three "Parables for Church Performance" as a group. Coming to Wagner's *Ring,* for example, we know that we are about to be presented with an organic sequence of music dramas chronologically arranged and with an integrated leitmotif system that binds the four operas together. The *Church Parables,* on the other hand, may be viewed as quite separate and discrete variations on a musico-dramatic form that is established in *Curlew River,* each with its own vocal characterization and distinctive chamber orchestra sound. They are companion pieces rather than an organic entity, sharing certain conventions derived from the Japanese No drama *Sumidagawa,* which Britten had seen in Tokyo in January 1956. As Britten's programme note to the first production explained, "The whole occasion made a tremendous impression upon me: the simple, touching story, the economy of the style, the intense slowness of the action, the marvelous skill and control of the performers, the beautiful costumes, the mixture of chanting, speech, singing which, with the three instruments, made up the strange music—it all offered a totally new 'operatic' experience."

Curlew River is the miraculous story of a madwoman in search of her lost son who regains her sanity on beholding the vision of his spirit at the place where he died. It is presented by an all-male cast in the form of a priestly ritual. Its two successors, *The Burning Fiery Furnace* and *The Prodigal Son,* arguably less austere but no less concentrated and ritualistically objective in style, are based on the well-known Bible stories from the Old and New Testaments. If *The Burning Fiery Furnace,* taking its point of departure from the bright D major of the plainsong 'Salus aeterna' is something of a colorful, exuberant divertissement based on the defiant stand of Shadrach, Meshach, and Abednego at the court of King Nebuchadnezzar in sixth-century B.C. Babylon, then *The Prodigal Son* is a contemplative meditation on peace and forgiveness that is memorably symbolized by the father's twin sound-image of plain B-flat major chord and alto flute arabesque. While it remains open to question whether the three works are heard to advantage in a continuous presentation, any full appreciation must take its bearings from *Curlew River,* considered by some to be the strongest member of the trilogy.

The Oriental origins of *Curlew River* present a subject of great fascination, but Britten and his librettist William Plomer intended a complete transformation of the original model for their English audience. In the process of transformation it became a new genre rooted in the idea of a revival of the English medieval religious drama for church performance at Orford. On the face of things this may seem rather parochial, but any one familiar with Britten's output knows his genius to invest the local with universal import. And it was typical of his always unpretentiously practical approach that a radically new departure in his work (a necessary reaction, perhaps, to the epic scale of the *War Requiem*) should have found its stimulus in the very limitations of performing conditions in Britten's own corner of rural England, far removed from those obtaining in centers of metropolitan culture. Britten's music has always thrived on limitations. If the *Church Parables* have a direct precedent in his oeuvre it is to be found in two works which likewise used limited vocal and instrumental resources and which took into account the acoustic properties of the buildings in which they were to be performed. These are *Noye's Fludde* (Orford, 1957) and the cantata *St Nicholas* (Aldeburgh Parish Church, 1948). Both these works involved audience participation in the hymns. There is no such participation in *Curlew River*, but the audience is made to feel part of the drama from the outset through the processional plainsong, through the shared courtesy of priestly ritual which proceeds to enact for our enlightenment a "sign of God's good grace." And the audience continues to feel a sense of involvement through the ceremonial preparation, the donning of masks, costumes, the return at the end to monk's habits, and the recessional. Nor is the orchestra separated from the stage as in the opera house, but the musicians go to their instruments on the acting area. (Indeed, the orchestra becomes portable and is heard literally "in the round" in *The Burning Fiery Furnace,* where there is the brilliant spatial effect of the music accompanying the worship of Merodak actually moving round the church.)

The *Church Parables*, as already stated, depend on a theater of strict conventions of form and musico-dramatic gesture, and these conventions are established in *Curlew River*. Take, for example, the "triple frame" of Plainsong, Abbot's invocation with chorus (a convention that is dramatically broken at the beginning of *The Prodigal Son*), and the ceremonial music which is given in reverse at the end. Together they make a small symmetrical form, for the ritual music of the ceremonial preparation is a treatment of the plainsong melody in which its notes are played by the orchestra in free-sounding nonalignment over a regular percussion ostinato. This so-called "heterophony" (anticipated as early in Britten's music as the *Sinfonia da Requiem, Paul Bunyan* and the *Ceremony of Carols*) is fundamental to the style of the *Church Parables* and, adopted in parts of *Owen Wingrave* and much of *Death in Venice,* becomes something of a late-style fingerprint. (Heterophony, by the way, was not an exoticism in Britten's music, but grew out of a natural liking for the sound of major seconds before he even began to take the techniques of Oriental music seriously.)

Britten was concerned with the necessity of convention, restraint, and ritual in his music. The *Church Parables*, conceived during a period in Western music of radical reappraisal, represent Britten's own reappraisal of methods and means that could lead to a sharper realization of his vision of high ideals in conflict with the powers of darkness. Their God-seeking and (in the first and last parables) essentially Christian message is characteristic of a composer who, like Shostakovich, believed in music as a moral force. (*The Prodigal Son* is dedicated to Shostakovich.) This aim is strengthened by the emphasis Britten places on the control of feeling by form, the importance to him of a stylistic objectivity that after the excesses of Romanticism and subjectivity in art always seemed to him worth striving for. (In this there is a strong affinity with Stravinsky's aesthetic.) The tonal/rhythmic freedom and fluidity of this music certainly represents an escape from traditional Western concepts of formal control through meter, tonality, sonata forms, etc. But, miraculously, Britten's own technical control is as strict, as precisely imagined in terms of sound, as ever, despite the freedoms allowed to the performers. In this respect, Britten is as progressive an artist as any of his time, freeing music from the threat of the over-exercise of individual power, questioning the surrender demanded by the (narcotic?) Wagnerian aesthetic of art and releasing the creativity latent in all of us. The *Church Parables*, despite their Oriental provenance, are also a reminder of Britten's essential modesty and generous acknowledgement of his debt to the whole of Western music. Taking in their sweep a range of reference that goes back to the very origins of music in our culture, this trilogy of one-act "church operas" represents a reconstitution of music as a language that remains contemporary in essence without the avant garde's arrogance of rejecting the past, a music that is simple in expression yet subtly made and deeply organic.

—Eric Roseberry

CICERI, Pierre-Luc-Charles.

Designer. Born 17 August 1782, in Saint-Cloud, France. Died 22 August 1868, in Saint-Chéron, Seine-et-Oise. Trained as a singer at the Paris Conservatoire, began instruction in drawing and painting under stage designer F.J. Belanger, 1802; entered Paris Opéra studio as *peintre des paysages,* 1806; accepted as one of the *peintres en chef* around 1818; became virtual head of group from 1824-47; founded commercial scenic studio, 1822; incorporated progressive techniques into settings such as gas lighting in *Aladin ou La lampe merveilleuse,* 1822; the new panorama and diorama in *Alfred le Grand,* 1822; the moving panorama in *La belle au bois dormant,* 1829; and a volcanic eruption in *La muette de Portici,* 1828.

Opera Productions (Selected)

Olimpie, Paris, Opéra, 1819 (with Eugenio Degotti).
Aladin ou La lampe merveilleuse, Paris, Opéra, 1822 (with Louis Daguerre).
Don Sanche, Paris, Opéra, 1825.
La muette de Portici, Paris, Opéra, 1828.
Le Comte Ory, Paris, Opéra, 1828.
Guillaume Tell, Paris, Opéra, 1829.
Manon Lescaut, Paris, Opéra, 1830.
Robert le diable, Paris, Opéra, 1831.

Publications

About CICERI: books–

Allevy, M.-A. *La mise en scène en France dans la première moitié du dix-neuvième siècle.* Paris, 1938.

Guest, Ivor. *The Romantic Ballet in France.* London, 1966.

Carlson, Marvin. *The French Stage in the Nineteenth Century.* Metuchen, New Jersey, 1972.

Crosten, William. *French Grand Opera: An Art and a Business.* New York, 1972.

Fulcher, Jane. *Nation's Image: French Grand Opera as Politics and As Politicized Art.* New York, 1987.

articles–

Blumer, M.L. "Pierre-Luc-Charles Ciceri." In *Dictionaire de biographie française.* Paris, 1933.

Guest, Ivor. "Pierre Ciceri." *Ballet and Opera 7* (1949).

Chevalley, S. "L'atelier Philastre et Cambon et la Comédie Française." In *Anatomy of an Illusion: 4th International Congress on Theatre Research: Amsterdam 1965,* 13.

Cohen-Stratyner, Barbara Naomi. "Ciceri, Pierre-Luc-Charles." In *Biographical Dictionary of Dance.* New York, 1982.

Pierre-Luc-Charles Ciceri is generally acknowledged as the primary trend-setter of Romantic stage art, especially in French grand opera. His set for Halévy's *Manon Lescaut* in 1830 led Théophile Gautier to declare that the "time of purely ocular spectacles has come." According to William Crosten, Ciceri's sets for *La muette de Portici* and *Robert le diable* "became the standards by which other works were judged."

A contemporary review of *Robert le diable* in *Le Journal de Débats* (23 November, 1831) noted that "the *mise en scène* of this opera cost nearly 200,000 francs; but it is money well spent." Chopin, who had just arrived in Paris that fall, wrote home to Tytus Woyciechowski : "I don't know whether there has ever been such magnificence in a theatre, whether it has ever before attained to the pomp of the new five-act opera 'Robert le Diable'. . . . It is a masterpiece of the new school, in which devils sing through speaking-trumpets, and souls rise from graves; in which there is a diorama in the theatre, in which at the end you see the *intérieur* of a church, the whole church, at Christmas or Easter, lighted up, with monks, and all the congregation on the benches, and censors—even with the organ . . . nothing of the sort could be put on anywhere else."

Recent reevaluation of Ciceri's achievement has placed his work in a sociopolitical context. Marvin Carlson (*The French Stage,* 1972) found that Ciceri's "career suggested in miniature the changing tastes of the period." Jane Fulcher (*Nation's Image: French Grand Opera as Politics and as Politicized Art,* 1987) speculated that his staging style, which drew on populist boulevard theater techniques, attempted to transform the essentially conservative opera form into a more democratic ideal.

—Kiko Nobusawa

CICOGNINI, Giacinto Andrea.

Librettist. Born 1606, in Florence. Died 1651, in Venice. Son of the playwright and actor Jacopo Cicognini; also wrote prose tragedies and comedies; transformed plays by Spanish dramatists, including Calderón, into Italian dramas and librettos.

Librettos (selected)

Il Celio, 1646, Baglioni and Sapiti; *Il Giasone,* 1649, Cavalli; *L'Orontea,* 1649, Cesti; *Gli amori di Alessandro Magneo e di Rossane* (unfinished; subsequently set by Luci, 1651, Ferrari, 1656, and Boretti, 1667).

Publications

About CICOGNINI: books–

Grashey, L. *Giacinto Andrea Cicogninis Leben und Werke, unter besonderer Berücksichtigung seines Dramas 'La Marienne ovvero il maggior mostro del mondo'.* Leipzig, 1909.

Verde, R. *G.A. Cicognini.* Catania, 1912.

articles–

Holmes, W.C. "Giacinto Andrea Cicognini's and Antonio Cesti's *Orontea* (1649)." In *New Looks at Italian Opera: Essays in Honor of Donald J. Grout,* Ithaca, 1968.

As the author of the libretto to Cavalli's opera *Giasone,* likely the most popular and widely performed of all seventeenth-century operas, Cicognini was one of the creators of a style of libretto that would dominate the opera of Venice—and thus much of the rest of Europe—for the second half of the seventeenth century. Yet, the critical dilemma surrounding Cicognini's librettos results from the general censure to which this style of libretto has long been subjected, instigated perhaps by this famous passage penned by the eighteenth-century poet Giovanni Crescembeni, member of the Arcadian Academy:

"Around the middle of that century, Giacinto Andrea Cicognini[. . .]introduced drama with his *Giasone,* which, to tell the truth is the first and the most perfect drama there is; and with it he brought the end of acting and consequently, of true and good comedy as well as tragedy. Since to stimulate to a greater degree with novelty the jaded taste of the spectators, equally nauseated by the vileness of comic things and the seriousness of tragic ones, the inventor of drama united them, mixing kings and heroes and other illustrious personages with buffoons and servants and the lowest men with unheard of monstrousness. This concoction of characters was the reason for the complete ruin of poetry, which went so far into disuse that not even locution was considered, which, forced to serve music, lost its purity and became filled with idiocies" (translation by Ellen Rosand).

It is likely that Crescembeni attaches both too much credit and too much blame to Cicognini; nevertheless, his observations are not without some validity. Cicognini's librettos are a masterful blend of the numerous devices that intrigued, fascinated, and pleased opera audiences, contributing to the enormous commercial success enjoyed by the young genre in Venice and elsewhere. Unlike many of his fellow-librettists, Cicognini was first and foremost a highly successful playwright. Two of his librettos, *Giasone* and *Gli amori di Alessandro Magneo e di Rossane,* existed as plays prior to their musical setting. Cicognini was likely one of the more important links between the Spanish theater and the Venetian opera libretto. His accomplishments included, for example, the Italian translation of Calderon de la Barca's *Life is a Dream.* Indeed, the combination of comedy and tragedy and variety of verse forms which so disconcerted Crescembeni and his fellow Arcadians may in part be attributed to this Spanish influence.

The libretto to *Giasone* contains many elements that appear in numerous other librettos of the period. As with other Venetian librettos based on myth or history, *Giasone* is far from faithful to its classical source. We first view the heroic Jason in bed after a passionate night with Medea (who has remained disguised to him throughout the year long liaison, despite having born him twins). Like many a mid-seventeenth century Venetian hero, Jason neglects his heroic responsibilities for the delights of love, thus earning Hercule's ridicule for his "weak effeminate nature," and relying upon the women characters for his physical and moral strength. Medea's magic power leads Jason to victory, and it is his abandoned wife Hypsiphyle who lays claim to dignity and moral stature. As can be seen in his popular *L'Orontea,* set by Antonio Cesti, Cicognini—like his fellow librettists—adds secondary plot lines with comic characters, including such stock Venetian favorites as the stuttering drunk and the elderly, sexually frustrated nurse. Yet despite the claims of Crescembeni and other critics, these secondary plots and comic characters do not function solely to provide comic relief or pander to popular taste. Rather, they add to the drama a second layer that often parodies the central action, thereby interpreting and commenting upon its meaning for the audience. The varied verse forms employed by Cicognini to express the differences among these characters were of fundamental importance in the development of an increasingly varied aria style that characterized the operas of Cesti and Cavalli.

Cicognini's undignified treatment of myth and rejection of Aristotelean unities undoubtedly offended Crescembeni and his colleagues. Yet, like many other librettists, Cicognini was only slightly abashed in his description of the straightforward nature of his aesthetic goals. "I write out of mere whim; my whim has no other aim than to give pleasure. To bring pleasure to myself is nothing other than to accommodate the inclination and taste of those who listen or read." In this aim, Cicognini and his contemporaries apparently succeeded.

—Wendy Heller

LE CID.

Composer: Jules Massenet.

Librettists: Adolphe Philippe d'Ennery, Louis Gallet, and Edouard Blau (after Corneille).

First Performance: Paris, Opéra, 30 November 1885.

Roles: Chimène (soprano); The Infanta (soprano); Don Rodrigue (tenor); Don Diègue (bass); Don Fernand, The King (baritone); Don Gomès (bass); Saint Jacques (baritone); The Moorish Ambassador (bass); Don Arias (tenor); Don Alonzo (bass); chorus.

Publications

book—

Hanslick, E. *Musikalisches und Litterarisches,* 79 ff. Berlin, 1889.

*   *   *

Le Cid followed immediately after Massenet's great triumph with *Manon,* and, for a time, rivaled it in popularity, although by the early years of this century it had begun to flag and eventually disappeared from the repertory. This is probably because, despite its contemporary success, it is something of a hybrid and suffers from an inadequate libretto. There have been at least twenty-six operas based on the Spanish national hero, many of them Italian, including one by Paisiello whose attempt on the Cid was to be outdistanced by Massenet.

The libretto for *Le Cid* is based on a French source, the great classical tragedy by Corneille. The three librettists interpolated many of the poet's original lines into their own dialogue. Additionally, Massenet insisted on putting in not only an extra scene inspired by his reading of the work but also a fifth act of another tragedy which he rescued from the bottom

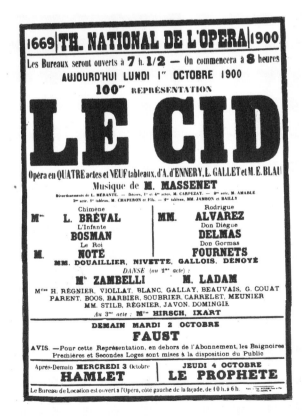

AFFICHE DE LA 100ᵉ DU « CID ».

A poster for the 100th performance of Massenet's *Le Cid*, Paris, 1900

of a drawer somewhere. The result is a plot of clumsy dimensions and clumsier language, where Corneille's stolen gems shine all the more incongruously for being surrounded with paste of the most derisory nature.

Massenet was probably not the ideal choice for composing an opera on this subject. Much of the opera's initial success was due to the brilliance of the stars Jean and Edouard De Reszke, the two brothers who had served Massenet well before, and of Fidès Devriès as the heroine Chimène. Quite apart, however, from the shortcomings of the libretto, the music is rarely at one with the setting and the characterization. Heroic attitudes and Castilian haughtiness were strangers to Massenet's music. He lacked ability to convey the fierce and passionate emotions which *Le Cid* demanded, and his insight into Spanish music was by no means as profound as Debussy's or even Bizet's. All that remains today of *Le Cid* is the showpiece aria "Pleurez, pleurez mes yeux," sung by Chimène. Yet even this, effective as it is when considered in isolation, is not wholly appropriate, for, while it is neatly written in the style of *Manon,* it strikes a false note in a score which ought to be striving for something else.

One other legacy of *Le Cid* may be mentioned, and that is the suite of ballet music which was drawn from it and which may still be heard today. It is an appealing example of Massenet's gift for light music and for the picturesque. He heard the tune of the *Castillane* while traveling in Spain as a young student, and, faithful to his thrifty habit, carefully noted it down. Guitars and flutes had played the theme to accompany a wedding celebration, and he had already used it, though less adroitly, in his second opera, *Don César de Bazan.* If, on the whole, *Le Cid* is not an example of Massenet at his best, at least one fine aria and a charming ballet suite survive.

—James Harding

CIGNA, Gina.

Soprano. Born 6 March 1900, in Angères. Studied at the Paris Conservatory; debut at Teatro alla Scala, 1927; sang there every season from 1929 to 1943; Metropolitan Opera debut as Aida, 1937; returned to Milan as a voice teacher; abandoned her singing career following an automobile accident in 1947; taught at the Royal Conservatory in Toronto, 1953-57.

*　　*　　*

Gina Cigna reigned the opera stages of Italy and beyond during the 1930s. Between her debut at La Scala in 1927 and an automobile accident that ended her stage career in 1947, she specialized in heavy, dramatic Italian heroines, particularly those of Verdi and Puccini, Mascagni and Zandonai, Giordano and Ponchielli.

Her debut as Aida at New York's Metropolitan Opera was broadcast in February 1937. The performance was representative of Gina Cigna at midpoint in her career. We hear from her a serious, concentrated, controlled, often exciting performance, an honest, restrained, somewhat generalized dramatic intensity. Her voice is a naturally clean, sensitively colored instrument with a sound redolent of trumpets and violas, modulated by a prominent, pleasing vibrato. She demonstrates an alertness to pulse and rhythm in setting a context

for careful shaping of phrases, draping upon that scaffold a simple, unforced, natural-sounding rubato.

Cigna's voice was not always perfectly even and connected throughout its range. She would at times exploit the break between the middle and lower registers, pouncing on that low note and relishing it with a growl for a dramatic effect. As Cigna's career progressed, those notes would tend more often to escape capture. She would on occasion simplify a low fioratura, covering it with a stylized, aspirant, dramatic "point."

An example of a positive employment of Cigna's vocal articulations can be heard in her rendition of "Morrò, ma prima in grazia," from *Ballo in maschera,* in which Amelia is waiting to be put to death at the hands of her husband as punishment for a supposed infidelity. A hardening of tone on the low notes at the ends of phrases, a subtle sharpening of the rhythm pointing to these cadences conveys, beyond sadness and desolation, an underlying bitterness, resentment, and strength in the character. This impression is a result of Cigna's deliberate interpretive choices.

One of Cigna's most celebrated roles was as Bellini's Norma. Considering today her account of that part can perhaps teach us something of the performance values of a past era. In the aria "Casta diva," while the singing is often beautiful, it is not universally so. We don't hear her sustaining a smooth, even, controlled legato. The long line is subdivided into shorter phrases of characteristically Verdian length, although each of these phrases is endowed with definition and vitality. But the voice as a whole seems not to be supported, tones are not sustained, and dynamics are not controlled according to the tenets of *bel canto* familiar to us. An important element of Bellini's expressive universe is compromised.

Norma's soliloqy in which she contemplates murdering her children is potent and splendid as delivered by Gina Cigna, a valid and consistent interpretation in its context, but not as highly inflected—not hair-raising—as we can hear from other divas. Arguably, Cigna's most satisfactory work in *Norma* comes out in the ensembles. Here her singing is focussed, deliberate, responsive; earnest and intense, intelligent, she listens to the performance around her. Her character stands out in these conflicts and contrasts. It is an integrated conception: with the conductor, she imparts a monumentality that serves the performing ensemble and the piece as a whole rather than primarily advancing the character of a particular *prima donna.* It also serves a particular conception of opera as a form of musical drama, a conception that deemphasizes the role of the beautiful voice in favor of what that voice might express, something more sensational, perhaps more accessible to that audience.

It is probably easier to hear Cigna's interpretive strengths in the later, more overtly dramatic composers who point to *verismo*—a different musical style in which the contrasting emotions are simple, ardent, clearly laid out, together with more directed, less ornamented melodic shapes and more fluid musical forms.

When Cigna's Gioconda sings to us of her impending "Suicidio!" a hot, contained rage sears across the footlights, but with such mastery of vocal resources, with such flexibility, craft, and impetus, that the aria gains a generative nature, the momentum of which carries us through the final act. As Cigna's Gioconda shows us many faces among complex emotional layers, these she will also present to her protagonists in the remaining thirty minutes of the opera.

In "La mamma morta" from *Andrea Chénier,* Maddalena recounts her mother's murder at the hands of the Revolution, flight with her maid and subsequent adversities, and finally describes a benediction bestowed by a celestial voice personifying her earthly love. These shifts of contrasting mood and meaning are depicted by Gina Cigna with striking clarity through musical means—modulating tone, tempo, consonants, vowels, discarding pitch altogether for a line or two when appropriate for expressing the agitated sense of the text, all used to express unspeakable (but singable) loss and despair, a turbulent journey from innocence to worldliness through pain and fear. She achieves a sense of resolution and closure in the final lyrical section by increasing her vocal weight and expanding the tone, creating a second voice for this second section of the aria.

We can see from these examples—and others in which she demonstrates a gorgeously controlled and inflected cantabile—that she had the vocal resources and intelligence to control her interpretive options, at least early on in her career. It is in this context that we consider the centrality of the role of Turandot in her career. Cigna's detached, intellectual, idealized sense of "dramatic" expression she so often projects in many ways weaves through the fundamental conception of Puccini's *Turandot* as opera; this is an illustration of several currents of aesthetic elements coinciding in a single event. *Turandot* was considered New Music at that time.

Her characterization of the Princess is imperious, competitive, hugely scaled, gestures tremendous, appropriate for a festival occasion. Part of our thrill in this spectacle may be inadvertent, based on our awareness that Cigna's control over her voice is not absolute. The sense of latent vulnerability resounds in the real-life soprano as well as the stage character, all contributing to our experience of suspense in the outcome of the Riddle contest.

The core in Turandot's part is her narrative "In questa reggia," the still center of the opera where the drama reposes for a short while, plot and motivations are explained, and the stage is reset, literally and figuratively, for the subsequent conflict to take off again. The form and meaning in this aria are shifting, restless, linear, in which an ancient history and the present of the opera performance, as well as constant vertical layers of meaning, interchange consecutively but freely, all through the voice of the soprano. Gina Cigna presents these various moods in many ways as a series of masks, each powerfully and richly portrayed, yet revealed statically, one by one. Here the externalized sense of drama is made clear, in which stage histrionics begin to take on independent meanings of their own, and all reverberating, through performer and audience, across experience and memory, against all the other grand, controlled, stylized gestures—in other performances, in other operas—this soprano has shared with us.

—Michael Cherniss

CILÈA, Francesco.

Composer. Born 23 July 1866, in Palmi, Calabria. Died 20 November 1950, in Varazze. Studied piano with Beniamino Cesi and composition with Paolo Serrao at the San Pietro di Majella Conservatory in Naples, 1881-89; knight of the Order of the Crown of Italy, 1893; piano teacher at the Naples conservatory, 1894-96; taught harmony at the Istituto Musicale in Florence, 1896-1904; member of the Reale Accademia Musicale in Florence, 1898; head of the Bellini Conservatory

in Palermo, 1913-16; director of the San Pietro di Majella Conservatory in Naples, 1916-35.

Operas

Publisher: Sonzogno.

Gina, Enrico Golisciani, Naples, Conservatory, 9 February 1889.
La Tilda, Angelo Zanardini ["A. Graziani"], Florence, Pagliano, 7 April 1892.
L'arlesiana, L. Marenco (after Alphonse Daudet), Milan, Lirico, 27 November 1897; revised 1898, 1910, 1937.
Adriana Lecouvreur, Arturo Colautti (after Scribe and Legouvé), Milan, Lirico, 6 November 1902.
Gloria, Arturo Colautti, Milan, Teatro alla Scala, 15 April 1907; revised 1932 (with libretto revisions by E. Moschini).
Il matrimonio selvaggio, G. di Bognasco, 1909 [not performed].
La rosa di Pompei, E. Moschini [unfinished].

Other works: chamber music, piano music.

Publications

About CILÈA: books–

Moschini, Ettore. *Sulle opere di Francesco Cilea.* Milan, 1932.
Gaianus, Cesare Paglia. *Francesco Cilea e la sua nuova ora.* Bologna-Rocca S. Casciano, 1939.
Rensis, R. de. *Francesco Cilea.* Palmi, 1950.
Amico, T.d'. *Francesco Cilea.* Milan, 1960.
Nicolasen, Jay. *Italian Opera in Transition, 1871-1893.* Ann Arbor, 1980.

articles–

Olivero, Magda. "Cilea and *Adriana Lecouvreur.*" *Opera* July (1963).
Klein, John W. "Cilea—A Centenary Tribute." *Opera* July (1966).
Nicolaisen, Jay. "Cilèa's 'Lamento di Federico' and the Puccinian Aria." *Musical Newsletter* 7/no. 4 (1977): 20.
Carpitella, Diego. "Populismo, nazionalismo e italianità nelle avanguardie musicali italiane." *Chigiana* 35 (1982): 59.

* * *

Modest, shy, and retiring, Francesco Cilèa was a conscientious musician who, on first appearances, would seem to have been suited by temperament more to academic than to theater life. As happened to so many composers-to-be, his family wished to see him in a career in law or medicine, but Cilèa was attracted early to music, his motivation supported by his maternal aunt's tenacious approval of the boy's desires. Overcoming opposition, he entered the San Pietro di Majella conservatory in Naples in 1881. His greatest inspiration there was Francesco Florimo, the librarian as well as a teacher, who also helped reconcile Cilèa's family to the boy's aim of having a musical career. Among other teachers particularly influencing the future composer were Cesi, Serrao, and Martucci. Cilèa proceeded rapidly and steadily in his studies, and, while still pursuing them, he became a student master, the first step along the way to his later calling as an educator. In 1889 he graduated, but straightforth became an auxiliary professor of harmony and piano, thereby launching his long professional teaching career, in which he achieved much distinction quite apart from his accomplishments as a composer.

Cilèa's first opera, an idyll in three acts to Enrico Golisciani's text, was a student work, *Gina,* first given 9 February 1889 at the conservatory in Naples. This score already was notable for the warmth, refinement, and fresh, copious melody that would characterize Cilèa's mature works. It also drew the attention of Edoardo Sonzogno, the publisher, who encouraged Cilèa to set *Tilda* (three acts, libretto by Angelo Zanardini writing under the pseudonym "A. Graziani"). *Tilda* was first mounted at the Teatro Pagliano in Florence on 7 March 1892 and quickly made a modest rounds of some theaters in and outside Italy. *Tilda* was a full-fledged work in the *verismo* idiom, remaining, however, the only one of the composer's stage works that could be so described. Tilda herself, in this mode of theatrical realism, is a prostitute, whose self-denying efforts to save her rival result in her own stabbing. The subject was not truly congenial to Cilèa's inclinations as a composer, and he had not yet developed the skill in composition to surmount the hurdle of setting such a subject convincingly. His last staged work, *Gloria,* itself on a stiff and conventional subject little to Cilèa's bent, was an artistic success despite its libretto, due to the composer's acquired skill and stagecraft, but *Tilda* was too premature to so succeed.

With his next libretto, however, Cilèa found a text ideally suited to his particular dramatic gifts. Leopoldo Marenco based his libretto for *L'Arlesiana* on Alphonse Daudet's French play, *L'Arlésienne.* Although ostensibly about matters of love and passion among people of humble origin, concerns true to the *verismo* movement's charter of realism, the libretto provided Cilèa the many moments of intimacy and reflection best calculated to engage his real sympathies and his talent for elegiac expression. Premiered in 4 acts in Milan on 27 February 1897, it appeared at the same theater, the Teatro Lirico, in a three act revision, with greater success, on 22 October 1898. Cilèa undertook the revision due to pressure from Sonzogno's firm, which was manifesting a lack of enthusiasm in promoting the work, but the changes were at the expense of the music's integrity.

Cilèa kept working away at the score of *L'Arlesiana* over the years, in 1910 restoring some of the music previously cut, and *L'Arlesiana* began to approach its familiar form by the time of the 1912 revival at the Teatro San Carlo, Naples. Cilèa added the aria, "Esser madre è un inferno" in the 1910 revision, as well as a scene for the same character (Rosa Mammai) with the "Innocente." The 1936 production at the Teatro alla Scala, Milan, did much to enhance the reputation of the opera through the efforts of a superb cast (Carosio, Schipa, Pederzini, Basiola). Even after that production, Cilèa continued to tinker at *L'Arlesiana,* in 1937 adding a new prelude to the score. The result of these changes was to strengthen the work's structure, which had been too rambling and diffuse.

L'Arlesiana remains essentially a lyrical work, lovably but perhaps too unrelievedly elegiac and melancholy in sentiment. It persisted as Cilèa's favorite among his own operas. Two arias from *L'Arlesiana* have held their place in the recital repertoire, "Esser madre è un inferno" and "Anch'io vorrei dormir così" (the famous "Lamento di Federico"); they typify the lyrical beauty of the work. Indeed, one can say that the simple strophic bipartite structure (AA') of the "Lamento di Federico" influenced Puccini to use the same formal device in his operas from *Tosca* onwards, which all postdate Cilèa's *L'Arlesiana.*

After *L'Arlesiana,* Cilèa, discouraged at its spotty reception, accepted a position as harmony instructor at Florence's musical institute. At about the time that he was losing heart, however, Sonzogno offered him *Adriana Lecouvreur,* which would prove a more decisive success, and a more enduring one, than *L'Arlesiana.* Arturo Colautti based his libretto, in four acts, on the play by Scribe and Legouvé. Certain ambiguities in the action, which have caused the libretto to suffer derision from some, actually derive from the perceived need to compress not only the play but also the draft of Colautti's text of the libretto, originally rather intricate but at least minimally logical, for the needs of the lyric stage. The subject exerted a strong grip on the composer, having many of the elements that kindled his imagination, including a sympathetic artist-heroine of deep feeling and sensitivity, as well as much humor and aristocratic etiquette to which Cilèa's elegance of style were well suited.

Adriana Lecouvreur saw its premiere on 6 November 1902 at the Teatro Lirico, Milan, with Caruso, Pandolfini, and De Luca, under Cleofonte Campanini's direction. *Adriana Lecouvreur* quickly became Cilèa's one sure success and justly remains at least on the margins of the standard repertory. It was immediately staged all over Italy, and within five years had spread from Lisbon (1903) west to Buenos Aires (1903), New Orleans, and New York (both 1907), as well as east to St. Petersburg (1906).

After *Adriana Lecouvreur,* Cilèa considered setting D'Annunzio's *Francesca da Rimini,* but negotiations over the libretto failed; the composer also pondered Renato Simoni's libretto to *Ritorno d'amore,* but rejected it. Cilèa settled on *Gloria,* to another three act libretto by Colautti. The text was already undeniably old-fashioned at the time of the work's composition. Its tale of heroic valor, love-instigated war and politics is redolent of the kind of libretto which Cammarano or Solera had cobbled for such works of Verdi as *Il Trovatore* or *I Lombardi.* There is little room in Colautti's text for character development, beyond Gloria's capitulation to her feelings for Lionetto. In spite of this, Cilèa, the complete professional, threw himself whole-heartedly into his work on the opera, clothing this turgid tale with music of the splendor and color needed to bring its creaking plot to life.

Toscanini conducted the premiere of *Gloria* on 15 April 1907 at the Teatro alla Scala. After *Gloria,* Cilèa resumed teaching more actively than ever, leaving Palermo for Naples in 1916 to teach at the San Pietro di Majella conservatory until 1935. He fashioned a revised version of *Gloria,* with the libretto revised by E. Moschini, for a production in Naples (20 April 1932). The fact that *Gloria*'s subject was not conducive to Cilèa's refined and delicate sensibilities, however, may account for the opera's lack of any truly memorable set pieces, despite considerable beauties in the score. All is well accomplished, and the orchestration, especially, has many felicities, such as the depiction of surging water in the fountain scene and the imitation of bells tolling in the wedding scene. The choral writing in *Gloria,* as usual with Cilèa, is exquisite.

Gloria's music is on a large scale and, taken as a whole, very impressively clothes the grand scenes of public ritual, battle, and similar happenings. Perhaps Cilèa's only real miscalculation is in the handling of Bardo's assassination of Lionetto, after which the action bustles along to other matters too quickly for such an important turn of the plot to register its impact fully enough. *Gloria,* although a solid success at the 1907 premiere, has held the stage less well than either *L'Arlesiana* or *Adriana Lecouvreur.* When *Gloria* has been revived occasionally, it is the 1932 score that has been used.

Cilèa set his last completed opera, *Il matrimonio selvaggio,* to a text by G. di Bagnasco in 1909, but the work was never staged or published. Cilèa broached one last opera, *La Rosa di Pompei,* to a text by E. Moschini, but left off work on it in a very preliminary stage. Although *Gloria* had terminated his career as a composer for the stage, Cilèa kept on composing while pursuing his calling as a teacher, even after his retirement. He had always devoted himself to instrumental music and continued to do so. His vocal works after *Gloria,* besides the two unstaged operas, include songs, a *Canto della vita* (a symphonic poem for solo voice, chorus, and orchestra, 1913) and the *Vocalizzi da concerto* (a wordless concerto for voice, 1932).

Cilèa is accounted one of the "Giovane Scuola" or, less aptly labelled, *verismo* school figures. He shared the fondness of his contemporaries (Giordano, Zandonai, Mascagni, et al.) for the "costume drama" (e.g. his own *Adriana Lecouvreur* or Giordano's *Andrea Chénier*) and, less widely perceived among these men, a late-blooming Mannerist sensibility, more than a real affinity for these composers' occasional forays into the realism known in Italian opera as *verismo.* Cilèa's *Tilda* and, to some extent, *L'Arlesiana* are his contributions to *verismo,* per se. On the whole, Cilèa leans towards the Mannerist aspect, with its cultivation of a refined but very expressive aestheticism, rather than the merely intermittent *verismo* of the "Giovane Scuola." What Cilèa does share with his contemporaries, for all his refined sensibility, aloof temperament, and his more elegantly diaphanous orchestration, is their harmonic language, exploitation of richly sensual orchestral palette, and highly charged lyricism.

Cilèa's experience in chamber music and instrumental writing is obvious in the finesse and refinement of much of his orchestration. Cilèa's harmony and orchestration, even more so than with others of the "Giovane Scuola," reflect the influence of the French school of the period. Cilèa, like many Italian composers both of his own time and before, did succumb perhaps too often to the use of *tremolandi* and arpeggiation to flesh out his orchestration at times, but such devices only rarely appear to any really crude or arbitrary effect. Cilèa carefully gauged the voicing of his harmonies (a concern no doubt influenced by study of French scores), each added or altered note making its fullest impact by being situated in the instrumental section or taken by an individual instrument which would most highlight its harmonic color and desired degree of prominence. While not so daring as Puccini, neither was Cilèa so reticent as Giordano in exploiting new harmonic pathways in his time.

Cilèa made more than passing use of the motif (something readily observable in *Adriana Lecouvreur*) as a unitary and dramatic device, even if his handling of motifs, often bits from arias or other musical numbers, was like that of many *veristi,* rudimentary compared to Wagner. As were most Italian composers (Puccini excepted) Cilèa was content to repeat motifs rather than to develop or modify them through symphonic synthesis.

More distinctive than even his harmonic style or orchestration, however, are Cilèa's melodies. At their best, they are noteworthy for their elegiac lyricism, melancholy, and for their sinuously decorative contours. Cilèa could write music powerful and blunt in effect, as, for example, the music with which he provides the formidable Princesse de Bouillon in *Adriana Lecouvreur.* In many ways, Cilèa summed up in one last, glorious burst the abundant lyricism of Naples and of southern Italy, with a strongly Gallic harmonic language (from the influence of such masters as Gounod, Bizet, and Massenet) underpinning it. The structure, dramatic and musical, of Cilèa's operas is at times faulty, but the rich melodic invention and fragrant orchestration more than compensate in holding the listener's attention and interest.

—C. P. Gerald Parker

CIMAROSA, Domenico.

Composer. Born 17 December 1749, in Aversa, near Naples. Died 11 January 1801, in Venice. First music teacher was Polcano, organist of the monastery overseeing the charity school of the Minorites; scholarship to the Conservatorio Santa Maria di Loreto, where he studied singing with Manna and Sacchini, counterpoint with Fenaroli, and composition with Piccinni, 1761-72; his oratorio *Giuditta* performed in Rome, 1770; first opera, *Le stravaganza del conte* performed in Naples, 1772; in Rome and Naples, 1778-1781; succeeded Paisiello as court composer at St Petersburg, 1787-91; success in Florence, Vienna, and Warsaw on the way to St Petersburg; Kapellmeister of the court at Vienna, 1791; Cimarosa's *Il matrimonio segreto* a huge success in Vienna, 1792, and later Naples, 1793; in Venice, Rome, and Naples, 1794-1801. Cimarosa went to prison in Naples in 1799 for his open support of the French republican army.

Operas

Le stravaganze del conte, P. Mililotti, Naples, Teatro dei Fiorentini, carnival 1772.
La finta parigina, F. Cerlone, Naples, Nuovo, carnival 1773.
I sdegni per amore, P. Mililotti, Naples, Nuovo, January 1776.
I matrimoni in ballo, P. Mililotti, Naples, Nuovo, January 1776.
La frascatana nobile, P. Mililotti, Naples, Nuovo, winter 1776.
I tre amanti, Giuseppe Petrosellini, Rome, Valle, carnival 1777.
Il fanatico per gli antichi romani, Giovanni Palomba, Naples, Teatro dei Fiorentini, spring 1777.
L'Armida immaginaria, Giovanni Palomba, Naples, Teatro dei Fiorentini, summer 1777.
Gli amanti comici, o sia La famiglia in scompiglio. Giuseppe Petrosellini, Naples, Teatro dei Fiorentini?, 1778?.
Il ritorno di Don Calandro, Giovanni Petrosellini?, Rome, Valle, carnival, 1778.
Le stravaganze d'amore, P. Mililotti, Naples, Teatro dei Fiorentini, 1778.
Il matrimonio per raggiro, c. 1778-79?; later performance in Rome, Valle, 1802.
L'italiana in London, Giuseppe Petrosellini, Rome, Valle, carnival 1779.
L'infedeltà fedele, Giovanni Battista Lorenzi, Naples, Teatro del Fondo, 20 July 1779.
Le donne rivali, Rome, Valle, carnival 1780.
Caio Mario, Gaetano Roccaforte, Rome, January 1780.
I finti nobili, Giovanni Palomba, Naples, Teatro dei Fiorentini, Carnival 1780.
Il falegname, Giovanni Palomba, Naples, Teatro dei Fiorentini, 1780.
Il capriccio drammatico, Giuseppe Maria Diodati, Turin?, 1781?.
Il pittor parigino, Giuseppe Petrosellini, Rome, Valle, 4 January 1781.

Domenico Cimarosa, c. 1815

Alessandro nell'Indie, Pietro Metastasio, Rome, Torre Argentina, carnival 1781.

L'amante combattuto dalle donne di punto, Giovanni Palomba, Naples, Teatro dei Fiorentini, 1781.

Giunio Bruto, G. Pindemonte ("Eschilo Acanzio"), Verona, Accademia Filarmonica, autumn 1781.

Giannina e Bernardone, Filippo Livigni, Venice, San Samuele, November 1781.

Il convito, Filippo Livigni, Venice, San Samuele, 27 December 1781.

L'amor costante, Rome, Valle, carnival 1782.

L'eroe cinese, Pietro Metastasio, Naples, San Carlo, 13 August 1782.

La ballerina amante, Cesare Augusto Casini and/or Giovanni Palomba, October 1782, Naples, Teatro dei Fiorentini, 1782.

La Circe, D. Perelli, Milan, Teatro alla Scala, carnival 1783.

I due baroni di Rocca Azurra, Giovanni Palomba, Rome, Valle, February 1783.

Oreste, L. Serio, Naples, San Carlo, 13 August 1783.

La villana riconosciuta, Giovanni Palomba, June 1783, Naples, Teatro del Fondo, fall 1783.

Chi dell' altrui si veste presto si spoglia, Giovanni Palomba, Naples, Teatro dei Fiorentini, 1783.

I matrimoni impensati, Rome, Valle, carnival 1784.

L'apparenza inganna, ossia La villeggiatura, Giovanni Battista Lorenzi, Naples, Teatro dei Fiorentini, spring 1784.

La vanità delusa, Carlo Goldoni, Florence, Teatro della Pergola, June 1784.

L'Olimpiade, Pietro Metastasio, Vicenza, Eretenio, 10 July 1784.

I due supposti conti, ossia Lo sposo senza moglie, Angelo Anelli, Milan, Teatro alla Scala, 10 October 1784.

Artaserse, Pietro Metastasio, Turin, Reggio, 26 December 1784.

Il marito disperato, Giovanni Battista Lorenzi, Naples, Teatro dei Fiorentini, 1785.

La donna sempre al suo peggior s' appiglia, Giovanni Palomba, Naples, Nuovo, 1785.

Il credulo, Giuseppe Maria Diodati, Naples, Nuovo, carnival 1786.

Le trame deluse, Giuseppe Maria Diodati, Naples, Nuovo, 1786.

L'impressario in angustie, Giuseppe Maria Diodati, Naples, Nuovo, 1786.

Volodimiro, G. Boggio, Turin, Regio, January 1787.

Il fanatico burlato, Saverio Zini, Naples, Teatro del Fondo, 1787.

La felicità inaspettata, Fernando Moretti, St Petersburg, Hermitage, March 1788.

La vergine del sole, Fernando Moretti, St Petersburg, Hermitage?, 1788?; St Petersburg, Kamennïy, 6 November 1789.

La Cleopatra, Fernando Moretti, St Petersburg, Hermitage, 8 October 1789.

Il matrimonio segreto, Giovanni Bertati (after Colman and Garrick, *The Clandestine Marriage*), Vienna, Burgtheater, 7 February 1792.

Amor rende sagace, Giovanni Bertati, Vienna, Burgtheater, 1 April 1793.

I traci amanti, Giovanni Palomba, Naples, Nuovo, 19 June 1793.

Le astuzie femminili, Giovanni Palomba (after Bertati, *Amor rende sagace*), Naples, Teatro del Fondo, 26 August 1794.

Penelope, Giuseppe Maria Diodati, Naples, Teatro del Fondo, carnival 1795.

Le nozze in garbuglio, Giuseppe Maria Diodati, Messina, Monizione, 1795.

L'impegno superato, Giuseppe Maria Diodati, Naples, Teatro del Fondo, 1795.

La finta ammalata, Lisbon, San Carlo, 1796.

I nemici generosi, Giuseppi Petrosellini, Rome, Valle, carnival 1796.

Gli Orazi ed i Curiazi, Antonio Simone Sografi, Venice, La Fenice, 26 December 1796.

Achille all' assedio di Troia, Rome, Torre Argentina, carnival 1797.

L'imprudente fortunato, Rome, Valle, carnival 1797.

Artemisia regina di Caria, Marcello Marchesini, Naples, San Carlo, 25 June 1797.

L'apprensivo raggirato, Giuseppe Maria Diodati, Naples, Teatro dei Fiorentini, 1798.

Il secreto, Turin, Carignano, autumn 1798.

Artemisia (left unfinished by the composer; finished for production by an unknown hand), Giovanni Battista Colloredo ("Cratisto Jamejo"), Venice, La Fenice, carnival 1801.

Other works: cantatas, oratorios, sacred vocal works, instrumental music, keyboard works.

Publications

About CIMAROSA: books–

Manfredonia, T. Terracina de. *Domenico Cimarosa. Biographia degli uomini illustri del regno di Napoli,* vol. 5, edited by Martuscelli. Naples, 1818.

Stendhal. *Vie de Rossini.* Paris, 1824; English translation 1956, 2nd ed. 1970.

Rosa, C. de [Marchese di Villarosa]. *Memorie dei compositori di musica del regno di Napoli.* Naples, 1840.

Croce, B. *I teatri di Napoli.* Naples, 1891.

Trevisan, M.S. *Nel primo centenario di Domenico Cimarosa.* Venice, 1900.

Hirschfeld, R. Biography in *Catalogue of the Vienna Exhibition for the Cimarosa Centenary.* Vienna, 1901.

Polidoro, F. *La vita, le opere di D. Cimarosa.* Naples, 1902.

Della Corte, A. *L'opera comica italiana nel '700.* Bari, 1923.

Vitale, Roberto. *Domenico Cimarosa: la vita e le opere.* Aversa, 1929.

Baimonti, G. *Il matrimonio segreto di Domenico Cimarosa.* Rome, 1930.

Tibaldi-Chiesa, Maria. *Cimarosa ed il suo tempo.* Milan, 1939.

Chailly, Luciano. *Il matromonio segreto.* Milan, 1949.

Hirschfeld, R. *Per il bicentenario della nascita di Domenico Cimarosa* [symposium]. Aversa, 1949.

Schlitzer, F. *Goethe and Cimarosa.* Siena, 1950.

Mooser, R.A. *Annales de la musique et des musiciens en Russie au XVIIIe siècle,* vol. 2. Geneva, 1951.

articles–

Arnold, I.T.F.C. "Domenico Cimarosa." *Gallerie der berühmtesten Tonkünstler des achtzehnten und neunzehnten Jahrhunderts* 2 (1810).

Cambiasi, Pompeo. "Notizie sulla vita e sulle opere di Domenico Cimarosa." *Gazzetta musicale di Milano* no. 55 (1900): 639; no. 66 (1901): 6.

Polidoro, F. "La vita e le opere di Domenico Cimarosa." *Atti della Accademia Pontaniana* 32 (1902): 1.

Engel, C. "A Note on Domenico Cimarosa's Il matrimonio segreto." *Musical Quarterly* 33 (1947): 201.

Dean, Winton. "The Libretto of 'The Secret Marriage' ".
    Music Survey 3 (1950): 33.
Mondolfi, A. "Cimarosa copista di Handel." *Gazzetta musicale di Napoli* 2 (1956): 125.
Mondolfi-Bossarelli. "Due varianti dovute a Mozart nel testo
    del *Matrimonio segreto.*" *Analecta musicologica* no. 4
    (1967): 124.
Bartha, D. "Haydn's Italian Opera Repertory at Esterháza
    Palace." In *New Looks at Italian Opera; Essays in Honor
    of Donald J. Grout,* edited by William Austin. Ithaca,
    1968.
Dietz, Hanns-Bertold. "Die Varianten in Domenico Cimarosas Autograph zu *Il matrimonio segreto* und ihr Ursprung." *Die Musikforschung* 31 (1978): 273.
Degrada, Francesco. "Dal *Marriage à la mode* al *Matrimonio
    segreto:* genesi di un tema drammatico nel Settecento." In
    Il palazzo incantato. Studi sulla tradizione del melodramma dal Barocco al Romanticismo. Fiesole, 1979.
Lippmann, Friedrich. "Mozart und Cimarosa." In *Die frühdeutsche Oper und ihre Beziehungen zu Italien, England
    und Frankreich. Mozart und die Oper seiner Zeit (Opernsymposium 1978 Hamburg,* edited by Martin Ruhnke,
    187. *Hamburger Jahrbuch für Musikwissenschaft* 5.
    Laaber, 1981.
————. "Haydns *La fedeltà premiata* und Cimarosas
    L'infedeltà fedele." *Haydn-Studien* 5 (1982): 1.
————. "Über Cimarosas *Opere serie.*" *Analecta musicologica* 21 (1982): 21.
————. "Mozart und die italienischen Komponisten des 19.
    Jahrhunderts." *Mozart-Jahrbuch* (1980-83): 104.

*   *   *

It was in his native Naples that Cimarosa first attracted attention as an opera composer. The established presence of Piccinni and Paisiello prevented him from making a significant breakthrough for several years, however, for it was not until these two composers both left the city in 1776—for Paris and St. Petersburg respectively—that Cimarosa's qualities were fully recognized. Soon his operas were heard in all the major Italian centers, beginning with the intermezzo *I tre amanti,* which was staged in Rome in 1777.

Within a few years Cimarosa's reputation had become international, and he responded by writing operas of various stylistic types. His first serious opera was *Caio Mario,* performed in Rome in 1780 in the two-act design he had by then come to prefer. Seven years later Catherine II invited him to take up the post of maestro di capella at her court in St. Petersburg, and there he remained until 1791. During these years his style developed toward the contemporary trend of complex finales containing a variety of musical structures, and each of the three operas he wrote in St. Petersburg moved impressively to a closing chorus.

Cimarosa chose to leave Russia once his contract there expired, making his way to Vienna, where he was well received by the Emperor Leopold II. Such was his reputation that Cimarosa was soon appointed Kapellmeister, and his creative response was the opera which posterity has judged to be his masterpiece, the opera buffa *Il matrimonio segreto.* With due respect for his new artistic environment, he worked with the Viennese Imperial Court Poet, Giovanni Bertati, as his librettist. Bertati was an experienced librettist who had previously worked with Salieri and Paisiello, and his plot concerning a wealthy merchant's daughter's secret marriage to her father's employee proved an excellent vehicle for Cimarosa's lively and entertaining music. So pleased was the

Emperor that he treated the entire cast to dinner after the premiere, in order that they could perform the opera again for him that same evening.

Leopold died soon after the premiere of *Il matrimonio segreto* and Cimarosa responded to the many invitations he received from his native Italy by returning to Naples in 1793, soon presenting a new opera, *I traci amanti.* His creative strength remained, and he returned successfully to serious opera three years later with *Gli orazi ed i curiazi.* In this, probably his best such work, he wrote skilfully and dramatically not only for solo voices but also for the chorus, which in fact plays a prominent and integral part in the evolution of the plot. An unusual feature of this opera is that the chorus is for male voices only.

During 1799, Naples was occupied by republican forces, and Cimarosa publicly sympathized with their cause. When the city was regained by King Ferdinand, the composer was arrested and spent a few months in prison. The intervention of eminent friends eventually secured his release, and he moved on to Venice, where he began composing a new opera, *Artemisia.* He did not live to complete it, however, for he died in January 1801. Throughout his career, in the course of which he completed more than sixty operas, Cimarosa was an accomplished master of dramatic pacing and of the depiction of individual characters. For these reasons he excelled in comic opera, writing in a style that reflected the prevailing taste but that also had integrity. His orchestral writing was skilful and well balanced, using contrasts of instrumental groupings and rhythmic phrases to enhance the movement of the plot. A typical feature, found generally in this style of opera, is how it is conveyed by means of short repetitive figurations. In his later works especially, his lyrical writing could be most expressive, and not merely in the vocal line, for his sense of orchestral color grew more acute, as did the range of his harmony. Accordingly, Cimarosa's later operas enhance their dramatic content with subtlety.

In the last decade of his life Cimarosa became the leading international exponent of Italian opera. He was ultimately more successful in comic opera than in serious works, though the latter cannot be judged insignificant. Only the arrival of Rossini would eclipse him.

—Terry Barfoot

CINDERELLA
See CENDRILLON

CINDERELLA
See LA CENERENTOLA

LA CLEMENZA DI TITO [The Mercy of Titus].

Composer: Wolfgang Amadeus Mozart.

Librettist: Caterino Mazzolà (after Metastasio).

First Performance: Prague, National Theater, 6 September 1791.

Roles: Tito (tenor); Sesto (contralto or mezzo-soprano); Vitellia (soprano); Servilia (soprano); Annio (countertenor or tenor); Publio (bass); chorus (SATB).

Publications

book–

Hocquard, Jean-Victor. *"La clemenza di Tito" et les opéras de jeunesse.* Paris, 1987.

articles–

Volek, T. "Über den Ursprung von Mozarts Oper 'La Clemenza di Tito'." *Mozart-Jahrbuch* (1959): 274.
Giegling, F. "Metastasios Oper *La clemenza di Tito* in der Bearbeitung durch Mazzolà." *Mozart-Jahrbuch* (1962-63).
Moberly, R.B. "The Influence of French Classical Drama on Mozart's "La clemenza di Tito'." *Music and Letters* 55 (1974): 286.

Neville, Don J. *"La clemenza di Tito:* Metastasio, Mazzolà, and Mozart." *Studies in Music from the University of Western Ontario* 1 (1976).
_____. "*Idomeneo* and *La clemenza di Tito:* Opera Seria and Vera Opera." *Studies in Music* [Canada] 5 (1978): 99.

unpublished–

Weichlein, William. "A Comprehensive Study of Five Musical Settings of *La clemenza di Tito.*" Ph.D. dissertation, University of Michigan, 1957.

*   *   *

Mozart's setting of Metastasio's *La clemenza di Tito* is perhaps his most controversial opera. Written for the coronation of Leopold II as King of Bohemia in Prague, its initial reception was lukewarm. The empress' barb condemning the work as a "porcheria tedesca" (German dirty trick) after she heard it was supported by many early nineteenth-century writers, who (while avoiding such out and out slander) found the work sterile, lacking in invention and creativity. That hardly reflects its proper evaluation, however, for soon after the composer's death the opera steadily gained popularity. It is now seen as an important culmination of Mozart's dramatic compositions and as revealing his affinity for serious opera; it is not like his Da Ponte comedies, but neither ought it to have been. It is a different genre, written for different circumstances, exhibiting different aesthetic proprieties.

Mozart's early biographer Niemetschek (1798) claimed that *La clemenza di Tito* was composed in eighteen days; that fact, along with Mozart's illness, were often offered as justification for shortcomings in the work. Recent studies have shown that Mozart probably began composing as early as July of 1791, with his attention directed first to the ensemble pieces and the arias for Tito. The other arias were written later. The work *was* written in a short time, therefore, and some compromises were made: it is fairly certain that Mozart's student, Sussmayr, set the recitatives (yet this practice was fairly common, as can be seen in the scores of such composers as Cimarosa and Paisiello).

This was the third time that Mozart had set a Metastasio text to music, but his last attempt (*Il rè pastore,* for Salzburg) had occurred over fifteen years earlier. Metastasio's *Tito,* loosely inspired by the reports of Titus's magnanimity in Suetonius and other Roman historians (but more directly modeled on several plays by Corneille and Racine), was one of his most popular texts. First set in 1734 by Caldara, over seventy other settings preceded Mozart's of 1791. Caterino Mazzolà—who served as Dresden court poet from 1782 until the spring of 1791, when he came to Vienna as court poet (replacing Da Ponte)—was engaged as the arranging librettist for Mozart's production by Guardasoni, the impresario. Mazzolà followed the pattern he had set in Dresden, altering Metastasio's texts to conform to the *dramma giocoso* model, i.e., collapsing the three acts into two (largely by deleting twelve scenes from the second act) and supplying a variety of extra ensembles (two duets, three trios), including act-ending finales, by then a tradition well established in comedies. His ideas pleased Mozart, who called his arrangement a transformation of the out-of-date Metastasio original into "vera opera," and whose musical setting underscores the integrity of Mazzolà's ideas.

The plot revolves around the disturbance of the natural order caused by Vitellia's irascible jealousy. Vitellia, the daughter of the deposed Roman emperor Vitellio, loves Tito,

La clemenza di Tito, **title-page of libretto, 1791**

but, believing that he is about to marry another, swears Sesto (confidant to the emperor and her ardent admirer) to slay him. Too late, she learns of her error; the palace is in flames and reports bear news of Tito's death. Fate has turned the tables, however: the wrong man was struck down. Annio, Sesto's friend and engaged to Sesto's sister, Servilia, at first appears to bear the blame, but the evidence soon shows Sesto the author of the conspiracy. Tito mourns for his friend and desperately hopes for some explanation, some new evidence. When that fails, he decides to forgive him, yet at the last moment Vitellia reveals her own fault. Still, Tito proclaims that his clemency is stronger than the irrational acts of passion now repented and forgives all. He proclaims that he will have no other consort but Rome, and all join in praise of Tito's virtue.

The act-ending ensembles for both acts are reminiscent of other operas from the 1780s. That for the first act, which culminates in the revelation of Sesto's guilt, is particularly effective. Unified tonally in E-flat, its harmonic plan strays abruptly to support dramatic events: Publio's declaration that Tito is feared dead is underlaid with diminished seventh chords; and the final chorus, in E-flat, is colored by movement to the minor subdominant and all its borrowed chords to underscore such emotive text as "tradimento" and "dolor." Mozart's lifelong sensitivity to his text setting is also well evident in his solo numbers. Sesto's aria, "Parto, ma tu ben mio," shows a three-part division of the two stanza Metastasio text. Each section accelerates the tempo (a not uncommon device in general), but with textual repetition that creates a truly rising passion. The basset horn obbligato part, written for Anton Stadler, is one of Mozart's most beautiful settings.

—Dale E. Monson

CLEOPATRA
See DIE UNGLÜCKSELIGE CLEOPATRA

THE CLOWNS
See I PAGLIACCI

CLUYTENS, André.

Conductor. Born 26 March 1905, in Antwerp. Died 3 June 1967, in Neuilly, near Paris. Studied piano at the Antwerp Conservatory; assistant to his father (conductor) at the Théâtre Royal in Antwerp, 1921; conducted at the Théâtre Royal, 1927-32; became a French citizen in 1932; music director of the Toulouse Opera, 1932-35; opera conductor in Lyons, 1935; conducted the Paris Opéra, 1941, and became music director, 1944; music director of the Opéra-Comique, Paris, 1947; conductor of the Société des Concerts du Conservatoire de Paris, 1949; conducted at the Bayreuth Festival, 1955; United States debut in Washington, D.C. as a guest conductor

of the Vienna Philharmonic; principal conductor of the Orchestre National de Belgique, Brussels, 1960-67.

Publications

About CLUYTENS: books—

Gavoty, B. *André Cluytens.* Geneva, 1955.

*   *   *

A specialist in the operas of the French repertoire, Belgian conductor André Cluytens held his first post at the Royal Theater, Antwerp from 1927 to 1932, making his debut with Bizet's *Les pêcheurs de perles.* He served as music director of the opera house in Toulouse, 1932-35, of Lyon, Bordeaux and Vichy from 1935, of the Paris Opéra orchestra in 1941 (music director from 1944), and of the Paris Opéra-Comique in 1947. He also conducted the Vienna State Opera orchestra.

Cluytens was the first French conductor at the Bayreuth Festival, leading *Tannhäuser* there in 1955 as a replacement for Eugen Jochum and returning for *Die Meistersinger* and *Lohengrin* between 1955 and 1958. He also conducted Wagner at the Teatro alla Scala in Milan, leading the *Ring* cycle and *Parsifal.*

Cluytens's conducting was straightforward and often rather stolid, dependable rather than inspired or imaginative, with a somewhat anonymous quality. He tended toward rapid tempos and somewhat slack rhythms. His soft-edged approach is more appropriate to the nineteenth-century French style than to the German and Russian operas he also led, and the French school brought out the more stylish, spontaneous, and sympathetic aspects of his conducting.

His recordings include Offenbach's *Les contes d'Hoffmann* (1948, 1964), Bizet's *Carmen* (1950, the first recording to use the spoken dialogue of the original Opéra-Comique version), Ravel's *L'heure espagnole* (1953), *Les pêcheurs de perles* (1954), Gounod's *Faust* (1954, 1958), Stravinsky's *Le rossignol* (1955), Debussy's *Pelléas et Mélisande* (1957), Musorgsky's *Boris Godunov* (1962), Humperdinck's *Hänsel und Gretel* (1964), Lalo's *Le roi d'Ys* (1964), Gounod's *Mireille,* and Poulenc's *Les mamelles de Tirésias.*

—Michael Sims

THE COACHMAN OF LONGJUMEAU
See LE POSTILLON DE LONGJUMEAU

COATES, Albert.

Conductor. Born 23 April 1882, in St Petersburg. Died 11 December 1953, in Milnerton, near Cape Town, South Africa. Studied organ with his brother while enrolled in Liverpool University; studied cello with Klengel, piano with Robert Teichmüller, and conducting with Arthur Nikisch at the Leipzig Conservatory, beginning 1902; debut as conductor of Offenbach's *Les contes d'Hoffmann* at the Leipzig Opera; chief conductor of the Elberfeld opera house, 1905; joint conductor with Schuch at the Dresden Opera, 1907-09; joint conductor with Bodanzky at the Mannheim opera house, 1909-10; conductor at the Imperial Opera of St Petersburg, 1911; conducted extensively in England, beginning 1913; United States debut as guest conductor of the New York Symphony Orchestra, 1920; taught conducting classes at the Eastman School of Music, 1923-25; conductor at the Berlin State Opera, 1931; conducted concerts with the Vienna Philharmonic, 1935; conducted the Johannesburg Symphony Orchestra and taught at the University of South Africa, Cape Town, 1946.

Publications

About COATES: articles–

Stroff, M. "Albert Coates." *Le Grand Baton* March (1980).

*   *   *

Albert Coates must be one of the most cosmopolitan conductors in recent times. In spite of English parentage, he spent his formative years in Russia and in Germany, he worked mainly in Russia, England and America, and he died in South Africa. A decade before Adrian Boult, Coates became a member of Nikisch's conducting class in Leipzig, and, as his assistant, made his debut at the Opera there with Offenbach's *Les contes d'Hoffmann* in 1904. He was also influenced by Ernst von Schuch, in charge at Dresden, where Coates went in 1907. After guest conducting *Siegfried* in St Petersburg, he accepted a post with the Imperial Opera at the Mariinsky Theater there until the turbulent events of 1917 (together with blood poisoning from eating bad food) forced him to return to England. Although he was offered the musical directorship in Mannheim (where he had also spent some apprentice years before going to Russia), he opted to remain in London, where he not only became associated with the recently formed London Symphony Orchestra, but also collaborated closely with Beecham as a champion of an English national opera, the impetus for which had already been given by Richter's seasons of Wagner's *Ring* in English at Covent Garden in 1908 and 1909. Coates had already made his London debut in 1914 with *Tristan und Isolde* and shared performances of the *Ring* with Nikisch, but from 1919 he became a regular figure on the operatic podium in England.

Of his *Prince Igor* at Covent Garden (performed soon after his arrival in 1919) Philip Heseltine (the composer Peter Warlock) observed that he "conducted the work with the most admirable verve and complete command not only of the orchestra, but of the immense crowd of singers. . . . The choruses were wonderfully done, the difficult chattering chorus in 5/4 for the women being especially good. . . . One may find his interpretations a bit coarse and unsubtle but of his command over the players there can be no question." Sir Dan Godfrey, while acknowledging Coates's brilliance as a conductor, also described him as an "illustrative," one who went for the "body" of the composer rather than the "mind" when presenting his interpretations. Godfrey had a point. Coates, large of body himself, gave uninhibited physical performances with electrifying crescendos and unrestrained dynamics of both extremes, and was happiest in programmes or operas full of emotion and warmth. Although he excelled in Russian music (Scriabin and Kabalevsky were composers whom he championed in particular), Coates's readings of the Wagnerian music dramas were imbued with a massive dignity

combined with a sensitivity to the inner pulse and architectural pacing of the music which place him among the greatest British conductors of the first half of the twentieth century.

Coates recording legacy is a fortunate testimony to this greatness, although it is a matter of regret that he never worked in the LP era. Among those artists with whom he did record were Chaliapin, Schorr, Leider and Melchior, who between them featured in recordings of extracts from the Wagner operas, *Boris Godunov, Salome, Carmen, Faust,* and Boito's two operas *Nerone* and *Mefistofele* as well as countless orchestral extracts from many Russian operas. Coates was also a prolific composer, and among his works are the operas *Mr Pickwick* (Covent Garden, 1936) and *Samuel Pepys* (Munich 1929). The former, staged by the short-lived British Music Drama Opera Company, had the distinction of being the first televised opera when extracts were filmed by the nascent British Broadcasting Corporation in 1936.

—Christopher Fifield

COLAS BREUGNON.

Composer: Dimitry Borisovich Kabalevsky.

Librettist: V. Gragin (after Romain Rolland, *Le maître de Clamécy*).

First Performance: Leningrad, 1938; revised, 1953, 1968.

Publications

article–

Danilevich, Lev. "Vremya, tvorchestvo, zhizn'." *Sovetskaya Muzyka* 12 (1979): 3.

*   *   *

The opera *Colas Breugnon,* originally called *The Master of Clamécy* and based on the novel of the same name by Romain Rolland, exists in three forms: the first version of 1936 (premiere 1938), the revision of 1953, and the final version of 1968, which consists of a prologue and eight scenes.

The 1968 version opens with the well-known, energetic, and industrious overture, which may certainly be regarded as a musical portrait of Colas Breugnon himself; indeed, several of its themes appear later in the work. A prologue introduces Breugnon with a pen in his hand, writing an account of his life. This leads directly into act I, scene i, which takes place in the pleasant landscape of Burgundy, near Clamécy, where peasant girls are working in the vineyards. Among them is Selina, joined by Colas, who is a gifted woodcarver and sculptor. The two engage in lively banter, but though they love each other, Colas will not propose to her. Gifliard, the Duke's equerry, appears and tells Colas, whom he hates, that he is going to marry Selina. They fight and the peasant girls encourage Breugnon, especially Jacqueline, who also loves him. But the sound of a bell announces that the Duke has returned from Paris with his unruly soldiers and guests. In the short intermezzo separating scenes one and two, the citizens of Clamécy engage the soldiers in witty verbal exchanges.

Scene ii opens in a meadow near Clamécy, where the citizens have assembled to meet the Duke, as custom demands. There is tension in the air. Four musicians start to play, and Colas joins in with his flute. One of the guests, Madamoiselle de Term, is struck by Colas and, learning that he is a craftsman, asks more precisely what he does. Colas replies, as always, in a self-effacing, humorous manner (to music which has previously been heard in the overture). The Duke points out a fountain that Breugnon has made and all are astounded at the quality of the craftsmanship. Colas is invited into the castle. The citizens are not happy at his "hob-nobbing" with the "upper classes," and Selina is filled with apprehension and sadness. She expresses her feelings in a poignant ballad, accompanied by the chorus to increasingly dissonant harmonies. Gifliard appears to tell the crowd that Colas has been invited to Paris to study. In a fit of pique, Selina agrees to dance with Gifliard and calls upon the drunken Priest to bless them. To the people's horror and astonishment Selina agrees to marry Gifliard.

Act II (scene iii) opens in Colas's workshop, where he is putting the final touches to his sculpture of Selina, aided by his young apprentice. He is visited first by Jacqueline, then by the Duke, who, when the sculpture is drawn to his attention by Gifliard, insists on taking it to the castle. Left alone, he broods on his misfortune and is joined in a most effective number by the drunken Priest and later by Jacqueline and the apprentice. The revelry is interrupted dramatically by the sound of a drum and pipe outside the window and two voices (a child's and an adult's) singing the words of the *Dies Irae* (though not the tune). Plague, brought in by the soldiers, has broken out in the town. All start to leave, but Colas decides to stay. An intermezzo, taking the form of a funeral procession, separates scenes iii and iv.

Breugnon, too, falls victim to the plague, and the fourth scene describes his delirium as he wanders through an abandoned vineyard, filled with visions of death. But his sturdy constitution prevails, and when he is visited by the Priest and his apprentice, even though he is told that his home and studio have been burnt at the Duke's orders and only his flute has survived, he replies with characteristic good humour. An intermezzo represents him limping along the road, where, in scene v, he meets Jacqueline, who is at the point of death. Scene vi takes place in the environs of Clamécy, where he encounters Selina, who reminiscences over past happiness and reproaches him for his backwardness in proposing.

Following another intermezzo, Colas meets the Clamécy inhabitants, who warn him not to enter the town, where a fire is raging. Scene vii is set in the castle, where all Colas's masterpieces are to be seen, including the statue of Selina, which the Duke calls his "Danaë". When the Duke asks if Colas is alive, the treacherous Gifliard informs him that Breugnon is inflaming the masses, and this so incenses the Duke that he orders all the craftsman's works to be burnt. A knock is heard at the door, announcing Colas's arrival, but when he enters and sees the destruction, his only reaction is to laugh. Not understanding Breugnon's behaviour, the Duke goes out. A short orchestral intermezzo leads into the final scene, which represents a procession of the citizens of Clamécy on the town's feast-day. The Duke and his retinue are present and, to celebrate the Feast of St Martin, a monument made by Colas is to be unveiled. When this is done, it proves to be a depiction of the Duke himself, seated on an ass. Unable to bear the humiliation, the Duke and his guests run to the castle for shelter to the mocking laughter of the citizens of Clamécy.

There are considerable differences between the three versions of the opera, especially in the final scenes of the work, while there are substantial changes to the personages themselves. Though Romain Rolland was charmed by Kabalevsky's music, he is said to have been worried by the ideological shifts of emphasis made to his own work, which took the form of fourteen separate stories and which he declared to be written "without politics." He was also concerned at the lack of any real French Burgundian character, for although the composer had studied French folk-songs before commencing composition, in the final version there is little French flavor present. Nevertheless, musically there are some extremely effective numbers, especially Colas's reply to Mademoiselle de Term in scene ii, Selina's ballad, Colas's sadness in scene iii and the fine ensemble that follows it, the delirium episode in the vineyard, the poignant scene of Jacqueline's death, the final meeting with Selina and the destruction of the craftsman's works, in all of which Kabalevsky's melodic gifts, strong musical harmonies, and scintillating orchestration are seen to full advantage. The music of the Suite *Colas Breugnon,* Op.24, derives from the first version of the opera, which has some excellent numbers omitted from the 1968 edition.

—Gerald Seaman

COMEDY ON THE BRIDGE [Veselohr na moste].

Composer: Bohuslav Martinů.

Librettist: Bohuslav Martinů (after Václav Kličpera).

First Performance: Czech Radio, 18 March 1937; revised c 1950.

Roles: Josephine (soprano); Bedron (bass); Nancy (contralto); Johnny (baritone); Schoolmaster (tenor); Captain (speaking); Soldier (speaking); Sentry (speaking).

*　　*　　*

In 1935 Martinů wrote two short operas for Radio Prague. The favorable reception accorded to *The Voice of the Forest* generated the stimulus to compose *The Comedy on the Bridge*, which he based on an eighteenth-century play by Václav Kličpera.

Although the original source was some one hundred and fifty years old, it provided a plot whose timeless qualities made it relevant and even topical for contemporary audiences. During a war, the opposite banks of a river are held by rival forces. There is a bridge, each end of which is controlled by the opposing sentries, and when friends and neighbors living on either side of the river wish to visit one another or travel on business, they find that the sentries issue permits for exit, but not for entry or re-entry. Thus, various characters become stranded on the bridge: the maid Popelka, her fiancee Sykoš the fisherman, his neighbor Bedroň the brewer with his wife Eva, and finally the local schoolmaster. Inevitably, tensions build up among them, not only because of their plight, but through personal jealousies that surface. From time to time bursts of shell- and gunfire bring moments of fear and crisis, as a result of which past indiscretions are revealed, until at last an armistice is signed and all can make their way safely home.

The Comedy on the Bridge is as suited to stage presentation as to the radio broadcast for which it was originally intended. The single act lasts less than an hour, and the opera has great unity in terms of time, place, and action. There are ample opportunities for an atmospheric setting and a distinctive musical imagery, as well as for imaginative stage movement in matters of perspective.

The restrictions imposed by a radio studio may have been responsible for the chamber orchestra scoring, but Martinů's imaginative colors and textures make this a positive virtue, since the instrumental music is always related to the dramatic context. For instance, the work opens with a short military march, and the side-drum and trumpet fanfares remain important throughout. A percussion battery is used to evoke the sounds of gunfire and explosions.

The six scenes flow continuously; each one, representing a new character's entry, marks a turning point in the plot—a device broken up only by the spoken roles of the rival guards, whose lack of sympathy with the plight of the locals is thereby expressed. An arioso style prevails in the dialogues, and the characters are cleverly drawn by means of their different voice types, though Martinů avoids developing the characterization beyond the initial stages of presenting each personality. The music abounds in wit and the drama is brilliantly paced, until at the end the news of the armistice is greeted by a triumphal march.

The Comedy on the Bridge played an important part in Martinů's life. Soon after its radio premiere, he left Europe for the United States, and during the 1940s he wrote no more operas. The new American production of this work, of which he spoke enthusiastically, took place in 1951 and revived the composer's interest in opera. Martinů wrote, *"The Comedy on the Bridge* was a tremendous success on the stage. It is Czech, in folk style, simple and informal, and it seems to contain a message for the people." Evidently the New York critics shared his enthusiasm, for the comedy was awarded their prize as the best new opera of the year. Feeling that the libretto had been crucial to the work's success, they also recommended a special award for Kličpera, who alas was unable to receive it in person, since he had been dead for some ninety-two years.

—Terry Barfoot

LE COMTE ORY [Count Ory].

Composer: Gioachino Rossini.

Librettists: E. Scribe and C.G. Delestre-Poirson (after their play).

First Performance: Paris, Opéra, 20 August 1828.

Roles: Countess Adèle (soprano); Isolier (mezzo-soprano); Count Ory (tenor); Robert (bass); Ragonde (contralto); Tutor (bass); Alice (soprano); Young Nobleman (tenor); chorus (SSAATTBB).

Publications

article–

Porter, A. *"Le Comte Ory." Opera* 5 (1954).

*　　*　　*

Rossini's last two operas, *Le comte Ory* and *Guillaume Tell*, can be considered as a pair: they are complementary in much the same way as *Tancredi* and *Italiana in Algeri*. Rossini made an international name for himself with *Tancredi* and *Italiana,* revealing himself to European audiences as a composer equally skilled in serious and comic opera; both works were first performed in Venice, site of most of his early operatic activity, in 1813. He bade farewell to the hectic world of operatic composition in Paris less than two decades later with two works, again one serious and one comic, that showed how much his artistic personality had evolved and matured during his short but intensely prolific progress from Venice to Naples to Paris.

Le comte Ory takes place in thirteenth-century France, in and around the castle of Adèle, Countess of Formoutiers. The countess's brother and all his male courtiers are away on a crusade. Count Ory, an adventurous youth always in search of amorous conquests, finds the countess attractive; he disguises himself as a hermit so as to gain entrance to the castle. The countess is melancholy; Count Ory convinces her that she will be happy if she falls in love. She welcomes this advice. Count Ory and his page Isolier, who also loves the countess, compete for her affections; but their efforts are thwarted by the return of the crusaders. The opera ends, somewhat unsatisfactorily, with Count Ory and his men making a hasty retreat from the castle.

Like many of Rossini's other operas, *Le comte Ory* borrows much from an early work, in this case *Il viaggio a Reims* (Rossini's first opera for Paris, 1825). But the adaptation of the earlier music to new words and dramatic situations is worked out so skillfully by Rossini and his librettist Scribe that the borrowing never detracts from the opera's freshness, charm, and wit.

Much of what is most attractive about *Le comte Ory* can be found in its many ensembles, some of which rival the best ensembles in the *opere buffe.* The opening ensemble grows directly out of the overture; here is an example of Rossini working, with many of his operatic contemporaries, towards a gradual breaking-down of the "number opera" in which overture, recitatives, arias, and ensembles are treated as separate and distinct musical units. Another example of the same tendency is the musical unit that begins as a relatively straightforward aria for the countess, "En proie à la tristesse," but goes on to incorporate chorus and soloists in a great, finale-like ensemble (actually the cabaletta of the countess's aria) in which the countess maintains her role as principal soloist. "Moi, je réclame," in which a credulous crowd asks the "hermit" to grant them their wishes, sparkles with energy and wit. No one could compose patter-song more effectively than Rossini: here he is at his most brilliant and amusing. Another remarkable ensemble, "O terreur! o peine extrême," expresses the general shock and dismay (exaggerated enough so that we do not take it too seriously) at the revelation that the "hermit" is in fact Count Ory. This thirteen-part unaccompanied ensemble is the high-point of the first-act finale. But the finest ensemble of all, and the number that crowns the entire opera, is the beautiful trio for Isolier, Count Ory, and the countess, "A la faveur de cette nuit obscure," in whose music one can sense a combination of nobility and charm such as only Rossini could achieve.

—John A. Rice

THE CONGENIAL INDIES
See LES INDES GALANTES

THE CONSUL.

Composer: Gian Carlo Menotti.

Librettist: Gian Carlo Menotti.

First Performance: Philadelphia, 1 March 1950.

Roles: Magda Sorel (soprano); John Sorel (baritone); Mother (contralto); Secretary (mezzo-soprano); Secret Police Agent (bass); Mr Kofner (bass-baritone); Foreign Woman (soprano); Anna Gomez (soprano); Vera Boronel (contralto); Nika Magdaoff (tenor); Assan (baritone).

*   *   *

The Consul is a disturbing political opera about the plight of a woman trying to obtain a visa to leave a totalitarian state. Following the tradition of its predecessor, *The Medium,* it is a true "musical drama" in three acts and six scenes. It was Menotti's first full-length work, and its libretto is one of his finest.

Magda Sorel is a woman left stranded in a police state, when her husband, John Sorel, barely escaping capture, flees across the frontier to gain asylum in a neighboring country. Trying to obtain a visa for her family, Magda virtually haunts the foreign consulate, but is endlessly thwarted by red tape. The consul himself never makes an appearance. He is represented by his secretary, who is the personification of governmental indifference and intrigue. At the consulate, Magda waits with other impoverished people, among them Nika Magdaoff, a magician with hypnotic powers.

As time passes, Magda's situation grows steadily more desperate. The secret police agent interrogates her, hoping she will betray other patriots. He watches her movements constantly, setting her up as bait in a trap for her husband. Magda's child dies of undernourishment, and the health of John's mother deteriorates from despair and worry. Assan, the window mender, is the only real contact Magda has to the underground; he brings news of her husband.

In the end, the pressure from Assan and the underground acts as the catalyst to real tragedy. Assan is concerned about the lives of all the underground members should John try to return and risk capture. He pleads with Magda to find a way to prevent John from rescuing her; John must not come back or the underground will be exposed. Magda agrees and resolves to end her life in order to eliminate any need for John to return.

In the last scene, Magda lies down by the gas stove while the telephone rings in the background; the unanswered call bears new of her husband's capture. As she drifts toward death, she dreams—of her husband as he comes to woo her, of John's mother still young, and of the magician saying "Look into my eyes, look into my eyes. You feel tired. You want to sleep. Breathe deeply." The visions recede; the room is empty; Magda falls back unconscious. The telephone continues to ring as the curtain falls.

The Consul, like it's predecessor *The Medium,* was presented on Broadway at the Ethel Barrymore Theater on March 15, 1950. The actual premiere took place two weeks earlier in Philadelphia. This original production, which was extremely well cast, ran for 269 performances, almost eight months. Among the cast can be found names such as baritone Cornell MacNeil, making his opera debut as John Sorel, soprano Patricia Neway, riveting as Magda Sorel, and contralto Marie Powers, who created the title role in *The Medium,* as the mother. Olin Downes of the *New York Times* (March 16, 1950) said each member of the cast "blended so excellently in the dramatic ensemble" that none was inadequate to the task. Speaking of Magda's "nobly fashioned" second act aria, he said it "simply stopped the show."

The Consul received The New York Drama Critics' Circle Award for the Best Musical of the Year and the Pulitzer Prize for Music in 1950. Productions were mounted in London, Zurich, Berlin, Vienna, and Italy in 1951, in Hamburg in 1952, and at Sadler's Wells, London, in 1954. It has since become standard operatic fare and has been translated into twelve languages. Though Menotti does not identify the police state in which his drama is set, it was a timely subject that remains current today.

Although originally a theater piece, it is opera in the finest tradition, and Menotti's training is clearly seen in the manner in which he creates musical shapes for the human voice. The melodies are tonal and easily remembered. Melodic repetition is common but with a sense of natural speech-like inflection. His melodic passages are often Puccini-like in their expanse of line and their singing quality. Recitative, ensemble, and aria seem to flow together with such ease that there are only two excerpts which can be pulled from the score without difficulty: the grandmother's lullaby to the dying child, and Magda's tragic recitative and aria from the second act.

Menotti is often compared to Puccini because, like Puccini, he is sensitive to techniques that make the dramatic intentions of the music stand out. He is not afraid of using musical techniques and devices—the dramatic levels of a Mozartian ensemble, the verismo of Puccini, or even the dissonance and atonality of the twentieth century—to create and sustain his dramatic purpose.

—Patricia Robertson

LES CONTES D'HOFFMANN [The Tales of Hoffmann].

Composer: Jacques Offenbach [unfinished; completed by Guiraud].

Librettist: J. Barbier.

First Performance: Paris, Opéra-Comique, 10 February 1881.

Roles: Hoffmann (tenor); Lindorf, Coppélius, Dappertutto, Dr Miracle, four manifestations of Hoffmann's evil genius (should be sung by the same bass-baritone); Stella (speaking); Olympia (soprano); Giulietta (mezzo-soprano); Antonia (soprano); Spalanzani (tenor); Crespel (bass or baritone); Pitichinaccio (tenor); Schlemil (bass or baritone); Frantz (tenor); Nicklausse (mezzo-soprano); A Voice (mezzo-soprano); Muse (speaking); Luther (bass or baritone); Hermann (bass or baritone); Wilhelm (tenor or baritone); Nathaniel (tenor); Andres (tenor); Cochenille (tenor); chorus (SATTBB).

Menotti's *The Consul*, production by Göran Gentele for the Royal Opera, Stockholm, 1952

Publications

book–

Lyon, Raymond, and Louis Saguer. *Les Contes d'Hoffmann: Etude et analyse.* Paris, 1947.

articles–

Avant-scène opéra January-February (1980) [*Les Contes d'Hoffmann* issue].

Peschel, Enid Rhodes, and Richard E. Peschel. "Medecine, Music, and Literature: The Figure of Dr Miracle in Offenbach's *Les Contes d'Hoffmann.*" *Opera Quarterly* summer (1985).

*   *   *

All his life Jacques Offenbach wanted to be accepted as a serious composer, though the bulk of his output had consisted of a lifelong flood of light comic operettas. Many of these had been extremely successful, but Offenbach wanted to write something that would gain him the respect of the serious musical establishment. He finally got his wish, albeit posthumously, with *Les Contes d'Hoffmann*. In this his last opera,

Les contes d'Hoffmann, **Berlin, 1910**

he strove for a level of seriousness seldom if ever evident in the operettas; Antonia's lovely, mournful "Elle a fui, la tourterelle," (The Turtledove has flown) is one of the few sad songs Offenbach ever wrote.

Offenbach had used E.T.A. Hoffmann as a literary source once already, with *Le Roi Carotte,* based on the story of "Kleinzaches, gennant Zinnober." Having seen a play based on some short stories of Hoffmann by Jules Barbier and Michel Carré, writers who had written other librettos, Offenbach decided to use it for an opera. The composer worked more slowly than usual, wanting this to be a serious piece of work. But he continued to turn out lighter pieces, and died without finishing the score. Léon Carvalho, director of the Opéra-Comique, was eager to mount the show anyway. Ernest Guiraud was asked to complete and orchestrate the work, and Carvalho himself made extensive alterations. As a result, there have been many conflicting editions appearing over the years. Although it is impossible to reconstruct it fully, since Offenbach always made changes depending on the audience's reaction to the first performance, *Les Contes d'Hoffmann* remains his most popular work.

The opera is loosely based on three short stories by E.T.A. Hoffmann, in which the main character is Hoffmann himself, living out his own peculiar adventures. This arrangement is justified by Hoffmann's practice of modeling his fictional characters after himself. A lengthy prologue introduces Hoffmann in a tavern with a rowdy group, drinking and singing ("Glug, glug, glug, I am wine, Glug, glug, glug, I am beer!"). A performance of Mozart's *Don Giovanni* is going on next

door. The subject of women comes up, and Hoffmann promises to tell the story of three women whom he has loved: Olympia, Giulietta, and Antonia. But there is a sinister twist to each story.

Act I, drawn from *Der Sandmann,* details Hoffmann's adventure with Olympia, falling madly in love only to learn that the woman is an automaton, smashed in the end by a disgruntled co-creator. Based on *Die Abenteuer der Sylvester-Nacht,* act II introduces the courtesan Giulietta, who, working for Dapertutto, steals the enamored Hoffmann's reflection; she is poisoned with drugged wine intended for Nicklausse. Act III features Antonia from *Rat Krespel;* she is a girl with a lovely voice who becomes ill and fevered when she sings. She agrees to renounce singing, but the evil Dr Miracle invokes the portrait of the girl's dead mother, tempting Antonia to sing, whereupon she collapses and dies.

Throughout these adventures, Hoffmann is accompanied by his one faithful friend, Nicklausse, who tries to protect him. The epilogue returns to the tavern, where Hoffmann's three loves are revealed as incarnations of Stella, who leaves with Lindorf. Nicklausse, on the other hand, reappears as the Muse, who consoles the despondent Hoffmann. "And what of me, your faithful friend, whose hand has dried your tears? I love you, Hoffmann! Be mine!" He replies: "Beloved Muse, I am yours!"

The opera is unified by parallel figures in each act, beginning with Hoffmann's three ill-advised loves, each a manifestation of Stella. (The four roles are often played by the same singer.) Within each of the stories, there is also someone to prevent Hoffmann from being with the woman he loves: Coppélius destroys Olympia, Dapertutto plants the poisoned wine that kills Giulietta, and Dr Miracle causes Antonia to sing herself to death. In the epilogue, Hoffmann's rival Lindorf intercepts Stella. Each of these is a parallel manifestation of the devil (again, usually sung by the same singer).

The libretto does not always live up to the promise of the source. If the women seem shallow, it is perhaps due to their nature as figments of Hoffmann's imagination. But the incarnations of the devil, while increasingly threatening through the course of the three acts, are not always convincing. The evil nature of Lindorf, who appears in the epilogue and prologue, is made ridiculous through self-aggrandizement. "I have the spirit of a devil, of a devil! My eyes flash lightning, and my whole appearance become diabolic," he sings.

Nor is Hoffmann's characterization in the opera profound; he is a pathetic and lonely spirit, yearning in vain for the ideal human woman but not achieving the level of the heroic, tortured Romantic soul. His persona is developed through brief references to a few well-known facts about E.T.A. Hoffmann's life, such as his love of Mozart (which Offenbach shared) and his Romantic reinterpretation of *Don Giovanni,* or veiled references to the beloved Julia Marc. Offenbach sought, and to a degree found, serious legitimacy by using Hoffmann as a source, but the opera does not fully escape the composer's habit of parody.

Whatever the shortcomings of the opera, especially when compared with the genius of E.T.A. Hoffmann, it is redeemed by Offenbach's brilliant music. The harmony is often standard, though there are also inspired touches of chromaticism. But Offenbach's typical tunefulness is raised to new dramatic heights, as in the setting of the prologue, when Hoffmann's dreamy reverie interrupts his energetic description of the misshaped dwarf Kleinzach. Again, the thrilling act III ensemble finale with Antonia, Dr Miracle, and the mother is a well-constructed dramatic admixture of accompanied recitative, lyricism, and trio as the three voices sing increasingly in step with one another. *Les Contes d'Hoffmann* has been acknowledged as Offenbach's masterpiece, and it has gained him more respect and historical attention than would have been the case without it. Offenbach would undoubtedly have been pleased.

—Elizabeth W. Patton

COPLAND, Aaron.

Composer. Born 14 November 1900, in Brooklyn. Died 2 December 1991, in North Tarrytown, New York. Studied piano with Victor Wittgenstein and Clarence Adler in his youth; lessons in harmony and counterpoint with Rubin Goldmark in New York, 1917; studied composition and orches-

tration with Nadia Boulanger in Paris, 1921-24; his early compositions, including *Music for the Theatre* of 1925, were performed by the Boston Symphony under Koussevitzky; member of the board of directors of the League of Composers in New York; organized the Copland-Sessions Concerts with Roger Sessions, 1928-31; founder of the Yaddo Festivals, 1932; lectures and courses at The New School for Social Research, 1935; founder of the American Composers' Alliance, 1937, and the American Music Center, 1939; participant in the Koussevitzky Music Foundation, the Composers' Forum, the Cos Cob Press, and others; head of the composition department at the Berkshire Music Center at Tanglewood, 1940-65; Charles Eliot Norton Lecturer at Harvard University, 1951-52; chairman of the faculty, Berkshire Music Center at Tanglewood, 1957-1965. Guggenheim fellowship, 1925-27; RCA Victor award for his *Dance Symphony;* Pulitzer Prize and New York Music Critics' Circle Award for *Appalachian Spring,* 1945; New York Music Critics' Circle Award for his *3rd Symphony,* 1947; Oscar for the film score of *The Heiress* from the Academy of Motion Picture Arts and Sciences, 1950; Gold Medal for Music from the American Academy of Arts and Letters, 1956; Creative Arts Award, Brandeis University, 1960; MacDowell Medal, 1961; Presidential Medal of Freedom, 1964; Howland Memorial Prize of Yale University, 1970; Commander's Cross of the Order of Merit in West Germany; honorary member of the Santa Cecilia Academy in Rome; Kennedy Center Honors, 1979; Presidential Medal of the Arts and Congressional Gold Medal, 1986; many honorary doctorates. Copland also had a successful career as a conductor, conducting leading orchestras in Europe, South America, Mexico, Russia, Israel, Japan, and the United States.

Aaron Copland, c. 1958

Operas

Publisher: Boosey and Hawkes.

The Second Hurricane (play-opera for high school), E. Denby, 1936, New York, Henry Street Settlement Music School, 21 April 1937.

The Tender Land, H. Everett (after E. Johns), 1952-54, New York, New York City Opera, 1 April 1954; revised 1955, Oberlin, Ohio, 20 May 1955.

Other works: ballets, film scores, orchestral music including symphonies, incidental music to plays, choral works, songs, chamber music, piano pieces.

Publications

By COPLAND: books–

What to Listen for in Music. New York, 1939; 2nd ed., 1957; 3rd ed., 1988.

Our New Music. New York, 1941; revised and enlarged 2nd edition as *The New Music 1900-1960,* 1968.

Music and Imagination. Cambridge, Massachusetts, 1952, 1959.

Copland on Music. New York, 1960.

With Vivian Perlis. *Copland: 1900 Through 1942.* New York and London, 1984.

With Vivian Perlis. *Copland Since 1943.* New York and London, 1989.

articles–

For a bibliography of Copland's many articles, see Gleason and Becker, listed under "About COPLAND: books."

interviews–

Cone, Edward T. "Conversations with Aaron Copland." *Perspectives of New Music* 6 (1968): 57.

Kenyon, Nicholas. "The Scene Surveyed: Nicholas Kenyon Talks to Aaron Copland." *Music and Musicians* 24 (1975): 22.

Interviews by Vivian Perlis, 1975-76. Oral History, American Music, Yale University, New Haven, Connecticut.

Rosenwald, P. "Aaron Copland Talks about a Life in Music." *Wall Street Journal* 14 November (1980): 31.

Smit, L. "A Conversation with Aaron Copland." *Keyboard* 6 (1980): 6.

Gagne, C. and T. Caras, "Aaron Copland." In *Soundpieces: Interviews with American Composers,* 101. Metuchen, New Jersey, 1982.

About COPLAND: books–

Berger, Arthur. *Aaron Copland.* New York, 1953.

Smith, Julia F. *Aaron Copland: His Work and Contribution to American Music.* New York, 1955.

Mellers, W.H. *Music in a New Found Land* [p. 81 ff]. London, 1964.

Zuck, Barbara. *A History of Musical Americanisms.* Ann Arbor, 1980.

Gleason, H. and W. Becker. *Aaron Copland. 20th-century American Composers, Music Literature Outlines,* series iv. Revised 2nd edition, Bloomington, Indiana, 1981.

Skowronski, J. *Aaron Copland: a Bio-bibliography.* Westport, Connecticut, 1985.

Butterworth, Neil. *The Music of Aaron Copland.* London, 1985; New York, 1986.

articles–

Thomson, Virgil. "Aaron Copland." *Modern Music* 9 (1932): 67.

———. "The Teenager's World." [*The Second Hurricane*] *Musical Times* 105 (1964): 500.

Hitchcock, H. Wiley. "Aaron Copland and American Music." *Perspectives of New Music* 19 (1980-81): 31.

*　　*　　*

Aaron Copland, recognized as a leading figure in American music of the twentieth century, had a long and distinguished career. His music has come to be thought of as quintessentially American. As a young man returning from his studies in France in 1924, Copland, with the support of his mentors Nadia Boulanger and Serge Koussevitzky, soon became the leading figure of American avant garde music. From early on, he was interested in the music of his colleagues and was active and effective in encouraging and promoting performances of their music. In order to create an American sound, Copland's early works incorporated jazz idioms, shocking concert audiences and critics. He then turned to a more abstract and difficult compositional style for several years. As pianist, Copland premiered his early keyboard works and performed the difficult piano parts in his orchestral and chamber music scores. In the late thirties, to reach a wider audience, he adopted a more accessible tonal style of composing and became interested in music to be used for ballet, film, radio, and theater. He frequently incorporated folk tunes into his works. Orchestral suites derived from the ballet scores, such as *Appalachian Spring, Billy the Kid,* and *Rodeo,* are among his most popular pieces.

Copland's first opera, *The Second Hurricane,* in two acts, ninety minutes duration, was composed for high school students, as a "play-opera," using vernacular speech rather than operatic recitative between the set pieces. Copland's intention was to create a work in a simple tonal style that could be performed by young non-professional musicians. *The Second Hurricane* calls for seven soloists, three spoken parts, a mixed chorus, and an orchestra that includes saxophone and musical saw. The premiere was at the Henry Street Settlement Music School, New York City, 21 April 1937, conducted by L. Engel, directed by O. Welles. Reviews were mixed and especially critical of the libretto. Occasional performances of *The Second Hurricane* followed the premiere. Leonard Bernstein directed the opera in Boston in 1942, and in 1960 produced a television version, later recorded, which he conducted and narrated.

Although Copland composed songs, arranged folk songs, and created a song cycle, *Twelve Poems of Emily Dickinson,* 1950, he wrote only one full-length opera, *The Tender Land* [see separate entry]. Following the premiere in 1954, Copland expressed his intention to compose more opera. He discussed ideas with various writers, but none came to fruition.

—Vivian Perlis

COPLEY, John (Michael Harold).

Director. Born 12 June 1933, in Birmingham, England. Attended Sadler's Wells Ballet School; diploma, honors in theater design, Central School of Arts and Crafts, London; studied at National School of Opera with Joan Cross; created the Apprentice in *Peter Grimes,* 1950; stage manager at Sadler's Wells Theatre (opera and ballet), 1953-57, and other theaters; deputy stage manager at Royal Opera House, Covent Garden, 1960-63, then assistant resident producer, 1963-66, associate, 1966-72, resident producer, 1972-75, and principal resident producer, 1975-88; stage direction debut in *Le nozze di Figaro,* Hintlesham Festival; particularly associated with the staging of Mozart's operas; has taught at the Royal Academy of Music and the London Opera Center.

Opera Productions (selected)

Le nozze di Figaro, Hintlesham Festival.
Il tabarro, Sadler's Wells, 1957.
Suor Angelica, Covent Garden, 1965.
Così fan tutte, Covent Garden, 1968 and 1981.
Orfeo ed Euridice, Covent Garden, 1969.
Carmen, Sadler's Wells, 1970.
Le nozze di Figaro, Covent Garden, 1971.
Lucia di Lammermoor, Dallas Opera, 1972.
Don Giovanni, Covent Garden, 1973.
La bohème, Covent Garden, 1974 and 1975.
Faust, Covent Garden, 1974.
Belle Hélène, London, Coliseum, 1975.
L'elisir d'amore, Covent Garden, 1975, 1981, and 1985.
Benvenuto Cellini, Covent Garden, 1976.
Ariadne auf Naxos, Covent Garden, 1976.
Maria Stuarda, Royal Silver Jubilee Gala, 1977.
Werther, Covent Garden, 1979.
Manon, London, Coliseum, 1979.
Aida, London, Coliseum, 1979.
Julius Caesar, London, Coliseum, 1979.
Le mamelles de Tirésias, London, Coliseum, 1979.
La traviata, Covent Garden, 1980.
Lucrezia Borgia, Covent Garden, 1980.
Alceste, Covent Garden, 1981.
Semele, Covent Garden, 1982 and 1988.
Peter Grimes, Welsh National Opera, 1983.
Midsummer Night's Dream, Ottawa Festival, 1983.
Eugene Onegin, Ottawa Festival, 1983.
The Midsummer Marriage, San Francisco Opera, 1983.
Adriana Lecouvreur, Munich, Staatsoper, 1984.
Orlando, Chicago, Lyric Opera, 1986.
Norma, Covent Garden, 1987.
La forza del destino, Toronto, Canadian Opera, 1987.
Carmen, Australian Opera, 1987.
Ariodante, Santa Fe Opera, 1987.
Semiramide, Metropolitan Opera, 1991.

Publications

By COPLEY: articles–

"Rehearsed By (Interview with Ande Anderson and John Copley)." *About the House* 2, no. 1 (1966): 18-21.

John Copley's production of Puccini's *La bohème*, Royal Opera, London, 1987 (with Thomas Allen, Plácido Domingo and Ilona Tokody)

"The Producer Speaks (Conversation with Harold Rosenthal)." *Opera* 24 (May 1973): 413-17.
"Handel in Performance (Conversation with Harold Rosenthal)." *Opera* (March 1985).

About COPLEY: articles–

"John Copley—Max Loppert Attends a Rehearsal for *Mary Stuart.*" *Music and Musicians* 22 (January 1974): 30-32.
Kentridge, C. "Soundings: John Copley Speaks Out (On Renting Opera Productions)." *Opera Canada* 29, no. 2 (1988): 24-25.

* * *

Director John Copley has been active in the operatic world since the 1960s, initially in England and more recently in the United States and Australia. Associated with Covent Garden since 1960, he became resident producer in 1972. His first Covent Garden production was Puccini's *Suor Angelica,* in 1965. This was followed by Mozart's *Così fan tutte* in 1968; it was hailed as one of the first successful Mozart productions in the house, achieving an appropriate intimacy despite the size of the theater. He later produced Gluck's *Orfeo ed Euridice* (1969), Donizetti's *L'elisir d'amore* (1975), Berlioz's *Benvenuto Cellini* (1976), and Handel's *Semele* (1982) there. His American debut was with a production of Donizetti's *Lucia di Lammermoor* in Dallas (1972).

Copley's productions are marked by a wealth of detail and properly thought-out movement, and an attention to the requirements of staging intimate scenes in the expanses of the opera stage. Copley's staging of Bizet's *Carmen* at the London Coliseum was the first production at that theater to take advantage of its capabilities as an opera house.

Copley has said that he approaches the direction of an opera from the starting point of the musical notes and their interpretation rather than from an extraneous "concept." He is opposed to directorial touches involving stage business that makes it difficult for singers to perform their roles. Although he takes a traditional, even conservative, approach to opera production, he feels that overly elaborate sets are unnecessary and tends toward what he calls the "simplification" of productions.

During the 1970s, Copley mounted productions at most of the world's major opera companies—including Welsh National Opera, the Scottish Opera, the English National Opera, the Australian Opera, the Washington Opera, the New York City Opera, the San Francisco Opera, Houston Grand Opera, Lyric Opera of Chicago, Festival Ottawa, Canadian Opera, Covent Garden, Opera North, and the Bavarian Staatsoper—in a repertory ranging from Handel to Poulenc. At the Metropolitan Opera, Copley directed Rossini's *Semiramide* (1991), the first production of the work there since 1895. For the 1991-92 season Copley mounted a new production of *L'elisir d'amore.*

—Michael Sims

CORELLI, Franco.

Tenor. Born 4 August 1921, in Ancona. Married singer Loretta di Lelio. Attended Liceo Musicale, Pesaro. Debut as

Don José in *Carmen,* Spoleto, 1951; Teatro alla Scala debut as Licinio in *Vestale,* 1954, and continued to sing there until 1965; Covent Garden debut as Cavaradossi in *Tosca,* 1957; Metropolitan Opera debut as Manrico, 1961, and sang there regularly until 1975; appeared at Berlin Städtische Oper, 1961, Vienna Staatsoper, 1963, and Paris Opéra, 1970.

Publications

About CORELLI: books–

Celletti, R. *Le grandi voci.* Rome, 1964.

articles–

Osborne, C.L. "Franco Corelli." *High Fidelity,* 17/no. 2 (1967): 63.
Celletti, R. "Franco Corelli." *Discoteca* no. 111 (1971): 14.

* * *

Some operatic voices suggest color associations or personalities. Franco Corelli's voice is unusual in that his recordings have an immediacy which suggests actual physical presence. Some admire Pavarotti's flexibility and strength; others may appreciate Domingo's clarity or Carreras's refinement. Corelli was of a different breed. A contemporary of del Monaco and di Stefano, his tenor was one of the most remarkable, with a ringing and potent force that sounds as if its possessor could sustain his notes indefinitely. It is also a beautiful voice offering great strength as well as heart-breaking tenderness.

Franco Corelli in *Les Huguenots*

Compared to many other singers, Corelli came to opera rather late in his life: he began to study voice at twenty-three. He comes from the same region of Italy by the Adriatic Sea as Tebaldi, del Monaco, Cerquetti and Gigli, and according to all sources, the people of Ancona have long said "Beautiful voices are born in this area." The Corelli family did not have a particularly musical background, and Franco began his young adulthood as a student of naval engineering. Impressed with his natural ability, friends encouraged him to train his voice, and after some study at the Pesaro Conservatory of Music, he entered and won a vocal competition at the Maggio Musicale in 1951.

At this point, his study took an unusual turn. Twice he studied with voice teachers, once before and once after winning the vocal competition; he found vocal studies unsatisfactory. Deciding he was his own best teacher, he became virtually self-taught. He learned about vocal technique from the recordings of Caruso, Lauri-Volpi and Gigli, gleaning from them details of style and projection to complement his natural technique. He apparently memorized roles through the phonograph, making him purely a tenor of the recording age. Singers traditionally rely on one or two mentors to guide their development. Since a recorded voice provides no critique or interaction, it may seem like an ineffective teacher. However, the results are impressive in Corelli's case. By shaping his voice along the lines of legendary tenors of the past, Corelli perfected a style of singing suited to the age of the long-playing record. It is certainly no wonder that his voice suggests physical presence.

The "physical presence" of his voice stems from his surety, firmness and phenomenal reserves of power. One is tempted to attribute his dramatic capabilities to his non-musical background, and correlate the strength he shows on stage to his resolution and determination to teach himself. Mainly, though, his voice carries the drama in a role. Though reviewers periodically claimed he was stiff in performance and substituted posing for acting, the roles in which he specialized do not call for intricacies of feeling. However, videotapes reveal him to have been a performer who concentrated on creating drama rather than just projecting voice. He is very satisfying. Many of his numerous performances spanning the 1950s and 1960s are available on broadcast tapes, and he has been credited with reviving many obscure operas including Donizetti's *Poliuto* and Allegra's *Romulus*.

Four roles show off Corelli's power, stamina and vibrancy to their best advantage: the title role in Giordano's *Andrea Chénier*, Manrico and Radamès in Verdi's *Il trovatore* and *Aida*, and Calaf in Puccini's *Turandot*. These are such operatic standards that the singer who can make them distinctive stands out from other tenors. Corelli differentiates himself from others in these works, and fills the roles superbly with ample, free-flowing voice. Although many can perform them, few can sound as if they inhabit Calaf or Manrico by sheer vocal force. As an example of that force, Corelli is in peak form in the recording of *Turandot* with Birgit Nilsson as his voice manifests the exuberance and hubris of Calaf.

Corelli certainly had his detractors, though, who note a sameness to his approach in various roles, a tendency to hold high notes too long, and, as Paul Henry Lang wrote in the *New York Herald Tribune* in the early 1960s, "inadequate" legato and pianissimo. While much of the criticism of his career is well-founded, he has inspired a core group of admirers who believe the strength and magnitude of his voice render such criticism superfluous. While he does sound miraculous in a specialized repertory, his voice is not so pliable that he can assume any tenor role with equal results.

Corelli has, not surprisingly, what some consider the most Italianate of traits, the tendency to embed a note with a throaty sob. Perhaps the greatest example of this is his recording of Leoncavallo's *I pagliacci*. Both detractors and admirers focus on this ability. Often critics maintain his way with a sob sacrifices music for the sake of cheap effect. But for music in which sentiment precedes other considerations, the sob is appropriate. His recording of the most familiar of Neapolitan songs, " 'O sole mio," bears this out. The poem equates the sun in the daytime to a lover's eyes at night, and while the conclusion has not the all-out sob you hear in "Vesti la giubba," the result is nonetheless compelling.

Corelli is nearly always compelling, and to hear him at his best, one should listen to his three recordings with Birgit Nilsson: *Turandot, Aida,* and *Tosca*. These show him off as the perfect match for another singer with a big voice and great reserves of power. Any operatic recording will reveal his individual timbre and exciting presence, but his readings of Neapolitan songs have an authority and charming conviction that are telling, too. Even if one is bothered by his tendency to sob, or his lack of pianissimo, the richness, vibrancy and presence of his voice place it among the most satisfying.

In Corelli we hear how a voice can be as individual as a face, and how that individuality transforms some of the most-performed roles in the tenor repertoire into fresh experiences.

—Timothy O. Gray

CORENA, Fernando.

Bass-baritone. Born 22 December 1916. Died November 1984, in Lugano; studied for holy orders in Fribourg University, but won a music competition, and studied music in Geneva, 1937-38, and with Enrico Romani in Milan; Italian debut in Tricote, 1947; appeared regularly throughout Italy; sang in 1949 premiere of Petrassi's *Cordovano* at Teatro alla Scala; debut at Metropolitan Opera as Leporello, 1954; debut at Covent Garden as Rossini's Bartolo; sang Osmin in *Die Entführung aus dem Serail* at Salzburg, 1965.

*　　*　　*

The basso buffo tradition began in Naples in the early eighteenth century with the Casaccia family, who dominated buffo singing there for four generations, generally performing in dialect. Some members went in for broad comedy. Stendahl had this to say of Carlo Casaccia in connection with his appearance at the city's Teatro dei Fiorentini in Pietro Carlo Guglielmi's *Paolo e Virginia* in 1817: "[T]he famous Casaccia . . . is enormous, a fact that gives him opportunity for considerable pleasant buffoonery. When seated, he undertakes to give himself an appearance of ease by crossing his legs; impossible; the effort that he goes through topples him onto his neighbor; a general collapse. This actor, commonly called Casacciello, is adored by the public; he has the nasal voice of a Capuchin. At this theater, everyone sings through his nose."

During the eighteenth century two types of buffo emerged: the "buffo nobile," or noble comic, and the "buffo caricato," or exaggerated comic. The same singers who undertook "basso cantante" or non-comic lyric bass roles also frequently sang those for buffo nobile, for they are similar in vocal demands, often requiring virtuosity. Buffo caricato parts, on the other hand, were a specialty, calling for falsetto singing in imitation of women and, above all, patter singing or chatter. Beauty of tone is of small consequence for a buffo caricato, mastery of comic effect essential. The part of Don Basilio in *Il barbiere di Siviglia* is for buffo nobile, that for Don Bartolo in the same opera for buffo caricato. The florid passages for Mustafà in *L'Italiana in Algeri* are not very different than those for Assur in *Semiramide,* and in fact both roles were written for Filippo Galli, who moved comfortably between the nobile and cantante genres. On the other hand Taddeo in *L'Italiana* is a patter part.

Fernando Corena had wonderful flair as a buffo caricato, and his best role was Bartolo—at first grand and expansive, exuding self-importance and pomposity, then sputtering with outrage. He invariably stole the show. But when he crossed over into parts for basso cantante, such as Il conte Rodolfo in *La sonnambula* or those for buffo nobile, such as Mustafà, he sounded ungainly—labored in coloratura and spread in pitch. Still, his voice was truer than that of Salvatore Baccaloni, his immediate predecessor. Corena was able to swat out Mustafà's Gs, beyond the range of many basses; however, particularly in later years, he sounded strained in the high tessitura of the *L'elisir d'amore* entrance aria, with its many Es. His voice retained substance no matter how quickly he chattered. And he was masterful at caricaturing women in falsetto, for example, at the interpolated words "sul tamburo" in *Barbiere.*

On stage, Baccaloni, a comedian, was never out of character. He claimed to have prepared five ways to play each moment, once remarking, "I choose. Only a fool improvises." Corena, a clown, often improvised—and frequently amused himself by playing pranks on other singers. He was better at expressing extroverted feelings than deep dark emotions. Portraying Falstaff as a clown, he failed to capture the character's reflective side. As Leporello (*Don Giovanni*) he was a delight in the "Catalogue" aria, somewhat of a disappointment toward the opera's end. As Don Pasquale he was a triumph—except in those passages calling for pathos. Above all, Corena excelled at detailing foibles and pomposity. He was pre-eminent in his repertoire from the mid-fifties until the late seventies.

—Stefan Zucker

CORNELIUS, Peter.

Composer. Born 24 December 1824, in Mainz. Died 26 October 1874, in Mainz. Married: Bertha Jung. Trained as an actor by his father; music lessons with Josef Panny and Heinrich Esser; violinist with the Mainz theater orchestra, 1840; actor with the Nassau court theater troupe, 1842-43; studied theory with Siegfried Wilhelm Dehn in Berlin, 1845-52; studied with Liszt in Weimar, 1852; met Wagner in Basle, 1853; composed lieder, 1853-54, and *Der Barbier von Bagdad,* 1855-58; in Vienna, 1859-65; contributed many articles to the *Neue Zeitschrift für Musik;* appointed reader to King Ludwig II and professor of harmony and rhetoric at the Royal Music School, 1865. Cornelius' circle of friends included Bülow, Bronsart, Damrosch, Draeseke, Joachim, Raff, Berlioz, Brahms, and the poet Friedrich Hebbel.

Operas

Edition: *P. Cornelius: Musikalische Werke.* Edited by M. Hasse. Leipzig, 1905-06.

Der Barbier von Bagdad, Cornelius, 1855-58, Weimar, 15 December 1858.
Der Cid, Cornelius, 1860-62, Weimar, 21 May 1865.
Gunlöd, Cornelius, 1866-74 [unfinished; completed and orchestrated by W. von Bauszern in vol. V of the Hasse edition]

Other works: vocal music.

Publications/Writings

By CORNELIUS: books–

Literarische Werke. Edited by C.M. Cornelius, E. Istel, and A. Stern. 4 vols. Leipzig, 1904-05.

About CORNELIUS: books–

Kretzschmar, H. *Peter Cornelius,* Leipzig, 1880.
Sandberger, A. *Leben und Werke des Dichterkomponisten Peter Cornelius.* Leipzig, 1887.
Hasse, Max. *Peter Cornelius und sein "Barbier von Bagdad."* Leipzig, 1904.
————. *Der Dichtermusiker Peter Cornelius.* 2 vols. Leipzig, 1922-23.
Cornelius, Carl Maria. *Peter Cornelius: Der Wort- und Tondichter.* Regensburg, 1925.
Glauert, B. *Spuren eines bewegten Lebens: Verschollenes und Unveröffentlichtes von Peter Cornelius.* Mainz, 1974.
Jacob, Walter. *Der beschwerliche Weg des Peter Cornelius zu Liszt und Wagner.* Mainz, 1974.
Federhofer, H., ed. *Peter Cornelius als Komponist, Dichter, Kritiker und Essayist.* Regensburg, forthcoming.
Wagner, G. *Peter Cornelius: ein Verzeichnis seiner musikalischen und literarischen Werke.* Tutzing, forthcoming.

articles–

Bartlett, K.W. "Peter Cornelius and *The Barber of Bagdad.*" *Opera* August (1956).
Wurmser, Leo. "Cornelius and his *Barber.*" *Opera* December (1965).

unpublished–

Pricken, K. "Peter Cornelius als Dichter und Musiker in seinem Liedschaffen." Ph.D. dissertation, University of Cologne, 1951.

*   *   *

Peter Cornelius lived in the very heyday of nineteenth-century Romanticism. In many ways a typical product of his time, his romantic, gentle nature was singularly suited to artistic ideals fostered by that tumultuous period. Also in common with other great musicians of the period, Cornelius was literarily motivated and able to transform poetry into exquisite sound images. In fact he was known as a poet as well as a musician, and he even had done some acting. Given the requisite talent, which he certainly had, this combination of abilities suited him perfectly for the operatic stage.

He produced three operas during his lifetime, all of which met with much criticism and received very few performances. The first of these, *Der Barbier von Bagdad,* has since achieved the status of a masterpiece, at least in Germany, while the others, *Der Cid* and *Gunlöd,* are largely unknown and almost never performed.

Cornelius, the non-heroic lyricist, was something of an anomaly in an age which produced such larger than life artists as Schumann, Liszt, and Wagner. Yet Cornelius was fascinated by and learned much from men like Liszt and Wagner, and he also took careful note of Berlioz's work. Mainly the influences show up in certain harmonic subtleties, and in his brilliant orchestrations. A composer of strong tonal tendencies, his frequent touches of chromaticism create a piquant, curious atmosphere, at once charming and surprising. However, Liszt's and Wagner's heavy trowel is replaced in Cornelius by the air brush, and a spirit of evanescence reigns supreme. Similarly, Cornelius's orchestra is remarkably colorful, and in this he admitted the strong influence of Berlioz, as well as the other two giants. But whereas there are lightning flashes in the Berlioz orchestra, Cornelius's merely flickers. Again, lyricism and subtlety are the operative principles.

While Cornelius didn't compose a great deal of music, there is much more than is generally realized. His many songs (of which only the *Weihnachtslieder* are generally known) are outstanding, and he has produced some exceptionally beautiful church music. But if his name has any other than an historical importance it is because of his most famous work, *Der Barbier von Bagdad.* With a highly polished libretto of his own creation, Cornelius has borrowed from the stories of the *Arabian Nights* to produce a generally comic opera which yet has many moments of pathos and even tragedy. The barber, unlike Rossini's Hispanic version, can only ruin whatever he touches. Aged and ragged, he is at once pitiful and maddening, and he talks incessantly, usually in absurd rhymed couplets! The young lovers seem like deliberate paste-board characters whom one can only laugh at until they turn surprisingly vital and quite serious. For them in particular Cornelius provides gloriously beautiful melodies lightly supported by an always luminous orchestra, after which the characters are made to look and act like parodies of themselves and their operatic types again. The result is a quietly out-of-kilter picture with several sly smiles and a tear every so often. Not a formula for great fame, *Barber* is still a unique opera.

—Harris Crohn

THE CORONATION OF POPPEA
See L'INCORONAZIONE DI POPPEA

DER CORREGIDOR [The Magistrate].

Composer: Hugo Wolf.

Librettist: R. Mayreder (after Alarcón, *El sombrero de tres picos*).

First Performance: Mannheim, 7 June 1896; revised, Strasbourg, 29 April 1898.

Roles: Don Eugenio (tenor); Juan Lopez (bass); Pedro (tenor); Tonuelo (bass); Repela (bass); Tio Lukas (baritone); Donna Mercedes (soprano); Frasquita (mezzo-soprano); Duenna (contralto); Manuela (mezzo-soprano); chorus.

Publications

book–

Cook, P. *Hugo Wolf's Der Corregidor.* London, 1976.

* * *

The composition of *Der Corregidor* represented for Hugo Wolf the fulfillment of his life's dream. Since the early 1880s, at least, he was obsessed with the idea of writing an opera. As early as the winter of 1882-83 Wolf drafted the libretto for an opera set in Spain. In 1890 he was offered, and initially rejected, a text based on Pedro de Alarcón's novel *El sombrero de tres picos* (The Three-Cornered Hat) by Rosa Mayreder, a writer who was active in the Austrian women's movement. Early in 1895 Wolf read a version of Alarcón's story by the chairman of the Wagner-Verein, Franz Schaumann. Although he rejected it, the new libretto reminded Wolf of the earlier one by Mayreder. When he read it for the second time, Wolf reversed his earlier decision and decided to use her libretto. The piano score was composed in fourteen weeks of intensive work during the spring and summer of 1895; the orchestration occupied the rest of the year.

The opera takes place in Andalusia in 1804. An amiable, hunchbacked miller, Tio Lukas, lives happily with his beautiful wife, Frasquita. Don Eugenio de Zuniga, the corregidor (magistrate), who is old and also hunchbacked, visits the mill and tries unsuccessfully to seduce Frasquita. After his first failed attempt, he arranges for Lukas to be called away that night to the house of the alcalde (mayor), and Frasquita is left alone at the mill. While she is alone, she hears a cry for help outside. Thinking it is Lukas, she opens the door and finds that it is the corregidor, who has accidentally fallen into the brook. He enters the house dripping wet and continues to pursue Frasquita, first by offering her an official appointment for her nephew, then by threatening her with a pistol. When she counters with Lukas's blunderbuss, the corregidor faints and is put to bed at the mill, and Frasquita leaves to search for Lukas at the alcalde's house. Meanwhile, Lukas has escaped by tricking the alcalde and his friends into drinking heavily. When he arrives home, he finds the door unlocked, the corregidor's clothes spread out before the fire, the document of appointment for Frasquita's nephew, and through a keyhole he sees the corregidor asleep in the bedroom. He assumes the worst and conceives a form of vengeance involving the corregidor's lovely wife. Lukas leaves for the corregidor's house wearing the corregidor's clothes. When the corregidor awakens and discovers that his clothes are gone, he puts on Lukas's. He is then attacked both by his own followers, who mistake him for the miller, and by his servants at his own home. The corregidor's wife, Donna Mercedes, tells him that her husband has long been home and in bed beside her. While the corregidor changes into his own clothes, we learn that Lukas told his story to the corregidor's wife and that she decided to teach him a lesson by pretending that Lukas's venture was successful.

Despite the fact that its level of musical craftsmanship is quite high, *Der Corregidor* is rarely performed and has never been part of the standard operatic repertoire. Much of the work's lack of success is attributable to its weak libretto, which Wolf's biographer, Frank Walker, has characterized as an "amateurish, hopelessly undramatic piece of poetic carpentry." The shortcomings of the text are especially acute in act IV, most of which does not advance the drama appreciably but instead recapitulates themes and events that were presented earlier. The work has also been criticized for the excessive rapidity of the action on stage and the concomitant failure to establish firmly the atmosphere of the various scenes. To some, it has seemed more like an expanded song cycle with orchestral accompaniment than an opera (indeed, two songs from the *Spanisches Liederbuch* [Spanish Songbook] were incorporated into *Der Corregidor*). These problems are clearly the consequences of Wolf's indifference to the details of staging. This attitude was especially evident in the rehearsals preceding the work's premiere, when it was discovered that he was completely uninterested in what was happening on the stage.

Despite these drawbacks, *Der Corregidor* contains some wonderful dramatic moments. The best scene of the opera is Lukas's monologue of jealousy in act III, scene iii. Each stage of his internal struggle—from shock and disbelief, to despair and the desire for revenge—is depicted vividly and powerfully. Walker has called it "one of the greatest scenes in all operatic literature . . . Wolf's unique masterpiece in the domain of opera."

There is also much to admire in the music of *Der Corregidor*. One of the most beautiful numbers is the tender love duet of Lukas and Frasquita in the first scene of act II. The orchestral interlude ("Zwischenspiel") between scenes vi and vii later in the same act—which shares the light texture and rhythmic drive of the scherzo from Mendelssohn's incidental music to *A Midsummer Night's Dream*—is another memorable section. Unfortunately, however, the thick, Wagnerian orchestration which dominates most of the work—and which seems incompatible with the sunny mood and milieu of the story—often overwhelms and weighs down the voices.

In recent years, *Der Corregidor* has occasionally been performed in unstaged concert versions. As much as this would have pained its composer, this manner of presentation—with cuts, especially in act IV—is the one most likely to ensure the work a place in modern musical life.

—Stephen A. Crist

CORSARO, Frank Andrew

Director. Born 22 December 1924, in New York, Married: singer Mary Cross "Bonnie" Lueders, 1971; one son. Educated at Yale School of Drama, graduated 1947; Actors Studio, New York 1954-67; opera debut, *Susannah*, New York City Opera 1958; resident director of the New York City Opera, since 1965-; directed world premiers of Floyd's *Of Mice and Men*, 1970, and *Flower and Hawk*, 1972; Hoiby's

Summer and Smoke, 1971; and Pasatieri's *The Seagull*, 1974; produced *Prince Igor* for video; Broadway productions include *Night of the Iguana*, 1961.

Opera Productions (selected)

Susannah, New York City Opera, 1958.
The Fiery Angel, Spoleto Festival, Teatro Caio Melisso, 1959.
Katerina Ismailova, New York City Opera, 1965.
Prince Igor, New York, State Theatre, 1969.
Faust, New York, State Theatre, 1969.
Koanga, Washington, DC, Lisner Auditorium, 1970.
The Makropoulos Affair (Vec Makropoulos), New York, State Theatre, 1970.
Pelléas et Mélisande, New York, State Theatre, 1970.
Of Mice and Men, Seattle Opera, 1970.
Summer and Smoke, St. Paul, 1971.
Flower and Hawk, Jacksonville Symphony, 1972.
Don Giovanni, New York City Opera, 1972.
Village Romeo and Juliet, Washington, DC, Kennedy Center, 1972.
L'incoronazione di Poppea, Washington, DC, 1972.
Cervantes, Washington, DC, 1973.
Manon Lescaut, New York City Opera, 1974.
The Seagull, Houston, 1974.
Lulu, Houston Grand Opera, 1975.
Die tote Stadt, New York, State Theatre, 1975.
Rinaldo, Houston Grand Opera, 1975.
L'Ormindo, Caramoor Music Festival, 1975.
Treemonisha, Houston, Miller Theater, 1975.
Doktor Faustus, Wolf Trap, 1977.
Die Zauberflöte, Houston, 1981.
La fanciulla del west, Deutsche Oper, Berlin, 1983.
Fennimore and Gerda, Edinburgh Festival, 1983.
The Love of Three Oranges, Glyndebourne, 1983.
Where the Wild Things Are, Glyndebourne, 1984.
Carmen, New York City Opera, 1984.
Higgledy, Piggledy, Pop, Glyndebourne, 1985.
L'heure espagnole, Glyndebourne, 1988.
L'enfant et les sortilèges, Glyndebourne, 1988.
Idomeneo, Los Angeles, 1991.

Publications

By CORSARO: books–

Maverick, a director's personal experience in opera and theater. New York, 1978.
with Maurice Sendak. *The Love for Three Oranges: the Glyndebourne version.* New York, 1984.
Libretto to *Before Breakfast.* Belwin-Mills.

articles–

"*Of Mice and Men*—the direction." *Opera Journal* 4/1 (1971): 12.
"Parings on Pasatieri." *Opera Journal* 9/2 (1976): 29.
" 'Malinscenation?' No!" *Opera News* 45 (7 March 1981): 9.

About CORSARO: books–

Guttman, Gilda Rae. *Multi-media projected scenery: Three New York City Opera productions directed by Frank Corsaro.* Ph.D. Dissertation, New York University, 1981.

articles–

"Avoiding the patterns." *Opera News* 31 (25 March 1967): 16.

Osborne, C.L. "Frank Corsaro vs. 'the great theatrical crimes'." *Hi Fidelity/Musical America* 19/May (1969): 24.

Kolodin, Irving. "Music to my ears." *The Saturday Review* 53 (21 November 1970): 86.

Cumming, R. "Corsaro, the operatic maverick." *Music Journal* 29/May (1971): 48.

Zachary, R. "Corsaro." *Opera News* 32/August (1972): 16.

Osborne, C.L. "Frank Corsaro." *Hi Fidelity/Musical America* 24/June (1974): MA6.

Seabury, D. "In a class with Corsaro—how a noted director helps young singers unlock their art." *Opera News* 39 (8 March 1975): 26.

"Let's make an opera: the collaboration (roundtable discussion at the New York Opera Club)." *Opera Digest* 4/1 (1984): 2.

"Uj szelek—uj rendezok az amerikai operahazakban." *Muzsika* 31/May (1988): 18.

Duffie, B. "Conversation piece: Frank Corsaro." *Opera Journal* 23/4 (1990): 51.

*   *   *

As a director, Frank Corsaro feels that "the prime task in bringing a work to life is the search for its psychologic and spiritual reality. . . . Initial emphasis is placed on fleshing out the lives of the characters in the work—paying particular regard to their ambivalences and contradictions." If these words recall the manifesto of that style of acting known as "The Method," there is a reason. Corsaro himself was an integral part of The Method's American home, the Actors Studio in New York, from 1954 to 1967. He had become involved in directing as an undergraduate at the Yale School of Drama, and at the Actors Studio he worked with young actors (among them James Dean, Steve McQueen, and, briefly, Marilyn Monroe) to unlock the motivations behind their characters' actions and to devise a stage presentation which would elucidate those motivations.

As a child, Corsaro was exposed to opera through his mother's singing and through the Saturday afternoon Metropolitan Opera radio broadcasts. He loved the music, but as an adolescent he became disillusioned by the productions he attended at the Met, especially by the poor acting. However, a performance by Maria Callas in *Lucia di Lammermoor* rekindled his interest in opera. To him, her acting realized the dramatic possibilities of opera he had felt but never seen.

In the late 1950s Corsaro directed two operas, Floyd's *Susannah* at the New York City Opera and Prokofiev's *The Fiery Angel* at the Spoleto Festival, but he considered them disconnected and ultimately frustrating ventures. When he felt prepared to tackle opera again, he contacted the New York City Opera. In 1965, he began his long-term association with that company with Shostakovich's *Katerina Ismailova*.

Corsaro works closely with his singers, creating histories and motivations for their characters, stressing the psychological reality of the drama. More often than not, this approach includes a strong sexual slant ("We are all Freud's children," he says). As Julius Rudel, head of the New York City Opera, has noted, all opera is obsessed with sex and violence. Both his supporters and his detractors would agree that Corsaro does tend to emphasize those elements in his productions.

Although Corsaro considers stage design secondary to the singer-actors' performances in the realization of a production, it is often the visual aspect of his staging which excites the most comment. His 1970 *Pelléas et Mélisande* was played behind a gauze scrim to "diffuse matters further" and to lend the opera a "patina of long ago and far away." However, it was *The Makropoulos Affair* of the same year which introduced a major element of the Corsaro style—the multi-media production. The combination of live stage action with projections had been used in ballet and theater, but Corsaro's was the first use in opera in America. In his staging of the Janáček opera, which unfolds backward in time, the entire look was influenced by German expressionist films. The present action took place on a stage set done in shades of gray to match the black-and-white film shot by Corsaro and Emile Ardolino. The film, which related the flashbacks, was projected onto nine jigsaw-puzzle-shaped screens designed by Gardner Compton.

After the success of *The Makropoulos Affair*, Corsaro was set to direct the Broadway premiere of *Jesus Christ Superstar*. He worked closely with Andrew Lloyd Webber and Tim Rice on the staging of their work, but a fractured vertebra from a car crash took him out of the production.

The leap from Janáček to Lloyd Webber is indicative of the broad range of Corsaro's activities. In addition to drama and ballet, Corsaro has staged operas ranging from Monteverdi's *L'incoronazione di Poppea* to the world premieres of American operas, such as Pasatieri's *The Seagull* and Floyd's *Of Mice and Men*. He has also revived long-unheard operas of Delius—*Koanga, Fennimore and Gerda*—and the Scott Joplin opera *Treemonisha*, which was a success in Washington, D.C. but struggled for acceptance on Broadway.

Corsaro was also part of the Carmen "wave." In the early 1980s, Peter Brook's stripped-down *La tragédie de Carmen* excited considerable controversy, Francesco Rosi's film with Placido Domingo and Julia Migenes Johnson brought the opera to a broad audience, and that film's choreographer, Antonio Gades, collaborated with filmmaker Carlos Saura to produce an acclaimed flamenco version. Somewhat less controversial than Brook's production and less unorthodox than the reality-bending Gades/Saura interpretation, Corsaro's *Carmen* still came in for a fair amount of criticism. In his staging, the action was moved up to the Spanish Civil War, with Carmen's motivations political as well as amorous.

Among Corsaro's other productions of the 1980s, several were designed by Maurice Sendak. *The Love For Three Oranges* was a marked success and led to their collaboration on two new operas, *Where the Wild Things Are* and *Higgledy, Piggledy, Pop,* with music by Oliver Knussen. Sendak also designed Corsaro's productions of Ravel's two rarely performed operas, *L'heure espagnole* and *L'enfant et les sortilèges*.

Although the visual aspects of Corsaro's productions have sometimes been considered "overwhelming" and the stage action "too busy" by the critics, many commentators also acknowledge the director's innate sense of theatricality and the success of individual elements of the staging, even when overarching concepts seem to fail (and, at times, the success of overarching concepts when individual elements fail). One critic, Patrick J. Smith, has noted more than once, however, that Corsaro's true strength lies in guiding the singer-actors— the part of his work Corsaro himself regards as the most important.

—Robynn J. Stilwell

UNA COSA RARA ossia Bellezza ed onestà [A Rare Occurrence, or Beauty and Virtue].

Composer: Vicente Martín y Soler.

Librettist: Lorenzo Da Ponte (after L. Vélez de Guevera).

First Performance: Vienna, Burgtheater, 17 November 1786.

Roles: Isabella (soprano); Giovanni (tenor); Corrado (tenor); Lilla (soprano): Ghita (soprano); Lubino (bass); Tita (bass); Lisargo (bass); chorus.

Publications

articles–

Genée, R. " 'Una cosa rara' in Mozarts 'Don Juan'." *Mitteilungen für die Mozart-Gemeinde Berlin* 1 (1900): 63.
"Vinzenz Martin, der Komponist von 'Una cosa rara'." *Mitteilungen für die Mozart-Gemeinde Berlin* 2 (1906): 23.
Walter, E. "Vicente Martin i Soler i la seva òpera. 'Una cosa raro o sia bellezza ed onestà'." *Revista musical catalana* 33 (1936): 144.
Jesson R. "Una cosa rara." *Musical Times* 109 (1968): 619.

*   *   *

This light romantic comedy is set in a village in rural Spain. At the center of the drama is Lilla, a beautiful and virtuous peasant girl (the role was created by Nancy Storace, Mozart's first Susanna in *Le nozze di Figaro*), who is engaged to another peasant, Lubino. Her fidelity is tested when she becomes the object of amorous advances from several men: Prince Giovanni, in the country on a hunting expedition with his mother Queen Isabella; Corrado, the royal equerry; and Lisargo, the local governor. Despite misunderstandings that inflame Lubino's jealousy, Lilla successfully defends her virtue with the help of Queen Isabella, and her wedding with Lubino is happily celebrated. Interwoven with this simple story are the quarrels and reconciliations of another pair of peasants, Tita (the role was created by Francesco Benucci, Mozart's first Figaro and Guglielmo) and Ghita, whose spirited romance gives the opera some of its more lively comic moments.

Martín y Soler skillfully evokes the sound and color of rural life. Dance-like rhythms in the "light" meters of 6/8 and 3/8 are common. Simple accompaniments often incorporate drones. Delicate orchestral effects include frequent use of pizzicato and some *sul ponticello* writing for violins. The occasional appearance of the mandolin and a seguidilla danced by Lilla and Ghita contribute to the opera's Spanish flavor.

The composer clearly differentiates the personalities and social classes of his characters, showing himself in command in a wide variety of modes of musical expression. The lively buffo patter of the duet for the quarreling Tita and Ghita, "Un briccone senza core," is an effective foil to the sentimental melancholy of Lilla's aria "Dolce mi parve un dì." The exotic and seductive strains of Prince Giovanni's off-stage serenade and Queen Isabella's exalted yet tender rondo show that Martín y Soler could bring his noble characters as vividly to life as his rural ones.

Performed in Spanish costumes donated by Martín y Soler's patroness, the wife of the Spanish ambassador, *Una cosa rara* won enthusiastic applause in Vienna. According to Da Ponte, "everyone praised such grace, such sweetness, such melody in the music, and therewith such novelty and interest in the words, that the audience was caught up in an ecstasy of pleasure. . . . The ladies in particular . . . could see nothing but the *Cosa rara* and dress only in the styles of the *Cosa rara*."

The opera was soon translated into several languages and performed in theaters throughout Europe, its popularity further attested to by the publication of many vocal scores and of many of its arias and ensembles. The reconciliation duet for Lilla and Lubino, "Pace, mio caro sposo," a copy of which can be seen in the engraved portrait of Martín y Soler published in Vienna in 1787 (see article on Martín y Soler), was especially beloved (according to Kelly, it was "completely the rage all over Ireland, England and Scotland for many, many years"); but the only part of the opera familiar today is a melody from the finale of act I that Mozart quoted in the dinner music for *Don Giovanni*.

—John A. Rice

———————

COSÌ FAN TUTTE, ossia La scuola degli amanti [All Women do Thus, or The School for Lovers].

Composer: Wolfgang Amadeus Mozart.

Librettist: Lorenzo Da Ponte.

First Performance: Vienna, Burgtheater, 26 January 1790.

Roles: Fiordiligi (soprano); Dorabella (soprano): Guglielmo (baritone); Ferrando (tenor); Despina (soprano); Don Alfonso (bass); chorus (SATB).

Publications

books–

Hocquard, Jean-Victor. *Così fan tutte*. Paris, 1978.
Vill, Susanne, ed. *Così fan tutte: Beiträge zur Wirkungsgeschichte von Mozarts Oper*. Bayreuth, 1978.
John, Nicholas, ed. *Wolfgang Amadeus Mozart: Così fan tutte*. London and New York, 1983.
Steptoe, Andrew. *The Mozart-Da Ponte Operas: The Cultural and Musical Background to "Le Nozze di Figaro," "Don Giovanni," and "Così fan tutte"*. Oxford, 1989.

articles–

Friedrich, Götz. "Zur Inszenierungskonzeption *Così fan tutte*: Komische Oper Berlin 1962." *Jahrbuch der Komische Oper Berlin* 3 (1962-63).
Keahey, D.J. "*Così fan tutte*: Parody or Irony." In *Paul A. Pisk: Essays in His Honor*, 116. Austin, 1966.
Williams, B. "Passion and Cynicism: Remarks on 'Così fan tutte'." *Musical Times* 114 (1973): 361.
Porena, Boris. "La Parola intonata in *Così fan tutte*, ovvero l'esplorazione musicale di una lingua e del suo uso sociale." *Analecta musicologica* 18 (1978): 198.
Branscombe, Peter J. "*Così* in Context." *Musical Times* 122 (1981): 461.
Steptoe, Andrew. "The Sources of *Così fan tutte*: A Reappraisal." *Music and Letters* 62 (1981): 281.

Così fan tutte, **English National Opera, London, 1984**

. "Mozart, Mesmer, and Così fan tutte." *Music and Letters* 67 (1986): 248.
Farnsworth, Rodney. "*Così fan tutte* as Parody and Burlesque." *Opera Quarterly* winter (1988-89).

* * *

Così fan tutte was Mozart's fourth opera since moving to Vienna, and his third major collaboration with the librettist Lorenzo Da Ponte (1749-1838). It has often been perceived as "problematic": there were few performances during the nineteenth century, and the opera gained recognition only in the more sympathetic climate of the 1920s. Even today, many feel uneasy with the work.

The question of immorality that so exercized the Romantics merits some exploration. Two pairs of lovers—Fiordiligi and Guglielmo; Dorabella and Ferrando—swap partners with feigned or (and increasingly) real conviction and then abruptly shift back (we assume) to their original attachments. This belies what are often felt to be crucial messages in Mozart's operas, the moral and emotional power of love and fidelity, and the significant place of women in the commonwealth of humanity. Moreover, the cynical machinations of Don Alfonso—the puppet-master of the intrigue—and the maid Despina are not what we expect in Mozart. Why should he have chosen such a frivolous plot for some of his greatest music?

Mozart's choice of subject (if the choice was his) is difficult to explain: there is little evidence on the genesis of *Così* either in Mozart's letters, Da Ponte's *Memoirs,* or other contemporary records. Moreover, the opera has no clear basis in pre-existing literary or dramatic sources. Mozart's first collaboration with Da Ponte, *Le nozze di Figaro* (1786), reworked a fashionable play by Beaumarchais, and their second, *Don Giovanni* (1787), involves characters with a clear history in seventeenth- and eighteenth-century drama. In both cases, contemporary audiences would have been sufficiently informed about the characters to understand and assess their motives, actions, and dramatic significance.

But the sources for *Così* are unclear. Certainly, the characters are rooted in the *commedia dell'arte,* as are the trappings of the plot (Albanian disguises, playful references to Mesmerism, a maid dressing up as a medical, then legal, quack). Similarly, fickle relationships can be traced back to classical myth—Procris and Cephalus offer one source—and the didactic message presented by this "School for Lovers" (the subtitle of *Così*) echoes Ovid's *Ars amatoria.* The action also had contemporary resonances: some commentators claim origins for the plot in a recent scandal at the court of Emperor Joseph II, and even in Mozart's own currently fraught relationship with his wife, Constanze Weber (he had originally fallen in love with her sister, Aloysia). Moreover, the Albanian elements (compare with Mozart's "Turkish" *Die Entführung aus dem Serail*) evoke Joseph II's recent military campaigns in the Balkans. But none of the characters in *Così* has the clear history of, say, Figaro or Don Giovanni. Thus they have a pasteboard quality, making it difficult for us to empathize with their predicament. And even when Mozart does explore his characters—Fiordiligi's wholehearted submission to Ferrando (in the magnificent duet "Fra gli amplessi in pochi istanti" in act II) well illustrates how he could focus on the human psyche—this seems the exception rather than the rule.

A second criticism of *Così fan tutte* is that Mozart's music is surprisingly and unusually inconsistent in terms both of style and quality, and of matching music to drama. Veering between the profundity of, say, the trio "Soave sia il vento" (act I) and Guglielmo's rather vapid "Donne mie, la fate a tanti" in act II sits uneasily in our minds. Further difficulties are caused by the parody-like nature of much of the opera: Fiordiligi's "Come scoglio immoto resta" (act I), a glorious pastiche of an *opera seria* aria, is only the most obvious example. Is this satire, irony, or real emotion? It is difficult to tell.

Of course, one can find explanations, or at least excuses, for the problems of *Così*. The original cast contained singers of whom Mozart was not particularly fond. Adriana Ferrarese del Bene (Fiordiligi) was Da Ponte's mistress, and Mozart disliked both her and her voice. Similarly, Francesco Bussani (Don Alfonso: his wife, Dorotea Sardi, played Despina) had proved unhelpful to the composer and librettist during their difficult careers in Vienna (he was Bartolo and Antonio in *Figaro,* and Masetto and the Commendatore in *Don Giovanni.*) Moreover, his voice was apparently in decline: witness the absence of a *bona fide* aria for him. As for Ferrando, although Mozart could rely on the acknowledged talents of Vincenzo Calvesi, the composer never seems to have liked writing for a tenor voice (compare Don Ottavio in *Don Giovanni*). And although Guglielmo was played by that Mozart stalwart, Francesco Benucci (the first Figaro and Leporello), even his presence may not have been enough to attract Mozart to do his best in *Così*.

Another explanation for *Così* may lie in the generally unfavorable reception afforded to Mozart's operas in Vienna: *Figaro* had only nine performances in 1786, and *Don Giovanni,* an opera conceived with Prague tastes in mind, was hardly successful when staged in Vienna in 1788. To be sure, multiple performances of operas in Vienna were less the norm than an exception: opera was an essentially transitory entertainment. But contemporary audiences did not always take kindly to the questionable politics of *Figaro,* the confusing mixture of genres in *Don Giovanni,* and, in general, the apparent complexity of Mozart's operatic style: Joseph II's comment on *Die Entführung*—"Too beautiful for our ears, and far too many notes, my dear Mozart"—may be apocryphal, but it represents a common view of the composer. Thus Mozart was perhaps struggling to meet the tastes of an audience that had failed to appreciate his best efforts: the work has by far the simplest plot of the three Mozart-Da Ponte operas, and the music, too, exhibits concessions to somewhat frivolous Viennese tastes.

It is convenient to blame the problems of *Così* on his singers and audience. But perhaps this misses a crucial point: the undoubted inconsistencies in the music of *Così* may instead reflect Mozart's changing perception of the nature and function of operatic music. In both *Figaro* and *Don Giovanni,* he had transfered essentially symphonic styles to the stage. This is most obviously apparent in his use of sonata-form structures: sonata form, often found in, say, the first movements of symphonies, is based on the establishing and resolution of tonal dissonances between different keys (often tonic and dominant), and also on thematic repetition for the sake of balance. But thematic repetition seems fundamentally unsuited to dramatic situations, where the action (and therefore the music) must look forwards rather than backwards. This creates problems for a composer seeking to use sonata form in an operatic context.

It is striking, however, that there is an almost total absence of sonata form is *Così fan tutte.* At several points where, were this *Figaro,* one might have found a sonata-form movement (e.i., the act I sextet, "Alla bella Despinetta," or "Fra gli amplessi in pochi istanti," Mozart produces instead more processive structures to match the forward-march of the action. Something is lost in the process (thematic unity and tonal coherence suffer) but the result is a more operatic, rather than symphonic, mode of dramatic composition.

The notion of Mozart experimenting with new kinds of operatic writing may seem an abstruse explanation of the musical problems of *Così fan tutte,* but it is entirely consistent with Mozart's own compositional development: his brief life encompassed an extraordinarily rapid growth in musical technique and emotional perception. But one might equally argue that the difficulties of the opera are due less to Mozart than to our own misguided expectations. Neither the drama nor the music of *Così fan tutte* are untypical of contemporary *opera buffa*—Domenico Cimarosa's *Il matrimonio segreto* (1792) provides a useful comparison—and its general opera embodies an aristocratic, slightly cynical and detached wit that is entirely consistent with late eighteenth-century aesthetics. We would perhaps do better to accept things for what they are rather than expect them to be what they are not. But is that not the lesson of this "School for Lovers"?

—Tim Carter

COSSUTTA, Carlo.

Tenor. Born 8 May 1932, in Trieste. Studied with Manfredo Miselli, Mario Melani, and Arturo Wolken in Buenos Aires; debut as Cassio at Teatro Colón, Buenos Aires, 1958, where he spent five seasons; created Ginastro's Don Rodrigo there in 1964; Chicago debut as Cassio, 1963; Covent Garden debut as Duke of Mantua, 1964; debut at Metropolitan Opera as Pollione, 1973.

*   *   *

The tenor voice is relatively rare among male singers: the *tenore robusto* (dramatic tenor) is rarer still. The voice type is characterised by a dark, baritonal timbre, often of considerable size and ideally combined with a ringing upper register and innate histrionic ability. For such singers were written roles such as Radames (*Aïda*), Manrico (*Il trovatore*), Don Alvaro (*La forza del destino*), many of Wagner's tenor parts and the ultimate role in the *robusto* repertoire, Otello. We do not usually look to the dramatic tenor, however, for the subtlety, style or sensitivity more usual in his lighter-voiced colleagues. Rarely, a robusto combines all these qualities; the result is an exceptional artist indeed.

Carlo Cossutta *is* such an artist, yet his career and achievements have been curiously undervalued. His career has been steady rather than spectacular and, most regrettable of all, he has been sadly neglected by the record companies. The result is that his exceptional art will be preserved for posterity in not even a handful of recordings, while some of his less accomplished colleagues record roles for the second or even a third time.

It is difficult to understand why a singer of such accomplishment has not had a more illustrious career, but even so, Cossutta's success has been considerable. In the late 50s and early 60s, as house tenor at the Teatro Colón in Buenos Aires, he was entrusted with leading roles but often also sang Cassio there to many of the most famous Otellos of the day, experience that was to prove invaluable in the future. As the voice darkened during the next decade, he became one of the most sought-after dramatic tenors, and eventually for his own assumption of the role of the Moor. Few tenors have combined all the requirements of this colossus amongst tenor roles more successfully than he.

It is in the singing of Verdi that Cossutta has most excelled. Few dramatic tenors have so exceptionally risen to every requirement of Verdi's writing for the tenor voice. Cossutta's technique permits adaptation of style from the most dramatic to the finest lyricism, while always demonstrating musicality and the scrupulous observation of the directions in the score. Exceptionally for this type of voice, he can sing pianissimo when required, as demonstrated in his commercial recording of the Verdi Requiem. During his career, Cossutta has been admired not only in such Verdi roles as the Duke of Mantua (*Rigoletto*), Radames, Don Alvaro, Gabriele Adorno (*Simon Boccanegra*) and Riccardo (*Un ballo in maschera*) but also in Puccini's, as Rodolfo (*La Bohème*) and Dick Johnson (*La Fanciulla del West*).

However, it will always be for the role of Otello that Cossutta will be best remembered. Perhaps there have been Otellos more gifted histrionically, but few have sung the part more beautifully or have been so technically the equal of one of the most difficult roles in the tenor repertoire. His commercial recording of Otello is a little disappointing. Though well-sung, Cossutta is not successful in compensating for the lack of a stage persona that makes his interpretation all the more convincing in the theatre.

Cossutta is possibly one of many exceptionally gifted singers in operatic history who have lacked the temperament and relentless ambition necessary to strive for the very highest operatic accomplishment. He has in addition eschewed the frenetic career tolerated by some of his colleagues, preferring to limit the number of his performances. Perhaps this may to some degree explain why Cossutta has never achieved just recognition. But, whatever the reason, it is unlikely that those who heard this fine singer in the theater would have been unaware of hearing an artist of anything other than the first rank.

—Larry Lustig

COTRUBAS, Ileana.

Soprano. Born 9 June 1939 in Galati, Romania. Married Manfred Ramin, 1972. Studied with Constantin Stroescu at Bucharest Conservatory and at Vienna Music Academy. Debut as Yniold in *Pelléas* in Bucharest, 1964; won first prize in the 's-Hertogenbosch competition, 1965; joined Frankfurt Opera, 1968; Glyndebourne debut as Mélisande, 1970; Vienna Staatsoper debut at Vienna, 1971, as Violetta; Covent Garden debut as Tatiana, 1971; Chicago debut as Mimi, 1973; Teatro alla Scala (1975) and Metropolitan Opera (1977) debuts in same role.

Publications

About COTRUBAS: articles–

Blyth, Alan. "Ileana Cotrubas." *Opera* May (1976): 428.

* * *

The Romanian soprano Ileana Cotrubas won the admiration and affection of opera lovers throughout the world during her relatively short career on the international operatic stage. Her roles were many and varied, extending chronologically from Cavalli's *Callisto* to Debussy's Mélisande. Her voice was not heavy enough for Wagner, making his operas one of the few major parts of the standard repertory into which she rarely ventured. Truly cosmopolitan in her repertory, she sang Mimi (Puccini's *La bohème,* Tatyana (Tchaikowsky's *Eugene Onegin*) and Micaela (Bizet's *Carmen*) with equal success. Her many recordings represent a valuable testament to her musical and dramatic skills.

In general Cotrubas tended towards the portrayal of good characters. There was something gentle and sweet in her stage personality that encouraged opera directors to cast her in the roles of young, innocent and essentially virtuous heroines, such as Ilia (in *Idomeneo*), Susanna, and Pamina, among others. She rarely had the opportunity to sing such villainous roles as Mozart's Queen of the Night (*Die Zauberflöte*), Electra (*Idomeneo*) or Vitellia (*La clemenza di Tito*).

When she sang Pamina at Covent Garden in 1979 her portrayal won praise from one critic as "a delectably phrased and coloured Pamina." Her performance of Ilia at the Metropolitan Opera, opposite Frederika von Stade's Idamante, can be admired on a video tape recorded in 1982 under the direction of James Levine. The opera opens with a big solo *scena* for Ilia in which we can see Cotrubas's strengths and her weaknesses. Among her strengths is the beautiful, uniform sound of her voice as well as her effective use of gestures and facial expressions to communicate feelings. Her excessive vibrato, however, often distorts the pitch. In the aria "Padre, germani, addio" a wider variety of vocal timbres would be welcome: it seems that Cotrubas's uniformity of tone comes at the expense of dramatic color. At the words "Grecia, cagion tu sei" (Greece, it is your fault), Mozart's music and Cotrubas's gestures and face express the intensity of Ilia's feelings, but Cotrubas's voice does not.

Among Cotrubas's best roles in nineteenth-century Italian opera was Norina in Donizetti's *Don Pasquale*. When she portrayed Norina at Covent Garden in 1979 a critic described her as "enticing", and praised the "effortless flow of liquid tone" with which she executed Donizetti's coloratura. She also won much praise for her performances of two of Verdi's best soprano roles, Violetta in *La traviata* and Gilda in *Rigoletto*. One critic who heard her perform Gilda at Covent Garden in 1976 called her portrayal "ideal," not only vocally but also in the way in which she conveyed the innocent and youthful personality of her character. Two years later a critic at Covent Garden described her Gilda as "peerless."

—John A. Rice

COUNT ORY
  See LE COMTE ORY

THE COUNTRY PHILOSOPHER
  See IL FILOSOFO DI CAMPAGNA

COX, John.

Director. Born 12 March 1935, in Bristol, England. Earned
B.A. at Oxford; studied with Walter Felsenstein in Germany;
directorial debut with *Ernani,* at the Oxford University Opera
Club, in 1957; directed the British stage premiere of Ravel's
L'enfant et les sortilèges at Oxford, 1958; became assistant to
Günther Rennert at Glyndebourne Festival, 1959; director of
production, Glyndebourne Festival, 1971-81; administrator,
Scottish National Opera, 1982-85; artistic director, Scottish
National Opera, 1985-; production director, Royal Opera,
Covent Garden, 1988-; world premieres staged by Cox in-
clude Daniel Jones's *The Knife* (1964), Phyllis Tate's *The
What D'ye Call It* (1966), Harrison Birtwistle's *Down by the
Greenwood Side* (1967), Malcolm Williamson's *Lucky Peter's
Journey* (1969), and Alexander Goehr's *Triptych* (1971); be-
ginning in 1959 Cox also worked extensively as a freelance
director, mounting productions throughout Europe and the
United States.

Opera Productions (selected)

Ernani, Oxford, 1957.
L'enfant et les sortilèges, Oxford, 1958.
The Peasant Rogue (Dvorak), Oxford, 1963.
The Knife (Jones), Sadler's Wells, 1964.
The What D'ye Call It (Tate), New Opera, 1966.
Down by the Greenwood Side (Birtwistle), Brighton, 1967.
Patience, English National Opera, 1969.
Lucky Peter's Journey (Williamson), English National Opera,
  1969.
Triptych (Goehr), Brighton Festival, 1971.
Il turco in Italia, Glyndebourne Festival, 1972.
La Bohème, Glyndebourne Festival, 1972.
Ariadne auf Naxos, Glyndebourne Festival, 1972.
Capriccio, Glyndebourne Festival, 1973.
Idomeneo, Glyndebourne Festival, 1974.
Intermezzo, Glyndebourne Festival, 1974.
Die schweigsame Frau, Glyndebourne Festival, 1977.
Die Zauberflöte, Glyndebourne Festival, 1978.
Tannhäuser, Netherlands Opera, 1978.
The Rake's Progress, Teatro alla Piccola Scala, 1978.
La fedeltà premiata, Glyndebourne Festival, 1979.
Arabella, San Francisco Opera, 1980.
Der Rosenkavalier, Glyndebourne Festival, 1980.
Così fan tutte, English National Opera, 1980.
Il barbiere di Siviglia, Glyndebourne Festival, 1981.
L'Egisto, Scottish National Opera, 1981.
Manon Lescaut, Edinburgh Festival, 1982.
Il barbiere di Siviglia, Metropolitan Opera, 1982.
The Rake's Progress, San Francisco Opera, 1982.

Capriccio, Brussels, 1983.
La Cenerentola, Glyndebourne Festival, 1983.
Arabella, Glyndebourne Festival, 1984.
A Midsummer Marriage (Tippett), San Francisco Opera,
  1984.
Un ballo in maschera, Australian Opera, 1985.
Don Carlo, San Francisco Opera, 1986.
Le nozze di Figaro, Scottish National Opera, 1986.
Daphne (Strauss), Munich, 1987.
Die fliegende Holländer, Scottish National Opera, 1987.
Lulu, Scottish National Opera, 1987.
Le Comte Ory (Rossini), Nice, 1988.
Manon, Covent Garden, 1988.
Die Fledermaus, Covent Garden, 1989.
Don Carlo, Covent Garden, 1989.
L'Egisto, Santa Fe, 1989.
Idomeneo, Teatro della Pergola, 1989.
Il re pastore, Salzburg, 1989.
Die Meistersinger von Nürnberg, Covent Garden, 1990.
Guillaume Tell, Covent Garden, 1990.
Capriccio, San Francisco Opera, 1990.
Die Frau ohne Schatten, Covent Garden, 1991-92.

Publications

By COX: articles–

"Standing Up for Strauss." *Opera* 30 (June 1979): 529.

About COX: books–

Friedman, Martin. *Hockney Paints the Stage.* Minneapolis,
  1983.
Higgins, John, ed. *Glyndebourne: A Celebration.* London,
  1984.

articles–

Milnes, R. "John Cox at Glyndebourne" (interview). *Opera*
  29 (July 1978): 662; (August 1978): 772.
O'Connor, T. "Testing the Element of Conviction" (interview). *San Francisco Opera Magazine* (Fall 1980): 74.
"John Cox to Relinquish Glyndebourne Post." *Opera* 32 (December 1981): 1226.
Clark, A. "Das Theaterporträt: Scottish Opera." *Opernwelt*
  27/6 (1986): 52.
"John Cox." *About The House* 8/1 (1988): 57.
Goodwin, N. "John Cox: Making It Happen." *Opera* 41 (January 1990): 23.
"Artist Profiles." *San Francisco Opera Magazine,* 69/2
  (1991): 46.

* * *

Director John Cox has been primarily associated with the
Glyndebourne Festival, where he was assistant director (with
Carl Ebert and Günther Rennert) and, from 1971 to 1981,
director of production, and the Scottish National Opera,
where he was administrator from 1982 to 1985 and artistic
director since 1985. A supporter of opera in English, he has
made a specialty of the operas of Richard Strauss.

After working in Germany with Walter Felsenstein, he
made his operatic debut directing Verdi's *Ernani* at Oxford
in 1957. This was followed in 1963 by a production of Dvořák's *The Peasant Rogue* (*Selma sedlák*).

At the 1971 Brighton Festival he directed Alexander Goehr's *Triptych*. Other directorial assignments have included Wagner's *Tannhäuser* for the Netherlands Opera (1978), Stravinsky's *The Rake's Progress* for La Piccola Scala (1978), and Gilbert and Sullivan's *Patience* (1969), Lehar's *The Merry Widow* (for which he was also the translator), and Mozart's *Così fan tutte* (1980), all for the English National Opera.

As production director at the Royal Opera, Covent Garden, a position he assumed in 1988, he is responsible for all revivals; he has rethought and restaged Massenet's *Manon* (1988), Johann Strauss's *Die Fledermaus* (1989), Verdi's *Don Carlo* (1989, the 1958 Visconti production); and Wagner's *Die Meistersinger* (1990). In 1990 he created a new production of Rossini's *Guillaume Tell*, the first British production since 1889. Richard Strauss's *Capriccio* was presented in a production shared with, and first seen at, the San Francisco Opera (1990). A new production of Richard Strauss's *Die Frau ohne Schatten* was staged for the 1991-92 season.

As director of production at Glyndebourne he has seen several of his productions travel to other opera houses in Europe. His productions for Glyndebourne include Rossini's *Il turco in Italia* (1972), Puccini's *La bohème* (1972), Richard Strauss's *Ariadne auf Naxos* (1972) and *Capriccio* (1973), Mozart's *Idomeneo* (1974), Richard Strauss's *Intermezzo* (1974) and *Die schweigsame Frau* (1977), Mozart's *Die Zauberflöte* (1978); Haydn's *La fedeltà premiata* (1979, the first Haydn opera to be performed at Glyndebourne), Richard Strauss's *Der Rosenkavalier* (1980), Rossini's *Il barbiere di Siviglia* (1981), Rossini's *La Cenerentola* (1983), and Richard Strauss's *Arabella* (1984).

As general administrator of the Scottish Opera he has directed productions of Cavalli's *L'Egisto* (1981), Mozart's *Le nozze di Figaro* (1986), Wagner's *Der fliegende Holländer* (1987), and Berg's *Lulu* (1987).

The 1982 Edinburgh Festival saw his mounting of Puccini's *Manon Lescaut.*

Other European opera companies that have presented Cox's productions include the Maggio Musicale Fiorentino at the Teatro della Pergola (*Idomeneo*, 1989), Salzburg (Mozart's *Il re pastore*, 1989), Cologne (Offenbach's *La périchole*, 1979), Brussels (*Capriccio*, 1983), the Australian Opera (Verdi's *Un ballo in maschera*, 1985), Munich (Richard Strauss's *Daphne*, 1987), and Nice (Rossini's *Le Comte Ory*, 1988).

Cox's American assignments have included productions at the New York City Opera (*Die Meistersinger*), Houston (*Der Rosenkavalier*), Santa Fe (*L'Egisto*, 1989), San Francisco (*Arabella*, 1980), Michael Tippett's *A Midsummer Marriage*, 1984, *The Rake's Progress*, 1982, and *Don Carlos*, 1986), the Metropolitan Opera (Rossini's *Il barbiere di Siviglia*, 1982), and Honolulu (*The Rake's Progress*, 1986). At Carnegie Hall in 1985 Cox oversaw a semi-staged performance of *Capriccio.*

Cox's directorial style is traditional and conservative, although he is not above updating productions, as in his *Capriccio*. He has said that productions are organisms that should change over time, to reflect, apparently, changes in taste and levels of musicological knowledge. His approach has been described as elegant and polished—detailed, with a sense of tableau. It is a style more suited to the operas of Richard Strauss and Mozart than to Italian verismo, and more successful in smaller opera houses (such as Glyndebourne) than at the Metropolitan or even Covent Garden.

The Met's *Il barbiere di Siviglia* is representative of Cox's approach. Cox avoided any imposition of sociopolitical elements, despite the play's origins as a work that articulated the playwright's social concerns, feeling that Rossini's intention, unlike that of Beaumarchais, was not social commentary. He staged the work as a comedy, not a farce, and paid careful attention to its characters' occupations—a reflection of its nineteenth-century origins.

—Michael Sims

THE CRADLE WILL ROCK.

Composer: Marc Blitzstein.

Librettist: Marc Blitzstein.

First Performance: New York, 16 June 1937.

Publications

articles–

Hunter, J.O. "Marc Blitzstein's 'The Cradle Will Rock' as a Document of America, 1937." *American Quarterly* 16 (1964): 227.

Oja, C.J. "Marc Blitzstein's *The Cradle Will Rock* and Mass-Song Style of the 1930s." *Musical Quarterly* 73 (1989): 445.

*   *   *

The text of Marc Blitzstein's *The Cradle Will Rock,* biting and satirical, involves the efforts of the workers in Steeltown, USA to unionize, as well as the actions of the capitalistic establishment to thwart them. Mr Mister controls Steeltown and its citizenry. In order to stop the workers, he organizes a so-called "Liberty Committee," comprised of stereotypical "good people" of the community; they are symbolic representations of the Press, the Groves of Academe, the Medical Establishment, the Church, the Arts, and the Legal Profession. The action takes place in a night court, and the plot unfolds through a series of flashbacks.

Mr Mister's efforts to thwart the union include bribing the local newspaper to help frame Larry Foreman, the union organizer, and using his leverage as owner of the mortgage of Harry Druggist's drug store to coerce the mild-mannered apothecary to help frame the innocent Gus Polack for the bombing of union headquarters. Polack and his wife Sadie, who is expecting a child, are to be killed in the blast. The Druggist's son, Steve, in an effort to prevent the tragedy, is himself killed along with the young couple. In the end, however, all the workers unite; virtue triumphs.

In this, his first full-length stage work, Blitzstein was clearly influenced by Kurt Weill, Bertolt Brecht, and Hanns Eisler. Aaron Copland aptly characterized *The Cradle Will Rock* as "something of a cross between social drama, musical review, and opera." The musical material includes parody and satire as well as popular songs in the style of Weill's *Three-Penny Opera.*

—David Z. Kushner

CRAIG, Edward Gordon.

Producer and designer. Born 16 January 1872, in Stevenage, Herts, England. Died 29 July 1966, in Vence, France. Best known for his revolutionary theories and his use of nonrepresentational settings and atmospheric effects such as the play of light on background screens. Attended Bradfield College; Heidelberg, Germany, 1886-87; made his first appearance on the stage in *Olivia* at the Court Theatre, London, 1878; founded *The Page* in which he published his wood cuts, 1898; after a time as an actor, he directed and designed *The Vikings at Helgeland* and *Much Ado About Nothing,* produced by his mother, Ellen Terry, 1903; contributed designs for *Venice Preserv'd,* 1904, *Rosmersholm,* 1906, *The Hour Glass,* 1911, and *Hamlet,* 1911; settled in Florence and founded the journal *The Mask,* 1908, to which he contributed, 1908-29; designed *St Matthew's Passion,* Florence, 1913; founded School for the Art of the Theatre at the Arena Goldoni, Florence, 1913; founded *The Marionette,* 1918; opened the first International Exhibition of Theatrical Art, State Museum, Amsterdam, 1922; directed *The Pretenders,* State Theatre, Copenhagen and received the Order of Dannebrog, 1926. Elected Royal Designer of Industry of the Royal Society of Arts, 1938; Companion of Honour in the Birthday Honours, 1956; award from the United Scenic Artists (United States) for his contributions to theatrical lighting, 1961; president of Theatre Trust, 1964.

Opera Productions (selected)

Dido and Aeneas, Hampstead Conservatoire, 1900.
The Masque of Love, Coronet Theatre, 1901.
Acis and Galatea, Great Queen Street Theatre, 1902.
Unrealized staging of the *St Matthew Passion.*

Publications

By CRAIG: books (selected)–

On the Art of the Theatre. London, 1911.
Towards a New Theatre: Forty Designs for Stage Scenes with Critical Notes by the Inventor Edward Gordon Craig. London, 1913.
The Theatre Advancing. London, 1921.
The Liar: A Comedy in Three Acts. Translated by Grace Lovat Fraser. London, 1922.
Scene. London, 1923.
Design in the Theater. London, 1927 (with George Sheringham).
Henry Irving. New York, 1930.
Hamlet. Weimar, 1930.
Fourteen Notes. Seattle, 1931.
Ellen Terry and Her Secret Self, Together with a Plea for G.B.S. New York, 1932.
Index to the Story of My Days. London, 1957.
Gordon Craig on Movement and Dance, ed. by Arnold Rood. New York, 1977.

About CRAIG: books–

Shaw, M.F. *Up to Now.* London, 1929.
Rose, Enid. *Gordon Craig and the Theatre: A Record and an Interpretation.* 1931.
Acterian, Haig. *Gordon Craig, is Ideia in Teatru.* Bucharest, 1936.
Leeper, J. *Edward Gordon Craig: Designs for the Theatre.* Harmondsworth, 1948.

Marotti, Ferrucio. *Edward Gordon Craig.* Italy, 1961.
Gordon Craig. Paris, 1962.
Bablet, Denis. *Edward Gordon Craig.* Translated by Daphne Woodward. New York, 1966.
Fletcher, I.W.K., and A. Rood. *Edward Gordon Craig: A Bibliography.* London, 1967.
Craig, Edward A. *Gordon Craig: The Story of His Life.* New York, 1968.
Loeffler, M.P. *Gordon Craigs frühe Versuche zur Überwindung des Bühnenrealismus.* Berne, 1969.
Steegmuller, F. *Your Isadora.* New York, 1974.

articles–

Marbach, G. "Aufbruch zu Raum und Licht; Bühnengestaltung um 1900." *Neue Zeitschrift für Musik* 122 (September 1961): 345-48.
Berthold, M. "Repäsentant einer Theaterepoche—Erinnerungen ab einen Besuch bei Edward Gordon Craig." *Musikalische Jugend* 16, no. 1 (1967): 4.
Craig, Edward A. "Gordon Craig and Bach's *St Matthew Passion.*" *Theatre Notebook* 26 (1972): 147.
Obraszowa, A. "Die Duncan und Craig." *Kunst und Literatur* 30 (July 1982): 744-60.

Most theater directors come to opera after work in the nonmusical theater. Edward Gordon Craig had undertaken no more than five stage productions, and those negligible, before joining with the musician Martin Shaw in directing Purcell's *Dido and Aeneas* for the Purcell Operatic Society. Craig was twenty-seven, and the opening of the production, on 17 May 1900 at the Hampstead Conservatoire, marked the first of the only three operatic productions he was ever to mount. *Dido and Aeneas* was revived in March 1901, at the Coronet Theatre alongside *The Masque of Love,* from Purcell's music for *The Prophetess or The History of Dioclesian. The Masque of Love* was, in its turn, revived a year later at the Great Queen Street Theatre, this time in tandem with Handel's *Acis and Galatea.*

Such a meager creative output would hardly seem to merit serious attention were it not for the main corpus of Craig's work as a director, and especially as a designer and as a theorist. The best known of his stage productions, *The Vikings,* under the management of his mother, Ellen Terry, in 1903; *Hamlet* with Stanislavsky at the Moscow Arts Theatre in 1912, and *The Pretenders* with the Poulsen brothers at the Royal Theatre in Copenhagen in 1926, were noted for an operatic touch which eschewed the dramatic movements of the times, naturalism, expressionism, and constructivism, in favor of a monumental approach which looked back to the theater of ancient Greece and forward to a new vision of a theater of gesture and essence.

The opera productions were fundamental in establishing Craig's sense of stage space, and the venues he used contributed to this sense. The Hampstead Conservatoire was a concert hall, not a theater, with a shallow stage. Craig chose to rely heavily on overhead lighting and had a bridge constructed above the stage for the lights. Spectacular effects were created by the use of scrims and the arrangement of the large cast of principals and chorus in a series of tableaux. The use of contrast between the horizontal and the vertical was to become a feature of all his later design work. Stage steps and levels in *Dido and Aeneas* were complemented and contrasted by poles and ropes, suggesting masts and rigging, and the pikes and lances of the Roman soldiers.

The set for *The Masque of Love* was less complex, with Craig relying more for effect on the elaborate post-Commedia costumes of Pierrot and Harlequin. Closer to ballet, perhaps, than opera, *The Masque of Love* used its visual images to trigger the imagination. The same is true of *Acis and Galatea*. The abiding image from that production is the renowned design for act II, scene 1, with the doomed lovers clasping each other tightly at center stage and a series of shadowy figures silhouetted behind. A closer look at the lowering shadows that tower over the pair reveals the shape of an enormous bear, a force of nature, poised to strike.

If choreography and scenic effect were the legacy of Craig's opera productions, these are not to be dismissed lightly. Craig felt it was unlikely that the importance of his work would be recognized in his own lifetime. He died in 1966, and it is the contemporary generation of opera designers and directors who look to his work for their inspiration.

—Michael Walton

CRESPIN, Régine.

Soprano. Born 23 March 1927, in Marseilles. Married writer Lou Bruder, 1962. Debut as Elsa in Mulhouse and at Paris Opera, 1950; Bayreuth debut as Kundry, 1958; Glyndebourne debut as Marschallin, 1959-60; Covent Garden debut as Marschallin, 1960; Chicago debut as Tosca, 1962; in Buenos Aires since 1962; Metropolitan Opera debut as Marschallin, 1962; entered mezzo repertory after 1971.

Publications

By CRESPIN: books–

Crespin, R. *La vie et l'amour d'une femme.* Paris, 1982.

About CRESPIN: books–

Natan, A. *Primadonna.* Basle, 1962.
Steane, J.B. *The Grand Tradition.* London, 1974.

articles–

Tubeuf, A. "Régine Crespin." *Opera* April (1963).
Rosenthal, H.D. "Régine Crespin." *Opera News* 30/no. 22 (1966): 14.

*   *   *

Régine Crespin is undoubtedly the greatest mid–twentieth-century singer produced by France; she is also, according to Henry Pleasants in *The Grand Tradition,* "one of the great singers on record." She is all the more remarkable that, like her great predecessor Germaine Lubin, she made her reputation in the German repertoire. Crespin's singing, however, is not to everyone's taste. Some critics, while recognizing the eloquent artistry of her dramatic soprano, have called the voice itself "flawed"; indeed, even Pleasants thinks of her as an "acquired taste that becomes addictive."

Crespin, in fact, had what may be almost thought of as two careers. Her busy international round of appearances as a dramatic soprano was interrupted by a personal crisis in the late 1960s and early 1970s which brought, in its turn, a vocal crisis about which she herself has written most frankly and movingly in the autobiographical *La vie et L'amour d'une femme* in 1982, and about which she has talked freely in interviews. As a result of the crisis she stopped singing during 1973-74 and reworked her vocal technique from the ground up with a "vocal rehabilitator," as she describes him, in Cologne. When she resumed her career in 1974 she moved toward (or returned to) roles more associated with mezzos (though continuing to sing them as a soprano): Carmen, Charlotte in *Werther,* and the Old Prioress in *Dialogues des Carmelites,* enjoying great success in them in New York and elsewhere.

But it was in what she calls *"les Wagneriennes blondes,"* that she began her career, making her debut in 1950 as Elsa at Mulhouse, quickly following that by her debut in the same role at the Paris Opéra. Seven years of singing such diverse roles as Tosca, Desdemona, Amelia (*Un ballo in maschera*) and the Marschallin in France brought her to Bayreuth in 1958 to work with Wieland Wagner as his "Mediterranean" Kundry. This marked the start of an international career which quickly took her to the major houses of Europe and North and South America where she won great renown in other Wagner roles: Elizabeth, Senta, Sieglinde (a special favourite with herself and audiences), the *Walküre* Brünnhilde—with Karajan only, for the recording and for nine live performances; in major Verdi roles; and as Fidelio, Ariadne and Pizzetti's *Fedra* among others. Her French roles included the role of the Second Prioress (which Poulenc wrote for her) in the Paris premiere of *Dialogues,* Fauré's Pénélope, Berlioz's Marguerite and Dido, as well as a number of Offenbach roles. Her debut at the Metropolitan Opera (1962) was as the Marschallin, for which she was coached by Lotte Lehmann.

Crespin could dominate the stage even when not actually singing, rivetting one's attention from her entrance. While her voice sometimes acquired a slightly acidulous quality under pressure, the use she made of it assures her a high place in the history of vocal art. Her striking femininity and personal elegance were reflected in the refinement of her singing; high intelligence and profound emotional comprehension lay behind her exquisite diction, her subtle phrasing, and the variety of her tone color. At her best the voice was lustrous, smooth, seductive, strong and even throughout its range; her high pianissimo was of a beauty and eloquence few of her rivals could approach. She could transform herself onstage into a magisterial Marschallin; a Sieglinde matching Lehmann's in its tender womanliness; a Carmen full of stark fatalism, humour, insouciance, sexiness; a Grande Duchesse of witty élan; an Old Prioress—a role she performed frequently towards the end of her career—of elemental power.

Crespin was a notably accomplished recitalist, singing Schumann and Wolf with subtle insight. The French repertoire, notably Berlioz, Fauré, Duparc, Ravel and Poulenc, provided some of her greatest moments in the concert hall. Some of them—not nearly enough—along with Brünnhilde, Sieglinde and Marschallin, provide some of her greatest testimonials on record. Her *Nuits d'Été,* not yet surpassed, contains many exquisite moments, not least the ethereally gentle expiration on the final word of the song, *"jalouser"* ("*que tous les rois vont jalouser*").

Wit, intelligence, sensitivity, integrity, dramatic concentration, all working through a voice capable of expressing noble defiance or exquisitely tender resignation—this was the art for which Régine Crespin will be long remembered.

—Peter Dyson

*   *   *

CROSSE, Gordon.

Composer. Born 1 December 1937, in Bury, Lancashire. Studied music history with Egon Wellesz at Oxford; postgraduate work on medieval music; took classes with Goffredo Petrassi at the Santa Cecilia Academy in Rome, 1962; taught at Birmingham University; on the faculty of the Essex University, 1969; composer in residence, King's College, Cambridge, 1976; visiting professor of composition, University of California, 1977.

Operas

Publisher: Oxford University Press.

Purgatory, Yeats, 1966, Cheltenham, Everyman, 7 July 1966.
The Grace of Todd, D. Rudkin, 1967-68, Aldeburgh, Jubilee Hall, 7 June 1969.
The Story of Vasco, T. Hughes (after Schehadé), 1968-73, London, Coliseum, 13 March 1974.
Holly from the Bongs [children's opera], A. Garner, 1973, Manchester, 9 December 1974.
Potter Thompson, A. Garner, 1972-73, London, St Mary Magdalene, Munster Square, 9 January 1975.

Other works: orchestral works, concertos, choral works, vocal works, chamber music.

Publications

By CROSSE: articles–

"A Setting of W.B. Yeats." *Opera* 17 (1966): 534.
"My Second Violin Concerto." *The Listener* 83 (1970): 156.
"Potter Thompson—an Introduction." *Opera* 26 (1975): 22.

About CROSSE: articles–

Waterhouse, J.C.G. "The Music of Gordon Crosse." *Musical Times* 106 (1965): 342.
Trevor, W. "The Arts." *The Listener* 76 (1966): 141.
Walsh, S. "First Performances: Gordon Crosse's *Purgatory.*" *Tempo* (1966): 23.
Bowen, M. "Gordon Crosse." *Music and Musicians* 20 (1971): 42.
Ford, C. "Gordon Crosse." *Guardian* 3 (1972).
Northcott, B. "The Story of Vasco." *Opera* 25 (1974): 188.
East, L. "The Problem of Communication—Two Solutions: Thea Musgrave and Gordon Crosse." In *British Music Now,* edited by L. Foreman, 19 ff. London, 1975.
Blacker, Terry. "Gordon Crosse: Towards a Style." *Tempo* December (1985): 22.

*   *   *

In order to develop a perspective on the compositional style of Gordon Crosse, it is helpful to consider some of his philosophical commentaries on the function of music in the world of the twentieth century, and the importance of literary and musical models for composers. As part of his tribute to Igor Stravinsky on the occasion of his 85th birthday, Crosse wrote the following: "I believe increasingly that music can, and should, be harnessed to those forces that can change the world. Yet, as the work of Stravinsky constantly reminds me, music must first become aware of itself; of its separateness from the world." Indeed, Crosse believed that Stravinsky's music was "capable of changing the world." Crosse also admits to having "elevated . . . [Stravinsky] to the status of a private saint."

For the text of his compositional homage to Stravinsky, Crosse appropriately selected Latin verses from *De rerum naturae, (On the Nature of Things),* book III, a poem in dactylic hexameter written in the first century B.C. by Titus Lucretius Carus, in honor of Epicurus: "E tenebris tantis tam clarum extollere lumen/qui primus potuisti inlustrans commoda vitae,/te sequor, . . ./. . .tuisque ex, inclute, chartis,/floriferis ut apes in saltibusomnia libant,/omnia nos itidem depascimur aurea dicta,/aurea, perpetua semper dignissima vita" Thee, who first wast able amid such thick darkness to raise on high so bright a beacon and shed a light on the true interests of life, thee I follow. . . . . . . and like as bees sip of all things in the flowery lawns, we, o glorious being, in like manner feed from out thy pages upon all the golden maxims, golden I say, most worthy ever of endless life). In book I of *De rerum naturae,* Lucretius began with an invocation to Venus. This is likely to have influenced Crosse to entitle his piece *Invocation (Lucretius) For Igor Stravinsky Upon His 85th Birthday.*

Just as Crosse expressed a deep reverence towards Stravinsky in his *Invocation,* so too did Lucretius affirm his belief in the teachings of Epicurus in *De rerum naturae.* With such a distinctive parallelism established between Crosse/Stravinsky, and Lucretius/Epicurus, it seems appropriate to explore the implications of Crosse's literary and musical models on the final outcome of *Invocation.* Was Crosse "overpowered" by these awesome models? On the contrary, Crosse's "will" prevailed in this brief work, just as it does in his other compositions, and these are the precise traits that Crosse admires in Stravinsky. "His [Stravinsky's] own refusal to be overpowered by the models he has taken, his demonstration of the need to take models, this is one of the most important things we can learn. . . . We can hear the supremely individual will of Stravinsky. . . . functioning in the music; it is the agent of expression."

What are some of the other literary and musical models that influenced Crosse's mature works? In his first opera *Purgatory* (1966), based on the play by W.B. Yeats, themusical influences of Webern and Stravinsky can be detected in the development of motivic ideas in this atonal context. As Crosse himself has said in reference to the inspiration of the Yeats play: "A play has usually to be compressed, with disastrous results, if the opera is not to be of unwieldy length. This question does not arise with W.B. Yeats's *Purgatory* which is, if anything, too compressed already. . . . Music here can relieve the compression of the play, give one time to take in its wealth of meaning, and actually increase its dramatic tension and its atmosphere." Crosse added, "*Purgatory* is not only a poetic drama but a play in verse. Such a play is already closer to the world of opera, which by its very nature cannot afford to be prosaic." Thus, for Crosse, the Yeats play was a perfect vehicle of expression for his own compositional style.

It seems that Crosse was trying to decide which path to take in the compositional world when he became a student of Goffredo Petrassi in 1962 in Rome. "When the 24-year-old Gordon Crosse arrived in Rome in 1962 to study with Petrassi, he carried with him the first movement of a Concerto da Camera written in the serene, faintly medieval vein of counterpoint that had characterized most of his earlier works. Petrassi liked it but suggested that the style was limited in its possibilities. So Crosse composed a second movement as different from the first as he knew how. "The remainder of the Concerto," he has written, "became a kind of dialogue between the two manners—the one, calm, lyrical and static, the other violent, spiky, dynamic. In retrospect I see the Concerto as the first work in which I became interested in music as drama—an interest that has now led me to opera itself." More than any other work, the first violin concerto serves as a microcosm of Crosse's stylistic evolution. Not only does it summarize his earlier style, but it predicts some of the philosophical issues which were to occupy his mind in the Second Violin Concerto.

In the Composer's Note for the Second Violin Concerto, Crosse writes the following: "The formal structure and, to a limited extent, the expressive manner of this concerto are derived from Vladimir Nabokov's novel *Pale Fire*. In the novel a lyrical poem is subjected to an elaborate and grotesque misreading by its editor, whose notes provide the narrative vehicle of the book. Much of the musical material, however, is derived from my opera *The Story of Vasco* and I have quoted a chanson Ockeghem which appears in its original form in the closing pages." Crosse was quite successful in establishing the contrast between stasis and development in this Concerto—a work in which he was careful to acknowledge his own literary models in the preface to the orchestral score. His resistance to using virtuosic concerto models of the past is in keeping with his view of 20th-century composition as a reaction against 19th-century expressiveness.

In recent years, Crosse has continued his evolution as a composer. It is impossible to make a global statement on all of his contributions because of his vast array of compositions. Suffice it to say that just as the music of Stravinsky and Webern have served as models for Crosse's mature works, so too will Crosse inspire other composers for years to come.

—Maureen A. Carr

THE CRUCIBLE.

Composer: Robert Ward.

Librettist: B. Stambler (after A. Miller).

First Performance: New York, 26 October 1961.

Roles: John Proctor (baritone); Elizabeth Proctor (mezzo-soprano); Abigail Williams (soprano); Reverend John Hale (bass); Judge Danforth (tenor); Reverend Samuel Parris (tenor); Tituba (contralto); Rebecca Nurse (contralto); Giles Corey (tenor); Mary Warren (soprano); Ann Putnam (soprano); Thomas Putnam (baritone); Ezekiel Cheever (tenor); Francis Nurse (bass); Sarah Good (soprano); Betty Parris (mezzo-soprano); Ruth Putnam (soprano); Susanna Walcott (contralto); Mercy Lewis (contralto); Martha Seldon (soprano); Bridget Booth (soprano); chorus (SATB).

*   *   *

In 1962 Robert Ward received both the Pulitzer Prize and the New York Critics Circle Citation for *The Crucible*. The opera, a large work in four acts, was based on Arthur Miller's play of the same name with the libretto adapted by Bernard Stambler. Ward's setting of Miller's powerful play about the witch trials of Salem, Massachusetts of the 1690s was a success at its New York premiere on 26 October 1961. The play and opera recreate the frenzy and anguish of the witch hunts of that strange period in American history. Winthrop Sargeant, writing in the *New Yorker* after the premiere, stated: "[Ward's] music, though quite accessible to the average listener, is everywhere dignified and nowhere banal. It is continuously expressive, and it intensifies all the nuances of the drama. . . . he has created an imposing work that will, I suspect, take its place among the classics of the standard repertory."

The central theme of the plot concerns the love affair between Abigail Williams and John Proctor. John, married to Elizabeth Proctor, will eventually be discovered for his adulterous behavior. The story opens with the Reverend Samuel Parris kneeling distraught at the bed of his daughter Betty. Betty and her cousin Abigail had been found dancing in the woods the night before. Abigail enters to tell him that the town is whispering about witchcraft. Accusations are made about compacts with the devil, and the citizens claim that these evil spirits must be removed from the community. The Reverend Hale, the leading inquisitor, arrives and begins his trials to seek out those who are bewitched. John Proctor and Rebecca Nurse are accused of witchcraft and sentenced to be executed.

Since its premiere performance, the opera has become one of the most frequently performed of American operas. Ward skillfully combines modern dissonance with his conservative tonal musical style. The result is a terse musical texture which creates great tension and anxiety for the unfolding drama. Ward utilizes a recitative-like style throughout the opera with occasional moments of lyricism. The orchestra provides much color and rhythmical punctuation to the quick-paced dramatic action. Ward's lyrical skill is especially evident in the close of act I. A hymn-like melody in $\frac{7}{8}$ is sung by all the main characters beginning with the words, "Allelulia. Jesus, my consolation, . . . " bringing the first act to a dramatic conclusion. The melody also reappears in the last three acts and provides motivic cohesion for the entire work.

The Crucible remains Ward's outstanding opera. His conservative tonal style with occasional incursions into twentieth-century dissonance was an ideal musical style for this historical drama. The story is one that will continue to hold an audience's attention. This work gives Ward an important role in the development of American opera.

—Robert F. Nisbett

THE CRY OF CLYTAEMNESTRA.

Composer: John Eaton.

Librettist: P. Creagh.

First Performance: Bloomington, Indiana University Open Theater, 1 March 1980.

*   *   *

The Cry of Clytaemnestra is perhaps John Eaton's quintessential operatic statement. It treats events from antiquity with contemporary immediacy and searing, unrelenting agony. Eaton sets this almost cinematically-conceived story of sordid deeds and depraved emotions in an atmosphere of shock and horror. Though it is largely atonal, *The Cry of Clytaemnestra* is far removed in its emotionalism from the dry, cerebral music that one might expect from an academic composer.

Patrick Creagh's libretto (loosely derived from Aeschylus) depicts, through the eyes of Clytaemnestra, the events immediately prior to Agamemnon's return to Argos from the Trojan Wars. The opera begins with the "cry" of the title, Clytaemnestra's shriek of grief as she recalls (in flashback) the sacrifice of her daughter Iphigeneia at the hands of Agamemnon, for "reasons of state." In a series of terse, crisply-rendered scenes, we see the factors—some real, some imaginary—that drive Clytaemnestra to take revenge on Agamemnon: her coarse lover Aegisthus, who tells Clytaemnestra of Agamemnon's adultery, bullies her children, and makes crude advances toward her daughter Electra; a vision of Agamemnon at Troy, as his mistress and prophetess Cassandra foretells his violent death; and Electra's bitter renunciation of her unfaithful mother. The overwhelmed Clytaemnestra falls unconscious and dreams of murdering Agamemnon upon his return. She wakes, sees the beacon heralding Agamemnon's arrival, and awaits him with a cold, nihilistic determination. Her final utterance is a restatement of the opening "cry"—now a cry of bitter triumph.

The opera is scored for a relatively small chamber orchestra augmented with electronics, a huge percussion group, and two pianos tuned a quarter-tone apart; like all of Eaton's operas, *The Cry of Clytaemnestra* makes extensive use of microtonal intervals, always employed for their profound expressive effects. Eaton's setting of this tale of domestic violence is similarly violent; the orchestral writing, which conspicuously avoids doubling voices, is highly coloristic and replete with jagged, shocking effects. The highly melismatic, microtonally-inflected vocal lines, which constantly emphasize the upper range (in a musical analog of agonized screams), demand singers of astounding flexibility and endurance.

In Patrick Creagh Eaton found the ideal librettist for his tortured sound; the libretto of *The Cry of Clytaemnestra* depicts a quasi-mythological world on an intimate scale reminiscent of television serial drama. Eschewing the sprawl and grandiosity of his earlier operas such as *Heracles* and *Danton and Robespierre,* Eaton presents a highly concentrated image of powerful, tormented characters. Even in its few moments of relative calm, such as Iphigeneia's tender and ethereal aria, "Gentle is heaven today, tender the flowering earth," there is a discernible element of pain. *The Cry of Clytaemnestra,* with its searing dissonance and immense palette of sound, operates at a level of sheer intensity that few twentieth-century operas have achieved.

—H. Stephen Wright

CUÉNOD, Hugues (Adhémar).

Tenor. Born 26 June 1902, Corseaux-sur-Vevey. Concert debut in Paris, 1928; debut at Teatro alla Scala, 1951; Glyndebourne debut, 1954; Covent Garden debut, 1954, as Astrologer in *The Golden Cockerel*; created Sellem in *The Rake's*

Progress, 1951; Metropolitan Opera debut as Emperor in *Turandot,* 1987, at age 85; appeared at Geneva Opera as Monsieur Taupe in *Capriccio* in 1989.

Publications

About CUÉNOD: books–

Spycket, J. *Un diable de musicien: Hugues Cuénod.* Lausanne, 1979.

Born at Vevey in the canton of Vaud, Switzerland, Cuénod's musical education was at first French, and later German at the Basel Conservatory and as a private student in Vienna. His light, natural tenor voice, pure in tone yet penetrating enough to ensure the success of his Metropolitan Opera debut at the age of 84 (as the Emperor in Puccini's *Turandot*) served him well throughout a long career in a much wider repertoire than is attempted by most tenors.

His interpretation of early music, greatly admired in the 1930s when he sang with Nadia Boulanger's group, found new success when he appeared at Glyndebourne from 1954 onwards in Monteverdi's *Poppea* and Cavalli's *L'Ormindo,* as well as other operas of the early 17th century. Much of his appeal is undoubtedly due as much to the flexibility of his voice—and his exquisite ability to sing a true *pianissimo* while still projecting his words—as to its remarkable aptitude for ornamentation. At the same time his acting ability, especially in humorous roles, is outstanding for its sharpness of vision and its ready insight into the quirks of a given character.

In works related in diverse ways to opera he has found new avenues for lyrical and dramatic expression. When Noel Coward's operetta *Bitter Sweet* opened on Broadway in 1939, Cuénod proved that he had exactly the right voice for the genre; and when he later gave concert performances of Monteverdi's *Combattimento di Tancredi e Clorinda* his declamatory powers in the Testo (Narrator's) part needed no emphasizing. His control of tone color combined with his wide range of dynamics invariably served him as valuable assets.

His debut as an opera singer took place at the Théâtre des Champs-Elysées in 1928, and he subsequently sang in many major European houses. In Rimsky-Korsakov's *Le coq d'or* (*The Golden Cockerel*) at Covent Garden in 1954, he sang the part of the Astrologer, overcoming with ease the difficulties of its high tessitura. When Stravinsky's *The Rake's Progress* was given its premiere in Venice in 1951, Cuénod created the role of Sellem, the auctioneer, in which once again his acting ability joined with his vocal prowess to leave a lasting impression.

Even smaller parts gain in prestige and purpose when he interprets them, as for example Triquet's song in act II of Tchaikovsky's *Eugene Onegin,* where his way of singing the final verse in hushed tones is marvelously effective. Similarly the part of the Emperor in *Turandot,* although not a long one, demands a sustained dignity of tone and an ability to project the text across a vast stage, and this Cuénod was most successful in doing at the Metropolitan Opera House in 1987.

He has often been quoted as saying that he has never lost his voice because he never had one to begin with, but this is an obvious over-simplification. What is more true is that since he has never had to force his voice he has therefore never

spoiled it, and so it has always remained an expressive and malleable instrument apt for many different kinds of music.
—Denis Stevens

THE CUNNING LITTLE VIXEN [Príhody Lišky Bystroušky].

Composer: Leoš Janáček.

Librettist: Leoš Janáček (after Rudolf Těsnohlidek).

First Performance: Brno, National Theater, 6 November 1924.

Roles: Forester (baritone); His Wife (contralto); Schoolmaster (tenor); Priest (bass); Harasta (bass); Vixen/Bystrouska (soprano); The Fox, Goldenmane (tenor or soprano); Lapák, Forester's Dog (mezzo-soprano); Pasak (tenor); His Wife (soprano); Badger (bass); Rooster (soprano); Hen (soprano); Screechowl (contralto); Jay (soprano); Woodpecker (contralto); various animals; chorus (SATB).

Publications

articles–

Sádecký, Z. "Celotónový character hudební řeči v Janáčkově 'Lišce Bystroušce' " [whole-tone aspects of *Cunning Little Vixen*]. *Živá hudba* 2 (1962): 95 [summary in German].

Warrack, John. "*The Cunning Little Vixen.*" *Opera* March (1961).

*   *   *

The Cunning Little Vixen is a striking example of Janáček's pantheism. His patchwork methods of story-telling are used less to form a coherent plot than to create a certain ambience, or to develop a vitalist philosophy. It is no coincidence that the most beautiful music of the opera occurs in the love scene between The Fox, Goldenmane, and The Vixen, Bystrouska, and in the finale, in which Forester pronounces a benediction on the beauty of nature, and the eternity of Life itself.

Janáček's musical setting for this story is remarkable. He avoids long melodic lines at almost all points in the score. As is now well known, Janáček believed that all music finds its ultimate source in the spoken word. This crucial aspect of his music is often misrepresented. He was as interested in reflecting the psychological realities of speech as he was in recreating the particular accents and other characteristics of the language. Like the composer's other operas, *The Cunning Little Vixen* contains a great deal of melodic writing, but it is usually of the short rhapsodic sort, as would be expected from the naturalistic word setting described here.

The orchestra for this opera is large and has a special luminosity that is even more pronounced than in most of Janáček's other operatic works. Janáček's orchestra is one of alternating choirs and brilliant colors, rarely blended in the

The Cunning Little Vixen, **with Thomas Allen as the Forester, Royal Opera, London, 1990**

nineteenth century style; it is sharp, clean, and utterly personal. He has a liking for wide orchestral spaces, often using extreme registers both in combination and alternately. Although the orchestra is very active, its scoring makes it quite easy for voices and words to be heard.

Superficially, it is possible to make a comparison between Janáček's methods and those of Wagner. It was the great German who militantly rejected (but not always) the "number opera." He also opted for a more naturalistic kind of expressive recitative. In the narrow sense, this could also describe the methods used by Janáček. But he goes further; each person is represented by music which reflects *his* particular use of language, governed by his personality and its particular idiosyncrasies. The criterion for Janáček was what the character would sound like if he were only speaking the lines.

—Harris Crohn

CURLEW RIVER
See CHURCH PARABLES

CURTIN, Phyllis.

Soprano. Born 3 December 1921 in Clarksburg, West Virginia; studied in Boston with Boris Goldovsky and Joseph Regneas; sang with New England Opera Theatre, 1946; debut with New York City Opera as Fraulein Burstner in Einem's *Der Prozess*; Glyndebourne debut, 1959; debut at Metropolitan Opera as Fiordiligi, 1961; created roles in Floyd operas: Susanna, 1955, and Cathy in *Wuthering Heights,* 1958.

*   *   *

Long associated with the furtherance of contemporary music, Phyllis Curtin has championed American music throughout the world. Although she was exposed to the study of the violin as a child, serious study in music and vocal technique began in association with her studies in political science at Wellesley College. By her own admission Curtin, even as a student with the Russian soprano Olga Averino at the Longy School and later with the bass Joseph Regneas, found the preparation of contemporary music extremely easy. This affinity may have been possible because of the background she had as a string player; whatever the reason, Curtin combined intelligence, sensitive musicality, and her desire to perform into a springboard for gaining stature as an international figure in opera. Appearances as Lisa in Tchaikovsky's *The Queen of Spades* and Lady Billows in Britten's *Albert Herring* in the New England Opera Theatre in Boston were her first substantial roles in opera.

Most closely associated with the New York City Opera, Curtin sang there virtually all the Mozart heroines as well as Salome, Violetta (*La traviata*), and Mistress Ford (*Falstaff*) in the standard operatic literature; however, she began her career in that opera house in *Der Prozess* by Gottfried von Einem in 1953. It was with Mozart (Fiordiligi in *Così fan tutte*) that she made her debut at the Metropolitan Opera in 1961. It was her creation of the title role in Carlisle Floyd's

opera *Susannah* that catapulted her into national fame and eventually international exposure as a singer. Her association with Floyd resulted in her singing in first performances of two other operas of his—*Wuthering Heights* (Santa Fe Opera) and *The Passion of Jonathan Wade* (New York City Opera). She also sang American premieres of Walton's *Troilus and Cressida* and Milhaud's *Medea.*

Curtin's European debut came in Floyd's *Susannah* at the Brussels World's Fair in 1958. A year with the Vienna State Opera in 1960-61 was her longest European engagement; but she also made appearances in Italy, Germany, England, Scotland, Scandinavia, Israel, and Argentina.

Curtin was the first singer to portray three operatic Rosina Almavivas: Mozart's, Rossini's, and Milhaud's. During the 1963-64 season she established a record in the United States for orchestral appearances by a singer. In 1950 she appeared with the National Broadcasting Corporation Opera in a production of *Carmen,* the first complete production televised in America. During her singing career she appeared in some seventy operatic roles; and over fifty musical works were composed specifically for her. She was in one sense a musician's musician, as is evidenced by her support from conductors, composers, and fellow singers. Her failure to attain greater renown as an international star may possibly have been due to her lack of stage charisma and her inability to project enough sound in the larger operatic houses.

Since her retirement from major public performances in 1984, Curtin has continued to use her singing expertise to influence the musical world, first in her position as a teacher at Yale University and later as Dean of Boston University's School of the Arts.

—Rose Mary Owens

CUZZONI, Francesca.

Soprano. Born c.1698 in Parma. Died 1770 in Bologna. Married composer and harpsichordist Pietro Giuseppe Sandoni, 1722. Studied with Lanzi; earliest known appearance in *Dafni* at Parma, 1716; sang in Bologna, Genoa, and Venice, 1716-19; first sang with her rival Faustina Bordoni in Venice, 1718, in Pollorolo's *Ariodante*; London debut as Teofane in Handel's *Ottone,* 1723; created Handel roles of Cleopatra in *Giulio Cesare,* title role in *Rodelinda,* Asteria in *Tamerlano,* and other works; spent the winter of 1728-29 in Vienna; sang at Modena and Venice, 1729; sang in Hasse's *Ezio* in Naples, 1730; sang in Genoa and for the last time in Venice, 1733-34; returned to London to sing for the Opera of the Nobility, 1734-36; sang Leo's *Olimpiade* and Caldara's *Ormisda* in Florence, 1737-38; sang in Hamburg in 1740 and in Amsterdam 1742; in Stuttgart for three years beginning in 1745, absconding to Bologna because of debts in 1748; returned to London for benefit concerts, 1750; arrested for debt in the Netherlands; spent her final years in Bologna making buttons.

Publications

About CUZZONI: books—

Tosi, P.F. *Opinioni de' cantori antichi e moderni.* Bologna, 1723; English translation, 1742; 1743.

Mancini, G. *Pensieri e riflessioni pratiche sopra il canto figurato.* Vienna, 1774; English translation, 1967.

Francesca Cuzzoni and Farinelli singing a duet, with Heidegger seated in the background. Caricature by Joseph Goupy after Marco Ricci, c. 1730

Deutsch, O.E. *Handel: a Documentary Biography.* London, 1955; New York, 1974.

Dean, Winton, and J. Merrill Knapp. *Handel's Operas: 1704-26.* Oxford, 1987.

articles–

Quantz, J.J. [Autobiography]. In F.W. Marpurg, *Historisch-Kritische Beyträge zur Aufnahme der Musik,* vol. 1, pp. 240-41. Berlin, 1755; 1970; English translation in Paul Nettl, *Forgotten Musicians,* New York, 1951; 1969.

Termini, Olga. "From Ariodante to Ariodante." Introduction to C.F. Pollarolo and A. Salvi, *Ariodante,* edited by Olga Termini, ix. Milan, 1986.

unpublished–

LaRue, C.S. "The Composer's Choice: Aspects of Compositional Context and Creative Process in Selected Operas from Handel's Royal Academy Period." Ph.D. dissertation, University of Chicago, 1990.

* * *

At a time when vocal virtuosity reigned supreme in the opera houses of all of western Europe, Francesca Cuzzoni was one of the most successful and significant prima donnas of the first half of the eighteenth century. While this statement can be supported by contemporary accounts of her abilities by such notable commentators as F. Tosi and J.J. Quantz, much more important is the fact that the greatest opera composers of the day, including Leo, Porpora, Hasse, and Handel created leading parts for her in the important opera centers of Italy, Austria, Germany, and England. While few autograph manuscripts of the composers who wrote for Cuzzoni survive, those of Handel during his tenure as "Master of the Orchestra" and composer of the Royal Academy of Music in London during the 1720s attest to Cuzzoni's abilities not just as a fabulously gifted virtuosa, but as a talented musico-dramatic interpreter in an era in which opera was regularly accused of being simply a showcase for vocal display.

Cuzzoni's strengths lay not just in her outstanding technique, but in her abilities to convey the role of the melancholy heroine through performances of pathetic arias capable of reducing the audience to tears. As the eighteenth-century music historian Charles Burney relates in his description (albeit second hand) of Cuzzoni's debut in London (*General History of Music,* London, 1789): "The slow air, *Falsa imagine* [in Handel's *Ottone,* 1723], the first which Cuzzoni sung in this country, fixed her reputation as an expressive and pathetic singer; as *Affanni del pensier* [also from *Ottone*] did Handel's, as a composer of such songs." If one traces Cuzzoni's five year career with the Royal Academy of Music, it becomes clear that Handel created roles for Cuzzoni based on her ability to play the wronged lover, the deceived wife, and other roles in which laments and songs of sorrow were dramatically appropriate. Throughout Handel's roles for Cuzzoni, she played the part of the unrequited lover (*Alessandro, Admeto, Siroe*), or the forlorn lover separated from her beloved (*Ottone, Riccardo primo, Tolomeo*). In keeping with these dramatic roles are arias in andante or larghetto time signatures (often in siciliano twelve-eight meters) frequently containing languishing suspensions and expressive appoggiaturas. These musico-dramatic abilities of Cuzzoni's are particularly apparent in the operas Handel composed for the Royal Academy after the arrival of Faustina Bordoni in 1726, who provided a very different type of virtuoso vocal type.

The famous on-stage battle between Cuzzoni and Faustina Bordoni in Bononcini's *Astianatte* (10 June 1727) is much less an example of the vanity of the leading opera singers of the day and the competition among them than it is a demonstration of how the British press could inflate antagonisms that may or may not have existed between these two stars prior to their engagement by the Royal Academy of Music. In fact, Cuzzoni and Bordoni were very different voice types; as the famous singing master Francesco Tosi states in his *Observations on the Florid Song,* "The one is inimitable for a privileg'd Gift of Singing, and for enchanting the World with a prodigious Felicity in executing, and with a singular Brilliant (I know not whether from Nature of Art) which pleases to Excess [Bordoni]. The delightful soothing Cantabile of the other, joined with the Sweetness of a fine Voice, a perfect Intonation, Strictness of Time, and the rarest Productions of a Genius, are Qualifications as particular and uncommon, as they are difficult to be imitated [Cuzzoni]. The Pathetic of the one, and the Allegro of the other, are the Qualities the most to be admired respectively in each of them" [London edition, 1742]. Cuzzoni's voice was that of a high soprano, with a range from middle "c" to the "c" two octaves above, whereas Bordoni's voice was lower and more restricted, ranging from "b flat" below middle "c" to "g" above the staff [Quantz]. Furthermore, these differences in their voices had distinct musico-dramatic implications, which Handel consistently took advantage of in all the operas he composed for them.

Although much of what eighteenth-century audiences went to the opera to hear was the beauty of the voices of the famous singers of the day, it seems clear that even the greatest and most versatile singers had particular strengths and weaknesses that, in the hands of the best composers, shaped the dramatic as well as the musical nature of the parts created for them. In this sense, Francesca Cuzzoni was not just a brilliant virtuosa but an integral part of the complex creative process in eighteenth-century *opera seria,* and perhaps one of the greatest pathetic heroines in the history of opera.

—C. Steven LaRue

D

LA DAFNE.

Composer: Marco da Gagliano.

Librettist: Ottavio Rinuccini.

First Performance: Mantua, 1608.

Roles: Ovid (tenor); Venus (soprano); Amore (soprano); Apollo (tenor); Dafne (soprano); Thirsus (contralto); Three Shepherds (bass, two tenors); Two nymphs (sopranos); chorus.

* * *

La Dafne is an early masterpiece of the new monodic style of the early seventeenth century. First produced at Mantua in 1608, the work followed on the heels of the first great work of the style, Monteverdi's *L'Orfeo* of 1607. *La Dafne* was ordered as a replacement work for Monteverdi's previously-commissioned *L'Arianna,* which was not available for performance until later in 1608. In *La Dafne* Gagliano followed the successful practice of Monteverdi in making use of a number of musical styles and textures to contrast with the expressive recitative.

The librettist Rinuccini drew upon Ovid's *Metamorphoses* for the story of Daphne, who, pursued by Apollo, becomes a laurel tree in order to escape him. After a prologue in which Ovid himself extols the patrons of the production, shepherds and nymphs implore Jove to deliver them from the serpent which is tormenting them. The shepherds' complaints continue at length, cast in the form of an echo song and a madrigal-like chorus. Apollo appears and kills the Python, which earns him a vigorous round of praise from the chorus. Cupid and Venus appear and, in response to the teasing of Apollo, cause him to be afflicted by the arrows of love. Dafne enters, in pursuit of game, but she soon encounters a love-smitten Apollo and becomes the pursued. Cupid and Venus gloat upon their victory over Apollo. Thirsus relates the rest of the story—how Dafne was transformed into a laurel and how Apollo embraced her. Apollo decrees that nothing shall disturb his beloved tree. The chorus, after delivering a blessing to Dafne, declares that, unlike Dafne, it will respond to true love.

In composing *La Dafne* Gagliano set a revised version of Rinuccini's libretto. The shorter, original form of the libretto had been set to music (now mostly lost) by Jacopo Peri and Jacopo Corsi and performed in Florence in 1598. In 1627 Schütz also set this important libretto to music (now lost), in a translation and revision by Martin Opitz. Rinuccini defined the narrative sections of his text by writing lines of seven and eleven syllables, freely mixed. Gagliano set these to music in the expressive recitative style already developed by Peri and Caccini in Florence, although the recitative of Gagliano is richer, more focused, and often livelier than that of Peri or Caccini. Gagliano also uses a greater range of expression than either Peri or Caccini and excels when he finds opportunities for lyrical effusion. These latter moments are always inspired by a careful reading of the text, adherence to the spirit of the words being one of Gagliano's great strengths and a subject about which he felt strongly. Choruses are frequent and varied. They can be either dance-like or madrigalesque in style, and serve either as commentary or as a means to help advance the action of the plot. There are effective settings of genres which were fast becoming conventions, namely the echo song, the lament, and the prayer. In the score only the voice parts and the bass line are notated, so that the modern-day editor must make numerous decisions about disposition of instruments and filling out of accompaniments. Although there is no overture contained in the score, the composer suggested that an instrumental sinfonia should be added.

Gagliano's contribution to the history of early opera in *La Dafne* is to have narrated a story convincingly by means of music and with a good deal of variety in order to compel his listeners' attention. In doing so he surpassed his fellow Florentines Peri and Caccini.

—Edward Rutschman

LA
DAFNE DI MARCO
DA GAGLIANO
NELL'ACCADEMIA DE GL'ELEVATI
L'AFFANNATO
. RAPPRESENTATA
IN MANTOVA

. IN FIRENZE·

APPRESSO CRISTOFANO MARESCOTTI. MDCVIII.
CON LICENZA DE'SVPERIORI

Title-page of first edition of score to Gagliano's *La Dafne*, Florence, 1608

d'ALBERT, Eugen ([Eugène] Francis Charles).

Composer. Born 10 April 1864, in Glasgow. Died 3 March 1932, in Riga. Married: 1) the pianist Teresa Carreño (1892-95); 2) the singer Hermine Finck; 4 other wives. Early instruction in music from father Charles Louis Napoléon d'Albert, a dancing master and composer of popular music; studied piano with Pauer and theory with Stainer, Prout and Sir Arthur Sullivan at the New Music School in London, beginning 1874; performed his piano concerto under Hans Richter, 24 October 1881; travelled to Vienna on a Mendelssohn fellowship; studied with Liszt; conductor at Weimar, 1895; director of the Hochschule für Musik in Berlin, 1907; adopted German citizenship and spent the rest of his life in Germany and Austria.

Operas

Publisher: Bote and Bock.

Der Rubin, d'Albert (after F. Hebbel), Carlsruhe, 12 October 1893.

Ghismonda, d'Albert (after K. Immermann), Dresden, 28 November 1895.

Gernot, Gustav Kastropp, Mannheim, 11 April 1897.

Die Abreise, Ferdinand von Sporck (after a play by August von Steigentesch), Frankfurt, 20 October 1898.

Kain, Heinrich Bulthaupt, Berlin, Court Opera, 17 February 1900.

Der Improvisator, Gustav Kastropp, Berlin, Court Opera, 20 February 1902.

Tiefland, Rudolph Lothar (after the play by Angel Guimerá *Terra baixa*), Prague, German Opera, 15 November 1903; revised 1905.

Flauto solo, Hans von Wolzogen, Prague, German Opera, 12 November 1905.

Tragaldabas (Der geborgte Ehemann), Rudolph Lothar (after a play by Auguste Vacquerie), Hamburg, 3 December 1907.

Izeÿl, Rudolph Lothar (after a play by Armand Silvestre and Eugène Morand), Hamburg, 6 November 1909.

Die verschenkte Frau, Rudolph Lothar and Richard Batka, Vienna, Court Opera, 6 February 1912.

Liebesketten, Rudolph Lothar (after a play by Angel Guimerá), Vienna, 12 November 1912.

Die toten Augen, Hanns Heinz Ewers (after Mark Henry, *Les yeux morts*), Dresden, 5 March 1916.

Der Stier von Olivera, Richard Batka (after a play by Heinrich Lilienfein), Leipzig, 10 May 1918.

Revolutionshochzeit, Ferdinand Lion (after the play by Sophus Michaelis), Leipzig, 26 October 1919.

Sirocco, Leo Feld and Karl Michael von Levetzow, Darmstadt, 18 May 1921.

Mareike von Nymwegen, Herbert Alberti, Hamburg, 31 October 1923.

Der Golem, Ferdinand Lion, Frankfurt, 14 November 1926.

Die schwarze Orchidee, Karl Michael von Levetzow, Leipzig, 1 December 1928.

Mister Wu [unfinished; completed by Leo Blech], Karl Michael von Levetzow (after the play by H.M. Vernon and Harold Owen), posthumous production, Dresden, 29 September 1932.

Other works: orchestral works, concertos, incidental music for plays, choral works, chamber music, piano music.

Publications/Writings

About d'ALBERT: books -

Hanslick, E. *Der Mensch und das Leben.* Berlin, 1896.

Korngold, J. *Deutsches Opernschaffen der Gegenwart.* Leipzig and Vienna, 1921.

Istel, E. *Die moderne Oper vom Tode Richard Wagners bis zur Gegenwart.* Leipzig, 2nd edition 1923.

Raupp. W. *Eugen d'Albert: ein Künstler-und-Menschen Schicksal.* Leipzig, 1930.

Pangels, Charlotte, *Eugen d'Albert Wunderpianist und Komponist, Eine Biographie.* Zurich, 1981.

articles–

Aber, A. "Eugene d'Albert 'Die schwarze Orchidee'." *Die Musik* (1928-29).

Sterl, Raimund Walter. "Komponisten im historischen Regensburg." *Regensburg Almanach 1980* 45 (1979).

Williamson, John. "Eugen d'Albert: Wagner and Verismo." *Music Review* 45 (1984): 26.

unpublished–

Heisig, H. "D'Alberts Opernschaffen." Ph.D. dissertation, University of Leipzig, 1942.

*   *   *

D'Albert had the talent of a film-composer *avant la lettre* and something of the temperament and life-style to match. Of cosmopolitan background and inclination, he composed twenty operas that explored the range of popular theatrical taste of his time. The extent of his success was nevertheless questioned by some of the higher-minded critics of his adopted Germany (as a young man he had published an open letter in the German press condemning his English musical education and praising German culture). He could readily slip from a light operetta style into Wagnerian romantic mannerisms that were nevertheless affected by his lively taste for the "verismo" operas of his young Italian contemporaries. It was easy to denounce him as an eclectic, bent on a "merely theatrical" kind of operatic entertainment; it was hard, however, to deny that he could on occasion achieve his ends with great skill and a measure of genuine inspiration.

Apart from *Tiefland* (1903/5), which is his best-known opera, his two most successful works are both in one-act format: *Die Abreise* (1898) and *Die toten Augen* (1916). The first of these won critical acclaim for its success in pioneering a post-*Meistersinger* type of German comic opera in an eighteenth century setting (nearly a decade before Strauss' *Der Rosenkavalier*). Based on a play by Steigentesch, it presented a cleverly worked version of the familiar love-triangle. A married couple have grown apart; the husband contemplates effecting a departure ("Abreise") in order to leave the way clear for his friend, but in the end it is the friend who departs, leaving the couple reunited. When the work was performed in Vienna its economy and skill in the conversational setting of alexandrines were welcomed by Julius Korngold, who valued its simple and "natural" style, given the Wagnerian reputation of d'Albert's earlier operas (e.g. *Der Rubin,* 1983 and *Ghismonda,* 1895). "At last," he exclaimed, "a light comic tone in German opera again!" Less successful, Korngold felt, was d'Albert's next one-acter: *Flauto solo,* whose plot, symbolically celebrating the rapprochement of German and Franco-Italian music, drew on a story from the biography of Frederick the Great. Rather surprisingly, the author of its libretto was the Wagnerian theorist Hans von Wolzogen.

For all the interest of the subject matter of the otherwise over-inflated *Flauto solo,* it was the revised and shortened version of *Tiefland,* premiered in the same year (1905), that achieved the popular success which established d'Albert's reputation as a composer. There is, however, no question that he was too prolific for his own good and unable consistently to focus his uneven talent. Attempts to repeat the success of *Tiefland* largely failed, although *Liebesketten* (1912), based on another play by Guimerá and dealing with smouldering passion in a Breton fishing-village, contained powerful scenes and effectively incorporated actual Breton folksongs.

Of the operas in many genres that the indefatigable d'Albert produced up to his death in 1932 (*Mister Wu,* his last, was completed by Leo Blech), only *Die toten Augen* (1916), an extended one-act melodrama with prologue, achieved a success comparable to that of *Tiefland.* Fashionably decadent and shocking in content, it relates the story of Myrtocle, the blind wife of a Roman legate in Jerusalem at the time of Christ. The idealistic Greek woman has her sight miraculously restored by Jesus (discreetly off-stage). She returns home and enthusiastically embraces her (ugly) husband's good-looking friend as the man she has always imagined her husband to be. Her actual husband angrily murders his friend even as his wife embraces him. The truth so shocks Myrtocle that she stares fully into the sun until she becomes blind again—and able to conclude the opera, with her husband, in a love-duet of regained, if psychologically improbable, ardor. Even the sternest critics of such theatrical material had to admit that it worked on stage and that the musical treatment of it was successful and craftsmanlike to a fault.

By any standards, d'Albert's operatic successes place him in the select company of only a few outstanding performers (Liszt and possibly Busoni are others) to have produced significant compositions for other than their own instrument. A master of the stock operatic mannerisms of his day, d'Albert certainly had an individual feeling for orchestral color (he relied on a Verdian succession of differentiated sonorities, rather than the kaleidoscopic textures of Strauss or Schreker). His strong melodic contours and unusually inflected chromatic harmony contributed to the entertainment of a widely constituted audience that never seriously mistook him for a "highbrow."

—Peter Franklin

DALIBOR.

Composer: Bedřich Smetana.

Librettist: J. Wenzig (Czech translation by E. Spindler).

First Performance: Prague, New Town Theater, 16 May 1868.

Roles: Dalibor (tenor); Milada (soprano); Vladislav (baritone); Budivoj (baritone); Beneš (bass); Vitek (tenor); Jitka (soprano); Zdeněk's Ghost (mute); chorus (SATB).

Publications

book–

Honolka, Kurt. *Bedřich Smetana in Selbstzeugnissen und Bilddokumenten* [includes analysis of *Dalibor*]. Reinbek bei Hamburg, 1978.

articles–

Clapham, John. " 'Dalibor': an Introduction." *Opera* 27 (1976): 890.
_____. "Smetana's Sketches for *Dalibor* and *The Secret*." *Music and Letters* 61 (1980): 136.

*   *   *

Dalibor, Smetana's third opera, was given its premiere in Prague in May 1868. Its stance is heroic and serious, a nationalist expression of the rescue opera concept, whose plot bears striking resemblances to that of Beethoven's *Fidelio*.

The action, set in the fifteenth century, is based on legend rather than historical fact. The knight Dalibor has been captured by his enemies, having killed the Burgrave in order to avenge the murder of his close friend Zdeněk. Vladislav, King of Bohemia, calls upon the Burgrave's daughter Milada to substantiate the charges, and judgment is found against Dalibor. Milada, however, feels pity for the knight and is impressed by his fearless, noble character. The people, represented by the chorus, share this view, but nevertheless Dalibor is led off to the dungeon. Inspired by his nobility, Milada determines to rescue him by disguising herself as a boy and becoming apprenticed to the gaolor Beneš; and when she takes Dalibor his beloved violin, the scene leads to a soprano-tenor love duet of extraordinary lyrical power. However, fearing a popular uprising in support of Dalibor, the king's advisers recommend the knight's immediate execution. Therefore Milada must rescue him, but she is wounded in the attempt. She dies in Dalibor's arms, and the hero takes his own life rather than submit to his enemies.

The opera was poorly received, a fact which distressed the composer and led him to revise the ending, so that Dalibor is executed and Milada dies in her rescue attempt. Smetana's heroic concept led to misconceptions that his music was Wagnerian, which it is not. Its vivid drama is closer in style to Verdi, and the most important musical idea, Dalibor's own theme, is subjected to many transformations in a manner reminiscent of Liszt's principle of metamorphosis.

This theme is itself wholly appropriate to the needs of both the dramatic situation and the musical treatment. It is first heard immediately after the opening fanfare, marked *largo maestoso,* and on its subsequent appearances it remains in the orchestra rather than in vocal presentation. It proves to be most flexible in expressive terms, representing both the hero's proud nature and, more introspectively, his love for his dead friend Zdeněk. It is even transformed into a fanfare figure in connection with the rescue attempt, and there is no doubt that musically this theme is the focal point of the opera.

The closing part of act II is one of the most inspired scenes Smetana created. Dalibor sings tenderly of Zdeněk, with whom the solo violin is associated throughout the opera, and this vision precedes the arrival of Milada, who begs the knight's forgiveness. He responds sympathetically, and their music builds strongly into an intense love duet.

The sophistication and range of Smetana's music and characterization were well ahead of contemporary taste. Even a potentially one-dimensional figure, King Vladislav, acquires depth through the sensitivity of his solo utterances, while the scene-setting is always strongly atmospheric. For example, the entrance of the king and his court is built as a majestic passacaglia (variations on a recurring idea in the bass), while the gloomy depths of the dungeons are realistically evoked. The musical structures, beyond those involving transformations of Dalibor's theme, include a broad tonal scheme and subtle linking devices, in which ideas are anticipated or recalled across scenes. There is room, also, for a wide range of expression, with lively choral dances in the tavern scene at the beginning of act II, in addition to the powerful ensembles and solos, which can be either introspective or ecstatic.

Smetana conceived *Dalibor* as a vehicle for the most noble feelings, as a work central to his desire to create a national operatic style and tradition, presenting his hero as a freedom fighter "who defended freedom at the cost of his own life." He explained that his opera was composed "with conscientiousness and truth." And so it was, though in his lifetime it received only fifteen performances. Smetana believed "the time of recognition of Dalibor would yet arrive," for he knew he had created a masterpiece.

—Terry Barfoot

DALLAPICCOLA, Luigi.

Composer. Born 3 February 1904, in Pisino (Pazin), Istria (now part of Yugoslavia). Died 19 February 1975, in Florence. Early education at the Pisino Gymnasium, 1914-21; studied piano and harmony in Trieste, 1919-21; studied piano with Ernesto Consolo and composition with Vito Frazzi at the Cherubini Conservatory in Florence, beginning 1922; active in the International Society for Contemporary Music from 1930s; on the faculty of the Cherubini Conservatory, 1934-67; visited London, 1946; taught at the Berkshire Music Center, 1951, Queens College, New York, 1956, 1959, the University of California, Berkeley, 1962, Dartmouth College, summer 1969, Aspen Music School, 1969, and Marlboro, 1969.

Operas

Publishers: Ars Viva, Carisch, Suvini Zerboni, Universal.

Volo di notte, Dallapiccola (after the novel by St-Exupéry), 1937-39, Florence, Teatro della Pergola, 18 May 1940.
Il prigioniero, Dallapiccola (after Villiers de l'Isle Adam and Charles de Coster), 1944-48 [revised for reduced orchestra 1950], Radio Audizioni Italiana, 1 December 1949; stage premiere: Florence, Comunale, 20 May 1950.
Ulisse, Dallapiccola (after Homer, *The Odyssey*), 1960-68, premiered in German as *Odysseus,* Berlin, Deutsche Oper, 29 September 1968; in Italian, Milan, 1969.

Other works: a ballet, orchestral works, choral works, concertos, various works for voices and instrumental combinations, violin and piano music, solo violoncello music, piano music, songs.

Publications

By DALLAPICCOLA: books–

Appunti, incontri, meditazioni. Milan, 1970; new edition as *Parole e musica,* edited by Fiamma Nicolodi and with an introduction by Gianandrea Gavazzeni, Milan, 1980.

La mia protest-music. Florence, 1971.
Dallapiccola on Opera. Edited by Rudy Shackelford, London, 1988.

articles–

"Praga: il XIII festival della SIMC." *Emporium* 82 (1935): 338.
"Musicisti del nostro tempo: Vito Frazzi." *La rassegna musicale* 10 (1937): 220.
"Di un aspetto della musica contemporanea." *Atti dell' Accademia del Regio Conservatorio di musica Luigi Cherubini* 60 (1938): 35.
"Per un' esecuzione de L'enfant et les sortilèges." *Letturatura* 3 (1939): 154.
"Volo di notte di L. Dallapiccola." *Scenario* 60 (1940): 176.
"Per la prima rappresentazione di Volo di notte." *Letturatura* 6 (1942): 10.
"Per una rappresentazione de Il ritorno di Ulisse in patria di Claudio Monteverdi." *Musica* 2 (1942): 121.
Articles in *Il Mondo* (1945-47).
"In memoria di Anton Webern." *Emporium* 55 (1947): 18.
"Kompositionsunterricht und neue Musik." *Melos* 16 (1949): 231.
"Appunti sulla scena della statua nel Don Giovanni." *La rassegna musicale* 20 (1950): 107; revised in *Appunti* (1970); English translation in *Music Survey* 3-4 (1950-52): 89.
"Sulla strada della dodecafonia." *Aut-Aut* 1 (1951): 30; reprinted in *Appunti* (1970); English translation in *Music Survey* 3-4 (1950-52): 318.
"The Genesis of the Canti di prigionia and Il prigioniero." *Musical Quarterly* 39 (1953): 355.
"Der Künstler und die Wahrhaftigkeit." *Musikalische Jugend* 4 (1955): 1.
"The Birth-pangs of Job." *Musical Events* 15 (1960): 26.
"A Composer's Problem." *Opera* 12 (1961): 8; in Italian, *Appunti* (1970).
"What is the Answer to 'The Prisoner'?" *San Francisco Sunday Chronicle* 2 December (1962): 27,36.
"My Choral Music," In *The Composer's Point of View,* edited by R.S. Hines, 151. Norman, Oklahoma, 1963.
"Parole e musica nel melodramma." *Quaderni della rassegna musicale* no. 2 (1962): 117; revised in *Appunti* (1970); English translation in *Perspectives of New Music* 5 (1966): 121.
"Encounters with Edgard Varèse." *Perspectives of New Music* 4 (1966): 1; in Italian in *Appunti* (1970).
"Nascita di un libretto d'opera." *Nuova rivista musicale italiana* 2 (1968): 605; reprinted in *Appunti* (1970); German translation in *Melos* 35 (1968): 265; abridged English translation in *The Listener* 82 (1969): 553.
"Betrachtungen über Simon Boccanegra." *Opera Journal* [Berlin] no. 7 (1968-69): 2.
"Meeting with Webern (Pages from a Diary)." *Tempo* no. 99 (1972): 2; Italian original in *Appunti* (1970).
"Arnold Schönberg: 'Premessa a un centenario'." *Chigiana* 29-30 (1972-73): 197; revised German translation in *Beiträge 74/75: Österreichische Gesellschaft für Musik* (1974): 9.
"Der Geist der italienischen Musik—Gian Francesco Malipiero zum Gedenken." *Österreichische Musikzeitschrift* 29 (1974): 3.
"Su Ferruccio Busoni: a Empoli il 29 agosto 1974." *Empoli* 1 (1974): 13.

"Un inedito di Dallapiccola: schema di una trasmissione televisiva su L.D." *Nuova rivista musicale italiana* 9 (1975): 248.

"Qualche nota in memoria di Gian Francesco Malipiero (18 marzo 1882-1 agosto 1973)." In *Miscellanea del Cinquantenario; Die Stellung der italienischen Avantgarde in der Entwicklung der neuen Musik.* Milan, 1978.

"Musicisti del nostro tempo: Vito Frazzi." In *L'Accademia musicale Chigiana ricorda Vito Frazzi e Valentino Bucchi,* edited by Luciano Alberti, et. al. *Chigiana* 34 (1981).

"Reflections on Three Verdi Operas." *19th-Century Music* 7 (1983): 55; in Italian in *Parole e musica.* Milan, 1980.

"Luigi Dallapiccola on Arnold Schoenberg." *Journal of the Arnold Schoenberg Institute* 7 (1983): 93; in Italian in *Parole e musica.* Milan, 1980.

editions–

M. Mussorgsky: Pictures at an Exhibition. 1940; revised 2nd edition, 1970.

C. Monteverdi: Il ritorno di Ulisse in patria. 1941-42.

A. Vivaldi: 6 sonatas. 1955.

30 Italian songs of the 17th-18th centuries. 1960.

About DALLAPICCOLA: books–

Ballo, F. *Arlecchino di Ferruccio Busoni, Volo di notte di Luigi Dallapiccola, Coro di morti di Goffredo Petrassi* [p. 22 ff], Milan, 1942.

Nicolodi, F. ed. *Luigi Dallapiccola: saggi, testimonianze, carteggio, biografia e bibliografia.* Milan, 1976.

Kämper, Dietrich. *Gefangenschaft und Freiheit: Leben und Werk des Komponisten Luigi Dallapiccola.* Cologne, 1984.

articles–

Gatti, G.M. "Modern Italian Composers, ii: Luigi Dallapiccola." *Monthly Musical Record* 67 (1937): 25.

Paoli, D. de'. "An Italian Musician: Luigi Dallapiccola." *The Chesterian* 19 (1937-38): 157.

Mantelli, A. "Lettura da Firenze: Volo di notte di Dallapiccola." *La rassegna musicale* 13 (1940): 274.

Mila, M. "Il prigioniero di Luigi Dallapiccola." *La rassegna musicale* 20 (1950): 303; French translation in *Musique contemporaine* no. 1 (1951): 53.

Pestalozza, L. "Pour l'étranger: Il prigioniero de Dallapiccola au XIII Maggio Musicale Fiorentino." *Il diapason* [Milan] 1 (1950): 22.

Goldman, R.F. "Current Chronicle: New York" [*Il prigioniero*]. *Musical Quarterly* 37 (1951): 405.

Gavazzeni, G. "Volo di notte di Dallapiccola." In *La musica e il teatro,* 221. Pisa, 1954.

Rufer, J. "Luigi Dallapiccola: 'Il prigioniero'." In *Oper im XX Jahrhundert,* edited by H. Lindlar, *Musik der Zeit* 6, 56. Bonn, 1954.

D'Amico, F. "Liberazione e prigionia." In *I casi della musica,* 139. Milan, 1962.

Ugolini, G. "Il prigioniero di Luigi Dallapiccola." *La rassegna musicale* 32 (1962): 233.

Waterhouse, J.C.G. "Dallapiccola, Luigi: Volo di notte." *Music and Letters* 46 (1965): 86.

Drew, D. "Dallapiccola's Odyssey." *The Listener* 80 (1968): 514.

Kaufmann, H. *Spurlinien* [p. 67ff on *Il prigioniero*]. Vienna, 1969.

Pestelli, G., and A. Gentilucci. *La musica moderna* [Milan] v (1969): 161-92 [two special issues].

Anon. "I commenti della stampa italiana alla prima in Italia dell' Ulisse di Luigi Dallapiccola." *Nuova rivista musicale italiana* 4 (1970): 205.

Zurletti, M. "Ulisse." *Quaderno 3 del 35° maggio musicale fiorentino* (1972): 41.

Kämper, Dietrich. "Uno squardo nell' officina: gli schizzi e gli abbozzi del *Prigioniero* di Luigi Dallapiccola." *Nuova rivista musicale italiana* 14 (1980): 227.

Shackelford, Rudy. "A Dallapiccola Chronology." *Musical Quarterly* 67 (1981): 405.

Várnai, Péter. "Die Opern Luigi Dallappiccolas." In *Oper heute: Ein Almanach der Musikbühne,* edited by Horst Seeger and Mathias Rank. Berlin, 1983.

Kämper, Dietrich. "Luigi Dallapiccola und die italienische Musik der dreissiger Jahre." In *Gesellschaft für Musikforschung, Report, Bayreuth 1981,* edited by Christoph-Hellmut Mahling and Sigrid Wiesmann, 158. Kassel, 1984.

Petrobelli, Perluigi. "On Dante and Italian music: Three movements." [on *Ulisse*]. *Cambridge Opera Journal* 2 (1990): 219.

*　　*　　*

Despite the fact that Italian music of the nineteenth century is almost synonymous with opera, large-scale theatrical works in the twentieth century have been consistently marginal to the main thrust of compositional developments. Several figures produced large numbers of operas, such as Respighi and Malipiero, but their reputations rest primarily on instrumental or small-scale vocal music. Dallapiccola is probably the only major Italian composer after Puccini for whom opera was clearly central to his output, and yet he produced only three operas (four if one includes the "Sacra rappresentazione" *Job*) the first two of which are in single acts lasting one hour or less.

The key to Dallapiccola's individual position may be found in his keen appreciation of both the native operatic tradition extending back to Monteverdi and the output of his foreign contemporaries, as his many writings on opera eloquently testify. His "practical edition" of Monteverdi's *Il ritorno d'Ulisse in patria* is both a classic of its kind and a benchmark for subsequent realizations. As a composer, Dallapiccola drew extensively from the examples of Debussy, Malipiero, Busoni and Berg, although later in his career, Webern's music came to occupy an increasingly dominant position in his thought. Malipiero was a key figure in the resurgence of interest in ancient as well as modern instrumental composition in Italy (along with Respighi, Pizzetti, Casella and others); Busoni's transalpine heritage and aesthetic principles chimed in well with Dallapiccola's own instincts; Berg and Webern were potent embodiments of the modern Austro-German tradition that so attracted him. These influences can all be heard to varying degrees in Dallapiccola's first two operas *Volo di notte* (1937-9) and *Il prigioniero* (1944-8). With the assumption of a more out-and-out (if unorthodox) dodecaphony in *Job* (1950; analogous in many ways to Stravinsky's opera-oratorios *Oedipus Rex* and *Perséphone*) and *Ulisse* (1960-8), the Second Viennese School clearly became increasingly important to Dallapiccola, but never at the expense of his essentially Italian sensibilities; indeed, *Ulisse* is in many ways his most Busonian conception.

The driving theme behind all of Dallapiccola's stage works (including his ballet *Marsia*) is that of the imprisonment of the individual within his fate, and the individual's attempts at reconciliation with it. For this burning theme, expressed in so many different ways in his *oeuvre,* Dallapiccola found in opera the perfect vehicle, and few of his other works (*Canti di prigionia* and *Canti di liberazione* being notable exceptions) attained comparable significance. In his first opera, *Volo di notte,* Rivière is trapped (not entirely without his own volition) into the sacrifice of a pilot's life to further the cause of night flying. He is just as much a prisoner, albeit of his technological ambitions, as the eponyms of *Il prigioniero* and *Job* by their particular circumstances. Unlike them, however, Rivière is able to exercise a measure of control: his ensnarement is ultimately by choice. In contrast, the Prisoner, Job and Ulisse are all victims, playthings even, of deliberate cruelty by other agents with which only the last is able to come to terms.

Two recurrent and vital ingredients of Dallapiccola's theatrical style which he used to point up the most crucial moments in his operas are the symbolic role of stars, usually associated with the keys—or at least triads—of B minor or major, and the chorus. In *Volo di notte,* the pilot Fabien relates, via the radio-telegraphist, how he deliberately breaks through the clouds to view the stars, achieving an ecstatic vision, before his aeroplane plunges into the sea. The sight of the open night sky is a symbol of the prisoner's desire for and seeming acquisition of liberty; and Ulisse's final revelation takes place in a boat beneath—and by contemplation of—the stars. Dallapiccola's orchestration was generally more expert than that of most of his operatic contemporaries, and this applies as much to his use of the chorus, which is frequently sparing (except in the oratorio-like *Job*). His ability to unite musical and dramatic purpose in the placing of choral passages to achieve the maximum cathartic effect, as in the "revolt" of the airport workers in *Volo di notte* or the two choral intermezzi in *Il prigioniero,* is masterly.

No matter how bleak the conception behind Dallapiccola's operas (in *Il prigioniero* there is no redemption or hope of it whatsoever), there is never any doubt of the positivism of the composer's intent. At the very least his sense of injustice shines constant even in the blackest night; despite torment, despite persecution (whether human or divine), his characters reflect his unbreakable belief in the dignity of the human spirit and the right to freedom, as expressed with peerless eloquence in his music.

—Guy Rickards

DAL MONTE, Toti (born Antonietta Meneghel).

Soprano. Born 27 June 1893, in Magliano Veneto. Died 26 January 1975, in Treviso. Married singer Enzo de Muro Lomanto, one daughter. Studied with Barbara Marchesio for five years; debut at Teatro alla Scala as Biancofiore in *Fran-*

cesca di Rimini, 1916; engaged by Toscanini to sing Lucia at La Scala, 1921; Metropolitan Opera debut as Lucia, 1924; Covent Garden debut as Lucia and Rosina, 1926; retired from the operatic stage in 1949, but continued to act.

Publications

By DAL MONTE: books–

Una voce nel mondo. Milan, 1962.

About DAL MONTE: articles–

Renton, A.C. "Toti dal Monte." *Record Collector* 6 (1947): 147.

*   *   *

Toti dal Monte is one of those rare and fortunate singers who made her debut at the foremost opera house of Europe. After five years of study with the celebrated mezzo-soprano Barbara Marchisio, and following a series of auditions with the leading conductors of the day, dal Monte was engaged for three months at the Teatro alla Scala, at ten lire a day. She made her debut as Biancofiore in Zandonai's *Francesca da Rimini* on 22 February 1916. Her colleagues were Rosa Raisa (another Marchisio pupil), Aureliano Pertile, and Giuseppe Danise. During rehearsals conductor Gino Marinuzzi suggested that she should change her name, Antonietta Meneghel. She chose her nickname—Toti—and her grandmother's maiden name.

Toti Dal Monte as Rosina in *Il barbiere di Siviglia*

After this promising start, dal Monte spent the next three years building a repertoire and gaining much needed experience in the lesser theaters of Italy. Her new roles included Norina, Oscar, Lisette in Puccini's *La Rondine,* Gilda, Nedda, the title role of Mascagni's *Lodoletta,* Zerlina in Auber's *Fra Diavolo,* Musetta, Leila in the *Les pêcheurs de perles,* and Lauretta in *Gianni Schicchi.* She sang her first Cio-Cio-San in *Madama Butterfly* on 14 September 1918, at the Teatro Lirico of Milan; after a total of six performances she did not assay the role again until 1938. Her tours soon made her a favorite of audiences everywhere, and her reputation grew accordingly.

During her first foreign engagement she sang Gilda, Philine *(Mignon),* Nannetta in *Falstaff,* the Countess in Gomes' *Lo Schiavo,* and Musetta in *La bohème* in the major South American cities of Argentina, Uruguay, and Brazil. Between her first two South American seasons she returned to La Scala in June 1922, as a soloist in Beethoven's Ninth Symphony under the baton of Arturo Toscanini. The Maestro then invited her for the following season to sing Gilda opposite Carlo Galeffi and Giacomo Lauri-Volpi in the cast. This endorsement and her success established her as a permanent member of that illustrious company. Her assignments at La Scala included the plum roles of the coloratura repertory: the title roles of *Lucia di Lammermoor, La sonnambula, La fille du régiment,* and *Linda di Chamounix,* along with Rosina, Gilda, and Norina. She also sang Rosalina in the world premiere of *Il re,* on 29 January 1929, a role Giordano had expressly composed for her.

Established as a major artist of international caliber, she received many invitations from the major operatic centers of the world. Among the many cities where she performed, her most important engagements were her debuts at the Teatro Colón in Buenos Aires (1923), Paris Opéra (1924), Metropolitan Opera (1924), Covent Garden (1925), San Carlo in Naples (1929), and the Verona Arena (1934). In 1924 and 1928, Nellie Melba took her on the Melba-Williamson tours to Melbourne and Sydney. In 1926 she was engaged for a four-month concert tour of Australia and New Zealand, and in 1929, when Toscanini took the La Scala company on tour to Germany and Austria, dal Monte was his choice for the title role of *Lucia di Lammermoor* in Berlin and Vienna. Another five-month concert tour took her in 1931 from Moscow to Hong Kong, Manila, Shanghai, and five cities in Japan. She sang only two Lucias and one Gilda in her single season at the Metropolitan (1924-25), but she was a member of the Chicago Civic Opera Company from 1924 to 1928, and toured United States coast to coast.

Later in her career she took on heavier roles: Mimi, Butterfly, Manon, Violetta. In spite of her initial apprehensions, Cio-Cio-San became one of her most successful and most often requested roles. In her own words, "I could have sung nothing else, so many were the requests." A list of her partners through her career read like the operatic who's who of the period: Gigli, Pertile, Lauri-Volpi, Schipa, Battistini, Stracciari, Galeffi, Chaliapin, Pinza. Her last operatic engagement was a series of Rosinas in four small Italian cities in 1947, and she also continued to give recitals until 1950. She also appeared as an actress in speaking roles on stage (in Goldoni's *Buona madre*) and in films, among the latter *Il carnevale di Venezia* (1940), *Fiori d'arancio* (1944), *Una voce nel tuo cuore* (1950) and *Cuore di mamma* (1955). Following her retirement, she taught singing in Milan, Rome, Venice, and the USSR. Her pupils included Gianna d'Angelo (*née* Jane Angelovic) and Dolores Wilson.

Dal Monte credited her teacher, Marchisio, with developing her voice, giving it power and agility, extending its range, and teaching her correct breathing and an exceptional coloratura technique. Light, clear, and brilliant, dal Monte's voice had more weight than the coloratura sopranos who preceded her or were her contemporaries. In fact, at first she thought of herself as a light mezzo, and was able to darken her voice sufficiently to persuade the management to let her sing Lola in *Cavalleria rusticana,* her second role at La Scala in 1916. The spectrum of her vocal palette and her sound musical instinct enabled her to shade her voice according to the dramatic demands of the role. Her well-executed coloratura ornamentations and *staccatti* as preserved on disc are accurate but not flashy, more devices of expression than vocal exhibitionism. Her voice had great purity; she could float a note and produce a well-supported, focused tone at any pitch or dynamic level. She was an accomplished actress, and although small and plump, her attractive face, expressive and beautiful large eyes, charm, grace, and innate femininity made her impersonations credible and appealing.

Dal Monte's recordings for Victor and His Master's Voice command respect among collectors. Writing in the *Gramophone,* the well-known author, critic, and voice teacher Herman Klein had high praise for her mad scene from *Lucia* (DB 1015): "The vocalization is worthy of Toti dal Monte at her best. . . . The duets with the flute are flawlessly executed; but even more astonishing to my ear are those long, gigantic E flats in *alt.*" Upon the release of her *Carnevale di Venezia* (DB 1004) Klein wrote "That this gifted *soprano leggiero* is the best singer of her class Italy has produced since Tetrazzini there can be no manner of doubt." Her only complete recording—*Madama Butterfly* (His Master's Voice, 1939), with Beniamino Gigli—was received with some ambivalence. Dal Monte purposefully and successfully colored her voice in the first act to create the vocal image of the fifteen-year-old geisha, a sound not associated with the role as sung by other sopranos. Her approach is well-conceived, her delivery honest, and her dramatic involvement complete.

Dal Monte suffered from high blood pressure all her life and she retired because of it. In January 1975 she was hospitalized in Florence and treated for circulatory problems. She died at Pieve di Soligo, on 26 January 1975. Her entertaining autobiography, *Una voce nel mondo,* first appeared in 1962; it was posthumously republished under the editorship of Rodolfo Celletti, with an added chronology and discography.

—Andrew Farkas

LA DAME BLANCHE [The White Lady].

Composer: Adrien Boieldieu.

Librettist: Eugène Scribe (after Walter Scott, *The Monastery, Guy Mannering* and *The Abbott*).

First Performance: Paris, Opéra-Comique, 10 December 1825.

Roles: Gaveston (bass); Anna (soprano); George Brown (tenor); Dikson (tenor); Jenny (soprano); Marguerite (soprano); Gabriel (bass); MacIrton (bass).

Publications

articles–

Liszt, Franz. "Boieldieus 'Weisse Dame'." In *Gesammelte Schriften,* ed. Lina Ramann, vol. 3, p. 99. Leipzig, 1881.

La dame blanche, **etching after T. Johannot, 1838**

Schaeffner, A. "A propos de *La dame blanche.*" *La revue
    musicale* 7 (1926): 97.

*   *   *

Boieldieu's next-to-last completed opera, *La dame blanche*
was at the same time one of the early triumphs of the prolific
librettist and playwright Eugène Scribe. It proved to be one of
the most widely performed operas of the nineteenth century,
reaching stages as far afield as Jakarta (1836) and Surabaya
(1866). The text is freely derived from motifs in Walter Scott's
Guy Mannering, The Monestary, and *The Abbott.* Unlike
many other operas inspired by the novels of Scott during this
period, Boieldieu's actually does incorporate several traditional Scottish tunes, notably "Robin Adair," which plays an
important role in act III.

In the first act an unknown officer going by the name of
George Brown arrives in a Scottish village, where he is asked
to act as godfather to the newborn child of the farmer Dikson
and his wife Jenny. From the latter he learns of the mysterious
White Lady who haunts the nearby castle ruins and watches
over the interests of the House of Avenel (*ballade,* "D'ici
voyez ce beau domaine"). The timid Dikson has received a
summons to meet the White Lady that very night, but George
offers to go in his stead (trio-finale to act I). George is received
by Anna, an orphaned girl who was left behind by the Count
of Avenel when he was forced, as a Stuart partisan, to flee
his estate some years ago. That night Anna appears to George
in the guise of the White Lady, instructing him to outbid the
greedy retainer, Gaveston, in the auction of the estate to be
held the next day. In the extensive ensemble finale to act II,

George obeys the apparition's command, to the outrage of
Gaveston and the astonishment of all. As the new landowner,
George receives tribute from the townspeople, who sing the
traditional song of the Avenel clan ("Chantez, joyeux ménestrel"). George recognizes the song from his earliest youth,
and it is gradually revealed that he is none other than Julien,
the missing son of Count Avenel and heir to the estate. Anna's
disguise as the White Lady is also revealed when she arrives
with the hidden family fortune to pay off the auctioned estate.
She is further revealed as the childhood love of Julien, who
now takes her as his wife.

La dame blanche belongs to a brand of popular Romanticism—represented by the works of Scott, from which it is
drawn—blending elements of historicism, local color, and the
supernatural. It is typical of the librettist Scribe that the
supernatural element is "rationalized" through Anna's impersonation of the spectral lady. Similarly, the ballad recounting the tale of this apparition defuses, as it were, the
mysterious tone of the B-flat minor introduction (with harp)
and principal verse by a rather trivial refrain in B-flat major.
The eight measures of uninterrupted tonic harmony that close
this refrain are emblematic of a general weakness of harmonic
imagination afflicting many of Boieldieu's works. This same
failing is encountered in the overture, which was pieced together at the last moment (using themes mainly from the first
act) with the help of Boieldieu's pupil, Adolphe Adam.

To some extent the simplicity of the musical idiom may
account for the immense popularity of the opera in its own
day. In the act-III Scottish chorus this simplicity serves to
convey a certain naïve sincerity as well as the kind of Romantic nostalgia that fueled the popularity of traditional Scottish,
Irish and other folk tunes throughout this era. This kind of
simplicity is balanced elsewhere by more ambitious musical
structures such as the extended "storm" trio ending act I and
especially the well-crafted auction scene that constitutes the
finale to act II. This finale contains elements that could be
considered a kind of parody, *avant la lettre,* of the dramatic
finale-tableau in later Scribe operas: the elaborate slow-tempo
ensemble at the moment George first outbids Gaveston (Mod-
erato, A-flat, "O ciel! Quel est donc ce mystère") and the
latter's enraged asides during the C-major stretta which ends
the number.

Two of George's numbers—the well-known military aria,
"Ah, quel plaisir d'être soldat" within the introduction and
the act-II cavatina, "Viens, gentile dame"—remained favorite
vehicles of the French tenor repertory even after the opera
itself had disappeared from the stage. The cavatina, sung in
anticipation of the White Lady's nocturnal visitation, includes an experimental use of $\frac{5}{4}$ meter expressive of George's
agitated frame of mind (". . . still she does not come, and my
heart beats with impatience"). Boieldieu's score was intended,
and received, as a native answer to the *Rossinisme* that had
overwhelmed the Parisian musical scene especially since the
Italian maestro had taken up permanent residence in the
French capital in 1823. In fact, Boieldieu succeeds in combining Rossinian traits (the "Rossini crescendo" in the closing
groups of the overture and the aria, "Quel plaisir," and the
somewhat mechanical *fioritura* of the duet for George and
Jenny in act I, or of Anna's aria, "Je vous revois, séjour de
mon enfance") with the classic traditions of the *opéra comique.* Scribe and Boieldieu were able to transplant a greater
than usual amount of action from the dialogue to the musical
numbers, and the technique of action-ensemble finales already cultivated by Cherubini and Boieldieu in earlier works

reaches a fitting culmination of its "classic" phase in the nimbly executed auction scene closing act II.

—Thomas S. Grey

DAMROSCH, Leopold.

Conductor. Born 22 October 1832, in Posen. Died 15 February 1885, in New York. Married: the singer Helene von Heimburg, 1857. M.D. from Berlin University, 1854; studied music with Ries, Dehn, and Böhmer; solo violinist and conductor at minor theaters in various German cities; solo violinist in the Weimar Court Orchestra, 1857; conductor of the Breslau Philharmonic Concerts, 1858-60; toured with Bülow and Tausig; organized the Breslau Orchestral Society, 1862; conducted the Society for Classical Music, and made frequent appearances as a violin soloist; conductored the Arion Society in New York, April 1871; attended the opening of Bayreuth, 1876; conductor of the New York Philharmonic, 1876-77; founded the Symphonic Society, 1878; honorary D. Mus. from Columbia College, 1880; founded the German Opera Company, 1884-85; conducted a season of German Opera with Anton Seidl at the Metropolitan Opera that included the United States premieres of Wagner's *Ring, Tristan und Isolde,* and *Die Meistersinger von Nürnberg.* Damrosch's circle of friends included Liszt and Wagner.

Publications

About DAMROSCH: books–

Martin, G. *The Damrosch Dynasty: America's First Family of Music.* New York, 1983.

articles–

Rice, E. "Personal Recollections of Leopold Damrosch." *Musical Quarterly* July (1942).

*   *   *

In the preface to his study of the Damrosch family, George Martin states that the book represents ". . . a history of the first three generations of an immigrant family that contributed more than any other to the development of serious music in the United States." Leopold Damrosch was the first of that family line which influenced significantly the course and shape of American musical life.

Undoubtedly the most important contribution of Leopold Damrosch to American musical life was the importation of German opera and its introduction to the American public. Although as early as 1859 there had been a staged production of *Tannhäuser* in New York City (by the Arion Society under the direction of Carl Bergmann), Damrosch's efforts represent the original motivating force behind establishing German opera in America, most conspicuously at the Metropolitan Opera.

The initial season of Italian opera at the Metropolitan had proved a near disaster and almost spelled financial ruin for the company. Until this time Italian opera had always been fashionable and successful. In order to keep the company operating, Damrosch devised a plan for German opera, went

to Germany to engage a company of German singers and technical experts, and then conducted most of the 1884-85 opera season at the Metropolitan (including *Tannhäuser, Lohengrin,* and *Die Walküre,* among others). He put into effect a scheme essentially German by dispensing with the traditional star system, substituting a good ensemble, and by paying unusual attention to dramatic effects. For the previous twelve years he had been a "vigorous factor" in the musical life of New York, but never before had he been associated exclusively in the public mind with opera. Nevertheless, his impact on the operatic life of New York would prove enormous.

As his son Walter stated in his autobiography (*My Musical Life*): "Opera in German was rather looked down upon and Wagner's genius was as yet too imperfectly known or recognized to exercise much influence on the opera-going folks of that time." Even though German opera was not yet to succeed unequivocally in America—within a few years it faltered—Leopold had laid the foundation for its eventual success.

The 1884-85 Damrosch season established the Metropolitan briefly as one of the greatest Wagnerian houses in the world. German opera survived for seven years at the Metropolitan; by 1891 Wagner had virtually disappeared from its stage, to be replaced by the traditional French and Italian opera. Again Walter commented on this phenomenon: "It was a natural reaction from the seven years of opera in German and the pendulum swung far to the other side." However, Wagner's operas had started a revolution in operatic taste in America that eventually helped even Italian opera "to recover the lost values of drama" (Martin). Shortly after his father's death in 1885, Walter's *Damrosch Opera Company,* founded solely for the purpose of producing Wagner throughout America, introduced Chicago, Cincinnati, Boston, and other major cities to "their first concentrated doses of staged Wagner" (Martin).

Damrosch also exerted tremendous influence in raising the standards of musical taste and appreciation in America. Before arriving in America he had been a well-respected musician in Europe. In 1942, E.T. Rice wrote of him that "The first mature European musician of high distinction and versatility to acquire a permanent residence in New York and to decide to make his future career in America was Dr. Leopold Damrosch." He recommended in America his work already begun in Europe and which his sons Frank and Walter would carry on in his place.

With a generous loan from the music dealer Gustav Schirmer, Leopold attended the grand opening of Bayreuth in 1876 where he heard the first cyclic performance of the *Ring.* Charles A. Dana, the editor of the *New York Sun,* paid him $500 for a series of articles on his Bayreuth experiences. If the articles did not represent exalted music criticism, they nevertheless promoted the music and a composer not yet familiar in the United States. Unfortunately, only after his death was his plan executed to produce the entire *Ring, Tristan,* and *Meistersinger.* In later years his son Walter would give an entire series of successful lectures on Wagner and *The Ring.*

Rice also wrote that in the summer of 1882, Walter had traveled to Bayreuth to hear some of the first performances of *Parsifal.* Upon his return he presented to Leopold as a gift from Wagner the *Vorspiel* and the finale of the first act of *Parsifal* in manuscript that would enable him to play this music for the first time in America (November 1882).

Central to Leopold Damrosch's importance in the United States was the legacy of opera he handed down to his successors, especially his son Walter, who followed in his steps at the Metropolitan Opera. Although his stature has waned somewhat in the twentieth century, perhaps the reevaluation that Walter's reputation has undergone would prove appropriate also in Leopold's case. He raised the standards of the repertoire and its performance to heights never before associated with American musical life by attempting to impose a European standard. Eventually the entire Damrosch family would exert an influence on American opera and musical life still felt to the present day. While he wrote no operas himself, his son Walter proved one of the foremost advocates of opera in English and contributed four operas, including *The Scarlet Letter* and *Man Without a Country.*

Most contemporary critics tend to agree that Damrosch's most important personal attributes were his energy, his strong musical temperament, and the organizing ability that brought him immediate influence and respect in New York's musical life. Shortly after he first arrived in New York he introduced the newer German school of composition represented by Wagner, Liszt, and Schumann and had little difficulty winning over his audiences.

Music critic Henry Edward Krehbiel best summarized Damrosch's career when he stated that although Damrosch had established a brilliant European reputation before coming to the United States, "his best and most enduring work was accomplished here. . . . The establishment of German opera, though it did not endure, was yet his crowning achievement, and at the culmination of the glory which it brought him he died."

—William Thornhill

DANCO, Suzanne.

Soprano. Born 22 January 1911, in Brussels. Studied at the Brussels Conservatory, and with Fernando Carpi in Prague; won the International Bel Canto Prize in Venice, 1936; debut as Fiordiligi in Mozart's *Così fan tutte,* Genoa Opera, 1941; Italian premier of Britten's *Peter Grimes,* Milan, Teatro alla Scala, 1941; Italian premier of Stravinsky's *Oedipus Rex,* Teatro alla Scala, 1948; appeared at Glyndebourne, 1948-51; U.S. debut, 1950; Covent Garden debut as Mimi, 1951.

Publications

About DANCO: articles–

Scott, M. "In harmony (a visit with Suzanne Danco)." *Opera News* 53 (15 April 1989): 30.

*   *   *

Today we remember Suzanne Danco primarily as a recitalist. Her silvery tone, excellent diction and elegant sense of line made her an ideal miniaturist, rather like Elly Ameling in more recent times, and her performances of German Lieder and in particular of the songs of Debussy, Berlioz and Ravel were among the finest of her generation. Recordings of this literature testify to her rare artistry and support her reputation in the forefront of post-war concert singers.

It thus comes as something of a surprise to us to learn just how much opera Danco sang and how diverse and wide-ranging her roles were. Perhaps it is her very excellence as a recitalist that causes us to undervalue her as an opera performer. Also, we might suspect that Danco lacked some of the

temperament and glamour for much of the standard operatic repertoire. Although her appearance as Mimi at Covent Garden was highly praised for both singing and acting, she performed almost no other Italian opera and recorded little from this repertoire. Probably wisely, Danco chose instead to concentrate much of her attention on modern music, where her strong technique and musical preparation were especially valuable. Popular acclaim did not come easily in this repertoire, however, and Danco had little opportunity to record her modern roles for posterity. We must, therefore, rely on contemporary critical accounts of her excellence as Ellen Orford in *Peter Grimes,* Marie in *Wozzeck,* and Jocasta in *Oedipus Rex.* And paradoxically, what recorded evidence we do have of Danco as an opera singer is often in parts that were perhaps not her best.

Much of Danco's current reputation is derived from her Mozart roles, a number of which she recorded. As polished and technically expert as many of these performances are, however, they do not completely satisfy. In Joseph Krips' recording of *Don Giovanni,* Danco offers a fluently sung account of Donna Anna, culminating in one of the few perfectly vocalized accounts of the difficult aria "Non Mi Dir," but the voice is too light for this dramatic role, and Danco offers no compensatory sense of weight and scale in her characterization. Almost perversely, this Donna Anna, one of the best on records, leaves virtually no impression on the listener. We turn to her Aix-en-Provence performance of Donna Elvira in the same opera and the virtues are similar—meticulous musicianship, supple and attractive singing—but once again the character never seems fully formed. As Cherubino in *Le nozze di Figaro,* her slender soprano ought to be perfect yet she is simply too feminine, her insights too non-specific to make the young page come to life. But as Fiordiligi in a live performance of *Così fan tutte* under Karl Böhm, we at last hear Danco as the singing actress she could be. Here the beguiling femininity is utterly appropriate and she responds positively to every nuance of her turbulent character. As always, the liquid tone quality and fluid coloratura singing are a joy.

French opera finds Danco even more at home, particularly in the music of those composers whose songs she served so well. She is a fragile and charming Princess in Ravel's *L'heure espagnole,* her Marguerite in *La damnation de Faust* is a trifle small-scale but beautifully sung, and she brings the word-pointing and coloristic skills of the recitalist to her Mélisande, where she is superb. A Decca recital offers us a glimpse of her in the more central French repertoire—as Louise, Micaela, and Manon—and makes us regret what we missed, for she is predictably idiomatic and winning. And this same recital also surprises with what may be the finest performance on records of Dido's "When I Am Laid in Earth." Danco's lyric soprano, lighter than one usually encounters in this music, paints an aristocratic Dido all the more poignant for her youth, and her characteristically elegant phrasing and crystalline diction are tellingly used. At her very best, as here, Suzanne Danco earns her reputation as one of the most aristocratic and accomplished of post-war sopranos.

—David Anthony Fox

DANTON'S DEATH
   See DANTONS TOD

DANTONS TOD [Danton's Death].

Composer: Gottfried von Einem.

Librettists: Boris Blacher and Gottfried von Einem (after Büchner).

First Performance: Salzburg, 6 August 1947; revised 1955.

Roles: Georges Danton (baritone); Camille Desmoulins (tenor); Herault de Sechelles (tenor); Robespierre (tenor); St. Just (bass); Lucille (soprano); Herrmann (baritone); Simon (bass); Julie (mezzo-soprano); Simon's Wife (contralto); Young Man (tenor); Two Executioners (tenor, bass); Woman (soprano); chorus (SATB).

Publications

book–

Rütz, H. *Neue Oper: G. von Einem und seine Oper "Dantons Tod"*. Vienna, 1947.

articles–

Rütz, H. " 'Danton's Death': Music Drama or Music Theater." *Musicology* 2 (1948): 182.
Schuh, O. " 'Danton's Death' and the Problem of Modern Opera." *Musicology* 2 (1948): 177.

*   *   *

The successful premiere of Gottfried von Einem's opera *Dantons Tod* at the 1947 Salzburg Festival and its quick staging by European houses were due to more than the strong drama of Einem's score. This was a first step toward the rehabilitation of German musicians after the war: an opera by a young Austrian composer who had not collaborated in the former regime's cultural policies. *Dantons Tod* dramatizes legalized governmental terror, a plague which the world at that time realized had not been eradicated with the end of the war.

Dantons Tod was adapted from Georg Büchner's play by Einem and his teacher, composer Boris Blacher. The protagonist is Georges Danton, a leader in the French government during the Revolution. When he turned against Robespierre's tactics—including the Terror—he was guillotined in April 1794. The opera's first act establishes Danton's confrontation with Robespierre. In the first scene Danton and Camille Desmoulins express their desire for an end of the daily executions to a group of their friends playing cards. Scene ii introduces the volatile crowd. Robespierre enters and in an aria sways the crowd and promises more executions. Danton confronts him. After Danton leaves, Robespierre and his colleague Saint-Just decide that he and Camille must be killed. In the last scene of the act Danton announces to Camille and his wife Lucille that he is to be arrested, but he refuses to flee.

Act II depicts Danton's trial and death. Two scenes before the Revolutionary Tribunal are separated by one with Danton and Camille in prison. Lucille comes to see Camille; she has lost her reason. In the trial scenes the crowd swings between demanding Danton's death and falling under the spell of his eloquent oratory. At the end, in the Place de la Revolution, the condemned prisoners sing the Marseillaise in counterpoint to the crowd dancing the Carmagnole. Danton and Camille are guillotined. After the crowd disperses, Lucille enters and sits on the steps of the guillotine. She cries "Es lebe der König" (Long live the king) and is arrested as the curtain falls.

Einem and Blacher collapse the four acts of Büchner's play to two. Most of their changes in the first act consist of pruning speeches and removing minor scenes and characters. The second act contains more substantial dramatic changes, the scenes with the crowd and in the prison being moved before the tribunal scene. The most newly penned lines in the opera occur in the passage where Lucille calls to Camille in prison. In making these changes, the authors unfortunately removed much explanatory material. For example, at the end of the trial scene with Danton's soaring oratory and acclaim by the crowd, one would think that he would be released, but in the next scene we find him at the guillotine. This is one of those historical- and literary-based operas with which it is helpful to be familiar with either the historical background of the plot or else the play on which it is based.

The power of Einem's musical expression makes up for the failings in the libretto. Throughout his career his chosen idiom has been tonal, "post-romantic." The most noticeable influence is Stravinsky, heard in the repeated wind chords and in the liberally sprinkled "wrong" notes over a diatonic foundation. In this opera Einem follows the stage works of Hindemith more than those of Berg or Strauss; he does not use a leitmotif complex. *Dantons Tod* is clearly conceived in terms of the orchestra: each scene is based around a clearly defined orchestral figure, as in the scene before the court with the sixty-fourth-note runs. Orchestral interludes between scenes play an important role in the mood of the opera and in conveying the progress of the drama. The quiet interlude before the chaotic counterpoint of the Carmagnole and the Marseillaise is a masterstroke. As Strauss used the waltz as an anachronism in *Der Rosenkavalier,* here Einem favors the tango, a dance form also found in other of his compositions.

Although the orchestra is predominant, the vocal line is not reduced to an expressionist recitative. Einem lets the voice take over in lyrical and dramatic moments: Robespierre's aria, the scenes for Lucille, Danton's address to the court. In his declamatory lines one hears the influence of Hindemith, Hugo Wolf, Othmar Schoeck, and others. His later practice of setting text to one repeated note is occasionally found here. One fault may be that at many points the orchestra is more interesting than the voice, although in Robespierre's aria, for example, Einem shows he can spin out an exquisite cantilena. Einem makes the crowd into a major character in the opera, but it often seems that it is better delineated than some of the characters.

Einem revised the score slightly after the premiere, replacing an orchestral prelude with the chords that now open the opera, cutting an orchestral passage after Danton's death, and revising the final scene with Lucille. These changes make for a more dramatic beginning and ending and add to a score that deserves more frequent revivals than it has seen to date.

—David Anderson

DAPHNE.

Composer: Richard Strauss.

Librettist: J. Gregor.

First Performance: Dresden, Staatsoper, 15 October 1938.

Roles: Peneios (bass); Gaea (contralto); Daphne (soprano); Leukippos (tenor); Apollo (tenor); Four Shepherds (baritone, tenor, two basses); Two Maids (sopranos); chorus (SATB).

Publications

book–

Birkin, Kenneth W. *"Friedenstag" and "Daphne": an Interpretive Study of the Literary and Dramatic Sources of the Two Operas by Richard Strauss.* New York, 1989.

article–

Gregor, J. "Zur Entstehung von Richard Strauss' Daphne." In *Almanach zum 35. Jahr des Verlags R. Piper and Co., München,* 104. Munich, 1939.
Birkin, Kenneth W. "Zweig-Strauss-Gregor Part 2. *Daphne.*" *Richard Strauss-Blätter* new series/no. 12 (1984).

* * *

Daphne was the second opera of the Richard Strauss/Joseph Gregor collaboration. Unlike the Zweig inspired *Friedenstag,* its immediate predecessor and team running-mate, Gregor was responsible both for the initial concept and for its textual working out. Zweig had withdrawn from collaboration with Strauss in the mid-1930s, pledging himself to monitor Gregor's librettist activities, but his retreat to England and subsequent self-exile in Brazil inevitably reduced both the opportunity for active participation and the level of his commitment. Gregor's original design ran parallel to that of *Friedenstag,* envisaging a similarly oratorio-like conclusion which portrayed the transformed Daphne as mediator between gods and men. The ultimate solution, as it emerged over the months of collaboration, was more complex owing to an injection of new ideas by the composer who, a life-long admirer of Nietzsche's *The Birth Of Tragedy,* re-interpreted Gregor's symbolism in terms of Nietzschean (Apollo/Dionysos) theory. It was these additions that contributed to the excessive combined length of *Daphne* and *Friedenstag,* which have, after the Dresden joint-premiere of 1938, generally been performed separately.

Daphne, daughter of Peneios (river) and Gaea (earth), is wooed by the shepherd Leukippos, her childhood playmate. She, however, eschews earthly passion, identifying with nature and glorying in sunlight, which she worships. Shepherds gather to celebrate the feast of Dionysos where bacchanalian rites are traditionally enacted. Leukippos, disappointed at his rejection, plans to approach Daphne in female disguise during the festal dances. Meanwhile, the sun god Apollo, also enamored of Daphne, takes human form, pressing his suit disguised as a cowherd. At first intrigued, she is shocked by his passionate embrace. During the feast, Apollo observes Leukippos' successful ruse to partner Daphne in the dance. In a fit of jealousy he exposes his rival's deceit. Leukippos replies in kind, enraging the god, who deals him a mortal blow. Daphne, distraught, mourns her lost playmate. Praying for

death, she decks Leukippos' bier with flowers. Overcome with remorse, Apollo intercedes with Zeus to grant Daphne's innermost nature longings: during the course of a wondrous orchestral postlude she is transformed into a flowering laurel tree.

Strauss's revived interest in ancient Greek mythology is not without significance. Increasingly isolated by events and official attitudes in the political climate of the mid-1930s, he perhaps found safety and greater security in a symbolic means of expression. Without doubt it was disillusionment with the contemporary world that led him, through re-identification with his cultural roots, to reaffirm his allegiance to the great German/European tradition which he saw in danger of eclipse. To this end, as a result of a profound inner compulsion, he set himself a comprehensive re-reading schedule which embraced Nietzsche, Wagner and, in chronological order, the entire Goethe opus.

Under the circumstances it is hardly surprising that the final group of operas, written between 1935 and 1942, reflect, comment on, and relate to an artistic heritage which he deemed, culturally, of paramount importance and which he set out, in practice and application, to preserve for future generations. The intensely autobiographical *Die Liebe der Danae* summarized the inheritance in terms of Mozart and Wagner. *Friedenstag,* modeled on *Fidelio,* had an explicit message to the world from which Strauss had ostensibly withdrawn, since it celebrates the peace and brotherhood of mankind—a fitting corollary to Daphne's mediation between the gods and men. The *Daphne* symbolism as Strauss eventually conceived it, however, goes much further than this. Opening with an inspired woodwind pastorale and sun invocation, the opera concludes with the wordless, hushed serenity of Daphne's transformation. "Touched by both Apollo and Dionysos," she is, as Strauss himself pointed out, representative, in the Nietzschean sense, of the perfect, the eternal, art work.

Within the framework of this consistently lyrical and almost perfectly structured opera, the Apollonian conflict is played out granting the composer ample opportunity for those illustrative effects in which he reveled and which so delighted his audiences. The Daphne role itself embodies some of Strauss's finest writing for soprano, while for once, it seems—in the case of Leukippos and Apollo—he conquered his wonted antipathy to the tenor voice. As the composer pointed out, each of his stage works inhabits its own sound world, each responds directly to the individual qualities, atmosphere, and ethos of its text. *Daphne* is no exception. Its perceived balance and lucidity of form, its linear plasticity dominated by the high lyric timbre of soprano and tenor voice, combine with radiantly glowing orchestral textures to personify that popular Germanic concept of Hellenism so dear to the composer's heart. It is this idiomatic serenity and restraint that presages the refined instrumental manner of Strauss's final years.

—Kenneth W. Birkin

DA PONTE, Lorenzo (born Emanuele Conegliano).

Librettist/Poet. Born 10 March 1749, in Ceneda, near Venice. Died 17 August 1838, in New York. Converted from Judaism to Catholicism, 1753; studied at the Ceneda Seminary and the Portogruaro Seminary, later teaching there (1770-73);

ordained as a priest, and administered sacraments for the first time in 1773; professor of rhetoric at Treviso, 1774-76; in Venice, 1776, but banished for adultery, 1779; official poet to the Imperial Theater, Vienna, 1782, where he met and worked with Mozart; poet for the King's Theatre in London, 1793-98; in the United States, 1805, where he taught Italian in New Jersey, Pennsylvania, and ultimately at Columbia College in New York, 1825.

Librettos (selected)

Il ricco d'un giorno, A. Salieri, 1784.
Il burbero di buon cuore (after Goldoni, *Le bourr bienfaisant*), V. Martín y Soler, 1786.
Le nozze di Figaro (after Beaumarchais), W.A. Mozart, 1786.
Il demogorgone ovvero il filosofo confuso, V. Righini, 1786.
Una cosa rara o sia Bellezz ed onestà (after Velez de Guevara, *La luna della sierra*), V. Martín y Soler, 1786.
Gli equivoci (after Shakespeare, *Comedy of Errors*), S. Storace, 1786.
Il Bertoldo (after Brunati), Piticchio, 1787.
L'arbore di Diana, V. Martín y Soler, 1787.
Il dissoluto punito ossia Il Don Giovanni (after G. Bertati, *Il convitato di pietra*), W.A. Mozart, 1787.
Axur, rè d'Ormus (after Beaumarchais, *Tarare*), A. Salieri, 1788.
Il talismano (after Goldoni), A. Salieri, 1788.
Il pastor fido (after Guarini), A. Salieri, 1789.
La cifra (after G. Petrosellini, *Dama pastorella*), A. Salieri, 1789.
Così fan tutte ossia La scuola degli amanti, W.A. Mozart, 1790.

Lorenzo Da Ponte

Nina o sia La pazza per amore (after B. Lorenzi), G. Paisiello and J. Weigl, 1790.
La caffettiera bizzarra (after Goldoni), J. Weigl, 1790.
I contadini bizzarri (after T. Grandi, *Le gelose villane*), G. Sarti G. Paisiello, 1794.
Il capriccio drammatico (after G.M. Diodati), D. Cimarosa, 1794.
La bella pescatrice (after Maldonati), P.C. Guglielmi, 1794.
La Semiramide (after F. Moretti), F. Bianchi, 1794.
La capricciosa corretta o La scuola dei maritati (also called *Gli sposi in contrasto* and *La moglie corretta*) (after Shakespeare, *The Taming of the Shrew*), V. Martín y Soler, 1795.
L'isola del piacere or The Island of Pleasure, Martín y Soler, 1795.
La bella Arsène (after Favart), Mazzinghi and P.A. Monsigny, 1795.
Antigona, F. Bianchi, 1796.
Il tesoro, Mazzinghi, 1796.
Il consiglio imprudente (after Goldoni, *Un curioso accidente*), F. Bianchi, 1796.
Merope (after Voltaire), F. Bianchi, 1797.
Cinna (? after A. Anelli), F. Bianchi, 1798.
L'Angelina (after C.P. Defranceschi), A. Salieri, 1801.
Armida, F. Bianchi, 1802.
La grotta di Calipso, P. Winter, 1803.
Castor e Polluce o Il trionfo dell' amor fraterno or The Triumph of Fraternal Love, P. Winter, 1804.
Il ratto di Proserpina or The Rape of Proserpine, P. Winter, 1804.

Publications

By DA PONTE: books—

Epistola al Abate Casti. Vienna, 1786.
Storia compendiosa della vita di Lorenzo Da Ponte scritta da lui medesimo a cui si aggiunge la prima letteraria conversazione tenuta in sua casa, il giorno 10 di marzo dell' anno 1807, in New York, consistente in alcune composizioni italiane . . . tradotto in inglese da suoi allievi. New York, 1807.
An Extract from the Life of Lorenzo Da Ponte, with the History of Several Dramas written by Him, and among others, il Figaro, il Don Giovanni and La scola degli amanti, set to music by Mozart. New York, 1819.
Memorie di Lorenzo Da Ponte da Ceneda scritte da esso. New York, 1823-27; 2nd ed., 1829-30; English translation by Elisabeth Abbott, Philadelphia, 1929; 1967.
Storia dell compagnia dell' Opera italiana condotta da Giacomo Montresor in America. New York, 1833.

About DA PONTE: books—

Casanova, G. *Mémoires.* Leipzig, 1826-38.
Masi, E. *L'abbate L. Da Ponte.* Bologna, 1881.
Marchesan, A. *Della vita e delle opere di Lorenzo Da Ponte.* Treviso, 1900.
Istel, E. *Das Libretto: Wesen, Aufbau und Wirkung des Opernbuches nebst einer dramatischen Analyse des Librettos von Figaros Hochzeit.* Berlin and Leipzig, 1914.
Payer von Thurn, R. *Joseph II als Theaterdirektor: ungedruckte Briefe und Aktenstücke aus den Kinderjahren des Burgtheaters.* Vienna, 1920.
Russo, J.L. *Lorenzo Da Ponte, Poet and Adventurer.* New York, 1922.
Gugitz, G. *Denkwürdigkeiten des Venezianers Lorenzo Da Ponte.* Dresden, 1924.
Livingston, A. *Da Ponte in America.* Philadelphia, 1930.

Andrees, G. *Mozart und Da Ponte.* Leipzig, 1936.

Fitzlyon, April. *The Libertine Librettist: a Biography of Mozart's Librettist Lorenzo Da Ponte.* London, 1955; 1982.

Lecaldano, P. *Lorenzo Da Ponte: tre libretti per Mozart.* Milan, 1956.

Rosenberg, A. *Don Giovanni: Don Juans Gestalt und Mozarts Oper.* Munich, 1968.

Michtner, O. *Das alte Burgtheater als Opernbühne: von der Einführung des deutschen Singspiels (1778) bis zum Tod Kaiser Leopolds II. (1792).* Vienna, 1970.

Smith, P.J. *The Tenth Muse: a Historical Study of the Opera Libretto.* New York, 1970.

Kunze, S. *Don Giovanni vor Mozart: die Tradition der Don-Giovanni-Opern im italienischen Buffa-Theater des 18. Jahrhunderts.* Munich, 1972.

Gallarati, Paolo. *Musica e maschera.* Torino, 1984.

Hodges, Sheila. *Lorenzo Da Ponte: the Life and Times of Mozart's Librettist.* London, 1985.

articles–

Chrysander, F. "Die Oper Don Juan von Gazzaniga und von Mozart." *Vierteljahrsschrift für Musikwissenschaft* 4 (1888): 351.

Boas, H. "Lorenzo Da Ponte als Wiener Theaterdichter." *Sammelbände der Internationalen Musik-Gesellschaft* 15 (1913-14): 325.

Loewenberg, A. "Lorenzo Da Ponte in London: a Bibliographical Account of his Literary Activity, 1793-1804." *Music Review* 4 (1943): 171.

Nettl, P. "Frühe Mozartpflege in Amerika." *Mozart-Jahrbuch* (1954): 78.

Freitag, W. "Lorenzo da Ponte in Amerika." *Musica* 14 (1960): 560.

Pisarowitz, K.M. "Da Ponte in Augsburg." *Acta mozartiana* 9 (1962): 68.

Livermore, A. "*Così fan tutte:* a Well-Kept Secret." *Music and Letters* 46 (1965): 316.

Michtner, O. "Der Fall Abbe Da Ponte." *Mitteilungen des Österreichischen Staatsarchivs* 19 (1966): 170.

Goldin, D. "Mozart, Da Ponte e il linguaggio dell' opera buffa." In *Venezia e il melodramma nel settecento,* vol. 2, edited by M.T. Muraro. Florence, 1981.

Kunze, S. "Elementi veneziani nella librettistica di Lorenzo Da Ponte." In *Venezia e il melodramma nel settecento,* vol. 2, edited by M.T. Muraro. Florence, 1981.

Zorzi, L. " 'Teatralità' di Lorenzo Da Ponte tra 'Memorie' e libretti d'opera." In *Venezia e il melodramma nel settecento,* vol. 2, edited by M.T. Muraro. Florence, 1981.

Bernic, J. "*The Marriage of Figaro:* Genesis of a Dramatic Masterpiece." *Opera Quarterly* 1/no. 2 (1983): 79.

Hodges, Sheila. "Mozart and Da Ponte: A Historic Partnership." *Opera Quarterly* 8 (1991): 9.

*   *   *

For nearly 150 years after his death the name of Lorenzo Da Ponte languished in relative obscurity. It was only in the 1980s that he began to be recognized as one of the greatest librettists who ever lived, worthy to be put beside Boito and Hofmannsthal. Perhaps one reason why he was forgotten was that, of his eighty-nine years, fewer than twenty were devoted to writing opera texts. Yet during this period, as poet first to the court of Joseph II in Vienna and then to the King's

Theatre, the home of Italian opera in London, he wrote or adapted nearly fifty libretti for nineteen different composers, including Salieri, Martín y Soler, Cimarosa, Gluck, and above all Mozart.

Da Ponte's texts can be divided into four categories: translations, of which there are only a handful; adaptations from "straight" plays, especially those of Goldoni; adaptations from existing libretti (*Don Giovanni,* partly based on a text by Bertati, is the best-known example); and original texts, of which there were few (for example, *L'arbore di Diana,* to music by Martín y Soler, and *Così fan tutte,* set by Mozart).

In his memoirs and in other writings, Da Ponte lists the many qualities which in his view were needed to make a good librettist: among them were feeling and heart, liveliness of affection, truth of characterization, grace of language, poetic imagery, and an understanding of how to alternate "the gentle and the fierce," "the light-hearted and the pathetic," "the pastoral and the heroic." He was a born versifier, turning out rhymes as easily as he could breathe, and he had a vast knowledge of classical and contemporary literature to which he could turn for inspiration. He also had an ear attuned to verbal and musical harmony.

One of Da Ponte's favorite composers was Martín y Soler, for whom he wrote the text of *Una cosa rara,* which was among the most popular and successful operas of the last quarter of the eighteenth century. This was an *opera buffa,* like most of the works put on at the Burgtheater during the reign of Joseph II. Another excellent collaboration with Martín y Soler was *L'arbore di Diana,* though some critics lambasted it as being indecent. One of the few serious operas he wrote was *Axur, re d'Ormus,* based on a play by Beaumarchais, and set to music by Antonio Salieri, director of music at the court. The text is at its best when the action involves intrigue, disguise and misunderstanding; nevertheless, Da Ponte's adaptation is typically skillful and dexterous. Whether writing *seria* or *buffa* texts, one of his greatest skills was his versatility and his ability to adjust to the needs of his composer.

It was in his partnership with Mozart that Da Ponte produced his best libretti. It is tantalizing that almost nothing is known of how the two men worked together. Since it is clear from Mozart's letters to his father how exacting the composer was in what he required from his collaborators, and that he liked to have a large hand in the libretti he set, it is revealing that the texts of *Le nozze di Figaro, Don Giovanni* and *Così fan tutte* all, in important respects, contradict his views. He believed, for instance, that Italian opera should be as comic as possible, whereas Da Ponte was convinced that changes of mood were essential if the listener's sympathies were to be engaged. Such changes occur in all three operas, and it is partly this which has made them immortal, giving us the feeling that we are watching human beings with real emotions rather than stock characters. Mozart felt, too, that the comic element in *opera buffa* should be violent and often absurd, as it is in *Die Zauberflöte,* whereas Da Ponte never forgot the literary and cultured tradition which was so fundamental a part of his being.

Mozart detested rhymes for their own sake. "Verses are indeed the most indispensable element for music," he wrote to his father, "but rhymes, solely for the sake of rhyming, the most detrimental." Yet rhymes abound in all three operas, and to accompany them Mozart composed some of the most ravishing music that has ever been written. In *Così fan tutte* in particular, the complex rhyming pattern is so skillful that the words almost sing themselves.

All three Da Ponte librettos for Mozart show an intimate knowledge of literary and theatrical Italian tradition which

Mozart can hardly have possessed. From the time he was fourteen, Da Ponte had read voraciously, including the Italian classics, Latin and French masterpieces, modern dramatists such as Goldoni, prose, poetry, and history. To help him in his search for source material he had also read hundreds of opera libretti, and he knew some of the greatest writers of the day, including Gasparo Gozzi, famous as one of the ablest critics in Italy, as well as one of the purest and most elegant stylists. Thus all the evidence seems to show that Mozart was influenced by him to an extent which the composer would never have tolerated from any of his other librettists.

That the two men were friends outside their professional collaboration is improbable, so unlike were their personalities; but as working partners they had an extraordinary empathy. For indifferent composers Da Ponte sometimes wrote indifferent texts; but for "the divine Mozart," as he called the composer in later years, he wrote libretti which are miracles of skill, poetry and knowledge of the human heart.

—Sheila Hodges

DARDANUS.

Composer: Jean-Philippe Rameau.

Librettist: C.-A. Le Clerc de la Bruyère.

First Performance: Paris, Opéra, 19 November 1739; revised 23 April 1744.

Roles: Venus (soprano); L'Amour (soprano); Iphise (soprano); Dardanus (tenor); Antenor (bass); Teucer (bass); Ismenor (bass); chorus.

Publications

book–

Beaussant, Philippe. *"Dardanus" de Rameau.* Paris, 1980.

articles–

Dacier, E. "L'opéra au XVIIIe siecle: les premières représentations de Dardanus." *La revue musicale* 3 (1903): 163.
Masson, P.-M. "Les deux versions du 'Dardanus' de Rameau." *Anuario musical* 26 (1954): 36.

*   *   *

Rameau's fifth opera, *Dardanus,* a *"tragédie mise en musique,"*—that is, a "tragedy set to music"—concerns the love, and the many obstacles that love must surmount, between Dardanus (son of the god Jupiter and of Electra, mythical founder of Troy) and Iphise, daughter of Teucer, king of Phrygia. At the opera's start, however, the two lovers do not know each other; Teucer is at war with Dardanus, and Iphise has been promised to Antenor, a neighboring king who joins forces with Teucer against Dardanus. With the help of the magician Ismenor, Dardanus meets Iphise, whereupon he is promptly captured and sentenced to death, a fate he is spared thanks to the intervention of the goddess Venus, guardian of lovers. Other mythological deities also lend him a helping

hand. So too does a monster sent to ravage Teucer's domain. Inexplicably unappreciative, Dardanus slays the creature, thus saving his rival Antenor from certain death. After yet another intercession by Venus, Antenor withdraws, Teucer acquiesces, and Dardanus and Iphise are wed.

After twenty-six performances the opera was withdrawn. Judging from the tenor of contemporaneous reviews, the main shortcoming was the story cooked up by librettist Le Clerc de la Bruyère and its uninspired reliance on stock figures and situations. Placed in context, the objections seem for the most part to have been leveled by a small but vociferous claque of conservative devotees of Lully (dead since 1687) bent on seeing the opera fail. They derided the music as being so densely written that for three whole hours no one in the orchestra had time even to sneeze. Dardanus' act IV sleep scene they mercilessly lampooned in numerous caricatures that circulated throughout Paris and which invariably depicted the composer being lulled to sleep by his own music, and this despite the fact that Lully's 1676 *Atys* and 1686 *Armide* both feature famous examples of sleep scenes. A letter written by a certain Monsieur Dubuisson on 30 November, twelve days into the opera's production, reveals that measures had already been taken to forestall additional criticism: "The music, it strikes me, is admirable, but so far it has not captivated everyone, and perhaps never will owing to the wretchedness of the text. The libretto in fact has already been significantly trimmed, but the cuts have only removed some of the more superfluous word-spinning without creating any real interest." Such cosmetic repairs evidently were not enough to save the opera, for when Rameau revived it in 1744 he decided to compose the last three acts anew. Although la Bruyère was retained as librettist, he was aided this time around by the Abbé Simon-Joseph Pellegrin, librettist of Rameau's first opera, the 1733 *Hippolyte et Aricie.* Dramatically, the major change involved eliminating Dardanus' sleep scene along with the initial appearance of Venus. Thus in the 1744 version Dardanus, when captured by Teucer's forces, is visited by Iphise, who is about to set him free when a successful attack by his own forces brings about his liberation. During the battle Teucer is taken prisoner and Antenor is mortally wounded. The old king refuses at first to grant his daughter to his captor but at length gives his permission. The opera ends with the *deus ex machina* of Venus descending from on high to officiate at the wedding. Revisions notwithstanding, the Lullists only renewed their assault and the opera failed to win any more favorable a reception than the first version. This state of affairs remained unchanged until the opera was revived once more in 1760, at which time Rameau was acknowledged as France's leading composer.

Rickety libretto or not, the score offers a wealth of enchanting music. Indeed, Cuthbert Girdlestone, the composer's indefatigable twentieth-century champion, has emphatically declared that "*Dardanus* contains more first-rate music, and of greater variety, than any other work of Rameau's except perhaps *Les Fêtes d'Hébé*" (the composer's previous opera, an *opéra-ballet* first given in May of 1739). Encountering the rare production or concert performance, one readily is inclined to agree. And it is easy to be torn between the music of the 1739 and 1744 versions. "Lieux funestes" ("O dreadful place"), the soliloquy with which Dardanus, chained in his enemy's dungeon, opens the new fourth act, ranks among the great moments of all French opera. With its anguished, slowly-moving F-minor harmonies and dark-hued accompaniment set off by an extraordinary bit of writing for solo bassoon, Rameau gives vent to Dardanus' despair with almost physical intensity. On the other hand, the original music for act IV, Dardanus' sleep sequence, the same number

The prison scene in Rameau's *Dardanus,* engraving by Daumont, Paris, 1760

that so amused Rameau's contemporaries (and which he omitted in the 1744 revival), is by no means as preposterous as his detractors sought to depict it. As luck would have it, a great deal of it is included in the 1981 Paris Opéra performance presided over by conductor Raymond Leppard and recorded for Erato, a performance bound to raise the hackles of those of us today who demand "authenticity"—in this case to either the 1739 or 1744 version, but not both at once. Such questionable authenticity to the contrary, that performance nonetheless gives credence to what Girdlestone endorsed way back in 1957. A staunch admirer of a great deal of the music Rameau composed for the earlier version, Girdlestone reflected: "It is deplorable that so much life and beauty should lie unknown, and one wonders whether a modern version, based on that of 1744 but incorporating some of the best parts from the earlier score . . . could not be put together. A prolonged acquaintance with his three greatest *tragédies* [according to Girdlestone *Hippolyte et Aricie,* the 1737 *Castor et Pollux,* as well as *Dardanus*] convinces me that much in them is still alive, awaiting merely the magic wand of an . . . Ismenor."

—James Parsons

DARGOMÏZHSKY, Alexander (Sergeyevich).

Composer. Born 14 February 1813, in Tula province. Died 17 January 1869, in St Petersburg. Lived in St Petersburg from 1817, where he studied piano with Schoberlechner and Danilevsky, and violin with Vorontsov; he became an excellent pianist by the age of 20; government position, 1827-43; studied music from 1843-51; visited Germany, Brussels, and Paris in 1845; produced his first opera, *Esmeralda,* in Moscow, 1847; published many songs and piano pieces, 1845-55; president of the Russian Music Society, 1867. Became an early advocate of realism and nationalism in Russian music.

Operas

Esmeralda, Dargomïzhsky (after Victor Hugo, *Notre-Dame de Paris*), 1838-41, Moscow, Bol'shoy, 17 December 1847.
The Triumph of Bacchus (*Torzhestvo Vakha*) (opera-ballet), after Pushkin, 1848, Moscow, Bol'shoy, 23 January 1867.
Rusalka, Dargomïzhsky (after Pushkin), 1848-55, St Petersburg, 16 May 1856.
The Stone Guest (*Kamenniy gost*), Pushkin (set directly to his poem), 1860s [unfinished: completed by C. Cui and scored by Rimsky-Korsakov], St Petersburg, Mariinsky, 28 February 1872.
Mazepa [fragments only].
Rogdana [sketches only].

Other works: orchestral works, vocal pieces, piano pieces.

Publications

By DARGOMÏZHSKY: books–

Findeyzen, N., ed. *Aleksandr Sergeyvich Dargomïzhsky (1813-1869): avtobiografiya; pis'ma; vospominaniya sovremennikov* [autobiography, letters, contemporary recollections]. Petrograd, 1921.

Pekelis, M.S., ed. *A.S. Dargomïzjsky: izbrannïye pis'ma* [selected letters]. Moscow, 1952.

articles–

Pekelis, M.S., ed. "Pis'ma Dargomïzhskovo Stanislavu Monyushko" [Dargomizhsky's letters to Stanislav Moniuszko]. *Sovetskaya muzyka* no. 2 (1963): 50.

About DARGOMÏZHSKY: books–

Newmarch, Rosa. *The Russian Opera.* London, 1914.
Riesemann, Oscar Von. *Monographien zur russischen Musik.* Vol 1. Leipzig, 1923.
Martinov, I. *A.S. Dargomizhsky.* Moscow and Leningrad, 1944.
Levik, B. *'Kammeniy gost' Dargomïzhskovo—'Mozart i Salieri' N. Rimskovo-Korsakovo—'Skupoy rïstar' S. Rakhmaninova* [Dargomïzhsky's *Stone Guest*—Rimsky Korsakov's *Mozart and Salieri*—Rachmaninov's *The Miserly Knight*]. Moscow and Leningrad, 1949.
Yakovlev, V. *Pushkin i muzïka* [Pushkin in music; p. 64 ff]. Moscow and Leningrad, 1949.
Pekelis, M.S. *Dargomïzhsky i narodnaya pesnya* [Dargomïzhsky and folksong]. Moscow, 1951.
Serov, A.N. *Ruskala: Opera Dargomyzhskogo.* Moscow, 1953.
Ogolevets. A.S. ed. *Materialï dokumentï po istorii russkoy relisticheskoy muzïkal'noy estetiki* [materials and documents on the history of Russian realist musical aesthetics], i. Moscow, 1954.
Livanova, T. *Stassov i russkaya klassicheskaya opera* [Stassov and Russian classical opera]. Moscow, 1957.
Taruskin, Richard. *Opera and Drama in Russia as Preached and Practiced in the 1860s.* Ann Arbor, 1981.
Pekelis, M.S. *A.S. Dargomyzskij i ego okruzenije III* [Dargomïzhsky and his environment]. Moscow, 1983.

articles–

Pekelis, M.S. "O realizme Dargomïzhskovo." [Dargomïzhsky's realism]. *Sovetskaya muzyka* no. 4 (1934): 47.
Abraham, Gerald. "*The Stone Guest.*" In *Studies in Russian Music,* 68. London, 1936.
Calvocoressi, M.D. and Gerald Abraham. "Dargomizhsky." In *Masters of Russian Music.* 65. London, 1936.
Abraham, Gerald. "Glinka, Dargomizhsky and 'The Russalka.'" In *On Russian Music,* 43. London, 1939.
Serov, A.N. *Izbrannïye stat'i, i* [selected articles, some of which are on *Rusalka*]. Moscow, 1950.
S.K. "Esmeralda A.S. Dargomïzhskovo efir" [*Esmeralda*]. *Sovetskaya muzyka* no. 5 (1950): 76.
Cui, C.A. *Izbrannïye stat'i, i* [selected articles, some of which are on *Rusalka* and *The Stone Guest*]. Leningrad, 1952.
Pekelis, M.S. "Russkiye klassiki o realizme" [Russian classics on realism]. *Sovetskaya muzyka* no. 2 (1953): 22.
Smith Brindle, Reginald. "The Sagra Musicale Umbra at Perugia." *Musical Times* 96 (1955): 661. [*The Stone Guest*]
Ivanova, K. "*Esmeralda.*" *Sovetskaya muzyka* no. 12 (1958): 64.
Livanova, T. "Dargomïzhsky i Glinka." In *Pamyati Glinki* [memories of Glinka], edited by V.A. Kiselyov. Moscow, 1958.
Pekelis, M.S. "Stsenicheskaya istoriya Esmeraldï" [stage history of *Esmeralda*]. *Musykal'naya zhizn* no. 15 (1958): 20.

Rabinovich, D. "K. vozobnovlenniyu *Kammenovo gostya* [the revival of *The Stone Guest*]. *Sovetskaya muzyka* no. 1 (1960): 62.

Velimirovic, M. "Russian Autographs at Harvard." *Notes* 18 (1960-61): 539.

Blagovidova, N. "Kammenïy gost" [*The Stone Guest*]. *Sovetskaya muzyka* no. 7 (1963): 87.

Allorto, R. "Aleksandr Sergievic Dargomiski e la conquista del recitativo melodico." *Chigiana* 26-27 (1969-70): 105.

Bremini, I. "Trieste." *Opera* 20 (1969): 535. [*The Stone Guest*].

Taruskin, Richard. "Realism as Preached and Practiced: the Russian Opera Dialogue." *Musical Quarterly* 56 (1970): 431.

Baker, Jennifer. "Dargomizhsky, Realism, and *The Stone Guest.*" *Music Review* 37 (1976): 193.

Monfort, Franz. "Quelques mots au sujet du personnage de Don Juan et de l'opéra *L'hôte de pierre* de Dargomijsky." *Bulletin de la Société liégeoise de musicologie* 27 (1979): 11.

Cuker, Anatolij. "*Kamennyi gost*' kak muzykal'naja koncepcija" [*The Stone Guest* as a musical work]. *Sovetskaya muzyka* 5 (1980): 108.

Pekelis, M.S. "Dramaturgiceskie iskanija pozdnego" [dramaturgic experiments of the late period]. *Sovetskaya muzyka* 5 (1980): 100.

Mikseeva, Galina. "O dramaturgiceskoj roli garmonii v *Kamennom goste* Dargomyzskogo" [dramaturgical function of harmony in *The Stone Guest*]. In *Problemy stilevogo obnovlenija v russkoj klassiceskoj i sovetskoj muzyke. Sbornik naucnyh trudov Moskovskoi konservatorii,* edited by Irina Stepanova and Irina Brezneva. Moscow, 1983.

*　　*　　*

The son of a wealthy landowner and a noblewoman with a modest reputation as a poetess, Dargomïzhsky studied piano, violin, and singing as a youth. His compositional development, however, was rather limited until he met Mikhail Ivanovich Glinka in 1833. From this master, he borrowed the harmony and counterpoint notebooks which Glinka compiled during his studies in Berlin with Siegfried Wilhelm Dehn. With Glinka, Dargomïzhsky also studied the early overtures of Felix Mendelssohn and the symphonies of Ludwig van Beethoven.

During the period 1827 to 1843, Dargomïzhsky toiled as a civil servant in the treasury department in St Petersburg, achieving the rank of honorary counselor. Immediately following his resignation, he went to France for a six-month stay, and in Paris he became acquainted with Auber, Halévy, and Meyerbeer; he had also met Fétis in Brussels. His first opera, *Esmeralda,* (1841) was influenced by the French grand opera style, and Dargomïzhsky became enchanted with the *vaudeville* as well. Upon his return to his native land, however, he developed a keen interest in Russian folk music.

During the 1850s, Dargomïzhsky was strongly influenced by a combination of folk tradition and the realist philosophy of the literary critic Nikolay Gavrilovich Chernyshevsky. The opera *Rusalka,* completed in 1855, exemplifies this artistic leaning. The folk song imprint is seen in melodic contours and in the accentuation of both words and music, while the Russian realist canon is manifested in the "natural" declamatory approach to text setting. In a letter of 1857, Dargomïzhsky declared that truthful expression was the paramount consideration for him as a creative artist. Following Glinka's death in the same year, Dargomïzhsky assumed a leadership role among the various factions that permeated the musical scene in St Petersburg. Although he maintained a good relationship with Anton Rubinstein and the Conservatory crowd, he also acted as a mentor for members of the "Mighty Five," notably Mussorgsky.

After a trip to Warsaw, Leipzig, Paris, London, and Brussels during 1864-1865, during which he met Liszt, the now recognized composer set to work on his masterwork, *The Stone Guest,* based on the Don Juan legend as set by Pushkin. With the exception of Laura's songs in act I, scene 2, which are prescribed in Pushkin's play, Dargomïzhsky abandons operatic convention and presents instead a style dominated by continuous arioso, limited variety in note-values and rhythms, and occasional melodic distortions of normal speech patterns for purposes of expressivity or heightened dramatic effect. Irregular harmonies and dissonance are employed particularly in the expression of terror or fright, as in the scene at the end in which the statue, the stone guest of the title, appears. Although this opera is the most frequently mentioned stage work of its creator, it was left unfinished at his death and completed by Cui and Rimsky-Korsakov. It should be mentioned that Cui's music is limited to the final sixty-three measures of the first act and the prelude. The orchestration, as might be expected, was the work of Rimsky-Korsakov.

Of Dargomïzhsky's other works, the songs are important, particularly those with declamatory settings, but the language has been a barrier to their acceptance in the West. The orchestral and piano pieces are generally light and derivative, but mention should be made of the two piano scherzi and the "Snuffbox Waltz," compositions which do display a degree of originality.

Dargomïzhsky is generally thought of as a precursor of Mussorgsky because of the latter's adoption of the realistic treatment of speech patterns. A review of his music, the operas in particular, reveals him to be a significant figure in his own right.

—David Z. Kushner

THE DAUGHTER OF THE REGIMENT
See LA FILLE DU RÉGIMENT

DAVIES, (Sir) Peter Maxwell.

Composer. Born 8 September 1934, in Manchester. Attended Leigh Grammar School, then the Royal Manchester College of Music and Manchester University; in Rome on a scholarship from the Italian government, where he studied with Goffredo Petrassi, 1957; Olivetti Prize for his orchestral work *Prolation,* 1958; director of music at Cirencester Grammar School, 1959-62; in the United States on a Harkness fellowship, where he studied with Sessions, 1962; joined the UNESCO Conference on Music in Education, and toured the world lecturing, 1965; composer-in-residence at the University of Adelaide, Australia, 1966-67; organized the Pierrot Players (renamed The Fires of London, 1970) with Harrison Birtwistle, 1967; professor of composition, Royal Northern College of Music, 1975-80; organized the annual St Magnus

Festival on the Orkney Islands, 1977; honorary doctorate of music from Edinburgh University, 1979; successor to Sir William Glock as director of music at Dartington Summer School, 1979; named Composer of the Year by the Composers' Guild of Great Britain, 1979; commissioned to write a symphony for the Boston Symphony Orchestra for its centennial, 1981; associate conductor, Scottish Chamber Orchestra, 1985-. Davies was knighted in 1987.

Operas/Masques

Publisher: Boosey and Hawkes.

Cinderella.
Blind Man's Buff (masque), Davies (after G. Büchner, *Leonce und Lena*), 1972, London, Round House, 29 May 1972; alternate version, 1972, London, The Place, 24 November, 1972.
Taverner, Davies, (libretto written 1956-64; set 1964-70), London, Covent Garden, 12 July 1972.
Notre Dame des fleurs (mini-opera), Davies, 1966, London, Queen Elizabeth Hall, 17 March 1973.
The Martyrdom of Saint Magnus, Davies (after G. MacKay Brown), 1976, Kirkwall, Orkney, St Magnus Cathedral, 18 June 1977.
The Two Fiddlers (children's opera), Davies (after MacKay Brown), 1978, Kirkwall, Orkney, 16 June 1978.
Le jongleur de Notre Dame (masque), Davies, 1978, Kirkwall, Orkney, 18 June 1978.
The Lighthouse, Davies (after a story by Craig Mair), 1979, Edinburgh, 2 September 1980.
Resurrection, Davies, Darmstadt, 25 September 1988.

Publications/Writings

By DAVIES: articles–

"The Young British Composer." *Score* no. 15 (1956): 84.
"Problems of a British Composer Today." *The Listener* 62 (1959): 563.
"Composing Music for School Use." *Making Music* no. 46 (1961): 7.
"Music Composition for Children." In *Music in Education,* edited by W. Grant, 108. London, 1963.
"The Young Composer in America." *Tempo* no. 72 (1965): 2.
"Where our Colleges Fail." [London] *Times Educational Supplement* no. 2699 (1967): 463.
"Sets or Series." *The Listener* 79 (1968): 250.
"Peter Maxwell Davies on Some of his Recent Work." *The Listener* 81 (1969): 121.
"*Taverner:* Synopsis and Documentation." *Tempo* no. 101 (1972): 4.
"Pax Orcadiensis." *Tempo* no. 119 (1976): 20.
"Symphony." *Tempo* no. 124 (1978): 2.

unpublished–

"An Introduction to Indian Music." Dissertation, University of Manchester, 1956.

About DAVIES: books–

Pruslin, Stephen, compiler. *Peter Maxwell Davies: Studies from Two Decades. Tempo* booklet 2. London, 1979.
Pirie, Peter John. *The English Musical Renaissance.* London: 1979.

Griffiths, Paul. *Peter Maxwell Davies. The Contemporary Composers.* London, 1982.
Jeutner, Renate. *Peter Maxwell Davies: Ein Komponistenporträt. Musik der Zeit: Dokumentationen und Studien,* vol. 3. Bonn, 1983.

articles–

Waterhouse, J. C. G. "Peter Maxwell Davies: Towards and Opera." *Tempo* no. 69 (1964): 18.
Arnold, S. "The Music of *Taverner.*" *Tempo* no. 101 (1972): 20.
Josipovici, G. "*Taverner:* Thoughts on the Libretto." *Tempo* no. 101 (1972): 12.
Pruslin, S. "An Anatomy of Betrayal." *Music and Musicians* 20, no. 11 (1972): 28.
Sutcliffe, T. "A Question of Identity: *Blind Man's Buff* and *Taverner.*" *Music and Musicians* 20, no. 10 (1972): 26.
Walsh, S. "Taverner." *Musical Times* 113 (1972): 653.
Roberts, D. "Maxwell Davies in Orkney: *The Martyrdom of St Magnus.*" *Musical Times* 118 (1977): 633.

* * *

As a composer, Peter Maxwell Davies has been both remarkably prolific and remarkably versatile, composing works in a wide variety of forms and even a wide range of styles. Six of his works (as of this writing) are operas, each of them a unique and original work, though some common threads do exist among them. But any account of his operas must also make some mention of his ten or so other dramatic works, including music-theatre pieces (the most famous of which is *Eight Songs for a Mad King*), the 1984 *No. 11 Bus,* and the 'mono-drama' *The Medium:* all these incorporate operatic elements.

Davies's operas may be grouped into three classes: first, the two large-scale works *Taverner* and *Resurrection;* next, the chamber operas *The Lighthouse* and *The Martyrdom of Saint Magnus;* and finally, the two operas *Cinderella* and *The Two Fiddlers* written to be played and sung entirely by children.

Certainly the most celebrated of these works is *Taverner,* the story of John Taverner (1490-1545), a man in crisis with both his art and his religion. Davies began work on this composition, one of the most important of his early years, in 1956; it was first performed in 1972. In *Taverner,* the composer makes use of music by Taverner (principally his *In Nomine*), weaving it in and out and permuting it throughout the opera. Renaissance and medieval compositional forms appear in the work alongside highly contemporary music. *Resurrection,* Davies's most recent opera, was commissioned by the city of Darmstadt and premiered there 25 September 1988. As in the case of *Taverner,* the composer wrote his own libretto. *Resurrection* is centered around a character, the "Hero," portrayed by a dummy. The Hero is tormented by the endless pressures and shallow values of contemporary society, represented by various characters and events (for instance, twenty-four television commercials and eight popular songs are included). Eventually, he is "resurrected" into an acceptable conformist, a truly "modern" man. The work calls for eight solo singers, an electronically amplified vocal quartet, dancers, a rock group, a Salvation Army band, and a main ensemble of 17 players.

Davies's two chamber operas are also very different in character from one another. *The Martyrdom of Saint Magnus* launched the first Saint Magnus Festival when it was premiered in the Cathedral of Saint Magnus in Orkney, 18 June 1977. Again, Davies provided his own libretto (basing it on the novel *Magnus* by George MacKay Brown, an author whose writings have served as the basis for a number of Davies's works). The musical material is open, bare, and stark: again, as in *Taverner,* a somewhat medieval treatment. Davies's other chamber opera, *The Lighthouse,* strikes quite a different note: it is the composer's interpretation of an event in a story by Craig Mair which tells the story of three lighthouse keepers who vanished from the Flannon lighthouse in December 1890. Davies overlays the events with religious imagery and ghosts; the lighting directions included in the score, as well as the spare scoring, serve to convey an aura of mystery and horror.

The two operas for children reflect Davies's interest in and concern with producing quality music for children to perform, as well as his commitment to music education. *The Two Fiddlers,* based on another novel by George MacKay Brown, is a moral tale, cautioning against the dangers of complacency, laziness, and succumbing to popular culture and fads. Its delightful score includes folk and folk-like themes, such as a square dance accompanied only by a solo violin; there is also a good deal of modal writing. *Cinderella,* composed for the Kirkwall Grammar School, is a retelling of Perault's classic fairy tale. The music, including a small ensemble consisting of three recorders, various percussion instruments and a string quintet, is primarily tonal and quite accessible to young performers. Rather than try to deal with expensive sets and props, the composer has thoughtfully included in the score directions calling for the use of cardboard cut-outs for such props as the carriage. In these two operas for young people, the same attention to detail found in all Davies's music is much in evidence: nothing is left to chance.

—Carolyn J. Smith

DAVIS, (Sir) Colin (Rex).

Conductor. Born 25 September 1927, in Weybridge, Surrey. Studied the clarinet at the Royal College of Music, London; conductor of the Household Cavalry band while serving in the military; conductor with the semi-pro Chelsea Opera Group; music director at Sadler's Wells, 1959-65; guest conductor with the Minneapolis Symphony Orchestra, 1960, and other American orchestras; conducted at the Royal Opera at Covent Garden, 1965; Commander of the Order of the British Empire, 1965; conducted *Peter Grimes* at the Metropolitan Opera, 20 January 1967; chief conductor of the British Broadcasting Corporation Symphony Orchestra, London, 1967-70; music director of the Royal Opera at Covent Garden (succeeded Solti), 1970-85; principal guest conductor of the Boston Symphony Orchestra, 1972-83; conducted at the Bayreuth Festival, 1977; toured with the Royal Opera in South Korea and Japan, 1979, and the United States, 1984; knighted, 1980; music director of the Bavarian Radio Symphony Orchestra in Munich, 1983.

Publications

About DAVIS: books–

Blyth, A. *Colin Davis.* London, 1972.

articles–

Wheen, N. "Colin Davis." *Ovation* April (1986).

*   *   *

Colin Rex Davis was the youngest of three brothers in a family of seven. Both his parents were musical, although neither was a professional musician. His father had a large collection of 78s by composers such as Elgar, Delius, Debussy, Sibelius and Wagner, and his earliest musical education really consisted in listening to these.

After attending primary school, Davis won a place at Christ's Hospital, a school with a very strong musical tradition, where he took up the clarinet. He won a scholarship to the Royal College of Music, where he studied with Frederick Thurston. Military service as a bandsman in the band of the Household Cavalry followed, and on his release from the army, he set about organizing a small chamber orchestra, the Kalmar, out of which developed the Chelsea Opera Group, which gave concert performances of Mozart operas in London, Oxford and Cambridge. These immediately attracted attention, but Davis still had to earn his living as an orchestral musician, playing in orchestras in London and at Glyndebourne under Fritz Busch.

Further conducting experience with the Ballet Russe and with the Ipswich Orchestral Society followed before Davis became assistant conductor of the British Broadcasting Corporation Scottish Orchestra in 1957. He also broadened his experience in opera by conducting works like *Der Freischütz, Falstaff, Fidelio* and Nicolai's *The Merry Wives of Windsor.*

On 18 October 1959 came Davis's great opportunity, when he stood in at very short notice for Otto Klemperer at a concert performance of *Don Giovanni* at the Royal Festival Hall. The success of the performance established him with the London public, and appointments followed at the Sadler's Wells Opera (1959-65), Glyndebourne (1960), the British Broadcasting Corporation Symphony (1967-70) and the Royal Opera, Covent Garden (1970-85). During his time there he introduced Tippett's operas *The Knot Garden* (1970) and *The Ice Break* (1972) as well as Hans-Werner Henze's *Tristan* (1974). He is now a free-lance conductor working much with the Bavarian Radio Orchestra, of which he became music director in 1983.

Davis's interpretations impress above all by their fire, rhythmic drive and clarity of line and texture. An outstanding Mozart conductor, he is also one of the greatest interpreters of Berlioz, a sympathetic conductor of Stravinsky and a specialist in the music of Michael Tippett, whose operas he conducts with a fine insight into both the musical and the psycho-dramatic argument. His Wagner performances—he was the first British conductor ever to appear at Bayreuth, in 1977, with *Tannhäuser*—impress by their unhysterical intensity, their onward drive and their eschewal of all self-indulgence as well as a close attention, evident in all his work, to the detail of the score. His liberal humanitarian sympathies also make him an ideal interpreter of works like Beethoven's *Fidelio*.

—James Day

THE DEAD CITY
See DIE TOTE STADT

DEATH IN VENICE.

Composer: Benjamin Britten.

Librettist: M. Piper (after Thomas Mann).

First Performance: Snape Maltings, 16 June 1973.

Roles: Gustav von Aschenbach (tenor); Traveller (baritone); Elderly Fop (baritone); Old Gondolier (baritone); Hotel Manager (baritone); Hotel Barber (baritone); Leader of the Players (baritone); Dionysus (baritone); Voice of Apollo (counter tenor); Polish Mother (dancer); Tadzio (dancer); Two Daughters (dancers); Governess (dancer); Jaschiu (dancer); Hotel Porter (tenor); Lido Boatman (baritone); Hotel Waiter (baritone); Strawberry-seller (soprano); Guide (baritone); Glass-maker (tenor); Lace-seller (soprano); Beggar-woman (mezzo-soprano); Newspaper-seller (soprano); Strolling Players (soprano, tenor); English Clerk (baritone); Two Acrobats (dancers); Russian Mother and Father (soprano, bass); Russian Nanny (soprano); German Mother (mezzo-soprano); Gondoliers (tenor, baritone).

Publications

articles–

Evans, Peter. "Britten's *Death in Venice*." *Opera* 24 (1973): 490.
Hindley, Clifford. "Contemplation and Reality: A Study in Britten's 'Death in Venice'." *Music and Letters* November (1990).

unpublished–

Milliman, Joan Ann. "Benjamin Britten's Symbolic Treatment of Sleep, Dream, and Death as Manifest in his Opera *Death in Venice*." Ph.D. dissertation, University of Southern California, 1977.

*   *   *

Benjamin Britten and his librettist Myfanwy Piper follow, in *Death in Venice,* the plot and theme of Thomas Mann's novella closely. The plot begins in Munich, where Gustav von Aschenbach (Mann gave him the first name and physical description of Mahler) is walking, taking a break from his work. He is known as an accomplished writer of prose fiction which emphasizes formal perfection of language and thus requires great concentration and self-discipline from the author. Seeing a strange figure in a graveyard, Aschenbach is overcome suddenly by an uncharacteristic desire to travel to the South. He soon arrives in Venice, where he begins to observe a Polish family on vacation—a mother, daughters, and an extremely beautiful boy. The boy, Tadzio, becomes a symbol for the writer of absolute beauty, and calls to his mind the Greek ideal of beauty discussed in Plato's *Phaedrus.* In spite of his pleasure in the boy's beauty, however, his vacation does not seem to be working out; Venice is too hot and seems somehow sinister. Aschenbach decides to leave. But at the last minute he finds he cannot leave the boy and aborts his departure. Remaining in Venice, then, Aschenbach becomes more and more interested in the boy as the days pass, and finally realizes that he has rather ridiculously fallen in love with him. Belatedly he also comes to understand, after various inquiries, that a cholera epidemic has struck the city. The visitors at the hotel have begun to leave, in spite of the efforts of the city officials to keep knowledge of the sickness hidden. Aschenbach stays on because of his infatuation with Tadzio, however; at last the boy's family decides to leave but it is too late for Aschenbach. He dies, presumably of the cholera, lying in his beach chair watching the boy walking on the beach.

Mann's story is usually interpreted as an exploration of the radical effects of separating reason and feeling. Britten adopts this interpretation, adding the offstage voices of Apollo and Dionysus to articulate the ideas of the story. As his opening aria makes clear, Aschenbach has always been an Apollonian artist, interested in form, reason, and restraint. But as the opera progresses, his love for Tadzio begins to allow him to see that passion is closely related to beauty, and finally, in a dream sequence, he understands that the irony of his life has been that the worship of beauty and perfection of form, removed from feeling, is not possible. He grasps at last that his life-long devotion to formalism is in its own way a type of sensualism, and leads one to submit to passion as surely as does a more direct love of beauty. Aschenbach learns inevitably that even the most disciplined artist cannot avoid passion or feeling, and that the more repressed passion is, the greater strength it has when it finally surfaces.

Britten makes these ideas clear in seventeen short scenes, with the overture inserted after the second scene. The fatigue and self-discipline with which Aschenbach works are indicated musically in the opening scene by a cell of melodic half-steps, a motif that returns frequently. The vague threat of the strange people Aschenbach meets is indicated dramatically by the fact that all—the man in the graveyard, the gondolier, a grotesque old fop he meets on the way to Venice, the barber who near the end makes Aschenbach up to resemble the fop, the hotel clerk—are played by the same actor and use the same musical motif, one that Aschenbach himself, after his admission of love for Tadzio, takes up. The sea has its own motif, of large intervals and rhythmic sweep, which near the end is transformed as it too becomes associated with the sensuality that begins to overwhelm Aschenbach. The boy Tadzio and his family are also indicated by their own music, and the boy is always accompanied by the vibraphone when he is on stage. In addition, the family are dancers, not singers, emphasizing the lack of communication between them and Aschenbach; several times the writer tries to naturalize his relationship with them simply by opening a conversation, feeling that would end his infatuation. But he is unable to do so, since Tadzio occupies a different world. Casting Tadzio as a dancer also allows for several dance scenes that make clear just how physical Aschenbach's attraction is and points up the body/mind dichotomy in which he is caught. For finally the opera shows that Aschenbach has tried to deny the body, not only to suppress passion, but to suppress even the body's natural desire for recreation and rest. The story suggests from the beginning the artificiality of this denial; self-discipline begins to break down in the first scene, when the mind inexplicably desires the South as a symbol of relaxation and sensuousness, and continues in the infatuation with the boy. Finally the South comes to represent the revenge of the senses, and Aschenbach succumbs to a death wish—pleasure and death become one for him. *Death in Venice* suggests that the radical separation of mind and body, reason and feeling, work and social life so common in Western culture is untenable and leads finally to total disintegration of the individual.

—Sandra Corse

DEBUSSY, (Achille-) Claude.

Composer. Born 22 August 1862, in St-Germain-en-Laye. Died 25 March 1918, in Paris. Married: 1) Rosalie Texier, 19 October 1899 (divorced, 2 August 1904); 2) Madame Emma Bardac, 15 October 1905 (daughter; died 14 July 1919). Studied with Madame de Fleurville, a student of Chopin; studied piano with Marmontel, solfeggio with Lavignac, and harmony with Emile Durand at the Paris Conservatory, 1872-1880; became the family piano teacher to Madame Nadezhda von Meck, Tchaikovsky's patron, and travelled to Switzerland, Italy, and Russia with her family, 1880-82; in Moscow,

Claude Debussy, c. 1900

became acquainted with the music of Borodin and Mussorgsky; second Prix de Rome, 1883; Grand Prix de Rome for his cantata *L'enfant prodigue,* 1884; heard *Parsifal* in Bayreuth, 1888; returned to Bayreuth in 1889; interest in Oriental music, which was presented at the Paris Exposition, 1889; his only opera, *Pelléas et Mélisande* composed between 1892 and its premiere at the Opéra-Comique on April 30, 1902; most of his well known orchestral compositions composed between 1892-1908; contributions to numerous journals, including *La revue blanche, Gil Blas, Musica, Le mercure de France, Le Figaro,* and others between 1901-17; various conducting engagements in Paris, Vienna, Budapest, Turin, Moscow, St Petersburg, The Hague, Amsterdam, and Rome between 1910-14; Debussy's last public appearance on 5 May 1917, when he played the piano part of his *Violin Sonata* with Gaston Poulet.

Operas

Publishers: Choudens, Durand, Fromont, Hamelle, Jobert, Schott/Eschig.

Axël, Auguste de Villiers de L'Isle–Adam, c. 1888 [one scene only].
Roderigue et Chimène, C. Mendès (after G. de Castro and Corneille), 1890-92 [unfinished].
Pelléas et Mélisande, Debussy (after Maeterlinck), 1893-95, 1901-02, Paris, Opéra-Comique, 30 April 1902.
Le diable dans le beffroi, Debussy (after Poe), 1902-11 [unfinished].
La chute de la maison Usher, Debussy (after Poe), 1908-17 [unfinished].

Publications/Writings

By DEBUSSY: books–

Durand, J., ed. *Lettres de Claude Debussy à son éditeur.* Paris, 1927.
André-Messager, J. ed. *La jeunesse de Pelléas: lettres de Claude Debussy à André Messager.* Paris, 1938.
Claude Debussy: lettres à deux amis: 78 lettres inédites à Robert Godet et G. Jean-Aubry. Paris, 1942.
Borgeaud, H., ed. *Correspondance de Claude Debussy et Pierre Louÿs.* Paris, 1945.
Tosi, G. ed. *Debussy et d'Annunzio.* Paris, 1948.
Lockspeiser, E. ed. *Lettres inédites de Claude Debussy à André Caplet.* Monaco, 1957.
Vallery-Radot, P. ed. *Lettres de Claude Debussy à sa femme Emma.* Paris, 1957.
Catalogue Nicolas Rauch no. 20, 24: Letters to Gabriel Mourey. Geneva, 1958.
Monsieur Croche antidilettante. Paris, 1921; 1926; English translation, 2nd ed., 1962.
Monsieur Croche et autres écrits. Edited by François Lesure. Paris, 1971, 1988; English translation as *Debussy on Music,* edited by Richard Langham Smith, London and New York, 1976.
Lettres 1884-1918. Edited by François Lesure. Paris, 1980; English translation as *Debussy Letters,* edited by Roger Nichols, London and Cambridge, Massachusetts, 1987.

articles–

"Preface." In the Durand edition of Chopin's piano works. Paris, 1915.

"Correspondance inédite de Claude Debussy et Ernest Chausson." *Revue musicale* 6 (1925): 116.
"3 lettres à B. Molinari." *Suisse romande* 2 (1939).
Lesure, F. ed. "Claude Debussy: textes et documents inédits." *Revue de musicologie* 48 (1963).

unpublished—

With R. Peter. *F.E.A.* [*Frères en art*], c. 1899; *L'eerbe tendre*, c. 1899, *L'utile aventure*, c. 1899; *Esther et la maison de fous*, 1900; *Les mille et une nuits de n'importe où et d'ailleurs*, 1901 [Plays].

About DEBUSSY: books—

Gilman, Lawrence. *Debussy's "Pelléas et Mélisande": A Guide to the Opera.* New York, 1907.
Emmanuel, Maurice. *Pelléas et Mélisande.* Paris, 1926.
Jardillier, R. *Pelléas.* Paris, 1927.
Denis, M. *H. Lerolle et ses amis.* Paris 1932. [letters]
Inghelbrecht, D.-E. *Comment on ne doit pas interpréter Carmen, Faust, Pelléas.* Paris, 1933.
Ysaÿe, A. *Eugene Ysaÿe: sa vie, son oeuvre, son influence.* Brussels, 1947.
Ackere, Jules van. *Pelléas et Mélisande.* Brussels, 1952.
Gauthier, A. *Debussy: documents iconographiques.* Geneva, 1952.
Goléa, Antoine. *Pelléas et Mélisande: analyse poétique et musicale.* Paris, 1952.
Büsser, H. *De Pelléas aux Indes galantes.* Paris, 1955.
Kerman, Joseph. *Opera as Drama.* New York, 1956; 2nd ed., 1988.
Stravinsky, I. et al. *Avec Stravinsky.* Monaco, 1958. [letters]
Vallery-Radot, P. *Tel était Claude Debussy.* Paris, 1958. [letters]
Lerberghe, C. van. *Pelléas et Mélisande: notes critiques.* Liege, 1962.
Lockspeiser, Edward. *Debussy et Edgar Poe.* Monaco, 1962.
Joly, A. and A. Schaeffer. *Ségalen et Debussy.* Monaco, 1962. [letters]
Lockspeiser, E. *Debussy: His Life and Mind.* Cambridge, 1965, 1966, 1978; revised edition by Richard Langham Smith, London, 1980; French translation by Leó Dilé, Paris, 1980.
Nichols, Roger. *Debussy.* London, 1973.
Abravanel, Claude. *Claude Debussy: A Bibliography.* Detroit, 1974.
Lesure, François. *Claude Debussy.* Geneva, 1975.
Wenk, Arthur B. *Debussy and the Poets.* Berkeley, 1976.
Lesure, François. *Esquisses de Pelléas et Mélisande.* Paris, 1977.
————. *Iconographie musicale: Debussy.* Geneva, 1977.
Metzger, H.-K., and R. Riehn. *Claude Debussy.* Munich, 1977. [*La chute de la maison Usher*]
Holloway, Robin. *Debussy and Wagner.* London, 1979.
Hirsbrunner, T. *Claude Debussy und seine Zeit.* Laaber, 1981.
Cobb, M.C. *The Poetic Debussy: A Collection of His Song Texts and Selected Letters.* Boston, 1982.
John, Nicholas, ed. *Claude Debussy: Pelléas et Mélisande. English National Opera Guides,* vol. 9. London and New York, 1982.
Orledge, Robert. *Debussy and the Theatre.* Cambridge, 1982.
Terrasson, René. *Pelléas et Mélisande; ou, L'initiation.* Paris, 1982.
Howat, Roy. *Debussy in Proportion: A Musical Analysis.* Cambridge, 1983.

Wenk, Arthur B. *Claude Debussy and Twentieth-Century Music.* Boston, 1983.
Grayson, David A. *The Genesis of Debussy's "Pelléas et Mélisande.* Ann Arbor, 1986.
Nichols, Roger, and Richard Langham Smith. *Claude Debussy: Pelléas et Mélisande.* Cambridge, 1989.
Dietschy, Marcel. *A Portrait of Claude Debussy.* Oxford, 1990.
Holmes, Paul. *Debussy.* London, 1990.
Parks, Richard. *The Music of Claude Debussy.* New Haven, 1990.

articles—

D'Indy, Vincent. "A propos de Pelléas et Mélisande: essai de psychologie du critique d'art." *L'occident* June (1902).
Evans, E. "Pelléas et Mélisande." *Musical Standard* 29 May (1909).
Doret, G. "Lettres et billets inédits de C. A. Debussy." *Lettres romandes* 23 November (1934).
Oulmont, C. "Deux amis: Claude Debussy et Ernest Chausson: documents inédits." *Mercure de France* 1 December (1934).
Peter, R. "Ce que fut la 'générale' de Pelléas et Mélisande." In *Inédits sur Claude Debussy,* Collection Comoedia Charpentier, 3. Paris, 1942.
Dukas, Paul. "Pelléas et Mélisande. In *Les écrits de Paul Dukas sur la musique.* Paris, 1948.
Abraham, M. "Sous le signe de Pelléas." *Annales du Centre Universitaire Mediterranéen* 7 (1953-54).
Mondor, H. "Mallarmé et Debussy." *Cahiers de marottes et violons d'Ingres* September-October (1954).
D'Estrade-Guerra, O. "Les manuscrits de Pelléas et Mélisande." *Revue musicale* no. 235 (1957): 5.
Leibowitz, R. "*Pelléas et Mélisande;* ou, le 'No-Man's Land' de l'art lyrique." *Critique* 13 (1957).
Lesure, F. "Lettres inédites de Claude Debussy." *Candide* 21 June (1962).
Stewart, Madear. "The First Mélisande: Mary Garden on Debussy, Debussy on Mary Garden." *Opera* May (1962).
Lesure, F. " 'L'affaire' Debussy-Ravel: lettres inédites." In *Festschrift Friedrich Blume.* Kassel, 1963.
————. "Claude Debussy, Ernest Chausson et Henri Lerolle." *Mélanges d'art et de littérature offerts à Julien Cain.* Paris, 1968.
————. "Lettres inédites de Claude Debussy à Pierre Louÿs." *Revue de musicologie* 57 (1971): 29.
Tinan, G. de. "Memoires of Debussy and his Circle." *Recorded Sound* nos. 50, 51 (1973): 158, 176.
Williams, B. "L'Envers des destinées: Remarks on Debussy's *Pelléas et Mélisande.*" *Cambridge University Quarterly* (1975).
Orledge, R. "Debussy's *House of Usher* Revisited." *Musical Quarterly* 62 (1976): 536.
Avant-scène-opéra, March-April (1977) [*Pelléas et Mélisande* Issue].
Myers, R. "The Opera that never was: Debussy's Collaboration with Victor Segalen in the Preparation of *Orphée.*" *Musical Quarterly* 64 (1978): 495.
Hirsbrunner, Theo. "Frankreichs Opern um 1900. Auf den Spuren von Richard Wagners Einfluss." *Neue Zürcher 3/* no. 52 (1979): 67.
Stirnemann, Kurt. "Zur Frage des Leitmotivs in Debussys *Pelléas et Mélisande.*" In *Schweizer Beiträge zur Musikwissenschaft, IV: Studien zur Musik des 19. und 20. Jahrhunderts,* edited by Jürg Stenzel. Bern and Stuttgart, 1980.

White, David A. "Echoes of Silence: The Structure of Destiny in Debussy's *Pelléas et Mélisande.*" *Music Review* 41 (1980): 266.

Abbate, Carolyn. "*Tristan* in the Composition of *Pelléas.*" *Nineteenth-Century Music* 5 (1981): 117.

Smith, Richard Langham. "Debussy and the Pre-Raphaelites." *Nineteenth-Century Music* 5 (1981).

Tammaro, Ferruccio. "Mélisande dai quattro volti." *Nuovo rivista musicale italiana* 15 (1981): 95.

Spieth-Weissenbacher, Christiane. "Prosodes et symboles mélodiques dans le récitatif de Pelléas et Mélisande ou place du figuralisme dans l'écriture vocale de Debussy." *International Review of the Aesthetics and Sociology of Music* 13 (1982): 82.

Kunz, Stefan. "Der Sprechgesang und das Unsagbare: Bemerkungen zu *Pelléas et Mélisande.*" In *Analysen: Beiträge zu einer Problemgeschichte des Komponierens. Festschrift für Hans Heinrich Eggebrecht zum 65, Geburtstag,* edited by Werner Breig, et al., 338. Weisbaden, 1984.

Wenk, Arthur. "Claude Debussy and the Art Nouveau Image of Woman." *Miscellanea musicologica* [Australia] 13 (1984): 67.

Grayson, David A. "The Libretto of Debussy's *Pelléas et Melisande.*" *Music and Letters* (1985).

Boulez, Pierre. "Reflections on *Pelléas et Mélisande.*" In *Orientations.* London, 1986.

unpublished–

Grayson, David Alan. "The Genesis of Debussy's *Pelléas et Mélisande:* a Documentary History of the Opera, a Study of its Sources, and 'Wagnerian' Aspects of its Thematic Revisions." Ph.D. dissertation, Harvard University, 1983.

*　　*　　*

Despite the fact that Debussy's total output in the genre of opera was quite limited, he made an immense impact on opera with his monumental work, *Pelléas et Mélisande.* Although none of his other operatic works survive in their complete form, Debussy worked on a number of opera projects throughout his life.

Debussy's early aborted opera projects include passages from two comedies of de Banville, *Hymnis* and *Diane au Bois,* which are both unpublished works, and a scene from Villiers de L'Isle–Adam's *Axël,* which is also unpublished. After working on these scores, Debussy realized he had overextended his abilities, which may be why he chose to abandon the works. Some say that the use of the dream world in *Diane,* in a general sense, foreshadows *L'Apres-midi d'un faune.*

After *Axël,* Debussy wrote *Rodrigue et Chimène,* a grand opera with a libretto by Catulle Mendès. The work remains in an unfinished, unpublished short score. Supposedly, Debussy undertook the project due to parental pressure, with the personal hope that his association with Mendès would open doors for him at the Paris Opéra. After two years of work on the project, however, he abandoned it, claiming that the manuscript had been destroyed in a fire.

Debussy's only completed opera score was set to the libretto, *Pelléas et Mélisande,* a slightly adapted version of Maeterlinck's play. Debussy began working on *Pelléas* in 1893, and the work was completed a decade later. *Pelléas et Mélisande* represents the height of Debussy's art and is one of the monuments in post-Wagnerian opera.

Opinions on *Pelléas et Mélisande* tend to be divided into two schools. Igor Stravinsky once said that it is "a great bore on the whole, in spite of many wonderful pages." On the other hand, Oscar Thomson once said that "*Pelléas et Mélisande* is of all lyric dramas the most objective and the most convincingly human."

Despite Debussy's admiration for Wagner, he rejected Wagner's symphonic method of composing operas. Debussy once had a conversation with his teacher, Guiraud, in which he stated that, "Music in opera is far too predominant. My idea is of a short libretto with mobile scenes, no discussion or argument between the characters, whom I see at the mercy of life or destiny." This aesthetic principle is in direct opposition to the ideas of Wagner. To compare the two, Wagner tended towards opera as symphonic poem, Debussy towards opera as sung play. Critics have generally compared *Pelléas et Mélisande* to Wagner's *Tristan und Isolde,* saying that *Pelléas* is the more refined, self-conscious, constrained work; *Tristan* is much more radical, much more difficult to come to terms with. Both of these operas are significant, however, for an understanding of the famous operatic "reform" of the nineteenth century.

After *Pelléas et Mélisande,* Debussy devoted a great deal of time to two operas: *Le diable dans le beffroi* and *La chute de la maison Usher.* Both of these are tales of Poe. In *Le diable,* Debussy was attempting to find a style of writing that embraced the conglomerate sentiments found in a crowd. In addition, Debussy decided to have the part of the Devil whistled rather than sung. The opera was never completed.

La chute is a study of pathological melancholia. It has been written that Debussy, to some extent, saw himself mirrored in the oversensitive person of Roderick Usher in *La chute.* In 1908 Debussy wrote to his editor: ". . . there are times when I lose contact with my surroundings and if Roderick Usher's sister were suddenly to appear I should not be all that surprised."

It is difficult to summarize either Debussy's contribution to the genre of opera or his musical process. As Debussy himself once said: "We must agree that the beauty of a work of art will always remain a mystery, in other words we can never be absolutely sure 'how it's made.' We must at all costs preserve this magic which is peculiar to music and to which, by its nature, music is of all arts the most receptive."

—Kathleen A. Abromeit

DEL BENE, ADRIANA GABRIELI
See BENE, ADRIANA GABRIELI DEL

DELIBES, (Clément-Philibert-) Léo.

Composer. Born 21 February 1836, in St-Germain-du-Val, Sarthe. Died 16 January 1891, in Paris. Enrolled in the Paris Conservatory, 1847; studied solfège with Tariot (first prize in 1850), organ with Benoist, and composition with Adam; organist of St Pierre de Chaillot and accompanist at the Théâtre-Lyrique, 1853; chorus master of the Paris Opéra, 1864; professor of composition at the Paris Conservatory, 1881; member of the Institut, 1884. Delibes is renowned for his ballets *Coppelia, ou La fille aux yeux d'émail* (1870), and

Sylvia, ou La nymphe de Diane (1876), as well as for his operas.

Operas

Deux sous de charbon, ou Le suicide de bigorneau, J. Moinaux, Paris, Théâtre des Folies-Nouvelles, 9 February 1856.

Les deux vieilles gardes, Villeneuve and Alphonse Lemonnier, Paris, Théâtre des Bouffes-Parisiens, 8 August 1856.

Six demoiselles à marier, E. Jaime and A. Choler, Paris, Théâtre des Bouffes-Parisiens, 12 November 1856.

Maître Griffard, Mestépès and Adolphe Jaime, Paris, Théâtre-Lyrique, 3 October 1857.

La fille du golfe, C. Nuitter [vocal score published 1859].

L'omelette à la Follembuche, Marc Michel and Eugène Labiche, Paris, Théâtre des Bouffes-Parisiens, 8 June 1859.

Monsieur de Bonne-Étoile, Philippe Gille, Théâtre des Bouffes-Parisiens, 4 February 1860.

Les musiciens de l'orchestre (with Offenbach, Erlanger and Hignard), de Forges and A. Bourdois, Paris, Théâtre des Bouffes-Parisiens, 25 January 1861.

Les eaux d'Ems, H. Crémieux and L. Hálevy, Ems, Kursaal, July 1861.

Mon ami Pierrot, Lockroy, Ems, Kursaal, July 1862.

Le jardinier et son seigneur, M. Carré and T. Barrière, Paris, Théâtre-Lyrique, 1 May 1863.

La tradition (prologue), H. Derville, Paris, Théâtre des Bouffes-Parisiens, 5 January 1864.

Grande nouvelle, A. Boisgontier [vocal score published 1864].

Le serpent à plumes. Philippe Gille and Cham, Paris, Théâtre des Bouffes-Parisiens, 16 December 1864.

Le boeuf Apis, Philippe Gille and Furpille, Paris, Théâtre des Bouffes-Parisiens, 25 April 1865.

Malbrough s'en va-t-en guerre (with Bizet, Jonas, and Legouix), Paul Siraudin and William Busnach, Paris, Théâtre de l'Athénée, 13 December 1867.

L'écossais de Chatou, Adolphe Jaime and Philippe Gille, Paris, Théâtre des Bouffes-Parisiens, 16 January 1869.

La cour du roi Pétaud, Adolphe Jaime and Philippe Gille, Paris, Théâtre des Variétés, 24 April 1869.

Fleur-de-lys, H. B. Farnie.

Le roi l'a dit, Edmond Gondinet, Paris, Opéra-Comique, 24 May 1873.

Jean de Nivelle, Edmond Gondinet and Philippe Gille, Paris, Opéra-Comique, 8 March 1880.

Lakmé, Edmond Gondinet and Philippe Gille, Paris, Opéra-Comique, 14 April 1883.

Kassya (unfinished: scoring and recitatives by Massenet), Henri Meilhac and Philippe Gille (after L. von Sacher-Masoch, *Frinko Balaban*), Paris, Opéra-Comique, 24 March 1893 [posthumous performance].

Le Don Juan suisse [lost].

La princesse Ravigote [lost].

Le roi des montagnes [sketches].

Jacques Callot [unfinished].

Publications

About DELIBES: books–

Guiraud, E. *Notice sur la vie et les oeuvres de Léo Delibes.* Paris, 1892.

Jullien, A. *Musiciens d'aujourd'hui.* 2nd series, 261. Paris 1894.

Maréchal, A. *Souvenirs d'un musicien.* Paris, 1907.

Pougin, A. *Musiciens du XIXe siècle.* Paris, 1911.

Downes, Olin. *The Lure of Music* [101 ff.]. New York, 1918.

Tiersot, J. *Un demi-siècle de musique française (1870-1917).* Paris, 1918.

Séré, O. *Musiciens français d'aujourd'hui.* Paris, 1921.

Loisel, Joseph. *"Lakmé" de Léo Delibes: étude historique et critique: analyse musicale.* Paris, 1924.

Curzon, Henri de. *Léo Delibes.* Paris, 1926.

Landormy, P. *La musique française de Franck à Debussy.* Paris, 1943.

Boschot, A. *Portraits de musiciens,* 2nd series. Paris, 1947.

Lalo, P. *De Rameau à Ravel.* Paris, 1947.

Coquis, André. *Léo Delibes: sa vie et son oeuvre (1836-1891).* Paris, 1957.

Curtiss, M. *Bizet and his World.* New York, 1958.

Studwell, William E. *Chaikovskii, Delibes, Stravinskii: Four Essays on Three Masters.* Chicago, 1977.

———. *Adolphe Adam and Léo Delibes: A Guide to Research.* New York, 1987.

articles–

Hanslick, H. "Jean de Nivelle von Léo Delibes." In *Aus dem Opernleben der Gegenwart,* 57. Berlin, 1885.

Pougin, A. "Léo Delibes." *Revue encyclopédique* 1 March (1891): 294.

Van Vechten, Carl. "Back to Delibes." *Musical Quarterly* October (1922): 605.

Miller, Philip Lieson. "The Orientalism of Lakmé." *Opera News* 22 December (1941): 18.

Hughes, G. "Delibes and Le roi l'a dit." In *Sidelights on a Century of Music 1825-1924,* 116. London, 1969.

unpublished–

Sharp, Stuart Walter. "The Twilight of French Opéra Lyrique, 1880-1900." DMA dissertation, University of Kentucky, 1975.

Boston, Margie Viola. "An Essay on the Life and Works of Leo Delibes." DMA dissertation, University of Iowa, 1981.

* * *

Léo Delibes is one of those figures in the history of French music in the nineteenth century whose reputation rests securely on but a few compositions, namely, three ballets, one opera, and several songs. He was talented enough to be admitted to the Paris Conservatory at the age of twelve but sufficiently unremarkable so as to pass four years as a composition student without distinction. Yet, such was his level of competency that when only sixteen he secured a position as staff accompanist at the Théâtre Lyrique where he tried his hand at operetta composition; several of these efforts were modestly successful and enjoyed a modicum of popularity. In time, he joined the choral staff at the Opéra and simultaneously held a similar position at the Théâtre Bouffes-Parisiennes, Offenbach's theater.

Delibes' disciplined training at the Conservatory served him admirably, and he learned the intricacies of the music theater inside out. His keen sensitivity to the taste of the middle class audience of the day enabled his continuing success, however modest, until almost by accident he was engaged by a leading Polish dancer to prepare a ballet score. *La Source,* 1866, was enormously successfully and was followed a little over three years later by an even more esteemed work, *Coppelia.* It has been noted that Delibes's musical abilities were as *ballabile* (dance worthy) as Italian opera was *cantabile* for the singer. With another enormously successful ballet, *Sylvia*, in 1876, Delibes reached the apex of his fame in the dance theater.

Finally, in 1883, after many years of effort, Delibes achieved the critical success in opera which had long eluded him. *Lakmé* was a triumph at its premiere and within twelve years had been performed 200 times at the Paris Opéra; it celebrated its 1000th appearance in 1931 and continues to be produced on occasion in France.

The story of *Lakmé* was ready-made for a respectably bourgeois clientele. The scene is India, and the work redounds with elements of the fashionable orientalism of the time as found in many Gerôme paintings and operas by Bizet (*Pearl Fishers*) and Saint-Saëns (*Samson and Delilah*). Lakmé, the beautiful daughter of a Brahmin priest, falls in love with an English officer. Determined to avenge this dishonor her father uses Lakmé to lure Gerald into the open in order to kill him (the seductive song employed for this purpose in act II is the famous "Bell Song" beloved by many a soprano since its premiere). Gerald is seriously wounded, and Lakmé nurses him back to health. Their secret haven is discovered by a fellow officer who persuades Gerald to rejoin his regiment. Lakmé, heart broken, commits suicide in a bower of poisonous datura plants.

This slightly scandalous tale was sufficiently genteel to be acceptable to late nineteenth-century French audiences. Delibes was not to repeat this success, but he had the honor of being elected to the Institut de France in 1884 to fill the vacancy left by Victor Massé. To his end he remained the epitome of the fashionable musician, confident in his craft, esteemed for the elegance and charm of his fashionable music, and conservative to the core with respect to compositional practice.

—Aubrey S. Garlington

DELIUS, Frederick (born Fritz Theodor Albert Delius).

Composer. Born 29 January 1862, in Bradford. Died 10 June 1934, in Grez-sur-Loing, France. Married: the painter Jelka Rosen, 1903. In Solana, near Jacksonville, Florida, 1884, to manage an orange plantation bought by his father; met and studied with the organist, Thomas F. Ward; taught in Danville, Virginia, 1885; studied counterpoint and harmony with Reinecke, Sitt, and Jadassohn at the Leipzig Conservatory, 1886, and met Grieg there; in Paris, 1888; in Grez-sur-Loing, near Paris, 1897; Companion of Honour awarded by King George V, 1929; honorary Mus.D. by Oxford, 1929. Sir Thomas Beecham organized a Delius festival in 1929.

Operas

Publishers: Augener, Boosey and Hawkes, Harmonie, Leuckart, Oxford University Press, Universal.

Irmelin, Delius, 1890-92, Oxford, New Theatre, 4 May 1953.
The Magic Fountain, Delius, 1893-95.
Koanga, Charles Francis Keary (after George Washington Cable, *The Grandissimes*, 1895-97, Elberfeld, Stadttheater, 30 March 1904.
A Village Romeo and Juliet, Delius (after Gottfried Keller, *Romeo und Julia auf dem Dorfe*), 1900-01, Berlin, Komische Oper, 21 February 1907.

Margot la Rouge, Mme Rosenval, 1902.
Fennimore and Gerda, Delius (after Jens Peter Jacobsen's novel *Niels Lyhne*), 1909-11, Frankfurt am Main, Opernhaus, 21 October 1919.

Other works: orchestral works, vocal works, chamber music, piano songs.

Publications

By DELIUS: books–

With Papus. *Anatomie et physiologie de l'orchestre*. Paris, 1894.

About DELIUS: books–

Chop, Max. *Frederick Delius*. Berlin, 1907.
Heseltine, Philip. *Frederick Delius*. London, 1923; revised 1952, 1974.
Hull, Robin H. *Delius*. London, 1928.
Holland, A.K. *Essays and Notes for the Delius Society Records*. London, 1934.
Delius, Clare. *Frederick Delius: Memories of my Brother*. London, 1935.
Fenby, Eric. *Delius as I Knew Him*. London, 1936; 2nd ed., 1948, 1975; 3rd ed., 1966; 4th ed., 1981.
Hutchings, Arthur. *Delius: A Critical Biography*. London, 1948.
Warlock, Peter. *Frederick Delius*. New York, 1952.
Beecham, Thomas. *Frederick Delius*. London, 1959; revised ed., 1975.
Frederick Delius: Centenary Festival Exhibition. London, 1962.
Jahoda, G. *The Road to Samarkand: Fredrick Delius and his Music*. New York, 1969.
Fenby, Eric. *Delius*. London, 1971.
Carley, Lionel, and R. Threlfall. *Delius and America*. 1972.
Jefferson, Alan. *Delius*. London and New York, 1972.
Carley, Lionel. *Delius: The Paris Years*. London, 1975.
Palmer, C. *Delius: Portrait of a Cosmopolitan*. London, 1976.
Redwood, Christopher, ed. *A Delius Companion*. London, 1976, 1980.
Tomlinson, F. *Warlock and Delius*. London, 1976.
Carley, Lionel, and R. Threlfall, *Delius: A Life in Pictures*. London, 1977, 1984.
Carley, Lionel, *Delius: A Life in Letters I 1862-1908*. London, 1983; *Delius: A Life in Letters II 1909-1934*. Aldershot, 1988.
Smith, John Boulton. *Frederick Delius and Edvard Munch: Their Friendship and Their Correspondence*. Rickmansworth, 1983.

articles–

Abraham, Gerald. "Delius and his Literary Sources." *Music and Letters* 10 (1929): 182.
Hutchings, Arthur. "Nietzsche, Wagner, and Delius." *Music and Letters* 22 (1941): 235.
Hull, Robin H. "The Scope of Delius." *Music Review* 3 (1942): 257.
Lyle, Robert. "Delius and the Philosophy of Romanticism." *Music and Letters* 29 (1948): 158.
Tempo no. 26 winter (1952-53) [Delius issue].
Cooke, Deryck. "Delius's Operatic Masterpiece." *Opera* April (1962).
Delius Society Journal (1963-)[London].

Threlfall, R. "Delius in Eric Fenby's MSS." *Composer* 31 (1969): 19.

Randel, William. "*Koanga* and Its Libretto." *Music and Letters* April (1971).

The subject-matter of Delius's first operatic experiment, *Irmelin* (1890-92), seems now more English and Victorian than the composer's later iconoclastic cosmopolitanism might have countenanced: a fairy-tale princess hears a "voice in the air" that encourages her to long for a fairy-tale prince, who duly arrives in the form of Nils, a dispossessed prince who has been reduced to acting as swineherd to a Nordic robber-lord. In the final scene their individual fantasies entwine and love blossoms; the sun rises as they wander playfully, hand in hand, into the forest "like two children." The later revised *Irmelin Prelude* captures the essence of the opera's evanescent lyricism, focussed by the idyllic vision of the young men and women Irmelin sees running into the forest at sunset. She is bound by duty and her lack of a partner to watch from afar in this essential Delian moment: the "free" young folk distantly singing and dancing their dreamy "tra-la-la" in an archetypally "English" nine-eight rhythm. Irmelin's own music, however, is typically cast in a slower tempo, its rhythm and manner that of the sentimental ballad of discreetly repressed Victorian ladies.

Although repeatedly criticized for the monotony of his declamation, Delius's idealistic purpose was to transform this manner into an ever more subtle reflection of a certain kind of bourgeois subjectivity in an art uncluttered by the inauthentic formulae and clichés of what he regarded as arid musical convention. His aim was for unbroken melodic continuity in his vocal lines, and he deliberately avoided the realism that might have been attained by more rapid vocal delivery over the complex orchestral underlay which was in itself consistently admired before the First World War in Germany for its subtly nuanced post-Wagnerian lyricism.

The "fantasy" Delius avowedly aimed for in his composition was influenced by memories of his Florida experiences. In his next two operas, Delius explored the late-Victorian tendency to link the Romantic Idyll with the lost freedom of oppressed colonial peoples like the American Indians or the black slaves. The improvised harmony of black field hands, heard in the distance at sunset, remained with Delius as an intense musical image of paradise recalled, and inspired him to write a trilogy of operas based respectively on the Indians, the negroes and the gypsies. The first of these was *The Magic Fountain,* through whose elaborate, filmic scene-changes we follow the shipwrecked Spanish explorer Solano and the Seminole Indian girl Watawa in search of the Fountain of Eternal Youth. Once found, its powerfully magical waters kill the unprepared couple, for whom love had blossomed out of initial racial suspicion (Watawa had intended to kill the white man as symbolic oppressor of her people).

That the problems of *Irmelin* were only partially solved in *The Magic Fountain* (neither was staged in Delius's lifetime) makes all the more remarkable the achievement of *Koanga*. This "negro" opera was indeed opera in a much more fully realized sense of the term. Above all Delius had found the pretext for a really integrated role for the chorus, whose richly harmonized spirituals and work-songs contribute to the strong effect of this drama. The story concerns Koanga, a Voodoo prince captured as a slave and "tamed" by his Mississippi owner, who offers him the beautiful mixed-race Palmyra as a wife. Other whites conspire to prevent the marriage, however, and the enraged Koanga escapes with followers into the swamps after placing a curse upon the plantation. The structurally-defining choruses of the slave workers and the fine set-piece "wedding" (including the dance-episode "La Calinda") are succeeded by a magnificent scene of Voodoo invocation. However, Koanga's remorseful longing for Palmyra leads the slave back to his capture and death. Palmyra commits suicide after denouncing Koanga's killers and their Christian faith.

In *Koanga* the Romantic Idyll is doubly historicized: first, as the memory of an oppressed people whose troubles are manifest in the forces that separate Koanga and Palmyra, and secondly, in that the three-act opera itself is framed by a prologue and epilogue in which "Uncle Joe" is persuaded by the daughters of a southern plantation house owner to retell the old story. As a key late-nineteenth-century expression of liberal-colonial Romanticism, it is only to be regretted that the opera's inept and historically naive libretto (by Keary after George Cable—it has been "improved" with some success in a new edition by Douglas Craig and Andrew Page), combined with unintentional racist implications, makes it unlikely that it will be revived, although it is arguably a masterpiece of its kind.

There should really be no argument about *A Village Romeo and Juliet,* which Delius deliberately called a "Lyric Drama in six scenes" (*Lyrisches Drama in sechs Bildern*—like *Koanga* and *Fennimore and Gerda,* this opera was first performed in German). The scenes are of varying length and avoid larger "act" divisions; they present six episodes from Gottfried Keller's tragic tale of Sali and Vrenchen, children of two farmers who get into conflict over an overgrown field whose rightful owner is a strange gypsy (The Dark Fiddler). Jealousy and litigation separate and finally ruin the two farmers whose grown-up children fall passionately in love with each other. Symbolically denied access to the luxuriantly overgrown "wildland" where they had played long ago, and recoiling from the sexual freedom of the gypsy folk, they finally consummate their love in a river barge which they deliberately sink as the opera concludes. Filled with strongly characterized music of considerable variety, it includes some of Delius's most successfully judged melodic declamation, but also functions as a seamlessly rhapsodic orchestral fantasy, whose initial descending motif of summer childhood abandonment is slowly replaced by the rising arpeggio whose apotheosis comes in the famous interlude between scenes five and six (which accompanies the partly-mimed "walk to the Paradise Garden," symbolic name of a country tavern). More than any other, this work clarifies Delius's conception of operatic fantasy as embodied dream in which the symbolic and the real meet in the musical language of subjective experience. Delius's stage characters are created *by* the impulse of his music, which has secondary concern for individual characterization.

Neither the one-act *Margot la Rouge* (a nevertheless interesting Delian interpretation of *verismo,* set amongst Parisian "vagabonds" of the kind that Sali and Vrenchen shun) nor the structurally problematic but stylistically flawless *Fennimore and Gerda* (1909-11) significantly extended Delius's range as an opera composer. Already by 1919, when *Fennimore and Gerda* was premiered in Frankfurt, his style had become that of a past era before it had ever fully been appreciated.

—Peter Franklin

DELLA CASA, Lisa.

Soprano. Born 2 February 1919, in Burgdorf, near Berne. Married Dragan Debeljevic, 1947 (one daughter). Studied with Margaret Haeser in Bern and Zurich; debut as Cio-Cio-San in Solothurn-Biel, 1941; sang in Zurich, 1943-50; debut at Salzburg as Zdenka, 1947; British debut at Glyndebourne as Countess, 1951; joined Vienna State Opera, 1947-73; debut at Metropolitan Opera as Countess, 1953, where she sang for fifteen seasons until 1968.

Publications

About DELLA CASA: books–

Natan, A. *Prima Donna.* Basle, 1962.
Celletti, R. *Le grandi voci.* Rome, 1964.
Debeljevic, D. *In dem Schatten ihrer Locken: ein Leben mit Lisa della Casa.* Zurich, 1975.
Rasponi, L. *The Last Prima Donnas.* New York, 1982.

articles–

Fitzgerald, G. "Lisa della Casa." *Opera* March (1968): 185.

*   *   *

In the 1950s, 60s and early 70s, Swiss-born soprano Lisa Della Casa shared repertoire with some of the centuries finest singers: her contemporaries include Elisabeth Schwarzkopf, Sena Jurinac, and Elisabeth Grümmer. Della Casa's natural

Lisa Della Casa as Arabella

vocal gifts were probably not comparable, but her willowy, raven-haired beauty and telling muscial artistry earn her a place in even this elite pantheon.

Della Casa's lyric soprano was a fascinatingly inconsistent instrument—Giacomo Lauri Volpi's famous description of Claudia Muzio's voice ". . . made up of tears and sighs" is equally appropriate here. Her voice was never completely equalized; the upper notes were always gloriously light and easy, but the bottom of the range was rather tinny and weak, and the middle voice—not dependable nor strong even in her earliest recordings—became increasingly threadbare over time. Yet it was Della Casa's gift to manipulate this rather patchy tone to a positive end, lending an ageless, touchingly frail and feminine quality to her performances. She seemed at once innocent and experienced, young and old, and Della Casa was able to turn what was a natural limitation into an asset.

That these fragile means could serve so well in a wide variety of music was again a tribute to Della Casa's artistry. She pushed her limited resources to encompass with some success the difficulties of Strauss' Chrysothemis in *Elektra* and even *Salome,* although she wisely limited her appearances in these roles. Della Casa greatly enjoyed singing Italian opera—her repertoire included Gilda in *Rigoletto,* Mimì in *La Bohème,* Tosca and Butterfly, but she was rarely cast in these roles in international opera houses. Some German language highlights recordings of the latter two may explain why; the singing is lovely and Della Casa's touching femininity is much in evidence, but a curious reticence and reserve leave the listener unsatisfied, and finally a warmer, more Italianate sound is needed.

Della Casa was in great demand as an interpreter of Mozart, though the lack of homogenous tone color was noticeable in this demanding music. She frequently performed and recorded the roles of Donna Elvira in *Don Giovanni,* the Countess in *Figaro,* and Fiordiligi in *Così fan tutte.* In each she exhibits lovely tone color, a clean sense of line and some personal charm, but all three performances lack the technical perfection of her contemporary Elisabeth Schwarzkopf. In the operas of Richard Strauss, Della Casa was something of a specialist—in addition to the two roles previously noted, her repertoire included Zdenka in *Arabella,* Ariadne, the Countess in *Capriccio* and all three principal parts (Octavian, Sophie and the Marschallin) in *Der Rosenkavalier.* Some exerpts from *Der Rosenkavalier,* recorded perhaps a bit too late to show Della Casa at her best are nonetheless a worthy souvenir of her fine Marschallin, altogether more youthful and natural than Schwarzkopf's, less specific in her word painting but always expressive and alive to nuances.

But no comparisons are necessary in judging Della Casa's assumption of the title role of Strauss's *Arabella,* of which she is the century's acknowledged master interpreter, and both of her complete recordings (Decca, 1957 and DG, 1963) more than adequately preserve this renowned portrayal. No other singer has negotiated the climactic high pianissimo phrases of "Und du wirst mein Gebieter sein" with such radiance. No other singer has invested the little "Aber die richtige" duet, in which Arabella dreams of a perfect lover, with more poignancy, and none has invested the oddly ambivalent character with such compassion—even the slightly chilly, aloof quality which limited some of Della Casa's portrayals was wholly consistent with this strange, serious, romantic girl.

Lisa Della Casa virtually owned the role of Arabella after she sang it for the first time; it is altogether appropriate and fitting that it was as Arabella that Della Casa performed for the last time in 1974.

—David Anthony Fox

DEL MONACO, Mario.

Tenor. Born 27 July 1915, in Florence. Died 16 October 1982, in Mestre. Largely self-taught before brief study with Melocchi at Pesaro Conservatory, Rome Opera School, 1935; debut as Turiddu in Pesaro, 1939; international appearances (including Mexico City, Buenos Aires, Rio) 1945-46; United States debut in San Francisco as Radames, 1950; debut at Metropolitan Opera as Des Grieux, 1950; sang more than one hundred performances at the Met in the 1950s; retired from the stage in 1973.

Publications

by DEL MONACO: books–

La mia vita e i miei successi. Milan, 1982.

About DEL MONACO: books–

Chedorge, A. *Mario del Monaco.* Paris, 1963.
Celletti, R. *Le grandi voci.* Rome, 1964.
Segond, A. and D. Sebille. *Mario del Monaco; ou, un Tenor de Legende.* Lyons, 1981.

articles–

Nuzzo, F. "Mario del Monaco." *Opera* 6 (June 1962).

*   *   *

Mario Del Monaco was a leading Italian dramatic tenor in the period from the 1940s to the early 1960s. Those who believe that the Italian dramatic tenorial ideal is represented by loud, intensely powerful, full-throated, virile singing in which emotion is at the forefront—the epitome of the verismo style—may hear its realization in his voice. Others, desiring elegance, subtlety, and nuance—approaching the so-called bel canto style—may perceive Del Monaco as monotonous, coarse, and insensitive. The true nature of his voice resides somewhere in between, although Del Monaco's reputation is of a singer employing the former style.

Del Monaco made his professional debut in 1940 as Turridu in Mascagni's *Cavalleria rusticana* in Cagli, Italy. His first major performance was as Pinkerton in Puccini's *Madama Butterfly* in Milan at the Teatro Puccini in 1941. Subsequent performances, especially those at the Verona Arena as Radames in Verdi's *Aida* and with the San Carlo opera company on tour at Covent Garden during the 1945-46 season, established Del Monaco's international career. He first appeared at the Teatro alla Scala as Pinkerton in 1945. His American debut was as Radames opposite Renata Tebaldi's Aida (in her American debut) in San Francisco in 1950, and he then sang extensively with the Metropolitan Opera in New York.

Del Monaco has often been described as a singer of unremitting loudness and unrelenting intensity, more the warrior

than the philosopher. His most frequently cited fault was a disinclination (or apparent inability) to sing below mezzo-forte. Critics complained that he demonstrated force without subtlety, and a brash, hard vocal quality. As one critic has remarked, he frequently gave the impression that the character he was portraying was not taking time to think; his style has been called the vocal equivalent of machismo. Some have found his singing boring because of an insufficient variation of tonal color and a lack of suppleness in the phrasing; others complain of a whining quality. He was also capable of sloppy, undisciplined singing, with excessive sliding between notes and some carelessness about pitch.

At times, however, Del Monaco displayed sufficient virtues to justify, at least in part, the high reputation he held in Italy. His voice had a bright, attractive surface with substantial body of tone and occasional moments of vocal splendor—a vibrant, heroic sound with strong visceral appeal. He had the ability to produce the kind of thrilling high notes that sustain listeners through the monotonous stretches. Del Monaco employed a firm legato and sense of line to produce an even flow of rich tone. Despite his voice's size and power he was able to sing beautifully, even sensitively, when required. Recordings show he was capable of some delicacy, and in his prime he managed to execute diminuendos, although his *piano* singing lacked body. He demonstrated a sense of drama and was able to convey honest emotion, not being afraid to be crude when the role demanded it and able to generate animal excitement when it was required (if also, frequently, when it was not). Toward the end of his career his voice became thinner and more nasal. As with many singers, however, he improved in artistry as his vocal prowess began to decline, making dramatic advantage out of increasing vocal difficulties. He never developed into a great actor—the relative inflexibility of his voice was probably a limiting factor.

Verdi's Otello was probably his greatest role; in it he combined dramatic power with depth of feeling. Other roles span the dramatic roles of the Italian and French repertoire: Don José in Bizet's *Carmen,* Aeneas in Berlioz's *Les Troyens,* Canio in Leoncavallo's *I pagliacci,* Verdi's Ernani, Don Alvaro in Verdi's *La forza del destino,* Radames, Pollione in Bellini's *Norma,* Samson in Saint-Saëns's *Samson et Dalila,* Manrico in Verdi's *Il trovatore,* Des Grieux in Puccini's *Manon Lescaut,* Dick Johnson in Puccini's *La fanciulla del West,* Giordano's Andrea Chénier, and Enzo Grimaldo in Ponchielli's *La gioconda,* the last two being especially well suited to his style. He also was successful, remarkably so for an Italian tenor, in two Wagnerian roles—Lohengrin and Siegmund (in *Die Walküre*), the latter of which he sang in its original language.

Many of these roles were recorded, often with the partnership of Renata Tebaldi: Canio in 1953 under Erede, Des Grieux in 1954 under Molinari-Pradelli, Otello in 1954 under Erede and in 1960 under Karajan, Don Alvaro in 1955 under Molinari-Pradelli in 1955, Manrico in 1956 under Erede, Enzo Grimaldo in 1957 under Gavazzeni, Andrea Chénier in 1957 under Gavazzeni, Dick Johnson in 1958 under Capuana, and Don José in 1962 under Schippers. Other recorded performances include Turiddu in Mascagni's *Cavalleria rusticana* in 1953 under Ghione, Calaf in Puccini's *Turandot* in 1955 under Erede, Maurizio in Cilèa's *Adriana Lecouvreur* in 1961 under Capuana, Luigi in Puccini's *Il tabarro* in 1962 under Gardelli, Loris in Giordano's *Fedora* in 1969 under Gardelli, and Hagenbach in Cilèa's *La Wally* in 1969 under Cleva.

Del Monaco's studio recordings are, in general, more disciplined than the recordings made at staged performances, as if the presence of an audience brought out the aggressive qualities of his singing.

—Michael Sims

DE LOS ANGELES, Victoria (born Lopez Cima).

Soprano. Born 1 November 1923, in Barcelona. Married Enrique Magrina, 1948 (two sons). Studied with Dolores Frau at Barcelona Conservatory to 1944; debut as Mimì in Barcelona, 1941; formal debut as the Countess in *Le nozze di Figaro* at Teatro Liceo in Barcelona, 1945; won Geneva International Singing Competition, 1947; debut at Paris as Marguerite, 1949; Teatro alla Scala debut as Ariadne, 1950; Covent Garden debut as Mimì, 1950; Metropolitan Opera debut as Marguerite, 1951, and she sang more than one hundred performances there until 1961; appeared as Elisabeth at Bayreuth, 1961-62.

Publications

About DE LOS ANGELES: books–

Gavoty, B. *Victoria de los Angeles*. Geneva, 1956.
Moore, G. *Am I too Loud?* London, 1962.
Natan, A. *Prima Donna*. Stuttgart, 1966.
Fernandez-Cid, A. *Victoria de los Angeles*. Madrid, 1970.
Roberts, P. *Victoria de los Angeles*. London, 1982.

Victoria de Los Angeles as Manon

articles–

Hardy, C. "Victoria de los Angeles." *Opera* April (1957): 210.
James, B. "Victoria de los Angeles." *Audio and Record Review* 2/no. 6 (1963): 14.
Avant-scène opéra August (1985).

*   *   *

With a musical family background, Victoria de Los Angeles seems to have first learned to sing as a mere natural expression of childhood happiness. Although the Spanish Civil War shadowed her formative years it did not interrupt her development, and after university and conservatory study it was clear that her future lay in opera, so much so that in 1941 she was invited at the age of eighteen to sing Mimì in *La bohème* at the Teatro Victoria in her native city of Barcelona. With surprising maturity, she refused the offer because she felt herself unready. Her official debut came four years later in another theater in the same city, as the Countess in Mozart's *Le nozze di Figaro*—an older role, which suggests that her voice and stage personality were already recognized as mature for her years.

In the immediate post-war years, helped by her success in the Geneva Singing Competition in 1947, de Los Angeles quickly gained international acceptance. British audiences were among the first outside Spain to appreciate her vivid personality and fine musicianship, not least in a 1949 British Broadcasting Corporation broadcast in which she played the fiery heroine Salud in Falla's *La vida breve*. Though Spanish music was an obvious field for her, she must have known from the start that it was limited, and she soon gave evidence of her mastery of several languages and a wide repertory, playing at Covent Garden as Mimì, Cio-Cio-San in *Madama Butterfly*, Nedda in *I pagliacci*, Santuzza in *Cavalleria rusticana*, Manon in Massenet's opera of that name and two Wagner roles, Elsa in *Lohengrin* and Eva in *Die Meistersinger*. She also sang the role of Rosina in Rossini's *Il barbiere di Siviglia*.

It has been said that "a voice is a person," but as an opera singer de Los Angeles had to be not just herself but also a singing actress, and during her career of more than two decades she gave abundant and consistent evidence of dramatic force and presence, together with real imaginative flexibility. The accompanist Gerald Moore declared that she sang with "total involvement in the emotions" as well as a lovely voice and keen musicianship. She gave further evidence of her musical and dramatic range in her performances of roles as diverse as Debussy's elusive Princess Mélisande in *Pelléas et Mélisande*, the virtuous but vocally agile Marguerite in Gounod's *Faust* and the loving and too-trusting Desdemona in Verdi's *Otello*. There was some suprise in Britain when the conductor Sir John Barbirolli chose her to sing (in English, alongside British singers) the role of Dido, the ill-fated Queen of Carthage in his recording of Purcell's *Dido and Aeneas*, but she rose magnificently to the occasion and did memorable justice to Purcell's style and the tragic role.

De Los Angeles' voice was sweet and vibrant as well as somewhat Mediterranean in quality, with a rich lower register. The upper soprano range was not quite so easy for her, particularly later in her career, and there could be a touch of hardness in some notes, but she could nearly always vary her tone so as to suit the music and her characterization of a role. By 1970 she had more or less brought her stage appearances to an end, but she continued with concert work and recordings. Her recording career was remarkably full, with no less than twenty-two operas committed to disc as well as an even larger number of recitals. Her personality seems to have been easy-going; she was charmingly modest in the British Broadcasting Corporation's long-running *Desert Island Discs* program in which she was invited to choose favorite records—in contrast with some other singers who have seemed only interested in their own voices. On the other hand, she was firm where artistic standards were concerned, and once refused to continue with a recording of Bizet's *Carmen* under Sir Thomas Beecham until she was given what she felt to be adequate recording time; Beecham took her side, and their famous 1960 recording offers proof of their successful collaboration. Perhaps it took her some time to get inside this particular role of a Spanish *femme fatale;* she did not sing it on stage until fairly late in her career.

—Christopher Headington

DE LUCA, Giuseppe.

Baritone. Born 25 December 1876. Died 26 August 1950. Studied with Venceslao Persichini in Rome and with Contogni; debut in Piacenza as Valentine in *Faust,* 1897; created Michonnet in *Adriana Lecouvreur,* Milan, 1902; debut at Teatro alla Scala as Alberich, 1903; created Gleby in Giordano's *Siberia,* 1903, and Sharpless, 1904; Covent Garden

Giuseppe De Luca as Figaro in *Il barbiere di Siviglia*

debut as Sharpless, 1907; Metropolitan Opera debut as Rossini's Figaro, 1915, and sang there until 1935; created Paquiro (in *Goyescas*) and Gianni Schicchi, 1918; taught at Juilliard.

Publications

About DE LUCA: books–

Shaman, William. *Giuseppe De Luca: A Discography.* London, 1992.

articles–

Current Biography. 1947 cumulation. New York, 1948.
Favia-Artsay, A. "Giuseppe De Luca." *Record Collector* 5 (1950): 56.

*   *   *

Baritone Giuseppe De Luca may not have been the last authentic exponent of bel canto as legend would have it, but he was certainly one of its most celebrated spokesmen, and a formidable representative of its principles long after most other bel canto singers had vanished. During De Luca's 1947 Golden Jubilee Concert, soprano Frances Alda commented "I've heard many voices *bigger* . . . Amato, Titta Ruffo, Battistini, and many others—but none of them could compare with the magnificent *bel canto* of De Luca." Few would dispute her. In 1946, as De Luca was undertaking a final wave of recitals, Irving Kolodin offered a similar assessment of him with even greater precision, observing that "There were some who considered the amount of voice he had to work with a small part of its original splendor; but they remember incorrectly. It was never a voice distinguished by size, rather by quality and the deftness with which it was used." To be sure, De Luca's was not an especially large voice, but it was beautifully modulated, effortlessly produced and skillfully handled. It may have lacked some of Ruffo's flexibility, but his singing was altogether more refined; it did not have Amato's dramatic consistency, but in the repertory that suited it best, it was sweeter and more sympathetic. Only Battistini can perhaps be seen as having been the more cultivated artist, possessing as he did an instrument of unrivaled agility. De Luca's was a low baritone of great dramatic potential, without Battistini's vast upper resources. It had considerably less weight in the first decades of his career, and seemed then to be propelled by a vibrant, almost tremulous intensity later absorbed into the darker, full-bodied timbre of his authentic prime. His technique was immaculate, capable of transforming the humblest material into a virtuosic display of classical phrasing and exemplary legato. Recordings make it equally clear, however, that De Luca's voice was neither small or second-rate, any more than his artistry was simply a triumph of technique and interpretation.

De Luca cultivated and maintained a large and varied repertory throughout his career, but did so cautiously. He certainly made no attempt to dominate so commanding a repertory as many of his contemporaries did, choosing instead to adopt only those roles which his voice could accommodate with complete authority. Avoiding the kind of destructive shouting that prematurely ruined the voices of Ruffo and Amato, his career—like Battistini's—was unusually long. Although he had created major roles of Giordano, Cilèa, and Puccini during his stay at the Teatro alla Scala, and continued to perform others as dramatically demanding as Tonio (*I pagliacci*) during his prime, his patronage of the verismo repertory was more or less incidental. His scant Wagnerian repertory, which consisted of Alberich (*Das Rheingold*), Wolfram (*Tannhaüser*), and Beckmesser (*Die Meistersinger*), though it brought him much success, was abandoned when he left the Teatro alla Scala after the 1914-1915 season. It was in fact with misgivings that he first performed Beckmesser under Toscanini's direction during a 1903 South American tour, complaining to his agent that such roles were ruinous to the voice. He eventually settled into the earlier nineteenth-century Italian repertoire, was a notable interpreter of Mozart, and gained his greatest recognition in the leading early and middle Verdi baritone roles. Here the size and disposition of his voice, as well as his skills as an actor—most notable, contemporary accounts suggest, in the extremes of high melodrama and buffo comedy—were particularly well suited. Hence his renown as Rigoletto, Germont (*La traviata*), Malatesta (*Don Pasquale*), and Rossini's Figaro (*Il barbiere di Siviglia*). Over the course of his career he also created a number of important roles, including the Devil in the 1902 Italian premiere of Massenet's *Griselda,* Michonnet and Gleby in the world premieres of Cilèa's *Adriana Lecouvreur* (1902) and Giordano's *Siberia* (1903), Sharpless in the chaotic first production of Puccini's *Madama Butterfly* (1904), and at New York's Metropolitan Opera, Paquiro in Granados' *Goyescas* (1916) and Puccini's Gianni Schicchi (1918). His American stage premieres—the title role in *Eugene Onegin* (1920), Guglielmo in *Così fan tutte* (1922), Ping in *Turandot* (1926), and the elder Bruschino in Rossini's *Il Signor Bruschino* (1932)—were equally impressive. He was also Don Carlos in *La forza del destino* (1918), Rodrigo in *Don Carlos* (1920), Sancho Panza to Chaliapin's Don Quixote in Massenet's *Don Quixote* (1926), and Miller in *Luisa Miller* (1929) in the first Met presentations of these works. De Luca was a commanding interpreter of song as well, his vast repertory accommodating Italian, French, English and Russian works spanning four centuries. With characteristic ease and assurance, he was able to invest in these the same evocative details that distinguished his operatic interpretations.

Like Battistini (and very briefly, Ruffo), he was a pupil of Venceslao Persichini (1827-1897), with whom he studied for five years at Rome's Academia di Santa Cecilia. He made his professional debut as Valentin (*Faust*) in Piacenza in 1897, and by 1904 had already embarked upon successful starring seasons at the Teatro Lirico, the Teatro San Carlo, and the Teatro alla Scala, where he remained for eight illustrious seasons. Giulio Gatti-Casazza, for whom De Luca sang both at the Teatro alla Scala and the Met, recalled him with restrained appreciation in his memoirs: "our admirable singer of *bel canto,*" he wrote of him, ". . . a reliable, versatile and serious artist, and distinctly a fine stylist." De Luca spent much of the first two decades of the century touring the major operatic centers of the world, enjoying particular success in Eastern Europe and South America. Prior to his coming to New York in 1915, he sang three guest seasons at Covent Garden between 1907 and 1910, yet he returned there only once for a single appearance as Figaro in 1935. At the Met he flourished for nineteen consecutive seasons, singing fifty-two roles in some 700 performances. Like a number of other notable Met imports, he went back to Europe in the midst of the Depression, but returned briefly in 1940 for performances of works closely associated with him—*La traviata, Rigoletto, Il barbiere di Siviglia* and *La Bohème.* He was again in fleeting residence at the Teatro alla Scala in 1936 and 1937 for performances of *Manon, L'elisir d'amore,* and *Don Pasquale.*

After nearly four decades of unceasing professional activity, he spent the war years at his estate in Italy. "For five years I was playing cards," he told a *Time* interviewer in

March, 1946, "I refused to sing because I was not in a good humor." But in fact, he did manage to perform sporadically throughout the hostilities. Returning to America in 1945, he gave a number of well-received concert performances in New York, culminating in a poignant farewell recital at New York's Town Hall on 7 November, 1947 in celebration of the "Golden Jubilee" of his career. He continued broadcasting and recording up until the year of his death at age 73. His professional activities never really allowed him to devote his energy entirely to teaching as he had anticipated, and we are only left to wonder at the vast influence he might have exerted had he lived to enjoy a long retirement.

De Luca recorded prolifically over a period of forty-eight years, leaving 156 published commercial recordings, forty-five live concert items, and nine surviving broadcasts. His first recordings were made in Milan for the Gramophone & Typewriter Ltd. in December, 1902, and his last, issued on a long-playing disc by the Continental Record Company of New York, in the winter of 1950. His principal output, made for Victor during his years at the Met, amounted to nearly seventy published titles. Few other major singers enjoyed such extraordinary artistic endurance, or managed to produce a recorded legacy as satisfying. The only significant gap in his recording activities was between 1908 and 1915, rendering inaccessible the transition into his prime. Several of his most important roles—Rigoletto, Germont (*La traviata*), Rossini's Figaro, are documented rather sparsely, though fortunately, there is an ebullient "Largo al factotum" among his three Vitaphone films of 1927 and 1928 to illustrate just how irresistible his Figaro must have been. Less fortunate is the fact that, apart from three published versions of Michonnet's Monologue from the first act of *Adriana Lecouvreur,* and three exerpts from *Siberia,* he was somehow never induced to record from the many important roles he created. Even among his American and Metropolitan Opera premiere vehicles, there remains only a handful of scenes from *La forza del destino* and *Don Carlos.* He left only one Wagner title, a 1907 "O tu bell' astro" from *Tannhäuser,* leaving little by which to judge his early success in this repertory.

It is only after the Second World War, in the commercial recordings he made for Decca (1946) and Continental (1950) and in the 1947 Town Hall recitals, that we begin to see signs of serious vocal decline. His last important recordings, duets from *Rigoletto* and *Il Barbiere di Siviglia* with Lily Pons, were recorded for Victor in March, 1940, and these, along with two Met broadcasts from the 1939-1940 season, give astonishing testimony to the fact that forty years of singing were powerless to diminish the stylistic vitality that so distinguished him among his contemporaries.

—William Shaman

DE LUCIA, Fernando.

Tenor. Born 11 October 1860, in Naples. Died 21 February 1925, in Naples. Studied with Vincenzo Lombardi and Beniamino Carelli at Naples Conservatory; debut at Teatro San Carlo in Naples as Faust, 1885; in London at Drury Lane in

1887 and at Covent Garden, 1892-1900; appeared in premieres of *L'amico Fritz, I Ranzau, Silvano,* and *Iris*; first to sing Puccini's Rodolfo in Italian at Covent Garden (with Melba); debut at Metropolitan Opera as Fritz, 1893-94; last stage appearance in *L'amico Fritz,* Naples 1917; sang at Caruso's funeral, 1921; pupils include Georges Thill, Maria Nemeth and Gianni Pederzini.

Publications

About DE LUCIA: books–

Henstock, M. *Fernando De Lucia.* London, 1990.

articles–

Shawe-Taylor, D. "Fernando de Lucia." *Opera* July (1955).
Williams, C. and E. Hain. "Fernando de Lucia." *Record Collector* 10 (1957): 125.
Henstock, M. "The London Career of Fernando de Lucia." *Record Collector* 17 (1967): 160.

*   *   *

Although Fernando de Lucia was successful as a leading tenor in the new operas of his time by composers such as Mascagni and Leoncavallo, his importance for present-day listeners lies mainly in the manner in which he performed the music of Rossini, Bellini, and Donizetti. Born in Naples and trained there in the classical Italian vocal method, de Lucia made more than 400 recordings, many of which demonstrate

Fernando De Lucia as Turridu in *Cavalleria rusticana*

the nearly lost art of free embellishment of the written operatic score. Just as significant is the manner in which he could (when he chose) actually sing the notes written by these early nineteenth-century composers with classical vocal poise and a true legato style. To hear such an unusual singer in our age of by-the-book performances and emphasis upon vocal beauty rather than technique strikes many as nothing short of a revelation.

Interpretive freedom represented for de Lucia (at his best) a means of expression, not an opportunity for meaningless vocal display. Regarding his performances of Rossini, John Steane (*The Grand Tradition,* p. 31) wrote that "he seems to have known exactly when to linger, when to soften, when to add an ornament, when to join one phrase to another." In his recordings of arias from *Il barbiere di Siviglia,* for example, in which the vocal technique is astounding, one savors above all his ability to enhance the music by escaping from the narrow dimension of metrical time. In "Ecco ridente," the embellishments are treated precisely as such, permitting expansive treatment of selected phrases of text and the creation of a romantic mood. By way of contrast, the singer pushes right through a written rest after the word *momento,* creating an affective moment by carrying the line over to the next word (*istante*). De Lucia's use of rubato to establish the introspective mood of a young man in love is exemplified beautifully in repertory as late as Verdi's *La traviata,* from which he recorded Alfredo's "Dei miei bollenti spiriti." Rhythmic freedom, especially in the middle as well as at the end of a phrase, distinguishes all of de Lucia's recordings of music from the first part of the nineteenth century.

The style of de Lucia presumes that vocal artistry rests firmly upon mastery of vocal technique, one aspect of which was appropriate use of ornaments, figuration, and scale passages. Some of de Lucia's embellishments result from the use of a true legato, a connection between sung notes so smooth that one hears the pitches in between, as in his recordings of Ernesto's arias from Donizetti's *Don Pasquale.* Most of his embellishments float lightly in the head voice, for another aspect of de Lucia's vocal mastery lay in his expressive use of *pianissimo* singing at the top of the voice. How moving Nemorino (*L'elisir d'amour*), Elvino (*Sonnambula*), and Arturo (*Puritani*) can be when the tenor can express the vulnerability of these characters by diminishing his volume at will.

Many critics have found it difficult to appreciate de Lucia's artistry because of the rapid vibrato always present (and nearly always under perfect control) in the voice. It is certainly true that he was not a perfect singer. His full voice singing on high notes tends to be strident, an impression that is reinforced by his frequent recourse to altered vowel sounds in that range. Too often there is an obvious contrast in the quality of the sound between his head and chest registers, almost as if he possessed two different voices. When he does manage a smooth decrescendo from loud to soft, a *ritardando* (slowing down of the tempo) seems to be required. His habit of using *rubato* at the ends of phrases requires him to break normal phrase-lengths in half (or into even smaller fragments), a practice that undermines the structure of the melody. In "A te, o cara" (Bellini, *Puritani*), for example, after carrying over one partial phrase to the beginning of the next, he breathes after the word *fra* and before the words *la gioia.* Extra breaths are also routinely taken in cadences so as to make it possible for him to sustain the final note or notes, and sometimes, as in "Dalla sua pace" at the return of those words (Mozart, *Don Giovanni*), a phrase is rushed in order to get to a breath. Another mannerism employed much too often in de Lucia's recordings is the introduction of an aspirate (an "h" sound) into the line as a special vocal effect, as in "Quando le sere al placido" (Verdi, *Luisa Miller*) on certain (but not all) occurrences of the words *"mi tradia"* (which become mi tradihia). All of these problems occur in nearly every one of his recordings; some, but certainly not all, of them may have been accentuated by the acoustic recording process and by hearing his recordings (or transfers from them) at inaccurate playing speeds. His custom of singing virtually everything in downward transpositions (sometimes by as much as a third) makes it difficult to work with his recordings, and it must have had a significant effect in complete opera performances.

De Lucia sang with considerable success in Italy, appearing for more than thirty years at the San Carlo in Naples. Outside of Italy, he encountered a mixed reception. Although his interpretation of Canio (Leoncavallo, *I pagliacci*) in pre-Caruso New York was ranked by Philip Hale on a par with de Reszke's Romeo, Maurel's Iago, and Calvé's Carmen, he remained at the Metropolitan Opera for only one season. In London he was by and large successful: whereas his Almaviva of 1887 was regarded as "more than indifferent" (and "Ecco ridente" as "detestable") by the London *Times,* his portrayal of Canio in *I pagliacci* was judged by Herman Klein as "a triumph of realism." From the evidence of the critics and of his recordings, it would seem that de Lucia might better be regarded as providing a glimpse (imperfect though it may be) of an age before specialization of roles and standardization of performing styles overtook operatic singing than as a paragon of bel canto.

—David Poultney

THE DEMON.

Composer: Anton Rubinstein.

Librettist: A.N. Maikov (after Lermontov).

First Performance: St Petersburg, Maryinsky, 1875.

*   *   *

Anton Rubinstein, one of the greatest virtuoso pianists of his day, was also an influential educator and a prolific composer. While his importance to musical education in Russia through his activity as founder and director of the St Petersburg Conservatory is universally acknowledged, his music is often all but ignored. Included in his sizeable compositional output are more than a dozen operas, of which the fourth, *The Demon,* has had the greatest measure of success.

Rubinstein's failure with the genre was not for lack of trying. Some of his other operas were popular for a few years. But after the initial poor reception of *Dmitri Donskoi,* his first Russian opera, he turned to writing operas in German and Italian. Bitter over repeated failures, he rejected opera in general and nationalist opera in particular. "To me the opera is altogether a subordinate branch of our art," he wrote in *Music and its Masters.* He nonetheless continued to write, returning later to the idea of a Russian opera, and in 1875 *The Demon* had its premiere at the Maryinsky Theater in St Petersburg. In spite of the worst predictions by management and friends, the production was a success. *The Demon* was in fact the most successful of Rubinstein's operas, receiving

many performances in Russia and abroad. It has the distinction of being the first Russian opera to be staged in England—albeit sung in Italian, as *Il Demonio.* With a libretto by Apollon Nikolayevich Maikov, the opera is based on a poem by Lermontov, outstanding Russian writer and poet.

The opera opens as the demon flies in on the wings of a great storm. He curses the world, but an angel appears to tell him that he should love rather than curse, and he will be pardoned and allowed into heaven. When the demon later spies the lovely Tamara, feelings begin to stir in him. Fearful and uncomprehending, Tamara hears the voice of the demon inviting her to join him and become the queen of the world. Then the demon incites wandering marauders to murder Tamara's betrothed, Prince Sinodal, and again approaches her with his tempting offers. When Tamara, distraught, retires into a convent, the demon follows her even there. Struck with compassion, Tamara requires the demon to forswear evil; but when they kiss, she dies. Angels carry Tamara to heaven while the demon descends into the eternal fire.

Lermontov, infamous for blasphemy and Satanism, foreshadowed in "The Demon" a Dostoyevskian interest in the mental process of a doomed hero. Not surprisingly, the opera was criticized by the censors as "incompatible with the teachings of our church." It was perhaps more surprising that the opera was also received poorly by the nationalist "kuchka" composers, including Balakirev, Rimsky-Korsakov, and the others of their circle. For a variety of reasons, including background, upbringing, educational ideology, and even personal rivalry, Rubinstein was frequently in opposition with the kuchkists. Rubinstein seemed to think that this new opera would gain him respect in their eyes, and he invited these hostile colleagues to a private recital to hear him sing and play through it. But they were not impressed: silence, recorded Rubinstein, was their reaction after each number.

Perhaps they noticed the unmistakable parallel with Gounod's *Faust,* one of the most popular operas of the latter nineteenth century. Both operas begin with a male protagonist cursing the world, both are offered potential redemption through human love, and both end up in hell with the female love interest carried to heaven. Though Rubinstein's opera was based on a poem by Lermontov, who was in turn inspired by an ancient Goergian legend, this blatant reminder of an old German tale popularized by Goethe would not have appealed to the anti-German kuchkists. And of course the premise of the redemptive power of human love was the very epitome of a romantic notion grown perhaps somewhat stale by the 1870s.

Perhaps too the kuchkists noticed that the music was not especially original. Rubinstein used much of the same spurious orientalism so in vogue with Russian composers at that time; it is particularly noticeable in the ballet sequences. The style shifts back and forth between this and an uneven romantic idiom, wherein a great deal of the singing is accompanied by lush strings which add nothing to the frequently forgettable melodies. Some of the more appealing tunes live on in the recital repertoire, notably the Demon's aria "Weep not, my child."

Rubinstein spent a great deal of creative energy on many compositions. He wanted to make his own contribution to the culture of Russia actively, not just vicariously by educating the next generation. But in spite of his best efforts to legitimize himself as a composer, his main contribution is still that of educational leader and legendary virtuoso. Although he was essentially a staunch conservative, he eventually came around to the trends of modernism and nationalism, and the marginal success of *The Demon* may serve as a reminder of the pervasive interest in Russian musical nationalism in the latter half of the nineteenth century.

—Elizabeth W. Patton

DE RESZKE, Edouard.

Bass. Born 22 December 1853, in Warsaw. Died 25 May 1917, in Garnek. Studied with Ciaffei in Warsaw, and with his brother, the tenor Jean de Reszke; also studied in Italy with Steller and Alba in Milan, and Coletti; debut as the King in *Aïda* under Verdi's direction at the Théâtre des Italiens in Paris, 1876; appeared in Paris for two seasons, then at Teatro alla Scala; sang in London 1880-84; American debut as the King in *Lohengrin*, Chicago, 1891; Metropolitan Opera debut as Frère Laurent in *Roméo et Juliette*, 1891; greatest role was as Méphistophélès in *Faust*, the last act of which he sang for his last appearance, at a Metropolitan gala in 1903.

Publications

About DE RESZKE: articles—

Klein, H. "Edouard de Reszke: the Career of a Famous Basso." *Musical Times* July (1917).
Dennis, J., "Edouard de Reszke." *Record Collector* 6 (1951): 101.

*   *   *

The De Reszke family is legendary in *fin de siècle* operatic history. Of the two brothers and one sister who had important careers, Josephine was a soprano, Jean a tenor, and Edouard, arguably the most gifted of the three, was a bass.

Edouard's voice, according to contemporary reports, was a high bass, capable of singing the bass-baritone repertoire with considerable sonority in the lower register. Its size was remarkable, and not long after his debut he was already being compared with the great Lablache, who was endowed with a similarly phenomenal organ.

The De Reszke brothers were inseparable. Together they conquered the major opera houses of the world but were especially admired at the Metropolitan Opera and at Covent Garden, where they both appeared practically every season during the 1890s. Edouard was a gentle giant of a man and a character of considerable bonhomie, a quality for which he was loved by his colleagues. His *laissez-aller* attitude and lack of discipline might easily have become his eventual artistic undoing. But the very qualities which he lacked were to be found in abundance in Jean, who watched over and guided his career with brotherly affection.

Edouard merely needed to find a role congenial to want to perform it. His technique and vocal range afforded him considerable versatility, a quality which also endeared him to managements. He appeared with considerable regularity in a great variety of roles. In his first New York season, for example, he appeared in fourteen different roles in less than five months. He could turn with ease from a florid Rossini role like Assur (*Semiramide*) to the heaviest Wagnerian role, but was particularly happy in those parts where his personality and enormous voice could be allowed their full rein, such as Méphistophélès (*Faust*), Mefistofele in Boïto's opera of that name and Leporello (*Don Giovanni*). According to the critic of the *New York Times,* he was as Leporello "simply superb. It is a joy without alloy to hear him read the recitative with all the skill of a perfect actor and vocalist, and with such brimming and unctious humour that every line is funny. As for his 'Madamina', it is one of the most admirable of all achievements in the art of buffo singing."

No doubt Jean's increasing forays into the Wagnerian repertoire were responsible also for Edouard's assumption of many of Wagner's bass roles in the latter part of his career. He continued to elicit high praise from the critics in roles such as Hagen (*Götterdämmerung*), König Marke (*Tristan und Isolde*), Hans Sachs (*Die Meistersinger*) and Wotan (*Siegfried*).

If the operatic careers of the De Reszke brothers could be described as unique, lamentable would be an appropriate description of their recording careers. Jean made two test recordings, disliked what he heard and forbade their release. Edouard was coaxed into the studios of Columbia in 1903, but by then the voice was well past its best. Though he was only forty-nine (an age at which the bass voice should be at its most mature), a career of overworking the voice and frequent appearances had obviously taken its toll. Matters are not improved by the technically poor nature of the recording. The results are perhaps the most disappointing records ever to have been made by a singer of major importance. The voice as recorded sounds weak, the lower register colorless and the breath short. There were just three titles: the best of them is probably Plunkett's aria from *Marta,* which at least shows agility, an excellent trill and evidence of obvious good schooling. The others, Tchaikovsky's Don Juan's Serenade and the aria "infelice" from *Ernani,* do not even begin to give an idea of the voice of one of the finest basses in operatic history.

—Larry Lustig

DE RESZKE, Jean.

Tenor. Born 14 January 1850, in Warsaw. Died 3 April 1935, in Nice. Brother of baritone Edouard and soprano Josephine. Studied with his mother, and with Ciaffei in Warsaw, then with Cotogni in Milan. Began career as a baritone, using name Giovanni di Reschi at his debut as Alphonse in Donizetti's *La favorite* in Venice, 1874; debut in Paris under his own name as Melitone in *La forza del destino,* 1876; left stage for three years to study tenor roles with Sbriglia in Paris; tenor debut as Robert le Diable in Madrid, 1879; appeared as Jean in first performance of *Herodiade,* 1884; Massenet composed *Cid* for him the following year; Metropolitan Opera debut as Lohengrin in Chicago, 1891; New York Metropolitan Opera debut as Romeo, 1891; remained at Metropolitan Opera until 1901; became a teacher in Paris; students include Sayao, Teyte, Saltzmann-Stevens and Maria-Louise Edvina.

Publications

About DE RESZKE: books–

Leister, C. *Jean de Reszke and the Great Days of Opera.* London, 1933.
Hurst, P. *The Age of Jean de Reszke: Forty Years of Opera 1874-1914.* London, 1958; as *The Operatic Age of Jean de Reszke.* New York, 1959.

Jean De Reszke as Romeo in Gounod's *Roméo et Juliette*

articles–

Shawe-Taylor, D. "Jean and Edouard de Reszke." *Opera* January (1955).

*   *   *

Born into a music-loving, financially comfortable family, and largely self-taught, Jean De Reszke profited from the international success of his elder sister, Josephine, who sang leading roles in the major opera houses of Europe in the 1870s and 80s. He made his debut as a baritone (on the advice of his only teacher, Sbriglia) in Donizetti's *La favorite* in 1874, and in two years had built an international career of his own, winning praise even from London's notoriously fastidious critic, "Corno di Bassetto" (George Bernard Shaw).

From the start, however, Shaw and others argued that De Reszke was in fact a natural tenor. De Reszke paid them heed, retiring for eight years (except for a brief foray into Meyerbeer tenor parts opposite Josephine in Madrid, 1879). It took the persuasion of Jules Massenet, who had withheld from Paris production his new opera *Herodiade* (1884) for lack of a suitable tenor to sing John the Baptist, to bring Jean back to the opera stage. De Reszke's creation of Massenet's *Le Cid* (1885) confirmed his preeminent place in the French capitol, one which he never relinquished, and paved the way for his triumphs in London and New York, where he soon became the favorite singer for French romantic parts, to which he often added selected Verdi roles in Italian.

Though not uncommon among intelligent singers today, De Reszke's method of preparation was unique for his time,

especially among tenors. He would read voluminously about the historical period and if applicable, the character he was to portray. He was meticulous in ordering correct period costumes (most principal singers of his time provided their own, integrated staging being almost unknown outside Germany), even to specifying authentic underwear. He required months of preparation for a new role, studying the music (all of it, not just his part) phrase by phrase and the text for whatever nuances of character might be found there. On stage he was not afraid to allow immobility to convey what he felt to be the proper emotion, never succumbing to the "semaphore school" of acting employed by so many of his contemporaries.

Sometimes his methods proved too subtle. In a London *Lohengrin* his Van Dyck beard was criticized. In fact, believing that his unadorned mouth was overly sensual for the ascetic Grail Knight, he had decided to mitigate that sensuality by covering it. Years later, as Siegfried, he shaved off his cherished moustache to make the opposite effect.

A visit to Bayreuth in 1888 left him with an overpowering desire to sing his Wagner roles (at that time Lohengrin and Walther in *Die Meistersinger*) in the original German instead of the Italian mandated by New York and London. Finally in 1895 he sang his first German Lohengrin and Tristan. The acclaim with which these performances were met persuaded London to alter its language policy in 1896. More than any other singer, De Reszke broke down the language ghetto which divided opera houses into German and Franco-Italian "wings," with no possibility of crossover except by singers of smaller roles. While the lighter Wagner operas might be given in Italian or French for a De Reszke, a Maurel, or a Melba, only the Germans approached the heavier *Ring* and *Tristan*. Once listeners heard his Tristan in German, however, they wanted his Siegfried, and were not long denied it. His brother Edouard, a fine basso, and sopranos Lillian Nordica and Milka Ternina, also admired initially in the Italian-French repertoire, proved that they too could sing in German successfully, and once accustomed to the idea that a singer need not be restricted to either Germanic or Mediterranean languages, audiences began to demand that singers who wished to appear in Wagner operas learn German to do so.

The ability of a tenor who continued to sing Roméo successfully also to portray Tristan and the two Siegfrieds better than anyone of his time was analyzed by Shaw in his description of de Reszke as Massenet's Werther: "he attacks [declamatory passages accompanied by the full orchestra] with triumphant force, and the next moment is singing quietly with his voice as unrestrained as responsive, as rich in quality as if it had been wrapped in cotton wool for a week." Wagner had insisted that his most strenuous tenor roles, Tristan and Siegfried, needed to be *sung*, not declaimed or ranted. Only de Reszke seems to have understood how to pace the voice so as to take advantage of the orchestration. His brief study with the famous Sbriglia during his baritone years certainly helped him to place the voice suavely amid the challenging orchestration. From what we can gather listening to the "live" fragments of his performances recorded backstage in New York in 1901, his projection resembles the apparent effortlessness of other Sbriglia pupils, notably the baritone Jean Lassalle and the basso Pol Plancon.

As to the recordings, some dozen two-minute snatches recorded by the Metropolitan's librarian Lionel Mapleson on a cylinder phonograph given him by Thomas Edison, they are probably all we shall ever hear of the de Reszke voice. He is known to have made two (possibly three) Fonotipia recordings in Paris, probably in 1905, but refused to allow their issue (a purported copy claimed for some decades as the possession of a prominent Paris collector has been proven bogus). Luckily, some of Mapleson's cylinders escaped the ravages of time and bad needles. What they convey of de Reszke's voice confirms the descriptions of his contemporaries. A brief, clear moment in the "O paradis" from Meyerbeer's *L'Africaine* displays his ease of emission and absolute security in moving up to an exposed B-flat. A bravura passage from Roderigue's apostrophe to his sword in the role de Reszke created in *Le Cid* demonstrates his agility and what sounds like an uncanny ability to place the voice so that it resonates over the orchestra. Excerpts from his farewell to New York, as *Lohengrin*, faintly reveal a bel canto approach to Wagner. Finally, in excerpts from Siegfried's forging song, the qualities described by Shaw in the passage quoted above are much in evidence, as he projects over the brass fanfares, his voice floats when not challenged by the orchestra. Clearly posterity is much the poorer for lack of professionally-made recordings of de Reszke's voice.

Following his retirement from the stage in 1905 he became a teacher, his most successful pupils being Maggie Teyte, Richard Bonelli, and Arthur Endrèze. Major singers sought him out as a coach for a particular role, but more than one suffered the fate of Johannes Sembach, who after studying *Lohengrin* with its greatest exponent found that conductors wedded to the literal score would not countenance musical nuances, especially when suggested by a mere singer. De Reszke's relative lack of success as a teacher lay most prominently in the undeniable fact that none of his pupils approached him in the combination of innate stage presence, musicianship, intelligence, and beauty of voice that had distinguished his own career during its two decades at the apex of the operatic firmament.

—William J. Collins

DERMOTA, Anton.

Tenor. Born 4 June 1910, in Kropa, Yugoslavia. Died June 1989, in Vienna. Studied organ and composition, Ljubljana, then voice with Rado, in Vienna; operatic debut in Cluj, Transylvania, 1934; Vienna Opera debut as an armed man in *Die Zauberflöte,* 1936; appeared as Zorn in *Die Meistersinger* at Salzburg under Toscanini, 1936; remained in Vienna and Salzburg for most of his career; made a Kammersänger in 1946; sang Florestan in the *Fidelio* that reopened the Vienna Staatsoper, 1955.

Publications

By DERMOTA: books–

Tausendundein Abend: Mein Sangerleben. Vienna, 1978.

About DERMOTA: books–

Celletti, R. *Le grandi voci.* Rome, 1964.

*   *   *

Anton Dermota was born in Kropa (then Serbia, now Yugoslavia) and studied composition and organ in Ljubljana, and voice with Elisabeth Rado in Vienna. He made his debut as the First Armed Man in *Die Zauberflöte* at the small opera

house in Cluj, Transylvania in 1934. His reputation swiftly grew until Bruno Walter called him to Vienna in 1936 to sing Don Ottavio in *Don Giovanni,* and there he remained for the rest of his operatic life as principal lyric tenor, together with Julius Patzak, at the Vienna Staatsoper.

Dermota will be remembered as one of the great Mozart tenors of this century, eclipsed at first only by Richard Tauber, for whom Dermota held great reverence. During the visit of the Vienna Staatsoper to Covent Garden, London in 1947, Dermota had the grace to stand down and allow his senior colleague to sing one performance (and his last as it turned out) of Don Ottavio among old, pre-war friends.

Dermota was a famous Ferrando in *Così fan tutte* and Tamino in *Die Zauberflöte,* making him a "natural" for Salzburg. He first sang there in 1936 as Zorn in *Die Meistersinger* under Toscanini and then as the Young Seaman in *Tristan und Isolde* under Bruno Walter. Belmonte in *Die Entführung aus dem Serail* and Don Ottavio followed in subsequent years and with a variety of casts. He also sang Jacquino in *Fidelio* and Cassio in *Otello*, both under Furtwängler, Flamand in *Capriccio,* and for his last Salzburg season in 1956, Tamino under Solti. If one adds the Tenor Singer in *Der Rosenkavalier,* it becomes obvious that Dermota's voice was lyrically expressive, full of warmth and the kind of musical quality typical of Viennese training and inclination.

These were only a few of the fifty roles that he had thoroughly prepared and interpreted during his thirty years in Vienna, where he was regarded first and foremost as the leading Mozartian of all Austria. Additionally, his Des Grieux in Massenet's *Manon* had much of Piccaver's smooth line and persuasive approach, enabling him to take over this, and other famous Piccaver roles while retaining the support of "Piccy's" admirers.

Coming into prominence, as Dermota did, following Tauber and Piccaver, and contemporary with Patzak, he managed by self-control, firm discipline and total dedication, combined with his winning, very musical voice, to assert and maintain his own presence.

Lensky in *Eugen Onegin* was a role which Dermota made his own, partly on account of his Slavic background which understood the morose nature of the character. But his care with Tchaikovsky's nuances while singing the role made his performance unforgettable.

Palestrina in Pfitzner's opera of that name had been one of Patzak's triumphs until Dermota began singing it. His own success as Palestrina was certain, but he stopped singing for some time, then took it up again. He also flirted with the more "modern" operatic trend such as his assumption of Josef K. in von Einem's *Der Prozess.*

Apart from his title of Kammersänger, awarded in 1946, Dermota's even greater accolade was when he was cast as Florestan in *Fidelio* in the first performance to open the rebuilt Vienna State Opera in 1955, an enormous, celebratory gala occasion.

Wisely, he did not keep singing after his voice had declined in power and beauty but taught at the Vienna Academy of Music until shortly before his death in 1989.

—Alan Jefferson

DERNESCH, Helga.

Soprano and mezzo–soprano. Born 3 February 1939, in Vienna. Studied at Vienna Conservatory, 1957-61; debut in mezzo soprano role of Marina in *Boris Godunov,* Berne Opera, 1961, where she performed until 1963; appeared in Wiesbaden and Cologne, 1965-69; at Bayreuth, 1965-69; shifted to soprano roles; appeared with Scottish Opera, where she sang Gutrune (1968) and Leonore in *Fidelio* (1970); Salzburg debut, 1969; made her Chicago (1971) and Vienna Staatsoper (1972) debuts in *Fidelio*; returned to mezzo roles, 1979; Metropolitan Opera debut as Marfa in *Khovanschina,* 1985.

Publications

About DERNESCH: articles–

Smillie, T. "Helga Dernesch" *Opera* 25 May (1973): 407.

*   *   *

Helga Dernesch is one of the few singers to have considerable success as both a soprano and a mezzo-soprano. Though the voice itself has never achieved a particularly individualistic sound, it is a more than adequate vehicle for an exceptional musical and dramatic intelligence. With her handsome appearance, this theatrically thrilling artist is able to make even minor character roles take on a dominating force in any given opera. This is perhaps why she is best experienced onstage rather than on recordings. Similarly, her broad strokes and bold characterizations have made her more of an operatic than a concert artist.

Dernesch's early years as a Wagnerian soprano under Herbert von Karajan brought her to some of the finest opera capitals of the world. Yet in listening to her recordings of Brünnhilde in *Götterdämmerung* and Isolde in *Tristan und Isolde,* it seems inevitable that she would eventually be a mezzo. Her high notes never had the ease and openness of a true soprano.

This is not to minimize her achievements in the soprano repertoire. Though her *Ring* recordings have a certain interpretive blandness that afflicts many of Karajan's opera recordings, her Isolde, also under Karajan, is a memorable interpretation that alone guarantees her a chapter—albeit a brief one—in the history of 20th-century dramatic sopranos. She has an unsparing, dramatic fearlessness that gives Isolde's curse in act I ample dramatic weight, even if she lacked the heft or color to make such a moment convincing from a purely vocal standpoint. Though she loses some of the more ecstatic aspects of the role because of the limitations in her upper range, her "Liebestod" is unusually articulate. Rather than simply letting the music carry the moment, she infused the words with meaning and conveys a feeling of being overwhelmed with the forces of passion more than anyone since Lotte Lehman.

Following a vocal breakdown of sorts during rehearsals for *Die Frau ohne Schatten* in Hamburg in 1979, Dernesch went home to Vienna on the advice of conductor Christoph von Dohnanyi and reworked her voice in the mezzo soprano range. She did so with such remarkable speed and vigor, it's fair to say that her career as a mezzo soprano has been considerably more interesting than her soprano career. She has embraced a wide range of roles, including Herodias in *Salome,* Adelaide in *Arabella* and Marfa in Mussorgsky's *Khovanchina,* and sung in the original Russian. Her interpretations of these extremely different roles—a decadent queen, a penniless socialite and a religious fanatic—are all so complete in their own way, it is sometimes difficult to imagine another singer in them.

Her most important legacy came out of her relationship with the 20th-century composer Aribert Reimann, whose Requiem (1983) and operas *Lear* (1978) and *Troades* (1986) she premiered. Though Reimann's idiom is atonal and frequently thorny (in keeping with the subject matter he choses), Dernesch maintained a dramatic sense in her vocal lines, as is apparent in her performance as Goneril in *Lear.* In the first scene when she proclaims her love for her father, her slightly exaggerated stylization of the wide-leaping vocal lines tell the listener she is not being sincere. Her background as a Wagnerian was particularly appropriate in this role. As she shuts her father out into the stormy night, she does so with a steely confidence perhaps only a Wagnerian could muster. Though the role does not have a great emotional range, Dernesch gives even the most hysterical moments a musical dignity that reveal her character as a cool manipulator, even in the most emotionally charged situations.

Possibly her finest achievement with Reimann is *Troades,* a retelling of the Trojan war whose score is more spare and vocal lines more graceful than its predecessors. Her voice was in prime condition for the premiere at the Bavarian State Opera, and the role of Hekabe, the mother of Hector, offered her monologues with only spare accompaniment from the tympani and lower brass, gives her a tailor-made platform for her sense of theatricality. She dominates the opera, culminating in an immolation scene, the comparisons with the Wagnerian counterpart illustrating how much she has grown in dramatic depth from her early years with Karajan, and suggesting that her career as a soprano is perhaps best considered a period of preparation for her real career as a mezzo.

—David Patrick Stearns

DE SABATA, Victor [Vittorio].

Conductor/Composer. Born 10 April 1892, in Trieste. Died 11 December 1967, in Santa Margherita, Ligure. Studied with Michele Saladino and Giacomo Orefice at the Milan Conservatory, 1901-11; performances of his opera *Il macigno,* 1917, and his tone poem *Juventus,* 1919, at the Teatro alla Scala; conducting debut at the first performance of Ravel's *L'enfant et les sortilèges,* 1925; conducted concerts in New York and Cincinnati, 1927; conducted at the Vienna State Opera, 1936; guest conductor with the Berlin Philharmonic, 1939; conducted in Switzerland and England, 1946; conducted the Chicago Symphony Orchestra, 1949; conducted a series of concerts at Carnegie Hall with the New York Philharmonic, 1950; guest conductor with the Boston Symphony Orchestra, summer 1950; conducted in numerous American cities, 1952-53; conducted at the funeral of Toscanini, 18 February 1957.

Publications

About DE SABATA: books–

Mucci, R. *Vittorio de Sabata.* Lanciano, 1937.
Celli, T. *L'arte di Vittorio de Sabata.* Turin, 1978.

*   *   *

"Toscanini was the magician who illuminated my youth." Thus Victor De Sabata, speaking on the death of his elder colleague in 1957. In much of De Sabata's career one can discern the influence of Toscanini—in De Sabata's musical taste, his approach to conducting, and his sense of theater. Like Toscanini, he divided his professional life equally between the operatic and the symphonic repertoire, but unlike Toscanini, De Sabata came to conducting at the relatively late age of twenty-six, after studying composition, even having an opera, *Il macigno*, performed at the Teatro alla Scala in Milan.

Following a ten-year apprenticeship in charge of the Italian wing of the Monte Carlo Opera, where his father had long-been the chorus master, and where he conducted the world premiere of Ravel's *L'enfant et les sortilèges*, De Sabata was called on to replace Toscanini at La Scala. Though as staunchly antifascist as his predecessor (he later became the first former "enemy" musician to perform in London after World War II), De Sabata's innate diplomatic reserve protected him almost to the end of the war, when for a time he was obliged to hide from the authorities in Rome.

At La Scala, De Sabata inherited Toscanini's repertoire, one which he himself preferred as well—late Verdi, Wagner, contemporary Italians such as Pizzetti, and masters of orchestration such as Berlioz and Richard Strauss. After the war he resumed his connection with La Scala, broadening his repertoire to include more Puccini and middle-period Verdi, and evenhandedly supporting the careers of both Renata Tebaldi and Maria Callas at a time when their partisans were becoming alarmingly bellicose. A major heart attack in late 1953 effectively ended his conducting career. Following it, he appeared once in the recording studio for Verdi's *Messa da Requiem* (and "to show that I'm still alive," as he later said), and once in public, conducting the La Scala orchestra at Toscanini's Milan funeral.

De Sabata's few opera recordings include the miraculous Callas-Di Stefano *Tosca*, which Leonard Bernstein was not alone in calling "the best recording of an Italian opera ever made," a thrillingly conducted but erratically sung "live" *Tristan und Isolde*, an effervescent *Falstaff* marred by the limitations of home-recorded broadcasts in 1950, and an overly-tense, heavily-cut *Il barbiere di Siviglia*. These recordings reveal De Sabata's understanding of orchestral texture and his ability to convey the most complex orchestration with extraordinary clarity and without sacrificing dramatic force and architectural tension, especially the *Tosca* and the *Tristan*. Unlike his hero, however, De Sabata could be remarkably responsive to an intelligent singer's interpretive powers. Renata Tebaldi recalls that during a rehearsal of Verdi's *Otello*, he instructed the orchestra "to breathe the way Tebaldi breathes."

Though ahead of (perhaps "above" is a better word) his time in many ways, De Sabata shared Toscanini's acceptance of certain traditional cuts, even in his favorite works, as the *Barbiere* and *Tristan* recordings reveal. On the podium he was demonstrative rather than reserved, but in a naturally kinetic response to the music rather than as an affectation. Both singers and orchestra players remember his ability to give cues with only a flash of his eloquent, piercing eyes. In rehearsal, those eyes and his caustic tongue were feared, though with his innate dignity he was not prone to the sometimes infantile behavior of his hero.

Besides leaving behind a too-small but remarkably revelatory group of recordings, both operatic and symphonic, De Sabata's influence is as evident on the subsequent generation of Italian conductors as Toscanini's was on him. Carlo Maria

Giulini and Gianandrea Gavazzeni have given touching testimonies to that fact, and De Sabata's mark can also be felt in the dedication and selflessness with which Claudio Abbado and Riccardo Muti approach their commitments. De Sabata bore the flame and increased its light.

—William J. Collins

DESTINN, Emmy [born Ema Pavlína Kittlová].

Soprano. Born 26 February 1878, in Prague. Died 28 January 1930, in Česke Budějovice. Married air force officer Joseph Halsbach, 1923. Studied with Marie Loewe-Destinn, whose name she adopted; debut as Santuzza in Berlin Kroll Opera, 1898, launched her international career; remained in Berlin until 1908, where she sang the first Salome in 1906; her debut as Senta at Bayreuth in 1901; Covent Garden debut as Donna Anna, 1904, and returned every season until 1914; debut at Metropolitan Opera as Aida, 1908, and sang regularly at Met until 1916 and in 1919-21; created Minnie in *La fanciulla del West*, Met, 1910; Chicago debut as Gioconda, 1915; return to native Bohemia during World War I; arrested for her Czech nationalist views during war; wrote the drama *Rahel* as well as novels and poetry; also a composer.

Publications

About DESTINN: books–

Rektorys, A. *Emy Destinnová*. Prague 1936.
Martinkova, M. *Život Emy Destinnové* [Life of Emma Destinn]. Plzeň, 1946.
Rektorys, A., ed. *Korespondence Leoše Janáčka s Gabrielou Horvátovou*. Prague, 1950.
Kopecký, E. and V. Pospíšil. *Slavni pěvci Národniho divadla* [National Theater singers]. Prague, 1968.
Pospíšil, M. *Veliké srdce: život a uměni Emy Destinové* [Destinn's life and art]. Prague, 1974.

articles–

Prexlerova, B. and M. Beutlova. "Ema Destinnová jako ucitelka" (Destinn as teacher). *Hudebni rozhledy* 11 (1958): 1031.
Rektorys, A. and J. Dennis. "Emma Destinn." *Record Collector* 20 (1971): 5.

*   *   *

Emmy Destinn ranks as one of the very greatest dramatic sopranos of the twentieth century. Born Ema Kittlová she adopted the name Destinn as a tribute to her teacher Marie Loewe Destinn. In this she was probably impelled by a need in the German operatic world to divert attention from her Czech origin. She remained a fervent Czech nationalist and after the creation of independent Czechoslovakia in 1918 she used the name Destinnova.

After being rejected by the Czech opera in Prague and at Dresden, she was engaged by the Berlin Opera and made her debut in the role of Santuzza in *Cavalleria rusticana* in 1898 at the age of 20 at the Kroll Theater. She was hailed by critics and compared favorably to the great Bellincioni, who had

Emmy Destinn as Carmen, Königliche Oper, Berlin, 1906

created the role. She soon appeared at the main Berlin house, the Hofoper and was to remain there for a decade, appearing in more than fifty different roles, usually singing several times a week. Throughout her career Destinn was a prodigous worker. She was later to complain of infrequency of appearances during her time with the Metropolitan Opera and looked back blissfully to singing several times a week in Berlin. In fact she appeared in 339 Metropolitan performances between 1908 and 1920, extensively at Covent Garden during the same period, and still giving some guest performances in Berlin and a few elsewhere. It seems probable that in her career on the operatic stage Destinn gave well over 1500 performances.

Destinn's versatility was also remarkable. Her debut in Berlin was in verismo. In 1901 she sang the role of Senta in *Die fliegende Holländer* at Bayreuth. According to the critic Oskar Bie her "silver toned instrument, full of sensuous charm throughout its entire compass was allied to impeccable technique in attack." In 1904 her first role at Covent Garden was Donna Anna in *Don Giovanni*. Hermann Klein thought her very nearly perfect—"surely, I thought, an artist capable of success at the outset in this most exacting of roles will one day stand in the royal line of dramatic sopranos." Although Destinn was to become an enormous popular favorite at Covent Garden, her career did not proceed quite in the direction anticipated by Klein. She was to appear in nearly 200 performances of 17 operas of which 60 were as Madame Butterfly, which she was the first to sing in London. Her debut in the USA was in yet another operatic role as Aïda. According

to Sydney Homer, whose wife Louise was singing Amneris that night, Destinn's was "a new and unique voice . . . the medium like some new woodwind instrument . . . a legato like a river of sound."

The year 1908 stands out as a kind of *annus mirabilis* in Destinn's career. In that year she had to break with the Berlin Hofoper when she was refused leave to sing with the Metropolitan Opera. Before crossing the Atlantic for the first time, she returned in triumph to Prague. She had left in 1898 unable to secure a contract and had given only a smattering of performances there since, but now returned as an international star. She appeared in *Aïda, Der fliegende Holländer, The Bartered Bride, Cavalleria rusticana, I pagliacci* and *Dalibor*. In the dungeon scene of *Dalibor* she was "strong, heroic, carrying all before her . . . voice ringing out like a church bell." During the same year Destinn also made 83 records—a third of her total output.

The voice on the best of her records is instantly recognizable. There is a warm throb in the middle of her voice allied to an exciting dramatic intensity, much in evidence in a recording of Tosca's prayer. Evenness throughout the register is demonstrated in early recordings, particularly as Donna Anna and Aïda. There is a rare lyric beauty in one of the lesser known arias from *Der Freischütz* "Und ob die Wolke." By way of contrast there is incredible verve and bite in Destinn's rendition of Milada's aria from *Dalibor*—the Czech language version has a peculiarly blazing intensity.

Destinn gave prodigously of her talents. The war had a considerable impact on her life and career and for a time she was interned by the Austro-Hungarian government as a Czech national sympathizer. She returned to Covent Garden in 1919 but without the same success as previously. She made a number of appearances at the Czech National Opera in Prague, and there were also concerts although this was hardly the medium for Destinn's talents.

Evidence of a singer's status can be derived from records and published criticism. But a further acid test of status lies in the testimony of fellow artists. Geraldine Farrar commented on Destinn's fine voice and musicianship. Lotte Lehmann was "nearly distracted (as) I had listened to that angelic voice." Frances Alda remarked: "hers was one of the greatest voices and she was one of the greatest singers . . . nobody ever sang Butterfly as Destinn did . . . her manner of singing was so perfect, her voice so divine . . . all these made her unforgettable."

—Stanley Henig

LES DEUX JOURNÉES [The Two Days].

Composer: Luigi Cherubini.

Librettist: Jean-Nicolas Bouilly.

First Performance: Théâtre Feydeau, 16 January 1800.

Roles: Armand (tenor); Constance (soprano); Mikéli (bass); Daniel (bass); Antonio (tenor); Marcellina (soprano); Sémos (bass); Angélina (soprano); Two Officers (basses); Officer of the Guard (mute); Two Italian Soldiers (basses); A Young Woman (soprano); chorus.

Publications

book–

Selden, Margery J.S. *The French Operas of Luigi Cherubini.* New Haven, Connecticut, 1951; 1972.

article–

Cianchi, Emilio. "Cenno analitico sopra *Le Due Giornate,* opera teatrale di Luigi Cherubini." *Atti dell' Accademia del Regio Istituto musicale de Firenze* 1 (1863): 31.

* * *

Act I of Cherubini's *Les Deux Journées,* set in Paris in the year 1647, shows three people waiting at home for the water carrier Mikéli: his ailing father, his daughter Marcellina, and his son Antonio. In a chanson Antonio tells the story of a Frenchman who saved the life of a Savoyard. Antonio, himself a Savoyard, was saved by a Frenchman six years ago without ever discovering the identity of his rescuer. Mikéli arrives and the others leave to obtain passports for their journey to Gonesse, where Antonio's wedding is to take place. Having been invited to stay by Mikéli, Armand, the president of the French parliament, and his wife Constance reach the house pursued by Mazarin's soldiers. Mikéli presents the couple as his own father and daughter when the police arrive

to search the house. On his return Antonio recognizes Armand as the man who saved his life. They persuade Marcellina to hand her passport over to Constance so that she can try to escape from Paris.

In act II, which takes place the next morning, Constance and Antonio are stopped at the city gate by the police as her appearance does not match the description in the passport; but the officer who had led the search of their house on the previous evening confirms that she is Mikéli's daughter. Mikéli himself appears with a large water barrel on a cart. Asked whether he has seen any enemy, he directs the soldiers towards the city. Unobserved by the soldiers he opens the barrel and Armand jumps out to escape from Paris.

In act III, set in Gonesse, a village near Paris, the village people assemble to celebrate Antonio's forthcoming marriage to Angélina. Antonio, who has brought Armand and Constance with him on a secret path, hides Armand in a hollow tree and presents Constance as his sister to Angélina's family. Soldiers arrive demanding free board and lodging at her father's house. Constance attempts to bring some food to her husband, but she is interrupted by two soldiers who want to abduct her. Armand rushes to her rescue, both are captured, and their identity is revealed. As Armand and Constance are led to prison, Mikéli arrives with a letter of amnesty granted to Armand by the queen. All unite to celebrate the victory of "humanité."

After *Médée* (1797) which was Cherubini's greatest achievement in the genre of serious opera, he turned towards comic opera in *L'hôtellerie portugaise* (1798). His change in subject matter and compositional style was confirmed when *Les deux journées* became his greatest overall success. *Les deux journées* resembles an *opéra-comique* in that musical numbers are separated by spoken dialogue. In fact, some of the most dramatic scenes take place in spoken form. The musical setting also rejects the high drama characteristic of *Médée.* Except for the good natured, patriarchal, and witty Mikéli, the characters do not display much personality. Neither has the couple Antonio and Angélina the opportunity to manifest their longing for each other, nor are Armand and Constance given the chance to protest against their enemies as do, for example, Fidelio and Florestan in Beethoven's opera. Arias are noticeably absent from Cherubini's opera. Rather, the protagonists express themselves in *chansons* with easy tunes, *mélodrames* or as part of ensembles. It is quite possible that such a distribution of roles was intended as a musical demonstration of the reconciliation between social classes in the aftermath of the French Revolution: not only the nobility but people of all classes should be given a chance to sing. However, the expression of individual sentiments seems intentionally subordinated to an ethical ideal which lies at the heart of this opera. To this end Cherubini used the refrain of the opening chanson as the reminiscence-motif of the opera (it further occurs in numbers 8 and 14). While the plot unfolds the refrain reminds us of the moral of *Les deux journées:* "A good action is never done in vain" ("Un bienfait n'est jamais perdu").

The use of non-operatic vocal forms is to a certain degree compensated for by a dramatic duo in act I, written in the style of Gluck, and above all by the ensemble finales to all three acts, which clearly form the musical highlights of this opera. In the first and third act the ensemble finales are composed with attention being paid to every detail in the dramatic development. Cherubini's orchestration is particularly remarkable. Yet in the finale to the first act there is a lack of real action, which composer and librettist compensated for with an ensemble of singers pressing the obstinate Marcellina to change her mind. The finale to the third act is very effective. The tension builds up to a *tableau générale* when Armand draws his pistol. The *choeur générale* at the end cannot disguise the fact that the happy ending is achieved by a *deus ex machina* of monarchic origin.

The opera was highly acclaimed at the time of its premiere, and it was particularly successful in France and Germany throughout the nineteenth century. Goethe found "the subject so perfect that, if given as a mere drama, without music, it could be seen with pleasure." It is still occasionally revived, for example in Paris at the Opéra-Comique in 1980.

—Michael Fend

THE DEVIL AND KATE [Čert a Káča].

Composer: Antonín Dvořák.

Librettist: A. Wenig (after a Czech fairy tale).

First Performance: Prague, National Theater, 23 November 1899.

Roles: Kate (mezzo-soprano); Princess (soprano); Marbuel (bass or bass-baritone); Jirka (tenor); Kate's Mother (contralto); Chambermaid (soprano); Lucifer (bass); Gatekeeper (baritone); Marshal (baritone); Musician (baritone); chorus (SATB) (TTBB).

Publications

article–

Bykovskih, Majja. "Narodno-fantastičeskaja osnova soderžanija opery *Čert a Káča*" [Folk and fairy tale elements in *Kate and the Devil*]. In *Issledovanie istoričeskogo processa klassičeskoj i sovremennoj zarubežnoj musyki,* edited by Tamara Cytovic. Moscow, 1980.

unpublished–

Bykovskih, Majja. "Principy dramaturgii pozdnih oper Antonína Dvorzaka *Čert i Káča* i *Rusalka*" [principles of dramaturgy in Antonín Dvořák's later operas *Kate and the Devil* and *Rusalka*]. Ph.D. dissertation, Gosudarstvennaja Konservatorija, Moscow, 1984.

The first act of *The Devil and Kate* takes place in the village of Mokra Lhota. After the overture, a gathering of farm hands and peasants performs dances at the county fair. With the entrance of the shepherd Jirka, the conversation turns to the treatment they all receive from the ruling Princess and her right-hand man. The crowd agrees that their employers are cruel people who drive them mercilessly.

Kate enters with her mother and sits down at a table. She is angry that nobody will ask her to dance, until a stranger dressed as a hunter approaches. Something about him makes everyone uneasy, particularly when he inquires casually about the treatment they receive at the hands of the Princess and the Steward. On hearing their negative reactions to his questions, the man, who identifies himself as Marbuel, turns to Kate and proceeds to charm her. He invites her to dance and she accepts enthusiastically. They dance with a strange intensity and the people are fascinated. Finally the dance ends and Kate is totally exhausted but very happy. Seeing this, Marbuel invites her to live in his town, which he describes as a place of delightful warmth, bright lights, and constant exciting activity. After some momentary doubts, Kate accepts the invitation and jumps onto Marbuel's back to be carried away. Suddenly Marbuel stamps his foot and in a haze of fire and smoke, the earth opens under his feet. To the intense dismay of all present, he and Kate disappear into the bowels of the earth. Jirka volunteers to descend the gaping hole in the earth to Hell, there to rescue Kate.

The second act is set in Hell, where card-playing and generally coarse behavior are the main activities, and the scene is noisy. The assembled crowd breaks into a ribald hymn to gold and its power to corrupt human beings, at which point Lucifer enters much irritated by the noise. He demands silence and then asks whether Marbuel has returned. Marbuel enters, still carrying Kate on his back. He can't get her off his back because of a cross she wears; it is making his load terribly heavy. Kate is not amused that "his town" has turned out to be Hell, and demands to be taken back as she came, on his back. He will do this, but must first rest. Jirka arrives, the rescue of Kate uppermost in his mind, but she is still stubbornly on Marbuel's back and too mad to think of rescue or the shepherd. Lucifer suggests diverting her with gold, so Marbuel gets the gold and she pounces on it, thus releasing Marbuel. In the meantime, Lucifer asks for a report from Marbuel about the Princess and the Steward. Marbuel relates that they are both pretty poor rulers but that the Princess is the worst of the two. Lucifer rules that she must be consigned to Hell, and that the Steward will be given one last chance.

Act III takes us back to the Princess' castle. The Princess is unhappy at hearing (erroneously) that the Steward has been taken to Hell. Full of remorse for her past actions and attitudes, she longs now to rule justly. The Shepherd appears and she pleads with him to save her from Marbuel. The Shepherd makes her promise that she will deal fairly with the townfolk, and her marshal makes a public announcement to that effect.

But Marbuel is to arrive soon, so the Shepherd arranges to hide Kate in a corner, and use her as a secret weapon against Marbuel. He arrives and announces to the Princess that she must return to Hell with him. Kate jumps out at Marbuel who is suddenly paralyzed with fear. The Princess and her evil ways he can handle, but Kate is just too much, so he flees for his life. All congratulate the Shepherd for his clever plan which has rescued the Princess, and he is now in a position to receive all the riches he desires. The Princess offers Kate much the same reward, and Kate observes that, looks or no looks, she will no longer lack dancing partners or marriage proposals. The opera ends with shouts of "slava" to the reconstructed Princess.

The Devil and Kate belongs to an unusual operatic genre, the fantasy-comedy. Neither Dvořák nor his librettist attempts any serious portrayal of Hell, and the characters and scenes found there are comic, or, at most, ironic. As for the village folk, they are just that—salt of the earth. It is their spirit that Dvořák mines, their dances, their music, their prosaic concerns. As with so many Czech operas, the people are Czech national types, and they are sympathetically depicted in *The Devil and Kate.* Curiously, even the underworld people project an aura of "Czechishness."

This is important to remember, for it gives Dvořák a chance to write music which is strongly dance and folk-inspired. One sees this in two places, in the orchestral writing and in the choral music. Surprisingly, Dvořák's inimitable melodic gifts are not usually to be found in the solo vocal lines. In fact, there is only one set piece, the Princess' third act aria, and the rest is in, for lack of better terminology, a sort of expressive recitative style. Meanwhile, however, there is that shimmering orchestra, a richness of melody in the dances, and a developmental skill available only to a master symphonist. And there are those marvelous choruses. This is not, then, a typical singer's opera—no thrilling vocal acrobatics, exciting high notes, and so forth. If a singer is to be effective, it must be by sharp character portrayal. The role of Kate is an exceptional vehicle for any mezzo-soprano with gifts for comedy. Marbuel, too, is a role of immense charm laced with moments of comic villainy. Lucifer's is a cameo role which can be truly terrifying if done well.

—Harris Crohn

THE DEVILS OF LOUDON [Diably z Loudon].

Composer: Krzysztof Penderecki.

Librettist: Krzysztof Penderecki (after Huxley/Whiting).

First Performance: Hamburg, Staatsoper, 20 June 1969.

Roles: Sister Jeanne of the Angels (soprano); Urbain Grandier (baritone); Father Barré (bass); De Laubardemont (tenor); Father Rangier (bass); Adam (tenor); Mannoury (baritone); Ninon (contralto); Philippe (soprano); Prince Henri de Condé (tenor); Gabrielle (soprano); Claire (mezzo-soprano); Louise (contralto); Father Mignon (bass); Father Ambrose (bass); Bontemps (bass-baritone); Mayor Jean D'Armagnac (speaking); Guillaume de Cerisay (speaking); chorus (SATB).

Publications

article–

interview in *Opera News* 33/no. 27 (1969).

*   *   *

The Devils of Loudon, Krzysztof Penderecki's first opera, was commissioned by the Hamburg Opera, which premiered it on 20 June 1969. The composer wrote his own libretto based on Aldous Huxley's documentary novel *The Devils of Loudon* (published in 1952 with a translation by Erich Fried) and John Whiting's play *The Devils,* first produced in London at the Aldwych Theatre in 1961. Although Penderecki depended substantially on Whiting's dramatization, he kept close to historical facts rather than the dramatic means employed by the playwright.

Penderecki's penchant for seeking momentous subject matter for his compositional activity suggests the impact on his social consciousness of many tragic events in the contemporary world. In *The Devils of Loudon* he addresses such topics as intolerance, the manipulation of truth, and the persecution of the individual by external forces and by the ignorance and injustice of society. The composer prefaced his score with the political and religious truth "DAEMONI, ETIAM VERA DICENTI, NON EST CREDENDUM (The devil cannot be believed even when he tells the truth)." The tragedy of all men is present in the intolerance shown to one man.

The story deals with the witchcraft trial, torture, and execution of Father Urbain Grandier, who was burned at the stake in Loudon on 18 August 1634. Ostensibly, Grandier was found guilty because of his confession under torture (actually, he refused repeatedly to confess despite the fact that his legs were smashed until the marrow ran from his bones); but in reality, it was Grandier's self-destructive egotism and powerful political prowess, dangerous to both church and state in seventeenth-century France, which condemned him.

According to Huxley's study of the morbid psychology underlying the circumstances, Grandier's flaunting of his sexual adventures, his making personal enemies with his cutting wit, enraging the Carmelites and Capuchins with his pulpit eloquence, and assuming an oppositional political position, all led him to martyrdom. Ironically, he was accused of demonic possession by a neurotic hunchbacked prioress he had never even met. Enticed by the rumors of his sexual indiscretions, she had invited Grandier to take a position in her convent. When Grandier rejected her, her love turned quickly to hate and vengeful action.

Thus Penderecki's highly charged libretto supports many levels of action and characterization interwoven with multifarious political, religious, and social ramifications. In an interview published in *Opera News* (1969), the composer explains that he approached writing the libretto like a movie script. Attracted to dramatic-literary sources, he wrote any number of scores for film and theater from 1955 to 1966. For his first operatic venture he stretched his various musical, dramatic, and linguistic resources completely, often to the most extreme ends.

Penderecki decided to work with the Erich Fried translation since German is an operatic language and the work would be premiered in a German opera house. (In the American premiere at Santa Fe, the English version adapted from Whiting's play was used.) However, Latin is always the language of the chorus in every version, not only because phonetically it was attractive to the composer, but also because it gave him an aesthetic distance from the text, which he needed in order to project its multi-functional and actively atmospheric role, reminiscent of Greek tragedy.

In his search for the creation of an authentic musical environment as background for the dramatic action, Penderecki describes his use of quotations from a Black Mass, which he found "on a dusty shelf of a monastery in Cracow," as well as from the Mass Book, "The Gruesome *Litany of Christ's Blood*," which is sung during the torture scene.

Penderecki finds nothing irreligious in his opera, although some audiences took exception to the love scene between Grandier and the young Widow Ninon, naked in an old bath tub. The nudity in this scene and in the exorcism sequence, during which the nuns rip off their habits, shocked some viewers (particularly after the Stuttgart premiere) and prompted criticism of the composer for seeking sensational effects.

Although the opera was commissioned after the premiere and worldwide acclaim of his *St Luke's Passion,* Penderecki stated that he had contemplated this opera long before the *Passion* and that both works are, in a sense, related in their focus on the elements of religious mystery and exorcism. The passion of St Luke, conceived as Stations of the Cross, parallels the passion of Grandier.

In the flow of the opera's thirty brief, self-contained scenes (suggestive in concept of Berg's *Wozzeck*), each vignette presents the composer with a vehicle for the fullest exploitation of his dynamic and expressionist musical language. According to Penderecki, of paramount importance is the creation of an atmosphere with a spectrum of sound supportive of the dramatic environment and circumstances in which the individual characters find themselves. However, critically speaking, against this intensely illustrative sonic background, character definition tends to become unfocused instead of being developed. It is as if this spectrum of sound as an extended musical means proportioned according to the great range of dramatic situations becomes an essential and powerful constituent to heighten the effect of the drama and to clarify the complexities of the plot. However, it often overshadows the characterization of the human participants.

Vocally, in addition to both free and rhythmically measured dialogue and monologue, declamatory recitative, solo and ensemble singing, Penderecki requires the chorus to scream, roar, laugh, chatter, as well as intone Gregorian chant. The huge orchestra—forty-two strings, thirty-two wind instruments including saxophones, a large battery of percussion plus organ, harmonium, piano, harp, electric guitar—is seldom used at full strength but provides a plethora of musical sound-painting with its individual instrumental combinations, tone clusters in quarter tones, glissandi, extreme ranges, and is designed to respond to whatever intensity or expressivity is demanded. The invention of special notational signs by the composer was necessary in order to accommodate his innovative vocal and instrumental techniques. Thus, having exploited and developed new sonic resources originated by Boulez, Xenakis, Stockhausen, and other avant-gardists, as well as his extensions of microtonality and the post-serialism of the Vienna School, Penderecki has been called the complete eclectic.

Predictably, the climax of this music drama is reached in the Aristotelian manner of a catharsis of fear and pity. At the end, the protagonist Grandier, who had previously squandered his honor, is prepared to endure excruciating agony and go to the stake forgiving his enemies for the sake of his own self-respect. Moreover, according to Huxley's sociopsychological theory of transcendence, Grandier's search for God, which led him to pursue life experience at all of its levels, is finally realized, in his passion for the truth.

—Muriel Hebert Wolf

LE DEVIN DU VILLAGE [The Village Soothsayer].

Composer: Jean-Jacques Rousseau.

First Performance: Fontainebleau, 18 October 1752.

Publications

book–

Mooser, A. *Pygmalion et Le devin du village en Russie au XVIIIe siècle.* Geneva, 1946.

Frontispiece to Rousseau's *Le devin du village,* first edition of score, 1753

articles–

Arnheim, A. "Le devin du village von J.J. Rousseau und die Parodie 'Les amours de Bastien et Bastienne'." *Sammelbände der Internationalen Musik-Gesellschaft* 4 (1902-03): 686.
Lichtenhahn, Ernst. "Jean Jacques Rousseau: *Le devin du village.*" *Schweizerische Musikzeitung/Revue musicale suisse* 119 (1979): 299.
Thacher, Christopher. "Rousseau's *Devin du village.*" In *Das deutsche Singspiel im 18. Jahrhundert,* edited by Renate Schusky, 119. Heidelberg, 1981.

*　　*　　*

Le devin du Village, the only surviving opera by Rousseau, has been sufficient to earn him a place in the history of music. It was composed during 1751, and was first performed the following year. At once a great success, its light, tuneful style, together with the pastoral comic plot, kept it in the repertoire in Paris until well into the nineteenth century. It was written at a time when public taste was turning away from the highly ornamented and formal style of the baroque towards a simpler style, based on folk melodies.

Le devin du Village was one of two works which were held up as models of the new style, the other being *La Serva Padrona* by Pergolesi. This Italian style was opposed to the French style of Rameau as seen in the *tragédie lyrique.* While for Rousseau the central issue was to reinstate the primacy of melody over harmony, a second distinction can be found in the subject matter. Opera had gradually turned into a spectacle, where the dramatic line was buried under a series of set pieces and ballet scenes, loosely tied to a story concerned with classical myths. By contrast *Le devin du Village*, set in a country village, has as its central characters a shepherd and shepherdess and requires the simplest means for its performance. In its idealized portrait of rural life, it is virtually as artificial as the scenes it replaced, but within its limits it marks a move back to nature. It is also very short, like an Italian intermezzo, lasting about an hour, and the drama unfolds at a reasonably fast pace. While there was a French tradition of light opera in the vaudeville, Rousseau broke with its conventions by linking the songs with sung recitatives rather than with spoken dialogue.

The story of *Le devin du Village* centers on Colin and Colette. As the opera opens, Colette laments the fact that Colin has deserted her for another. Oddly, the melody is pastoral and in a major key, so that the effect is above all charming rather than tragic. Colette visits the village soothsayer, who tells her that Colin, while having been led astray by another woman, in actuality still loves Colette. She reflects that it is easy, even without beauty, to win a man through the artifices of elegant clothes and jewels. The Soothsayer advises her to feign indifference, and Colin will be sure to return. She leaves, and in a little monologue the Soothsayer reveals that this gives him an opportunity to pay back the lady of the town, though for what reason we are not told. We are clearly expected to feel sympathy for the true emotions of the countrydwellers, as opposed to the superficiality of those who live in the town.

Colin returns, expecting to resume his relationship with Colette. He is dumbfounded when the Soothsayer tells him she prefers another, a man from the town. Colin pleads for help from the Soothsayer, who casts a spell to make Colette pass by. The fraud is transparent to the audience, for in an aside he makes it clear that she is nearby, waiting for him to tell her how to respond. Nevertheless, he offers Colin, and us, the homily that "with a kind and faithful heart all is possible." While Colin awaits her entrance, he has a song in which he claims that her favors mean more to him than all the wealth of the world.

Colette then appears, and Colin tells her that he has recognized the error of his ways, and that he will be faithful to her. Not so easily won, she tells him of her new lover in the town. There follows a simple duet in a minor key, which avoids any real intensity. In desperation Colin throws himself at her feet, at which point she relents, presenting him with a ribbon as a token of their union. There is a second duet, as might be expected in the major, on their happiness and the joys of marriage.

The Soothsayer returns, claiming to be responsible for opening their eyes to the truth, and a chorus of villagers sing his praises and celebrate the reunion of the lovers. At this point the drama really has finished, but appended to this is a series of dances, solos for Colin and Colette, a pantomime, set to a series of musical dances in which a version of the story is acted out again, a rondeau in which each of the characters comes forward in the verse to sum up the story from his or her point of view, and then all join in the chorus. The entertainment is rounded off by yet more dancing.

—Robin Hartwell

DEXTER, John.

Director. Born 2 August 1925, in Derby, England. Died 23 March 1990. Worked as actor for BBC; director of English Stage Company, 1957; director of National Theatre 1963-66, 1971-75; operatic debut, *Benvenuto Cellini*, Royal Opera, Covent Garden, 1966; subsequent productions in London, Paris and Hamburg included *Billy Budd, Boris Godunov, Les vêpres siciliennes, Aida* and *Un ballo in maschera;* director of productions, Metropolitan Opera, 1974-1981, where his productions included *Lulu* (1977), *Parade* (1981), and *Dialogues of the Carmelites.*

Publications

About DEXTER: books–

Jacobsen, Robert. *Magnificence: Onstage at the Met.* New York, 1985.

articles–

Marx, Robert. "Working Radical: John Dexter, 1925-1990." *Opera News* May (1990).

John Dexter's first involvement in opera production was at Covent Garden in 1966, when he produced Berlioz's *Benvenuto Cellini,* the lavish, spectacular staging of a highly dramatic work. It was three years before he directed another opera, this time Verdi's *Les vêpres siciliennes* for the Hamburg State Opera. His approach was very different: an abstract set forced him to concentrate, not on spectacle or violent action, but on the complex relationships between the chief characters. Despite its austerity, this production was highly successful; recreated at the Metropolitan Opera, and the Paris Opera in 1974, the staging still aroused admiration; but revived by English National Opera at the London Coliseum ten years later, it appeared somewhat dated.

Dexter staged three other operas at Hamburg: two twentieth-century works with powerfully dramatic plots laid in all-male establishments, the Siberian prison camp of Janáček's *From the House of the Dead* and the scarcely less brutal scene on board HMS Indomitable in Britten's *Billy Budd;* and Verdi's *Un ballo in maschera,* set in the Southern States during the American Civil War. These productions all demonstrated the director's superb handling of large crowds on stage. In London Dexter staged the first British production of *The Devils* (opera by Penderecki based on John Whiting's play) for English National Opera, a subtle treatment of a difficult and, to some members of the audience, a shocking subject.

Appointed director of productions at the Metropolitan Opera after the success of *Les vêpres siciliennes,* Dexter first re-staged an old production of Verdi's *La forza del destino,* then produced a new *Aida,* widely renowned for its torch-lit procession in the triumphal scene. In Meyerbeer's grand opera *Le prophète* and the five-act version of Verdi's *Don Carlos,* his management of large-scale crowd scenes was once more greatly admired, but the most highly acclaimed productions of his years at the Metropolitan were undoubtedly Berg's *Lulu* (given originally in the two-act version and later adapted for the complete, three-act version) and Kurt Weill's *Rise and Fall of the City of Mahagonny,* sung in English. These operas gave him ample opportunity to employ the tautly

John Dexter's production of *Billy Budd* for Hamburg Oper, 1972

dramatic style evolved during the latter part of his career. In sharp contrast, two triple bills, staged in collaboration with David Hockney, provided few chances for the director to exercise his unique talent for characterization.

After he left the Metropolitan Opera Dexter worked only rarely in the lyric theater, but his twenty years of involvement in opera had a wholly beneficial influence on his contemporaries and successors. His careful attention to detail was legendary, while an acute dramatic perception enabled him to discern instantly the essential spirit of an opera or play. An example of this perception was offered by *Les dialogues des Carmélites* first staged in New York, then in San Francisco and finally in Paris. Poulenc's moving account of the nuns guillotined during the French Revolution was treated with fastidious restraint as well as sympathy, thereby gaining greatly in effectiveness.

—Elizabeth Forbes

DIALOGUES DES CARMÉLITES [Dialogues of the Carmelites].

Composer: Francis Poulenc.

Librettist: Francis Poulenc (after Georges Bernanos).

First Performance: Milan, Teatro alla Scala, 26 January 1957.

Roles: Blanche de la Force (soprano); Prioress (contralto); Madame Lidoine (soprano); Mother Marie (mezzo-soprano); Sister Constance (soprano); Chevalier de la Force (tenor); Marquis de la Force (baritone); Mother Jeanne (contralto); Sister Mathilde (mezzo-soprano); Father Confessor (tenor); Two Officers (tenor, baritone); Jailer (baritone); Thierry (baritone); M Javelinot (baritone); chorus (SSAATTBB).

Publications

books–

Catalogue de l'exposition à Tours: Georges Bernanos, Francis Poulenc et les "Dialogues des Carmélites." Paris, 1970.
Bernanos, Georges. *Francis Poulenc et les "Dialogues des Carmélites."* Paris, 1970.

articles–

La Maestre, André Espiau de. "Francis Poulenc und seine Bernanos-Oper." *Österreichische Musikzeitschrift* 14 (1959).
Avant-scène opéra 52 (1983) [*Dialogues des Carmélites* and *La voix humaine* issue].

*   *   *

In March of 1953, Francis Poulenc arrived in Milan while on a brief concert tour with Pierre Fournier, the cellist for whom he had written a 1948 sonata. He called at the offices of Ricordi to discuss a ballet on the life of Saint Margaret of Cortona, which the publishing company had commissioned from him for a premiere at the Teatro alla Scala. He informed the director that Saint Margaret simply did not inspire him; Ricordi countered with George Bernanos' *Dialogues des Carmélites,* a play Poulenc had seen. Suddenly, it seemed like the perfect libretto: "I can see myself sitting in a café, devouring Bernanos' drama, and saying to myself at each scene, 'But of course, it's made for me, it's made for me.' "

Poulenc made the few cuts he felt were necessary to adapt the play into a libretto during his train ride back to Paris. He then immersed himself in the lives and thoughts of the Carmelite nuns, reading extensively about them and visiting their convents. His letters to friends during the fall of 1953 reveal his obsession with the subject matter: "I am working like a madman—I don't go out, I see no one—I am composing a tableau (scene) each week. I no longer recognize myself. I am so obsessed with my subject that I am beginning to believe that I knew these women."

The "women" were the entire order of Carmelite nuns from the Compiègne convent, who, having been found "enemies of the people," were publicly guillotined in Paris on 17 July 1794, during the last days of the Reign of Terror. Their story leading up to this execution is contained in the memoirs of Mother Marie, the only member of the order not to face the blade that day. Her memoirs were expanded into a novella, *Die Letzte am Schafott* (*The Last on the Scaffold*), by the German novelist Gertrud von Le Fort. In 1947, the Reverend Raymond Bruckberger and French producer Philippe Agostini decided to make a film version of Le Fort's novella. They called upon Georges Bernanos to write the dialogue, and he agreed reluctantly, for he had never before worked in the film medium. But the producers soon canceled the project, expressing dissatisfaction with the screenplay. Bernanos' "dialogues" survived, however, and were arranged for the stage after his death by his friend and executor, Albert Beguin.

Bernanos's story focuses on a fictitious character, the aristocratic Blanche de la Force, who enters the Carmelite convent to seek refuge from the horrors of the French Revolution and her own fear of death. As Sister Blanche of the Agony of Christ, however, she struggles to cope with the exigencies of religious life, with the death of her beloved Mother Superior, and with an imposed vow of martyrdom. She makes the ultimate sacrifice in a stirring conclusion, joining her fellow Sisters as they are beheaded while singing a Salve Regina which fluctuates from a quiet, sensual prayer to a sweeping cry of anguish. In a brilliant *coup de théâtre,* Poulenc has the nuns' voices drop out one by one as the blade falls, leaving Blanche's friend Constance alone as Blanche dramatically joins the procession. As the blade descends for the final time, the hushed crowd murmurs a final minor seventh chord, a harmonic "signature" of Poulenc.

The dedication of the opera tells us much about the musical sources of *Dialogues:* "to Debussy, who inspired me to compose, and to Claudio Monteverdi, Giuseppe Verdi, and Modeste Mussorgsky, who served here as my models." The emphasis on interior, psychological drama, as well as the consistently subdued mood, recall Debussy's masterful *Pelléas et Mélisande.* Furthermore, Poulenc's vocal style, which occupies a middle ground between accompanied recitative and lyric aria, owes much to the extended arioso style developed by Debussy.

The influence of Monteverdi appears in several passages, such as the introductions to act I, scene ii and act III, scene i, which are reminiscent of early seventeenth-century Italian music. In the case of Musorgsky, the influence is felt particularly in the harmonic style—various chord progressions can be traced directly to *Boris Godunov.* The same can be said of Stravinsky, a pervasive influence on Poulenc who was probably not mentioned because it was such instrumental works as the *Symphonies of Wind Instruments* (see the opening of act I, scene iii) rather than Stravinsky's operas which influenced *Dialogues.*

The imprint of Verdi is the most significant, for *Dialogues* is clearly singers' opera in the best Italian tradition. Everything in the opera is designed to glorify the solo voice: the orchestra is subtle and subdued, there is little action to detract from the singing, and ensembles are avoided (in fact, there are only two short choruses before the final choral scene). Even when an obvious opportunity for a duet presents itself, as in the scene between Blanche and her brother, Poulenc resolutely retains a dialogue format. His thirty-five years of experience as France's leading art song composer certainly served him well in this opera.

Three other striking musical characteristics of *Dialogues* bear mentioning. The opera is irrepressibly tonal, though many of the harmonies are highly colored, and parallel diminished seventh chords create an ambiguity in some of the less lyrical passages. Secondly, several phrases have taken on the role of unifying leading motives, referring, for example, to Blanche's father, to the imminence of danger, or to the concept of redemption through grace. These motives are entrusted to the orchestra, and each appears in several different tonalities. The orchestra also sets the mood for many of the twelve scenes with short preludes or more substantial interludes, reminding the listener of Britten's *Peter Grimes.*

In fact, like *Grimes, Dialogues des Carmélites* is one of the last great tonal operas in the nineteenth-century tradition. It provided Poulenc with a fine outlet to express his deep, personal religious fervor, and it remains a viable dramatic stage work with a place in the standard repertoire.

—Keith W. Daniel

DIALOGUES OF THE CARMELITES
See DIALOGUES DES CARMÉLITES

DIDO AND AENEAS.

Composer: Henry Purcell.

Librettist: Nahum Tate (after Virgil).

First Performance: London, Josias Priest's Boarding School for Young Ladies, Chelsea, December 1689.

Roles: Dido (soprano or mezzo-soprano); Aeneas (baritone); Belinda (soprano); First Woman (soprano); Second Woman (mezzo-soprano); Sorceress (mezzo-soprano); First Witch (soprano); Second Witch (soprano); Sorcerer (soprano); Sailor (tenor); chorus (SATB); chorus (SATB).

Publications

books—

Price, Curtis A., ed. *Purcell: Dido and Aeneas: an Opera.* New York, 1986.

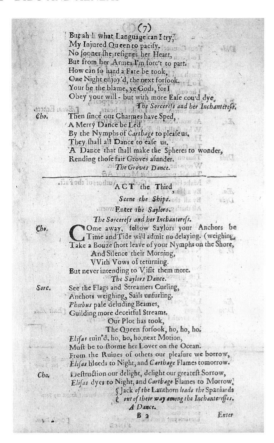

A page from the 1689 libretto of Purcell's *Dido and Aeneas* (end of act II showing Aeneas' monologue, and beginning of act III)

Harris, Ellen T. *Henry Purcell's Dido and Aeneas.* Oxford, 1987.

articles–

Squire, William Barclay. "Purcell's 'Dido and Aeneas'." *Musical Times* June (1918).
Buttrey, John. "Dating Purcell's *Dido and Aeneas.*" *Proceedings of the Royal Musical Association* 94 (1967-68): 51.
Savage, Roger, "Producing Dido and Aeneas: an Investigation into Sixteen Problems." *Early Music* 4 (1976): 393.
Avant-scène opéra November-December (1978) [*Didon et Enée* issue].
Craven, Robert R. "Nahum Tate's Third *Dido and Aeneas:* The Sources of the Libreto to Purcell's Opera." In *The World of Opera.* 1979.
Harris, Ellen T. "Recitative and Aria in *Dido and Aeneas.*" *Studies in the History of Music* 2 (1987).

*   *   *

Dido and Aeneas is Henry Purcell's only opera with continuous music. More than that, it is his only theatrical work in which the main characters are delineated directly through musical expression. His other theatrical compositions, such as *The Fairy Queen* and *King Arthur,* consist rather of a spoken play with musical interpolations of varying relevance to the drama. *Dido and Aeneas,* however, is not merely exceptional for its period and for Purcell's oeuvre in terms of its

form; it is also exceptional for all time in terms of its literary and musical quality.

The libretto of *Dido and Aeneas* was written by Nahum Tate based on the original story in Virgil's *Aeneid.* In Virgil, Aeneas leaves the destroyed city of Troy with a band of devoted followers in hopes of founding a new state in Italy. After seven tempest-tossed years, the ragged and diminished fleet takes harbor at the city of Carthage. Aeneas and the Queen of Carthage, Dido, quickly fall in love, due at least in part to the interference of the goddesses Juno and Venus. When Jove (the king of the gods) discovers Aeneas's dalliance, he sends his messenger Mercury to remind him of his destiny to found a kingdom at Rome. Although stunned by this order, Aeneas obeys. He leaves Dido, and she, in despair, kills herself on his sword.

Tate's libretto makes a number of changes in this outline, of which two stand out. He replaces the mythological characters who are aware of and concerned with Aeneas's destiny with a Sorceress and a coven of witches who plot Dido's downfall. Secondly, he omits Dido's violent suicide, replacing it with a scene in which the Queen dies from grief. Both changes had been previewed in Tate's play *Brutus of Alba* (1678), which as Tate himself writes in the preface was "begun and finish . . . under the Name of *Dido and Aeneas.*" *Brutus of Alba* is thus the direct source for *Dido and Aeneas,* the major differences between the two texts being that the play is much longer, has more characters, and is written in decasyllabic blank verse (unrhymed lines of ten syllables), whereas the libretto limits the actions and characters to the main story and is written in rhymed verse with varied but generally shorter line lengths appropriate for musical setting. Despite his stature as poet laureate (which position he attained three years before *Dido and Aeneas*), Nahum Tate has not been kindly treated by posterity. He is especially criticized for his adaptation of Shakespeare's *King Lear,* in which he gives the play a happy ending. However, Tate's ability to write dramatic English verse well-suited to musical setting is rivaled by none in the seventeenth century.

Because no definitive source for this opera survives, questions have been raised about its original content and form. The only seventeenth-century source is an undated, printed libretto that is assumed to derive from the original performance, thought to have taken place in 1689. The earliest musical score dates from no earlier than 1777. These two sources present sometimes strikingly different versions of the work. The libretto contains an allegorical prologue depicting the arrival and ascension of William and Mary, King and Queen of England (21 April 1689). No musical setting of this survives. The remainder of the libretto is divided into three equal acts, whereas the musical sources contain a lopsided division into three acts that indicates an underlying division into two equal parts. Many lines in the libretto are assigned differently in the musical sources, and a chorus and dance at the end of the second act in the libretto are lacking altogether. Because of these and other discrepancies, it is impossible to recreate an absolutely authoritative version of this work.

Some modern writers have interpreted all of *Dido and Aeneas,* like its prologue, as a political allegory. According to one such theory, William, the Dutch Prince of Orange, was (like Aeneas) a foreign king whose allegiance to Mary, the native queen (like Dido), might be questioned. The libretto might therefore illustrate "the possible fate of the British nation should Dutch William fail in his responsibilities to his English queen." Alternatively, the libretto has been seen to illustrate the Protestant fear that the Catholics (represented by the Sorceress and her witches) would undermine the joint sovereignty of William and Mary (Dido and Aeneas) and reestablish the Catholic James II on the throne. However, given that it was written for a girls' school in Chelsea and never performed publicly, it is also possible that the opera was intended as a morality play for the female performers and the audience. The Epilogue, written by Thomas D'Urfey and spoken by Lady Dorothy Burke, significantly asks "Great Providence . . . To save us from those grand deceivers, men."

Dido and Aeneas illustrates Purcell's particularly sensitive setting of English text through word painting, dissonance, and proper rhythmic declamation. For example, in "Whence could so much virtue spring," the word "storms" is set with hurried runs of sixteenth notes, while "valour" receives a pompous dotted note figure. Dissonance is used to express the pain of "woe" and "distress." Most distinctive to the modern ear, however, is Purcell's use of short-long rhythmic patterns (with the short note accented) to set the many English words, such as "pity" and "stubborn," with this accentuation.

Purcell's opera is also justly famous for its use of ground bass (repetitive bass patterns). Such pieces would seem to have a built-in rigidity, as the regularity of the repeated bass exerts a powerful influence over harmony, melody, and phrase structure. Purcell, however, takes this apparent compositional limitation and creates continually different and imaginative solutions. The four ground bass pieces in the opera: "Ah, Belinda," "The Triumphing Dance," "Oft she visits," and "When I am laid in earth" (Dido's Lament), are all remarkable in different ways. Dido's Lament particularly stands out. The voice line never coincides with the regular cadences of the five-bar recurring bass until the last word, when Dido, echoed by the music, meets her fate.

—Ellen T. Harris

---

d'INDY, (Paul-Marie-Théodore-) Vincent.

Composer. Born 27 March 1851, in Paris. Died 2 December 1931, in Paris. Studied piano with Diémer, and harmony and theory with Marmontel and Lavignac, 1862-65; met Henri Duparc in 1869, and studied the works of Bach, Beethoven, Berlioz, and Wagner with him; served in the Garde Mobile in the Franco-Prussian War; studied composition and organ with César Franck, 1872-80; organist at St-Leu, 1872-76; met Liszt and Wagner in Germany, and was introduced to Brahms, 1873; heard the premiere of Wagner's *Ring*, 1876, and *Parsifal*, 1882, in Bayreuth; chorus master and timpanist with the Colonne Orchestra, 1873-78; secretary of the Société Nationale de Musique, 1876-90, president, 1890; City of Paris Prize for *Le chant de la cloche*, 1885; chorus coach and assistant to Lamoureux for the Paris premiere of *Lohengrin*, 1887; founded the Schola Cantorum with Bordes and Guilmant, 1896; conducting engagements in Spain, 1897, Russia, 1903 and 1907 and the United States, 1905; member of the commission to revise the curriculum of the Paris Conservatory, 1892, and refused a post as professor of composition; professor of ensemble class at the Paris Conservatory, 1912; inspector of musical instruction in Paris, 1899; Chevalier of the Legion of Honor, 1892, and officer in 1912; member of many academies and artistic societies.

Operas

Publishers: Durand, Hamelle, Heugel.

Les burgraves du Rhin, R. de Bonnières, 1869-72 [unfinished].
Attendez-moi sous l'orme, J. Prével and de Bonnières (after Régnard), 1876-82, Paris, Opéra-Comique, 11 February 1882.
Le chant de la cloche (staged version of a choral work), 1879-83, Brussels, Monnaie, 21 November 1912.
Fervaal, d'Indy, 1889-95, Brussels, Monnaie, 12 March 1897.
L'étranger, d'Indy, 1898-1901, Brussels, Monnaie, 7 January 1903.
La légende de Saint Christophe, d'Indy (after J. de Voragine, *Golden Legend*), 1908-15, Paris, Opéra, 9 June 1920.
Le rêve de Cinyras, X. de Courville, 1922-23, Paris, Petite Scène, 10 June 1927.

Other works: orchestral works, vocal works, chamber music, band music, songs, keyboard works.

Publications

By d'INDY: books–

Histoire du 105ème Bataillon de la Garde nationale de Paris, en l'année 1870-71. Paris, 1872.
Projet d'organisation des études du Conservatoire de musique de Paris. Paris, 1892.
De Bach à Beethoven. Paris, 1899.
Une école de musique répondant aux besoins modernes: discours d'inauguration de l'école de chant liturgique . . . fondée par la Schola Cantorum en 1896. Paris, 1900.
Cours de composition musicale. Paris, 1903-50 [fourth volume edited by G. de Lioncourt].
César Franck. Paris, 1906; English translation, 1909.
Beethoven. Paris, 1911; English translation, 1913; 1970.
Emmanuel Chabrier et Paul Dukas. Paris, 1920.
La Schola Cantorum en 1925. Paris, 1927.
Richard Wagner et son influence sur l'art musical français. Paris, 1930.
Introduction à l'étude de "Parsifal" de Wagner. Paris, 1937 [incomplete].
Sérieyx, M.L., ed. *Vincent d'Indy, Henri Duparc, Albert Roussel: lettres à Auguste Sérieyx*. Lausanne, 1961.

articles–

Le figaro (1892-1900).
Guide musical (1897-1904).
Tribune de St Gervais (1897-1909).
L'art moderne (1900-03).
Courrier musical (1902-31).
Musica (1902-13).
Comoedia (1907-28).
Bulletin français de la Société Internationale de Musique (1909-14).
Tablettes de la Schola (1900-24).
A. van der Linden, ed. "Lettres de Vincent d'Indy à Octave Maus." *Revue belge de musicologie* 14 (1960): 87.

About d'INDY: books–

Imbert, H. *Vincent d'Indy. Profils de musiciens*. Paris, 1888.
Destranges, E. *Le chant de la cloche*. Paris, 1890.
Willy [H. Gauthier-Villars]. *Lettres de l'ouvreuse*. Paris, 1890.
Destranges, E. *Fervaal*. Paris, 1896.

Bréville, P. de, and H. Gauthier-Villars. *Fervaal: étude analytique et thématique.* Paris, 1897.

Bruneau, A. *Musiques d'hier et de demain.* Paris, 1900.

Deniau, E. *Vincent d'Indy.* Toulouse, 1903.

Destranges, E. *L'étranger.* Paris, 1904.

Borgex, L. *Vincent d'Indy.* Paris, 1913.

Sérieyx, A. *Vincent d'Indy.* Paris, 1914.

Mason, Daniel Gregory. *Contemporary Composers.* Paris, 1918; 1974.

Vallas, L. *Vincent d'Indy,* i: *La jeunesse (1851-86).* Paris, 1946.

———. *Vincent d'Indy,* ii: *La maturité, la viellesse (1886-1931).* Paris, 1950.

Canteloube, J. *Vincent d'Indy.* Paris, 1951.

Cooper, Martin. *French Music from the Death of Berlioz to the Death of Fauré.* London, 1951.

Demuth, N. *Vincent d'Indy 1851-1931, Champion of Classicism.* London, 1951.

Fauré, Gabriel. *Correspondance.* Edited by Jean-Michel Nectoux. Paris, 1980.

Hirsbrunner, Theo, *Claude Debussy und seine Zeit.* Laaber, 1981.

articles–

Ravel, Maurice. "Fervaal-poème et musique de Vincent d'Indy." *Comoedia illustré* 5/20 January (1913): 361.

La revue musicale no. 122 (1932) [d'Indy issue].

La revue musicale no. 176 (1937) [*Autour de Vincent d'Indy*].

Kufferath, M. "Fervaal." *Rivista musicale italiana* 4 (1897): 313.

Lalo, P. "Fervaal et la musique française." *Revue de Paris* 15 May (1898).

Rolland, R. "Vincent d'Indy." *Revue d'art dramatique* 5 February (1899); reprinted in *Musiciens d'aujourd'hui,* Paris, 1908.

La Laurencie, L. de. "L'oeuvre de Vincent d'Indy." *Durendal* April (1902); reprinted in *Courrier musical* December (1903).

Debussy, C. "L'étranger, à Bruxelles," *Gil Blas* 12 January (1903).

Laloy, L. "Le drame musical moderne: Vincent d'Indy." *Bulletin français de la Société Internationale de Musique* 1, 15 May (1905).

Davies, L. "The French Wagnerians." *Opera* 19 (1968): 351.

Paul, G.B. "Rameau, d'Indy and French Nationalism." *Musical Quarterly* 58 (1972): 46.

Hoérée, Arthur. "Lettres de Vincent d'Indy à Roussel." *Cahiers Albert Roussel* 1 (1978): 11.

Longyear, Rey M. "Political and Social Criticism in French Opera 1827-1920." In *Essays on the Music of J.S. Bach and Other Divers Subjects: A Tribute to Gerhard Herz,* edited by Robert L. Weaver, 245. Louisville, 1981.

Fulcher, Jane. "Vincent d'Indy's 'Drame Anti-Juif' and its meaning in Paris, 1920." *Cambridge Opera Journal* 2 (1990): 295.

*   *   *

Vincent d'Indy (1851-1931) is better known as a symphonic composer and director of the Parisian Schola Cantorum (established 1896) than as an opera composer. D'Indy was heavily influenced in general by his mentor César Franck and in particular by the music dramas of Richard Wagner. The combination of compositional Germanophilia and aristocratic lineage caused d'Indy to be associated with the conservative artistic element that was battling with the artistic modernists for cultural dominance in Paris during the first quarter of the 20th century. In such a highly charged politico-artistic environment it is not surprising that d'Indy's music came under extreme criticism in the hands of Camille Saint-Säens and Gabriel Fauré.

D'Indy's compositional technique may be loosely characterized as classical, that is, classical in the sense of having a transparent formal structure and expressing a reverence for the great musical masters of the past. His rigorous study of counterpoint played an essential part in both his music and his compositional pedagogy, the latter of which is revealed in his *Cours de composition musicale,* 3 volumes (1903, 1909, posthumous), which served as the foundation of the composition curriculum at the Schola Cantorum.

Of d'Indy's six operas, two are forgettable comic works, *Attendez-moi sous l'orme* (1882) and *Le rêve de Cinyras* (1923). Better known are the three staged works, *Le chant de la cloche* (1883), *Fervaal* (1895), *L'étranger* (1901), and the opera-oratorio *La légende de Saint Christophe* (1915). Of these works, only *Fervaal* has managed to secure a place in the opera repertoire.

D'Indy's libretti, most of which he wrote himself, exhibit a high-minded seriousness that is the result of fervent religious beliefs. The religious element is seen most prominently in *Fervaal* (sometimes dubbed the "French Parsifal") and, of course, *La légende de Saint-Christophe.* Other Wagnerian elements include leitmotivic structures, continuous melodies, and extravagant orchestrations. The last element may play a significant role in the small number of performances that d'Indy's operas have received. For example, *Fervaal* require four flutes, two piccolos, three oboes, English horn, four clarinets, bass clarinet, contra-bass clarinet, four bassoons, four saxophones, four horns, four trumpets, eight saxhorns, four trombones, tuba, and a mountain horn with the name of "cornet à Bouquin."

Although d'Indy's operas have had few performances in the sixty years following the composer's death, his influence is apparent in the works of his many students. D'Indy's students who attained reputations as opera composers include Leevi Madetoja (1887-1947), Bohuslav Martinu (1890-1959), Déodat de Séverac (1873-1921), and Albert Roussel (1869-1937). Additionally, d'Indy's compositional ideas have had a significant impact upon the operas of Arthur Honegger (1892-1955), Darius Milhaud (1892-1974), and Olivier Messiaen (b. 1908).

—William E. Grim

THE DISGUISED GARDENER
See LA FINTA GIARDINIERA

THE DISTANT SOUND
See DER FERNE KLANG

DI STEFANO, Giuseppe.

Tenor. Born 24 July 1921, near Catania, Sicily. Educated in Sicily. Studied with Adriano Torchi and Luigi Montesanto in Milan; three years of military service, then escaped to Switzerland, 1943, interned as refugee; debut as Massenet's Des Grieux, Reggio Emilia, 1946; Teatro alla Scala debut in same role, 1947; Metropolitan Opera debut as Duke of Mantua in *Rigoletto,* 1948; appeared at Met 1948-52, 1955-56 and 1964-65; San Francisco debut as Rodolfo, 1950; at La Scala 1952-60, often appearing with Callas; created Giuliano in Pizzetti's *Calzare d'Argento*; Chicago debut as Edgardo, 1954; British debut at Edinburgh, 1957; Covent Garden debut as Cavaradossi, 1961; world tour with Callas, 1973-74.

Publications

By DI STEFANO: books–

L'Arte del canto. Milan, 1989.

*   *   *

Giuseppe di Stefano's beautiful, warm voice places him among the best lyric tenors since World War II. In fact, di Stefano's voice may easily be rated one of the best tenor voices of this century. In the late 1940s he began to make some of the best recordings by a lyric tenor in some two decades. Unfortunately the voice had lost its youthful freshness by 1960 and along the way there had been blatant problems. Like his contemporary Franco Corelli, di Stefano could sometimes be crude, singing with open vowels, lifting to notes, shouting, and aspirating. "A te, o cara" from the *I Puritani* recording of 1953 with Maria Callas already shows some clear faults. Yet at his best—as Pinkerton, Cavaradossi, and Rodolfo (the latter two also recorded with Callas), in some early aria discs, and in Neapolitan songs and in tunes from his native Sicily—di Stefano was incomparable. Above all, there was the warm, ardent sound, the embodiment of how an Italian tenor should sound. However, di Stefano was too prodigal, singing on the edge, giving away far too much too quickly.

It was a large enough voice, yet di Stefano took on a number of roles that were too heavy for him. These included Manrico (preserved in a fine recording with Callas), Riccardo in *Un ballo in maschera,* and Enzo in a recording with Milanov in which di Stefano performs at the limit of his capabilities. As is common with a voice of such richness and beauty, di Stefano's high notes never sound effortless. In this regard Placido Domingo is his closest contemporary counterpart.

After a number of radio broadcasts, di Stefano made his operatic debut in 1946, in a production of Massenet's *Manon* with Mafalda Favero at Reggio Emilia. His Metropolitan Opera debut came in 1948 and it was in 1951 that he sang with Callas for the first time, a partnership that became legendary both in the opera house and on recordings throughout the 1950s, sadly revived in a worldwide recital tour in 1973-74. A number of the recordings he and Callas made together were conducted by Tullio Serafin; others were led by Victor De Sabata, Antonino Votto, and Herbert von Karajan. The 1953 *Tosca* with Callas, di Stefano, and Gobbi, conducted by De Sabata, is still considered not only the most stirring *Tosca* ever committed to discs, but also one of the finest opera recordings ever made.

Although di Stefano continued to sing for many years after his voice began showing signs of deterioration in the late 1950s, eventually limiting himself to Viennese operetta, he was never the same artist. Incipient flaws previously masked by the almost erotic warmth of his sound could no longer be disguised or ignored. Aspirating seemed to become a necessity to make it through even the most elementary of florid passages, lifting to notes became more pronounced, as did register breaks. Taking on increasingly heavier roles throughout the 1950s, by the mid-1960s he had sung Radames, Alvaro, Calaf, and Otello. One serious consequence of the overuse and abuse of the voice was di Stefano's eventual inability to sing, not *piano,* but even *mezzo-forte:* the later recorded examples are painfully stentorian. This tendency can be heard on the "live" recordings di Stefano and Callas on their 1973-74 tour and on a duet album of 1974 with Montserrat Caballé. The general feeling was that one of the most glorious Italian tenor voices of the century had been misused to the point of early destruction. Yet without this prodigality, this outpouring of passion, would he have been such a sensation in his prime? In his willingness to give everything with little regard to the future he was the perfect match for Callas; perhaps working with her alerted him to dramatic possibilities and refinements, although, as in the famous 1957 Teatro alla Scala production of Verdi's *La traviata,* di Stefano voiced loud complaints about the long, painstaking rehearsal process.

The final impression of di Stefano must be a positive one. Even with the faults there is still much to praise: the earliest aria recordings, such as "Ah dispar, vision" from *Manon,* are stunning and even in the 1960s, with all the problems, the tone is still gorgeous on many notes. The ever-present ardor, the yearning sound, the "tears in the voice" made di Stefano incomparable.

—Stephen Willier

DOKTOR FAUST.

Composer: Ferruccio Busoni [completed by Busoni's pupil Philipp Jarnach after Busoni died in 1924].

Librettist: Ferruccio Busoni (after Marlowe and other treatments of the Faust legend).

First Performance: 21 May 1925.

Roles: Doktor Faust (baritone); Mephistopheles (tenor); Nightwatchman (tenor); Wagner (baritone); Duchess of Parma (soprano); Duke of Parma (tenor); Master of Ceremonies (bass); Girl's Brother (baritone); Lieutenant (tenor); Three Students (tenor, two bass); Theologian (bass); Jurist (bass); Doctor of Natural History (baritone); Four Students (four tenor); Gravis (bass); Levis (bass); Asmodus (baritone); Beelzebub (tenor); Megarus (tenor); chorus (SSATTBB).

Publications

books–

Guerrini, Guido and Paolo Fragapane. Il "Doctor Faust" di Ferruccio Busoni. Florence, 1942.

articles–

Dent, Edward J. "Busoni's 'Doktor Faust'." Music and Letters 7 (1926): 196.
Baricelli, Jean Pierre. "Faust and the Music of Evil." Journal of European Studies (1983): 1.
Roberge, Marc-André. "Le retour au catalogue du Doktor Faust de Busoni." Sonances [Canada] 2 (1983): 24.

Doktor Faust is considered by most critics to be Ferruccio Busoni's masterpiece. The composition of this opera occupied the last fifteen years of the composer's life, and many of his earlier compositions were conceived as studies for the technical problems he thought he would encounter in Doktor Faust. Busoni first contemplated Leonardo da Vinci as the subject of this opera, abandoned that idea in favor of Merlin before finally settling upon Faust. Through his acquaintance with Arrigo Boito and his knowledge of the latter's great difficulties with Mefistofele, Busoni wisely decided to eschew setting Goethe's Faust and instead fashioned a libretto based upon the traditional Faust Puppenspiel. The opera was fully complete at the time of Busoni's death except for the final scene, which was realized by the composer's protégé Philipp Jarnach.

The opera is prefaced by a prologue in which Busoni's operatic philosophy is recited in verse. Faust is first seen in his study and is visited by three students who present him with a book of magic, a key, and a deed assigning ownership of the items. Faust then invokes the Devil who appears in six manifestations, the final being Mephistopheles. After Faust requests Mephistopheles' assistance in disposing of his creditors and pursuers, a pact is signed to the ironic accompaniment of the Easter Chorus. Valentine, the brother of the unnamed girl Faust has seduced, is killed in church. Faust and Mephistopheles then intrude upon the wedding festivities of the Duke of Parma. After conjuring up the images of various historical personages, Faust runs off with the Duchess before the wedding is complete. The scene then shifts to a tavern in Wittenberg in which rival groups of Protestant and Catholic students are holding forth in an intellectual debate. Faust thinks wistfully of the Duchess whom he has abandoned. Mephistopheles arrives and announces that the Duchess has sent Faust a child, whose dead body Mephistopheles drops at Faust's feet; however, Mephistopheles transforms the corpse into straw which is then burned and transformed into a vision of Helen of Troy, which vanishes as Faust attempts to embrace it. The three students from Cracow return and demand their gifts back, but Faust is unable to honor their request because he has lost them. The three students prophesy Faust's death at midnight and depart. In the final scene, Wagner has been named Rector of the University and now resides in Faust's former house. Faust sees a beggar woman who turns out to be the Duchess. She gives Faust their dead child and tells him that there is still time to complete his task. Kneeling before a cross, Faust is unable to remember any prayers. He puts the child on the ground and makes a magic circle. In his last living act, Faust transfers his will to the child who rises up and flies across the town. Mephistopheles, in the guise of a night watchman, sees Faust's body and asks rhetorically: "Sollte dieser Mann verunglückt sein?" ("Has this man met with some misfortune?").

Busoni's conception of the Faust legend is both dramatically effective and conspicuously modern. Influenced by the philosophy of Friedrich Nietzsche, Busoni has altered the traditional Faust story from the level of morality play to an examination of a being truly beyond good and evil, a musical Bildungsroman of the Übermensch as it were. Busoni's atheistic impulses, indeed his rejection of both the sacred and the demonic, is most forcefully in evidence in that portion of Faust's final monologue which was left unset at his death and which Jarnach felt too controversial to realize, especially the lines: "So let the work be finished,/ in defiance of you,/ of you all,/ who hold yourselves for good,/ whom we call evil,/ who, for the sake of old quarrels/ take mankind as a pretext/ and pile upon him/ the consequences of your discord./ Upon this highest insight of my wisdom/ is your malice now broken to pieces/ and in my self-won freedom/ expire both God and Devil at once."

Unlike other Faust operas, Busoni never allows other characters to dominate Faust, nor is there even a suggestion of sentimentality in the opera. This latter phenomenon is seen in the downplaying of the "Gretchen" episode to the point that it is only mentioned as already having occurred; the woman seduced by Faust is never seen nor mentioned by name, and the episode's only pretext in the opera is to provide a motivation for the appearance and eventual murder of Valentine. Additionally, the episodic dramaturgy of Doktor Faust, while reminiscent of Berlioz's La damnation de Faust and other works, suggests on the part of Busoni an awareness of the editing techniques of cinema.

From a purely musical standpoint, Doktor Faust is remarkable for the composer's rejection of the Wagnerian leitmotif. Although the music of the opera is continuous in the Wagnerian sense, there are no meaningful repetitions of melodic fragments in conjunction with readily identifiable characters, objects, ideas, or emotions. Indeed, in his theoretical writings, Busoni emphasized his belief that the organic development of the music and the text of an opera should not be contingent upon one another. Unlike other Faust operas, Busoni's Doktor Faust employs almost no word-painting except for a few instances of melodic tritones (the "diabolus in musica") at appropriate places in the text. From a stylistic standpoint, Doktor Faust is indicative of the hyper-romantic sensibilities of the late nineteenth-early twentieth-century period which led to the collapse of the traditional system of harmonic relationships and provided the impetus for the development of expressionist and dodecaphonic techniques. Busoni utilizes a curious admixture of the old and new in Doktor Faust; modern chromatic harmonies are placed within the context of traditional musical forms and techniques such as the sarabande and the fugue.

Although seldom performed, Doktor Faust deserves its place of honor alongside other breakthrough operas of the early twentieth century, such as Berg's Wozzeck and the Salome and Elektra of the Strauss-Hofmannsthal collaboration.

—William E. Grim

DOMINGO, Plácido.

Tenor. Born 21 January 1941, in Madrid. Lived in Mexico from age seven. Studied singing with Iglesias and Morelli in Mexico City. Debut as Borsa in *Rigoletto* in Mexico City, 1959; United States debut in Dallas, 1961; with Israel National Opera in Tel Aviv, 1962-65; operatic debut at Metropolitan Opera as Maurizio in *Adriana Lecouvreur,* 1968; Teatro alla Scala debut as Ernani, 1969; appeared at Covent Garden as Cavaradossi, 1971; appeared at Salzburg as Don Carlos, 1975; created title roles of Morena Torroba's *El poeta* (Madrid, 1980), and Menotti's *Goya* (Washington, DC, 1986); has appeared in films of *La traviata* (1983), *Carmen* (1984) and *Otello* (1986).

Publications

By DOMINGO: books–

My First Forty Years. New York and London, 1983.

articles–

"Domingo on Hoffman." *Opera* November (1982).

About DOMINGO: books–

Steane, J.B. *The Grand Tradition.* London, 1974.

Snowman, D. *The World of Placido Domingo.* London and New York, 1985.

articles–

Rosenthal, H. "Placido Domingo." *Opera* 23 (1972): 18.

*   *   *

Plácido Domingo is the most gifted all-around operatic artist of his generation, combining musical, vocal and dramatic talents to a rare degree. Although specializing in late nineteenth-century Italian and French opera, Domingo has a vast repertoire (including more than eighty operas) that ranges from light romantic Spanish "zarzuelas" and the songs of popular composers like Andrew Lloyd Webber to some of the most demanding roles of Wagner. No other basically "Italianate" tenor in this century has worked with such consummate success through so wide a repertoire.

Domingo's voice quality is in many ways reminiscent of the later, darker Caruso (minus the "protruding jaw" mannerisms and with a cleaner *portamento*): a powerful, burnished, often almost baritonal sound which Domingo characteristically uses with impeccable musicianship. In this integration of qualities, he is the natural successor to Bjorling. With his tall, dark good looks and powerful stage presence, Domingo is superb in the standard romantic tenor parts: Hoffmann, Don Carlo, Cavaradossi in *Tosca,* Don José in *Carmen,* Gustavo (or Riccardo) in *Un ballo in maschera,*

Plácido Domingo with Ilona Tokody in *La bohème,* Royal Opera, London, 1987

Rodolfo in *La bohème,* Radames in *Aïda.* A conscientious actor, Domingo is capable of making each role develop during performance. There is a twinkle in the eye, and in the voice, in the opening scenes of an opera like *Ballo* or *Bohème,* for example, that makes the tragic final scenes of these operas all the more poignant. In *Carmen,* Domingo will typically portray a shy young man whose nervous infatuation grows gradually towards a homicidal passion.

The part with which Domingo has come to be most associated is the title role in Verdi's *Otello.* His assumption of this role is essentially a lyrical, internalized interpretation in contrast to the stentorian vocalism of Mario del Monaco, the eye-popping madness of James McCracken, or the terrifying desperation portrayed by Jon Vickers. Domingo's Otello retained greater dignity than these, a quality of yearning after the unattainable that suggested tragedy on an epic scale. The only Domingo performance of *Otello* in which frenetic movement took the place of inner turbulence was the one filmed by Franco Zeffirelli.

Domingo has made a number of operatic films, and is also one of the most recorded classical artists in the history of the gramophone. He has committed the entire standard operatic repertoire to disc, much of it two or three times. In addition, he has recorded a number of operas that are only rarely performed (Charpentier's *Louise,* Montemezzi's *L'Amore dei Tre Re* and Mascagni's *Iris,* for example) and a great many light and popular songs in English, French, German, Italian and Spanish. Domingo has also starred in well over fifty operatic videos and telecasts. He has also given some 2,500 live performances during a quarter century on the operatic stage.

Inevitably an artist so exposed will lay himself open to criticism. Some have found Domingo's performances undifferentiated, his Cavaradossi too like his Andrea Chénier, his Canio too like his Otello. There is certainly a recognizable Domingo style of stagecraft: the quick, short steps as a way of suggesting energy or resolve, or the furrowed brow, stooped shoulders and buckled knees to indicate yearning or pleading. Vocally, too, Domingo's invariably covered tone, his characteristic qualities of legato phrasing and clean *portamento,* are evident whether he is singing *Lohengrin* or *L'elisir d'Amore.* Even in Domingo's lighter, more popular recordings—zarzuela, German operetta or the songs of John Denver, Henry Mancini or Lloyd Webber—his characteristic style is in evidence, including a reluctance either to press the voice too hard or to resort too often to head tones. Critics have asked whether an occasional slide or tear in the voice, a suggestion of desperation (or even of vulgarity), perhaps, would add an extra dramatic *frisson?* These questions miss the point. Domingo's art, for all the magnetism of the man and the muscular glory of his vocalism, is essentially that of a refined and sensitive artist who uses his voice as an instrument in the service of music rather as Casals treated his cello.

At the height of his career, Domingo was criticized by some for spreading himself too thin—taking on too many operatic commitments, appearing on too many television chat shows, recording popular music unworthy of his talents, etc. His energy, and ubiquity, are legendary. Was Domingo motivated by a desire for fame? For money? Some supposed he was goaded by the growing celebrity of Luciano Pavarotti, his supposed rival, into these undertakings. Domingo's own answer is unequivocal: he was brought up in an atmosphere of popular song, and he liked the music he sang. He also felt that by reaching out to a wider audience he could help bring millions to opera. Domingo is by no means the first top-level opera singer to perform a more popular repertoire.

He is, however, the first major operatic singer with serious aspirations as a conductor. A versatile musician quite capable of teaching himself difficult operatic roles at the piano, Domingo has conducted something like a dozen different works and appeared on the podium in most of the world's major opera houses. He has also begun conducting symphonic repertoire. Domingo's calling card as a conductor is Johann Strauss' *Die Fledermaus* (which he has recorded), and he has also conducted a number of the operas with which he is associated as a singer, including *Tosca* and *Bohème.* He has a large, clear, somewhat curvilinear beat, with a tendency to use more arm and less wrist or eye than might be ideal. Performances tend to be thoroughly professional, though lacking the kind of freedom from the page that he regularly achieves as a singer.

Into his fifties, Domingo shows little sign of reducing his commitments, though he is scheduling more concerts than formerly, some in places new to him like Norway, Belgium, and Australia. But there is perhaps a greater change, both in the man and in the artist: more Wagner and fewer press and television interviews. Domingo is Artistic Consultant to the Los Angeles Opera and has become increasingly identified over the years with the Hispanic world, devoting time to Mexican earthquake relief, singing Spanish and Latin American music, and helping to direct the ambitious musical programme for the 1992 Seville International Festival. The greatest singer-actor of recent times clearly enjoys the emerging role of operatic elder statesman.

—Daniel Snowman

DON CARLOS.

Composer: Giuseppe Verdi.

Librettists: François Joseph Méry and Camille du Locle (after Schiller, W.H. Prescott, *History of Philip II,* and E. Cormon, *Philippe II, roi d'Espagne*).

First Performance: Paris, Opéra, 11 March 1867; translated into Italian by A. de Lauzières and A. Zanardini for Milan, Teatro alla Scala, 10 January 1884.

Roles: Elisabeth de Valois (soprano); Princess Eboli (mezzo-soprano); Don Carlo (tenor); Rodrigo (baritone); Philip II (bass); Grand Inquisitor (bass); Friar (bass); Theobaldo (soprano); Count of Lerma (tenor); Royal Herald (tenor); Celestial Voice (soprano); Countess of Aremberg (mute); chorus (SATB).

Publications

book—

Degrada, Francesco. *Il palazzo incantato.* Fiesole, 1979.

articles–

Porter, Andrew. "A Sketch for *Don Carlo.*" *Musical Times* 111 (1970).
_____. "The Making of *Don Carlos.*" *Proceedings of the Royal Musical Association* 98 (1971-72).

Don Carlos, **title page of score, Paris, 1867**

Günther, Ursula. "Zur Entstehung der zweiten französischen Fassung von Verdis *Don Carlos.*" In *International Musicological Society Congress Report 11. Copenhagen 1972.*

———. "La genèse de *Don Carlos.*" *Revue de Musicologie* 58 (1972): 16; 60 (1974): 87.

Porter, Andrew. "Prelude to a New *Don Carlos.*" *Opera* 25 (1974): 665.

Günther, Ursula, and Carrara Verdi. "Der Briefwechsel Verdi-Nuitter-Du Locle zur Revision des *Don Carlo.*" *Analecta Musicologica* 14, 15 (1974, 1975).

Clémeur, M. "Eine neuentdeckte Quelle für das Libretto von Verdis *Don Carlos.*" *Melos/Neue Zeitschrift für Musik* 3 (1977).

Porter, Andrew. "Observations on *Don Carlos.*" *World of Opera* 1/ no. 3 (1978-79): 1.

Günther, Ursula. "Zur Revision des *Don Carlos.* Postscriptum zu Teil II." *Analecta Musicologica* 19 (1979): 373.

Sutcliffe, James Helme. "Die sechs 'Fassungen' des *Don Carlos:* Versuch einer Bilanz." *Oper Heute* 7 (1984): 69.

Avant-scène opéra September-October (1986) [*Don Carlos* issue].

*   *   *

Verdi's *Don Carlos* is, in its original French version, the longest of Verdi's operas. The work was to be a showpiece for the Paris Opéra during Napoléon III's 1867 Universal Exhibition and was thus for Verdi a challenge to produce French grand opera in the Meyerbeerian manner in Paris itself. When Verdi's French publisher, Léon Escudier, brought the scenario for *Don Carlos* to Sant' Agata for Verdi's perusal in 1865, the composer was extremely enthusiastic but wanted to add some elements of spectacle, an important component of French grand opera. In addition to the act I scene at Fontainebleau and the appearance of the emperor Charles V, Verdi, who played a large role in shaping this libretto, also demanded a scene, found in Schiller, between Philip and the blind and aged Inquisitor, and a duet between Philip and Rodrigo. One of the most spectacular scenes of the entire opera was the coronation-*auto da fe* in act III.

As befitting the French grand opera mould, the opera is in five acts. Act I begins in the forest of Fontainebleau. The Infante Don Carlo of Spain is to wed Elisabeth, daughter of Henri II of France. Carlo has come to France incognito to see her; they meet in the Fontainebleau forest and fall passionately in love. The scene ends, however, with the news that Elisabeth is not to wed Carlo, but his father, Philip II. Act II, scene i is set at the cloister of the monastery of San Yuste, to which Carlo's grandfather, Charles V, has retreated from earthly cares. Carlo meets his friend Rodrigo, the Marquis of Posa, who has just returned from Flanders. Carlo tells of his love for Elisabeth, and the two men swear friendship and devotion to liberty in a rousing duet. In scene ii, outside the gates of the convent, Princess Eboli sings the "Veil Song" with the court ladies as chorus. Elisabeth and Rodrigo join them; the latter distracts Eboli's attention so that Elisabeth may read a note from Carlo. Rodrigo leads Eboli away, Carlo enters to talk to Elisabeth, but he ends up delirious; when she reminds him that she is now his mother he leaves in despair. Philip and Rodrigo have a long exchange in which the latter criticizes the king's cruelty to the Flemings. The king confesses his suspicions about the queen and his son to Rodrigo and asks him to pay attention to the situation.

Act III begins in the queen's gardens in Madrid. Carlo is reading a letter about a midnight tryst. He thinks Elisabeth wrote it, but it was actually Eboli, who becomes extremely angry and swears vengeance. Scene ii shows Philip's coronation in conjunction with an *auto da fe*. During the procession a group of Flemish deputies, led by Carlo, asks for pity for Flanders. Carlo draws a sword on his father, but is persuaded to yield it to Rodrigo. In act IV, scene i Philip reveals in soliloquy that his wife will never love him. The Grand Inquisitor enters: Philip speaks of sacrificing his own son, and the Inquisitor asks for Rodrigo's life. Philip eventually acquiesces. Elisabeth enters, distraught that her jewel-case is missing; Philip has it, with the picture of Carlo inside. The queen swoons. Eboli, left alone with her, confesses that she was the one who betrayed her to the king because of her own love for Carlo. Elisabeth forgives her this, but when Eboli then confesses to being Philip's erstwhile mistress, Elisabeth forces her to choose between exile and the veil. Eboli chooses the latter, but in the one day left to her she vows to save Carlo. In scene ii Carlo is visited in prison by Rodrigo. Incriminating letters have been found on Rodrigo; he must die and Carlo, freed, must go to save Flanders. Rodrigo is then killed by a shot, the king enters to free his son but Carlo recoils from him. Act V takes place at the cloister again. Elisabeth addresses the tomb of Charles V, recalling her happiness at Fontainebleau. Carlo comes to bid her farewell; he will go to Flanders and they will meet in another world. Philip and the Inquisitor interrupt them and the gates of Charles V's tomb open as the Emperor appears to lead Carlo back into the cloister with him.

Both Schiller's play and Verdi's operatic setting have had the charge of historical inaccuracy leveled against them, yet accuracy was not a primary consideration for either. In 1883 Verdi wrote a letter to Giulio Ricordi addressing this issue: "In short, nothing in the drama is historical, but it contains a Shakespearean truth and profundity of characterizations." Previously, in 1876, he had remarked to Andrei Maffei that "To copy truth can be good, but to invent truth is better, far better." Typical Verdian themes that are found in *Don Carlos* are the depiction and criticism of ecclesiastical narrowness and cruelty (also found in *La forza del destino, Aida,* and *Simon Boccanegra*) and the destruction of personal lives against the background of larger forces: religious, political, and dynastic. Thus *Don Carlos,* as with other Verdi operas, e.g., *La forza del destino, Un ballo in maschera, Aida,* and *Otello,* and as with French grand opera and Metastasian *opera seria,* is revelatory of personal happiness destroyed by exigencies of public duty.

A number of versions of *Don Carlos* exist. Because of the length of the original and the need for the Parisian audiences to catch the last train back to the suburbs, cuts were already being made during Opéra rehearsals for the premiere. Those passages cut—among them a prelude and introduction, a duet for Elisabeth and Eboli, and a duet for Carlo and Philip that eventually became the "Lacrymosa" of the *Messa da Requiem*—were never published. They were physically cut from the score; in 1969 Andrew Porter and David Rosen discovered and reconstructed them from 1867 performance materials. Verdi made small revisions in 1872 and revised the score heavily in 1882, with a Viennese revival in mind. Aims of this revision were first to cut a very long opera, and also to repair some of the damage of the 1867 cuts and to bring the drama closer to Schiller (a goal of Verdi's from the very beginning), and finally to excise purely musical moments that impeded the action. With these in mind, Verdi cut out all of act I, placing Carlo's *romanza* in act II so that he would not be without a solo aria; cut the ballet (which had been obligatory for Paris) and the mask-changing episode preceding it; shortened the great act IV quartet; and recomposed the ending insurrection in act IV in a much more concise manner. These revisions were completed in February of 1883 and the result was published both in French (du Locle had helped Verdi) and in Italian; this version premiered at the Teatro alla Scala in Italian in January 1884 with Francesco Tamagno in the title role. Two years later another version was performed and published in which, with Verdi's consent, the 1867 Fontainebleau act preceded the four acts of the 1883 revision. This 1886 version is the one most often performed and recorded today. It is well to keep in mind that Verdi actually composed none of *Don Carlos* to an Italian text. Although this opera was not always appreciated, *Don Carlos* is now considered by many to be one of Verdi's greatest operas.

—Stephen Willier

DON GIOVANNI (Il Dissoluto Punito).

Composer: Wolfgang Amadeus Mozart.

Librettist: Lorenzo Da Ponte.

First Performance: Prague, National Theater, 29 October 1787.

Roles: Don Giovanni (bass-baritone); Leporello (bass); Donna Anna (soprano); Don Ottavio (tenor); Donna Elvira (soprano); Masetto (bass or baritone); Zerlina (soprano); Commendatore (bass); chorus (SATB).

Publications

books–

Gounod, C. *Le Don Juan de Mozart*. Paris, 1890; English translation, 1895; 1970.
Dumesnil, R. *Le "Don Juan" de Mozart*. Paris, 1927.
Jouve, P.J. *Le Don Juan de Mozart*. Fribourg, 1942; English translation, 1957.
Moberly, Robert B. *Three Mozart Operas: Figaro, Don Giovanni, The Magic Flute*. London, 1967.
Eggebrecht, Hans H. *Versuch über die Wiener Klassik: Die Tanzszene in Mozarts "Don Giovanni"*. Wiesbaden, 1972.
Kunze, Stefan. *Don Giovanni vor Mozart: die Tradition der Don Giovanni-Opern im italienischen Buffo-Theater des 18. Jahrhunderts*. Munich, 1972.
Amico, Fedele d'. *Attorno al "Don Giovanni" di Mozart*. Paris, 1978.
Hocquard, Jean-Victor. *Le "Don Giovanni" de Mozart*. Paris, 1978.
Massin, Jean, ed. *Don Juan, mythe littéraire et musical*. Paris, 1979.
Csampai, Attila, and Dietmar Holland, eds. *Wolfgang Amadeus Mozart. "Don Giovanni." Texte, Materialien, Kommentare*. Reinbek, 1981.
Rushton, Julian, ed. *W.A. Mozart: Don Giovanni: Cambridge Opera Guides*. Cambridge, 1981.

Rickmann, Sonja P. *Mozart: Ein bürgerlicher Künstler: Studien zu den Libretti "Le Nozze di Figaro," "Don Giovanni," und "Così fan tutte"*. Vienna, 1982.
Allenbrook, Wye J. *Rhythmic Gesture in Mozart: "Le nozze di Figaro" and "Don Giovanni"*. Chicago, 1983.
John, Nicholas, ed. *Wolfgang Amadeus Mozart: Don Giovanni*. London and New York, 1983.
Henze-Döhring, Sabine. *Opera seria, Opera buffa und Mozarts "Don Giovanni": Zur Gattungsconvergenz in der italienischen Oper des 18. Jahrhunderts*. Laaber, 1986.
Steptoe, Andrew. *The Mozart-Da Ponte operas: The Cultural and Musical Background to "Le Nozze di Figaro," "Don Giovanni," and "Così fan tutte"*. Oxford, 1989.
Miller, Jonathan, ed. *The Don Giovanni Book*. London, 1990.

articles–

Einstein, Alfred. "Das erste Libretto des 'Don Giovanni'." *Acta musicologica* 9 (1937): 149.
Wellesz, E. "Don Giovanni and the dramma giocoso." *Music Review* 4 (1943): 121.
Livermore, A. "The Origins of Don Juan." *Music and Letters* 44 (1963): 257.
Henning, C. "Thematic Metamorphoses in Don Giovanni." *Music Review* 30 (1969): 22.
Noske, F.R. "Don Giovanni: Musical Affinities and Dramatic Structure." *Studia musicologica Academiae scientiarum hungaricae* 12 (1970): 167; reprinted in *Theatre Research/Recherches théâtrales* 13 (1973): 60.
Kunze, Stefan. "Mozarts Don Giovanni und die Tanzszene im ersten Finale." *Analecta musicologica* 18 (1978).
Agmon, Eytan. "The Descending Fourth and its Symbolic Significance in *Don Giovanni*." *Theory and Practice* 4 (1979): 3.
Heartz, Daniel. "Goldoni, *Don Giovanni* and the *dramma giocoso*." *Musical Times* 120 (1979): 993.
Valentin, Erich. "'Don Ottavio balla Menuetto.' Anmerkungen zum *Don Giovanni*." *Acta mozartiana* 26 (1979): 66.
Heartz, Daniel. "'Che mi sembra morir': Donna Elvira and the Sextet." *Musical Times* 122 (1981): 448.
Osthoff, Wolfgang. "Gli endecasillabi Villostistici in *Don Giovanni* e *Nozze di Figaro*." In *Venezia e il melodramma nel settecento*, edited by Maria Teresa Muraro, vol. 2, p. 293. Florence, 1981.
Pirotta, Nino. "The Tradition of Don Juan Plays and Comic Operas." *Pamphlet of the Royal Musical Association* 107 (1981): 60.
Autexier, Philippe A. "Rhapsodie philologique à propos du *Don Giovanni* de Mozart." *Studia musicologica* 24 (1982): 21.
Staehelin, Martin. "'Ah fuggi il traditor . . .' Bemerkungen zur zweiten Donna-Elvira-Arie in Mozarts *Don Giovanni*." In *Festschrift Heinz Becker zum 60. Geburtstag am 26. Juni 1982*, edited by Jürgen Schläder and Reinhold Quandt, 67. Laaber, 1982.
Wilkens, Lorenz. "Mozarts *Don Giovanni*." In *Notizbuch 5/6. Musik*, edited by Reinhard Kapp, 59. Berlin, 1982.
Hirsbrunner, Theo. "Struktur und Dramaturgie in Mozarts *Don Giovanni*." *Universitas* 38 (1983): 985.
Stone, John. "The Making of 'Don Giovanni' and Its Ethos." *Mozart-Jahrbuch* (1984-85): 130.

Don Giovanni, **Luigi Bassi in the title role, Prague, 1787**

Volek, Tomislav. "Prague Operatic Traditions and Mozart's *Don Giovanni.*" In *Divadelní ústav* [Prague] no. 334 (1987): 23.

* * *

The Don Juan theme had appeared in Western literature even before Tirso de Molina (if indeed it was he) immortalized the great seducer's legendary powers in *El burlador de Sevilla* (*The Prankster from Seville*) around the turn of the sixteenth century. It was part of a corpus of tales inherited from the late middle ages, which included also the story of the quasi-historical Don Juan Tenorio, and may be seen as counterpart to another great legend of masculine prowess, that of Dr Faustus, which also harks back to medieval times.

The story line was primitively simple in the beginning, merely describing Don Juan's unending series of sexual exploits. But it grew deeper and more complicated as the tradition grew, as did the character of Don Juan himself. Originally merely a libidinous womanizer, Don Juan in time took on new psychological dimensions, offering a basis for philosophical speculations on the daemonic in romanticism, on the universality of the Don's persuasion, and so forth, as the tradition developed.

By 1787, when Lorenzo Da Ponte prepared a libretto for Mozart to set as *Don Giovanni, ovvero il dissoluto punito* (*Don Juan, or the Roué punished*), both the play and its principal character had reached maximum depth and complication. Truth to tell, these qualities were virtually copied from a libretto which Giovanni Bertati had produced in 1775 for a setting by Gazzaniga with the title *Don Giovanni Tenorio, o sia Il convitato di pietro* (*Don Juan Tenorio, or The Stone Guest*). Indeed, Da Ponte's recommendation that Mozart set his new libretto was probably prompted by his close familiarity with Bertati's script, which gave him basis for a new libretto with minimum labor on his part.

Mozart's Overture sets in motion both tragic and comic elements of this *dramma giocoso,* as the composer named it, building these upon two basic motives. The tragic element is expressed throughout by an ominous scalar figure in d-minor, which recurs as a psychological flashback at a key point in the drama, when Donna Anna first suspects that Don Giovanni is the mysterious rapist who murdered her father. The same scalar motive, with its aura of the supernatural, returns again at the end when Don Giovanni is consumed by hell-fire after his last encounter with the stone statue of the Commendatore. The second motive is a light-hearted tune which captures the merriment that brightens festive scenes throughout the drama.

Act I of the tragicomedy opens in the garden of the Commendatore, where Leporello, Don Giovanni's serving man, laments his underprivileged social status as he stands guard, while his master attempts to seduce Donna Anna, the Commendatore's daughter. How he longs to achieve the Don's status! Suddenly, much to Leporello's disquietude, a commotion begins as Don Giovanni appears, still masked, and hotly pursued by Anna, the angry object of his seduction. Awakened by the disturbance, the Commendatore enters, sword in hand, to challenge the intruder, who promptly dispatches the old man. Leporello, commenting on the fact that neither father nor daughter asked for what they got, flees with his master, as Donna Anna returns with Don Ottavio, her fiancé, to find her father already dead. It is a remarkable opening scene, introducing the two basic topics that are treated in the opera: Don Giovanni's ruling passion for sexual conquest,

and Leporello's revolutionary aspiration for equality. However, nothing in this opening scene is more remarkable than Mozart's music, which vividly mirrors every nuance of human feeling, every psychological reaction, with utmost reality. The musical portrayal of the dying Commendatore is one of the most masterful expressions of a human condition in all of operatic literature.

As Leporello and his master escape to make their way back to Seville, a brief duo-recitative reflects their ambivalent relationship. Don Giovanni is jubilant and unremorseful for his most recent acts, but nevertheless shows a strange dependence upon his minion, Leporello, who remains in the Don's service. The tone of the recitative veers suddenly as Don Giovanni senses a female presence and all his instincts are awakened.

Scene ii reveals Donna Elvira, whose presence had aroused the Don's hopes for another romantic adventure—hopes intensified when he hears her singing of finding the villain who had ruined her, "to carve out his heart." He does not recognize that Elvira is a former conquest until the end of her song, when she turns and recognizes him, the man who had ruined her life. In her surprise, her feelings of vengeance falter, giving way to soulful entreaty that they resume their old relationship. Don Giovanni, unheedful of the strength of character revealed in her virtuoso aria, slips away, after charging his servant to acquaint her with his illustrious record of sexual conquest. Leporello complies, singing a mocking "catalog aria," classifying, characterizing and enumerating all his exploits, nation by nation: there were 640 in Italy, 231 in Germany, 100 in France, 91 in Turkey, but 1003 in Spain! Mozart's music again subtly delineates every psychological nuance, with orchestral *bizzarrie* which catch the mocking tone of Leporello's aria most adroitly.

Even as Elvira, shocked by the Don's sheer effrontery, reaffirms her feelings of vengeance, the amorous Don is off on another romantic adventure, as Zerlina and Masetto, a peasant pair, enter to celebrate prenuptial festivities. Don Giovanni, deciding at once to exercise his "*droit de seigneur*" where Zerlina is concerned, orders Leporello to invite the wedding party to his castle, at the same time instructing him to keep Masetto well occupied. Immediately, he applies his seductive arts to Zerlina, and wins her over in a lively duet that faithfully mirrors her ebbing resistance and eventual capitulation. He is about to set off with her to a convenient cottage nearby, when Donna Elvira catches up with him, preventing the seduction. She warns Zerlina with the voice of bitter experience and upbraids the Don, still arguing passionately for reconciliation. Donna Anna and Don Ottavio arrive to witness the end of this scene. Disbelieving Don Giovanni's explanation that Donna Elvira is love-mad, they join forces with her, in growing doubt of his credibility. As he leaves, Donna Anna suffers a feeling of *dejà vu,* as the music recalls the scene of her father's death. At that moment she recognizes Don Giovanni as the rapist who killed her father.

Still intent on seducing Zerlina, and perhaps a dozen more that same evening, Don Giovanni gloats over prospects created by the great ball he has organized at his palace. Meanwhile, Zerlina manages at least partially to quiet Masetto's fears concerning her fidelity. But just as she does, Don Giovanni returns, and her reactions awaken all his fears again. So he decides to hide and watch; but the wily Don dissimulates, inviting both to the ball, now in full swing in the palace. Just then Donna Anna, Don Ottavio, and Donna Elvira arrive in masks, and Leporello, upon his master's instructions, invites them all to the ball. Inside, as the dance begins, Leporello again keeps Masetto occupied, while Don Giovanni dances off into a nearby bedroom with Zerlina. No longer compliant, she screams for help as he attempts to force her, and the crowd comes to her rescue. Cleverly, the Don emerges prodding Leporello forth at sword's point and branding him as the would-be rapist. No one is fooled, but Don Giovanni nevertheless makes good his escape in the confusion.

As act II begins, Leporello serves notice on his master: He will quit unless his master gives up women altogether. "Impossible," says the Don, "I need them more than the food I eat, more than the very air I breathe." He then quickly persuades Leporello to aid him with his next conquest. Don Giovanni now has settled his amorous attention upon Elvira's maid-servant. To lure Elvira away that evening, he disguises Leporello as himself by exchanging hats and cloaks, then stands behind his gesticulating servant while he sings a seductive aria underneath her window. Taken in by the ruse, Elvira descends to disappear into the shrubbery with Leporello, who under cover of night now undertakes the pleasant task of seducing her.

Meanwhile, Don Giovanni, dressed in Leporello's clothes, openly serenades Elvira's maid. But his seduction is forestalled by Masetto, at the head of a posse of peasants who seek to capture the aristocratic felon. Taking advantage of the darkness and using his servant's disguise, the Don pretends to join forces with the band and immediately sends off all the other peasants on various missions, tricking Masetto to give up his musket and pistol, with which he promptly beats him before making good his escape. Zerlina arrives with a lantern to find Masetto sorely wounded, and offers to cure him, magically, with a certain balm she carries with her always. As usual, Mozart's musical accompaniment is apt and highly suggestive.

Meanwhile, Donna Elvira, still mistaking Leporello for Don Giovanni, seeks what she supposes to be an amorous reconciliation, while he desperately tries to escape. Suddenly, Donna Anna and Don Ottavio come upon the pair, and they too mistake the servant for the master. To save his skin, Leporello reveals his true identity, then quickly runs off, leaping over the wall of the cemetery in which the Commendatore lies buried, to find Don Giovanni there before him. As the Don chortles over his latest conquest, a sepulchral voice interrupts, commanding both to be silent. Leporello is terrified, but Don Giovanni remains nonchalant, forcing his servant to read the inscription on the Commendatore's tomb: "Revenge awaits the villain who killed me." The Don, laughing, orders Leporello to invite the statue to dine with him that same evening. To the latter's dismay, the statue accepts. In the next scene, inserted after the first performance, Don Ottavio upbraids Donna Anna for postponing their wedding day by a year, but at last accepts her decision.

In the final scene, Don Giovanni, well entertained by music from several operas, including one of his own, prepares to dine in his apartment as Leporello waits to serve him. Just then Donna Elvira rushes in, in vainly urging the Don to repent. As she departs in total distress, the statue from the Commendatore's mausoleum treads heavily up the steps to the Don's apartment. He too urges the Don to repent, and, upon his resolute refusal, consigns him to his fate. The flames of hell rise up to surround him, and Don Giovanni falls headlong, to join the infernal chorus.

In a brief epilogue, all the remaining characters arrive to question Leporello about his master. When they learn of his fate, Donna Anna and Don Ottavio rejoice, Donna Elvira retires to a convent, Zerlina and Masetto go home to have their dinner, and Leporello goes off in search of a new master. Before going their several ways, they all sing a final chorus

on the fate of evildoers, whose punishment always suits their crimes.

—Franklin B. Zimmerman

DONIZETTI, (Domenico) Gaetano (Maria).

Composer. Born 29 November 1797, in Bergamo. Died 8 April 1848, in Bergamo. Married: Virginia Vasselli, 1828 (died 30 July 1837). Studied singing with Salari, piano with Gonzales, and harmony with J.S. Mayr at the Bergamo school of music; studied counterpoint with Pilotti and Mattei at the Bologna Liceo Filarmonico, 1815; 30 operas between 1816-29; *Anna Bolena* (1830) a huge success; visited Paris, 1835; succeeded Zingarelli as the director of the Naples Conservatory, 1837; *Poliuto* not performed in Naples due to censorship; numerous successful productions in France, including *La fille du régiment,* and *La favorite,* 1840; in Rome and Milan, 1841; court composer and master of the imperial chapel, Vienna, 1842; a stroke suffered in 1845 led to his death.

Operas

Il Pigmalione (scena drammatica), 1816, Bergamo, 13 October 1960.

L'ira d'Achille, 1817 [not performed].

Olimpiade, Metastasio, 1817 [unfinished].

Enrico di Borgogna, B. Merelli (after Kotzebue), Venice, San Luca, 14 November 1818.

Una folia, B. Merelli, Venice, San Luca, 15 December 1818 [also performed as *Il ritratto parlante*].

Le nozze in villa, B. Merelli, 1819, Mantua, Vecchio, carnival 1820-21 [also performed as *I provinciali*].

Il falegname di Livonia, o Pietro il grande, czar delle Russia, G. Bevilacqua-Aldovrandini (after A. Duval), Venice, San Samuele, 26 December 1819.

Zoraida di Granata, B. Merelli (after F. Gonzales), Rome, Torre Argentina, 28 January 1822; revised, with libretto revisions by J. Ferretti, Rome, 1824.

La zingara, A.L. Tottola, Naples, Nuovo, 12 May 1822.

La lettera anonima, G. Genoino, Naples, Fondo, 29 June 1822.

Chiara e Serafina, o I pirati, Felice Romani (after R.C.G. de Pixérécourt, *La cisterne*), Milan, Teatro alla Scala, 26 October 1822.

Alfredo il grande, A.L. Tottola, Naples, San Carlo, 2 July 1823.

Il fortunato inganno, A.L. Tottola, Naples, Nuovo, 3 September 1823.

L'ajo nell'imbarazzo, o Don Gregorio, Ferretti (after G. Giraud), Rome, Valle, 4 February 1824; revised, 1826 and 1828.

Emilia di Liverpool, Scatizzi, Naples, Nuovo, 28 July 1824; revised 1828; also performed as *L'eremitaggio di Liwerpool.*

Alahor in Granata, Palermo, Carolion, 7 January 1826.

La bella prigioniera, 1826 [unfinished].

Elvida, G.F. Schmidt, Naples, San Carlo, 6 July 1826.

Gabriella di Vergy, Tottola (after Du Belloy), 1826; second version composed 1838.

Olivio e Pasquale, Ferretti (after A.S. Sografi), Rome, Valle, 7 January 1827.

Gaetano Donizetti, portrait by Girolamo Induno

Otto mesi in due ore, ossia, Gli esiliati in Siberia, D. Gilardoni (after Pixérécourt, *La fille de l'exilé*), Naples, Nuovo, 13 May 1827; revised 1833.

Il borgomastro di Saardam, D. Gilardoni (after A.H.J. Mélesville, J.T. Merle, and E. Cantiran de Boire), Naples, Nuovo, 19 August 1827.

Le convenienze ed inconvenienze teatrali, Donizetti (after Sografi), Naples, Nuovo, 21 November 1827; revised 1840.

L'esule di Roma, ossia Il proscritto, D. Gilardoni, Naples, San Carlo, 1 January 1828 [also performed as *Settimio il proscritto*].

Alina, regina di Golconda, Felice Romani (after S.J. de Boufflers), Genoa, Carlo Felice, 12 May 1828; revised 1833.

Gianni di Calais, D. Gilardoni (after C.V. d'Arlincourt), Naples, Fondo, 2 August 1828.

Il Giovedi Grasso, o Il nuovo Pourceaugnac, D. Gilardoni, Naples, Fondo, fall 1828.

Il paria, Gilardoni (after C. Delavigne), Naples, San Carlo, 12 January 1829.

Elizabeth, o Il castello di Kenilworth, A.L. Tottola (after Hugo, *Amy Robsart;* Scribe, and Scott, *Leicester*) Naples, San Carlo, 6 July 1829.

I pazzi per progetto, D. Gilardoni (after Scribe and Poirson), Naples, Fondo, 7 February 1830.

Il diluvio universale, D. Gilardoni (after Byron, *Heaven and Earth,* and Ringhieri, *Il diluvio*), Naples, San Carlo, 28 February 1830.

Imelda de' Lambertazzi, A.L. Tottola (after Sperduti), Naples, San Carlo, 23 August 1830.

Anna Bolena, Felice Romani (after Pindemonte and Pepoli), Milan, Carcano, 26 December 1830.

Gianni di Parigi, Felice Romani (after Saint-Just), 1831, Milan, Teatro alla Scala, 10 September 1839.

Francesca di Foix, D. Gilardoni (after Favart and Saint-Amans, *Ninette à la cour*), Naples, San Carlo, 30 May 1831.

La romanziera e l'uomo nero, D. Gilardoni, Naples, Fondo, 18 June 1831.

Fausta, D. Gilardoni and Donizetti, Naples, San Carlo, 12 January 1832.

Ugo, conte di Parigi, Felice Romani (after Bis, *Blanche d'Acquitaine*), Milan, Teatro alla Scala, 13 March 1832.

L'elisir d'amore, Felice Romani (after Scribe, *Le philtre*), Milan, Canobbiana, 12 May 1832.

Sancia di Castiglia, P. Salatino, Naples, San Carlo, 4 November 1832.

Il furioso all'isola di San Domingo, Ferretti (after an anonymous *Don Quixote* play), Rome, Valle, 2 January 1833; revised 1833.

Parisina, Felice Romani (after Byron), Florence, Teatro della Pergola, 17 March 1833.

Torquato Tasso, Ferretti (after G. Rosini), Rome, Valle, 9 September 1833 [also performed as *Sordello il trovatore*].

Adelaide, 1834 [unfinished; partly used in *L'ange de Nisida*].

Lucrezia Borgia, Felice Romani (after Hugo), Milan, Teatro alla Scala, 26 December 1833; revised 1840.

Rosamonda d'Inghilterra, Felice Romani, Florence, Teatro della Pergola, 27 February 1834; revised as *Eleonora di Gujenna,* Naples, 1837.

Maria Stuarda, G. Bardi (after Schiller), 1834 [for Naples], Milan, Teatro alla Scala, 30 December 1835; second version [new libretto, Naples music], *Buondelmonte,* P. Saltino, Naples, San Carlo, 18 October 1834.

Gemma di Vergy, E. Bidera (after Dumas, *Charles VII*), Milan, Teatro alla Scala, 26 December 1834.

Marino Faliero, E. Bidera (after C. Delavigne and Byron), Paris, Théâtre Italien, 12 March 1835.

Lucia di Lammermoor, S. Cammarano (after Scott), Naples, San Carlo, 26 September 1835; revised 1839.

Belisario, S. Cammarano (after J.F. Marmontel), Venice, La Fenice, 4 February 1836.

Il campanello di notte, Donizetti (after L.L. Brunswick, M.B. Troin, and V. Lhérie, *La sonnette de nuit*), Naples, Nuovo, 1 June 1836.

Betly, ossia La capanna svizzera, Donizetti (after Scribe, *Le chalet*), Naples, Nuovo, 24 August 1836; revised, 1837.

L'assedio di Calais, S. Cammarano (after Du Belloy), Naples, San Carlo, 19 November 1836.

Pia de' Tolomei, S. Cammarano (after Sestini), Venice, Apollo, 18 February 1837; revised with libretto revisions by Sinigaglia, 1837.

Roberto Devereux, ossia Il conte de Essex, S. Cammarano (after F. Ancelot, *Elisabeth d'Angleterre*), Naples, San Carlo, 29 October 1837.

Maria di Rudenz, S. Cammarano (after Anicet-Bourgeois and Mellian, *La nonne sanglante*), Venice, La Fenice, 30 January 1838.

Le duc d'Albe, Eugène Scribe and Duveyrier, 1839 [unfinished].

Poliuto, S. Cammarano (after Corneille), 1838, Naples, San Carlo, 30 November 1848; second version, *Les martyrs,* Eugène Scribe, Paris, Opéra, 10 April 1840.

La fille du régiment, J.H.V. de Saint-Georges and J.F.A. Bayard, Paris, Opéra Comique, 11 February 1840.

L'ange de Nisida, A. Royer and G. Vaëz, 1839 [not performed]; also as *Silvia;* revised as *La favorite* [below].

La favorite, A. Royer and G. Vaëz (after Baculard d'Arnaud, *Le comte de Comminges*), Paris, Opéra, 2 December 1840; revised and expanded from *L'ange de Nisida* [above].

Adelia, o La figlia dell'arciere, Felice Romani and G. Marini (after an anonymous French play), Rome, Apollo, 11 February 1841.

Rita, ou Le mari battu, G. Vaëz, 1841, Paris, Opéra-Comique, 7 May 1860 [also performed as *Deux hommes et une femme*].

Maria Padilla, G. Rossi (after Ancelot), Milan, Teatro alla Scala, 26 December 1841.

Linda di Chamounix, G. Rossi (after D'Ennery and Lemoine, *La grâce de Dieu*), Vienna, Kärntnertor, 19 May 1842; revised 1842.

Ne m'oubliez pas, J.H.V. de Saint-Georges, 1842 [unfinished].

Caterina Cornaro, G. Sacchero (after Saint-Georges, *La reine de Chypre*), 1842, Naples, San Carlo, 18 January 1844.

Don Pasquale, G. Ruffini and Donizetti (after A. Anelli, *Ser Marc' Antonio*), Paris, Théâtre Italien, 3 January 1843.

Maria di Rohan, S. Cammarano (after Lockroy [J.P. Simon], *Un duel sous le cardinal de Richelieu*), Vienna, Kärntnertor, 5 June 1843; revised 1844.

Dom Sébastien, roi de Portugal, Eugène Scribe (after Barbossa Machado, *Memoires . . . o governo del Rey D. Sebastiao*), Paris, Opéra, 13 November 1843.

Publications

By DONIZETTI: books—

A. Eisner-Eisenhof, ed. *Lettere.* Bergamo, 1897.

About DONIZETTI: books—

Bellotti, A. *Donizetti e i suoi contemporanei.* Bergamo, 1866.
Alborghetti, F., and M. Galli. *Gaetano Donizetti e G. Simone Mayr: notizie e documenti.* Bergamo, 1875.

Branca, E. *Felice Romani ed i più riputi maestri di musica del suo tempo.* Turin, Florence, and Rome, 1882.

Calzado, A. *Donizetti e l'opera italiana in Spagna.* Paris, 1897.

Verzino, E.C. *Le opere di Gaetano Donizetti: contributo allo loro storia.* Bergamo and Milan, 1897.

Klefeld, W.J. *Don Pasquale von Gaetano Donizetti.* Leipzig, 1901.

Cametti, A. *Donizetti a Roma.* Turin, 1907.

Pougin, A. "Donizetti." In *Musiciens du XIXe siècle.* Paris, 1911.

Miragoli, L. *Il melodramma italiana nell' ottocento.* Rome, 1924.

Bonetti, G. *Gaetano Donizetti.* Naples, 1926.

Donati-Pettèni, G. *Studi e documenti donizettiani.* Bergamo, 1929.

———. *Donizetti.* Milan, 1930; 3rd ed. 1947.

Gavazzeni, G. *Gaetano Donizetti: vita e musiche.* Milan, 1937.

Pinetti, G. *Le opere di Donizetti nei teatri di Bergamo.* Bergamo, 1942.

Baccaro, M. *"Lucia di Lammermoor" prima al S. Carlo di Napoli.* Naples, 1948.

Barblan, G. *L' opera di Donizetti nell' età romantica.* Bergamo, 1948.

Zavadini, G. *Donizetti: vita, musiche, epistolario.* Bergamo, 1948.

Bossi, L. *Donizetti.* Brescia, 1956.

Geddo, A. *Donizetti: l' uomo, le musiche.* Bergamo, 1956.

Walker, Frank. *The Man Verdi.* London, 1962.

Weinstock, H. *Donizetti and the World of Opera in Italy, Paris, and Vienna in the First Half of the Nineteenth Century.* London, 1964.

Ashbrook, William. *Donizetti.* London, 1965; revised as *Donizetti and His Operas,* Cambridge, 1982.

Barblan, G. *La favorita: mito e realtà.* Venice, 1965.

Bleiler, H. *Lucia di Lammermoor by Gaetano Donizetti.* New York, 1972.

Allit, J. *Donizetti and the Tradition of Romantic Love: a Collection of Essays on a Theme.* London, 1975.

Primo l'convegno internazionale di studi donizettiani: Bergamo 1975.

Mitchell, J. *The Walter Scott Operas.* Tuscaloosa, Alabama, 1977.

Studi Donizettiani 1. 1962.

Studi Donizettiani 2. 1972.

Studi Donizettiani 3. 1978.

Hauser, Richard. *Felice Romani—Gaetano Donizetti—"Anna Bolena." Zur Ästhetik politischer Opern in Italien zwischen 1826 und 1831.* Emmendingen, 1980.

Black, John. *Donizetti's Operas in Naples.* London, 1982.

Steiner-Isenmann, Robert. *Gaetano Donizetti. Sein Leben und seine Opern.* Bern, 1982.

Gossett, Philip, et al. *Masters of Italian Opera: Rossini, Donizetti, Bellini, Verdi, Puccini. The New Grove Composer Biography Series.* London and New York, 1983.

Gossett, Philip. *Anna Bolena and the Artistic Maturity of Gaetano Donizetti.* Oxford, 1985.

articles–

Berlioz, H. "La fille du régiment." *Journal des débats* 16 February (1840); reprinted in *Les musiciens et la musique,* 145. Paris, 1903.

Scudo, P. "Donizetti et l'école italienne depuis Rossini." In *Critique et littérature musicales,* 75. Paris, 1850.

Chorley, H.F. "Donizetti's Operas." In *Thirty Years' Musical Recollection,* vol. 1, 153. London, 1862.

Bettòli, P. "Le opere di Gaetano Donizetti: errori e lacunae." In *Gaetano Donizetti: numero unico nel primo centenario della sua nascita 1797-1897,* ed. P. Bettoli, 26. Bergamo, 1897.

Pougin, A. "Les opéras de Donizetti en France." In *Gaetano Donizetti: numero unico nel primo centenario della sua nascita 1797-1897,* ed. P. Bettòli, 20. Bergamo, 1897.

Ricci, C. "Donizetti a Bologna: a appunti e documenti." In *Gaetano Donizetti: numero unico nel primo centenario della sua nascita 1797-1897,* ed. P. Bettòli, 10. Bergamo, 1897.

Prout, E. "Auber's 'Le philtre' and Donizetti's 'L'elisir d' amore': a Comparison." *Monthly Musical Record* 30 (1900): 25, 49, 73.

Lazzari, A. "Giovanni Ruffini, Gaetano Donizetti e il *Don Pasquale." Rassegna nazionale* 1-16 October, 1915.

Barbiera, R. "Chi ispirò la 'Lucia'." In *Vite ardenti nel teatro (1700-1900).* Milan, 1930.

Micca, C.B. "Giovanni Ruffini e il libretto del 'Don Pasquale'." *Rivista di Bergamo* 10 (1931): 537.

Gavazzeni, G. "Donizetti e l' Elisir d' amore." *La rassegna musicale* 6 (1933): 44.

Pizetti, I. "Un autografo di Donizetti." *La musica italiana dell' ottocento,* 231. Turin, 1947.

Schlitzer, F. "Curiosità epistolari inedite nella vita teatrale di Gaetano Donizetti." *Rivista musicale italiana* 1 (1948): 273.

Gallini, N. "Inediti donizettiani: ultima scena dell' opera 'Caterina Cornaro'." *Rivista musicale italiana* 55 (1953): 257.

Dal Fabbro, B. "Donizetti e l' opera buffa." In *I bidelli del Valhalla.* Florence, 1954.

Dent, E.J. "Donizetti: an Italian Romantic." In *Fanfare for Ernest Newman,* 86. London, 1955; reprinted in *Journal of the Donizetti Society* 2 (1975): 249.

Barblan, G. "Un personaggio di Cervantes nel melodramma italiano: 'Il furioso all' isole di San Domingo'." *Chigiana* 15 (1958): 85.

Walker, Frank. "The Librettist of 'Don Pasquale'." *Monthly Musical Record* 88 (1958): 85.

Commons, J. "An Introduction to 'Il duca d' alba'." *Opera* x (1959): 421.

———. "Emilia di Liverpool." *Music and Letters* 40 (1959): 207.

Lievsch, H. "Eine Oper—zwei Texte: textkritische Bemerkungen zu Donizettis 'Don Pasquale'." *Musik und Gesellschaft* 13 (1963): 91.

Barblan, G. "Alla ribalta un' ottocentesca tragedia lirica: 'Parisina d' Este' di Donizetti." *Chigiana* 21 (1964): 207-38.

Cella, F. "Indagini sulle fonte francesi dei libretti di Gaetano Donizetti." *Contributi dell' Istituto di filologia moderna* French series 4 (1966): 343-590.

Barblan, B. "Lettura di un' opera dimenticata: 'Pia de' Tolomei' di Donizetti (1836)." *Chigiana* 24 (1967): 221.

Celliti, R. "Il vocalismo italiano da Rossini a Donizetti." *Analecta musicologica* 5 (1968): 267; 7 (1969): 214-47.

Lippmann, F. "Gaetano Donizetti." In *Vincenzo Bellini und die italienische opera seria seiner Zeit. Analecta musicologica* 6 (1969): 304.

Rattalino, P. "Il processo compositivo nel 'Don Pasquale' di Donizetti." *Nuova Rivista Musicale Italiana* 1 (1970): 51, 263.

Schmid, Patric. "*Maria Stuarda* and Buondelmonte." *Opera* 24 (1973).

Dean, Winton. "Donizetti's Serious Operas." *Proceedings of the Royal Musical Association* 100 (1973-74): 123.

————. "Some Echos of Donizetti in Verdi's Operas." *3° congresso internazionale di studi verdiana: Milano 1972*, 122.

Barblan, G. "Donizetti in Naples." *Journal of the Donizetti Society* July (1974).

Schaap, J. "Il burgomastro di Saardam." *Journal of the Donizetti Society* 1 (1974): 51.

Watts, J. 'L'ajo nell' imbarazzo.' *Journal of the Donizetti Society* 1 (1974): 41.

Barblan, G. "Maria di Rohan." *Journal of the Donizetti Society* 2 (1975): 199.

Commons, Jeremy. "The Authorship of 'I picciolo virtuosi ambulanti'." *Journal of the Donizetti Society* 2 (1975): 199.

————. "Unknown Donizetti Items in the Neapolitan Journal 'Il sibilo'." *Journal of the Donizetti Society* 2 (1975): 145.

Guaricci, J. "Lucrezia Borgia." *Journal of the Donizetti Society* 2 (1975): 161.

Leavis, R. "*La favorite* and *La favorita:* One Opera, Two Librettos." *Journal of the Donizetti Society* 2 (1975): 117.

Lippmann, F. "Verdi und Donizetti." In *Opernstudien: Anna Amalie Abert zum 65. Geburtstag,* 153. Tutzing, 1975.

Messenger, M.F. "Donizetti, 1840: 3 'French' Operas and their Italian Counterparts." *Journal of the Donizetti Society* 2 (1975): 99.

Ashbrook, William. "Maria Stuarda: The Vindication of a Queen." *About the House* (1977).

Commons, Jeremy. "*Maria Stuarda* and the Neopolitan Censorship." *Journal of the Donizetti Society* 3 (1977).

————. "19th Century Performances of Maria Stuarda." *Journal of the Donizetti Society* 3 (1977).

White, Don. "Donizetti and the Three 'Gabriellas'." *Opera* October (1978).

Gazzaniga, Arrigo. "Un intervallo nelle ultime scene di *Lucia.*" *Nuova rivista musicale italiana* 13 (1979): 620.

Lippmann, Friedrich. "Briefe Rossinis und Donizettis in der Bibliothek Massimo, Rome." *Analecta musicologica* 19 (1979): 330-35.

Black, John N. "Notes for the Staging of *Lucia di Lammermoor.*" *Journal of the Donizetti Society* 4 (1980).

————. "Cammarano's Self-Borrowings: The Libretto of *Poliuto.*" *Journal of the Donizetti Society* 4 (1980).

Budden, Julian. "Verdi and Meyerbeer in relation to *Les vêpres siciliennes.*" *Studi Verdiana* 1 (1982): 11.

Avant-scène opéra September 1983 [*Lucia di Lammermoor* issue].

Gazzaniga, Arrigo. "Le geminazione nel linguaggio di Donizetti." *Nuova revista musicale italiana* 18 (1984): 420.

Morey, Carl. "Donizetti Revised the Rules." *Opera Canada* 23 (1984): 24.

Avant-scène opéra February 1987 [*L'elixir d'amour* issue].

Avant-scène opéra April 1988 [*Don Pasquale* issue].

Ashbrook, William. "Popular Success, the Critics and Fame: the Early Careers of *Lucia di Lammermoor* and *Belisario.*" *Cambridge Opera Journal* 2 (1990): 65.

*　　*　　*

The reputation of Gaetano Donizetti has undergone remarkable fluctuations. At the outset of his career he was regarded as merely one of a number of people imitating Rossini; later, even in the first years after *Anna Bolena* had made his name known in Paris, London, and Vienna, he was apt to be ranked as inferior to Bellini. It was not until *Lucia di Lammermoor,* which ironically had its premiere three days after Bellini's untimely death, that Donizetti became generally recognized as the leading Italian composer of his day, and this was in part because *Lucia* spoke persuasively to the romantic sensibility of its time.

Until his death, Donizetti was the most widely performed composer of the day, even though his declining health cut short his active career in 1845. His reputation lost ground during the remaining years of the nineteenth century, in part because of the influx of newer works (by Verdi, Wagner, and the *veristi*) and in part because singers capable of doing full justice to his music were becoming scarcer. Up through the time of World War II, he had come to be regarded as hopelessly old-fashioned, a composer for canaries. It was not until the 1950s that the tide began to turn, and today he is generally acknowledged as one of the most important Italian composers of his time and a key figure in the development of Italian opera.

The reasons for this shift are not hard to find. Most importantly, since World War II the influx of new works that enter the repertory and are performed internationally with any frequency has so shrunk as to become barely perceptible. To introduce variety into their offerings, the directors of large, expensive-to-run opera houses found no alternative but to turn to neglected works from the past. Further, in those years after World War II there emerged a number of singers, sopranos principally, with Maria Callas heading the procession, who made a popular and artistic success of revivals of some largely forgotten operas by Donizetti, among them *Anna Bolena, Maria Stuarda,* and *Lucrezia Borgia.* Further, the case for opera composers in particular has been boosted considerably by the emergence of newer and handier methods of not merely auditory recording but visual recording as well, improvements which make a whole cornucopia of attractive material easily accessible to a steadily increasing public. Donizetti's reputation has profited from these developments because of the sheer number of viable operas in the whole gamut of genres to be found in his extensive *oeuvre.*

The conditions under which Donizetti was forced to pursue his career were unfavorable in certain respects. In his time composers were primarily concerned with providing material for singers, tailored to show off their strong points and disguise their weak ones. In those days before the repertory concept was well established, the opera houses of Italy constantly demanded new material, preferably fresh but not too far out, much in the way television requires it today. By training, Donizetti was equipped better to meet this requirement than most of his contemporaries, but what raised him above them was his craftsmanship, his good taste, and his deep concern with dramatic values.

In Italy in Donizetti's time every new stagework had to conform to the stringent limits imposed by religious as well as political censors, imposed in the rather naive hope that if theaters were places that uplifted morals they would also affirm the status quo politically. This purpose rather seriously limited the subjects available for musico-dramatic treatment. As actively as he could as a private citizen dependent upon state-regulated theaters for his livelihood, Donizetti waged a campaign to try to liberalize these censorious restrictions in the interest of providing powerful dramatic fare in the form of romantic lyric tragedies. In Naples both *Maria Stuarda* and *Poliuto* were banned before they received what would have been their first performances. *Lucrezia Borgia,* to cite another instance, was regarded as such a volatile subject (its heroine a pope's daughter who is presented as a mass poisoner) that two years elapsed after its successful premiere in Milan before another Italian opera house would stage it and then only in a bowdlerized form. Also at Milan, then slightly more liberal than Naples, Maria Malibran sought to get away with using the pre-censored text and action of *Maria Stuarda*, with the result that the opera was banned there as well after only a handful of performances.

As a composer, Donizetti excelled both in tragic works and comic, the most consistently popular of the latter being *L'elisir d'amore*, *La fille du régiment*, and *Don Pasquale*, but serious works dominated his last decade of activity. He was particularly famous for his skill at writing powerful ensembles, the most famous of them being the "sextet" from *Lucia*, but there are a number of others that are equally effective: the whole temple scene from *Poliuto* (which anticipates many of the effects of the triumphal scene in Verdi's *Aïda*) and the septet in act IV of *Dom Sébastien*. One of his greatest achievements, serious or comic, is the quartet-finale to act II of *Don Pasquale*.

Donizetti frequently experimented with modifying the convention of quadri-partite structure he inherited from Rossini. This pattern consisted of: 1) *tempo d'attacco* or active build-up, 2) *cantabile*, a static lyric section (often reflective), 3) *tempo di mezzo*, active, shift of mood (often a message arrives or a decision is reached), and 4) *cabaletta* or *stretta*, a static piece, often a two-statement aria with opportunities for vocal display, or, in an ensemble, involving the intensification of some confrontation. This four-section pattern could be employed in solo arias, duets, and large ensembles. In its totality the mad scene from *Lucia* is a familiar example of this structure. Donizetti, however, frequently modified this basic pattern. As one who was much concerned with dramatic values, Donizetti shifted the whole emphasis of the mid-point finale in *Maria Stuarda*, for example, to the third section, the confrontation between Queen Elizabeth and Mary, Queen of Scots. Sometimes he would introduce a second voice into what would traditionally have been a solo, as when he inserts a mezzo-soprano line into the entrance aria of the heroine of *Rosamonda d'Inghilterra*. In two of his later works, *Linda di Chamounix* and *Caterina Cornaro*, he experimented with eliminating or telescoping parts of this compound structure, even dividing its sections between different soloists, all in the interest of sustaining dramatic tension and momentum.

One characteristic peculiar to his style was his ability to write sad elegiac numbers using major instead of minor tonalities: Edgardo's 'Tu che al Dio spiegasti l'ali' from the tomb scene in *Lucia* is a good example of this, as is the arioso for the dying Gennaro in the final scene of *Lucrezia*. In many ways, Donizetti can be seen to anticipate certain aspects of Verdi's practice: increased importance of baritone parts, as with the title roles in *Il furioso*, *Torquato Tasso*, and *Belisario*. There is a general movement away from the emphasis on solo arias toward confrontational duets as points of major focus: the encounter between the Duke of Nottingham and his wife Sara at the beginning of act III of *Roberto Devereux*, for instance, or the father-daughter encounter in act II of *Linda*, or the tragic duet that climaxes act IV of *La favorite*. The treatment of the voices in the famous trio in *Lucrezia Borgia* provided a model that lingered in the back of Verdi's mind as late as *Otello*. Indeed, *Lucrezia Borgia* was receiving its first round of performances at the Teatro alla Scala when Verdi came to Milan to study composition, and the impact of this work upon his formative imagination is difficult to overestimate.

It used to be wondered at that a few of Donizetti's works stubbornly survived even when his reputation was at its lowest ebb. Prejudices and fashions have modified the repertory in the century and a half since his death. As the so-called "music of the future" (a phrase associated with the introduction of Wagner's works) has receded into the past and, later, various anti-romantic stances have come to seem mere posturing, the musical consistency and unfailing good taste of Donizetti have come to seem more valuable virtues than once they did. The operatic repertory we have grown accustomed to today is more extensive chronologically than it was even a quarter of a century ago. In its context the combination of vocal melody, solid structure, and dramatic intensity to be found in a surprising number of Donizetti's operas have won him new respect and admiration.

—William Ashbrook

LA DONNA DEL LAGO [The Lady of the Lake].

Composer: Gioachino Rossini.

Librettist: A.L. Tottola (after Scott, *The Lady of the Lake*).

First Performance: Naples, San Carlo, 24 September 1819.

Roles: Elena (soprano); Malcolm (mezzo-soprano); Rodrigo (tenor); Uberto (tenor); Douglas of Angus (bass); Albina (soprano); Serano (tenor); Bertram (tenor); chorus.

Publications

articles–

Bonaccorsi, A. "*La donna del lago.*" *La rassegna musicale* (1958).
Melica, A. "L'aria in rondò de *La donna del lago.*" *Bollettino del Centro rossiniano di studi* (1958).
Isotta, P. "*La donna del lago* e la drammaturgica di Rossini." *Bollettino del Centro rossiniano di studi* (1970).

*   *   *

La donna del lago, one of Rossini's most frequently revived operas in the nineteenth century, was premiered at the Teatro San Carlo in Naples on 24 September 1819. It is an *opera seria* in two acts with a libretto by Andrea Leone Tottola based on Sir Walter Scott's poem *The Lady of the Lake*. In the original cast, the title role was sung by Isabella-Angela Colbrán, who created a number of Rossini's heroines. The action takes place in Scotland during the time when the Highlanders were in conflict with James V, who was planning to subdue them. *La donna del lago* is thus one of the several Italian operas from the early nineteenth century with a Scottish setting. In act I, Elena, the "lady of the lake" and daughter of the rebel leader Douglas of Angus, sings pensively of her love for Malcolm as she crosses the lake. Elena's father, however, has promised her to Rodrigo. Elena encounters Uberto, who is actually the king in disguise, separated from his hunting party, and offers him shelter. He falls in love with her practically at first sight and is mistakenly convinced that she returns his feelings. As Elena is about to be married to Rodrigo, Malcolm arrives with forces to repel the advancing royal army. In act II, Elena is forced to tell Uberto the truth about her feelings for him; he gives her a ring that he claims will obtain for her anything she wishes from the king. Rodrigo

A scene from Rossini's *La donna del lago,* Royal Italian Opera, Covent Garden, 1847

surprises them and challenges Uberto to a duel, which Rodrigo loses. The rebels are defeated and Elena's father, Douglas of Angus, is captured. Elena recognizes Uberto's true identity, the king releases Douglas and gives Elena in marriage to Malcolm.

La donna del lago, the first opera in Italy based on a work by Walter Scott was a landmark opera in its use of such romantic elements as local color and characteristic choruses. Scott's poem seemed to cry out for operatic treatment: it had a strong narrative line, vividly contrasting characters, picturesque lake and mountain scenery, in addition to numerous cues for choruses and folk songs, ballads, and laments. Ellen's "Ave Maria" was set by Franz Schubert and became one of his most popular songs. The focus on landscape, atmosphere, and setting is captured by Rossini especially well in the large ensembles at both the beginning and the end of the first act. The orchestral prelude consists of a mere sixteen bars before the chorus of countrymen begin to sing. Pastoral-idyllic elements such as a chorus of shepherds and hunters are evoked by lyrical music and by the prominence of hunting-horns. Elena appears in a boat on the lake, a stage picture that prompted the following response from Stendahl in his *Life of Rossini:* "The décor of the opening scene showed a wild and lonely loch in the Highlands of Scotland, upon whose waters, the *Lady of the Lake,* faithful to her name, was seen gliding gracefully along, upright beside the helm of a small boat. This set was a masterpiece of the art of stage-design. The mind turned instantly towards Scotland, and

waited expectantly for the magic of some Ossianic adventure." The conclusion of the first act features the Scots bards singing a hymn to a harp accompaniment as suggested by Scott's "Harp of the North! that mouldering long hast hung/ On the witch-elm that shades Saint Fillian's spring." The warriors sing a martial chorus to a brass band accompaniment; eventually the two melodies are contrapuntally combined.

La donna del lago was not well received at its premiere. The second night's audience was considerably more responsive, however, and the work quickly became appreciated. Colbrán's powers were on the decline at this time; Rossini thus gave Elena only one brilliant solo scene (the finale, "Tanti affetti") and relatively little ensemble singing. On the other hand, the two tenors must sing a number of high Cs, several C-sharps, and extensive coloratura passages. When Rossini wrote the role of Elena's lover, Malcolm, for a mezzo-soprano, he was employing an operatic convention that was already outmoded. There is general agreement that *La donna del lago* begins better than it finishes. The static second act was labeled a "costume in concert" by the nineteenth-century English critic, Henry Chorley.

—Stephen Willier

DON PASQUALE.

Composer: Gaetano Donizetti.

Librettists: G. Ruffini and Gaetano Donizetti (after A. Anelli, *Ser Marc' Antonio*).

First Performance: Paris, Théâtre-Italien, 3 January 1843.

Roles: Don Pasquale (bass); Ernesto (tenor); Dr Malatesta (baritone); Norina (soprano); Notary (tenor, baritone, or bass); chorus (SATB).

Publications

book–

Klefeld, W.J. *Don Pasquale von Gaetano Donizetti.* Leipzig, 1901.

articles–

Lazzari, A. "Giovanni Ruffini, Gaetano Donizetti e il *Don Pasquale.*" *Rassegna nazionale* 1-16 October, 1915.
Micca, C.B. "Giovanni Ruffini e il libretto del 'Don Pasquale'." *Rivista di Bergamo* 10 (1931): 537.
Walker, Frank. "The Librettist of 'Don Pasquale'." *Monthly Musical Record* 88 (1958): 85.
Lievsch, H. "Eine Oper—zwei Texte: textkritische Bemerkungen zu Donizettis 'Don Pasquale'." *Musik und Gesellschaft* 13 (1963): 91.
Rattalino, P. "Il processo compositivo nel 'Don Pasquale' di Donizetti." *Nuova rivista musicale italiana* 1 (1970): 51, 263.
Avant-scène opéra April 1988 [*Don Pasquale* issue].

*　　*　　*

The last of Donizetti's comic operas, *Don Pasquale* is also the last work in the original *opera buffa* tradition to have remained in the repertory. It was written for the Théâtre-Italien, where it enjoyed immediate success, thanks to the supple wit of its score and a cast including the greatest stars of the international Italian opera circuit: Lablache, Tamburini, Grisi, and the tenor Mario. Luigi Lablache's characterization of the portly old Pasquale trying to play the gallant suitor in act II was especially appreciated. The text was a re-working by Giovanni Ruffini of an 1810 *buffa* libretto, *Ser Marc'Antonio,* with an unusual amount of input from Donizetti himself.

Don Pasquale is determined to disinherit his nephew, Ernesto, who has refused the sensible liaison proposed by his uncle. To effect this disinheritance, he decides to get married himself, with the help of his doctor and confidant, Malatesta. The doctor assures him that he has the perfect candidate in the person of his sister, "Sofronia," a meek and obedient girl fresh from the convent. In the meantime he contrives with the high-spirited Norina, the real object of Ernesto's affection, to have her play the part of the sister in such a way as to cure Pasquale of his matrimonial ambitions forever. Norina arrives with Malatesta, feigning the utmost timidity until the moment the (sham) contract is signed. Thereupon she immediately begins to play the brazen hussy, to the consternation of Pasquale and the amusement of Ernesto, who is present as a witness.

In act III "Sofronia" compounds her new-found impertinence with outrageous extravagance. Don Pasquale is finally defeated when his uncontrollable new wife delivers him a slap in the face on her way out to the theater, where she goes in defiance of his commands. Now Pasquale is ready to fall in with the next stage of the plot against him. Dr Malatesta arranges a rendezvous between Sofronia/Norina and a secret admirer for that evening in the garden and alerts her husband to this assignation. Pasquale tries to snare his guilty wife. Although he fails even at this, the masks are soon dropped, and in his relief the old man quickly assents to the marriage of the young lovers.

The enduring popularity of *Don Pasquale* is probably due to several factors. The work is simple and concise without being vapid. The vocal roles and the orchestration are grateful and elegant but not over-taxing (with the possible exception of the consistently high tessitura of the tenor role). The comic situations are well-defined and easily conveyed, whether in Italian or in translation, as, for example, Norina's sudden character reversal in the act-II finale, her clowning with Malatesta as they rehearse her role as Sofronia, or the ever-popular Rossinian patter style of Malatesta and Pasquale as they plot to surprise the guilty lovers in act III. All of the roles (again with the exception of Ernesto) offer ample opportunity for engaging comic acting. Donizetti usually provides these situations with foolproof cues by means of apt declamatory inflections and gestures in the vocal line. Yet every character is afforded at least one opportunity for expansive lyricism, even the affable prankster Malatesta ("Bella siccome un angelo," act I), and the cunning, roguish Norina (her opening cavatina and the "notturno" with Ernesto in the garden scene of act III).

Although Donizetti claimed to have completed *Don Pasquale* in eleven days—fast work even for this facile composer—the evidence suggests that this figure does not include the time spent on orchestration and—in the case of Ernesto's principal number, "Cercherò lontana terra"—even a considerable amount of sketching and revision. Some time was saved by means of the typical procedure of borrowing earlier material: Don Pasquale's bouncy $\frac{3}{8}$ cabaletta, "Un foco insolito," was transposed down from a tenor aria in *Gianni di Parigi* (1831), and the final ensemble rondo is a re-working of a *mélodie* for voice and piano, "La bohémienne" (1842).

The characters in *Don Pasquale* are all clearly drawn from stock buffa types: the over-aged suitor, the strong-willed and rebellious young woman, the young tenor lover prone to amorous lament, the neutrally situated figure directing the course of the intrigue. Naturally, the style of their music is also indebted to the analogous vocal types and styles, such as the characteristic syllabic patter of the *basso buffo* in ensemble contexts, or the pert coloratura *soubrette* of Norina, immediately recalling Rosina in *Il barbiere di Siviglia*. The element of pathos, often cited as a trademark of Donizetti's mature comic operas, is focused here in the A-minor larghetto, "E finita, Don Pasquale," in act III. The following section, in C major (with Norina), is notable for its expressive excursions into the neapolitan-relation of D flat. The "Mozartean" quality that has been attributed to Donizetti's last *opera buffa* may reside in the intimacy and deftness of its musical characterizations in general, or in the specific musical character of such passages as the bustling D-major "vivace" ending act II, whose rhythmic and melodic gestures suggest a deliberate evocation of the finales of Mozart or Cimarosa. On the other hand, Donizetti also makes repeated use of a quick, $\frac{3}{8}$ or $\frac{6}{8}$ waltz rhythm (e.g., Norina's "Via, caro sposino," the chorus's "Quel nipotino," and the rondo-finale, "Bravo, bravo, Don

The London premiere of *Don Pasquale*, Her Majesty's Theatre, 1843, with (from left to right) Giovanni Mario as Ernesto, Giulia Grisi as Norina, Luciano Fornasari as Malatesta, and Luigi Lablache as Don Pasquale

Pasquale!" all in act III), lending the score a distinctly "modern" imprint. This contrast of styles seems appropriate to a work standing, as it does, at the end of a tradition.

—Thomas S. Grey

DON QUICHOTTE [Don Quixote].

Composer: Jules Massenet.

Librettist: Henri Cain (after Jacques Le Lorrain, *Le chevalier de la longue figure*).

First Performance: Monte Carlo, Opera, 19 February 1910.

Roles: Don Quixote (bass); Sancho (baritone); Dulcinea (contralto); Juan (tenor); Pedro (soprano); Garcia (soprano); Rodriguez (tenor); Two Servants (baritones); Bandit Chief (speaking); Four Bandits (speaking); chorus (SAATTBB).

Publications

articles—

Schlegel, Klaus. "Don Quichotte: die Fabellesart in der Inszenierung der Komischen Oper Berlin." In *Jahrbuch der Komischen Oper Berlin* 12 (1973).

THÉÂTRE LYRIQUE MUNICIPAL (GAÎTÉ)

DON QUICHOTTE

Comédie héroïque en 5 actes
de HENRI CAIN d'après LE LORRAIN
Musique de J. MASSENET

A poster for Massenet's *Don Quichotte*, 1910

Avant-scène opéra December (1986) [*Don Quichotte* issue].

*　　*　　*

Don Quichotte is a late work taken from a contemporary poetic drama by Jacques Le Lorrain, which in turn was based on the Spanish masterpiece by Cervantes. In this operatic version Don Quixote becomes a champion of goodness and idealism, while Dulcinea is transformed from a tavern servant into a sophisticated lady of fashion. The famous windmill incident is preserved from Cervantes, but the main episode concerns Quixote's gallant retrieval of the lady's necklace from a gang of bandits: they are so moved by his blessed simplicity that they meekly hand it over to him. When the haughty Dulcinea rejects his offer of marriage, the old man realizes his futility and dies, lance in hand, leaning against a tree.

This "comédie héroïque," as Massenet called it, has a genial warmth that sets it apart from his other works. The brilliance of *Manon* and *Thaïs* is replaced by a more relaxed mood, and the music he wrote for Dulcinea in particular strikes a delicate balance between irony and true emotion. Sometimes his touch is so light that the style hints at operetta, although Don Quixote himself is always portrayed with sympathy. Written as a starring role for Chaliapin, the central character is given many opportunities himself, among them the famous mandoline serenade which is a tender statement of romantic idealism and which returns at various points throughout the action.

The humor of the score expresses itself in various different ways. One example is Sancho Panza's boisterous diatribe against women, "those hussies, those jades!" Another, more subtle and reaching a plane where idiocy becomes sublime, is Quixote's aria when he attacks the windmills. By the fifth act, however, which shows him dying in the starry night, sympathetic amusement at him has turned into pity. The faithful Sancho addresses him, "O mon maître, O mon Grand!" (O my master, O my Great One), in a few bars of pathetic *grisaille,* and the knightly apotheosis takes place to a flowing accompaniment which repeats the fourth-act motif of Dulcinea's regret that the time of love has flown.

To a certain extent the original drama on which the opera is founded presents a self-portrait of its author Jacques Le Lorrain, foolhardy to the point of nobleness, eccentric to a degree of genius. His version of the knight of the doleful countenance inspired a late flowering of Massenet's art, as mellow as it is attractive. The music written for Dulcinea shows an advance on his earlier techniques of constructing his heroine's melodic lines: particularly noticeable are the plangent tones of her lament referred to above ("Lorsque le temps d'amour a fini"), which gains still more from the contrast it makes with the bright festive music immediately before and after it. Only in the fourth act, where she gently disabuses the amorous knight, does the too-expansive bloom seem a little out of place. This is only a small blemish on a score which in general is remarkable for its sustained charm and attractiveness. Although much of its initial success was due inevitably to the presence of Chaliapin, revivals of *Don Quichotte* have shown that the opera can stand on its own merits and that the music still preserves its vitality and its ability to move the listener.

—James Harding

DON QUIXOTE
See DON QUICHOTTE

DIE DREIGROSCHENOPER [The Threepenny Opera].

Composer: Kurt Weill.

Librettists: B. Brecht and E. Hauptmann (after John Gay, *The Beggar's Opera*).

First Performance: Berlin, Theater am Schiffbauerdamm, 31 August 1928.

Roles: Jenny (chanteuse-style singer); Polly (soprano); Macheath (tenor); Mr Peachum (bass); Mrs Peachum (mezzo-soprano); Lucy (soprano); Streetsinger (tenor); Tiger Brown (bass); chorus (SATB).

Publications

book—

Hilton, Stephen. *Kurt Weill: The Threepenny Opera.* Cambridge, 1990.

articles—

Einstein, A. "A German Version of 'The Beggar's Opera'." *Radio Times* 1 February (1935): 13.

Mitchell, D. "Kurt Weill's 'Dreigroschenoper' and the German Cabaret-opera in the 1920s. *The Chesterian* 25 (1950): 1.

Kowalke, Kim H. "Accounting for Success: Misunderstanding *Die Dreigroschenoper.*" *Opera Quarterly* spring (1989).

*   *   *

Die Dreigroschenoper, the second collaboration of Bertolt Brecht and Kurt Weill (they had already completed the *Mahagonny Songspiel*), not only created a new style somewhere between opera and popular theater, but was to set the type for much of Brecht's later theatrical practice. Although based on John Gay's *The Beggar's Opera* (in a German translation provided for Brecht by Elisabeth Hauptmann), *The Threepenny Opera* differed in spirit from its original; musically, it owes much not only to Pepusch's ballads, but also to operatic models such as *Die Zauberflöte* and *Fidelio,* German cabaret styles, and American jazz.

The story follows the outlines of Gay's play but with a Brechtian twist. Macheath, affectionately known as Mack the Knife (Mackie Messer) has married, in a mock ceremony, Polly Peachum, the daughter of a man who runs a front for beggars in Victorian London. In doing so, however, Mac-

The Threepenny Opera, **English Music Theatre, London, 1976 (Susan Daniel as Lucy Brown and Nigel Douglas as Macheath)**

heath angers not only her parents but also his former lover, the prostitute Jenny, who with Mrs Peachum conspires to turn him in to the authorities for his many crimes. However, this is not easy, since Macheath has a long-standing agreement with the Chief of Police, Tiger Brown, who overlooks his crimes in return for payoffs. Peachum, however, forces Brown to arrest Macheath this time by threatening to organize a march of beggars to disrupt the he Queen's coronation. Macheath escapes, but he is betrayed and arrested again. Brought to the gallows, he sings a ballad asking forgiveness for his crimes but is rescued at the last moment by operatic convention—Peachum announces that the opera demands a better ending. Promptly a Riding Messenger from the Queen arrives and announces Macheath's reprieve in an elaborate burlesque of rescue operas. All characters then step forward and sing a final chorale prelude, ironically exhorting the audience to combat injustice, but in moderation.

The theatrical and operatic style, which owes much to the moralistic commentary in *Die Zauberflöte* as well as *The Beggar's Opera,* is intended to provide what Brecht later called estrangement (*Verfremdung*). He and Weill intended not simply to parody operatic conventions but to provide social commentary which engages the audience in new ways, later elaborated by Brecht as part of what he called epic theater. The songs consciously interrupt the action, their titles announced on letter boards and the actors stepping out of character in order to sing; the singing style is rough, with many lines spoken "against" the music rather than sung with it. The texts of the songs, influenced by François Villon and Rudyard Kipling, comment on the action, though often very obliquely. The point is to disallow the usual identification an audience has with the characters in illusionist theater and to force the audience to view them as actors and to see theater as social space. Brecht and Weill attempt to call into question the easy middle-class assumptions of audience members; the songs emphasize the injustice and pain of a bourgeois world in which every person is a commodity.

Gay's opera depends on the motivations of individual characters. For Brecht and Weill, the individuals are, rather, examples of an economic system which forces them to become property, things to be bought and sold. For example, Macheath wants Polly less for herself than for her business acumen; he plans to turn in his followers and go into banking (the obvious point is that there is no difference between thieves and bankers). Similarly, Peachum uses the beggars to provide his own income, forcing them to exploit the inadequate pity of the middle class by donning false limbs and rubber wounds. Jenny sells Macheath just as he, her pimp, sells her; the other prostitutes, like Peachum's beggars and Macheath's thieves, sell themselves and their work. Though this work is usually classified as pre-Marxist Brecht, the message is clear: bourgeois society is structured on the exploitation of the workers, who reproduce their own exploitation by failing to question the discrepancy between the easy sentimentality advocating justice and love, ironically presented in the songs, and their own reality. The final parody of baroque opera's *deus ex machina* points out that the bourgeois system cannot fail its own members: Macheath is needed by the Queen to keep the system of commodification going, so he is spared.

Musically, Weill's score places itself firmly in the various movements in Germany in the twenties to renounce an individualist and elitist aesthetic for a new style of music that included popular and dance elements, a simplification of musical means, and an overall montage effect which highlights the artificiality of each of its elements. The music is characterized by a ballad style, beginning with the famous opening *Moritat* (a type of ballad sung by street singers who illustrated

their lurid tales with pictures, which may have suggested Brecht's use of title-boards for the songs throughout). Weill's music employs monotonous Alberti basses, simple melodic lines, texts and melodies that often don't quite "fit" together, small melodic ranges in keeping with the untrained voices of the actors, and dance and jazz rhythms. The music was described by Adorno as surrealist, designed to shock the decadent bourgeoisie, as was the text. However, the work was and remains extremely popular with exactly the middle-class audience it was supposed to shock.

—Sandra Corse

I DUE FOSCARI [The Two Foscari].

Composer: Giuseppe Verdi.

Librettist: Francesco Maria Piave (after Byron, *The Two Foscari*).

First Performance: Rome, Torre Argentina, 3 November 1844.

Roles: Francesco Foscari (baritone); Jacopo (tenor); Lucrezia Contarini (soprano); Jacopo Loredano (bass); Barbarigo (tenor); Pisana (soprano); Officer of the Council of Ten (bass); Servant of Doge (bass); Messer Grande (mute); Two Small Sons of Jacopo (mute); Officer (mute); Jailor (mute); chorus (SATB).

Publications

articles—

Simone, C. "Lettere al tenore Mario de Candia sulla cabaletta de *I due Foscari.*" *Nuova Antologia* 69 (1934).
Biddlecombre, George. "The Revision of 'No, non morrai, che' i perfidi'. Verdi's Compositional Process in *I due Foscari.*" *Studi verdiani* 2 (1983): 59.

*   *   *

I due Foscari (1844) was Verdi's sixth opera, coming immediately after his Venice triumph earlier the same year with *Ernani.* The opera is based on Lord Byron's play, *The Two Foscari,* a rather static exploration of the hidden malevolence of fifteenth-century Venice that was never intended for stage performance. It nevertheless attracted Verdi, who described it to his librettist Francesco Piave as "a fine subject, delicate and full of pathos," while noting that it would need some changes since it didn't quite have the "theatrical grandeur needed for an opera." The work was enthusiastically received at its opening performances in Rome and appeared everywhere until the 1870s, when it fell into disfavor. Dismissed, usually by critics who had never seen it, in the 1930s and 40s as an inferior work that could never be resuscitated, it began, as part of a reawakening interest in early Verdi, to reappear onstage to favorable audience and critical response only in the 1950s.

The action, set in the Venice of 1457, traces the final stages in the misfortunes of the elder Foscari, the Doge, and his last living son, Jacopo, who has been brought back out of exile to

A scene from Verdi's *I due Foscari,* **Royal Italian Opera, London, 1847**

stand trial for further crimes against Venice. An enemy of the Foscari family, one Loredano, a member of the Council of Ten, pursues father and son relentlessly for injuries he believes the Foscari have done his family. The old Doge, urged on by Jacopo's wife, Lucrezia, desires to aid his son, but is rendered impotent by his duty (and perhaps his weakness) to uphold the laws of Venice. Jacopo is again unjustly condemned by the Council to further exile but dies as he sets sail, while his father, crushed by this loss of his last son and forced by the Council (urged on by Loredano) to abdicate, collapses and dies as he hears the bells of San Marco saluting his successor, at which Loredano is observed to write in his notebook, "I am paid."

There are three dramatic drawbacks to the work which, while causing difficulty, by no means render it ineffective: first, being no Iago, the villain Loredano and his hatred, which is the driving force of the action, remain unfocused both dramatically and musically; second, the struggle between the old Doge's paternal desire to save his son and the restrictions imposed on him by his position as Doge is not clearly articulated until late in the opera, leaving his motivation unclear; and third, the dramatic situation is such that it has no direction in which to develop. Jacopo begins and ends condemned; the struggle to save him is merely a series of stops and starts. Important moments are not part of the stage-action: Jacopo's condemnation by the Council happens between the scenes; the arrival of the letter from Erizzo (whoever he may be since he figures otherwise not at all in the drama) absolving Jacopo of guilt is given no context; indeed,

the death of Jacopo himself is merely reported—and in a perfunctory manner—by his long-suffering wife. The scenes which stir the excitement of the audience, e.g., act I, scene iv, in which Lucrezia pleads with her father-in-law, the Doge, to save her husband, have musical but not dramatic momentum. Other stageworthy moments such as Lucrezia's sudden appearance with her children before the Council to plead for her husband allow an exciting musical climax which fails to carry the action forward. There is little overall sense of dramatic necessity. Not surprisingly perhaps, Verdi, who tended to be dismissive of his past accomplishments, described *Foscari* a few years later as too unvarying in color.

Nevertheless, *I due Foscari* is stageworthy; recent productions have shown that whatever the dramatic problems, the music makes it eminently viable. No one can hear it in the theater without recognizing that Verdi has caught the sombre gloom of the Venice conjured up by Byron's drama. Sensitive from the beginning to the dramatic function of orchestral coloring, Verdi makes an advance in *I due Foscari* in his use of woodwinds to create atmospheric darkness and, in combination with harp and strings, to produce moments (e.g., the prison scene of act II) of the most delicate texture. The level of workmanship throughout is high; stylistically the work marks a movement toward the intimate style which Verdi was later to develop in *Luisa Miller* and, especially, *La traviata.* The duet between Lucrezia and the Doge points toward the latter while the prison ensembles point toward *Rigoletto;* if the comparisons are apt to highlight the shortcomings of *I due Foscari,* they also place this earlier work in a line of major Verdian development.

The musical characteristic of *I Due Foscari* most often pointed out is Verdi's use of quasi-*Leitmotivs,* not developed systematically in the Wagnerian manner but used almost as static signature tunes. Their success is variable. For example, the motiv associated with most of Lucrezia's entrances constantly suggests her haste and energy without adding to her stature; meanwhile the Doge's motiv does precisely that, establishing him in his first appearance ("Eccomi solo alfine") as a figure of suffering majesty far more than Piave's text would appear to warrant; suggestions of that later Doge, Simon Boccanegra, are unmistakable.

I due Foscari contains a number of fine Verdian numbers: Jacopo's opening aria with its evocative accompaniment suggesting the Venetian waterside; Lucrezia's act I cavatina ("Tu al cui sguardo onnipossente") and cabaletta in which the solo voice is most effectively floated above the chorus; the tender duet ("No, non morrai") for Lucrezia and Jacopo in the prison which evolves into a magnificent trio at the entrance of the Doge; and the Doge's splendid outpouring ("Questa dunque") to the Council when they demand his resignation.

—Peter Dyson

DUKAS, Paul.

Composer. Born 1 October 1865, in Paris. Died 17 May 1935, in Paris. Studied piano with G. Mathias, harmony with T. Dubois, and composition with R. Guiraud at the Paris Conservatory, 1882-88 (first prize for counterpoint and fugue, 1886); second Prix de Rome for his cantata *Velléda,* 1888; music critic of the *Revue Hebdomadaire* and *Gazette des Beaux-Arts:* Chevalier of the Légion d'Honneur, 1906; professor of orchestration at the Paris Conservatory, 1910-13; elected Debussy's successor as a member of the *Conseil de l'enseignement supérieur,* 1918; professor of composition at the Paris Conservatory, 1927, and professor of orchestration, 1928; taught at the École Normale de Musique. Dukas was involved in editing Rameau's complete works for the publisher Durand.

Operas

Publisher: Durand.

Horn et Rimenhild, Dukas, 1892 [unfinished].
L'arbre de science, Dukas 1899 [unfinished].
Ariane et Barbe-bleue, Maeterlinck, 1899-1906, Paris, Opéra-Comique, 10 May 1907.
Le nouveau monde, 1908-10? [destroyed].

Other works: overtures, cantatas, orchestral works, chamber music, piano works.

Publications

By DUKAS: books–

Chroniques musicales sur deux siècles 1892-1932. Paris, 1948; partial reprint, 1980.
Ecrits sur la musique. Paris, 1948.
Favre, G., ed. *Correspondence de Paul Dukas.* Paris, 1971.
Preckler, Mercedes Tricias, ed. *Cartas de Paul Dukas a Laura Albeniz.* Barcelona, 1983.

articles–

Fauve, G., ed. "Paul Dukas et le Théâtre-Lyrique." *Revue d'histoire du théâtre* 1 (1978): 55.

About DUKAS: books–

Samazeuilh, G. *Paul Dukas.* Paris, 1913; 2nd ed. 1936.
d'Indy, Vincent. *Emmanuel Chabrier et Paul Dukas.* Paris, 1920.
Revue musicale 166 (1936) [Dukas issue].
Favre, G. *Paul Dukas: sa vie, son oeuvre.* Paris, 1948.
Lesure, F. *Catalogue de l'exposition Paul Dukas.* Paris, 1965.
Favre, G. *L'oeuvre de Paul Dukas.* Paris, 1969.
Helbé, Jacques. *Paul Dukas (1865-1935).* Paris, 1975.
Hirsbrunner, T. *Claude Debussy und seine Zeit.* Laaber, 1981.

articles–

Favre, G. "Les débuts de Paul Dukas dans la critique musicale." *Revue de musicologie* 56 (1970): 54-85.
Nicolodi, Fiamma. "Parigi e l' opera versita: dibatti, riflessioni, polemiche." *Nuova rivista musicale italiana* 15 (1981): 577.

* * *

One of the most enigmatic personalities in the history of French music, Paul Dukas has come down to us primarily as the composer of the tone poem *The Sorceror's Apprentice.* That this work is rather atypical of his output is an irony in a musical life where ironies abound.

From his earliest years Dukas had an intellectual bent coupled with a love for art which manifested itself (as it did with his friend and classmate Debussy) in his choice of companions, drawn almost entirely from painters, poets and the like rather than fellow music students. This was accompanied in Dukas' case by an intensely personal sense of rigorous craftsmanship, first evinced when the teenager taught himself solfeggio before ever setting foot in the Conservatory. Later, having been awarded the second Prix de Rome in 1888 but piqued over his failure to do so the following year, Dukas withdrew from his classes and embarked on the discipline of teaching himself to compose by assiduously studying the scores of the masters.

If he was hard on his teachers he was doubly hard on himself, a trait reflected by the extreme brevity of the list of his completed works. In later years this penchant for perfection became nothing short of an obsession, resulting in the composer burning several major works (a symphonic poem, his second symphony, an opera and two ballet scores) before his death rather than release to the world music which he deemed unworthy. As he communicated to his friend Georges Enesco: "Mon cher Georges, j'ai tout brûlé" ("My dear Georges, I have burned everything.").

Thus Dukas' greatest strength (intellectual rigor) was also the weakness which eventually paralyzed his creative energies. It is probably no accident that much of the charm of *The Sorceror's Apprentice* lies in its uncharacteristic spontaneity, the result of a stringent performance deadline which for once in his life Dukas had to race to meet. This spontaneity is not easily detected elsewhere in his finely chiseled and minutely crafted scores.

One can only admire the very real strengths of Dukas' surviving works, however. Dukas possessed a wonderful grasp of orchestral color (his palette being more blended in the Straussian sense than soloistic as with Debussy) and an infallible sense of musical structure. It is very likely that Dukas was most energized and inspired by writing music for the theater. His first practical stage experience was in 1895 when he and his friend Saint-Saëns edited and brought to performance *Frédégonde,* an unfinished opera by their recently deceased mutual teacher Guiraud. Dukas entertained two operatic projects of his own between 1892 and 1899 only to grow dissatisfied and leave them in fragments.

A congenial subject finally emerged when Maurice Maeterlinck's libretto to *Ariane et Barbe-bleue* came his way. Possibly the greatest music Dukas ever penned, *Ariane* had its premiere in 1907 and is a treasure trove of the composer's finest music. More theater music in the form of a major ballet, *La Peri,* followed in 1912, after which a great silence descended, broken only by a few occasional pieces and lasting until Dukas' death in 1935.

Justly famed as an author and teacher, Dukas wrote extensively for several of the French music journals of his day and was a professor at the Conservatoire and elsewhere from 1910 until his death. One of his more noted admirers and composition students, Olivier Messiaen, tellingly described his mentor in the following words: "... he embodied the intellectual achievements of his own time. Out of an almost overwhelming knowledge sprung doubts, anxieties and a frightful scepticism which, spreading out even into his work, condemned his last twenty years to silence.... Who can gauge the inner heartbreak of that solitary man, who forsook himself to the point of destroying his own works while ceaselessly encouraging those of his younger colleagues? There is so much love and so much faith to be detected in that tragic search for Truth" (*La revue musicale,* May-June 1986).

—Dennis W. Wakeling

DUKE BLUEBEARD'S CASTLE [A Kékszakállú herceg vara].

Composer: Béla Bartók.

Librettist: Béla Balázs.

First Performance: Budapest, Budapest Opera, 24 May 1918.

Roles: Judith (soprano or mezzo-soprano); Bluebeard (bass-baritone); The Bard (speaking part); Bluebeard's Three Former Wives (mute); ballet.

Publications

articles–

Nüll, Edwin von der. "Stilelemente in Bartóks Opera." *Melos* May-June (1929).
Oláh, Gustáv. "Bartok and the Theatre." *Tempo* 13-14 (1949-50).
Veress, Sándor. "Bluebeard's Castle." *Tempo* 13-14 (1949-50).
Kroó, György. "Duke Bluebeard's Castle." *Studia Musicologica Academiae Scientiarum Hungaricae* 1 (1961): 251.
———. "Data on The Genesis of *Duke Bluebeard's Castle.*" *Studia Musicologica Academiae Scientiarum Hungaricae* 23 (1981).

Béla Bartók's opera, *Duke Bluebeard's Castle,* is exemplary of the radical transformation in opera that occurred during the first decade of the twentieth century. Despite its status as the first genuinely Hungarian opera, *Bluebeard* did not find national public support in its early years, a condition which was largely due to the conservative tastes of the Hungarian public. It was originally rejected in a competition for a national opera in 1911 because its true Hungarian qualities were unrecognizable to an audience accustomed to hearing Italianate and Germanized settings of Hungarian texts. *Bluebeard* finally had its premiere in Budapest on May 24, 1918, but, with the collapse of the post-war revolutionary regime in 1919, the opera was banned because of the political exile of its librettist, Béla Balázs, and was not performed again in Budapest until 1937.

As part of an evolution toward new musical styles and techniques in the early part of the century, this opera, based on the symbolist play by Maurice Maeterlinck, is far removed from the ultra-chromaticism of German late-Romantic music as well as from the major-minor scale system of Classical functional tonality. Originating in the pentatonic-diatonic modality of Hungarian peasant music, it is inevitable that the musical language of *Bluebeard* should reveal irreconcilable differences from the prevailing supranational German and Italian operas of the nineteenth century in details of phrase, rhythm, and pitch organization as well as large-scale formal construction. In its general stylistic and technical assumptions, one finds fundamental connections rather with the musical impressionism of Debussy's *Pelléas et Mélisande* (1893-1902), another revolutionary opera from the same symbolist trilogy by Maeterlinck. An affinity between *Bluebeard* and *Pelléas* is partly suggested in their common absorption of pentatonic-diatonic modality into a kind of twelve-tone language, a fusion which is revealed by Bartók's own statement: "it became clear to me that the old [folk] modes, which had been forgotten in our music, had lost nothing of their vigor. Their employment made new rhythmic combinations possible. This new way of using the diatonic scale brought freedom from the rigid use of the major and minor keys, and eventually led to a new conception of the chromatic scale, every tone of which came to be considered of equal value and could be used freely and independently." Bartók realized that Debussy's music was based on the same "pentatonic phrases" that he had found in his own Hungarian folk music, and he attributed this to the influences of folk music from Eastern Europe, particularly Russia.

With the reaction around the turn of the century against the naturalism of nineteenth-century theater, many authors began to develop a new interest in psychological motivation and a level of consciousness manifested in metaphor, ambiguity, and symbolism. In his symbolist plays, Maeterlinck was to transform the internal concept of subconscious motivation into an external one, in which human action is entirely controlled by fate. *Bluebeard* represents a significant manifestation of this transformation. Theodor Adorno's assessment of musical modernism is particularly relevant to the *Bluebeard* idiom, in which "the concept of shock is one aspect of the unifying principle of the epoch.... Through such shocks the individual becomes aware of his nothingness." Bartók's opera, limited to a bare minimum of characters, introduces the shock element and a level of reality entirely steeped in metaphor. "Blood," as a symbol of Bluebeard's inner soul, vividly appears in each of his chambers as the seven doors are forced open by Judith, who relentlessly pries into her husband's hidden life. Judith herself represents the "fatalistic" element of relentless time and Bluebeard's inevitable move toward "endless darkness."

Bartók's personal symbolist musical language is set within a clearly architectural framework in both its overall form as well as local phrasal details, an approach which is in keeping with the composer's understanding of the folk-music structures themselves. The entire opera consists of distinct forms (often based on folk-like quatrain structures that sometimes suggest a rondo type of format) within scenes. Furthermore, much of the melodic and harmonic fabric is generated by means of modal elaboration and transformation, a principle that appears to be derived from the process of thematic variation found in the folk-music sources. From the modal material of the opera, Bartók derives the basic leitmotifs and pitch cells, which are central in generating the musico-dramatic fabric. The basic "Blood" motif, characterized by half-steps, is gradually manifested in the intrusion of this dissonant element into the opening pentatonic folk mode as Judith becomes aware of blood on the castle walls. However, psychological tension in the unbroken musical fabric is created not so much by the manifest details, but by the latent symbolic and metaphorical questions that these details invoke with regard to our own perception of reality. Such questions are explicit in the Prologue: "The curtains of our eye-lids are raised. But where is the stage? In me? In you?"

Psychological development, which is also fundamental to the symbolic meaning of the opera, is realized by means of two inextricably connected and overlapping formal concepts, one sectional, and the other unfolding the dynamic spiritual evolution and transformation of the two characters. Sándor Veress has shown how the large-scale form of the opera is a closed symmetrical construction, an arch-form in three parts: (1) an introduction initially established by a folk-like, brooding, F-sharp pentatonic theme and the "menacing" motif; (2) seven scenes demarcated by Doors I-VII, which peak at the uncovering of Bluebeard's vast domain behind Door V in the contrastingly bright key of C major (the most distant key from the opening F sharp); and (3) a recapitulation of the "menacing" motif and F-sharp pentatonic. The shape of the sectional arch-form is heightened by the dramatic psychological process. The distinct vocal styles and personalities of the two characters are established at the outset. Judith's first vocal entry, a prominent (whole-tone related) wide-ranging figure in a characteristically strong Magyar rhythm, contrasts with Bluebeard's reserved (pentatonic-diatonic) repeated-note line in even durational values. By the time Door V (opening on Bluebeard's vast domain) is reached, this contrast is reversed: the man has progressed from quietness to increasingly intense and passionate utterance, while the woman has moved in decrescendo toward her own extinction. Only with the inevitable loss of Judith does Bluebeard become emotionally resigned.

The symbolism of Bluebeard is derived directly from that of Debussy's Pelléas, both operas belonging to the same dramatic trilogy of Maeterlinck. The woman as "fatalistic" symbol—the siren of destruction—is first evident in the Debussy opera. This is represented musically by the intrusion of the whole-tone scale ("fate" motif) into the diatonic sphere ("human" motifs); the interaction between these two types of pitch-sets also underlies the same dramatic symbolism in Bartók's opera. Bluebeard's opening vocal sections are primarily diatonic, Judith's primarily whole-tone, Judith thus "fatalistically" intruding into Bluebeard's inner life. The subject of Bluebeard suggests the eternally problematical relation of the two sexes. The relation between the two as depicted in the opera is one that the contemporary feminist movement would deplore, but all the more do we have to understand this relation. There are only two characters, a man and a woman. The man is the central character, who is reticent to reveal his inner self, while Judith symbolizes the passionate and demanding woman who, through her love, is in the man's power.

Both the Debussy and Bartók operas also find common ground in their approaches to the relationship between music and language. Both operas are based on a kind of contemporary "recitative" style pioneered by Debussy. The music-text relationships of both operas are based on special premises that could only have been established by the liberation of meter and rhythm that became possible after the disappearance of traditional tonal functions in the early twentieth century. In Bartók's case, exploration of the old Hungarian folk tunes permitted him to break with the established nineteenth-century tradition of translating Western languages into Hungarian for opera performance, a tradition which had inevitably led to distortions in Hungarian accentuation. Just as Debussy had been faithful to the French language in his musical setting, Bartók strictly preserved the Hungarian language accents in his musical setting of the Balázs libretto, in which the archaic syllabic structure is set almost entirely in the old "parlando-rubato" folk style. The Hungarian text—and this is true of the orchestral phrases as well—is appropriately based on eight syllables per line, which is one of the isometric stanzaic patterns that the composer found in the oldest of the Hungarian folk melodies. Thus, as the intended inception of a new and genuinely Hungarian tradition based on the fusion of folk elements and French impressionism, the Bluebeard idiom permitted an expansion of the possibilities for symbolic representation that were first manifested in Debussy's opera.

—Elliott Antokoletz

DUPREZ, Gilbert-Louis.

Tenor. Born 6 December 1806, in Paris. Died 23 September 1896. Tenor debut in Il barbiere di Siviglia at the Odéon, 1825; went to Italy to continue studies, 1828; created Edgardo in Lucia di Lammermoor, Naples, 1835; Paris Opera debut in Guillaume Tell, in 1837; sang in London in 1844-5 and toured Germany in 1850; taught at Paris Conservatory from 1842 to 1850; founded his Ecole Spéciale de Chant in 1853.

Publications

About DUPREZ: books–

Elwart, A. Duprez: sa vie artistique. Paris, 1838.
Devrient, E. Galerie des artistes dramatiques de Paris. Paris, 1840-42.

Gilbert-Louis Duprez as Arnold in *Guillaume Tell,* **1837**

articles—

Celletti, R. "Duprez, Gilbert-Louis." *Enciclopédia dello spettacolo.*

*　　*　　*

Gilbert-Louis Duprez is one of the most important forerunners of the dramatic tenor of today. Remembered principally as the first tenor to sing the high C "from the chest," in his own time he was also prized as a dramatic interpreter. This reputation was achieved by overcoming a number of obstacles. Initially his voice was a light lyric tenor of very limited volume. When he made his debut in the Odéon Theatre in Paris as Almaviva in *Il barbiere di Siviglia* (1825), he was said to have been barely audible. After subsequent engagements there and at the Opéra Comique, he went to Italy in 1828, where he continued to sing light tenor roles without attracting particular notice.

In 1831, however, he was called to replace an indisposed singer as Arnold in *Guillaume Tell.* For this heavier role, Duprez adopted the *voix sombrée,* a darkened tonal quality recently introduced by the Italian tenor Domenico Donzelli, and, as he recalled in his memoirs, summoned "every resource of will power and physical strength" to carry chest resonance up to the high C's that would soon bring him much success. As his reputation in Italy grew, he was asked to create the leading tenor roles in a number of operas, including several by Donizetti. (Apparently he did not abandon the traditional method of producing falsetto tones above the high C, for Donizetti's *Parisina* and *Lucia di Lammermoor,* both written

for Duprez during this period, contain E-flats above high C.) When he made his debut at the Paris Opéra in 1837 as Arnold, his high C's and dramatic approach produced controversy and sold-out houses.

Over the next decade, Duprez was the leading dramatic tenor of the Paris Opéra, creating roles in operas by Halévy, Berlioz, Donizetti, Auber, and Verdi, and singing important parts in such works as *La Juive* and *Les Huguenots.* His voice soon began to decline, however. As early as 1838, during the first performances of *Benvenuto Cellini,* Berlioz had commented on the singer's inability to sing softly or sustain long notes; three years later the composer wrote to his sister that Duprez no longer retained any voice at all. Nevertheless, he continued to sing at the Opéra until 1849, and the following year toured the French provinces and gave concerts in Germany and England.

Despite his success, Duprez seems to have had a number of limitations as a singer throughout his career. Contemporary writers suggest that Duprez's delivery became violent (caricatures of him almost invariably show Herculean effort on his part) and that his range of tonal color was increasingly restricted to the *voix sombrée,* except above the high C. In his *Memoirs* Berlioz points to the tenor's occasional carelessness over musical details, relating that Duprez consistently sang an F instead of a G-flat in a particular passage in *Guillaume Tell,* even after he had been asked to correct it. In a thinly disguised account of Duprez's career in *Evenings in the Orchestra,* Berlioz also presents unflattering pictures of the singer's unvaried dramatic approach to his roles and of his dealings with composers and managers of opera houses.

Against this assessment should be set that of Henry Chorley, who relates having heard the singer in Paris in 1837. He concedes that Duprez's voice was "thick" and comparatively inflexible and notes that his stage appearance was unprepossessing, but he also gives vivid accounts of his dramatic power on stage in such operas as *Guillaume Tell,* Auber's *Masaniello,* and Halévy's *La Juive.* Later, hearing him sing *Messiah* in English in 1845, Chorley once more praised Duprez's "feeling for dramatic truth," calling him "the finest dramatic tenor singer I have ever heard and seen on the stage."

Duprez lived to a great age and published a vocal method and several volumes of memoirs, composed a number of operas and other musical works, and trained a number of singers both at the Paris Conservatory and his own school (among them Marie Miolan-Carvalho, who created Gounod's Marguerite and Juliette). His most lasting contribution to opera, however, was as the first dramatic tenor in the modern sense of that term. The dark tone, stentorian high notes, and dramatic intensity that were combined in his performances have gradually become the expected norm in the repertoire that he helped create.

—Joe K. Law

DVOŘÁK, Antonín (Leopold).

Composer. Born 8 September 1841, in Mühlhausen. Died 1 May 1904, in Prague. Married: Anna Cermáková, 1873 (7 children). Studied with Pitzsch at the Prague Organ School; violist in the orchestra of the National Theater in Prague, 1861-71; Austrian State Prize for his Symphony in E-flat, 1875; organist at St Adalbert's Church in Prague; professor of composition at the Prague Conservatory; in London, 1884;

Dvořák's autograph score of *Rusalka*, 1901

commissioned to write a new work for the Birmingham Festival of 1885 (*The Spectre's Bride*); made honorary Mus. D. by Cambridge University, and honorary Ph.D. by the Czech University in Prague, 1891; headed the National Conservatory in New York, 1892; symphony *From the New World* premiered by the New York Philharmonic, 15 December 1893; artistic director of the Prague Conservatory, 1901; life member of the Austrian House of Lords.

Operas

Edition: *A. Dvořák: souborné vydání,* edited by O. Šourek et al. Prague, 1955-.

Alfred, K.T. Körner, 1870, Olomouc, Czech Theater, 10 December 1938.
King and Charcoal Burner [*Král a uhlíř*], B.J. Lobeský, 1871, Prague, National Theater, 28 May 1929; revised, 1874; further revised and performed, 1887.
The Stubborn Lovers [*Tvrdé palice*], J. Štolba, 1874, Prague, New Czech Theater, 2 October 1881.
Vanda, V.B. Šumavský (after J. Surzycki), 1875, Prague, Provisional, 17 April 1876; revised 1879, 1883.
The Cunning Peasant [*Šelma sedlák*], J.O. Veselý, 1877, Prague, Provisional, 27 January 1878.
Dimitrij, Cervinková-Riegrová, 1881-82, Prague, New Czech Theater, 8 October 1882; revised 1883, 1885, 1894-95.
The Jacobin [*Jakobin*], Cervinková-Riegrová, 1887-88, Prague, National Theater, 12 February 1889; revised, 1897.
Kate and the Devil [*Čert a Káča*], A. Wenig (after Czech fairy tale), 1898-99, Prague, National Theater, 23 November 1899.
Rusalka, J. Kvapil, 1900, Prague, National Theater, 31 March 1901.
Armida, J. Vrchlický (after Tasso, *Gerusalemme liberata*), 1902-03, Prague, National Theater, 25 March 1904.

Publications/Writings

By DVOŘÁK: books—

Šourek, O., ed. *Dvořák ve vzpomínkách a dopisech.* Prague, 1938; 9th ed. 1951; English translation as *Antonín Dvořák: Letters and Reminiscences,* 1954.
———. *Antonín Dvořák přátelům doma.* Prague, 1941.
———. *Antonín Dvořák a Hans Richter.* Prague, 1942.

articles—

"Antonín Dvořák on Negro Melodies." *New York Herald* 25 May (1893).
"Franz Schubert." *Century Illustrated Monthly Magazine* 48 (1894): 341; reprinted in Clapham, 1966.
"Music in America." *Harper's* 90 *(1895): 428.*

About DVOŘÁK: books—

Šourek, O. *Antonín Dvořák.* Prague, 1929; 3rd ed. 1947; English translation 1952.
———. *Dvořákova čítanka: články a skadby* [Dvorák reader]. Prague, 1929.
Šourek, O., and P. Stefan. *Dvořák: Leben und Werk.* Vienna, 1935; English translation 1941; reprint as *Anton Dvořák,* 1971.
Robertson, Alec. *Dvořák.* London, 1945, 1977.

Hořejš, A. *Antonín Dvořák: the Composer's Life and Work in Pictures.* Prague, 1955.
Smetana, R. *Antonín Dvořák: o místo a výsnam Dvořákova skladatel ského díla v českém hudebním vývoji* [Dvořák's works and Czech music]. Prague, 1956.
Burghauser, J. *Král a uhlíř* [critical edition of the libretto]. Prague, 1957.
———. *Antonín Dvořák: thematický katalog, bibliografie, přehled života a díla* [thematic catalogue, bibliography, survey]. Prague, 1960.
———. *Dimitrij* [critical edition of the libretto]. Prague, 1961.
Clapham, John. *Antonín Dvořák. Musician and Craftsman.* London, 1966.
Hughes, Gervase. *Dvořák: his Life and Music.* London, 1967.
Clapham, John. *Dvořák.* Newton Abbot and London, 1979.
Butterworth, Neil. *Dvořák: his Life and Times.* Tunbridge Wells, 1980.
Schönzler, Hans-Hubert. *Dvořák.* London, 1984.
Cadieu, Martine. *Musiques tchèques.* Paris, 1984.

articles—

Hudebni revue 4 (1910-11): 409-96 [Dvořák memorial issue].
Newmarch, Rosa. "The Letters of Dvořák to Hans Richter." *Musical Times* 73 (1932): 605, 698, 795.
Colles, H.C. "Antonín Dvořák: Opera at Home." *Musical Times* 82 (1941).
Šourek, O. "Z neznamych dopisů Antonína Dvořák nakladateli Simrockovi" [Dvořák's letters to Simrock]. *Smetana* 37 (1944): 119, 131.
Kiselev, V.A. "Perepiska A Dvorzhaka s V.I. Safonovim" [correspondence with Safonov]. *Kratkiye soobscheniya* [Moscow] no. 17 (1955): 57.
Clapham, John. "The Operas of Antonín Dvořák." *Proceedings of the Royal Musical Association* 84 (1958).
Geist, B. "Dva nezámé Dvořákovy dopisy" [two unknown Dvořák letters]. *Hudebni věda* 5 (1968): 316; 7 (1970): 497.
Kiselev, V.A., ed. "Pis'ma A. Dvorzhaka iz Moskvi." In *Puti razvitiya i vzaymosvyazi russkovo i cheshkoslovatskovo iskusstva,* 183. Moscow, 1970.
Smaczny, J. "*Armida*—Dvořák's Wrong Turning?" *Zpráva* [London] 3 (1977): 10.
Seaman, Gerald. "The Rise of Slavonic Opera, I." *New Zealand Slavonic Journal* 2 (1978): 1.
Kuna, Milan, and Milan Pospíšil. "Dvořák's *Dimitrij.*" *Musical Times* 120 (1979): 23.
Pospíšil, Milan. "Balada v České opeře 19. stoleti" [Ballads in nineteenth-century Czech opera] *Hudebni věda* 16 (1979): 3.
Bykovskih, Majja. "Narodno-fantastičeskaja osnova soderžanija opery *Čert a Káča*" [Folk and fairy tale elements in *Kate and the Devil*]. In *Issledovanie istoričeskogo processa klassičeskoj i sovremennoj zarubežnoj musyki,* edited by Tamara Cytovic. Moscow, 1980.
Clapham, John. "Dva neznámé Dvořákovy dopisy E Hanslickovi" [two unknown letters from Dvořák to E. Hanslick]. *Hudebni věda* 17 (1980): 154.
Kuna, Milan. "Ke vzniku Dvořákova Dimitrije" [the genesis of *Dimitrij*]. *Hudebni věda* 18 (1981): 326.
Schläder, Jürgen. "Märchenoper oder symbolistisches Musikdrama? Zum Interpretationsrahm der Titelrolle in Dvořáks *Rusalka.*" *Die Musikforschung* 34 (1981): 25.
Kuna, Milan. "Ke zrodu Dvořákova Jakobína" [the origins of *The Jacobin*] *Hudebni věda* 19 (1982): 245.

_____. "Od 'Matčiny písně' k Dvořákovu *Jakobínu*" [From "mother's song" to *Jacobin*]. *Hudebni věda* 21 (1984): 32.

Pospíšil, Milan. "Dvořákova operné představivost" [Dvořák's imagination in the realm of opera]. *Opus musicum* [Czechoslovakia] 6 (1984): 182.

_____. "Dramatická úloha Meyerbeerovy harmonie" [dramatic function of Meyerbeer's harmony]. *Hudebni věda* 21 (1984): 323.

Stich, Alexandr. "O libretu Dvořákova Dimitrije" [libretto of *Dimitrij*]. *Hudebni věda* 21 (1984): 339.

Smaczny, J. "*Alfred:* Dvořák's First Operatic Endeavor Surveyed." *Journal of the Royal Musical Association* spring (1990).

unpublished–

Bykovskih, Majja. "Principy dramaturgii pozdnih oper Antonína Dvorzaka *Čert i Kača* i *Rusalka*" [principles of dramaturgy in Antonín Dvořák's later operas *Kate and the Devil* and *Rusalka*]. Ph.D. dissertation, Gosudarstvennaja Konservatorija, Moscow, 1984.

*   *   *

Of all Dvořák's operas, *Rusalka* is the only one which has achieved a degree of international recognition. Why this is so is complicated, but a major part of the reason is the rather long period of development which Dvořák seemed to need.

Dvořák reached the point of total mastery in the genre of opera with *The Jacobin,* a product of the mid 1880s, which was further revised in the late 1890s. Before that, we observe Dvořák running from his roots, so to speak, in an attempt to address a wider audience. The results were often striking, as in *Vanda,* a story about the Polish nobility that takes place in the 16th century. It has many affecting moments as well as much fine vocal writing, but it also has a curiously static, even formal quality.

One might be critical of the formal quality of *Vanda,* but it is a fact that Dvořák wrote it that way deliberately. The Prague National Opera was to have a triumphal opening in 1876, and the call went out to create something new and impressive. Smetana had just finished his positively statuesque masterpiece, *Libuse,* and there is evidence that Dvořák had seen the score. He countered with *Vanda,* and its "static" quality was almost an exact duplication of the style found in *Libuse.* In any case, if it was indeed a contest between Prague's two best composers, Smetana won, and his was the first opera presented at the new opera house. It should be said that Smetana (older and more experienced) was a past master at this kind of ceremonial music, whereas for Dvořák, it was a new departure. Consequently, it is hardly surprising that, on balance, *Libuse* is the more effective work.

After *Vanda,* Dvořák was preoccupied with *Dimitrij,* the story of which can be characterized as a quasi-historical sequel to Mussorgsky's quasi-historical opera, *Boris Godunov.* In *Dimitrij,* as in almost all of Dvořák's operas, there are wonderful choruses, as well as vocal parts which are quite demanding, but also quite effective dramatically. *Dimitrij* and *Vanda* are spoken of by many of today's critics with great respect, even though both are marginally uneven, and yet they have been performed rarely, even in Czechoslovakia.

Kate and The Devil was written just prior to *The Jacobin* and approaches it in quality. Here the potent mix of peasants, a ruling aristocracy, a tenor hero, Hell, and the admirable, plain but rude Kate create a mix of comedy, pathos, and social conflict which seems to have excited Dvořák's imagination. This is a serio-comic opera in which the music is consistently strong, and the frequently used technique of through-composition works really well. There are some problems, however. The libretto, though effective, is occasionally unclear and it all but eliminates Kate, one of the title characters, before the last act begins.

The problems of the earlier operas are notably absent from *The Jacobin.* Written at the same general time as his 7th and 8th symphonies, this opera shares the strengths of those works and gives us the quintessential Dvořák. The story is a good one, involving a pair of young lovers, an older man of high station who threatens the young pair with his libidenous demands on the young girl, a father who has denounced his son and daughter-in-law, and, oddly pivotal to the rest, the choir-master Benda, who speaks constantly of ideals, particularly those of the "devine" art of music. This latter element seems to have inspired Dvořák to compose a veritable flood of gorgeous music, utilizing brilliant orchestral sonorities, and some of his finest melodies.

Rusalka, based on a Czech re-working of the old Undine legend, marks a rather new path for the composer. It is a fairy-tale-fantasy-opera for adults, and is in many ways the most Romantic music Dvořák penned. He was, of course, a Romantic composer, but his music retained the formal clarity, and clean-limbed rhythmic drive of an earlier period. In *Rusalka,* these stylistic fingerprints are modified by a kind of aural voluptuousness. The opera, a grand tragedy, provides many opportunities for exquisite vocalism, as well as the kind of high drama of which Verdi might have been proud. In spite of some minor difficulties in the matter of sustained musical invention, *Rusalka* is a masterpiece, and has become known as such throughout the world.

In the 1930s and 40s not much of Dvořák's music was known. For whatever reasons the situation today has changed markedly. Dvořák is now one of the most respected and performed composers of the instrumental repertoire. One is reminded of what Gustav Mahler once said: "My time will come." Perhaps Dvořák's operas will find their "time" soon.

—Harris Crohn

E

EAMES, Emma.

Soprano. Born 13 August 1865, in Shanghai. Died 13 June 1952, in New York. Studied with Clara Munger in Boston and Mathilde Marchesi in Paris. Debut as Juliette in Gounod's *Romeo et Juliette*; Covent Garden debut as Marguerite, 1891; Metropolitan Opera debut as Juliette, 1891; sang over 250 performances at Metropolitan Opera until 1909; after her retirement from the Met she made concert tours with her second husband, the baritone Emilio de Gogorza.

Publications

By EAMES: books–

Some Memories and Reflections. New York, 1927.

About EAMES: articles–

Dennis, J. and L. Migliorini. "Emma Eames." *Record Collector* 8 (1953): 77.
Shawe-Taylor, D. "Emma Eames." *Opera* January (1957).
Lawrence, A.F.R. and S. Smolian. "Emma Eames." *American Record Guide* 29 (1962): 210.

*　　*　　*

Emma Eames' career on the operatic stage was relatively short, only twenty years, and her activities were confined largely to New York and London, but there were few singers of the "Golden Age" who wore the mantle of *prima donna* with greater authority. Between 1891 and 1901 she sang more than a dozen leading roles in eight seasons at Covent Garden, although her celebrated rivalry with Nellie Melba did not allow her to enjoy the kind of absolute domination over her repertory that she felt was her due. She fared better in her sixteen seasons at the Metropolitan Opera as one of the highest paid artists on the roster, singing some twenty-one roles in more than 250 performances. She did not have an especially large repertory, but she was certainly the most versatile of the star Marchesi pupils. In addition to the predictable lyric heroines of Gounod, Bizet and Massenet, she quickly assumed a number of heavier roles which eventually came to include Aïda, Leonora (*Il trovatore*), Alice Ford (*Falstaff*), and Amelia (*Un ballo in maschera*). In December 1902 she added *Tosca* to her growing dramatic repertory, following Milka Ternina in the title role. She was also entrusted with the first Met productions of Mascagni's *Cavalleria rusticana* and *Iris*. Her Desdemona, which she sang in both New York and London to the Otello of Francesco Tamagno, the role's creator, received stunning reviews, and as early as 1891 she made her way with great assurance into the Wagnerian repertory, first as Elsa in *Lohengrin,* and later as Elisabeth (*Tannhäuser*), Eva (*Die Meistersinger*), and most remarkably, Sieg-

linde (*Die Walküre*). Throughout her career, she was a notable interpreter of Mozart as well, singing the Countess (*Le nozze di Figaro*), both Donna Elvira and Donna Anna (*Don Giovanni*), and Pamina (*Die Zauberflöte*).

Few *prima donnas,* even of that era, went to such lengths to compose so stern and defensive a public profile as did Eames. With certain determination she offered this sober prelude to her 1927 autobiography, *Some Memories and Reflections:* "Great fixity of purpose, absolute absorption in the task at hand, and a complete obsession concerning the duty to be accomplished, have been the fundamental laws governing my career and life." Her career, forged by self-denial and nurtured by self-discipline, is portrayed as a constant challenge of temptations, met with a consuming suspicion of all external forces beyond her control. "I was so obsessed and absorbed by my work," she commented in 1939, "that it proves to me that the wisest course is to mind one's own business exclusively. I had to detach myself from outside influences in order to find simplicity, sincerity, and truth in my interpretations."

In spite of her subsequent rejection of Mathilde Marchesi's instruction and her merciless public recriminations of her as a teacher, Eames possessed in abundance virtually all of the stylistic characteristics associated with the Marchesi method. Like Melba's, hers was a perfectly sculpted instrument, with an exquisite, even scale, a highly disciplined precision of attack, immaculate intonation, and the fluidity necessary to cope with the most demanding passage work. It was only in the upper extremes that she seemed to have lacked Melba's consummate fluency, and this proved a burden from the outset of her career. Bernard Shaw pointed it out in his review of her Covent Garden debut in April, 1891, noting that the upper register, "though bright, does not come so easily as the rest," and her recordings demonstrate—in some cases, painfully—that she was never able to fully overcome this deficiency.

Eames has been unjustly labeled a cold and unfeeling singer, an accomplished yet unemotional interpreter. Shaw found her an "intelligent, ladylike" actress, but "somewhat cold and colorless . . . The best that can be said for her playing in the last two acts [of *Faust*] is, that she was able to devise quietly pathetic business to cover her deficiency in tragic conviction." He later wrote of her: "I never saw such a well-conducted person as Miss Eames. She casts her propriety like a Sunday frock over the whole stage." Even her celebrated beauty and her patrician bearing were conveniently summoned in contrast to her staunch emotional reserve, especially by colleagues making light of their many unpleasant encounters with her. Eames scurried to her own defense in a February 1939 New York radio broadcast, using some of her recordings as tools of reconciliation. She described her Gounod numbers in particular as "documents as well as interpretations . . . for with him," she explains, "I studied at the beginning of my career, *Faust, Mireille,* and *Roméo and Juliette.*" Her 1906 recording of the "Jeux vivre dans ce rêve" from *Roméo et Juliette* is offered as an example "sung as Gounod taught it to me, absolutely in time and without the meaningless holds and *retards* that one so often hears," as if to caution against mistaking what she felt was purity and authority of style for lack of involvement. But like most of her recorded performances, the "Waltz" is in fact saturated with all of the affectations she professes to eschew, just as the tempo she invokes is breached throughout by clear and frequent departures.

Her last appearances in opera, single performances of *Tosca* and *Otello* at the Boston Opera, were made in December, 1911, two years after her official retirement from the stage. She continued to give occasional recitals for several years, but these were not always received enthusiastically.

Like so many other brilliant-voiced lyric sopranos of her day (the Marchesi pupils in particular), Eames was not well-served by the acoustical method of recording. She fully realized the consequences of her activity in the primitive studios and lived longer than most to regret it. She disliked the process of record making: "With even the most satisfactory results," she felt, "my voice would be diminished and deformed, and the softer vibrations eliminated completely." But in spite of her fears, the brilliance and warmth of her voice are still unmistakable. The recordings certainly attest to the fact that there was little in Eames' singing of the "monotony of beautiful, even tones" that dissuaded Geraldine Farrar from studying at the *École Marchesi* on Melba's advise.

Between 1905 and 1911, Eames made nearly fifty commercial recordings, resulting in thirty-five published titles divided almost equally between opera and song. Only a few of the dramatic roles with which she was associated—Tosca, Leonora, and Santuzza (*Cavalleria rusticana*)—are represented

by major arias, along with a good deal of the Mozart and Gounod. There is even a faint but persuasive sample of her Elsa in the second-act duet "Du Ärmste kannst wohl" from *Lohengrin,* sung with contralto Louise Homer. In addition, there are five Mapleson cylinders recorded live from the stage of the Met in 1902 and 1903, the most remarkable of these being four excerpts from the last act of *Tosca.* The most sympathetic performances, however, are drawn from her extensive repertory of French and Italian song. While her manner with songs was neither vibrant nor caressing, it was rarely wanting of color and warmth of expression. She recorded works of Hermann Bemberg, George Henschel, Horatio Parker, and Charles Koechlin in 1908, and as early as 1905, songs of Amy Beach, Reynaldo Hahn and Schubert. Her final recording sessions of November, 1911 yielded a superb rendition of Tosti's "Dopo," and what may be the definitive acoustical recording of Schubert's "Gretchen am Spinnrade." Had she left nothing else in the way of recorded evidence, these would dispel any doubt as to her contemporary stature.

—William Shaman

EATON, John.

Composer. Born 30 March 1935, in Bryn Mawr, Pennsylvania. Studied composition with Milton Babbitt, Edward Cone, and Roger Sessions, Princeton University (A.B., M.F.A.); three American Prix de Rome awards, two Guggenheim fellowships; professor of music at Indiana University, 1970-91;

Emma Eames as Juliette in Gounod's *Roméo et Juliette*

The Tempest by John Eaton, performed by Santa Fe Opera, 1985

won the Peabody and Ohio State awards for *Myshkin,* 1973; composer in residence at the American Academy in Rome, 1974; lectured at the Salzburg Center in American Studies, 1976; Santa Fe Opera Commission, 1982; National Endowment for the Arts opera commission, 1987; visiting professor of music, University of Chicago, 1990-91; professor of music, University of Chicago, 1991-.

Operas

Publishers: Bote and Bock, Carisch, Faber, Malcolm, Ricordi, G. Schirmer.

Ma Barker, A. Gold, 1957.
Heracles, M. Fried, 1964, Turin, Bloomington, Indiana University Opera Theater, May 1972.
Myshkin, P. Creagh (after Dostoyevsky, *The Idiot*), 1971, televised 23 April 1973.
The Lion and Androcles (children's opera), E. Walter and D. Anderson, 1973, Indianapolis, Public School no. 47, 1 May 1974.
Danton and Robespierre, P. Creagh, 1978, Bloomington, Indiana University Opera Theater, 21 April 1978.
The Cry of Clytaemnestra, P. Creagh, 1979, Bloomington, Indiana University Opera Theater, 1 March 1980.
The Tempest, A. Porter (after Shakespeare), 1983-85, Santa Fe, 27 July 1985.
The Reverend Jim Jones, J. Reston, Jr., 1988.
Il Divino Narciso (dramatic cantata), N. Nelson (after Sor Juana Inez de la Cruz). Chicago [scenes ii-vi], 20 May 1990.

Other works: vocal and instrumental works for various combinations of voices and conventional and electronic instruments.

Publications

By EATON: books–

Involvements with Music: New Music since 1950. New York, 1976.

articles–

"Stories that Break into Song." *Kenyon Review* 4 (1982): 71.

About EATON: articles–

Monson, K. "Eaton: Danton and Robespierre." *HiFi* 30 (1980): 67.
Morgan, R.P. "Alchemist." *Opera News* 1 (1985): 28.

*   *   *

The music of John Eaton spans the full spectrum of serious music, including chamber music, solo works, songs, and large-scale orchestral works, but it is for his operas that he has received the widest attention and acclaim. This is no accident, for Eaton's complex, intricately-wrought music has always exhibited a powerful dramatic sense, a sense that has found its clearest expression in opera.

Eaton avails himself of a huge range of compositional concepts; describing his early epic opera *Heracles,* Eaton declared that it "completely exhausts every traditional technique of contemporary music." Throughout his career, Eaton has made frequent use of electronics; in his operas, they are skillfully deployed in conjunction with traditional acoustic instruments. In *Myshkin,* Eaton utilizes the SynKet, a synthesizer developed by the Italian engineer Paolo Ketoff; in *Danton and Robespierre,* Eaton employs the more commercially-viable Moog synthesizer. Eaton's operas since *Heracles* are also strongly characterized by their use of microtonal intervals; his singers must frequently negotiate quarter sharps and flats in addition to coping with extremely wide ranges, and his accompanying ensembles usually incorporate pairs of instruments or opposing groups of instruments tuned a quarter-tone apart.

Eaton has consistently shown a preference for historical subjects and stories with strong psychological and personal conflicts. *Heracles,* ostensibly an epic, deals not with the mythical twelve labors but with Heracles's personal frustrations as he nears the end of his life; similarly, *The Cry of Clytaemnestra* depicts the inner torment of Agamemnon's queen. *Myshkin,* based on Dostoyevsky's *The Idiot,* takes the audience into Myshkin's fragmented mind via Eaton's wide range of avant-garde devices.

Danton and Robespierre, an operatic treatment of the Reign of Terror of the French Revolution (and the only Eaton opera to be commercially recorded), represents the elevation of Eaton's aesthetic of horror and violence to a truly grand scale (over 400 performers were involved in the CRI recording). *Danton* utilizes not only quarter tones but sixth tones as well, and features the brilliant device of a synthesizer tuned in "just intonation," a tuning scheme in which the "home" key is pure, but the more remote keys sound increasingly awry; this is vividly used to express Robespierre's descent into madness.

Eaton's most recently performed opera, *The Tempest,* represents something of a departure from the intensity of his earlier operas, though the technical range and complexity of his work continues to expand. *The Tempest* contains remarkable juxtapositions of style: Ariel is accompanied by a group of Renaissance instruments (lute, recorder, and shawm) tuned a quarter-tone apart from the orchestra; Caliban scat-sings with a jazz trio of alto saxophone, electric guitar, and electric bass. Furthermore, each character (except the dominant Prospero) sings in an independent tempo, often contradicted by the orchestra. With its elegant libretto, deftly compressed from Shakespeare by Andrew Porter, *The Tempest* is clearly Eaton's most complex and ambitious work.

Eaton's development as one of America's leading opera composers continues, and he has received increasing praise from critics and audiences. He has recently completed a new opera about the Reverend Jim Jones and the Jonestown massacre; though this work has not yet been performed, it will undoubtedly contain a broader spectrum of musical ideas and bring Eaton an even wider audience than before.

—H. Stephen Wright

EBERT, (Anton) Carl.

Director. Born 20 February 1887, in Berlin. Died 14 May 1980, in Santa Monica. Trained as an actor with Max Reinhardt; general director of the Landestheater, Darmstadt, 1927-31; general director of Berlin Städtische Oper 1931-33; co-founder and artistic director of Glyndebourne Music Festival, 1934-39 and 1947-59; founder and director of Turkish State School for Opera and Drama, 1936-47; director of

University of Southern California Opera Department, 1948-56; rejoined Berlin Städtische Oper as general administrator, 1956-61; New York Metropolitan Opera, 1959-62. Staged world premiere of *The Rake's Progress*, 1951; Commander of the British Empire (C.B.E.), 1960; honorary doctorates at University of Edinburgh, 1954, and University of Southern California, 1955; his assistant at Darmstadt was Rudolph Bing; his son Peter is also an opera director.

Opera Productions (selected)

Le nozze di Figaro, Darmstadt, Hessisches Landestheater, 1927.
Wozzeck, Darmstadt, Hessisches Landestheater, 1931.
Die Bürgschaft, Berlin, Charlottenburg Oper, 1931.
Macbeth, Berlin, Charlottenburg Oper, 1931.
Un ballo in maschera, Berlin, 1932.
Die Entführung aus dem Serail, Salzburg, 1932.
Don Giovanni, Glyndebourne, 1936.
The Rake's Progress, Venice, La Fenice, 1951.
Martha, New York, Metropolitan Opera, 1961.
Così fan tutti, New York, Metropolitan Opera, 1961.
Ariadne auf Naxos, New York, Metropolitan Opera, 1962.
Pelléas et Mélisande, Glyndebourne, 1962.

Publications

About EBERT: articles–

Carson, Elizabeth. "Carl Ebert." *Opera* 1/August (1950): 25.
Taubman, H. "Interesting People." *The New York Times* 101 (14 October 1951): 7, section 2.
Hickman, C.S. "In the Key of C Sharp." *Music of the West* 7/January (1952): 10.
Bollert, W. "Die Ära Ebert." *Musica* 9/April 19 (1955): 165.
———. "Carl Ebert." *Neue Zeitschrift für Musik* 118/ February (1957): 97.
———. "Porträt." *Musica* 11/February (1957): 98.
Besch, Anthony. "A Triptych of Producers." *Opera* 9/April (1958): 224.
Cushing, M.W. "Carl Ebert." *Opera News*. 23 (16 February 1959): 12.
Stuckenschmidt, H.H. "Streit um Carl Ebert in Berlin." *Melos* 26/April (1959): 127.
List of productions in Berlin and Glyndebourne. *Opera* 10/ July (1959): 437.
Faulkner, M. "Ebert and Fond Memories." *The Music Magazine* 164/April (1962): 23.
"Dirigenten, Regisseur und Bühnenbildner." *Opernwelt* 4/ April (1967): 2.
Stuckenschmidt, H.H. "Das Leben eines Unverwüstlichen: Carl Ebert wieder in Berlin." *Melos* 34/July-August (1967): 260.
Geitel, K. "Doppelte Ehrung." *Opernwelt* 8/August (1967): 37.
Spingel, H.O. "Mozart ist für mich die Vollendung." *Opernwelt* 9/September (1967): 30.
"The Musical Whirl." *Hi Fidelity/Musical American* 20/October (1970): MA19.
"Carl Ebert zum Gruss." *Acta Mozartiana* 19/1 (1972): 22.
"Carl Ebert 90" *Acta Mozartiana* 24/1 (1977): 34.
Steinbeck, D. "Künstlerische Maximen, die gültig blieben; zum Tode von Carl Ebert." *Neue Zeitschrift für Musik* 4/ July-August (1980): 373.
Hughes, S. "Glyndebourne, 50 Years On: The Heartbeat of the Performance." *Musical Times* 125/May (1984): 255.

Crichton, R. "A Glyndebourne Retrospective." *Musical Times* 125/May (1984): 262.

*   *   *

Carl Ebert was one of the century's most important and influential producers of opera. Ebert's status is a consequence of his multifaceted art and career. His extensively rehearsed productions with their fastidious matching of movement to music, precise ensembles, and attention to detail; the role he played in the Verdi revival in Germany while at the Berlin Städtische (Charlottenburg) Oper; his participation in the establishment of the Glyndebourne Festival, which revolutionized opera in England; ground-breaking, ensemble-based productions of Mozart both in Germany and in England; and his training of young singers and producers, both at the Turkish State School for Opera and Drama, which he founded, and at the University of Southern California—these features contributed to his significance as an opera producer.

Ebert brought skills acquired as an actor—he enjoyed a brief but distinguished career in Frankfurt and at the Staatsschauspiel in Berlin—to the operatic stage. He did not stage his first opera, Mozart's *Le nozze di Figaro*, until after his appointment as Generalintendant of the Hessische Landestheater in Darmstadt in 1927. His assistant there, Rudolph Bing, later became a distinguished opera administrator in his own right. Many of Ebert's Darmstadt productions and the artists he hired were controversial; this became more of a problem after he moved to Berlin in 1931 with the growing Nazi presence in both national and local government. Ebert sought out new works: his Darmstadt staging of Alban Berg's *Wozzeck* was the first outside Berlin, and his creation of Kurt Weill's *Die Bürgschaft* after his move to the capital created a great furor in the city council. Even in his later years he produced new works, staging the premiere of Stravinsky's *The Rake's Progress* (in 1951).

Ebert's initial production at the Charlottenburg Oper was Verdi's *Macbeth*, a startling choice, as the opera was almost unknown in Germany. Ebert later revived his staging at both Glyndebourne and the Metropolitan Opera. Ebert's production of Verdi's *Un ballo in maschera* with conductor Fritz Busch in 1932 was another milestone in the German Verdi revival. Ebert and Busch had worked together earlier that year at the Salzburg Festival on a production of Mozart's *Die Entführung aus dem Serail*. Busch had been impressed—"in spite of occasional over-subtleties," as he put it—by Ebert's Berlin production, which treated the opera as real drama, rather than in the story-book, sing-and-mug-to-the-audience style then in fashion.

After Ebert left Germany in 1933 because of his political opposition to the Nazis, he worked in Buenos Aires, Salzburg, Florence, Vienna, and elsewhere. A major milestone in his career occurred when an obscure English landowner named John Christie interested Ebert's colleague Busch in a scheme to produce Mozart on his estate, Glyndebourne, and they brought Ebert in to be the producer. He was artistic director there from 1936 until 1939, and again from 1946 until 1959.

Ebert's productions at Glyndebourne from 1934 onward were a revelation to the English audiences, who at that time were accustomed to productions for which the singers might have had perhaps one rehearsal. The first Glyndebourne *Figaro* saw twenty-four three-hour orchestral rehearsals. Ebert instilled an ensemble spirit into these early productions of Mozart that, with Busch's musical leadership, immediately established Glyndebourne as the *ne plus ultra* for productions of Mozart at the time. Ebert himself performed speaking roles in some of the productions: the Speaker in *Die Zauberflöte* and Pasha Selim in *Die Entführung.* Not all of his touches were universally admired—the bevy of semi-naked courtesans in the final scene of *Don Giovanni* came in for severe criticism in 1936—and his productions at times were afflicted by too much stage business. As a German producer who had made his name with Mozart and Verdi, it is ironic that one of his finest Glyndebourne productions was of the quintessential French opera, Debussy's *Pelléas et Mélisande,* which he returned to direct in 1962. Ebert's son Peter also established himself as a producer and staged a number of works for Glyndebourne.

Carl Ebert's productions, especially those for Glyndebourne, together with those by Wieland Wagner at Bayreuth in the 1950s, formed the basis for post-war opera stagings. Ebert was so widely copied that it was often forgotten that many of the original concepts were his. In the early 1960s he was reunited with his old colleague Bing at the Metropolitan Opera. One of the operas he staged there had been seen recently in a production by another producer. Some of the reviewers noted that Ebert had borrowed ideas from the other production. But, in fact, it was the other producer who had based his production on Ebert's Glyndebourne staging. Ebert had become the *lingua franca* for the opera stage.

—David Anderson

EDGAR.

Composer: Giacomo Puccini.

Librettist: Ferdinando Fontana (after A. de Musset, *La coupe et les lèvres*).

First Performance: Milan, Teatro alla Scala, 21 April 1889; revised, Ferrara, 28 February 1892; further revised, Buenos Aires, 8 July 1905.

Roles: Edgar (tenor); Gualtiero (bass); Frank (baritone); Fidelia (soprano); Tigrana (mezzo-soprano); chorus.

* * *

First staged at the Teatro alla Scala in 1889, *Edgar* was withdrawn after its third performance. Like Puccini's *Le villi* of 1884, it suffered from a weak libretto by Ferdinando Fontana, who adapted Alfred de Musset's play *La coupe et les lèvres* (1832). Fontana reset the tale in medieval Flanders rather than the Tyrol, creating four exaggerated leading characters who have little in common with those of Musset's original. Puccini attempted to improve the libretto but to no avail, since Fontana was adamant about the quality of his verse. Although the composer later revised the work in 1892, compressing acts III and IV into one, this later version was no more successful.

Act I begins at daybreak in a Flemish village. The opera opens as Fidelia, a pure and innocent girl, expresses her love for the sleeping Edgar. She withdraws at the approach of Tigrana, a gipsy girl who was abandoned as a child and brought up by Fidelia's father. Tigrana tries to convert Edgar to her own sensual way of life, but he denounces her and returns home. The gypsy insults Fidelia's brother Frank, who

secretly loves her. After he departs she reappears, this time outraging the approaching congregation with her taunts about religion and her defence of the erotic life. Edgar, by now besotted with Tigrana, protects her against the hostile crowd. He resolves to take her away from the village and, in a gesture of defiance, sets fire to his own house. Following a fight with Frank, Edgar flees with Tigrana.

The second act, which takes place at night on the terrace of a palace, concerns the deteriorating relationship of Edgar and Tigrana. Although Tigrana adores him, Edgar now finds her tiresome. Towards the end of this short act, Frank and some soldiers appear. He and Edgar resolve their quarrel and depart together. Tigrana, deserted, swears vengeance.

Act III, set in a fortress, opens with a choral *Requiem aeternam* during which a suit of armor is borne in, supposedly Edgar's coffin. As Frank proclaims Edgar a hero, he is interrupted by a monk who accuses Edgar of villainy, so that all but Fidelia turn against him. As the people depart, Frank and the monk try to tempt Tigrana to discredit Edgar. She is eventually persuaded when jewels are put in front of her. The monk calls back the crowd. His claim that Edgar had betrayed his country is confirmed by Tigrana. As the people break into the suit of armor, the monk tears off his costume, revealing himself as Edgar. Condemning Tigrana, he embraces Fidelia, who is stabbed by her rival. All demand Tigrana's execution and the curtain falls as Edgar, in despair, throws himself on Fidelia's dead body.

If it were not for the quality of the music, an opera with such an inane plot would be forgotten. From the opening bars Puccini's superior talent is clearly apparent. His melodies have a character that is both sensuous and haunting, while his use of lower instruments to double high-lying vocal lines gives them a unique quality. It is a sign of the general excellence of his melodies that he was able to reuse one aria, discarded from the 1892 version, in *Tosca* as Cavaradossi's leading final aria "Amaro sol per te." He avoided the standard number system, making the music continuous. Puccini's choral writing is fluent, frequently conceived in the contrapuntal manner. Some, indeed, is borrowed from his earlier *Messa di gloria* (1880). The chorus plays an important part in generating the necessary dramatic power, in particular at the climax of act I and the beginning of act III.

One weakness can be found in Puccini in extreme dramatic moments when the music accompanies the *verismo* passages of violent and realistic action in an over-indulgent manner, for example as in the fight near the end of act I, or at the end of the work, in Frank's summary condemnation of Tigrana to execution.

The most effective section of the whole opera is in act II, where the growing disharmony between Tigrana and Edgar is expressed in a passage comparable with the best of *La bohème.* Such moments outweigh the opera's occasional crudities, making it well worthy of occasional revival.

—Alan Laing

EGK, Werner (born Werner Mayer).

Composer. Born 17 May 1901, in Auchsesheim, near Donauwörth. Died 10 July 1983, in Inning, near Munich. Married: Elisabeth Karl. Studied piano with Anna Hirzel-Langenhan and composition with Carl Orff in Munich; conductor at the Berlin State Opera, 1938-41; head of the German Union of Composers, 1941-45; commissioned to compose music for the 1936 Berlin Olympics; commissioned to compose music for the Nazi Ministry of Propaganda; stood trial before the Allied Committee for his involvement with the Nazis, 1947, but was not convicted of any crimes; director of the Berlin Hochschule für Musik, 1950-53.

Operas

Publisher: Schott.

Columbus, Egk, 1932, radio performance: Munich, 13 July 1933; staged performance: Frankfurt, 13 January 1942; revised, 1951.
Die Zaubergeige, Egk (after Pocci), 1935, Frankfurt, 19 May 1935; revised, Stuttgart, 1954.
Peer Gynt, Egk (after Ibsen), Berlin, 24 November 1938.
Circe, Egk (after Calderón, *El mayor encanto amor*), 1945, Berlin, 18 December 1948; revised as *17 Tage und 4 Minuten,* Stuttgart, 2 June 1966.
Irische Legende, Egk (after Yeats, *The Countess Cathleen*), Salzburg, 17 August 1955; revised 1970.
Der Revisor, Egk (after Gogol), Schwetzingen, 9 May 1957.
Der Verlobung in San Domingo, Egk (after Kleist), Munich, 27 November 1963.

Other works: ballets, orchestral works (including two orchestral sonatas), vocal works, a piano sonata.

Publications

By EGK: books–

Die Zeit wartet nicht. Künstlerisches, Zeitgeschichtliches, Privates aus meinem Leben. Munich, 1981.
Musik, Wort, Bild. Munich, 1960.

Werner Egk discussing the set for *Peer Gynt* with producer H. Arnold (center) and set designer Helmut Jürgens (left), Munich, 1952

articles–

numerous articles in *Melos, Neue Zeitschrift für Musik, Das Orchester, Österreichische Musikzeitschrift,* and others.

About EGK: books–

Kohl, B. and E. Nölle, eds. *Werner Egk: das Bühnenwerk.* Munich, 1971.
Krause, E., *Werner Egk: Oper und Ballet.* Wilhelmshaven, 1971.

articles–

Werba, Erik. "Geburtskalendarium: Werner Egk." *Österreichische Musikzeitschrift* 36 (1981): 347.
Blätter der Bayerischen Staatsoper no. 4 (1981-82).
Klein, Hans-Günter. "Ideologisierung von Werken Kleists in Opern aus dem 20. Jahrhunderts." *Norddeutsche Beiträge* 1 (1984): 44.
————. "Viel Konformität und wenig Verweigerung: Zur Komposition neuer Opern 1933-1944." In *Musik un Musikpolitik im faschistischen Deutschland,* edited by Hanns-Werner Heister and Hans-Günter Klein, 145. Frankfurt am Main, 1984.

*   *   *

It has been claimed (by dietrich fischer-dieskau) that the three most special operas in German of the present century are Pfitzner's *Palestrina,* Busoni's unfinished *Doktor Faust* and Hindemith's *Mathis der Maler.* Apart from these composers, and leaving aside the operas of Richard Strauss and the New Viennese School, only Carl Orff and Hans Werner Henze have scored any sustained albeit inconsistent success outside of Germany, but it is clear that, as a body of work, Werner Egk's seven operas deserve to share as much (if not more) attention as these others, and in *Peer Gynt* (1938), he composed an outstanding opera deserving the widest attention.

Egk was an accomplished painter and writer as well as a composer; he wrote a fairy-tale play, *Das Zauberbett* (*The Magic Bed*), and fashioned his own libretti from the wide range of sources that he drew on for his operatic subjects. *Das Zauberbett* was written as a parergon to Calderon's *El mayor encanto amor,* the source for his opera, *Circe* (revised 1966, as *Siebzehn Tage und vier Minuten*). He also provided the phonetic "libretto" for Boris Blacher's highly experimental *Abstract Opera no. 1* (1953). This remarkable and very odd work seeks to portray standard human emotional and psychological situations purely through the medium of music, but in a theatrical context. No plot exists to motivate the various scenes, and no actual words express them, beyond basic syllabic representations related only in mood.

Apart from his operas, Egk composed four original ballets of which the second, his "Faust-ballet" *Abraxas* (1948), was banned for obscenity after five performances; several other works have been choreographed as well. His music for the stage and for the voice is his most enduring legacy, his other purely concert music being small in quantity.

The plots of Egk's stage works all share common themes and concerns, involving outlandish characters of an often magical or mythical bearing, such as Kaspar (in *Die Zaubergeige*), the trolls and Peer Gynt himself, Don Juan and Doctor Faustus (in the ballets *Joan von Zarissa* and *Abraxas*), Ulysses and the eponymous Circe. Cast into elemental situations, the beguiling of these characters and the consequences of their choices are recurrent themes which inspired his music to portray their emotions with great skill and power. These elements can be seen to best effect in *Peer Gynt,* where the hero is enticed into the trolls' lair and later flees from Norway and the only woman he can love, to escape from the inopportune dalliance with the daughter of the Old Man. Although there is often a sardonic, even caustic, edge to his music, there is genuine humor in it as well, as the satirical opera after Gogol *Der Revisor* (*The Government Inspector,* 1956) and *Peer Gynt* well illustrate.

The sources of Egk's operas show the wide range of his knowledge as well as his ruthlessness in extracting precisely those aspects of a story he wished to utilize, not being content merely to transcribe for the stage. *Die Zaubergeige*'s text derives from Pocci's fairy tale of illusion and magic; in *Peer Gynt,* Egk distilled successfully certain facets from the plot but ignored the wider philosophical (and ironic) implications of Ibsen's outlandish drama. In his fourth opera, *Irische Legende* (after a story by W. B. Yeats 1955; revised 1970), Egk responded with relish to the challenge of portraying demonic possession and created an allegory in which temptation leads to extortion. After Gogol and *Der Revisor,* Egk turned (in 1963) to Heinrich von Kleist's *Die Verlobung in San Domingo* (*The Betrothal in San Domingo*), accentuating and encapsulating the conflict between black and white.

Egk's first opera, *Columbus* (1932), is the only one with an "original" storyline, i.e. one culled directly from history and not from a pre-existing play or book. It was actually written for radio, bearing the appropriately journalistic subtitle of "Report and Portrait," only being adapted for the stage in 1942 (and subsequently revised in 1951), following the success, initially at least, of his first stage operas (*Peer Gynt* was finally banned by the Nazis). *Columbus,* along with the oratorio *Furchtlosigeit und Wohlwollen* (*Fearlessness and Goodwill*), showed Egk as very much a young and vital composer, learning from the many disparate types of music around him.

"Egk's music is direct; sometimes racy ... It directly touches the listener, and is broadly full of charm." So said Arthur Honegger, and the operas *Peer Gynt, Der Revisor* and *Circe* (as well as the ballet *Abraxas*) affirm Egk's ability to imbue theatrical forms with color within existing traditions. It was his superb dramatic sense that was the cornerstone of his success as a composer for the stage, coupled with a compositional ear to match.

—Guy Rickards

EINEM, Gottfried von.

Composer. Born 24 January 1918, in Bern, Switzerland. Studied at Plön, Holstein (Germany); opera coach at the Berlin Staatsoper; arrested by the Gestapo in 1938, imprisoned for four months; studied composition with Boris Blacher in Berlin, 1941-43; resident composer and music adviser, Dresden State Opera, 1944; visited the United States in 1953; settled in Vienna; professor at the Hochschule für Musik, 1965-72.

Operas

Publishers: Boosey and Hawkes, Bote and Bock, Schott, Universal.

Dantons Tod, Blacher and von Einem (after Büchner), 1944-46, Salzburg, 6 August 1947; revised 1955.
Der Prozess, Blacher and von Cramer (after Kafka, *The Trial*), 1950-52, Salzburg, 17 August 1953.
Der Zerrissene, Blacher (after Nestroy), 1961-64, Hamburg, 17 September 1964.
Der Besuch der alten Dame, Dürrenmatt, 1970, Vienna, 23 May 1971.
Kabale und Liebe, Blacher and L. Ingrisch (after Schiller), 1975, Vienna, 17 December 1976.
Jesu Hochzeit, L. Ingrisch, 1980, Vienna, 18 May 1980.
Der Tulifant, L. Ingrisch, 1989-90, Vienna, 30 October, 1990.

Other works: ballets, orchestral works, vocal works, chamber music, a piano concerto.

Publications

By EINEM: books–

Das musikalische Selbstporträt von Komponisten, Dirigenten, Sängerinnen und Sänger unserer Zeit. Hamburg, 1963.
Komponist und Gesellschaft. Schriftenreihe Musik und Gesellschaft, i. Karlsrühe, 1967.

articles–

"Ein Komponist im Turm." *Melos* 31 (1964): 113.
"Die Freiheit des Komponisten." *Österreichische Musikzeitschrift* 20 (1965): 278.
"Vier Fragen an die Komponisten" [a response to a questionnaire by 14 contemporary composers, including Einem.] *Österreichische Musikzeitschrift* 36 (1981): 208.
"Über Igor Stravinsky (1952)." *Musikblätter der Wiener Philharmoniker* 36 (1982): 304.
"Die Symphonie nach Anton Bruckner. Vom Standpunkt des Komponisten." In *Die österreichische Symphonie nach Anton Bruckner Symposion, 12 bis 14 September 1981. Bericht,* edited by Uwe Harten, 11. Linz and Graz, 1983.
"Versuch über Mozart, C. Abbado und anderen." *Österreichische Musikzeitschrift* 46 (1991): 4.

About EINEM: books–

Rütz, H. *Neue Oper: G. von Einem und seine Oper "Dantons Tod."* Vienna, 1947.
Hartmann, D. *Gottfried von Einem.* Vienna, 1967.
Stuckeschmidt, H.H. *Die Grossen Komponisten unseres Jahrhunderts.* Munich, 1971.
Wagner, Manfred, ed. *Geschichte der österreichischen Musikkritik in Beispielen. Publikationen des Instituts für Österreichische Musikdokumentation* 5. Tutzing, 1979.
Dietrich, Margot, and Wolfgang Greisenegger, eds. *Pro und Contra "Jesu Hochzeit": Dokumentation eines Opernskandals.* Vienna, 1980.
Saathen, Friedrich. *Einem-Chronik: Dokumentation und Deutung.* Vienna, Cologne, Graz, 1982.

Brosche, Günther, ed. *Musikalische Dokumentation: Gott-fried von Einem.* Vienna, 1984.

articles–

Rütz, H. " 'Danton's Death': Music Drama or Music The-ater." *Musicology* 2 (1948): 188.

Schneditz, W. "From Drama to Libretto." *Musicology* 2 (1948): 182.

Schuh, O. " 'Danton's Death' and the Problem of Modern Opera." *Musicology* 2 (1948): 177.

Graf, M. " 'Der Prozess' von G. v. Einem." *Österreichische Musikzeitschrift* 8 (1953): 259.

Reich, W. "Der Prozess." *Musical Quarterly* 40 (1954): 62.

Hajas, D. " 'Dantons Tod' nach 16 Jahren." *Österreichische Musikzeitschrift* 18 (1963): 204.

Schuh, W. "Gottfried von Einem's 'Der Zerrissene'." *Tempo* no. 71 (1964-65).

Hartmann, D. "Bekenntnisoper unserer Zeit." *Österreichische Musikzeitschrift* 22 (1967): 594.

Klein, R. "Von Einems Dürrenmatt-Oper 'Der Besuch der alten Dame'." *Österreichische Musikzeitschrift* 26 (1971): 302.

Stuckenschmidt, H.H. "Von Einem's *Der Besuch der alten Damen.*" *Tempo* no. 98 (1971-72): 28.

Klein, R. "Der Symphoniker Gottfried von Einem. Versuch einer Identitätsabgrenzung." *Österreichische Musik-zeitschrift* 33 (1978): 3.

Weismann, Sigrid. "Neues Musiktheater in Österreich." *Österreichische Musikzeitschrift* 35 (1980): 273.

Klein, R. "Gottfried von Einems Oper *Jesu Hochzeit.* Zur Uraufführung der Wiener Festwochen." *Österreichische Musikzeitschrift* 35 (1980): 189.

Klein, R., and P. Cosse. " 'Die Kunst ihre Freiheit': Zur Uraufführung von *Jesu Hochzeit.*" *Österreichische Musik-zeitschrift* 35 (1980): 309.

Rubin, Marcel. "Gottfried von Einem—65 Jahre." *Österreichische Autorenzeitung* 35 (1983): 14.

Werba, E. "Der Lyriker Gottfried von Einem." *Österreichische Musikzeitschrift* 38 (1983): 394.

Blaukopf, K. "Gottfried von Einem zum 70. Geburtstag." *Musik und Bildung* 20 (1988): 27.

Klein, R. "*Tulifant* von Einem und Ingrisch: eine verspielte und zugleich weise Parabel." *Österreichische Musik-zeitschrift* 45 (1990): 708.

*   *   *

Austrian composer Gottfried von Einem emerged in the after-math of World War II as one of Europe's most promising opera composers. Beginning with *Dantons Tod* in 1947 and progressing through *Der Prozess* (1953), *Der Zerrissene* (1964), *Der Besuch der alten Dame, Kabale und Liebe* (1976), and *Jesu Hochzeit* (1980), Einem produced a series of stage works popular with European audiences, although they have not proved to be popular exports.

Einem did not join the serial juggernaut but continued composing in an unashamedly romantic style, probably one major reason for his success. His style has always demon-strated strong neoclassical influences, especially that of Stra-vinsky. The spirit of the dance is felt in many of his composi-tions, which doubtlessly also contributed to the success of Einem's ballet scores. Another factor in Einem's favor with Cold War audiences is his choice of libretti. Throughout his career he has shown an interest in themes of alienation and of the individual against the crowd—witness Danton, Josef K. in *Der Prozess,* and Alfred Ill in *Der Besuch.*

Einem's early works, *Dantons Tod* and *Der Prozess,* are heavily indebted to Hindemith and Berg rather than to Strauss and Wagner. Einem has never been one to use leitmo-tifs (leading motives) or tone rows in his operas; he depends more on symphonic development within self-contained scenes. In *Dantons Tod,* he shows himself to be at an early stage of this procedure, with individual orchestral figures often the basis of blocks of a scene; for example, the ornament-like figure in the first scene before the tribunal. Einem exhibits his ability here to construct effective scenes for chorus—the first crowd in act I, the scenes before the tribunal, and the final frenzy at Danton's death are all vividly portrayed. Large-scale orchestral interludes are also important, as in his later operas, to the progression of the drama as much as for covering scene changes.

Der Prozess incorporates Einem's first large-scale use of singers singing long passages of text on a single tone, a tech-nique which he improved on in later operas and songs. This opera also shows an advancement in developing and con-trasting orchestral materials within a scene, perhaps fur-thered by Einem's work in purely symphonic idioms in the years since *Dantons Tod. Der Zerrissene* is lighter in charac-ter, tending more toward a Singspiel style appropriate for Nestroy's farce. *Der Besuch* is still divided into self-contained scenes, separated by interludes, but the scenes are now thor-oughly through-composed and demonstrate Einem's fully de-veloped, personal style. *Kabale und Liebe* is notable for his identification of instruments with characters in the opera. In *Jesu Hochzeit,* his "mystery opera" with a text by his wife Lotte Ingrisch, Einem turned more toward a chamber style, one of his interests in his purely instrumental works of the last decade.

Einem's *Der Besuch der alten Dame* enjoyed one of the composer's greatest successes at its Vienna premiere in 1971, but it seems unlikely that it will demonstrate lasting success. Most of the opera's strength comes from the libretto by Friedrich Dürrenmatt, adapted from his play. Einem, in all of his operas, gives the orchestra the primary musical and dramatic impetus, but the unevenness of his ideas here causes the drama to unravel to some extent. The score almost seems to be a series of studies or excerpts from Einem's orchestral compositions of the 1950s or early 1960s. Often it demon-strates a peculiar detachment from what is happening on stage, especially when the composer falls back on his ever-favorite dance figures and rhythms. *Der Besuch* illustrates one problem encountered when a composer is not using a "system" such as a motif-complex—namely, how to ensure both musical cohesion and dramatic portrayal.

As in other Einem operas, the chorus is often given the most interesting material, but the *Totentanz* (dance of death) at the end, which should be the apotheosis of the chorus/ townspeople, is barely half the length it needs to be. To Einem's credit, his percussion interludes between scenes and when Ill meets his fate are brilliant. *Der Besuch* may be the contemporary "winner" among his operas, but one suspects that posterity will judge his fine first work, *Dantons Tod,* to be his best.

—David E. Anderson

EINSTEIN ON THE BEACH
See TRIPTYCH

ELEGY FOR YOUNG LOVERS.

Composer: Hans Werner Henze.

Librettists: W.H. Auden and C. Kallman.

First Performance: Schwetzingen, 20 May 1961; English Premiere, Glyndebourne, 13 July 1961.

Roles: Gregor Mittenhofer (baritone); Hilda Mack (soprano); Elisabeth Zimmer (soprano); Carolina (contralto); Dr Wilhelm Reischmann (bass); Toni (tenor); Joseph Mauer (speaking part); Servants (mute).

*   *   *

Elegy for Young Lovers is the first of the two opera collaborations between composer Hans Werner Henze and librettists W.H. Auden and Chester Kallman. The story takes place in 1910 at the mountain inn "The Black Eagle" at the base of the "Hammerhorn." Every summer the great poet Gregor Mittenhofer comes here to receive inspiration from the visions of the inn's proprietress, Hilda Mack. Hilda's husband disappeared on the mountain on their wedding day forty years before, and since then she believes she hears his voice and that he will return one day. Mittenhofer is a supreme egoist who manipulates those around him—Hilda and his entourage—to get material for his poetry. This year his doctor's son Toni has joined them. When Toni is introduced to Mittenhofer's mistress, Elisabeth, Hilda has a vision in which she foresees the fate of Toni and Elisabeth.

The opera revolves around Mittenhofer's writing of his poem and Toni and Elisabeth's falling into an illusory love. The body of Hilda's husband is found by the retreating glacier, left exposed, on the mountain, and her visions leave her. After Elisabeth falls in love with Toni, Mittenhofer wins her back with a powerful monologue in which he expounds on the joys and sorrows of being a poet. This and the ensemble reading of his poem-in-progress later in the act form the central points, dramatically and musically, of the opera. Mittenhofer sacrifices Toni and Elisabeth to a sudden blizzard, so he can call his poem an elegy. His secretary, Carolina, acquiesces in the deed and slips into madness. In the last scene, Mittenhofer gives a reading of his newest poem, based on the fate of the young lovers. As he reads, the voices of all who played a part in the poem's creation are heard in a wordless ensemble.

Auden and Kallman's libretto tackles the romantic myth of the artist as isolated hero who uses all those around him to create his art. Mittenhofer has more than a little of Auden himself drawn in him (tongue in cheek for the most part), with his secretary/patroness, his doctor with daily medications, and his overbearing attitude. The librettists fashioned the libretto on Italian models: Felice Romani's stanzas for the *Lucia di Lammermoor* mad scene are parodied for Hilda's; each act and each scene is given a title, usually prefigured in the last line of the preceding scene; there is a "servant number," here the duet early in act I for Carolina and the

doctor, Reischmann. The second act, except for Mittenhofer's central monologue, is taken up with ensembles.

Henze's score uses twelve-tone techniques, although not strictly applied; many passages could better be described as atonal, almost tending toward tonality, rather than dodecaphonic. The orchestration is delicate and complex, and the vocal writing is carefully differentiated between the various characters. Hilda's line uses leaps of wide intervals and coloratura, for example. Henze meticulously distinguishes between spoken lines, singing speech or *Sprechstimme,* "rhythmically fixed speech without definite pitch," and "rhythmically fixed speech on three levels of pitch (high, middle, low)." There are many passages of breathtaking beauty and great dramatic power: the ensemble reading of Mittenhofer's poem is an example of the former; Mittenhofer's showpiece aria, of the latter.

If the opera is marred by a certain consistency of tone in many places, this is an unfortunate result of the twelve-tone style Henze employs. Even at this late date in musical history, listeners find it easier to distinguish between major and minor than among various pitch class sets. Henze's later opera, *Der junge Lord,* shows a more tonal emphasis that has contributed to its wider acceptance. Dramatically, *Elegy for Young Lovers* would benefit by a cut or cuts toward the end of the last act. We know that Elizabeth and Toni are going to die in the blizzard; the "playing house" scene on the mountain that Auden and Kallman gave them is anticlimactic. Revising or cutting part of the scenes on the mountain would strengthen the ending.

Elegy for Young Lovers requires a strong ensemble—particularly in Mittenhofer and in Hilda, who emerges as his nemesis—and a skilled conductor. Many companies have probably been frightened away from the work by its poorly received English premiere at Glyndebourne. But this is a powerful opera. It is distinguished by a libretto laden with both humor and pathos, by ravishing lyrical passages in nontonal settings, and marvelous orchestration.

—David Anderson

ELEKTRA.

Composer: Richard Strauss.

Librettist: Hugo von Hofmannsthal.

First Performance: Dresden, Court Opera, 25 January 1909.

Roles: Elektra (soprano); Chrysothemis (soprano); Klytemnestra (mezzo-soprano); Aegisthus (tenor); Orestes (baritone); Klytemnestra's Confidante (soprano); Trainbearer (soprano); Overseer of Servants (soprano); Young Servant (tenor); Old Servant (bass); Guardian of Orestes (bass); Five Maidservants (two sopranos, two mezzo-sopranos, contralto); chorus (SATB).

Publications

books–

Fischer-Plasser, E. *Einführung in die Musik von Richard Strauss und Elektra.* Leipzig, 1909.

The first production of *Elektra*, Berlin, 1909 (Marie Götze as Klytemnestra and Thila Plaichinger as Elektra)

Hutcheson, E. *Elektra by Richard Strauss: a Guide to the Opera with Musical Examples from the Score.* New York, 1910.

Overhoff, K. *Die "Elektra"-Partitur von Richard Strauss.* Salzburg, 1978.

John, Nicholas, ed. *Richard Strauss: Salome, Elektra.* London and New York, 1988.

Puffett, Derrick, ed. *Richard Strauss: Elektra.* Cambridge, 1989.

articles–

Bekker, P. "*Elektra:* Studie." *Neue Musik-Zeitung* 30 (1909): 293, 330, 387.

Mennicke, C. "Richard Strauss: *Elektra.*" In *Riemann-Festschrift,* 503. Leipzig, 1909.

Klein, W. "Die Harmonisation in *Elektra* von Richard Strauss: ein Beitrag zur modernen Harmonisationslehre." *Der Merkur* 2 (1911): 512, 540, 590.

Enix, M. "A Reassessment of *Elektra* by Strauss." *Indiana Theory Review* 2 (1979).

Schnitzler, Günter. "Kongenialität und Divergenz. Zum Eingang der Oper *Elektra* von Hugo von Hofmannsthal und Richard Strauss." In *Dichtung und Musik,* edited by Günter Schnitzler, 175. Moscow, 1979.

Avant-scène opéra November (1986) [*Elektra* issue].

unpublished–

Kaplan, Richard Andrew. "The Musical Language of *Elektra:* a Study in Chromatic Harmony." Ph.D. dissertation, University of Michigan, 1985.

* * *

In *Elektra,* Strauss creates a new level of demands for female voices and for singers remaining on-stage for extended periods of time. For example, after the short opening scene in which the servants describe her, Elektra is present on stage for the rest of the opera. The size of the orchestra and the ways in which it is used require singers who can project well in the lower registers more so than in his other operas. In fact, with its leitmotivic use of themes, the orchestra itself becomes another character in the drama. Because of the orchestra, the singers must on several occasions employ "Sprechstimme" (speaking in the direction of the pitch of a melody line) rather than actually sing the notes as they ordinarily would.

The plot, adapted from the Greek plays of Aeschylus, is continuous, without changes of stage. In scene i the servants describe Elektra as insanely blood-thirsty, eager to avenge her father Agamemnon's death. Scene ii opens with Elektra's entrance and first words, "alone" (melodic intervals which occur again after her death) and connects to scene iii with her sister, Chrysothemis. In scene iv Elektra confronts her mother, Klytemnestra, and both receive the false news of Orestes' death. Scene v is another Elektra-Chrysothemis conflict with Elektra demanding that Chrysothemis help her avenge their father's death. Scene vi is the gentle recognition scene between Elektra and her brother, Orestes; but it connects with the off-stage vengeance—Klytemnestra's death for Agamemnon's murder. Scene vii is between Aegisthus (Klytemnestra's lover and now husband) and Elektra; he too goes off-stage to be killed. The final scene shows Elektra claiming her triumph. Chrysothemis calls on their brother Orestes with the same two melodic intervals Elektra sang in her first

scene; but Elektra is dead; and the Agamemnon and the murder motives end the opera.

Elektra, Chrysothemis, and Klytemnestra are required to have two-octave ranges in order to be able to project the text, especially in the lower register. Strauss, a master of orchestration, generally reduces the orchestration when he writes for the singers' lower registers. However, due to the symphonic poem aspects of the orchestra-as-character in this work, occasionally the singers are secondary to the orchestra. Since this orchestra-as-character continually states both the Agamemnon and murder motives, the opera could almost be retitled *Agamemnon.* The dead king dominates the opera musically through the orchestra.

—Samuel B. Schulken, Jr.

ELIAS, Rosalind.

Mezzo-soprano. Born 13 March 1930, in Lowell, Massachusetts. Studied at New England Conservatory, Boston, and at the Accademia di Santa Cecilia, Rome; joined the Metropolitan Opera, 1954; sang role of Erika in premiere of Barber's *Vanessa,* 1958.

* * *

Rarely, but by good fortune every so often, a singer and a role come together as one entity for posterity. Of all the roles she has sung on the world's stages in a long career, mezzo-soprano Rosalind Elias will always be associated with Erika, the niece of Vanessa in the Samuel Barber-Gian Carlo Menotti opera of that name. *Vanessa* premiered at the Metropolitan in 1958, and received limited performances at the Salzburg Festival (where critics were upset about having to hear an American opera). Elias's single-minded intensity and her identification with Erika became almost legendary even in those relatively few appearances.

American-born and almost completely American trained, Elias has sung all manner of roles, large and small. At the Metropolitan Opera, where she debuted in 1954, she has sung the Second Esquire in *Parsifal,* Octavian, the Second Peasant Girl in *Le Nozze di Figaro* and Carmen. (To round out a trio of "seconds" she has also sung the Second Lady in *Die Zauberflöte.*) She branched out at the Metropolitan to sing Zerlina (*Zauberflöte*), a role not usually recognized as part of the mezzo's repertoire. She has sung over 45 roles in the New York house alone.

In Europe Rosalind Elias has appeared from Hamburg to Lisbon, and at many festivals, including Glyndebourne. She has also appeared at the Teatro Colón in Buenos Aires. She became part of Leonard Bernstein's traveling casts, singing his works with him or under other conductors. She has also concertized extensively. While never known as a reigning star, Elias was always recognized as a reliable, hard-working artist—and a survivor.

First among her recordings is with the "original cast" on RCA (now BMG) of Barber's *Vanessa* with Eleanor Steber, Regina Resnik, Nicolai Gedda, and Giorgio Tozzi, conducted by Dimitri Mitropoulos, which duplicates the original performances. Elias also appears on other RCA complete opera recordings such as *La forza del destino, Il trovatore,* and *Falstaff* in roles of varying sizes. There are also excerpts from

Werther with Elias as Charlotte opposite Cesare Valletti in the title role, conducted by René Liebowitz, which show off her vocal and dramatic gifts to fine advantage.

—Bert Wechsler

L'ELISIR D'AMORE [The Elixir of Love].

Composer: Gaetano Donizetti.

Librettist: Felice Romani (after Scribe, *Le philtre*).

First Performance: Milan, Canobbiana, 12 May 1832.

Roles: Dr Dulcamara (bass); Adina (soprano); Nemorino (tenor); Sergeant Belcore (baritone); Gianetta (soprano); chorus (SATTB).

Publications

articles–

Prout, E. "Auber's 'Le Philtre' and Donizetti's 'L'elisir d'amore': a Comparison." *Monthly Musical Record* 30 (1900): 25, 49, 73.
Gavazzeni, G. "Donizetti e l'Elisir d'amore." *La rassegna musicale* 6 (1933): 44.

Luigi Lablache and Giovanni Mario in *L'elisir d'amore*

Avant-scène opéra February (1987) [*L'elisir d'amour* issue].

*   *   *

Gaetano Donizetti wrote dozens of tragic and dramatic operas and created the most durable of all musical madwomen, Lucia di Lammermoor. But he also was a comic genius, producing three warm and cheerful works, *L'elisir d'amore, La fille du régiment* and *Don Pasquale,* which have spread sunshine through the operatic world for a century and a half.

Of these, *L'elisir d'amore* was the earliest, and the only one composed in Italian, the others being designed originally for production in Paris and set to French texts (though they have long been given in Italian versions). Donizetti had already written thirty-five operas when, at the age of thirty-four, he completed *L'elisir d'amore* in two weeks' time. Showing no signs of haste in its graceful melodies and sparkling ensembles, it was an instant hit when given on 12 May 1832 at the Teatro della Canobbiana, a rival of the Teatro alla Scala in Milan.

Its plot was adapted—not to say stolen—by the librettist Felice Romani from *Le philtre,* a successful French opera by Auber with a text by Eugène Scribe. In the Donizetti version, a young and rather simple villager named Nemorino is hopelessly in love with Adina, daughter of a wealthy landowner and a flighty girl much given to reading romances, such as that of Tristan and Isolde. A quack doctor named Dulcamara arrives in town, genially peddling an elixir guaranteed to cure all ills from aches to love-sickness. Nemorino eagerly buys a flagon, hoping it will work like Isolde's love-potion. A troop of soldiers arrives, led by Sergeant Belcore who promptly pays court to Adina. She promises to marry him that very night, mainly to spite Nemorino, who has deliberately begun acting indifferently to her while he waits for the potion to exercise its magic. Shocked by the impending nuptials, Nemorino purchases a second bottle, raising the money by enlisting in Belcore's regiment for "venti scudi"—twenty crowns. Suddenly word arrives that Nemorino's uncle has died leaving him a fortune, but even before hearing this news, Adina relents, buys back Nemorino's enlistment contract, and confesses that she loves him. The villagers, led by Dulcamara, rejoice in the happy outcome.

Donizetti's buoyant score became a favorite wherever it was presented; in Paris, for example, it played at the Théâtre des Italiens while Auber's *Le philtre* continued to be given at the Opéra. When someone suggested to Auber that the two versions be presented on the same evening as a double-bill he replied: "That's an idea. But it might suit Donizetti better than me." And indeed, *Le philtre* has long since evaporated while *L'elisir* has never lost its potency as one of the supreme achievements of opera buffa.

L'elisir d'amore is something more than a straight comedy, however; thanks to Donizetti's lyric gifts, it also is a warm and touching story about people who, while they may not be particularly original or strikingly individual in character, nevertheless represent some thoroughly recognizable and sympathetic human types. Lovesick tenors, for instance, are anything but an operatic rarity, yet Nemorino turns out to be one of the most likable of the species. Long before he gets to sing his famous aria "Una furtiva lagrima" in the second act, he has the audience on his side; clearly he is far more entitled to get the girl than the belligerent Belcore. As for that mellifluous aria just named, beloved of tenors from Caruso to Pavarotti, we owe it strictly to Donizetti the composer rather than Romani the librettist, who objected that a melancholy *romanza* might dampen the comic spirit of the work. But

Donizetti insisted and prevailed, thus producing one of Italian opera's all-time hit numbers.

Adina is a more conventional figure; her opening aria, in which she mockingly reads the story of Tristan and Isolde from a book, establishes her as a mixture of the worldly and the romantic, but we never quite see the reason for her obduracy in refusing to accept her village swain—except, of course, to establish some sort of excuse for the young man to grasp so avidly at Dr Dulcamara's magical drink.

Dulcamara himself—"quel gran medico, Dottore enciclopedico," as he portentously announces himself—is a true descendant of the basso buffo line, as pompous as any, friendlier than most, and, at the end, an honest man—for has his elixir, after all, failed to deliver the promised goods? He is one of Donizetti's supreme creations, and he is blended into the musical landscape with consummate ease and mastery. Observe, for instance, the act I scene between Dulcamara and Nemorino when the quack is selling the youth his magical bottle of "bordo" wine, all the time commenting on his gullibility. The episode builds up from a *recitativo secco* (with keyboard) to accompanied recitative (with the orchestra joining in) to a full-fledged comic duet with the two voices intertwining in a splendid example of Italian patter ensemble.

—Herbert Kupferberg

THE ELIXIR OF LOVE
See L'ELISIR D'AMORE

THE EMPEROR JONES.

Composer: Louis Gruenberg.

Librettists: Louis Gruenberg and K. de Jaffa (after Eugene O'Neill).

First Performance: New York, Metropolitan Opera, 7 January 1932.

Roles: Brutus Jones (baritone); Henry Smithers (tenor); An Old Nativewoman (soprano); Witch-Doctor (dancer); several non-singing parts; chorus.

*　　*　　*

The importance of *The Emperor Jones* in the history of American opera cannot be underestimated. After the opera's premiere in 1932, the consensus of opinion was that the work was the most epoch-making of all attempts at an American opera up to this time. Olin Downes, writing in *The New York Times,* stated "The Emperor Jones, an American opera, American in its dramatic and musical origins, its text, its swiftness and tensity, and all the principle elements of the interpretation, was given its world premiere, with instant and sweeping success." Soon after this first performance Gruenberg was given the David Bispham Medal for his contributions in American opera. This distinguished award brought

Gruenberg into national prominence and established his reputation as an important operatic composer.

In adapting Eugene O'Neill's play into an opera, Gruenberg was confronted with a very difficult task. The play, O'Neill's earliest success, had a continuous run of 204 performances in 1920. O'Neill intensified the drama by requiring the steady beat of a tom-tom throughout the play. Thus Gruenberg was undertaking a text which already had musical effects as part of the stage directions. The story is that of an ex-Pullman porter who makes himself emperor of a West Indian island by combining an appeal to superstition with the white man's cunning. Jones cynically exploits the natives, or bush-niggers as he calls them, until they rebel and he is forced to flee. Making his escape into the jungle, Jones loses his way, panics, and returns in a circle to where he began and is shot by his rebelling subjects. Most important is O'Neill's expressionistic treatment of the torment Jones undergoes when he escapes into the jungle, with the result that he is gradually destroyed by fear.

The libretto differs only slightly from the original play. For the most part Gruenberg uses O'Neill's text verbatim with an occasional omission or repetition of dialogue for emphasis. Other important changes include the use of a chorus that comments on the events taking place (with text written by Gruenberg), the insertion of the Black spiritual "It's Me, O Lord," and the manner in which Jones dies. Gruenberg's treatment of Jones' death is a significant alteration from the original play. Rather than having the natives kill him, Gruenberg has Jones commit suicide. This changed ending brought forth a mixed reaction but was accepted by many critics as an important element that contributed to the opera's dramatic success. Throughout the opera the orchestra provides a background of syncopated dissonances to the fast moving drama. Except for one lyrical, dramatic moment when Jones sings the interpolated spiritual, the singers recite and shout their words in a speech-like manner. The demands of the title role are great, and in the premiere Lawrence Tibbett received rave reviews for his portrayal of Jones.

The Emperor Jones remains Gruenberg's most important opera. Although the work enjoyed immediate recognition after its premiere, performances have become infrequent and rare in recent years, partly owing to the work's controversial subject matter—the exploitation of Blacks by a Black—and the difficulty in casting the lead role of Brutus Jones.

—Robert F. Nisbett

L'ENFANT ET LES SORTILÈGES [The Bewitched Child].

Composer: Maurice Ravel.

Librettist: Colette.

First Performance: Monte Carlo, 21 March 1925.

Roles (some of the following may be doubled): The Child (mezzo-soprano); Mama (contralto); The Bergère (soprano); The Chinese Cup (mezzo-contralto); The Fire (soprano); The Princess (soprano); The White Cat (mezzo-soprano); The Dragonfly (mezzo-soprano); The Nightingale (soprano); The Bat (soprano); The Screech-owl (soprano); The Squirrel (mezzo-soprano); A Country Lass (soprano); A Herdsman (contralto); The Armchair (bass); The Comtoise Clock (baritone); The Teapot (black Wedgwood) (tenor); The Little Old Man; The Black Cat (baritone); A Tree (bass); The Tree Frog (tenor); The Bench, The Sofa, The Stool, The Wicker Chair (chorus of children); The Numbers (chorus of children); The Shepherds, The Herdsmen (chorus); The Tree Frogs, The Animals, The Trees (chorus).

Publications

articles–

Orenstein, Arbie. "*L'enfant et les sortilèges:* correspondence inédite de Ravel et Colette." *Revue de musicologie* 52 (1966): 215.
Green, Marcia S. "Ravel and Krenek: Cosmic Music Makers." *College Music Symposium* 24 (1984): 96.

Ravel—like Satie, Stravinsky, Milhaud, Hindemith, Weill, and many other European composers—was fascinated by the chic vitality of the popular music (mostly ragtime and jazz) coming from the United States in the 1910s and 1920s. In writing *L'enfant et les sortilèges,* Ravel consciously tried for a style akin to the feel of American musical-comedy and operetta. And while *L'enfant* bears little resemblance to, say, the Gershwin or Kern shows being produced in the mid-1920s, there remain the lightness, the satire, the genuine but unwrenching emotion that wed American spunk to French sentimentality.

America, to Europeans, was a young, restless country, and it suited Ravel's musical aims that his librettist, Colette, took as the central character a naughty little boy who hasn't been doing his homework. (Though the scene is set in Normandy, might not the choice of subject have been inspired by the little American girl in Satie's *Parade?*) His mother confines him to his room to reflect on his poor behavior. And what should happen? His behavior gets worse, as he flies into a rage, smashing and abusing everything around him (and all the while feeling triumphantly wicked).

Magically, the objects of his fury come to life, and, in retribution, begin to taunt him. The first scene of the one-act opera takes place in the boy's room, while the second scene whisks us out into the moonlit garden, where the insects and animals continue the harassment only, by accident, to discover the boy's fundamental goodness.

Constructed something in the manner of French eighteenth-century opera-ballet, with its series of "entrées" (Colette's original title for the opera was *Ballet pour ma fille*), *L'enfant* moves from one essentially self-contained episode to another. Unfortunately, the supernatural succession begins with the least interesting vignette of the entire work, the duet for chair and sofa, but following this tentative beginning, the opera continues at an amazingly high level of musical and dramatic inspiration.

The wonderfully comic "ding, ding, ding" of the grandfather clock from which the Boy yanked the pendulum gives way to the jaunty fox-trot of the black Wedgwood teapot (who struts around in the manner of an American boxer) and the Chinese cup. Ravel and Colette use pidgin American and Chinese here to charming effect ("How's your mug?" "Rotten"; "I knock out you, stupid chose, I marm'lade you"; "Hara-kiri, Sessue Hayakawa"), with the polytonal jazziness of the teapot's music (one of the few overt Americanisms of the score) juxtaposed with the parallel-4th pentatonicisms of the cup.

Next, from the fireplace, appears Fire, who, as a coloratura soprano, informs the Boy that she warms good boys but burns the bad ones. The shepherds and shepherdesses slip off the torn wallpaper in a mournful little dance, which Ravel imbues with a centuries-old flavor by means of Renaissance modalism. The Princess emerges plaintively from out of the pages of the ripped storybook (another soprano, accompanied only by flute), followed by little Mr Arithmetic, complete with a squadron of numerical demons who menace the boy with insoluble mathematical problems. (Even the Boy's homework is getting back at him.)

Two cats croon a meowing duet (considered scandalously suggestive at the opera's premiere), whereupon we find ourselves transported to the garden, in which trees cry out in pain and in which frogs, dragonflies, bats, owls, and squirrels commingle. When the animals, as a group, finally attack the Boy (as he utters the strange word "Maman") and a squirrel is injured in the mélée, the Boy demonstrates compassion by binding its wounds. The animals' anger toward the Boy now abates, and the work ends with a fugal chorus in praise of his goodness and wisdom. The Boy calls out one final time to his mother.

What makes *L'enfant* so refreshing and absorbing to modern audiences is its combination of impudence and warmth, communicated through its continually varied set of musical episodes. Ravel uses a large orchestra mostly for the range of colorings it offers him, and he for the most part eschews tutti scoring in favor of chamber-music-like settings. His restraint is nowhere more apparent than in the opera's opening bars, where two oboes play langorously in parallel 5ths and 4ths until they are joined by a single string-bass. The orchestral coloring changes with each vignette, never more enchantingly than in the "night music" and dances in the garden. It is also here that the opera takes an unexpectedly expressionist turn: the animals, stunned at the boy's show of humanity, sing in choral *Sprechstimme.* Schoenberg's influence on Ravel dates back to *Pierrot Lunaire,* and moonlit Pierrot makes a symbolic appearance here in *L'enfant*'s moonlit garden. The expressionist tone of this one episode deepens and enriches the psychological resonance of the entire work.

It is well known that Ravel, unmarried throughout life, held his mother in especial reverence and that he, small in stature, had an affinity for child-like simplicities. It is thus particularly understandable that Colette's libretto should have brought out in Ravel the choicest and most poetic compositional thoughts of his entire career. *L'enfant* is sometimes ranked, after Alban Berg's *Wozzeck,* as the finest and most irreplaceable twentieth-century opera. That ranking hardly seems amiss.

—Gerald Moshell

DIE ENTFÜHRUNG AUS DEM SERAIL [The Abduction from the Seraglio].

Composer: Wolfgang Amadeus Mozart.

Librettist: J. Gottlieb Stephanie, Jr (after C.F. Bretzner, *Belmonte und Constanze*).

First Performance: Vienna, Burgtheater, 16 July 1782.

Die Entführung aus dem Serail, **illustration showing characters, c. 1800**

Roles: Constanze (soprano); Blonde (soprano); Belmonte (tenor); Pedrillo (tenor); Osmin (bass); Pasha Selim (speaking); chorus (SATB).

Publications

books–

Pahlen, Kurt, ed. *Wolfgang Amadeus Mozart: Die Entführung aus dem Serail.* Munich, 1980.
Csampai, Attila, and Dietmar Holland, eds. *Wolfgang Amadeus Mozart: Die Entführung aus dem Serail.* Reinbek, 1983.
Bauman, Thomas. *W.A. Mozart: Die Entführung aus dem Serail. Cambridge Opera Guides.* Cambridge, 1987.

articles–

Keller, Hans. "The *Entführung*'s Vaudeville." *Music Review* 17 (1956): 304.
Raeburn, C. "Die Entführungsszene aus 'Die Entführung aus dem Serail'." *Mozart-Jahrbuch* (1964): 130.
Mahling, Christoph-Hellmut. "Die Gestalt des Osmin in Mozarts *Entführung:* Vom Typus zur Individualität." *Archiv für Musikwissenschaft* 30 (1973).
Avant-scène opéra 59 (1984) [*Die Entführung aus dem Serail* issue].

*   *   *

Posterity has agreed that the operas Mozart composed during the last decade of his life surpass those of his contemporaries. *Die Entführung aus dem Serail,* the first of these operas, is a *Singspiel,* in other words, an essentially German treatment of a plot, although the story has an exotic setting in a Pasha's palace in Turkey. The *Singspiel* tradition, which in some ways continues in modern musicals, also demanded that many of the exchanges between the characters be in speech rather than music, thus dispensing with the rather artificial use of recitative that belonged to Italian-language operas including Mozart's own. However, the singers made up for this when they did have solo numbers, duets, and ensembles, for since these tended to occur at key points of the drama, they were often powerful and florid. The remark made by the Austrian Emperor after the first performance, "Too many notes, my dear Mozart," has gone down to posterity unexplained: it may well be that he felt there were too many sung numbers relative to speech, or that they were too long. He may also have thought Mozart's orchestra too big, for the composer had used "Turkish"-type instruments (piccolo, triangle, cymbals and bass drum) in addition to the normal ones of the orchestra in order to set the scene already in the first bars of the overture.

Much of the story—though not the ending—pokes fun at the Ottoman Empire, something the Austrians always enjoyed doing. At the start of act I, the Spanish nobleman Belmonte is outside the house of the Pasha Selim (a speaking role), seeking his beloved Constanze, who has been taken captive with her English maid, Blonde. The name Constanze was that of the composer's own wife, and it suggests too that the character in the opera shall prove herself to be faithful: indeed, the Pasha courts her but respects her virtue. Pedrillo is Belmonte's servant just as Blonde is Constanze's, and he loves Blonde; he aids his master in a plan for the rescue of Constanze, and Belmonte meets the Pasha in the guise of a visiting architect. In the meantime the Pasha's comic chief servant Osmin is at odds with Pedrillo, who has also gained admittance to the house, and with Blonde herself, whom he fancies. Act II includes a vivid exchange between Osmin and Blonde as well as Constanze's large-scale aria "Martern aller Arten" ("Martyrs of all kinds"), in which she tells the Pasha that death itself shall not make her give herself to a man she does not love. Pedrillo devises a plan to make Osmin drunk and facilitate the escape of both couples, which he does after overcoming his adversary's religious scruples, and he and Belmonte reassure themselves of the ladies' virtue in a quartet with Constanze and Blonde.

But the unhurried preparations of the two couples are overheard by a guard. Osmin is awakened and appears to sing a celebrated aria of comic and gloating rage, "Ha! wie will ich triumphieren" ("Oh, how I will triumph"). The Pasha enters and pronounces a sentence of torture on Belmonte, now revealed as the son of an old enemy. Belmonte and Constanze are left to sing a duet, "Welch' ein Geschick" ("What fate is this"), in which they bravely face punishment and parting, but now the Pasha returns to tell them that he has decided on clemency: he will not carry out his sentence and they are free to go. The opera ends with an ensemble of general happiness.

The busy plot of *Die Entführung,* together with the essentially light-hearted nature of the *Singspiel* tradition in which Mozart wrote, makes it a thoroughly entertaining opera, and it is well supplied not only with memorable arias (such as those already mentioned as well as Belmonte's fearful "O wie ängstlich, o wie feurig" in act I and Pedrillo's charming act III serenade "Im Mohrenland") but also with ample stage action together with broad comedy as provided by Pedrillo and Osmin. But Osmin is especially well drawn, a fearsome character as well as a comic one, and his aria of triumph in act III requires a bass singer to offer a range of over two octaves upwards from a low D. Carl Maria von Weber said of *Die Entführung* that in this opera Mozart reached maturity: "With the best will in the world he could not have written another *Entführung.*"

—Christopher Headington

ERKEL, Ferenc (Franz).

Composer. Born 7 November 1810, in Gyula, Hungary. Died 15 June 1893, in Budapest. Studied with his father; director of the Kaschau opera troupe, 1834; conductor of the National Theater in Pest at its opening, 1837; founder and director of the Budapest Philharmonic Concerts, 1853; first professor of piano and instrumentation at the National Musical Academy. Erkel composed the Hungarian national anthem in 1845.

Operas

Editions:

Erkel Ferenc áriák [arias]. Edited by J. Kenessey, Budapest, 1954-5.
Erkel-kórusok [choral works]. Edited by M. Forrai. Budapest, 1960.

Bátori Mária, Béni Egressy (after András Dugonics), Pest, National Theater, 8 August 1840.

Ferenc Erkel, 1841

Hunyadi László, Béni Egressy (after Lörinc Tóth), 1842-44, Pest, National Theater, 27 January 1844.

Erzsébet (with Ferenc and Károly Doppler), Jósef Czanyuga, Pest, National Theater, 6 May 1857.

Bánk bán, Béni Egressy (after József Katona), 1844-52, Pest, National Theater, 9 March 1861.

Sarolta, Jósef Czanyuga, Pest, National Theater, 26 June 1862.

Dózsa György (with G. and S. Erkel), Ede Szigligeti (after Mór Jókai), 1864-67, Pest, National Theater, 6 April 1867.

Brankovics György (with G. And S. Erkel), Lethel Odry and Ferenc Ormai (after Károly Obernyik), Budapest, National Theater, 20 May 1874.

Névtelen hösök [*Anonymous heros*] (with G., S., E., and L. Erkel), Ede Tóth, 1875-80, Budapest, National Theater, 30 November 1880.

István király [*King István*], Anatal Váradi (after Lajos Dobsa), 1874-84, Budapest, Royal Hungarian Opera, 14 March 1885.

Kemény Simon, Jókai [lost].

Other works: orchestral works, chamber works, piano music, incidental music, songs.

Publications

About ERKEL: books–

Abrányi, K. *Erkel Ferenc élete és müködése* [life and works] Budapest, 1895.

Scherer, F. *Erkel Ferenc.* Gyula, 1944.

Maróthy, J. *Erkel Ferenc opera-dramaturgiája.* Budapest, 1954.

László, Z. *Erkel Ferenc élete Képekben* [life in pictures]. Budapest, 1958.

Nagy, I.V., and P. Várnai. *Bánk bán az operaszin padon.* Budapest, 1960.

Bartha, D., and B. Szabolcsi, eds. *Az opera történ etéböl* [history of opera]. *Zenetudományi tanulmányok,* vol. 9, Budapest, 1961.

Németh, A. *Erkel Ferenc.* Budapest, 1967.

Legány, D. *Erkel Ferenc müvei* [works]. Budapest, 1974.

Vébev, G. *Ungarische Elemente in der Opernmusik Ferenc Erkels.* Budapest, 1976.

Németh, A. *Ferenc Erkel. Sein Leben und Wirken.* Budapest, 1979.

articles–

Isoz, K. "Kisérletek Erkel Hunyadìm László-jázak párisi szinrehozatalára" [attempts to produce *Hunyadi László* in Paris: letters of Liszt, Erkel, and others]. *Musika* (1929): 16.

Valkó, A. "Szemelvények a fòrárosì levéltár Erkel-Liszt leveleiböl" [letters of Erkel and Liszt]. *Magyar zene* 1 (1960-61): 70; 3 (1962): 46.

Maróthy, J. "Erkels Weg von der 'heroisch-lyrischen' Oper zum kritischen Realismus." *Studia musicologica Academiae scientiarum hungaricae* 1 (1961): 161.

Volly, I, "Népdalváltozatok egy Erkel operadallamra" [folk tunes on an Erkel opera melody]. *Magyar zene* 6 (1965): 237.

Badacsonyi, George, "Bánk Bán—Hungary's National Opera." *Opera* February (1968).

Bónis, F. "Erkel über seine Oper Bánk bán." *Studia musicologica Academiae scientiarum hungaricae* 11 (1969): 69.

* * *

In the wake of the realignment of post-Napoleonic Europe, the frustrated forces of republicanism and revolution turned increasingly to music, literature and the theater to express the sense of nationhood that might otherwise have been realized through political means. In many countries this process was accelerated by the discovery of folk music, or what passed for folk music, since this had unambiguous national connotations. The movement was strongest in the empires of Central and Eastern Europe: in Poland, Bohemia and the Balkans, where indigenous cultures had been suppressed by alien rulers anxious to discourage any demonstration of individuality. Being the largest and most diverse of these conglomerates, the Austro-Hungarian empire spawned the greatest and most potent of the national movements.

The songs and dances performed by rural communities in connection with traditional country pursuits spread rapidly to the towns and were processed for consumption by more sophisticated audiences. When combined with drama and spectacle in the form of opera, especially opera celebrating national myths or historical events, the mixture was found to be an explosive political weapon. Thus it was that Auber's *La muette de Portici* aroused the Belgians to independence in 1830, and Verdi fanned the flames of Italian revolt. The standard of Bohemian nationalism, savagely repressed by Austria, was tentatively raised by Škroup's *Drátenik* (*The Tinker*) in 1826 and firmly hoisted by Smetana with *The Brandenburgers in Bohemia* (1862). In Poland, Moniuszko did the same with *Halka* (1847) while in Russia Glinka and

Dargomïzhsky prepared the ground for Musorgsky and Rimsky-Korsakov.

The Hungarian part of the Hapsburg domains held fervently to its individuality. As a race that had no relationship with any other in Europe and a language which had no recognizable links with those of their neighbors (Slav, Ottoman or Teuton), the Hungarians were dominated by a feudal aristocracy that ruthlessly controlled the peasant population and maintained fiscal independence from their theoretical overlords in Vienna. In 1848 Kossuth led a short-lived rising against the Austrians, but for nearly a decade before that, Ferenc Erkel had been promoting the national cause on the operatic stage.

It is difficult now to appreciate just how important Erkel was in the firmament of the Hungarian National movement, since he has been overshadowed by Liszt. Favored by a long and active career extending from the 1830s to 1892, he aspired from the outset to a specifically "Hungarian" style which he expressed in the Hungarian national hymn (1845), his arrangements of the *Rákóczy* march and the incorporation into his music of elements of the *verbunkos* music made popular by gypsy bands and used as an adjunct to recruiting, and the *csárdás* which supplanted it after about 1830. Both were accepted as genuine Hungarian folk music until the early twentieth century when Kodály and Bartók proved otherwise.

Erkel's use of such material was not exactly original—Jozsef Ruzitska's *Béla futasa* (1822) must claim that privilege—but his first opera, *Bátori Mária* (1840) established him as a leading Hungarian composer, and the intensely nationalistic *Hunyadi László* (1844), immensely successful throughout Hungary, confirmed his preeminence. After this Erkel seems to have undergone a fallow period in which he experimented with a form of ballad opera incorporating popular Hungarian songs, often unaltered. He was, however, active as the conductor and later director of the Hungarian National Theater, a post he held from 1838 until 1874 when Richter took over. He also enjoyed other distinctions, administrative as well as academic, and remained active until his death.

Erkel's most famous opera outside Hungary is *Bánk bán* which appeared in 1861. This historical drama ends the first and most significant stage of his development. He tried two comic operas without success (*Sarolta,* 1862, and *Névtelen hösök,* 1880) and also turned his hand to a high Romantic style that increasingly owed a debt to Wagner. The best and most innovative of these is *Brankovics György* (1874), which incorporates Balkan and Turkish material in addition to the by now familiar Hungarian influences and treats them in a way that uncannily anticipates the late Liszt and Bartók. His last opera, *István király* (1874-84), composed in close collaboration with his son Gyula and enthusiastically received, suggests that by this time Erkel had completely surrendered his individuality to his adulation of Wagner.

Among Erkel's contemporaries, Mosonyi, Huber, Csaszar, and the two Dopplers made significant contributions to the growth and popularity of Hungarian nationalism, but Erkel alone must take credit for having established a universally recognized Hungarian style that has found expression in the music of composers as diverse as Berlioz, Liszt, Kálmán, Kodály and Szokolay.

—Kenneth Dommett

ERNANI.

Composer: Giuseppe Verdi.

Librettist: Francesco Maria Piave (after Hugo, *Hernani*).

First Performance: Venice, La Fenice, 9 March 1844.

Roles: Ernani (tenor); Don Carlo (baritone); Don Ruy Gomez de Silva (bass); Elvira (soprano); Giovanna (soprano); Don Riccardo (tenor); Jago (bass); chorus (SSATTBB).

Publications

articles–

Kerman, Joseph. "Notes on an Early Verdi Opera." *Soundings* 3 (1973): 56.
Parker, Roger. "Levels of Motivic Definition in Verdi's *Ernani.*" *Nineteenth-Century Music* 6 (1982).
Parsons, James. "Made to Measure: Verdi's Aria for Tenor Nicola Ivanoff." *Opera News* December (1983), vol. 48/ no. 6: 19.

Accustomed as we are nowadays to all manner of theatrical fare, it seems hard to believe that a play such as Victor Hugo's *Hernani* could ever have been deemed even potentially seditious. Yet at its 1830 Paris premiere it very nearly provoked a riot. And why? The list of infractions against tradition in the name of Romanticism, or "Liberalism in literature" as Hugo preferred to put it, was lengthy: flagrant disregard for the classical unities of time and place; mixing the comic and the tragic; irregular verse forms; and, arguably the greatest sacrilege of all in the precarious political climate in France immediately preceding the July 1830 revolution against King Charles X, portraying a nobleman turned bandit (Don Juan of Aragon, better known as Hernani). But for Verdi in 1843, buoyed by the recent success of his *Nabucco* and *I Lombardi,* the freedom of expression *Hernani* offered must have seemed heaven-sent, particularly since he was then bent on expanding his horizons—heretofore limited to Milan's Teatro alla Scala—by accepting the commission of northern Italy's other leading opera company, Venice's Gran Teatro la Fenice.

Radical though *Hernani* surely was, then, at bottom what it offered Verdi and his librettist Francesco Maria Piave was the utterly fundamental conflict between love and honor—what Verdi called "immensely good theater." Or, to take a different tact as has the daringly unorthodox but perceptive Verdi critic Gabriele Baldini, the "story" afforded the pretense for "an ideal musical subject" that "requires nothing but the vaguest explanation. . . . A youthful, passionate female voice is besieged by three male voices, each of which establishes a specific relationship with her." Baldini continues, "the siege is fruitless. The male voices, or rather registers, meet with various fates, and each is granted a relationship with the woman, although on different levels. This relationship varies in intensity of passion according to the distance between the soprano register and the particular male voice" (*The Story of Giuseppe Verdi,* 1980). What an inventive way to make the point that *Ernani* is first and foremost an opera about *music,* and incredibly forceful music at that. Small wonder, too, that George Bernard Shaw was moved to write of Verdi's first collaboration with Piave: "*Falstaff* [Verdi's

A scene from Verdi's *Ernani,* Her Majesty's Theatre, London, 1845

last opera] is lighted and warmed only by the afterglow of the fierce noonday sun of *Ernani.*"

Verdi and Piave tailored their reworking of Hugo's amatory quadrangle into four acts, each of which bears a subtitle: "The Bandit," "The Guest," "The Pardon," and "The Mask." The first introduces all four principals, the tenor Ernani, the soprano Elvira, the baritone Don Carlo (King of Spain), and the bass Don Ruy Gomez de Silva. While all three men have designs on Elvira, she has pledged to marry her uncle Silva though she loves Ernani alone. The complications generated by the four-way romantic entanglement continue in act II with an interrupted impromptu rendezvous between Elvira and Ernani on the eve of her marriage to Silva, Silva learning that the king is also a suitor for the lady's hand, and the unexpected alliance between Ernani and Silva against Carlo. The act is capped, however implausibly, by Ernani giving his hunting horn to Silva as a token of good faith, promising to kill himself whenever the old man sounds it. Silva is given a reason to do exactly that when in act III Carlo is elected Emperor Charles V of the Holy Roman Empire; among his first acts is to condone the marriage of Ernani and Elvira. In act IV the two do marry yet their happiness is brief; hardly has the ceremony taken place when Silva sounds the horn. Ernani pleads for a moment of happiness at the end of his life of misery, but Silva insists the pact be honored forthwith. Offered a dagger, Ernani slays himself and falls dying into Elvira's arms.

Shaw's judgment of *Ernani* was not misplaced. Indeed, the score abounds with a special kind of memorable and highly-charged music aptly characterized by his phrase "fierce noonday sun." The first evidence of this comes in the second scene of act I, in Elvira's impassioned "Ernani, involami" when she dreams of being carried away by her beloved. As Baldini nimbly characterizes this showcase of vocal bravura that demands of the soprano a range of over two octaves (from high C to B-flat below middle C): "So overwhelming is the expressive force here that the passion seems to consume and destroy the woman." Other instances from among the many in this one of Verdi's most tune-drenched of scores include the baritone's third-act "O dei verd' anni miei," the conspirator's chorus "Si ridesti" and Elvira's "Ah! signor, se t'è concesso" in the same act, and—as an example of what could be called the very substance of early Verdi—the whole of the last-act trio.

Perhaps surprisingly, given Verdi's well-known diatribes against mere "entertainment, artifice and the system" when it threatened to obscure what to him was "art," on at least two occasions he deigned to supply *Ernani* with insert arias, one of the chief mediums by which singers traditionally sought to assert their dominance in the "system" that was nineteenth-century Italian opera. The first, the addition of the cabaletta "Infin che un brando vindice" for Silva in act I, was made in order to make the role more appealing to star bass singers; in the event, Verdi's authorship has been questioned, although the piece appeared in printed scores of the opera during his lifetime. Unequivocally authentic, however, is the act II double aria for Ernani that begins "Odi il voto, o grande Iddio." The aria was commissioned by none other than Gioacchino Rossini who had shortly before taken on the role of mentor for the tenor Nicola Ivanoff; the latter first sang the new number 26 December 1844 in a performance of the opera in Parma. Luciano Pavarotti revived the piece in 1983 at the Metropolitan Opera. Verdi's autograph for the aria is preserved at New York's Pierpont Morgan Library.

—James Parsons

ERWARTUNG [Expectation].

Composer: Arnold Schoenberg.

Librettist: Marie Pappenheim.

First Performance: Prague, Neues Deutsches Theater, 6 June 1924.

Roles: A Woman (soprano or mezzo-soprano).

Publications

book–

Garcia-Laborda, José Maria. *Studien zu Schönbergs Monodram "Erwartung" op. 17.* 2 vols. Laaber, 1981.

articles–

Buchanan, H. "A Key to Schoenberg's 'Erwartung'." *Journal of the American Musicological Society* 20 (1967): 434.
Wörner, K.H. "Schonberg's 'Erwartung' und das Ariadne-Thema." In *Die Musik in der Geistesgeschichte,* 91. Bonn, 1970.
Budde, E. "Arnold Schönbergs Monodrama 'Erwartung': Versuch einer Analyse der ersten Szene." *Archiv für Musikwissenschaft* 36 (1979): 1.
Mauser, Siegfried. "Forschungsbericht zu Schönbergs 'Erwartung'." *Österreichische Musikzeitung* 35 (1980): 215.
Weissweiler, Eva. "Schreiben Sie mir doch einen Operntext, Fräulein!' Marie Pappenheims Text zur Arnold Schönbergs *Erwartung.*" *Neue Zeitschrift für Musik* 145 (1984): 4.

unpublished–

Mauser, Siegfried. "Das expressionistische Musiktheater der Wiener Schule. Stilistische und entwicklunggeschichtliche Untersuchungen zu Arnold Schönbergs *Erwartung* op. 17, *Die glückliche Hand* op. 18 und Alban Bergs *Wozzeck* op. 7." Ph.D. dissertation, University of Salzburg, 1981.

*   *   *

Erwartung, which Schoenberg himself called "a monodrama in one act," was written in a seventeen-day period between 27 August and 12 September 1909 using a libretto written for Schoenberg by his friend Marie Pappenheim, a physician in Vienna. The premier, however, did not take place until fifteen years later in Prague on 6 June 1924 at the second International Society for Contemporary Music Festival at the Neue Deutsche Theater with Marie Gutheil-Schröder, soprano, and conducted by Schoenberg's teacher (and brother-in-law), Alexander von Zemlinsky. It was performed subsequently in Wiesbaden on 22 January 1928, in Berlin on 7 June 1930, and in Brussels on 6 May 1936 in a French translation by J. Weterings. More recent performances include those in London on 4 April 1960, with Heather Harper, and the American stage premiere in Washington, D.C. on 28 December 1960 with Helga Pilarczyk, conducted by Robert Craft.

While the term "nightmare" is often used to describe this opera, Schoenberg's "Angst-traum" is more precise. Lasting only twenty-seven minutes, it is comprised of four scenes marked by the entrance and exit of a solitary woman. The plot, if we may use the term at all, unfolds by memory association as if the woman were a patient on an analyst's couch. The woman enters, walking along the moonlit path of the garden, searching for "the man." The night is full of sinister intimations, but she finds the courage to rush into the wood in her search. In the second scene she is deep in the forest's interior darkness; she sees apparitions, imagines she hears strange noises and is being attacked. Suddenly calmed, she ventures deeper still. The speech now becomes in part a dialogue with the imagined man, and in part a confession. As the scene closes, she stumbles into a tree trunk which she mistakes for a body. The third scene brings her to a clearing. She is even more frightened by the specters of the night and now identifies "him" as her lover. She imagines him calling; a shadow reminds her of his shadow on a wall. She complains because he must leave her so quickly, and plunges deeper into the wood, crying for her lover's protection against the imagined wild beasts.

The final scene presents a dark and shuttered house. She stumbles in, dress torn, face and hands now bleeding. Now the night symbolizes death. There is no living thing, no breath of air, no sound. Only death and the pallid, bloodless moon. She approaches a bench but fears that a strange woman will chase her away. Her foot strikes something—a bloody corpse. She swoons as she recognizes the body of her lover, and attempts to call him awake in a hymn-like passage. We learn that of late the beloved's attentions have slacked off, and she suspects him of betraying her with another, the white-armed woman. The kisses and embraces with which she first greeted the imagined corpse (there is no corpse in Schoenberg's stage directions; everything is imagined) turn to kicks and jealous tantrums. Finally, as dawn colors the sky, she rises, exhausted, saying "I was seeking . . ." and slips away into the shadows, the quest unsatisfied, and her memory already slipping away from her conscious mind. The music ends with one of the most amazing passages ever written— an orchestral "shiver" which seems not to stop but to vanish beyond audible sound.

Although direct connections between Schoenberg and Freud are difficult to make, *Erwartung* can surely be called the first psychoanalytic opera. The reality plumbed in the short, intense drama is purely psychological, and the only dramatic event is the discovery of the body. This occurs quite early in the opera, and the remainder of the monologue passes from recall of the past love through heightened emotions and ends in a kind of posthumous reconciliation brought about by exhaustion. There is only a vestigial sense of real time. Past and present seem to cross and recross in a way that mirrors the confused state of mind of the nightmare victim. Conventional tonal music could not have convincingly supported the interplay of conflicting emotions. Although there are identifiable repetitions of musical themes—the ostinato figures used as the woman walks along the path, for instance—the score appears athematic. The level of repetition is so subtly disguised within the surface fabric that whatever repetition exists contributes but little to the overall coherence of the music. Certainly this is Schoenberg's most daring and furthest venture into athematicism, a path he chose not to pursue further.

The extreme compression of this work, both in actual time and in the almost continuous level of harmonic intensity, seem somehow inexorably tied to the subject matter itself: the confused state of the hysterical mind. It is not generally known that the librettist, Marie Pappenheim, was the cousin of "Anna O." (Bertha Pappenheim, whose initials were transposed backward one place to arrive at the name Freud used in his case study, the first classic documented case of hysteria). While the symptoms displayed by Anna O. differ markedly from those apparitions and phantoms that appear in the opera, comparing the cases tempts one to make suppositions that Schoenberg knew at least something about Freud's investigations. On the other hand, Schoenberg himself was no stranger to the tortured state of mind. Furthermore, Viennese culture was fixated on repression, despair, and suicide, and any number of plays, poems, and other art works can be identified that spring from these dark psychic roots. We may never know exactly which influences were uppermost in Schoenberg's mind as he worked so feverishly on this opera, but there is no doubt that *Erwartung* is a direct expression of its time and place.

—Robert H. Danes

—————

ESCLARMONDE.

Composer: Jules Massenet.

Librettists: Alfred Blau and Louis de Gramont.

First Performance: Paris, Opéra-Comique, 14 May 1889.

Roles: Esclarmonde (soprano); Parséis (mezzo-soprano); Roland (tenor); Phorcas (bass-baritone); Bishop of Blois (bass); Enéas (tenor); Cléomer (bass); Byzantine Ambassador (bass); Byzantine Herald (tenor); chorus.

Publications

books–

Malherbe, C. *Notice sur "Esclarmonde".* Paris, 1890.
Augenot, R. *Esclarmonde ou Une forme divine de l'expression musicale au théâtre.* Brussels, 1939.

article–

Crichton, Ronald. "*Mireille* and *Esclarmonde.*" *Opera* December (1983).

The modern revival of Jules Massenet's "opéra romanesque," *Esclarmonde,* took place at the San Francisco Opera on 23

October 1974 with Joan Sutherland in the title role; the production was then taken to the Metropolitan Opera in New York City. Only a very few great sopranos before Sutherland had taken the role, among them Gabrielli Ritter-Ciampi and Fanny Heldy, the latter in a revival in Paris that held the stage from 1925 to 1934. The opera was created for the American soprano Sibyl Sanderson (also the first Thaïs) for the Universal Exposition of 1889. It had great initial success, achieving ninety-one performances during the Exposition from May through October. Massenet always declared it his favorite of his own operas. A work involving magic, voluptuous eroticism, and chivalry, it has been called by Henry T. Finck "Massenet's Wagnerian confession of faith." Camille Bellaigue noted that "One might define *Esclarmonde* as at the same time a small French *Tristan* and a small French *Parsifal.*" In a number of its features *Esclarmonde* rather strikingly anticipates Strauss's *Die Frau ohne Schatten* and Puccini's *Turandot.*

The prologue takes place in the Basilica at Byzantium. Emperor Phorcas, a magician, intends to abdicate the throne in favor of his daughter Esclarmonde, whom he has instructed in the art of magic. She must, however, remain veiled to all men until the age of twenty, at which time the winner of a tournament will be allowed to marry her and rule with her. Phorcas bids Esclarmonde's sister, Parséis, to act as her guardian as he hands over the crown and sceptre to Esclarmonde before the assembled court. In act I Parséis learns that Esclarmonde pines for Roland, a French knight she has seen and fallen in love with. Parséis suggests that Esclarmonde use her magical powers to bring Roland to her. Enéas, Parséis's knight-errant, reveals however that Roland is soon to wed the daughter of Cléomer, King of France. Distressed by this news, Esclarmonde invokes the spirits of air, water, and fire to lead Roland to an enchanted island where she will join him. Act II, scene i takes place on the island. Esclarmonde awakens the sleeping Roland with a kiss. She declares her love, enjoins him never to try to lift her veil, and the two spend a glorious *Liebesnacht* together. In scene ii Esclarmonde gives Roland the sword of St George, which will render him invincible in battle as long as he keeps his vows to her. She will join him each night. In act III, scene i, Roland is victorious in battle for King Cléomer over the Saracens; Cléomer thus offers him the hand of his daughter Bathilde. Roland refuses and declines to explain. The Bishop of Blois determines to learn the reason. In scene ii, in a room in the palace of King Cléomer, the bishop demands of Roland the reason for refusing Bathilde. Eventually Roland confesses his union with the mysterious, veiled Esclarmonde. The bishop judges him guilty of sacrilegious possession by a demon. As the bishop leaves, Esclarmonde appears; the bishop returns with monks, torch-bearers, and executioners. He tears the veil from Esclarmonde's face and begins to exorcise demons from her. She reproaches Roland for betraying her and protects herself by summoning the spirits of fire. As Roland draws the sword of St George on the bishop it splinters in his hand. Esclarmonde curses Roland again for his betrayal and disappears in a burst of flames.

Act IV begins with the tournament in Byzantium for the hand of Esclarmonde. Phorcas is extremely upset over Esclarmonde's experience with Roland; he commands the spirits to bring her to him and she appears through thunder and lightning, surrounded by flames. Phorcas strips her of her powers and declares that Roland will die unless Esclarmonde renounces him. She submits to save his life. She now faces Roland alone; he begs for and is granted forgiveness but must now, she insists, forget her. Roland, learning that she has lost her magical powers because of him, asks Esclarmonde to flee with him. She agrees but her father's power, demonstrated in a thunderclap, stops her. She renounces Roland, is expiated and disappears with her father in a magic cloud. Roland, desiring only death, goes off to the tournament. The epilogue, like the prologue, takes place in the Basilica of Byzantium. Phorcas commands Esclarmonde to appear to be presented to the victor of the tournament. When the champion is led in he gives his names as Despair, declaring that he sought only death and refuses his prize. Esclarmonde recognizes his voice—it is Roland. She unveils and the two are united, to the delight of the court.

The libretto of *Esclarmonde,* by Alfred Blau and Louis de Gramont, is based on a story from *Parthénopoeus de Blois,* a Medieval metrical romance. Some of the earliest critics of the opera liked neither the magical ambience nor the Wagnerian aspects of the score, which included Massenet's adoption of a system of *Leitmotifs,* of which seven are especially prominent: two for magic, one for Esclarmonde, one for Roland, one for the Tournament, one for the Nuptials, and one for Possession. Yet Wagner's is not the only voice to be found echoed in *Esclarmonde.* It is, to say the least, an eclectic work; one early critic heard in it traces of Wagner, Gounod, Meyerbeer, Verdi, Reyer, and features of operetta. Yet *Esclarmonde* does not sound in the least Germanic, especially in the melodic writing and in its luminous orchestration, which are especially French.

Massenet had a supreme knowledge of the human voice. His setting of the French text throughout is masterly in the correctness of inflections and rhythms, e.g., Esclarmonde's *parlato* in the act IV quartet, beginning with the words "Donc . . . pour sauver la vie à celui que j'adore." In his vocal writing Massenet was known for the inspired, arching "mélodie éternelle," examples of which may be found in the melody to which he set the words "Va . . . je suis belle et désirable!" in act II, scene i, and on the words "Chaque nuit, cher amant" in act II, scene ii. The role of Esclarmonde, designed specifically for the much-admired Sibyl Sanderson, was not for a typical French soprano, but for a voice with great power, a glowing, full, round voice.

The "magic carpet" orchestration, as the noted French opera authority Robert Lawrence called it, matches the plot and setting in its exoticism and voluptuousness. Massenet includes three of all winds (the bass clarinet and tuba are especially prominent). Exotic or unusual instruments are not called for; instead, Massenet combines familiar instruments in unfamiliar combinations and exploits unusual registers to arrive at the striking orchestral colors intrinsic to the score. In terms of Massenet's brilliant orchestration, another name needs to be added to the previous list of influences, that of Berlioz. As Robert Lawrence explains of Massenet's work: "There is a tremendous difference between the piano-vocal reduction and the full orchestral score. The vigor and exuberance of the first-act hunt, the *démonisme* of the scene for the hero, Roland, the princess and the fanatical Bishop of Blois reveal a side of Massenet . . . not to be found elsewhere, in which the orchestral texture, rather than a brilliant *appliqué,* is—as in Berlioz's *Troyens*—an outgrowth of organic musical thought." Although there will be doubts about the opera's total worth, for the magical orchestral sound, the opulent vocal writing, the sense of magical transport, and numerous striking musical ideas, *Esclarmonde* deserves to be heard. There is a recording on Decca-London starring Joan Sutherland, with Richard Bonynge conducting.

—Stephen Willier

EUGENE ONEGIN [Evgeny Onegin].

Composer: Piotr Ilyich Tchaikovsky.

Librettists: K. Shilovsky and Piotr Ilyich Tchaikovsky (after Pushkin).

First Performance: Moscow, Malïy, 29 March 1879.

Roles: Tatyana (soprano); Lensky (tenor); Eugene Onegin (baritone); Madame Larina (mezzo-soprano); Olga (contralto); Filippevna (mezzo-soprano); Prince Gremin (bass); Triquet (tenor); Zaretski (bass); A Captain (bass); Gillot (mute); chorus (SSAATTBB).

Publications

articles—

Abraham, Gerald. "*Eugene Onegin* and Tchaikovsky's Marriage." In *On Russian Music,* 225. London, 1939.

Berlin, I. "Tchaikovsky, Pushkin, and Onegin." *Musical Times* 60 (1979).

Avant-scène opéra September (1982) [*Eugène Onéguine* issue].

Gliede, Edmund. "*Eugen Onegin*—Metamorphosen eines Stoffes." *Musik und Bildung* 15 (1983): 18.

Schläder, Jürgen. "Operndramaturgie und musikalische Konzeption zu Tschaikowskijs Opern *Eugen Onegin* und *Pique Dame* und ihren literarischen Vorlagen." *Deutsche Vierteljahrsschrift für Literaturwissenschaft und Geistesgeschichte* 57 (1983): 525 [summary in English].

*   *   *

When a singer named Elizaveta Lavrovskaya first suggested Pushkin's *Eugene Onegin* to Tchaikovsky as a subject for an opera, he thought the idea peculiar. But a short time later, reading over the poet's popular "novel in verse," he changed his mind, and eagerly sketched out a scenario for the opera that is largely a blueprint for the finished product.

Tchaikovsky had tried his hand at opera many times with varying degrees of success. He set ten librettos and considered many other subjects that never came to anything. But this time, something clicked. Pushkin's verses about a naive young girl named Tatyana, cruelly spurned by the worldly, sophisticated Onegin, fired his imagination as had no other source.

In a letter from 1877 he wrote, "How delightful to avoid the commonplace Pharaohs, Ethiopian princesses, poisoned cups and all the rest of these dolls' tales! *Eugene Onegin* is full of poetry. I am not blind to its defects. I know well enough the work gives little scope for treatment, and will be deficient in stage effects; but the wealth of poetry, the human quality and simplicity of the subject, joined to Pushkin's inspired verses, will compensate for what it lacks in other respects."

Pushkin's *Eugene Onegin,* a "novel in verse," is imbued with his special sarcastic touch. He had started the tale intending a satire on Byron's *Don Juan,* but over the years it took him to complete it, the work developed instead into a merciless satire on Russian society of Pushkin's time. The narrator's snide remarks and long asides create an ironic distance, discouraging deep sympathy for the characters on the part of the reader. By poking fun at the troubles of his characters, Pushkin made his tract an anti-Romantic caricature of emotional idealism.

Tchaikovsky by contrast identified deeply with the characters, especially the sensitive Tatyana. In constructing the libretto, he eliminated the ironic tone of the original. A great deal of Pushkin's beautiful poetry is used as written, but with the narrator's asides excised or restated as the words of the characters. For example, Lensky, who was "in the flower of youthful looks and lyric power," "mourned the wilt of life's young green, when he had almost turned eighteen." The first phrase appears in the libretto, but the comical remark about the jaded youth's real age does not. By thus eliminating the sarcasm, the characters' emotional vagaries are accepted at face value.

These were calculated changes made by a composer who knew the language of opera to be one of strong, visceral feeling. Operatic characters must be larger than life and experience intense emotions: hence the importance of Tatyana's love. Pushkin's dry, intellectual sarcasm had exactly the opposite effect. Pushkin deflated his characters; Tchaikovsky re-inflated them.

In the opera, Madame Larina has two daughters, Olga and Tatyana. Lensky, who is courting Olga, brings his friend Eugene Onegin to meet the girls. Tatyana is immediately attracted to the worldly Onegin. Later, in private, she writes him a long letter confessing her love. Tatyana is devastated when Onegin rebuffs her love coolly, telling her that he is unsuitable for marriage and suggesting that she learn to control her emotions.

Act II opens with a ball. Irritated with Lensky after overhearing gossip about himself and Tatyana, Onegin flirts and dances with Olga, who is not unresponsive to his attentions. The fiery Lensky is furiously jealous and challenges Onegin to a duel. When Lensky is killed in the duel, Onegin is grief-stricken. Act III takes place three years later, when Onegin by chance meets Tatyana at another ball. Now married to Prince Gremin, Tatyana is transformed from a naive girl into a sophisticated lady. It is Onegin's turn to be smitten. But when he professes his love, Tatyana in turn rejects his overtures, saying that whatever her true feelings she must remain faithful to her husband.

Pushkin's tale has little to recommend it to grand theatrical effects, a problem of which Tchaikovsky was keenly aware. Acknowledging the non-dramatic nature of his work, the composer did not even call it an opera, but rather "lyric scenes in three acts." Some of the rewriting of the libretto, such as the contrived confrontation between Onegin and Lensky at the ball, was designed to inject a bit of drama. But significant portions of the story are left out entirely, making the plot a little confusing. The disjointed progression is particularly noticeable in the gap between the second and third acts. Tchaikovsky could safely assume that most of his listeners would be familiar with Pushkin's novel, but today, for non-Russian audiences, such familiarity is unlikely.

The most important of the scenes, and the first that Tchaikovsky wrote, was the crucial letter scene from act I. Freed of Pushkin's long preamble, which in the novel trivializes Tatyana's distress, Tchaikovsky makes it into a drama in miniature of the rollercoaster ride of the girl's emotions. Tatyana boldly begins the letter, then falters, tears it up, and starts again. After pouring out her feelings, she finally finishes writing, throwing herself on Onegin's mercy. This scene underscores the heights to which Tchaikovsky fanned Tatyana's passion, supported musically by the obsessive sequential repetitions of a chromatic descending four-note theme.

Throughout his creative life, Tchaikovsky was usually involved in some way with dramatic music. He found his subjects in sources as varied as Shakespeare (*Hamlet*), Joan of Arc (*The Maid of Orleans*), and mythology (*Undine*). But

that was not where Tchaikovsky's strengths lay. His powers lay in characterization, not in depicting the fantastic, and his lyric gifts were most effective in direct emotional expression. It was with *Eugene Onegin,* a tale of ordinary people and real passions, that Tchaikovsky achieved his greatest success and created a staple of the Russian operatic repertory.

—Elizabeth W. Patton

L'EURIDICE.

Composer: Giulio Caccini.

Librettist: Ottavio Rinuccini.

First Performance: Florence, Palazzo Pitti, 5 December 1602.

Roles: Tragedy (soprano); Euridice (soprano); Orfeo (tenor); Arcetro (contralto); Tirsi (tenor); Aminta (tenor); Dafne (soprano); Venus (soprano); Pluto (bass); Proserpina (soprano); Radamanto (bass); Caronte (tenor); chorus.

Publications

articles–

Palisca, Claude V. "The First Performance of *Euridice.*" *Queen's College Department of Music Twenty-fifth Anniversary Festschrift, 1937-62.* New York, 1964.
Brown, Howard M. "How Opera Began: an Introduction to Jacopo Peri's Euridice (1600)." *The Late Italian Renaissance,* edited by Eric Cochrane, 401. New York, 1970.

*　　*　　*

L'Euridice, an important example of the application of the ideals of the Florentine monodists to the setting of a full-scale drama to music, is one of the two earliest surviving operas, the other being Jacopo Peri's setting of the same libretto. Caccini's work was performed in Florence in 1602, but the score was published earlier, in 1600. Peri's work had been performed in Florence in 1600 but appeared in print only after the publication of Caccini's score.

The librettist Rinuccini drew his plot from Greek myth but did not hesitate to change the ending of the story. After a prologue in which the personification of tragedy sets the scene and praises the nobles in the audience, nymphs and shepherds sing and dance in honor of Euridice on her wedding day. Orfeo enters and calls for Euridice, but soon Dafne comes to inform him that Euridice has died of a snake's bite. Extensive lamentation follows, including Orfeo's lament and commentaries by the chorus. Arcetro describes Orfeo's grief upon visiting the scene of Euridice's death. Venus arrives and convinces Orfeo to seek Euridice in Hades, where Orfeo finally convinces Pluto to release Euridice. All ends well as nymphs and shepherds celebrate the return of Orfeo and Euridice. Rinuccini's happy ending is an alteration of the ending of the myth. In the traditional version Orfeo loses Euridice once more, because he fails to meet the requirement that he keep Euridice out of his sight until they have escaped from Hades.

Caccini dedicated the printed score of *L'Euridice* to Count Giovanni de' Bardi, who had sponsored the Florentine group known as the "Camerata" in the 1570s and 1580s. On his title page and in the dedication Caccini introduced the term "stile rappresentativo" ("theatrical style") to describe the new genre, and he made several important statements in his dedication. He claimed to have cultivated the new style already for a number of years (and soon became embroiled in a dispute with Peri over primacy of place). He mentions the Camerata and the discussions concerning the proper means of imitating the ancient Greeks' use of singing in the performance of dramas. He points out that the style of recitation in his opera has been calculated to tend toward ordinary speech. He describes use of "basso continuato," as he calls it, by means of which the bass line determines the harmony but the details of voicing are left to the performer. Implicit are certain points from Bardi's *Discourse* addressed to Caccini and published some twenty years earlier. Bardi had counseled Caccini to observe natural declamation and to avoid counterpoint in the name of clarity in text-setting. Much of this is borne out in the music of *L'Euridice,* and the novel aspects of the work are indeed striking. Caccini carries out most of the story in recitative, which occasionally becomes heightened in a passage such as Dafne's description of the death of Euridice. Choral commentaries and occasional metrically-regular songs provide contrast to the recitative. Caccini notated only an instrumental bass line and the voice parts. He composed an instrumental *ritornello* as part of the prologue, but there is no independent instrumental music. On the basis of written and musical evidence, however, it seems likely that at least a short sinfonia should be supplied in performance of the work.

The cumulative effect of Caccini's *L'Euridice* must have seemed quite novel when the work was written and produced, but the effect pales when compared with Monteverdi's handling of the same legend in his *L'Orfeo.*

—Edward Rutschman

L'EURIDICE.

Composer: Jacopo Peri.

Librettist: O. Rinuccini.

First Performance: Florence, Palazzo Pitti, 6 October 1600.

Roles: Euridice (soprano); Daphne (soprano); Proserpina (soprano); Venus (soprano); Orpheus (tenor); Amyntas (tenor); Arcetro (tenor); Thyrsis (tenor); Pluto (bass); Caronte (bass); chorus (SATB).

Publications

articles–

Palisca, C.V. "The First Performance of 'Euridice'." *Queens College Twenty-fifth Anniversary Festschrift,* 1. New York, 1964.

Monterosso Vacchelli, A.M. "Elementi stilistici nell' 'Euridice' di J. Peri in rapporto al 'Orfeo' di Monteverdi." In *Congresso internazionale sul tema Claudio Monteverdi e il suo tempo: venezia, Mantova e Cremona 1968,* 117.

Brown, Howard M. "How Opera Began: An Introduction to Jacopo Peri's *Euridice.*" In *The Late Italian Renaissance 1525-1630,* edited by Eric Cochrane, 401. London, 1970.

————. Preface to *Jacopo Peri: Euridice.* Madison, Wisconsin, 1981.

Carter, Tim. "Jacopo Peri's *Euridice* (1600): A Contextual Study." *Music Review* 43 (1982): 83.

McGee, Timothy. "*Orfeo* and *Euridice,* the First Two Operas." In *Orpheus, the Metamorphosis of a Myth,* edited by John Warden, 163. Toronto, 1982.

*   *   *

Encouraged by the "pleasure and astonishment" that greeted the "simple trial" of *Dafne* in 1598 (all music lost save for six numbers), the composer Jacopo Peri and the librettist Ottavio Rinuccini continued their efforts in the fledgling genre of opera two years later with *Euridice,* a *favola per musica* (or "tale [written] for music"). First performed in a small room of the Pitti Palace before a select audience of nobility, the work was but one of the many splendid entertainments given in Florence in October 1600 to celebrate the marriage by proxy of Maria de' Medici and King Henri IV of France. Among those who first heard the work was the composer Marco da Gagliano, whose remarks seem particularly well chosen in describing the first opera for which music has survived.

"I shall not grow tired of lauding it," Gagliano wrote; "indeed there is no one who does not bestow infinite praise upon it, no lover of music who does not have constantly before him the songs of Orfeo. Let me say truthfully that no one can completely understand the gentleness and the force of [Peri's] airs if he has not heard him sing them himself. He gives to them such grace and so impresses on the listener the affection of the words, that he is compelled to weep and rejoice, as the composer wills."

As in the previous *Dafne,* the story of *Euridice* is simply constructed. In the opening prologue the character of "*La Tragedia*" (Tragedy) sings that she has abandoned her customary role as the specter of pity and terror in exchange for a more "pleasing mien for the royal nuptials," and so "I tune my song to happier strings to give sweet pleasure to the noble heart." In the first scene, nymphs and shepherds rejoice at the impending wedding of Orpheus and Euridice. Euridice enters, expressing her happiness, and suggests that she and those present retreat "to the pleasing shade of that flowering wood, and there to the sound of the limpid stream let us sing happy songs and dance." Orpheus appears in scene ii and delivers a monologue in praise of nature, telling the flora and fauna around him that they will henceforth hear from him no songs of sadness: "No longer will my noble lyre/ Move you to tears with its plaintive song: / With ineffable mercy, into great delight/ Courtly Love has today changed my plaint." Arcetro, Orpheus's friend, joins him and the two reflect on the comforts and joys of love. Interrupting their conversation, the rustic Thyrsis begins to play his panpipes and dance in anticipation of the coming wedding. Thyrsis has scarcely finished his song when Daphne breaks in to recount the tragic news of Euridice's death. The inconsolable Orpheus sings of his sorrow and hurries off in search of his beloved, followed by Arcetro, who goes to comfort him; the nymphs and shepherds thereupon return from the forest, bewailing the loss of their mistress. In the third scene, Arcetro describes how Orpheus threw himself down on the spot where Euridice expired and how a goddess (later revealed as Venus) descended in a golden chariot and carried him away. In scene

Peri's *L'Euridice,* opening prologue from first edition of score, Florence, 1600

iv, Venus leads Orpheus to the gates of hell, where he sings a lament for the departed Euridice. The passion of his song forces open the gates; following a protracted discussion, Pluto, moved by Orpheus's entreaties, agrees to return Euridice to the living. (In so departing here from the traditional version of the myth, Rinuccini states in the dedication of the libretto that since the opera was to be performed at a wedding he was compelled to alter the ending to one befitting "a time of such great rejoicing.") In the concluding scene the shepherd Amyntas announces the joyous news to the other shepherds and nymphs. Following the arrival of Orpheus and Euridice, the opera ends with an elaborate chorus of rejoicing.

Comparing the libretto for *Euridice* with that of *Dafne,* Rinuccini remarked that "greater favor and fortune have been bestowed upon *Euridice,*" for it was "set to music by Peri with wonderful art." Peri himself, in describing his aims in composing the work (set forth in the forward to the printed edition of the score of *Euridice,* 1600/1601), laid considerable emphasis on his efforts at "imitating speech in song" in a style "lying between the slow and suspended movements of song and the swift and rapid movements of speech." Such was Peri's confidence in the expressive power of recitative that he even used it in setting Orpheus's solemn invocation to the powers of the Underworld. And one must say the effect is extraordinarily convincing. Indeed, Peri's "artful manner of reciting in song"—as the composer Marco da Gagliano wrote elsewhere—was to have a considerable influence on opera in the years to come. But for all its indisputable historical consequence, the significance of *Euridice* does not reside solely in the fact that it is the first opera for which the music is extant. In the hands of performers willing to devote themselves to mastering its expressive demands, the work is indeed capable, as Gagliano asserted, of so impressing the listener "that he is compelled to weep and rejoice, as the composer wills." Although it would be wrong to claim that the work is on the same level with Monteverdi's *Orfeo* (composed just seven years later), *Euridice* nevertheless can provoke astonishment that the inventor of opera got most things right the first time round, spelling out and turning to dramatic effect the tensions between speech and song, solo and chorus, voice and instruments, singing and scenery, acting and dance—all the things in which opera, that most all-encompassing of the arts, has lived ever since. Whereas Peri and Rinuccini's first work *Dafne* was likely little more than the "simple trial" they said it was, with *Euridice,* which treats yet again the compelling story of the power of music, opera was unequivocally and wholly established.

—James Parsons

EURYANTHE.

Composer: Carl Maria von Weber.

Librettist: H. von Chezy.

First Performance: Vienna, Kärntnertor, 25 October 1823.

Roles: Euryanthe de Savoy (soprano); Eglantine de Puiset (mezzo-soprano); Count Adolar de Nevers (tenor); Count Lysiart de Forêt (baritone); King Louis VI of France (bass); Rudolph (tenor); Bertha (soprano); chorus (SATTBB).

Publications

articles—

Chezy, H. von. "Carl Maria von Webers Euryanthe: ein Beitrag zur Geschichte der Deutschen Oper." *Neue Zeitschrift für Musik* 13 (1840): 1, 9.

Abert, A.A. "Webers *Euryanthe* und Spohr's *Jessonda* als grosse Opern." In *Festschrift für Walter Wiora,* 435. Kassel, 1967.

Tusa, Michael C. "Weber's *Grosse Oper:* a Note on the Origins of *Euryanthe.*" *Nineteenth-Century Music* 8 (1984): 119.

Euryanthe, a "grand heroic-romantic opera," as Weber called it, has an entirely implausible and fanciful libretto. Even such an admirer of the composer as Mahler made some cuts in the score when he conducted it in Vienna, with the intention of making the drama more convincing. But it now seems that the opera should be accepted on its own terms as a kind of pageant.

The time is the twelfth century. Act I is set in the French court of King Louis VI. Adolar de Nevers loves Euryanthe and sings a troubadour song in her praise, but Lysiart de Forêt cynically tells him that he can prove she lacks virtue, persuading Adolar into a bet of their respective estates pledged upon her fidelity and chastity. In the second scene we meet Euryanthe herself in the castle at Nevers, telling her guest Eglantine of her love for Adolar, revealing foolishly to Eglantine that she and Adolar share the guilty secret (which they have sworn to keep) of his sister Emma's suicide and that the ghost of Emma cannot rest until the tears of an innocent maid have been shed on her ring, lying in her tomb. Eglantine, who has also loved Adolar, is jealous and determines to obtain the ring and show him that his beloved Euryanthe has betrayed the secret. Lysiart arrives to escort Euryanthe back to court and is welcomed by her and her peasants.

In act II Lysiart quickly realizes that his bet is vain and hopeless, recognizing the goodness of Euryanthe, though in an angry aria he vents feelings of frustration and a desire to avenge himself. Learning of Eglantine's plot, he tells her that he will aid her in the betrayal of Euryanthe and that they will marry and together enjoy the possession of Adolar's lands. Scene ii reveals Adolar alone, singing rapturously of Euryanthe. When Euryanthe enters, the lovers unite in a lyrical duet. But now the king and court enter, and Lysiart announces that he has won his bet, producing the dead Emma's ring and saying that he knows the precious secret on which Euryanthe and Adolar had vowed eternal silence. The court accepts what Lysiart says, and even Adolar is now convinced that his rival has seduced her; but instead of abandoning her, he leads her away to kill her.

The last act begins in a wilderness. Adolar reproaches Euryanthe, who protests her innocence and love but is left in the desert. Alone, she awaits death, but the king and court now appear on a hunt, and she convinces the king that she is guiltless. He assures her that Adolar will be restored to her, and the act ends with an ecstatic short aria for Euryanthe in which the chorus echoes her happiness. However, at the end of the scene she collapses. Scene ii shows us Lysiart and Eglantine in possession of Nevers and its lands, and preparing for their wedding in dances and a joyful chorus. But when Adolar reappears, the peasants pledge their renewed loyalty to their former lord. In the meantime, the guilty Eglantine is visited by a vision of the dead Emma. The king arrives just in time to prevent Adolar and Lysiart from fighting. He tells them that Euryanthe is dead, and on hearing this Eglantine confesses her plot and is at once killed by Lysiart. Adolar says that his own guilt is worse, but when a revived Euryanthe is restored to him, her tears falling on Emma's ring assure us, together with smooth harmonies, that the troubled ghost of Emma may at last rest.

Euryanthe's qualities are mainly musical rather than dramatic, although several commentators have suggested that the story of Wagner's *Lohengrin* owes something to this work. The overture sets the tone by foreshadowing later music such as Adolar's aria of love in act II and the ghostly muted string harmonies associated with the dead Emma and her ring; and among the memorable numbers that follow are Adolar's troubadour-style song and Eglantine's confession of jealous anger (both in act I), Adolar's loving soliloquy in act II and some of the choruses such as the wedding chorus in act III. The opening of this final act, set in the wilderness, is remarkable for its uncannily shifting harmonies which create an eerie atmosphere.

It is such imaginative touches that make *Euryanthe* special. In 1847 Schumann called the music "noble," indeed the noblest that Weber could offer. But it was Liszt—who though not himself an opera composer knew more about it than most—who perceptively said that here was "a marvelous divination of the future shaping of the drama and the endeavour to unite with opera the whole wealth of instrumental development"—in other words that Weber, with his rich instrumental imagination, showed future composers, and Wagner above all, how to make the operatic orchestra itself part of the drama.

—Christopher Headington

EVANS, (Sir) Geraint (Llewellyn).

Baritone. Born 16 February 1922, in Pontypridd, Wales. Died 20 September 1992, in Bronglais, Wales. Married: Brenda Evans Davies, 1948 (two sons). Military service in Royal Air Force, then studied with Walter Hyde at the Guildhall School of Music, with Theo Hermann in Hamburg, and with Fernando Carpi in Genoa; debut at Covent Garden as Night Watchman in *Die Meistersinger*, 1948; sang at Glyndebourne, 1950-61; San Francisco debut as Beckmesser, 1959; debut at Teatro alla Scala (1960) and Vienna Staatsoper (1961) as Figaro; debut at Chicago as Lem in Giannini's *The Harvest*, 1961; Salzburg debut as Figaro, 1962; debut at the Metropolitan Opera as Falstaff, 1964; debut at Paris Opera as Leporello in *Don Giovanni*, 1975; created Flint in *Billy Budd* (1951), Mountjoy in *Gloriana* (1953); Evadne and Antenor in Walton's *Troilus and Cressida* (1954); began to produce operas in mid-1970s.

Publications

By EVANS: books–

Sir Geraint Evans: A Knight at the Opera. London, 1984.

About EVANS: books–

Cairns, D. *Responses.* London, 1973.

Geraint Evans as Falstaff

articles–

Dunlop, L. "Geraint Evans." *Opera* 12 (1961): 231.

* * *

The compact but energetic figure of Geraint Evans became a familiar one on the British operatic stage and in many other centers during a career which lasted not much short of forty years. Like so many British singers, he began his professional life in oratorio, but his studies in Hamburg and Geneva revealed to him that his strengths lay in opera. From the start his typically Welsh vitality and confidence, together with a mercurial sparkle, made him a future star in a profession where such stardom is often reserved for tenors rather than baritones—although not always so, as the case of Tito Gobbi reminds us.

The mention of Gobbi makes it worth saying that Evans was a different kind of artist from that Italian baritone. His innate geniality, a vocal matter as well as one of physical presence, made him less than convincing in the role of Scarpia, the cruel and corrupt police chief in Puccini's *Tosca*, a role in which Gobbi excelled—but it is also fair to say that however well Evans had acted, his public might not have accepted him as a villain. Nor would they see him as a darkly brooding, wronged and vengeful Rigoletto, Verdi's court jester; and although his musicianship allowed him to sing Berg's downtrodden soldier protagonist in *Wozzeck* he may have found it hard to portray a man so weak and wanting in initiative. By contrast, his wit and bravado made him an ideal Figaro in Mozart's *Le nozze di Figaro*. After he had sung this role at Covent Garden in the 1949-50 season he became closely identified with it, and it was not surprising that Herbert von Karajan singled him out to sing it at the Teatro alla Scala, Milan, in 1960 and he sang it again at the Vienna Staatsoper.

At this time, Evans was approaching forty and at the height of his powers, having already had considerable experience. Somewhat earlier Benjamin Britten, always more interested in vocal personality than mere vocal beauty, saw Evans' warmth and essential goodness and wanted him in the title role of *Billy Budd* in its first performance in 1951 but the singer thought the music lay too high for his voice (he sometimes referred to himself as a bass-baritone). Instead he sang the sailing master Mr Flint in what the producer Basil Coleman later called "a performance full of individuality and character." However, he did sing Mountjoy in the premiere of Britten's *Gloriana*.

It is above all for his skilful acting of genial and comedy roles that Evans remains famous. He was a playful yet believable Papageno in Mozart's *Die Zauberflöte* and a likably cynical Leporello in *Don Giovanni*. As Beckmesser in Wagner's *Die Meistersinger* he was pompous but comic, while he was a kindly American consul Sharpless in Puccini's *Madama Butterfly*. He was best of all in middle-aged roles, particularly where humor was to the fore. His portrayal of the title role in Verdi's *Falstaff* was one of his finest, and it was as Shakespeare's fat knight that he made his Metropolitan Opera debut in 1964, while in 1973 he returned to Covent Garden to play Donizetti's crusty old bachelor Don Pasquale with vigour and relish.

Evans' voice was unfailingly pleasant in tone and carried well although it was not exceptionally powerful. In later years he continued to work as a producer and operatic coach and he held some effective master classes for television, including some on Britten's *Peter Grimes*, which showed his enthusiasm and ability to communicate with young students.

—Christopher Headington

EVERDING, August.

Director. Born 31 October 1928, in Bottrop, Germany. Married: Gustava Everding, 1963. Studied philosophy, theology, dramaturgy, Germanics and music at the Universities of Bonn and Munich; opera debut *La traviata*, Bayerische Staatsoper, Munich; intendant, Münchner Kammerspiele 1963-73; intendant and resident stage director, Hamburgische Staatsoper, 1973-77; general intendant Bayerische Staatsoper, Munich, 1977-1982; 1982- general intendant of all three Munich state theaters; professor, Munich University.

Opera Productions (selected)

La traviata, Munich, 1965.
Tristan und Isolde, Vienna, 1967.
Hamlet, Hamburg Staatsoper, 1968 (world premiere).
Der fliegende Holländer, Bayreuth, 1969.
Salome, Royal Opera, London, 1970.
Tristan und Isolde, Metropolitan Opera, 1971.
De temporum fine comoedia, Salzburg, 1973 (world premiere).
Tristan und Isolde, Bayreuth, 1974.
Paradise Lost, Stuttgart, 1979.

Boris Godunov, Lyric Opera of Chicago, 1980.
Die Zauberflöte, Lyric Opera of Chicago, 1986.
Wagner's Ring cycle, Warsaw, 1989.
Der fliegende Holländer, Metropolitan Opera, 1990.
Wagner's Ring cycle, Lyric Opera of Chicago, 1992 (planned).

Publications

About EVERDING: books—

Kieh, Sabine. *Die Regie has die Wort: Meinungen zum Musiktheater* [interview with Everding]. Brunswick, 1988.

* * *

August Everding's experience as a stage director had its foundation in his years as artistic director (1959-63) and, later, intendant (1963-73) of the Kammerspiele, Munich. After nearly twenty years of directing legitimate theater, he was invited by Rudolf Hartmann, then head of the Bavarian State Opera in Munich, to create a new staging of Verdi's *La traviata* (Munich, 1965). He was subsequently asked to mount a new production of Musorgsky's *Boris Godunov* (1968), the opera that also figured in his Metropolitan Opera debut (1974). Everding has also directed Metropolitan Opera productions of Wagner's *Lohengrin* (1974), Musorgsky's *Khovanshchina* (1985), and Wagner's *Der fliegende Holländer* (1989).

The first director at Bayreuth who was not a member of the Wagner family, Everding produced *Der fliegende Holländer* there in 1969 and *Tristan und Isolde* in 1974. Other major stagings included a Covent Garden *Salome,* 1970; a production (with Jean-Pierre Ponnelle) of Landi's 1634 *Il sant' Alessio* that opened the 1977 Salzburg Festival; Wagner's *Parsifal* at the Vienna State Opera (1979); a 1979 Stuttgart *Paradise Lost* (Penderecki); Mozart's *Die Schuldigkeit des ersten Gebotes* at the St Johannes Basilica in Berlin in 1980; Richard Strauss's *Elektra* in Cologne in 1983; Orff's *Antigonae* at the Congress House in Zurich (1983); a season-opening Mozart *Die Zauberflöte* in Chicago in 1986; Verdi's *Rigoletto* in Cologne, 1987; Richard Strauss's *Salome* at the Munich Opera Festival, 1987; and Beethoven's *Fidelio* in Düsseldorf in 1990. He is scheduled to produce Wagner's *Ring* in Chicago in the 1992-93 season.

Everding served as general manager and stage director of the Hamburg State Opera from 1973 to 1977. A notable staging of that period was Verdi's *Otello* with Placido Domingo in the title role.

Everding was intendant of the Bavarian State Opera in Munich from 1977 to 1982. For the 1978-79 season he created a new production of Mozart's *Die Zauberflöte*. His 1973 production of Mozart's *Die Zauberflöte* for Munich was seen for more than fifteen seasons at Finland's Savonlinna Festival, which he had founded in 1973 with bass Martti Talvela. He also presented Peter von Winter's 1798 *Das Labyrinth,* not seen in 180 years, with a libretto by *Zauberflöte*'s Emanuel Schikaneder at the Covilliés-Theater. In 1984 he produced Honegger's *Jeanne d'Arc au bûcher*. He also directed a film of Humperdinck's *Hänsel und Gretel* in 1981.

Everding's years in Munich were not without their problems. A new production of Wagner's *Die Meistersinger* in 1979 was set at a Bavarian Oktoberfest; critics wondered why Bavarians would care about the rules of the *Tabulatur* that form the basis for the story. A live telecast (the first from the Deutsche Oper) of Lehár's *Die lustige Witwe* provoked

August Everding's production of *Tristan und Isolde,* **Bayreuth, 1976**

controversy because of political dialogue added for the character of Njegus. A production of Mozart's *Die Entführung aus dem Serail* in 1980—also telecast—was poorly received. As critical and popular opinion of Everding's productions declined, and as relations with conductor Wolfgang Sawallisch deteriorated, it was decided to put Sawallisch in charge of the opera as of 1983 and raise Everding to general intendant of Munich's three state theaters. A wildcat strike by the chorus disrupted the 1981 Munich Festival performance of Everding's *Meistersinger* production.

Everding's Metropolitan Opera productions exhibit many characteristics of his style. In his Metropolitan production of *Boris Godunov* Everding ended many scenes with a spotlit solo figure, focusing the audience's attention on the individual's emotional dilemma. The production alternated the individual and his ambitions, disappointments, and tragedies with the larger canvas of Russian politics, contrasting the massive and the intimate, the rich and the poverty-striken. Everding was especially interested in certain aspects of the story: the political relationship of Shuisky and the others; the familial relationship between the father and his two children; the theological aspects of the Jesuits in the Russia of that time; and the influence of Poland on Russia. His direction is sparse to reflect the starkness of Musorgsky's original orchestration, which the Met introduced with this production, rather, than Rimsky-Korsakov's more elaborate rescoring. He uses props such as maps and globes to indicate the individual characters' quest for power and elaborate costumes to isolate the rulers from the masses. The tsar's downfall is graphically portrayed:

in the throes of his hallucinations Boris pulls down the huge drapes in his study and writhes on the floor under a massive table. The original staging, for Martti Talvela, had the tsar fall headlong down the Kremlin steps at the moment of his death, his son, the heir to the throne, immediately being carried up these same steps to the throne.

Everding has produced five different productions of Wagner's *Tristan und Isolde* (Vienna, 1967 and 1971, Metropolitan Opera, 1971, Bayreuth, 1974, and Munich, 1980). In his otherworldly Met production, one influenced by the space exploration and drug experimentation of the era, the central theme he expresses is transformation, the shift between reality and unreality. With spare sets, abstract images, a generous use of projections, and the effective exploitation of the stage elevator, Everding emphasizes the infinite, dreamlike character of the story. Although much of the production is grounded in realism, he has Tristan and Isolde soar heavenwards after ingesting the love potion, spotlighted against a background of darkness like two stars in the cosmos. In act two, during the love duet, the lovers again soar above the stage until King Marke's return literally brings them back down to earth. At Isolde's final transfiguration she ascends one last time, escaping from earthly reality.

Everding has said that his primary concern is to tell the story. He prefers that the set designs be only semirealistic to leave room for the story to unfold without giving too much away at the outset. He sees opera as "an amalgam of text and music and behavior and art and singing." He derives his interpretation of the opera from the music. He sees his task as staging an opera, not making a social comment.

Everding's training as a director of legitimate theater has helped him deal with the problems of stage movement and in the treatment of spoken dialogue. His productions are in the traditional mold, although he has used updated stagings in a few operas (his Metropolitan *Fliegende Holländer* is set in the late nineteenth century, as was his 1987 Cologne *Rigoletto*). He makes substantial use of stage machinery and technology, as in his *Zauberflöte* productions; this has led to some accusations of gimmickry. His psychological approach has led to a use of symbolism, which is sometimes handled in a heavy-handed manner, with ideas being unnecessarily underlined.

—Michael Sims

EWING, Maria.

Soprano. Born 27 March 1950, in Detroit. Married producer Peter Reginald Frederick Hall, artistic director at Glyndebourne (one daughter). Studied with Eleanor Steber at the Cleveland Institute of Music, and later with Jennie Tourel and Otto Guth; appeared at Meadowbrook Festival, 1968; debut at Ravinia Festival with Chicago Symphony Orchestra, 1973; Metropolitan Opera debut as Cherubino, 1976, where she has also sung Zerlina, Dorabella, Rosina, and Carmen, among others; debut in *Pelléas et Mélisande* at Teatro alla Scala, 1976; at Glyndebourne from 1978; Covent Garden debut as Salome, 1988.

*   *   *

The story of Maria Ewing's career is still unfolding with great interest and an element of surprise. Born in 1950 (in Detroit, Mich.), she has left a distinguished reputation as a mezzosoprano behind, and is now singing roles such as Salome and Tosca.

American trained, she studied in Cleveland with two superb teachers, Jennie Tourel and Eleanor Steber, both of whom were concerned not only with singing but also with dramatic declamation and acting. Ewing's professional debut was at the Ravinia Chicago Symphony Summer Festival in 1973. Her Metropolitan Opera debut came three years later, as Cherubino in *Le nozze di Figaro*.

Throughout several seasons, her appearances at the Metropolitan were unfathomably spotty: Blanche in *The Dialogue of the Carmelites* alternating seasons in French and English, an extremely funny Dorabella (*Così fan tutte*) and a *Barbiere* Rosina in the same mold, an impassioned *Ariadne* Composer, and a poorly received Carmen (the production was excoriated in the New York press) that had originated at Glyndebourne. Once a protégée of Music Director James Levine, but long chafing at his refusal to cast her more extensively and more often, Ewing publicly denounced him and left the Metropolitan Opera. Her American appearances are now only with other opera companies or as soloist with symphony orchestras.

She has long been a favorite at Glyndebourne: among the roles she has sung there are Carmen and Monteverdi's Poppea (*L'incoronazione di Poppea*), both later released commercially on video tape. She has sung Zerlina and recorded Donna Elvira in different productions of *Don Giovanni*. As early in her career as 1976, she sang Mélisande at the Teatro alla Scala. Ewing has appeared at the Salzburg Festival, the Paris Opéra, Brussels, and sang a particularly successful Perichole in Geneva.

Maria Ewing is a dedicated artist whose voice can be velvety and can negotiate florid passages. She is a striking woman with a particularly sensuous face who is not afraid to look a bit daft, should the role call for it, or should her interpretation of the role require it. She can be hilarious or a spitfire. Her Salome actually removes the seventh veil, as well as the other six.

Ewing's recorded Donna Elvira has its faults, but the videos from Glyndebourne, including the *Carmen* so hated in New York, are superb. She is a Poppea, in or out of the stage bath, for whom any Caesar would leave home.

More is to be heard and seen from Maria Ewing.

—Bert Wechsler

EXPECTATION
See ERWARTUNG

Maria Ewing in *Carmen,* **Royal Opera, London, 1991**

F

THE FABLE OF ORPHEUS
See LA FAVOLA D'ORFEO

FACCIO, Franco (Francesco Antonio).

Conductor/Composer. Born 8 March 1840, in Verona. Died 21 July 1891, near Monza. Studied with G. Bernasconi; studied at the Milan Conservatory, 1855-64; collaborated with Boito on a number of operas; military service under Garibaldi, 1866; Scandinavian tour as a symphony conductor, 1866-68; professor at the Milan Conservatory, 1868; succeeded Terziani as a conductor at the Teatro alla Scala, Milan, 1871; conducted the premiere of Verdi's *Otello* at the Teatro alla Scala, 1887.

Publications

About FACCIO: books–

Rensis, R. de, ed. *Franco Faccio e Verdi: Carteggi e documenti inediti.* Milan, 1934.

*   *   *

Franco Faccio, a composer and friend of Giuseppe Verdi, was known principally as one of the most active Italian conductors of opera in the nineteenth century. Verdi first met him and Arrigo Boito in Paris at the salon of his friend Clarina Maffei in the early 1860s. On 31 July 1863 Verdi wrote to Maffei: "Last year in Paris I saw Boito and Faccio often, and they are surely two young men of great intelligence, but I can say nothing of their musical talent, because of [Faccio] I have . . . heard . . . only a few things that he came and played for me one day." Faccio's working association with Verdi did not begin until 1869, when, working as an assistant at the Teatro alla Scala in Milan, he helped prepare the composer's revised *La forza del destino.*

Faccio was admitted to the Milan Conservatory in 1855, where he and Boito met and became lifelong associates. The two collaborated in 1860 on the patriotic cantata *Il quatro giugno* and in the following year on another patriotic essay, *Le sorelle d'Italia.* These were produced at the Conservatory and earned the two a reputation for modernism, a charge of which Verdi was well aware and spoke of in the same letter quoted from above: "These two young men are accused of being very warm admirers of Vagner [sic]. Nothing wrong with that, provided admiration does not degenerate into imitation. Vagner is made and it is useless to remake him." It was in 1863, when Faccio returned to Milan after study in Paris, that his first opera, *I profughi fiamminghi,* to a libretto by the veristic author Emilio Praga, was premiered at La Scala, producing charges of Wagnerianism. To honor Faccio,

Boito wrote an ode and read it aloud in public, to the effect that Faccio was the Italian composer destined to "cleanse the altar of Italian opera, now defiled like the walls of a brothel." This phrase incensed Verdi, who took it personally and was still referring to it caustically in letters to friends some fifteen years later. In 1863, having received a letter from Faccio relating "the news of the good outcome of my first opera," Verdi wrote a rather cold, formal reply and then for some years shunned Faccio and Boito, both of whom played such vital roles in the creation of *Otello* many years later.

Faccio's second opera, premiered on 30 May 1865, was *Amleto,* to a text by Boito. Given in Genoa, it was a *succès d'estime.* Soon after, Faccio took up conducting, embarking on a two-year tour of Germany and Denmark from 1866-68. When he returned to Milan in 1868, two significant events occurred: he was hired to conduct the autumn season at the Teatro Carcano, and he won the competition for the chair of composition at the Milan Conservatory. In 1869 he was appointed a deputy conductor at La Scala, beginning his fruitful association with Verdi; when in 1871 the chief conductor, Terziani, retired, Faccio took his place. A revival at La Scala on 9 February 1871 of Faccio's *Amleto* proved so disastrous that he abandoned further hopes of writing opera and instead resolved to focus on conducting, a relatively new role in Italian musical life at that time. Aside from his regular schedule at La Scala, important events in Faccio's conducting career included the 1878 Paris Exhibition, where he led the La Scala forces not only in representative Italian vocal works, but also in symphonic works by Beethoven and Berlioz. In 1879 the Società Orchestrale della Scala was founded with Faccio as its director, an important group in promoting instrumental music by Italians.

On 25 April 1886 Faccio conducted for the 1,000th time at La Scala. Notable performances and premieres include the Italian premiere of *Aida* in 1872, *Lohengrin* in 1873, the 1876 premiere of Ponchielli's *La gioconda,* Massenet's *Le roi de Lahore* in 1878, the premiere of the revised, definitive version of Verdi's *Simon Boccanegra* in 1881, the Italian premiere of Massenet's *Hérodiade* in 1882, the 1883 premiere of Catalani's *Dejanice,* the premiere of the four-act Italian version of Verdi's *Don Carlo,* in 1884, Puccini's *Le villi* in 1885, and the most prestigious, the premiere of Verdi's *Otello* in 1887.

Faccio's final period as a conductor was devoted primarily to promoting the works of Wagner; he revived *Lohengrin* in 1889, the first time it was successful in Italy. In that same year he traveled with Puccini and Giulio Ricordi to Bayreuth to hear Wagner's *Die Meistersinger* in order to decide on cuts for the Italian premiere, given on 26 December 1889, the last triumph of Faccio's illustrious career. The following year he died in an insane asylum in Monza.

—Stephen Willier

Caricatures of Franco Faccio conducting, Milan, 1882

THE FAIR MAID OF PERTH
See LA JOLIE FILLE DE PERTH

THE FAIRY QUEEN.

Composer: Henry Purcell.

Librettist: Elkanah Settle? (after Shakespeare, *A Midsummer Night's Dream*).

First Performance: London, Dorset Gardens Theater, April 1692.

Publications

articles—

Squire, William Barclay. "Purcell's 'Fairy Queen'." *Musical Times* January (1920).
Savage, Roger. "The Shakespeare-Purcell *Fairy Queen:* a Defence and Recommendation." *Early Music* 1 (1973): 200.

* * *

The attribution of *The Fairy Queen*'s libretto to Elkanah Settle may or may not be correct, but it is certainly one of the more lunatic of the libretti used for seventeenth-century opera in England. Attempts have been made to replace it by using most of the text of *A Midsummer Night's Dream* and so present Shakespeare-Purcell as it might or could be in an ideal theatrical world, but the fact is that Purcell did not set a single line of Shakespeare to music.

In the main Purcell's music forms part of the masques which elaborate or conclude the acts amidst scenery of remarkable beauty and mystery, and since he was less concerned with what he termed "a perfect opera" than with a hangover from Renaissance styles—the old masque in which music, song, dance, and audience participation were cheerfully intermingled—he had a reasonably free hand. Indeed, Purcell may have had a hand in the actual preparation of the masque texts.

The main plot of the play has been ruthlessly butchered. Hippolyta is omitted entirely, Theseus is mostly cut, the wrangling of the lovers is reduced, and the Pyramus-Thisbe play is moved forward to act III (where it is treated as a rehearsal). First given in 1692, the opera was repeated in the following year (Queen Mary attending on 16 February) with various additions.

The manuscript full score, lost for over 200 years, finally turned up in the library of the Royal Academy of Music just in time for it to be published as Volume 12 of the Purcell Society in place of the reconstructed fragments which had in fact already been engraved. The extant printed libretti reveal however that music for certain sections of the work have still not been found—notably the Clown's Dance and "The woosel cock" in act III, the Entry and Dance of the Four Seasons in act IV, a "hunt" sonata and Entry of Oberon, Titania, Robin and the Fairies in act V.

The masques offer atmosphere and mood more than plot and depiction. The moonlit wood in act II, for example, changes to a vision of "grottos, arbors, and delightful walks"

as Titania commands a fairy prospect, and an invocation to the song-birds leads to a wonderfully effective echo piece for instruments. Later come four of Purcell's most inspired shorter songs, for Night, Mystery, Secrecy, and Sleep.

In act III Titania conjures up an enchanted lake, the bridge composed of dragons and swans gliding in the background. But the swans become fairies and dance, while songs of a romantic or evocative nature lead suddenly to a duet in which buffoonery takes over, Corydon and his lady Mopsa both being played by men. The masque in act IV presents a garden of fountains, where the chief participants are the four seasons, their group of songs corresponding strategically to the quartet in the previous act.

The most elaborate masque of all (act V) gives Juno a splendid solo ("Thrice happy lovers") after which Oberon expresses a wish to hear "the Plaint that did so nobly move, when Laura mourned for her departed love." This soprano song, with violin obbligato, provides a high point in the structure before the scene changes to a Chinese Garden, in which songs and choruses divert the assembled throng until Hymen, god of marriage, is summoned to bring the play to a joyful conclusion.

This melodious melange of many theatrical elements can only be brought to life in a production which emphasizes the romantic or fantastic aspect of the fairy drama. In 1947 it enjoyed notable success at Covent Garden Opera, where Michael Ayrton designed sets and costumes based on the work of Inigo Jones. Both the space and mechanical resources of an opera house are needed for this kind of production, yet the orchestral resources require much modification if Purcell's score is to be properly realized. As one of his really outstanding works, *The Fairy Queen* deserves the best possible ingredients of music, dance, song, and acting, yet a successful combination of the four is difficult to bring off. Fortunately the music will continue to sing for itself as ready proof of Purcell's theatrical genius.

—Denis Stevens

THE FAITHFUL NYMPH
See LA FIDA NINFA

FALCON, Marie Cornélie.

Soprano. Born 28 January 1814, in Paris. Died 25 February 1897, in Paris. Studied with Bordogni and A. Nourrit at Paris Conservatory; debut as Alice in *Robert le Diable,* Paris, Opéra, 1832; lost her voice during a performance in 1838; after several efforts to regain it, she retired to her villa near Paris.

Publications

About FALCON: books–

Bouvet, C. *Cornélie Falcon.* Paris, 1927.

*   *   *

Marie Cornélie Falcon possessed a voice so individual in its weight, timbre, and compass that it defied normal classification. In France certain roles came to be spoken of as "falcon," roles that demand a combination of dramatic soprano and dramatic mezzo-soprano singing. Margared in Lalo's *Le roi d'Ys* is one example, being labeled as for "mezzo-soprano or falcon." The situation is by no means straight-forward; there is a great deal of overlap between the standard soprano and mezzo-soprano repertory in the roles that Falcon herself performed. Her voice was a powerful instrument that collapsed far too soon after a few years of overuse. She entered the Paris Conservatory at the age of thirteen, where the great Nourrit taught her singing and coached her in dramatic action. Four years later, in 1831, she took first prizes in singing and lyric declamation and made her debut at the Paris Opéra as Alice in Meyerbeer's *Robert le diable* in 1832, a role indicated in the score as being for mezzo-soprano. Later, the roles of Valentine in Meyerbeer's *Les huguenots* of 1836 and Rachel in Halévy's *La Juive* of 1835 were created expressly for Falcon; both are indisputably soprano parts. Additional roles that Falcon created were those of Mrs. Ankarström in Au-

Marie Cornélie Falcon in *La Juive*

ber's *Gustave III;* Morgiani in Cherubini's *Ali Baba;* the heroine in Louise Bertin's *Esmeralda;* and Léonor in Niedermeyer's *Stradella.* She also performed Mozart's Donna Anna (*Don Giovanni*) in Paris, the heroines in Rossini's *Moïse, Le siège de Corinthe* and *Guillaume Tell,* and Giulia in Spontini's *La vestale.*

Falcon's presence on the stage was later compared to that of the renowned actress Elisa Rachel (1821-58). A contemporary characterized Falcon's voice as being of "an incomparable metal, a timbre like nothing that has ever been heard." Yet there were certain glaring vocal problems: the coloratura was not easily produced nor was the top register. In short, she did not have the assets of an Italian-trained soprano, yet she may have had, at least for a few years, something better. Her rich, dark timbre was especially apt at expressing ardor and grief and her influence was by no means confined to French opera and French singers. As Rupert Christiansen notes in his *Prima Donna,* her voice was "the image strongly received into Verdi's middle-period operas—Falcon is, as it were, French for *spinto.*"

Some six years after her premiere at the Paris Opéra, Falcon's voice gave out in the middle of a performance of *Stradella.* In time-honored fashion she repaired to Italy for an extended holiday and further vocal training. Her return to the Opéra came in 1840, when she sang in the first two acts of *La Juive* and in act IV of *Les huguenots,* both parts that she had created. Her return was greeted with so much enthusiasm and such rapturous applause that she fainted. After her study in Italy both her chest and head voices were greatly strengthened, but the hole in the middle of the voice was so glaring that it forced her premature retirement at the age of twenty-six. François-Joseph Fetis, the noted nineteenth-century critic and lexicographer, spoke of Falcon as "... beautiful ... possessing a splendid voice, great intelligence, and profound dramatic feeling, she made every year remarkable by her progress and by the development of her talent."

—Stephen Willier

FALLA, Manuel de.

Composer. Born 23 November 1876, in Cádiz. Died 14 November 1946, in Alta Gracia (province of Córdoba, Argentina). Studied piano with J. Tragó and composition with F. Pedrell in Madrid; won the prize of the Academia de Bellas Artes, Madrid, for his opera *La vida breve,* 1905; Ortiz y Cussó Prize for pianists, 1905; met Debussy, Dukas, and Ravel in Paris, 1907; returned to Spain, 1914; his ballet *El Sombrero de tres picos* produced by Diaghilev, 1919; toured Europe as a conductor of his own works; president of the Instituto de España, 1938; in Argentina, 1939. Falla taught composition to Ernesto Halffter and Joaquin Nin-Culmell.

Operas/Zarzuelas

Publishers: Chester, Eschig, Ricordi.

El conde de Villamediana, Falla, 1887 [lost].
La casa de Tócame Roque (zarzuela), D. Ramón de la Cruz, 1900 [lost].
Límosna de amor (zarzuela), Jackson Veyan, 1901.

Los amores de la Inés (zarzuela), E. Duggi, 1902, Madrid, Comico, 12 April 1902.

El cornetín de órdenes (zarzuela), A. Vives, 1903 [lost].

La cruz de Malta (zarzuela), A. Vives, 1903 [lost].

La vida breve, Carlos Fernández Shaw, 1904-05; revised, Nice, Casino Municipal, 1 April 1913.

Fuego fatuo, Martinez Sierra (after music by Chopin), 1918-19 [parts lost].

El retablo de maese Pedro (puppet opera), Falla (based on part of Cervantes, *Don Quixote*), 1919-22, concert performance Seville, San Fernando, 23 March 1923; staged performance Paris, home of Princesse Edmond de Polignac, 25 June 1923.

Other works: orchestral works, vocal works, chamber and instrumental music, piano pieces.

Publications

By FALLA: books–

Sopeña, Federico, ed. *Escritos sobra música y músicos.* Madrid, 1950; 3rd ed., 1972; English translation by John Thomson and David Urman, London, 1979.

Recuero, P., ed. *Cartas a Segismondo Romero.* Granada, 1976.

Franco, E., ed. *Correspondencia de Manuel de Falla.* Madrid, 1978.

Craft, Robert, ed. *Stravinsky: Selected Correspondence, II.* London and New York, 1984.

articles–

"La musique française contemporaine." *Revista Musical Hispano-Americana* July (1916).

"Claude Debussy et L'Espagne." *La revue musicale* December (1920).

"Felipe Pedrell." *La revue musicale* February (1923).

"Notes on Richard Wagner, for the Fiftieth Anniversary of his Death." *Revue Cruz y Rayas* [Madrid] September (1933); reprint in *Pauta* 2 (1983): 121.

"Notes sur Ravel." *La revue musicale* March (1939).

About FALLA: books–

Trend, J.B. *Manuel de Falla and Spanish Music.* New York, 1929, 1935.

Roland-Manuel. *Manuel de Falla.* Paris, 1930; Spanish translation, 1945.

Chase, Gilbert. *The Music of Spain.* New York, 1941.

Sagardia, Angel. *Manuel de Falla.* Madrid, 1946.

Pahissa, Jaime. *Vida y Obra de Manuel de Falla.* Buenos Aires, 1947; 2nd edition, 1956; English translation by Jean Wagnstaff as *Manuel de Falla: His Life and Works,* London, 1954.

Thomas, Juan Mariá. *Manuel de Falla en la isla.* Palma de Mallorca, 1947.

Jaenisch, J. *Manuel de Falla und die spanische Musik.* Zurich and Freiburg, 1952.

Pahlen, K. *Manuel de Falla und die Musik in Spanien.* Olten and Freiburg, 1953.

Campodonico, L. *Falla.* Paris, 1959; 1980.

Arizaga, R. *Manuel de Falla.* Buenos Aires, 1961.

Mila, M., et al. *Manuel de Falla.* Milan, 1962.

Molina Fajardo, E. *Manuel de Falla y el "cane jondo".* Granada, 1962, 1976.

Demarques, Suzanne. *Manuel de Falla.* Paris, 1963; English and Spanish translations 1968.

Gauthier, A. *Manuel de Falla: l'homme et son oeuvre.* Paris, 1966.

Viniegra, J. *Manuel de Falla: su vida intima.* Cádiz, 1966.

Grunfeld, J. *Manuel de Falla: Spanien und die neue Musik.* Zurich, 1968.

Orozco, M. *Manuel de Falla: biografia illustrada.* Barcelona, 1968.

Fernandez-Shaw, G. *Larga historia de 'La vida breve'.* Madrid, 1972.

Franco, E. *Manuel de Falla.* Madrid, 1977.

Burnett, James. *Manuel de Falla and the Spanish Musical Renaissance.* London, 1979.

Hirsbrunner, Theo. *Claude Debussy und seine Zeit.* Laaber, 1981.

Crichton, Ronald. *Falla.* London, 1982.

Li-Koechlin, Madeleine, ed. *Charles Koechlin 1867-1950. Correspondance.* Paris, 1983.

Chase, Gilbert, and Andrew Budwig. *Manuel de Falla: A Guide to Research.* New York, 1986.

Pinamonti, Paolo, ed. *Manuel de Falla tra la Spagna e l'Europa.* Florence, 1989.

articles–

————, "Manuel de Falla." In *The Book of Modern Composers.* New York, 1942.

Mayer-Serra, Otto. "Falla's Musical Nationalism." *Musical Quarterly* 29 (1943): 1.

Matos, M. Garcia. "Folklore in Falla." *Musica* [Madrid] 1, 2 (1953).

Orenstein, Arbie. "Ravel and Falla: An Unpublished Correspondence, 1914-1933." In *Music and Civilization: Essays in Honor of Paul Henry Lang,* edited by Edmond Strainchamps et al., 335. New York and London, 1984.

*   *   *

While Manuel de Falla was born and raised in Spain, it was actually a series of events much after his birth which helped to shape the composer's own "Spanish" style. His early musical training on the piano was provided by his mother, an accomplished pianist, who introduced him to the standard keyboard works of composers such as Beethoven and Chopin, leaving little if any contact with the folk music of his native people. Among those influences which actually directed Falla to the music of Spain were the popular *zarzuelas* of the day, his teacher Felipe Pedrell, the Spanish pianist Ricardo Viñes, the famous Spanish poet Garcia Lorca, and a book entitled *L'acoustique nouvelle* by Louis Lucas.

Falla's earliest works of an operatic nature were his youthful *zarzuelas,* most of which were never performed. The *zarzuela* is a form of comic opera that was very popular in Spain during the late nineteenth century. It was through this genre that he was first introduced to Spanish music, albeit at a rather superficial level. None of Falla's *zarzuelas* could be deemed successes, but they did provide a foundation for the young composer to explore more serious opera composition.

The next influence that propelled the composer toward his native music was his teacher Felipe Pedrell, a composer and folklorist. Pedrell had issued his manifesto, *Por nuestra música,* in 1891, at which time he called upon Spanish composers to look toward their own national folk traditions as a musical foundation. He wrote, "Let us aspire to the essence of an ideal and purely human form, but seated in the shade of our southern gardens." As a result of Falla's studies with Pedrell, he became intensely interested in Spanish folk idioms and set forth on a clear direction with his music. The authentic music of Spain was to provide him with a rhythmic, harmonic and melodic basis in all of his writing, not through incorporation of actual native songs into his music, but through adaptation of the stylistic qualities of those folk songs. At the same time that Falla came to assimilate the ideas of Pedrell, he happened to come across a book in a secondhand bookstall in Madrid written by Louis Lucas entitled *L'acoustique nouvelle*. Written in the middle of the nineteenth century, it went beyond the theories of Rameau and suggested the exploration of scales beyond the major and minor. These writings gave Falla the insight and incentive to explore the "nontraditional" sounds of Spanish folk music and to incorporate them into his own musical expression.

After Falla moved to Paris he was to find many of the teachings of Pedrell and Lucas reinforced and expanded by such individuals as the Spanish pianist Ricardo Viñes and the French composers Maurice Ravel and Claude Debussy. In later years Falla would explore authentic Spanish folk music even further in conjunction with the Spanish poet Garcia Lorca, with whom he held a competition for Spanish folk singers in 1919. By 1904, the year in which *La vida breve* was completed, Manuel de Falla had a thorough understanding of the unique sound of Spanish folk music and captured it masterfully within the score.

Falla's only other operatic venture was *El retablo de maese Pedro*, completed in 1923. This chamber work is a delightful venture with singers and puppets, which matches the great wit of Cervantes in its adaptation of a "play within a play" taken from an episode of *Don Quixote*. After completing his *Concerto for Harpsichord* in 1926, he began to work on a massive dramatic cantata, *Atlántida*, based on an epic poem in the Catalan language by Jacinto Verdaguer. With the upheaval of the Spanish Civil War and Falla's deteriorating health, little work was done on the piece. He left Spain in 1939 in order to conduct four concerts of his music in Buenos Aires. The concerts were a great success and he was persuaded to remain in Argentina where he could work on *Atlántida* and avoid the war in Spain. He moved to the resort town of Alta Gracia de Córdoba where he spent his last years living with a sister and continuing to compose in peace.

—Roger E. Foltz

FALSTAFF.

Composer: Giuseppe Verdi.

Librettist: Arrigo Boito (after Shakespeare, *The Merry Wives of Windsor* and *King Henry IV*).

First Performance: Milan, Teatro alla Scala, 9 February 1893.

Roles: Sir John Falstaff (baritone); Mr Ford (baritone); Mrs Ford (soprano); Nanetta (soprano); Dame Quickly (mezzo-contralto or contralto); Fenton (tenor); Mrs Page (mezzo-soprano); Dr Caius (tenor); Bardolph (tenor); Pistol (bass); Host (mute); Robin (mute); chorus (SATB).

Publications

books—

Barblan, Guglielmo. *Un prezioso spartito di Falstaff*. Milan, 1957.

John, Nicholas, ed. *Giuseppe Verdi: Falstaff*. London, 1982.
Hepokoski, James A. *Giuseppe Verdi: Falstaff*. Cambridge, 1983.

articles—

Cone, E.T. "The Stature of *Falstaff*: Technique and Content in Verdi's Last Opera." *Center* 1 (1954).
Roncaglia, Gino. "Annotazioni sul *Falstaff* di Verdi." In *Volti musicali di Falstaff*. Siena, 1961.
Aycock, Roy Edwin. "Shakespeare, Boito, and Verdi." *Musical Quarterly* October (1972).
Sabbeth, Daniel. "Dramatic and Musical Organization in Falstaff." In *3° congresso internazionale di studi verdiani, Milan, 1972*. Parma, 1974.
Osthoff, Wolfgang. "Il sonetto nel *Falstaff* di Verdi." In *Il melodramma italiano dell' ottocento: studi e richerche per Massimo Mila*, 157. Turin, 1977.
Linthicun, David. "Verdi's *Falstaff* and Classical Sonata Form." *Music Review* February (1978).
Hepokoski, James A. "Verdi, Giuseppina Pasqua, and the Composition of *Falstaff*." *Nineteenth-Century Music* 3 (1980): 239.
Busch, Hans. "Apropos of a Revision in Verdi's *Falstaff*." In *Music East and West: Essays in Honor of Walter Kaufmann*, edited by Thomas Noblitt, 339. New York, 1981.
Marek, George R. "*Falstaff*—Boito's Alchemy." *Opera Quarterly* 1/no. 2 (1983): 69.
Bauman, Thomas. "The Young Lovers in Falstaff." *Nineteenth-Century Music* 9 (1985): 62.
Hepokoski, James A. "Under the Eye of the Verdian Bear: Notes on the Rehearsals and Premiere of *Falstaff*." *Musical Quarterly* 71 (1985): 135.
Avant-scène opéra May-June (1986) [*Falstaff* issue].

*   *   *

After the disastrous failure of his first comic opera, *Un giorno di regno* in 1840, Verdi had been naturally reluctant to try another. However, following the satisfaction of successfully completing the Shakespearean *Otello* with librettist Arrigo Boito in 1887, and, with the sense at the age of almost eighty of little to lose and the gifted services of Boito on which to draw, the composer once again turned to comedy. Boito actually suggested the subject and sent Verdi a proposed scenario in the summer of 1889: it was a study of another powerful old man, the Shakespearean character of Falstaff as he appears in the *Merry Wives of Windsor* and the *Henry IV* histories. The subject attracted Verdi immediately, possibly because it promised the composer a broad, career-summing opportunity to comment on life through the extravagant, comic alter ego of Falstaff.

The plot is as follows: Sir John Falstaff has written the same love letter to two different married women of Windsor, Alice Ford and Meg Page, in the hope of seducing them and thereby gaining access to their husbands' money as well. His comrades Bardolph and Pistol refuse to carry the letters, and instead reveal his plans to the husbands, who then plot revenge against the ridiculous fat knight. Meanwhile, the wives have compared the love letters and also plan comic revenge with the other women of Windsor, including Dame Quickly, who is engaged to set up an appointment between Sir John and Alice. In the midst of the planning, Alice's daughter Nannetta steals moments of love with young Fenton, although her father wants her to marry his friend Dr Caius.

Falstaff, **Glyndebourne Festival production with Claudio Desderi in the title role, 1988**

In act II, Falstaff receives Dame Quickly's instructions to attend Alice at their home between two and three o'clock, when her husband will be out. He also receives a visit from Ford, in his disguise as Mr Fontana, a man who wants to pay Falstaff to seduce Alice, after which he hopes to have an easier time doing the same. Laughing at the poor cuckolded husband in the affair, Falstaff reveals that he already has an appointment with Alice, leaving husband Ford (unaware of the women's plot) in a jealous rage. When Falstaff follows Quickly's instructions and attends Alice, Ford unexpectedly comes home to catch them in the act, but the women hide Falstaff in a laundry basket. Instead of Alice and Falstaff making love, Ford finds Nannetta and Fenton, and the servants accidentally dump Falstaff, still in the laundry basket, out the window into the stream below.

In act III, Falstaff drinks away his shame and falls for another trap when Dame Quickly tells him to meet Alice in Windsor forest at midnight, dressed as the legendary Black Hunter with horns. Falstaff meets Alice as instructed, but they are interrupted by The Queen of the Fairies and her band (Nanetta and the disguised Windsorites), who beat and insult the frightened Falstaff until he finally admits his stupidity. Now Ford proposes his plan, a wedding between his friend Caius and the Queen of the Fairies, and he in turn agrees to his wife's request of a marriage for two other disguised lovers. To Ford's chagrin, when the wedding is over and the disguises are off, the mates turn out to be Caius and Bardolph—now dressed as the Queen of the Fairies instead of Nanetta—and Nanetta and Fenton; after which Ford admits to being as big a fool as Falstaff, and all join in a final fugue, "Tutto nel mondo e burla" ("All the world's a joke").

In terms of musical language, *Falstaff* is a marvelous culmination of Verdi's career-long experimentation and evolution, beginning out of the singer-oriented, *bel canto* traditions of the early nineteenth-century, moving towards a more organic, dramatically-oriented approach to musical theater. In *Falstaff* Verdi's expressive vocal lines work together with the words, the scenography, and the orchestral accompaniment to convey the composer's dramatic ideas, very often through the lightning-quick action and conflict of duets and ensembles. The square thematic phrase groups of Verdi's middle period give way in *Falstaff* to a more flexible syntax of irregular phrase-groups, which in turn are given larger-scale coherence through a combination of thematic and motivic recurrence, and harmonic symmetry. Perhaps the best example of this flexible syntax is found in the delightfully concise scene ii of act I, where the composer makes a unified whole of amazingly disparate characters and incidents, ending in a simultaneous polyphonic reprise of mens' and womens' choruses as they plot their separate revenges against Falstaff.

Another unique aspect of *Falstaff* is Verdi's success at focusing attention on the central words of Boito's libretto with deft musico-poetic imagery and repetition. Thus in act II, scene i, for example, the ornamental flourish and repetition of Dame Quickly's line "reverenza" ("your reverence") captures both Falstaff's grandiosity and Quickly's mocking of it in a single musico-poetic image, which, in its repetitions, helps to infuse the whole scene with dramatic color and unity.

Moreover, the orchestration of *Falstaff* is the most careful and evocative of Verdi's career, especially in the act III tone paintings of Falstaff's drunken trance and the sublime fairy scene in Windsor forest.

Falstaff had a successful premiere run at the Teatro alla Scala with twenty-two performances, a European tour, and subsequent appearances at every major opera house in the world, with translations into every modern European language. Nonetheless, audiences and critics gradually cooled to the opera, uncomfortable with the lightning-quick complexity of the musical language. Verdi made revisions for the Rome and Paris productions of April 1893 and 1894 respectively, but he gradually gave up hopes for an ultimate triumph, particularly after a difficult run in Genoa in the winter of 1894-95. Still, the conductor of that run, Arturo Toscanini, continued to program and perform *Falstaff* as often as he could during his influential career, featuring it eight seasons in a row during his reign as artistic director at La Scala in the 1920s. Today *Falstaff* is widely recognized as a work of greatness, and although it requires an unusual number of exceptional singers, among other heavy production demands, it has become a solid part of the operatic repertory.

—Claire Detels

LA FANCIULLA DEL WEST [The Girl of the West].

Composer: Giacomo Puccini.

Librettists: Guelfo Civinini and Carlo Zangarini (after David Belasco, *The Girl of the Golden West*).

First Performance: New York, Metropolitan Opera, 10 December 1910.

Roles: Minnie (soprano); Dick Johnson/Ramerrez (tenor); Jack Rance (baritone); Nick (tenor); Ashby (bass); Sonora (baritone); Trin (tenor); Sid (baritone); Handsome (baritone); Harry (tenor); Joe (tenor); Happy (baritone); Larkens (bass); Billy Jackrabbit (bass); Wowkle (mezzo-soprano); Jake Wallace (baritone); Jose Castro (bass); Courier (tenor); chorus (TTBBB).

Publications

article–

DiGaetani, John Louis. "Comedy and Redemption in *La fanciulla del West.*" *Opera Quarterly* 2 (1984): 88.

*   *   *

Based on a play by David Belasco, *La fanciulla del West* has only recently been getting the attention it deserves. After a highly successful premiere at the Metropolitan Opera in New York in 1910, it quickly sank out of sight. Since the 1960s, on the other hand, the opera has been regularly revived—often for a particular soprano who wants to sing the role of Minnie—and regularly appreciated.

Act I takes place in the Polka Saloon in California during the Gold Rush. The men are miners who come to the saloon to forget their loneliness through gambling and drink. Minnie, the owner of the saloon, conducts a Bible class there for the miners, who enjoy it very much. Minnie tries to protect the miners' gold by guarding it in the saloon, but she also tries to remind them of religion and God. The miners are also hunting for one Ramerrez, a bandit and outlaw. Jack Rance, the town sheriff, is especially eager to hang Ramerrez and also to win Minnie for a wife. Ramerrez enters, disguised as Dick Johnson, and Minnie is immediately attracted to him and invites him to dinner the next night.

Act II occurs in Minnie's log cabin. Dick Johnson enters, while Jack Rance and the other miners are hunting the woods for the bandit Ramerrez. During their dinner together, Minnie and Dick seem to fall in love, but then Johnson leaves suddenly and, recognized as the bandit by the sheriff, is shot. Johnson once again enters Minnie's cabin, bleeding from his wound. Jack Rance enters, demanding possession of Dick Johnson. Minnie offers to play a hand of poker for him, and she wins, but only by cheating.

In Act III, set in a California forest, Johnson has been caught and is brought onstage by the miners to be lynched. The noose is around his neck, and just as Jack Rance orders his execution, Minnie rushes in to save him. The opera ends with Minnie and Dick riding off into the dawn, seeking a new life away from the greed of the California Gold Rush.

Aside from its thriller plot, the opera contrasts the materialism of the California Gold Rush with the spiritual qualities of Minnie, who seeks a more religious and less materialistic life. On another level, the opera is also a comic parody of Wagner's *Ring* cycle, which also contrasts material with spiritual values. The opera has some lovely arias, but its ensemble singing, use of chorus, and orchestration remain especially remarkable.

—John Louis DiGaetani

FARINELLI [real name Carlo Broschi].

Soprano castrato. Born 24 January 1705, in Apulia. Died 15 July 1782, in Bologna. Studied with Nicolo Porpora; first public performance in 1720 in Naples, in *Angelica e Medoro* by Porpora; sang in Naples and Rome, 1720-34; sang in London, 1734-37; sang in Paris, 1736; sang at the court of the Spanish Kings Philip V (1700-46) and Ferdinand VI (1746-59), 1737-59; retired to Bologna in 1759.

Publications

About FARINELLI: books–

Burney, C. *The Present State of Music in France and Italy.* London, 1771.
Sacchi, G. *Vita del Cavaliere Don Carlo Broschi.* Milan, 1784.
Bouvier, R. *Farinelli, le chanteur des rois.* Paris, 1946.

articles–

Freeman, R. "Farinelli and his repertory." *Studies in Renaissance and Baroque Music in honor of Arthur Mendel.* Kassel and Hackensack, 1974.
Heartz, D. "Farinelli and Metastasio, rival twins of public favour." *Early Music* 12 (1984): 358.
Scott, M. "On wings of song." *Opera News* 48 (1984): 18.

The premiere of *La fanciulla del West*, Metropolitan Opera, New York, 1910, with Enrico Caruso (center) as Dick Johnson, Emmy Destinn as Minnie and Pasquale Amato as Jack Rance

Peschel, E.R. and R.E. "Medicine and music: the castrati in opera." *Opera Quarterly* 4/4 (1986-1987): 21.

Roselli, J. "The castrati as a professional group and a social phenomenon 1550-1850." *Acta Musicologica* 60 (1988): 164.

Hoeft, T. and W. Lempfrid. "Virtuosen der Barockzeit." *Concerto* 6 (1989): 24.

*   *   *

Perhaps the most famous of all castrato singers, Farinelli appears in literature, letters and art to such an extent that even non-musical members of the public had heard of him well before the middle of the 18th century. At fifteen he had already made a successful debut as a soprano in an occasional cantata by his teacher Porpora, with whom he was later associated in Rome and London.

Contemporary reports on his singing emphasize particular features of his tone and technique. Giambattista Mancini, court singing-teacher in Vienna, found his voice powerful, sonorous and rich throughout its range. A supreme master of ornamentation, he exploited it to the full, ever inventing new flourishes and conceits which contributed vastly towards his reputation. His breathing seemed little short of miraculous, for he was able to take in quietly and sustain almost endlessly an air supply more than adequate for the most elaborate and taxing of arias.

His other qualities included evenness of voice, total control of the *messa di voce* (swelling out and back again on one long note), *portamento* (gliding lightly from one note to another) and a truly remarkable trill. At first an exponent of the heroic style, full of brilliance and bravura, he later cultivated a gentler aspect of his art, in which the voice became an instrument of pathos and simplicity.

It was these features which caused an abrupt change in his career, when after experiencing triumphs in Italy, France and England he set his sights on Spain, intending only a fleeting visit. In fact this lasted for almost twenty-five years, as chamber singer and first favorite at the royal court. His duties in alleviating the melancholic disposition of Philip V might be termed monotonous, since he sang the same few songs whenever the king required them, but his spare time saw him actively engaged in politics, the importation of Hungarian horses and the redirection on the river Tagus. Aside from this, he greatly influenced the music performed at the royal chapel and opera house, altogether wielding powers such as few ministers ever enjoyed. Such was his acceptance that he remained there in the reign of Ferdinand VI and continued to receive a generous pension from Charles III, who nevertheless asked him to leave in view of the political importance of dealing with Naples and France, to which Farinelli was opposed.

He lived the last twenty years of his life at a magnificent villa near Bologna where he developed his considerable gallery of paintings and played on his collection of instruments,

Carlo Farinelli, engraving after Amigoni, 1735

which included the viola d'amore, harpsichord, and forte-piano. Burney and others visited him there, commenting on his courtesy and hospitality. George Sand mentions him in her novel *Consuelo,* and Voltaire obviously had him in mind when he wrote in *Candide* that the Neapolitan castrato who survived the operation could look forward to fame, fortune and political power. Among those who painted his portrait were Jacopo Amigoni and Bartolommeo Nazari, while carica-tures exist by such artists as Zanetti, Ghezzi and Hogarth. Stage works about his life and adventures have been written by August Roeckel, Hermann Zumpe, and Auber, in whose operetta *La part du diable* the part of Farinelli is sung by a soprano.

—Denis Stevens

FARRAR, Geraldine.

Soprano. Born 28 February 1882, in Melrose, Massachusetts. Died 11 March 1967, in Ridgefield, Connecticut. Studied voice with Mrs John H. Long, Emma Thursby, Trabadello,

Francesco Graziani, and Lilli Lehmann; studied stage presen-tation with Sarah Bernhardt, David Belasco, Jules Massenet. Operatic debut as Marguerite in *Faust,* Berlin Royal Opera, 1901; sang in first performance of Mascagni's *Amica,* Monte Carlo, 1905; Metropolitan Opera debut as Juliette in *Roméo et Juliette,* 1906; sang in American premiere of *Ariane et Barbe-bleue,* 1911; created the roles of the Goose Girl in Humperdinck's *Königskinder,* 1910, and Louise in Charpen-tier's *Julien,* 1914; twenty-nine roles at the Metropolitan Op-era, 1906-22, including Butterfly, Tosca, Thaïs, Zazà, Gilda, Manon, and Carmen; frequent partner of Enrico Caruso; retired 1922; also worked in silent films and as a radio com-mentator.

Publications:

By FARRAR: books—

Geraldine Farrar: The Story of an American Singer By Herself. 1916.
Such Sweet Compulsion: The Autobiography of Geraldine Far-rar. New York, 1938.

About FARRAR: books—

Wagenknecht. *Geraldine Farrar.* Seattle, 1929.
Nash, E. *Always First Class: The Career of Geraldine Farrar.* Washington, DC, 1982.

articles—

Moran, W.R. "Geraldine Farrar." *Record Collector* 13 (n.d.): 194.
van Vechten, Carl. "Geraldine Farrar." In *Interpreters and Interpretations.* New York, 1917.
Baxter, R. "Duelling Divas." *Fugue* December (1979): 24.
Ardoin, J. "Operatic Shadows." *Opera Quarterly* 6/1 (1988): 52.
Green, L. "Some Words About the Great Verismo Singers." *Opera Quarterly* 7/4 (1990-91): 74.

*   *   *

From 1906 until 1922, Geraldine Farrar was the Metropoli-tan Opera's most popular prima donna. Convinced that music must always serve the drama, she often sacrificed tonal beauty to dramatic effect. Nevertheless, Farrar was a superb singer, possessing a beautiful lyric soprano voice, as evidenced on her numerous recordings. She studied singing in Boston with Mrs John H. Long, in New York with Emma Thursby, in Paris with Trabadello, and in Berlin with Francesco Graziani and later Lilli Lehmann. But it was in large part due to Lehmann's training that Farrar was to be noted for the even-ness of her voice, vibrant forward production, and impeccable diction.

On 15 October, 1901, Farrar made her operatic debut at the Berlin Royal Opera as Gounod's Marguerite. She was an instant success. Contracts followed in Monte Carlo, Paris, Munich, Warsaw and finally New York. The beautiful and magnetic young singer opened the Metropolitan Opera's 1906/1907 season on 26 November as Gounod's Juliette. During her sixteen year reign as the Metropolitan's leading singing actress, Farrar performed 493 times in twenty-nine roles, the most popular of which were Puccini's Madama Butterfly and Tosca, Humperdinck's Goose Girl, Bizet's Car-men and Leoncavallo's Zazà.

Geraldine Farrar as Cho-Cho-San in *Madama Butterfly,* **1907**

Farrar was meticulous in the preparation of her roles. She studied Madama Butterfly with the Japanese actress, Fu-ji-Ko; Tosca with the French actress Sarah Bernhardt, for whom Victorien Sardou had written the play upon which the opera's libretto is based; Zazá with the stage version's director and producer, David Belasco; and Manon with its composer, Jules Massenet. Farrar's characterizations were highly individualized. She frequently introduced radically new staging and costuming into her performances of the standard repertory. Her acting was noted for its intensity and realism. Farrar's voice was sufficiently flexible for the rapid vocal passages of Gounod's Juliette and yet adequately powerful for the dramatic outbursts of Wagner's Elisabeth. Her vocal range was extensive, with the brilliant upper register necessary for the high tessitura of Puccini's Madama Butterfly and the rich middle and lower registers required for Bizet's Carmen. She could produce almost limitless contrasts of tonal coloration, from the soft caressing notes of Massenet's Manon, to the raucous laughs of Dukas' la Fille. Despite a tendency to force the upper register of her voice during moments of emotional intensity, she was a brilliant vocal technician.

With petite figure, refined features, and warm sympathetic personality, Farrar was ideally suited to the romantic heroines of the Italian, French and German lyric repertoires. Visually and emotionally, she virtually embodied Gounod's Marguerite, Puccini's Madama Butterfly, and Humperdinck's Goose Girl, imbuing them with her own grace and charm. Farrar, however, was not limited to these roles alone. In later years she won acclaim for a flamboyant Carmen and Zazà as well as for a realistically brutal Dukas' la Fille. She was a versatile actress both on stage and in films.

Farrar's frequent operatic partner was the tenor Enrico Caruso. Their joint performances of *Madama Butterfly, Tosca, Manon* and *Carmen* guaranteed sold-out houses. They were undoubtedly the most dynamic duo in the annals of the Metropolitan.

Farrar's farewell performance at the Metropolitan Opera on 22 April 1922, as Zazà occasioned one of the most tumultuous demonstrations in the history of American opera. During the 1934/1935 season, she was intermission commentator for the Metropolitan Opera's Saturday afternoon broadcasts. Her first autobiography, *Geraldine Farrar: the Story of an American Singer by Herself,* was published in 1916, and her second, *Such Sweet Compulsion,* in 1938.

—Elizabeth H. Nash

FARRELL, Eileen.

Soprano. Born 13 February 1920, in Willimantic, Connecticut. Married: Robert V. Reagan in 1976; one son and one daughter. Studied with Merle Alcock and Eleanor McLellan; professional debut with Columbia Broadcasting Company, 1941; opera debut as Santuzza in Mascagni's *Cavalleria rusticana* with the San Carlo Opera in Tampa, Florida, 1956; San Francisco debut as Leonora in Verdi's *Il trovatore,* 1957; Metropolitan Opera debut as Alceste in Gluck's *Alceste,* 1960; Distinguished Professor of Music at Indiana University's School of Music, 1971-80; Distinguished Professor of Music at the University of Maine, 1984.

Publications

About FARRELL: books–

Sargeant, W. *Divas.* New York, 1973.

articles–

Sargeant, W. "Doing what comes naturally." *Opera News* 32 (1967): 28.
Soria, D.J. "Artist Life." *High Fidelity/Musical America* 19 (1969).
Davis, P.G. "Stars ascendant—an observer follows the steady rise of our native singers." *Opera News* 40 (1976): 28.
Lucano, R.V. "An interview with Eileen Farrell. *Fanfare Magazine* 12/2 (1988): 444.

*   *   *

Eileen Farrell possessed one of the most powerful and beautifully agile dramatic soprano voices of the second half of this century. Her parents, of Irish descent, both had successful careers in vaudeville and church music. As a child, Farrell received informal but serious training in singing from her mother. Her mother also arranged for her to study with Merle Alcock, former Metropolitan Opera contralto, after Farrell's graduation from high school and a brief stint in an art school in 1939. She remained under the stern tutelage of this teacher until she began to study with Eleanor McLellan, to whom she has given almost total credit for her subsequent successes.

Farrell's breakthrough as an artist came when James Fassett of CBS made her a member of the choruses and ensembles of that broadcasting company. In 1941 she sang on a program in which she impersonated Rosa Ponselle, a soprano to whom she would be most favorably compared in future years. This appearance eventually led to the establishment of her own radio program, *Eileen Farrell Sings,* where she presented operatic arias, art songs, and popular music to eager listeners. In the late 1940s she began singing in numerous concert appearances—both as a recitalist and as a soloist with orchestra. Her close association with the New York Philharmonic allowed her to establish a record sixty-one appearances with this famed ensemble during the 1950-1951 season. She distinguished herself by singing with the Philharmonic in American premiere performances of Milhaud's *Les Choëphures* and Berg's *Wozzeck.* It was her concert performances and recordings of Wagner with this and other orchestras that encouraged fans of opera to anticipate Farrell's entering this arena. Her first appearance singing in a complete work did not come until 1955, however; and it was not a staged performance but rather a concert version of Cherubini's *Medea* by the American Opera Society in New York's Town Hall. Critics wrote lavish praise of this performance and a new era in her career appeared to have begun.

Although she appeared as Santuzza in a staged production of Mascagni's *Cavalleria rusticana* in Tampa, Florida, in 1956, it was later in that same year that she made her first appearance with a major company, the San Francisco Opera. Her performance there of Leonora in Verdi's *Il trovatore* brought her rave reviews. She made subsequent appearances in San Francisco and in Chicago with the Chicago Lyric Opera. Her entry to the New York stage occurred on Staten Island with the Richmond Opera Company production of *Il trovatore* in 1959. Her debut at the Metropolitan Opera came in Gluck's *Alceste* late in 1960 some fifteen years after Edward Johnson, then managing director of the Metropolitan, had invited her to sing. In addition to this role, Farrell appeared at the Metropolitan as Santuzza in *Cavalleria rusticana,* La Gioconda in Ponchielli's opera by the same name, Leonora in *La forza del destino,* and Maddalena in Giordano's *Andrea Chénier.* Her career began in the old opera house, but her contract was not renewed when the company moved into its new quarters at Lincoln Center.

The fact that Farrell was never heard in a staged production of Wagnerian opera is a loss to opera-goers, but Rudolf Bing, managing director of the Metropolitan opera during her tenure, did not like Wagner. Farrell did not have the professional temperament to propel herself into performing more than excerpts from these roles on recordings and in concert. Had she determined to do so, Farrell could have had an enormous impact upon the international scene even without recording, because her concert appearances in Berlin, London, Spoleto, and South America were well received.

Very frequently artists who successfully perform in opera are consumed by it and never become satiated, but this has not been the case with Farrell. Despite having the talent for such a challenging career, her priorities lay in her devotion to family life rather than to learning and performing additional roles on a regular basis. Her performing satisfaction came in other musical mediums—the dubbing of her voice in the motion picture *Interrupted Melody,* a biography of the life of Marjorie Lawrence, is but one example. Of large stature, she may have been self-conscious about her appearance on stage, but her weight apparently never detracted from her effectiveness in the roles she portrayed and would have served her well in Wagner. Her work with radio gave her a clarity of diction envied by many on the operatic stage, and her earlier association in New York with William Scheide's Bach Aria Group gave her interpretative powers an added dimension.

Farrell's singing career has been complemented by one in teaching, with positions as Distinguished Professor of Music at Indiana University from 1971-1980 and at the University of Maine, Orono, from 1984. She has also been the recipient of several honorary doctorates and other awards.

—Rose Mary Owens

FASSBAENDER, Brigitte.

Mezzo-soprano. Born 3 July 1939, in Berlin. Studied with her father, baritone Willi Domgraf-Fassbaender, at Nuremberg Conservatory, 1957-61; debut as Nicklausse in *Les contes d'Hoffmann* at Bayerische Staatsoper, Munich, 1961; debut at Covent Garden as Octavian, 1971; debut at Salzburg as Fricka in *Das Rheingold,* 1973; debut at Metropolitan Opera as Octavian, 1974; has sung in Paris, Milan and Vienna; made a Bavarian Kammersängerin, 1970.

Publications

About FASSBAENDER: articles–

Gould, S. "Brigitte Fassbaender." *Opera* August (1981).

*   *   *

Opera singers, like sports figures, usually achieve fame and critical recognition while they are young. The prime years of a career generally fall between the ages of twenty-five and forty-five, and a singer with a beautiful voice may make a great impact on the musical world right away. Sadly, it also often happens that as a voice inevitably loses youthful beauty and bloom, the singer's career itself may lose some of its lustre, and critics and audiences turn their attentions elsewhere—to other, younger, artists.

Rarer and more treasurable is the performer whose artistic imagination and musicianship grows year by year, so that reputation and appreciation also increase over time. Such is the case of the remarkable German mezzo-soprano Brigitte Fassbaender. In the decades following her 1962 debut, Fassbaender has matured steadily from one of a rather large number of capable though perhaps not especially distinctive mezzos into the magnificent singing-actress that she is today. At the time of this writing, Fassbaender is just over fifty years old, yet today she is widely regarded as the finest female Lieder singer on the concert stage, and her increasingly infrequent appearances in opera are celebrated by critics and public alike.

That Fassbaender's great fame has been somewhat late in coming may be explained in part by a voice which, while highly distinctive and skillfully deployed, is not conventionally beautiful. Hers is a rather lean, reedy sound, with a pronounced vibrato; the high notes in particular are not always easily nor cleanly produced. Fassbaender cannot muster the sheer power and plush sense of amplitude of Christa Ludwig, for example, much of whose repertoire she shares. Nor has she the silvery sheen which is such an essential and delectable part of the voice of Frederica Von Stade, her near-contemporary. And, over time, Fassbaender's vocal idiosyncracies have become more exaggerated, so that now in louder musical passages the voice can take on a pronounced beat and sound threadbare and hollow; high notes frequently turn sour and have an almost "wailing" quality in the tone.

Perhaps this is a reason that Fassbaender has recorded so few of the standard operatic roles with which she was associated in her early career. Carmen, Princess Eboli in *Don Carlo,* Cherubino in *Le nozze di Figaro,* Sextus in *La clemenza di Tito,* Rosina in *Il barbiere di Siviglia,* Amneris in *Aïda*—all of these she performed with critical success yet recorded none of them. She was probably the premier Octavian in *Der Rosenkavalier* of her generation, yet this splendid portrayal too was not recorded commercially, although a much-heralded televised performance under Carlos Kleiber is available and confirms her great reputation in the part.

Not that Fassbaender made few records—quite the contrary, for from very early on recording played a major part in her career. It is instead that she turned her attention primarily to concert music and in particular the Lied, where her outstanding musicality and interpretive gifts were best displayed—and where, perhaps, her purely vocal limitations mattered less. In recitals of the songs of Schubert, Schumann, Brahms and others, Fassbaender demonstrates an actor's natural ability to color and inflect words and phrases, as well as a surprising boldness; she always shapes music in a startling and individual way, yet such is her skill that these performances never sound forced or mannered. As time has passed and Fassbaender's vocal gifts have waned, her interpretive mastery continues to grow; like Maria Callas in a much different repertoire, Fassbaender is able to capitalize on her own weaknesses, to make the odd and sometimes infirm sounds seem to be artistic choice rather than enforced limitations.

In the last several years, Fassbaender's operatic career has focused on Wagner: she has sung Fricka in *Das Rheingold* and

Brigitte Fassbaender (right) with Lilian Sukis in *Così fan tutte,* **Royal Opera, London, 1979**

Die Walküre, Waltraute in *Götterdämmerung,* Brangaene in *Tristan und Isolde,* all with great success. Much of this music is extended narrative, and to it Fassbaender brings her Lieder singer's sense of detail and word painting; rarely have these passages seemed so acted, the texts so illuminated. She has also sung to acclaim some of the character mezzo roles in the operas of Richard Strauss—in particular Klytemnestra in *Elektra* and Herodias in *Salome*—where these same gifts are even more welcome.

Fassbaender's explorations of the song repertoire continue, and with each new recital it seems that her already exalted critical reputation increases. Recently, in collaboration with pianist and composer Aribert Reimann, she has performed Schubert's *Die Winterreise,* the bleak, epic song cycle which is the Lieder singer's ultimate challenge. Few women have attempted this monumental work; fewer still have met with success. For Fassbaender it has been a triumph. She brings an operatic sense of size and scope to the twenty-four songs, vividly characterizing the narrative of the wanderer, achieving through varied tone color and an ever-attentive rhythmic sense an almost unbearable pathos as well as a remarkable feeling of perspective—for once we really sense the time and progression of the cycle. In Fassbaender's singing, and in the highly individual accompaniment of Aribert Reimann, *Die Winterreise* sounds almost modern, and rarely if ever has seemed more heartbreaking. Brigitte Fassbaender's recording of this cycle is one of the remarkable records of recent years, and a fitting document of this extraordinary vocal artist.

—David Anthony Fox

FAURÉ, Gabriel (Urbain).

Composer. Born 12 May 1845, in Pamiers (Ariège, France). Died 4 November 1924, in Paris. Studied with Louis Niedermeyer and Saint-Saëns in Paris; organist at the church of Saint-Sauveur, Rennes, 1866; light infantryman in the Franco-Prussian War; organist at Notre-Dame de Clignancourt, Saint-Honoré d'Eylau, and Saint-Sulpice, 1871-74; second organist, 1875, and choirmaster, 1877, at the Madeleine; first organist at the Madeleine, 1896; professor of composition at the Paris Conservatory, 1896; succeeded Théodore Dubois as director of the Paris Conservatory, 1905 (resigned 1920); member of the Académie des Beaux Arts, 1909; Commander of the Légion d'Honneur, 1910. Fauré's students included Ravel, Enesco, Koechlin, Roger-Ducasse, Laparra, Florent Schmitt, Louis Aubert, and Nadia Boulanger.

Operas

Barnabé, J. Moineaux, 1879 [unfinished].
Prométhée, Jean Lorrain and A.F. Hérold, Béziers, Arènes, 27 August 1900; revised 1917.
Pénélope, René Fauchois, 1907-13, Monte Carlo, 4 March 1913.
Masques et bergamasques, René Fauchois, Monte Carlo, 10 April 1919.

Other works: orchestral works, vocal works, chamber music, piano pieces.

Publications

By FAURÉ: books–

Hommage à Eugène Gigout. Paris, 1923.
Opinions musicales [articles from *Le Figaro,* 1903-21]. Paris, 1930.
Gabriel Fauré. Paris and Grenoble, 1946.
Fauré-Fremiet, Philippe, ed. *Lettres intimes (1885-1924).* Paris, 1951.
Nectoux, Jean-Michel, ed. *Correspondance.* Paris, 1973, 1978, 1980; English translation as *Fauré: his Life Through his Letters.* London, 1984.
_____. *Saint-Saëns, Fauré, correspondance, soixante ans d'unité.* Paris, 1973.
_____. *Visages de Gabriel Fauré.* Neufchâtel, 1978.
_____. *Correspondance.* Paris, 1980.

articles–

"Lettres à propos de la réforme religieuse." *Monde musical* 16 (1904): 35.
"Joachim." *Musica* April (1906).
"Edouard Lalo." *Courrier musical* 2 (1908): 245.
"André Messager." *Musica* September (1908).
"La musique étrangère et les compositeurs français." *Le Gaulois* 10 January (1911).
"Sous la musique que faut-il mettre." *Musica* February (1911): 38.
Preface to G.J. Aubry. *La musique française d'aujourd'hui.* Paris, 1916.
"Camille Saint-Saëns." *La revue musicale* 3 (1922): 97.
"Souvenirs." *La revue musicale* 3 (1922): 3.
Bellaigue, C., ed. "Lettres à une fiancée." *Revue des deux mondes* 46 (1928): 911.
Nectoux, Jean-Michel, ed. "Correspondance Saint-Saëns, Fauré." *Revue de musicologie* 58 (1972): 65, 190; 59 (1973): 60.

interviews–

Comoedia 31 January (1910): 1; 20 April (1910): 1; 10 November (1924): 4.
Excelsior 12 June (1922): 2.
Candide 9 December (1937): 19.
Paris-Comoedia 3 March (1954): 106.
Études fauréennes 19 (1982): 3.

About FAURÉ: books–

Imbert, H. *Profils de musiciens.* Paris, 1888.
Vuillemin, Louis. *Gabriel Fauré et son oeuvre.* Paris, 1914.
Séré, Octave. *Musiciens français aujourd'hui,* 183-98. Paris, 1911; 8th ed., 1921.
Marliave, J. de. *Études musicales.* Paris, 1917.
Aguettant, L. *Le génie de Gabriel Fauré.* Lyons, 1924.
Koechlin, Charles. *Gabriel Fauré.* Paris, 1929; 2nd ed., 1957; English translation by Leslie Orrey, London, 1945.
Bruneau, Alfred. *La vie et les oeuvres de Gabriel Fauré.* Paris, 1925.
Rohozinski, L. ed. *Cinquante ans de musique française.* Paris, 1925-26.
Fauré-Fremiet, Philippe. *Gabriel Fauré.* Paris, 1929, 1957.
Servières, G. *Gabriel Fauré.* Paris, 1930.
Dumesnil, René. *Portraits de musiciens français,* 77. Paris, 1938.
Favre, G. *Gabriel Fauré.* Paris, 1945.

Rostand, Claude. *L'oeuvre de Gabriel Fauré.* Paris, 1945; German translation, 1950.
Suckling, Norman. *Fauré.* London, 1946.
Vuillermoz, Emile. *Gabriel Fauré.* Paris, 1960; English translation, Philadelphia, 1969.
Nectoux, Jean-Michel. *Gabriel Fauré.* Paris, 1972, 1986.
_____. *Phonographie de Gabriel Fauré.* Paris, 1979.
Orledge, Robert. *Gabriel Fauré.* London, 1979.
Jones, J. Barrie. *Fauré: a Life in Letters.* London, 1989.
Tait, Robin. *The Musical Language of Gabriel Fauré.* New York, 1989.

articles–

Dukas, Paul. "Prométhée de G. Fauré." *Revue hebdomadaire* 6 October (1900); reprinted in Paul Dukas, *Les écrits sur la musique,* Paris, 1948.
Musica no. 77 (1909) [Fauré issue].
La revue musicale 3 (1922) [Fauré issue].
Copland, Aaron. "Gabriel Fauré: a Neglected Master." *Musical Quarterly* 10 (1924): 573.
Jankelevitch, V. "Pelléas et Pénélope." *Revue du Languedoc* 6 (1945): 123.
La revue musicale May (1945) [Fauré issue].
Orrey, L. "Gabriel Fauré: 1845-1924." *Musical Opinion* 68 (1945): 197.
_____. "Gabriel Fauré, 1845-1924." *Musical Times* 86 (1945): 137.
Suckling, Norman. "Gabriel Fauré, Classic of Modern Times." *Music Review* May (1945).
Bulletin de l'Association des amis de Gabriel Fauré (1972-).
Nectoux, Jean-Michel. "Flaubert/Gallet/Fauré ou le démon du théâtre." *Bulletin du bibliophile* 1 (1976): 33.
_____. "Gabriel Fauré et l'esthétique de son oeuvre théâtrale." *Revue Musicale de Suisse Romande* 33 (1980).
Loppert, Max. "Fauré's *Pénélope.*" *Opera* March (1982).

* * *

Fauré wrote but one opera, and that has never taken its rightful place in the repertoire; so far it remains an enthusiasm for cognoscenti only. His reputation continues to rest firmly (the perennially popular *Requiem* apart) on his output of chamber music, piano pieces, and songs. Yet like practically every French composer of his time, he was fascinated by the theater, the operatic stage, and Wagnerian music-drama in particular. Opera, especially opera on some archetypal, mythic subject, represented for him one of the ultimate goals of a composer's career—just as it did for his contemporaries d'Indy (with *Fervaal*), Chausson *(Le Roi Arthus)*, Lalo *(Le Roi d'Ys)*, and Magnard *(Guercoeur, Bérénice)*. Yet none of these admirable works attains the radical adaptation and wholly personal absorption of Wagnerian techniques that Fauré achieved in *Pénélope;* among French operas of the period perhaps only Debussy's *Pelléas et Mélisande* represents an even more original creative answer to the challenge of post-Wagnerian music-drama.

Pénélope, whose composition occupied Fauré from 1907 to 1913, undoubtedly benefited from being slightly later than all the above mentioned works (except Magnard's *Bérénice*, 1905-09, its nearest contemporary and closest sister in aesthetic outlook). Fauré finally came to opera on the threshold of his ultra-refined "late period," by which time he had pondered the role of music in relation to words and drama over many years. As early as 1885 he had contemplated an opera on Pushkin's *Mazeppa,* and during the next 15 years he composed a number of extremely accomplished theater-scores which contain strong hints of his potential operatic strength. Indeed these works can be viewed as a long apprenticeship in the skills which a full-scale opera would demand.

Fauré's music for Alexandre Dumas's *Caligula* (1888) already shows skilled handling of choruses in a banqueting scene, and though both this and the *Shylock* music (1889, to a French adaptation of Shakespeare's *As You Like It*) are comparatively light-weight, they also contain effective and charming movements of scene-setting and atmosphere. The score for a London production of Maeterlinck's *Pelléas et Mélisande* (1898, orchestrated by Charles Koechlin under Fauré's direction) strikes a much deeper note, especially in the quasi-symphonic Prelude and Funeral March, which unite an utterly personal lyricism with a "Wagnerian" atmosphere and sense of tragedy.

The most important of Fauré's "operatic preparations," however, was his extraordinary score for the lyric tragedy *Prométhée* (1900) by Jean Lorraine and A.F. Hérold. The play—written in imitation of a Greek tragedy, on the legend of Prometheus's theft of fire from the gods to bestow its power upon humanity—was specifically designed for performance in the gigantic natural arena at Béziers in southern France, in a conscious attempt on the part of a local art patron to revive the ancient classical theater (in the event, *Prométhée* was performed before an audience of nearly 15,000). Fauré's score was in no sense through-composed: most of the dialogue was spoken and it was his task to provide songs, choruses, and orchestral preludes. The orchestra for this open-air venue consisted of a huge body of strings supported by two military bands and a large number of harps. Fauré entrusted the orchestration to an experienced band-master, Charles Eustace. However, he clearly took the instrumental forces and the open-air resonance into account in composing the short score, and the result was a music of epic simplicity and enormous impressiveness, virile and monumental in its handling of large choral and orchestral groups. The Olympian gods are delineated, in Wagnerian fashion, by leitmotifs, shuffled in an almost mosaic manner to create a music akin to relief sculpture. To a large extent this distinctive character is retained in the version for conventional orchestra which Fauré allocated, for a 1916 Paris revival, to Roger Ducasse.

In accepting such subjects as *Caligula* and *Prométhée,* Fauré gave evidence of his strong imaginative affinity with the Graeco-Roman classical world. (It is not without significance that in 1894 he provided an accompaniment for the musical fragment of the "Hymn to Apollo" recently discovered at Delphi.) This was a milieu to which most of his contemporaries turned for decadence and exoticism, but which for Fauré seems to have represented the ultimate in Attic clarity and poise. It is this aspect above all which is embodied and celebrated in his Homeric opera *Pénélope,* the supreme masterpiece of French musical appreciation of the Hellenic ideal. Here the post-Wagnerian leitmotivic technique appears stripped of all inessentials in a basically through-composed, almost symphonic, continuous development, combined with all Fauré's strict contrapuntal skill and the austerely ecstatic cantabile writing of his late song-cycles.

—Malcolm MacDonald

FAURE, Jean-Baptiste.

Baritone. Born 15 January 1830, in Moulins. Died 9 November 1914, in Paris. Entered Paris Conservatory in 1851; debut as Pygmalion in Massé's *Galathée,* Paris, Opéra-Comique, 1852; created the role of Malipieri in Auber's *Haydée,* 1853, and of Hoël in Meyerbeer's *Dinorah,* 1859; Covent Garden debut as Hoël, 1860; sang there and at Drury Lane and Her Majesty's Theatre until 1875; Paris Opéra debut as Julien in Poniatowsky's *Pierre de Médicis,* 1861; continued to sing at the Paris Opéra regularly until 1869, then again from 1872-76; created many roles there, including Nelusko in Meyerbeer's *L'Africaine,* 1865, Posa in Verdi's *Don Carlos,* 1867, and Hamlet in Thomas's opera, 1868.

Publications

About FAURE: books–

Curzon, H. de. *Jean-Baptiste Faure.* Paris, 1923.

articles–

Curzon, H. de. "Jean-Baptiste Faure." *Musical Quarterly* April (1918).

*   *   *

In his book *The Reign of Patti* (1920), that doyen of opera critics, Hermann Klein, recalled the art of Jean-Baptiste

Jean-Baptiste Faure as Méphistophélès in *Faust,* London, 1864

Faure, "that consummate artist, Faure, King of French baritones and prince of Don Giovannis." With these words Klein, who had heard many of the greatest singers from the 1870s onward, succinctly accords Faure his place as one of the greatest operatic artists of his day.

A prolific composer and teacher of singing (he wrote two books on vocal technique) as well as a baritone, Faure lived at a time of operatic plenitude. His association with many of the greatest 19th-century composers of opera is, in itself, sufficient to assure him a place of importance in musical history. His fellow student at the Paris Conservatory, under the direction of Auber, was Bizet. Meyerbeer wrote several of his great baritone roles with Faure's voice expressly in mind. For Rossini, Faure alone championed the preservation of all the grand traditions of bel canto at a time when other singers epitomized vocal decadence.

Faure reigned supreme at the Opéra Comique and later at the Opéra, where he was chosen to create the main baritone roles in the world premieres of many important new compositions. In little more than a decade, Faure created the baritone parts in *Manon Lescaut* (Auber), *Dinorah* (Meyerbeer), *L'Africaine* (Meyerbeer), *Don Carlos* (Verdi) and *Hamlet* (Thomas), and many other roles by important composers of their time who, for one reason or another, are largely forgotten today. He was especially admired in Vienna, Belgium, Monaco and London where he numbered among his colleagues many singers now legendary. His performances, a combination of exceptional histrionic ability and superior vocalism, in such diverse roles as Don Giovanni, Alfonse (*La favorite*), Guillaume Tell and Nelusko (*L'Africaine*), usually elicited the praise of the critics whenever he appeared. In Germany, however, he was not liked, for, according to contemporary accounts of his singing, his voice was occasionally afflicted with a strong vibrato, a characteristic not usually to Teutonic taste.

Sadly, the invention of the gramophone occurred too late to preserve Faure's voice for posterity. He had largely finished his career before the full commercial potential of the gramophone had begun to be realised. He had heard the results of some of the crude, early attempts at recording and categorically refused tempting offers to allow his voice to be captured by the primitive equipment of the time. As a result, we have only contemporary descriptions of his singing from which to gain some idea of how he must have sounded. However, two unauthenticated cylinders, thought to have been made in Paris around the turn of the century, have been ascribed to him. Crude in sound and technically imperfect, they preserve two items that were especially associated with Faure: "Cantique de Noël" (Adam), a favourite concert encore, and an oddly abridged and truncated version of Alfonse's aria "Viens Léonore" from *La favorite.* The cylinders dimly reveal the voice of a baritone undoubtedly well past his best but of obvious authority. It is unlikely that these cylinder recordings will ever be incontestably authenticated; but even if they were they afford but a faint echo of a singer who was one of the most gifted musicians of all time.

—Larry Lustig

FAUST.

Composer: Charles Gounod.

Librettists: Jules Barbier and Michel Carré (after Goethe).

First Performance: Paris, Théâtre-Lyrique, 19 March 1859; revised to include recitatives, Strasbourg, April 1860, and ballet, Paris, Opéra, 3 March 1869.

Roles: Faust (tenor); Mephistopheles (bass or bass-baritone); Marguerite (soprano); Valentine (baritone); Martha (mezzo-soprano or contralto); Siebel (mezzo-soprano or soprano); Wagner (baritone); chorus (SSAATTBB).

Publications

books–

Soubies, Albert, and Henri Curzon, editors. *Documents inédits sur le "Faust" de Gounod.* Paris, 1912.
Marinelli, Carlo. *"Faust" e "Mefistofele" nelle opere teatrali e sinfonico—vocali o discografia.* Rome, 1986.

articles–

Saint-Saëns, Camille. "Le Livret de 'Faust'." *Monde musicale* (1914-19).
Hopkinson, C. "Notes on the Earliest Editions of Gounod's Faust." In *Festschrift Otto Erich Deutsch,* 245. Kassel, 1963.
Avant-scène opéra March-April (1976) [*Faust* issue].

*   *   *

Faust is arguably the most popular opera of all time. By 1934, it had been performed over 2,000 times in Paris alone, and the work was the first opera performed at the Metropolitan Opera House (New York City) on the occasion of its opening on 22 October 1883. For all of its popularity with general audiences, *Faust* has been reviled as an unliterary perversion of Goethe's *Faust,* a work so estranged from its original source that it is commonly referred to in German-speaking countries by the title *Margarete.*

Act I begins with Faust alone in his study, lamenting his loss of youth and lack of love. A chorus singing the glories of nature does nothing to rouse Faust from his spiritual torpor. Still despairing, Faust cries out for Satan to appear. Mephistopheles appears, offers to wait upon Faust in exchange for his soul, and entices Faust with a vision of Marguerite at her spinning wheel. Faust then signs the demonic pact and is transformed into a young man. The setting switches to a village fair with a festive peasant chorus performing. Valentine (Marguerite's brother), Wagner (Faust's assistant), Siebel (a youth infatuated with Marguerite), and Mephistopheles appear at the fair. The "Song of the Golden Calf," the "Chorale of the Swords," and the "Waltz and Chorus" ensue. Faust sees Marguerite and immediately falls in love with her.

Act II shows Siebel proclaiming his love for Marguerite before Faust in turn sings her praises. He leaves a box of jewels for Marguerite, who sings the "King of Thule" and "The Bijou Song." Faust meets Marguerite at an encounter arranged by Mephistopheles and Martha, Marguerite's friend and neighbor. Faust and Marguerite become enamored of one another and pledge eternal love.

Act III begins with Marguerite lamenting her loss of innocence, and a chorus informs the audience that Marguerite has been abandoned by Faust. She then sings the dolorous "Spinning-Wheel Song." Siebel arrives and tells Marguerite that he will avenge her honor. Marguerite goes to church

Faust, **Covent Garden, 1864 (Adelina Patti as Marguerite, Giovanni Mario as Faust, and Jean-Baptiste Faure as Méphistophélès)**

where she is accosted by a chorus of demons. Valentine returns with his fellow soldiers and follows Siebel to the church where Marguerite is praying. Valentine engages in swordplay with Faust in order to avenge his sister's honor. Faust's sword, however, is guided by Mephistopheles, and Valentine is mortally wounded. Before dying, Valentine curses Marguerite and tells her to repent. Act IV commences with Faust and Mephistopheles' attendance at the "Walpurgis Night." Faust, however, desires to return to Marguerite, who is now in prison for the murder of her child by Faust. Faust attempts to rescue Marguerite, but she rejects his offer. Marguerite prays for forgiveness, dies, and ascends to Heaven.

Although it has become a commonplace of operatic criticism to disparage the libretto of *Faust,* in fairness to Barbier and Carré we must consider their work in relation to the unique demands of opera. Barbier and Carré only utilized portions of eight of the twenty-six scenes of Part I of Goethe's *Faust.* Those who criticize the libretto often deplore the omission of the "Prologue in Heaven," whereby Goethe altered the traditional Faust story from a personal relationship between the supplicant Faust and the procurer Mephistopheles into a cosmic "wager" between God and the Devil. Goethe's lofty conception is lost in the libretto, but there is a very important practical reason for doing so. In Goethe's *Faust* the full implications of the "Prologue in Heaven" are not realized until the final scene of Part II, some 12,000 lines later. Including Part II would not only have been too vast an undertaking, but it would also have proved to be especially problematic in view of the religious sensibilities of the potential audience. Goethe's Faust never begs for forgiveness, yet he is saved. Gretchen's rediscovery of her moral substance (and her subsequent transcendence) along with the melodramatic nature of her descent into sinfulness, were precisely those features of the Faust legend that appealed most directly to the conventional (and public) morality of the opera-going bourgeoisie.

Barbier and Carré also give increased emphasis to characters and situations which are only briefly utilized by Goethe. The most notable example is the importance given to the character Siebel. In Goethe's drama, Siebel (along with Altmayer, Brander, and Frosch) is one of Faust and Mephistopheles' student drinking companions at Auerbach's Tavern. Barbier and Carré have transformed Siebel from a drunken collegian into a youthful defender of Marguerite's honor. He is completely ineffectual but his intentions are entirely noble.

Other additions to the opera include choral sections designed to be crowd-pleasing spectacles, such as the "Song of the Golden Calf" and the "Chorale of the Swords." But this type of material is precisely what was required by Parisian audiences of the time, for it not only satisfied the audience's appetite for visual spectacle, but also provided the extravagance of heightened emotionality that is opera's métier.

Barbier and Carré also change drastically Goethe's conception of the title character. Youth and love are all that Gounod's Faust wants from life. The lofty conception of the struggle for perfection exemplified in Goethe's phrase "verweile doch, du bist so schön," the desire for a truly transcendent moment of being, is completely absent. Faust does enjoin Marguerite to linger during their duet "Il se fait tard," but the relationship between Gounod's opera and Goethe's drama has become so attenuated that the text of the duet cannot be considered as anything more than the importuning of a desperate lover.

From a musical standpoint Gounod does adhere to Goethe's preference for strophic settings of poetic texts; this is seen particularly in Gounod's settings of Goethe's song lyrics. Although Gounod does not generally employ tonalities

< in a unifying and consistent manner, there are a few notable exceptions; for instance, when Marguerite recalls in prison her first meeting with Faust, a short reprise of the waltz music from their initial encounter is given.

Sometimes, however, the demands of the music alter Goethe's staging intentions. In Gounod's setting of Goethe's "Garden" scene ("Seigneur Dieu"), Faust, Mephistopheles, Marguerite, and Martha at times sing simultaneously. This type of ensemble is very popular with audiences and has a long history in opera, yet it effaces the original concept of Goethe's in which two couples (Faust-Gretchen and Mephistopheles-Martha) were to stroll in a circular pattern and alternately come into view and listening range of the audience.

Ultimately, the critical dilemma that *Faust* presents, its overwhelming popularity in the face of severe and long-standing criticism, belongs more to the realm of *Rezeptionsgeschichte* than to the criticism and history of opera per se. For better or worse, Gounod's *Faust* is a permanent fixture in the operatic repertory; its beautiful arias live separate existences on the concert stage, and its affective qualities are such that authors as diverse as Ivan Turgenev (in *Faust: A Story in Nine Letters,* 1856) and Estanislao del Campo (in *Fausto,* 1866) have utilized the opera as the catalyst for profound emotional and spiritual upheavals in their literary protagonists.

—William E. Grim

LA FAVOLA D'ORFEO (Orfeo) [The Fable of Orpheus].

Composer: Claudio Monteverdi.

Librettist: Alessandro Striggio.

First Performance: Mantua, February 1607.

Roles: Orfeo (tenor); Euridice (soprano); La Musica (mezzo-soprano); Sylvia (mezzo-soprano); Hope (mezzo-soprano); Charon (bass); Persephone (contralto); Pluto (bass); Apollo (tenor); Echo (soprano or mezzo-soprano); Shepherd (tenor); Other Shepherds (soprano, contralto, mezzo-soprano); Spirits (soprano, mezzo-soprano, tenor, bass); chorus (SSATB).

Publications

books—

Pirrotta, Nino. *I due Orfei: da Poliziano a Monteverdi.* Turin, 1969; English translation, Cambridge, 1982.

Müller, Reinhard. *Der "stile recitativo" in Claudio Monteverdis "Orfeo": Dramatischer Gesang und Instrumentalsatz.* Tutzing, 1984.

Whenham, John. *Claudio Monteverdi: Orfeo.* Cambridge, 1986.

articles—

Westrup, J.A. "Two First Performances: Monteverdi's *Orfeo* and Mozart's *La clemenza di Tito.*" *Music and Letters* 39 (1958): 327.

L'ORFEO

FAVOLA IN MVSICA

DA CLAVDIO MONTEVERDI

RAPPRESENTATA IN MANTOVA

Anno 1607 & nouamente data in luce

AL SERENISSIMO SIGNOR

D. FRANCESCO GONZAGA

Prencipe di Mantoua, & di Monferato, &c

In Venetia Appreſſo Ricciardo Amadino.

M D C I X.

The title page from the first printed score of Monteverdi's *Orfeo*, Venice, 1609

Frobenius, W. "Zur Notation eines Ritornellos in Monteverdis 'L'Orfeo'." *Archiv für Musikwissenschaft* 28 (1971): 201.

Avant-scène opéra September-October (1976) [*Orfeo* issue].

McGee, Timothy J. "*Orfeo* and *Euridice,* the First Two Operas." In *Orpheus, the Metamorphosis of a Myth,* edited by John Warden, 163. Toronto, 1982.

Fenlon, Iain. "Monteverdi's Mantuan *Orfeo:* Some New Documentation." *Early Music* 12 (1984): 163.

Osthoff, Wolfgang. "Contro le legge de' Fati: Polizianos und Monteverdis *Orfeo* als Sinnbild künstlerischen Wettkampfs mit der Natur." *Analecta musicologica* 22 (1984): 11.

*   *   *

The Mantuan councillor Alessandro Striggio based his libretto for *La favola d'Orfeo* on passages from Virgil's *Georgics* and Ovid's *Metamorphoses.* Typical of the haste and hurry surrounding Mantuan productions, that of *Orfeo* suffered a worse fate than most, because it was the first opera that Striggio and Monteverdi had ever written (and the first thorough-going opera in history). The tension and time-shortage were such that as each section of the libretto was completed it would be handed over to the composer for setting to music. But the libretto had already gone to press when Striggio and Monteverdi were reminded by a Florentine visitor that one essential element had been omitted—the *deus ex machina.* Even fledgling opera had to have two things, a castrato and a *deus,* and eventually *Orfeo* had both. Striggio, ignoring the printed libretto, re-wrote the ending of act V, so providing a peroration with overtones of divine intervention and earthly rejoicing—infinitely more satisfactory than the original destructive bacchanalia with its fivefold repeats of a drunken chorus.

After the overture, played by Mantua's brass ensemble (muted), the Spirit of Music introduces the story of Orpheus in a prologue. As act I begins, nymphs and shepherds announce the wedding of Orpheus and Euridice, who enter to the sounds of a choral invocation to Hymen. A light-hearted sung ballet prefaces a request for a love-song, and Orpheus naturally obliges. After a brief reply by Euridice, the choral numbers are heard again, in reverse order, whereupon a shepherd suggests that everyone go to the temple to offer thanks and prayers. The bridal pair and the chorus slowly leave the stage, while shepherds sing of happiness and springtime. An off-stage chorus hails Orpheus and Euridice at the temple.

Act II sees the return of Orpheus in a cheerful mood, while Euridice goes for a walk with her confidante, Sylvia. But unexpectedly and suddenly Sylvia returns with the terrible news that Euridice, bitten by a snake, is dead. Shepherds commiserate while Orpheus vows to bring her back from the dead or die with her. Sylvia resigns herself to the life of a recluse; the shepherds go to find Euridice. In act III, Hope guides Orpheus to Hades but retreats as Charon appears, saying that he cannot help live mortals to cross the Styx. Orpheus delivers a magnificently ornate aria, and while Charon nods off to sleep the singer steps into the boat and crosses the river, pleading with the Tartarean gods to give him back his beloved. Underworld spirits praise the determination of mankind.

Act IV begins with a scene between Proserpine (Persephone) and Pluto. He is moved by her to help Orpheus, and agrees only on condition that the singer not look back as he leads his beloved from hell, or he will lose her forever. As they move earthwards, Orpheus sings several verses of a touching song, but on hearing the Furies he turns round, and Euridice disappears into the gloom, singing her farewell. The chorus of spirits warn men to keep control of their emotions.

In act V, once again in the countryside, Orpheus praises Euridice but renounces all other women. Apollo's voice is heard, echoing the sentiment expressed by the previous chorus, and invites Orpheus to join him in heaven. A final chorus in the manner of a *moresca* (moorish dance) tells us that those who sow in sorrow will reap in joy.

La favola d'Orfeo is an unusually satisfying opera because the action is clear and concise. If acts I and II are performed in sequence, followed by a short interval before acts III and IV, the last act stands on its own as the scene returns to the countryside after the gloomier passages in the underworld. The whole work should last only about two hours, but within that time-span Monteverdi provides a great wealth and variety of forms and styles. In fact he had brought together in his score generous samples of everything that was current in the musical world of his day: full-voiced choruses doubled by suitable groups of instruments, echoes of the time-honored madrigal and the more modern balletto, ritornels and symphonies using a wide range of timbre, duets, trios, ariosos, and a virtuoso aria.

Orfeo provides a foretaste of modern opera, especially when one takes into account the transference of musical paragraphs from one section to another, as in the case of the ritornel first used in the verses for the Spirit of Music, and later heard at the close of act II and the beginning of act V. Throughout the opera, Monteverdi's choice of key relates well to the character or situation, the total effect being of refined perception and a subtle feeling for mood.

—Denis Stevens

LA FAVORITE [The Favorite].

Composer: Gaetano Donizetti.

Librettists: A. Royer and G. Vaëz (after Baculard d'Arnaud, *Le comte de Comminges*).

First Performance: Paris, Opéra, 2 December 1840 [revised and expanded from *L'ange de Nisida,* 1839].

Roles: Leonora di Guzman (soprano or mezzo-soprano); Alfonso XI (baritone); Fernando (tenor); Baldassare (bass); Don Gasparo (tenor); Ines (soprano); Gentleman (tenor); chorus (SATB).

Publications

article–

Leavis, R. "*La favorite* and *La favorita:* One Opera, Two Librettos." *Journal of the Donizetti Society* 2 (1975): 117.

*   *   *

It was with *La favorite* that the *French* Donizetti finally emerged. In this opera, the Italian composer had, in Wagner's opinion, acquired a "skill and dignity that you would search for in vain in the other works of the inexhaustible maestro."

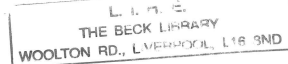

The final scene from *La favorite,* **Royal Italian Opera, London, 1848**

He had had an eye on Paris since 1830 or so, when Rossini's residence there and the vogue for *grand-opéra* captured the attention of all Europe. His first tentative effort had been *Marino Faliero* at the Théâtre-Italien in 1835, but this had proved an unappreciated sacrifice at the Parisian alter. In 1838 he moved to the French capital more or less for good. Operas with French texts, *La fille du régiment* and *Les martyrs* (both 1840), soon followed, but these were thoroughly Italianate in everything except language. It was *La favorite* that actually realized Donizetti's Parisian ambitions to the full. It has a four-act score, with a properly integrated ballet, replete with the processions, the scenic wonders, the adultery, cloisters, cowls and religiosity that made the Meyerbeerian exemplar so fascinating to all aspiring Italian *maestri* seeking international fame. But *La favorite* was far from being an original score; the opera showed that a really professional operatic composer could add and subtract any number of ingredients to the musical stew and still end up with a perfect assimilation of flavors. *La favorite* was cobbled together in haste from two unfinished scores, *Adelaide* of 1835, and *L'ange de Nisida* of 1839, to which were added some fragments from other operas, and six or seven new pieces.

The opera is set in Castille in 1340. Fernando, a novice in the Monastery of Santiago de Compostela, protests his love for the beautiful Leonora before his Father Superior (who is incidentally his own father). But Leonora, unbeknownst to Fernando, is the mistress of the king, Alfonso XI.

Expelled from the monastery, Fernando goes off to seek fame and fortune and the hand of Leonora. With notable cynicism, Alfonso renounces Leonora, who marries Fernando. When the nature of his misalliance is explained to him, Fernando breaks his sword before the court and returns to the cloister. After taking orders, he is horrified to discover the disguised Leonora at his knees begging forgiveness. Repentant, she dies in his arms.

To those familiar with Donizetti's Italian scores, the music of *La favorite* is at once plainer, lower-keyed, more expansive melodically, eschewing predictable transitions and cadences, and with a grander orchestration. Indeed, Donizetti employed as many Parisian mannerisms as he dared. Even the *vocalità* has been pruned: Italian in volume and sheen, it is Gallic in its choice of range. Leonora is a *falcon;* Fernand a tenor inching up into an *haut-contre* register; Alfonso is a baritone honeyed as never before. All these roles are devoid of superfluous ornament, and there are only some isolated passages of florid singing. The lyrical flow is nearly unbroken throughout. Everything is flexible, more responsive to words and setting, and arias are not allowed to obtrude out of context.

Even a relatively seamless score can have its sterling moments. *La favorite* has three great arias to its credit: Alfonso's *andante* section of the act III trio, "Pour tant d'amour"; Leonora's *air* which almost immediately follows, "O mon Fernand" (both composed especially for the opera and not derived from earlier music); and Fernando's "Ange si pur" (famous also as "Spirto gentil" in the various bowdlerized Italian versions of the opera), taken from the unfinished *Le duc d'Albe* of 1839. It is, however, the ballet music, used by

Carlotta Grisi to make her sensational stage debut in Paris, that shows Donizetti at his most versatile, his most truly adaptable, relishing France and its traditions, even embracing with enthusiasm the dilution of this music with a "ballabile," at home a task given to lesser composers.

—Alexander Weatherson

LA FEDELTÀ PREMIATA [Fidelity Rewarded].

Composer: Franz Joseph Haydn.

Librettist: unknown, after G. Lorenzi, L'infedeltà fedele.

First Performance: Esterháza, 25 February 1781.

Roles: Fillide/Celia (soprano); Fileno (tenor); Amarante (soprano); Count Perrucchetto (bass); Nerina (soprano); Lindoro (tenor); Melibeo (bass); Diana (soprano); chorus.

Publications

articles–

Thomas, Günter. "Zu 'Il mondo della luna' und 'La fedeltà premiata': Fassungen und Pasticcios." Haydn-Studien 2 (1969): 122.
Porter, A. "Haydn and 'La fedeltà premiata'." Musical Times 112 (1971): 331.
Landon, H.C. Robbins. "A New Authentic Source for La Fedeltà Premiata by Haydn." Soundings 2 (1971-72): 6.
Smith, Erik. "Haydn and La fedeltà premiata." Musical Times 120 (1979): 567.
Lippmann, Friedrich. "Haydns La fedeltà premiata und Cimarosas L'infedeltà fedele." Haydn-Studien 5 (1982): 1.

*   *   *

Composed for the 1781 inauguration of Esterháza's new and enlarged opera house, La fedeltà premiata is based on Giambattista Lorenzi's libretto L'infedeltà fedele which, in a setting by Domenico Cimarosa, opened Naples' Teatro del Fondo in 1779. While Cimarosa's setting is the more comic of the two, both operas unite comedy and solemnity to create, in Lorenzi's words, "an in-between entertainment, partaking discreetly of elements from both 'serio' and 'giocoso,' so that everyone . . . might find a theatrical event corresponding to his taste."

In the first scene, Amarante, the prima buffa, reads aloud an inscription on the Temple of Diana that outlines the plot: every year two faithful lovers will be sacrificed to the sea monster until a heroic soul offers his own life. Only then will peace return to the land of Cumae. Thus begins the "hunt"— so vividly presented in the "La chasse" overture (subsequently adapted as the closing movement of Haydn's Symphony no. 73)—for the sacrificial victims to be offered to Diana, the Roman goddess of the hunt. Unlike other librettos where love intrigues predominate, the characters in this piece are given ample justification for their coy and felicitous actions since, to be in love without the consent of the devious

high priest, Melibeo, means certain disaster. Amarante accepts Melibeo's favor, thereby receiving immunity, while simultaneously pursuing the ever-comic Count Perrucchetto (literally Count Wigmaker), whom she sees as her ticket to the ranks of the nobility. Her weak-willed brother, Lindoro, is convinced to switch his allegiances from the wood-nymph Nerina to the noble Celia. Because of Diana's curse, Celia, whose real name is Fillide, must hide her love for Fileno, the long-lost lover who presumed her dead. The oscillation between private and professed pairings is enough to make one dizzy; for instance, over the course of the first act Count Perrucchetto woos all three women, while in the act I finale Celia is almost forced into accepting Lindoro's marriage proposal in front of a despairing Fileno. In the second act Melibeo, angry at having failed to unite Lindoro and Celia, and jealous of the love vows exchanged by Amarante and the Count, contrives to have Celia and Count Perrucchetto brought forth as the sacrificial couple. In the next act Fileno announces that, rather than see Celia devoured by the sea monster, he will offer himself as the single sacrificial victim, a noble deed worthy of a Metastasian hero. Moved by Fileno's devotion, Diana arrives magically amid clamorous thunder and lightning to save Fileno. She unites Celia with Fileno, Nerina with Lindoro, and Amarante with Count Perrucchetto, taking Melibeo as her victim for having contrived events to his own benefit.

The convoluted plot and disjointed multi-scenic structure of this opera are in part responsible for the traditional view that Haydn set poor librettos. However, La fedeltà premiata was Haydn's most successful comic opera at Esterháza in terms of the number of performances (ranking second to Armida, Haydn's last opera seria for the court), remaining in the repertory until 1785. The opera also received highly acclaimed German-language productions in Vienna (1784) and Pressburg (1785). Furthermore, Celia's famous act II scena "Ah come il core" was published in a solo concert version in 1782, and a lengthy analytical review of the "Cantata" appeared in Cramer's Magazin der Musik in 1783. These measures of the opera's success, as well as Haydn's own pride in the work recorded in a letter to his publisher, Artaria, in May 1781 (". . . I assure you that no such work has been heard in Paris up to now, nor perhaps in Vienna either") ought not be overlooked, in spite of differing aesthetic values.

The story's fantastic and spectacular elements, including the festive hunt for the feast of Diana and her appearance "dea ex machina," can be rendered very appealing on stage to modern-day audiences. The espoused virtues of honesty and faithfulness are timeless, and the poignancy of these virtues for Haydn, who by late 1780 was involved in an affair with the mezzo-soprano Luigia Polzelli, may in part explain the high level of musical sensitivity and competence demonstrated throughout the score.

That Haydn derived compositional impetus from Cimarosa's L'infedeltà fedele is indisputable. He possessed a copy of this score and modeled parts of his setting on the Neapolitan version, although the debt is probably not as large as previously believed, since some similarities result from common period, not individual, practices. Lippmann's conclusion that Haydn sometimes used Cimarosa's score as a springboard is particularly apt for the act I finale; the tonal progression based on descending thirds is derived from Cimarosa's setting, but the linking of the parti serie couple's situations through tempo, meter, and key in sections 3 and 7 (presto, $\frac{3}{4}$, G minor) has no counterpart in Cimarosa's setting. Similarly Haydn's parody of the famous chorus of the furies from Gluck's Orfeo ed Euridice (1762) in the act II finale (sections 3-7), while perhaps triggered by the brief rhythmic reference in Cimarosa's score, was probably calculated to tickle the fancy of his musically-astute patron. After all, Prince Nicholas initiated regular operatic productions at Esterháza in 1776 with Gluck's opera.

A large number of the arias in *La fedeltà premiata* are sectional in structure. The music's built-in flexibility is particularly suitable for mirroring the wide-ranging emotional states of a character, and is used to great effect in the act II solo scenes for the *parti serie*. Here Fileno's attempted suicide ("Bastano i pianti") followed by Celia's desperate contemplation of events in the above-mentioned scena ("Ah come il core"), which together constitute the dramatic highpoint of the opera, are amply served by a constantly adaptive musical structure. Once again Haydn's setting of Celia's scena goes beyond Cimarosa's conception, showing that *La fedeltà premiata*'s success owes very little to *L'infedeltà fedele*.

—Caryl Clark

FEDORA.

Composer: Umberto Giordano.

Librettist: A. Colautti (after Sardou).

First Performance: Milan, Lirico, 17 November 1898.

Roles: Princess Fedora Romazoff (soprano); Count Loris Ipanoff (tenor); De Siriex (baritone); Countess Olga Sukarev (soprano); Grech (bass); Borov (baritone); Cirillo (baritone); Lorek (baritone); Dimitri (contralto); Desire (tenor); Little Savoyard (mezzo-soprano); Baron Rouvel (tenor); Boleslao Lazinski (mime); chorus (SATB).

*   *   *

Fedora was written toward the end of the *verismo* decade opened by Mascagni's *Cavalleria rusticana,* and remained in the repertories as Giordano's most successful opera after *Andrea Chénier* (1896). It displays the composer's unerring sense of the theater and his ability to create suspense and convey strong emotions while exercising restraint and formal control over his musical resources.

Sardou's four-act play exploiting a fashionable subject (love among Russian aristocrats) is turned into a tight, action-packed, operatic thriller. The wealthy princess Fedora Romazoff is to marry count Vladimir Andreyevich, but he is wounded in a shooting and dies. Count Loris Ipanoff is named as a strong suspect and Fedora vows to pursue the murderer by herself. At a reception in her Paris house, Fedora makes Loris fall in love with her and extorts a confession of guilt from him. Loris promises to return after all the guests have departed and reveal his good reasons for the murder. Meanwhile Fedora writes a letter to the police authorities in Petersburg accusing Loris and his brother Valeriano who has been mentioned as an accomplice by a Russian agent. Loris returns and explains that Vladimir was having an affair with Loris' own wife Wanda, so his murder was in fact an act of revenge. As a proof, he shows Vladimir's love letters to Wanda; in one of them Fedora reads that her fiancé was marrying her only for her money. All this turns Loris from a murderer into her own avenger. Fedora takes him to her retreat in the Bernese

Enrico Caruso with Lina Cavalieri in *Fedora*

Oberland. But her dilatory letter reaches the police in Petersburg and Valeriano Ipanoff is arrested. In the fortress on the Neva the waters rise overnight and drown the young prisoner. His old mother dies of a shock. The idyll in the Oberland is soon shattered by such tidings. Fedora admits her responsibility to Loris, takes poison and dies in the arms of her distressed lover.

Giordano's approach in devising a suitable musical medium was to support the quick pace of the action and enhance the well calculated theatrical effects of Sardou's drama. This resulted in a tense orchestral continuum interspersed with few recurring motifs which either identify a character (e.g., Fedora's love theme in act I) or provide dramatic depth for crucial narrative sequences (e.g., the sombre figure of the strings accompanying the account of Valeriano's drowning and his mother's death in act III). Loris and Fedora are given very short lyrical solos fully integrated in the action: e.g., Fedora's fond description of Vladimir as she contemplates his photograph in act I ("O grandi occhi lucenti di fede"— "Oh large, shining, truthful eyes"), or Loris passionate statement "Amor ti vieta di non amar" ("Love forbids you not to love," act II); its warm, straightforward melody is then used as an orchestral interlude to distance Loris' second meeting with Fedora, and quoted at the end of the opera to counterbalance Fedora's dramatic *parlato* in her death scene.

The first two acts of *Fedora* have none of the turgid orchestration and vocal paroxysm of a Mascagni opera. The musical comment is always neat and adroit. The dialogue between Fedora and Loris (act II), in the course of which he confesses his killing of Vladimir, has no orchestral accompaniment. A simple and effective solution is adopted by Giordano to add realism and tension to the scene and avoid the conventional form of a duet. The main attraction of the reception in Fedora's Parisian residence is a young Polish pianist who plays a pseudo-Chopin nocturne. The orchestra stops and the guests listen attentively while, in the foreground, Loris and Fedora keep themselves apart from the stage audience and sing *a mezzavoce*, in a subdued tone. Their conversation is thus indirectly supported by the piano solo and terminates on the last, slightly ironic, virtuoso passage of the nocturne. A totally different treatment is chosen for the second part of the dialogue which closes the act: the description of the murder, Fedora's realization of Vladimir's deceitfulness and her response to Loris' love are built up into a duet with impassioned, soaring phrases shared by the full orchestra. In act III, Loris' vocal outbursts supported by string tremolos and the predictable, picturesque, off-stage mountain songs fall within the common practice of *verismo* composers.

Fedora ranks with other minor nineteenth-century operas for its conventional harmonic language, but it also exhibits an individual character in the dynamic, agile structures anticipating, at their best, the future techniques of film music.

—Matteo Sansone

FELSENSTEIN, Walter.

Director and producer. Born 30 May 1901, in Vienna; died 8 October 1975, in Berlin. Studied at a technical college in Graz; then studied acting at the Vienna Burgtheater, 1921-23; made acting debut in Lübeck in 1923; in 1925 became dramatic advisor and producer in Beuthen, Silesia, where he staged his first operatic productions, including *La bohème* in 1926 and *Fidelio* in 1927; in 1927 appointed chief opera and drama producer at the Stadttheater in Basel; worked as dramatic advisor and producer in Freiburg, 1929-32; chief producer of the Cologne Opera, 1932-34; chief producer at Frankfurt am Main, 1934-36; worked as producer in Zurich, 1938-40, and at the Schiller-Theater in Berlin, 1940-44; enlisted in armed forces 1944-45; appointed director of the Komische Oper in Berlin, 1947; continued to stage highly acclaimed productions in Berlin up until his final production for the Komische Oper, *Le nozze di Figaro*, eight months before his death. During these years he also staged productions throughout Germany and abroad, and worked as a film maker and teacher; he was appointed professor (1959) and vice-president (1962) of the Akademie der Künste in Berlin; he also served as chairman of the music-theatre committee of the International Theatre Institute and won numerous awards, including the Nationalpreis der D.D.R. in 1950, 1951, 1956, 1960 and 1972. As a teacher Felsenstein had a profound influence on younger producers and directors such as Götz Friedrich, Joachim Herz, and Ruth Berghaus.

Opera Productions (selected)

La bohème, Beuthen, Vereinigte Städtische Bühnen, 1926.
Fidelio, Beuthen, Vereinigte Städtische Bühnen, 1927.
Die Meistersinger von Nürnberg, Basel, Stadttheater, 1927.
Turandot, Basel, Stadttheater, 1928.
Hänsel und Gretel, Freiburg, Stadttheater, 1929.
Cardillac, Freiburg, Stadttheater, 1930.
Rienzi, Cologne, Opernhaus, 1932.
Die Entführung aus dem Serail, Cologne, Opernhaus, 1932.
Parsifal, Cologne, Opernhaus, 1933.

Tannhäuser, Frankfurt am Main, Opernhaus, 1934.
La traviata, Frankfurt am Main, Opernhaus, 1934.
Euryanthe, Frankfurt am Main, Opernhaus, 1935.
Rigoletto, Frankfurt am Main, Opernhaus, 1936.
La vie parisienne, Zurich, Stadttheater, 1939.
Der Zigeunerbaron, Friedrichshagen, Naturtheater, 1939.
Madama Butterfly, Zurich, Stadttheater, 1940.
Falstaff, Aachen, Stadttheater, 1941.
Le nozze di Figaro, Salzburg Festival, 1942.
La vie parisienne, Berlin, Hebbel-Theater, 1945.
Die Fledermaus, Berlin, Komische Oper, 1947.
Orphée aux enfers, Berlin, Komische Oper, 1948.
Carmen, Berlin, Komische Oper, 1949.
Der Freischütz, Berlin, Komische Oper, 1951.
Die Zauberflöte, Berlin, Komische Oper, 1954.
The Cunning Little Vixen, Berlin, Komische Oper, 1956.
Othello, Berlin, Komische Oper, 1959.
Il barbiere di Siviglia (Paisiello), Berlin, Komische Oper, 1960.
A Midsummer Night's Dream (Britten), Berlin, Komische Oper, 1961.
Rigoletto, Hamburg, Staatsoper, 1962.
Don Giovanni, Berlin, Komische Oper, 1966.
La traviata, Berlin, Komische Oper, 1967.
Háry János (Kodály), Berlin, Komische Oper, 1973.
Le nozze di Figaro, Berlin, Komische Oper, 1975.

Publications

By FELSENTEIN: books–

With S. Melchinger. *Musiktheater.* Bremen, 1961.
With G. Friedrich and J. Herz; Stephan Stompor, ed. *Musiktheater: Beiträge zur Methodik und zu Inszenierungs-Konzeptionen.* Leipzig, 1970.
Stompor, Stephan, ed. *Schriften zum Musiktheater.* Berlin, 1976.

articles–

"Partnerschaft mit dem Publikum." In *Festschrift 1817-1967 Akademie für Musik und darstellende Kunst in Wien,* 26. Vienna, 1967.
"The Road to Improvement" (interview). *Opera* 21/1 (January 1970): 8. Reprinted from *World Theatre.*

About FELSENSTEIN: books–

Ott, W., and G. Friedrich, eds. *Die Komische Oper 1947-54.* Berlin, 1954.
Friedrich, G. *Walter Felsenstein: Weg und Werk.* Berlin, 1967.
Fuchs, Peter Paul, ed. *The Music Theater of Walter Felsenstein.* New York, 1975.
Kranz, Dieter. *Gespräche mit Felsenstein.* Berlin, 1976.
Körte, Konrad. *Die Oper im Film.* Frankfurt am Main, c. 1989.

article–

McMurray, John. "Die Komische Oper, Berlin." *Musical Times* 130/1758 (August 1989): 452.

unpublished–

Münz, R. "Untersuchungen zum realistischen Musiktheater Walter Felsensteins." Ph.D. diss., Humboldt University, Berlin, 1964.

The shadow of Walter Felsenstein's directorial genius falls across opera production of the second half of the twentieth century. His own productions at the Komische Oper Berlin and his pronouncements (essays, lectures, master classes) on his work were, for many practitioners of the art as well as devotees of it, signposts on the road to operatic perfection.

Felsenstein's guiding principle was always to be at the service of the work itself, producing a *Gesamtkunstwerk* in which all contributions were equal—design, performance, musical direction. He insisted that the "human truth" of an opera's action should "attain such power of conviction that the spectator . . . experiences a more intense feeling of reality and community than he has known before."

He called for a seamless combination of drama and music which he dubbed *"realistisches Musiktheater."* These productions were to be "humanly believable and convincing," with the singers transformed into the characters they were portraying. They must convince the audience that they sing because they "cannot sufficiently express themselves through speech and gesture alone," thus making "singing and music making . . . a convincing, truthful and absolutely essential human statement."

The search for human truth on the operatic stage was, of course, not unique to Felsenstein, but he was uniquely placed to pursue his vision at the Komische Oper, one of the two cultural flagships of post-war East Germany (the other being Brecht's Berliner Ensemble). Although Felsenstein's aims were not politically oriented, the socialist regime realized early on the propaganda value of allowing the producer to work in freedom and welcomed the prestige that accrued from the acclaim accorded the Komische Oper, to the extent that the producer was allowed to live in the West and commute to the East to work. In the heavily-subsidized house he was able to rehearse his productions as long as he deemed necessary, and his concentration on only a few bars of music in the course of several hours' intense study became the stuff of journalists' amazed reportage and of other producers' dreams.

Not only were rehearsal periods open-ended, but a first night could be postponed indefinitely until every element was as close as possible to Felsenstein's conception. As long as the work remained in the repertoire, it would be re-rehearsed; Felsenstein emphasized the "necessity of maintaining a quality of production which admits of neither routine nor slackness"—thus ensuring the retention of the production's initial freshness and spontaneity.

In addition, if a performer were ill, the performance would be cancelled. Felsenstein was unwilling to allow the appearance of a substitute, who might know the notes but not have the same working experience of the opera as his fellow performers.

In an essay on the preparation of a Felsenstein *Carmen,* Stephan Stompor gives a vivid picture of the way the Komische Oper company was involved in a production from its conception: "As a prelude to the musical rehearsals it is necessary to have a detailed understanding between the stage director and the conductor, as well as with the conductor's close collaborators, such as the director of musical studies, the chorus director, and all the assistant conductors and coaches. . . all these people, as well as the Dramaturgs and assistant stage directors, were assembled at the piano for a joint reading of the work; on those occasions dramatic and scenic problems, and also the determination of tempos and even questions of casting, were discussed. . . . When the musical rehearsals began, an exact scenic and musical concept had already been formed."

Felsenstein demanded that "each person should know why he stands on stage and for whom he stands there." With "every note a scenic direction," rehearsals entailed a detailed exploration of music and libretto, so that the singers learned not just their own roles but every note of the score: "A singer who knows only his vocal part and not the entire instrumental substance, is bound to be a slave to the conductor's beat." Note by note, the opera would be mined for intention and motivation.

A vivid insight into his working methods is given by Felsenstein as he describes his work on the first phrase of Tamino's aria "Dies Bildnis" (*Zauberflöte*, act I). He begins with the Prince's actions: Tamino reluctantly looks at the portrait of Pamina which the First Lady has thrust into his hand, and falls instantly in love, crying "This portrait is extraordinarily beautiful!" Felsenstein delineates the Prince's complex emotional and psychological make-up at the moment of this *coup de foudre,* but he also is mindful of the "devilishly difficult tessitura" of the sung phrase that underlies this moment. To tackle the technical problems, he suggests that the singer imagine a high E flat above his first high G. This would make the high G seem less formidable, the imagined high E flat corresponding to the heightened emotion produced by Tamino's glimpse of Pamina's portrait. This juxtaposition of the character's emotion with the singer's technical means of dealing with the musical phrase makes clear how Felsenstein could animate for himself and his performers each note of the score, and suggests why—with this kind of painstaking dissection—Komische Oper rehearsals could take so long.

Preparing a role in this manner, Felsenstein claimed, prevented it from becoming "a vocal exercise," allowing instead the music to become the expression of the drama within.

Felsenstein did not come to the work as a theoretician. He had begun his career as an actor, had played many of the German provincial playhouses during the 1930s, and had begun directing by accident: "We were rehearsing Schnitzler's *Liebelei,* and I had a role I didn't want to give up, but we suddenly had no director and in order to save the play I had to direct it, against my will. . . the company unanimously decided that I should replace the same vanished director in staging *La bohème.* . . . I definitely had a future (as an actor) but that future got sabotaged by my getting recommended in Basel as a director."

By the end of the war he had directed plays and produced operas throughout Germany and in German-speaking Switzerland. These experiences led to another important Felsenstein tenet of operatic production: use of the vernacular for all operas presented at the Komische Oper. Working from the original texts (of non-Germanic operas), he re-translated their libretti, sweeping away all the textural accretions and musical adaptations that had been a feature of pre-War German opera production. A text must be presented in the language of its listeners, he declared, in order that the composer's intentions are clearly apparent to the audience.

The audience was ultimately the focus of Felsenstein's work. He deplored the "invisible wall" which usually developed between stage and auditorium. What he wished to achieve was a "fusion" between performer and spectator, so that the spectator would "never recognise singing as the practicing of a professional skill" but rather as the expression of emotion on the highest level.

Felsenstein's ideas have had an enormous impact on younger producers, including his pupils Joachim Herz and Götz Friedrich, as well as on Harry Kupfer who succeeded him as head of the Komische Oper. But he had his detractors too. While applauding his constant search for dramatic truth, his critics felt that Felsenstein's highly accomplished dramatic performers were not always equal to the vocal demands of the music and that the music was therefore sacrificed for the dramatic moment. They were quick to point out that despite his insistence on equality between production elements, too often it was a Felsenstein-led production, with musical direction following his lead.

Even his detractors, however, conceded that his methods kept alive the freshness of his productions, and that his ability to inspire singers to a dramatic reality was rare on other stages. At his best his genius made familiar works look new-minted, revealing new meaning in a work that had become clichéd or dulled by decades of traditional production. With only an unsatisfactory filmed record of a few Felsenstein productions, opera historians and practitioners will be limited to his written and oral statements—but the vision contained in them is inspiring.

—Louise Stein

DER FERNE KLANG [The Distant Sound].

Composer: Franz Schreker.

Librettist: Franz Schreker.

First Performance: Frankfurt am Main, 18 August 1912.

Publications

articles–

Dahlhaus, Carl. "Schreker and Modernism: On the Dramaturgy of *Der ferne Klang.*" In *Schoenberg and the New Music.* Cambridge, 1987; original German, 1978, as "Schreker und die Moderne: zur Dramaturgie des *Fernen Klangs,*" in *Franz Schreker am Beginn der neuen Musik,* edited by O. Kolleritsch, 9. Graz, 1978.
Franklin, Peter R. "Distant sounds-Fallen music: *Der ferne Klang* as 'woman's opera'?" *Cambridge Opera Journal* 3 (1991): 159.

*   *   *

The considerable success of Franz Schreker's first staged opera, *Der ferne Klang,* nearly ten years in the making, was justified not least by its marriage of German Romanticism with striking elements of theatrical and musical Modernism in a format that was both idealistic and popular. The composer's libretto was criticized for being derivative and lacking in discipline, but its originality and effectiveness on the operatic stage have been demonstrated in a number of revivals in European opera houses since the 1960s. The story of Fritz, the village boy who longs to find "the distant sound" whose artistic expression might bring him fame and fortune, is rooted in the literature of nineteenth-century Romanticism. Closer to the contemporary worlds of Hauptmann and Wedekind, however, is the ultimately more dominant role of Grete, the girl Fritz leaves behind: she escapes her feckless father and runs away in search of Fritz, only to be drawn into prostitution by a grotesque variant of the conventional fairy godmother.

Act II finds Grete the central attraction in a grand bordello near Venice. By chance, Fritz visits the place, recognizes her, but rejects her as a whore. He thus abandons her once again to face the real world while going off to celebrate his fantasy in the opera whose premiere is being given (often audibly; it is *Der ferne Klang* of course) in the nearby theatre during act III, set on an adjoining street with an open-air cafe. Grete, now no more than a sickly street-walker, has been overcome by emotion in the theatre and is brought to the cafe, where a former acquaintance tends to her and offers to take her to Fritz. They are reunited in the final scene, set in Fritz's study, where the ill and dissatisfied composer has already come to realize that the "distant sound" had all along surrounded him in the natural world. Grete herself, as embodiment of that world, arrives in time for a mutual protestation of love before Fritz fails her for the last time by dying in her arms.

Much has been made of the opera's influence on a wide circle of younger composers before the First World War, and it can certainly be viewed as an exemplary compendium of experimental techniques and devices, particularly musical ones (including scales of alternate tones and semitones, whole-tone chords, and a wide vocabulary of both dissonant and consonant chromatic harmony). Schreker seems deliberately to have married a broadly symphonic post-Wagnerian style, employing a rich fund of recurring *leitmotifs,* with a theatrical naturalism, even proto-expressionism, that is closer to the manner of Italian *verismo.* His use of the orchestra went far beyond Wagner, however, in its partly French-inspired concern to achieve a highly nuanced palette of timbres and textures with which to furnish a kind of three-dimensional psychological backdrop to the finely judged melodic arioso of the singers—as in the initial scene, where Schreker provides Fritz and Grete with vocal lines whose natural declamatory rhythms retain a strong melodic identity.

Equally striking, however, is Schreker's daring manipulation of the large ensemble, and his operas typically have dramatically important roles for the chorus. Here the opening of the second act is remarkable for its multi-layer collage of disparate elements: the girls of the bordello beckoning their clients in mysterious siren-voices while "Venetian music" is heard above an apparently independently motivated orchestral underlay of festive bustle, to which is added an on-stage gypsy ensemble (including cimbalom) which Schreker provides with fully-notated improvisational gypsy music of some complexity.

The fundamental sound of Schreker's operas undoubtedly derives from the composer's experiments with richly-varied orchestral sonorities, but it is not enough to brand his style simply as decadent or self-indulgent. The equally collage-like manner in which the music progresses in time—particularly in key orchestral interludes like that in the third act of *Der ferne Klang*—relies upon techniques of spliced and displaced continuity that would become common in later, less tonally-oriented expressionist music. This stream-of-consciousness effect can undermine the grand Romantic rhetoric, which is directly questioned in the work's self-reflexive tendency as focused in the final act: Grete's emotional response to the opera we are watching (whose music is heard sporadically from the off-stage theatre orchestra) here becomes a concrete element in the drama, whose larger theme is the deluding aspect of art-as-wish-fulfillment and the value of a humane, creative response to life.

—Peter Franklin

FERRIER, Kathleen.

Contralto. Born 22 April 1912, in Lancashire. Died 8 October 1953, in London. Studied voice and piano in Blackburn; studied voice with J.E. Hutchinson in Newcastle upon Tyne and with Roy Henderson in London; engaged as a soloist in *Messiah*, Westminster Abbey, 1943; created title role in Britten's *Rape of Lucretia*, Glyndebourne, 1946; also sang Orfeo in Gluck's *Orfeo ed Euridice*, Glyndebourne, 1947, and Covent Garden, 1953; made Commander of the Order of the British Empire, 1953.

Publications

About FERRIER: books–

Cardus, N., ed. *Kathleen Ferrier: a Memoir* [with discography]. London, 1954; revised edition, 1969.
Ferrier, W. *The Life of Kathleen Ferrier.* London, 1955.
Rigby, C. *Kathleen Ferrier: A Biography.* London, 1955.

Kathleen Ferrier

Campion, P. *Ferrier—a Career Recorded* [with discography]. London, 1992.

*   *   *

Kathleen Ferrier is one of those artists (James Dean and John Lennon are others) whose tragic early death makes critical objectivity difficult. She was just over forty when she succumbed to the cancer against which she had fought for some time, and it is hard to hear her recording of Mahler's *Das Lied von der Erde* with its final tearladen repetitions of the German word *ewig* ("forever") without thinking of the dying woman as well as the artist. She apologized for her tears to the conductor Bruno Walter, but he told her that he and his orchestra too would have wept if they had had her nobility and sensitivity, and elsewhere he said of her that it was music of spiritual meaning that seemed her most personal domain. Nevertheless Walter, who also played for her in Lieder recitals, declared too that Ferrier should be remembered "in a major key." Despite an unhappy early marriage hers was not a sad life. Her unsophisticated Lancashire background, from which she emerged as a solo singer during her late twenties, gave her a practical attitude to life and she never ceased to find a provincial's excitement in her success in opera and the concert hall.

At the end of the Second World War Ferrier was known mainly as an oratorio singer, not at all in opera. Benjamin Britten heard and liked her in Bach, and Britten and his librettist Ronald Duncan gave her her first really big chance by choosing her for the title role in *The Rape of Lucretia* after auditioning her in Britten's London flat: this, Duncan later said, was a Lucretia who was not only vocally right but also had the "genuine feeling of purity" necessary for the role. The premiere at Glyndebourne, her memorable operatic debut, led to her recognition as a singing actress of real presence and power, but her stage appearances remained limited. She never played in nineteenth-century romantic opera, for which her voice and personality seem to have been thought unsuited—though we cannot be certain that she lacked the dramatic versatility to take on a wholly different kind of role such as Dalila in Saint-Saëns' *Samson et Dalila,* for which the mezzo register would have presented her with no difficulty. However, her only other operatic role besides that of Lucretia was that of Orpheus in Gluck's *Orfeo,* again a work where both music and story demanded an evident nobility of soul from the protagonist. She performed *Orfeo* at Glyndebourne and in Holland, and then in London with Sir John Barbirolli, another conductor who could draw from her her best work, as he did in the music of the Angel in Elgar's oratorio *The Dream of Gerontius.* It was in *Orfeo* that she made her last stage appearances before her illness forced her to cancel the remaining scheduled performances.

The critic Neville Cardus called Ferrier Britain's "only one truly great singer since the war," but this seems too great a claim when one considers such other names as Peter Pears and Janet Baker. (To the public, Baker seemed Ferrier's successor, and Britten chose her also to play Lucretia in a recording of his opera.) Her voice was full and rich, and a laryngologist who examined her is said to have found her throat a perfect example of vocal architecture. But not everyone cared for it, and one critic called her "this goitrous singer with the contralto hoot," a comment which she took with humor and quoted to friends. There was a certain heaviness about the Ferrier sound and the way she used her voice, and there was a self-conscious provinciality about her perform-ances of English folk songs such as "Blow the Wind South-erly," although there was also an attractive warmth and some humour. Her repertory was limited compared to that of most singers, though what she sang was usually memorable and in Mahler's rich autumnal moods she was unequalled. She left few recordings, but some private or semi-private ones have surfaced since her death. One such is of Lennox Berkeley's *Four Poems of St. Teresa of Avila,* a work written for her in which her spiritual quality was to the fore, just as it was in the canticle *Abraham and Isaac* that Britten composed for her and Peter Pears. She did not record the Handel and Bach oratorios to which she also brought a telling dramatic quality, and we only have her as Lucretia in part of a performance recovered from a broadcast.

—Christopher Headington

FERVAAL.

Composer: Vincent d'Indy.

Librettist: Vincent d'Indy (after Esaïas Tegner, *Axel*).

First Performance: Brussels, Théâtre de la Monnaie, 12 March 1897.

Roles: Fervaal (tenor); Arfagard (baritone); Guilhen (mezzo-soprano); Kaïto (contralto); Lennsmor (tenor); Grympuig (bass); Edwig (tenor); Chennos (tenor); Ilbert (tenor); Fer-kemnat (tenor); Gwell Kingubar (bass); Geywhir (bass); Ber-ddret (bass); Penvald (bass); Helwrig (bass); Buduann (bass); Moussah (tenor); a shepherd (tenor); a messenger (baritone); a bard (tenor); five peasants (two tenors, three basses); two Saracen peasants (tenor, bass); four Gallic priests (two tenors, two basses).

Publications

books–

Destranges, E. *Fervaal.* Paris, 1896.
Bréville, P. de and H. Gauthier-Villars. *Fervaal: étude ana-lytique et thématique.* Paris, 1897.

articles–

Kufferath, M. "Fervaal." *Rivista musicale italiana* 4 (1897): 313.
Lalo, P. "Fervaal et la musique française." *Revue de Paris* 15 May 1898.
Ravel, Maurice. "Fervaal—poème et musique de Vincent d'Indy." *Comoedia illustre* 5/20 January (1913): 361.

*　　*　　*

During the last decades of the nineteenth century, Wagner was practically a code word in France for everything that was daring and new. Avant-garde composers like Vincent d'Indy flocked to Bayreuth to hear Wagner's operas and found in them the key to their own works. D'Indy's *Fervaal* is one such French opera cast in the Wagnerian mold. Its

resemblance to *Parsifal,* in particular, is so striking that it has been dubbed the "French *Parsifal.*" Yet this label is somewhat misleading; though *Fervaal* does derive from *Parsifal,* it is also a vehicle for d'Indy's personal musical style and religious beliefs.

D'Indy's source for the libretto was Esaïas Tegner's poem, *Axel,* which is about a chaste and brave Swedish soldier who is torn between his love for a beautiful woman and his career. The struggle between love and duty remains intact in *Fervaal,* but the action in this three-act opera takes place on French soil during the time of the medieval Crusades.

The protagonist, Fervaal (whose name means "Free Choice"), is the last descendant of the leaders of Cravann, a Celtic-like region in the mountains of Cévennes. When the opera begins, he is attacked and wounded by a group of peasants in southern France; it is Guilhen, the beautiful daughter of a Saracen emir, who nurses him back to health. They fall madly in love, but an old Celtic druid named Arfa-gard reminds Fervaal of his oath of chastity to the pagan gods. Fervaal quickly abandons Guilhen, who then plots revenge by directing the Saracen army north to Cravann. A bloody battle ensues and Fervaal's army is crushed.

In the final act, Fervaal intends to sacrifice himself to the gods and asks Arfagard to kill him. At the crucial moment, Guilhen calls out to Fervaal and begs forgiveness. Once again, Arfagard interferes and tries to separate the two lovers, but this time Fervaal slays him and then rushes headlong into Guilhen's arms. As she lies dying from the cold mountainous climate, Guilhen reveals her own destiny, namely that her love was intended to give Fervaal a new life by liberating his once-enslaved soul and by offering him the gift of choice. The opera ends with Fervaal carrying the body of Guilhen up the mountain and into the clouds while a heavenly chorus sings the medieval chant for Good Friday, the *Pange lingua.*

As is all too clear, many aspects of the plot are straight out of *Parsifal.* The quasi-mythic context, Fervaal's injury and subsequent recovery under Guilhen's care, his oath of chas-tity, the extraordinary setting of the *Pange lingua*—these are just a few of the derivative aspects of the story line. Even some of the main conflicts and ideas in *Fervaal*— such as the triumph of Christianity over paganism, redemption through death, and rebirth through love—are familiar Wagnerian sub-jects. In *Parsifal,* however, the hero rejects his lover, Kundry, whereas in *Fervaal* the exact opposite is true: the hero ulti-mately chooses his lover. Herein lies the most important difference between the two operas: the goal in *Parsifal* is renunciation, whereas the goals in *Fervaal* are love, forgive-ness and, of course, free choice. One can't help but think that d'Indy, who was a strict Catholic, was trying to inject some of his own religious beliefs into his libretto and, in so doing, constructed a late nineteenth-century version of a medieval morality play.

D'Indy also looked to Wagner for the musical techniques and structures that would hold his opera together. Like Wagner, he uses leitmotifs and tonalities to symbolize specific characters, emotions, and situations. The key of F major is reserved for Guilhen, A-flat major is symbolic of the birth of love, love is either F-sharp or G-flat major, and so on. Fur-ther, both composers constructed tightly-knit symmetrical designs that span the entirety of their operas, with the third acts representing a reworking of the material of the first, and the middle acts serving as a contrasting unit.

D'Indy's harmonic language and his treatment of the vocal line and orchestra are much more personal. Though both he and Wagner employ mammoth orchestral forces, d'Indy never allows his orchestra to overpower the singers, whereas Wagner does. For d'Indy, the instructive messages of the text were all-important. The fact that he nearly always restricts the melodies to the vocal parts also draws attention to the singers' words rather than to the orchestra. As for the harmonic vocabulary, both Wagner and d'Indy favor a continuous stream of chromatic harmonies, but d'Indy ventures much further. In one scene, where the oracle Kaïto is summoned, he uses harmonies based on the whole-tone scale, a particularly effective move since the lack of tonal focus inherent in whole-tone chords wonderfully conveys the strange, mysterious world of the supernatural.

The 1897 premiere of *Fervaal* was an immediate success. Many contemporary critics admired d'Indy's superb craftsmanship and considered his work to be strikingly innovative. By the time *Fervaal* had its premiere at the Paris Opera shortly before World War I, however, the prevailing musical style had changed. Ravel and Stravinsky were all the rage, and there was a violent backlash against anything Germanic. Understandably, d'Indy, who wore his debt to Wagner on his sleeve, was seen in many fashionable circles as a throwback to an earlier period and his music no longer relevant.

Today, *Fervaal* is remembered as an important and serious achievement by one of the leading French Wagnerians of the *fin de siècle*. In his zeal to incorporate Wagner's thought and musical techniques, d'Indy went overboard, and much of the opera sounds forced and contrived. We do get glimpses of what it might have been, such as in the prelude to act I, where everything we hear flows smoothly and easily into everything else. Nonetheless, the overall impression is of rigidity, and it is precisely this lack of spontaneity that is the crowning irony in an epic tale of passion and freedom.

—Teresa Davidian

FEUERSNOT [Fire Famine; St John's Eve].

Composer: Richard Strauss.

Librettist: H. von Wolzogen.

First Performance: Dresden, Court Opera, 21 November 1901.

Roles: Schweiker von Gundelfingen (tenor); Ortolf Sentlinger (bass); Diemut (soprano); Margret (soprano); Elsbeth (mezzo-soprano); Wigelis (contralto); Kunrad (baritone); Jor Poschel (bass); Hamerlein (baritone); Kofel (bass); Kunz Gilgenstock (bass); Ortlieb Tulbeck (tenor); Ursula (contralto); Ruger Aspeck (tenor); Walpurg (soprano); chorus (SATB).

Publications

book–

Schultz, K. and S. Kohler, eds. *Richard Strauss: "Feuersnot"*. Munich, 1980.

*   *   *

The librettist for *Feuersnot* was a young German poet later famed for his cabaret verses, Hans von Wolzogen. He found his inspiration in a medieval Dutch story, but prudently jettisoned some of the more salacious details and transfered events

to his and Strauss' own Munich, casting the text in a broad (and often untranslatable) Bavarian dialect. Simultaneously (and with Strauss' connivance), he manipulated the situation in order to both make a polemic comment on the shabby way the town had treated Richard Wagner in the previous century and to create a hymn to the power of all-conquering love (read: sex).

Feuersnot, the first of Strauss' many stage works to be written in the form of a longish single act, is set in a medieval Munich of fairy tale ambience. The title is difficult to render gracefully into English; while it has sometimes appeared as "Fire Famine," it might be literally rendered as "Fire's Need." We find ourselves in a moondrenched street on Midsummer Eve, similar in atmosphere to the second act of Wagner's *Die Meistersinger*. It was (and still is) the custom in the area to light huge solstice bonfires over which young couples were supposed to leap in what must be the remnants of an ancient fertility ritual. To that end a crowd of raucous and nervy children are collecting firewood from door to door. To one side is the home of the mayor and his beautiful daughter Diemut, on the other the dwelling once occupied by a great sorcerer, Meister Reichardt (i.e., Wagner). Despite his many good works the sorcerer was driven from town by a group of petty citizens, and the house is now occupied by his darkly handsome yet moody young apprentice, Kunrad (Strauss). When the youngsters knock on Kunrad's door, he is startled by the news that it is solstice eve, but rapidly enters the festive mood proclaiming that books and study must yield to the ardent glow of desire in order for life to be fully tasted. His own eye falls on Diemut, who rather coldly spurns him, even as a few of the more small-minded townspeople have chattered darkly on his reputedly evil ways. Diemut, who feels that she has been insulted and compromised by Kunrad's admittedly rather brazen declarations of love, quickly finds the means of revenge. Her house is equipped with a basket rigged to a winch and used to haul provisions to the upper stories. Thus when the street empties, she appears high on a balcony and encourages Kunrad's lovemaking. At her urging he climbs in the basket which she purposefully hauls only half way up, leaving him literally hanging to the mockery of those who have surreptitiously returned to the street below.

In the ensuing darkness Kunrad inexplicably materializes on the balcony and, calling on his old master's sorcery, extinguishes every fire in the city, plunging all into a terrified "Feuersnot." Thus he is avenged both for Diemut's cruelty and his master's ostracism, and in a lengthy solo riddled with both verbal and musical puns (allusions to Wagner, Strauss, and even Wolzogen himself) he iterates the shortcomings of the citizenry, with emphasis on Diemut's failure to respond to the fire of true love. He concludes with the opera's moral: "All' Wärme quillt vom Weibe, all' Licht vom Liebe stammt, aus heiss-jungfraulichem Leibe einzig das Feuer Euch neu entflammt!" (All warmth comes from woman, all light stems from love, only from the body of a warm young virgin shall your fire flame up anew!). The terrified crowd urges Diemut to capitulate and in total darkness Strauss begins his orchestrally graphic depiction of those (offstage) events which will end Munich's flameless predicament. At the climax every fire in town bursts into spectacular life, and the chorus intones a jingle which had been heard earlier in an innocent context but which is now overlaid with new meaning: "Imma, Ursel, Lisaweth, alle Mädeln mögen Meth!" (Roughly: Every maiden on the street has a taste for something sweet).

The score is one of protean inventiveness, yet (especially in the first third of the opera) Strauss is so concerned with textual clarity that the opera seems to go in fits and starts. Also, Kunrad's overlong solo has lost its timeliness and the result is labored. These factors, plus the terribly difficult music assigned the children's chorus, make repertoire status unlikely. On the other hand, the erotic interlude, first of many such in the Straussian stage works, is also one of the finest and has become a welcome concert item. In Kunrad the composer has created his first great baritone romantic hero, and much of the love music has the ardent glow one expects of Strauss.

Feuersnot was Strauss' first opera (after the ill-fated *Guntram*) to enjoy even a modicum of success. While it is far too topical ever to rival his next stage work (*Salome*) in popular appeal, the opera nonetheless contains more than its share of wit, charm and unabashed erotic effusion, and will assuredly continue to hover on the fringes of the Straussian canon as worthy festival fare.

—Dennis Wakeling

LA FIDA NINFA [The Faithful Nymph].

Composer: Antonio Vivaldi.

Librettist: S. Maffei.

First Performance: Verona, Filarmonico, 6 January 1732; revised as *Il giorno felice,* Venice, 1737 [lost].

Roles: Oralto (bass); Narete (tenor); Licori (soprano); Elpina (contralto); Morasto (soprano); Osmino (contralto); Giunone (contralto); Eolo (bass).

Publications

article–

Muraro, Maria T. and Elena Povoledo. "Le scene della *Fida ninfa:* Scipione Maffei, Vivaldi, e Francesco Bibiena." In *Studi di musica veneta,* edited by Francesco Degrada, 235. Florence, 1980.

*   *   *

Between 1712 and 1715 the celebrated Bolognese architect Francesco Bibiena designed for the Accademia Filarmonica of Verona an imposing theater conceived along classical lines, the Teatro Filarmonico. Its building took several years, and the official inauguration was planned for May 1730. The academicians entrusted the libretto of the opening work to one of their members, the eminent scholar and man of letters Scipione Maffei. Maffei decided not to write an entirely new text but to revise *La fida ninfa,* a pastoral drama that he had written as a young man in 1694. The music was entrusted to the Florentine composer Giuseppe Maria Orlandini, who came to Verona to work on the score under Maffei's supervision.

For reasons that are still unclear, the scheduled production of *La fida ninfa* was prohibited by the Venetian state and the work was not heard until carnival 1732 (probably in late January or February), by which time—again in obscure circumstances—Vivaldi had replaced Orlandini as composer. Shortly after the cancelation of the 1730 performance, Maffei published *La fida ninfa* together with his two other stage

works. A preface to the volume by his colleague Giulio Cesare Beccelli comments on the dramaturgical ideas behind the pastoral work. Two points are of direct relevance to Vivaldi's musical setting. Obviously echoing Maffei himself, Beccelli notes that each of the three acts (not merely the last act as was customary at the time) ends with an ensemble and that several of the arias are positioned in the middle of a scene rather than at the end, which makes them best suited to a brief setting without the conventional *da capo.*

The inspiration for operatic works in the pastoral genre can be found in sixteenth-century classics such as Tasso's *Aminta,* where tragedy is skirted rather than confronted directly and the general tone is light-hearted and amorous. Maffei adds a slightly extraneous element derived from the ordinary *dramma per musica* by introducing the character Oralto, a corsair who has made himself lord of the Aegean island of Naxos. When the action begins, Oralto has just captured and brought back to Naxos a shepherd from the island of Scyros, Narete, together with his daughters Licori and Elpina. Oralto's lieutenant Morasto recognizes Licori as his old betrothed; he too comes from Scyros, although he has been captured "at second hand" by the corsair after having first been taken to Thrace by raiding soldiers. Morasto's original name, which is how Licori remembers him, is Osmino, but there is another Osmino on the island already. The plot develops along several lines: Morasto's decision not to reveal his identity to Licori immediately in order to test her fidelity; Licori's confusion of Tirsi-Osmino with her original sweetheart; Elpina's flirtation with both brothers; Oralto's unrequited passion for Licori. Eventually, all confusions are resolved and the five natives of Scyros escape from Naxos by sea, having tricked Oralto into departing on a new expedition in the belief that Licori has drowned herself. A storm appears to block their way, but a prayer to Juno (Giunone) brings the goddess herself onto the stage; she persuades Aeolus (Eolo) to calm the winds so that the five can regain their homeland.

The poetic quality of Maffei's libretto is high, particularly in the carefully structured recitatives. However, the dramatic structure is not without its defects. The passion of Oralto for Licori is not integrated thoroughly enough into the main plot and is too easily resolved by his convenient departure. The storm and its quelling by Juno and Aeolus (not present in Maffei's original version) form a too obviously artificial appendage to the drama.

Rather untypically for him, Vivaldi, whose autograph score of *La fida ninfa* is preserved in the Biblioteca Nazionale of Turin, set the libretto exactly in the form in which it was presented to him. The possible problems of discrepancies between the underlaid text in the score and the libretto text or of alternative versions relating to different productions are therefore non-existent. He took Beccelli's hint by casting no fewer than eight of the twenty-seven solo arias in a non-*da capo* form and lavished particular care on the terzet ending act I, the quartet ending act II and the pair of choruses at the end of act III. The terzet, which comments on the revolving wheel of fate, has an appropriately contrapuntal texture; Vivaldi seems to have based it on a movement from a setting of the psalm *Confitebor tibi Domine* preserved among the manuscripts of his sacred music. Not all the solo arias are of the same high quality, but they include memorable numbers with symphonically worked accompaniments (e.g., Licori's "Alma oppressa da sorte crudele" in act I, scene ix) or brilliant coloratura writing (e.g., Morasto's "Fra inospite rupi" in act III, scene xi, in a tempo marked "Allegro molto più che si può"—an "impossibly fast" speed!). With one brief exception (Juno's invocation to Aeolus), all the recitatives are of the simple type with a plain continuo accompaniment, but they are sensitively wrought and certainly do not deserve to be cut on musical grounds. Vivaldi's skill as a composer of purely instrumental music is exploited in three numbers towards the end: a symphony preceding Juno's appearance that depicts a storm at sea, assembled from the material of at least three concertos including *La tempesta di mare* from Op. 8, another symphony to introduce the realm of Aeolus that bears more than a passing resemblance to the "Spring" concerto from *The Four Seasons,* and a graceful minuet for the calming of the winds.

Periodic modern revivals since 1958 have shown that *La fida ninfa* is one of Vivaldi's operas best suited to a staged or concert performance today. The differentiation between the "star" (Licori and Morasto), "intermediate" (Oralto and Elpina) and "minor" (Narete and Osmino) roles is not as extreme as in many late baroque operas, and there is plenty of variety in the scoring, style, and form of the music. The roles of Juno and Aeolus can easily be taken—as they seem to have been at the original performance in Verona—by the appropriate singers in the main cast. The autograph score lacks the opening quire containing the overture (since overtures were unconnected thematically with the rest of the opera, they were often "borrowed" from one work for another and never returned), but it is easy to find a suitable three-movement work among Vivaldi's numerous sinfonias and concertos; alternatively, the sinfonia to his later pasticcio-opera *Tamerlano,* which is in the right key (F major) and has parts for two horns just like the storm sinfonia in act III, will serve excellently.

—Michael Talbot

FIDELIO, oder Die eheliche Liebe [Fidelio, or Conjugal Love].

Composer: Ludwig van Beethoven.

Librettist: J. Sonnleithner (after J.N. Bouilly, *Léonore ou L'amour conjugal*).

First Performance: Vienna, Theater an der Wien, 20 November 1805; revised 1805-06, Vienna, Theater an der Wien, 29 March 1806; revised 1814, Vienna, Kärntnertor, 23 May 1814.

Roles: Florestan (tenor); Leonore (soprano); Don Pizarro (bass-baritone); Rocco (bass); Marzeline (soprano); Jaquino (tenor); Don Fernando (bass); chorus (SATTBB).

Publications

books—

Kufferath, M. *Fidelio de L. van Beethoven.* Paris, 1913.
Hess, W. *Beethovens Oper Fidelio und ihre drei Fassungen.* Zurich, 1953.
———. *Beethovens Bühnenwerke.* Göttingen, 1962.
Pahlen, Kurt. *Ludwig van Beethoven—"Fidelio" Ein Opernführer.* Munich, 1978.
Csampai, Attila, and Dietmar Holland, eds. *Ludwig van Beethoven. "Fidelio." Texte, Materialien, Kommentare.* Reinbek bei Hamburg, 1981.
Mayer, Hans. *Versuch über die Oper.* Frankfurt am Main, 1981.

John, Nicholas, ed. *Ludwig van Beethoven. "Fidelio." English National Opera Guides* 4. London, 1988.

articles—

Schiederman, L. "Über Beethovens 'Lenore'." *Zeitschrift der Internationalen Musik-Gesellschaft* 8 (1906-07): 115.
Engländer, R. "Paers *Lenora* und Beethovens *Fidelio.*" *Neues Beethoven-Jahrbuch* 4 (1930): 118.
Anderson, Emily. "Beethoven's Operatic Plans." *Proceedings of the Royal Musical Association* 88 (1961-62): 61.
Dean, Winton. "Beethoven and Opera." In *The Beethoven Companion,* edited by Denis Arnold and Nigel Fortune, 374. London, 1971.
Ruhnke, Martin. "Die Librettisten des *Fidelio.*" In *Opernstudien: Anna Amalie Abert zum 65. Geburtstag.* 121. Tutzing, 1975.
Tyson, Alan. "The Problem of Beethoven's 'First' *Lenore* Overture." *Journal of the American Musicological Society* 28 (1975): 292.
———. "Das Leonoreskizzenbuch (Mendelssohn 15): Probleme der Rekonstruktion und der Chronologie." *Beethoven-Jahrbuch* (1977): 469.
Avant-scène opéra May-June (1977) [*Fidelio* issue].
Tyson, Alan. "Yet Another 'Leonore' Overture?" *Music and Letters* 58 (1977): 192.
Pulkert, Oldrich. "Die Partitur der zweiten Fassung von Beethovens Oper *Lenore* im Musikarchiv des Nationaltheaters in Prag." In *Bericht über dem Internationalen Beethoven-Kongress 20,* edited by Harry Goldschmidt, Karl-Heinz Kohler, and Konrad Niemann, 247. Leipzig, 1978.
Carner, Mosco. "Fidelio." In *Major and minor* [a collection of essays by Carner]. London, 1980.
Schuler, Manfred. "Zwei unbekannte *Fidelio*-Partiturabschriften aus dem Jahre 1814." *Archiv für Musikwissenschaft* 39 (1982): 151.
Wagner, Manfred. "Rocco, Beethovens Zeichnung eines Funktionärs." *Österreichische Musikzeitschrift* 37 (1982): 369.
Gossett, Philip. "The arias of Marzelline: Beethoven as a Composer of Opera." *Beethoven-Jahrbuch* 10 (1983): 141.
Pulkert, Oldrich. "Historische Aspekte des Fidelio-Subjekts." In *Ars jocundissimo: Festschrift für Kurt Dorfmüller zum 60. Geburtstag,* edited by Horst Leuchtmann and Robert Münster, 257. Tutzing, 1984.
Robinson, Paul. "*Fidelio* and the French Revolution." *Cambridge Opera Journal* 3 (1991): 23.

*   *   *

Although the story of Beethoven's only completed opera is based on a 1798 French libretto by Jean-Nicolas Bouilly (set to music by Pierre Gaveaux and subsequently by two Italians, Ferdinando Paer in 1804 and Simone Mayr in 1805), Beethoven's interest in that story may be traced to his arguably larger fondness for a subcategory of operatic entertainment immensely popular with French audiences for some two decades following the French Revolution: the "rescue opera." More often than not such works were based on actual historical incident, the plot typically centering on a comparatively defenseless person who challenges the unjust use of power and ancient privilege on the part of another, one moreover who not only defies that power but triumphs over it in the end. But what saves the victim is the strength and ingenuity of another, prompted into action by the conviction of his or her personal feelings—variously love, compassion, gratitude

Fidelio, **English National Opera, 1980**

or loyalty. Indeed, Beethoven's admiration for such operas—and for French opera in general—was very great. Of the master of the genre, Luigi Cherubini, he declared as late as 1823: "I value your works more highly than all other compositions for the theater"; elsewhere we know that Beethoven considered Cherubini the greatest living composer. As it happens, Cherubini was to a large extent the originator of the "rescue opera" as well, having brought out *Lodoïska* in 1791, *Eliza* in 1794, and *Les deux journées* in 1800, each one involving the deliverance of an individual from some injustice. And when *Lodoïska* and *Les deux journées* arrived in the Austrian capital in 1802, Beethoven, like the rest of Vienna, must have been startled by the sureness of technique and contemporary realism expressed in both works, traits worlds removed from the conservatism of most Viennese operas.

The rescue opera in general together with the story of *Fidelio* seem fated to have appealed to Beethoven, who held fast to the Enlightenment ideals of a benevolent social order devoted to spiritual and physical freedom as well as to secular reform. True to most of the details of Bouilly's libretto, Beethoven and his librettist Joseph Sonnleithner concerned themselves with an account of how the brave wife Leonore disguises herself as a man—thereby assuming the name Fidelio—in order to rescue her husband Florestan from the dungeon of the tyrant Pizaro. While the story is set in Spain, the plot nevertheless was drawn from a true event that had taken place in France during the Reign of Terror, a period of particular cruelty in the first turbulent days of the French Revolution.

Yet for all Beethoven's devotion to the subject, in the end he would see the opera through three separate versions and four different overtures over a period of ten years. (Stephan von Breuning was called in as librettist for the 1806 version, Georg Frierich Treitschke for that of 1814.) In the event, the premiere in 1805 was less than encouraging given that a great many of the composer's friends, as well as most of the aristocracy, had fled Vienna in the wake of Napoleon's occupation of the city; after only three performances the opera was withdrawn. The critics were decidedly unenthusiastic. The few friends of Beethoven's who did hear the work urged that it be severely revised, particularly the first act, which was judged too long and static. Thus Beethoven and Breuning combined acts one and two (reducing the work from the original three acts to two), condensed several numbers and removed others. The 1806 version was performed twice but again failed to find favor. Profoundly disappointed, Beethoven accused the theater management of having cheated him and angrily withdrew the work with the remark: "I don't write for the galleries!" Following an eight-year hiatus, he was induced to take up the opera a third time when he learned three singers wished to revive it. Insisting on still further changes, he wrote his third and final librettist Treitschke: "I could compose something new far more quickly than patch up the old. . . . I have to think out the entire work again. . . . This opera will win for me a martyr's crown. If you had not given yourself so much pains with it and revised everything so successfully . . . I would scarcely have been able to bring myself to it. You have thereby saved some good remainders of a ship that was stranded." The outcome, especially in the first act, was well worth the toil, a point reflected on the one hand in the success accorded the 1814 version and, on the other, in the fact that it is in this version most listeners know the opera today. (Nevertheless, as revivals have convincingly shown, the 1805 version is not the slight work it is oftentimes claimed; in fact, for many listeners—especially scholars and critics—it expresses individuality of character far better than do the subsequent versions.) If the opera (i.e., the 1814 version) has not become a repertory staple, it is not because it is musically or dramatically ineffectual (far from it), but rather because it lies outside the norm of operatic tradition. *Fidelio* is an exceptional work, one in which character delineation is secondary to the larger goal of addressing a philosophical ideal: namely faith in the nobility of the human spirit and the unswerving conviction that good will triumph over evil.

As for the various overtures Beethoven supplied for the opera, *Leonore* no. 2 was composed for the November 1805 premiere while *Leonore* no. 3 was written for the 1806 revival. The misleadingly-entitled *Leonore* no. 1 was composed in 1807 for a hoped-for yet never realized performance of the opera in Prague. The *Fidelio* overture dates from the 1814 version. The practice of performing *Leonore* no. 3 between the two scenes of act II was inaugurated by Gustav Mahler and followed by Toscanini and Klemperer as well as many other conductors.

—James Parsons

FIDELITY REWARDED
See LA FEDELTÀ PREMIATA

FIERABRAS.

Composer: Franz Schubert.

Librettist: J. Kupelwieser.

First Performance: Karlsruhe, 9 February 1897.

Roles: Fierabras (tenor); Charlemagne (bass); Emma (soprano); Roland (baritone); Eginhard (tenor); Boland (bass); Florinda (soprano); Maragond (soprano); Brutamonte (bass); chorus.

Publications

articles–

Brown, M.J.E. "Schubert's *Fierabras*." *Musical Times* 112 (1971): 338.
Dieckmann, Friedrich. "*Fidelios* Erben: *Fierabras* und das biedermeierliche Bewusstsein." *Oper heute* 8 (1985): 77.
Thomas, Werner. "Bild und Aktion in *Fierabras:* ein Beitrag zu Schuberts musikalischer Dramaturgie." In *Franz Schubert: Jahre der Krise, 1818-1823. Arnold Feil zum 60. Geburtstag,* edited by W. Aderhold et al., 85. Kassel, 1985.

*　　*　　*

Fierabras, a Moorish prince, is taken captive by Charlemagne's knights. After converting to Christianity, he is given the freedom of the castle. He loves the king's daughter Emma, having met her years before in Rome. Likewise, Roland, the king's son, and the Moorish princess Florinda, pine for each other. Eginhard, a poor young knight, and Emma are secretly in love. To protect them, Fierabras pretends to have wooed Emma, and is imprisoned. The knights ride to conquer the Moors. First Eginhard and then the others are taken prisoner. Florinda recognizes Roland and supplies the imprisoned knights with arms. Roland is taken prisoner again. Eginhard, who has escaped, mobilizes Charlemagne's forces, who rescue Roland in the nick of time. The pairs of lovers are united, Fierabras becomes a French warrior, and the Moorish king converts.

Schubert's last completed opera was not performed until 1897, though it was scheduled to go into rehearsal shortly after its completion in 1823. Had the composer been given the opportunity to make adjustments during rehearsals, the work might have become his operatic breakthrough and a milestone in German Romantic opera; instead, it effectively marked the end of Schubert's operatic career.

Fierabras is a Singspiel in the grand manner. Its heroic subject is treated with dramatic scenes, melodramas (i.e., words spoken over musical accompaniment), and the usual arias, choruses, and spoken dialogue. Only two of the roles receive any notable amount of characterization; the rest are either stock figures or lack sufficient motivation. Florinda begins by pining for her lover; when she sees him taken captive by her father, she acts quickly and heroically. Eginhard, on the other hand, grows from being a shy, indecisive young lover to a hero. The title role is the most perplexing one. Fierabras willingly gives up his religion, his family, and finally the object of his affections out of sheer nobility of spirit; and his role in the drama is largely passive. He is little more than a device to set the plot in motion and allow the other characters to portray themselves.

Schubert, never a great dramatist, achieves mixed success in setting the unwieldy libretto. Sometimes he produces genuine dramatic excitement, as in the second and third scenes of act II. In the second scene, after a quintet with trio and double male chorus, in which the Moors take the knights captive while Florinda prays for mercy for her beloved while her father rages, she ends the scene alone with a bravura aria (over an orchestra that uses a full complement of nine brass instruments), expressing her rage and determination. The climactic battle scene at the end of the act is a melodrama. We do not see the battle; instead, Florinda looks out of the tower and describes the action. She faints as the knights burst in and announce Roland's capture.

But other parts of the opera are far less effective. Act I presents the convoluted situation, but consists mainly of setpieces that neither further the action nor illuminate any more than the most obvious features of the characters. Only the secret love of Eginhard and Emma, and Fierabras' nobility in assisting them, rise above the dramatically routine. In act III, on the other hand, the drama is concluded so rapidly, with so many threads being tied up one after another in the short finale, that credibility and proportion are lost. Schubert was probably under pressure to finish this act in order to have the work considered for a performance that never came.

—Roger L. Lustig

THE FIERY ANGEL [Ognennïy angel].

Composer: Sergei Prokofiev.

Librettist: Sergei Prokofiev (after V. Bryusov).

First Performance: act II concert performance, Paris, 14 June 1928; complete concert performance, Paris, Champs-Elysées, 25 November 1954; staged, Venice, La Fenice, 14 September 1955.

Roles: Ruprecht (baritone); Renata (soprano); Mephistopheles (tenor); Faust (baritone); Innkeeper (mezzo-soprano); Fortune-teller (soprano); Jacob Glock (tenor); Agrippa (tenor); The Inquisitor (bass); Laborer/Matthew (mute); Abbess (mute); Physician (mute); Innkeeper (mute); Count Heinrich (mute); chorus (SATB).

Publications

articles–

Bruch, C. " 'Ognennïy angel' Parizhe." *Sovetskaya muzïka* no. 7 (1955).

Swarenki, H. "Prokofiev's *The Flaming Angel.*" *Tempo* 39 (1956): 16.

Jefferson, A. "The Angel of Fire." *Music and Musicians* 13 (1965): 32.

McAllister, R. "Natural and Supernatural in *The Fiery Angel.*" *Musical Times* 111 (1970): 785.

*   *   *

The Fiery Angel was written in the period 1919-1923. Based on a novel by the Russian Symbolist writer Valery Bryusov (published in 1907), the opera in its original form consisted of three acts and eleven scenes, though Prokofiev subsequently altered this to five acts and seven scenes. Though some parts of the opera were performed at a concert conducted by Koussevitsky in Paris in 1929, the first complete performance did not take place until 25 November 1954, when it was given at the Théâtre des Champs-Elysées under Charles Bruck. The full stage premiere occurred at the Venice Festival in 1955.

The action of *The Fiery Angel* is set in sixteenth-century Germany. In act I Ruprecht, a wandering knight, takes a room at an inn, but is disturbed by a woman's cries in the next room. Her agitation is so great that Ruprecht breaks down the door and discovers a young girl, Renata. Ruprecht calms her and she tells him her story: since childhood she has been in love with an angel, Madiel, who encouraged her to do good deeds. When she was seventeen, however, she asked him to love her physically, upon which the angel glowed in anger but finally promised to return in human

Set design by L. Damiani for the premiere of Prokofiev's *The Fiery Angel*, Venice, 1955

form. Renata met Count Heinrich von Otterheim, whom she believed to be the angel, and they lived together for a year before he left her. Since then she has searched for the Count without success, and she begs Ruprecht to help her find him.

In act II Renata and Ruprecht are in Cologne. Ruprecht has fallen in love with Renata, who, still infatuated with Heinrich, repels his advances. They attempt to invoke Heinrich's spirit by means of sorcery, but though three knocks are heard (the thought that it is Heinrich excites Renata to the point of hysteria), there is no one there. Ruprecht decides to consult the famous magician, Agrippa von Nettesheim, and, following a short orchestral interlude, Ruprecht finds himself in the necromancer's room. Agrippa, fearing the power of the Inquisition, will not help Ruprecht.

In act III Ruprecht returns to discover that Renata has found Heinrich, who has spurned her; she pleads with Ruprecht to avenge her. Heinrich is not Madiel, she says, but an impostor. The hapless Ruprecht fights an impossible duel with Heinrich and is severely wounded. In act IV Ruprecht has almost recovered and is living with Renata, who tells him that she must enter a convent in order to save her soul. At this point Faust and Mephistopheles enter and provide a bizarre comic scene (which is sometimes cut). In the final act Renata is in the convent, where she is accused of being possessed by the devil and brought before the Inquisitor. In a scene of indescribable frenzy, perhaps unparalleled in opera, the nuns are possessed and Renata is condemned by the Inquisitor to be burnt at the stake.

The fact that Prokofiev devoted so much time to composing *The Fiery Angel* suggests that the theme had a special fascination for him. *The Fiery Angel* is a brilliant, enigmatic, psychological study in which the theme of erotic schizophrenia is enhanced by orchestral music that is strident, dissonant, energetic and vital.

—Gerald Seaman

FIGNER, MEDEA
  See MEI-FIGNER, MEDEA

FIGNER, Nikolay Nikolayevich.

Tenor. Born 21 February 1857, in Nikiforovka, near Kazan. Died 13 December 1918, near Kiev. Married soprano Medea Mei in 1889 (divorced 1904). Studied at St Petersburg Conservatory and with Lamperti in Italy; debut in Gounod's *Philémon et Baucis,* Teatro Sannazaro in Naples, 1882; sang in Latin America in 1884 and 1886; sang Raoul in *Les Huguenots* at Imperial Opera, St Petersburg, 1887; Covent Garden debut as Duke in *Rigoletto,* 1887; joined Imperial Opera, 1887-1904; director and soloist with Narodniy Dom Opera, 1910-15; from 1915 taught singing.

Publications

About FIGNER: books—

Figner, M. *Moi vaspominaniya* [My memories]. St Petersburg, 1912.
Levik, S. Yu. *Zapiski opernovo pevtsa* [Notes of an opera singer]. Moscow, 1955; 1962.
Yankovsky, M., ed. *Figner vospominaniya, pis'ma, materialï* [Recollections, correspondence, material]. Leningrad, 1968.

articles—

Yankovsky, M. O., James Dennis, and Boris Semeonoff. "Nikolai N. Figner." *Record Collector* 35 no. 1-2 (1990): 2.

*   *   *

Nikolay Nikolayevich Figner was the leading tenor of Imperial Russia a generation before the rise of Erschov, Sobinov, Labinsky, and Davidov. Arriving on the scene at a time when Russia was flooded with touring artists, Figner was a native-born contestant in an operatic arena more or less dominated by foreigners, and this exerted great appeal, as did his Italian training and European credentials.

Much of his success can be attributed to his lengthy association with his second wife, soprano Medea Mei. Returning to Russia together in the spring of 1887, they began a long and important association with the Imperial Opera at the Mariinsky Theater in St Petersburg where, from their first

Nicolay Figner as Enzo in *La Gioconda*

seasons together, they were enormously successful. Indeed, throughout the 1880s and 1890s, they were among the highest paid performers in Russia. Earlier they had toured Europe and South America together, making an especially noteworthy appearance in a production of *Aïda* with the Claudio Rossi Company at Rio de Janeiro's Teatro Imperial on 30 June, 1886, which marked the legendary, unannounced conducting debut of the 19-year-old Arturo Toscanini, then a cellist in the orchestra (years later the Maestro claimed that he owed his career in part to Figner's subsequent intervention on his behalf).

Figner's voice frequently provoked criticism. Its timbre was often described as strident, its middle register uncommonly weak and unresponsive, and its scale uneven. By consensus it was a small instrument, though judging from the breadth of his repertory, it must have been a remarkably flexible one in its prime. He was certainly capable of adapting himself to an impressive variety of roles, which eventually came to include Hermann in *The Queen of Spades,* Lenski in *Eugene Onegin,* Alfredo in *La traviata,* and Gounod's Roméo; Faust in both the Gounod and Boito settings, Don José in *Carmen,* and Canio in *I pagliacci;* Raoul in *Les Huguenots,* Radames in *Aïda,* and Verdi's *Otello*—in short, many of the principal lyric, dramatic, and heroic vehicles of the international tenor repertory. His acting was considered extraordinary for the time, being described as vivid, intelligent, harshly realistic, and consumed with detail, allowing him to somehow transcend his inherent vocal shortcomings—certainly to the satisfaction of an adoring public. This was another of the happy circumstances that assisted his career, coming at a time when the Russian public in particular, as if poised for the new dramatic requirements of *verismo,* was tiring of the crude theatrical antics of Italian singers. He was evidently hindered only by his unwillingness, or perhaps inability, to alter his physical appearance significantly.

Though he assumed a number of leading roles in Russian opera, and participated in four important domestic premieres—Eduard Napravnik's *Dubrovsky* and *Francesca da Rimini,* and Tchaikowsky's *Iolanta* and *The Queen of Spades*—his commercial intuition, like that of Medea Mei's, impelled a greater commitment to the Italian and French repertory that had established his career and maintained his popularity. His concert repertory, rich in songs of Borodin, Dargomyzhsky, and Rimsky-Korsakov, was not enough to insulate him from charges of patriotic neglect.

After their divorce in 1904, Figner continued to appear on the stage with Medea Mei, but he also performed with his third wife, Renée Efimovna Radina-Figner, whom he had married in 1905. Overwhelmed by a rash of new tenor idols, he retired from the Imperial Theater in 1907 after two decades of distinguished service. His final years were spent variously as the manager of his own theater in Nizhny Novgorod, the director of the Narodny Dom Theater in St Petersburg, and as a teacher of singing in Kiev.

At least forty-one recordings of Nikolay Figner have survived, all made for the Gramophone Company in St Petersburg between the winter of 1901 and late November, 1909. Collectively they give a less than flattering account of an artist at the margin of his prime. The timbre of the voice is certainly characteristic of the Russian lyric sound so closely associated with his successors, but its production is markedly more Italianate in style. Its distinct lack of size and body, not wholly attributable to age, is evident even in the earliest group of recordings and there is little smoothness or control. His *mezza voce* was by then poorly fused to the rest of his voice and, from its clumsiness, seems to have been used more often out of necessity than by choice. But there is still something

distinctive about his singing, and it is obvious that a keen dramatic instinct is struggling to surmount fatigue. He is at his most stylish in the many songs he recorded, which included works of Cui, Schumann, Tchaikowsky, Glinka, and even Denza. The operatic excerpts, while they do not quite yield a comprehensive overview of his stage repertory, include arias and duets from *The Queen of Spades, Dubrovsky, Oprichnik, Mefistofele, Les Huguenots, Fra Diavolo, La bohème, Roméo et Juliette, Tosca, I pagliacci,* and a most dramatic "Ora e per sempre addio" from *Otello.* He is clearly overshadowed in his duets with Medea Mei, her voice being the more striking of the two and her singing more adroit, but these are perhaps the most compelling documents of all, as much for the historic partnership they preserve as for the delightful blend of two remarkably consonant voices.

—William Shaman

LA FILLE DU RÉGIMENT [The Daughter of the Regiment].

Composer: Gaetano Donizetti.

Librettists: J.H.V. de Saint-Georges and J.F.A. Bayard.

First Performance: Paris, Opéra-Comique, 11 February 1840.

Roles: Marie (soprano); Tonio (tenor); Sulpice (bass); Marquise of Birkenfeld (mezzo-soprano); Duchess of Krakentorp (speaking part); Hortensio (bass); Corporal (bass); Peasant (tenor); Notary (mute); chorus (SSATTB).

Publications

articles–

Berlioz, H. "La fille du régiment." *Journal des débats* 16 February (1840); reprinted in *Les musiciens et la musique,* 145, Paris, 1903.

*   *   *

Gaetano Donizetti's *La fille du régiment* was the composer's first attempt at French comic opera. The setting, as in a number of comic operas of the period, is a Swiss village. In act I, set in the Marquise of Birkenfeld's castle, Sulpice, sergeant in the Savoyard regiment, arrives with Marie, the young *vivandière,* the "daughter of the regiment." Marie had been found in a battlefield and raised by the soldiers. Young Tonio has been following the troops out of love for Marie. He is arrested as a spy, but Marie intervenes and relates how Tonio saved her from falling over a precipice. When the regiment insists that she may only marry a grenadier, Tonio enlists and becomes one of them. Sulpice recounts that years ago a certain Captain Roberto de Birkenfeld had entrusted Marie to the soldiers before his death. Upon hearing this, the Marquise declares that Marie must be her niece and takes her off to the castle to be raised properly. Marie is sad to leave the regiment, especially Tonio.

Act II takes place in a salon in the castle. Marie is dressed so elegantly that Sulpice barely recognizes her. She enjoys the luxury of living in the castle but loathes having to learn

Jenny Lind in *La fille du régiment*, **Her Majesty's Theatre, London, 1847**

singing and dancing. There is a hilarious singing lesson with the Marquise during which Marie rebels, preferring fanfares to the poignant love songs she is forced to learn. The Marquise has arranged for Marie to marry the Duke of Krakentorp; she has confided to Sulpice that she is actually Marie's mother. Upon hearing this, Marie decides that she must comply with her mother's wishes and marry the Duke. The Marquise, however, realizes how much Marie and Tonio love each other and allows them to be married.

At the time of the premiere of *La fille du régiment*, a number of other operas by Donizetti were playing in Paris, a situation that prompted Berlioz to write in the *Journal des débats:* "What, two major scores at the Opéra, *Les Martyrs* [a French reworking of his *Poliuto*] and *Le Duc d'Albe*, two others at the Renaissance, *Lucie* [*sic*] *di Lammermoor* and *L'Ange de Nisida*, [really his *La favorite*], two at the Opéra-Comique, *La Fille du régiment* and another whose title is unknown, and still another for the Théâtre-Italien, will have been written or transcribed in one year by the same composer! M. Donizetti seems to treat us like a conquered country; it is a veritable invasion. One can no longer speak of the opera houses of Paris, but only of the opera houses of M. Donizetti!" Berlioz' diatribe notwithstanding, *La fille* was a great popular success: it was given at the Opéra-Comique forty-four times in 1840, eleven in 1841, achieving a total of 1044 performances at that theater alone by the turn of the century. In France it became customary, because of the opera's lively military tunes and jingoistic nature, to perform it on Bastille Day. It has always been more popular in France than in Italy; for the Italian version that premiered at the Teatro alla Scala in December of 1840, the French text was adapted by Callisto Bassi, and Donizetti supplied recitatives to replace the spoken dialogue.

Despite its great success with the French public, *La fille* was nearly a failure at its premiere, a situation recounted by the great tenor Duprez in his *Souvenirs d'un chanteur* (*A Singer's Recollections*). Apparently there was a French cabal organized against Donizetti. Berlioz judged the opera's defects thus: "The score of *La fille du régiment* is not at all one that either composer or the public takes seriously. There is some harmony, some melody, some rhythmic effects, some instrumental and vocal combinations; it is music, if one will, but not new music. . . . One discovers the style of M. Adam next to that of M. Meyerbeer." Nor was the music of *La fille*, despite the fact that it was Donizetti's first essay in the opéra-comique genre, new in terms of his own style and output. The combination of vivacious comic musical style and *larmoyante* arias (exemplified by "Il faut partir" in this score, sung when Marie must leave the regiment to live in the castle) is a hallmark of Donizetti's comic operas, traits found as well in his Italian operas *Don Pasquale* and *L'elisir d'amore* (*The Elixir of Love*). Giuseppe Verdi was evidently greatly influenced in a general way by Donizetti's operatic style; one specific instance is surely the model of "Il faut partir" for Violetta's "Ah fors'è lui" in act I of Verdi's *La traviata:* both arias begin in F minor and, through a series of short, detached phrases, proceed to F major, at which point a broad, descending melody begins from the F at the top of the stave.

La fille du régiment has been favored by some of the most famous "nightingales" in opera history, including Jenny Lind, Henriette Sontag, Marcella Sembrich, Toti Dal Monte, and Lily Pons. Recent revivals have featured Mirella Freni and, especially successfully, Joan Sutherland, who has also recorded the role for London-Decca. It was Tonio's "Pour mon âme quel destin" with its string of high Cs that helped to bring the young Luciano Pavarotti to international prominence.

—Stephen Willier

IL FILOSOFO DI CAMPAGNA [The Country Philosopher].

Composer: Baldassare Galuppi.

Librettist: Carlo Goldoni.

First Performance: Venice, San Samuele, 26 October 1754.

Roles: Eugenia (soprano); Rinaldo (soprano); Nardo (tenor); Lesbina (soprano); Don Tritemio (bass); Lena (soprano); Capocchio (tenor).

* * *

Don Tritemio, a wealthy landowner (the role's creator, Francesco Carrattoli, was one of the most famous comic singers of his day), has arranged for the marriage of his daughter Eugenia to Nardo, a well-to-do farmer and dispenser of homespun philosophy (likewise, Nardo was originally sung by another famous comic singer and actor, Francesco Baglioni). Nardo, who personifies a thinly-veiled jab at Arcadian musings, always chooses the path of least resistance in situations

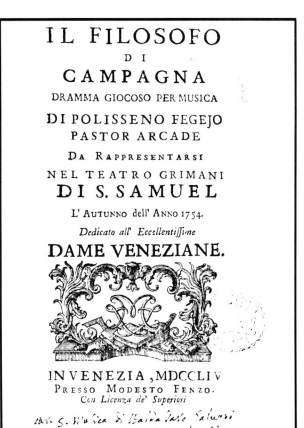

Il filosofo di campagna, **title page of libretto, Venice, 1754**

of conflict. Eugenia, of course, loves another (Rinaldo, a wealthy nobleman). The housemaid Lesbina tries to plead her cause to Tritemio, to no avail. When Nardo comes to call, he strikes Lesbina's own fancy, so she decides to present herself to him as the Eugenia he has come to court. In act II this leads to complications; Lesbina has passed the engagement ring to Eugenia, to appease Tritemio, but it is unfortunately seen by Rinaldo, who storms away in anger. All seems about to come apart. Rinaldo proceeds straight to Nardo and threatens him with death should he marry Eugenia; Nardo, true to form, freely gives her up and muses on the foolishness of sacrificing comfort (not to mention physical well-being) merely for a wife. Lena, Nardo's daughter, has learned of the switch of identity, and when Lesbina comes to call (still presenting herself as Eugenia), Lena exposes Lesbina's true identity. Her station makes no difference to Nardo, however; whether servant or wealthy, he aspires only to preserve peace and harmony—so the marriage plans resume. To complete her designs, Lesbina convinces Don Tritemio that she is in love with him, and Tritemio then plans a double wedding, bringing in a notary to draw up the contract: Eugenia is to be married to Nardo, and Lesbina to himself—yet while his back is turned, Lesbina substitutes the names of Rinaldo for Nardo, and Nardo for Tritemio. Unaware of all this, Rinaldo and Eugenia decide to elope and flee for temporary asylum to Nardo's estate. When Tritemio arrives in pursuit he is convinced that everything is as he originally intended, and the contract is signed. Too late, he sees his error, but decides to marry Lena as a consolation.

Of the many collaborations between Galuppi and Goldoni in the *drammi giocosi* that spread across Europe none was more successful or more brilliantly comic than this Venetian work of 1754. There were dozens of new productions through the 1750s and 1760s, although in some restagings much was changed, including the insertion of new arias and the reshaping of the work into a two-act comic intermezzo. In capsule *Il filosofo di campagna* contains all of the most characteristic features of their comedies: witty poetry, satire, and simple slapstick, clothed in elegant and tuneful melodies, facile orchestral writing, and unobtrusive texture. The act-ending ensemble finales (also known as "chain finales"), which had been pioneered by Galuppi and Goldoni in *L'arcadia in Brenta* five years earlier, are well paced and dramatically effective; they represent some of the earliest attempts at shifting the musical style and structure to accommodate the varied dramatic situations of a comic ensemble. The dramatic surprises at the conclusion of act I, as various characters slip back and forth across the stage without meeting, reinforced by Galuppi's flexible music, are wonderfully comic. Yet his lyric melodies (several in a "pastoral" mode, such as "La pastorella al prato," for Lena in act II) reveal the roots of the contemporary praise for his elegant style.

—Dale E. Monson

LA FINTA GIARDINIERA [The Disguised Gardener].

Composer: Wolfgang Amadeus Mozart.

Librettist: attributed to Ranieri de Calzabigi (revised by M. Coltellini).

First Performance: Munich, Assembly Rooms, 13 January 1775.

Roles: Countess Violante/Sandrina (soprano); Count Belfiore (tenor); Arminda (soprano); Serpetta (soprano); Podestà, Don Anchise (baritone); Ramiro (mezzo-soprano); Nardo/Roberto (bass-baritone); Doctor (speaking).

Publications

articles—

Münster, R. "Die verstellte Gärtnerin: neue Quellen zur authentischen Singspielfassung von W.A. Mozarts *La finta giardiniera*." *Die Musikforschung* 18 (1965): 138.
Abert, Anna Amalie. " 'La finta giardiniera' und 'Zaide' als Quellen für spätere Opern Mozarts." In *Musik und Verlag: Karl Vötterle zum 65. Geburtstag,* 113. Kassel, 1968.
Angermüller, Rudolf. "Wer war der Librettist von *La finta giardiniera?*" *Mozart-Jahrbuch* 1976-77 (1978): 1.

*   *   *

It was long believed that the libretto for *La finta giardiniera* was written by Ranieri de Calzabigi for Pasquale Anfossi, revised for Munich by Marco Coltellini. Anfossi's setting was known to Mozart. More recent scholarship (by Rudolf Angermüller, among others), however, has suggested the name of Giuseppe Petrosellini, a Groom of the Chamber at the Papal Court. The libretto appears in neither the 1774 nor the 1793 editions of Calzabigi's works.

The action of the opera, which takes place in the fictitious land of Lagonero, proceeds as follows. Don Anchise, the podestà (a provincial mayor), is a foolish old man in love with his gardener Sandrina, who is in reality the Countess Violante Onesti. She is disguised as a gardener in order to search for her former betrothed, Count Belfiore, who stabbed her in a jealous quarrel and left her for dead. Amorous complications abound. The podestà's maid Serpetta is adamant about marrying her master. She rejects the attentions of the aging Nardo, who is in reality the countess's servant Roberto but is now, like his mistress, disguised as a gardener. Arminda, the niece of the podestà, likewise spurns her admirer Ramiro in favor of Count Belfiore, who has rejected the countess for her.

In act II the countess reveals her true identity in order to save Belfiore from a charge of murdering her. Soon after, however, she resumes the guise of Sandrina, retracting her former statement. Arminda arranges for Sandrina to be taken away to a lonely wood. Serpetta informs the podestà that Sandrina has run away; Nardo rushes to tell the count of this. They all repair to the wood to search. As it grows dark they can no longer recognize each other, which leads to confusion and strange couplings among the characters. Accusations fly, and Sandrina and the count lose their reason and imagine they are mythical figures. Act III provides a happy ending. Sandrina and the count recover their reason and are betrothed once again; Arminda returns to Ramiro, and finally Serpetta even accepts Nardo. Only the podestà resolves to remain single.

When the nineteen-year-old Mozart accepted a commission from Maximillian III, Elector of Bavaria, to produce an opera for the Munich carnival season of 1774-75, he was given this rather chaotic libretto with a plot that is complicated, inconsistent, full of secondary characters, disguises, mad scenes, mistaken identity, and farce. Yet, with his extraordinary insight into the human psyche, Mozart was able to cut through the confusion and to breathe life into the characters and to illuminate their motivations through his music. In providing music for these characters, Mozart went against comic opera tradition in a number of ways. Ramiro is drawn directly from *opera seria* and thus the role was written for a castrato, a most uncommon hero for comic opera. It would seem likely that the podestà, as ruler and father figure, would be a *basso buffo,* but Mozart made him a baritone. Nor is Nardo (Roberto) the typical *basso buffo* servant; there is nothing very comic about his role. Others, however, fall more neatly into expected categories. Serpetta is the wily servant soubrette of Neapolitan opera, sister to Pergolesi's Serpina of *La serva padrona,* and Arminda, like Donna Anna after her, is recognizable as a high-born soprano from *opera seria.* Sandrina, really a countess but disguised as a gardener, presents a more complicated situation. Mozart has been criticized (by Donald Grout among others) for lack of musical unity in portraying her, but that is precisely the point: she must be shown as two different characters, the fatuous young girl from the world of *opera buffa* and the tragic heroine, stabbed and left for dead by her lover. Just as she assumes a material disguise, so Mozart gives her a musical disguise.

This mixture of tragedy and comedy is only one of the several "problems" associated with *La finta giardiniera.* Mozart's great trio of comic operas abound in chiaroscuro, situations in which the characters and the audience smile through tears. So it is, too, with *La finta giardiniera.* Thus the designation of the work in the Neue Mozart Ausgabe as "dramma giocoso" is more apt than the traditional "opera buffa." The term "dramma giocoso" suggests a mixture of light and dark, of comedy and tragedy. It was Da Ponte's description of the *Don Giovanni* libretto he wrote for Mozart in 1787, a tale, like *La finta giardiniera,* replete with unrequited love, lust, disguises, stabbing, the aristocracy pitted against the peasants, and scenes in darkness contrasted with outdoor scenes of festivity. More complicated is the fact that, after the first successful run of performances, *La finta giardiniera* was revived in the 1779-80 season, but in German to a text by Stierle (as *Die verstellte Gärtnerin*) with spoken dialogue substituted for the sung recitatives, in the manner of a *Singspiel.* In 1789 the work was performed in Frankfurt as *Die Gärtnerin aus Liebe,* which version has been recorded in modern times. Until recently, the Italian text of act I was lost. Such Mozart scholars as Wyzewa, Saint-Foix, and Alfred Einstein believed that the succeeding versions were not merely German translations but contemporary revisions by Mozart himself. Einstein saw this as the explanation for the "strange inequality of style" of the score, with arias ranging from the older, simpler *buffa* style to entire sections looking forward to *Le nozze di Figaro* or *Don Giovanni.* Particularly advanced are the several arias in minor keys expressing agitation or pathos, most of act III, and the symphonically-conceived ensemble finale of act II, in which the characters are lost in a forest in the middle of the night.

Despite the unevenness of the score, its mixture of Germanic and Italianate styles, and the considerable problems besetting a modern performance, *La finta giardiniera* is eminently worth reviving. Much to the discomfiture of Mozart's patron, the Archbishop Colloredo, who wanted to keep the young genius tied to menial musical tasks in Salzburg, there was little doubt about the enthusiasm of the first Munich audiences. Mozart wrote his mother on 14 January 1775: "God be praised! My opera was performed yesterday the 13th, and it had such a success that it would be impossible to describe the applause to you. First of all, the theater was so full that many people had to return home; after each aria there was a terrific din of applause and cries of 'Vivo Maestro'. . . . scarcely had the applause stopped when somebody would start again—and so it went on."

—Stephen A. Willier

FIRE FAMINE
See FEUERSNOT

FISCHER-DIESKAU, Dietrich.

Baritone. Born 28 May 1925, in Zehlendorf. Studied in Berlin with Georg Walter and Hermann Weissenborn; in German army; prisoner of war in Italy, 1945; concert debut in *Ein deutsches Requiem,* in Freiburg, 1947; opera debut as Posa in *Don Carlos*; in Berlin, 1948, in Vienna and Munich from 1949 and Salzburg from 1952; appeared at Bayreuth, 1954-56 as Herald in *Lohengrin* (1954); Covent Garden debut as Mandryka in *Arabella,* 1965; created Mittenhofer in Henze's *Elegy for Young Lovers,* Schwetzingen Festival 1961.

Publications

By FISCHER-DIESKAU: books–

Texte deutscher Lieder: Ein Handbuch. Munich, 1968.
Auf den Spuren der Schubert-Lieder: Werden-Wesen-Wirkung. Wiesbaden, 1971.
Wagner und Nietzsche: Der Mystagoge und sein Abtrünniger. Stuttgart, 1974.
Schubert: A Biographical Study of His Songs. London, 1976.
Robert Schumann: Wort und Musik. 1981
Töne sprechen, Worte klingen. 1985.
Nachklang. 1987.
Echoes of a Lifetime. London, 1989.

About FISCHER-DIESKAU: books–

Herzfeld, F. *Dietrich Fischer-Dieskau.* Berlin, 1958.
Moore, G. *Am I Too Loud?* London, 1962.
Whitton, K.S. *Dietrich Fischer-Dieskau: Mastersinger: A Documented Study.* New York and London, 1981.
Von Lewinski, W. E. *Dietrich Fischer–Dieskau.* Mainz and München, 1988.

articles–

Whitton, K. P. "Dietrich Fischer-Dieskau." *The European Teacher* October (1985).

* * *

While there are now a few Anglo-Saxon critics/record-reviewers who are hesitant to grant Dietrich Fischer-Dieskau even the status of one of the greatest Lieder singers of the twentieth century, there are still more, it seems, who are wary of ranking him among the most distinguished operatic

Dietrich Fischer-Dieskau with Erika Köth in *Don Giovanni*, **Deutsche Oper, Berlin, 1961**

baritones of the century. The reasons for this prejudice in the USA and Great Britain are varied, but stem possibly from his relatively rare operatic appearances on British stages and his complete absence from American ones. His operatic performances have therefore to be judged from the limited cultural experience of his many recordings; only the Germanic countries have seen him in countless stage productions.

It has always been the custom in German-speaking countries for Lieder singers also to appear regularly in opera. Frieda Hempel, Lotte Lehmann, Hans Hotter, Heinrich Schlusnus, Elisabeth Schumann, Elisabeth Schwarzkopf and many others enjoyed great reputations in the opera houses of the world as well as in the concert halls. Dietrich Fischer-Dieskau is no exception; from his first operatic appearance as Posa in Verdi's *Don Carlos* in the Berlin Städtische Oper on 18 November 1948, he has been a regular member of the great opera houses in Berlin, Munich and Vienna, and has sung all the leading baritone roles in the repertoire. Britain has seen him only as the Count in *Le nozze di Figaro,* as Mandryka in Strauss' *Arabella,* and as a very controversial Falstaff at Covent Garden in February 1967. Although some critics have since written that the faults (mainly the overdone "stage business") in that *Falstaff* production were to be laid at the door of the producer rather than at that of the singer, Fischer-Dieskau was sufficiently disgusted by the views of the critics to wish never to return to Covent Garden—in opera, at any rate. A recording of *Falstaff* (January 1967) had been made during the six performances in Vienna where Fischer-Dieskau had been compared to "the Falstaff of the century," Mariano Stabile. It is a performance full of fire, wit and pathos crowned by a superb rendition of Falstaff's great "Ehi! Taverniere!" monologue at the beginning of Act III which proves that Sir John was indeed *the* creative spirit of the opera: "L'arguzia mia crea l'arguzia degli altri" ("My cleverness creates the cleverness of others"). Many felt that the Covent Garden performance retained that vocal magnificence.

Of his many other Verdian performances, I should select his 1970 Italian version of *Macbeth,* where his ability to depict the text and his knowledge of Italian gained from his two years' imprisonment in Bologna during 1945-1947 enabled him to create a chilling interpretation of the great Scottish rogue. All his skills as a great interpreter of Lieder went into the moving performance of Macbeth's last aria and, in particular, of that melting phrase "sol la bestemmia, ahi lasso! la nenia tua sarà" ("Blasphemy alone, alas, shall be your epitaph!") where Fischer-Dieskau's celebrated *mezza voce* served to underline his oft-repeated reminder that Verdi worshipped Schubert and his heartfelt melodies "based on rhythm."

As in the Britain of Carl Rosa's and Sadler's Wells' times, opera in German-speaking countries is often given in the native tongue, and there are many recordings of Italian operas in German, unknown to the largely non-German speaking Anglo-American public, which feature Dietrich Fischer-Dieskau. He has also recorded almost every lyric baritone role (and some *Heldenbariton* ones as well) in the Wagner repertoire. German speakers rate highly his Wotan for Karajan's *Rheingold* (1968), and I was always most impressed by the majesty of the performance which Karajan himself (in a private letter to the singer) felt had "the fascination of a late Renaissance prince." The re-issue of the celebrated *Tristan und Isolde* recording of 1952, with Flagstad and Suthaus, conducted by Furtwängler, allowed the younger record reviewers who had grown up to accept Fischer-Dieskau as an aging wonder now a little *passé* to marvel at his Kurwenal

which, as one of them wrote, "is what Wagner singing is all about."

The major recent criticism of Fischer-Dieskau concerned his practice of highlighting specific words and the overly forceful, emphatic delivery of much of his singing. A great singer, however, lives a role whether in opera or in song and will emphasize a word with special meaning for him or her as one would do in speech. ("Oh, how *lovely . . .* !). Listen for example to Fischer-Dieskau's caressing of the erotic "gioiello mio" phrase in the introduction to his duet with Zerlina in *Don Giovanni.* The second objection was dealt with by Suvi Raj Grubb in his book *Music on Record,* where he describes how difficult Fischer-Dieskau's voice is to record and to balance because of its enormous dynamic range, "much greater than that of any other singer I have recorded" (p. 106). I am sure that this is the major cause of many of the reviewers' complaints since one is not aware of this "fault" in concert hall or opera house. The voice is simply an enormous one, with the range of a Titta Ruffo.

Is *all* perfection by no means; perfection is unattainable. Some of Fischer-Dieskau's rather weak notes at the top and bottom of the range have always disappointed his admirers, and his willingness to record almost every genre of music, his unwillingness to say "No" to an agent or a record-producer, has led him into recording music unsuited to his particular, if impressively versatile, genius. One thinks of roles such as Handel's *Giulio Cesare* or Golaud in Debussy's *Pelléas et Mélisande,* where the voice and the delivery do not seem to be quite right.

However, when one looks back over a career now spanning over forty years and listens, for example, to Fischer-Dieskau's matchless Count in *Le nozze di Figaro,* his Mandryka in *Arabella,* his Rigoletto, his Amfortas in *Parsifal,* his magisterial Hans Sachs in *Die Meistersinger,* recorded at the age of fifty, among his countless operatic roles, then one is inclined to wonder, with John Steane, whether Fischer-Dieskau has ever sung anything "without shedding some new light on it." Such a thought alone surely places a singer among the greatest artists of his day.

—Kenneth Whitton

FLAGSTAD, Kirsten.

Soprano. Born 12 July 1895, in Hamar. Died 7 December 1962, in Oslo. Studied voice with her mother and with Ellen Schytte-Jacobsen in Christiana; debut as Nuri in d'Albert's *Tiefland,* Oslo, 1913; sang throughout Scandinavia until 1933, when she began to sing minor roles at Bayreuth; first major success as Sieglinde, Bayreuth, 1934; Metropolitan Opera debut as same, 1935; Covent Garden debut as Isolde, 1936; guest appearances at San Francisco Opera, 1935-38, and Chicago Opera, 1937; returned to Nazi-occupied homeland to be with her husband, 1941; resumed her career after the war; sang Leonore and Isolde at Metropolitan Opera, 1951; director of the Norwegian Opera, Oslo, 1958-60.

Publications

By FLAGSTAD: books–

The Flagstad Manuscript, ed. by L. Biancolli. New York, 1952.

About FLAGSTAD: books–

McArthur, E. *Flagstad: A Personal Memoir.* New York, 1965.
Vogt, H. *Flagstad.* London, 1987.

articles–

Dennis, J. "Kirsten Flagstad." *Record Collector* 7 (1952): 173.

* * *

Kirsten Flagstad's career took her to a position as one of the greatest Wagnerian sopranos of the mid-20th century. But it started slowly, and it was some twenty years from her Oslo debut at eighteen in d'Albert's verismo opera *Tiefland* (when she played the young girl Nuri) to her first Isolde in *Tristan und Isolde* in Oslo in 1932. However, during these years she gained vast stage experience in operetta, musical comedy and even revues, though singing nearly always in Norwegian. But as Isolde she sang in German, and her fellow Scandinavian Ellen Gulbranson, Bayreuth's regular Brünnhilde in Wagner's *Ring* cycle from 1897-1914, heard her and recognized her potential, recommending her to the management at Bayreuth. Flagstad was now approaching forty and had recently married for the second time, and she had even contemplated retirement from active singing. But now instead she found herself catapulted into a new start in different surroundings, and small roles at Bayreuth during 1933 and 1934 led to her going to the New York Metropolitan Opera in the following year to sing Sieglinde in *Die Walküre* and

Kirsten Flagstad as Senta in *Der fliegende Holländer*

Isolde in *Tristan und Isolde.* From now on, she was in demand internationally. Soon she added Brünnhilde to her Wagner roles, singing this one as well as those of Isolde and Senta in *Der fliegende Holländer* at Covent Garden in London.

The Second World War found Flagstad in the United States, but her return to occupied Norway in 1941 and her husband's arrest as a collaborator after the end of the war cast a temporary cloud over her career, though this resumed in the late 1940s when she sang a memorable Isolde at Covent Garden and she continued to please British and American audiences in the major Wagnerian soprano roles (including now the enchantress Kundry in *Parsifal*) until her last appearance as Isolde at the age of fifty-five in 1951. Her British following also gave her an opportunity in new repertory when she was offered the chance to play Dido, the tragic Queen of Carthage in Purcell's opera *Dido and Aeneas,* in a production that took place in the small Mermaid Theatre in London, which was directed by the actor-producer Bernard Miles. This is traditionally a somewhat mature role (though it is unclear why this should be so) and she brought to it a tremendous presence and pathos, not least in the final Lament over a ground bass which crowns her role and which precedes the final suicide. It was as Dido that she made her farewell to the operatic stage in 1953. However, she continued to sing occasionally in concerts, for example in the songs of Grieg and Sibelius, and went on to direct the Norwegian State Opera. She also recorded *Dido and Aeneas* and a Wagner role new to her, that of the god Wotan's wife Fricka in *Das Rheingold,* the first opera in the *Ring* tetralogy.

Beside the Wagner roles already mentioned, Flagstad's career also included Elsa in *Lohengrin* and Elizabeth in *Tannhäuser.* But her powerful and splendidly focused voice made her suited above all to heroic roles, and another such by Beethoven was that of Leonore (disguised as the young man Fidelio) in *Fidelio.* Unfortunately, she did not record the complete role of Brünnhilde, but her recordings include a famous performance as Isolde, opposite Ludwig Suthaus as Tristan, that was conducted by Wilhelm Furtwängler. Here she is heard at her best and most characteristic, as a Northern princess of great dignity and depth of feeling, with a voice of remarkable and inimitable natural beauty which stood up magnificently to the demands Wagner placed upon it.

—Christopher Headington

FLETA, Miguel.

Tenor. Born 1 December 1897, in Albalate de Cinca, Spain. Died 29 May 1938, in La Coruña. Married singer Luisa Pierrich. Studied at Barcelona Conservatory with Luisa Pierrich; debut as Paolo in *Francesca da Rimini* in Trieste, 1919; in Vienna, 1920; in Rome 1920-21; appeared at Monte Carlo,

1921; in Madrid 1921-21; in Buenos Aires, 1922; at Metropolitan Opera 1923-25, first appearing as Cavadorossi; created Zandoni's Romeo, 1922, and Calaf in Puccini's *Turandot,* 1926.

Publications

About FLETA: books–

Torres, L. et al. *Miguel Fleta: El hombre, el "divo" y su musa.* Zaragoza, 1940.
Lauri-Volpi, G. *Voci paralleli.* Milan, 1955.
Saiz Valdivielso, A., *Fleta, Memoria de una voz Albia Grupo.* Madrid, 1986.

articles–

Gualerzi, G., ed. "Tavola rotonda su Fleta." *Discoteca* no. 41(1964): 17.
Dzazópoulos, J., "Miguel Fleta." *Record Collector* 37 (1992): 161.

*　　*　　*

There can be few examples of singers more idolised in their lifetime than the tenor Miguel Fleta. In his native Spain, his name was a household word and even today he is still largely remembered there. Yet his was one of the shortest careers of any major singer of importance. His style of singing was highly individual, but his vocalism was as imperfect as it was unique. Nevertheless, a flawed diamond can still excite the

Miguel Fleta as Don José in *Carmen*

senses, and the achievements of his spectacular career assure Fleta of a place as one of the most important Spanish tenors of this century.

In order to comprehend the enigma that was Fleta, one needs to understand the nature of the voice itself. It was a ringing lyric-dramatic tenor of great richness and individuality of timbre, with an ease in the upper register often characteristic of Spanish tenors. His style and great intelligence combined with a flexibility of voice enabled him to sing a wide variety of roles, from the lyric, such as Des Grieux (*Manon*), Elvino (*La Sonnambula*) and the Duke (*Rigoletto*), to the dramatic, such as Radames (*Aïda*) and Canio (*Pagliacci*). His control over his voice was formidable and he would delight audiences by spinning out notes and the use of morendo (a long, sustained decrescendo on a note) until the sound was sustained on the breath by the merest whisper. At times, his singing could be mannered almost to the point of self-parody. Yet, despite his mastery, his technique was flawed. Even in his earliest records, made not three years after his debut, his vibrato can create a feeling of unease in the listener. Within less than a decade, that vibrato had widened to a wobble, an alarming flap in the tone. The records made around this time are unpleasant listening. More than a half century after his death, it is difficult to comprehend exactly what was wrong: it was often said that Fleta led an undisciplined, self-indulgent life-style which was reflected in his singing. Perhaps there is an element of truth in this, in view of his tragically early death. Others speculate that some of the roles he undertook were possibly too heavy for his voice.

However, during his short career his achievements were remarkable. He held his own during a period of considerable tenor talent. At the Teatro alla Scala alone, Pertile, Merli and Lauri-Volpi were on the roster, competing for the very roles in which Fleta excelled. Indeed, Pertile was always thought of as Toscanini's favorite tenor, yet it was Fleta whom Puccini and Toscanini chose to create the role of Calaf in the world premiere of *Turandot.*

Fleta's voice appealed mostly to Spanish-speaking countries, where his self-indulgent manner was accepted and probably appreciated. In Spain, he could revel in vocal display and exhibitionism to the delight of his audience. Scott, in his book *The Record of Singing,* describes how during a performance of *Carmen* the tenor, having aroused the audience to a frenzy with his aria, arranged for a piano to be wheeled on to the stage so that he could give an impromptu recital of popular songs.

As his vocal deterioration progressed, appearances outside his native Spain diminished in number and his repertoire increasingly concentrated more on the zarzuela, the Spanish equivalent of operetta, where popular appeal is perhaps more greatly valued than the discipline and rigidity of opera. And popular appeal is what Fleta possessed in abundance. He was a handsome man and there is little doubt that Fleta's stage persona and singing could mesmerize an adoring public. It is this Fleta that has not been forgotten and whose records sold in abundance.

For the serious collector, Fleta's records repay careful selection. He recorded exclusively for HMV and Victor towards the end of the acoustic era (1922-1925) and electrically over a period of another decade. In the best of them, his highly individual style and mastery of his voice is bewitching. Yet the recordings made late in his career can be grotesquely bad. All, however, display the instability of pitch that increased as his career progressed.

In his earliest records, the vibrato is successfully controlled, and as a group they make rewarding listening. Few tenors exhibit such a fascination of style and an intensity that is extraordinary. Few could have displayed such beautiful lyricism in "Che gelida manina" (*La bohème*) and still achieve the dark, brooding intensity and drama of his "Vesti la giubba". From the martial fervor and romanticism of his "Celeste Aïda" (*Aïda*), to his long-breathed, ravishingly sung "Il fior" (*Carmen*), each of his recordings bears the stamp of a master of his instrument and the immediately recognizable hallmarks of a great singer.

The many admirable qualities of his acoustics far outweigh their faults. However, with his electrics, the listener must tread more warily. In his later recordings the vibrato becomes more obtrusive and the pitch wavers constantly. Until about 1928, there is still much to admire. The ability to play with the voice is unimpaired, as is the intensity and beauty of the tone.

After 1930 it is significant that Fleta recorded no more operatic music, concentrating instead on the zarzuela repertoire. These are probably best avoided except by those who have fallen under the spell of the artist.

In his short career Fleta's impact was considerable. Perhaps it is as well not to speculate on what he might have been had his artistry been less flawed. It is preferable, perhaps, to be thankful for the remarkable legacy of arguably one of the greatest singers to have emerged from Spain this century.

—Larry Lustig

DER FLIEGENDE HOLLÄNDER [The Flying Dutchman].

Composer: Richard Wagner.

Librettist: Richard Wagner (after Heine, *Aus den Memoiren des Herrn von Schnabelewopski*).

First Performance: Dresden, Königliches Hoftheater, 2 January 1843; revised, 1846; revised, 1852; revised, 1860.

Roles: Senta (soprano); The Dutchman (baritone); Daland (bass); Erik (tenor); A Steersman (tenor); Mary (mezzo-soprano); chorus (SSAATTBB).

Publications

books–

Wolzogen, H. von. *Richard Wagner über den 'Fliegenden Holländer': die Entstehung, Gestaltung und Darstellung des Werkes aus den Schriften und Briefen des Meisters zusammengestellt*. Leipzig, 1914.
Deathridge, John. *An Introduction to "The Flying Dutchman"*. London, 1982.
John, Nicholas, ed. *Richard Wagner: "Der fliegende Holländer"*. London, 1982.

articles–

Altmann, W. "Richard Wagner und die Berliner General-Intendantur: Verhandlungen über den 'Fliegenden Holländer' und 'Tannhäuser'." *Die Musik* 2/no. 11 (1902-03): 331; no. 14 (1902-03): 92; no. 16 (1902-03): 304.

Heuss, A. "Zum Thema, Musik und Szene bei Wagner: im Anschluss an Wagners Aufsatz, Bemerkungen zur Aufführung der Oper 'Der fliegende Holländer'." *Die Musik* 10 (1910-11): 3, 81.
Istel, E. "Autographe Regiebemerkungen Wagners zum 'Fliegende Holländer'." *Die Musik* 12 (1912-13): 214.
Mehler, E. "Beiträge zur Wagner-Forschung: unveröffentlichte Stücke aus 'Rienzi,' 'Holländer' und 'Tannhäuser'." *Die Musik* 12 (1912-13): 195.
Strobel, O. "Wagners Prosaentwurf zum 'Fliegende Holländer'." *Bayreuther Blätter* 56 (1933): 157.
Abraham, G. " 'The Flying Dutchman': Original Version." *Music and Letters* 20 (1939): 412.
Vetter, Isolde. "Holländer-Metamorphosen." *Melos/Neue Zeitschrift für Musik* 4 (1978).
Avant-scène opéra November-December (1980) [*Le vaisseau fantôme* issue].
Vetter, Isolde. "Die Entstehung des *Fliegenden Holländers* von Richard Wagner." In *Bericht über den Internationalen Musikwissenschaftlichen Kongress Bayreuth, 1981*, edited by Christoph Hellmut Mahling and Sigrid Wiesmann, 436. Kassel, 1984.

unpublished–

Machlin, P.S. "The Flying Dutchman: Sketches, Revisions and Analysis." Ph.D. dissertation, University of California, Berkeley, 1976.

*   *   *

Cursed by Satan, the Dutchman is doomed to sail the seas forever, unless he can find a woman who will be faithful to him until death. He hopes to have found his redeemer in Senta, who agrees to marry him out of compassion. Overhearing and misunderstanding a conversation between Senta and Erik, the Dutchman assumes she has been unfaithful and sets sail. Senta declares her loyalty and leaps into the sea; the Dutchman's ship sinks with all hands. The transfigured forms of Senta and the Dutchman rise from the sea and soar upward.

Der fliegende Holländer revolves around three central elements: cosmic conflict, redemption, and transfiguration. The dramatic/musical relevance of these concepts is intimately connected with the opera's compositional history.

In early May 1850, Wagner drafted a prose scenario for a one-act opera based upon the legend of the Flying Dutchman. Hoping for a commission from the Paris Opéra, he submitted this draft to the librettist Eugène Scribe. Sometime before the end of July, he composed three numbers from the projected opera for a Paris audition: the chorus of Norwegian (originally Scottish) sailors, the "phantom chorus" of the Dutchman's crew, and Senta's ballad. Wagner did not require a libretto in order to give musical expression to three of the drama's crucial elements: the world of everyday reality (sailor's chorus), the realm of the supernatural (phantom chorus), and redemption through eternal fidelity (Senta's ballad). Apparently he had conceived the dramatic argument in essentially musical terms from the very beginning.

When he realized that the Opéra was not about to offer him a contract, Wagner sold his scenario to the Opéra's director, Léon Pillet, but not before he had finished his own libretto. He then composed two more numbers—the Steersman's Song and the Spinning Chorus—each of which depicts yet another facet of the "normal" everyday world. These five songs, all cast in three-verse strophic form, lie at the heart

Der fliegende Holländer, act I, Städtische Oper, Berlin, 1933 (produced by Carl Ebert with designs by Caspar Neher)

of the opera's musical structure, and form the basis of the following discussion.

In act I, Daland's steersman whiles away his watch by singing the first of the opera's five strophic songs, about a sailor returning home to his sweetheart. He sings the first verse to a tune whose regular phraseology and melodic symmetry evoke the mundane, everyday world. Beginning the second verse, he gradually succumbs to drowsiness; the orchestra fills in his involuntary pauses with agitated storm music signaling the arrival of the Dutchman's ship. Thus Wagner musically depicts the interpenetration of the normal world by the spectral realm. After the Dutchman's apocalyptic aria and his buffa-like duet with Daland, the sailors round out the act by vigorously declaiming the long-awaited third verse of the Steersman's Song—now revealed as a trite parody of the Dutchman's tremendous quest for salvation.

The Spinning Chorus which opens act II is a female counterpart to the Steersman's Song: encouraged by Mary, the girls sing about the return of their seafaring lovers. Unable to bear this "stupid song" any longer, Senta angrily interrupts its third verse to sing the ballad of the Flying Dutchman, whose brooding portrait hangs on the wall. By doing this, Daland's daughter verbally and musically summons the spectral, storm-tossed world into her father's comfortable sitting room. Each of Senta's three verses begins in a rather agitated manner but concludes with a lyrical theme expressing the promise of redemption. At the end of the third verse, the maidens alone sing this tune as Senta sinks back exhausted. Suddenly inspired, the girl leaps to her feet and interrupts

her own song to declare, in a passionate variant of the "Redemption" theme, "Let me be the one who through her faith redeems thee!" Although Senta has presumably sung the ballad before, this represents the first time she has attempted to catapult herself into the legend, to become a part of the story she unfolds.

At the opening of act III, the drama's cosmic conflict erupts into a duel of song between the Norwegian sailors and the Dutchman's crew. After the former have sung the first verse of a rollicking C major tune, their girlfriends appear bearing refreshments, and the merrymakers comment upon the unnatural silence of the Dutch ship. To calm their jitters, the sailors sing verse two above an increasingly restless accompaniment. Suddenly the Dutchmen interrupt and roar out two verses of their own grisly song, in a demonic b minor. Both crews sing their third verses simultaneously, C major and b minor fighting for supremacy. This tremendous tonal conflict is finally resolved in favor of b minor, as the terrified Norwegians quit the deck and the Dutchmen burst into shrill laughter. The demonic element has triumphed.

The catastrophe follows swiftly. After Senta leaps into the sea and the Dutchman's ship sinks, the variant of the "Redemption" theme with which Senta interrupted her own ballad reappears in D major, followed (in the original version of the opera) by a sonorous major-mode rendition of the Dutchman's motive. However, the final tableau—the transfigured forms of Senta and the Dutchman rising from the sea in close embrace—at first found no counterpart in the music.

In 1860, Wagner changed the ending of the overture for a Paris concert. Originally the overture ended like the opera, with no hint of transfiguration. However, by 1860 Wagner had composed *Tristan und Isolde,* whose transfigured lovers transcend the physical world and become one with each other and the universe. He replaced the ending of the *Holländer* overture with an ecstatic development of the "Redemption-Variant"; its rising sequences and "celestial" orchestration express the couple's transcendence of both the natural and the supernatural world. He then grafted the final portion of this ending, with its Tristanesque plagal cadence, onto the end of act III, whereby the concept of transfiguration—previously present in the stage directions alone—finally received full musical expression.

Although some critics have denigrated *Der fliegende Holländer,* recent scholarship has begun to reveal what a fascinating, multifaceted work it really is. Of all the composer's pre-*Rheingold* operas, this one alone contains a dramatic-musical expression of cosmic conflict, redemption, transfiguration, and transcendence—elements Wagner was later to work out on a colossal scale in *Der Ring des Nibelungen.*

—Warren Darcy

A FLORENTINE TRAGEDY
See EINE FLORENTINISCHE TRAGÖDIE

EINE FLORENTINISCHE TRAGÖDIE [A Florentine Tragedy].

Composer: Alexander von Zemlinsky.

Librettist: Oscar Wilde (translated by M. Meyerfeld).

First Performance: Stuttgart, 30 January 1917.

Roles: Guido Bardi (tenor); Simone (bass); Bianca (mezzo-soprano).

*   *   *

European painters, writers, and dramatists of the early twentieth century drew frequent inspiration from Renaissance Italy. The cultural splendor and violent intrigue of its city-states suggested a Freudian mirror-image of the modern bourgeois metropolis: fifteenth- and sixteenth-century Florence or Venice offered the historical costume-setting beloved of popular theater, while permitting the treatment of art and psychology as much as of battles and the lessons of political power. The First World War period saw the premieres, in successive years, of four significant operas that mark the climax of popular interest in such material: Schillings's *Mona Lisa* (1915), Erich Wolfgang Korngold's *Violanta* (1916), Zemlinsky's *Eine florentinische Tragödie* (1917) and, most extravagant of all, Schreker's *Die Gezeichneten* (1918).

Zemlinsky's one-act setting of a fragmentary play by Oscar Wilde is not the best of these, but it is striking in many ways and was successfully revived in the 1980s with *Die Geburtstag*

der Infantin (originally *Der Zwerg*). It represents his most sustained essay in the virtuoso style of Strauss' *Salome* and *Elektra* and boasts an appropriately large orchestra (including six horns, four trumpets, three trombones and a mass of percussion, along with harp, mandoline and celesta). This is unleashed at full tilt in the prelude, which follows Strauss' *Der Rosenkavalier* in graphically depicting the love-making of the two characters seen when the curtain rises: Guido Bardi, Prince of Florence, and Bianca, wife of Simone, a "bürgerlich" merchant who trades in fine clothes and fabrics. The cataclysmic excitement of Guido and Bianca has barely subsided before Simone returns. The ensuing action involves the transformation of his at first apparently sycophantic behavior towards the haughty young prince. Having manoeuvered Guido into buying all his merchandise for a considerable sum, Simone permits his metaphorical allusions to power and adultery to grow ever more direct, until the off-hand Guido is cornered into a sword-fight and encouraged by Bianca to kill her husband. But Simone kills *him* in the ensuing fight and turns on his faithless wife, only to find that Bianca's love for him has been reawakened by his strength. Somewhat improbably, they kiss as the curtain descends.

The critic Julius Korngold likened Wilde's strategy in the play, *vis à vis* this conclusion, to that of a man who sets his house on fire in order to light a cigar. Undoubtedly the play suggests operatic treatment at many points, but where Zemlinsky succeeds in sustaining a tense, near-hysterical emotional atmosphere, depicted in ever-changing orchestral colors and a dazzling display of elliptical and often dissonantly harmonized "continuous melody," he fails to clarify the drama. In *Kleider machen Leute* he had succeeded in finding a lighter, melodically contoured style in which to depict petit-bourgeois mediocrity. He here, however, makes little or no attempt at a musical characterization of the older merchant Simone. Instead, he is drawn from the start into the rather high-flown passionate rhetoric of Guido, the princely young lover. Simone's ultimate victory might have been to hijack that rhetoric and make it his own. Instead, he is given no other manner in which musically to confirm his status as a "poor burgher." As a result, psychology follows morality out of the window at the end of the opera. The radiant A flat major conclusion might light a box of cigars but it threatens to obscure the socio-critical implications Wilde had smuggled into Simone's subtle verbal assault upon his prince. Does the bourgeois composer spread out his musical cloth-of-gold only at the prompting of some Nietzschean "master-amorality"? Zemlinsky claimed that his intention was to underline the terrible sanctity of the marriage-bond; if psychology and symbolism nevertheless short-circuit each other here, the resultant musical explosion is unquestionably electrifying.

—Peter Franklin

FLOTOW, Friedrich (Adolf Ferdinand) von.

Composer. Born 27 April 1813, in Teutendorf. Died 24 January 1883, in Darmstadt. In the choir at Gustrow; studied piano with J.P. Pixis and composition with Reicha at the Paris Conservatory, 1829; collaborations with various composers on a number of operas produced in Paris, 1836-39;

first big success *Alessandro Stradella,* 1844; intendant at the grand ducal court theater in Schwerin, 1855-63; in Austria and then Germany, 1873-.

Operas

Pierre et Catherine, J.H. Vernoy de Saint-Georges, 1831-32; performed in German, Ludwigslust and Schwerin, 1835.

Die Bergknappen, Theodor Körner, c. 1833.

Alfred der Grosse. Theodore Körner, c. 1833.

Rob Roy, P. Duport and Pierre Jean Baptiste Choudard Desforges (after Walter Scott), Paris, Royaument Castle, September 1836.

Sérafine, Pierre Jean Baptiste Choudard Desforges (after Soulier), Royaumont Castle, 30 October 1836.

Alice, Comte de Sussy and D. de Laperriere, Paris, Hôtel de Castellane, 8 April 1837.

La lettre du préfet, E. Bergounioux, Paris, Salon Gressler, 1837; revised 1868.

Le comte de Saint-Mégrin (*La duchesse de Guise*), F. and C. de la Bouillerie (after Dumas, *Henri III et sa cour*), Royaumont Castle, 10 June 1838; revised as *Le duc de Guise,* Paris, Ventadour, 3 April 1840; German translation, Schwerin, 24 February 1841.

Le naufrage de la Méduse (with Grisar), Hippolyte and Théodore Cogniard, Paris, Théâtre de la Renaissance, 31 May 1839; revised and enlarged as *Die Matrosen,* Hamburg, 23 December 1845.

L'esclave de Camoëns, J.H. Vernoy de Saint-Georges, Paris, Opéra-Comique, 1 December 1843; second version: *Indra, das Schlangemädchen,* Gustav Gans zu Putlitz, Vienna, 18 December 1852; third version: *Alma, L'incantrice*

Friedrich von Flotow

(*L'enchanteresse*), J.H. Vernoy de Saint-Georges, Paris, Théâtre-Italien, 6 April 1878; fourth version: *Die Hexe,* 1879.

Alessandro Stradella, F.W. Riese, Hamburg, Stadttheater, 30 December 1844 [recomposed from incidental music to the play by P.A.A. Pittaud de Forges and P. Duport].

L'âme en peine (*Der Förster*) (*Leoline*), J.H. Vernoy de Saint-Georges, Paris, Opéra, 29 June 1846.

Martha, oder, Der Markt zu Richmond, F.W. Riese (after the Ballet, *Lady Harriette*), Vienna, Kärntnertor, 25 November 1847.

Sophia Katharina, oder Die Grossfürstin, C. Birch-Pfeiffen, Berlin, Hofoper, 19 November 1850.

Rübezahl, Gustav Gans zu Putlitz, Retzien, 13 August 1852 (private performance); Frankfurt am Main, 26 November 1853.

Albin, oder Der Pflegesohn, Salomon H. Mosenthal (after *Les deux savoyards*), Vienna, Kärntnertor, 12 February 1856; revised as *Der Müller von Meran,* Königsberg, 1859, Gotha, 15 January 1860.

Herzog Johann Albrecht von Mecklenburg, oder Andreas Mylius, Hobein, Schwerin, 27 May 1857.

Pianella, Emil Pohl (after Federico, *La serva padrona*). Schwerin. 27 December 1857.

La veuve Grapin, P.A.A. Pittaud de Forges, Paris, Théâtre des Bouffes-Parisiens, 21 September 1859; performed in German, Vienna, Theater am Franz-Josephs-Kai, 1 June 1861.

Naida (*Le vannier*) translated into Russian from J.H. Vernoy de Saint-Georges and Léon Hálevy, St. Petersburg, 11 December 1865.

La châtelaine (*Der Märchensucher*), M.A. Grandjean, Vienna, Karl Theater, September 1865; revised K. Treumann as *Das Burgfräulein.*

Zilda, ou La nuit des dupes, J.H. Vernoy de Saint-Georges, Henri Charles Chivot, and A. Duru, Paris, Opéra-Comique, 28 May 1866.

Am Runenstein, Richard Genée, Prague, 13 April 1868.

Die Musikanten (*La Jeunesse de Mozart*), Richard Genée, Mannheim, 19 June 1887.

L'ombre, J.H. Vernoy de Saint-Georges and Adolphe de Leuven, Paris, Opéra-Comique, 7 July 1870; German translation as *Sein Schatten,* Vienna, Theater an der Wien, 10 November 1871.

La fleur de Harlem, J.H. Vernoy de Saint-Georges (after Dumas); in Italian as *Il fiore di Harlem,* Turin, 18 November 1876.

Rosellana, c. 1878, Achille de Lauzières de Thémines [unfinished].

Sakuntala, c. 1878-81 C. d'Ormeville (after Kalidasa).

Other works: ballets, incidental music, instrumental works, choral works, songs.

Publications/Writings

By FLOTOW: articles–

"Erinnerungen aus meinem Leben." In *Vor dem Coulissen,* edited by J. Lewinsky, ii. Berlin, 1882; reprint in *Deutsche Revue* 8 (1883): 61.

About FLOTOW: books–

Bussensius, A.F. *Friedrich von Flotow: eine Biographie.* Kassel, 1855.

Gleich, F. *Wegweiser für Opernfreunde.* Leipzig, 1857.

————. *Pracht-Album für Theater und Musik.* Vienna, Leipzig, and Dresden, 1861.

————. *Charakterbilder aus der neueren Geschichte der Tonkunst,* 1. Leipzig, 1863.

Svoboda, R. *Friedrich von Flotow's Leben: von seiner Witwe.* Leipzig, 1892.

Beyer, R. von. *Meine Begegnung mit Goethe und anderen grossen Zeitgenossen,* edited by R. Schade. Berlin, 1930.

Henseler, A. *Jakob Offenbach.* Berlin, 1930.

Weissmann, J.S. *Flotow.* London, 1950.

articles–

Grandjean, M.A. "Klein Reminiszensen." *Deutsche Kunst- und Musikzeitung* 10, 7 April (1883).

Breakspeare, E.J. "F. v. Flotow." *Musical Opinion* 23 (1899).

Dent, Edward. "A Best-Seller in Opera." *Music and Letters* 22 (1941): 139.

Stockhammer, R. "Friedrich von Flotows Beziehungen zu Wien" *Österreichische Musikzeitschrift* 17 (1962): 175.

Hübner, W. "Martha, Martha, komm doch wieder." *Musik und Gesellschaft* 13 (1963): 618.

Kaiser, Fritz, "Flotow in Darmstadt. Zum 100. Todestag des Komponisten der *Martha.*" In *Mitteilungen der Arbeitgemeinschaft für mittelrheinische Musik-geschichte* 47 (1983): 278.

————. "Von hundert Jahren starb Friedrich von Flotow." *Deutsches Adelsblatt* 22 (1983): 7.

unpublished–

Bardi-Poswiansky, B. "Flotow als Opernkomponist." Ph.D. dissertation, University of Königsberg, 1924.

*   *   *

Although Flotow was born in Mecklenberg, and composed his two most famous works, *Martha* and *Alessandro Stradella,* to German libretti, it would be a mistake to judge him as a "German" composer. Of an ancient aristocratic family, he came to Paris at the age of sixteen to study under Anton Reicha, whose other pupils would include Berlioz, Gounod, and César Franck. Except for a short time in 1830 when he returned home in the aftermath of the 1830 Revolution against Charles X, Flotow was seldom far from Paris for almost two decades. He knew the foremost French composers of the day, Auber, Cherubini, and Halévy, as well as the two Germans who redefined French theater music in the mid-19th century, Meyerbeer and Offenbach.

Most of Flotow's earliest works were written for, and in the style preferred by, the salons of the rich and titled, where talented amateurs performed them. His stylistic influences were not Beethoven, Weber, and Marschner, but Boieldieu, Auber, and Cherubini. As his two best-known operas show, he was not unmindful of the tradition within which his German contemporaries Lortzing and Nicolai were writing successfully, but musically his allegiance was to France (and, to a lesser extent, to the Rossinian influence from Paris).

Alessandro Stradella, Flotow's first international success, reveals both his strengths and his weaknesses. Like the later *Martha,* it contains one unforgettable aria, the eponymous tenor's "Jungfrau Maria," a prayer he has composed to the Virgin, the performance of which saves him from assassins. Otherwise, the score demonstrates Flotow's capacity to produce facile melody, his thoroughly professional orchestral writing, and his unevenness of invention. Some of the arias

and ensembles, notably the quartet "Italia, mein Vaterland," have an undeniable charm, but they are linked by other numbers which, though pleasant, possess little individuality.

With *Martha,* an expansion of music he had previously composed for a cooperative ballet, Flotow found a subject which inspired him to compose his most consistently inventive score. Using a succession of finely-wrought duets and intricate ensembles punctuated only three times by solo arias (the tenor's "Ach so fromm," Lady Harriet's "The Last Rose of Summer," and Plunkett's drinking song), he paces the work masterfully, leading up to the third act finale, its main melody heard earlier in the conclusion of the overture, "Mag der Himmel euch vergeben."

His international reputation assured in his thirty-fifth year, Flotow continued to write for both the German and French stages until his death. Whereas his contemporary Meyerbeer explored the dramatic possibilities of the orchestra as protagonist, and massive changes were being wrought by Wagner and Verdi, Flotow was content to reflect the conservative simplicity which had served him so well. There are no neglected masterpieces among his forgotten works, though *L'âme en peine* (1846), which contains the first use of the "Ach so fromm" melody, the once highly popular *La veuve Grapin* (1859), and his last success, *L'ombre* (1870), deserve an occasional hearing. The latter especially is much superior overall to the overrated (at least at one time) *Stradella,* and is an outstanding example, perhaps the last of its genre, of the kind of opéra-comique produced by Auber and his school.

—William J. Collins

————

FLOYD, Carlisle.

Composer. Born 11 June 1926, in Latta, South Carolina. Studied composition with Ernst Bacon at Syracuse University, A.B. 1946, M.A. 1949; private lessons with Rudolf Firkusny and Sidney Foster; on the staff of the School of Music, Florida State University at Tallahassee, 1947; professor of music at the University of Houston, 1976; his opera *Susannah* received the New York Music Critics Circle Award as the best opera of 1956.

Operas

Publishers: Belwin-Mills, Boosey and Hawkes.

Slow Dusk, Floyd, 1949, Syracuse, New York, May 1949.
The Fugitives, Floyd, 1951, Tallahassee, Florida, 1951.
Susannah, Floyd, 1954, Tallahassee, Florida, 24 February 1955.
Wuthering Heights, Floyd (after Brontë), 1958, Santa Fe, 16 July 1958; revised, 1959.
The Passion of Jonathan Wade, Floyd, 1962, New York, 11 October 1962.
The Sojourner and Mollie Sinclair, Floyd, 1963, Raleigh, North Carolina, 2 December 1963.
Markheim, Floyd (after Stevenson), 1966, New Orleans, 31 March 1966.
Of Mice and Men, Floyd (after Steinbeck), 1969, Seattle, Washington, 22 January 1970.
Bilby's Doll, Floyd (after E. Forbes, *A Mirror for Witches*), 1976, Houston, 29 February 1976.

Willie Stark, Floyd (after R.P. Warren, *All the King's Men*), 1981, Houston, 24 April 1981.

Publications/Writings

By FLOYD: articles–

"Bronte Heroine: the Cathy of Wuthering Heights posed Problems for Opera Setting." *New York Times* 13 July (1958).
"The Composer as Librettist." *Opera News* 27/no. 3(1962): 9.
"Victorian Gothic" [interview]. *Opera News* 30/no. 22 (1966): 17.
"Of Mice and Men." *Opera News* 34/no. 1 (1969): 20.
Review of *Richard Strauss: A Chronicle of the Early Years, 1864-1898,* by Willi Schuh (translated by Mary Whittall). In *Opera Quarterly* 2 (1984): 132.

About FLOYD: articles–

Mordden, Ethan C. "Unprotected Poet." *Opera News* 40/no. 13 (1976): 12.
Porter, Andrew. "Musical Events: Down in the Valley." *New Yorker* 58/no. 5 April (1982): 172.

unpublished–

McDevitt, F.J. "The Stage Works of Carlisle Floyd, 1949-72." Ph.D. dissertation, Juilliard School of Music, 1975.

*   *   *

Carlisle Floyd's career spans over thirty years and includes nine full length productions, yet his place in the history of American opera remains unclear. Despite several critical successes, including *Susannah,* which won the New York Critics Circle Award in 1956, he has not attained the status level of other prominent American composers. As Andrew Porter has noted (*New Yorker* 5 April 1982), "If there is a national repertory to be discerned here, it is—at any rate, on the far shores of the Hudson—founded largely on Floyd's work. . . . [Yet] there is something about Floyd's operas that pleases the public but often inhibits simple, unreserved praise from critics." Though Floyd's own librettos often excel in the ability to convey high drama, according to most critics the composer has never succeeded in developing a bold music language which sustains its own internal development and momentum.

At their best, Floyd's works offer a compelling and complete drama centered around highly charged scenes. He focuses on American themes, and the plots usually pit an individualistic protagonist against society's norms with tragic results. The subject matter may often relate directly to profound conflicts within contemporary America: *The Passion of Jonathan Wade,* in which a Northerner works in the South during Reconstruction, appeared at the onset of the civil rights movement in the early 1960s. The music is often eclectic in style and combines traditions and techniques such as American folk music, Wagnerian leitmotif effects, Puccini's lyrical sense, and sometimes even Broadway. Winthrop

Sargeant (*New Yorker* 27 October 1956) wrote of *Susannah:* "This style owes a great deal to the homely idioms of real American religious and folk music, but Mr. Floyd's work is by no means the dreary essay in musical ethnology that American 'folk operas' have usually turned out to be. The language he employs in telling a story that moves forward with enthralling intensity is clearly his own, and he uses it with the intellectual control and the theatrical flair that bespeak both the serious composer and the born musical dramatist."

Some critics, however, find that this eclecticism leads Floyd astray. Irving Kolodin, who was enthusiastic about *Susannah* as well, expressed disappointment with *The Passion of Jonathan Wade:* "My conclusion is that Floyd is conducting a search for identity which has led him into a kind of musical Everglades. What he needs is the vantage point of perspective from which one can chart the way out of such dilemmas, artistic as well as geographic." (*Saturday Review* 27 October 1962).

Floyd's operas pose aesthetic problems beyond the merely technical. In his writings, Floyd displays a greater concern over the libretto than the music. He states (*Opera News* 10 November 1962) that "Perhaps the greatest advantage enjoyed by a composer-librettist is his tremendously increased awareness of dramatic elements, a general sharpening of his theatrical acuity. By necessity he is forced to think in dramatic terms, both in structure and content." Concerning *Wuthering Heights,* (*New York Times* 13 July 1958) "I have tried to tackle head-on with this opera a basic aesthetic difficulty that composing music for this medium presents us with. That is, I have tried to strike a balance between two polarities, symphonically conceived music on the one hand that is essentially theatrical effect on the other." Not surprisingly, Floyd has also been directly involved in the stage direction. As Frank Merkling of *Opera News* (1 December 1962) has perceptively commented: "*The Passion of Jonathan Wade . . .* suggests that there are two Carlisle Floyds. One writes plays; the other wants to compose stirring operas."

Critics echo Floyd's conception of music as "theatrical effect", but often find the results to be less than satisfying. Thus, Andrew Porter has written of *Susannah* that "most of the time the music is an accompaniment to the drama, not really dramatic in itself. To justify that charge, I'd point (as I did when writing about *Bilby's Doll*) to the reluctance of the harmonies to move, to impel and not merely follow the drama; and also to the way that Floyd, when he gets hold of a good idea, works it out thoroughly, doggedly, without the flights of imaginative fancy that suggest the music has taken on a life of its own. . . . . . *Susannah* depends a lot on its acting. In elaborate rubrics, Floyd spells out what his music alone does not convey."

This charge has been repeated with *Of Mice and Men,* adapted from the Steinbeck novel. Robert Commanday (*New York Times* 1 February 1970) found that "Floyd's orchestral score does not develop the deeper more powerful qualities that should comment on the drama; this is still opera dominated by text and vocal line—a musical play. It's as if the prose and melody had been set and the orchestral music created as accompaniment." And Phillip Gainsley (*Opera News* 12 December 1970) specifically pointed out how "Part of the blame falls on the lack of melody and the repetition of phrases in the score. Crescendoes and sudden changes in tempo, even in the more subdued scenes tend to vitiate the compassion and sensitivity of the libretto. Thus, whether a particular work succeeds, depends seemingly on one's critical view point, and the extent to which the music integrates into the drama, rather than perhaps the other way around."

The issue recurred with Floyd's last full length score *Willie Stark*. Here, Floyd employs long passages of dialogue over a small thirty-six piece Broadway-style orchestra, and at the premiere preferred lightly amplified singers to a full voice production. The most vitriolic response came from Donal Henehan of the *New York Times:* "Mr Floyd's work . . . retold Mr. Warren's many-leveled tale in a one-dimensional Broadway musical style, which relied for most of its appeal on period flavor and tricky staging ideas. The music was pushed into the background rather effectively." Not all critics disliked the overall effect, however, and Andrew Porter felt it to be "a dexterous and accomplished piece," noting that "*Willie Stark* is a political opera that picks up some threads from Marc Blitzstein's political operas, some of its dramaturgy (I think) from *Evita,* and some of its musical manners from Broadway ballads. It is a bold and adventurous work. Over the air . . . it seemed to me brilliant."

Though critics have yet to agree on Floyd's work, *Susannah* and *Of Mice and Men* continue to be performed and remain among the most successful and popular of American operas. Despite some aesthetic confusion and the lack of consistent critical success, "Floyd's music speaks to the contemporary American operagoer" (Frank Warnke, *Opera News* 14 March 1970).

—David Pacun

THE FLYING DUTCHMAN
See DER FLIEGENDE HOLLÄNDER

THE FORCE OF DESTINY
See LA FORZA DEL DESTINO

THE FOREIGN LADY
See LA STRANIERA

LA FORZA DEL DESTINO [The Force of Destiny].

Composer: Giuseppe Verdi.

Librettist: Francesco Maria Piave (after Angelo Pérez de Saavedra, *Don Alvaro, o La fuerze de Sino,* and Schiller, *Wallensteins Lager*).

First Performance: St Petersburg, Imperial Theater, 10 November 1862; revised, libretto by A. Ghislanzoni, Milan, Teatro alla Scala, 27 February 1869.

Roles: Leonora (soprano); Don Alviro (tenor); Don Carlo (baritone); Padre Guardiano (bass); Preziosilla (mezzo-soprano); Curra (soprano); Trabucco (tenor); Fra Melitone (baritone); Alcalde (bass); Surgeon (baritone); Marquis di Calatrava (bass); chorus (SSSATTTBBB).

Publications

book–

Rescigno, E. *"La Forza del destino" di Verdi.* Milan, 1981.

articles–

Bollettino dell' Institute de Studi Verdiani [Parma] 2 (1961-66) [*La forza del destino* issue].
Porter, A. "Destination Unknown; or, How Should *Forza* End?" *Opera* November (1981).

*   *   *

With the sole exception of *Don Carlos,* none of Verdi's operas is on the epic scale of *La forza del destino.* The action takes place over an indeterminate number of years in both Spain and Italy and requires a large cast. Unlike several operas of middle period Verdi, such as *La traviata, Rigoletto* and *Luisa Miller, Forza* is not really about people. The theme of the opera is fate, which determines the lives of the three major protagonists. Heroic characters in a tragedy seek to determine their destinies but are undermined by their own character faults. *Forza* is not like this: Leonora, Don Alvaro, and Don Carlos have no control over circumstance.

It is sometimes suggested that the opera is made unwieldy by Verdi's mixing of sources. The opera is formally based on a play by the Duke of Rivas, but the encampment scene which involves a major enhancement of the role of the gypsy, Preziosilla, is derived from Schiller's Wallenstein plays. The very length of the opera and its apparent unwieldiness have inspired editors to make various cuts, but Verdi knew his business. It is, of course, the case that the "high born" and "low born" characters know little about each other and probably care less. But if Don Alvaro knows nothing of Melitone's soup kitchen, he has little more appreciation of Don Carlos' motivations, and in the first version of the opera he has little time for Padre Guardiano's sanctimoniousness. The opera has been described as a long duet, but in the first-act love scene and the later duel scenes the protagonists communicate at, rather than with, each other. Only between Guardiano and Melitone is there some real communication and, perhaps, a little understanding.

The ending was a problem for Verdi. There were simply too many dead bodies for the critics at the first performance in St Petersburg and in early productions in Italy. Verdi's 1869 revision introduces the fine last trio in which Alvaro is urged by Guardiano to accept God's comfort. Perhaps to make this a more likely denouement Verdi removed Alvaro's "blood and thunder" aria from the end of act IV—a real musical loss—and also re-arranged the sequencing of acts III and IV, making the dramatic flow even less comprehensible. However, various small compositional changes were almost all for the better. The famous 1869 overture replacing the 1862 prelude is probably Verdi's masterpiece of the genre.

Once the 1869 version entered the repertoire, the original version was almost forgotten. Producers tampered with the order of events in the middle scenes and made various cuts, but surprisingly in an age of interest in the first thoughts of composers there was no interest in the 1862 *Forza*. However, in the early 1970s the British Broadcasting Corporation gave a studio performance. In 1990 The Scottish National Opera mounted a production including the 1862 prelude, Alvaro's "additional" aria and the original ordering of acts III and IV, but otherwise using the musical score of 1869. The result was a performance of great musical and dramatic impact.

—Stanley Henig

FORZANO, Giovacchino.

Librettist. Born 19 November 1884, in Borgo San Lorenzo, Florence. Died 18 October 1970, in Rome. Director of the *Giornale apucano* and collaborator on *La Mazione, La Stampa,* and *Il Corriere della Sera;* scenic director at the Teatro alla Scala, 1920-30, then at the Teatro San Carlo in Naples and the Teatro Regio in Turin.

A poster for Puccini's *Suor Angelica,* from *Il trittico,* set to a libretto by Giovacchino Forzano

Librettos

Galvina, L. Ferrari-Trecate, 1904.
Fiorella, L. Ferrari-Trecate, 1904.
Santa Poesia, D. Cortopassi, 1909.
La reginetta delle rose, R. Leoncavallo, 1912.
L'aquila e le colombe, G. Luporini, 1914.
Notte di leggenda, A. Franchetti, 1915.
La candidata, R. Leoncavallo, 1915.
Lodoletta (after Ouida), P. Mascagni, 1917.
Gianni Schicchi, G. Puccini, 1918.
Suor Angelica, G. Puccini, 1918.
Edipo re, R. Leoncavallo, 1920.
Il piccolo Marat, P. Mascagni, 1921.
Ciottolino, L. Ferrari-Trecate, 1922.
Glauco (after E.L. Morselli), A. Franchetti, 1922.
I compagnacci, P. Riccitelli, 1923.
Giocondo e il suo re (after Ariosto), C. Jachino, 1924.
Gli amanti sposi (with I. Sugana, G. Pizzola, and E. Golisciani, after Goldoni, *Ventaglio*) [libretto completed 1904, E. Wolf-Ferrari], E. Wolf-Ferrari, 1925.
I carnasciali, G. Laccetti, 1925.
Delitto e castigo (after Dostoyevsky), A. Pedrollo, 1926.
Sly ovvero La legenda del dormiente risvegliato (after Shakespeare), E. Wolf-Ferrari, 1927.
Tien-Hoa, G. Bianchini, 1928.
Il Re, U. Giordano, 1929.
Fiori del Brabante, various composers, 1930.
Madonna Oretta, P. Riccitelli, 1932.
Palla de'Mozzi, G. Marinuzzi, 1932.
Ginevra degli Almieri, M. Peragallo, 1937.
Lo stendardo di San Giorgio, M. Peragallo, 1941.
Lisistrata, V. De Sabata [not performed].

Publications

By FORZANO: books–

Mussolini autore drammatico. Florence, 1954.
Come li ho conosciuti. Turin, 1957.

About FORZANO: articles–

Klein, John W. "Giovacchino Forzano, 1884-1970." *Opera* April (1971).
Fischer-Williams, Barbara. "Forzano Remembered." *Opera News* 41 (1977): 14.
Ashbrook, William. "*Turandot* and its Posthumous *prima.*" *Opera Quarterly* 2/no. 3 (1984): 126.

* * *

In his study of operatic dramaturgy entitled *The Tenth Muse,* Patrick Smith writes that "the modern Italian libretto . . . was remarkable not only for its quality but also for its scope. . . . The contrasts in tone and spirit within the Italian libretto are well encapsulated in Puccini's *Il Trittico.* . . . Any study of the differing texts set by Mascagni, Montemezzi, Franchetti, Puccini, and Leoncavallo will demonstrate the strength of the Italian libretto of its time, and if many of the conceits of the period have ceased to appeal with the power they once had, the vitality of the period is evident" (p. 360). Despite being the librettist for two thirds of the *Trittico* and having worked with four out of the five aforementioned composers, in addition to maintaining a prominent career as stage director of Teatro alla Scala, little has been written about

Giovacchino Forzano's contribution to Italian opera. He appears in neither *The New Grove Dictionary of Music and Musicians* nor *Baker's Biographical Dictionary of Musicians.*

Forzano is generally praised for his *Suor Angelica* and *Gianni Schicchi* librettos. As Spike Hughes notes in *Famous Puccini Operas,* both "were conceived . . . as operatic subjects custom built for Puccini right from the start, and . . . the composer seems to have had far less trouble writing the music for these two one-acters . . . than ever before in his career" (p. 173). Hughes sees particular talent in Forzano's adaptive and creative abilities: "[with *Gianni Schicchi*] Forzano took no more than the bare facts mentioned by Dante and elaborated and developed the situation into a comedy of great wit and ingenuity." William Ashbrook (*The Operas of Puccini*) also sees both works as "among the best that Puccini set to music" (p. 181), but nevertheless sees a weakness in the "loose" structure of *Suor Angelica:* "The exposition consists of a series of vignettes that establishes a picture of convent life. These scenes with their seemingly random sequence provide the necessary contrast for the main plot. The looseness of structure is confirmed by Puccini's cuts and changes." In contrast, "the libretto of *Gianni Schicchi* is tart and vivid." Richard Sprecht, a Puccini biographer, views Forzano's work as "terse and effective dramatic anecdotes and at the same time presenting brilliant contrast to each other."

More recent critical attention has been paid to Forzano's role as stage director for the premier of Puccini's *Turandot* (and also Boito's *Nerone*) at La Scala under Toscanini. Forzano's notes for the production have been preserved in the *disposizione scenica* and have been discussed in detail by Ashbrook, who states that Forzano "impresses by his resourcefulness in revealing motivation and character, in heightening conflict through movement" (*Puccini's "Turandot": The End of the Great Tradition*). In an article published in the autumn 1984 issue of *Opera Quarterly,* Ashbrook wrote that Forzano "stress[es] an aura of massive and spectacular chinoiserie. . . . [The crowds then] serve as a living backdrop for the great confrontation between Turandot and Calaf, yet not an impassive one, for Forzano was concerned that the group's partisanship should be clearly projected." Ashbrook concludes that though "there is something that, perhaps, strikes us today as old-fashioned and flamboyant about many of these directions, no one could for a minute deny the clarity and consistency of Forzano's approach, nor find it inappropriate to the far-flung rhetoric of the music and text."

Forzano's later career as a playwright and film director in Fascist Italy have come under far harsher criticism. James Hay (*Popular Film Culture in Fascist Italy*) finds that Forzano's film *Camicia nera* (1933), though complex in its use of silent film techniques and in its interrelationship with other historical films, nevertheless "clearly stands as an example of political propaganda." Edward Tannenbaum describes Forzano as "a thirdrate playwright who sometimes served as a mouthpiece for Mussolini," and whose plays were "vulgar and pretentious" (*The Fascist Experience: Italian Society and Culture 1922-45*).

—David Pacun

FOSS, Lukas (born Lukas Fuchs).

Composer. Born 15 August 1922, in Berlin. Studied piano and music theory with Julius Goldstein-Herford in Berlin; studied piano with Lazare Lévy, flute with Marcel Moÿse, composition with Noël Gallon, and orchestration with Felix Wolfes in Paris at the Lycée Pasteur, 1933-37; studied piano with Isabelle Vengerova, composition with Rosario Scalero, and conducting with Fritz Reiner at the Curtis Institute in Philadelphia, beginning 1937; studied conducting with Koussevitzky at the Berkshire Music Center in Tanglewood, Massachusetts, 1940-43; studied composition with Hindemith at Yale University, 1940-41; naturalized American citizen, 1942; two Guggenheim fellowships for composition, 1945 and 1960; as internationally acclaimed pianist, premiered his own works; conducting debut with Pittsburgh Symphony Orchestra, 1939; pianist of the Boston Symphony Orchestra, 1944-1950; in Rome on a Fulbright fellowship and as a fellow of the American Academy, 1950-52; professor of composition and conducting, and established the Improvisation Chamber Ensemble at the University of California Los Angeles, 1953-62; State Department tour of Russia, 1960; music director and conductor, Buffalo Philharmonic Orchestra, 1963-1970; led the concert series "Evenings of New Music," New York, 1964-65; music director of the American-French Festival, Lincoln Center, 1965; principal conductor of the Brooklyn Philharmonic, 1971-90, where he established a "Meet the Moderns" concert series; conductor, Jerusalem Symphony Orchestra, 1972-76; director of the Milwaukee Symphony Orchestra, 1980-86; composer in residence, Tanglewood, 1989-90; professor of composition, Boston University, 1991-.

Operas

Publishers: C. Fischer, Salabert, G. Schirmer, Boosey and Hawkes.

The Jumping Frog of Calaveras County, J. Karsavina (after Twain), 1949, Bloomington, Indiana, 18 May 1950.
Griffelkin, A. Reed (after H. Foss), 1955, NBC television, 6 November 1956.
Introductions and Goodbyes, G. Menotti, New York, 5 May 1960.

Other works: orchestral works, chamber music, choral works, solo vocal.

Publications

By FOSS: interviews

Gagne, Cole, and Tracy Caras, eds. *Soundpieces: Interviews with American Composers,* 193 ff. Metuchen, New Jersey, 1982.
Interviews by Vivian Perlis, 1988. Oral History, American Music, Yale University, New Haven, Connecticut.

About FOSS: books–

Perone, Karen L. *Lukas Foss; A Bio-Bibliography.* Westport, Connecticut, 1991.

articles–

Berger, A. "Spotlight on the Moderns." *Saturday Review* 34/no. 63 (1951).
Mellers, W. "Today and Tomorrow: Lukas Foss and the Younger Generation." In *Music in a New Found Land,* 220. New York, 1965.

Salzman, E. "The Many Lives of Lukas Foss." *Saturday Review* 1 (1967): 73.

Waugh, J. "Chance, Choice and Lukas Foss." In *1st American Music Conference: Keele 1975,* edited by P. Dickinson, 37. Keele, England, 1977.

*   *   *

Lukas Foss has become one of the leading musical figures of the twentieth century, realizing the extraordinary gifts evident from the time he was a youthful prodigy in Germany. Never content to limit himself, Foss became a pianist and conductor as well as composer. In recent years, he has given more of his time and efforts to conducting. His curiosity and his wide-ranging interests are qualities that show themselves in his music and have frequently brought forth charges of eclecticism. Not content to develop one recognizable musical style, Foss views his use of varied sources as a positive element. His natural talents and technical mastery of many styles and periods have resulted in works that range from neoclassical, such as the Symphony in G, to American folkloristic as *The Prairie* and the comic opera, *The Jumping Frog of Calaveras County,* which makes use of folk music and a text by Mark Twain. It is the most recognized of his three vocal stage works and is characteristic of his diversified approach: a synthesizing of early twentieth-century European cynicism as in early Kurt Weill with American popular idioms. Foss' other stage works, *Griffelkin* (1955) and the one-act *Introductions and Goodbyes* (1959), are unpretentious and informal rather than of grand operatic tradition.

During Lukas Foss' long career, he turned to improvisation, particularly while at UCLA in the 1950s, and these experiments turned him away from neoclassicism and tonality to a use of various advanced systems such as serialism, indeterminacy, and electronic music. Foss is similar to Charles Ives in his inclusivity: no musical idea need be excluded as a source of expression. Contrary to Ives, Foss' active involvement in the world of music as performer, conductor and promoter of contemporary music adds to his stature as one of the significant figures of twentieth-century music.

—Vivian Perlis

FOUR SAINTS IN THREE ACTS.

Composer: Virgil Thomson.

Librettist: Gertrude Stein.

First Performance: Hartford, Connecticut, 8 February 1934.

Roles: St Teresa I (soprano); St Teresa II (mezzo-soprano); St Settlement (soprano); St Chavez (tenor); St Ignatius (baritone); Commère (mezzo-soprano); Compère (bass); St Plan (bass); St Stephen (tenor); small chorus of named saints with solo lines (SATB); large chorus (SATB).

Publications

articles–

Smith, C. "Thomson's Four Saints Live again on Broadway." *Musical America* 72/no. 7 (1952): 7.

Garvin, H.R. "Sound and Sense in *Four Saints in Three Acts.*" *Bucknell Review* 5/no. 1 (1954): 1.

Helm, E. "Virgil Thomson's *Four Saints in Three Acts.*" *Music Review* 15 (1954): 127.

unpublished–

Ward, K.M. "An Analysis of the Relationship between Text and Musical Shape: an Investigation of the Relationship between Text and Surface Rhythmic Details in 'Four Saints in Three Acts' by Virgil Thomson." Ph.D. dissertation, University of Texas, Austin, 1978.

*   *   *

Despite its name, Virgil Thomson's first opera features approximately thirty saints in a prologue and four acts. Set in Spain, the plotless and free-wheeling work with its vivid stream-of-consciousness libretto by Gertrude Stein is, according to Thomson in his autobiography, about "the religious life—peace between the sexes, community of faith, the production of miracles." Lacking a logical story progression, the opera presents a course of tableaux and processions which are dominated by two major saints, Teresa of Avila and Ignatius Loyola. An uninhibited blend of gravely devout episodes and theatrical choruses, piety and circus parades, sense and nonsense, the work amuses and amazes. As John Cage explains in his *Virgil Thomson: His Life and Music,* the hearer of *Four Saints in Three Acts* must "leap into that irrational world from which it sprang, the world in which the matter-of-fact and the irrational are one, where mirth and metaphysics marry to beget comedy."

It would have been interesting indeed to have been with Thomson in Paris during the work's composition. In the mornings he sat at his piano, text before him, and sang, improvising act by act. He wrote nothing down until an act had been repeated several times in the same way, placing great faith in the ability of his unconscious mind to shape the music to the text, including the stage directions which he felt formed a part of the poetic whole. Thomson's score is mainly diatonic and filled with snatches drawn from a wide musical range: Anglican chant, popular songs, ballads, nursery tunes, and dance melodies. The work often has a tongue-in-cheek resonance as Thomson weaves these varying musics into witty parodies of the conventional arias, recitatives, choruses, and ballets of grand opera. Moments of grandeur do surface here and there, but there is also much musical wit amidst the word play of Stein's poetry. Ever sensitive to prosody, Thomson's declamation is superb; he imbues the startling and seemingly incoherent text with energy. Having previously set Stein's "Susie Asado" and "Capital, Capitals," Thomson was in tune with her sensibilities and delighted by her poetic ear, finding her words quite often closer to music than to speech. The two were an imaginative, compatible team that could scarcely fail to produce a work of originality, flair, and odd magic.

The resounding success of the premiere was more than a parlor trick, however. The strange but tonal music and unorthodox libretto jarred the 1934 season and toppled the conventions of opera. With its famous and innovative collaborators, its all Black cast, and its sets of cellophane, feathers, shells, lace, and glitzy colored lights, *Four Saints in Three Acts* catapulted its composer into fame and fashion. Store windows imitated the sets, and the names of both the composer and the work were buzzwords among the society and intellectual sets that year. The opera toured in New York and Chicago, but Thomson went back to Paris a few months after the premiere and continued to compose and write extensively. It would, however, be more than a decade before he and Stein worked together again on his second opera, *The Mother of Us All*.

—Michael Meckna

FRA DIAVOLO, ou L'hôtellerie de Terracine [Brother Devil, or The Inn at Terracine].

Composer: Daniel-François-Esprit Auber.

Librettist: Eugène Scribe.

First Performance: Paris, Opéra-Comique, 28 January 1830.

Roles: Fra Diavolo (tenor); Lord Cockburn (baritone); Lady Pamela (mezzo-soprano); Zerlina (soprano); Lorenzo (tenor); Giacomo (tenor); Beppo (bass); Matteo (bass); Francesco (bass); a Miller (bass); chorus (SATB).

Fra Diavolo, **title page from a piano arrangement**

Publications

books—

Kirk, B.L. *The Role of Zerline in Auber's "Fra Diavolo": A Mirror of Her Age.* Ann Arbor, 1982.

articles—

Ringer, Alexander. "Fra Diavolo." *The Musical Quarterly* 38 (1952): 642.

*   *   *

The most widely known of D.F.E. Auber's thirty-six *opéras comiques, Fra Diavolo* is the only one to have remained popular up to the present day. The title character is based on a historical figure—Michele Pezza, an Italian outlaw and mercenary during the period of the Napoleonic occupation—and on the popular literature which grew up around this semi-legendary outlaw after his execution in 1806. Auber's opera had received over 900 performances in Paris alone by the beginning of the twentieth century (fewer, however, than his *Le domino noir,* which has since disappeared from the repertory).

Zerlina, the daughter of the innkeeper Matteo, is hoping to marry the young officer Lorenzo, but has been promised to a wealthy local farmer. Following the spirited overture and a drinking chorus for Lorenzo and his *carabinieri* (during which they also discuss the price placed on the head of the notorious Fra Diavolo), Zerlina and Lorenzo reflect on their sad plight. Amidst much commotion a wealthy English couple arrives, Lord Coekburn (whose name appears in a confusing array of variants in different sources—in the text he is usually referred to simply as "Milord") and Lady Pamela, who have just been accosted by the outlaw and his band. They give expression to their marital difficulties in a humorous set of couplets ("Je voulais bien"). Fra Diavolo then arrives, presenting himself as the "Marquis de San Marco," in which guise he has been trailing the English couple for some time. In response to the disingenuous questions of the "Marquis," Zerlina sings her famous ballade ("Voyez sur cette roche"). With its mock-sinister refrain, "Diavolo, Diavolo, Diavolo!," it becomes a kind of signature tune for the opera. The Marquis renews his earlier attempts at seducing Lady Pamela, in hopes of acquiring her remaining money and jewels. In the finale to act I, Lorenzo announces his victory over the outlaw band (without their leader, of course) and the recovery of Pamela's jewel-case. Lorenzo and Zerlina rejoice over the reward bestowed upon them for this service, which will enable them to marry. Fra Diavolo and his cohorts, Giacomo and Beppo, contemplate their revenge.

Act II takes place in the evening, as the residents of the inn are preparing to retire. When all is quiet, Diavolo sings a barcarolle ("Agnes la jouvencelle") as a signal to his henchmen. The three of them hide in Zerlina's closet, with an eye to filching her new-found dowry. She sings to herself as she dons her nightclothes, admiring her figure in the mirror, to the amusement of the three men. Her simple and affecting prayer ("O vierge sainte en qui j'ai foi") causes them to hesitate in their attack, when suddenly Lorenzo and his men return, seeking food and shelter. In the finale, Diavolo is discovered in his hiding place and pretends to have made assignations with both Pamela and Zerlina. Lorenzo challenges him to a duel.

Act III opens with Diavolo's only solo number (recitative and aria, "Je vais marcher sous ma bannière") in which he merrily reflects on his outlaw existence. He contemplates his schemes to rob the Englishman and to ambush Lorenzo at the moment of their duel. Giacomo and Beppo encounter a chorus of peasants singing an Easter hymn, after which Lorenzo appears and laments his fiancée's apparent faithlessness in a Romance. As the act-III Finale begins, Zerlina is in despair at Lorenzo's accusations. When Giacomo and Beppo, sitting outside the inn, mockingly repeat Zerlina's words of the previous night (in front of the mirror), her suspicions are aroused. A note they carry reveals their complicity with Fra Diavolo, who is also apprehended upon returning to the scene, so that peace and order are restored (reprise of the chorus from finale, act I, "Victoire, victoire! Ils sont tombés sur nos coups!").

The success of *Fra Diavolo*, like that of most of Auber's comic operas in his own time, is due both to Eugène Scribe's entertaining, cleverly crafted text and to the easy charm of the composer's typical style: an abundance of simple, attractive tunes, brisk, toe-tapping ensembles and choruses, and a facility for smooth, natural musical dialogue in ensembles and finales. Since 1825, Auber had been striving to perfect a native French alternative to the Rossinian style that had recently conquered Paris and the rest of Europe. Thus the part of Zerlina is provided with enough coloratura writing to create a satisfying vehicle for a light, agile soprano voice without imposing demands that would restrict the casting of "provincial" performances. The rhythmic verve of Rossinian comedy is translated here into contemporary Parisian dance types, such as the quick waltz (three-eight or six-eight time) and the contredanse or quadrille. Auber also incorporates such fashionable genres as the vocal barcarolle—used to comic effect in the Marquis's seduction of Pamela in act I, and as a purely lyrical opportunity for the tenor in act II—and the sentimental Romance (Lorenzo's "Pour toujours, toujours, disait-elle" in act III). The major mode, dotted rhythms and allegretto tempo of the latter number are indicative of the composer's general disinclination for deep pathos or weighty expression of any kind, a disinclination for which he has been frequently chided by his critics. Certainly the jaunty swaggering of Fra Diavolo and the brisk marching-tunes of the *carabinieri* seem to lie at the heart of Auber's musical personality. On the other hand, Zerlina's "bedtime" aria and scene in act II, perhaps the finest number in the score, demonstrates Auber's ability to integrate within a continuous scene moments of sincere expression (Zerlina's touching seven-measure "litany" to the Virgin) with typical lightweight tunefulness (the opening aria) and frankly comic ensemble writing (the interjections of her would-be assailants). Scribe's witty parody in the portrayal of the English gentleman and his wife doubtless contributed something to the popularity of the opera, especially among French audiences.

Within the first decade of its premiere, *Fra Diavolo* had made its way as far as Budapest, Zagreb, Stockholm, St Petersburg, Warsaw, New York, Philadelphia, Bucharest, Calcutta, and Helsinki. The work still receives occasional performances in France and Germany, although it has become rare elsewhere. A studio recording including Nicolai Gedda (Fra Diavolo) and Mady Mesplé (Zerlina), conducted by Marc Soustrot, was released in 1984.

—Thomas S. Grey

FRANCESCA DA RIMINI.

Composer: Riccardo Zandonai.

Librettist: G. d'Annunzio (abridged by T. Ricordi).

First Performance: Turin, 1914.

Roles: Francesca (soprano); Samaritana (mezzo-soprano); Ostasio (baritone); Gianciotti (baritone); Paolo (tenor); Ma-

Francesca da Rimini, **poster by Giuseppe Palanti, 1914**

latestino (tenor); Biancofiore (soprano); Garsenda (soprano); Donella (soprano); Altichiara (mezzo-soprano); Smaragdi (mezzo-soprano); Ser Toldo Berardengo (tenor); Jester (baritone); chorus (SSAATTBB).

*   *   *

Zandonai's fourth opera, based on d'Annunzio's play of the same name from 1900, is the composer's most popular work, and the only one to have made any lasting international impact. The reduction of the play into a libretto was done by Tito Ricordi, after the rights had been secured from the poet at the enormous cost of twenty-five thousand lire. Later, when the composition was in progress, Zandonai and Ricordi together went to visit d'Annunzio in France to request and receive a new text for the third-act duet between the two lovers.

The setting of the opera is Italy at the end of the thirteenth century. Francesca, the daughter of Guido Minore da Polenta, is to be married to one of Malatesta da Verucchio's three sons. The husband chosen for her is the lame Giovanni lo Sciancato (Gianciotti), but she is tricked into believing that she will marry the handsome Paolo il Bello. After the marriage has taken place, Francesca and Paolo are unable to deny their love for each other, and drawing together while reading the story of Lancelot and Queen Guinevere, they kiss. The wicked third brother, Malatestino dall' Occhio, himself makes advances to Francesca and when she rejects him he tells Gianciotti of his suspicions about Paolo. Acting on this information, Gianciotti surprises the two lovers and kills them both.

The influences of recent operas on both librettist and composer are fairly audible in this work. Nevertheless, with the rhetoric and archaicism of d'Annunzio's text, the result is a satisfyingly confident example of the rosy-tinted view of the Renaissance current at the time (the designs for the premiere, in which Renaissance palaces were subtly transformed into bourgeois early twentieth-century homes, were striking).

As with other operas of the period, the immediate points of reference for *Francesca da Rimini* are Verdi's last two operas, *Otello* and *Falstaff*. (Zandonai, according to his biographer Vittoria Tarquini, intended the libretto to be the equal of Boito's text of *Falstaff*.) The sonata structure of the opening scene of Verdi's opera and the tossing of motifs between orchestra and singers set the standard for the composers of the *verismo* period and their successors.

Zandonai's method, developed from this model, relies on a network of significant themes, and he is more likely to favor the orchestra rather than the singer's line in driving a dramatic point home. Thus the *coup de théâtre* of the first act is the moment when Francesca and Paolo see each other for the first time and gaze in silence from either side of a gate. Above a static open chord in the bass and murmuring strings on top, a viola shapes a broad, rhapsodic theme as a wordless comment on the scene. When text does appear and voices re-enter, it is only Francesca's ladies singing yet another quaint song.

Strauss and Debussy are frequently named as the composers with most recognizable influence on Zandonai's scores, yet the influence has been absorbed into a fundamentally Italian musical idiom. The rhythmic fluidity of Debussy is missing, as is the sheer energy and free tonality of Strauss, whose *Elektra*, first performed in Italy in 1909, influenced the violent first scene of Zandonai's fourth act. One other work which resonates through *Francesca da Rimini* is

Wagner's *Tristan und Isolde*, not simply in the subject matter, but also in the sonorous B-major close to the love duet.

Perhaps the most interesting element of Zandonai's writing in *Francesca* is his harmonic idiom. He rarely writes a key signature, but where he does (and usually it is one of exaggerated sharpness or flatness), the major-key tonality arrived at is emphasized in its plainness, after a period of troubled chromaticism. Vocal and instrumental lines often move in tritones, and the composer exploits this interval and the whole tones contained in the French 6th chord, which will often be extended for many bars before resolving.

Elsewhere, relations at the third are used to propel the harmonic sense forward. These can be interspersed with chords created by adding whole tones to an existing harmony. The progression in the last scene on Francesca's words "Perdonami! / Un sonno duro più d'una percossa / mi spezzò l'anima" is typical in this respect. Zandonai, however, is not able to break out of conventional four-square melodic and harmonic periods to anything like the extent of *Elektra*. In addition, the self-conscious archaic quality of the text is often simply illustrated with apt music, rather than providing a springboard for the music to take flight. The exceptions are the mime at the end of the first act, the long love duet, and the two scenes of the fourth act. And sometimes Zandonai provides colorful touches of his own (a tiny sketch of the sea at the words "Guardate il mare come si fa bianco") which show him to be a composer with a keen theatrical imagination.

—Kenneth Chalmers

DIE FRAU OHNE SCHATTEN [The Woman Without a Shadow].

Composer: Richard Strauss.

Librettist: Hugo von Hofmannsthal.

First Performance: Vienna, Staatsoper, 10 October 1919.

Roles: The Emperor (tenor); The Empress (soprano); The Empress' Nurse (contralto); Barak, the Dyer (baritone); The Dyer's Wife (soprano); Spirit Messenger (baritone); Falcon (soprano); Hunchback (tenor); One-Eye (bass); One-Arm (bass); Apparition of Youth (tenor); Keeper of Temple (soprano); chorus (SSAATTBB).

Publications

books—

Röttger, H. *Das Formproblem bei Richard Strauss gezeigt an der "Die Frau ohne Schatten"*. Berlin, 1937.

Knaus, J. *Hugo von Hofmannsthal und sein Weg zur Oper Die Frau ohne Schatten*. Berlin, 1971.

Ascher, G.I. *Die Zauberflöte und die Frau ohne Schatten: ein Vergleich zwischen zwei Operndichtungen der Humanität*. Bern, 1972.

Pantle, Sherrill Hahn. *"Die Frau ohne Schatten" by Hugo von Hofmannsthal and Richard Strauss: an Analysis of Text, Music, and their Relationship*. Bern, 1978.

Set design by Alfred Roller for act II of *Die Frau ohne Schatten,* **first production, Vienna, 1919**

Konrad, Claudia. *Studien zu "Die Frau ohne Schatten" von Hugo von Hofmannsthal und Richard Strauss.* Hamburg, 1988.

articles–

Specht, R. "Vom *Guntram* zur *Frau ohne Schatten.*" In *Almanach der Deutschen Musikbücherei auf das Jahr 1923,* 150. Regensburg, 1923.
Erhart, O. "Richard Strauss's Die Frau ohne Schatten." *Tempo* 17 (1950).
Beinl, S. "A Producer's Viewpoint: Notes on Die Frau ohne Schatten." *Tempo* 24 (1952).
Gurewitsch, Matthew. "In the Mazes of Light and Shadow: a Thematic Comparison of *The Magic Flute* and *Die Frau ohne Schatten.*" *Opera Quarterly* 1/no. 2 (1983): 11.

*   *   *

Die Frau ohne Schatten, completed in 1917 and first performed in 1919, represents a climax of sorts for Strauss and Hofmannsthal. This elaborate allegorical fairy tale follows on the heels of *Ariadne auf Naxos,* and, like its predecessor, mixes mythology and domestic drama, although *Die Frau ohne Schatten* attains a size and scope that are unique in the Strauss-Hofmannsthal canon. After *Die Frau,* composer and librettist would abandon this intriguing mix of elements in favor of more straightforward works with less overtly symbolic references. Their subsequent operas are primarily settings of contemporary and historical domestic themes: the autobiographical *Intermezzo* (1924), and *Arabella* (1933), their final collaboration, are little more than a gloss on *Der Rosenkavalier.* Strauss and Hofmannsthal would return only once to the grandeur of a mythological theme, with *Die ägyptische Helena* (1928), a stiff and awkward piece which met with less than rapturous public acclaim. So *Die Frau* is the last of Strauss and Hofmannsthal's truly ambitious works, and it also serves as a critical transitional piece in our understanding of the team: in the vivid words of Ernst Kraus, *Die Frau ohne Schatten* "rears up like an immense mountain massif between the one-act tragedies of the first decade of the century and the sunlit slopes of the later operas."

It seems scarcely possible to imagine a more grandiose conception than that which lies behind this opera. Hofmannsthal's libretto drew on an immense and complex series of sources, from Grimm fairy tales and folk stories of China, Persia, and India, to the works of Goethe, Rückert, and other German Romantic poets. Strauss' music is of Wagnerian proportions: even heavily cut (as the opera invariably is in performance), it can run nearly four hours in length, and requires five star singers of almost superhuman stamina and power. These elements, coupled with the need for extraordinary and spectacular production effects, have prohibited *Die Frau* from being presented by any but the most ambitious opera companies—although in truth, even if the staging requirements were less limiting, the abstract and often murky symbolism of the opera probably rules it out for most popular tastes.

Hofmannsthal's libretto is a tale of two mythical couples—in particular, of two wives. One is a fairy empress who is too much a part of the spirit world: she has not achieved humanity. The other, the dyer's wife, is a mortal who is too much bound by earthly desires. For both women, their inability to integrate spiritual and human values is exemplified by their barrenness: the empress cannot have children, and the dyer's wife will not. The latter character, in fact, offers her shadow (a representation of fertility) to the empress in return for worldly riches. What follows in the action of the opera is a series of trials and rituals of purification for the two couples which resemble those undergone by Tamino and Pamina in Mozart's *Die Zauberflöte,* an opera which served as a conscious model for Strauss and Hofmannsthal in *Die Frau ohne Schatten,* just as in *Der Rosenkavalier* seven years before the two had paid homage to *Le nozze di Figaro.*

As with *Die Zauberflöte,* the densely allegorical nature of *Die Frau ohne Schatten* invites complex interpretation. Critics have written extensively on the meaning of Hofmannsthal's libretto, often giving particular significance to the fact that the opera was composed so soon after World War I, and suggesting that the ability to conceive, an issue so central to *Die Frau,* should be read broadly as referring to the survival of mankind rather than as a representation of purely personal fulfillment. In this view, the themes of creation, humanity, and survival are inexorably linked: perpetuation of the species can be ensured only by uniting the earthliness of man with the higher values of the spiritual realm. Hofmannsthal's letters to Strauss make clear that this idea was a primary theme in his libretto, but—again as with *Die Zauberflöte*—the end result is not wholly satisfying as an allegory. Too much of *Die Frau ohne Schatten* is merely obtuse and heavy-handed; worse, equating women's worth with childbearing, even in this special historical context, is depressingly antiquated and bourgeois, even—in light of the often overblown libretto—pretentious. Strauss himself questioned the wisdom of overlaying the text so heavily with symbols, insisting that the central issues were really quite clear and simple.

Hofmannsthal's response, as it always was when he felt Strauss had misunderstood a crucial point, was to despair that his composer was not a real intellectual. It is especially ironic, then, that Strauss' score seems to complement Hofmannsthal's libretto perfectly and in truth the music often more successfully realizes the scope and size of the poet's intention than the text itself does. In keeping with the Wagnerian style of *Die Frau ohne Schatten,* Strauss uses leitmotifs to define characters and ideas, and it is these themes which illuminate and clarify the story, guiding listeners through the often convoluted plot.

The music itself is some of Strauss' lushest and most demanding, combining the long melismatic vocal lines which are typical of his later operas with the jagged, often dissonant writing found in his early settings of mythology. The dense orchestration, reminiscent of Mahler and Wagner, further emphasizes the large scale of the work, and—coupled with the difficult vocal parts—makes extraordinary demands on the singers.

Strauss is justly celebrated for his ability to write marvelous music for sopranos, and *Die Frau* certainly has its share. The three female leads—the empress, the dyer's wife, and the nurse—are each given highly individualized treatments, but they share the gorgeous chromatic harmonies which are a Strauss trademark. The superb music for the male characters in *Die Frau* is more of a surprise. Most of Strauss' music for men's voices is of the character or buffo variety; he rarely

seemed interested in composing for a principal tenor or baritone. Yet the roles of the emperor and Barak, the dyer (tenor and baritone respectively) are executed with the same detail and sense of melody which characterize their spouses; the resulting duets and ensembles are quite beautiful.

It is the music of *Die Frau ohne Schatten* which is responsible for its continued place in opera theaters. And as difficult as the principal roles are to sing, several opera stars in recent years have made something of a specialty of the work. Leonie Rysanek was strongly identified with the part of the empress, and Christa Ludwig and Walter Berry had a joint triumph in performances as the dyer and his wife. Occasionally, these three singers came together, as in a now-legendary production at the Metropolitan Opera during the 1960s. Such performances, and the memory of them, ensure that *Die Frau ohne Schatten* will retain a place in the repertoire, but it is highly unlikely that this odd and difficult work will ever displace *Der Rosenkavalier* or *Elektra* in the public's affections.

—David Anthony Fox

FREEMAN, David.

Director and producer. Born 1 May 1951. Married: Marie Angel, 1985; one daughter. Education at Sydney University; founded and directed the Opera Factory in Sydney from 1973-76; founded the Opera Factory in Zurich in 1976 where he has since directed nineteen productions, appearing in five, and writing the text for three; founded the Opera Factory in London in 1981 where he has directed fifteen productions, seven of which were televised, and wrote the text for one; directed Johann Wolfgang von Goethe's *Faust* parts I and II at the Lyric, Hammersmith, 1980; Associate Artist, English National Opera beginning in 1981; adapted Malory's *Morte d'Arthur,* Lyric, Hammersmith, 1990; has produced operas in New York City, Houston, Paris, and Germany. Awards include Chevalier de l'Ordre des Arts et des Lettres, France, 1985.

Opera Productions (selected)

Orfeo ed Euridice, Sydney University, 1970.
Acis and Galatea, London, 1979.
Orfeo ed Euridice, English National Opera, 1981.
The Beggar's Opera, Drill Hall, London, 1981.
Così fan tutte, Zurich, 1982.
Happy End, 1982.
Punch and Judy, Drill Hall, London, 1982-83 season.
Eight Songs for a Mad King, Théâtre Musical de Paris, 1983.
Calisto, Royal Court Theatre, London, 1984.
The Knot Garden, Wilde Theatre, Bracknell, 1984.
Akhnaten, Houston Grand Opera, 1984.
Iphigénie en Aulide, Adelaide Festival, 1986.
Iphigénie en Tauride, Adelaide Festival, 1986.
Yan Tan Tethera, Queen Elizabeth Hall, London, 1986.
The Mask of Orpheus, English National Opera, 1986.
La bohème, Opera North, 1988.
Così fan tutte, Queen Elizabeth Hall, London, 1988.
Il ritorno d'Ulisse in patria, English National Opera, 1989.
Ghost Sonata, Queen Elizabeth Hall, London, 1989.
Don Giovanni, 1990.
Le nozze di Figaro, Queen Elizabeth Hall, 1991.
Manon Lescaut, Théâtre Français de la Musique, Paris.

David Freeman's production of *Così fan tutte,* **Opera Factory, London, 1991 (from left: Marie Angel as Fiordiligi, Marilyn Bennett as Dorabella and Susannah Waters as Despina)**

Publications

About FREEMAN: articles–

Robertson, A. "Adventurer: David Freeman Believes Tradition Must Be Confronted." *Opera News* 49 (October 1984): 30.
Clements, A. "David Freeman." *Opera* 40 (November 1989): 1297.

*   *   *

Called "the most controversial director working regularly in London," David Freeman is the founder of the Opera Factory concept. Freeman has explained the Opera Factory as "essentially an experimental performance group, looking for a new opera/drama rationale. . . . It will have the luxury of being able to question every premise on which opera is based." Freeman has assembled an ensemble of singers, an artistic director, and a stage manager who work together intensively for approximately thirty-five weeks, using training based on improvisation and physical and mental exercise. They employ the principles of method acting and aim for productions that can be adapted to any performing space. Their repertory is mostly baroque, classical, and contemporary music.

Freeman directed his first opera at age nineteen: Monteverdi's *Orfeo ed Euridice* at Sydney University. He founded the Opera Factory in Australia in 1973. This was followed by

Opera Factory Zurich in 1976, which brought its production of *Acis and Galatea* to London in 1979 and has performed Karl Amadeus Hartmann's *Simplicius Simplicissimus,* Mozart's *Così fan tutte* (1982), and Weill's *Happy End* (1982). It also presented a double bill of abridged versions of Gluck's *Iphigénie en Aulide* and *Iphigénie en Tauride* at the Adelaide Festival (1986). Opera Factory London was founded in 1981; it began with Gay's *Beggar's Opera* and Birtwistle's *Punch and Judy* in its first British staging since the 1968 Aldeburgh premiere, and continued with Tippett's *The Knot Garden,* Cavalli's *La Calisto,* Mozart's *Così fan tutte,* Osborne's *Hell's Angels,* the premiere of Birtwistle's *Yan Tan Tethera* (1986), Maxwell Davies's *Eight Songs for a Mad King,* Reimann's *Ghost Sonata* (1989), alternating with August Strindberg's play, and Mozart's *Don Giovanni* (1990) and *Le nozze di Figaro* (1991).

The Opera Factory immediately stirred up controversy with its depictions of violence and graphic sex. Some English critics were disturbed by what they termed the "arrogant exhibitionism" of the *Acis and Galatea* production, in which the Arcadians perform simulated sexual acts and Polyphemus kills Acis by striking him over the head with a wine bottle. The divide remains between those who see the Opera Factory as a stimulating and creative rethinking of operas (what one critic has called Freeman's "radical assault on opera") and those who find the productions pretentious, self-indulgent, and unnecessarily sordid. Freeman is careful, however, to maintain respectable performance quality and high musicological standards in choices such as performing editions.

Freeman calls opera "the unique collaborative art." He finds performances by stars boring and feels that theater is about "doing things together. That's why it has some relevance to society and there's a point to it." He prefers a small, tight-knit company and is suspicious of big-theater opera and the "travelling circus" aspect of interchangeable casts where productions are just sets and costumes. "What we care about is the level of performance, not the level of ideas. . . . There is no such thing as an original idea in the theatre; it's a reflection." His productions reduce the operas to what he considers to be their essentials, allowing the audience to concentrate on the characters.

Freeman has also produced opera outside of his affiliation with the Opera Factory: Cowie's *Commaedia* with the New Opera Company (London); Glass's *Akhnaten* with the New York City Opera (a coproduction with Houston, later seen in a revised version for the English National Opera); Monteverdi's *Orfeo ed Euridice* (1981), Birtwistle's *Mask of Orpheus* (1986), Monteverdi's *Ritorno d'Ulisse in patria* (1989), all for the English National Opera; Puccini's *La bohème* for Opera North, Leeds (in which Schaunard, in flashbacks, speaks lines from Henri Murger's novel); and Auber's *Manon Lescaut* at the Théâtre Français de la Musique in Paris.

—Michael Sims

THE FREE-SHOOTER
See DER FREISCHÜTZ

DER FREISCHÜTZ [The Free-Shooter].

Composer: Carl Maria von Weber.

Librettist: J. F. Kind (after J.A. Apel and F. Laun, *Gespensterbuch*).

First Performance: Berlin, Schauspielhaus, 18 June 1821.

Roles: Agathe (soprano); Aennchen (soprano); Max (tenor); Caspar (baritone); Kilian (bass); Cuno (bass); Prince Ottokar (baritone); Hermit (bass); Bridesmaid (soprano); Samiel (speaking); chorus (SATTTBB).

Publications

books—

Kind, Friedrich. *Freischütz-Buch*. Leipzig, 1843.
Servières, G. *Freischütz*. Paris, 1913.
Cornelissen, T. *Carl Maria von Webers Freischütz als Beispiel einer Opernbehandlung*. Berlin, 1940.
Schnoor, H. *Weber auf dem Welttheater: ein Freischützbuch*. Dresden, 1942; 4th ed., 1963.
Kron, W. *Die angeblichen Freischütz-Kritiken E.T.A. Hoffmanns*. Munich, 1957.
Mayerhofer, G. *Abermals vom Freischützen: Der Münchener Freischütze von 1812*. Regensburg, 1959.
Csampai, Attila, and Dietmar Holland, eds. *Carl Maria von Weber. Der Freischütz: Texte, Materialien, Kommentare*. Reinbek bei Hamburg, 1987.

articles—

Berlioz, H. "Le Freyschütz de Weber." *Voyage musicale en Allemagne et en Italie,* vol. 1, 369. Paris, 1844.
Wagner, R. "Der Freischütz in Paris." In *Gesammelte Schriften und Dichtungen,* vol. 1. Leipzig, 1871; English translation in *Richard Wagner's Prose Works,* edited and translated by W.A. Ellis, vol. 7, London, 1898.
Kapp, J. "Die Uraufführung des Freischütz." *Blätter der Staatsoper* [Berlin] 1/no. 8 (1921): 9.
Abert, H. "Carl Maria von Weber und sein Freischütz." *Jahrbuch der Musikbibliothek Peters* (1926): 9; reprinted in *Gesammelte Schriften und Vorträge,* edited by H. Blume, Halle, 1929; 2nd ed., 1968.
Dent, Edward J. "Der Freischütz." *Opera* 5 no. 3 (1954): 137.
Maehder, Jürgen. "Die Poetisierung der Klangfarben in Dichtung und Musik der deutschen Romantik" [*Der Freischütz*]. *Aurora* 38 (1978): 9.
Stephan, Rudolf. "Bemerkungen zur *Freischütz*-Musik." In *Studien zur Musikgeschichte Berlins im frühen 19. Jahrhundert,* edited by Carl Dahlhaus, 491. Regensburg, 1980.
Dahlhaus, Carl. "Webers Freischütz und die Idee der romantischen Oper." *Österreichische Musikzeitschrift* 38 (1983): 381.
Finscher, Ludwig. "Weber's *Freischütz*: Conceptions and Misconceptions." *Proceedings of the Royal Musical Association* 110 (1983-84): 79.
Avant-scène opéra January-February (1988).

*　　　*　　　*

The seventh of Carl Maria von Weber's ten operas, *Der Freischütz* is a *Singspiel,* an alternation of musical numbers and spoken dialogue. Weber and his librettist, Johann Friedrich Kind (1768-1843), recount the legend of the marksman who makes a pact with the forces of evil to obtain magic bullets. The plot unfolds in the great Bohemian forest shortly after the end of the Thirty Years' War (1618-48). Local custom dictates that the young hunter Max must pass a shooting trial in order to marry his beloved Agathe. Caspar, a hunter in league with the heathen world represented by Samiel, persuades Max to use "free bullets," which streak magically to their targets. Casting such bullets involves forbidden rites conducted in a terrifying abyss, the Wolf's Glen. Samiel controls one of these bullets. Caspar expects it to strike Agathe; instead it mortally wounds him. For Max's transgression, Prince Ottokar decrees banishment. A hermit, who represents the Christian world, recommends clemency. The secular ruler accepts heaven's will. The shooting trial is abolished. Max, if he proves worthy, can marry Agathe in a year. The opera ends with general rejoicing.

For the libretto (1817), Kind consulted earlier versions of the tale, chiefly a short story in the *Gespensterbuch* (Book of Ghosts, 1810) by Johann August Apel and Friedrich Laun [Friedrich August Schulze] and *Der Freyschütze* by Franz Xaver von Caspar (1812; 1813; music by Carl Neuner). He adds bridesmaids and huntsmen, the villain Caspar, the soubrette Aennchen, and the peasant Kilian, reduces the number of magic bullets from sixty-three to seven, shifts the forbidden rites from a crossroads to the Wolf's Glen, and substitutes a happy ending (Apel's story ends tragically, as does Caspar's

Der Freischütz, engraving after illustration by J. H. Ramburg, 1821

1813 version). Weber contributed various details and, over Kind's objections, accepted his fiancé Caroline's recommendation to eliminate two opening scenes involving the hermit. Thus, the action begins *in medias res* with the entire village assembled at a shooting contest.

Simple, brave, and motivated by love, the well-intentioned Max is an early Heldentenor. Agathe, pure, patient, domestic, faithful, and pious, is nicely complemented by Aennchen, her charming, lively, good-natured relative. Beyond the individual characters stands a lovingly portrayed community of simple folk. This community, in turn, exists within the vast forest, an environment both hospitable and threatening.

"There are in *Der Freischütz* two principal elements that can be recognized at first sight—hunting life and the rule of demonic powers as personified by Samiel." In this bit of conversation with J.C. Lobe, Weber underscores the chief dramatic theme of the opera: a struggle between the forces of good and evil. Important also are the themes of religion, love, and nature: its dark, sinister side (the Wolf's Glen); its idealized side (the huntsmen and the farmers); and its ordered, beautiful side (nature in harmony with God and humanity).

Having contemplated a *Freischütz* setting as early as 1810, Weber enthusiastically set Kind's libretto during the years 1817-20, adding in 1821 the Romance and Aria for the first Aennchen, Johanna Eunicke. Not only was the material consonant with Weber's own personal triad of God, family, and music; it also afforded him a welcome opportunity to create the kind of opera he thought Germans desired: "an art work complete in itself, in which the partial contributions of the related and collaborating arts blend together, disappear, and, in disappearing, somehow form a new world" (Weber, "On the Opera 'Undine'," trans. Strunk).

Weber drew inspiration from several musical traditions: the *Singspiel,* to include Beethoven's *Fidelio;* Italian opera, as in Max's great scene, waltz and aria, "Durch die Wälder, durch die Auen" (no. 3, Through the Forests, through the Meadows), and Agathe's scene and aria, "Wie nahte mir der Schlummer" (no. 8, How tranquilly I slumbered); *opéra comique,* with its realistic out-of-doors scenes, choruses and dances, and soubrette roles; and folksong, drawn into the realm of art and functioning intrinsically, not incidentally. He incorporated actual melodies, for example, the refrain of the Bridesmaids' Chorus (no. 14) and "Marlborough," embedded in the Huntsmen's Chorus (no. 15). Conversely, original Weber tunes, such as the opening of the Huntsmen's Chorus, quickly became popular songs. Whatever the influence of the moment, vocal production ranges from speech and melodrama (speech accompanied by the orchestra) at one extreme to exquisite lyricism at the other.

Reinforcing the opera's dramatic plan and the dark-light curve it suggests are unifying musical plans of motive, tone color, and key. Identified with characters or states of mind, certain themes and harmonies recur throughout the opera. Weber explained his tone color plan as follows: for the forest and hunting life, horns; for the dark powers, "the lowest register of the violins, violas and basses, particularly the lowest register of the clarinet, which seemed especially suitable for depicting the sinister, then the mournful sound of the bassoon, the lowest notes of the horns, the hollow roll of drums or single hollow strokes on them" (Warrack, *Carl Maria von Weber,* p. 221). Commentators have tended to exaggerate Weber's key architecture. C minor does indeed represent a specific force in the opera, the demonic. Otherwise, the most that can realistically be said about tonal planning is that good generally is associated with bright major keys, evil with minor keys.

Distributed throughout the three acts are an overture and sixteen musical numbers: an introductory complex, an entr'acte, simple songs, ariettas, elaborate arias, ensembles, choruses, and two great ensemble finales. In evoking the forest, the demonic powers, Max, Agathe, and the triumph of love and faith, the overture is a symphonic synthesis of the drama. Within the *Singspiel* format, Weber builds some remarkable structures by combining separate components into large form-complexes, as in the introduction (no. 1; see also the linking of Caspar's drinking song [no. 4], which Beethoven admired, with his aria of rage and triumph [no. 5]). "Half the opera plays in darkness. . . . These dark forms of the outer world are underlined and strengthened in the musical forms." The Wolf's Glen scene (no. 10) dramatically illustrates Weber's observation. Elements of chorus, recitative, aria, melodrama, and symphonic music coalesce into an innovative, yet unified whole. Here, where the work reaches its profoundest depth before the resolution into light, he realized musically a "real, palpable, and unmistakable scene of horror" (report of his son, Max Maria von Weber).

Count Carl von Brühl, the Berlin Intendant and Weber's friend, oversaw the preparations for the premiere. Although some negative criticisms were voiced, by Hoffmann, Zelter, Tieck, and Spohr, for example, *Der Freischütz* was fabulously successful from the outset. For a host of commentators, it epitomizes German Romantic opera. Indeed, Kind and Weber have emphasized nature and the "folk," blurred the distinctions between humans, nature, and the supernatural, integrated the overture with the opera, allotted the orchestra a role in the drama, and aimed the music at the listener's emotions. But is the opera a high Romantic product, in the manner of the Hoffmann-Fouqué *Undine* of 1816? Given its basic format of innocence, fall, and redemption, does it offer a questioning, probing, and expansive world view? Is it even truly nationalistic? Without diminishing the importance or stature of the opera, one specialist has argued persuasively that *Der Freischütz* has as its goal the reinforcement of established norms: "Man remains oriented towards the church and hence towards a universal conception of man" (Doerner, "The Influence of the 'Kunstmärchen' on German Romantic Opera, 1814-1825"). As a mixture of morality play and melodrama, Doerner argues, it illustrates a later, more tamed phase of Romanticism, a blend of Romantic and Enlightenment values: "dogma and religious moralizing take the place of a complex secular philosophy. . . . The jubilation expressed at the conclusion . . . is focused on the modest prospect of a more secure and comfortable worldly existence." Whatever its interpretation, in Austria and Germany especially, *Der Freischütz* continues to hold the stage.

—Malcolm S. Cole

FREMSTAD, Olive [born Olivia Rundquist].

Mezzo-soprano and soprano. Born 14 March 1871, in Stockholm. Died 21 April 1951, in Irvington-on-Hudson, New York. Studied piano in Minneapolis; studied singing with F.E. Bristol in New York and later with Lilli Lehmann in Berlin; debut as Lady Saphir in Sullivan's *Patience* in Boston, 1890; opera debut as Azucena in Cologne, 1895, and remained there for three years; sang contralto roles in Bayreuth, 1896; joined Munich Court Opera, 1900-03; Metropolitan Opera debut as Sieglinde, 1903; remained at Met until 1914;

left Met after arguing with Gatti-Casazza, and sang in Boston, Chicago and for the Manhattan Company; appeared in recital, 1920; taught in New York at the end of her career.

Publications

About FREMSTAD: books–

Cushing, M. *The Rainbow Bridge.* New York, 1954; 1977.

articles–

Dennis, J. "Olive Fremstad." *Record Collector* 7 (1952): 53.

Remembered principally as one of opera's great Wagnerians, Olive Fremstad was also one of its most extraordinary international tragedians. She was considerably larger than life, both on and off the stage, "an epic sort of creature," as she was described by her biographer, Mary Watkins Cushing, "moving most comfortably somewhere between heaven and earth."

She studied initially as a contralto with Frederick E. Bristol in New York before journeying to Berlin in 1893 for instruction with Lilli Lehmann, who immediately set about the task of directing what she considered to be the correct placement of her pupil's voice, extending the upper register, without sacrificing the already well-developed lower tones. Fremstad made her operatic debut as a mezzo-soprano in Cologne as Azucena (*Il trovatore*) in May, 1895, and remained there for nearly four years, assuming a variety of principal roles. Between 1896 and 1903 she was engaged at the Vienna Hofoper, made guest appearances in Bayreuth, Antwerp, and Amsterdam, spent three successful seasons at the Munich Hofoper, and was well received in two Royal Opera Seasons at Covent Garden. She is said to have mastered some seventy roles in the mezzo-contralto repertory during this busy, formative period of her career.

Thereafter her principal artistic home was New York's Metropolitan Opera House. Her debut as Sieglinde in *Die Walküre* on 25 November, 1903 was something of a qualified success: Henry Krehbiel expressed passing dissatisfaction with her "Teutonic stride and pose," but he was quick to add that even in a city accustomed to greatness, she "took rank with most of her predecessors." Over the next decade Fremstad would gradually cultivate an uncommonly varied international repertory that came to include nearly all of the important Wagner heroines—Venus, Fricka, Kundry, the three Brünnhildes, and most notably, Isolde, after years of portraying Brangäne in Europe. Emma Calvé's departure after the 1903-1904 season brought her the opportunity to add Carmen, a role she had played very successfully in Munich, just as Emma Eames' retirement in 1909 permitted her to assume Tosca, which turned out to be one of her less well-received roles. She took part in a number of important debuts at the Met: Carmen to Caruso's first Don José, Selika to his first Vasco da Gama (*L'africana*), and Giulietta in the Met's first production of *Les contes d'Hoffmann*. Her debut as Isolde on 1 January, 1908 coincided with Mahler's American debut as a conductor, just as Toscanini's first Wagnerian production in America, *Die Götterdämmerung* on 10 December, 1910, featured her celebrated Brünnhilde. Also under Toscanini's direction she sang the title role in the first American production of Gluck's *Armide* on 14 November, 1910. In 1907, she created Strauss's Salome in both the American and

French premieres, a role she prepared under the guidance of both the composer and Alfred Hertz, conductor of the Met production. Though her Kundry and Isolde were held in the highest esteem, Salome was rated by some as her finest achievement, both vocally and dramatically. Krehbiel called it "a miracle," while Richard Aldrich was content merely to say that it represented "the crown to all that she has done at the Metropolitan," her Kundry notwithstanding. Her two public performances of the role in late January, 1907 (one of them an especially uninhibited dress rehearsal) were enough to banish the opera from the Met for the next quarter of a century.

She left the Metropolitan Opera during the 1913-1914 season under troubled circumstances that were never fully explained. But her departure was heroic, despite the fact that the management, perhaps deliberately, assigned Elsa (*Lohengrin*), one of her least effective roles, as her farewell performance. In all, she had sung eleven seasons at the Met, essaying eighteen roles in just over two hundred performances. A proposed re-engagement for the 1917-1918 season was announced but never came to pass, possibly because of the suspension of the Wagner repertory during the war. She undertook an impressive succession of guest seasons from 1915, notably with the Boston and Chicago Opera Companies, but in both houses confined herself to Isolde, Tosca, and the three Brünnhildes. Thereafter, concert tours occupied much of her time. Her last major public appearance came on the afternoon on 19 January, 1920 in New York City's Aeolian Hall, where she sang a varied if not especially demanding program of songs to respectful reviews. The remaining years of her life were spent in tragic obscurity.

In her prime, Fremstad undertook relatively few major roles, the majority of them Wagnerian. But her eagerness to expand the depth of her repertory, to deny herself no compelling opportunity even if it meant overtaxing her voice, was apparently insatiable, and this, coupled with a profound sense of dramatic purpose seems to be the final explanation of her extraordinary career. Beginning as a contralto and establishing her reputation as a mezzo-contralto, she climbed steadily upward to dramatic soprano in her authentic prime. Her success in extending the working range of her voice was uncanny, and she undertook the task with great relish in full view of the public. Even as early as 1902, when she first appeared at Covent Garden, her voice was praised for its unusually wide range. In an oft-quoted 1913 interview published in *McClure's Magazine*, Fremstad declared in a grand manner, "I do not claim this or that for my voice. I do not sing contralto or soprano. I sing Isolde. What voice is necessary for the part I undertake, I will produce." Her vocal prime as a soprano was indeed prodigious, and the expansion of her repertory never went unnoticed or unappreciated, but the price she paid was formidable. By the teens, even her interpretative diligence was powerless to fend off a premature retirement.

Fremstad's recorded legacy is an especially fragile one, consisting of only fourteen published titles recorded for American Columbia in the winter of 1911 and the autumn of 1913. These have long been considered unworthy of so great an artist, not so much for their technical limitations as for their scant representation of her repertory, and the fact that there is not a flawless performance among them. Like Emma Calvé, Mary Garden, Geraldine Farrar, and the other preeminent singing actresses of her age, Fremstad was incapable of committing to wax anything even approaching a complete portrait of her art, so consuming was her merging of voice, drama, and characterization. The voice we hear is expansive and well balanced throughout its vast range, and though there is much to deceive us into thinking otherwise, especially in the songs she recorded, its overall character is that of an authentic dramatic soprano. The most tempting of her recordings, but perhaps ultimately least revealing, are the five Wagner excerpts, which were especially displeasing to the singer. Most reassuring among them, however, is the "Dich, teure Halle" from *Tannhäuser*, a thoroughly absorbing performance spoiled only by faulty intonation in the opening bars. The finest of all is perhaps the "O don fatale" from *Don Carlos*, a well-defined reading that offers more than a passing glimpse of what was certainly a large, resonant voice with an agile and accommodating working range, and an uncommon breadth of dramatic intensity.

—William Shaman

FRENI, Mirella.

Soprano. Born 27 February 1935, in Modena. Married: 1) Leone Magiera (one daughter); 2) bass Nicolai Ghiaurov in 1981. Studied at Mantua and at Bologna Conservatory with Ettore Campogalliani; debut as Micaela in *Carmen* at Modena, 1955; sang with Netherlands Opera; Covent Garden debut as Nannetta in *Falstaff,* 1961; Teatro all Scala debut in same role, 1962 and has appeared there regularly since; Metropolitan Opera debut as Mimi, 1965; appeared at Salzburg, 1966–72 and 1974–80.

Publications

About FRENI: books–

Chedorge, A. *Mirella Freni.* Paris, 1979.
Magiera, Leone. *Mirella Freni—Metodo e Mito.* Milan, 1990.

articles–

Gualerzi, G. "Mirella Freni." *Opera* April (1967).

*   *   *

In the 1960s Mirella Freni emerged as one of the world's leading sopranos; she has maintained her preeminent position during the following two decades. Much of her early career was devoted to eighteenth-century opera and to some of the lighter roles in opera of the nineteenth century, but as her voice and acting ability have matured she has gradually taken on heavier nineteenth-century roles. At the same time she has managed to maintain a youthful face and figure, causing one critic who witnessed her performance of Elisabetta in Verdi's *Don Carlos* in 1979 to call her "something of a miracle, since she does not seem to get older."

A recording of *Don Giovanni* made in the mid 1960s under Klemperer shows the young Freni in good voice. As Zerlina she sings with attractive clarity and freshness. In the duet "La ci darem la mano" her singing is simple and beautiful; it perfectly conveys Zerlina's sweetness, and at the same time hints at her seductive power. We understand why Don Giovanni is attracted to her. Freni's arias are just as charming, though "Batti, batti" is marred by an annoying mannerism: Freni's excessive scooping eventually wears on the listener's patience.

Freni brought all her youthful talents to bear in another great eighteenth-century role, this one much less familiar to today's opera-goers. She is perfect in the title role of Picinni's *La buona figliuola* (or *La Cecchina*), as recorded under Franco Caracciolo in the 1960s. In her beautiful, sentimental showpiece "Una povera ragazza" she sings with moving tenderness and simplicity. Even more memorable is her performance of the aria "Vieni, il mio seno," sung by Cecchina as she goes to sleep. Freni sings the aria's long lines with exquisite delicacy.

Another recording from early in Freni's career reveals her as a fine singer of baroque opera: Handel's *Alcina,* recorded under Bonynge. In the role of Oberto, Freni stands out as an outstanding declaimer of recitative. She sings recitative as if it means something: there is real pathos in Oberto's words as he tells of his attempt to find his father. Freni's arias are no less vivid. In "Chi m'insegna il caro padre" one can hear a fresh, light soprano voice of beautiful tone. Gliding over melismas with ease and grace, Freni seems to caress Handel's melodies.

Freni's versatility in the performance of nineteenth-century opera is extraordinary. Whether the opera is in Italian, French or Russian, she is able to bring her character to life with unsurpassed vividness and musical perfection. One of her best roles is Tatyana in Tchaikovsky's *Eugene Onegin*— "the Tatyana of one's dreams," one critic raved after her performance of the role in Bordeaux. The subtlety and variety that she brings to this role have astonished and delighted audiences in many of the world's leading opera houses. One of the Verdi roles in which Freni has been particularly successful is the title role of *Aida.* She triumphed in the role at Salzburg, winning praise for her rich tone, her intelligent, expressive phrasing, and for the intensity of her acting. Freni has been equally successful as Desdemona, a role she has sung in Salzburg and elsewhere. She has brought to lighter, more cheerful roles in nineteenth-century opera as much energy as she brings to her portrayals of the great tragic heroines, winning praise for her many performances of Micaela in Bizet's *Carmen* (the role with which she made her operatic debut in the mid 1950s), Nannetta in Verdi's *Falstaff* and Marie in Donizetti's *La fille du regiment.*

—John A. Rice

FRICK, Gottlob.

Bass. Born 28 July 1906, in Olbronn, Württemberg. Studied with Neudörfer-Opitz and at Stuttgart Conservatory. Debut as Daland in *Der fliegende Holländer* at Coburg, 1934; sang in Freiburg and Königsberg, then in Dresden, where he created Caliban in Sutermeister's *Die Zauberinsel* and the Carpenter in Haas's *Die Hochzeit des Jobs,* 1941-52; at Berlin State Opera, 1950-53; Bavarian State Opera from 1953; Metropolitan Opera debut as Fafner in *Das Rheingold,* 1961; appeared as Sarastro at Salzburg, 1955; Bayreuth from 1957.

Mirella Freni in *Eugene Onegin,* **Royal Opera, 1988**

Publications

About FRICK: books–

Hey, H. *Gottlob Frick.* Munich, 1968.

articles–

Schwinger, W. "Gottlob Frick." *Opera* 17 (1966): 188.

*   *   *

In an era rich in dark-voiced bassos, Gottlob Frick possessed his own distinctive majesty and greatness. Born in 1908, Frick studied voice in Stuttgart and in 1927 became a member of the Stuttgart Opera Chorus. His solo debut was as Daland in Coburg, in 1934, beginning a distinguished career as a leading Wagnerian bass.

After further seasons in Freiburg and Königsberg, Frick joined the Dresden company where he remained a valued member until 1950, singing repertoire roles and appearing in several world premieres. He then moved to the Berlin Opera and in 1953 became a member of the Munich and Vienna companies, and a regular guest in Hamburg. In 1951 he first appeared at Covent Garden where he sang Rocco (*Fidelio*) and important Wagner bass roles there during the next twenty years.

In 1953 he was in Rome participating in the grand recording of Wagner's Ring under Furtwängler for Italian Radio. He was a regular at the Bayreuth Festival. At the Salzburg Festival, Frick sang Mozart, Pfitzner, and Egk. He was a guest at the Teatro alla Scala, the Paris Opéra, and in Amsterdam and Brussels.

Frick first came to the Metropolitan Opera in 1961 for a Ring cycle under Erich Leinsdorf. This engagement was belated perhaps due to the plethora of fine basses at the time.

Frick officially retired from the stage in 1970, but actually continued to appear. Further roles were Philip in *Don Carlos* and Padre Guardiano in *La forza del destino* of Verdi, Kaspar in *Der Freischütz*, Osmin in *Die Entführung aus dem Serail*, Kezal in *The Bartered Bride*, and van Bett in *Zar und Zimmermann*.

From his Dresden days, Gottlob Frick is represented on recordings of Dvorak's *Rusalka, Tristan, Fra Diavolo,* Hugo Wolf's *Der Corrigidor,* and Goetz' *The Taming of the Shrew.* He appears in performance recordings from Bayreuth, and in other commercial complete Wagnerian opera accounts. He also sings in complete recordings of *Entführung, Zar und Zimmermann, The Merry Wives of Windsor, Fidelio, Don Giovanni* and is especially delightful in Orff's *Die Kluge.*

Frick had a well-schooled, even voice, and was noted for his interpretive ability. He was equally at home and enjoyable as a villain or as a comedian.

—Bert Wechsler

FRIEDRICH, Götz.

Director. Born 4 August 1930, in Naumburg. Studied stagecraft at Weimar Theater Institut, 1949-53; successive positions at the Berlin Komische Oper: assistant stage director, 1953-56; assistant to Felsenstein, 1957-59; producer, 1959-72; production director, Hamburg Opera, 1973-74; chief of productions, Netherlands Opera Amsterdam, 1973-74; professor of theater, Hamburg University; principal producer at Covent Garden 1976-81; general director, Deutsche Oper, Berlin 1981-. Staged world premieres of Matthus's *Der letzte Schuss,* 1967; Berio's *Un re in ascolto,* 1984; Henze's *Das verratene Meer,* 1990.

Opera Productions (selected)

Così fan tutte, Weimar, 1958.
La bohème, Berlin, Komische Oper, 1959.
Die Zauberflöte, Cassel, 1960.
Il ritorno d'Ulisse in patria, Berlin, Komische Oper, 1967.
Der letzte Schuss, Berlin, Komische Oper, 1968.
Porgy and Bess, Berlin, Komische Oper, 1968.
Noch ein Löffel Gift, Liebling, Berlin, Komische Oper, 1972.
Tannhäuser, Bayreuth, 1972.
Jenůfa, Stockholm, 1972.
Falstaff, Holland Festival, 1972.
Moses und Aron, Vienna State Opera, 1973.
Aida, Amsterdam, Cirque Carré, 1973.
Orphée aux enfers, Amsterdam, Cirque Carré, 1973.
Le nozze di Figaro, Hamburg Opera, 1974.
Don Quichotte, Hamburg Opera, 1975.
Der Ring des Nibelungen, Covent Garden, 1976.
Die Soldaten, Hamburg Opera, 1976.
Tosca, Munich, 1976.
Parsifal, Stuttgart, 1976.
Der Freischütz, Hamburg Opera, 1977.
Ein Engel kommt nach Babylon, Zurich, 1977.
Lohengrin, Bayreuth, 1979.
Lulu, Zurich, 1979.
From the House of the Dead (Z mrtvého domu), Berlin, Deutsche Oper, 1981.
Parsifal, Bayreuth, 1982.
Wozzeck, Houston Grand Opera, 1982.
Un re in ascolto, Salzburg Festival, 1984.
Boris Godunov, Zurich, Sports Stadium, 1984.
Pelléas et Mélisande, Berlin, Deutsche Oper, 1984.
Otello, Los Angeles.
Katya Kabanová, Paris, Opéra.
Elektra, London, Covent Garden.
Der Ring des Nibelungen, Berlin, Deutsche Oper, 1985.
Die Frau ohne Schatten, Stuttgart, 1987.
Die Bassariden, Stuttgart, 1990.
Der Rosenkavalier, Hannover, 1990.
Das verratene Meer, Berlin, Deutsche Oper, 1990.
Mathis der Maler, Berlin, Deutsche Oper, 1990.

Publications

By FRIEDRICH: books–

Die humanistische Idee der "Zauberflöte": ein Beitrag zur Dramaturgie der Oper. Dresden, 1954.
"Die Zauberflöte" in der Inszenierung Walter Felsensteins an der Komischen Oper Berlin 1954. Berlin, 1958.
Walter Felsenstein: Weg und Werk. Berlin, 1961.
with Walter Felsenstein and J. Herz. *Musiktheater: Beiträge zur Methodik und zu Inszenierungs-Konzeptionen.* Leipzig, 1970.
Wagner-Regie. Zurich, 1983.

Götz Friedrich's production of *Tannhäuser,* **Bayreuth, 1978**

articles–

"Der Theaterman Schikaneder als Dramatiker und als Director." *Theater der Zeit* 11 (1956).

"Zur Inszenierungskonzeption *Cosi fan tutte:* Komische Oper Berlin 1962." *Jahrbuch der Komische Oper Berlin* 3 (1962-63).

"Zwanzig Notizen zu eines Aufführungskonzeption von *Porgy und Bess.*" *Jahrbuch des Komischer Oper Berlin* 9 (1968-69).

"Statt grosser Oper die Oper des grossen Gegenstands." *Opernwelt* 9/September (1969): 38.

with H. Seeger. "Eine sozusagen neue Art von Schauspiel." *Opernwelt* 3/March (1971): 14.

"Unaufgehobene Polaritäten; die Oper as 'Lyrische Szene'." *Opernwelt* 4/April (1971): 21.

"*Le nozze di Figaro,* een nieuw type theater." *Opera Journaal* 9 (1973-74): 4.

"Die Sehnsucht nach szenischem Musizieren." *Opernwelt* 12/December (1975): 26.

"Welttheater als bürgerliches Parabelspiel—Aspekte des Londoner *Ring;* Konzeptes." *Opernwelt* Yearbook 1976: 16.

"*Der Freischütz* in 1977." *Opera* (February 1977).

"Komödie und demokratisches Modell." *Opernwelt* 18/2 (1977): 28.

Introduction to Remus, M., *Mozart.* Stuttgart, 1991.

interviews–

"Musiktheater und neues opernschaffen." *Musik und Gesellschaft* 13/March (1963): 136; April: 205.

"Schüsse aus der Hüfte." *Opernwelt* 2/February (1968): 15.

Ludwig, H. "Oper als permanentes Plaidoyer für die Humanität: ein Gespräch mit Götz Friedrich." *Opernwelt* 9/September (1973): 30.

"Gespräch mit Professor Götz Friedrich über den 'Studiengang Musiktheater' in Hamburg." *Opernwelt* 5/May (1975): 32.

"Gespräch mit Götz Friedrich." *Oper und Konzert* 15/1 (1977): 9.

Fleming, M. *Hi Fidelity/Musical American* 33/May (1983): MA6.

"Berlin ist auch eine Chance; Professor Götz Friedrich, Generalintendant der Deutsche Oper Berlin, im Gespräch mit Imre Fabian." *Opernwelt* 25/11 (1984): 52.

"Die Oper zeigt sich in den Medien von einer neuen Seite; Gespräch mit Götz Friedrich." *Opernwelt* 26 (Yearbook 1985): 75.

"Oper für alle Berliner: Gespräch mit Götz Friedrich." *Opernwelt* 31/March (1990): 18.

About FRIEDRICH: book–

Barz, P. *Götz Friedrich—Abenteuer Musiktheater: Konzepte, Versuche, Erfahrungen.* Bonn, 1978.

articles–

Lehmann, D. "Muzick i teatar kao model realnost-misli iz seminara 'Nove teme na muzickoj pozornici' u Berlin." *Zvuk* 90 (1968): 662.

"Götz Friedrich." *Bühne* 177 (1973): 10.

Schwinger, W. "Die seltsame Träume des Peter Hacks: zu einem metaphorischen Pamphlet gegen Götz Friedrich und Felsensteins Komische Oper." *Opernwelt* 3/March (1973): 10.

Loney, Glenn. "Götz Friedrich: 'One Must Also Know What Freud Meant'." *Hi Fidelity/Musical American* 24/April (1974): MA38.

Loppert, M. "Götz Friedrich Interviewed About Producing Opera in General and 'The Ring' in Particular." *Music and Musicians* 23/October (1974): 30.

Koch, H.W. "Ponnelle, Götz Friedrich, Chéreau und andere." *Opernwelt* Yearbook 1977: 97.

Schmidt, D.N. "Die Angst und die Utopie." *Opernwelt* 19/3 (1978): 13.

Barz, P. "Irgendwie ein irrsinnig schönes Leben." *Opernwelt* 19/8 (1978): 33.

Barz, P. "Zum 25-jährigen Bühnenjubilaeum von Götz Friedrich—Porträt eines Regisseurs." *Orchester* 27/January (1979): 31.

Rohde, G. "Götz Friedrich." *Neue Musikzeitung* 1/February-March (1980): 2.

Steinbeck, D. "Von Siegfried Palm zu Götz Friedrich: zur Situation der Deutschen Oper Berlin." *Neue Zeitschrift für Musik* 2/3-4 (1980): 146.

Fabian, Imre. "Der Sängerdarsteller im Mittelpunkt." *Opernwelt* Yearbook 1980: 65.

Gerhartz, L.K. "Regietheater im Opernhaus—Sakrileg oder Auftrag." *Österreichische Musikzeitschrift* 35/October-November (1981): 531.

Stuckenschmidt, H.H. "Mrtvy dum plny zivota." *Hudebni Rozhledy* 35/3 (1982): 125.

Loney, Glenn. "Götz Friedrich: The Political Activist." *Opera News* 47/May (1983): 16.

Sutcliffe, James Helme. "Götz Friedrich." *Opera* 36/January (1985): 28.

Koltai, Tamas. "Az opera mint tarsadalmi pszichoterapia: beszelgetes Götz Friedrichhel." *Muzsika* 29/April (1986): 13.

Vituba, J. "O Janackovi s Götzem Friedrichem." *Hudebni Rozhledy* 41/6 (1988): 280.

Tallian, T. "Mese, mitosz, moralitas: Götz Friedrich a Deutsche operben." *Muzsika* 32/July (1989): 14.

Fuhrmann, P. "Umstrukturierungen im längeren Dreierspiel: Perspektiven und Pläne im Berliner Kulturleben—die Einheit im Visier." *Neue Musikzeitung,* 39/February-March (1990): 10.

Weber, D. "Rückkehr ins Haus am Ring." *Bühne* 387/December (1990): 5.

Ausserhofer, G. "Rückkehr zu den Quellen." *Opernwelt* 32/June (1991): 67.

*　　*　　*

While still a student, Götz Friedrich was given the chance to watch director Walter Felsenstein rehearse his productions for the Komische Oper, East Berlin. In 1953, at the age of 23, Friedrich joined the Komische Oper as an assistant director, later becoming first assistant to Felsenstein. Those years, during which he learned his craft from a consummate master, were of inestimable value to the young director, who retained many of Felsenstein's ideas and beliefs after he had left East Germany.

Friedrich directed his own first production in 1958; it was *Così fan tutte,* which he staged at Weimar, where he had attended university. The following year he directed *La bohème* at the Komische Oper, the first of 13 productions for which he was responsible over the next dozen years. Even at that date, Friedrich was a workaholic (which he has remained all his life) and, combined with his duties as Felsenstein's assistant and the staging of his own productions, he began to direct in West German theaters. After tackling *Die Zauberflöte* in 1960 at Cassel, in 1963 he formed an association with Bremen, where during the next five years he staged operas such as *Rigoletto, Ariadne auf Naxos, La forza del destino, Le nozze di Figaro* and *Don Giovanni,* which he had not had occasion to direct in Berlin.

The Komische Oper had a comparatively small repertory; many large-scale works could not be given because of the small size of the theater, while Felsenstein, believing that nothing that happened on the operatic stage should be without connection to life, refused to stage certain popular operas (*Madama Butterfly,* for instance) that he found dramatically "unreal." *Tosca, Salome* and *Jenůfa,* on the other hand, were considered "real," as was *Il trovatore,* despite its often ludicrous plot. Friedrich's powerful production exhibited the ultra-realism combined with vividly imaginative detail that characterized much of his more recent work. He also directed Monteverdi's *Il ritorno d'Ulisse,* realized by composer Siegfried Matthus, and the premiere of a new opera by Matthus, *Der letzte Schuss,* in 1967.

Venturing for the first time outside Germany, Friedrich recreated the Monteverdi production in Copenhagen, where he also directed *Simon Boccanegra* and *Eugene Onegin.* In Oslo he staged *Falstaff,* an opera for which he has a particular affection, for the first time. Back in Berlin the new breadth of his sympathy was evident in an immensely successful production of *Porgy and Bess.* In April 1972 another Matthus premiere, *Noch ein Löffel Gift, Liebling,* (based on an American comedy, *Risky Marriage,* by Saul O'Hara), was Friedrich's last production for the Komische Oper. In June he re-staged *Falstaff* for the Holland Festival; in July he directed his first Wagner opera, *Tannhäuser,* at the Bayreuth Festival; in August he produced *Così fan tutte* at the Court Theater, Drottningholm; then, instead of returning to East Berlin, in December he staged *Jenůfa* at Stockholm.

Friedrich's decision to stay in the West was not made in haste. While aware that he would never again work in the ideal conditions afforded by the Komische Oper, he was ambitious to try out Felsenstein's principles and theories in the different atmosphere of the West. His fascination with Wagner undoubtedly played a considerable part in his decision; equipped with the necessary intellectual power and stagecraft, Friedrich was now ready to tackle Wagner's mature masterpieces. In 1973, after a spectacular production of Schoenberg's *Moses und Aron* at the Vienna State Opera, he returned to Amsterdam to stage *Aida* in the Cirque Carré. He also acquired a new post, being appointed director of productions at the Hamburg State Opera.

Friedrich remained in Hamburg for seven seasons. His work there included several Mozart productions; a second, even more successful staging of *Falstaff;* an unconventional presentation of *Der Freischütz,* completely lacking in the folk element, that later appeared at Covent Garden; an exciting, original reading of *Macbeth;* and, finest of all his Hamburg stagings, Zimmermann's *Die Soldaten* (1976), in which Friedrich's great technical and dramatic skills were magnificently displayed. Continuing with his explorations of Wagner, he directed *Tristan und Isolde* in Amsterdam and *Parsifal* at Stuttgart, both for the first time; at Covent Garden he staged his first cycle of *Der Ring des Nibelungen,* which was completed in 1976. With its view of the gods as effete and powerless, *Das Rheingold* was especially interesting. Friedrich returned to Bayreuth in 1979 to stage *Lohengrin,* and later that year he directed *Lulu* (the three-act version) for the first time in Zurich. Berg's operas, as *Lulu* for Covent Garden and *Wozzeck* in Zurich were to demonstrate, suited Friedrich's talents particularly well.

Friedrich was appointed intendant of the Deutsche Oper, West Berlin in 1981. His first production there, Janáček's *From the House of the Dead,* was followed by another *Lulu.* Because of his administrative duties at the Deutsche Oper, his work for other theaters was curtailed, but he found time for an unexpectedly warm-hearted *Der Rosenkavalier* at Stuttgart; a much-criticized *Parsifal* at Bayreuth, that was nonetheless frequently revived; a bleak but effective staging of *Les Troyens* at Hamburg and the world premiere of Berio's *Un re in ascolto* at the Salzburg Festival (1984), which was repeated in Vienna and at the Teatro alla Scala, Milan. Friedrich made his American debut in 1982 at Houston, restaging his Zurich production of *Wozzeck.* He also restaged a production of *Manon Lescaut* from Hamburg at Covent Garden.

Meanwhile, in Berlin Friedrich successfully attempted the art-deco style with Korngold's *Die tote Stadt,* which traveled to Los Angeles and Vienna. He also began to build up another *Ring* cycle, ten years after the first. Completed in 1985, this *Ring* took place in a "time tunnel" and developed many of the ideas broached in the earlier version. Adapted for the wider, shallower stage of Covent Garden (1989-91), the "time tunnel" was less impressive; in contrast, the Amsterdam *Tristan,* revived for English National Opera, fitted the London Coliseum stage to perfection. Notable productions during the 1980s included his first stagings of *Boris Godunov* in the Zurich Sports Stadium; of *Otello* in Los Angeles; of *Die Frau ohne Schatten* and *Die Bassariden* in Stuttgart; of *Katya Kabanová* at the Paris Opéra and *Elektra* at Covent Garden. After the unification of Germany the Deutsche Oper suffered some financial cuts, but Friedrich's contract was renewed until 1996. His staging of the premiere of Henze's *Das verratene Meer* in 1990 raised a certain amount of controversy, but the production of *Mathis der Maler,* set partly in 1525 (the peasants' revolt) and partly in 1933 (the last days of the Weimar Republic), was greatly admired.

—Elizabeth Forbes

FRIEND FRITZ
See L'AMICO FRITZ

FROM THE HOUSE OF THE DEAD [Z mrtvého domu].

Composer: Leoš Janáček.

Librettist: Leoš Janáček (after Dostoevsky).

First Performance: Brno, National Theater, 12 April 1930 (posthumous; revised and reorchestrated by O. Chlubna and B. Bakala).

Roles: Goryančikov (baritone); Alyei (tenor); Šiškov (baritone); Shapkin (baritone); Skuratov (tenor); Commandant (bass); Prostitute (soprano or mezzo-soprano); Four Men and Four Women (mute); chorus (TTBB).

Publications

article–

Nepomnjaščaja, Tat'jana. "Poslednjaja opera L. Janačeka" [*House of the Dead*]. *Sovetskaya muzyka* 1 (1979): 108.

* * *

The House of the Dead (1860-62) was Dostoevsky's first novel. He was arrested in 1849 as a political prisoner, and—after a mock execution and reprieve—was sent to Siberia for ten years. The novel is a thinly disguised autobiographical record in which Dostoevsky repeatedly shows how the strength of the human heart and the quality of the soul may transcend humiliation and oppression. This was the aspect of the novel which appealed to Janáček, who summed up the whole of his life's work in *From The House of the Dead,* completed just after his 74th birthday. It was far ahead of its time in its musical style, its brevity, the absence of a coherent plot and the composer's disregard for most of the conventions of opera.

Janáček entitled his opera *From the House of the Dead,* and the message which he brings from the prison to his audience is summed up in the motto: "in every creature a spark of God." The quest to understand the human soul, and vindicate our existence by seeking that "spark of God" even among convicted murderers, is the essence of the opera. There is a tension throughout (most eloquently expressed in the orchestral introduction) between the music of oppression and human suffering and the exultant music in which Janáček asserts and celebrates the essential, inner freedom of all humanity.

Janáček had focused four of his previous operas—*Jenůfa, Katia Kabanová, The Cunning Little Vixen* and *The Makropoulos Case*—on the developing character of one central female figure. In *From the House of the Dead,* by contrast, there are no women (except a raddled prostitute who sings a few bars in act II). There is also no plot, in any conventional sense. Janáček developed still further the discursive, almost cinematic narrative techniques with which he had experimented in *Osud* and *The Excursions of Mr Brouček.* He wrote no formal libretto, but simply excerpted episodes, narratives and anecdotes from Dostoevsky's novel and arranged them, sometimes synthesizing characters and incidents, to create his text.

The fortunes of one character, the political prisoner Alexandr Petrovič Goryančikov, form a loose framework. He is admitted into the prison and savagely flogged early in act I; the opera ends with his release. There is also an implied sequence of seasons or moods; act I is set in winter, act II in spring, and act III, after opening in the gloom of the prison hospital at night, escapes for the final scene, in which Goryan-čikov is freed, into the light of a sunny day.

Dostoevsky observed the prisoners' habit of obsessively telling their own stories to one other. From *Jenůfa* onwards, Janáček had crystallized the meaning of each of his tragic operas through the medium of a monologue just before the close. In *From the House of the Dead* he used his gift for narrative more extensively, and gave a strangely compelling unity to this opera by setting in each act a prisoner's story of the events which led him to be imprisoned.

This device introduces into the camp glimpses of the normal, outside world. Each story is more expansive than the one before, and Šiškov's narrative in act III, in the prison hospital, leads to the central climax of the opera. One of the more depraved and brutal convicts tells how, tormented by his young wife Akulina's declaration of love for one Filka Morozov, he cut her throat. As the story ends, another convict dies, and Šiškov recognizes him in death as Filka.

Šiškov curses the corpse repeatedly, but an old convict comments that "even he was some mother's child." Janáček used these words as the springboard for a music which expresses his compassion for and understanding even of men like Šiškov and Filka. By comprehending acts of violence which are almost incomprehensible, Janáček finds the "spark of God" in the most apparently worthless of human beings, and so vindicates our own common humanity.

To match this extraordinary subject-matter, Janáček devised an extraordinary musical style. It proved to be beyond the understanding even of his own pupils; two of them reorchestrated the opera for the posthumous premiere, and substituted a jubilant closing chorus in praise of freedom for Janáček's grimmer finale, in which the prisoners are forced to march back to work. This adaptation seriously distorts the composer's meaning; the sound of the whole opera is softened, and the ending imposes a sentimental idealism where the original has taught us to accept the cruel realities of separation and imprisonment, and to glory in the tenacity of the human spirit. In recent years performances have reverted more to Janáček's original scoring.

Janáček's orchestration in *From the House of the Dead* is extremely spartan, with often bizarre combinations between extremes of pitch and timbre. The music is more dissonant than any of his earlier works; and there is a striking alternation between the stylized use of the prisoners as a chorus and the realism—heightened almost to the level of expressionism by Janáček's laconic, gestural style—in the interchanges between individuals.

Despite its forbidding title and almost all-male cast, *From the House of the Dead* has attracted memorable productions both inside Czechoslovakia and elsewhere. Many theatrical styles have proved effective, ranging from the detailed realism of Colin Graham's version when Charles Mackerras first conducted the score in England for Sadler's Wells Opera to the stylization and abstraction of Götz Friedrich's production for the Berliner Staatsoper. This is certainly Janáček's most original score, and possibly his greatest opera.

—Michael Ewans

FROM TODAY TILL TOMORROW
See VON HEUTE AUF MORGEN

FURTWÄNGLER, (Gustav Heinrich Ernst Martin) Wilhelm.

Conductor. Born 25 January 1886, in Berlin. Died 30 November 1954, in Ebersteinburg. Studied with Schillings, Rheinberger, and Beer-Walbrunn; studied piano with Conrad Ansorge; worked as a vocal coach with Mottl in Munich, 1907-09; third conductor at the Strasbourg Opera, 1909-11; conducted in Lübeck, 1911-15; conducted in Mannheim, 1915-20; conducted the Vienna Tonkünstler Orchestra, 1919-24; director of the Gesellschaft der Musikfreunde in Vienna, from 1921; conducted the Berlin Staatskapelle, 1920-22; succeeded Nikisch as principal conductor of the Berlin Philharmonic and of the Leipzig Gewandhaus Orchestra, 1922; United States debut with the New York Philharmonic, 3 January 1925; succeeded Weingartner as conductor of the Vienna Philharmonic, 1927-30; honorary Ph.D., University of Heidelberg, 1927; Generalmusikdirektor of the city of Berlin, 1928; conducted at Bayreuth, 1931; Goethe Gold Medal, 1932; director of the Berlin State Opera, and vice president of the Reichsmusikkammer, 1933; conducted Hindemith's *Mathis der Maler*, 12 March 1934; resigned all of his positions 4 December 1934 as a result of Nazi interference; returned

Wilhelm Furtwängler, c. 1927

to the conductorship of the Berlin Philharmonic, 1935; declined a permanent post succeeding Toscanini as conductor of the New York Philharmonic, 1936; in London to participate in the musical celebrations surrounding the coronation of George VI; Commander of the Legion of Honor in France, 1939; in Germany during the war; exonerated by the Allied denazification court of charges of pro-Nazi activity, 1946; took the Vienna and the Berlin Philharmonic Orchestras on a number of Western European tours; regular conductor of the Philharmonia Orchestra of London; reinaugurated the Bayreuth Festival with Beethoven's Ninth Symphony, 1951; resumed as principal conductor of the Berlin Philharmonic, 1952.

Publications

By FURTWÄNGLER: books–

Johannes Brahms und Anton Bruckner. Leipzig, 1941; 2nd ed., 1952.
Gespräche über Musik. Zurich, 1948; English translation as *Concerning Music,* London, 1953.
Ton und Wort. Wiesbaden, 1954.
Der Musiker und sein Publikum. Zurich, 1954.
Vermächtnis. Wiesbaden, 1956.
Thiess, Frank, ed. *Wilhelm Furtwängler: Briefe.* Wiesbaden, 1964.
Whiteside, S., trans., and M. Tanner, ed. *Notebooks 1924-1954 by Wilhelm Furtwängler.* London, 1989.

About FURTWÄNGLER: books–

Specht, R. *Wilhelm Furtwängler.* Vienna, 1922.
Schrenck, O. *Wilhelm Furtwängler.* Berlin, 1940.
Herzfeld, F. *Wilhelm Furtwängler, Weg und Wesen.* Leipzig, 1941.
Geissmar, B. *Two Worlds of Music.* New York, 1946.
Siebert, W. *Furtwängler, Mensch und Künstler.* Buenos Aires, 1950.
Riess, C. *Furtwängler: Musik und Politik.* Bern, 1953.
Gavoty, Bernard. *Furtwängler.* Geneva, 1956.
Hoecker, Karla. *Wilhelm Furtwängler: Begegnungen und Gespräche.* Berlin, 1961.
Gillis, D., ed. *Furtwängler Recalled.* Tuckahoe, New York, 1966.
Schonberg, Harold C. *The Great Conductors.* New York, 1967.
Hoecker, Karla. *Wilhelm Furtwängler: Dokumente—Berichte und Bilder—Aufzeichnungen.* Berlin, 1968.
Gillis, D. *Furtwängler and America.* Woodhaven, New York, 1970.
Olsen, H.S. *Wilhelm Furtwängler: a Discography.* Copenhagen, 1970.
_____. *Wilhelm Furtwängler: Konzertprogramme Opern und Vorträge 1947 bis 1954.* Wiesbaden, 1972.
Furtwängler, E. *Über Wilhelm Furtwängler.* Wiesbaden, 1979.
Hoecker, Karla. *Die nie vergessenen Klänge: Erinnerungen an Wilhelm Furtwängler.* Berlin, 1979.
Pirie, Peter. *Furtwängler and the Art of Conducting.* London, 1980.
Hunt, J. *The Furtwängler Sound.* London, 1985.
Squire, J. and J. Hunt. *Furtwängler and Great Britain.* London, 1985.
Wessling, B. *Wilhelm Furtwängler: Eine kritische Biographie.* Stuttgart, 1985.

Matzner, J. *Furtwängler: Analyse, Dokument, Protokoll.* Zurich, 1986.
Schönzeler, H.-H. *Furtwängler.* London, 1987.

articles–

Einstein, A. "Wilhelm Furtwängler." *Monthly Musical Record* January (1934).
Ardoin, John. "Furtwängler and Opera, Part One: Gluck, Beethoven, and Weber." *Opera Quarterly* spring (1984).
_____. "Furtwängler and Opera, Part Two: Mozart." *Opera Quarterly* summer (1984).
_____. "Furtwängler and Opera, Part Three: Verdi and Wagner." *Opera Quarterly* winter (1984-85).

*　　*　　*

Wilhelm Furtwängler was one of the most renowned conductors of the first half of the twentieth century. Like many other conductors of his generation, Furtwängler's first professional conducting experience was in opera. In 1905-6 he was engaged as a vocal coach at the Breslau Municipal Theater. Following this was a year (1906-7) spent as a vocal coach and assistant conductor in Zurich, and from 1907-9, Furtwängler worked under the famous Wagner conductor, Felix Mottl. Furtwängler's first full position was as third conductor in the Strasbourg Opera from 1909-11. The music director in Strasbourg, Hans Pfitzner, was a great influence on Furtwängler—both as a composer and a conductor. In 1911, Furtwängler was appointed chief conductor in Lübeck, where he stayed until 1915. During this time he conducted Beethoven's *Fidelio* and Wagner's *Die Meistersinger* with the Lübeck Opera.

After appearances with several symphony orchestras, including five years (1915-20) as successor to Arthur Bodansky in Mannheim, Furtwängler was appointed conductor of the Berlin Staatsoper, taking over from Richard Strauss. Furtwängler then succeeded Arthur Nikisch as music director of the Berlin Philharmonic and Leipzig Gewandhaus orchestras in 1922, and thus began his extensive concert career with these two orchestras.

In 1928 Furtwängler conducted Wagner's *Das Rheingold* at the Vienna Opera. Subsequently he was invited to direct there, but refused. In June 1933 he became chief conductor at the Berlin Staatsoper, but resigned all his posts in 1934 as a protest against the Nazi regime.

Furtwängler conducted at the Bayreuth Festival on three occasions. This first was in 1931, when he conducted three performances of *Tristan.* The second engagement was in 1936, when he conducted *Parsifal, Lohengrin,* and the *Ring.* The third time was in 1944, this time conducting *Die Meistersinger.*

Furtwängler also conducted at Covent Garden in London several times during the 1930s. He conducted *Tristan* in 1935 and the *Ring* a total of four times—twice in both 1937 and 1938.

Following the Second World War and his denazification, Furtwängler moved to Switzerland. Regular work at the Salzburg and Lucerne festivals continued for the rest of his life. In addition, he conducted the *Ring* three times at the Teatro alla Scala in Milan during 1950, made a London Philharmonic Orchestra recording of *Tristan* in 1952, a recording of the *Ring* with Radio Audizioni Italiana in 1953, and a recording of Wagner's *Die Walküre* in Vienna shortly before his death in 1954.

Furtwängler's vast experience in opera manifests itself on several of his recorded performances. His 1950 Salzburg recording of *Fidelio* is almost unparalleled in intensity and drama. It is with Wagner's works, however, that Furtwängler's genius is perhaps most apparent. Being a master of musical transitions, Furtwängler was able to give Wagner's music dramas a sense of unity that few other conductors have been able to achieve. His 1953 RAI *Ring* recordings are especially brilliant in their organic unity.

Furtwängler's aesthetic sense favored Wagner's concept of the "melos"—or, in other words, allowing the melody to be readily perceived by the listener. Furthermore, Furtwängler avoided sharp musical accents—except for very deliberate occasions (cf: *Fidelio,* act II, Pizzaro's entrance). Thus Furtwängler's baton technique developed to what some musicians regarded as disorienting—but was in Furtwängler's own words "shaped to the expressive needs of the music."

The mellifluous nature and logical acoustic balance combined to create a distinctive "Furtwängler sound." This quality of sound is already apparent on a 1933 Berlin Philharmonic recording of "Siegfried's Funeral March." In many ways it is similar to the same section in the RAI recording of twenty years later, but if anything it is even a bit less impetuous. This contradicts the tendency of most other recordings (particularly symphonic works) to be slower in later versions than in earlier.

Although the sonic quality of most Furtwängler recordings is less than ideal, the performances themselves are testimony to the achievements of one of the century's most distinguished conductors.

—Richard Niezen

G

GADSKI, Johanna.

Soprano. Born 15 June 1872, in Anklam, Prussia. Died 22 February 1932, in Berlin. Studied with Schroeder-Chaloupka in Stettin; debut in Lortzing's *Undine* at the Kroll Opera, Berlin, 1889; American debut as Elsa in *Lohengrin* at Damrosch Opera Company's season at the Metropolitan Opera, 1895, and remained with company for three years; engaged by Covent Garden, 1898-1901; debut as a member of Metropolitan Opera Company as Senta in *Der fliegende Holländer,* 1900, and remained at Met until 1917; concert tours of the United States, 1904-06; appeared in Munich, 1905-06; appeared at Salzburg in 1906 and 1910; after 1917 did not appear in opera until 1929, when she was leader of a Wagnerian touring company.

Publications

About GADSKI: books–

Hurok, S. *Impresario.* New York, 1946.

articles–

Ridley, N. and L. Migliorini. "Johanna Gadski." *Record Collector* 11 (1957): 197.

Although recorded only on pre-electronic records which sound tinny and fuzzy to modern ears, Johanna Gadski is still a pleasure to hear more than fifty years after her death. J.B. Steane called her "one of the most sensitive and musical singers of her day." Yet Gadski did not always receive such praise in live performance. Audiences loved her, but the critics were less impressed. The reviews were so mixed that sometimes it seemed as if the critics were contradicting each other, and themselves, with each subsequent report. Her reputation, like that of many artists, has fared better after death than during her life.

Gadski debuted at age seventeen in Lortzing's *Undine* at the Kroll Opera in Berlin; she sang in Germany between 1889 and 1894 before her United States debut in 1895 with the Damrosch Opera company in *Lohengrin* at the Metropolitan Opera House in New York. She joined the Metropolitan Opera Company in 1900. While she was one of their leading Wagnerian sopranos, her repertoire was not limited to Wagner. She had roles in Verdi's *Aïda, Il trovatore,* and *Rigoletto,* Meyerbeer's *Les Huguenots,* Mozart's *Zauberflöte* and *Le nozze di Figaro;* she sang in Mahler's production of *Don Giovanni* at the Met in 1908 as well as in Toscanini's revival of *Orfeo,* and performed in some lesser known works such as Ethel Smyth's *Der Wald,* Boieldieu's *La Dame Blanche,* Mancinelli's *Ero e Leanero,* and Damrosch's *Scarlet Letter.* She sang recitals as well as opera, programming Mozart and Wagner arias, and German lieder; she was one of the few recitalists of her day to regularly include songs by American composers. The burgeoning record industry saw her potential early. She was one of the first Victor Red Seal artists, and made almost 100 records during her career. In 1917, when German nationals had grown out of political favor during the first world war, she was asked to leave the Met. In the 1920s, she formed her own opera company in Germany and toured the United States several times before her death in an auto accident in 1932.

Her live performances received mixed reviews and contradictory criticism. Richard Aldrich, reviewing for the *New York Times,* wrote of a recital in 1904 "She is, first of all, a singer in the real sense of the word; an uncommonly beautiful voice, in which the evidences of full control and skillful use are rarely lacking, is at her disposition. She has the dramatic instinct, guided by intelligence and artistic understanding, and she has sincere sentiment and a serious view of the artist's task." Audiences agreed, and she was an extremely popular recitalist. Aldrich had less positive things to say as well, however. He continued in the same article in a less complimentary vein that "with much that is beautiful in her singing she has not always a perception of the finer differences of values, [nor] the subtler elements of characteristic expression that go to the proper singing of songs." Eleven years later he reviewed her again and complained that her voice was not what it used to be and that she was "not infrequently at variance with the pitch." Another New York critic, W.J. Henderson, did not like her at all. In 1917, he attributed her retirement from the Metropolitan Opera, a purely politically-induced move, to "the deterioration of Mme Gadski's voice and art." He said she was merely "an honest, hardworking . . . soprano" who has had "much admiration from easy going opera patrons." Yet when she toured in the United States after the war, he wrote that she was in "astonishingly good condition." While one critic maintained that she did not have "the creative imagination of an interpreter," Herman Klein in London disagreed: "[She is] the finest Eva we have had in London . . . [due to her] rare vocal and histrionic attainments."

Gadski fared better in recordings than she apparently did in live performance, for her recordings are considered vocal classics. They reflect her versatility: she recorded the lieder of Schubert, Mendelssohn and Strauss, Rossini's *Stabat Mater,* operas of Wagner, Strauss, Verdi, and Mozart, and American songs. She had a large voice with a beautifully pure tone. She could sing strongly when needed without the "Bayreuth Bark" of some other Wagnerians. Her "*Liebestod,*" "Immolation," and "Battle Cry" all ring out with power and vibrancy, yet she could also float her tones when warranted; her performance of Pamina was young and light. While she showed an occasional tendency towards shrillness at the top of her range, she also had a lovely, round, high pianissimo. Her chest voice was well blended and even. In most of her recordings, at least, her musicianship was unquestionable. Even in the most difficult of passages, her accuracy showed her thorough knowledge of her scores.

During her life, Gadski's critics accused her of expressive monotony. Aldrich wrote that she had a very limited emotional range. One modern critic labeled her "worthy if not exciting." Yet her recordings prove her to be a sensitive interpreter with a real depth and frankness of emotion. Critics of her live performances complained of her stolid and unchanging interpretations, but her records belie this. She recorded some pieces more than once; the differences and variety of these performances are striking. She shaded and colored her tone to create moods. Her expressive use of the *portamento* lent a tragic inflection to her singing. She could command a driving energy, or a tender pathos.

Her later records also illustrate that some of the criticisms received were justified. Towards the end of her career she lost some of her vocal consistency. Her middle register occasionally sounded colorless; her vibrato grew wider and more fluttery. Sometimes her highest notes went flat, and her phrasing seemed slightly short breathed. Her rubato occasionally gave way to rhythmic inaccuracies. But as J.B. Steane concluded, "with so many strengths, . . . she can carry a few weaknesses."

Modern listeners are fortunate that the early days of the recording industry caught Gadski for posterity. The recordings that have been periodically reissued have kept her voice alive and have given us the pleasure of evaluating her singing and the criticism she received. Recordings, which have insured immortality to many musicians, provided a new vehicle for Gadski—a second, if posthumous, career, which has fared better and been less controversial than the reception of her live performances.

—Robin Armstrong

GAGLIANO, Marco da.

Composer. Born 1 May 1582, in Florence. Died 25 February 1643, in Florence. Studied with L. Bati; established the Accademia degli Elevati, 1607; maestro di cappella at San Lorenzo in Florence, 1608; maestro di cappella at the Medici court, Florence; became a canon in 1610; Apostolic Protonotary, 1615.

Operas

La Dafne, Ottavio Rinuccini, Mantua, 1608.
La Flora (with J. Peri), A. Salvadori, Florence, 1628.

Other works: intermedii, madrigals, monodies, sacred vocal music.

Publications

By GAGLIANO: articles–

29 letters printed in Vogel, E. "Marco da Gagliano: zur Geschichte des Florentiner Musiklebens von 1570-1650." *Vierteljahrsschrift für Musikwissenschaft* 5 (1889): 550.

About GAGLIANO: books–

Ademollo, A. *La bell' Adriana ed altre virtuose del suo tempo alla corte di Mantova,* 41, 53ff, 57f, 141, 146, 235, 270f. Città di Castello, 1888.
Bertolotti, A. *Musici alla corte dei Gonzaga dal secolo XV al XVIII,* 76, 82, 89, 90. Milan, 1890, 1969.
Goldschmidt, H. *Studien zur Geschichte der italienischen Oper im 17. Jahrhundert,* vol. 1, 29ff, 141. Leipzig, 1901, 1967.
Solerti, A. *Le origini del melodramma,* 76ff, 138. Turin, 1903, 1969.
_____. *Gli albori del melodramma,* vol. 1, 73ff. Milan, 1904, 1969.
_____. *Musica, ballo e drammatica alla corte medicea dal 1600 al 1637.* Florence, 1905, 1968, 1969.
Daugnan, F.F. de. *Gli italiani in Polonia dal IX secolo al XVII,* vol. 2, 295f, 303f. Crema, 1907.
Einstein, Alfred. *The Italian Madrigal,* 729ff, 849. Princeton, 1949, 1971.
Abert, A.A. *Claudio Monteverdi und das musikalische Drama.* Lippstadt, 1954.
Nagler, A.M. *Theatre Festivals of the Medici, 1539-1637,* 118, 131ff, 139ff, 177ff. New Haven, 1964.

articles–

Picchianti, L. "Cenni biografici di Marco da Gagliano e di alcuni altri valenti compositori di musica." *Gazzetta musicale di Milano* 3 (1844): 2.
Vogel, E. "Marco da Gagliano: zur Geschichte des Florentiner Musiklebens von 1570-1650." *Vierteljahrsschrift für Musikwissenschaft* 5 (1889): 396, 509.
Fortune, Nigel. "Italian Secular Monody from 1600 to 1635: an Introductory Survey." *Musical Quarterly* 39 (1953): 184.
Valabrega, C. "Antiche schermaglie." *La Scala* 114 (1959): 28, 77.
Fabbri, M. and E. Settesoldi. "Aggiunte e rettifiche alle biografie di Marco e Giovanni Battista da Gagliano: il luogo e le date di nascita e di morte dei due fratelli musicisti." *Chigiana* 21 (1964): 131.
Cortellazzo, A.T. "Il melodramma di Marco da Gagliano." In *Congresso internazionale sul tema Claudio Monteverdi e il suo tempo,* 583. Venice, Mantua, and Cremona, 1968.
_____. "New Light on the Accademia degli Elevati of Florence." *Musical Quarterly* 62 (1976): 507.
_____. "Marco da Gagliano and the *Compagnia dell' Arcangelo Raffaello* in Florence: an Unknown Episode in the Composer's Life." In *Essays in Honor of Myron P. Gilmore.* Florence, 1977.
Sternfeld, Frederick W. "The First Printed Opera Libretto." *Music and Letters* 59 (1978): 121.
Carter, Tim. "Jacopo Peri." *Music and Letters* 61 (1980): 122.

*　　　*　　　*

Gagliano is, with the composers Jacopo Peri and Giulio Caccini, an important figure in the early development of opera in Florence at the beginning of the seventeenth century. Although the older composers Peri and Caccini were in the true vanguard of the new style, it was Gagliano who, of the Florentine composers, provided the new genre with a minor masterpiece.

Gagliano is now primarily remembered for his opera *La Dafne* (Mantua, 1608), but in his lifetime he was widely revered as a composer of vocal chamber music and sacred music as well. He spent most of his career in his native city of Florence, serving the Medici court and the cathedral of Florence. The Accademia degli Elevati, which Gagliano founded for the purpose of advancing the serious study of music, included in its membership many prominent Florentine musicians and men of letters.

Gagliano achieved his first and most lasting success, however, in Mantua, early in his career, with his setting of Ottavio Rinuccini's libretto *La Dafne*. When it became clear that Monteverdi's *L'Arianna*, originally scheduled for production during the carnival season of 1608, could not be produced at that time, Gagliano was chosen to provide a replacement work. That Gagliano was chosen even after Jacopo Peri's *Tetide* had been turned down in favor of Monteverdi's *L'Arianna* is a measure of Gagliano's emerging stature. For this occasion Gagliano's Florentine associate Rinuccini revised and expanded the libretto for *La Dafne,* which had already been set to music by Peri a decade earlier.

Gagliano composed other stage works for Mantua (an *intermedio* and a *ballo*) before returning to Florence. Accepting appointments at the court and the cathedral, he remained in Florence as composer and performer for more than three decades until his death. There is only one additional surviving opera by Gagliano, *La Flora,* composed to celebrate the wedding of Maria de' Medici and the Duke of Parma in 1628. For this work Gagliano collaborated with Peri, who wrote the music for the role of Clori. Both extant operas have been reprinted in modern editions.

In the important and highly-quotable preface to the printed score of *La Dafne* (1608), Gagliano gives useful information about contemporary staging and performance practice. He argues for the importance of integrating all of the elements of a production in order for the work to be effective, specifically mentioning plot, text, music, gesture, dancing, sets, and costumes. He describes how Apollo's onstage, mimed lyre playing should be coordinated with offstage musicians playing viols. Singers should be easily visible to the accompanying instrumentalists in order to aid the ensemble. The instrumentalists, in realizing the *basso continuo,* should leave melodic embellishment to the singers, who should themselves apply embellishments only when it is appropriate to the text. The text is, therefore, the governing force which should control the music. Gagliano suggests that an instrumental *sinfonia* be supplied in order to begin the work, as there is none in the score.

Gagliano, the most accomplished of the three early Florentine opera composers, provided the genre with an early masterwork, and he would be even better remembered if his operas were not overshadowed by the work of Monteverdi.

—Edward Rutschman

GALLET, Louis.

Librettist/Novelist/Poet. Born 1835, in Valence, Drôme. Died 16 October 1898, in Paris.

Librettos

La coupe du roi de Thulé, J. Massenet, c. 1866 [not performed].
Le kobold, E. Guiraud, 1870.
Djamileh, G. Bizet, 1872.
La princesse jaune, C. Saint-Saëns, 1872.
L'adorable bel'-boul', J. Massenet, 1874.
Le roi de Lahore, J. Massenet, 1877.
Cinq-Mars (with Paul Poirson), C. Gounod, 1877.
Étienne Marcel, C. Saint-Saëns, 1879.
Le Chevalier Jean, V. de Joncières, 1885.

Le Cid (with A.P. d'Ennery and E. Blau, after Corneille), J. Massenet, 1885.
Proserpine, C. Saint-Saëns, 14 March 1887.
Ascanio, C. Saint-Saëns, 1890.
Thamara, Bourgault-Decoudray, 1891.
L'attaque du moulin (after Zola), A. Bruneau, 1893.
Thaïs, J. Massenet, 1894.
Frédégonde (with E. Guiraud) [unfinished; completed by Saint-Saëns], 1895.
Déjanire, C. Saint-Saëns, 1911.

Publications

By GALLET: books—

Notes d'un librettiste. Paris, 1891.

*   *   *

Louis Gallet was, by profession, a bursar in a Paris hospital. Short, moon-faced with a big beard and a bald, dome-like forehead, he was also very deaf. His deafness prevented a full appreciation of music, for which he did not much care any way, although during the last thirty years of the nineteenth century he provided libretti for over a dozen operas by leading French composers. He was an all around literary man, with the literary man's typical distrust of music. Novels, articles, poems, addresses, inaugural speeches and a voluminous correspondence flowed readily from his pen. He was also a competent artist who painted seascapes at his holiday cottage in Wimereux where, on a clear day, he could see the English coast. The desert scene in Massenet's *Le roi de Lahore,* for which he wrote the libretto, had decor based on a water color of his, as did the convent scene in Saint-Saëns's *Proserpine.*

Gallet's libretti were solid and workmanlike. The verse played its essentially modest part without drawing too much attention away from the music, and he, good-natured and accommodating, was always ready to make changes when a composer required them. In *Thaïs,* however, he departed from convention for once and replaced formal meters with a looser, more conversational style. Anatole France, who wrote the novel, did not think much of Gallet's libretto. Gallet confessed that he could not find enough dignified rhymes for the hero's name, which was Paphnuce. All he had thought of so far were *puce* and *prépuce.* Could he change the name to Athanaël, which rhymed with more respectable words like *ciel* and *autel?* France agreed, adding sardonically: "Between ourselves I prefer Paphnuce."

A collaboration with Alfred Bruneau resulted in *L'attaque du moulin* based on a Zola short story, though in later years Zola himself supplied the libretti of three more Bruneau operas. Gallet also wrote the words of Gounod's *Cinq-Mars,* an overblown grand opera. More interestingly, for Gounod's unfinished opera *Maître Pierre,* which aimed to retell the story of Héloïse and Abelard, Gallet continued the experiment begun with *Thaïs* of using a more flexible style that aspired to prose. His work for Massenet included an exotic *Roi de Lahore* and the words of two oratorios, one of them, *Marie Magdeleine,* being given in a stage version at the Opéra-Comique in 1906. He found Bizet a particularly congenial associate and collaborated with him on *Djamileh* and *Don Rodrigue.* In his memoirs, *Notes d'un librettiste* (Paris, 1891), he gives some very interesting sidelights on Bizet the man.

Gallet was especially close to Saint-Saëns who thought him "an ideal collaborator, the sort I had always dreamt of meeting but never dared hope I would." They did five operas together, ranging from the witty *Princesse jaune* to the tragic *Déjanire.* The latter, premiered at an open-air festival in Béziers sponsored by a rich wine merchant, brought Gallet an honor rarely accorded to humble librettists: a thoroughfare in that torrid Southern town was named the avenue Louis Gallet.

—James Harding

GALLI-CURCI, Amelita.

Soprano. Born 18 November 1882, in Milan. Died 26 November 1963, in La Jolla, California. Married Luigi Curci, 1910 (divorced 1920) and pianist Homer Samuels, 1921. Studied piano at Milan Conservatory. Took up singing at Mascagni's suggestion. Studied briefly with Carignani and Sara Dufes, but mainly self-taught; debut as Gilda at Trani, 1906; then appeared in Italy, Spain, and South America; in Rome she appeared in premiere of Bizet's *Don Procopio,* 1908; United States debut as Gilda in Chicago, 1916, where she remained until 1924; Metropolitan Opera debut as Violetta, 1921, and became a regular member of Metropolitan Opera until 1930; underwent surgery for a goiter, 1935; attempted to return to stage in *La bohème,* Chicago, 1936.

Publications

About GALLI-CURCI: books–

La Massena, C. *Galli-Curci's Life of Song.* New York, 1945 (reprinted 1978).

articles–

Favia-Artsay, A. "Amelita Galli-Curci." *Record Collector* 4 (1949): 163.

Originally trained as a pianist at the Milan Conservatory, Amelita Galli-Curci was encouraged to become a singer by the opera composer Pietro Mascagni, who admired the unique timbre of her voice. It appears that her preparation for a career in opera consisted of a few voice lessons, the study of opera scores, and her own natural ability to imitate the serene singing of birds outside her home. She made her operatic debut as Gilda, singing a series of *Rigoletto*s in Trani and Rome.

During the next decade she carefully selected roles which would highlight her natural agility and bird-like timbre. She consistently performed that group of heroines which we now consider to be the property of the coloratura soprano. She sang Rosina in Rossini's *Il barbiere di Siviglia,* Amina in Bellini's *La sonnambula* and Donizetti heroines *Lucia di Lammermoor* and *Linda di Chamounix.* She also included in her repertoire such roles as *Lakme, Dinorah* and *Manon.* In his book *The Great Singers,* Henry Pleasants suggests that Galli-Curci, as well as her contemporary Luisa Tetrazzini, succeeded in distinguishing themselves from other sopranos of their time by specializing in these particular roles and

creating a new phenomenon by "crowning" their performances with the electrifying high notes (E-flat, E and F) that we have come to expect from "coloratura" sopranos. Although she sang primarily these roles, from time to time she did perform more lyrical repertoire, including Sophie in *Der Rosenkavalier,* Mimi in *La bohème* and Violetta in *La traviata.* She performed continually during these early years, but did not really achieve international status until her American debut in 1916.

She sang in the United States for the first time on 18 November 1916 in a performance by the Chicago Opera. She again chose Gilda as her debut vehicle. Her performance there electrified the unprepared audience and she was an overnight sensation. Critics and audiences alike adored her. During her first season with the Chicago Opera she sang *Lucia di Lammermoor, Roméo et Juliette,* and *Il barbiere di Siviglia* as well as *Rigoletto.*

She had come to the United States, after a performance tour in South America, primarily because she had a letter of recommendation to Victor Records in New York City. She would record throughout these next few years on the Victor Records label, and some of her best recordings are from this early acoustic period. After her Chicago triumph, a quickly arranged tour of American cities solidified her popularity in the United States. Her phonograph records, distributed in huge editions, sold as fast as they reached the dealers; "Caro nome" sold 10,000 copies of the first edition in Chicago alone.

Two years later, during a tour designed to show off the roster of the blossoming Chicago Opera, Galli-Curci performed at the Lexington Theater in New York City. Singing Meyerbeer's *Dinorah* for this much-publicized New York performance, she took the town by storm. The audience demanded twenty-four curtain calls after the "Shadow Song" and sixty curtain calls at the end of the opera. She was heard five more times during this rather lengthy season in New York, each performance drawing more patrons than the theatre could hold. In addition to a second Dinorah, she sang Lucia, Gilda, Rosina and Violetta. James Alfonte in his *Opera News* tribute to Galli-Curci (March 1958) relates the incredible circumstances surrounding her last appearance at the Lexington Theater. Undaunted by the fact that the performance was "long since sold out," 10,000 hopeful admirers remained outside the theater, and the capacity crowd inside simply "refused to go home" until "a piano was wheeled on stage" and Galli-Curci serenaded them from the piano. The unprecedented reaction of the public to these and other performances demonstrates the astounding effect of Galli-Curci's voice and personality. Her Metropolitan Opera debut, this time as Violetta, took place on 14 November 1921. From 1921 until 1924 she was a permanent member of both the Metropolitan and Chicago Operas, but after that she made the decision to remain permanently in New York and withdrew from the Chicago roster.

Throughout her career Galli-Curci's popularity never flagged. However, many critics commented about her increasing tendency to sing under pitch. We can only assume that she sang better, at least more consistently, earlier in her career. It is important to note that the height of her career came well before her actual Metropolitan debut, and that at this age, she was in all probability feeling the first effects of a thyroid condition which would worsen as the years progressed.

Her voice, most often described as "limpid" and "natural," was said to have been of remarkable beauty. She had the ability to produce sustained tones with a seemingly effortless floating quality. The unique timbre is said to have been reminiscent of birds and not necessarily the metallic quality that one hears on recordings. The crystalline quality of her upper notes remained unspoiled despite the increasing intonation problems. She was said to have an extraordinary, warm and graceful stage presence.

A throat ailment, diagnosed as a goiter, compelled her to bring her career to a temporary end. She was operated on in 1935 and in November of the following year she attempted a comeback with the Chicago Opera as Mimì. She then went into complete retirement in California, where she remained until her death in 1963.

—Patricia Robertson

GALLI-MARIÉ, Célestine Laurence [born Marié de l'Isle].

Mezzo-soprano. Born November 1840, in Paris. Died 22 September 1905, in Vence, France. Studied with father Felix Mécène Marié de l'Isle; debut in Strasbourg, 1859; sang in Toulouse, 1860; appeared in Lisbon, 1861; appeared in Rouen, 1862; debut at Opéra-Comique, as Serpina in *La serva padrona*, 1862, and sang there until 1885; performed at Her Majesty's Theatre, London, 1886; returned to Opéra-Comique as Carmen, 1885; created Thomas's Mignon (1866) and Bizet's Carmen (1875).

Publications

About GALLI-MARIÉ: books–

Curzon, H. de. *Croquis d'artistes.* Paris, 1897.
Malherbe, H. *Carmen.* Paris, 1951.
Curtiss, M. *Bizet and his World.* New York, 1958.

*   *   *

Célestine Galli-Marié was a mezzo-soprano with a voice described in 1863 as having no range or volume, but an exceptional timbre combined with clear diction and fine musical phrasing. It was her dramatic ability that seemed to be most striking in her performances when through her voice and person she was able to create exciting characters often entirely opposed to her own. She could excite audiences so as to induce tears or laughter with equal facility. Her contribution to the Paris Opéra–Comique between 1862 and about 1902 was considered of "incontestable dramatic worth." She was "small, vivacious and had a cat-like grace."

Her debut was at Strasbourg (as Célestine Marié) in 1859. She moved to the Toulouse Opera in 1860, then to Lisbon in 1861, singing in Italian. There she met and married a sculptor called Galli, whose name she took and kept, although he died very soon. She never remarried.

Her first big success came at Rouen in 1862 when she sang the mezzo role of the Gipsy Queen in the first French production of Balfe's *Bohemian Girl* (called, at the time, *La bohème*). The director of the Paris Opéra–Comique heard her and immediately engaged her for his house, where her debut was in the OC's first performance of Pergolesi's intermezzo *La serva padrona* (called *La servante maîtresse*), under her name of Galli-Marié, singing the soprano role of Serpina.

She created Mignon in Ambroise Thomas's opera in 1866 (and sang in its 500th presentation in 1878); the two mezzo roles of Taven and Andrelou in *Mireille*, 1874; Dorothée

(mezzo) in *Cendrillon*, 1899 as Marié de l'Isle; and Camille (soprano) in *Louise*, 1900. She later sang the Mother in *Louise*, a contralto role, and was a famous Charlotte in *Werther* and Lola in *Cavalleria rusticana*, both mezzo roles, at the end of her career, though she created neither.

The part with which she was most closely associated was Carmen. She created it at the Opéra-Comique on 3 March 1875 (as Galli-Marié) with Paul Lhérie as Don José and Jacques-Joseph Bouhy as Escamillo. Her performance, according to Tchaikovsky's brother Modeste, was characterized by intense passion and a mystical sense of fatalism. She again sang in many subsequent performances and in the 100th, in 1883, followed in 1890 by a charity *Carmen*, to raise funds for a Bizet monument, when her partners were Nellie Melba, Jean de Reszke and Jean Lassalle. As time went on, Galli-Marié changed to the deeper roles such as Mercédès, and also gave some memorable performances of Lola in *Cavalleria rusticana*.

She visited London in 1886 and sang at Her Majesty's Theatre, with an indifferent French company, in *Carmen* and as Gilda in *Rigoletto*, seeming to challenge the early opinion that her voice lacked range.

She continued to sing at the Opéra–Comique (though never at the Paris Opéra) until she retired to Vence and died there on 22 September 1905. She made no recordings.

—Alan Jefferson

GALUPPI, Baldassare.

Composer. Born 18 October 1706, on the island of Burano, near Venice. Died 3 January 1785, in Venice. Studied with his father; first opera, *La fede nell' incostanza*, performed in Vicenza, 1722; studied with Lotti in Venice; appointed maestro del coro at the Ospizio dei Mendicanti, 1740; in London, 1741-43; second maestro at San Marco, Venice, 1748; principal maestro at San Marco, 1762-64; maestro del coro, Ospedali degl' Incurabili, 1762; maestro to the Russian court, 1765-68; returned to Venice. Galuppi and the librettist and playwright Carlo Goldoni pioneered a number of important techniques in comic opera; Galuppi taught a number of Russian singers and composers, including Bortniansky.

Operas

La fede nell' incostanza, ossia Gli amici rivali, Neri?, Vicenza, Teatro delle Grazie, 1722.
Gl' odi delusi dal sangue (with Pescetti), Lucchini, Venice, Sant' Angelo, 4 February 1728.
Dorinda (with Pescetti), Benedetto Pasqualigo?, Marcello?, Venice, San Samuele, 9 June 1729.
L'odio placato, Silvani, Venice, San Samuele, 27 December 1729.
Argenide, Giusti, Venice, Sant' Angelo, 15 January 1733.
L'ambizione depressa, Papis, Venice, Sant' Angelo, Ascension 1733.
La ninfa Apollo, Lemene (with additions by Boldini), Venice, San Samuele, 30 May 1734.
Tamiri, Vitturi, Venice, Sant' Angelo, 17 November 1734.
Elisa, regina di Tiro, Zeno and Pariati, Venice, Sant' Angelo, 27 January 1736.
Ergilda, Vitturi, Venice, Sant' Angelo, 12 November 1736.

L'Alvilda, Zeno (with additions by Lalli), Venice, San Samuele, 29 May 1737.

Issipile, Metastasio, Turin, Regio, 26 December 1737.

Alessandro nell' Indie, Metastasio, Mantua, Nuovo Arciducale, carnival 1738.

Adriano in Siria, Metastasio, Turin, Regio, January? 1740.

Gustavo primo, re di Svezia, Goldoni, Venice, San Samuele, 25 May 1740.

Oronte, re de' Sciti, Goldoni, Venice, San Giovanni Grisostomo, 26 December 1740.

Berenice, Vitturi, Venice, Sant' Angelo, 27 January 1741.

Didone abbandonata, Metastasio, Modena, Molzo, carnival 1741.

Penelope, Rolli, London, King's Theatre in the Haymarket, 23 December 1741.

Scipione in Cartagine, Vanneschi, London, King's Theatre in the Haymarket, 13 March 1742.

Enrico, Vanneschi, London, King's Theatre in the Haymarket, 12 January 1743.

Sirbace, Stampa, London, King's Theatre in the Haymarket, 20 April 1743.

Ricimero, Silvani, Milan, Regio Ducal, 26 December 1744.

La forza d'amore, Panicelli, Venice, San Cassiano, 30 January 1745.

Ciro riconosciuto, Caldará, Milan, Regio Ducal, 26 December 1745.

Antigono, Metastasio, London, King's Theatre in the Haymarket, 24 May 1746.

Scipione nelle Spagne, Piovene, Venice, Sant' Angelo, November 1746.

Evergete, Silvani and Lalli, Rome, Capranica, 2 January 1747.

L'Arminio, Salvi, Venice, San Cassiano, 26 November 1747.

L'Olimpiade, Metastasio, Milan, Regio Ducal, 26 December 1747.

Vologeso, Zeno, Rome, Torre Argentina, 13 or 14 February 1748.

Demetrio, Metastasio, Vienna, Burgtheater, 16 or 27 October 1748.

Clotilde, Passarini, Venice, San Cassiano, November 1748.

Semiramide riconosciuta, Metastasio, Milan, Regio Ducal, 25 January 1749.

Artaserse, Metastasio, Vienna, Burgtheater, 27 January 1749.

L'Arcadia in Brenta, Goldoni, Venice, Sant' Angelo, 14 May 1749.

Il conte Caramella, Goldoni, Verona, Teatro dell' Accademia Vecchia, 18 December 1749.

Il Demofoonte, Metastasio, Madrid, Teatro del Buon Retiro, 18 December 1749.

Olimpia, Trabucco, Naples, San Carlo, 18? December 1749.

Alcimena, principessa dell' Isole Fortunate, ossia L'amore fortunato ne' suoi disprezzi, Chiari (after Molière, *Princesse d'Élide*), Venice, San Cassiano, 26 December 1749.

Arcifanfano, re dei matti, Goldoni, Venice, San Moisè, 27 December 1749.

Il mondo della luna, Goldoni, Venice, San Moisè, 29 January 1750.

Il paese della Cuccagna, Goldoni, Venice, San Moisè, 7 May 1750.

Il mondo alla roversa, ossia Le donne che comandano, Goldoni, Venice, San Cassiano, 14 November 1750.

La mascherata, Goldoni, Venice, San Cassiano, 26? December 1750.

Antigona, Roccaforte, Rome, Teatro delle Dame, 9 January 1751.

Dario, Baldanza, Turin, Regio Ducal, carnival 1751.

Lucio Papirio, Zeno, Reggio Emilia, Teatro del Pubblico, fair 1751.

Artaserse, Metastasio, Padua, Nuovo, 11 June 1751.

Le virtuose ridicole, Goldoni (after Molière, *Les précieuses ridicules*), Venice, San Samuele, carnival 1752.

La calamità de' cuori, Goldoni, Venice, San Samuele, 26 December 1752.

I bagni d'Abano (with Bertoni), Goldoni, Venice, San Samuele, 10 February 1753.

Sofonisba, Roccaforte, Rome, Teatro delle Dame, c. 24 February 1753.

L'eroe cinese, Metastasio, Naples, San Carlo, 10 July 1753.

Siroe, Metastasio, Rome, Torre Argentina, 10 February 1754.

Il filosofo di campagna, Goldoni, Venice, San Samuele, 26 October 1754.

Il povero superbo, Goldoni, Venice, San Samuele, February 1755.

Attalo, Papi?, Silvani?, Padua, Nuovo, 11 June 1755.

Le nozze, Goldoni, Bologna, Formagliari, 14 September 1755.

La diavolessa, Goldoni, Venice, San Samuele, November 1755.

Idomeneo, Rome, Torre Argentina, 7 January 1756.

La cantarina, Goldoni, Rome, Capranica, 26 February 1756.

Le pescatrici, Goldoni, Modena, Rangoni, carnival 1756?

Ezio, Metastasio, Milan, Regio Ducal, 22 January 1757.

Sesostri, Zeno and Pariati, Venice, San Benedetto, 26 November 1757.

L'Ipermestra, Metastasio, Milan, Regio Ducal, 14 January 1758.

Adriano in Siria, Metastasio, Livorno, spring 1758.

Melite riconosciuto, Roccaforte, Rome, Teatro delle Dame, 13 January 1759.

La ritornata di Londra, Goldoni, Rome, Valle, c. 19 February 1759.

La clemenza di Tito, Metastasio, Venice, San Salvatore, Ascension 1760.

Solimano, Migliavacca, Padua, Nuovo, fair 1760.

L'amante di tutte, Antonio Galuppi, Venice, San Moisè, 15 November 1760.

Li tre amanti ridicoli, Antonio Galuppi, Venice, San Moisè, 18 January 1761.

Il caffè di campagna, Chiari, Venice, San Moisè, 18 November 1761.

Antigono, Metastasio, Venice, San Benedetto, carnival 1762.

Il marchese villano, Chiari, Venice, San Moisè, 2 February 1762.

L'orfana onorata (intermezzo), Rome, Valle, carnival 1762.

Il re pastore, Metastasio, Parma, Ducal, spring 1762.

Viriate, after Metastasio, *Silface,* Venice, San Salvatore, 19 May 1762.

Il Muzio Scevola, Lanfranchi-Rossi, Padua, Nuovo, June 1762.

L'uomo femmina, Venice, San Moisè, fall 1762.

Il puntiglio amoroso, Carlo or Gasparo Gozzi, Venice, San Moisè, 26 December 1762.

Arianna e Teseo, Pariati, Padua, Nuovo, 12 June 1763.

Il re alla caccia, Goldoni, Venice, San Samuele, fall 1763.

La donna di governo, Goldoni, Prague, 1763.

Sofonisba, Verazi, Turin, Regio, carnival 1764.

Caio Mario, Roccaforte, Venice, San Giovanni Grisostomo, 31 May 1764.

La partenza il ritorno de' marinari, Venice, San Moisè, 26 December 1764.

La cameriera spiritosa, Goldoni, Milan, Regio Ducal, 4 October 1766.

Ifigenia in Tauride, Coltellini, St Petersburg, court, 2 May 1768.

Il villano geloso, Bertati, Venice, San Moisè, November 1769.

Amor lunatico, Chiari, Venice, San Moisè, January 1770.

L'inimico delle donne, Bertati, Venice, San Samuele, fall 1771.

Gl'intrighi amorosi, Petrosellini, Venice, San Samuele, January 1772.

Montezuma, Cigna-Santi, Venice, San Benedetto, 27 May 1772.

La serva per amore, Livigni, Venice, San Samuele, fall 1773.

Other works: oratorios, sacred music, keyboard sonatas.

Publications

About GALUPPI: books–

Wotquenne, Alfred. *Baldassare Galuppi: étude bibliographique sur ses oeuvres dramatiques.* Brussels, 1902.

Cheshikhin, V.G. *Istoriya russko opery (s 1674-1903g)* [74f]. 2nd ed., Moscow, 1905.

Abert, H. *W.A. Mozart* [vol. 1, 450ff]. Leipzig, 1919.

Blom, Eric. *Stepchildren of Music* [23ff]. London, 1923.

Della Corte, A. *L'opera comica italiana nel '700* [vol. 1, 141ff; vol. 2, 216ff]. Bari, 1923.

Torrefranca, F. *Le origini italiane del romanticismo musicale* [180ff]. Turin, 1930, 1969.

Bollert, W. *Die Buffo-Opern B. Galuppis: Ein Beitrag zur Geschichte der italienischen komischen Oper im 18. Jahrhundert.* Bottrop, 1935.

B. Galuppi detto Il Buranello (1706-1785): note e documenti raccolti in occasione della settimana celebrativa. Siena, 1948.

Della Corte, Andrea. *Baldassare Galuppi: profilo critico.* Siena, 1948.

Mooser, R.-A. *Annales de la musique et des musiciens en Russie au XVIIIme siècle* [vol. 2, 69ff]. Geneva, 1951.

Livanova, T. *Russkaya muzykal'naya kul'tura XVIII veka v eyo svyazyak h s literatury teatrom i bytom* [Russian musical culture of the 18th century and its links with literature, the theater, and everyday life] [vol. 1, 421, 445; vol. 2, 405f]. Moscow, 1952-53.

Strohm, Reinhard. *Die italienische Oper im 18. Jahrhundert.* Wilhelmshaven, 1979.

Wiesend, Reinhard. *Studien zur Opera seria von Baldassare Galuppi* [2 vols]. Tutzing, 1984.

articles–

Molmenti, P. "Il Buranello." *Gazetta musicale di Milano* 1 (1899): 59.

Bernardi, G.G. *L'opera comica veneziana del sec. XVIII.* In *Atti dell' Accademia virgiliana di Mantova.* Mantua, 1908.

Piovano, Francesco. "Baldassare Galuppi: note bio-bibliografiche." *Rivista musicale italiana* 13 (1906): 676; 14 (1907): 333; 15 (1908): 233.

Dent, E.J. "Ensembles and Finales in 18th Century Italian Opera." *Sammelbände der Internationalen Musik-Gesellschaft* 11 (1909-10): 543; 12 (1910-11): 112.

———. "Giuseppe Maria Buini." *Sammelbände der Internationalen Musik-Gesellschaft* 13 (1911-12): 329.

Bollert, W. "Tre opere di Galuppi, Haydn e Paisiello sul Mondo della luna di Goldoni." *Musica d'oggi* August/September (1939).

"B. Galuppi detto 'Il Buranello': note e documenti raccolti in occasione della settimana celebrativa (20-26 settembre 1948)." *Chigiana* 14 (1948).

Heartz, Daniel. "The Creation of the Buffo Finale in Italian Opera." *Proceedings of the Royal Musical Association* 104 (1977-78): 67.

———. "Hasse, Galuppi and Metastasio." In *Venezia e il melodramma nel settecento I,* edited by Maria T. Muraro, 309. Florence, 1978.

———. "Goldoni, Don Giovanni and the dramma giocoso." *Musical Times* 120 (1979): 993.

———. "Vis comica: Goldoni, Galuppi and L'Arcadia in Brenta (Venice 1749)." In *Venezia e il melodramma nel settocento II,* edited by Maria T. Muraro, 33. Florence, 1981.

Kolk, Joel. " 'Sturm und Drang' and Haydn's Operas." In *Haydn Studies: Proceedings of the International Haydn Conference, Washington, D.C. 1975,* edited by Jens Peter Larsen, Howard Serwer, and James Webster, 440. New York and London, 1981.

Leopold, Silke. "Zur Szenographie der Türkenoper." In *Die stilistische Entwicklung der italienischen Musik zwischen 1770 und 1830 und ihre Beziehungen zum Norden. Colloquium, Rom, 20.-30. März 1978,* edited by Friedrich Lippmann, 370. Laaber, 1982.

Wiesend, Reinhard. "Die arie: 'Già si sa ch'un empio sei': von Vivaldi oder von Galuppi?" *Informazioni e studi vivaldiani* 4 (1983): 76.

———. "Il giovane Galuppi e l'opera: materiali per gli anni 1722-1741" [translated from German by Maria Antonella Balsano]. *Nuova rivista musicale italiana* 17 (1983): 383.

Bimberg, Guido. "Die italienische Opera seria im russischen Musiktheater des 18. Jahrhunderts. II." *Händel-Jahrbuch* 30 (1984): 121.

unpublished–

Fuchs, M. "Die Entwicklung des Finales in der italienischen opera buffa vor Mozart." Ph. D. dissertation, University of Vienna, 1932.

Weichlein, W.J. "A Comparative Study of Five Musical Settings of 'La Clemenza di Tito' " [vol. 1, chapters 3, 4]. Ph. D. dissertation, University of Michigan, 1956.

Sprague, Cherl Ruth. "A Comparison of Five Musical Settings of Metastasio's *Artaserse.*" Ph. D. dissertation, University of California at Los Angeles, 1979.

Wiesend, Reinhard. "Studien zur opera seria von Baldassare Galuppi: Werksituation und Überlieferung, Form und Satztechnik, Inhaltsdarstellung." Ph. D. dissertation, University of Würzburg, 1981.

Wilson, J. Kenneth. "*L'Olimpiade:* Selected Eighteenth Century Settings of Metastasio's Libretto." Ph. D. dissertation, Harvard University, 1982.

*   *   *

Baldassare ("Baldissera" in Venetian records) Galuppi was, for a time in the 1750s and early 1760s, the most performed composer of Italian opera in Europe. While he has long been praised for his collaboration with Goldoni in the development of the *dramma giocoso,* he is now known to have played a central role in serious opera as well.

His first opera, composed at age 16, was *Gli amici rivali* (*La fede nell' incostanza* at a later performance); its poor reception (a "scandal") led him to approach Benedetto Marcello for advice. Galuppi committed himself to extended study with the first organist in San Marco, Antonio Lotti, and to abstain from the stage for three years. The boy was arranging operas and composing substitute arias (as well as playing cembalo) for theaters in Venice and Florence before two years were out, however, and his career rose steadily through the 1730s and 40s.

In 1741-43 he was in London, where he oversaw the production of numerous operas, both his own works and many arranged from other composers. Horace Walpole and Handel criticized his music, but his light, tuneful melodies captured much public attention; his music was printed and reprinted by London publishers, and his operas continued to be staged after his return to Italy. Back in Venice, he took up his old professions of arranging, performing, and composing, and his prestige continued to climb.

His genius fully blossomed only late in the 1740s. In *opera seria* he saw enormous success. *L'Olimpiade* (Milan, 1747) and *Vologeso* (Rome, 1748) were followed by *Demetrio* and *Artaserse,* both for Vienna, which broke all box office records. While he remained within the traditional formal constraints of the opera of the day, both in recitatives and arias, his charming and graceful melodies were everywhere praised. His orchestration (he was a hard taskmaster over those orchestras under his control) was always clear and unobtrusive.

His success proved only to be an omen of greater things to come, for 1749 saw the beginning of his collaboration with the father of Italian comedy, Carlo Goldoni. Their first joint venture in comic opera, *L'Arcadia in Brenta* (Goldoni had supplied Galuppi with two serious librettos in 1740, neither of which was particularly successful), was rapidly followed by a long series of similar works, all of which were quickly adapted and performed throughout Europe. Goldoni's elegant poetry, witty dialogue, and sometimes biting satire were ideally matched with Galuppi's remarkable comic pacing, his facile, tuneful melodies, and his lucid orchestration. Together they largely pioneered the development of the ensemble finale (or "chain" finale), in which all aspects of the musical structure, including tempo, mode, key, accompaniment, formal design, etc., shift fluidly and easily according to the dictates of the drama; ensembles and solo sections freely alternate, usually presenting a variety of comic situations, and (particularly) the reactions of the protagonists to these changing developments. The second act finale of *La diavolessa* (Venice, 1755) is a good example; here a farcical seance evoking dark spirits is juxtaposed with pointed laughter, amazement, ridicule, and confusion when the lights go out. Similarly, the sneezing ensemble that closes the first act of *L'arcadia in Brenta* (Venice, 1749) is a masterpiece of comic effect.

In both his serious and comic compositions, Galuppi was particularly sensitive to the needs and abilities of his singers, and in this he enjoyed the collaboration of the finest singers of his day, including two of the most gifted comic performers: Francesco Baglioni and Francesco Carrattoli. Among his serious cast members were Caffarelli, Manzuoli, Gizziello, Gabrieli, Guadagni, and Amorevoli. His vocal writing changed to suit the abilities and inclinations of his singers; it was at times brilliantly florid, and at other times subdued, but always elegant and refined.

Climaxing his unimpeded rise to international prominence over the 1750s and 1760s, Galuppi accepted the post of maestro di coro of St. Marks in Venice in April, 1762 (with a high salary), and was elected maestro di coro at the Ospedale degli' Incurabili. Despite his advanced years, Galuppi petitioned the Venetian senate in early 1764 to allow his travel to Russia, which was reluctantly granted a year later. He served both in St Petersburg and Moscow from September 1765 to late in 1768, completing his *Ifigenia in Tauride* and reviving *Didone abbandonata* and *Il re pastore,* all to great success, while arranging other operas and providing religious and occasional music. Upon his return to Venice, laden with

many gifts, he dedicated himself exclusively to sacred music until his death.

—Dale E. Monson

THE GAMBLER [Igrok].

Composer: Sergei Prokofiev.

Librettist: Sergei Prokofiev (after Dostoevsky).

First Performance: Brussels, Théâtre de la Monnaie, 29 April 1929.

Roles: The General (bass); Pauline (soprano); Alexey (tenor); Grandmother (mezzo-soprano); Marquis (tenor); Mr Astley (baritone); Blanche (contralto); Prince Nilsky (tenor); Baron Wurmerhelm (bass); Potapich (baritone); several bit roles which may be doubled; chorus (SATB).

Publications

articles–

Potapova, Natal'ja. "Contribution to the History of the Second Version of the Opera *Igrok* by Sergej Prokof'ev." In

Prokofiev's *The Gambler,* Lyric Opera of Chicago, 1991 production

Vosprosy muzhkal'nogo stilja, edited by Mark Aranovskij. Leningrad, 1978.

Konieczna, Aleksandra. "Postac przestrzen i czas w finalowym akcie *Gracza* Sergiusza Prokofiewa" [last act of *The gambler*]. *Muzyka* 28 (1983): 31.

Robinson, Harlow. "Dostoevsky and Opera: Prokofiev's *The gambler.*" *Musical Quarterly* 70 (1984): 96.

* * *

Prokofiev shared with Tchaikovsky both a lifelong passion for opera and a high failure-rate in the genre. Three Prokofiev operas, *Maddalena* (1911-13), *Khan Buzay* (1942) and *Distant Seas* (1948), were abandoned unfinished. Three more, *The Fiery Angel* (1919-27), *War and Peace* (1941-52) and *The Story of a Real Man* (1947-48), were denied complete staged performances in his lifetime. Following decades of neglect, the reputation of *The Gambler* has been much enhanced by recent revivals.

Prokofiev long had it in mind to compose an opera based on Dostoevsky's novel *Igrok* or *The Gambler*—the first such Dostoevsky adaptation. Rebuffed by his patron Sergey Diaghilev, he took the project to the Maryinsky Theater where there was a real prospect of operatic performance from the end of 1915. Aware that a sensation was expected of him and eager to restore a fluid, theatrical dimension to the form, Prokofiev reacted sharply against operatic convention. He put together his own text and opted for a supple conversational style, leaving no room for anything as orthodox as an aria to hold up the action.

The story (a curtailed version of Dostoevsky's) is set in the imaginary German spa town of Roulettenburg, where a retired Russian general eagerly awaits the news that Babulenka, a rich relative, has died leaving him her fortune. He is surrounded by a crowd of fellow-gamblers, plus his young children, his step-daughter Pauline, and Alexey, the children's tutor. Alexey is in love with Pauline, while Pauline has in the past had a liaison with the marquis from whom the general has had to borrow large sums of money. Unfortunately for the family finances, Babulenka turns up in her wheel-chair. Reports of her death have been greatly exaggerated. She too becomes infected with the passion for roulette and loses a fortune before leaving for home. Now Pauline is faced with marriage to her father's creditor, the marquis. In order to rescue her from this situation, Alexey vows to win the money for her at roulette. He has fantastic luck and breaks the bank. But when he brings her the cash, she throws it back in his face, crying that money is an insulting payment for love. The opera ends with Alexey raving, lost to his obsession.

For too long, *The Gambler* was generally dismissed as a problem piece. The drama lacks any genuinely sympathetic characters, and its almost relentless cynicism is not for all tastes. On the other hand, Prokofiev builds to a stunning last act: "I make bold to believe that the scene in the gambling-house is totally new in operatic literature both in idea and structure. And I feel that in this scene I succeeded in accomplishing what I had planned," he wrote. Instead of treating the gamblers and croupiers as a chorus, Prokofiev gives them individual lines and characters. The effect is appropriately feverish: the track of mounting tension will culminate in hysteria and madness. It would be absurd to present a non-political composer as having revolutionary ambitions, yet the collective intoxication of Russia on the brink is aptly symbolized in this idiosyncratic score. Prokofiev's *Gambler*

seems to hold up a mirror to a society corrupted by the pursuit of easy money and racing toward oblivion.

The work's chequered career was not unaffected by the spirit of revolution. Rehearsals began at the Maryinsky in January 1917. But, as the press reported, "The prevailing sentiment among the artists is that Prokofiev's opera *The Gambler* should be dropped from the repertory, for while this cacophony of sounds, with its incredible intervals and enharmonic tones, may be very interesting to those who love powerful musical sensations, it is completely uninteresting to the singers, who in the course of a whole season have scarcely managed to learn their parts" (*Vecherniye Birzheviye Vedomosti,* 10 May 1917). By the time of the world premiere, given in French at the Théâtre de la Monnaie, Brussels, in April 1929, Prokofiev had revised the work thoroughly, softening the edges in the process. *The Gambler* had to wait until 1962 for its first British performance, given in Serbo-Croat by a touring company of Belgrade Opera. And until Gennady Rozhdestvensky's pioneering radio broadcast of March 1963, it was unknown in its native Russia. In April 1974, *The Gambler* finally entered the repertoire of the Bolshoi and, in 1983, David Pountney's brilliantly effective production came to English National Opera, giving UK opera-goers their first real chance to assess one of Prokofiev's most compelling operatic achievements.

—David Gutman

GARCIA, Manuel.

Tenor. Born 22 January 1775, in Seville. Died 9 June 1832, in Paris. Liaison with Manuela Morales (one daughter). Married singer Joaquina Sitches (daughters were Maria Malibran and Pauline Viardot-Garcia; son Manuel Garcia). Studied with Antonio Ripa. By 1798 he had established a career in Spain as a composer and tenor; sang in Paris, 1808-11, then went to Italy; created Norfolk in Rossini's *Elisabetta, regina d'Inghilterra* in Naples in 1815 and Almaviva in *Il barbiere di Siviglia* in Rome, 1816; sang and taught in London, 1817-19; in Paris, 1819-24; students include Nourrit, Meric-Lalande, and Maria Malibran.

Publications

About GARCIA: books–

Levien, J. *The Garcia Family,* London 1932; reprinted as *Six Sovereigns of Song.* London, 1948.

Malvern, G. *The Great Garcias.* New York, 1958.

* * *

Manuel Garcia's youth was spent in Spain where he established himself as that country's leading tenor, as well as the composer of countless *tonadillas.* His wildly temperamental character left legends of murders, fights, sexual escapades, jail terms, and other excesses which may have hastened his departure from his native country in early 1807, at the age of 32. Ambition led him to Paris where, after several disheartening months, the composer Ferdinando Paër noticed him and cast the new tenor in his *Griselda,* given at the Théâtre-Italien on 11 February 1808. Garcia's success with both public and

Manuel Garcia as Don Giovanni, Paris, 1824

critics was great. His voice, "sweet, pleasing, of great range and extreme flexibility" was praised, as was his "Andalusian passion." Having conquered Paris, Garcia accepted an engagement in Naples, making his Italian debut in 1811. There his success was such that King Joachim Murat made him Primo Tenore of the Royal Chapel. During his Italian sojourn he created the tenor roles in many new operas written by composers long forgotten, and two for the young Rossini: Norfolk in *Elisabetta, regina d' Inghilterra* (Naples, October 1815) and, more important, Almaviva in *Il barbiere di Siviglia* (Rome, January 1816). He also continued his vocal studies, further refining his art under the tutelage of Giovanni Ansani, a great singer then in retirement.

In 1816 Garcia returned to Paris and in 1817 made his English debut as Almaviva, introducing Rossini's *Barbiere* to London, which received him as the great tenor of the day. Over the next several years his fame and fortune grew ever greater, as did his arrogance and quarrels with theater management. His disputes with John Ebers, intendant of King's Theatre, London, were published in the public press and make hilarious reading. His brutal treatment of his children, both in public and in private, was not so easily dismissed.

Perhaps the apogee of Garcia's career was his performances as Rossini's Otello in Paris, 1821, in which he played the moor to the Desdemona of the great Giuditta Pasta, then at the peak of her considerable powers. For these performances Rossini had reworked his opera, adapting it for the voices of Pasta and Garcia, neither of whom had been in the original cast. (Even now musicologists and critics write that Rossini composed the role of Otello for Garcia, and that Garcia created the part. But at the time of the opera's premiere [Naples, December 1816] Garcia had long since departed for

Paris, and the first Otello was the admirable Andrea Nozzari, another great tenor for whom Rossini wrote many roles.) A reviewer of the Paris performances wrote that "never before has opera in France been seen at such clear advantage, nor has it been performed by so exceptional a company. . . . . Garcia, as Otello, shows unusual powers, not only as a remarkable singer, but as a considerable tragic actor; no one could show a finer grasp of every thread in the infinitely subtle web of thought and feeling which goes to make up the violent and impassioned character of Desdemona's lover."

By 1825, when Garcia was 50, the signs of his vocal deterioration became impossible to ignore. At precisely this time, fate offered an opportunity: to bring Italian opera to the New World. Assembling a troupe consisting of his family and secondary singers, including his daughter Maria, who had just made her debut, Garcia sailed for New York. There and in Mexico he produced operas for the next three years. He lost Maria to Eugene Malibran, and his scores, which he rewrote from memory, and his earnings to bandits in Mexico. Returning to France in early 1829, he found his daughter, now Maria Malibran, the sensation of Paris and well on her way to becoming the greatest singer of the age. Destitute and with diminished vocal resources, he continued to sing sporadically, but his career as a performer was over and he devoted himself to teaching, at which he excelled. Among his pupils were his son Manuel Jr. (later the greatest vocal pedagogue of that century and perhaps of all time), his daughters Maria and Pauline (famous as Pauline Viardot-Garcia), as well as Adolphe Nourrit and Henriette Méric-Lalande. He died at the age of 57, three years after his return from the new world.

Throughout his career, Garcia composed scores of operas, operettas, and *tonadillas,* but once beyond Spanish borders, his successes as a composer were infrequent. His insistence that the theaters enjoying his services as the great tenor also stage his works led one critic to scoff at this "musical rent" and at one point he was paid *not* to compose. Still, he was responsible for carrying the Spanish musical idiom into Europe where it found favor with many important composers. Bizet used some of Garcia's musical ideas, most notably the "fate" theme, in *Carmen.*

Both as a singer and actor Garcia had "an irresistible verve," and if critics sometimes ridiculed him for excessive ornamentation ("every crotchet was literally suffocated with quavers [trills], like the flutterings of so many mosquitos"), they were also willing to praise him for an art that was superlative, both vocally and dramatically. One critic wrote: "A more commanding actor or a more gifted singer has rarely appeared . . . . Signor Garcia's voice is a tenor of great volume and compass. It is so powerful indeed as to leave most others at a distance. It is formed according to the manner of the best schools, but perhaps is not so rich in quality nor so beautifully perfect as that of [Gaetano] Crivelli . . . . He is an admirable musician, and his invention is more fertile than that of any other singer we ever heard. But what chiefly exalts his style is the sensibility with which he penetrates into the meaning of his songs. He enters heart and soul into the music . . . ."

In the summer of 1824, Garcia appeared with Giuditta Pasta in Zingarelli's *Romeo e Giulietta*, and a London critic wrote: "His soul is in every note—he seems let loose from earth, and the more boundless his flight, the more full of ecstasy is his song, for herein lies the grand difference between Garcia and every other florid singer it has fallen to our lot to hear. He makes every passage expressive by the ardour and the ease and the feeling with which he 'wantons in the wiles of sound.' His last aria, 'misero che faro' gave proofs never to be forgotten of the deep sensibility with which he entered

into passages of pathos. The words *misero* and *mia figlia* were uttered with a tone and emphasis that touched the very soul."
—Howard Bushnell

GARDEN, Mary.

Soprano. Born 20 February 1874, in Aberdeen. Died 3 January 1967, in Inverurie. Studied in Chicago with Mrs. Robinson Duff and in Paris with Sbriglia, Bouhy, Trabadello, Marchesi, and Fugère; debut as replacement in *Louise* at Opéra-Comique, 1900; at Covent Garden, 1902-03; Hammerstein's Manhattan Opera House debut in United States premiere of *Thaïs,* 1907; Chicago debut as Mélisande, 1910, and remained with Chicago for twenty years; director of Chicago's 1921-22 season; last Chicago appearance as Jean in Massenet's *Le jongleur de Notre Dame,* 1931; appeared in Cleveland, 1932; appearance at Opéra-Comique, 1934; in United States for Debussy recital-lectures in 1934-35, and Debussy lectures, 1949-55; created roles in Massenet's *Chérubin,* Pierne's *La fille du Tabarin,* d'Erlanger's *Camille,* Leroux's *La reine fiammette,* and Debussy's *Pélleas et Mélisande.*

Publications.

By GARDEN: books–

Mary Garden's Story. New York, 1951.
Souvenirs de Mélisande. Liège, 1962.

About GARDEN: books–

Huneker, J. *Bedouins.* New York, 1920.
Kahn, O. *Of Many Things.* New York, 1926.
Moore, E.C. *Forty Years of Opera in Chicago.* New York, 1930.
Barnes, H. *Mary Garden on Records.* San Angelo, 1947.
Wagenknecht, E.C. *Seven Daughters of the Theatre.* Norman, Oklahoma, 1964.
Davis, R.L. *Opera in Chicago.* New York, 1966.

articles–

Whelan, G. "The Recorded Art of Mary Garden." *Gramophone* 29 (1952): 367.
Fletcher, R.D. "The Mary Garden of Record." *Saturday Review* February (1954): 47.
_____. "The Short, Mad Reign of Mary the First." *Panorama* September (1963).
Cuenod, H. "Remembrances of an Enchantress." *High Fidelity* 14/no. 7 (1964): 36.
Fletcher, R.D. " 'Our Own' Mary Garden." *Chicago History* 2/no. 1 (1972): 34.
Shawe-Taylor, D. "Mary Garden." *Opera* October (1984).
Pennino, J. "Mary Garden and the American Press." *Opera Quarterly* summer (1989).

*   *   *

Once, when confounded by a critic's comment that her upper notes were like the snakes in Ireland, Mary Garden turned to her father for an explanation. "Why, Mary," he responded, "there are no snakes in Ireland." The story may be apocryphal, but it illustrates the problems Garden faced with critics throughout her professional life. Mary Garden was known as a "singing-actress" long before the term was popularized by Maria Callas. The stress was on "actress," and Garden professed to be enamored of the dramatic stage just as much as the operatic. Like Callas, however, she was not an actress per se, as both discovered when they attempted straight drama in unsuccessful films.

In order to appreciate Garden better, we must depend on contemporary reviews of her performances which constantly drive home the fact that for her word and gesture were paramount. Garden's voice followed along like an obedient servant ready to bow to her will to make the note telling, the scene more riveting. Was this not Callas's aim also? The analogy is apt since both aspired to the same end—the vivid recreation of a character according to the composer's intentions. The comparison can be extended even further since Callas possessed a hauntingly beautiful voice finely schooled in the art of bel canto, and Garden (at least toward the beginning, if one judges by the recordings prior to 1926) one of gleaming silver, perhaps less well schooled than Callas's, but no less effective.

In her own time Garden was unique. When other sopranos were emulating the legendary Adelina Patti in their tonal perfection, Garden, by her own admission, was trained (albeit briefly) in all the finer points of vocal techniques, but left most of what she learned in the studio. We must take this statement on faith, however, since apart from her recording of "Semper libra" (in French) which she executes unembellished but quite neatly, we have no other example of what she could do with florid singing. Her recordings, in general, reveal only a small part of what was the essential Mary Garden. Without the visual element, we can only guess at what she looked like on stage. Her voice is nonetheless telling, from the purity of "Mes longs cheveux" from *Pelléas et Mélisande,* which so eloquently and simply captures the childlike quality of Debussy's waif, to the dark, tortured tones of Katusha's aria from *Risurezzione* (again, sung in French), which so pointedly depicts the despair of a woman facing an emotional crisis.

Another source for capturing a glimmer of what Garden was like are her photographs. The pains she took to resemble the character she portrayed are clearly reflected in these—from the steely stare of a hoydenish Carmen, the aloof beauty of Thais, black-clad Marguerite "after the fall", the Renaissance grace of Mélisande, the jeweled gossamer dress of Salome to the plain, simple Jongleur. The photograph of Garden's Katusha is arguably the most telling, and after one has viewed the torture in her eyes, the unkempt hair, the haggard face, one has almost been witness to Garden on stage.

Today Teresa Stratas most closely resembles Garden in intent. It is doubtful that the two sopranos mirror one another's acting style, for styles change, though their purpose remains the same. When one has seen Stratas bare her soul as Suor Angelica or suffer the grand passions of Violetta in *La traviata,* one has also fit another piece in the Garden puzzle. Even if Garden's films were available, they would not give more than a hint as to what she was like; they were silent films and, like her recordings, therefore, tell us only half the story.

Where does all this leave us? The art of Mary Garden is as elusive as the voices of Jean de Reszke or Emma Eames, Adelina Patti in her prime or Jenny Lind, or the great castrati. Although there are those who can still recall the rose strewing

L'Art du Théâtre

Mary Garden as Mélisande in the premiere of Debussy's *Pelléas et Mélisande*, Paris, 1902

Thaïs of their youths, there are a multitude who can not. The disembodied voice of Garden only begins to tell the story.

—John Pennino

GAY, John.

Librettist: Baptized 16 September 1685, in Barnstaple, Devon. Died 4 December 1732, in London.

Librettos

The Beggar's Opera, Gay and Pepusch, 1728.

Publications

About GAY: books–

Pearce, C. *Polly Peachum: The Story of "Polly" and "The Beggar's Opera."* London, 1923.
Schultz, W. *Gay's Beggar's Opera.* New Haven, Connecticut, 1923.
Sherwin, O. *Mr. Gay: Being a Picture of the Life and Times of the Author of The Beggar's Opera.* New York, 1929.
Tolksdorf, C. *John Gays Beggar's Opera und Bert Brechts Dreigroschenoper,* Rheinberg, 1934.
Gaye, P. *Ballad Opera.* New York, 1937.
———. *John Gay.* London, 1938.

* * *

John Gay's most important contribution to the history of opera was as the writer of the text to *The Beggar's Opera,* first performed in London in 1728. Gay, known in London primarily as a poet and playwright, surrounded himself with many of Britain's greatest contemporary writers, including such figures as Pope, Swift, and Congreve. His first major operatic effort was as the librettist for Handel's two-act masque *Acis and Galatea,* with additional text by Pope and Dryden; it is considered to be one of the better English texts set by Handel. While Gay's literary efforts prior to *The Beggar's Opera* met with only limited success, it is likely that this earlier theatrical experience was an important factor in the eventual triumph of this highly unique work.

The Beggar's Opera was not only an immediate hit, running for an unprecedented sixty-three nights, but it also established the genre of ballad opera, which was to enjoy enormous success in London during the next decade. *The Beggar's Opera,* however, did little to further the cause of London's conventional opera theaters, which at that time presented primarily Italian operas by such composers as Handel and Bononcini. These were primarily serious works based on historical or mythological subjects, performed in a language that was inaccessible to much of the audience. With *The Beggar's Opera,* Gay discovered a formula that engaged the popular taste of a far broader audience. It was sung in English rather than Italian, and it was comic rather than serious. More importantly, Gay set *The Beggar's Opera* in lower class London, focusing his libretto on the activities of a highly astute, albeit corrupt, underworld. In the highwayman MacHeath, the villainous but pragmatic Peachum, and his trusting daughter Polly—one of two women in love with the dashing

MacHeath—Gay created characters that were quite distant from the dignified heroes and heroines that populated the Italian operas, and who likely seemed more realistic to contemporary audiences. Yet it was not the underworld itself which was the object of Gay's satire, but the upper classes—such important figures as then-Prime Minister Sir Robert Walpole and his wife—who were so accurately mimicked by the anti-heroes of *The Beggar's Opera.*

Gay's originality was not limited solely to the text of *The Beggar's Opera.* From a musical point of view, *The Beggar's Opera* differed considerably from the Italian opera that it often satirized. For the songs, Gay used short, simple, and often familiar tunes—borrowed from pub, parlor, or even opera house—for which he wrote new and daring words. While composer Johann Christian Pepusch wrote the overture and arranged much of the music, it was Gay who was responsible for the choice of melodies and for the music's comfortable meshing with his new texts. These straightforward tunes must have contrasted strikingly with the more lengthy, elegant, and ornate arias of Italian opera that so beautifully demonstrated the skill of the reigning—and/or feuding—prima donnas. As has since been the practice in many types of popular musical theater, audience accessibility was further enhanced by the use of spoken dialogue rather than sung recitative.

The success of *The Beggar's Opera* contributed to—or was perhaps itself precipitated by—a decline in the fortunes of Italian opera in London, a decline that eventually led Handel, for example, to redirect his efforts to the English oratorio. Yet while *The Beggar's Opera* was in some respects a product of its time, its has continued to be popular well into this century, reworked and rearranged by many writers and composers, most notably Bertolt Brecht and Kurt Weill in *Die Dreigroschenoper. The Beggar's Opera,* with its anti-heroes and inverted sense of morality, undoubtedly expresses a message that transcends the specific satirical intent of its creator.

—Wendy Heller

GEDDA, NICOLAI [born Harry Gustaf Ustinoff].

Tenor. Born 11 July 1925, in Stockholm. Married Anastasia Caraviotis, 1965 (one son, one daughter). Studied with his father in Leipzig, in Stockholm with Carl Martin Oehmann, and later in New York with Paola Novikova; military service, then worked in a bank for five years; debut in Stockholm as Chapelou in Adam's *Le postillon de Longjumeau,* 1952; debut at the Teatro alla Scala as Don Ottavio, 1952-53; debut at Paris Opéra, 1954; Covent Garden debut as Duke in *Rigoletto,* 1954; Metropolitan Opera debut as Faust, 1957; created role of the Bridegroom in Orff's *Il trionfo d'Afrodite* and Anatol in Barber's *Vanessa.*

Publications

By GEDDA: books–

Gåvan är inte gratis. Stockholm, 1978.

About GEDDA: books–

Steane, J. B. *The Grand Tradition.* London, 1974.
Matheopoulos, H. *Bravo.* London, 1986.

articles–

Storjohann, G. "Nicolai Gedda." *Opera* 17 (1969): 939.

Throughout his long career, tenor Nicolai Gedda has been known for his versatility, style, intelligence, and taste, characteristics in small supply in the stereotypical operatic tenor. He made his operatic debut in 1952 as Chapelou in Adam's *Le postillon de Longjumeau* in Stockholm; his success was such that he was invited almost immediately to make his first recording, as Dmitri in Musorgsky's *Boris Godunov,* a recording that starred Boris Christoff in the title role (and that cut one of Dmitri's arias).

Gedda's debut at the Teatro alla Scala, as Ottavio in Mozart's *Don Giovanni,* followed in 1953. He created the role of the Bridegroom in Orff's *Il trionfo dell' Afrodite* at the composer's request. He made his debut at Covent Garden (as the Duke in Verdi's *Rigoletto*) and at the Paris Opéra (as Huon in Weber's *Oberon*) in 1954, followed quickly by his debuts in Rome (in Stravinsky's *Oedipus Rex*) and Vienna. He gave his first performances at the Metropolitan Opera (as Gounod's Faust) and Salzburg in 1957; at the Metropolitan he created the role of Anatol in Barber's *Vanessa* in 1958 and, in its American premiere, sang Kodanda in Menotti's *Le dernier sauvage* in 1964.

A highly accomplished singer, Gedda is renowned for his musicianship, insight, sensitive phrasing, and attention to detail. A specialist in the lyric and spinto tenor repertoire who rarely attempts heavier roles (although he sang Wagner's Lohengrin in Stockholm in 1966 and has sung and recorded Don José in Bizet's *Carmen*), Gedda possesses a voice that can be described as sturdy, sweet, centered, and firmly focused. His proficiency with languages (he is fluent in Swedish, Russian, English, French, and German) and excellent diction, combined with his apparent intelligence and taste, have been significant assets in his unusually extensive repertoire. He has the ability to convey or suggest personality through his singing. His acting is vivid and enthusiastic yet nuanced; his ability to sing mezzavoce and even pianissimo is a skill that contributes to his vocal acting ability. He generally follows the composer's score markings scrupulously. At his best, his tone is liquid, limpid, his phrasing aristocratic, his interpretations stylish, charming, even bewitching.

This intelligent approach has led some critics to fault Gedda for what they consider to be overstudied, unspontaneous interpretations, ones imposed from without rather than growing naturally out of the words. He is sometimes more reliable than exciting; his singing can be mannered, the enunciation exaggerated, the characterizations too sophisticated. He has also been criticized for a lack of smoothness in his line, for an explosive attack on certain notes that disrupts the flow. In later performances he has sometimes sounded cautious and labored, unable to conceal the effort of singing. Even in his prime he was sometimes criticized for a lack of Italianate tone in his Italian roles, a result of his rather lean timbre.

Gedda is especially associated with the French repertoire, including such roles as Des Grieux in Massenet's *Manon,* Hoffmann in Offenbach's *Les contes d'Hoffmann,* Berlioz's Benvenuto Cellini, Gounod's Faust and Roméo, and Raoul in Meyerbeer's *Les Huguenots.* Among his Slavic roles are Gherman in Tchaikovsky's *Queen of Spades,* Jeník in Smetana's *The Bartered Bride,* Dmitri, and Lensky in Tchaikovsky's *Eugene Onegin.* His Mozart portrayals include Don Ottavio in *Don Giovanni,* Belmonte in *Die Entführung aus dem Serail,* and Tamino in *Die Zauberflöte.* In the Italian lyric repertoire he has sung Nemorino in Donizetti's *L'elisir d'amore,* Ernesto in Donizetti's *Don Pasquale,* Edgardo in Donizetti's *Lucia di Lammermoor,* and, among Verdi roles, the Duke in *Rigoletto,* Alfredo in *La traviata,* and Riccardo in *Un ballo in maschera.* His Puccini roles include Rodolfo in *La bohème* and Pinkerton in *Madama Butterfly.* He has also performed and recorded operettas, particularly Johann Strauss's *Die Fledermaus* and *The Gypsy Baron,* and Lehar's *The Merry Widow.*

Lensky in Tchaikovsky's *Eugene Onegin* is arguably Gedda's greatest role, and was the role that marked his debut in Russia in 1980. He brings to it both the youthful ardor and the sadness and resignation of Pushkin's character.

Gedda has been a prolific recording artist; he has perhaps recorded a greater range of works than any other tenor. Among the roles he has performed in complete opera recordings are Gounod's Faust, Don Narciso in Rossini's *Il turco in Italia,* Orfeo in Gluck's *Orfeo ed Euridice,* Pinkerton, Eisenstein in Johann Strauss's *Die Fledermaus,* Don José, Rodolfo, Tamino in Mozart's *Die Zauberflöte,* Don Ottavio, Hoffmann, Belmonte, Max in Weber's *Der Freischütz,* Des Grieux in Massenet's *Manon,* Alfredo, Benvenuto Cellini, Arturo in Bellini's *I Puritani,* Mozart's Idomeneo, Ferrando in Mozart's *Così fan tutte,* Nicias in Massenet's *Thaïs,* Auber's Fra Diavolo, and Vaudémont in Tchaikovsky's *Iolanta.*

—Michael Sims

GENOVEVA.

Composer: Robert Schumann.

Librettist: R. Reinick (after L. Tieck and C.F. Hebbel, as altered by Schumann).

First Performance: Leipzig, 25 June 1850.

Roles: Hidulfus (baritone); Siegfried (baritone); Genoveva (soprano); Golo (tenor); Margaretha (soprano); Drago (bass); Balthasar (bass); Caspar (baritone); Angelo (baritone); Conrad (baritone); chorus.

Publications

book–

Oliver, Willie-Earl. *Robert Schumanns vergessene Oper "Genoveva".* Freiburg im Breisgau, 1978.

articles–

Hanslick, E. "R. Schumann als Opernkomponist." In *Die moderne Oper,* 256. Berlin, 1875; 3rd ed., 1911.
Abert, H. "R. Schumanns Genoveva." *Zeitschrift der Internationalen Musik-Gesellschaft* 11 (1910): 227.
Wolff, H. "Schumanns 'Genoveva' und der Manierismus des 19. Jahrhunderts." In *Beiträge zur Geschichte der Oper,* 89. Regensburg, 1969.
Cooper, F. "Operatic and Dramatic Music." In *Robert Schumann: the Man and His Music,* edited by A. Walker, 324. London, 1972; 2nd ed., 1976.

Siegel, L. "A Second Look at Schumann's *Genoveva.*" *Music Review* 36 (1975): 17.
Avant-scène opéra January (1985) [*Genoveva* issue].

* * *

In act I of Schumann's *Genoveva,* Count Siegfried rides off to battle, entrusting his wife Genoveva to the care of his friend Golo. Golo, disappointed at being left behind, kisses Genoveva, who has fainted. Margaretha, a witch who was once Golo's nursemaid, sees him and offers to aid him in his attempt to win Genoveva. In act II, Golo confesses his love to Genoveva, who rejects him in horror. Drago, the chaplain, tells Golo that Genoveva is rumored to be unfaithful. Golo tells Drago to secret himself in Genoveva's chamber that night. Mobilizing the castle, Golo enters the chamber, runs Drago through with a sword, and imprisons Genoveva to await her husband's judgment.

In act III, Siegfried, wounded, is being nursed by the disguised Margaretha, whose potions hinder his recovery. She describes a magic mirror which she claims can show past events. Siegfried is aloof until Golo appears with a letter describing Genoveva's supposed unfaithfulness. Siegfried now demands the magic mirror, which falsely shows Genoveva betraying him. He departs, breaking the mirror; Drago's ghost rises from its shards and threatens Margaretha with fiery death unless she confesses her trick to Siegfried.

In act IV, Genoveva, being led to her execution, prays for strength. Golo offers to spare her if she yields to him. She refuses. Golo, departing, orders her immediate execution. His servants hesitate since she is standing under a cross; Margaretha leads in Siegfried and disappears. The couple is reunited amid rejoicing.

Schumann's only opera is a failure, despite interesting and often beautiful musical features. His libretto, based on a conflation of Tieck's (1779) and Hebbel's (1841) dramas on the same subject, gives its main characters inadequate motivation or interest. Genoveva displays only Christian and marital fidelity; and Golo's torment and path to evil, though the focus of careful musical underlining, are not supported by enough specifics to become believable. Margaretha and Siegfried barely attain even one-dimensional characterization. As Margaretha confesses between acts, and Golo simply disappears after ordering Genoveva's execution, one sees virtue triumphant, but not evil defeated.

Schumann's goal was to create an innovative German opera with a Romantic subject; his medium was a symphonic style using motivic reminiscence and transformation. Unlike Wagner, Schumann saw Germanness in music as deriving from folkish elements, and free from foreign influence; accordingly, he included chorale and folk-melody in the score as well as choosing a popular folk-tale as his dramatic source. Although the score is structured in numbers, the opera is effectively through-composed; dialogue is set with orchestral accompaniment in a freely modulating, endless-melody style, and there are only a few set-pieces, mainly choruses and soliloquies. Ironically, these last (Golo's tormented outburst in act I and Genoveva's prayer in act II) contain the most memorable music in the opera, and are very much in the style of Schumann's art songs. The motivic technique works best in underlining Golo's character; but most of the motives are neither as memorable as Wagner's nor as tellingly applied.

Much of the music, moreover, fails to make dramatic sense. The choruses that frame the work and the drinking chorus in act II are among the worst offenders; and the spirits that accompany the magic mirror in act III are not nearly eerie or characteristic enough to make a dramatic climax. Schumann's musical language is lyrical and often highly chromatic, and perhaps more advanced even than Wagner's was at the time, but it does not suit itself to musical drama.

—Roger L. Lustig

GENTELE, Göran.

Producer. Born 20 September 1917, in Stockholm; died 18 July 1972, on Sardinia. Married second wife Marit Bergson, 15 April 1951. Three children, Jeannette, Cecilia, Beatrice. Studied romance languages in Paris at the Sorbonne, and political science and economics at Stockholm University; began training at Royal Dramatic Theater in Stockholm in 1941; beginning in the mid-1940s began working as actor and stage manager for the Royal Theater, and directed first plays there in 1946; during the 1950s collaborated on films with his wife; engaged as guest director at Royal Opera of Stockholm in 1951, for a production of Menotti's *The Consul,* and became a staff director of the opera in 1952; succeeded Set Svanholm as managing director of Royal Opera in 1963, holding position until 1971; appointed general manager at New York's Metropolitan Opera in 1972, but died in automobile accident in July of that year.

Opera Productions (selected)

The Consul, Stockholm, Royal Opera, 1951.
Salome, Stockholm, Royal Opera, 1954.
Aniara (Blomdahl), Stockholm, Royal Opera, 1959.
Un ballo in maschera, Stockholm, Royal Opera, 1959.
Iphigénie en Tauride, London, Covent Garden, 1961.
The Rake's Progress, Stockholm, Royal Opera, 1961.
Pelléas et Mélisande, Stockholm, Royal Opera, 1971.
Carmen, New York, Metropolitan Opera, 1972 (posthumous).

Publications

About GENTELE: articles–

"Northern Exposure." *Opera News* 29 (January 30, 1965): 13.
Kolodin, I. "Music to My Ears." *Saturday Review* 53 (December 26, 1970): 34.
Soria, D.J. "Artist Life." *High-Fidelity/Musical America* 21 (September 1971): MA6.
Rosenthal, H. "Göran Gentele." *Opera* 23 (1972): 782.
Jenkins, S. "Gentele Greets the Press." *Opera News* 36 (February 19, 1972): 3.
"In Memoriam." *Opera News* 37 (September 1972): 8.

* * *

A regular producer at the Royal Opera, Stockholm, beginning in 1951, Göran Gentele became managing director in 1963, succeeding Set Svanholm when he stepped down due to illness. His first production in Stockholm was Menotti's *The Consul,* in 1951, one of many collaborations with conductor Sixten Ehrling. He created a production of Richard Strauss's *Salome* that marked soprano Birgit Nilsson's first major success. His controversial and influential production of Verdi's

Göran Gentele's production of *Un ballo in maschera*, Royal Opera, Stockholm, 1958

Un ballo in maschera portrayed King Gustavus III as a homosexual (apparently a historical fact, although unknown to Verdi). He also produced Blomdahl's *Aniara* at the Royal Opera in its world premiere performance. He persuaded Ingmar Bergman to direct Stravinsky's *The Rake's Progress* at the Stockholm Opera. During his tenure, the Royal Opera toured England, Holland, Denmark, and Finland. In keeping with the tradition of the company, all operas were sung in Swedish (with the exception of Wagner, whose operas were sung in German) and designers were selected from the ranks of Sweden's artists. A supporter of modern music, he included one contemporary work in each subscription series. He left the Royal Opera in 1971 when he was named as successor of Rudolf Bing as general manager of the Metropolitan Opera.

Gentele created a single production for Covent Garden: Gluck's *Iphigénie en Tauride,* which opened on 14 September 1961, the first production of the Solti administration. He also produced operas in Amsterdam and Brussels.

Gentele was selected to succeed Bing as of June, 1972. One of his first acts was to select James Levine as principal conductor. His plans for the Metropolitan included a collaboration between the various components of Lincoln Center (such as the New York Philharmonic and the New York City Ballet), an active campaign for government subsidy, the introduction of more contemporary operas, and the creation of a "mini-Met," akin to the Piccola Scala in Milan for the production of nonstandard repertoire. He was scheduled to direct the opening production of Bizet's *Carmen,* which he had suggested as a replacement for an aging production of

Wagner's *Tannhäuser.* The *Carmen* production reinstated the spoken dialogue used in the original Opéra-Comique version.

A few weeks before the opening of the 1972-73 season, Gentele was killed in a car accident in Sardinia. The Met had planned to put on a new production of *Un ballo in maschera* based on Gentele's Stockholm staging, but they decided not to proceed in his absence.

Gentele said that human beings and their voices are more important than elaborate stagings. Described in the press as an outgoing, energetic man, a former actor as well as a cinema director, he appreciated the need for give-and-take between artists and directors. His reputation was that of a director and administrator who fostered cooperation, a successful negotiator, and an inspirational leader.

—Michael Sims

GERSHWIN, George (born Jacob Gershvin).

Composer. Born 26 September 1898, in Brooklyn, New York. Died 11 July 1937, in Beverly Hills, California. Studied piano with Ernest Hutcheson and Charles Hambitzer in New York; studied harmony with Edward Kilenyi and Rubin Goldmark; studied counterpoint with Henry Cowell and Wallingford Riegger; also studied with Joseph Schillinger in the last years of his life. Gershwin enjoyed enormous success throughout

George Gershwin with DuBose Heyward and Ira Gershwin, 1935

his career; song *Swanee* sold over a million copies, 1917; *Rhapsody in Blue* conducted by Paul Whiteman with Gershwin playing the solo part, Aeolian Hall, New York, 12 February 1924; numerous orchestral compositions, including Piano Concerto in F, *An American in Paris, Cuban Overture,* and *Variations for Piano and Orchestra* on his song, "I Got Rhythm," 1925-1934, as well as many musicals.

Operas

Publishers: Chappell, New World.

Blue Monday (retitled *135th Street*), Globe Theater, 28 August 1922.
Song of the Flame (operetta), O. Hammerstein II and O. Harbach, New York, 44th Street Theater, 30 December 1925.
Porgy and Bess, DuBose Heyward (after Dubose and Dorothy Heyward), New York, Alvin Theater, 10 October 1935.

Other works: orchestral works, musicals, piano pieces, songs.

Publications/Writings

By GERSHWIN: articles–

"The Relation of Jazz to American Music." In *American Composers on American Music,* edited by Henry Cowell. Palo, Alto, California, 1933, 1962.

About GERSHWIN: books–

Goldberg, Isaac. *George Gershwin.* New York, 1931.
Armitage, Merle, ed. *George Gershwin.* New York, 1938.
Ewen, George. *The Story of George Gershwin.* New York, 1943.
———. *George Gershwin: a Journey to Greatness.* New York and London, 1956; 2nd ed. as *George Gershwin: his Journey to Greatness,* Englewood Cliffs, New Jersey, 1970.
Armitage, Merle. *George Gershwin: Man and Legend.* New York, 1958.
Jablonski, Edward, and Lawrence D. Stewart. *The Gershwin Years.* New York, 1958, 1973; London, 1974.
Gershwin, Ira. *Lyrics on Several Occasions.* New York, 1959.
Payne, Robert. *Gershwin.* New York, 1960; London, 1962.
Mellers, W. *Music in a New Found Land.* New York, 1965.
Rushmore, Robert. *The Life of George Gershwin.* New York and London, 1966.
Kimball, Robert, and Alfred Simon. *The Gershwins.* New York, 1973.
Schwartz, Charles M. *Gershwin: his Life and Music.* Indianapolis, 1973.
Brown, Anne. *Sang fra frossen gren* [autobiography of Anne Brown, who created the role of Bess in *Porgy and Bess,* 1935]. Oslo, 1979.
Jeambar, Denis. *George Gershwin.* Paris, 1982.
Lipmann, Eric. *L'Amérique de George Gershwin.* Paris, 1982.
Kendall, Alan. *George Gershwin: a Biography.* London, 1987.

Jablonski, Edward. *Gershwin.* New York, 1987; London, 1988.

articles–

Kolodin, I. "Porgy and Bess: American Opera in the Theatre." *Theatre Arts Monthly* 19 (1935): 853.
Thomson, Virgil. "George Gershwin." *Modern Music* 13 (1935-36): 13.
Levant, O. "My Life, or The Story of George Gershwin." In *A Smattering of Ignorance,* 147. New York, 1940.
Arvey, V. "George Gershwin through the Eyes of a Friend." *Opera and Concert* 13 (1948): 10, 27.
Jablonski, Edward. "Gershwin on Music." *Musical America* 82 (1962): 32.
———. "George Gershwin." *Hi Fi/Stereo Review* 12 (1967): 49.
Crawford, R. "It ain't necessarily Soul: Gershwin's *Porgy and Bess* as Symbol." *Yearbook for Inter-American Musical Research* 8 (1972): 17.
Shirley, W.D. "Porgy and Bess." *Library of Congress Quarterly Journal* 31 (1974): 97.
Jablonski, Edward. "Gershwin at 80: Observations, Discographical and Otherwise, on the 80th Anniversary of the Birth of George Gershwin, American Composer." *American Record Guide* 41/no. 11 (1977-78): 6, 58; no. 12: 8, 57.
Crawford, R. "Gershwin's Reputation: a Note on Porgy and Bess." *Musical Quarterly* 65 (1979): 257.
Shirley, W.D. "Reconciliation on Catfish Row: Bess, Serena, and the Short Score of Porgy and Bess." *Library of Congress Quarterly Journal* 38 (1981).
———. "Notes of Gershwin's First Opera" [*Blue Monday*]. *Institute for Studies in American Music Newsletter* 11 (1982): 8.
Starr, L. "Toward a Reevaluation of Gershwin's Porgy and Bess." *American Music* 2 (1984): 25.
Youngren, William H. "Gershwin's Genius." *Atlantic* 253 (1984): 132.

unpublished—

Baskerville, D. "Jazz Influence on Art Music to Mid-century." Ph.D. dissertation, University of California at Los Angeles, 1965.

*   *   *

Irving Berlin said of Gershwin: "He is the only songwriter I know who became a 'composer.'" For Gershwin, to be a "composer" meant to accomplish much more than achieving phenomenal commercial success as a tunesmith for Broadway's musical theater scene. It meant engaging larger, more traditional forms such as ballet, opera and the symphony, and it meant producing music—contrary to the Broadway norm—in which every note would in fact be written by him. Through Charles Hambitzer, with whom he took piano lessons from 1912 to 1914, he had been exposed early on to the world of classical music. Later he studied composition with, among others, Wallingford Riegger, Joseph Schillinger, Rubin Goldmark and Henry Cowell. But his involvement with composition teachers was typically intermittent and short-lived. For the most part, Gershwin was self-taught in both songwriting and in what he regarded as his "serious" work.

Products of the latter include the 1924 *Rhapsody in Blue* for piano and jazz band, the 1925 *Concerto in F* for piano and

orchestra, the 1928 tone-poem *An American in Paris,* the 1931 *Second Rhapsody for Piano and Orchestra,* the 1932 *Cuban Overture,* the 1934 set of *Variations for Piano and Orchestra* based on his song "I Got Rhythm" and—perhaps his best-known work—the 1935 opera *Porgy and Bess.* All of these have been, and continue to be, performed in orchestrations other than Gershwin's. Except for *Rhapsody in Blue* (written by Gershwin only in "short score" and then arranged, originally for Paul Whiteman's jazz band and later for full orchestra, by Ferde Grofé), however, all of them do have scores that are entirely Gershwin's own.

Commissioned and premiered by Walter Damrosch and the New York Symphony Orchestra, *An American in Paris* proved enormously popular, and its reception prompted New York's Metropolitan Opera in 1929 to commission a full-length theatrical work from Gershwin. A contract was signed for "a Jewish opera" to be titled *The Dybbuk,* but the commission was never fulfilled. *Porgy and Bess,* based on a play by DuBose Heyward, with libretto by Heyward and lyrics by Gershwin's brother Ira, was not a commissioned work; its first production, heavily invested in by Gershwin himself, took place in New York's Alvin Theater. It ran only for 124 performances and was considered a financial failure.

Gershwin died less than two years after the premiere of *Porgy and Bess,* the victim—at age 38—of a brain tumor. Along with a ballet titled *Swing Symphony,* a string quartet, another piano concerto and a classically structured symphony, his plans included a second full-length opera to be made in collaboration with Heyward.

—James Wierzbicki

GHIAUROV, Nicolai.

Bass. Born 13 September 1929, in Lydjene, near Velingrad, Bulgaria. Married Mirella Freni in 1981. Studied with Christo Brambarov at Sofia Conservatory, 1949-50, and Moscow Conservatory, 1950-55; debut as Basilio in *Il barbiere di Siviglia,* Sofia, 1955-56; Bolshoi Opera debut as Pimen, 1957-58; Teatro alla Scala debut as Varlaam, 1959; appeared at Covent Garden as Padre Guardiano in *La forza del destino,* 1962; Chicago debut as Mephistopheles, 1963-64; Metropolitan Opera debut in *Faust,* 1965.

Publications

About GHIAUROV: books–

Kazaka, T. *Nicolai Ghiaurov.* Sofia, 1972.
Greneche, P. *Nicolai Ghiaurov.* Paris, 1979.
Matheopoulos, H. *Bravo.* London, 1986.

*   *   *

During his long and highly successful career Nicolai Ghiaurov has established a firm reputation as one of the leading basses of the second half of the twentieth century. His repertory is restricted chronologically: he has sung comparatively few roles composed before 1850 or after 1900. Nor is he particularly effective in comic roles. But in serious operas of the second half of the nineteenth century Ghiaurov is unsurpassed in the richness and power of his deep voice and the vividness of his acting.

One can hear the qualities that have brought Ghiaurov such success in one of his rare eighteenth-century roles, the title role of *Don Giovanni* (as recorded under Klemperer). Ghiaurov is a strong, threatening Don Giovanni; the power of his voice seems to convey an almost superhuman strength against which all resistance by women (or men) is futile. And yet he can be lyrical and suave. When he praises Zerlina's face in the recitative preceding "La ci darem la mano," he caresses her with his gentle words. We can understand how Zerlina (sung in the recording by Mirella Freni, later to become Ghiaurov's wife) allows herself to be seduced.

Ghiaurov has sung many Verdi roles. As Fiesco in *Simon Boccanegra* (Paris, 1978) he won praise for his "rich bass tone and great dignity," and at the Teatro alla Scala he was greatly applauded in the same role. A recording of the opera under Abbado shows why Ghiaurov has been so successful a Fiesco. His performance of the great aria "Il lacerato spirito" is deeply felt, and intensely lyrical (in spite of an imperfection in the voice that produces thin, hard-edged tones on the syllable "o"; listen, for example, to the second "o" in "dolore" as Ghiaurov holds this syllable). His low register is rich and strong; he uses it to wonderful effect in the duet "Vieni a me, ti benedico."

Among Ghiaurov's other Verdi roles are Philip II in *Don Carlos* and Ramphis in *Aida* (his Ramphis as recorded under Muti was praised by one critic as "magnificent") He has sung several more unusual Verdi roles as well, winning applause as Silva in *Ernani* (Chicago) and as Banquo in *Macbeth* (La Scala).

Ghiaurov's roles are not limited to opera in Italian. He has achieved considerable success in nineteenth-century French and Russian opera. One of his early international triumphs, at La Scala in 1962, was in the role of Marcel in Meyerbeer's *Les Huguenots*. In the title role of Massenet's *Don Quichotte* at Chicago he was praised as a "funny—yet very unfunny—and lovable Quixote." Less successful was his portrayal of Mephistopheles in a recording of Gounod's *Faust;* a critic found fault with the "worn patches" in Ghiaurov's tone (perhaps alluding to the same weakness mentioned above). He is one of the best recent portrayers of the title role in Mussorgsky's *Boris Godunov;* he has also sung the role of Gremin in Tchaikovsky's *Eugene Onegin*. Reviewing a recording of Tchaikovsky's opera a critic praised Ghiaurov as "a tower of strength"; but when he sang the role in Chicago in 1984 a critic pointed out that Ghiaurov's voice had lost some of its former richness.

—John A. Rice.

GHISLANZONI, Antonio.

Librettist. Born 25 November 1824, in Lecco. Died 16 July 1893, in Caprino Bergamasco. Studied medicine and singing; career as an opera baritone in France and Italy, 1846-55; from 1850, librettist, journalist, publisher, and editor (*Gazzetta musicale di Milano, Italia musicale, Rivista minima*).

Librettos (selected)

revision of *La forza del destino* with G. Verdi (after Piave), 1869.
I promessi sposi, E. Petrella, 1869.
Aïda, G. Verdi, 1871.
Fosca, A.C. Gomes, 1873.
Il parlatore eterno, A. Ponchielli, 1873.
I lituani, A. Ponchielli, 1874.
Salvator Rosa, A.C. Gomes, 21 March 1874.
I Mori di Valenza, A. Ponchielli 1874 [unfinished; completed by Annibale Ponchielli and A. Cadore, and performed 1914]
Edmea, A. Catalani, 1886.

Publications

By GHISLANZONI: books–

Gli artisti da teatro. Milan, 1856.
Il Mefistofele di A. Boito. Milan, 1868.
Reminiscenze artistiche. Milan, 1869.
Libro serio. Milan, 1879.

articles–

Numerous articles in *Gazzetta musicale di Milano, Italia musicale,* and others.

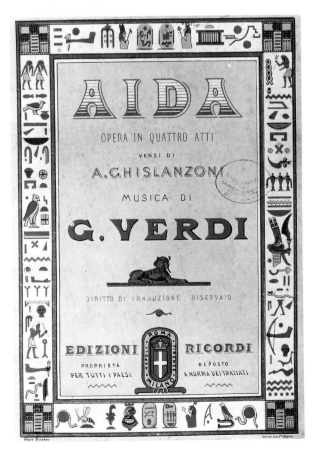

Title page of vocal score of *Aida,* **1871: libretto by Antonio Ghislanzoni**

About GHISLANZONI: books–

Miragoli, S. *Il melodramma italiano nell'ottocento.* Rome, 1924.
Corte, A. della. *Satire e grotteschi.* Turin, 1946.

articles–

Mantovani, T. "Librettisti verdiani: Antonio Ghislanzoni." *Musica d'oggi* 11 (1929): 112, 156.
Weaver, W. "A Librettist's Novel." *Opera News* 26 December (1955).
Morini, M. "Antonio Ghislanzoni, librettista di Verdi." *Musica d'oggi* new series, 4 (1961): 56, 98.
Weaver, W. "Aida's Poet." *About the House* 2/no. 8 (1967): 34.
Gossett, P. "Verdi, Ghislanzoni, and *Aïda:* the Uses of Convention." *Critical Inquiry* 1 (1974): 291.
Weaver, W. "Verdi and His Librettists." In *The Verdi Companion,* ed. by W. Weaver and M. Chusid. New York, 1979.

* * *

Despite being a prolific writer and the creator of eighty-five librettos, Antonio Ghislanzoni has received scant attention from critics. He remains best known as the "versifier" for Verdi's *Aïda,* but is typically viewed as the somewhat incompetent recipient of Verdi's correspondence during *Aïda*'s composition. Alessandro Luzio calls the Verdi-Ghislanzoni correspondence over *Aïda* "the most marvelous course in musical aesthetics in action" (quoted from Gossett, p. 293).

William Weaver, one of the few critics to attempt a complete assessment, finds Ghislanzoni "the most professional" of all of Verdi's poets (*Verdi Companion,* p. 128). Though his verses are not on a "spectacularly high level, they are still the work of a man of letters" ("*Aïda's* Poet" p. 34). Weaver also sees value in his other writings: "Ghislanzoni's wit is often still pungent. His *Storia di Milano dal 1836 al 1848* gives a lively picture of the city Verdi knew as a young man; and his *Libro serio* contains an affectionate and penetrating word-portrait of Verdi at the time of *Aïda.*" (1979, p. 128) Ultimately for Weaver, while "Ghislanzoni [was] not a profound observer . . . he had a gift: the ability to depict, to draw a scene. And it was this ability that Verdi leaned upon to create the first of his last operas, *Aïda,* where local color is as important as plot and character" ("A Librettist's Novel," p. 9). Hans Busch (*Verdi's Aïda*) concurs, finding that "Ghislanzoni emerges from the general mediocrity of Italy's nineteenth-century librettists as a great talent, in company with Donizetti and Bellini's collaborator Felice Romani and, later, Arrigo Boito" (639).

Other critics are less generous and see Ghislanzoni as essentially a conservative figure. Julian Budden, in *The Operas of Verdi,* notes that the design of Ghislanzoni's librettos, such as that for Catalani's *Edmea,* are "curiously old-fashioned" (vol. 3, p. 288), often "fall[ing] back on . . . time-honoured conversational gambits" (vol. 2, p. 27) and refusing to break free from traditional structures such as "the habit of giving straightforward narrative to a chorus" (vol. 3, p. 173). For Patrick Smith (*The Tenth Muse*), Ghislanzoni hardly figures in late romantic Italian opera, and for William Ashbrook, who wrote the *New Grove* essay on Catalani, the libretto for Catalani's *Edmea* is "preposterous . . . bombastic, [and] crudely motivated."

The Verdi-Ghislanzoni correspondence during the composition of *Aïda* has generated the greatest attention. This correspondence, as many critics have noted, shows Verdi clearly in control and tends to display Ghislanzoni's poor understanding of dramaturgy. Philip Gossett is slightly more sympathetic, though, noting that although Ghislanzoni was "nurtured by [the conventions of Italian opera] and unable to proffer anything truly new and yet musical, Verdi's bullying was by no means consistently along 'reformist' lines. In this duet [act IV duet between Radames and Amneris], at least, the most conventional aspects spring directly from the composer" (p. 320).

—David Pacun

GIACOSA, Giuseppe.

Librettist/Dramatist. Born 21 October 1847, in Colleretto Parella, near Turin. Died 2 September 1906, in Colleretto Parella. Studied law at the University of Turin; teacher at the Accademia di Belle Arti, Turin, 1877; moved to Milan, 1888; visited the United States in 1891.

Giuseppe Giacosa (left) with Puccini and Illica

Librettos

La bohème (with L. Illica; after Murger), G. Puccini, 1896.
Tosca (with L. Illica; after Sardou), G. Puccini, 1900.
Madama Butterfly (with L. Illica), G. Puccini, 1904.

Publications

About GIACOSA: books–

Croce, B. "Giuseppe Giacosa." *La letteratura della nuova Italia.* Bari, 1914.
Toscanini, G. *Giacosa.* Florence, 1924.
Garaio Armò, L. *Il teatro di giuseppe Giacosa.* Palermo, 1925.
Rumor, M. *Giuseppe Giacosa.* Padua, 1940.
Nardi, P. *Vita e tempo di Giuseppe Giacosa.* Milan, 1949.
Barsotti, A. *Giuseppe Giacosa.* Florence, 1973.

Unlike his collaborator, Luigi Illica, Giacosa never had any dealings with opera except for his part in the libretti of Puccini's *La bohème, Tosca* and *Madama Butterfly.* He was a successful and distinguished comic dramatist and regarded his operatic work as a sideline. Indeed, his involvement was only brought about with Giulio Ricordi's persuasion, and he continually complained of the long, painstaking, thankless task of condensation. After *Bohème,* he wrote, "I assure you that I shall never again apply myself to such an undertaking, not at any price at all." Nevertheless, he soon embarked on *Tosca,* later becoming convinced that it was unsuitable for setting as an opera, being all action with no lyric moments.

It seems that Illica, an impetuous worker with a fluent improvisatory genius, would sketch the scenario and perhaps some of the text. Giacosa would then write the final draft, beginning with the lyric passages. Next there would be a meeting of the four men, Giacosa, Illica, Puccini and Ricordi. These meetings were "real struggles in which whole acts were torn to pieces, scenes sacrificed, ideas disowned that were fine and brilliant a moment before, and the long and arduous work of months ruined in a minute" (Illica). But Giacosa was a calming force, "a rainbow on a stormy day." Even when a libretto had been finalized, Puccini would write to Giacosa requesting extra material and specifying exactly the meter in which it was to be written.

It is miraculous that the resulting librettos are such models of theatrical dexterity and linguistic purity. They are, however, very different one from another. Probably the collection of funny, tender vignettes by Henry Murger, originally called *Scènes de la vie de Bohème,* which had been turned into a play by Théodore Barrière, was the most initially appealing to Giacosa, whose best plays were works of *verismo borghese,* full of romantic pathos and psychological probing expressed in exquisite language. The unforgettable scene of Mimi's death, taken in essence from Barrière's play, seems to be mostly Giacosa.

Tosca is a different matter, for it was based on a famous play by Victorien Sardou. The aged Verdi had toyed with the idea of writing a *Tosca* opera; doubtless the "operatic" aspects attracted him. Illica suppressed these, however, turning it into a drama of essentially three characters only. Giacosa grumbled that the first act ended with a monologue and the second began with another—and for the same character, Scarpia. Nevertheless, he preserved this arrangement. His lyric insertions occur at unexpected moments; right at the start, Cavaradossi philosophizes on the mysterious harmony

of light and dark in the hair colors of two women ("Recondita armonia"); Tosca suddenly pauses in the midst of fighting off Scarpia's advances to tell of her life dedicated to art and love ("Vissi d'arte"). These lyrics are metrically more varied than those in *Bohème* and more sparing with rhyme. While writing this libretto Giacosa was also engaged on his masterpiece *Come le foglie,* in which the language is singularly poetic. Somehow, the playwright succeeded in writing a lyric work for the spoken theater, and a dramatic work for the lyric theater.

For Giacosa and Illica, the worst came with *Butterfly.* After composing act I, Puccini changed his mind about the whole drift of the opera, which he had envisaged as an encounter between two cultures, the American and the Japanese. He now realized that it was turning into the personal tragedy of Butterfly herself. Illica had devised a scene in act II in the American consulate in Nagasaki; this was jettisoned, the two remaining scenes being divided by the "Humming Chorus." The result was an enormous second act, with the roles of Sharpless and Pinkerton reduced to the level of secondary characters, and this contributed to the failure of the opera at Milan in 1904. Significantly, in rewriting this score, Puccini called on Giacosa for his final lyric effusion, Pinkerton's aria "Addio fiorito asil."

The craft of the librettist has generally been a specialized area; except where composers have chosen to use stage plays intact, playwrights have stayed out of this difficult arena. Though it cost Giacosa so much pain, his contribution shows the advantages of having a professional literary dramatist as a member of the operatic team.

—Raymond Monelle

GIANNI SCHICCHI
See TRITTICO

GIANNINI, Dusolina.

Soprano. Born 19 December 1900, in Philadelphia. Died 29 June 1986, in Zurich. Studied with her father (the tenor Ferruccio Giannini), and with Marcella Sembrich; made her concert debut in 1923; opera debut as Aida, Hamburg, 1925; sang in Berlin, London, Vienna; appeared at Salzburg as Donna Elvira in *Don Giovanni* under Walter and in *Faust* under Toscanini; Metropolitan Opera debut as Aïda, 1936; appeared at New York City Opera from 1944; sang in Europe again, 1947-50; retired in 1961-62 and became a teacher; created Hester Prynne in her brother Vittorio Giannini's *The Scarlet Letter.*

Publications

Moran, W. "Dusolina Giannini and Her Recordings." *Record Collector* 9 (1954): 29.
Steane, J.B. *The Grand Tradition.* London, 1974.

Dusolina Giannini could not remember her first singing lesson; her entire childhood was marked by musical training. Her father, Ferruccio (1868-1948) was an operatic tenor and impresario; her mother was an accomplished instrumentalist. An older sister, Euphemia, a soprano whose early career in opera was cut short by the war, became a well-known voice teacher at the Curtis Institute in Philadelphia; a younger brother, Vittorio, was a composer of merit. Dusolina began her stage career in her father's theater at the age of nine with a recital of Neopolitan songs, followed by her assumption at age eleven of the role of La Cieca in *Gioconda* to her father's Enzo, later singing Azucena to his Manrico in *Trovatore*. Her childhood performances won her the title of "The Little Duse" in the Philadelphia Italian colony; in later years she was to become known as "The Musician's Singer."

The family could not decide if Dusolina was a soprano or contralto, so she was sent to Marcella Sembrich and became a pupil of the great singer at the age of sixteen. In an interview in 1953, Dusolina said: "What a truly great woman she was! And how much she taught above and beyond the technique of singing! The emphasis in the Sembrich studio was on learning . . . always learning. Learning to be humble, and have a great reverence towards the music I was singing. Learning that it was a privilege to be able to interpret great music, and learning never to be satisfied until I had given the best that was in me. Those things I *did* learn, and I have always had those goals before me throughout my career." The *credo* of Marcella Sembrich did indeed govern Dusolina Giannini's life and career, and, in later years, her own teaching.

On 14 March 1923, Anna Case was scheduled for a concert at Carnegie Hall at which some new songs by Genei Sadero were to be introduced. When Case became ill and neither Alma Gluck nor Hulda Lashanska was available, Giannini was plucked out of her class at the Sembrich studio to learn the songs in one day. "It seems as though nearly everyone who was to have a hand in the launching of my career was present at that concert," Giannini later recalled. Offers to appear as soloist with major orchestras and conductors poured in, along with a contract to make records exclusively for the Victor Talking Machine Co. The young singer relished the challenge to develop programs of unusual merit and content, under the guidance of such musicians as Bruno Walter and Henri Verbrugghen. Her London debut was at a concert in Queen's Hall 19 June 1924, followed by an extensive concert tour which took her from Montreal to Havana, embracing sixteen states and Washington, D.C.

Her first German concert tour opened in Berlin in May 1925, with her operatic debut taking place in Hamburg on 12 September 1925 as Aida. *Aida* was repeated a month later under Bruno Walter in Berlin, where Dr Frieder Weissmann hailed her as the greatest Aida since Destinn. More concerts followed in Europe and the United States, with her Covent Garden debut as a guest with the La Scala Company in June 1928, singing Aida to Pertile's Radames, Santuzza, and her first *Butterfly*. She was offered a contract at Covent Garden the following season for *Butterfly, Cavalleria Rusticana, Aida, Manon Lescaut* and Donna Anna in *Don Giovanni*. "I had not been happy in my first season at Covent Garden," Giannini recalled some years later. "I had appeared as a guest star with the La Scala company, and I suppose it was more or less inevitable that there was some resentment in the company to my success during the season. So, I really wasn't looking forward to a season in which I was to be given several important roles. [Thus] when I was approached by an Australian impresario and offered the opportunity of an Australia-New Zealand concert tour, I didn't even think twice about giving up my Covent Garden contract. Everyone told me I was

committing artistic suicide . . . that I was ruining my career . . . but I never regretted that decision for one minute." Her original contract called for fifteen concerts, but it was extended to twice that number. So popular was she that The Gramophone Company's Sydney branch came out with a special release of recordings which she had made in London, even including some issued nowhere else in the world.

Giannini's London success in *Aida* at the time of her debut with the La Scala company led to a contract with The Gramophone Company (through her exclusive contract with Victor) for a complete recording of *Aida* to be made in Milan with the same all-star cast as the London production. The recording took place at the La Scala Opera House in Milan in 1929, and she took advantage of her first visit to Italy to schedule a number of concerts. It was at this time that she was offered a contract for the following La Scala season. When she was told by the La Scala management that it would be necessary to conform to the current Milan protocol with official meetings with the press and arrangements for a personal claque, she once again asserted her artistic independence, and refused the contract. She then decided that she would never become a formal member of *any* opera company, but would only appear as a guest artist, contracting individually for roles which she wanted to sing under conditions which she considered artistically favorable. So it was as a guest at the Berlin Staatsoper that she gave her first *Carmen* under Leo Blech, a role repeated in Hamburg; and as a guest at the Vienna Staatsoper she was heard in *Aida* and *Butterfly*. She was also a guest artist at the 1934 Salzburg festival, where she sang Donna Anna in *Don Giovanni* with Lotte Schoene, Maria Muller, Dino Borgioli, Emmanuel List and Ezio Pinza, and again the following year when her fellow artists were Helletsgruber, Mildmay, Borgioli, Lazzari and Pinza, both under Bruno Walter. The critics said that not since Lilli Lehmann had the role of Donna Anna been sung with such authority.

Her debut at the Metropolitan in New York was as Aida on 12 February 1936, with Bampton, Martinelli, and Tibbett, conducted by Ettore Panizza. She went onto the Metropolitan stage for the first time with no rehearsal, and she had never sung with most of the artists before. Even so, she managed such rapport with the other artists, especially Tibbett, that Olin Downes remarked the following day that ". . . the whole [Nile] scene was treated with such authority and dramatic spirit and . . . carried through with such sureness and effect that the audience was stirred to an unusual demonstration after the curtain. . . ."

A revival of *Norma* was scheduled for 26 February 1936, under Panizza's direction, but Giannini withdrew from the part after the first rehearsal. She had studied the role with great care under Sembrich, and she found that her understanding and interpretation of the title role were so different from Panizza's that sufficient rehearsal time was not allowed for them to work out their differences. "There is no *correct* or *incorrect* way to interpret any role," Mme Giannini remarked, "but singers and conductor must be allowed to work out compromises so that there is complete artistic understanding between them of form and style. In those days, the Metropolitan just could not afford to allow enough rehearsal time for a new production, especially for an opera like *Norma* which is such a unique work in any case. I just did not feel that I could be a part of a revival of this great operatic masterpiece which was anything short of perfection."

Once again, Giannini had insisted on appearing at the Metropolitan as a guest artist, and not as a regular member of the company. As a result, her six seasons with the New York company were not very rewarding. She sang only four roles at the Metropolitan: Aida, Donna Anna, Santuzza and Tosca, for a total of twelve appearances in the New York house (plus two concerts) and eight performances on tour. Her performances were hailed by press and public, but she felt that most of the work at the house during this period was more or less routine, in spite of the excellent artists available, largely because of lack of rehearsal time.

It was also in 1936 that Giannini returned to Salzburg, this time at the request of Toscanini, to sing Mistress Ford in the festival production of Verdi's *Falstaff.* "In Salzburg, unlike the Metropolitan, we had from eight to ten weeks of rehearsal. Toscanini had worked with the orchestra for weeks, and the cast had studied their roles separately with him before the first rehearsals with the orchestra. . . ."

Giannini continued her work as a concert artist, with a few operatic performances each year. In 1946 she sang two concert performances as Kundry in *Parsifal* with Pierre Monteux and the San Francisco Symphony. She considered that one of the greatest honors she received was an invitation from Siegfried Wagner to sing Kundry at Bayreuth. "This, I think would have been the culminating point of my career . . . an American singer asked to sing at Bayreuth in these days was a most unusual thing, and I felt this was a supreme honor. However, a man named Hitler interfered with my plans. . . ." After the war, Giannini settled in Zurich where she gave master classes, trying to pass on, as she said, the wonderful heritage which was hers.

Giannini described her voice as "lirico dramatico"; her range was from A below C to E flat above high C. Her voice had a distinct quality, instantly recognizable, and while big enough to fill the largest hall, it could project sustained pianissimos with a firm steadiness of tone. Her Sembrich training can be heard in her precise runs and impeccable reading of the score in her recording of "Casta diva" from *Norma* on the one hand, and her interpretation of Strauss and Brahms songs on the other. She is a fiery Santuzza to Gigli's Turiddu, and gives a reading of the *Carmen* card scene which is highly dramatic and forceful with beautiful lush tone.

Giannini's work is well represented on recordings, her first having been made in 1924 by the acoustic process. Unfortunately, none of her Metropolitan performances were broadcast, so they were not preserved, but we do have her complete 1929 *Aida* with the La Scala forces. She has left us recordings of operatic arias (especially fine are those from *Forza del destino*), Mexican folk songs, Neapolitan songs (several in arrangements by her brother), English songs, and German Lied. The early electrical recordings (especially those made in Milan but to a lesser degree in those made in London and Berlin) tend to add a steely quality to the voice which was not evident when the singer was heard in person. Her farewell concert tour, which took her to Berlin, Hamburg and Vienna in 1956, was recorded on tape, with excerpts released on UORC and ROCOCO lps.

Dusolina Giannini never had a publicity agent. She was a very serious musician who approached her work with a certain sense of awe. Sembrich had given Giannini a goal of artistic integrity and stressed the importance of humility. In reviewing her career, she stressed her great privilege in having had the opportunity to work with "all the great conductors of my time. One does not learn the great traditions of artistry alone and by oneself." Giannini was proud of the title of "The Musician's Singer" which was given her by her peers. She

was a fitting successor to her great teacher, Marcella Sembrich, and to her, as it was to Sembrich, the phrase *Great Artist . . . Noble Woman* can truly be applied.

—William R. Moran

GIGLI, Beniamino.

Tenor. Born 20 March 1890, in Recanati, Italy. Died 30 November 1957, in Rome. Married Costanza (one daughter, singer Rina Gigli; one son, Enzo; and three other children). Studied with Agnese Bonucci in Rome, and at Liceo Musicale with Antonio Cotogni and Enrico Rosati; debut as Enzo in *La gioconda,* Rovigo, 1914; appeared in Bologna and Naples as Boito's Faust, 1915; appeared in same role under Toscanini at the Teatro alla Scala, 1918; at Metropolitan Opera, 1920-32, and returned for 1938-39 season; Covent Garden debut as Andrea Chénier, 1930, and sang there in 1931, 1938, and 1946; appeared primarily in concert after World War II; final tour of North America, 1955; appeared in seventeen films.

Publications

By GIGLI: books

Confidenze. Rome, 1942.
Memorie. Milan 1957; translated as *Memoirs,* London, 1957.
La verità sul mio "caso." Rome, 1945.

About GIGLI: books—

Rosner, R. *Beniamino Gigli und die Kunst des Belcanto.* Vienna, 1929.
Rensis, R. de. *Il cantore del popolo, Beniamino Gigli.* Rome, 1933.
Silvestrini, D. *Beniamino Gigli e l'anima delle folle.* Bologna, 1937.
Halm, H. *Heute wird es nicht regnen—es singt ja Beniamino Gigli.* Stuttgart, 1940.
Herbert-Caesari, E. *Tradition and Gigli 1600-1955: A Panegyric.* London, 1958.
Halm, H. *Un anima cantava, eine Seele sang: Begegnungen mit Beniamino Gigli.* Stuttgart, 1966.
Foschi, F. *Primavera del tenore: Il giovane Beniamino Gigli.* Milan, 1978.
Flamini, L. *Beniamino Gigli: E la sua gente che parla.* Recanati, 1979.
Gigli, R. *Beniamino Gigli: A cura di Celso Minestroni.* Parma, 1986.

articles—

Blyth, A. "Gigli and Melchior—Blessed by the Gods." *Opera* April (1990).

*   *   *

The foremost Italian operatic tenor of the 1920s, 30s, and 40s, Beniamino Gigli is said to have possessed "the finest lyric tenor voice of this century." His voice was indeed one of extraordinary beauty; its texture was warm, lush, velvety, and mellifluous. It was also a large voice, and Gigli could

Beniamino Gigli as Lionel in Flotow's *Martha*

sing with passion and vigor and with ringing, thrilling top tones. To these qualities can be added his excellent diction, his absolutely accurate sense of pitch, and his perfect breathing technique. One critic noted that he sang "as naturally as a gamecock fights." He best exhibited his talents when a role called for both lyricism and dramatic vitality. While his stage acting was old-fashioned, he was capable of expressing through his singing a wide range of emotions. One might say that he acted with his voice. To all his roles and performances he brought a conviction, an emotional intensity, and a total commitment that never failed to electrify his audiences.

In addition to his appearances all over Italy, he was leading tenor at the Metropolitan Opera between 1920 and 1932, returning for a few performances in 1939. He sang often at Covent Garden. As a young man he sang in Spain and in South America; he returned to enthusiastic audiences in Rio de Janeiro and Buenos Aires after World War II. He was a popular recitalist as well as an opera singer. More than 300 commercial recordings are to his credit and perhaps an equal number of recordings not to be bought on commercial labels, including complete or substantially complete operas that were recorded sometimes from live performances. He also appeared in several films.

Gigli's repertoire was enormous, although it was primarily within the vast realm of Italian opera and song. He might have said as did Andrea Chénier, "Colla mia voce ho cantato mia patria!" (With my voice I have sung my country!). The most notable exceptions were his excursions into French opera, which he sang usually in Italian. Early in his career he sang Des Grieux in Massenet's *Manon,* and later he excelled in Gounod's *Faust,* as his fine recording of "Salve, dimora casta e pura" bears witness. After World War II he sang Don José in *Carmen,* with his daughter Rina, a highly gifted soprano, in the role of Micaela. To this list one can add the tenor roles in Gounod's *Romeo and Juliet,* Thomas's *Mignon,* and Lalo's *Le roi d'Ys.*

Gigli's recitals were full of Italian songs ranging from those of the 16th-, 17th-, and 18th-century masters through the traditional Neapolitan songs to those of contemporary composers. These pieces endeared him to his audiences and were a delightful appendage to his truly herculean accomplishments in opera, where his fame chiefly rests.

As an interpreter of Puccini roles, Gigli has not been surpassed. The complete recordings on 78 of *La bohème, Tosca,* and *Madama Butterfly,* made in the late 1930s, have set a standard for all future tenors. Although we have no complete commercial recording of *Manon Lescaut,* the arias that he recorded and a live performance from Rio in 1951 indicate that Puccini's Des Grieux was one of his best roles. His artistic temperament is best exemplified in the scene at Le Havre leading into the impassioned aria "No! Pazzo son! Guardate." The excessive sobbing for which he was frequently criticized is very appropriate here as Des Grieux implores the captain to let him board the ship to go with Manon to Louisiana. The captain agrees, and there is a crashing E-major chord in the orchestra, to which Gigli interpolates a high B sung to the name "Manon." The effect is absolutely electrifying; it is vintage Gigli.

Among Verdi operas one should first cite *La traviata,* in which Gigli's fine lyricism stood him in good stead as Alfredo. A complete live performance from Covent Garden (in 1939) has come down to us in which Gigli sings with Maria Caniglia, a favorite partner, in the title role. The war-time commercial recording of *Un ballo in maschera* (1943), again with Caniglia and under the baton of Serafin, is another testimony of Gigli's excellence. He and Caniglia also had sung solo parts, along with Ebe Stignani and Ezio Pinza, in Serafin's

1939 complete recording of the *Requiem.* Gigli sang Radames in the 1930s and 1940s and recorded a complete *Aïda* (1946), the last of the complete commercial operatic recordings, but in *Aïda,* as well as in *Il trovatore* and *Rigoletto,* he shares honors with other great tenors. Heroic tenors like Caruso and Mario del Monaco come first to mind when one thinks of Alvaro in *La forza del destino,* but Gigli's recording from 1927 with Giuseppe de Luca of the famous tenor/baritone duet, "Solenne in quest'ora," is an everlasting monument to his memory; never has Verdi's beautiful tenor line been sung so expansively and with such vocal splendor.

In Leoncavallo's *I pagliacci* Gigli's inspired rendition of "No, Pagliaccio non son" is unforgettable; a complete commercial recording was made in 1939. Unfortunately we have no complete recordings of his performances in *La gioconda* and *Mefistofele;* the arias and excerpts that do exist suggest that he has no peer. There is no question that his complete commercial recordings of *Cavalleria rusticana* (1940), with Mascagni conducting, and of *Andrea Chénier* (1941)—his favorite role, for which he received high praise from Giordano himself—will remain the standards by which all later interpretations can be measured.

Two of Gigli's interpretations of Donizetti are particularly noteworthy: *L'elisir d'amore* and *Lucia di Lammermoor.* Gigli was singing Nemorino as late as 1953, with daughter Rina as Adina. Although the complete recording has rather bad sound, the celebrated aria "Una furtiva lagrima" and the aria from Act I have been well preserved in earlier studio recordings. Gigli's finest electrical 78 RPM recordings also include the Sextette from *Lucia* and the entire Tomb Scene, with Pinza. The Fountain Scene (from Edgardo's entrance to the end of the act) exists on a private label; Gigli sings with Marion Talley in this collector's item from 1927.

Gigli also starred in famous operas that are seldom performed today, including Meyerbeer's *L'Africaine* and Flotow's *Martha;* his recordings of "O Paradiso" (1928) and "M'appari" (1929) are superb. Finally, he sang the leading tenor roles in operas not well known outside of Italy; these include Mascagni's *Iris* and *L'amico Fritz* (of which there is a complete recording), Giordano's *La cena delle beffe* and *Fedora* (Gigli sang "Amor ti vieta" extremely well), and operas by Catalani, Cilèa, and Montemezzi.

In April of 1955 at the age of 65, Beniamino Gigli returned to New York, after an absence of sixteen years, for three farewell recitals at Carnegie Hall. Although his vocal prowess was beginning to wane, as is evident from the RCA Victor recording, his adoring audiences called him back on stage for encore after encore, one of which was "E lucevan le stelle." While he had recorded *Tosca* completely and the aria separately when in his prime, his rendition of the famous aria on these memorable occasions—especially the poignant closing line: "E non ho amato mai tanto la vita, tanto la vita!" ("And never have I loved life so much!")—would have thrilled Puccini as much as it did everyone present, judging from the spontaneous burst of enthusiastic applause before he finished.

—Jerome Mitchell

GINASTERA, Alberto.

Composer. Born 11 April 1916, in Buenos Aires. Died 25 June 1983, in Geneva. Married: 1) Mercedes de Toro, pianist,

1941 (divorced 1965; one son, one daughter), 2) Aurora Natola, cellist, 1965. Studied composition with José Gil, Athos Palma, and José André at the National Conservatory of Music in Buenos Aires; studied piano with Argenziani; awarded first prize by El Unisono for his *Piezas infantiles* for piano, 1934; commissioned to write the ballet *Estancia* for the American Ballet Caravan, 1941; in United States on a Guggenheim fellowship, 1945-47; on the faculty of the National Conservatory of Music in Buenos Aires, 1948-58; dean of the faculty of music, Argentine Catholic University; cantata *Bomarzo* commissioned by the Elizabeth Sprague Coolidge Foundation, 1964; in Geneva from 1969; opera *Beatrix Cenci* commissioned by the Opera Society of Washington D.C.

Operas

Publisher: Boosey and Hawkes.

Don Rodrigo, A. Casona, 1963-64, Buenos Aires, Colón, 24 July 1964.
Bomarzo, after Manuel Mujica Láinez, 1966-67, Washington D.C., 19 May 1967.
Beatrix Cenci, W. Shand and A. Girri, 1971, Washington D.C., Kennedy Center, 10 September 1971.
Barabbas, after Ghelderode, 1977-.

Other works: ballets, orchestral works, chamber music, choral and solo vocal works, piano music, film music, incidental music.

Publications

About GINASTERA: books–

Suárez Urtubey, Pola. *Alberto Ginastera.* Buenos Aires, 1967.
———. *Alberto Ginastera en cinco movimientos.* Buenos Aires, 1972.
Spangemacher, F., ed. *Alberto Ginastera.* Bonn, 1984.

articles–

Chase, Gilbert. "Alberto Ginastera: Argentine Composer." *Musical Quarterly* 43 (1957): 439.
Hume, P. "Alberto Ginastera." *Inter-American Music Bulletin* no. 48 (1965).
Suárez Urtubey, Pola. "Ginastera's Don Rodrigo," *Tempo* no. 74 (1965): 11.
Orrero-Salas, Juan. "An Opera in Latin America: *Don Rodrigo* by Ginastera." *Artes Hispánicas* (1967).
Lowens, I. "Ginastera's Beatrix Cenci." *Tempo* no. 105 (1973): 48.
La Vega, Aurelio de. "The Artist in Latin America." *Canadian Association of University Schools of Music/Association Canadienne des Ecoles Universitaires de Musique journal* 8 (1978): 40.
Kuss, Malena. "Type, Derivation, and Use of Folk Idioms in Ginastera's *Don Rodrigo.*" *Latin American Music Review* 1 (1980): 176.
La Vega, Aurelio de. "Latin American Composers in the United States." *Latin American Music Review* 1 (1980): 162.

unpublished–

Wallace, D. "Alberto Ginastera: an Analysis of his Style and Techniques of Composition." Dissertation, Northwestern University, 1964.

Unlike the work of many a nationalist composer, Ginastera's music is never merely a naive evocation of folk music. Rather, like Bartók, he is able to reconcile the influences of his native culture with the ideals he was taught through his study of the European masters. His work displays the sophisticated structure and development based on European models yet uses melodies and rhythms drawn from Argentine popular music. While South American composers before him (notably the Brazilian Carlos Gomes) introduced native music into theatrical scores, Ginastera integrates indigenous music more thoroughly into the fabric of his compositions. The soul of Argentina is deeply rooted in his music, yet he is no provincial; his forms and technique prove him an accomplished and cosmopolitan artist of international importance.

In the 1960s Ginastera received numerous important commissions in the United States, from, among others, the Fromm Foundation and the Koussevitzky Foundation. In 1962 his first opera, *Don Rodrigo*, was commissioned by the city of Buenos Aires. At this time he gave up two teaching posts to assume the directorship of the newly-formed Latin American Center for Advanced Musical Studies in Buenos Aires. In this position Ginastera influenced a generation of younger Latin American composers.

Don Rodrigo was premiered at the Teatro Colón in July of 1964. Its spectacular success established Ginastera as an important composer of grand opera, no small feat in the latter half of the twentieth century. This success led to the commissioning of *Bomarzo* by the Opera Society of Washington in 1967.

Thoroughly modern in temperament yet set in Renaissance Italy, the plot of *Bomarzo* was marked by explicitly sexual material; so shocking was its content that it was banned in Buenos Aires until 1972. Cast in fifteen scenes in two acts, it stands as an early example of musical postmodernism, drawing on Renaissance music and musical forms together with intensely expressive instrumental writing of a distinctly modern vein.

Throughout this time Ginastera was traveling widely. In 1970 he went to Europe, and eventually made his home in Geneva (where he remained until his death in 1983). In the same year his third opera, *Beatrix Cenci*, was premiered at the Kennedy Center for the Performing Arts in Washington D.C. In this opera, the sexuality first witnessed in *Bomarzo* was compounded by explicit violence and incest. In all his operas Ginastera retained the spectacle of Verdian grand opera, but coupled it with the disturbing expressionism unique to the twentieth century.

The development of Ginastera's musical style follows a clear path, in which overt nationalism featuring material modeled after Argentine *musica criolla* gradually gave way to a much more formalist modern idiom, what he himself viewed as neoexpressionism. This path reflects his evolution from an essentially provincial composer to an international, cosmopolitan artist with a nationalistic bent. The evocation of Argentine folk music, very much in the foreground in his early works, becomes gradually sublimated in favor of a more abstract approach; nevertheless he maintained a predilection for propulsive rhythm, theatricality and liveliness that is distinctly Latin American in character. In this way he is truly the product of his culture, although not a provincial composer by any stretch.

Ginastera himself saw his oeuvre falling into three periods. In his early works he embraced overt nationalism, using native music coupled with traditional European development and structure. The works written between 1948 and 1954, the term he viewed as his "middle period," display a more subjective nationalism, borrowing rhythms and motives from Argentine music but using these materials more discreetly than before. Evocations of traditional native instruments, chiefly the guitar, are used structurally to create referential harmonies in a number of works. In this period Ginastera internalized the sounds of his culture and allowed his own individuality to feature more prominently.

In the music written after 1954 Ginastera concerned himself more deeply with problems of construction, no doubt because of his growing interest in twelve-tone composition (which he claimed had first figured in his earliest works). Beginning with his second String Quartet (1958), he embraced serialism and did so until his death. Modernist resources such as polytonality, microtonality, chance procedures, and extended instrumental techniques were used, often in the service of evoking supernatural worlds. Ginastera's brand of serialism recalls that of Schoenberg and Berg rather than that of Webern, for it is characterized by its lyric expressionism rather than intellectual rigor. At the same time, like Berg, Ginastera was fascinated with formalism, creating symmetrically structured groups of scenes in his opera *Don Rodrigo* which recall *Wozzeck* and *Lulu*.

While Ginastera embraced many of the techniques of musical modernism, he did so in the service of traditionalism, striving to reinvent traditional forms and genres rather than disintegrate them. His operas display this orientation most clearly, for they reveal the influence of the Verdian *verismo* with the surrealism of much European music of the 1950s and 1960s. In his operas the inherent theatricality present throughout his output is given full freedom. The composition of opera was the ideal medium for his talents and compositional concerns: lyricism, drama, and formalism.

—Jonathan Elliott

LA GIOCONDA [The Joyful Girl].

Composer: Amilcare Ponchielli.

Librettist: Tobia Gorrio [=Arrigo Boito] (after Hugo, *Angelo, tyran de Padoue*).

First Performance: Milan, Teatro alla Scala, 8 April 1876; revised, Venice, Rossini, 18 October 1876; final revision, Milan, Teatro alla Scala, 12 February 1880.

Roles: La Gioconda (soprano); Laura (mezzo-soprano); La Cieca (contralto); Enzo (tenor); Barnaba (baritone); Alvise (bass); Zuane (bass); Isepo (tenor); Pilot (bass); A Monk (bass); Two Streetsingers (baritones); Two Voices (tenor, bass); chorus (SSATTBB).

Publications

article—

Hanslick, E. "Gioconda." In *Die moderne Oper,* vol. 4. *Musikalisches Skizzenbuch.* Berlin, 1888; 3rd ed., 1911; 1971.

*   *   *

Amilcare Ponchielli's *La Gioconda* was premiered at the Teatro alla Scala on 8 April 1876 but did not assume precisely the form we know it in today until 1880, when Ponchielli made the revised, definitive version. The libretto is by Tobia Gorrio, an anagram of Arrigo Boito. The action is set in Venice in the seventeenth century. In act I, set in the courtyard of the ducal palace, a traveling singer, La Gioconda, rejects the advances of Barnaba, a spy of the Council of Ten. In retaliation he accuses her blind mother, La Cieca, of being a witch. If Enzo Grimaldo, a Genoese prince whom La Gioconda secretly loves, had not intervened, Gioconda's mother would have been killed by the crowd after Barnaba's accusation. Enzo had been banished from Venice but has returned in disguise because he is in love with Laura Adorno, wife of Alvise Badoero, one of the chiefs of the Venetian state inquisition. Alvise arrests La Cieca despite Enzo's intervention, but Laura obtains a pardon for her. In gratitude La Cieca gives Laura a rosary. Meanwhile, hoping to keep Enzo away from La Gioconda, Barnaba promises to help him elope with Laura. When La Gioconda discovers this, she determines to kill her rival.

In act II, La Gioconda hides in the ship in which Enzo and Laura plan to escape. As La Gioconda is about to stab Laura, she notices her mother's rosary and realizes that it was Laura who saved La Cieca. La Gioconda now resolves to help the lovers escape. Alvise appears; as Laura and La Gioconda flee together, Enzo sets fire to the ship and swims ashore.

Act III begins at the Ca' d'Oro in Laura's room. A magnificent ball is taking place while Alvise accuses his wife of adultery and demands that she drink poison. La Gioconda, however, substitutes a sleeping draught for the poison; she instructs Laura to drink it and merely pretend to be dead. After the ball, during which the famous ballet, "Dance of the Hours," is heard, Alvise raises a curtain to show the shocked guests Laura lying, as it were, dead. The masked Enzo is at the ball, but when he sees Laura thus he betrays himself and is arrested. To save Enzo, La Gioconda realizes her only recourse is to give in to Barnaba's lust in exchange for Enzo's safety. Barnaba agrees but hauls away La Cieca as a hostage.

In act IV, La Gioconda has the sleeping Laura brought to a ruined palace. Because she has lost both her mother and Enzo, La Gioconda contemplates suicide. With Barnaba's help Enzo has escaped from prison; although he is grateful for La Gioconda's sacrifices, he nevertheless leaves with Laura. Barnaba arrives to claim his part of the bargain from Gioconda; she pretends to consent but instead stabs herself. He cries out that he has killed her mother, but La Gioconda is past hearing.

La Gioconda is the only opera by Ponchielli still to be heard on a regular basis. It is an old-fashioned standard grand opera with a full complement of voice types, each given a solo aria, a large chorus that adds local color, a lengthy ballet, and several instances of theatrical spectacle. In fashioning the libretto Boito drew on Victor Hugo's play *Angelo, tyran de Padoue* (1835); although it was not one of Hugo's stronger dramas, it also served as the basis for operas by composers

La Gioconda, set design by Carlo Ferrario for first production, Teatro alla Scala, Milan, 1876

as diverse as Mercadante (*Il giuramento* of 1837) and César Cui. Boito changed the locale to Venice, where there were greater opportunities for intrigue and spectacle than in Hugo's Paduan setting. Boito's libretto featured the play of sharply drawn opposites and the portrayal of one of the first genuinely evil characters in Italian opera—Barnaba—whom one cannot help seeing as a model for Iago in Boito's libretto for Verdi's *Otello.*

It has been said that Boito's libretto for *La Gioconda* relies heavily on coincidence and hysteria, and in general terms it has been so roundly criticized as to make his assumption of an anagram of his own name readily understandable. Boito and Ponchielli were in many ways an ill-matched pair: Boito's literary conceits were not ideal for the rather unsophisticated Ponchielli, as he himself recognized. "I compose more easily when the verse is more commonplace. The public wants smooth, clear things, melody, simplicity." At Ponchielli's request, Boito constantly had to revise and simplify. He was asked to make changes, however, that were not always improvements. In cutting La Gioconda's aria in act III, scene ii (in which she explains why she has shown up at Alvise's party) in favor of the long ballet, for example, dramatic motivation is lost. When *La Gioconda* was given in Rome (December 1877) and in Genoa (December 1879) it was substantially altered from the original. The final version, representing the work as we know it today, was staged in Milan at the Teatro alla Scala on 12 February 1880. With each revision much of the complexity of the story and the music was discarded.

For Ponchielli was indeed a master of "melody, simplicity." His opera, with its melodramatic situations, its expressive arias (full of wide leaps and vocal acrobatics), and its masterly handling of huge crowd scenes, all against the backdrop of the Venice of opulent palaces and sinister little alleys, is extremely popular with the public but loathed by the snobs. It is a remarkably well-crafted piece. Rather than compose separate numbers, in *La Gioconda* Ponchielli joined arias and ensembles and *declamato* passages so skillfully that each act holds together as an entity. Act I, for example, is skillfully wrought in introducing the six main characters, showing the relationships among them, and portraying the vitality and shifting moods of the Venetian crowds. In act II the music vividly heightens the scenic element, and in act III there is the famous ballet, "Dance of the Hours." If *La Gioconda* leans heavily on the incredible, the music, although not to everyone's taste, compensates handsomely.

—Stephen Willier

I GIOIELLI DELLA MADONNA [The Jewels of the Madonna].

Composer: Ermanno Wolf-Ferrari.

Librettists: E. Golisciani and C. Zangarini.

First Performance: Berlin, Kurfürstenoper, 23 December 1911.

Roles: Gennaro (tenor); Carmela (mezzo-soprano); Maliella (soprano); Rafaele (baritone); Biasco (bass); Ciccillo (tenor); Rocco (bass); Stella (soprano); Serena (contralto); Concetta (soprano); Grazia (the dancer "La Biondina," soprano); Totonno (tenor); chorus (SSATTBB).

Publications

article–

Vigolo, G. "Pudori perduti." In *Mille e una sera all' opera e al concerto,* 255. Florence, 1971.

I gioielli della Madonna is a belated product of the fashion for low-life, sensational melodramas inaugurated by Mascagni's *Cavalleria rusticana* in the 1890s and generally referred to as *verismo.* The vogue of such operas was particularly strong in Germany where Wolf-Ferrari was well-known for his elegant settings of two Goldoni comedies and the charming intermezzo *Il segreto di Susanna* (1909). When it was first performed at the Kurfürstenoper of Berlin, sung in German, *I gioielli* won an immediate success and was soon exported to the United States, where it appeared in all the major opera houses, arousing popular enthusiasm and the critics' interest. The link between *Cavalleria* and *I gioielli* is hardly more than an historical one, since their actual similarity is limited to the adoption of a low-life subject. The dramatic tension and ethical undertones of the prototype opera, which where transposed from a valuable literary source, are missing in Wolf-Ferrari's artful imitation. The music also evidences the distance in time and the difference in style between the two operas. With all its garish trappings and the skilful echoes of authentic Neapolitan tunes, *I gioielli* never strikes a genuinely dramatic note; its music has none of the elemental strength characterizing Mascagni's one-act opera.

The closest precedents of *I gioielli* are two lesser veristic operas set in Naples and successfully premiered in Germany: P. Tasca's *A Santa Lucia* (Berlin, Krolloper, 1892; revived in 1905) and N. Spinelli's *A Basso Porto* (Stadttheater, Cologne, 1895, sung in German). Most of the environmental ingredients of *I gioielli* are derived from these two operas, but some details can be traced back to a third Neapolitan work of the same period, Giordano's *Mala vita* (1892). The linguistic and musical peculiarities of these operas cannot be fully appreciated if they are not connected to one of the most popular Neapolitan works of the mid-nineteenth century, the "commedia per musica" *La festa di Piedigrotta* (later simply *Piedigrotta,* 1852) by Luigi Ricci. Its celebrated "tarantella" is echoed in a similar dance of *I gioielli.*

The libretto of *I gioielli della Madonna* was sketched out by Wolf-Ferrari and then developed by the two librettists of *A Santa Lucia,* C. Zangarini and E. Golisciani. They assembled all the stereotypes about Naples espoused by earlier *verismo* operas: open-air revels on a picturesque square by the sea, macaroni-eaters, ragged urchins playing popular instruments or smoking cigarettes, street-cries, a religious procession accompanied by ritual fireworks and music, a "Pazzariello" (a type of clown who shouts and mimes witty advertisements for local shops and products) with his scratch band, assorted songs and dances. A feeble story unfolds through the three acts of the opera: the blacksmith Gennaro loves Maliella, an adopted girl living in his home. She becomes infatuated with the camorra boss Rafaele who pesters her. The camorrist boasts that he would even steal the jewels from the statue of the Madonna to please Maliella. The desperate Gennaro actually does so and offers the jewels to the spiteful girl. The moment Maliella wears the shiny ornaments she is seized by an erotic frenzy; her thoughts are for Rafaele, but she does not resist Gennaro's lovemaking. In the camorrists' den, Rafaele praises Maliella's greatest asset, her virginity. Presently the distraught girl arrives, still wearing the stolen jewels and begging for protection as she is pursued by Gennaro. The camorrists are horrified by the sacrilegious theft. They fear they may be accused of it and abandon their hide-out. Maliella, in despair, rushes to drown herself in the sea, and the wretched Gennaro, overwhelmed by shame and remorse, stabs himself in front of a painting of the Madonna.

The opera suffers from the weakness of the plot and the number of veristic sketches overcrowding acts I and III. The second act is built on the unlikely effects of the jewels on Gennaro and Maliella. The most questionable aspect of the opera is the sympathetic and lighthearted presentation of the camorrists. In *A Basso Porto,* also dealing with camorrists and women, the gang was depicted as a bunch of despicable thugs. In *I gioielli,* violence and intimidation are tinged with self-righteousness and a sinister charm. At the end of the opera, the camorrists' sense of outrage at the theft of the jewels isolates the blasphemous, working-class Gennaro as the only villain of the story. His suicide is a necessary atonement.

Wolf-Ferrari's music does little to conceal the basic flimsiness of the plot, particularly in act I. The *Times* review of the London premiere (Covent Garden, 30 May 1912) commented on the plot and music noting that "It stakes everything on the capacity to make it all seem true, from the festival antics of the Neapolitan crowd to the contrasted characters of the chief personages. So during large parts of the first act the music is literally crowded out in order to make real the shouts of the people, the whistles and drums and bands playing in different keys. . . . When at last we do get to the music which belongs to the essentials of the drama and not to its trimmings, it is disappointing." Two enjoyable intermezzos are perhaps all that could be salvaged from Wolf-Ferrari's redundant score.

I gioielli della Madonna may have earned the composer the most substantial royalties in his career, but it did nothing to improve his reputation. This rests safely on his Goldonian musical comedies where his technical abilities, humor, and inventiveness are put to their best advantage.

—Matteo Sansone

GIORDANO, Umberto.

Composer. Born 28 August 1867, in Foggia. Died 12 November 1948, in Milan. Studied with Gaetano Briganti in Foggia, and with Paolo Serrao at the Naples Conservatory, 1881-90; his opera *Marina* given honorable mention at the Sonzogno competition, 1888; opera composition until 1929. Giordano was elected a member of the Accademia Luigi Cherubini in Florence.

Operas

Publisher: Sonzogno.

Marina, E. Golisciani, 1888.
Mala vita, N. Daspuro (after Salvatore Di Giacomo), Rome, Torre Argentina, 21 February 1892; revised as *Il voto,* Milan, Lirico, 10 November 1897.
Regina Diaz, G. Targioni-Tozzetti and G. Menasci (after Lockroy, *Un duel sous le cardinal de Richelieu*), Naples, Mercadante, 5 March 1894.
Andrea Chénier, Luigi Illica, Milan, Teatro alla Scala, 28 March 1896.
Fedora, A. Colautti (after Sardou), Milan, Lirico, 17 November 1898.
Siberia, Luigi Illica, Milan, Teatro alla Scala, 19 December 1903; revised 1921, Milan, Teatro alla Scala, 5 December 1927.
Marcella, L. Stecchetti (after H. Cain, J. Adenis), Milan, Lirico, 9 November 1907.
Mese Mariano, Salvatore Di Giacomo, Palermo, Massimo, 17 March 1910.
Madame Sans-Gêne, R. Simoni (after Sardou and Moreau), New York, Metropolitan Opera, 25 January 1915.
Giove a Pompei (with Franchetti), Luigi Illica and E. Romagnoli, Rome, La Pariola, 5 July 1921.
La cena delle beffe, S. Benelli, Milan, Teatro alla Scala, 20 December 1924.
Il Re, G. Forzano, Milan, Teatro alla Scala, 12 January 1929.
La festa del Nilo, Sardou and Moreau [unfinished].

Other works: the symphony *Delizia,* some instrumental music, incidental music, chamber works, piano pieces, songs.

Publications

About GIORDANO: books–

Galli, A., G. Macchi, and G.C. Paribeni. *Umberto Giordano nell' arte e nelle vita.* Milan, 1915.
Paribeni, G.C. *Madame Sans-Gêne.* Milan, 1923.
Cellamare, D. *Umberto Giordano: la vita e le opere.* Milan, 1949.
Giazotto, R. *Umberto Giordano.* Milan, 1949.
Confalonieri, G. *Umberto Giordano.* Milan, 1958.
Umberto Giordano dieci anni dopo la morte. Foggia, 1959.
Morini, M., ed. *Umberto Giordano.* Milan, 1968.
Mariani, R. *Verismo in musica e altri studi.* Edited by C. Orselli. Florence, 1976.
Tedeschi, R. *Addio, fiorito asil. Il melodramma italiano da Boito al Verismo.* Milan, 1978.
Nicolodi, F. *Musica e musicisti nel ventennio fascista.* Fiesole, 1984.

articles–

Musica e scena [Milan] (1926) [special issue].
Nicolodi, F. "Parigi e l'opera verista: dibattiti, riflessioni, polemiche." *Nuova rivista musicale italiana* 15 (1981): 577.
Pinzauti, Leonardo. "Le ragioni di *Andrea Chénier.*" *Nuova rivista musicale italiana* 15 (1981): 216.
Carpitella, Diego. "Populismo, Nazionalismo e italianitá nelle avanguardie musicali italiane." *Chigiana* 15 (1982): 59.

Avant-scène opéra June (1989) [*Andrea Chénier* issue].

*　　*　　*

Giordano's early operas can appropriately be defined by the term *verismo,* which has been loosely applied to the production of the Young Italian School. *Verismo* should be understood, however, as indicating a new musico-dramatic conception not necessarily connected with a particular subject matter.

Like his colleagues Mascagni and Leoncavallo, Giordano first achieved success with a low-life story, *Mala vita (A wretched life),* derived from a veristic play by the Neapolitan poet Salvatore Di Giacomo. Written in the wake of the sensational success of *Cavalleria rusticana,* it was the first opera to deal with the superstitions and moral weaknesses of the Neapolitan working classes.

A dyer suffering from tuberculosis vows to marry and redeem a prostitute so that God may help him recover his health. In the event, his former mistress does not let him keep his word and the young prostitute he has chosen returns to her brothel while the whole city revels in the Piedigrotta festival. *Mala vita* has an authentic Neapolitan flavor not simply for its musical folklore (a fiery "tarantella" and some songs skillfully inserted in the action) but for the unabashed realism of its characters and situations.

Sung by the first interpreters of *Cavalleria,* Gemma Bellincioni and Roberto Stagno, the opera was well received in Rome but failed hopelessly on its first and only performance in Naples (San Carlo, 26 April 1892) where the audience and the press took it as an insult to the city and its glorious opera house. Away from its natural milieu, *Mala vita* enjoyed an ephemeral popularity. In September 1892, it was presented at the Vienna International Theater and Music Exhibition with other veristic operas such as *Cavalleria* and *Pagliacci.* In his review, the critic E. Hanslick pointed out what would become a typical characteristic of Giordano's music: "[it] makes its effects through its rough-hewn ability to achieve a tone appropriate to the situation . . . the music is the obedient, all too eager servant of the dialogue." A few years later, Giordano tried to reshape *Mala vita* and tone down its pungent *verismo.* The revised version, presented as *Il voto (The vow)* at the Teatro Lirico of Milan in 1897, with E. Caruso and R. Storchio in the leading roles, no longer moved or outraged anybody and the opera was soon forgotten.

In 1910 Giordano turned again to the vernacular theater of Di Giacomo for a one-act opera with a Neapolitan setting, *Mese mariano (Our Lady's month).* It featured nuns and children in a poor-house. Pathos, diatonic harmonies and an intimate conversation style characterized the music of this short lyrical episode. It was not a belated return to the youthful *verismo* of *Mala vita,* but rather a disavowal of its sensational, cruder connotations.

Giordano made a more appreciable and lasting contribution to *verismo* with two operas written in the late 1890s, *Andrea Chénier* and *Fedora.* A poet guillotined during the French Revolution and a fictitious Russian princess should be clear evidence of a shift of Giordano's taste and interests. In fact, Sardou's four-act drama *Fedora* had been a pet project of the composer's since he had seen it played by Sarah Bernhardt in Naples where he was a student at the Conservatory. In 1894, fruitless negotiations with the French playwright on *Fedora* determined the choice of an alternative subject.

Luigi Illica's libretto on Chénier had originally been intended for Alberto Franchetti who then sold his rights to Giordano. Borrowing from various sources (the Goncourts,

Barbier, Houssaye, Méry, Renan), the skilled librettist managed to strike the right balance between fiction and history, individual feelings and collective moods, and produced four "tableaux" with strong, dramatic situations: i. reception at the castle of the Countess of Coigny (1789); ii. Paris under the Reign of Terror (1794); iii. revolutionary tribunal; iv. prison of St. Lazare. After their first meeting at the castle, Chénier and Maddalena of Coigny go through the horrors of the Revolution and fall victim to the machinations of Gérard, formerly a servant in the Coigny household and secretly in love with Maddalena, then a revolutionary leader. Chénier is sentenced to death and Maddalena volunteers to die with him taking the place of a female prisoner. Reunited in prison the night before the execution, they sing a passionate hymn to love and death, and move "with enthusiasm" to the guillotine.

Some twenty years earlier, such a libretto would have been set as a "grand-opéra" featuring choruses, ballet, colorful historical pageants, great love duets and full-hearted lyrical solos. Such components can indeed be found in Chénier, but the format is different. The novelty of Giordano's opera consists in the subordination of all those ingredients to the tense rhythm of the action, in the predominance of the situation over the musical form. Giordano's orchestra gives the plot impelling energy and dramatic cohesion. A musical continuum enfolds each "tableau," tightening the frivolous amusements of the aristocrats and the lament of tattered peasants, the grand gestures of Chénier and Gérard and the sneering interjections of the Parisian mob, vocal emphasis and revolutionary songs. Chénier's splendid "Improvviso" in act I, "Un dì all'azzurro spazio" ("One day I gazed at the blue sky"), exemplifies the dynamic nature of most of the vocal pieces in the opera. It is not simply an entry song for the tenor to introduce his character; it gradually upsets the aristocrats with its reference to social inequality and prepares the arrival of the peasants whose chorus spoils a graceful gavotte.

In his next opera, Fedora, Giordano had to deal with a murder case set in an exotic environment. The unusual subject stimulated his imagination to explore new ways of transposing the characters and situations of a modern play onto the operatic stage. The solution he adopted was to write a musical commentary which supports the long dialogue sections of the libretto and keeps lyrical expansion at a minimum level. This is particularly evident in act I where, in just over twenty minutes of performing time, a wounded man is brought in, a police interrogation is conducted, the fruitless search of a suspect takes place, and the wounded man dies.

Of the composer's remaining works, Siberia was particularly successful for some time in Italy and abroad. After Fedora, Giordano chose a second Russian story set in St. Petersburg and featuring aristocrats and officers. The local color was partly due to Illica's own readings and partly derived from the photographs and newspaper reports of Luigi Barzini. Illica's libretto concentrates on the courtisan Stephana, whose genuine passion for a young officer, Vassili, gives her the strength to redeem herself. Vassili fights and wounds her former lover, Prince Alexis, and is arrested and deported to Siberia where Stephana joins him to share a life of misery and hard labor. As they try to escape from the prison camp, the woman is shot by the guards. The second act, set at the frontier between Russia and Siberia, contains highly suggestive music (incorporating the song of the Volga boatmen) and a passionate duet between Stephana and Vassili.

In 1905, during a short season organized by the publisher E. Sonzogno at the Théâtre Sarah Bernhardt in Paris, Andrea Chénier, Fedora and Siberia were presented with other operas by Mascagni, Leoncavallo and Cilèa. Siberia received the best reviews from French critics, and composers like Bruneau and Fauré praised unreservedly its second act. The opera, however, has not survived, nor has the musical comedy Madame Sans-Gêne (from a well-known play by Sardou and Moreau) or La cena delle beffe (The mockery supper), a decadent drama turned into a libretto by its own author, the D'Annunzian playwright Sem Benelli.

Although Giordano tried to update his harmonic language in his last two operas, he was confined to being a survivor in the twentieth century. His distinctive contribution to late nineteenth-century musical dramaturgy was to consist only of the romantic Chénier and the gripping Fedora.

—Matteo Sansone

THE GIRL OF THE GOLDEN WEST
See LA FANCIULLA DEL WEST

THE GIRL OF THE WEST
See LA FANCIULLA DEL WEST

GIULINI, Carlo Maria.

Conductor. Born 9 May 1914, in Barletta. Studied violin and viola with Remy Principe, composition with Alessandro Bustini, and conducting with Bernardino Molinari at the Conservatorio di Musica di Santa Cecilia in Rome, beginning 1930; studied conducting with Casella at the Accademia Chigiana in Siena; in the viola section of the Augusteo Orchestra, Rome, under such conductors as Furtwängler, Mengelberg, Walter, and Richard Strauss; drafted into the Italian army during World War II, but went into hiding as an anti-Fascist; conducted the Augusteo Orchestra in 1944; assistant conductor of the Radio Audizioni Italiana Orchestra in Rome, and the chief conductor, 1946; helped found the Radio Audizioni Italiana Orchestra in Milan, 1950; assistant conductor to Victor De Sabata at the Teatro alla Scala, Milan, 1952; principal conductor at La Scala, 1954; conducted Verdi's Falstaff at the Edinburgh Festival, 1955; guest conductor of the Chicago Symphony Orchestra, 1955, and principal guest conductor, 1969-72; principal conductor of the Vienna Symphony Orchestra, 1973-76; led the Vienna Symphony on a world tour, 1976; succeeded Zubin Mehta as music director of the Los Angeles Philharmonic, 1978-84.

Publications

By GIULINI: articles–

"Carlo Maria Giulini on Brahms." In Conductors on Conducting, edited by Bernard Jacobson. Frenchtown, New Jersey, 1979.

Carlo Maria Giulini

interviews–

Chesterman, Robert, ed. *Conductors in Conversation.* London, 1990.
Matheopoulos, Helena. *Maestro: Encounters with Conductors of Today.* London, 1982.

About GIULINI: articles–

Harewood, Marion. "Carlo Maria Giulini." *Opera* November (1964).
Le Grand Baton September (1977) [special Giulini issue].
Bernheimer, Martin. "Giulini and *Falstaff.*" *Opera* July (1982).

Few conductors have experienced such a radical artistic metamorphosis as Carlo Maria Giulini. The Italian conductor first came to fame in the early 1950s as a fiery interpreter of Verdi, particularly in a production of Verdi's *Don Carlo* at Covent Garden in 1958 that did much to rehabilitate the then-neglected opera. His tempos were lively and his rhythms emphatic and precise, giving a highly dramatic effect.

Giulini was also a noted Mozart conductor during this period: his recordings of *Don Giovanni* and *Le nozze di Figaro* burn with a unique, Italianate fire, more concerned with an immediate, vital expression than gracefulness. Unlike Herbert von Karajan, whose Mozart performances at the time were rushed and driven, Giulini achieved a similarly masculine, volatile impression with moderate tempi that were more flattering to the music's sense of lyricism.

Giulini's Rossini interpretations at that time almost adamantly refused to sparkle for their own sake, so interested was Giulini in looking past the opera conventions in search for the dramatic truth, even in comedies such as *L'italiana in Algeri.* Throughout, Giulini was always careful not to expose the music's limitations by exceeding them.

In 1968, Giulini retired indefinitely from opera performances, aside from a recording of *Don Carlo* the following year. Comparisons between it and the performances he gave twelve years before in the Covent Garden production demonstrate Giulini's shift in emphasis from an artist whose values were primarily visceral to one whose values were predominantly contemplative and philosophical.

Even more changes were apparent when Giulini returned to live performance of opera in 1982, when he conducted the Los Angeles Philharmonic in a production of Verdi's *Falstaff.* Tempi were slow, searching, and one critic described the recording made from those performances as "Parsifalstaff." Elsewhere in Verdi, Giulini's interpretations do not accept even a single bar as a mere operatic convention, and later performances and recordings continued this approach. Even with the most simple, guitar-like accompaniments to the arias, Giulini searched for the poetic intention rather than acknowledging where Verdi found his materials for expressing it. In *Rigoletto,* Gilda's aria "Caro nome" is, more than ever, a nocturnal mood piece rather than a typical operatic cavatina. His treatment of Rigoletto's music has a rare monumentality.

Giulini's tempos have grown so stately that his 1989 recording of the Verdi Requiem, for example, is a full ten minutes longer than his 1964 recording. Giulini has polarized many critics: some consider him revelatory, others find his performances overripe. His symphonic interpretations (he specializes in Bruckner, Brahms and Mahler) suggest a preoccupation with smooth, warm surfaces and homogeneous textures, and some of this has carried over into his opera performances. Yet his Verdi interpretations have retained a certain fire that makes them deeply satisfying, unique musical statements, perhaps similar to how Wilhelm Furtwängler would have conducted Verdi had he conducted more of his operas. Giulini also tends to bring out the best in singers. Vocalists who often seem bland elsewhere take on a passion, style and taste under his baton.

—David Patrick Stearns

GIULIO CESARE IN EGITTO [Julius Caesar in Egypt].

Composer: George Frideric Handel.

Librettist: Nicola F. Haym (after G.F. Bussani).

First Performance: London, King's Theatre in the Haymarket, 20 February 1724; revised 2 January 1725, 17 January 1730.

Roles: Giulio Cesare (contralto); Cornelia (contralto); Sesto (soprano); Tolomeo (contralto); Cleopatra (soprano); Curio (bass); Achilla (bass-baritone); Nirenos (alto); chorus (SATB).

Publications

articles–

Dean, Winton. "Handel's *Giulio Cesare.*" *Musical Times* 104 (1963): 402.
Knapp, J. Merrill. "Handel's *Giulio Cesare in Egitto.*" In *Studies in Music History: Essays for Oliver Strunk,* edited by Harold S. Powers, 389. Princeton, 1968.
Monson, Craig. "*Giulio Cesare in Egitto:* from Sartorio (1677) to Handel (1724)." *Music and Letters* fall (1985).
Avant-scène opéra April (1987) [*Giulio Cesare* issue].

*   *   *

Italian opera in England had developed only in a lackluster, spasmodic fashion until the arrival of Handel in England in 1710. Through connections with Aaron Hill, English poet, dramatist and entrepreneur, and aided by the vocal skill and international reputation of his Italian star, Nicolini, Handel enjoyed his first London triumph in 1711 with *Rinaldo,* which ran for fifteen performances. In the next season, he produced two new operas, *Teseo* and *Il pastor fido,* works thus making it clear that he had chosen to stay in London, rather than return to Hanover, where he was the newly appointed court composer to George Ludwig, future King of England.

Within that decade, Handel's efforts were so successful as to lead to the establishment of a Royal Academy of Music, under the guidance of the Duke of Newcastle, with Handel as principal composer. Under the terms of his contract, he was required to produce a full season of operas for the London public each year. Handel took on this prestigious, though laborious responsibility with customary energy and enthusiasm, producing over the next two decades one masterwork after another in rapid succession. *Radamisto,* his first opera for the Royal Academy, was followed by *Muzio Scevola* (a "contest opera" of which he wrote only the third act), *Il Floridante, Ottone,* and *Flavio.* In dramatic worth, as in literary quality, the libretti for these first Royal Academy operas were not uniformly inspiring. Nonetheless, Handel outshone both Attilio Ariosto and Giovanni Maria Bononcini, his Italian colleagues, and competitors, at the Academy. Then, late in 1723, he finished *Giulio Cesare,* performing it in February the following year. Its success was astonishing, sufficient to drive Ariosti into the shadows and Bononcini out of the country.

Haym's plot and scenario are simple, Handel's characterizations vivid: The Roman Emperor Giulio Cesare, an athletic hero and lover, arrives in an Egypt now controlled by his enemy, Tolomeo, who has usurped the throne belonging rightfully to his sister, Cleopatra. Tolomeo orders Achilla, his chief general, to deliver Pompey's head on a charger, to his son Sesto and his wife, Cornelia, upon whom the usurper has sexual designs. Cesare denounces him as an impious villain, and Sesto vows revenge. Cleopatra, who soon establishes a romantic as well as a political liaison with Cesare, is alarmed when he is cornered by Achilla and his armed guards, and saddened by news of his death when he leaps into the sea to make his escape. However, the news proves false. After swimming to safety, Cesare returns in the nick of time to oust Tolomeo, and to restore the rights of Sesto, Cornelia, and, especially, of Cleopatra, who becomes his wife, as well as his political ally.

Haym's libretto presents a fine story, and Handel's musical characterizations are superb. Cesare's music is imperious, bold and impassioned, while that of Cleopatra is seductive, charming, plaintive, and witty by turns. Tolomeo's expressions are properly villainous, and Achilla's loutish. Cornelia sings of her tragic grief with a quiet dignity that is immensely moving, and Sesto projects vengeance in a manner most touching. *Giulio Cesare* emerged as one of Handel's best heroic operas to date. It is small wonder that it should have brought defeat to his rivals, new popularity to Handel, and frequent revivals, particularly in the twentieth century.

—Franklin B. Zimmerman

GLASS, Philip.

Composer. Born 31 January 1937, in Baltimore. Married: 1) JoAnne Akalaitis, actress (divorced), 2) Luba Burtyk, doctor, 1980. Studied flute at the Peabody Conservatory; studied piano at the University of Chicago, 1952-56; studied composition with Persichetti at Juilliard (M.A., 1962); in Paris on a Fulbright grant, 1964; studied counterpoint with Nadia Boulanger; met and studied with Ravi Shankar, 1965; travel in Morocco and across Asia; returned to New York, 1967; co-founded the recording company Chatham Square Productions; organized the Glass Ensemble, 1968; eight European

Giulio Cesare, title page of printed score, London, 1724

The Making of the Representative of Planet 8, by Philip Glass, English National Opera, 1988

tours, 1969-75; in India, 1970, 1973; Rockefeller Foundation grant, 1978; recording contract with CBS records, 1982; *Musical America* Musician of the Year, 1985.

Operas

Publishers: Peters, Dunvagen (Presser), Chester.

Einstein on the Beach (with Robert Wilson), Glass, 1975, France, Avignon, 25 July 1976.
The Panther (madrigal opera), 1980.
Satyagraha, C. DeJong (after *Bhagavad Gita*), 1980, Rotterdam, 5 September 1980.
The Photographer (chamber opera), 1982, Amsterdam, June 1982.
Akhnaten, Glass and others, 1983, Stuttgart, 24 March 1984.
The Juniper Tree (with R. Moran), A. Yorinks (after Grimm), 1986.
The Making of the Representative for Planet 8, Lessing, 1987.
The Fall of the House of Usher, A. Yorinks (after Poe), 1988.
1000 Airplanes on the Roof, Hwang, 1988, Vienna, July 1988.
The Voyage, Hwang, 1991-92, New York, 1992.

Other works: various works for conventional and electronic instruments.

Publications

By GLASS: books–

With R. Palmer. *Einstein on the Beach* [liner notes for Tomato 4-2901], 1979.
With C. DeJong. *Satyagraha, M.K. Ghandi in South Africa, 1893-1914: the Historical Material and Libretto Comprising the Opera's Book*. New York, 1980.
Robert T. Jones, ed. *Music by Philip Glass*. New York, 1987.
————. *Opera on the Beach*. London, 1988.

articles–

"Creating *Einstein on the Beach*: Philip Glass and Robert Wilson speak to Maxime de la Falaise." *On the Next Wave: the Audience Magazine of BAM's Next Wave Festival* 2/no. 4 (1984): 5.

interviews–

Porter, K. and D. Smith. "Interview with Philip Glass." *Contact* no. 12 (1976): 25.
Zimmermann, W. "Philip Glass." in *Desert Plants: Conversations with 23 American Musicians*. Vancouver, 1976.
Lentin, J. "Interview with Philip Glass." In *Le monde de musique*. Paris, 1978.
Gagne, C. and T. Caras. "Philip Glass." In *Soundpieces: Interviews with American Composers*. Metuchen, New Jersey, 1982.
Calres, P. "Entretien avec Philip Glass." *Jazz magazine* no. 317 (1983): 28.

About GLASS: articles–

Quander, Georg. "Schauplätz für Musik. Tendenzen im amerikanischen Musiktheater der Gegenwart." *Musiktheater heute. Sechs Kongressbeiträge. Jahrestagung Darmstadt, 1982,* edited by Hellmut Kühn, 104. Mainz, 1981.
Garland, D. "Philip Glass: Theater of Glass." *Down Beat* 50/no. 12 (1983): 16.

Jones, R.T. "*Einstein on the Beach:* Return of a Legend." *On the Next Wave: the Audience Magazine of BAM's Next Wave Festival* 2/no. 4 (1984): 1.
Taylor, S. "*Einstein* on the Stage." *Brooklyn Academy of Music* (1984): 3.
Rockwell, John. "Glass at the Crossroads." *Opera* November (1988).

*   *   *

Opera is almost by definition a multi-faceted art form composed and produced on a grand scale, and the concept of Minimalism seems ill-suited to it. But so-called Minimalism in music is just a technical term that has to do not with a work's substance but merely with its materials; its prominent features are relatively static harmony and extended repetition of relatively short, but not necessarily simple, melodic-rhythmic figures. Musical Minimalism can yield results that are extraordinarily complex; it can, as in the case of the operas of Philip Glass, be writ large.

Glass's involvement with music in theatrical contexts dates back to the mid 1960s, when he regularly produced incidental music for the avant-garde New York acting company called Mabou Mines. The first work he opted to call an opera, however, was the 1976 work *Einstein on the Beach,* a curiously iconoclastic "portrait" of the scientist that lasts some five hours and whose high-decibel, high-speed instrumental music—played for the most part on synthesizers and electronic organs—is offset by very little singing. Vocal elements in *Einstein on the Beach* are many, but for the most part they take the form of narrations or rhythmic choral recitations of numbers and solfege syllables.

Glass's second major opera, the 1980 work *Satyagraha,* stands in marked contrast to *Einstein on the Beach,* as does the 1984 *Akhnaten* and subsequent works. In these later examples, Glass retains many of his trademark chord progressions and rhythmic patterns, but he varies their rate of flow, and—using the full resources of the conventional orchestra—he softens both their textures and their colors. Musical Minimalism in the later operas is confined largely to accompaniments over which are set lyric lines of often rhapsodic character.

Like *Einstein on the Beach, Satyagraha* and *Akhnaten* are "portrait" operas, the one focusing on Mohandas K. Gandhi and the other on the ancient Egyptian pharaoh named in the title. Neither work, however, features a traditional story-line; they are considerably less abstract in their representations than is *Einstein on the Beach,* but both consist only of isolated scenes from their protagonist's lives, arranged in an order other than chronological. Their texts, too, are deliberately cryptic; *Satyagraha*'s is in Sanskrit, and *Akhnaten*'s is in a variety of archaic languages, and both works have had productions in which translations—at the composer's request—have not been made available to the audience.

Along with operas built of shuffled vignettes, Glass has written a number of operas in traditional narrative format. These are viable works, dynamic and well crafted. On the whole, though, Glass's skills at storytelling, exemplified in such works as the *The Juniper Tree* (1985) and *The Fall of the House of Usher* (1988), seem not so great as his ability to conjure up vague yet potent images of his heroes.

—James Wierzbicki

GLINKA, Mikhail Ivanovich.

Composer. Born 1 June 1804, in Novospasskoye, Smolensk district. Died 15 February 1857, in Berlin. Married: Mariya Petrovna Ivanova, 1835 (divorced 1846). Studied piano with Carl Meyer in Novospasskoye; briefly studied piano with John Field when he was in St Petersburg; worked for the Ministry of Communications in St Petersburg, 1824-28; studied singing with Belloli; in Milan, 1830, and visited Naples, Rome, and Bologna, meeting Donizetti and Bellini; studied counterpoint and composition with Siegfried Wilhelm Dehn in Berlin, 1833; *A Life for the Tsar* produced in St Petersburg, 1836; met Berlioz in Paris, 1844; collected folk songs in Spain; in Warsaw for three years. Glinka was friends with the famous Russian poets Zhukovsky and Pushkin.

Operas

Edition: *M.I. Glinka: Polnoye sobraniye sochineniv.* Edited by V. Ya. Shebalin et al. Moscow, 1955-69.

Rokeby, after Scott, 1824 [sketches only].
Sketches for an opera on V. Zhukovsky's *Mar'ina Grove,* 1834 [used in *A Life for the Tsar*].
A Life for the Tsar (Zhizn'za tsarya), G.F. Rosen, 1834-36, St Petersburg, Bol'shoy, 9 December 1836.
Ruslan and Lyudmila (Ruslan i Lyudmila), V.F. Shirkov, N.V. Kukol'nik, M.A. Gedeonov, N.A. Markevich (after Pushkin), 1837-42, St Petersburg, Bol'shoy, 9 December 1842.
The Bigamist (Dvumuzhnitsa), A.A. Shakhovsky, 1855 [sketches only; lost].

Mikhail Glinka

Other works: incidental music, sacred music, choral and vocal works, orchestral works, chamber music, ballets, piano works, songs with piano accompaniment.

Publications

By GLINKA: books–

Lapiski. St Petersburg, 1871; English translation as *Memoirs,* edited by Richard B. Mudge, Norman, Oklahoma, 1963.
Stasov, V., ed. *Zapiski M.I. Glinki i perepiska evo s rodnïmi i druz'yami* [memoirs and correspondence]. St Petersburg, 1887.
Findeyzen, N.F., ed. *M.I. Glinka: polnoye sobraniye pisem* [letters]. St Petersburg, 1907.
Ginsburg, S.A., ed. *Autobiography and Notes on Instrumentation.* Leningrad, 1937.
Lyapunov, A.S., ed. *M.I. Glinka: Literaturnïye proizvedeniya i perepiska* [writings and correspondence]. Moscow, 1973-77.

articles–

"Zametki ob instrumentovke" [notes on orchestration], "Prilozheniye instrumentovki k musïkal'nomu sochineniyu" [orchestration]. *Muzïkal'nïy i teatral'nïy vestnik* no. 2 (1856): 21; no. 6 (1856): 99.
Musïkal'nïy Sovremennik 1/no. 6, 2/no. 1 (1916) [letters].

About GLINKA: books–

Fouque, Octave. *Michel Ivanovitch Glinka d'après ses mémoires et sa correspondance.* Paris, 1880.
Weimarn, P. *M.I. Glinka.* Moscow, 1892.
Shestakova, L. *Glinka as he Was.* St Petersburg, 1894.
Serov, A.N. *Reminiscences of M.I. Glinka.* In *Critical Essays,* vol. 3. St Petersburg, 1895.
Findeyzen, N. *Mikhail Ivanovich Glinka: evo zhizn'i tvorcheskaya deyatel'nost'* [life and creative activity]. St Petersburg, 1896.
Calvocoressi, M.D. *Glinka: biographie critique.* Paris, 1911.
Montagu-Nathan, M. *Glinka.* London, 1916; 1977.
Riesemann, Oskar von. *Glinka. Monographien zur russischen Musik,* vol. 1. Munich, 1923.
Rimsky-Korsakov, A.N., ed. *M.I. Glinka: zapiski.* Moscow and Leningrad, 1930.
Asaf'yev, B. *M.I. Glinka.* Moscow, 1947; 1978.
Martinov, I.I. *M.I. Glinka.* Moscow, 1947.
Zagursky, B.I. *M.I. Glinka.* Leningrad, 1948.
Kann-Novikova, E. *M.I. Glinka: novïye materialï i dokumentï* [new material and documents]. Moscow, 1950-55.
Livanova, T., ed. *M.I. Glinka: sbornik materialov i stat'yey* [collection of material and articles]. Moscow, 1950.
Ossovsky, A., ed. *M.I. Glinka issledovaniya i materialï* [researches and material]. Leningrad and Moscow, 1950.
Orlova, A., and B. Asaf'yev, eds. *Letopis' zhizni i tvorchestva Glinki* [Glinka's life and work]. Moscow, 1952.
Livanova, T., and V. Protopopov, eds. *Glinka: tvorcheskiy put'* [Glinka's creative path]. Moscow, 1955.
Orlova, A. ed. *Glinka v vospominaniyakh sovremennikov* [Glinka in the reminiscences of his contemporaries]. Moscow, 1955.
Petzoldt, R. *Mikhail Glinka: sein Leben in Bildern.* Leipzig, 1955.
Gordeyeva, E. ed. *M.I. Glinka: sbornik stat'yey* [collection of articles; includes complete bibliography of Russian books and articles]. Moscow, 1958.

Kiselyov, V.A., et. al., eds. *Pamyati Glinki 1857-1957: issledo-vaniya i materialï* [in memory of Glinka 1857-1957; research and material]. Moscow, 1958.

Brown, David. *Glinka: a Biographical and Critical Study.* London, 1974, 1985.

Orlova, A., comp. *Letopis'zhizni i tvorchestva M.I. Glinki. I: 1804-1843* [chronicle of Glinka's life and works]. Leningrad, 1978.

Vasina-Grossman, Vera. *Mikhail Ivanovich Glinka.* Moscow, 1979.

Taruskin, Richard. *Opera and Drama in Russia as Preached and Practiced in the 1860s.* Ann Arbor, 1981.

Olkhosvsky, Yuri. *Vladimir Stasov and Russian National Culture. Russian Music Studies* 6. Ann Arbor, 1983.

Swolkień, Henryk. *Michal Glinka.* Warsaw, 1984.

Orlova, A. *Glinka's Life in Music: a Chronicle.* Ann Arbor, 1988.

articles–

Stasov, V. "M.I. Glinka." *Russkiy vestnik* (1857).

Shestakova, L., ed. "M.I. Glinka: zapiski." *Russkaya starina* 1 (1870): 380, 474, 562; 2 (1870): 56, 266, 372, 419; English translation, 1963.

Stasov, V. "M.I. Glinka: novïye materialï dlya evo biografii" [new biographical material]. *Russkaya starina* 61 (1889): 387.

Abraham, Gerald. "Glinka and his Achievement." In *Studies in Russian Music,* 21. London, 1935.

———. "Michael Glinka." In *Masters of Russian Music,* edited by Gerald Abraham and M.D. Calvocoressi, 13. London, 1936.

———. "A Life for the Tsar." In *On Russian Music,* 1. London, 1939.

———. "Glinka, Dargomïzhsky and *The Rusalka.*" In *On Russian Music,* 43. London, 1939.

———. "Ruslan and Lyudmila." In *On Russian Music,* 20. London, 1939.

Taruskin, Richard. "Glinka's Ambiguous Legacy and the Birth Pangs of Russian Opera." *Nineteenth-Century Music* 1 (1977-78).

Seaman, Gerald. "The Rise of Slavonic Opera, I." *New Zealand Slavonic Journal* 2 (1978): 1.

Aranovskij, Mark. "Dva očerka o *Ruslane.*" *Sovetskaya muzyka* 7 (1979): 68.

Levaševa, Ol'ga, "Čitaja pis'ma Glinki" [reading Glinka's letters]. *Sovetskaya muzyka* 6 (1979): 74.

Rahmanova, Marina. "Hudožestvennyj genij v Rossii" [an artistic genius in Russia]. *Sovetskaya Muzyka* 6 (1979): 71.

Homjakov, A. "Opera Glinki *Zhizn'za tsarya*" [A Life for the Tsar]. *Sovetskaya muzyka* 1 (1980): 91.

Bjoørkvold, Jon-Roar. "*Ivan Susanni,* en russisk nasjonalopera under to despotier" [*Ivan Susanin* (*A Life for the Tsar*): a Russian national opera under two rulers]. *Studia musicologica Norvegica* 8 (1982): 9.

Mihajlov, Mihail. "Pol'skaja muzykal'naja citata v *Ivane Susanine* Glinki" [quotation of Polish music in *Ivan Susanin* (*A Life for the Tsar*)]. In *Stilevye osobennosti russkoj muzyki XIX-XX vekov,* edited by Mihail Mihajlov, Leningrad, 1983.

Vasina-Grossman, Vera. "K istorii libretto *Ivana Susanina* Glinki" [history of the libretto of *Ivana Susanina* (*A Life for the Tsar*)]. In *Stilevye osobennosti russkoj muzyki XIX-XX vekov,* edited by Mihail Mihajlov. Leningrad, 1983.

Taruskin, Richard. "Some Thoughts on the History and Historiography of Russian Music." *Journal of Musicology* 3 (1984): 321.

Rowen, Ruth Halle. "Glinka's Tour of Folk Modes on the Wheel of Harmony." In *Russian and Soviet Music: Essays for Boris Schwarz,* edited by Malcolm H. Brown, *Russian Music Studies* 11, p. 35. Ann Arbor, 1984.

———. "Christian themes in Russian opera: A millenial essay." *Cambridge Opera Journal* 2 (1990): 83.

*   *   *

Assessing the operatic legacy of Mikhail Glinka is more difficult that it might seem at first. His two completed operas inhabit very different aesthetic worlds: the oriental, exotic atmosphere of *Ruslan and Lyudmila* strongly contrasts to the grand historical setting of *A Life for the Tsar.* This diversity can in part be explained, however, by both Glinka's musical education and his exposure to a wide variety of western and non-western musical styles.

Glinka began his musical career as a dilettante, but he traveled with first-rate professional musicians in Italy and Germany, and studied with the famous German theorist Siegfried Dehn in Berlin. Glinka's exposure to various uncles' and friends' serf orchestras (comprised not of folk musicians, but of competent classically trained musicians who performed works by Haydn, Mozart, and Beethoven) provided him not only with exposure to western classical music, but with a laboratory in which to try out various orchestral effects in his own compositions.

Up to the composition of *A Life for the Tsar,* almost all of Glinka's works are Italianate in style, as are the pieces for the character Farlaf in *A Life for the Tsar.* With this composition, however, Glinka developed a number of folk characteristics in various different ways. One of the most prevalent techniques (used extensively in *A Life for the Tsar*) is the use of unison or near-unison accompaniment for a folk tune, clearly exposing the tonal ambiguities inherent in the melody. Another common technique (clearly evident in the act II "Persian Chorus" of *Ruslan and Lyudmila*) is a type of cantus firmus technique that consists of setting the source tune literally as the melody, but providing a constantly varying background accompaniment. Glinka also used a number of devices common to western operatic music, such as the recurring theme technique (not the leitmotif techniques associated with Wagner) found in contemporary and slightly earlier French operas by Méhul, Catel, and Berton (the Poles in *A Life for the Tsar,* for example, are represented by the characteristic dances that make up their act II divertimento).

Perhaps Glinka's greatest strength as an opera composer is his expertise at characterization. If the Poles in *A Life for the Tsar* are caricatures overdrawn to the point that the overall dramatic effect is threatened, Farlaf and Naina in *Ruslan* are effective comedic types, as demonstrated in Farlaf's aria and scene with Naina. (Less effective is the character of Sobinin, a stereotypical Italianate primo uomo.) Similarly, an effective heroic manner is created for Susanin and Ruslan. In addition, Glinka's heroines are often notable for the strength of their roles, such as Lyudmila, who displays both determination and playfulness.

Ultimately, the greatest asset of Glinka's style is its flexibility, as *Ruslan and Lyudmila* clearly demonstrates. The difference between *A Life for the Tsar* and *Ruslan and Lyudmila* is not only due to the greater maturity of the composer when he wrote the latter, but also to the very different demands of the subjects. Paradoxically, the more successful opera was *A Life,* which proved to be less influential than *Ruslan* (a disappointment at its premiere). With these two works, however, Glinka provided models for Russian opera to follow:

the grand historical opera on a national subject (adopted by Tchaikovsky), and the magic opera (adopted by the "The Five": Balakirev, Borodin, Cui, Musorgsky, and Rimsky-Korsakov). He also set a precedent for succeeding composers by creating the admittedly undramatic works of the "lyrical scene" type, demonstrating both exoticism and Orientalism. In addition, Glinka's treatment of the orchestra, such as his seemingly transparent orchestration, creates great effects on its own terms, and affected the work of Tchaikovsky and Rimsky-Korsakov in particular.

If Glinka's music is not yet thoroughly "Russian" in style, in that native style patterns often dissolve into conventional Italianate phrases, he more than provided the model for succeeding generations of Russian composers, breaking as he did from the practice of mere quotation of national elements into an integration of those elements with traditional European musical practices.

—Gregory Salmon

GLORIANA

Composer: Benjamin Britten.

Librettist: W. Plomer.

First Performance: London, Covent Garden, 8 June 1953.

Roles: Elizabeth (soprano); Robert Devereux, Earl of Essex (tenor); Frances, Countess of Essex (mezzo-soprano); Charles Blount, Lord Mountjoy (baritone); Penelope, Lady Rich (soprano); Sir Robert Cecil (baritone); Sir Walter Raleigh (bass); Henry Cuffe (baritone); Lady-in-Waiting (soprano); Recorder of Norwich (bass); Housewife (mezzo-soprano); Spirit of Masque (tenor); Master of Ceremonies (tenor); City Crier (baritone); chorus (SSATTB).

Publications

books–

John, Nicholas, ed. *Benjamin Britten: Peter Grimes and Gloriana. Opera Guide 24.* London and New York, 1983.

articles–

"*Gloriana*: A Symposium." *Opera* August (1953).
Tempo no. 28 (1953) [*Gloriana* issue].
Klein, J. "Reflections on 'Gloriana'." *Tempo* no. 29 (1953): 16.
Porter, Andrew. "Britten's 'Gloriana'." *Music and Letters* 34 (1953): 277.
Alexander, Peter F. "The Process of Composition of the Libretto of Britten's *Gloriana*." *Music and Letters* 67 (1986).

*   *   *

Of all Benjamin Britten's large scale operas, *Gloriana* was the composer's child of sorrow. It was written in response to a royal commission for a piece to celebrate the coronation of Her Majesty Queen Elizabeth II, and was first performed at

Covent Garden on 8 June 1953 before an audience mainly comprised of national and international personages who had congregated in London to participate in the festive events.

That such people possess the attributes of wealth and power is a truism, but they do not tend to be a particularly knowledgeable crowd when it comes to modern music and probably would have been far happier with a production of *Aida* or *La bohème.* In the event, Britten's new opera was judged a resounding fiasco at the time, and had to await a resuscitation by the English National Opera (then Sadler's Wells) in 1966 to have its true merits at last displayed and clarified out of the glare of mean-spirited criticism and hostile publicity.

In keeping with the purpose of the initial occasion, the plot of *Gloriana* is dynastic and deals primarily with the time-tested story of Queen Elizabeth I (the opera's title is a contemporaneous laudatory epithet for that ruler) and Robert Devereux, Earl of Essex; the self-same material that was used by Donizetti for *Roberto Devereux,* to say nothing of well known treatments by other media, especially the cinema.

Britten and his librettist William Plomer went to Lytton Strachey's book *Elizabeth and Essex* for their immediate source, but properly utilized that somewhat unsatisfactory work rather loosely. Among other results, Essex's role in the events—while important—is not so central as to detract from what is essentially a probing character study of the Queen in all her various facets as both ruler and woman.

We first meet Elizabeth in a public setting, in the act of restoring harmony between Essex and Lord Mountjoy, who have quarreled after a jousting tourney. This scene of pageantry and homage is followed by a private one in which she discusses affairs of state with her adviser Cecil, enjoys a touching rendezvous with Essex (including the well-known Lute Songs) and finally, alone, prays for divine guidance in steering the realm.

Act II finds her in Norwich being entertained by the locals with a Masque. This is followed by a short scene in which Essex, Mountjoy and Penelope Rich (Mountjoy's lover) plot to seize power while Lady Essex voices her fears. The act ends with a dancing party at Whitehall, during which the Queen publicly humiliates Lady Essex, then partially atones by granting (at long last) Essex's desire to be named leader of the forces being sent to Ireland to put down Tyrone's rebellion. In the last act it becomes fatally clear that Essex has failed in his Irish mission and consequently fallen from royal favor. He attempts to incite a rebellion but is soon taken prisoner. The Queen, caught between personal desires and political necessities, decides for the latter and orders Essex's execution: the final scene movingly depicts her in lonely splendor on the great stage of history, inexorably inching toward her own death.

In many ways *Gloriana* is quite different from the usual Britten stage work. It is the closest the composer ever came to traditional grand opera, inasmuch as it calls for full scale orchestra, chorus, corps de ballet and a good deal of scenic panoply. Also, in contrast to the through-composition he usually employed, it is constructed using a format of individual numbers, these being carefully demarcated in the printed score, as an example from act I scene ii will show: "3. Cecil's Song of Government. 4. Recitative and Essex's Entry. 5. First Lute Song." etc.

Several moments use an appropriate quasi-Elizabethan musical vocabulary, particularly the Masque, the Courtly Dances and the Lute Songs. None of these, however, could be described as mere pastiche but instead are graced with an unmistakably twentieth-century tang not unlike, say, the cross-fertilization between Stravinsky and various eighteenth-century composers in *Pulcinella.* On the other hand the great chorus of homage, the Queen's prayer with its plainchant cadences, the act II quartet and the final scene are all pure Britten at his finest. Thus the music may be said to reflect all of the composer's justly famous skills at word setting, thematic organization, theatricality and beauty of vocal line and in no way deserves to remain in the limbo to which it was initially consigned.

—Dennis Wakeling

GLOSSOP, Peter.

Baritone. Born 6 July 1928, in Sheffield. Studied with Joseph Hislop, Leonard Mosley, and Eva Rich. Joined Sadler's Wells Opera Chorus, but assumed leading roles and sang with company until 1962; Covent Garden debut as Demetrius in *A Midsummer Night's Dream,* 1961; Teatro alla Scala debut as Rigoletto, 1964-65; Metropolitan Opera debut in *Rigoletto,* 1967; sang under Karajan at Salzburg, 1970-72; also has appeared in Vienna, Salzburg, San Francisco, and Buenos Aires.

Publications.

About GLOSSOP: articles–

Granville Barker, F. "Peter Glossop." *Opera* May (1969).

* * *

Peter Glossop as the Marquis of Posa in *Don Carlos*

Peter Glossop began singing with his local Amateur Operatic Society in Sheffield before joining the Sadler's Wells Opera company in London as a member of the chorus. His talent was soon recognised and he began to sing the principal baritone roles, including Rigoletto, Count di Luna (*Il Trovatore*), Gerard (*Andrea Chénier*), Scarpia (*Tosca*) and Eugene Onegin. In his *The Grand Tradition* (1974), J.B. Steane recalls, "I remember a principal tenor of Sadler's Wells at this time telling me how he would leave the stage during *Pagliacci,* passing through the chorus and always hearing a voice that would raise goose-pimples on his skin as he heard it. The voice was Glossop's."

As his career developed, Glossop worked principally at Covent Garden, and his international standing became considerable. In 1961 he won the first prize in the International Competition for Young Singers in Sofia, Bulgaria, his performance of the Count di Luna making a particularly strong impression. Later that year he made his Covent Garden debut, singing the role of Demetrius in Britten's *A Midsummer Night's Dream,* and the following year he confirmed his special affinity with the baritone roles of Verdi with a highly praised performance as Renato in *Un ballo in maschera.* An international career soon followed, with appearances from 1964 at the Teatro alla Scala, Milan, and other Italian houses, as well as in the United States and Canada. It was as Rigoletto that he made his debut at the Metropolitan Opera in New York in 1967, and this had been the role in which he had first appeared at La Scala three years before. In 1968 he appeared at the Vienna Staatsoper, and he sang Iago in the performances of *Otello* conducted by Karajan at the 1970 Salzburg Festival, an achievement preserved on an acclaimed recording.

These successes not only represent an outstanding personal achievement, but also played a significant part in establishing a new international recognition for British singers generally. Glossop was especially identified with Verdi through a wide range of different characters portrayed with the utmost commitment, including Renato, Rodrigo (*Don Carlo*), Iago, Di Luna, Germont (*La traviata*) and Simon Boccanegra. While not as extensive as his Verdi roles, Glossop's association with the operas of Benjamin Britten will surely rank as equally important. This judgment stems particularly from his outstanding recording of the title role in *Billy Budd,* under the direction of the composer, in which Glossop's extrovert style seems ideally suited to the part. This, together with his fine Iago recorded for Karajan, makes one regret the lack of major recordings, for at his peak in the 1960s and early 70s, Glossop's sensitive musicianship and his richly colored tone made him an artist of the highest calibre.

—Terry Barfoot

GLUCK, Alma [born Reba Fiersohn].

Soprano. Born 11 May 1884, in Bucharest. Died 27 October 1938, in New York. Married Bernard Gluck, 1902 (divorced 1912; one daughter, the author Marcia Davenport); married violinist Efrem Zimbalist (one son). Studied with Arturo

Buzzi-Peccia, New York, and then with Jean de Reszke and Marcella Sembrich; debut as Sophie in *Werther* at the Metropolitan Opera, 1909; remained at Metropolitan Opera until 1912; after 1913 sang only in concert.

Publications

About GLUCK: books–

Davenport, M. *Too Strong for Fantasy.* New York, 1967.

articles–

Eke, B.T. "Alma Gluck." *Record Collector* 6 (1951): 33.

*   *   *

For American record buyers, soprano Alma Gluck was the female Caruso. Not that their voices or styles were in any way similar—Gluck's airy lyricism and delicate sense of concert deportment could not have resembled less that most passionate and Italianate of tenors! What they did share was commercial success unparalleled among classical musicians of the time. Actually Gluck's recording of "Carry me back to old Virginny" was the first RCA Victor Red Seal record to sell one million copies, and she was able to live quite lavishly on her royalties alone: something that could be said about no opera singer before her and very few since.

So today it comes as no surprise that Gluck is remembered almost exclusively as a recital and recording artist, and it seems difficult to grasp that she did, in fact, have a rather

Alma Gluck

substantial career at the Metropolitan Opera, where she performed some of the standard operatic repertoire—Violetta in *La traviata,* Mimì in *La bohème* among others—many times with the aforementioned Enrico Caruso. And it is true that Gluck's "operatic years" were short (after 1918 she returned to the Metropolitan only to sing in concert) and her recordings document few of her roles.

Listening to these records today, Gluck's apparent choice—to veer away from the standard opera singer fare and concentrate instead on song, with only occasional forays into operatic music—seems wise. Not that she lacked anything in the way of appropriate vocal equipment; quite the contrary, for she was an uncommonly accomplished lyric soprano with a purity and tonal bloom that were special even during the years in which she performed, that much discussed and lamented golden age. She was even a pupil of the great Marcella Sembrich, who passed on to Gluck much of her breathtaking sense of line and perfect musical attack—but not her own glamour and affinity for the stage, for Gluck simply lacked an inclination for the theatre, the kind of natural temperament we associate with opera singers.

Her very few records of operatic music from what we think of as the central repertoire (little of it was central to her) are impressively sung, thoughtfully conceived and characterized, and have a graceful and fluent sense of style—but there is always a sense of the recital hall about them and the feeling that the music is removed from a dramatic context. A good example is her performance of Musetta's little waltz song from *La bohème.* This seems an odd choice for her, as Mimì was the role she performed and certainly the one that would seem to fit better her unaffectedness and gift for pathos. Sure enough, the lovely and poised singing is marvelous in its way, but so lacking in the seductiveness which underlies this aria that we almost do not recognize it. Even stranger is her performance of the "Mira O Norma" duet, where she very surprisingly sings Adalgisa to the Norma of contralto Louise Homer. The voices are as well matched and the singing as precise and fluid as we would wish, but we smile at the reverence and decorum of the two artists—it sounds more like Mendelssohn than Bellini.

Gluck is much better in her records of more out-of-the-way operatic music. There is a superb performance of Ljuba's aria from Rimsky-Korsakov's *The Tsar's Bride,* perfect in its intonation and sweetness of tone. Her performance of "Rossignols amoureux" from Rameau's *Hippolyte et Aricie* too is justly celebrated for these qualities as well as the elegant phrasing we associate with a true musician. Gluck also recorded "Le bonheur est chose légère" from Saint-Saëns *Le timbre d'argent,* this one with her husband, the famous violinist Efrem Zimbalist, and no greater praise can be offered than to say that their instruments are managed with equal suavity.

All three of these examples of music which was seldom heard in Gluck's day, and in particular was rarely performed by an artist of her popular fame. It speaks well for her taste and musicality, and is reassuring in the face of her overwhelming discography of sentimental song, much of it less than first rate. But even in this repertoire Gluck's artistry is exquisite. Michael Arne's rather silly "Lass with the delicate air," for example, is a thing of real charm in Gluck's record, filled with delicious rhythmic play and delivered with a bewitching smile in the tone. And to bring us full circle, there is again that famous "Carry me back to old Virginny." In lesser hands such a piece could easily turn maudlin; Gluck invests it with all the scrupulous musicianship and discernment that she offers in "great music," with the result that even this trifle becomes something affecting and treasurable.

It is a wonderful example of how to sing a parlor song— and as good an example as any of the refined art of Alma Gluck.
—David Anthony Fox

GLUCK, Christoph Willibald Ritter von.

Composer. Born 2 July 1714, in Erasbach. Died 15 November 1787, in Vienna. Married: Marianna Pergin, 1750. In Prague, 1732; chamber musician to Prince Lobkowitz in Vienna, 1736; taken to Milan by Prince Melzi, 1737, where he met and worked with Sammartini; successful production of his first opera, *Artaserse,* to a libretto by Metastasio, 1741; commissioned to write two operas for the King's Theatre in the Haymarket in London, 1745; met Handel in London; conducted Mingotti's opera company in Hamburg, Leipzig, and Dresden, 1746-47; in Vienna, 1750, where many of his operas were premiered; statement of the "reform" of opera in the preface to *Alceste,* 1767 [published 1769]; in Paris, 1773, where he produced many successful operas; returned to Vienna, 1779. Gluck taught singing and harpsichord to Marie Antoinette.

Operas

Editions: *C. W. Gluck: Sämtliche Werke.* Edited by R. Gerber, G. Croll, et al. Kassel and Basle, 1951-.

Artaserse, Metastasio, Milan, Regio Ducal, 26 December 1741.
Demetrio, Metastasio, Venice, San Samuele, 2 May 1742.
Demofoonte, Metastasio, Milan, Regio Ducal, 6 January 1743.
Il Tigrane, Francesco Silvani (after Goldoni, *La virtù trionfante dell' amore e dell' odio*), Crema, 26 September 1743.
La Sofonisba, Francesco Silvani, with arias by Metastasio, Milan, Regio Ducal, 18 January 1744.
Ipermestra, Metastasio, Venice, San Giovanni Grisostomo, 21 November 1744.
Poro, after Metastasio, *Alessandro nell' Indie,* Turin, Regio, 26 December 1744.
Ippolito, Gioseffo Gorino Corio, Milan, Regio Ducal, 31 January 1745.
La caduta de' giganti, Francesco Vanneschi, London, King's Theatre in the Haymarket, 7 January 1746.
Artamene, Vanneschi (after Bartolomeo Vitturi), London, King's Theatre in the Haymarket, 4 March 1746.
Le nozze d'Ercole e d' Ebe, Pillnitz [near Dresden], 29 June 1747.
La Semiramide riconosciuta, Metastasio, Vienna, Burgtheater, 14 May 1748.
La contesa de' numi, Metastasio, Copenhagen, Charlottenborg Castle, 9 April 1749.
Ezio, Metastasio, Prague, carnival 1750; revised, Vienna, Burgtheater, 26 December 1763.
Issipile, Metastasio, Prague, carnival 1752.
La clemenza di Tito, Metastasio, Naples, San Carlo, 4 November 1752.
Le cinesi, Metastasio, Schlosshof [near Vienna], 24 September 1754.
Les amours champestres, Schönbrunn, 1755.
La danza, Metastasio, Laxenburg [near Vienna], 5 May 1755.

L'innocenza giustificata, Giacomo Durazzo, with arias by Metastasio, Vienna, Burgtheater, 8 December 1755 revised as *La Vestale,* Vienna, Burgtheater, summer 1768.
Antigono, Metastasio, Rome, Torre Argentina, 9 February 1756.
Il rè pastore, Metastasio, Vienna, Burgtheater, 8 December 1756.
La fausse esclave, Louis Anseaume and Marcouville, Vienna, Burgtheater, 8 January 1758.
L'île de Merlin, ou Le monde renversé, Louis Anseaume (after Le Sage and D'Orneval), Vienna, Schönbrunn, 3 October 1758.
La Cythère assiégée, Charles-Simon Favart, Vienna, Burgtheater, spring 1759; revised, Paris, Académie Royale, 1 August 1775.
Le diable à quatre, ou La double métamorphose, Jean Michael Sedaine, Laxenburg (Vienna), 28 May 1759.
L'arbre enchanté, ou Le tuteur dupé, Pierre-Louis Moline (after J. Vadé), Vienna, Schönbrunn, 3 October 1759; revised Versailles, 27 February 1775.
L'ivrogne corrigé [*Der bekehrte Trunkenbold*], Louis Anseaume and L. de Sarterre, Vienna, Burgtheater, April 1760.
Tetide, Gianambrosio Migliavacca, Vienna, Hofburg 10 October 1760.
Le cadi dupé, Pierre René Le Monnier, Vienna, Burgtheater, 9 December 1761.
Arianna (pasticcio), Gianambrosio Migliavacca, Laxenburg, 27 May 1762.
Orfeo ed Euridice, Ranieri Calzabigi, Vienna, Burgtheater, 5 October 1762; revised as *Orphée et Eurydice,* Pierre-Louis Moline (translated and adapted from Calzabigi), Paris, Académie Royale, 2 August 1774.
Il trionfo di Clelia, Metastasio, Bologna, Comunale, 14 May 1763.
La rencontre imprévue, L.H. Dancourt (after Le Sage and d'Orneval, *Les pélerins de la Mecque*), Vienna, Burgtheater, 7 January 1764.
Il Parnaso confuso, Metastasio, Vienna, Schönbrunn, 24 January 1765.
Il Telemaco ossia L'isola di Circe, Marco Coltellini (after Carlo Sigismondo Capece), Vienna, Burgtheater, 30 January 1765.
La corona, Metastasio, for the emperor's name day, 4 October 1765 [not performed].
Il prologo, Lorenzo Ottavio del Rosso, Florence, Teatro della Pergola, 22 February 1767.
Alceste, Ranieri Calzabigi, Vienna, Burgtheater, 26 December 1767; revised, François Louis Grand Lebland du Roullet (translation and revision of Calzabigi), Paris, Académie Royale, 23 April 1776.
Le feste d' Apollo, Carlo Innocenzio Frugoni and Ranieri Calzabigi, Parma, Corte, 24 August 1769.
Paride ed Elena, Ranieri Calzabigi, Vienna, Burgtheater, 3 November 1770.
Iphigénie en Aulide, François Louis Grand Lebland du Roullet (after Racine), Paris, Académie Royale, 19 April 1774.
Armide, Philippe Quinault, Paris, Académie Royale, 23 September 1777.
Iphigénie en Tauride, Nicolas-François Guillard and François Louis Grand Lebland du Roullet (after Euripides), Paris, Académie Royale, 18 May 1779; revised in German, translated by J.B. von Alxinger and Gluck), Vienna, Burgtheater, 23 October 1781.
Écho et Narcisse, L.T. von Tshoudi, Paris, Académie Royale, 24 September 1779.

Christoph Willibald Ritter von Gluck, portrait by Joseph Duplessis, 1775

Other works: ballets, vocal works, symphonies, chamber music.

Publications

By GLUCK: books–

Mueller von Asow, H. and E.H., eds. *The Collected Correspondence and Papers of Christoph Willibald Gluck.* Translated by S. Thomson. London, 1962.

About GLUCK: books–

Ditters von Dittersdorf, C. *Lebensbeschreibung.* Leipzig, 1801; English translation, 1896, 1970; edited by N. Miller, Munich, 1967.

Siegmeyer, J.G. *Über den Ritter Gluck und seine Werke: Briefe von ihm und andern berühmten Männern seiner Zeit.* Berlin, 1837.

Schmid, Anton. *C.W. Ritter von Gluck: dessen Leben und künstlerisches Wirken.* Leipzig, 1854.

Marx, Adolf Bernhard. *Gluck und die Oper.* 2 vols. Berlin, 1863, 1970; in one volume, 1980.

Desnoiresterres, Gustave. *Gluck et Piccinni.* Paris, 1872; 2nd ed. 1875.

Bitter, C.H. *Reform der Oper durch Gluck und Richard Wagner.* Brunswick, 1884.

Newman, Ernest. *Gluck and the Opera.* London, 1895, 1964.

Udine, Jean D'. *Gluck.* Paris, 1906.

Tiersot, Julien F. *Gluck.* Paris, 1910; 4th ed. 1919.

Kurth, Ernst. *Die Jugendopern Glucks.* Vienna, 1913.

Berlioz, Hector. *Gluck and his Operas.* Translated by E. Evans. New York, 1915.

Arend, Max. *Gluck: eine Biographie.* Berlin, 1921.

Haas, Robert. *Gluck und Durazzo im Burgtheater: die Opera comique in Wien.* Zurich, Vienna, and Leipzig, 1925.

Kinsky, Georg. *Glucks Briefe an Franz Kruthoffer.* Vienna, 1929.

La Laurencie, L. de. *Orphée de Gluck: étude et analyse* Paris, 1932.

Cooper, Martin. *Gluck.* London, 1935.

Einstein, Alfred. *Gluck.* London, 1936, 1964.

Tenschert, Roland. *Christoph Willibald Gluck: sein Leben in Bildern.* Leipzig, 1938.

Gerber, Rudolf. *Christoph Willibald Gluck.* Potsdam, 1941, 1950.

Della Corte, Andrea. *Gluck e suoi tempi.* Florence, 1948.

Prod'homme, J.-G. *Gluck.* Paris, 1948.

Mannlich, J.C. von. *Mémoires, 1740-1822.* Paris, 1948.

Tenschert, R. *Christoph Willibald Gluck: der grosse Reformator der Oper.* Olten and Freiburg, 1951.

Albert, A.A. *Gluck.* Munich, 1959.

Howard, Patricia. *Gluck and the Birth of Modern Opera.* London, 1963.

Felix, W. *Christoph Willibald Gluck.* Leipzig, 1965.

Hortschansky, Klaus. *Parodie und Entlehnung im Schaffen Christoph Willibald Glucks.* Cologne, 1973.

Gallarati, P. *Gluck e Mozart.* Turin, 1975.

Degrada, Francesco. *Il palazzo incantato, Studi sulla tradizione del melodramma dal Barocco al Romanticismo.* Fiesole, 1979.

Strohm, Reinhard. *Die italienische Oper im 18. Jahrhundert.* Wilhelmshaven, 1979.

Howard, Patricia. *Christoph Willibald von Gluck: Orfeo.* Cambridge, 1981.

Gallarati, Paolo. *Musica e maschera: Il libretto italiano del settecento.* Turin, 1984.

Gülke, Peter. *Rousseau und die Musik.* Wilhelmshaven, 1984.

Lesure, François. *Querelle des Gluckistes et des Piccinnistes.* 2 vols. Geneva, 1984.

Howard, Patricia. *Gluck: A Guide to Research.* New York, 1987.

Pozzoli, Barbara Eleonora. *Dell' alma amato oggetto: gli affetti nel "Orfeo ed Euridice" di Gluck a Calzabigi.* Milan, 1989.

Brown, Bruce Alan. *Gluck and the French Theatre in Vienna.* Oxford, 1991.

articles–

Rousseau, J.-J. "Extrait d'une résponse du petit faiseur á son prête-nom, sur un morceau de L'*Orphée* de M. le Chevalier Gluck." In *Lettre à M. Burney sur la musique avec fragmens.* Geneva, 1781; reprint in *Oeuvres complètes,* vol. 4, 475, Paris, 1857.

————. "Fragment d'observations sur l'*Alceste* italien de M. le Chevalier Gluck." in *Projet concernant de nouveaux signes pour la musique.* Geneva, 1781; reprint in *Oeuvres complètes,* vol. 4, 463. Paris, 1857.

Reichardt, J.F. "Ueber Gluck und dessen Armide." *Berlinische musikalische Zeitung* 1 (1805): 109; 2 (1806): 57.

Favart, C.S. "Etwas über Glucks Iphigenia in Tauris und dessen Armide." In *Mémoires et correspondance,* edited by A.P.C. Favart and H.F. Dumolard. Paris, 1808.

Fürstenau, M. "Das Festspiel 'Il Parnaso confuso' von Gluck." *Berliner Musikzeitung Echo* 19 (1869): 205.

————. "Die Oper 'Ezio' von Gluck." *Berliner Musikzeitung Echo* 19 (1869): 157, 165, 173.

————. "Über die schluss-Arie des ersten Aktes aus Gluck's französischem Orpheus." *Berliner Musikzeitung Echo* 19 (1869): 261, 269.

————. "Gluck's Orpheus in München 1773." *Monatshefte für Musikgeschichte* 4 (1872): 218.

————. "Le Nozze d'Ercole e d'Ebe von Gluck." *Monatshefte für Musikgeschichte* 5 (1873): 2.

Gugler, B. "Urform einer Nummer in Gluck's 'Orpheus'." *Leipziger allgemeine musikalische Zeitung* 11 (1876): 516.

Welti, H. "Gluck und Calsabigi." *Vierteljahrsschrift für Musikwissenschaft* 7 (1891): 26.

Tiersot, J. "Etude sur Orphée de Gluck." *Le ménestrel* 62 (1896): 273.

————. "L'ultima opera di Gluck 'Eco e Narciso'." *Rivista musicale italiana* 9 (1902): 264.

Kretzschmar, H. "Zum Verständnis Glucks." *Jahrbuch der Musikbibliothek Peters* (1903): 61.

Piovano, F. "Un opéra inconnu de Gluck." *Sammelbände der Internationalen Musik-Gesellschaft* 9 (1907-08): 231, 448.

Abert, H. "Zu Glucks 'Ippolito'." *Gluck-Jahrbuch* 1 (1913): 47.

Englander, R. "Gluck's 'Cinesi' und 'Orfano della China'." *Gluck-Jahrbuch* 1 (1913): 54.

Kurth, E. "Die Jugendopern Glucks bis 'Orfeo'." *Studien zur Musikwissenschaft* 1 (1913): 193.

Tiersot, J. "Les premiers opéras de Gluck." *Gluck-Jahrbuch* 1 (1913): 9.

Keller, O. "Gluck-Bibliographie." *Die Music* 13 (1913-14): 23, 85.

Gluck-Jahrbuch 1-4 [Leipzig] (1913-18); reprint 1969.

Arend, M. "Unbekannte Werke Glucks." *Die Musik* 14 (1914-15): 171.

Abert, H. "Glucks italienische Opern bis zum 'Orfeo'." *Gluck-Jahrbuch* 2 (1915): 1; reprinted in *Gesammelte Schriften,* edited by F. Blume, 287, Halle, 1929.

Arend, M. "Glucks erste Oper. 'Artaxerxes'." *Neue Zeitschrift für Musik* 82 (1915); 201.

Engländer, R. "Zu den Münchener Orfeo-Aufführungen 1773 und 1775." *Gluck-Jahrbuch* 2 (1915): 26.

Squire, W. Barclay. "Gluck's London Operas." *Musical Quarterly* 1 (1915): 397.

Unger, M. "Zur Entstehungsgeschichte des 'Trionfo di Clelia'." *Neue Zeitschrift für Musik* 82 (1915): 269.

Arend, M. "Das vollständige Textbuch zu Glucks 'Tigrane.' *Die Stimme* 10 (1915-16): 130.

Prod'homme, J.-G. "Gluck's French Collaborators." *Musical Quarterly* 3 (1917): 249.

Meyer, R. "Die Behandlung des Rezitativs in Glucks italienischen Reformopern." *Gluck-Jahrbuch* 4 (1918): 1.

Arend, M. "Ein wiedergewonnenes Meisterwerk Glucks [Semiramis]," *Kunstwart* 33 (1920): 278, supplement i-iv.

Vetter, Walther. "Stilkritische Bemerkungen zur Arienmelodik in Glucks 'Orfeo'." *Zeitschrift für Musikwissenschaft* 4 (1921): 27.

_____. "Glucks Entwicklung zum Opernreformator." *Archiv für Musikwissenschaft* 6 (1924): 165; reprinted in *Mythos—Melos—Musica* 2 [Leipzig] (1961): 180.

_____. "Glucks Stellung zur Tragédie lyrique und Opéra-comique." *Zeitschrift für Musikwissenschaft* 7 (1924-25): 321; reprinted in *Mythos—Melos—Musica* 1 [Leipzig] (1957): 309.

_____. "Gluck und seine italienischen Zeitgenossen." *Zeitschrift für Musikwissenschaft* 7 (1924-25): 609; reprinted in *Mythos—Melos—Musica* 2 [Leipzig] (1961): 225.

Brück, P. "Glucks Orpheus." *Archiv für Musikwissenschaft* 7 (1925): 436.

Holzer, L. "Die komischen Opern Glucks." *Studien zur Musikwissenschaft* 13 (1926): 3.

Abert, H. "Mozart and Gluck." *Music and Letters* 10 (1929): 256.

Haas, R. "Zwei Arien aus Glucks 'Poro'." *Mozart Jahrbuch* 3 (1929): 307.

Gastoué, A. "Gossec et Gluck à l'Opéra de Paris: le ballet final d'Iphigénie en Tauride." *Revue de musicologie* 19 (1935): 87.

Loewenberg, Alfred. "Gluck's *Orfeo* on the Stage with some Notes on Other Orpheus Operas." *Musical Quarterly* 26 (1940): 311.

Müller-Blattau. "Gluck and Racine." *Annales Universitatis Saraviensis* 3 (1954): 219.

Weismann, W. "Der Deus ex machina in Glucks 'Iphigenie in Aulis'." *Deutsches Jahrbuch der Musikwissenschaft* 7 (1962): 7.

Finscher, L. "Der verstümmelte Orpheus: über die Urgestalt und die Bearbeitung von Glucks 'Orfeo'." *Neue Zeitschrift für Musik* 124 (1963): 7.

Geiringer, Karl. "Gluck und Haydn." In *Festschrift Otto Erich Deutsch,* 75. Kassel, 1963.

Finscher L. "Che farò senza Euridice? ein Beitrag zur Gluck-Interpretation." In *Festschrift Hans Engel,* 96. Kassel, 1964.

Hortschansky, K. "Gluck und Lampugnani in Italien: zum Pasticcio 'Arsace'." *Analecta musicologica* no. 3 (1966): 9.

Sternfeld, F.W. "Expression and Revision in Gluck's *Orfeo* and *Alceste*." In *Essays Presented to Egon Wellesz,* edited by Jack Westrup, 114. London, 1966.

Hortschansky, K. "Doppelvertonungen in den italienischen Opern Glucks: ein Beitrag zu Glucks Schaffensprozess." *Archiv für Musikwissenschaft* 24 (1967).

Heartz, Daniel. "From Garrick to Gluck: the Reform of Theatre and Opera in the Mid-eighteenth Century." *Proceedings of the Royal Musical Association* 94 (1967-68): 111.

Hortschansky, K. "Glucks Sendungsbewusstsein dargestellt an einem unbekannten Gluck-Brief." *Die Musikforschung* 21 (1968): 30.

Hammelmann, H. and M. Rose. "New Light on Calzabigi and Gluck." *Musical Times* 110 (1969): 604.

Winternitz, E. "A Homage of Piccini to Gluck." In *Studies in Eighteenth-century Music: a Tribute to Karl Geiringer,* 397. New York and London, 1970.

Hortschansky, K. " 'Arianna' (1762), ein Pasticcio von Gluck." *Die Musikforschung* 24 (1971): 407.

Angermüller, R. "Opernreform im Lichte der wirtschaftlichen Verhältnisse an der Académie royale de Musique von 1775 bis 1780." *Die Musikforschung* 25 (1972): 267.

Rushton, Julian. " 'Iphigénie en Tauride': the Operas of Gluck and Piccinni." *Music and Letters* 53 (1972): 411.

Dahlhaus, Carl. "Ethos und Pathos in Glucks Iphigenie auf Tauris." *Die Musikforschung* 28 (1974): 289.

Hortschansky, K. "Unbekanntes aus Glucks 'Poro' (1744)." *Die Musikforschung* 28 (1974): 460.

Howard, Patricia. "Gluck's Two Alcestes." *Musical Times* 115 (1974): 642.

Allroggen, G. "La scena degli Elisi nell' 'Orfeo'." *Chigiana* 29-30 (1975): 369.

Ballola, G.C. " 'Paride ed Elena'." *Chigiana* 29-30 (1975): 465.

Finscher, L. "Gluck e la tradizione dell'opera seria; il problema del lieto fine nei drammi della riforma." *Chigiana* 29-30 (1975): 263.

Fubini, E. "Presupposti estetici e letterari della riforma di Gluck." *Chigiana* 29-30 (1975): 235.

Gallarati, P. "Metastasio e Gluck: per una collocazione storica della 'riforma'." *Chigiana* 29-30 (1975): 299.

Heartz, Daniel. " 'Orfeo ed Euridice': some Criticisms, Revisions, and Stage-realizations during Gluck's Lifetime." *Chigiana* 29-30 (1975): 383.

Joly, J. "Deux fêtes théâtrales de Métastase: 'Le cinesi' et 'L'isola disabitata'." *Chigiana* 29-30 (1975): 15.

Rushton, Julian. "From Vienna to Paris: Gluck and the French Opera." *Chigiana* 29-30 (1975): 283.

Sternfeld, F.W. "Gluck's Operas and Italian Tradition." *Chigiana* 29-30 (1975): 275.

Stoll, A. and K. "Affect und Moral:zu Glucks Iphigenie auf Tauris." *Die Musikforschung* 28 (1975): 305.

Kaplan, James Maurice. "Eine Ergänzung zu Glucks Korrespondenz." *Dei Musikforschung* 31 (1978): 314.

Croll, Gerhard. "Giacomo Durazzo a Vienna: la vita musicale e la politica (1754-1764)." *Atti della Soc. Figure di Storia Patria* [new series] 20 (1979): 71.

Paduano, Guido. "La 'costanza' di Orfeo. Sul lieto fine dell' *Orfeo* di Gluck." *Rivista italiana di musicologia* 14 (1979): 349.

Churgin, Bathia. "Alterations in Gluck's borrowings from Sammartini." *Studi musicali* 9 (1980): 117.

Robinson, Michael F. "The Ancient and the Modern: A Comparison of Metastasio and Calzabigi." *Studies in Music* [Canada] 7 (1982): 137.

Brown, Bruce Alan. "Gluck's *Rencontre imprévue* and its Revisions." *Journal of the American Musicological Society* 36 (1983): 498.

Hartung, Günther. "Die Iphigenien—Thematik in Musik und Dichtung des 18. Jahrhunderts." In *Thematik und*

Ideenwelt der Antike bei Georg Friedrich Händel, edited by Walther Siegmund-Schultze, 100. Halle, 1983.

Candiani, Rosy, "L'*Alceste* da Vienna a Milano." *Giornale storico della letteratura italiana* 159 (1984): 227.

Croll, Gerhard. "Anmerkungen zu 'Gluck in Wien'." In *Musik am Hof Maria Theresias. In Memoriam Vera Schwarz,* edited by R.V. Karpf, *Beitrage für Aufführungspraxis* 6, p. 51. Munich and Salzburg, 1984.

Heartz, Daniel. "Haydn und Gluck im Burgtheater an 1760." In *Gesellschaft für Musikforschung, Report, Bayreuth 1981,* ed. Cristoph-Hellmut Mahling and Sigrid Wiesmann, 120. Kassel, 1984.

* * *

Gluck is certain of a place in any history of music. The nature of his achievements ensures that no account of opera in the eighteenth century can ignore his unique contribution: after Gluck, opera was a changed artform.

Gluck's response to his environment was influenced by a climate of thought affecting the whole of eighteenth century Europe. Gluck translated the Enlightenment into music. He addressed many interests of that movement in the course of his life: neo-classicism was integral to his concept of opera, sensibility informed his redefinition of the aria, and the imitation of nature was the goal of each of his reforms, which also tended deliberately and explicitly towards a new internationalism in music, eliminating "the ridiculous distinctions" between national styles, to create "music belonging to all nations" (letter, 1 February 1773).

Gluck is always identified as a reformer, though his reputation credits him with more initiative than the facts substantiate. His apparent satisfaction with traditional forms of opera for the first 48 years of his life does nothing to strengthen his revisionist image. It might be truer to say that he attracted reforming spirits to him, by his readiness to follow where they led. Yet other composers had the same opportunities to collaborate with the reformers, and only Gluck took up the challenge. His association with the choreographer Angiolini led to radical changes in the ballet: *Don Juan* showed how natural gesture and acting could replace a more abstract, geometric approach to dance. Friendship with the poet Klopstock led him to devise a new declamatory style for the German language: his settings of eight of Klopstock's *Odes* played a part in the birth of the German art-song, the Lied. Prompted by the theater director Giacomo Durazzo, he discovered he had a genius for comedy: some ten French comic operas resulted. He is associated with two distinct reforms of serious opera, and in both cases the impetus came from a librettist. In Vienna, Ranieri Calzabigi must take the credit (and he did) for much that was new in the three operas, *Orfeo, Alceste* and *Paride ed Elena,* through which Gluck breathed new life into the old *opera seria*. And in Paris, François Louis Grand Lebland du Roullet, the librettist of *Iphigénie en Aulide,* was responsible for strengthening the tired conventions of French opera by blending the lyrical skills Gluck learned in Italy and Austria with the native tradition, although the finest fruits of this reform were not seen until *Iphigénie en Tauride,* a collaboration with yet another librettist, Guillard.

There is a unity of concept in all these developments which can only be explained by attributing a crucial, if selfless, role to Gluck. In each genre that he renewed, everything was to be subordinated to "simplicity, truth and nature" (*Alceste*

preface). For opera this meant the smoothly flowing presentation of the drama, with as much continuity between the disparate elements as an eighteenth century musician could conceive. The overture, earlier regarded as a detachable extra, at best an irrelevance to the opera which was to follow, at worst, disconcertingly inappropriate in mood, became incorporated into the drama. Gluck required the overture to "apprise the spectators of the nature of the action which is to be represented," to form a psychological or pictorial preparation, continuous with the first scene, as in *Iphigénie en Aulide,* where the overture begins with a taut Andante of searing suspensions whose meaning is revealed when it returns at the beginning of the first scene to accompany a recitative in which the suspensions seem to crush Agamemnon between the millstones of kingship and conscience. Gluck's reform of the overture was one of his most widely influential acts: few composers of serious operas ignored his lead. Beethoven's struggle through four versions to find the right prelude to *Fidelio* shows the same concerns, and his overtures to *Coriolan* and *Egmont* are links in a chain which led directly from Gluck to the symphonic poem.

In the interest of continuity, Gluck also sought to diminish the differences between aria and recitative. He often substituted a strophic or through-composed air for the prevalent da capo aria form (there are no da capo arias in *Orfeo*). Nevertheless, Gluck understood singers: his anxiety to tame the worst excesses of the virtuosi, ever eager to "display the agility of a fine voice," did not hinder his telling use of vocal registers to enhance dramatic expression. Just when, in *Alceste,* it is most difficult and most necessary for the audience to believe in Admetus's capacity for feeling, Gluck wrote one of his finest arias, "Nò crudel, non posso vivere," capturing almost by pitch changes alone both the king's passion and his enforced passivity in the face of his wife's sacrifice. Gluck is rarely given credit for his mastery of lyrical styles, but he possessed a wide melodic range, from the opulent "O malheureuse Iphigénie" (*Iphigénie en Tauride*) to the intimate, lied-like "Chiamo il mio ben così" (*Orfeo*). Recitative in the reform operas is accompanied by the orchestra, and often flowers into an expressive arioso which can hardly be distinguished from the short airs. "Che puro ciel" (*Orfeo*) shows how musically substantial a medium Gluck made the *accompagnato,* while Iphigenia's dream-narration, "Cette nuit j'ai revu le palais de mon père," (*Tauride*) demonstrates the expressive force of his style.

The orchestra plays an increasingly important role throughout the reform operas. Some of Gluck's moments of greatest tension are created with a few bars of instrumental music, dropped into an air or ensemble. These passages create an opportunity for the protagonists to act—always a priority with Gluck—but they also obviate the need for gesture, by matching heightened emotions with graphically expressive music. Such an instance is created in the trio "Je pourrais du Tyran" in *Tauride,* where the priestess's indecision (as she hesitates between two captives, which one is to live and which to die) is marvellously painted in two brief orchestral interpolations. The celebrated portrayal of Orestes haunted by the Furies, in the same opera, is only one among many telling uses of the orchestra to reveal to the audience truths of which the character on stage is ignorant. A further remarkable example is the oracle scene in *Alceste,* which so impressed the eleven-year-old Mozart, watching the first production, that the haunting trombone chords reappear in the ghostly Commendatore's music in *Don Giovanni.*

The lavish choral writing in Gluck's first reform opera came about by accident. *Orfeo* is not an *opera seria* but a *festa teatrale,* a court entertainment in which the chorus traditionally played a substantial role. Seeing the impact of the choruses of mourning shepherds, dancing furies and blessed spirits in this work, Gluck decided to enhance the chorus role in his serious operas, and so in *Alceste* the chorus becomes almost the most important character—the people for whom the king must live, and for whom the queen must die. When Gluck revised this opera for Paris, he augmented their role further. Persuading his librettist to add more choruses to the last act, Gluck urged Du Roullet, "The piece cannot finish before these poor people have been consoled" (letter, 2 December 1775). Gluck's choruses are never passive bystanders. All are strongly characterized—frightened Thessalonians in *Alceste,* angry Greeks in *Aulide*—and often contrasted: Phrygians and Spartans in *Paride,* priestesses and barbarians in *Tauride.* Gluck required his chorus, like all his cast, to act. Although the chorus had always played a substantial role in French opera, Gluck found his Parisian choir expecting to stand motionless at each side of the stage, men with folded arms, the women carrying fans. Teaching these singers to act was by no means the least of his opera reforms.

Shortly after his death, Gluck was identified as one who "belonged to no school and who founded no tradition" (*Allgemeine musikalische Zeitung,* 1804). His strong individual personality isolated him from his contemporaries, and though many of his achievements were imitated by his immediate successors, Mozart, Spontini, and Cherubini, his influence was perhaps even stronger on his more distant heirs, Berlioz and Wagner. Gluck was accused by a contemporary, perhaps accurately, of devising his unique style in order to hide shortcomings in his technique. His harmonic and melodic vocabulary was limited by the times in which he lived. He is one of the "lost generation" of composers (C.P.E. Bach and Jommelli share the year of his birth, and Pergolesi, Wagenseil and Stamitz were close contemporaries) who seem never quite to have achieved their full potential as a result of living through the great stylistic upheaval of the middle decades of the century. Gluck rose above this limitation by harmonizing his talents and his aims. In an age dedicated to dismantling the complexities of the late baroque, Gluck advocated simplicity and produced his best work with direct melodies and spare textures: "Che farò" was for many years the only song from early opera to capture the public's hearts, while his ravishing flute solo, "Dance of the Blessed Spirits" has never been out of favor.

—Patricia Howard

DIE GLÜCKLICHE HAND [The Lucky Hand].

Composer: Arnold Schoenberg.

Librettist: Arnold Schoenberg.

First Performance: Vienna, Volksoper, 14 October 1924.

Roles: A Man (baritone); A Woman (mute); A Gentleman (mute); Six Women (three sopranos, three contraltos); Six Men (three tenors, three basses).

Publications

articles–

Wörner, K.H. "Die glückliche Hand, Arnold Schönbergs Drama mit Musik." *Schweizerische Musikzeitung/Revue musicale suisse* 204 (1964): 274.

Crawford, J. "Die glückliche Hand: Schoenberg's Gesamtkunstwerk." *Musical Quarterly* 60 (1974): 583.

Beck, Richard Thomas. "The Sources and Significance of *Die glückliche Hand.*" In *Bericht über den Internationalen Musikwissenschaftlichen Kongress Berlin 1974,* edited by Helmut Kühn and Peter Nitsche, 427. Kassel, 1980.

Crawford, J. "*Die glückliche Hand:* Further Notes." *Journal of the Arnold Schoenberg Institute* 4 (1980): 68.

Steiner, E. "The 'Happy' Hand: Genesis and Interpretation of Schoenberg's Monumentalkunstwerk." *Music Review* 41 (1980): 207.

Mauser, Siegfried. "Die musikdramatische Konzeption in *Herzong Blaubarts Burg*" [compares Bartok's *Bluebeard's Castle* to Schoenberg's *Die glückliche Hand*]. *Musik-Konzepte* 22 (1981): 169.

unpublished–

Mauser, Siegfried. "Das expressionistische Musiktheater der Wiener Schule. Stilistische und entwicklunggeschichtliche Untersuchungen zu Arnold Schönbergs *Erwartung* op. 17, *Die glückliche Hand* op. 18 und Alban Bergs *Wozzeck* op. 7." Ph.D. dissertation, University of Salzburg, 1981.

Auner, Joseph. "Schoenberg's Compositional and Aesthetic Transformations 1910-1913: the Genesis of *Die Glückliche Hand.*" Ph.D. dissertation, University of Chicago, 1991.

* * *

Composed between 1910 and 1913 to a text and scenario of his own making, *Die glückliche Hand,* Schoenberg's "drama with music" (as he subtitled it), portrays the artist as one who is both blessed with the fortune of creativity and cursed with its martyrdom. This vision has unmistakable autobiographical undertones, given the composer's increasingly isolated and difficult personal situation at the time, coupled with an elevated sense of his own artistic mission.

The work is compressed and intensely symbolic. Cast in four short scenes, it opens and closes in the style of Greek tragedy: two six-part choruses chastise the protagonist, an anonymous Man, for seeking earthly rather than spiritual happiness. In scene ii the Man's artistic potency, his "lucky hand" of the title, is given to him by a Woman proffering a cup of love; consequently he is able, in the workshop scene that follows, to create a beautiful diadem, to the outrage of the artisans whom, as a true artist, he so clearly excels. The jewel, however, is counterfeit for true, spiritual beauty, and the Woman deserts him for a Gentleman. In the final scene she returns to crush him with a boulder. The Man has been betrayed by his own all-too-human desires and actions.

Schoenberg's scoring for large orchestra is marked by an extraordinary range of sonorities which, though certainly novel, also show Mahler's feeling for soloistic and small-ensemble differentiation. Vocal resources for the choruses are stretched to include "Sprechstimme" and whispering, while the Man's part is limited to brief exclamations. Other parts are silent, expressing themselves through pantomime. Detailed directions are given throughout the score for the coordination of stage action, gesture, lighting and color effects, which together with the sounds themselves are all important to the work's symbolism. The third scene's "wind-light-tone" crescendo, accompanying the making of the jewel and the mounting exaltation of its creator, is quite unique in all opera. Historically the conception of the work as a whole, of which that crescendo is a climax, derives from the correlation of lighting effects with expression in turn-of-the-century stagings of Wagner (particularly those in Vienna of Alfred Roller), but can also be linked to the color theories of the painter Wassily Kandinksy, with whom Schoenberg was in close contact during the work's composition, and, not least, to the composer's own activity at the time as a painter.

In its integration of word, visual image, and tone for the purpose of representing a personal yet spiritual worldview, *Die glückliche Hand* is perhaps the most significant musical manifestation of early twentieth-century Expressionism. Yet it also bears the legacy of Wagner, one that goes beyond the obvious borrowing of such symbols as the love potion of *Tristan* as well as Siegfried's forging of the sword (now the jewel). Schoenberg threads through his intricate orchestral web a number of leitmotifs which are to be associated with each of the characters and dramatic situations. These elements, consisting mostly of small intervallic cells or even just single chords and sonorities, are however rarely emphasized or subjected to straightforward repetition. The work is essentially atonal, requiring that motivic elements be submerged in a constantly varied and renewed texture; their effect, therefore, is mostly subliminal. The dramatic force of the work hinges on the abundance of mainly mimed gestures on stage, supported by explicitly (perhaps even naively) descriptive music. The melodramatic nature of the whole is not inconsistent with the tendencies of Expressionist drama and theatre.

One might well ask whether an opera with such essentially philosophical content is suitable for the stage. On the other hand, Schoenberg's intent, as he himself once explained, was to reduce everything to "the play of color and forms," and hence to translate that content into pure art. With that in mind, the composer became interested in a proposal to recast the work as a film, this medium being even better suited than the stage (so he believed) at portraying what he described as the "unreality" of the opera. Nothing came of the idea, and indeed the work has only rarely been performed since its premiere in Vienna in 1924. It is perhaps too personal and idiosyncratic a creation to win broad acceptance, but it can be appreciated in its proper context: as a landmark of the period preceding the First World War that saw the arts attempting to join forces in a common quest for spiritual regeneration.

—Alan Lessem

GOBBI, Tito.

Baritone. Born 24 October 1913, in Bassano del Grappa, Italy. Died 5 March 1984, in Rome. Studied law at Padua University, then studied singing with Giulio Crimi in Rome; debut as Rodolfo in *La sonnambula*, Gubbio, 1935; appeared as Germont in *La traviata* at the Teatro Adriano in Rome, 1937; debut at Teatro alla Scala as Belcore in *L'elisir d'amore*, 1942; American debut in San Francisco, 1948; appeared frequently in Chicago, 1954-73; Covent Garden debut, 1955; debut at Metropolitan Opera as Scarpia, 1956; guest in most leading opera houses; also appeared in films, especially early in his career.

Publications

By GOBBI: books–

Tito Gobbi: My Life. London, 1979.
Tito Gobbi on His World of Italian Opera. New York, 1984.

About GOBBI: books–

Schiavo, R. *Costumi per un museo: Tito Gobbi e la sua città.* Bassano, 1980.

articles–

De Paoli, D. "Tito Gobbi." *Opera* October (1955).
Lauri-Volpi, G. "Un grande artista, un amico reale." *Musica e dischi* 24 (1968): 49.
Freeman, J.W. "Tito Gobbi Talks." *Opera News* 36/no. 19 (1972): 14.
Blyth, A. "Gobbi: the Singer and the Man." In *British Music Yearbook 1975.*
Rosenthal, H. et al. "Tito Gobbi." *Opera* May (1984).

*   *   *

Even in the decade after his death, Tito Gobbi remains by common consent the great Italian singing actor of our age—in many ways the successor to such singers as Scotti, De Luca, and Stabile. Gobbi, though, was not merely the brilliant student of past traditions, but an authentic creator in a large

Tito Gobbi as Macbeth

number of styles, from Monteverdi to Alban Berg. To consider for a moment only the fringes of his repertory, Gobbi's *Wozzeck* (in Italian) was a creation of astonishing bitterness, his controversial *Don Giovanni* was a figure of alienating misanthropy, and his recording of Orfeo's "Rosa del ciel," though it might contradict current ideas of seventeenth-century singing practice, showed a fearless conviction that indeed qualified the character for myth.

Gobbi's creative method combined the motivational scrutiny of Stanislavsky with the inventive sweep of the great actors of the previous century—the century in which most of the baritone's major roles were created. In addition to intuition and intelligence, he brought to opera a superbly responsive presence, as quick in *Barbiere* as it was grand in *Simon Boccanegra;* a handsome and expressive face; a painstaking genius in makeup; and a vocal technique which preserved his very individual sound over a long career and yet allowed him maximum capacity for emotional coloring. His Figaro and Rigoletto, filmed in the 1940s, reflect all of this. The other singers (Tagliavini and Sinimberghi among them) are dramatically earnest and a little embarrassing, however well they may sing. Gobbi is dazzlingly quick, attractive, and amused in the Rossini, and at once theatrically extravagant and deeply touching in a quite modern sense in the Verdi. He revives some of the grand dramatic rituals of Verdi's time with exhilarating conviction; there is a legato of gesture and style in his performance (he writes of this element in his autobiography), a sense of histrionic proportion that leads us, if we will allow it, to the values of the theatre for which Verdi composed. Such a style contradicts most of the commonplaces about film acting, but it presents to us some truths about the profundity of the Italian operatic genre at its worthiest.

Gobbi began on the operatic stage in the late 1930s and made his last recordings (including a fine *Gianni Schicchi*) in 1977. His earliest records show a lyric tone of amazing beauty and vitality, a remarkable legato style, and already a masterly dramatic command. For intimate nobility, his 1942 recording of Roderigo's farewell and death (*Don Carlo*) is equalled only by his own later performance (1955) in the complete set. His 1950 Credo (*Otello*) has a dead vitality of tone astonishingly apt for the music, and his "Era la notte" of 1948 is, as seldom in other performances, ravishingly insinuating. Throughout his career the voice remained uniquely expressive and steady, though the top was sometimes dry. Despite a basic sound that was not always ideally roomy in the big Verdi roles for which his theatrical genius and musicianship fitted him so beautifully, his Rigoletto, Simon Boccanegra, Nabucco, and Scarpia, to name only a few, are still among the definitive interpretations on records, and have been analyzed as such by many critics.

A fascinating instance of Gobbi's ability to immortalize even a minor moment is his less famous performance of the smitten stage manager Michonnet's ecstatic description of the actress Adriana Lecouvreur's opening scene in Racine's *Bajazet*. As he watches her from the wings, Michonnet expresses his hidden feelings quite unaware that he is in fact speaking aloud. The intimacy, the jealousy, the hesitancy, the forthrightness, the musing frustration are all there in Gobbi's remarkably subtle realization of Cilea's touching passage. It is as if Gobbi (and this is quite possible) took as guidelines for his own work Michonnet's reverent words about Adriana's performance: "What charm! What tone! What simplicity! How profound and yet how human!" And finally, as he says, "The truth itself!"

—London Green

GOEHR, Alexander.

Composer. Born 10 August 1932, in Berlin. Studied with Richard Hall at the Royal Manchester College of Music, 1952-53; studied with Messiaen at the Paris Conservatory, 1955-57, produced BBC orchestra concerts, 1960-67; composer-in-residence at the New England Conservatory, 1968-69; visiting professor, Yale University, 1969-70; West Riding Professor of Music, Leeds University, 1972-76; artistic director of the Leeds Festival, 1975; professor of music, Cambridge University, since 1976; visiting professor, Peking Conservatory, 1980.

Operas/Theater Works

Publisher: Schott (London).

Arden Must Die, E. Fried (after 16th century *Arden of Faversham*), 1966, Hamburg, 1967.
Naboth's Vineyard (dramatic madrigal), after I Kings xxi, 1968, London, 1968.
Shadowplay, K. Cavander (after Plato, *Republic*), 1970, London, 1970.
Sonata about Jerusalem, Goehr and R. Freir (after Obadiah the Proselyte, *Autobiography,* and Samuel ben Yahya ben al Maghviti, *Chronicle*), 1970, Jerusalem, 1971.
Behold the Sun, 1987.

Other works: ballets, orchestral works, vocal works, chamber music, piano music.

Publications

By GOEHR: books–

Musical Ideas and Ideas About Music. Birbeck College Foundation Orations. London, 1978.

articles–

"Poetics of my Music." *University of Leeds Review* 116 (1973): 170.
"The Study of Music at University." *Musical Times* 114 (1973): 588.
"The Theoretical Writings of Arnold Schoenberg." *Proceedings of the Royal Musical Association* 100 (1973-74): 85.
Review of Monteverdi, Claudio, *The Letters of Claudio Monteverdi,* introduced and translated by Denis Stevens. *Tempo* 136 (1981): 32.
"Schoenberg and Krauss: the Idea behind the Music." *Music Analysis* 4/nos. 1-2 (1985): 59.
"Working on *Die Wiedertäufer*" [conversation with Bayan Northcott]. *Opera* April (1985).
"Goehr: Reith Lectures 1987." *Listener* 118 (1987): 3038.
"Music as Communication." In. D.H. Mellor, *Ways of Communicating.* Cambridge, 1990.

About GOEHR: books–

Northcott, Bayan, ed. *The Music of Alexander Goehr: Interviews and Articles.* London, 1980; Mainz, 1981.

articles–

Wood, H. "The Music of Alexander Goehr." *Musical Times* 103 (1962): 312.
Schafer, M. "Alexander Goehr." In *British Composers in Inverview.* London, 1963.

Drew, D. "Why Must Arden Die?" *The Listener* 78 (1967): 412, 445.

Fried, Erich. "Mein Libretto für Goehr." Melos 34/no. 4 (1967): 110.

Northcott, Bayan, "Goehr the Progressive." *Music and Musicians* 18 (1969): 36.

———. "Alexander Goehr's Triptych" [*Naboth's Vineyard, Shadowplay, Sonata about Jerusalem*]. *The Listener* 86 (1971): 739.

Harrán, Don. "Report from Israel: Testimonium II." *Current Musicology* 15 (1973): 38.

———. "... most wickedlye murdered ..." [*Arden Must Die*]. *Music and Musicians* 22 (1974): 26.

Protheroe, G. "Alexander Goehr." In *British Music Now*, edited by L. Foreman, 41. London, 1975.

Northcott, Bayan. "Alexander Goehr: the Recent Music." *Tempo* 124 (1978): 10; 125 (1978): 12.

Schiffer, Brigitte. "Die Folgen der Kulturrevolution. Interview mit Alexander Goehr über seine Lehrtätigkeit in China." *Neue Zeitschrift für Musik* 142 (1981): 155.

Williams, Nicholas. "Hope That Is Seen: Goehr's *Behold the Sun*." *Musical Times* October (1987).

———. "Behold the Sun: the Politics of Music Production." In C. Norris, *Music and the Politics of Culture*, 150. Lawrence and Wishart, 1989.

*   *   *

Alexander Goehr's musical roots lie firmly grounded in the fertile soil of Judeo-Germanic modernist culture. His father, the conductor Walter Goehr, had studied composition with Schoenberg at his Berlin masterclass, whilst his mother, a pianist of some talent, had trained with Scharwenka and Leonid Kreutzer at the Berlin Hochschule. The family moved to Britain as refugees in 1933 when Goehr was about four months old, and the English language became his vernacular.

A conventional British middle-class education at Berkhamsted School could have led Goehr to classical scholarship at Oxford University where he had won a place, had it not been for his fortuitous discovery of the unexpected musical opportunities offered by Manchester, a Northern, provincial, industrial town. Goehr's conscientious objections meant that his National Service was to be spent working as an agricultural laborer and in mental hospitals, duties which took him to Manchester, and thus to encounter the Royal Manchester College of Music.

His good fortune was to find there, in Richard Hall, a teacher who could perceive his potential as a composer, and, in a group of contemporary students including Peter Maxwell Davies, Harrison Birtwistle, John Ogden and Elgar Howarth, an enthusiasm for and a seriousness about both the technical discipline and expressive means of the new musical language. Under Hall's guidance, he mastered classical Schoenbergian serialism, explored Indian and Oriental music, and assimilated medieval techniques such as isorhythm, whilst discovering the new music of the Darmstadt school of composers. These diverse early influences and his later period of study with Messiaen in his Paris Conservatory classes formed the mould for Goehr's development as a composer.

While some of his early music had dramatic origins (for example the 1961 Leeds Festival commissioned cantata *Sutter's Gold*, with text after Eisenstein), *Arden muss Sterben* (*Arden Must Die*), opus 21, presents his first foray into the field of opera, and demonstrates his growing maturity as a composer. *Arden*'s theme is serious, and in Goehr's terms

political, in that it deals with the way people behave towards each other.

The emotional detachment which marks *Arden* is maintained in the three music theater pieces written between 1968 and 1970; *Naboth's Vineyard, Shadowplay* and *Sonata about Jerusalem*. These three works scored for a few soloists and a small ensemble are by no means miniature operas, being almost anti-dramatic in effect, at least in the western sense. One is reminded both of the Church operas of Benjamin Britten (and surely Britten's influence on Goehr can already be heard in the ferryman scene of *Arden*), and of the Japanese No theater.

Naboth's Vineyard has as its theme the biblical story of the stoning to death of Achab (Kings I, 21), because of his unwillingness to sell Naboth his land. The twist lies at the end of the work, for Achab prostrates himself before God, and is forgiven just as the hypocritical Mrs. Bradshaw is in *Arden*. The musical language is less wide ranging than the opera and has a certain hieratic quality partly generated by the use of Latin for the direct speech of the protagonists; only when the three soloists act as a chorus is the audience addressed in the vernacular, setting the scene, but drawing no conclusions. In Elijah's aria of condemnation we find Goehr utilising a kind of aleatoric technique, not for radical effect, but to stand as a dramatic statement in stark relief to the measured rhythms of the rest of the work, and as a practical gesture to simplify the notation of complex rhythmic events.

For *Shadowplay*, whose text is drawn from Plato's *Republic* (Book 7), Socrates' analogy of the mind's ascent to enlightenment, and the difficulty of discriminating illusion and reality, Goehr produces a musical structure that mirrors the bridge-like shape of the libretto. As in *Naboth's Vineyard*, the use of controlled aleatoricism contributes to the musico-dramatic effect, especially in the central intermezzo in which the Prisoner emerges from the dark cave peopled by shadows to the real corporeal and natural world.

Sonata about Jerusalem, the final work of the trilogy, pursues a theme that has had a continuing influence on Goehr's musical output, that of false prophecy. Commissioned by Testimonium, Jerusalem, it uses texts adapted from the autobiography of Obadiah the Proselyte and the twelfth century chronicle of Samuel ben Yahya ben al Maghribi. It concerns the persecuted Jewish community of twelfth century Baghdad, who were persuaded by a demented boy that the Messiah was about to appear to free them from their oppression and bring them to Jerusalem. Although the Jews of Baghdad were regarded as the wisest in the world, they believed the crazed youth and went to the roofs of their houses to await the miracle with prayer and rejoicing. Their joy dissolved in the morning with the dawning of the truth, and humiliated they descended to the mockery of their neighbors.

The melodic and harmonic language of the music from the middle sixties to early seventies was governed by the technique of modal serialism whose method was described by Goehr in his inaugural lecture as professor of music at Leeds University in October 1972. In his address (called "Poetics of my Music") he makes clear his own interest in the material of music and the primacy of the idea. "The problems of language, meaning and form must remain central to the composer and he has to constantly set himself against the history of his own art." It is interesting to note that Goehr's technical apparatus was to be radically transformed soon after taking up this academic post, and a method of composition emerged which derived much more clearly from diatonic modality, a language whose hieratic severity is presaged by the refrain from *Sonata about Jerusalem*.

Goehr's most recent opera *Behold the Sun*, which took some ten years from conception to performance, presents a further development of ideas which run throughout his oeuvre: the conflict between individuals and their social environment and the discontinuity between reality and our perception of it. In this as in all his dramatic work we find an artist who pursues themes of universal relevance with a seriousness, intelligence and restrained passion.

—David Cooper

THE GOLDEN APPLE
See IL POMO D'ORO

THE GOLDEN COCKEREL [Zolotoy petushok].

Composer: Nicolai Rimsky-Korsakov.

Librettist: V.I. Bel'sky (after Pushkin).

First Performance: Moscow, Solodovnikov, 7 October 1909.

Roles: King Dodon (bass); Prince Guidon (tenor); Prince Aphron (baritone); General Polkan (bass); Astrologer (tenor); Princess Shemakha (soprano); Golden Cockerel (soprano); chorus (SATB).

* * *

The Golden Cockerel was Rimsky-Korsakov's last completed opera. Not performed in his lifetime, it was never given on the Russian Imperial stage, and there is no doubt that the work was conceived as a satire on the Russian autocracy and the bumbling incompetence of its generals.

Act I is set in the luxurious palace of the elderly King Dodon, where the king and his two sons, Guidon and Aphron, are in council with his ministers to find an answer to the invasions that constantly threaten them. Guidon suggests that they withdraw the army and place it around the capital and there retire with ample provisions until they can catch the enemy unawares. All approve the idea except General Polkan (the stage direction reads: "speaks always as if he were swearing"), who finds it useless advice. Dodon next calls upon Prince Aphron, who ridicules his brother and suggests that the army be dismissed and then reassembled a month later to attack the enemy. Dodon and the noblemen are delighted, but Polkan again points out the dangers. Dodon is furious and there is widespread disagreement. Suddenly the old astrologer appears, magnificently attired, saying that he has brought a gift—a golden cockerel that will announce both when all is well and when there is impending danger. The king is delighted and asks how he can be rewarded. The astrologer says that he requires no immediate reward but would like the king's written promise that he will reward him when requested. But Dodon is indignant: his word is sufficient! The astrologer departs and the king is relieved.

The king lies down, talks to his parrot, and, to the sound of the slumber motive (which is connected with the cockerel's

theme that all is well), falls asleep. The Princess Shemakha's theme appears, suggesting the king's thoughts. Suddenly the cockerel's warning motif is heard. The people in front of the palace are frightened. The king is roused with difficulty, and an army under his two sons is dispatched to the sounds of a military march. The cockerel crows that all is well, and the king goes back to bed and tries to remember his dream. The cockerel's warning cry sounds again, and the people are terrified. Polkan says that since the king himself is now threatened, he must go in person, and even though Dodon complains that his armor is rather tight and his shield rusty, he sets out on the campaign to popular acclaim.

Act II opens on a dark night with a blood-red moon. In a narrow gorge lie the bodies of Dodon's defeated forces, including the corpses of his two sons. The army is frightened at the sight and Dodon passionately laments the death of Guidon and Aphron. The mist lifts to reveal an oriental pavilion. Polkan wonders if it belongs to the enemy's chief and decides to fire at it. To everyone's astonishment, from out of the tent steps a beautiful princess, with four slaves carrying musical instruments, at which point she sings the well-known "Hymn to the Sun." Dodon and Polkan are now the only ones left, since the rest of the army has fled. On questioning her, they learn that she is the Princess Shemakha and she offers them refreshment. Polkan distrusts the princess. Irritated by Polkan's blunt comments, she asks Dodon to dismiss him. The princess vividly describes her personal attributes to him, to which the king responds enthusiastically. Completely besotted, he asks the princess to marry him. She agrees, provided that Polkan be dealt with. The king offers to have him beheaded. Flanked by the army, the bizarre wedding procession sets off for the capital.

Act III opens in the capital, where the crowd is waiting for the forces' return. The procession arrives, at the climax of which the king and the queen appear in a golden carriage. But at that moment the astrologer enters and states that he has come to claim his reward: he desires the princess! Dodon refuses angrily and tries to persuade him to accept something else. But the astrologer insists, and Dodon strikes him dead with his sceptre. The queen laughs; when Dodon tries to kiss her, she repels him. Now the cockerel appears and pecks the king, who falls down lifeless. The sky goes completely black; only thunder and the princess' laughter are heard. When light returns, the princess and the cockerel have disappeared. The crowd sings a sad lament to the prophetic words: "What will life be without a Tsar?"

The Golden Cockerel was the culmination of Rimsky-Korsakov's work as an opera composer. Full of ingenious sonorities, chromatic harmonies, exotic melismata and sparkling orchestration, the score skillfully underlines the witty brilliance of Pushkin's verses. Outstanding numbers include the celebrated "Hymn to the Sun," the king's lament for his fallen sons, and the great folk chorus at the end of act III. The splendid orchestral passages are well-known from the orchestral suite.

—Gerald Seaman

GOLDMARK, Karl.

Born 18 May 1830, in Keszthely, Hungary. Died 2 Jnauary 1915, in Vienna. Studied at the Musical Society of Sopron, 1842-44; studied violin with L. Jansa in Vienna, 1844-45;

The Golden Cockerel, **set design by Natalia Goncharova, 1914**

studied harmony with Preyer and violin with Böhm at the Vienna Conservatory.

Operas

Die Königin von Saba, Salomon Hermann Mosenthal, Vienna, Opera, 10 March 1875.
Merlin. Siegfried Lipiner, Vienna, Opera, 19 November 1886; revised 1904.
Das Heimchen am Herd, Alfred Maria Willner (after Dickens, *The Cricket on the Hearth*), Vienna, Opera, 21 March 1896.
Die Kriegsgefangene [originally *Briseïs*], E. Schlicht [A. Formey], Vienna, Opera, 17 January 1899.
Götz von Berlichingen, Alfred Maria Willner (after Goethe), Budapest, 16 December 1902; revised Frankfurt am Main, 1903, and Vienna, 1910.
Ein Wintermärchen, Alfred Maria Willner (after Shakespeare, *Winter's Tale*), Vienna, Opera, 2 January 1908.

Publications

By GOLDMARK: books–

Erinnerungen aus meinem Leben. Vienna, 1922; 2nd ed., 1929; English translation by Alice Goldmark Brandeis as *Notes from the Life of a Viennese Composer,* New York, 1927.

About GOLDMARK: books–

Hanslick, E. *Die moderne Oper.* Berlin, 1875-1900.
Keller, O. *Carl Goldmark.* Leipzig, n.d.
Batka, R. *Aus der Opernwelt.* 107ff, 185f. Munich, 1907.
Niemann, W. *Die Musik seit Wagner.* 70f, 107, 238, Berlin, 1913.
Korngold, J. *Deutsches Opernschaffen der Gegenwart.* 224ff. Leipzig and Vienna, 1921.
Kapp, J. *Die Oper der Gegenwart.* 19ff. Berlin, 1922.
Schwarz, Hermina. *Ignaz Brüll und sein Freundeskreis: Erinnerungen an Brüll, Goldmark und Brahms.* Vienna, 1922.
Kálmán, E. *Károly Goldmark.* Budapest, 1930.
Klempá, J. *Károly Goldmark.* Budapest, 1930.
Koch, L., ed. *Karl Goldmark, 1830-1930; 18. Mai.* Budapest, 1930.
Káldor, M., and P. Várnai. *Goldmark Károly élete és müvészete* [Karl Goldmark: life and music]. Budapest, 1956.
Helm, T. *Fünfzig Jahre Wiener Musikleben (1866-1916),* edited by M. Schönherr. Vienna, 1977.

articles–

Perger, R. Von. "Karl Goldmark." *Die Musik* 7 (1907-08): 131.
Truscott, H. "Carl Goldmark." *Monthly Musical Record* 90 (1960): 62.

Werba, Robert. "*Königin* für 277 Abende. Goldmarks Oper und ihr wienerisches Schicksal." *Österreichische Musik-zeitschrift* 34 (1979): 192.

*   *   *

Well known in his day for a number of orchestral and chamber music compositions (the *Sakuntula* Overture, Op. 13, the "Rustic Wedding" Symphony, Op. 26, two piano trios and a string quintet, among other works), Goldmark's operatic reputation is confined largely to the first of his six operas, *Die Königin von Saba* (premiered in Vienna, 1875). He was sometimes jokingly referred to as the "court composer to the Queen of Sheba," so strongly was his name identified with this one work. Stylistically it can be said to take the Paris version of Wagner's *Tannhäuser* as a point of departure. Its central dramatic relationship between the youthful Assad and the quasi-supernatural seductress Sheba closely parallels that of *Tannhäuser* and Venus in Wagner's opera. To Wagner's through-composed grand opera structure (based on a linking of solo, ensemble, and choral scene units) and the sensual chromaticism and instrumental timbres of the Venusberg music Goldmark adds a heavy dose of sultry exoticism in colorfully scored ballet sequences, choral tableaux, and "oriental" melodic inflections. He never attempted to recapture this exotic element in subsequent operas, although it remained in fashion to the end of the century; this may in part explain the failure of his later operas.

Goldmark grew up in a large German-speaking Jewish family in rural Hungary. Although he wrote no explicitly Hungarian or Gypsy style music it seems likely that characteristic elements of his early musical environment helped to color his most successful works, the *Königin* and the "Rustic Wedding" Symphony. Goldmark received scant formal training in music, and no formal schooling at all. He did become an accomplished violinist, however, and was later enabled to study violin and some elementary theory at the Vienna Conservatory until the outbreak of the 1848 revolution. For a long time he was forced to earn a meager living by playing in small theater orchestras and giving lessons (the theater orchestra in Odenburg [Sopron], near Goldmark's home town, boasted a total of two first violins). His D major string quartet of 1860 made his name known in Vienna, but only after *Die Königin von Saba*, in the 1880s and '90s, did he achieve anything approaching international celebrity. The opera was, incidentally, quite popular in Italy; Toscanini conducted it at the Teatro alla Scala in 1901.

The success of this work was enough to gain premieres at the Vienna *Hofoper* [Court Theater] for four of the subsequent five operas; the second-to-last, *Götz von Berlichingen* (based on Goethe's *Sturm und Drang* drama), was first produced in Budapest in 1902, but also reached Vienna eight years later. For all its popularity—it continued to play in Vienna and Budapest through the 1930s—*Die Königin von Saba* now seems something of a period piece, recalling the sumptuous, exotic ostentation of Hans Makart, whose paintings, stage sets, and *objets d'art* greatly appealed to late nineteenth-century Viennese society.

Goldmark's next opera, *Merlin*, fell still more strongly under the all-pervasive influence of Wagner. The librettist (Siegfried Lipiner) was an ardent Wagnerian and youthful intimate of Gustav Mahler. The Arthurian setting, like that of so many operas of the time, derives from the example of *Tristan* and *Parsifal*, but musically and dramaturgically it wavers between Wagnerian models and more conventional grand opera. The "round of flower-spirits" conjured up in act II, for example, is clearly reminiscent of the flower-maidens of *Parsifal*, yet its music veers between the style of an Austrian *Ländler* and harmonic progressions of the most extreme chromaticism. Where Wagner's score for *Parsifal* establishes a subtle balance between the anguished chromatic prolongations of Amfortas's or Kundry's music and an enriched diatonic language for Parsifal and the realm of the Grail temple, Goldmark's *Merlin* remains rooted in the stiffer declamatory style of *Lohengrin*, shifting uncomfortably from self-consciously plain diatonicism (Merlin's "bardic" style, Viviane's *scherzando* hunting music, and various choral and recitative passages), seemingly uncontrolled modulatory passages and frequently dense chromatic textures.

Das Heimchen am Herd (The Cricket on the Hearth, 1896, libretto by A. M. Willner after Charles Dickens) was considerably more successful than *Merlin*, at least for a short period around the turn of the century. Here Goldmark lightened his style in accordance with the subject matter, recalling elements of the bourgeois comedy or *Spieloper* of Lortzing and Nicolai. Being through-composed and not completely eschewing aspects of a Wagnerian motivic orchestral texture, however, *Das Heimchen* might best be compared to the contemporaneous *Märchenoper* of Humperdinck (*Hänsel und Gretel*, *Königskinder*).

The last opera, *Ein Wintermärchen* (after Shakespeare's *A Winter's Tale*, a third collaboration with Willner) is a more ambitious work than *Das Heimchen*. As in *Merlin*, however, Goldmark gives the impression of over-reaching his powers. The orchestral prelude—utilizing material from the final scene, the re-vivification of Hermione's petrified form—is characterized by restless modulations and complex, sometimes turgid orchestral textures in the style of Max Reger. Nonetheless this prelude, like that to *Merlin* (with its echoes of the *Lohengrin* prelude) demonstrates Goldmark's mastery of the late Romantic orchestra. The cheerfully rustic music of Perdita, Florizel and the Bohemian shepherd folk in act II (Shakespeare's act IV) offers some relief from the heavier idiom of the surrounding acts. The premiere of *Ein Wintermärchen* at the Vienna *Hofoper* in 1908 enjoyed the participation of a first-rate cast: Leo Slezak, Anna Bahr-Mildenburg, Selma Kurz (as Perdita, a role containing some brilliant fioratura, perhaps expressly devised for her), Leopold Demuth and Fritz Schrödter, with Bruno Walter conducting. Nonetheless, like most German operas of its time, it made little headway; Goldmark was to be remembered only for his first opera of some thirty years earlier.

—Thomas S. Grey

GOLDONI, Carlo.

Librettist/Dramatist. Born 25 February 1707, in Venice. Died 6 or 7 February 1793, in Paris. Comic writer in Venice, 1734-43 (at some point up to 1741 he was directing poet for the Teatro San Giovanni Grisostomo in Venice); practiced law in Tuscany; wrote for the comic theater in Venice, 1748-62; commissioned to write three librettos for the Bourbon court, 1756, where he was awarded the title of court poet; moved to Paris, and wrote for the Comédie-Italienne, 1762; Italian tutor to Princess Adelaïde, daughter of Louis XV.

DOCTOR CAROIVS GOLDONI
POETA COMICVS

Carlo Goldoni, portrait by Alessandro Longhi

Librettos

Il buon vecchio (intermezzo), 1730 [lost].

La cantatrice (intermezzo), 1730 [lost].

Amalasunta, 1732-33 [destroyed by Goldoni].

I sdegni amorosi tra Bettina Putta de Campielo e Buleghin barcariol Venezian (intermezzo), 1733.

La pupilla (intermezzo), Maccari, 1734; also set by Gialdini, and F. Mancini.

Aristide (intermezzo), A. Vivaldi, 1735.

La birba (intermezzo), Maccari?, Appoloni?, 1735.

L'ippocondriaco (intermezzo), Maccari?, Appoloni?, 1735.

Il filosofo (intermezzo), Maccari?, 1735.

La bottega da caffè (intermezzo), Maccari?, 1736; also set by V. Righini.

L'amante cabala (intermezzo), Maccari?, 1736.

La fondazion di Venezia, Maccari, 1736.

La generosità politica (after Lalli, *Pisistrato*), Marchi, 1736.

Monsieur Petiton (intermezzo), Maccari?, Appoloni?, 1736; also set by Corbisiero (as revised by A. Palomba), and N. Piccinni.

Lugrezia Romana in Costantinopoli, Maccari?, 1737.

Germondo, composer?, 1739?; also set by T. Traetta.

Gustavo Primo, re di Svezia, B. Galuppi, 1740.

Oronte, re de' Sciti, B. Galuppi, 1740; also set by P. Scalabrini, and B. Galuppi with additions by N. Jommelli and J.A. Hasse.

Statira, Chiarini, 1741; also set by Maggiore and others, and G. Scolari.

Tigrane, Arena, 1741; also set by C.W. Gluck, Barba, G.B. Lampugnani, Carcano, and Tozzi.

Amor fa l'uomo cieco (intermezzo, after Mariani, *La contadina astuta ossia Livietta e Tracollo*), Chiarini, 1742.

La contessina, Maccari, 1743; also set by Kurzinger, G.B. Lampugnani, Gherardeschi, Astaritta, M. Bernardini, F.L. Gassmann, Mährisch-Neustadt, Rust (revised by Calzabigi), and N. Piccinni.

Il quartiere fortunato (intermezzo), Maggiore, 1744.

La scuola moderna o sia La maestra di buon gusto (after Palomba, *La maestra*), V.L. Ciampi, 1748.

Bertoldo, Bertoldini e Cacasenna, V.L. Ciampi, 1749.

L'Arcadia in Brenta, B. Galuppi, 1749; also set by Meneghetti, Silva, and Bosi.

Il negligente, V.L. Ciampi, 1749; also set by G. Paisiello.

La favola de' tre gobbi (intermezzo), V.L. Ciampi, 1749; also set by Ciami in a revised version by Goldoni, and in a revised version by Fabrizi.

Il conte Caramella, B. Galuppi, Verona?, 1749?; also set by G. Scolari.

Arcifanfano, re dei matti, B. Galuppi, 1749; also set by Duni, G. Scolari, and F.L. Gassmann.

Il mondo della luna, B. Galuppi, 1750; also set by Avondano, N. Piccinni, Astaritta, G. Paisiello, J. Haydn, and Portogallo.

Il paese della Cuccagna, B. Galuppi, 1750; also set by Mango, N. Piccinni, Tozzi, G. Paisiello, and Astaritta.

Il mondo alla roversa, ossia Le donne che comandano, B. Galuppi, 1750; also set by G. Paisiello, D'Antoine, and A. Salieri.

La mascherata, G. Cocchi, 1750-51.

Le donne vendicate, G. Cocchi, 1751; also set by G. Scolari and N. Piccinni.

Le pescatrici, B. Galuppi, 1752?; also set by Gioanetti, J. Haydn, and F.L. Gassmann.

Le virtuose ridicole, B. Galuppi, 1752; also set by Cordella, Rinaldo di Capua, G. Paisiello, Ottani.

I portentosi effetti della Madre Natura, G. Scarlatti, 1752; also set by N. Piccinni.

La calamità de' cuori, B. Galuppi, 1752; also set by De Gamerra, A. Salieri, and D. Cimarosa.

I bagni d'Abano, B. Galuppi, F.G. Bertoni, 1753; also set by G. Paisiello.

De gustibus non est disputandum, G. Scarlatti, 1754.

Il filosofo di campagna, B. Galuppi, 1754.

Lo speziale, V. Pallavicini and D. Fischietti, 1754; also set by J. Haydn.

Il povero superbo, B. Galuppi, 1755.

Le nozze, B. Galuppi, 1755; G. Scolari, 1757; also set by G. Cocchi, and G. Sarti.

La diavolessa, B. Galuppi, 1755; also set by Bartha.

La cacina, G. Scolari, 1755; also set by G.F. Brusa.

La ritornata di Londra, D. Fischietti, 1756; also set by B. Galuppi (revised as an intermezzo).

La buona figliuola, E.R. Duni, 1756; also set by N. Piccinni, Perillo, F.L. Gassmann, and Graffigna.

Il matrimonio discorde (farsetta), Lorenzini, 1756.

La cantarina (farsetta), B. Galuppi, 1756.

Il festino, G. Ferradini, 1757.

Il viaggiatore ridicolo, Mazzoni, 1757; also set by Perillo, G. Scolari, Magroni, F.L. Gassmann, Caramanica, and P.C. Guglielmi (?).

L'isola disabitata, G. Scarlatti, 1757.

Il mercato di Malmantile, G. Scarlatti, 1757; also set by D. Fischietti, Lauri, D. Cimarosa (revised), Bartha, and N.A. Zingarelli (revised).

La conversazione, G. Scolari, 1758.

Il signor dottore, D. Fischietti, 1758.

Buovo d'Antona, T. Traetta, 1758.

Gli uccellatori, F.L. Gassmann, 1759; also set by N. Piccinni, P.C. Guglielmi, and Marinelli.

Il conte Chiccera, G.B. Lampugnani, 1759.

Filosofia ed Amore, F.L. Gassmann, 1760.

La fiera di Sinigaglia, D. Fischietti, 1760.

Amor contadino, G.B. Lampugnani, 1760.

La vendemmia (intermezzo), A.M.G. Sacchini, 1760.

L'amore artigiano, G. Latilla, 1761; also set by F.L. Gassmann, Gherardeschi, J. Schuster, and Accorimbeni.

Amore in caricatura, V.L. Ciampi, 1761; also set by Notte.

La buona figliuola maritata, N. Piccinni, 1761; also set by G. Scolari (?), and T. Traetta.

La bella verità, N. Piccinni, 1762.

Il re alla caccia, B. Galuppi, 1763; F. Alessandri, Ponzio.

La finta semplice, Perillo, 1764; also set by W.A. Mozart.

La notte critica, A. Boroni, 1766; also set by N. Piccinni, F.L. Gassmann, Gherardeschi, Fortunati, and Lasser.

La cameriera spiritosa, B. Galuppi, 1766; also set by Gherardeschi.

La nozze in campagne, Sciroli, 1768.

Vittorina, N. Piccinni, 1777; also set by Farinelli as revised by Foppa.

I volponi, 1777 [not performed?].

Il talismano, A. Salieri, 1779; set by Salieri as revised by Da Ponte, 1788.

Publications/Writings

By GOLDONI: books–

Mémoires pour servir à l'histoire de sa vie et à celle de son théâtre. Paris, 1787.

Ortolani, G., ed. *Tutte le opere di Carlo Goldoni.* Verona, 1935-56.

About GOLDONI: books–

Wotquenne, A. Zeno, Metastasio et Goldoni. *Table alphabétique des morceaux mesurés contenus dans les oeuvres dramatiques.* Leipzig, 1905.
Gallarati, P. *Musica e maschera. Il libretto italiano del settecento.* Turin, 1984.

articles–

Musatti, C. "Drammi musicali di Goldoni e d'Altri tratti dalle sue commedie." *L'ateneo Veneto* 21 (1898): 51.
———. "I drammi musicali di Carlo Goldoni: appunti bibliografiche-cronologici." *L'ateneo Veneto* 25 (1902): 6.
Parini, G. "Il Goldoni e la musica." *La fanfulla della domenica* 24 February (1907): 2.
Musatti, C. "I melodrammi goldoniani." *Antiquarium* 1/no. 2 (1922): 6.
Bustico, G. "Drammi, cantate, intermezzi musicali di Carlo Goldoni." *Rivista della biblioteche e degli archivi* 3/January-June (1925): 51; 3/July-December (1925): 128.
Malamanni, V. "Il teatro lirico a Venezia nel secolo XVIII." *Archivio Veneto* 1 (1927): 191.
Ortolani, G. "Appunti sui melodrammi giocosi del Goldoni." *Rivista della città di Venezia* 13/no. 4 (1934): 141; reprinted in *Mélanges de philologie, d'histoire et de littérature offerts à Henri Hauvette,* 437, Paris, 1934; also reprinted in *La riforma del teatro nel settecento a altri scritti da Giuseppe Ortolani,* edited by G. Damerini, 199, Venice, 1962.
Paoli, D. de. "Goldoni librettista." *Il veltro* 1/no. 2 (1957): 21.
Folena, G. "Goldoni librettista comico." In *Venezia e il melodramma nel settecento,* edited by M.T. Muraro. Florence, 1981.
Heartz, D. "Goldoni, Don Giovanni and the Drama Giocoso." *Musical Times* 120 (1979): 993.
———. "Vis comica: Goldoni, Galuppi and *L'Arcadia in Brenta.*" In *Venezia e il melodramma nel settecento,* edited by M.T. Muraro. Florence, 1981.
Robinson, M.F. "Three Versions of Goldoni's *Il filosofo di campagna.*" In *Venezia e il melodramma nel settecento,* edited by M.T. Muraro. Florence, 1981.

unpublished–

Weiss, P.E. "Carlo Goldoni, Librettist: the Early Years." Ph.D. dissertation, Columbia University, 1970.

*   *   *

Carlo Goldoni is most widely known as the "father of Italian comedy"; from the 1730s to the 1760s, he revolutionized Italian spoken theater, purging many of the most affected, stylized traits of the *commedia dell'arte* (along with its improvisatory nature), and developing characters of more natural expression with believable and identifiable personalities. In opera, he wrote both serious and comic librettos over these same years, but achieved his greatest success, again, in comedy.

Goldoni's efforts in serious opera had an inauspicious beginning. By his own account he brought a new drama, *Amalasunta,* to Milan in 1732 in hopes of selling it to an opera impresario. During an informal gathering of a group of friends, including the great singer Caffarelli, he gave the drama its first public reading—and it was laughed to scorn.

He had ignored most of the conventional "rules" of the genre: the rank and prestige of different singers were not observed in parcelling arias, there were too many characters, aria types were not mixed properly, there weren't enough scene changes, etc. (the whole account is made somewhat less credible by Goldoni's repeated citation of a contemporaneous performance of Metastasio's *Demofoonte* in Milan, which libretto the Imperial poet had not yet written; however, Caffarelli did sing in two other Milanese productions during the 1732-33 carnival). Goldoni later wrote six additional serious libretti, of which only *Statira* and *Tigrane* showed any lasting success.

It was in comedy that Goldoni's true genius excelled. In the 1730s and early 1740s he merely dabbled in theatrical poetry, while otherwise practicing law; it was only after 1748 that his career in the theater was assured. Contracted to write six spoken comedies for Venice, he simultaneously began a long and fruitful opera collaboration with Baldassare Galuppi in writing *drammi giocosi* for Venetian audiences. Their first effort, *L'Arcadia in Brenta,* was an enormous success. In this work, which satirizes the summer retreats of the Venetian aristocracy and the affectatious behavior of cultivated society, Goldoni's elegant poetry and witty, fast-paced dialogue was ideally matched with Galuppi's comic musical pacing, his facile, tuneful melodies, and lucid orchestration. Over the ensuing years a long stream of collaborative works followed, including *Il conte Caramella, Il mondo della luna, Il mondo alla roversa,* and particularly *Il filosofo di campagna.*

Goldoni's plots are varied, but all play on the follies of society and the weaknesses of men and women. In the ridiculously comic ones, such as his *Il mondo della luna,* there are no truly serious characters at all; such old, reliable devices as subterfuge, disguise, greed, and misunderstandings motivate the plot, and slapstick often gets the laugh. In his more subtle works, such as *Il filosofo di campagna* and *La buona figliuola,* serious characters motivate much of the action, although even they are not immune from comic situations. In *Il filosofo* the country philosopher uses a very "common sense" and (above all) pragmatic approach to solve life's dilemmas, and particularly to poke fun at arcane, idealistic conventions of opera seria.

A number of innovative features, inherent in Goldoni's poetic texts, created exciting new effects. The previous history of full-length comic opera, as it rose from dialect comedies in Naples through Rome to Venice, was largely based on serious opera, with da capo arias, similar dramaturgy, and casts. Goldoni rejected these constraints and allowed the motivation of the action itself to guide his poetic forms and dramatic integrity. As a result, aria structures were increasingly varied: short ariette (momentary interjections not demanding that a character exit), ensembles of all types (both to begin and end scenes), and a significant decline in the amount of recitative (by about half), all combined to create a flexible, fast-paced, and persuasive design. The so-called "chain finale," which was generally gaining ascendency through the 1750s, saw significant development through the Goldoni-Galuppi creations. In this scheme each act ends with repeated twists of plot as additional characters are added, until (in Goldoni's later comedies) everyone is on stage. The musical structure becomes fluid (reflecting the poetic changes), altering keys, tempo, rhythmic or melodic motives, etc., as demanded by circumstance and poetry. These concluding scenes became longer, funnier, and more convincing through the 1750s.

Goldoni's most successful libretto was written for Parma, where in 1756 he wrote three librettos for the court. *La buona figliuola,* originally set by Dunì, was later reset by the young Piccinni; this version proved to be the most popular comic opera of its day. This work, as well as the other Galuppi-Goldoni collaborations from Venice, was disseminated throughout Europe and created much of the framework emulated by others in comic opera, as well as establishing many of the effects incorporated into serious opera in the late eighteenth century.

—Dale E. Monson

GOMES, Antonio Carlos.

Composer. Born 11 July 1836, in Campinas, Brazil. Died 16 September 1896, in Pará (Belém). Studied with his father, and then at the Conservatory of Rio de Janeiro; granted a stipend by Emperor Don Pedro II for study in Milan; productions of his operas in Italy, 1867-72; returned to Rio de Janeiro, 1872; wrote the hymn "Il saluto del Brasile" for the centenary of American independence, 1876; cantata *Colombo* for the Columbus Festival, 1892; director of the new conservatory at Pará, 1895.

Operas

A noite do castelo, A.J. Fernandes dos Reis, Rio de Janeiro, 4 September 1861.
Joana de Flandres, S. de Mendonça, Rio de Janeiro, 15 September 1863.
Il Guarany, A. Scalvini and C. d'Ormeville (after Jose de Alencar, *O Guarani*), Milan, Teatro alla Scala, 19 March 1870.
Fosca, A. Ghislanzoni, Milan, Teatro alla Scala, 16 February 1873; revised, 1878.
Salvator Rosa, A. Ghislanzoni, Genoa, 21 March 1874.
Maria Tudor, E. Praga (after Hugo), Milan, 27 March 1879.
Lo schiavo, R. Paravicini (after Taunay), Rio de Janeiro, 27 September 1889.
Condor, M. Canti, Milan, Teatro alla Scala, 21 February 1891.

Other works: songs, choruses, piano pieces.

Publications

By GOMES: books–

Vetro, Gaspare Nello, ed. *Carteggi italiani.* Milan, 1977; Portuguese translation as *Correspondencias italianas,* Rio de Janeiro, 1982.

About GOMES: books–

Boccanera, S. *Um artista brasiliero: in memoriam.* Bahia, 1904.
Tauney, A. *Dois artistas maximos: Jose Mauricio e Carlos Gomes.* Sao Paulo, 1930.
Vieira, H.P. *Carlos Gomes: sua arte e sua obra.* Sao Paulo, 1934.
Seidl, R. *Carlos Gomes: brasiliero e patriota.* Rio de Janeiro, 1935.
Guimares, A. Pereira. *Antonio Carlos Gomes.* Bahia, 1936.
Souto, L.F. Viera. *Antonio Carlos Gomes.* Rio de Janeiro, 1936.
Almeida, R. *Carlos Gomes.* Rio de Janeiro, 1937.

Castro, E. de Freitas e. *Carlos Gomes.* Porto Alegre, 1937.
Azevedo, L.H. Corrêa de. *Relação das óperas de autores brasileiros.* Rio de Janeiro, 1938.
Andrade, M. de. *Carlos Gomes.* Rio de Janeiro, 1939.
Cerquera, P. *Carlos Gomes: Com uma biografia.* Sao Paulo, 1944.
Bettencourt, G. de. *A vida ansiosa e atormentada de um gênio.* Lisbon, 1945.
Carvalho, I. Gomes Vaz de. *A vida de Carlos Gomes.* Rio de Janeiro, 3rd ed., 1946.
Rinaldi, G. Da Rocha. *Carlos Gomes. Nho fonico de Campinas.* Sao Paulo, 1955.
Roberti, S. *Carlos Gomes: Rapido escorco de sua vida atormentada e da sua arte triunfadora.* Brazil, 1955.
Azevedo, L.H. Corrêa de. *150 Anos de Música no Brasil (1800-1950).* Rio de Janeiro, 1956.
Brito, J. *Carlos Gomes.* Rio de Janeiro, 1956.
Mariz, V. *A canção brasileira.* Rio de Janeiro, 1959.
Marques, G. *O homem da cabeça de leão.* Sao Paulo, 1971.
Fernandes, Juvenal. *Do sonho à conquista: revivendo um gênio da musica—Carlos Gomes.* Sao Paulo, 1978.
Mariz, Vasco. *História da música no Brasil.* 2nd ed., Rio de Janeiro, 1983.
Penalvo, J. *Carlos Gomes: o compositor.* Campinas, 1986.
Angelo, A. *O brasiliero Carlos Gomes.* Sao Paulo, 1987.

* * *

Born into a family which contained the town bandmaster (his father), the leader of the opera house orchestra (his brother), and the leading female singer (an aunt), Gomes seems to have been destined for a career in music. At the Conservatory in Rio de Janeiro, his work attracted the attention of the director of the Opera Nacional de Lirica, Jose Amat, who entrusted him with a libretto based on a popular Portuguese gothic horror poem, *A noite do Castel* (1860). The music, for *A noite,* like that of its successor, *Joanna de Flandres* (1863), reflects what a talented amateur composer had been able to learn not so much from his teachers as from the operas he had been able to hear, those of Bellini, Rossini, and early Donizetti. Though derivative, his scores demonstrated an inventiveness and persona appropriation of the already outmoded form which garnered him a government scholarship to the Milan Conservatory.

Gomes was a passionate listener; on his trip to Milan he stopped off in Paris, where hearing the operas of Meyerbeer and of the young Bizet made an indelible mark on his approach to orchestration. His keen ear is probably also responsible for the success of his first works for the Italian stage, not operas but musical comedies ("reviews" would be closer to the mark) set in Milanese dialect. As a liberal and patriotic Brazilian, his choice of an opera topic based on a novel by his countryman, Jose de Alencar, *O Guarani,* which had just appeared in Italian translation, constitutes an eminently just historical accident, as he first read it in Italian translation in Milan. Perhaps the fact that one of his grandmothers had been a fullblooded Guarani indian assisted Gomes in his choice, but Alencar's embodiment of the cutting-edge intellectual preoccupation of the time, *indianismo,* with its idealized combination of Rousseau's noble savage and Fenimore Cooper's canny (*North* American) native possessed its own appeal.

Il Guarany reveals how much Gomes had learned of contemporary Italian and French opera since his arrival in Europe. The orchestration owes much to Meyerbeer's example, the structure to Verdi's middle-period operas, which had not yet appeared in Brazil prior to Gomes's departure. Above all he demonstrated an individual gift for melody which, unlike that of his Italian contemporaries, could not be mistaken for Verdi on a bad day. The plot of *Il Guarany,* with its enslaved natives versus imperialist Europeans, owed not a little to Meyerbeer's posthumous masterpiece, *L'Africaine,* but Gomes, following Alencar, introduced a shocking variation. For the first time the theme of love between white and dark skinned people involved not the acceptable European model of white male/native female, but the reverse. Perhaps the Meyerbeerian structure and Verdian sweep of the act I duet between the Indian Pery and the Portuguese noblewoman Cecilia won the sympathy of an audience which might otherwise have rejected the opera's central love interest out of hand.

Having heard the opera in Ferrara, Verdi called Gomes "a true musical genius." Boito, not yet the great man's librettist, publically expressed the opinion that Gomes might be Verdi's heir apparent. The Brazilian's next two operas, *Fosca* (1873) and *Salvator Rosa* (1874) confirmed the possibility. *Fosca* is Gomes's most contemporary Italianate, Verdian score, sublimating his obvious infatuation with Meyerbeer's idea of using and abandoning a plethora of melodic inventions as the dramatic emphasis of the text is shifted, to a remarkable understanding of the development of aria and ensemble themes that Verdi had begun to incorporate into his scores following his conquest of French style in *Don Carlos.* In imitation of the latter, Gomes included a few obvious *Leitmotiven* (leading themes) in *Fosca,* for which he was immediately accused of "Wagnerismo" by conservative operagoers. This controversy ruined the chances of *Fosca,* perhaps Gomes's most viable score in retrospect, to enter the standard repertoire.

Obviously in response to the criticism of his previous opera, Gomes retreated to the safer ground of middle-Verdi/late-Donizetti for his next work, *Salvator Rosa,* that of uncomplicated melody and predictable development. At the time, his decision proved financially beneficial; the opera remained his most popular in Italy for three decades. *Maria Tudor* (1879) shows him betwixt and between. He attempted the popular approach of *Salvator Rosa* but could no longer sublimate his particular genius to the exigencies of popular taste. A return visit to Brazil in 1880 put him again in touch with the most significant liberal movements of his homeland, specifically the struggle to become the last major power to outlaw slavery. He accepted a libretto from the Vicomte de Taunay, a leading abolitionist, dealing with the origin of the odious institution in the early 1600s, *Lo Schiavo.*

Though it became the first of Gomes's mature operas to have its first performance in his native Brazil, by the time he had composed it the subject had become passé; Brazil had become a republic and abolished slavery. Its sophisticated orchestration, especially the prelude to act IV, depicting dawn over Guanabara Bay, and Gomes's return to the Meyerbeerian model of orchestra at the service of dramatic exigency, produced his most personal lyric effusion. Its success was immediate but transitory on European stages.

In the interim, Wagner had conquered Italy and the indigenous response of verismo had been begun by Catalani and Puccini. Gomes tried to respond to the musical demands of the new wave in *Condor* (1891), but could not successfully meld his particular genius to the task. His last stage work, *Colombo,* a scenic cantata commissioned for the four-hundredth anniversary of the discovery of the New World, showed him still in possession of the ability to write effectively for voice and chorus, but he died, as head of the Belém Conservatory, a few months later.

Though still performed in Brazil, as much as a civic duty as otherwise, Gomes's operas have been singularly overlooked in the continuing investigation of forgotten operas which has resulted in our reacquaintance with significant music by Rossini, Donizetti, and Meyerbeer. Even the centennial revival of works by his less-gifted contemporary Mercadante has not focussed much interest in the Brazilian master's operas. His dramatic sensibility, his thoroughly professional and often astonishing orchestration, and his considerable melodic gifts have not yet occasioned a merited reappraisal by opera companies or critics.

—William J. Collins

THE GOOD DAUGHTER
See LA BUONA FIGLIUOLA

THE GOOD SOLDIER SCHWEIK.

Composer: Robert Kurka.

Librettist: Lewis Allan (after Jaroslav Hašek).

First Performance: New York, City Opera, 23 April 1958 [unfinished: completed by Hershey Kay].

Roles (these may be doubled, as indicated by slashes): Schweik (tenor); Bretschneider/First Psychiatrist/First Doctor (tenor); A Guard/A Sergeant/Mr Wendler (tenor); Palivec/General von Schwarzburg/Mr Kakonyi (baritone); Second Psychiatrist/Second Doctor/Army Doctor/Lt Lukash (baritone); Police Officer/Third Psychiatrist/Col. Kraus von Zillergut (bass); Mrs Muller/Katy/Mrs Kakonyi (soprano); Baroness von Botzenheim (contralto); Prologue/The Dog/Voditchka/Sergeant Vorek (speaking); chorus (TB).

Publications

articles–

Allan, L. "Czech Opera by American Czech." *New York Times* 20 April 1958.
Kolodin, I. "Kurka's 'Schweik'." *Saturday Review* 41/no. 24 (1958).
Bloch, H. [Review of piano-vocal score of *The Good Soldier Schweik*]. *Notes* 21 (1963-64): 229.

*   *   *

The Good Soldier Schweik is drawn from Jaroslav Hašek's novel about a poignantly comical Czech soldier of World War I who makes the best of sad circumstances. He is a kind of comic *Wozzeck* in this episodic treatment (two acts, eighteen short scenes) who cheerfully survives many humiliations to remain a kind-hearted, uncomplicated man of indestructible optimism retaining a positive attitude about life.

The good-natured Schweik hears of the assassination of the Archduke Ferdinand of Sarajavo from his cleaning woman and goes as usual to "The Flagon" tavern. He is arrested after a conversation with a secret service policeman looking for people expressing anti-Austrian opinion. Later, in jail with the tavern landlord, Schweik is pulled out for questioning by three psychiatrists who have different points of view. His bland good nature convince them Schweik is an idiot, and they commit him to a mental institution. Schweik enjoys the institutional life, but two other doctors conclude that Schweik is feigning idiocy to escape military service and throw him out. At home in bed suffering from chronic rheumatism, Schweik receives his draft call. Patriotism impels him to report. Mrs Muller, his cleaning lady, tearfully wheels his wheelchair along the street as he shouts "On to Belgrade" to a gleeful crowd, brandishing his crutches.

Schweik's mishaps continue in act II as he is confined to a hut with other suspected malingerers. A baroness arrives with food for Schweik, whose patriotic story has captured newspaper headlines. After eating heartily, Schweik and his companions are thrown into the guardhouse. There Schweik breaks into tears when the chaplain storms at them. The chaplain makes him his orderly, but loses him shortly to Lieutenant Henry Lukash in a poker game. More chaotic episodes follow, and we last see Schweik disagreeing with the lieutenant (having been sent together to the front) on the correctness of a map. Schweik, following his own inclination, takes another road and disappears.

Kurka applies a small orchestra (16 pieces) of winds and percussion to a rhythmic, cabaret-like score that is more gentle than biting. Hershey Kay, a friend of Kurka's, completed the score after Kurka's early death. There are jazz influences and also moments of lyricism when Schweik sings "Who will go to the war when it comes" and "Wait for the Ragged Soldiers." At the conclusion, Schweik wanders away singing, "I'll take a quiet road, and I'll be in the sun. For birds and butterflies I won't need a gun." Although the opera conveyed an attitude that was popular, it is an idea that is somewhat dated, and Eastern Europeans have expressed their concern with what they think is a superficial treatment of a favorite novel. But over 500 performances in Europe and 100 performances in America suggest the staying power of the work.

—Andrew H. Drummond

GOODALL, (Sir) Reginald.

Conductor. Born 13 July 1901, in Lincoln, England. Died 5 May 1990, near Canterbury. Studied at the Royal College of Music in London; assistant conductor at Covent Garden, 1936-39; assistant to Furtwängler with the Berlin Philharmonic; conducted the premiere of Britten's *Peter Grimes*, 1945; conducted Wagner's *Ring* at Sadler's Wells Opera, London, 1973; Commander of the Order of the British Empire, 1975; knighted, 1985.

*   *   *

There was an odd shape to the career of this distinguished British conductor. His earliest musical training was as a boy chorister in Lincoln Cathedral, and he then went on to study conducting and piano at the Royal College of Music, London.

But it was above all his pre-war operatic pilgrimages to Munich, Salzburg and Vienna which gave him an all-around knowledge of the repertory and crowned his already acquired skills with experience of the finest European opera.

From time to time at Covent Garden during the 1930s, Goodall assisted the conductor Albert Coates, but did not take charge of a major new production until after he joined the Sadler's Wells Company and conducted the premiere of Britten's *Peter Grimes*. That celebrated occasion changed the face of British opera and launched Britten and his leading singer Peter Pears into long-lasting star careers. Yet it did not do the same for Goodall, though Pears always said, admiringly, that "no one conducted *Grimes* like Reggie," and Britten chose Goodall to alternate with Ernest Ansermet as the conductor of *The Rape of Lucretia* at Glyndebourne. Certainly he became a staff conductor at Covent Garden and conducted *Die Meistersinger* there, but he was overshadowed by Karl Rankl, who held the post of music director there from 1946-51. Goodall's quiet personality (some said "self-effacing") may have contributed to his staying in a secondary role, which continued during Rafael Kubelik's reign (1955-58), and after the dynamic George Solti arrived in 1961 Goodall was unpardonably demoted to the duties of a vocal coach. Later he told a singer colleague that he felt he had been overlooked by the management—a considerable understatement, though typical of the man. It is not being chauvinistic to wonder whether at this time the mere fact of his being British caused his talents to be undervalued by the general administrator Sir David Webster and his advisers.

The re-emergence of Goodall as a major opera conductor came in 1968, when he returned as a guest to Sadler's Wells and conducted *Die Meistersinger*. Stephen Arlen of the Wells deserves credit here, not merely for issuing the invitation but also for empowering him to take the amount of rehearsal time which he deemed necessary (which was more than some of his colleagues, for he always coached his singers personally). This successful production, sung in English, led eventually to his triumphant *Ring* cycle for the same company at the London Coliseum, also in English (for the first time in over forty years). These productions showed him as a musician with a deep understanding of the shaping and imaginative weighing of music and story alike, who could draw the best from his orchestra as well as his singers. His recording, taken from live performances, was widely saluted and has kept its place in the catalogue. Goodall found himself at last acclaimed as a master of time and tone in these great works, and a Wagner conductor worthy of comparison with Furtwängler. Covent Garden made belated amends for its long neglect of his skills by inviting him to conduct *Parsifal* but his eagerly awaited *Tristan and Isolde* was given with the Welsh National Opera, with which company he also recorded *Parsifal*.

With his singers, Goodall insisted on evenness of sound in all registers as well as tonal "beauty and youthfulness" of sound. He also demanded a clear articulation and projection of the text, flexibly expressive coloration of the voice, and rhythmical accuracy. His tempos were notoriously broad (he even got into the *Guinness Book of Records*), but the singer Norman Bailey (a famous Wotan in the *Ring*) said that he filled them with so much orchestral detail that they were never simply "slow." Nevertheless, we may admit that his *Parsifal* recording takes one compact disc more (five in all) than is required by four other conductors.

Away from the rostrum, Goodall seemed slightly built, poor-sighted and delicate, but artists usually found that once in charge of a performance he became "a lion." He may have regretted that he did not conduct more operas by composers other than Wagner, and told a friend that he thought Mozart the greater composer, though "Wagner had so much more breadth." His Commander of the Order of the British Empire and, later, knighthood came in time to mark the full recognition of his stature by the British establishment. When he became too frail and elderly to work, he continued to enjoy music in the opera house and on record, and appropriately he was listening to a recording of *Götterdämmerung* a few hours before his death.

—Christopher Headington

GORR, Rita (born Marguerite Geirnaert).

Mezzo-soprano. Born 18 February 1926, in Zelzaete, Belgium. Studied in Ghent and Brussels; debut as Fricka in *Die Walküre*, Antwerp, 1949; sang in Strasbourg Opera, 1949-52; debut at Paris Opéra and Opéra-Comique, 1952; debut at Bayreuth, 1958; appeared at Covent Garden as Amneris in *Aïda*, 1959, and sang there regularly until 1971; Teatro alla Scala debut as Kundry, 1960; Metropolitan Opera debut as Amneris in *Aïda*, 1962.

Publications

About GORR: articles—

Bourgeois, J. "Rita Gorr." *Opera* 12 (1961): 637.

*   *   *

One of the casualties of operatic style in recent times has been the grand tradition of French singing. At the turn of the century, many marvelous artists kept French operas in the core repertoire of every international house; today, the native French-speaking opera singer of distinction has all but disappeared. The 1950s and 60s saw the last wave of the tradition, as a small but significant group of fine French and Francophone singers—including sopranos Régine Crespin and Mady Mesplé, tenor Alain Vanzo, and baritones Michel Dens, Gabriel Bacquier and Gérard Souzay—gave opera audiences a last, glorious "Indian summer" before the current chill set in.

There was no finer artist in this rarified group than Belgian mezzo-soprano Rita Gorr, who used her prodigious resources to illuminate a variety of music. To French opera from Gluck to Massenet she brought a velvety timbre and nobility of phrase that placed her as the successor to such legendary interpreters as Félia Litvinne and Alice Raveau. In the operas of Verdi and Mascagni's *Cavalleria rusticana*, Gorr could provide an Italianate bite and theatricality which were the equal of those to the manner born. And her singing of Wagnerian roles was similarly idiomatic: Gorr's plangent voice and telling sensitivity to words share something of the style and sound of Christa Ludwig.

Like Ludwig's, Gorr's was an unusually large vocal range, and her skills as a colorist allowed her to sound comfortable in contralto, mezzo-soprano, and even some soprano roles. As Orphée, for example, the richness and dark glow of Gorr's tone sound like that of a natural alto; so it may surprise us that, as Amneris, the voice has brightness and a good deal of thrust at the top. The role of Cherubini's Medée (which Gorr sang both on record and in the theater) lies rather high for

her, but we sense the strain only in a few isolated passages; for the most part the music is splendidly and easily sung, and her grandeur of scale and commitment are stamped with greatness.

It is these latter qualities, even more than the voice itself, which are the hallmarks of Gorr's artistic mien. French roles in the "classical" style (like Medée, Didon, and Orphée) are notoriously difficult to bring off, for they require a careful balance: if an artist goes too far in one direction, the character becomes almost comically overwrought, while if she goes too far in the other direction the result is a performance that is lifeless and merely statuesque. Gorr's portrayals always found the ideal blend of humanity and heroic size, and her superbly clear enunciation of the language was a particular joy. In recent years, Jessye Norman has brought to a similar repertoire something resembling Gorr's artistry and finesse, but—perhaps inevitably—the younger American singer cannot achieve the natural and idiomatic sense of style of her predecessor.

Records provide a reasonable sampling of Gorr's career, though we might wish for more and particularly for a better representation of her French roles. Her fiery Amneris (with Georg Solti) may be the finest performance of the part on record. The RCA recording of *Lohengrin* finds Gorr sadly out of form as Ortrud (one of her finest parts in the theater), but her recording of Fricka in *Die Walküre* (with Eric Leinsdorf) is a worthy souvenir of her Wagner. Perhaps best of all is her Dalila (with Georges Prêtre), where she is partnered by the stentorian Samson of Jon Vickers. Here is Gorr's voice at its lushest and most sensual, and the crystalline diction is unmistakably that of a native speaker. It is a performance which will not be rivaled—and a style which may not be heard again—in our time.

—David Anthony Fox

GÖTTERDÄMMERUNG (TWILIGHT OF THE GODS) See DER RING DES NIBELUNGEN

GOUNOD, Charles François.

Composer. Born 17 June 1818, in St. Cloud. Died 17 October 1893, in Paris. Studied piano with his mother; studied with Halévy, Lesueur, and Paër at the Paris Conservatory, beginning 1835; second Prix de Rome for his cantata *Marie Stuart et Rizzio*, 1837; Grand Prix de Rome for his cantata *Fernand*, 1839; studied sacred music in Rome, and composed a Mass for 3 voices and orchestra; his Requiem performed in Vienna, 1842; precentor and organist of the Missions Etrangères; studied theology for two years; conducted the choral society Orphéon, 1852-60; first successful opera, *Faust*, 1859; organized Gounod's Choir in London, 1870; returned to Paris, 1874, and primarily composed sacred music.

Operas

Sapho, Emile Augier, 1850, Paris, Opéra, 16 April 1851; revised, Paris, Opéra, 2 April 1884.

La nonne sanglante, Eugène Scribe and Germain Delavigne (after Matthew Gregory Lewis, *The Monk*), 1852-54, Paris, Opéra, 18 October 1854.

Le médecin malgré lui, Jules Barbier and Michael Carré (after Molière), 1857, Paris, Théâtre-Lyrique, 15 January 1858.

Faust, Jules Barbier and Michel Carré (after Goethe), 1852-59, Paris, Théâtre-Lyrique, 19 March 1859; revised to include recitatives, Strasbourg, April 1860, and ballet, Paris, Opéra, 3 March 1869.

Philémon et Baucis, Jules Barbier and Michel Carré, 1859, Paris, Théâtre-Lyrique, 18 February 1860; revised, Paris, Opéra-Comique, 16 May 1876.

La colombe, Jules Barbier and Michel Carré (after La Fontaine, *Le faucon*), 1859, Baden-Baden, 3 August 1860.

La reine de Saba, Jules Barbier and Michel Carré (after Gérard de Nerval), 1861, Paris, Opéra, 29 February 1862.

Mireille, Michel Carré (after Frédéric Mistral, *Mirèio*), 1863, Paris, Théâtre-Lyrique, 19 March 1864; revised, performed 15 December 1864; restored, Henri Büsser, Paris, Opéra-Comique, 6 June 1939.

Roméo et Juliette, Jules Barbier and Michel Carré (after Shakespeare), 1864, Paris, Théâtre-Lyrique, 27 April 1867; revised to include ballet, Paris, Opéra, 28 November 1888.

George Dandin, after Molière, 1873 [unfinished].

Cinq–Mars, Louis Gallet and Paul Poirson (after a novel by Alfred de Vigny), 1876-77, Paris, Opéra-Comique, 5 April 1877; revised as grand opera, Lyon, 1 December 1877.

Polyeucte, Jules Barbier and Michel Carré (after Corneille), 1870-78, Paris, Opéra, 7 October 1878.

Le tribut de Zamora, Adolphe Philippe d'Ennery and Jules Brésil, 1878-80, Paris, Opéra, 1 April 1881.

Charles Gounod

Maître Pierre, Louis Gallet (on the subject of Abelard and Héloïse), 1877 [unfinished].

Publications

By GOUNOD: books–

Autobiographie de Charles Gounod et articles sur la routine en matière d'art, édités et compilés, avec une préface, par Mme Georgina Weldon. London, 1875.

Le Don Juan de Mozart. Paris, 1890; 5th ed. 1909; English translation, 1895.

articles–

"L'allaitement musical." *Le nouveau-né* January (1882).

Preface to A. Mortier, *Les soirées parisiennes de 1883, par un monsieur de l'orchestre.* Paris, 1884.

Preface to R. Mulholland, *Une idée fantasque.* Paris, 1885.

"Considérations sur le théâtre contemporain." Preface to E. Noël and E. Stoullig, *Les annales du théâtre et de la musique* 9. Paris, 1886.

Review of Saint-Saëns, *Prosperine. Le Figaro* 18 March (1887).

Review of Saint-Saëns, *Ascanio. La France* 23 March (1890).

Preface to *Mors et vita: a Sacred Trilogy . . . Book of Words.* London, 1890.

Preface to S. Frère, *Maman Jean.* Paris, 1891.

"Mémoires d'un artiste." *Revue de Paris* 2/nos 3, 4 (1895); enlarged and published separately, Paris, 1896; English translation, 1896.

Revue de Paris 6 (1899): 677 [correspondence with Bizet].

Revue hebdomadaire 26 December (1908): 451; 2 January (1909): 23 [correspondence with Richomme].

"Lettres de la jeunesse de Charles Gounod: Rome et Vienne 1840-43." *Revue bleue* 48 (1910): 833; 49 (1911): 8.

About GOUNOD: books–

Dancla, C. *Les compositeurs chefs d'orchestre: réponse à M. Charles Gounod.* Paris, 1873.

Weldon, G. *La destruction du "Polyeucte" de Charles Gounod: mémoire justicatif.* Paris, 1875; English translation, 1875?.

————. *Mon orphelinat et Gounod en Angleterre: lettres de M. Gounod et autres lettres et documents originaux.* London?, 1875; English translation, 1875?.

Lasalle, A. *Mémoires du Théâtre-Lyrique.* Paris, 1877.

Blaze de Bury, H. *Musiciens du passé, du présent et de l'avenir.* Paris, 1880.

Pagnerre, L. *Charles Gounod.* Paris, 1890.

Imbert, Hugues. *Nouveaux profils de musiciens.* Paris, 1892.

Bovet, M.A. de. *Charles Gounod: sa vie et ses oeuvres.* Paris, 1890; English translation, London, 1891.

Saint-Saëns, Camille. *Charles Gounod et le Don Juan de Mozart.* Paris, 1893.

Soubies, A., and C. Malherbe. *Histoire de l'Opéra Comique, la seconde Salle Favart, ii: 1860 à 1887.* Paris, 1893.

Hervey, A. *Masters of French Music.* London, 1894.

Delaborde, H. *Notice sur la vie et les oeuvres de Charles Gounod.* Paris, 1895.

Dubois, Théodore. *Notice sur Charles Gounod.* Paris, 1895.

Voss, P. *Charles Gounod: ein Lebensbild.* Leipzig, 1895.

Saint-Saëns, Camille. *Portraits et souvenirs.* Paris, 1899; 3rd ed., 1909.

Soubies, Albert. *Histoire des Théâres-Lyriques 1851-1870.* Paris, 1899.

Hillemacher, P.L. *Charles Gounod.* Paris, 1906; 2nd ed., 1914.

Tolhurst, H. *Gounod.* London, 1905.

Bizet, G. *Lettres: impressions de Rome (1857-1860); la Commune (1871).* Paris, 1908.

Bellaigue, Camille. *Gounod.* Paris, 1910.

Prod'homme, Jacques Gabriel, and A. Dandelot. *Gounod: sa vie et ses oeuvres,* 2 vols. Paris, 1911.

Soubies, Albert, and Henri Curzon, eds. *Documents inédits sur le "Faust" de Gounod.* Paris, 1912.

Northcott, R. *Gounod's Operas in London.* London, 1918.

Hartleb, H. *Einführung zur Oper Margarethe von Gounod.* Berlin, 1939.

Pincherle, M., ed. *Musiciens peints par eux-mêmes: lettres de compositeurs écrits en français,* 138f. Paris, 1939.

Landormy, Paul. *Gounod.* Paris, 1942.

————. *Faust de Gounod: étude et analyse.* Paris, 1944.

Demut, H. *Introduction to the Music of Gounod.* London, 1950.

Noske, F. *La mélodie française de Berlioz à Duparc: essai de critique historique,* 145ff. Amsterdam, 1954; English translation, revised, 1970.

Büsser, H. *Charles Gounod.* Lyon, 1961.

Davies, L. *César Franck and his Circle.* London, 1970.

Harding, James. *Gounod.* New York and London, 1973.

Bertier de Sauvigny, Emmanuel de, ed. *Quelques photographies et lettres inédites de Gounod, Massenet et Saint-Saëns.* La Jourdane, 1980.

Berlioz, Hector. *Cauchemars et passions.* Edited by Gerard Condé, *Musiques et musiciens.* Paris, 1981.

Walsh, Thomas Joseph. *Second Empire Opera: the Théâtre Lyrique, Paris, 1851-1870.* London and New York, 1981.

Mack, Dietrich, ed. *Richard Wagner, Das Betroffensein der Nachwelt: Beiträge zur Wirkungsgeschichte.* Darmstadt, 1982.

Marinelli, Carlo. *"Faust" e "Mefistofele" nelle opere teatrali e sinfonico–vocali o discografia.* Rome, 1986.

articles–

Debillemont, J.J. "Charles Gounod," *Nouvelle revue de Paris* 2 (1864): 559.

Ehlert, L. "Gounod contra Wagner." In *Aus der Tonwelt: Essays.* Berlin, 1877; 2nd ed. 1882.

Pougin, A. "Les ascendants de Charles Gounod." *Revue libérale* 3/no. 8 (1884); reprint in *Gazette de France* 12 July (1884).

Erlich, A.H. "Charles Gounod." *Nord und Süd* 34 (1885): 339; reprinted in *Aus allen Tonarten: Studien über Musik,* Berlin, 1888.

Hanslick, E. "Charles Gounod." In *Die moderne Oper, vii: Fünf Jahre Musik (1891-1895): Kritiken,* 361. Berlin, 1896, 1971.

Julien, A. "A propos de la mort de Charles Gounod." *Rivista musicale italiana* 1 (1894): 60; reprinted in A. Julien, *Musique: mélanges d'histoire et de critique musicales et dramatiques.* Paris, 1896.

————."Gounod causeur et écrivain: I. Sur *Mors et vita* et *Héloise et Abélard.* II. Sur *Le Don Juan de Mozart.*" In *Musique: mélanges d'histoire et de critique musicales et dramatiques.* Paris, 1896.

Imbert, H. "Les *Mémoires d'un artiste et autobiographie.*" *Guide musical* (1896-7); published separately, Paris, 1897.

Servières, G. "La version originale de *Mireille.*" *Quinzaine musicale* 1 April (1901).

————. "La légende de la reine de Saba et l'opéra de Charles Gounod." *Guide musical* 2 December (1909).

Pougin, A. "Gounod écrivain: I. Gounod littérateur." *Rivista musicale italiana* 17 (1910): 590; "II, Gounod critique et polémiste." 18 (1911): 747.

Debussy, Claude. "A propos de Charles Gounod," *Musica* July (1906); reprint in *Monsieur Croche et autres écrits* 192, Paris, 1971.

Clouzut, G. "Pierre Dupont et Charles Gounod." *Pages modernes* October (1909).

Prod'homme, Jacques G. "Une famille d'artistes: les Gounod." *Revue d'histoire et de critique musicales* 9 (1910).

Pougin, A. "Gounod écrivain: III, Gounod épistolaire." *Rivista musicale italiana* 19 (1912): 239, 637; 20 (1913): 453, 792.

Saint-Saëns, Camille. "Le Livret de 'Faust'." *Monde musicale* (1914-19).

Prod'homme, Jacques, G. "Miscellaneous Letters by Charles Gounod." *Musical Quarterly* 4 (1918): 630.

Tiersot, J. "Charles Gounod: a Centennial Tribute." *Musical Quarterly* 4 (1918): 409.

————. "Gounod's Letters." *Musical Quarterly* 5 (1919): 40.

d'Ollone, M. "Gounod et l'opéra comique." *La revue musicale* no. 140 (1933): 303.

Cooper, Martin. "Charles Gounod and his Influence on French Music." *Music and Letters* 21 (1940): 50.

Brancour, R. "Gounod." *Rivisita musicale italiana* 48 (1946): 361.

Hahn, R. "La vraie *Mireille.*" In *Thèmes variés,* 101. Paris, 1946.

Samazeuilh, G. "Charles Gounod: à propos du cinquantenaire de sa mort." In *Musiciens de mon temps: chroniques et souvenirs,* 28, Paris, 1947.

Dukas, Paul. "Gounod." in *Ecrits sur la musique.* Paris 1948.

Curtiss, M. "Gounod before *Faust.*" *Musical Quarterly* 38 (1952): 48.

Büsser, H. "Mon Maître Charles Gounod." *Revue des deux mondes* September (1955): 36.

Hopkinson, C. "Notes on the Earliest Editions of Gounod's *Faust.*" In *Festschrift Otto Erich Deutsch,* 245. Kassel, 1963.

Avant-scène opéra March-April (1976) [*Faust* issue].

Schneider, Herbert. "Probleme der Mozart-Rezeption im Frankreich der ersten Hälfte des 19. Jahrhunderts." *Mozart-Jahrbuch* (1980-83): 23.

Avant-scène opéra 41 May-June (1982) [*Roméo et Juliette* issue].

Crichton, Ronald. "*Mirelle* and *Esclarmonde.*" *Opera* December (1983).

Huebner, Steven. "*Mireille* revisited." *Musical Times* 124 (1983): 737.

*   *   *

Faust is so much taken for granted that its vast popularity has made it overfamiliar. Yet it is a landmark in the history of French music. In spite of the obvious flaws—the trivial libretto compared to the profundity of Goethe's original, the blaring soldiers' chorus—*Faust* explains Debussy's remark that Gounod represents an important phase in the evolution of French sensibility. It replaced the traditional pomposity of grand opera with a more poetic and intimate approach. Gounod introduced a technique of conversational exchange rather than declamation. True feeling took over from rant, and proportion was restored. The play of emotion was controlled with a subtle touch. The music suggests perpetual nuance.

The triumph of *Faust,* however, contained a danger. Its overwhelming success often led Gounod to emphasize in his later works those very elements in it which are weakest: the showy and the grandiose. These came to the fore in *Polyeucte,* a lofty "fresco" (Gounod's own word) about an early Christian martyr; in *La reine de Saba,* an epic featuring the Queen of Sheba; in *Cinq-Mars,* an historical piece taken from Vigny's novel about a conspiracy against Cardinal Richelieu; and in *Le tribut de Zamora,* an improbable melodrama with a heroine who is, in turn, a bloodthirsty madwoman, a fiercely devoted mother, and in the end a determined murderess. To these operas, which represent Gounod's weaker side, must be added *La nonne sanglante,* an early work based on Matthew Lewis's Gothic thriller *The Monk,* where the ambitious young composer, in vain as it turned out, tried for success by collaborating on the nineteenth-century equivalent of a modern horror film.

The first glimmer of his true originality shines through in *Sapho.* It is bathed in a Hellenic radiance and that pastoral simplicity which thirteen years later characterised *Mireille.* When he turned to Molière for *Le médecin malgré lui* he found the perfect vehicle for his delicate wit, humor and tenderness. The score abounds in clever orchestral detail and exquisite vocal writing which impressed Diaghilev, who revived it sumptuously with recitatives by Erik Satie and Debussy (who chose it as his favorite Gounod opera). Equally light of touch are *Philémon et Baucis* and *La colombe,* which Diaghilev also revived in the 1920s.

Among Gounod's finest achievements must be counted *Mireille.* Its faults—the heroine's rather too edifying death scene and an occasional over-emphasis on melodrama—are far outweighed by the idyllic portrait Gounod draws of the womanly Mireille and by the skillfully blended chiaroscuro in the picture he gives of her native Provence. The music is filled with sunshine, although Gounod has caught as well the tragedy that broods under the bright coloring of the Provençal countryside.

Juliet was another heroine who inspired some of Gounod's best writing. The score of *Roméo et Juliette* flows with a naturalness of speech and a sharpness of youthful feeling that evokes a moving and innocent beauty. The three simple bars accompanying Juliet's "C'est le doux rossignol de l'amour" ("It is the sweet nightingale of love") carry the poignant touch of genius. "Melody alone counts in music," Gounod once said. "Melody, always melody, that is the sole, the unique secret of our art," and clear, flowing, spontaneous melody is characteristic of Gounod at his best.

—James Harding

GOYESCAS.

Composer: Enrique Granados.

Librettist: Fernando Periquet y Zuaznabar.

First Performance: New York, Metropolitan Opera, 28 January 1916.

Roles: Rosario (soprano); Fernando (tenor); Paquiro (baritone); Pepa (mezzo-soprano); A Voice (soprano or tenor); chorus.

Publications

book–

Granados and Goyescas: the Catalogue of an Exhibition Honoring Enrique Granados and the American Premiere of *Goyescas, Boston Athenaeum Gallery, January 18-20, 1982.* Boston, 1982.

articles–

Chase, W.B. "Opera founded on paintings." *Opera Magazine* March (1916): 10.
Newman, E. "The Granados of the 'Goyescas'." *Musical Times* August 1 (1916): 343.
Periquet, F. "La opera española moderna: 'Goyesca'." *World's Work* April (1916): 178.
Periquet, F. "'Goyescas'; how the opera was conceived." Translated by S. de Silva. *Opera News* 29 January (1916): 12.
Van de Broekhoven, J. "'Goyescas' (The Rival Lovers) A Spanish Opera in Three Pictures." *Musical Observer* 13/no.3 (1916): 134.
Vernon, Grenville. "New York hears its first Spanish opera." *Opera News* 7/no.13 (1916): 2,5.
Abbado, M. *"Goyescas." Rassegna della Istruzione Artistica* 8 (1938): 116.
Longland, J.R. "Granados and the opera 'Goyescas'." *Notes Hispanic* 5 (1945): 95.
Wilson, C. "The Two Versions of the 'Goyescas'." *Monthly Musical Record* 81 (1951): 203.
Rozenshil'd, K. "'Goyeski' Granados." *Sovetskaya muzyka* no. 1 (1968): 87.

*　　*　　*

In the wake of the New York premier of *Goyescas,* most critics concurred that its greatest failing was a lack of any real dramatic action. The critic of *Musical America* claimed: "It is . . . neither drama nor character nor ideas in which Granados is interested—it is the expression of a certain spirit, the spirit he found in the paintings of Goya." Indeed, *Goyescas* was an attempt, literally, to bring to life scenes from Goya's paintings in a vivid visual and musical recreation, as suggested by the opera's descriptive title. Granados even uses the word *cuadro* (tableau), rather than act, to describe each main section. A parallel could be made with the contemporary vogue for *tableaux vivants.* Although Goya is more famous for his grim depictions of the peninsula war or his visionary Black paintings, in Granados' day his idealistic studies of *Majos* and *Majas* (colorful, lower-class characters who lived in Madrid during the eighteenth century) were a popular source of inspiration for writers and artists alike. Whatever the realities of their existence, in Goya's paintings they were usually depicted singing or dancing, or participating in some flirtatious encounter. Granados was fascinated with Goya's *Majos* and *Majas.* At the time of composing *Goyescas* he claimed: "Goya's masterpieces immortalize him by exalting our national life. I subordinate my inspiration to that of the man who knew so well how to depict the actions and times peculiar to the people of Spain." In his music Granados attempted to convey the spirit of the popular music and dance of Goya's Spain, and he even incorporates a theme from a well-known *tonadilla* (a kind of musical entertainment which was popular in the eighteenth century).

Enacted in three short tableaux (the first and second tableaux only last about ten minutes each), the plot of *Goyescas* is a simple tale of jealousy and wounded pride for four main characters, supported, in the first and second tableaux, by a chorus of *Majos* and *Majas.* Paquiro (a bull-fighter) asks Rosario (a high-born lady) to the ball. In doing so he not only incenses his girlfriend, Pepa, but also Rosario's lover,

The first production of Granados's *Goyescas,* **Metropolitan Opera, New York, 1916**

Fernando (a captain of the Royal Guard), who insists on taking her himself. At the ball Fernando and Paquiro argue and, much to Rosario's dismay, resolve to fight a duel later that night. Alone in her garden, she sings a sad lament to the nightingale (this section is an adaptation of his well-known piano piece "The Maiden and the Nightingale"). Fernando arrives and they sing a duet, mutually declaring their undying love. But Paquiro keeps his appointment, and in the ensuing duel (heard off-stage) Fernando is mortally wounded, and he dies in Rosario's arms. Granados claimed before the premier that the characters of Fernando and Rosario were actually based on Goya and his mistress the Duchess of Alba. The total running time (including two intermezzi) is less than an hour. The original performance also featured ballet dancers.

Granados's piano suite *Goyescas* (1909-11) formed the musical basis of the opera (though the final "Epilogo" is excluded), but it also contains music from other sources, including his youthful *zarzuela Ovillejos* (1897) as well as some original music. The orchestral intermezzo which Granados composed at the behest of the Metropolitan directors a few days before the first performance was to be his last work. Uniquely in the history of opera, the complete music of *Goyescas* was composed before the libretto, which had to be tailor-made by Fernando Periquet y Zuaznabar to fit the music. Not surprisingly, given these unusual circumstances, the on-stage drama is, in reality, virtually non-existent, and the words often seem awkwardly cramped together. Similarly, owing to Granados's penchant for ensembles, Periquet's dialogue, consisting largely of abstract thoughts of the characters

rather than direct exchanges, is frequently incomprehensible. From a purely dramatic perspective, these are clearly drawbacks, yet the text fulfills an important coloristic function in the choral exclamations, which reinforce the strongly-marked rhythmic character of the music.

Musically speaking, the most serious faults in *Goyescas* are the result of Granados's tendency to rely too heavily on his piano work as the basis of the opera. Although some of the tunes in the piano suite are suitable as vocal material (having been originally adapted from popular song), Granados shows little discretion in his tendency to extrapolate extra voice parts from the surrounding harmonic structure, and much of the vocal music (especially in the chorus) presents real technical difficulties. Perhaps deliberately, *Goyescas* contains little true recitative, and at times the continuous melodic material for the soloists creates a monotonous effect when not relieved by the chorus. Granados's orchestration shows little of the ingenuity and boldness which is a feature of the Catalan works, and in those sections based on the piano music, it is barely more than adequate transcription. His inability to successfully adapt the contrapuntal lines which are a characteristic feature of the piano score is particularly evident.

In *Goyescas* Granados fulfilled his aim of creating a series of musical *tableaux vivants* based on Goya's paintings. Yet, deprived of the vivid stage effects, as in a concert performance, *Goyescas* is a work which fails absolutely. In the wake of its premier, few critics omitted to mention the authentic national color the music possessed, yet the opera does little to improve the brilliant synthesis of folk and popular elements already obtained in the superior piano suite. *Goyescas* failed to live up to the theater managers' expectations and was abandoned after only five performances in New York. A few years after Granados's death, a critic wrote: "the idea of making an opera with these piano pieces was a sin of commercialism, which met with the fate it well deserves." It is a shame, in many ways, that Granados's operatic reputation should hang on this piece. His Catalan works are far superior. Even so, despite its technical failings, *Goyescas* remains an enthusiastic testament to Granados's obsession with the masterpieces of Goya.

—Mark Larrad

GRAF, Herbert.

Director, producer. Born 10 April 1904, in Vienna; son of the music critic Max Graf. Died 5 April 1973, in Geneva. Married: Liselotte Austerlitz, 1927. Studied with Guido Adler at the University of Vienna, Ph.D. 1925; also studied at the Opera School of the State Academy for Music; began career at opera house in Münster, Germany, 1925; worked as director in Münster, Breslau, Frankfurt am Main, and Basel; moved to the United States and worked for the Philadelphia Opera, 1934-35; stage director, Metropolitan Opera, 1936-60; naturalized American citizen, 1943; head of the opera department at the Curtis Institute in Philadelphia, 1949-60; produced Canadian premiere of *Tristan und Isolde;* returned to Europe and became the artistic director at Zürich Opernhaus, 1960-62; artistic director, Grand Théâtre, Geneva, 1965-73.

Opera Productions (selected)

Die Meistersinger von Nürnberg, Salzburg, 1936.
Samson et Delila, Metropolitan Opera, 1936.
Salome, Metropolitan Opera, 1938.
Falstaff, Metropolitan Opera, 1938.
Otello, Metropolitan Opera, 1937 and 1963.
Orfeo ed Euridice, Metropolitan Opera, 1938.
Le nozze di Figaro, Metropolitan Opera, 1940.
Un ballo in maschera, Metropolitan Opera, 1940.
La fille du régiment, Metropolitan Opera, 1940.
Il trovatore, Metropolitan Opera, 1940 and 1959.
Alceste, Metropolitan Opera, 1941.
Die Zauberflöte, Metropolitan Opera, 1941.
Der Streit zwischen Phoebus und Pan, Metropolitan Opera, 1942.
Die Entführung aus dem Serail, Metropolitan Opera, 1946.
Il tabarro, Metropolitan Opera, 1946.
The Warrior, Metropolitan Opera, 1947.
Das Rheingold, Metropolitan Opera, 1948.
Die Walküre, Metropolitan Opera, 1948.
Siegfried, Metropolitan Opera, 1948.
Götterdämmerung, Metropolitan Opera, 1948.
Manon Lescaut, Metropolitan Opera, 1949.
Der fliegende Holländer, Metropolitan Opera, 1950.
La forza del destino, Metropolitan Opera, 1952.
Tannhäuser, Metropolitan Opera, 1953.
Arabella, Metropolitan Opera, 1955.
Parsifal, Metropolitan Opera, 1956.

Der Rosenkavalier, Metropolitan Opera, 1956.
Don Giovanni, Metropolitan Opera, 1957.
Samson, Covent Garden, 1958-59 season.
Boris Godunov, Covent Garden, 1958-59 season.
Parsifal, Covent Garden, 1958-59 season.
Wozzeck, Metropolitan Opera, 1959.
Tristan und Isolde, Metropolitan Opera, 1959.
Fidelio, Metropolitan Opera, 1960.
Elektra, Metropolitan Opera, 1966.
Ernani, Verona Arena, 1972.

Publications

By GRAF: books–

The Opera and its Future in America. New York, 1941.
Opera for the People. Minneapolis, 1951.
Producing Opera for America. New York, 1961.

articles–

"New Opera Theatre Concepts." *Musical America* 78 (February 1958): 18-19.
"Letter and Spirit in Staging." *Opera News* 22 (7 April 1958): 26-28.
"On Staging *Wozzeck*." *Opera News* 23 (9 March 1959): 6-7.
"Staging *Othello*." *Opera News* 27 (23 March 1963): 8-11.
"Opera az uj Oroszorszagban." *Magyar Zene, Zenetudomanyi folyoirt* 18, no. 3 (1977): 298-308.
"Operska rezija kao nauka; pokusaj njene teorije (1927)." *Zvuk; Jugoslovenska muzicka revija* no. 4 (Winter 1983): 67-71.
"Pokusaj njene teorije (1927)." *Zvuk; Jugoslovenska muzicka revija* no. 2 (Summer 1984): 34-38.

About GRAF: articles–

Freeman, F.J. "Torch Bearers of Opera." *Opera News* 15 (30 October 1950): 8-10.
"Graf on Wing." *Opera News* 18 (19 October 1953): 28.
"Graf's Summer Projects." *Opera News* 18 (5 April 1954): 32.
"Herbert Graf." *London Musical Events* 13 (November 1958): 21.
Helm, E. "Graf in Zurich." *The New York Times* 110 (26 February 1961): 11, Section 2.
Regitz, H. "Das Interview: Herbert Graf." *Opernwelt* no. 7 (July 1972): 28-29.

*   *   *

Herbert Graf was a prominent member of the large group of German- and Austrian-born operatic producers/stage directors who came to their profession with a thorough musical background and sound academic training in the art of stagecraft. Unlike some more recent recruits from the legitimate stage, from films and television, or from academe who have found opera a diverting personal plaything, Graf began by being well grounded in operatic tradition and, with a fertile imagination and understanding of the requirements of singers and musicians, proceeded from there.

A seven-year apprenticeship as producer in Münster, Breslau, and Frankfurt am Main occurred when experimentation vied with traditionalism in Europe's state-subsidized opera houses, so that when Graf came to America in 1934, he brought with him many ideas new and untried there. His first assignment, as producer of the Philadelphia Orchestra's initial season of staged opera, proved to be an eyeopener to operagoers in the United States: an uncut *Tristan und Isolde,* *Carmen* on a revolving stage, *Le nozze di Figaro* and *Falstaff* in English translation, and the American premieres of Christoph Willibald Gluck's *Iphigénie en Aulid* and Igor Stravinsky's *Mavra* were all presented with fresh staging concepts unfamiliar in established American companies. The season generated warm audience and press acclaim, especially for Graf, but a large deficit forced the company to stop productions after that year. Graf returned to Europe to produce *Die Entführung aus dem Serail* for Bruno Walter in Florence, *Tannhäuser* for Wilhelm Furtwängler in Vienna, and *Die Meistersinger von Nürnberg* for Arturo Toscanini in Salzburg.

From 1936 to 1967, Dr Graf was closely associated with the Metropolitan Opera, staging new productions and revivals. Given the restrictions of the repertory system, as opposed to the luxury of festival preparations, he admittedly "learned the hard way how to deal in some fashion with the problems of producing opera with solo artists who are not available for rehearsals . . . the handicap of casts that are constantly changing . . . the hard task of adopting action to existing sets . . . and particularly the lack of rehearsals." However, with characteristic patience, he did not admonish principal singers who had done a role a certain way somewhere else, or browbeat a chorus molded into a long-practiced routine. His approach was low-keyed, reasonable, understanding, and ultimately convincing, resulting over the years in many notable performances: a legendary *Otello* with Giovanni Martinelli and Lawrence Tibbett; a sparkling *Nozze di Figaro* in which he cleverly adapted the intimacies of the work to the large Metropolitan Opera stage and a cast of major grand opera artists (Ezio Pinza, Bidu Sayão, Elisabeth Rethberg, John Brownlee and Risë Stevens); and a series of collaborations with the artist Eugene Berman (*Don Giovanni, Rigoletto, Otello,* and *La forza del destino*) where stage action and handsome design were skillfully combined.

Dr Graf remained active in Europe, where the chosen venue often inspired new and spectacular staging methods: *Oberon* with singing mermaids in the Boboli Gardens, Florence; *Otello* before the Ducal Palace in Venice; *Don Giovanni* in Salzburg's Rocky Riding School; *Aida* (four different stagings), *Carmen,* and *Mefistofele* at the 25,000-seat Roman Arena in Verona, and a staged version of Johann Sebastian Bach's *St Matthew Passion* in Palermo. At Covent Garden, Graf staged new productions of *Boris Godunov, Parsifal* and George Frideric Handel's *Samson.*

In 1960, Dr Graf was engaged as general manager of the opera in Zurich, where he proceeded to enliven the repertory and build an ensemble of young singers including James McCracken, Gwyneth Jones, Sandra Warfield, Reri Grist, and James Pease, among others. As his then-assistant Lotfi Mansouri wrote: "He knew voices, he loved them, and he could work with them. He was a 'star-maker', recognizing talent, and most important, giving employment."

With the restoration of the Grand Théâtre in Geneva, Dr Graf became its manager and was permitted to carry out his original Zurich proposals: opera in the original language; complete artistic authority within a given budget; use of radio and television facilities, and formation of a studio group of young artists to supplement the "name singers" engaged. As Mansouri indicated "His dream materialized in Geneva." Graf remained there as manager from 1965 until his death in 1973.

—Louis Snyder

GRAHAM, Colin.

Director. Born 22 September 1931, in Hove, Sussex. Educated at Stowe School, Royal Academy of Dramatic Art 1949-51; began career as actor and stage manager; opera debut, *Il re pastore,* London, 1954; stage manager, stage director English Opera Group 1953-63; artistic director of English Opera Group, 1963-75; associate director of production, Sadler's Wells, 1964-79; English National Opera 1968-83, director of productions, 1978-83; artistic director Aldeburgh Festival, 1968-; co-founder and artistic director English Music Theatre, 1976-; associate artistic director Opera Theatre of St Louis, 1978-84; artistic director Banff Opera Programme, 1984-; artistic director, Opera Theatre of St Louis, 1985-. Wrote libretti and directed world premieres for Bennett's *Penny for a Song,* 1967; Paulus's *The Postman Always Rings Twice,* 1981, and *The Woodlanders,* 1984; revised libretto for Purcell's *King Arthur;* directed world premieres of Britten's *Noye's Fludde,* 1957, *Curlew River,* 1964, *The Burning Fiery Furnace,* 1966, *The Prodigal Son,* 1968, *The Golden Vanity,* 1970, *Death in Venice,* 1973, and *Owen Wingrave* (for BBC-TV), 1970; Bennett's *The Mines of Sulphur,* 1965, and *Victory,* 1970; Walton's *The Bear,* 1967; Musgrave's *The Decision,* 1967, and *Voice of Ariadne,* 1974; Crosse's *The Grace of Todd,* 1968; Maw's *The Rising of the Moon,* 1970; and Corigliano's *The Ghosts of Versailles,* 1991.

Opera Productions (selected)

Il re pastore, London, 1954.
Noye's Fludde, Aldeburgh, 1957.
Curlew River, Aldeburgh, 1964.

Colin Graham

The Mines of Sulphur, London, Sadler's Wells, 1965.
The Burning Fiery Furnace, Aldeburgh, 1966.
Penny for a Song, London, Sadler's Wells, 1967.
The Bear, Aldeburgh, 1967.
The Decision, New Opera Company, 1967.
The Prodigal Son, Aldeburgh, 1968.
The Grace of Todd, Aldeburgh, 1968.
Peter Grimes, Scottish Opera, 1968.
La forza del destino, London, Sadler's Wells, 1969.
The Rising of the Moon, Glyndebourne, 1970.
Victory, London, Covent Garden, 1970.
The Golden Vanity, Vienna Boys' Choir, 1970.
Death in Venice, Aldeburgh, 1973.
Voice of Ariadne, Aldeburgh, 1974.
Troilus and Cressida, London, Covent Garden, 1977.
From the House of the Dead (Z mrtvého domu), London Coliseum, 1978.
Lulu, Santa Fe, 1979.
An Actor's Revenge, Opera Theatre of St Louis, 1981.
La traviata, New York, Metropolitan Opera, 1981.
Così fan tutte, New York, Metropolitan Opera, 1982.
Curlew River, St Louis, Christ Church Cathedral, 1986.
Il viaggio a Reims, St Louis.
Peter Grimes, St Louis, 1990.
Albert Herring, San Diego Opera, 1991.
The Ghosts of Versailles, New York, Metropolitan Opera, 1991.

Publications:

By GRAHAM: librettos

Libretto to Britten, *The Golden Vanity.* New York, 1967.
Libretto to Bennett, *A Penny for a Song,* 1969.
Revised libretto to Purcell, *King Arthur,* 1971.
Libretto to Paulus, *The Postman Always Rings Twice.* Valley Forge, 1982.
Libretto to Paulus, *The Woodlanders,* 1984.
Libretto to Miki, *Joruri,* 1985.

articles—

"On Tour in the Soviet Union." *Opera* 15/December (1964): 784.
"*King Arthur* Revised and Revived." *Opera* 21/October (1970): 904.
Production notes to Britten, Benjamin, *The Prodigal Son: Third Parable for Church Performance, Op. 81.* London, 1971.
"Walter Felsenstein." *Opera* 27/January (1976): 29.
"Working with Britten." *Opera* 28/February (1977): 130.
Graham, Colin et al. "English Music Theatre's Kabuki Opera." *Opera* 30/October (1979): 948.
Production notes to Britten, Benjamin, *The Curlew River: A Parable for Church Performance, Op. 71.* London, 1980.
"Opera as Theatre: A Conversation between Colin Graham and Harold Rosenthal." *Opera* 32/June (1981): 577.
Production notes to Britten, Benjamin, *Burning Fiery Furnace: Second Parable for Church Performance, Op. 77.* London, 1983.
"Stand and Sing vs. Today's Expectations." *Opera Canada* 30/1 (1989): 15.

About GRAHAM: articles—

Senior, E. "Producer's Librettos." *Music and Musicians* 14/April (1966): 46.

Trilling, O. "Zweimal Britten." *Opernwelt* 20/6 (1979): 47.
Rosenthal, Harold. "Opera as Theatre: Towards an Ideal Company." *Opera* 32/May (1981): 452.
Heymont, G. "All in the Family." *Opera News* 50/June (1986): 14.
Citron, P. "On the Cover." *Opera Canada* 28/2 (1987): 4.
Reisman, J. "The Creative Spark." *Opera Canada* 30/4 (1989): 16.
Caswell, E. "Curlew River." *The RCM* 87/3 (1990): 30.

* * *

Colin Graham is a man of the theater. He studied at the Royal Academy of Dramatic Art, and worked for a short time at the Nottingham Playhouse, but quickly moved into the world of opera. Early in his career he became associated with Benjamin Britten and directed as many as seven Britten premieres (*Noye's Fludde, Golden Vanity,* for which he wrote the libretto, the three church parables, *Owen Wingrave,* and *Death in Venice*). He has subsequently directed all of Britten's operas, with the exception of *Billy Budd.* His association with Britten has had a profound effect on Graham's artistic and spiritual development. Graham himself says that Britten "taught me the organic nature of music, how everything had to spring from it, and yet at the same time he would always say that if it hadn't been for the words, the composer would never have written the music in the first place." Joan Cross was another formative influence on Graham's work; she insisted he keep focused on the legitimate theater and not let his style become "ossified" within opera and its conventions.

Aside from *Golden Vanity,* Graham also prepared a libretto for Britten based on *Anna Karenina;* the opera was specifically intended for Galina Vishnevskaya, Peter Pears, and Mstislav Rostropovich to present at the Bolshoi. Plans were well underway, but they were scrapped when the Russians marched into Czechoslovakia. Later there was talk of presenting the work at Snape with Heather Harper in the title role, but this never materialized. The libretto is still extant. Graham wrote the libretti for an adaptation of Hardy's *The Woodlanders, The Postman Always Rings Twice* (both by Stephen Paulus) and for *Jōruri* (Minoru Miki). More controversial have been Graham's performing adaptations of works such as Weber's *Oberon* and Purcell's *King Arthur.* When the latter was first presented by the English Opera Group it was hailed as a masterwork; when it was revived in St Louis in 1989 some purists found it excessive. Audiences, however, loved it, and responded to Graham's sense of what actually works in the theater. Thus he is not reluctant to supply additional words to such pieces as *Les contes d' Hoffmann* and *Béatrice et Bénédict.*

As a director of opera, Graham always thinks in theatrical terms; this can readily be seen in his treatment of the chorus, which he rarely uses as a collective but as a group of individuals. He sometimes goes so far as to give chorus members a written biography/character sketch, so that each can find an identity within the group.

In the early 1980s, Graham began study for the ministry and almost left the theater. He was ordained by the non-denominational Covenant Ministries in 1987, and now spends a good deal of his time counseling artists, for whom he has a great deal of empathy. This spiritual dimension to his life seems to inform his theatrical work. His 1986 presentation of Britten's *Curlew River* in Christ Church Cathedral in St Louis made a profound impression because of its measured and moving simplicity. It shows up also in his 1990 presentation of *Peter Grimes,* where there is demonstrable tension between soul and body, between Grimes's self-love and self-hate. Graham himself believes that it is also revealed in a growing simplicity in his work. "Economy of means, maximum of effect" is a phrase he likes to use, and it certainly is not an empty one. His attraction to Japanese theater is probably another side of this spiritual quest. Graham spent some time in Japan in the early 1970s under the auspices of the British Council studying noh and kabuki, and the two Miki operas (*Actor's Revenge* and *Jōruri*) reflect this directly. Not surprisingly, Graham is less successful with an opera such as *Carmen.*

Graham's work is not, of course, always serious. His was the first modern presentation of Rossini's *Il viaggio a Reims;* the production was joyous and sparkling. But there is a sense that when dealing with the world of the imagination, the fairy worlds of, for example, *King Arthur* and *Oberon,* his spirituality is also evident. Through comparatively simple means, Graham can conjure a world of ravishing beauty. Frequently in the past he has acted as his own designer to achieve these ends, although he is less inclined to do so now.

Graham's current positions in St Louis and Banff seem to fill his artistic needs and give him the opportunity to control the total artistic venture and to experiment with new works and styles. He is particularly interested in working with young singers in order to develop their sense of the theater. In a way, he views himself as a teaching director, reflecting his early interest in acting itself. He has had no formal training in music beyond his school days, and his work at the Royal Academy of Dramatic Art was as an actor; thus the task of training singers to move, to project, and to fill a role, is close to his heart.

Although he is through-and-through an operatic director, he heeded Joan Cross's advice and has worked occasionally in the theater. He still hopes for the opportunity to direct more Shakespeare. Doubtless the music he finds there is as fascinating as the music he finds in the worlds of Purcell, Tchaikovsky, and Britten.

—Lawrence J. Dennis

GRANADOS, Enrique.

Composer. Born 27 July 1867, in Lérida. Died 24 March 1916, aboard the S.S. Sussex (sunk by a German submarine in the English Channel). Studied piano with Pedrell and Pujol at the Barcelona Conservatory; studied composition with Pedrell at the conservatory, 1884-87; studied with Beriot in Paris, 1887; recital debut in Barcelona, 1890; his zarzuela *María del Carmen* successful, 1898; established the Academia Granados in 1901.

Operas/Dramatic Works

Publishers: G. Schirmer, Union Musical Española.

Los Ovillejos (zarzuela), José Feliú y Codina, 1897 [unperformed]; revised as *Ovillejos* (sainete lírico) [unperformed].
María del Carmen, José Feliú y Codina, Madrid, Parish, 12 November 1898.
La leyenda de la fada (drama liric), c. 1898-1900 [unperformed].
Petrarca (poema dramàtic), Apeles Mestres, 1899-1900 [unperformed].

Gaziel by Enrique Granados, Barcelona, 1906

Picarol (drama liric), Apeles Mestres, Barcelona, Tivoli, 23 February 1901.
Follet (drama liric), Apeles Mestres, Barcelona, Liceu, 4 April 1903.
Gaziel (drama liric), Apeles Mestres, Barcelona, Principal, 27 October 1906.
Liliana (poema lirico), Apeles Mestres, Barcelona, Palau de Bellas Artes, 9 July 1911.
El portalico de Belén (children's opera), Gabriel Miró, Vallcarca (near Barcelona), Christmas 1914-15.
Goyescas (largely based on the piano pieces of the same name, which were inspired by paintings and etchings of Goya), Fernando Periquet y Zuaznabar, New York, Metropolitan Opera, 28 January 1916.

Other works: orchestral works, choral works, chamber music, songs, piano pieces.

Publications/Writings

By GRANADOS: articles–

"La opera española moderna: 'Goyesca'." *World's Work* April (1916): 177.

About GRANADOS: books–

Ibern, G. de Boladeres. *Enrique Granados.* Barcelona, 1921.
Collet, H. *Albéniz et Granados.* Paris, 1926; 2nd ed. 1948.
Subirá, J. *Enrique Granados.* Madrid, 1926.
Rafols, J.F. *Modernismo y Modernistas.* Barcelona, 1949.

Pahissa, J. *Sendas y cumbres de la música española.* Buenos Aires, 1955.

Fernández-Cid, A. *Granados.* Madrid, 1956.

Curet, F. *Història del teatre Català.* Barcelona, 1967.

Rozenshil'd, K. *Enrike Granados: iz ispanskoy muziki.* Moscow, 1971.

Burnett, James. *Manuel de Falla and the Spanish Musical Renaissance.* London, 1979.

Granados and Goyescas: the Catalogue of an Exhibition Honoring Enrique Granados and the American Premiere of Goyescas, Boston Athenaeum Gallery, January 18-20, 1982. Boston, 1982.

Aviñoa, X. *La música i el modernisme.* Barcelona, 1985.

Hess, C.A. *Enrique Granados: a Bio-Bibliography.* Westport, Connecticut, 1991.

articles–

Pillois, J. "Un entretien avec Granados." *Revue musicale S.I.M.* 15 April (1914): 1.

Revista musical catalana 15 June (1916) [Granados issue].

Chase, W.B. "Opera founded on paintings." *Opera Magazine* March (1916): 10.

Newman, E. "The Granados of the 'Goyescas'." *Musical Times* August 1 (1916): 343.

Periquet, F. "La opera española moderna: 'Goyesca'." *World's Work* April (1916): 178.

Periquet, F., translated by S. de Silva. " 'Goyescas'; how the opera was conceived." *Opera News* 29 January (1916): 12.

Van de Broekhoven, J. " 'Goyescas' (The Rival Lovers) A Spanish Opera in Three Pictures." *Musical Observer* 13/no. 3 (1916): 134.

Vernon, Grenville. "New York hears its first Spanish opera." *Opera News* 7/no. 13 (1916): 2, 5.

Mason, E.L. "Enrique Granados." *Music and Letters* 14 (1933): 231.

Abbado, M. "*Goyescas.*" *Rassegna della istruzione artistica* 8 (1938): 116.

Longland, J.R. "Granados and the opera 'Goyesca'." *Notes Hispanic* 5 (1945): 95.

Livermore, A. "Granados and the 19th Century in Spain." *Music Review* 7 (1946): 80.

Wilson, C. "The Two Versions of the 'Goyescas'." *Monthly Musical Record* 81 (1951): 203.

Martinez, P.J. "Enrique Granados." *Temas españolas* no. 6 (1952): 12.

Rozenshil'd, K. " 'Goyeski' Granados." *Sovetskaya muzika* no. 1 (1968): 87.

Sandelewski, W. "Spotkanie z corka Enrique Granadosa." *Ruch Muzyczny* 16 (1977): 7.

Mas-Lopez, E. "Apeles Mestres: poetic lyricist." *Opera Journal* 13 (1980): 24.

Larrad, Mark. "The Lyric Dramas of Enric Granados." *Revista de musicologia* [forthcoming].

unpublished–

Riva, J.D. "The Goyescas for Piano by Enrique Granados: a critical edition." Ph.D. dissertation, New York University, 1983.

Larrad, Mark. "The Catalan Theatre Works of Enric Granados." Ph.D. dissertation, University of Liverpool, 1992.

* * *

Even within his lifetime Granados was more famous as a composer of piano music than of operas. At that time the domination of Spanish opera houses by main-stream European (and, above all, Italian) works presented a formidable challenge to native opera composers, few of whom achieved enduring success. Although Granados's operas were received rapturously at the time, they failed to remain in the repertory. Only two, *María del Carmen* and *Goyescas*, were performed outside Spain, and until recently, his operas were largely ignored by musicologists. However, the recent rediscovery of several "lost" operas has led to a re-evaluation of Granados as a composer. Far from being peripheral works, his operas occupy a unique place in his output and within the development of national opera in Spain.

The flowering of a native opera tradition in Spain in the late nineteenth century was inspired by Felipe Pedrell (1841-1922), the "father of Spanish music." Pedrell, whose teachings had a profound influence on Granados, believed that the art and folk music of Spain's past could form the basis of a uniquely national style. Based on librettos which depict scenes from everyday Spanish life, Granados's first stage works, *Ovillejos* and *María del Carmen*, are the most overtly national in style and content. *Ovillejos* is Granados's only *zarzuela* (a type of operetta with spoken dialogue) and the music invokes some of the distinctive melodic and rhythmic idioms of popular Spanish music. It was never performed, but some of the music was incorporated in his last conspicuously national work, *Goyescas*. The success of *María del Carmen* was undoubtedly fostered by the galvanizing of national feelings which followed Spain's loss of her remaining overseas colonies in 1898. Musically, it represents a rapprochement between the "popular" Hispanism of his earlier work with elements derived from the folk music of Murcia (the score includes at least one identifiable folk song from the region, which Granados had copied from a collection of folk songs). The rousing final chorus of act II invokes the color and sounds of a village celebration (complete with guitars and mandolines) to the tune of a lively dance called a *malagueña*. Popular elements proliferate too in Granados's last major stage work, *Goyescas* (inspired by the paintings of Goya), which is largely an adaptation of his piano suite of the same name.

Forming a corollary to Pedrell's quest for a national opera, the growth of a tradition of operas in the Catalan language (which reached its apogee around 1900) had been strongly influenced by Catalonia's striving towards cultural and political autonomy from the rest of Spain. A feature of the Catalan modernist movement as a whole was its fervent desire to embrace the latest artistic currents emanating from northern Europe. This was balanced by its rejection of Hispanic traditions, however, and in his Catalan works Granados carefully avoided the musical idioms which give his nationalist works their distinctive Hispanic flavor.

The texts Apeles Mestres wrote for Granados reveal his romantic preoccupation with an imaginary and idealised past, as in *Petrarca*, which is based on the events surrounding the last day of the poet Petrarch, whose idealised love for Laura is a central theme of the work. Mestres (1854-1936) was a poet rather than a dramatist, and all his works lack developed on-stage action. Yet it was the very naturalness and directness of Mestre's language that appealed to Granados's essentially romantic nature.

In terms of musical invention and internal dramatic coherence, *Petrarca* and *Follet* are Granados's greatest works for the stage, yet they still remain unknown. In both operas the use of continuous dramatic recitative and the expanded symphonic sections betray a debt to Wagner, yet the originality of Granados's musical language is indisputable and astonishing. The bold and ingenious orchestral effects come as a surprise from a composer usually associated with the piano. In the final scene of *Petrarca* (an imaginative dream sequence) the sparse combination of a high solo violin with double basses creates an effect of striking modernity which contradicts our usual conception of Granados as a composer of lushly romantic music. *Follet,* his most meticulously prepared opera, contains several Catalan folk tunes which are worked into the symphonic texture and function as reminiscence motives. Act III is preceded by a prelude which powerfully evokes a storm symbolizing the tragic events at the end of the opera, suggesting parallels with Verdi.

Picarol, Gaziel and *Liliana* (which all contain spoken dialogue) represent part of a tradition of operettas that were composed specifically to fill the need for a type of popular entertainment in the Catalan language that could compete with the Hispanic *genero chico* (a kind of one-act *zarzuela*). Containing direct, tuneful music, they represent a secondary facet of Granados's theatrical production. In *Gaziel* (a subtle adaption of the Faust story with a female devil), trilling woodwinds and strings are graphically used to represent the sound of the raging wind in the opening song. *Liliana* is a curious hybrid work containing a mixture of spoken drama, songs, symphonic interludes and dance, that could be regarded as a rather sophisticated form of pantomime. A product of the contemporary "naturistic" vogue for gnomes and fairies, *Liliana* even contains a frogs' chorus.

Granados composed two other minor theater works of which only fragments remain. Although previously listed as an orchestral work, the drama *La leyenda de la fada* contained songs as well as orchestral music, and the existence of a few professionaly copied parts suggests that a performance had been planned. *El portalico de Belén* is a drama with songs for children based on the nativity scene. The music of both works is reminiscent of the naive folklike style of his Catalan operettas.

Viewed synoptically, Granados's operas reveal great diversities, stylistically and qualitatively, and they form an essential and consistent thread throughout his musical output. Granados is a miniaturist and he lacks the Verdian flair for stage effects, but his innate tendency to develop programmatic ideas in his compositions found its logical expression in his stage works, where he excelled in capturing the mood and atmosphere of his texts. Because *María del Carmen* and *Goyescas* measure up to the international conception of a Spanish opera, they have remained (albeit tenuously) in the repertory. Granados's great Catalan operas, *Petrarca* and *Follet,* remain to be discovered by today's opera-going public.

Although sometimes erroneously listed as operas, Granados's incidental music to Feliú y Codina's comedy *Miel de la Alcarria* (1895) and Gual's drama *Blancaflor* (1899) is essentially non-operatic, and neither work contains significant vocal material.

—Mark Larrad

LE GRAND MACABRE.

Composer: György Ligeti.

Librettist: M. Meschke (after Ghelderode).

First Performance: Stockholm, Royal Opera, 12 April 1978.

Roles: Chief of the Secret Police (soprano); Venus (soprano); Clitoria (soprano); Spermando (mezzo-soprano); Prince Go-Go (soprano); Mescalina (mezzo-soprano); Piet the Pot (tenor); Nekrotzar (baritone); Astradamors (bass); Ruffiak (baritone); Schobiak (baritone); Schabernak (baritone); White Minister (speaking); Black Minister (speaking).

Publications

articles—

Jungheinrich, Hans-Klaus. "György Ligetis *Le grand macabre.* Ein Avantgardist auf dem Seil und in der Manege." *Hi-Fi-Stereophonic* 17 (1978): 694.
Fabian, Imre. " 'Ein unendliches Erbarmen mit der Kreatur.' Zu György Ligetis *Le grande macabre.*" *Österreichische Musikzeitschrift* 36 (1981): 570.
Wiesmann, Sigrid. "Bedingungen der Komponierbarkeit. Bernd Alois Zimmermanns *Die Soldaten,* György Ligetis *Le grande macabre.*" In *Für und wider die Literaturoper. Zur Situation nach 1945,* edited by Sigrid Wiesmann, 27. Laaber, 1982.
Fanselau, Rainer. "György Ligeti: *Le grand macabre.* Gesichtspunkte für eine Behandlung im Musikunterricht." *Musik und Bildung* 15 (1983): 17.

The most striking aspect of Ligeti's only opera, *Le grand macabre,* is its anti-rationalism, which while reminiscent of surrealism, has more in common with the works of Alfred Jarry. The opera is based on a play by the Belgian writer Michel de Ghelderode, though Ligeti has treated the text with great freedom, sometimes even writing the music first and then adding the words to it.

Ligeti claims to have written, not an anti-opera, but an anti-anti-opera. Indeed, under the comic and scatological surface can be traced a fairly constant theme, the relationship between love (or sex) and death. The opera even suggests a philosophical attitude, which is that since life is absurd, cruel, and bestial, and there is little to be expected of the afterlife— one had better live for the moment. This message is underlined by being presented near the end of the opera as if in conclusion, but Ligeti has said that he does not believe that the adoption of this attitude can overcome the sensation of meaninglessness. For him, a life utterly devoid of fear, and devoted entirely to pleasure, is profoundly sad.

The opera opens with an overture, unforgettably scored for twelve motor horns. Piet the Pot enters, drunk, singing of death and pleasure. He is joined by a pair of lovers who spend the entire opera absorbed in erotic activities. Originally Ligeti named them Clitoria and Spermando, which indicates their essential characteristics, but before reaching the stage in England they were renamed, disappointingly, Miranda and Amando. Both roles are to be sung by sopranos, recalling the castrati roles of the Baroque era. The lovers retire to a burial chamber in which to find some privacy to consummate their lovemaking, and as they depart Nekrotzar appears.

He is the central figure of the drama. From his appearance we recognize him as Death, but we are also aware of an undercurrent of pantomime, of theatrical falsehood. It is this ambiguity of death—whether it is really frightening and to be taken seriously, or is just a bogeyman of the imagination—which forms the central theme of the work.

Nekrotzar tells Piet, in the dramatic style of the worst of nineteenth-century Italian opera, that he has come to destroy the world. Piet's down-to-earth responses mark him as the descendant of Papageno from Mozart's *Zauberflöte*. The scene ends with Nekrotzar riding off on Piet, whom he uses as a horse, while the chorus sings a mock chorale. The lovers have the last word from the tomb, where they are singing of their love, which will last until death.

The second scene opens with the astronomer, Astradamors, being whipped by his wife Mescalina, though he has taken the precaution of hiding a saucepan lid in his trousers. They join in a grotesque dance based on the days of the week; morbid Monday, tiresome Tuesday, etc. In this miserable marriage both suffer "dreary nights, dark with bitterness," she for lack of sexual activity, he for the impenetrable mysteries of astronomy. She falls asleep dreaming of a virile lover.

Nekrotzar appears and is warmly greeted by the astronomer, who had predicted his arrival from the stars. Nekrotzar claims to be the man Mescalina had been waiting for, and makes love to her, but so violently that she is killed.

The second act opens in the court of Prince Go-Go. Two ministers are engaged in ritual insults, working their way through the alphabet for terms of abuse. The thirteen-year-old Prince Go-Go (a role that can be sung by a countertenor), calls on his ministers to show more restraint. The head of the secret service (a coloratura soprano) enters in the absurd disguise of a bird. She cryptically warns the prince that the populace is planning a demonstration, but when we hear the people of Brueghelland singing, it is in honor of Go-Go, although the meaning of the text is subverted by the innumerable repetitions. She also warns Go-Go of *le grand macabre*, but with such a heavy stutter that the meaning is obscured.

Astradamors arrives with the words, "my wife is dead, hurray!" There is an extended orchestral passage, based on the theme Beethoven composed for Prometheus and the Eroica symphony, on top of which Ligeti piles up layer on layer of contrasting music, each in a different tempo. This leads to the entrance of Nekrotzar, still riding Piet. He announces the end of the world in a solemn quasi-religious fashion, accompanied by brass fanfares. The chorus, some of whom are placed in the stalls, plead to be spared; "Punish all the rest, but not me, me, me!" Piet decides they should all have a drink, including Nekrotzar, who ends up unable to find his scythe.

In the final scene Piet and Astradamors ascend to heaven. Prince Go-Go meets up with Nekrotzar, who, realizing that he has failed to kill everyone, heads off towards his tomb, exhausted. As he nears it, Mescalina appears, keen to continue their sexual antics. Piet and Astradamors enter, wondering if that was the end of the world, for the after-life seems to be identical with the life before. The two lovers reappear, still oblivious to everything but each other, and from their indifference the moral is drawn that it is futile to worry about death: it is better to live in the here and now.

It is appropriate that, given the nihilistic message of the opera, Ligeti should write a score which avoids the consolation of coherence. There is no single musical style, but music ranging from parodies of earlier historical styles, to expressionistic outbursts, to finely wrought detailed orchestral textures. Any one style rarely runs for more than a few minutes. The scoring is frequently very thin, using a large percussion section, and the greatest prominence is given to the wind and brass, which is accentuated by using the strings as soloists. Further, the opera contains a great deal of speech, which again breaks up the musical flow. The total effect is somewhat bleak and desultory, which while perfectly appropriate for the subject matter, has perhaps restricted the number of Ligeti's admirers.

—Robin Hartwell

GRAUN, Carl Heinrich.

Composer. Born 7 May 1704, in Wahrenbrück, near Dresden. Died 8 August 1759, in Berlin. Studied voice with Grundig and organ with Petzold at the Kreuzschule in Dresden, 1713-21; sang soprano in the town council choir; studied composition with Johann Christoph Schmidt; entered the University of Leipzig, 1717; employed as an opera tenor at the Brunswick court, 1725, and composed operas to German librettos; first Italian opera, *Lo specchio della fedeltà*, 1733; invited by Frederick the Great to become music director at Rheinsberg, 1735; went to Berlin with Frederick when he became king, 1740, and established an Italian opera troupe there; remained in the employ of the court for the rest of his life, composing primarily Italian operas, but important sacred music as well.

Operas

Sancio und Sinilde, J.U. König (after Silvani), Brunswick, 3 February 1727.
Polydorus, J.S. Müller, Brunswick, summer of 1726 or 1728.
Iphigenia in Aulis, C.H. Postel, Brunswick, winter 1731.
Scipio Africanus, Fiedeler and C.H. Postel, Wolfenbüttel, summer 1732.
Lo specchio della fedeltà (*Timareta*), Zeno, Salzdahlum, Brunswick, 13 June 1733.
Pharao Tubaetes, Müller (after Zeno), Brunswick, February 1735.
Rodelinda, regina de' langobardi, G.G. Botarelli (after Salvi), Potsdam, Schlosstheater, 13 December 1741.
Venere e Cupido (prologue), G.G. Botarelli, Potsdam, Schlosstheater, 6 January 1742.
Cesare e Cleopatra, G.G. Botarelli (after Corneille), Berlin, Opera, 7 December 1742.
Artaserse, Metastasio, Berlin, Opera, 2 December 1743.
Catone in Utica, Metastasio, Berlin, Opera, 24 January 1744.
La festa del Imeneo (prologue), G.G. Botarelli, Berlin, Opera, 18 July 1744.
Lucio Papirio, Zeno, Berlin, Opera, 4 January 1745.
Ariano in Siria, Metastasio, Berlin, Opera, 7 January 1746.
Demofoonte, re di Tracia, Metastasio, Berlin, Opera, 17 January 1746.
Cajo Fabricio, Zeno, Berlin, Opera, 2 December 1746.
Le feste galanti, Villati (after Duché de Vancy), Berlin, Opera, 6 April 1747.
Il rè pastore (with Frederick II, Quantz, Nichelmann), Villati, Charlottenburg, 4 August 1747.
L'Europa galante, Villati (after Houdard de la Motte), Schloss Monbijou, 27 March 1748.
Galatea ed Acide (pasticcio), Villati, Potsdam, Schlosstheater, 11 July 1748.
Ifigenia in Aulide, Villati and Frederick II (after Racine), Berlin, Opera, 13 December 1748.

Angelica e Medoro, Villati (after Quinault), Berlin, Opera, 27 March 1749.

Coriolano, Villati (after Frederick II), Berlin, Opera, 19 December 1749.

Fetonte, Villati (after Quinault), Berlin, Opera, 29 March 1750.

Il Mitridate, Villati (after Racine?), Berlin, Opera, 18 December 1750.

L'Armide, Villati (after Quinault), Berlin, Opera, 27 March 1751.

Britannico, Villati (after Racine), Berlin, Opera, 17 December 1751.

L'Orfeo, Villati (after M. du Boulair), Berlin, Opera, 27 March 1752.

Il giudizio di Paride, Villati, Charlottenburg, 25 June 1752.

Silla, Frederick II (translated Tagliazucchi), Berlin, Opera, 27 March 1753.

Il trionfo della fedeltà (with Frederick II, G. Benda, Hasse, Princess Maria Antonia of Saxony), Charlottenburg, August 1753.

Semiramide, Tagliazucchi (after Voltaire), Berlin, Opera, 27 March 1754.

Montezuma, Frederick II (translated Tagliazucchi), Berlin, Opera, 6 January 1755.

Ezio, Tagliazucchi? (after Metastasio), Berlin, Opera, 1 April 1755.

I fratelli nemici, Frederick II (after Racine, translated Tagliazucchi), 9 January 1756.

La Merope, Frederick II (after Voltaire, translated Tagliazucchi), 27 March 1756.

Publications/Writings

About GRAUN: books—

Algarotti, F. *Saggio sopra l'opera in musica.* 1755; partial English translation in *Source Readings in Music History,* edited by O. Strunk, New York, 1950; 1965.

Reichardt, J.F. *Briefe eines aufmerksamen Reisenden.* Frankfurt and Leipzig, 1774; partial English translation in *Source Readings in Music History,* edited by O. Strunk, New York, 1950; 1965.

Schneider, L. *Geschichte des Berliner Opernhauses.* Berlin, 1852.

Thouret, Georg. *Friedrich der Grosse als Musikfreunde und Musiker.* Leipzig, 1898.

Meyer-Reinach. *Denkmäler der Deutschen Tonkunst.* Vol. 15. Leipzig, 1904; Wiesbaden/Graz, 1958.

Helm, Ernest Eugene. *Music at the Court of Frederick the Great.* Norman, Oklahoma, 1960.

articles—

Agricola, J.F. Introduction to Kirnberger, *Duetti, terzetti, quintetti, sestetti ed alcuni chori.* Berlin and Königsberg, 1773-74; reprint in J.N. Forkel, *Musikalisch-kritische Bibliothek,* vol. 3, 286. Gotha, 1779.

Mayer-Reinach, A. "C.A. Graun als Opernkomponist." *Sammelbände der Internationalen Musik-Gessellschaft* 1 (1899-1900): 446.

Mennicke, C. "Zur Biographie der Brüder Graun." *Neue Zeitschrift für Musik* 71 (1904): 129.

Quander, Georg. "Montezuma als Gegenbild des grossen Friedrich—oder: Die Empfindungen dreier Zeitgenossen beim Anblick der Oper *Montezuma* von Friedrich dem Grossen und Carl Heinrich Graun." In *Preussen-Dein Spree-Athen. Beiträge zu Literatur, Theater und Musik in*

Berlin, edited by Hellmut Kühn. Reinbek bei Hamburg, 1981.

Wolff, Hellmuth Christian. "Die erste italienische Oper in Berlin: Carl Heinrich Grauns *Rodelinda* (1741)." *Beiträge zur Musikwissenschaft* 23 (1981): 195.

Klüppelholz, Heinz. "Die Eroberung Mexicos aus preussischer Sicht. Zum Libretto der Oper 'Montezuma' von Friedrich dem Grossen." In *Oper als Text. Romanistische Beiträge zur Libretto-Forschung,* edited by Albert Gier. Heidelberg, 1986.

Maehder, Jürgen. "Mythologizing the Encounter—Columbus, Motecuzoma, Cortés and Representation of the 'Discovery' on the Opera Stage." In *Musical Repercussions of 1492,* edited by Carol E. Robertson. Washington, D.C., 1992.

unpublished—

Mallard, James Harry. "A Translation of Christian Gottfried Krause's *Von der musikalischen Poesie,* with a Critical Essay on his Sources and the Aesthetic Views of his Time." Ph.D. dissertation, University of Texas at Austin, 1978.

Sprague, Cherl Ruth. "A Comparison of Five Musical Settings of Metastasio's *Artaserse.*" Ph.D. dissertation, University of California at Los Angeles, 1979.

* * *

In his youth, Carl Heinrich Graun received a broad and varied music education. Between 1713 and 1721 he attended the Kreuzschule in Dresden, where he studied singing with cantor Johann Zacharias Grundig and clavier with cembalist Christian Petzold. Recognized for his exceptional soprano voice, Graun sang in the Dresden town council choir until his voice changed (1717), when he joined the Kreuzchor. In addition, he sang in the opera chorus, studied composition with the Kapellmeister of the Dresden opera, Johann Christoph Schmidt, and observed the establishment of *opera seria* in Dresden under the direction of Antonio Lotti and Johann David Heinichen. While continuing to attend the Kreuzschule in Dresden, Graun entered the University of Leipzig in 1717. He also studied the operas of Reinhard Keiser and in 1723 journeyed to Prague, where he acquainted himself with the operas of Johann Joseph Fux. These formative years in Dresden would influence Graun's development as an opera composer.

In 1725, Graun was hired as a tenor for the Brunswick court opera. During his ten-year stay at Brunswick, Graun, while working under the patronage of Dukes August Wilhelm and Ludwig Rudolf, composed his first six operas (the first five were set to German texts) and developed his Italian opera style. His first opera, *Sancio und Sinilde,* was premiered on 3 February 1727, and following its success, Graun was promoted to the position of vice-Kapellmeister. Graun's first Italian opera, *Lo specchio della fedeltà,* was written for the occasion of Prince Frederick's marriage to Elizabeth Christine of Brunswick on 12 June 1733. That same year Graun was invited by Prince Frederick of Prussia to join his musical establishment. Owing to his commitments as vice-Kapellmeister, Graun was unable to leave his position at Brunswick until Ludwig Rudolf's death in 1735, following which he joined Frederick in Ruppin as a singer and composer. Months later Graun was appointed to the position of Kapellmeister, and in 1736 was among the seventeen musicians who moved with Frederick from Ruppin to Rheinsberg.

In Rheinsberg, Graun composed Italian chamber cantatas and a few instrumental works, conducted the court orchestra, and taught music theory to Frederick and Franz Benda, and composition to Prince Frederick himself.

In 1740 Frederick moved to Berlin, where he was crowned King of Prussia. Graun followed him to Berlin, where he was given the title of Royal Kapellmeister. Under the patronage of Frederick, Berlin became an important North German musical center, employing Graun and the composers C.P.E. Bach, Johann Philipp Kirnberger, and Johann Joachim Quantz. Graun's first assignment, following the composition of a Trauerkantate for the deceased Friedrich Wilhelm I, was to travel to the major cities of Italy (Bologna, Florence, Naples, Rome and Venice) to recruit singers for Frederick's new court opera. Upon his return, Graun presented his first opera for Berlin, *Rodelinda,* on 13 December 1741 at the Schlosstheater. A year later, on 7 December 1742, Graun's opera *Cesare e Cleopatra* was premiered at the opening of the Royal Berlin Opera House ('Linden-Opera'). In 1745, music critic Johann Adolph Scheibe described both these operas as leading works in the "new" musical style—clear, singable and sensitive, in opposition to the old contrapuntal practices of J.S. Bach, Christoph Graupner and Fux.

With unfailing regularity, Graun composed approximately thirty operas for Frederick and the Berlin Opera between the years 1742 and 1756. Among the last great examples of Baroque *opera seria,* Graun's operas were based on Italian libretti, and written in the Italianate style that venerated the solo voice (in particular, the castrato) and emphasized the lyrical moments of the dramatic performance. The music adheres to the formulaic alternation of recitatives (mostly secco) and arias, to which a duet, trio, quartet, sextet or chorus may be added. Graun also composed short ballets that usually had little connection to the plot, but which were performed between acts and at the end of the operas. Customarily, the music of these ballets was not included in the opera score, so most of that music is lost. While the majority of Graun's opera libretti—written by Metastasio, Zeno, and librettists under Frederick's employment (Botarelli, Villati, and Tagliazucchi)—are tragedies that deal with mythological subjects or ancient historical themes, *Montezuma* (1755) is a noteworthy exception in that it draws on a comparatively modern historical subject.

Graun's development as an opera composer was molded by Frederick the Great, who frequently exercised control over the musical productions in his court. Frederick not only edited many of the libretti used by Graun, but he also wrote several libretti himself. In keeping with the trends of the time and Frederick's wishes, Graun opened his operas after 1745 with the three-movement Italian sinfonia, and thus abandoned the French overture used in his own previous works and by Handel and earlier composers. Graun often rewrote arias at the king's request. Possibly influenced by Lotti, Graun substituted cavatinas for da capo arias in several of his operas, including *Artaserse* (1743), *L'Europa galante* (1748), *Angelica e Medoro* (1749), *Semiramide* (1754) and *Montezuma* (1755). The unusually large number of cavatinas in *Montezuma* were added at the recommendation of Frederick. After 1755 Graun incorporated cavatinas into all of his operas.

The year 1756 witnessed the outbreak of the Seven Years' War and the Berlin Opera closed its doors. Graun returned to the composition of sacred music and wrote a Te Deum (1757) commemorating Frederick's victory in the Battle of Prague. On 8 August 1759, Graun died in Berlin.

In his travel journals of 1774, Johann Friedrich Reichardt, who in 1775 became Kapellmeister for Frederick the Great, gave this assessment of Graun as an opera composer: "He worked only according to the king's taste. Whatever did not please Frederick was struck out, even if it happened to be the best piece in the opera. Since the king adhered stubbornly to his own unchanging preferences, he could not allow Graun the slightest variety or freedom" (Thouret, 69).

It is ironic that while Graun was recognized foremost as an opera composer in his own time, today he is most often remembered for his sacred works.

—Anne Lineback Seshadri

THE GREEK PASSION [Řecke pasije].

Composer: Bohuslav Martinů.

Librettist: Bohuslav Martinů (after Nikos Kazantzakis, *Christ Recrucified*).

First Performance: Zurich, 9 June 1961.

Roles: Grigori (bass); Manolios (tenor); Yannakos (tenor); Katerina (mezzo-soprano or soprano); Fotis (baritone); Kostandis (bass); Panait (tenor); Lenio (soprano); Michelis (tenor); Despinio (soprano); Nikolio (tenor); Adonis (tenor); Archon Patriarcheas (bass); Old Man (bass); Old Woman (contralto); Ladas (speaking); Narrator (speaking); chorus (SATTB).

*   *   *

Much of our knowledge of the genesis of Martinů's last and most prestigious opera stems from the reminiscences of two friends, Zdenka Podhajsky and Milos Šafránek, his first biographer. Mme Podhajsky recalled that Martinů wrote to her in 1954 saying he been bowled over by Kazantzakis's novel *Zorba.* He was then looking for a subject for a dramatic opera. *Zorba* was unsuitable, but Kazantzakis's other great work, *Christ Recrucified* (in America, *The Greek Passion*), suited his purpose admirably. He had, he wrote, "no idea that a book like [it] existed." Martinů's influence over authors seems to have been potent, for when he met Kazantzakis in Antibes later that same year he received unqualified permission to adapt the book, and using Jonathan Griffin's English translation had, by the autumn of 1955, reduced the 400-odd pages to a mere forty.

Martinů's initial pleasure dimmed when he started to compose the music. He normally did this in tandem with work on his librettos, but here he began to encounter difficulties. Some of these stemmed from a reluctance to abandon Kazantzakis's many felicitous phrases and, as he described them to Šafránek in 1956, "wise sayings." Other difficulties arose because he felt confined by Griffin's text though he was loath to change it. Progress was unusually slow. Rafael Kubelík, then musical director of the Royal Opera House, Covent Garden, planned to premiere the work, but his enthusiasm soon cooled. Next Herbert von Karajan was persuaded to take an interest. He demanded changes to libretto and score and a German translation. Martinů agreed, but Kazantzakis's death in 1957 severed a vital connection and slowed progress even further. Karajan in turn withdrew.

In February 1958 Martinů began a complete revision. The libretto was spared, but the music was radically altered. By mid-January 1959 the opera was declared complete, though Martinů was still revising it when he died eight months later. "I just did it wrong," he told Zdenka. "It was *so* difficult." The first performance, in German, took place in Zurich in June 1961 under the direction of the composer's long-standing friend and patron, Paul Sacher.

In devising the plot for *The Greek Passion,* Martinů's problem lay in the realization of the conflicts reflected in Kazantzakis's recreation of the Passion. In a submission to the Guggenheim Foundation in 1956 he outlined the problem: "In our time the artist goes about with a confused grasp of values and seeks an order, a system, in which human and artistic values are preserved and confirmed . . . that is why I have chosen [the novel] as the text of a tragic opera." No mention, we observe, of spiritual (i.e. Christian) values. Martinů was not noticeably religious: what concerned him was the humanistic aspect of the struggle between good and evil. Christ's betrayal and death happened to be the most graphic context in which this cosmic drama might be expressed.

In the Greek village of Lycovrissi, after Easter Mass, the priest Grigori announces the names of the actors chosen for next year's Passion play—three Apostles (the café proprietor, a pedlar, and a farmer's son), Judas (an ugly fellow named Panait who resents being chosen for the role), Mary Magdalene (Katerina, the village prostitute) and, of course, Christ (Manolios, a shepherd destined to marry Lenio, the illegitimate daughter of a wealthy farmer). All are bidden to prepare themselves during the coming year, and gradually each, but especially Manolios, begins to assume the character of their biblical counterparts.

A group of starving refugees from a neighboring village arrives and their priest Fotis, who has promised them a new life, pleads for succour. Grigori and his villagers are suspicious. A young woman refugee falls dead of starvation. Grigori seizes the opportunity to drive out the intruders by raising the cry of "cholera!" At Manolios's suggestion, the fugitives seek shelter on a nearby mountain.

The four scenes of act II illustrate the transformation of the actors. Manolios experiences pains suggestive of the crucifixion. Katerina discovers love. Yannakos, the peddlar who is to play Peter, has been bribed by a villager to get the refugees to part with their wealth, but has been won over by their faith and has given the money away. The first four scenes of act III reflect Manolios's agonized assumption of the mantle of Christ. In dreams Lenio reproaches him, Grigori admonishes him, Katerina declares her love for him, and Yannakos reminds him that he is to be Christ and should not be thinking of women. Lenio and Nikolios, a jealous fellow shepherd, deride him. Manolios departs for the hills where he is heard proclaiming "Christ is in the hills!"

Grigori, sensing Manolios's threat to his authority, demands that he be stopped from acting as if he were indeed Christ. Panait-Judas declares Manolios a dangerous influence. Manolios appears in the village square and begins to preach, and people wonder if he is not really the reincarnated Christ. Grigori denounces him and his followers, and Manolios departs.

Lenio has rejected Manolios in favor of Nikolios. Act IV begins with the wedding. Grigori appears at the church door and in the midst of the festivities excommunicates Manolios. Manolios's "Apostles" all declare their adherance to him. Manolios appears and confesses that he thought he had been tempted by Satan but the plight of the refugees has convinced him. The refugees are coming to claim their rights. "Nothing," Manolios proclaims, "is achieved without blood. . . .

Let us purify the world." The crowd, goaded on by Grigori, rushes upon him and Panait kills him. Everyone is horror-struck. The refugees enter and Fotis brings both communities together in prayer. Katerina utters a valediction, and the opera ends with a Kyrie as Fotis leads his people off.

In his desire to remain true to Kazantzakis's (and his own) vision of *The Greek Passion,* Martinů searched for and studied Russian church music and Greek folk song. Such dedication was rare. He usually felt able to rely on his natural inventiveness. The chorus in the wedding scene was particularly difficult. Kazantzakis had described these ceremonies to him, but the nearest Martinů could get to authenticity was to set verses from the *Song of Solomon.* Šafránek says Martinů told him the music was "Czech." It is true that during the years of its composition thoughts of home preoccupied the composer, and he wrote several nostalgic works, notably the four folk cantatas on poems by Bureš (1955-59), but there is little ostensibly Czech in *The Greek Passion.* Nor are there any echoes of *Julietta* even in the dream scenes (except perhaps the on-stage accordion). Neither *Ariadne* (1958), Martinů's brief return to the fantasy world of Neveux, nor *Mirandolina,* a lively excursion into the world of Goldoni (1954) had anything to offer this tense tragic opera either. For *The Greek Passion,* Martinů had to evolve an entirely new language. Its accents may be familiar, but the syntax is not.

—Kenneth Dommett

GREGOR, Joseph.

Librettist/Novelist/Dramatist/Scholar. Born 26 October 1888, in Czernowitz, Bukovina. Died 12 October 1960, in Vienna. Studied musicology with G. Adler and philosophy at the University of Vienna beginning 1907, then at the University of Berlin; further music education at the Konservatorium der Musikfreunde in Vienna, 1908, and private study with R. Fuchs; librarian at the Nationalbibliothek di Vienna, where he founded the Archiv für Filmkunde, 1929; teacher at the Reinhardt School of Dramatic Art, 1929; honorary professor of the Wiener Akademie der Bildende Künste, 1932.

Librettos

Friedenstag, R. Strauss, 1938.
Daphne, R. Strauss, 1938.
Die Liebe der Danaë, R. Strauss, 1944 (dress rehearsal for canceled premiere).
Semiramis [manuscript].

Publications

By GREGOR: books–

Das Wiener Barocktheater. Vienna, 1922.
Wiener Szenische Kunst. 2 vols. Vienna, 1924-25.
Mozart-Geist österreichischen Theaters, eine Festrede. Vienna, 1931.
Weltgeschichte des Theaters. Zurich, 1933.
Richard Strauss, der Meister der Oper. Monaco, 1939.
Kulturgeschichte des Ballets. Vienna, 1944.
C. Krauss. Seine musikalische Sendung. Vienna, 1953.

with R. Strauss. *R. Strauss und J. Gregor. Briefwechsel.* Edited by R. Tenschert. Salzburg, 1955.
Die Theaterregie in der Welt unseres Jahrhunderts. Vienna, 1958.
Editor. *Denkmäler des Theaters.* 12 vols. Monaco, 1926-30; new series, Vienna, 1954-.

Various volumes of short stories and poetry.

*   *   *

Joseph Gregor followed illustrious predecessors—Hugo von Hofmannsthal and Stefan Zweig—as librettist for Richard Strauss. In this role he penned the libretti for three of Strauss's last four operas—*Friedenstag, Daphne,* and *Die Liebe der Danaë*—and began work on the last, *Capriccio,* before Strauss and later conductor Clemens Krauss took it over. Gregor is usually described as a "theater historian," and critics deride his work for Strauss when compared to the libretti of the earlier Strauss operas. Yet it must be remembered that Gregor was an internationally known expert on the theater; he had published novels and volumes of short stories and poetry; his own plays had been produced in Vienna; and he was a close friend of Zweig, who held him in high esteem. *Daphne* turned into one of Strauss's most beautiful operas and looks forward to his Indian Summer works of the 1940s.

Friedenstag and *Die Liebe der Danaë* are not successful libretti; they are probably Strauss's weakest operas. Their failure is due in large part to the fact that Gregor took over material first developed by other librettists (Zweig and Hofmannsthal, respectively). He did not have as much of a personal interest in them as he did in *Daphne,* which was his own idea. *Friedenstag* suffers from a certain lack of expansiveness. The characters are not fully developed, and the text is more philosophy than drama. Strauss had complained to Hofmannsthal while composing *Die Frau ohne Schatten* that it was difficult to compose when he was not inspired by the characters. He was also uninspired by the characters in *Friedenstag,* and that worked to the detriment of the score. Themes of war and peace were not Strauss's forte; his suggestion to Zweig early on for a subsidiary love affair had been quickly rejected.

Die Liebe der Danaë also suffers from a lack of interest on Gregor's part. Hofmannsthal had submitted the original scenario to Strauss many years before. By this point in their collaboration, Gregor had a thorough fear of Strauss and was willing to revise on demand. But this did not make for a coherent libretto. Strauss composed text he never would have considered otherwise to take his mind off the difficult times. Producer Rudolf Hartmann, who created the first performances, admitted that he had trouble making the convoluted and even contradictory libretto coherent on stage. This was a classical subject suitable to them both; under better circumstances it surely could have been developed into a fine opera.

Gregor's libretto for *Daphne,* while not without its longueurs, inspired Strauss by its treatment of the Greek myth. The librettist succeeded here where he had failed in the other two works because this was his own idea, not a hand-me-down from another librettist. With his extensive classical background, he weaved gods and demigods together from various myths to make a coherent story. Also, Strauss and Gregor worked on the libretto over a substantial period of time, so they were able to develop it more fully than *Friedenstag* or *Danaë.* This was a subject congenial to both men. Strauss had often pestered Hofmannsthal for a libretto on classical themes, and here he finally found his text.

"Theater und keine Literatur!" (Theater not Literature!) was Strauss's frequent reminder to Gregor. As a theater historian, Gregor tended to overwrite his libretti and overload them philosophically (a problem that also afflicted Hofmannsthal at times). Even with Strauss's constant demands for revisions and his own rewriting (the final form of Daphne's opening aria "O bleib, geliebter Tag!" was Strauss's own invention) and the input of Zweig, Krauss, and Wallerstein, these libretti are Gregor's creations and show passages of great beauty. Maria's aria and the "Magdeburg" ballad in *Friedenstag* are undoubtedly effective, and Strauss rejected Zweig's rewriting of the final confrontation in favor of one by Gregor. There are effective passages scattered among the dross in *Danaë*—some of the ensembles and Jupiter's farewell, one of Strauss's favorite passages, for example. Another farewell scene in *Daphne,* that of Apollo, is not the work of an amateur, nor is Daphne's lament for the slain Leukippos.

Much of Gregor's trouble with Strauss and the resulting difficulties with development of the libretti he wrote for the composer stemmed from a basic personality conflict. Strauss needed a combative fellow artist with whom to argue ideas. Hofmannsthal had rarely avoided expressing his opinions strongly. Gregor, on the other hand, was too submissive, too servile toward Strauss. He considered it a great honor to have been almost forced on Strauss by Zweig as his successor, and to be working with the most renowned composer at all. Strauss, upset by losing Zweig because the latter was a Jew, exasperated by Gregor's lack of the immediate grasp of the theater that he expected, and finding that he could bully him, often treated Gregor roughly. The composer eventually turned to his more outspoken and more operatically experienced colleagues Clemens Krauss and producer Lothar Wallerstein for advice, and even sent Gregor to consult with them. It was Krauss who came up with the idea of the solo closing scene in *Daphne.*

In the final analysis Gregor was perhaps the right man at the wrong time, or for the wrong composer. Yet his libretti kept Strauss active at one of the most difficult periods of his life and resulted in some glorious music before the final outpouring in the last orchestral works and the *Four Last Songs.*

—David E. Anderson

GRÉTRY, André-Ernest-Modeste.

Composer. Born 8 February 1741, in Liège. Died 24 September 1813, in Montmorency, near Paris. Grétry's daughter Angélique-Dorothée-Lucie [Lucille] (born 15 July 1772; died 25 August 1790) was also a composer. Chorister at the St Denis Church, 1750; studied with François Leclerc and H.F. Renkin; studied composition with Henri Moreau; composed 6 symphonies in 1758; studied at the College de Liège in Rome, 1761-65; taught music in Geneva, 1766, where he met Voltaire; in Paris, 1767, where he continuously composed operas; privy councillor of Liège, 1784; Parisian street named after him, 1785; admitted to the Institut de France, 1795; appointed inspector of the Paris Conservatory, 1795; made Chevalier of the Legion of Honor by Napoleon, 1802.

Operas

Edition: *A.-E.-M. Grétry: Collection complète des oeuvres.* Edited by F.A. Gevaert, E. Fétis, A. Wotquenne, et al. Leipzig, 1884-1936.

La vendemmiatrice (2 intermezzi), Labbate, Rome, Aliberti, carnival 1765.

Isabelle et Gertrude, ou Les sylphes supposés, Charles Simon Favart (after Voltaire), Geneva, December 1766.

Le connaisseur, Jean François Marmontel (after his *Conte*) [for Paris, Comédie-Italienne, 1768; unfinished]

Les mariages samnites, Pierre Légier (after Jean François Marmontel), Paris, Prince of Conti's, c. January 1768; revised, 12 June 1776, 1782.

Le huron, Jean François Marmontel (after Voltaire, *L'ingénu*), Paris, Comédie-Ialienne, 20 August 1768.

Momus sur la terre (prologue), C.H. Watelet, Château de la Roche-Guyon, 1769?.

Lucile, Jean François Marmontel, Paris, Comédie-Italienne, 5 January 1769.

Le tableau parlant, Louis Anseaume, Paris, Comédie-Italienne, 20 September 1769.

Silvain, Jean François Marmontel (after S. Gessner, *Erast*), Paris, Comédie-Italienne, 19 February 1770.

Les deux avares, Charles Georges Fenouillot de Falbaire, Fontainebleau, 27 October 1770; revised 6 December 1770, 1773.

L'amitié à l'épreuve, Charles Simon Favart and Claude Henri Fusée de Voisenon (after Jean François Marmontel), Paris, Comédie-Italienne, 13 November 1771; revised 1775, 1776, 1786.

André-Ernest-Modeste Grétry

L'ami de la maison, Jean François Marmontel, Fontainebleau, 26 October 1771; revised 1772.

Zémire et Azor, Jean François Marmontel (after Beaumont, *La belle et la bête*), Fontainebleau, 9 November 1771.

Le magnifique, Jean Michel Sedaine (after La Fontaine), Paris, Comédie-Italienne, 4 March 1773.

La rosière de Salency, Alexandre Frédéric Jacques Masson de Pézay, Fontainebleau, 23 October 1773; revised 1774.

Céphale et Procris, ou L'amour conjugal (opéra-ballet), Jean François Marmontel (after Ovid), Versailles, 30 December 1773; revised 1775, 1777.

La fausse magie, Jean François Marmontel, Paris, Comédie-Italienne, 1 February 1775; revised 16 February 1775.

Pygmalion, B.F. de Rosoi, 1776 [unfinished].

Les statues, Jean François Marmontel (after *Arabian Nights*), 1776-78, for Paris, Comédie-Italienne [unfinished].

Amour pour amour, intermezzi by Pierre Laujon in the comedy by P.C.N. de La Chaussée, Versailles, 10 March 1777.

Matroco, Pierre Laujon, Chantilly, Prince of Condé's, 3 November 1777; revised 21 November 1777, 1778.

Le jugement de Midas, Thomas d'Hèle (versification partly by Louis Anseaume), Paris, at the home of Mme de Montesson, 28 March 1778; revised 27 June 1778.

Les trois âges de l'opéra (*Le génie de l'opéra; Les trois âges de la musique*) (prologue, including music by Lully, Rameau, and Gluck), Alphonse Marie Denis Devismes de Saint-Alphonse, Paris, Opéra, 27 April 1778.

Les fausses apparences, ou L'amant jaloux, Thomas d'Hèle (versification by Francis Levasseur) (after S. Centlivre, *The Wonder a Woman Keeps a Secret,* Versailles, 20 November 1778; revised 23 December 1778.

Les événemens imprévus, Thomas d'Hèle, Versailles, 11 November 1779; revised 1780.

Aucassin et Nicolette, ou Les moeurs du bon vieux temps, Michel-Jean Sedaine (after a fable edited by J.B. de la Curne de Sainte-Palaye, Versailles, 30 December 1779; revised 1782.

Andromaque, Louis Guillaume Pitra (after Racine), Paris, Opéra, 6 June 1780; revised 1781.

Emilie, ou La belle esclave (opéra-ballet), Nicolas François Guillard, Paris, Opéra, 22 February 1781 [act V of the ballet pantomime *La fête de Mirza*].

Electre, Jean Charles Thilorier [composed for the Paris Opéra, 1782; not performed].

Les colonnes d'Alcide, Pitra, for the Paris Opéra, 1782 [unfinished].

La double épreuve, ou Colinette à la cour, Jean Baptiste Lourdet de Santerre (after Charles Simon Favart), Paris, Opéra, 1 January 1782.

Le sage dans sa retraite, L.J.C.S. d'Allainval (after a comedy by Linguet), The Hague, 19 September 1782.

L'embarras des richesses, Jean Baptiste Lourdet de Santerre (after L.J.C.S. d'Allainval), Paris, Opéra, 26 November 1782.

Thalie au nouveau théâtre (prologue), Michel-Jean Sedaine, Paris, Comédie-Italienne, 28 April 1783.

La caravane du Caïre (opéra-ballet), Étienne Morel de Chédeville, Fontainebleau, 30 October 1783; revised 1784.

Théodore et Paulin, Pierre Jean Baptiste Choudard (Desforges), Versailles, 5 March 1784; revised and performed as *L'epreuve villageoise,* Paris, Comédie-Italienne, 24 June 1784.

Richard coeur-de-lion, Michel-Jean Sedaine (after La Curne de Sainte-Palaye), Paris, Comédie-Italienne, 21 October 1784; revised 1785.

Oedipus à Colonne, Nicolas François Guillard, for Paris, Opéra, 1785 [unfinished].

Panurge dans l'île des lanternes, Morel de Chédeville (after F. Parfaict), Paris, Opéra, 25 January 1785.

Amphitryon, Michel-Jean Sedaine (after Molière), Versailles, 15 March 1786; revised 1788.

Les méprises par ressemblance, Joseph Patrat (after Plautus, *Menacchmi*), Fontainebleau, 7 November 1786; revised 3 December 1786.

Le comte d'Albert, Michel-Jean Sedaine (after La Fontaine, *Le lion et le rat*), Fontainebleau, 13 November 1786; revised as *Albert et Antoine, ou Le service récompensé,* Paris, Opéra-Comique, 7 December 1794.

Le prisonnier anglais, F.G. Fouques (François Guillaume Desfontaines), Paris, Comédie-Italienne, 26 December 1787; revised 1788, and as *Clarice et Belton, ou Le prisonnier anglais,* 23 March 1793.

Le rival confident, Nicholas Julien Forgeot, Paris, Comédie-Italienne, 26 June 1788; revised 6 October 1788.

Raoul Barbe-bleue, Michel-Jean Sedaine (after C. Perrault), Paris, Comédie-Italienne, 2 March 1789.

Aspasie, Morel de Chédeville, Paris, Opéra, 17 March 1789.

Roger et Olivier, after L. d'Ussieux, *Victor et Roger de Shabran,* for Paris, Comédie-Italienne, c. 1790.

Pierre le Grand, Jean Nicolas Bouilly, Paris, Comédie-Italienne, 13 January 1790; revised 2 November 1790.

Guillaume Tell, Michel-Jean Sedaine (after A.M. Lemierre), Paris, Comédie-Italienne, 9 April 1791.

Séraphine, ou Absente et présente, André Joseph Grétry, for Paris, Comédie-Italienne, c. 1792 [not performed].

Cécile et Ermancé, ou Les deux couvents, C.J. Rouget de Lisle and Jean Baptiste Denis Després, Paris, Comédie-Italienne, 16 January 1792; revised as *Le despotisme monacal,* 1 November 1792.

Basile, ou A trompeur, trompeur et demi, Michel-Jean Sedaine (after Cervantes), Paris, Comédie-Italienne, 17 October 1792.

Diogène et Alexandre, Pierre Sylvain Maréchal, 1794, for Paris, Opéra [unfinished].

Le congrès des rois (with 11 other composers), Antoine François Éve (Desmaillot), Paris, Opéra-Comique, 26 February 1794.

Joseph Barra, Guillaume Denis Thomas Levrier Champ-Rion, Paris, Opéra-Comique, 5 June 1794.

Denys le tyran, maître d'école à Corinthe, Pierre Sylvain Maréchal, Paris, Opéra, 23 August 1794.

La rosière républicane, ou La fête de la vertu, Pierre Sylvain Maréchal, Paris, Opéra, 2 September 1794.

Callias, ou Nature et patrie, François Benoît Hoffman, Paris, Opéra-Comique, 19 September 1794.

Lisbeth, Edmond Guillaume François Favières (after J.P.C. de Florian, *Claudine*), Paris, Opéra-Comique, 10 January 1797.

Anacréon chez Polycrate, Jean Henri Guy, Paris, Opéra, 17 January 1797.

Le barbier du village, ou Le revenant, André Joseph Grétry, Paris, Théâtre Feydeau, 6 May 1797.

Élisca, ou l'amour maternel, Edmond Guillaume François Favières, Paris, Opéra-Comique, 1 January 1799; revised as *Elisca, ou L'habitante de Madagascar,* libretto revised by André Joseph Grétry, Paris, Comédie-Italienne, 5 May 1812.

Zelmar, ou l'Asyle, André Joseph Grétry, for Paris, Opéra, 1801.

Le casque et les colombes (opéra-ballet), Nicolas François Guillard, Paris, Opéra, 7 November 1801.

Delphis et Mopsa, Jean Henri Guy, Paris, Opéra, 15 February 1803.

Les filles pourvues, Louis Anseaume, Comédie-Italienne, ?.

Other works: romances, sacred works, songs, chamber music.

Publications/Writings

By GRÉTRY: books–

Mémoires, ou Essais sur la musique. Paris, 1789; enlarged 2nd ed. 1797, 1973.

De la Verité, ce que nous fûmes, ce que nous sommes, ce que nous devrions être. Paris, 1801.

Méthode simple pour apprendre à préluder en peu de temps, avec toutes les resources de l'harmonie. Paris, 1803, 1968.

Closson, E. and L. Solvay, eds. *Réflexions d'un solitaire.* Brussels and Paris, 1919-22.

Froidecourt, G. de, ed. *La correspondance générale de Grétry.* Brussels, 1962.

About GRÉTRY: books–

La Harpe, J.F. *Correspondance littéraire.* Paris, 1801.

———. *Lycée ou Cours de littéraire ancienne et moderne, xii: De l'opéra.* Paris, 1801.

Livry, Comte de. *Recueil de lettres écrits à Grétry, ou à son sujet.* Paris 1809.

Grétry, A.J. *Grétry en famille.* Paris, 1814.

Van Hulst, F. *Grétry.* Liège, 1842.

Grégoir, E.G.J. *Grétry, célèbre compositeur belge.* Brussels, 1883.

Rongé, J.B., and F. Delhasse. *Grétry.* Brussels, 1883.

Brenet, Michel, *Grétry.* Paris, 1884.

Dietz, M. *Geschichte des musikalischen Dramas in Frankreich wärend der Revolution.* Vienna, 1885; 2nd ed. 1886, 1893.

Curzon, Henri de. *Grétry.* Paris, 1907.

Abert, H. *W.A. Mozart,* vol. 1, 547ff. Leipzig, 1919; 3rd ed., 1965.

Closson, Ernest, *André-Modeste Grétry.* Turnhout and Brussels, 1920.

Long des Clavières, P. *La jeunesse de Grétry et ses débuts à Paris.* Besançon, 1921.

Wichmann, Heinz. *Grétry und das musikalische Theater in Frankreich.* Halle, 1929.

Rolland, Romain. *La musique dans l'histoire générale: Grétry, Mozart.* Berlin, 1930.

Bruyr, José E. *Grétry.* Paris, 1931.

Sauvenier, J. *André Grétry.* Brussels, 1934.

Froidcourt, J. de. *43 lettres inédites de Grétry à A. Rousselin, 1806-12.* Liége, 1937.

Gérard-Gailly. *Grétry à Honfleur.* Paris, 1938.

Clercx, Suzanne. *Grétry, 1741-1813.* Brussels, 1944.

Berlioz, Hector. *Cauchemars et passions.* Edited by Gerard Condé, *Musiques et musiciens.* Paris, 1981.

L'opéra aux XVIIIe siècle. Aix-en Provence, 1982.

Charlton, David. *Grétry and the Growth of Opéra-Comique.* Cambridge, 1986.

articles–

Rolland, Romain, "Grétry." *Revue de Paris* 15 March (1908): 305; reprinted in *Musiciens d'autrefois,* Paris, 1908; English translation, 1915.

Alexis, G.L.J. "Grétry arrangé, revu et corrigé." *La vie wallonne* 9 (1929): 308.

Degey, M. "Les échos imprévus de la mort Grétry." *La vie wallonne* 18 (1938): 197, 229, 305; 19 (1939): 37; published separately as *André-Modeste Grétry,* Brussels, 1939.

Closson, E. "Les notes marginales de Grétry dans l'Essai sur la musique' de Labourde." *Revue belge de musicologie* 2 (1948): 106.

Van der Linden, A. "La première version d'"Elisca' de Grétry." *Académie royale de Belgique: bulletin de la classe des beaux-arts* 35 (1953): 135.

———. "Broutilles au sujet de Grétry." *Revue belge de musicologie* 12 (1958): 74.

Clercx, Suzanne. "Le rôle de l'Académie Philharmonique de Bologne dans la formation d'A.M. Grétry." *Quadrivium* 8 (1967): 75.

Koch, C.F. Jr. "The Dramatic Ensemble Finale in the Opéra Comique of the Eighteenth Century." *Acta musicologica* 39 (1967): 72.

Pendle, K. "The Opéras Comiques of Grétry and Marmontel." *Musical Quarterly* 62 (1976): 409.

Charlton, David. "The Appeal of the Beast: a Note on Grétry and *Zémire et Azor.*" *Musical Times* 121 (1980): 169.

Heartz, Daniel. "The Beginnings of the Operatic Romance: Rousseau, Sedaine, and Monsigny." *Eighteenth-Century Studies* 15 (1981): 149.

Bartlet, M. Elizabeth. "Politics and the Fate of *Roger et Olivier,* A Newly Recovered Opera." *Journal of the American Musicological Society* 37 (1984): 98.

Hyart, Charles. "Grétry et Bouilly: Le musicien et son librettiste." *R. Générale* 10 (1984): 21.

Joly, Jacques. "Avant Rossini, Grétry" [on *Guillaume Tell*], *Avant-scène opéra* March (1989).

unpublished–

Jobe, R.D. "The Operas of André-Ernest-Modeste Grétry." Ph.D. dissertation, University of Michigan, 1965.

Kopp, James Butler. "The *drame lyrique:* a study in the esthetics of *opéra-comique.*" Ph.D. dissertation, University of Pennsylvania, 1982.

Stones, Linda M. "Musical Characterization in Eighteenth-century opéra-comique: *Tom Jones, Le déserteur,* and *Richard coeur-de-lion.*" DMA dissertation, University of Illinois, urbana-Champaign, 1985.

* * *

André-Ernest-Modeste Grétry was born into a modest environment. His father, first violinist at the collegiate church of St Denis in Liège, helped him gain entrance into the choir school for musical boys in 1750. The choirmaster, H. F. Devillers, was responsible his general music studies from age 6 to 9. Grétry, of feeble constitution, found the teaching despotic, too severe and prejudiced, so his father found an able private teacher, the cathedral musician François Leclerc, to continue the boy's studies. In 1754 an Italian traveling operatic troupe established itself in Liège with works of Pergolesi and Galuppi. Maestro Resta allowed Grétry to assist at all performances and at many rehearsals for a year. Grétry wrote in his memoirs: "It is there I gained a passionate taste for music"; when he returned to the St Denis choir, his public audition showed just how much he had learned while assisting the Italian troupe.

At the choir school Grétry studied keyboard and harmony with H. F. Renkin and counterpoint with Henri Moreau, who was then chapel master at St Paul Cathedral. In 1758 he began to play second violin at the St Denis school, which provided instrumental lessons for boys with changing voices. The provost eventually underwrote Grétry's studies in Italy.

In Rome his contrapuntal studies with Giovanni Casali produced a few sacred works, but severe deficiencies in polyphony coupled with an intense interest in opera hampered Grétry's progress in liturgical composition. He was enchanted by Piccinni's *La buona Figliuola ossia la Cecchina,* 1760, which mixed comic and sentimental elements, traits that would appear later in Grétry's own dramatic works. *La vendemmiatrice,* two Italian intermezzi written for the Aliberti Theater during the 1765 carnival season, displayed Grétry's strong penchant for Italianate melody.

He left Rome early in 1766 for Geneva, where he met Voltaire and certain of his disciples, notably the librettist Marmontel, and this association facilitated Grétry's entry into the literary and enlightened circles in Paris, where he arrived in the fall of 1767, anxious to try his hand at opéra-comique. *Les mariages samnites* was a failure, but Grétry's career took off with *Le huron* set to a libretto by Marmontel after Voltaire's politically-oriented *L'Ingénu.* Marmontel and Grétry successfully combined sentiment and pathos in *Lucile* and the tearful comedy *Le tableau parlant* ensured his lasting fame.

Zémire et Azor (1771) a moral tale on an excellent libretto by Marmontel, earned Grétry a royal pension and established his name internationally. With *Le magnifique* based on a tale by Boccaccio, Grétry began a long, fruitful collaboration with Michel-Jean Sedaine, with whom he also produced *La rosière de Salency* and *Céphale et Procris,* 1773. The librettist Thomas Hales (a.k.a. d'Hèle) provided Grétry libretti for three of his greatest opera-comiques: *Le jugement de Midas, L'amant jaloux,* and *Les événements imprévus.*

The successful opéra-ballet *La Caravane du Caïre* (1783) was followed by *Richard coeur-de-lion,* with a rescue plot by Sedaine. Grétry concluded his striking career with two political opera-comiques: *Pierre le Grand,* on a Bouilly libretto, and *Guillaume Tell,* on a libretto by Sedaine. Both of the libretti alluded to specific events of the revolution. Grétry's music for *Tell* was energetic and passionate, but Sedaine, labeled a constitutional monarchist, watered down the rebel role of Tell. The last of his thirty-four opéra-comiques enjoyed only scant success, and Grétry retired to the Ermitage in Montmorency to write his memoirs.

Grétry's music reveals Italianate melody, uncomplicated harmonies, an avoidance of contrapuntal texture, rhythmic vivacity, motivic coherence, correct declamation and especially genial musical characterization which carefully followed the contingencies of the text. The correct tone of declamation was central to his composition. His characters emerged as sincere and true-to-life through an accompanying instrumental solo, a given rhythm or melodic motive. Elements of musical association, such as a fanfare for a King's entrance or a chromatically falling scale symbolizing tears, would complete a portrait. He created new instruments for a given dramatic situation. He enlarged the ensembles with spectacle, and provided local color. Grétry was an original, an experimentalist. He dissolved barriers between comedy and tragedy, forming a solid foundation for nineteenth-century opera. He was an enlightened man of literature with a refined sense of drama and unerring taste. Grétry helped to develop opéra-comique into a large-scale unified genre reflecting the changing tastes of the public.

—Linda M. Stones

GRISI, Giuditta.

Mezzo-soprano. Born 28 July 1805, in Milan. Died 1 May 1840, in Robecco d'Oglio, near Cremona. Sister of Giulia Grisi. Studied with her aunt, the contralto Josephina Grassini, and at Milan Conservatory; debut in Rossini's *Bianca e Faliero,* Vienna, 1825; then sang in Florence, Parma, Turin, and Venice, where she sang in the premiere of *I Capuleti e i Montecchi,* 1830; in London and Paris, 1832; retired 1839 after an engagement at the Teatro Argentina, Rome.

*   *   *

Although Giuditta Grisi is probably best known today as being Giulia Grisi's elder sister, she also had a brief, but important career of her own. This career took her to many of the world's most important cities including Vienna (where she made her debut), Naples, Milan, Venice, Rome, Florence, Madrid, Paris and London. She created roles in a number of operas, the most important of these being Romeo in Bellini's *I Capuleti ed i Montecchi,* and the title role in Luigi Ricci's once tremendously successful, but now forgotten *Chiara di Rosembergh.*

She is generally thought of as a mezzo-soprano, perhaps because she created the previously mentioned role of Romeo, and because she primarily sang mezzo roles early in her career. However, she sang soprano roles almost as often, especially when a contralto or mezzo-soprano of greater fame than her own was in the company. These soprano roles included Semiramide, Elena (in *La donna del lago*) Desdemona, Norma, Imogene, Parisina d'Este and Gemma di Vergy. But she never earned much of a reputation for her work as a soprano, and even as a mezzo-soprano she was in the shadow of singers like Rosmunda Pisaroni and Marietta Brambilla.

She and her sister sang together during only two seasons: the 1830 autumn season at the Teatro alla Scala, and the 1832-33 Paris season. While in Paris, the two sisters shared the stage in Bellini's *I Capuleti ed i Montecchi,* Vaccai's opera on the subject, *Giulietta e Romeo,* and Rossini's *La donna del lago.*

Giuditta started to decline towards the end of her career, when she tended to sing in smaller houses in the Italian provinces, specializing in the dramatic soprano repertory, especially roles like Norma, Antonina in *Belisario,* Parisina d'Este, and Gemma di Vergy.

She was known as a singer of much cultivation and considerable stage experience, as well as for the power of her voice. But her voice was considered neither particularly beautiful nor sweet. She has to be regarded as being in the second tier of singers.

—Tom Kaufman

Giuditta and Giulia Grisi

GRISI, Giulia.

Soprano. Born 22 May 1811, in Milan. Died 29 November 1869, in Berlin. Studied with her sister, the mezzo-soprano Giuditta Grisi, and with Filippo Celli and Pietro Guglielmi; also studied with Marliani in Milan and with Giacomelli in Bologna; debut as Emma in Rossini's *Zelmira,* Bologna, 1828; created role of Adalgisa in *Norma,* Milan, 1831; sang in Milan until 1832; Paris debut as Semiramide, 1832; London debut in Rossini's *La gazza ladra,* 1834; lived with the tenor Mario from c. 1842; toured the U.S. with him in 1854.

Publications

About GRISI: books–

Forbes, E. *Mario and Grisi.* London, 1985.

* * *

Posterity has been extremely unkind to Giulia Grisi. During her lifetime she was universally regarded as the reigning Italian prima donna of the mid-nineteenth century. But no single biography has been devoted exclusively to her, although one book on Grisi and Mario is available and another is in preparation. Worse, a number of historians have stated that she gained most of her fame by imitating her predecessors (most notably Giuditta Pasta). Worse still, she reportedly waged a petty and malicious campaign against her arch-rival, Pauline Viardot, using her companion of many years, the tenor Mario, as her key weapon.

That there was a serious rivalry between Grisi and Viardot cannot be doubted, but the blame should be shared equally by the two prima donnas, not placed entirely on Grisi's shoulders. Viardot remembered, with lasting resentment, that Grisi had replaced Viardot's half sister Maria Malibran in both Paris and London while the latter was still in her prime. The war between the prima donnas started due to a reappearance by Viardot at Covent Garden in *La sonnambula* in 1848. Mario canceled due to illness and a substitute had to be found. Viardot took this as a personal insult, claiming that the illness was feigned, and a plot on Grisi's part. The *Musical World,* a contemporary London periodical stated that Mario was truly sick, and had made every effort to sing. Later that year, Viardot was scheduled to sing Valentine in *Les Huguenots* for her benefit, and Mario again had to cancel due to illness. Grisi offered to sing *Norma* in Viardot's honor; Viardot agreed to *Norma,* but insisted that she sing the title role, leaving Grisi to sing Adalgisa. They finally found a substitute tenor for Mario, the famous Gustave Roger who was to create Jean in *Le prophète* a year later. The opera was a huge success, although Roger sang in French. Again, there is substantive evidence that Mario was truly ill.

Things came to a head in 1850, when on hearing Pasta in scenes from *Anna Bolena,* Viardot said "Now I know where Grisi got all her greatness." Even though this remark was not widely publicized at the time, it must have spread fuel on the fire. Then, once more, in 1852 Mario cancelled an appearance in *La Juive* when Viardot was singing. Again, Grisi was blamed, although Mario's illness was confirmed by a review of the second performance, two nights later. Then, finally, when in 1852 Viardot was not engaged at Covent Garden, Grisi took over the role of Fidès. Instead of being credited by historians for being a good trooper and singing a role which lay too low for her voice so that the show could go on, she was criticized for daring to take on one of her rival's roles.

The charge that Grisi's talent was primarily that of an imitator also deserves brief comment, even when one realizes that it originated with a rival jealous of her success. An examination of numerous contemporary reviews of her in *Norma* reveals no suggestion of any plagiarism. Yet, Viardot's accusation that Grisi plagiarized was taken up years later by Chorley, a great admirer of Viardot's, and even printed in Grisi's obituary in the *Musical World.* The latter is easily explained—Grisi's death was a sudden one; the editors of *Musical World* had a deadline to meet, and it is unlikely that they would have had the time to check the facts, even in the backfiles of their own magazine.

To put it in as few words as possible, Grisi had everything. According to Chorley, "She was known for her great beauty, although she was never known to be a coquette on stage. Her soprano voice was rich, sweet, equal throughout its compass of two octaves (from C to C) without a break, or a note which had to be managed. Nor has any woman ever more thoroughly commanded every gradation of force than she, being capable of any required violence or of any desired delicacy."

Her best role was Norma, and while it had to be modeled to some extent on Pasta's, it was regarded (even by Chorley) as an improvement because of its greater animal passion. She was so ferocious in the part that many tenors took her violence personally. Her acting ability was compared favorably to that of great dramatic actresses such as Sarah Siddons.

Grisi also was famous for her Lucrezia Borgia, Donna Anna and Anna Bolena. She created a number of major *bel canto* roles, including among others, Adalgisa in *Norma,* Elvira in *I Puritani* and Norina in *Don Pasquale.* Oddly, none of these were destined to be among her favorites. In its early years, Adalgisa was usually sung by lesser sopranos, although it eventually became the province of great mezzos and contraltos. Elvira was frequently taken over by Fanny Persiani, while *Don Pasquale* was not fully a repertory work in those years. Important as these were, they probably were less so than the roles created by Pasta.

How important, then, was Grisi? That she learned from Pasta, Malibran, and others is certainly to her credit—she would have been foolish not to do so. That she was little more than an imitator, as some historians suggest, is totally untrue. Assertions that she attempted to fight off challenges from rivals, whether to her or to Mario, are probably partially true, and, if so, are understandable. That she was neurotic, or even fanatical is difficult to believe, although it makes a good story. She accepted Persiani into the *vieille garde,* and even sang Elisetta in Cimarosa's *Matrimonio segreto* while Persiani sang the much more important role of Carolina. Nor is there any record of Grisi or Mario making trouble for his most serious rival, Enrico Tamberlick.

The question of Grisi's importance can best be answered by remembering that she reigned supreme in Paris for 18 seasons, and in London for close to 20, withstanding challenges from Lind, Sontag, Frezzolini, Barbieri-Nini and others in opera seria, although Lind did do better in the light repertory. Only Viardot was able to rival her successfully in some roles and in some seasons, but a comparison of the two careers shows that Grisi's was much more distinguished. This record of supremacy by a single singer in cities of such importance has been equaled in later years only by the likes of Patti and Melba in London, Tamberlick and Battistini in St Petersburg, and Caruso in New York.

Grisi's place in history is secure as the second in a line of great dramatic coloratura sopranos starting with Giuditta

Pasta, continuing with Teresa Tietjens and Rosa Ponselle and culminating with Maria Callas, Joan Sutherland and Montserrat Caballé.

—Tom Kaufman

GRIST, Reri.

Soprano. Born about 1934 in New York. From childhood performed in musicals. Studied singing with Claire Gelda; appeared on Broadway in *West Side Story,* 1957; opera debut as Blonde in *Die Entführung aus dem Serail,* Santa Fe, 1959; sang Königin der Nacht in *Die Zauberflöte* in Cologne and Zurich, 1960; Covent Garden debut in *The Golden Cockerel,* 1962; Metropolitan Opera debut as Rosina in *Il barbiere di Siviglia,* 1966; appeared at Salzburg as Blonde in 1965 and Despina in 1972; appeared as Adina in *L'elisir d'amore,* Vienna, 1973.

*　　*　　*

Reri Grist is one of several twentieth-century singers (Teresa Stich-Randall and Rita Streich are others) whose repertory was based firmly on the operas of Mozart and Richard Strauss. This aspect of her repertory may be related to the fact that, like Stich-Randall, Grist is an American singer who spent most of career singing in German-speaking parts of Europe. Her voice and stage personality were quite similar to those of her older contemporary Streich, with whom she shared much the same repertory.

With her light, high, and focused soprano voice, and her capacity for impressive flights of coloratura, Grist won applause as the Queen of the Night (in Mozart's *Die Zauberflöte*) and Zerbinetta (in Strauss's *Ariadne auf Naxos*), as Despina (*Così fan tutte*) and Sophie (*Rosenkavalier*). Comic roles were her speciality: she won audiences over with her soubrettish wit and lively charm, even after age robbed her voice of much of its sweetness and warmth.

When she was not singing Mozart or Strauss, Grist gave fine performances of some of the lighter roles in nineteenth-century opera. She was praised for both her singing and her acting in the role of Adina when she sang in Donizetti's *Elisir d'amore* at the Metropolitan in 1971. She was also successful as Oscar in Verdi's *Un ballo in maschera* and as Marie in Donizetti's *La fille du regiment.*

A certain shrillness entered Grist's voice in the 1970s; critics began to describe her voice as edgy and thin. Sometimes her performances were marred by a tendency to exaggerate the playfulness of a role at the expense of vocal quality. She was criticized in 1972 for her portrayal, in Munich, of Aminta in Strauss's *Die schweigsame Frau.* Although her infectious high spirits won applause, critics found her voice lacking in the warmth and lyricism that the role demanded. A recording of Mozart's *Der Schauspieldirektor* with Grist in the role of Madame Herz shows the singer well past her prime. Her portrayal of Strauss's Sophie at the Metropolitan in 1978 was criticized as "hard-edged and brittle." Yet the same year she was still able to triumph as Despina, a role in which she could make the most of her talents as a soubrette.

Grist's interpretation of the page Oscar in *Ballo in maschera* was applauded in many of the world's leading opera houses. "Charming"; "boyish"; "bouncy": these are some of the adjectives that critics used to describe Grist's Oscar. The playful song "Volta la terrea fronte" in act I of *Un ballo in maschera,* recorded in the 1960s under Erich Leinsdorf, shows Grist at her charming best. Listen to the way she pertly leaps, with perfect accuracy of pitch, to the high notes at the words "È con Lucifero." Listen to the subtle change in vocal color as she responds to the chromatic descending line in the orchestra at the words "Quando alle belle." Grist's light, detached articulation and bright vocal color seem to be perfectly in tune with the character of the music.

—John A. Rice

GRUBEROVA, Edita.

Soprano. Born 23 December 1946. Studied music in Prague and Vienna; debut with the Slovak National Theater in Bratislava, 1968; appeared at Vienna State Opera, 1972; has also appeared at Bayreuth, Hamburg State Opera, Frankfurt Opera, the Bavarian State Opera in Munich, and other major opera houses.

*　　*　　*

After making her debut at the Slovak National Theater in Bratislava in 1968, Edita Gruberova quickly emerged as one of Europe's leading coloratura sopranos. Her career has developed, for the most part, in central Europe; Salzburg, Vienna and Munich have witnessed many of her triumphs. Her appearances in the United States and Great Britain have been relatively rare. Like Rita Streich, a soprano whose voice Gruberova's resembles somewhat, her repertory is dominated by operas in German; again like Streich, Gruberova specializes in the music of Mozart and Richard Strauss. Gruberova's voice has remarkable dexterity. Her tessitura is high; her lower notes are comparatively weak. When she sings *piano* her voice can be beautiful; in *forte* passages a shrillness, a kind of acid quality often mars her singing.

One of Gruberova's best Mozart roles is the Queen of the Night in *Die Zauberflöte.* In Munich in 1978 Gruberova's Queen was praised (in *Opera*) for her "glittering coloratura cascades"; in Salzburg the following year Gruberova won applause (again in *Opera*), for the "glittering menace" of her portrayal. Among her other Mozart roles is Constanze in *Die Entführung aus dem Serail.* She has also sung and recorded many of Mozart's concert arias.

Some of Gruberova's best qualities can be admired in her portrayal of Marcellina in Paer's *Leonora* (recorded under Peter Maag in 1979). Gruberova executes delicate melismas and tosses off high notes lightly and beautifully in her first aria, "Fedele, mio diletto." Her performance of the aria "Corri, corri" is just as fine: she sings the aria's teasing, playful coloratura with admirable gracefulness.

Less successful is Gruberova's performance of the aria "No, che non sei capace," written by Mozart in 1783 for insertion in Anfossi's opera *Il curioso indiscreto.* Gruberova is to be thanked for bringing this rarely sung aria to the attention of music-lovers in a recording conducted by Leopold Hager (1983); but her performance does not show the music at its best. The voice is often shrill and unpleasant to the ear. The high notes, when sung lightly, are beautiful; but Gruberova executes the climactic coloratura, so reminiscent of the Queen of the Night, with a heavy hand, singing *legato* and *forte* passages that Mozart surely wanted to be sung with a light *staccato.*

Gruberova has won much praise for her many portrayals of Zerbinetta in Strauss's *Ariadne auf Naxos,* a role that she has sung in Salzburg, Vienna and New York, among other cities. A recording made under Solti in 1977 shows why Gruberova has been so successful as Zerbinetta. Her performance of the great aria "Grossmächtige Prinzessin" reveals a voice fuller and richer than those of Streich and Grist, two earlier specialists in this role. At the same time one sometimes misses the dexterity and lightness that Streich and Grist could bring to the coloratura passages. But sometimes Gruberova's coloratura is undeniably beautiful: she does the long cadenza with extraordinary delicacy and charm.

—John A. Rice

GRUENBERG, Louis.

Composer. Born 3 August 1884, near Brest Litovsk. Died 19 June 1964, in Los Angeles. Studied piano with Adele Margulies in New York; studied piano and composition with Busoni in Berlin; debut as a pianist with the Berlin Philharmonic, 1912; took courses at the Vienna conservatory, and tutored there; returned to United States, 1919; organizer and active member of the League of Composers from 1923; taught composition at the Chicago Music College, 1933-36; settled in Santa Monica, California.

Operas

Publishers: Birchard, Cos Cob, Universal.

Signor Formica, Gruenberg (after E.T.A. Hoffmann), 1912.
The Witch of Brocken (children's opera), E.F. Malkowski (translated by L. Vandevere), 1912.
Piccadillymädel (operetta), 1913.
The Bride of the Gods, Busoni (after the ancient Hindu epic, *Mahabharata,* translated by C.H. Meltzer), 1913.
The Dumb Wife (chamber opera), after A. France, 1922-23.
Hallo! Tommy! (operetta), L. Herzer, 1920s [composed under the pseudonym George Edwards].
Lady X (operetta), L. Herzer. c. 1927 [published under the pseudonym George Edwards].
Jack and the Beanstalk, J. Erskine, 20 November 1931.
The Emperor Jones, Gruenberg and K. de Jaffa (after Eugene O'Neill), 1930-31, New York, Metropolitan Opera, January 1932.
Green Mansions (radio opera), after W.H. Hudson, 1937, Columbia Broadcasting System, 17 October 1937.
Helena's Husband, P. Moeller, 1938.
Volpone, Gruenberg (after Ben Jonson), 1949; revised, 1963.
One Night of Cleopatra, Gruenberg (after T. Gautier).
The Miracle of Flanders [(legend with narrator, actors, music], Gruenberg (after Balzac), 1954.
The Delicate King, Gruenberg (after Dumas), 1955.
Antony and Cleopatra, Gruenberg (after Shakespeare), 1955; revised 1958, 1961.

Other works: film scores, incidental music, orchestral works, chamber music, vocal works.

Publications/Writings

About GRUENBERG: articles–

Kramer, A.W. "Louis Gruenberg," *Modern Music* 7 (1930): 3.
Nisbett, R.F. "Louis Gruenberg: a Forgotten Figure of American Music." *Current Musicology* no. 18 (1974): 90.
———. "Louis Gruenberg's American Idiom." *American Music* 3 (1985): 25.

unpublished–

Nisbett, R.F. "Louis Gruenberg: his Life and Works." Ph.D. dissertation, Ohio State University, 1979.

* * *

Louis Gruenberg started his career as a concert pianist and composer under the guidance of Ferruccio Busoni. This great composer-teacher was an important influence on Gruenberg, and their association continued from 1908 until Busoni's death in 1924. Busoni encouraged Gruenberg to experiment in his compositions and search for new means of expression. Eventually Gruenberg evolved a musical style based on melodic and rhythmic traits of Black spirituals and the popular jazz of the 1920s. Although Gruenberg's jazz style characterized only one group of his compositions, the popularity of these jazz-influenced works made him known as an important innovator of jazz.

Gruenberg's first operas were *The Witch of Brocken* and *The Bride of the Gods. The Witch of Brocken* was a children's opera completed in 1912. *The Bride of the Gods,* composed in 1913, used a libretto written by Busoni. Adapted from the ancient Hindu epic, the *Mahabharata,* Gruenberg was never satisfied with the work and the opera remains unperformed. In 1922 Gruenberg completed *The Dumb Wife,* a chamber opera in two acts. The work was based on Anatole France's play *The Man Who Married a Dumb Wife.* Regrettably Gruenberg wrote the opera before securing permission to use the play, and the work was not performed. Gruenberg did not complete his next opera until 1930. In the intervening years he devoted most of his efforts towards writing chamber and symphonic music, and it was during this time that his reputation as a jazz composer was established.

In 1930 Gruenberg received a commission from the Juilliard School to write an opera which could be performed by students as part of the celebration for Juilliard's new music building. The result was the opera *Jack and the Beanstalk.* This well-known fairy tale was suggested by John Erskine who was also the librettist. Erskine, a writer and musician, was the president of the Juilliard School. The premiere was given on 20 November 1931, and the opera proved so successful that it was moved to a theater on Broadway, where it continued to play for two additional weeks. The opera is in a lyrical, tonal style well suited to young singers. In his review in *Modern Music,* Randall Thompson wrote "The music bubbles and shimmers. . . . That he wrote an opera practicable for such performers, without once writing down to them, is greatly to his credit."

While working on *Jack and the Beanstalk,* Gruenberg also began composing his most important opera, *The Emperor Jones.* After a lengthy period in which he sought permission from Eugene O'Neill to use his play, Gruenberg finally received approval and began the work in 1930. The opera was completed in 1931. After the premiere in January 1932 by the Metropolitan Opera Company, Giulio Gatti-Casazza, the Metropolitan's director, hailed the work as "an American achievement."

Gruenberg's next opera was *Helena's Husband* which was based on the play by Philip Moeller. Like the earlier opera *The Bride of the Gods,* Gruenberg was not satisfied with the work. Although it was completed in 1938, he never sought to have it performed. In 1937 Gruenberg received a commission from the Columbia Broadcasting Company to write a radio opera. For this unusual medium Gruenberg chose William Hudson's novel *Green Mansions.* Since the work was to be a non-visual opera, Gruenberg experimented with the technology available at that time to achieve a jungle atmosphere. Microphone amplification was used to increase the volume of sound for selected instruments, and phonograph records were used for the jungle sounds. The jungle girl's voice was represented by a musical saw. Although the 17 October 1937 broadcast was the only performance the opera received, it was given praise for its interesting innovations.

Just before the performance of *Green Mansions,* Gruenberg moved to California, where he began a career in film composition. During this period, in which he completed ten film scores, Gruenberg did not complete any more operas until he left the film industry in 1950. In this last period of his life, Gruenberg returned to opera and completed two large and three chamber operas. The large scale operas were *Volpone* (1949) after Ben Jonson and *Antony and Cleopatra* (1961) after Shakespeare. Both operas consist of three acts, and demand large casts and orchestras. Gruenberg's chamber operas were intended for television performance. These works are *One Night of Cleopatra* (after Gautier), *The Miracle of Flanders* (after Balzac) and *The Delicate King* (after Dumas). To most opera companies these later works are unknown, and when Gruenberg died in 1964 he was largely forgotten by his musical colleagues.

Gruenberg remains known for his operatic works primarily through the significance of *The Emperor Jones.* This opera was recognized after its first performance as the most important American opera up to that time. Unfortunately, the work has been neglected for many years, and it is difficult to appreciate its earlier importance. All of Gruenberg's operas written after 1950 remain in manuscript. An examination of these works reveals a mature, well-crafted musical style. It is hoped that future opera companies will take an interest in Gruenberg's works, and that his unperformed operas and a revival of his earlier works will find their way into the operatic repertoire.

—Robert F. Nisbett

GUADAGNI, Gaetano.

Castrato contralto. Born c.1725, in Lodi or Vicenza. Died November 1792, in Padua. Began career in Parma, 1746; went to London, 1748, where he sang for Handel; many successful appearances in London; sang in Dublin, 1751-52, Paris, 1754, and Lisbon, 1755, where he studied with Gizziello; engaged by Gluck to sing Orfeo, Vienna, 1762; appeared in London, Munich and Venice, 1769-72; summoned

by Frederick the Great to Potsdam, 1776; settled in Padua, 1777, where he sang at the Basilica del Santo.

*　　*　　*

As one of the foremost singers of the eighteenth century, Guadagni is notable for the roles he created, the composers he worked with, and for the part he played in rescuing opera from its mid-century nadir, when drama had been sacrificed to a display of the vanity of singers. After holding minor posts in churches and opera houses in northern Italy, a turning point in his career was the visit to London in 1748, where he attracted the attention of Handel, who engaged him to sing Mrs Cibber's solos in *Messiah,* Micah in *Samson,* and created for him the role of Didimus in *Theodora.* The climax of Guadagni's career came in 1762, when he created the title role in Gluck's *Orfeo,* and throughout the 1760s he is identified as the principal singer in Vienna. Although he owed his greatest success to Gluck, Guadagni also owed his eventual decline to having identified too closely with Gluck's reforming principles, finally antagonizing his public by refusing to hold up an opera to acknowledge applause, or to indulge them with encores. His obstinate personality attracted comment: even Burney, always one to whitewash a character with whom he had been associated, asserted that his generous nature was marred by a tendency to provoke quarrels; defending the race of castratos from a generalized charge of cowardice, he claimed that Guadagni "so far from timid and pusillanimous . . . would seek danger rather than shun it." The librettist Calzabigi described him as a knave. He was reportedly the finest billiards player in Europe.

The clearest evidence of Guadagni's particular talents lies in the role of Orpheus, devised, according to Calzabigi, to fit the singer like a glove. Calzabigi went so far as to say that the opera "went well because there we had Guadagni . . . otherwise it would have been terrible." The range is not wide (a to e″) and from the isolated anguished cries in the first chorus, to the great aria "Che farò senza Euridice" Orpheus's music is punctuated throughout by pauses, allowing the singer time to run through his repertory of expressive gestures. Guadagni's mastery of gesture is often mentioned: "a few notes with frequent pauses, and opportunities of being liberated from the composer and the band, were all he wanted" (Burney). Significantly, one of Guadagni's many illustrious teachers was David Garrick, celebrated for his powerful use of gesture, and among routine descriptions of Guadagni's "uncommonly elegant" figure, Burney notes that the singer's movements "would have been excellent studies for a statuary." Despite Gluck's celebrated antipathy to singers' ornamentation, three arias from *Orfeo* were published in decorated form, as "sung by Signor Guadagni," though the ornaments are modest and expressive rather than athletic and virtuosic.

His singing technique was rebuilt in the 1750s by the castrato Gizziello Conti, who had retired from the stage in a fit of religious devotion after narrowly surviving the Lisbon earthquake. Guadagni's seems to have been a small voice, and while most eighteenth-century castratos were praised for their powers of crescendo, he, "after beginning a note or passage with all the force he could safely exert, fined it off to a thread, and gave it all the effect of extreme distance." Later in life he extended his range to sing soprano roles, up to g″. Burney graphically describes the consequent weakening of tone: "Let a fluid of six feet in depth be spread over more than double its usual surface, and it will necessarily be shallower, though of greater extent."

Like many eighteenth-century singers, Guadagni was also a composer in a small way. He dared to replace "Men tiranne," Gluck's agitated air in which Orpheus tries to convince the Furies of the power of his love, with a tuneful minuet which he composed for a pastiche version of *Orfeo* in London in 1770. It is hard to see how a singer who preferred this slight, prettified air could have been the chosen vehicle for bringing Gluck's dramatic reforms to life.

—Patricia Howard

GUEDEN, Hilde.

Soprano. Born 15 September 1917, in Vienna. Died 17 September 1988, in Vienna. Studied with Wetzelsberger at Vienna Conservatory; operetta debut in Stolz's *Servus servus,* Vienna, 1939; opera debut as Cherubino in *Le nozze di Figaro* in Zurich, 1939-41; at Bavarian Staatsoper in Munich, 1941-42; Rome, 1942-46; appeared at Salzburg as Zerlina, 1946; associated with Vienna Staatsoper until 1972; Covent Garden, 1947; debut at Metropolitan Opera as Gilda, 1951; made an Austrian Kammersängerin, 1951.

Publications

About GUEDEN: articles–

Rosenthal, H. "Hilde Gueden." *Sopranos of Today.* London, 1956.
Liversidge, H. "Hilde Gueden." *Gramophone Record Review* 58 (1958): 809.
Rosenthal, H. "Hilde Gueden." *Great Singers of Today.* London, 1966.

*   *   *

The light lyric soprano may be the least memorable of all operatic voices. Even very good ones are not, for the most part, in short supply; even during periods when audiences and critics lament the paucity of great voices there seems to be a virtual plethora of talented artists of this vocal type. Moreover, it is a voice type which, while pleasing, is not often especially distinctive, and many excellent lyric sopranos sound much alike. So it follows that only a small number of these singers have ever achieved genuine star status, and those who have offered something quite special and distinctive in addition to their voices.

Hilde Gueden is one of that select company. No doubt her exceptional physical beauty had something to do with it—blond, slender and graceful, her loveliness was heightened by a slightly exotic, Eastern European quality that gave her stage presence a particular glamour. There was an exotic touch of "spice" in Gueden's creamy voice as well, lending it personality and allure.

Had she not possessed these very individual qualities, Gueden's career might have been rather less distinguished than it was, for she was a great charmeuse rather than one of the most accomplished of vocalists. Her intonation was not always true, and sustained notes often flattened into an unattractive whine, an inclination which became more exaggerated as she grew older. This plagues certain critical passages in Gueden's several recorded performances as Sophie

in *Der Rosenkavalier,* though much of the singing is lovely. Equally troublesome is her sloppiness and imprecision which emerges specifically as rhythmic laziness, a tendency to sing behind the beat. This lack of energetic thrust and alertness compromises some of Gueden's Mozart singing, where her individual tone otherwise gives much pleasure. A characteristic example is her recording of the motet "Exsultate, Jubilate." The slow middle section is handled with skill and caresses the ear just as it should—but both the outer movements make considerable demands on her coloratura singing, and she seems barely able to keep up with conductor Alberto Erede's rather moderate tempo.

Elsewhere in Gueden's performances of Mozart this tendency is less troubling. As Susanna in *Le nozze di Figaro,* there is less need for virtuoso vocalism and more for real personal charm, and here she is often marvelous. Even the tendency to lag behind the beat pays a certain dividend, as in the climactic aria "Deh vieni, non tardar," where she achieves just the right quality of dreamy rapture, which eludes many fine singers of this role. It is no surprise, particularly with her good looks and formidable skills as an actress, that Gueden became such a favorite in this part—and in the similar roles of Pamina in *Die Zauberflöte* and Zerlina in *Don Giovanni.*

Still it is in the light music of Johann Strauss and Franz Lehár that Hilde Gueden is at her best. Here too the lazy, dreamy quality is beguiling and even the coloratura passages seem to work well for her. Many records preserve memorable examples of Gueden in songs and arias as well as complete operettas. Especially noteworthy are her performances as Rosalinde in *Die Fledermaus,* where her touch of Eastern European panache is just right, and her humor and vivacity fairly leap off the turntable. She may be the best exponent of this delectable part on record.

—David Anthony Fox

GUILLAUME TELL [William Tell].

Composer: Gioachino Rossini.

Librettists: E. de Jouy, H.-L.-F. Bis, et al. (after Schiller).

First Performance: Paris, Opéra, 3 August 1829.

Roles: Guillaume Tell (baritone); Arnold (tenor); Mathilde (soprano); Melcthal (bass); Jemmy (mezzo-soprano); Hedwig (contralto); Walter Furst (bass); Ruedi (tenor); Leuthold (bass); Gesler (bass); Rudolph (tenor); A Hunter (tenor or baritone); chorus (SSATTBB).

Publications

books–

Staeten, E. van der. *La mélodie populaire dans l'opéra "Guillaume Tell" de Rossini.* Paris, 1879.
Cagli, B. *"Guglielmo Tell": La guida all'opera.* Milan, 1971.

articles–

Berlioz, Hector. "Guillaume Tell." *Gazzette musicale* 1/October-November (1834): 326, 336, 341, 349; English translation in *Source Readings in Music History,* edited by Oliver Strunk, New York, 1950.

Cametti, A. "Il 'Guglielmo Tell' e le sue prime rappresentazioni in Italia." *Rivista musicale italiana* 6 (1899): 580.

Kirby, P.R. "Rossini's Overture to 'William Tell'." *Music and Letters* 33 (1952): 132.

Porter, A. "William Tell." *Opera* 9 (1958).

Viale Ferrero, M. *"Guglielmo Tell* a Torino (1839-1840) ovvero una *Procella* scenografica." *Rivista italiana musicale* 14 (1979): 378.

Gerhard, Anselm. "L'eroe titubante e il finale aperto: un dilemma insolubile nel *Guillaume Tell* di Rossini." *Rivista italiana di musicologia* 19 (1984): 113.

Avant-scène opéra March (1989) [*Guillaume Tell* issue].

Crichton, Ronald. "An Overture to *Guillaume Tell.*" *Opera* June (1990).

Guillaume Tell was the last opera of Rossini, but it was the first of a proposed series of works by the composer for the Opéra in Paris. Although Rossini previously had written three other French operas, and strains of their influence may be traced in *Guillaume Tell,* the latter work is one of immeasurably greater genius. It exceeds in scope and power the earlier French works and in fundamental style the Italian works upon which Rossini's lasting fame rests. *Guillaume Tell* is one of the first examples of what came to be known as *grand opéra,* a genre whose other early examples are Auber's *La muette de Portici* (1828), Halévy's *La juive* (1830), and Meyerbeer's *Robert le diable* (1831) and *Les Huguenots* (1836).

Popular from the outset, *Guillaume Tell* quickly surpassed the box-office receipts of its major competitor, *La muette de Portici.* However, it soon suffered drastic cuts, and in two years its five acts characteristic of French grand opera were reduced to three. Ultimately, *Guillaume Tell* endured the indignity of reaching the public in the form of act II alone. Nevertheless, it was an important part of the repertory of the Opéra in Paris throughout the nineteenth century and had received 648 performances there by the end of 1880. Its popularity stemmed from several sources: its libretto, local color, orchestration, and, of course, Rossini's inimitable grasp of musico-dramatic principles.

The plot is loosely based upon the well-known medieval legend of the Swiss patriot, the chronicles of whose exploits have attracted generations of poets. Friedrich von Schiller's play of 1804 furnished the basis of the adaptation by Etienne de Jouy, Hippolyte Bis, and others, who made substantial alterations in Schiller's structure, primarily pruning and simplifying it. The central threads of the plot are: 1) the personal opposition of the opera's namesake to the oppressive Hapsburg governor, Gesler, and ultimately the latter's death at Tell's hands; 2) the complications arising from the liaison between the lovers Arnold, son of Melcthal, the peasant conspirator, and Mathilde, daughter of whom else but the tyrannical Gesler; and 3) the triumph of Arnold and his compatriots in rousing the peasants to successful revolution.

These themes of patriotism and liberation from tyranny appealed immensely to the French audiences of the time. The beginning of the revolution of 1830 in Belgium has been attributed in some respects to the riotous audience's reaction

at the premiere of Auber's stormy *La muette de Portici.* Always responsive to the times, Rossini had exploited elements of these themes in his previous Parisian works, *Le siège de Corinthe* and *Moïse et Pharaon.*

Among the defining attributes of the Romantic movement of the early nineteenth century is the infusion of the power and picturesque qualities of nature into art. Along with this came an increasing interest in local color—that is, the unique qualities of specific cultures and locales. Clearly, the Swiss peasantry and spectacular scenery of their cantons of Schwyz, Uri, and Unterwalden provided ample resources for exploitation by Rossini. Exotic atmospheres and unusual settings were common in French opera in the early nineteenth century, but few composers exceeded Rossini in successfully melding these elements into the music itself. The famous *ranz des vaches* (song of the Swiss herdsmen) played by the English horn in the overture; the choruses of hunters, wedding celebrants, and conspirators; and the fisherman's song are all informed by atmosphere and characterization adroitly shaped by instrumentation and orchestration. Rossini previously had shown this kind of mastery in other works, notably *La donna del lago.* Edward Dannreuther (*The Oxford History of Music,* 1905) contends that "Local color so perfect was not again seen or heard in opera till 1875, when Bizet's *Carmen* was produced." Bizet's fondness for act II of *Tell* is well documented.

Today, among the least recognized of the important attributes of *Guillaume Tell* is the fine orchestration that most know only from the overture, but which in fact is excelled easily by many sections of the opera itself. Rossini's contemporaries acknowledged the genius of his orchestration, despite the infamous criticism of his brass and percussion "noisiness." Later, the great French scholar, Arthur Pougin (*Musiciens du XIXe siècle,* 1911) observes that "it is finally to Rossini that is owed the innovation and richness of the splendors of the modern dramatic orchestra. Who knows if Wagner's orchestra, that admirable orchestra to which unfortunately everything is sacrificed, would exist today without the advent of Rossini?" The score of *Guillaume Tell* is a model of imagination and mastery in orchestration, but special mention may be made of the writing for horns and for violoncellos.

A horn player himself, Rossini chose that instrument as the key element in the creation of local color. The depiction of the bucolic atmosphere of the Swiss countryside, the virtuoso paean of the hunting chorus, and the antiphonal, on-stage horn calls that rally the Swiss peasants—all contribute to the establishment of the horn as the central instrument of the opera.

The sub-divided solo violoncellos of the opening of the overture portend their creative use in most of the opera. Perhaps most striking, and yet typical, is their aspiring sixteenth-note passage that sets the tone of the aria of the famous archery scene, "Sois immobile" ("Be still").

The florid arias and dazzling set pieces well-known to lovers of Rossini's Italian operas do not dominate his last work for the stage, although the arias are demanding—especially those of the tenor, Melcthal. Rather, we find that a superb coordination of ensembles, choruses, dances, evocative instrumental sections, and solos and duets informed by dramatic lyricism carry the whole in a marvelous unity of expression. Striking scenes abound, but perhaps the most arresting is the entirety of the second act, where Rossini carefully builds to a smashing climax, with soloists, chorus, and orchestra all propelling the drama forward.

Guillaume Tell is Rossini's neglected masterpiece of early French romantic opera. Although it was popular during the nineteenth century, it did not enjoy unqualified success. Today, performances of it are rare, but the meritorious qualities of *Guillaume Tell* easily outstrip the hindrances imposed by a libretto that is occasionally awkward. The ever-popular overture, enduring though it may be, is only a presage of far richer treasures in the opera proper.

—William E. Runyan

GUTHRIE, Tyrone.

Director. Born 2 July 1900, in Tunbridge Wells, England; died 15 May 1971, in Newbliss, Ireland. Married: Judith Bretherton, 30 August 1930. Received a degree in ancient history and philosophy from St. John's College, Oxford, in 1923; in same year made professional debut as actor and stage manager at the Oxford Playhouse, working under James Bernard Fagan; during the 1920s worked as an announcer, script writer and director for the BBC; director Scottish National Theatre, 1926-27; director at Festival Theatre in Cambridge, 1929-30; staged dramatic productions (especially Shakespeare) in England and New York during 1930s; administrator at Old Vic and Sadler's Wells theaters 1939-45; directed Britten's *Peter Grimes* at Covent Garden (1947); director, Old Vic, 1951-52; founding director, Shakespeare Festival, Stratford, Ontario, 1953-57; helped plan Guthrie Theater, Minneapolis, which opened in 1963 and for which he staged several productions. Guthrie was knighted in 1961.

Opera Productions (selected)

Peter Grimes, London, Covent Garden, 1947.
La traviata, London, Covent Garden, 1947.
Carmen, London, Sadler's Wells, 1949.
Il barbieri di Siviglia, London, Sadler's Wells, 1950.
Falstaff, London, Sadler's Wells, 1950.
Carmen, New York, Metropolitan Opera, 1952.
La traviata, New York, Metropolitan Opera, 1957.
HMS Pinafore, Stratford, Ontario, Avon Theater, 1960.
The Pirates of Penzance, Stratford, Ontario, Avon Theater, 1960.
Carmen, New York, Metropolitan Opera, 1967.
Peter Grimes, Metropolitan Opera, 1967.

Publications

By GUTHRIE: books–

Theatre Prospect. London, 1932.
With Robertson Davies and Grant MacDonald. *Renown at Stratford.* Toronto, 1953.
With Robertson Davies and Grant MacDonald. *Twice Have the Trumpets Sounded.* Toronto, 1954.
With Robertson Davies. *Thrice the Brinded Cat Hath Mew'd.* Toronto, 1955.
A Life in the Theatre. London, 1959.
A New Theatre. New York, 1964.
In Various Directions. New York, 1966.
Tyrone Guthrie on Acting. London, 1971.

About GUTHRIE: books–

Joseph, Stephen, ed. *Actor and Architect.* Toronto, 1964.

Morison, Bradley G. *In Search of an Audience: How an Audience Was Found for the Tyrone Guthrie Theatre.* New York, 1968.
Rossi, Alfred. *Minneapolis Rehearsals: Tyrone Guthrie Directs Hamlet.* Berkeley, CA, 1970.
Forsyth, James. *Tyrone Guthrie: A Biography.* London, 1976.
Rossi, Alfred. *Astonish Us in the Morning: Tyrone Guthrie Remembered.* London, 1977.

*　　*　　*

Tyrone Guthrie divided his work between the straight theater and the opera house, with the latter only playing a secondary role. According to the actor Sir Alec Guinness, a colleague who became a close family friend, he was the true *enfant terrible* of the British stage during the 1930s and 1940s, although with his stature of well over six feet, military bearing and brisk orders to artists this was an *enfant* to be reckoned with.

Opera occupied Guthrie mainly in the early and middle periods of his career. He made his first major contribution as the administrator of the Sadler's Wells Opera Company in the wartime years, following his appointment in 1941 as overall director of the Vic-Wells partnership, producing the popular operas *La bohème* and *La traviata* and bringing to them a certain freshness which remained, however, acceptable rather than radical or avant-garde. His boldest decision, vigorously supported by his artistic director Joan Cross, was to accept the young Benjamin Britten's *Peter Grimes* as the opera which should reopen the Sadler's Wells Opera House in London at the end of the European war in 1945. Before the curtain rose on the opening night he told Joan Cross, "Whatever happens, we were quite right to do this piece." As it transpired, the production was a triumph, although several members of the company opposed the opera and all those associated with it. Guthrie went on to produce *Peter Grimes* at Covent Garden in its 1947-48 season.

Characteristically, Guthrie aimed to banish the stiff, stock movements (or lack of them) of solo singers and the operatic chorus and to achieve dramatic verisimilitude. His production of Bizet's *Carmen* for Sadler's Wells and the New York Metropolitan Opera was more realistic than audiences were used to, and antagonized some people while winning vociferous admiration from others. He was especially strong with a chorus and crowd scenes, recognizing (and making audiences recognize too) that even when a crowd is seemingly moved by one basic emotion and acts in a single direction it is still made up of individuals whose various natures interact. For example, he made it clear that while nearly all the Borough folk join in the final hounding to death of the outsider fisherman Peter Grimes in Britten's powerful opera, such persons as the inquisitive Mrs. Sedley, the pompous Lawyer Swallow and the religious zealot Bob Boles all have their slightly different reasons for doing so.

Guthrie set the fashion for many later directors of opera in that he was a strong artistic personality who tended to sweep all before him. His rehearsals were always spontaneous and stimulating and sometimes "great fun," but he was not a trained professional musician. The delicate balance of music and drama, in this most vivid of alliances between the two, needs constant care; and it is arguable that directors who think above all in terms of words, stage action and visual presentation cannot plumb the depths which a musician can see and reveal in an operatic score. It is perhaps because of such artists as these that today we often speak of Franco Zeffirelli's *Traviata* and Jonathan Miller's *Tosca,* putting the producer's name where before we only placed that of the composer or very occasionally that of a great singer like Maria Callas. It is a fact of modern operatic life that when new productions prove controversial the controversy often has little or nothing to do with the music or the way it is sung and played; it is sometimes as if that were of secondary importance. But this comment is in no way intended to detract from Guthrie's achievement as a much needed pioneer of naturalism in opera in the English-speaking world at a time when its presentation had become artificial.

—Christopher Headington

GWENDOLINE.

Composer: Emmanuel Chabrier.

Librettist: Catulle Mendès.

First Performance: Brussels, Théâtre de la Monnaie, 10 April 1886.

Roles: Harald (baritone); Armel (tenor); Gwendoline (soprano); Aella; Erik; chorus.

Publications

book–

Desaymard, Joseph. *Emmanuel Chabrier et 'Gwendoline'.* Paris, 1904.

*   *   *

The plot of *Gwendoline,* while somewhat melodramatic, is no more so than that of many better-known operas. The action takes place on the coast of eighth-century Britain, where a peace-loving community of Saxons is invaded by a band of Danish pirates, headed by their chieftain Harald. He falls in love with Gwendoline, a Saxon princess and daughter of the chief, Armel. Harald seeks the hand of Gwendoline, who despite initial repugnance at the invasion of her land, falls deeply in love with Harald. Armel pretends to agree to their marriage, while at the same time ordering his warriors to slay the Danish invaders during the nuptial celebrations. Armel hands his daughter a dagger with which to murder her husband on their wedding night. She pleads with Harald to flee, but he refuses and is mortally wounded by Armel. Gwendoline immediately commits suicide with the dagger her father has given her, and the opera ends with a passionate duet between the doomed bridal pair.

A number of misconceptions seem to have arisen about this opera. It is commonly described as "Wagnerian" work in which it was impossible for Chabrier to be himself. In *A Hundred Years of Music,* Gerald Abraham comments,

"There is some really fine music in *Gwendoline,* but it is far from being the essential Chabrier." Even the composer seems to have had some doubts about the work. Writing to a friend, he remarked that "*Gwendoline* is a kind of musical Liebig [Justus von Liebig, German chemist]; it's too compact; I ought to have taken a little piece of it and added some good old honest water and given it a good stir before serving it up." However, Chabrier made these comments while he was still working on the opera. There can be no doubt that he labored long and hard over the work, and that on its completion, it represented for him his most ambitious and satisfying achievement to date.

The enthusiasm for Wagner's music during the 1880s was widespread among French composers, and Chabrier was no exception. The influence is unquestionably there in *Gwendoline.* The Wagnerian sense of drama, the harmonic vocabulary with such devices as the use of unprepared ninths and extended pedal points, and the use of leitmotives, all these techniques seem peculiarly apt to the opera's setting, an exceptional one in Chabrier's output. (Ironically, the overture—the only familiar movement in the score for many—is the most Wagnerian part of the opera, and in one sense invites comparison with Glinka's *Russlan and Ludmila,* another work whose overture is familiar, albeit untypical of the little-known opera that follows.) Against all this must be set the fact that *Gwendoline* was the only opera by Chabrier to employ continuous music. Its avoidance of spoken dialogue made it suitable for presentation at the Paris Opéra, where indeed it was eventually staged in December 1893, by which time its composer was seriously ill. This continuity inevitably puts the work onto a different plane from the remainder of Chabrier's stage works. If *Gwendoline* is unlike them, it is still characteristic of Chabrier's musical attitudes: the traditional operatic constructive devices of recitatives, arias, duets, ensembles and choruses were both congenial to Chabrier and essential for the traditionally-minded Parisian opera-going public.

Gwendoline was conceived and performed during the 1880s, when French musical taste of the period was possessed of a strong intellectual streak, epitomized by the short-lived *Revue Wagnérienne* (Wagnerian Journal). The periodical was supported principally by a group of Paris intellectuals who regarded solidity of substance and musical "weight" as a necessary prerequisite to counter-balance the Teutonic musical aspirations and achievements of the time. The journal coincided with and indeed was a direct outcome of this "Wagner fever." Although it never became a general epidemic, this fever was sufficiently all-embracing to marry with the long-established ideals of the Paris Opéra, where works of grandiloquence and magnificence were frequently *de rigueur.* Seen in this light, Chabrier's *Gwendoline* fits well into the French musical climate of the period. At the same time it is infinitely superior to a host of stage works which it may not have yet entirely supplanted, although eventually its music will surely receive due recognition.

—J. Barrie Jones

H

HADRIAN IN SYRIA
See ADRIANO IN SIRIA

HALÉVY, Jacques-François-Fromental-Elie.

Composer. Born 27 May 1799, in Paris. Died 17 March 1862, in Nice. Studied elementary music with Cazot, 1809, piano with Lambert, 1810, harmony with Berton, 1811, and counterpoint for five years with Cherubini at the Paris Conservatory; won the second Prix de Rome for his cantata, *Les derniers moments du Tasse,* 1816, and for his cantata *La mort d'Adonis,* 1817; won the Grand Prix de Rome for his *Herminie,* 1819; vocal coach at the Italian Opera, 1827; succeeded Daussoigne as professor of harmony and accompaniment at the Paris Conservatory, 1827; first successful opera *Clari,* 1828; appointed "chef du chant" at the Paris Opéra, 1830; succeeded Fétis as professor of counterpoint and fugue at the Paris Conservatory, 1833; *La Juive* an international success, 1835; succeeded Reicha as a member of the Académie, 1836; taught an advanced composition class at the Paris Conservatory, 1840; appointed Secretary for life of the Académie, 1854; Chevalier of the Legion of Honor. Halévy's students included Gounod and Bizet (who married Halévy's daughter in 1869).

Operas

Les bohémiennes, 1819-20.
Marco Curzio, 1822.
Les deux pavillons, ou Le jaloux et le méfiant, J.B.C. Vial, c. 1824.
Pygmalion, Patin and Arnoult, c. 1824.
Erostrate, Arnoult, Léon Halévy, c. 1825 [unfinished].
L'artisan, J.H. Vernoy de Saint-Georges, Paris, Opéra-Comique, 30 January 1827.
Le roi et le batelier (with V.E. Rifaut), J.H. Vernoy de Saint-Georges, Paris, Opéra-Comique, 8 November 1827.
Clari, Pietro Giannone, Paris, Théâtre-Italien, 9 December 1828.
Le dilettante d'Avignon, François Benoît Hoffman and Léon Halévy, Paris, Opéra-Comique, 7 November 1829.
Attendre et courir (with H. de Ruolz), Fulgence and Henri, Paris, Opéra-Comique, 28 May 1830.
La langue musicale, Saint-Yves, Paris, Opéra-Comique, 11 December 1830.
La tentation (ballet-opera, with Casimir Gide), Cavé and J. Coralli, Paris, Opéra, 20 June 1832.
Yella. Moreau and P. Duport, 1832.
Les souvenirs de Lafleur, P.F.A. Carmouche and de Courcy, Paris, Opéra-Comique, 4 March 1833.
Ludovic (completion of Hérold's last opera), J.H. Vernoy de Saint-Georges, Paris, Opéra-Comique, 16 May 1833.
La Juive, Eugène Scribe, Paris, Opéra, 23 February 1835.

L'éclair, J.H. Vernoy de Saint-Georges and F.A.E. de Planard, Paris, Opéra-Comique, 16 December 1835.
Guido et Ginevra, ou La peste de Florence, Eugène Scribe, Paris, Opéra, 5 March 1838.
Les treize, Eugène Scribe and P. Duport, Paris, Opéra-Comique, 15 April 1839.
Le shérif, Eugène Scribe (after Balzac), Paris, Opéra-Comique, 2 September 1839.
Le drapier, Eugène Scribe, Paris, Opéra, 6 January 1840.
Le guitarrero, Eugène Scribe, Paris, Opéra-Comique, 21 January 1841.
Le reine de Chypre, J.H. Vernoy de Saint-Georges, Paris, Opéra, 22 December 1841.
Charles VI, Casimir and Germain Delavigne, Paris, Opéra, 15 March 1843.
Le lazzarone, ou Le bien vient en dormant. J.H. Vernoy de Saint-Georges, Paris, Opéra, 23 March 1844.
Les mousquetaires de la reine, J.H. Vernoy de Saint-Georges, Paris, Opéra-Comique, 3 February 1846.
Les premiers pas (with Auber, Adam, Carafa), A. Royer, G. Vaëz, Paris, Opéra-National, 15 November 1847.
Le val d'Andorre, J.H. Vernoy de Saint-Georges, Paris, Opéra-Comique, 11 November 1848.
La fée aux roses, Eugène Scribe and J.H. Vernoy de Saint-Georges, Paris, Opéra-Comique, 1 October 1849.
La tempesta, Pietro Giannone (translated from Scribe's French libretto after Shakespeare), London, Her Majesty's Theatre, 8 June 1850.
La dame de pique, Eugène Scribe, Paris, Opéra-Comique, 28 December 1850.
Le juif errant, Eugène Scribe and J.H. Vernoy de Saint-Georges (after E. Sue), Paris, Opéra, 23 April 1852.
Le nabab, Eugène Scribe and J.H. Vernoy de Saint-Georges, Paris, Opéra-Comique, 1 September 1853.
Jaguarita l'indienne, J.H. Vernoy de Saint-Georges and Adolphe de Leuven, Paris, Théâtre-Lyrique, 14 May 1855.
L'inconsolable, Paris, Théâtre-Lyrique, 13 June 1855.
Valentine d'Aubigny, J. Barbier, M. Carré, Paris, Opéra-Comique, 26 April 1856.
La magicienne, J.H. Vernoy de Saint-Georges, Paris, Opéra, 17 March 1858.
Noé, [unfinished, completed by Bizet as *Le déluge*], J.H. Vernoy de Saint-Georges, Karlsruhe [in German], 5 April 1885.
Vanina d'Ornono, Léon Halévy [unfinished].

Other works: ballets, incidental music, cantatas.

Publications

By HALÉVY: books–

Leçons de lecture musicale . . . pour les écoles de la ville de Paris. Paris, 1857.
Souvenirs et portraits. Paris, 1861.
Derniers souvenirs et portraits. Paris, 1863.

Set design by P. Chaperon for Halévy's *La Juive*, Paris, 1898

About HALÉVY: books–

Halévy, Léon. *F. Halévy: sa vie et ses oeuvres*. Paris, 1862; 2nd ed., 1863.
Lorbac, C. de. *Fromenthal Halévy: sa vie, ses oeuvres*. Paris, 1862.
Catelin, A. *F. Halévy: notice biographique*. Paris, 1863.
Escudier, L. *Mes souvenirs*. Paris, 1863.
Monnais, E. *F. Halévy: souvenirs d'un ami pour joindre à ceux d'un frère*. Paris, 1863.
Sainte-Beuve, C.A. *Nouveaux lundis*, ii. Paris, 1864.
Pougin, A. *F. Halévy: écrivain*. Paris, 1865.
Saint-Saëns, C. *Ecole buissonnière: notes et souvenirs*. Paris, 1913.
Pendle, Karin. *Eugène Scribe and French Opera of the Nineteenth Century*. Ann Arbor, 1979.
Fulcher, Jane F. *The Nation's Image: French Grand Opera as Politics and Politicized Art*. Cambridge, 1987.

articles–

[Numerous contemporary reviews of Halévy's works by Hector Berlioz; for a complete list, see the *New Grove Dictionary of Music and Musicians*, 1980 ed.]
Wagner, Richard. "Bericht uber eine neue Pariser Oper: La reine de Chypre von Halévy." *Dresdener Abend-Zeitung* 26 (1842); English translation in *Richard Wagner's Prose Works*, edited by W.A. Ellis, vol. 7, p. 205. London, 1898; 1979.

————. "Halévy et La reine de Chypre." *Revue et gazette musicale de Paris* 9 (1842): 75, 100, 179, 187; English translation in *Richard Wagner's Prose Works*, edited by W.A. Ellis, vol. 8, p. 175. London, 1899; 1979.
Curtiss, Mina. "Fromental Halévy." *Musical Quarterly* 39 (1953): 196.
Klein, J.W. "Jacques Fromental Halévy (1799-1862)." *Music Review* 23 (1962): 13.
Gregor-Dellin, M., ed. *Richard Wagner: Mein Leben*. Munich, 1963.
Wolff, H.C. "Halévy als Kunst-und Musikschriftsteller." In *Musicae scientiae collectanea: Festschrift Kal Gustav Fellerer*, 697. Cologne, 1973.
Leich-Galland, Karl. "Quelques observations sur les autographes des grandes opéras de Fromenthal Halévy." In *Les sources en musicologie*, edited by Michel Huglo, 159. Paris, 1981.
Avant-scène opéra July 1987 [*La Juive* issue].

*   *   *

Together with Auber and Meyerbeer, Halévy was one of the leading figures in French opera from the period of the July monarchy to the middle of the 19th century. Although his posthumous reputation rests almost entirely on the 5-act grand opera, *La Juive* (*The Jewess*, 1835), most of his 37 completed stage works were produced at the Opéra-Comique.

Le dilettante d'Avignon (1829) was Halévy's first significant success, an *opéra comique* to a text arranged by his brother

Léon Halévy. The twin success of *La Juive* and *L'éclair* (*The Lightening-Bolt*) at the Opéra and the Opéra-Comique, respectively, in February and December of 1835 established him as a leading figure in French music. While he had consistently to contend with the rivalry of Auber in the area of comic opera and with Meyerbeer in grand opera, neither of them could match Halévy's versatile command of both fields. Throughout his career Halévy collaborated in about equal measure with the two most prominent French librettists of the day, Augustin Eugène Scribe and J. H. Vernoy de Saint-Georges, each providing texts in both comic and serious genres.

Following *L'éclair* (with Saint-Georges)—a somewhat experimental comedy of manners set "in the vicinity of Boston, 1797" with a cast consisting only of 2 sopranos and 2 tenors, without chorus—Halévy's most successful *opéras comiques* include *Le guitarrero* (1841), *Les mousquetaires de la reine* (1846), *Le val d'Andorre* (1848), and *Jaguarita l'indienne* (1855), the latter produced at the newly-opened Théâtre-Lyrique. Certainly Halévy was most comfortable working in this genre, while his few full-scale grand operas, by his own testimony, cost him protracted labor and mental anguish. Eduard Hanslick was still impressed by the "elegance, charm, spirit" and "brilliant technical facility" of *L'éclair* in its 1881 Viennese revival, also commenting on the quality of its instrumentation, the deftness of its musical characterizations, and of its "transitions from cheerful to sentimental musical numbers." No less an authority than Berlioz—no great admirer of Halévy in general—also praised the composer's orchestration in *Le val d'Andorre,* declaring the act-II finale to be a "masterpiece" and the score of the opera as a whole to be so closely matched to its text that both seemed to emanate from one and the same mind.

Critical response to the grand operas—despite the enduring popularity of *La Juive* into the 20th century—has been less enthusiastic on the whole. After that first essay in the genre Halévy was never able to rival Meyerbeer's successes. He did garner the admiration of the young Wagner, who reviewed the 1841 premiere of *Le reine de Chypre* as well as providing arrangements of the score for the publisher Schlesinger. In his work, but above all in *La Juive,* Wagner found a "concentrated energy and varied richness of freely developed yet artfully ordered forms," which came close to fulfilling his youthful operatic ideal. Wagner's praise for Halévy (which he never retracted) stands in striking contrast to his vehement rejection of Meyerbeer. Halévy, he felt, was able to achieve imposing theatrical effects and vivid dramatic contrasts without sacrificing an underlying sense of stylistic unity, and to evoke characteristic, exotic, or historical settings without resorting to jarring or trivial details. The musical-dramaturgical influence of the Scribe-Halévy collaboration is clearly detectable in *Rienzi.*

Halévy can be credited, along with Meyerbeer, with the perfection of the influential choral/ensemble movement type that unfolds at great length from a single moment of dramatic revelation or reversal (e.g., *La Juive,* finale to act III). While many other choral movements in his operas merely serve as obligatory elements of stage spectacle, lacking either dramatic or musical conviction, the composer did maintain a talent for more individualized dramatic expression, as in the musical depiction of the dying Lusigan in act V of *La reine de Chypre* or of the mentally afflicted French monarch in *Charles VI.* Halévy was never able to repeat the popular success of *La Juive,* however. *Guido et Ginevra,* which introduced Gilbert Duprez and Julie Dorus-Gras to the Opéra stage in 1836, continued to appear in opera houses through the 1880s. But

the remaining grand operas, though usually well-received at their premieres, received only scattered revivals. If a modern revival of any of these other grand operas seems unlikely, it is to be hoped that the lesser demands and the genuine musical merits of Halévy's better *opéras comiques* may elicit the attention of smaller opera companies in search of worthy new repertoire.

—Thomas S. Grey

HALKA.

Composer: Stanisław Moniuszko.

Librettist: W. Wolski.

First Performance: concert performance, Vilnius, 1 January 1848; revised, 1857; staged performance, Warsaw, 1 January 1858.

Roles: Halka (soprano); Jontek (tenor); Stolnik (bass); Zofia (mezzo-soprano); Janusz (baritone); Dziemba (bass); A bagpiper (baritone); chorus.

Publications

book–

Kaczyński, T. *Dzieje sceniczne "Halka" Stanislawa Moniuszki* [performance history of *Halka*]. Cracow, 1969.

articles–

Bator, Zbigniew. "Halka- o czym to ject?" [dramaturgy of *Halka*]. *Ruch muzyczny* 15, 16 (1983): 3,22.
Nowaczyk, Erwin. "Stanislawa Moniuszki *Halka.*" *Ruch muzyczny* 18/no. 21 (1984): 1,24.

*　　*　　*

Halka exists in two versions, a two-act opera written for Vilnius, and a four-act "Grand Opera" written for the Warsaw performance in 1858. For the later (now standard) version Moniuszko divided each of the original acts into two and made several major additions, including Stolnik's polonaise aria in act I, Halka's opening aria and the duet between Jontek and Janusz in act II, the Highlander Dances in act III and Jontek's aria in act IV. Independent orchestral movements were also added—the concluding mazurka of act I and the preludes to acts II, III and IV.

The curtain rises on a betrothal party in Stolnik's manor house. His daughter Zofia is to marry Janusz, a young nobleman who has seduced and abandoned Halka, a peasant girl from his estate. She arrives at the manor house, unaware of his duplicity. Jontek, a mountaineer from Halka's village, is in love with Halka and tells her of Janusz's treachery, begging her to return to the village. Act III is set in the village, where the people prepare for the forthcoming wedding of their lord of the manor. As the wedding procession arrives (act IV), Halka laments for her child who died of starvation but also declares her unchanging love for Janusz. Finally she resolves to end her life, throwing herself over the precipice before Jontek can stop her. The opera ends as Jontek confronts Janusz with news of the tragedy.

Plots which centered on the relationships between social classes were popular in the early nineteenth century, and *Halka* invites comparison in this respect with works such as Cherubini's *Les deux journées* (1800), Auber's *La Muette di Portici* (1828) and Verdi's *Luisa Miller* (1849). The Auber work, an early example of French "Grand Opera," was well-known to Moniuszko, and its plot is especially close to *Halka*, with the dumb peasant girl Fanella present at her seducer's wedding and committing suicide by leaping into the crater of Vesuvius. The overall construction of *Halka* also owes much to French Grand Opera, specifically in its use of dramatic recitatives and extended scenic tableaux. The whole of act III, for instance, is a (balletic) scenic tableau with no significant dramatic action. Italian opera was also a major influence on *Halka*, notably in the two-part Rossini-like overture and in much of the solo vocal writing. Halka's double-aria in act II, described by Hans von Bulow as "a little masterpiece, full of warmth and tenderness," is characteristic, not least in its use of the Italianate device of embellishing a melody with woodwind figuration. A further influence was Weber, whose *Der Freischütz* greatly impressed Moniuszko. The folk-like choruses in the first and third acts of *Halka* are reminiscent of *Der Freischütz*, and much of the orchestral writing throughout was clearly inspired by Weber's example.

From a European viewpoint it is above all the Polish elements in the opera which give it its distinctive flavor. The rousing choral polonaise which opens the work, immediately recreating the world of the Polish aristocratic manor house, is balanced later in the act by Stolnik's polonaise aria and contrasted with the lively orchestral mazurka with which the act ends. In act II Jontek's tenor aria has a folk-bravura character with krakowiak rhythms, while in act III there is a sequence of Highlander Dances based on the distinctive folk music of the Tatra highlands of southern Poland. Most striking of all is Jontek's lament (*Dumka*) in the final act. The slow mazurka (*kujawiak*) rhythms of this lament are the foundation for some of the most expressive solo vocal writing in the opera.

Despite numerous foreign productions, beginning with a Prague performance in 1868 conducted by Smetana, *Halka* has never succeeded in establishing itself outside Poland. But its popularity there can be compared to that of *The Bartered Bride* in Prague and *Faust* in Paris. Following its initial triumph, *Halka* has been permanently in the repertoire of the Grand Theatre in Warsaw, and it has been produced at least once in every opera house in Poland.

—Jim Samson

HALL, (Sir) Peter (Reginald Frederick).

Director. Born 22 November 1930, in Bury St. Edmunds, England. Married: Leslie Caron (divorced); Jacqueline Taylor (divorced); Maria Ewing (mezzo-soprano); four children. Educated at Perse School and St. Catharine's, Cambridge, M.A., 1964. Director, Oxford Playhouse, 1954-55; director, Arts Theatre, London, 1955-57; founder, International Playwrights' Theatre, 1957; founder and managing director of the Royal Shakespeare Company, 1960-68; Associate Professor of Drama, Warwick University; director of National Theatre, 1973-; artistic director, Glyndebourne, 1984-90. Opera debut, world premiere of Gardner's *The Moon and Sixpence*, Sadler's Wells, 1957; produced world premiere of Tippett's *The Knot Garden*, Covent Garden, 1970; awards: Chevalier de l'ordre des Arts et des Lettres, 1965; Commander of the British Empire (C.B.E.), 1973; Knight of the British Empire, 1977; several honorary doctorates, two Antoinette Perry Awards (*The Homecoming*, 1967; *Amadeus*, 1981), two London Theatre Critic Awards.

Opera Productions (selected)

The Moon and Sixpence, London, Sadler's Wells, 1957.
Moses und Aron, London, Covent Garden, 1965.
Die Zauberflöte, London, Covent Garden, 1966.
Benvenuto Cellini, London, Covent Garden, 1967.
The Knot Garden, London, Covent Garden, 1970.
La Calisto, Glyndebourne, 1970.
Tristan und Isolde, London, Covent Garden, 1971.
Eugene Onegin, London, Covent Garden, 1971.
Il ritorno d'Ulisse in patria, Glyndebourne, 1972.
Don Giovanni, Glyndebourne, 1977.
Così fan tutte, Glyndebourne, 1978.
Fidelio, Glyndebourne, 1979.
Le nozze di Figaro, Glyndebourne, 1981.
A Midsummer Night's Dream, Glyndebourne, 1981.
Macbeth, Glyndebourne, 1982.
Orfeo ed Euridice, Glyndebourne, 1983.
Der Ring des Nibelungen, Bayreuth, 1983.
Albert Herring, Glyndebourne, 1985.
Carmen, Glyndebourne, 1985.
Simon Boccanegra, Glyndebourne, 1986.
La traviata, Glyndebourne, 1987.
Falstaff, Glyndebourne, 1988.
Katya Kabanová, Glyndebourne, 1988.
Salome, London, Covent Garden, 1988.
New Year, Glyndebourne, 1990.

Publications

By HALL: book–

Peter Hall's Diaries: The Story of a Dramatic Battle. London, 1983.

articles–

"Living Figures." *Opera News* 29 (14 November 1964): 6.
with Michael Tippett. "*The Knot Garden*." *About the House* 3/7 (February 1971): 44.
Foreword to Addenbrooke, David, *The Royal Shakespeare Company: The Peter Hall Years.* London, 1974.
"Thoughts on Opera." *Opera* 26/February (1975): 132.
"Peter Hall's Statements Given to the Critics." *Opera* 34/Autumn (1983): 28.

interviews–

"Peter Hall Talks." *About the House* 2/4 (1966): 22.
"Approaching the 'Flute'." *Opera* 17/July (1966): 522.
"Producing a New *Ring;* Sir Peter Hall Talks to Bryan Magee about *The Ring* at Bayreuth This Summer." *Musical Times* 124/February (1983): 86.
Trilling, O. *Opernwelt* 26/8 (1985): 25.

About HALL: books–

Addenbrooke, David. *The Royal Shakespeare Company: The Peter Hall Years.* London, 1974.
Higgins, J. *The Making of an Opera: Don Giovanni at Glyndebourne.* London, 1978.
Fay, S. *The Ring: Anatomy of an Opera.* London, 1984.

Peter Hall's production of *Das Rheingold,* **from** *Der Ring des Nibelungen,* **Bayreuth, 1983**

articles–

"Peter the Second." *Opera* 20/August (1969): 664.

Wocker, K.H. "Neue Konstellationen in London." *Neue Zeitschrift für Musik* 130/October (1969): 447.

Hobson, H. "Bearded Brilliance." *Christian Science Monitor* 62 (29 October 1970): 13.

Sutcliffe, T. "Opera: That Bastard Medium." *Theatre* 72 (1972): 198.

Marx, R. "Can Opera Houses Become Lyric Theatres?" *Music News* 5/4 (1975): 18.

Jacobson, R. "Great Directors: Sir Peter Hall, Practicing Craftsman." *Opera News* 47 (18 December 1982): 10.

Woddis, Carole. "Sir Peter Hall." *Drama* 150/Winter (1983): 9.

Loppert, M. "Travelling from Z to A." *Opera* 35/June (1984): 596; July: 715.

Thorn, F. "Glyndebourne: Die stille Reform eines Festivals." *Bühne* 323/August (1985): 55.

Mann, W. "Verdi, der Shakespeare-Kenner." *Opernwelt* 29/ November (1988): 45.

Levine, R. "Sir Peter Hall's 'How-To' Traviata." *Classical: The Musical Experience* 2/March (1990): 35.

*　　　*　　　*

Producer Sir Peter Hall has had a long and important career in which opera productions have played only a part. Hall's operatic productions have spanned the whole chronology of

opera, from Monteverdi to such twentieth-century composers as Schoenberg and Britten. He first directed opera at Sadler's Wells, a production of Gardner's *The Moon and Sixpence* in 1957. Temporarily turning away from opera to found the Royal Shakespeare Company in 1959, he joined the Royal Opera, Covent Garden, in 1965, where he mounted productions of Schoenberg's *Moses und Aron* (a production remembered for the sensuality of the "Dance around the Golden Calf" sequence), Mozart's *Die Zauberflöte* (1966), Tippett's *The Knot Garden* (1970), Tchaikovsky's *Eugene Onegin* (1971), and Wagner's *Tristan und Isolde* (1971). His productions at Glyndebourne have included Cavalli's *La Calisto,* Monteverdi's *L'incoronazione di Poppea,* Monteverdi's *Il ritorno d'Ulisse in patria* (1972), Mozart's *Così fan tutte* (1978), Beethoven's *Fidelio* (1979), Mozart's *Le nozze di Figaro* (1981, redirected in 1989), Britten's *A Midsummer Night's Dream* (1981), Gluck's *Orfeo ed Euridice* (1983), Mozart's *Don Giovanni* (1983), Britten's *Albert Herring* (1985), Bizet's *Carmen* (1985), Verdi's *Simon Boccanegra* (1986), Verdi's *La traviata* (1987), Verdi's *Falstaff* (1988), and Tippett's *New Year* (1990). He became Glyndebourne's artistic director in 1984, but resigned in 1990 because director Peter Sellars chose, without consulting Hall, to dispense entirely with the dialogue in a production of *Die Zauberflöte.* He has produced Verdi's *Macbeth* and Bizet's *Carmen* at the Metropolitan Opera, as well as Richard Strauss's *Salome,* starring Maria Ewing (at the time Hall's wife), for the Chicago Lyric Opera.

In 1983 Hall's production of Wagner's *Der Ring des Nibelungen* was seen at Bayreuth, the sixth staging of the *Ring* since the reopening of Bayreuth after World War II in 1951. The production was an attempt to create a fairy-tale *Ring* on the assumption that Wagner had fashioned the equivalent of a fairy tale for adults—an adult myth. It represented a return to a romantic, realistic, naturalistic style of staging not seen in any Bayreuth *Ring* since before the war. Hall preferred to de-emphasize the political connotations of the work—the socialist slant popularized by George Bernard Shaw and seen in Patrice Chéreau's staging—and the Freudian elements highlighted by Wieland Wagner in his productions. Hall stressed the inherent naïveté of the story, seeing as the basic element the power of heroic love to redeem those corrupted by power. He attempted to follow Wagner's stage directions as closely as possible, with sets that permitted the transition from the depths of the Rhine and Nibelheim to the gods' mountaintop, and providing believable giants and dragons. Despite Hall's typically well-thought-out approach, the production was not a success, although revivals in subsequent Bayreuth festivals were more successful. Hall found that the task of mounting the entire work—four separate operas—in one summer did not provide him with adequate time to work with all of the singers to the extent he desired, nor did it allow enough opportunity to perfect the workings of the stage machinery. The production was further undermined by the problems inherent in creating a realistic production of an unrealistic work; Hall could not use the vague, abstract images employed by most *Ring* producers to hide the difficulties presented by Wagner's stage directions. Despite the fine efforts by several members of the cast, especially in the area of acting, the critics felt that Hall had not been able to realize his stated aims.

Hall's selection of *Moses und Aron* for his Covent Garden debut had the advantage of being a work without a long tradition and performance history at the house against which his production would be compared. It also had the advantage of being a collaboration with Georg Solti, and he was granted both his choice of designer, John Bury, and his request for seven weeks of rehearsal. Adequate rehearsal time has been one of Hall's consistent demands; when he was being considered by General Administrator David Webster as director of productions at Covent Garden in 1971—where he would have been the first to hold the title since Peter Brook's departure in 1950—he also expressed his view that the company should do more performances of fewer operas, expanding a work's run from six or eight performances to sixteen, with the same cast performing throughout a run. Hall eventually decided not to assume the post, becoming instead the successor to Laurence Olivier as director of London's National Theatre. His decision was based on his feeling that an international opera house, one that depends on revivals for most of its performances, is incompatible with a director who would not want to see his or her productions diluted by different revival directors, casts, and conductors over the seasons.

Hall prefers to work under festival conditions—with casts consistent through the run and with the luxury of restudying and redirecting productions in later seasons. He disapproves of star singers who cannot be available for extensive rehearsals. His goal is seamless opera, where all participants work as a team, and where the director and the conductor have equal authority. The collaboration of the director, the conductor, the singers, and the designer is crucial to the success of the production. He has largely avoided working in international houses, limiting himself to assignments that will allow him to work under controlled conditions.

To Hall, the most important aspect of a director's task is to convey meaning—meaning that comes from an exploration of the score and that leads to the words. He prefers to work back from the music to what the actors should feel in order to communicate the meaning. In Mozart, for example, the orchestration—even more than the text—informs the listener as to what the characters are thinking and doing at any given moment. In early operas, he is concerned with making the works accessible to modern audiences, blending traditional stagings with a modern aesthetic; in contemporary works, he concentrates on character delineation and the clarification of relationships. He believes that singers, who might find it difficult to accomplish complex or strenuous stage business while sustaining a vocal line, often enjoy rising to the challenge and should be encouraged to do so; however, he feels that many directors encourage singers to move too much on stage and that movements should be contained, as demonstrated by such singers as Maria Callas and Janet Baker.

Hall has a preference for opera in the original language, feeling that words that are different from the ones the composer heard misrepresent the nature of the music. He sees opera as a museum art, and feels that we need to perform opera in a way that is as close as possible to the original. He believes that the relatively limited size of the standard operatic repertoire has led directors to mount eccentric stagings that call attention to themselves rather than illuminate the work. Although he feels that operas do not speak for themselves, he does not like to reinterpret works, to impose his own interpretation on them. He begins with the composer's stage directions as a clue to the composer's aspirations, even where, as frequently in Wagner, the directions are virtually impossible to follow exactly. His method usually involves learning the work beforehand but not planning the direction until the actors are present. He wants the singers to do what they feel is appropriate, and then he will respond to it, changing the direction as necessary to find out what works. His aim is to make the action seem natural and inevitable.

—Michael Sims

HAMLET.

Composer: Ambroise Thomas.

Librettists: J. Barbier and M. Carré (after Shakespeare).

First Performance: Paris, Opéra, 9 March 1868.

Roles: Hamlet (baritone); Claudius (bass); Ophelia (soprano); Gertrude (mezzo-soprano); Laertes (tenor); Horatio (bass); Polonius (bass); Marcellus (tenor); Ghost (bass); Two Gravediggers (baritone, tenor); Players in the Pantomime: King, Queen, Villain; chorus (SSTTBB).

Publications

article–

Porter, Andrew. "Translating Shakespeare Operas: Thomas's *Hamlet.*" *Opera* July (1980).

*   *   *

Premiering at the Paris Opéra shortly after his highly successful *Mignon,* Ambroise Thomas's *Hamlet* consolidated its composer's stature in French music and propelled him into the Directorship of the Conservatoire when the position became vacant several years later.

Shakespeare's play had been set as an opera by at least nine composers before Thomas, and was to receive another five attempts afterwards. None has approached Thomas's in initial popularity (no doubt prompted by a nationalist French desire to compete operatically with Wagner and especially Verdi) or in longevity. Despite some major flaws (especially the ending), inventions, omissions, and differences, Thomas's *Hamlet* resembles Shakespeare's more often than not, and maintains a remarkable measure of the original's introspection and intensity.

In the first scene of the opera's act I, Claudius's and Gertrude's nuptials are celebrated at the Danish court. Hamlet expresses displeasure at his mother's hasty remarriage, and then pledges his love to Ophelia. Her brother Laertes announces his departure on a diplomatic mission, after which Marcellus and Horatio report to Hamlet their sighting of his father's ghost. The second scene takes place on the palace esplanade, where Hamlet encounters the ghost. During this interview the ghost demands that Hamlet avenge his death, but take pity upon Gertrude.

The first scene of act II is set in the palace gardens, where Ophelia is musing over Hamlet's inattention and seeming hostility. Gertrude attempts to console her, and agrees, along with Claudius, to Hamlet's suggestion that a troupe of actors perform at the palace. Hamlet meets with the players, and instructs them to present "The Murder of Gonzago" that evening. Scene two is the performance, in the course of which Claudius explodes in anger and stalks from the hall. Hamlet feigns insanity and accuses Claudius before the assembled court.

In act III, Hamlet is discovered alone in his mother's bedchamber (where he sings the "To be or not to be" aria). He forgoes an opportunity to strike Claudius, but overhears him with Polonius, Ophelia's father, implicating himself in the murder of the former king. Hamlet confronts and threatens Gertrude, during which the ghost reappears and reminds him to spare his mother. Since the ghost is visible only to Hamlet, Gertrude is convinced of her son's madness.

Act IV begins with an extended ballet. Set before a lake, the dance celebrates the "festival of spring." At its conclusion, Ophelia wanders in for her well-known mad scene. After recalling Hamlet's broken promises of love, the deranged heroine drowns herself in the lake.

The final act takes place in a cemetery, where two gravediggers are preparing a tomb. Hamlet meets Laertes, who holds the hero responsible for his sister's suicide. As the two men cross swords, their duel is interrupted by an approaching cortège, and Hamlet first learns of Ophelia's death. Hamlet tries to stab himself, and the ghost appears again, this time visible to all. Finally Hamlet hesitates no longer, kills Claudius, and orders Gertrude to a nunnery. Hamlet is proclaimed the new king.

In addition to Ophelia's famous mad scene from act IV, several other musical items deserve mention. The love-duet between Hamlet and Ophelia in act I, "Doute de la lumière," must rank among the finest examples of the genre. As a substitute for Hamlet's "instructions to the players" found in the original, the opera presents Hamlet's drinking song "Ô vin, dissipe la tristesse." And Thomas sets Hamlet's monologue ("Être ou ne pas être") with surprising effectiveness and sensitivity. Touches of innovative orchestration are evident throughout the opera, including the use of both alto and

baritone saxophones, and the bass saxhorn to emphasize the darker tone colors.

Although *Hamlet* is sometimes performed with an ending that approximates Shakespeare's, Thomas's original conclusion is very much in keeping with the relatively non-violent conventions of early French opéra-lyrique. Given the abundant strengths of the score and a generally valid libretto by Carré and Barbier, it is regrettable that the "happy ending" has so compromised the work's reputation.

—Morton Achter

HAMMOND, Joan.

Soprano. Born 24 May 1912, in Christchurch, New Zealand. Studied at the Sydney Conservatory; debut in Sydney, 1929; studied in London with Dino Borgioli; also studied in Vienna; London debut, 1938; member of the Carl Rosa Opera Company, 1942-45; Covent Garden debut, 1948; also sang with Sadler's Wells Opera; appeared with the New York City Center Opera, 1949.

Publications

By HAMMOND: books–

A Voice, a Life [with discography]. London, 1970.

About HAMMOND: articles–

Celletti, R. and C. Williams. "Hammond, Joan." In *Le grandi voci,* Rome, 1964.

*   *   *

Although the first opera performance by local artists took place early in the 19th century, Australasia mostly knew opera only from visiting companies until after the Second World War. However, Australia produced a number of successful soprano singers such as Nellie Melba and Joan Sutherland; Hammond's most famous operatic compatriot from New Zealand was Frances Alda. Hammond began her studies in Sydney and made her debut there in small roles when she was still under twenty, unwisely young by today's standards. She then went on to seek consolidation and further development of her vocal and interpretative skills in Vienna and London, and began her international career when she sang with the Vienna Staatsoper in 1938.

From this time onwards, her vocal personality was fairly well defined: it was above all warm and vibrant, and her physical presence on stage was equally attractive. Her four seasons in wartime Britain with the Carl Rosa Company reflected not only their popular choice of Italian and French opera but also her style, and she could always win an audience's sympathy as Gounod's Marguerite in *Faust,* as Puccini's doomed heroines Cio-Cio-San, Mimì and Tosca (in *Madama Butterfly, La Bohème* and *Tosca*), or as the equally ill-fated courtesan Violetta in Verdi's *La traviata.* Even these roles made varied demands on her ability as a singing actress: to take only one example, the innocent, too-trusting Butterfly is very different from the sophisticated though vulnerable Tosca. Hammond was never a great actress, nor did she have the physical magnetism of a Maria Callas, but as she gained stage experience she became equal to still other kinds of roles. One such was Beethoven's Leonore in *Fidelio,* where she was required to disguise herself as a young man. Similarly, she could be at least reasonably convincing in the title role of Verdi's *Aïda* and as Desdemona in his highly dramatic *Otello,* as Tchaikovsky's youthful Tatyana in *Eugene Onegin* and as Purcell's Queen Dido in *Dido and Aeneas.* This last came late in her career, when she also finally brought herself to play the Princess Turandot in Puccini's opera of that name, a character at first intolerably cold and cruel who only melts with love at the end of the last act.

Joan Hammond's voice had considerable power, but it was not of a Wagnerian kind, and she sang hardly any German opera, although in Australia towards the end of her career (1960), she did play the lead in Richard Strauss's *Salome*—which must in any case have been something of a miscasting since Salome is supposed to be sixteen and the singer was approaching fifty. She was always too mature-sounding for some Mozart roles such as those of Susanna or Cherubino in *Le nozze di Figaro,* but although she might have played the Countess in the same opera, Mozart was another area of the repertory which she hardly touched. Still, she and her public doubtless knew where her strengths lay, and her record of "O, my beloved father" from Puccini's *Gianni Schicchi* had sold over a million copies by 1969 and seems to sum up her warm, expansive style. It did much, too, to open up today's popular interest in opera which makes best-selling international stars of singers such as Luciano Pavarotti and Placido Domingo.

—Christopher Headington

HANDEL, George Frideric [born Georg Friederich Händel].

Composer. Born 23 February 1685, in Halle. Died 14 April 1759, in London. Studied harpsichord, organ and composition with Wilhelm Zachau, organist of the Liebfrauenkirche in Halle; entered the University of Halle, 1702; in Hamburg, 1703, where he was hired as a violinist by Reinhard Keiser for the Hamburg Opera orchestra; met Mattheson in Hamburg; first opera *Almira,* produced at the Hamburg Opera, 1705; traveled to Italy, where he lived and worked in Florence, Rome (under the patronage of the Marquis Francesco Ruspoli), Naples, and Venice; first Italian opera *Rodrigo,* 1709; succeeded Agostino Steffani as Kapellmeister to the Elector of Hannover, 1710; visited England, and produced his opera *Rinaldo* at the Queen's Theatre in the Haymarket, London, 1711; began permanent residence in England, 1714; composer in residence to the Duke of Chandos, 1717-19; composer and master of the orchestra for the Royal Academy of Music, an Italian opera company established in London at the King's Theatre in the Haymarket, 1719-28; became a naturalized British subject, 1727; second Royal Academy, 1728-1733; honorary doctorate, Oxford University, 1733; Handel continued to compose Italian operas in London until 1741; oratorios *Deborah* and *Athalia,* 1733; ode *Alexander's Feast,* 1736; Handel increasingly composed oratorios from 1737-1752. Handel's circle included the poets and writers Rolli, Haym, Gay, Pope, Jennings, and the composers Mattheson, Telemann, G. Bononcini, Ariosti, and the Scarlattis.

Operas

Editions:

G.F. Händels Werke: Ausgabe der Deutschen Händelgesellschaft. Edited by Friedrich W. Chrysander. Leipzig and Bergedorf bei Hamburg, 1858-94, 1902; reprint 1965.
Hallische Händel-Ausgabe im Auftrage der Georg Friedrich Händel-Gesellschaft. Edited by M. Schneider, R. Steiglich et al. Kassel, 1955-.

Der in Krohnen erlangte Glücks-Wechsel oder Almira, Königin von Castilien [Almira], F.C. Feustking (after G. Pancieri), Hamburg, Theater am Gänsemarkt, 8 January 1705.
Die durch Blut und Mord erlangte Liebe [Nero], F.C. Feustking, Hamburg, Theater am Gänsemarkt, 25 February 1705.
Vincer se stesso è la maggior vittoria [Rodrigo], after F. Silvani, *Il duello d'Amore e di Vendetta,* Florence, Cocomero, November c. 1707.
Der beglückte Florindo; Die verwandelte Daphne, H. Hinsch, Hamburg, Theater am Gänsemarkt, January 1708.
Agrippina, V. Grimani, Venice, San Giovanni Grisostomo, c. January 1709.
Rinaldo, Giacomo Rossi (after a scenario by A. Hill based on Tasso, *La Gerusalemme liberata*), London, Queen's Theatre in the Haymarket, 24 February 1711; revised 1717, 1731.
Il pastor fido, Giacomo Rossi (after B. Guarini), London, Queen's Theatre in the Haymarket, 22 November 1712; revised 18 May 1734, 9 November 1734.
Teseo, Nicola F. Haym (after P. Quinault, *Thésée*), London, Queen's Theatre in the Haymarket, 10 January 1713.
Silla, Giacomo Rossi, London, Burlington House?, 2 June 1713.
Amadigi di Gaula, Nicola F. Haym (after A.H. de la Motte, *Amadis de Grèce*), London, King's Theatre in the Haymarket, 25 May 1715; revised 16 February 1716, 16 February 1717.
Radamisto, Nicola F. Haym (after D. Lalli, *L'amor tirannico, o Zenobia,* Florence, 1712), London, King's Theatre in the Haymarket, 27 April 1720; revised 28 December 1720, January-February 1728.
Muzio Scevola (with F. Amadei and G. Bononcini), Paolo A. Rolli (after S. Stampiglia, Venice, 1710), London, King's Theatre in the Haymarket, 15 April 1721; revised 7 November 1722.
Floridante, Paolo A. Rolli (after Silvani, *La costanza in trionfo,* Livorno, 1706), London, King's Theatre in the Haymarket, 9 December 1721; revised 4 December 1722, 29 April 1727.
Ottone, Rè di Germania, Nicola F. Haym (after S.B. Pallavicino, *Teofane*), London, King's Theatre in the Haymarket, 12 January 1723; revised 8 February 1726, 13 November 1733.
Flavio, Rè di Longobardi, Nicola F. Haym (after M. Noris, *Flavio Cuniberto,* Rome, 1696), London, King's Theatre in the Haymarket, 14 May 1723; revised 18 April 1732.
Giulio Cesare in Egitto, Nicola F. Haym (after G.F. Bussani), London, King's Theatre in the Haymarket, 20 February 1724; revised 2 January 1725, 17 January 1730.
Tamerlano, Nicola F. Haym (after A. Piovene, *Il Bajazet,* 1710, and as revised for 1719, based on J. Pradon, *Tamerlan, ou La mort de Bajazet*), London, King's Theatre in

George Frideric Handel, portrait attributed to Balthasar Denner, c. 1730

the Haymarket, 31 October 1724; revised 13 November 1731.

Rodelinda, Regina de' Longobardi, Nicola F. Haym (after A. Salvi, based on P. Corneille, *Pertharite*), London, King's Theatre in the Haymarket, 13 February 1725; revised 18 December 1725, 4 May 1731.

Scipione, Paolo A. Rolli (after A. Salvi), London, King's Theatre in the Haymarket, 12 March 1726; revised 3 November 1730.

Alessandro, Paolo A. Rolli (after O. Mauro, *La superbia d' Alessandro*), London, King's Theatre in the Haymarket, 5 May 1726; 25 November 1732; as *Rossane,* 1743, 1744, 1748.

Admeto, Rè di Tessaglia (after O. Mauro, *L'Antigona delusa da Alceste,* based on A. Aureli), London, King's Theatre in the Haymarket, 31 January 1727; revised 25 May 1728, 7 December 1731.

Riccardo Primo, Rè d' Inghilterra, Paolo A. Rolli (after F. Briani, *Isacio tiranno*), London, King's Theatre in the Haymarket, 11 November 1727.

Genserico [unfinished; music used in *Siroe* and *Tolomeo*].

Siroe, Rè di Persia, Nicola F. Haym (after Metastasio, Naples, 1727), London, King's Theatre in the Haymarket, 17 February 1728.

Tolomeo, Rè di Egitto, Nicola F. Haym (after C.S. Capece, *Tolomeo et Alessandro*), London, King's Theatre in the Haymarket, 30 April 1728; revised 19 May 1730, 2 January 1733.

Lotario, after A. Salvi, *Adelaide* (Venice, 1729), London, King's Theatre in the Haymarket, 2 December, 1729.

Partenope, after S. Stampiglia (Venice, 1707), London, King's Theatre in the Haymarket, 24 February 1730; revised 12 December 1730, Covent Garden, 29 January 1737.

Poro, Rè dell' Indie, after Metastasio, *Alessandro nell' Indie,* London, King's Theatre in the Haymarket, 2 February 1731; revised 23 November 1731, 8 December 1736.

Tito, after Racine, *Bérénice* [unfinished; some music used in *Ezio*].

Ezio, after Metastasio, London, King's Theatre in the Haymarket, 15 January 1732.

Sosarme, Rè di Media, after A. Salvi, *Dionisio, Rè di Portogallo,* London, King's Theatre in the Haymarket, 15 February 1732; revised 27 April 1734.

Orlando, after C.S. Capece (based on Ariosto, *Orlando furioso*), London, King's Theatre in the Haymarket, 27 January 1733.

Arianna in Creta, after P. Pariati, *Arianna e Teseo* (Naples, 1721; Rome, 1729), London, King's Theatre in the Haymarket, 26 January 1734; revised, Covent Garden, 27 November 1734.

Oreste (pasticcio), after G. Barlocci, London, Covent Garden, 18 December 1734.

Ariodante, after A. Salvi, *Ginevra, Principessa di Scozia* (based on Ariosto, *Orlando furioso*), London, Covent Garden, 8 January 1735; revised 5 May 1736.

Alcina, after *L'isola di Alcina* (1728, based on Ariosto, *Orlando furioso*), London, Covent Garden, 16 April 1735; revised 6 November 1736.

Atalanta, after B. Valeriano, *La caccia in Etolia,* London, Covent Garden, 12 May 1736.

Arminio, after A. Salvi, London, Covent Garden, 12 January 1737.

Giustino, after Pariati (Rome, 1724; based on N. Beregan), London, Covent Garden, 16 February 1737.

Berenice, after A. Salvi, London, Covent Garden, 18 May 1737.

Faramondo, after Zeno (Rome, 1720), London, King's Theatre in the Haymarket, 3 January 1738.

Alessandro Severo (pasticcio), after Zeno (Milan, 1723), London, King's Theatre in the Haymarket, 25 February 1738.

Serse, after S. Stampiglia (Rome, 1694; based on N. Minato), London, King's Theatre in the Haymarket, 15 April 1738.

Imeneo, after S. Stampiglia, London, Lincoln's Inn Fields, 22 November 1740; revised for concert performance, Dublin, New Music Hall, 24 March 1742.

Deidamia, Paolo A. Rolli, London, Lincoln's Inn Fields, 10 January 1741.

Other works: cantatas, oratorios, odes, anthems, songs, concertos, sonatas, keyboard works, music for musical clock.

Publications/Writings

By HANDEL: books–

Müller, E.H., ed. *The Letters and Writings of George Frideric Handel.* London, 1935.

About HANDEL: books–

Mainwaring, John. *Memoirs of the Life of the Late George Frederic Handel.* London, 1760; reprint 1964, 1967.

Winterfeld, C. von. *"Alceste" von Lully, Händel und Gluck.* Berlin, 1851.

Schoelcher, Victor. *The Life of Handel.* London, 1857; reprint 1979.

Chrysander, Friedrich W. *G.F. Händel.* Leipzig, 1858-66; 1967.

Delany, Mary. *Autobiography and Correspondence of Mary Granville, Mrs. Delany.* London, 1861-62.

Leichentritt, Hugo. *Händel.* Stuttgart, 1924.

Eisenschmidt, Joachim. *Die szenische Darstellung der Opern Händels auf der Londoner Bühne seiner Zeit.* Wolfenbüttel, 1940-41.

Wolff, H.C. *"Agrippina": eine italienische Jugendoper Händels.* Wolfenbüttel, 1943.

Mueller von Asow, H. and E.H. *Georg Friedrich Händel: Briefe und Schriften.* Lindau, 1949.

Brockpähler, R. *Handbuch zur Geschichte der Barockoper in Deutschland.* Emsdetten, 1954.

Deutsch, Otto Erich. *Handel: a Documentary Biography.* London, 1955; New York, 1974.

Wolff, H.C. *Die Händel-Oper auf der modernen Bühne.* Leipzig, 1957.

Sasse, Konrad. *Händel Bibliographie.* Leipzig, 1963; supplement, 1967.

Lang, Paul Henry. *Handel.* New York, 1966.

King, Alex Hyatt. *Handel and his Autographs.* London, 1967.

Dean, Winton. *Handel and the Opera Seria.* Berkeley and Los Angeles, 1969.

Strohm, Reinhard. *Die italienischen Oper im 18. Jahrhundert.* Wilhelmshaven, 1979.

Harris, Ellen T. *Handel and the Pastoral Tradition.* London and New York, 1980.

Kubik, Reinhold. *Händels "Rinaldo". Geschichte—Werk—Wirkung.* Neuhausen, 1981.

Dean, Winton and Anthony Hicks. *The New Grove Handel.* London and New York, 1983.

Editionsleitung der Hallischen Händel-Ausgabe, ed. *Händel-Handbuch IV: Dokumente zu Leben und Schaffen.* Kassel, 1985.

Hogwood, Christopher. *Handel.* London, 1984; New York, 1985.

Bimberg, Guido. *Dramaturgie der Händel-Opern.* Halle, 1985.

Strohm, Reinhard. *Essays on Handel and Italian opera.* Cambridge, 1985.

Dean, Winton, and John Merrill Knapp. *Handel's Operas: 1704-1726.* Oxford, 1987.

Hill, Cecil. *Handel's 'Imeneo': a Pre-Edition Study.* Armidale, New South Wales, Australia, 1987.

Sadie, Stanley, and Anthony Hicks, eds. *Handel Tercentenary Collection.* Ann Arbor and London, 1987.

Parker-Hale, Mary Ann. *G.F. Handel: a Guide to Research.* New York, 1988.

Gibson, Elizabeth. *The Royal Academy of Music (1719-1728): the Institution and its Directors.* New York, 1989.

Harris, Ellen T. *The Librettos of Handel's Operas.* 13 vols. New York, 1989.

articles–

Ellinger, G. "Händels *Admet* und seine Quelle." *Vierteljahrsschrift für Musikwissenschaft* 1 (1885): 201.

Streatfield, R.A. "Handel, Rolli, and Italian Opera in London in the Eighteenth Century." *Musical Quarterly* 3 (1917): 428.

Spitz, Charlotte. "Die Oper *Ottone* von Händel und *Teofane* von Lotti: ein Stilvergleich." in *Festschrift zum 50. Geburtstag Adolf Sandberger,* 265. Munich, 1918.

Coopersmith, J.M. "A List of Portraits, Sculptures, etc. of Georg Friedrich Handel." *Music and Letters* 12 (1932): 156.

Dent, Edward J. "Handel on the Stage." *Music and Letters* 16 (1935): 174.

Schulze, W. *Die Quellen der Hamburger Oper (1678-1738).* Hamburg, 1938.

Dahnk-Baroffio, E. "Nicola Hayms Anteil an Händels Rodelinde-Libretto." *Die Musikforschung* 7 (1954): 295.

Knapp, J. Merrill. "Handel, the Royal Academy of Music, and its First Opera Season in London." *Musical Quarterly* 45 (1959): 145.

Serauky, W. "Handel und die Oper seiner Zeit." *Händel-Honor* 5 (1959): 27.

Dahnk-Baroffio, E. "Zur Stoffgeschichte des *Ariodante.*" *Händel-Jahrbuch* 6 (1960): 151.

Finscher, L. "Händels 'Alceste'." *Göttinger Händel-Tage* (1960): 10.

Flesch, S. "Händels 'Orlando'." In *Festschrift der Händel–Festspiele,* 42. Halle, 1961.

Powers, Harold, S. "*Il Serse* trasformato." *Musical Quarterly* 47 (1961): 481; 48 (1962): 73.

Trowell, B. "Handel as a Man of the Theatre." *Proceedings of the Royal Musical Association* 88 (1961-62): 17.

Dean, Winton. "Handel's *Giulio Cesare.*" *Musical Times* 104 (1963): 402.

Kimbell, D.R.B. "The Libretto of Handel's *Teseo.*" *Music and Letters* 44 (1963): 371.

Dean, Winton. "Handel's *Riccardo primo.*" *Musical Times* 105 (1964): 498.

Siegmund-Schultze, W. "Händels 'Muzio Scevola'." In *Festschrift der Händelfestspiele,* 27. Halle, 1965.

Dahnk-Baroffio, E. "Zum Textbuch von Händels *Flavio.*" In *Festschrift der Händel-Festspiele,* 37. Göttingen, 1967.

Dean, Winton. "Handel's *Scipione.*" *Musical Times* 108 (1967): 902.

Knapp, J. Merrill. "Händels Oper Flavio." In *Festschrift der Händel-Festspiele,* 25. Göttingen, 1967.

Dean, Winton. "Handel's *Amadigi.*" *Musical Times* 109 (1968): 324.

Kimbell, David R.B. "The 'Amadis' Operas of Destouches and Handel." *Music and Letters* 49 (1968): 329.

Knapp, J. Merrill. "Handel's *Giulio Cesare in Egitto.*" In *Studies in Music History: Essays for Oliver Strunk,* edited by Harold S. Powers, 389. Princeton, 1968.

Celletti, Rodolfo. "Il virtuosismo vocale nel melodramma di Haendel." *Rivista italiana di musicologica* 4 (1969): 77.

Dean, Winton. "A Handel Tragicomedy" [*Flavio*]. *Musical Times* 110 (1969): 819.

Knapp, J. Merrill. "The Libretto of Handel's 'Silla'." *Music and Letters* 1 (1969): 68.

Dahnk-Baroffio, E. "Händels 'Riccardo primo' in Deutschland," In *50 Jahre Göttinger Händel-Festspiele,* edited by W. Meyerhoff, 150. Kassel, 1970.

Dean, Winton. "Handel's Wedding Opera" [*Atalanta*]. *Musical Times* 111 (1970): 705.

——. "Vocal Embellishment in a Handel Aria." In *Studies in Eighteenth-Century Music: a Tribute to Karl Geiringer,* 151. New York and London, 1970.

Gerlach, R. and E. Dahnk-Baroffio. "Über Georg Friedrich Händels Oper *Riccardo I.*" In *Festschrift der Händel-Festspiele,* 75. Göttingen, 1970.

Knapp, J. Merrill. "Handel's *Tamerlano:* the Creation of an Opera." *Musical Quarterly* 56 (1970): 405.

Knapp, J. Merrill and E. Dahnk-Baroffio. "Titus l'Empereur." In *Festschrift der Händel-Festspiele,* 27. Göttingen, 1970.

Smith, William C. "The 1754 Revival of Handel's *Admeto.*" *Music and Letters* April (1970).

Dean, Winton, "Handel's *Ottone.*" *Musical Times* 112 (1971): 955.

Knapp, J. Merrill. "The Autograph Manuscripts of Handel's 'Ottone'." In *Festschrift Jens Peter Larsen,* 167. Copenhagen, 1972.

Chisholm, Duncan. "The English Origins of Handel's *Il pastor fido.*" *Musical Times* 115 (1974).

Dean, Winton. "A French Traveller's View of Handel's Operas." *Music and Letters* 55 (1974): 172.

Knapp, J. Merrill. "The Autograph of Handel's *Riccardo primo.*" In *Studies in Renaissance and Baroque Music in Honor of Arthur Mendel,* 331. Kassel and Hackensack, New Jersey, 1974.

Baselt, Bernd. "Zum Parodieverfahren in Händels frühen Opern." *Händel-Jahrbuch* 21 (1975): 19.

Dean, Winton. "Handel's *Sosarme,* a Puzzle Opera," In *Essays on Opera and English Music in Honour of Sir Jack Westrup,* 115. Oxford, 1975.

——. "Twenty Years of Handel Opera." *Opera* 26 (1975): 924.

——. "The Performance of Recitative in Late Baroque Opera." *Music and Letters* 58 (1977): 389.

Lindgren, Lowell. "Parisian Patronage of Performers from the Royal Academy of Music (1719-1728)." *Music and Letters* 58 (1977): 4.

Knapp, J. Merrill. "Handel's First Italian Opera: 'Vincer se stesso è la maggior vittoria' or 'Rodrigo'." *Music and Letters* 62 (1981): 12.

Baselt, Bernd, "Zur Gestaltung des Alceste-Stoffes in Händels Oper *Admeto.*" In *Thematik und Ideenwelt der Antike bei Georg Friedrich Händel,* edited by Walther Siegmund-Schultze, 74. Halle, 1982.

Bimberg, Guido. "Notate zu einer Dramaturgie der Händel-Opern." *Händel-Jahrbuch* 28 (1982): 35.

Jorgens, Elise B. "*Orlando* metamorphosed: Handel's Operas after Ariosto." *Parnassus* 10/no. 2 (1982): 45.

Cummings, Graham. "Reminiscence and Recall in Three Early Settings of Metastasio's *Alessandro nell' Indie*"

[*Poro*]. *Proceedings of the Royal Musical Association* 109 (1982-83): 80.

Baselt, Bernd. "Wiederentdeckung von Fragmenten aus Händels verschollenen Hamburger Opern." *Händel-Jahrbuch* 29 (1983): 7.

Dean, Winton. "The Recovery of Handel's Opera." In *Music in Eighteenth-Century England: Essays in Memory of Charles Cudworth,* edited by Christopher Hogwood and Richard Luckett, 103. Cambridge, 1983.

Solomon, John. "Polyphemus's Whistle in Handel's *Acis and Galatea.*" *Music and Letters* (1983).

Wolff, H.C. "Eine englische Händel-Parodie: *The dragon of Wantley,* 1737." *Händel-Jahrbuch* 29 (1983): 43.

Baselt, Bernd. "Vorbemerkung zum Libretto von Händels verschollener Oper *Der beglückte Florindo.*" *Händel-Jahrbuch* 30 (1984): 21 [includes facsimile of original libretto].

Avant-scène opéra February (1985) [*Rinaldo* issue].

Monson, Craig. "*Giulio Cesare in Egitto:* from Sartorio (1677) to Handel (1724)." *Music and Letters* fall (1985).

Rossi, Nick, "Handel's *Muzio Scevola.*" *Opera Quarterly* fall (1985).

Edlemann, Bernd. "Die zweite Fassung von Händels Oper 'Radamisto' (HWV 12b)." *Göttinger Händel-Beiträge* 2 (1986): 99.

Milhous, Judith, and Robert D. Hume. "A Prompt Copy of Handel's *Radamisto.*" *Musical Times* June (1986).

Avant-scène opéra April (1987) [*Giulio Cesare* issue].

Fenton, Robin F.C. "Almira (Hamburg, 1705): the Birth of G.F. Handel's Genius for Characterization." *Händel-Jahrbuch* 33 (1987): 109.

Lindgren, Lowell. "The Staging of Handel's Operas in London." In *Handel Tercentenary Collection,* edited by Stanley Sadie and Anthony Hicks. Ann Arbor and London, 1987.

Price, Curtis. "English Traditions in Handel's *Rinaldo.*" In *Handel Tercentenary Collection,* edited by Stanley Sadie and Anthony Hicks. Ann Arbor and London, 1987.

Roberts, John H. "Handel and Charles Jennens's Italian Opera Manuscripts." In *Music and Theatre: Essays in Honour of Winton Dean,* edited by Nigel Fortune, 159. Cambridge, 1987.

―――. "Handel and Vinci's 'Didone Abbandonata': Revisions and Borrowings." *Music and Letters* 68 (1987): 141.

Siegmund-Schultze, Walther. " 'Deidamis' und 'Zauberflöte'." *Händel-Jahrbuch* 33 (1987): 73.

Trowell, Brian. "Acis, Galatea, and Polyphemus: a 'Serenata a tre voci'?" In *Music and Theatre: Essays in Honour of Winton Dean.* Cambridge, 1987.

Baselt, Bernd. "Libretto (mit deutscher Übersetzung) des Händelschen Pasticcio 'Oreste' (mit Einleitung)." *Händel-Jahrbuch* 34 (1988): 7.

Hill, John Walter. "Handel's Retexting as a Test of his Conception of Connections between Music, Text, and Drama." *Göttinger Händel-Beiträge* 3 (1989): 284.

Händel-Jahrbuch 36 (1990) [many articles on Handel, Keiser, and the Hamburg opera].

unpublished―

Kimbell, David R.B. "A Critical Study of Handel's Early Operas." Ph.D. dissertation, Oxford University, 1968.

LaRue, C. Steven. "The Composer's Choice: Aspects of Compositional Context and Creative Process in Selected Operas from Handel's Royal Academy Period." Ph.D. dissertation, University of Chicago, 1990.

* * *

Perhaps best known today for his English oratorios (especially *Messiah*) and orchestral music (such as *Water Music*), George Frideric Handel was primarily a man of the theater. Between 1705 and 1741, Handel composed and, with the exception of three, produced forty-two operas. He also produced eleven *pasticcio* operas (in effect, "casserole" operas created by arranging old music): three using his own music and eight using the music of contemporary composers. Furthermore, Handel's twenty-four oratorios are surely dramatic works, even if they are not theatrical. As opposed to the operas, many contain elaborate choruses, having contemplative or reflective, rather than dramatic, functions. However, Handel regularly continued to write stage directions in his dramatic oratorio manuscripts, and certainly his secular oratorios, *Semele* (1744) and *Hercules* (1745), as well as the apocryphal *Susanna* (1749), were seen as directly competitive with contemporary opera.

Whereas Handel's oratorio texts were frequently newly written for the composer in close collaboration with his librettist (such as *Judas Maccabaeus* and *Jephtha* by Thomas Morell), Handel's operas are mostly adaptations of older librettos. The adaptors of his opera texts are not always known, but two of his collaborators stand out, Nicola Haym and Paolo Rolli. Rolli's work illustrates a greater poetic artistry, but Haym, although a rougher poet, forged dramatic scenes that awakened Handel's creative powers. Many of Handel's greatest operas had librettos adapted by Haym, including *Radamisto* (1720), *Ottone* (1723), *Giulio Cesare* (1724), *Tamerlano* (1724), and *Rodelinda* (1725).

It is not known what role Handel played in the choice and adaptation of his opera librettos, although what evidence exists suggests that the composer was intimately involved at every stage. First, there is testimony from Handel's oratorio librettists. Second, many of the operas whose librettos were adapted for him are among those Handel had earlier heard performed. For example, *Radamisto, Tamerlano, Sosarme* (1732), *Ariodante* (1735), and *Berenice* (1737) are based on operas the composer probably heard in Florence between 1706 and 1709. *Ottone* is adapted from an opera Handel certainly heard in Dresden in 1719, *Partenope* (1730) from an opera the composer most likely heard in Venice in 1708, and *Lotario* (1729) from an opera Handel had heard in Venice in 1729.

Handel's librettos are typified by the style of construction and composition known as *opera seria* ("serious opera"). In content, these librettos are distinguished by a lack of comic characters and by a high moral tone illustrating characters coming to grips with their own inadequacies, balancing their positions, responsibilities, and duties against their illegitimate (frequently sexual, but sometimes war-like) desires, and, in the case of Handel's librettos especially, acting within the bonds of familial (parental, fraternal, or marital) devotion. In structure, they illustrate a rigid design in which individual scenes generally begin with recitative (typified by blank, or unrhymed, verse of varying lengths) and conclude with a solo aria (in rhymed verse with regular, and generally shorter, line lengths). Individual scenes were defined at their ends by the exit of the character who had sung the aria; frequently, scene beginnings were marked by the entrance of a new character. Within a single scenic backdrop, a number of these scenes would be grouped together by a linked chain of entrances and exits, referred to as the *liaison de scènes* ("tying together of scenes"), so that the stage was never bare of actors except at the change of backdrop.

Musically, these structures elicited a similar rigidity. The recitative text was generally set in *recitativo semplice* ("simple recitative"), with the singers performing (reciting) in a musically heightened speech style, supported only by punctuating chords played by harpsichord and cello. The arias were in *da capo* ("from-the-beginning") form, in which two distinct sections of music were followed by a repeat of the first with elaborate ornamentation added. Ensembles and choruses were very rare. In Handel's operas, this structure became a strong framework of expectation against which the slightest changes had extraordinary dramatic effect.

Handel's operatic career falls into discrete periods defined both by geography and venue and by the structure and content of the librettos. The pre-London operas, composed between 1704 and 1709 for performance in Hamburg, Florence, and Venice, all display a somewhat antiquated style. Both *Almira* (1705), Handel's only surviving opera from Germany, and *Agrippina* (1709), Handel's only opera for Venice, contain comic servant characters, a throwback to the seventeenth century tradition. Furthermore, the surviving librettos from Germany all indicate a dependence on pageantry and ballet that derives from the French tradition. Handel's early English operas (1711-1715), on the other hand, display a style that combines the Italian operatic tradition with the English tradition of dramatic opera, in which there was a heavy reliance on the supernatural and extravagent scenery. *Rinaldo* (1711), *Silla* (1713), and *Teseo* (1713) all include flying dragons and furies; *Rinaldo, Teseo,* and *Amadigi* (1715) all have important roles for sorceresses.

With the opening of the Royal Academy of Music in 1720, Handel can be said to have achieved his mature style. Although this Academy failed financially in 1728, Handel quickly regrouped his forces and reopened the so-called second Academy in the 1729-1730 season. Handel's three operas based on earlier librettos by Pietro Metastasio all derive from late in the first Academy period or early in the second Academy period: *Siroe* (1728), *Poro* (1731), and *Ezio* (1732), but all the operas from this period, especially from *Radamisto* (1720) to *Ezio* reflect the growing trend toward reform style. Arias generally occur at the ends of scenes, after which the singer exits, a structure that is known as the "exit convention," and arias are longer, so that these operas contain approximately thirty or fewer arias, or only about half the number in *Almira*. With the exception of the first Academy's *Admeto* (1727), in which act II opens with Ercole (Hercules) rescuing Alceste from Hell, they lack magical, mythological, and legendary elements, and, at least partially due to that, there are no spectacular stage effects. The librettos are historical and political, and they tend to emphasize parental, sibling, and marital relationships. Mutual concern and respect between parents and children, for example, are especially important to *Radamisto, Giulio Cesare,* and *Tamerlano.*

Beginning with his last opera for the second Academy, *Orlando* (1732), and extending to 1736, Handel returned to the magic, mythological, and legendary operas of the early English period. In part this reflects the intense competition Handel faced during these years from rival companies. In March of 1732 a new company under the direction of Thomas Arne (father of the composer) began producing English operas; in May of that year they produced Handel's *Acis and Galatea.* In autumn of 1733 a rival Italian opera company opened its doors, forcing Handel for the first time out of the Haymarket Theatre. This company not only stole most of

Handel's singers and his librettist Rolli, but in 1734, they produced Handel's *Ottone.* Despite the intense competition that sometimes pitted Handel against himself, or perhaps because of it, Handel composed some of his most spectacular scores, including the trilogy of operas based on Ariosto's *Orlando furioso: Orlando, Ariodante* (1734) and *Alcina* (1735). The mad scenes for Orlando exist totally outside the *da capo* tradition and thus define musically the hero's unbalanced state. In *Ariodante* Handel used a full chorus for the first time since *Amadigi,* and for the first time perhaps since his earliest German operas, he had the availability of a ballet troupe. *Ariodante* and *Alcina* are notable for their extended ballets.

After 1736, Handel's last seven operas revert somewhat to the heroic and historical type of libretto. Although the rival companies remained open, by 1736 Handel's superiority was manifest. Perhaps not surprisingly, after the intensely competitive period of 1732 to 1736, there is initially a drop in quality. Handel's last three operas, however, can be set apart from the vast majority of his operas in that they contain decidedly comic characters and situations. The Argument for *Serse* (*Xerxes,* 1738) specifically mentions that "the basis of the story" resides partially in "some imbicilities," and the cast list describes Serse's servant, Elviro, as "a facetious Fellow." Many commentators have described these comic elements as pre-Mozartean, but they look backward more clearly than they look forward. Not only are they reminiscent of Handel's earliest surviving operas, *Almira* and *Agrippina,* but the source libretto for *Serse* derives from 1694.

Throughout his career, Handel created his operatic roles for specific singers whose special abilities strongly influenced the musical characterizations of their roles. Margherita Durastanti was the only soloist regularly employed by the Marquis Ruspoli in Rome, where Handel resided for much of 1707 and 1708. Handel not only wrote many cantatas for her, but he also created for her the role of Santa Maria Maddalena (Mary Magdalene) in *La resurrezione* (*The Resurrection,* 1708) and the title role of *Agrippina* (Venice, 1709). She specialized in parts for strong women (Armida, Agrippina) and "pants roles" (male roles played by a woman). The title male role of *Radamisto* was first performed by her in London, 1720, but the castrato Senesino replaced her at the second set of *Radamisto* performances, after which Handel composed his most famous heroic roles for this singer, including the title roles in *Giulio Cesare, Ottone, Alessandro,* and *Orlando.* For the soprano Francesca Cuzzoni, Handel created, among many others, the role of Cleopatra in *Giulio Cesare,* including the arias "V'adoro pupille" ("Beloved eyes") and "Piangerò" ("I shall weep"). After the arrival of soprano Faustina Bordoni, Handel wrote five operas (*Alessandro* to *Tolomeo*) that balanced distinct roles for both women, Faustina playing the coquette against Cuzzoni's favored pathetic style. For the tenor Francesco Borosini, Handel rewrote the title role of *Tamerlano* to include an extended death scene freed from the constraints of the *da capo* and typical scenic construction. The bass singer Giuseppe Boschi, like Durastanti, performed for Handel in Italy (including the role of Narciso in *Agrippina*) and followed him to London, where he sang Argante in *Rinaldo.* During the Royal Academy, thirteen more, mostly villanous, roles were created for him, leading to the contemporary quip "And Boschi-like be always in a rage." Even during the 1730s, Handel's operas were based largely on the concept of a repertoire company. After Senesino moved into the Opera of Nobility, he was replaced by the castrato Carestini. Soprano Anna Strada was the one singer who stayed with Handel throughout this competitive period, and for her he created thirteen roles, including the title roles of *Arianna, Alcina,* and *Atalanta* (1736).

Handel frequently reused his own music in different contexts, and he borrowed from other composers as well. Sometimes he was able to transform this pre-existent material, often with the simplest changes; other times he transferred music by himself or others unchanged, but even then the change of context seems to change the nature of the music. In some cases Handel borrows ideas from earlier settings of the librettos he uses. For example, some of Bajazet's music in *Tamerlano,* including the opening aria "Forte e lieto" ("Bravely and happily"), derives from Gasparini's setting of the same texts. Similarly the famous Larghetto of *Serse,* "Ombra mai fu" ("Never was there shade more soothing"; often referred to as "Handel's Largo") is based on Bononcini's setting. Three of Handel's earlier operas, *Agrippina, Rinaldo,* and *Il pastor fido,* are so heavily dependent on his earlier music that they could be called *pasticcio* operas. Thus the famous aria "Lascia ch'io pianga" ("Leave me to weep") from *Rinaldo* (London), had earlier been heard as "Lascia la spina" ("Leave the thorns") in *Il trionfo del tempo* (*The Triumph of Time;* 1707, Rome) and as a Sarabande in *Almira* (Hamburg). In this and many other cases, however, the borrowings seem to be Handel's way of preserving his music in an age when composers could not assume their music would be heard more than once within their own lifetimes, much less saved for posterity.

—Ellen T. Harris

HANSEL AND GRETEL
See HÄNSEL UND GRETEL

HÄNSEL UND GRETEL [Hansel and Gretel].

Composer: Engelbert Humperdinck.

Librettist: Adelheid Wette (after the tale by the Brothers Grimm).

First Performance: Weimar, Court Theater, 23 December 1893.

Roles: Gretel (soprano); Hänsel (mezzo-soprano); Gertrud (mezzo-soprano); Peter (baritone); Witch (mezzo-soprano); Sandman (soprano); Dew Fairy (soprano); chorus (children, SA).

Publications

book–

Kuhlmann, Hans. *Stil und Form in der Musik von Humperdincks Oper "Hänsel und Gretel".* Marburg, 1930.

articles–

Hanslick, E. "Hänsel und Gretel." In *Die moderne Oper* 7: *Fünf Jahre Musik (1891-1895).* Berlin, 1896.
Batka, R. "Von Hänsel und Gretel." In *Musikalische Streifzuge.* Leipzig, 1899.
Avant-scène opéra December (1987) [*Hänsel und Gretel* issue].

*   *   *

The very title of *Hänsel und Gretel* informs us that it tells a homely tale of old Germany rather than one of gods or heroes. It took some time to develop into a fully-fledged opera, however, for it grew from music that Humperdinck composed for his two young nieces Isolde and Gudrun, who had a homemade puppet theater at their house in Cologne and liked to stage little domestic performances of plays devised by their mother Adelheid Wette. One of these plays was based on the Grimm Brothers' fairy tale of two children who are captured by a wicked witch but outwit her and escape, and besides the immediate family a number of local friends and musicians saw it and were delighted by the story and by Humperdinck's music, not least the lilting dance song "Brother, will you dance with me?" which now comes early in act I. Eventually Frau Wette and her brother the composer turned *Hänsel und Gretel* into the Singspiel or music drama that had its first performance under Richard Strauss at Weimar at Christmas-tide 1893 and soon won fame elsewhere in Germany and in other centers such as London and New York.

Although usually performed with adult singers, and with a mezzo-soprano singing the role of the young boy Hänsel, the opera is of course about children and to be enjoyed by them. It has therefore to be simple in its appeal but at the same time varied and subtle enough musically and dramatically, so as not to bore audiences of any age in the course of its three acts. Humperdinck and his sister (who supplied the libretto) succeeded remarkably well, and the composer's direct musical language allowed him to include a few traditional children's songs and folksongs without disturbing the overall style. A good production of *Hänsel und Gretel* avoids sentimentality and *kitsch.* Indeed, a German critic has called it "a true German folk opera . . . that awakens, especially in children, affection and at least a little understanding of the art sacred to the Muses, that of Music."

The story is set in medieval Germany, where at the start of act I the two children are alone working at household tasks in the hut of their parents, the broom-maker Peter and his wife Gertrud. But they forget their work and start playing, and when their mother returns she scolds them for idleness. In her anger she accidentally knocks over a jug of precious milk, and so she sends them out into the nearby forest to gather strawberries for supper. When Peter returns unexpectedly laden with provisions, it is too late to recall the children, and he tells her of the danger of the witch of the Ilsenstein who catches children and turns them into gingerbread. The parents rush out in search of their children.

Act II commences with a not-too-scary orchestral "Witch's Ride" and the curtain rises to find the children in the forest with their basket filled. Unfortunately they now start to play and to eat the fruit, and realize too late, and with dismay, that it is getting dark and they can no longer find their way home. When the Sandman appears before them they sing an evening prayer (a touching duet) and fall asleep, protected by fourteen angels from heaven. But when act III begins with their awakening at morning by the Dew Fairy, they espy a little house made entirely of gingerbread and other cookies.

Hänsel und Gretel, **Cathryn Pope as Gretel and Ethna Robinson as Hänsel, English National Opera, London, 1987**

Hänsel plucks up courage to break off and eat a piece, but now the witch whose house it is (whose name is Rosina Leckermaul) captures both children and places a spell on them with her wand which prevents them from running away, her idea being to bake them both for gingerbread, just as she has done with others who have got into her clutches. But by a stratagem, the resourceful Gretel persuades the witch to show her how to get into the oven to inspect its contents, and then with great daring she and her brother manage to push their captor inside and to shut the door on her. The oven soon explodes, and by using the witch's wand the children restore to life all the gingerbread children that the witch had previously turned into biscuits, while she herself has been transformed once and for all into a big cake. The children's parents now appear and everyone sings a joyful song of thanksgiving.

—Christopher Headington

HANS HEILING.

Composer: Heinrich Marschner.

Librettist: Eduard Devrient (after Theodor Körner).

First Performance: Berlin, Court Opera, 24 May 1833.

Roles: The Queen (soprano); Hans Heiling (baritone); Anna (soprano); Konrad (tenor); Gertrud (contralto); Stephan (bass); Kiklas (speaking part); chorus (SATB).

Publications

book–

Gnirs, Anton. *Hans Heiling.* Karlsbad, 1931.

article–

"Die Uraufführung des Hans Heiling." *Blätter der Staatsoper* 10/no. 7 (1929).

*   *   *

Hans Heiling was the eleventh of Marschner's sixteen stage works. The libretto, by Eduard Devrient, was an adaptation of the *Hans-Heiling-Felsen* by Theodor Körner (1791-1813), with elements borrowed from other Bohemian folk tales. Intended for Mendelssohn in 1827, it was eventually accepted by Marschner four years later and first performed in 1833. Devrient himself took the role of Heiling at its first performances.

In his own lifetime Marschner's operas were well regarded by many, including Schumann, von Bülow and even Hanslick; Wagner, who conducted *Hans Heiling*, commented that Marschner was "most unfairly taken as a mere imitator of

Weber." Despite this high regard, his works faded from the repertory, and *Hans Heiling* is nowadays regarded as a rarity. Nevertheless, it retains some importance within the German operatic tradition on account of the composer's character development and approach to formal construction.

The start of the opera is unusual: it begins not with an overture but with a dramatic prelude, set in the underworld. A chorus of gnomes toils over gold and other treasures (an anticipation of Wagner's *Nibelungen*). Their Queen tells her son Heiling that he will lose his kingdom if he should ever leave the underworld. These entreaties are of no avail, however, since Heiling has already decided to marry a mortal, Anna. He leaves, taking a magic book by which he retains power over the gnomes. There follows the overture (representing Heiling's journey), after which music from the prelude recurs briefly at the start of act I, accompanying the Queen's distant cries as Heiling appears from the underworld.

Thereafter, the work's construction is more orthodox, maintaining the established "number" system, with clear divisions between sections. In linking the set pieces Marschner chose to use spoken dialogue rather than recitative, but instead of following the *Singspiel* tradition he developed the technique of melodrama where the orchestra accompanies the dialogue, as in Beethoven's *Fidelio* and Weber's *Der Freischütz*.

As Heiling emerges from the underworld, he is greeted by Anna and her mother. Left alone, Anna opens Heiling's magic book, but the pages begin to turn by themselves. When Heiling sees what she has done he becomes angry, and against his better judgment burns the book. Anna leaves in a terrified state. Now alone, Heiling declares his passionate love for Anna in an aria not unlike early Wagner in style. Anna reappears, and Heiling throws himself at her feet, the dialogue beginning before the aria's orchestral postlude is over. Heiling agrees to visit the village fair, but only on condition that Anna does not dance. In rustic music, the villagers are enjoying the fun of the fair. The mood darkens as Anna's suitor Konrad asks her to dance. When Heiling refuses permission, Anna torments him and leaves with Konrad. Heiling gives vent to feelings of rage at such fickleness.

Act II begins in a wild forest, where Anna expresses her indecision between Heiling and Konrad. She suddenly finds herself surrounded by the gnomes, while their Queen tells her of Heiling's ancestry. The passionate nature of this passage encouraged Wagner to borrow the melody and harmony for the motive of the Intimation of Death in *Die Walküre*.

In scene ii Gertrud, alone in her cottage, is frightened by Anna's absence and by the remoteness of the cottage. Her aria is a melodrama including not only speaking but humming and singing. Arriving with Anna, Konrad tries to dissuade her from marrying his rival. When Heiling appears, offering jewelry as a dowry, Anna tells Konrad and Gertrud what she has learned from the Queen and states that she would rather die than marry Heiling. Heiling then stabs Konrad, departing with a maniacal laugh.

In act III, Heiling learns from the gnomes that Anna and Konrad intend to marry. Villagers are heard in the church, while Anna and Konrad deliver a short, almost Mozartean love duet. When Heiling arrives demanding vengeance, Konrad attacks him with a sword, but as the blade enters his body Heiling merely laughs. The Queen appears and finally persuades Heiling to return to the underworld. After he has departed, the peasants thank God for their deliverance.

Marschner could produce impressive large-scale scenes, which sometimes combine soloists with two choruses (of gnomes and villagers). Although the orchestra is a conventional one, his orchestration is original: in Gertrud's anxious

soliloquy in act II, scene ii, for example, he confines himself to the lowest instruments with a wind machine, while horns represent wild dogs. In the folk dancing, he captures the effect of guitars with repetitive chords for the strings; elsewhere he writes a brass fanfare with very low horns, and adds an unmistakably romantic touch to the final ensemble by means of a sensuously chromatic solo violin line when Heiling returns to the underworld.

The opera's subject matter, and particularly its use of the supernatural, is in the tradition of works like *Der Freischütz*. In its musical style, however, it comes closer to Wagner: this is certainly true of the role of Heiling, and the vocal writing as a whole often has an intensity that seems ahead of its time.

There are obvious weak moments in the opera. The lighter style of music for the villagers, which is deliberately contrasted with that representing the supernatural, is sometimes disappointingly trite. But such miscalculations do not seriously detract from the work's undoubted dramatic power, and the opera deserves more than the occasional airing it receives.

—Alan Laing

HARLEQUIN, OR THE WINDOWS
See ARLECCHINO, ODER, DIE FENSTER

DIE HARMONIE DER WELT [The Harmony of the World].

Composer: Paul Hindemith.

Librettist: Paul Hindemith.

First Performance: Munich, Prinzregententheater, 11 August 1957,

Roles (doubled as indicated): Rudolf II/Ferdinand II/Sol (bass); Johannes Kepler/Earth (baritone); Wallenstein/Jupiter (tenor); Ulrich/Soldier/Mars (tenor); Daniel Hizler/Parson/ Mercury (bass); Tansur/Saturn (bass); Baron Starhemberg (baritone); Christoph (tenor); Susanna/Venus (soprano); Katharina/Luna (contralto); Little Susanna (soprano); Bailiff (baritone); Solicitor (baritone); Four Women (two sopranos, two contraltos); Three Assassins (tenor, two basses); chorus.

Publications

articles—

Briner, Andres. "Eine Bekenntnisoper Paul Hindemiths: zu seiner Oper *Die Harmonie der Welt*." *Schweizerische Musikzeitung* January-February (1959).
———. "Die erste Textfassung von Paul Hindemiths Oper 'Die Harmonie der Welt'." In *Festschrift für einen Verleger: Ludwig Strecker*, 203. Mainz, 1973.

Rubeli, Alfred. "Johannes Keplers Harmonik in Paul Hindemiths Oper *Die Harmonie der Welt.*" In *Kepler-Symposion zu J. Keplers 350. Todestag Linz 1980,* edited by Rudolf Hasse, 107. Linz, 1982.

unpublished–

D'Angelo, James P. "Tonality and its Symbolic Association in Paul Hindemith's Opera *Die Harmonie der Welt.*" Ph.D. dissertation, New York University, 1983.

* * *

Die Harmonie der Welt is Hindemith's last large-scale opera forming a thematic trilogy with the earlier *Cardillac* (1926) and *Mathis der Maler* (1933-35). The principal work of Hindemith's last period (1955-63), it reflects his artistic, philosophical, and artistic credo and can be construed as his musical autobiography. It is a unique and neglected work yet to be staged outside Germany and Austria.

For many years Hindemith was preoccupied with the nature of the creative artist, be it a goldsmith (Cardillac), a painter (Mathis), or a scientist (Kepler). Therefore (as in the case of *Mathis*), he felt it necessary to write his own libretto for *Die Harmonie der Welt,* employing unusual rhyme schemes and occasional archaic German words. The opera's title is taken from the astronomer Johannes Kepler's magnum opus *Harmonices Mundi* (1619) in which Kepler propounded the three laws of planetary motion and speculated upon the actual sounds emitted by the orbiting planets. Hindemith strongly identified with Kepler, the opera's central figure, because both of them believed they had discovered universal laws in their respective disciplines and were devoted to the belief that the harmony of the universe existed and could be made manifest to the intellect of mankind. In addition, Hindemith drew a number of parallels between the circumstances of their lives.

During a long gestation period (1939-57), Hindemith composed a series of sonatas as preparatory exercises, as well as the symphony *Die Harmonie der Welt* (1951), whose three movements were later incorporated into the opera. The final movement, *Musica Mundana,* meaning "the music of the spheres," with vocal parts superimposed, became the opera's final scene. The work is comprised of tableaux, which chronologically depict important events in or surrounding the life of Kepler. It begins in 1608, shortly after the appearance of Halley's comet (used as a symbol of destruction), and ends in 1630, the year of Kepler's death. There is no dramatic progression from scene to scene or character development as such; rather, the opera builds to the final scene in which Hindemith unfolds his vision of the harmony of the world. During the opera a gallery of Kepler's associates and relatives is presented, all of whom have their symbolic meaning in this essentially allegorical work. These characters either impede or assist the steadfast Kepler in his quest to find union with the universal harmony. Those detrimental to Kepler's search are General Wallenstein, the famous military commander during the Thirty Years War (1618-48), which serves as a backdrop to the opera; Tansur, a charlatan and Wallenstein's recruiter; Emperors Rudolf II and Ferdinand II, Kepler's wayward patrons; Pastor Hizler, who denies Kepler the holy sacrament; Ulrich, his ambitious assistant; and his mother Katharina, accused of witchcraft. Only the two Susannas—his second wife and his little daughter—are completely inspirational figures for Kepler.

Each character is associated with the astrological meaning of the sun, moon, and six planets known in Kepler's time. Occasionally there are glimpses of their pure essence but more often they display their negative, lesser selves in opposition to such qualities as love, service, humility, and faith. This polarization was symbolized in part by the juxtaposition of "leit" tonalities a tritone apart, e.g., C and F sharp. For example, the tonality of E stands for the Harmony while the tonality of B flat represents Chaos, all those forces exerted by the imperfection of human nature. This polarity is also highlighted by Hindemith's use of dual scenes in which two distinct events are both alternately and simultaneously presented.

All the obstructions to Kepler's desired union with the Harmony are removed at his death. This opens the door for the purification of not only Kepler but also all the other flawed characters in a kind of heavenly purgatorial world that leads to the source of the Harmony. This final scene of *Musica Mundana* is in the form of a passacaglia, with the constant repetition of its theme symbolizing the constancy of the heavenly world. During the twenty-two variations, each character, transformed into a member of the solar system, repents his errors and expresses his higher self. The final E-major chord is much more than a conventional ending for Hindemith: it is the harmonious portal which leads to the ultimate Harmony.

Hindemith's overriding theme is that the life of humanity on earth cannot be resolved by efforts of will. Rather than ever being reconciled, the polarization of positive versus negative attributes in man must be transcended and resolved in an afterlife state. Hindemith's rather pessimistic view of life on earth and his optimistic view of an afterlife point to the inspiration he found in Catholicism.

—James D'Angelo

THE HARMONY OF THE WORLD
See DIE HARMONIE DER WELT

HARTMANN, Rudolf.

Producer. Born 11 October 1900, in Ingolstadt, Bavaria. Died 26 August 1988, in Munich. Studied art and stage design in Munich and Bamberg; resident producer in Altenburg, 1924-27; Gera, 1927-28; Nuremburg, 1928-34; Berlin Staatsoper, 1934-37; chief producer, Bavarian State Opera, 1937-45 where he staged the premieres of Richard Strauss's *Friedenstag,* 1938, and *Capriccio,* 1942; Nuremberg, 1946-53; Staatsintendant at Munich, 1952-67; Guest at Covent Garden, Bayreuth, Vienna State Opera, Düsseldorf, Mannheim, and Teatro alla Scala.

Opera Productions (selected)

Die Azubergeige, Berlin Staatsoper, 1935.
Friedenstag, Bavarian State Opera, 1938.
Capriccio, Bavarian State Opera, 1942.
Die Meistersinger von Nürnberg, Bayreuth, 1951.
Liebe der Danae, Salzburg, 1952.
Elektra, Covent Garden, 1953.
Ring, Covent Garden, 1954.
Arabella, Covent Garden, 1965.
Die Frau ohne Schatten, Covent Garden, 1967.

Publications

By HARTMANN: books–

Das geliebte Haus; mein Leben mit der Oper. Munich, 1975.
Opera. Translated by Arnold J. Pomerons. New York, 1976.
Oper: Regie und Bühnenbild heute. Stuttgart, 1977.
Richard Strauss: The Staging of His Operas and Ballets. Translated by Graham Davies. New York, 1980.
Richard Strauss, Rudolf Hartmann: ein Briefwechsel mit Aufsatzen und Regiearbeiten. Tutzing, 1984.

articles–

"Instrumentiertes Secco-Rezitativ." *Musikerziehung; Zeitschrift zur Erneuerung der Musikpflege* 13 (December 1959): 119-21.
"Richard Strauss och hans sista skaparperiod." *Musikrevy* 19, no. 3 (1964): 81-84.
"Joseph Keilberth, 1908-1968." *Opera* 19 (October 1968): 799-802.
"Marginalia on *Capriccio.*" *Opera* 23 (March 1972): 203-06.
"Meine Lebensaufgabe—der Wiederaufbau der Münchner Oper." *Opernwelt* no. 10 (October 1975): 38-40.
"*Don Juan* oder *Don Giovanni?*" *Acta Mozartiana* 37, no. 2 (1990): 24-27.

About HARTMANN: articles–

Lange, M. "Rudolph Otto Hartmann; zu seiner Berufung nach München." *Musica* 6 (May 1952): 207-08.
"Covent Garden Newcomers." *Opera* 4 (May 1953): 279-80.
Jaretzki, P. "Munich Stresses Strauss." *Opera News* 18 (19 October 1953): 18.
Friess, H. "Richard Strauss and the Bavarian State Opera." *Tempo* no. 43 (Spring 1957): 26-29.
Breuer, R. "Munich's Grand Seigneur." *Opera News* 24 (26 March 1960): 14.
Schuh, W. "Rudolph Hartmann 60 Jahre alt." *Neue Zeitschrift für Musik* 121 (October 1960): 34.
Faulkner, M. "Four European Men of Opera." *Music Magazine* 164 (February 1962): 20-21.
Schmidt-Garre, H. "Doppel premiere soll Ensembletheater retten." *Neue Zeitschrift für Musik* 123 (April 1962): 180-81.
Keim, W. "Zehn Jahre Müncher Festspiele unter Stadtsintendant Rudolph Hartmann." *Internationale Richard Strauss-Gesellschaft* no. 34 (September 1962): 1-3.
Friess, Herman. "Rudolf Hartmann." *Opera* 16 (September 1965): 622-25.
"Hartmann's Farewell at Munich." *Opera* 18 (October 1967): 834.
Ruppel, K.H. "Rudolf Hartmanns Abschied." *Opern Welt* no. 10 (October 1967): 30-32.

Lüdicke, H. "In München letzmals Hartmann-Festspiele." *Musik und Gesellschaft* 18 (February 1968): 129-30.
"Rudolf Hartmann's New Production." *Musical Events* 24 (February 1969): 15.
"Rudolf Hartmann zum 70 Geburtstag." *Oper und Konzert* 8 (October 1970): 25-29.
"Gespräch mit Rudolf Hartmann." *Oper und Konzert* 9 (March 1971): 29-31.
Schmidt-Garre, H. "Der entmythologisierte *Lohengrin.*" *Neue Zeitschrift für Musik* 132 (April 1971): 205.
Sutcliffe, J.H. "Hartmann inszeniert Strauss—*Der Rosenkavalier* und *Don Pasquale* in Kassel." *Opernwelt* no. 12 (December 1975): 45.
"Rudolf Hartmann wird 80." *Oper und Konzert* 18, no. 10 (1980): 17-18.
Schreiber, U. "Du holde Kunst, hast mich in eine bessre Welt entrückt; zum Realitätsverhältnis in den Memoiren berühmter Kunstwalter." *Hifi-Stereophonie; Musik-Musikwiedergabe* 20 (February 1981): 115.
Asche, G. "Rudolf Hartmann: Die Festwiese wurde demokratisiert (interview)." *Opernwelt* Yearbook (1981): 11-12.

*　　*　　*

Opera producer and administrator Rudolf Hartmann was an influential figure in European musical life from the late 1930s through the 1960s. Hartmann established his name through his collaboration with conductor Clemens Krauss, first in Hartmann's years in Berlin (1934-37) and then in Munich (1937-45). He was most closely associated with the operas of Richard Strauss. After the Second World War he worked in Nuremberg and Zurich and on various guest engagements. From 1952 to 1967 Hartmann was Staatsintendant (Administrator) of the Bavarian State Opera in Munich. He retired in 1972.

Hartmann's apprenticeship years in Bamberg, Altenburg, and Nuremberg gave him good training for his meeting with Krauss a year after his arrival in Berlin in 1934. Hartmann's star was already rising: an innovative staging of Handel's *Giulio Cesare in Egitto* in Bamberg had attracted much attention. Krauss, with his keen sense of theater, was the ideal co-worker for the young Hartmann. He took his protégé with him when he moved to Munich, and with designer Ludwig Sievert they formed a team responsible for many acclaimed productions.

After the war Hartmann worked primarily in Zurich, with guest productions in various European houses, including Bayreuth (*Die Meistersinger von Nürnberg*). Much of his work up to this time may be seen as preparation for his most important position, his return to Munich as head of the State Opera in 1952. Hartmann restored its prewar reputation as one of the great houses of Europe. Their guest performances in London helped in the restoration of English-German relations. Hartmann oversaw the reopening of the Cuvilliéstheater in 1958 and then the rebuilt National Theater in 1963 after years of postponements and delays. Ballet received more attention from Hartmann than from most opera administrators; an annual ballet festival was inaugurated during his tenure. He also reestablished the summer Munich Festivals. To avoid duplicating the offerings of Bayreuth and Salzburg, Hartmann organized the festival repertory around the trio of Wolfgang Amadeus Mozart, Richard Wagner, and Strauss. Although he was unsuccessful in obtaining Hans Knappertsbusch, his first choice, for musical director when he returned to Munich, Hartmann enjoyed a succession of talented conductors in that position: Rudolf Kempe, Ferenc Fricsay, and Joseph Keilberth.

Hartmann was strongly influenced by Krauss's philosophy of tinkering with a score when he thought it would improve the dramatic values of a production. This was particularly true with the works of Strauss, and Hartmann and Krauss had the composer's approval for many of their changes. For example, Krauss and his Vienna producer Lothar Wallerstein had previously reworked the second act of *Die ägyptische Helena,* but Krauss and Hartmann decided the first act also required clarification, so they divided it into two scenes in their 1935 Berlin production. In the 1938-39 season in Munich, Krauss and Hartmann prepared a production of *Carmen* which went back to the original dialogue and incorporated recently discovered material for the third act.

Although Hartmann took a romantic, naturalistic approach to opera production, his work was characterized by insightful consideration of the text and its relation to the music, often resulting in striking new views of characters (e.g., Beckmesser) and their motivations. He did not follow the innovations of Wieland Wagner, techniques which he admired but considered a one-man phenomenon, or the ideological approach of many producers in the 1950s and 1960s, yet he did not hesitate to update operas, for example setting *Der Freischütz* in the period immediately following the Thirty Years War. Most of his work was well received, but he also had less successful conceptions: his *Ring* at Covent Garden in the 1950s received mixed reviews, as did his production of the premiere of Hindemith's *Die Harmonie der Welt* in 1957.

Hartmann championed new works, and he also maintained a lifelong interest in baroque and classical period opera.

During his tenures in Munich he was closely associated with the works of Carl Orff, Werner Egk, and Arthur Honneger—principally conservative composers—but Hartmann also championed works by Hans Werner Henze and other young experimental composers of the postwar period.

Years after his Bamberg production of *Giulio Cesare* he won another success with this opera in a striking production that placed the characters on a central platform on a raked, staircased stage. One of his last productions in Munich was Handel's *Agrippina,* designed by Jean-Pierre Ponnelle. Hartmann was also in charge of the yearly Baroque Weeks at the Opera House in Bayreuth.

Hartmann developed a close friendship with Strauss during his production of the premiere of *Friedenstag* in 1938. Hartmann worked with Strauss on the premieres of *Capriccio* in 1942 and the Generalprobe (dress rehearsal; the premiere was canceled) of *Die Liebe der Danae* at Salzburg in 1944. Toward the end of his life, Strauss considered Krauss and Hartmann to be the authoritative conductor and producer of his works. Strauss saw Hartmann as the means of perpetuating his own views of his operas.

Hartmann wrote prolifically on matters of opera production for program notes, newspaper and journal articles, and books. He published his production book for the premiere of *Capriccio.* It was to have been followed by similar volumes for other Strauss operas, but this, like the study of opera production that Strauss urged him to write, never came to be. His lifelong association with Strauss's operas culminated in his definitive book on the subject. Hartmann's pedagogical tendencies also included the training of young producers and singers. He coaxed now well-known opera director August Everding from the straight theater to opera. Hartmann's

work can be seen in the video cassette recording of *Der Rosenkavalier* conducted by Herbert von Karajan, based on their 1960 Salzburg production.

—David E. Anderson

HÁRY JÁNOS.

Composer: Zoltán Kodály.

Librettists: Béla Paulini and Zsolt Harsányi.

First Performance: Budapest, Royal Hungarian Opera, 16 October 1926.

Roles: Háry János (baritone); Örzse (mezzo-soprano); Marczi (bass-baritone); Marie-Louise (contralto); Empress of Austria (soprano); several non-singing roles; chorus.

Publications

article–

Hundt, Theodor. "Zoltán Kodály in eigener Sache." *Musica* 38 (1984): 139.

*   *   *

Kodály's *Háry János,* cover of piano-vocal score, 1931

Háry János is difficult to categorize. It is officially a *Singspiel* in five scenes, but there are elements of the musical in it; it has rather more in common with Bernstein's *Candide* than with Mozart's *Entführung aus dem Serail.* The libretto is divided into four "adventures" with a prologue and epilogue. Its source is a nineteenth-century narrative poem by János Garáy, the hero of which, Háry János, became something of a national emblem, a peasant hero, ex-soldier, braggart and dreamer, or, as some would see him, a symbol of Hungary itself, "a great credulous self-deceiving child." Kodály firmly believed that every Hungarian liked to think he had in him something of Háry's benevolence, fidelity, valor and patriotism, and the enthusiasm which greeted the work on its first performance on 16 October 1926 and which has continued ever since suggests that he was probably right. In some respects Háry can be compared with Jaroslav Hasek's great comic creation in *The Good Soldier Schweik,* but he lacks the earthy cunning that characterizes the Czech hero's running battles with Austrian authority and relies more on native charm, braggadoccio, and sentiment to see him through.

The overture introduces us to the village inn at Nagybony, the scene of Háry's picaresque imaginings. The tale begins with the famous orchestral "sneeze" which assures Hungarian audiences that everything they are about to hear is absolutely true! In the first adventure Háry, the Hungarian hussar, and his betrothed Örzse (the diminutive of Erzebét, Elizabeth) are on the borders of Galicia and Muscovy. Marie-Louise, wife of Napoleon, arrives with her retinue but is prevented by the Russians from crossing the border. The party retires to a sentry-box which Háry promptly drags into imperial territory. The delighted empress invites him to join the Vienna Guard. Háry agrees, subject to certain conditions, one being that the empress's coachman Uncle Marci is permitted to wear Hungarian dress (forbidden before 1867). Marie-Louise agrees, and as they leave Háry pushes the sentry-box and the border guards back into Russia.

An orchestral intermezzo separates the first from the second adventure. Háry, now a sergeant, is happy except that a Count Ebelastin is persecuting him because Marie-Louise is taking too much interest in him. Has he not tamed a wild Austrian stallion and provided a cure for the emperor's gout? The "Viennese Musical Clock" is heard striking twelve. Örzse is feeding the Austrian double eagle and Ebelastin is trying unavailingly to arouse her jealousy. Piqued, he produces from his pocket Napoleon's declaration of war. In the third adventure Háry is with the Army in Italy. General Krucifix calls upon him for advice and the battle against Napoleon begins with parodies of the Marseillaise. The French, realizing they are faced by the invincible Háry, flee. The Imperial Hymn triumphs, and Napoleon pleads for mercy (to wailing saxophones). Marie-Louise wants to exchange her defeated husband for Háry. Napoleon sidles off dejectedly and the traitor Ebelastin is discredited. The Empress is anxious to make Háry a prince, but he reassures Örzse that he has no wish to become part of the Austrian royal family. He calls for a Recruiting Dance.

For the final adventure, the scene returns to the palace in Vienna and preparations for the wedding of Háry to Marie-Louise. A march heralds the appearance of the court, and everyone pays respect to Háry. He, however, makes it plain that he only wants to return home with his true love. He makes an impassioned plea on behalf of the emperor's downtrodden Hungarian subjects, then the pair leave for "a little hut with a poplar tree." The epilogue returns us to the inn at Nagybony where Háry sits, poor but apparently content, in the world of his imaginings.

Háry János is an expression of the urge for a national identity. Of the thirty musical numbers, the sixteen solo and choral items are arrangements of folksongs collected by Kodály that were still current in Hungary when the piece was composed. The orchestral and instrumental numbers are mainly original; those relating to the Hungarians rely heavily on Magyar idioms such as the "Verbunkos" (Recruiting) music and *csárdás* (the intermezzo and the Hussar's Song) and national instruments like the cimbalom. Several of these melodies had been introduced to the stage by Erkel some seventy years earlier. As in the latter's *Bánk Bán,* the music associated with the Austrians and French has a distinctive and recognizably "foreign" sound.

The opera has a political message as well as being a manifesto for national culture. At the time it was written, Hungary had been through a period of acute political chaos. The country had suffered dismemberment and was in the grip of raging inflation. The brutal excesses of Béla Kun's 1918 Communist regime were followed by a year of bloody political in-fighting, the coming to power of Admiral Horthy's pro-Fascist government and in 1921 by an abortive attempt by ex-King Karl (the last Hapsburg emperor) to restore the monarchy. The appearance of Kodály's comic testimony to the enduring spirit of the Hungarian people was therefore more than opportune and its enormous popularity predictable. So successful was it that Kodály may have been tempted to try something else along the same lines, but he did not attempt to hit the same bulls-eye twice. Instead he turned to the concert hall and pursued the cause of Hungarian nationalism through a series of idiomatic folk-inspired orchestral works—the *Háry János* Suite, the Dances of Galánta and of Marosszék, and the "Peacock" Variations—which beside cementing his reputation at home helped establish him abroad as *the* internationally acclaimed representative of Hungarian music.

—Kenneth Dommett

HASSE, Johann Adolph.

Composer. Baptized 25 March 1699, in Bergedorf, near Hamburg. Died 16 December 1783, in Venice. Married: the famous mezzo-soprano Faustina Bordoni (1730). Studied with his father and then in Hamburg, 1714-17; employed as a tenor at the Hamburg Opera, 1718; tenor at the Brunswick theater, 1719, and production of his opera *Antioco,* 1721; studied composition with Porpora and A. Scarlatti in Naples; on the staff of the Scuola degl' Incurabili, Venice, 1727; Kapellmeister to the Elector of Saxony at Dresden and lived mainly in Dresden, 1731-57; in Vienna, 1763-73; in Venice, 1773-83.

Operas

Antioco, B. Feind (after Zeno and Minato), Brunswick, court, 11 August 1721.
Il Sesostrate, A. Carasale (after Zeno and Pariati), Naples, San Bartolomeo, 13 May 1726; revised 28 August 1726.
L'Astarto, Zeno and Pariati, Naples, San Bartolomeo, December 1726.
Gerone tiranno di Siracusa, after A. Aureli, Naples, San Bartolomeo, 19 November 1727.
Attalo, re di Bitinia, F. Silvani?, Naples, San Bartolomeo, May 1728.
L'Ulderica, Naples, San Bartolomeo, 29 January 1729.

La sorella amante [*Lavinia*], B. Saddumene, Naples, Nuovo or Toledo, spring 1729.

Tigrane, F. Silvani, Naples, San Bartolomeo, 4 November 1729; revised A. Palella, Naples, San Carlo, 4 November 1745.

Artaserse, Boldini (after Metastasio), Venice, San Giovanni Grisostomo, February 1730; revised Dresden, court, 9 September 1740; revised Naples, San Carlo, 20 January 1760.

Dalisa, D. Lalli (after N. Minato), Parma, April 1730.

Arminio, A. Salvi, Milan, Regio Ducal, 28 August 1730.

Ezio, Metastasio, Naples, San Bartolomeo, fall 1730; revised Dresden, court, 20 January 1755.

Cleofide [*Alessandro nell' Indie*], M.A. Boccardi (after Metastasio), Dresden, court, 13 September 1731; revised Venice, San Giovanni Grisostomo, carnival 1736; revised carnival 1738, 1743.

Catone in Utica, Metastasio, Turin, Regio, 26 December 1731.

Cajo Fabricio, after Zeno, Rome, Capranica, 12 January 1732; revised Naples, San Bartolomeo, winter 1733; revised Dresden, court, 8 July 1734; performed as *Pirro,* Jaromeritz, Schloss Questenberg, fall 1734; revised Berlin, court, September 1766.

Demetrio, Metastasio, Venice, San Giovanni Grisostomo, January 1732; performed as *Cleonice,* Vienna, court?, February 1734; as *Demetrio,* Venice, San Cassiano, carnival 1737; as *Cleonice,* Dresden, court, 8 February 1740; as *Demetrio,* Venice, San Giovanni Grisostomo, carnival 1747.

Euristeo, D. Lalli (after Zeno), Venice, San Samuele, May 1732.

Issipile, Metastasio, Naples, San Bartolomeo, 1 October 1732.

Siroe rè di Persia, Metastasio, Bologna, Malvezzi, 2 May 1733; revised Naples, San Carlo, 4 November 1747; revised Warsaw, Imperial, carnival 1763.

Tito Vespasiano [*La clemenza di Tito*], Metastasio, Pesaro, Pubblico, 24 September 1735; revised Dresden, court, 17 January 1738; revised Naples, San Carlo, 20 January 1759.

Senocrita, S.B. Pallavicino, Dresden, court, 27 February 1737.

Atalanta, S.B. Pallavicino, Dresden, court, 26 July 1737.

Asteria (favola pastorale), S.B. Pallavicino, Dresden, court, 3 August 1737.

Irene, S.B. Pallavicino, Dresden, court, 8 February 1738.

Alfonso, S.B. Pallavicino, Dresden, court, 11 May 1738.

Viriate [*Siface*], D. Lalli (after Metastasio), Venice, San Giovanni Grisostomo, carnival 1739.

Numa Pompilio (with intermezzo *Pimpinella e Marcantonio*), S.B. Pallavicino, Hubertusburg, 7 October 1741.

Lucio Papirio, Pallavicino, Dresden, court, 18 January 1742; revised G. de Majo, Naples, San Carlo, 4 November 1746; revised Hasse or Graun, Berlin, court, 24 January 1766.

L'Asilo d'Amore (festa teatrale), Metastasio, Naples, court?, July 1742.

Didone abbandonata, F. Algarotti (after Metastasio), Hubertusburg, 7 October 1742; revised Berlin, court, 29 December 1752; revised Versailles, court, 28 August 1753.

Endimione (festa teatrale), Metastasio, Naples?, court, July 1743.

Antigono, Metastasio, Dresden, court, 10 October 1743 or 20 January 1744.

Ipermestra, Metastasio, Vienna, court, 8 January 1744; revised Hubertusburg, 7 October 1751.

Semiramide riconosciuta, Metastasio, Naples, San Carlo, 4 November 1744 and/or Venice, San Giovanni Grisostomo, 26 December 1744; revised Dresden, court, 11 January 1747; revised Warsaw, Imperial, 7 October 1760.

Arminio, G.C. Pasquini, Dresden, court, 7 October 1745; revised Dresden, court, 8 January 1753.

La spartana generosa, ovvero Archidamia, G.C. Pasquini, Dresden, court, 14 June 1747.

Leucippo (favola pastorale), G.C. Pasquini, Hubertusburg, court, 7 October 1747; revised? Venice, San Samuele, May 1749; revised Dresden, Zwinger, 7 January 1751; revised Berlin, court, 7 January 1765.

Demofoonte, Metastasio, Dresden, court, 9 February 1748; revised, Venice, San Giovanni Grisostomo, carnival 1749; revised Naples, San Carlo, 4 November 1758.

Attilio Regolo, Metastasio, Dresden, court, 12 January 1750.

Ciro riconosciuto, Metastasio, Dresden, court, 20 January 1751.

Adriano in Siria, Metastasio, Dresden, court, 17 January 1752.

Solimano, G.A. Migliavacca, Dresden, court, 5 February 1753; revised Dresden, court, 7 January 1754.

L'eroe cinese, Metastasio, Hubertusburg, court, 7 October 1753; revised Potsdam, court, 18 July 1773.

Artemisia, G.A. Migliavacca, Dresden, court, 6 February 1754.

Il rè pastore, Metastasio, Hubertusburg, court, 7 October 1755; revised Warsaw, Imperial, 7 October 1762, or Vienna, 1760.

L'Olimpiade, Metastasio, Dresden, court, 16 February 1756; revised Warsaw, Imperial, carnival 1761; revised Turin, Regio, 26 December 1764.

Nitteti, Metastasio, Venice, San Benedetto, January 1758; revised Vienna, court?, 1762.

Il sogno di Scipione (azione teatrale), Metastasio, Warsaw?, court, 7 October 1758 [lost].

Achille in Sciro, Metastasio, Naples, San Carlo, 4 November 1759.

Alcide al bivio (festa teatrale), Metastasio, Vienna, Palace Redoutensaal, 8 October 1760.

Zenobia, Metastasio, Vienna, court?, carnival 1761.

Il trionfo di Clelia, Metastasio, Vienna, Burgtheater, 27 April 1762.

Egeria (festa teatrale), Metastasio, Vienna, court, 24 April 1764.

Romolo ed Ersilia, Metastasio, Innsbruck, Imperial Palace, 6 August 1765.

Partenope (festa teatrale), Metastasio, Vienna, Burgtheater, 9 September 1767; revised Berlin, Sans-souci, 18 July 1775.

Piramo e Tisbe (intermezzo tragico), M. Coltellini, Vienna, Burg, November 1768; revised Vienna, Luxemburg, September 1770.

Il Ruggiero ovvero L'eroica gratitudine, Metastasio, Milan, Regio Ducal, 16 October 1771.

Other works: arias, intermezzos, oratorios, cantatas, instrumental works, keyboard works.

Publications/Writings

About HASSE: books–

Agricola, J.F. *Anleitung zur Singekunst.* Berlin, 1757; 1966.

Mancini, G.B. *Riflessioni pratiche sul canto figurato,* 29. Milan, 3rd ed. 1775.

Hiller, J.A. *Über Alt und Neu in der Musik,* 11. Leipzig, 1787.

Kandler, F.S. *Cenni storico-critici intorno alla vita ed alle opere del cel. Gio. Adolfo Hasse detto il Sassone.* Venice, 1820.

Fürstenau, M. *Zur Geschichte der Musik und des Theaters am Hofe zu Dresden,* vol. 2, 173, 204ff, 375ff. Dresden, 1861-62; 1971.

Ricci, C. *I teatri di Bologna nei secoli XVII e XVIII,* 438, 447, 456ff, 495, 507, 538ff. Bologna, 1888; 1965.

Gheltof, U. de. *La 'nuova Sirena' e il 'caro Sassone': note biografiche.* Venice, 1890.

Zeller, B. *Das Recitativo accompagnato in den Opern J.A. Hasses.* Halle, 1911.

Haböck, F. *Die Gesangskunst der Kastraten.* Vienna, 1923.

Gerber, R. *Der Operntypus J.A. Hasse und seine textlichen Grundlagen.* Leipzig, 1925.

Högg, M. *Die Gesangskunst der Faustina Hasse und das Sängerinnenwesen ihrer Zeit in Deutschland.* Königsbrück, 1931.

Prosnak, J. *Kultura muzyczna Warzawy w XVIII wieku* [musical culture in eighteenth century Warsaw]. Cracow, 1955.

Strohm, Reinhard. *Italienische Opernarien des frühen Settecento (1720-1730).* Cologne, 1976.

Degrada, Francesco. *Il palazzo incantato. Studi sulla tradizione del melodramma dal Barocco al Romanticismo.* Fiesole, 1979.

Strohm, Reinhard. *Die italienische Oper im 18. Jahrhundert.* Wilhelmshaven, 1979.

Lühning, Helga. *"Titus" Vertonung im 18. Jahrhundert: Untersuchungen zur Tradition der Opera Seria von Hasse bis Mozart.* Rome, 1983.

Weimer, Eric Douglas. *Opera Seria and the Evolution of Classical Style, 1755-1772. Studies in Musicology* 78. Ann Arbor, 1984.

articles–

Quantz, J.J. "Lebenslauf, von ihm selbst entworfen [1725]." In F.W. Marpurg, *Historische-kritische Beyträge zur Aufnahme der Musik,* vol. 1, p. 227. Berlin, 1754; 1970; English translation in Paul Nettl, *Forgotten Musicians,* New York, 1951; 1969.

Marpurg, F.W. "Die Königl. Capell. und Cammer Music zu Dresden 1756." *Historische-kritische Beyträge zur Aufnahme der Musik,* vol. 2, p. 475. Berlin, 1754; 1970.

Kretzschmar, H. "Aus Deutschlands italienischer Zeit." *Jahrbuch der Musikbibliothek Peters* (1901): 47.

Sonneck, O.G.T. "Die drei Fassungen des Hasse'schen Artaserse." *Sammelbände der Internationalen Musik-Gesellschaft* 14 (1912-13): 226.

Downes, E.O.D. "Secco Recitative in Early Classical Opera Seria (1720-80)." *Journal of the American Musicological Society* 14 (1961): 50.

Prota-Giurleo, U. "Notizie nel settecento." *Analecta Musicologica* no. 2 (1965): 124.

Torcellan, G. "Scritti su Ortes," "Documenti su Mozart a Venezia: dal carteggio di G.A. Hasse e Ortes." In *Settecento Veneto a altri scritti storici,* 35, 149. Turin, 1969.

Abert, A.A. "Opera in Italy and the Holy Roman Empire." In *New Oxford History of Music,* vol. 7, pp. 13, 36. London, 1973.

Viertel, K.-H. "Neue Dokumente zu Leben und Werk J.A. Hasses." *Analecta Musicologica* no. 12 (1973): 209.

Heartz, Daniel. "Raaff's Last Aria: a Mozartian Idyll in the Spirit of Hasse." *Musical Quarterly* 60 (1974): 517.

Millner, F.L. "Hasse and London's Opera of the Nobility." *Music Review* 35 (1974): 240.

Strohm, Reinhard, "Hasse, Scarlatti, Rolli." *Analecta Musicologica* no. 15 (1975): 220.

Heartz, Daniel. "Hasse, Galuppi and Metastasio." In *Venezia e il melodramma nel settecento,* edited by Maria T. Muraro, 309. Florence, 1978.

Monelle, Raymond. "Recitative and Dramaturgy in the Dramma per Musica." *Music and Letters* 59 (1978): 245.

Strohm, Reinhard. "Zu Vivaldis Opernschaffen." In *Venezia il melodramma nel settecento.* edited by Maria T. Muraro, 237. Florence, 1978.

Surian, Elvidio. "Metastasio, i nuovi cantanti, il nuovo stile: verso il Classicismo. Osservazioni sull *Artaserse.*" *Venezia e il melodramma nel settecento,* edited by Maria T. Muraro, 341. Florence, 1978.

Wolff, H.C. "Johann Adolf Hasse und Venedig." *Venezia e il melodramma nel settecento,* edited by Maria T. Muraro, 295. Florence, 1978.

Zeim, E. "Musikzentrum Dresden: Einige Notizien zur Ära Hasse." In *Musikzentren in der ersten Hälfte des 18. Jahrhunderts,* edited by Eitelfriedrich Thom, 64. Magdeburg, 1979.

Sachsen, Albert Herzog zu. "Die Barocke Hofmusik in Dresden und ihre Beziehungen zu Berlin und München." *Musik in Bayern* 2 (1980): 25.

Cummings, Graham. "Reminiscence and Recall in Three Early Settings of Metastasio's *Alessandro nell' Indie*" [*Poro*]. *Proceedings of the Royal Musical Association* 109 (1982-83): 80.

Analecta Musicologica 20 (1983) [an issue devoted to essays on *Tito* settings from Hasse to Mozart].

Landmann, Ortrun. "Ein deutscher 'italienischer' Komponist. Zum zweihundertsten Todestag von Johann Adolf Hasse." *Neue Zürcher Zeitschrift* 293 (1983): 35.

Haider-Pregler, Hilde. "Festopern am Wiener Hof im theresianischer Zeit" [*Ipermestra*]. In *Musik am Hof Maria Theresias. In Memoriam Vera Schwartz,* edited by Roswitha Vera Karpf, 41. Munich and Salzburg, 1984.

Lazarevich, Gordana. "Pasticcio Revisited: Hasse and his *parti buffe.*" In *Music and Civilization: Essays in Honor of Paul Henry Lang,* edited by Edmond Strainchamps, Maria Rika Marriates, and Christopher Hatch, 141. New York and London, 1984.

Lippmann, Friedrich. "Motivische Arbeit bei Hasse." *Analecta Musicologica* 22 (1984): 197.

Viertel, Karl-Heinz. "Zur Bedeutung von Johann Adolfe Hasse (1699-1783)." *Wissenschaft Beiträge der Martin-Luther-Universtät Halle* 38 (1984): 122.

unpublished–

Wilson, J. Kenneth. "*L' Olimpiade:* Selected Eighteenth-Century Settings of Metastasio's Libretto." Ph.D. dissertation, Harvard University, 1982.

*   *   *

Perhaps the most stable form in the history of opera was the so-called *opera seria* (a late term) of the eighteenth century, associated with a group of composers whom Charles Burney called the "Neapolitan school." It was already coming into being in the 1720s, yet it was still the point of reference for the young Mozart in the 1770s and even lies behind the serious Italian operas of Rossini. It has a better right to be called "classical" than, for example, the *dramme giocose* of Mozart, because it was so tightly organized and standardized, and because, superficially at least, it embodied the high moral ideals of classical drama. Nowadays it is little known about, because apart from Handel (whose Italian operas are not typical) there were no composers of the first rank who specialized in *opera seria*. The dominant figure was not a composer, in fact, but a librettist, Pietro Metastasio, whose dramas were set again and again by different composers.

Most *opera seria* composers had Neapolitan connections; Niccolo Porpora was born there, Leonardo Leo and Leonardo Vinci were born nearby and worked there for much of their lives. J. A. Hasse was an exception in being German, born near Hamburg, and in spending much of his creative life in Dresden. But even he worked in Naples during his formative years, from 1722 onward. Throughout his life he was known as "Il Sassone," some of his title pages bearing this name alone.

Hasse's operas are exclusively Italian in style, settings of libretti by Metastasio (his first setting of this poet was *Artaserse*, produced in Venice in 1730) and by other librettists such as Zeno, Stefano Benedetto Pallavicino and Claudio Pasquini. He married Faustina Bordoni, one of the century's greatest singers. His first Dresden opera was *Cleofide*, an adaptation of Metastasio's *Alessandro nell'Indie*. Since Metastasio was working in Vienna, Hasse was seldom the first composer of his librettos; naturally the job went to the Viennese kapellmeisters Caldara and Bonno. However, in 1744 Hasse was favored with two, *Antigono* (produced in Dresden) and *Ipermestra* (written for Vienna). An interesting correspondence occurred over the next Metastasio text to be written for the composer, *Attilio Regolo* (1750), in which the poet described in detail exactly how he wished the piece to be set to music; Hasse followed his instructions.

In Vienna after 1760 he became the first composer of several more Metastasio texts. His last opera *Ruggiero* was performed in Milan in 1771 during the same festivity as *Ascanio in Alba*, a serenata by the fifteen-year-old Mozart. The boy was so impressed that he learned almost all of the *Ruggiero* arias by heart.

Hasse was a fluent, elegant composer whose style altered very little during his long career. Arias were almost always in *da capo* form, and there are standard types which recur, not only the *aria patetica, aria di bravura, aria parlante, aria di mezzo carattere* and *aria brillante* listed by Goldoni, though these are easy to discern, but also pastoral arias, with imitations of doves, nightingales and sunrises, and arias of high drama, of anger, despair and love. In spite of the formulaic nature of many arias—similar themes constantly reappear—Hasse was truly a great melodist, and wrote several arias of surpassing beauty.

The twenty-two to thirty arias of a typical score were separated by long stretches of *recitativo semplice* accompanied only by continuo instruments. The orchestra played very largely in three parts; a modest wind section was added to the basic strings in the later works. There are some very fine *recitativi stromentati*, accompanied by the full orchestra, but these almost always appear in solo scenes at the ends of acts; they do not embrace dialogue or action.

Hasse's operas have six or seven characters, with arias allotted according to their importance—more for the *primo uomo* than for the *secondo uomo* or the *tenore*, for example. All four leading roles are sung by high voices, *castrati* in the case of the males. When there is a chorus, it is given very little to sing; the final ensemble, marked *coro*, is sung by the principals only.

Hasse boasted to Burney that he had set every opera of Metastasio at least once, except *Temistocle*. Because he often revised and adapted his scores it is impossible to say how many operas he composed in all; if adaptations are excluded the figure is about 50.

The reputation of Hasse as the definitive setter of Metastasio rests not so much on the superior quality of his music—there were other excellent *opera seria* composers—as on the length of his career; undoubtedly he was a model for Mozart's early operas, such as *Il re pastore*, and the "reform" of Gluck and Calzabigi was aimed principally at Metastasio and Hasse, by then the conservative wing of Viennese music. Also, the German scholars who unearthed *opera seria* in the early twentieth century tended to favor their compatriot, even suggesting there was something German, therefore profound, about his style. But the most remarkable thing about Hasse was his preservation of the classic *opera seria* type, with some modifications, throughout the half-century of his composing life.

—Raymond Monelle

HAYDN, Franz Joseph.

Born 31 March 1732? (baptized 1 April 1732), in Rohrau. Died 31 May 1809, in Vienna. Married: Maria Anna Keller, 26 November 1760. Studied with his paternal cousin Johann Mathias Franck in Hainburg; soprano in the choir of St Stephen's Cathedral in Vienna under the direction of Karl Georg Reutter, 1740; became a music tutor to a private family on the recommendation of Pietro Metastasio; accompanied students of Nicola Antonio Porpora in exchange for composition lessons; harpsichordist and singing teacher to Countess Thun, 1751; Kapellmeister to Count Ferdinand Maximilian von Morzin at his estate in Lukavec, 1759; second Kapellmeister at the Esterházy estate in Eisenstadt, 1761; first Kapellmeister at Esterháza, 1766; elected a member of the Modena Philharmonic Society, 1780; received a gold medal from Prince Henry of Prussia, 1784; commissioned to write *The Seven Last Words* for the Cathedral of Cádiz, 1785; given a diamond ring by King Friedrich Wilhelm II, 1787; took up permanent residence in Vienna, 1790; in London at the invitation of Johann Peter Salomon, 1791; honarary Mus.D. from Oxford University, 1791; met Beethoven in Bonn, 1792, and accepted him as a student; in London, 1794; became Kapellmeister once again to the Esterházy family; composition of sacred works, including 6 masses, 1796-1802; composition of *The Creation*, 1796-98; composition of *The Seasons*, 1799-1801; due to illness, resigned as Kapellmeister at Esterháza, 1802.

Operas

Editions:

J. Haydn's Werke. Edited by E. Mandyczewski et al. Leipzig, 1907-33.
J. Haydn: Kritische Gesamtausgabe. Edited by J.P. Larsen. Boston, Leipzig, and Vienna, 1950-1951.
J. Haydn: Werke. Edited by the J. Haydn-Institut, Cologne. Munich, 1958-.

Der krumme Teufel (Singspiel), J. Kurz, 1751?, Vienna, 29 May 1753 [lost].
Der neue krumme Teufel (Singspiel), J. Kurz, c. 1758? [lost].
Acide (festa teatrale), G.A. Migliavacca, 1762, Eisenstadt, 11 January 1763; revised 1773.

Franz Joseph Haydn, drawing by George Dance, 1794

La Marchesa Nespola, 1763 [fragmentary].
[opera buffa or Italian comedy]. 1762? [an aria and recitative survive]
Il dottore, c. 1761-65? [lost].
La vedova, c. 1761-65? [lost].
Il scanarello, c. 1761-65? [lost].
La canterina (intermezzo), G. Palomba (after the intermezzo *La canterina* in Niccolo Piccinni, *Origille*), 1760.
Lo speziale (*Der Apotheker*), C. Goldoni, 1768, Esterháza, fall 1768.
Le pescatrici (*Die Fischerinnen*), C. Goldoni, 1769, Esterháza, 16, 18 September 1770.
L'infedeltà delusa, (*Liebe macht erfinderisch, Untreue lohnt sich nicht*), M. Coltellini, 1773, Esterháza, 26 July 1773.
Philemon und Baucis oder Jupiters Reise auf die Erde (Singspiel/marionette opera), G.K. Pfeffel, 1773; revised, Esterháza, 2 September 1773.
Hexenschabbas (marionette opera), 1773? [lost].
L'incontro improvviso (*Die unverhoffte Zusammenkunft, Unverhofftes Begegnen*), K. Friebert (after Dancourt, *La rencontre imprévue*), 1775, Esterháza, 29 August 1775.
Dido (Singspiel/marionette opera), Bader, 1776?-78, Esterháza, March 1776, fall 1778.
Opéra comique vom abgebrannten Haus, c. 1773-79 [lost; may be identical to either *Hexenschabbas* or *Die bestrafte Rachbegierde*].
Die Feuersbrunst? (Singspiel/marionette opera), 1775?-78.
Genovefens vierter Theil, 1777.
Il mondo della luna (*Die Welt auf dem Monde*), C. Goldoni, 1777, Esterháza, 3 August 1777.
Die bestrafte Rachbegierde (Singspiel/marionette opera), Bader, 1779?, Esterháza, 1779.
La vera costanza, F. Puttini, 1778?-79, Esterháza, 25 April 1779; revised as *Der flatterhafte Liebhaber* (*Der Sieg der Beständigkeit, Die wahre Beständigkeit, List und Liebe, Laurette*), P.U. Dubuisson, 1785.
L'isola disabitata (*Die wüste Insel*) (azione teatral), Metastasio, 1779, Esterháza, 6 December 1779; finale revised, 1802.
La fedeltà premiata (*Die belohnte Treue*), after G. Lorenzi, *L'infedeltà fedele,* 1780, Esterháza, 25 February 1781.
Orlando paladino (*Der Ritter Roland*), C.F. Badini, N. Porta (after Ariosto), 1782, Esterháza, 6 December 1782.
Armida, 1783, Esterháza, 26 February 1784.
L'anima del filosofo ossia Orfeo ed Euridice, C.F. Badini, 1791.

Other works: oratorios, symphonies, chamber music, piano works, choruses, songs.

Publications/Writings

By HAYDN: books–

Landon, H.C. Robbins, ed. *The Collected Correspondence and London Notebooks of Joseph Haydn.* London, 1959.
Bartha, Dénes, ed. *Gesammelte Briefe und Aufzeichnungen.* Kassel, 1965.

About HAYDN: books–

Wendschuh. *Über Joseph Haydn's Opern.* Halle, 1896.
Geiringer, K. *Joseph Haydn.* Potsdam, 1932.
Wirth, H. *Joseph Haydn als Dramatiker: sein Bühnenschaffen als Beitrag zur Geschichte der deutschen Oper.* Wolfenbüttel and Berlin, 1940.

Geiringer, K. *Haydn: a Creative Life in Music.* New York, 1946; enlarged 2nd ed., 1963; 1968; revised and enlarged, Berkeley and Los Angeles, 1982; translated into French, 1984.
Hughes, Rosemary. *Haydn.* London, 1950; 5th ed., 1975.
Wirth, H. *Joseph Haydn: Orfeo ed Euridice: Analytical Notes.* Boston, 1951.
Bartha, Dénes, and Laszlo Somfai. *Handel als Opernkapellmeister.* Budapest, 1960.
Redfern, B. *Haydn: a Biography, with a Survey of Books, Editions and Recordings.* London, 1970.
Landon, H.C. Robbins. *Haydn.* London, 1972.
Zeman, Herbert, ed. *Joseph Haydn und die Literatur seiner Zeit.* Eisenstadt, 1976.
Landon, H.C. Robbins. *Haydn: Chronicle and Works.* London, 1976-80.
_____. *Haydn: A Documentary Study.* London and New York, 1981.
Larsen, Jens Peter. *The New Grove Haydn.* London and New York, 1982.
Mraz, Gerda, Gottfried Mraz and Gerald Schlag, eds. *Joseph Haydn in seiner Zeit.* Eisenstadt, 1982.
Feder, Georg, Heinrich Hüschen and Ulrich Tank, eds. *Joseph Haydn: Tradition und Rezeption.* Regensburg, 1985.
Badura-Skoda, Eva, ed. *Proceedings of the International Joseph Haydn Congress: Vienna 1982.* Munich, 1986.
Landon, H.C. Robbins, and David Wyn Jones. *Haydn: His Life and Music.* London, 1988.

articles–

Prefaces and critical commentaries to *La canterina* (25/2), *Lo speziale* (25/3), *L'incontro improvviso* (25/6), *L'infedeltà delusa* (25/5), *Armide* (25/12), *La fedeltà premiata* (25/10), *Philemon und Baucis* (24/1), *Le pescatrici* (25/4), *Orlando Paladino* (25/11), *L'anima del filosofo ossia Orfeo ed Euridice* (25/13), *La vera costanza* (25/8), *Textbücher verschollener Singspiele* (24/2), *Die Feuersbrunst* (24/3), *Acide und andere Fragmente* (25/1). In *J. Haydn: Werke,* edited by the J. Haydn-Institut, Cologne. Munich, 1959-76.
Haas, R. "Teutsche Comedie Arien." *Zeitschrift für Musikwissenschaft* 3 (1921): 405.
Geiringer, Karl. "Haydn as an Opera Composer." *Proceedings of the Royal Musical Association* 66 (1940).
_____. "The Operas of Haydn." *Musical America* (1940).
Landon, H.C. Robbins. "Some Notes on Haydn's Opera 'L'infedeltà delusa'." *Musical Times* 102 (1961): 356; in German, *Österreichische Musikzeitschrift* 16 (1961): 481.
_____. "Haydn's Marionette Operas and the Repertoire of the Marionette Theatre at Esterház Castle." *Haydn-Yearbook* 1 (1962): 111.
_____. "Haydn and his Operas." *Opera* August (1965).
Porter, A. "L'incontro improvviso." *Musical Times* 107 (1966): 202.
Feder, Georg. "Einige Thesen zu dem Thema: Haydn als Dramatiker." *Haydn-Studien* 2 (1969): 126.
_____. "Ein Kolloquium über Haydns Opern." *Haydn-Studien* 2 (1969): 113.
Müller-Blattau. "Zu Haydns Philemon und Baucis." *Haydn-Studien* 2 (1969): 66.
Thomas, Günter. "Zu 'Il mondo della luna' und 'La fedeltà premiata': Fassungen und Pasticcios." *Haydn-Studien* 2 (1969): 122.
Badura-Skoda, Eva. "Teutsche Comoedie-Arien' und Joseph Haydn." In *Der junge Haydn: International Arbeitstagung des Instituts für Aufführungspraxis,* 59. Graz, 1970.

Porter, A. "Haydn and 'La fedeltà premiata'." *Musical Times* 112 (1971): 331.

Hoboken, A. van. "Nunziato Porta und der Text von Joseph Haydns Oper 'Orlando Paladino'." In *Symbolae historiae musicae: Hellmut Federhofer zum 60. Geburtstag,* 170. Mainz, 1971.

Landon, H.C. Robbins. "A New Authentic Source for La Fedeltà Premiata by Haydn." *Soundings* 2 (1971-2): 6; in German, *Beiträge zur Musikdokumentation: Franz Grasberger zum 60. Geburtstag,* 213. Tutzing, 1975.

Geiringer, K. "From Guglielmi to Haydn: the Transformation of an Opera." *International Musicological Society Report* 11 (1972): 391.

Landon, H.C. Robbins. "The Operas of Haydn." In *New Oxford History of Music,* vol. 7, 172. London, 1973.

Allroggen, G. "Piccinni's 'Origille'." *Analecta Musicologica* no. 15 (1975): 258 [discusses libretto of *La canterina*].

Feder, Georg. "Opera seria, opera buffa und opera semiseria bei Haydn." In *Opernstudien: Anna Amalie Abert zum 65. Geburtstag,* 37. Tutzing, 1975.

Smith, Erik. "Haydn and *Le fedeltà premiata*." *Musical Times* 120 (1979): 567.

Kolk, Joel. " 'Sturm und Drang' and Haydn's Opera." In *Haydn Studies,* edited by Jens Peter Larsen, Howard Serwer, and James Webster, 440. New York and London, 1981.

Thomas, Günter. "Observations on *Il Mondo della luna.*" In *Haydn Studies,* edited by Jens Peter Larsen, Howard Serwer, and James Webster, 144. New York and London, 1981.

Walter, Horst. "On the History of the Composition and Performance of *La vera costanza*." In *Haydn Studies,* edited by Jens Peter Larsen, Howard Serwer, and James Webster, 154. New York and London, 1981.

Klein, Rudolf. "Joseph Haydn und die Oper." *Wiener Journal* 15-16 (1981-82): 36.

Avant-scène opéra July-August (1982) [*Orlando paladino* issue].

Badura-Skoda, Eva. "Zur Entstehungsgeschichte von Haydns Oper *La vera costanza.*" *Österreichische Musikzeitung* 37 (1982): 487.

Geyer-Kiefl, Helen. "Haydns vis comica." *Österreichische Musikzeitschrift* 37 (1982): 22.

Feder, Georg. "Bermerkung zu Haydns Opern." *Österreichische Musikzeitung* 37 (1982): 154.

Landon, H.C. Robbins. "Joseph Haydn als Opernkomponist und Kapellmeister." In *Joseph Haydn in seiner Zeit,* edited by Gerda Msaz et al., 249. Eisenstadt, 1982.

————. "Out of Haydn." *Opera News* 47 (1982): 9.

Leopold, Silke. "Haydn und die Tradition der Orpheus-Opern." *Musica* 36 (1982): 131.

Lippmann, Friedrich. "Haydns *La fedeltà premiata* und Cimarosas *L'infedeltà fedele*." *Haydn-Studien* 5 (1982): 1.

Thomas, Günter. "Kostüme und Requisiten für die Uraufführung von Haydns *Le pescatrice*." *Haydn-Studien* 5 (1982): 62.

Lippmann, Friedrich. "Haydn e l'opera buffa: tre confronti con opere italiane coeve sullo stesso testo." *Nuova rivista musicale italiana* 17 (1983): 223.

Rossi, Nick. "Haydn and Opera." *Opera Quarterly* spring (1983).

Thomas, Günter. "Anmerkungen zum Libretto von Haydns *festa teatrale Acide*." *Haydn Studien* 5 (1983): 118.

Braga, Michael. "Haydn, Goldoni and *Il mondo della luna*." *Eighteenth Century Studies* 17 (1983-84).

Carli Ballola, Giovanni. "Metastasio secondo Haydn." *Chigiana* 36 (1984): 79.

Feder, Georg. "I melodrammi di Haydn e le loro edizioni." *Chigiana* 36 (1984): 5.

Hunter, Mary. "Haydn's Sonata Form Arias." *Current Musicology* 37-38 (1984): 19.

Rice, John A. "Sarti's *Giulio Sabino,* Haydn's *Armida,* and the Arrival of Opera Seria at Esterháza." *Haydn Yearbook* 15 (1984): 181.

Thomas, Günter. "Zur Frage der Fassungen in Haydns *Il mondo della luna*." *Analecta Musicologica* 22 (1984): 405.

Hunter, Mary Kathleen. "Text, Music and Drama in the Italian Opera Arias of Joseph Haydn: Four Case Studies." *Journal of Musicology* 7 (1989): 29.

unpublished–

Hunter, Mary Kathleen. "Haydn's Aria Forms: A Study of the Arias in the Italian Operas Written at Esterházy, 1766-1783." Ph.D. dissertation, Cornell University, 1982.

Clark, Caryl. *The Opera Buffa Finales of Joseph Haydn.* Ph.D. dissertation, Cornell University, 1991.

*   *   *

Haydn's production of operas spans the majority of his working life. His earliest German *Singspiele* were written before he began working for Prince Esterházy, while his last Italian opera was written (but never performed) in 1791 during his first sojourn in London. *Philemon und Baucis* is the only fully-authenticated complete German *Singspiel* that has survived; the remainder are either of doubtful authenticity or lost. By contrast, all but the very earliest Italian-language works survive complete. The German-language works are all comic; some of them were written for the marionette theater at Eszterháza, which was capable of spectacular scenic effects. The storm at the beginning of *Philemon und Baucis* is only one small example of this phenomenon. The Italian-language works range from relatively short, completely comic intermezzi like *La canterina,* through comic operas with serious or sentimental characters, to fully-fledged examples of *opera seria.* Over the course of Haydn's career, there is a general progression from the former type of opera to the latter; this may be largely connected to changes in Prince Nicholas Esterházy's taste.

With the exception of the earliest *Singspiele,* and the late *L'anima del filosofo,* Haydn's operas were written in the limited but significant social context of the Esterházy court. Before 1776, Prince Nicholas commissioned Haydn to write operas for particular celebratory occasions, and there were few if any other operas performed during these years. *Lo speziale* was written for the opening of the Esterháza opera house in 1768, for example, and *L'infedeltà delusa* was written to celebrate the visit of the Empress Maria Theresia to Esterháza. From 1776 until 1790, operas were a major part of the regular season of entertainment, and Haydn's took their place alongside works by Anfossi, Cimarosa, Righini, Paisiello, Piccinni, Sarti, Salieri and other successful Italian opera composers. Haydn rearranged, rehearsed, and directed multiple performances of these works, and clearly knew them all intimately. Even before this immersion, however, Haydn's proximity to poet laureate Metastasio and his lessons with the older Italian operatic master Porpora suggest that he was well acquainted with the tradition of Italian opera, both serious and comic. It is therefore relevant and important to see his own operas in this context.

All of Haydn's libretti had been set previously by other composers. Three (see works list) are texts by Goldoni set by several composers before him. The majority of his remaining operas are resettings of libretti with connections to Vienna; *L'incontro improvviso* is a resetting of Gluck's *La rencontre imprévue,* given in Vienna numerous times in the 1760s. A group of works performed in Vienna in 1777 resurface in settings by Haydn over the next 7 years. These include *L'isola disabitata* (Haydn, 1779), a much-set short work by Metastasio, performed in Vienna as a benefit for the singer Metilde Bologna in a setting by Luigi Bologna (Madame Bologna became one of the leading singers at Esterháza from 1781-1790); Puttini's *La vera costanza,* set by Pasquale Anfossi; Badini's *Orlando paladino,* reworked by Nunziato Porta (Esterháza house librettist from 1781) and set by Guglielmi with possible additions by Anfossi; and the much-beloved story of Armida, in a version by Giovanni Bertati and Johann Gottlieb Naumann (Haydn did not in fact set this version of *Armida,* but a variant of it). The origins of the libretto of *L'infedeltà delusa* are not so clear; however, a work of the same title was performed by a company of noble young ladies in the garden of the Imperial Palace in Vienna in 1765, and this may shed new light on the choice of this libretto for Maria Theresia's visit to Esterháza in 1773. Of Haydn's later operas for Esterháza, only *La fedeltà premiata* bears no relation to Vienna; this is a reworking of a text by Giambattista Lorenzi, set first by Cimarosa as *L'infedeltà fedele* (Naples, 1779).

In addition to having clear connections to the Viennese repertory, the operas Haydn composed after 1776 also reflect trends within the Esterháza repertory itself, and often have clear similarities to at least one other work premiered in the same season. For example, the sentimental comedy *La vera costanza* (1779) has much in common with Anfossi's *L'incognita perseguitata* (1779), or the same composer's *La finta giardiniera* (1780). The "dramma eroicomico" *Orlando paladino* (1782) has clear connections with Traëtta's *Il cavaliere errante* (1782). Like *Orlando paladino, Armida* (1784) reflects a growing interest in heroic subject matter and in *opera seria;* Sarti's *Giulio Sabino* was the first opera seria performed at Esterháza in 1783. *Armida* also connects thematically with Luigi Bologna's *L'isola di Calipso abbandonata* (1784).

It has frequently been noted about Haydn's operas that they are "insufficiently dramatic"—that despite their undoubted musical value, they fail to articulate and flesh out their texts. There is little evidence that Haydn badgered his librettists with the insistence and intensity of a Mozart, and it is true that the relatively relentless alternation of recitative and aria seems "undramatic" to modern taste. On the other hand, within the constraints of the genre as Haydn knew it in the late 1770s and early 1780s (before Mozart had started on *The Marriage of Figaro*), there is much to value in his operas.

Haydn's music is invariably beautiful, and on occasion this beauty is put to impressive dramatic effect. For example, in the first act finale of *Il mondo della luna,* where the dupe Buonafede believes himself to be going to the moon and his daughter and maid believe he is dying, the orchestral music weaves a web around the broken utterances of the characters, and gives emotional plausibility to a superficially trivial situation in a manner which directly anticipates Mozart's *Così fan tutte.* Haydn is also to be valued for his ability to embody a dramatic or psychological situation in music. For example, when the blustering Rodomonte arrives on the scene in act II of *Orlando paladino,* Haydn writes an aria with a single thematic idea which vividly encapsulates the inarticulate and apparently pointless fury of this character. In the first-act finale of the same opera, a sudden modulation from Bb major to B major, accompanied by a change in tempo and meter, brings home to the audience the affective distance between

the world dominated by Rodomonte's pursuit of the princess Angelica, and the world shaped by Angelica's own thoughts and emotions.

In general, Haydn's shaping and deployment of musical form in his arias vividly projects both character and situation. Haydn's well-known propensity for word-painting is also present in his operas, particularly where nature images are invoked. A few of the many examples include the *Sturm und Drang* beginning to *Philemon und Baucis,* the ideal garden imagined by Buonafede in *Il mondo della luna,* or Rinaldo's final temptation in *Armida.*

Haydn's operas did not achieve the contemporary pan-European success of Paisiello's or Cimarosa's; nevertheless, the later works (from *La vera costanza* on) all enjoyed modest success in German-speaking countries (mostly in German translation). *La vera costanza* was performed, much altered, in Paris in 1791 as *Laurette,* and *Armida* was given in Turin in 1804. All of Haydn's operas were consigned to oblivion through the nineteenth century and well into the twentieth, with the exception of *Lo speziale,* which had some modest success in a one-act German-language version. There have been modern revivals of all the Italian operas, of *Philemon und Baucis* and of the unauthenticated *Die Feuersbrunst;* most have been commercially recorded.

—Mary Hunter

HAYM, Nicola Francesco.

Librettist/Musician/Scholar. Born 6 July 1678, in Rome. Died 11 August 1729, in London. Violone player in Cardinal Ottoboni's private orchestra under Corelli, Rome, 1694-1700; chamber musician to the second Duke of Bedford, London, 1701-11; played in the orchestra of the Queen's Theatre in the Haymarket, 1708; assisted in the preparation of Clayton's all-Italian opera *Arsinoe,* 1705; arranged Bononcini's *Camilla,* 1706, A. Scarlatti's *Pirro e Demetrio,* 1708, Bononcini's *Etearco,* 1711, and the pasticcios *Dorinda* (1712), *Creso* (1714), and *Lucio Vero* (1715); bass player for the Duke of Chandos, Cannons, 1718; secretary of the Royal Academy of Music, 1722-28, providing many librettos for the composers of the company (Ariosti, Bononcini, Handel); member of the Academy of Ancient Music, 1726-27. In addition to Haym's activities as a performer, teacher, librettist, and scholar, he composed a considerable amount of music and edited music for the firm of Estienne Roger in Amsterdam.

Librettos

Teseo, G.F. Handel, 1713.
Amadigi (Haym?), G.F. Handel, 1715.
Radamisto (Haym?), G.F. Handel, 1720.
Ottone, G.F. Handel, 1723.
Flavio, G.F. Handel, 1723.
Caio Marzio Coriolano, A. Ariosti, 1723.
Vespasiano, A. Ariosti, 1724.
Artaserse, A. Ariosti, 1724.
Calpurnia, G. Bononcini, 1724.
Giulio Cesare, G.F. Handel, 1724.
Tamerlano, G.F. Handel, 1724.
Rodelinda, G.F. Handel, 1725.
Elisa (pasticcio), 1726.
Admeto (Haym?), G.F. Handel, 1727.

Lucio Vero, imperator di Roma (Haym?), A. Ariosti, 1727.
Teuzzone (Haym?), A. Ariosti, 1727.
Astianatte, G. Bononcini, 1727.
Siroe, G.F. Handel, 1728.
Tolomeo, G.F. Handel, 1728.

Publications

By HAYM: books and articles–

For Haym's writings, see Lindgren, "Accomplishments," 1987.

About HAYM: books–

Deutsch, O.E. *Handel: a Documentary Biography.* London, 1955; New York, 1974.
Lindgren, Lowell. *A Bibliographic Scrutiny of Dramatic Works set by Giovanni and his Brother Antonio Maria Bononcini.* Ann Arbor, Michigan, 1974.
Dean, Winton, and John Merrill Knapp. *Handel's Operas: 1704-1726.* Oxford, 1987.
Gibson, Elizabeth. *The Royal Academy of Music 1719-1728: the Institution and its Directors.* New York, 1989.
Harris, Ellen T. *The Librettos of Handel's Operas.* 13 vols. New York, 1989.

articles–

Dahnk-Baroffio, E. "Nicola Hayms Anteil an Händels Rodelinde-Libretto." *Die Musikforschung* 7 (1954): 295.
Monson, Craig. " 'Giulio Cesare in Egitto': from Sartorio (1677) to Handel (1724)." *Music and Letters* 66 (1985): 313.
Lindgren, Lowell. "The Accomplishments of the Learned and Ingenious Nicola Francesco Haym." *Studi musicali* 16 (1987): 247.

*   *   *

Although little known today, Nicola Haym was surely Handel's most important librettist; he stands in the same relation to Handel as Arrigo Boito stands to Verdi. Both Haym and Boito understood the nature of opera not only as librettists but as composers, and both prepared librettos for operas considered among the best written by their composer-collaborators. Haym's librettos for Handel include *Ottone, Giulio Cesare, Tamerlano,* and *Rodelinda,* operas from 1723-25 that mark the high point of the Royal Academy of Music. Like practically all of Handel's texts, these and all of Haym's librettos are adaptations of earlier operatic texts, which vary from a 1675 French text by Philippe Quinault for *Teseo* (1713) to a 1727 Italian text by Pietro Metastasio for *Siroe* (1725). In addition to his work as a librettist and composer, Haym was also a first-rate cellist and a scholar. Unfortunately, his two-volume *History of Musick* that was advertised in 1726 does not survive.

Haym played an important role in the production of operas in London from the time of his arrival in 1701. For the extremely popular London production of Giovanni Bononcini's *Camilla* (1706), Haym not only adapted the opera, but composed new settings for the recitatives. Alessandro Scarlatti's *Pyrrhus and Demetrius* (1708) was also adapted by Haym, who this time not only provided new recitatives but also composed a new overture and twenty-one songs. The anonymous "A Critical Discourse on Opera's and Musick in England" (1709), which offers a devastating attack on London operatic productions of the immediately preceding period, reserves praise only for *Camilla* and *Pyrrhus;* this led the contemporary producer Charles Gildon to identify the author of the "Discourse" as "Seignior H[aym] or some Creature of his."

Given his prominence it is not surprising that Handel collaborated with Haym soon after his arrival in London: *Teseo* (1713) definitely has a text by Haym; and *Amadigi* (1715) has been attributed to Haym because of a payment made to him for the revival in 1717 and also the similarity of the adaptation to that of *Teseo.* With the opening of the Royal Academy in 1719, Haym was hired as one of two first cellists, a role he continued to play until his death in 1729. In 1722, he also acceded to the position of Secretary and principal librettist, displacing Paolo Rolli.

The typical opera libretto from this period follows a relatively rigid pattern of construction that consists of a succession of scenes; each scene is typically delineated by entrances of characters at its beginning and exits at the end. Formally these scenes generally consist of recitative leading up to a concluding aria, and the arias generally follow the *da capo* form in which the text is divided into two usually symmetrical parts; the first part is repeated with its original music ornamented by the singer after the second part is heard, generating the large-scale ABA form. Each of the three acts of such operas frequently contain twelve or more scenes, with each scene following a similar format and ending with a *da capo* aria, after which the singer exits the stage. The advantage of this repetitive and predictable structure was that relatively simple changes to it could be dramatically very effective.

Haym's style of adaptation is typified by few alterations. By and large he retained about half of the arias from his source librettos; the unused arias were eliminated altogether, altered, or replaced with new text. Recitative was heavily cut. More importantly, however, the drama was often condensed and intensified by structural changes, providing Handel with theatrically charged scenes that inspired some of his best operatic composition. At the end of act II in *Tamerlano,* for example, five scenes are compressed into one, with main characters exiting in mid-scene after participating in a trio or singing an aria, none of which are composed in *da capo* form until the final, culminating aria of the act.

Haym's style is also recognizable by a preference for short aria texts, typically of two or three lines in each part of the *da capo,* and rarely more than four. Further, the two parts of the text are usually balanced and symmetrical in terms of their rhyme schemes. Haym's favorite pattern, aab/ccb, offers both a closed rhyme in each section and a rhyme tagged across the sections. Four-line schemes are typically variations on this pattern, such as abbc/addc. Shorter texts, such as ab/ab, are typical of an older style; they appear in Haym's texts both because Haym left these unchanged from his source libretto and because he sometimes emulated them in his additions.

Copies of the source librettos for Haym's adaptations generally appear in the printed sale catalogue for Haym's library of books compiled immediately after his death and "Sold by Auction, on Monday the 9th of March 1929-30." Haym's library may therefore have been a major resource for the Royal Academy of Music. On the other hand, Handel certainly participated in the choice of operatic subject, and in some cases may have provided the libretto as well. For example, the composer was probably present at the Dresden 1719 production of Lotti's setting of Pallavincino's *Teofane* on which *Ottone* (1723) is based. The copy of *Teofane* in Haym's library may therefore have been the copy Handel acquired at the performance, the composer himself having decided to set this text and given it to Haym for adaptation.

All Handel operas definitely attributable to Haym include a dedicatory letter signed by him in the printed libretto. A few librettos lacking this dedication have also been attributed to Haym. *Amadigi,* discussed above, is one. *Radamisto* (1720) was attributed to Haym by Charles Burney in *A General History of Music* (1789), and the source libretto exists in two copies in the list of Haym's library. That Handel would choose a known collaborator for his first opera for the Royal Academy seems likely, and the style of adaptation matches Haym's. On the other hand, *Admeto* (1727) has sometimes been attributed to Haym, but the style is rather that of Rolli. Three of Handel's operas produced after Haym's death have also been considered possibly Haym's work. Although the stylistic evidence argues strongly against his authorship of *Sosarme* (1732), the operas *Partenope* (1730) and *Orlando* (1732) may well be based on adaptations he prepared.

—Ellen T. Harris

HELDY, Fanny (born Marguerite Virginia Emma Clementine Deceuninck).

Soprano. Born 29 February 1888, in Ath, near Liège. Died 13 December 1973, in Paris. Studied at Liège Conservatory; debut at Théatre de la Monnaie, Brussels, 1910, and remained there until 1912; appeared in Monte Carlo, Warsaw and St Petersburg; debut in Paris at Opéra-Comique as Violetta, 1917; debut at Paris Opéra as Gounod's Juliette, 1920-21 season; appeared at Teatro alla Scala, sang Manon at Covent Garden, 1926; created Portia in Hahn's *Le marchand de Venise* and the Duke of Reichstad in Ibert and Honegger's *L'aiglon.*

*   *   *

"The soprano is young, comely and an accomplished artist; her voice of clear, ringing quality and delightfully even throughout": the words are not particularly memorable in themselves, but they carry some weight as coming from the veteran critic Herman Klein. He was writing of Fanny Heldy in *Manon* at Covent Garden in 1926, and he could do so in the light of experience that took him back well into the age when the opera was written.

Klein's enthusiasm for Fanny Heldy has not always been shared by record-collectors, who have tended to find a hardness in the ringing quality and a tone too bright for comfort. Some critics, it must be said, gained that impression too. Newman reported on her voice as "an excellent instrument that is played on sometimes badly and others none too well." Sorabji, an acute if testy observer, found her "too French, too fidgety": "she sings in a typical French way—that dreadful tight, hard, 'dans la masque' business pushed to extremes." Some who thought her Manon unsympathetic considered her right for her second London role, that of Concepcion in *L'heure espagnole,* though again Sorabji objected: "When *will* that Northern superstition die out that Spanish women pass through life with their hands on their hips?" Others liked her better. The *Daily Telegraph* spoke of "perfect clarity, plenty of power, pure as a bell, produced with consummate ease,"

and another even described it as a "rich-toned voice." The *Musical Times* was either more fair or more diplomatic: according to this account, the voice was "never hard but always with a very bright, forward production that would infallibly make for hardness in a less skilful artist." She was, they said, "a charming creature, and it was a delight to watch her successful skating on the thin ice of her method."

London effectively had only one season to debate her merits (she appeared briefly in 1928 but was ill); Paris had a period of twenty years (from 1917 to 1937) during which she was the acknowledged star first of the Opéra-Comique and then the Opéra. This is a substantial career, and such "thin ice" as was described by the London critic could hardly have withstood the weight of twenty years skating without mishap. She had a reasonably enterprising repertoire—Mélisande and the three women in *Les contes d'Hoffmann* were among her great successes. She won the regard of Toscanini, who invited her to the Teatro alla Scala, and she took her fair share of the new operas, unpromising as much of the material was. Though it sometimes seemed that she cared more for her racehorses than for the more serious aspects of her art, she nevertheless took her acting seriously enough to be coached for *La traviata* by Sarah Bernhardt. A scholarship founded in her name is still awarded to promising young singers to this day.

What we hear of her on records remains a mixed pleasure. The earliest have the freshness and charm with less tendency to the hardness on high notes which mars her better-known solos and duets with the admirable Fernand Ansseau. One of her virtues is certainly that of steadiness, unimpaired as late as 1935 at least; and at the very least the Gallic brightness makes, as the *Musical Times* remarked, "a change from the fruity Germans."

—J. B. Steane

HELEN IN EGYPT
See DIE ÄGYPTISCHE HELENA

HEMPEL, Frieda.

Soprano. Born 26 June 1885, in Leipzig. Died 7 October 1955, in Berlin. Married William B. Kahn, 1918 (divorced 1926). Studied piano at Leipzig Conservatory; studied voice with Selma Nicklass-Kempner in Berlin at Stern Conservatory, 1902-05; debut as Frau Fluth in *Die lustigen Weiber von Windsor,* Berlin, 1905; sang at Schwerin, 1905-07; Covent Garden debut as Mozart's Bastienne and Humperdinck's Gretel, 1907; in Berlin, 1907-12; Metropolitan Opera debut as Queen in *Les Huguenots,* 1912.

Publications

By HEMPEL: books–

Mein Leben dem Gesang: Erinnerungen. Berlin, 1955.

About HEMPEL: articles–

Reed, P. et al. "The Recorded Art of Frieda Hempel." *Record Collector* 10 (1955): 53.

*   *   *

Frieda Hempel made a brilliant Berlin Opera debut in 1905 as Frau Fluth in Nicolai's *Die lustigen Weiber von Windsor;* she stayed there for five years, winning special acclaim in Mozart operas. In 1911, Richard Strauss offered Hempel her choice of the three leading women's roles in *Der Rosenkavalier* for its Berlin premiere. She chose that of the Marschallin. Strauss was delighted with her lyric voice and gracious interpretation. The following year he wanted her to create Zerbinetta in the Stuttgart launching of *Ariadne auf Naxos,* and composed with her in mind probably the most difficult bravura coloratura aria ever written, "Als ein Gott kam jeder gegangen." Gatti-Casazza, however, had been trying to persuade Hempel to join the Metropolitan Opera. His terms proved irresistible and Hempel accepted—much to Strauss's chagrin, for he knew of no other soprano capable of singing the aria and was forced to simplify it to the form now in the printed score.

On 27 December 1912, Hempel made her Metropolitan Opera debut as Marguerite de Valois in *Les Huguenots,* and the critics commended her voice's agility and ease. Of her Rosina in *Il barbiere di Siviglia* W.J. Henderson wrote that her facility in coloratura had not been surpassed "within the memory of the present generation." There followed her triumphant Queen of the Night, a role in which European critics had ranked her as the greatest exponent since Ilma di Murska. At Richard Strauss's request, she was the first to sing the Marschallin in America (9 December 1913) and in England (4 June 1914).

In the seven seasons spent singing for Gatti-Casazza, Hempel gave some 150 performances of seventeen leading parts. In 1915 Richard Aldrich wrote of her Rosina, "not for a good while has so pure and vibrant a soprano voice delivered the florid measures with so great ease and certainty." Then suddenly in 1919 she left the Metropolitan. No official reason was given for this, causing rumours to spread that Gatti-Casazza wanted Galli-Curci to join his company and that she had accepted conditional on Hempel's being jettisoned. Some thought that having given her best years to the opera public and made her name, she, like other prima donnas before and since, thought it wise to switch to the less arduous work of the concert platform and thus preserve her vocal skills for as long as possible.

Much profitable publicity was gained for Hempel through being selected to impersonate Jenny Lind at the Centennial Concert held in Carnegie Hall on 6 October 1920, when she sang the same program that the Swedish Nightingale had at her American debut in 1850. Opening with "Casta diva" from Bellini's *Norma,* Hempel enchanted her audience and, as a result, an enterprising impresario then arranged for her to repeat the program in costume at all the places Jenny had visited during her historic tour of 1850-51. Over the next decade Hempel gave some 300 such concerts in the United States and the British Isles. Actually she hardly resembled Lind.

Quite apart from these popular programs, Frieda Hempel held more serious recitals selecting what was then regarded as "advanced" music—songs by Brahms, Wolf, Mozart, Schubert and Schumann. It had been becoming increasingly difficult for her to reach high notes and this change made it possible for her to retire gracefully from attempting to compete with younger sopranos in opera houses. After her first recital on 5 January 1921, Richard Aldrich declared in the *New York Times* next day: "Her voice has rarely sounded more beautiful in its rounded smoothness, its color, its equality throughout its range." Hempel's finest achievement in this concert was her singing of the recitative and aria "Non mi dir" from *Don Giovanni.* "Here was the true Mozart style in as near perfection as it is now to be heard; a limpid and translucent delivery of the melody in the most equable tones, in artistic and well-considered phrasings; and, in the few measures at the end, in finished coloratura."

From then on, Hempel appeared nearly every season at Carnegie Hall or the New York Town Hall, giving at the latter her last recital on 7 November 1951. In Britain, besides touring, she sang at both the Queen's Hall and the Royal Albert Hall. Gerald Moore in *Am I Too Loud?* wrote that she asked him, as she did others, to omit the preludes to Wolf's "Er ist's" and "Ich hab' in Penna" because it made a better effect for her, and at the end just to play on for a chord when the voice part ends, saying that if he went on longer it might spoil her applause. Moore, however, would not give in to her.

Frieda Hempel's voice was a naturally brilliant soprano extending at least to the F *in alt* at the start of her career. It was animated and vibrant. Michael Scott in *The Record of Singing* compares her first recordings for Odeon in 1906 with the later series completed for H.M.V. and Victor. In the former, mostly in German, he finds the style "very provincial" with too elaborate ornamentation, but the top clearly more responsive. By 1911, in Adam's variations, Scott regards the passage work as fluent and the staccati as dazzlingly effective but points out that sometimes the "squeezed out" head notes fail to hit the mark and the intonation is occasionally sharp or flat. His final judgment is that while her voice is musical and often attractive it misses having the distinctive character that would place her among the great singers of her era.

The Record Collector for August 1955 contains a detailed discography of Frieda Hempel's art. Asked what were the best, George T. Keating chose: *Traviata* (Victor 88471), *Puritani* (Victor 87179 and 88470), *Bohème* (Gram. 053327), *Die Stumme von Portici* (Odeon 76904/5), *Huguenots* (Victor 88382, Gram. 033125), the Adam *Variations* (Victor 88404, Gram. 033114), *Die Zauberflöte* (Gram. 053260 and 043185) and *Robert le diable* (Gram. 033165). He especially recommended listening to Elvira's exacting aria and recitative from Auber's *Die Stumme von Portici* because it was a fine example of Hempel's technique and artistry in 1910.

—Charles Neilson Gattey

HENZE, Hans Werner.

Composer. Born 1 July 1926, in Gütersloh, Westphalia. Studied at the Braunschweig School of Music; military service in the Second World War; studied at the Kirchenmusikalisches Institut in Heidelberg and privately with Wolfgang Fortner; attended seminars on Schoenberg's twelve-tone system given by René Leibowitz at Darmstadt; lived in Ischia, Italy, 1953-56, then in Naples, and Marino; withdrew from membership in the Academy of the Arts of West Berlin; became a member of the Italian Communist Party; artistic director at the Music Institute, Montepulciano, 1976-81; has taught at the Hochschüle für Musik, Cologne, since 1980, and at the Philharmonic Academy, Rome, since 1981.

Operas

Publisher: Schott.

Das Wundertheater, after Cervantes (translated by A. Graf von Schack), 1948, Heidelberg, Stadttheater, 7 May 1949; revised 1964, Frankfurt Städtische Bühnen, 30 November 1965.

Boulevard Solitude (lyric drama), W. Jokisch (after G. Weil and Prévost), 1951, Hannover, Landestheater, 17 February 1952.

Ein Landarzt (radio opera), after Kafka, 1951, Hamburg, 29 November 1951; revised for the stage, 1964, Frankfurt, Städtische Bühnen, 30 November 1965.

Das Ende einer Welt (radio opera), W. Hildesheimer, 1953, Hamburg, 4 December 1953; revised for the stage, 1964, Frankfurt, Städtische Bühnen, 30 November 1965.

König Hirsch, H. von Cramer, 1952-55, Berlin, Städtische Oper, 23 September 1956; revised as *Il re cervo, or The Errantries of Truth,* Kassel, Staatstheater, 10 March 1963.

Hans Werner Henze, 1955

Der Prinz von Homburg, J. Bachmann (after Kleist), 1958, Hamburg, Staatsoper, 22 May 1960.

Elegy for Young Lovers, W. H. Auden and C. Kallman, 1959-61, Schwetzingen, 20 May 1961.

Der junge Lord, J. Bachmann (after W. Hauff), 1964, Berlin, Deutsche Oper, 7 April 1965.

Die Bassariden, W.H. Auden and C. Kallman (after Euripides), 1965, Salzburg, 6 August 1966.

Moralities (three scenic cantatas), W.H. Auden (after Aesop), 1967, Cincinnati, May Festival 18 May 1968.

Der langwierige Weg in die Wohnung der Natascha Ungeheuer (show), G. Salvatore, 1971, Rome, Radio Audizioni Italiana, 17 May 1971.

La cubana, oder Ein Leben für die Kunst (vaudeville), M.M. Enzensberger (after M. Barnet), 1973, New York, National Educational Television Opera Theater, 4 March 1974.

We Come to the River (actions for music), E. Bond, 1974-76, London, Royal Opera House, 12 July 1976.

Pollicino (children's opera). G. Di Leva (after Collodi, Grim, and Perault), 1979-80, Montepulciano, 2 August 1980.

The English Cat, E. Bond, 1980-83, Schwetzingen, 2 June 1983.

Ödipus der Tyrann (Spiel), Henze et al., 1983, Kindberg, 30 October 1983.

Das verratene Meer, H.-U. Treichel (after Y. Mishima), West Berlin, Deutsche Oper, 5 May 1990.

Other works: ballets, incidental music, film scores, orchestral works, choral works, solo vocal works, chamber music.

Publications

By HENZE: books–

Undine: Tagebuch eines Balletts. Munich, 1959.
Essays. Mainz, 1964.
With M.M. Enzensberger. *El Cimarrón: ein Werkbericht.* Edited by C.H. Henneberg. Mainz, 1971.
Brockmeier, Jens, ed. *Musik und Politik: Schriften und Gespräche 1955-1975.* Munich, 1976; translated into English by Peter Labanyi as *Music and Politics: Collected Writings 1953-81,* London, 1982.
Henze, Hans Werner, ed. *Zwischen den Kulturen. Neue Aspekte der musikalischen Ästhetik.* Frankfurt am Main, 1979; 1986.
——, ed. *Die Zeichen. Neue Aspekte der musikalischen Ästhetik.* Frankfurt am Main, 1981.
Müller, Hans-Peter, ed. *Schriften und Gespräche: 1955-1979.* Berlin, 1981.
"Die englische Katze." Ein Arbeitstagebuch, 1978-1982. Frankfurt am Main, 1983.
Mürztaler Musikwerkstatt, Steirischer Herbst '83, Mürzzuschlag, 1983.
Henze, Hans Werner, ed. *Neues Musiktheater.* Munich, 1988.

articles–

"Exkurs über den Populismus." In *Zwischen den Kulturen. Neue Aspekte der musikalischen Ästhetik,* edited by Hans Werner Henze, 7 Frankfurt am Main, 1979.
"*Pollicino:* eine Oper für Kinder." *Musik und Bildung* 13 (1981): 216.

interviews–

Baruch, G.-W. "Hans Werner Henze am Tyrrhenischen Meer: süd-italienischer Dialog." *Melos* 23 (1956): 70.

Heyworth, P. "I can imagine a Future . . . : Conversation with Hans Werner Henze." *The Observer* 23 August (1970).

Lück, H. "Der lange Weg zur Musik der Revolution." *Neue Musikzeitung* (1971).

Jungheinrich, H.K. "4 Stunden auf Henzes neuem Weg." *Melos* 39 (1972): 207.

Stürzbecher, U. *Werkstattgespräche mit Komponisten.* Cologne, 1972.

"The Bassarids: Hans Werner Henze talks to Paul Griffiths." *Musical Times* 115 (1974): 831.

Holland, Hubert. "Die Schwierigkeit, ein Bundesdeutscher Komponist zu sein: Neue Musik zwischen Isolierung und Engagement. Gespräch mit Hans Werner Henze." In *Musik 50er Jahre,* edited by Hanns-Werner Heister and Dietrich Stern, 50. Berlin, 1980.

Malmros, Anna-Lise. "Elitekunst og folkfestivaler: Interview med komponisten Hans Werner Henze." *Politisk revy* 17 (1980): 14.

Bachmann, C.H. " 'Ich wolte gern, dass es mir einmal glückt. . . .'" *Neue Zeitschrift für Musik* no. 3 (1985): 24.

Rexroth, D. " 'Ich begreife mich in der Schoenberg-Tradition'." *Neue Zeitschrift für Musik* no. 11 (1986): 23.

About HENZE: books–

Koeppen, W. *Der Tod in Rom.* Stuttgart, 1954; English translation, 1956.

Motte, D. de la. *Hans Werner Henze: Der Prinz von Homburg.* Mainz, 1960.

Geitel, K. *Hans Werner Henze.* Berlin, 1968.

Petersen, Peter. *Hans Werner Henze: Ein politischer Musiker.* Hamburg, 1986.

Rexroth, D., ed. *Der Komponist Hans Werner Henze.* Mainz, 1986.

articles–

Kuntz, E. "Hans Werner Henze." *Melos* 17 (1950): 341.

Wörner, K.H. "Hans Werner Henze." *Neue Zeitschrift für Musik* 112 (1951): 240.

Stephan, R. "Hans Werner Henze." *Die Reihe* 4 (1958): 32, English translation in *Die Reihe* 4 (1960): 32.

Pauli, H. "Hans Werner Henze." *Musica* 13 (1959): 761.

––––––. "Hans Werner Henze's Italian Music." *Score* no. 25 (1959): 26.

Melos 32 (1965) [special issue].

Österreichische Musikzeitung 21/no. 369 (1966) [*The Bassarids* issue].

Heyworth, P. "Henze and the Revolution." *Music and Musicians* 19 (1970): 36.

Henderson, Robert. "Henze's Progess: From *Boulevard Solitude* to *The Bassarids.*" *Opera* October (1974).

Burde, W. "Tradition und Revolution in Henzes musikalischem Theater." *Melos/Neue Zeitschrift für Musik* 2 (1976): 271.

Henderson, R. "Hans Werner Henze." *Musical Times* 117 (1976): 566.

Borris, Siegfried, compiler. "Bibliographie Hans Werner Henze. Eigene Schriften Bibliographie, Discographie." *Musik und Bildung* 10 (1978): 111.

Klein, Hans-Günter. "Ideologisierung von Werken Kleists in Opern aus dem 20. Jahrhunderts." *Norddeutsche Beiträge* 1 (1978): 44.

Barry, M. "Bedford, Cardew and Henze." *Music and Musicians* 27 (1979): 65.

Klüppelholz, Werner. "Zur Soziologie der neuen Musik." *International Review of the Aesthetics and Sociology of Music* 10 (1979): 73.

Rutz, Hans. "Hans Werner Henzes Werk und seine Stellung in der Musikentwicklung heute." *Universitas* 34 (1979): 143.

Dziewulska, Malgorzata. "Da Ponte naszyck czasów." *Ruch muzyczny* 10 (1980): 3.

Gronemayer, Gisela. "Zu Hans Werner Henzes *El rey de Harlem.*" *Österreichische Musikzeitung* 17 (1980): 14.

Miller, Norbert. "Geborgte Tonfälle aus der Zeit. Ingeborg Bachmanns *Der junge Lord* oder, Keine Schwierigkeiten mit der komischen Oper." In *Für und Wider der Literaturoper,* edited by Sigrid Wiesmann, 87. Laaber, 1982.

Schiffer, B. "Imaginäres Theater oder Programmusik?" *Neue Zeitschrift für Musik* no. 8 (1982): 50.

Vill, Susanne. "Über Opernrezeption im zeitgenössischen Tanztheater." In *Für und Wider der Literaturoper,* edited by Sigrid Wiesmann, 211. Laaber, 1982.

Nyffeler, M. "Einem neuen Realismus auf der Spur." *Neue Zeitschrift für Musik* no. 1 (1984): 15.

Stoianova, I. "*El Cimarron* de Henze." *Revue d'esthetique* no. 16 (1989): 135.

Clements, A. "Hans across the Ocean." *Opera* 41 (1990): 928.

Hatten, R.S. "Pluralism of Theatrical Genre and Musical Style in Henze's *We Come to the River.*" *Perspectives of New Music* 28 (1990): 292.

Hans Werner Henze is one of the preeminent composers of opera, and indeed of compositions in all genres, in the last half of the twentieth century. Part chameleon, part magpie, Henze changes his colors from opera to opera, lifting devices from various stylistic nests to construct vivid and effective musical theater. Henze's language and style are always identifiably his own, but from one opera to another one experiences striking contrasts. In two early operas the kaleidoscopic, fantastic *König Hirsch* (*King Stag*) follows the cosmopolitan, eclectic amalgamation of styles in *Boulevard Solitude.*

Next come his four works of the 1960s: *Der Prinz von Homburg* (*The Prince of Homburg*), in which Henze turned toward early nineteenth century bel canto style; *Elegy for Young Lovers,* a number opera using a free serial technique; *Der junge Lord* (*The Young Lord*), which begins on an E-flat chord and slips into more atonal harmonies as the comedy blackens; and *Die Bassariden* (*The Bassarids*), through-composed in four symphonic movements and returning to the use of tone rows.

In Henze's later works, inspired by social/revolutionary themes, he follows the bleak *Wir kommen zum Fluss* (*We Come to the River*) with the lighter *Die englische Katze* (*The English Cat*). We should not forget his politically informed theater pieces, *La Cubana, El Cimarrón,* and *Der langwierige Weg in die Wohnung der Natascha Ungeheuer* (*The Tedious Way to Natascha Ungeheuer's Flat*), and the oratorio *Der Floss vom Medusa* (*The Raft of the Medusa*), which some refer to as operas.

Although Henze was one of the first of the post-World War II composers to turn to serialism, he was also the first to move on to his own personal style in which tone rows are treated freely, and polytonality, atonality, jazz, and even tonality are interspersed, all in support of the musical and dramatic effect. In the earlier operas, the radio piece *Ein*

Landarzt (*A Country Doctor*) for example, Henze's twelve-tone writing seems more contrapuntal, less reliant on vertical structures, than in his later works. Chords and harmonies are still structured in thirds and fifths, although often not used in a tonal context. By the 1960s one finds more use of quartal harmonies in Henze's writing, which has, overall, become more vertical, although he is still a master of delicate chamber effects. Ostinatos are now more important, as are cluster effects. In many operas tonality is used to depict the world of the bourgeois, of decay, often in closed "parody" forms like Rachel's and the Emperor's arias in *Wir kommen zum Fluss.*

Form, as contrasted between numbers and large-scale symphonic structures, has been an important concern of Henze's throughout his career. In *König Hirsch* each piece forms a scene, and the finale from the original version became his Fourth Symphony. While sections are self-contained, bridge passages give the effect of the music's being through-composed. *Der Prinz von Homburg* is made up of scenes that are transformations of older genres such as rondo or fugue. For *Elegy for Young Lovers* Henze switched to a deliberately archaic number style, inspired in part by Hofmannsthal's experiments in integrating number and through-composed styles. Whereas *Elegy* is a succession of arias and ensembles, *Der junge Lord* contains only one aria and one duet, and the last act opens with a huge passacaglia that encompasses various smaller forms or numbers. Henze writes that his models for his ensembles here were Rossini and Mozart—*Barber, Figaro,* and especially *Così. Die Bassariden* returned to large-scale, through-composed structures; the opera takes the form of a four-movement symphony with sonata movement, scherzo, adagio and fugue with an interpolated intermezzo, and passacaglia.

A hallmark of Henze's work is his brilliant use of the orchestra, in developing chamber combinations and especially in creating inventive combinations of percussion instruments for new and intriguing sonorities. *Der Prinz von Homburg* utilizes a large chamber orchestra, with each scene given an individual instrumental grouping as well as a particular symphonic form. *Elegy* is scored for only single strings and winds, but a huge percussion ensemble assumes many of the functions normally assigned to the strings. For the succeeding opera, *Der junge Lord,* Henze went back to a string-based ensemble, inspired by the simplicity of Mozart's orchestra in *Die Entführung aus dem Serail. Wir kommen zum Fluss* incorporates three orchestras, each with unique groupings and styles.

Henze is one of the few contemporary composers attracted to various forms of comedy in his operas, although these elements are usually informed by social concerns. *König Hirsch* is more a phantasmagoria than a comedy, but *Elegy* is shot through with comic elements to relieve the basic tone of neurosis and tragedy. *Der junge Lord* is a black comedy, a morality play, with the ape dictating the customs of society. As Henze says, it is an *opéra comique*, not opera buffa. *Die englische Katze,* after Balzac, returns from the prevailing tragic tone of the previous two operas to combine comedy with social commentary, the motivating force in much of Henze's later work.

Henze's social statements have perhaps been more vividly expressed in the theater pieces than in the later operas because in the former he is free of the conventions of opera and of opera audiences' desire to be entertained. In the theater pieces he could blur the distinctions between actors/singers, instrumentalists, and audience so that, for example, the instrumentalists become actors in the drama. Henze developed here the lessons he learned writing opera, creating new ensembles of expression with which to proclaim his message of human dignity.

—David E. Anderson

HÉRODIADE [Herodias].

Composer: Jules Massenet.

Librettists: Paul Milliet, Henri Gremont [=Georges Hartmann] and Zamadini (after Flaubert).

First Performance: Brussels, Théâtre de la Monnaie, 19 December 1881

Roles: Hérode (baritone); Jean (tenor); Phanuel (bass); Vitellius (baritone); Salomé (soprano); Hérodiade (mezzo-soprano); High Priest (baritone); Voice (tenor); Young Babylonian (soprano); chorus (SSTTBB).

In his monumental *Annals of Opera* Alfred Loewenberg describes *Hérodiade* as "one of Massenet's most successful works; still performed on French stages." The judgment is eccentric but apt. Massenet's libretto was prepared by Milliet with help from the publisher Hartmann (under the pseudonym Gremont), based on a story by Flaubert, itself a very free adaptation from the bible; any similarities with Oscar Wilde's play and Strauss's opera are coincidental.

Massenet had anticipated a premiere at the Paris Opéra only to be faced with indifference. The Théâtre de la Monnaie in Brussels, under much more astute leadership, quickly snapped up the work for an enormously successful premiere in December 1881 with the composer conducting. Just two months later it was produced in an Italian version at the Teatro alla Scala, and there were early performances in Budapest and Hamburg before the first French production at Nantes. The opera only reached Paris in 1884, when it was presented in Italian at the Théâtre Italien with a stunning cast including Jean De Reszke in his tenor debut as Jean, his brother Edouard as Phanuel, Maurel as Hérode and Devries as Salomé. Subsequently the latter was substituted by Josephine De Reszke—the first occasion on which the three De Reszkes appeared together.

Despite the success of these performances, the opera did not really "take off." Its only Covent Garden production was in 1904 when it was retitled *Salomé.* Hammerstein introduced it to New York with a cast including Lina Cavalieri—no doubt a bewitching Salomé—and Maurice Renaud, and he also gave some performances in London. There have never been any performances at the Metropolitan and apparently none in Vienna. *Hérodiade* finally arrived at the Paris Opéra in 1921, and it was thenceforth performed reasonably frequently until the 1940s.

Much of the opera represents the best of Massenet. There is a sense in which the music of operas such as *Hérodiade, Esclarmonde* and *Le roi de Lahore* may seem interchangeable. However, *Hérodiade* has more showpiece arias than any of his operas outside *Manon* and *Werther.* Among many moments of rare beauty is Herod's aria "Vision fugitive"—an unforgettable paean to the unattainable. Salomé, a love-struck teenager rather than a nymphet or nymphomaniac, has a gracious aria of pure affection for Jean, himself almost the archetypal French heroic tenor. Hérodiade may be an unsympathetic character, but she has some fine music as she schemes and pleads for her evil ends, and this is perhaps symptomatic of the opera's real problem. The score is not lacking in dramatic impact, but somehow everything is too nice. All too often, as with the arias for Hérode and Hérodiade, the music does not really reflect some of the nastier goings-on even in this version of the story.

Possibly it is his predilection for such lush and evocative music which helped push Massenet out of fashion, with the exception of *Manon* and *Werther.* Nor is *Hérodiade* helped by a story which veers between the improbable and the incredible. Not surprisingly, Massenet ran into trouble with the Catholic authorities over this reworking of the Bible. He was virtually excommunicated after performances in Lyons in 1885, although there is no evidence that this made any difference to the popularity, or subsequent lack thereof, of the opera.

Massenet's operas have not been helped by decline in the French singing style, and the recorded history of the work certainly bears this out. There has never been a complete commercial recording, although at least one has been mooted. There are extant versions of live performances, of which only one recorded by the forces of French radio in 1974 is in tolerable sound. However, if this is compared to a single LP of highlights recorded under Georges Prêtre with Régine Crespin, Rita Gorr and Michael Dens, it emerges as little more than workmanlike. In turn the performances on the early LP bear no comparison with versions of the major arias from the days of 78s. Tamagno is thrilling and heroic, if somewhat unidiomatic, in Jean's aria and a snippet from one of the duets. Ansseau is far more lyrical in the aria, but the outstanding Jean is Vezzani, who recorded the aria and two duets. There is an interesting if slightly ghostly sounding recording of Salomé's aria "Il est doux" by Mary Garden, as well as fine performances by Calvé and Vallin. There are wonderful versions of Hérode's aria by Couzinou, Endrèze and Renaud, although for sheer beauty of singing Renaud is unmatched.

It is voices like those of Renaud, Vallin and Vezzani which bring out the lyric beauty of the score, and which suggest that reinstatement of *Hérodiade* in the repertoire will ultimately depend on the availability of appropriate singers.

—Stanley Henig

HERODIAS
See **HÉRODIADE**

HÉROLD, (Louis-Joseph) Ferdinand.

Composer. Born 28 January 1791, in Paris. Died 19 January 1833, in Thernes, near Paris. His father François-Joseph Hérold was a pupil of C.P.E. Bach, and a piano teacher and composer. Studied with Fétis at the Hix school; studied piano with Louis Adam, harmony with Catel, and composition with Méhul at the Paris Conservatory, 1806-1812; won the Prix de Rome for his cantata *Mlle de la Vallière,* 1812; pianist for Queen Caroline, Naples; first opera produced in Naples, 1815; in Vienna briefly before returning to Paris; chorus master of the Italian Opera, 1824; on the staff of the Grand Opéra, 1826; his opera *Zampa* (1831) very successful, and established his reputation as one of the best contemporary French composers.

Operas

La gioventù di Enrico quinto, Hérold (translated by Landriani, after Alexandre Duval, *La jeunesse de Henry V*), Naples, Teatro del Fondo, 5 January 1815.
Charles de France, ou Amour et gloire (with Boieldieu), Rancé, Marguerite Théaulon de Lambert and Armand d'Artois de Bournonville, Paris, Opéra-Comique, 18 June 1816.
Les rosières, Marguerite Théaulon de Lambert, Paris, Opéra-Comique, 27 January 1817.
La clochette, ou Le diable page, Marguerite Théaulon de Lambert, Paris, Opéra-Comique, 18 October 1817.
Le premier venu, ou Six lieus de chemin, Jean Baptiste Charles Vial and François Antoine Eugène de Planard, Paris, Opéra-Comique, 28 September 1818.
Les troquers, Achille and Armand d'Artois de Bournonville (after J.J. Vadé, 1753, based on Lafontaine), Paris, Opéra-Comique, 18 February 1819.
L'amour platonique, Auguste Rousseau, 1819.

Ferdinand Hérold

L'auteur mort et vivant, François Antoine Eugène de Planard, Paris, Opéra-Comique, 18 December 1820.

Le muletier, Paul de Kock (after Lafontaine, based on Boccaccio), Paris, Opéra-Comique, 12 May 1823.

Lasthénie, de Chaillou, Paris, Opéra, 8 September 1823.

Vendôme en Espagne (with Auber), E. Mennechet and Adolphe d'Empis, Paris, Opéra, 5 December 1823.

Le roi René, ou La Provence au XVe siècle, Belle and Charles Augustin Sewrin, Paris, Opéra-Comique, 24 August 1824.

Le lapin blanc, Anne Honoré Joseph Mélesville and Pierre Carmouch, Paris, Opéra-Comique, 21 May 1825.

Marie, François Antoine Eugène de Planard, Paris, Opéra-Comique, 12 August 1826.

L'illusion, J.H. Vernoy de Saint-Georges and C. Ménissier, Paris, Opéra-Comique, 18 July 1829.

Emmeline, François Antoine Eugène de Planard, Paris, Opéra-Comique, 28 November 1829.

L'auberge d'Auray (with Carafa), Moreau and d'Epagny, Paris, Opéra-Comique, 11 May 1830.

Zampa, ou La fiancée de marbre, Anne Honoré Joseph Mélesville, Paris, Opéra-Comique, 3 May 1831.

La marquise de Brinvilliers (with Auber, Batton, Berton, Blangini, Boieldieu, Carafa, Cherubini, and Paër), Eugène Scribe and F.H.J. Castil-Blaze, Paris, Opéra-Comique, 31 October 1831.

La médecine sans médecin, Eugène Scribe and J.F.A. Bayard, Paris, Opéra-Comique, 15 October 1832.

Le pré aux clercs, François Antoine Eugène de Planard (after Mérimée), Paris, Opéra-Comique, 15 December 1832.

Ludovic, J.H. Vernoy de Saint-Georges, Paris, Opéra-Comique, 16 May 1833 [posthumous; completed by F. Halévy].

Other works: vocal pieces, orchestral works, chamber music, piano works (including four piano concertos).

Publications

By HÉROLD: books–

Souvenirs inédits. Sammelbände der Internationalen Musikgesellschaft, 1910.

About HÉROLD: books–

Fétis, F.J. *Biographie universelle des musiciens et bibliographie générale.* Paris, 1835-44.

Adam, A. *E.H. Méhul. L.J.F. Hérold: Biographien.* Kassel, 1855.

————. *Souvenirs d'un musicien.* Paris, 1857.

Clement, F., and P. Larousse. *Dictionnaire lyrique, ou Histoire des opéras.* Paris, 1867-69; enlarged 3rd ed., 1905; edited by Arthur Pougin, 1969.

Clement, F. *Les musiciens célèbres depuis le seizième siècle jusqu'à nos jours.* Paris, 1868; 4th ed., 1887.

Fouqué, G. *Histoire du Théâtre-Ventadour 1829-1879.* Paris, 1881.

Berthelot. M. *F. Hérold.* Paris, 1882.

Jouvin, B. *Hérold: sa vie et ses oeuvres.* Paris, 1868.

Berlioz, Hector. *Les musiciens et la musique.* Paris, 1903.

Pougin, Arthur. *Hérold.* Paris, 1906.

Chantavoine, J. *Cent opéras célèbres.* Paris, 1948.

articles–

Berlioz, Hector. "De la partition de *Zampa.*" *Journal des débats* 27 September (1835).

Pougin, A. "La jeunesse d'Hérold." *Revue et gazette musicale* 47 (1880): 138.

Hérold, E. "Souvenirs inédits." *Bulletin français de la Société Internationale de Musique* 7 (1910): 100, 156.

Desbruères, Michel. "Le *Promethée* de Jean Lorrain et André - Ferdinand Hérold." *Études fauréennes* 20-21 (1983-84): 7.

Budden, Julian. "*Le pre aux clercs.*" *Musical Times* 129 (1985).

Tiersot, J. "Victor Hugo musicien." *Revue musicale* no. 378 (1985): 13.

Hérold settled in Paris in 1815 after three years of active involvement in Italian theaters (primarily in Naples) and immediately became a *maestro al cembalo* at the Théâtre Italiènne, where he served with distinction. Such was his success at this theater that he was selected by Boieldieu to collaborate on an *opéra-comique, Charles de France,* which premiered with modest success in 1816. Between 1816 and 1819 Hérold composed several operas none of which were highly successful, but the composer continued to be favorably regarded. After 1820 he worked in various capacities at the Opéra-Comique and Opéra while he continued to be on the staff at the Théâtre Italiènne. In general, his stage works did not enjoy great success, and only in 1826 did he score a genuine triumph with an *opéra-comique, Marie,* which had been adapted from a popular novel of the day. (*Marie* was to receive its 100th performance by the end of the year and its 400th performance within the decade.)

It was only with *Zampa,* however, which premiered at the Opéra-Comique in 1831, some sixteen years after he had launched his career in Paris, that Hérold found the acclaim he had so long desired. *Zampa's* enormous popularity was to be exceeded the following year when *Le pré aux clercs* became the brilliant success of the season. *Zampa* was performed over 200 times within the next twenty-five years whereas *Le pré aux clercs* reached its 1500th performance by the end of the century. (The modern world awaits proper revivals of both *Zampa* and *Le pré aux clercs.*) With music in his genes and the theater in his blood after his years in Italy, Hérold was uniquely equipped to challenge French musical theatrical conventions.

Zampa is significant in the history of opera not only because of its elegant craftsmanship, but because it is one of few major works which reflect Mozart's and da Ponte's *Don Giovanni.* Zampa, a dissolute rogue, is a nobleman turned pirate. Having caused the death of Albena, his first wife, he forces himself upon Camilla by threatening to kill Alfonso, her fiancé, as well as her father if she will not marry him. He mocks a statue of Albena, and when he places a ring upon its finger, the statue closes its hand upon the ring. Zampa is only momentarily intimidated and later has his henchmen throw the statue into the sea. But when he scorns Camilla, Albena reappears and carries him to a watery grave. If the shades of *Don Giovanni* are recalled in the confrontations between statue and rogue, de la Motte Fouqué's famous novella *Undine* comes to mind as well, although Hérold would not have known Hoffmann's opera on this subject.

Hérold was a master of the urbane, sophisticated style demanded by the *opéra-comique* as the genre developed in Paris in the first decades of the nineteenth century. If anything, his melodic style was even more tuneful than that of other native Frenchmen, probably because he had such extensive experience in the Italian theater. Since his dream was to be a successful composer of serious French *opéra,* it is believed that in time Hérold would have been able to bring fresh Ideas and renewal to the serious music theater. His untimely death from tuberculosis in 1833 robbed French opera of a major talent.

—Aubrey S. Garlington

HERZ, Joachim.

Producer. Born 15 June 1924, in Dresden. Educated at the State Academy for Music and Theater in Dresden and Humboldt University in Berlin; staged first production, Richard Mohaupt's *Die Bremer Stadtmusikanten,* in 1950; producer, Landesbühnen Sachsen, 1951-53; worked as assistant to Walter Felsenstein at the Komische Oper Berlin, 1953-56; producer at Cologne, 1956-57; appointed chief producer at the Städtische Theater Leipzig in 1957; director of opera, Städtische Theater Leipzig, 1959-76; inaugurated the Leipzig Opera House with a production of *Die Meistersinger von Nürnberg,* 1960; became member of Akademie der Künste der D.D.R. in 1969; awarded the Leipzig Kunstpreis in 1973; while at Leipzig directed first German language productions of several operas, and staged a highly successful production of *Der Ring des Nibelungen* (1973-76); director of Komische Oper in Berlin, 1976-81; became director of productions at the Dresden Semper Oper in 1982. Awarded the Nationalpreis der D.D.R. in 1961 and 1974.

Opera Productions (selected)

Die Bremer Stadtmusikanten (Mohaupt), Dresden, Staatstheater, 1950.
Rigoletto, Landesbühnen Sachsen, 1952.
Die Hochzeit des Jobs (Haas), Berlin, Komische Oper, 1953.
Albert Herring, Dresden, Staatstheater, 1955.
Manon Lescaut, Berlin, Komische Oper, 1955.
Turandot, Berlin, Komische Oper, 1958.
Prince Igor, Leipzig, Städtische Theater, 1959.
Falstaff, Leipzig, Städtische Theater, 1959.
Die Meistersinger von Nürnberg, Leipzig, Städtische Theater, 1960.
War and Peace, Leipzig, Städtische Theater, 1961.
Don Giovanni, Leipzig, Städtische Theater, 1962.
Der fliegende Holländer, Berlin, Komische Oper, 1962.
Katya Kabanová (Janáček), Berlin, Komische Oper, 1963.
Lohengrin, Leipzig, Städtische Theater, 1965.
Le nozze di Figaro, Leipzig, Städtische Theater, 1966.
Don Giovanni, Buenos Aires, Teatro Colón, 1966.
Aufstieg und Fall der Stadt Mahagonny, Leipzig, Städtische Theater (Kleines Haus), 1967.
Don Carlo, Leipzig, Städtische Theater, 1967.
Così fan tutte, Buenos Aires, Teatro Colón, 1967.
Der junge Lord (Henze), Berlin, Komische Oper, 1968.
Griechische Hochzeit (Hanell), Leipzig, Städtische Theater, 1969.
The Maid of Orleans, Leipzig, Städtische Theater, 1970.
Die Zaubergeige (Egk), Leipzig, Städtische Theater, 1970.
Die Zauberflöte, Beograd, Narodno Pozorište, 1971.
Die Entführung aus dem Serail, Leipzig, Städtische Theater, 1972.
Der Ring des Nibelungen, Leipzig, Städtische Theater, 1973-76.

Les Huguenots, Leipzig, Städtische Theater, 1974.
Lulu, Berlin, Komische Oper, 1975.
Salome, English National Opera, 1975.
Aufstieg und Fall der Stadt Mahagonny, Berlin, Komische Oper, 1977.
Das Land Bum-Bum (Katzer), Berlin, Komische Oper, 1978.
Madama Butterfly, Berlin, Komische Oper, 1978.
Fidelio, English National Opera, 1980.
Die ägyptische Helena, Munich Opernfestspielen, 1981.
Peter Grimes, Berlin, Komische Oper, 1981.
Ariadne auf Naxos, Dresden, 1982.
Così fan tutte, Dresden, 1983.
Wozzeck, Dresden, 1984.
Der Freischütz, Dresden, Semper Oper, 1985.
Der Rosenkavalier, Dresden, Semper Oper, 1985.
The Nose, Dresden, Semper Oper, 1986.
Parsifal, English National Opera, 1986.
Madama Butterfly, Zurich, 1987.
Salome, Dresden, Semper Oper, 1988.
Don Giovanni, Salzburg, 1989.
Der goldene Topf, Dresden, 1989.
The Love of Three Oranges, Dresden Musikfestspielen, 1990.
Osud (Janáček), Dresden, Staatsoper, 1991.

Publications

By HERZ: books–

. . . und Figaro lässt sich scheiden: Oper als Idee und Interpretation. Munich, 1985.
Theater—Kunst des erfüllten Augenblicks: Briefe, Vorträge, Notate, Gespräche, Essays. Berlin, 1989.

articles–

"Das Theater Richard Wagners: Utopie oder Realität?" *Theater der Zeit* 39/1,2 (1984): 36, 25.
"Richard Wagner und der Mythos." *Beiträge zur Musikwissenschaft* 26/2 (1984): 91.
"Richard Wagners Dresdener Opern: Fragen der Interpretation." *Reihe Musiktheater* 36 (1984): 3.
"Was du ererbt von deinen Vätern." *Opernwelt* 25 (1984): 13.
"Tradition und Fortschritt." *Musik und Gesellschaft* 35 (December 1985): 641.
"Aspekte der Freischütz-Interpretation." *Beiträge zur Musikwissenschaft* 30/1-2 (1988): 37.
"Unverantwortliche Gedanken und zu verantwortende Erfahrungen mit Giacomo Meyerbeer." *Musik und Gesellschaft* 39 (May 1989): 238.

About HERZ: book–

Irmer, Hans-Jochen, ed. *Joachim Herz: Regisseur im Musiktheater.* Berlin, 1977.

articles–

Krause, E. "Das Interview: Joachim Herz." *Opernwelt* 19/2 (1978): 24.
Schroeder, H. "Widerspruch zwischen Musik und Szene?" (interview). *Musik und Gesellschaft* 30 (November 1980): 665.
Elisabeth-Renk, H. "Das Interview." *Opernwelt* 22/8-9 (1981): 22.
Mueller, U. "Seminar an den Universitäten in Salzburg und München mit Joachim Herz." *Opernwelt* 25/8-9 (1984): 25.

Joachim Herz's production of *Salome* for English National Opera, London, 1987 (Josephine Barstow as Salome)

Schneider, Frank. "Drei Wege zu Berg: Joachim Herz über seine Inszenierungen der Opern *Lulu* und *Wozzeck*" (interview). *Bulletin des Musikrat der D.D.R.* 22/3 (1985): 26.

*   *   *

Born in Dresden, where he studied conducting as well as stage production, Joachim Herz worked, while himself a student, as a *repetiteur* with the Dresden Opera School. After further study in Berlin and experience as director with a touring opera company, he became assistant to Walter Felsenstein at the Komische Oper, East Berlin in 1953. The same year he directed Joseph Haas's *Die Hochzeit des Jobs,* and his productions for the Komische Oper in the next two decades included *Manon Lescaut, Albert Herring, Turandot, Der fliegende Holländer,* Henze's *Der junge Lord* and *Katya Kabanová.* Meanwhile, after a year at Cologne, he was appointed chief producer in 1957 and director of opera at the Leipzig Opera in 1959.

During the nineteen years that he worked in Leipzig, Herz evolved a personal style of direction that, while it owed much to the dramatic realism of Felsenstein, was more stylized in form and less rigid in concept. His first production there, Borodin's *Prince Igor,* displayed his mastery of large-scale crowd scenes, while his next, of Verdi's *Falstaff,* demonstrated his affinity for comedy. A much-praised staging of *Die Meistersinger,* his first direction of a Wagner opera, with which the new Leipzig Opera House was inaugurated in 1960, brought both these skills into prominence. Other Leipzig productions included the first staging in the German language of *War and Peace, Don Giovanni, Lohengrin, Le nozze di Figaro, Don Carlos,* the premiere of *Griechische Hochzeit* (Hanell), *The Maid of Orleans,* Egk's *Die Zaubergeige,* and Handel's *Serse,* which was later seen in the United Kingdom. The climax of his work in Leipzig, however, was the staging of *Der Ring des Nibelungen.* Herz's *Ring* cycle, built up between 1973 and 1976, was a magnificently dramatic realization of Wagner's great work that, while it contrasted the bourgeois world of the gods with the proletarian world of the giants and Nibelungs in true Marxist fashion, also drew graphic portraits of individual characters, in particular that of Siegfried.

During the Leipzig years, Herz also staged many productions in the West: at Hamburg, Frankfurt, Buenos Aires, Vienna and in London, where he directed *Salome* with great success in 1975 for English National Opera. After the death of Felsenstein and the defection of his most likely successor, Götz Friedrich, to West Germany, Herz was appointed *Intendant* of the Komische Oper, East Berlin, in 1976, a post he retained for five years. Notable productions he directed during that period included the two-act version of Berg's *Lulu,* which he later converted into the three-act version; a superb staging of Weill's *Aufstieg und Fall der Stadt Mahagonny;* the premiere of an amusing opera for children by Georg Katzer, *Das Land Bum-Bum,* in 1978; and in the same year, *Madama Butterfly.* Felsenstein had always refused to produce *Butterfly* at the Komische Oper, claiming that it lacked drama and realism. Herz, by reverting to the original, two-act version, with its unflattering view of Pinkerton, proved that Puccini's tear-jerker could be both dramatic and realistic. When restaged for Welsh National Opera, this production became extremely popular. Herz also directed *La forza del destino* for the Welsh National Opera, Strauss's *Die ägyptische Helena* (1981) at Munich, as well as *Fidelio* and *Parsifal*

(1986), his first attempt at Wagner's sacred drama and his 100th production to date, for English National Opera.

In 1982 Herz returned to Dresden, his birthplace, as director of productions at the State Opera. His first new production, of *Ariadne auf Naxos,* was also presented at the Edinburgh Festival; his second, of *Così fan tutte,* was later staged in Helsinki. The reconstructed Semper Oper, destroyed in the bombing of Dresden on the night of 13 February 1945, reopened exactly 40 years later with *Der Freischütz,* followed the next evening by *Der Rosenkavalier,* both directed in traditional style by Herz. His subsequent work in Dresden has included *Falstaff; Salome;* the premiere of Eckehard Mayer's *Der goldene Topf* (1989), adapted from a tale set in Dresden by E.T.A. Hoffmann; and Prokofiev's *The Love of Three Oranges* (1990). Herz's finest productions—the Leipzig *Meistersinger* and *Ring* cycle; the English National Opera *Salome* and *Fidelio;* the Berlin *Lulu* and *Mahagonny;* the Welsh National Opera *Butterfly* and *Forza del destino;* the Dresden *Freischütz* and *Rosenkavalier*—are among the most interesting to be seen in Europe during the last 40 years.

—Elizabeth Forbes

L'HEURE ESPAGNOLE [The Spanish Hour].

Composer: Maurice Ravel.

Librettist: Franc-Nohain.

First Performance: Paris, Opéra-Comique, 19 May 1911.

Roles: Concepcion (soprano); Gonzalve (tenor); Torquemada (tenor); Ramiro (baritone); Don Inigo Gomez (bass).

*   *   *

Maurice Ravel's *L'heure espagnole* is a funny and provocative work. Set in eighteenth-century Toledo, Spain, it is about a clockmaker named Torquemada, his wife Concepcion, and the three other men in her life. The first lover to visit Concepcion while her husband is away from his shop is Gonzalve, a young poet full of hot air and empty promises. The second is Don Inigo Gomez, a fat and pompous banker who is ethically bankrupt. Both lovers prove to be substandard, leading Concepcion to complain, "Oh! What a pathetic adventure! And of my two lovers, one lacks the temperament and the other is ridiculous. . . . And to think they call themselves Spaniards." Then a third man comes into the shop, a brawny muleteer named Ramiro. Simple and straightforward, healthy and robust, Ramiro is the opposite of both Gonzalve and Don Inigo, and he's always at Concepcion's beck and call. For her he gladly minds the shop while she attends to her lovers upstairs in her bedroom, and he effortlessly carries heavy grandfather clocks (sometimes with a lover hidden inside) up and down stairs. Because of his constancy and feats of endurance, Concepcion ultimately drops Gonzalve and Don Inigo for Ramiro.

Clearly, this comic and uninhibited opera contains elements of cruelty, although none of the characters ever gets hurt; they are, after all, one-dimensional. The plentiful witticisms, puns and silly situations keep the tone of the story light and nonchalant. Just in case we do disapprove of all the machinations and deceptions, the librettist Franc-Nohain provides a tidy moral from Boccaccio at the end of the story that lets us off the hook: "Among all lovers, only the effective one matters. There comes a moment in the pursuit of love when the muleteer has his turn."

Ravel's music is lighthearted as well, serving as a witty commentator on the action. At times the orchestra is smarter than the characters, such as when Don Inigo, alone in the shop, hears footsteps and hastily assumes they belong to Concepcion. The dissonant tritones sounded on kettledrums, however, signify Ramiro's clumsy footsteps. Sure enough, the muleteer, and not Concepcion, reappears on stage.

Ravel's music never drags. The entire opera lasts only an hour and avoids anything so lingering as a soulful melody since the predominant vocal style is declamatory rather than tuneful. With the exception of the extraordinary orchestral introduction, which Ravel called a "mischievous hubbub" of ticking and chiming clocks, there isn't anything particularly haunting about the score.

On recordings, the prevailing chattiness of the vocal line can sound monotonous, and to a certain extent the opera owes its effectiveness to clever staging and interpretation. At the 1911 premiere, the costumes were inspired by models by Goya, and the singer Jean Périer portrayed Ramiro with a Montmartre accent that the audience found hilarious. According to press reports, Périer helped carry the opera.

—Teresa Davidian

Elvira de Hidalgo as Rosina in *Il barbiere di Siviglia*

HIDALGO, Elvira de.

Soprano. Born 27 December 1892, in Aragón. Died 21 January 1980, in Milan. Debut in Naples as Rosina, 1908; Metropolitan Opera debut in same role, 1910; sang at Metropolitan Opera, 1924-25; Covent Garden debut as Gilda, 1924; retired from singing, 1932; taught in Athens, where her most famous pupil was Maria Callas.

Publications

About HIDALGO: articles–

Celletti, R. "Hidalgo, Elvira de." In *Le grandi voci,* Rome, 1964.

*   *   *

Elvira de Hidalgo was a light coloratura soprano of the type familiar to record collectors in the voices of Luisa Tetrazzini and Amelita Galli-Curci. De Hidalgo's career lasted from approximately 1910 to 1930. Listening to her crisp, intelligently-sung excerpt as Adina from Donizetti's *L'elisir d'amore* one can readily hear why she was so highly prized as a *bel canto* singer. Today she is best known as the principal teacher of Maria Callas at the Athens Conservatory beginning in 1937; de Hidalgo's recordings demonstrate that she had certain valuable lessons to impart and that Callas indeed learned much from her. In the accuracy of the embellishments and the tantalizing play of light and shade in de Hidalgo's voice the influence on Callas is manifest. There is also the temperament, de Hidalgo's a recognizably Spanish one of the type associated with singers who came after her, such as

Conchita Supervia. Moreover, de Hidalgo, like Callas, was not afraid to use sufficient, some might say excessive, chest voice.

Born in Spain in 1892, de Hidalgo was a pupil of Concetta Bordalba and Melchiorre Vidal. Her 1908 Rosina in Rossini's *Il barbiere di Siviglia* was a great success. Following her debut she then conquered the Sarah Bernhardt Theater in Paris, the Khedive in Cairo (1909) and there followed successes in Monte Carlo, Prague, New York (at the Metropolitan Opera), Baltimore, Vienna, and Florence (at the Teatro della Pergola). Roles sung in these cities, in addition to Rosina, were Gilda in Verdi's *Rigoletto* (the only role in which she appeared at Covent Garden), Zerlina in Mozart's *Don Giovanni,* and the title-role in Donizetti's *Linda di Chamounix.* In 1916 de Hidalgo appeared at the Teatro alla Scala as Rosina for the centenary of Rossini's comic opera masterpiece and in 1918 sang Marie from Donizetti's *La figlia del reggimento* in Trieste. During the 1924-25 and 1925-26 seasons she returned to the Metropolitan Opera in New York. After her retirement from the stage in 1932, de Hidalgo went to the Athens Conservatory to teach; later she taught at the Conservatory in Ankara.

De Hidalgo was, along with Mercedes Caspir, the end of a line of illustrious Spanish *soprani d'agilità* from the nineteenth century, including Regina Pacini (who was actually Portuguese) and Maria Galvany, continuing into the twentieth century with Josefina Huguet and Maria Barrientos. De Hidalgo's voice had an attractive timbre, limpid and silvery. It reached to a top D and her manner of performing was outgoing and vivacious. She left a number of recordings of arias. On Columbia in 1907-08 she recorded "Una voce poco fa" from *Il barbiere di Siviglia,* "Ah non giunge" from Bellini's *La sonnambula,* and "Son vergin vezzosa" from Bellini's *I Puritani.* For Fonotipia in 1909-10 she once again recorded "Una voce poco fa"; during these sessions she also made discs of Adina's aria from *L'elisir d'amore,* "Quel guardo il cavaliere-So anch'io la virtu magica," two arias from *La sonnambula,* "Come per me sereno" and "Ah! non credea," selections from Gounod's *Roméo et Juliette,* the "Shadow Song" ("Ombra leggera") from Meyerbeer's *Dinorah,* and the duet for Giovanni and Zerlina from *Don Giovanni,* "Là ci darem la mano," with Magini Coletti. De Hidalgo died in Milan in 1980.

—Stephen Willier

HINDEMITH, Paul.

Composer. Born 16 November 1895, in Hanau, near Frankfurt. Died 28 December 1963, in Frankfurt. Married: Gertrud Rottenberg (daughter of the conductor Ludwig Rottenberg). Studied violin with A. Rebner and composition with Arnold Mendelssohn and Sekles at the Hochschule für Musik in Frankfurt; concertmaster of the orchestra of the Frankfurt Opera House, 1915-23; violist with the Amar String Quartet, 1922-29; participated in the contemporary music concerts at Donaueschingen and Baden-Baden; instructor of composition at the Berlin Hochschule für Musik, 1927; problems in Germany with the Nazis; three visits to Ankara, Turkey, beginning in 1934, where he helped organize the curriculum of the Ankara Conservatory; first American appearance with his unaccompanied viola sonata at the Library of Congress, 1937; in Switzerland briefly, then emigrated to the United States; instructor at the Berkshire Music Center in Tanglewood, summer 1940; professor at Yale University, 1940-53; became an American citizen, 1946; elected a member of the National Institute of Arts and Letters; conducting engagements in Europe, 1947-49; appointed Charles Eliot Norton Lecturer at Harvard University, 1950-51; taught at the University of Zurich, 1953; received the Sibelius Award, 1954; guest conducting appearances in the United States, 1959-61.

Operas

Edition:

P. Hindemith: Sämtliche Werke. Edited by Kurt von Fischer and Ludwig Finscher. Mainz, 1975-.

Mörder, Hoffnung der Frauen, Kokoschka, 1919, Stuttgart, Landestheater, 4 June 1921.
Das Nusch-Nuschi (marionette opera), Franz Blei, 1920, Stuttgart, Landestheater, 4 June 1921.
Sancta Susanna, Stramm, 1921, Frankfurt, Opernhaus, 26 March 1922.
Cardillac, Ferdinand Lion (after Hoffmann, *Das Fräulein von Scuderi*), 1926, Dresden, Staatsoper, 9 November 1926; Hindemith (after Lion), 1952, Zurich, Stadttheater, 20 June 1952.
Hin und zurück (sketch), Marcellus Schiffer, 1927, Baden-Baden, 15 July 1927.
Neues vom Tage, Marcellus Schiffer, 1928-29, Berlin, Kroll, 8 June 1929; revised 1953.
Lehrstück, Brecht, 1929.
Mathis der Maler, Hindemith, 1934-35, Zurich, Stadttheater, 28 May 1938.
Die Harmonie der Welt, Hindemith, 1956-57, Munich, Prinzregententheater, 11 August 1957.
The Long Christmas Dinner, Thornton Wilder, 1960, Mannheim, Nationaltheater, 17 December 1961.

Other works: ballets, orchestral works, choral works, solo vocal works, chamber music, piano pieces.

Publications/Writings

By HINDEMITH: books–

Unterweisung im Tonsatz, i: *Theoretischer Teil.* Mainz, 1937; revised 2nd ed., 1940; English translation as *The Craft of Musical Composition,* 1941.
Unterweisung im Tonsatz, ii: *Übungsbuch für den zweistimmigen Satz.* Mainz, 1939; English translation as *The Craft of Musical Composition,* 1941.
A Concentrated Course in Traditional Harmony, i. New York, 1943; 2nd ed., 1949; German translation, 1949.
Elementary Training for Musicians. New York, 1946; revised 2nd ed., 1949.
Rexroth, D., ed. *Briefe.* Frankfurt, 1982.
A Concentrated Course in Traditional Harmony, ii: *Exercises for Advanced Students.* New York, 1948; German translation, 1949; 2nd ed., 1953.
A Composer's World. Cambridge, Massachusetts, 1952; revised and in German, 1959; English translation of revised German version in *Journal of Music Theory* 5 (1961): 109.
Johann Sebastian Bach: ein verpflichtendes Erbe. Frankfurt, 1951; English translation, 1952.
Unterweisung im Tonsatz, iii: *Der dreistimmige Satz.* Mainz, 1970.

About HINDEMITH: books–

Schilling, H.L. *Paul Hindemiths Cardillac.* Würzburg, 1962.
Kemp, Ian. *Hindemith.* London, 1970.
Briner, A. *Paul Hindemith.* Zurich and Mainz, 1971.
Skelton, Geoffrey. *Paul Hindemith: The Man Behind the Music.* London, 1975.
Schubert, G. *Hindemith.* Hamburg, 1981.
Preussner, Eberhard. *Paul Hindemith: Ein Lebensbild.* Innsbruck, 1984.
Neumeyer, David. *The Music of Paul Hindemith.* New Haven, 1986.
Cook, Susan C. *Opera for a New Republic: The "Zeitopern" of Krenek, Weill, and Hindemith.* Ann Arbor, 1988.
Noss, Luther. *Paul Hindemith in the United States.* Champaign, Illinois, 1989.

articles–

Lion, F. "Cardillac I und II." *Akzente* 4 (1957): 126.
Briner, A. "Eine Bekenntnisoper Paul Hindemiths: zu seiner Oper *Die Harmonie der Welt.*" *Schweizerische Musikzeitung* January-February (1959).
Rösner, H. "Zur Hindemith-Bibliographie." *Hindemith-Jahrbuch* 1 (1971): 161.
Padmore, Elaine. "Hindemith und Grünewald." *Music Review* 33 (1972).
Briner, A. "Die erste Textfassung von Paul Hindemiths Oper 'Die Harmonie der Welt'." In *Festschrift für einen Verleger: Ludwig Strecker,* 203. Mainz, 1973.

Zickenheimer, O. "Hindemith-Bibliographie." *Hindemith-Jahrbuch* 3 (1974): 155.

Paulding, James E. "*Mathis der Maler*—The Politics of Music." *Hindemith-Jahrbuch* 5 (1976): 102.

Laubenthal, A. "Hindemith-Bibliographie 1974-78." *Hindemith-Jahrbuch* 7 (1978): 229.

Rexroth Dieter. "Zum Stellenwert der Oper *Cardillac* im Schaffen Hindemiths." In *Erprobungen und Erfahrungen. Zu Paul Hindemiths Schaffen in den Zwanziger Jahren,* edited by Dieter Rexroth, 56. Mainz, 1978.

———. "Hindemith and *Mathis der Maler.*" Booklet accompanying Angel, SZCX-3869 (1979).

Schneider, Norbert J. "Prinzipien der rhythmische Gestaltung in Hindemiths Oper *Mathis der Maler.*" *Hindemith-Jahrbuch* 8 (1979): 7.

Hitchcock, H. Wiley. "Trinitarian Symbolism in the 'Engelkonzert' of Hindemith's *Mathis der Maler.*" In *A Festschrift for Albert Seay,* edited by M. Grace, 217. Colorado Springs, 1982.

Rubeli, Alfred. "Johannes Keplers Harmonik in Paul Hindemiths Oper *Die Harmonie der Welt.*" In *Kepler-Symposion zu J. Keplers 350. Todestag Linz 1980,* edited by Rudolf Haase, 107. Linz, 1982.

Sinjavskaja, Nadezda. "*Garmoniji mira* P. Hindemitha kak filosofskaja muzykal'naja drama." In *Ocerki po isorij zarubeznoj muzyki XX veca.* Leningrad, 1983.

Laubenthal, A. "Ausgerechnet der frühe Hindemith." *Hindemith-Jahrbuch* 12 (1983): 7.

Kemp, Ian. "Hindemith." In *Modern Masters. The New Grove Composer Biography Series,* p. 229. New York and London, 1984.

Mainka, Jürgen. "Von innerer zu äusserer Emigration: Eine Szene in Paul Hindemiths Oper *Mathis der Maler.*" In *Musik und Musikpolitik im faschistischen Deutschland,* edited by Hanns-Werner Heister and Hans-Günter Klein, 265. Frankfurt am Main, 1984.

unpublished–

D'Angelo, James, P. "Tonality and its Symbolic Association in Paul Hindemith's Opera *Die Harmonie der Welt.*" Ph.D. dissertation, New York University, 1983.

*   *   *

Hindemith's connection with the operatic world began early in his career when, at nineteen, he became a violinist with the Frankfurt Opera (1915-1923). During this period his earliest operas emerged—a set of three one-act operas. These works attracted attention to Hindemith's music but also earned him the reputation of a radical. All the libretti are provocative and sensational, products of high German expressionism.

Mörder, Hoffnung der Frauen (*Murderers, the Hope of Women*) (1919) revolves around the sexual conflicts which flare up between men and women. Despite the feverish expressionism of Oscar Kokoschka's autobiographical libretto, Hindemith resisted the temptation to employ heavy-handed polyphonic writing. Nonetheless the work suffers from an inconsistency between the derivative music (Wagner, Strauss and Puccini) and Kokoschka's obscure text.

Das Nusch-Nuschi (1920), intended to be acted by Burmese marionettes, reflects Hindemith's intent to curb the excesses of late German romanticism. The text by Franz Blei is a blend of whimsy, moderate eroticism and general absurdity. The central figures of this oriental story are a lustful, drunken field marshal, accused of seducing the emperor's four wives, and a strange creature, half-rat and half-alligator (Nusch-Nuschi) who frightens the soldier into submission. Dancing plays a large role in this opera and hence Hindemith's rhythmic style is much stronger than in the other one-act operas. Throughout Hindemith derides late nineteenth century music and romantic dance music by his use of stinging chords and unexpected accents in the manner of Bartok and Stravinsky. He satirizes nineteenth century musical practice by composing a choral fugue that fails to follow the "rules" and by quoting a passage from Wagner's *Tristan und Isolde* whose accompaniment is purposely marred by a persistent wrong note in the bass.

By far the most controversial and explicitly erotic of these one-act operas is *Sancta Susanna* (1921) with text by August Stramm. Its theme is the triumph of Eros over inhibited religious training. A young nun, aroused by a spring evening, a glimpse of peasant love and the sexual experiences of another nun, frenetically strips off her garments and embraces the altar crucifix; at the opera's climax she tears the loin cloth from the Christ figure. Although the opera is tightly controlled and dramatically and stylistically more integrated than his previous operas, it still reveals Hindemith searching for his own language in this experimental period. Undoubtedly these works served as vehicles for his powerful, youthful emotions under the guise of expressionism. Eventually he saw them as such and disowned them. However, the Nazis cited these works in their case against Hindemith as a decadent artist.

Hindemith's first full-length opera *Cardillac* (1926) is based upon a short story by E.T.A. Hoffmann, *Das Fräulein von Scuderi* and adapted by Ferdinand Lion. The librettist made substantial alterations emphasizing the action and even dispensing with the Fräulein of the title. Lion created precise situations of mood that complemented the Baroque forms Hindemith favored, such as the passacaglia. This approach parallels the construction of Berg's *Wozzeck* (1925), based also on classical forms. However, Hindemith's procedures are far more evident, and his application of strict forms to such a dramatic text establishes *Cardillac* as a significant twentieth century opera.

The subject of *Cardillac*—the nature of the artist—was to preoccupy Hindemith for many years, later giving rise to *Mathis der Maler* and *Die Harmonie der Welt*. Cardillac is a goldsmith so attached to his handiwork and indifferent to human relationships and social values that he is compelled to kill his customers and retrieve their purchases. Throughout the opera no moral judgment is passed on Cardillac. Hindemith holds to a consistent objectivity, putting his neo-Baroque style to wonderful dramatic effect as a counterbalance to the dark expressionistic subject. Hindemith eventually decided the libretto was unsatisfactory, and in 1952 wrote an entirely new libretto that is closer to the original play, but cannot be considered an improvement on Lion's text. Because of the textual changes and the retention of the original music with new overlaid vocal parts, the strength and directness of the original are undermined and the character of Cardillac substantially weakened.

After *Cardillac* Hindemith returned to the character of the earlier one-act operas and produced two works on comic themes. The brief chamber opera *Hin und zurück* (*There and Back*) (1927) is a charming miniature, far lighter than most of Hindemith's output and considerably less contrapuntal. The opera's action, written by Marcellus Schiffer, progresses to its central climax in which a jealous husband shoots his wife. Then, through an intervening *deus ex machina*, the action is exactly reversed. This structure undoubtedly intrigued Hindemith who, instead of composing exact retrograde music, reversed the sequence of sections. In *Neues vom Tage* (*News of the Day*) (1929) with a libretto by Schiffer, Hindemith satirizes divorce, journalism, show business and opera itself. This full-length piece revolves around a couple who file for divorce, become celebrities and in the end are not allowed a reconciliation by their public. The opera was only partially successful because Hindemith's highly contrapuntal music stifled the quite simple and high-spirited plot. Also, even though Hindemith possessed a great sense of humor, he lacked the bite necessary to create real satire. In 1953, in another act of repentance, Hindemith revised *Neues vom Tage* making substantial alterations to the music and allowing the couple to save their marriage.

Neues vom Tage was the last work of Hindemith's first creative period. All of these early operas were, in Hindemith's view, the sins of his youth. In 1923 he had momentarily glimpsed his true path in relation to his song cycle *Das Marienleben*. Certainly the subject—the life of the Virgin Mary—was in stark contrast to his operas at that time. Hindemith observed that "the strong impression which the first performance made on the audience . . . made me aware for the first time in my musical existence of the ethical qualities of music and the moral obligations of the composer." This outlook, combined with Hindemith's growing interest in German folk song, produced a new idiom, first heard in the *Konzertmusik* works (1930), that was characterized by strong tonality, clear linear writing and a broad lyricism.

The opera *Mathis der Maler* (1934-35), based upon the life of the painter Matthias Grünewald (?1480-?1528), marks the culmination of this spiritual metamorphosis in Hindemith. In contemplating the life of Grünewald, Hindemith discovered his true nature, seeing parallels between himself and Grünewald as estranged, dedicated artists caught up in an unsettling political world. Such a text demanded that Hindemith write his own libretto.

The backdrop for Hindemith's undertaking was the rising Nazi regime which, by the end of 1934, had effectively banned performances of his music including the *Mathis* opera. The conductor Wilhelm Furtwangler, who pleaded Hindemith's case in a leading German newspaper, presented the premiere of the symphony *Mathis der Maler,* the movements of which were later incorporated into the opera. It was not until 1938 that *Mathis* was staged in Zurich.

Despite the parallels drawn between the political environment of Grünewald's time and Nazi doctrine, the deeper issue for Hindemith was the role of the creative artist and the purpose for which his works are created. In the end St Paul tells Mathis that he can serve God best by cultivating his gifts with humility and reverence. Thereupon Mathis unlocks his blocked creative force, paints a stream of great works and, completely drained, resigns himself to death.

Structurally *Mathis* represents a major departure from the strict self-contained forms of *Cardillac*. Hindemith often employs the conventional aria, ensemble and chorus while varying the degrees of musical tension. There are some set musical forms that never intrude upon the action. Overall he put aside much of his neo-Baroque style and found his classical and romantic heritage. This was especially revealed in his new harmonic language with its tonal and often triadic harmony, postulated by Hindemith in his music theory text *The Craft of Musical Composition* (written 1934-36; published 1937).

By 1937 Hindemith had already conceived another opera in the mold of *Mathis*. He had come particularly under the influence of the astronomer/mystic Johannes Kepler (1571-1630) and the early music theorist, Boethius (d. 524), who had described three levels of music—*musica instrumentalis, musica humana* and *musica mundana* or "the music of the spheres." Kepler believed that he had scientifically uncovered these celestial harmonies which he delineated in his *Harmonices Mundi* (1619). It was this work that inspired Hindemith to compose the opera *Die Harmonie der Welt* (*The Harmony of the World*), for he was convinced that in his own musical theory he had found laws that related *musica mundana* to the actual sounds of instruments and voices (*musica instrumentalis*) and the music sounding between two souls (*musica humana*).

After a long gestation period during which he composed the symphony *Die Harmonie der Welt* (1951) (later incorporated into the opera), Hindemith finally undertook the work in 1956, completing it in 1957. Again Hindemith wrote his own libretto so as to use the figure of Kepler as an alter ego and the other characters as his mouthpieces. *Die Harmonie der Welt* is a complete reflection of his artistic, philosophical and religious credo and is, in effect, a musical autobiography. It is a unique work in which episodes of the scientist's life are presented in tableaux form, each dramatic in itself but without cumulative tension. Underpinning the work is not only the whole of Hindemith's music theory, but also a vast network of tonality symbolism. In the final scene the characters, transformed into the solar system and purged of their errors, find their redemption in the postulated World Harmony. This was to have been Hindemith's greatest work, but in the view of most critics it was simply a noble effort. It has yet to be seen outside of Germany and Austria.

Three years before his death Hindemith embarked upon his last opera, *The Long Christmas Dinner* (1960) with a libretto by Thornton Wilder. It is a one-act chamber opera lasting only an hour. Its subjects, death and the passage to an afterlife, are recurring themes in Hindemith's vocal works. In this respect there is a link between the finale of *Die Harmonie der Welt* and *The Long Christmas Dinner*. Both are concerned with endless death and rebirth, an infinite world without beginning or end; both reflect Hindemith's essentially Roman Catholic perspective. The simple plot of *The Long Christmas Dinner* focuses on a family gathered round a table at Christmas. Three generations come and go, their conversation revealing the passage of time. Their births and deaths are represented by two portals at stage right and left. The opera ends with a certainty that this sequence of events will continue without change. Hindemith's music is seamless and unobtrusively complements the text. The opera contains some of his most delicate, transparent music including a sextet harmonized exclusively in triads. In no other work of his late period did the triad play such an important role.

Hindemith's operatic music, like much of his vocal and instrumental music, is currently out of fashion principally because it does not conform to contemporary musical values. His was a music of synthesis, retaining the values of past musical epochs in conjunction with his own twentieth century musical language. His last three operas, with their spiritual and metaphysical themes, are especially at odds with the typical psychological plots of most contemporary operas. Perhaps in 1995, the year of his centenary, Hindemith's operas will be re-evaluated and again be appreciated for their many praiseworthy qualities.

—James D'Angelo

HINES, Jerome Albert Link (born Heinz).

Bass. Born 8 November 1921, in Los Angeles. Married singer Lucia Evangelista. Studied with Gennaro Curci in Los Angeles, and later with Samuel Margolis in New York; opera debut as Monterone in *Rigoletto,* San Francisco, 1941; employed as chemist during the war; Metropolitan Opera debut as the Sergeant in *Boris Godunov,* 1946; appeared at Edinburgh as Nick Shadow in *The Rake's Progress,* 1953; appeared in Munich as Don Giovanni, 1954; sang the role of Boris Godunov at the Bol'shoy, Moscow, 1962; composed the opera *I Am the Way.*

Publications

By HINES: books–

This is My Story: This is My Song. Westwood, New Jersey, 1968.
Great Singers on Great Singing. London, 1982.

* * *

Standing as perhaps America's only truly great bass of the second half of this century, Jerome Hines has brought numerous distinctions to the art of singing. His early life was consumed with the study of science—an undergraduate degree in chemistry with a minor in mathematics from the University of California in Los Angeles confirms the fact that his approach to life and singing has been, in one sense, an analytical one. In fact, he was successful in developing a non-toxic, special-effects solution to be used as Méphistophélès' youth potion in the opera *Faust.* This development has eliminated a physical danger encountered by the character playing the role of Faust in Metropolitan Opera productions. His interest in vocal techniques led to the publication in 1982 of a book entitled *Great Singers on Great Singing.* The book is a compendium of comments on the production of vocal tone, acquired from interviews with well-known singers, one speech therapist, and a medical doctor.

His almost clinical approach to developing the various operatic roles he has portrayed throughout the years has involved extensive score study on his part and scheduled conferences with psychiatrists regarding character analysis of the roles he is preparing. For example, his portrayal of Boris Godunov has shown a remarkable evolution through the years as he has pursued an intensive character probe. His interest in hypnotism has allowed him an amateur exploration of the benefits this method of introspection and relaxation can give to singing. During the breaks between the acts of an opera he is performing, he frequently practices self-hypnotism in an effort to completely withdraw from the pressures at hand.

A totally American-taught singer, Hines took lessons for years from Gennaro Curci who recognized early the potential in his young pupil. After Curci's death in 1955, Hines received coaching from both Samuel Margolis and Rocco Pandiscio. His professional stage debut came after his first year in college when he sang Bill Bobstay in *H.M.S. Pinafore* for the Los Angeles Civic Light Opera Association. It was for this performance that he changed the spelling of his last name from Heinz to Hines. His debut for the San Francisco Opera came in 1941 as Biterolf in Wagner's *Tannhäuser.* Performances of Ramfis in Verdi's *Aida* for the San Carlo Opera, Méphistophélès in Gounod's *Faust* for the New Orleans Opera, Osmin in Mozart's *Die Entführung aus dem Serail* for the Central

City, Colorado, Opera preceded his debut with the Metropolitan Opera in March 1946. Upon winning the $1000 Caruso Award for that year, he was assured a Metropolitan contract and was awarded it the day after his audition. His debut as the Sergeant in *Boris Godunov,* although a brief role, afforded him immediate recognition from the critics.

He has achieved many firsts at the Metropolitan Opera. He was the first American-born bass to sing the title role in *Boris Godunov* and the roles of Philip II in *Don Carlos* and Wotan in *Die Walküre* and *Das Rheingold.* By composing the opera *I Am the Way,* a work based upon the life of Jesus and staged at the Metropolitan Opera in 1968, he became the first composer to write for himself an opera that has been produced at the Metropolitan. The popularity of the work is evidenced by its being given over fifty times following the initial performance in 1956.

Internationally, Hines distinguished himself by being the first American-born bass to sing the role of Philip II (*Don Carlos*) in Buenos Aires and Palermo. The same distinction was awarded him for portrayals of Gurnemanz in *Parsifal,* King Mark in *Tristan and Isolde,* and Wotan in *Die Walküre* in Bayreuth at the Wagner Festival. These appearances came after his establishment as a singer of international repute through performances at Glyndebourne, Edinburgh, Munich, and Milan. His greatest international triumph, however, came with his 1962 performance of the title role in *Boris Godunov* at the Bolshoi in Moscow and other Soviet cities. He was the first American to sing the role in that country in Russian. This conquest came at the height of the Cuban missile crisis when the political climate between the United States and Russia was especially tenuous. Premier Nikita Khrushchev, who was in the audience on the evening of his debut, joined others in giving him a standing ovation.

Hines has been an imposing figure on the stage in several ways. His towering height (over 6'6") has served him best, according to most critics, in the role of Boris. He has also been a physical stalwart of the Metropolitan Opera by setting a record for longevity of an American-born singer interpreting leading roles. This feat has not been attained without criticism, however. It appeared in the mid-1970s that his voice had literally been spent as a result of the arduous schedules he was forced to assume because he was, at times, the only bass performing leading roles at the Metropolitan Opera. Another result of this relentless schedule was his failure to have sufficient time to have adequate exposure on the international scene either through performances or recordings. The wear and tear did not go unnoticed by either the critics or the audiences, and the deterioration was openly criticized in the 1970s. In addition, the onset of a severe bout with osteoarthritis threatened to shorten his career even further. In recent years, however, he has undertaken an exhaustive physical fitness and nutrition program with surprisingly good results. Apparently his singing voice had a noticeable rejuvenation that has allowed him to enjoy further productive years.

—Rose Mary Owens

HOCKNEY, David.

Designer. Born 9 July 1937, in Bradford, Yorkshire, England. Attended Bradford College of Art, 1953-57; Royal College of Art, 1959-62; lecturer at University of Iowa, 1964, University of Colorado, 1965, University of California at Los

Angeles, 1966, University of California at Berkeley, 1967, and other universities; exhibited in one-man shows, 1963-present; designed sets and costumes for the Metropolitan Opera House, 1980.

Opera Productions (selected)

The Rake's Progress, Glyndebourne, 1975.
Die Zauberflöte, Glyndebourne, 1978.
The Rake's Progress, Teatro alla Scala, 1979.
L'enfant et les sortilèges, Metropolitan Opera, 1981.
Les mamelles de Tirésias, Metropolitan Opera, 1981.
Le rossignol, Metropolitan Opera, 1981.
Oedipus Rex, Metropolitan Opera, 1981.
L'enfant et les sortilèges, Covent Garden, 1983.
The Nightingale, Covent Garden, 1983.
Varii Capricci, Covent Garden, 1983.
Tristan und Isolde, Los Angeles Music Center Opera, 1987.

Publications

By HOCKNEY: books and illustrations–

Six Fairy Tales of the Brothers Grimm. Illustrated by David Hockney. 1969.
David Hockney: Travels with Pen, Pencil, and Ink. London, 1978.
Pictures. Edited by Nikos Stangos. New York, 1979.

Seidler, Tor. *The Dulcimer Boy.* Illustrated by David Hockney. New York, 1979.
Paper Pools. Edited by Nikos Strangos. New York, 1980.
David Hockney: Looking at Pictures in a Book. New York, 1981.
David Hockney Photographs. New York, 1982.
Hockney Paints the Stage. Minneapolis, 1983.
David Hockney: Martha's Vineyard—My Third Sketchbook from the Summer of 1982. New York, 1985.
_____, with Larry Stanton. *Larry Stanton: Painting and Drawing.* Pasadena, Calif., 1986.
David Hockney, Faces 1966-84. Los Angeles, 1987.
David Hockney. Edited by Nikos Stangos. New York, 1988.
David Hockney: A Retrospective. London, 1988.
Picasso. New York, 1990.

About HOCKNEY: books–

Friedman, Martin. *Hockney Paints the Stage.* With Contributions by J. Cox and Others. New York, 1983.
Livingston, Marco. *David Hockney.* London, 1987.
Webb, Peter. *Portrait of David Hockney.* New York, 1989.

articles–

Langton, B. "Game for the Stage; Realist Painter David Hockney Is Drawn into the World of Theatrical Illusion." *Opera News* 44 (May 1980): 12-14.

David Hockney's set for *The Rake's Progress,* **Glyndebourne Festival, 1975**

Smith, P.J. "*Parade:* An Evening of French Musical Theater; A Folio of Designs by David Hockney." *Opera News* 45 (28 February 1981): 20-21.

Steinbrink, M. "David Hockney Reinvents Himself." *Saturday Review* 8 (December 1981): 30-31.

Kolodin, I. "Stravinsky à la Hockney (*Le Sacre du Printemps; Le Rossignol; Oedipus Rex*)." *Saturday Review* 9 (February 1982): 46.

O'Connor, T. "Ad Hockney (Interview)." *San Francisco Opera Magazine* no. 5 (Summer 1982): 47-48.

Robertson, B. "David Hockney and the Theatre." *About the House* 6, no. 9 (1983): 26-28.

"David Hockney Paints the Stage." *Saturday Review* 9 (November-December 1983): 8.

Neubauer, S. "Piekfeine Moritat: Stawinsky's *The Rake's Progress*" in David Hockneys legendaerer Ausstattung in Bremen. *Opernwelt* 28, no. 6 (1987): 41-2.

Huck, W. "Recalling Fantasy: David Hockney and *The Rake's Progress.*" *San Francisco Opera Magazine* no. 2 (Fall 1988): 48-50.

Weschler, Lawrence. "Hockney on the Beach." *Interview* 19 (August 1989): 91.

Sheff, D. "The *Rolling Stone* Interview: David Hockney." *Rolling Stone* no. 593-94 (13 December 1990): 178-83.

Hanson, Henry. "Hockney Paints the Town Bright for Opera and Art." *Chicago* 41 (January 1991): 21.

Rockwell, John. "David Hockney Is Back in Opera, with a Few Ifs, Ands and Buts." *The New York Times* 140 (10 January 1991): B1.

Newhall, Edith. "David Hockney." *ARTnews* 90 (March 1991): 137.

Adams, Brooks. "Musical Mystery Flute." *Art in America* 79 (May 1991): 50.

Littell, Philip. "Opera Magician David Hockney and His Sorcerer's Apprentice." *The Advocate* (14 January 1992): 61.

*   *   *

David Hockney's first designs for an opera, Stravinsky's *The Rake's Progress* at Glyndebourne in 1975, seemed to grow quite naturally out of his well-known graphic work of the late 1960s and early 1970s. The predominantly black-and-white sets and costumes, with deliberately stylized cross hatching drawn on to the clothes and backdrops, use of written slogans, and tilted perspectives all harked back to his illustrations, among which was a series on the same theme. However, with the Glyndebourne *Die Zauberflöte* in 1978, and especially with the French triple bill at the Metropolitan Opera in 1981 (*Parade, Les mamelles de Tirésias* and *L'enfant et les sortilèges*), he developed a much more stagy and bold use of color and lighting, less an illustrator's and much more a painter's vision. These productions have proved remarkably durable and adaptable, and have been seen in several other theaters over quite a long period (*Die Zauberflöte* came to the Metropolitan Opera in 1990, *Parade* to the Paris Opéra-Comique in 1991). At the same time, Hockney developed a technique of working out his schemes for the productions which would begin with paintings, more or less connected with the theme in hand, then more specific designs, and finally integrated models to a scale of approximately one foot equals one inch. Hockney says that he was initially advised to work with models, in order to maintain a degree of control over the space and thus the lighting on stage—rather than just providing sketches for costumes and backdrops which might then be re-adapted by other hands.

Hockney's work with John Cox at Glyndebourne (a partnership to be renewed with *Die Frau ohne Schatten* at Covent Garden in late 1992), and especially with John Dexter for the French triple bill and a subsequent Stravinsky trio (*Oedipus Rex, Le rossignol* and *Le sacre du printemps*), evinced a theatricality which no other major postwar collaboration has produced. The transformation scene in *L'enfant et les sortilèges,* in which the child's room and its walls move away to reveal the huge tree in the garden, complete with bird and insect sounds and changes of color, is one of the simplest, yet most effective pieces of stage design in recent years.

For *Tristan und Isolde* at Los Angeles in 1987, in a production by Jonathan Miller, Hockney experimented with light boxes similar to ones that had been developed for large discotheques. His early studies for the opera seemed to take their starting point from late works of Picasso; the players dressed in brilliant reds and greens glowing through dark canvas. Isolde's curtain was a circus-painted flat, her bed like a fairground swing boat. The deck and ship's rails were daubed with Celtic crosses and stripes, the sails grey quarter moons, and the masts of the boat, tree trunks with peeling bark. In act II, the deep perspective of the forest was linked by an aquamarine-dappled lawn. As the climax of the love duet approached, dawn crept across the sky, turned green, and the castle turret was illuminated with a pinpoint spotlight.

With *Turandot* in Chicago in 1992, Hockney took the elaborate lighting scheme a step further, using not only the spotlights but juxtapositions of costumes to build up successive "paintings." Although he claimed *Turandot* as one of his favorite operas, it did not seem a natural for his style—the banishment of obvious chinoiserie leaving room for only an abstraction of forms and colors that hampered the possible interpretation of the drama. In the preliminary paintings (exhibited in January 1992) which were to become designs for *Die Frau ohne Schatten,* he seems to have moved towards a more obviously surrealist mood, somewhat in the manner of MacKnight-Kauffer or de Chirico. Tackling the problems of the use of light and space on stage, Hockney takes the early productions of Wieland Wagner as his ideal. In his always intense, sometimes oppressive, use of strong colors, Hockney harks back to the most extravagant creations of Bakst or Benois. Unlike them, though, he is always working with established pieces, and thus his contribution depends much more upon the individual strengths of the stage directors involved. One of the most good-natured and idealistic of modern artists, Hockney's example has yet to be followed by a younger generation of painters—to the loss of opera in general.

—Patrick O'Connor

HOFFMANN, E(rnst) T(heodor) A(madeus) (born Ernst Theodor Wilhelm Hoffman).

Composer. Born 24 January 1776, in Königsberg. Died 25 June 1822, in Berlin. Law student; assessor at Poznan; studied music with the organist Podbielski; music director of the theater in Bamberg; conducted opera performances in Leipzig and Dresden, 1813-14; settled in Berlin, 1814; series of articles in the *Allgemeine Musikalische Zeitung* under the name "Kapellmeister Johannes Kreisler."

Operas

Editions:

E.T.A. Hoffmann: Musikalische Werke, edited by G. Becking. Leipzig, 1922-27.
E.T.A. Hoffmann: Ausgewählte musikalische Werke, edited by G. von Dadelsen et al. Mainz, 1970-.

Die Maske (Singspiel), Hoffmann, 1799.
Scherz, List und Rache (Singspiel), Hoffmann (after Goethe), Poznan, 1801-02? [lost].
Die lustígen Musikanten (Singspiel), Brentano, Warsaw, 6 April 1805.
Die ungebetenen Gäste oder Der Kanonikus von Mailand (Singspiel), Rohrmann (after A. Duval, *Le souper imprévu*), 1805.
Liebe und Eifersucht, Hoffmann (after Calderón, *La banda y la flor,* translated by A.W. Schlegel), 1807.
Der Trank der Unsterblichkeit, J. von Soden, 1808.
Dirna (melodrama), J. von Soden, Bamberg, 11 October 1809.
Sabinus (melodrama), J. von Soden, 1810.
Aurora, F. von Holbein, 1811-12, Bamberg, 5 November 1933.
Saul, König in Israel (melodrama), J. Seyfried (after L.C. Caigniez, *Le triomphe de David*), Bamberg, 29 June 1811.
Undine, F. Fouqué, 1814, Berlin, 3 August 1816.
Der Liebhaber nach dem Tode, C.W. Salice-Contessa (after Calderón, *El galan fantasma*), 1818-22 [unfinished; lost].

E. T. A. Hoffmann, self-portrait engraved by L. Buchhorn, 1823

Other works: sacred and secular vocal music, orchestral works, chamber music, piano pieces.

Publications/Writings

For a complete listing of HOFFMANN's extensive writings on music, see the *New Grove Dictionary of Music and Musicians,* 1980 ed.

By HOFFMANN: books–

Schnapp, F., ed. *E.T.A. Hoffmanns Briefwechsel,* i-iii. Munich, 1967-69.
––––––, ed. *E.T.A. Hoffmann; Tagebücher.* Munich, 1971.
––––––, ed. *Schriften zur Musik.* Munich, 1977.
––––––, ed. *Der Musiker E.T.A. Hoffmann. Ein Dokumentenband.* Hildesheim, 1981.
Charlton, David, ed. *E.T.A. Hoffmann's Musical Writings.* Translated by Martyn Clarke. Cambridge, 1989.

articles–

Max Knight, trans. "Johannes Kreisler's Certificate of Apprenticeship." *19th Century Music* 5 (1982): 189.

About HOFFMANN: books–

Chezy, H. von. *Unvergessenes,* vol. 2, pp. 162 ff. Leipzig, 1858 [*Der Liebhaber nach dem Tode*].
Salomon, G. *E.T.A. Hoffmann: Bibliographie.* Weimar, 1924; 2nd ed. 1927, 1963.
Greeff, P. *E.T.A. Hoffmann als Musiker und Musikschriftsteller.* Cologne and Krefeld, 1948.
Ehinger, H. *E.T.A. Hoffmann als Musiker und Musikschriftsteller.* Olten and Cologne, 1954.
Voerster, J. *160 Jahre E.T.A. Hoffmann-Forschung 1805-1965: eine Bibliographie mit Inhaltserfassung und Erläuterungen.* Stuttgart, 1967.
Dechant, H. *E.T.A. Hoffmanns Oper "Aurora".* Regensburg, 1975.
Schläder, Jürgen. *Undine auf dem Musiktheater. Zur Entwicklungs-geschichte der deutschen Spieloper.* Bonn-Bad Godesberg, 1979.
Mistler, Jean. *Hoffmann le fantastique.* Paris, 1927; revised 2nd ed., 1950; revised 3rd ed., 1982.
Rohr, J. *E.T.A. Hoffmanns Theorie des musikalischen Dramas; Untersuchungen zum musikalisches Romantikbegriff in Umkreis der Leipziger "Allgemeine musikalische Zeitung."* Baden-Baden, 1985.

articles–

Weber, Carl Maria von. Review of *Undine. Allgemeine musikalische Zeitung* 19 (1817): column 201; reprinted in *Sämtliche Schriften von Carl Maria von Weber,* edited by G. Keiser, Berlin and Leipzig, 1908.
Truhn, H. "E.T.A. Hoffmann als Musiker: mit Beziehung auf die bevorstehende Herausgabe seines musikalischen Nachlasses." *Freihafen* ii/no. 3 (1839): 66.
Marschalk, E. von. "Die Bamberger Hof-Musik unter den drei letzen Fürstbischofen." In *Festschrift zum 50 jährigen Jubiläum des Liederkranzes Bamberg,* 20f, 44. Bamberg, 1885.
Leist, F. "Geschichte des Theaters in Bamberg." In *Historischer Verein zu Bamberg* 55 (1893): 130, 168.
Curzon, H. de. "La musique d'Hoffmann." *Revue internationale de musique* 15 May (1898): 321.

Pfitzner, H. "E.T.A. Hoffmanns Undine." *Süddeutsche Monatshefte* 3 (1906): 307; reprinted in *Gesammelte Schriften* vol. 1, p. 55, Munich, 1926.

Thiessen, K. "E.T.A. Hoffmanns Zauberoper Undine und ihre Bedeutung für die Entwicklung der deutschen romantischen Oper." *Neue Musikzeitung* 28 (1907): 491.

Kroll, E. "E.T.A. Hoffmann als Bühnenkomponist." *Die Musik* 15/no. 1 (1922): 99 [*Aurora*].

———. "E.T.A. Hoffmanns Opern" [*Aurora*]. In *Almanach der Deutschen Musikbücherei 1924-25*, 178.

———. "Über den Musiker E.T.A. Hoffmann." *Zeitschrift für Musikwissenschaft* 4 (1922): 530; corrections, 644.

Becking, G. "Zur musikalischen Romantik." *Deutsche Vierteljahrsschrift für Literaturwissenschaft und Geistesgeschichte* 2 (1924): 581-615.

Abraham, Gerald. "Hoffman as a Composer." *Musical Times* 83 (1942): 233; reprinted in *Slavonic and Romantic Music*, 233ff. London, 1968.

Schnapp, F. "E.T.A. Hoffmanns letzte Oper." *Schweizerische Musikzeitung/Revue musicale suisse* 88 (1948): 339.

Neumann, A.R. "Musician or Author? - E.T.A. Hoffmann's Decision." *Journal of English and Germanic Philology* 52 (1953): 174.

Fellerer, K.G. "Der Musiker E.T.A. Hoffmann." *Literaturwissenschaftliches Jahrbuch der Görres-Gesellschaft* new series (1963): 43.

Lichtenhahn, E. "Über einen Ausspruch Hoffmanns und über das Romantische in der Musik." In *Musik und Geschichte: Leo Schrade zum sechzigsten Geburtstag*, 178. Cologne, 1963.

Sölle, D. and W. Seifert. "In Dresden und in Atlantis: E.T.A. Hoffmann und die Musik." *Neue Zeitschrift für Musik* 124 (1963): 260.

Giraud, J. "Die Maske' ein bereits typisches Hoffmann-Werk." *Mitteilungen der E.T.A. Hoffmann-Gesellschaft* 14 (1968): 18.

Allroggen, G. "E.T.A. Hoffmanns Musik zur 'Dirna'." *Mitteilungen der E.T.A. Hoffmann-Gesellschaft* 15 (1969): 31.

———. "Die Opern-Ästhetik E.T.A. Hoffmanns." In *Beiträge zur Geschichte der Oper*, edited by H. Becker, 25. Regensburg, 1969.

Herd, R. "Hoffmanns 'Dirna' wieder aufgetaucht: ein Bericht." *Mitteilungen der E.T.A. Hoffmann-Gesellschaft* 15 (1969): 2.

Schnapp, F. "Die Quelle von Sodens Melodram 'Dirna'." *Mitteilungen der E.T.A. Hoffmann-Gesellschaft* 15 (1969): 4.

Garlington, Aubrey S. Jr. "Notes on Dramatic Motives in Opera: Hoffmann's *Undine*." *Music Review* 32 (1971): 136.

Zhitomirsky, D.V. "Ideal'noye i real'noye v muzikal'noy estetike E.T.A. Gofmana" [ideology and reality in Hoffmann's musical aesthetics]. *Sovetskaya muzyka* no. 8 (1973): 97.

Allroggen, G. "Hoffmanns Musik zum 'Sabinus'." *Mitteilungen der E.T.A. Hoffmann-Gesellschaft* 20 (1974): 41.

Schnapp, F., ed. "*Sabinus*: Melodram in Drei Aufzügen von Julius Reichsgrafen von Soden mit Abänderungen von E.T.A. Hoffmann." *Mitteilungen der E.T.A. Hoffmann-Gesellschaft* 20 (1974): 1 [complete text of the melodrama].

Sams, E. "E.T.A. Hoffmann, 1776-1822." *Musical Times* 117 (1976): 29.

Maehder, Jürgen. "Die Poetisierung der Klangfarben in Dichtung und Musik der deutschen Romantik." *Aurora* 38 (1978): 9.

Garlington, Aubrey S. Jr. "E.T.A. Hoffmann's *Der Dichter und der Komponist* and the creation of the German Romantic Opera." *Musical Quarterly* 55 (1979): 22.

Miller, Norbert. "Hoffmann und Spontini. Vorüberlegungen zu einer Ästhetik der romantischen *opera seria*." In *Studien zur Musikgeschichte Berlins in frühen 19. Jahrhundert*, ed. Carl Dahlhaus, 451. Regensburg, 1980.

Becker, Max. "Spezialisierung auf den Totaleffekt -Absolute Musik im Gesamtkunstwerk bei E.T.A. Hoffmann." In *2. Romantikkonferenz 1982*, edited by Günther Stephan and Hans John, 48. Dresden, 1983; also published in *Beiträge zur Musikwissenschaft* 25 (1983): 293.

Köhler, Ingeborg. "Richard Wagner und E.T.A. Hoffmann." *Mitteilungen der E.T.A. Hoffmann Gesellschaft* 29 (1983): 36.

unpublished–

Wilson, Richard L. "Text and Music in the Operas of E.T.A. Hoffmann." Ph.D. dissertation, University of Southern California, 1988.

E.T.A. Hoffmann is one of the most brilliant of early-nineteenth century German Romantic figures, being the only trained musician among such near-contemporaries as Wackenroder, Tieck, Novalis, August and Ferdinand von Schlegel. Posterity concurs with his contemporaries in that he was more gifted as a writer than as a musician.

Hoffmann's childhood years were unhappy due to his father, who was violently opposed to the young boy's interest in music. Because of economic necessities, he completed law studies in Königsberg in 1795, but only a year later began a desultory series of musical studies which continued off and on until 1798 when he moved to Berlin, where J.F. Reichardt gave him composition lessons. In 1799 his first theatrical work, *Die Maske*, a Singspiel in three acts for which he wrote his own text, was produced privately. By 1808 he had composed at least seven stage works. Two more, *Aurora* and *Undine*, followed in 1811 and 1816, respectively. Hoffmann was also responsible for incidental music for approximately twenty plays between 1804 and 1812.

Hoffmann's personality was such that he had great difficulty in holding a position, but in 1804 he was successful enough with music to be able to give up his legal career. In 1809 the first of his gifted tales in which music served as the center appeared when Rochlitz published *Ritter Gluck* in the *Algemeine musikalische Zeitung*. Other stories, polemics, criticisms, fantasies, etc., quickly followed, and Hoffmann's literary fame grew rapidly. His essay on Beethoven's Fifth Symphony, 1815, one of the best contemporary articles written about this work, was admired by Beethoven himself.

Hoffmann became deeply concerned over the lack of a German Romantic Opera. His seminal essay, *Der Dichter und der Komponist*, 1813, appeared the same year he began work on *Undine*, after the famed novella by de la Motte Fouqué, which was destined to be his final opera and last major compositional effort. In *Der Dichter* Hoffmann argued that the poet and composer would ideally be two separate creative intelligences who would explore the wondrous realm of the imagination together in order to create new images of truth. Only the most sophisticated fantasies were to be the substance of the new German Romantic opera. Unlike other Romantics Hoffmann was suspicious of popular culture, and the new German Romantic Opera was *not* to cater to the lower classes

(*Der Freischütz* would not please him.) Paradoxically, *Undine* was an entirely different kind of creative actuality as opposed to the brilliant theoretical speculations offered in this major essay.

During this period, Hoffmann came to recognize his deficiencies as a composer and gave up music. He returned to the Prussian civil service in 1814 when he obtained a legal post in Berlin. *Undine* premiered in 1816 with limited acclaim, but after only 14 performances the theater burned, and *Undine* was not to be staged again until the twentieth century. Hoffmann's last years in Berlin also saw his greatest literary effort, *Kater Murr,* and the final collection of many of his brilliant stories and tales into a definitive four volume edition, as *Die Serapionsbrüder.* While his devotion to music was never doubted, his undisciplined and eratic behavior kept him from acquiring the technical discipline necessary for him to become a major composer.

—Aubrey S. Garlington

HOFMANNSTHAL, Hugo von.

Librettist/Poet/Dramatist. Born 1 February 1874, in Vienna. Died 15 July 1929, in Vienna. Successful career as a poet, 1890s; approached Strauss with the scenario for the ballet *Der Triumph der Zeit,* 1900, but never set; collaboration with Strauss began with the adaptation of Hofmannsthal's play *Elektra* as an opera libretto, 1906; established the Salzburg Festival with Max Reinhardt, 1920. In addition to his famous collaborations with Strauss, Hofmannsthal's texts were set by many other composers, including Wellesz, Varèse, and Zemlinsky.

Librettos

Elektra, R. Strauss, 1909.
Oedipus und die Sphinx, E. Varèse, 1908-14 [unfinished; lost].
Der Rosenkavalier, R. Strauss, 1911.
Ariadne auf Naxos, R. Strauss, 1912; revised, 1915-16.
Die Frau ohne Schatten, R. Strauss, 1919.
Alkestis (after Hofmannsthal's play), E. Wellesz, 1924.
Die ägyptische Helena, R. Strauss, 1928.
Die Hochzeit der Sobeide (after Hofmannsthal's play), A. Tcherepnin, 1930.
Arabella, R. Strauss, 1933.
Die Liebe der Danaë (completed by J. Gregor), R. Strauss, 1944 (dress rehearsal for canceled premiere).
Das Bergwerk zu Falun (after Hofmannsthal's play), R. Wagner-Régeny, 1961.

Publications/Writings

By HOFMANNSTHAL: books–

Strauss, F., ed. *Richard Strauss: Briefwechsel mit Hugo von Hofmannsthal.* Berlin, 1925; English translation, 1928.

Hugo von Hofmannsthal (left) with Richard Strauss, silhouette by W. Bithorn, 1914

Steiner, H., ed. *H. von Hofmannsthal: Gesammelte Werke.* Stockholm and Frankfurt am Main, 1946-49.

Hottinger, M., and T. and J. Stern, eds. *H. von Hofmannsthal: Selected Writings.* London and New York, 1952.

Schuh, W., ed. *Hugo von Hofmannsthal: Danae oder die Vernunftheirat: Szenarium und Notizen.* Frankfurt, 1952.

———. *Richard Strauss und Hugo von Hofmannsthal: Briefwechsel: Gesamtausgabe.* Zurich, 1952; 2nd ed., 1955; English translation, 1961, 1980.

Gilbert, M.E., ed. *H. von Hofmannsthal: Selected Essays.* Oxford, 1955.

Burger, H., ed. *Hugo von Hofmannsthal und Harry, Graf Kessler: Briefwechsel 1898-1929.* Frankfurt am Main, 1969.

About HOFMANNSTHAL: books–

Krüger, K.J. *Hugo von Hofmannsthal und Richard Strauss.* Berlin, 1935.

Naef, Karl J. *Hugo von Hofmannsthal: Wesen und Werk.* Zurich, 1938.

Hammelmann, H. *Hofmannsthal.* Cambridge, 1957.

Baum, G. *"Hab' mir gelobt, ihn lieb zu haben . . .": Richard Strauss und Hugo von Hofmannsthal nach ihrem Briefwechsel dargestellt.* Berlin, 1962.

Rösch, Ewald. *Die Komödien Hofmannsthals: Die Entfaltung ihrer Sinnstruktur aus dem Thema der Daseinstufen.* Marburg, 1963.

Baum, G. *Richard Strauss und Hugo von Hofmannsthal.* Berlin, 1964.

Haas, Willy. *Hugo von Hofmannsthal.* Berlin, 1964.

Pörnbacher. *H. von Hofmannsthal-R. Strauss: "Der Rosenkavalier". Interpretation.* Monaco, 1964.

Schuh, W. *Hugo von Hofmannsthal und Richard Strauss: Legende und Wirklichkeit.* Munich, 1964.

Schäfer, Rudolph H. *Hugo von Hofmannsthals "Arabella".* Bern, 1967.

Knaus, J. *Hugo von Hofmannsthal und sein Weg zur Oper Die Frau ohne Schatten.* Berlin, 1971.

Schuh, W., ed. *Hugo von Hofmannsthal, Richard Strauss: Der Rosenkavalier: Fassungen, Filmszenarium, Briefe.* Frankfurt am Main, 1971.

Smith, P.J. *The Tenth Muse.* New York, 1970.

Lenz, Eva-Maria. *Hugo von Hofmannsthals mythologische Oper "Die ägyptische Helene".* Tübingen, 1972.

Fuhrich-Leisler, Edde. *Hugo von Hofmannsthal auf dem Theater seiner Zeit: Katalog der Ausstellung.* Salzburg, 1974.

Forsyth, Karen. *"Ariadne auf Naxos" by Hugo von Hofmannsthal and Richard Strauss: its Genesis and Meaning.* Oxford, 1982.

articles–

Wellesz, E. "Hofmannsthal and Strauss." *Music and Letters* 33 (1952): 239.

Keith-Smith, B. "Hugo von Hofmannsthal." In *German Men of Letters,* vol. 1, edited by A. Natan. London, 1961.

Winder, Marianne. "The Psychological Significance of Hofmannsthal's *Ariadne auf Naxos.*" *German Life and Letters* 15 (1961).

Cohn, Hilde D. "Hofmannsthals Libretti." *German Quarterly* 35 (1962).

Mühler, Robert. "Hugo von Hofmannsthals Oper *Ariadne auf Naxos.*" *Interpretationen zur Österreichischen Literatur* 6 (1971).

Könneker, Barbara. "Die Funktion des Vorspiels in Hofmannsthals *Ariadne auf Naxos.*" *Germanisch-Romanische Monatsschrift* 12 (1972).

Auden, W.H. "A Marriage of 'True Minds'." In *Forwards and Afterwards.* London, 1973.

Stenberg, Peter S. "Silence, Ceremony, and Song in Hofmannsthal's Libretti." *Seminar* 11 (1975).

Borchmeyer, Dieter. "Der Mythos als Oper. Hofmannsthal und Richard Wagner." *Hofmannsthal-Forschungen* 7 (1983): 19.

Gurewitsch, M. "In the Mazes of Light and Shadow: a Thematic Comparison of *The Magic Flute* and *Die Frau ohne Schatten.*" *Opera Quarterly* 1/no. 2 (1983): 11.

Hoppe, Manfred. "Das 'Musikalische Gespräch' in *Der Bürger als Edelmann:* Ein 'richtiges Gedicht' Hofmannsthals?" *Modern Philology* 81 (1983): 159.

———. "Fromme Parodien. Hugo von Hofmannsthals Opernlibretti als Stilexperimente." *Hofmannsthal-Forschungen* 7 (1983): 67.

Kessler, Harry. "Die Entstehung der Josef-Legende." *Hofmannsthal-Blätter* 27 (1983): 53.

Pix, Gunther. "Die Operndramaturgie des *Rosenkavalier* zwischen Hofmannsthals Libretto und Strauss' musikalischer Komposition." *Sprache im Technischen Zeitalter* 3/no. 91 (1984): 179.

Schuh, W. "Hofmannsthal, Kessler und die *Josephslegende.*" *Hofmannsthal-Blätter* 27 (1983): 48.

unpublished–

Partsch, E.W. "Artifizialität und Manipulation. Studien zur Genese und Konstitution der 'Spieloper' bei Richard Strauss unter besonderer Berücksichtigung der *Schweigsamen Frau.*" Ph.D. dissertation, University of Vienna, 1983.

Hofmannsthal's early work is instinctively cognizant of a "cultural synthesis" indigenous to Vienna, a city traditionally, geographically, and historically situated at the East/West "crossroads" of Europe. The symbolist imagery characterizing the early poems, overlaid by a finely controlled, almost virtuosic lyricism, had dangers and limitations which Hofmannsthal himself recognized. Indeed, the so-called "Chandos letter" (1902) registers an artistic crisis which led to the abandonment of purely poetic forms. Hofmannsthal turned to theater, whose "collaborative unity" added a new, expressive dimension to his work; the dramatic instinct inherent in his lyric verse found an outlet in plays such as the Sophocles *Elektra* re-working (1903), *König Oedipus* (1910), and the moralities *Jedermann* (1906) and *Das grosse Welttheater* (1921). These developments in Hofmannsthal's career were inspired both by a desire to reach a wider audience with his works, and by an emergent social and political conscience. The Habsburg decline and the dissipatory effects of post-First World War diplomacy upon Austria aroused patriotic feelings resulting in a series of historical lectures designed by Hofmannsthal to revive the traditional Austrian mediatory role as a factor in the spiritual restructuring of modern Europe. Theater it seemed, was the perfect and obvious medium for the propagation of such ideas. In religious allegory— through the symbolic and festive ritual of the morality plays—Hofmannsthal sought to re-establish the spiritual identity of the Austro-Bavarian race.

The final stage in this process of artistic synthesis, cultural dissemination and spiritual regeneration was inevitably opera with its formal combination of musical and theatrical elements. Thus, Hofmannsthal's collaborative decision was no diversionary experiment in an illustrious literary career but a deliberate step toward a clearly envisaged socio-political and cultural goal. Baroque orientated, his preferred concept of "theater" as a festive institution could best be realized in opera. Ceremonial in aspect, uplifting of spirit, popular in appeal, opera, as a celebration of artistic unity, approached the ultimate cultural phenomenon. Sensing his collaborative destiny, Hofmannsthal approached Strauss with a ballet sketch as early as 1900. It was their meeting in 1906, however, that launched a twenty-three year long collaboration that began with *Elektra* and ended with *Arabella* (1929).

Naturally, a partnership between two such individually distinguished and independent artists ran into difficulties from time to time. The *Elektra* adaptation and the composition of *Der Rosenkavalier* went smoothly enough, but the ideological abstractions of *Ariadne* presented problems to the practically-minded Strauss. This was a testing time as poet and composer struggled to define the extent of their individual artistic freedom within the collaborative environment. The net result, however, was real gain; *Ariadne*'s deployment of ballet, pantomime, speech, poetry, drama, music, and its juxtaposition of tragedy and comedy constitutes a seminal experiment in theatrical integration. Musically speaking it initiated a neo-classic style indicative of the new direction which Hofmannsthal had set for the composer.

Strauss recognized the opportunity to work alongside a writer of Hofmannsthal's calibre as an intellectual and artistic challenge of the highest order. Inspired, as ever, by poetry, he was acutely aware of the problems inherent in combining text and music. The avowed aim of the partnership—to seek with delicacy and imagination new ways of expression—was, indeed, characteristically realized in the "declamatory" pace of *Der Rosenkavalier, Ariadne* and *Arabella*. These works, depending upon textual comprehensibility for their success, are, by virtue of their "conversational" *genre*, closely related to Viennese stage comedy (of which Hofmannsthal was so persuasive an exponent). They deliberately tackle, and (each in its own way) solve, the perennial problem of musical and textual balance: the employment of interchangeable declamatory techniques (between poetry and music) within a lyric framework grants *Rosenkavalier, Ariadne* and *Arabella* an innovatory significance in the context of the Strauss/Hofmannsthal opus.

Hofmannsthal's strength as a librettist lies, indeed, in a lyricism whose loosely woven verbal texture allows space for, and is cognizant of, the music which underlies it and which it evokes. In *Die Frau ohne Schatten,* however, the poet essayed an esoteric symbolism whose psychological complexity and concentration of ideas led, both textually and musically, to a more formal and weighty style. Taking its starting point from Mozart's *Magic Flute, Die Frau,* whose ideas spilled over into a separate literary work, was destined—despite its compelling power—to outgrow its original terms of reference. A further experiment, *Die Aegyptische Helena,* promoted in a light "operetta vein," suffered similarly.

The Strauss/Hofmannsthal collaboration, undoubtedly one of the most important in musical history, contributed materially to the artistic development of both poet and composer. Each recognized the other's value as a spur to inspiration and achievement, and as a sounding board for ideas. In many ways theirs was the perfect partnership, in which it might be said that Strauss, the musician, through his practical instinct for theater, approached the status of dramatist, while Hofmannsthal, the dramatist, through his evocative "sound" language, approached that of the musician. Creative achievement apart—a total of five operas and a ballet—their association had, for Strauss, implications far beyond Hofmannsthal's death: it is inconceivable, without his stimulation, vision and guidance that Strauss's last opera *Capriccio* could have been written. Not the least important aspect of the collaboration was the voluminous correspondence, published in numerous editions over the years, a detailed record of the creative imagination at work on its subject, it remains, as a literary document, a lasting testimony to a unique collaborative venture.

—Kenneth Birkin

HOLST, Gustav [born Gustavus Theodore von Holst].

Composer. Born 21 September 1874, in Cheltenham. Died 25 May 1934, in London. Married: Isobel Harrison, 1901 (daughter: Imogen Clare Holst, musician and chronicler of her father's life, born 12 April 1907, in Richmond, Surrey; died 9 March 1984, in Aldeburgh). Studied music with his mother, a piano teacher, and his father, an organist; studied trombone, piano with Herbert Sharpe, composition with Charles Villiers Stanford and William Smyth Rockstro at the Royal College of Music in London, beginning 1893; trombonist in various London orchestras; music master at St Paul's Girls' School, 1905; music director of Morley College in London, 1907; organized musical activities among British troops in Salonika and Constantinople during World War I; composition teacher, Royal College of Music, London, 1919; on the faculty of Reading College, 1919-23; lecturer and conductor in the United States, 1923 and 1932. Holst studied both Sanskrit and eastern philosophy throughout his life.

Operas/Masques

Editions: *Collected Facsimile Edition.* London, 1974.

Publishers: Boosey and Hawkes, Faber, Novello, Stainer and Bell.

The Revoke, Fritz Hart, 1895.
The Idea (children's operetta), Fritz Hart, 1898.
The Youth's Choice, Holst, 1902.
Sita, Holst (after an episode from the Ramayana, translated by Holst), 1900-1906.
Savitri (chamber opera), Holst (after an episode from the Mahabharata), 1908, London, Wellington Hall, 5 December 1916.
The Vision of Dame Christian (masque), 1909.
The Perfect Fool, Holst, 1918-22, London, Covent Garden, 14 May 1923.
At the Boar's Head, after Shakespeare, *Henry IV,* 1924, Manchester, 3 April 1925.
The Wandering Scholar (chamber opera), Clifford Bax, 1929-30, Liverpool, David Lewis Theatre, 31 January 1934.

Other works: orchestral works, choral works, chamber music, piano pieces.

Publications

By HOLST: books—

Short, M., ed. *Gustav Holst (1874-1934): a Centenary Documentation.* London, 1974.

Gustav Holst

_____. *Collected Essays on Gustav Holst.* London, 1974.
Short, M., ed. *Gustav Holst: Letters to W.G. Whittaker.* Glasgow, 1974.

About HOLST: books–

Holst, Imogen. *Gustav Holst: A Biography.* London, 1938; 2nd ed., 1969.
Rubbra, E. *Gustav Holst.* Monaco, 1947, 1973.
Holst, Imogen. *The Music of Gustav Holst.* London, 1951; revised 3rd ed., 1975; 4th ed., 1986?.
Vaughan Williams, U., and Imogen Holst. *Heirs and Rebels.* London, 1959, 1974.
Holst, Imogen. *Holst. The Great Composers.* London, 1975; 2nd ed., 1981.
Pirie, Peter John. *The English Musical Renaissance.* London, 1979.

articles–

Evans, E. "Modern British Composers: 6. Gustav Holst," *Musical Times* 9 (1919): 524, 588, 657.
Vaughan Williams, Ralph. "Gustav Holst." *Music and Letters* 1 (1920): 181, 305.
Capell, R. "Gustav Holst: Notes for a Biography." *Musical Times* 67 (1926): 1073; 68 (1927): 17.
Evans, E. "Gustav Holst." *Musical Times* 75 (1934): 593.
Bax, C. "Recollections of Gustav Holst." *Music and Letters* 20 (1939): 1.
Mellers, W. "Holst and the English Language." *Music Review* 2 (1941): 228; reprinted in *Studies in Contemporary Music*, London, 1947.
Tippett, Michael. "Holst: Figure of Our Time." *Listener* 13 November (1958).
Warrack, John. "A New Look at Gustav Holst." *Musical Times* February (1963).
Holst, Imogen, A.C. Boult, F. Wilkinson, and R. Spearing. "Commemorative Essays," *Royal College of Music Magazine* 70 (1974): 49.
Ottaway, Hugh. "Holst as an Opera Composer." *Musical Times* June (1974).
Warrack, John. "Holst and the Linear Principle." *Musical Times* 115 (1974): 732.
Holst, Imogen. "Holst's *At the Boar's Head.*" *Musical Times* 123 (1982): 321.
Head, Raymond. "Holst and India." *Tempo* September (1986); March (1987); September (1988).

*   *   *

While he was a student, Holst was greatly affected by the music of Wagner, by the guild socialism of William Morris and by the poetry of Walt Whitman. It was not until after he left college in 1897, however, that he came across the ancient Hindu legends and the Indian sacred scriptures, the *Rig Veda,* which became a lifelong interest, providing the plot for at least two of his operas as well as being a source for some of his other important works. Finding no adequate translation of them, he set to and learned Sanskrit so as to translate them himself.

During this period of his life, Holst was obliged to earn his living as a trombonist and *repetiteur* in the Carl Rosa Opera Company, gaining further experience of operatic conditions first hand by playing under Richter at Covent Garden. He also played in the Scottish Orchestra, and this experience of orchestral life from the inside was invaluable to him. However, he never lost sight of his vocation as a composer. His opera *Sita,* to his own libretto, and based on an episode from the *Bhagavad-Gita,* was composed between 1900 and 1906, and was unsuccessfully entered for the Ricordi prize in 1908. It was never performed, and Holst later dismissed it as "good old Wagnerian bawling".

Holst's *Savitri,* however, is quite another matter; it has remained the only one of his stage pieces to achieve regular performance. For all his experience in the opera house and his interest in the theater, Holst's reputation as a composer was felt by the critics and the public at large to rest mainly on his choral and orchestral music. He developed a characteristic musical idiom of his own, absorbing stylistic elements from English folk-song, from the brilliant orchestral writing of the impressionists, and from the sensitivity to the rhythm and sense of English prosody found in the works of Henry Purcell and the Elizabethan madrigal composers (Weelkes was his especial favorite) to which he added his own peculiar blend of forthright craftsmanship and gentle but never sentimental mysticism.

The mystical element is particularly evident in works such as *Savitri,* and it may well have puzzled early audiences. But this is only part of the story; the lack of recognition of his operas was due at least in part to the haphazard manner in which opera in Britain was financed and administered at that time, as well as the unconventional subjects for stage presentation that aroused Holst's interest. None the less, his orchestral music attracted some attention during the period before the first World War even if his operas remained unperformed.

In December 1916, *Savitri* was performed for the first time at the London School of Opera. Its first professional performance came at the Lyric Theatre, Hammersmith, on 23 June 1921. This encouraged Holst to work on another opera, *The Perfect Fool,* a light-hearted and satirical surrealist one-acter first performed by the recently-established British National Opera Company on the opening night of its 1923 season at Covent Garden. Holst's parodies of Wagner and Verdi in *The Perfect Fool* have failed to stay the course, but the vigorous ballet music has become a favorite concert piece.

With the successful production of works such as *The Planets* and *The Hymn of Jesus* (1920), Holst was one of the foremost musical figures of the post-war generation, and in 1923, he paid the first of his visits to the United States, lecturing and conducting for three months at the University of Michigan. He was also now on the staff of the Royal College of Music and of University College, Reading. But overwork led to an enforced rest from teaching and conducting, and for some months in 1924, he went to live at Thaxted in Essex, where he worked on his *Choral Symphony* and his comic opera, *At the Boar's Head,* an interlude based on the Falstaff scenes from *King Henry IV* and making much use of traditional tunes that fitted the Shakespeare text with amazing aptness. It was first performed in Manchester on 3 April 1925.

Holst's music following *At the Boar's Head* tended to be much more austere, as is evident in such works as the *Fugal Concerto* (1925) and *Egdon Heath* (1928), based on a passage in Hardy's *The Return of the Native.* This was, however, no neoclassicist, Stravinskian reaction, as some critics mistakenly took it to be; similar economy of means can be found as early as *Savitri.* Holst was merely developing an aspect of his musical personality that had lain dormant for some time, and which puzzled the British critics, some of whom dismissed his later music as being in decline. But he was still welcomed in the United States, where he spent the first six months of

1932 lecturing in composition at Harvard. While he was there, he was operated on for a duodenal ulcer; his health, never robust, gradually deteriorated and he was unable to attend the premiere of his last opera, *The Wandering Scholar,* at the David Lewis Theatre, Liverpool, on 31 January 1934. He died on 25 May of that year.

Holst's operas are unconventional. They lack the stock components of the standard operatic plot, such as flamboyant, passionate characters and full-blooded love-music; and though their composer had a fertile melodic and harmonic gift, the two most striking of them—*Savitri* and *The Wandering Scholar*—are notable more for their reticence and half-light atmosphere than for any spectacular stage effects. His gift for parody, evident in *The Perfect Fool,* and his sense of fun, notable in *At the Boar's Head,* are qualities not always appreciated by the unsophisticated among opera-goers, and his questing spirit, always firmly avoiding the beaten track, was stimulated more by transcendental issues rather than purely human ones. Thus his portrayal of character is at its best and most profound in situations such as the prolonged encounter with and eventual conquest of Death in *Savitri,* where the inner core of the heroine's tender devotion to her husband is revealed, rather than any passionate protestation of sexual desire. It is this, plus a fine consistency and intensity of mood, that makes *Savitri* in particular the moving little masterpiece that it is. With the interest in chamber opera resulting from Britten's success in the genre after World War II, at least it and *The Wandering Scholar* should come into their own, even if his other operas do not.

—James Day

HOMER, Louise [née Beatty].

Contralto. Born 30 April 1871, in Pittsburgh. Died 6 May 1947, in Winter Park, Florida. Married: Sidney Homer in 1895; six children. Studied in Paris with Fidèle Koenig and Paul Lhérie; debut as Leonora in *La favorite* in Vichy, 1898; Covent Garden debut as Lola in *Cavalleria rusticana,* 1899; Metropolitan Opera debut as Amneris, 1900; premiered Humperdinck's *Königskinder* in 1910; premiered Parker's *Mona;* sang with the Chicago Opera Company, 1920-25; sang with the Metropolitan Opera, 1927-1929.

Publications:

About HOMER: books–

Homer, S. *My Wife and I.* New York, 1939.
Homer, A. *Louise Homer and the Golden Age of Opera.* New York, 1973.

* * *

Few artists have successfully combined a fulfilling domestic life with a triumphant performing career. Few have even tried. But one who both tried and succeeded was the noted American contralto, Louise Homer.

Daughter of a Pennsylvania minister, Louise Dilworth Beatty was raised in a large family where equal affection, common effort, and strict moral values prevailed. When Louise's voice was "discovered" in high school, no one at home

paid much attention. On her own, she ventured to Philadelphia where she studied to become "Miss Beatty, Stenographer and Typewriter," successful enough, with a church choir salary, to pay for singing lessons with several uncomprehending teachers, none of whom knew what to do with her rich, deep, cumbersome voice. Frustrated by her lack of progress, Louise went to Boston to enroll in the New England Conservatory of Music. There she met Sidney Homer, a Boston-born private teacher of harmony and would-be composer who had studied abroad. Henceforward, both their lives changed. He introduced her to opera and ambitions she had never dreamed of; she inspired in him "the truth that I have sought and never found."

The Homers were married in January, 1895, and in November of that year, Louise, the first of six children, was born. Meanwhile plans were being made to go abroad, to find a proper teacher for Louise and to provide Sidney with freedom to compose. With borrowed funds and Baby Louise, they embarked for Paris to seek their fortunes.

In these unfamiliar surroundings events moved swiftly. Finally Louise met a teacher in Fidèle König who found the key to her vocal problems, so that life at home could be more relaxed. Within a year, the voice was "floating free," its range miraculously extended and such staples as octave leaps, pianissimi, trills, and sustained coloratura became second nature. When at a routine audition in 1898 she was offered a summer engagement for leading roles at Vichy, she was as amazed as the seasoned impresario who discovered her.

From then on, with the singing career successfully launched, there were always equally important family problems: In busy Vichy would there be a safe place for the baby to play? Could Louise convince the family back home that it wasn't "sinful" to appear in opera? In Angers, the next stop, could they find a modest house of their own instead of the cramped quarters provided? In London during two prestigious international summer seasons at Covent Garden, finding appropriate quarters for themselves and Sidney's visiting relatives was a top priority.

Perhaps the most serious crisis of all took place when in Maurice Grau's offer of a Metropolitan Opera contract for the 1900 season there appeared in Louise's repertory list two boy's roles, Siebel in *Faust* and Urbain in *Les Huguenots.* Sidney, envisioning Louise in close-fitting tights so uncharacteristic of her usual majestic appearance, was outraged, and a feverish trans-Atlantic correspondence with family and friends followed. However, the matter was settled to the satisfaction of all by the Théatre de la Monnaie's costumer who, with tunics, cloaks, and knee-high boots, made Louise look boyish yet modest. Ironically, in later years, she scored one of her greatest successes in male attire—the title role in Toscanini's legendary revival of Gluck's *Orfeo.*

From 1900 to 1919, Louise Homer sang with the Metropolitan Opera—over 700 performances of forty-two roles in seasons interrupted only once by the birth of the youngest of their six children. The family remained together during those years, in New York and at their summer home at Bolton on Lake George, New York. There she sponsored Sunday hymn-sings which drew families from the surrounding country, and brought back echoes of less affluent days in her minister-father's parish. Her concert tours were planned, often to the consternation of her managers, so that she would never be long away from home, and when her daughter Louise proved to have a pleasing lyric soprano, mother and daughter toured successfully in joint recitals, often programming Sidney's well known songs as solos and duets.

As Anne, Louise's biographer-daughter wrote: "A career in singing and a tranquil life—that had been their unlikely goal . . ." and when in later years, she received offers "that might have enhanced her reputation . . . she had refused, not wanting to disturb their life at home and perhaps diminish the stability and contentment they had managed to achieve."

—Louis Snyder

HONEGGER, Arthur (Oscar).

Composer. Born 10 March 1892, in Le Havre. Died 27 November 1955, in Paris. Married: Andrée Vaurabourg (1894-1980), pianist and composer, 1926. Studied violin with Lucien Capet in Paris; studied with L. Kempter and F. Hegar at the Zurich Conservatory, 1909-11; studied with André Gédalge and Charles-Marie Widor at the Paris Conservatory, beginning 1912, and took private lessons with Vincent d'Indy; composed the well known "machine" piece *Pacific 231,* 1923; visited the United States in 1929, and again in 1947, when he taught summer classes at the Berkshire Music Center at Tanglewood. Honegger was one of "Les Six," which included Milhaud, Poulenc, Auric, Durey, and Tailleferre.

Operas

Publisher: Salabert.

Antigone, Jean Cocteau (after Sophocles), 1924-27, Brussels, Théâtre de la Monnaie, 28 December 1927.
Judith (biblical opera), René Morax, 1926, Monte Carlo, 13 February 1926.
Amphion (ballet-melodrama), Paul Valéry, 1929, Paris, Opéra, 23 June 1931.
Les aventures du roi Pausole (operetta), Albert Willemetz (after a novel by Pierre Louÿs), 1930, Paris, Théâtre des Bouffes-Parisiens, 12 December 1930.
La belle de Moudon (vaudeville), René Morax, 1933, Mézières, Théâtre du Jorat, 1933.
L'aiglon (with Ibert), Henri Cain (based on a play by Edmond Rostand), 1935, Monte Carlo, 11 March 1937.
Les petites cardinales (operetta), Albert Willemetz, 1937, Paris, Théâtre des Bouffes-Parisiens, 12 February 1938.
Nicholas de Flue (dramatic legend), Denis de Rougemont, 1939, Neuchâtel, 1941.
Charles le téméraire, René Morax, 1943-44, Mézières, Théâtre du Jorat, May 1944.

Other works: incidental music, radio and film scores, orchestral works, vocal works, chamber music, songs.

Publications

By HONEGGER: books–

Incantation aux fossiles. Lausanne, 1948.
Reich, Willi, ed. *Arthur Honegger: Nachklang: Schriften, Photos, Dokumente.* Zurich, 1957.
Je suis compositeur. Paris, 1951; English translation, London, 1966.
Klemm, Eberhardt, ed. *Beruf und Handwerk des Komponisten: Illusionslose Gespräche, Kritiken, Aufsätze,* Leipzig, 1980.

About HONEGGER: books–

George, A. *Arthur Honegger.* Paris, 1925.
Tappolet, Willy. *Arthur Honegger.* Zurich, 1933.
Claudel, Paul, et al. *Arthur Honegger.* Paris, 1943.
Bruyr, José. *Honegger et son oeuvre.* Paris, 1947.
Delannoy, Marcel. *Honegger.* Paris, 1953.
Matter, J. *Honegger ou la quête de joie.* London and Paris, 1956.
Gauthier, A. *Arthur Honegger.* London, 1957.
Landowski, M. *Honegger.* Paris, 1957.
Meylan, P. *Arthur Honegger: humanitäre Botschaft der Musik. Wirkung und Gestalt, viii.* Frauenfeld, 1970.
Fischer, Kurt von. *Arthur Honegger. Neujahrsblatt der Allgemeine Musikgesellschaft Zurich.* vol. 162. Zurich, 1978.
Spratt, Geoffrey, K. *The Music of Arthur Honneger.* Cork, 1987.

articles–

Browne, A.G. "Arthur Honegger." *Music and Letters* 10 (1929): 372.
Blagodatov, G. "Honegger's 'King David'." *Vosprosï teorii i estetiki muzïki,* edited by Yu N. Tulin. Leningrad, 1967.
Schrade, Leo. "Von Sinn der Musik in Honegger's Werk." In *De scientia musicae studia atque orationes,* 556. Berne, 1967.

*   *   *

Arthur Honegger's operas belong to a period of French musical history during which the opera reached a sort of impasse; the audience was more conservative than ever and the music that French composers were writing, whether innovatory or traditional, seemed unsuited to the requirements of the operatic stage (Poulenc did not compose his first opera until after the occupation). Honegger declared that "The public is composed of old folk: they don't want to hear anything but successes." Of his stage works, the only ones which carry the title "opera" are *Antigone, Judith, L'aiglon,* and *Charles le téméraire.* But it is his "stage oratorio" *Jeanne d'Arc au bûcher* that has had the widest currency, has been recorded several times, and still attracts producers and performers because of the universal appeal of its subject, and also, perhaps, because the central role of the Maid of Orleans is for an actress who declaims but does not sing (it was written for the great dancer and mime, Ida Rubinstein, who was also Debussy's first St Sebastien, and has attracted such interpreters as Ingrid Bergman, Vera Zorina and Mia Farrow.)

L'aiglon is particularly interesting, as it is one of the few relatively successful examples of an opera composed by collaborating composers. It was commissioned by Raoul Gunsburg of the Monte Carlo Opéra. The five-act drama by Edmond Rostand concerning the brief life of Napoleon's son, the Duke of Reichstadt, known as L'aiglon (the eaglet), was one of the most celebrated vehicles written for Sarah Bernhardt, who played the young man when she herself was in her fifties. Gunsburg first asked Honegger, who declined, and then Jacques Ibert, to undertake the work. The two friends decided, as a wager, to compose it together.

The audience at the first performance of *L'aiglon* was enthusiastic but naturally curious as to which sections each composer had written. They are said to have replied, "We fairly shared the job, one wrote the flats, the other wrote the sharps." A claim has been made that the first and fifth acts were by Ibert and the others by Honegger. In *L'aiglon,* there are no formal arias or duets; the music is through-composed, with waltzes and marches evoking the faraway places and victories of which the Duke and the old campaigner, Flambeau, talk. The style is not unlike that of Charpentier's *Louise*, with a dash of *Manon;* both operas, like *L'aiglon*, deal with characters who are longing to go to Paris.

Just as the title role had been a tour de force for Bernhardt, so the soprano part of *L'aiglon* provides a high-lying vocal line and an opportunity for histrionic display. The general pomposity of the subject is gently lampooned by the imaginative yet quite conventional orchestration. It is difficult to associate the mixture of Parisian romanticism and verismo-style declamation with the late 1930s. For all the influence that "Les Six" had drawn from Satie and later from American, Russian and German music of the 1920s, the direction that *L'aiglon* takes is definitely reactionary.

The role of Metternich is as important as that of the Duke and Flambeau; he has a scene of meditation and hallucination, the music for which, with much sighing of strings, resembles a movie score for one of the historical dramas that were popular at the time and which were, dramatically, the thirties' equivalent of the boulevard melodramas, of which *L'aiglon* is such an extreme example. If Honegger and Ibert had hoped to achieve the same success that Puccini, Cilèa and Giordano had had in adapting other Bernhardt vehicles for the lyric stage *(Tosca, Adriana, Fedora),* however, they failed to provide sufficiently striking music. The climax of the opera (act IV), set on the plain of Wagram, was Bernhardt's most famous scene in the play; her recording of it can still be heard, with a background of wailing voices suggesting the ghosts of the fallen; it seems oddly to be more "operatic" than Honegger's version, with its shifts of tempo, a sort of battle symphony with recitative and the strains of well-known French songs ("La Carmagnole," "La Marseilleise," "Il pleut, il pleut, berger").

Honegger was most successful in vocal music with a form of oratorio; the times in which he lived did not demand a full-time devotion to opera and his stage works must remain curiosities.

—Patrick O'Connor

HORNE, Marilyn (Bernice).

Mezzo-soprano. Born 16 January 1934, in Bradford, Pennsylvania. Married conductor Henry Lewis in 1960 (separated 1976; one daughter). Studied with William Vennard at the University of Southern California in Los Angeles and attended Lotte Lehmann's master classes; debut as Hata in *The Bartered Bride,* Los Angeles, 1954; appeared as Giulietta at Gelsenkirchen Opera, 1957, where she remained until 1960; Covent Garden debut as Marie in *Wozzeck,* 1965; appeared at the Teatro alla Scala as Neocles in *Le siège de Corinthe,* 1969; Metropolitan Opera debut as Adalgisa in *Norma,* 1970, where she remains a principal singer.

Publications

By HORNE: books–

(with J. Scovell) *My Life.* New York, 1983.

About HORNE: books–

Sargeant, W. *Divas.* New York, 1973.
Dodge, E. *Marilyn Horne.* New York, 1979.

articles–

Scott, M.R. "Marilyn Horne." *Opera* 18 (1967): 963.
Zakariasen, B. "Marilyn Horne." *Ovation* July (1983).

*　　*　　*

It is commonplace to attribute the "rediscovery" of the bel canto operas of Donizetti and Bellini first to Maria Callas and later to Joan Sutherland, but Marilyn Horne has been equally inspirational in the more recent revival of interest in the huge and, until recently, generally neglected output of Rossini.

Marilyn Horne's first performances in Los Angeles were largely unheralded—a minor role in Smetana's *The Bartered Bride* and, more significantly, Rossini's *Cenerentola* for Carl Ebert. Her 'galley years' were spent with the small opera company of Gelsenkirchen where she mostly sang soprano territory—Mimì, Minnie in *La fanciulla del West,* Amelia in *Simon Boccanegra* and Tatiana in *Eugene Onegin.* In 1960 she began a long association with the San Francisco Opera by performing Marie in Berg's *Wozzeck.*

Throughout a lengthy career Horne has been attracted to a wide range of musical genres. Her first recording assignment was to dub the voice of Dorothy Dandridge in *Carmen Jones.* Her French repertoire includes Fidès in *Le prophète* and Thomas' *Mignon,* as well as Carmen. Her Verdi roles include Amneris (*Aïda*), Azucena (*Il trovatore*) and Eboli (*Don Carlos*). She has sung many of the Handel operas and several of Mahler's song cycles. Early in her career she recorded an astonishing two LP tribute to Malibran and Viardot. This includes pieces from no less than five operas by Rossini, one of which is an aria of Semiramide's and Horne has subsequently become an outstanding Arsace in the same opera.

Despite this catholicity of repertoire Horne's international career has been increasingly identified with early nineteenth-century Italian opera and above all with Rossini. Given her superb mezzo voice and professional status, it is hardly surprising that the world's opera houses have continued to press her to sing the basic repertoire. Andrew Porter found her Amneris in *Aïda* at the Metropolitan "curiously unimpressive," which did not deter Salzburg and Karajan from asking her to undertake the same role some months later. Although recognizing the pressure that singing Verdi roles placed on her voice—"I don't want to fight to be heard over the orchestra"—Horne could not resist, but in her own words "it was one of my monumental failures".

In 1961 Horne appeared in Bellini's *Beatrice di Tenda* at New York Town Hall. Sutherland sang the title role and a great operatic partnership was inaugurated. They sang *Norma* together in Vancouver in 1963 and at Covent Garden in 1967 and *Semiramide* in Boston in 1964. In 1969 Horne scored a sensational success at the Teatro alla Scala in Rossini's *Le siège de Corinthe.* The final, belated accolade of success for an American singer came with her first appearance at the

Marilyn Horne in *L'italiana in Algeri,* **Royal Opera, London, 1989**

Metropolitan in 1970 in *Norma,* again with Sutherland in the title role.

Horne's autobiography suggests an element of "hit and miss" about her training but there can be no doubt of her intense commitment to work. By 1990 she had been singing for three and a half decades. Almost imperceptibly, the career has become ever more dominated by the florid mezzo roles of Rossini. It is here that Horne's incredible technique—replete with runs and roulades, unrivalled in modern times—has come into its own. Andrew Porter's reaction has been very different from that quoted previously—"When Miss Horne sings, Rossini's florid writing doesn't sound automatic, and not only because it is embellished and made even more florid: piquant unpredictability enlivens both the musical text and her delivery of it." Many of Horne's greatest performances of Rossini have been in concert versions and Porter makes a tactful reference to Horne's physique and the nature of the "breeches" roles she frequently undertakes—"Her concert presence is warm and winning. She seems far more attractive, far more dramatic, more of a character, than when in boots and plumed helmet; she stomps around and gesticulates on the stage." In 1978 Porter thought her "a vocally brilliant Tancred, singing the music with matchless energy, accuracy and bravura." By 1983 he felt she had added "a new command of the words and of the mood."

Horne's recorded legacy encompasses her range of musical interests, even if not all equally successfully. Thus there is a fine recital of Handel arias and some delicious performances of American songs; in contrast she never seems to "get inside" the Mahler song cycles. There is much fascinating French material: pride of place goes to her Fidès in *Le prophète.* This is one of the glories of the nineteenth-century contralto repertoire; at times the quality of Horne's voice is almost cello-like. In contrast she does not really project as Azucena in *Il trovatore.* Otherwise the legacy of collaboration with Sutherland is superb; Horne features as Adalgisa in *Norma,* Maffeo Orsini in *Lucrezia Borgia* and Arsace in *Semiramide.*

Pride of place has to go to Rossini. Oddly her Rosina in *Il barbiere di Siviglia* seems uninspired compared to some others, but her Isabella in *L'italiana in Algeri* offers bravura singing hardly otherwise encountered on records. The whole is a tour de force. Her Arsace and Tancred are almost as impressive and there is a magnificent recital of pieces from *Donna del lago* and *Le siège de Corinthe.* As with other modern singers, much of Horne's career has been preserved by radio and television and this is true for her performances in the Rossini festivals in Pesaro. In the revival of *Bianca e Falliero,* she sets a new standard of controlled virtuoso singing. We may speculate as to whether Rossini himself ever heard the quality of florid singing required for such roles; in our time this particular art has been rediscovered by Marilyn Horne.

—Stanley Henig

HOTTER, Hans.

Bass-baritone. Born 19 January 1909, in Offenbach am Main. Married Helga Fischer, 1936 (one son, one daughter). Studied with Matthäus Roemer in Munich; worked as organist and choirmaster; debut at Troppau, 1930; has appeared in Breslau (1931), Prague (1932-34), Hamburg (1934-35), and Munich (1937-72); Metropolitan debut as the Dutchman in *Der fliegende Holländer,* 1950, where he appeared until 1954; produced a *Ring* cycle at Covent Garden, 1961-62; retired from stage in 1972; became a member of the Vienna Hochschule für Musik, 1977; created the Kommandant in Strauss's *Friedenstag,* Olivier in *Capriccio,* and Jupiter in *Die Liebe der Danaë.*

Publications

By HOTTER: articles–

"On Producing *Die Walküre.*" *Opera* November (1961).
"Die Oper: Das unmögliche Kunstwerk." *Österreichische Musikzeitschrift* (1965).
"Hans Hotter Remembers." *Opera* July (1976).

About HOTTER: books–

Wessling, B. *Hans Hotter.* Bremen, 1966.
Turing, P. *Hans Hotter: Man and Artist.* London, 1983.

articles–

Francis, P. "Hans Hotter." *Opera* 4 (1953): 589.
Cairns, D. "Hotter's Farewell." In *Responses.* London, 1973.
Tubeuf, A. "Hans Hotter: le long voyage de Wotan." *Avant-scène opéra* September (1984).

For many, the voice of German bass-baritone Hans Hotter *is* the voice of Wotan. Even those who never saw him in the theater, where he virtually owned the role in the two decades following World War II, came through recordings to identify Hotter's as the true voice of Wagner's anguished god—perhaps these at-home listeners most of all, given the universal currency of the famous Solti performances, which feature Hotter as the *Walküre* Wotan and the Wanderer. That Hotter is so richly satisfying on these records, despite being undeniably past his vocal prime, is a testament to his intelligence and long experience in the role, experience provided through a long career of a kind well-nigh vanished from today's opera scene.

Hotter's early musical inclinations led him to study as an organist and choirmaster; his initial vocal studies arose from the conviction that knowing something about singing would be useful to him as a conductor. It was soon apparent, however, that his future lay on the opera stage. He made his debut at Troppau in 1930, and stayed there three seasons absorbing

Hans Hotter as Wotan in *Die Walküre,* 1955

a wide variety of repertoire. Seasons at Breslau and Prague followed, where among the roles he essayed were Escamillo, Iago, Falstaff, Boris, and, in 1938, his first *Das Rheingold* Wotan. The milieu in which Hotter moved in the first part of his career was extraordinary. Among the conductors he worked with were Furtwängler, Knappertsbusch, Karajan, Kleiber, and Clemens Krauss (who led Hotter in the premieres of Strauss' *Friedenstag* and *Capriccio*); among his role models in the repertoire he would make his own were Friedrich Schorr, Wilhelm Rode, and Rudolf Bockelmann. A comparable school for Wagnerians would be impossible to assemble today. Though soon established as one of Germany's leading singers, Hotter's international career did not begin until after the war, when he visited London with the Vienna State Opera in 1947. His New York Metropolitan debut came in 1950, and by this time the world encountered in Hotter a fully mature artist at the peak of his vocal powers.

Hotter combined a Lieder singer's sensitivity to words and colors with a voice large enough to sing in the biggest houses over Wagnerian orchestras. His voice was instantly recognizable, very dark in color, and projected with a uniquely warm resonance, equally effective in conveying paternal love or godly wrath. One might expect a voice like Hotter's to be prone to muddiness, and though it was not always ideally focused, the basic quality and color were rarely compromised. Despite occasional unsteadiness, distortion rarely crept in, owing most likely to the primacy of the word in Hotter's traversal of even the most vocally demanding operatic literature. His care in communicating the text tends to ensure natural, unexaggerated vocalism.

It is a sad fact that while there are many Hotter recording, too few of them caught him in his absolute prime, and some of his greatest roles are documented only in piecemeal fashion, if at all. Would that, in the Fifties, some enterprising company had recorded his Hans Sachs or Dutchman, let alone his Cardinal Borromeo in Pfitzner's *Palestrina*. Remarkable documents remain: of course the Solti *Der Ring des Nibelungen* with Hotter's vocally aged but peerlessly expressive Wotan, but also a 1957 record of the duet "Wie aus der Ferne" from *Der fliegende Holländer* with Birgit Nilsson, which for sheer vocal beauty combined with vivid character projection stands among his most memorable achievements; a 1976 Viennese studio recording of *Lulu,* Hotter as a Schigolch comic and sinister, with a core of toughness appropriate for the principal survivor of Berg's *femme fatale;* and, remarkably enough, a *Guerrelieder* recorded in New York in 1991, with Hotter in his eighties giving a mesmerizing account of the narration, the voice still unmistakable, the authority unquestioned. Hearing Hotter, one is reminded afresh that opera, even the rarified world of Wagnerian music-drama, depends on the incantatory power of the human voice. Hotter was a master singer and a master enchanter.

—Michael Kotze

HUGH THE DROVER, or, Love in the Stocks.

Composer: Ralph Vaughan Williams.

Librettist: H. Child.

First Performance: London, His Majesty's, 14 July 1924; revised, 1956.

Roles: Hugh (tenor); Mary (soprano); John (bass-baritone); Susan (soprano); Nancy (contralto); William (tenor); Robert (bass); Aunt Jane (contralto); The Turnkey (tenor); The Constable (bass); A Fool (baritone); An Innkeeper (bass); A Sergeant (baritone); chorus.

Publications

article–

Wilson, S. "Hugh the Drover." *Opera* 1 (1950): 29.

*   *   *

Set in the small town of Cotsall in the west of England during the Napoleonic Wars, *Hugh the Drover* deals with the love of Mary, the daughter of the town constable, betrothed to John the town butcher, at her father's behest. Mary falls in love with the mysterious Hugh, a drover who roams the country rounding up horses for the army. All he can offer her is a roving life of probable hardship, but at least she will be free, rather than having to endure caged comfort with John. A prize fight is set up with a prize of £20 for any man who can beat John. Hugh sees his chance, stakes £50 on the result, and challenges John to add Mary's hand in marriage to the bet. Hugh wins; but John instantly accuses him of being a French spy; how else could he have come by as large a sum as £50? The crowd turns against Hugh; he is arrested and put in the stocks.

In act II, on May Day, Mary brings the key to the stocks and is about to release Hugh so that they can elope together, but they are interrupted by the May revelers. She gets into the stocks beside Hugh. Finding his daughter missing, the constable arouses the townspeople. The lovers are discovered. Mary refuses to abandon Hugh, and her father disowns her. A troop of soldiers arrives to take the "spy" away. The sergeant in charge of the detachment recognizes Hugh as a man who once saved his life; and instead of arresting Hugh, the soldiers conscript John. Mary hesitates to go off with Hugh, but he wins her over. The lovers bid the townsfolk farewell and go off together.

Hugh the Drover is a conscious attempt to write a kind of English equivalent of Smetana's *Bartered Bride;* but for all its sturdy tunefulness and defiantly "English" idiom, it does not quite manage to do so. This is at least as much Vaughan Williams' fault as that of his librettist Harold Child. There is much fine music in the score: Hugh's stirring ballad "Horse Hooves" in act I and the love music are certainly full-blooded and finely characterized; but the "villain," John, never really comes to life; and the two main figures, though credible as romantic symbols of true love and the desire to challenge the unknown, are not three-dimensional creatures of flesh and blood. The musical construction is straightforward, the scoring effective, and the musical idiom bracing, drawing its sometimes Pucciniesque soaring melodic line from the contours of English folksong, and basing its harmonic procedures on the modal implications of the tunes. Dramatically, the work suffers from Vaughan Williams' inexperience in welding the constituent parts of the action into a coherent whole, an example of which is the prize-fight in the finale of the first act (Vaughan Williams' starting point for the plot of the opera), which never really quite "jells," though the tension is skillfully built up in the individual sections. Nonetheless, the work is easy on the ear and shows a distinct sense of the theater, which was to be more fully realized in *Sir John in Love* and especially in *Riders to the Sea*.

—James Day

LES HUGUENOTS [The Huguenots].

Composer: Giacomo Meyerbeer.

Librettists: Eugène Scribe and Émile Deschamps.

First Performance: Paris, Opéra, 29 February 1836.

Roles: Marguerite de Valois (soprano); Valentine (soprano); Raoul de Nangis (tenor); Comte de Nevers (baritone); Comte de St Bris (baritone or bass-baritone); Marcel (bass); Urbain (mezzo-soprano or contralto); Catholic Noblemen (tenors, basses, baritones); Page of Nevers (soprano); Ladies of Honor (sopranos, mezzo-soprano); Huguenot Soldiers (tenor, bass); Archer (tenor); Three Monks (tenors, bass); Two Gypsies (sopranos); chorus (SSAATTBB).

Publications

books–

Frese, Christhard. *Meyerbeer: Les Huguenots: Materialien zum Werk.* Leipzig, 1974.
Walter, Michael. *"Hugenotten"—Studien.* Frankfurt, 1987.

articles–

Prod'homme, J.G. "Die Hugenotten-Premiere." *Die Musik* 3/no. 1 (1903-04): 187.
Istel, E. "Act IV of *Les Huguenots.*" *Musical Quarterly* 22 (1936): 87.
Frederichs, H. "Das Rezitativ in den Hugenotten G. Meyerbeers." In *Beiträge zur Geschichte der Oper,* edited by H. Backer, 55. Regensburg, 1969.
Walter, Michael. "'Man überlege sich nur alles, sehe, wo alles hinausläuft!' Zu Robert Schumanns *Hugenotten*-Rezension." *Die Musikforschung* 36 (1983): 127.

Les Huguenots ensued from the second collaboration between Meyerbeer and the chief librettist of French grand opera, Eugène Scribe. Its premiere came more than four years after that of Meyerbeer's extraordinarily successful *Robert le diable* (1831). The earlier work was a triumph of orchestral innovation and imagination, spectacular staging, and lurid drama. With *Robert* Meyerbeer had taken full advantage of the popular achievement of Auber's *La muette de Portici* (1827) and Rossini's *Guillaume Tell* (1828). These three earlier works collectively defined French grand opera, but as a genre whose mature realization was reached only in *Les Huguenots*. In the creation of *Les Huguenots* Meyerbeer labored with the same unhurried care and attention to detail that had characterized his work on the earlier opera. He has suffered more than the usual criticism accorded those who

garner popular success, but whose works are not of transcendent quality. Nonetheless, one cannot accuse him of quickly-wrought hackwork, for he typically labored long, constantly revising in an era when composers of opera were not known for that.

The work's libretto is based upon the St Bartholomew's massacre of the Huguenots by the Catholics in 1572 and revolves around related events in Touraine and Paris. Religious strife between Protestants and Catholics drives the action, complicated, of course, by the love between Raoul, a prominent Huguenot, and Valentine, daughter of the Conte de St Bris, a leader of the Catholics. Queen Marguerite de Valois envisions Valentine as agent for making peace between the two factions by arranging her marriage to Raoul. Unfortunately, Valentine is the fiancée of the Count de Nevers, one of the Catholic leaders. Marcel, rough-hewn old retainer of Raoul, and Urbain, page to the Queen, round out the list of principals.

The on again, off again, relationship between Raoul and Valentine ultimately leads to the marriage of Valentine and Nevers—despite her continuing love for Raoul—all played against a background of imminent bloodshed between the factions. Raoul's visit to newly-wed Valentine's home to try to relight their mutual fire results in his entanglement in the launching of the Catholic plot to slay all Huguenots. Noble husband Nevers virtuously demurs participation and is turned upon by his coreligionists. Bloodshed begins, and Raoul flees knowing of Valentine's continuing love for him. As the massacre proceeds, Raoul and Marcel take refuge in a churchyard, joined by Valentine, whose husband has already perished. Valentine declares allegiance to the Huguenots and all are slain by vengeful Catholics, led by St Bris, who thus orders the murder of his own daughter in ironic error.

The immediate success of *Les Huguenots,* while not quite approaching that of *Robert le diable,* was considerable and the opera soon became Meyerbeer's most important and influential work. By 1880 it had been performed 693 times at the Paris Opéra alone, not to speak of myriad performances the world over. Of the earlier examples of French grand opera, only *Les Huguenots* enjoys many revivals in the twentieth century. Critics generally view it as Meyerbeer's first work that was essentially non-derivative: *Il crociato in Egitto* was considered Italianate, almost Rossinian, and *Robert le diable* possessed more than a few attributes of German romanticism, specifically those of Carl Maria von Weber. But in *Les Huguenots,* Meyerbeer reached the definition of his personal style that, for better or worse, has come to be his cachet.

The characteristic elements of grand opera are present, of course: 1) a structure of five acts of increasing tension which generates a lengthy work; 2) a libretto based upon relatively recent historical incident; 3) important ballet and choral scenes; 4) lavish, spectacular staging; and 5) vivid, colorful orchestration. But in Meyerbeer's hands these elements are executed with an intuitive adroitness and flair that transcend their easy imitation by others. His gift for innovative instrumentation and orchestration, for composing broad, appealing melodies, and for the creation of entertaining drama that moves at a smooth and tightly-constructed pace, all contributed to the immense popularity of *Les Huguenots* with the opera-going public. Critics and scholars have often been ruthless in their analyses of Meyerbeer's creation, but they have not deterred its popularity, especially during the nineteenth century.

Les Huguenots requires exceptional solo voices, and not just a few. There are seven major roles, and all demand singers of world-class ability who have a mastery of *bel canto* technique, as well as an understanding of the nineteenth-century French school. These impressive standards make revivals problematic; perhaps the heyday of performances of *Les Huguenots* during this century was reached early on, at the Metropolitan Opera. The work was a staple of the Metropolitan's repertoire, and performances there were known as "nights of the seven stars." From Marcel's colorful "Piff, paff" account of his wars with the Catholics, accompanied only by piccolo, low instruments, and percussion, to the well-known "Romance" of Raoul, with its extensive part for solo viola d'amore, the arias of *Les Huguenots* are appealing. They succeed because they achieve a memorable quality wrought by a combination of an innate understanding of the *bel canto* voice, a rare ear for orchestra color, and a flair for dramatic insight. Many of the major arias have achieved lives of their own in recital programs, as representatives of the best aspects of the nineteenth-century French school.

It is not upon the coattails of the arias taken alone that the success of the opera rides. Rather, its achievement stems also from their apt juxtaposition with solo ensembles and extraordinarily effective writing for chorus, all placed within a context of scene complexes that drive to forceful, entertaining dénouements.

The young Wagner saw *Les Huguenots* in Paris and praised it effusively, especially its orchestral treatment and staging. It should be more widely acknowledged that he, as well as Berlioz, was immensely influenced by *Les Huguenots*'s example. The evidence clearly is present not only in the straightforward admiration expressed in their own essays, but also in their musical works. Their artistic achievement, as well as that of Verdi, Bizet, and others, owes much to Meyerbeer, whatever his commercial success at pleasing the operatic bourgeoisie.

—William E. Runyan

THE HUMAN VOICE
See LA VOIX HUMAINE

HUMPERDINCK, Engelbert.

Composer. Born 1 September 1854, in Siegburg, near Bonn. Died 27 September 1921, in Neustrelitz. Studied architecture in Cologne; studied with Ferdinand Hiller, Friedrich Gernsheim, and Gustav Jensen, piano with Seiss and Mertke, and cello with Rensberg and Ehlert at the Cologne Conservatory; Mozart Prize of Frankfurt, 1876; studied with Franz Lachner and Rheinberger in Munich; Mendelssohn Prize for the chorus *Die Wallfahrt nach Kevelaar,* 1879; Meyerbeer Prize of Berlin, 1881, and travel to France and Italy; met Wagner in Italy, who invited him to Bayreuth, where Humperdinck assisted in the preparation of the score of *Parsifal* for performance and publication; later taught Siegfried Wagner (Wagner's son); professor at the Conservatory in Barcelona, 1885-87; taught in Cologne; hired by the publishing firm Schott in Mainz; professor at the Hochschule für Musik in Frankfurt and music critic for the *Frankfurter Zeitung,* 1890; *Hänsel und Gretel* enormously successful, 1893; retired to Boppard on the Rhine to devote himself exclusively to composition, 1896; director of the Akademische Meisterschule in Berlin, 1900.

Operas

Hänsel und Gretel, Adelheid Wette (after the tale by the brothers Grimm), Weimar, Court Theater, 23 December 1893.
Die sieben Geislein, Adelheid Wette (after the brothers Grimm), Berlin, Schiller Theater, 19 December 1895.
Königskinder (incidental music for the melodrama), Ernst Rosmer [Elsa Bernstein-Porges], Munich, Court Theater, 23 January 1897; revised as an opera, New York, Metropolitan Opera, 28 December 1910.
Dornröschen, E. Ebeling and B. Filhès (after Perrault), Frankfurt am Main, Municipal Theater, 12 November 1902.
Die Heirat wider Willen, Hedwig Humperdinck (after Dumas, *Les demoiselles de Saint-Cyr,* Berlin, Royal Opera, 14 April 1905.
Bübchens Weihnachtstraum (melodramatisches Krippenspiel), G. Falke, Berlin, 30 December 1906.
Die Marketenderin, Robert Misch, Cologne, Municipal Theater, 10 May 1914.
Gaudeamus: Szenen aus dem deutschen Studentenleben, Robert Misch, Darmstadt, Provincial Theater, 18 March 1919.

Other works: incidental music, choral works, songs, orchestral works, chamber music.

Publications/Writings

By HUMPERDINCK: books–

Grundlage für eine Schönheitslehre in der Kunst. Incomplete manuscript.
Essayo de un metodo de armonia. Manuscript, 1885.
J. Haydn: Symphonie Es-dur: Musikführer. Frankfurt, 1895.
Die Zeitlose: Modernes Traummärchen: Siegburger Kindheits-erinnerungern. Siegburg, 1948.
Irmen, H.J., ed. *Engelbert Humperdinck: Briefe und Tagebücher I.* Cologne, 1975; *Engelbert Humperdinck: Briefe und Tagebücher II,* Cologne, 1976; *Engelbert Humperdinck: Briefe und Tagebücher III: 1883-1886,* Berlin and Kassel, 1983.

articles–

"Parsifal-Skizzen: persönliche Erinnerungen an R. Wagner und an die erste Aufführung des Bühnenweihfestspiels." *Die Zeit* [Vienna] (1907); published separately, Siegburg, 1949.

About HUMPERDINCK: books–

Niemann, W. *Die Musik seit Richard Wagner.* Berlin, 1913.
Besch, Otto. *Engelbert Humperdinck.* Leipzig, 1914.
Kuhlmann, Hans. *Stil und Form in der Musik von Humperdincks Oper "Hänsel und Gretel".* Marburg, 1930.
Bitter, W. *Die deutsche komische Oper der Gegenwart.* Leipzig, 1932.
Mahler, A. *Gustav Mahler: Erinnerungen und Briefe.* Amsterdam, 1940 [letters from Humperdinck to Mahler].
Humperdinck, W. *Engelbert Humperdinck.* Frankfurt am Main, 1965.
Irmen, H.J. *Die Odyssee des Engelbert Humperdinck: eine biographische Dokumentation.* Siegburg, 1975.

Engelbert Humperdinck, 1912

articles–

Hanslick, E. "Hänsel und Gretel." In *Die moderne Oper 7: Fünf Jahre Musik (1891-1895)*. Berlin, 1896.

Batka, R. "Der Kampf um's Melodram." *Musikalische Rundschau* March (1897).

––––––. "Von Hänsel und Gretel." In *Musikalische Streifzüge*. Leipzig, 1899.

Pastor, W. "Engelbert Humperdincks 'Heirat wider Willen'." *Kunstwart* 18 (1905-06).

Münzer, G. "Engelbert Humperdinck." In *Monographien moderner Musiker*, i, 59. Leipzig, 1906.

Batka, R. "Engelbert Humperdinck." *Die Musik* 8/no. 3 (1908-09): 20.

Humperdinck, W. "Aus der Entstehungszeit der 'Königskinder'." *Zeitschrift für Musik* 115 (1954): 715.

Avant-scène opéra December (1987) [*Hänsel und Gretel* issue].

Kravitt, E.F. "The Joining of Words and Music in Late Romantic Melodrama." *Musical Quarterly* 62 (1976): 571.

Roberge, Marc-André. "*Königskinder:* L'autre chef-d'oeuvre de Humperdinck." *Sonances. Revue musicale québécoise* 4/no. 1 (1984): 2.

unpublished–

Kirsten, L. "Motivik und Form in der Musik zu Engelbert Humperdincks Oper 'Königskinder'." Ph.D. dissertation, University of Jena, 1942.

*   *   *

It is above all for his "children's fairy tale" *Hänsel und Gretel* that Humperdinck holds his place in the repertory, while in second place comes his *Königskinder,* which has a young prince as its hero but is also set in an old German forest with its wicked witch. Of his other stage works, four more are also called fairy tales or children's pieces, and it is clear that the nature of his genius led him towards the world of childhood and children's tales to an extent that is unique in opera, although Ravel and Britten also wrote pieces in the same genre.

In fact, *Hänsel und Gretel* is usually performed to adult audiences by adult singers, and the role of the young lad Hänsel is designated as for a mezzo soprano although it has sometimes been sung by a boy treble. Nevertheless, the genesis of *Hänsel und Gretel* was in the right surroundings, for it began to take shape in a children's nursery in which two young girls with good voices liked to sing verses written by their mother Adelheid Wette and set to music by their "uncle Entepent"—who was Engelbert Humperdinck himself. He was then in his thirties, and, as well as teaching music in the Cologne Conservatory, he had a firm association with the musical stage and had assisted Wagner at Bayreuth. Most of his compositions had been for voices, but he had also written incidental music for the theater, and little by little one particular nursery song inspired by the Grimm brothers' fairy tale of the two children turned itself into a *Singspiel* or German opera with a libretto by Adelheid herself, the idea for this having been put forward by her husband Dr Hermann Wette. Another enthusiastic supporter of the project was the composer Hugo Wolf.

Richard Strauss conducted the première of *Hänsel und Gretel* in 1893 at Weimar and in a letter to the composer he called the new work "a masterpiece of the first water . . . you have bestowed upon our fellow citizens a work that they hardly deserve, though one hopes that very soon they will be worthy of it." Its immense success came when Humperdinck was forty, and he followed it with nine more stage works of which the earliest version of *Königskinder* was the third, though he later reshaped it considerably. It was always the world of childhood which inspired this genial and melodious composer to give of his best, as in his *Bübchens Weihnachtstraum* of 1906—with its title meaning "Baby boy's Christmas Dream" and its designation as a "musical crib play"—and the pantomime *Das Mirakel* (*The Miracle*), which had its premiere in London five years later.

Later in life, Humperdinck was laid low by ill-health, and he may have been discouraged by the feeling that contemporary music had moved in a way that had left him behind. Nevertheless, the warmth and freshness of his musical inspiration, expressed above all in attractive and memorable themes, together with the unobtrusive but impressive skill with which he constructed his "children's music dramas" (he had learned much from Wagner) won the lasting affection and admiration not only of ordinary operagoers but also of such conductors as Levi, Mahler, Weingartner and Karajan, all of whom performed *Hänsel und Gretel* in the secure knowledge that it would find a ready response with audiences of all ages. This work also helped to show composers and librettists at the turn of the century another way forward for opera besides Wagnerian music drama and Italian *verismo.*

—Christopher Headington

I

THE ICE BREAK.

Composer: Michael Tippett.

Librettist: Michael Tippett.

First Performance: London, Covent Garden, 7 July 1977.

Roles: Lev (bass); Nadia (soprano); Yuri (baritone); Gayle (soprano); Hannah (mezzo-soprano); Olympion (tenor); Luke (tenor); Lieutenant of Police (baritone); Astron (mezzo-soprano).

Publications

article–

Warrack, John. "The Ice Break." *Musical Times* 118 (1977): 553.

*   *   *

In depicting the quest of a handful of individuals for personal wholeness, *The Ice Break* resembles its predecessors among Tippett's operatic works. Its dramatization of the effects that stereotypical mob psychology and violence have on individuals makes this opera unique, however.

Stage place is defined (an airport, an apartment, the street, a "Paradise Garden," and a hospital), but time is deliberately unspecified. All mob actions burst in upon the private encounters of individuals and as suddenly disperse. Short scenes elide into each other (as in *The Knot Garden*). For the first time in Tippett's operas, amplified spoken and sung sound off-stage blends into or is juxtaposed to stage music. "Black Mob" and "White Mob" are as forcefully characterized as are Lev, Nadia, and Yuri, the father, mother, and son who seek reconciliation after twenty years of enforced separation; or the young couples Yuri and his girlfriend Gayle and Hannah and Olympion, a Black nurse and the leader of the Black mob, respectively. Each of these gentle or idealistic people is deeply disturbed by mob conflict.

In acts I and II, the chorus represents two mobs "each of whom acts with blind and arbitrary behavior," as Ian Kemp has stated (*Tippett: The Composer and His Music*); in Act III, the chorus portrays a group of seekers looking for the thrill of a psychological "trip." The choral writing resembles that in *King Priam* in the use of doubled male and female voices singing in two-note intervals to one another, or the creation of heterophony of similar choral phrases. This clear sound and simple textural device suits well the naive or stubbornly fixated attitudes of the mobs. Gone from both *King Priam* and *The Ice Break* are the luxuriant contrapuntal lines in traditional SATB balance of parts found in *The Midsummer Marriage*, because gone too is that chorus' exuberant unanimity with the main characters.

The structure of *The Ice Break* appears to be one long scene constantly interrupted, choral music barging in upon arias and duets. One example from act I demonstrates this unique structure. In scene ix of act I, the chorus interrupts the husband-wife conversation of scenes viii and x; better, scene ix can be seen as the enactment of mob turmoil into which Yuri, the son, is drawn and about which Lev and Nadia are singing in xiii and x.

Musical language and musical-dramatic techniques of *The Ice Break* logically follow the procedures found to be successful in Tippett's second and third operas. Use of motives, of distinctive tone colors, of musical allusion and quotation (especially in the Black-White mob scenes), and the construction of short musical forms in which evolving variation and other traditional thematic processes take shape are the outstanding factors responsible for the cumulative dramatic effect. Musical encapsulation of events and emotional reactions is even more succinct in *The Ice Break* than in *The Knot Garden*. *The Ice Break* is 75 minutes in total performing time as compared to 87 minutes for *The Knot Garden*.

The most graphic technique used to conjure the surreal in *The Ice Break* is the use of noise. Noise predominates in act II, scene viii, for example, where the mob's violence reaches a climax as its victims are kicked to death. Boot stamping, screaming, gun shots, and police-car and ambulance sirens completely overwhelm the clusters of major and minor seconds in woodwinds and strings. So convincingly fierce is the noise that it transforms the surrealism back into a dreadful realism. The short scene is not easily forgotten.

The opera's greatest strength lies in Tippett's depiction of a world in which society's untamed acceptance of stereotypical heroes repeatedly imposes itself upon the individual's search for meaning. This very strength is also the opera's weakness. The musical and non-musical evocation of mob behavior has generally stronger dramatic impact than the music that evokes the numinous world of the individual characters.

This is not to say, however, that the characterization of the real people of the opera is without dramatic weight. Tippett's techniques of motives, distinctive tone colors, and pitch-focus to depict psychological states work to especially effective dramatic impact in act II, scene v and scene x, to take but two examples. Scene v, Hannah's aria "Blue night of my soul" is the jewel in the opera's crown—a masterpiece of haunting, agonizing soul-searching. Scene x, using musical reference to scene v, delineates, through instrumental music alone, the consolation Hannah brings to Lev in the wake of the violence that has deeply touched their lives.

Unfortunately, the dramatic impact of these scenes is not quite matched at the conclusion of the opera. There, the musical reiteration of a motive-cum-instrumental sound that has stood for hope elsewhere in the opera is Tippett's way of reasserting his belief in the power of the human psyche to be healed. That *The Ice Break* is a product of a time when Tippett was more appalled by the violence of our world than certain of our ability to rise above it may be evidenced by the lingering effect of act II, scene viii, even as the opera closes.

—Margaret Scheppach

IDOMENEO, KING OF CRETE
See IDOMENEO, RÈ DI CRETA

IDOMENEO, RÈ DI CRETA[Idomeneo, King of Crete].

Composer: Wolfgang Amadeus Mozart.

Librettist: Giambattista Varesco (after Danchet, *Idomenée*).

First Performance: Munich, Hoftheather, 29 January 1781.

Roles: Ilia (soprano); Electra (soprano); Idamante (soprano, later tenor); Idomeneo (tenor); Arbaces (baritone); High Priest (tenor); Voice of Neptune (bass); chorus (SSAATB).

Publications

books–

Angermüller, Rudolf, and Robert Münster, eds. *Wolfgang Amadeus Mozart: "Idomeneo" 1781-1981.* Munich, 1981.
Hocquard, Jean-Victor. *Idoménée.* Paris, 1982.

articles–

Neville, Don J. "*Idomeneo* and *La clemenza di Tito:* Opera Seria and Vera Opera." *Studies in Music* [Canada] 5 (1978): 99.
Gerstenberg, Walter. "Betrachtung über Mozarts *Idomeneo.*" In *Festschrift Georg von Dadelsen zum 60. Geburtstag,* edited by Thomas Kohlhase and Volker Scherliess, 148. Stuttgart, 1978.
Heartz, Daniel. "Mozart, His Father, and *Idomeneo.*" *Musical Times* 119 (1978).
Kramer, Kurt. "Antike und christliches Mittelalter in Varescos *Idomeneo,* dem Libretto zu Mozarts gleichnamiger Oper." *Mitteilungen der Internationalen Stiftung Mozarteum* 28/no. 1-2 (1980): 6.
———. "Frauengestalten in Varescos *Idomeneo.* Ilia, die opferbereite Priamustochter und ihre dämonische Gegenspielerin Elektra." *Mitteilungen der Internationalen Stiftung Mozarteum* 28/no. 3-4 (1980): 16.
———. "Zur Entstehung von Mozarts *Idomeneo.*" *Mitteilungen der Internationalen Stiftung Mozarteum* 29 (1981): 23.
Plath, Wolfgang. "*Idomeneo:* Miszellen." *Acta mozartiana* 31 (1984): 5.
Platoff, John. "Writing about Influences: *Idomeneo,* a Case Study." In *Explorations in Music, the Arts, and Ideas: Essays in Honor of Leonard B. Meyer,* edited by Eugene Narmour and Ruth A. Solie, 43. New York, 1988.

*   *   *

The original tale of Idomeneo (Idomeneus) described how the shipwrecked Cretan general, upon his return from the ten-year siege at Troy, vowed to Neptune (Poseidon) to sacrifice the first human he might encounter upon his hoped-for return to the Cretan shore. This human turned out to be Idomeneo's (nameless) son. The popularity of this myth derived not from Homer's tale of the Trojan War, in which Idomeneo plays a distinguished role, but from Virgil and early medieval Latin sources, including the Trojan saga of Diktys. The myth received little artistic attention thereafter, however, until Crébillon's drama (1705) and Danchet's five-act libretto which was set to music by André Campra and produced at the Paris Opéra in 1712. Abbé Giambattista Varesco adapted Danchet's libretto and rendered the tale in Italian, reducing it to three acts, for Mozart late in 1780.

To the ancient myth eighteenth-century taste necessarily applied additional dramatic layers. Idomeneo's son, given the name Idamante, falls in love with Ilia, a Trojan princess kept in Crete as a hostage. Their romance irks the fiery daughter of Agamemnon, Electra, who has fled to Crete after the notorious Argive patricide. Varesco and Mozart have given each of these roles a vivid characterization, most memorable in the guilt-ridden fear ever apparent in Idomeneo and the relentless jealousy of Electra. They also provided a *deus ex machina* substitution for Idomeneo's avowed sacrifice, which he spends the entire opera carefully averting.

Commissioned by Karl Theodor, Elector of Bavaria, for the Munich carnival in 1781, *Idomeneo* has become universally recognized as Mozart's first great opera. In applying his natural dramatic sense to the *opera seria* form, Mozart replaced the popular *da capo* exit arias with carefully engineered musical bridges connecting aria, recitativo accompagnato, recitativo secco, smaller ensemble, and chorus. By allowing almost nothing (including applause) to interrupt the dramatic tension, Mozart could develop his graceful if determined fix on the drama at hand and establish greater musical consistency. The emotion Mozart sensed in the libretto he recreated either in the vocal score or in the instrumental accompaniment. Except for the advisor Arbaces, who does not seem to belong to this opera, very few of the numbers are irrelevant to the drama. With such Gluckian control of the drama itself, Mozart immediately demonstrated his early mastery— the dress rehearsal was held on his twenty-fifth birthday—of large dramatic form. It must be said, however, that Mozart himself interrupted his own dramatic unity by the additions he composed for the 1786 Vienna production of the same opera, which was the occasion for which he also recast the soprano Idamante as a tenor.

Besides its musical importance, Mozart's *Idomeneo* is of great biographical importance as well because of the many extant letters exchanged between Wolfgang and Leopold Mozart during the late fall and winter of 1780-81, when Wolfgang was in Munich working on *Idomeneo* and Leopold remained in Salzburg. Among a number of interesting episodes described in the letters, one reveals to us Mozart's great disappointment in having the aging tenor Anton Raaff sing the role of Idomeneo. Mozart, although at times insulting, also showed sensitivity in his description of Raaff's abilities and condition. The modern reader is then all the more impressed with how able and determined Mozart was as composer to tailor the part to Raaff's artistic temperament, his personal vanity, his limited acting style and failing vocal ability. Because Varesco himself had remained in Salzburg as well and Mozart had therefore to communicate with him through Leopold, we learn much about what kinds of textual alterations Mozart required or permitted during the early stages of an operatic production.

Despite the success of the Munich *Idomeneo,* this was to be Mozart's last attempt at composing an *opera seria* until he penned *La clemenza di Tito* in the last year of his life. Subsequent productions were limited. Of recent note have been the reconstruction by Richard Strauss and Lothar Wallerstein in

Idomeneus.

Ein musikalisches

Schauspiel,

welches

auf gnädigsten Befehl

Sr. kurfl. Durchl.

Carl Theodor

in

Ober = und Niederbaiern , wie auch der
obern Pfalz Herzogen, Pfalzgrafen bey Rhein,
des H. R. R. Erztruchseffen , und
Kurfürsten rc. rc.

im neuen Opernhause

zur

Faschingszeit

1781

aufgeführt worden.

Die Poesie ist vom Herrn Johann Baptist Vares-
ko, Sr. hochfürstl. Gnaden Erzbischofen und Fürsten
zu Salzburg Hofkapellan.

Die Musik vom Herrn Wolfgang Gottlieb Mozart,
akademischen Mitgliede von Bologna und Verona, in
wirklichen Diensten Sr. hochfürstl. Gnaden zu Salzburg.

Die Uebersetzung vom Herrn Andre Schachtner,
ebenfalls in wirkl. hochfürstl. salzburgischen Diensten.

München,

gedruckt bey Franz Joseph Thuille.

Idomeneo, title page of libretto, 1781

1931, Fritz Busch's revival at Glyndebourne in 1951, and the Metropolitan Opera and television premiere of 1982.

—Jon Solomon

ILLICA, Luigi.

Librettist/Dramatist. Born 9 May 1857, in Castell' Arquato, near Piacenza. Died 16 December 1919, in Colombarone. Fought against the Turks, 1876; founded a radical literary review with the help of the poet Carducci, 1881; first collection of prose sketches published in Milan, 1882; wrote ten plays, 1883-93; concentrated on libretto writing from 1892-1904.

Librettos (selected)

Il vassallo di Szigeth (with F. Pozzi), A. Smareglio, 1889.
La Wally, A. Catalani, 1892.
Cristoforo Colombo, A. Franchetti, 1892.
Manon Lescaut (with others), G. Puccini, 1893.
Cornelio Schutt, A. Smareglia, 1893.
Nozze istriane, A. Smareglia, 1893.
La martire, S. Samaras, 1894.
Andrea Chénier, U. Giordano, 1896.
La collana di Pasqua, G. Luporini, 1896.
La bohème (with G. Giacosa), G. Puccini, 1896.
Iris, P. Mascagni, 1898.
La fonte di Enschir, F. Alfano, 1898.
La Rosalba, E. Pizzi, 1899.
Medioevo latino, E. Panizza, 1900.
Tosca (with G. Giacosa), G. Puccini, 1900.
Le maschere, P. Mascagni, 1901.
Lorenza, E. Mascheroni, 1901.
Germania, A. Franchetti, 1902.
Cassandra, V. Gnecchi, 1902.
Siberia, U. Giordano, 1903.
Madama Butterfly (with G. Giacosa), G. Puccini, 1904.
Tess, F. d'Erlanger, 1906.
Il principe Zilah, F. Alfano, 1909.
La perugina, E. Mascheroni, 1909.
Isabeau, P. Mascagni, 1911.
Giove a Pompei (with E. Romagnoli), U. Giordano and A. Franchetti, 1921 [posthumous production].

Publications

By ILLICA: books–

Farfalle, effetti di luci. Milan, 1882.

About ILLICA: books–

Adami, G. *Giulio Ricordi e i suoi musicisti.* Milan and Rome, 1933.
Donelli, D. *G. Giacosa.* Milan, 1948.
Nardi, P. *Vita e tempo di Giuseppe Giacosa.* Milan, 1949.
Gara, E., and M. Morini, eds. *Carteggi pucciniani.* Milan, 1958.
Morini, M. *Luigi Illica.* Piacenza, 1961.

articles–

De Angelis, A. "Luigi Illica." *Tribuna* (1919).
Morini, M. "Profilo di Illica." *La Scala* (1956).
Morini, M. "Illica e Mascagni nell' esperienza dell' *Iris.*" *Musica d'oggi* new series 6 (1963): 58.

*   *   *

When Puccini became dissatisfied with Marco Praga's original libretto for *Manon Lescaut,* his publisher, Giulio Ricordi, enlisted the help of several other writers, including Domenico Oliva and Leoncavallo. Finally he approached the celebrated dramatist Giuseppe Giacosa, probably hoping that the great man would himself lend a hand. In fact, Giacosa recommended Luigi Illica, whose libretto for Catalani's *La Wally* had impressed him. Illica was able to get the *Manon* libretto into better shape, and he then became Giacosa's collaborator on the librettos for Puccini's next three operas.

Although he had begun his career as a playwright, after his work on *Manon Lescaut* Illica devoted himself to opera texts. He wrote several of his own during the period of the Giacosa collaboration, including *Andrea Chénier* for Giordano and *Iris* for Mascagni, and was still active after Giacosa's death in 1906, providing *Isabeau* for Mascagni in 1911.

Illica was a fiery and impetuous character, with a rapid improvisatory ability and an excellent theatrical sense. His ear for language, however, was unrefined, and he fell easily into cliché and empty rhetoric. Composing within the short meters required by operatic numbers, he could not avoid chanting rhythms and jingling rhymes. During the 1890s he started to affect the fashionable *dannunzianesimo,* the decadent and flowery style of D'Annunzio; this led him to write long, self-indulgent stage directions. *Iris* begins with a full-page description of a sunrise: "Ecco! i primi albori che si diffondono rispecchiandosi in scintille adamantine entro a le rugiade sui fiori, sulle erbe!" (Lo! the first streaks of dawn, which fall, reflected in adamantine glitter, on the dew-drenched flowers, on the grass!)

It is noticeable that whenever Giacosa discusses his problems, it is always matters of language and prosody which concern him. Illica, on the other hand, discusses nothing but dramaturgy, motivation, and scene-construction. In act I of *Iris,* the heroine is abducted during a marionette-show. Her father is blind. "Thus she is snatched away under his eyes and the scene is not interrupted. After she is gone the blind man continues speaking to her . . . Thus, without interruptions, we convey the public from the scene of the puppet-theatre to the end of the act" (letter to Giulio Ricordi).

Illica had a scrupulous concern for historical accuracy, and his best libretto (apart from the collaborations) was undoubtedly *Andrea Chénier.* It is ostentatiously full of accurate historical detail; Madeleine de Choigny speaks of the "cassa di sconto," the "Basilio" and the "Montgolfier," three styles of bonnet fashionable in the 1790s. This opera brings together the themes of love and conspiracy, fidelity and betrayal, and politics and poetry, balancing two social tableaux (aristocratic in act I, revolutionary in act III) with two passages of dialogue and lyricism (acts II and IV both end with a love-duet). The rapidity and naturalism of dialogue, the complex ensembles, and the telling use of the chorus provide a rich framework for Giordano's score. The enormous cast is deployed without any character seeming redundant. Perhaps it was a pity that

Luigi Illica (right) with Puccini

Illica's other French Revolutionary libretto, *Maria Antoinetta,* was rejected by Puccini.

—Raymond Monelle

THE IMPRESARIO
See DER SCHAUSPIELDIREKTOR

L'INCORONAZIONE DI POPPEA [The Coronation of Poppea].

Composer: Claudio Monteverdi.

Librettist: G.F. Busenello.

First Performance: Venice, 1642.

Roles: Poppea (mezzo-soprano); Nero (tenor); Ottavia (mezzo-soprano or soprano); Ottone (baritone); Seneca (bass); Drusilla (soprano); Arnalta (contralto); Valetto (soprano); Damigella (soprano); Two Soldiers (tenor); Pallas (soprano); Mercury (tenor); Nutrice (contralto); Amore (soprano); Liberto (tenor); Lictor (bass); chorus (SATTBB).

Publications

articles–

Benvenuti, G. "Il manuscritto veneziano della 'Incoronazione di Poppea'." *Rivista musicale italiana* 41 (1937): 176.

Redlich, H.F. "Notationsprobleme in Cl. Monteverdis 'Incoronazione di Poppea'." *Acta musicologica* 10 (1938): 129.

Osthoff, W. "Die venezianische und neapolitanische Fassung von Monteverdis 'Incoronazione di Poppea'." *Acta musicologica* 26 (1954): 88.

―――. "Neue Beobachtungen zu Quellen und Geschichte von Monteverdis 'Incoronazione di Poppea'." *Die Musikforschung* 11 (1958): 129.

Arnold, Denis. " 'L'incoronazione di Poppea' and its Orchestral Requirements." *Musical Times* 104 (1963).

Fano, Fabio. "*Il combattimento di Tancredi e Clorinda* e *L'incoronazione di Poppea* di Claudio Monteverdi." In *Studi sul teatro veneto fra rinascimento ed età barocca.* Florence, 1971.

Chiarelli, Alessandra. "*L'incoronazione di Poppea* o *Il Nerone:* Problemi di filologia testuale." *Rivista italiana di musicologia* 9 (1974): 117.

Bragard, Anne-Marie. "Deux portraits de femmes dans l'oeuvre de Monteverdi: Ariane et Popée." *Bulletin de la Société liégeoise de musicologie* 24 (1979): 1.

Müller, Reinhard. "Basso ostinato und die 'imitatione del parlare' in Monteverdis *Incoronazione di Poppea*." *Archiv für Musikwissenschaft* 40 (1983): 1.

Avant-scène opéra December (1988) [*L'incoronazione di Poppea* issue].

Rosand, Ellen. "Monteverdi's Mimetic Art: *L'incoronazione di Poppea.*" *Cambridge Opera Journal* 1 (1989): 113.

*   *   *

There can be no discussion of Monteverdi's *L'incoronazione di Poppea* without mention of the editions according to which it is usually performed. These, in 1990, offer a choice between a somewhat free interpretation of the sources by Raymond Leppard (1962) and a more accurate and scholarly one by Alan Curtis (1967). The former is much cut, the scoring lush and romantic, while the latter provides the full and complete text with lighter scoring typical of the operatic scene in the early 17th century.

An understanding of the original sources is also of importance, in that the Venice manuscript (1646) is not even partly an autograph, and shows signs of having been cut, transposed, and in other ways spoiled. The Naples manuscript is more reliable and complete, containing newly composed material to enlarge the role of Ottavia and give the stage machinery a chance to shine. Both scores derive from a lost autograph.

A copy of the libretto at Treviso, first studied from a scholarly point of view in 1902, shows that Monteverdi followed the libretto very carefully, so that the legend about his having changed the ending and written his own verse for the final duet can be disregarded.

The opera begins with a prologue in which Fortune, Virtue, and Love sing of their influence on human affairs, Love being predominant. Act I, set in first-century Rome, introduces the Emperor Nero who, infatuated with the courtesan Poppea, is intent upon making her his empress. Ottavia, the reigning empress, both jealous and vindictive, is no more moved by the philosopher Seneca's advice than is Nero. A nobleman, Ottone, still in love with Poppea, finds his way to her room blocked by guards. He tries to console himself with Drusilla, a court lady.

In act II we see Seneca go to his death, mourned by his disciples. Poppea's murder is planned by Ottone and Ottavia, with Drusilla's assistance. But as Ottone lingers over the sleeping woman, Love (Amore) appears and foils his attempt. As light relief, we witness the first intimations of love between a page and a lady-in-waiting. Nero and his friend Lucan, a poet, sing a duet in celebration of Seneca's death and Poppea's beauty. Act III sees the banishment of the conspirators, with Ottavia's farewell to the city, while the old nurse Arnalta is raised to the status of confidante to the empress. The final scene consists of Nero and Poppea's radiant love-duet.

L'incoronazione di Poppea has gone down in history as perhaps the first example of a plot in which evil triumphs over good, resulting from a procession of suicide, attempted murder, banishment, and exile. Such a story displays the triumph of power and vaulting ambition, the harshness and corruption of politics, and the venalities of court life, all of which Monteverdi knew well, notably in Cremona, Mantua, and Venice, where he was exposed to the machinery of corruption and the chicanery of musical life. His letters reveal his sufferings, and his music in *L'incoronazione di Poppea* shows him rising above those lowly intrigues. He has left us a musical legacy purified of evil, although he is perfectly capable of representing it.

There are wonderful moments in the character portrayals, notably in Nero's overbearing manner and his all-consuming pride; in Seneca's quiet stoicism and his acceptance of the folly of those set to govern over us; in Ottone's duplicity, transformed "not from Ottone into Drusilla but from a man into a serpent." All these traits are revealed in music that, in the original, relies not on instrumental coloring so much as refinement of melodic expression, vitality of rhythm, and expert word-painting.

Other felicities include the luscious ariosos given to Poppea, whose music certainly reflects her sensuality; the touching pronouncements of the repudiated Ottavia; the helplessness of Drusilla, caught in a plot of increasing complexity; and the superficially amusing yet basically serious attitude of Arnalta, whose change of station shows her to be a changed personality. Monteverdi also deals with his lesser figures in a masterly manner, especially the conversations between the Praetorian Guards and the naive but moving encounter of the page and the lady-in-waiting.

His grasp of musical style is such that he is never at a loss for a situation or a character, and when certain events central to the story are raised aloft by the librettist, Busenello, it is as if the musician followed the lighted flame and used its beckoning glimmer to inspire his musical thought. It is never less than intense, so that even in a mutilated or cut version we are bound to experience a feeling of illumination, even incandescence. Within a year of its production, Monteverdi was dead, and the first great chapter in the history of opera had come to an end.

—Denis Stevens

LES INDES GALANTES [The Congenial Indies].

Composer: Jean-Philippe Rameau.

Librettist: L. Fuzelier.

First Performance: Paris, Opéra, 23 August 1735; revised 10 March 1736, 28 May 1743, 8 June 1751, and 14 July 1761.

Roles: Hébé (soprano); Bellone (bass); L'Amour (soprano); Osman (bass); Smilie (soprano); Valère (tenor); Huascar (bass); Phani (soprano); Don Carlos (tenor); Tacmas (tenor); Ali (bass); Zaïre (soprano); Fatime (soprano); Adario (tenor); Damon (tenor); Don Alvar (bass); Zima (soprano); chorus.

Publications

book–

Bertrando-Patier, Marie-Claire. *L'exoticisme dans la musique française du XVIIIe siècle: "Les Indes galantes" du Jean-Philippe Rameau.* Strasbourg, 1974.

articles–

Sadler, G. "Rameau's Harpsichord Transcriptions from *Les Indes galantes.*" *Early Music* 7 (1979): 18.
Avant-scène opéra December (1982) [*Les Indes galantes* issue].

Weary of the moralizing posturing symptomatic of the *tragédie lyrique,* French audiences in the years following the death, in 1687, of Jean-Baptiste Lully—the genre's leading practitioner—began to desire more down-to-earth fare. Reflecting this change in taste, the November 1714 *Mercure de*

France reported that Lully's "*Bellérophon* nowadays appears too tragic, *Thésée* too unfeeling." Similar sentiments were noted—and lamented—by Rémond de Saint-Mard in his 1741 *Réflexions sur l'opéra.* "There is no longer any need for the strong and the pathetic action of the tragic. People want only sensuous spectacles that are easy to follow," for "the French public is no longer inclined toward entertainment that requires concentration." The shift, really one of degree, was motivated, one imagines, by the desire for novelty. Louis de Cahusac, librettist, *littérateur,* and successful man of the theater, said precisely this when he wrote: "the opera conceived by Lully is composed of one principal dramatic action over the course of five acts. It is a vast concept, such as that of Raphael or Michelangelo." In its place, Cahusac continues, spectators wanted an opera of "piquant miniatures of pretty Watteau's," with "precision of draftsmanship, grace of brushstrokes, and brilliance of color."

The cry for the agreeable, graceful, and colorful was soon to be answered by the *opéra-ballet,* of which Rameau's *Les Indes galantes,* his second venture into the realm of dramatic music, is a textbook example. (The title defies exact translation—"The Congenial Indies" is one possibility, the less-literal "The Allure of Exotic Places" is another.) In the hands of the genre's creator, André Campra, the *opéra-ballet,* as Pierre-Charles Roy remarked in his 1749 *Lettre sur l'opéra,* "corresponds to French capriciousness"—a capriciousness perhaps best typified by the title of the opening act of Campra's *Les fêtes vénitiennes* ("Venetian Festival," 1710): "Le triomphe de la folie sur la raison" ("The triumph of folly over reason"). The public had spoken, and Saint-Mard confessed self-consciously: "we have reached the point where one desires only [opéra-]ballets. Each act must be composed of a fast-moving, light, and *galante* intrigue.... You will find there the portrait of our mores. They are, to be sure, rather vile, but they are, nonetheless, ours."

As with many a critic, Saint-Mard perhaps protests too much. The real appeal of the *opéra-ballet,* or so it would seem, was the banishment of mythological and allegorical figures in favor of real humans in recognizable, or at least plausible, settings. Nevertheless, the genre brought with it a new set of problems: to oblige the demand for "sensuous spectacles," dramatic breadth necessarily was diminished. Yet the poets' loss became the musicians' gain, for in reducing the drama the opportunity to increase music and dance presented itself, thereby allowing composers both greater musical freedom and room for experimentation. Dramatically, the *opéra-ballet* consists of a prologue and three or four *entrées* (acts), each with its own characters and independent actions, but all loosely related to the collective idea expressed in the work's title. In *Les Indes galantes,* the unifying theme is love; its setting is in remote corners of the world—the first act in Turkey, the second in Peru, the third in Persia, and the fourth in a North American forest. The prologue, a celebration of the universal appeal of love, does, however, make use of mythological figures—most prominently the ballet mistress Hébé, overseer of the god's pleasures. (As first performed in Paris on 23 August 1735 the work contained only a prologue and two *entrées;* for the third performance Rameau and his librettist, Louis Fuzelier, added the present third *entrée;* the following year they added the present fourth.)

In *Les Indes galantes* the increased reliance on the purely musical may be illustrated by a brief look at its *première entrée,* "Le turc généreux." The setting is the garden of the generous Turk mentioned in the title, Osman Pasha. In the background is the sea. Émilie, a French captive, pledged from birth to Valère, sings to the pasha of her abduction by cruel bandits and imprisonment by pirates "on the vast seas near all that I hate, far from the one I love." Thus separated from Valère, she goes on to relate his many courageous attempts to rescue her. Presently, "the sky darkens with clouds, the winds roar, and the seas rise." From the storm emerges a wind-tossed chorus of sailors who have narrowly escaped death. Scarcely believing it, Émilie sees Valère among their number. The pasha's generosity is manifest by his willingness to forsake his own love for Émilie in order that she might at last be reunited with Valère.

It is the "Tempeste" that elicits Rameau's most arresting music. Graphically depicting the raging storm, the scene is rich with abrupt changes of harmonies, enharmonic modulations, and vivid orchestral effects of violin tremolos and rapid scales for the flutes—all of which provide a remarkably picturesque expression of the sailors' terror in the grip of nature. Rameau's love of such nature depictions is to be discovered as well in the second *entrée*, "Les Incas," with its representation of an earthquake in which he again, as in the "Tempeste," deploys an impressive array of harmonic tricks. In the event, the public took a while to warm to such realistic portrayals of natural catastrophes. Indeed, Desfontaines, editor of the *Observations sur les écrits modernes,* complained that "the music is a perpetual witchery; nature has no share in it. Its airs are fit to stir up the benumbed nerves of a paralytic. I am racked, flayed, dislocated by this devilish *Les Indes galantes.*" And yet as Cahusac, who was to become Rameau's most steadfast librettist, boasted years later: "six months after the first performance, every tune from the overture to the last gavotte had been parodied [i.e., set to new words for popular consumption]. At the 1751 revival the pit sang the chorus 'Brillant Soleil' [from act II] as easily as our fathers sang Lully's 'Armide est encor plus aimable.' "

—James Parsons

INTERMEZZO.

Composer: Richard Strauss.

Librettist: Richard Strauss.

First Performance: Dresden, Staatsoper, 4 November 1924.

Roles: Christine Storch (soprano); Robert Storch (baritone); Baron Lummer (tenor); Anna (soprano); Notary (baritone); Notary's Wife (soprano); Conductor Stroh (tenor); Businessman (baritone); Judge (baritone); Singer (bass); Little Franzl (speaking part); Resi (speaking part); Therese (speaking part); Marie (speaking part); Cook (speaking part).

Publications

article–

Graf, E. "Die Bedeutung von Richard Strauss's *Intermezzo.*" *Österreichische Musikzeitschrift* 18 (1963).

* * *

In 1919 Strauss completed the composition of *Die Frau ohne Schatten.* That enormous and symbolically laden work had taken its toll on the composer both in terms of sheer length and emotional weight, and he longed for the lightness of comic spoofery as an antidote. This urge took form presently with the ballet *Schlagobers,* but found its ultimate outlet in *Intermezzo.*

An autobiographical penchant had long played a significant role in Strauss's music, including *Feuersnot* as well as the better known allusions of *Ein Heldenleben* and *Sinfonia domestica.* Thus an episode from his own personal life seemed an ideal topic for an opera, especially dealing as it did with his marriage to a rather notorious termagant of an ex-prima donna, Pauline de Ahna. Strauss in fact loved his wife very much, and in retrospect it would seem that her tantrums and nagging (along with other more positive qualities) fulfilled a deep need in the composer's psyche. In any case theirs was a lengthy and happy union by all accounts. *Die Frau ohne Schatten* had also dealt with marriage, and thus *Intermezzo* stands in relationship to the monumental earlier work comparable to that of a satyr play, and Strauss even allows the two operas to share one all-important musical idea.

It was predictable, given his intellectual aloofness and distaste for Frau Strauss, that long-time collaborator Hugo von Hofmannsthal found the concept vulgar and refused to participate in the new project. After some false starts with critic and author Hermann Bahr, Strauss was finally convinced to write the text himself, a logical decision since he was, after all, a participant in the events to be related and wanted the words to reflect ordinary conversation and avoid all hints of poetry.

Thus we are in the household of famous conductor and composer Robert Storch and his wife, the rather notorious termagant of an ex-prima donna, Christine. In brief, the plot conflates two episodes. Robert leaves home for Vienna, where he has some concert engagements. In his absence Christine almost accidentally develops an innocent relationship with a featherbrained young man, one Baron Lummer, who takes her dancing but bores her with his vapidity. He finally ruins whatever friendship they might have had by asking her for a considerable sum of money, a request she rightfully refuses to consider. More serious and central to the story is the saga of Mieze Maier. This young lady of dubious reputation (who never appears on stage) sends a letter to the composer which addresses him affectionately ("Lieber Schatz"), asks for some opera tickets and closes with "meet me afterwards in the bar as usual." Christine opens the letter, suspects the worst, and immediately files for divorce. Robert, severely disadvantaged by being out of town, finally unscrambles the situation. He learns that Mieze had confused him with another conductor with a similar last name, and returns home to mollify Christine and revel in a happy ending, his marriage back on track.

The charm of the work, however, lies not in its slender plot but in the wonderfully witty repartee with which Strauss characterized all of the roles, especially the endless chatterbox banter and tantrums of the wife. Written in two acts, the opera's many brief scenes are linked with evocative interludes, virtually the only places where Strauss allows the orchestra to have its head. This is the direct result of those experiments in the conversational style which he deployed in the recently completed prologue to *Ariadne auf Naxos.* Deeming his efforts at textual clarity and effortless passage from speech through recitative to arioso to have been successful, he devotes virtually all of *Intermezzo* to the newly minted technique, allowing the voices to blossom into cantilena only at a few emotionally crucial finales.

Following the lead of Gluck in *Alceste,* Strauss wrote a foreword to the opera which is printed in the *Intermezzo* piano score and is an important statement on his theories of word-setting and indeed operatic composition and performance in general. Thus a harmless and trenchant comedy of manners becomes simultaneously yet unobtrusively a professional tract. *Intermezzo* is probably too specialized to enter the standard repertoire, and there are still those who find the autobiographical element distasteful. Nonetheless it remains an important work in Strauss' operatic canon and will undoubtedly continue to delight and reward the conoisseur.

—Dennis Wakeling

IOLANTA.

Composer: Piotr Ilyich Tchaikovsky.

Librettist: M. Tchaikovsky (after V. Zotov's translation of H. Hertz's *King René's Daughter*).

First Performance: St Petersburg, Mariinsky, 18 December 1892.

Roles: Iolanta (soprano); King René (bass); Count Vaudémont (tenor); Duke Robert (baritone); Bertram (bass); Martha (contralto); Brigitta (soprano); Laura (mezzo-soprano); Ibn-Hakia (baritone); Almerik (tenor); chorus (SATB).

Publications

article–

Lloyd-Jones, D. "A Background to Iolanta." *Musical Times* 109 (1968): 225.

* * *

Both Tchaikovsky's ballet *The Nutcracker* and the opera *Iolanta* belong to the last years of the composer's life. When the ballet and the opera were performed together on 18 December 1892, it was the opera that was successful, not the ballet, though subsequent years have reversed this verdict.

Following the introductory orchestral prelude, marked *piano espressivo,* which may well be suggestive of Iolanta's blindness, the opera opens in a luxurious garden. To a background of four musicians, Princess Iolanta gropes for fruit, which, assisted by her friends Brigitta, Martha, and Laura, she plucks and puts into baskets. Although she is blind, her father, King René, has forbidden anyone to discuss the fact. Iolanta, though unaware of her handicap, realizes instinctively that she is different from other people. She wonders how her friends know she is crying if they do not touch her eyes. She is sad at heart and in an arioso reflects on her former happiness. In the following scene, the sound of hunting horns is heard, announcing the imminent arrival of the king. A discussion between Almerik, the king's armor-bearer, and Bertram, keeper of the castle, discloses that King René is bringing with him a famous Moorish doctor and that Iolanta is engaged to Robert, Duke of Burgundy. The king, wanting to conceal Iolanta's blindness, keeps her isolated in the remote castle where they are now staying.

Another fanfare announces the entry of the king and the Moorish doctor, Ibn-Hakia, who has been summoned as the last hope of curing the princess. The doctor goes to look at the sleeping Iolanta and in his absence René, in a poignant aria, prays to the Lord, asking why he and his daughter have been so punished, and calls for divine assistance. When Ibn-Hakia returns, he tells the king that Iolanta must be made aware of her condition and that only her will-power can save her. But René will not even consider this, and both depart.

Now through the forest appear Robert, Duke of Burgundy, and his friend Count Vaudémont. Vaudémont cannot believe his eyes at the beauty of the garden, which they have come across by accident. Robert, though betrothed to Iolanta, whom he has never seen, wishes to break his engagement, having fallen in love with Mathilde. Both come across the sleeping Iolanta, whose beauty immediately captivates Vaudémont, But Robert, alarmed by the whole business and fearing sorcery, wishes to leave. The sound of their voices wakes Iolanta. Vaudémont begins to talk to her, and while the princess goes to fetch wine, Robert departs to find his retinue. The following duet between Iolanta and Vaudémont, which reveals the growing warmth of their affection, is the highlight of the whole opera, especially the moment when Vaudémont asks for a red rose and is given a white one. When this action is repeated, he suddenly realizes that she is blind. His stunned silence disturbs Iolanta, but Vaudémont reassures her, explaining to her the meaning of light, the first-born gift of the Creator. Iolanta replies in ecstatic terms.

Their reverie is interrupted by the sudden arrival of the king, Ibn-Hakia, and their entourage. The king is alarmed to find his daughter talking to a strange knight and even more so when he discovers that he has told her about the concept of light. René wishes to put Vaudémont to death, but Ibn-Hakia sees the event as reason for hope. René agrees to Ibn-Hakia attempting to cure Iolanta, but tells the knight that if the treatment is unsuccessful, he will forfeit his life. Iolanta, aghast, expresses her love for Vaudémont, and their duet, reintroducing earlier material, forms another climactic moment. Iolanta and the doctor depart, and the king admits to the knight that the threat of death was a ploy to stir Iolanta to action. Robert, Duke of Burgundy, returns and explains all the circumstances to the king, who agrees to release him from his bond, thus enabling Vaudémont to marry Iolanta. To a great chord of C major comes the news that Iolanta has regained her sight. The opera ends with a big ensemble, in which all give thanks to Heaven.

It is surprising that *Iolanta* is not more frequently performed, since it contains many attractive numbers—Iolanta's arioso, René's supplicatory aria, Ibn-Hakia's aria, Robert's aria in praise of Mathilde, as well as the impressive duet between Iolanta and Vaudémont. The scene between René and the doctor in the first part of the work is highly dramatic, and the use of the women's chorus in the opening scene in the garden is charming in its skillful part-writing and novel timbres. The orchestration is effective throughout, the texture unified by a number of recurrent themes.

—Gerald Seaman

IPHIGENIA IN AULIS
See IPHIGÉNIE EN AULIDE

IPHIGENIA IN TAURIS
 See IPHIGÉNIE EN TAURIDE

IPHIGÉNIE EN AULIDE [Iphigenia in Aulis].

Composer: Christoph Willibald von Gluck.

Librettist: François-Louis Lebland du Roullet (after Racine).

First Performance: Paris, Académie Royale, 19 April 1774.

Roles: Iphigenia (soprano); Clytemnestra (mezzo-soprano); Achilles (tenor); Agamemnon (baritone); Patroclas (bass); Calchas (bass); Arkas (bass); Artemis [Diana] (soprano); chorus (SATTBB).

Publications

articles—

Weismann, W. "Der Deus ex machina in Glucks 'Iphigenie in Aulis'." *Deutsches Jahrbuch der Musikwissenschaft* 7 (1962): 7.

Iphigénie en Aulide, **title page of first edition of the score, Paris, 1774**

Hartung, Günther. "Die Iphigenien-Thematik in Musik und Dichtung des 18. Jahrhunderts." In *Thematik und Ideenwelt der Antike bei Georg Friedrich Händel,* edited by Walther Siegmund-Schultze, 100. Halle, 1983.

* * *

To see *Iphigénie en Aulide,* as many critics have, as an inferior preparation for the later opera, *Iphigénie en Tauride,* is to do it an injustice. This is the opera with which Gluck conquered Paris, at a stroke releasing French opera from its stifling national traditions and launching a new synthesis of Italian, French, and German styles which was to be an inspiration for many nineteenth-century opera composers. Wagner acknowledged his debt by partially rewriting the work, a form of homage from which the opera has been trying to escape ever since.

The plot relates an incident from the beginning of the Trojan war. Having offended the goddess Diana, the Greek king Agamemnon is ordered to sacrifice his daughter, Iphigenia, so that a favorable wind may be granted to transport his fleet to Troy. Unaware of the crisis, Iphigenia arrives in Aulis with her mother Clytemnestra, to marry the Greek hero Achilles. Only as Iphigenia approaches the altar is the news of the king's vow revealed; Clytemnestra and Achilles rage against Agamemnon, but Iphigenia submits obediently to her fate. After an agonized struggle with his conscience, Agamemnon decides to save his daughter by sending her back to Greece, but the Greeks angrily demand that the vow be fulfilled. As the sacrifice is about to take place, Achilles arrives with an army to rescue his bride. A battle is averted by the priest Calchas, who announces that Diana is appeased, and will raise a wind to carry the fleet to Troy. The work ends with general reconciliation.

It is remarkable that an opera dealing with human sacrifice and supernatural intervention should sound so modern today. This is partly due to its structure—a continuous stream of music, reflecting the changing moods of the drama. *Iphigénie en Aulide* is the second opera which Gluck invested with an integrated overture, hinting at the mood of the story and running directly into the first scene, where the poignant dissonances of the opening are revealed to be the voice of Agamemnon, wrestling in prayer. The libretto by François-Louis Lebland du Roullet (derived from Racine) allows Gluck to integrate short airs, recitatives, chorus and dance into a seamless web of musical drama, held together by expressive orchestral passages, which allow characters space to act and react to the dramatic sequence of events. (This unprecedented continuity clearly appealed to Wagner.)

The chorus has a major role in the opera. Here, as in *Alceste,* Gluck understood that the pressures of kingship are only credible if the people for whom the king is responsible are brought convincingly to life. When Agamemnon promises that he will sacrifice his daughter, he does so in the knowledge that he has sent a secret messenger to prevent her arrival in Aulis, but as he gives Calchas his promise, he is interrupted by welcoming shouts from the army announcing Iphigenia's approach. Gluck extracts the full irony from the situation; he also uses it to build a complex texture as the king's agonized cries are superimposed on the rejoicing chorus; additionally, the stage is filled with brilliant spectacle as the army and its general are swept aside by the chorus and ballet of Clytemnestra's suite. The airs are perhaps too brief to allow a full exploration of the extreme emotions of the protagonists, which swing rapidly between elation and despair. A listener might well say with Iphigenia, "How sweet and yet how difficult to pass so suddenly from cruelest torture to supreme happiness." Agamemnon alone is a fully developed character; his dilemma is the subject of several powerful scenes, written in that expressive blend of recitative and air which Gluck made his own. Here the role of the orchestra is enhanced so that it makes a telling commentary on the words: Agamemnon sings that he hears within his heart the voice of his conscience, and the orchestra brings this to life with a plaintive oboe phrase, reiterated throughout the air. By such vivid details of scoring, and through his intensity of response to human situations, Gluck brings opera into the world of late eighteenth-century sensibility.

—Patricia Howard

IPHIGÉNIE EN TAURIDE [Iphigenia in Tauris].

Composer: Christoph Willibald von Gluck.

Librettists: Nicolas-François Guillard and François-Louis Grand Lebland du Roullet (after Euripides).

First Performance: Paris, Académie Royale, 18 May 1779; revised in German, translated by J.B. von Alxinger and Gluck, Vienna, Burgtheater, 23 October 1781.

Roles: Iphigenia (soprano); Pylades (tenor); Orestes (baritone); Thoas (bass or baritone); Diana (soprano); Greek Woman (soprano); Two priestesses (sopranos); Minister of the Sanctuary (bass); A Scyth (baritone); chorus (SATTB).

Publications

articles–

Favart, C.S. "Etwas über Glucks Iphigenia in Tauris und dessen Armide." In *Mémoires et correspondance,* edited by A.P.C. Favart amd H.F. Dumolard. Paris, 1808.

Gastoué, A. "Gossec et Gluck à l'Opéra de Paris: le ballet final d'Iphigénie en Tauride." *Revue de musicologie* 19 (1935): 87.

Rushton, Julian. " 'Iphigénie en Tauride': the Operas of Gluck and Piccinni." *Music and Letters* 53 (1972): 411.

Dahlhaus, Carl. "Ethos und Pathos in Glucks Iphigenie auf Tauris." *Die Musikforschung* 28 (1974): 289.

Stoll, A. and K. "Affekt und Moral: zu Glucks Iphigenie auf Tauris." *Die Musikforschung* 31 (1975): 305.

Hartung, Günther. "Die Iphigenien-Thematik in Musik und Dichtung des 18. Jahrhunderts." In *Thematik und Ideenwelt der Antike bei Georg Friedrich Händel,* edited by Walther Siegmund-Schultze, 100. Halle, 1983.

* * *

The operatic aims of Christoph Willibald von Gluck are perhaps most effectively realized in *Iphigénie en Tauride,* an impressive work of musical and dramatic power, which is important in the history of opera as well as a significant achievement in its own right. In an open letter published in the *Journal de Paris* two years before the premiere of 1779, Gluck had avowed his desire to revitalize the drama through a search for strong expression and the interconnection of all

parts of his works. He accomplished these goals in *Iphigénie en Tauride* by means of vivid dramatic characterizations, fluid musical structures, and a balance between vocal and instrumental components that integrated dance and chorus within a cohesive entity.

The libretto, written by Nicolas-François Guillard on a drama by Euripides, involves a decision by the Greek Iphigenia, who had been brought to the island of Tauris to serve as high priestess to the goddess Diana. King Thoas, barbaric ruler of the Scythians, has decreed that the oracles can be appeased and his life saved only if all strangers to the island are killed. Iphigenia and her priestesses are to carry out these sacrifices. The storm opening the lyric tragedy brings to Tauris two Greek friends, Orestes and Pylades. Both must be killed, but Iphigenia risks Thoas' wrath by determining to spare the life of one. Feeling a tender sentiment toward Orestes, who reminds Iphigenia of her brother, she resolves that Pylades be sacrificed and Orestes be saved to carry a message to her sister in Mycenae.

Orestes has been tormented by guilt and pursued by the Eumenides for having avenged the murder of his father, King Agamemnon, by killing his mother, Clytemnestra. Believing that he must expiate his crime, Orestes urges Pylades to exchange places and let him die, but Pylades refuses and expresses heroic acceptance of the destiny enabling his friend to live. Orestes then implores Iphigenia to reconsider and sacrifice him instead of Pylades; with the greatest reluctance, she accedes. As Orestes is being prepared for the sacrifice, he names his sister, Iphigenia. A joyful recognition scene ensues. King Thoas angrily tries to destroy both Orestes and Iphigenia but is killed by Pylades, who arrives with soldiers from Greece in time to rescue Orestes. The goddess Diana assures Orestes that remorse has assuaged his guilt; he is to reign in Mycenae with Iphigenia restored to her homeland. The final chorus celebrates the return of peace.

Gluck responded with varied musical means to the striking situations, images, and universal themes. A French late-eighteenth century perspective on ancient Greece produced an emphasis on the conflict between Iphigenia's duty and her human response to nature and individual feeling. Gluck and Guillard intensified the drama between sister, brother, and friend by delineating bonds of family love, friendship, courage, and heroic rescue set against the strife between Scythian and Greek civilizations. Gluck's techniques include the use of unadorned arias, shorter expressive ariosos, dramatically motivated accompanied recitatives, choruses heightening contrast and mood, ballets in the new style that advance rather than impede action, and active orchestral passages that provide a sense of musical continuity.

Concentrated exchanges occur between the three main figures in the second and third acts of the four-act work. The characterization of Orestes is especially successful because the dramatic element of his obsessive guilt has its parallel in Gluck's desire to achieve musical unity through the reiteration of short rhythmic figures that build in intensity. Thus, for example, an inexorable sense of momentum is attained in the first aria of act II, in which Orestes sings in allegro tempo of the gods who pursue him, while oboes, clarinets, horns, trumpets, and timpani reinforce his vocal line with persistent motives as bassoons and strings play vigorous scale-like passages. The next scene has been noted for the psychological insight revealed by Gluck in setting accented orchestral syncopations that reveal the troubled disorientation of Orestes as he sings of calm returning to his heart. There follow a dramatic chorus and ballet-pantomime of terror by the Eumenides punctuated by the cries of Orestes and an intense dialogue in recitative during which Iphigenia hears of her

Iphigénie en Tauride, autograph manuscript of a portion of the recitatives from act II, scene 3, German version, 1781

family's fate from Orestes. In the final scene, Iphigenia instructs her priestesses to combine laments for their fallen king with her expression of private grief; their plaintive lines are supported by sustained dissonances in the oboes.

Act III celebrates friendship. Its third scene includes an unusual ensemble between Iphigenia and the two men. Her noble decision to spare one of the victims is set to music whose tempo, rhythmic patterns, instrumentation, and dynamics differ substantially from those in the harmonious accord of the unselfish friends. Three times they exchange statements and responses until the moment when Iphigenia's fateful choice leads the flowing lines to merge into a recitative, an orchestral passage expressive of her despair, and Orestes' anguished solo phrase on learning that it is Pylades who is to be sacrificed.

The duet in C minor between Orestes and Pylades in the next scene is an impassioned dialogue whose first part stresses the intensity felt by each in attempting to convince the other through brief overlapping phrases that accumulate power by means of their sequential repetition in an insistent increase in volume. It is musically stirring and it also serves the crucial dramatic function of lending additional stature to the figure of Pylades, whose steadfast heroism emerges. When later he finds himself free to live, his resolute determination to save Orestes is fully credible. The paean to *amitié*, friendship, in C major with which Pylades closes the act sustains the weight of its position as an effective culmination.

Iphigénie en Tauride balances dramatic expression through truthful characterization with musical concision through deftly conceived structures. Its majestic sweep and energetic vigor admirably convey the new dramatic musical style for which Gluck became renowned.

—Ora Frishberg Saloman

IRIS.

Composer: Pietro Mascagni.

Librettist: Luigi Illica.

First Performance: Rome, Costanzi, 22 November 1898; revised, Milan, Teatro alla Scala, 19 January 1899.

Roles: Iris (soprano); Il Cieco, Iris's blind father (bass); Osaka (tenor); Kyoto (baritone); Geisha (soprano); Dealer (tenor); Ragpicker (tenor); chorus (SSAATTBB).

Publications

books–

Mantovani, T. *Iris di Mascagni.* Rome, 1929.
Morini, M., and P. Ostali, eds. *Mascagni e l'"Iris" fra simbolismo e floreale. Atti del 2° Convegno di studi su Pietro Mascagni.* Milan, 1989.

article–

Torchi, L. " 'Iris' di Mascagni." *Rivista musicale italiana* 2 (1895): 287.

*   *   *

Pietro Mascagni's *Iris,* a *melodramma* in three acts, was first given at the Teatro Costanzi in Rome in 1898 under the baton of Arturo Toscanini. The premiere was attended by such notables as Giacomo Puccini, Alberto Franchetti, Leopoldo Mugnone, Arrigo Boito, Giovanni Sgambati, and critics from the most important newspapers all over the world. The subject of the opera and its musical treatment reflect the turn-of-the-century fascination with the exoticism of the Far East, in particular China and Japan. *Iris* was the first collaboration between Mascagni and one of Puccini's favored librettists, Luigi Illica. The action takes place in a Japanese village. In act I Osaka, a young, wealthy ladies' man, falls in love with Iris, a laundry girl. Osaka asks Kyoto, the owner of a teahouse, to abduct Iris. The two men prepare a marionette show that features the love between Dhia and Jor. As Osaka sings the role of Jor (the son of the God of the Sun) Iris becomes interested in his portrayal and joins the crowd to watch the show. Kyoto seizes her and carries her away; he sends her blind father, Il Cieco, some money and a message that Iris has decided on her own to go to Yoshiwari, the district of ill-repute. Iris's father wants to find her, so that he may put a curse on her.

In act II Iris wakes up in Osaka's sumptuous apartment and recognizes his voice as that of Jor in the marionette show. He tells her that he is Pleasure; frightened, she relates that one day in the temple a priest told her that pleasure and death were one. This aria ("Un dì—ero piccina—al tempio") is one of the several musical highlights of the score. Osaka has no luck in conquering Iris and eventually tires of trying. Kyoto dresses Iris up and displays her to the crowd, who lead her blind father to her so that he may throw mud at her and curse her. Despairing, she throws herself into a sewer. Her body is found there by some rag-pickers, who try to remove her clothing and jewelry. When they realize she is alive they run away in terror. Iris is comforted in her last moments by the light of the rising sun. Flowers bloom around her as she ascends into the heavens bathed in light and color.

Iris achieved an enormous success with the public—the greatest of any of Mascagni's operas aside from *Cavalleria rusticana* of 1890—but it was found wanting on a number of counts by the critics. The libretto was considered empty and inconclusive, and it was believed that Mascagni put too many abstruse ideas and harmonic subtleties into the music. *Iris* never rivaled *Cavalleria's* popularity, because it lacks that opera's memorable tunes; yet *Iris* is a technically accomplished score with intriguing colors and harmonies and opportunities for exotic spectacle. There are several fine moments, among them a few arias, an attractive duet, and especially the final apotheosis, the "Hymn to the Sun," a choral piece of great effectiveness. The act I tenor serenade displays Mascagni's propensity for writing extremely demanding music for his tenor heros, a fact evidenced already in his *Guglielmo Ratcliff*, premiered in 1895 but composed before *Cavalleria.*

The plot and characters of *Iris* were intended to be symbolic: Iris herself represents Art, Osaka Romance, and Kyoto Commerce. That the events of the plot are especially sordid is typical of *verismo* opera and of the period. Mascagni wrote that "Iris is the symbol of immortal art, triumphing over all the filth of the base world, but what graceful contours, what delicacy, what sweetness surround this symbol!" If Mascagni's musical ideas seem diffuse, perhaps the following explanation by the composer sheds some light: "I did not content myself with two or three ideas that return . . . and are repeated, reproduced and concealed. . . . Instead, I always searched for melody, and hoped I would be accused of even having found too much."

—Stephen Willier

L'ITALIANA IN ALGERI [The Italian Girl in Algiers].

Composer: Gioachino Rossini.

Librettist: A. Anelli (for L. Mosca).

First Performance: Venice, San Benedetto, 22 May 1813.

Roles: Mustafà (bass); Elvira (soprano); Lindoro (tenor); Isabella (contralto); Taddeo (bass); Zulma (mezzo-soprano); Haly (bass); chorus (TTBB).

Publications

article–

Gallarati, P. "Dramma e ludus dall' *Italiana* al *Barbiere*." In *Il melodramma italiano dell' ottocento: studi e ricerche per Massimo Mila*. Turin, 1977.

*   *   *

Between 1810, when Rossini's operatic career began in earnest, and 1813 the composer was occupied much of the time with writing one-act *farse* for the Teatro San Moisè in Venice. This work gave Rossini the experience he needed to be able to write effective comic operas on a larger scale. With *La pietra del paragone* (Milan, 1812), he proved that he was ready to compete with the best composers of full-length *opere buffe;* with *L'italiana in Algeri* (1813), the twenty-one-year-old composer confirmed his reputation as one of Italy's leading young composers of comic opera, only four months after having made a name for himself in the world of *opera seria* with the success of *Tancredi*.

L'italiana in Algeri is a delightfully humorous treatment of that favorite eighteenth-century theme: the escape of Europeans from a Turkish or Middle-Eastern harem. Mustafà, the pompous and blustering Bey of Algiers, is tired of his wife, timid Elvira, and longs for a spirited Italian woman. Just such a woman, the courageous and lively Isabella, happens to be shipwrecked nearby; she is brought to the Bey's court where she finds Lindoro, her long-lost lover, who happens to be a slave of the Bey. Their astonishment sets in motion Rossini's wild and hilarious first-act finale.

Mustafà, infatuated with Isabella, grants Taddeo, Isabella's ineffectual suitor now posing as Isabella's uncle, the honorary title of Kaimakan; this gives Isabella and Lindoro an idea of how to escape Mustafà's clutches. They convince him to accept the title of Papatacci and, as part of the initiation rite, to promise to do nothing but eat and sleep. As Mustafà enjoys his initiation meal, Isabella, Lindoro, and the rest of the Italians make their escape. Mustafà discovers the trick, but too late to foil the Italians' escape; he gives up his hopes for an Italian wife and returns to Elvira.

L'italiana in Algeri shows Rossini at his freshest and most charming. The overture, with its lovely woodwind solos and artfully constructed crescendos, is a perfect example of the Rossini overture. Lindoro's aria "Languir per una bella" breathes youthful impetuousness and ardor. "Se inclinasse a prender moglie," the duet for Lindoro and Mustafà in which the Bey tries to persuade Lindoro to marry Elvira, delights listeners with its witty repartee. Perhaps the most remarkable part of the opera is the first-act finale, a memorable celebration of the absurd in which all the characters express their confusion in nonsense syllables. The harem-operas by Jommelli (*La schiava liberata*), Gluck (*La rencontre imprévue*), Mozart (*Die Entführung aus dem Serail*), and Salieri (*Tarare* and *Axur, re d'Ormus*) are all successful in their own way; but none contains as much wit and hilarity as Rossini's; none contains more pure musical beauty.

—John A. Rice

THE ITALIAN GIRL IN ALGIERS
See L'ITALIANA IN ALGERI

IVOGÜN, Maria (real name, Ilse Kempner).

Soprano. Born 18 November 1891, in Budapest. Died 2 October 1987, in Beatenberg, Lake Thun. Married: 1) the tenor Karl Erb, 1921-32; 2) Michael Raucheisen, her accompanist, in 1933. Daughter of the singer Ida von Günther; studied voice with Schlemmer-Ambros in Vienna, and with Schöner in Munich; debut as Mimi at the Bavarian Court Opera, Munich, 1913; created the role of Ighino in Pfitzner's *Palestrina,* 1917; sang with the Chicago Opera Company, 1921-22; appeared as Rosina in New York with the Chicago Opera, 1922; appeared at Covent Garden, 1924 and 1927; joined the Berlin State Opera, 1925; appeared at the Salzburg Festivals, 1925 and 1930; taught at the Vienna Academy of Music, 1948-50, and at the Berlin Hochschule für Musik, 1950-58; teacher of Elisabeth Schwarzkopf.

Publications

About IVOGÜN: articles–

Frankenstein, A. "Maria Ivoguen." *Record Collector* 20 (1978): 98.

*   *   *

Born Ilse Kempner in Budapest in 1891, the coloratura soprano Maria Ivogün devised her stage name from her operetta singer mother's maiden name: *Ida von Gün*ther. Many connoisseurs of fine singing consider Ivogün to be one of the most accomplished singers on record, similar in vocal timbre and coloratura ability to her near contemporary, Lotte Schöne (b. 1894). After vocal studies at the Vienna Music

Maria Ivogün in *Eugene Onegin*

Academy and in Munich, Ivogün made her debut at the Bavarian Court Opera in Munich in 1913 as Mimi in Puccini's *La bohème.* She sang in Munich from 1913 to 1925, often under the baton of Bruno Walter, appearing in such roles as the Queen of the Night, Constanze, Zerlina, Marzelline, Norina, Oscar, Gilda, and Nannetta. In Munich she premiered a number of now-forgotten operas, including two by Hans Pfitzner, *Palestrina* (with the tenor Karl Erb, her husband from 1921 to 1932, in the title role) and *Christ-Elflein.* In 1916 she participated in the premiere of Korngold's *Der Ring des Polykrates.*

When Bruno Walter went to Berlin to conduct opera, Ivogün followed him, eventually appearing at both the Städtische Oper and the Staatsoper. In Berlin she sang, in addition to her coloratura repertory, heavier parts such as Manon, Mignon, and Tchaikovsky's Tatiana. Her most famous role was Zerbinetta in *Ariadne auf Naxos* by Strauss, in which the composer himself commented that she was "unique and without rival." Ivogün's most famous recording has likewise been of Zerbinetta's aria, "Grossmächtige Prinzessin." It is not a technically perfect execution of the aria, showing, for example, a tendency to slide over certain of the high notes.

Although the trill on the high D does not come off well—Rita Streich, one of Ivogün's most illustrious pupils, wisely omits the trill entirely on her recording—Ivogün's performance displays great charm and the glittering *staccati* for which she was known.

Although Ivogün's recorded output is fairly limited, there is enough now issued on compact disc in good sound to show what an accomplished, valuable singer she was. She made both acoustical and electrical recordings, more of the former. For a number of arias there is more than one version, sometimes a few years apart, sometimes in different languages. Both of the Queen of the Night's arias from *Die Zauberflöte* are excellent, showing her pinpoint accuracy in leaps and runs. John Steane characterizes her, along with Schöne, as a singer who "conveys happiness" and of her heavily decorated "Una voce poco fa" from Rossini's *Il barbiere di Siviglia,* Richard Osborne noted that she "sings the cavatina with great sweetness and beauty, with smiling descents from the high Cs, perceptibly Viennese in style, *Fledermaus* just around the corner." She made two versions of Norina's act I *Don Pasquale* aria, in German and in Italian. Ivogün appeared in this opera with Erb at Salzburg under Walter in 1925 and in 1930. She and Erb recorded the duet "Tornamo a dir" in German; Harold Rosenthal believed that their "vocal partnership remains one of the classic ones in recorded history."

Typical of the German-trained coloratura soprano, Ivogün in her recordings shows ease of production but a concomitant lack of force and energy on the high notes. Such qualities can be heard on, among others, her recorded excerpts from Verdi's *La traviata* and Donizetti's *Lucia di Lammermoor,* both of which also display her ability to convey pathos. Other recordings full of charm and technical accomplishment are Mozart's "Martern aller Arten," Handel's "Il penseroso," and "Ah, non giunge" from Bellini's *La sonnambula.* Steane claims that her recording of "Caro nome" is "probably the best of any on 78s," and that "her encores may be the best of all." These include Swiss folk songs and waltz tunes such as "Frühlingsstimmen" (Voices of Spring) and "An der schönen blauen Donau" (On the Beautiful Blue Danube), of which there are two recordings.

Ivogün's operatic career ended in 1932, although she sang Zerbinetta once again in 1934 in Berlin. In 1933 she married the noted accompanist Michael Raucheisen with whom she continued an extensive recital career. She never sang at the Metropolitan Opera, appearing in New York in opera only as Rosina with the Chicago Opera; she sang with that company in the 1921-22 season. She was a favorite at Covent Garden and at Salzburg. In Ivogün's 1987 *Opera* obituary, Alan Blyth conjectured that "a single record on a desert island might have to be the two Swiss folksongs, which were later adopted by Schwarzkopf, though she couldn't quite match the simplicity and sheer ingenuous freshness of her renowned teacher."

—Stephen A. Willier

J

JADLOWKER, Hermann.

Tenor. Born 5 July 1877, in Riga. Died 13 May 1953, in Tel Aviv. Studied with J. Gänsbacher at the Vienna Conservatory; sang in Karlsruhe, 1906-10; sang in Berlin's Kroll Opera from 1907; Metropolitan Opera debut as Faust, 1910; sang there until 1913; in Boston, 1910-12; at the Berlin Hofoper, 1911-12; created the role of the King's son in Humperdinck's *Königskinder,* 1910, and Bacchus in *Ariadne auf Naxos,* Stuttgart, 1912; with Berlin State Opera, 1922-23; chief cantor of the Riga synagogue, 1929-38; taught at the Riga Conservatory, 1936-38.

Publications

About JADLOWKER: articles–

Frankenstein, A. "Hermann Jadlowker." *Record Collector* 19/nos. 1-2 (1970): 4.

*　　*　　*

A number of great singers received their first training in synagogue choirs, thus forging an interesting link between cantorial tradition and operatic profession. The most outstanding of these singers was Hermann Jadlowker. His father disapproved of professional singing as a career so that the young man virtually ran away from Riga to Vienna, nonetheless seeking advice there from the chief cantor, Schorr, father of Friedrich Schorr. That cantor must have specialized in spotting fine voices, for at about the same time he also helped another Jewish boy from Riga, Joseph Schwarz.

Four years at the Vienna conservatory led to a debut in Cologne but after a few desultory appearances elsewhere in Germany he returned to Riga in 1901. Jadlowker's career proper started only in 1906 with a contract as first tenor for the Karlsruhe Opera. He remained a member of that company until 1914 but the nature of the contract is unclear since he seems also to have been a member of the Berlin Staatsoper from 1911 until 1919.

During these early years a major international career seemed to beckon. Jadlowker was singing extensively throughout Germany and he participated in the premiere at Stuttgart of Strauss's *Ariadne auf Naxos* alongside such artists as Siems and Jeritza. From 1910 until 1913 he was also on the roster of the Metropolitan Opera where he held his own against a plethora of fine tenors led by Caruso, although ultimately his popular and critical success were limited. His first performance in the USA was as Faust when "he truly sang with justice of intonation, with heed of melodic design, with musical shapeliness of phrase, with unforced and intelligently ordered quality of tone." He also appeared in Boston, Chicago, Detroit, Indianapolis, Philadelphia and St Paul whilst as early as May 1910 he appeared with the Metropolitan Opera in its Paris season. Record companies competed for his services and his discs were internationally available.

It seems curious that this phase of Jadlowker's career was effectively over by 1913 for thereafter his appearances were almost exclusively confined to Germany and from 1919 mostly in concert performance rather than opera. Returning to Riga in 1929 he devoted himself to both teaching and cantorial duties which latter may well explain how he was still able in 1943 to undertake the role of Riccardo in *Un ballo in maschera* in Jerusalem, his final appearance. Nonetheless, it seems likely that the brevity of his main career as an operatic tenor resulted from singing heavy dramatic roles, including Wagner, which were quite unsuited to his fine lyric voice.

Jadlowker's recorded legacy is of the greatest importance in demonstrating an almost unique style of singing. With a baritone-like timbre he produces effortless and unforced high notes. There is a wonderful smoothness and evenness to the line and moments of rare lyric beauty. Additionally, and probably the result of his synagogue training, Jadlowker demonstrates on records an incredible agility. Trills and runs abound in a record of the opening aria from *Il barbiere di Siviglia;* there is an unbelievably, magical sustained note in Liszt's "Fischerknabe"; and above all, stunning coloratura in the fiendishly difficult aria "Fuor del mar" from Mozart's *Idomeneo*—a performance which will surely never be equalled. Particular interest can be attached to Jadlowker's highly enterprising repertoire on records as well as a series of duets with other fine singers, especially Frieda Hempel. Pride of place goes to their recordings from *Les Huguenots, Romeó et Juliette* and *La fille du régiment.*

The lack of a protracted international career may best be explained by operatic fashion. Jadlowker excelled in Mozart when both the opera and record companies seemed more interested in Wagner. A wonderful series of Mozart records were hardly available outside Germany. The Wagner items which were released internationally are solid, dull and show a kind of woodenness in the centre of the voice. Jadlowker's was a voice for bel canto in an age when verismo predominated. He probably had difficulty with languages: many of his recordings of French and Italian arias are sung in German. In Boston he sang the tenor lead in *La traviata.* Finally he was a poor actor, which again would not help in an age of verismo. A friendly comment on his US debut—that he was the "first Faust in living memory who could wear the doublet, hose and blond beard without looking like a tailor's dummy"—seems a bit of a back-handed compliment!

—Stanley Henig

JANÁČEK, Leoš.

Composer. Born 3 July 1854, in Hukvaldy, Moravia. Died 12 August 1928, in Ostrava. Sang in the choir of the Augustine monastery in Brno; studied at the Brno Teacher's Training College, 1872-74; studied organ with Skuhersky at the Organ

School in Prague, 1874-75; studied composition with L. Grill at the Leipzig Conservatory and with Franz Krenn at the Vienna Conservatory, 1879-80; conductor of the Czech Philharmonic, 1881-88; taught at the Conservatory of Brno, 1919-1925. Janáček was very interested in Russian literature and music, and visited Russia three times.

Operas

Edition: *L. Janáček: Souborné kritické vydání.* Edited by J. Vyslouzil et al. Prague, 1978-.

Šárka. Julius Zeyer, 1887-88, Brno, National Theater, 11 November 1925; revised 1918-19 (act III orchestrated by O. Chlubna), 1924-25.

The Beginning of a Romance [Počátek románu], Jaroslav Tichý (after a story by Gabriela Preissová), 1891, Brno, National Theater, 10 February 1894.

Jenůfa [Její pastorkyňa], Janáček (after a play by Gabriela Preissová), 1894-1903, Brno, National Theater, 21 January 1904; revised before 1908.

Fate [Osud], Fedora Bartošová and Janáček, 1903-05 (revised 1906-07), radio broadcast from Brno, 1 September 1934; staged, Brno, National Theater, 25 October 1958.

Mr Brouček's Excursion to the Moon [Výlet pana Broučka do mĕsíce], Janáček, Viktor Dyk, F.G. Gellner and F.S. Procházka (after a satire by Svatopluk Čech), 1908-17, Prague, National Theater, 23 April 1920.

Mr Brouček's Excursion to the 15th Century [Výlet pana Broučka do XV. století], Frantisek S. Procházka (after a satire by Svatopluk Čech), 1917, Prague, National Theater, 23 April 1920.

Leoš Janáček, c. 1925

Katia Kabanová, Janáček (after A.N. Ostrovsky, *The Storm,* translated by Vincenc Červinka), 1919-21, Brno, National Theater, 23 November 1921.

The Cunning Little Vixen [Příhody Líšky Bystroušky], Janáček (after Rudolf Tĕsnohlídek), 1921-23, Brno, National Theater, 6 November 1924.

The Makropoulos Case [Vĕc Makropulos], Janáček (after a play by Karel Čapek), 1923-25, Brno, National Theater, 18 December 1926.

From the House of the Dead [Z mrtvého domu], Janáček (after Dostoyevsky), 1927-28; revised and reorchestrated by O. Chlubna and B. Bakala, Brno, National Theater, 12 April 1930.

Other works: sacred and secular choral works, orchestral works, chamber music, piano pieces.

Publications

By JANÁČEK: books–

Note: for a complete list of Janáček's writings, see *The New Grove Dictionary of Music and Musicians,* 1980 ed.

Firkušný, L. *Leoš Janáček kritikem brnĕnské opery* [reviews of the Brno opera]. Brno, 1935.
Rektorys, A., et al., eds. *Janáčekův archiv.* Prague, 1934-53.
Štĕdroň, B., ed. *Letters and Reminiscences.* Prague, 1955.
Straková, Theadora ed. *Leoš Janáček: Musik des Lebens: Skizzen, Feuilletons, Studien.* Leipzig, 1979.
Tausky, Villem, and Margaret Tausky, eds. *Janáček: Leaves from his Life.* London, 1982.
Fischmann, Zdenka, E., ed. *Janáček-Newmarch Correspondence.* Rockville, Maryland, 1988.
Zemanová, Mirka, ed. *Janáček's Uncollected Essays on Music.* London, 1989.

About JANÁČEK: books–

Muller, Daniel. *Leoš Janáček.* Paris, 1930.
Brod, Max. *Leoš Janáček.* Vienna, 1925; 2nd ed. 1956.
Firkušný, L. *Odkaz Leoše Janáčka české opeře* [Janáček's legacy to Czech opera]. Brno, 1939.
Newmarch, R. *The Music of Czechoslovakia,* 211 ff. London, 1942; 1969.
Leoš Janáček na svĕtových jevištích [Janáček on the world's stages]. Brno, 1958.
Hollander, H. *Leoš Janáček.* Zurich, 1954; English translation as *Leoš Janáček: his Life and Work.* London, 1963.
Vogel, Jaroslav, *Leoš Janáček: his Life and Works.* London and New York, 1962; revised by Karel Janovicky, 1981; Russian translation by Jurji Ritcik and Jurji Skarina, Moscow, 1982; Polish translation by Henryk Szwedo, Cracow, 1983.
Černohorská, Milena. *Leoš Janáček.* Prague, 1966.
Polyakova, L. *Opernoye tvorchestvo Leosha Janachka* [Janáček's operas]. Moscow, 1968.
Štĕdroň, B. *Zur Genesis von Leoš Janáčeks Oper Jenufa.* Brno, 1968; revised, 1971; English extracts in *Sborník prací filosofiké fakulty brnĕnské university* (1968): 43.
Chisholm, Erik. *The Operas of Leoš Janáček.* Oxford, 1971.
Štĕdroň, B. *Zur Genesis von Leoš Janáčeks Oper Jenufa.* Brno, 1968, 1972.
Kneif, T. *Die Bühnenwerke von Leoš Janáček.* Vienna, 1974.
Ströbel, B. *Motiv und Figur in den Kompositionen den Jenufa-Werkgruppe.* Freiburg, 1975.

Martin, George. *The Opera Companion to the Twentieth Century Opera.* New York, 1979.

Ewans, Michael. *Janáček's Tragic Operas.* London, 1977; German translation, Stuttgart, 1981.

Curtis, William D. *Leoš Janáček.* Utica, New York, 1978.

Poljakova, Ljudmila. *Českaja i slovackaja opera XX veka, I* [Czech and Slovic opera of the 20th century]. Moscow, 1978.

Leoš Janáček, sa personnalité, son oeuvre. Issued by Art Centrum, Prague. Paris, 1980.

Erisman, Guy. *Janáček ou la passion de la vérité.* Paris, 1980.

Dahlhaus, Carl. *Musikalischer Realismus. Zur Musikgeschichte des 19. Jahrhunderts.* Munich, 1982.

Honolka, Kurt. *Leoš Janáček. Sein Leben, sein Werk, seine Zeit.* Stuttgart, 1982.

Horsbrugh, Ian. *Leoš Janáček: the Field That Prospered.* Newton Abbott, 1981; New York, 1982.

Knaus, J., ed. *Leoš Janáček: Materialien: Aufsätze zu Leben und Werk.* Zurich, 1982.

Tyrrell, John, compiler. *Leoš Janáček: Káťa Kabanová. Cambridge Opera Handbooks.* Cambridge, 1982.

Nicholas, John, ed. *Jenufa and Katya Kabanova.* London and New York, 1985.

Susskind, Charles. *Janáček and Brod.* New Haven, 1985.

Tyrell, John. *Czech Opera.* Cambridge, 1988.

articles–

Newmarch, R. "Leos Janácek and the Moravian Music Drama." *Slavonic Review* 1 (1922-23): 362.

Stuart, C. "*Katya Kabanová* Reconsidered." *Music Review* 12 (1951).

Shawe-Taylor, Desmond. "Janáček in Prague and Berlin." *Opera* September (1956).

———. "An Introduction to Janáček's Jenůfa." *Opera* November (1956).

Staková, T. "Janáčkova opera Osud" [Janáčeks opera *Fate*]. *Časopis Moraského musea* 41 (1956): 209; 42 (1957): 133 [summary in German].

Shawe-Taylor, Desmond. "The Operas of Leoš Janáček." *Proceedings of the Royal Musical Association* 85 (1958-59): 49.

Pala, F. "Postavy a prostředí v Její pastorkyni" [Characters and environment in *Jenůfa*]. In *Leoš Janáček sborník stati a studii,* 29. Prague, 1959.

Štědroň, B. "K Janáčkově opeře Osud" [Janáček's opera *Fate*]. *Živá hudba* 1 (1959): 159.

Wörner, K. "Katjas Tod: die Schlußszene der Oper 'Katja Kabanova' von Janáček." *Schweizerische Muzikzeitung/Revue musicale suisse* 99 (1959): 91.

Očadlík, M. "Dvě kapitoly k Janáčkovým Výletům pana Broučka na měsíc" [on *Mr Brouček's Excursion to the Moon*] *Miscellanea musicologica* [Czechoslovakia] no. 12 (1960): 133.

Sádecký, Z. "Celotónový character hudební řeči v Janáčkově 'Lišce Bystroušce'" [whole-tone aspects of *Cunning Little Vixen*]. *Živá hudba* 2 (1962): 95 [summary in German].

Fiala, O. "Libreto k Janáčkově opeře Počátek románu" [libretto of *The Beginning of a Romance*]. *Časopis Moravského musea* 49 (1964): 192 [summary in German].

Warrack, John. "*The Cunning Little Vixen.*" *Opera* March (1961).

Československý hudební slovník [list of works and bibliography to 1962].

Mackerras, Charles. "Janáček's *Makropoulos.*" *Opera* February (1964).

Tyrrell, John. "Mr Brouček's Excursion to the Moon." *Časopis Moravského musea* 53-54 (1968-69): 89 [summary in Czech].

———. "The Musical Prehistory of Janáček's Počátek románu and its Importance in Shaping the Composer's Dramatic Style." *Časopis Moravského musea* 52 (1967): 245 [summary in Czech].

Abraham, Gerald. "Realism in Janáček's Operas." In *Slavonic and Romantic Music,* 83. London, 1968.

Mazlová, A. "Zeyerova a Janáčkova Šárka" [Zeyer's and Janáček's *Šárka*]. *Časopis Moravského musea* 53-54 (1968-69): 71 [summary in English].

Sádecký, Z. "Výstava dialogu a monologu v Janáčkavoě Jeji pastorkyni" [dialogue and monologue structure in *Jenůfa*]. *Živá hudba* 4 (1968): 73 [summary in German].

Tyrrell, John. "How Domšík became a Bass." *Musical Times* 114 (1973): 29; Czech translation in *Österreichische Musikzeitung* 5 (1973): 201.

Polyakova, L. "O "ruských' operách Leoše Janáčka" [Janáček's "Russian" operas]. In *Cesty rozvoje a vzájemné vztahy ruského a československého uměni,* 247. Prague, 1974.

Straková, Theodora. "Janáčkova opera Její pastorkyňa: pokus o analýzu díla" [an attempt at an analysis of *Jenůfa*]. *Časopis Moravského musea* 59 (1974): 119 [summary in German].

Pulcini, Francesco. "Le opere teatrali inedite di Leoš Janáček." *Nuova rivista musicale italiana* 9 (1975): 552.

Blaukopf, Kurt. "Gustav Mahler und die tschechische Oper." *Österreichische Musikzeitschrift* 34 (1979): 285.

Nepomnjaščaja, Tat'jana. "Poslednjaja opera L. Janačeka" [*House of the Dead*]. *Sovetskaja muzyka* 1 (1979): 108.

Pečman, Rudolf. "Janáčeks Oper vom ewigen Leben" [*Makropulos Case*]. *Österreichische Musikzeitschrift* 34 (1979): 201.

Seaman, Gerald. "The Rise of Slavonic Opera, I." *New Zealand Slavonic Journal* 2 (1978): 1.

Němcová, Alena. "Na okraj Janáčkovy Její pastorkyně" [sources for *Jenůfa*]. *Časopis Moravského musea* 65 (1980): 159.

Přibáňová, Svatava. "Operní dílo Janáčkova vrcholného, údobí" [Janáček's late operas]. *Časopis Moravského musea* 65 (1980): 165.

Straková, Theodora. "Janáčkovy opery Šárka, Počátek, Románu, Osud a hudebnědramatická torza" [*Sarka, The Beginning of a Romance, Fate,* and Janáček's unfinished operas]. *Časopis Moravského musea* 65 (1980): 149.

Tyrrell, John. "Mr. Broucek at Home: an Epilogue to Janáček's Opera." *Musical Times* 120 (1980).

Plamenac, Dragan. "Nepoznati komentari Leoš a Janáčka operi Katja Kabanova" [Unknown comments of Janáček on his opera *Katja Kabanova*]. *Musiko/Zbornik* 17 (1981): 122 [summary in English].

Holubová, Eliška. "Kompositionstechnische und musikdramatische Aspekte der Schlusszenen in den Opern Janáčeks." In *Colloquium Leoš Janáček ac tempora nostra, Brno 2.-5.10, 1978,* edited by Rudolf Pečman. Brno, 1983.

Němcová, Alena. "Janáček - libretista. Úvaha o Janáčkově účasti na tvorbě libret k vlastním operám. Cást I." In *Hubda a literatura,* edited by Rudolf Pečman. Frýdek-Místek, 1983.

Pulcini, Francesco. "Da Dostoevskij a Janácek. *Da una casa di morti* e la sua genesi librettistici." *Rivista italiana di musicologia* 18 (1983): 220.

Abraham, Gerald. "Dostoevsky in Music." In *Russian and Soviet Music: Essays for Boris Schwartz,* edited by Malcolm H. Brown, 193. Ann Arbor, 1984.

unpublished—

Pulcini, Francesco. "Per una recognizione italiana del teatro musicale di Leoš Janáček. Aspetti della drammaturgia di *Da una casa di morti.*" Ph.D. dissertation, University of Turin, 1983.

Europe of the mid-nineteenth century was experiencing the consequences of tidal changes that had started about one hundred years before, first as a philosophical movement, and then as a social and military upheaval. Janáček was born (1854) into the time of the mass man, the industrial revolution, and, paradoxically, the growing importance of the individual.

Shaped by his own excitable nature and the rapid, destabilizing changes in European society, Janáček developed his brilliant gifts to the point that, unlike other musicians, he almost seemed to be an active participant in the changes taking place around him. It might be noted that this is exactly the function of all successful artists, to reflect and intensify the world in which they live, but with many artists this role seems more subconscious than deliberate. With Janáček, the impression is that he spent much of his life and creativity involving himself in his surroundings, and although this aspect of Janáček's work could be illustrated with any of his most significant works, it becomes most apparent when we turn to his operas.

Jenůfa, Janáček's first real success, was first performed in Brno in 1904. While *Jenůfa* was favorably received by many, however, it also shocked some of those who first heard it. On the surface, *Jenůfa* is directly related to the operas of Smetana, Dvořák, and Fibich: it deals with the people and their problems in a small-town, rural setting. But where the work of the earlier masters generally idealizes this lifestyle, Janáček's opera is about the churning conflicts these people really experience.

Jenůfa is about two men in love with the title character, and the conflicts which result. The music is extremely dramatic and quite unforgettably original. Its originality resides in Janáček's treatment of melodic motifs. These are constantly repeated at different pitch levels, and a kind of dissolution by diminution of the material occurs, both metrically and melodically. Janáček creates a musical fabric at once high-strung and exceptionally dramatic. It is difficult to describe, but once experienced, it is not easily forgotten. Its power is obvious, and, listened to carefully, its melodic content is compelling.

Part of this strange score's sound, as well as that of all of Janáček's later scores, is due to his principles of word-setting. As is well known by now, Janáček attempted to notate the natural sound of speech as it was spoken rather than sung. This is a matter of accents, speed, pitch of voice, and speech idiosyncrasies. Janáček was convinced that the usual practice of creating flowing musical lines was wrong. He advocated, rather, that music should mirror, yet heighten the sound and emotion of actual speech. Thus, in *Jenůfa*, it is the interaction of the main characters and their rapid-fire speech which Janáček's music heightens with startling success, and it is the extremely flexible treatment of that musical fabric which sets Janáček's efforts in stark contrast to anyone else's, until the later non-tonal composers of the twentieth century. Later composers had similar ideas, but without the verbal rationale that is so integral to Janáček's work.

Jenůfa also illustrates some other aspects of Janáček's methods. His orchestra is capable of the most brilliant effects, but they are not at all the same as, for example, Wagner's orchestral sonorities. Wagner usually creates orchestral effects of rich opulence by blending his instrumental colors, while Janáček's effects are created more by the brilliance of primary colors played against each other, and by using the extreme registers of instruments. Thus, despite the hyperactivity of the sonorities, there is a prevailing orchestral clarity. Also, voices have little trouble riding over this kind of sound.

As for Janáček's vocal writing, he rarely asks for sustained sound, but rather for an extreme intensity of utterance. If, as happens in the roles of Laca or Kostelnicka, the tessitura is mostly high, there are difficulties, but the relative absence of sustained (and slow) singing mitigates those difficulties. What is exceedingly demanding for the singers is the psychological element. As an extrapolation of the word-setting practices described above, Janáček managed to write music to the texts which sharply mirrored the mental state as well as the personality-types represented. Slimy characters have jagged chromatic music, and madmen have music which is harmonically deranged. Janáček's operas make it imperative for singers to be first rate actors, capable of seeing the verbally realistic elements in the composer's music. Here, the first need is not vocal beauty, but skillful musical-dramatic declamation of naturalistic intensity.

Jenůfa, the only opera so far mentioned, is Janáček's first successful effort to carry out his word-centered theories. He was to follow these principles throughout his later operas, but they were to be more varied and reflective of wider varieties of moods. Thus, in *Katia Kabanova* we see a set of dramatic circumstances similar to *Jenůfa*, but Janáček creates a score of inward, quiet isolation. Katia's tragic situation elicits music of compassion, but Kabanichka, Katia's mother-in-law, visits a kind of casual cruelty on both her son and Katia which is chillingly caught by Janáček's muted but loudly played brass. It should be said that *Katia Kabanova* is perhaps Janáček's most intimate, romantic opera. A product of 1919, it might have heralded a new direction in Janáček's work. In fact, it did not, for in *The Cunning Little Vixen, The Makropulous Case*, and finally, *From the House of the Dead*, there are more violent ways of looking at the tragedy of human existence, as well as its frequent humor and even whimsy.

From the House of the Dead is Janáček's last work, and considering its date of composition, it is often seen as ominously prophetic of the world we were about to enter at that time. In point of fact, however, it derives its libretto directly from the two-volume novel of the same name by F. Dostoyevsky, and that novel reports on circumstances that were common in the nineteenth century. Set in a prison camp, it describes, through the narrations of four people, what brought them to their captivity, and what that life is like. Everyone except one political prisoner has committed a serious crime, but their punishments are seen as crimes of infinitely greater proportions. That is the main point, perhaps, of Dostoyevsky's masterpiece. What is prophetic about Janáček's opera is the ferocity, the brutality of his setting, which smacks of the twentieth century as we have come to know it. He views the cruelty of the camp as something to be depicted in very harsh sounds. His orchestra rages in anger at the inhuman treatment accorded the prisoners by the guard, or it wails in horror at the way the inmates torment each other. It is this raw vividness which, with the aid of hindsight, is so descriptive of what was to happen in Europe fifteen years later. Since the composer died in 1928, he could have had little idea of the future, but his score is so disturbing that it is difficult *not* to think of 1942.

Janáček's art seems to be more a part of his time than is often the case with opera composers. It is a fact that all of the operas discussed here, as well as those not mentioned, constitute some form of social criticism (even the *Vixen*), and it is a measure of Janáček's mastery that they are all effective as social criticism and musical drama. As such, the more we know his operas the more we recognize them as part of the twentieth century's finest artistic products.

—Harris Crohn

JANOWITZ, Gundula.

Soprano. Born 2 August 1937, in Berlin. Studied at Graz Conservatory with Herbert Thöny; debut as Barbarina in *Le nozze di Figaro,* Vienna Staatsoper, 1959; appeared at Bayreuth, 1960-63; member of Frankfurt Opera, 1963-66; Metropolitan Opera debut as Sieglinde, 1967; sang Countess in *Le nozze di Figaro* at reopening of Paris Opéra, 1973; Covent Garden debut as Donna Anna in *Don Giovanni,* 1976; became director of Graz Opera, 1990.

*   *   *

The Berlin-born soprano Gundula Janowitz won a student contract at the Vienna State Opera on finishing her studies at the Graz Conservatory in 1959 at the age of twenty-two, and within two years she had appeared not only in Vienna but Bayreuth, Aix-en-Provence and Glyndebourne. She quickly came under the notice of Herbert von Karajan, who became a major influence in her career; under his guidance she made her mark as Marzelline, Agathe and, at the age of twenty-seven, the Empress in a new Staatsoper production of Strauss's *Die Frau ohne Schatten.*

Although her career took her to the major European houses as well as to America and elsewhere, she divided her time principally between Berlin and Vienna, singing a variety of roles which included not only the Mozart and Strauss for which she became celebrated but Micaela, Fidelio and a number of Verdi roles such as Aïda, Amelia and Odabella in *Atilla.* First attracting attention as Pamina, she progressed through all the major female roles in *Le nozze di Figaro* to achieve a Susanna, Cherubino and Countess of great distinction, to major roles in other Mozart operas, including Donna Anna in *Don Giovanni,* Ilia in *Idomeneo,* and Fiordiligi in *Così fan tutte* as well as mastering a large number of the concert arias. Purity of tone, cleanness of line and aristocratic phrasing were her great gifts in this repertoire, qualities which she brought also to her Wagner and Strauss roles.

An example of the pure "white" soprano tone associated with central European sopranos such as Tiana Lemnitz and the early Schwarzkopf, her voice had a tight vibrato, making it almost instrumental—and very beautiful—in its texture. Janowitz, recognizing these qualities in her own voice and exploiting them with great intelligence and sensitivity, rarely attempted to push it beyond the bounds nature provided it with. Consequently she sang only the lighter Wagner roles—Eva, Elsa and Elizabeth—until Karajan persuaded her to sing (a very successful) Sieglinde for his Salzburg *Ring* in 1967, the role in which she made her debut at the Metropolitan

Opera. Her Wagner was fascinating in its rare combination of purity of tone (rarely distorted) and brilliance in the climaxes.

Her performances were sometimes described as cool, some critics tending (as with Birgit Nilsson) to mistake the narrow, brilliant column of tone—J.B. Steane describes it as a "pure 'tube' of sound"—for a personality trait which translated onstage into a dramatic deficiency. But Janowitz, though a very controlled artist, was accurate in describing herself in an interview as *"ein ganz, ganz, normal Mensch,"* ("a very, very usual kind of person"). Her normality was the opposite of flamboyance but did not inhibit, as many of her records will testify, her warmth and communicative power.

Her greatest achievements were perhaps in Strauss, beginning with her interpretation of the Four Last Songs with Karajan and running through her Marschallin, Arabella and, perhaps most of all, her Ariadne. Her recording of this opera with Rudolph Kempe is exquisite from first to last. "Ein Schönes war" becomes almost a dialogue between the instrumental quality—which paradoxically emphasizes the humanity—of her tone and the instruments of the orchestra; the solo violin at the repeat of "Und ging im Licht" is an uncannily beautiful echo of the voice. The elegiac lament for a lost world of love is profoundly moving. So also with "Es gibt ein Reich," superbly shaped both in terms of sound and emotion, rising to the climatic B flat at "Du nimm es von mir."

Janowitz always devoted a large portion of her time to concert activity with orchestra and in recital, achieving real distinction in both. She retired from the opera stage in the spring of 1990 to assume the directorship of the Opera at Graz, where she grew up and pursued her musical studies, while planning to continue with her concert career.

—Peter Dyson

JANSSEN, Herbert.

Baritone. Born 22 September 1892, in Cologne. Died 3 June 1965, in New York. Studied in Cologne, then with Oskar Daniel in Berlin; debut in Schreker's *Der Schatzgräber,* Berlin State Opera, 1922; remained on Berlin State Opera's roster until 1938; appeared regularly at Covent Garden, 1926-39, and at Bayreuth, 1930-37; Metropolitan Opera touring debut as Wotan, Philadelphia, 1939; New York debut as Wolfram, Metropolitan Opera, 1939; remained on the Met's roster until 1952; became American citizen, 1946.

*   *   *

Herbert Janssen was perhaps the most cherishable of German baritones in the interwar years: on stage his performances had a nobility and mastery that distinguished them in whatever company, and on records his voice possesses an entirely personal timbre, warm and gently resonant, giving it an inherent depth of character beyond that of his many gifted contemporaries.

In the 1940s when he appeared at the Metropolitan Opera and based his career in the United States, the velvet was beginning to wear thin and the steadiness was not the reliable absolute known previously to audiences at Covent Garden. At his New York house debut in 1939 his voice was considered beautiful and his performance exemplary; but that was as Wolfram, one of the lighter, more lyrical Wagnerian roles, and when he came later to undertake Wotan and Hans Sachs the sheer power was lacking. Off-the-air recordings show something of the deterioration. In 1941 a *Fidelio* conducted by Bruno Walter finds him in his element, portraying the benevolent authority of Don Fernando, but when three years later he was cast as Don Pizarro in a broadcast performance under Toscanini it is not simply in response to the villainy of the character that his voice has lost its attractiveness; by 1949 when he sang Jokanaan to Ljuba Welitsch's Salome, however admirable the performance in some ways, it is no longer identifiable as the voice we remember from the previous decade.

In his best years, roughly from 1925 to 1940, Janssen won not only the admiration of the public but also the respect of the critics to a degree which was probably unique in London. From 1926 onwards he returned for every summer season at Covent Garden, and year after year the characteristic touches came to be held in deeper affection and the art itself grew in mastery till it was recognized as the most consummate of its kind that was then to be found on the lyric stage. "Turning that fine jeweller's art of his upon the music of Kurwenal", as Ernest Newman said, he provided what everyone came to see as the classic portrayal. At first it had seemed a curious piece of casting, that this particularly sensitive, subtle singer with the soft grain in his voice should be chosen for the bluff Kurwenal, but he deepened people's perception of the part, so that he made of it the moving tragedy of a generous faithful soul whose dying words "Schilt mich nicht, dass der Treue auch mit kommt" remained in the mind almost to rank with the more famous love-death that was to follow. As Telramund in *Lohengrin* he would darken his tone, said the *Daily Telegraph's* critic, "yet without ever producing an ugly sound." As the Dutchman, wrote Newman, he presented "one of the truly great things of the operatic stage today; here is a sufferer who carries on his shoulders not only his own but the whole world's woe." To Walter Legge, Janssen's Gunther in *Götterdämmerung* was the most consummate achievement before the public. Even when he sang a secondary role such as the Speaker in *Die Zauberflöte* it registered as "a noble piece of work" (Newman), and his Kothner in *Die Meistersinger* was a masterpiece of comical self-importance.

The voice itself and the way he produced it remain a subject of some fascination. On records the tone often seems to be so gentle that one wonders how well it carried. A reminiscence on the part of one of those stalwart British singers often brought in to the international seasons to fill a suitably inconspicuous gap tells how his colleague on stage asked *sotto voce* who was that singing just now. "Herbert Janssen." "Well, I don't think much of him." "Right," said the other, "you go down there to the back of the stalls and see what you think from there"—which he did, only to hear the most perfect projection of sound, and a remarkable growth of power in the process. The critic of the *Daily Telegraph* made a similar observation in 1930: "his *mezza voce* is quite remarkable for its carrying power."

To listeners in the present day he is no more than a voice on records, a Wagnerian singer with the smoothness and technique of one who (as he said) would practice the aria "Il balen" from *Il trovatore* every day for one whole year, and a Lieder singer belonging to a sensitive but less analytical school than that of the post-war generation. Nobody hearing him sing Wolfram's music in *Tannhäuser*, Schumann's *Die Lotosblume,* Strauss's *Zueignung* or the *Harfenspielerlieder* of Wolf is likely to miss the special quality of his voice; and,

once lodged in the mind, it quickly becomes a treasured possession.

—J.B. Steane

JENŮFA [Její pastorkyňa].

Composer: Leoš Janáček.

Librettist: Leoš Janáček (after a play by Gabriela Preissová).

First Performance: Brno, National Theater, 21 January 1904.

Roles: Grandmother Buryja (contralto); Laca (tenor); Števa (tenor); Kostelnička (soprano); Jenůfa (soprano); Old Foreman (baritone); Mayor (bass); His Wife (mezzo-soprano); Karolka (mezzo-soprano); Maid (mezzo-soprano); Barena (soprano); Jano (soprano); Aunt (contralto); chorus (SATTBB).

Publications

books—

Ströbel, B. *Motiv und Figur in den Kompositionen den Jenufa-Werkgruppe.* Freiburg, 1975.
Nicholas, John, editor. *Jenufa and Katya Kabanova.* London and New York, 1985.

articles—

Shawe-Taylor, Desmond. "An Introduction to Janáček's Jenůfa." *Opera* November (1956).
Pala, F. "Postavy a prostředí v Její pastorkyni" [Characters and environment in *Jenůfa*]. In *Leoš Janáček sborník stati a studii,* 29. Prague, 1959.
Sádecký, Z. "Výstava dialogu a monologu v Janáčkavoě Její pastorkyni" [dialogue and monologue structure in *Jenůfa*]. *Živá hudba* 4 (1968): 73 [summary in German].
Straková, Theadora. "Janáčkova opera Její pastorkyňa: pokus o analýzu díla" [an attempt at an analysis of *Jenůfa*]. *Časopis-Moravskéhomusea* 59 (1974): 119 [summary in German].
Němcová, Alena. "Na okraj Janáčkovy Její pastorkyně" [sources for *Jenůfa*]. *Časopis-Moravskéhomusea* 65 (1980): 159.

* * *

Gabriela Preissová's play *Her Foster-Daughter* (1890) was widely attacked, since it undermined the Prague nationalists' idealized picture of peasant life. But Preissová's uncompromising realism, her personal knowledge of the character of Moravian Slovakia, and her use of his own native dialect appealed powerfully to Janáček; this text liberated his musical imagination, and enabled him to create his first masterpiece—the opera which is known outside Czechoslovakia as *Jenůfa*

At the opening of act I, we find Jenůfa pregnant by Števa, the feckless heir to an isolated mill in the mountains of Moravia. If he is conscripted into the army, her predicament will be discovered, and she will be disgraced; if not, she hopes to

Jenůfa, with (left to right) Jan Blinkhof as Laca, Eva Randova as Kostelnica and Ashley Putnam as Jenůfa, Royal Opera, London, 1988

marry him. Števa returns from the recruiting board, unconscripted but also drunk; Jenůfa's foster-mother, the Kostelnička or sextoness of the village, forbids them to marry unless he can stay sober for a year. Števa's half-brother Laca loves Jenůfa deeply, and is bitterly jealous of her affection for Števa, who admires her only for her good looks. Laca destroys Jenůfa's beauty, slashing her cheek with his knife.

By the opening of act II, Jenůfa has secretly given birth to her child, a boy. The Kostelnička is tormented by its existence. She tries to persuade Števa to marry Jenůfa, but fails. Laca is full of remorse, and wants to marry Jenůfa. The baby would be the only obstacle to this marriage; the Kostelnička murders it by throwing it into the freezing river, lies to Jenůfa that it died when she was sick with fever, and brings the couple together.

In act III, on the morning of Jenůfa's wedding day, the baby's body is discovered under the ice. To prevent the villagers from stoning Jenůfa to death, the Kostelnička confesses. After a moment of initial revulsion, Jenůfa forgives her, and gives her the strength to accept her punishment. Left alone with Laca, Jenůfa gives him his freedom; but he insists that they should remain together.

Preissová evokes two themes which became fundamental to Janáček's operatic output; the eternal pattern of life, death and renewal, and the ideal of a morality and spiritual growth which are based on self-knowledge and harmony with nature. In the final outcome three people rise; Jenůfa and Laca to a mature, adult understanding of themselves and others, and the Kostelnička to a true humility in which she can accept the outside world's verdict on her crime. Community standards—in particular those of traditional religious morality—are shown to be useless; the forgiveness and love which resolve the action spread outwards from Jenůfa, who has gained her strength from a hard-won harmony with nature.

Jenůfa obliged Janáček to free himself from traditional ways of setting words to music, and to forge a new operatic style. The composer had to devise an idiom in which he could set the prose text direct, in which the realism of the text would not be marred by excesses of false emotion, and in which Janáček's own visionary portrait of spiritual growth could be convincingly displayed.

In *Jenůfa,* short but intense motifs in the orchestra dominate each successive section of the score. They are repeated as long as is required to illuminate their particular part of the action, and are not usually heard again. There are no arias; there is one traditional ensemble, a quartet with chorus in act I, but otherwise the prose text is set direct, without formal structures. The vocal style is a richly expressive arioso which, for clarity, avoids melisma. Vocal phrases are often repeated, partly to accent the nervous brooding exhibited by many of the characters in this story, and partly because in this opera Janáček had not yet perfected the difficult mesh between the dramatic timing and the musical timing of his action.

In *Jenůfa* Janáček established new standards for opera, in the depth and detail with which the orchestra can illuminate human psychology in action. (Richard Strauss made a corresponding advance, using a symbolist text, at exactly the same time. Both *Salome* and *Jenůfa* were completed in 1903.) The power of Preissová's plot, the strength of the dramatic structure, and the truthfulness, insight and emotional range of Janáček's musical response ensure that a committed performance of this opera is a shattering experience for the audience.

Because of the novelty of the idiom, and certain antagonisms which Janáček's forthrightness had created in Prague, *Jenůfa* was not heard outside his home town of Brno until 1916, and then only in a reorchestration which for many years blurred the stark outlines of the score and romanticized the sound. Charles Mackerras' 1983 Decca recording reverts to the original orchestration, which is also increasingly heard in live performances.

The great success of *Jenůfa* in Prague in 1916, and then in Vienna in 1918, led to its subsequent adoption throughout central Europe. In the English-speaking world recognition took longer (the first British performance was in 1956), but *Jenůfa* now occupies a central place in the twentieth-century repertoire.

—Michael Ewans

JERITZA, Maria (born Marie Jedlizka).

Soprano. Born 6 October 1887, in Brno. Died 10 July 1982, in Orange, New Jersey. Married Baron von Popper. Studied in Brno, with Auspitz in Prague, and later with Sembrich in New York; debut as Elsa in *Lohengrin,* Olomouc, 1910; Vienna debut as Elisabeth, Volksoper, 1911; first appeared with Vienna Court Opera in Oberleitner's *Aphrodite,* 1912; appeared at Covent Garden, 1925 and 1926; Metropolitan Opera debut as Marietta in Korngold's *Die tote Stadt,* 1921, and appeared at Metropolitan Opera until 1932; created Ariadne in both versions of *Ariadne auf Naxos;* created the Empress in *Die Frau ohne Schatten.*

Publications

By JERITZA: books–

Sunlight and Song: A Singer's Life. New York, 1924.

About JERITZA: books–

Decsey, E. *Maria Jeritza.* Vienna, 1931.
Werba, R. *Maria Jeritza: Primadonna des Verismo.* Vienna, 1981.

*   *   *

The Moravian soprano Maria Jeritza was possessed of all possible attributes to become a successful prima donna: an impressive, well-produced and luxurious voice; exceptional personal beauty and presence; and steadfast devotion to her art. Details of her personal life remain elusive (except that she married three times) and her autobiography goes no further than 1929, omitting many details about herself and her colleagues that one would like to have known. It tends to stress her puritanical diet and blameless early nights in pursuit of her all-important career.

Jeritza came up the hard way through a provincial opera chorus and her official debut was as Elsa in *Lohengrin* in the provincial opera house at Olomouc, north of Brno, where she

was born. She then joined the Vienna Volksoper, a thorough training-ground for promotion. While singing Rosalinde in a performance of *Die Fledermaus* before the Emperor Franz Josef in 1912, her personality and physical appearance appealed to him so much that he arranged for her immediate transfer to his Hofoper in Vienna, where she remained until 1935, soon receiving a far higher salary than any other singer there.

Jeritza's spectacular successes included the Empress in *Die Frau ohne Schatten,* Giorgetta in *Il tabarro,* Minnie in *La Fanciulla del West* and Violanta. She was also a famous Thaïs, Jenufa, Salome, Fedora and Carmen, and her Wagner roles were Senta, Elsa, Elisabeth and Sieglinde. The wide range of her roles indicates her vocal capabilities and how much she was valued as a prima donna. She was known for her temperament and autocratic treatment of possible rivals (notably Lotte Lehmann in Vienna). Strauss and Hofmannsthal engaged her to sing *Ariadne* but failed to obtain her services in Dresden for an opera for which she would have been eminently qualified—*Die ägyptische Helena*—but she finally sang it in Vienna. Strauss paid her the huge compliment of dedicating one of his *Four Last Songs* to her, too late for her to be able to sing it.

Eyewitnesses have described Jeritza's zany sense of humor, usually unexpected and therefore breathtaking when it happened on stage. Her glorious presence as Elisabeth on her first entrance in *Tannhäuser,* as Turandot going up and down the staircase, and as Tosca singing "Vissi d'arte" lying flat on the stage were three show-stoppers. As Minnie, she rode a horse and gamboled among the cowboys; as Carmen she smoked a cigarette and danced on a table. She was also entirely at home in operetta.

Jeritza's voice on gramophone records seems impaired by the uninteresting, sterile atmosphere of recording studios which minimized her gift for effective dramatic characterization. One exception is Ariadne's monologue, beautifully sung in its coolness and assurance, giving some idea of how it must have sounded in performance. All the same, as time went on, an initial fault in training produced increasingly obvious scooping in phrases, but even the critical reviewer of her Met *Tosca* had to admit that she "scooped to conquer." This *Tosca* was the second of her appearances at the Metropolitan Opera, the first having been Marietta in Korngold's *Die tote Stadt,* also receiving its first appearance in that house.

She remained at the Metropolitan Opera until 1932, finally taking up American residence. Her offstage entourage was always large, and even at the age of ninety, Jeritza continued to hold court at her estate in New Jersey. It was not until after her death that among her effects was found the manuscript of the very last song by Richard Strauss called "Malven," which had never been heard. The glamour and mystery surrounding one of the last great prima donnas accompanied her to the grave.

—Alan Jefferson

JERUSALEM, Siegfried.

Tenor. Born 17 April 1940, in Oberhausen. Studied in Essen, and in 1961 began his career as a bassoonist; member of Stuttgart Radio Orchestra, 1972-77; studied singing in Stuttgart with Hertha Kalcher; sang in Stuttgart, Aachen and

Hamburg; Bayreuth debut as Froh, 1977; Metropolitan Opera debut as Lohengrin, 1980; London Coliseum debut as Parsifal, 1986; Covent Garden debut as Erik, 1986.

*   *   *

During the 1970s and 1980s Siegfried Jerusalem established a well earned reputation as a fine heroic tenor, especially effective in the operas of Richard Wagner. Among his best Wagner roles are those of Siegmund in *Die Walküre,* Siegfried and Parsifal. Jerusalem has not traveled as much as many leading opera singers: he has given most of his performances in the German-speaking parts of Europe, winning equal applause in the major opera houses of Germany (including Bayreuth), Austria (including Salzburg), and Switzerland.

Parsifal was one of the first Wagner roles that Jerusalem mastered. He won applause for his portrayal of Parsifal in Vienna in 1979; in the same year he brought the role to Salzburg, where critics applauded both his good looks and his beautiful, expressive voice. When Jerusalem performed Siegmund in Zurich in 1988 his singing was loudly applauded, but his acting did not receive unanimous approval; one critic described him as "a bit clod-footed." He triumphed as the young Siegfried at Bayreuth a few months later, winning praise for his fine musicianship and beautiful tone.

One can hear the strengths of Jerusalem's voice in his portrayal of Siegmund in *Die Walküre,* recorded under Marek Janowski in 1981. Jerusalem's Siegmund has a clear, manly voice, firm and strong. A slight vibrato gives the voice richness without effecting its accuracy of pitch. He pronounces the words distinctly, thereby enhancing the vividness of his characterization. His voice can be sweetly lyrical, but he can also express anger and violence. For example, in the soliloquy beginning "Ein Schwert verhiess mir der Vater," Jerusalem sings the words "ein Weib" (a woman) with a warmth and gentleness that communicate his feelings with great immediacy. He sings out "Wälse! Wälse!" with resounding power, as his voice conveys his excitement and anticipation. Jerusalem brings a distinctly darker tone to his voice as he sings the words "nächtiges Dunkel" (darkness of night).

Jerusalem has not limited his performances to Wagner's operas. His portrayal of Florestano in Paer's *Leonora* (recorded under Peter Maag in 1979), shows another side of Jerusalem's artistic personality. This is a fine, virile performance, proving that Jerusalem has a real talent and flair for Italian opera, and making a good case for the dramatic potential of Paer's rarely performed opera. Alone in the dungeon at the beginning of Act II, Jerusalem's Florestano sings the recitative "Ciel! che profonda oscurità tirrana" with intense feeling. In the big aria "Dolce oggetto del mio amore," we can admire Jerusalem's beautiful, rich tone. Lyrical lines, when not too high, he sings with grace and warmth. Yet the performance has weaknesses. Jerusalem does not seem to be completely in control of his high notes, and he cannot master the coloratura near the end of the aria, which seems to demand a light, Rossini-type tenor rather than a *Heldentenor.* But the performance is such as to make us wish that he devoted more of his artistic energy to Italian opera.

—John A. Rice

JESSONDA.

Composer: Ludewig Spohr.

Librettist: E. Gehe (after A.M. Lemièrre, *La veuve de Malabar*).

First Performance: Kassel, 28 July 1823.

Roles: Jessonda (soprano); Amazili (soprano); Dandau (bass); Nadori (tenor); Tristan (baritone); Pedro Lopes (tenor); Indian Officer (tenor); First and Second Bajadere (sopranos).

Publications

articles–

Abert, A.A. "Webers 'Euryanthe' und Spohrs 'Jessonda' als grosse Opern." In *Festschrift für Walter Wiora,* 35. Kassel, 1967.
Brown, Clive. "Spohr's *Jessonda.*" *Musical Times* 121 (1980): 94.

*   *   *

Writing in the *Allgemeine musikalische Zeitung* in 1823, Spohr heralded the forthcoming premiere of his *Jessonda* by issuing an "Appeal to German composers" that opened with

Costume designs by Girolamo Franceschini for Spohr's *Jessonda*, 1856

the words: "The long-awaited moment seems finally to have arrived, when the German public, cloyed with the insipid sweetness of the new Italian music, longs for what is of real and essential value." Of all his operas, Spohr's *Jessonda* is generally recognized as his masterpiece. Adapted from Antoine Lemièrre's drama *La veuve de Malabar* (1770), it is a superbly crafted rescue opera in the tradition of such works as Cherubini's *Les deux Journées.*

The plot centers on the eponymous heroine, a young widow of the Rajah of Goa who has been condemned to the funeral pyre. But already in the opening scene there is a juxtaposition of two diametrically opposed characters: the High Priest, Dandau, rigid and unshakable, and a young priest, Nadori, idealistic and impressionable. In the second scene, set in Jessonda's apartments, her sister Amazili reveals that Jessonda's had been a forced marriage, arranged after she had been torn from her true love, the Portuguese general, Tristan d'Achuna. Nadori, sent as a messenger of death, falters, so smitten is he by the beauty of the two sisters. By the end of the scene he has not only fallen in love with Amazili, but has also made a vow to do whatever he can to save Jessonda.

The second act opens with military exercises of the Portuguese army, which is under the command of none other than the general himself. It becomes apparent that the purpose of the campaign is to avenge the deaths of Portuguese traders cruelly murdered by the natives. At the same time, Tristan mourns the loss of his true love of a few years earlier. He has also allowed the local Indians to perform what he believes is an innocent purification ritual, only to learn the truth soon from Nadori. Tristan investigates the situation, discovers his Jessonda and is on the verge of saving her when Dandau intervenes. Jessonda is taken away. As the third and final act opens Tristan is in despair as he realizes that he is helpless in the face of Jessonda's fate. But Nadori arrives to reveal that Dandau has broken his trust by organizing an attack on the Portuguese ships. Tristan decides to retaliate, and Nadori volunteers to guide his forces through a secret passage into the city. While final preparations for the sacrifice are underway, a lightning storm is raging; a huge image of Brahma is struck and destroyed, a sure sign of the god's displeasure. But the Portuguese army saves the day; Tristan and Nadori are happily united with Jessonda and Amazili respectively.

The formal structure of Spohr's score is notable for its extensive scene-complexes, including choral and ballet sections that were possibly inspired by what Spohr had recently seen in Paris. Acts I and II are continuous with the exception of one break each (a scene change and a duet for Amazili and Nadori respectively). Act III is essentially continuous with a transition being straddled by a sustained note on the French horn. Individual components of scene-complexes are open-ended and tied together by a fluid mixture of *secco* recitative and *arioso*. In achieving this virtually continuous writing Spohr anticipates what was later to become a characteristic feature of Wagner's music dramas. But even more strikingly proto-Wagnerian is the treatment of Tristan's vision, so suggestive of Tannhäuser's, which comes at the beginning of the third act. In addition, the details of rhythm and orchestration at such moments as the delivery of the message of death in the first finale are essentially the same as those of Wagner in *Die Walküre* when Brünnhilde warns Siegmund of his imminent death. This was no mere coincidence, in that Wagner conducted *Jessonda* a number of times.

Also worthy of mention is Spohr's use of reminiscence motifs, among them Tristan's oath and the love motif associated with Nadori and Amazili. In addition, the Indians and Portuguese are sharply differentiated in terms of instrumental color, rhythm, and choice of key. Trombones in E-flat become a Brahmin signature, while in the case of the Portuguese in general and Tristan and Jessonda's recognition duet in particular, D major is the key of choice. Elsewhere Spohr displays an acute sense of color as when, for example, he writes in a low register for flutes, clarinets and horn as Jessonda is prepared for sacrifice. There is a corresponding change to percussion instruments when he writes music to accompany the dances of the Bayaderes.

As a work that remained an operatic staple and the embodiment of high German ideals until World War I, *Jessonda* had its share of conductor-champions—among them Franz Lachner, Wagner, Hans von Bülow, Mahler, and Richard Strauss; and no less a composer than Brahms found it magnificent.

—Joshua Berrett

THE JEWELS OF THE MADONNA
See I GIOIELLI DELLA MADONNA

THE JEWESS
See LA JUIVE

JOHNSON, Edward.

Tenor. Born 22 August 1878, in Guelph, Ontario. Died 20 April 1959, in Guelph, Ontario. Married Viscountess Beatrice d'Arneiro, 1909. Attended University of Toronto, then studied singing with Mme von Feilitsch; sang on Broadway in Oscar Straus's *Walzertraum,* 1908; studied in Florence with Vincenzo Lombardi, 1909; opera debut under the name Edoardo Di Giovanni as Andrea Chénier at the Teatro Verdi, Padua, 1912; Teatro all Scala debut as Parsifal, 1914; sang in Chicago, 1919-22; Metropolitan Opera debut as Avito in *Amore di tre re,* 1922; last Metropolitan Opera performance, 1935; served as general manager of the Metropolitan Opera until 1950.

Publications

About JOHNSON: books–

Mercer, R. *The Tenor of His Time: Edward Johnson of the Met.* Toronto, 1976.

articles–

Simon, R. "Profile: General Director." *New Yorker* 14 December (1935).

Bauer, E. "Edward Johnson." *Canadian Review and Musical Art* 7 and 8 (1944).

Benson, E. "Edward Johnson." *Opera Canada* May (1958).

* * *

In the realm of opera, the name of Edward Johnson is most immediately associated with his role as general manager of the Metropolitan Opera, a position which he held from 1935 until his retirement in 1950. This administrative post was, however, only the final consummation of a long career in opera as a dramatic tenor in Italy, Chicago, and finally in New York at the Metropolitan Opera itself.

Using the stage name Edoardo Di Giovanni (a direct Italian translation of his real name), Johnson made his operatic debut at Padua in 1912, in a production of Giordano's *Andrea Chénier*. Several important Italian appearances followed, including his debut at the Teatro alla Scala in 1914, for which he sang the title role in Wagner's *Parsifal* in the first Italian production of the opera. For five seasons he was principal tenor of Teatro alla Scala, and toured with the company to Latin America and Spain. During this time he created several leading tenor roles and in 1919 he sang in the premieres of two Puccini operas (*Gianni Schicchi* and *Il tabarro*) at the request of the composer. The same year, he first sang Pelléas in the Rome production of Debussy's *Pelléas et Mélisande,* a role with which he was to be particularly associated in his later career.

Throughout this Italian period, critical reaction to Johnson's singing was consistently laudatory. In particular, he was acclaimed for the intensity of his dramatic interpretations of operatic roles and for the intelligence and skill with which he used his voice. Recordings from this period illustrate his fine sense of control. Although Johnson was billed as a dramatic tenor, his voice was not particularly heavy; his ease in the upper registers was often noted, especially in his early years.

After the death of his wife in 1919, Johnson—resuming the anglicized spelling of his name—returned to the United States. He had earlier established a strong reputation in North America as a singer of oratorio, both in his native Ontario and later in New York where he had also starred in operetta (his performance in Oscar Straus's *Walzertraum* in 1908 had been highly acclaimed). On his return, however, he sang only opera, first with the Chicago Opera for three years, then with the Metropolitan Opera, where he made his debut in 1922 as Avito in Montemezzi's *L'amore dei tre re*. Richard Aldrich, reviewing the performance in the *New York Times* (17 November 1922), commented both on the "warm tenor quality" of Johnson's singing and on his intelligence and musical understanding, observing that "here is a tenor who is something more than a voice, who is an artistic personality." This natural artistic presence continued to serve Johnson well for the next twelve seasons, during which time he was one of the most popular tenors at the Met. While he sang a large number of contrasting roles, he was most celebrated for his portrayal of Pelléas, Roméo (Gounod's *Roméo et Juliette*), Sadko (Rimsky-Korsakov's *Sadko*), and especially for the title role that he created in the Deems Taylor opera, *Peter Ibbetson* (1931). Many of his greatest successes were in performances with the Spanish soprano, Lucrezia Bori.

Johnson's tenure as general manager of the Met was clouded by several problems, largely resulting from the economic pressures of the late 1930s and the war years. The most significant change that he oversaw was the gradual shift from acclaimed European stars to native American talent. Under his leadership, the Met became more genuinely a North American company.

Even upon retirement in 1950, Johnson continued to be involved with music. He returned to Canada, where he helped to establish the Edward Johnson Music Foundation, which sponsors the annual Guelph Spring Festival in Ontario. In 1962, the University of Toronto honoured his memory by the posthumous dedication of its new music building and library, the Edward Johnson Building.

—Joan Backus

LA JOLIE FILLE DE PERTH [The Fair Maid of Perth].

Composer: Georges Bizet.

Librettists: Jules-Henry Vernoy de Saint-Georges and Jules Adenis (after Walter Scott).

First Performance: Paris, Théâtre-Lyrique, 26 December 1867.

Roles: Catherine (soprano); Mab (soprano); Henry Smith (tenor); Le Duc de Rothsay (baritone or tenor); Ralph (bass or baritone); Simon Glover (bass); Le Majordome, Guyot (bass).

Publications

article–

Westrup, Jack. "Bizet's *La Jolie Fille de Perth.*" In *Essays Presented to Egon Wellesz,* 157. Oxford, 1966.

* * *

Despite a promising start, *La jolie fille de Perth* has never attained a secure place in the repertory, unlike Bizet's previous opera *Les pêcheurs de perles* (1863). It will probably remain a work that is revived only occasionally, even though the score has improved upon many of the weaknesses of its predecessor. It has a strong second act and a substantial number of fine pieces in the first and third acts; however, its overall impact onstage is greatly weakened by a hackneyed final act and a libretto that is probably the worst Bizet ever set. Shortly after receiving his text, even Bizet had to admit to a friend, "I am not using the words to compose; I wouldn't find a note!"

In July 1866 Bizet signed a contract with Carvalho, director of the Théâtre-Lyrique, and despite many obligations to various publishers, he finished and delivered his score by 29 December. Budget and casting problems delayed the production. Finally, after the successful dress rehearsal in September 1867, the premiere was unexpectedly postponed until later in the season when a more sophisticated public would have returned to the city. Following the opening night in December, most critics were fairly positive, but both Ernest Reyer (*Le journal des débats*) and Johannès Weber (*Le temps*) pointed out the eclectic style and concessions made for the public and the prima donna. To the latter Bizet confessed: "All my concessions failed! . . . I am delighted with that! The school of oom-pahs, trills and falsehood is dead, quite dead. Let us bury it without tears, without regrets, without emotion and . . . onward!" By February 1868, however, when Bizet saw the possibility of a success evaporating and the run of eighteen performances coming to a close, he described himself to his friend Galabert as sick, discouraged, and worn down by work.

Only the title and some of the characters' names come from the Sir Walter Scott novel, but the convoluted plot depends much more on clichés that had succeeded in other libretti. As arbitrarily strung together here, they create stereotypical characters devoid of believable motivation. The first act involves the protagonists in jealousy and argument. Scarcely have the coquettish Catherine and Henry Smith, an armorer, pledged their love but the lecherous Duke of Rothsay arrives to invite Catherine to that evening's masked carnival celebration. Smith becomes jealous of what he perceives as Catherine's flirtation and starts to attack the duke. Mab, the gypsy queen, prevents disaster, and it is then Catherine's turn to be jealous, for she incorrectly assumes that Mab is Smith's mistress. Act II is driven by disguise and further misunderstanding. Smith serenades his betrothed in the hope that she has forgiven him, but leaves, discouraged, for a nearby tavern when she does not reply. Mab, a former conquest of the duke's, disguises herself as Catherine. Despite his sherry-induced stupor, lovesick Ralph, the apprentice of Simon Glover, notices "Catherine" stepping into the duke's litter and rouses himself to warn Smith. However, before Ralph himself can stumble offstage, the real Catherine appears at her window singing part of Smith's serenade. The third act features an ironic seduction scene in which Mab in disguise hears the duke use some of the same lines to woo "Catherine" that he had earlier used with her. It closes with a public confrontation between the furious Smith and a bewildered Catherine. For the final act, the librettists contrive to include both a mad scene and a reconciliation. Ralph tries to convince Smith of Catherine's innocence, but Smith challenges him to a duel. In the following duet Smith explains to Catherine that his death will restore her honor. She snaps from the stress and may thus sing a fashionably ornate ballade. It is Mab who dreams up the device to restore her reason. Once again the gypsy queen dresses up as Catherine, and once again Smith sings his serenade. Catherine's sanity miraculously returns as she protests that he is singing to the wrong person. The duke never appears in this act, but Mab reports that it is he who has stopped the duel. To conclude, all praise love and Saint Valentine.

Like the plot itself, much of the score comes close to the *opéra comique* style of the 1850s and 60s, although Catherine's music, largely unsuccessful, regularly incorporates Italianate coloratura. Bizet's gift for orchestration is immediately demonstrated in a lyrically elegant prelude. Act I also contains a strong series of ensembles, beginning with a tender duo for the young lovers that shows some similarities to the Micaela-Don José duet in *Carmen*. It is followed by a dramatically effective trio in which Smith's rising anger, underlined by the banging of his anvil, alternates with the suave, wooing tune of the duke (here presented in three of the half dozen uses scattered through the opera and imaginatively scored). The succeeding quartet is effective, but reminiscent of Auber. In this score Bizet has not only created some dramatically effective numbers but has also found his own voice at times. A striking example appears in act III, where a small instrumental group plus harp plays a minuet backstage while the duke makes his practiced advances on the false Catherine. (Since *La jolie fille* was largely forgotten by 1880, Guiraud felt

free to borrow the charming minuet for the second *Arlésienne* suite.)

More often than elsewhere in *La jolie fille* Bizet's distinctive sound appears in act II. The main theme for the opening chorus features his characteristic woodwinds—dark bassoons that are then joined by higher pitched winds; then the men of the watch sing a square march tune with full orchestra until they scatter in fear at the slightest noise. Though the harmonies are not as piquant as the "Danse bohème" in *Carmen*, a delightful gypsy dance features a great crescendo (starting from *ppp* for flute and harp alone) and acceleration that eventually doubles the pulse. The two finest solos of the opera follow one another near the end of this act. The opening of Smith's serenade is Italianate and memorable, borrowed in part from Bizet's earlier *Don Procopio*. Still more original is Ralph's drunken air, where accents on weak beats create a lurching rhythm and dark bassoons, brass, and low strings underline his maudlin and tragic self-pity.

The score contains fine pieces of every type. The climactic finale of act III even begins to develop a true pathetic and dramatic power that forecasts the equivalent scene in *Carmen*. Yet both score and libretto fall flat in act IV, where only the Saint Valentine's chorus has a fresh, Gounod-like charm. If it did not limp to a close, *La jolie fille de Perth* would have to be ranked one of the finest works of its decade.

—Lesley A. Wright

JOMMELLI, Niccolò.

Composer. Born 10 September 1714, in Aversa, near Naples. Died 25 August 1774, in Naples. Studied with Canon Muzzillo, director of the Cathedral Choir in Aversa; studied with Prota and Feo at the Conservatorio San Onofrio in Naples, 1725-28; studied with Fago, Sarcuni, and Basso at the Conservatorio Pietà dei Turchini in Naples, 1728; first comic opera produced in Naples, 1737; first serious opera produced in Rome, 1740; studied with Padre Martini in Bologna, 1741; membership in the Accademia Filarmonica; in Venice, December 1741; music director of the Ospedale degli Incurabili, 1743; in Rome, 1747; in Vienna, 1749; commissioned to compose an opera for Karl Eugen, Duke of Württemberg; became Ober-Kapellmeister in Stuttgart, 1754; accepted a commission to write operas and sacred music for King José of Portugal at the court of Lisbon, 1768; in Italy, 1768.

Operas

L'errore amoroso, A. Palomba, Naples, Nuovo, spring 1737.
Odoardo, Naples, Fiorentini, winter 1738.
Ricimero rè de' Goti, Zeno and P. Pariati, Rome, Torre Argentina, 16 January 1740.
Astianatte, A. Salvi, Rome, Torre Argentina, 4 February 1741.
Ezio, Metastasio, Bologna, Malevezzi, 29 April 1741.
Merope, Zeno, Venice, San Giovanni Grisostomo, 26 December 1741.
Semiramide riconosciuta, Metastasio, Turin, Royal, 26 December 1741.
Don Chichibio (intermezzo), Rome, Teatro della Valle, 1742.
Eumene, Zeno, Bologna, Malevezzi, 5 May 1742.
Semiramide, F. Silvani, Venice, San Giovanni Grisostomo, 26 December 1742.

Niccolò Jommelli

Tito Manlio, G. Roccaforte, Turin, Royal, carnival 1743.

Demofoonte, Metastasio, Padua, Obizzi, 13 June 1743.

Alessandro nell'Indie, Metastasio, Ferrara, Bonocossi, carnival 1744.

Ciro riconosciuto, Metastasio, Bologna, Formagliari, 4 May 1744.

Sofonisba, A. and G. Zanetti, Venice, San Giovanni Grisostomo, carnival 1746.

Cajo Mario, Roccaforte, Rome, Torre Argentina, 6 February 1746.

Antigono, Metastasio, Lucca, Teatro di Lucca, 24 August 1746.

Tito Manilio, Sanvitale (after M. Noris), Venice, San Giovanni Grisostomo, fall 1746.

Ciro riconosciuto, Metastasio, c. 1747.

Didone abbandonata, Metastasio, Rome, Torre Argentina, 28 January 1747.

Eumene, Zeno, Naples, San Carlo, 30 May 1747.

L'amore in maschera, A. Palomba, Naples, Fiorentini, carnival 1748.

Ezio, Metastasio, Naples, San Carlo, 4 November 1748.

Artaserse, Metastasio, Rome, Torre Argentina, c. 1747; revised, 4 February 1749.

La cantata e disfida di Don Trastullo (intermezzo), Rome, Teatro della Valle, carnival 1749.

Demetrio, Metastasio, Parma, Royal Ducal, spring 1749.

Achille in Sciro, Metastasio, Vienna, Burgtheater, 30 August 1749.

Didone abbandonata [pasticcio], Vienna, Burg, 8 December 1749.

Ciro riconosciuto, Metastasio, Venice, San Giovanni Grisostomo, fall 1749; revised for Pisa, 1751, for Mantua, 1758.

Cesare in Egitto, G. Bussani, Rome, Torre Argentina, carnival 1751.

Cajo Mario, Roccaforte, Bologna, Formagliari, carnival 1751.

La villana nobile, Palermo, de' Valguarneri di San Lucia, carnival 1751.

Ifigenia in Aulide, M. Verazi, Rome, Torre Argentina, 9 February 1751; revised, Naples, San Carlo, 18 December 1753.

L'uccellatrice (intermezzo), Venice, San Samuele, 6 May 1751; revised as *Il paratajo, overro La pipée,* Paris, Opéra, 25 September 1753.

Ipermestra, Metastasio, Spoleto, Comunale, October 1751.

Talestri, Roccaforte, Rome, Teatro delle Dame, 28 December 1751.

I rivali delusi (intermezzo), Rome, Teatro della Valle, carnival 1752.

Demofoonte, Metastasio, Milan, Royal Ducal, carnival 1753.

Attilio Regolo, Metastasio, Rome, Teatro delle Dame, 8 January 1753; revised as pasticcio, Naples, San Carlo, 23 March 1761.

Fetonte, L. Villati, Stuttgart, Ducal, 11 February 1753.

Semiramide riconosciuta, Metastasio, Piacenza, Ducal, fiera d'Aprile 1753.

La Clemenza di Tito, Metastasio, Stuttgart, Ducal, 30 August 1753.

Bajazette, A. Piovene, Turin, Royal, 26 December 1753.

Lucio Vero, after Zeno, Milan, Royal Ducal, carnival 1754.

Don Falcone (intermezzo), Bologna, Rossi, 22 January 1754.

Catone in Utica, Metastasio, Stuttgart, Ducal, 30 August 1754.

Pelope, Verazi, Stuttgart, Ducal, 11 February 1755; revised, J. Cordeiro da Silava, Salvaterra, Palace, carnival 1768.

Enea nel Lazio, Verazi, Stuttgart, Ducal, 30 August 1755; revised, da Silva, Salvaterra, Palace, carnival 1767.

Artaserse, Metastasio, Stuttgart, Ducal, 30 August 1756.

Creso, G. Pizzi, Rome, Torre Argentina, 5 February 1757.

Temistocle, Metastasio, Naples, San Carlo, 18 December 1757.

Tito Manlio, Stuttgart, Ducal, 6 January 1758.

Ezio, Metastasio, Stuttgart, Ducal, 11 February 1758.

Endimione, ovvero Il trionfo d'amore, Metastasio, Stuttgart, Ducal, spring 1759; revised, Queluz, Palace, 29 June 1780.

Nitteti, Metastasio, Stuttgart, Opera, 11 February 1759; revised, da Silva, Lisbon, Ajuda, 6 June 1770.

Alessandro nell'Indie, Metastasio, Stuttgart, Opera, 11 February 1760; revised, da Silva, Lisbon, Ajuda, 6 June 1776.

Cajo Fabrizio, Verazi, Mannheim, 4 November 1760.

L'Olimpiade, Metastasio, Stuttgart, Opera, 11 February 1761; revised, da Silva, Lisbon, Ajuda, 31 March 1774.

L'isola disabitata, Metastasio, Ludwigsburg, Ducal, 4 November 1761; revised, Queluz, Palace, 31 March 1780.

Semiramide riconosciuta, Metastasio, Stuttgart, Opera, 11 February 1762.

Didone abbandonata, Metastasio, Stuttgart, Opera, 11 February 1763; revised for Stuttgart, 1777-83.

Il trionfo d'amore, Tagliazucchi, Ludwigsburg, improvised stage, 16 February 1763.

La pastorella illustre, Tagliazucchi, Stuttgart, Ducal, 4 November 1763; revised, da Silva, Salvaterra, Palace, carnival 1773.

Demofoonte, Metastasio, Stuttgart, Opera, 11 February 1764; revised, da Silva, Lisbon, Ajuda, 6 June 1775.

Il rè pastore, Metastasio, Ludwigsburg, Ducal, 4 November 1764; revised, da Silva, Salvaterra, Palace, carnival 1770.

La clemenza di Tito, Metastasio, Ludwigsburg, Ducal, 6 January 1765; revised, da Silva, Lisbon, Ajuda, 6 June 1771.

Temistocle, Metastasio, Ludwigsburg, Ducal, November 1765.
Imeneo in Atene, after Stampiglia, Ludwigsburg, Ducal, 4 November 1765; revised, da Silva, Lisbon, Ajuda, 19 March 1773.
La critica, G. Martinelli, Ludwigsburg, Ducal, 1766; revised as *Il giucco di picchetto,* Koblenz, Palace, spring 1772; revised as *La conversazione e L'accademia di musica,* Salvaterra, Palace, carnival 1775.
Enea nel Lazio, Verazi, Ludwigsburg, Ducal, 6 January 1766.
Vologeso, Verazi, Ludwigsburg, Ducal, 11 February 1766; revised, da Silva, Salvaterra, Palace, Carnival 1769.
Il matrimonio per concorso, Martinelli, Ludwigsburg, Palace, 4 November 1766; revised, da Silva, Salvaterra, Palace, carnival 1770.
Il cacciatore deluso, ovvero La Semiramide in bernesco, Martinelli, Tübingen, New, 4 November 1767; revised, da Silva, Salvaterra, Palace, carnival 1771.
Fetonte, Verazi, Ludwigsburg, Ducal, 11 February 1768.
La schiava liberata, Martinelli, Ludwigsburg, Ducal, 18 December 1768; revised, da Silva, Lisbon, Ajuda, 31 March 1770.
Armida abbandonata, F.S. de Rogati, Naples, San Carlo, 30 May 1770; revised, da Silva, Lisbon, Ajuda, 31 March 1773.
Demofoonte, Metastasio, Naples, San Carlo, 4 November 1770.
L'amante cacciatore, A. Gatta, Rome, Palla a Corda, carnival 1771.
Achille in Sciro, Metastasio, Rome, Teatro delle Dame, 26 January 1771.
Le avventure di Cleomede, Martinelli, finished Naples, April 1771; revised, da Silva, Lisbon, Ajuda, 6 June 1772.
Ifigenia in Tauride, Verazi, Naples, San Carlo, 30 May 1771; revised, da Silva, Salvaterra, Palace, carnival 1776.
Ezio, Metastasio, finished in Naples, July 1771; revised, da Silva, Lisbon, Ajuda, 20 April, 1772.
Il trionfo di Clelia, Metastasio, finished in Naples, early 1774; revised, da Silva, Lisbon, Ajuda, 6 June 1774.
La pellegrina.
La Griselda, after Zeno.

Other works: serentatas, sacred and secular vocal works, instrumental music.

Publications/Writings

About JOMMELLI: books–

Mattei, S. *Elogio del Jommelli.* Colle, 1785.
Sigismondo, G. *Descrizione della città di Napoli,* vol. 2, 19 ff. Naples, 1788.
Burney, Charles. *Memoires of the Life and Writings of Metastasio.* London, 1796.
Villamors, C. *Memorie dei compositori di musica del regno di Napoli.* Naples, 1840.
Alfieri, P. *Notizie biografiche di Nicolò Jommelli.* Rome, 1845.
Abert, Hermann. *Niccolo Jommelli als Opernkomponist.* Halle, 1908.
Krauss, R. *Das Stuttgart Hoftheater.* Stuttgart, 1908.
Corte, A. della. *L'opera comica italiana nel '700.* Bari, 1923.
Robinson, M. *Naples and Neapolitan Opera.* Oxford, 1972.
Strohm, Reinhard. *Die italienische Oper im 18. Jahrhundert.* Wilhelmshaven, 1979.
McClymonds, Marita P. *Niccolo Jommelli: The Last Years 1769-1774.* Ann Arbor, 1980.
Weimer, Eric Douglas. *Opera Seria and the Evolution of Classical Style, 1755-1772. Studies in Musicology* 78. Ann Arbor, 1984.

articles–

Abert, Hermann. "Vorwort." *Fetonte.* In *Denkmäler deutscher Tonkunst,* vols. 32-33. Leipzig, 1907.
Goldschmidt, H. "Die Reform der italienischen Oper des 18 Jahrhunderts." In *International Musical Society Congress Report,* vol. 3. Vienna, 1909.
Fehr, M. "Zeno, Pergolesi und Jommelli." *Zeitschrift für Musik* 1 (1918-19): 281.
Abert, Hermann. "Die Stuttgarter Oper unter Jommelli." *Neue Musikzeitung* 46/no. 24 (1925).
Brofsky, H. "Jommelli e Padre Martini." *Rivista musicale italiana* 8 (1973): 132.
Carli Ballola, Giovanni. "Mozart e l'opera seria di Jommelli, De Majo e Traetta." *Analecta musicologica* 18 (1978): 138.
McClymonds, Marita P. "The Evolution of Jommelli's Operatic Style." *Journal of the American Musicological Society* 33 (1980): 326.
McCredie, Andrew. "La informa operatistica prima di Gluck e il teatre musicale eroico tedesco dello *Sturm und Drang.*" *Richerche musicali* 5 (1981): 86.
Henze, Sabine. "Zur Instrumentalbegleitung in Jommellis dramatischen Kompositionen." *Archiv für Musikwissenschaft* 39 (1982): 168.
McClymonds, Marita P. "Mattia Verazi and the Opera at Mannheim, Stuttgart, and Ludwigsburg." *Studies in Music* [Canada] 7 (1982): 99.

unpublished–

Tolkoff, L. "The Stuttgart Operas of Nicolò Jommelli." Ph.D. dissertation, Yale University, 1974.
Sprague, C. "A Comparison of Five Settings of Metastasio's *Artaserse.* Ph.D. dissertation, University of California, Los Angeles, 1978.
Wilson, J. Kenneth. "*L'Olimpiade:* Selected Eighteenth-Century Settings of Metastasio's Libretto." Ph.D. dissertation, Harvard University, 1982.

* * *

Niccolò Jommelli's operas, though largely unknown today, are among the most dramatic and effective theater works of the mid-eighteenth century. His frequent experimentation with new textures and musical contexts for expression, his great sensitivity to singers, the admiration and affinity he felt for Hasse, and the fortunate and cosmopolitan circumstances under which he composed for many years, all converged to mold works that are astonishingly progressive and effective. Though his influence or fame may not have rivaled that of Gluck, Jommelli's operas often far exceed in brilliance, complexity, and effectiveness the so-called "reform" operas of his more studied contemporary.

Jommelli's early education was a traditional one, first in Aversa and then, at age 11, in two different Neapolitan conservatories: the San Onofrio and the Pietà dei Turchini. Naples in the 1720s and 30s, as one of the largest cities in Europe, fostered a rich musical environment, including a new theater for *opera seria* (the Teatro San Carlo), which opened in 1734. Pergolesi, Hasse, Leo, Porpora, Sarro, and others were popular on the stage; it was around the style of such composers that Jommelli fashioned his early works. His first operas, beginning with two comedies (a traditional pattern), appeared slowly, but by the 1740s his music was in great demand. Jommelli had works performed widely throughout Italy, including Rome, Bologna (where Jommelli met and studied with Padre Martini), Florence, and Venice; in Venice he was appointed (with the help of Hasse) to the Ospedale degli Incurabili in 1743, which gave rise to numerous sacred compositions. By 1749 he took a post in Rome as *maestro coadiutore* to the papal chapel. Over the next several years his fame in opera continued to rise, and he became particularly distinguished for his ability to infuse musical support for dramatic conceits.

Jommelli's greatest efforts blossomed in environments that were sympathetic to French opera (as was also true for Gluck in Vienna and Traetta in Parma); these operas included a wider and more varied use of chorus and ballet, richer orchestration, a more flexible approach to recitative (Jommelli had already far exceeded the Italian limited use of accompanied recitative), and an increasingly experimental attitude towards the formal design of arias and ensembles. To this was added his emulation of German chromatic harmony. From 1754 until 1769 Jommelli served as Ober-Kapellmeister to Duke Karl Eugen, who held court imitating Versailles at his palace in Ludwigsburg, near Stuttgart. Jommelli experimented widely over these years, having enormous financial resources at his disposal, some of the best singers of his day (Schubart reports how closely he worked with them, particularly Giuseppe Aprile, in writing for the voice), a virtuoso orchestra (which he nearly doubled in size and trained to a high level), and the assistance of Jean Georges Noverre (among other great ballet choreographers of the time). The subjects for libretti were usually chosen by the Duke; some were traditional (several Metastasio libretti were used), and others much less so (at the special request of the Duke), particularly those penned by the court poet Mattia Verazi. Such works as *Enea nel Lazio* (1755), *Vologeso* (1766), and *Fetonte* (1768) were organized in new ways, with greater spectacle and act-ending climaxes in the manner of comic opera. Even in the more traditional libretti, however (such as *Didone abbandonata* of 1763), long and complex accompanied recitatives intertwine with evocative and forceful arias. Jommelli's sense for drama in opera was unsurpassed. By *Vologeso* almost no secco recitative remained. Two comic works appeared in 1766, in acknowledgement of the fashion for comic operas elsewhere, and this was followed in 1768 by *La schiava liberata,* in the manner of a *dramma-giocoso* (which often included serious, tragic elements as well as comedy).

By 1769 the Stuttgart court was in decline. Jommelli was given leave to return to Italy with his ailing wife, but after he departed the Duke refused him his promised pension and hoarded the composer's opera scores. His return to Naples was not successful; Neapolitan taste did not take well to his progressive ideas. When Jommelli tried to adapt his style to lighter Neapolitan fashion he was criticized by Mozart, who found his *Armida abbandonata* (1770) "too old fashioned." From 1769 until 1777 Jommelli was under contract, by correspondence, with the court in Lisbon, where the composer's operas were frequently feted, with as many as four works a year performed. Jommelli revised many of his earlier compositions for its new casts, composed three new works, and was well rewarded for his efforts.

—Dale E. Monson

JONES, Gwyneth.

Soprano. Born 7 November 1936, in Pontnewyndd, Wales. Married Till Haberfeld (one daughter). Studied as mezzo-soprano at Royal College of Music with Ruth Parker; at Accademia Chigiana, Siena; in Zurich; and with Maria Carpi in Geneva; debut as Gluck's Orfeo, Zurich, 1962; at Covent Garden since 1963; moved to soprano roles; Vienna debut as Fidelio, 1966; Bayreuth debut, 1966; Metropolitan Opera debut as Sieglinde, 1972.

Publications

About JONES: books–

Mutafian, C. *Gwyneth Jones.* Paris, 1980.

articles–

Loveland, K. "Gwyneth Jones." *Opera* February (1970).

*   *   *

As with the soprano Leonie Rysanek and a few others, Gwyneth Jones may be characterized as an erratic singer who, when at her best, provides the audience with thrilling vocalism and a powerful theatrical experience. Jones went through a severe vocal crisis in the early 1970s, a period when, unfortunately, she was involved in many recordings of complete operas. That many of these recordings produced results that are unacceptable as pure singing cannot be denied. Her Ortrud under Kubelik, which Charles Osborne termed "a pain in the ears," was perhaps the nadir. There are, however, fine performances from this period, such as a strongly characterized Medea even against the touchstone of Maria Callas, a gorgeously sung "D'amor sull'ali rosee," and a touching portrayal of Desdemona under the languorous baton of Barbirolli. Much less successful are an Octavian under Bernstein with Christa Ludwig as the Marschallin (a role that Jones later successfully undertook), a Salome, partly live from Hamburg under Böhm, and a Kundry from Bayreuth with Boulez. This is a "theatrical" performance in every sense of the word, full of groans, shrieks, and maniacal laughter.

The voice is naturally beautiful, as shown by some of her fine Verdi singing and by a 1969 *Fidelio* with Böhm, although in this role she lacks total control of her large instrument. Yet it is a very feminine voice, which goes a long way in projecting the dramatic and emotional situation in Beethoven's opera. Also with Böhm there is a Senta with Thomas Stewart as the Dutchman. Here she is once again the embodiment of femininity; she engages in lovely soft singing but in the grand, emotional moments it is a bumpy ride.

Jones began her studies as a mezzo-soprano, but Nello Santi in Zurich convinced her to essay the soprano roles. She developed into a true lirico-spinto, taking on Verdi roles at Covent Garden. Her first Wagnerian role in London, Sieglinde in 1965, provoked comparison with Lotte Lehmann and from 1966 she was a regular singer at Vienna and at Bayreuth. The assumption of a taxing schedule, along with intense emotional onstage involvement, took a heavy toll on the production of the voice, causing it, for example, to develop a beat. After her initial Sieglinde at Covent Garden she began to sing regularly at Bayreuth, not only Sieglinde but Eva, Kundry, both Venus and Elisabeth in *Tannhäuser,* and eventually (in 1976) Brünnhilde. She performed all three Wagner Brünnhildes at Bayreuth in the internationally-televised *Ring* cycle

Gwyneth Jones in *Die Walküre*, Bayreuth, 1976

in Patrice Chéreau's controversial production conducted by Boulez.

Although the vocal crisis has been largely surmounted, a Jones night in the theater is never predictable, ranging from squally, unpleasant singing to thrilling theater. Despite any vocal problems, she continued to be in constant demand and has now been in the international spotlight for a quarter of a century and has amassed an extremely diverse repertoire. Recent undertakings have included Poulenc's *La voix humaine* for the Théâtre du Chatelet and a series of Turandots in various venues. For counsel in performing this role she went to Dame Eva Turner, an illustrious Turandot of the past. There is no doubt that a Turandot must have power and volume; the secret to those things seemed to be what Jones was most interested in garnering from Turner. As Jones explains: "It was like getting it from the horse's mouth, and she gave me a wonderful *attacca*, having the voice in front of the mask, the necessary cutting edge, so it comes out like knives." One has to speculate that perhaps an interest in volume has not helped any vocal problems Jones had developed; that she purposely chose volume over steadiness.

Yet, as with Rysanek, she is a mesmerizing, supreme singing-actress and one for whom the opera world should be most grateful. She explains that the emotion in performing a role "comes from the inside and from the face and the eyes, which are the most important thing about your interpretation. With your eyes you can transmit thoughts to the public." From the evidence of her stage performances and the several opera films she has participated in—*The Ring, Tannhäuser, Der*

Rosenkavalier—Jones' contribution to opera over a quarter of a century has been a very special one, greatly contributing to the exultation and magic of the genre.

—Stephen A. Willier

LE JONGLEUR DE NOTRE DAME [The Juggler of Our Lady].

Composer: Jules Massenet.

Librettist: Maurice Léna (after Anatole France).

First Performance: Monte Carlo, 18 February 1902.

Roles: Jean (tenor or soprano); Boniface (baritone); Prior (bass); Poet (tenor); Painter (baritone); Musician (baritone); Sculptor (bass); Two Angels (soprano, mezzo-soprano); The Virgin (mute); chorus (SATBB).

*   *   *

Based on the medieval legend, Anatole France's short story *Le jongleur* features the humble juggler Jean, who is taken in and given shelter in a welcoming monastery. Unlike the

Poster for the premiere of Massenet's *Le jongleur de Notre-Dame*, Monte Carlo, 1902

Jean conceives his great idea of worshiping the Virgin with his own modest skills.

Simplicity is the tone of *Le jongleur*—a simplicity which is only achieved, however, through cunning art. The motto of the work is a chorale theme which emerges triumphantly in the prior's words "Heureux les simples car ils verront Dieu" ("Happy are the pure in heart for they shall see God") when Mary descends from the altar to bless Jean. Another element is the "Légende de la sauge" which appears again, passing through some enchanting modulations, in the "Pastorale mystique" linking acts II and III.

Le jongleur glows with the rosy light of stained glass windows. Its characters are like those primitive figures depicted in glistening colors on the pages of illuminated manuscripts. In creating the atmosphere he wanted, Massenet used his material shrewdly. The monks' "Ave coeleste lilium" at the beginning of act III, in the chapel where Jean is about to pay tribute after his fashion to Mary, comes from a sequence formerly sung at Assumption. Jean's impious "Alleluia du vin" in act I was written after close study of the *chansons farcies,* which used to be a speciality of the old minstrels. All these strands are woven together with skilful judgment and blended into a satisfying unity with the rest of the work. The changing moods of the action are imperceptibly fused into a seamless whole, and in few of his other operas did Massenet achieve such a perfect balance.

—James Harding

JONNY SPIELT AUF [Jonny Strikes up the Band].

Composer: Ernst Krenek.

Librettist: Ernst Krenek.

First Performance: Leipzig, 10 February 1927.

Roles: Max (tenor); Anita (soprano); Jonny (baritone); Daniello (baritone); Yvonne (soprano); The Manager (bass); The Hotel Director (tenor); three Policemen (tenor, baritone, bass); several mute roles; chorus.

Publications

article–

Sams, Jeremy. "*Jonny*—The First Jazz Opera." *Opera* October (1984).

*　　　*　　　*

learned and talented monks, Jean can only express his adoration of the Virgin Mary through his juggling, and, each evening, he performs his tricks before the chapel altar. One night the prior is scandalized to see him doing this and is about to stop the "sacrilege" when the Virgin Mary herself appears and gently wipes the sweat from his brow. Jean dies, haloed with glory.

Written by a composer best known for his seductive heroines, *Le jongleur* is unusual in that it has no role for a woman—except, that is, for the brief and silent appearance of the Virgin Mary, who was, as Massenet slyly remarked, the sublimest of all women. The libretto is pleasantly archaic, and the score achieves a happy balance of interest. The impression, as Fauré observed, is one of uniformity throughout. Massenet moves with smoothness from the boisterous couplets of Jean's "Le vin, c'est Dieu le Père" ("Wine, 'tis God Almighty") to the serenity of Friar Boniface's "Pour la Vierge d'abord" ("For the Virgin first of all"), and there is no incongruity in the quick transition from the hearty teasing of the monks to the gentleness of the "Légende de la sauge" ("Legend of the Sage") which tells the story of how the common sage gave the hospitality of its calyx to the infant Jesus.

The set piece which provides the focal point of act II begins with a music lesson given by the musician monk, which is followed by a good-humored contest between the other monks as they vaunt their individual skills as sculptor, painter, and poet. Friar Boniface has the last word when he hymns the Virgin Mary in an aria which links gastronomy with mysticism in the most tactful way. It is at this point that

Ernst Krenek was not yet twenty-seven years old when the Leipzig Neues Theater produced *Jonny spielt auf.* Although he had already composed two operas to some critical acclaim, *Jonny spielt auf* met with an unexpected success that brought Krenek fame and financial security and secured the reputation of the Leipzig Opera as a center for operatic experimentation. In its first season, *Jonny* was staged in Hamburg and Prague, and in the following season (1927-28) it was the most performed work of the year, receiving well over 400 performances at forty-five houses throughout eastern and western Europe. It was never, however, produced in England. The New York Metropolitan Opera staged the work in January 1929 at the urging of American composer John Alden

Jonny spielt auf, title page of score, Vienna, 1900

Carpenter. In recent years it has been successfully revived in Europe.

Much of the opera's success came from its unabashed celebration of modern post-war culture, which led critics who supported avant-garde experimentation to hail it as the first *Zeitoper* or "topical opera." The opera's title translates as "Jonny strikes up [the band]," and the title hero is an African American jazz band leader and violinist. Jonny's race and his characterization as the hero and artistic role model elicited public outcry and earned Krenek negative, even vitriolic, reviews in the growing fascist musical press. Performances in Budapest and Munich were marked by disturbances bordering on riots. The Metropolitan chose to cast Jonny as a buffoonish blackface performer rather than risk the controversy of a mixed-race cast.

The two-act work on Krenek's own libretto opens with Max, a composer of "serious" music and a parody of Schoenberg and his student Webern, alone in the alps. He is found by Anita, an opera singer; they fall in love and move in together. Anita goes to Paris for a performance and in her hotel, where Jonny's band is employed, she meets Daniello, a concert violinist. Daniello seduces Anita, and while he is thus engaged, Jonny steals his priceless violin. The following morning Anita decides to return to Max, leaving Daniello seeking revenge both for this rejection and his stolen violin. Max learns of Anita's affair and returns to the isolation of his mountains; a radio broadcast of Anita singing one of his arias, however, sends him back to her. The same radio, broadcasting Jonny's band featuring his violin solo, sends Daniello after Jonny. All is resolved in a train station where Max hopes to be reunited with Anita, who is about to depart for a tour of the United States, and where Daniello plans to retrieve his violin. Daniello falsely accuses Max of the theft and is pushed in front of the on-coming train by Anita's maid Yvonne, who has attempted to reason with him. Jonny knocks out the police officer waiting to drive Max to jail and returns Max, who has had a change of heart about his relation to both Anita and his art, to the station, and the entire company honors Jonny and his "new world" of music as he plays his jazz violin atop the railroad clock.

Krenek's choice of settings, properties, and staging added greatly to the work's topical *Zeitgeist.* Krenek contrasted Max's alpine world with scenes set in chic modern apartments, a hotel lobby and terrace, a police car, and the final scene in the railroad station. Properties include giant loudspeakers, an on-coming express train and large station clock, which for Jonny's apotheosis was transformed into a spinning record. Krenek specified that the last four scenes, from Max's arrival at the train station to Jonny's triumph, were to move in quick succession in the manner of film, and the Leipzig production used rudimentary animation to give the allusion of the moving police car. The reliance on modern technology for his unusual and demanding staging both added to the work's popularity and suggest Krenek's awareness of current theatrical experiments, particularly the documentary techniques of Erwin Piscator.

Musically, the work demonstrates Krenek's shift from his earlier highly chromatic idiom to an awareness of the possibilities of American popular music, which had been embraced by young German composers following the war as part of a greater infatuation with American culture. Highly dissonant sections contrast with those designated as "shimmy," "blues," "jazz," or "tango," incorporating characteristic dance rhythms and blues harmonies of the flat third and seventh. Krenek's use of a tango for the seduction scene between Daniello and Anita is particularly skillful. Krenek also created music for Jonny that evoked his ethnic heritage through imitation of the African American spiritual. The orchestration included saxophones, banjo, and drums with wire brushes [*Jazzbesen*], all associated with popular dance music; his use of the violin as a solo jazz instrument, as with the misspelling of Jonny's name, betrays Krenek's lack of much experience with an authentic American musical product. Several of the opera's numbers, in particular Jonny's "blues" solo "Leb wohl, mein Schatz," became quite popular and were released on commercial recordings.

Historians have represented *Jonny spielt auf* as either an example of faddishness or the misguided and naive work of a young composer. The opera, however, was the result of a sincere belief on Krenek's part, articulated as well in his essays from the time, that modern music should be redefined to meet the needs of its audience. The dichotomy between the fun-loving Jonny, producer of functional music, and the isolated composer of atonal music, Max, demonstrated this aesthetic stance, and it was taken seriously by many critics in its own time and by those composers who followed Krenek's lead. Today the opera remains as an important reflection of aesthetic concerns and issues of the short-lived artistic experimentation of the Weimar Republic.

—Susan C. Cook

JONNY STRIKES UP THE BAND
See JONNY SPIELT AUF

———————

JOPLIN, Scott.

Composer. Born 24 November 1868, in Texarkana, Texas. Died 1 April 1917, in New York. Learned piano at home as a child, and studied classical music with Julius Weiss, a local German musician; played piano for a living in St. Louis, 1885; at the Columbian Exhibition and World's Fair, Chicago, 1893; studied music at George Smith College in Sedalia, Missouri, 1894; enormous success with *Maple Leaf Rag,* published 1899; settled in St. Louis, where he taught piano and music theory, and composed many of his piano rags; in New York, 1907, where he worked on his grand opera, *Treemonisha;* awarded exceptional posthumous recognition by the Pulitzer Prize Committee, 1976.

Operas

Edition: *The Collected Works of Scott Joplin.* Edited by V.B. Lawrence. New York, 1971; revised 2nd ed. as *The Complete Works of Scott Joplin.* New York, 1981.

A Guest of Honor, Joplin, St Louis, 1903 [lost].
Treemonisha, Joplin, 1908-11, New York, 1915.

Publications/Writings

About JOPLIN: books–

Blesh, R. and H. Janis. *They All Played Ragtime.* New York, 1950; revised 4th ed., 1971.
Gammond, Peter. *Scott Joplin and the Ragtime Era.* London, 1975.
Haskins, James and Katheen Benson. *Scott Joplin.* Garden City, New York, 1978.
Berlin, E.A. *Ragtime; a Musical and Cultural History.* Berkeley, 1980; reprint 1984 with addenda.
Dasilva, Fabio, Anthony Blasi, and David Dees. *The Sociology of Music.* Notre Dame, Indiana, 1984.

articles–

Fuld, James J. "The Few Known Autographs of Scott Joplin." *American Music* 1 (1983): 41.
Reed, A.W. "Scott Joplin: Pioneer." In *Ragtime: its History, Composers, and Music,* edited by J.E. Hasse, 117. New York, 1985.

unpublished–

Reed, A.W. "The Life and Works of Scott Joplin." Ph.D. dissertation, University of North Carolina, 1973.

*   *   *

Scott Joplin was given the title "King of Ragtime Writers" in 1899 after the publication of his most famous ragtime composition, the *Maple Leaf Rag.* This composition was published by John Stark, and its publication promoted a relationship between composer and publisher in the late nineteenth century which was to last to the end of the first decade of the twentieth century. Throughout this association, John Stark, in diaries and other writings, continued to espouse the uniqueness of classic ragtime and its contributions to American musical culture. All of this was at the beginning of the century. It took approximately sixty to seventy years for scholars and performers to recognize ragtime, created and produced by blacks, as a formidable art form.

To aid in ragtime's legitimacy, in the late 1960's Vera Brodsky Lawrence, with the support of various ragtime enthusiasts, began a search for the compositions written by Scott Joplin. Ultimately their endeavors produced *The Collected Works of Scott Joplin* in 1971, and in 1981 the *Complete Works* were published by such a noteworthy establishment as the New York Public Library. Later in 1974, ragtime gained even more eminence with the production of the movie, *The Sting,* with such notable actors as Robert Redford and Paul Newman. The score for the movie consisted exclusively of the compositions of Scott Joplin. The *Entertainer,* which was the theme of the movie, became so popular that it climbed to number one on the popularity charts. In the midst of all this popularity, another Joplin piece was given its premiere in Atlanta, Georgia in 1972. This was Joplin's final effort at extended composition, *Treemonisha,* a folk opera. Although Joplin was never to see a successful performance, the opera was later performed at Wolf Trap in Washington, D.C., in Houston, Texas by the Houston Grand Opera company, and on Broadway at the Uris Theater. In its final form, the opera was recorded by the Deutsche Grammophon recording company.

Despite these accomplishments, the ultimate goal of Scott Joplin, at least during his lifetime, was never realized. For Joplin, his creations were in the category of the "Mazurkas" by Chopin, the "Moments Musicale" by Schubert, or the "Bagatelles" by Beethoven. The rags, two steps, marches, and waltzes were concert music to Joplin, although ragtime's origin was in the red light districts and brothels. Much of this seriousness of purpose may be ascertained from Joplin's efforts through the years to compose extended works. In 1902 he composed a ballet entitled *The Rag Time Dance* for which he provided the choreography, and around the same period he wrote his first opera, *A Guest of Honor.* The latter work is known to have toured extensively throughout the midwest during the first decade of the twentieth century. Almost immediately after completing *A Guest of Honor* Joplin began work on what may be considered his magnum opus: *Treemonisha.* Again his seriousness of purpose was promoted in the plot of the opera: education would be the salvation of the Negro race.

Scott Joplin's early life was beset by the usual difficulties encountered during the period following the demise of slavery, the emancipation proclamation, and the advent of reconstructionism. But, despite the single parent household in which he was reared, education was constantly impressed upon the six children to the extent that all achieved some degree of success during their lifetimes. Of course Scott Joplin was the most notable in that he achieved success during his lifetime and is now considered to be one of the premiere composers of a form that scholars have pronounced as the first art music of the United States.

As an itinerant performer in the late nineteenth century, Scott Joplin traveled throughout the midwest, to New York state, and to various towns in Texas. Basically he learned his art as most jazz pianists have done over the years. They listen, and then they imitate until finally they have developed their own style. This was basically Joplin's approach in his early travels until he met Otis Saunders at the Chicago World's Fair in 1893. It was through Saunders's influence, among others, that Joplin returned to Sedalia, Missouri around 1894, and entered one of the first schools established above the Mason Dixon line for Negroes, the George R. Smith College. Here Joplin was able to obtain the basic knowledge necessary for the notation of musical ideas that had been in his mind over the years.

Joplin's first efforts at composition and publication are indicative of late nineteenth century taste. Marches, waltzes, and minstrel type songs were the vogue of the day. Examples of these forms are found in the early efforts of Scott Joplin, which include two marches and a waltz published in 1896 and two songs published in 1895. They are typical of the times and do not, in any way, reflect what was to come in just a few years.

In general, the surviving work of Scott Joplin, although fairly modest in size, speaks of an era long since forgotten by many, yet very much in the present for some. The works are composed in a form which was the most popular means of entertainment as the twentieth century began. To some the works are a blight on America's past, for they signify an era which was decadent and replete with illicit activities. Then for some the works bespeak a tradition or an institution which is probably best forgotten, or is at least considered to be one of the world's many instances of man's inhumanity to man.

Joplin's primary creative activity throughout his career was the composition of rags. Even though the compositions are termed ragtime and contain those formal and stylistic elements which characterize rag, the titles and the content indicate a viable form of pianistic endeavor. Besides the two operas, Joplin composed ten songs, two of which are arrangements of previously published rags. He also wrote seven rags in collaboration with other composers. In addition he wrote an exercise booklet entitled "School of Ragtime," "Sensation Rag" by Joseph F. Lamb, arranged by S. Joplin, and "Silver Swan Rag," attributed to Joplin. It is interesting to note that most of the covers for the rags, marches, and waltzes contain advertisements indicating that the compositions are available for other combinations of instruments.

An evaluation of Joplin's works must take into consideration compositional progress; however, progress or development in composition is usually judged on the existence of dated manuscripts. No original manuscripts by Joplin have been found or seem to be in existence. Nevertheless ragtime scholars either place Joplin's rags in particular style periods or argue over what transpired in Joplin's compositional process toward the last years of his life. Progression in Joplin's rag style may be ascertained relative to the periodic changes which occur in his horizontal and vertical structures, but the progression is not stable or clear, and to place one or two compositions as dividing lines is altogether misleading. Folk-like melodies are in early and late compositions. Chromaticism and the use of minor tonalities so very plentiful in his later rags and in his last opera can also be found in his early works preceeding the "Maple Leaf Rag," but it is true that a greater amount of chromaticism occurs in Joplin's later rags. Another factor, ragtime's defining factor, that of syncopation, indicates his preoccupation with rhythmic subtleties especially in the rags of 1907 through 1909. The rags of this period continue the characteristic tonal relations, dispense in unique ways the oompah bass, experiment with minor tonalities, explore chromaticism, and use shifting textures within a chorus and between choruses. It was as if Joplin was experimenting with various facets of the smaller form to enhance

the extended works, thereby bringing the elements of ragtime to respectability.

—Addison W. Reed

JOSEPH.

Composer: Etienne-Nicolas Méhul.

Librettist: A. Duval.

First Performance: Paris, Opéra-Comique, 17 February 1807.

Roles: Jacob (bass); Joseph (tenor); Siméon (tenor); Benjamin (soprano); Ruben (tenor); Naphtali (baritone); Utobal (baritone); chorus.

Publications

article–

Weckerlin, J.-B. "Les quatre versions de la romance de Joseph, opéra de Méhul." *Revue et gazette musicale de Paris* 42 (1875): 252.

Joseph, the most famous of Méhul's operas, came about as the consequence of a wager made at a dinner. The dinner guests were discussing a recent tragedy, the *Omasis ou Joseph en Egypte* of one Baour-Lormian. It seems that Baour-Lormian had introduced a love-interest and elements of sorcery into the familiar Biblical tale. Alexandre Duval, a librettist in attendance at the dinner, argued that introducing the love interest spoiled the clear outlines of the Biblical story, obscuring the parable of filial piety. Méhul maintained that the story of Joseph was too simple a story to furnish the basis for an opera, claiming that some further episode had to be introduced for the story to form such a basis. Duval persisted in his views until he was challenged by the assemblage to produce a libretto that would support his claims. He agreed to write the libretto within two weeks, and Méhul found himself with a new libretto to set.

The first performance of the Méhul-Duval *Joseph* was sold out and the work was a great success, but the libretto was severely criticized nonetheless. In any case, *Joseph* exerted an influence on many of the most important operatic composers of the nineteenth century, and it remained in the repertory in both France and Germany throughout the nineteenth century. Charles Rosen has well summarized the position of *Joseph* in operatic history, writing that "Méhul's music for *Joseph* lacks the vigor and passion of his earlier work, such as *Ariodant,* but *Joseph* suited both the sober neoclassical aesthetic of the Empire and the religious revival of the early nineteenth century. It remained an influential example of classical taste in France and Germany throughout the nineteenth century, and was much admired by Weber, Cherubini, and—with reservations—Berlioz."

Naturally enough, the libretto of *Joseph* remained faithful to the Biblical account, given the history of its genesis. Joseph was the favorite son of the Israelite, Jacob. Their jealousy thus having been excited, Joseph's brothers sold him into slavery. Eventually, Joseph was bought by an Egyptian to whom he brought great prosperity, but when Joseph rejected the advances of his Master's wife, he was thrown into prison. There Joseph interpreted the dreams of the Chief Butler and the Chief Baker with such accuracy that rumors of his skill in interpreting dreams began to spread. Finally, the Pharaoh himself summoned Joseph in order that Joseph might interpret his dreams. Pharaoh told Joseph of a dream in which seven fat cattle had been eaten by seven lean cattle. Joseph advised Pharaoh to lay in stores for the seven lean years that—as Joseph predicted—would follow seven good years, whereupon Pharaoh made Joseph his governor.

The seven lean years are upon them when the opera opens, and Joseph's brothers have come to Egypt during the famine to seek aid from Cléophas, the name Joseph has been given by the Egyptians. One of Joseph's brothers, Siméon, believes that the famine is a punishment from God for the sale of Joseph into slavery. Joseph/Cléophas, whom the brothers no longer recognize, grants the Hebrews refuge in Egypt, even as conflicting feelings of anger and affection well up inside him. At dawn the next day, the Hebrews are rendering thanks to the God of Abraham for the beneficence of Cléophas when Joseph/Cléophas comes to their encampment in disguise. The remorseful Siméon confesses his crime to the disguised Joseph, and Benjamin, who has supplanted Joseph as Jacob's favorite, tells the stranger that Jacob has gone blind. Joseph leaves before Jacob awakens to tell Siméon, Benjamin, and Joseph's other brothers that he has seen Joseph in a dream. When an emissary from Joseph/Cléophas comes to announce that Cléophas wishes to acclaim the family in public, the two brothers realize that the stranger who had visited them was none other than Cléophas. Realizing that he has confessed his crime to the governor of the Pharaoh of Egypt, Siméon flees. During the celebration that unfolds in the Pharaoh's palace, Siméon, who has been captured, is dragged in. Siméon confesses his crime to his father, and Jacob curses all of his sons except the young Benjamin. Cléophas attempts to appease the enraged old man before unveiling his true identity, but Jacob will only forgive his other sons when Cléophas reveals himself to be Joseph. There is a general reconciliation and rejoicing when the Hebrews are invited to settle in Egypt.

Joseph was remote in subject matter from Méhul's other operas, and there is no subplot within the opera, while the only role for a woman is the "trousers" role of Benjamin. In all other respects, *Joseph* fits in with the rest of Méhul's operatic output. The operas that Méhul wrote after the pinnacle of Revolutionary opera represented by *Ariodant* were more conservative and less experimental in nature, efforts of consolidation rather than vehicles of exploration, and the deliberately modest *Joseph* is no exception: *Joseph* is a less ambitious and less accomplished work than the greatest *opéras comiques* of the 1790s. Nevertheless, Méhul staunchly maintained an independence of style in the face of the growing appreciation for Mozart and Italian opera in France after 1800, although Méhul admired Mozart more than any other composer, and *Joseph* largely maintained the style that Méhul had developed in the earlier period. In *Joseph*, we find the same range of forms and devices as in his other *opéras comiques*. Méhul's formal range can be gauged from the first two numbers for Joseph within the opera, the celebrated *Air*, "Champs paternels! [Fields of my fatherland]" and Joseph's *Romance*, "A peine au sortir de l'enfance [Barely grown up from childhood]." The latter is the simplest of strophic songs, touching in its deliberately naive simplicity, as befits its pastoral character, and there is not even a modulation from the original key of C major. "Champs paternels," on the other hand, is an elaborate two-part form prefaced with a turbulent accompanied recitative. The slow first section of the *Air* proper is in regular periods and modulates to the key of the dominant. The second section in quick tempo returns to the opening tonic key but has a design that is *sui generis* and touches on remote tonalities.

Weber, who was surprisingly beholden to the French master in his development of a new German Romantic opera, was a fervent admirer of Méhul's operas, and he remains one of the most astute critics of *Joseph*. More than anything else, it was Méhul's handling of the orchestra within his operas that struck Weber, who admired *Joseph* above all for the "ingenuous clarity" of its instrumentation. In *Joseph*, we find little of the elaborate contrapuntal displays and detailed motivic development so characteristic of the operas of the 1790s, but Weber appreciated the extent to which this was a conscious refusal in the service of a deliberately simple and even austere religious manner on Méhul's part. Weber admired "the patriarchal color and life allied with the pure candor of an ingenuous religiosity" that he discovered in the work. In any case, it was the distillation of Méhul's style that we find in *Joseph* that kept Méhul's influence alive down to the twentieth century. More than any other work, *Joseph* spread Méhul's influence throughout the operatic capitals of Europe, and echoes of its style can be found in Rossini's *Guillaume Tell*, in Wagner's operas, and above all in that direct descendant of *Joseph*, Berlioz's *L'Enfance du Christe*. Berlioz's oratorio exhibits a number of parallels to *Joseph*, down to the specific characters of various numbers within the two works and the purportedly "antique" style that the two works share.

—David Gable

JOURNET, Marcel.

Bass. Born 25 July 1867, in Grasse. Died 5 September 1933, in Vittel. Studied with Obin and Seghettini at Paris Conservatory; debut as Balthaser in *La favorite*, 1891; in Brussels, 1894-1900; Covent Garden debut as Duke of Mendoza in d'Erlanger's *Inez Mendo*, 1897; Metropolitan Opera debut as Ramfis, 1900, and remained until 1908; appeared at Paris Opéra, 1908-32; at Monte Carlo, 1912-20; at Buenos Aires, 1916-18, 1923, 1927; at Teatro alla Scala, 1917-27; created Simon Mago in Boito's *Nerone*.

Publications

About JOURNET: articles—

Celletti, R. "Marcel Journet." *Le grandi voci*. Rome, 1964.

In the ranks of French basses known to us through recordings, Marcel Journet stands second only to Pol Plançon. Although he was an extremely fine singer, he seemed, as Michael Scott points out in *The Record of Singing*, doomed throughout his career to come second to somebody. At the start it was Edouard de Reszke, later Chaliapin, and then back in France he found the mercurial Vanni-Marcoux, a singing-actor of infinite resource. His career was highly successful by any standards, but quite possibly some of the greatest personal triumphs came to him in its last phase, when he was an honored guest at the Teatro alla Scala. He net a young and aspiring bass there, one Ezio Pinza, who later remembered the impression the veteran Journet had made upon him. In his autobiography Pinza recalled the older singer "covered with glory," one of those rare artists who never stopped growing. More specifically, he wrote: "I have never heard anyone go from high notes to low ones with the ease and sonority of the middle-aged Journet."

This we also hear on records. Journet made a large number over a period of some thirty years, the earliest having him barely audible among the clatter and hiss of the Mapleson cylinders made during performances at the Metropolitan in 1903; the last was a complete recording of *Faust* made in 1932. In his prime the voice was absolutely solid: there is a marvellous early recording of Hagen's Watch in *Götterdämmerung,* an unexpected selection but sounding the very embodiment of ruthless, brooding determination; a voice as 'black' as any of the German specialists in the role, but with an even, finely produced resonance such as few of those possessed. In the later years of his career the depth diminished and the solidity dissolved somewhat. He still presented a mightily sonorous, authoritative Mephistopheles, but the timbre had become more baritone-like and less firm.

The English critics noted a deterioration on his return to Covent Garden, after long absence, in 1928. He sang Escamillo (normally a baritone role) and, said *Musical Opinion,* "in aiming at the target of correct pitch, he scored more 'inners' and 'outers' than 'bulls'. " Some years earlier, in 1921, the Paris correspondent of *Musical Times* had remarked that since Covent Garden days Journet's voice "has taken an upward tendency" and that he was now to be heard singing Tonio in *I pagliacci.* He also sang Hans Sachs in this period, and there is a record (in French) of the 'Wahn' Monologue, again with much to admire though the firmness of former days has passed away.

In Journet's early recordings, particularly in the 1910s, he is one of the finest of singers. In the courtly French tradition he is less fastidious than Plançon but still immensely accomplished: the air from Adam's *Le chalet* is a fine example. In Italian opera (such as *Ernani* and *Don Carlos*) he cultivates a full-bodied, even resonance and adds a little French grace. In 'character' parts (Mefistofele, Leporello, Marcel in *Les huguenots*) he may not be subtle but has the know-how of the seasoned practitioner. In simple melodies, such as the lullabies in *Mignon* and *Louise,* he can be touchingly gentle. One also gets the measure of his power and sonority in the duets and ensembles he recorded, many of them with Caruso.

—J.B. Steane

THE JOYFUL GIRL
See LA GIOCONDA

THE JUGGLER OF OUR LADY
See LA JONGLEUR DE NOTRE DAME

LA JUIVE [The Jewess].

Composer: Jacques-François-Fromental-Elie Halévy.

Librettist: Eugène Scribe.

First Performance: Paris, Opéra, 23 February 1835.

Roles: Princess Eudoxie (soprano); Rachel (soprano); Eléazar (tenor); Cardinal de Brogni (bass); Léopold (tenor); Ruggiero (baritone); Albert (bass); Herald (baritone); Officer (tenor); Majordomo (baritone); Executioner (baritone); chorus (SATTBB).

Publications

articles—

Avant-scène opéra July (1987) [*La Juive* issue].

*　　*　　*

The first and best-known of Halévy's six full-scale grand operas, *La Juive* premiered at the Rue Le Peletier (Opéra) 23 February 1835 and remained in the repertory through the turn of the century, receiving its 500th Parisian performance in 1886. Despite the composer's Jewish ancestry on both sides of his family, there is little evidence that he was inspired by any direct identification with the subject matter, although some critics have claimed to perceive an element of "authenticity" in the realization of the Passover scene in act II with its responsorial prayer, "O Dieu de nos pères." Produced one year before *Les Huguenots, La Juive* can be credited along with Meyerbeer's opera (both to texts by Scribe) with establishing the distinctive musical-theatrical idiom of French grand opera which, unlike Auber's *Muette de Portici,* was no longer strongly indebted to the style of Rossini.

As with many of Scribe's librettos, important events have taken place before the curtain rises which are either recalled or alluded to in the course of acts I and II. The goldsmith Eléazar was banished from Rome some twenty years ago by a decree of Count de Brogni, who was also responsible for the deaths of Eléazar's children under the Inquisition. Before leaving Rome Eléazar happened to rescue Brogni's infant daughter from a burning house. Fleeing north to Constance, Eléazar has raised the girl as his own, in the Hebrew faith and under the name of Rachel. Prince Léopold, heir to the throne of the Holy Roman Empire, has recently fallen in love with Rachel and continues to see her under the disguise of a Jewish artisan apprenticed to her father.

As the opera begins, a Te Deum is being sung in honor of Léopold's recent victory over the Hussites and of the ecclesiastical council about to convene in Constance. (The motif of the Hussite "heresy" and the ensuing, giddy chorus, "Hosanna, plaisir, ivresse, gloire à l'Eternel," are clearly meant to reinforce the larger theme of religious intolerance and the hypocrisy or ethical naïveté of the populace.) The sound of hammering from Eléazar's workshop on a day of sacred

The final scene from Halévy's *La Juive*, Royal Italian Opera, London, 1850

festivities arouses the ire of the people and city officials (Ruggiero). Eléazar and Rachel are saved from persecution by the intervention of Brogni, now a high-ranking Cardinal disposed to seek reconciliation with his former victim. At the end of the act, the pair is saved from another outburst of popular rage, this time by a sign from the incognito prince Léopold. During a Passover celebration (act II) Léopold accidentally betrays himself to Rachel, to whom he is forced to reveal his disguise, though not yet his true identity. He tries to convince Rachel to flee with him, but they are stopped by Eléazar. When Léopold further admits that he is betrothed to another (the princess Eudoxie), both Rachel and Eléazar are outraged. Following more celebrations in honor of Léopold (chorus, pantomime and ballet, act III), the princess Eudoxie is about to bestow a fabulous jeweled medallion upon her

fiancé when he is recognized by Rachel, who publicly denounces him. Brogni condemns Léopold and the two Jews. In act IV Eudoxie pleads with the imprisoned Rachel to recant her accusation and thus save Léopold. Meanwhile Eléazar, scorning Brogni's plea to save himself by converting, reveals his knowledge of the Cardinal's missing daughter. Afterwards, in the famous aria, "Rachel, quand du seigneur," he deliberates with himself whether he is justified in sacrificing the girl in order to be revenged upon Brogni and the rest of Christian society. As act V begins Eléazar and Rachel are led to the stake with grim pomp and ceremony. In response to Brogni's desperate entreaties, Eléazar reveals the identity of his lost daughter just as she is engulfed by the flames.

Like most French grand operas, *La Juive* contains an enormous amount of music, not all of it of equal quality. When the original full score was published by Schlesinger, several numbers were excised from the beginning of act III (an aria, a duet, and a strophic "Bolero" for Eudoxie) along with the extensive overture. Yet the essential "grandeur" of the idiom depends not only on the scenic splendor of the staging, but also on the expansive, occasionally repetitious musical idiom in which the eventful drama is given ample space to unfold— stately, lyrical, and impassioned, by turns. The tendency to make still further cuts to the score—whether as a measure of fiscal or of aesthetic economy—impairs the potential impact of the work, as it does others of this genre. Yet Halévy is able to maintain a fairly consistent level of quality and interest, even in the large choral tableaux. The chorus of townspeople at the beginning of act V, for instance, in which they express their grotesque elation in anticipation of the upcoming execution, contains some of the opera's most imaginative music in its use of spare textures, silences, and orchestral dissonance (contrasted with the deliberately trivial refrain, "Plus de travaux et plus d'ouvrage").

The unusual casting of the father figure as a tenor was due, in part, to the input of the role's creator, Adolphe Nourrit, who had originally been cast as the young prince Léopold. The bass role was consequently transferred from Eléazar to Cardinal de Brogni. It was also Nourrit's suggestion to end act IV with a solo scene for Eléazar, which came to be the opera's most celebrated excerpt ("Rachel, quand du seigneur"). The plangeant duo of English horns over pizzicato bass that introduces the aria, in addition to the faintly ethnic quality of the augmented seconds in the melody, may have influenced one of the opera's greatest champions, Gustav Mahler (Mahler conducted the opera, among other occasions, in Vienna in 1903 with Leo Slezak).

La Juive was also much admired by Richard Wagner, despite his pronounced antipathies toward the Jews, the French, and Parisian grand opera. In Wagner's opinion Halévy managed to break away from the conventional rhythms and vocal *fioritura* of composers like Rossini and Auber and to take a "truly poetic approach" to his material. Besides the greater breadth and continuity of Halévy's general musical conception, by comparison with earlier operas, Wagner was doubtless also impressed by the highly charged silences and sustained single notes following Léopold's confession to Rachel in act II, a passage which seems to be recalled in the meeting of Wagner's Senta and the Flying Dutchman, written at the end of his years in Paris.

Probably Halévy's most characteristic and influential achievement in this score, however, is the massive tableau of the act-III finale, gradually built up from the horrified reactions to the explosive accusation with which Rachel interrupts the splendid festivities ("Je frisonne et succombe"). If Halévy cannot match the contrapuntal intricacies of comparable ensembles in the works of Berlioz or Wagner, he nonetheless displays a fine sense for the musical opportunities of such forceful theatrical climaxes.

—Thomas S. Grey

JULIETTA, or The Key to Dreams.

Composer: Bohuslav Martinů.

Librettist: Bohuslav Martinů (after Georges Neveux, *Juliette ou la clé des songes*).

First Performance: Prague, National Theater, 16 March 1938.

Roles: Michel (tenor); Julietta (soprano); Old Arab (bass); many unnamed roles, covering all voice ranges.

The subtitle of Georges Neveux's play, *Juliette ou la clé des songes* ("The Key to Dreams"), may help us to understand what Martinů's opera, based on Neveux's play, is about. Martinů himself confessed that "to give the story of *Julietta* is almost impossible." It is an opera out of time, existing in an unending present, without past or future, where illusion becomes reality and vice versa.

Julietta is herself an illusion, an unrealizable ideal towards whom all aspire. She may be the focus of the opera, but she is not the central character; that is Michel, a commercial traveler who came long before to a nameless seaside town where, in the evening, as he was about to take the train home, he heard a girl singing from a window. In dreams he returns, seeking her, and finds himself in a familiar but baffling world where events take place inconsequentially and people converse in *non sequiturs*. In a world where everything is forgotten as soon as it happens, memory is valued above all and, like the one-eyed man in the country of the blind, he who can recall even so mundane a fact that as a child he had a toy duck is fit to be mayor. Michel is that man. Struggling to retain a hold on reality, he is acclaimed and decked out with meaningless symbols of a meaningless authority. He meets Julietta, who arranges to see him in a wood. There he encounters a fortune teller who predicts the past, and party-goers who do not know where they are going. A man tells pointless stories and a policeman turned postman delivers letters full of other people's memories. When the couple meets, Julietta pretends to remember but ridicules his talk of an earlier meeting. She leaves him. He draws his mayoral revolver and shoots at her: she cries out. Did he really shoot her? A gamekeeper claims to have fired at a snipe. A crowd gathers. They deny ever having seen Michel and threaten him with death. He asks the way to the railway station only to be told there is no railway. A man urges him to board a ship on which he is booked as a passenger. He sends sailors to look for Julietta; they return with only a veil. Michel boards the vessel and finds himself in a Bureau of Dreams where men are buying the dream of their choice. Michel is warned that he has had his dream and the office is closing. As the door shuts he hears the voice he heard so long ago. The door-keeper opens the door to reveal an empty room. Michel enters and finds himself back at the beginning. He is trapped in his land of dreams where every girl is called Julietta, the object of every desire, endlessly sought but never found.

Produced at the Théatre de l'Avenue in Paris in 1930, the play *Juliette ou la clé des songes* enjoyed a modest success. Georges Neveux was more poet than dramatist and it was the crystal clear, unemphatic language of his play that caused Martinů to seek permission to set it to music. The two men became friends, and Neveux generously gave Martinů carte blanche to adapt the work as freely as he chose. In the play Michel is uncertain whether to choose reality or dream; Martinů's revised ending won the author's approval and reinforced Neveux's fantasy by enclosing Michel totally in his dream life.

Martinů's involvement with fantasy can be traced back to the ballet *Istar* (1918-22), but recurred more powerfully in *Les larmes de couteau* (Tears of the Knife, 1928) and again in *Sister Pascaline,* the fourth of the "Plays of Mary" (1934). In the midst of composing this he wrote an orchestral work, *Inventions,* which anticipated both the emotional climate and the technical means that crystallize in *Julietta.* The nature of *Julietta* demanded an unorthodox approach, and Martinů deliberately dispensed with all the traditional appurtenances of opera: arias, ensembles, choruses, etc. The only "melody" is Julietta's song. Nor, despite the opera's theme of love and longing, are there any passionate scenes or languishing declamations such as one might find in, say, Delius or Richard Strauss. Using instead ordinary speech and an evolutionary form of speech-song skillfully and imaginatively combined with the large orchestra (including an off-stage accordion), Martinů created music of unexpected variety and intensity.

Julietta is the masterpiece of the mid-phase of Martinů's career, as *The Greek Passion* is of his final years. In 1939 he began a Czech translation of Neveux's French text with the idea of rephrasing the music to fit more easily the accents of his native tongue. He worked on this right up to the time of his death but never completed it. The Prague premiere on 16 March 1938 under Vaclav Talich was memorable, a triumph of coordination between music, acting, and design. "Whenever I think about it," Martinů wrote from Paris, "the whole play appears all at once before me in a single instant, like a single chord."

Julietta was not Martinů's only involvement with Neveux. In 1953 he began but did not complete *La plainte contre inconnu* ("Complaint Against an Unknown"), and in 1958 he wrote the one-act *Ariadne,* to an adaptation of Neveux's *Le voyage de Thésée.*

—Kenneth Dommett

JULIUS CAESAR IN EGYPT
See GIULIO CESARE IN EGITTO

DER JUNGE LORD [The Young Lord].

Composer: Hans Werner Henze.

Librettist: J. Bachmann (after W. Hauff).

First Performance: Berlin, Deutsche Oper, 7 April 1965.

Roles: Sir Edgar (mime); Secretary (baritone); Lord Barrat (tenor); Baroness von Greenweasel (mezzo-soprano); Luise (soprano); Ida (soprano); Wilhelm (tenor); Begonia (mezzo-soprano); The Burgomaster (bass-baritone); Chief Magistrate Harethrasher (baritone); Town Comptroller Sharp (baritone); Professor von Mucker (tenor); Frau von Hoofnail (mezzo-soprano); Frau Harethrasher (soprano); Parlormaid (soprano); Amintore la Rocca (tenor); Lamplighter (baritone); mimes and dancers; chorus (SATB).

Publications

article–

Miller, Norbert. "Gegorgte Tonfälle aus der Zeit. Ingeborg Bachmanns *Der junge Lord,* oder, Keine Schwierigkeiten

mit der komischen Oper." In *Für und Wider der Literaturoper,* edited by Sigrid Wiesmann, 87. Laaber, 1982.

* * *

Der Junge Lord is among Hans Werner Henze's most graceful, uncomplicated and immediately listenable works for the stage. It was initially conceived as an *opera buffa,* for which Henze developed a homogenous mixture of nineteenth-century operatic traditions, such as arias and ensembles, and popular music styles, such as waltzes and salon music, used to satirize the opera's provincial, middle-class characters.

The libretto portrays the small German town of Hulsdorf-Gotha and its excitement over its new, enigmatic resident, an English doctor named Sir Edgar. He insults even the wealthiest members of the community by failing to take them up on their social invitations, but welcomes various members of a traveling circus into his home. In the second act, the town is again aflutter over the arrival of Sir Edgar's nephew, Lord Barrat. At a grand party to introduce him to the community, the young lord displays eccentric manners that the rest of the townspeople attempt to imitate, until they realize he is simply an ape from the circus who has been trained to approximate human behavior.

The characters bear a clear resemblance to fashion-conscious people of our own time. Perhaps the satire would be satisfying if there was a sense of absolution in the ridiculous behavior of the townspeople. Instead, the curtain comes down as the true identity of the young lord is revealed, and we have no idea what if anything the townspeople have learned from their experience.

This resonant satire has parallels ranging from the ancient Israelites worshipping the gold calf to the modern fashion industry. But the baldness of the satire is offset by the charm and invention of Henze's music. It slips deftly between atonality and polytonality but has a lightness, transparency, richness of sounds, and general air of playfulness that occasionally suggest distant influences from Stravinsky's *L'Histoire du Soldat.*

Benjamin Britten once said that the key to being a first-rate opera composer is having the flexibility to write many different kinds of music, and Henze seems to revel in that. The libretto provides him with opportunities for a great variety of exotic musical characterization, from Sir Edgar's Creole maid Begonia to the music of the circus performers. Perhaps the most imaginative passages are in act II, with the eerie, otherworldly cries Henze wrote for the young lord as he is being forcibly taught German and social graces.

Henze also takes the opportunity to balance the satirical elements with some spare but lyrical love music (scored for voice and harp) in a romantic subplot that concerns the characters Wilhelm and Luise, who are operatic descendants of Fenton and Nanetta in Verdi's *Falstaff.* The opera's extended orchestral interludes, which often crystallize the action in the previous scene, would be welcome in concert.

—David Patrick Stearns

JURINAC, Sena [born Srebrenka Jurinac].

Soprano. Born 24 October, 1921, in Travnik, Yugoslavia. Married the baritone Sesto Bruscantini, 1953 (divorced 1957);

married Josef Lederle, 1965. Studied with Milka Kostrenčić in Zagreb; debut as Mimì, Zagreb, 1942; Vienna Staatsoper debut as Cherubino, 1945; Salzburg debut as Dorabella, 1947; Teatro alla Scala debut as Cherubino, 1948; at Glyndebourne as Dorabella, 1949; in Chicago as Desdemona, 1963.

Publications

About JURINAC: books–

Tamussino, U. *Sena Jurinac.* Augsburg, 1971.
Rasponi, L. *The Last Prima Donnas.* New York, 1982.

articles–

Earl of Harewood. "Sena Jurinac." *Opera* 1 (1950): 26.
Tamussino, U. "Sena Jurinac." *Opera* 17 (1966): 265.
Tubeuf, A. "Entretien avec Sena Jurinac." *Opera* September-October (1985).

*   *   *

Sena Jurinac first came to international prominence as one of several fine Mozart sopranos championed by Herbert von Karajan. Amid this very select and excellent company—including Elisabeth Schwarzkopf, Irmgard Seefried, Lisa Della Casa and Hilde Gueden—Jurinac's distinction is obvious, for she is also successful and idiomatic in the heavier Italian repertoire of Verdi and Puccini. It is surprisingly rare for a soprano to demonstrate equal skills in these very different arenas, and Jurinac achieves special status through exceptional resources. Hers was certainly one of the most beautiful voices of her time, combining a creamy tonal richness and perfect legato line that is intrinsic to all great Mozart voices with a power and size that sets her quite apart. The color too is unusual, darker than that of her silvery-toned colleagues, and yet shaded with great delicacy and femininity, so that as Butterfly, for example, she combined the necessary stamina and force with a marvelously girlish frailty that was unique and memorable.

Jurinac was also a naturally gifted actress with an affinity for an audience, the kind of charisma with which it seems a stage personality must be born. Seefried had it too, and shared with Jurinac a similar sense of fragility and charm. But where Seefried's persona seemed rooted in a childlike sense of joy, Jurinac was, by contrast, immediately identified with pathos and tragedy. Though she sang a number of comic roles with

considerable success—Fiordiligi in *Così fan tutte* is one good example among many—one always sensed the underlying sadness of the character. In parts which were themselves of a more serious and pensive nature—Butterfly and Tosca or Donna Anna and Ilia in *Idomeneo*—Jurinac could create a heartbreaking sense of theater; yet this vulnerability was never achieved at the expense of a shining, well-nourished tone.

There are many recorded examples of Jurinac in Mozart which support her fine reputation. She appears as Ilia in highlights of *Idomeneo* under Fritz Busch as well as in a complete performance with John Pritchard, and surely the role has never been better sung or more elegantly and movingly interpreted. As Fiordiligi the competition is stiffer (including her colleagues Schwarzkopf and Della Casa), here the voice per se is wonderfully rich, but with its size and thrust comes a certain awkwardness; she is not entirely up to the florid passages of the role. Better are her Donna Anna and Elvira and her Countess in *Le nozze di Figaro,* all of which display her gracious sense of style and show off the voice at its lustrous best.

Like many other fine Mozarteans, Jurinac was also highly regarded in the operas of Richard Strauss. She made something of a specialty of the roles of Octavian in *Der Rosenkavalier* and the Composer in *Ariadne auf Naxos,* as did Seefried. Comparing the two singers, particularly in the latter role, does not entirely flatter Jurinac, who is less impassioned and imaginative than her colleague, but on her own terms she is noble and involving. The generous, radiant tone is a constant source of pleasure. On records she is probably best heard in Strauss's *Vier letzte Lieder,* where the sultry tone makes us more than usually aware of the grandeur and scope of these songs, and her superbly steady line is especially welcome.

Regrettably, Jurinac committed few of her Italian roles to disc, perhaps because quite a few formidable Italianate sopranos—including Callas and Tebaldi—were also kept busy in the recording studios. Still, the loss is ours, as a broadcast performance of *Don Carlos* under Herbert von Karajan amply illustrates. Here Jurinac is the Elisabetta of one's dreams; no soprano before or since has launched the last act scene "Tu che le vanità" with such perfectly poised attack and incandescent tone. We may lament that there are not more such unforgettable souvenirs, but we may also rejoice in what we have—a significant legacy of a unique and thrilling artist.

—David Anthony Fox

K

KABALEVSKY, Dimitry Borisovich.

Composer. Born 30 December 1904, in St Petersburg. Studied at the Scriabin Music School, 1919-25; studied music theory privately with Gregory Catoire; studied composition with Miaskovsky and piano with Goldenweiser at the Moscow Conservatory, beginning 1925; instructor of composition at the Moscow Conservatory, 1932, and full professor, 1939; head of the Commission of Musical Esthetic Education of Children, 1962; president of the Scientific Council of Educational Esthetics in the Academy of Pedogical Sciences of the U.S.S.R., 1969; president of the International Society of Musical Education, 1972. Appearances in Europe and America as a pianist, composer, and conductor.

Operas

Publisher; Mezhkniga

Colas Breugnon, V. Gragin (after Romain Rolland, *Le maître de Clamécy*), 1936-38, Leningrad, 1938; revised, 1953, 1969.
Into the Fire [*V ogne*], Solodar, 1942.
The Taras Family [*Semya Tarasa*], S. Tsenin (after B. Gorbatov, *The Unconquerables*), 1947; revised, 1950, 1967.
Nikita Vershinin, S. Tsenin (after V. Ivanov), 1954-55, first performance 1955.
Spring Sings [*Vesna poët*] (operetta), 1957.
The Sisters [*Sestry*], S. Bogomazov (after I. Lavrov, *The Encounter with a Miracle*), 1967, Perm State Academic Opera and Ballet Theater, 1969.

Other works: orchestral works, works for voice and orchestra, chamber music, choral works, piano pieces.

Publications

By KABALEVSKY: books—

Izbrannye stat'i o muzyke [collected articles on music]. Moscow, 1963.
Dorogie moi druz'ya [address]. Moscow, 1977.
Vospitanie uma i serdtsa: kniga dlya uchitelya. Moscow, 1981.

articles—

"On Educating the Composer." *International Society for Musical Education* 4 (1977): 24.
"Round-Table Statement on the Education of the Professional Musician." *International Society for Musical Education* 4 (1977): 14.
"The Main Principles and Methods of an Experimental Music Program for the Schools of General Education." In *Muzykal'noe vospitanie,* compiled by Lev Barenboym. Moscow, 1978.
"The Piano Concerto of German Galynin," and "The Second String Quartet." In *German Galynin,* ed. Vladimir Tscndrovsky. Moscow, 1979.

"Grundprinzipien und Methoden des Lehrplans im Fach Musik der allgemeinbildenden Schule" [elementary school education]. In *Beiträge zur Musikkultur,* edited by Carl Dahlhaus and Givi Ordzonikidze, 51. Hamburg, Sikorski, Wilhelmshaven, 1982.
"Iz perepiski" [correspondence]. *Sovetskaya Muzyka* 12 (1984): 16.

About KABALEVSKY: books—

Abraham, Gerald, *Eight Soviet Composers,* 70 ff. London, 1943.
Grosheva, E. *Dimitry Kabalevsky.* Moscow, 1956.
Abramovsky, G.D. *Kabalevsky.* Moscow, 1960.
Nazarevsky, P., ed. *D.B. Kabalevsky: notografichesky i bibliografichesky spravochnik* [bibliography and list of works]. Moscow, 1969.
Krebs, S.D. *Soviet Composers and the Development of Soviet Music,* 233 ff. London and New York, 1970.
Bernandt, G.B. and I.M. *Yampol'sky: Kto pisal o muzïke,* vol. 2 [includes complete list of Kabalevsky's writings]. Moscow, 1974.
Pozhidaev, G.A. *D. Kabalevsky.* 4th ed. Moscow, 1987.

articles—

Danilevich, Lev. "Vremya, tvorchestvo, zhizn' . . ." [*Colas Breugnon*]. *Sovetskaya muzyka* no. 12 (1979): 3.
———. "Tema neiscerpaemaja, vecnaja" [*The Taras Family*]. *Sovetskaya muzyka* no. 5 (1980): 10.

* * *

Kabalevsky composed in all four operas and a lyric opera, which is virtually an operetta. Of these, however, only the first, *Colas Breugnon,* is at all known outside Russia and, even then, it is familiar mostly in the form of the overture and the colorful suite. This is a pity, for within the pages of at least three of his operatic works one finds many striking arias and splendid choral ensembles.

The opera *Colas Breugnon,* based on Romain Rolland's story *Le maître de Clamécy* (*The Master of Clamécy*), was completed in 1938 and was given with great success. Since this work is described in fuller detail elsewhere, suffice it to say here that it was essentially a product of the young composer, full of verve and *esprit.*

Although Kabalevsky's first opera is based on a French subject, his succeeding operatic works all utilize Russian subject matter. His second opera *V ogne* (*Into the Fire*) was written in 1942 to a libretto by Solodar. A topical work, dealing with the Red Army's defense of Russia against the German invasion, its main shortcoming is the poor libretto, and, after a few performances, the composer became dissatisfied, and the work was withdrawn. Some of the music, however, was transferred to his next and, in some ways, most successful opera *Semyu Turasa* (*The Taras Family*), written originally in 1947.

Like most of his operas, *The Taras Family* underwent several revisions, first as a result of the Party Decree of 1948, then again in 1950 and once more in 1967. The source of the opera is a story by B. Gorbatov entitled *The Unconquerables,* which was published in *Pravda* in 1942 and awarded a Stalin Prize. The story was adapted by S. Tsenin. Not only did the opera win a Stalin Prize when first given, but (most unusually) so did the two opera companies that performed it (the Kirov Theater in Leningrad and the Nemirovich-Danchenko Theater in Moscow). Like its predecessor, the theme is based on events in the Second World War. In Soviet history this is referred to as "The Great Patriotic War," and the themes of patriotism and self-sacrifice are very much to the fore. Somewhat like a modern Ivan Susanin, the action centers on the figure of old Taras, whose sons and daughters are underground resistance fighters. Even though his daughter, Nastya, is captured, tortured and eventually put to death by the Nazis, her spirit remains unbroken. Running through the whole opera is a quite complex system of motto themes— the motif of indomitability (which is connected with the themes of Taras and Nastya), the Nazis' theme, and others. Conceived in monumental terms, the work opens with a massive overture, which introduces a number of the key themes. The Russian folk idiom is present throughout, much use being made of powerful choruses, dramatic arias and orchestral interludes (a favorite Kabalevsky device). Among the high points are Taras's defiant aria at the end of act I, and the aria of Stepan (one of Taras's sons) in act II. The approach of the Nazis at the end of act II is most effective, as is also the orchestral intermezzo preceding the burning by the partisans of the school where the Nazis have made their headquarters. The scene in act IV where Nastya is interrogated is realistic and overpowering.

Following *The Taras Family,* Kabalevsky again turned to a political theme, this being the opera *Nikita Vershinin,* using a libretto by S. Tsenin after a story by V. Ivanov. Written in 1954-55, the opera draws its inspiration from the Civil War in the first years of the Revolution, being set in far-eastern Siberia. The hero, Nikita Vershinin, a dedicated Communist, finds himself in conflict with the anti-Soviet powers, which involves his whole family (including his daughter, Katya), a young Bolshevik named Peklevanov, and others. The action recalls Glinka's *A Life for the Tsar,* and like its nineteenth century prototype contains much choral writing and numbers in the folk spirit. On the whole the music is less effective than that of *Colas Breugnon* and *The Taras Family,* and the work has not retained a place in the Russian repertoire.

Kabalevsky's final opera *Sestry* (*The Sisters*) was written in 1967 to a libretto by S. Bogomazov. Based on a story by I. Lavrov entitled *The Encounter with a Miracle,* it received its premiere at the Perm State Academic Opera and Ballet Theater in 1969. A lyric opera, the action centers on the adventures of two sisters, Asya and Slava, who leave home in order to travel to the sea, but find themselves instead on a farm. The work is obviously written for performance by young people and is simple and melodic throughout. Consisting of three acts, it is framed by a chorus about the sea, which occurs in the prologue and epilogue, and which the composer instructs to be played through loudspeakers placed among the audience. Among the attractive numbers are Anatoly's song with guitar in act II and the effective sound painting in act I of the scene in Red Square.

Although Kabalevsky's operas may lack the strength and originality of those of Prokofiev and Shostakovich, they are by no means void of interest, and *Colas Breugnon* and *The Taras Family* certainly deserve to be more widely performed.

—Gerald Seaman

KAGEL, Mauricio.

Composer. Born 24 December 1931, in Buenos Aires. Studied with Juan Carlos Paz and Alfredo Schiuma in Buenos Aires; studied literature and philosophy at the University of Buenos Aires; associated with the Agrupación Nueva Música, 1949; choral director at the Teatro Colón, 1949-56; in Cologne on a stipend from the Academic Cultural Exchange with West Germany, 1957, and established permanent residence; guest lecturer at the International Festival Courses for New Music in Darmstadt, 1960-66; lectures and demonstrations of modern music in the United States, 1961, 1963; professor of composition at the State University of New York, Buffalo, 1965; guest lecturer at the Academy for Film and Television in Berlin, 1967; director of the Institute of New Music at the Musikschule in Cologne, 1969; professor at the Musikschule in Cologne, 1974–.

Operas/Dramatic Works [partial list]

Publishers: Universal, Peters.

Anagrama, 1955-58, Cologne, 11 June 1960.
Sur scène, 1958-60, Bremen, 6 May 1962.
Pas de cinq, 1965, Munich, 14 June 1966.
Staatstheater, 1967-70, Hamburg, 25 April 1971.
Die Erschöpfung der Welt, 1979, Stuttgart, 8 February 1980.
Aus Deutschland (lieder opera), 1981.

Other works: various experimental works.

Publications

By KAGEL: books–

Scmidt, F., ed. *Tantam: Dialoge und Monologe zur Musik.* Munich, 1975; French translation by Lucie Touzin-Bauer et al., Paris, 1983.

articles–

"Ton-Cluster, Anschläge, Übergänge." *Die Reihe* no. 5 (1959): 23; English translation in *Die Reihe* no. 5 (1961): 40.
"Translation-Rotation." *Die Reihe* no. 7 (1960): 31; English translation in *Die Reihe* no. 7 (1965): 32.
"Möte med en ny musikalisk tid: Kommentarer kring Transicion I och II." *Nutida musik* 4/no. 3 (1960-61): 5.
"Den instrumentala teatern." *Nutida musik* 5/no. 3 (1961-62) 1.
"Om ord och röst i Anagrama." *Nutida musik* 5/no. 3 (1961-62): 13.
"Komposition - Notation - Interpretation." *Darmstädter Beiträge zur neuen Musik,* 9 (1965): 55.
"Komposition + Decomposition," " Notation heute," "Analyse der analysirens." In *Collage* vol. 3. Palermo, 1964.
"Fünf Antworten auf fünf Fragen." *Melos* 33 (1966): 305.

"Über Form." *Darmstädter Beiträge zur neuen Musik* 10 (1966): 51.
"Musikalische Form." In *Collage,* vol. 7. Palermo, 1967.
"Om Tremens, Pandorasbox och Match." *Nutida musik* 11 (1967-68): 29.
"Sobre Match." *Sonda* (1968).
"Über Montage." In *Collage,* vol. 8. Palermo, 1968.
"A proposito de Ludwig van." *Spettatore musicale* no. 2 (1970).
"Der Umweg zur höheren Sub-Fidelität." *Interfunktionen* no. 4 [Cologne] (1970).

About KAGEL: books–

Prieberg, F.K. *Musica ex machina.* Berlin, 1960.
Schnebel, D. *Mauricio Kagel: Musik, Theater, Film.* Cologne, 1970.
Klüppelholz, Werner. *Mauricio Kagel 1970-1980.* Cologne, 1981.

articles–

Stockhausen, K. "Musik und Graphik." *Darmstädter Beiträge zur neuen Musik* 3 (1960): 5.
Carlson, S. "Mauricio Kagel: Anagrama." *Nutida musik* 4/ no. 3 (1960-61): 1.
Muggler, F. "Instrumentales Theater: 'Sur scène'." *Magnum* no. 47 (1963).
Schnebel, D. "Die Musik Mauricio Kagels." *Neue Musik* 9-10 (1964).
Jenny, U. "Über 'Pas de cinq'." In *Theater 1966.* Hanover, 1966.
Kesting, M. "Musikalisierung des Theaters -Theatralisierung der Musik." *Melos* 36 (1969): 101.
Oehlschlägel, R. "Mixed Media, Collage und Montage." *Opernwelt* 3 (1969): 38.
Nyffeler, M. "Gespräch mit Mauricio Kagel," "Zu Mauricio Kagels 'Unter Strom'." In *Dissonanz,* vol. 4. Zurich, 1970.
Krellman, H. "Mauricio Kagel." *Schweizerische Musikzeitung/ Revue musicale suisse* 111 (1971): 327.
Klüppelholz, Werner. "Kagels Musiktheater im Musikunterricht" [*Pas de cinq*]. *Musik and Bildung* 12 (1980): 218.
Stegemann, Michael. "Komponieren heute: 'Aus Deutschland' . . . ?! Ein Gespräch mit Mauricio Kagel." *Neue Zeitschrift für Musik* 144 (1983): 18.

*   *   *

Although he has not composed any operas in the traditional sense of the word, Mauricio Kagel has been preoccupied throughout his career both with the visual and theatrical aspects of concert music and with the development of what amounts to a new musical theater. As a composer, he is entirely self-taught. At the University of Buenos Aires, philosophy and literature were his chosen fields of study, although he also studied piano, organ, cello, music theory, and conducting privately. After completing his education, he worked for a time as a choral coach and conductor at the Teatro Colón. These varied experiences were the perfect crucible for Kagel's output, which poses "metamusical" and "metaphilosophical" questions in a manner at once witty and disturbing. The author of radio plays and a film director as well as a composer, Kagel has attempted to keep the boundaries between philosophical inquiry and various theatrical and musical media fluid.

Kagel is a difficult figure to pigeon-hole, and this is reflected in the eclectic influences that his work exhibits. He has been influenced by the expressionism of Arnold Schoenberg, Anton Webern, and Alban Berg on the one hand and by John Cage's acceptance and exploitation of chance on the other. Both the absurdist theater of Samuel Beckett and Eugène Ionesco and the German expressionist cinema have been preponderant influences on Kagel's theatrical conceptions, while in some ways, Kagel may be viewed as a latter-day dadaist or surrealist. Kagel's goal has never been the "masterwork," the closed self-contained whole characteristic of traditional Western conceptions of the artwork. Rather his output embodies a specific manner of criticism. Kagel's works are provocations, whether understated or outrageous, implicitly designed to induce or reveal unsettling insights.

While still in Argentina, Kagel wrote some precisely structured works—the *String Sextet* of 1953 subjects several independent rhythmic processes to strict compositional control— but he also began to experiment with more freely organized works. As the composer himself has indicated, he has tended toward strict composition with elements that are not themselves pure. The experimental side of Kagel really emerged after he emigrated to Cologne in 1957, and his works from the later 1950s began to have a pronounced theatrical aspect. For example, *Anagrama* (1955-58), which is based on systematic transformations of the sounds (at the expense of the sense) of a Latin palindrome, calls for whispering and screaming from the singers and for wild noises from the instrumentalists as well.

In the 1960s, visual and theatrical elements became central to Kagel's work, and the concept of "music" was stretched to the limit. In *Sur scène* (1958-60), a mime improvises gestures while musicians play on keyboard and percussion instruments, a speaker delivers a lecture, and a singer delivers nonverbal commentaries. Dieter Schnebel, a German composer closely associated with Kagel, has suggested that this work is intended as a commentary on the futility of musical communication. Later, Kagel specifically referred to many of his works as "theater pieces." One of these is *Pas de cinq* (1965), in which five carefully choreographed actors walk around the stage, the "musical" quotient of the work being provided by the sound qualities and patterns of the actors' footfalls. On the other hand, in Kagel's films and theater pieces, gesture and motion are often submitted to quasi-musical control. Kagel manipulates the editing, camera angles, and placement of actors to produce quasi-musical effects of rhythm, repetition, and contrast in his films and there is, as in life, an interpenetration of visual and aural experience.

Some of Kagel's works embody more specific critiques of aspects of our musical heritage. These include *Musik für Renaissanceinstrumente* (1965-66), heterophonic music for an "alienated" collection of historical instruments, *Variationen ohne Fugue* for orchestra (1971-72), which fragments the "Handel Variations" of Brahms, and Kagel's film, *Ludwig Van* (1969-70). The soundtrack of *Ludwig Van* utilizes fragments of Beethoven's music, which are also subjected to distortion by electronic means, while, embodying a critique of social aspects of Western musical culture, the visual aspect of the film humorously exploits such social aspects of Beethoven iconography as the "hero-worship" of "Beethoven the Creator."

—David Gable

KARAJAN, Herbert von.

Conductor. Born 5 April 1908, in Salzburg. Died 16 July 1989, in Anif, near Salzburg. Married: 1) Elmy Holgerloef, operetta singer, 1938 (divorced, 1942); 2) Anita Gütermann, 1942 (divorced, 1958); 3) Eliette Mouret, French fashion model, 1958. Studied piano with Franz Ledwinka and conducting with Bernhard Paumgartner at the Salzburg Mozarteum; studied at a technical college in Vienna, and studied piano with J. Hofmann; studied conducting with Clemens Krauss and Alexander Wunderer at the Vienna Academy of Music; conducted with the Salzburg Orchestra, 1929; conductor of the Ulm Stadttheater, 1929-34; became a registered member of the Nazi party, 1933; conductor of the Stadttheater in Aix and Generalmusikdirektor there, 1935-42; conducted with the Berlin Philharmonic, 9 April 1938; conducted at the Berlin Staatsoper, as well as at the Teatro alla Scala in Milan, 1938; conductor of the symphony concerts of the Berlin Staatsoper Orchestra, 1939; denazified by the Allied occupation after the war; conducted the Vienna Philharmonic, 1948-58; conductor of the Philharmonia Orchestra of London, 1948-54; succeeded Furtwängler as conductor of the Berlin Philharmonic, 1955, after the first United States tour of the orchestra; artistic director of the Vienna Staatsoper, 1956-64; artistic director of the Salzburg Festival, 1957-60; artistic adviser of the Orchestre de Paris, 1969-71; organized the Salzburg Easter Festival, 1967; named conductor for life of the Berlin Philharmonic, 1967; Metropolitan Opera debut with *Die Walküre,* 21 November 1967; celebrated thirty years as conductor of the Berlin Philharmonic, 1985, and retired from that post in 1989.

Publications

By KARAJAN: books—

with Franz Endler. *Mein Lebensbericht.* Vienna, 1988; English translation as *My Autobiography,* London, 1989.

interviews—

"The Karajan Interview" [with F. Karwin]. *Opera* May and June (1978).
Chesterman, R. *Conductors in Conversation.* London, 1990.

About KARAJAN: books—

Häusserman, E. *Herbert von Karajan Biographie.* Gütersloh, 1968; 2nd ed., 1978.
Spiel, C., ed. *Anekdoten um Herbert von Karajan.* Munich, 1968.
Robinson, P. *Karajan.* London and New York, 1976.
Fuhrich-Leisler, E., and G. Prossnitz, eds. *Herbert von Karajan in Salzburg* [exhibition catalogue]. Salzburg, 1978.
Lorcey, Jacques. *Herbert von Karajan.* Paris, 1978.
Bachmann, R. *Anmerkungen zu einer Karriere.* Düsseldorf, 1983.
Kröber, H. *Herbert von Karajan: Der Magier mit dem Taktstock.* Munich, 1986.
Vaughan, R. *Herbert von Karajan: a Biographical Portrait.* New York and London, 1986.
Götze, H., and W. Simon, eds. *Wo sprache aufhört . . . Herbert von Karajan zum 5. April 1988.* Berlin, 1988.
Osborne, R. *Conversations with Karajan.* Oxford, 1989.

articles—

Goldsmith, H. "Karajan's Early Years Reappraised." *Musical Times* May (1989).

*   *   *

Herbert von Karajan was one of the most talented as well as influential and controversial conductors of his generation. Though he won fame and preeminence in the years immediately following the Second World War as an orchestral conductor, he had learned his trade in the 1930s in the provincial opera houses of Ulm and Aix, and he was to remain, first and foremost, a theater-oriented musician. As such, he involved himself not only in conducting but also in stage production, and film and video work. In the late 1950s, during his seven-year period as head of the Vienna State Opera, he oversaw the building of Salzburg's Grosse Festspielhaus and in 1967 established his own Easter Festival in the new Salzburg theater. In effect, Karajan had acquired his own opera house, staffed and equipped as he wanted it, with loyal design teams, his own orchestra (the Berlin Philharmonic), changing groups of hand-picked singers, and regular sources of subsidy from lucrative recording and video contracts. It was the logical outcome of a patiently built career that one of his record producers Walter Legge likened to a "ruseful act of paramilitary planning."

As an interpreter, Karajan was considered by fellow-musicians to be at his finest in the operas of Wagner, later Verdi (though he was always a powerful exponent of *Il trovatore),* Puccini, Debussy, and Richard Strauss. His Mozart was more variable. He recorded an exquisitely stylish account of *Così fan tutte* in 1954 but declined to conduct the work in the theater. For the most part, the humor of *Le nozze di Figaro* eluded him (his own sense of humor took a more sardonic turn), though he did conduct successful performances and recordings of *Die Zauberflöte,* beginning in Berlin in 1938 with a celebrated production by Gustav Gründgens. No musical snob, Karajan also conducted a good deal of operetta. Early recordings included outstanding accounts of *Die Fledermaus* and Humperdinck's *Hänsel und Gretel,* and though works like Flotow's *Martha* and Lortzing's *Der Wildschütz* dropped from his repertory with his departure from Aix in 1942, as late as 1989 he was planning concert performances of Kálmán's *Gräfin Maritza.*

Karajan was a master of the orchestra and orchestral sonority, and was widely regarded as an incomparable accompanist, breathing with singers and anticipating their every gesture and inflection. As one singer put it, "he stuck to you like gum to a shoe." Throughout his long career, he established close artistic relationships with many great singers. When working with artists like Schwarzkopf, Callas, or Vickers, the results were rarely less than extraordinary. Appalled by the dramatic ineptitude of many second-rank singers in Germany and Italy in the 1930s and 40s, he came increasingly to favor young and dramatically credible artists. There were those who accused him in later years of prematurely exposing favored young artists to unduly heavy roles. In fact, Karajan's own work with them was usually sympathetically conceived and sensitively accomplished; that problems arose for singers when working on a role with Karajan was taken as a sign of more indiscriminate exploitation.

Karajan's career as stage director for productions he was conducting began in Aix in 1940 with *Die Meistersinger.* Though he was to work with Felsenstein (in Aix), Wieland Wagner (for the memorable 1952 Bayreuth *Tristan und*

Herbert von Karajan

Isolde), Zeffirelli (a legendary *La bohème* at the Teatro alla Scala in Milan, 1963), Ponnelle, Strehler, Hampe, and Schlesinger, his own production methods were thought to be both conservative and conventional at a time when the phenomenon of "producer's opera" was increasingly in the ascendant. For Karajan, the music came first, something that won the equivocal admiration of Zeffirelli when in 1954 Karajan directed Callas in *Lucia di Lammermoor* in Milan: "Karajan didn't even try to direct. He just arranged everything around her. She did the Mad Scene with a follow-spot like a ballerina against black. Nothing else. He let her be music, absolute music." Karajan did, however, have a highly developed visual sense. Characteristically loyal to a chosen and tested team, he worked from 1962 onwards more or less exclusively with stage-designer Günther Schneider-Siemssen and costume-designer Georges Wakhevitch, and with them helped to create nearly twenty scenically memorable productions, beginning in Vienna with *Pelléas et Mélisande* (costumes by Charlotte Flemming) and including, for the Salzburg Easter and Summer festivals, *Der Ring* (1967-70), *Otello* (1974), *Lohengrin* (1976), *Salome* (1977), and *Der fliegende Holländer* (1982). It is, however, the gramophone that leaves the more complete impression of Karajan in opera, with outstanding recordings made in London and Milan in 1950s (including *Il trovatore* and *Madama Butterfly* with Callas and *Der Rosenkavalier* with Schwarzkopf and Edelmann), a complete *Ring* cycle, and a wonderfully searching and humane 1970 Dresden recording of *Die Meistersinger* which makes an instructive contrast with the more theatrically extrovert recording taped live in Bayreuth in 1951.

—Richard Osborne

KATIA KABANOVÁ [also Kát'a Kabanová].

Composer: Leoš Janáček.

Librettist: Leoš Janáček (after A.N. Ostrovsky, "The Thunderstorm," translated by Vincenc Červinka).

First Performance: Brno, National Theater, 23 November 1921.

Roles: Kát'a (soprano); Kabanicha (contralto); Boris (tenor); Dikoj (bass); Varvara (soprano); Váňa Kudrjáš (tenor); Tichon (tenor); Glasha (mezzo-soprano); Feklusha (mezzo-soprano); Kudrjáš (baritone); chorus (SATB).

Publications

books—

Tyrrell, John, compiler. *Leoš Janáček: Kát'a Kabanová.* Cambridge Opera Handbooks. Cambridge, 1982.
Nicholas, John, editor. *Jenufa and Katya Kabanova.* London and New York, 1985.

articles—

Stuart, C. "*Katya Kabanová* Reconsidered." *Music Review* 12 (1951).

Wörner, K. "Katjas Tod: die Schlussszene der Oper 'Katja Kabanova' von Janáček." *Schweizerische Musikzeitung/ Revue musicale suisse* 99 (1959): 91.
Plamenac, Dragan. "Nepoznati komentari Leoš Janáčka operi Katja Kabanova" [Unknown comments of Janáček on his opera *Katia Kabanova*]. *Musiko/Zbornik* 17 (1981): 122 [summary in English].

*   *   *

After *Jenůfa,* the best-known, most frequently performed, and most dramatically successful of Leoš Janáček's nine operas, *Kát'a Kabanová* is only one of four major works the composer wrote in response to Russian literature. These include the 1918 orchestral rhapsody *Taras Bulba* (after Gogol), the 1923 String Quartet No. 1, "Kreutzer Sonata" (after Tolstoy) and two operas: *Kát'a Kabanová,* from a play by Alexander Ostrovsky, and *From the House of the Dead,* based on Fyodor Dostoevsky's prison memoirs, *The House of the Dead.* Like most Czechs of his generation, Janáček looked to Russia and Russian culture as positive nationalistic alternatives to the non-Slavic Austrian civilization that had oppressed Bohemia for centuries. Even more important, the composer found in Russian literature the same passionate concern for the large spiritual questions that so deeply disturbed him, especially the relationship between sin and virtue, guilt and innocence, sexuality and fidelity.

Janáček himself wrote the libretto for *Kát'a,* using Vincenc Červinka's Czech translation of Ostrovsky's powerful 1859 play, "The Thunderstorm." The prolific author of 50 plays, Ostrovsky (1823-86) almost single-handedly created a modern professional theater in Russia. The gloomy and powerful "Thunderstorm," describing the hopeless struggle between enlightenment and ignorance in a remote, backward, and repressive merchant town on the Volga in the 1850s—on the eve of the emancipation of the serfs—has achieved the greatest popular success both in Russia and elsewhere.

Kát'a Kabanová contains three acts, each with two scenes. In act I, scene i, we meet all the main characters as they gather in a park on the steep Volga riverbank: Dikoj, a rich and brutal merchant; his nephew Boris; the domineering and shrewish merchant's widow Kabanicha; her timid son Tichon; his wife, the naively pious and spiritually vulnerable Kát'a; her friend Varvara; and Varvara's boyfriend Váňa Kudrjáš. Dikoj and Kabanicha abuse the others for their supposed disrespect. In the following scene, Kát'a shares her ecstatic visions with Varvara before Kabanicha bullies Tichon, about to leave on a business trip, into extracting a pledge of fidelity from his humiliated wife. In act II, Varvara persuades Kát'a to overcome her hesitation and meet secretly in the garden with Boris, with whom she has become infatuated. The two couples enjoy a romantic nocturnal interlude. In act III, Tichon returns as a thunderstorm breaks over the town, and the overwrought Kát'a makes an unprovoked hysterical public confession of her adultery. The opera's final scene brings Kát'a and Boris together for a final reunion, followed by her farewell lament. Kát'a then throws herself in the Volga, unable to live with her guilt and shame.

Kát'a's "natural" personality, expressed through her love for birds and flowers and, ultimately, by her merging, rather like a doomed water sprite, with the eternal stream of the

Katia Kabanová, with Nancy Gustafson as Katia and Felicity Palmer as Kabanicha, Glyndebourne Festival, 1988

Volga, exercised a strong appeal over the pantheistic Janáček. (In *Jenůfa,* too, nature is an important agent: the ice conceals, and then the spring thaw reveals, the body of Jenůfa's illegitimate baby.) In a letter to Kamila Stoesslová, the composer described the genesis of *Kát'a Kabanová.* "It was in the sunshine of summer. The sun-warmed slope of the hill where the flowers wilted. That was when the first thoughts about poor Kát'a Kabanová and her great love came to my mind. She calls to the flowers, she calls to the birds—flowers to bow down to her, birds to sing for her the last song of love. My Kát'a grows in you, in Kamila! This will be the most gentle and tender of my works." In 1928, the year he died, Janáček formally dedicated the opera to Kamila, with whom he seems to have had nothing more than a platonic relationship.

Like Musorgsky—whom he greatly admired—and Prokofiev, Janáček welcomed the challenge of prose texts, believing they could be dramatized more easily and effectively. Also like them, he attempted to find a kind of musical "intonation" or "phrase" for each character or idea. Usually, this is a very short motif—no more than three or four measures—that goes through endless harmonic, metrical, and dynamic changes, in an extended theme-and-variations process. Two examples from *Kát'a* are the ominous "fate" theme, heavy with timpani, that sounds first in the overture's fifth measure; and the lighter, "trivial" Russian theme associated primarily with Kát'a's cowardly husband Tichon. Later, in the magnificent garden scene (act II, scene ii), Janáček makes superb use of Russian-style folk melodies to characterize Varvara and Kudrjáš, the carefree, if morally inferior, counterparts to

Kát'a and Boris. The opera succeeds brilliantly at conveying in musical terms the growing atmosphere of doom and tragedy that finally suffocates the ethereal title character.

Two musical worlds coexist in *Kát'a Kabanová:* Kát'a's, and that of the "kingdom of darkness." Kát'a's vocal line is frequently accompanied by flute or clarinet, producing a light, open, airy texture in contrast to the heavier, lower music associated with Dikoj and Kabanicha. First stated in the overture, her simple, soaring lyrical theme appears in small stuttering bits until its complete unfolding at Kát'a's first appearance. Boris, on the other hand, sings mundane, unimaginative phrases, including his act I solo, which demonstrate his lack of complexity and romantic depth. Because they have no souls to express, Kabanicha and Dikoj do not receive defined themes; Dikoj's blustering line comes the closest to actual speech, since his prosaic and destructive personality lacks spirituality and love.

From start to finish, both onstage and off, Kát'a, fragile and fascinating, dominates the action. One of the most rewarding and completely realized soprano roles created in the twentieth century, she recalls (in her hopeless love, passionate nature, and riverbank suicide) the heroine of Janáček's favorite Tchaikovsky opera, *The Queen of Spades.* Another operatic suicide, the hara-kiri of Puccini's Madama Butterfly, who is incapable, like Kát'a, of reconciling her ecstatic visions and romantic delusions with oppressive social realities, also influenced Janáček here. A wise and universal empathy propels *Kát'a Kabanová* on its dark and doomed course, dispensing pain and compassion, celebrating Kát'a's spiritual beauty even as it mourns her inevitable destruction at the hands of savage small-town Philistines.

—Harlow Robinson

KEILBERTH, Joseph.

Conductor. Born 19 April 1908, in Karlsruhe. Died (while conducting *Tristan und Isolde*) 20 July 1968, in Munich (Nationaltheater). Studied in Karlsruhe; became a vocal coach, 1925, and then Generalmusikdirektor, 1935-40, of the State Opera in Karlsruhe; principal conductor of the German Philharmonic Orchestra of Prague, 1940-45; Generalmusikdirektor of the Dresden Staatskapelle, 1945-49; principal conductor of the Bamberg Symphony Orchestra, 1949-68; conductor of the Bavarian State Opera, 1951; toured with the Bamberg Symphony in Europe, 1951, and the United States and Latin America, 1954; conductor at Bayreuth, 1952-56; Generalmusikdirektor of the Hamburg State Philharmonic Orchestra, 1950-59; Generalmusikdirektor of the Bavarian State Opera in Munich, 1959-68.

Publications

About KEILBERTH: book–

Lewinski, W.-E. von. *Joseph Keilberth*. Berlin, 1968.

$$*\quad\quad*\quad\quad*$$

Conductor Joseph Keilberth was a specialist in the German repertoire who made only infrequent excursions outside that sphere. He served as chief conductor of the Karlsruhe Opera from 1935 to 1940, and during the 1940s served as guest conductor at the Berlin State Opera, becoming conductor of the Dresden State Opera in 1945 and remaining there until 1949. He was named conductor of the Bavarian State Opera in 1951, and music director in 1959, succeeding Ferenc Fricsay. In 1952 he conducted Richard Strauss's *Der Rosenkavalier* and Weber's *Der Freischütz* with the Hamburg Opera at the Edinburgh Festival and, later in the decade, appeared at the Salzburg Festival and the Lucerne Festival. His first appearance at the Bayreuth Festival came in 1952, and he conducted the *Ring* cycle there every year until 1956; he also led *Lohengrin* (1953), and *Der fliegende Holländer* there in 1955 and 1956. At the Bavarian State Opera his performances included Wagner's *Die Meistersinger* and Richard Strauss's *Die ägyptische Helena* (1956) and *Arabella* (1963). He collapsed and died while conducting a performance of Wagner's *Tristan und Isolde* in Munich in 1968.

Keilberth rarely strayed from the German repertoire, the works for which he had particular insight and to which his conducting style was especially appropriate. This style has been described as firm, direct, dynamic, energetic, solidly robust, intelligent, committed, exhibiting a great understanding of musical style and purpose. He also, however, has been accused of dullness, reticence, a lack of thrust and impetuosity, despite his predilection for fast tempos; yet his performances were often atmospheric, lyrical, forceful, and well shaped. A rather inconsistent conductor, he was capable of leading eloquent performances, especially in the Wagnerian repertoire. At his best, he was capable of maintaining firm

control over his orchestras and creating intense performances that brought out the best in his singers. He has been faulted, however, for making substantial cuts to many of the scores he conducted.

His recordings of complete operas, other than those taken from live performances at the Bayreuth Festival and in Munich, include Dvořak's *Rusalka, Lohengrin,* Richard Strauss's *Die Frau ohne Schatten,* Verdi's *Aida,* and the first complete recordings of Richard Strauss's *Salome,* Weber's *Der Freischütz,* and Hindemith's *Cardillac.* A complete Bayreuth *Ring* was recorded by English Decca in 1955, but because of contractual difficulties the records were not released.

—Michael Sims

KEISER, Reinhard.

Composer. Born 9 January 1674, in Teuchern, near Weissenfels. Died 12 September 1739, in Hamburg. Studied with his father, Gottfried Keiser, an organist; studied at the Thomasschule in Leipzig; in Braunschweig, where his first opera was performed, 1693; Kammer-Komponist in Braunschweig, 1694; in Hamburg, where he established permanent residence, 1695; Kapellmeister of the Hamburg Opera, 1696; co-director of the Hamburg Opera, 1702-07; guest Kapellmeister to the Duke of Württemberg in Stuttgart, 1718; in Copenhagen to supervise productions of his operas, 1721; returned to Hamburg, 1723; Canonicus minor and Cantor of the Katharinekirche in Hamburg, 1728.

Operas

Der königliche Schäfer oder Basilius in Arcadien, Bressand (after Parisetti), Brunswick, 1693?.

Procris und Cephalus (Singspiel), Bressand, Brunswick, 1694.

Die Wiedergefundenen Verliebten [Die beständige und getreue Ismene] (Scäferspiel), Bressand, Brunswick, 1695.

Mahumet II (Trauerspiel), Heinrich Hinsch, Hamburg, 1696.

Der geliebte Adonis (Postel), Hamburg, 1697.

Die durch Wilhelm den Grossen in Britannien wieder eingeführte Treue, Postel, Hamburg, 1698.

Aller-unterhänigster Gehorsam (Tanz- und Sing-Spiel), Postel, Hamburg, 15 November 1698.

Der aus Hyperboreen nach Cymbrien überbrachte güldene Apfel zu Ehren Friedrichs und Hedwig Sophiens zu Holstein, Postel, Hamburg, 1698.

Der bey dem allgemeinen Welt-Friede und dem Grossen Augustus geschlossene Tempel des Janus, Postel, Hamburg, 1699.

Die wunderbahr-errettete Iphigenia, Postel (after Euripides), Hamburg, 1699.

Die Werbindung des grossen Hercules mit der Schönen Hebe (Singspiel), Postel, Hamburg, 1699.

Die Wiederkehr der güldnen Zeit, Bressand, Lüneburg?, 1699.

La forza della virtù, oder Die Macht der Tugend, Bressand, Hamburg, 1700.

Der gedemüthigte Endymion (Phaeton), Nothnagel, Hamburg, 1700.

Das höchstpreissliche Crönungsfest Ihrer Kgl. Majestät zu Preussen (ballet opera), Hotter and Nothangel, Hamburg, 1701.

Störtebecker und Jödge Michaels I, Hotter?, Hamburg, 1701.

Störtebecker und Jödge Michaels II, Hamburg, 1701.

Die wunder-schöne Psyche (Singspiel), Postel, Hamburg, 20 October 1701.

Circe oder Des Ulisses erster Theil, Bressand, Hamburg, 1702.

Penelope oder Des Ulysses ander Theil, Bressand, Hamburg, 1702.

Sieg der fruchtbaren Pomona, Postel, Hamburg, 1702.

Die sterbende Eurydice oder Orpheus erster Theil, Bressand, Hamburg, 1702; combined with *Orpheus ander Theil* and revised as *Die bis und nach dem Todt unerhörte Treue des Orpheus,* Bressand, Hamburg, 1709.

Orpheus ander Theil, Bressand, Hamburg, 1702; combined with *Die sterbende Eurydice oder Orpheus erster Theil* and revised as *Die bis und nach dem Todt unerhörte Treue des Orpheus,* Bressand, Hamburg, 1709.

Neues preussiches Ballet, Heinrich Hinsch, Hamburg, 1702.

Die verdammte Staat-Sucht, oder Der verführte Claudius, Heinrich Hinsch, Hamburg, 1703.

Die Geburt der Minerva, Hinsch, Hamburg, 1703.

Die über die Liebe triumphierende Weissheit oder Salomon, Hunold, Hamburg, 1703.

Der gestürzte und wieder erhönte Nebucadnezar, König zu Babylon, Hunold, Hamburg, 1704.

Die römische Unruhe oder Die edelmüthige Octavia, Barthold Feind, Hamburg, 5 August 1705.

Die kleinmüthige Selbstmörderinn Lucretia oder Die Staats-Thorheit des Brutus (Trauerspiel), Barthold Feind, Hamburg, 29 November 1705.

La fedeltà coronata oder Die gekrönte Treue, Heinrich Hinsch, Hamburg, 1706.

Masagniello furioso, Die Neapolitanische Fischer-Empörung, Barthold Feind, Hamburg, June 1706.

La costanza sforzata, Die gewungene Beständigkeit oder Die listige Rache des Sueno, Barthold Feind, Hamburg, 11 October 1706.

Il genio d'Holsatia, Bartold Feind, Hamburg, 1706 [used as a prologue to *Der durchlauchtige Secretarius, oder Almira, Königin von Castilien*].

Der durchlauchtige Secretarius, oder Almira, Königin von Castilien, Feustking, Hamburg, 1706.

Der angenehme Betrug oder Der Carneval von Venedig (some arias by Graupner), Meister and Curro, Hamburg, 1707.

La forza dell' amore oder Die von Paris entührte Helena, Keiser, Hamburg, 1709.

Die blutdürstige Rache oder Heliates und Olympia (with Graupner), Hamburg, 1709.

Desiderius, König der Langobarden, Barthold Feind, Hamburg, 26 July 1709.

La grandezza d' animo oder Arsinoe, Breymann, Hamburg, 1710.

Le bon vivant oder Die Leipziger Messe, Weidermann, Hamburg, 1710.

Der Morgan des europäischen Glückes oder Aurora (Schäferspiel), Bremann, Hamburg, 16 July 1710.

Der durch den Fall des grossen Pompejus erhöhte Julius Casear, Barthold Feind, Hamburg, November 1710.

Der hochmüthige, gestürtzte und wieder erhabene Croesus, Postel, Hamburg, 1710; revised, 1730.

Die oesterreichische Grossmuth oder Carolus V, König, Hamburg, 1712.

Die entdeckte Verstellund oder Die geheime Liebe der Diana (Schäferspiel), König, Hamburg, April 1712; revised as *Der sich rächende Cupido,* Hamburg, 1724.

Die wiederhergestellte Ruh oder Die gecrönte Tapferkeit des Heraclius, König, Hamburg, June 1712.

L'inganno fedele oder Der getreue Betrug, König, Hamburg, October 1714.

Die gecrönte Tugend, König, Hamburg, 15 November 1714.

Fredegunda, König, Hamburg, March 1715.

L'amore verso la patria oder Der sterbende Cato, Barthold Feind, Hamburg, 1715.

Artemisia, (several librettists), Hamburg, 1715.

Das zerstörte Troja oder Der durch den Tod Helenen versöhnte Achilles, Hoe, Hamburg, November 1716.

Die durch Verstellung und Grossmuth über die Grausamkeit siegende Liebe oder Julia, Hoe, Hamburg, February 1717.

Die grossmüthige Tomyris, Hoe, Hamburg, February 1717.

Der die Festung Siebenbürghisch-Weissenburg erobernde und über Dacier triumphiernde Kayser Trajanus, Hoe, Hamburg, November 1717.

Das bey seiner Ruh und Gebuhrt eines Printzen frolockende Lycien unter der Regierung des Königs Jacobates und Bellerophon, Hoe, Hamburg, 28 December 1717.

Die unvergleichliche Psyche, Copenhagen, 16 April 1722.

Ulysses, Lersner, Copenhagen, October 1722.

Der Armenier, Lersner?, Copenhagen, November 1722.

Die betrogene und nochmahls vergötterte Ariadne, Postel, Hamburg, 25 November 1722; adaptation of Conradi, 1691.

Sancio oder Die siegende Grossmuth, Lersner, c.1723 [unfinished?].

Bretislaus oder Die siegende Beständigkeit, Prätorius, Hamburg, February 1725.

Der Hamburger Jahrmarkt oder Der glückliche Betrug, Prätorius, Hamburg, 1725.

Die Hamburber Schlachtzeit oder Der misslungene Betrug, Prätorius, Hamburg, 1725.

Mistevojus König der Obotriten oder Wenden, Müller, Hamburg, 1726.

Der lächerliche Printz Jodelet, Prätorius, Hamburg, 1726.

Buchhofer der stumme Printz Atis (intermezzo), Hamburg, 1726.

Barbacola (intermezzo), Hamburg, 1726; some music by Lully.

Lucius Verus oder Die siegende Treue, Heinrich Hinsch (after Bronner, *Berenice,* 1702), Hamburg, 1728.

Jauchzen der Künste, 1733.

Circe (collaboration with other composers), Maurizius and Prätorius, Hamburg, 1734.

Other works: sacred vocal works, secular cantatas, serenatas, instrumental music.

Publications/Writings

About KEISER: books—

Mattheson, Johann. *Das neu-eröffnete Orchestre....* Hamburg, 1713.

———. *Grundlage einer Ehren-Pforte.* Hamburg, 1740; edited by M. Schneider, Berlin, 1910, 1969.

Burney, C. *The Present State of Music in Germany, the Netherlands and the United Provinces.* London, 1773

Scheibe, J.A. *Über die musikalische Komposition.* Leipzig, 1773.

Schmidt, G.F. *Die frühdeutsche Oper und die musikdramatische Kunst G.K. Schürmanns.* Regensburg, 1933.

Schulze, W. *Die Quellen der Hamburger Oper.* Hamburg and Oldenburg, 1938.

Wolff, H.C. *Die Barockoper in Hamburg.* Wolfenbüttel, 1957.

Brockpähler, R. *Handbuch zur Geschichte der Barockoper in Deutschland.* Emsdetten, 1964.

Zelm, K. *Die Opern Reinhard Keisers.* Munich, 1975.

Harris, E. *Handel and the Pastoral Tradition.* Oxford, 1980

Bianconi, L. *Music in the Seventeenth Century,* translated by David Bryant. Cambridge, 1987

articles–

Kretzschmar, H. "Das erste Jahrhundert der deutschen Oper." *Sammelbände der Internationalen Musik-Gesellschaft,* 3 (1901-02): 270.

Krogh, T. "Reinhard Keiser in Kopenhagen." In *Musikwissenschaftliche Beiträge: Festschrift für Johannes Wolf,* 79. Berlin, 1929, 1973.

Becker, H. "Die frühe Hamburgische Tagespresse als musikgeschichtliche Quelle." In *Beiträge zur Hamburgischen Musikgeschichte,* edited by H. Husmann, Hamburg, 1956.

Rudolph, J. "Probleme der Hamburger deutschen Frühoper." *Händel-Jahrbuch* (1969-70): 7.

Brenner, R.D. "Emotional Expression in Keiser's Operas." *Music Review* 33 (1972): 222.

Buelow, George J. "Opera in Hamburg 300 Years Ago." *Musical Times* 119 (1978): 26.

Marx, Hans Joachim. "Geschichte der Hamburger Barock Oper: ein Forschungsbericht." *Hamburger Jahrbuch für Musikwissenschaft* 3 (1978): 7.

Zelm, K. "Die Sänger der Hamburger Gänsenmarkt-Oper." *Hamburger Jahrbuch für Musikwissenschaft* 3 (1978): 35.

Baselt, Bernd. "Händel auf dem Wege nach Italien." In *G.F. Händel und seine italienischen Zeitgenossen,* 10. Halle, 1979.

Dahlhaus, Carl. "Zum Affektbegriff der frühdeutschen Oper." In *Opernsymposium 1978 Hamburg,* edited by Martin Ruhnke, 107. Laaber, 1981.

Zelm, Klaus. "Stilkritische Untersuchungen an einem Opernpasticcio. Reinhard Keisers *Jodelet.*" In *Festschrift Heinz Becker zum 60. Geburtstag am 26. Juni 1982,* edited by Jürgen Schläder and Reinhold Quandt, 10. Laaber, 1982.

――――. "Reinhard Keiser und Georg Philipp Telemann—zum Stilwandel an der früdeutschen Oper in Hamburg." In *Die Bedeutung Georg Philipp Telemanns,* edited by Günter Fleischhauer et al., 104, Magdeburg, 1983.

unpublished–

Leichtentritt, Hugo. "Reinhard Keiser in seinen Opern." Ph.D. dissertation, University of Berlin, 1901.

Bartmuss, A.W. "Die Hamburger Barockoper und ihre Bedeutung für die Entwicklung der deutschen Dichtung." Ph.D. dissertation, University of Jena, 1926.

Brenner, R.D. "The Operas of Reinhard Keiser in their Relationship to the Affektenlehre." Ph.D. dissertation, Brandeis University, 1968.

*   *   *

Reinhard Keiser was one of the most important Baroque composers and today perhaps the most undeservedly neglected. This claim might at first seem merely one more example of what C.S. Lewis in *The Allegory of Love* called "that itch for 'revival', that refusal to leave any corpse ungalvanized, which is among the more distressing accidents of scholarship." Keiser's importance, however, can be established by a multitude of factors: his historical importance as the leading composer of German opera in the Baroque period; the esteem awarded him by the great men of his own day, including Johann Sebastian Bach, who directed Keiser's St Mark Passion in Leipzig in 1726; his influence on George Frideric Handel, who "borrowed" extensively from Keiser;

and above all, the strength and magnitude of his musical output.

Public opera at the Theater-am-Gänsemarkt in Hamburg began in 1678 and continued until 1738. Unlike most other European opera houses, which presented operas in Italian, Hamburg offered German-language operas, either original productions or Italian operas in German translation, similar to the *drammi per musica* of Venetian theaters. The principal Hamburg opera composers include Strungk, Kusser, Krieger, Mattheson, Handel (who composed his first operas for Hamburg), Keiser, and Telemann. Although Keiser began his career in Brunswick, where his first opera, *Basilius in Arcadien,* was performed in 1693, he spent the bulk of his creative life in Hamburg (where he moved some time between 1695 and 1702) with relatively brief sojourns at Weissenfels, Stuttgart, and Copenhagen.

Keiser's operas apparently were not performed outside of Germany and Denmark; there is no record of productions even at other important operatic centers in German-speaking lands, such as Vienna or Munich. Nonetheless, Keiser's importance was noted by several eighteenth-century theorists and composers. In *Das neu-eröffnete Orchestre* of 1713, for instance, Johann Mattheson of Hamburg called Keiser the "premier homme du monde." According to Charles Burney's *The Present State of Music in Germany, the Netherlands and the United Provinces* of 1773, the composer Johann Adolph Hasse regarded Keiser as "one of the greatest musicians the world ever saw. His compositions are more voluminous than those of [Alessandro] Scarlatti, and his melodies, though more than fifty years old, are such as would be thought modern and graceful." In the same year J.A. Scheibe's *Über die musikalische Komposition* hailed Keiser as an "inexhaustably inventive" composer and "perhaps the most original genius Germany has produced." C.P.E. Bach listed Keiser among the composers highly esteemed by Johann Sebastian Bach in his last years, and a letter of 1788 attributed to C.P.E. Bach tells us that "as an opera composer there was another great man besides Handel: Kaiser [Keiser], who, be it mentioned in passing, in the beauty, novelty, expression, and pleasing qualities of his melody, need have no fear of comparison with Handel" (translation by Hans T. David, *The Bach Reader,* New York, 1966). Today the musicologist Lorenzo Bianconi calls Keiser "a musician of truly 'European' stature," praising "the truly extraordinary quality of his music."

As is the case with other Hamburg operas, the subjects of Keiser's (aside from a few comic works) are serious, in spite of comic episodes characteristic of seventeenth-century opera. They are drawn from numerous sources, including Greek mythology and literature (*Circe oder Ulisses erster Theil*), Roman history (*Octavia*), the Old Testament (*Nebucadnezar*), and European sources, including current political subjects (*Masagniello furioso*) and local themes (*Störtebecker und Jödge Michaels*). In structure and style Keiser's grand operas draw on elements of seventeenth-century Venetian opera with comic episodes and a tendency to cut historical figures "down to size"; they also draw on the emerging Metastasian *opera seria* with its pervasive *da capo* arias followed by the exit of the singer, and on French *tragédie-lyrique* with its spectacular *divertissements* and dances. The interaction of these conventions can best be understood by analysis of specific operas.

Keiser's *Octavia* is based on an earlier libretto by Conradi, *Il Nerone,* first performed with music by Pallavicino in Venice in 1695. Barthold Feind, who collaborated with Keiser on several operas, translated much of the libretto into German (Ormoena has four arias in Italian, Nero and Octavia have two apiece, and Piso, Tiridates, Clelia, and Livia have one each). Such polyglot performances became common in Hamburg after 1703, when Keiser first used Italian arias in his *Claudius.*

Like earlier Venetian opera, *Octavia* has comic scenes, such as act III scene iii, where Nero's servant Davus, a comic character, reads excerpts from Seneca's books and misinterprets them. Such comic episodes remained popular in Hamburg. In his *Gedanken von der Oper* of 1708 Feind deplores the persistant popularity of the clown in Hamburg operas. Like French opera, *Octavia* also contains *divertissements,* such as court dances in the final scene of act I and a dance of gravediggers and ghosts in the last scene of act II.

While arias ending scenes followed by the exit of a character are a staple of Metastasian *opera seria,* they form a minority in *Octavia.* Of more than fifty arias and choruses only eight—or fifteen per cent—are scene-ending exit arias. *Octavia* contains ten scene-ending arias that are not followed by an exit, ten arias sung at the beginnings of scenes when a character enters, and twenty-five arias sung in the midst of a scene and not followed by an exit. At the end of act I of *Octavia,* all of the characters are on stage. Rather than singing individual arias or an ensemble, the characters leave one by one in recitative, quite unlike Metastasian *opera seria.* Twenty-five arias (just half) are *da capo* arias, the predominant form in Metastasian opera, with many operas in through-composed, binary and a-b-a forms. The distinction between recitative and aria, the mainstay of Metastasian opera, is altered in Keiser with arias interrupted by recitative and recitative interwoven with arioso sections. On the whole, then, this particular opera is closer to its Venetian model than to Metastasian reform opera.

Not surprisingly for so prolific a composer, Keiser's output is varied in regard to formal structure. As musicologist John Roberts points out, *La forza della virtù* of 1700 contains only one aria that is not in *da capo* form. Although the later opera *Die grossmüthige Tomyris* of 1717, on a libretto by Johann Joachim Hoe, is more closely based on the scene-ending exit aria convention and *da capo* aria forms of contemporary *opera seria,* the influence of Metastasian *opera seria* is still not pervasive. Many scene-ending arias are not followed by an exit, and characters sometimes leave the stage without singing arias. As with *Octavia,* act I opens with a chorus (a common feature of German opera singled out as a positive trait by Feind). *Tomyris* contains dances, and the action is interwoven with a comic subplot—both characteristics of German opera.

Paul Henry Lang's claim that Keiser influenced Handel in his "felicity in the musical setting of words, his observance of natural inflections, the rise and fall of the prosody, his deft use of recitative, in which he had no peer, and his colorful orchestration," is difficult to substantiate, for no music by Handel written before his arrival in Hamburg in 1703 survives. Nonetheless, Lang singles out some of the most notable features of Keiser's style. Particularly noteworthy is Keiser's colorful and inventive orchestration, probably a reflection of the capabilities and availability of instrumentalists in Hamburg. Keiser's most unique and eccentric type of scoring is the use of numerous instruments in the same family, for instance five bassoons in an aria in *Octavia,* and the use of unusual instruments such as the zuffolo in *Croesus* and the carillon in the oratorio *Der Siegende David.*

Ironically, Keiser's survival today rests primarily on scholarly recognition of his importance to Handel. *Octavia,* from which Handel borrowed, appeared in an appendix to Chrysander's edition of the complete works of Handel, and most of the handful of works by Keiser available in modern publications form part of the facsimile series of Handel sources edited by John Roberts. Only one of Keiser's operas, *Croesus,* is currently (1992) available on compact disc. Keiser's obscurity is no doubt partly a reflection of the fate of late Baroque opera on the whole, which until now has been dismissed as hopelessly contrived and artificial. With the current revival of interest in Handel's operas, now regarded with the oratorios as that composer's most viable masterpieces, we can hope that the future will bring wider interest in the works of Keiser.

—David Ross Hurley

KELLY, Michael.

Tenor. Born 25 December 1762, in Dublin. Died 9 October 1826, in Margate, Kent. Studied with Passerini and Rauzzini; debut as Count in Piccinni's *La buona figliuola,* Dublin, 1779; then went to Milan and studied with Finaroli and Aprile; sang in several Italian cities, including Florence and Venice; at Vienna Court Opera, 1783-87, where he created Don Curzio and Don Basilio in *Le nozze di Figaro;* sang at Drury Lane in London from 1787; stage manager for King's Theatre in the Haymarket, 1793-1824; also composer and wine trader.

Publications

By KELLY: books—

Fiske, R., ed. *Reminiscences.* London, 1975.

About KELLY: books—

Ellis, S. *The Life of Michael Kelly, Musician, Actor, and Bon Viveur.* London, 1930.

*   *   *

Michael Kelly, singer and composer, was the son of a Dublin wine merchant. He was born on Christmas Day, 1762, and died in Margate, England, 9 October 1826, apparently from the complications of gout. There were fourteen children in the family, all of whom seem to have been musical. Michael was the most precocious and talented. His musical training, which began at age seven, included piano lessons with Philip Cogan (who had studied with Clementi), Michael Arne, and others. After training as a boy soprano, he decided quite early on a singing career, and was taught by Rauzzini, who recommended to his father that he be sent to Italy, where he was to study with Passerini, Santo Giorgio, Aprile, and others.

As a result, after appearing several times on stage in Dublin, in 1779 Kelly sailed for Naples, where he attended the Conservatory, La Madonna di Loreto, studying there with Finaroli, teacher of Cimarosa. Then, by happy accident, he made the acquaintance of Giuseppe Aprile, a famous singer, who took him on his travels as a protégé, sometimes giving him lessons every day of the week. By 1781 Kelly began to get small engagements, and was at last given the part of the Frenchman in *Il Francese in Italia,* for a performance in Florence, in which he had a great success. Afterward he was engaged at the Teatro San Moisè in Venice.

Apart from his career as a talented operatic singer, Michael Kelly's chief claim to fame arose from his personal and professional acquaintances with such important composers as

Michael Kelly

Haydn, whom he visited at Esterhazy for three days, and Mozart, who worked with him frequently over a period of four years. Kelly's copious memory of all these events is recorded in the pleasant literary style of Thomas Hooke, who provided the prose for Kelly's *Reminiscences,* published in 1826, shortly before his death.

From *Reminiscences* we learn that Kelly spent four years in Vienna, where he had an appointment at the Court Theatre. With Nancy and Stephen Storace, whom he had met in Italy, and Thomas Attwood, he became part of an English musical coterie, all of whom worked with Mozart. Attwood took lessons in musical composition, while the two Storaces and Michael Kelly concentrated on singing. In 1786, Kelly created the roles of both Basilio and Don Curzio, and Nancy Storace sang the part of Susanna. Mozart was pleased with both.

In 1787 Kelly returned to London, as did the other members of the coterie. There, for the rest of his life, he continued his career as an operatic tenor, occasionally appearing in oratorios as well, in London and throughout England. During this period he was engaged by Joah Bates and the Directors of Ancient Concerts as principal tenor. Shortly thereafter, he also joined Dr Arnold's Academy of Ancient Music. From 1793-1824 he managed King's Theater, for which he composed and arranged musical stage pieces. He was also proprietor of a wine shop in London, a fact which prompted Richard Sheridan to suggest that he should style himself a "Composer of wines and importer of music."

—Franklin B. Zimmerman

KEMPE, Rudolf.

Conductor. Born 14 June 1910, in Niederpoyritz, near Dresden. Died 11 May 1976, in Zurich. Studied oboe at the Orchestral School of the Dresden Staatskapelle; first oboist of the Gewandhaus Orchestra of Leipzig, 1929; conducted at the Leipzig Opera, 1936; served in the German army during World War II; director of the Chemnitz Opera, 1945-48; director of the Weimar National Theater, 1948-49; Generalmusikdirektor of the Dresden Staatskapelle, 1949-52; Generalmusikdirektor of the Bavarian State Opera in Munich, 1952-54; conducted in Vienna, London, New York, and at the Bayreuth Festival (1960, 1962-64, 1967); associate conductor, 1960, principal conductor (succeeding Beecham), 1961, and artistic director, 1963-75, of the Royal Philharmonic Orchestra, London; principal conductor of the Tonhalle Orchestra in Zurich, 1965-72; principal conductor of the Munich Philharmonic, beginning 1967; conducted the British Broadcasting Corporation Symphony Orchestra, 1975-76.

Publications

About KEMPE: books—

Kempe-Oettinger, C. *Rudolf Kempe.* Munich, 1977; English translation, London, 1979.

articles—

Rosenthal, Harold. "Rudolf Kempe." *Opera* November (1959).
Le Grand Baton March-June (1978) [Kempe memorial issue].

* * *

Rudolf Kempe was one of the preeminent conductors of the Austro-Germanic Romantic repertoire, especially the operas of Wagner and Richard Strauss. Especially associated with the orchestra and opera company of Dresden, Kempe began his conducting career in 1935 at the Leipzig Opera, where he led Lortzing's *Der Wildschütz.* Starting during his military service he worked for the Chemnitz Opera, where he returned after the war as conductor and music director, and where he remained until 1948. After a year at the Weimar National Theater, he became general music director of the Dresden State Opera, where he served from 1949 until 1952; he succeeded Georg Solti at the Bavarian State Opera in Munich, remaining there from 1952 to 1954. His first performances outside Germany were with the Vienna State Opera in 1951, where he conducted the season opener. In 1953 he led the Bavarian Staatsoper at Covent Garden and made guest appearances in South America. In 1955 he led Pfitzner's *Palestrina* at the Salzburg Festival. Kempe made his Metropolitan Opera debut conducting Richard Strauss's *Arabella* in 1955; he also led Wagner's *Tristan und Isolde* and *Tannhäuser* in 1955 and Richard Strauss's *Der Rosenkavalier* and Wagner's *Die Meistersinger* in 1956.

In 1960 he conducted at the Bayreuth Festival, leading Wagner's *Ring des Nibelungen,* which he had first conducted in Barcelona in 1954; he returned to Bayreuth in 1962, 1963, 1964, and 1967.

When Sir David Webster was searching for a new music director for the Royal Opera in 1954, Kempe was one of the conductors under consideration for the position. He had come to Covent Garden with the Bavarian State Opera of Munich in 1953 to conduct two Richard Strauss operas, including the little-known *Die Liebe der Danaë* (which he had already led in Munich the year after its world premiere), and he returned that October to lead *Salome.* Shortly afterward he led *Elektra* and, in the summer of 1954, *Der Rosenkavalier.* Although he had only conducted Strauss up to this time, Webster saw Kempe's potential. When Kempe returned that autumn to lead another *Rosenkavalier,* followed by Wagner's *Tristan und Isolde* and Beethoven's *Fidelio,* his abilities, at least within the German repertoire, were made clear. In 1955 he conducted two *Ring* cycles, performances described as characterized by "lyricism, delicacy, beauty of texture." These were followed by his first excursions into Italian repertoire at Covent Garden with Puccini's *Madama Butterfly,* performances that demonstrated his abilities in that sphere, and that critic Andrew Porter praised for "eschewing mere continuance of the 'Puccini' tradition" and making audiences "listen with fresh ears."

Webster was not able to convince Kempe to take the position at Covent Garden, however; although the conductor had recently relinquished his post in Munich, he was not ready to commit himself to a new long-term position. During the 1960s he continued to conduct at Covent Garden, leading Verdi's *Aida* and *Un ballo in maschera,* Bizet's *Carmen,* Wagner's *Ring,* Strauss's *Elektra, Salome,* and *Die schweigsame Frau,* Weber's *Der Freischütz,* Wagner's *Die Meistersinger* and *Parsifal,* and Mozart's *Don Giovanni.* During his years as guest conductor he supported British singers, a point that no doubt contributed to his popularity in England.

Within his relatively limited repertoire, Kempe reached an extraordinary level of achievement. His performances were memorable for their subtle phrasing and delicacy, and for their feeling of naturalness, inevitability, rightness. His conducting technique employed small but clear gestures; his approach was energetic but unidiosyncratic and unmannered, exhibiting a constant lyric flow while paying close attention to the architectural elements of his scores. The quality of his performances was due in part to his concern with texture and structural matters, as well as his careful attention to problems of balance between the various sections of the orchestra and the singers. He tried to recreate the effect possible at Bayreuth (with its covered orchestra pit) at other theaters, which required the orchestra, especially the brass, to play more softly than was comfortable for them. Most important, however, was what might be termed the authenticity of his readings. Through careful attention to the demands of the scores but without an overly literal approach, Kempe was able to bring out both the dramatic and the emotional content of the operas he led. He chose his tempos carefully, avoiding extremes without descending into dullness. He was occasionally criticized for smoothing out dramatic peaks, a trait discernible, for example, in his chamber music approach to the *Ring,* but this was probably a manifestation of his self-effacing stance. His best work, as seen, for example, in the operas of Richard Strauss and in *Die Meistersinger,* ranks with the finest conducting of the post-World War II period.

Kempe's recordings include *Der Rosenkavalier* (1950, the first virtually complete studio recording), *Der Freischütz* (1950), *Die Meistersinger* (1951 [from a broadcast], 1956), Smetana's *The Bartered Bride* (1962), Wagner's *Lohengrin* (1951, 1963), and Richard Strauss's *Ariadne auf Naxos* (1968).

—Michael Sims

KHOVANSHCHINA [The Khovansky Plot].

Composer: Modest Musorgsky [completed and orchestrated by Rimsky-Korsakov; later re-worked by Ravel, Stravinsky, and Shostakovich].

Librettist: Modest Musorgsky.

First Performance: St Petersburg, 21 February 1886.

Roles: Ivan Khovansky (bass); Marfa (contralto); Andrei Khovansky (tenor); Vassily Golitsyn (tenor); Dosifei (bass); Shaklovity (baritone); Emma (soprano); Scrivener (tenor); Susanna (soprano); Varsonofiev (baritone); Kuzka (tenor); Streshniev (tenor); Three Streltsy (basses, tenor); chorus (SSAATTBB).

Publications

book–

Lopashev, S., et al. *Musorgskiy i evo "Khovanshchina": sbornik statey.* Moscow, 1928.

articles–

Lloyd-Jones, David. "Musorgsky's *Khovanshchina. Opera* December (1959).
Vul'fson, Aleksej. "K problemann tekstologii" [on *Khovanshchina*]. *Sovetskaja muzyka* 3 (1981): 103.
Baroni, Mario. "La nozione de 'realismo' nella *Chovanscina di Musorgskij." Nuova rivista musicale italiana* 16 (1982): 313.
Avant-scène opéra November-December (1983) [*La Khovantchina* issue].

* * *

Already in 1872, while he was still completing *Boris Godunov,* Musorgsky began gathering materials for his historical opera on the political problems associated with the reign of Peter the Great. Philosophically, this period (the 1680s) is dominated by the friction between Peter's modernist orientation and the conservative beliefs of "old" Russia. It was just this turbulence that so fascinated Musorgsky and his friend Vladimir Stasov, whom Musorgsky credited with introducing the idea of this opera to him. He worked on the music for *Khovanshchina* from 1873 until his death, leaving a fairly complete piano-vocal score but with most of the orchestration still to be done. Rimsky-Korsakov, Ravel, and Stravinsky all worked at completing this opera, but it is in the 1959 Shostakovich scoring that the work is currently best known.

The opera begins with a strikingly visual orchestral prelude, "Dawn on the Moscow River," then moves to St Basil's Square, on the morning after a bloody raid by a quasi-police force called the Streltsy, led by Ivan Khovansky. He and his son Andrei would like to depose Peter, perhaps using an alliance of the Streltsy and the Old Believers, a religious sect, to achieve this end. Shaklovity, a boyar prince, informs the tsar of the impending treachery, while the leader of the Old Believers, Dosifei, warns of the troubles that undoubtedly lie in the future for Russia's people. This first act forms the basis against which subsequent scenes may be understood in relation to the opera's central conflicts.

Other characters who give shape to these conflicts are Marfa, an Old Believer, a fortune teller, and also Andrei

Khovansky's former lover; and Golitsyn, a prince trying to bring the various elements of society together to achieve Peter's modernization. As the opera concludes, the Streltsy have been threatened with execution, and the Old Believers, also facing certain persecution and death, gather themselves, Marfa and Andrei included, into their hermitage for the ritualistic cleansing of self-immolation.

The interwoven political, religious, and social conflicts that lie at the heart of *Khovanshchina,* while certainly suggestive of grand opera, gave Musorgsky great difficulties in plot organization. The resultant libretto is more like a sequence of excerpts from a larger story, as it were, than a logical unfolding of a compelling drama. While Marfa, who embodies many of the opera's conflicts, is perhaps the most interesting character, it is really the Russian people who are central in this opera. Elements of action and character development play a distinctly secondary role.

As a giant canvas depicting the Russian psyche during this important historical period, the work is a significant accomplishment. As an opera, it is most certainly flawed, in part because of Musorgsky's problems with the libretto, in part because he was unable to complete the work. It nonetheless contains moments of great musical portraiture, including the prelude, Shaklovity's prayer for his country in act III, and the final chorus of Old Believers. While *Boris Godunov* may be the greater work of art, *Khovanshchina* makes a most important contribution to our fuller understanding of Musorgsky's aesthetic and cultural identity.

—Roy J. Guenther

THE KHOVANSKY PLOT
See KHOVANSHCHINA

KIEPURA, Jan.

Tenor. Born 16 May 1902, in Sosnowiec, Poland. Died 15 August 1966, in Rye, New York. Married soprano Marta Eggerth. Studied with Leliva in Warsaw; debut as Gounod's Faust in Lwow, 1924; appeared as Cavaradossi at Vienna Staatsoper, 1926; also appeared in Berlin, Milan, Paris and Budapest; United States debut in Chicago as Cavaradossi, 1931; Metropolitan Opera debut as Rodolfo in *La bohème,* 1938; appeared in films; created role in Korngold's *Das Wunder der Heliane.*

Publications

About KIEPURA: books–

Ramage, J. *Jan Kiepura.* Paris, 1968.
Waldorf, J. *Jan Kiepura.* Cracow, 1974.

*   *   *

Jan Kiepura was the most popular, self-aggrandizing tenor of his era. It is possible that, if he lived in today's world of

media, Luciano Pavarotti would be only a guest on Kiepura's television specials.

Kiepura was, in addition, a dedicated, serious singer who possessed a most beautiful, flexible voice. His was an incredibly successful and varied career almost from its beginning. In time, the name Kiepura became a synonym both for "tenor" and "operetta."

He was born in Sosnowiec, Poland, in 1902. At 22 he made his debut as Gounod's Faust in Lwów; and by 1926 he was singing with Maria Jeritza in Vienna. In 1927 he partnered Lotte Lehmann in the American premiere of Korngold's *Das Wunder der Heliane,* and sang first in London, at Covent Garden and Albert Hall. In 1928 he was at the Paris Opéra. Kiepura then went on to the Teatro alla Scala, the Berlin State Opera, Paris' Opéra-Comique, Teatro Colón, Chicago (where he sang in the American premiere of the Polish composer Moniusko's *Halka*), and the Metropolitan Opera. His debut at the Metropolitan was in 1938, as Rudolfo: he also sang there Don José, Duke of Mantua, Des Grieux (Massenet), and Cavaradossi for a total of 29 performances in New York and on tours.

He was a celebrated film star, a concert favorite, and starred on Broadway in a revival of *The Merry Widow* with his wife, Martha Eggerth, which ran for three years. One of his films, Léhar's *Land of Smiles* (1952) was a remake 20 years after Tauber had starred in the original. An earlier film was *The Charm of La Bohème* in 1936.

Jan Kiepura recorded prodigiously in opera and operetta all through his career. It is moot, however, how many of his recordings, popular as they were at the time, can be found today. After his death in 1966, "Memorial" LP's were published, and then little, if any, further re-releases. Tauber has taken the CD imagination, with Kiepura and Joseph Schmidt waiting in the wings with several other equally gifted tenors.

There is an air check extant of the 1939 *Rigoletto* Metropolitan Opera broadcast with Kiepura, Lily Pons, and Lawrence Tibbett. It is impressive.

—Bert Wechsler

KING, James.

Tenor. Born 22 May 1925, in Dodge City, Kansas. Studied at University of Kansas City as a baritone; trained as a tenor with Singher in New York; also studied with Max Lorenz; European debut as Cavaradossi at Teatro della Pergola, Florence, 1961; joined Deutsche Oper, Berlin, 1962; appeared as Achilles in *Iphigénie en Aulide* at Salzburg, 1962; Bacchus in *Ariadne auf Naxos,* Vienna, 1963; appeared at Bayreuth as Siegmund, 1965; London, 1966; debut at Metropolitan opera as Florestan, 1966; has taught at Indiana University from 1984.

Publications

About KING: articles–

Forbes, E. "James King." *Opera* July (1986).

*   *   *

In these post-Melchior decades in which opera has lacked true heldentenors, opera audiences have had to make do with lyric tenors who have pushed themselves to the limit in attempting to cope with dramatic roles. There has been, however, a small number of singers who have been able to fill the gap, despite vocal endowments smaller than the ideal. James King is one of these: possessor of a dependable, potentially exciting voice, with sufficient stamina and power to sustain the longer, more dramatic roles without collapse. In hindsight, given the current state of dramatic tenor singing, it appears that the quality of his singing may have been underestimated over the course of his long career.

King's proficiency in the Wagnerian roles derives in part from his possession of a baritonal quality in his lower notes, a characteristic found in most successful—that is, long-lived—Wagnerian tenors; like many such tenors, King began singing as a baritone before the start of his professional career. He moved on to tenor roles when he was thirty-one; however, he was advised to restrict himself to high Italian roles for as long as possible before moving on to the heavier dramatic parts.

As his career progressed, King moved to the heroic repertoire from lyric and spinto Italian roles. He has made a specialty of the taxing, usually thankless tenor roles of the Richard Strauss operas, such as Bacchus in *Ariadne auf Naxos,* Apollo in *Daphne,* the Emperor in *Die Frau ohne Schatten,* and Aegisth in *Elektra,* and the lighter Wagnerian repertoire, most notably Walther in *Die Meistersinger von Nürnberg,* Parsifal, and Lohengrin. The possessor of a voice with a distinctive, immediately recognizable timbre and, at least in his earlier years, an easy top, he lacks only an exceptionally beautiful tone.

Aside from his core repertoire of Wagner and Strauss, King has sung a limited number of Italian roles, notably Calaf in Puccini's *Turandot,* Cavaradossi in Puccini's *Tosca,* Des Grieux in Puccini's *Manon Lescaut,* Verdi's Don Carlos, and Canio in Leoncavallo's *I pagliacci.* After an early performance in Gluck's *Iphigénie en Aulide,* he has sung few French roles, including Samson in Saint-Saëns's *Samson et Dalila* and Cherubini's *Anacréon.*

After his debut at the Teatro della Pergola in Florence (as Cavaradossi) in 1961, King has sung in Berlin (beginning with the Emperor in *Die Frau ohne Schatten*), Salzburg, Bayreuth (first as Siegmund in *Die Walküre*), La Scala, Paris (as Calaf), and Covent Garden (as the Emperor).

In Vienna King made his debut as Bacchus in 1963. For the Vienna Festival in 1964, Strauss's centennial year, he sang Apollo, an especially high-lying role, and one that he had to learn within three months of another difficult Strauss role, the Emperor.

King has appeared at the Metropolitan Opera since 1966, beginning in the last season held at the old house, singing such roles as Bacchus, Don José in Bizet's *Carmen,* Aegisth, Florestan in Beethoven's *Fidelio,* Erik in Wagner's *Der fliegende Holländer,* the Emperor, Lohengrin, Walther, Cavaradossi, Calaf, Siegmund in Wagner's *Die Walküre,* Captain Vere in Britten's *Billy Budd,* and the Drum Major in Berg's *Wozzeck.*

In San Francisco King added Verdi's Otello to his repertoire, but this venture into the heaviest end of the operatic spectrum was not fully successful, his voice being rather too light for the role. In recent years he has sung a number of character roles, most notably Aegisth. Despite his many years of singing, his voice has remained remarkably fresh and has retained its basic quality.

King's voice has been described as burly, honest, virile, and accurate. It contains a touch of metal, useful in his chosen repertoire. It is not an ingratiating, beguiling sound, nor is

it an especially heroic one, although it can take on heroic proportions at times. His high notes occasionally bely some strain. He can sing softly, not a common trait among dramatic tenors, but he is not an elegant, stylish singer. Yet, within its limits, it is a reliable, strong, sometimes thrilling voice. Interpretively, King lacks the ability to phrase with subtlety—his phrasing is somewhat wooden—and acting is not his strongest area.

King's recordings of complete operas, not including those derived from stage performances, include Mozart's *Die Zauberflöte* (as one of the Armed Men, 1965, under Böhm), Siegmund (1966, under Solti), Strauss's *Salome* (as Narraboth, 1968, under Leinsdorf), *Ariadne auf Naxos* (as Bacchus, 1968, under Kempe), *Fidelio* (as Florestan, 1969, under Böhm), *Lohengrin* (1971, under Kubelik), *Samson et Dalila* (as Samson, 1973, under Patané), Berlioz's *La damnation de Faust* (as Brander, 1980, under Solti), and Schmidt's *Notre Dame* (as Phoebus, 1988, under Perick).

—Michael Sims

KING ARTHUR
See LE ROI ARTHUS

KING ARTHUR, or The British Worthy.

Composer: Henry Purcell.

Librettist: John Dryden.

First Performance: London, Dorset Gardens Theater, spring 1691.

Publications

articles–

Alssid, Michael. "The Impossible Form of Art: Dryden, Purcell, and King Arthur." *Studies in the Literary Imagination* spring (1977).
Charlton, David. "King Arthur: Dramatick Opera." *Music and Letters* July-October (1983).

Henry Purcell's semi-opera, *King Arthur,* produced in the spring of 1691, marked his second attempt to create a compromise musical drama for the operatic stage. *The Prophetess, or the History of Dioclesian,* which appeared in the previous year, had been his first experiment with this new hybrid form, intermixing operatic formulas with elements of spoken drama, drawn from England's beloved stage tradition. In both these dynastic operas, John Dryden's gentle guidance is apparent: he appears to have been the actual author of the oft-quoted preface to *Dioclesian,* which was credited to Henry Purcell in the original printed edition. And it is clear from Dryden's foreword to Purcell's *Amphitryon* that he had lent his considerable influence to Purcell's career as an opera composer, which accelerated so impressively after the premiere of *Dido and Aeneas,* his only true opera.

For Dryden, the creation of *King Arthur* brought welcome opportunity to repair his reputation as librettist, sadly tarnished by the miserable failure of an earlier attempt on this subject, with Louis Grabu's ill-fated allegory *Albion and Albanius.* This was originally planned as a prologue to *King Arthur,* but the death of King Charles seven years earlier had undone all efforts to perform it. Then, when a revised version was ready in 1686, Monmouth's rebellion forestalled it for a second time. Actually these two mischances may have been fortunate. Given Dryden's jumbled, allegorical plots and overblown metaphors, neither *Albion and Albanius* nor its sequel, *King Arthur,* could have succeeded.

However, by 1691 Dryden had managed to clarify the story line in *King Arthur* and to improve poetry and imagery. The plot, as it may be pieced together from both spoken and sung lines, is as follows: the British king, Arthur, with the help of his officers, Albanacht, Aurelius, and Conon, and of the sorceror Merlin, had retaken all his kingdom from the Saxon Oswald and his able assistants, the magician Osmond and the earth-spirit Grimbald. An aerial spirit, Philidel, unhappy with the brutal Saxons, defects to the Britons. In a crucial eleventh battle, the Saxons are again defeated in the field. But Grimbald leads the pursuing Britons astray, and only Philidel's timely guidance saves them from being lost in the bogs. Moreover Oswald still holds prisoner Emmeline, who has been blinded. When Merlin and Arthur go to save her, Philidel magically restores her sight. Then Osmond, having cast Oswald into prison, renews his ardent suit to Emmeline. To impress her with Love's power, he conjures up a scene of frozen people, who are promptly thawed and warmed by Cupid. When she still resists, he strengthens his suit with a forceful couplet: "But if you will not fairly be enjoy'd,/A little honest force is well employ'd."

Just in the nick of time, Merlin foils his plan by ensnaring Grimbald and breaking Osmond's spell. Meanwhile Oswald, now free, reappears, only to be challenged to single combat by King Arthur. The defeat of the Saxon king opens the way to a magnificent "Vision of Britain," which, of course, glorifies Dryden's England.

All was not plain sailing for Dryden in this venture, as we may judge from his complaint in the preface: "The numbers of Poetry and Vocal Musick are sometimes so contrary, that in many places I have been oblig'd to cramp my Verses, and make them rugged to the reader, that they may be harmonious to the hearer."

Whatever discomfort Dryden may have felt from Purcell's cramping strictures, he nevertheless created a libretto providing rich scope for musical depiction of picturesque actions, sacrificial and battle scenes charged with music and atmosphere, and national pageantry on a grand scale. Purcell rose brilliantly to the occasion, realizing all these opportunities with consummate artistry.

—Franklin B. Zimmerman

THE KING IN SPITE OF HIMSELF
See LE ROI MALGRÉ LUI

A KING LISTENS
See UN RÈ IN ASCOLTO

THE KING OF LAHORE
See LE ROI DE LAHORE

THE KING OF YS
See LE ROI D'YS

KING PRIAM.

Composer: Michael Tippett.

Librettist: Michael Tippett.

First Performance: Coventry, Belgrade, 29 May 1962.

Roles: Priam (bass-baritone); Hecuba (soprano); Hector (baritone); Andromache (soprano); Paris (tenor); Helen (mezzo-soprano); Achilles (tenor); Patroclus (baritone); Hermes (tenor); Nurse (mezzo-soprano); Old Man (bass); Young Guard (tenor); Athene (soprano); Hera (soprano); Aphrodite (mezzo-soprano); chorus (SSATTBB).

Publications

articles–

Tippett, Michael. "At Work on King Priam." *Score* no. 28 (1961): 58.
Tippett, Michael. "King Priam: some Questions Answered." *Opera* 13 (1962): 297.

*   *   *

Tippett's subject in *King Priam* is, in his own words, "the mysterious nature of human choice." For Tippett, as the Ancients sing in his first opera *The Midsummer Marriage,* "Fate and freedom propound a paradox; choose your fate but yet the God speaks through whatever acts ensue."

In act I, a wise Old Man tells the young King Priam that his newborn son Paris will inevitably cause his father's death. Priam decides to have the child killed; but Paris is saved, and returns to Troy to become a young warrior. Paris seduces Menelaus' wife Helen, and so causes the Trojan War. Acts II and III show the tide of war turning from initial success for the Trojans towards their inevitable defeat. Finally, Priam, alone, in the flaming ruins of Troy, learns to accept his choice, his fate and his death.

King Priam, written as a commission from the Koussevitsky Foundation, was first performed on 29 May 1962 to mark the opening of Coventry Cathedral. Its impact was muted, both by the novelty of Tippett's style, and by the immediate success of Benjamin Britten's *War Requiem,* which was also given its world premiere to mark that occasion. *King Priam* won early esteem in Germany, and found many new admirers in the 1980s through David Atherton's powerful recording for Decca and Nicholas Hytner's remarkable production for Kent Opera, which has been released on videotape.

After the complex, Jungian collage of images in *The Midsummer Marriage,* Tippett accepted Peter Brook's advice to seek a story drawn from traditional mythical material. He had been much impressed by the visits to London in 1956 of the Compagnie Renaud Barrault with Claudel's *Christophe Colomb,* and the Berliner Ensemble with *Mother Courage* and *The Caucasian Chalk Circle.* Their epic style of theater gave him the confidence to adopt a dramatic style in which there is no unity of time, place, or action. In his second opera Tippett dramatizes only those short episodes from the story of Troy which he requires to present his own vision.

During close consultations with the director Günther Rennert, Tippett evolved a libretto in which the stage directions are minimal, allowing much more freedom to directors and designers than in *The Midsummer Marriage.* Three minor characters become a Brechtian chorus, stepping out of role in the interludes between scenes to address the audience, to discuss and comment on the drama. (This aspect of *King Priam* prefigures the cinematic technique of the "dissolve," which is used between scenes in Tippett's third opera, *The Knot Garden.*)

The stark subject-matter of *King Priam* and the economy and directness of the text are both matched by the music. Tippett has written that for this opera's subject-matter "the lyrical and sustained language that I'd used in *The Midsummer Marriage,* concentrating on melody and line, had to give way to a stark quality, with the accent on harmony and rhythm." For *King Priam* the orchestra is deconstructed into its individual parts, and the rich, post-Romantic vertical chording of the earlier opera is completely avoided. Individual moments are characterized by terse melodic fragments, which express the impact of the situation as concisely as possible.

Tippett represents the isolation and single-mindedness of his characters by assigning one group of instruments to each of them; only Priam himself is complex enough to be excepted from this rule. The conflicts between characters are rarely resolved; and the composer symbolizes the tragic frustration this generates by thematic material that does not develop in any way. Where characters sing together, Tippett simply creates a collage, in which their groups of instruments are heard simultaneously, playing their characteristic melodic fragments without any interaction.

Tippett was initially influenced by Brecht's presentational style; but he totally opposes Brecht's ideal of "estranging" the audience from the action. Tippett involves the audience in this opera immediately, by the sheer physical power of the opening fanfares, drumrolls, and female outcries. And his Aristotelian ethos is openly declared in the final scene, where Hermes first appeals to the audience to feel "the pity and the terror" as Priam dies, then sings an apostrophe to "divine music," which alone has power to heal our wounds.

The idea of spiritual healing is a major theme in all Tippett's operas. So too is the sense of numinous, magical worlds beyond our normal apprehension, represented in *King Priam* when Hermes appears to link the world of human action with the gods. This feature of the work is particularly evident in the final scene of act I; Zeus obliges Paris to choose between three goddesses (played on stage by the three women in his

life—mother, wife, and mistress), and he is irresistibly drawn to the goddess of sexual desire.

Fate or freedom? In the opening scene, the Old Man prophesies that Paris will cause *as by an inexorable fate* his father's death. Destiny, in Tippett's opera, is overwhelming; and the colloquy of Priam with Achilles in his tent becomes a pale reflection of its original in *The Iliad,* book XXIV, simply because Tippett's characters have nothing to do but accept their imminent deaths with bleak resignation. Also, the opening scene of act III—for the women of Troy—is unduly protracted. But overall, the new style which Tippett evolved for this opera is totally consistent and extremely powerful. For all its austerity, *King Priam* is one of the richest operas composed in Britain since 1945.

—Michael Ewans

KING ROGER
See KRÓL ROGER

THE KING'S CHILDREN
See DIE KÖNIGSKINDER

KIPNIS, Alexander.

Bass. Born 13 February 1891, in Zhitomir, Ukraine. Died 14 May 1978, in Westport, Connecticut. Father of the harpsichordist Igor Kipnis. Studied conducting at Warsaw until 1912 and then served as a bandmaster in Russian army; studied voice with Ernst Grenzebach at Klindworth-Scharwenka Conservatory, in Berlin; opera debut in Hamburg, 1915/16; at Wiesbaden, 1917-22; leading bass in Berlin Charlottenburg (later Städtische) Oper, 1919-29, and the Staatsoper, 1930-35; in Vienna to 1938; United States debut as Pogner in *Die Meistersinger von Nürnberg,* Baltimore, 1923; in Chicago, 1923-32; appeared at Covent Garden, 1927, 1929, and 1933-35; appeared at Bayreuth, 1927, 1930, and 1933; Glyndebourne, 1936; Salzburg, 1937; Metropolitan Opera debut as Gurnemanz, 1940, and remained there until his retirement in 1946; taught singing in New York.

Publications

About KIPNIS: articles–

Frankenstein, A. et al. "Alexander Kipnis." *Record Collector* 22 (1974): 53.

*   *   *

Alexander Kipnis is a prime example of the artist-musician who had everything: the respect and admiration of audiences, critics, and his peers. His large recorded legacy contains many

Alexander Kipnis, early 1940s

performances of arias and Lieder that are unsurpassed, only a few that are unremarkable, and almost no failures. This appraisal could equally describe his career, which was on the very highest plane. Although some engagements were of routine quality, there was never a failure.

Kipnis was to a large degree both a victim and a representative of his background. As a Russian Jew who matured at the beginning of World War I he had gravitated to Germany for his musical schooling and apprenticeship. Throughout his career he dabbled in Russian repertoire, but he was never considered a Russian singer in style, vocal quality, or instinct. He was, in fact, the finest German-style bass of his epoch. The smooth voice, spacious phrasing, and sheer vocal resource, however, were a marked departure from the accepted German bass school of his time, which emphasized cavernous black sound at the bottom and "barking" the upper register with disregard for pitch. Instead of black sound Kipnis produced a deep rich velvety sound, never "barked" the upper register, and was scrupulous in matters of pitch. This vocal culture enabled him to sing the big Italian roles with extraordinary smoothness.

In many ways Kipnis was a performing nomad; there was no central theater where he was a dominating force. Instead his career was marked by steady engagements of high quality and prestigious guest appearances. Other than an ongoing but sporadic association with Berlin, at least up to 1935, his closest operatic associations were a decade at the Chicago Opera (1923-1932) and seven seasons at the Metropolitan Opera (1940-1946). The American phase of his activities is important both artistically and personally. In Chicago he evolved from a utility artist to a genuine star. By the time he came to the Metropolitan he was nearing the end of his career, and he specialized in the Wagner bass parts.

In Chicago in 1925 he married the daughter of the distinguished composer-pianist Heniot Levy. This helped firm up his American ties, and he later became an American citizen.

His periodic visits to Berlin would see him featured in Wagner casts that were the best of his time; in a 1929 Furtwängler production of *Tristan und Isolde,* for example, he played King Marke in a cast that featured Leider, Onegin, Melchior and Schorr. In his wanderings as a guest artist a drop-in performance in Oslo in 1932 introduced him to the then completely unknown Kirsten Flagstad, who deeply impressed him. He immediately spread the word about her unique voice, thus helping lay the groundwork for her fateful encounter two years later with Gatti-Casazza of the Metropolitan.

His recorded legacy is mostly of the highest calibre. Mozart arias of Sarastro, Osmin, and Bartolo are virtually definitive; his Wotan Farewell noteworthy; and his Parsifal Good Friday Spell from Bayreuth under Siegfried Wagner unsurpassed to this day. His *Simon Boccanegra* aria is a lesson in classically broad phrasing and vocal control. There are hardly any of his recordings that are not definitive or at least so good as to be almost definitive. The one drawback is the lack of an overriding vocal personality such as distinguishes Chaliapin and Pinza. Kipnis is ultimately a textbook study of correct and musical rather than inspiring singing. His artistry thus reflects his career: prestigious in the extreme, but ultimately not as unique or impressive as the handful of other great bassos of the century.

—Charles B. Mintzer

KITEZH
See LEGEND OF THE INVISIBLE CITY OF KITEZH AND THE MAIDEN FEVRONIYA

KLEIBER, Carlos.

Conductor. Born 3 July 1930, in Berlin. Married: Stanislava Brezovar, dancer. Son of conductor Erich Kleiber. Left Nazi Germany in 1935 with his parents; lived in South America, 1940; studied chemistry in Zurich, 1949-50; studied music in Buenos Aires; vocal coach and stage assistant at the Theater am Gärtnerplatz, Munich, 1952; conducting debut in Potsdam, 1954; vocal coach, 1956, and conductor, 1958, at the Deutsche Oper am Rhein, Düsseldorf; conductor at the Zurich Opera, 1964-66; conducted Berg's *Wozzeck* at the Edinburgh Festival, 1966; principal conductor of the Württemberg State Theater in Stuttgart, 1966-68; conductor of the Bavarian State Opera in Munich, 1968-78; conducted *Tristan und Isolde* at the Vienna State Opera, 1973, and at Bayreuth, 1974; conducted *Der Rosenkavalier* at Covent Garden, London and at the Teatro alla Scala, Milan, 1974; conducted *Otello* at the San Francisco Opera, 1977; became a naturalized Austrian citizen, 1980; has conducted the Chicago Symphony Orchestra, the Vienna Philharmonic Orchestra, and the Berlin Philharmonic Orchestra; Metropolitan Opera debut with Puccini's *La bohème*, 1988.

Publications

About KLEIBER: articles–

Flowers, W. "Carlos Kleiber—A Legend at 50." *Le Grand Baton* March (1982).
Rhein, J. von. "The Unpredictable Carlos Kleiber." *Ovation* September (1983).

For many modern operagoers, Carlos Kleiber exists among the exalted few. This is true despite his self-imposed limit on the number of his operatic performances and recordings; his performances are rare enough to be eagerly anticipated events. His specialties have been the operas of Wagner, Strauss, Verdi, Weber, and Berg, but he has also had significant success in Puccini and Bizet. The son of conductor Erich Kleiber, Carlos Kleiber first conducted opera at the Theater am Gärtnerplatz in Munich in 1953. Throughout the 1950s he conducted at various opera houses in Germany and elsewhere, notably in Potsdam, at the Deutsche Oper am Rhein, Düsseldorf and Duisburg, Zurich, and Stuttgart, finally reaching international prominence by the late 1960s.

Kleiber began conducting at the Bavarian Staatsoper, Munich, in 1968, where he developed a relationship with intendant Günther Rennert that led to a ten-year period now called a "golden age" for opera in Munich; Kleiber's relations with Rennert's successor, August Everding, were less productive. He conducted at the Vienna Staatsoper initially in 1973. His first Bayreuth appearance was in 1974, when he led *Tristan und Isolde.* Outside the German-speaking countries he has conducted at La Scala and at Covent Garden, among other theaters, leading the relatively small group of works with which he has become associated: Richard Strauss's *Der Rosenkavalier* and *Elektra,* Puccini's *La bohème,* Bizet's *Carmen,* Weber's *Der Freischütz,* Wagner's *Tristan und Isolde,* and Verdi's *Otello* and *La traviata.*

His Metropolitan Opera debut came in 1988 with *La bohème,* which was a critical and popular triumph. This was followed by *Otello,* a performance that many critics thought the finest they had heard, and *La traviata* in 1989. In 1990 he returned to the Met to conduct *Der Rosenkavalier.*

In recent years Kleiber has become both highly respected among the cognoscenti and something of a cult figure, an identity enhanced by the relative infrequency of his performances. He is known as a perfectionist who will perform only when conditions are exactly as he wants, and he has a reputation for canceling engagements. Critics have made reference to his "infinitely expressive left hand" and point out its importance in his communicating with the singers and orchestra. His baton technique is clear; his gestures do not convey every marking in the score but are used to clarify the music. He is known as a creative, imaginative musician who is willing to take chances and one who can be spontaneous because of his deep knowledge of his scores. Less self-effacing than many modern conductors, he is able to impose his own personality on the works he conducts without self-indulgence, a trait some may feel connects Kleiber to an earlier school of conductors. He has preferred not to accept an appointment as resident conductor at any one opera house, preferring to conduct a limited number of performances. This is dictated by his insistence on a restricted repertoire on which he can concentrate, by his rigorously high standards, and by the provision of sufficient rehearsal time.

A highly intellectual conductor, Kleiber is capable of great eloquence and strongly passionate expression. He has been praised for his close attention to detail and careful adherence to the instructions in the score, while still being able to superimpose his own personality on the work he is leading. Beauty of sound takes second place to structure and architecture, yet tonal beauty is not slighted. It is through such attention to structure that he feels he can reveal the dramatic truth of the work. He encompasses the lyrical as well as the impassioned in his work. His performances are marked by a combination of tension and elegance, as well as spirituality, tenderness, fervor, and a sense of dramatic purpose. He is especially successful in delineating the various strands of ensembles, clarifying detail while not losing sight of the whole. He is known as a supportive accompanist to his singers. Because he often chooses fast tempos, he avoids the sentimentalizing that can result from leisurely pacing. His approach is analytical, but this does not impede sweep and passion. Finally, he is adept at creating atmosphere and at inspiring his orchestras to greatness. Some critics, however, accuse him of being overly meticulous, sophisticated where he should be spontaneous and of adopting extremes of tempo, especially fast ones, with a tendency to hurry through certain passages of scores.

Kleiber has recorded only four complete operas: Weber's *Der Freischütz* (1973), Johann Strauss, Jr.'s *Die Fledermaus*

(1976), Verdi's *La traviata* (1977), and Wagner's *Tristan und Isolde* (1982).

—Michael Sims

KLEIBER, Erich.

Conductor. Born 5 August 1890, in Vienna. Died 27 January 1956, in Zurich. Married: Ruth Goodrich, 1926 (one son [the conductor Carlos Kleiber], one daughter). Studied at the Prague Conservatory and the University of Prague, 1908; conducted at the German Theater in Prague, 1911; conducted opera at Darmstadt, 1912-19, Barmen-Elberfeld, 1919-21, Düsseldorf, 1921-22, and Mannheim, 1922-23; Generalmusikdirektor of the Berlin State Opera, 1923; conducted the premiere of Berg's *Wozzeck,* 14 December 1925; resigned his position with the Berlin State Opera as an anti-Nazi protest, 1934; emigrated to South America; conducted at the Teatro Colón in Buenos Aires, 1936-49; conducted at Covent Garden, London, 1937, and 1950-53; reinstated as Generalmusikdirektor of the Berlin State Opera, 1954, but resigned before the season opened due to disagreements with the Communist party.

Publications

About KLEIBER: books–

Russell, J. *Erich Kleiber: a Memoir.* London, 1957.

articles–

Prerauer, Curt. "Erich Kleiber." *Opera* January (1952).

*   *   *

Erich Kleiber's rather small but choice recorded legacy and the contemporary accounts of his conducting have made him into a legendary figure among opera conductors. He was known to be the utmost perfectionist, the enemy of compromise and sloppy performance traditions, believing in the sanctity of the composer's intentions. Many of his great virtues and musical values were imparted to his son, Carlos, himself now an esteemed opera conductor.

Erich Kleiber was born Viennese and his musical tastes and outlooks reflected this. He had a special affinity for interpreting the works of Mozart, Beethoven, and Richard Strauss. It seems fitting that Kleiber was able to see Gustav Mahler conduct at the Vienna Hofoper during his final years there. In 1908 the young Kleiber left Vienna to study in Prague, both at the Conservatory and at the University. In 1911 he won a prize for a symphonic poem and received early conducting appointments at the German Theater in Prague (1911) and Darmstadt (1912). He remained in Darmstadt for seven years, conducting principally operetta and opéra-comique. His great chance came in 1916 when he conducted *Der Rosenkavalier* flawlessly from sight at a dress rehearsal. For the remainder of his career he was closely associated with this work, imparting to the score a special luminescence and Straussian "Aufschwung." His 1953 recording of the opera on Decca with Reining, Jurinac, Gueden, and Weber is an especially gorgeous reading in which Kleiber elicits glowing tone from the Vienna Philharmonic.

In 1923 Kleiber had a great success in Berlin with a performance of *Fidelio* in which Leider and Schorr were the principals; only a few days after this premiere he was chosen to succeed Leo Blech as Generalmusikdirektor of the Berlin State Opera. At that house he was instrumental in premiering new works or presenting operas that were little-known. His conducting of Janáček's *Jenůfa* in 1924 helped to further wider knowledge and acceptance of Janáček's works, and in 1925 Kleiber gave the world premiere of Berg's *Wozzeck* after 137 exhaustive rehearsals. Other new works that he introduced include Schreker's *Der singende Teufel* in 1928 and Milhaud's *Christophe Colombe* in 1930. Kleiber's tenure in Berlin came to a close when he resigned in 1934 due to the rise of the Nazis; he did not return to Berlin until 1951.

During the 1920s and 1930s Kleiber traveled far as a guest conductor. His Covent Garden debut came in 1938 with *Der Rosenkavalier* with Lotte Lehmann as the Marschallin. He became especially active in South America, not only at the Teatro Colón in Buenos Aires but also in theaters in Chile, Uruguay, Mexico, and Cuba. Not until after World War II did Kleiber resume his connections with the opera houses of Europe; he was an important musical director at the postwar Covent Garden. Plans for an appointment to the Vienna Staatsoper unfortunately never materialized.

Among the prizes of Kleiber's all too small number of recordings are the Decca *Rosenkavalier* with the Vienna Philharmonic and a 1955 *Le nozze di Figaro,* also on Decca and also with the Vienna Philharmonic. William Mann has characterized the latter performance by saying that "It remains Kleiber's set, spacious but not laggard, lively yet loving, musical and dramatic at once." Kleiber draws the best from the Viennese players: a legato, cantabile string sound and delightful woodwind playing, perfectly phrased. Lisa Della Casa is the Countess; her "Dove sono," is exquisitely accompanied. The set includes every musical number and all the recitative. The live performances under Kleiber's baton that have been preserved include a pirate set of Verdi's *I vespri siciliani* from the 1951 Florence May Festival with Maria Callas as Elena. Although there are a number of cuts in the score, it is a very fine performance, both vocally and on Kleiber's part. There is a 1955 *Der Freischütz,* recorded in a studio for broadcast, with Elisabeth Grümmer as Agathe and Rita Streich as Ännchen. A broadcast of *Fidelio* from Cologne Radio was made within a few days of Kleiber's death in January of 1956. The cast includes Nilsson, Frick, and Schöffler. Kleiber emphasizes the *Singspiel* rather than the heroic aspect in his choice of tempi; as usual his sense of proportion and attention to detail are masterly.

In sum, Kleiber was a great interpreter of the Viennese classics, yet a musician whose ideas transcended geographical boundaries. He is the embodiment, in the words of Kurt Blaukopf, of the "tempestuous, the unbending, the independent artist," in whose hands music, while using the materials of humanity, becomes spiritual in the sense of always being created anew. Blaukopf wrote of Kleiber's Mozart: "It is not the *theme* which rules his [Mozart's] music [as interpreted by Kleiber], but its *exposition;* not its existence, but its *development;* not its being, but its *coming into being.*"

—Stephen Willier

KLEMPERER, Otto.

Conductor. Born 14 May 1885, in Breslau. Died 6 July 1973, in Zurich. Studied piano with Kwast and theory with Knorr at the conservatory in Frankfurt, 1901; studied composition and conducting with Pfitzner in Berlin; debut conducting Max Reinhardt's production of Offenbach's *Orphée aux enfers* in Berlin, 1905; chorus master and subsequently conductor of the German Theater in Prague; assisted Mahler with preparations for the premiere of *Symphony of a Thousand,* Munich, 1910; conductor at the Hamburg Opera, 1910-12; conducted in Barmen, 1913-14, and Strasbourg (under Pfitzner), 1914-17; music director of the Cologne Opera, 1917; music director of the Wiesbaden Opera, 1924; guest conductor of the New York Symphony Orchestra, 1926; director of the Kroll Opera, Berlin, 1927-31; conducted the premiere of Hindemith's *Neues vom Tage,* 8 June 1929; conducted the first Berlin performances of Hindemith's *Cardillac,* Stravinsky's *Oedipus Rex,* and Schoenberg's *Die glückliche Hand;* conducted the first performance of Schoenberg's *Begleitungsmusik;* conductor of the Berlin State Opera, 1931; emigrated to the United States when the Nazi's came to power in 1933; music director of the Los Angeles Philharmonic, 1933; underwent surgery for a brain tumor, 1939; conductor at the Budapest State Opera, 1947-50; guest conductor with the Philharmonia Orchestra, London, 1951, and principal conductor, 1959; conducted in Jerusalem and became an Israeli citizen, 1970; retired 1972. Klemperer was also a composer, and studied composition with Schoenberg when they were both in America.

Publications

By KLEMPERER: books–

Meine Erinnerungen an Gustav Mahler und andere autobiographische Skizzen. Zurich, 1960.
Minor Recollections. London, 1964.
Stomper, Stephan, ed. *Otto Klemperer über Musik und Theater: Erinnerungen, Gespräche, Skizzen.* Berlin, 1982.
Anderson, M., ed. *Klemperer on Music: Shavings from a Musician's Workbench.* London, 1986.

interviews–

Heyworth, P., ed. *Conversations with Klemperer.* London, 1973.
"Otto Klemperer in Conversation with Peter Heyworth." In *Conversations with Conductors,* edited by Robert Chesterman. London, 1976.

About KLEMPERER: books–

Curjel, Hans. *Experiment Krolloper 1927-1931.* Munich, 1975.

Otto Klemperer with members of the Kölner Rundfunk-Symphonie-Orchester, 1954

Osborne, C. and K. Thomson, eds. *Klemperer Stories: Anecdotes, Sayings and Impressions of Otto Klemperer.* London, 1980.

Heyworth, P. *Otto Klemperer: his Life and Times. Volume 1, 1885-1933.* London, 1983.

articles–

Stomper, Stephan. " 'Die Idee kann Mann nicht töten! . . .': Otto Klemperer und die Berlin Kroll-Oper 1927-31." *Jahrbuch der Komischen Oper Berlin* (1963).

*   *   *

Otto Klemperer's career in opera began in 1905 with fifty performances of Offenbach's *Orphée aux enfers* in Berlin. He returned to Berlin after a period of over twenty years (spent in various appointments in several German opera houses) to take the musical world by storm with his direction of the capital's Kroll Opera House. The Kroll was considered the center of both experimental productions of the established repertoire and for the presentation of new operas, and at the time of Klemperer's work there (1927-31) Kleiber was at the State Opera, Walter was at the Charlottenburg Opera and Furtwängler was in charge of the Berlin Philharmonic Orchestra—a rich period in Germany's history of performances in the twentieth century. The new works Klemperer presented included Hindemith's *Cardillac* and *Neues vom Tage,* Stravinsky's *Oedipus Rex* and *Mavra,* Janáček's *From the House of the Dead,* Krenek's *Lebendes Orest,* Weill's *Der Jasager* (Klemperer rejected the chance to premiere the same composer's *Aufstieg und Fall der Stadt Mahagonny*) and Schoenberg's *Erwartung* and *Die glückliche Hand.* Controversial productions of *Fidelio, Die Zauberflöte, Carmen, Les contes d'Hoffmann* and *Madama Butterfly* were eclipsed by an infamous *Fliegende Holländer* in modern dress and with revolutionary stage designs, whose influence persisted until after the Second World War with Wieland Wagner's new approach to the staging of his grandfather's music dramas at Bayreuth (where Klemperer never conducted) and even further ahead to the 1970s with such directors as Götz Friedrich and Patrice Chéreau. In some quarters Klemperer was labeled a cultural Bolshevik, and the production was later pilloried by the Nazis as a leading example of the cultural excesses and outrages of the preceding Weimar Republic.

Klemperer was dogged throughout his life by a series of mental problems and physical accidents which would have laid a lesser man low. As well as being the victim of both Nazism in the 1930s and McCarthyism in the 1950s, he was subject to severe depressions that affected his temperament and made him a very difficult man to work with. It was not until 1947 that he worked regularly in an opera house again, this time in Budapest where he devoted himself to the Mozart operas and much of the standard repertoire (an exception was Musorgsky's *Sorochintsy Fair,* which he himself called "a really unimportant work").

Klemperer's career enjoyed a magnificent Indian summer in the last decade of his life, and brought him fairly frequently to Covent Garden (*Fidelio, Zauberflöte* and *Lohengrin*), but appearances at the opera houses of Berlin and New York were thwarted (as was a proposed *Meistersinger* to be directed by Wieland Wagner at Bayreuth) by ill-health. On occasion (such as at the Kroll and in his last appearances in London) he directed the operas he conducted in order to forestall any overshadowing of the musical conception by the stage production. Unlike the debate in Strauss' *Capriccio,* there was no doubt in Klemperer's mind that the music dominated the text.

Klemperer's technique, limited by dreadful accidents over the years, was largely based on an overpowering charisma and presence. Immensely tall and imposing with a fixed and sometimes manic stare, he would dominate his players and singers by sheer personality and power of suggestion and yet give both the opportunity to breathe within the phrase. He colored his sound by emphasising the woodwind chorus in his orchestras and unerringly found his tempo with a firmly established up-beat.

—Christopher Fifield

DIE KLUGE [The Wise Woman].

Composer: Carl Orff.

Librettist: Carl Orff (after the Brothers Grimm, *Die kluge Bauerntochter*).

First Performance: Frankfurt, 20 February 1943.

Roles: The King (baritone); The Farmer (bass); His Daughter (soprano); Jailer (bass); Donkey Boy (tenor); Muleteer (baritone); Three Vagabonds (tenor, baritone, bass).

*   *   *

The literary source for *Die Kluge,* which Orff called simply "The Story of the King and the Wise Woman," was, like its predecessor, *Der Mond,* from the collection of Grimm's fairy tales. Grimm's version differs from those cited by Leo Frobenius in his multi-volume collection of African folk literature; the German story is more brief and childlike in its sentimental rendition. Orff began a libretto for *Die Kluge,* but soon recognized it as what he termed a "false start," so he put it aside, to start afresh after finding an old collection of more than 12,000 German folk proverbs, published in 1846 by H.L. Brönner. Orff's first glance at a few pages of the book brought whole scenes to mind, and his ultimate setting of *Die Kluge* used no narrator, but added the Shakespearean-like figures of the three ruffians, the muleteer, and the donkey boy— perfect vehicles for scattering old proverbs like raisins throughout the sections of spoken dialogue, and fleshing out the dramatic action with contrasts of high humor and pathos.

The fable itself is based on one such proverb: one cannot be wise and also love. The Wise Woman is the daughter of a poor farmer, who at the opening curtain is in prison, bewailing his fate and regretting aloud that he didn't listen to his daughter's advice. While plowing, he'd found a golden mortar, which he was determined to take to the king, but she said, "Throw it away . . . if you give it to him, he'll want the pestle, too, and since you don't have it, he'll call you a liar and a thief and cast you into the palace dungeon." Overhearing the prisoner's loud cries, the king has the man brought before him to hear the sorry tale. Such wisdom in a young girl intrigues the king, who commands her to appear, and offers her a wager: answer three riddles, and freedom will be given her and her father, with the daughter marrying the king. Lose, and both die. The girl succeeds, to His Highness'

The premiere of Orff's *Die Kluge*, Frankfurt, 1943

amazement and delight. He calls for celebration and a release of *all* prisoners for the festivities. Later, the queen (in disguise) gives some advice to the donkey boy; the king learns of it, and, enraged to think she is usurping his governing powers, banishes her from the court, but gives her a trunk in which she may take what is dearest to her. A measure of poppyseed in the supper wine puts the king to sleep, and when the queen leaves the palace with her trunk, the king is in it. The musical drama ends with the king's revival, the reuniting of the married couple, and the release of the donkey boy with a sack of gold as a present from the king. But the queen says to her husband, "My wisdom was just a pose; no one can both love and be wise." And seeing them together once more, her father remarks, "Aha! . . . she found the pestle after all."

The music for *Die Kluge* is stripped to bare essentials, prompting a disgruntled reviewer to call it "ten minutes of music stretched into ninety." By means of a few simple melodic motives, passed from voice to voice in dialogue and recast later here and there in the orchestral underlay, Orff provides a unifying element that adds cohesion. Great dynamic contrasts, a Renaissance use of fanfares, repeated instrumental *Intratas,* modal vocal lines with occasional oriental touches, and octave leaps in motivic solo lines and repeated phrases, together with snatches of rustic folk song, give the work "the appropriate anonymity of time and place." Musical settings glide in and out of spoken dialogue, and rhythmic

contrasts, *ostinati,* and judicious repetition are used to carefully shape the action on stage.

—Jean C. Sloop

KNAPPERTSBUSCH, Hans.

Conductor. Born 12 March 1888, in Elberfeld. Died 25 October 1965, in Munich. Studied with Steinbach and Lohse at the Cologne Conservatory, 1908-12; assistant conductor at the Bayreuth Festival, 1910-13; conducted in Bochum, 1912-13; conducted opera at Elberfeld, 1913-18, Leipzig, 1918-19, and Dessau, 1919-22; Generalmusikdirektor of the Bavarian State Opera in Munich, 1922-36 (resigned as a result of Nazi pressure); conductor at the Vienna State Opera, 1936-45; conductor of the Vienna Philharmonic, 1937-44; conductor at the Salzburg Festival, 1947-50, 1954-55; guest conductor at the Bayreuth Festival, beginning 1951-64; guest conductor with the Vienna Philharmonic, 1947-64.

Publications

About KNAPPERTSBUSCH: books–

Knappertsbusch, W.G. *Die Knappertsbusch und ihre Vorfahren.* Elberfeld, 1943.
Betz, R., and W. Panofsky. *Knappertsbusch.* Ingolstadt, 1958.

articles–

Dawson-Bowling, Paul. "Knappertsbusch: the Recorded Legacy." *Opera* March (1988).

*   *   *

Hans Knappertsbusch was solid in his musical interpretations, the antithesis of Felix Weingartner, whose tempi were swift. Not for nothing was Knappertsbusch Hans Richter's assistant at Bayreuth at the 1912 festival for *Die Meistersinger,* and not for nothing did the master present his pupil with the full score after the last performance (which was also Richter's last public appearance). It was probably also from Richter that Knappertsbusch developed an aversion to rehearsals; tales are legion in Vienna of a short 'top-and-tail' rehearsal in which the conductor forgot to clarify the matter of repeats within a work, and the resultant confusion during the performance only confirmed Knappertsbusch in his belief that even that short rehearsal had been the cause. In the same city he omitted the overture at the final rehearsal of an entirely new production of *Die Zauberflöte,* preferring to leave it to the opening night, and he avoided attending rehearsals of a new *Lohengrin.* When he did see it (even as he conducted its premiere) he loathed it so much that he refused to conduct any further performances.

Knappertsbusch's view of rehearsals inevitably led to an improvised way of music-making that produced an air of spontaneity in performance. His philosophy was based on four precepts: if the conductor knew the work well, if the orchestra knew the work well, if the conductor knew the orchestra well and if the orchestra knew the conductor well, then rehearsals became superfluous. At the same time this attitude made Knappertsbusch a very difficult conductor for the recording industry, for he hated the endless repetition of the recording process as much as he disliked rehearsing. He was the natural first choice for the famous Decca *Ring,* but was passed over in favor of Solti.

Knappertsbusch's career was, by his own choice, effectively limited to three centers: Vienna, Munich and Bayreuth (his mentor Richter had been similarly limited to Vienna, London and Bayreuth, and both men shared a dislike of traveling). His association with the famous Wagner festival only began with the reopening of the Bayreuth theater after the Second World War in 1951, and he was largely responsible for rebuilding orchestral standards after the festival's seven year closure.

Knappertsbusch was entrusted with the mantle of *Parsifal* like Hermann Levi and Karl Muck before him, and conducted it each year (except in 1953) until his last appearance in 1964. The 1951 performances have become legendary, for in spite of Knappertsbusch's profound dislike of Wieland Wagner's new ideas of stage design and production, he directed his energies toward creating a magical superlative orchestral sound to match his concept of Wagner's music drama. During that same season he also conducted both the *Ring* cycle and *Die Meistersinger,* and was universally praised

for the warmth and tonal purity he extracted from his orchestra, many commenting in particular upon the chamber-music quality of the balance between stage and pit which permitted the text to be heard. In 1956 Knappertsbusch said that the orchestra, which he described as the eighth wonder of the world, was the magnet that drew him annually to the Bayreuth Festival.

Knappertsbusch's manner was brusque and he never minced words. In many respects his performances were modeled on musical traditions handed down by Hans Richter, even if the results, rather than the methods, were often more in keeping with von Bülow or Nikisch, impulsive and born more of feeling than thought.

—Christopher Fifield

THE KNIGHT OF THE ROSE
See DER ROSENKAVALIER

THE KNOT GARDEN.

Composer: Michael Tippett.

Librettist: Michael Tippett.

First Performance: London, Covent Garden, 2 December 1970.

Roles: Faber (baritone); Thea (mezzo-soprano); Flora (soprano); Denise (soprano); Mel (bass-baritone); Dov (tenor); Mangus (baritone); chorus (offstage voices and whistles).

Publications

articles–

Sutcliffe, T. "Tippett and the Knot Garden." *Music and Musicians* 19/no. 4 (1970): 52.
Tippett, Michael. "The Knot Garden." *About the House* 3/no. 7 (1970).
Warrack, John. *"The Knot Garden." Musical Times* 111 (1970): 1092.

*   *   *

Tippett was drawn to write an opera about the universal psychological problem of relativity of identity by his reading of Christopher Fry's play, *A Sleep of Prisoners.* Tippett's starting point was to present a group of contemporary characters each of whom was of equal importance; therefore, there would be no leading man, no leading woman, and no chorus. This would be an ironic comedy, to use Tippett's phrase; human situations are depicted in such a way that they remind us of the dichotomy between ideal and real situations on the human and psychological levels. The idea of placing the action in a garden is Tippett's adaptation of the notion of the Renaissance garden—one which can also be viewed as a maze.

For the first time in his operas, Tippett's imagination is influenced by cinematic techniques. There are several short scenes in each act, all handled like collage, one scene cutting into another.

In act I, the scene is a rose garden. All of the characters are introduced. Mangus is the analyst and would-be-healer. Thea and Faber are a young couple whose marriage is troubled. She is self-preoccupied and indifferent to Faber's needs, going so far as to flirt with Mel, a Black author. In his frustration, Faber first makes sexual advances to Flora, his naive young ward, then to Dov, an insecure musician and the homosexual lover of Mel. Denise, Thea's younger sister, is a belligerent, proud freedom fighter, who has just come home disfigured from the torture she has undergone.

In act II, Mangus is only an observer. The garden becomes a maze which throws or whirls the characters into a series of seemingly chance confrontations in which their pairings continually change. The brief, intense encounters show increasingly more violent dichotomies between love and hate as the act progresses. At the end of the act, the two characters most lost, Flora and Dov, are thrown clear of the maze onto the forestage, where they try to comfort each other as the maze recedes.

Having silently observed the encounters of act II, Mangus in act III resumes his part in the action. The scene is once again a rose garden. The act is called "Charade," because Mangus, as Prospero, allots roles based on figures from Shakespeare's *The Tempest* to four of the characters, so that all the characters—those who role-play and those who observe—may have a chance to see themselves more truthfully. Tippett would have the observer of *The Knot Garden* recognize the notion of "forgiveness scenes" in these charades: forgiveness between Mangus and Mel and Dov after Mangus has manipulated them to the point of indignity (fourth charade, scene ix), to take but one example. The idea of forgiveness, hard to come by until the end, is essential to the irony of the comedy. When the fourth charade fails to demonstrate Mel's and Dov's potential for healing, Mangus abdicates his role of Prospero and joins the others in their first common admission that acceptance of the bittersweetness of the human condition is the only hope.

As the opera draws to a close, Mel and Denise exit together, having found healing and hope in their budding love. Dov, still uncertain of himself, needs a sign from Mel to follow after them. Flora exits alone, dancing happily; she has understood the message of the charades and shed some of her naiveté. Before he exits alone, Mangus points out that only Thea and Faber remain to express their newly revitalized respect and love. Alone together, they face each other honestly and with acceptance. The opera is over, but for them and the others "the curtain rises" (as the last words of their duet say) on the beginning of a new life.

Musical allusion is another of Tippett's strong dramatic techniques. The most outstanding example occurs in the finale of act I. Here he creates an original blues form, harmony, and instrumentation that accompany the dense vocal counterpoint of six of the characters. The sound creates a kind of human howling. To use the blues as a metaphor for suffering is nothing new. To use it to this poignant effect in opera is highly original.

One of the several other musically significant techniques that Tippett uses as dramatist is distinctive timbre and harmony to create moments of magic and mystery. The instrumentation of Mangus' "Magic" motif is a case in point. This motif appears whenever Mangus portrays Prospero. Its peculiar timbre gives the motif its numinous effect: flutes repeat a high E-flat staccato; celeste and harp play an isorhythmic arpeggio on two seventh chords—E, Mm and D, AM; the bass clarinet and horn reiterate a quiet low B-flat. This sound immediately conjures the magic.

Nowhere are distinctive tone-color and harmony more felicitously apparent than in the opera's epilogue. Thea and Faber are alone, mostly speaking their text of mutual acceptance as the motif used to designate the garden-as-stage functions in the orchestra. When they sing the final "the curtain rises," the words could be lost in the angularity and melisma of the vocal line with heavy brass accompaniment. But the final wash of sound that spirals upward to a stunning orchestral climax removes all doubt. The thrill of the music convinces the listener that a new beginning is at hand.

—Margaret Scheppach

KNUSSEN, (Stuart) Oliver.

Composer. Born 12 June 1952, in Glasgow. Married: Susan Freedman, 1972 (one daughter). Early studies in piano and theory with John Lambert; conducted his First Symphony with the London Symphony Orchestra at the age of 15 (7 April 1968); studied advanced composition with Gunther Schuller on Tanglewood fellowships 1970-73; Margaret Grant Composition Prize at Tanglewood for his Second Symphony, 1976; on the faculty of the Royal College, 1976-80; artistic director of the Aldeburgh Festival, 1983-; composer in residence, Tanglewood, 1986; Coordinator of Contemporary Music, Tanglewood, 1986-91; composer in residence, Chamber Music Society of Lincoln Center, 1990-92. Knussen has been commissioned by the Melos Ensemble, the Aldeburgh Festival, the Florida International Festival, the London Sinfonietta, the Koussevitzky Centennial Commission, and the British Broadcasting Company.

Operas

Publisher: Faber.

Where the Wild Things Are, Maurice Sendak and Knussen, 1979-83, Brussels National Opera, 28 November 1980; revised, London, National Theatre, 9 January 1984.
Higglety Pigglety Pop! Maurice Sendak, 1984-85, Glyndebourne, 8 May 1985.

Publications

By KNUSSEN: articles–

"Peter Maxwell Davies's *Five Klee Pictures.*" *Tempo* 124 (1978): 17.
"Cirencester and the *Five Klee Pictures.*" In *Peter Maxwell Davies: Studies from Two Decades,* compiled by Stephan Pruslin, 102. London, 1979.

interviews–

Griffiths, Paul. *New Sounds, New Personalities: British Composers of the 1980s.* London, 1985.

About KNUSSEN: articles–

Northcott, Bayan. "Oliver Knussen." *Musical Times* 120 (1979): 729.
Sand, Barbara L. "Oliver Knussen." *Musical America* 3/no. 3 (1991): 8-11.

*   *   *

The British composer generally considered heir to Benjamin Britten's legacy, Oliver Knussen has already had considerable success in both vocal and instrumental genres. Whether his accomplishments will eventually parallel Britten's is as yet unknown, but Knussen has so far show himself as a prodigious and gifted composer with a wide range of works, many performed and recorded. Knussen's life and works have been closely connected to the London Symphony Orchestra through his father, who was principal bassist, and to the London Sinfonietta, for which he has composed and conducted frequently. Associations and influences from the United States are also strong, especially through Gunther Schuller, with whom Knussen studied, and with the Tanglewood Music Center, where he has organized the contemporary music festival since 1986.

During the 1980s, Knussen was preoccupied with the creation of two operas in collaboration with Maurice Sendak, acclaimed American artist and author of children's books. The operas, *Where the Wild Things Are* (1979-83) and *Higglety Pigglety Pop!* (1984-85) are similar in character. *Wild Things* had remarkable critical and popular success in Europe and the U.S. More recently it has been paired with *Higglety* as a double bill. Both operas have been cited as attempts at reviving the Fantasy Opera, filled with magic and with a fey quality and an obvious desire to delight that is unmistakably childlike in effect. Sendak's animal figures converse with humans as they do in the minds of children. For example, the principal role in *Higglety* is a terrier sung by a mezzo-soprano. The large, hairy, larger-than-life characters in *Wild Things* are imbued with a spirit of enthusiasm and humor that bears resemblance to the composer himself. Amusing as they are, a mature and sophisticated musical spoofing is part of the mix as well as a depth of philosophical ideas.

Although Knussen's stated intent was to compose in as immediate and colorful a musical style as possible, his melodies are not typical of traditional operas. A contemporary sound that is characteristic of Knussen's work prevails in the operas. Rather than arias and set pieces, vocal lines are brisk and declamatory, and the operatic form flows out of the text and story line. Use of natural speech and vernacular expressions add to the present-day atmosphere. Segments of *Wild Things* have been extracted for a suite, "Songs and a Sea Interlude."

In addition to composing and conducting his own pieces, Knussen has a deep commitment to the performance of new music. In such responsible positions as co-director of the Aldeburgh Festival and composer-in-residence of the Chamber Music Society of Lincoln Center, he is responsible for the performances of many new works. In his own music and in presenting the works of others, Knussen's ever-inquiring mind combines with an exceptional musicianship to make a major contribution to the entire field of contemporary music.

—Vivian Perlis

KOANGA.

Composer: Frederick Delius.

Librettist: Charles Francis Keary (after George Washington Cable, *The Grandissimes*).

First Performance: Elberfeld, Stadttheater, 30 March 1904.

Roles: Uncle Joe (bass); Renée (soprano); Hélène (soprano); Jeanne (soprano); Marie (soprano); Aurore (contralto); Hortense (contralto); Olive (contralto); Paulette (contralto); Don José Martinez (bass); Simon Perez (tenor); Koanga (baritone); Rangwan (bass); Palmyra (soprano); Clotilda (contralto); chorus.

Publications

articles–

Randel, William. "*Koanga* and Its Libretto." *Music and Letters* April (1971).

*   *   *

Delius's *Koanga,* like Cable's original, is a frame-narrative, beginning and ending with action that takes place several years after the main events of the opera. A short prologue has the story-teller, an old slave, about to tell the tale of Koanga to a group of young planters' daughters on the verandah of a Southern plantation-house. A similarly short epilogue shows the girls' reaction to the story, which is set on a sugar plantation on the Mississippi in Louisiana in the second half of the eighteenth century.

Act I proper of the opera introduces the quadroon heroine Palmyra, her unwelcome suitor and overseer of the plantation Simon Perez, and the slaves soon to be heard singing their worksongs on the plantation. Palmyra rejects Perez's advances. Koanga, a prize slave newly arrived from Africa, is brought in. Originally both a prince and voodoo priest in his own country, he refuses to do work unworthy of his exalted rank. Don José Martinez, the plantation's owner, decides that Palmyra must use her beauty and seductive charm to make Koanga accept his status as a slave. The idea works well, and Don José decides that they shall marry. His wife, Clotilda, however, knows the secret that her own father is also Palmyra's father. Moreover, she and her half-sister have both been brought up as Christians. She determines that Palmyra must be prevented from marrying the heathen Koanga.

Act II sees the wedding preparations. Clotilda tells Simon Perez the truth about Palmyra's birth. If Perez can somehow prevent the marriage, she tells him that Palmyra shall be his. He reveals the secret to Palmyra, insisting that she must forget Koanga, "a negro slave, and you a planter's daughter." Palmyra refuses, the wedding feast begins and the slaves dance La Calinda. But before the bond can be sealed, Perez and his servants seize Palmyra and drag her away. Koanga angrily demands that Don José bring her back, but the planter will not be challenged by a slave and draws his whip. After a brief struggle he falls injured, and Koanga escapes to the forest, invoking a voodoo curse on his oppressors.

Time has passed, and act III opens at nightfall with a voodoo ceremony in the forest, with Koanga and the voodoo priest Rangwan calling for freedom and protection for the slaves. However, Koanga's curse has worked, and fever and death now stalk the plantation. Koanga fears that Palmyra, too, may die, and determines to return for her. He reappears on the plantation just as Perez again tries to force his attentions on her. Urged on by Palmyra, he kills Perez. But the hunt is on for Koanga. He is caught, overcome, and mortally wounded. Dying, he again invokes God Voodoo's protection of the slaves and promises that they shall one day have their freedom and be avenged. Palmyra denounces in turn the "white tyrants" and the Christian faith and, embracing voodoo, kills herself.

Koanga represents a considerable step forward from Delius' two earlier operas. Even so, the composer's muse had to do battle with a remarkably poor libretto, written in almost archaic English. It is a measure of his fast-approaching maturity that Delius surmounted most of the hurdles erected by his collaborator, C.F. Keary, to produce an opera that is colorful, full of drama and packed with much fine music. A thoroughgoing and notably successful revision of the libretto by Douglas Craig and Andrew Page (prepared for the 1972 Sadler's Wells production and used in the EMI recording of the opera the following year) has made *Koanga* fully viable for most stages. Productions have nonetheless been few, from the Elberfeld premiere in 1904, through Beecham's Covent Garden performances in 1935, to Corsaro's eye-opening and highly successful staging in Washington in 1970 and subsequently elsewhere in the United States.

Delius's clear sympathies with his hero and heroine, and with the plight of blacks generally, today confer upon his work both integrity and credibility. Through the writings of George Washington Cable he had found a fellow-spirit, for Cable was a campaigner against the various forms of slavery still widespread in the South in the late nineteenth century. Certainly, the exotic local color conjured up by Delius in his score, pointed as it is by authentic-sounding slave choruses and by banjo-like effects summoned from plucked strings, owes much to his own two extended stays in the American South. His music and, in particular, elements of his choral writing are generally acknowledged to owe much to his contacts with blacks and with their spirituals and worksongs in Florida and Virginia. And even earlier he would probably have been more than familiar with such kinds of music in their more vulgarized and then fashionable form as performed by the Christy minstrels and similar troupes who were popular in England in his young years.

With the completion of *Koanga* in 1895, there can be no doubt that Delius had finally arrived as a fully-fledged composer of opera. The work has considerable musical and dramatic impact and is, after all, a highly original conception, with strong claims to be the first major American black opera. Nevertheless, Delius was to write two more operas in fairly rapid succession before *Koanga* became, in 1904, the first of his works in the genre to be produced.

—Lionel Carley

————————

KODÁLY, Zoltán.

Composer. Born 16 December 1882, in Kecskemét, Hungary. Died 6 March 1967, in Budapest. Married: 1) Emma Gruber Sandor, 1910 (died 1958); 2) Sarolta Péczely (born 1940), 18

December 1959. Studied piano, violin, viola, and cello as a child; studied composition with Hans Koessler at the Budapest Academy of Music; Ph.D. dissertation *Strophic Structure in the Hungarian Folk Song*, 1906; worked with Béla Bartók in collecting and editing folk songs; in Berlin, 1906; studied with Charles-Marie Widor in Paris, 1907; instructor at the Budapest Academy, 1907; contributor to several newspapers in Budapest, as well as the *Revue musicale* and the *Musical Courier;* assistant director of the Academy of Music in Budapest, 1919; lost assistant directorship of the Academy for political reasons, but resumed teaching in 1922; *Psalmus Hungaricus* commissioned as a work commemorating the uniting of Buda and Pest, 1923; worked on his compilations of folksongs in Budapest, 1939-45; conducted concerts of his works in the United States, 1946-47; lecturer in the United States, 1965.

Operas

Publishers: Boosey and Hawkes, Magyar Kórus, Universal.

Háry János (Singspiel), Béla Paulini and Zsolt Harsányi, 1925-27, Budapest, Royal Hungarian Opera, 16 October 1926.
The spinning room [*Székely fonó*], 1924-32, Budapest, Royal Hungarian Opera, 24 April 1932.
Czinka Panna, (Singspiel) Béla Balázs, 1946-48, Budapest, Hungarian State Opera, 15 March 1948.

Other works: orchestral works, choral works, solo vocal works, chamber music, educational pieces.

Publications

By KODÁLY: books–

With Béla Bartók. *Erdélyi magyarság: népdalok* [folksongs of the Hungarians of Transylvania; preface in English and French]. Budapest, 1923.
A magyar népzene [Hungarian folk music]. Budapest, 1937; 2nd ed., 1943; 3rd ed., 1952; English translation, 1960.
With A. Gyulai. *Arany János népdalgyüjteménye* [folksong collection of Arany]. Budapest, 1953.
Szöllösy, A., ed. *A zene mindenkié*. Budapest, 1954; 2nd ed., 1975.
Mein Weg zur Musik: fünf Gespräche mit Lutz Besch. Zurich, 1966
Bónis, Ferenc. *Visszatekintés. Magyar zenetudomány*, v-vi. Budapest, 1964; 2nd ed., 1974; partial German translation, Budapest, 1983.
The Selected Writings of Zoltán Kodály. Budapest, 1974.
Bartók, Béla. *The Hungarian Folk Song*. Edited by Benjamin Suchoff, translated by M.D. Calvocoressi, annotated by Zoltán Kodály. Albany, New York, 1981.
Legány, Dezsö, ed. *Kodály Zoltán levelei* [letters]. Budapest, 1982.
Szekeres-Farkas, ed. *Kodály: Voyage en Hongrie*. Budapest, 1983.

articles–

In *Magyar zenei szemle* and *Zenei szemle*.

About KODÁLY: books–

Molnár, A. *Kodály Zoltán*. Budapest, 1936.
Szöllösy, A. *Kodály müvészete*. Budapest, 1943.

Zoltán Kodály, 1930

Sonkoly, I. *Kodály, az ember, a müvész, a nevelö* [Kodály: man, artist, educator]. Nyiregyháza, 1948.

Gergely, J. *Zoltán Kodály, musico hungaro e mestro universal.* Lisbon, 1954.

Eösze, László. *Zoltán Kodály élete és munkássága.* Budapest, 1956; English translation as *Zoltán Kodály: his Life and Work,* London, 1962.

Young, Percy M. *Zoltán Kodály: a Hungarian Musician.* London, 1964.

Szabolcsi, B. *Uton Kodályhoz* [toward Kodály]. Budapest, 1972.

Szönyi, E. *Kodály's Principles in Practice.* Budapest, 1973.

Lendvai, E. *Bartók és Kodály harmóniavilága* [harmonic world of Bartók and Kodály]. Budapest, 1975.

Breuer, J. *Kodály-dokumentumok,* i. Budapest, 1976.

Eösze, László. *Kodály Zoltán életének krónikája* [chronology of Kodály's life]. Budapest, 1977.

articles–

Pollatsek, L. "Háry János." *Musikblätter des Anbruch* 9 (1927): 138.

Hundt, Theodor. "Zoltán Kodály in eigener Sache" [*Háry János*]. *Musica* 38 (1984): 139.

Though Kodály was not an instinctive man of the theater, he was not unacquainted with it. At college he contributed incidental music to three student plays *Notre Dame de Paris* (1902), *Le Cid* (1903), and *A nagybácsi* (*The Uncle,* 1904, but it was 1917 before he had his first encounter with the professional stage when he wrote music for Zsigismond Móricz's *Pacsirtaszó* (*Lark Song*), first performed in Budapest on 14th September that year.

Almost from the outset of his career Kodály was immersed in the collection and study of Hungarian folksongs, a preoccupation which came to dominate his work as a composer. In 1905 his folksong studies brought him into contact with Béla Bartók, and the two composers began a lifelong friendship. For Bartók, folk music was the key that unlocked the doors of his originality. He absorbed it and forged from it a new and individual language, whereas Kodaly seemed content to act as a funnel from which it flowed, filtered but otherwise unchanged. By nature a conservative, Kodály lacked Bartók's breadth of vision and would have been incapable of writing anything as adventurous as *Bluebeard's Castle* or as daemonic as *The Miraculous Mandarin.* Kodály always considered it preferable to woo his audience rather than challenge it, and the lamentable fate of Bartók's two masterpieces when set before Hungarian audiences undoubtedly dissuaded Kodály from attempting to follow in his friend's footsteps.

Bartók championed Kodály's music unceasingly, and in 1928 proclaimed it "the purest expression of the Hungarian spirit." For Kodály that spirit was embodied in the human voice, and the bulk of his work is in the form of solo song and choral music designed for amateur as well as professional use. During and after the Second World War (which he spent in Hungary), and right up to his death, Kodály devoted himself to educational music, an occupation that won the approval of the post-war Communist government. His purpose, though, was didactic rather than political, and always had been; even in his most ambitious works he aimed to direct the attention of the Hungarian people to the rich heritage of their folk music. This is essentially the raison d'être of *Székely fonó* and the prime objective of *Háry János.*

Kodaly's three original stage works are difficult to describe since they are not operas in the accepted sense and fall into no readily definable category. The first, *Székely fonó* (*The Spinning Room*) (1924-32), has been called a 'lyric play," but it is more like an action cantata in which the flimsiest and most static of plots is combined with songs and dances. Its antecedents may be found among such nineteenth century comic operas as Erkel's *Névtelen hösök* (*Anonymous Heroes*), and it utilizes material from the composer's own collection of Hungarian folk music. In some ways it resembles Stravinsky's *Les noces,* though it lacks both the originality and impact of that seminal work. Kodaly hoped it would remind town dwellers of the rich fund of music then still thriving in the rural areas of Transylvania. *Székely fonó* had a modest but genuine success in its original version, and in 1932 Kodaly revised and extended it to some eighty minutes. After the war, he added yet another song, "Te tul rozsám" ("O my love") (No.10a). Prompted by this initial success he began work in 1925 on the infinitely more varied and popular *Háry János,* which was to bring him international recognition.

Háry János (1925-27) is described as a Singspiel, and this is as good a description as any. It has become a firm favorite in Hungary, and the celebrated orchestral suite Kodaly arranged from the music in 1927 made him famous worldwide, although even now the opera itself cannot be said to have gained entrée to the repertory of foreign opera houses.

Czinka Panna (1946-48), a Singspiel in three acts, was intended to be a celebration of the centenary of Kossuth's 1848 uprising against Austria, but has so far made little impression anywhere because the libretto, by Bela Balázs (author of Bartók's *Bluebeard's Castle* and *The Wooden Prince*), was deemed ideologically unacceptable, and the work was suppressed. Recent changes in the political climate in Hungary may give us an opportunity to assess its merits, but until it can be seen and heard one must reserve judgment.

—Kenneth Dommett

KOLLO, René.

Tenor. Born 20 November 1937, in Berlin. Studied with Elsa Varena, Berlin. Debut in triple bill of *Oedipus Rex, Mavra,* and *Renard,* Brunswick, 1965, where he remained until 1967; at Düsseldorf, 1967-71; Bayreuth debut as Steersman in *Tristan und Isolde,* 1969; Metropolitan Opera debut as Lohengrin, 1976; Covent Garden debut as Siegmund, 1976; sang both Siegfrieds in San Francisco, 1985.

Publications

By KOLLO: books–

Imre Fabian im Gespräch mit René Kollo. Zurich, 1982.

About KOLLO: books–

Matheopoulos, H. *Bravo.* London, 1986.

* * *

René Kollo began his career as a successful pop singer, but in 1958 he began to study voice with Elsa Verena in Berlin. In

1965 he signed a beginner's contract with the Braunschweig Opera where he made his debut in *Oedipus Rex*. Two years later he joined the German Opera on the Rhine in Düsseldorf where he sang a number of lyric tenor roles including Froh, Eisenstein, Titus, Pinkerton, and the Steuermann (*Tristan und Isolde*). It was with the latter part that he made his Bayreuth debut in 1969. Since then he has been one of the most important tenors on the Bayreuth festival rosters. His leading roles there included Erik (1970), Lohengrin (1971), Stolzing (1973), Parsifal (1975), the Young Siegfried (1976), and Tristan (1981). For such major tenor roles, René Kollo's voice was somewhat light, but he was so believable a stage figure and such an intelligent and musical singer that during the 1970s and 80s his successes in Bayreuth were overwhelming. In 1974 René Kollo sang in both the Salzburg Easter Festival (Stolzing) and the summer performances of *Die Zauberflöte* (Tamino). Covent Garden heard his Siegmund in 1976, and Max in *Der Freischütz* and Lohengrin a year later. In 1968 Kollo made his Munich debut as Lohengrin and followed that the next year with Stolzing. In 1981 Lohengrin was his introduction to the Teatro alla Scala, as it had been in 1976 at New York's Metropolitan Opera. In 1984 he sang Walter in the first performance at the newly renovated opera house in Zurich. Tristan was his debut role at the Paris Opéra during the 1985 season.

Side by side with his Wagnerian tenor roles, Kollo also sang a number of lyric parts including Lensky (*Eugene Onegin*), Matteo (*Arabella*), Vladimir (*Prince Igor*), Laca in *Jenufa* and the dramatic roles of Hermann in *Pique Dame* and Otello in Frankfurt (1988). In 1990 he sang Siegfried in the San Francisco *Der Ring des Nibelungen*, Walther in the Munich Festival's *Die Meistersinger von Nürnberg* and Tannhäuser in Hamburg.

René Kollo has continued with the family tradition of operetta and has appeared in countless television programs in that genre. His recordings for major European labels are also extensive. They include HMV-Electrola (*Die Meistersinger von Nürnberg* and *Lohengrin*), DGG (*Die Lustige Witwe*, *Fidelio*, and *Tristan und Isolde*), Eurodisc (*The Bartered Bride* and Siegfried in the complete *Ring*), CBS (operetta arias, Stravinsky's *Oedipus Rex*) and Decca (*The Magic Flute*, Walther in *Die Meistersinger von Nürnberg*, *Tannhäuser*, *Parsifal*, *Der fliegende Holländer*, *Ariadne auf Naxos*, and *Freischütz*), and RCA (*Die tote Stadt* by Korngold).

—Suzanne Summerville

KOLTAI, Ralph.

Designer. Born 31 July 1924, in Berlin. Married: Andrea Stubbs, 1956. Educated at Berlin and Central School of the Arts and Crafts, Holborn, London; associate of the Royal Shakespeare Company; head of Theatre Department, Central School of Art and Design, 1965-73; opera debut: *Angélique*, 1950; has designed over 130 operas, plays and ballets worldwide. Students have included John Gunter, John Napier, Maria Bjornson.

Opera Productions (selected)

Angélique, London, Fortune Theatre, 1950.
Tannhäuser, London, Covent Garden, 1955.
Carmen, English National Opera, 1961.
Assassinio nella Cattedrale, English National Opera, 1962.
Aufstieg und Fall der Stadt Mahagonny, English National Opera, 1963.
Don Giovanni, Scottish National Opera, 1964.
Otello, Scottish National Opera, 1964.
Boris Godunov, Scottish National Opera, 1965.
The Rake's Progress, Scottish National Opera, 1967.
Elegy for Young Lovers, Scottish National Opera, 1970.
Der Ring des Nibelungen, English National Opera, 1970.
Duke Bluebeard's Castle, English National Opera, 1972.
Taverner, London, Covent Garden, 1972.
Lulu, Kassel, 1973.
The Midsummer Marriage, Cardiff, 1976.
The Icebreak, London, Covent Garden, 1979.
Anna Karenina, English National Opera, 1981.
Die Soldaten, 1983.
Der fliegende Holländer, Hong Kong, 1987.
La traviata, Hong Kong, 1990.

Publications

By KOLTAI: articles–

"Weill Bodies." *Music and Musicians*. 11/January (1963): 17.
"Opera on the Drawing Board." *Musical Events* 18/November (1963): 20.

About KOLTAI: articles–

Sadie, S. "The Twilight of the Gods." *The Music Times* 112/March (1971): 252.
Burian, Jarka M. "Contemporary British Stage Design: Three Representative Scenographers." *Theatre Journal* 35/May (1983): 213.
Fingleton, David. "Stage Design." *Arts Review* 38 (31 January 1986): 34.
Fingleton, David. "Stage Design." *Arts Review* 38 (23 May 1986): 270.
Wolfe, Debbie. "Design for Acting." *Drama* 160 (1986): 13.
Fingleton, David. "Stage Design." *Arts Review* 42 (7 September 1990): 468.

* * *

Although he has come to be identified with productions by England's National Theatre and the Royal Shakespeare Company, Ralph Koltai actually designed more than forty operas and many ballets before designing any dramas. His work in opera, which has continued over the years, reflects his basic concerns with aesthetic form and his concept-centered approach to all his stage productions, whether opera, ballet, or drama. Equally important to Koltai is the special flavor and spirit of the time in which a production is presented, which he tries to convey not only in the style of his design but also in his use of contemporary materials and instruments.

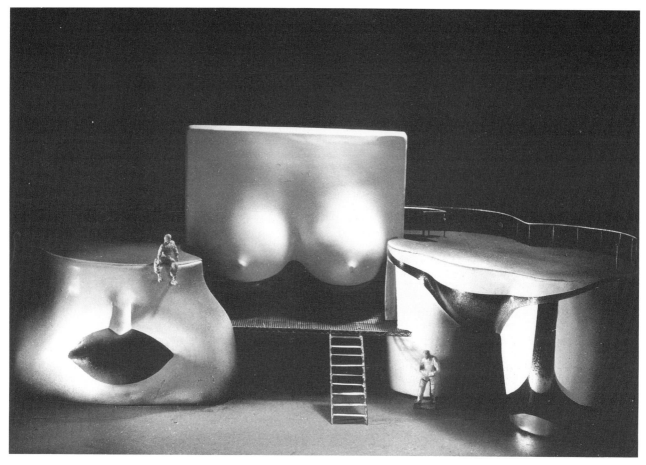

Ralph Koltai's set design (model) for Zimmermann's *Die Soldaten,* **Opéra Lyon, 1982**

A sense of deliberate design is present in all of Koltai's work ("Stage design is an art, and I am an artist"), yet his starting point is usually an intuitive response to an image or metaphor inherent in the work itself or in the director's views of the work. Finding a concept that will make a production work is crucial: "I'm totally concerned with concept . . . I don't like to 'design scenery.' Once I have an idea I get excited." He also prefers to work with directors who want him to contribute ideas; he wants an active role in determining the essential idea underlying the whole production.

Koltai's opera productions reveal considerable variety, but they have in common a boldness and imagination that find an outlet in works that demand creative fantasy and metaphoric expressiveness more than realistic detail. More often than not, Koltai's work reveals a sculptor's talent, perhaps nowhere so purely in opera as in his *Tannhäuser* in the early 1970s in Australia. On a very deep stage, Koltai extended a bare, raked platform that had no embellishment except for two simple, graceful curves that peeled up from its surface, one downstage left, the upper upstage right. Changes of locale were conveyed primarily by projections.

More complex sculptured effects were evident in Koltai's production of Wagner's *Ring* for the English National Opera in the early 1970s. In a production that emphasized futuristic magical and fairy tale elements rather than philosophy, Koltai employed fiberglass and transparent and translucent plastics in the form of striated, crystalline panels to form clouds, as well as trees and foliage; spheres of various sizes dotted a black and silver landscape resembling that of an alien planet.

The total visual impact was heightened by a tilted mirror at the back, which reflected the circular acting area. Mirrors played an even stronger role in his production of Bartók's *Duke Bluebeard's Castle* in the early 1970s, for which Koltai had two large paneled, vertical, mirrored surfaces meeting at the rear and slightly tilted forward, in order to reflect whatever objects, figures, or projections were on the crumpled silvery floor in front of the surfaces.

Projections became the dominant scenographic element in Hamilton's *Anna Karenina* for the English National Opera in the early 1980s. Koltai set up two projection surfaces: a downstage scrim for front projections and a special translucent screen upstage for rear projections. The projections could alternate or blend, creating an atmospheric reality and facilitating a continuous flow of action.

Two other examples of a sculptural, architectonic approach are worth mentioning. For Maxwell-Davies' *Taverner* in the early 1970s at Covent Garden, Koltai erected a constructivistic central structure consisting of a simple, stark pylon of two vertical steel members, with a cross bar or girder that functioned like a teeter-totter and could support up to five people at each end. A large, tilted ring enclosed the entire structure, and small lights outlined all the elements. The whole structure, which could also rotate, was totally abstract, yet it also suggested a cross, a sword, Renaissance science, and, indeed, a teeter-totter, symbolically representing the changing tides of power between church and state in 16th-century England.

A strikingly different sculptured setting and dramatic effect occurred in Zimmerman's *Die Soldaten* in the early 1980s. Three massive, pop-art-like sections of a woman's anatomy (mouth, breasts, and gartered loins), joined by a gantry, formed acting platforms to supplement the bare floor. It was, as Koltai put it, "a surreal composition . . . a metaphor for a story essentially about the degradation of women by men." Almost luridly literal in its impact, the set is of course aesthetically distanced by its greatly exaggerated scale as well as its highly theatrical functionality. It reminds one of yet another Koltai characteristic: his tacit wit.

A significant contemporary designer, Koltai has also been a notable teacher of designers. Three of England's most important younger designers, John Gunter, John Napier, and Maria Bjornson, were among his students at London's Central School of Design during Koltai's eight-year tenure there. In recent years he has also become increasingly interested in directing, reflecting not only his conceptual orientation but his sense that designers are both undervalued and underrecognized within the British system. In 1987, he directed Wagner's *Der fliegende Holländer* and in 1990, Verdi's *La traviata,* both in Hong Kong.

The primary and lasting impression of Koltai's work is that of distinctive artistry and inventive imagery in his embodiment of the essential concept underlying a given work. An advocate of simplicity, he is never merely plain, simple, or weak. Instead, he creates works that convey the effect of great selectivity, distillation, and complex inner tension.

—Jarka M. Burian

KONETZNI, Anny.

Soprano. Born 12 February 1902, in Ungarisch-Weisskirchen. Died 6 September 1968, in Vienna. Sister of soprano Hilde Konetzni. Studied with Erik Schmedes in Vienna and Jacques Stückgold in Berlin; debut as contralto in Vienna Volksoper, 1925; sang as soprano at Staatsoper in Berlin, 1931-34; member of Vienna Staatsoper, 1935-54; Metropolitan Opera debut as Brünnhilde in *Die Walküre,* 1934; London, 1935; Salzburg, 1934-36 and 1941; retired 1955; taught at the Viennese Music Academy until 1957.

* * *

Anny Konetzni began vocal studies at the Vienna Conservatory with Erik Schmedes and continued with Jacques Stückgold in Berlin. Her first professional singing was as a chorister at the Vienna Volksoper in 1923. She was let go from that position because of lack of voice. Three years later she made her debut as contralto soloist at that same theater in the role of Adriano in Wagner's *Rienzi.* She sang at the theaters in Augsburg and Elberfeld and in 1929 she was engaged as a dramatic soprano in Chemnitz. Between 1931 and 1934 she was a member of the Berlin State Opera and in 1932 she sang the first performance at that theater of Verdi's *I vespri Siciliani.* In 1933 she began her long association with the Vienna State Opera and soon was one of that theater's best known artists. From her home base in Vienna she was hailed in Milan's Teatro alla Scala, Rome, Paris, Covent Garden (1935-39 and again in 1951), Brussels, Amsterdam,

and Buenos Aires. During the 1934-35 season she was a member of the Metropolitan Opera.

Anny Konetzni was engaged at the Salzburg Festival between 1934-36 and again during the summer of 1941. Her roles included Isolde under Toscanini in 1936, Rezia in *Oberon,* Leonore in *Fidelio,* and the Marschallin in *Der Rosenkavalier.* In 1951 she sang the title role in Richard Strauss' *Elektra* at the Maggio musicale in Florence. She was also Ortrud at the festival in Verona.

Anny Konetzni took part in the two major historical events of the revival of opera in Vienna after World War II. She sang Leonore in the opening performance held in the Theater an der Wien on 6 October 1945 under the baton of Josef Krips. Ten years later, she, her sister, Lotte Lehmann, and Bruno Walter were among the honored guests at the gala reopening of the Vienna Staatsoper in November 1955.

—Suzanne Summerville

KONETZNI, Hilde.

Soprano. Born 21 March 1905, in Vienna. Died there 20 April 1980. Sister of soprano Anny Konetzni. Married: Mirko Urbanic, 1940 (one daughter). Studied at Vienna Conservatory; debut as Sieglinde in *Die Walküre,* Chemnitz, 1929; in Prague for four years; Vienna Staatsoper debut as Elisabeth, 1935, and soon joined the company; retired 1974, but continued to teach.

* * *

Hilde Konetzni (born Konerczny) was the younger of two Austrian sisters who became sopranos. In their youth they were champion swimmers, and this developed their breathing capacity and stamina, laying a solid foundation for their later careers. Hilde began singing lessons at the New Vienna Conservatory after Anny, who was three years older, was already engaged to sing at the Chemnitz Opera. Hilde was not progressing well enough and turned to her sister for advice and help; she moved to Chemnitz and became such a successful student that in 1929 she was suddenly asked by the intendant at Chemnitz to take on Sieglinde in *Die Walküre* with only three days' notice. This she did, with Anny's considerable help, but refused a contract there.

After further tuition in Vienna for eighteen months, Hilde was engaged by the small but excellent Gablonz Opera in Czechoslovakia, and a year later joined the German Theater in Prague. She remained in Prague for four years, learning and singing a wide variety of roles and with a new, ideal teacher, Ludmilla Prochaska-Neumann.

Hilde Konetzni was called to the Vienna Opera in 1933 (debut Elisabeth in *Tannhäuser,* which was enthusiastically received). For three years she divided her engagements between Prague and Vienna, eventually settling in the city of her birth in 1936. Bruno Walter cast her as Donna Elvira and took her to Paris, with Elisabeth Rethberg and Ezio Pinza, in the celebrated production of *Don Giovanni.* Konetzni instantly showed that she was as well-suited to Mozart as to Wagner and Richard Strauss. She repeated Donna Elvira at the Salzburg Festival that year, and returned there in 1937. She was cast to sing one performance of the Marschallin in *Der Rosenkavalier* with the most famous exponent of the time, Lotte Lehmann. Konetzni also sang Chrysothemis in *Elektra* and the First Lady in *Die Zauberflöte* under Toscanini's baton.

Anny Konetzni had never been an easy-going person, and now she became envious of her younger sister's successes. Although the Marschallin and (later) Leonore in *Fidelio* were the only roles that they shared, Anny attempted, as far as possible, never to allow herself to appear with Hilde in the same opera. Their interpretations were, in any case, quite different: Anny's were more heroic in stature while Hilde's were lyrical and sympathetic.

Hilde's tender heart encouraged her to sing roles like Gutrune in *Götterdämmerung* and Chrysothemis in *Elektra,* partly because she felt sorry for the characters. She greatly enjoyed singing Senta in *Der fliegende Holländer,* whom she found fascinating whereas other sopranos often considered her tiresome. But she never sang Eva in *Die Meistersinger,* nor Jenufa, nor Aïda. She studied both of the latter roles, but considered that the tessitura was beyond her, especially in the third act of *Aïda.* Nor did she perform any of Puccini's operas on stage even though she recorded excerpts from many of them; she was wise enough to recognize her limitations.

Her voice, strong though not enormous, had great warmth and beauty of tone, making it ideal for the lighter Wagnerian roles and, with its flexibility, for Mozart. Combined with intelligence, the capacity for quick and accurate learning, and a strong frame, her voice lasted for almost as long as she did and is one of the more recent classic examples of careful vocal preservation.

In 1938, Sir Thomas Beecham engaged both Konetzni sisters for his London summer season at Covent Garden. Hilde sang her famous Sieglinde (thought by some to be preferable even to Lotte Lehmann's) while Anny sang Brünnhilde. When Lotte Lehmann collapsed during act I of *Der Rosenkavalier,* Hilde Konetzni stepped in without notice, greatly increasing her prestige in England; only two weeks later she performed another rescue operation at Glyndebourne as Donna Elvira.

At the Salzburg Festival of 1938, Hilde Konetzni sang Leonore in *Fidelio,* the role in which she was heard when the Vienna Staatsoper visited Covent Garden after the war in 1947. Beethoven's Leonore suited her perfectly; unlike most sopranos, she regarded Leonore's "Abscheulicher!" aria and its treacherous last seven bars as no ordeal.

As a result of the war, Konetzni lost everything she owned, but when European opera began to recover, she was much in demand. She sang in the USA with a touring company as one of a quartet of German and Austrian singers. In 1946 she created Niobe in Sutermeister's opera of that name in Zürich. In 1951 she sang Sieglinde in a concert performance of act I of *Die Walküre* at the Royal Albert Hall under Furtwängler. The voice had grown richer since her last appearance and her interpretation had deepened and was most moving, even in an evening gown.

Again she was called to the rescue at Covent Garden when Leonie Rysanek was taken ill, and Konetzni sang her famous Sieglinde for the last time in Britain, opposite Ramon Vinay with Hans Hotter as Wotan in Rudolf Kempe's *Ring* cycle.

From 1954 she taught voice at the Vienna Music Academy, though she continued to sing in cameo roles at the Volksoper, re-creating old characters with enormous skill, charm, often humor, and still in good voice. Her last performance was in *Der Zigeunerbaron* in January 1974. She died in Vienna, after a lingering illness, on 20 April 1980.

—Alan Jefferson

DIE KÖNIGIN VON SABA [The Queen of Sheba].

Composer: Karl Goldmark.

Librettist: Salomon Hermann Mosenthal.

First Performance: Vienna, Court Opera, 10 March 1875.

Roles: King Solomon (baritone); Baal-Hanan (baritone); Assad (tenor); High Priest (bass); Sulamith (soprano); The Queen of Sheba (mezzo-soprano); Astaroth (soprano); Voice of the Temple Guard (bass); Four Voices (soprano, contralto, tenor, bass); chorus.

Publications

article–

Werba, Robert. " 'Königin' für 277 Abende: Goldmarks Oper und ihr wienerisches Schicksal." *Österreichische Musikzeitung* 34 (1979): 192.

*　　*　　*

The first and only widely performed of Goldmark's six operas capitalized on the popularity of "exotic" near-eastern and oriental subjects during the second half of the nineteenth century, as manifested in such other works as Verdi's *Aïda,* Bizet's *Djamileh,* Saint-Saëns *Samson et Dalila,* Massenet's *Le roi de Lahore,* Ponchielli's *Il figliuol prodigo,* Rubinstein's *Demon, Die Maccabäer,* and *Sulamith,* or Delibes's *Lakmé—* all from the 1870s and '80s. Gounod's earlier opera on the same subject, *La reine de Saba* (1862), makes less use of exotic local color than do most of these later works. Goldmark sketched his own scenario for the opera as early as 1863, but it was some time before he could extract a satisfactory libretto from his collaborators (Mosenthal was the second to work on it). Even so, the text constitutes one of the work's principal weaknesses, as most early critics pointed out. The score was complete by the end of 1871, but it took several more years before the authorities of the Vienna Court Opera could be persuaded to mount the new work. When it did reach the stage, *Die Königin von Saba* enjoyed the participation of Vienna's best singers, including Amalie Materna in the title role, who would become Wagner's first Brünnhilde at Bayreuth the following year.

Act I is centered on the arrival of the Queen of Sheba at Solomon's court. Sulamith eagerly awaits her betrothed, Assad, who has been sent to escort the regal guest. When he arrives to announce the queen, Assad is noticeably disturbed, confessing to Solomon a strange nocturnal tryst he has had with a mysterious, seductive woman. Sheba arrives with her sumptuous retinue, bearing costly gifts (entry march and ballet). When she lifts her veil, Assad recognizes his mysterious seductress. She pretends not to know him. After a large ensemble expressing the general perplexity and dismay, Solomon does his best to smooth things out. Act II begins with a grand *scena* for the Queen alone, in a moonlit garden. Her spirit-like handmaiden, Astaroth, summons Assad to the garden in an unaccompanied, rhapsodic incantation. After a passionate duet, Sheba suddenly disappears at the break of dawn. The marriage ceremonies for Assad and Sulamith in the following scene (temple of Solomon) are interrupted when the Queen enters and Assad is thrown into a new fit of consternation. The high priest unveils the Holy of Holies, in an attempt to exorcise whatever demon has possessed Assad, but the latter throws himself at the Queen's feet, to the horror of the congregation. Following an elaborate ballet and pantomime (act III), in which a woman is chased by a bee, Sheba attempts to intercede with Solomon to save Assad. She fails, and departs in a rage. Solomon is touched, however, by Sulamith's doleful pleas, and agrees to commute the sentence to exile. In the final act, the outcast Assad encounters Sheba in the desert, on her homeward journey. He repulses her advances, and she disappears with her entourage into a sandstorm. Sulamith and her followers appear, and Assad dies in her arms, receiving her pardon and blessing.

The strength of *Die Königin von Saba* lies not in its dramatic content, which is negligible, but in the colorfully evocative "orientalism" of its score and the rich opportunities it provides for vocal and scenic display. The musical style owes something to *Tannhäuser* and *Lohengrin*. While more "advanced" than these in terms of harmonic idiom and orchestration, it bears little resemblance to Wagner's later music (although the words of the act-II nocturnal duet may echo *Tristan und Isolde*). Goldmark develops the combination of dramatic arioso, semi-closed forms and large choral-ensemble scenes of Wagner's earlier operas within a more traditional grand-operatic framework: descriptive ballet, liturgical scenes, and elaborate *mise en scène*. The musical style of *Tannhäuser* is especially evident in Assad's first scene (confrontation with Solomon), with its propulsive, modulatory arioso. Elsewhere the dramatic situations themselves are highly reminiscent of that work: the outraged assembly of the temple scene (act-II finale) when Assad invokes Sheba, Venus-like, as his "goddess," Sulamith's religious resignation after this catastrophe (Elisabeth), her pleas on his behalf, and Sheba's attempt to win back the wretched, penitent Assad in the fourth act.

Goldmark is most successful in his descriptive and "spectacle" music—the lushly scored "fountain" music of Assad's narrative (act I) and Sheba's aria (act II), the march and divertissement at her entrance, the grandiose temple scene, and the act-III ballet. Besides the exotic pseudo-historical touches provided by harps, bells, tambourines and other percussion, he makes frequent use of *divisi* strings in many combinations, up to fourteen parts at a time. Such textures anticipate the orchestral technique of Richard Strauss, as does the softly glowing orchestral counterpoint of the G-flat postlude to act III, with its melodic inner-voice horn parts. A discreet use of augmented intervals (entry of the slave-women in the act-I ballet, Astaroth's "incantation") contributes to the sense of exotic locale. Goldmark tries to invest his large ensembles with energetic harmonic activity, in the German tradition, but both these and the dramatic encounters of individual figures often sound forced. Like many post-Wagnerians, he lacked the ability to give convincing shape to free-form, declamatory material. Within the generally progressive context of the score, some conventional phrases (the "cabaletta" to the queen's big aria, "Durch das Herz zuckt mir ein Blitzen") stand out uncomfortably. That Goldmark's talents were best suited to the lyrical and the picturesque—and the development of conventional structures—seems borne out by the popularity of his first opera in comparison to more dramatically ambitious later works like *Merlin* (1886) or *Ein Wintermärchen* ("A Winter's Tale," 1908).

—Thomas S. Grey

DIE KÖNIGSKINDER [The King's Children].

Composer: Engelbert Humperdinck.

Librettist: Ernst Rosmer [Elsa Bernstein-Porges].

First Performance: New York, Metropolitan Opera, 28 December 1910.

Roles: Prince (tenor); Goose Girl (soprano); Fiddler (baritone); Witch (contralto); Woodcutter (bass); Broommaker (tenor); Innkeeper's Daughter (soprano); Innkeeper (bass); Stable Maid (mezzo-soprano); Broommaker's Daughter (child); Tailor (tenor); Senior Councillor (bass); Two Gatekeepers (baritones); chorus (SAATTBBB); chorus (3-part children's chorus or additional SAA).

Publications

articles—

Humperdinck, W. "Aus der Entstehungszeit der 'Königskinder'." *Zeitschrift für Musik* 115 (1954): 715.
Roberge, Marc-André. "*Königskinder:* L'autre chef-d'oeuvre de Humperdinck." *Sonances, Revue musicale québécoise* 4/no. 1 (1984): 2.

unpublished—

Kirsten, L. "Motivik und Form in der Musik zu Engelbert Humperdincks Oper 'Königskinder'." Ph.D. dissertation, University of Jena, 1942.

*   *   *

Soon after the enormous success of his first opera, *Hänsel und Gretel*, Humperdinck wrote incidental music for a play called *Die Königskinder* by "Ernst Rosmer" (the pseudonym of the Viennese-born woman writer Else Bernstein-Porges, 1866-1949), which had its premiere in 1897. It was a rather serious, moralistic piece, but a decade later the composer and writer decided to take the play and the existing music (which included some songs) and to turn it into what *Hänsel und Gretel* had been, a *Märchenoper* or "fairy tale opera." In this form it was first seen at the New York Metropolitan Opera, with the American soprano Geraldine Farrar as the Goose Girl and the Latvian tenor Hermann Jadlowker as the Prince.

Just as in the case of *Hänsel und Gretel*, the setting is again Humperdinck's favorite one of medieval Germany, and although here the two principal characters are young adults rather than children, and there is a love interest, the story still has the element of the supernatural which is important not only in his work but also in earlier German operas such as Weber's *Der Freischütz* and Marschner's *Hans Heiling*. Indeed, the Goose Girl is a King's daughter under the spell of a witch in whose house she is forced to live and work. Once again, as in *Hänsel und Gretel*, cooking plays a part in the story, for the witch compels the girl to bake a magic loaf which will bring death to those who eat it. In act I, the Prince, disguised as a commoner, comes upon her and they fall in love, and although she cannot escape from the witch's custody, before they part he gives her his crown in exchange for a garland of flowers that she has been wearing.

Now a wandering fiddler comes with two other men (a broommaker and a woodcutter) to the witch's hut, and he

A page from Humperdinck's autograph score of *Die Königskinder,* **act III**

recognizes the Goose Girl's royal blood. On hearing of her meeting with the Prince, he helps her to break the spell that has bound her. In act II, the townsfolk of nearby Hellabrunn await their new King, who, according to the witch, shall be the first person to enter the town after its bells have rung at noon. The Prince is already there, still dreaming of the beautiful Goose Girl and indifferent to the advances of the innkeeper's daughter. He decides to stay in the town and to accept work as a swineherd. At midday, the town gates are opened and the Goose Girl herself enters, wearing her royal crown and accompanied by the fiddler and her geese. The lovers embrace and the Prince greets his beloved as his future queen. However, the townsfolk are angry at what they believe to be a trick, and the lovers are driven out and the fiddler beaten.

After a lengthy prelude to act III, the curtain rises to reveal a winter scene and the fiddler now living in the hut formerly occupied by the witch. The broommaker from Hellabrunn comes to beg him to return to the town, and he agrees to do so once he has found the Prince and Princess, setting off on his quest accompanied by a number of the town's children. In the final scene, the lovers are seen approaching the hut, cold and starving. In the hut is the woodcutter, to whom the Prince gives the crown in exchange for bread. Alas, in return he receives the witch's deadly magic loaf and after eating it the two lovers fall, although happily, into their last sleep. They are now found by the returning fiddler and the children, who together mourn them and set off for the town with their bodies.

Die Königskinder is the only one of Humperdinck's operas besides *Hänsel und Gretel* to hold a place in the repertory, and that is really only in the German-speaking world. It was an ambitious work for him, and since it is a kind of tragedy it represented a big departure from the simple optimism of *Hänsel und Gretel*. Possibly the fundamental hopefulness and affirmation of his art, one drawn at its best in simple outlines, was overstretched by a tale which is far more complex than that of the earlier opera. For all that we find the familiar fairy-tale elements here, the witch is now much more than a nursery concept, and she disappears early from the story although it is her evil magic that brings the dénouement, while the good fiddler too seems something of a mystery man. But what is never in doubt is Humperdinck's ability to write singable and memorable melodies and to make his orchestra serve the drama at all points so that our attention is held and our hearts are touched.

—Christopher Headington

KORNGOLD, Erich Wolfgang.

Composer. Born 29 May 1897, in Brno, Czechoslovakia. Died 29 November 1957, in Hollywood. Early music education with his father, Julius Korngold, a music critic; studied with Fuchs, Zemlinsky, and Grädener in Vienna; published compositions, 1909; public success in Vienna, Leipzig, Berlin, and Munich, 1910-20; collaborated with the film director Max Reinhardt beginning in 1929; taught at the Vienna Academy of Music, 1930-34; in Hollywood arranging Mendelssohn's *A Midsummer Night's Dream* for the Reinhardt film of Shakespeare's play, 1934; numerous film scores; conducted at the

New York Opera Company, 1942 and 1944; American citizen, 1943; lived in the United States and Europe after 1945.

Operas

Publisher: Schott.

Der Ring des Polykrates, after Heinrich Teweles, Munich, 28 March 1916.
Violanta, Hans Müller, Munich, 28 March 1916.
Die tote Stadt, Paul Schott [=E.W. and J. Korngold] (after Georges Rodenbach, *Bruges la morte*), Hamburg and Cologne, 4 December 1920.
Das Wunder der Heliane, Hans Müller (after Hans Kaltneker), Hamburg, 10 October 1927.
Die Kathrin, E. Decsey, Stockholm, 7 October 1939.
The Silent Serenade, E.W. Korngold and H. Reisfeld, 1946.

Other works: film scores, orchestral works, chamber music, songs.

Publications/Writings

About KORNGOLD: books–

Hoffmann, R.S. *Erich Wolfgang Korngold.* Vienna, 1922.
Korngold, Luzi. *Erich Wolfgang Korngold: Ein Lebensbild.* Vienna, 1967.
Carroll, Brendan G. *Erich Wolfgang Korngold 1897-1957: his Life and Works.* Edited by Konrad Hopkins and Ronald van Roekel. Paisley, Scotland, 1984.

articles–

Lingg, Ann M. "Master of Melody." *Opera News* 39/5 April (1975): 8.
Porter, Andrew. "Musical Events: A Tale of Two Cities." *New Yorker* 51/14 April (1975): 120.
Sargeant, Winthrop. "Concert Records: Romantic and Gothic." *New Yorker* 51/26 January (1976): 91.
Smith, Patrick J. "New York City Opera." *High Fidelity/Musical America* July (1975): 26.
Brown, Royal S. "Record Reviews." *High Fidelity* January (1977).
Carroll, Brendan G. "Korngold's *Violanta.*" *Musical Times* 122 (1980): 695.
Heinsheimer, Hans. "Gone with the Wind." *Opera News* 49/July (1984): 19.
Ashbrook, William. "Recordings." *Opera Quarterly* 17/no. 4 (1991): 188.

unpublished–

Carroll, Brendan G. "The Operas of Erich Wolfgang Korngold." Ph. D. dissertation, University of Liverpool, 1975.

*   *   *

Gustav Mahler called Erich Korngold a "genius"; Richard Strauss wrote to his father upon hearing the fourteen year-old's *Schauspiel-Ouverture* that "Such mastery fills me with awe and fear"; and Giacomo Puccini noted that "He has so much talent, he could easily give us half and still have enough left for himself." Throughout Korngold's career, Europe's most prominent conductors and musicians, including Bruno Walter, Arthur Nikisch, Artur Schnabel, Jasha Heifetz, and

Erich Korngold, 1916

Maria Jeritza premiered his works. Yet despite extraordinary public success, Korngold's operas have not attained the level of interest and critical enthusiasm which sustain great masterpieces. Even with the recent resurgence of Neo-Romantic compositional idioms and the fact that critics no longer dismiss Korngold outright because of his Hollywood film scores, revivals of his most successful early works, *Violanta* and *Die tote Stadt,* have often met with lukewarm and oven hostile reviews.

Korngold's defenders claim that his voice is bold, expressive and original. Brendan Carroll, Korngold's most recent biographer, writes: "He composed in a densely chromatic style, which is the logical extension of the post-Wagnerian school, beyond Richard Strauss and Franz Schreker, but not into the territory explored by the serialists. His musical language is idiosyncratic and receives its impetus from his frenetic rhythms. The combination of these elements, deployed on a large orchestra with brilliant technique, and coupled with an exceptional melodic gift, identifies his artistic uniqueness." (Carroll, 1984) Many critics view Korngold's operas as an alternative to the atonal vocal works of Schoenberg, Berg, and Webern. In reviewing Korngold's first mature and best known opera *Die tote Stadt,* Ann Lingg cites the "colorful yet lucid [orchestration], with full sonorities, telling leitmotifs, uncanny musical characterization and bold harmonies that never manage to offend the ear. Above all, Korngold was a master of melody, untouched by the Viennese School's new fad for atonality." Lingg also finds that the opera's positive outlook announces "the triumph of life over death, the fallacy of living in the past." Winthrop Sargeant concurs that "[Korngold wrote] rich, melodious music that communicated something to his listeners. . . . [*Die tote Stadt*] has been clothed by Korngold in the most ravishing score—music of the effulgent and vocally knowing sort that Strauss wrote—but . . . is quite original and extremely beautiful, and the pre-Schoenberg Viennese idiom is employed in a manner all Korngold's own."

While acknowledging the colorful nature of Korngold's scores, other critics have questioned the relationship of the music to the drama. William Ashbrook writes that in *Die tote Stadt,* "the composer, for all his cleverness, is rarely able to invoke visually credible atmosphere through his music alone. The score is crammed chockablock with 'effects', but they do not add up to much." At the 1975 revival of this same work, Patrick J. Smith commented more harshly: "[One hears] lushly orchestrated seas of velveteen with every emotion made shamelessly obvious. . . . [though] Korngold's orchestrational ear was sound enough, if not particularly inspired . . . [h]is extremely limited inventional ability . . . tell more heavily with each passing moment."

In a review of the 1975 recording, Royal Brown also found fault with Korngold's decision to rework portions of Rodenbach's original novel—the protagonist's murder of his lover—as a dream sequence: "[E]ither you work within the limits of a certain domain envisaged by an author or you turn to a different writer; by tacking a happy ending onto Rodenbach's lugubrious vision, and by applying a nicely Germanic, logical distinction between "real" life and dream to a work that assumes an ambiguity between the two, the libretto very simply emasculates the work's narrative as well as its thematic impact." Andrew Porter, dismissing the music as "tawdry—Strauss and Puccini, plus dashes of Mahler and Debussy, served in syrup," also found fault with the dramaturgy: "So

it *is* a pretty tale after all; the eroticism and violence are spices, not substance."

—David Pacun

KÖTH, Erika.

Soprano. Born 15 September 1925, in Darmstadt. Died 20 February 1989. Studied in Darmstadt with Elsa Blank; debut as Philine in *Mignon,* Kaiserslautern, 1948; sang in Karlsruhe, 1950-53; in Munich from 1954; made a Bavarian Kammersängerin, 1956; in Berlin from 1961; in Salzburg, 1955-64; appeared at Bayreuth as the Forest Bird, 1965-68; made a Berlin Kammersängerin, 1970; became professor at the Hochschule für Musik, Cologne, 1973.

Publications

About KÖTH: books–

K. Adam. *Herzlichst! Erika Köth.* Darmstadt, 1969.

* * *

Erika Köth studied with Elsa Blank at the Hochschule in Darmstadt and sang with a dance orchestra to pay for her education. In 1947 she won a singing competition sponsored by the Radio in Hesse and made her debut the following year as Philine in Thomas' *Mignon* at the Pfalztheater in Kaiserslautern. Even before her stage debut Erika Köth sang the role of Adele in *Die Fledermaus* for a Darmstadt broadcast. From 1950 through 1953 she was engaged by the City Theater in Karlsruhe and in 1954 she joined the roster of the Munich State Opera. From Munich she soon began her meteoric rise to international prominence at the Vienna State Opera and Hamburg. In 1955 she first sang the role of Costanza in Mozart's *Die Entführung aus dem Serail* with sensational reviews. She was equally successful in the same role there in 1955-57 and 1962-63. Between 1955 and 1960 she also sang the Queen of the Night and was the soprano soloist in a number of Festival concerts. In 1957 Köth returned to Munich for a production of Donizetti's *Lucia di Lammermoor* which was put in the repertoire especially for her. Guest performances took Köth to Milan's Teatro alla Scala, the Opera in Rome, Hollywood, San Francisco, and Budapest. She was especially praised for her performances as the Fiakermilli in *Arabella* and the Italian singer in *Capriccio* during the Munich ensemble's guest season at Covent Garden. In 1961 Erika Köth toured Russia and from 1965 through 1968 she was heard at the Bayreuth Festival in the role of the Waldvogel in *Siegfried.*

Köth made many recordings for Columbia, Electrola, Decca, Philips, Eurodisc, and DGG of both complete operas and highlights of her best opera roles. Among these are the leading coloratura parts in *Die Entführung aus dem Serail, Die Fledermaus, Die Zauberflöte, Der Freischütz, Così fan tutte, Zar und Zimmermann, Siegfried,* and *Der Rosenkavalier.* On Melodrama there are performances recorded in Munich in 1954 and 1957 of the Queen of the Night from *Die Zauberflöte* and Sophie in *Der Rosenkavalier.* Other major roles which she did not record included Gilda, Violetta, Rosina, Donna Elvira, and Zerbinetta.

Erika Köth's voice was best described as exquisitely beautiful with an especially luminous top. Her technical ability was of the highest virtuoso quality. Besides her success on the opera and operetta stages and on television, she was beloved for her singing of coloratura waltzes and chansons. Köth was the most important German coloratura soprano in the generation after the Second World War.

—Suzanne Summerville

KRAUS, Alfredo.

Tenor. Born 24 November 1927, in Las Palmas, Canary Islands. Studied in Barcelona with Gali Markoff, in Valencia with Francisco Andres, and in Milan with Mercedes Llopart; debut as Duke in *Rigoletto,* Cairo, 1956; European debut as Cavaradossi, 1956; Covent Garden debut as Edgardo in *Lucia di Lammermoor,* 1959; Teatro alla Scala debut as Elvino in *La sonnambula,* 1960; in Chicago as Nemorino in *L'elisir d'amore,* 1962, and has returned regularly; Metropolitan Opera debut as the Duke, *Rigoletto* 1966.

Alfredo Kraus as Gennaro in *Lucrezia Borgia*, Royal Opera, London, 1980

Publications

About KRAUS: books–

Vitali, G. *Alfredo Kraus.* Bologna, 1992.

articles–

Celletti, R. "Alfredo Kraus." *Opera* June (1975).
Current Biography June (1987).

*   *   *

Alfredo Kraus is an aristocrat among modern tenors, never forcing his voice or singing roles too big for him. The result is that to an amazing degree he sounds as fresh as he did twenty-five years ago. His timbre and style have little in common with most other post-war tenors such as Del Monaco, Di Stefano, Corelli, or Domingo; instead, critics are forced to make comparisons with tenors of a much earlier age—Tito Schipa and Fernando De Lucia—although not always to Kraus's advantage. Kraus himself reverts to this earlier period in naming his own models. His idol is Schipa, "an artist because of his limitations," and he also admires Aureliano Pertile.

Not only does Kraus never damage his voice by venturing outside of a somewhat circumscribed range of roles, but he also limits himself to roughly fifty performances a year. He will not perform operas like *La bohème* or *Tosca* because of the thick orchestration; rather, his great successes are Don Ottavio, Count Almaviva, Alfredo, the Duke of Mantua, Massenet's Des Grieux, and Werther. The voice itself is not of the warm, melting variety of a Di Stefano or a Gigli, but is bright, penetrating, dry, and somewhat thin. The remarkable aspect of his artistry lies in the elegant manner in which he phrases and shapes a musical line. Another facet of his artistry is the great upward range of the voice, up to a high D; in this regard he has been compared to Giacomo Lauri-Volpi, a famous high-note tenor of the past. These high notes are a great asset in works such as *La favorita* by Donizetti and Bellini's *I Puritani.* Kraus worked with Tullio Serafin, a conductor who was very knowledgeable about the human voice, on the role of Arturo in *I Puritani* and sang it untransposed for twenty years. Furthermore, Kraus's stage presence is elegant; he is a matinee idol in his native Spain and Rodolfo Celletti has written that "It is difficult to imagine Kraus portraying a character who does not wear sumptuous costumes and whose language is not noble and in a certain sense idealized, because the smooth gentleness of his singing, the elegance of his phrasing and his good stage looks make Kraus the only *grand seigneur* tenor of our time."

Kraus' vocal longevity may also be attributed in part to the fact that his career began fairly late in life; he is the antithesis of the over-achiever singer who burns himself out in a few thrilling seasons or the superstar tenors such as Domingo and Pavarotti. Kraus was in his late twenties when he came to the stage in Turin as Alfredo Germont after study with Mercedes Llopart in Milan. He sang Alfredo also in the famous 1958 "Lisbon Traviata" with Maria Callas, a performance that has for some time been available in recorded form and which shows Kraus as a perfect Alfredo, vocally and dramatically youthful, passionate and impetuous. He has recorded extensively, not only his most celebrated roles, but others as well. These include Ferrando in *Così fan tutte;* Gennaro in *Lucrezia Borgia* with Caballé and Verrett; Des Grieux to Cotrubas' Manon, Edgardo to Gruberova's Lucia di Lammermoor, and a number of recordings with Beverly Sills: the Duke of Mantua, Almaviva, and Ernesto in *Don Pasquale* among them.

Although he is equally renowned in the Italian and French repertoires, it is to the latter that Kraus, with his particular qualities of voice—the color, the lack of portamento, the scrupulous observance of rhythmic values—is suited. If his voice does not possess the heft or the velvet for many Italian roles, it must be borne in mind that the qualities that make for an ideal French singer are rather more rare. Thus Kraus is a connoisseur's singer, yet a *tenore di grazia* who pleases critics and public alike. At a 1975 performance of *La favorite* in Carnegie Hall, with Eve Queler, Andrew Porter reported that Kraus's "Spirto gentil" elicited "the longest mid-scene ovation I have ever heard any singer receive anywhere," and went on to say that Kraus had "no inhibitions about accepting applause," that "in this repertory he is peerless," exhibiting a "finer-drawn distinction of style than Pavarotti."

—Stephen Willier

KRAUSS, Clemens (Heinrich).

Conductor. Born 31 March 1893, in Vienna. Died 16 May 1954, in Mexico City. Married: the soprano Viorica Ursuleac. Singer in the Imperial Choir; studied piano with Reinhold, composition with Grädener, and theory with Heuberger at the Vienna Conservatory, graduating 1912; chorus master at the Brno Theater, 1912-13; conducting debut at the Brno Theater with Lortzing's *Zar und Zimmermann,* 1913; second conductor of Riga's German Theater, 1913-14; second conductor at Nuremberg, 1915-16; first conductor at Stettin, 1916-21; conducted in Graz, 1921-22; assistant to Schalk at the Vienna State Opera, 1922; taught conducting at the Vienna Academy of Music, 1922-24; conductor of the Vienna Tonkünstlerkonzerte, 1923-27; director of the Frankfurt Opera, 1924-29; conducted the premiere of Hindemith's *Cardillac,* 1928; director of the Vienna State Opera, 1929-34; conductor of the Vienna Philharmonic, 1930-33; conductor at the Salzburg Festival, 1926, 1929-34; conducted in South America, 1927; guest conductor with the New York Philharmonic and the Philadelphia Orchestra, 1929; conducted at Covent Garden, London, 1934; director of the Berlin State Opera, 1934-37; Generalmusikdirektor of the Bavarian State Opera in Munich, 1937-44; conducted at the Salzburg Mozarteum, 1939-45; conducted with the Vienna Philharmonic, 1944-45; tried by the Allied authorities for his association with the Nazis, and not allowed to resume his career until 1947; took the Vienna State Opera to London, 1947; conductor with the Vienna Philharmonic, 1947; conducted at Covent Garden, London, 1951-53; conducted at the Bayreuth Festival, 1953-54.

Publications

By KRAUSS: books–

Kende, G.K., and W. Schuh, eds. *Richard Strauss, Clemens Krauss: Briefwechsel.* Munich, 1963; 2nd ed., 1964.

Clemens Krauss

About KRAUSS: books–

Berger, A. *Clemens Krauss.* Graz, 1924; 3rd ed., 1929.

Gregor, Joseph. *Clemens Krauss: seine musikalische Sendung.* 1953.

Pander, O. van. *Clemens Krauss in München.* Munich, 1955.

Kende, G.K. *Höchste Leistung aus begeistertem Herzen: Clemens als Direktor der Wiener Staatsoper.* Salzburg, 1971.

Kende, G.K., S. Scanzoni. *Der Prinzipal. Clemens Krauss: Fakten, Vergleiche, Rückschlüsse.* Tutzing, 1988.

articles–

Cook, Ida. "Clemens Krauss." *Opera* February (1954).

Flowers, B. "Clemens Krauss (1893-1954): An Evolution." *Le Grand Baton* November (1986) [includes discography].

*   *   *

Despite his growing reputation as a conductor in the years up to 1929, the achievements of Krauss's maturity went largely unrecognized outside the German speaking countries due to the unsettled state of Europe from the 1930s on. "Hitler politics" and the outbreak of World War Two overtook him on the brink of a brilliant international career. Since, like Furtwängler, he remained in Nazi-occupied Europe, the inevitable, and retrospective, linking of his name with National Socialism, together with implicit charges of opportunism, tarnished his image in the immediate post-war environment.

Of "theater" stock, Krauss was raised in Vienna during the "Mahler era." After completing his formal musical education (at the Vienna Academy) he was engaged as assistant vocal coach at the Stadttheater in Brno where, in 1913, he conducted his first opera, Lortzing's *Zar und Zimmermann.* Further appointments at a string of provincial opera houses culminated in the post of first Kapellmeister in Vienna during the Strauss-Schalk regime. By this time he had directed most major repertoire works, including Strauss's *Der Rosenkavalier, Salome, Ariadne* and *Elektra,* performances whose excellence made a considerable impression on their composer. This first, interim, Viennese appointment (1922-24) constituted a milestone in Krauss's career. As a Strauss protégé, he "took on board" precepts learned from the Master which he subsequently put into practice in Frankfurt.

Frankfurt was the first modern opera house over which Krauss had full control. Here, with a company whose artists were contractually available to him throughout the year, he confirmed his allegiance to the "ensemble" tradition. These years were marked by exemplary performances of the repertoire classics in which no dramaturgical or musical detail was left to chance. Harnessing available technical facilities, and supported by the formidable Wallerstein/Sievert production/design team, he was poised to make good his contention that an opera house chief, while keeping abreast of new developments, should not neglect the works of older masters. Thus, he deliberately advocated a traditional format within the context of which he championed Busoni's *Faust* (1927), gave the world premiere of Hindemith's *Cardillac* (1928), and later mounted performances of Berg's *Wozzeck* (Vienna 1930) which the composer himself regarded as definitive.

Krauss was best known for his Strauss interpretations, and it is his association with Strauss, not least as co-librettist of *Capriccio,* that has kept his name alive today. The Frankfurt years saw their relationship develop into a collegial friendship (to which a voluminous correspondence bears witness), and

it was Strauss's influence that helped to secure for Krauss the directorship of the Vienna Opera in 1929. In 1933 he was entrusted with his first Strauss premiere, *Arabella,* in Dresden—to be followed, in due course, by those of *Friedenstag, Capriccio* (Munich, 1938 and 1942 respectively), and *Die Liebe der Danaë* in 1944 (Salzburg *Generalprobe*). His determined advocacy of "ensemble" opera as opposed to the ascendent modern star system fueled musico-political intrigue which led to the abandonment of Krenek's *Karl V* premiere—a cherished project. For Krauss, who made a steadfast refusal to sully music with politics, it was an unbearable blow and drove him from Vienna—first to Berlin and then, in 1937, to the Bavarian capital, Munich.

While it is difficult to view dispassionately an appointment which was so directly in Hitler's gift, there can be no doubt that Krauss was primarily motivated by the musical opportunities this new post afforded. His Munich deeds are legendary. In the space of eight years, and under war-time conditions, he initiated forty-eight new productions, gathering round him a team which included Sievert and Hartmann, and singers of the calibre of Hotter, von Milankovic and Ursuleac, who, along with other Krauss faithfuls, converged on the city, adding lustre to the era. Here it was that he collaborated with Strauss on *Capriccio,* an opera about opera—a testimony to their common aesthetic, musical and theatrical beliefs.

Despite his Munich success, Krauss's ultimate goal was reinstatement as Generalmusikdirektor in Vienna. As early as April 1945, undaunted by post-war chaos, he demonstrated unselfish commitment drawing up detailed reorganizational plans for the Opera and conducting the Philharmonic Orchestra in morale-boosting concerts. His indictment by the allies (Sept 1945) ended such activities. Rehabilitated in April 1947, he returned to participate in the city's musical life but again political intrigue deprived him of the promised and expected opportunity to lead it. He died on a South American tour in May 1954, spared the 1955 inauguration of the rebuilt Vienna Opera, which opened with *Fidelio* under the directorship of Karl Böhm.

Krauss performances were authoritative and unidiosyncratic, demonstrating consummate technique and musicianship. A thorough professional and recognized as an outstanding orchestral trainer he was tireless and exacting in rehearsal, achieving outstanding results, not only in the opera house, but also in concert programs, which embraced a forward-looking modernity. His recording activities have preserved many outstanding performances for posterity, particularly the music of Richard Strauss, of which he was certainly the foremost interpreter. By nature innovative, his unprecedented sanctioning of rehearsal recordings (by the technical staff at the Vienna Opera for the House archive) was epoch-making. These, now commercially available, preserve many valuable "historic" performances of the 1930s. It is, perhaps, the Munich years which testify most comprehensively to his gifts and abilities. Here, his friendship with Strauss flowered into collaborative partnership in *Capriccio,* and here, faithful to the "ensemble" tradition, and against all war-time odds, he realized standards of administration and performance which laid the foundation for the international reputation that the Munich Opera enjoys today.

—Kenneth Birkin

KRENEK, Ernst.

Composer. Born 23 August 1900, in Vienna. Died 23 December 1991, in Palm Springs, California. Married: 1) Anna Mahler, daughter of Gustav Mahler, 1924 (divorced 1924); 2) Berta Hermann, actress, 1928 (divorced 1949); 3) Gladys Nordenstrom, 1950. Studied with Franz Schreker in Vienna and Berlin; in Zurich, 1923-25; opera coach in Kassel under Paul Bekker, 1925-27; in Vienna, a correspondent for the *Frankfurter Zeitung,* 1928; toured Europe as a lecturer and accompanist in concerts of his songs; in the United States, 1937; professor of music at Vassar College, 1939-42; chairman of the music department at Hamline University, St. Paul, Minnesota, 1942-47; American citizen, 24 January 1945; in Hollywood, 1947-50; tours of Germany during the summers from 1950 on as a lecturer and conductor of his own works; Grand State Prize of Austria, 1963; visiting professor, Brandeis University, 1965; Peabody Institute, 1967; University of Hawaii, 1967; Regents Lecturer, University of California, San Diego, 1970; Ring of Honor, Vienna, 1970; honorary citation for arts and sciences, Austria, 1975; honorary citizenship, Vienna, 1982.

Operas

Publisher: Bärenreiter, Schott, Universal.

Zwingburg (scenic cantata), Franz Werfel, 1922, Berlin, 20 October 1924.
Der Sprung über den Schatten, Krenek, 1923, Frankfurt, 9 June 1924.

Ernst Krenek, 1937

Orpheus und Eurydike, Oskar Kokoschka, 1923, Kassel, 27 November 1926.
Jonny spielt auf, Krenek, 1925-26, Leipzig, 10 February 1927.
Der Diktator, Krenek, 1926, Wiesbaden, 6 May 1928.
Das geheime Königreich (fairy-tale opera), Krenek, 1926-27, Wiesbaden, 6 May 1928.
Schwergewicht, oder Die Ehre der Nation (burlesque operetta), Krenek, 1926-27, Wiesbaden, 6 May 1928.
Leben des Orest, Krenek, 1928-29. Leipzig, 19 January 1930.
Karl V. (play with music), Krenek, 1930-33, Prague, Deutsches Theater, 22 June 1938.
Cefalo e Procri, R. Küfferle, 1933-34, Venice, 1934.
Tarquin (drama with music), Emmet Lavery, 1940.
What Price Confidence? (comic chamber opera), Krenek, 1945-46, Saarbrücken, 1960.
Dark Waters, Krenek, 1950, Los Angeles, 1950.
Pallas Athene weint, Krenek, 1952-55, Hamburg, 1955.
The Belltower, Krenek (after Melville), 1955-56, Urbana, Illinois, 1957.
Ausgerechnet und verspielt (television opera), Krenek, 1961, Vienna, 1962.
Der goldene Bock, Krenek, 1963, Hamburg, 1964.
Der Zauberspiegel (television opera), Krenek, 1966, Munich, 1967.
Sardakai, Krenek, 1967-69, Hamburg, 1970.
Flaschenpost vom Paradies, oder der englisch Ausflug (television play with music), Krenek, 1972-73, Vienna, under the auspices of the Austrian Radio, 8 March 1974.

Other works: ballets, incidental music, choral works, orchestral works, vocal chamber works, chamber music, instrumental music, music for tape, piano pieces.

Publications

By KRENEK: books–

Über neue Musik: sechs Vorlesungen zur Einführung in die theoretischen Grundlagen. Vienna, 1937; revised and in English as *Music Here and Now,* New York, 1939; 1967.
Selbstdarstellung. Zurich, 1948; revised and enlarged as "Self Analysis," *University of New Mexico Quarterly* 23 (1953).
Studies in Counterpoint. New York, 1940; German translation, 1952.
Musik im goldenen Westen. Vienna, 1949.
Johannes Okeghem. New York, 1953.
De rebus prius factis. Frankfurt, 1956.
Zu Sprache gebracht [essays]. Munich, 1958.
Tonal Counterpoint. New York, 1958.
Gedanken unterwegs [essays]. Munich, 1959.
Modal Counterpoint. New York, 1959.
Komponist und Hörer. Kassel, 1964.
Prosa, Drama, Verse. Munich, 1965.
Exploring Music [essays]. London, 1966.
Horizons Circled: Reflections on my Music. Berkeley, 1974.
Das musikdramatische Werk. Vienna, 1974-82.
Electro Ton und Spärenklang. Festrede zur Eröffnung des Internationalen Brucknerfestes Linz 1980. Linz, 1980.
Im Zweifelsfalle; Aufsätze über Musik. Vienna, 1984.

articles–

"Problemi di stile nell' opera." *La rassegna musicale* 7 (1934).
"Zur musikalischen Bearbeitung von Monteverdis Poppea." *Schweizerische Musikzeitung/Revue musicale suisse* 76 (1936): 545.

"The New Music and To-day's Theater." *Modern Music* 14 (1937).

"Gustav Mahler." In *Gustav Mahler,* by B. Walter. English translation, New York, 1941.

"New Developments of the 12-tone Technique." *Music Review* 4 (1943): 81.

"Opera Between the Wars." *Modern Music* 20 (1943).

"The Treatment of Dissonance in Okeghem." In *Hamline Studies in Musicology,* edited by Ernst Krenek. St. Paul, Minnesota, 1945; 1947.

"Extents and Limits of Serial Techniques." *Musical Quarterly* 46 (1960): 210.

"Vom Geiste der geistlichen Musik." *Sagittarius* 3 (1970): 17.

"Parvula corona musicalis." *Bach* 2/no. 4 (1971): 18.

"Postscript to the Parvula corona." *Bach* 3/no. 3 (1972): 21.

"Jonny erinnert sich." *Österreichische Musikzeitschrift* 35 (1980): 187.

"Programnotizen zum Musikprotokoll Graz 1980." *Österreichische Musikzeitschrift* 35 (1980): 430.

"Marginal Remarks to *Lulu.*" In *Alban Berg Symposium, Wien 1980,* edited by Rudolf Klein, 272. Vienna, 1981.

"Von Krenek über Krenek zu Protokoll gegeben." In *Ernst Krenek,* edited by Otto Kolleritsch. Vienna and Graz, 1982.

"Wie es zu *Karl V.* kam und wie es mit *Karl V.* ging." *Jahrbuch des wiener Goethe-Vereins* 86-88 (1982-84): 21.

"Zu Anton Weberns 100. Geburtstag." *Musik-Konzepte* [Munich] (1983): 427 [special issue].

"Aus der Mappe eines Opernschreibers." *Österreichische Musikzeitschrift* 39 (1984): 6.

"Meine Zusammenarbeit mit Oskar Kokoschka." *Österreichische Musikzeitschrift* 45 (1990): 337.

Other articles in *Melos, Musica, Musical America, Musical Quarterly, Perspectives of New Music, Prisma,* and other publications.

interviews–

Antoniou, Theodore. "Das Interview. Theodore Antoniou im Gespräch mit Ernst Krenek." *Musica* 34 (1980): 145.

Gabrielli, Siegfried. "Ein 'Grosser' lehrte in Voduz. Interview mit Ernst Krenek anlässlich der 13. Internationalen Meisterkurse." *Kultur Journal* 2 (1983): 5.

About KRENEK: books–

Rogge, W. *Ernst Kreneks Opern: Spiegel der zwanziger Jahre.* Wolfenbüttel, 1970.

Adorno, Theodor W. *Theodor W. Adorno und Ernst Krenek: Briefwechsel.* Frankfurt, 1974.

Knoch, Hans. *Orpheus und Eurydike.* Regensburg, 1977.

Zenck, Claudia Maurer. *Ernst Krenek-ein Komponist im Exil.* Vienna, 1980.

Kolleritsch, Otto, ed. *Ernst Krenek.* Vienna, 1982.

Metzger, Heinz-Klaus and Rainer Riehn, eds. *Ernst Krenek.* Munich, 1984.

Cook, Susan C. *Opera for a New Republic: the "Zeitopern" of Krenek, Weill, and Hindemith.* Ann Arbor, 1988.

Bowles, Garrett H. *Ernst Krenek: a Bio-Bibliography.* Westport, Connecticut, 1989.

Stewart, John L. *Ernst Krenek: the Man and his Music.* Berkeley, 1991.

articles–

Tschulik, Norbert. "Die verhinderte Uraufführung von Kreneks Karl V." *Österreichische Musikzeitschrift* 34 (1979): 121.

Zenk, Claudia Maurer. "Unbewältigte Vergangenheit: Kreneks *Karl V.* in Wien. Zur nicht bevorstehenden Wiener Erstaufführung." *Die Musikforschung* 32 (1979): 273.

Molkow, Wolfgang. "Der Sprung über den Schatten. Zum Opernschaffen Ernst Kreneks in den 20er und 30er Jahren." *Musica* 34 (1980): 132.

Rogge, Wolfgang. "Oper als Quadratur des Kreises. Zum Opernschaffen Ernst Kreneks." *Österreichische Musikzeitschrift* 35 (1980): 453.

Stadlen, Peter. "Krenek: A Lifetime of Opera."*Opera* September (1980).

Stewart, John L. "Frauen in den Opern Ernst Kreneks." *Musica* 34 (1980): 136.

———. "Ernst Krenek Masken." *Österreichische Musikzeitschrift* 35 (1980): 437.

Zenck, Claudia Maurer. "Musikalisches Welttheater: Kreneks *Karl V.* Zur konzertanten Wiedergabe der Oper bei den Salzburger Festspielen." *Österreichische Musikzeitschrift* 35 (1980): 370.

Musik-Konzepte [Munich] 39/40 (1984) [Ernst Krenek issue].

Green, Marcia S. "Ravel and Krenek: Cosmic Music Makers." *College Music Symposium* 24 (1984): 96.

Sams, Jeremy, "*Jonny*–The First Jazz Opera." *Opera* October (1984).

*   *   *

Throughout his distinguished and prolific career Ernst Krenek (1900-1991) demonstrated an abiding commitment to opera as a central genre of the twentieth century. Although best known for his early work *Jonny spielt auf* (1927), Krenek composed some nineteen operas in his long career as well as writing numerous essays on issues of opera composition and performance. His operas include comic works, traditional grand operas, one-act and chamber operas, and television operas.

Typically set to his own German and later English libretti, Krenek's operas reflect many of the stylistic trends and dramatic concerns of this century. The early works, in particular, received prestigious premieres at the leading houses of Berlin, Leipzig, and Frankfurt am Main, testifying to Krenek's early recognition as an important post-World War I composer. Many of these works were both critical and (often surprisingly) commercial successes, and they continue to be performed with some regularity in Germany and Austria.

Born in Vienna, Krenek began composition studies with Franz Schreker, whose *Die Ferne Klang* and some eight other operas may well have been early influences on Krenek, although Krenek's adoption of a highly dissonant style caused a break between teacher and pupil. Krenek's first opera or "scenic cantata," *Zwingburg* (1922), demonstrated this new dissonant idiom, and its libretto by Franz Werfel explored the theme of individual freedom popular with expressionist theater of the time. His third opera, *Orpheus und Eurydike* (1923), was similar to *Zwingburg* in style and suggests in its mythological subject the Greco-revivalism shared by others as well; Krenek would maintain an interest in Greek myth as a starting place for later operas.

Between 1925 and 1927, following an influential visit to Paris, Krenek became an assistant to Paul Bekker (noted writer and ardent supporter of new music) and then director of opera houses first in Kassel and later Wiesbaden. During his time with Bekker, Krenek received practical and invaluable experience in all areas of theatrical production. He described the opera house as his "fabulous toy," and this first-hand knowledge of live theater contributed markedly to the success of his fourth opera, *Jonny spielt auf,* with its innovative staging demands.

Although *Jonny spielt auf* was the unexpected success of the 1926-27 German season, Krenek's second opera, *Der Sprung über den Schatten* (1923), foreshadowed *Jonny* and its new aesthetic of tonal and dramatic accessibility. Both works show Krenek's ability to write his own witty librettos and his desire to depict modern life on stage. In *Der Sprung,* Krenek made use of popular music idioms such as a duple meter fox-trot, and this musical feature came to the fore in *Jonny spielt auf* and accounted for much of its popular success. Krenek continued to draw upon such popular music and dance idioms for dramatic purposes in *Schwergewicht,* one of his three one-act operas of 1926-27, and in *Leben des Orest,* his grand opera (1930).

In the early 1930s, Krenek was invited to compose a work for the Vienna Staatsoper and chose as his subject the life of Emperor Charles V. Of more importance, he decided to use the twelve-tone technique for this new opera, entitled *Karl V,* again set to his own libretto. Krenek thus became one of the first composers outside of Schoenberg's immediate circle of pupils to adopt this compositional method, a surprising move given that the two composers had openly condemned each other in the 1920s. With the rising power of National Socialism, *Karl V* and its celebration of an embracing national Catholicism came to be seen as a political work not in keeping with Nazi tenets. Political pressure intervened, and rehearsals were stopped. By the time the opera received a first performance in Prague in 1938, Krenek had been branded a "Cultural Bolshevik" in Germany and had emigrated to the United States. In the 1938 exhibition of "Entartete Musik" held in Düsseldorf, Krenek and his character Jonny received prominent attention as representatives of "degenerate" musical trends being purged under Nazi rule. *Karl V* was not performed in Vienna until 1984.

Following *Karl V* and his move to the United States, Krenek composed several chamber works for performance by University students, and then reestablished contact with his operatic past with *Pallas Athene weint.* A three-act work on a mythological subject with overt political overtones in its discussion of democracy, the opera was the success of the 1955 opening of the Hamburg Opera House. Krenek again wrote his own libretto and continued his exploration of serial techniques now marked by his study of medieval counterpoint.

In the decade of the 60s, Krenek composed five more works, including three one-act operas for television performance. *Ausgerechnet und verspielt* (1961) and *Der Zauberspiegel* (1966) continued his exploration of serial composition as well as chance procedures and show Krenek's awareness of contemporary science fiction literature. His third work for television, *Flaschenpost vom Paradies,* combined electronic tape with percussion and piano. Performed by the Vienna Radio in 1974, it remains unpublished.

Krenek's two remaining large-scale operas, *Der goldene Bock* (1963) and *Sardakai* (1969), were again written on commissions from the Hamburg Opera and received premieres there during meetings of the International Congress of Contemporary Music. In them Krenek demonstrated his turn to a freer kind of twelve tone composition influenced by his interest in electronic music. *Der goldene Bock* once again shows his fondness for mythological subject matter.

Although Krenek composed no operas during his final two decades, later works such as the baritone solo on autobiographical texts *Spätlese* op. 218 and the Latin- and German-texted *Opus sine nomine* show a continued desire to work with texts and devise new kinds of musico-dramatic forums. Upon his death in December of 1991, writers remembered Krenek foremost as the composer of the stunningly successful *Jonny spielt auf,* and for his prolific output, and a personal musical language that changed and developed with other currents of this century. However, it was in his operatic works that Krenek often made the grandest demonstrations of his stylistic and aesthetic development. Opera, as a genre itself, served as an abiding inspiration throughout his life.

—Susan C. Cook

KRIPS, Josef.

Conductor. Born 8 April 1902, in Vienna. Died 13 October 1974, in Geneva. Studied with Mandyczewski and Weingartner in Vienna; first violin in the Volksoper orchestra in Vienna, 1918-21; vocal coach and chorus master at the Volksoper, then conductor, 1921; conducted opera in Aussig an der Elbe, 1924-25, and in Dortmund, 1925-26; Generalmusikdirektor in Karlsruhe, 1926-33; conductor at the Vienna State Opera, 1933; professor at the Vienna Academy of Music; lost his various posts when Austria was annexed to Germany, 1938; conducted at Belgrade, 1938-39; principal conductor of the Vienna State Opera, 1945; conducted the Vienna State Opera at Covent Garden, London, 1947; principal conductor of the London Symphony Orchestra, 1950-54; United States debut as guest conductor with the Buffalo Philharmonic, and then music director, 1954-63; music director of the San Francisco Symphony Orchestra, 1963-70; numerous guest appearances, including performances at the Lyric Opera, Chicago, 1960, 1964, Covent Garden, London, 1963, 1971-74, and the Metropolitan Opera, New York, 1966-67, 1969-70.

*　　*　　*

At the time of his death at the age of seventy-two in 1974, Josef Krips was widely regarded as the last in a long line of illustrious Viennese conductors. Although in 1953 he turned to the symphonic repertoire, he was trained as a vocal coach and opera conductor, and he spent his early career conducting opera. Krips knew and conducted some 130 operas ranging from Pergolesi to Richard Strauss, Pfitzner, and beyond, but it was to the operas of Mozart that he was most drawn and which best displayed his considerable talents.

In an interview late in his life, Krips stated that "Mozart is, of all composers, the most difficult to conduct. And I can tell you why: two bars, and you are suddenly transported to heaven. It is very hard to keep your bearings when you are up there." In an *Opera News* article written in 1971 entitled "Becoming a Conductor," Krips advised would-be conductors to begin by studying the Mozart operas, preferably *Die Entführung aus dem Serail.* He further noted that it "takes at least twenty years of constant study and restudy to conduct a good performance" of a Mozart opera.

Krips cited Toscanini, with his admonition that "instruments must sing," as his greatest musical influence. Numerous conductors have attempted to get a singing tone from their orchestral players, but Krips put the idea into practice with splendid results. He developed the theory that the players must breathe with the conductor to achieve real unity: ". . . an orchestra will play exactly the way the conductor feels the music. If his feeling is imprecise, then the performance will suffer. It will lack focus. Nor can the feeling be faked; the musicians will invariably know." He tells his players to "sing the music into your instruments. Breathe it in." From this he gets a soft, warm, glowing quality, as if the instruments were actually tuned lower in pitch—the antithesis of the "brilliant" playing that he detests.

Krips's life ran a far from smooth course, but perhaps no more so than anyone else's who was caught in the web of political upheaval and war of the 1930s and 1940s. Born in 1902 in Vienna, Krips entered the Academy of Music after a stint as Vienna choir boy; there, in addition to taking courses from Eusebius Mandyczewski, he engaged in special conducting studies under Felix Weingartner. Krips's first position was as chorus director and voice coach for the Vienna Volksoper, in 1921. When the regular conductor for a performance of Verdi's *Un ballo in maschera* fell ill, Krips, who knew the score perfectly, was able to fill in. "I conducted without the score and I would advise any ambitious youngster to do exactly as I did." By that, Krips meant that a young conductor should coach the singers himself and know the score by memory. Engagements in Germany followed: 1925-26 in Dortmund, and from 1926-33 as music director at Karlsruhe. He was forced to leave Germany in 1933 because of the rise to power of Hitler; not only was Krips politically at odds with Nazi philosophy, he also had some Jewish blood. His career at the Vienna Staatsoper began in 1933, but with the Anschluss he had to give up his position there in 1938. After a year conducting in Belgrade he spent the war years working in a factory. It was as early as 1 May 1945, however—only a few weeks after the cessation of hostilities in Europe—that Krips began rebuilding musical, especially operatic, life in Vienna. The first performance he conducted was of Mozart's *Le nozze di Figaro,* at the Volksoper (due to the Allied bombing of the Staatsoper). Subsequent operas conducted by Krips during this uncertain yet exciting period included *La bohème, Il barbiere di Siviglia, Madama Butterfly, The Bartered Bride,* and *Così fan tutte.* In 1946 Krips helped to reopen the Salzburg Festival by conducting *Don Giovanni* with Ljuba Welitsch as Donna Anna; he returned on several occasions. In the years after the war he also toured with the Staatsoper and the Vienna Philharmonic to several European countries, including Britain in 1947, where his performances made a great impact. Krips had built up a remarkable ensemble, including such singers as Welitsch, Gueden, Seefried, Schwarzkopf, London, Kunz, and Schoeffler. These postwar performances are still prized by those fortunate enough to have heard them.

Only in the 1950s did Krips turn to concert work. From 1950 to 1954 he led the London Symphony; from 1954-63 the Buffalo (New York) Philharmonic, and in 1963 he became the conductor of the San Francisco Symphony, a position he held until 1970. In 1960 he led a stellar cast, including Schwarzkopf, Wächter, Berry, Corena, Ludwig, and Streich, in *Le nozze di figaro* at the Lyric Opera of Chicago, a production that critic Claudia Cassidy lauded as "right out of Vienna's top drawer." From 1966, when he conducted *Die Zauberflöte* with Chagall's sets at Lincoln Center, Krips was a guest at the Metropolitan Opera in New York, where he also conducted a production of *Le nozze di Figaro* in the 1969-70

season. Krips's return to the Vienna Staatsoper in 1963 was heralded with great enthusiasm. Writing of this event in *Opera,* Joseph Wechsberg characterized Krips as "the man with no artistic compromise and with great taste and style who knows the problems of instrumentalists and singers."

Later in life Krips conducted a number of operas at Covent Garden, among them *Die Meistersinger, Der Rosenkavalier,* and *Fidelio.* Of a 14 May 1973 performance of *Fidelio,* Harold Rosenthal wrote: "Josef Krips was obviously the hero of the evening, and the orchestra certainly were playing at their very best. His reading is gentler than some we have heard in recent years, but there was much to admire in the loving way he shaped phrases and judged his tempos. The *Leonore 3* was excitingly played." Of the *Rosenkavalier* in November of 1972, Rosenthal noted that "Josef Krips's way with the score is far gentler, and more Viennese than Solti's, and the orchestra played ravishingly for him. He never oversentimentalized the music, and some of the playing was of the utmost delicacy." Krips conducted guest performances of operas in Paris, Amsterdam, Rome, and Florence.

Krips claimed a long list of premieres: the first German performances of Janáček's *The Makropoulos Case* in 1929, the Continental premiere of Britten's *Rape of Lucretia,* and the world premiere of Bartók's Violin Concerto, and literally dozens of new works by Blacher (e.g., his opera *Romeo und Julia*), Einem, Hindemith, and Shostakovich. Krips was anything but a routine conductor; he was forever creating anew, even with a warhorse like Puccini's *Tosca.* He was known as a benevolent despot, a conductor who, in spite of his reserve and discretion, had great vitality. He was a passionate maker of music who often got extraordinary results. Of the *Don Giovanni* in September 1963 at the Vienna Staatsoper, Wechsberg wrote that Krips "had obviously worked with the singers and gave help to those who needed it, and made them sound much better than they usually do." He left two of his Mozart opera interpretations on disc—*Don Giovanni* and *Die Entführung aus dem Serail.* For Philips he recorded a remarkable cycle of Mozart symphonies. Of twentieth-century conductors perhaps only Sir Thomas Beecham, Bruno Walter, and (at times) Herbert von Karajan equaled Krips as an interpreter of Mozart.

—Stephen Willier

KRÓL ROGER [King Roger].

Composer: Karol Szymanowski.

Librettists: Karol Szymanowski and J. Iwaszkiewicz.

First Performance: Warsaw, 19 June 1926.

Roles: King Roger (baritone); Roxana (soprano); Edrisi (tenor); The Shepherd (tenor); Archbishop (bass); Diakonissa (contralto); chorus.

*   *   *

Król Roger, to a libretto by Jarosław Iwaszkiewicz (modified by the composer), is often considered to be Szymanowski's masterpiece. Ostensibly it concerns the conflict between the Christian church in medieval Sicily and a pagan creed of beauty and pleasure proclaimed by a young shepherd-prophet. Queen Roxana is seduced by the allurements of the shepherd and his faith and leaves with him and his followers. King Roger eventually follows the shepherd as a pilgrim, but in the end stands alone. This provides the framework for a Nietzschean reworking of Euripides' *Bacchae,* which Szymanowski knew in Zieliński's Russian translation, where Roger (Pentheus) emerges "strong enough for freedom," having "overcome" the enriching but dangerous Dionysian forces within himself.

The ending (in which Roger alone resists the Shepherd's influence) marked a crucial modification by Szymanowski himself of the original version of the libretto (where Roger followed the shepherd as a disciple). The change was symptomatic of a change in Szymanowski's attitude to the hedonistic private world inhabited by his earlier music. In *Król Roger* that private world is symbolized above all by the "Bacchic singing and dancing" of the second act, built as it is around two extended set numbers: Roxana's aria, in which she pleads for clemency for the shepherd, and the ritual dance of the shepherd's followers. Yet the seductions of this second act are given distance and perspective by means of a gentle stylistic counterpoint arising naturally out of specific stylizations of Byzantine, Arabic, and Hellenic elements in the opera.

It is possible in fact to view the three acts as vast static *tableaux*—Byzantine, Oriental, and Hellenic respectively—in a way which suggests oratorio as much as opera. The first act stylizes the Byzantine religious-cultural world. Its first formal unit presents the deliberate archaisms of a solemn mass, while its second is the shepherd's *apologia*. The motivic links between these two units help to clarify the symbolic meaning of the opera and of its *dramatis personae*. It is apparent already that the conflict between medieval scholasticism and the Dionysian cult of self-abandoning beauty is an externalization of opposing forces within Roger himself. Much of the opera works on this symbolic level. Edrisi, the Arabian advisor, might be viewed as a symbol of rationality, for instance, and Roxana as an embodiment of the allurements of love.

The second act is an Oriental (Arabic-Indian) tableau whose sumptuous orchestral impressionism (recalling the Ravel of *Daphnis et Chloë*) and Oriental stylizations are in sharp contrast to the archaisms of the first act. Here the attractions of Dionysus are presented without dilution in a musical language which recalls—often in close detail—the most opulent of Szymanowski's middle-period works. In act III the symbolism of the opera becomes explicit. Here, in the ruins of a Greek temple, the shepherd appears to Roger as Dionysus and the King makes a sacrifice to him, no longer suppressing the Dionysian within himself. At the end, recognizing that the "dream is over . . . the beautiful illusion passed," Roger sings a hymn to the rising sun and his vocal line achieves a strength and dignity which had formerly eluded it. He stands alone, enriched and transformed by the truths of Dionysus but no slave to them, a powerful symbol of modern Nietzschean man.

—Jim Samson

KUBELÍK, (Jeronym) Rafael.

Conductor. Born 29 June 1914, in Býchory, near Kolín. Married: 1) Ludmila Bertlova, violinist, 1942 (one son); 2) Elsie Morison, soprano, 1963. Studied violin with his father, the violinist Jan Kubelík, and then entered the Prague Conservatory; conducting debut with the Czech Philharmonic, 1934; music director at the National Theater in Brno, 1939-41; principal conductor of the Czech Philharmonic, 1942-48; conducted in England and Europe, 1948-50; guest conductor, 1949, and then principal conductor of the Chicago Symphony Orchestra, 1950-53; director of the Royal Opera, Covent Garden, 1955-58, where he presented Musorgsky's *Boris Godunov* in its original version; principal conductor of the Bavarian Radio Symphony Orchestra, Munich, 1961-79; toured with the Bavarian Radio Symphony Orchestra in Japan, 1965, and the United States, 1968; became a Swiss citizen, 1966; guest appearances with the New York Philharmonic, 1967; music director of the Metropolitan Opera, New York, 1971-74; retired in 1985; returned to Czechoslovakia, 1990.

Publications

About KUBELÍK: articles–

Arundell, Dennis. "Rafael Kubelik." *Opera* May 1955.

* * *

Rafael Kubelík, the son of violinist Jan Kubelík, first conducted opera at the Brno Opera in Czechoslovakia, where he was music director from 1939 to 1941. It was at Brno that Kubelík first led performances of Berlioz's *Les Troyens,* an opera that later brought him triumphs at Covent Garden in London, the Teatro alla Scala in Milan, and the Metropolitan Opera in New York.

Conductor Bruno Walter recommended Kubelík to Carl Ebert for the Glyndebourne performances of *Don Giovanni* in 1948. These performances, which also toured to the Edinburgh Festival, as well as Smetana's *Bartered Bride* in English at Covent Garden, introduced Kubelík to the British musical establishment. Performances of Janáček's *Katya Kabanová* with the Sadler's Wells Opera in 1954, chosen to celebrate the composer's centenary, marked a turning point in Janáček's popularity with audiences and demonstrated Kubelík's ability to improve the virtuosity of the orchestra, even in unfamiliar music. The positive publicity generated by these performances precipitated his selection by Sir David Webster, general administrator of the Royal Opera, Covent Garden, to become its music director in 1955 despite his relatively limited experience in opera. His first season as director opened with Verdi's *Otello* with a cast of international stars, despite his preference for casts (in the interest of ensemble work) composed of resident artists. He led a new production of Verdi's *Aida* in 1957. The English stage premiere of Janáček's *Jenůfa* was a milestone in Kubelík's Covent Garden career; he returned to conduct it again in 1970.

During Kubelík's tenure at Covent Garden he emphasized the importance of the company over the individual performer. He insisted on all singers being present at all rehearsals and refused to take solo curtain calls except on opening night and at the last performance of the season. He also championed young British singers, relatively unknown artists many of whom have gone on to have important careers.

If a performance of Wagner's *Die Meistersinger* in 1957 was less than a success, *Les Troyens* later that season was a triumph. According to Lord Harewood, with this performance "Kubelik made a great contribution to music in London," adding that he demonstrated "his ability to give unstintingly to colleagues, company, audience, and above all to music." Part of the importance of this production was that, in accordance with Kubelík's emphasis on ensemble, it was put on with only one guest artist.

Kubelík was deeply hurt by a series of scathing letters submitted to the *Times* by conductor Sir Thomas Beecham in 1956. Beecham attacked Kubelík as a "foreigner" who lacked the qualifications to create a national opera at Covent Garden, despite Kubelík's reputation for being a champion of English singers and his belief that operas in England should be performed in English.

Kubelík's resignation from Covent Garden after three seasons may have been related to the critical failure of *Die Meistersinger.* Beyond this, however, lies Webster's belief that Kubelík lacked the stamina and driving ambition to manage an opera company. Walter Legge expressed misgivings about Kubelík's knowledge of the repertoire and his judgment about singers, and felt that he lacked a firm enough will to get the desired and necessary results. His sensitivity and lack of ambition, while they may have contributed to the quality of his performances, were potentially detrimental in his role as administrator of an opera company.

Kubelík's next operatic appointment was similarly short-lived. In 1971, Göran Gentele, Rudolf Bing's successor as general manager of the Metropolitan Opera, selected Kubelík as the Met's first music director, with Schuyler Chapin as his assistant manager. The first season planned by this troika, that for 1973-74, included *Les Troyens,* which Kubelík had conducted at both Covent Garden and La Scala. The season also had Kubelík conducting *Götterdämmerung,* the last segment of the Wagner *Ring* cycle, which was initiated by Herbert von Karajan in 1969.

Kubelík's plan for the Met was to attempt to maintain the same ensemble casts for multiple performances of each opera because he felt that high quality could only be ensured if all performers rehearsed and performed together many times. He wanted to have the same cast perform throughout the run of each opera, or to have two separate casts with adequate—if not generous—rehearsal time for both.

Gentele's death in an automobile accident in 1972 was the first step in the dissolution of the management troika; Kubelík's resignation in February 1974 was the second. A combination of disagreements with Schuyler Chapin, the pressures of his commitments in Munich (he was often absent from the Met during his tenure), and health problems, all contributed to Kubelík's departure, which led to the promotion of James Levine to the position of artistic director. Plans for the 1974-75 season would have had Kubelík leading Britten's *Death in Venice* (an American premiere), Janáček's *Jenůfa* (which had not been mounted at the Met since the 1924-25 season), and Wagner's *Ring* cycle; as it transpired, Kubelík conducted none of these works. His influence was felt, however, in the decision to perform Musorgsky's *Boris Godunov* in the new production (1974) using the Lamm edition based on the composer's original scoring rather than in the version by Rimsky-Korsakov that was customarily employed.

Kubelík led performances of *Katya Kabanová* in San Francisco in 1977. On the basis of his own research on Janáček's manuscripts, he dropped the orchestral interludes (rediscovered by Charles Mackerras) that cover the opera's scene changes on the grounds—apparently mistaken—that they were inauthentic.

Kubelík's performances are marked by a lack of eccentricity and a reluctance to impose his own personality on the music. This is not meant to imply that there is dullness in his work; his combination of energy and sensitivity to the composer's markings prevents his performances from being mere literal readings.

Kubelík has made few opera recordings. They include Verdi's *Rigoletto* (1963), Weber's *Oberon* (1970), Wagner's *Lohengrin* (1971), Pfitzner's *Palestrina* (1974), and Mozart's *Don Giovanni* (1985).

—Michael Sims

KUNZ, Erich.

Bass-baritone. Born 20 May 1909, in Vienna. Studied with Hans Duhan and Theo Lierhammer, Vienna Music Academy; debut in Troppau, 1933; in Vienna from 1940, when he became a member of the Staatsoper; sang at Salzburg; appeared at Glyndebourne, 1948 and 1950; Metropolitan Opera debut as Leporello, 1952, and appeared there until 1954.

*   *   *

Most classical singers make at least occasional forays into light music, and when they do it is often the music of their homelands. Placido Domingo's audiences have come to expect and delight in his inevitable Zarzuela aria encores; Jessye Norman is the latest in a long line of distinguished black artists to offer spirituals as part of a concert program; and a number of prominent Germans and Austrians have made a "sub-specialty" of operetta and Viennese song. For most of them—Richard Tauber was a notable exception—the lighter repertoire offers a charming way to reach new audiences which never threatens the preeminence of their "serious" careers nor their primary identification as opera singers.

Erich Kunz, was, like Tauber, an anomaly in this company, for as widely admired as he was in German opera and especially in Mozart, his great reputation with a public who adored him was based largely on performances of light opera and volkslieder. Long after he retired from the opera stage he continued to give concerts of light music, and even now, when many of his excellent operatic recordings have disappeared from circulation, Kunz remains alive and well in record stores dispensing reissues on which he sings hearty German university songs, cozy ballads praising the charms of Vienna, and operetta arias of Lehár and the Strauss family.

Kunz certainly did not select this pursuit because of any musical limitations, for he possessed one of the finest and most mellifluous voices of his era. Often billed as a bass-baritone (and the voice did darken over the years), he easily encompassed the top notes of lyric baritone roles as well, and the supple, creamy tone was even and unforced throughout his considerable range. And today we may be surprised to realize that his operatic repertoire was significant, including not only all of the major Mozart baritone parts (Figaro, Papageno in *Die Zauberflöte* and both Don Giovanni and Leporello were specialties) but such serious and diverse roles as Gianni Schicchi, Varlaam in *Boris Godunov,* Fra Melitone in *La forza del destino* and Beckmesser in *Meistersinger.*

His experience in the light repertoire did lend a very individual *boulevardier* style to Kunz's opera performances, and this individuality was both an asset and a liability. At his best, Kunz brought a lilt and a smile to his roles which was incomparable. Much of Papageno's music makes the desired effect only in the hands of a singer who offers just the right lightness of touch, and here Kunz has a charm that is quite unique. The same qualities beguile us in some of his other operatic roles.

Some, but not all, for it must also be said that the "gemütlichkeit" can quickly wear thin: the beautiful voice becomes a croon, the manner insufferably coy and we are all too conscious of what John Steane calls Kunz "slithery Viennese vowels [which] compliment the snakelike attraction." We are also reminded of some of the criticisms which plague Kunz' fine colleague Elisabeth Schwarzkopf, with whom he recorded several operettas. The comparison is useful and not always favorable to Kunz. He has, for example, a way—as Schwarzkopf absolutely does not—of abandoning the written musical line in an attempt to create character. This even compromises some of his Papageno, as in "Ein Mädchen oder Weibchen," where the character is delightful but the way the turns and grace notes are manhandled is not.

Still, far more is good than bad, and perhaps we are so conscious of Kunz' limitations and mannerisms because so much of his singing borders on perfection. Has any other baritone in our time captured the twinkle and sarcasm that underlies Figaro's "Non più andrai," and at the same time sung it with such an unbroken stream of gorgeous tone? Has any other baritone in our experience sung—really sung—Beckmesser at all? And there are, of course, those songs and operettas, which captivate as no other singer since Tauber has, and which are as good examples as any of one of the loveliest voices of his era.

—David Anthony Fox

KUPFER, Harry.

Director. Born 12 August 1935, in Berlin. Married: Marianne Fischer (one child). Studied at the Theaterhochschule "Hans Otto" in Leipzig; began career as assistant stage director at the Landestheater Halle, 1953-1957; operatic debut *Rusalka,* Landestheater Halle, 17 August 1958; assistant director at the Stralsund Theater, 1958-1962; chief director at the Karl Marx Stadt Theater, 1966-1972, Weimar; instructor at the Musikhochschule "Franz Liszt," 1967-1972; director at the Dresden State Opera, 1973-1981; professor at the Musikhochschule "Carl Maria von Weber," 1977-1981; chief director, Komische Oper Berlin, 1981- ; professor at the Musikhochschule "Hanns Eisler"; Kunstpreis, DDR, 1968; Nationalpreis, third class, DDR, 1975; Martin-Andersen-Nexo-Kunstpreis, 1980; Nationalpreis, first class, DDR, 1983; member, National Academy of Arts, 1983.

Opera Productions (selected)

Rusalka, Halle, 1958.
Enoch Arden, Stralsund, 1959.
Die lustige Weiber von Windsor Stralsund, 1960.
Die fliegende Holländer, Stralsund, 1961.
Ottone, Stralsund, 1961.
Legend of Tsar Soltan, Stralsund, 1962.
Nabucco, Karl Marx Stadt Theater, 1963.
Wie Tiere des Waldes, Stralsund, 1964.
Arabella, Karl Marx Stadt Theater, 1965.
Les Contes d'Hoffmann, Karl Marx Stadt Theater, 1966.
Die Blumen von Hiroshima Weimar, 1967 (world premiere).
Jacobowsky und der Oberst Weimar, 1968.
Der Rosenkavalier Weimar, 1969.

Die Frau ohne Schatten, Berlin Deutsche Staatsoper, 1971.
Le nozze di Figaro, Dresden, 1972.
Levins Mühle, Dresden, 1973 (World Premiere).
Don Giovanni, Graz, 1974.
Prince Igor, Copenhagen, 1976.
Parsifal, Copenhagen, 1977.
Die fliegende Holländer, Bayreuth, 1978.
Simon Boccanegra, Dresden, 1980.
Pelléas et Mélisande, English National Opera, 1981.
Rigoletto, Berlin Komische Oper, 1983.
La bohème, Vienna Volksoper, 1984.
The Black Mask, Salzburg, 1986.
Der Ring des Nibelungen, Bayreuth, 1988.

Publications

About KUPFER: books–

Lewin, Michael. *Harry Kupfer.* Vienna, 1988.

articles–

Boutwell, Jane. "Complex and Dangerous." *Opera News* August (1988).

* * *

Harry Kupfer was born in Berlin and studied in Leipzig. Unlike his slightly older contemporaries, Joachim Herz and Götz Friedrich, he never worked for Walter Felsenstein at the Komische Oper, Berlin, but he was allowed to attend rehearsals there and to watch Felsenstein's methods of direction. Having directed his first production at Halle in 1958 when he was 23, he was engaged at Stralsund and Chemnitz before becoming opera director at Weimar. He first worked at the Berlin Staatsoper in 1971, directing Strauss's *Die Frau ohne Schatten.* Two years later he became opera director at Dresden, where he remained for eight years.

They were very fruitful years for Kupfer. At Leipzig he directed a wide variety of operas, ranging from Mozart's *Le nozze di Figaro, Die Zauberflöte* and *Die Entführung aus dem Serail,* to Schoenberg's *Moses und Aron,* and three premieres: Udo Zimmermann's *Levins Mühle* (1973) and *Die Schuhu und die fliegende Prinzessin* (1976), and R. Kunad's *Vincent* (1979). He tackled an opera by Wagner for the first time, staging *Tristan und Isolde,* followed later by *Tannhäuser.* During that period he also worked extensively outside Germany, directing *Prince Igor* and *Parsifal* in Copenhagen and *Elektra* in Amsterdam and for Welsh National Opera. The Welsh National Opera production was an enormous success, confirming Kupfer as one of the most interesting and original directors in Europe.

His controversial production of *Der fliegende Holländer* at Bayreuth in 1978, caused a scandal at its first performances, but continued to be performed until 1985, by which time it had become acceptable. At Frankfurt, Kupfer directed the three-act-version of *Lulu,* one of his best and most successful productions, and *Madama Butterfly.* In 1981 he inaugurated a Janáček cycle at Cologne with *Jenůfa,* returned to Welsh National Opera for *Fidelio* and staged *Pelléas et Mélisande* for English National Opera. That year he also became opera director at the Komische Oper, Berlin. Among his early productions there were *Die Meistersinger, La bohème* and a new version of *Die Entführung,* later seen in Edinburgh.

Kupfer's particular gift for staging twentieth-century opera was frequently exercized during the next decade. After a very

Harry Kupfer's production of Gluck's *Orfeo ed Euridice*, Royal Opera, 1991

fine *Wozzeck* in Stuttgart, he returned there to direct *Die Soldaten* in possibly the finest production that Zimmermann's opera has ever received; later it was restaged at Strasbourg and at the Vienna Staatsoper. Reimann's *Lear,* originally produced at the Komische Oper, Berlin, was successfully transferred to Zurich. Kupfer directed the world premieres of Matthaus' *Judith* (1985) in Berlin, and Penderecki's *Die schwarze Maske* at the 1986 Salzburg Festival; he followed *Katya Kabanova* (second in his Janáček cycle) in Cologne with a powerful staging of Shostakovich's *Lady Macbeth of Mtsensk.*

Kupfer also directed many works of the 18th century. After Handel's *Alcina* at Graz and *Belshazzar* at Hamburg, he staged the same composer's *Giustino* in Berlin, Hamburg, Amsterdam and Vienna. For the Komische Oper he provided new productions of several Mozart operas, including a thought-provoking *Don Giovanni;* and, most interesting of all, the original version of Gluck's *Orfeo e Euridice.* This was performed by the Komische Oper on a visit to Covent Garden, then restaged by Kupfer in 1991 as part of the company's repertory. In this production Kupfer saw Orpheus as a modern pop-star whose injured girl-friend is taken to the hospital, from whence he tries to rescue her.

In 1988 Kupfer returned to Bayreuth, this time to direct *Der Ring des Nibelungen.* As with *Der fliegende Holländer,* his production was not at first liked, but by the fourth year it had become acknowledged as one of the finest and most original stagings of the cycle in the post-second-world-war period. The director's ability to evoke and control vast spaces

as well as vast crowds, which he had frequently demonstrated in operas as diverse as *Boris Godunov* and *Die Soldaten,* was crucial to his staging of *Der Ring,* where the huge, cosmic proportions of the work were, for once, fully understood and completely realized.

—Elizabeth Forbes

KURKA, Robert.

Composer. Born 22 December 1921, in Cicero, Illinois. Died 12 December 1957, in New York. Studied violin with Kathleen Parlow and Hans Letz, and composition with Otto Luening and Darius Milhaud; Guggenheim fellowships, 1951, 1952; his sole opera, *The Good Soldier Schweik,* an enormous international success. Kurka died of leukemia.

Opera

Publisher: Weintraub.

The Good Soldier Schweik, Lewis Allan (after Jaroslav Hašek), 1957, New York, City Opera, 23 April 1958 [unfinished: completed by Hershey Kay].

Other works: orchestral works, choral works, songs, chamber music, instrumental music, violin sonatas.

Publications

About KURKA: articles–

Allan, L. "Czech Opera by American Czech." *New York Times* 20 April 1958.
Kolodin, I. "Kurka's 'Schweik'." *Saturday Review* 41/no. 24 (1958).
Freeman, J.W. "Robert Kurka, 1923-1958." *Opera News* 23/no. 8 (1958).
Bloch, H. [Review of piano-vocal score of *The Good Soldier Schweik*]. *Notes* 21 (1963-64): 229.
Freeman, J.W. *Opera News* 32/no. 31 (1967).

Robert Kurka worked primarily in instrumental idioms and composed only one opera, *The Good Soldier Schweik*, before dying of leukemia at the age of thirty five. Kurka managed to complete the entire vocal/piano score of *The Good Soldier Schweik* and most of the orchestration; Hershey Kay finished the instrumentation based upon notes by the composer. The first performance took place after the composer's death. Though his suite for band by the same title predates the opera, Kurka appears to have conceived of the music in operatic terms from the start. Only upon meeting Lewis Allan in 1955 was he able to bring his project to fruition.

Reaction to *The Good Soldier Schweik* has been both highly critical and essentially laudatory. The central question has been whether the work resides fully in the operatic tradition, or is best viewed as an extension of musical theater. Most of the negative criticism takes the former view, the positive the latter.

Many have noted the influence of Kurt Weill and Bertold Brecht on both the subject matter and its musical treatment. The influence of jazz and blues harmonies, Czech folk music, and dance band music is clearly discernable as well. Not surprisingly, Kurka retained the same instrumentation when he expanded the suite into the stage form. The emphasis thus clearly lies in rhythmic drive over lyrical writing, and as a result narrow ranged melodies predominate. On the larger scale, the music consists of a series of brief scenes or episodes rather than the broad, sweeping gestures typical of grand opera. The harshest criticism views *The Good Soldier Schweik* as a derivative work, whose music, though well-crafted and entirely appropriate to the subject matter, never manages to rise above the commonplace. Many have also noted the rather uneven quality of the libretto.

Nevertheless, critics have been impressed by the variety of color achieved with limited forces. J.W. Freeman—one of the most ardent supporters of *Schweik*—has noted that the music often turns on subtle shadings "between what is funny in the score and what is serious." Freeman further rejects the influence of Weill, finding a more compelling connection between "the musical and dramatic structure."

In performance, the opera demands a first rate tenor/actor for the role of Schweik, a bill fulfilled admirably in the past by Norman Kelly, who created the role. Past productions have been notable for both staging and design, with somewhat mixed results as the tendency to go over-board has often drowned out the music's ironies.

The Good Soldier Schweik has received numerous successful performances throughout the United States and Europe, and continues to be revived every few years. The first European productions in Dresden in 1959 were especially notable, due in part to the political climate of the day and in part to Van Cliburn's first place finish at the Tchaikovsky competition, causing an upsurge in interest in American classical music.

—David Pacun

KURZ, Selma.

Soprano. Born 15 November 1874, in Bielitz, Silesia. Died 10 May 1933, in Vienna. Married: gynecologist Josef Halban in 1910 (daughter Dési Halban). Studied in Vienna with Johannes Ress and in Paris with Mathilde Marchesi; debut as Mignon, Hamburg, 1895; sang in Frankfurt, 1896-99; with Vienna Staatsoper, 1899-1927; created Zerbinetta in the revised version of *Ariadne auf Naxos*, 1916; appeared at Covent Garden in 1904, 1905, 1907, and 1924; appeared at Monte Carlo and Salzburg.

Publications

About KURZ: books–

Goldmann, H. *Selma Kurz: Der Werdegang einer Sängerin*. Bielsko, 1934.
Halban, D. and U. Ebbers. *Selma Kurz: Die Sängerin und ihre Zeit*. Stuttgart, 1983.

articles–

Halban, D. et al. "Selma Kurz." *Record Collector* 13 (1960): 53.
Halban, D. "My Mother Selma Kurz." *Recorded Sound* 49 (1973): 128.

Selma Kurz was one of the group of singers who made up Mahler's unforgettable ensemble at the Vienna Opera, where she was to remain a permanent member of the company until 1927 with occasional guest appearances until 1929. In all she gave almost one thousand performances at the Vienna Opera.

The conventional view, reinforced by her more readily available recordings—that Kurz was a light lyrical soprano with a striking coloratura and an incredible trill—is not totally borne out by her career. She began in 1895 at Hamburg in the role of Mignon, but her contract was bought out by the Frankfurt Opera where her debut was as Elisabeth in *Tannhäuser*. She also sang Carmen, and Siebel in *Faust*, and she studied the role of Fidès in *Le Prophète*.

Kurz's first Vienna performance in September 1897 was again as Mignon, soon followed by Marguerite in *Faust*. The coloratura side of her vocal accomplishments was reflected in her assumption of the Queen of the Night in *Die Zauberflöte* and Olympia in *Les contes d'Hoffmann*, but she went on to sing the other heroines in the same opera. She also appeared as "an exquisite Eva, fresh and youthful" in *Die Meistersinger* and undertook the role of Sieglinde in *Die Walküre*, for which

Mahler arranged coaching by Anna Bahr-Mildenburg. Mahler's interest in Kurz's career was at this stage multi-faceted. She gave a highly successful performance of some of his songs in January 1901 and they also had a brief love affair.

In 1904 Kurz made her first appearances at Covent Garden as Gilda in *Rigoletto,* Oscar in *Un ballo in maschera* and again Elisabeth. According to P.G. Hurst "her triumph was immediate and emphatic." There is an evocative description of the "most liquid and exquisite shake (in the Masked Ball) that seemed to grow in volume as it proceeded, filling the whole house with its vibrant tones." Kurz re-appeared at Covent Garden in 1905 and 1907 and also sang in Monte Carlo and in Paris. She did not cross the Atlantic until 1921, but serious illness forced her to cancel all except the first of a series of concerts.

In all, Kurz's repertoire extended to some sixty roles, and they indicate an impressive range of musical genres. Her Verdi included Elvira in *Ernani* and Leonora in *Il trovatore;* there are a significant number of roles in French operas by Massenet, Gounod and others; there are also many contemporary works.

Kurz left a considerable legacy of recordings made over a period stretching from 1900 to 1925. Some of the earliest demonstrate clearly that she was not purely a lyrical soprano. In Elvira's aria her attack is that of a dramatic soprano. Nonetheless, Kurz is better remembered for her lyrical singing and coloratura feats on record. There is great verve in a piece from *Les diamants de la couronne* that remained unpublished for fifty years, and a stunning rendition of Oscar's aria from *Un ballo in maschera.* The single most extraordinary record is from Goldmark's *Queen of Sheba*—the "Lockruf" sung by Astaroth, the third soprano in the opera. The opening is itself magical and contains towards the end the most incredible, sustained trill—perhaps the longest on record.

There is, however, a deficit to Kurz's singing which is clearly brought out by her records. For all the technical proficiency and frequent pyrotechnics, the records often lack excitement. Unlike many of her great contemporaries Kurz lacked expressiveness and this is demonstrated by her records, impressive though they may be. There is wonderful singing on a series of records from *La Bohème,* but they never efface the memory of Melba, certainly no greater an actress but possessing in abundance that expressiveness which Kurz lacks. Such a view is also consistent with Mahler's own known preference for the greater acting abilities of Gutheil-Schoder. In the last analysis it suggests that Kurz was an important singer who enjoyed a major career at one of the world's leading opera houses rather than one of the great international artists.

—Stanley Henig

WITHDRAWN